THE UNIVERSAL ALMANAC 1996

Edited by
JOHN W. WRIGHT

ANDREWS AND McMEEL
A Universal Press Syndicate Company
Kansas City

Staff and Contributors

General Editor, John W. Wright
Executive Editor, John Rosenthal

Section Editors
Bryan Bunch (Science and Technology); John Connelly and John Major (Nations of the World); Patricia Szczerba (World Topics and Statistics); James Pallot (Media); Don Clippinger (States); Lawrence Lorimer (Religion); Jenny Tesar (Health and Medicine); Allison Paxton Paine (Economy)

Senior Writers
Deborah Kaple, Lincoln Paine, Glen Gendzel, Ellen Chodosh, Thomas LaRosa, Stephen Lichtman, Lincoln Paine, Lisa Renaud, John Rosenthal, Marilyn Rosenthal

Staff Writers
Jerold Kappes, Eugene McCaffrey, Charles Myers, Strom Thacker

Fact Checkers and Proofreaders
Maureen Chiofalo, Byrgen Finkelman, David Harford, Richard Crowe, Robert L. Spring, Raymond Sullivan, Victoria Wright

Maps
David Lindroth, West Milford, N.J.

Data Entry
Dorothy Green, Raymond Sullivan

Editorial Director, Donna Martin
Executive Editor, Jean Lowe
Associate Editor, Matt Lombardi
Production Manager, Carol Coe
Production Editors, Sharon Garrett, Katie Mace
Chief Copyeditor/Proofreader, Myia Williams
Designers, Barrie Maguire, Cameron Poulter

The manuscript for this book was prepared in electronic form.
Typography by Connell-Zeko Type & Graphics, Kansas City, Missouri.
Printing and binding by The Banta Company/Harrisonburg, Virginia.

The Universal Almanac™
is a trademark of Andrews and McMeel and John W. Wright.

The Universal Almanac 1996

For information, write Andrews and McMeel,
a Universal Press Syndicate Company,
4900 Main Street, Kansas City, Missouri 64112.

ISBN: 0–8362–0555–3 (hd)
ISBN: 0–8362–0549–9 (ppb)
ISSN: 1045–9820

Contents

1996

JANUARY

S	M	T	W	T	F	S
	1	2	3	4	5	6
7	8	9	10	11	12	13
14	15	16	17	18	19	20
21	22	23	24	25	26	27
28	29	30	31			

FEBRUARY

S	M	T	W	T	F	S
				1	2	3
4	5	6	7	8	9	10
11	12	13	14	15	16	17
18	19	20	21	22	23	24
25	26	27	28	29		

MARCH

S	M	T	W	T	F	S
					1	2
3	4	5	6	7	8	9
10	11	12	13	14	15	16
17	18	19	20	21	22	23
24	25	26	27	28	29	30
31						

APRIL

S	M	T	W	T	F	S
	1	2	3	4	5	6
7	8	9	10	11	12	13
14	15	16	17	18	19	20
21	22	23	24	25	26	27
28	29	30				

MAY

S	M	T	W	T	F	S
			1	2	3	4
5	6	7	8	9	10	11
12	13	14	15	16	17	18
19	20	21	22	23	24	25
26	27	28	29	30	31	

JUNE

S	M	T	W	T	F	S
						1
2	3	4	5	6	7	8
9	10	11	12	13	14	15
16	17	18	19	20	21	22
23	24	25	26	27	28	29
30						

JULY

S	M	T	W	T	F	S
	1	2	3	4	5	6
7	8	9	10	11	12	13
14	15	16	17	18	19	20
21	22	23	24	25	26	27
28	29	30	31			

AUGUST

S	M	T	W	T	F	S
				1	2	3
4	5	6	7	8	9	10
11	12	13	14	15	16	17
18	19	20	21	22	23	24
25	26	27	28	29	30	31

SEPTEMBER

S	M	T	W	T	F	S
1	2	3	4	5	6	7
8	9	10	11	12	13	14
15	16	17	18	19	20	21
22	23	24	25	26	27	28
29	30					

OCTOBER

S	M	T	W	T	F	S
		1	2	3	4	5
6	7	8	9	10	11	12
13	14	15	16	17	18	19
20	21	22	23	24	25	26
27	28	29	30	31		

NOVEMBER

S	M	T	W	T	F	S
					1	2
3	4	5	6	7	8	9
10	11	12	13	14	15	16
17	18	19	20	21	22	23
24	25	26	27	28	29	30

DECEMBER

S	M	T	W	T	F	S
1	2	3	4	5	6	7
8	9	10	11	12	13	14
15	16	17	18	19	20	21
22	23	24	25	26	27	28
29	30	31				

1997

JANUARY

S	M	T	W	T	F	S
			1	2	3	4
5	6	7	8	9	10	11
12	13	14	15	16	17	18
19	20	21	22	23	24	25
26	27	28	29	30	31	

FEBRUARY

S	M	T	W	T	F	S
						1
2	3	4	5	6	7	8
9	10	11	12	13	14	15
16	17	18	19	20	21	22
23	24	25	26	27	28	

MARCH

S	M	T	W	T	F	S
						1
2	3	4	5	6	7	8
9	10	11	12	13	14	15
16	17	18	19	20	21	22
23	24	25	26	27	28	29
30	31					

APRIL

S	M	T	W	T	F	S
		1	2	3	4	5
6	7	8	9	10	11	12
13	14	15	16	17	18	19
20	21	22	23	24	25	26
27	28	29	30			

MAY

S	M	T	W	T	F	S
				1	2	3
4	5	6	7	8	9	10
11	12	13	14	15	16	17
18	19	20	21	22	23	24
25	26	27	28	29	30	31

JUNE

S	M	T	W	T	F	S
1	2	3	4	5	6	7
8	9	10	11	12	13	14
15	16	17	18	19	20	21
22	23	24	25	26	27	28
29	30					

JULY

S	M	T	W	T	F	S
		1	2	3	4	5
6	7	8	9	10	11	12
13	14	15	16	17	18	19
20	21	22	23	24	25	26
27	28	29	30	31		

AUGUST

S	M	T	W	T	F	S
					1	2
3	4	5	6	7	8	9
10	11	12	13	14	15	16
17	18	19	20	21	22	23
24	25	26	27	28	29	30
31						

SEPTEMBER

S	M	T	W	T	F	S
	1	2	3	4	5	6
7	8	9	10	11	12	13
14	15	16	17	18	19	20
21	22	23	24	25	26	27
28	29	30				

OCTOBER

S	M	T	W	T	F	S
			1	2	3	4
5	6	7	8	9	10	11
12	13	14	15	16	17	18
19	20	21	22	23	24	25
26	27	28	29	30	31	

NOVEMBER

S	M	T	W	T	F	S
						1
2	3	4	5	6	7	8
9	10	11	12	13	14	15
16	17	18	19	20	21	22
23	24	25	26	27	28	29
30						

DECEMBER

S	M	T	W	T	F	S
	1	2	3	4	5	6
7	8	9	10	11	12	13
14	15	16	17	18	19	20
21	22	23	24	25	26	27
28	29	30	31			

1998

JANUARY

S	M	T	W	T	F	S
				1	2	3
4	5	6	7	8	9	10
11	12	13	14	15	16	17
18	19	20	21	22	23	24
25	26	27	28	29	30	31

FEBRUARY

S	M	T	W	T	F	S
1	2	3	4	5	6	7
8	9	10	11	12	13	14
15	16	17	18	19	20	21
22	23	24	25	26	27	28

MARCH

S	M	T	W	T	F	S
1	2	3	4	5	6	7
8	9	10	11	12	13	14
15	16	17	18	19	20	21
22	23	24	25	26	27	28
29	30	31				

APRIL

S	M	T	W	T	F	S
			1	2	3	4
5	6	7	8	9	10	11
12	13	14	15	16	17	18
19	20	21	22	23	24	25
26	27	28	29	30		

MAY

S	M	T	W	T	F	S
					1	2
3	4	5	6	7	8	9
10	11	12	13	14	15	16
17	18	19	20	21	22	23
24	25	26	27	28	29	30
31						

JUNE

S	M	T	W	T	F	S
	1	2	3	4	5	6
7	8	9	10	11	12	13
14	15	16	17	18	19	20
21	22	23	24	25	26	27
28	29	30				

JULY

S	M	T	W	T	F	S
			1	2	3	4
5	6	7	8	9	10	11
12	13	14	15	16	17	18
19	20	21	22	23	24	25
26	27	28	29	30	31	

AUGUST

S	M	T	W	T	F	S
						1
2	3	4	5	6	7	8
9	10	11	12	13	14	15
16	17	18	19	20	21	22
23	24	25	26	27	28	29
30	31					

SEPTEMBER

S	M	T	W	T	F	S
		1	2	3	4	5
6	7	8	9	10	11	12
13	14	15	16	17	18	19
20	21	22	23	24	25	26
27	28	29	30			

OCTOBER

S	M	T	W	T	F	S
				1	2	3
4	5	6	7	8	9	10
11	12	13	14	15	16	17
18	19	20	21	22	23	24
25	26	27	28	29	30	31

NOVEMBER

S	M	T	W	T	F	S
1	2	3	4	5	6	7
8	9	10	11	12	13	14
15	16	17	18	19	20	21
22	23	24	25	26	27	28
29	30					

DECEMBER

S	M	T	W	T	F	S
		1	2	3	4	5
6	7	8	9	10	11	12
13	14	15	16	17	18	19
20	21	22	23	24	25	26
27	28	29	30	31		

1999

JANUARY

S	M	T	W	T	F	S
					1	2
3	4	5	6	7	8	9
10	11	12	13	14	15	16
17	18	19	20	21	22	23
24	25	26	27	28	29	30
31						

FEBRUARY

S	M	T	W	T	F	S
	1	2	3	4	5	6
7	8	9	10	11	12	13
14	15	16	17	18	19	20
21	22	23	24	25	26	27
28						

MARCH

S	M	T	W	T	F	S
	1	2	3	4	5	6
7	8	9	10	11	12	13
14	15	16	17	18	19	20
21	22	23	24	25	26	27
28	29	30	31			

APRIL

S	M	T	W	T	F	S
				1	2	3
4	5	6	7	8	9	10
11	12	13	14	15	16	17
18	19	20	21	22	23	24
25	26	27	28	29	30	

MAY

S	M	T	W	T	F	S
						1
2	3	4	5	6	7	8
9	10	11	12	13	14	15
16	17	18	19	20	21	22
23	24	25	26	27	28	29
30	31					

JUNE

S	M	T	W	T	F	S
		1	2	3	4	5
6	7	8	9	10	11	12
13	14	15	16	17	18	19
20	21	22	23	24	25	26
27	28	29	30			

JULY

S	M	T	W	T	F	S
				1	2	3
4	5	6	7	8	9	10
11	12	13	14	15	16	17
18	19	20	21	22	23	24
25	26	27	28	29	30	31

AUGUST

S	M	T	W	T	F	S
1	2	3	4	5	6	7
8	9	10	11	12	13	14
15	16	17	18	19	20	21
22	23	24	25	26	27	28
29	30	31				

SEPTEMBER

S	M	T	W	T	F	S
			1	2	3	4
5	6	7	8	9	10	11
12	13	14	15	16	17	18
19	20	21	22	23	24	25
26	27	28	29	30		

OCTOBER

S	M	T	W	T	F	S
					1	2
3	4	5	6	7	8	9
10	11	12	13	14	15	16
17	18	19	20	21	22	23
24	25	26	27	28	29	30
31						

NOVEMBER

S	M	T	W	T	F	S
	1	2	3	4	5	6
7	8	9	10	11	12	13
14	15	16	17	18	19	20
21	22	23	24	25	26	27
28	29	30				

DECEMBER

S	M	T	W	T	F	S
			1	2	3	4
5	6	7	8	9	10	11
12	13	14	15	16	17	18
19	20	21	22	23	24	25
26	27	28	29	30	31	

2000

JANUARY

S	M	T	W	T	F	S
						1
2	3	4	5	6	7	8
9	10	11	12	13	14	15
16	17	18	19	20	21	22
23	24	25	26	27	28	29
30	31					

FEBRUARY

S	M	T	W	T	F	S
		1	2	3	4	5
6	7	8	9	10	11	12
13	14	15	16	17	18	19
20	21	22	23	24	25	26
27	28	29				

MARCH

S	M	T	W	T	F	S
			1	2	3	4
5	6	7	8	9	10	11
12	13	14	15	16	17	18
19	20	21	22	23	24	25
26	27	28	29	30	31	

APRIL

S	M	T	W	T	F	S
						1
2	3	4	5	6	7	8
9	10	11	12	13	14	15
16	17	18	19	20	21	22
23	24	25	26	27	28	29
30						

MAY

S	M	T	W	T	F	S
	1	2	3	4	5	6
7	8	9	10	11	12	13
14	15	16	17	18	19	20
21	22	23	24	25	26	27
28	29	30	31			

JUNE

S	M	T	W	T	F	S
				1	2	3
4	5	6	7	8	9	10
11	12	13	14	15	16	17
18	19	20	21	22	23	24
25	26	27	28	29	30	

JULY

S	M	T	W	T	F	S
						1
2	3	4	5	6	7	8
9	10	11	12	13	14	15
16	17	18	19	20	21	22
23	24	25	26	27	28	29
30	31					

AUGUST

S	M	T	W	T	F	S
		1	2	3	4	5
6	7	8	9	10	11	12
13	14	15	16	17	18	19
20	21	22	23	24	25	26
27	28	29	30	31		

SEPTEMBER

S	M	T	W	T	F	S
					1	2
3	4	5	6	7	8	9
10	11	12	13	14	15	16
17	18	19	20	21	22	23
24	25	26	27	28	29	30

OCTOBER

S	M	T	W	T	F	S
1	2	3	4	5	6	7
8	9	10	11	12	13	14
15	16	17	18	19	20	21
22	23	24	25	26	27	28
29	30	31				

NOVEMBER

S	M	T	W	T	F	S
			1	2	3	4
5	6	7	8	9	10	11
12	13	14	15	16	17	18
19	20	21	22	23	24	25
26	27	28	29	30		

DECEMBER

S	M	T	W	T	F	S
					1	2
3	4	5	6	7	8	9
10	11	12	13	14	15	16
17	18	19	20	21	22	23
24	25	26	27	28	29	30
31						

2001

JANUARY

S	M	T	W	T	F	S
	1	2	3	4	5	6
7	8	9	10	11	12	13
14	15	16	17	18	19	20
21	22	23	24	25	26	27
28	29	30	31			

FEBRUARY

S	M	T	W	T	F	S
				1	2	3
4	5	6	7	8	9	10
11	12	13	14	15	16	17
18	19	20	21	22	23	24
25	26	27	28			

MARCH

S	M	T	W	T	F	S
				1	2	3
4	5	6	7	8	9	10
11	12	13	14	15	16	17
18	19	20	21	22	23	24
25	26	27	28	29	30	31

APRIL

S	M	T	W	T	F	S
1	2	3	4	5	6	7
8	9	10	11	12	13	14
15	16	17	18	19	20	21
22	23	24	25	26	27	28
29	30					

MAY

S	M	T	W	T	F	S
		1	2	3	4	5
6	7	8	9	10	11	12
13	14	15	16	17	18	19
20	21	22	23	24	25	26
27	28	29	30	31		

JUNE

S	M	T	W	T	F	S
					1	2
3	4	5	6	7	8	9
10	11	12	13	14	15	16
17	18	19	20	21	22	23
24	25	26	27	28	29	30

JULY

S	M	T	W	T	F	S
1	2	3	4	5	6	7
8	9	10	11	12	13	14
15	16	17	18	19	20	21
22	23	24	25	26	27	28
29	30	31				

AUGUST

S	M	T	W	T	F	S
			1	2	3	4
5	6	7	8	9	10	11
12	13	14	15	16	17	18
19	20	21	22	23	24	25
26	27	28	29	30	31	

SEPTEMBER

S	M	T	W	T	F	S
						1
2	3	4	5	6	7	8
9	10	11	12	13	14	15
16	17	18	19	20	21	22
23	24	25	26	27	28	29
30						

OCTOBER

S	M	T	W	T	F	S
	1	2	3	4	5	6
7	8	9	10	11	12	13
14	15	16	17	18	19	20
21	22	23	24	25	26	27
28	29	30	31			

NOVEMBER

S	M	T	W	T	F	S
				1	2	3
4	5	6	7	8	9	10
11	12	13	14	15	16	17
18	19	20	21	22	23	24
25	26	27	28	29	30	

DECEMBER

S	M	T	W	T	F	S
						1
2	3	4	5	6	7	8
9	10	11	12	13	14	15
16	17	18	19	20	21	22
23	24	25	26	27	28	29
30	31					

THE 1996 PRESIDENTIAL ELECTION

After their sweeping victory in November 1994, Republicans took aim on recapturing the White House in 1996. With Pres. Clinton forced into a strategic retreat, his standing in the polls weakening, many Republicans seized the opportunity to make a run for the Oval Office. By September 1995, no fewer than 11 men had declared themselves candidates for president. Only Senate Majority Leader Bob Dole had anything like a national reputation, and he immediately became the front-runner in the polls and in the race for raising funds. But many saw Dole's age (71) and his moderate views (but not so moderate temperament) as serious drawbacks that could deprive him of the nomination. Chief among his rivals was a little-known senator from Texas, Phil Gramm, whose militant, antiabortion positions and strong demand for deep tax cuts appealed to the party's right wing, which funded Gramm's candidacy despite his inability to cut into Dole's lead.

Perhaps more intriguing than the Republican nominee-seekers were the handful of public figures entertaining third-party candidacies. Foremost among them was Ross Perot, the billionaire populist whose on-again off-again candidacy in 1992 nevertheless attracted nearly 20 percent of the vote, more than any third-party candidate since Theodore Roosevelt garnered 27 percent in 1912. On Sept. 25, Perot went on his favorite podium, CNN's "Larry King Live," to announce that he was forming a new third party called the Independence party that would field its own presidential candidate in 1996 as well as in selected congressional races. He did not, however, say whether he would be the party's presidential candidate.

But it was Colin Powell, the former chairman of the Joint Chiefs of Staff, who seemed to strike the most fear in both Republican and Democratic presidential hopefuls alike, when he revealed in September that he was thinking about making a run for the presidency. Powell did not say whether he would seek office as a Republican, Democrat, or third-party candidate, but he finally revealed how he stands on a number of issues. He described himself as pro-choice, pro–gun control, and pro–death penalty, thus aligning himself with the majority of Americans on each issue.

As of October 1995, however, none of these figures had officially declared a candidacy, nor had any Democrats come forward to challenge the incumbent president. (Clinton is not expected to declare his reelection bid officially until 1996.)

1996 Presidential Candidates (as of Nov. 1, 1995)

Clinton/Gore '96 Primary Committee, 2100 M St. NW, Washington, D.C. 20036, (202) 331-1996

Alexander for President Inc., P.O. Box 23071, Nashville, Tenn. 37202, (615) 327-3350, (declared Feb. 28, 1995)

Buchanan for President Inc., 6862 Elm St., Ste. 210, McLean, Va. 22101, (703) 848-1996, (800) GOPATGO, (Mar. 20, 1995)

Dole for President Inc., 810 First St. NE, Washington, D.C. 20002, (202) 414-6400, (Apr. 10, 1995)

Dornan for President Inc., 6320 Augusta Dr., Ste. 1101, Springfield, Va. 22150, (703) 644-2600, (Apr. 13, 1995)

Forbes for President Inc., P.O. Box 1009, Bedminster, N.J. 07921, (908) 781-5111, (Sept. 22, 1995)

Phil Gramm for President Inc., P.O. Box 33119, Washington, D.C. 20033, (202) 467-8600, (Feb. 24, 1995)

Alan Keyes for President '96 Inc., 611 Pennsylvania Ave. SE, Washington, D.C. 20003, (800) 792-1222, (Mar. 26, 1995)

Lugar for President Committee Inc., 3921 North Meridian St., Indianapolis, Ind. 46208, (317) 923-1996, (Apr. 19, 1995)

Arlen Specter '96, 1503 Locust St., Box 1996, Philadelphia, Pa. 19102, (215) 564-1996, (Mar. 30, 1995)

Taylor for President Inc., 2345 Market St., Des Moines, Iowa 50317, (515) 264-1996, (800) USA BEAR, (May 6, 1995)

1996 PRESIDENTIAL PRIMARY SCHEDULE

The following is an unofficial list of the 1996 presidential primaries and caucuses. The list was accurate as of Oct. 20, 1995. But because local politics can play havoc with the best-laid plans, many dates may change.

Date	Republican primary or caucus (delegates at stake)	Democratic primary or caucus (delegates at stake)
Feb. 6	Louisiana caucus[1] (28)	—
Feb. 19	Iowa caucus[1,2] (25)	Iowa caucus[1,2] (56)
Feb. 20	New Hampshire[1,2] (16)	New Hampshire[1,2] (26)
Feb. 24	Delaware[1,2] (12)	Delaware[1,2] (22)
Feb. 27	Arizona[1] (39)	Arizona (52)
	North Dakota (18)	North Dakota (22)
	South Dakota (18)	—
Mar. 2	South Carolina (37)	—
Mar. 5	Colorado (27)	Colorado (58)
Super	Connecticut (27)	Connecticut (66)
Tuesday	Georgia (42)	Georgia (91)
	—	Idaho caucus (24)
	Maine caucus (15)	Maine (32)
	Maryland (32)	Maryland (86)
	Massachusetts (37)	Massachusetts (115)
	Minnesota caucus (33)	Minnesota caucus (92)
	Rhode Island (16)	Rhode Island (31)
	—	South Carolina (52)
	Vermont (12)	Vermont (22)
Mar. 7	—	Missouri caucus (93)
	New York (102)	New York (289)
Mar. 9	—	Alaska caucus (19)
	—	South Dakota caucus (22)
Mar. 10	—	Nevada caucus[1] (27)
Mar. 12	Florida (98)	Florida (177)
	—	Hawaii caucus (30)
	—	Louisiana (75)
	Mississippi (32)	Mississippi (48)
	Oklahoma (38)	Oklahoma (52)
	Oregon[1] (23)	Oregon (56)
	Tennessee (37)	Tennessee (83)
	Texas (123)	Texas (229)

Date	Republican primary or caucus (delegates at stake)	Democratic primary or caucus (delegates at stake)
Mar. 16	—	Michigan caucus (157)
Mar. 19	Illinois (69)	Illinois (194)
	Michigan (57)	—
	Ohio (67)	Ohio (172)
	Wisconsin (36)	Wisconsin (93)
Mar. 23	—	Wyoming caucus (19)
Mar. 25	Utah caucus (28)	Utah caucus (30)
Mar. 26	California (163)	California (423)
	Washington (36)	—
Mar. 28	—	Washington (90)
Apr. 2	Kansas (31)	Kansas (41)
Apr. 13, 15	—	Virginia caucus (96)
Apr. 23	Pennsylvania (73)	Pennsylvania (195)
Apr. 27	Alaska caucus (19)	—
May 2	Nevada caucus (14)	—
May 4	Wyoming caucus (20)	—
May 7	District of Columbia (14)	District of Columbia (37)
	Indiana (52)	Indiana (89)
	North Carolina (58)	North Carolina (98)
May 14	Nebraska (24)	Nebraska (33)
	West Virginia (18)	West Virginia (43)
May 17	Missouri caucus (36)	—
May 21	Arkansas (20)	Arkansas (48)
May 28	Idaho (23)	—
	Kentucky (26)	Kentucky (61)
June 4	Alabama (40)	Alabama (66)
	Montana (14)	Montana (25)
	New Jersey (48)	New Jersey (120)
	New Mexico (18)	New Mexico (34)
Aug. 10–16[1]	Republican National Convention, San Diego Convention Center	
Aug. 26–29		Democratic National Convention, United Center, Chicago
	1,984 total delegates	**4,326 total delegates**

Note: At press time, Hawaii (14 delegates) had not set a date for its Republican primary. Virginia elects its 53 Republican delegates through local district conventions, which by state law are held between May 10 and June 11. 1. Date subject to change. 2. Iowa traditionally holds its caucuses eight days before the New Hampshire primary. By state law, New Hampshire's primary must be the earliest in the country, falling on the Tuesday immediately before the next-earliest primary. Delaware's primary is on the first Saturday after the New Hampshire primary.

OBITUARIES

Oct. 1, 1994–Oct. 15, 1995

Abbott, George, 107, legendary U.S. theater director and playwright, famed for no-nonsense methods developing material and sure instincts finding hits; involved in more than 100 productions, *Pal Joey, Wonderful Town, Pajama Game, Fiorello!* and *A Funny Thing Happened on the Way to the Forum,* among many others. Awarded Pulitzer, two Tonys, and Kennedy honors. Of a stroke, Miami Beach, Fla., Jan. 31, 1995.

Alfven, Hannes, 86, Swedish scientist, cowinner 1970 Nobel Prize in Physics for study of magnetohydrodynamics, the phenomenon of thin plasmas and magnetic fields stretching throughout space. Of influenza, Djursholm, Sweden, Apr. 2, 1995.

Anfinsen, Christian, 79, U.S. scientist, cowinner 1972 Nobel Prize in Chemistry for research in structural properties of proteins; laboratory director National Institutes of Health 1963–82; 1958 Guggenheim Fellow. Of a heart attack, Randallstown, Md., May 14, 1995.

Aspin, Les, 56, Wisconsin Democratic congressman 1970–92, chairman Armed Services Committee; Sec. of Defense under Clinton; early foe of Vietnam War and Pentagon policies who later supported 1980s arms buildup and Gulf War. After a stroke, Washington, D.C., May 21, 1995.

Ballantine, Ian, 79, U.S. publisher who began paperback movement; founder of Penguin USA, Bantam Books, and Ballantine Books. Of cardiac arrest, Bearsville, N.Y., Mar. 9, 1995.

Barre, Mohammed Siad, ca. 74, president of Somalia 1969–91 whose dictatorial rule brought war with Ethiopia, severe economic problems, and serious human rights abuses leading to his overthrow and subsequent civil war and mass civilian starvation. Of undisclosed causes, Lagos, Nigeria, Jan. 2, 1995.

Begelman, David, 73, U.S. movie executive. President of Columbia Pictures, later fired after a 1978 check-forging incident. An apparent suicide, Los Angeles, Aug. 8, 1995.

Bernays, Edward, 103, Vienna-born public opinion expert, nephew of Sigmund Freud, pioneered methods of using celebrities and opinion polls to sell numerous brand-name products. Of old age, Cambridge, Mass., Mar. 9, 1995.

Bolt, Robert, 70, British writer, best known for *A Man For All Seasons,* winning Tony and Academy Awards; wrote screenplays for *Lawrence of Arabia* and *Dr. Zhivago.* Of heart disease, Hampshire, England, Feb. 20, 1995.

Burger, Warren E., 87, 15th chief justice of the U.S., 1969–86. Appointed by Pres. Nixon to promote conservative judicial restraint, but in whose tenure the Supreme Court continued in a liberal direction with validation of busing, abortion rights, etc. Devoted to improving judicial administration in national courts. Of congestive heart failure, Washington, D.C., June 25, 1995.

Butenandt, Adolf, 91, German scientist, won 1939 Nobel Prize in Chemistry for sex hormone research, which led to later developments of cortisone and birth control pills. After a long illness, Munich, Jan. 18, 1995.

Calloway, Cab, 86, legendary U.S. jazz band leader famed for lithe grace and scat-singing exuberance, notably in his signature tune "Minnie the Moocher." He appeared as Sportin' Life in *Porgy and Bess* on Broadway in 1952. After a stroke, Hockessin, Del., Nov. 18, 1994.

Camras, Marvin, 79, U.S. electrical engineer who developed magnetic tape for sound recordings and the forerunners of modern tape recorders. A member of the Inventors Hall of Fame. Of kidney failure, Evanston, Ill., June 23, 1995.

Chandrasekhar, Subrahmanyan, 84, India-born U.S. scientist awarded 1983 Nobel Prize in Physics for discovery of collapsed stars that became white dwarfs, leading to development of the theory of black holes. Of a heart attack, Chicago, Aug. 21, 1995.

Congar, Rev. Yves, 91, French theologian and writer, promoter of worker-priest and ecumenical movements; disciplined by Vatican for liberal views, though later achieved wide recognition in Second Vatican Council; named cardinal 1994. Of old age, Paris, June 22, 1995.

Cook, Peter, 57, British comedian, the sometimes manic tall man in *Beyond the Fringe* and later with the short Dudley Moore in *Good Evening,* both hits on Broadway. Of an internal hemorrhage, London, Jan. 9, 1995.

Cosell, Howard, 77, U.S. sports analyst and commentator on radio and TV, known for his arrogant style and outspoken views, notably on boxing and football shows. Of heart embolism after cancer surgery, New York, Apr. 23, 1995.

Day, Leon, 78, U.S. baseball pitcher in the Negro Leagues who beat Satchel Paige three of the four times they faced each other. Elected to the Baseball Hall of Fame a week before his death. Of a heart condition, Baltimore, Mar. 13, 1995.

Delany, Annie Elizabeth (Bessie), 104, U.S. centenarian who along with her older sister Sadie became a famous author after both passed their 100th birthdays. Their 1993 bestseller, *Having Our Say: The Delany Sisters' First 100 Years,* was adapted into a Tony Award–nominated Broadway play of the same name in 1995. Of old age, Mount Vernon, N.Y., Sept. 25, 1995.

Desai, Morarji, 99, Indian politician who unseated Indira Gandhi to become the first prime minister of India not from the Congress party. During his two years in office, he decreased the power of the Congress party in favor of regional and other opposition parties. Of undisclosed causes, Bombay, India, Apr. 10, 1995.

Djilas, Milovan, 83, Yugoslavian Communist revolutionary-turned-critic, who in 1957 denounced his colleagues for becoming a privileged and self-serving new class of bureaucrats. A close lieutenant to Marshal Tito, but later expelled from the party, he spent much of his life in prison. Of a heart condition, Belgrade, Yugoslavia, Apr. 20, 1995.

Duke, Angier Biddle, 79, U.S. heir to the American Tobacco Company fortune and the scion of two aristocratic American families who served as ambassador to several countries. After being hit by a car while in-line skating, Southhampton, N.Y., Apr. 30, 1995.

Eazy-E (Eric Wright), 31, U.S. rap singer and founding member of the rap group N.W.A. (Niggaz Wit' Attitude). The group's 1988 album *Straight Outta Compton,* was criticized for its glorification of gang life, rape, guns, violence, and drugs, but its immense popularity paved the way for the commercial success of gangsta rap. Of AIDS, Los Angeles, Mar. 26, 1995.

Eckert, J. Presper, 76, U.S. engineer and computer pioneer, coinvented giant Electronic Numerical Integrator and Computer, ENIAC, in 1945, credited as the first digital computer. Of leukemia, Bryn Mawr, Pa., June 3, 1995.

Eisenstaedt, Alfred, 96, German-born photojournalist, notably for *Life* magazine with thousands of picture stories and almost 100 covers. The most famous was a V-J Day photo of a sailor kissing a nurse, the "storytelling moment" that expressed the euphoria felt at the close of World War II. Of natural causes, Martha's Vineyard, Mass., Aug. 23, 1995.

Elkin, Stanley, 65, U.S. writer praised for fiction blending dark humor, real life, extravagant fantasy, and overwrought language; won National Book Critics Circle Award for 1982 novel *George Mills.* Of heart failure, St. Louis, May 31, 1995.

Faubus, Orval, 84, Arkansas Democratic governor 1955–67, best known for defying federal orders to desegregate Little Rock schools after the Supreme Court's *Brown v. Board of Education* decision. Otherwise considered a progressive populist. Of cancer, Conway, Ark., Dec. 14, 1995.

Flanders, Ed, 60, U.S. actor, Tony winner for *Moon for the Misbegotten* and Emmy winner for "St. Elsewhere." Of undisclosed causes, Denny, Calif., Feb. 22, 1995.

Fleming, Art, 70, U.S. actor best known for hosting the original television quiz show "Jeopardy!" Of pancreatic cancer, Apr. 25, 1995.

Fowler, William A., 83, U.S. scientist, cowinner 1983 Nobel Prize in Physics for demonstrating astrophysical theory that all elements are produced within the stars. Of kidney failure, Pasadena, Calif., Mar. 14, 1995.

Frondizi, Arturo, 86, former president of Argentina who propped up the country's economy during a period of financial austerity from 1958 to 1962. An outspoken opponent of the exiled Juan Perón. Of a heart ailment, Buenos Aires, Apr. 18, 1995.

Fukuda, Takeo, 90, Japanese prime minister 1976–78, led movement toward formal peace with China and more open relations with other Asian countries. Of emphysema, Tokyo, July 5, 1995.

Fulbright, J. William, 89, Arkansas Democratic senator 1945–74, chairman of Senate Foreign Relations Committee 15 years; architect and critic of U.S. foreign policy, outspoken foe of Vietnam War; created influential Fulbright exchange program for scholars in 1946; wrote censure motion that ended Joseph McCarthy's career. After a stroke, Washington, D.C., Feb. 9, 1995.

Gabor, Eva, 74, Hungarian-born actress, one of the Gabor sisters, familiar as the ditzy socialite in TV's "Green Acres." Of respiratory failure after a fall, Los Angeles, July 4, 1995.

Garcia, Jerry, 53, U.S. rock musician and founding member for the Grateful Dead. His personality and technique embodied the group known for its improvisational spontaneity, affability and the loyalty of its dedicated tie-dyed fans. Author of hundreds of songs, including "Truckin'" and "Casey Jones." Of a heart attack after years of drug use, Forest Knolls, Calif., Aug. 9, 1995.

Godunov, Alexander, 45, flamboyant Russian-born ballet dancer and movie actor. The youngest dancer in the Bolshoi Ballet when he joined in 1971. He defected to the U.S. in 1979 while on tour. Of undisclosed causes, West Hollywood, Calif., May 18, 1995.

Gonzalez, Pancho, 67, U.S. tennis player, 1948 and 1949 national champion, later dominant professional (1954–62) acclaimed for natural ability and combative style. Of stomach cancer, Las Vegas, Nev., July 3, 1995.

Gordon, Gale, 89, U.S. radio, film, and TV actor, master of bluster and the slow burn, notably opposite Eve Arden and Lucille Ball. Of cancer, Escondido, Calif., June 30, 1995.

Griswold, Erwin, 90, U.S. law professor, Harvard Law School dean 1946–67; U.S. solicitor general under Johnson and Nixon; strong foe of Sen. Joseph McCarthy. Of undisclosed causes, Nov. 19, 1994.

Hackett, Albert, 95, Pulitzer Prize–winning U.S. playwright best known for *The Diary of Anne Frank,* which he wrote with his first wife, Frances Goodrich. They were a successful screenwriting team during the 1930s and 1940s; their scripts include *Father of the Bride, The Thin Man, It's a Wonderful Life,* and *Seven Brides for Seven Brothers.* Of pneumonia, New York City, Mar. 16, 1995.

Harris, Phil, 91, U.S. bandleader, best known as a comic personality on radio with Jack Benny and later with his wife, Alice Faye; the voice of Baloo the Bear in Disney's *Jungle Book.* Of natural causes, Rancho Mirage, Calif., Aug. 11, 1995.

Hawkins, Erick, 85, U.S. modern dancer and choreographer who formed his own company after breaking with Martha Graham. He created a new flowing dance language articulating natural body movements. Of prostate cancer, Nov. 23, 1994.

Herriot, James, 78, Scottish veterinarian and author, many of whose books about animals have been best-sellers, notably *All Creatures Great and Small* and *Every Living Thing.* Of cancer, Yorkshire, England, Feb. 23, 1995.

Hobby, Oveta Culp, 90, Texas newspaper executive and founding organizer of the Women's Army Corps (the WACs) in World War II. Pres. Eisenhower named her the first secretary of the newly created Dept. of Health, Education, and Welfare. After a stroke, Houston, Aug. 16, 1995.

Holman, Nat, 98, famed U.S. basketball player and coach. Led championship teams at City College of New York, winning both NCAA and NIT titles in 1950; elected to Basketball Hall of Fame. Of natural causes, New York, Feb. 12, 1995.

Horgan, Paul, 91, U.S. writer of fiction, history, and biography, noted for rich details of the Southwest and eloquent style; won two Pulitzer Prizes: 1955 for history of the Rio Grande and 1975 for *Lamy of Santa Fe,* biography of an antislavery archbishop. Of cardiac arrest, Middletown, Conn., Mar. 8, 1995.

Ives, Burl, 85, U.S. folk singer and Academy Award–winning actor best remembered for his stage and screen performance of Big Daddy in *Cat on a Hot Tin Roof* and numerous other roles. Of mouth cancer, Anacortes, Wash., Apr. 14, 1995.

Jobim, Antonio Carlos, 67, Brazilian composer of bossa nova, noted for "The Girl from Ipanema" and *Black Orpheus* film score. Of heart failure, New York, Dec. 8, 1994.

Julia, Raul, 54, U.S. stage and film actor who moved easily from Shakespeare to Broadway musicals to hit movies like *The Kiss of the Spider Woman* and *The Addams Family.* Of stroke complications, Manhasset, N.Y., Oct. 24, 1994.

Kennedy, Rose, 104, daughter of Boston mayor, wife to wily financier and presidential adviser, and mother to U.S. president and two senators, known for the strict religious fervor and astute political instincts that bore her through a life of fortune as well as wrenching loss. Of pneumonia complications, Hyannis Port, Mass., Jan. 22, 1995.

Kingsley, Sydney, 88, U.S. playwright of sharp, realistic dramas, notably *Men in White* (winner of the Pulitzer Prize), *Dead End, Detective Story,* and *Darkness at Noon.* After a stroke, Oakland, N.J., Mar. 20, 1995.

Koch, Howard, 93, U.S. screenwriter and Academy Award–winning coauthor of *Casablanca.* Wrote numerous other films as well as the radio script for Orson Welles's *The War of the Worlds.* Of natural causes, Kingston, N.Y., Aug. 17, 1995.

Köhler, Georges, 48, German scientist, cowinner of 1984 Nobel Prize in Medicine for developing a method of forcing immune cells to produce pure antibodies, paving the way for extensive commercial use in diagnosing and curing specific disease organisms. Of heart failure, Freiburg, Germany, Mar. 1, 1995.

Kuchel, Thomas, 84, California Republican senator 1952–68, a liberal who supported Civil Rights Act and Medicare. Of lung cancer, Beverly Hills, Nov. 21, 1994.

Kuhn, Maggie, 89, U.S. founder of the Gray Panthers, a group committed to "fundamental social change that would eliminate injustice, discrimination and oppression in our present society," especially against the elderly. Of natural causes, Philadelphia, Apr. 22, 1995.

Kunstler, William, 76, U.S. lawyer and defender of unpopular people and causes. His clients included civil rights leader Martin Luther King, Jr., Long Island Railroad mass murderer Colin Ferguson, and the terrorists accused of the World Trade Center bombing. His most famous case, however, was his successful defense of the Chicago Seven, the social activists accused of conspiring to incite riots at the 1968 Democratic National Convention in Chicago. Of heart failure, New York, Sept. 4, 1995.

Lamont, Corliss, 93, U.S. humanist philosopher who left a life of privilege to battle for social causes. As director of the American Civil Liberties Union for 22 years, he fought against Sen. Joseph McCarthy and against mail censorship by the CIA. Of heart failure, Apr. 26, 1995.

Luciano, Ron, 57, U.S. baseball umpire known more for his theatrical, confrontational style on the field than for his ball and strike-calling abilities. Later the author of several successful books recounting his major league experiences. An apparent suicide, Endicott, N.Y., Jan. 18, 1995.

Lupino, Ida, 77, London-born U.S. movie actress, noted for strong performances, often in villainous or neurotic roles. Director of several social-minded films and numerous TV episodes. Of cancer after a stroke, Burbank, Calif. Aug. 3, 1995.

Mantle, Mickey, 63, U.S. baseball player with the N.Y. Yankees (1951–68). He achieved legendary status for his power, speed in the field, and his ability to hit in big games (his 18 World Series home runs are a record). He won the triple crown in 1956 and the MVP three times. Elected to the Hall of Fame in 1974. Of cancer after a liver transplant, Dallas, Aug. 13, 1995.

Maxwell, Vera, 93, U.S. fashion designer known for her classic comfortable styles popular in 1940s and 1950s. After a brief illness, Rincon, Puerto Rico, Jan. 15, 1995.

May, Rollo, 85, U. S. psychologist, one of the first to emphasize humanistic approach that helps people grow; author of several influential books, notably *Love and Will.* Of congestive heart failure, Tiburon, Calif., Oct. 22, 1994.

McNeil, George, 86, U.S. painter of abstract expressionism whose later work became charged with violent energy and extreme use of color and materials; winner of Guggenheim Fellowship and American Academy and Institute of Arts and Letters prize. Of congestive heart failure, New York, Jan. 10, 1995.

McRae, Carmen, 74, U.S. jazz singer, early protégé of Billie Holiday, much appreciated for her sensitive interpretation of lyrics. After stroke, Beverly Hills, Calif., Nov. 10, 1994.

Merrill, James, 68, U.S. poet known for polished style that mingled lyricism with common speech. Awarded Pulitzer and Bollingen Prizes and two National Book Awards; member National Institute of Arts and Letters. After a heart attack, Tucson, Ariz., Feb. 6, 1995.

Montgomery, Elizabeth, 57, U.S. television actress best known as the star of the long-running series "Bewitched." She went on to a successful career in made-for-TV movies. Of an undisclosed form of cancer, Los Angeles, May 18, 1995.

Nelson, Lindsey, 76 U.S. sportscaster known as much for his loud sportsjackets as for his versatility in calling many different kinds of sporting events. A member of the broadcasters' wing of the Baseball Hall of Fame. Of Parkinson's disease, Atlanta, June 14, 1995.

Nizer, Louis, 92, U.S. celebrity lawyer known for his flamboyant style and meticulous methods; specialist in libel cases and the entertainment industry; author of best-selling *My Life in Court.* Of kidney failure, New York, Nov. 10, 1995.

Nu, U, 87, first prime minister of Burma after independence from Britain. In his 12 years in office, he promoted democracy and helped found the nonaligned nations movement before being forced from office in a 1962 coup. Of undisclosed causes, Yangon, Myanmar, Feb. 14, 1995.

Onganía, Gen. Juan Carlos, 81, president of Argentina 1966–70; headed repressive and unpopular military regime. Of a heart attack, Buenos Aires, June 8, 1995.

Osborne, John, 65, British playwright whose acid views of nation and family in *Look Back in Anger* brought a new voice and direction to English-speaking theater. Of diabetes, Shropshire, England, Dec. 24, 1994.

Penick, Harvey, 90, U.S. golf coach to champions; author of best-selling golf advice books, including *Harvey Penick's Little Red Book.* Of old age, Austin, Tex., Apr. 2, 1995.

Pleasence, Donald, 75, British stage and film actor known for the accuracy and immediacy of his characters, whether sinister or poignant. After heart surgery, St. Paul de Vence, France, Feb. 2, 1995.

Redenbacher, Orville, 88, U.S. farmer and entrepreneur whose funny name and trademark bowtied appearance helped him revolutionize the popcorn industry. He created a lighter, fluffier kind of hybrid corn that expanded twice as much as ordinary popcorn kernels. Of a heart attack, Coronado, Calif., Sept. 19, 1995.

Reynolds, Allie ("The Chief"), 79, pitcher for New York Yankees 1947–54; famed for throwing two no-hitters in 1951 and a remarkable 15 Yankee World Series appearances. Of lymphoma and diabetes, Oklahoma City, Okla., Dec. 27, 1994.

Riesel, Victor, 81, U.S. journalist, wrote a syndicated column documenting labor corruption. Blinded in 1956 acid attack, allegedly by garment district thugs, he continued to write until 1990. After a heart attack, New York, Jan. 4, 1995.

Rogers, Ginger, 83, U.S. screen icon of the 1930s and 1940s who blended sophisticated dancing with Fred Astaire, working-girl grit, and sly humor in numerous movies. She won an Oscar for drama *Kitty Foyle* and later had success on the stage as Dolly and Mame. Of undisclosed causes, Rancho Mirage, Calif., Apr. 26, 1995.

Romney, George, 88, Republican governor of Michigan 1962–68 and secretary of Housing and Urban Development under Pres. Nixon. A serious presidential candidate in 1968, he advocated liberal policies. Of natural causes, Bloomfield Hills, Mich., July 26, 1995.

Rozsa, Miklos, 88, Hungarian-born composer of music for movies, including *Spellbound, A Double Life,* and *Ben-Hur,* all Academy Award winners. After a stroke, Los Angeles, July 27, 1995.

Rubin, Jerry, 56, U.S. radical, Vietnam War protester, and cofounder of the Yippies; one of the Chicago Seven, indicted but acquitted of conspiracy, 1969. Later worked on Wall Street. Of car accident injuries, Los Angeles, Nov. 28, 1994.

Rudolph, Wilma, 54, U.S. Olympic runner, winner of three gold medals in 1960 games, first woman to do so; 1961 Sullivan Award winner as outstanding U.S. amateur athlete. Of a brain tumor, Brentwood, Tenn., Nov. 12, 1994.

Rusk, Dean, 85, U.S. politician who as secretary of state in the Johnson and Kennedy administrations consistently defended American involvement in the Vietnam War. Of congestive heart failure, Athens, Ga., Dec. 20, 1994.

Salk, Jonas, 80, U.S. scientist, world-renowned for developing first effective polio vaccine in 1955, using killed virus. It was later replaced by Sabin live virus vaccine, promoting lengthy scientific controversy and rivalry. Of heart failure, La Jolla, Calif., June 23, 1995.

Sarton, May, 83, Belgian-born U.S. poet and writer of numerous novels and autobiographical journals. All of her writing was grounded in the solitary life and a quest for understanding the nature of love and individuality. Of breast cancer, York, Maine, July 16, 1995.

Seldes, George, 104, U.S. author, journalist, and independent critic of the press who protested suppression of news by powerful business interests during the 1930s and 1940s. He reveled in reporting stories of corruption that had been overlooked or covered up by leading newspapers. Of natural causes, Windsor, Vt., July 2, 1995.

Selena (Selena Quintanilla Perez), 23, Mexican-American singer regarded as the queen of Tejano-style music popular on Spanish-language radio stations throughout southern Texas and northern Mexico. Winner of a Grammy Award for best Mexican-American album in 1994. Shot by the president of her fan club, Corpus Christi, Tex., Mar. 31, 1995.

Shapp, Milton, 82, Pennsylvania Democratic governor, 1971–79, whose policies favored consumers, seniors, and the handicapped; suggested Peace Corps to President Kennedy. Of Alzheimer's disease, Wynnewood, Pa., Nov. 24, 1994.

Shulman, Irving, 81, U.S. writer best known for novels *The Amboy Dukes* and *Cry Tough* and original story for film *Rebel Without a Cause,* all studies of juvenile problems. Of undisclosed causes, Sherman Oaks, Calif., Mar. 23, 1995.

Slovo, Joe, 68, Lithuanian-born South African Communist who led guerrilla efforts against apartheid; later a key player in bringing black and white factions together leading to open elections and the triumph of Nelson Mandela. Of bone marrow cancer, South Africa, Jan. 6, 1995.

Smith, Margaret Chase, 97, Maine Republican congresswoman 1941–49, senator 1949–75, first woman elected to both houses; noted for diligence and independence; supported New Deal and Medicare, opposed Joseph McCarthy; first woman considered for presidential ticket. After a stroke, Skowhegan, Maine, May 29, 1995.

Spender, Stephen, 86, British poet and critic whose lyrical verse often focused on contemporary events and politics of the 1930s and 1940s. Cofounder of magazines *Horizon* and *Encounter.* Of undisclosed causes, London, July 16, 1995.

Stennis, John, 93, Mississippi Democratic senator 1948–89, expert on military affairs; highly regarded for personal integrity and diligence; second longest in Senate service. Of pnuemonia complications, Jackson, Miss., Apr. 23, 1995.

Stevens, Brooks, 83, U.S. industrial designer of numerous familiar products like clothes dryers and Harley Davidson motorcycles; cofounder of Industrial Designers Society of America. Of heart failure, Milwaukee, Wis., Jan. 4, 1995.

Stibitz, George, 90, U.S. scientist who invented first digital computer, 1940; later applied computer science to numerous medical problems. Of natural causes, Hanover, N.H., Jan. 30, 1995.

Swayze, John Cameron, 89, U.S. journalist. He was one of the first TV anchormen (1949–56), but is perhaps best known as the spokesman in the Timex "takes a licking but keeps on ticking" watch commercials. Of natural causes, Sarasota, Fla., Aug. 15, 1995.

Taylor, Peter, 77, U.S. writer of finely wrought fiction praised for its emotional depth and precision; 1986 Pulitzer Prize–winner for novel *A Summons to Memphis;* best known for *New Yorker* short stories. After a stroke, Charlottesville, Va., Nov. 2, 1995.

Townsend, Peter, 80, Royal Air Force group captain forced in 1955 to give up love affair with Princess Margaret, sister of Queen Elizabeth. After long illness, Paris, June 19, 1995.

Turner, Lana, 75, U.S. film star whose glamorous studio image over a long career sometimes overshadowed her acting ability, especially in *The Postman Always Rings Twice, The Bad and the Beautiful,* and *Peyton Place.* Also famed for tempestuous private life and many marriages. Of throat cancer, Los Angeles, June 29, 1995.

Versalles, Zoilo, 55, Cuban-born baseball player. A shortstop for the Minnesota Twins, he was the first Latin MVP, but injuries hampered his career after that. Of undisclosed causes but suspected suicide, Bloomington, Minn., June 9, 1995.

Volpe, John A., 85, Republican Massachusetts governor 1960–62; later transportation secretary under Nixon. Of natural causes, Nahunt, Mass., Nov. 11, 1994.

Walton, Ernest, 91, Irish scientist. Cowinner of the 1951 Nobel Prize in Physics for development of first atom-smashing device (1932), leading to verification of Einstein's $E = mc^2$. Of undisclosed causes, Belfast, N. Ireland, June 25, 1995.

Wayne, David, 81, U.S. stage, film, and TV actor, winner of Tony Awards for *Finian's Rainbow* and *Teahouse of the August Moon.* Of lung cancer, Santa Monica, Calif., Feb. 9, 1995.

Wiesner, Jerome, 79, U.S. engineer and analyst of military technology. As science adviser to Pres. John F. Kennedy, he advocated the ban of all nuclear tests except those conducted underground. Later president of the Massachusetts Institute of Technology. Of an unspecified illness, Watertown, Mass. Oct. 21, 1994.

Wigner, Eugene, 92, Budapest-born scientist who won 1963 Nobel Prize in Physics for his study of the essential symmetry of subatomic particles, insights that led to development of nuclear weapons and reactors. Of pneumonia, Princeton, N.J., Jan. 1, 1995.

Wilson, Harold, 79, British Labor prime minister 1964–70, 1974–76, economist who solidified Britian's Common Market membership amid expanded educational opportunities. Of cancer, London, May 24, 1995.

Wolfman Jack (Robert Smith), 57, U.S. radio disc jockey whose raspy voice and flamboyant personality attracted national attention when he was a host on Mexican "border radio" station XERB, which broadcast at 250,000 watts—five times the legal U.S. limit—to audiences across the U.S. and Mexico. Of a heart attack, Belvidere, N.C., July 1, 1995.

Zamora, Pedro, 22, Cuban-born U.S. AIDS educator whose direct attitude about his own transmission of the disease, especially on MTV's "The Real World," persuaded many not to have unprotected sex. Of complications from AIDS, Miami, Nov. 11, 1994.

Zelazny, Roger, 58, U.S. science fiction writer; novels include *Lord of Life* and *Damnation Alley;* winner of two Nebula Awards. Of cancer, Santa Fe, N.Mex., June 14, 1995.

PART I THE ALMANAC OF THE YEAR

THE YEAR IN REVIEW

MAJOR NEWS STORIES OF THE YEAR Oct. 1, 1994–Oct. 25, 1995

The Oklahoma City Bombing

The deadliest terrorist bombing in U.S. history shocked the nation in the spring of 1995, demonstrating that terrorist attacks on human life could not only come on U.S. soil, but at the hands of fellow American citizens.

The blast, a 5,000-pound car bomb, ripped a huge hole in the Alfred Murrah Federal Building in Oklahoma City just after 9:00 A.M. on Apr. 19. The timing of the explosion—just as thousands of people were arriving for work—maximized its lethal effect: 169 people were killed, including 15 young children whose parents had just dropped them off at a day-care center within the building. The blast cut a crater out of the building's front entrance measuring six feet deep and 20 feet in diameter.

In the first few hours after the bombing, suspicion first centered on Muslim extremists of the sort responsible for the 1993 World Trade Center bombing. Pres. Clinton went on national television to warn against stereotyping Muslims, but also promised that punishment for the "evil cowards" responsible for the bombing would be "swift and severe."

But the day after the blast, FBI agents uncovered evidence that pointed not to an Islamic terrorist group, but to American citizens. They tracked a fragment of the truck that had housed the bomb to a Ryder rental agency in Junction City, Kans., 245 miles north of the bombing site, where eyewitnesses described two white men who rented the truck in question. The following day (Apr. 21), federal authorities arrested Timothy McVeigh, a 27-year-old army veteran said to be enraged over the federal raid on the Branch Davidian compound near Waco, Tex., exactly two years to the day before the Oklahoma City blast.

Ironically, McVeigh had been arrested by local authorities in Perry, Okla., less than two hours after the bombing, for driving a vehicle without license plates. Police found that he had a 9-millimeter pistol with "cop-killer" bullets, and detained him on a concealed weapons charge, but they had no idea McVeigh was being hunted by the FBI. Not until two days later, a mere 30 minutes before McVeigh was scheduled for release, did a routine Social Security number check reveal him to be one of the FBI's suspects in the bombing. So instead of being released on bail, McVeigh was handed over to the FBI. He refused to talk to federal investigators, who said they had no leads on the second suspect.

The same day (Apr. 21), federal agents in Michigan took into custody James and Terry Nichols, two farmers believed to be material witnesses in the case. But four days later (Apr. 25), the FBI charged both brothers with conspiring with McVeigh to build explosives from 1992 to 1995. The FBI did not immediately charge either Nichols brother for the Oklahoma City blast, however.

As the FBI and other federal agencies stepped up their pursuit of the bombers, emergency rescue crews toiled night and day through heavy rains, wind, and the very real possibility that the rest of the building might collapse, in hopes of finding survivors trapped in the rubble. After three days, they brought in heavy machinery to plow through the debris rather than combing through it by hand as they had been doing. On May 5, 17 days after the blast, the rescue workers gave up their search, with two bodies still buried in the rubble. Workers at the site turned a page by holding a memorial service signaling the end of hope and the beginning of healing from the bombing. Finally, on May 23 the remnants of the building were dynamited.

Other sectors of the government were also hard at work trying to prevent future such attacks.

(Continued)

Late Breaking News

THE NOBEL PRIZES, 1995

PEACE Joseph Rotblat (UK) Pugwash Conferences on Science and World Affairs. A Polish-born physicist who was a member of the Manhattan Project that created the first atomic bomb, Rotblat has spent the past 40 years campaigning to eliminate nuclear weapons. In giving the award to Rotblat, the Nobel Committee intended to send a message of protest to France and China for their continued nuclear weapons testing in the face of worldwide opposition.

PHYSIOLOGY AND MEDICINE Edward B. Lewis (U.S.) California Institute of Technology, **Eric F. Wieschaus** (U.S.) Princeton Univ., and **Christiane Nüsslein-Volhard** (Germany) Max-Planck Institute in Tübingen, for their discovery of how genes control structural development of the body. Their research, performed on fruit flies, helps explain birth defects in humans.

ECONOMIC SCIENCE Robert E. Lucas, Jr. (U.S.) Univ. of Chicago, "the economist who has had the greatest influence on macroeconomic research since 1970." His work challenges the Keynesian belief that the government is able to fine-tune the economy.

CHEMISTRY F. Sherwood Roland (U.S.) Univ. of California–Irvine, **Mario Molina** (U.S.) MIT, and **Paul Crutzen** (Netherlands) Max-Planck Institute for Chemistry in Mainz, Germany, for their pioneering work in explaining how production and use of refrigerants, plastic foams, aerosol propellants, and other chlorofluorocarbons deplete the ozone layer, thus increasing the risk of skin cancer, cataracts, and damage to human immune systems.

PHYSICS Martin L. Perl (U.S.) Stanford Univ. Linear Accelerator Center, and **Frederick Reines** (U.S.) Los Alamos National Laboratory, for their separate discoveries of "two of nature's most remarkable subatomic particles." Perl's discovery of the tau in the 1970s and Reines's discovery of the neutrino in the 1950s are watershed events in scientists' understanding of elementary particle physics.

LITERATURE Seamus Heaney (Ireland), poet and essayist, "for works of lyrical beauty and ethical depth, which exalt everyday miracles and the living past." His works include *Station Island, Lightenings viii, Death of a Naturalist,* and *Door Into the Dark.*

THE EMMY AWARDS, 1994–95

Outstanding Comedy Series: *Frasier* (NBC)
Outstanding Drama Series: *NYPD Blue* (ABC)
Outstanding Variety, Music, or Comedy Series: *The Tonight Show with Jay Leno* (NBC)
Outstanding Lead Actor in a Comedy Series: Kelsey Grammer, *Frasier* (NBC)
Outstanding Lead Actor in a Drama Series: Mandy Patinkin, *Chicago Hope* (CBS)
Outstanding Lead Actress in a Comedy Series: Candice Bergen, *Murphy Brown* (CBS)
Outstanding Lead Actress in a Drama Series: Kathy Baker, *Picket Fences* (CBS)

MTV VIDEO MUSIC AWARDS, 1995

Best video of the year: TLC, *Waterfalls*
Best male video: Tom Petty & the Heartbreakers, *You Don't Know How it Feels*
Best female video: Madonna, *Take a Bow*
Best group video: TLC, *Waterfalls*
Best new artist in a video: Hootie & the Blowfish, *Hold My Hand*
Best rap video: Dr. Dre, *Keep Their Heads Ringin*
Best alternative music video: Weezer, *Buddy Holly*

On Apr. 23, Pres. Clinton asked Congress to grant him broad powers to combat terrorism in the United States and to create a domestic antiterrorism force under the aegis of the FBI. On June 7, over the objections of civil liberties advocates who warned of a hysterical overreaction, the Senate sweepingly (91–8) approved an antiterrorism bill that gave the government broad powers to monitor the activities of suspected terrorists and to deport illegal aliens suspected of terrorism.

While the FBI continued to look for the second suspect in the blast, the government began to piece together its case against McVeigh and the Nichols brothers. They officially detained McVeigh on Apr. 27, citing an "indelible trail of evidence" linking him to the bombing. Terry Nichols was charged two weeks later with direct involvement in the bombing, as well as with aiding and abetting the attack, a sign that the government's case against him was not as strong as it was against McVeigh.

Finally, on Aug. 10, a federal grand jury indicted McVeigh and Nichols on 11 counts, three concerning the actual bombing and eight of murdering federal law enforcment officials. As promised, the government announced plans to seek the death penalty for the murder counts. A third man, Michael Fortier, an army buddy of both McVeigh and Terry Nichols, negotiated a plea bargain in which prosecutors agreed to a reduced charge in exchange for Fortier's testimony that he and McVeigh inspected the federal building as a bombing target several days before the blast. Fortier had previously told federal authorities that McVeigh had talked about plans to bomb the building months earlier when both men lived in Kingman, Ariz. He was expected to be the government's lead witness. The government dropped all charges against James Nichols.

On Aug. 15, McVeigh and Terry Nichols pled not guilty to all charges. Although the trial was not scheduled to begin until spring of 1996, defense lawyers succeeded in gaining a change of venue to Lawton, Okla., where potential jurors would be less personally influenced by the bombing.

O.J. Simpson Is Acquitted

In a decision that shocked millions of white Americans but that elated blacks around the country, the jury in the O.J. Simpson double murder trial on Oct. 3 found the former football star not guilty of murdering his ex-wife Nicole Brown Simpson and her friend Ronald Goldman. After a trial that lasted more than nine months, exhausted 126 witnesses, paraded 1,105 pieces of evidence, filled 45,000 pages of transcripts, and cost taxpayers an estimated $9 million, the jury took less than four hours to reach its verdict. The entire nation watched the verdict as it was broadcast live, but reactions were divided largely along racial lines. Blacks were more likely to believe the defense's contention that police planted evidence in an attempt to frame Simpson. Most whites, on the other hand, believed that a jury composed of eight black women, one black man, two white women, and a Hispanic man simply ignored an overwhelming amount of evidence implicating Simpson. Following is a summary of highlights from the so-called trial of the century.

December

8 After nearly six months of legal wrangling, a panel of 12 jurors and 12 alternates is finally selected. The composition of the jury will change several times throughout the trial, but will always remain mostly black and mostly female.

January

18 Judge Lance A. Ito allows the prosecution to introduce testimony about O.J. Simpson's attacks on and abusive treatment of his ex-wife, including the tape and transcript of a 911 call Nicole Brown Simpson made during one attack a mere eight months before she was killed.

24 Lead prosecutor Marcia Clark begins her opening argument, painting a picture of O.J. Simpson as a jealous, abusive, possessive husband who ultimately killed his ex-wife once she threatened to leave him for good.

25 In his opening statements, lead defense attorney Johnnie Cochran alleges a sloppy police investigation and hints at incidents of police misconduct and a "rush to judgment."

30 Judge Ito reprimands the defense for failing to reveal all of its witnesses before its opening arguments. Ito grants the prosecution the opportunity to revisit its opening argument; it is the first time any judge in California history has made such an extraordinary exception.

31 The prosecution plays the tape of Nicole Brown Simpson's frantic 911 call as O.J. Simpson was attacking her on New Year's Eve 1989.

February

1 Ronald G. Shipp, a longtime friend of O.J. Simpson, testifies that on the day after the murders of Ronald Goldman and Nicole Simpson, O.J. confided to him that he had dreamed of slaying his ex-wife.

3 Denise Brown testifies that O.J. Simpson once lifted her sister Nicole Brown Simpson and physically threw her against a wall and then tossed her out of their house.

March

9–10 Det. Mark Fuhrman, a key prosecution witness, testifies that the crime scene was well secured by other officers by the time he arrived, that he had a police chaperone with him at all times, and that another officer was the first to spot a bloody glove and knit cap implicating O.J. Simpson in the murders. The cap was later revealed to have fibers and hairs that matched Simpson's; the glove was later revealed to be a match for one found behind O.J. Simpson's estate.

13–16 The defense cross-examines Det. Mark Fuhrman, painting him as a racist cop obsessed with Nicole Brown Simpson and virulently opposed to interracial marriage. They suggest that Fuhrman picked up one of two bloody gloves at the crime scene, rubbed it around the Bronco, and then planted it behind O.J.'s house. Under repeated questioning, Fuhrman testifies that he has not used the word "nigger" in the past 10 years. He also admits that there was a short period in which he was alone at the crime scene, and a period of about 15 minutes in which he was investigating alone at O.J. Simpson's house during which he found the bloody right glove matching the one found at the crime scene.

17–21 Philip Vannatter, one of the two lead detectives in the case, testifies that the trail of blood from the crime scene to the Bronco to Simpson's home, plus a bandage on the middle finger of Simpson's left hand made O.J. a "very strong suspect." The prosecution plays a videotape of Vannatter making the drive between Nicole and O.J. Simpson's houses in under six minutes both ways to show that Simpson had plenty of time to commit the murders at around 10:45 P.M. and return home by 11:00 P.M. Vannatter also acknowledges he did not immediately book a sample of Simpson's blood, but instead carried it with him from police headquarters to Simpson's home, 20 miles away. Vannatter claims there was no time to book the blood, and that the criminologist was at Simpson's home.

22 O.J. Simpson's houseguest Brian (Kato) Kaelin testifies that he heard several loud thumps on the rear wall of the guest house on the night of the murders. He also testifies that he never saw Simpson return to his house after they went to McDonald's at 9:40 P.M., and that Simpson appeared not to be home at 11:00 P.M.

28 Allan Park, the limousine driver who picked up Simpson on the night of the murders, testifies that Simpson's Ford Bronco was not on the street and that Simpson did not answer when Park rang the bell at Simpson's estate at 10:22. He says he saw a black man enter Simpson's completely dark house at around 10:56 P.M. and turn on the lights. When Park buzzed again at 11:00, Simpson answered, said he had overslept, and that he would be down in a minute.

29 A skycap at Los Angeles International Airport testifies that O.J. Simpson checked only three bags on his flight to Chicago—the limousine driver said he had loaded four into the car—and that he saw Simpson near a trash can at the airport; the prosecution suggests that Simpson might have disposed of the bag of bloody clothes at the airport to discard evidence of his guilt in the murder.

April

3–4 The prosecution shifts its focus to the physical evidence from the crime scene. Dennis Fung, chief criminalist at the Los Angeles Police Dept., testifies how he and his assistant removed spots of blood from Simpson's Bronco, the ground near the car, the bloody glove found on the Simpson estate, and the bloody socks found in Simpson's bedroom. He testifies that all evidence was under lock and key by the time Det. Vannatter handed him a vial of Simpson's blood taken at police headquarters.

4 On cross-examination, defense attorney and DNA expert Barry Scheck plays a videotape of the criminalists' work at the murder scene, showing not Fung, but his assistant Andrea Mazzola, a trainee with little experience, picking up the bloody glove and the knit cap (without changing her latex gloves). In previous testimony to the grand jury, Fung claimed he himself had collected this evidence and never mentioned

Mazzola's existence. Scheck also attempts to show that Fung did not receive the vial of Simpson's blood on June 13, as he and Vannatter have claimed. Rather, Scheck asserts, Vannatter did not give Fung the blood until the following day, giving police time to spread the blood on the various pieces of evidence implicating Simpson in the murders.

7 Judge Lance Ito rejects a request by the defense to exclude DNA evidence linking Simpson to the murders.

14–18 Prosecutors attempt to rehabilitate Fung by trying to show that mistakes he might have made during evidence collection were innocent, minor, and did nothing to change the essential facts of the case.

26 On cross-examination, defense lawyer Peter Neufeld reminds evidence collector Andrea Mazzola of her earlier testimony that she never saw Vannatter hand the vial of Simpson's blood to Dennis Fung (as both men have testified) even though she accompanied Fung throughout the time they were at Simpson's house, when the exchange was said to have taken place. The defense seeks to use this information to prove that the police held onto Simpson's blood for a half day longer and sprinkled it on the Bronco, his socks, and on a glove found on the Simpson estate, all in an attempt to frame him.

May

10 Dr. Robin Cotton, a forensic expert in DNA evidence, testifies that there is a genetic match between the blood of O.J. Simpson and blood splotches found near the bodies. Cotton says there is a 1-in-9.7 billion chance that the blood stains on a sock found in Simpson's bedroom came from anybody else except Nicole Simpson.

16–18 Gary Sims, a California state forensic expert, testifies that the Bronco was splattered with Simpson's blood as well as the blood of his ex-wife and Ronald Goldman. He also testifies that blood on the glove found at O.J.'s house matches Goldman's. On cross-examination, he rejects all suggestions by defense lawyers that the DNA evidence was mishandled. Instead, he testifies that the state's rigorous testing methods make its results even more accurate than those cited by Dr. Robin Cotton's independent Cellmark Laboratories. Sims says there is only a 1-in-21 billion chance that blood found on O.J. Simpson's socks came from any white person besides Nicole Brown Simpson.

June

15 At the prosecution's request, O.J. Simpson tries on the bloody gloves, but claims they are "too tight." Legal experts say this is a devastating blow from which the prosecution may never recover.

27 A technician in the Los Angeles Police Department's special investigations unit testifies that hairs and fibers from the knit cap found near the bodies implicate Simpson in the murders.

July

6 After 92 days of testimony, the prosecution rests. Prosecutors called 58 witnesses, presented 488 exhibits, and ran the length of the trial's transcript to 34,500 pages.

11 A young couple on a blind date testify that they walked past Nicole Simpson's home at 10:25 P.M. on June 12 and saw nothing unusual at the site like bloody paw prints, nor did they hear sounds of a scuffle or dogs barking. A witness for the prosecution had testified that he heard the "plaintive wail" of Ms. Simpson's dog at around 10:15 or 10:20 P.M., suggesting that this was about the time the murders had occurred.

12 A defense witness testifies on cross-examination that he saw a white vehicle similar to a Bronco leaving the crime scene at around 10:40 P.M. on June 12.

17 Countering the defense's assertion that O.J. Simpson was too infirm from football injuries and arthritis to have committed the murders, the prosecution plays footage from an exercise video Simpson shot just two weeks beforehand, in which Simpson performs jumping jacks, push-ups, and other strenuous physical activities.

24–25 Fredric Rieders, a defense expert on forensic toxicology, testifies that blood found on the rear gate of Nicole Brown Simpson's house and on the sock found in O.J. Simpson's bedroom both contained a preservative not normally found in blood, thus suggesting that the blood had been planted. But the FBI agent who actually conducted the tests on the blood evidence contradicts this claim.

31 Blood splatter expert Herbert MacDonnell testifies the bloody sock discovered in O.J. Simpson's bedroom had Nicole Brown Simpson's blood on both sides, suggesting that the sock was not on a person's foot when it was stained, but lying flat, thus supporting the defense's theory that the blood was planted.

August

2 John Gerdes, a molecular biologist who examined the LAPD evidence investigation laboratory for the defense, testifies that the lab was riddled with chronic cases of cross-contamination. The defense uses the testimony to show that even if the police did not intentionally try to frame O.J. Simpson for the murders, their bungling and incompetence could produce the same botched result.

10 Dr. Michael Baden, a forensic pathologist for the defense, testifies that both murder victims put up a struggle. He says Ronald Goldman could have fought for "5, 10, or 15 minutes" after his jugular vein was cut. The defense hopes this testimony, which contradicts the claim by the prosecution and the L.A. coroner that the murders were quick surgical strikes, will demonstrate that O.J. Simpson did not have time to commit the murders.

23 Dr. Henry Lee, a criminalist from the Connecticut State Police and a nationally recognized expert, uses engaging blood-splatter demonstrations to show that blood had been rubbed onto the inside of one of the bloody socks, and had not seeped through from the outside. Lee also testifies for the defense that a series of imprints at the crime scene and on Ronald Goldman's jeans bolsters the defense's assertion of a second killer.

29 Laura Hart McKinny, a would-be screenwriter and college professor, testifies with the jury absent that Det. Mark Fuhrman repeatedly used the word "nigger" over the course of a series of taped interviews, contradicting Fuhrman's claim that he hadn't used the "n-word" in the past 10 years, and bolstering the defense's theory that Fuhrman is a racist who planted evidence.

31 After listening to McKinny's tapes, Ito rules that the jury may hear only two of the 41 tape-recorded instances in which Fuhrman refers to blacks as "niggers" and none of Fuhrman's remarks about how cops plant evidence when necessary.

September

6 With the jury absent, Fuhrman returns to the stand and invokes his Fifth Amendment right against self-incrimination rather than answer questions about whether he lied about his use of the word "nigger" in previous testimony. Ito rules that Fuhrman does not need to appear before the jury, which will not be told why Fuhrman did not testify.

26 Marcia Clark begins the prosecution's closing arguments by focusing the jury's attention on the 78 minutes during which O.J. Simpson could not account for his whereabouts on June 12. With exhaustive graphs and charts, Clark labors to show that Simpson was busy committing the two murders during this time. She then reminds the jury about the pieces of evidence that she says add up to prove Simpson's guilt: the injury to Simpson's hand, the knit cap with Simpson's hair and Ron Goldman's shirt fibers on it, the size-12 Bruno Magli shoeprints on the walkway, the DNA evidence, the blood in Simpson's Bronco, the bloody gloves, the bloody socks, and the blood in Simpson's bathroom.

27–28 In closing arguments for the defense, Johnnie Cochran repeatedly tells the jury: "If it [the prosecution's case] doesn't fit, you must acquit." Defense attorney Barry Scheck reminds the jury of the "contaminated, corrupted, and compromised" physical evidence presented by the prosecution. He tells the jury if they believe the police manufactured one piece of evidence—he cites the bloody socks—then they have to question every piece of evidence in the prosecution's case. Completing the defense's case, Cochran compares Mark Fuhrman to Adolf Hitler and then presents the jury and Marcia Clark with a list of 15 questions he says are unanswered by the prosecution's case. He urges the jury to "do the right thing," and "stop this coverup."

29 Marcia Clark completes her rebuttal argument by replaying the tape of Nicole Brown Simpson's 911 call to police just eight months before her murder. Finally, the case goes to the jury.

October

3 After deliberating for less than four hours, the jury returns a verdict of not guilty on both counts. Jurors interviewed after the verdict indicate that they believed the defense's contention that the police planted evidence to frame Simpson. This was all the "reasonable doubt" they needed to find Simpson not guilty.

Newt Gingrich Leads the Republican Takeover of Congress

After 40 years of wandering in a political desert where Democrats treated their opinions with disdain and their mere existence as an occasional nuisance, Republicans across the country scored one of the most sweeping political victories in U.S. history. On Nov. 8, 1994, the Republicans gained control of both houses of Congress for the first time since the Eisenhower administration.

The victory was so widespread that no sitting Republican governor, senator, or representative was defeated. Voters threw out Democratic governors in New York and Texas and 10 other states, while Tennessee went from having two Democratic senators to two Republicans overnight. Virginia's Chuck Robb barely survived a challenge from Iran-Contra conspirator Oliver North, even though several prominent leaders from North's own party repudiated his candidacy. Even House Speaker Tom Foley lost his seat. In all, Republicans increased their numbers by eight in the Senate (from 44 to 52) and by 52 (from 178 to 230) in the House. After the election, Democratic senators Richard Shelby (Ala.) and Ben Nighthorse Campbell (Colo.) switched parties, as did three Democrats in the House.

Although only 85 million people (less than half of the voting age population) actually cast ballots, Republican leaders quickly claimed a powerful mandate from the people to shrink the size of the government by dismantling much of the social legislation passed since the 1960s. Led by new Speaker Newt Gingrich (R-Ga.), House Republicans immediately set out to pass as many items in the now famous "Contract With America" *(see box)* as possible during the first 100 days of the new Congress.

Early in the year, the two least controversial items in the contract—Congressional Accountability and unfunded mandates—were quickly passed by both the House and Senate and signed by Pres. Clinton. It should be noted that part of the Congressional Accountability Act (holding Congress accountable to the same laws, especially equal opportunity laws, that it passes for the rest of the country) had already been passed by the Democratic-controlled Congress several years earlier. Moreover, a close look at the unfunded mandates provision reveals that Congress left itself a few loopholes to pass an unfunded mandate whenever it thinks necessary.

Throughout the winter and spring, Gingrich and his followers raced through the provisions of the contract, passing a balanced budget amendment to the Constitution, a sweeping package of antiregulatory measures that would prevent the federal government from enforcing environmental, health, and safety laws such as the Clean Air Act and the Clean Water Act, a new crime bill, and an overhaul of the welfare system that included dramatic cuts to the food stamp program. The only major setback in the House came over term limits, when four separate proposals went down to defeat, primarily at the hands of entrenched Republicans who had been there for many years (Mar. 29). Even Gingrich himself seemed less enthusiastic about this idea than most of the other provisions of the contract.

The euphoria in the House began to diminish when the Republcan-controlled Senate defeated the balanced-budget amendment (Mar. 2), and the plan to change the rules in civil litigation by limiting civil damage awards. (Pres. Clinton had threatened a veto and had garnered public support by labeling the Republican bill "The Drunk Driver Protection Act.")

But on May 25, the Senate did sign off on the most important element of the House plan: a bill to eliminate the federal deficit by 2002 through spending cuts of $1.1 trillion while simultaneously enacting tax cuts. The Senate's proposed tax reduction was far more judicious than the $354 billion cut proposed by the House, but the idea of major tax cuts during a time of fiscal austerity carried political risks, forcing the House and Senate leadership to settle on a less ambitious cut of $245 billion.

The Budget Battle When Congress returned in September, the battle over spending cuts was immediately engaged as all the major congressional committees—Appropriations, Finance, Ways and Means—fought over allocations for almost every government program. Only the enormous defense budget ($243 billion) went unchallenged; in fact, the Republicans added $7 bil. more than the Pentagon requested, despite the fact that there seemed to be no serious military threat to the U.S. from anywhere in the world.

By the middle of October, the only other major legislation passed by both houses of Congress concerned the restructuring of the welfare system. The House passed its bill, largely along party lines, in late March, promising to cut $102 billion from the welfare program over seven years. The Senate waited until Sept. 19 to pass its version, but it did so with much more bipartisan support (87–12), albeit less savings ($65 billion) than its House counterpart. Like the House bill, the Senate plan would require welfare recipients to work after two years of assistance, but it would give the states more leeway in allocating benefits to unwed teenage mothers and women who have more children while on welfare. Both plans propose simple block grants to the states, which would then be free to dispense the money in any way they thought best. Pres. Clinton indicated that he would be likely to sign a final bill that resembles the less harsh Senate plan, but that he would veto it if in conference it "moves in any way toward the original House position."

Surprisingly, another place the GOP sought savings was Medicare, long considered politically untouchable because of the voting power wielded by the elderly population the program serves. Nevertheless, Republicans in the House pledged to cut $270 billion (14 percent) from the Medicare budget over the next seven years. Although the Republicans insisted they were simply trying to save Medicare from insolvency, the Democrats made this the central issue in the fierce battle over the budget. Many criticized the plan as long on rhetoric, but short on details about where the savings would come from. Pres. Clinton pledged to veto the bill less than 24 hours after it was announced; Democrats in the House asserted that the $270 billion was how the GOP planned to pay for its $245 billion tax cut; and Senate Democrats offered their own $89 billion overhaul, which would keep Medicare solvent through 2006.

On Oct. 19, Gingrich and his followers led the House in what would be the most significant vote of the year, as they made the first major cuts to Medicare. Whether the Senate would follow was harder to predict.

Newt Gingrich The most dramatic political development of the year was the emergence of Newt Gingrich as the titular head of the Republican party. For good or ill, he was driving the new agenda relentlessly. How Senate Majority Leader Bob Dole countered this impression, either through compromise with the president or confrontation with Gingrich, would directly affect his presidential bid. In either case, Gingrich couldn't lose, and let it be known he might make his own presidential bid.

Gingrich had planned his ascendancy for a number of years. He had won the support of many Republican members because of his organizing skill and because his political action commitee, GOPAC, provided campaign funds for Republicans seeking reelection and for GOP candidates who had a good chance of unseating Democrats. After the election, he used his new power as Speaker to stifle opposition in the influential committees by overturning the seniority system and appointing his loyal followers—including John Kasich (R-Ohio), William Archer (R-Tex.), and Robert Livingston (R-La.)—to powerful positions on the major funding committees. If Gingrich doesn't run himself in 1996, he will still be a powerful force in the election. In either case, he will most likely be a key issue in the campaign.

Election Issues, 1996

In the last five presidential elections, only one incumbent, Ronald Reagan, won reelection. For Bill Clinton to avoid the same fate as Ford, Carter, and Bush, he must position himself as the mainstream candidate, the one solidly in touch with the views of most Americans. So it is entirely possible that the Republican takeover will work to his advantage. Throughout 1995, the Republicans dominated the political news, in large part because they attempted to transform their electoral victory into an ideological one. By trying to recast radically the role of government that had evolved over 30 years in a few legislative sessions, they have disturbed many important sectors of the electorate, including senior citizens, environmentalists, and teachers.

So the most important issue of 1996 will most likely be the Republicans themselves. With their newly won power, will they show themselves able to govern? When Pres. Clinton, as is his custom, makes concessions, offers compromises, and generally gives the impression he cares more about the welfare of the nation than partisan politics, will the radical parts of the Republican party be able to do the same? Obviously, the eventual Republican nominee will determine the course of the campaign and the issues to be addressed, but the broad outlines of the coming campaign can be drawn. Below are several issues that will play a key role throughout 1996.

Abortion Unless the Republicans nominate Colin Powell, their candidate will be bound to take a strong antiabortion position, one that hurt them in 1992 as Clinton kept a firm pro-choice stance.

The economy Clinton will be in the odd position of claiming credit for the strong economy (low unemployment and inflation) while attacking the erosion of middle-class incomes. He will most likely gain labor's support by arguing for a higher minimum wage and by calling for a ban on replacement workers.

The environment During the last weeks of 1995, Republican moderates in Congress were working to stop leadership proposals that would effectively halt governmental regulation of the environment. If they fail, Democrats will make this a key issue.

Foreign policy Despite Republican sniping, Clinton will claim several major achievements, including Haiti, the Middle East peace, and continued good relations with Russia and Ukraine. Clinton can also point to progress in international trade (especially with China, the p.r. victory over Japan, and the passage of NAFTA). Only a false step in the use of troops in Bosnia could hurt him.

Medicare This could become the most important issue of the campaign. No matter what kind of bill emerges from the 1995 debate, the Republicans will have to answer to a politically powerful audience—the elderly population—for their decision to cut one of the nation's most successful programs.

Other important issues—welfare, tax cuts, the balanced budget, and crime—will be less critical because both sides have essentially agreed on them with only small variations in the details. Others such as Whitewater and Gingrich's problems before the House Ethics Committee will be playing out over the year.

The blueprint for the Republican revolution of 1994 was the* Contract With America, *a document first published in* TV Guide, *and later signed with great fanfare by 367 GOP candidates for House seats. It is reprinted here.

Contract With America

As Republican Members of the House of Representatives and as citizens seeking to join that body we propose not just to change its policies, but even more important, to restore the bonds of trust between the people and their elected representatives. That is why, in this era of official evasion and posturing, we offer instead a detailed agenda for national renewal, a written commitment with no fine print. This year's election offers the chance, after four decades of one-party control, to bring to the House a new majority that will transform the way Congress works. That historic change would be the end of government that is too big, too intrusive, and too easy with the public's money. It can be the beginning of a Congress that respects the values and shares the faith of the American family.

Like Lincoln, our first Republican president, we intend to act "with firmness in the right, as God gives us to see the right." To restore accountability to Congress. To end its cycle of scandal and disgrace. To make us all proud again of the way free people govern themselves.

On the first day of the 104th Congress, the new Republican majority will immediately pass the following major reforms, aimed at restoring the faith and trust of the American people in their government:

First, require all laws that apply to the rest of the country also apply equally in Congress;

Second, select a major, independent auditing firm to conduct a comprehensive audit of Congress for waste, fraud, or abuse;

Third, cut the number of house committees, and cut committee staff by one-third;

Fourth, limit the terms of all committee chairs;

Fifth, ban the casting of proxy votes in committee;

Sixth, require committee meetings to be open to the public;

Seventh, require a three-fifths majority vote to pass a tax increase;

Eighth, guarantee an honest accounting of our federal budget by implementing zero baseline budgeting.

Thereafter, within the first one hundred days of the 104th Congress, we shall bring to the House Floor the following bills, each to be given full and open debate, each to be given a clear and fair vote, and each to be immediately available this day for public inspection and scrutiny.

1. The Fiscal Responsibility Act. A balanced budget/tax limitation amendment and a legislative line-item veto to restore fiscal responsibility to an out-of-control Congress, requiring them to live under the same budget constraints as families and businesses.

2. The Taking Back Our Streets Act. An anti-crime package including stronger truth-in-sentencing, "good faith" exclusionary rule exemptions, effective death penalty provisions, and cuts in social spending from this summer's crime bill to fund prison construction and additional law enforcement to keep people secure in their neighborhoods and kids safe in their schools.

3. The Personal Responsibility Act. Discourage illegitimacy and teen pregnancy by prohibiting welfare to minor mothers and denying increased AFDC (Aid to Families with Dependent Children) for additional children while on welfare, cut spending for welfare programs, and enact a tough two-years-and-out provision with work requirements to promote individual responsibility.

4. The Family Reinforcement Act. Child support enforcement, tax incentives for adoption, strengthening rights of parents in their child's education, stronger child pornography laws, and an elderly-dependent-care tax credit to reinforce the central role of families in American society.

5. The American Dream Restoration Act. A $500-per-child-tax credit, begin repeal of the marriage tax penalty, and creation of American Dream Savings Accounts to provide middle-class tax relief.

6. The National Security Restoration Act. No U.S. troops under UN command and restoration of the essential parts of our national security funding to strengthen our national defense and maintain our credibility around the world.

7. The Senior Citizens Fairness Act. Raise the Social Security earnings limit, which currently forces seniors out of the work force, repeal the 1993 tax hikes on Social Security benefits, and provide tax incentives for private long-term-care insurance to let older Americans keep more of what they have earned over the years.

8. The Job Creation and Wage Enhancement Act. Small business incentives, capital gains cut and indexation, neutral cost recovery, risk assessment/cost-benefit analysis, strengthening of the Regulatory Flexibility Act and unfunded mandate reform to create jobs and raise worker wages.

9. The Common Sense Legal Reform Act. "Loser pays" laws, reasonable limits on punitive damages, and reform of product liability laws to stem the endless tide of litigation.

10. The Citizen Legislature Act. A first-ever vote on term limits to replace career politicians with citizen legislators.

Further, we will instruct the House Budget Committee to report to the floor and we will work to enact additional budget savings, beyond the budget cuts specifically included in the legislation described above, to ensure that the federal budget deficit will be less than it would have been without the enactment of these bills.

Respecting the judgment of our fellow citizens as we seek their mandate for reform, we hereby pledge our names to this Contract With America.

Russia Subdues Chechnya

Russia's four-year-long dispute with Chechnya over the republic's independence came to a head at the end of 1994 as Russian president Boris Yeltsin finally decided to use military force to bring the breakaway region back into the fold, and to discourage other republics from seeking independence from Russia. In the process, Yeltsin risked the wrath of leading western nations, which disapproved of a military solution, and was forced back to the bargaining table when a group of Chechen rebel commandoes humiliated him by seizing a Russian hospital.

The dispute began back in 1991, shortly after the coup that sparked the breakup of the Soviet Union. Under the leadership of Dzhokar Dudayev, a former Soviet Air Force general, Chechnya declared its own independence, sparking civil war in the region. Three years of negotiations, threats, and even sporadic military flareups did not resolve the conflict, so on Dec. 11, 1994, Yeltsin sent 40,000 Russian troops and tanks to Chechnya to quell the secessionist movement and maintain Russia's territorial integrity.

Initially reluctant to press the invasion for fear of killing civilians, the military did not begin a full-scale assault on the capital city of Grozny until Dec. 31, after peace talks, threats, and even isolated bombing raids proved fruitless. The assault resulted in heavy civilian casualties, leaving the streets littered with hundreds of dead bodies, and drawing the ire of the U.S. and several prominent European nations, which had previously regarded the dispute as an internal Russian affair. German chancellor Helmut Kohl went so far as to refer to the Russian army's "unparalleled brutality."

The assault also drew criticism at home. Yeltsin's enemies in both the Russian Parliament and the military opposed the invasion openly. But the government was determined to wage the war to a successful conclusion.

By Jan. 19, 1995, the Russian troops had captured the Presidential Palace and controlled most of the capital. Yeltsin declared the war over, and used the opportunity to oust four senior defense ministry officials with whom he had disagreed. Nevertheless, fighting continued intermittently throughout the winter and spring, with Russian troops seemingly content to win a battle of attrition. By April, Russia controlled all of Chechnya's urban centers, with the rebels fleeing to the Caucasus.

What looked like a Russian victory was suddenly altered, however, on June 14, when Chechen rebels stormed across the border into the Russian town of Budyonnovsk, shooting civilians, taking more than 2,000 hostages (and shooting some of them as well), and seizing a hospital complex. Yeltsin again attempted to resolve the situation by military means, again was unsuccessful, and again drew stern warnings from the leaders of the seven major industrialized nations. Only delicate negotiations by Russian prime minister Viktor Chernomyrdin avoided further bloodshed. With almost all of their demands met, the commandoes returned to Chechnya and released the remaining hostages. The defeat was particularly humbling to the Russian government, especially Yeltsin, and it hurried Russia to the bargaining table.

After six weeks of negotiations, the two sides finally reached an agreement on July 30. The accord called for an immediate end to the fighting, the withdrawal of Russian troops from Chechnya, the disarmament of the Chechen soldiers, and an exchange of prisoners. From his mountain hideout in the southwest, Chechen president Dudayev at first rejected the agreement, but reversed himself on Aug. 2, approving the truce and ordering Chechen soldiers to cease fighting. Skirmishes nonetheless continued for two more weeks until Yeltsin threatened to resume military action to compel the Chechen soldiers to lay down their arms.

What the truce failed to address at all, however, was the question that started the civil war in the first place: Chechnya's independence. Something short of complete independence (with separate foreign and military policies) might prove acceptable to both sides. But it would have to include a Chechen flag and legislature and freedom from the Russian draft. Both sides were looking to elections in Chechnya by early November 1995.

Japan's Most Difficult Year

In addition to marking the 50th anniversary of Japan's defeat in World War II, 1995 will be remembered as one of the most difficult years in recent Japanese history. The assaults on the far eastern nation came from the United States, from religious cult leaders within the country's borders, and from mother nature herself.

The natural disaster was the first chronologically and perhaps the most crippling. A massive earthquake measuring 7.2 on the Richter scale ripped through the port city of Kobe, sixth largest in Japan, just before 6 A.M. on Jan. 17. More than 5,000 people were killed throughout the region of Kansai, making it the deadliest earthquake in Japan since 1923. An additional 300,000 people (15 percent of the city's population) were left homeless as more than 1,000 buildings collapsed. A million people were left without water, and hundreds of thousands had no electricity or gas. Over 30,000 buildings were damaged, at a cost of more than $100 billion. Entire sections of highways, including the Hanshin Expressway between Osaka and Kobe, fell over on their sides. Long stretches of rail lines for the country's "bullet trains" were destroyed. Fortunately, no tsunamis or giant tidal waves followed the tremor and its aftershocks, as often happens with earthquakes around Japan.

Kobe had been a major port on the Osaka Bay, handling about one-eighth of Japan's export trade. It was also a center for many multinational conglomerates. In an emergency session, the Japanese cabinet set aside more than $1 billion to fund aid and the initial recovery work. The serious damage to structures both old and new (and purportedly earthquake resistant) raised questions about Japan's preparedness for a major earthquake. Many critics complained that the government had grown complacent in recent years as the earthquake-prone country had not been hit by a major quake in some time.

Just two months later, on Mar. 20, the capital city of Tokyo was jarred by a deadly terrorist nerve gas attack on a main interchange of the city's subway system (Mar. 21). Twelve people were killed and more than 5,000 commuters were injured by the morning rush-hour attack, in which open canisters leaked the deadly nerve gas sarin on five separate cars on three subway lines. Cleanup crews decontaminated the area within a day and by the following morning, service had been restored on the entire subway system.

Two days after the attack, police raided the offices of the religious sect known as Aum Shinrikyo, which had been linked to the production of sarin in the past. The raid proved successful in discovering more than two tons of chemicals that could be used to produce sarin, as well as more than $7 million in cash and 22 pounds of gold ingots. But police were unable to apprehend the group's leader Shoko Asahara, who went into hiding immediately after the attack.

It wasn't until May 16 that the Japanese police finally nabbed Asahara, whom they found in a secret chamber between two floors of a building in the cult's compound in Kamikuishiki, some 100 miles from Tokyo. They charged him and 40 other cult members with murder for their participation in the attack; they also named all 41 as chief suspects in a June 1994 incident in which seven people died and 200 were injured in a sarin attack on the city of Matsumoto.

The third jolt was of a more predictable nature. On May 10, 20 months of trade negotiations between Japan and the U.S. broke off with Japan continuing to refuse to open its automobile and auto parts markets to U.S. imports. Citing Japan's intransigence in helping to reduce the U.S.'s record $12 billion trade deficit, U.S. Trade Rep. Mickey Kantor filed a grievance with the newly formed World Trade Organization. On May 16, the same day police captured Asahara, the U.S. announced that it would impose a 100 percent tariff on imports of 13 models of luxury Japanese automobiles if Japan did not settle the trade dispute by June 28.

Hours before the tariff was scheduled to take effect, the two countries agreed on a vaguely worded accord in which Japanese automakers agreed to adopt "voluntary plans" to increase purchases of U.S. auto parts and to expand the number of dealerships selling American cars. In exchange, the U.S. agreed not to impose trade quotas on Japan. In addition, the Japanese government agreed to loosen regulations that had unfairly burdened U.S. auto parts makers trying to sell replacement parts to Japanese repair shops. The Clinton administration estimated that the nonbinding agreement would add $9 billion to U.S. auto sales over the next three years, though Japan disputed the specific numbers. The primary beneficiaries would be U.S. plants of Japanese auto companies, which would increase their exports of cars and parts back to Japan.

Civil War in the Balkans: Year Five

Just as it appeared that the situation in Bosnia was improving, the reentry of Croatia into the conflict during the spring of 1995 inflamed the fighting and further muddied the Balkan waters. But Croatia's reappearance in the ongoing conflict may prove to be the development that helps speed the five-year-long civil war to a peaceful conclusion.

Thanks in part to the efforts of former U.S. president Jimmy Carter, who visited Sarajevo in December 1994 and helped to broker a cease-fire, the new year opened with circumstances "promising for peace negotiations," according to Sir Michael Rose, UN commander in Bosnia. Shuttling between Sarajevo and Pale, Rose had negotiated a complete cessation of hostilities between the government of Bosnia and Radovan Karadzik's "Bosnian Serb Republic," to last for the first four months of the year. It was the Bosnians, not the Serbs, who broke the truce on Mar. 20 with offensives against Serbian troop concentrations near Tuzla and Travnik, provoking Serbian retaliation against the UN-designated "safe areas" of Tuzla, Gorazde, and Sarajevo, retaliation that brought the threat of UN air strikes against the Serbs. With Croatian assistance, Bosnia captured Mount Vlasik near Travnik on Apr. 5, while the level of hostilities swelled at all the Muslim enclaves of eastern Bosnia.

Serious doubt was cast on the UN's continued presence in Bosnia when Croatian president Franjo Tudjman announced in April that all 12,000 UN peacekeepers in Croatia would have to leave by the end of June. By serving as a buffer between the Croatian and Bosnian Serb armies, the UN appeared to be establishing a virtual border, a border that Croatia did not recognize. But if the peacekeepers left Croatia, the "blue helmets" still in Bosnia would then be left in an untenable position. Under pressure from U.S. vice president Al Gore, Tudjman agreed to a new UN mandate for 5,000 troops to patrol "international borders"—i.e., not the de facto border they were currently policing—a significant harbinger of what was to come in August.

On May 1, a new front opened as Croatia hurled 3,000 troops across UN lines into western Slavonia, recapturing 200 square miles from the Serbs. By the end of the month, NATO air strikes were hitting weapons depots near Pale. In response, the Bosnian Serbs seized hundreds of "blue helmets," holding them as hostages and chaining them to poles to serve as human shields against further air attacks. The air strikes stopped almost immediately, and by mid-June, all the hostages had been released. The seizing of hostages seemed the desperate act of a cornered people, and the second half of June saw a new Bosnian government offensive to break the siege of Sarajevo.

But the tide of battle suddenly turned in July. Serbian troops of General Ratko Mladic attacked the UN-designated "safe area" of Srebrenica on July 6 and easily took the town. Although outnumbered by about three to one by the town's Muslim defenders, the Serbs were better armed. About 30,000 Muslims were driven out as refugees to Tuzla. On July 19, Zepa, another safe area, fell to the Serbs and was put to the torch. On the 25th, the Serbs began a major offensive against Bihac, one of the last four Muslim enclaves in eastern Bosnia. Momentum was now with the Serbs; UN and NATO blustering about "overwhelming" air strikes seemed the loud talk that would precede withdrawal.

Just as Serbian forces appeared to be on the brink of a decisive victory, Croatia, on Aug. 4, suddenly reopened the war against the Serbs in its region called Krajina. The Croatian army swept with lightning speed along a 700-mile front, destroying and scattering the Serbian forces and conquering in just three days the entire 3,500-square-mile region that had been lost in 1991. The "Serbian Republic of Krajina" was destroyed, its capital of Knin captured. The Croat assault drove 150,000 Serbs fleeing headlong into Bosnia and Serbia in an "ethnic cleansing," which undid the Serbian "ethnic cleansing" of 1991. The victory dramatically tipped the balance in the entire territory of the former Yugoslavia. The effect on the Serbs of Bosnia was devastating, for Pres. Milosevic of Serbia lifted not a finger to save Krajina.

By the end of August, a sufficient number of secret diplomatic agreements had most likely been agreed to so that when the Bosnian Serb army shelled Sarajevo (Aug. 28) killing 37 civilians and wounding 80, NATO planes, led by the U.S., immediately launched several days of intense bombing of Serb military positions; several Tomahawk missiles were also fired at them. On Aug. 31, chief U.S. negotiator Richard Holbrooke announced that the Bosnian Serbs agreed to follow the decisions of Yugoslavia's president Slobodan Milosevic in all peace talks.

In early September, in Geneva, Holbrooke brokered an accord on the fate of Bosnia that kept its borders intact theoretically, but divided it into two statelets (the accord calls them nothing more precise than "entities"), one of the Bosnian Serbs, the other of a Croat-Muslim federation. On Sept. 26, at the UN, the foreign ministers of Bosnia, Croatia, and the Serb-dominated Yugoslavia solidified that agreement but Bosnian and Croatian forces continued to attack the Serbs, driving them from the areas they had won earlier. A cease-fire was finally agreed to (Oct. 5) by the three major parties, although few observers were seriously optimistic about its chances of holding.

Intense fighting did continue in the days leading up to the effective date of the cease-fire (Oct. 12), as all sides—Muslims, Serbs, and Croats—attempted to expand their territorial holdings before the peace conference began. Skeptics were not surprised when western officials presented evidence (Oct. 19) that thousands of Muslims had been killed during the previous week, most likely by Serb paramilitary groups.

NEW NATIONS FROM THE FORMER YUGOSLAVIA

Note: Population statistics do not reflect the refugee problem throughout these new nations. Reliable economic statistics for every country are not available at this time, so general economic descriptions are given.

Bosnia and Herzegovina

Republic of Bosnia and Herzegovina

Geography Location: southeastern Europe. **Boundaries:** Croatia to N, S, W, Yugoslavia to E and SE, Adriatic Sea to S. **Total land area:** 19,776 sq. mi. (51,233 sq km). **Coastline:** 13 mi. (20 km). **Comparative area:** Slightly larger than Tennessee. **Land use:** 36% forest and woodland, 25% meadows and pastures, 20% arable land, 2% permanent crops, 17% other. **Major cities:** *Bosnia:* (1991) Sarajevo (capital) 525,980, Banja Luka 195,139. *Herzegovina:* (1991) Mostar 126,067.

People Population: 4,651,485 (July 1994 est.). **Nationality:** noun—Bosnian(s); adjective—Bosnian; noun—Herzegovine(s) or Herzegovinian(s); adjective—Herzegovine or Herzegovinian. **Ethnic groups:** 44% Bosnian, 31% Serb, 17% Croat, 8% other. **Languages:** Serbo-Croatian. **Religions:** 40% Muslim, 31% Orthodox, 15% Catholic, 4% Protestant, 10% other.

Government Type: emerging democracy. **Independence:** Mar. 1, 1992, popular referendum overwhelmingly approved independence. On Mar. 18, 1992, ethnic leaders met and agreed to secede from Yugoslavia. Recognized as independent state by European Community Apr. 6 and by U.S. Apr. 8, 1992. **Constitution:** being drafted. **National holiday:** N.A. **Heads of government:** Dr. Alija Izetbegovic, president (since Dec. 1990); Haris Silajdzic, prime minister (since Oct. 1993). **Structure:** executive—collective presidency, prime minister, cabinet; legislative—bicameral National Assembly with upper house (Chamber of Municipalities) and lower house (Chamber of Citizens); judicial—Supreme Court, Constitutional Court.

Economy Monetary unit: Yugoslavian dinar (Croatian dinar used in Croat areas). **Budget:** N.A. ***income:*** N.A. ***expend.:*** N.A. **GDP:** $14 bil. (1991); $3,200 per capita. Chief crops: corn, wheat, potatoes, plums, tobacco. **Livestock:** sheep, cattle, chicken, pigs. **Natural resources:** coal, iron, bauxite, manganese, timber, wood products, copper, chromium, lead, zinc. **Major industries:** steel production, mining, manufacturing, armaments, aircraft assembly, oil refining. **Labor force:** 1,026,254 (1991 est.) 45% mining, 45% industries, 2% agriculture. **Exports:** $2.054 mil. (1990); 31% manufactured goods, 20.8% machinery and transport equipment, 18% raw materials, 17.3% manufactured articles. **Imports:** $1,891 mil. (1990); 32% fuels and lubricants, 23.3% machinery and transport equipment, 21.3% other manufactures, 10% chemicals, 6.7% raw materials, 5.5% food and live animals. **Major trading partners:** Other former Yugoslav republics.

Intl. Orgs. CEI, ECE, OSCE, UN, UNCTAD, UNESCO, WHO.

Croatia

Republic of Croatia

Geography Location: southeastern Europe. **Boundaries:** Slovenia and Hungary to N, Yugoslavia and Bosnia and Herzegovina to E, Adriatic Sea to S, Slovenia to W. **Total land area:** 21,824 sq. mi. (56,538 sq km). **Coastline:** 1,105 mi. (1,778 km). **Comparative area:** Slightly smaller than West Virginia. **Land use:** 36% arable land, 20% permanent crops, 18% meadows and pastures, 15% forest and woodland, 10% other. **Major cities:** (1991 census) Zagreb (capital) 708,770; Split 189,388; Rijeka 167,064; Osijek 104,761; Zadar 76,343.

People Population: 4,697,614 (July 1994 est.). **Nationality:** noun—Croat(s); adjective—Croatian. **Ethnic groups:** 78% Croat, 12% Serb, 0.9% Muslim, 0.5% Hungarian, 0.5% Slovenian, 8.1% other. **Languages:** Serbo-Croatian. **Religions:** 76.5% Catholic, 11.1% Orthodox, 1.4% Protestant, 1.2% Slavic Muslim, 9.8% other.

Government Type: parliamentary democracy. **Independence:** Assembly (Parliament) declared itself in the process of "dissociation" on May 30, 1990 (from Yugoslavia). Seceded on Oct. 8, 1991. Recognized as independent state by Germany Dec. 23, 1991, and by European Community Jan. 15, 1992. **Constitution:** Dec. 22, 1990. **National holiday:** Independence Day, May 30. **Heads of government:** Dr. Franjo Tudjman, president (since May 1990); Nikica Valntic, prime minister (since Apr. 1993). **Structure:** executive—president, prime minister, cabinet; legislative—bicameral Assembly (sabor) of upper House of Districts and lower House of Representatives; judicial—Supreme Court, Constitutional Court.

Economy Monetary unit: Croatian dinar. **Budget:** N.A. ***income:*** N.A. ***expend.:*** N.A. **GDP:** $21.8 bil. (1992 est.); $4,500 per capita. **Chief crops:** corn, wheat, sugar beets, sunflowers, alfalfa, olives, citrus fruits, vegetables. **Livestock:** dairy cattle. **Natural resources:** oil, coal, bauxite, low-grade iron ore, calcium, silica, mica, clays, salt. **Major industries:** chemicals and plastics, machine tools, fabricated metal, electronics, pig iron, textiles, shipbuilding, petroleum and petroleum refining, food processing, and beverages. **Labor force:** 1,509,489 (1991 est.) 37% industry and mining, 16% agriculture. **Exports:** $3.9 bil. (f.o.b., 1990); 30% machinery and transport equipment, 37% other manufacturers, 11% chemicals, 9% food and live animals, 6.5% raw materials, 5% fuels and lubricants. **Imports:** $4.7 bil. (c.i.f., 1993); 21% machinery and transport equipment, 19% fuels and lubricants, 16% food and live animals, 14% chemicals, 13% manufactured foods. **Major trading partners:** EU countries, Slovenia, other former Yugoslav republics, republics of former Soviet Union.

Intl. Orgs. CEI, ECE, IBRD, ICAO, IMF, IMO, INTELSAT, INTERPOL, OSCE, UN, UNCTAD, UNESCO, UPU, WHO, WIPO, WMO.

Croatia is one of Europe's most ancient states, King Tomaslav having created an independent Catholic realm in 924. In the sixth century the Croats, led by their eponymous chieftain Chrovatos, had migrated to the old Roman province of Illyricum, south of the Danube, where they dwelt in practical independence of the Byzantine Empire. Pope Gregory VII sent a papal crown, and therewith international recognition, to King Zvonimir (1076–89), but the king's death spelt the demise of the native dynasty. In 1102 Hungary's king Kalman was recognized as king of Croatia as well, in a dynastic union in which Croatia retained its own nobility and institutions. From the 14th century, Croatia (along with Hungary and Serbia) formed Europe's bulwark against the Ottoman Empire. After the Turkish victory at Mohacs (1526), the Hungarian and Croatian crowns were added to the Habsburg dynasty. Escaping Turkish sway, Croatia became controlled by Austrian military authorities as the frontier district against the Ottomans.

With the proclamation of the Austrian Empire in 1804, amalgamating the Habsburg possessions into one unified state, the estates of Croatia resisted the royal absolutism, stressing their autonomous status and ties to the Hungarian kingdom, but to slight avail, even after the Croat army of Baron Josip Jellacid proved essential in suppressing the Hungarian revolt of 1848. However, after the 1867 Ausleich ("compromise"), which established a practically independent Hungary within the Dual Monarchy, a further compromise (Nagoda) in the following year recognized Croatian autonomy within the Hungarian realm.

When the Habsburg monarchy collapsed during World War I, Croatia joined the new Yugoslavia, but since that state proved to be no federation but rather a greater Serbia, Croatia resisted Serbian dominance. And after the ferocious ethnic hostility provoked a royal dictatorship in 1929, Ante Pavelic formed the Ustase, a terrorist organization similar to and having ties with the Macedonian IMRO, with the aim of attaining Croatian independence. Just a week before the outbreak of World War II, Croatia was again granted autonomy, but it was too late. With Hitler's 1941 conquest and dismemberment of Yugoslavia, an "Independent Croat State" was established under Italian protection. While Aimone, Duke of Spoleto was proclaimed king of Croatia under the preposterous name of Tomaslov II, he had the good sense never to enter "his" kingdom, whose governance was left to Pavelic and the Ustase. An "ethnic cleansing" of Croatia commenced, in which perhaps 100,000 Serbs and Jews lost their lives. Since the "chetniks" of Gen. Mihajlovic were Serbs and royalists, anti-Ustase Croats had nowhere to turn but to the Communist "partisans" of Tito (himself a Croat). Postwar vengeance against Tito's enemies, especially the Ustase, was severe but short-lived and Croatia in 1946 became one of the "republics" of the reconstituted Yugoslavia.

The old ethnic hatred, papered over during the Tito years and even in the decade following the dictator's death under "collegial" Communist party rule, erupted again after 1989. In June 1991 Croatia seceded from Yugoslavia, precipitating the many-sided civil war which continues to this day, even as Serbs and Croats war against each other while cooperating in the partitioning of Bosnia.

Slovenia

Republic of Slovenia

Geography Location: southeastern Europe. **Boundaries:** Austria to N, Hungary to NE, Croatia to E and S, Adriatic Sea and Italy to W. **Total land area:** 7,836 sq. mi. (20,296 sq km). **Coastline:** 20 mi. (32 km). **Comparative area:** Slightly larger than New Jersey. **Land use:** 45% forest and woodland, 20% meadows and pastures, 10% arable land, 2% permanent crops, 23% other. **Major cities:** (1991 census) Ljubljana (capital) 323,291; Maribor 153,053; Kranj 72,814; Ptuj 68,846.

People Population: 1,972,227 (July 1994 est.). **Nationality:** noun—Slovene(s); adjective—Slovenian. **Ethnic groups:** 91% Slovene, 3% Croat, 2% Serb, 1% Muslim, 3% other. **Languages:** Slovenian, Serbo-Croatian. **Religions:** 96% Catholic, 1% Muslim, 3% other.

Government Type: emerging democracy. **Independence:** June 25, 1991 (from Yugoslavia). **Constitution:** Dec. 23, 1991. **National holiday:** Statehood Day, June 25. **Heads of government:** Milan Kucan, president of the presidency (four other members) (since Apr. 1990); Janez Drnovsek, prime minister (since May 1992). **Structure:** executive—president, prime minister, cabinet; legislative—bicameral parliament (National Assembly) of State Assembly and State Council; judicial—Supreme Court, Constitutional Court.

Economy Monetary unit: tolar (SIT). **Budget:** N.A. ***income:*** N.A. ***expend.:*** N.A. **GDP:** $15 bil. (1993 est.); $7,600 per capita. **Chief crops:** potatoes, hops, hemp, flax. **Livestock:** sheep, cattle. **Natural resources:** lignite coal, lead, zinc, mercury, uranium, silver. **Major industries:** ferrous metallurgy and rolling mill products, aluminum reduction and rolled products, lead and zinc smelting, electronics, trucks, electric power equipment, wood products, textiles. **Labor force:** 786,036; 46% manufacturing and mining, 2% agriculture. **Exports:** $5.1 bil. (f.o.b., 1993); 38% machinery and transport equipment, 44% other manufactured goods, 9% chemicals, 4.6% food and live animals, 3% raw materials. **Imports:** $5.3 bil. (c.i.f., 1993); 35% machinery and transport equipment, 26.7% other manufactured goods, 14.5% chemicals, 7% fuels and lubricants, 6% food and live animals. **Major trading partners:** ***exports:*** 27% Germany, 14% Croatia, 13% Italy, 9% France; ***imports:*** 23% Germany, 14% Croatia, 14% Italy, 8% Austria, 8% France.

Intl. Orgs. CEI, EBRD, ECE, IAEA, IBRD, ICAO, ILO, OSCE, UN, UNCTAD, UNESCO, UPU, WHO, WIPO, WMO.

In the sixth century, as part of the great Slavic migrations out of the Vistula and Oder basins, the Slovene people crossed the Carpathians into the Danube plain, penetrating as far as the eastern Alps. In the eighth and ninth centuries the lands they inhabited were subject to Bavarian colonization as part of the Ostmark (Eastern March) of the Carolingian Empire. It is probable, although contested, that most current Austrians are German-speaking Slovenes while the Slovenes are Slavophone Austrians. In any case, for 1,000 years, Slovene history was Austrian history. Thus, like the Croats, Christianity came in its western (Roman Catholic) form.

Lacking their own nobility and even a burgher class for most of their history, the Slovenes tended to look to their priests for leadership, regularly electing them as their representatives to the Reichstag in Vienna (as they did later to the Skupstina in Belgrade after Slovenia became part of Yugoslavia). The 19th-century rise of a national consciousness, associated with literary collections of legend and folklore by learned amateurs, took a special turn in the Slovene case because of Napoleon's conquests from Austria. His "province of Illyria" was the first association of the Slovenes with Croats and Serbs and his minister of education there was the Slovene Franciscan Valentin Vodnik, so that Slovene "nationalism" had from a start a "Yugoslav" tinge.

In 1815 the Slovenes were again part of the Austrian Empire and were confirmed in the Ausgleich of 1867 as part of the Austrian, not Hungarian, part of the dual Monarchy. As that monarchy collapsed in World War I, it was the Slovene monsignor Anton Korosec who served as president of "The National Council of the Serbs, Croats, and Slovenes" out of which the new state of Yugoslavia emerged. Though the new Yugoslavia was a highly centralized, unitary state with no provision for Slovene autonomy, certain circumstances brought a kind of privileged position to Slovenia. First of all, their distinct language made Serbian administration a practical impossibility. Second, Serbian struggles against Croat separatism led them to favor the Slovenes to Croatia's north, forestalling any additional separatism there. And third, as a part of the long Austrian connection, the Slovenes were better educated and more industrially advanced than any other part of Yugoslavia.

After the interlude of Hitler's break-up of Yugoslavia (in which Slovenia itself was partitioned between Germany and Italy) Slovenia became a constituent "republic" in Tito's reconstructed Yugoslavia and, despite the enduring emnity provoked by the Communist slaughter of the Slovene Domobranci (Home Guard), again assumed a kind of priviliged status in Yugoslavia. After the dictator's death in 1980, the Slovene Socialist Republic took part in the "collegial rule" of Yugoslavia, but with the end of Communist rule in 1990, Slovenia became the first of the republics to secede, in June 1991. After the Slovene militia inflicted a humiliating defeat on the Yugoslav army in July and with EU recognition in December, Slovenia became independent for the first time in all of its history. Forging economic ties with Austria, Hungary, and Italy, it has remained prosperously apart from the debacle to its south.

Macedonia

Republic of Macedonia

Geography Location: southern part of the Balkan Peninsula. **Boundaries:** Serbia to N, Bulgaria to E, Greece to S, Albania to W, Yugoslavia to NE and N. **Total land area:** 9,781 sq. mi. (25,333 sq km.). **Coastline:** none. **Comparative area:** slightly larger than Vermont. **Land use:** 30% forest and woodland, 20% meadows and pastures, 5% arable land, 40% other. **Major cities:** (1991) Skopje (Skoplje or, in Turkish, Uskub) 450,000; Bitola 85,000; Kumanovo 70,000; Tetovo 51,000.

People Population: 2,213,785 (July 1994 est.). **Nationality:** noun—Macedonian(s); adj.—Macedonian. **Ethnic groups:** 65% Macedonian, 22% Albanian, 4% Turkish, 2% Serb, 7% other (includes gypsies). **Languages:** 70% Macedonian (official), 21% Albanian, 3% Turkish, 3% Serbo-Croatian, 3% other. **Religions:** 67% Eastern Orthodox, 30% Muslim, 3% other.

Government Type: emerging democracy. **Independence:** Nov. 20, 1991 (from Yugoslavia). **Constitution:** Nov. 17, 1991. **National holiday:** August 2, Ilinven (St. Elijas Day). **Heads of government:** Kiro Gligorov, president (since Jan. 1991); Branko Crvenkovski, prime minister (since Sept. 1992). **Structure:** executive—president and cabinet; legislative—unicameral parliament (Sobranje); judicial—Constitutional Court, Judicial Court of the Republic.

Economy Monetary Unit: denar. **Budget:** N.A. ***income:*** N.A. ***expend:*** N.A. **GDP:** $2.2 bil. (1993 est.); $1,000 per capita. **Chief crops:** rice, tobacco, wheat, corn, millet; legal cultivator of opium poppy for the world pharmaceutical industry. **Livestock:** sheep, cattle, pigs, horses, fowl. **Natural resources:** chrome, iron ore, marble, zinc. **Major industries:** metallurgy and metal processing, chemicals, textiles, timber. **Labor force:** (1991) 450,000 employed; 100,000 industry and mining; 47,000 trade, 42,000 construction; 35,000 agriculture, 35,000 education, culture, and media; 27% unemployed. **Exports:** $578 mil. (1990); 40% manufactured goods, 14% machinery and transport equipment, 7.6% raw materials, 5.7% food and live animals. **Imports:** $1.112 bil. (1990); 19% fuels and lubricants, 18% manufactured goods, 15% machinery and transport equipment, 14% food and live animals, 11.4% chemicals, 10% raw materials. **Major trading partners:** ***exports:*** Serbia and Montenegro, other former Yugoslav republics, Germany, Greece, Albania; ***imports:*** Other former Yugoslav republics, Greece, Albania, Germany, Bulgaria.

Intl. Orgs. EBRD, ICA, IMF, UN, UNCTAD, UNESCO, UPU, WHO, WIPO, WMO.

Located at the geographic center of the Balkan peninsula, Macedonia is an epitome of the entire region in its history and ethnic complexity as well. While there is a Macedonian language (a Slavic tongue more akin to Bulgarian than to Serbo-Croatian and codified in grammar and orthography only after World War II), the question of whether or not there is a Macedonian nation is contested: to Serbians, Macedonians are "south Serbs"; to Greeks, they are "Slavophone Greeks"; to Bulgars, they are kindred people, ethnic "cousins."

In any case, Macedonians are not related to the classical people of King Philip and Alexander the Great. Their realm had become a Roman province by 146 B.C. and remained part of the Byzantine Empire even after being invaded and settled by Slavic peoples in the sixth and seventh centuries. Contested in the Middle Ages by the Byzantine, Bulgarian, and Serbian empires, Macedonia fell at last to the Ottoman Turks in 1371. Well into the 19th century its population called itself "Christian" or "Slav," while Greek served as the language of culture and business until a literary awakening associated with scholarly collections of folk songs and heroic poetry brought a Macedonian consciousness. This found significant political expression with the formation in 1893 of the IMRO (Internal Macedonian Revolutionary Organization) that sought to unify all non-Turks—Bulgars, Greeks, Albanians, Vlacha—in an autonomous or independent state and which did not shrink from terrorism and revolution.

The peace treaties of Paris that concluded World War I divided Macedonia among three states: Greece, Bulgaria, and the newly created Yugoslavia. IMRO turned now against Serbian dominance in Yugoslavia and filled the 1930s with violent struggles against "denationalization." It was Bulgarian claims to Macedonia that led that state to ally with Hitler's Germany and to occupy Macedonia in 1941. With the victory of Tito's partisans and the reconstruction of the Yugoslav state as a federation of Communist "republics," a Macedonian People's Republic was established in 1946.

After the dictator's death in 1980, Macedonia took part in the "collegial rule" whereby the presidency of Yugoslavia and the chairmanship of the Communist party Presidium rotated annually among the republics. But as the separate republics declared independence in 1991 and civil war began, Macedonia at last declared its own independence in January 1992. The opposition of Greece, which viewed the very name and flag of Macedonian as menaces to the northern Greek province of the same name, prevented international recognition of the new statelet (except by Bulgaria) until April 1993, when Greece and Macedonia agreed upon the name "The Former Yugoslav Republic of Macedonia" until an arbitration committee led by EU mediator Lord Owen can settle the issue. With UN recognition came both UN "peacekeeping forces" (including 300 American troops) to patrol the frontier with rump Yugoslavia and the painful need to comply with the UN embargo against Serbia, to whose economy Macedonia has been closely tied.

CHRONOLOGY OF THE YEAR

CHRONOLOGY OF THE YEAR'S KEY EVENTS

November 1994

1 General Motors Corporation asks the Dept. of Transportation to call off a hearing on the safety of millions of GM pickup trucks. In return, GM promises to seek an immediate recall of the vehicles.

Complying with the terms of an Oct. 21 agreement with the U.S., North Korea reports it has halted construction of two nuclear reactors that could be used to produce weapons-grade plutonium. In return, the U.S. will create an international consortium to finance construction of nuclear plants in Korea that cannot be used to make nuclear arms.

2 After deliberating for only 20 minutes, a Florida jury convicts Paul J. Hill of shooting to death a doctor and his escort outside a Pensacola abortion clinic.

More than 400 people are killed in southern Egypt, after an explosion sends blazing fuel through the streets of a small village. The explosion is caused when a bridge collapses over a military fuel depot, and floodwaters carry more than 15,000 tons of fuel through the streets of Surunka, 200 miles south of Cairo.

Muslim gunmen shoot and kill the military commander of Algeria, Col. Djelloul Hadj Cherif, who had been negotiating the surrender of nine accused Islamic guerrillas captured earlier in the week by Algerian security forces.

3 Susan V. Smith is arrested for the murder of her two young sons, 14 months and 3 years old. A week earlier Smith claimed that a black man hijacked her car with her two sons in it and disappeared. But hours after Smith made the last of several televised appeals to have her children returned to her, police discover the drowned bodies of the two boys inside their mother's car deep under the waters of a lake near Smith's hometown of Union, S.C.

4 The Labor Dept. reports a four-year low in the unemployment rate and the largest increase in average hourly wages in over a decade.

Russian economics minister Aleksandr N. Shokhin resigns in protest over the appointment of a new finance minister, claiming the economy has become "hostage to politics."

5 In a handwritten letter to the American people, former president Ronald Reagan reveals that he has entered the early stages of Alzheimer's disease.

6 Rotund 45-year-old George Foreman becomes the oldest man to win a boxing title when he knocks out heavyweight champion Michael Moorer in the 10th round.

7 Pres. Clinton jets from Minnesota to Michigan to Delaware to round up votes for Democratic Senate candidates in trouble in a final push to keep Democratic control of the Senate.

Voters in Albania reject a new constitution that would have committed the country to observe international human rights standards and would have allowed it to join the Council of Europe.

8 In national elections, Republicans capture control of both houses of Congress for the first time in 40 years. No sitting Republican governor, senator, or representative is defeated. (For further details, see Part I: "Major News Stories of the Year.")

In Haiti, Pres. Jean-Bertrand Aristide swears in a prime minister and a cabinet and begins plans to return democracy to his country.

9 The Federal Aviation Administration bars small planes from going on autopilot in icy conditions. The move is in response to the crash of an American Eagle flight a week earlier, which had iced up while on autopilot.

The number of U.S. farms drops below two million for the first time since the Civil War, according to the Census Bureau. Crop sales, however, continue to rise even as the number and total acreage of all U.S. farms decrease.

Prime Minister Chandrika Bandaranaike Kumaratunga easily wins Sri Lanka's presidential election. She credits her victory to the peace talks she began with Tamil rebels in an effort to end their 11-year war against the government. She is the first woman to serve as president of Sri Lanka.

10 Iraq agrees to recognize Kuwait's independence and to honor its current borders. Iraq had invaded Kuwait after refusing to recognize its boundaries in 1991; the recognition of Kuwaiti independence will likely allow the removal of some UN sanctions against Iraq.

11 A rare notebook of Leonardo da Vinci's, containing more than 300 illustrations and scientific writings, is auctioned at Christie's for $30.8 million.

12 The House Ethics Panel opens an inquiry into links between a college course House Speaker–designate Newt Gingrich taught and a Republican political action committee he chairs.

More than a million Italians fill the ancient squares of Rome to protest an austerity budget proposed by the conservative government of Prime Minister Silvio Berlusconi.

The Angolan government reports that it has captured the rebel headquarters in the city of Huambo, and told the rebels to sign a peace treaty or face defeat. The rebels had agreed to a peace agreement with the government several weeks earlier, but rebel leader Jonas Savimbi called off the treaty when government troops began their attack on his main base in Huambo.

13 The U.S. offers to forgive China's violations of an international missile agreement and waive possible sanctions if China will admit that it sold missile technology to Pakistan.

Tamil Tiger rebels in Sri Lanka announce a cease-fire in their 11-year battle for a separate state hours after the inauguration of Prime Minister Chandrika Bandaranaike Kumaratunga as president. The cease-fire may end the Tamil war in which 34,000 people have died.

14 House Speaker–designate Newt Gingrich pledges to pass the provisions of the Contract with America in the new Congress's first 100 days. He says he will force Congress to work 20 hours a day, seven days a week if necessary.

At a conference in Indonesia, 18 nations from Asia and the Pacific region reach agreement on a sweeping economic growth pact that will remove trade barriers between the countries by the year 2020.

15 The Federal Reserve raises the prime interest rate by ¾ of a point, the largest jump since 1981. The increase, the sixth in 1994, is intended to curb inflation and pace economic growth. Critics say the constant rate hikes are clipping the economy and costing jobs.

German chancellor Helmut Kohl narrowly wins reelection to a fourth term, but by only a one-vote margin, suggesting a weak and perhaps short-lived rule.

Sri Lankan president Chandrika Bandaranaike Kumaratunga names her 78-year-old mother, Sirima Bandaranaike, as prime minister. It is her second stint as prime minister; the first was during the 1960s when she succeeded her husband, Solomon Bandaranaike, who was assassinated in 1959.

16 Pres. Clinton pledges to go forward and seek approval for the General Agreement on Tariffs and Trade (GATT), despite the battering he took at the polls a week earlier. He vows to cooperate with Republican leaders Bob Dole and Newt Gingrich, because the agreement, which took 12 years to negotiate with 123 nations, would surely die if put off until 1995.

A federal judge temporarily blocks California officials from enforcing Proposition 187, the harsh, hotly debated immigration control measure overwhelmingly approved by California voters a week earlier. The judge finds that the proposition, which would deny most government services to undocumented immigrants, raises serious constitutional questions.

Ukraine's Parliament votes to make the country nuclear free, clearing obstacles to Ukrainian signing of two arms control agreements.

The two-year-old coalition government of Irish prime minister Albert Reynolds collapses, forcing a general election before Christmas to select a new Parliament and a new government.

17 Sony Corporation announces it is taking a $3.2 billion loss on its investment in Tri-Star Pictures and Columbia Pictures, both of which it acquired only five years earlier.

Facing criticism from civil liberties groups, Pres. Clinton tries to clarify a stance he took earlier favoring a constitutional amendment allowing school prayer. He now says he prefers passage of a federal "moment of silence law."

A leftist coalition led by Communist party chairman Man Mohan Adhikari wins parliamentary elections in Nepal. The Communist victory is attributed to its promise to break up large farms and redistribute the land.

18 In the last Senate race to be decided, Sen. Dianne Feinstein (D-Calif.) retains her seat against a challenge from multi-millionaire Rep. Michael Huffington. Feinstein had to wait until absentee ballots were counted before declaring victory. The $28 million spent by Huffington and the $14 million spent by Feinstein is the costliest congressional election ever, easily surpassing the old mark of $26 million.

Yasir Arafat's police open fire on Palestinian protesters in Gaza, killing 12 and wounding more than 200 in street battles. It is the worst internal violence since the beginning of the six-month-old peace accord giving Palestinian autonomy over the West Bank and the Gaza Strip.

19 Mozambique's president Joachím A. Chissanó and his Frelimo party win the country's first multiparty elections, capturing 53 percent of the vote and 129 of the 250 seats in Parliament.

20 The Angolan government and Unita rebels agree on a peace treaty to end the country's 19-year-old war, the last war in southern Africa. Nevertheless, Unita leader Jonas Savimbi remains in hiding during the signing, because he fears the government will try to kill him.

21 The Republican House leadership proposes a bill to overhaul the welfare system by cutting spending and curtailing benefits to women and children.

Stepping up its role in Bosnia, NATO warplanes bomb a Serbian-controlled air base in Croatia. The air raid is the biggest in Europe since the end of World War II.

22 In his second inflammatory attack on Pres. Clinton in less than a week, Sen. Jesse Helms (R-N.C.) says the president "better have a bodyguard" if he comes to North Carolina because the president is so unpopular on military bases in the state. He does not explain his remarks; The next day, he calls them an "unwise and inappropriate" mistake.

Italian magistrates name Prime Minister Silvio Berlusconi in a corruption investigation because of bribes paid to tax inspectors by his business empire. Weakened by losses in local elections, Berlusconi proclaims his innocence and refuses to resign, claiming only Parliament can force him from his post.

Pres. Clinton thanks Ukraine for its decision to eliminate nuclear weapons by extending $200 million in economic aid to the financially troubled former Soviet Republic.

23 Pres. Clinton and Senate Republican leader Bob Dole reach a deal that will allow the U.S. to ratify the World Trade Organization (WTO) pact reducing trade barriers among 124 nations.

24 Finland becomes the first country in the world to eradicate all homegrown cases of measles, German measles, and mumps.

25 Akio Morita, the 73-year-old chairman and cofounder of Sony, who built the company into a multibillion-dollar enterprise, steps down because of poor health.

26 Hours after a law banning assisted suicide expires, Dr. Jack Kevorkian helps a 73-year-old woman die in her bedroom. It is the first time Kevorkian assists in a suicide in more than a year. The Michigan Supreme Court is still considering the constitutionality of the expired law.

A year after four decades of one-party rule came to an end in Japan, the country's political parties find themselves in an upheaval. Both the conservative rebels who brought down the old system, and the Socialist party of current prime minister Tomiichi Murayama vote to dissolve their parties.

27 A month after they signed a peace treaty ending 46 years of war, Israel and Jordan officially establish diplomatic relations. Jordan is the second Arab country to open diplomatic ties with Europe; Egypt was the first.

28 Serial killer Jeffrey Dahmer, serving 15 consecutive life sentences in a Wisconsin prison, is attacked and killed by a fellow inmate.

The U.S. abandons its attempts to oust a gay soldier from the Navy, but says it will retain its "don't ask, don't tell" policy about homosexuals in the armed services.

The European Union lifts an eight-year arms embargo against Syria. Israel calls the move a mistake.

In the closest election in Uruguayan history, Julio Sanguinetti of the opposition Colorado party wins the presidency. A moderate centrist, he pledges to slow the process of economic liberalization that was begun during five years of rule by the conservative National party.

Nepal's ruling Congress party's efforts to stop the Communist party from taking power collapse, clearing the way for the first democratically elected Communist government in Asia.

29 Haiti postpones parliamentary elections, originally scheduled for December, until March of 1995, saying the administrative confusion left by the military government makes it mechanically impossible to hold to the original date.

Norway becomes the first European nation to reject membership in the European Union. The country's rich reserve of oil, gas, and fishing stocks are cited as reasons the country spurned EU membership.

Russian president Boris Yeltsin threatens to declare a state of emergency in the breakaway Russian region of Chechnya if fighting there does not stop by December 1.

30 The Postal Rate Commission approves a three-cent increase in the price of a first-class stamp, from 29 to 32 cents, effective Jan. 1, 1995.

Both sides of the regional civil war in Chechnya ignore Russian president Boris Yeltsin's threats of intervention and continue fighting in the breakaway region.

December 1994

1 The Senate approves (76–24) U.S. participation in the World Trade Organization, the 124-nation expansion of the General Agreement on Tariffs and Trade that will lower trade barriers among most of the world's economies.

Webster Hubbell, a close friend of Pres. Clinton and a former Justice Dept. official, agrees to plead guilty to two felony counts stemming from his involvement in the Whitewater real estate scandal.

2 Senate Republicans reelect Bob Dole as party leader, but name the confrontational Trent Lott to replace Alan Simpson as assistant leader.

The Labor Dept. reports that unemployment fell to 5.6% in November, a four-year low. Fearing inflation, the Federal Reserve indicates it will raise interest rates again.

The United Nations and NATO agree to suspend flights over Bosnia in a conciliatory gesture aimed at persuading the Bosnian Serbs to accept a cease-fire and free close to 400 UN peacekeepers from captivity.

3 Japanese officials strongly criticize plans by the U.S. Postal Service to issue a stamp depicting the atomic bombings of Hiroshima and Nagasaki in celebration of the 50th anniversary of the end of World War II. At the White House's request, the Postal Service later drops the plans.

4 House Speaker–designate Newt Gingrich urges the allies to pull UN forces out of Bosnia, train the Muslim-led forces, and threaten an all-out attack against the Bosnian Serbs.

The FBI reports that serious crime declined 3 percent during the first half of 1994, even though public concern about crime remains high.

5 Treasury Secretary Lloyd Bentsen indicates he will resign before the end of the year, or as soon as his successor, Robert Rubin, can be confirmed by the Senate.

House Republicans unanimously choose Newt Gingrich as their leader. Gingrich, who takes much of the credit for the Republican landslide in the November elections, will become House Speaker in January.

6 Orange County, Calif., perennially one of the nation's wealthiest counties, files for bankruptcy protection. Officials cite an overaggressive investment strategy by treasurer Robert L. Citron for the county's disastrous $1.5 billion in losses.

The Hubble Space Telescope, its lens repaired, takes the first clear pictures of some of the earliest galaxies, giving an indication of what the infant universe looked like.

House Republicans pledge to withdraw financing to the caucuses, special interest groups created by members to lobby each other. The GOP claims the move is a cost-cutting measure; Democrats say it is a way to silence opposition, especially on issues affecting blacks, women, and other interest groups whose voice in the entire Congress is not so strong.

Mexico's new president Ernesto Zedillo Ponce de León proposes a broad overhaul of the country's justice system, including a revamping of the Supreme Court.

7 Republicans propose sweeping changes in House rules, including the dismantling of three House committees and 25 subcommittees, eliminating more than 600 employees from the chamber's payroll. Other proposed changes include ending closed-door hearings and requiring a three-fifths vote to approve any tax increase.

8 As hopes for a peace agreement in Bosnia fade, Pres. Clinton pledges to send 25,000 U.S. troops to supervise withdrawal of UN peacekeeping troops if a pullout becomes inevitable.

After nearly six months of legal wrangling, a jury of 12 members and 12 alternates is finally chosen for the O.J. Simpson double murder trial. The jury is predominantly black and predominantly female.

9 Pres. Clinton succumbs to Republican pressure and forces the resignation of Surgeon

General Joycelyn Elders. Elders had become a target of conservative Republicans who opposed her views on abortion, the legalization of drugs, and, most recently, her suggestion that teenagers use masturbation as a way of preventing the spread of AIDS.

Representatives of the British government and the Irish Republican Army meet publicly for the first time ever in talks aimed at ending 25 years of strife in Northern Ireland.

10 Pres. Clinton and leaders from Canada, Mexico, and 31 Central and South American nations agree to create a free-trade zone throughout the Americas. The pact, which will have to be approved by the U.S. Congress, would take effect by the year 2005.

Pres. Sam Nujoma and his South West African People's Organization (Swapo) party easily win Namibia's first elections since gaining independence from South Africa in 1989.

11 Russian tanks roll across the border into the breakaway republic of Chechnya to quell the rebellion: The region has been trying to secede since 1991. (For further details, see Part I: "Major News Stories of the Year.")

Jacques Delors, president of the European Union and the front-runner for the presidency of France, unexpectedly drops out of the presidential race.

Pres. Clinton and leaders from Canada and Mexico agree to admit Chile to the North American Free Trade Agreement.

12 The Justice Dept. reports that senior officials violated the Constitution and internal FBI policy in relaxing rules about shooting suspects during a 1992 standoff between Idaho white separatists and federal agents. Federal agents mistakenly shot Vicki Weaver, wife of separatist Randall Weaver, in the 10-day siege during a chaotic sequence of events, in which confusion and errors in judgment by FBI agents ruled.

IBM suspends sales of all personal computers using the Intel Pentium chip after Intel reveals a flaw in the device that causes incorrect calculations at high levels of precision. Although Intel contends the flaw is trivial, IBM says mistakes could result as often as once a month.

13 An American Eagle commuter plane crashes in North Carolina, killing 15 of the 20 people on board. The accident involved a different kind of plane than the American Eagle flight that crashed a month earlier, killing 68.

U.S. immigration officials report that increased patrols along a section of the Mexican border have succeeded in cutting the rate of illegal crossings by half. The program known as Operation Gatekeeper cost $25 million, and led to increased illegal crossings at other less-guarded border sections.

Italian prime minister Silvio Berlusconi is interrogated for seven hours by magistrates in Milan who suspect him of involvement in a corruption scandal.

Forty-six leaders from the former Marxist government of Ethiopia are brought to court to face charges of genocide and crimes against humanity. Twenty other leaders, including former president Mengitsu Haile Mariam, remain in hiding or in exile, and will be tried in absentia. All 66 defendants face the death penalty.

14 Amtrak announces sharp cutbacks in service and 5,500 layoffs in an effort to make up a $200 million deficit by September 1995. The most severe cuts in service will come in the heavily traveled Washington–NewYork–Boston corridor and service from New York to Montreal.

Transportation Secretary Federico Peña orders a safety audit for every U.S. airline and accelerates a timetable for stricter safety rules for commuter airlines.

15 Pres. Clinton, in a nationally televised Oval Office address, outlines a program to provide middleclass tax breaks, reduce the federal government, and create education and job training incentives. The tax breaks, he claims, will not exacerbate the budget deficit.

A coalition of centrist and leftist parties rally around farm owner John Bruton, leader of the centrist Fine Gael party, to be Ireland's prime minister. The country had been without a government since November, when Albert Reynolds resigned as prime minister.

16 The U.S. announces plans to send ships and several thousand marines to Somalia to help evacuate the remaining UN peacekeeping troops there early in 1995. The Pentagon stresses that there will be no further U.S. combat involvement in the war-torn nation.

17 Congressional Republicans unveil plans for sweeping cuts to federal welfare spending. The money would be spent instead on block grants to the states, which could decide how best to distribute the funds for social welfare programs.

In the second such incident in two months, shots are fired at the White House. One of the bullets strikes the mansion while Pres. Clinton and his family are sleeping inside. The Secret Service insists the president was never in danger, but they have no suspects.

The U.S. demands the release of two American pilots whose Army helicopter wandered into North Korean airspace and was either shot down or forced to make an emergency landing there. Pyongyang reveals that the pilots had been taken into custody for questioning, but no more about their condition is known. The following day, the White House reports that one of the aviators was killed in the incident.

18 The former Communist party returns to power in Bulgaria, claiming victory in parliamentary elections. Party leader Zhan Videnov, the likely next prime minister, says his party will reverse the country's deep economic decline since its move to democracy in 1989.

Peace efforts between rebel leaders of the breakaway republic of Chechnya and the Russian government falter as Moscow's deadline for the rebels to lay down their arms or face a Russian invasion passes. Russian troops resume their advance on the rebel capital of Grozny, but there is no indication of a full-scale assault yet.

Fresh from successful peace settlements in North Korea and Haiti, former president Jimmy Carter travels to Sarajevo in an attempt to negotiate a settlement in the Bosnian war, but reports little progress.

19 The Environmental Protection Agency allows 12 eastern states to impose California's auto emission standards, the strictest in the nation, on cars sold within their borders.

Russian jets bomb Grozny, the capital of the breakaway Chechen republic, as talks with rebel leaders break off.

20 Conceding that the flaw in its Pentium chip is more serious than it had originally admitted, the Intel corporation offers all customers a free replacement part on request.

State police officers in the southern Mexican state of Chiapas retake an isolated territory that had been taken the day before by rebel forces there. The rebel action was the first serious revolt since a cease-fire agreed to by both sides in January.

21 A federal judge approves a Clinton administration plan for logging old-growth forests in the Pacific Northwest. Three years earlier, the same judge, William L. Dwyer of the District Court in Seattle, had disallowed a Bush administration logging plan because the forests were the home of the the spotted owl and other endangered species.

After intense pressure from the U.S., North Korea's government returns the body of the U.S. pilot who was killed when his helicopter went down over North Korean air space.

Italy's embattled Prime Minister Silvio Berlusconi announces his resignation in the face of a rift within his coalition government. Berlusconi had been the subject of several corruption scandals during his seven-month tenure.

22 Mexico allows its currency to trade freely against the American dollar, causing the peso to drop 20 percent in a day, further plunging the country into economic crisis.

23 The Centers for Disease Control report that the percentage of pregnancies that end in legal abortion reached its lowest level in 15 years. The abortion-to-live-birth ratio, the Centers report, was about one to three, lower than any rate since 1977.

The president of HarperCollins adult trade division claims the $4 million book deal it signed with House Speaker–designate Newt Gingrich had no impact on the Georgia congressman's efforts to lift restrictions against foreign ownership of television networks. Rupert Murdoch, who controls both HarperCollins and the Fox TV Network, stands to benefit substantially if the ban on foreign ownership is lifted.

24 House Republicans announce plans to make it significantly more difficult for the government to regulate everything from automobile safety to the environment. Democrats criticize the plan as a benefit to business and a blow to consumer safety.

Four gunmen believed to be Islamic fundamentalists hijack an Air France plane at Algiers airport shortly before takeoff. They kill three and release 57 Algerians among the more than 230 passengers and crew, and demand clearance to fly to another, as yet unknown, destination.

25 Retailers report a lackluster Christmas shopping season. Sales exceeded the previous year, but revenues and profits were down because many shoppers waited until the last minute to make their purchases, when prices were slashed on much of the Christmas season merchandise.

The former Soviet Republic of Uzbekistan continues its move toward democracy, holding its first multiparty elections for a 250-seat national legislature.

26 French paratroopers storm the hijacked Air France jet at a Marseilles airport, killing all four Islamic militant gunmen who had seized the airliner and freeing the more than 170 passengers and crew who had been held hostage for two days.

27 The Mexican peso continues its free fall, dropping another 10 percent in value against the dollar.

Amid growing opposition to the war in the breakaway region of Chechnya, Russian president Boris Yeltsin says he will limit air raids on Grozny to avoid bombing more civilians. Nevertheless, he says, he will press on to seize the rebel capital.

28 CIA Director R. James Woolsey resigns unexpectedly after less than two years on the job. Woolsey presided over the intelligence agency as it tried to regroup after the devastating revelation that top officials knew about the double-agency of traitor Aldrich Ames long before it became public knowledge.

The U.S. pledges several billion dollars to help Mexico extricate itself from its financial crisis. The new money comes on top of a $6 billion line of credit the U.S. made available to Mexico a week earlier.

29 After holding him hostage for 13 days, Pyongyang releases the U.S. helicopter pilot who had strayed into North Korean airspace.

One day after most of the opposition members resign from Parliament, Bangladesh prime minister Khaleda Zia agrees to their demand that she step down before elections in 1996.

30 A lone gunman opens fire at two abortion clinics on the same street in Brookline, Mass., a Boston suburb, killing two receptionists and wounding five others before escaping by car.

In the face of criticism from the media, Democrats, and even leaders of his own party, Newt Gingrigh agrees to give up a $4.5 million advance on his forthcoming book, accepting a $1 advance instead (plus royalties).

31 Police in Norfolk, Va., seize John Salvi, the man who opened fire at two Massachusetts abortion clinics the day before, as he commits the same act at a Norfolk clinic. No one is hurt in the Norfolk incident.

In a move attributed to finances, not politics, the Clinton administration quietly decides not to rejoin UNESCO, the United Nations Educational, Scientific, and Cultural Organization. The U.S. broke with the organization in 1984, charging mismanagement and an anti-Western bias; but it is the $65 million dues that are cited as the reason for not rejoining in 1995.

January 1995

1 Russian troops enter the Chechnyan capital of Grozny, firing on soldiers of the breakaway republic and surrounding the presidential palace. Heavy casualties are reported on both sides.

Brazil inaugurates Fernando Henrique Cardoso as president. In his speech, Cardoso, the architect of Brazil's radical economic recovery, vows to wipe out inflation and open the country to increased foreign investment and trade.

2 Less than five years after being convicted for smoking crack, Marion Barry becomes the mayor of Washington, D.C., for the second time.

The U.S. puts up $9 billion in an overall loan package of $18 billion to help stabilize the Mexican economic crisis and to stabilize the peso.

3 Mexican president Ernesto Zedillo Ponce de León outlines a recovery plan for his country's sagging economy. The plan will reduce the purchasing power of workers, cut corporate profits, and trim the nation's budget by selling off some state-owned resources.

Sri Lanka's government reaches a new agreement with separatist Tamil rebels to end 12 years of warfare there.

4 Republicans take control of both houses of Congress for the first time in 40 years as the 104th Congress is seated. They pledge to undo much of the work done by the Democratic-led Congress, vowing cuts in everything "from Amtrak to zoological studies," according to Senate Majority Leader Bob Dole.

Russian president Boris Yeltsin orders a halt to the bombing of the capital of Grozny. Yeltsin had come under criticism both at home and abroad for the Russian attack on the rebel city.

O.J. Simpson's lawyers drop their challenge of the admissibility of DNA evidence. The defense also agrees the jury should be sequestered. (For further details, see Part I: "Major News Stories of the Year.")

5 Pres. Clinton meets with the new Republican leaders of Congress and pledges a spirit of compromise with the new regime on Capitol Hill.

The Library of Congress enters the information age by unveiling Thomas, an Internet site on the World Wide Web that allows users to call up myriad information from Congress. All bills introduced since 1992, as well as every word uttered on the floors of the House and Senate, will be available over the service.

6 The Dept. of Labor reports an increase of 3.5 million jobs for 1994, and says the jobless rate fell to 5.4 percent in December, its lowest level since July 1990.

7 In a sign of the fear instilled by the new budget-slashing Republican majority, the Dept. of Housing and Urban Development announces plans to cut more than one-third of its workforce (a reduction of 5,000 jobs) over the next five years to avoid being eliminated altogether.

O.J. Simpson announces a deal with Little, Brown & Co. to publish *I Want to Tell You,* his assertion of his innocence of killing his wife Nicole Brown Simpson and her friend Ronald Goldman. (For further details, see Part I: "Major News Stories of the Year.")

8 Russian troops intensify their attacks on the Chechnyan capital of Grozny, spraying mortar and rocket fire at virtually every building in the city and littering the streets with hundreds of dead bodies.

9 After intense pressure from House Democrats, Speaker Newt Gingrich dismisses Christina Jeffrey as House historian after it is revealed that she once denied federal funding to an educational program about the Holocaust on the grounds that it did not present the views of the Nazis or the Ku Klux Klan.

Pres. Clinton selects Sen. Christopher J. Dodd (D-Conn.) to head the Democratic National Committee and to help revive the staggering party.

The most important terrorism trial in the U.S. opens in New York, with prospective jurors filling out a 19-page questionnaire about their knowledge and opinions of the World Trade Center bombing of 1993. The trial is expected to last six to nine months.

10 Japan opens several financial markets to U.S. investment firms, allowing them to vie for the right to manage nearly a trillion dollars in Japanese pension funds. In a separate agreement, Japanese markets begin selling American apples for the first time after years of refusing to allow the imports.

11 Severe rainstorms continue to pound northern California, flooding the Napa and Russian Rivers, forcing thousands to evacuate areas threatened by flooding and mudslides; Pres. Clinton declares a disaster area in 24 counties.

12 Malcolm X's daugher Qubilah Bahiyah Shabazz is arrested in Minneapolis on federal charges of attempting to hire a hit man to kill Nation of Islam minister Louis Farrakhan. Farrakhan was originally a disciple of Malcolm X, but later turned into his bitter rival. Shabazz's mother Betty had previously asserted that Farrakhan was involved in the mysterious assassination of Malcolm X in 1965, an assertion Farrrakhan has consistently denied.

13 After nearly a month-long search, Italy's Parliament chooses Lamberto Dini, a 63-year-old banker and current treasury minister to replace former prime minister Silvio Berlusconi, who resigned in December. Dini, who has no political affiliations, says he will form a government of technicians "free of political ties" to complete the country's fiscal and political reforms.

Russia's head of domestic intelligence rules out any negotiations with the secessionist Chechnyan region as Russia launches one of its fiercest attacks yet on the rebel capital. Meanwhile, Pres. Clinton urges Moscow to end the onslaught against the Chechens, but he refuses to cut back U.S. aid to Russia.

14 California governor Pete Wilson calls an emergency session of the state legislature to handle the flooding that has killed 11 people and caused more than $300 million in damage.

15 Leaders of the rebel Zapatista National Liberation Army meet with Mexican president Ernesto Zedillo for the first time since his election in an attempt to bring about a peaceful resolution to the uprising in the southern state of Chiapas.

A crowd of close to four million greets Pope John Paul II in Manila on World Youth Day.

16 A devastating earthquake rips through the Japanese port city of Kobe, killing at least 2,000 people and injuring countless thousands more. (For further details, see Part I: "Major News Stories of the Year.")

17 The House of Representatives unanimously

approves a bill that would end Congress's exemption from laws against discrimination and sexual harassment in the workplace and from lawsuits by employees.

18 Judge Lance A. Ito allows the prosecution in the O.J. Simpson double murder trial to introduce into evidence the tape of a 911 call Nicole Brown Simpson made while O.J. Simpson was attacking her in 1989. (For further details, see Part I: "Major News Stories of the Year.")

19 Russian troops capture the presidential palace in Grozny and claim victory in their war with the secessionist republic of Chechnya 40 days after they began their assault. Russian president Boris Yeltsin declares the war over, and in an effort to tighten his grip over the military, he ousts four senior defense ministry officials. (For further details, see Part I: "Major News Stories of the Year.")

20 The U.S. eases its trade embargo slightly on North Korea for the first time since 1950, allowing direct telephone calls between the two countries and permitting travelers to use credit cards there.

21 Pres. Clinton announces he will seek to increase the budget for enforcing immigration laws and labor standards in an effort to curb the number of illegal aliens entering the country. He couples this plan with a proposal to increase the minimum wage.

22 At least one suicide bomber blows up a bus stop crowded with Israeli soldiers near the West Bank, killing at least 19, injuring 61, and casting a pall over fragile peace talks between Israel and the Palestinians.

23 Pres. Clinton signs into law the Congressional Accountability Act, which holds Congress to the same federal workplace laws as the rest of the world.

24 In his State of the Union address, Pres. Clinton pledges a spirit of cooperation with the new Republican majority on Capitol Hill, but vows to amend some of their proposals to make them more palatable to the centrist Democrats that elected him. He endorses proposals to shrink the federal bureaucracy, cut taxes, overhaul welfare, and crack down on illegal immigration, issues he addressed in his presidential campaign.

25 Federal Reserve chairman Alan Greenspan says he will raise short-term interest rates yet again in an effort to forestall inflation, claiming the economy is too robust.

Israeli police identify two Islamic Gazans as the suicide bombers who blew up a bus stop in Israel earlier in the week, killing 19 and wounding more than 60 others. The group Islamic Holy War took responsibility for the attack.

26 The House of Representatives votes, 300–132, in favor of a constitutional amendment for a balanced budget. The vote is 12 votes more than the two-thirds majority required to override Pres. Clinton's anticipated veto. The vote in the Senate is expected to be much closer.

Commerce Sec. Ron Brown is accused of violating federal financial disclosure requirements by failing to report $135,000 he received from a partnership in 1993. It is the third time Brown is questioned about financial improprieties in the past year.

27 The U.S. and Vietnam take a step toward full diplomatic relations by exchanging low-level diplomats for the first time since the end of U.S. involvement in the Vietnam War in April 1975.

Newly appointed House Majority Leader Dick Armey (R-Tex.) ignites a storm on Capitol Hill when he refers to Rep. Barney Frank (D-Mass.), an openly gay congressman, as "Barney Fag." Armey later apologizes and calls it a mispronunciation, but Frank says he sees it as part of "a climate of meanness and intolerance with the Republicans."

The National Governors' Association outlines a plan for Pres. Clinton giving states the option of receiving a single federal payment each year and designing their own welfare payment plans with few federal regulations. Pres. Clinton expresses opposition to this "block grant" program, saying "simply passing the buck to the states is not welfare reform."

28 Ecuador and Peru renew a historic conflict over a 130-square-mile piece of land within the Peruvian border as troops from each country clash. Ecuador has maintained a claim to the land, which would give it access to the Amazon River, and fought for it in 1941 and 1981.

29 The tide of American public opinion starts to turn against sending financial aid to bail out the Mexican economy as leaders of both houses of Congress declare that a $40 billion loan package is all but dead. They say the bailout will reward U.S. investors who speculated on the Mexican economy before it went sour, but will produce little benefit for most Americans.

30 The Mexican peso plummets as it appears unlikely that Congress will pass Pres. Clinton's $40 billion bailout package. Clinton scrambles to find support for his plans as the peso loses another 10 percent of its value.

The Smithsonian severely scales back a planned exhibit about the *Enola Gay,* the B-29 bomber that dropped the atomic bomb on Hiroshima. Veterans and members of Congress complained that the exhibit was revisionist history because it portrayed America as an aggressive, racist nation and Japan as a victim.

House Speaker Newt Gingrich says that even Medicare, the 30-year-old health care program for the elderly and long a sacred cow of congressional budgets, may not be spared the budget ax as the new majority on Capitol Hill looks for ways to balance the budget by the year 2002.

31 Pres. Clinton uses his emergency powers to lend $20 billion to Mexico without having to gain Congress's approval in an effort to rescue Mexico from economic decline. Congress had opposed Clinton's original $40 million loan package. News of Pres. Clinton's action sends Mexico's stock market soaring by more than 10 percent, recovering much of the ground it had lost in the past few days.

Myanmar continues its persecution of political insurgents, pushing more than 1,000 members of the Karen ethnic minority into refugee camps across the Thai border. A total of more than 15,000 insurgents have been driven across the border in a week.

The worst flooding in 40 years forces 100,000 Dutch from their homes between the Meuse and Waal Rivers in eastern Amsterdam.

February 1995

1 The Federal Reserve raises the prime rate for the seventh time in less than a year for fear of inflation. Major commercial banks followed the rate increase lockstep, raising their prime lending rates to 9 percent, up from 6 percent one year earlier.

Russian artillery troops pound the Chechen town of Samashki, 20 miles west of the capital of Grozny. Russian officials say they chose this small village because it harbored many soldiers loyal to rebel leader Dzhokhar M. Dudayev.

2 The leaders of Israel, Egypt, Jordan, and the PLO meet at a regional summit in Cairo and agree to hold talks to create lasting peace in the Middle East. It is the first time the four leaders have met at the same table.

Six key western allies rebuff Pres. Clinton by withholding their support of a $17.8 billion loan package to Mexico from the International Monetary Fund. Although the package is ultimately approved, Britain, Germany, Denmark, the Netherlands, Belgium and Switzerland abstain.

3 Congressional Republicans criticize Dr. Henry W. Foster, whom Pres. Clinton had nominated for surgeon general the day before, for performing abortions over his 30 years as a practicing obstetrician and gynecologist.

Pres. Clinton proposes a 90-cent raise in the minimum wage, to $5.15 an hour, to be phased in over two years. Clinton explained that without such an increase, the real buying power of the minimum wage (adjusting for inflation) would be at a 40-year low in 1996. Republicans vow to fight the proposal.

Negotiators for Peru and Ecuador announce a cease-fire in their dispute over a remote area of the Amazon jungle.

4 Pres. Clinton imposes steep sanctions totaling $1 billion on imports of Chinese goods in retaliation for China's refusal to crack down on rampant piracy of American software, movies, and music.

U.S. Border Patrol authorities report that illegal alien crossings from Mexico have risen dramatically in response to the plummeting Mexican peso. Increased patrols in San Diego and El Paso make Nogales, Ariz., the new hot spot for entering the U.S. illegally.

5 Talks break off between Ecuador and Peru in their border war over a piece of land in the Amazon jungle. Although Peruvian warplanes bomb some Ecuadorian positions, most fighting shifts to jungle-style guerrilla tactics.

6 One of the defendants in the trial of 12 Islamic fundamentalists accused of plotting to blow up several New York City buildings changes his plea to guilty and implicates his former codefendants. Siddig Ibrahim Siddig Ali tells the court that he and the others planned a campaign of bombings and assassinations, and he names Sheik Omar Abdel Rahman as the ideological ringleader of the group.

Pres. Clinton's budget shows him cutting the deficit to about $190 billion for each of the next

10 years and spending $1.6 trillion in 1996. The cuts do not go far enough, however, for the Republican majority on Capitol Hill, which wants a balanced budget by 2002. Clinton's budget proposes eliminating more than 130 programs (at a savings of $2 billion annually) and by consolidating close to 300 others.

7 After failing to convince baseball players and owners to resolve their dispute peacefully among themselves, Pres. Clinton calls on Congress to impose arbitration on the two sides in hopes of ending the six-month-long baseball work stoppage.

8 An Islamic militant accused of being the mastermind of the 1993 World Trade Center bombing is arrested in Pakistan and extradited to the U.S. for trial, where he is held as one of the world's most wanted terrorists. Ramzi Ahmed Yousef is suspected of buying and brewing the explosive chemicals used to create the gigantic bomb that blew up parts of the World Trade Center in February 1993.

9 Former vice president Dan Quayle, citing a distaste for the rigors of fund-raising, unexpectedly withdraws from contention for the 1996 Republican presidential nomination.

10 Law enforcement officials say they have uncovered a computer disk and documents left in a Manila apartment that link Ramzi Ahmed Yousef, the accused mastermind of the World Trade Center bombing, to an earlier airline bombing and a plot to assassinate the pope.

11 Police in the Philippines reveal that they were able to apprehend accused World Trade Center bombing mastermind Ramzi Ahmed Yousef after he accidentally set fire to his Manila apartment while mixing explosives in his kitchen sink. According to police, Yousef, living under the name Naji Haddad, fled the building, leaving behind containers of acid, timing devices, and a computer disk filled with details of his plots to kill Pope John Paul II and to blow up American jets flying routes in the Far East.

12 The White House steps up its defense of surgeon general nominee Henry Foster from critics on the right who objected to his performance of abortions during his 38 years as an obstetrician and gynecologist and allegations that he performed hysterectomies on severely mentally retarded women more than 20 years ago. After fumbling much of his defense, the White House paints Foster's opponents as right-wing extremists.

The United Nations begins a peacekeeping operation in Zaire to protect more than a million Rwandan refugees living in Zairean camps where former militia members had been ruling through violence and intimidation.

13 Russian and Chechen commanders agree to a cease-fire and an exchange of prisoners in the civil war in the secessionist republic of Chechnya, where fighting has raged since December. There is no indication of how long the truce might last. Pres. Clinton calls Russian president Boris Yeltsin to urge peace in the region.

14 The House of Representatives defies a veto threat from Pres. Clinton and easily passes a revised crime bill that would eliminate Clinton's program to put 100,000 more police officers on the street, in favor of a bill that would give money directly to the states and allow them to determine how best to spend it.

15 Moody's Investors Service, a Wall Street credit rating firm, lowers the bond rating of the city of Washington, D.C., to that of a junk bond, expressing serious doubt that the city can balance its budget.

16 Israel agrees to loosen border restrictions that have prevented many Palestinians from crossing into Israel and going to work for nearly a month. The tight border restrictions were imposed following a January suicide bombing of a bus stop in Gaza by an Islamic militant that killed 19 Israeli soldiers.

17 A New York jury finds Colin Ferguson guilty on 19 counts of attempted murder and six counts of second-degree murder for his rush-hour slayings on a Long Island commuter railroad in December 1993.

18 The NAACP narrowly votes to oust its chairman, Dr. William Gibson, in favor of Myrlie Evers-Williams, widow of slain civil rights leader Medgar Evers. Gibson had been accused of wasting NAACP money and using some of the organization's funds for his own personal use.

19 Nine Republican candidates for the party's nomination for president square off at a party fund-raising dinner in New Hampshire in what is seen as the unofficial start of the 1996 presidential campaign. The candidates take turns jabbing at Pres. Clinton, at front-runner Bob Dole, and at each other.

20 Several economic studies reveal that Americans age 55 or older are primarily responsible for the slump in savings by the nation's population. Once as high as 9 percent of national income during the 1950s, 1960s, and 1970s, the savings rate plummeted to 5 percent in the 1980s and currently stands at slightly over 3 percent.

21 The British and Irish governments approve a common approach aimed at reaching a settlement to end 25 years of violence in Northern Ireland. The joint position follows 14 months of talks between the two governments. The so-called Framework Document is expected to meet with opposition from the Protestant Unionists, who fear London will cede control of Northern Ireland to Dublin.

The U.S. and Mexico reach an official agreement on a broader-than-expected program to bolster the disastrous Mexican economy. The U.S. will provide $20 billion of international aid package worth about $50 million to restore investor confidence in the country's economy. The Mexican stock market drops nearly 5 percent in response to fears of the fiscal austerity required to carry out the plan.

22 France accuses five Americans, including the former CIA station chief there, of political and economic espionage and orders them to leave the country immediately. The Americans are charged with trying to bribe high-ranking French government officials into revealing the country's negotiating position with regard to movies and entertainment. The U.S. State Dept. calls the allegations unfounded.

Two-time Olympic gold medal diver Greg Louganis reveals that he has AIDS.

23 The Dow Jones industrial average tops the 4,000 mark for the first time. Market analysts say the surge decreases the likelihood of a recession soon.

The Clinton administration announces plans to step up patrols along the Mexican border to intercept more illegal drugs coming into the United States. The Customs Service will shift as many as 80 agents to crossing points in the Southwest and add new surveillance equipment such as helicopter patrols and cargo X-ray machines.

24 Ethnic fighting flares up between Hutus and Tutsis in Burundi, forcing more than 24,000 Burundian and Rwandan refugees to flee into northwest Tanzania.

The U.S. and Canada agree to open the skies between the two countries, allowing airlines from each country to fly any routes between the two. The agreement is the latest in a series designed to expand free trade.

25 An aide to the governing party in Mexico is arrested as the second gunman in the 1994 assassination of party presidential candidate Luis Donaldo Colosio. The arrest gives credence to widespread allegations that the assassination was part of a conspiracy by the ruling Institutional Revolutionary party to hold onto power. Colosio's campaign manager, Ernesto Zedillo, later became the party candidate and won the election.

26 The U.S. and China agree on a pact that will end a long-running dispute over Chinese piracy of American software, movies, music, and other intellectual property. The accord averts a trade war between the two countries.

Barings PLC, Britain's oldest and one of its most venerable investment firms, collapses after suffering a $750 million loss from an unauthorized gamble in the Japanese stock market. Most of the loss was sustained by a single trader, 28-year-old Nick Leeson, who risked more than $29 billion on Japanese stock prices. Leeson's whereabouts are unknown; financial markets in Europe and the Far East are severely shaken by the revelation.

27 A *New York Times*/CBS News poll shows that Americans are dubious about key parts of the Republican Contract with America. The poll finds that most Americans think Congress should focus more on issues like jobs and health care.

The U.S. sends nearly 2,000 marines to Mogadishu to protect UN forces as they pull out from their mission in Somalia. UN officials admit that the mission was a fiasco, as famine still plagues the country, which is without a government and ruled by heavily armed rival groups of thugs.

28 Fearing it does not have enough votes to pass the balanced budget amendment, Republican leaders in the Senate postpone the vote to allow some more arm-twisting.

Raul Salinas de Gortari, brother of former Mexican president Carlos Salinas de Gortari, is charged with having ordered and paid for the assassination of a former official of the ruling Institutional Revolutionary party. It is unclear why the PRI wanted the official, Jose Francisco Ruiz Massieu, killed. It is also unclear whether this assassination is related to the assassination of former PRI candidate Luis Donaldo Colosio, who, it was revealed earlier in the week, was murdered by yet another PRI aide. The arrest shatters a notion of immunity from prosecution for party leaders and their families.

March 1995

1 Nicholas W. Leeson, the 28-year-old trader whose risky investments in the Japanese stock market caused Britain's venerable Barings PLC investment bank to collapse into bankruptcy, is detained by German border police at Frankfurt airport. Leeson is not arrested, however, as it is unclear whether he has broken any laws.

One week after heavy fighting broke a ceasefire agreement between the two countries, Peru and Ecuador sign another truce to end a border war over a parcel of land in the Amazon jungle.

2 The Senate finally rejects a constitutional amendment to require a balanced federal budget. Fifty-one Republicans and 14 Democrats vote for the amendment, two votes short of the two-thirds majority necessary for passage. It is the first major setback to the new Republican majority on Capitol Hill.

Two competing groups of physicists announce that they have found the top quark, a fleeting building block of matter that may hold clues to the understanding of the universe.

3 The Justice Dept. files a federal civil rights suit against Illinois State University for a janitor-training program that excludes white men. It is the first civil rights case the administration has filed on behalf of white men.

In an attempt to alter radically the federal government's role, the House passes a package of antiregulatory measures that would suspend most new environmental, health, and safety regulations and subject future proposed regulations to strict cost-benefit analyses before they could be implemented. Democrats say the move would benefit land owners and developers at the expense of the health and safety of the public, and if passed, would limit the government's power to enforce regulations like the Clean Air and Clean Water Acts, the Endangered Species Act, and the Superfund law.

4 The last contingent of U.S. Marines evacuate Somalia after safely escorting UN peacekeepers from Mogadishu, ending the two-year mission to restore peace.

5 The Clinton administration attacks a Republican bill that would alter the nation's legal system by making it more difficult to sue for damages in injury cases. Clinton argues that the so-called "loser pays" legislation would "tilt the legal playing field dramatically to the disadvantage of consumers and middle-class citizens."

Republicans in the House of Representatives unveil a plan to cut $16.5 billion from the federal food stamps program over five years by requiring recipients without children to find work within 90 days of receiving benefits. The Democrats say the legislation, which would also the national school lunch program, is cruel to women and children.

6 The dollar continues its plunge against the Japanese yen and briefly hits a historic low against the German mark. Several economic pressures, ranging from the Mexican economic crisis to the failure of the balanced budget amendment threaten to shape the Clinton administration's response to the dollar's woes.

Conoco Inc. signs a $1 billion agreement with Iran to develop a huge offshore oil field in the Persian Gulf. It is the first energy agreement with Iran since the U.S. severed relations with Teheran in 1980.

Mario Ruiz Massieu, Mexico's former deputy attorney general, is charged with covering up evidence and impeding the investigation he conducted into the assassination the previous fall of his own brother, another member of the Mexican governing party. The brother of former Mexican president Carlos Salinas de Gortari has been charged with ordering the assassination.

7 The lead detective in the O.J. Simpson double murder trial testifies that the single set of footprints at the crime scene persuaded police that a single killer was responsible for both murders. (For further details, see Part I: "Major News Stories of the Year.")

8 Gunmen in Pakistan open fire on a van carrying three Americans to work at the U.S. Consulate in Karachi, killing two and wounding the third. The Pakistani government vows to do everything in its power to apprehend the gunmen, who disappeared into rush hour traffic in a taxi after the attack. Their identities and even their motives remain unclear.

9 Over the strong objections of the British government, Pres. Clinton permits Gerry Adams, the political leader of the Irish Republican Army, to make a money-raising tour of the U.S. Until 1994, the U.S. had condemned the IRA's political wing, Sinn Fein, as a terrorist organization.

10 Michael P.C. Carns, Pres. Clinton's choice for director of the CIA, suddenly abandons his quest for the job after the FBI uncovers evidence that he may have violated labor and immigration laws when he brought a young Filipino man into his household. Pres. Clinton immediately nominates Deputy Defense Sec. John M. Deutch to the post.

The Dept. of Labor reports a new four-year low in the unemployment rate of 5.4 percent, suggesting that the economic expansion in the U.S. is continuing.

11 Separate studies by the Bureau of Alcohol, Tobacco and Firearms, CBS News, and the International Association of Chiefs of Police demonstrate that the Brady law requiring background checks of handgun purchasers has stopped 45,000 felons from obtaining guns in the year since the law was passed.

12 At the request of his successor, former Mexican president Carlos Salinas de Gortari leaves his country for a life of exile in the United States. Once considered one of Mexico's strongest and most dynamic rulers, Salinas became embroiled in a scandal in which it is suggested that he may have played a part in one or more assassinations of key political figures.

A former officer in the Argentine Navy reveals for the first time, in lurid detail, how he and other officers pushed approximately 2,000 political activists out of planes flying over the Atlantic Ocean during the military government's "dirty war" of the 1970s.

13 The defense in the O.J. Simpson double murder tries to paint Detective Mark Fuhrman as a racist cop who planted evidence to frame Simpson for the murder of Nicole Brown Simpson and Ronald Goldman. (For further details, see Part I: "Major News Stories of the Year.")

Rainstorms pound California from Eureka to San Diego, causing some of the most expensive damages in state history, exceeding even the $1.3 billion in damages from floods in January.

14 Conoco Inc. backs off its $1 billion deal with Iran to develop two oil fields in the Persian Gulf. Pres. Clinton said the deal was technically legal under existing U.S. policy, but would have undermined U.S.sanctions against Iran. He says he will issue a directive barring all such agreements in the future.

Atty. Gen. Janet Reno appoints a special prosecutor to investigate the financial dealings of Housing Sec. Henry G. Cisneros after concluding that Cisneros lied to federal agents about payments he made to a former mistress.

In a move designed to speed up peace talks, Britain pulls 400 troops out of Northern Ireland, the largest reduction in British forces there in more than a decade. The action leaves about 18,000 British troops in Northern Ireland.

15 Democrats in the Senate score a victory for Pres. Clinton when they muster the necessary votes to stage a filibuster over a Senate plan to undo Clinton's executive order barring federal contracts to companies that replace striking workers with permanent employees.

The military junta in Myanmar releases 31 key political prisoners, including opposition leader U Tin Oo to commemorate the 50th anniversary of Armed Forces Day. Daw Aung San Suu Kyi, who won the 1991 Nobel Peace Prize for her attempts to bring democracy to Myanmar, remains under house arrest, however.

16 Norman E. Thagard becomes the first American astronaut to board the Russian space station *Mir.* Thagard, who was launched with two other Russian crewmates on a Russian Soyuz capsule from Kazakhstan two days earlier, will remain on the space station for three months.

17 A federal judge in Washington rules that the Bell Atlantic Corporation—and consequently all of the seven regional Baby Bell companies—may compete directly with cable operators and broadcasters by transmitting programs anywhere in the country. Regulations imposed during the 1984 breakup of the Bell System had prevented the Baby Bells from offering long-distance telephone service. But the judge, Harold H. Greene, rules that this restriction does not apply to long-distance transmission of television programs.

18 Ukraine's Parliament removes the separatist leader of the Crimean region and revokes the Crimean constitution in an effort to reassert Ukrainian control over the area. Separatists in Crimea, led by President Yuri Meshkov, have sought stronger ties with Russia because most of its residents are ethnic Russians.

19 Michael Jordan returns to the Chicago Bulls

21 months after retiring from basketball and an unsuccessful attempt to become a major league baseball player. Television ratings for the broadcast are the highest of the year.

20 After Russian president Boris Yeltsin says he will eliminate a show of arms from a military parade in Red Square, Pres. Clinton announces that he will attend May 9 V-E Day ceremonies in Moscow to celebrate the 50th anniversary of the Allied victory in Europe in World War II.

Turkish troops numbering nearly 35,000 attack the undefended border with Iraq in pursuit of separatist Kurdish rebels. The three-pronged attack, complete with tanks and jet fighters, is the largest military operation in the history of the Turkish republic. Prime Minister Tansu Ciller says the operation was an attempt to end the Kurdish rebels' terrorist attacks.

21 A guerrilla-style nerve gas attack on a subway station in Tokyo kills eight and hospitalizes nearly 5,000 others. (For further details see Part I: "Major News Stories of the Year.")

22 A former employee at the Montclair, N.J., post office is charged with the killing of four men in a robbery there the day before. A computer search revealed that the man, Christopher Green, was the registered owner of a handgun matching the caliber of the weapon used.

More than 2,500 police officers raid the offices of a religious sect that authorities say is responsible for the nerve gas attack on the Tokyo subway system. (For further details see Part I: "Major News Stories of the Year.")

23 The Senate overwhelmingly (69–29) approves the line-item veto, which would give the president the power to veto only specific portions of congressional spending bills without rejecting the entire package.

The Senate Commerce Committee approves a proposal to ban from the Internet all material it deems obscene, lewd, lascivious, filthy, or indecent.

A government informer who says that Malcolm X's daughter tried to hire him to kill Louis Farrakhan admits the government promised to pay him $45,000 for his help in the case. The defense for Qubilah Bahiyah Shabazz seeks to have the charges against her thrown out for "gross governmental misconduct."

24 In the wake of evidence that the CIA employed a Guatemalan colonel linked to the killing of an American and the husband of an American, Pres. Clinton warns of a radical shakeup at the intelligence agency. He removes a top-ranking official from his post and threatens further dismissals of any others who deliberately withhold information about the killings.

The House of Representatives passes legislation to cut $69 billion in spending on social welfare programs from the federal budget. The vote, largely along party lines, would give the states considerably more control over how to allocate federal monies to low-income people in need of federal assistance; welfare payments would be limited to five years of cash benefits. Pres. Clinton denounces the bill.

25 Former heavyweight boxing champion Mike Tyson leaves an Indiana prison after serving three years for raping an 18-year-old beauty contestant. He says nothing about his widely anticipated return to the ring.

26 The National Labor Relations Board seeks an injunction against major league baseball owners for unfair labor practices in its seven-month-long dispute with baseball players. The players have said they would return to work if the injuction is granted.

27 In a week of fighting in Algeria, government special forces step up their attacks on Islamic militants, killing between 300 and 600 rebels. In their pursuit of a pure Islamic state, the rebels continue to kill intellectuals, writers, artists, and journalists who oppose them, including the recent assassination of the executive editor of Algeria's oldest daily newspaper.

28 Two of Japan's largest banks merge to create the world's largest banking company, with a total of $819 billion in assets. Together, the Bank of Tokyo and the Mitsubishi Bank will be about a third larger than Sumitomo Bank, the next-largest bank, and more than three times the size of Citibank, the U.S.'s largest bank.

The limousine driver who took O.J. Simpson to the airport on June 12, 1994, contradicts Simpson's alibi that he was home during the time prosecutors say Simpson murdered his ex-wife and Ronald Goldman. (For further details see Part I: "Major News Stories of the Year.")

29 In a major defeat for the Contract with America, the House of Representatives rejects four separate proposals, all of which would have imposed term limits of some kind on members of Congress. It is the first measure from the Contract to fail in the House.

30 A federal judge strikes down the Pentagon's "don't ask, don't tell" policy on homosexuals in the military, saying it violates the First and Fifth Amendments and catered to fears and prejudices of heterosexual troops.

31 A federal judge in New York issues an injunction against major league baseball owners for unfair labor practices. The decision restores arbitration, free agency, and other provisions of the collective bargaining agreement that were in effect when the players went on strike Aug. 12, 1994. The players end their seven-month-long strike after the injunction is issued.

Pres. Clinton travels to Port-Au-Prince to oversee the withdrawal of U.S. troops from Haiti and the transition of security responsibilities for the country from the U.S. to the United Nations. He praises the Haitian government and the U.S. forces for engineering "the triumph of freedom over fear," but places the burden on the Haitians for maintaining a fair society.

April 1995

1 The U.S. Immigration and Naturalization Service reports that the number of legal immigrants applying for U.S. citizenship has nearly doubled in the past year. The INS attributes the surge to recent initiatives by Congress and by the state of California to deny benefits to noncitizens.

2 Owners of the 28 major league baseball teams fail to collect enough votes to lock out baseball players returning to work after gaining an injunction restoring the previous year's working conditions.

3 Ignoring the strong protest of the U.S. government, Russia's government announces it will proceed with the sale of light-water nuclear reactors to Iran. Russia says only that it will "take actions to reduce the proliferation risk."

A federal jury in Alexandria, Va., convicts former United Way chairman William Aramony of stealing more than $600,000 from the charity and using the money to pay for vacations, luxury apartments, and other perks for himself and his teenage girlfriend.

4 Ukraine's Parliament throws out the entire cabinet in an overwhelming vote of no-confidence. Pres. Leonid Kuchma seizes the opportunity to create a team of leaders willing to pursue his market reforms to modernize the country.

5 The House of Representatives passes a bill to cut taxes by $189 billion over five years, the biggest tax break in 14 years. The majority of the cuts will come in the form of a $500-per-child credit to taxpaying families. Democrats denounce the package as a reckless giveaway to rich people.

6 The Seagram company pays $7 billion for an 80 percent stake in the movie and entertainment giant MCA.

7 Displaying more assertiveness than he has since the GOP's sweeping electoral victory in November, Pres. Clinton threatens to veto a host of bills passed by the House unless they are altered substantially.

Congress approves legislation to create an oversight board to manage the finances of the District of Columbia for at least eight years. The Oversight Board will have authority to overrule decisions of the City Council and Mayor Marion Barry.

8 Robert S. McNamara, the defense secretary to Presidents Kennedy and Johnson who was a major supporter of escalating U.S. involvement in the Vietnam War, publishes a memoir in which he admits that he and others in the government knew as early as 1963 that the U.S. should have withdrawn from Southeast Asia. He is immediately criticized for trying to clear his conscience at so late a date and after so many thousands of Americans lost their lives fighting "McNamara's War."

9 The dollar continues its descent against the Japanese yen to a new postwar low, losing 4% of its value in a single day. It rebounds slightly when Japanese finance minister Masayoshi Takemura calls for a "fundamental review" of the global exchange rate system.

Amid allegations of widespread ballot-tampering, Peruvian president Alberto Fujimori overwhelmingly wins a bid for reelection, with approximately 60 percent of the vote, more than double that of his closest rival, former UN secretary general Javier Perez de Cuellar.

10 Palestinian police arrest more than 100 members of Hamas and Islamic Holy War, the two militant groups that took credit for a bombing the day before that killed eight Israelis in the Gaza Strip. The militant groups oppose talks with Israel to bring peace to the Middle East.

11 Russian government forces clash with militant Islamic rebels on the border between Tajikistan and Afghanistan. They kill close to 50 rebels in retaliation for repeated Islamic attacks on the remote border post.

12 Billionaire investor Kirk Kerkorian announces a $22.8 billion takeover offer of the Chrysler Corporation. The offer of $55 a share is 40 percent higher than current trading prices.

A group of Republican governors offers its own proposal to reform the welfare system, saying the bill passed by the House of Representatives places too many restrictions on them. They urge the Senate to give them more freedom to distribute federal funds to the needy.

Nelson Mandela quietly reinstates his estranged wife Winnie into his cabinet, saying her earlier dismissal was "technically and procedurally invalid." He intimates that he will again dismiss her with greater legal precision.

13 Tokyo approves a plan to stop the decline of the dollar against the yen. Japan's central bank will cut its discount lending rate by three-quarters of a percentage point from its current level of 1.75 percent.

14 The UN Security Council votes to ease sanctions against Iraq, making it easier for Baghdad to sell oil to meet its urgent need for medicine, food, and other humanitarian aid. If Iraq accepts the waiver, it would mark the first break in the embargo since Saddam Hussein invaded Kuwait in 1989.

15 Pres. Clinton lays out a three-pronged agenda for the next round of battles with the Republicans in Congress. He pledges to focus on tax cuts linked to education, an overhaul of the welfare system, and anticrime measures that will preserve the ban on assault weapons.

16 Several new studies show that the gap in wealth between the richest and poorest people is wider in the U.S. than in any other western nation. The studies show that far from being an egalitarian society, America is even more economically stratified than traditional class-based societies like Britain, where disparities in wealth have existed for hundreds of years.

Senate Majority Leader Bob Dole says he will oppose Dr. Henry Foster, Pres. Clinton's choice for surgeon general and may even prevent the nomination from coming to a vote.

17 Pres. Clinton signs an executive order that radically alters government regulations on secrecy of documents. Under the new rules, all but the most highly classified documents will be made public after 25 years.

A federal appeals court throws out a settlement in a class-action lawsuit between General Motors and owners of 5.7 million GM trucks suspected of posing a fire hazard in sideways crashes. The court says the settlement, which would have given consumers coupons of $1,000 toward the purchase of new GM trucks, was little more than "a sophisticated marketing program aimed at selling more GM trucks."

18 The dollar continues its steep descent, plunging to new post–World War II lows against the Japanese yen and the German mark, shaking both the stock and bond markets.

Pres. Clinton criticizes as too harsh on children the plan to overhaul the welfare system passed by the Republican-controlled House of Representatives. He calls on Congress to pass by the Fourth of July a comprehensive bill that would put the poor to work and give states more flexibility in extending benefits.

19 A massive car bomb blows up a federal building in Oklahoma City, killing 167 people, including 15 children whose parents had just dropped them off at a day-care center in the building. (See also Part I: "Major News Stories of the Year.")

A cease-fire in Sri Lanka's long ethnic war collapses as rebel commandos attack a key government naval base and blow up two gunboats, killing 11 sailors and injuring 21 others. The rebel leader, Vellupillai Prabakharan, cites the government's intransigence in peace talks to concede to several rebel demands.

20 The FBI releases sketches of two men it says are the primary suspects in the bombing of an Oklahoma City federal building.

21 Authorities in Oklahoma City apprehend Timothy McVeigh, one of the men it suspects of setting off the bomb at the Alfred Murrah Federal Building two days earlier. (See also Part I: "Major News Stories of the Year.")

A chemical plant in Lodi, N.J., explodes and burns, killing four workers and forcing the evacuation of hundreds of nearby residents who feared they might have been the victims of a blast similar to the Oklahoma City bombing.

22 Rwandan government officials open fire on a Hutu refugee camp in Kibeho, causing a panic in which 2,000 Hutus are killed by gunfire or trampled to death by fleeing refugees. The government says 300 were killed.

23 Pres. Clinton asks Congress to grant him broad powers to combat terrorism in the U.S. Foremost among his requests is the creation of a domestic antiterrorism force under the aegis of the FBI. Clinton also asks for authority to make it easier for federal agents to obtain wiretaps and monitor telephone calls and travel records of suspected terrorists. Clinton travels to Oklahoma City for a memorial service for victims of the bombing.

Socialist candidate Lionel Jospin places first in the preliminary round of presidential elections in France. He will face second-place finisher Jacques Chirac, the conservative mayor of Paris in the second-round runoff.

24 The court-appointed lawyers for bombing suspect Timothy McVeigh ask to be excused from defending him, saying that they knew people killed in the blast.

25 Federal officials say that the mysterious serial bomber known as the Unabomber, who has claimed responsibility for more than a dozen bombings in the past 17 years, sent several letters to major media outlets including the *New York Times,* prior to delivering a package bomb that killed the California Forestry Association president in Sacramento the day before.

26 The Supreme Court overturns a five-year-old federal law making it a crime to possess a gun within 1,000 feet of a school. The 5–4 decision limits the federal government's ability to play a larger role in local law enforcement.

Turkey claims victory in its five-week assault on separatist Kurdish rebels along the Iraqi border. The country now faces the more difficult task of maintaining peace and securing the mountainous border area that had become a launching pad for attacks on Turkey by the Kurdistan Workers' party.

27 The Justice Dept. files an antitrust lawsuit against Microsoft Corporation, blocking the software giant from acquiring Intuit, the maker of Quicken, the leading personal finance software program. The Justice Dept. contends that the merger, the largest ever in the software industry, would severely limit competition.

A new study by an archaeologist at George Washington University shows that Africans were the first society to use tools, not Europeans, as many experts have long believed. The study cites tools discovered in Zaire that predate similar tools found in Europe by more than 60,000 years.

28 A leaking gas main at a subway construction site in Taegu, South Korea, causes an explosion, killing more than 100 people, most of them students.

New federal studies show the success of a decade-long grassroots fund-raising program by the Republican party. GOP House and Senate candidates raised $50 million more than their Democratic counterparts in 1993–94, with most of the edge provided by individual contributors giving less than $500.

29 The National Academy of Sciences says it will recommend that Congress change the way it defines and measures poverty. The proposed change, which would define the poverty level using disposable income after taxes and essential expenses rather than cash income before taxes, would substantially increase the number of working poor.

30 Pres. Clinton says he will order a trade embargo against Iran, stepping up the government's effort to isolate Teheran as an "inspiration and paymaster to terrorists."

May 1995

1 Hours before she was to stand trial for an attempt to hire a hit man to kill Louis Farrakhan, Qubilah Bayihah Shabazz reaches a plea agreement with federal prosecutors in which she accepts responsibility for her involvement in the sketchy plot, but receives no jail time. Shabazz, the daughter of Farrakhan rival Malcolm X, will spend three months in a psychiatric and drug treatment program and receive two years' probation.

2 The Clinton administration reverses a 35-year-old policy of giving Cuban refugees special treatment when applying for political asylum in the U.S. The administration says it will admit a group of 20,000 refugees now held at Guantanamo Bay Naval Station, but after that, all Cuban boat people will be returned to Cuba.

Federal authorities apprehend and detain two men they were looking for as material witnesses in the Oklahoma City bombing but releases them just after midnight.

3 Police in Tokyo arrest a top official and lawyer for the Aum Shinrikyo religious cult on charges related to the nerve gas attack on the Tokyo subway system two months earlier. (See also Part I: "Major News Stories of the Year.")

4 Republicans in the Senate fail to pass legislation to make sweeping changes to the nation's civil litigation system. Termed "loser pays" legislation by some, but "The Drunk Drivers Protection Act of 1995" by Pres. Clinton (who threatened to veto the bill if passed), the bill would have limited civil damage awards in state and federal courts.

A former aide to Sheik Omar Abdel Rahman, suspected mastermind of the World Trade Center bombing, testifies that Rahman told him to assassinate Egyptian president Hosni Mubarak while Mubarak was in the U.S. two years ago. The aide, Abdo Mohammed Haggag, testifies against Rahman when federal prosecutors agree to drop conspiracy charges against Haggag for his involvement in a plot to blow up several New York City buildings and tunnels and assassinate key political leaders.

5 Rescue workers at the Oklahoma City federal building hold a memorial service signaling the end of hope of finding survivors in the rubble and the beginning of healing from the bombing. (See also Part I: "Major News Stories of the Year.")

The Bureau of Labor Statistics reports that the unemployment rate jumped three-tenths of a point, to 5.8 percent in April, and that the number of new jobs fell for the first time in two years. The report confirms signs that the economy is slowing its pace and raises fears that the Federal Reserve Bank's anti-inflationary interest rate hikes may have gone too far.

6 Allied leaders celebrate the 50th anniversary of V-E Day. In London, Queen Elizabeth calls on the young people of the world to stop the spread of prejudice and hatred.

7 Jacques Chirac, the conservative mayor of Paris who ran for president unsuccessfully twice before, wins this time, with more than 52 percent of the vote, defeating Lionel Jospin, who had hoped to succeed his fellow Socialist François Mitterand after 14 years in office.

House Speaker Newt Gingrich pledges that the House's proposed budget will include sharp cuts to Medicare spending, but will not significantly affect anyone now enrolled in the health program for America's elderly population.

8 Prosecutors in the O.J. Simpson trial begin the DNA evidence phase of their case, in which they will attempt to show that genetic fingerprints on key pieces of evidence prove Simpson's guilt in the double murder. (See also Part I: "Major News Stories of the Year.")

Ethiopia's ruling coalition government wins a new five-year term in the country's first multiparty general election. The victory by the People's Revolutionary Democratic Front is aided by a boycott of the election by many main opposition parties.

9 Federal prosecutors charge Terry Nichols with direct involvement in the Oklahoma City bombing. In a separate story, a federal magistrate appoints new counsel for Oklahoma City bombing suspect Timothy McVeigh after his first lawyers ask to be excused because they knew people killed in the blast. (See also Part I: "Major News Stories of the Year.")

Interest rates on long-term bonds fall below 7 percent for the first time in more than a year, signaling a boost to the economy that will likely deter a recession.

10 The House Budget Committee votes largely along party lines to approve a federal budget plan that would erase the national deficit over the next seven years. In addition to cutting more than $1.1 trillion in spending, the House bill would also have to dig deeper to pay for a $340 billion tax cut.

Former president George Bush angrily resigns from the National Rifle Association after reading a fund-raising letter in which the organization described federal law-enforcement agents as "jackbooted Government thugs." Pres. Clinton praises his predecessor and joins Bush in condemning the NRA.

11 More than 170 nations agree to extend indefinitely the Treaty on the Nonproliferation of Nuclear Weapons, which has limited the spread of nuclear weapons for 25 years already. The original treaty, signed in 1970, limited nuclear weapons to the five countries that had them at the time: the U.S., Britain, France, China, and the Soviet Union.

12 The World Health Organization, an arm of the UN, sends a team of scientists to Zaire to attempt to control the spread of the Ebola virus, a deadly virus that has killed 48 people. Scientists do not know what causes the virus, which has erupted in Africa for the third time since it was discovered in 1976, but they do know how to stop it from spreading.

13 Iran's top nuclear official says his country is planning 10 nucelar power reactors, but denies charges by the U.S. that Teheran is trying to build nuclear weapons. The official, Reza Amrollahi, reveals that Iran has signed an agreement with China for two nuclear reactors and was in negotiation for a third.

14 Argentina's president Carlos Menem survives a late surge by Senator José Octavio Bordón to win a second term in nationwide elections.

15 Japanese police storm the headquarters of the Aum Shinrikyo religious sect and arrest cult leader Shoko Asahara and 14 others for organizing the nerve gas attack on the Tokyo subway system two months earlier. (See also Part I: "Major News Stories of the Year.")

Overwhelmed by the number of personal injury claims filed against it by hundreds of women who used their silicone breast implants, the Dow Corning Corporation files for bankruptcy protection. The filing means that the bankruptcy court will decide how much the company will have to pay to compensate women who say they were harmed by the implants.

16 In a last-ditch effort to convince Japan to open its trading markets to American goods, the Clinton administration places a 100 percent tariff on imports of Japanese luxury cars. The sanctions are technically scheduled to go into effect in three days, but they would be reversible if the two countries reach a trade agreement by the end of June.

17 The Senate Ethics Committee accuses Sen. Bob Packwood (R-Oreg.) of bringing "discredit upon the United States Senate" for allegations of his sexual misconduct and for seeking help from lobbyists to get his wife a job.

Pres. Clinton vows to use the first veto of his presidency to block a bill that would cut $16.4 billion in spending. He accuses the Republicans of protecting pork-barrel projects at the expense of education, the environment, and crime prevention.

Atty. Gen. Janet Reno orders a special prosecutor to investigate the financial dealings of Commerce Sec. Ron Brown.

18 A state DNA evidence witness for the prosecution in the O.J. Simpson double murder trial testifies that there is only a 1 in 21 million chance blood found on O.J. Simpson's socks came from anybody except Nicole Brown Simpson. (See also Part I: "Major News Stories of the Year.")

19 Michael Fortier, an army buddy of Timothy McVeigh's, tells federal authorities that he and McVeigh inspected the federal building in Oklahoma City as a bombing target several days before the blast. (See also Part I: "Major News Stories of the Year.")

NASA says it will make deep cuts in its workforce to shrink the agency back to about the same size it was in 1961, before the Apollo space program. The agency plans to cut about 28,000 civil service and contractor jobs and ultimately turn over operation of the space shuttle program to private industry.

20 Citing security concerns long voiced by the Secret Service, Pres. Clinton closes the stretch of Pennsylvania Ave. in front of the White House to all but pedestrians in an attempt to deter a car or truck-bomb attack.

Former Italian prime minister Silvio Berlusconi is indicted for corruption. The indictment charges Berlusconi's company, Fininvest, with paying bribes totaling nearly $200,000 to government tax inspectors. Berlusconi continues to deny the allegations.

21 Heavy rains cause the Mississippi and Missouri Rivers to jump their banks, resulting in flooding throughout the Midwest. The floods are not as bad as those two years earlier, primarily because the government succeeded in persuading people to move permanently to higher ground.

Top Clinton administration aides say the president will break with a 16-year-old policy and issue a visa to Taiwanese president Li Teng-hui. In doing so, Clinton risks the wrath of Beijing, which the U.S. agreed in 1979 to recognize as the sole government of China.

22 The Supreme Court votes 5–4 that neither the states nor Congress may impose term limits on congressional office without a constitutional amendment. The sweeping decision wipes out term-limit legislation in 23 states but does not affect term limits for state offices.

In a separate decision, the Court rules unanimously that police must knock and announce their presence before entering a home with a search warrant.

23 An armed intruder climbs the fence of the

South Lawn of the White House before being shot and wounded by a Secret Service agent at about 10:45 P.M. Though the president was never in any danger, it was the third breach of security at the White House since September.

Germany's highest court rules that East German spymasters cannot be tried in a reunited Germany and that espionage officials already convicted do not have to serve their sentences. The ruling gives virtual amnesty to dozens of former Communist spymasters.

24 Syria makes a major concession in Middle East peace talks, abandoning its insistence that Israel and Syria withdraw their troops an equal distance from the Golan Heights. While the concession breaks an impasse in talks between the two countries, it does not address the core issues that continue to divide them, including Israel's demand that Syria consent to full peace with full diplomatic relations and open trade, and Syria's demand that Israel withdraw all troops from the Golan Heights.

25 The Senate approves a budget proposal that will eliminate the federal deficit by the year 2002. The legislation now goes to conference where differences between this bill and the one passed by the House, primarily a $183 billion difference in the amount of tax cuts, will be ironed out.

In response to the Bosnian Serbs' use of heavy weapons around Sarajevo, NATO warplanes, including eight U.S. jets, bomb an ammunition depot near Serbian political headquarters in Pale. It is the most direct NATO involvement to date in the ongoing civil war in the Balkans. Pres. Clinton warns the Serbs to stop shelling the Bosnian capital, but the Serbs respond by shelling five of the six Bosnian towns designated as "safe areas" by the UN.

26 In retaliation for a second NATO strike in as many days on Serbian headquarters in Pale, Bosnian Serbs chain UN officers to poles and other fixtures outside ammunition depots and other key installations, using them as human shields from further NATO bombings.

The Immigration and Naturalization Service announces that it will formally recognize rape, sexual abuse, and other forms of domestic violence against women as grounds for political asylum. In the past, the INS and immigration courts had considered sexual violence a private act, even when committed by soldiers or government officials.

27 The entire board of the troubled Chicago Housing Authority resigns, leaving the nation's second-largest housing agency in the hands of the federal government. The Dept. of Housing and Urban Development will take over Chicago's 40,000 public housing units in the largest federal takeover of a housing agency.

NATO and UN involvement in the war in the Balkans increases as UN troops attempt to recapture an observation post in central Sarajevo. Two French soldiers are killed in the exchange. Instead of halting their attacks, Serbs shell Muslim towns and begin seizing UN troops. (See also Part I: "Major News Stories of the Year.")

28 An earthquake on Russia's Sakhalin Island north of Japan kills at least 2,000 people, with thousands more buried in the rubble. The quake measures 7.5 on the Richter scale.

29 The U.S., Britain, France, Germany, and Russia resolve to expand the size of the UN force in Bosnia in response to Serbian attacks on UN forces in Bosnia-Herzegovina.

Bowing to threats of political violence by Muslim separatists, India's government cancels elections in the state of Kashmir. Violence in the state flared after a Muslim shrine in the region was razed during a confrontation between rebels and government troops.

30 Pres. Clinton says the U.S. is prepared to offer American troops to a combat role to reinforce UN peacekeeping troops in Bosnia, which currently number 22,500.

31 In move designed to enhance his standing with the religious right, Senate Majority Leader Bob Dole attacks the entertainment industry for inundating popular culture with violent images hostile to family values. Dole specifically singles out Time Warner for promoting gangsta rap recordings with lyrics that describe violence against the police. Critics immediately lambaste Dole for picking on Hollywood when it is Congress, not the entertainment industry, that has the power to control issues of violence through gun and crime control legislation.

California governor Pete Wilson condemns affirmative action as unfair and unjust and says he will abandon them throughout the state government wherever his power allows him to do so. In an open letter to the people of California, Wilson says "merit," not race or sex, will be the basis for decisions regarding state employment, contracting, and school admissions policies.

June 1995

1 The actor Christopher Reeve is thrown from his horse during a show jumping trial, leaving him paralyzed below the neck and unable to breathe without a mechanical respirator. His doctor says the damage is most likely irreversible.

California governor Pete Wilson moves quickly to dismantle affirmative action programs in his state. He signs an executive order that, among other things, reduces by half the amount of transportation money to be set aside for minority contractors and eliminates 150 boards that provide hiring advice based on race and sex to state agencies.

2 Bosnian Serbs shoot down a U.S. fighter plane flying a NATO mission over northern Bosnia, drawing the U.S. deeper into the conflict in the Balkans. The pilot ejects from the jet; his whereabouts remain unknown. Shortly after the attack, in a goodwill gesture, the Serbs relase 120 UN hostages they have held for the past week.

The Dept. of Labor reports that employers cut more than 100,000 jobs in May alone, the biggest monthly decline in employment since the spring of 1991. The news is an indication of a slowing economy.

3 In response to criticism from Congress and the public about earlier comments he made suggesting that the U.S. might step up its involvement in the Balkan region, Pres. Clinton says American troops would only be used if NATO allies "become stranded and could not get out of a particular place in Bosnia."

4 A member of the Los Angeles County Board of Supervisors tallies up the total cost of the O.J. Simpson double murder trial to California taxpayers: $5 million as of April 30, and spiraling at the rate of about $1 million per month. (For further details, see Part I: "Major News Stories of the Year.")

5 IBM makes a surprise $3.3 billion bid to acquire Lotus Development Corporation. The deal would be the computer industry giant's first-ever hostile takeover and the largest amount ever paid for a computer software company.

6 South Africa's Supreme Court, in its first major decision, abolishes capital punishment as unconstitutional. It ends the country's tradition of using the death penalty not only as punishment but as a means of terror in enforcing racial segregation.

Bosnian Serbs continue to release more UN peacekeepers, but Serbian officials say they are not holding the American pilot whose F-16 fighter plane was shot down by a Bosnian Serb missile. The Bosnian Serbs release 108 peacekeepers at the urging of Serbian president Slobodan Milosevic, and promise to release the remaining 149 "in the next few days."

7 A federal grand jury indicts Arkansas governor Jim Guy Tucker, charging him with falsifying statements in an attempt to hide from the IRS profits he made from a multimillion-dollar cable TV deal.

The *New York Times* obtains documents revealing that over 15 years of studies on nicotine, Philip Morris discovered that it produced "pharmacological" effects on the body and brain, contradicting the tobacco giant's current claim that nicotine should not be regulated by the Food and Drug Administration under laws that apply to body- and mind-altering drugs.

The Senate sweepingly (91–8) approves an antiterrorism bill that gives the government broad powers to monitor the activities of suspected terrorists and to deport illegal aliens suspected of terrorism. Civil liberties experts warn that the bill tramples constitutional rights in the hysteria to prevent future bombings like the one in Oklahoma City.

Pres. Clinton uses his first veto to strike down a $16.4 billion spending cut passed by both houses of Congress. "I cannot in good conscience sign a bill that cuts education to save pet congressional projects," Clinton says.

8 Scott O'Grady, the American pilot whose F-16 fighter plane was shot down by a Bosnian Serb missile while on a regular monitoring mission six days earlier, is found alive by an international rescue team and the U.S. Marines.

Ukraine's president Leonid Kuchma appoints Yevgeny Marchuk prime minister and forges ahead with several economic reforms. Under a power-sharing agreement reached earlier in the week, Kuchma retains full control over the government and all appointments.

9 Japan undercuts the U.S.'s attempts to isolate Iran by saying it will not join a trade embargo against Teheran. Because Japan is one of the largest consumers of Iranian oil—purchasing 400,000 barrels a day—its refusal to participate threatens to eviscerate the entire embargo.

Russia and Ukraine settle a bitter dispute over the Black Sea Fleet. Russian president Boris Yeltsin and Ukraine's president Leonid Kuchma meet in the Black Sea resort town of Sochi and agree to a 50–50 split of the 635-vessel fleet. Russia will then purchase 32 percent of the fleet back from Ukraine and pay Kiev rent for use of the Sevastopol naval base.

10 Capt. Scott O'Grady, the U.S. fighter pilot rescued from Bihac after his plane was shot down by a Serbian missile during a routine monitoring mission, tells a news conference audience how he ate bugs and drank rainwater from his socks to stay alive during the six days he was missing in a Bosnian forest.

11 IBM raises its offer to $3.5 billion, or $64 a share, to persuade Lotus Development Corporation to accept its hostile takeover bid. Under terms of the deal, Lotus will retain a degree of independence previously unseen at IBM.

12 The Supreme Court (5–4) rules that affirmative action programs can only survive constitutional scrutiny if they are "narrowly tailored" to accomplish a "compelling governmental interest." Although the standard the Court defines is difficult to meet, the justices stop short of invalidating all affirmative action programs.

In a separate ruling, the Court holds that lower federal courts had improperly ordered the state of Missouri to pay for a Kansas City desegregation plan that called for magnet schools and increases in teacher salaries.

13 Pres. Clinton proffers his own plan for balancing the federal budget. His proposal would take 10 years, not the seven proposed by Republicans, and would have a smaller tax cut, but also fewer reductions in Medicare spending.

14 The Senate votes overwhelmingly (84–16) to impose heavy penalties and lengthy prison terms on people who distribute explicit material over the Internet deemed "indecent." Civil liberties advocates criticize the measure, saying it would affect not only hard-core pornography, but also private communications among adults.

15 Chechen rebels cross the border into Russia, shooting civilians, taking hostages, and reportedly executing some of them. The commando-style attack on Budyonnovsk, 70 miles north of the Chechen border, is the first attack on Russian soil in the ongoing Chechen battle for independence. (See also Part I: "Major News Stories of the Year.")

Nicaraguan president Violeta Barrios de Chamorro ends a four-month stalemate with the National Assembly and agrees to a new constitution that gives the legislature greater powers at the expense of the executive.

O.J. Simpson tries on the bloody gloves found as evidence in the murders of Nicole Brown Simpson and Ronald Goldman, but claims they are "too tight." (See also Part I: "Major News Stories of the Year.")

16 Russian soldiers and tanks begin a counterattack on a hospital captured the day before by Chechen rebels in the Russian town of Budyonnovsk.

Salt Lake City, Utah, wins the right to host the 2002 Winter Olympics competition.

Still angry over a U.S. decision to grant a visa to Taiwan's president, China recalls its ambassador to the U.S. Ambassador Li Daoyu does not say that China is planning to downgrade diplomatic relations with the U.S.

17 Chechen rebels in Budyonnovsk continue to release hostages from the hospital it captured two days earlier, but repel two assaults by Russian troops seeking to retake the building. Leaders of the seven major industrialized nations, meeting at a Summit conference in Halifax, Nova Scotia, warn Russian president Boris Yeltsin not to resolve the situation in Chechnya by military means.

18 As Bosnian Serbs release the last 26 UN peacekeepers it has held hostage for more than two weeks, the UN announces it will abandon its attempt to protect Sarajevo from bombardment by heavy artillery. The sequence of events unwittingly rewards the Bosnian Serbs for using terrorist tactics to achieve almost all of their demands in the ongoing battle.

Russian prime minister Viktor Chernomyrdin orders a cease-fire throughout Chechnya and agrees to peace talks with rebel leaders.

19 The Supreme Court rules unanimously that the private sponsors of Boston's St. Patrick's Day Parade have a constitutional right to exclude gay and lesbian groups from marching.

The U.S. broadens its trade dispute with Japan, threatening to bar Japanese airlines from profitable cargo routes in the U.S. in retaliation for Japan's refusal to allow Federal Express to expand operations there. The threatened sanctions are separate from plans to impose 100 percent tariffs on imports of Japanese luxury automobiles, but are part of a U.S. plan to confront Japan directly on trade matters.

In a humiliating defeat, Russia allows the Chechen commandos who stormed a hospital complex in Budyonnovsk and took more than 2,000 hostages to return to Chechnya after almost all their demands are met. (For further details, see Part I: "The Year in Review.")

20 The Southern Baptist Convention, America's largest Protestant denomination, votes to apologize for slavery and ask forgiveness from "all African-Americans." The church was founded in the 19th century, largely in defense of slavery.

21 Senate Majority Leader Bob Dole finally brings the nomination of Dr. Henry Foster as surgeon general to the Senate floor. Although Foster has more than the required 51 votes for confirmation, he does not have the 60 supporters necessary to cut off debate and bring the nomination to a vote. Pres. Clinton denounces Dole for using parliamentary politics to quash the nomination.

The Commerce Dept. reports that the nation's trade deficit increased to a record $11.37 billion in April. It cites indicators that auto dealers are stockpiling Japanese cars, in anticipation of the steep 100 percent tariffs the U.S has threatened if Japan does not open its auto and auto parts markets to U.S. companies.

22 In a gamble designed to solidify his party, British prime minister John Major resigns as leader of the Conservative party. The move forces immediate party elections, which he expects to win and use as a vote of confidence to quash critics within the party. But if he loses, he would have to step down as prime minister.

23 Hong Kong passes several laws intended to protect freedom of the press even after China takes back control of the city in 1997.

24 Top negotiators for each side agree to meet in Geneva as trade talks between the U.S. and Japan stall just four days before the deadline the U.S. has set for imposing punitive 100 percent tariffs on imports of Japanese automobiles.

25 Voters in Haiti flock to the polls for the first open democratic elections since the restoration of Pres. Jean-Bertrand Aristide. More positions are up for election in this balloting than at any other time in Haitian history. At least 100,000 Haitians are unable to vote, however, as polling places open late, or not at all.

In his first public interview since being charged with the Oklahoma City federal building bombing, Timothy McVeigh does not directly answer when the interviewer asks if he had bombed the building. When the interviewer prods him, saying "you've got a chance right now to say 'hell no!'" McVeigh replies, "We can't do that."

26 The United Healthcare Corporation, an operator of health maintenance organizations, announces it will buy Metrahealth, a more traditional health insurance company, in a $1.65 billion deal. The new company will be the largest provider of health plans in the country.

The Supreme Court (6–3) upholds a random drug testing program for the first time in its history, when it allows public school officials to subject student-athletes to random urinalysis testing as a condition of being allowed to participate in sports programs.

Egyptian president Hosni Mubarak survives an assassination attempt when gunmen toting automatic weapons open fire on his motorcade as it travels to an African summit in Addis Ababa, Ethiopia. Mubarak is unhurt by the attempt, but two of the gunmen and two Ethiopian police are killed in the shootout.

27 Although their county government is bankrupt, voters in Orange County, Calif., go to the polls and overwhelmingly reject a half-cent increase in the sales tax to help bail the government out of its fiscal crisis.

28 At the eleventh hour, the U.S. and Japan reach a broad accord on automotive trade in which the U.S. will abandon its threat to impose 100 percent tariffs on imports of Japanese luxury automobiles and Japan will open its automobile and auto parts markets to U.S. companies. The vaguely worded agreement carries no numerical promises other than voluntary cooperation by the two countries.

The House of Representatives votes overwhelmingly to adopt a constitutional amendment outlawing flag burning. Nearly 100 Democrats join 219 Republicans to top the two-thirds (280 votes) majority to amend the Constitution.

29 The Supreme Court (5–4) rules that congressional districts drawn with race as a "predominant factor" are unconstitutional. The decision invalidates a congressional district in Georgia in question, but leaves uncertain how to determine when race is the predominant factor in drawing other congressional districts.

The Supreme Court (5–4) rules that the University of Virginia is constitutionally required to give the same amount of financial support to a religious magazine as to any other student publication. Free speech advocates contend that denying funding to the religious magazine would punish them for their beliefs. The minority argue that allowing a university to subsidize a religious venture would constitute the establishment of religion.

The Unabomber delivers a 35,000-word manifesto calling for a revolution against the government to the *New York Times* and the *Washington Post,* saying he will stop trying to kill people if they will print the document. However, he says in the letter that he will not stop his destruction of property.

The space shuttle *Atlantis* docks flawlessly with the Russian space station *Mir,* raising hopes of a future joint U.S.-Russian space program.

30 Russian president Boris Yeltsin moves decisively to silence his opposition by removing three ministers from his cabinet, blaming them for the humiliating series of events in which a Chechen commando group took over a Russian hospital and killed hostages.

July 1995

1 Russia's Parliament narrowly defeats a vote of no-confidence that would have forced Pres. Boris Yeltsin and Prime Minister Viktor Chernomyrdin to form a new government or hold elections.

2 In Sarajevo, Bosnian Serbs shell UN headquarters, culminating in two days of attacks that killed 13 and wounded 81.

3 In Thailand the Chart Thai, or Thai Nation party, moves to form a coalition government headed by new Prime Minister Banharn Silparcha after winning controversial elections several days earlier. Two leading members of this party have been denied U.S. visas because of alleged drug dealing.

4 In London, Prime Minister John Major is reelected as leader of the Conservative party by a comfortable margin, 218 to 89, over John Redwood; there were 22 abstentions.

In Jerusalem, Israel and the Palestine Liberation Organization announce the outline of an agreement calling for Israeli troop withdrawals in the West Bank, setting the stage for Palestinian elections and expanded self-rule.

The space shuttle *Atlantis* ends its five-day linkup with the Russian space station *Mir* and heads back to Earth.

5 The head of a UN inspection team tells the Security Council that Iraq has admitted for the first time that it produced offensive biological weapons in 1989–90, shortly before it invaded Kuwait.

6 In Washington, the Federal Reserve reduces short-term interest rates slightly for the first time since 1992; the federal funds rate is now 5.75 percent, down from 6 percent.

The prosecution in the O.J. Simpson double murder trial ends its 92-day presentation of the evidence against the former football star. (See also Part I: "Major News Stories of the Year.")

7 The U.S. Labor Department reports a downturn in unemployment to 5.6 percent, much stronger than most analysts predicted.

In the central Chinese city of Wuhan, the Chinese government arrests Harry Wu, a U.S. citizen, charging him with obtaining state secrets, a very serious political offense.

In northern Iraq, Turkish planes and helicopters bomb villages of Kurds, forcing thousands to flee. Tanks join in the assault.

8 The Chinese government officially charges Harry Wu with espionage three weeks after he was detained at a remote border crossing in Kazakhstan. Wu's arrest is seen as a serious threat to already strained U.S.-China relations.

9 In Sarajevo UN officials again threaten to have NATO bomb Bosnian Serbs if they attack a UN position in eastern Bosnia. Meanwhile 30 Dutch peacekeeping troops remain as hostages to prevent the bombing.

10 Pres. Clinton endorses congressional proposals to require TV manufacturers to install a computer chip (called a V-chip) that would block out programs precoded as violent.

In the eastern Bosnian town of Srebrenica, UN peace keepers clash with Bosnian Serb forces demanding that all UN troops and the 42,000 civilians (most of them refugees) leave the area.

Government officials in Yangon, Myanmar, release Nobel Peace Prize recipient Daw Aung San Suu Kyi after six years of confinement. The release does not require her to leave the country as the government had demanded earlier.

11 At the White House, Pres. Clinton announces full diplomatic recognition of Vietnam, 22 years after U.S. withdrawal from the most divisive war in American history. Clinton says the U.S. will continue to press Vietnam for a full accounting of the 2,202 U.S. servicemen officially listed as missing.

Bosnian Serb forces overwhelm the UN peacekeeping force at Srebrenica, a so-called "safe area," causing at least 20,000 civilians to flee.

In Moscow, Russian president Boris Yeltsin is hospitalized for "acute" heart pains but officials assert that he is fully conscious and in control of the government.

12 In a speech to students in Vienna, Virginia, Pres. Clinton asserts his belief that the First Amendment does not prevent religious expression in the schools and he announces that he has ordered government officials to distribute national guidelines explaining what is permitted.

The Food and Drug Administration announces that it believes nicotine is a drug that should be regulated as such; FDA officials submit proposed regulations to the White House.

Bosnian Serb forces seize Potocari, the last UN stronghold in the "safe area" and begin busing thousands of women, children, and the elderly out of the region. About 40,000 refugees are now in the area.

The Chinese government asks Pres. Clinton to reaffirm the U.S. position that Taiwan is part of China and that the president of Taiwan will not be allowed to make any more visits to the U.S.

13 As thousands of Bosnian Muslim refugees flee from Srebrenica, telling stories of atrocities, Bosnian Serb forces begin to attack Zepa, another UN "safe zone." France calls on the U.S. and Britain to join a military operation to prevent further attacks.

The government of South Korea announces that twice as many people as were previously estimated are missing in the collapse of a Seoul department store two weeks earlier, bringing the toll to over 700.

Two groups of physicists announce they have independently created a type of matter whose existence was first postulated by Albert Einstein 70 years ago. The so-called Bose-Einstein condensate, a gas of atoms that are chilled to halt their normal motion, may have profound effects on quantum mechanics.

14 In Washington, FBI director Louis J. Freeh demotes Deputy Director Larry Potts only two months after his promotion to that job, because of his role in the Waco debacle and the shootout at Ruby Ridge in Idaho.

In Sarajevo, Bosnian Serb forces disregard NATO threats of retaliation and launch a new attack on the town of Zepa, another UN "safe area."

15 On the final day of the Republican National Committee's meeting in Philadelphia, Bob Dole and Phil Gramm clash on welfare reform as underdog Gramm attacks front-runner Dole for compromising and deal-cutting.

UN officials in Bosnia say that about 20,000 refugees from Srebrenica, most of them young men, are unaccounted for. Officials believe some have escaped but others are now being held as hostages.

16 Iraq finally releases William Barloon and David Daliberti, the two American civilians held captive for four months after they strayed into Iraq from Kuwait. They had been sentenced to eight years in prison.

In a formal statement, newly elected French president Jacques Chirac officially acknowledges France's responsibility for the deportation of thousands of Jews to Nazi death camps during World War II.

17 City officials in Chicago report that 179 people died there during a week-long heat wave in which temperatures reached a record high of 106°F.

The last American-owned television manufacturer, Zenith Electronics, agrees to sell controlling interest in the company to the South Korean LG Electronics Inc.

18 A special Senate committee, chaired by Alfonse D'Amato (R-N.Y.), opens hearings on Whitewater with an investigation into the White House's handling of events following deputy White House counsel Vincent Foster's suicide.

Senate Democrats unite to stall debate on a key Republican proposal to limit federal health, safety, and environmental regulations.

Bosnian troops defending the embattled area around Zepa threaten to use UN peacekeepers as human shields against the advancing Bosnian Serbs unless NATO provides air power to protect the region.

In Moscow, Russian president Boris Yeltsin appears on TV from his hospital room assuring his people and the world that although he is ill his condition is not life threatening.

19 In a speech at the National Archives in Washington, Pres. Clinton asserts his strong support for affirmative action programs and says they have been good for America.

In Washington, Pres. Clinton again rejects a French plan to reinforce UN peacekeeping troops in Bosnia and seeks allied support for a large-scale program of air attacks.

The Bosnian Serb army captures the UN "safe area" of Zepa, which the UN reports was already empty of civilians, but the Bosnian government army refuses to surrender.

20 Documents presented to the Senate Whitewater Committee reveal that senior Justice Dept. officials were very disturbed by the limitations imposed by the White House on the investigation into Vincent Foster's office after his suicide.

In San Francisco, the governing regents of the University of California vote to stop admitting students, hiring professors, and awarding contracts on the basis of race and sex.

21 At congressional hearings on the raids at the Branch Davidian compound in Waco, Tex., witnesses tell of their failed warnings to federal authorities that any attack would precipitate a holocaust by sect leader David Koresh.

In London, the U.S., French, and British governments pledge "substantial" air strikes against the Bosnian Serbs if they attack the safe area of Gorazde in eastern Bosnia.

22 At the White House, Pres. Clinton and his wife Hillary are questioned under oath by special counsel Kenneth Starr about the Whitewater affair.

In Union, S.C., a jury finds Susan Smith guilty of two counts of murder for drowning her two sons last Oct. 23.

Despite NATO warnings about retaliation, Bosnian Serbs continue their attack against Zepa and their heavy shelling of Sarajevo; the shelling of Gorazde, however, subsides.

23 Over 800 heavily equipped British and French troops move toward Sarajevo as the UN attempts to relieve the Bosnian capital.

Military authorities of Taiwan say that China fired four test missiles off its southern coast over the last two days. The New China News Agency issues an official commentary accusing Taiwan's president, Li Heng-hui, of plotting with some people in the U.S. to declare the island independent of mainland China.

24 At congressional hearings on the raid in Waco, an undercover agent who had infiltrated the Branch Davidians testifies that his superiors ignored warnings that David Koresh knew government agents were about to arrest him.

The Senate overwhelmingly passes legislation requiring thousands of lobbyists to register if they wish to deal with the government.

A Palestinian suicide bomber sets off a bomb in a bus killing at least five passengers and wounding 32 more in a Tel Aviv suburb. Israeli prime minister Yitzhak Rabin asserts that peace talks with the Palestinians will continue.

25 The Justice Dept. convenes a grand jury in New York to investigate whether tobacco companies misled regulators about the contents and effects of cigarettes.

In Paris a bomb explodes on a crowded train near Notre Dame, killing four and wounding 62.

26 Led by Majority Leader Bob Dole, the Senate votes decisively (69–29) to lift the arms embargo against Bosnia. The Clinton administration had worked hard to defeat the proposal and the president continues to oppose the idea.

UN Sec. General Boutros Boutros-Ghali agrees to relinquish his authority to veto or approve NATO air attacks to UN field commanders.

At the Senate hearing on Whitewater, a Secret Service officer directly contradicts the White House's version of events on the night of Vincent Foster's death. Henry O'Neill testifies that he saw Hillary Clinton's top aide remove files from Foster's office. The aide, Margaret Williams, strongly denies doing so, citing a lie detector test she took earlier.

A new article in the journal *Science* asserts that researchers have discovered a hormone that makes overweight animals lose weight rapidly, giving promise for new therapies to treat obesity.

27 In Washington, D.C., the leaders of three large unions announce a plan to merge within five years. The United Automobile Workers (800,000 members), the United Steel Workers (700,000), and the International Association of Machinists and Aerospace Workers (500,000) hope to restore some of the power they have lost over the last 20 years as union membership has declined to less than 15 percent of the workforce.

A top FBI official, Larry Potts, tells a congressional committee that before the raid on the Branch Davidian compound in Waco, Tex., he did not know that the commander of the operation believed a tear gas attack was certain to escalate into a massive assault.

Speaker Newt Gingrich testifies in private before the House Ethics Committee concerning his book deal with a major New York publisher owned by media mogul Rupert Murdoch, some of whose business interests will be affected by pending legislation.

28 The U.S. Senate votes (98–0) to adopt new rules limiting the kinds of gifts, expense-paid trips, and meals senators and aides may receive from lobbyists.

Moderate Republicans join with Democrats in the House of Representatives to defeat the Republican leadership's proposal to limit the EPA's enforcement of pollution laws.

The Federal Communications Commission strikes down the 25-year-old prime-time access rule that prevented the major networks from supplying programs in the hour before prime time (8–11 P.M. eastern time), a rule that helped lead to the boom in syndicated game shows and tabloid magazine programs.

The jury in the Susan Smith trial rejects the prosecution's call for the death penalty and asks that she spend at least 30 years in prison.

29 In his weekly radio address, Pres. Clinton warns the nation that current Republican plans to slow the growth of Medicare could impoverish 500,000 elderly people.

The war in the Balkans threatens to widen as Croatian forces shell territory in Croatia held by rebel Serbs since the 1991 civil war.

French police say they have evidence that a militant Algerian group was responsible for the bombing of a commuter train on July 26.

30 Russia and Chechnya sign a treaty they say will end the fighting in Chechnya while they continue to negotiate the future status of the rebellious region.

Sec. of State Warren Christopher tells reporters Pres. Clinton may not hold a summit meeting with China's president Jiang Zemin unless Harry Wu, the American charged with stealing state secrets, is released.

31 Speaking at the National Governor's Association meeting in Burlington, Vt., Pres. Clinton and Senate Majority Leader Bob Dole present different plans to reform the current welfare system, although both call for less direct federal involvement. Clinton also announces he has just taken action to have the administration move quickly to approve state programs that put welfare recipients to work.

House Republican leaders succeed in reversing last week's defeat over cuts to the EPA budget to enforce pollution laws; Pres. Clinton has threatened to veto the bill.

In New York, the heads of Walt Disney Company and Capital Cities/ABC announce that Disney will acquire the television network for $19 bil., making it the second largest corporate takeover ever.

August 1995

1 In all-day testimony before a House committee on the Waco incident, Atty. Gen. Janet Reno asserts that "the finger of blame points . . . directly at David Koresh," head of the Branch Davidians. She also says that Pres. Clinton was not involved in the final decision to spray tear gas into the compound.

Pres. Clinton strongly criticizes Congress for failing to approve federal spending bills in a timely fashion. "This Congress is on the wrong track," he tells an informal news conference.

CBS, the last independent TV network, accepts a $5.4 bil. offer from the Westinghouse Electric Corp.

NATO allies extend air power protection to all the safe areas in Bosnia, including Sarajevo, saying that any Serb attack will trigger a bombing campaign.

2 The Senate votes (52–48) not to have public hearings about the accusations of sexual misconduct against Sen. Bob Packwood, but agrees to make public all the testimony against him.

At the Senate hearings on Whitewater, a former deputy attorney general testifies that the White House prevented a full investigation into the death of Vincent W. Foster, lawyer and close friend of the Clintons.

3 Two new complaints against Sen. Bob Packwood (R-Oreg.) delay release of the record against him until after the August recess.

Croatian forces launch a major attack against

rebel Serbs in the town of Knin, bringing the war in the Balkans to a new phase.

4 The House of Representatives votes overwhelmingly to approve sweeping legislation to rewrite the nation's communications laws. The bill, similar to one passed by the Senate in June, reduces regulations on cable TV, and on local and long-distance telephone services. Consumer advocates oppose the bill, saying it will cost consumers a lot more in the long run.

5 The Senate votes (50–44) to ban the use of government money to pay for most abortions for federal workers.

Croatian forces capture Knin from rebel Serbs who used the area as headquarters for four years.

6 Police in Cali, Colombia, arrest a top leader in the Cali drug cartel, Miguel Rodriguez Orejuela, one of the last remaining still at large.

7 The House Banking Committee opens hearings on Whitewater with Republicans saying that their investigators had found evidence of influence peddling by Pres. Clinton's partner, James B. McDougal, who received favors from Clinton when he was governer of Arkansas.

NBC agrees to pay $1.27 bil. for TV rights to the Summer Olympics in 2000 and the Winter Olympics in 2002.

As over 120,000 Croatian Serbs flee the Krajina region, relief officials say they face the most serious refugee problem of the war.

8 Senate Republican leaders decide to postpone the welfare bill that would produce sweeping changes in the way programs for the poor and disabled are funded.

Pres. Clinton issues an order saying companies doing business with the federal government must comply with disclosure requirements regarding chemical emissions, requirements the Republican Congress is trying to weaken.

Jean Lewis, a federal bank examiner, tells the House committee on Whitewater that her investigation was hindered at every turn by officials in Arkansas and Washington.

9 The U.S. State Dept. says it has aerial reconaissance photos indicating the presence of mass graves outside the Bosnian town of Srebrenica where Muslim men and boys were rounded up by Bosnian Serbs last month.

At the Senate hearings on Whitewater, former White House council Bernard Nussbaum asserts it was his duty to prevent investigators from searching Vincent Foster's files.

10 In Oklahoma City a federal grand jury indicts Timothy J. McVeigh and Terry L. Nichols on charges of blowing up the federal building there last April and killing 169 people, including 15 children. In a separate indictment, Michael J. Fortier, an army friend of McVeigh, is charged with knowledge of the bombing plans. Fortier pleads guilty to this charge; he is expected to be the prosecution's chief witness. (See also Part I, "Major News Stories of the Year.")

Pres. Clinton proposes sweeping regulations aimed at curtailing smoking among teenagers, including limitations on advertising and the banning of vending machine sales.

At the Senate Whitewater hearings, a top Justice Dept. official says the White House improperly restricted the initial investigation into the suicide of Vincent Foster.

The French government announces a change in its opposition to the comprehensive nuclear weapons test ban treaty, saying it will now support the ban but only after completing tests of its new submarine missile warheads next year.

11 Pres. Clinton calls for a permanent ban on all nuclear testing, thereby ending a debate within his administration concerning the Pentagon's request to test low-level nuclear weapons.

The FBI suspends four high-ranking officials after the Justice Dept. announces a new criminal investigation into the handling of the 1992 attack on white separatist Randy Weaver and his family in Idaho.

Pres. Clinton vetoes legislation that would end U.S. participation in the arms embargo against Bosnia.

In Dallas, at a convention of Ross Perot's group, United We Stand America, the nation's most powerful politicians, including most of the Republican presidential candidates, gather to speak to a group that may hold the key to victory in the 1996 election.

12 At a news conference in Amman, Jordan, Lt. Gen. Hussein Kamel, Pres. Saddam Hussein's son-in-law and a leading military figure in Iraq for over a decade, asserts that he and several other high-ranking military leaders who defected with him the day before will work actively to overthrow the Iraqi government.

13 In Dallas, Ross Perot's political convention ends with Perot asserting that he may still run for president in 1996. During the three-day meeting every Republican candidate for president spoke, as did over 30 congressional leaders.

A Luxembourg think-tank issues a report saying that poor children in the U.S. are poorer than those in other industrialized nations because the gap between rich and poor is greater and welfare programs less generous.

14 Japanese prime minister Tomiichi Murayama offers a "heart-felt apology" for atrocities committed by his country in World War II; he is the first Japanese leader to do so.

By issuing very critical evaluation letters, the U.S. Air Force effectively ends the careers of the seven officers involved in the accidental destruction of two army helicopters in Iraq on Apr. 14, 1994; 26 people, including 15 Americans, were killed when their aircraft were shot down by two U.S. F-15s.

15 In Oklahoma City, the two suspects in the bombing of the federal building there plead not guilty to all charges.

The federal government agrees to pay $3.1 million to the family of white separatist Randy Weaver, whose wife and son were killed by federal agents in a shootout at the Weaver cabin in Ruby Ridge, Idaho, in 1992. The family had filed a $200 million suit against the Justice Dept.

16 Sen. Bill Bradley (D-N.J.) announces he will not seek re-election in 1996, citing his frustration with government and both political parties as reasons. On the following day he says at a news conference that he will not challenge Pres. Clinton as a Democrat but leaves the door open for a possible third-party run.

In an article in *Nature* magazine, scientists announce fossil discoveries in Kenya that indicate a new species of human ancestors that lived four million years ago. The species was not much bigger than chimpanzees, resembled both apes and evolving man, and walked on two legs.

The Bureau of Justice Statistics more than doubles its annual estimate of the numbers of rapes or attempted rapes (from 133,000 in 1991 to 310,000 in 1993) after revising its survey questions to ask women more directly whether they have been the victim of a rape or sexual assault.

17 The Pentagon announces an immediate buildup of men and equipment in the Persian Gulf region because of unusual troop movements in Iraq and the assertions by two Iraqi defectors that Saddam Hussein was considering an attack on Kuwait and Saudi Arabia.

In Washington, D.C., a federal grand jury indicts Pres. Clinton's Whitewater business partners, James B. McDougal and his wife, Susan, on 21 charges of fraud, conspiracy, and making false statements to obtain federally secured loans for Madison Guarantee Savings and Loan in Arkansas. Gov. Jim Guy Tucker, who was indicted in June, is also named on 11 new counts.

In Paris, only three weeks after the subway bombing, a bomb explodes near the Arc de Triomphe, wounding 17 people. Police suspect Algerian Islamic fundamentalists.

18 Shannon Faulkner, who weeks earlier won a three-year battle to become the first woman cadet at the all-male military school The Citadel, abruptly withdraws from the Charleston, S.C., college after being physically unable to complete the rigorous training program.

The Algerian military government announces that a presidential election will be held on November 16 this year, three years after it had canceled general elections because it appeared Islamic fundamentalists would win easily.

19 On a winding road near Sarajevo, three U.S. diplomats who came to discuss the U.S. peace initiative are killed when their vehicle falls off the road and explodes when it hits two land mines.

After serving a three-year prison term for rape, former heavyweight champ Mike Tyson makes his return to boxing with a first-round decision over Peter McNeely. Tyson reportedly receives $25 million for the 89-second fight; McNeely gets $800,000 for a night's work.

20 In a nonbinding straw poll sponsored by the Iowa Republican party, Phil Gramm surprises Bob Dole by getting 24 percent of the vote, the same as Dole, the front-runner for the Republican nomination.

In northern India an estimated 350 people are killed and 400 injured when a crowded train slams into the rear of another train that had stalled after hitting a cow.

21 In Jerusalem a suicide bomber attacks a crowded bus, killing five and wounding 100; it is the second such attack in Israel in the last four weeks. Hamas, the Islamic resistance movement, again claims responsiblity.

ABC News surprisingly settles a libel suit filed against it by Philip Morris and R.J. Reynolds that calls for the news organization to apologize twice on prime time TV and to pay the tobacco companies' legal expenses of $3 million. ABC had asserted on its program "Day One" that the tobacco companies manipulated nicotine levels in cigarettes to addict smokers.

22 In a provincial election in Boris Yeltsin's home area, his new centrist party, Our Home Is Russia, suffers a humiliating defeat as an official dismissed by Yeltsin beats his hand-picked opponent 2–1. Parliamentary elections are scheduled for December 1995.

UN officials report that Iraq told an inspection team that its germ warfare program was much larger than previously revealed, and that biological agents and weapons it said were destroyed before the Persian Gulf War had in fact not been.

The government of Zaire sends troops to Goma to force thousands of refugees to return to Rwanda. About 10,000 leave but another 60,000 flee into the hills. About 750,000 Rwandans, almost all Hutus, remain in Zaire living in sprawling camps.

23 In Taiwan, Pres. Li Teng-hui announces his decision to run in the country's first democratic presidential election despite the deep distrust Beijing's leaders feel toward him.

The Israeli government announces the capture of at least 32 members of Hamas suspected of triggering the last two bus bombings.

24 The Chinese government announces that a court in the central city of Wuhan has convicted Chinese-American human rights activist Harry Wu of spying and sentenced him to 15 years in prison. In a concession to the U.S. government, which had protested China's detention of Wu, he will instead be expelled from the country as "punishment" for his crimes.

The government of Zaire honors the UN's request to cease deporting thousands of Rwandan refugees.

25 In a move that would prove to be a serious strategic error, Sen. Bob Packwood (R-Oreg.) changes his position and now requests that charges of sexual and official misconduct be aired in public hearings.

26 Bob Dole's presidential campaign returns a $1,000 donation made by the Log Cabin Republicans, a nationwide organization of gay Republicans. Dole says he disagrees with their agenda and that the money was taken by mistake (a charge quickly disproven by the group).

On the eastern half of Long Island, New York State's worst ground fire in 60 years is subdued after three days. Windblown flames destroyed more than 7,000 acres and a dozen homes, severely disrupted the Long Island Railroad, and caused miles of snarled traffic.

27 The Clinton administration's chief negotiator for the Balkans tells "Meet the Press" that Bosnian Serbs could face NATO air strikes that might entail a six-month plan to help the Bosnians defend themselves.

28 In a deal valued at $10 billion, Chase Manhattan Corporation announces it will merge with Chemical Banking Corporation, thereby creating the largest bank in the nation, with over $297 billion in assets, but cutting about 12,000 jobs in the process.

In a central market in Sarajevo, two shells fired by Bosnian Serbs explode, killing at least 37 and wounding 80. The Clinton administration urges the UN and NATO to respond militarily.

29 In Bosnia about 100 NATO planes bomb Bosnian Serb positions near Sarajevo. (See also Part I: "Major News Stories of the Year.")

The Investment Company Institute, a mutual fund trade group, reports that investors put $12.4 billion into equity funds in July, the most ever in a single month.

In Tblisi, Georgia, the nation's leader, Eduard Shevardnadze, narrowly escapes an assassination attempt when a car explodes, littering him with glass and debris. The next day he vows to run for the presidency in November.

30 The *New York Times* reports that Time Warner, Inc. is offering $8.5 billion to buy Turner Broadcasting Company, a deal that would create a huge media company with revenues of $18.7 billion.

In Bosnia, NATO planes fly over 200 sorties bombing Serb targets across the country.

A report in *The New England Journal of Medicine* describes a successful pilot program to have safe, early abortions by administering two prescription drugs already available.

Voters in Kazakhstan overwhelmingly approve a new constitution that gives Pres. Nazarbayev such broad powers—including the right to govern by decree—that many diplomats have called it autocratic and said it fails to meet democratic standards.

31 In Zagreb, the chief U.S. negotiator in the Bosnian conflict, Richard Holbrooke, announces that Bosnian Serbs have agreed to follow the decisions of Serbia's president, Slobodan Milosevic, in peace talks, a move Holbrooke calls a "dramatic advance."

September 1995

1 For the first time in two years, the foreign ministers of Bosnia, Croatia, and the Serb-dominated Yugoslav Federation agree to meet in Geneva for peace talks. The Serbs hold almost 70 percent of Bosnia and they will be expected to surrender some of this.

French commandos seize two ships owned by the environmental group Greenpeace trying to prevent France from conducting nuclear tests near the Mururoa Atoll in the South Pacific.

2 Several political groups, including the League of Women Voters, report that more than 5 million Americans have registered to vote in the eight months since the National Voter Registration Act, properly known as "The Motor Voter Law" because it allows people to register while obtaining a driver's licence. Experts say it is the greatest expansion of voter rolls in history.

In Huairou, China, leaders of the UN's fourth World Conference on Women demand that Chinese officials end their intense surveillance of participants—who will soon number 30,000—or they will cancel the forum.

3 NATO issues an ultimatum to Bosnian Serbs to remove their heavy artillery from around Sarajevo, open the airport there, and to cease all attacks against the city and other safe areas; NATO vows to resume bombing if the Serbs do not comply within 36 hours.

4 Speaking in Monterey, Calif., Pres. Clinton attacks the GOP agenda on immigration, welfare, and affirmative action, saying those issues have not caused the economic problems of the middle class; he calls for a higher minimum wage and education and training for workers.

The NATO deadline in Bosnia passes without the Serbs removing their weapons and no resumption of the bombing.

5 After a four-day pause for negotiations, NATO planes resume bombing of Bosnian Serb positions near Sarajevo.

Despite widespread international protests, France detonates a nuclear device buried deep beneath a coral reef atoll in the South Pacific, 750 miles southeast of Tahiti.

Speaking to the international women's conference in Beijing, Hillary Clinton assails human right abuses against girls and women, and criticizes the Chinese government for trying to censor the meeting.

In Little Rock, Ark., a federal judge rules that the Whitewater special prosecutor exceeded his jurisdiction in one of the two indictments against Gov. Jim Guy Tucker.

6 The Senate Ethics Committee votes unanimously to recommend that Bob Packwood be expelled from the Senate for official and sexual misconduct.

NATO officials say they will intensify their bombing campaign against Bosnian Serbs but are being hampered by bad weather.

Cal Ripken, Jr., plays in his 2,131st consecutive game, breaking the record held by Lou Gehrig since 1939.

7 Sen. Bob Packwood resigns from the Senate as the Ethics Committee releases over 10,000 pages of evidence that document his salacious behavior and reveals a level of financial corruption not suspected earlier.

As both sides prepare for U.S.-led peace talks, NATO expands its bombing campaign against Serb positions in Bosnia.

8 Even as NATO planes bomb Serb positions in Bosnia for a fourth straight day, leaders of the three main combatants in the four-year war—Serbia, Croatia, and Bosnia—reach an agreement at talks in Geneva that a Serbian republic will be created in Bosnia. (See also Part I: "Major News Stories of the Year.")

At the opening of the Christian Coalition's annual convention in Washington, the leading Republican presidential candidates, including front-runner Bob Dole, give speeches praising the agenda of the 1.7 million–member group that has been a powerful source in recent Republican primaries.

9 In response to criticisms made at the UN-sponsored Conference on Women, Chinese authorities issue a detailed report asserting that Chinese women enjoy greater personal safety, better career opportunities, and more legal protection than women in the United States.

10 In Bosnia, NATO expands its bombing

campaign to Serbian air defense networks in the northwest, and for the first time uses Tomahawk cruise missiles in an effort to convince Bosnian Serbs to obey its ultimatum to withdraw heavy artillery from around Sarajevo.

Delegates to the international women's conference in Beijing agree to declare a woman's right to make sexual decisions free of coercion or violence.

11 Sources close to the negotiations say the Mitsubishi Estate Co. of Japan will give up its $2 billion stake in New York's Rockefeller Center, the world's most prestigious piece of real estate, which is already under bankruptcy protection.

12 At the Senate hearings on the shootout in Ruby Ridge, Idaho, the FBI sharpshooter who killed the wife of a white separatist invokes his Fifth Amendment rights and refuses to testify.

In a quiet but significant victory for the Clinton administration, the U.S. dollar is valued above 100 Japanese yen for the first time in nine months. Market economists credit Treasury Sec. Robert Rubin's strategy for enabling the dollar to regain the 20 percent it lost earlier.

13 The Senate votes to eliminate the part of the Republican welfare bill that would have denied additional benefits to women who have more children while on the welfare rolls.

The Justice Dept. announces a dozen arrests after a two-year investigation into the distribution of child pornography over America OnLine, the nation's largest computer network. About 125 homes and offices were searched.

14 After two weeks of NATO bombings the Bosnian Serbs agree to pull back their heavy artillery from Sarajevo. NATO agrees to a "temporary pause" in bombing.

House Republican leaders announce their proposal to redesign Medicare and cut spending on the program by $270 bil., or 14 percent, over the next seven years. Details of the plan are sketchy. Pres. Clinton says he will veto it.

15 In Tokyo the major manufacturers of consumer electronic products—including Toshiba, Sony, and Phillips—agree to a single format for a new disk that will succeed both videocassettes and CD-ROMs. Although called a video disk (it will store a 133-minute movie) it also holds 4.7 gigabytes of information, and can be used for audio as well.

Bosnian Serbs begin to withdraw their guns and to open highways and the airport near Sarajevo as Pres. Clinton warns that airstrikes will resume if they don't continue to honor their commitments.

16 NATO warns Bosnian Serbs to speed up their removal of artillery or it will resume bombing.

During a tour of Africa, Pope John Paul II visits Johannesburg, South Africa to signal the Vatican's approval of the end of apartheid.

17 Following revelations in Bob Packwood's diaries, House Republican leaders agree to consider lobbyist registration requirements and a strict limitation on gifts and meals.

18 The *New York Times* and the *Washington Post* agree to publish the complete manifesto of the so-called Unabomber in hopes that he will stop sending deadly bombs to unsuspecting people.

Pres. Clinton attacks Republican plans to curb the earned income tax credit that benefits the poor, saying "we believe no one should be taxed into poverty."

The House Ethics Committee begins to interview lawyers to choose one who will serve as independent counsel to investigate Speaker Newt Gingrich.

19 The Senate overwhelmingly (87–12) approves a welfare plan that will restucture federal antipoverty programs and end the 60-year guarantee of assistance to needy families.

The National Acadamy of Sciences issues a report, commissioned by Congress, confirming the belief that encouraging drug addicts to exchange used needles for new ones greatly reduces the spread of the virus that causes AIDS but does not increase drug use.

20 AT&T Corp., valued at over $101 bil., divides itself into three separate companies: communications services, communications equipment, and computers. About 8,500 jobs will be cut.

NATO and UN officials say the bombing of Bosnian Serb positions will not resume because heavy weapons have been removed from around Sarajevo.

21 House Speaker Newt Gingrich threatens to hold up an increase in the federal debt limit if Pres. Clinton refuses to balance the budget on Republican terms. The tactic would send the U.S. government into default for the first time in history. The bond market grows skittish and the value of the dollar declines.

The first details of the House Republican plan for changing Medicare reveal steep increases in premiums and a limit on malpractice awards. With only one day of hearings scheduled, House Democrats say they will hold their own hearings on the lawn outside the Capitol.

22 After five weeks of negotiation, Time Warner Inc. announces it will buy 82 percent of Turner Broadcasting System, which includes CNN and New Line Cinema. The new firm will have revenues of $19.8 bil., making it even larger than the new company formed by Disney's purchase of Capital Cities/ABC, estimated at $16.4 bil.

23 The Clinton administration tells the press that Senate Foreign Relations Committee chairman Jesse Helms is blocking 30 ambassadorial appointments, more than a dozen treaties, and the hiring of more than 400 State Dept. employees, until the administration agrees that three small independent agencies are made part of the State Dept., a move Helms says will save $3 bil.

24 Sixteen months after signing an initial peace treaty, PLO leader Yasir Arafat and Israeli foreign minister Shimon Peres announce they have reached agreement on how and when control of the West Bank will be transferred to its Arab residents.

In a small town in southern France, a 16-year-old boy bludgeons his parents and stepbrother to death, then walks three miles to another town, where he opens fire with a rifle, killing eight people and wounding nine before shooting himself to death.

25 Appearing on the CNN program "Larry King Live," Ross Perot announces he is forming a new third party called the Independence party that will field its own presidential candidate in 1996 as well as in selected congressional races. Perot did not say whether or not he would be the candidate.

26 Leading senators from both major parties indicate that major budget problems can be solved if all government leaders will agree to reduce the cost-of-living adjustment paid to Social Security recipients. Sen. Daniel P. Moynihan (D-N.Y.) says the Consumer Price Index used to compute the adjustment always overstates the rise in the cost of living and that the government could save $281 bil. over seven years if the adjustment was reduced by 1 percent as a panel of famous economists recently recommended.

In Palermo, Sicily, Giulio Andreotti, the seven-time prime minister of Italy, goes on trial for charges that he aided the Mafia while in power. For most Italians it is a trial about the link between politics and organized crime in postwar Italy.

At UN headquarters in New York, the foreign ministers of Croatia, Bosnia, and Serb-dominated Yugoslavia agree in principle on a structure for a new government of Bosnia. No truce or cease-fire is signed, however, and fighting continues in Bosnia.

27 In a compromise to avoid a shutdown of the federal government on Oct. 1, Pres. Clinton and the Republican leaders of Congress agree to provide reduced funding to many agencies while 1996 appropiations bills are debated.

The Congressional Budget Office reports that the Republican plan to overhaul Medicare would achieve most of its projected savings of $270 bil. over seven years through higher costs for beneficiaries and lower fees for doctors and hospitals.

China tells the U.S. that it has decided not to sell two nuclear power reactors to Iran, a deal agreed to five months earlier and vigorously attacked by the Clinton administration.

28 In a formal ceremony in Washington, Yasir Arafat and Yitzhak Rabin sign the agreement that will transfer much of the West Bank to Arab control.

Despite the talk of peace for Bosnia, the army of the Bosnian government continues to hammer away at Bosnian Serb positions in the hope of driving them from the region.

29 Calif. governor Pete Wilson is the first Republican candidate to drop out of the race for president. A lack of funds, low poll numbers, and a backlash against him in California (where he had sworn he would not run for national office while governor) made his candidacy untenable. Many see Wilson's decision as a victory for Pres. Clinton, since it leaves Arlen Specter as the lone pro-choice Republican candidate.

30 The Senate Finance Committee approves, 11–9, the Republican plan to cut Medicaid spending by 19 percent over seven years and to reduce the growth of spending on Medicare by 14 percent. Hours later, Pres. Clinton condemns the bill in his weekly radio address and singles out a provision that would force a husband or wife to sell their home if their spouse went into a nursing home.

CALENDAR OF THE YEAR

UNDERSTANDING CALENDARS

The day Earth turns at a fairly steady pace about the imaginary line that defines the North and South Poles. This line through the poles is called Earth's axis. Each turn about the axis, called a rotation, takes slightly less than 24 hours. Since Earth is also traveling around the Sun, however, the time from noon to noon is longer than the time it takes for one rotation—about 3 minutes and 56 seconds longer, or almost exactly 24 hours. The time from noon to noon changes slightly during the year, depending on where Earth is in its path. If you average all the days in a year, the average time from noon to noon is exactly 24 hours.

The year All the nine planets of the solar system travel in nearly circular paths, called orbits, around the Sun. Each trip around the Sun is called a revolution. The planets all revolve in the same direction, which can be observed from Earth by noting the position the Sun has among the background stars, which are traditionally grouped into constellations. (Since you can't see the Sun and stars at the same time, you can observe where the Sun rises or sets each day and then note the stars that appear in the same region.) Over the course of a year, the Sun appears to pass through the 12 constellations that make up the zodiac.

Earth's trip around the Sun, reflected in the Sun's trip through the zodiac, takes about 365.25 days. This varies slightly from time to time, so astronomers add or delete a second in some years to keep their records in tune with Earth's motion. The last time this occurred was June 30, 1992, when a second was added at 7:59:59 P.M. Eastern daylight time. (See also "Precession of the equinoxes" below.)

Seasons Most of us have learned that the seasons change on the 21st of March, June, September, and December. However in some years the dates in these months may be as early as the 20th or as late as the 23rd.

The seasons do *not*, strictly speaking, coincide with climate changes. In the northeastern United States, it still snows after Mar. 21, it gets quite hot before June 21, and there is not much "winter" until sometime in January. What the seasons mark is the change in the pattern of daylight over the course of the year.

The Earth is tilted with respect to its path around the Sun; different parts receive different amounts of sunlight during Earth's annual orbit, the time we know as a year. Between late September (around the 21st) and late March, Earth's Northern Hemisphere is tilted away from the Sun. This period constitutes the fall and winter seasons for the Northern Hemisphere, during which there are less than 12 hours of daylight each day. For the rest of the year, spring and summer, the Northern Hemisphere is tilted toward the sun, and daylight hours constitute more than half of each day. In the Southern Hemisphere the situation is reversed: spring and summer last from late September to late March, while fall and winter make up the other half of the year.

At the points of transition from long days and short nights to short days and long nights, and vice versa, the *equinoxes* occur—the two days of the year when periods of daylight and darkness are equal. The *vernal equinox*, marking the first day of spring, takes place on or around Mar. 21 in the Northern Hemisphere, while the *autumnal equinox*, marking the beginning of fall, is on or around Sept. 21. Officially, summer begins on the day of the longest daytime during the year, about June 21 in the Northern Hemisphere, called the *summer solstice*. The *winter solstice*, about Dec. 21 in the Northern Hemisphere, has the shortest amount of daylight and the longest night of the year. The word *solstice* means "standing-still sun." These two days are so called because the apparent movement of where the Sun rises or sets reaches its extreme positions on the solstices and then reverses direction.

Precession of the equinoxes Ancient Greek astronomers determined that the direction of Earth's axis is constantly, but very slowly, changing in a regular pattern. The kind of change is similar to the way a spinning top slowly leans one way then another as its axis changes direction. This movement of the Earth is caused by several factors, the most dominant of which is called precession. The precession of the Earth results from its not being a perfect sphere. Earth's diameter is about 27 miles greater from one side of the equator to the other than it is from one pole to the other. (Earth is oblate, or fat around the middle, as a result of its rotation.)

Picture Earth without considering its revolution. Keep Earth's center in the same place mentally, and think about how the axis changes position during precession. Any point on Earth's axis (except the center of the planet) moves in a slow circle as a result of precession. This movement is so slow that it takes 26,000 years for a point to return to its original spot. In the meantime, the axis gradually changes its position in relation to the stars. While what we call the North Star (officially known as Polaris) is currently positioned above the North Pole about one degree off center, over time the axis will shift, so that at about A.D. 15,000 the star Vega will be above the North Pole within about four degrees of that axis. By about A.D. 28,000, Polaris will have returned to its present position.

As the precession continues, one of its effects is to change the times of the year that seasons occur. Our calendar is corrected for this; if it were not, the vernal equinox would, over 13,000 years, shift from around Mar. 21 to about Sept. 21, the date at which the autumnal equinox is now. For this reason, the precession of the Earth is generally known as the precession of the equinoxes.

Although the precession of the equinoxes is slow, it can be easily observed. The year of about 365.25 days is the time it takes from one vernal equinox to the next. Because of the precession of the equinoxes, however, the time it takes the Sun to appear in the same position with respect to the stars is 20 minutes, 24 seconds longer than the period from one equinox to the next. For this reason, accurate star maps have to specify both the date and year for which they are intended.

SOLAR PHENOMENA: THE SEASONS, 1996

Solar phenomenon	Month	Day	Hour	Min
Perigee[1]	Jan.	4	07	—
Vernal equinox	Mar.	20	08	03
Summer solstice	June	21	02	24
Apogee[2]	July	5	18	—
Autumnal equinox	Sept.	22	18	00
Winter solstice	Dec.	21	14	06

Note: Shown in universal time (UT). To convert to local time, see "Timing Planetary Phenomena." 1. Sun closest to the Earth (91.4 million miles). 2. Sun farthest from the Earth (94.5 million miles). **Source:** U.S. Naval Observatory, *Astronomical Phenomena for the Year 1996* (1994).

Lunar Calendar

There is some evidence that very early humans (c. 25,000 B.C.) used marks on bone to indicate the passage of time, which they may have measured by the Moon's phases. A calendar for the year can be based upon the Moon's phases, which gives a year of 12 periods from new moon to new moon (hence the word *month*) lasting about 354 days. This is about 11 days shorter than the time it takes Earth to revolve around the Sun. The Chinese, who still use a version of this calendar, resolve the discrepancy by inserting extra months at fixed intervals to bring the lunar and solar years into alignment. The Chinese year is divided into months that are either 29 or 30 days long, since the time from new moon to new moon is approximately 29.5 days. (The Moon takes about 27.33 days to orbit Earth, but Earth is moving with respect to the Sun during that time, so the combined movement produces the period of about 29.5 days.) The New Year begins at the first new moon over China between Jan. 21 and Feb. 19, and is celebrated for a four-day period. Each year has both a number and a name. The year 1996—or 4633 in the Chinese era—is the Year of the Rat.

Year/Calendar Number

Year	No.	Year	No.	Year	No.	Year	No.
1775	1	1844	9	1913	4	1982	6
1776	9	1845	4	1914	5	1983	7
1777	4	1846	5	1915	6	1984	8
1778	5	1847	6	1916	14	1985	3
1779	6	1848	14	1917	2	1986	4
1780	14	1849	2	1918	3	1987	5
1781	2	1850	3	1919	4	1988	13
1782	3	1851	4	1920	12	1989	1
1783	4	1852	12	1921	7	1990	2
1784	12	1853	7	1922	1	1991	3
1785	7	1854	1	1923	2	1992	11
1786	1	1855	2	1924	10	1993	6
1787	2	1856	10	1925	5	1994	7
1788	10	1857	5	1926	6	1995	1
1789	5	1858	6	1927	7	1996	9
1790	6	1859	7	1928	8	1997	4
1791	7	1860	8	1929	3	1998	5
1792	8	1861	3	1930	4	1999	6
1793	3	1862	4	1931	5	2000	14
1794	4	1863	5	1932	13	2001	2
1795	5	1864	13	1933	1	2002	3
1796	13	1865	1	1934	2	2003	4
1797	1	1866	2	1935	3	2004	12
1798	2	1867	3	1936	11	2005	7
1799	3	1868	11	1937	6	2006	1
1800	4	1869	6	1938	7	2007	2
1801	5	1870	7	1939	1	2008	10
1802	6	1871	1	1940	9	2009	5
1803	7	1872	9	1941	4	2010	6
1804	8	1873	4	1942	5	2011	7
1805	3	1874	5	1943	6	2012	8
1806	4	1875	6	1944	14	2013	3
1807	5	1876	14	1945	2	2014	4
1808	13	1877	2	1946	3	2015	5
1809	1	1878	3	1947	4	2016	13
1810	2	1879	4	1948	12	2017	1
1811	3	1880	12	1949	7	2018	2
1812	11	1881	7	1950	1	2019	3
1813	6	1882	1	1951	2	2020	11
1814	7	1883	2	1952	10	2021	6
1815	1	1884	10	1953	5	2022	7
1816	9	1885	5	1954	6	2023	1
1817	4	1886	6	1955	7	2024	9
1818	5	1887	7	1956	8	2025	4
1819	6	1888	8	1957	3	2026	5
1820	14	1889	3	1958	4	2027	6
1821	2	1890	4	1959	5	2028	14
1822	3	1891	5	1960	13	2029	2
1823	4	1892	13	1961	1	2030	3
1824	12	1893	1	1962	2	2031	4
1825	7	1894	2	1963	3	2032	12
1826	1	1895	3	1964	11	2033	7
1827	2	1896	11	1965	6	2034	1
1828	10	1897	6	1966	7	2035	2
1829	5	1898	7	1967	1	2036	10
1830	6	1899	1	1968	9	2037	5
1831	7	1900	2	1969	4	2038	6
1832	8	1901	3	1970	5	2039	7
1833	3	1902	4	1971	6	2040	8
1834	4	1903	5	1972	14	2041	3
1835	5	1904	13	1973	2	2042	4
1836	13	1905	1	1974	3	2043	5
1837	1	1906	2	1975	4	2044	13
1838	2	1907	3	1976	12	2045	1
1839	3	1908	11	1977	7	2046	2
1840	11	1909	6	1978	1	2047	3
1841	6	1910	7	1979	2	2048	11
1842	7	1911	1	1980	10	2049	6
1843	1	1912	9	1981	5	2050	7

PERPETUAL CALENDAR 1775–2050

A perpetual calendar lets you find the day of the week for any date in any year, past, present, or future. Since January 1 may fall on any of the seven days of the week, a perpetual calendar requires 14 different calendars to cover all possibilities, including leap and non–leap years.

To use the perpetual calendar, find the year desired in the table at the left. The number next to each year corresponds to one of the 14 calendars below. For example, calendar 9 (a leap year in which January 1 fell on a Monday) was in use during 1776, meaning that July 4 of that year was a Thursday. Calendar 9 was used again in 1816 and 1844 and will be used next in 1996. Calendar 1 was used in 1995.

1

JANUARY

S	M	T	W	T	F	S
1	2	3	4	5	6	7
8	9	10	11	12	13	14
15	16	17	18	19	20	21
22	23	24	25	26	27	28
29	30	31				

FEBRUARY

S	M	T	W	T	F	S
			1	2	3	4
5	6	7	8	9	10	11
12	13	14	15	16	17	18
19	20	21	22	23	24	25
26	27	28				

MARCH

S	M	T	W	T	F	S
			1	2	3	4
5	6	7	8	9	10	11
12	13	14	15	16	17	18
19	20	21	22	23	24	25
26	27	28	29	30	31	

APRIL

S	M	T	W	T	F	S
						1
2	3	4	5	6	7	8
9	10	11	12	13	14	15
16	17	18	19	20	21	22
23	24	25	26	27	28	29
30						

MAY

S	M	T	W	T	F	S
	1	2	3	4	5	6
7	8	9	10	11	12	13
14	15	16	17	18	19	20
21	22	23	24	25	26	27
28	29	30	31			

JUNE

S	M	T	W	T	F	S
				1	2	3
4	5	6	7	8	9	10
11	12	13	14	15	16	17
18	19	20	21	22	23	24
25	26	27	28	29	30	

JULY

S	M	T	W	T	F	S
						1
2	3	4	5	6	7	8
9	10	11	12	13	14	15
16	17	18	19	20	21	22
23	24	25	26	27	28	29
30	31					

AUGUST

S	M	T	W	T	F	S
		1	2	3	4	5
6	7	8	9	10	11	12
13	14	15	16	17	18	19
20	21	22	23	24	25	26
27	28	29	30	31		

SEPTEMBER

S	M	T	W	T	F	S
					1	2
3	4	5	6	7	8	9
10	11	12	13	14	15	16
17	18	19	20	21	22	23
24	25	26	27	28	29	30

OCTOBER

S	M	T	W	T	F	S
1	2	3	4	5	6	7
8	9	10	11	12	13	14
15	16	17	18	19	20	21
22	23	24	25	26	27	28
29	30	31				

NOVEMBER

S	M	T	W	T	F	S
			1	2	3	4
5	6	7	8	9	10	11
12	13	14	15	16	17	18
19	20	21	22	23	24	25
26	27	28	29	30		

DECEMBER

S	M	T	W	T	F	S
					1	2
3	4	5	6	7	8	9
10	11	12	13	14	15	16
17	18	19	20	21	22	23
24	25	26	27	28	29	30
31						

2

JANUARY

S	M	T	W	T	F	S
	1	2	3	4	5	6
7	8	9	10	11	12	13
14	15	16	17	18	19	20
21	22	23	24	25	26	27
28	29	30	31			

FEBRUARY

S	M	T	W	T	F	S
				1	2	3
4	5	6	7	8	9	10
11	12	13	14	15	16	17
18	19	20	21	22	23	24
25	26	27	28			

MARCH

S	M	T	W	T	F	S
				1	2	3
4	5	6	7	8	9	10
11	12	13	14	15	16	17
18	19	20	21	22	23	24
25	26	27	28	29	30	31

APRIL

S	M	T	W	T	F	S
1	2	3	4	5	6	7
8	9	10	11	12	13	14
15	16	17	18	19	20	21
22	23	24	25	26	27	28
29	30					

MAY

S	M	T	W	T	F	S
		1	2	3	4	5
6	7	8	9	10	11	12
13	14	15	16	17	18	19
20	21	22	23	24	25	26
27	28	29	30	31		

JUNE

S	M	T	W	T	F	S
					1	2
3	4	5	6	7	8	9
10	11	12	13	14	15	16
17	18	19	20	21	22	23
24	25	26	27	28	29	30

JULY

S	M	T	W	T	F	S
1	2	3	4	5	6	7
8	9	10	11	12	13	14
15	16	17	18	19	20	21
22	23	24	25	26	27	28
29	30	31				

AUGUST

S	M	T	W	T	F	S
			1	2	3	4
5	6	7	8	9	10	11
12	13	14	15	16	17	18
19	20	21	22	23	24	25
26	27	28	29	30	31	

SEPTEMBER

S	M	T	W	T	F	S
						1
2	3	4	5	6	7	8
9	10	11	12	13	14	15
16	17	18	19	20	21	22
23	24	25	26	27	28	29
30						

OCTOBER

S	M	T	W	T	F	S
	1	2	3	4	5	6
7	8	9	10	11	12	13
14	15	16	17	18	19	20
21	22	23	24	25	26	27
28	29	30	31			

NOVEMBER

S	M	T	W	T	F	S
				1	2	3
4	5	6	7	8	9	10
11	12	13	14	15	16	17
18	19	20	21	22	23	24
25	26	27	28	29	30	

DECEMBER

S	M	T	W	T	F	S
						1
2	3	4	5	6	7	8
9	10	11	12	13	14	15
16	17	18	19	20	21	22
23	24	25	26	27	28	29
30	31					

3

JANUARY

S	M	T	W	T	F	S
		1	2	3	4	5
6	7	8	9	10	11	12
13	14	15	16	17	18	19
20	21	22	23	24	25	26
27	28	29	30	31		

FEBRUARY

S	M	T	W	T	F	S
					1	2
3	4	5	6	7	8	9
10	11	12	13	14	15	16
17	18	19	20	21	22	23
24	25	26	27	28		

MARCH

S	M	T	W	T	F	S
					1	2
3	4	5	6	7	8	9
10	11	12	13	14	15	16
17	18	19	20	21	22	23
24	25	26	27	28	29	30
31						

APRIL

S	M	T	W	T	F	S
	1	2	3	4	5	6
7	8	9	10	11	12	13
14	15	16	17	18	19	20
21	22	23	24	25	26	27
28	29	30				

MAY

S	M	T	W	T	F	S
			1	2	3	4
5	6	7	8	9	10	11
12	13	14	15	16	17	18
19	20	21	22	23	24	25
26	27	28	29	30	31	

JUNE

S	M	T	W	T	F	S
						1
2	3	4	5	6	7	8
9	10	11	12	13	14	15
16	17	18	19	20	21	22
23	24	25	26	27	28	29
30						

JULY

S	M	T	W	T	F	S
	1	2	3	4	5	6
7	8	9	10	11	12	13
14	15	16	17	18	19	20
21	22	23	24	25	26	27
28	29	30	31			

AUGUST

S	M	T	W	T	F	S
				1	2	3
4	5	6	7	8	9	10
11	12	13	14	15	16	17
18	19	20	21	22	23	24
25	26	27	28	29	30	31

SEPTEMBER

S	M	T	W	T	F	S
1	2	3	4	5	6	7
8	9	10	11	12	13	14
15	16	17	18	19	20	21
22	23	24	25	26	27	28
29	30					

OCTOBER

S	M	T	W	T	F	S
		1	2	3	4	5
6	7	8	9	10	11	12
13	14	15	16	17	18	19
20	21	22	23	24	25	26
27	28	29	30	31		

NOVEMBER

S	M	T	W	T	F	S
					1	2
3	4	5	6	7	8	9
10	11	12	13	14	15	16
17	18	19	20	21	22	23
24	25	26	27	28	29	30

DECEMBER

S	M	T	W	T	F	S
1	2	3	4	5	6	7
8	9	10	11	12	13	14
15	16	17	18	19	20	21
22	23	24	25	26	27	28
29	30	31				

4

JANUARY

S	M	T	W	T	F	S
			1	2	3	4
5	6	7	8	9	10	11
12	13	14	15	16	17	18
19	20	21	22	23	24	25
26	27	28	29	30	31	

FEBRUARY

S	M	T	W	T	F	S
						1
2	3	4	5	6	7	8
9	10	11	12	13	14	15
16	17	18	19	20	21	22
23	24	25	26	27	28	

MARCH

S	M	T	W	T	F	S
						1
2	3	4	5	6	7	8
9	10	11	12	13	14	15
16	17	18	19	20	21	22
23	24	25	26	27	28	29
30	31					

APRIL

S	M	T	W	T	F	S
		1	2	3	4	5
6	7	8	9	10	11	12
13	14	15	16	17	18	19
20	21	22	23	24	25	26
27	28	29	30			

MAY

S	M	T	W	T	F	S
				1	2	3
4	5	6	7	8	9	10
11	12	13	14	15	16	17
18	19	20	21	22	23	24
25	26	27	28	29	30	31

JUNE

S	M	T	W	T	F	S
1	2	3	4	5	6	7
8	9	10	11	12	13	14
15	16	17	18	19	20	21
22	23	24	25	26	27	28
29	30					

JULY

S	M	T	W	T	F	S
		1	2	3	4	5
6	7	8	9	10	11	12
13	14	15	16	17	18	19
20	21	22	23	24	25	26
27	28	29	30	31		

AUGUST

S	M	T	W	T	F	S
					1	2
3	4	5	6	7	8	9
10	11	12	13	14	15	16
17	18	19	20	21	22	23
24	25	26	27	28	29	30
31						

SEPTEMBER

S	M	T	W	T	F	S
	1	2	3	4	5	6
7	8	9	10	11	12	13
14	15	16	17	18	19	20
21	22	23	24	25	26	27
28	29	30				

OCTOBER

S	M	T	W	T	F	S
			1	2	3	4
5	6	7	8	9	10	11
12	13	14	15	16	17	18
19	20	21	22	23	24	25
26	27	28	29	30	31	

NOVEMBER

S	M	T	W	T	F	S
						1
2	3	4	5	6	7	8
9	10	11	12	13	14	15
16	17	18	19	20	21	22
23	24	25	26	27	28	29
30						

DECEMBER

S	M	T	W	T	F	S
	1	2	3	4	5	6
7	8	9	10	11	12	13
14	15	16	17	18	19	20
21	22	23	24	25	26	27
28	29	30	31			

5

JANUARY

S	M	T	W	T	F	S
				1	2	3
4	5	6	7	8	9	10
11	12	13	14	15	16	17
18	19	20	21	22	23	24
25	26	27	28	29	30	31

FEBRUARY

S	M	T	W	T	F	S
1	2	3	4	5	6	7
8	9	10	11	12	13	14
15	16	17	18	19	20	21
22	23	24	25	26	27	28

MARCH

S	M	T	W	T	F	S
1	2	3	4	5	6	7
8	9	10	11	12	13	14
15	16	17	18	19	20	21
22	23	24	25	26	27	28
29	30	31				

APRIL

S	M	T	W	T	F	S
			1	2	3	4
5	6	7	8	9	10	11
12	13	14	15	16	17	18
19	20	21	22	23	24	25
26	27	28	29	30		

MAY

S	M	T	W	T	F	S
					1	2
3	4	5	6	7	8	9
10	11	12	13	14	15	16
17	18	19	20	21	22	23
24	25	26	27	28	29	30
31						

JUNE

S	M	T	W	T	F	S
	1	2	3	4	5	6
7	8	9	10	11	12	13
14	15	16	17	18	19	20
21	22	23	24	25	26	27
28	29	30				

JULY

S	M	T	W	T	F	S
			1	2	3	4
5	6	7	8	9	10	11
12	13	14	15	16	17	18
19	20	21	22	23	24	25
26	27	28	29	30	31	

AUGUST

S	M	T	W	T	F	S
						1
2	3	4	5	6	7	8
9	10	11	12	13	14	15
16	17	18	19	20	21	22
23	24	25	26	27	28	29
30	31					

SEPTEMBER

S	M	T	W	T	F	S
		1	2	3	4	5
6	7	8	9	10	11	12
13	14	15	16	17	18	19
20	21	22	23	24	25	26
27	28	29	30			

OCTOBER

S	M	T	W	T	F	S
				1	2	3
4	5	6	7	8	9	10
11	12	13	14	15	16	17
18	19	20	21	22	23	24
25	26	27	28	29	30	31

NOVEMBER

S	M	T	W	T	F	S
1	2	3	4	5	6	7
8	9	10	11	12	13	14
15	16	17	18	19	20	21
22	23	24	25	26	27	28
29	30					

DECEMBER

S	M	T	W	T	F	S
		1	2	3	4	5
6	7	8	9	10	11	12
13	14	15	16	17	18	19
20	21	22	23	24	25	26
27	28	29	30	31		

PERPETUAL CALENDAR 1775–2050 (continued)

6

JANUARY

S	M	T	W	T	F	S
					1	2
3	4	5	6	7	8	9
10	11	12	13	14	15	16
17	18	19	20	21	22	23
24	25	26	27	28	29	30
31						

FEBRUARY

S	M	T	W	T	F	S
	1	2	3	4	5	6
7	8	9	10	11	12	13
14	15	16	17	18	19	20
21	22	23	24	25	26	27
28						

MARCH

S	M	T	W	T	F	S
	1	2	3	4	5	6
7	8	9	10	11	12	13
14	15	16	17	18	19	20
21	22	23	24	25	26	27
28	29	30	31			

APRIL

S	M	T	W	T	F	S
				1	2	3
4	5	6	7	8	9	10
11	12	13	14	15	16	17
18	19	20	21	22	23	24
25	26	27	28	29	30	

MAY

S	M	T	W	T	F	S
						1
2	3	4	5	6	7	8
9	10	11	12	13	14	15
16	17	18	19	20	21	22
23	24	25	26	27	28	29
30	31					

JUNE

S	M	T	W	T	F	S
		1	2	3	4	5
6	7	8	9	10	11	12
13	14	15	16	17	18	19
20	21	22	23	24	25	26
27	28	29	30			

JULY

S	M	T	W	T	F	S
				1	2	3
4	5	6	7	8	9	10
11	12	13	14	15	16	17
18	19	20	21	22	23	24
25	26	27	28	29	30	31

AUGUST

S	M	T	W	T	F	S
1	2	3	4	5	6	7
8	9	10	11	12	13	14
15	16	17	18	19	20	21
22	23	24	25	26	27	28
29	30	31				

SEPTEMBER

S	M	T	W	T	F	S
			1	2	3	4
5	6	7	8	9	10	11
12	13	14	15	16	17	18
19	20	21	22	23	24	25
26	27	28	29	30		

OCTOBER

S	M	T	W	T	F	S
					1	2
3	4	5	6	7	8	9
10	11	12	13	14	15	16
17	18	19	20	21	22	23
24	25	26	27	28	29	30
31						

NOVEMBER

S	M	T	W	T	F	S
	1	2	3	4	5	6
7	8	9	10	11	12	13
14	15	16	17	18	19	20
21	22	23	24	25	26	27
28	29	30				

DECEMBER

S	M	T	W	T	F	S
			1	2	3	4
5	6	7	8	9	10	11
12	13	14	15	16	17	18
19	20	21	22	23	24	25
26	27	28	29	30	31	

7

JANUARY

S	M	T	W	T	F	S
						1
2	3	4	5	6	7	8
9	10	11	12	13	14	15
16	17	18	19	20	21	22
23	24	25	26	27	28	29
30	31					

FEBRUARY

S	M	T	W	T	F	S
		1	2	3	4	5
6	7	8	9	10	11	12
13	14	15	16	17	18	19
20	21	22	23	24	25	26
27	28					

MARCH

S	M	T	W	T	F	S
		1	2	3	4	5
6	7	8	9	10	11	12
13	14	15	16	17	18	19
20	21	22	23	24	25	26
27	28	29	30	31		

APRIL

S	M	T	W	T	F	S
					1	2
3	4	5	6	7	8	9
10	11	12	13	14	15	16
17	18	19	20	21	22	23
24	25	26	27	28	29	30

MAY

S	M	T	W	T	F	S
1	2	3	4	5	6	7
8	9	10	11	12	13	14
15	16	17	18	19	20	21
22	23	24	25	26	27	28
29	30	31				

JUNE

S	M	T	W	T	F	S
			1	2	3	4
5	6	7	8	9	10	11
12	13	14	15	16	17	18
19	20	21	22	23	24	25
26	27	28	29	30		

JULY

S	M	T	W	T	F	S
					1	2
3	4	5	6	7	8	9
10	11	12	13	14	15	16
17	18	19	20	21	22	23
24	25	26	27	28	29	30
31						

AUGUST

S	M	T	W	T	F	S
	1	2	3	4	5	6
7	8	9	10	11	12	13
14	15	16	17	18	19	20
21	22	23	24	25	26	27
28	29	30	31			

SEPTEMBER

S	M	T	W	T	F	S
				1	2	3
4	5	6	7	8	9	10
11	12	13	14	15	16	17
18	19	20	21	22	23	24
25	26	27	28	29	30	

OCTOBER

S	M	T	W	T	F	S
						1
2	3	4	5	6	7	8
9	10	11	12	13	14	15
16	17	18	19	20	21	22
23	24	25	26	27	28	29
30	31					

NOVEMBER

S	M	T	W	T	F	S
		1	2	3	4	5
6	7	8	9	10	11	12
13	14	15	16	17	18	19
20	21	22	23	24	25	26
27	28	29	30			

DECEMBER

S	M	T	W	T	F	S
				1	2	3
4	5	6	7	8	9	10
11	12	13	14	15	16	17
18	19	20	21	22	23	24
25	26	27	28	29	30	31

8

JANUARY

S	M	T	W	T	F	S
1	2	3	4	5	6	7
8	9	10	11	12	13	14
15	16	17	18	19	20	21
22	23	24	25	26	27	28
29	30	31				

FEBRUARY

S	M	T	W	T	F	S
			1	2	3	4
5	6	7	8	9	10	11
12	13	14	15	16	17	18
19	20	21	22	23	24	25
26	27	28	29			

MARCH

S	M	T	W	T	F	S
				1	2	3
4	5	6	7	8	9	10
11	12	13	14	15	16	17
18	19	20	21	22	23	24
25	26	27	28	29	30	31

APRIL

S	M	T	W	T	F	S
1	2	3	4	5	6	7
8	9	10	11	12	13	14
15	16	17	18	19	20	21
22	23	24	25	26	27	28
29	30					

MAY

S	M	T	W	T	F	S
		1	2	3	4	5
6	7	8	9	10	11	12
13	14	15	16	17	18	19
20	21	22	23	24	25	26
27	28	29	30	31		

JUNE

S	M	T	W	T	F	S
					1	2
3	4	5	6	7	8	9
10	11	12	13	14	15	16
17	18	19	20	21	22	23
24	25	26	27	28	29	30

JULY

S	M	T	W	T	F	S
1	2	3	4	5	6	7
8	9	10	11	12	13	14
15	16	17	18	19	20	21
22	23	24	25	26	27	28
29	30	31				

AUGUST

S	M	T	W	T	F	S
			1	2	3	4
5	6	7	8	9	10	11
12	13	14	15	16	17	18
19	20	21	22	23	24	25
26	27	28	29	30	31	

SEPTEMBER

S	M	T	W	T	F	S
						1
2	3	4	5	6	7	8
9	10	11	12	13	14	15
16	17	18	19	20	21	22
23	24	25	26	27	28	29
30						

OCTOBER

S	M	T	W	T	F	S
	1	2	3	4	5	6
7	8	9	10	11	12	13
14	15	16	17	18	19	20
21	22	23	24	25	26	27
28	29	30	31			

NOVEMBER

S	M	T	W	T	F	S
				1	2	3
4	5	6	7	8	9	10
11	12	13	14	15	16	17
18	19	20	21	22	23	24
25	26	27	28	29	30	

DECEMBER

S	M	T	W	T	F	S
						1
2	3	4	5	6	7	8
9	10	11	12	13	14	15
16	17	18	19	20	21	22
23	24	25	26	27	28	29
30	31					

9

JANUARY

S	M	T	W	T	F	S
	1	2	3	4	5	6
7	8	9	10	11	12	13
14	15	16	17	18	19	20
21	22	23	24	25	26	27
28	29	30	31			

FEBRUARY

S	M	T	W	T	F	S
				1	2	3
4	5	6	7	8	9	10
11	12	13	14	15	16	17
18	19	20	21	22	23	24
25	26	27	28	29		

MARCH

S	M	T	W	T	F	S
					1	2
3	4	5	6	7	8	9
10	11	12	13	14	15	16
17	18	19	20	21	22	23
24	25	26	27	28	29	30
31						

APRIL

S	M	T	W	T	F	S
	1	2	3	4	5	6
7	8	9	10	11	12	13
14	15	16	17	18	19	20
21	22	23	24	25	26	27
28	29	30				

MAY

S	M	T	W	T	F	S
			1	2	3	4
5	6	7	8	9	10	11
12	13	14	15	16	17	18
19	20	21	22	23	24	25
26	27	28	29	30	31	

JUNE

S	M	T	W	T	F	S
						1
2	3	4	5	6	7	8
9	10	11	12	13	14	15
16	17	18	19	20	21	22
23	24	25	26	27	28	29
30						

JULY

S	M	T	W	T	F	S
	1	2	3	4	5	6
7	8	9	10	11	12	13
14	15	16	17	18	19	20
21	22	23	24	25	26	27
28	29	30	31			

AUGUST

S	M	T	W	T	F	S
				1	2	3
4	5	6	7	8	9	10
11	12	13	14	15	16	17
18	19	20	21	22	23	24
25	26	27	28	29	30	31

SEPTEMBER

S	M	T	W	T	F	S
1	2	3	4	5	6	7
8	9	10	11	12	13	14
15	16	17	18	19	20	21
22	23	24	25	26	27	28
29	30					

OCTOBER

S	M	T	W	T	F	S
		1	2	3	4	5
6	7	8	9	10	11	12
13	14	15	16	17	18	19
20	21	22	23	24	25	26
27	28	29	30	31		

NOVEMBER

S	M	T	W	T	F	S
					1	2
3	4	5	6	7	8	9
10	11	12	13	14	15	16
17	18	19	20	21	22	23
24	25	26	27	28	29	30

DECEMBER

S	M	T	W	T	F	S
1	2	3	4	5	6	7
8	9	10	11	12	13	14
15	16	17	18	19	20	21
22	23	24	25	26	27	28
29	30	31				

10

JANUARY

S	M	T	W	T	F	S
		1	2	3	4	5
6	7	8	9	10	11	12
13	14	15	16	17	18	19
20	21	22	23	24	25	26
27	28	29	30	31		

FEBRUARY

S	M	T	W	T	F	S
					1	2
3	4	5	6	7	8	9
10	11	12	13	14	15	16
17	18	19	20	21	22	23
24	25	26	27	28	29	

MARCH

S	M	T	W	T	F	S
						1
2	3	4	5	6	7	8
9	10	11	12	13	14	15
16	17	18	19	20	21	22
23	24	25	26	27	28	29
30	31					

APRIL

S	M	T	W	T	F	S
		1	2	3	4	5
6	7	8	9	10	11	12
13	14	15	16	17	18	19
20	21	22	23	24	25	26
27	28	29	30			

MAY

S	M	T	W	T	F	S
				1	2	3
4	5	6	7	8	9	10
11	12	13	14	15	16	17
18	19	20	21	22	23	24
25	26	27	28	29	30	31

JUNE

S	M	T	W	T	F	S
1	2	3	4	5	6	7
8	9	10	11	12	13	14
15	16	17	18	19	20	21
22	23	24	25	26	27	28
29	30					

JULY

S	M	T	W	T	F	S
		1	2	3	4	5
6	7	8	9	10	11	12
13	14	15	16	17	18	19
20	21	22	23	24	25	26
27	28	29	30	31		

AUGUST

S	M	T	W	T	F	S
					1	2
3	4	5	6	7	8	9
10	11	12	13	14	15	16
17	18	19	20	21	22	23
24	25	26	27	28	29	30
31						

SEPTEMBER

S	M	T	W	T	F	S
	1	2	3	4	5	6
7	8	9	10	11	12	13
14	15	16	17	18	19	20
21	22	23	24	25	26	27
28	29	30				

OCTOBER

S	M	T	W	T	F	S
			1	2	3	4
5	6	7	8	9	10	11
12	13	14	15	16	17	18
19	20	21	22	23	24	25
26	27	28	29	30	31	

NOVEMBER

S	M	T	W	T	F	S
						1
2	3	4	5	6	7	8
9	10	11	12	13	14	15
16	17	18	19	20	21	22
23	24	25	26	27	28	29
30						

DECEMBER

S	M	T	W	T	F	S
	1	2	3	4	5	6
7	8	9	10	11	12	13
14	15	16	17	18	19	20
21	22	23	24	25	26	27
28	29	30	31			

11

JANUARY

S	M	T	W	T	F	S
			1	2	3	4
5	6	7	8	9	10	11
12	13	14	15	16	17	18
19	20	21	22	23	24	25
26	27	28	29	30	31	

FEBRUARY

S	M	T	W	T	F	S
						1
2	3	4	5	6	7	8
9	10	11	12	13	14	15
16	17	18	19	20	21	22
23	24	25	26	27	28	29

MARCH

S	M	T	W	T	F	S
1	2	3	4	5	6	7
8	9	10	11	12	13	14
15	16	17	18	19	20	21
22	23	24	25	26	27	28
29	30	31				

APRIL

S	M	T	W	T	F	S
			1	2	3	4
5	6	7	8	9	10	11
12	13	14	15	16	17	18
19	20	21	22	23	24	25
26	27	28	29	30		

MAY

S	M	T	W	T	F	S
					1	2
3	4	5	6	7	8	9
10	11	12	13	14	15	16
17	18	19	20	21	22	23
24	25	26	27	28	29	30
31						

JUNE

S	M	T	W	T	F	S
	1	2	3	4	5	6
7	8	9	10	11	12	13
14	15	16	17	18	19	20
21	22	23	24	25	26	27
28	29	30				

JULY

S	M	T	W	T	F	S
			1	2	3	4
5	6	7	8	9	10	11
12	13	14	15	16	17	18
19	20	21	22	23	24	25
26	27	28	29	30	31	

AUGUST

S	M	T	W	T	F	S
						1
2	3	4	5	6	7	8
9	10	11	12	13	14	15
16	17	18	19	20	21	22
23	24	25	26	27	28	29
30	31					

SEPTEMBER

S	M	T	W	T	F	S
		1	2	3	4	5
6	7	8	9	10	11	12
13	14	15	16	17	18	19
20	21	22	23	24	25	26
27	28	29	30			

OCTOBER

S	M	T	W	T	F	S
				1	2	3
4	5	6	7	8	9	10
11	12	13	14	15	16	17
18	19	20	21	22	23	24
25	26	27	28	29	30	31

NOVEMBER

S	M	T	W	T	F	S
1	2	3	4	5	6	7
8	9	10	11	12	13	14
15	16	17	18	19	20	21
22	23	24	25	26	27	28
29	30					

DECEMBER

S	M	T	W	T	F	S
		1	2	3	4	5
6	7	8	9	10	11	12
13	14	15	16	17	18	19
20	21	22	23	24	25	26
27	28	29	30	31		

12

JANUARY

S	M	T	W	T	F	S
				1	2	3
4	5	6	7	8	9	10
11	12	13	14	15	16	17
18	19	20	21	22	23	24
25	26	27	28	29	30	31

FEBRUARY

S	M	T	W	T	F	S
1	2	3	4	5	6	7
8	9	10	11	12	13	14
15	16	17	18	19	20	21
22	23	24	25	26	27	28
29						

MARCH

S	M	T	W	T	F	S
	1	2	3	4	5	6
7	8	9	10	11	12	13
14	15	16	17	18	19	20
21	22	23	24	25	26	27
28	29	30	31			

APRIL

S	M	T	W	T	F	S
				1	2	3
4	5	6	7	8	9	10
11	12	13	14	15	16	17
18	19	20	21	22	23	24
25	26	27	28	29	30	

MAY

S	M	T	W	T	F	S
						1
2	3	4	5	6	7	8
9	10	11	12	13	14	15
16	17	18	19	20	21	22
23	24	25	26	27	28	29
30	31					

JUNE

S	M	T	W	T	F	S
		1	2	3	4	5
6	7	8	9	10	11	12
13	14	15	16	17	18	19
20	21	22	23	24	25	26
27	28	29	30			

JULY

S	M	T	W	T	F	S
				1	2	3
4	5	6	7	8	9	10
11	12	13	14	15	16	17
18	19	20	21	22	23	24
25	26	27	28	29	30	31

AUGUST

S	M	T	W	T	F	S
1	2	3	4	5	6	7
8	9	10	11	12	13	14
15	16	17	18	19	20	21
22	23	24	25	26	27	28
29	30	31				

SEPTEMBER

S	M	T	W	T	F	S
			1	2	3	4
5	6	7	8	9	10	11
12	13	14	15	16	17	18
19	20	21	22	23	24	25
26	27	28	29	30		

OCTOBER

S	M	T	W	T	F	S
					1	2
3	4	5	6	7	8	9
10	11	12	13	14	15	16
17	18	19	20	21	22	23
24	25	26	27	28	29	30
31						

NOVEMBER

S	M	T	W	T	F	S
	1	2	3	4	5	6
7	8	9	10	11	12	13
14	15	16	17	18	19	20
21	22	23	24	25	26	27
28	29	30				

DECEMBER

S	M	T	W	T	F	S
			1	2	3	4
5	6	7	8	9	10	11
12	13	14	15	16	17	18
19	20	21	22	23	24	25
26	27	28	29	30	31	

13

JANUARY

S	M	T	W	T	F	S
					1	2
3	4	5	6	7	8	9
10	11	12	13	14	15	16
17	18	19	20	21	22	23
24	25	26	27	28	29	30
31						

FEBRUARY

S	M	T	W	T	F	S
	1	2	3	4	5	6
7	8	9	10	11	12	13
14	15	16	17	18	19	20
21	22	23	24	25	26	27
28	29					

MARCH

S	M	T	W	T	F	S
		1	2	3	4	5
6	7	8	9	10	11	12
13	14	15	16	17	18	19
20	21	22	23	24	25	26
27	28	29	30	31		

APRIL

S	M	T	W	T	F	S
					1	2
3	4	5	6	7	8	9
10	11	12	13	14	15	16
17	18	19	20	21	22	23
24	25	26	27	28	29	30

MAY

S	M	T	W	T	F	S
1	2	3	4	5	6	7
8	9	10	11	12	13	14
15	16	17	18	19	20	21
22	23	24	25	26	27	28
29	30	31				

JUNE

S	M	T	W	T	F	S
			1	2	3	4
5	6	7	8	9	10	11
12	13	14	15	16	17	18
19	20	21	22	23	24	25
26	27	28	29	30		

JULY

S	M	T	W	T	F	S
					1	2
3	4	5	6	7	8	9
10	11	12	13	14	15	16
17	18	19	20	21	22	23
24	25	26	27	28	29	30
31						

AUGUST

S	M	T	W	T	F	S
	1	2	3	4	5	6
7	8	9	10	11	12	13
14	15	16	17	18	19	20
21	22	23	24	25	26	27
28	29	30	31			

SEPTEMBER

S	M	T	W	T	F	S
				1	2	3
4	5	6	7	8	9	10
11	12	13	14	15	16	17
18	19	20	21	22	23	24
25	26	27	28	29	30	

OCTOBER

S	M	T	W	T	F	S
						1
2	3	4	5	6	7	8
9	10	11	12	13	14	15
16	17	18	19	20	21	22
23	24	25	26	27	28	29
30	31					

NOVEMBER

S	M	T	W	T	F	S
		1	2	3	4	5
6	7	8	9	10	11	12
13	14	15	16	17	18	19
20	21	22	23	24	25	26
27	28	29	30			

DECEMBER

S	M	T	W	T	F	S
				1	2	3
4	5	6	7	8	9	10
11	12	13	14	15	16	17
18	19	20	21	22	23	24
25	26	27	28	29	30	31

14

JANUARY

S	M	T	W	T	F	S
						1
2	3	4	5	6	7	8
9	10	11	12	13	14	15
16	17	18	19	20	21	22
23	24	25	26	27	28	29
30	31					

FEBRUARY

S	M	T	W	T	F	S
		1	2	3	4	5
6	7	8	9	10	11	12
13	14	15	16	17	18	19
20	21	22	23	24	25	26
27	28	29				

MARCH

S	M	T	W	T	F	S
			1	2	3	4
5	6	7	8	9	10	11
12	13	14	15	16	17	18
19	20	21	22	23	24	25
26	27	28	29	30	31	

APRIL

S	M	T	W	T	F	S
						1
2	3	4	5	6	7	8
9	10	11	12	13	14	15
16	17	18	19	20	21	22
23	24	25	26	27	28	29
30						

MAY

S	M	T	W	T	F	S
	1	2	3	4	5	6
7	8	9	10	11	12	13
14	15	16	17	18	19	20
21	22	23	24	25	26	27
28	29	30	31			

JUNE

S	M	T	W	T	F	S
				1	2	3
4	5	6	7	8	9	10
11	12	13	14	15	16	17
18	19	20	21	22	23	24
25	26	27	28	29	30	

JULY

S	M	T	W	T	F	S
						1
2	3	4	5	6	7	8
9	10	11	12	13	14	15
16	17	18	19	20	21	22
23	24	25	26	27	28	29
30	31					

AUGUST

S	M	T	W	T	F	S
		1	2	3	4	5
6	7	8	9	10	11	12
13	14	15	16	17	18	19
20	21	22	23	24	25	26
27	28	29	30	31		

SEPTEMBER

S	M	T	W	T	F	S
					1	2
3	4	5	6	7	8	9
10	11	12	13	14	15	16
17	18	19	20	21	22	23
24	25	26	27	28	29	30

OCTOBER

S	M	T	W	T	F	S
1	2	3	4	5	6	7
8	9	10	11	12	13	14
15	16	17	18	19	20	21
22	23	24	25	26	27	28
29	30	31				

NOVEMBER

S	M	T	W	T	F	S
			1	2	3	4
5	6	7	8	9	10	11
12	13	14	15	16	17	18
19	20	21	22	23	24	25
26	27	28	29	30		

DECEMBER

S	M	T	W	T	F	S
					1	2
3	4	5	6	7	8	9
10	11	12	13	14	15	16
17	18	19	20	21	22	23
24	25	26	27	28	29	30
31						

Solar Calendar

The ancient Egyptians were the first people known to have instituted a solar calendar. In actuality their calendar might be called a stellar calendar, since the year began with the rising of Sirius—the brightest star in the sky—at the same place the Sun rises, which generally happened at the same time the Nile flooded. The Egyptians determined that a year was 365 days, about 0.25 day short of the true solar year, so gradually the Egyptian calendar no longer coincided with the seasons. Historical records reveal when the Egyptian calendar and the rising of Sirius coincided, from which astronomers inferred that the Egyptian calendar must have been instituted in either 4241 B.C. or 2773 B.C. The Egyptian calendar had 12 30-day months and five days of festival, a system adopted by various early cultures, although some continued to use lunar calendars.

Julian Calendar

In 46 B.C. Julius Caesar realized that various parts of the land controlled by Rome used different calendars, so he asked the astronomer Sosigenes to develop a uniform calendar. Sosigenes proposed that since the year was 365.25 days long (which is not exact), a 365-day calendar be kept with one day added (a "leap day") every fourth year. When Caesar introduced the new system, he also added days to the year 46 B.C., to bring the seasons in line with the calendar. With a total of 445 days, 46 B.C. is the longest calendar year on record. A year at that time began in what we call March, and the months were numbered. *September, October, November,* and *December* derive from this system, and mean "seventh," "eighth," "ninth," and "tenth" months, respectively.

There was a little further adjustment of the calendar, however, by Augustus Caesar, the first Roman emperor. The name of the fifth month (our July) was changed from Quintilis to honor Julius Caesar. Augustus named the sixth month after himself, August. So that August would not be shorter than 31-day July, Augustus borrowed a day from February.

Because of the Roman Empire's great sphere of influence, the Julian calendar became the ordinary calendar of Western nations.

Gregorian Calendar

From at least A.D. 730, it was known that the solar year—measured from vernal equinox to vernal equinox—was somewhat short of 365.25 days. Each century the solar year gets about half a second shorter. In 1990 the solar year is calculated at 365 days 5 hours 48 minutes 45.5 seconds long, not 365 days 6 hours, which is what the Julian calendar assumes. Because the date of Easter (the Sunday following the first full Moon after the vernal equinox) was slipping, Pope Gregory XIII instituted calendrical reform in 1582. He proclaimed that the day following Oct. 4 would be Oct. 15, which dropped 10 days from the year. Furthermore, on the advice of astronomer Christoph Clavius, the new calendar would be kept in line by omitting the leap year in century years unless they were divisible by 400. Thus 1900 was not a leap year in the Gregorian calendar, as it came to be called, but 2000 would be.

Most Roman Catholic countries and some other Western countries adopted the new system, but England did not. Finally, in 1752, England and its colonies adopted the Gregorian calendar, but they had to drop 11 days to fit common Western practice. It was at this time that New Year's Day in England was moved from Mar. 25 to Jan. 1, changing the number of the year for the almost three months affected. Thus, George Washington was born according to the Julian calendar on Feb. 11, 1731, but came to celebrate his birth as Feb. 22, 1732, on the Gregorian calendar.

Because the solar year is shortening, astronomers today keep the Gregorian calendar in line by making a one-second adjustment as needed, usually on Dec. 31 at midnight, whenever the error's accumulation nears one second.

Julian Day Count

A year after the Gregorian calendar was first instituted, Joseph Justus Scaliger developed a system of counting days instead of years, which is still used by astronomers. Called the Julian Day Count (after his father, Julius Caesar Scaliger), it begins with 1 on Jan. 1, 4713 B.C. On this date the Julian calendar, the lunar calendar, and the Roman tax system (which had its own calendar) all coincided—something that won't happen again until A.D. 3267. Each day within such a 7,980-year period is numbered. Jan. 1, 1996, is Julian Day 2,450,082.

HOLIDAYS AND HOLY DAYS

Federal Holidays in the United States

Congress and the president have designated 10 days as federal holidays. Although these are so widely observed as to be considered "national" holidays, they technically apply only to federal employees and the District of Columbia. It is up to the individual states to designate their own holidays. When a federal holiday falls on a Saturday or a Sunday, it is observed on the preceding Friday or the following Monday.

New Year's Day (Jan. 1) The observance of the New Year dates back to pre-Christian times when rites were performed to ensure the return of spring. It was observed in England on Mar. 25 until 1752, when it was changed to Jan. 1.

Martin Luther King, Jr., Day (Third Monday in January) Before his assassination in 1968, Martin Luther King, Jr., was the foremost civil rights leader of the 1950s and 1960s, and in 1964 he won the Nobel Peace Prize. In 1983 Congress set aside this day to celebrate his life and accomplishments.

Presidents' Day (Third Monday in February) Presidents' Day combines the observance of George Washington's birthday (Feb. 22), first observed in 1796, and Abraham Lincoln's birthday (Feb. 12), which became a federal holiday in 1892.

Memorial Day (Last Monday in May) Memorial Day (also known as Decoration Day) honors soldiers fallen in battle. Dating from the Civil War, it is traditionally marked with parades and memorial services.

Independence Day (Fourth of July) The most important U.S. holiday, Independence Day commemorates the signing of the Declaration of Independence on July 4, 1776, an event that marked America's birth as a free nation. The holiday was first observed in 1777 and is celebrated with fireworks, parades, and oratory.

Labor Day (First Monday in September) The idea of Peter J. McGuire, president of the United Brotherhood of Carpenters and Joiners of America, the official observance of a day celebrating the American worker was signed into law on June 28, 1894.

Columbus Day (Second Monday in October) On Oct. 12, 1492, Christopher Columbus and his crew landed in the Bahama Islands after sailing across the Atlantic. First celebrated in 1792, Columbus Day was not officially recognized until 1909. Its observance is of special national pride to Italian-Americans who claim the Genoese Columbus for their own.

Veterans' Day (Nov. 11) Armistice Day, which marked the end of World War I on Nov. 11, 1918, was made a legal holiday in 1938. The name was changed to Veterans' Day in 1954 to honor all of America's veterans.

Thanksgiving Day (Fourth Thursday in November) Thanksgiving Day was first observed in Plymouth Colony (Mass.) in 1621, the year in which the Pilgrims landed in the New World and gave thanks for their first harvest and for the new land they had colonized. President Lincoln proclaimed Thanksgiving a national holiday in 1863.

Christmas Day is celebrated on Dec. 25. (See also "Christian Holy Days.")

U.S. Minor Holidays and Occasions

April Fools' Day (Apr. 1) A day for practical jokes; the origin of April Fools' Day is obscure, but it bears some resemblance to an ancient Roman festival honoring the goddess of nature.

Arbor Day (Last Friday in April) Dedicated to trees and their preservation; its observance is meant to encourage preservation of the environment. Internationally, it is observed on Dec. 22.

Armed Forces Day (Third Saturday in May) A day to honor members of the U.S. Armed Forces.

Citizenship Day (Sept. 17) First observed by presidential proclamation in 1952, Citizenship Day falls on the same day as the old Constitution Day, which it replaces, though the old name is still commonly used.

Daylight Savings Time During this period, clocks are set one hour ahead of standard time; daylight saving time lasts from the first Sunday in April to the last Sunday in October, when clocks are turned back one hour—"Spring ahead, fall back."

Election Day (The Tuesday after the first Monday in November) In years evenly divisible by

IMPORTANT DATES IN THE U.S. AND CANADA, 1995–2000

Event	1995	1996[1]	1997	1998	1999	2000[1]
New Year's Day[2]	Jan. 1	Jan. 1	Jan. 1	Jan. 1	Jan. 1	Jan. 1
Martin Luther King, Jr., Day[2]	Jan. 16	Jan. 15	Jan. 20	Jan. 19	Jan. 18	Jan. 16
Groundhog Day	Feb. 2	Feb. 2	Feb. 2	Feb. 2	Feb. 2	Feb. 2
St. Valentine's Day	Feb. 14	Feb. 14	Feb. 14	Feb. 14	Feb. 14	Feb. 14
Susan B. Anthony Day	Feb. 15	Feb. 15	Feb. 15	Feb. 15	Feb. 15	Feb. 15
Presidents' Day[2]	Feb. 20	Feb. 19	Feb. 17	Feb. 16	Feb. 15	Feb. 20
Mardi Gras	Feb. 28	Feb. 20	Feb. 11	Feb. 24	Feb. 16	Mar. 7
St. Patrick's Day	Mar. 17	Mar. 17	Mar. 17	Mar. 17	Mar. 17	Mar. 17
April Fool's Day	Apr. 1	Apr. 1	Apr. 1	Apr. 1	Apr. 1	Apr. 1
Daylight Savings begins	Apr. 2	Apr. 7	Apr. 6	Apr. 5	Apr. 4	Apr. 2
Arbor Day	Apr. 28	Apr. 26	Apr. 25	Apr. 24	Apr. 30	Apr. 28
National Teacher Day	May 9	May 7	May 6	May 5	May 4	May 9
Mother's Day	May 14	May 12	May 11	May 10	May 9	May 14
Armed Forces Day	May 20	May 18	May 17	May 16	May 15	May 20
Victoria Day[3]	May 22	May 20	May 19	May 18	May 24	May 22
National Maritime Day	May 22	May 22	May 22	May 22	May 22	May 22
Memorial Day[2]	May 29	May 27	May 26	May 25	May 31	May 29
Flag Day	June 14	June 14	June 14	June 14	June 14	June 14
Father's Day	June 18	June 16	June 15	June 21	June 20	June 18
Canada Day[3]	July 1	July 1	July 1	July 1	July 1	July 1
Independence Day[2]	July 4	July 4	July 4	July 4	July 4	July 4
Labor Day[2,3]	Sept. 4	Sept. 2	Sept. 1	Sept. 7	Sept. 6	Sept. 4
Citizenship Day	Sept. 17	Sept. 17	Sept. 17	Sept. 17	Sept. 17	Sept. 17
Columbus Day[2]	Oct. 9	Oct. 14	Oct. 13	Oct. 12	Oct. 11	Oct. 9
Thanksgiving Day (Can.)[3]	Oct. 9	Oct. 14	Oct. 13	Oct. 12	Oct. 11	Oct. 9
United Nations Day	Oct. 24	Oct. 24	Oct. 24	Oct. 24	Oct. 24	Oct. 24
Daylight Savings ends	Oct. 29	Oct. 27	Oct. 26	Oct. 25	Oct. 31	Oct. 29
Halloween	Oct. 31	Oct. 31	Oct. 31	Oct. 31	Oct. 31	Oct. 31
Election Day (U.S.)	Nov. 7	Nov. 5	Nov. 4	Nov. 3	Nov. 2	Nov. 7
Veterans' Day[2,4]	Nov. 11	Nov. 11	Nov. 11	Nov. 11	Nov. 11	Nov. 11
Remembrance Day[3]	Nov. 11	Nov. 11	Nov. 11	Nov. 11	Nov. 11	Nov. 11
Thanksgiving Day (U.S.)[2]	Nov. 23	Nov. 28	Nov. 27	Nov. 26	Nov. 25	Nov. 23
Christmas Day[2,3]	Dec. 25	Dec. 25	Dec. 25	Dec. 25	Dec. 25	Dec. 25
Boxing Day[3]	Dec. 26	Dec. 26	Dec. 26	Dec. 26	Dec. 26	Dec. 26
New Year's Eve	Dec. 31	Dec. 31	Dec. 31	Dec. 31	Dec. 31	Dec. 31

Note: For dates of Jewish, Christian, and Muslim holy days, see accompanying tables. 1. Leap year; February has 29 days. 2. Federal holiday in U.S. 3. Federal holiday in Canada. 4. Also known as Armistice Day.

four, presidential elections are held; in years evenly divisible by two, elections for all members of the House of Representatives and for one-third of the members of the Senate are held.

Father's Day (Third Sunday in June) A uniquely American institution, Father's Day was first observed in West Virginia in 1908, but it was not until 1972 that the president signed a congressional resolution designating its official observance.

Flag Day (June 14) The first observance of Flag Day was in 1877, the centenary of the Flag Resolution, which adopted the design of the American flag flown today. Pres. Harry Truman signed the Flag Day Bill in 1949.

Groundhog Day (Feb. 2) On this day, as legend has it, the groundhog peeks out of his burrow to look for his shadow, and if he sees his shadow, six weeks of winter will follow; if he doesn't, spring is just around the corner.

Halloween (Oct. 31) All Hallow's Eve began as a pagan custom honoring the dead and as a celebration of autumn. The wearing of costumes can be traced back to medieval religious practice in which parishioners dressed as saints and angels and paraded through the churchyard. The modern practice of "trick or treating" is of recent American origin.

Mother's Day (Second Sunday in May) Conceived by Anne M. Jarvis of Philadelphia, Pa., where it was first observed, as a day for children to pay tribute to their mothers, this was declared a national holiday by Congress in 1914.

National Maritime Day (May 22) Designated by presidential proclamation in 1935, this commemorates the anniversary of the departure of the SS *Savannah* on the first successful transoceanic voyage of a steam-powered vessel, in 1819. It is also a day of remembrance of merchant mariners who died in defense of their country.

National Teacher Day (Tuesday of the first full week in May) The day when students and communities around the country honor their teachers and the teaching profession.

St. Patrick's Day (Mar. 17) A day in honor of Ireland's patron saint, St. Patrick's Day is a religious, political, and social event rolled into one. In Ireland St. Patrick is honored by church ceremonies and a three-day period of devotion. In the United States, Mar. 17 is celebrated with parades and the "wearing of the green."

St. Valentine's Day (Feb. 14) Originally, an occasion to honor two Christian saints martyred by the Roman Emperor Claudius (214–270). Since the Middle Ages, the day has been dedicated to lovers, probably because it is believed to be the day birds choose their mates.

Susan B. Anthony Day (Feb. 15) Anthony (1820–1906) was one of the first women's rights advocates, working especially for equal suffrage. She was a cofounder and later president of the National Woman Suffrage Association.

United Nations Day (Oct. 24) Commemorates the ratification of the UN Charter on this date in 1945 by the five permanent members of the Security Council and a majority of the other charter signatories.

Christian Holy Days

Christmas is the celebration of Christ's birth. The exact date of his birth is unknown, but the date of Dec. 25 was probably chosen because it coincided with the ancient midwinter celebrations honoring pagan deities. The 12 days of Christmas fall between Christmas and Epiphany (Jan. 6), the day the Wise Men visited the Christ child.

Easter is the most important holy day in the Christian religion. It is the celebration of Christ's Resurrection from the dead, which gave Christians the hope of salvation and eternal life. Although Easter is only one day, the full observance of the holy day spans from Septuagesima Sunday (70 days before Easter Sunday), which may fall as early as January, to Pentecost, which can occur as late as June.

Shrove Tuesday (Mardi Gras; Fat Tuesday) Originally a day of penance, the last day before the beginning of Lent is now celebrated with feasting and merrymaking.

Ash Wednesday derives its name from the rite of burning the palms carried on the Palm Sunday of the year before and using the ashes to mark worshipers' foreheads with a cross.

Lent, a 40-day period of fasting and penitence beginning on Ash Wednesday and ending on Easter Sunday, is traditionally observed by fasting, performing acts of charity, and by giving up certain pleasures and amusements. (Note that the six Sundays that fall during Lent are not considered part of the 40-day period. Thus Easter occurs 46 calendar days after Ash Wednesday.)

Palm Sunday, the Sunday before Easter, celebrates Jesus' triumphant entry into Jerusalem, where palm branches were spread before him to honor his path.

CALENDAR OF CHRISTIAN HOLY DAYS

Year A.D.	Ash Wednesday	Good Friday	Easter Sunday	Pentecost	Trinity Sunday	Advent
1994	Feb. 16	Apr. 1	Apr. 3	May 22	May 29	Nov. 27
1995	Mar. 1	Apr. 14	Apr. 16	June 4	June 11	Dec. 3
1996	Feb. 21	Apr. 5	Apr. 7	May 26	June 2	Dec. 1
1997	Feb. 12	Mar. 28	Mar. 30	May 18	June 1	Nov. 30
1998	Feb. 25	Apr. 10	Apr. 12	May 31	June 7	Nov. 29
1999	Feb. 17	Apr. 2	Apr. 4	May 23	May 30	Nov. 28
2000	Mar. 8	Apr. 21	Apr. 23	June 11	June 18	Dec. 3
2001	Feb. 28	Apr. 13	Apr. 15	June 3	June 10	Dec. 2

Holy (Maundy) Thursday is the anniversary of the Last Supper. The traditional services mark three events that occurred during the week before Jesus was crucified: he washed the feet of his 12 disciples; he instituted the Eucharist (the sacrament of Holy Communion); and he was arrested and imprisoned.

Good Friday marks the day of Christ's Crucifixion. The holy day is observed with fasting, mourning, and penitence.

Holy Saturday is the day that anticipates the Resurrection. In the Catholic church, special vigils are held on Holy Saturday evening.

Easter Sunday marks the day of Christ's Resurrection. Many worshipers celebrate the holy day with sunrise services, a custom believed to be inspired by the example of Mary Magdalene, who went to Christ's tomb "early, while it was yet dark."

Pentecost (literally, 50th day) is the end of the full ecclesiastical observance of Easter. It takes place on the seventh Sunday after Easter Sunday and commemorates the descent of the Holy Spirit upon the Apostles.

The Annunciation This holy day marks the archangel Gabriel's announcement to Mary that she would conceive and give birth to Jesus. It is celebrated by Roman Catholics on Mar. 25; it is not observed by Protestant denominations.

Trinity Sunday The Sunday after Pentecost, this occasion honors the Father, Son, and Holy Ghost. It was declared a part of the church calendar in 1334 by Pope John XXII and is observed by Roman Catholics and by some Protestant denominations.

Corpus Christi This feast celebrates the presence of the body (corpus) of Christ in the Eucharist. At one time this was the principal feast of the church year, but today it is observed only by Catholic churches. Corpus Christi is celebrated on the Thursday following Trinity Sunday.

All Saints' Day, celebrated on Nov. 1, honors all of the Christian saints. In America many churches mark the Sunday nearest Nov. 1 as a day to pay tribute to those who have died during the year. All Saints' Day is observed primarily by Roman Catholics.

Advent, a religious season that begins on the Sunday closest to Nov. 30 and lasts until Christmas, both celebrates the birth of Jesus and anticipates his second coming. At one time Advent was a solemn season observed by fasting, but this is no longer the case.

Holy Days of Obligation are feast days in the Catholic calendar, observed by attendance at Mass and rest from unnecessary work. Six holy days of obligation are observed in the United States:

1. Solemnity of Mary, Jan. 1
2. Ascension Thursday (of Jesus to Heaven), 40 days after Easter
3. Assumption of the Blessed Virgin into Heaven, Aug. 15
4. All Saints' Day, Nov. 1
5. Mary's Immaculate Conception (honoring the Mother of God as the only person conceived without original sin), Dec. 8
6. Christmas, Dec. 25

The Jewish Calendar

The months of the Jewish year are Tishri, Heshvan, Kislev, Tebet, Shebat, Adar, Nisan, Iyar, Sivan, Tammuz, Ab, and Elul. The Jewish era dates from the year of the creation (*anno mundi*, or A.M.), which is equal to 3761 B.C.E. (before the Christian era). Thus 5756 began in 1995 and ends in 1996 of the Gregorian calendar. (Tishri, the first month of the Jewish year, falls in either September or October of the Gregorian calendar.)

Because the Jewish calendar is a blend of solar and lunar calendars, there are intercalated months to keep the lunar and solar years in alignment. (Intercalation is the insertion of an extra day, month, or other unit—Feb. 29 in a leap year, for example—into a calendar. The intercalated month here is called Adar Sheni, or Veadar—"Second Adar." The year 5749 was a leap year).

Jewish Holy Days

Sabbath is the first and most important Jewish holy day, occurring each week from sundown Friday to sundown Saturday. It is a day of rest and spiritual growth, given to men and women

HOW TO FIND EASTER SUNDAY, 1951–2050

Easter Sunday always falls on the first Sunday after the first full moon after the vernal equinox on Mar. 21. Thus, Easter can fall no earlier than Mar. 23 (if the first full moon is a Saturday, Mar. 22) and no later than Apr. 25 (if the first full moon is a Sunday, Apr. 17). The following table lists the days on which Easter falls between 1951 and 2050.

Year	Easter Sunday	Year	Easter Sunday	Year	Easter Sunday	Year	Easter Sunday	Year	Easter Sunday	Year	Easter Sunday
1951	March 25	1968	April 14	1985	April 7	2002	March 31	2019	April 21	2036	April 13
1952	April 13	1969	April 6	1986	March 30	2003	April 20	2020	April 12	2037	April 5
1953	April 5	1970	March 29	1987	April 19	2004	April 11	2021	April 4	2038	April 25
1954	April 18	1971	April 11	1988	April 3	2005	March 27	2022	April 17	2039	April 10
1955	April 10	1972	April 2	1989	March 26	2006	April 16	2023	April 9	2040	April 1
1956	April 1	1973	April 22	1990	April 15	2007	April 8	2024	March 31	2041	April 21
1957	April 21	1974	April 14	1991	March 31	2008	March 23	2025	April 20	2042	April 6
1958	April 6	1975	March 30	1992	April 19	2009	April 12	2026	April 5	2043	March 29
1959	March 29	1976	April 18	1993	April 11	2010	April 4	2027	March 28	2044	April 17
1960	April 17	1977	April 10	1994	April 3	2011	April 24	2028	April 16	2045	April 9
1961	April 2	1978	March 26	1995	April 16	2012	April 8	2029	April 1	2046	March 25
1962	April 22	1979	April 15	1996	April 7	2013	March 31	2030	April 21	2047	April 14
1963	April 14	1980	April 6	1997	March 30	2014	April 20	2031	April 13	2048	April 5
1964	March 29	1981	April 19	1998	April 12	2015	April 5	2032	March 28	2049	April 18
1965	April 18	1982	April 11	1999	April 4	2016	March 27	2033	April 17	2050	April 10
1966	April 10	1983	April 3	2000	April 23	2017	April 16	2034	April 9		
1967	March 26	1984	April 22	2001	April 15	2018	April 1	2035	March 25		

CALENDAR OF JEWISH HOLY DAYS, 5755–62

Year A.M.	Rosh Hashanah	Yom Kippur	Sukkoth	Hanukkah	Purim	Pesach	Shavuoth
5755	Sept. 6, 1994	Sept. 15, 1994	Sept. 20, 1994	Nov. 28, 1994	Mar. 16, 1995	Apr. 15, 1995	June 4, 1995
5756	Sept. 25, 1995	Oct. 4, 1995	Oct. 9, 1995	Dec. 18, 1995	Mar. 5, 1996	Apr. 4, 1996	May 24, 1996
5757	Sept. 23, 1996	Oct. 2, 1996	Sept. 28, 1996	Dec. 6, 1996	Mar. 23, 1997	Apr. 22, 1997	June 11, 1997
5758	Oct. 2, 1997	Oct. 11, 1997	Oct. 16, 1997	Dec. 24, 1997	Mar. 12, 1998	Apr. 11, 1998	May 31, 1998
5759	Sept. 21, 1998	Sept. 30, 1998	Oct. 5, 1998	Dec. 14, 1998	Mar. 2, 1999	Apr. 1, 1999	May 21, 1999
5760	Sept. 11, 1999	Sept. 20, 1999	Sept. 25, 1999	Dec. 4, 1999	Mar. 21, 2000	Apr. 20, 2000	June 9, 2000
5761	Sept. 30, 2000	Oct. 9, 2000	Oct. 14, 2000	Dec. 22, 2000	Mar. 9, 2001	Apr. 9, 2001	May 28, 2001
5762	Sept. 18, 2001	Sept. 27, 2001	Oct. 2, 2001	Dec. 10, 2001	Feb. 26, 2002	Apr. 3, 2002	May 17, 2002

Source: *Encyclopedia Judaica.*

so they will remember the sweetness of freedom and keep it. Sabbath takes precedence over all other observances.

Rosh Hashanah (New Year), held to be the birthday of the world, is also called the Day of Judgment and Remembrance, and the day of the shofar—a ram's horn—which is blown to remind Jews of Abraham's willingness to sacrifice his son Isaac. The holiday takes place on the first and second days of Tishri (in September or October).

Yom Kippur (Day of Atonement) concludes the 10 days of repentance that Rosh Hashanah begins and takes place from sundown on the ninth day of Tishri until sundown on the 10th. The observance begins with the recitation of the most famous passage in the Jewish liturgy—the *Kol Nidre*—which nullifies unfulfilled vows made in the past year. The entire day is spent praying and fasting.

Sukkoth (Tabernacles) is a harvest festival celebrated from the 15th through the 22nd of Tishri. Sukkoth also commemorates the journey of the Jewish people through the wilderness to the land of Israel. Jewish families take their meals this week in a roughly constructed *sukkah* (booth)—a reminder of an agricultural society, of the Exodus, and of how precarious and fragile life can be. On the Simchath Torah, the 23rd of Tishri, a congregation finishes reading the last book of the Torah and immediately starts again with the first.

Hanukkah (Feast of Dedication; Festival of Lights) The importance of the eight-day feast, which begins on the 25th day day of Kislev, is its commemoration of the first war in human history fought in the cause of religious freedom. The Maccabees vanquished not just the military threat to Judaism but also the internal forces for assimilation into the Hellenistic culture of Israel's rulers. Jews light candles for eight nights to mark a miracle: a day's supply of oil, found in the recaptured Temple, that burned for eight days.

Purim (Feast of Lots), set on the 14th day of Adar, is another celebration of survival, noting the events described in the Book of Esther. At Purim Jews rejoice at Queen Esther's and her cousin Mordecai's defeat of Haman, the Persian King Ahaseurus's adviser who plotted to slaughter all the Persian Jews. Ahaseurus ruled around 400 B.C.

Pesach (Passover), beginning on the 15th day of Nisan and lasting seven days, commemorates the exodus of the Hebrews from Egypt in about 1300 B.C. The name Passover also recalls God's sparing (passing over) the Jewish first-born during the plagues upon the land brought by God through Moses. The holiday is marked by eating only unleavened foods and participating in a seder, or special meal.

Shavuoth (Feast of Weeks) is observed on the sixth or seventh day of Sivan. Originally an agricultural festival, Shavuoth is a celebration of the revelation of the Torah at Mt. Sinai, by which God established his covenant with the Jewish people.

The Islamic Calendar

The 12 months of the Islamic year are: Muharram, Safar, Rabi I, Rabi II, Jumada I, Jumada II, Rajab, Sha'ban, Ramadan, Shawwal, Dhu'l-Qa'dah, Dhu'l-Hijja. The Islamic calendar is based on a lunar year of 12 months of 30 and 29 days (alternating every month), and the year is equal to 354 days. It runs in cycles of 30 years, of which the second, fifth, seventh, 10th, 13th, 16th, 18th, 21st, 24th, 26th, and 29th are leap years. Leap years have 355 days, the extra day being added to the last month, Dhu'l-Hijja. The year A.H. 1410 (*anno hegirae,* in the year of the hejira) is the 30th year in the cycle. There are no intercalated months or leap years, so the Islamic year does not keep a constant relationship to the solar year—which dictates the seasons—and months occur about 10 or 11 days earlier than in the year before.

The caliph Abu Bakr adopted A.D. 622—the year of the hejira (Muhammad's migration from Mecca to Medina)—as the first year of Islam. However, dating of the Muslim era varies throughout the Islamic world. In some countries the year of the Muslim era is obtained by subtracting 622 from the Gregorian year; A.D. 1990 equals A.H. 1368.

Other countries (Saudi Arabia, Yemen, and the principalities of the Persian Gulf) continue to use a purely lunar year. To approximate the

CALENDAR OF MUSLIM HOLY DAYS

Year A.H. (A.D.)	New Year's Day, 1 Muharram	1 Ramadan	Id al-Fitr, 1 Shawwal	Id al-Adha, 10 Dhu al-Hijja
1412 (1991–92)	July 13, 1991	Mar. 5, 1992	Apr. 4, 1992	June 11, 1992
1413 (1992–93)	July 2, 1992	Feb. 23, 1993	Mar. 25, 1993	June 1, 1993
1414 (1993–94)	June 20, 1993	Feb. 12, 1994	Mar. 14, 1994	May 21, 1994
1415 (1994–95)	June 9, 1994	Feb. 1, 1995	Mar. 3, 1995	May 10, 1995
1416 (1995–96)	May 28, 1995	Jan. 22, 1996	Feb. 20, 1996	Apr. 28, 1996
1417 (1996–97)	May 18, 1996	Jan. 10, 1997	Feb. 9, 1997	Apr. 18, 1997

CHINESE YEARS, 1900–2007

Rat	Ox	Tiger	Hare (Rabbit)	Dragon	Snake	Horse	Sheep (Goat)	Monkey	Rooster	Dog	Pig
1900	1901	1902	1903	1904	1905	1906	1907	1908	1909	1910	1911
1912	1913	1914	1915	1916	1917	1918	1919	1920	1921	1922	1923
1924	1925	1926	1927	1928	1929	1930	1931	1932	1933	1934	1935
1936	1937	1938	1939	1940	1941	1942	1943	1944	1945	1946	1947
1948	1949	1950	1951	1952	1953	1954	1955	1956	1957	1958	1959
1960	1961	1962	1963	1964	1965	1966	1967	1968	1969	1970	1971
1972	1973	1974	1975	1976	1977	1978	1979	1980	1981	1982	1983
1984	1985	1986	1987	1988	1989	1990	1991	1992	1993	1994	1995
1996	1997	1998	1999	2000	2001	2002	2003	2004	2005	2006	2007

Muslim era equivalent of the Gregorian year, subtract 622 (the year of hejira in the Gregorian calendar) from the current year and multiply the result by 1.031 (days in the year of the Gregorian calendar divided by days in the lunar year): A.D. 1990 = (1990 − 622) × 1.031 = A.H. 1410.

Muslim Holy Days

Ramadan, the ninth month of the Islamic calendar, is the Islamic faith's holiest period. To honor the month in which the Koran was revealed, all adult Muslims of sound body and mind observe fasting—eschewing food, water, or even a kiss—between the hours of sunrise and sunset. Exempted from the fast are women in menstruation or childbirth bleeding, the chronically ill, or people on a journey, all of whom must make up the fast days at a later date.

Id al-Fitr This day of feasting is celebrated at the end of Ramadan. To mark the fast's break, worshipers also attend an early morning service, Salat-ul-'Id, at which they give alms in staple foodstuffs or their monetary value.

Id al-Adha The Feast of Sacrifice takes place on the 10th day of Dhu'l-Hijja, the last month of the year and the season of the *haj*, or pilgrimage. The day begins with a service in the mosques or other places of gathering, and for those who are not pilgrims continues with the ritual slaughter of a sheep in commemoration of God's ransom of Abraham's son from sacrifice. At least a third of the meat of the animal is to be set aside for charity.

Fridays At noontime Muslims attend mosque or comparable gathering places to say the congregational Friday prayer that ends the week. While Friday—Jumuah—is the holy day of the weekly Muslim calendar, it is not a Sabbath comparable to Christian Sundays or Jewish Saturdays, and there are no restrictions on work or other worldly enterprises.

The Hindu Year

The Hindu year consists of 12 months: Caitra, Vaisakha, Jyaistha, Asadha, Sravana, Bhadrapada, Asvina, Karttika, Margasivsa, Pansa, Magha, and Phalguna. Calendrically, holidays are of two types, lunar and solar. Solar holidays in the Hindu calendar include the following:

Mesasamkranti is the beginning of the new astrological year, when the sun enters the constellation Aries.

Makaraj-Samkranti, the winter solstice, occurs when the sun enters the constellation Capricorn.

Mahavisuva Day is New Year's Eve.

Principal holidays determined by the lunar year are these:

Ramanavami (Caitra 9) celebrates the birth of Rama, in Hindu folklore the epitome of chivalry, courage, and obedience to sacred law. Rama is considered an incarnation of Vishnu, and his name is synonymous with God.

Rathayatra (Asadha 2) is the pilgrimage of the chariot festival of Orissa.

Janmastami (Sravana 8) is the birthday of Krishna, an incarnation of the supreme deity, Vishnu, celebrated as a philosopher-king and hero.

Dasahra (Asvina 7–10) commemorates Rama's victory over the demon Ravana.

Laksmipuja (Asvina 15) honors Laksmi, goddess of good fortune.

Dipavali (Karttika 15) occasions the festival of lights and exchanging of presents.

Mahasivaratri (Magha 13) honors the god Shiva, one of the three supreme Hindu gods. Shiva, whose name means "Auspicious One," is a god of both reproduction and destruction.

MONTHS OF THE YEAR

Gregorian	Hebrew	Hindu	Muslim
January	Shebat	Magha	*Muharram*
February	Adar	Phalguna	Safar
March	Nisan	*Caitra*	Rabi I
April	Iyar	Vaisakha	Rabi II
May	Sivan	Jyaistha	Jumada I
June	Tammuz	Asadha	Jumada II
July	Ab	Sravana	Rajab
August	Elul	Bhadrapada	Sha'ban
September	*Tishri*	Asvina	Ramadan
October	Heshvan	Karttika	Shawwal
November	Kislev	Margasivsa	Dhu'l-Qa'dah
December	Tebet	Pansa	Dhu'l-Hijja

Note: The months of the Gregorian, Hebrew, Hindu, and reformed Muslim calendars occur at roughly the same time of year, while those of the traditional (lunar) Muslim calendar occur at different times every year. Months in italics indicate the first month of the year in the respective calendars.

ASTROLOGICAL CALENDAR

Dates	Sign
January 20–February 18	Aquarius, the water bearer
February 19–March 20	Pisces, the fishes
March 21–April 19	Aries, the ram
April 20–May 20	Taurus, the bull
May 21–June 20	Gemini, the twins
June 21–July 22	Cancer, the crab
July 23–August 22	Leo, the lion
August 23–September 22	Virgo, the virgin
September 23–October 22	Libra, the scales
October 23–November 21	Scorpio, the scorpion
November 22–December 21	Sagittarius, the archer
December 22–January 19	Capricorn, the goat

WEDDING ANNIVERSARIES

Anniversary	Type of gift	Anniversary	Type of gift
1st	Cotton	14th	Ivory
2nd	Paper	15th	Crystal
3rd	Leather	20th	China
4th	Fruit, flowers	25th	Silver
5th	Wood	30th	Pearl
6th	Sugar	35th	Coral
7th	Copper, wool	40th	Ruby
8th	Bronze, pottery	45th	Sapphire
9th	Pottery, willow	50th	Gold
10th	Tin	55th	Emerald
11th	Steel	60th	Diamond
12th	Silk, linen	70th	Platinum
13th	Lace		

BIRTHSTONES

Month	Stone
January	Garnet
February	Amethyst
March	Aquamarine, Bloodstone
April	Diamond
May	Emerald
June	Alexandrite, Moonstone, Pearl
July	Ruby
August	Peridot, Sardonyx
September	Sapphire
October	Opal, Tourmaline
November	Topaz
December	Turquoise, Lapis Lazuli

ASTRONOMICAL EVENTS, 1996

The main astronomical events included in this section are the phases of the Moon, the Moon's perigee (when it is closest to the Earth) and apogee (when it is farthest away), lunar and solar eclipses, and the visibility of the planets.

Phases of the Moon

A lunation is the cycle from new moon to new moon and takes about 29.53 days. During this period, the relative position of the Earth, Moon, and Sun affect what, if any, part of the Moon we can see illuminated by the sun during our night. A *new moon* occurs when the Moon is in conjunction with the Sun, and the Moon is invisible from the Earth. When the Moon is at *first quarter* (90° from the Sun relative to the Earth), its sunlit part appears in the shape of a D (in the Southern Hemisphere, a backward D). A *full moon*, when the Moon shows an almost fully illuminated face, occurs when the Moon is 180° around the sky from the sun. The *last quarter* (or third quarter) is when the Moon is again moving toward a position between the Earth and the Sun, and it appears as a backward D (a normal D in the Southern Hemisphere). Intermediate phases are the *crescent moon*—between the new moon and first quarter (waxing), and between the last quarter and new moon (waning); and the *gibbous moon*, occurring before and after the full moon.

Visibility of the Planets

Mercury can only be seen low in the east before sunrise, or low in the west after sunset (about the time of the beginning or end of civil twilight). It is visible in the mornings between the following approximate dates: January 25–March 19, May 24–July 4, and September 25–October 20. The planet is brighter at the end of each period (the best conditions in northern latitudes occur from mid-October to just a few days before the end of that month, and in southern latitudes from the third week of February until the third week of March). It is visible in the evenings between the following approximate dates: January 1–13, April 6–May 5, July 19–September 11, and November 19–December 27. The planet is brighter at the beginning of each period (the best conditions in northern latitudes occur during the first half of May, and in the southern latitudes from the third week of August until the third week of September).

Venus is a brilliant object in the morning sky from the beginning of the year until the first week of June, when it becomes too close to the Sun for observation. During the middle of June, it reappears in the evening sky, where it stays until the end of the year. Venus is in conjunction with Saturn on February 3, with Mercury on June 23, and with Mars on June 30 and September 4.

PHASES OF THE MOON, 1996

New moon				First quarter				Full moon				Last quarter			
Month	d	h	m	Month	d	h	m	Month	d	h	m	Month	d	h	m
Jan.	20	12	50	Jan.	27	11	14	Jan.	5	20	51	Jan.	13	20	45
Feb.	18	23	30	Feb.	26	05	52	Feb.	4	15	58	Feb.	12	08	37
Mar.	19	10	45	Mar.	27	01	31	Mar.	5	09	23	Mar.	12	17	15
Apr.	17	22	49	Apr.	25	20	40	Apr.	4	00	07	Apr.	10	23	36
May	17	11	46	May	25	14	13	May	3	11	48	May	10	05	04
June	16	01	36	June	24	05	23	June	1	20	47	June	8	11	05
July	15	16	15	July	23	17	49	July	1	03	58	July	7	18	55
Aug.	14	07	34	Aug.	22	03	36	July	30	10	35	Aug.	6	05	25
Sept.	12	23	07	Sept.	20	11	23	Aug.	28	17	52	Sept.	4	19	06
Oct.	12	14	14	Oct.	19	18	09	Sept.	27	02	51	Oct.	4	12	04
Nov.	11	04	16	Nov.	18	01	09	Oct.	26	14	11	Nov.	3	07	50
Dec.	10	16	56	Dec.	17	09	31	Nov.	25	04	10	Dec.	3	05	06
								Dec.	24	20	41				

Note: Shown in universal time (UT). To convert to local time, see "Timing Planetary Phenomena." **Source:** U.S. Naval Observatory, *Astronomical Phenomena for the Year 1996* (1993).

Mars is too close to the Sun for observation until the middle of May, when it appears in the morning sky. Its westward elongation gradually increases, moving from Aries at the beginning of May, into Taurus in early June (passing 6°N of *Aldebaran* on June 27), and into Gemini in the last week of July (passing 6°S of Pollux on August 31). It then continues through Cancer, Leo (passing 1.2°N of Regulus on October 29), and into Virgo where after mid-December it can be seen for more than half the night. Mars is in conjunction with Mercury on May 31 and with Venus on June 30 and September 4.

Jupiter rises just before sunrise in Sagittarius, in which constellation it remains throughout the year. Its westward elongation gradually increases; from the second week of April it can be seen for more than half the night. It is at opposition on July 4, when it is visible throughout the night. Its eastward elongation then decreases; from the beginning of October until the end of the year, it can only be seen in the evening sky.

Saturn can be seen in the evening sky in Aquarius until mid-February, when it becomes too close to the Sun for observation. It reappears in the morning sky during the first week in April in Pisces. Its westward elongation gradually increases, passing into Cetus in early June and Pisces again from early September, in which constellation it remains for the rest of the year. It is at opposition on September 26, when it is visible throughout the night. Its eastward elongation then gradually decreases; in the second half of December, it can only be seen in the evening sky. Saturn is in conjunction with Venus on February 3.

Uranus is too close to the Sun for observation until mid-February, when it appears in the morning sky in Capricornus, in which constellation it remains throughout the year. Its westward elongation gradually increases until July 25, when it is at opposition and is visible throughout the night. Its eastward elongation then gradually decreases; from the second half of October it can only be seen in the evening sky.

VISIBILITY OF PLANETS IN MORNING AND EVENING TWILIGHT, 1996

Planet	Morning	Evening
Venus	June 17–Dec. 31	Jan. 1–June 4
Mars	May 14–Dec. 31	
Jupiter	Jan. 1–June 4	July 4–Dec. 31
Saturn	Apr. 4–Sept. 26	Jan. 1–Feb. 29; Sept. 26–Dec. 31

Source: U.S. Naval Observatory, *Astronomical Phenomena for the Year 1996* (1993).

Neptune is too close to the Sun for observation until the second week of February, when it appears in the morning sky in Sagittarius, in which constellation it remains throughout the year. It is at opposition on July 18 when it can be seen throughout the night. Its eastward elongation gradually decreases; from mid-October to late December, it can only be seen in the evening sky, after which it again becomes too close to the Sun for observation.

Do not confuse:

1) Venus with Saturn from the end of January to the end of the first week in February; Venus with Mars from late June to early July and from late August to mid-September; and Venus with Mercury in the fourth week of June. On all occasions, Venus is the brighter object.

2) Mercury with Mars from the last week of May to the end of the third week of June. Mercury is the brighter object except for the last week in May.

3) Jupiter with Mercury around mid-December, when Jupiter is the brighter object.

TOTAL SOLAR ECLIPSES IN THE 1990s

A total eclipse is one of nature's most spectacular sights, and many people will travel halfway around the world to see one. A total eclipse occurs when the Moon is close enough to Earth to cover the entire Sun. As the Earth turns below, the shadow of the Moon races roughly from west to east in a long curving path. People not near the midline of that path see only a partial eclipse. Since the period of totality is only a few minutes, weather along the path is especially important. The viewing notes here are based on historical records of cloud cover at the time of the eclipse for places along the path.

Date	Path	Remarks
July 22, 1990	Near Helsinki, Finland, along USSR's Arctic Coast, to Aleutian Islands	Best seen at dawn in Finland, where weather was best; cloud cover 99 percent of time in Aleutians
July 11, 1991	Island of Hawaii, over the Pacific to Baja California, through Mexico and Central America, into South America to Brazil's rain forest	Best eclipse of decade because of 3 excellent viewing sites: Hawaii, Baja California, and Brazil; longest total-eclipse period until 2137
June 30, 1992	From coast of South America to tip of South Africa, almost entirely in Atlantic Ocean	Over 5 min. long in mid-Atlantic; best seen from ship
Nov. 3, 1994	Started in eastern Pacific but reached land near Arequipa, Peru; crossed Chile, Bolivia, Paraguay, Brazil; and headed into Atlantic.	Best viewing in inland Peru in terms of clouds, but total-eclipse longest in Atlantic
Oct. 24, 1995	From Iran; across Afghanistan, Pakistan, India, Southeast Asia; and into western Pacific	Shortest eclipse of decade, lasting little over 2 minutes over China Sea; best viewing in Great Indian Desert near Calcutta, India
Mar. 9, 1997	From Mongolia, across Siberia, almost to North Pole	If you can stand the cold of March in Siberia, best viewing is between Magadan and Yakutsk on banks of frozen Lena
Feb. 26, 1998	From eastern Pacific; past Galapagos; across Panama, Colombia, and Venezuela; into Caribbean	North of Marcaibo, Venezuela, should provide good viewing, or vicinity of Leeward Islands in Caribbean
Aug. 11, 1999	From western Atlantic off Nova Scotia to Isles of Scilly and the southwest tip of Great Britain; through central Europe, Middle East, India, and Pakistan, to Bay of Bengal	First total eclipse for central Europe since 1961, but best viewing should be in Iran and Iraq; southeastern Europe and Turkey also should be good

Source: Jay Anderson, "Eclipse Prospects for the 1990s," *Astronomy* (February 1989).

ECLIPSES

Eclipses of the Moon

A lunar eclipse occurs when the Sun, Earth, and Moon are in a straight line and the shadow of the Earth falls on the Moon. There are three kinds of lunar eclipses. A *total eclipse* is when the moon passes completely into the Earth's umbra, or shadow, so the Sun cannot be seen from the moon. A *partial eclipse* occurs when only part of the Earth's umbra falls across the Moon and the Sun is partially visible from some places on the Moon. A *penumbral eclipse* occurs when only the Earth's penumbra (partial shadow) shades the moon, and from the Moon one's view of the Sun would be only partially blocked by the Earth. It is usually difficult to detect a penumbral eclipse from the Earth.

During 1996, there are two total eclipses of the Moon; both may be visible in parts of the United States. Whether the eclipse can be viewed depends on one's location and the time of day. Since the Moon must be on the opposite side of the Earth from the Sun for a lunar eclipse to occur, eclipses occurring during daylight hours cannot be seen.

April 3–4, 1996—Total eclipse *Moon enters penumbra* Apr. 3, 21:15.7. *Moon enters umbra* Apr. 3, 22:20.9. *Moon enters totality* Apr. 3, 23:26.5. *Middle of eclipse* Apr. 4, 0:09.7. *Moon leaves totality* Apr. 4, 0:53.0. *Moon leaves umbra* Apr. 4, 1:58.7. *Moon leaves penumbra* Apr. 4, 3:03.7. The beginning of the umbral phase is visible in extreme eastern North America, South America, Greenland, Europe, Africa, western and central Asia, the extreme western coast of Australia, Antarctica, most of the Atlantic Ocean, and the Indian Ocean. The end is visible in eastern and central U.S. and Canada, most of Mexico, Central America, South America, Greenland, Europe, Africa, western Asia, Antarctica, and the Pacific, Atlantic, and Indian Oceans.

September 27, 1996—Total eclipse *Moon enters penumbra* Sept. 27, 0:12.4. *Moon enters umbra* Sept. 27, 1:12.3. *Moon enters totality* Sept. 27, 2:19.3. *Middle of eclipse* Sept. 27, 2:54.4. *Moon leaves totality* Sept. 27, 3:29.4. *Moon leaves umbra* Sept. 27, 4:36.3. *Moon leaves penumbra* Sept. 27, 5:36.4. The beginning of the penumbral phase is visible in eastern and central U.S. and Canada, most of Mexico, Central America, South America, Greenland, Europe, Africa, western Asia, parts of Antarctica, the eastern South Pacific Ocean, the Atlantic Ocean, and the western half of the Indian Ocean. The end is visible in North America, Central America, South America, western Africa, Greenland, Antarctica, and the Pacific and Atlantic Oceans.

Eclipses of the Sun

A solar eclipse occurs when the Moon passes between the Earth and the Sun; there are three types. A *total eclipse* occurs when the Moon completely covers the Sun and the sky turns dark. Total eclipses occur along a narrow path (typically 100–200 miles wide) called the track of totality and last only a few minutes at any point on the track. During the 1990s, no total eclipse will be visible from the continental United States, but on July 11, 1991, an excellent one was visible from Hawaii to Mexico City. A *partial eclipse* occurs when the Moon covers only a portion of the Sun. Whether an eclipse is total or partial depends on where one is standing; the July 11, 1991, eclipse that was total over a narrow strip of Mexico was partial over much of North and Central America. An *annular* (ring-shaped) *eclipse* occurs when the Moon is too far from the Earth to cover the Sun completely, so that at the height of the eclipse a ring of light surrounds the Moon. The most prominent annular eclipse in the United States during the 1990s took place May 10, 1994, and was visible from Texas to Maine.

TIMING PLANETARY PHENOMENA

The times for astronomical data shown here are expressed in universal time (UT) which is the standard time of the Greenwich meridian (0° of longitude), also known as Greenwich mean time (GMT). To convert to local time, determine your longitude and subtract one hour for every 15° of longitude west of 0°; or add one hour for every 15° of longitude east of 0°.

The first new moon of 1996 occurs Jan. 20 at 1250 hours in UT. The equivalent time in New York (74°W) is 5 hours earlier, or Jan. 20 at 750 hours (7:50 A.M.); in Chicago (87°W), 6 hours earlier, or Jan. 20 at 6:50 A.M.; in Denver (105°W), 7 hours earlier, or Jan. 20 at 5:50 A.M.; and in San Francisco (122°W), 8 hours earlier, or Jan. 20 at 4:50 A.M. (To obtain the P.M. equivalent of UT times later than 1200, subtract 12: 1827 = 6:27 P.M.) Note that local clock times may differ from these standard times, especially in summer when clocks are often advanced by one hour.

PART II THE UNITED STATES

U.S. GEOGRAPHY

LOCATION

The United States of America shares the North American continent with Canada, Mexico, and the Central American nations. The 48 conterminous states lie in a broad landmass from approximately latitude 24° N to 49° N (south to north), and longitude 67° W to 124° W (east to west). It is bordered on the north by Canada, on the south by Mexico and the Gulf of Mexico, on the east by the Atlantic Ocean, and on the west by the Pacific Ocean. The state of Alaska is located to the northwest on the North American continent; Hawaii is in the Pacific Ocean Basin approximately 2,100 miles southwest of the state of California.

Political-Geographic Divisions

The Bureau of the Census groups the states in a number of divisions and subdivisions.

Northeast
New England Maine, New Hampshire, Vermont, Massachusetts, Rhode Island, Connecticut.
Middle Atlantic New York, New Jersey, Pennsylvania.

Midwest
East North-Central Ohio, Indiana, Illinois, Michigan, Wisconsin.
West North-Central Minnesota, Iowa, Missouri, North Dakota, South Dakota, Nebraska, Kansas.

South
South Atlantic Delaware, Maryland, District of Columbia, Virginia, West Virginia, North Carolina, South Carolina, Georgia, Florida.
East South-Central Kentucky, Tennessee, Alabama, Mississippi.
West South-Central Arkansas, Louisiana, Oklahoma, Texas.

Pacific
Mountain Montana, Idaho, Wyoming, Colorado, New Mexico, Arizona, Utah, Nevada.
Pacific Washington, Oregon, California, Alaska, Hawaii.

Physiographic Regions

The physiographic regions, that is, the primary geological features and landforms of the United States are:

Atlantic and Gulf Coast Plains Run from the islands of southern New England, Cape Cod, and Long Island through New Jersey, Delaware, Maryland, Virginia, North Carolina, South Carolina, Georgia, Florida, Alabama, Mississippi, Louisiana, Texas; include lower Mississippi Valley in Arkansas, Missouri, Tennessee.

Appalachian System Divided into five parts:
New England White Mountains (New Hampshire), Green Mountains (Vermont), Champlain Lowland and Hudson Valley (Vermont, New York), Catskill Mountains (New York).
The Piedmont Pennsylvania, Virginia, North Carolina, South Carolina, Georgia, Alabama.
Great Smoky and Blue Ridge Mountains Pennsylvania (Poconos), [discontinuous], Virginia, North Carolina, Georgia.
Ridge and Valley Pennsylvania, West Virginia, Virginia, Kentucky, Tennessee, Alabama.
Appalachian Plateau Pennsylvania, Ohio, West Virginia, Kentucky, Tennessee, Alabama.

Canadian (or Laurentian) Shield Covers much of eastern Canada and extends into the United States in two places:
Adirondack Mountains New York.
Superior Upland Upper Michigan, Wisconsin, Minnesota.

Central Lowland Includes most of the U.S. interior and is divided into four parts:
Interior Lowlands Ohio, Kentucky, Tennessee.
Mississippi Great Lakes Basin Ohio, Indiana, Illinois, Michigan, Wisconsin, Iowa, North Dakota, South Dakota.
Interior Highlands Ozark Mountains: Missouri, Arkansas, Oklahoma; Ouachita Mountains: Arkansas, Oklahoma.
Great Plains North Dakota, South Dakota, Nebraska, Kansas, Oklahoma, Texas, Montana, Wyoming, Colorado, New Mexico.

Cordilleran Province
Rocky Mountains New Mexico, Colorado, Wyoming, Montana.

Intermontane Range Divided into four sections:
Colorado Plateau Colorado, Utah, New Mexico, Arizona (including Grand Canyon).
Basin and Range Plateau Nevada, Utah (including Wasatch Range).
Desert Basin and Range California (including Death Valley), Arizona.
Snake and Columbia River Basins Idaho, Washington, Oregon.

Pacific Coastlands Divided into four sections, three oriented north-south, the other east-west.
Cascade Mountains and Sierra Nevada Washington, Oregon, California.
Puget Sound, Willamette Valley, and Central Valley Washington, Oregon, California.
Coast Ranges Washington, Oregon, California.
Los Angeles Extension Tehachapi Mountains (east-west), San Gabriel Mountains, San Bernardino Mountains.

Source: J.H. Paterson, *North America*, 8th ed. (New York: Oxford University Press, 1989).

NATIONAL PARK SYSTEM

The National Park System of the United States began in March 1872 with the establishment of Yellowstone National Park in the Territories of Montana and Wyoming "as a public park or pleasuring ground for the benefit and enjoyment of the people" and placed it "under exclusive control of the Secretary of the Interior." The founding of Yellowstone began a worldwide national park movement, and today more than 100 countries contain some 1,200 national parks or equivalent preserves.

The U.S. National Park System comprises 368 areas covering some 75 million acres (3% of total U.S. area) in 49 states (there are no areas in Delaware), the District of Columbia, Guam, Puerto Rico, Saipan, and the Virgin Islands. Additions to the National Park System are generally made through acts of Congress, and national parks can be created only through such acts. But under the Antiquities Act of 1906, the president has authority to proclaim national monuments on lands already under federal jurisdiction.

The diversity of the parks managed by the National Park Service (NPS) is reflected in the variety of titles given to them. Although the system is best known for its scenic parks, more than half the areas of the National Park System preserve places and commemorate persons, events, and activities important in the nation's history. Brief definitions of each type of park follow, together with the number of areas and total federal acreage. An additional 11 areas such as the White House, the National Mall, etc., totaling 37,497 acres of federal land are without designation.

National battlefields/battlefield parks/battlefield site/military parks cover a variety of areas associated with U.S. military history (Antietam National Battlefield, Md.). (1 battle site, 1 acre; 9 military parks, 34,471 acres; 11 battlefields, 10,110 acres; 3 battlefield parks, 8,007 acres)

National capital parks include more than 346 sites (The Ellipse; Lafayette Park) throughout the Washington, D.C., area. (6,482 acres)

National historical parks are commonly areas of greater physical extent and complexity than historic sites (Nez Perce, Idaho). (37; 112,268 acres)

National historic sites include areas of prehistoric and modern historical interest (Tuskegee Institute, Miss.), archaeological sites, historic structures, and the like. Because it is of importance to both the United States and Canada, St. Croix Island (35 acres) is designated an International Historic Site. (72; 17,404 acres)

National lakeshores/seashores (Cape Cod National Seashore, Mass.; Pictured Rocks National Lakeshore, Mich.) preserve shoreline areas and offshore islands while providing water-oriented recreation. (10 seashores, 477,372 acres; 4 lakeshores, 145,170 acres)

National memorial commonly designates an area or structure that is commemorative in nature (Mount Rushmore,S. Dak.). (25; 7,963 acres)

National monuments are intended to preserve at least one nationally significant resource (Rainbow Bridge, Utah). They are usually smaller than national parks and lack the diversity of attractions. (73; 1,742,065 acres)

National parks contain a variety of resources and encompass large land and water areas (Grand Canyon, Ariz.) to help provide adequate protection of resources. (54; 48,111,144 acres)

National parkways are ribbons of land flanking roadways (Natchez Trace, Miss.–Ala.–Tenn.) that offer an opportunity for leisurely driving through areas of scenic interest. (4; 163,038 acres)

National preserves serve primarily to protect certain resources (Big Thicket, Tex.). Activities such as hunting and fishing or mineral extraction may be permitted. (15; 20,198,156 acres)

National recreation areas were originally areas surrounding reservoirs (Lake Mead, Nev.–Ariz.), but now include other lands and waters set aside for recreational use. (18; 3,350,510 acres)

National reserves are similar to the preserves, but are administered by state or local authorities (City of Rocks, Idaho). (2; 9,952 acres)

National rivers/wild and scenic riverways preserve ribbons of land bordering on free-flowing streams that have not been dammed, channelized, or otherwise altered (Delaware River, Pa.–N.J.). Activities such as hiking, boating, and hunting may be permitted. (15; 368,089 acres)

National scenic trails are usually long-distance footpaths winding through areas of natural beauty (Appalachian Trail, Maine–Ga.). (3; 111,532 acres)

National wilderness areas are designated under the Wilderness Act of 1964, which provides that "there shall be no commercial enterprise and no permanent road within any wilderness area . . . and (except for emergency uses) no temporary road, no use of motor vehicles, motorized equipment or motorboats, no landing of aircraft, no other form of mechanical transport, and no structure or installation." Wilderness areas are usually part of other larger entities.

In addition to the National Park System, there are three groups of areas that are closely linked in importance and purpose to areas managed by the Park Service.

Affiliated areas (designated by act of Congress, 1970) are areas in the United States and Canada that preserve significant areas outside the National Park System but that rely on Park Service assistance.

Wild and scenic rivers system (designated by act of Congress, 1968) preserves undeveloped rivers as free-flowing streams accessible for public use. Wild rivers are free of dams and generally accessible only by trails; scenic rivers have relatively primitive shorelines and are largely undeveloped but may be accessible by road.

National trails system (designated by National Trails System Act of 1968) includes trails in both urban and rural settings for persons of all ages, interests, skills, and physical abilities. The Appalachian Trail and the Pacific Crest were the first two trails designated under the National Trails System. Today, there are more than 800 trails in every state, Puerto Rico, and the District of Columbia, totaling more than 9,000 miles in length.

Source: National Park Service, *The National Parks: Index 1993* (1993), *National Park Service Statistical Abstract*, 1994.

RIVERS AND LAKES

Major Navigable Waterways of the United States

The U.S. inland and intracoastal waterway system handles over 500 million tons of traffic each year, carried by a fleet of more than 5,000 towboats and 31,000 barges on over 11,000 miles of primary channels. Ninety percent of these channels have depths of between 9 and 14 feet. Maintenance and improvement of the waterways—including channel dredging, bridge and levee maintenance, and the construction of canals and locks—are in large measure the responsibility of the U.S. Army Corps of Engineers. The 522-mile New York State Barge Canal System is the only major nonfederal waterway in the country.

Mississippi River system The major inland river transportation network is the Mississippi River and its tributaries. This north-south–oriented system includes the Mississippi River, the Ohio River system, the Illinois Waterway, and the Arkansas and Missouri Rivers, among others. In this system there are about 7,000 miles of heavily used, improved navigable channels, 85 percent of which have at least nine-foot navigable channel depths.

Intracoastal waterways At its mouth the Mississippi River is intersected by the Gulf Intracoastal Waterway (GIWW), which parallels the Gulf Coast for 1,180 miles from St. Marks River, Fla., to Brownsville, Tex., at the Mexican border. The GIWW is intersected by a number of river systems in addition to the Mississippi, including the Mobile River, the Apalachicola, and the Houston Ship Channel.

This network of major inland and coastal waterways connects some of the largest Gulf Coast ports—New Orleans, La.; Houston, Beaumont, and Corpus Christi, Tex.; and Mobile, Ala.—with some of the largest inland ports—St. Louis, Mo.; Pittsburgh, Pa.; Huntington, W.Va.; Cincinnati, Ohio; Memphis, Tenn.; and Chicago, Ill. The 40-foot controlling depth of the Mississippi River between the Gulf of Mexico and Baton Rouge allows ocean shipping to join the barge traffic, making this segment especially vital to both the domestic and foreign commerce of the United States.

The Atlantic Intracoastal Waterway provides 1,329 miles of protected channels for commercial and recreational navigation along the Atlantic Coast from Key West, Fla., to Norfolk, Va. Partially protected segments of the waterway continue north from Norfolk along the Delmarva Peninsula, the New Jersey coast, and Long Island. Among the major Atlantic Coast ports located along this waterway are Miami, Fla.; Savannah, Ga.; Baltimore, Md.; Philadelphia, Pa.; and the Port of New York and New Jersey.

Pacific Coast In comparison with the Mississippi River system and the intracoastal waterways of the Atlantic and Gulf Coasts, the inland and coastal waterways of the Pacific are few. Shallow draft waterways include the Columbia-Snake Waterway and the Willamette River above Portland, Oreg.; the Sacramento River above Sacramento, Calif.; the San Joaquin River above Stockton, Calif.; and a few short navigable rivers stretching along the Washington and Oregon coasts.

The table on page 48 shows the major navigable rivers in the United States, their total length, the distance commercially navigable, the body of water they flow into and the head of navigation—the upriver point beyond which commercial ships cannot pass—and the states through or by which the rivers pass, from source to mouth.

The Great Lakes and St. Lawrence Seaway

The Great Lakes have been crucial to the development of the United States and Canada. They were the highways along which people and finished goods moved west, and along which raw materials such as lumber, minerals, and grains were transported to eastern markets. Later the cities of the Great Lakes, such as Chicago, Duluth, Detroit, and Buffalo, became important centers of finance, industry, and trade in their own right. So important was the maritime trade of the Great Lakes that in the 1890s, Chicago was the fourth-largest port in the world, despite being closed by ice for as many as five months a year.

An early obstacle to Great Lakes navigation was the fact that the lakes are not all at the same elevation: there is a difference of 354 feet between the level of westernmost Lake Superior and easternmost Lake Ontario, and there is another 246-foot descent from Lake Ontario down the St. Lawrence River to where it empties into the Atlantic Ocean.

AREA CODES OF THE UNITED STATES AND CANADA, BY STATE AND PROVINCE

State/Province	Area code
Alabama (Birmingham, Tuscaloosa)	205
Alabama (Mobile, Montgomery)	334
Alaska	907
Alberta, Canada	403
Arizona (Flagstaff, Tucson)	520
Arizona (Phoenix, Scottsdale)	602
Arkansas	501
Bermuda	441
British Columbia, Canada (Alaskan Highway)	403
British Columbia, Canada (all other points)	604
California (Fresno)	209
California (Los Angeles)	213
California (Long Beach, Santa Monica)	310
California (San Jose)	408
California (San Francisco)	415
California (Berkeley, Oakland)	510
California (San Diego)	619
California (Santa Rosa, Eureka)	707
California (Orange County)	714
California (Bakersfield)	805
California (Burbank, Pasadena)	818
California (Riverside, San Bernardino)	909
California (Sacramento)	916
Caribbean islands[1]	809
Colorado (Denver, Englewood)	303
Colorado (Colorado Springs, Pueblo)	719
Colorado (Aspen, Grand Junction)	970
Connecticut	203
Delaware	302
Florida (Fort Lauderdale, Miami)	305
Florida (Melbourne, Orlando)	407
Florida (St. Petersburg, Tampa)	813
Florida (Jacksonville, Tallahassee)	904
Florida (Fort Myers, Okeechobee)	941
Georgia (Atlanta)	404
Georgia (Augusta)	706
Georgia (Marietta, Smyrna)	770
Georgia (Macon, Savannah)	912
Hawaii	808
Idaho	208
Illinois (Decatur, Springfield)	217
Illinois (Moline, Peoria)	309
Illinois (Chicago)	312
Illinois (Centralia, East St. Louis)	618
Illinois (Elmhurst, Lombard)	630
Illinois (Lansing, Evergreen Park)	708
Illinois (Joliet, Rockford)	815
Illinois (Des Plaines, Evanston)	847
Indiana (Fort Wayne, Gary)	219
Indiana (Indianapolis, Muncie)	317
Indiana (Evansville, Terre Haute)	812
Iowa (Cedar Rapids, Dubuque)	319
Iowa (Ames, Des Moines)	515
Iowa (Council Bluffs, Sioux City)	712
Kansas (Emporia, Wichita)	316
Kansas (Kansas City, Salina, Topeka)	913
Kentucky (Bowling Green, Louisville)	502
Kentucky (Covington, Lexington)	606
Louisiana (Lafayette, Shreveport)	318
Louisiana (Baton Rouge, New Orleans)	504
Maine	207
Manitoba, Canada	204
Maryland (Rockville, Frederick, Bethesda)	301
Maryland (Baltimore, Annapolis)	410
Massachusetts (Amherst, Springfield)	413
Massachusetts (Cape Cod, Lowell, New Bedford)	508
Massachusetts (Boston)	617
Michigan (Ann Arbor, Detroit)	313
Michigan (Lansing, Saginaw)	517
Michigan (Grand Rapids, Kalamazoo)	616
Michigan (Flint, Pontiac)	810
Michigan (Escanaba, Upper Peninsula)	906
Minnesota (Duluth)	218
Minnesota (Rochester, Winona)	507
Minnesota (Minneapolis–St. Paul–Minnetonka)	612
Mississippi	601
Missouri (Jefferson City, St. Louis)	314
Missouri (Joplin, Springfield)	417
Missouri (Kansas City, St. Joseph)	816
Montana	406
Nebraska (Grand Island, North Platte)	308
Nebraska (Lincoln, Omaha)	402
Nevada	702
New Brunswick, Canada	506
Newfoundland, Canada	709
New Hampshire	603
New Jersey (Jersey City, Newark)	201
New Jersey (Atlantic City, Trenton)	609
New Jersey (Elizabeth, Middlesex)	908
New Mexico	505
New York City (Manhattan)	212
New York (Syracuse, Utica)	315
New York (Hempstead, Long Island)	516
New York (Schenectady, Albany)	518
New York (Binghampton, Elmira)	607
New York (Buffalo, Rochester)	716
New York City (Bronx, Brooklyn, Queens, Staten Island)	718
New York (White Plains, Yonkers)	914
New York (cellular phones, pagers)	917
North Carolina (Asheville, Charlotte)	704
North Carolina (Greensboro, Winston-Salem)	910
North Carolina (Raleigh, Durham)	919
North Dakota	701
Northwest Territories, Canada	403
Nova Scotia, Canada	902
Ohio (Akron, Cleveland)	216
Ohio (Sandusky, Toledo)	419
Ohio (Cincinnati, Dayton)	513
Ohio (Columbus, Steubenville)	614
Oklahoma (Lawton, Oklahoma City)	405
Oklahoma (Muskogee, Tulsa)	918
Ontario, Canada (Toronto)	416
Ontario, Canada (London)	519
Ontario, Canada (Ottawa)	613
Ontario, Canada (North Bay)	705
Ontario, Canada (Ft. William, Thunder Bay)	807
Ontario, Canada (Hamilton)	905
Oregon (Portland, Salem)	503
Oregon (Eugene, Medford)	541
Pennsylvania (Philadelphia)	215
Pennsylvania (Pittsburgh)	412
Pennsylvania (Allentown, Reading)	610
Pennsylvania (Harrisburg, Scranton)	717
Pennsylvania (Altoona, Erie)	814
Prince Edward Island, Canada	902
Puerto Rico	809
Quebec, Canada (Quebec City)	418
Quebec, Canada (Montreal)	514
Quebec, Canada (Sherbrooke)	819
Rhode Island	401
Saskatchewan, Canada (Creighton)	204
Saskatchewan, Canada (Regina, Saskatoon)	306
Saskatchewan, Canada (Aberfeldy, Greenstreet, Tangleflag)	403
South Carolina (Charleston, Columbia)	803
South Carolina (Greenville-Spartanburg)	864
South Dakota	605
Tennessee (Chattanooga, Knoxville)	423
Tennessee (Nashville)	615
Tennessee (Jackson, Memphis)	901
Texas (San Antonio)	210
Texas (Dallas)	214
Texas (Galveston)	409
Texas (Austin)	512
Texas (Houston)	713
Texas (Amarillo)	806
Texas (Arlington, Fort Worth)	817
Texas (Paris, Texarkana)	903
Texas (Abilene, El Paso)	915
Utah	801
Vermont	802
Virginia (Lynchburg, Roanoke)	540
Virginia (Alexandria, Fredericksburg)	703
Virginia (Richmond, Virginia Beach)	804
Virgin Islands	809
Washington (Seattle, Tacoma)	206
Washington (Bellingham, Vancouver)	360
Washington (Spokane, Yakima)	509
Washington, D.C.	202
West Virginia	304
Wisconsin (Green Bay, Milwaukee)	414
Wisconsin (La Crosse, Madison)	608
Wisconsin (Eau Claire, Wausau)	715
Wyoming	307
Yukon, Canada	403

Note: When no cities are listed, the area code is for the entire state or province. For area codes and dialing instructions for other countries, see Part III: "The World, World Geography." 1. Includes Anguilla, Antigua, Bahamas, Barbados, Bequia, Cayman Islands, Dominica, Dominican Republic, Jamaica, Montserrat, Mustique, Nevis, Puerto Rico, St. Kitts, St. Lucia, St. Vincent, Trinidad and Tobago, Virgin Islands.

THE GREAT LAKES

	Area		Depth		Height above sea level	
Lake	**Sq. mi.**	**Sq km**	**Feet**	**Meters**	**Feet**	**Meters**
Ontario	7,540	19,529	802	244	246	75
Erie	9,940	25,745	210	64	571	174
Michigan	22,400	58,016	923	281	577	176
Huron	23,010	59,596	750	229	577	176
Superior	31,820	82,414	1,333	406	600	183

Source: U.S. Environmental Protection Agency and Environment Canada, *The Great Lakes: An Environmental Atlas and Resource Book* (1987).

The first canal (1799) was built on the St. Marys River between Lake Superior and Lake Huron. (Today there are two Sault Sainte Marie [or Soo] Canals—one U.S. and one Canadian—along the 70-mile river.) In 1825 the United States opened the way between the upper lakes (all but Lake Ontario) and the Atlantic via the 353-mile Erie Canal between Buffalo, on Lake Erie, and Albany, on the Hudson River north of New York City. Canada followed with the 27-mile Welland Canal (1833) connecting Welland on Lake Erie and St. Catharines on Lake Ontario.

AREA CODES OF THE UNITED STATES AND CANADA, BY NUMBER CODE

201	New Jersey (Jersey City, Newark)
202	Washington, D.C.
203	Connecticut
204	Manitoba, Canada (plus Creighton, Saskatchewan)
205	Alabama (Birmingham, Tuscaloosa)
206	Washington (Seattle, Tacoma)
207	Maine
208	Idaho
209	California (Fresno)
210	Texas (San Antonio)
212	New York City (Manhattan)
213	California (Los Angeles)
214	Texas (Dallas)
215	Pennsylvania (Philadelphia)
216	Ohio (Akron, Cleveland)
217	Illinois (Decatur, Springfield)
218	Minnesota (Duluth)
219	Indiana (Fort Wayne, Gary)
301	Maryland (Rockville, Frederick, Bethesda)
302	Delaware
303	Colorado (Denver, Englewood)
304	West Virginia
305	Florida (Fort Lauderdale, Miami)
306	Saskatchewan, Canada (Regina, Saskatoon)
307	Wyoming
308	Nebraska (Grand Island, North Platte)
309	Illinois (Moline, Peoria)
310	California (Long Beach, Santa Monica)
312	Illinois (Chicago)
313	Michigan (Ann Arbor, Detroit)
314	Missouri (Jefferson City, St. Louis)
315	New York (Syracuse, Utica)
316	Kansas (Emporia, Wichita)
317	Indiana (Indianapolis, Muncie)
318	Louisiana (Lafayette, Shreveport)
319	Iowa (Cedar Rapids, Dubuque)
334	Alabama (Mobile, Montgomery)
360	Washington (Bellingham, Vancouver)
401	Rhode Island
402	Nebraska (Lincoln, Omaha)
403	Alberta, Northwest Territories, Canada (plus Aberfeldy, Greenstreet, and Tangleflag, Saskatchewan, Canada)
404	Georgia (Atlanta)
405	Oklahoma (Lawton, Oklahoma City)
406	Montana
407	Florida (Melbourne, Orlando)
408	California (San Jose)
409	Texas (Galveston)
410	Maryland (Baltimore, Annapolis)
412	Pennsylvania (Pittsburgh)
413	Massachusetts (Amherst, Springfield)
414	Wisconsin (Green Bay, Milwaukee)
415	California (San Francisco)
416	Ontario, Canada (Toronto)
417	Missouri (Joplin, Springfield)
418	Quebec, Canada (Quebec City)
419	Ohio (Sandusky, Toledo)
423	Tennessee (Chattanooga, Knoxville)
441	Bermuda
501	Arkansas
502	Kentucky (Bowling Green, Louisville)
503	Oregon (Portland, Salem)
504	Louisiana (Baton Rouge, New Orleans)
505	New Mexico
506	New Brunswick, Canada
507	Minnesota (Rochester, Winona)
508	Massachusetts (Cape Cod, Lowell, New Bedford)
509	Washington (Spokane, Yakima)
510	California (Berkeley, Oakland)
512	Texas (Austin)
513	Ohio (Cincinnati, Dayton)
514	Quebec, Canada (Montreal)
515	Iowa (Ames, Des Moines)
516	New York (Hempstead, Long Island)
517	Michigan (Lansing, Midland, Saginaw)
518	New York (Albany, Schenectady)
519	Ontario, Canada (London)
520	Arizona (Flagstaff, Tucson)
541	Oregon (Eugene, Medford)
601	Mississippi
602	Arizona (Phoenix, Scottsdale)
603	New Hampshire
604	British Columbia, Canada
605	South Dakota
606	Kentucky (Covington, Lexington)
607	New York (Binghampton, Elmira)
608	Wisconsin (La Crosse, Madison)
609	New Jersey (Atlantic City; Trenton)
610	Pennsylvania (Allentown, Reading)
612	Minnesota (Minneapolis–St. Paul, Minnetonka)
613	Ontario, Canada (Ottawa)
614	Ohio (Columbus, Steubenville)
615	Tennessee (Nashville)
616	Michigan (Grand Rapids, Kalamazoo)
617	Massachusetts (Boston)
618	Illinois (Centralia, East St. Louis)
619	California (San Diego)
630	Illinois, (Elmhurst, Lombard)
701	North Dakota
702	Nevada
703	Virginia (Alexandria, Roanoke)
704	North Carolina (Asheville, Charlotte)
705	Ontario, Canada (North Bay)
706	Georgia (Augusta)
707	California (Santa Rosa, Eureka)
708	Illinois (Lansing, Evergreen Park)
709	Newfoundland, Canada
712	Iowa (Council Bluffs, Sioux City)
713	Texas (Houston)
714	California (Orange County)
715	Wisconsin (Eau Claire, Wausau)
716	New York (Buffalo, Rochester)
717	Pennsylvania (Harrisburg, Scranton)
718	New York City (Bronx, Brooklyn, Queens, Staten Island)
719	Colorado (Colorado Springs, Pueblo)
770	Georgia (Marietta, Smyrna)
801	Utah
802	Vermont
803	South Carolina (Charleston, Columbia
804	Virginia (Richmond, Virginia Beach)
805	California (Bakersfield)
806	Texas (Amarillo)
807	Ontario, Canada (Fort William, Thunder Bay)
808	Hawaii
809	Caribbean islands[1]
810	Michigan (Flint, Pontiac)
812	Indiana (Evansville, Terre Haute)
813	Florida (St. Petersburg, Tampa)
814	Pennsylvania (Altoona, Erie)
815	Illinois (Joliet, Rockford)
816	Missouri (Kansas City, St. Joseph)
817	Texas (Arlington, Fort Worth)
818	California (Burbank, Pasadena)
819	Quebec, Canada (Sherbrooke)
847	Illinois (Des Plaines, Evanston)
864	South Carolina (Greenville–Spartanburg)
901	Tennessee (Jackson, Memphis)
902	Nova Scotia, Prince Edward Island, Canada
903	Texas (Paris, Texarkana)
904	Florida (Jacksonville, Tallahassee)
905	Ontario, Canada (Hamilton)
906	Michigan (Escanaba, Upper Peninsula)
907	Alaska
908	New Jersey (Elizabeth, Middlesex)
909	California (Riverside, San Bernardino)
910	North Carolina (Greensboro, Winston-Salem)
912	Georgia (Macon, Savannah)
913	Kansas (Kansas City, Salina, Topeka)
914	New York (White Plains, Yonkers)
915	Texas (Abilene, El Paso)
916	California (Sacramento)
917	New York (cellular phones and pagers only)
918	Oklahoma (Muskogee, Tulsa)
919	North Carolina (Raleigh, Durham)
941	Florida (Fort Myers, Okeechobee)
970	Colorado (Aspen, Grand Junction)

Note: When no cities are listed, area code is for entire state or province. 1. Includes Anguilla, Antigua, Bahamas, Barbados, Bequia, Cayman Islands, Dominica, Dominican Republic, Jamaica, Montserrat, Mustique, Nevis, Puerto Rico, St. Kitts, St. Lucia, St. Vincent, Trinidad and Tobago, Virgin Islands.

The most ambitious undertaking was the construction of the St. Lawrence Seaway, a joint Canadian-American effort to open the entire length of the St. Lawrence and the Great Lakes to oceangoing navigation. Started in 1955 and opened to navigation in 1959, the seaway's system of canals and locks allows ships of up to 730 feet in length and 27 feet draft to sail the entire 2,342 miles from the mouth of the St. Lawrence to Duluth, Minn., at the western end of Lake Superior. The seaway also provides hydroelectric power for Canada and the United States.

The Panama Canal

One of the great engineering feats of the world, the 44-mile Panama Canal bisects the continents of North and South America, making it possible for ships to sail between the Atlantic and Pacific Oceans without rounding the treacherous Cape Horn at the tip of South America. The U.S. government began construction of the canal in 1904, and it was opened to commercial navigation Aug. 15, 1914. For interocean shippers the savings in distance and time afforded by the canal are enormous. A ship sailing from New York to San Francisco via the Panama Canal travels a distance of 5,263 miles, a savings of more than 7,800 miles—or about 20 days—over the 13,100-mile route around Cape Horn. The minimum depth of the canal is 41 feet, the minimum width 300 feet, and the highest elevation above sea level 85 feet.

The Canal Zone, a 10-mile-wide strip of land around the canal in the Republic of Panama, was acquired in 1903 by the United States, who governed it until 1979. The Panama Canal Treaty of 1977 abolished the Canal Zone as an independent political entity, but the canal's maintenance and operation remain the responsibility of the U.S. Panama Canal Commission until 1999, when the Republic of Panama assumes full responsibility.

U.S. NATIONAL PARKS—ACREAGE, VISITS, AND OVERNIGHT STAYS, 1990–94

	Federal acres ('000s)	Visits ('000s)		Overnight stays ('000s)	
National park/state	1994	1990	1994	1990	1994
Acadia, Me.	41	2,413	2,711	223	169
Arches, Utah	66	621	777	58	52
Badlands, S.Dak.	233	1,326	1,130	35	61
Big Bend, Tex.	775	257	330	215	264
Biscayne, Fla.	170	573	25	29	0
Bryce Canyon, Utah	36	863	1,028	144	157
Canyonlands, Utah	338	277	430	78	103
Capitol Reef, Utah	223	562	605	48	43
Carlsbad Caverns, N.Mex.	46	747	617	0	3
Channel Islands, Calif.	64	144	175	32	60
Crater Lake, Oreg.	183	385	454	45	48
Death Valley, Calif.–Nev.	2,049	(1)	971	(1)	281
Denali, Alaska	4,725	547	490	118	131
Dry Tortugas, Fla.	61	19	17	25	43
Everglades, Fla.	1,451	958	886	128	75
Gates of the Arctic, Alaska	7,075	1	2	5	6
Glacier, Mont.	1,013	1,987	2,153	330	365
Glacier Bay, Alaska	3,225	204	251	36	53
Grand Canyon, Ariz.	1,181	3,777	4,364	908	1,164
Grand Teton, Wyo.	308	1,588	2,541	597	595
Great Basin, Nev.	77	65	88	44	30
Great Smoky Mountain, Tenn.–N.C.	520	8,152	8,628	463	489
Guadalupe Mountains, Tex.	77	193	204	18	24
Haleakala, Hawaii	27	1,261	1,527	19	26
Hawaii Volcanoes, Hawaii	208	1,097	1,174	112	95
Hot Springs, Ark.	5	1,123	1,619	8	11
Isle Royale, Mich.	539	23	25	56	65
Joshua Tree, Calif.	549	(1)	1,185	(1)	248
Katmai, Alaska	3,611	41	56	12	19
Kenai Fjords, Alaska	529	66	210	1	1
Kings Canyon, Calif.	462	1,063	726	302	266
Kobuk Valley, Alaska	1,670	3	3	0	1
Lake Clark, Alaska	2,574	10	12	1	3
Lassen Volcanic, Calif.	106	461	385	113	96
Mammoth Cave, Ky.	52	1,925	2,010	98	100
Mesa Verde, Colo.	52	611	685	159	152
Mount Rainier, Wash.	236	1,327	1,426	184	189
North Cascades, Wash.	505	456	19	97	17
Olympic, Wash.	913	2,795	3,382	404	542
Petrified Forest, Ariz.	94	845	923	1	1
Redwood, Calif.	75	348	475	16	73
Rocky Mountain, Colo.	265	2,647	2,968	209	248
Saguaro, Ariz.	83	(1)	769	(1)	2
Sequoia, Calif.	402	1,064	1,034	345	368
Shenandoah, Va.	196	1,772	1,927	323	313
Theodore Roosevelt, N.Dak.	70	461	505	26	33
Virgin Island, U.S. Virgin Islands	13	665	635	173	190
Voyageurs, Minn.	132	224	224	47	18
Wind Cave, S.Dak.	28	586	871	11	10
Wrangell–St. Elias, Alaska	7,656	36	50	3	11
Yellowstone, Mont.–Wyo.–Idaho	2,220	2,824	3,046	1,345	1,283
Yosemite, Calif.	760	3,125	3,962	2,220	2,248
Zion, Utah	143	2,102	2,271	292	286
Total national parks	**48,111**	**54,619**	**62,984**	**10,156**	**11,129**
Total national parks system[1]	**74,905**	**255,655**	**268,636**	**17,625**	**18,300**

1. Area was not a National Park in 1990. 2. Includes national historic sites, national memorials, national seashores, national parkways, and other areas under the jurisdiction of the National Park Service. **Source:** U.S. National Park Service, Land Resource Division, December 1994.

STATE PARKS AND RECREATION AREAS BY STATE, 1992

		Visitors ('000s)		Revenue	
State	Acreage ('000s)	Total[1]	Day[2]	Total ('000s)	Percent of operating budget
Alabama	50	6,268	4,985	$23,427	81.4%
Alaska	3,169	6,321	6,110	1,063	19.9
Arizona	33	1,750	1,891	3,734	35.9
Arkansas	47	6,725	6,312	12,046	56.0
California	1,323	67,301	64,487	73,563	49.3
Colorado	340	9,522	8,148	13,373	109.0
Connecticut	173	7,053	6,392	3,498	47.9
Delaware	13	3,619	2,961	4,176	43.0
Florida	444	12,232	12,063	18,061	38.9
Georgia	57	16,284	15,595	15,029	42.5
Hawaii	25	19,255	19,023	1,161	14.7
Idaho	42	2,697	2,193	1,958	79.8
Illinois	403	38,555	33,819	3,528	11.6
Indiana	57	10,570	8,600	9,111	73.7
Iowa	391	12,230	11,736	1,804	24.0
Kansas	324	4,425	2,470	2,523	45.5
Kentucky	43	27,831	26,207	36,529	63.3
Louisiana	39	1,226	788	2,142	25.0
Maine	75	2,005	2,211	1,478	34.9
Maryland	241	8,891	7,293	6,176	26.0
Massachusetts	274	11,549	11,206	9,256	64.9
Michigan	264	21,172	19,868	21,108	77.4
Minnesota	231	7,932	7,124	7,472	41.6
Mississippi	23	4,033	3,168	5,607	48.0
Missouri	122	16,103	13,919	4,300	22.4
Montana	41	4,491	1,099	1,330	48.6
Nebraska	142	9,227	7,754	8,600	71.1
Nevada	142	2,679	2,402	751	14.5
New Hampshire	75	1,737	2,655	4,341	51.5
New Jersey	305	10,607	10,492	6,123	22.8
New Mexico	122	4,089	1,700	2,932	29.0
New York	260	63,250	58,208	36,657	33.5
North Carolina	135	9,713	9,221	2,108	18.3
North Dakota	19	990	809	809	49.1
Ohio	208	49,861	64,730	13,178	30.8
Oklahoma	77	16,183	14,221	17,127	76.7
Oregon	91	42,334	37,288	9,171	38.5
Pennsylvania	277	35,542	34,585	8,053	15.4
Rhode Island	9	3,423	4,759	2,584	44.8
South Carolina	80	7,876	7,001	10,955	60.7
South Dakota	92	5,166	5,545	3,946	64.5
Tennessee	133	27,360	25,814	20,270	59.0
Texas	501	24,423	21,515	16,366	49.8
Utah	97	5,577	4,495	3,923	31.9
Vermont	64	839	586	4,222	96.2
Virginia	66	3,975	3,456	2,635	27.6
Washington	241	47,289	44,487	7,360	36.1
West Virginia	202	8,753	7,577	14,806	64.6
Wisconsin	125	11,646	10,787	8,338	70.0
Wyoming	120	1,949	652	275	10.2

1. Includes overnight visitors. 2. Figures for 1991. **Source:** National Association of State Park Directors (Austin, Tex.), *1993 Annual Information Exchange* (1993).

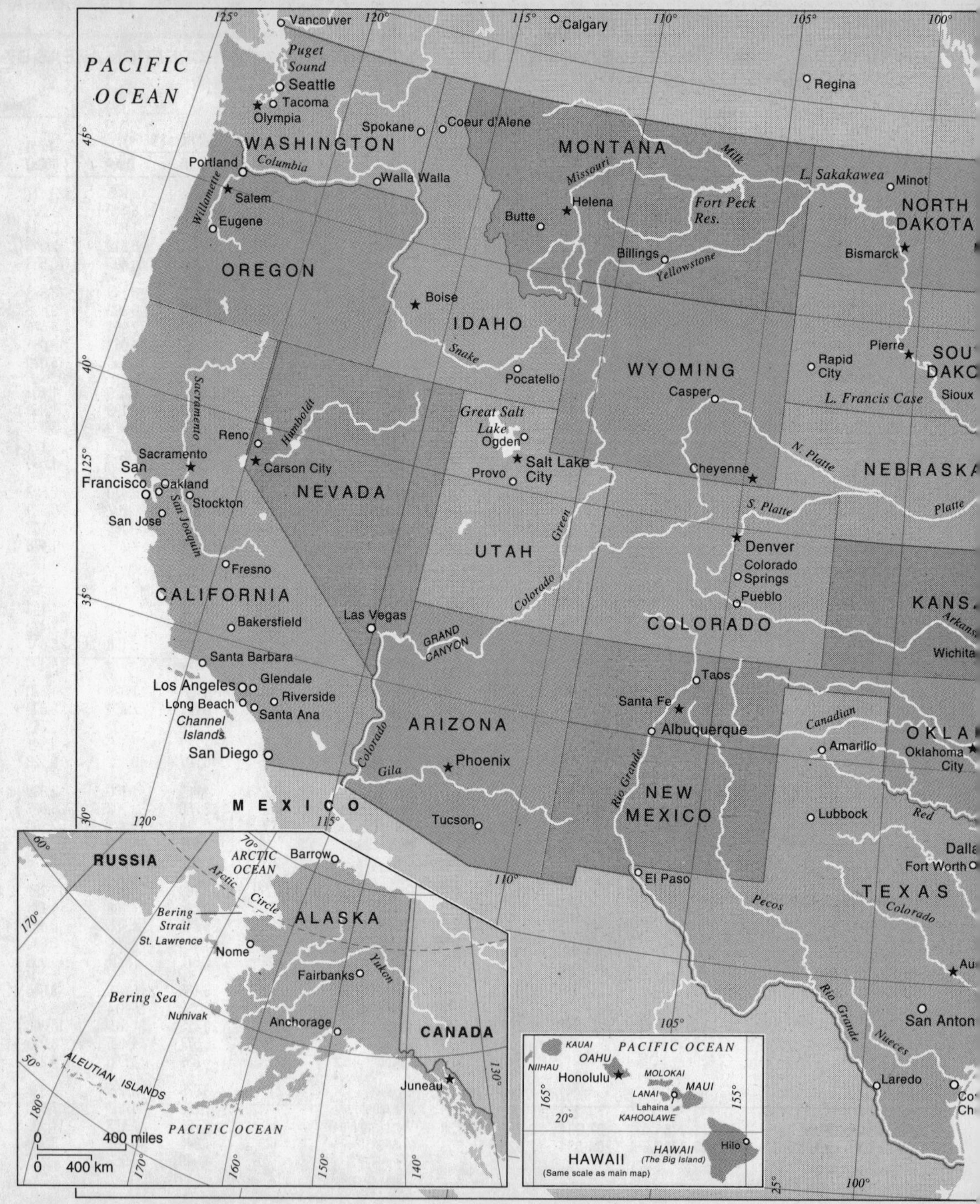
PACIFIC OCEAN
Vancouver
Calgary
Regina
Puget Sound
Seattle
Tacoma
Olympia
Spokane
Coeur d'Alene
WASHINGTON
MONTANA
Milk
Missouri
L. Sakakawea
Minot
Portland
Columbia
Walla Walla
Helena
Fort Peck Res.
NORTH DAKOTA
Salem
Willamette
Butte
Eugene
Billings
Yellowstone
Bismarck
OREGON
Boise
IDAHO
Snake
Pocatello
WYOMING
Pierre
Rapid City
SOUTH DAKOTA
Casper
L. Francis Case
Sioux
Sacramento
Humboldt
Great Salt Lake
Reno
Ogden
Sacramento
Carson City
Salt Lake City
Provo
N. Platte
Cheyenne
NEBRASKA
San Francisco
Oakland
Stockton
San Jose
San Joaquin
NEVADA
S. Platte
Platte
Green
UTAH
Denver
Fresno
Colorado
Colorado Springs
Pueblo
CALIFORNIA
KANSAS
Arkansas
Las Vegas
COLORADO
Bakersfield
GRAND CANYON
Wichita
Santa Barbara
Taos
Los Angeles
Glendale
Riverside
Long Beach
Santa Ana
Channel Islands
Santa Fe
Albuquerque
Canadian
ARIZONA
Amarillo
OKLAHOMA
Oklahoma City
San Diego
Colorado
Phoenix
Gila
Rio Grande
NEW MEXICO
MEXICO
Tucson
Lubbock
Red
Dallas
Fort Worth
El Paso
TEXAS
Pecos
Colorado
Austin
Rio Grande
San Antonio
Nueces
Laredo
Corpus Christi
125°
120°
115°
110°
105°
100°
45°
40°
35°
30°
25°
RUSSIA
ARCTIC OCEAN
Arctic Circle
Barrow
Bering Strait
St. Lawrence
ALASKA
Nome
Yukon
Fairbanks
Bering Sea
Nunivak
Anchorage
CANADA
ALEUTIAN ISLANDS
Juneau
PACIFIC OCEAN
0 400 miles
0 400 km
60°
70°
170°
50°
180°
160°
150°
140°
130°
KAUAI
PACIFIC OCEAN
NIIHAU
OAHU
Honolulu
MOLOKAI
MAUI
LANAI
Lahaina
KAHOOLAWE
165°
155°
20°
HAWAII
HAWAII (The Big Island)
Hilo
(Same scale as main map)

CANADA
L. Nipigon
Lake of the Woods
Thunder Bay
L. Superior
Duluth
Sault Ste. Marie
MICHIGAN
L. Huron
St. Lawrence
Québec
MAINE
Montréal
Ottawa
ST. LAWRENCE SEAWAY
Burlington
Montpelier
Augusta
NEW HAMPSHIRE
Portland
Lake Champlain
VERMONT
Concord
Portsmouth
MASSACHUSETTS
St. Paul
Minneapolis
Minnesota
Green Bay
WISCONSIN
L. Michigan
Toronto
L. Ontario
ERIE CANAL
NEW YORK
Albany
Boston
Rochester
Syracuse
Worcester
Cape Cod
Buffalo
Providence
Nantucket
Milwaukee
Madison
Lansing
Warren
Hudson
Delaware
Connecticut
Hartford
RHODE ISLAND
IOWA
Cedar Rapids
Mississippi
Grand Rapids
Detroit
L. Erie
Allegheny
New Haven
CONNECTICUT
Scranton
Long Island
Chicago
Toledo
Cleveland
PENNSYLVANIA
Newark
New York
NEW JERSEY
Trenton
Des Moines
Illinois
Fort Wayne
OHIO
Harrisburg
Pittsburgh
Philadelphia
Wilmington
INDIANA
Columbus
Baltimore
Dover
DELAWARE
ILLINOIS
Monongahela
WASHINGTON, D.C.
Annapolis
MARYLAND
Springfield
Indianapolis
Dayton
Cincinnati
Ohio
WEST VIRGINIA
Kansas City
Potomac
Chesapeake Bay
St. Louis
Wabash
VIRGINIA
Jefferson City
Louisville
Frankfort
Kentucky
Charleston
Kanawha
Richmond
James
Lexington
Roanoke
Norfolk
Virginia Beach
Green
MISSOURI
Ohio
KENTUCKY
Greensboro
Raleigh
Outer Banks
Cumberland
Nashville
Knoxville
NORTH CAROLINA
Tennessee
ARKANSAS
TENNESSEE
Asheville
Charlotte
Arkansas
Memphis
Chattanooga
Cape Fear
Wilmington
Greenville
ATLANTIC OCEAN
Cape Fear
Fort Smith
Little Rock
Huntsville
Columbia
Black Warrior
Atlanta
SOUTH CAROLINA
Yazoo
Tombigbee
Birmingham
Savannah
Macon
Charleston
Shreveport
MISSISSIPPI
ALABAMA
Columbus
Chattahoochee
Savannah
Jackson
Montgomery
GEORGIA
Sabine
Red
Pearl
Alabama
Mobile
Jacksonville
Baton Rouge
Pensacola
Tallahassee
New Orleans
Apalachicola
FLORIDA
Houston
LOUISIANA
Orlando
Cape Canaveral
Tampa
St. Petersburg
L. Okeechobee
West Palm Beach
Gulf of Mexico
Fort Myers
Fort Lauderdale
Naples
Miami
Miami Beach
Hialeah
0 200 miles
0 200 km
Key West
Florida Keys
CONICAL EQUAL-AREA PROJECTION

MAJOR NAVIGABLE RIVERS AND CANALS IN THE UNITED STATES

Ultimate outflow/River	Length (miles)	Navigable length (mi.)	Mouth to head of navigation	States/Provinces (from source to mouth)
Atlantic Ocean				
St. Lawrence	760	760	Gulf of St. Lawrence to Lake Ontario	N.Y.; Ontario, Québec (Can.)
Cape Cod Canal	17	17	Sandwich to Buzzards Bay, Mass.	Mass.
Connecticut	407	52	Long Island Sound to Hartford, Conn.	N.H., Vt., Mass., Conn.
Hudson	306	134	New York Bay to Troy, N.Y.; New York State Barge Canal (522 mi.) links to Lake Erie (353 mi. Troy to Buffalo) and to Lakes Champlain, Ontario, Cayuga, Seneca	N.Y.
Delaware	367	77	Delaware Bay to Trenton, N.J.	N.Y., Pa., N.J., Del.
Chesapeake and Delaware Canal	14	14	Delaware Bay to Chesapeake Bay	Del., Md.
Potomac	287	101	Chesapeake Bay to Washington, D.C.	Va., Md., D.C.
James	340	87	Chesapeake Bay to Richmond, Va.	Va.
Roanoke	410	112	Atlantic Ocean to Altavista, Va.	Va., N.C.
Cape Fear	202	111	Atlantic Ocean to Fayetteville, N.C.	N.C.
Savannah	314	181	Atlantic Ocean to Augusta, Ga.	S.C., Ga.
Saint Johns	285	160	Atlantic Ocean to Lake Harney, Fla.	Fla.
Gulf of Mexico				
Chattahoochee	436	194	Apalachicola River to Columbus, Ga.	Ga., Ala.
Apalachicola	90	90	Gulf of Mexico to Chattahoochee, Fla.	Fla.
Mobile	45	45	Mobile Bay to confluence of Alabama and Tombigbee Rivers	Ala.
Alabama	318	305	Mobile River to Montgomery, Ala.	Ala.
Tombigbee	362	362	Mobile River to Amory, Miss.; linked to Tennessee River by Tennessee-Tombigbee Waterway (253 mi.)	Miss., Ala.
Black Warrior	217	217	Tombigbee River to Birmingham, Ala.	Ala.
Houston Ship Channel	57	57	Galveston Bay to Houston, Tex.	Tex.
Rio Grande[1]	1,885	13	Gulf of Mexico to Brownsville, Tex.	Colo., N. Mex., Tex., Mexico
Mississippi River System				
Mississippi	2,348	1,807	Gulf of Mexico to Minneapolis, Minn.	Minn., Wis., Iowa, Ill., Mo., Ky., Tenn., Ark., Miss., La.
EASTERN TRIBUTARIES				
Illinois	273	271	Mississippi River to Joliet, Ill.; also linked to Mississippi by Illinois and Mississippi Canal, and to Lake Michigan (at Chicago, Calumet, East Chicago, Gary) by Illinois Waterway	Ill.
Ohio	981	981	Mississippi River to Pittsburgh, Pa.	Pa., Ohio, W.Va., Ind., Ky., Ill.
Monongahela	129	129	Ohio River to Fairmont, W.Va.	W.Va., Pa.
Allegheny	325	72	Ohio River to East Brady, Pa.	N.Y., Pa.
Kanawha	97	91	Ohio River to Charleston, W.Va.	W.Va.
Kentucky	259	82	Ohio River to Beattyville, Ky.	Ky.
Green	360	103	Ohio River to Bowling Green, Ky.	Ky.
Cumberland	694	387	Ohio River to Burnside, Ky.	Ky., Tenn.
Tennessee	652	648	Ohio River to Knoxville, Tenn.	Tenn., Ala., Miss., Ky.
Yazoo	169	165	Mississippi River to Greenwood, Miss.	Miss.
WESTERN TRIBUTARIES				
Missouri	2,315	753	Mississippi River to Ponca, Nebr.	Mont., N.Dak., S.Dak., Nebr., Iowa, Kans., Mo.
Arkansas	1,396	448	McClellan-Kerr Arkansas River system from Mississippi River to Catoosa, Okla.; incorporates sections of White, Arkansas, Verdigris Rivers	Colo., Kans., Okla., Ark.
Ouachita[2]	605	351	Mississippi River to Camden, Ark.	Ark., La.
Red	1,018	106	Mississippi River to Alexandria, La.	N.Mex., Tex., Okla., Ark., La.
Atchafalaya[3]	220	220	Atchafalaya Bay to Mississippi River	La.
Pacific Ocean and Arctic Ocean				
San Joaquin	340	103	Sacramento River to Hills Ferry, Calif.	Calif.
Sacramento	374	163	San Francisco Bay to Chico Landing, Calif.	Calif.
Columbia	1,210	285	Pacific Ocean to Pasco, Wash.	British Columbia (Can.), Wash., Oreg.
Snake	1,083	192	Columbia River to Johnson Bar Landing, Idaho	Wyo., Idaho, Oreg., Wash.
Willamette	294	133	Columbia River to Harrisburg, Oreg.	Oreg.
Yukon	1,979	1,699	Bering Sea to Whitehorse, Yukon	Yukon (Can.), Alaska

Note: All distances in nautical miles except for the Mississippi River system. One nautical mile = 1.151 statute miles. 1. In Mexico, known as the Río Bravo del Norte. 2. Lower 57 miles known as the Black River. 3. Flows from the Mississippi River to the Gulf of Mexico. **Source:** National Oceanic and Atmospheric Administration, *Distances between United States Ports, 1987* (1987).

LAND COVER AND USE, BY STATE, 1992 (in thousands of acres)

State	Total surface area[1]	Federal land area	Nonfederal land areas: Developed[2]	Nonfederal land areas: Rural cropland	Nonfederal land areas: Rural pastureland	Nonfederal land areas: Rural rangeland	Nonfederal land areas: Rural forestland
United States	**1,937,678**	**407,899**	**91,946**	**381,950**	**125,215**	**389,803**	**394,437**
Alabama	33,091	921	2,046	3,147	3,760	67	20,968
Arizona	72,960	30,280	1,404	1,198	76	32,227	4,718
Arkansas	34,040	3,207	1,322	7,730	5,727	159	14,267
California	101,572	46,792	5,001	10,052	1,161	17,140	14,794
Colorado	66,618	23,923	1,694	8,940	1,256	23,537	3,755
Connecticut	3,212	15	816	229	110	—	1,760
Delaware	1,309	33	205	499	26	—	353
Florida	37,545	3,791	4,645	2,997	4,373	3,476	12,378
Georgia	37,702	2,087	3,077	5,173	3,075	—	21,714
Hawaii	4,093	432	170	274	88	925	1,483
Idaho	53,481	33,298	587	5,600	1,243	6,668	4,024
Illinois	36,061	521	3,094	24,100	2,764	—	3,419
Indiana	23,159	487	2,095	13,513	1,866	—	3,626
Iowa	36,016	184	1,779	24,988	3,712	—	1,931
Kansas	52,658	606	1,997	26,565	2,306	15,723	1,331
Kentucky	25,862	1,201	1,653	5,092	5,859	—	10,312
Louisiana	30,561	1,264	1,764	5,972	2,269	227	12,961
Maine	21,290	164	697	448	111	—	17,557
Maryland	6,695	167	1,095	1,673	545	—	2,364
Massachusetts	5,302	89	1,309	272	170	—	2,778
Michigan	37,457	3,166	3,686	8,985	2,353	—	15,608
Minnesota	54,017	3,383	2,418	21,356	3,282	—	13,815
Mississippi	30,521	1,726	1,337	5,726	4,047	—	15,765
Missouri	44,606	2,017	2,336	13,347	11,911	126	11,656
Montana	94,109	27,122	1,096	15,035	3,370	36,835	5,156
Nebraska	49,507	739	1,252	19,239	2,066	22,669	777
Nevada	70,759	60,290	394	762	297	7,854	353
New Hampshire	5,938	747	563	142	98	—	3,932
New Jersey	4,984	159	1,588	650	159	—	1,766
New Mexico	77,819	27,394	866	1,892	212	39,792	4,600
New York	31,429	231	3,005	5,616	3,001	—	17,178
North Carolina	33,708	2,448	3,542	5,960	2,019	—	15,979
North Dakota	45,250	1,951	1,344	24,743	1,168	10,325	426
Ohio	26,451	375	3,558	11,929	2,269	—	6,624
Oklahoma	44,772	1,202	1,875	10,081	7,720	14,061	6,988
Oregon	62,127	32,291	1,125	3,776	1,900	9,375	11,839
Pennsylvania	28,997	682	3,432	5,596	2,326	—	15,316
Rhode Island	776	4	190	25	24	—	393
South Carolina	19,912	1,156	1,856	2,983	1,190	—	10,922
South Dakota	49,354	2,907	1,135	16,436	2,158	21,933	540
Tennessee	26,972	1,379	2,161	4,857	5,165	—	11,580
Texas	170,756	3,203	8,231	28,261	16,710	94,155	9,960
Utah	54,336	35,582	561	1,815	665	10,050	1,626
Vermont	6,153	368	324	635	349	—	4,138
Virginia	26,091	2,389	2,183	2,901	3,444	—	13,539
Washington	43,608	12,479	1,851	6,745	1,352	5,476	12,547
West Virginia	15,508	1,201	689	915	1,609	—	10,534
Wisconsin	35,938	1,829	2,357	10,813	2,954	—	13,410
Wyoming	62,598	30,020	541	2,272	901	26,015	975

Note: U.S. totals exclude Alaska and the District of Columbia. 1. Includes 107.9 million acres of water area, minor land cover, and uses not shown separately. 2. Includes urban and built-up areas in units of 10 acres or greater, and rural transportation areas. **Source:** U.S. Department of Agriculture, Soil Conservation Service, and Iowa State University, Statistical Laboratory, *Summary Report, 1992 National Resources Inventory* (December 1989).

U.S. TERRITORIAL EXPANSION

Accession	Acquisition date	Gross area (land and water): Sq. mi.	Gross area (land and water): Sq km
The 50 states	(X)	3,618,770	9,372,614
Territory in 1790[1]	(X)	3,536,288	9,158,960
Louisiana Purchase	1803	895,415	2,319,125
Purchase of Florida[2]	1819	58,666	151,945
Texas	1845	388,687	1,006,699
Oregon Territory	1846	286,541	742,141
Mexican Cession	1848	529,189	1,370,600
Gadsden Purchase	1853	29,670	76,845
Alaska	1867	570,374	1,477,267
Hawaii	1898	6,423	16,636
Other areas			
Puerto Rico	1898	3,427	8,875
Guam	1898	210	543
American Samoa	1899	77	200
Virgin Islands, U.S.	1917	134	346
Trust Territory of the Pacific Islands	1947	179	464
Northern Mariana Is.	1947	177	458
All other	(X)	16	41
Total U.S. territory	**(X)**	**3,540,558**	**9,170,043**

Note: Boundaries of all acquisitions listed here were indefinite, at least in part, at time of acquisition. Because different sources are used for land areas, the sums of the acquisitions will not equal the United States or the total. X = not applicable. 1. Includes that part of drainage basin of Red River of the North, south of 49th parallel, sometimes considered part of Louisiana Purchase. 2. The U.S. also acquired areas west of the Mississippi River amounting to 22,834 squae miles, but relinquished to Spain 97,150 square miles, resulting in a net loss of 15,650 square miles. **Source:** U.S. Bureau of the Census, *Statistical Abstract of the United States, 1994.*

URBAN PARKLAND IN SELECTED U.S. CITIES

City	Parkland as percent of area	City	Parkland as percent of area
Honolulu[1]	40.8%	Wichita, Kans.	6.0%
Washington, D.C.	20.6	Columbus, Ohio	5.8
Minneapolis	17.3	Los Angeles	5.3
Tulsa	14.0	Toledo, Ohio	5.3
St. Paul, Minn.	12.0	Miami	5.1
El Paso, Tex.	11.7	Indianapolis	5.0
Buffalo, N.Y.	11.5	Newark, N.J.	5.0
Portland, Oreg.	11.0	Fort Worth, Tex.	4.7
Chicago	10.5	Denver	4.0
Seattle	10.0	Oklahoma City	4.0
Omaha	9.8	New Orleans	3.6
Dallas	9.0	Arlington, Tex.	3.0
Cincinnati	9.0	Birmingham, Ala.	3.0
Pittsburgh	7.3	Tucson, Ariz.	2.9
Virginia Beach	7.1	Fresno	1.6
Oakland	7.0	Milwaukee	1.0
Austin, Tex.	6.8	Kansas City, Mo.	0.1

1. Includes the entire island of Oahu. **Source:** World Resources Institute.

EXTREME AND MEAN ELEVATIONS, STATES AND OUTLYING AREAS

State/Territory	Highest point			Lowest point			Approximate mean elevation	
		Elevation			Elevation			
	Name	Feet	Meters	Name	Feet	Meters	Feet	Meters
United States	**Mount McKinley (Alaska)**	**20,320**	**6,198**	**Death Valley (Calif.)**	**–282**	**–86**	**2,500**	**763**
Alabama	Cheaha Mountain	2,405	733	Gulf of Mexico	Sea level		500	153
Alaska	Mount McKinley	20,320	6,198	Pacific Ocean	Sea level		1,900	580
American Samoa	Lata Mountain	3,160	964	Pacific Ocean	Sea level		1,300	397
Arizona	Humphreys Peak	12,633	3,853	Colorado River	70	21	4,100	1,251
Arkansas	Magazine Mountain	2,753	840	Ouachita River	55	17	650	198
California	Mount Whitney[1]	14,494	4,421	Death Valley	–282	–86	2,900	885
Colorado	Mount Elbert	14,433	4,402	Arkansas River	3,350	1,022	6,800	2,074
Connecticut	Mount Frissell, on south slope	2,380	726	Long Island Sound	Sea level		500	153
Delaware	Elbright Rd., New Castle Co.	442	135	Atlantic Ocean	Sea level		60	18
Dist. of Columbia	Tenleytown	410	125	Potomac River	1	(Z)	150	46
Florida	Sec. 30, T6N, R20W, Walton Co.	345	105	Atlantic Ocean	Sea level		100	31
Georgia	Brasstown Bald	4,784	1,459	Atlantic Ocean	Sea level		600	183
Guam	Mount Lamlam	1,332	406	Pacific Ocean	Sea level		330	101
Hawaii	Puu Wekiu	13,796	4,208	Pacific Ocean	Sea level		3,030	924
Idaho	Borah Peak	12,662	3,862	Snake River	710	217	5,000	1,525
Illinois	Charles Mound	1,235	377	Mississippi River	279	85	600	183
Indiana	Franklin Township, Wayne Co.	1,257	383	Ohio River	320	98	700	214
Iowa	Sec. 29, T100N, R41W, Osceola Co.	1,670	509	Mississippi River	480	146	1,100	336
Kansas	Mount Sunflower	4,039	1,232	Verdigris River	679	207	2,000	610
Kentucky	Black Mountain	4,139	1,262	Mississippi River	257	78	750	229
Louisiana	Driskill Mountain	535	163	New Orleans	–8	–2	100	31
Maine	Mount Katahdin	5,267	1,606	Atlantic Ocean	Sea level		600	183
Maryland	Backbone Mountain	3,360	1,025	Atlantic Ocean	Sea level		350	107
Massachusetts	Mount Greylock	3,487	1,064	Atlantic Ocean	Sea level		500	153
Michigan	Mount Arvon	1,979	604	Lake Erie	571	174	900	275
Minnesota	Eagle Mountain, Cook Co.	2,301	702	Lake Superior	600	183	1,200	366
Mississippi	Woodall Mountain	806	246	Gulf of Mexico	Sea level		300	92
Missouri	Taum Sauk Mountain	1,772	540	St. Francis River	230	70	800	244
Montana	Granite Peak	12,799	3,904	Kootenai River	1,800	549	3,400	1,037
Nebraska	Johnson Township, Kimball Co.	5,426	1,655	Southeast corner of state	840	256	2,600	793
Nevada	Boundary Peak	13,140	4,007	Colorado River	479	146	5,500	1,678
New Hampshire	Mount Washington	6,288	1,918	Atlantic Ocean	Sea level		1,000	305
New Jersey	High Point	1,803	550	Atlantic Ocean	Sea level		250	76
New Mexico	Wheeler Peak	13,161	4,014	Red Bluff Reservoir	2,842	867	5,700	1,739
New York	Mount Marcy	5,344	1,630	Atlantic Ocean	Sea level		1,000	305
North Carolina	Mount Mitchell[2]	6,684	2,039	Atlantic Ocean	Sea level		700	214
North Dakota	White Butte, Slope Co.	3,506	1,069	Red River	750	229	1,900	580
Ohio	Campbell Hill	1,549	472	Ohio River	455	139	850	259
Oklahoma	Black Mesa	4,973	1,517	Little River	289	88	1,300	397
Oregon	Mount Hood	11,239	3,428	Pacific Ocean	Sea level		3,300	1,007
Pennsylvania	Mount Davis	3,213	980	Delaware River	Sea level		1,100	336
Puerto Rico	Cerro de Punta	4,390	1,339	Atlantic Ocean	Sea level		1,800	549
Rhode Island	Jerimoth Hill	812	248	Atlantic Ocean	Sea level		200	61
South Carolina	Sassafras Mountain	3,560	1,086	Atlantic Ocean	Sea level		350	107
South Dakota	Harney Peak	7,242	2,209	Big Stone Lake	966	295	2,200	671
Tennessee	Clingmans Dome	6,643	2,026	Mississippi River	178	54	900	275
Texas	Guadalupe Peak	8,749	2,668	Gulf of Mexico	Sea level		1,700	519
Utah	Kings Peak	13,528	4,126	Beaverdam Creek	2,000	610	6,100	1,861
Vermont	Mount Mansfield	4,393	1,340	Lake Champlain	95	29	1,000	305
Virginia	Mount Rogers	5,729	1,747	Atlantic Ocean	Sea level		950	290
Virgin Islands	Crown Mountain	1,556	475	Atlantic Ocean	Sea level		750	229
Washington	Mount Rainier	14,410	4,395	Pacific Ocean	Sea level		1,700	519
West Virginia	Spruce Knob	4,861	1,483	Potomac River	240	73	1,500	458
Wisconsin	Timms Hill	1,951	595	Lake Michigan	579	177	1,050	320
Wyoming	Gannett Peak	13,804	4,210	Belle Fourche River	3,009	945	6,700	2,044

Note: Z = less than 0.5 meter. Sec. = section; T = township; R = range; N = north; W = west. 1. Highest point in 48 conterminous states. 2. Highest point east of Mississippi River. **Source:** U.S. Geological Survey, *Elevations and Distances in the United States* (1990).

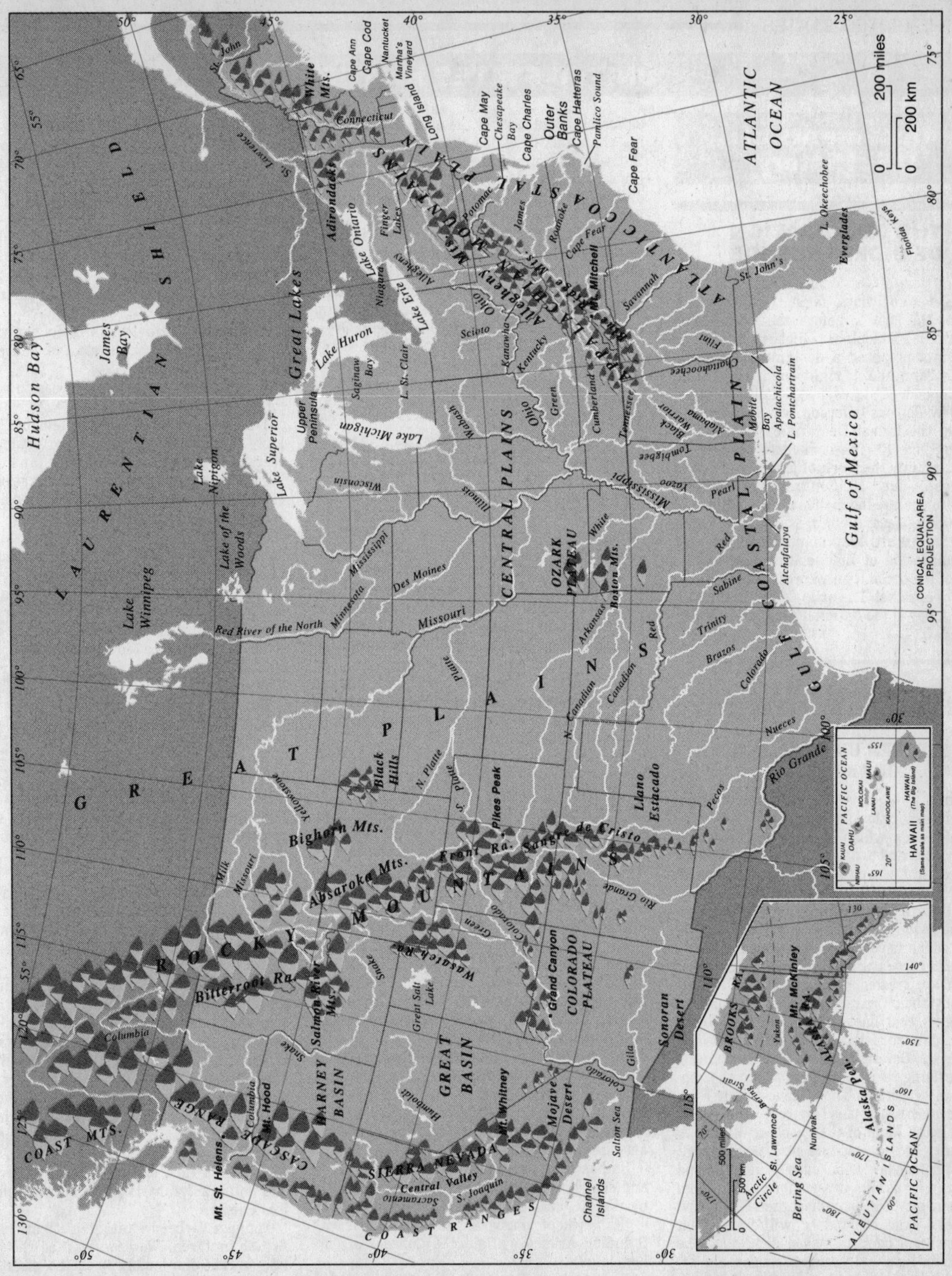

THE UNITED STATES PHYSICAL MAP

UNITED STATES HISTORY

Documents of U.S. History

THE DECLARATION OF INDEPENDENCE

After a year of war with Britain, American patriots were driven to make the final break in 1776. On June 7, before the Continental Congress in Philadelphia, Richard Henry Lee of Virginia proposed a declaration that the colonies "are, and of right ought to be, free and independent States." A committee of five, headed by Thomas Jefferson, was appointed to draw up the formal Declaration of Independence on June 10. The committee brought its version, mainly the work of Jefferson, back to Congress on June 28. Congress voted unanimously to declare independence on July 2, and after making several changes in the Jefferson committee's draft, they unanimously adopted the Declaration of Independence on July 4. Copies of the declaration were dispatched to the states for approval. The original document is on display today at the National Archives in Washington, D.C.

In Congress, July 4, 1776,
THE UNANIMOUS DECLARATION OF THE THIRTEEN UNITED STATES OF AMERICA,

When in the Course of human events, it becomes necessary for one people to dissolve the political bands which have connected them with another, and to assume among the Powers of the earth, the separate and equal station to which the Laws of Nature and of Nature's God entitle them, a decent respect to the opinions of mankind requires that they should declare the causes which impel them to the separation.

We hold these truths to be self-evident, that all men are created equal, that they are endowed by their Creator with certain unalienable Rights, that among these are Life, Liberty and the pursuit of Happiness. That to secure these rights, Governments are instituted among Men, deriving their just powers from the consent of the governed. That whenever any Form of Government becomes destructive of these ends, it is the Right of the People to alter or to abolish it, and to institute new Government, laying its foundation on such principles and organizing its powers in such form, as to them shall seem most likely to effect their Safety and Happiness. Prudence, indeed, will dictate that governments long established should not be changed for light and transient causes; and accordingly all experience hath shown, that mankind are more disposed to suffer, while evils are sufferable, than to right themselves by abolishing the forms to which they are accustomed. But when a long train of abuses and usurpations, pursuing invariably the same Object evinces a design to reduce them under absolute Despotism, it is their right, it is their duty, to throw off such Government, and to provide new Guards for their future security. Such has been the patient sufferance of these Colonies; and such is now the necessity which constrains them to alter their former Systems of Government. The history of the present King of Great Britain is a history of repeated injuries and usurpations, all having in direct object the establishment of an absolute Tyranny over these States. To prove this, let Facts be submitted to a candid world.

He has refused his Assent to Laws, the most wholesome and necessary for the public good.

He has forbidden his Governors to pass Laws of immediate and pressing importance, unless suspended in their operation till his Assent should be obtained; and when so suspended, he has utterly neglected to attend to them.

He has refused to pass other Laws for the accommodation of large districts of people, unless those people would relinquish the right of Representation in the Legislature, a right inestimable to them and formidable to tyrants only.

He has called together legislative bodies at places unusual, uncomfortable, and distant from the depository of their Public Records, for the sole purpose of fatiguing them into compliance with his measures.

He has dissolved Representative Houses repeatedly, for opposing with manly firmness his invasions on the rights of the people.

He has refused for a long time, after such dissolutions, to cause others to be elected; whereby the Legislative Powers, incapable of Annihilation, have returned to the People at large for their exercise; the State remaining in the mean time exposed to all the dangers of invasion from without, and convulsions within.

He has endeavoured to prevent the population of these States; for that purpose obstructing the Laws of Naturalization of Foreigners; refusing to pass others to encourage their migration hither, and raising the conditions of new Appropriations of Lands.

He has obstructed the Administration of Justice, by refusing his Assent to Laws for establishing Judiciary Powers.

He has made Judges dependent on his Will alone, for the tenure of their offices, and the amount and payment of their salaries.

He has erected a multitude of New Offices, and sent hither swarms of Officers to harass our People, and eat out their substance.

He has kept among us, in times of peace, Standing Armies without the Consent of our legislature.

He has affected to render the Military independent of and superior to the Civil Power.

He has combined with others to subject us to a jurisdiction foreign to our constitution, and unacknowledged by our laws; giving his Assent to their acts of pretended legislation:

For quartering large bodies of armed troops among us:

For protecting them, by a mock Trial, from Punishment for any Murders which they should commit on the Inhabitants of these States:

For cutting off our Trade with all parts of the world:

For imposing taxes on us without our consent:

For depriving us in many cases, of the benefits of Trial by Jury:

For transporting us beyond Seas to be tried for pretended offences:

For abolishing the free System of English Laws in a neighbouring Province, establishing therein an Arbitrary government, and enlarging its Boundaries so as to render it at once an example and fit instrument for introducing the same absolute rule into these Colonies:

For taking away our Charters, abolishing our most valuable Laws, and altering fundamentally the forms of our Government:

For suspending our own legislature, and declaring themselves invested with Power to legislate for us in all cases whatsoever.

He has abdicated Government here, by declaring us out of his Protection and waging War against us.

He has plundered our seas, ravaged our Coasts, burnt our towns, and destroyed the lives of our people.

He is at this time transporting large armies of foreign mercenaries to compleat the works of death, desolation and tyranny, already begun with circumstances of Cruelty & perfidy scarcely paralleled in the most barbarous ages, and totally unworthy of the Head of a civilized nation.

He has constrained our fellow Citizens taken Captive on the high Seas to bear Arms against their Country, to become the executioners of their friends and Brethren, or to fall themselves by their Hands.

He has excited domestic insurrections amongst us, and has endeavoured to bring on the inhabitants of our frontiers, the merciless Indian Savages, whose known rule of warfare, is an undistinguished destruction of all ages, sexes and conditions.

In every stage of these Oppressions We have Petitioned for Redress in the most humble terms: Our repeated Petitions have been answered only by repeated injury. A prince, whose character is thus marked by every act which may define a Tyrant, is unfit to be the ruler of a free People.

Nor have We been wanting in attention to our British brethren. We have warned them from time to time of attempts by their legislature to extend an unwarrantable jurisdiction over us. We have reminded them of the circumstances of our emigration and settlement here. We have appealed to their native justice and magnanimity, and we have conjured them by the ties of our common kindred to disavow these usurpations, which would inevitably interrupt our connections and correspondence. They too have been deaf to the voice of justice and of consanguinity. We must, therefore, acquiesce in the necessity, which denounces our Separation and hold them, as we hold the rest of mankind, Enemies in War, in Peace Friends.

We, therefore, the Representatives of the United States of America, in General Congress, Assembled, appealing to the Supreme Judge of the world for the rectitude of our intentions, do, in the Name, and by Authority of the good People of these Colonies, solemnly publish and declare, That these United Colonies are, and of Right ought to be Free and Independent States; that they are Absolved from all Allegiance to the British Crown, and that all political connection between them and the State of Great Britain, is and ought to be totally dissolved; and that as Free and Independent States, they have full Power to levy War, conclude Peace, contract Alliances, establish Commerce, and to do all other Acts and Things which Independent States may of right do. And for the support of this Declaration, with a firm reliance on the Protection of Divine Providence, we mutually pledge to each other our Lives, our Fortunes and our sacred Honor.

THE U.S. CONSTITUTION

During and after the Revolution, the United States was governed by the Continental Congress under the Articles of Confederation, which delegated very limited powers to the national government and reserved the rest to the states. Economic chaos, political confusion, and widespread dissatisfaction with the lack of central authority peaked after Shays's Rebellion in 1786. George Washington lent his prestige to the call for a convention to consider a new form of government. Congress endorsed the plan on Feb. 21, 1787, "for the sole and express purpose of revising the Articles of Confederation." All states but Rhode Island sent delegates to the convention, which opened in Philadelphia on May 14. The delegates moved at once to discard the articles, draw up a new Constitution, and conduct their meetings in secrecy, while Washington presided and James Madison took notes. A long summer of debate and compromise finally produced the document that most of the delegates signed on Sept. 17. Congress ordered the Constitution sent to the states for ratification on Sept. 28, requiring approval by at least nine of them to validate the new charter. Whether the Constitution would be adopted was in doubt until June 21, 1788, when New Hampshire became the ninth state to ratify it. The Constitution went into effect on Mar. 4, 1789. All of the original 13 states eventually ratified the Constitution, ending with Rhode Island on May 29, 1790. The U.S. Constitution remains the world's oldest written constitution.

Signers of the Declaration of Independence

Delegate	*Colony*	*Born/Died*	*Delegate*	*Colony*	*Born/Died*	*Delegate*	*Colony*	*Born/Died*
Adams, John	Massachusetts	1735–1826	Hooper, William	North Carolina	1742–90	Read, George	Delaware	1733–98
Adams, Samuel	Massachusetts	1722–1803	Hopkins, Stephen	Rhode Island	1707–85	Rodney, Caesar	Delaware	1728–84
Bartlett, Josiah	New Hampshire	1729–95	Hopkinson, Francis	New Jersey	1737–91	Ross, George	Pennsylvania	1730–79
Braxton, Carter	Virginia	1736–97	Huntington, Samuel	Connecticut	1731–96	Rush, Benjamin	Pennsylvania	1745–1813
Carroll, Charles	Maryland	1737–1832	Jefferson, Thomas	Virginia	1743–1826	Rutledge, Edward	South Carolina	1749–1800
Chase, Samuel	Maryland	1741–1811	Lee, Francis Lightfoot	Virginia	1734–97	Sherman, Roger	Connecticut	1721–93
Clark, Abraham	New Jersey	1726–94	Lee, Richard Henry	Virginia	1732–94	Smith, James	Pennsylvania	1713–1806
Clymer, George	Pennsylvania	1739–1813	Lewis, Francis	New York	1713–1803	Stockton, Richard	New Jersey	1730–81
Ellery, William	Rhode Island	1727–1820	Livingston, Philip	New York	1716–78	Stone, Thomas	Maryland	1743–87
Floyd, William	New York	1734–1821	Lynch, Thomas, Jr.	South Carolina	1749–79	Taylor, George	Pennsylvania	1716–81
Franklin, Benjamin	Pennsylvania	1706–90	McKean, Thomas	Delaware	1734–1817	Thornton, Matthew	New Hampshire	1714–1803
Gerry, Elbridge	Massachusetts	1744–1814	Middleton, Arthur	South Carolina	1742–87	Walton, George	Georgia	1741–1804
Gwinnett, Button	Georgia	1732–77	Morris, Lewis	New York	1726–98	Whipple, William	New Hampshire	1730–85
Hall, Lyman	Georgia	1724–90	Morris, Robert	Pennsylvania	1734–1806	Williams, William	Connecticut	1731–1811
Hancock, John	Massachusetts	1737–93	Morton, John	Pennsylvania	1724–77	Wilson, James	Pennsylvania	1742–98
Harrison, Benjamin	Virginia	1726–91	Nelson, Thomas, Jr.	Virginia	1738–89	Witherspoon, John	New Jersey	1723–94
Hart, John	New Jersey	?–1779	Paca, William	Maryland	1740–99	Wolcott, Oliver	Connecticut	1726–97
Hewes, Joseph	North Carolina	1730–79	Paine, Robert Treat	Massachusetts	1731–1814	Wythe, George	Virginia	1726–1806
Heyward, Thomas, Jr.	South Carolina	1746–1809	Penn, John	North Carolina	1741–88			

THE CONSTITUTION OF THE UNITED STATES OF AMERICA

Preamble

WE, THE PEOPLE OF THE UNITED STATES, in order to form a more perfect union, establish justice, insure domestic tranquillity, provide for the common defense, promote the general welfare, and secure the blessing of liberty to ourselves and our posterity, do ordain and establish this Constitution for the United States of America.

Article I

SECTION 1 All legislative powers herein granted shall be vested in a Congress of the United States, which shall consist of a Senate and House of Representatives.

SECTION 2 [1] The House of Representatives shall be composed of members chosen every second year by the people of the several States, and the electors in each State shall have the qualifications requisite for electors of the most numerous branch of the State legislature.

[2] No person shall be a Representative who shall not have attained to the age of twenty-five years, and been seven years a citizen of the United States, and who shall not, when elected, be an inhabitant of that State in which he shall be chosen.

[3] Representatives and direct taxes shall be apportioned among the several States which may be included within this Union, according to their respective numbers, which shall be determined by adding to the whole number of free persons, including those bound to service for a term of years, and excluding Indians not taxed, three-fifths of all other persons. The actual enumeration shall be made within three years after the first meeting of the Congress of the United States, and within every subsequent term of ten years, in such manner as they shall by law direct. The number of Representatives shall not exceed one for every thirty thousand, but each State shall have at least one Representative; and until such enumeration shall be made, the State of New Hampshire shall be entitled to choose three; Massachusetts, eight; Rhode Island and Providence Plantations, one; Connecticut, five; New York, six; New Jersey, four; Pennsylvania, eight; Delaware, one; Maryland, six; Virginia, ten; North Carolina, five; South Carolina, five; and Georgia, three.

[4] When vacancies happen in the representation from any State, the executive authority thereof shall issue writs of election to fill such vacancies.

[5] The House of Representatives shall choose their Speaker and other officers, and shall have the sole power of impeachment.

SECTION 3 [1] The Senate of the United States shall be composed of two Senators from each State, chosen by the legislature thereof for six years; and each Senator shall have one vote.

[2] Immediately after they shall be assembled in consequence of the first election, they shall be divided as equally as may be into three classes. The seats of the Senators of the first class shall be vacated at the expiration of the second year, of the second class at the expiration of the fourth year, and of the third class at the expiration of the sixth year, so that one-third may be chosen every second year; and if vacancies happen by resignation or otherwise during the recess of the legislature of any State, the executive thereof may make temporary appointments until the next meeting of the legislature, which shall then fill such vacancies.

[3] No person shall be a Senator who shall not have attained to the age of thirty years, and been nine years a citizen of the United States, and who shall not, when elected, be an inhabitant of that State for which he shall be chosen.

[4] The Vice-President of the United States shall be President of the Senate, but shall have no vote, unless they be equally divided.

[5] The Senate shall choose their other officers and also a President *pro tempore* in the absence of the Vice-President, or when he shall exercise the office of President of the United States.

[6] The Senate shall have the sole power to try all impeachments. When sitting for that purpose, they shall be on oath or affirmation. When the President of the United States is tried, the Chief Justice shall preside; and no person shall be convicted without the concurrence of two-thirds of the members present.

[7] Judgment in cases of impeachment shall not extend further than to removal from office, and disqualification to hold and enjoy any office of honor, trust, or profit under the United States; but the party convicted shall, nevertheless, be liable and subject to indictment, trial, judgment, and punishment, according to law.

SECTION 4 [1] The times, places, and manner of holding elections for Senators and Representatives shall be prescribed in each State by the legislature thereof; but the Congress may at any time by law make or alter such regulations, except as to the places of choosing Senators.

[2] The Congress shall assemble at least once in every year, and such meeting shall be on the first Monday in December, unless they shall by law appoint a different day.

SECTION 5 [1] Each House shall be the judge of the elections, returns, and qualification of its own members, and a majority of each shall constitute a quorum to do business; but a smaller number may adjourn from day to day, and may be authorized to compel the attendance of absent members, in such manner, and under such penalties, as each House may provide.

[2] Each House may determine the rules of its proceedings, punish its members for disorderly behavior, and with the concurrence of two-thirds, expel a member.

[3] Each House shall keep a journal of its proceedings, and from time to time publish the same, excepting such parts as may in their judgment require secrecy, and the yeas and nays of the members of either House on any question shall, at the desire of one-fifth of those present, be entered on the journal.

[4] Neither House, during the session of Congress, shall, without the consent of the other, adjourn for more than three days, nor to any other place than that in which the two Houses shall be sitting.

SECTION 6 [1] The Senators and Representatives shall receive a compensation for their services, to be ascertained by law and paid out of the Treasury of the United States. They shall, in all cases except treason, felony, and breach of the peace, be privileged from arrest during their attendance at the session of their respective Houses, and in going to and returning from the same; and for any speech or debate in either House they shall not be questioned in any other place.

[2] No Senator or Representative shall, during the time for which he was elected, be appointed to any civil office under the authority of the United States, which shall have been created, or the emoluments whereof shall have been increased during such time; and no person holding any office under the United States shall be a member of either House during his continuance in office.

SECTION 7 [1] All bills for raising revenue shall originate in the House of Representatives; but the Senate may propose or concur with amendments as on other bills.

[2] Every bill which shall have passed the House of Representatives and the Senate shall, before it becomes a law, be presented to the President of the United States; if he approves he shall sign it, but if not he shall return it, with his objections, to that House in which it shall have originated, who shall enter the objections at large on their journal and proceed to reconsider it. If after such reconsideration two-thirds of that House shall agree to pass the bill, it shall be sent, together with the objections, to the other House, by which it shall likewise be reconsidered, and if approved by two-thirds of that House it shall become a law. But in all such cases the vote of both Houses shall be determined by yeas and nays, and the names of the persons voting for and against the bill shall be entered on the journal of each House respectively. If any bill shall not be returned by the President within ten days (Sundays excepted) after it shall have been presented to him, the same shall be a law, in like manner as if he had signed it, unless the Congress by their adjournment prevent its return, in which case it shall not be a law.

[3] Every order, resolution or vote to which the concurrence of the Senate and House of Representatives may be necessary (except on a question of adjournment) shall be presented to the President of the United States; and before the same shall take effect shall be approved by him, or being disapproved by him, shall be repassed by two-thirds of the Senate and House of Representatives, according to the rules and limitations prescribed in the case of a bill.

SECTION 8 [1] The Congress shall have power to lay and collect taxes, duties, imposts and excises, to pay the debts and provide for the common defense and general welfare of the United States; but all duties, imposts and excises shall be uniform throughout the United States;

[2] To borrow money on the credit of the United States;

[3] To regulate commerce with foreign nations, and among the several States, and with the Indian tribes;

[4] To establish an uniform rule of naturalization, and uniform laws on the subject of bankruptcies throughout the United States;

[5] To coin money, regulate the value thereof, and of foreign coin, and fix the standard of weights and measures;

[6] To provide for the punishment of counterfeiting the securities and current coin of the United States;

[7] To establish post offices and post roads;

[8] To promote the progress of science and useful arts by securing for limited times to authors and inventors the exclusive right to their respective writings and discoveries;

[9] To constitute tribunals inferior to the Supreme Court;

[10] To define and punish piracies and felonies committed on the high seas and offenses against the law of nations.

[11] To declare war, grant letters of marque and reprisal, and make rules concerning captures on land and water;

[12] To raise and support armies, but no appropriation of money to that use shall be for a longer term than two years;

[13] To provide and maintain a navy;

[14] To make rules for the government and regulation of the land and naval forces;

[15] To provide for calling forth the militia to execute the laws of the Union, suppress insurrections, and repel invasions;

[16] To provide for organizing, arming and disciplining the militia, and for governing such part of them as may be employed in the service of the United States, reserving to the States respectively the appointment of the officers, and the authority of training the militia according to the discipline prescribed by Congress;

[17] To exercise exclusive legislation in all cases whatsoever over such district (not exceeding ten miles square) as may, by cession of particular States and the acceptance of Congress,

become the seat of the Government of the United States, and to exercise like authority over all places purchased by the consent of the legislature of the State in which the same shall be, for the erection of forts, magazines, arsenals, dockyards, and other needful buildings;

[18] To make all laws which shall be necessary and proper for carrying into execution the foregoing powers, and all other powers vested by this Constitution in the Government of the United States, or in any department or officer thereof.

SECTION 9 [1] The migration or importation of such persons as any of the States now existing shall think proper to admit shall not be prohibited by the Congress prior to the year one thousand eight hundred and eight, but a tax or duty may be imposed on such importation, not exceeding ten dollars for each person.

[2] The privilege of the writ of habeas corpus shall not be suspended, unless when in cases of rebellion or invasion the public safety may require it.

[3] No bill of attainder or ex post facto law shall be passed.

[4] No capitation or other direct tax shall be laid, unless in proportion to the census or enumeration hereinbefore directed to be taken.

[5] No tax or duty shall be laid on articles exported from any State.

[6] No preference shall be given by any regulation of commerce or revenue to the ports of one State over those of another; nor shall vessels bound to or from one State be obliged to enter, clear or pay duties in another.

[7] No money shall be drawn from the Treasury but in consequence of appropriations made by law; and a regular statement and account of the receipts and expenditures of all public money shall be published from time to time.

[8] No title of nobility shall be granted by the United States; and no person holding any office of profit or trust under them shall, without the consent of the Congress, accept of any present, emolument, office, or title of any kind whatever from any king, prince, or foreign state.

SECTION 10 [1] No State shall enter into any treaty, alliance, or confederation; grant letters of marque and reprisal; coin money, emit bills of credit, make anything but gold and silver coin a tender in payment of debts; pass any bill of attainder, ex post facto law or law impairing the obligation of contracts, or grant any title of nobility.

[2] No State shall, without the consent of the Congress, lay any imposts or duties on imports or exports, except what may be absolutely necessary for executing its inspection laws; and the net produce of all duties and imposts, laid by any State on imports or exports, shall be for the use of the Treasury of the United States; and all such laws shall be subject to the revision and control of the Congress.

[3] No State shall, without the consent of Congress, lay any duty of tonnage, keep troops and ships of war in time of peace, enter into any agreement or compact with another State or with a foreign power, or engage in war, unless actually invaded or in such imminent danger as will not admit of delay.

Article II

SECTION 1 [1] The executive power shall be vested in a President of the United States of America. He shall hold his office during the term of four years, and together with the Vice-President, chosen for the same term, be elected as follows:

[2] Each State shall appoint, in such manner as the legislature thereof may direct, a number of Electors, equal to the whole number of Senators and Representatives to which the State may be entitled in the Congress; but no Senator or Representative, or person holding an office of trust or profit under the United States shall be appointed an Elector.

[3] The Electors shall meet in their respective States and vote by ballot for two persons, of whom one at least shall not be an inhabitant of the same State with themselves. And they shall make a list of all the persons voted for, and of the number of votes for each; which list they shall sign and certify, and transmit sealed to the seat of government of the United States, directed to the President of the Senate. The President of the Senate shall, in the presence of the Senate and House of Representatives, open all the certificates, and the votes shall then be counted. The person having the greatest number of votes shall be the President, if such number be a majority of the whole number of Electors appointed; and if there be more than one who have such majority, and have an equal number of votes, then the House of Representatives shall immediately choose by ballot one of them for President; and if no person have a majority, then from the five highest on the list the said House shall in like manner choose the President. But in choosing the President the votes shall be taken by States, the representation from each State having one vote; a quorum for this purpose shall consist of a member or members from two-thirds of the States, and a majority of all the States shall be necessary to a choice. In every case, after the choice of the President, the person having the greatest number of votes of the Electors shall be the Vice-President. But if there should remain two or more who have equal votes, the Senate shall choose from them by ballot the Vice-President.

[4] The Congress may determine the time of choosing the Electors and the day on which they shall give their votes, which day shall be the same throughout the United States.

[5] No person except a natural-born citizen, or citizen of the United States at the time of the adoption of this Constitution, shall be eligible to the office of President; neither shall any person be eligible to that office who shall not have attained to the age of thirty-five years, and been fourteen years a resident within the United States.

[6] In case of the removal of the President from office, or of his death, resignation, or inability to discharge the powers and duties of the said office, the same shall devolve on the Vice-President, and the Congress may by law provide for the case of removal, death, resignation, or inability, both of the President and Vice-President, declaring what officer shall then act as President, and such officer shall act accordingly until the disability be removed or a President shall be elected.

[7] The President shall, at stated times, receive for his services a compensation, which shall neither be increased nor diminished during the period for which he shall have been elected, and he shall not receive within that period any other emolument from the United States or any of them.

[8] Before he enter on the execution of his office he shall take the following oath or affirmation:

"I do solemnly swear (or affirm) that I will faithfully execute the office of President of the United States, and will to the best of my ability preserve, protect, and defend the Constitution of the United States."

SECTION 2 [1] The President shall be Commander-in-Chief of the Army and Navy of the United States, and of the militia of the several States when called into the actual service of the United States; he may require the opinion, in writing, of the principal officer in each of the executive departments, upon any subject relating to the duties of their respective offices, and he shall have power to grant reprieves and pardons for offenses against the United States, except in cases of impeachment.

[2] He shall have power, by and with the advice and consent of the Senate, to make treaties, provided two-thirds of the Senators present concur; and he shall nominate, and, by and with the advice and consent of the Senate, shall appoint ambassadors, other public ministers and consuls, judges of the Supreme Court, and all other officers of the United States whose appointments are not herein otherwise provided for, and which shall be established by law; but the Congress may by law vest the appointment of such inferior officers, as they think proper, in the President alone, in the courts of law, or in the heads of departments.

[3] The President shall have power to fill up all vacancies that may happen during the recess of the Senate, by granting commissions which shall expire at the end of their next session.

SECTION 3 He shall from time to time give to the Congress information of the state of the Union, and recommend to their consideration such measures as he shall judge necessary and expedient; he may, on extraordinary occasions, convene both Houses, or either of them, and in case of disagreement between them with respect to the time of adjournment, he may adjourn them to such time as he shall think proper; he shall receive ambassadors and other public ministers; he shall take care that the laws be faithfully executed, and shall commission all the officers of the United States.

SECTION 4 The President, Vice-President and all civil officers of the United States shall be removed from office on impeachment for and conviction of treason, bribery, or other high crimes and misdemeanors.

Article III

SECTION 1 The judicial power of the United States shall be vested in one Supreme Court, and in such inferior courts as the Congress may from time to time ordain and establish. The judges, both of the Supreme and inferior courts, shall hold their offices during good behavior, and shall, at stated times, receive for their services a compensation which shall not be diminished during their continuance in office.

SECTION 2 [1] The judicial power shall extend to all cases, in law and equity, arising under this Constitution, the laws of the United States, and treaties made, or which shall be made, under their authority; to all cases affecting ambassadors, other public ministers, and consuls; to all cases of admiralty and maritime jurisdiction; to controversies to which the United States shall be a party; to controversies between two or more States; between a State and citizens of another State; between citizens of different States; between citizens of the same State claiming lands under grants of different States, and between a State, or the citizens thereof, and foreign states, citizens, or subjects.

[2] In all cases affecting ambassadors, other public ministers and consuls, and those in which a State shall be party, the Supreme Court shall have original jurisdiction. In all the other cases before mentioned the Supreme Court shall have appellate jurisdiction, both as to law and fact, with such exceptions and under such regulations as the Congress shall make.

[3] The trial of all crimes, except in cases of impeachment, shall be by jury; and such trial shall be held in the State where the said crimes shall have been committed; but when not committed within any State, the trial shall be at such place or places as the Congress may by law have directed.

SECTION 3 [1] Treason against the United States shall consist only in levying war against them, or in adhering to their enemies, giving them aid and comfort. No person shall be convicted of treason unless on the testimony of two witnesses to the same overt act, or on confession in open court.

[2] The Congress shall have power to declare the punishment of treason, but no attainder of treason shall work corruption of blood or forfeiture except during the life of the person attained.

Article IV

SECTION 1 Full faith and credit shall be given in each State to the public acts, records, and judicial proceedings of every other State. And the Congress may by general laws prescribe the manner in which such acts, records, and proceedings shall be proved, and the effect thereof.

SECTION 2 [1] The citizens of each State shall be entitled to all privileges and immunities of citizens in the several States.

[2] A person charged in any State with treason, felony, or other crime, who shall flee from justice, and be found in another State, shall, on demand of the executive authority of the State from which he fled, be delivered up, to be removed to the State having jurisdiction of the crime.

[3] No person held to service or labor in one State, under the laws thereof, escaping into another, shall, in consequence of any law or regulation therein, be discharged from such service or labor, but shall be delivered up on claim to the party to whom such service or labor may be due.

SECTION 3 [1] New States may be admitted by the Congress into this Union; but no new State shall be formed or erected within the jurisdiction of any other State; nor any State be formed by the junction of two or more States or parts of States, without the consent of the legislatures of the States concerned as well as of the Congress.

[2] The Congress shall have power to dispose of and make all needful rules and regulations respecting the territory or other property belonging to the United States; and nothing in this Constitution shall be so construed as to prejudice any claims of the United States or of any particular State.

SECTION 4 The United States shall guarantee to every State in this Union a republican form of government, and shall protect each of them against invasion, and on application of the legislature, or of the executive (when the legislature cannot be convened), against domestic violence.

Article V

The Congress, whenever two-thirds of both Houses shall deem it necessary, shall propose amendments to this Constitution, or, on the application of the legislatures of two-thirds of the several States, shall call a convention for proposing amendments, which in either case shall be valid to all intents and purposes as part of this Constitution, when ratified by the legislatures of three-fourths of the several States, or by conventions in three-fourths thereof, as the one or the other mode of ratification may be proposed by the Congress; provided that no amendment which may be made prior to the year one thousand eight hundred and eight shall in any manner affect the first and fourth clauses in the Ninth Section of the First Article; and that no State, without its consent shall be deprived of its equal suffrage in the Senate.

Article VI

[1] All debts contracted and engagements entered into, before the adoption of this Constitution, shall be as valid against the United States under this Constitution as under the Confederation.

[2] This Constitution, and the laws of the United States which shall be made in pursuance thereof, and all treaties made, or which shall be made, under the authority of the United States, shall be the supreme law of the land; and the judges in every State shall be bound thereby, anything in the Constitution or laws of any State to the contrary notwithstanding.

[3] The Senators and Representatives before mentioned and the members of the several State legislatures, and all executive and judicial officers both of the United States and of the several States, shall be bound by oath or affirmation to support this Constitution; but no religious test shall ever be required as a qualification to any office or public trust under the United States.

Article VII

The ratification of the conventions of nine States shall be sufficient for the establishment of this Constitution between the States so ratifying the same.

Amendments to the Constitution

[The first 10 amendments, known collectively as The Bill of Rights, were adopted in 1791.]

Amendment I

Congress shall make no law respecting an establishment of religion, or prohibiting the free exercise thereof; or abridging the freedom of speech or of the press; or the right of the people peaceably to assemble, and to petition the government for a redress of grievances.

Amendment II

A well-regulated militia being necessary to the security of a free State, the right of the people to keep and bear arms shall not be infringed.

Amendment III

No soldier shall, in time of peace, be quartered in any house without the consent of the owner, nor in time of war, but in a manner to be prescribed by law.

Amendment IV

The right of the people to be secure in their persons, houses, papers, and effects, against unreasonable searches and seizures, shall not be violated, and no warrants shall issue but upon probable cause, supported by oath or affirmation, and particularly describing the place to be searched, and the persons or things to be seized.

Amendment V

No person shall be held to answer for a capital, or otherwise infamous crime, unless on a presentment or indictment of a grand jury, except in cases arising in the land or naval forces, or in the militia, when in actual service in time of war or public danger; nor shall any person be subject for the same offense to be twice put in jeopardy of life or limb; nor shall be compelled in any criminal case to be a witness against himself, nor be deprived of life, liberty or property, without due process of law; nor shall private property be taken for public use without just compensation.

Amendment VI

In all criminal prosecutions, the accused shall enjoy the right to a speedy and public trial, by an impartial jury of the State and district wherein the crime shall have been committed, which district shall have been previously ascertained by law, and to be informed of the nature and cause of the accusation; to be confronted with the witnesses against him; to have compulsory process for obtaining witnesses in his favor, and to have the assistance of counsel for his defense.

Amendment VII

In suits at common law, where the value in controversy shall exceed twenty dollars, the right of trial by jury shall be preserved, and no fact tried by a jury shall be otherwise reexamined in any court of the United States, than according to the rules of the common law.

Amendment VIII

Excessive bail shall not be required, nor excessive fines imposed, nor cruel and unusual punishments inflicted.

Amendment IX

The enumeration in the Constitution of certain rights shall not be construed to deny or disparage others retained by the people.

Amendment X

The powers not delegated to the United States by the Constitution, nor prohibited by it to the States, are reserved to the States respectively, or to the people.

Amendment XI

[Adopted Jan. 8, 1798]

The judicial power of the United States shall not be construed to extend to any suit in law or equity, commenced or prosecuted against one of the United States by citizens of another State, or by citizens or subjects of any foreign state.

Amendment XII

[Adopted Sept. 25, 1804]

[1] The Electors shall meet in their respective States and vote by ballot for President and Vice-President, one of whom, at least, shall not be an inhabitant of the same State with themselves; they shall name in their ballots the person voted for as President, and in distinct ballots the person voted for as Vice-President, and they shall make distinct lists of all persons voted for as President and of all persons voted for as Vice-President, and of the number of votes for each; which lists they shall sign and certify, and transmit sealed to the seat of the government of the United States, directed to the President of the Senate. The President of the Senate shall, in the presence of the Senate and House of Representatives, open all the certificates and the votes shall then be counted. The person having the greatest number of votes for President shall be the President, if such number be a majority of the whole number of Electors appointed; and if no person have such majority, then from the persons having the highest numbers not exceeding three on the list of those voted for as President, the House of Representatives shall choose immediately, by ballot, the President. But in choosing the President the votes shall be taken by States, the representation from each State having one vote; a quorum for this purpose shall consist of a member or members from two-thirds of the States, and a majority of all the States shall be necessary to a choice. And if the House of Representatives shall not choose a President whenever the right of choice shall devolve upon them, before the fourth day of March next following, then the Vice-President shall act as President, as in the case of the death or other constitutional disability of the President.

[2] The person having the greatest number of votes as Vice-President shall be the Vice-President, if such number be a majority of the whole number of Electors appointed; and if no person have a majority, then from the two highest numbers on the list the Senate shall choose the Vice-President; a quorum for the purpose shall consist of two-thirds of the whole number of Senators, and a majority of the whole number shall be necessary to a choice. But no person constitutionally ineligible to the office of President shall be eligible to that of Vice-President of the United States.

Amendment XIII

[Adopted Dec. 18, 1865]

SECTION 1 Neither slavery nor involuntary servitude, except as a punishment for crime whereof the party shall have been duly convicted, shall exist within the United States, or any place subject to their jurisdiction.

SECTION 2 Congress shall have power to enforce this article by appropriate legislation.

Amendment XIV

[Adopted July 28, 1868]

SECTION 1 All persons born or naturalized in the United States, and subject to the jurisdiction thereof, are citizens of the United States and of the State wherein they reside. No State shall make or enforce any law which shall abridge the privileges or immunities of citizens of the United States; nor shall any State deprive any person of life, liberty or property, without due process of law; nor deny to any person within its jurisdiction the equal protection of the laws.

SECTION 2 Representatives shall be apportioned among the several States according to their respective numbers, counting the whole number of persons in each State, excluding Indians not taxed. But when the right to vote at any election for the choice of Electors for President and Vice-President of the United States, Representatives in Congress, the executive and judicial officers of a State, or the members of the legislature thereof, is denied to any of the male inhabitants of such State, being twenty-one years of age, and citizens of the United States, or in any way abridged except for participation in rebellion or other crime, the basis of representation therein shall be reduced in the proportion which the number of such male citizens shall bear to the whole number of male citizens twenty-one years of age in such State.

SECTION 3 No person shall be a Senator or Representative in Congress, or elector of President and Vice-President, or hold any office, civil or military, under the United States or under any State, who, having previously taken an oath as a member of Congress, or as an officer of the United States, or as a member of any State legislature, or as an executive or judicial officer of any State, to support the Constitution of the United States, shall have engaged in insurrection or rebellion against the same, or given aid or comfort to the enemies thereof. But Congress may, by a vote of two-thirds of each House, remove such disability.

SECTION 4 The validity of the public debt of the United States, authorized by law, including debts incurred for payment of pensions and bounties for services in suppressing insurrection or rebellion, shall not be questioned. But neither the United States nor any State shall assume or pay any debt or obligation incurred in aid of insurrection or rebellion against the United States, or any claim for the loss or emancipation of any slave; but all such debts, obligations, and claims shall be held illegal and void.

SECTION 5 The Congress shall have power to enforce, by appropriate legislation, the provisions of this article.

Amendment XV

[Adopted Mar. 30, 1870]

SECTION 1 The right of citizens of the United States to vote shall not be denied or abridged by the United States or by any State on account of race, color, or previous condition of servitude.

SECTION 2 The Congress shall have power to enforce this article by appropriate legislation.

Amendment XVI

[Adopted Feb. 25, 1913]

The Congress shall have power to lay and collect taxes on incomes, from whatever source derived, without apportionment among the several States, and without regard to any census or enumeration.

Amendment XVII

[Adopted May 31, 1913]

SECTION 1 The Senate of the United States shall be composed of two Senators from each State, elected by the people thereof, for six years; and each Senator shall have one vote. The electors in each State shall have the qualifications requisite for electors of the most numerous branch of the State legislatures.

SECTION 2 When vacancies happen in the representation of any State in the Senate, the executive authority of such State shall issue writs of election to fill such vacancies: Provided, that the legislature of any State may empower the executive thereof to make temporary appointments until the people fill the vacancies by election as the legislature may direct.

SECTION 3 This amendment shall not be so construed as to affect the election or term of any Senator chosen before it becomes valid as part of the Constitution.

Amendment XVIII

[Adopted Jan. 29, 1919]

SECTION 1 After one year from the ratification of this article the manufacture, sale or transportation of intoxicating liquors within, the importation thereof into, or the exportation thereof from the United States and all territory subject to the jurisdiction thereof, for beverage purposes, is hereby prohibited.

SECTION 2 The Congress and the several States shall have concurrent power to enforce this article by appropriate legislation.

SECTION 3 This article shall be inoperative unless it shall have been ratified as an amendment to the Constitution by the legislatures of the several States, as provided in the Constitution, within seven years from the date of the submission hereof to the States by the Congress.

Amendment XIX

[Adopted Aug. 26, 1920]

SECTION 1 The right of citizens of the United States to vote shall not be denied or abridged by the United States or by any State on account of sex.

SECTION 2 Congress shall have power to enforce this article by appropriate legislation.

Amendment XX

[Adopted Feb. 6, 1933]

SECTION 1 The terms of the President and Vice-President shall end at noon on the 20th day of January, and the terms of Senators and Representatives at noon on the 3d day of January, of the years in which such terms would have ended if this article had not been ratified; and the terms of their successors shall then begin.

SECTION 2 The Congress shall assemble at least once in every year, and such meeting shall begin at noon on the 3d day of January, unless they shall by law appoint a different day.

SECTION 3 If, at the time fixed for the beginning of the term of the President, the President-elect shall have died, the Vice-President-elect shall become President. If a President shall not have been chosen before the time fixed for the beginning of his term or if the President-elect shall have failed to qualify, then the Vice-President-elect shall act as President until a President shall have qualified; and the Congress may by law provide for the case wherein neither a President-elect nor a Vice-President-elect shall have qualified, declaring who shall then act as President, or the manner in which one who is to act shall be selected, and such person shall act accordingly until a President or Vice-President shall have qualified.

SECTION 4 The Congress may by law provide for the case of the death of any of the persons from whom the House of Representatives may choose a President whenever the right of choice shall have devolved upon them, and for the case of death of any of the persons from whom the Senate may choose a Vice-President whenever the right of choice shall have devolved upon them.

SECTION 5 Sections 1 and 2 shall take effect on the 15th day of October following the ratification of this article.

SECTION 6 This article shall be inoperative unless it shall have been ratified as an amendment to the Constitution by the legislatures of three-fourths of the several States within seven years from the date of its submission.

Amendment XXI

[Adopted Dec. 5, 1933]

SECTION 1 The eighteenth article of amendment to the Constitution of the United States is hereby repealed.

SECTION 2 The transportation or importation into any State, territory, or possession of the United States for delivery or use therein of intoxicating liquors, in violation of the laws thereof, is hereby prohibited.

SECTION 3 This article shall be inoperative unless it shall have been ratified as an amendment to the Constitution by conventions in the several States, as provided in the Constitution, within seven years from the date of the submission hereof to the States by the Congress.

Amendment XXII

[Adopted Feb. 26, 1951]

SECTION 1 No person shall be elected to the office of President more than twice, and no person who has held the office of President, or acted as President, for more than two years of a term to which some other person was elected President shall be elected to the office of President more than once. But this Article shall not apply to any person holding the office of President when this Article was proposed by the Congress, and shall not prevent any person who may be holding the office of President, or acting as President, during the term within which this Article becomes operative from holding the office of President or acting as President during the remainder of such term.

SECTION 2 This article shall be inoperative unless it shall have been ratified as an amendment to the Constitution by the legislatures of three-fourths of the several States within seven years from the date of its submission to the States by the Congress.

Amendment XXIII

[Adopted Apr. 3, 1961]

SECTION 1 The District constituting the seat of Government of the United States shall appoint in such manner as the Congress may direct:

A number of electors of President and Vice-President equal to the whole number of Senators and Representatives in Congress to which the District would be entitled if it were a State, but in no event more than the least populous State; they shall be in addition to those appointed by the States, but they shall be considered, for the purposes of the election of President and Vice-President, to be electors appointed by a State; and they shall meet in the District and perform such duties as provided by the twelfth article of amendment.

SECTION 2 The Congress shall have power to enforce this article by appropriate legislation.

Amendment XXIV

[Adopted Jan. 23, 1964]

SECTION 1 The right of citizens of the United States to vote in any primary or other election for President or Vice-President, for electors for President or Vice-President, or for Senator or Representative in Congress, shall not be denied or abridged by the United States or any State by reason of failure to pay any poll tax or other tax.

SECTION 2 The Congress shall have power to enforce this article by appropriate legislation.

Amendment XXV

[Adopted Feb. 10, 1967]

SECTION 1 In case of the removal of the President from office or of his death or resignation, the Vice-President shall become President.

SECTION 2 Whenever there is a vacancy in the office of the Vice-President, the President shall nominate a Vice-President who shall take office upon confirmation by a majority vote of both Houses of Congress.

SECTION 3 Whenever the President transmits to the President pro tempore of the Senate and the Speaker of the House of Representatives his written declaration that he is unable to discharge the powers and duties of his office, and until he transmits to them a written declaration to the contrary, such powers and duties shall be discharged by the Vice-President as Acting President.

SECTION 4 Whenever the Vice-President and a majority of either the principal officers of the executive departments or of such other body as Congress may by law provide, transmit to the President pro tempore of the Senate and the Speaker of the House of Representatives their written declaration that the President is unable to discharge the powers and duties of his office, the Vice-President shall immediately assume the powers and duties of the office as Acting President.

Thereafter, when the President transmits to the President pro tempore of the Senate and the Speaker of the House of Representatives his written declaration that no inability exists, he shall resume the powers and duties of his office unless the Vice-President and a majority of either the principal officers of the executive department or of such other body as Congress may by law provide, transmit within four days to the President pro tempore of the Senate and the Speaker of the House of Representatives their written declaration that the President is unable to discharge the powers and duties of his office. Thereupon Congress shall decide the issue, assembling within forty-eight hours for that purpose if not in session. If the Congress, within twenty-one days after receipt of the latter written declaration, or, if Congress is not in session, within twenty-one days after Congress is required to assemble, determines by two-thirds vote of both Houses that the President is unable to discharge the powers and duties of his office, the Vice-President shall continue to discharge the same as Acting President; otherwise the President shall resume the powers and duties of his office.

Amendment XXVI

[Adopted June 30, 1971]

SECTION 1 The right of citizens of the United States, who are eighteen years of age or older, to vote shall not be denied or abridged by the United States or by any State on account of age.

SECTION 2 The Congress shall have power to enforce this article by appropriate legislation.

Amendment XXVII

[Adopted May 18, 1992]

No law, varying the compensation for the services of the Senators and Representatives, shall take effect until an election of Representatives shall have intervened.

THE 27th AMENDMENT

The 27th Amendment was originally proposed by James Madison more than 200 years ago, but it did not win backing of the required three-quarters of the states until Michigan ratified it in 1992. Although Congress generally imposes a time limit, usually seven years, for amendment ratification, the first Congress set no such limit on Madison's proposal. Thus in the weeks before the amendment's adoption, there was some controversy over its validity. But in an election year already notable for voter outrage over the perks of elected office, Congress was quick to endorse the measure.

THE EMANCIPATION PROCLAMATION

On July 22, 1862, Abraham Lincoln read to his cabinet a preliminary draft of an emancipation proclamation. Secretary of State William Seward suggested that the proclamation not be issued until a military victory had been won. The battle of Antietam gave Lincoln his desired opportunity, and on Sept. 22, he read to his cabinet a second draft of the proclamation. After some changes this was issued as a preliminary proclamation; the formal and definite proclamation came Jan. 1, 1863.

THE PRESIDENT OF THE UNITED STATES OF AMERICA:

A Proclamation.

Whereas on the 22nd day of September, A.D. 1862, a proclamation was issued by the President of the United States, containing among other things, the following, to wit:

"That on the 1st day of January, A.D. 1863, all persons held as slaves within any State or designated part of a State the people whereof shall then be in rebellion against the United States shall be then, thenceforward, and forever free; and the executive government of the United States, including the military and naval authority thereof, will recognize and maintain the freedom of such persons and will do no act or acts to repress such persons, or any of them, in any efforts they may make for their actual freedom.

"That the executive will on the 1st day of January aforesaid, by proclamation, designate the States and parts of States, if any, in which the people thereof, respectively, shall then be in rebellion against the United States; and the fact that any State or the people thereof shall on that day be in good faith represented in the Congress of the United States by members chosen thereto at elections wherein a majority of the qualified voters of such States shall have participated shall, in the absence of strong countervailing testimony, be deemed conclusive evidence that such State and the people thereof are not then in rebellion against the United States."

Now, therefore, I, Abraham Lincoln, President of the United States, by virtue of the power in me vested as Commander-in-Chief of the Army and Navy of the United States in time of actual armed rebellion against the authority and government of the United States, and as a fit and necessary war measure for suppressing said rebellion, do, on this 1st day of January, A.D. 1863, and in accordance with my purpose so to do, publicly proclaimed for the full period of one hundred days from the first day above mentioned, order and designate as the States and parts of States wherein the people thereof, respectively, are this day in rebellion against the United States the following, to wit:

Arkansas, Texas, Louisiana (except the parishes of St. Bernard, Plaquemines, Jefferson, St. John, St. Charles, St. James, Ascension, Assumption, Terrebonne, Lafourche, St. Mary, St. Martin, and Orleans, including the city of New Orleans), Mississippi, Alabama, Florida, Georgia, South Carolina, North Carolina, and Virginia (except the forty-eight counties designated as West Virginia, and also the counties of Berkeley, Accomac, Northhampton, Elizabeth City, York, Princess Anne, and Norfolk, including the cities of Norfolk and Portsmouth), and which excepted parts are for the present left precisely as if this proclamation were not issued.

And by virtue of the power and for the purpose aforesaid, I do order and declare that all persons held as slaves within said designated States and parts of States are, and henceforward shall be, free; and that the Executive Government of the United States, including the military and naval authorities thereof, will recognize and maintain the freedom of said persons.

And I hereby enjoin upon the people so declared to be free to abstain from all violence, unless in necessary self-defense; and I recommend to them that, in all cases when allowed, they labor faithfully for reasonable wages.

And I further declare and make known that such persons of suitable condition will be received into the armed service of the United States to garrison forts, positions, stations, and other places, and to man vessels of all sorts in said service.

And upon this act, sincerely believed to be an act of justice, warranted by the Constitution upon military necessity, I invoke the considerate judgment of mankind and the gracious favor of Almighty God.

THE GETTYSBURG ADDRESS

Abraham Lincoln's most famous and most eloquent words were delivered on Nov. 19, 1863, at the dedication of the cemetery that held the remains of the 45,000 soldiers who fell at the Battle of Gettysburg, a significant Union victory. A powerful summation of Lincoln's war aims as well as a moving tribute to those who died for a just cause, the Gettysburg Address has become justly famous as a rhetorical masterpiece as well as a stirring example of Lincoln's statesmanship.

"Four score and seven years ago our fathers brought forth on this continent, a new nation, conceived in Liberty, and dedicated to the proposition that all men are created equal.

"Now we are engaged in a great civil war, testing whether that nation or any nation so conceived and so dedicated, can long endure. We are met on a great battle-field of that war. We have come to dedicate a portion of that field, as a final resting place for those who here gave their lives that that nation might live. It is altogether fitting and proper that we should do this.

"But, in a larger sense, we can not dedicate—we can not consecrate—we can not hallow—this ground. The brave men, living and dead, who struggled here, have consecrated it, far above our poor power to add or detract. The world will little note, nor long remember what we say here, but it can never forget what they did here. It is for us the living, rather, to be dedicated here to the unfinished work which they who fought here have thus far so nobly advanced. It is rather for us to be here dedicated to the great task remaining before us—that from these honored dead we take increased devotion to that cause for which they gave the last full measure of devotion—that we here highly resolve that these dead shall not have died in vain—that this nation, under God, shall have a new birth of freedom—and that government of the people, by the people, for the people, shall not perish from the earth."

PLEDGE OF ALLEGIANCE

The original version of the Pledge of Allegiance appeared in the Sept. 8, 1892, issue of *Youth's Companion* magazine. Authorship was disputed until 1939, when the United States Flag Association declared Francis Bellamy the author. Congress mandated two changes by substituting "the flag of the United States of America" for "my flag" in 1923 and adding "under God" in 1954. Public schools throughout the United States made the daily Pledge of Allegiance obligatory, until the Supreme Court ruled in *West Virginia Board of Education* v. *Barnette* (1943) that the First Amendment protected the "right of silence" as well as freedom of speech.

"I pledge allegiance to the flag of the United States of America, and to the Republic for which it stands, one nation, under God, indivisible, with liberty and justice for all."

Chronology of U.S. History

c. 1000 Viking explorer Leif Ericson explores North American coast and founds temporary colony called Vinland.

1492 On first voyage to America, Christopher Columbus lands at San Salvador island in Bahamas.

1493 Pope Alexander VI divides New World between Spain and Portugal.

1497 John Cabot claims Newfoundland for King Henry VII of England.

1499 Florentine merchant Amerigo Vespucci visits New World and begins writing popular accounts of his voyages.

1506 Columbus dies poor and embittered, convinced he found new route to Asia and refusing to believe he discovered new continent.

1507 German mapmaker Martin Waldseemüller, after reading Amerigo Vespucci's descriptions of New World, names it America after him.

1513 Juan Ponce de León discovers Florida. Vasco Nuñez de Balboa crosses Panama and sights Pacific Ocean.

1519 Hernán Cortés lands in Mexico.

1520 Ferdinand Magellan, first to sail around world, discovers South American straits, named after him.

1522 Cortés captures Mexico City and conquers Aztec empire.

1524 Giovanni de Verrazano, commissioned by King Francis I of France, discovers New York harbor and Hudson River.

1534 Jacques Cartier of France explores coast of Newfoundland and Gulf of St. Lawrence.

1536 Traveling overland from Gulf of Mexico, Alvar Núñez Cabeza de Vaca reaches Gulf of California.

1539 Fernando de Soto conquers Florida and begins three-year trek across Southeast.

1540 Francisco Vásquez de Coronado explores Southwest, discovering Grand Canyon and introducing horses to North America.

1541 Coronado discovers Mississippi River.

1542 João Rodrígues Cabrilho (Cabrillo) explores coast of California, missing San Francisco Bay.

1565 Don Pedro Menéndez de Aviles founds first permanent European settlement in North America, at St. Augustine, Florida.

1572 Sir Francis Drake of England makes first voyage to America, landing in Panama.

1576 English explorer Martin Frobisher searches for Northwest Passage.

1577 Drake begins voyage of plunder around world.

1579 Drake lands north of San Francisco Bay and claims region for Queen Elizabeth I.

1584 Sir Walter Raleigh discovers Roanoke Island and names land Virginia, after Queen Elizabeth.

1585 Raleigh establishes England's first American colony at Roanoke.

1586 Drake evacuates surviving Roanoke settlers.

1587 Raleigh resettles Roanoke with 150 new colonists. Virginia Dare first child of English parents born in America.

1591 Relief expedition returns to Roanoke colony; all settlers have disappeared without trace.

1602 Capt. Bartholomew Gosnold, first Englishman to set foot in New England, explores Cape Cod and Martha's Vineyard.

1603 Samuel de Champlain of France explores St. Lawrence River; later founds Quebec.

1607 First permanent English settlement in America established at Jamestown, Va. Only 32 of original 105 colonists survive first winter.

1608 Capt. John Smith imprisoned by Indians and saved by Pocahontas, daughter of Chief Powhatan.

1609 Henry Hudson sets out in search of Northwest Passage. Champlain sails into Great Lakes.

1611 Hudson cast adrift by mutinous crewmen to die in bay later named for him.

1612 First Dutch trading post appears on Manhattan Island.

1616 Smallpox epidemic decimates Indian tribes from Maine to Rhode Island.

1619 Dutch traders bring first African slaves to Virginia for sale. Americans hold first election when Virginia planters vote for House of Burgesses.

1620 Pilgrims and others arrive in Plymouth, Mass., aboard *Mayflower.* They draw up Mayflower Compact.

1622 Most of Virginia colony wiped out in Indian attack.

1624 King James I revokes Virginia's charter and makes it royal colony.

1626 Dutch colony of New Amsterdam founded on Manhattan Island, bought from Indian people for about $24.

1630 John Winthrop sets sail for Massachusetts with 900 Puritans and others, beginning Great Migration to New England.

1632 King Charles I of England grants Lord Baltimore charter to establish colony in Maryland.

1634 Massachusetts adopts representative government. Jean Nicolet of France begins trading with Indians in Wisconsin.

1635 Roger Williams, banished from Massachusetts, founds dissident colony of Rhode Island.

1636 New Englanders massacre hundreds of Indians in Pequot War. Harvard College established.

1638 First Swedish colony founded in Delaware.

1639 "Oath of a Free Man" the first English document printed in America. First public school appears in Dorchester, first post office in Boston, and Connecticut writes first colonial constitution.

1644 Indians make last, unsuccessful attempt to expel English settlers from Virginia. First American ship built in Boston.

1647 Margaret Brent of Maryland first American woman to demand right to vote. Massachusetts passes first compulsory education law. First witchcraft execution takes place in Hartford, Conn.

1648 Boston shoemakers and coopers establish first American labor unions.

1651 British Parliament passes first Navigation Act regulating colonial trade.

1652 Rhode Island first colony to outlaw slavery. First American coins minted in Boston.

1654 Jacob Barsimon, first American Jew, arrives in New Amsterdam, followed by 23 more Jews from Brazil.

1655 Dutch colonists capture Swedish colony in Delaware. Lady Deborah Moody of Long Island first American woman to vote.

1656 First Quakers arrive in America; imprisoned in Boston, beaten, and deported.

1659 Massachusetts hangs two Quakers on Boston Common.

1660 British Parliament forbids Americans to export goods to countries other than England. Massachusetts outlaws celebration of Christmas.

1661 Virginia first colony to recognize slavery as legal.

1662 Connecticut granted royal charter. Massachusetts appoints official press censors and institutes "half-way" covenant.

1663 British Parliament requires colonial imports from Europe to pass first through England. King Charles II grants charters to Carolina and Rhode Island.

1664 New Amsterdam captured by Richard Nicolls, who renames it New York. New Jersey established.

1670 Charles Town, later called Charleston, first permanent settlement in Carolina.

1672 British Parliament tightens trade restrictions on colonies and appoints American customs collectors.

1673 French explorers Jacques Marquette and Louis Jolliet paddle down Mississippi River to Arkansas. Regular mail service begins between Boston and New York. Dutch forces recapture New York.

1674 Treaty of Westminster restores New York to England. King Louis XIV of France sends Sieur de La Salle to explore Mississippi River.

1675 Thousands die in King Philip's War between New Englanders and five Indian tribes.

1676 Bacon's Rebellion overthrows government of Virginia and burns down Jamestown.

1680 New Hampshire separated from Massachusetts and made royal colony.

1681 King Charles II names William Penn proprietor of Pennsylvania.

1682 Penn founds Philadelphia. Sieur de La Salle claims North American interior for France, naming it Louisiana.

1683 First German-Americans, a group of Mennonites, arrive in Philadelphia.

1684 King Charles II revokes Massachusetts charter.

1686 King James II appoints Sir Edmund Andros governor-general of Dominion of New England, dissolving colonial governments.

1688 Quakers publish first antislavery tracts in Pennsylvania.

1689 Andros surrenders to Boston mobs, and colonial self-government is reestablished. Jacob Leisler seizes power in New York uprising. King William's War begins in America.

1690 Massachusetts issues first colonial paper money. American campaigns against French Canada fail. French and Indians burn Schenectady, N.Y.

1691 Jacob Leisler surrenders and is hanged. Massachusetts rechartered with religious freedom.

1692 Witchcraft hysteria breaks out in Salem, Mass., leading to 20 executions.

1693 College of William and Mary chartered, the second college in America.

1695 New York City organizes public relief for poor and homeless.

1696 British Parliament places more commercial restrictions on colonies. American merchants join slave trade.

1697 Treaty of Ryswick ends King William's War.

1701 Antoine de la Mothe Cadillac establishes French outpost at Detroit, Mich. Yale College founded. Delaware separated from Pennsylvania.

1702 Queen Anne's War breaks out.

1704 *Boston News-Letter* first regularly published newspaper in America.

1710 German migration to America begins. British and American forces capture Port Royal, Nova Scotia.

1711 Anglo-American attack on Quebec fails. Tuscarora Indian War breaks out in North Carolina.

1712 Militia quell slave rebellion in New York City. Pennsylvania prohibits importing slaves.

1713 Treaty of Utrecht ends Queen Anne's War.

1714 Americans begin drinking tea. *Androborus,* a political satire, first play written in America.

1716 First theater in America built in Williamsburg, Va. Slavery introduced to French Louisiana.

1718 Jean Baptiste Le Moyne founds French city of New Orleans.

1721 Sir Robert Walpole loosens colonial trade restrictions with policy of "salutary neglect."

1722 France declares New Orleans capital of Louisiana.

1723 America's first business corporation chartered in Connecticut.

1724 France expels all Jews from Louisiana.

1728 First American synagogue built in New York City.

1729 North and South Carolina receive royal charters.

1731 Benjamin Franklin founds first American library in Philadelphia.

1732 King George II grants charter to Georgia. Only Catholic church in colonial America opens in Philadelphia. Benjamin Franklin begins publishing *Poor Richard's Almanack.* George Washington born in Virginia.

1733 British Parliament passes Molasses Act, taxing imports from non-British sugar islands.

1734 Beginning of Great Awakening, widespread religious revival.

1735 French begin settling in Illinois.

1737 Boston holds its first public celebration of St. Patrick's Day.

1739 War of Jenkins' Ear begins. South Carolina slaves mount Stono Rebellion. French explorers Pierre and Paul Mallet discover Rocky Mountains.

1741 Danish navigator Vitus Bering, hired by Peter the Great of Russia, explores coast of Alaska. *American Magazine,* the first in colonies, begins publishing in Philadelphia. Slave insurrection panic sweeps New York City.

1742 First sugarcane planted in Louisiana.

1744 King George's War breaks out.

1745 British and Americans capture Ft. Louisbourg on Cape Breton Island. French and Indians raid Maine.

1748 Ft. Louisbourg restored to France by Treaty of Aix-la-Chapelle, ending King George's War.

1751 British Parliament forbids New England colonies to issue paper money.

1752 Benjamin Franklin conducts famous kite experiment. Liberty bell is cracked in Philadelphia.

1753 Gov. Robert Dinwiddie of Virginia sends George Washington into Ohio country to demand withdrawal of French. First steam engine arrives in America.

1754 Washington skirmishes with French patrol, touching off French and Indian War. Franklin presents Albany Plan of Union for colonies.

1755 Quakers withdraw from Pennsylvania assembly rather than vote for military spending. Washington leads retreat from Battle of the Wilderness.

1758 British and American forces lose Battle of Ticonderoga but capture Louisbourg and Ft. Duquesne. New Jersey sets aside first Indian reservation for Onami tribe.

1759 Gen. Wolfe defeats Gen. Montcalm as British capture Quebec. Both generals fall in battle.

1760 After fall of Montreal, all of New France surrenders to Britain. King George III crowned in England.

1762 King Louis XV of France secretly cedes Louisiana to Spain.

1763 Treaty of Paris ends French and Indian War. France cedes Canada to Britain. King George III prohibits Americans to settle in West. Conspiracy of Pontiac threatens frontier.

1764 British Parliament passes Sugar Act and forbids all colonies to issue paper money. French settlers found St. Louis. "Paxton Boys" march on Philadelphia. In Boston James Otis protests, "No taxation without representation."

1765 Parliament passes Stamp Act (tax on newspapers, legal documents, etc.) and Quartering

Act (requiring housing of British soldiers in homes). Sons of Liberty organize resistance and nonimportation throughout colonies. Stamp Act Congress meets in New York.

1766 Parliament repeals Stamp Act but passes Declaratory Act, affirming its right to pass laws binding on colonies. Chief Pontiac makes peace.

1767 Parliament enacts Townshend Duties and suspends New York assembly for resisting Quartering Act.

1768 "Regulators" rebel in North Carolina. Boston riots against Townshend Duties.

1769 Daniel Boone explores Kentucky. Father Junipero Serra founds San Diego, the first Spanish mission in California. Gaspar de Portola sails into San Francisco Bay.

1770 Five Americans perish in Boston Massacre (Mar. 5). British Parliament repeals Townshend Duties, except tax on tea.

1771 North Carolina "Regulators" defeated by militia.

1772 Rhode Island mob burns British revenue ship *Gaspee*. Boston appoints first Committee of Correspondence.

1773 British Parliament passes Tea Act, leading to Boston Tea Party (Dec. 16).

1774 Parliament passes "Intolerable Acts," punishing colonists for Tea Party. Boston is occupied by British forces under Gen. Thomas Gage. First Continental Congress meets in Philadelphia.

1775 American Revolution begins with Battle of Lexington and Concord (Apr. 19). Second Continental Congress appoints George Washington as commander of Continental Army. British win Battle of Bunker Hill. First abolition society organized in Pennsylvania.

1776 Tom Paine's *Common Sense* published. Declaration of Independence signed. Congress adopts name United States of America. British occupy New York City. George Washington crosses Delaware to win Battle of Trenton, N.J.

1777 Americans win battles at Princeton and Saratoga. British occupy Philadelphia. Congress adopts Stars and Stripes flag and endorses Articles of Confederation. Washington's army spends winter at Valley Forge, Pa.

1778 France makes alliance with U.S. and declares war on Britain. When French fleet arrives, British evacuate Philadelphia.

1779 Congress offers to make peace in exchange for independence. British withdraw from New York City.

1780 Pennsylvania first state to abolish slavery. British occupy Charleston, S.C. Washington quells Continental Army mutiny. Benedict Arnold defects to British.

1781 French and American victory at Battle of Yorktown ends American Revolution. Articles of Confederation take effect. Los Angeles founded by Spanish missionaries.

1782 British Parliament votes for peace with U.S. Negotiations in Paris lead to provisional Anglo-American peace treaty. First English Bible printed in America.

1783 Massachusetts, Connecticut, and Rhode Island abolish slavery. Treaty of Paris signed (Sept. 3), officially ending American Revolution. Washington retires to Mount Vernon, Va.

1784 Congress ratifies Treaty of Paris. Spain closes Mississippi River to American trade. First bale of American cotton shipped to Britain.

1785 First state university chartered in Georgia.

1786 Virginia proclaims religious freedom. Shays's Rebellion put down in Massachusetts. Annapolis Convention calls for revising Articles of Confederation. New Jersey abolishes slavery.

1787 Convention in Philadelphia writes Constitution. Congress passes Northwest Ordinance and submits Constitution for states' approval.

1788 Constitution ratified and takes effect.

1789 George Washington wins first presidential elections unopposed. Federal government begins meeting in New York City. Congress enacts first federal tariff.

1790 First antislavery petitions are submitted to Congress. Temporary capital moved to Philadelphia. Pope Pius VI appoints John Carroll first Catholic bishop in U.S. First U.S. census lists population at 3,929,625.

1791 Congress sets up First Bank of the United States and first internal revenue law, a tax on whiskey. Vermont enters Union as 14th state. Bill of Rights takes effect. Pres. Washington selects site of new U.S. capital on Potomac River.

1792 New York stock traders begin meeting under a tree on Wall Street. Pres. Washington unanimously reelected. Construction begins on White House.

1793 Eli Whitney invents cotton gin. Congress passes first Fugitive Slave Act. Pres. Washington holds first official cabinet meeting and lays cornerstone for Capitol. Britain begins confiscating American ships trading with France.

1794 Pres. Washington defeats Whiskey Rebellion in Pennsylvania. U.S. and Britain sign Jay's Treaty. Ohio Indians defeated at Battle of Fallen Timbers.

1795 Georgia stung by scandal of Yazoo land frauds. Senate ratifies Jay's Treaty with Britain.

1796 Pres. Washington delivers "Farewell Address." France begins to confiscate ships trading with Britain.

1797 France insults American diplomats in XYZ affair. Spanish begin building Mission San Juan Capistrano in California.

1798 Congress passes Alien and Sedition Acts. U.S. renounces alliance with France as unofficial naval war breaks out.

1799 Russian-American trading company set up in Alaska. New York abolishes slavery. George Washington dies.

1800 Library of Congress founded. Convention of 1800 signed, ending quasi-war between U.S. and France. Spain secretly cedes Louisiana to France. Congress begins meeting in Washington, D.C.

1801 Election of Thomas Jefferson results in first transfer of executive power between rival parties. Congress takes jurisdiction over District of Columbia. Tripoli pirates declare war on U.S. for not paying tribute.

1802 U.S. Military Academy established at West Point, N.Y.

1803 Louisiana Purchase from France doubles size of U.S. federal outpost founded at Ft. Dearborn, Ill., future site of Chicago.

1804 Lewis and Clark expedition sets out from St. Louis. New Jersey begins gradual emancipation. Alexander Hamilton killed in duel with Aaron Burr.

1805 Barbary War with Tripoli ends.

1806 Congress authorizes construction of Cumberland Road. Noah Webster's first dictionary published. Aaron Burr conspires to create private frontier empire.

1807 Britain and France enact blockades in Europe, confiscating American trading ships. British attack USS *Chesapeake*. Embargo Act forbids all American exports.

1808 Congress declares end to African slave trade.

1809 Embargo Act replaced with Non-Intercourse Act, outlawing exports to Britain and France. Henry Clay of Kentucky enters U.S. Senate. First steamboat sea voyage made from New York City to Philadelphia.

1810 Pres. James Madison annexes West Florida.

1811 Russians settle at Ft. Ross, Calif. First Bank of the United States fails to obtain recharter. Gen. William Henry Harrison defeats Indians at Battle of Tippecanoe. New Madrid earthquakes rock Ohio-Mississippi Valleys.

1812 War of 1812 begins by close vote in Congress. New England resists war. Daniel Webster of Massachusetts elected to Congress. British clamp blockade on U.S. ports, capture Detroit, and repel American attack on Canada at Queenstown.

1813 Americans regain Detroit, attack Toronto and Ft. George in Canada, but surrender to British at Beaver Dams, Ontario. Capt. Oliver H. Perry wins control of Great Lakes. British and Indians burn Buffalo, N.Y.

1814 British destroy Ft. Oswego, N.Y., and set fire to Washington, D.C. Francis Scott Key writes "The Star Spangled Banner." New Englanders opposed to war meet secretly at Hartford Convention. First textile mill established at Waltham, Mass. Treaty of Ghent ends War of 1812.

1815 Gen. Andrew Jackson routs British at Battle of New Orleans, before news arrives that War of 1812 is over.

1816 Congress charters Second Bank of the United States.

1817 Rush-Bagot Treaty between Britain and U.S. demilitarizes Great Lakes. Harvard Law School founded. New York Stock and Exchange Board organized. Work begins on Erie Canal. Indian attack touches off first Seminole War in Florida.

1818 Cumberland Road opened. Congress adopts present format for American flag. Canadian boundary dispute with Britain settled.

1819 Panic of 1819 plunges South and West into depression. U.S. obtains Florida from Spain in Adams-Onís Treaty, settling border of Louisiana. *Savannah* makes first successful transatlantic crossing under steam power.

1820 Missouri Compromise solves crisis over admission of Missouri as slave state. Abolitionists begin colonizing freed slaves in Africa.

1821 First Catholic cathedral in U.S. built in Baltimore.

1822 Denmark Vesey and 36 others executed for organizing rebel slave conspiracy in Charleston, S.C.

1823 Monroe Doctrine, masterminded by Sec. of State John Quincy Adams, announced by Pres. James Monroe.

1824 Russia and U.S. sign treaty settling territorial disputes in Pacific Northwest. First presidential nominating convention held in Utica, N.Y.

1825 John Quincy Adams chosen president in infamous "Corrupt Bargain" with Henry Clay, who becomes secretary of state. Erie Canal opened. Mexico invites Americans to settle in Texas.

1826 Anti-Mason party organized. John Adams and Thomas Jefferson die on 50th anniversary of Declaration of Independence. Jedediah Smith leads first overland expedition to California.

1827 Joseph Smith has visions of Book of Mormon. U.S. and Britain agree to joint occupation of Pacific Northwest.

1828 Congress passes protectionist "Tariff of Abominations" over southern protests.

1829 Mexico refuses Pres. Andrew Jackson's offer to buy Texas.

1830 Webster-Hayne Debate in U.S. Senate reveals sectional tension. Church of Latter-day Saints (the Mormons) founded by Joseph Smith in Fayette, N.Y. Mexico forbids further American immigration to Texas.

1831 Nat Turner leads bloodiest of all slave rebellions, killing 57 whites in Virginia.

1832 Black Hawk War fought in Illinois and Wisconsin. First nationwide Democratic party convention held in Baltimore. Pres. Jackson vetoes bill to recharter national bank. South Carolina nullifies "Tariff of Abominations."

1833 Massachusetts last state to end tax support for churches. Congress lowers tariff and passes "Force Bill" to pressure South Carolina, which rescinds nullification. American Anti-Slavery Society organized. Oberlin College becomes first coeducational college.

1834 Whig party organized by Senators Henry Clay and Daniel Webster in opposition to Pres. Jackson. Antiabolitionist riots break out in New York and Philadelphia.

1835 Samuel Morse invents telegraph. National debt completely paid off. Pres. Jackson survives first attempt to assassinate a president. Second Seminole War begins in Florida.

1836 Samuel Colt invents revolver. Texas declares independence from Mexico and requests U.S. annexation. Mexican army captures Alamo, but Texans are victorious at San Jacinto.

1837 Panic of 1837 begins lengthy economic depression.

1838 Joshua Giddings of Ohio is first abolitionist elected to Congress. Transatlantic steamship service established. Congress blocks abolitionist petitions with "Gag Rule."

1839 Abner Doubleday of Cooperstown, N.Y., codifies rules of baseball. Congress outlaws dueling in Washington, D.C.

1840 "Log Cabin Campaign" between William Henry Harrison and Martin Van Buren begins era of mass political participation. Liberty party founded by abolitionists in Albany, N.Y.

1841 First emigrant train of 48 covered wagons arrives in California. Pres. William Henry Harrison dies after month in office. First Japanese immigrant arrives in New Bedford, Mass.

1842 Webster-Ashburton Treaty settles Canada boundary disputes between U.S. and Britain. U.S. accidentally seizes California, then returns it with apology to Mexico.

1843 End of Second Seminole War. B'Nai B'rith founded in New York. Mormons begin practicing polygamy.

1844 Baptist is first church to split North and South over slavery. Samuel Morse sends first telegraph message. James K. Polk, first dark horse candidate, elected president.

1845 Potato Famine begins massive Irish immigration. U.S. annexes Texas over Mexican protests. U.S. Naval Academy opens at Annapolis, Md.

1846 Mexican War begins when U.S. troops are attacked in disputed Texas territory. American settlers in California stage Bear Flag Revolt. Oregon Treaty gives U.S. sole possession of Pacific Northwest up to 49th parallel. First recorded baseball game played in Hoboken, N.J.

1847 Wilmot Proviso, forbidding slavery expansion, passes House and sets off wave of panic in South. Gen. Winfield Scott conquers Mexico City. Brigham Young leads Mormons to Utah. Abraham Lincoln of Illinois arrives in Congress.

1848 Treaty of Guadalupe-Hidalgo ends Mexican War, ceding Southwest to U.S. Revolution of 1848 begins wave of German immigration. New York–Chicago telegraph line completed. Chicago Board of Trade established. Free Soil party organized. Gold discovered in California. First Chinese immigrants arrive in San Francisco. Lucretia Mott and Elizabeth Cady Stanton hold first Women's Rights Convention in Seneca Falls, N.Y.

1849 Gold Rush brings hundreds of thousands to California. Over 20 killed in New York City riot between fans of rival actors. Elizabeth Blackwell first American woman to receive medical degree.

1850 Sen. Henry Clay's Compromise of 1850 solves crisis over slavery expansion. Clayton-Bulwer Treaty pledges Anglo-American cooperation in building any Central American canal. John C. Calhoun of South Carolina delivers last address to Senate.

1851 Young Men's Christian Association (YMCA) established. Northern mobs resist Fugitive Slave Act. Maine is first state to pass prohibition laws. Hungarian patriot Louis Kossuth draws huge crowds touring country. *New York Times* founded. Herman Melville's *Moby-Dick* published.

1852 Harriet Beecher Stowe's *Uncle Tom's Cabin* published.

1853 U.S. buys Gila River Valley from Mexico in Gadsden Purchase. American, or "Know-Nothing," party founded. Commodore Matthew C. Perry opens trade with Japan.

1854 Congress passes Kansas-Nebraska Act, setting off mass protests across North. Republican party founded. U.S. threatens to seize Cuba from Spain in Ostend Manifesto.

1855 "Bleeding Kansas" fighting begins as proslavery and antislavery settlers hold rival state conventions. First railroad train crosses Mississippi River at Rock Island, Ill., into Davenport, Iowa.

1856 Congressman Preston Brooks of South Carolina beats Sen. Charles Sumner of Massachusetts unconscious on Senate floor for insulting a southern senator. John Brown leads Pottawatomie massacre in Kansas. First Republican national convention nominates John C. Frémont for president in Pittsburgh, Pa.

1857 New York–St. Louis railroad completed. Supreme Court hands down controversial *Dred Scott* decision protecting slavery. Panic of 1857 sends North into depression.

1858 Lincoln-Douglas debates dramatize issue of slavery expansion in Illinois race for Senate. First transatlantic telegraph cable laid.

1859 John Brown's raid on Harper's Ferry arsenal to launch abolitionist war against slavery ends in his capture and execution. Slave insurrection panic sweeps South. Comstock Lode discovered in Nevada. First producing oil well in U.S. flows in Titusville, Pa.

1860 Democratic party splits into northern and southern wings. South Carolina is first southern state to secede from Union after victory of Abraham Lincoln. Crittenden Compromise fails to preserve Union. Pony Express begins mail delivery between California and Missouri.

1861 Civil War begins with attack on Ft. Sumter in South Carolina (Apr. 12). Pres. Abraham Lincoln calls for 75,000 volunteers to put down rebellion. Jefferson Davis of Mississippi elected president of Confederate States of America. New York–San Francisco telegraph link completed. Yale awards first American Ph.D. Congress enacts first federal income tax.

1862 Congress issues "greenbacks," subsidizes transcontinental railroad, abolishes slavery in District of Columbia, and passes Homestead Act. Pres. Lincoln issues Emancipation Proclamation after Battle of Antietam, bloodiest fight of Civil War.

1863 Emancipation Proclamation takes effect (Jan. 1). Union victories at Vicksburg, Miss., and Gettysburg, Pa., signal turning point of Civil War. West Virginia secedes from Virginia and rejoins Union. Hundreds killed in New York City draft riot. Pres. Lincoln proclaims Thanksgiving national holiday.

1864 Pres. Lincoln names Gen. Ulysses S. Grant as commander of Union armies. Gen. William T. Sherman destroys Atlanta and conducts "March to the Sea." Confederate army of Gen. Robert E. Lee crippled in Wilderness Campaign. Cheyenne and Arapaho slaughtered in Sand Creek Massacre in Colorado.

1865 Gen. Lee surrenders to Gen. Grant at Appomattox Court House, Virginia (Apr. 9). Pres. Lincoln assassinated by John Wilkes Booth in Washington, D.C. (Apr. 14). Confederacy dissolved, ending Civil War. Pres. Andrew Johnson proclaims amnesty for most rebels. Slavery outlawed by adoption of 13th Amendment. Ku Klux Klan founded in Pulaski, Tenn.

1866 In the struggle over Reconstruction policy, Congress overrides Pres. Johnson's vetoes of Civil Rights Act and New Freedmen's Bureau Bill. Whites riot in New Orleans to protest black suffrage. Grand Army of the Republic organized by Union veterans. Young Women's Christian Association (YWCA) founded in Boston.

1867 Congress takes control of Reconstruction in South by passing First Reconstruction Act over Pres. Johnson's veto and Tenure of Office Act. U.S. purchases Alaska from Russia for $7.2 million (2 cents an acre). Farmers organize Patrons of Husbandry, beginning Granger movement. Cigarettes appear on American market. First elevated trains begin running in New York City.

1868 For violating Tenure of Office Act of 1867, Pres. Johnson is impeached in the House (Feb. 24), but acquitted in the Senate by a single vote (May 16). U.S. and China sign Burlingame Treaty to allow immigration. Fourteenth Amendment grants equal citizenship and protection to freedmen (July 28). Half a million black votes help elect Gen. Ulysses S. Grant to presidency. Typewriter invented. University of California chartered.

1869 "Hard Money" prevails when Congress passes Public Credit Act, promising repayment of government debts in gold. Transcontinental railroad completed when Union Pacific and Central Pacific lines meet at Promontory Point, Utah (May 10). Jay Gould and James Fisk cause financial panic by trying to corner gold market on "Black Friday" (Sept. 24). Knights of Labor national union organized. National Women's Suffrage Association formed in New York. Wyoming Territory grants first U.S. women's suffrage.

1870 Fifteenth Amendment guarantees right to vote for all U.S. citizens, though only Wyoming and Utah Territories allow women's suffrage (Mar. 30). Congress passes first Ku Klux Klan Act to enforce 15th Amendment. First black senator and black congressman elected. Yale and Harvard initiate first gruadate studies programs in U.S. All states represented in Congress for the first time since 1860.

1871 Congress passes second Ku Klux Klan Act to enforce 14th Amendment in South. U.S. and Britain resolve Civil War disputes with Treaty of Washington. Tammany Hall ring overthrown in New York City when *New York Times* begins publishing exposé of William Marcy "Boss" Tweed. Most of Chicago destroyed in Great Fire (Oct. 8–11). Anti-Chinese race riots in Los Angeles. Illinois enacts first railroad regulations.

1872 Liberal Republicans bolt from Pres. Grant and nominate newspaperman Horace Greeley for president. Crédit Mobilier scandal implicates Vice Pres. Schuyler Colfax and embarrasses Grant administration. Yellowstone National Park created. Susan B. Anthony arrested for leading suffragists to the polls. Jehovah's Witnesses, originally called Russellites, founded by Charles Taze Russell. Montgomery Ward opens for business in Chicago.

1873 Silver withdrawn from money supply in "Crime of '73." Congressmen raise their own salaries 50 percent, retroactive for two years, and double president's pay in "Salary Grab" Act. Panic of 1873, triggered by failure of Jay Cooke's banking house, begins depression of 1870s. New York Stock Exchange forced to close for 10 days. Great Bonanza silver lode discovered in Nevada. San Francisco installs first cable cars.

1874 Granger movement begins passing railroad regulations in midwestern states. Women's Christian Temperance Union founded in Cleveland, Ohio. Young Men's Hebrew Association organized in New York. Democrats recapture Congress for first time since Civil War. Greenback party formed in Indianapolis, Ind. Black rioters attack courthouse in Vicksburg, Miss. Chautauqua movement begins bringing educational speakers to rural communities across the country.

1875 Congress passes Specie Resumption Act to reduce money supply by redeeming greenbacks for gold, and Civil Rights Act to guarantee equal rights for freedmen. Whiskey Ring scandal casts further pall on Grant administration. Archbishop John McCloskey of New York first American bishop. Aristides wins first Kentucky Derby at Churchill Downs, Ky.

1876 U.S. awards patent to Alexander Graham Bell for telephone. Gen. George A. Custer and 265 men massacred by Sioux Indians at Little Big Horn, Mont. (June 25). Centennial of U.S. celebrated. Democrat Samuel Tilden outpolls Republican candidate Rutherford B. Hayes as presidential election is thrown into the House (Nov. 7). Professional baseball's National League established. Kappa Alpha opens first college fraternity house at Williams College. Central Park in New York completed.

1877 Congress appoints Electoral Commission to solve impasse over disputed 1876 election (Jan. 29). House votes 185 to 184 to declare Rutherford B. Hayes president-elect, three days before his inauguration (Mar. 2). Reconstruction officially ends with withdrawal of federal troops from South (Apr. 24). Pres. Hayes sends in troops as Great Railroad Strike paralyzes much of nation (July 17). Anti-Chinese riots break out in San Francisco. Colorado silver rush begins.

1878 Sen. A.A. Sargent introduces Women's Suffrage Amendment in Congress (Jan. 10). Greenback-Labor party formed in Toledo, Ohio. coinage of silver resumes with Bland-Allison Act. Democrats win control of both houses of Congress for first time since 1858. American Bar Association organized in Saratoga, N.Y. Edison Electric begins operating in New York City. New Haven, Conn., sets up first commercial telephone network.

1879 U.S. resumes specie payments for greenbacks. Pres. Hayes battles with Congress over use of federal troops in elections. F.W. Woolworth opens his first store in Utica, N.Y. First Church of Christ, Scientist, founded in Boston. Thomas Edison invents light bulb. California adopts state constitution forbidding employment of Chinese labor. Henry George's radical social critique, *Progress and Poverty,* becomes national best-seller.

1880 Pres. Hayes declares U.S. must control any Isthmian canal. Former president Grant fails in attempt to regain Republican nomination. U.S. and China agree to Chinese Exclusion Treaty (Nov. 17). National Farmers' Alliance organized in Chicago. American branch of Salvation Army founded in Philadelphia, Pa. Census lists U.S. population over 50 million for first time (50,155,783).

1881 Pres. James Garfield assassinated by Charles Guiteau in Washington, D.C. (July 2; dies Sept. 19). Chester A. Arthur becomes president (Sept. 20). Clara Barton creates American Red Cross. Booker T. Washington founds Tuskegee Institute for black education in Alabama. First summer camp for children opens in Squam Lake, N.H. Russian Jews begin immigrating to U.S. to escape pogroms.

1882 John D. Rockefeller organizes Standard Oil trust, first such combination. Congress passes first Chinese Exclusion Act (May 10), which would be renewed for decades, and legislates first immigration restrictions: no paupers, convicts, or mental defectives (Aug. 3). Polygamists forbidden to vote or hold office. Knights of Columbus founded with permission from Roman Catholic church.

1883 Congress passes Pendleton Act, requiring civil service competition for federal jobs. Brooklyn Bridge opened in New York. Supreme Court strikes down Civil Rights Act of 1875 (Oct. 15). New York–Chicago telephone service begins. Ohio River floods devastate Cincinnati. U.S. Navy builds its first steel ships. Railroads agree on standard time zones for North America.

1884 "Mugwumps" bolt Republican party. Statue of Liberty cornerstone laid (Aug. 5). Belva A. Lockwood of Equal Rights party first woman candidate for president. Grover Cleveland of New York first Democrat elected president since Civil War. Home Insurance building of Chicago first skyscraper in world. Moses Fleetwood Walker first black professional baseball player.

1885 Washington Monument completed after 36 years of construction. U.S. Post Office begins Special Delivery service. U.S. Marines land in Panama (Apr. 24). Senate refuses to ratify treaty for building canal across Nicaragua. Congress outlaws building fences on public lands in West. Stanford University founded in Palo Alto, Calif. Josiah Strong's best-seller *Our Country* argues for American imperialism.

1886 Knights of Labor rail strike sets off national wave of strikes for eight-hour day. Haymarket Riot in Chicago leads to execution of seven anarchists. Pres. Cleveland has first White House wedding (June 2). Statue of Liberty in New York Harbor dedicated (Oct. 28). American Federation of Labor (AFL) founded in Columbus, Ohio. Indian wars end with capture of Geronimo. U.S. Treasury begins accumulating large revenue surplus.

1887 Congress creates Interstate Commerce Commission, the first federal regulatory agency, but with weak enforcement powers. Pres. Cleveland orders Confederate battle flags returned to South, provoking outcry (June 7). Congress distributes reservation land to Indians; also bans opium imports. First electric trolley line built in Richmond, Va. U.S. Navy leases base at Pearl Harbor, Hawaii. First American golf club founded in Foxburg, Pa.

1888 Snow falls for 36 hours in New York, killing 400 people in Great Blizzard of '88 (Mar. 12). First secret-ballot election held in Louisville, Ky. George Eastman brings first Kodak camera onto market. National Geographic Society founded in Washington, D.C. Edward Bellamy's utopian novel, *Looking Backward*, becomes sensational best-seller.

1889 Four new states—N.Dak., S.Dak., Mont., Wash.—all admitted in one day (Feb. 22). Oklahoma Land Rush results when former Indian territory opened for settlement (Apr. 22). Johnstown flood claims thousands of lives in Pennsylvania (May 31). Kansas passes first antitrust law. Jane Addams founds Hull House in Chicago. First all-American college football players chosen. Tower Building, the first New York skyscraper, completed.

1890 Congress passes Sherman Antitrust Act (July 2) and Sherman Silver Purchase Act. Wyoming admitted as first state with women's suffrage (July 10). Sioux uprising ends at Battle of Wounded Knee (Dec. 29). Yosemite National Park created. Mormons renounce polygamy. Mississippi leads South in disfranchising black voters. Jacob Riis's *How the Other Half Lives* awakens Americans to problem of urban poverty. First Army-Navy football game played—Navy 24, Army 0.

1891 Pres. Grover Cleveland denounces "dangerous and reckless experiment" of silver coinage. New Orleans mob lynches 11 Italian immigrants. People's, or Populist, party organized in Cincinnati. U.S. and Chile nearly go to war over death of two American sailors in Valparaíso (Oct. 16). Dr. James A. Naismith invents basketball in Springfield, Mass. Thomas Edison patents first American-made motion picture camera.

1892 Immigrants begin landing at Ellis Island in New York (Jan. 1). Populist candidate James B. Weaver of Iowa receives over million votes for president. Violent strikes break out among steelworkers in Homestead, Pa., and among silver miners in Coeur d'Alene, Idaho. Chinese immigrants forced to register with federal government. George W.G. Ferris invents Ferris Wheel. First gasoline-powered American automobile built in Chicopee, Mass. Boll weevil first appears in Texas.

1893 U.S. gold reserve falls below $100 million (Apr. 21). Panic of 1893, touched off by New York stock market crash (June 27), begins second-worst depression in U.S. history. Congress repeals Sherman Silver Purchase Act (Oct. 30). Hawaii requests U.S. annexation. Mormon Temple dedicated in Salt Lake City, Utah. Thousands perish in Louisiana cyclone. Frank Lloyd Wright completes first solo project, the Winslow home in Chicago.

1894 Coxey's Army of unemployed march on Washington, D.C. (Apr. 30). U.S. Treasury issues two $50 million bond offerings to shore up dwindling gold reserves. Congress enacts first peacetime federal income tax, denounced as "socialism, communism, devilism" (Aug. 27). Pullman strike paralyzes railroads across nation. Senate refuses to annex Hawaii. Thomas Edison exhibits his kinetoscope.

1895 Billionaire banker J.P. Morgan bails out U.S. Treasury, faced with gold drain. "Silver Democrats" appeal for unlimited silver coinage as way out of depression. Supreme Court rules income tax unconstitutional (May 20). Venezuelan boundary dispute brings U.S. and Britain close to war. Cuban insurrection against Spanish rule begins, winning American sympathy. National Association of Manufacturers formed in Cincinnati. First professional football game played in Latrobe, Pa.

1896 Supreme Court approves segregation *(Plessy* v. *Ferguson).* William Jennings Bryan, "Silver Democrat" of Nebraska, wins nomination with "Cross of Gold" speech (July 7). Gold discovered in Klondike, Alaska, defusing money question (Aug. 16). American athletes sweep nine of 12 events at first International Olympics. Henry Ford builds his first automobile. First American motion pictures appear in theaters. "The Yellow Kid," first comic strip, begins running in New York *World*. First American hockey league organized in New York.

1897 U.S. and Britain consent to arbitration of boundary disputes in Olney-Paunceforte Convention (Jan. 11). Venezuelan boundary dispute ends with Britain accepting arbitration. Klondike gold rush to Alaska moves into full swing. Senate again refuses to annex Hawaii. U.S. offers to mediate Cuban rebellion; lodges official complaint against Spanish brutality. "Yellow press" newspapers keep up constant assault on Spain. First American subway completed in Boston.

1898 After mysterious explosion of battleship *Maine* in Havana harbor (Feb. 15), Spanish-American War breaks out (Apr. 21). Commodore George Dewey destroys Spanish fleet at Manila Bay (May 1), and U.S. takes Manila (Aug. 13). After Battle of San Juan Hill (July 1), Spanish garrison at Santiago, Cuba, surrenders (July 17). U.S. takes Cuba, Puerto Rico, Guam, Wake Island, and Philippines from Spain in Treaty of Paris (Dec. 10). Senate finally agrees to annex Hawaii.

1899 Philippine Revolt against U.S. rule erupts. Sec. of State John Hay issues Open Door notes to European powers and Japan, requesting no spheres of influence in China (Sept. 6). U.S. and Germany agree to partition Samoan Islands (Dec. 2). Congress investigates incompetence in War Department, revealed during Spanish-American War. William McKinley first president to ride in an automobile.

1900 "Hard Money" triumphs as U.S. returns to single gold standard (Mar. 14). Puerto Rico and Hawaii become U.S. territories by acts of Congress (Apr. 12 and 30). U.S. troops relieve foreign legations under siege in Peking, China, during Boxer Rebellion (Aug. 14). Olds Co. opens first Detroit, Mich., auto factory. Carrie Nation leads hatchet-wielding women into Kansas saloons to smash liquor barrels. Professional baseball's American League organized. Census lists U.S. population above 75 million for first time (75,994,575).

1901 J.P. Morgan creates U.S. Steel, first billion-dollar corporation. U.S. retains control over Cuba with Platt Amendment. Pres. McKinley shot by anarchist Leon Czolgosz in Buffalo, N.Y. (Sept. 6; dies Sept. 14). Hay-Paunceforte Treaty secures British approval for U.S.-built canal in Panama (Nov. 18). First great Texas oil strike made near Beaumont, Tex. Army War College opens in Washington, D.C. Pres. Theodore Roosevelt promises to "speak softly and carry a big stick."

1902 End of Philippine Insurrection. Reclamation Act initiates federal policy of conservation of natural resources (June 17). Congress declares Philippines an unorganized territory and its inhabitants non-U.S. citizens (July 1). Pres. Roosevelt escapes injury in trolley car accident near Pittsfield, Mass. First Tournament of Roses football game (later known as Rose Bowl) played—Michigan 49, Stanford 0. Pres. Roosevelt helps mediate Pennsylvania coal strike.

1903 U.S. prevails over Canada in Alaskan boundary dispute. Pres. Roosevelt helps Panama gain independence from Colombia, then negotiates treaty to build Panama Canal (Nov. 2–18). Orville and Wilbur Wright conduct first powered flight near Kitty Hawk, N.C. (Dec. 17). *The Great Train Robbery,* first feature-length motion picture, appears in theaters. Wisconsin holds first primary elections. Ford Motor Co. formed. Boston defeats Pittsburgh in first baseball World Series.

1904 Supreme Court upholds antitrust dissolution of Northern Securities company (Mar. 14). Pres. Roosevelt wins reelection and says he will not run again (Nov. 8). "Roosevelt Corollary" to Monroe Doctrine justifies U.S. intervention to keep other powers out of western hemisphere (Dec. 6). First New York City subway opened. New York State enacts first speed limit: 20 mph on open roads. Publication of Lincoln Steffens's *The Shame of the Cities,* well-known muckraking book. Deaf, dumb, and blind, Helen Keller graduates with honors from Radcliffe College.

1905 Supreme Court disallows limits on length of working day. Industrial Workers of the World, a radical labor union, formed in Chicago. Pres. Roosevelt mediates Treaty of Portsmouth, ending Russo-Japanese War (Sept. 5). U.S. takes control of Santo Domingo trade. Black leaders hold Niagara Falls Conference, calling for equal rights. Winslow's Soothing Syrup for babies found to contain morphine and poison.

1906 San Francisco destroyed by earthquake and fire (Apr. 18–19). Responding to consumer pressure, Congress passes Pure Food and Drug Act and Meat Inspection Act (June 30). Race riot breaks out in Atlanta (Sept. 22). Japan protests segregation of Asian students in California schools (Oct. 25). Pres. Roosevelt first American to win Nobel Peace Prize and first sitting president to leave U.S. on visit to Panama.

1907 Panic of 1907 triggers crash on Wall Street (Mar. 13) and run on banks across nation. Pres. Roosevelt orders exclusion of Japanese laborers (Mar. 14). U.S. Navy's Great White Fleet embarks on tour around world (Dec. 16). Congress outlaws corporate contributions to political campaigns. Hundreds killed in coal mine explosions in Monongah, W.Va., and Jacobs Creek, Pa. All-time-record 1,285,349 immigrants arrive in one year.

1908 U.S. and Japan conclude "Gentleman's Agreement" limiting immigration. Ford Model T appears on market (Oct. 1). Root-Takahira Agreement promises U.S. and Japan will respect each other's interests in Pacific. Pres. Roosevelt appoints National Conservation Commission. Federal Bureau of Investigation established. New York City outlaws women smoking in public. Lt. Thomas W. Selfridge, U.S. Army, first American air crash fatality. Gideons place their first Bible in hotel in Iron Mountain, Mont.

1909 Expedition team led by Robert E. Peary plants American flag at North Pole (Apr. 6). Pres. William Howard Taft opens 700,000 acres for settlement in West. W.E.B. DuBois founds National Association for the Advancement of Colored People (NAACP), advocating racial equality. U.S. Mint issues first Lincoln-head pennies. U.S. troops land in Nicaragua.

1910 Theodore Roosevelt calls for "New Nationalism" in speech at Osawatomie, Kans. (Aug. 31). *Los Angeles Times* building destroyed by terrorist bomb (Oct. 1). Glacier National Park created. Mann Act cracks down on "white slave" trade. Milwaukee, Wis., elects socialist mayor and congressman. Boy Scouts of America chartered. Ballinger-Pinchot controversy reveals major differences over conservation policy in Taft administration. Barney Oldfield sets land speed record (133 mph) in Daytona Beach, Fla.

1911 Sen. Robert M. LaFollette of Wisconsin founds National Progressive Republican League to promote reform (Jan. 21). Pres. Taft orders U.S. troops to border during Mexican Revolution. Supreme Court upholds antitrust breakups of Standard Oil (May 15) and American Tobacco (May 29). Calbraith P. Rodgers makes first transcontinental airplane flight. U.S. bankers take control of Nicaragua's finances. Steel magnate Andrew Carnegie donates $125 million for philanthropic purposes.

1912 *Titanic* sinks on maiden voyage from England (Apr. 15). Congress approves free-trade tariff reciprocity with Canada (July 22), rejected by Canadian Parliament (Sept. 21). Progressive, or "Bull Moose," party founded by Theodore Roosevelt, who survives assassination attempt by John Schrank in Milwaukee, Wis. (Oct. 14). Massachusetts adopts first minimum wage law. U.S. Marines land in Honduras, Cuba, Nicaragua, and Santo Domingo. Textile strike in Lawrence, Mass.

1913 Sixteenth Amendment empowers federal government to collect income taxes (Feb. 25), and 17th Amendment allows for popular election of U.S. senators (May 31). Congress creates Federal Reserve system. Ford Motor Co. introduces assembly line. John D. Rockefeller donates $100 million to philanthropic Rockefeller Foundation. Civil War veterans hold 50th anniversary reunion at Gettysburg. Grand Central Station opens in New York City.

1914 Pres. Woodrow Wilson nearly goes to war with Mexico over arrests of American sailors in Tampico (Apr. 14). U.S. Navy shells Vera Cruz and lands marines in retaliation (Apr. 21). U.S. declares neutrality in World War I (Aug. 4). Congress passes Clayton Act, toughening antitrust standards. Yale Bowl, the first full-size football stadium, opened in New Haven, Conn. Congress proclaims Mother's Day.

1915 *Birth of a Nation* first movie blockbuster. Panama-Pacific International Exposition opens in miraculously rebuilt San Francisco. Pres. Wilson strongly protests German sinking of *Lusitania* with 128 Americans aboard (May 7). U.S. Marines land in Haiti (July 28). J.P. Morgan arranges $500 million war loan to France and Britain. Ku Klux Klan revived in Atlanta, Ga. Coast-to-coast long-distance telephone service begins.

1916 House-Grey Memorandum warns Germany that refusal to negotiate may bring U.S. into World War I. Gen. John Pershing chases Pancho Villa into Mexico after border raid on Columbus, N.Mex. (Mar. 15). Britain blacklists U.S. firms doing business with Germany. U.S. acquires Virgin Islands from Denmark for $25 million (Aug. 4). Pres. Wilson wins reelection with slogan "He Kept Us Out of the War" (Nov. 7). Jeanette Rankin of Montana first woman elected to Congress. Louis D. Brandeis first Jewish member of Supreme Court. Margaret Sanger opens first birth-control clinic in Brooklyn, N.Y. National Park Service created.

1917 Germany resumes unrestricted submarine warfare, leading U.S. to sever diplomatic relations (Feb. 3). Gen. John Pershing withdraws from Mexico. Zimmerman Telegram, intercepted by British intelligence and made public, reveals German overtures to Mexico in case of war (Feb. 24). U.S. merchant ships armed for self-defense against German submarines (Mar. 13). After Pres. Wilson proclaims "world must be made safe for democracy," Congress declares war on Germany (Apr. 6) and Austria-Hungary (Dec. 7), bringing U.S. into World War I. Prohibition begins as wartime conservation measure (Aug. 10). Race riot breaks out in East St. Louis, Mo. American soldiers begin fighting in Europe.

1918 Pres. Wilson announces U.S. war aims in "Fourteen Points" speech (Jan. 8). U.S. troops join Allied intervention in Russian Revolution (Aug. 2). Congress passes Sedition Act. Over million U.S. troops participate in month-long Meuse-Argonne campaign (Sept. 26–Nov. 11). Republicans win control of Congress, a rebuke to Pres. Wilson (Nov. 5). Armistice Day ends World War I (Nov. 11); mass celebrations break out across country. Pres. Wilson goes to Europe for peace conference (Dec. 4). Supreme Court approves draft laws and strikes down child labor laws. Influenza epidemic takes hundreds of thousands of American lives.

1919 Eighteenth Amendment establishes Prohibition (Jan. 29). Strike wave sweeps country, triggering Red Scare. American Communist party organized in Chicago. Race riots in Washington, D.C., and Chicago (July 19 and 27). Pres. Wilson suffers incapacitating stroke during nationwide speaking tour (Sept. 26). Volstead Act implements national Prohibition enforcement. Versailles Treaty, including League of Nations, rejected by Senate (Nov. 19). Grand Canyon National Park created. New York–Chicago daily airmail service begins.

1920 Atty. Gen. A. Mitchell Palmer stages "Palmer Raids," arresting and deporting thousands of radicals and immigrants. Sacco and Vanzetti arrested for murder in Braintree, Mass. (May 5). Supreme Court upholds Prohibition. Nineteenth Amendment establishes women's suffrage (Aug. 26). National League of Women Voters organized. Wall Street rocked by terrorist bomb, killing 30 bystanders (Sept. 16). First regular radio broadcasts begin in East Pittsburgh, Pa. Pres. Wilson receives Nobel Peace Prize. U.S. population, more urban than rural for first time, tops 100 million (105,710,620).

1921 Pres. Warren G. Harding, promising "return to normalcy," takes office. U.S. agrees to compensate Colombia for supporting Panama revolution and seizing Panama Canal. Former president William Howard Taft receives job he wants most, chief justice of U.S. (June 30). U.S. negotiates separate peace with Germany, Austria, and Hungary. Ku Klux Klan spreads terror in South. International disarmament conference meets in Washington, D.C. Jack Dempsey defeats Georges Carpentier in first million-dollar prizefight.

1922 Washington Conference concludes with nine international treaties to limit naval arms race, relax tensions in Pacific, and protect China. Supreme Court upholds women's suffrage. Lincoln Memorial dedicated in Washington, D.C. (May 30). Pres. Harding vetoes "Bonus Bill" for World War I veterans. Congress passes joint resolution in favor of Jewish homeland in Palestine (Sept. 21). Narcotics Control Board established. First commercial radio show broadcast in New York.

1923 Last U.S. occupation troops leave Germany (Jan. 10). Senate begins investigating corruption in Veterans Bureau and Teapot Dome oil leases (Oct. 25). Pres. Harding dies mysteriously of "apoplexy" in San Francisco (Aug. 2). Pres. Calvin Coolidge's address to Congress, calling for economy in government, first radio broadcast of a presidential speech (Dec. 6). Oklahoma declares martial law to crack down on Ku Klux Klan. Yankee Stadium opens in New York.

1924 Congress provides bonuses for World War I veterans over Pres. Coolidge's veto. Congress passes Immigration Act, imposing strict national quota system. European powers accept Dawes Plan for repayment of war debts and reparations. U.S. Marines withdraw from Santo Domingo. Coast-to-coast airmail service begins. Tornadoes wreak havoc in Midwest. Ford Motor Co. turns out its 10-millionth automobile.

1925 Tennessee outlaws teaching evolution in school, leading to Scopes Trial in Dayton, Tenn. (July 10–21). Ku Klux Klan marches on Washington, D.C. (Aug. 8). Nellie Tayloe Ross of Wyoming first woman governor. Florida land boom draws hordes of speculators. Col. Billy Mitchell suspended from U.S. Army for advocating stronger air force. Chicago gang wars break out as Al Capone consolidates bootlegging operations.

1926 Sec. of Treasury Andrew Mellon's drastic tax cuts approved. Adm. Richard E. Byrd and Floyd Bennett first to fly over North Pole (May 9). Henry Ford institutes eight-hour day and five-day workweek at Ford Motor Co. factories (Sept. 25). Hurricane sweeps Florida, killing 372 people. Book of the Month Club founded. California evangelist Aimee Semple MacPherson fakes her own kidnapping to draw publicity. U.S. Marines return to Nicaragua.

1927 Charles Lindbergh completes nonstop solo flight from New York to Paris (May 20–21); returns home to huge welcoming crowds. Sacco and Vanzetti executed in Massachusetts, despite international protests (Aug. 23). *The Jazz Singer* with Al Jolson becomes first "talkie" motion picture (Oct. 6). Holland Tunnel in New York opened. Mississippi River floods, causes $300 million damage. Ford Model A unveiled. Mechanical cotton picker invented. New York–London commercial telephone service begins.

1928 U.S. joins 14 countries in signing Pact of Paris (aka Kellogg-Briand) for "outlawry of war" (Aug. 27). Clark Memorandum disavows future U.S. interventions in Latin America. Pres. Coolidge refuses to aid American farmers mired in agricultural depression. Walt Disney creates "Steamboat Willie," first Mickey Mouse cartoon. George Eastman demonstrates color motion-picture technology. Republicans promise a "chicken in every pot, a car in every garage."

1929 St. Valentine's Day Massacre claims six lives in Chicago gang wars. Young Plan replaces Dawes Plan for payment of war debts and reparations. Ramsay MacDonald first prime minister of Great Britain to address Congress (Oct. 7). Albert B. Fall, former secretary of interior, found guilty in Teapot Dome scandal (Oct. 25). Stock market crash on "Black Tuesday" (Oct. 29) ushers in Great Depression. Supreme Court upholds "pocket veto." Pres. Hoover insists business confidence is intact.

1930 Wave of bank failures sweeps U.S., wiping out millions of savings accounts and leading to private hoarding of gold. Chicago bootlegging outfit worth $50 million broken up. U.S., Britain, and Japan sign London Naval Treaty limiting naval arms race (Apr. 22). Hawley-Smoot Tariff raises barriers to world trade, worsening depression (June 17). Congress creates Veteran's Administration (July 3). Hoover Dam begun near Las Vegas, Nev. The planet Pluto discovered.

1931 World War I veterans offered "Bonus Loans" to combat Great Depression. "Star Spangled Banner" becomes national anthem. "Scottsboro Boys" arrested for rape in Alabama. Empire State Building, tallest building in world, opened in New York City. Pres. Herbert Hoover declares moratorium on international debt and reparations payments. George Washington Bridge over Hudson River completed.

1932 Stimson Doctrine announces U.S. disapproval of Japanese invasion of China. Congress approves Reconstruction Finance Corporation to help recovery. Norris-LaGuardia Act restricts use of injunctions against labor strikes. Franklin D. Roosevelt, promising "New Deal" for Americans, elected president in Democratic landslide. Stock market drops to 10 percent of its 1929 value; national income cut in half. "Bonus Army" of poor veterans marches on Washington, D.C. Amelia Earhart first woman to fly solo across Atlantic.

1933 Giuseppe Zangara kills Chicago mayor Anton J. Cermak in Miami, Fla., motorcade, narrowly missing president-elect Franklin D. Roosevelt (Feb. 15). Banks closed for four days by presidential order (Mar. 5). During "Hundred Days" (Mar. 9–June 16), Pres. Roosevelt pushes New Deal through Congress, conducts first "fireside chat" on radio, and takes U.S. off gold standard. Beer and wine made legal again (Mar. 22). Congress passes National Industrial Recovery Act (June 16). U.S. recognizes Soviet Union (Nov. 16). U.S. Marines withdraw from Nicaragua. Frances Perkins, secretary of labor, becomes first woman cabinet member.

1934 Dust storms inundate Southwest, driving "Okies" and "Arkies" to California. General strike paralyzes San Francisco (July 16). John Dillinger, public enemy number one, killed by FBI agents (July 22). Upton Sinclair mounts unsuccessful EPIC (End Poverty in California) campaign for governor. Sen. Gerald P. Nye of North Dakota begins investigating role of U.S. munitions manufacturers in World War I. U.S. releases Cuba from Platt Amendment. U.S. troops withdrawn from Haiti. Roman Catholic Legion of Decency begins censoring motion pictures.

1935 Supreme Court invalidates National Industrial Recovery Act. Pres. Roosevelt pushes more "Second New Deal" legislation through Congress, notably, Wagner Act protecting unions (July 5), Social Security Act (Aug. 14), and "soak-the-rich" Wealth Tax Act (Aug. 30). Sen. Huey P. Long of Louisiana assassinated (Sept. 8). Congress of Industrial Organization (CIO) formed (Nov. 9). Congress passes first Neutrality Act. Alcoholics Anonymous founded.

1936 Congress passes second Neutrality Act. France, Britain, and U.S. sign New London Naval Treaty (Mar. 25). U.S. declares neutrality in Spanish Civil War (Aug. 7). Congress of Industrial Organizations auto workers begin sit-down strikes in Flint, Mich. (Dec. 30). *Life* magazine begins publishing. William "Liberty Bell" Lemke, Republican of North Dakota, runs for president on Union party ticket endorsed by radio demagogue Father Charles E. Coughlin. Jesse Owens wins four gold medals at "Nazi Olympics" in Berlin.

1937 Congress passes third Neutrality Act. Pres. Roosevelt proposes controversial "court-packing" plan. German dirigible *Hindenburg* explodes and burns in Lakehurst, N.J. (May 6). Pres. Roosevelt angers isolationists with "Quarantine Speech" (Oct. 5). Japanese planes sink U.S. Navy gunboat *Panay* in China (Dec. 12). Golden Gate Bridge completed in San Francisco. Slow recovery ends abruptly as economic depression worsens.

1938 Republican gains in Congress signal end of New Deal. Pres. Roosevelt calls for military buildup (Jan. 28). Mexico seizes U.S.-owned oil wells (Mar. 18). Rep. Martin Dies of Texas begins House Un-American Activities Committee (HUAC) investigations of Communists and Fascists. Howard Hughes sets record for around-the-world flight in less than four days (July 14). "Invasion from Mars" radio broadcast by Orson Welles causes widespread panic (Oct. 30). Hurricane devastates Atlantic Coast, killing 700 people.

1939 Supreme Court upholds Tennessee Valley Authority. First food stamp program begins in Rochester, N.Y. (May 16). Pan Am begins first regular transatlantic passenger service from New York to Lisbon, Portugal (June 28). U.S. declares neutrality in World War II (Sept. 5). Congress passes fourth Neutrality Act, approving Pres. Roosevelt's request for "cash-and-carry" arms sales to belligerents. Nylon stockings appear on market.

1940 As World War II engulfs Europe, Pres. Roosevelt announces U.S. has moved from "neutrality" to "non-belligerency" (June 10). U.S. and Britain conclude Destroyers-for-Bases deal (Sept. 2). Congress enacts a peacetime draft (Sept. 16) and massive increases in military spending. Over 16 million men register for draft as Pres. Roosevelt's embargo on strategic exports takes effect. Roosevelt, reelected to unprecedented third term, calls for U.S. to become "arsenal of democracy" (Dec. 20). Both the Committee to Defend America by Aiding the Allies and the isolationist America First Committee organized.

1941 Congress appropriates $7 billion in Lend-Lease aid to Britain. German submarine sinks merchant ship *Robin Moor,* first U.S. casualty of war (May 21). Roosevelt responds by declaring "unlimited national emergency" (May 27), freezing German and Italian assets in U.S. (June 14) and promising aid to USSR (June 24). Roosevelt freezes Japanese assets in retaliation for invasion of Indochina (July 25). Pres. Roosevelt and Prime Minister Winston Churchill issue Atlantic Charter (Aug. 12). U.S. Navy is ordered to "shoot on sight" at German warships (Sept. 11). "America has been attacked, the shooting has started," Pres. Roosevelt informs nation (Oct. 27). Japanese planes attack Pearl Harbor, Hawaii, killing 2,400 U.S. servicemen and civilians (Dec. 7). U.S. declares war on Japan (Dec. 10). Germany and Italy declare war on U.S. (Dec. 11). U.S. declares war on Germany and Italy (Dec. 11).

1942 Roosevelt creates War Production Board, calls for mass mobilization, and puts New Deal on hold. U.S. troops land in North Ireland, first to arrive in Europe (Jan. 26). Pres. Roosevelt approves internment of Japanese-Americans for duration of war (Feb. 20). Japanese submarine shells an oil refinery in Santa Barbara, Calif. (Feb. 23). Maj. James H. Doolittle stages carrier-launched bombing raid on Tokyo (Apr. 18). U.S. forces surrender in Philippines (May 6) but win major naval victories over Japan in Coral Sea (May 4–8) and at Midway (June 3–6). U.S. offensive begins in Pacific with invasion of Guadalcanal Island (Aug. 7). First all-U.S. bombing attack launched against German forces at Rouen, France (Aug. 17). Congress approves "Victory Tax" on wartime incomes (Oct. 21). Allies land 400,000 men in North Africa (Nov. 7–8). Eight German saboteurs apprehended in New York; six executed. Cocoanut Grove nightclub fire in Boston claims lives of 492 patrons.

1943 Congress appropriates $100 billion for war effort. Roosevelt and Prime Minister Winston Churchill demand "unconditional surrender" at Casablanca conference in Morocco (Jan. 24). U.S. Marines drive last Japanese from Guadalcanal (Feb. 9). U.S. troops defeated in first battle with Germans at Kasserine Pass, Tunisia (Feb. 20). Pres. Roosevelt declares wage-and-price freeze to stem inflation (Apr. 8). U.S. and Britain invade Sicily (July 10) and Italy proper (Sept. 3). Roosevelt and Churchill meet with Chiang Kai-shek of China in Cairo, Egypt (Nov. 22), and with Josef Stalin of Soviet Union in Tehran, Iran (Dec. 4–6). Gen. Dwight D. Eisenhower named Supreme Commander of Allied Forces in Europe. Congress approves federal income tax withholding. Race riots in Detroit and Harlem leave 40 dead. Chicago opens its first subway.

1944 U.S. and British planes begin around-the-clock bombing of Berlin. Allied forces land at Anzio, Italy (Jan. 22). Congress approves $1.35 billion for UN Relief and Reconstruction Agency, first U.S. foreign aid (Mar. 29). Allied forces enter Rome (June 5) as reconquest of Europe begins with D-Day invasion of Normandy (June 6). Allied breakout from Normandy sends German forces reeling across France (July 25). Postwar financial arrangements made at international conference in Bretton Woods, N.H. (July 1–22). Plans for UN made at Dumbarton Oaks conference (Aug. 21–Oct. 7). Gen. Douglas MacArthur begins reconquest of Philippines with landings at Leyte Gulf (Oct. 20). Congress passes Servicemen's Readjustment Act, known as "GI Bill of Rights." Roosevelt wins fourth term.

1945 Roosevelt, Churchill, and Stalin meet for last time at Yalta in Soviet Crimea to begin postwar planning (Feb. 4–11). Allied forces cross Rhine River and drive into heart of Germany (Mar. 7). U.S. air raids destroy Tokyo (Mar. 10–11). Pres. Roosevelt dies suddenly of cerebral hemorrhage in Warm Springs, Ga. (Apr. 12). UN Conference begins meeting in San Francisco (Apr. 24). Germany surrenders, ending war in Europe (May 7). Fifty nations sign UN Charter (June 26). First atomic explosion occurs in test at Alamagordo, N. Mex. (July 16). Pres. Harry S Truman meets with Churchill and Stalin at Potsdam, Germany (July 17–Aug. 2). Atomic bombs dropped on Hiroshima (Aug. 6) and Nagasaki (Aug. 9); Japan surrenders (Aug. 14), ending World War II. Council of Allied Foreign Ministers meets in London, unable to agree on peace treaty (Dec. 16–27). Television channels are allotted for commercial use. Empire State Building hit by B-25 bomber in heavy fog.

1946 Strike wave sweeps U.S., idling 4.6 million U.S. workers. Congress passes Employment Act, committing federal government to postwar economic management. Winston Churchill warns Americans about Communist expansion with "Iron Curtain" speech at Westminster College in Fulton, Mo. (Mar. 5). Pres. Truman seizes control of railroads and coal mines during strikes. Paris Peace Conference ends in failure (July 29–Oct. 15). U.S. presents Baruch Plan for international control of atomic energy, grants independence to Philippines (July 4), and agrees to loan Britain $3.5 billion for postwar reconstruction. Congress creates Atomic Energy Commission. UN General Assembly begins meeting in New York. John D. Rockefeller, Jr., donates $8.5 million for UN Headquarters. Most wartime wage and price controls lifted. Dr. Benjamin Spock publishes influential guidebook on baby care.

1947 Council of Foreign Ministers meets in Moscow, again unable to agree on peace treaty (Mar. 10–Apr. 24). Pres. Truman announces Truman Doctrine, promising aid to countries threatened by subversion (May 12). Sec. of State George C. Marshall announces Marshall Plan for postwar reconstruction of Europe (June 5). Republican-dominated Congress restricts union organizing with Taft-Hartley Act. House Committee on Un-American Activities (HUAC) begins investigating communism in Hollywood (Oct. 20). Council of Foreign Ministers meets for last time in London (Nov. 25–Dec. 16). Texas City, Tex., wiped out when munitions ship explodes, killing over 500 people. Jackie Robinson of Brooklyn Dodgers breaks color line in baseball.

1948 Postwar inflation keeps prices rising fast. Congress approves $5.3 billion for Marshall Plan aid to Europe with Foreign Assistance Act. U.S. recognizes new state of Israel (May 14) and admits 205,000 war refugees from Europe. Britain and U.S. begin airlifting supplies into West Berlin after Soviets cut off all traffic into city (June 26). Pres. Truman orders peacetime draft and desegregation of U.S. armed forces. HUAC charges Alger Hiss with spying for Soviet Union. Pres. Truman wins upset reelection victory over Republican candidate Thomas E. Dewey of New York, despite Progressive and Dixiecrat walkouts from Democratic party. Idlewild International Airport, largest in world, opens in New York.

1949 Pres. Truman calls for "Fair Deal" domestic programs and "Point Four" foreign aid programs. U.S., Canada, and 10 Western European nations sign treaty that will lead to North Atlantic Treaty Organization (NATO). Berlin Airlift ends when Soviets finally lift blockade (May 12). State Department issues "white paper" disclaiming responsibility for Communist takeover in China. Pres. Truman announces Soviet atomic bomb test (Sept. 23). Eleven U.S. Communist leaders convicted of conspiring to overthrow government. UN Headquarters on East River dedicated in New York City (Oct. 24). Steel strike idles half a million workers nationwide (Oct. 1–Nov. 11). *Lucky Lady II* of U.S. Air Force completes first nonstop around-the-world flight.

1950 Sen. Joseph R. McCarthy of Wisconsin issues his first accusations of Communists in government at speech in Wheeling, W.Va. North Korea invades South Korea, beginning Korean War (June 25). Pres. Truman orders U.S. intervention (June 27), obtains UN support (July 7), asks Congress for a $10 billion rearmament program (July 20), and calls up reserves (Aug. 4). Inchon landing begins rout of North Korean invaders (Sept. 15). Congress passes Internal Security Act, requiring registration of Communist organizations, over Pres. Truman's veto (Sept. 23). UN troops recapture Seoul (Sept. 26) and invade North Korea (Oct. 7). Puerto Rican nationalists nearly assassinate Pres. Truman in Washington (Nov. 11). After China intervenes in Korean War, Pres. Truman proclaims national emergency (Dec. 16). U.S. population tops 150 million (150,697,361).

1951 Gen. Dwight D. Eisenhower comes out of retirement to accept command of Allied forces in Europe (Apr. 4). Julius and Ethel Rosenberg sentenced to death for spying (atom bomb secrets) for Soviets (Apr. 5). Pres. Truman removes Gen. Douglas MacArthur from command in Korea for insubordination (Apr. 11). MacArthur returns to U.S., greeted by exultant crowds, to deliver address to Congress. Missouri River floods devastate Kansas City, causing over $1 billion in damages (July 11–25). U.S. concludes a mutual defense pact with Australia and New Zealand and signs a peace treaty with Japan (Sept. 8). Congress passes Mutual Security Act, providing $7 billion for foreign aid and military cooperation with pro-U.S. nations. Sen. Estes Kefauver of Tennessee investigates gambling and organized crime. CBS transmits first color television broadcast from New York.

1952 Pres. Truman seizes steel mills paralyzed by strikes (Apr. 8). U.S., Britain, and France sign peace treaty with West Germany (May 26). GI Bill extended to Korean War veterans. Construction begins on USS *Nautilus*, first atomic submarine. Supreme Court upholds barring subversives from teaching in schools. Sen. Richard M. Nixon of California, Republican candidate for vice president, delivers "Checkers" speech on national television to explain his "secret slush fund." Republicans win control of White House and both houses of Congress for first time since 1928. Supreme Court rejects appeal of Julius and Ethel Rosenberg. U.S. announces first successful hydrogen bomb test at Eniwetok Atoll in Marshall Islands (Nov. 16). Pres.-elect Dwight D. Eisenhower visits U.S. troops in Korea.

1953 Sen. John W. Bricker of Ohio proposes sharp limits on presidential powers to make treaties. Thirteen more Communist leaders convicted of conspiring to overthrow government. Julius and Ethel Rosenberg executed in Ossining, N.Y. (June 19). Pres. Eisenhower lifts wage and price controls, increases U.S. support for French war effort in Indochina, negotiates armistice ending Korean War (June 27). Congress creates Department of Health, Education, and Welfare (Apr. 1). U.S. pledges aid to Spain in exchange for military bases (Sept. 26). First "atomic cannon" tested in Nevada. Maj. Chuck Yeager of U.S. Air Force sets new air speed record in rocket-powered X-1 jet plane. *The Robe* first motion picture in CinemaScope.

1954 Sec. of State John Foster Dulles vows "massive retaliation" against Soviet aggression (Jan. 12). Foreign Ministers Conference in Berlin fails to achieve reunification of Germany (Jan. 25–Feb. 18). Puerto Rican nationalists shoot five congressmen on floor of House of Representatives (Mar. 1). U.S. negotiates the Southeast Asia Treaty Organization (SEATO) security pact (Sept. 8). Army-McCarthy hearings discredit Sen. Joseph McCarthy and his methods. Supreme Court orders school desegregation in *Brown* decision (May 17). CIA helps overthrow Arbenz government in Guatemala (June 29). Congress passes Communist Control Act. Senate censures Sen. McCarthy. France announces that U.S. has paid for most of Indochina war. New York Stock Exchange prices finally reattain 1929 levels.

1955 Pres. Eisenhower promises to use atomic weapons in case of war and conducts first televised press conference. U.S., Soviet Union, and Allies agree on Austrian peace treaty to end occupation. Summit conference of U.S., British, French, and Soviet leaders in Switzerland produces "spirit of Geneva." Supreme Court orders school desegregation to proceed "with all deliberate speed." Pres. Eisenhower hospitalized for three weeks following heart attack. Interstate Commerce Commission orders desegregation on interstate trains and buses. AFL and CIO labor federations merge to form AFL-CIO, with 15 million members (Dec. 5). Dr. Jonas Salk perfects polio vaccine. Civil rights leader Dr. Martin Luther King, Jr., leads bus boycott in Montgomery, Ala.

1956 Pres. Eisenhower refuses to intervene against Soviet invasion of Hungary and exerts pressure on Allies to withdraw from Suez. Congressmen signing Southern Manifesto promise "massive resistance" to school desegregation. Atomic Energy Commission approves commercial nuclear power plants. Congress passes Highway Act, appropriating $32 billion for construction of vast nationwide road system. TWA and United airliners collide in midair and crash in Grand Canyon, killing 128 people (June 30). *Peyton Place* blockbuster best-seller of year. First transatlantic telephone cable begins operating. Albert Woolson, last Union veteran of Civil War, dies at age 109. American actress Grace Kelly marries Prince Rainier III of Monaco.

1957 Pres. Eisenhower announces Eisenhower Doctrine, promising aid to any Middle Eastern country threatened by communism. McClellan Committee begins investigating corruption and racketeering in International Brotherhood of Teamsters union. Sen. J. Strom Thurmond of South Carolina sets all-time filibuster record (24 hrs., 27 min.) with speech against civil rights (Aug. 30). Congress eventually approves first Civil Rights Act since Reconstruction (Sept. 9). Pres. Eisenhower sends troops to Little Rock, Ark., to enforce federal desegregation order (Sept. 24). First underground atomic test conducted in Nevada (Sept. 19). Sen. John F. Kennedy of Massachusetts wins Pulitzer Prize for *Profiles in Courage*.

1958 In response to Soviet launch of Sputnik, U.S. launches Explorer I, first American satellite; Congress creates National Aeronautics and Space Administration (NASA) and passes National Defense Education Act. Vice Pres. Richard M. Nixon nearly killed by angry mob in Caracas, Venezuela. At request of weak government in Beirut, Pres. Eisenhower orders U.S. Marines to land in Lebanon (July 15). Nuclear submarine *Nautilus* performs first undersea crossing of North Pole (Aug. 5). Presidential assistant Sherman Adams forced to resign in scandal over accepting favors (Sept. 22). Dr. Linus Pauling predicts five million birth defects from radioactivity already released into atmosphere by atomic tests.

1959 Fidel Castro's takeover of Cuba begins rapid deterioration of U.S.-Cuba relations (Jan. 1). Alaska becomes 49th state (Jan. 3), and Hawaii 50th (Aug. 21). Joint U.S.-Canada St. Lawrence Seaway project completed. Congress passes

Landrum-Griffin Act to suppress racketeering in labor unions. Vice Pres. Nixon holds impromptu "kitchen debate" in Moscow with Soviet premier Nikita Khrushchev, who later visits USS *George Washington,* the first U.S. Navy ballistic-missile submarine, launched. Charles Van Doren testifies that his victory on "$64,000 Question" TV game show was fixed. Walter Williams, last surviving Civil War veteran, dies at age 117.

1960 U.S. and Japan conclude new security treaty (Jan. 19). Black students stage first sit-in at Woolworth's lunch counter in Greensboro, N.C. (Feb. 1). U-2 spy plane, with American pilot Francis Gary Powers, shot down over Soviet Union (May 1). Congress passes second Civil Rights Act since Reconstruction. Congress investigates "payola" in radio industry, leading to arrest of Alan Freed, "father of rock 'n' roll." After Cuba rejects American protests over confiscated property, Pres. Eisenhower imposes trade embargo. John F. Kennedy and Richard M. Nixon hold first televised presidential campaign debates. Kennedy wins by 0.3 percent of popular vote, closest presidential election since 1884 (Nov. 8).

1961 Pres. Eisenhower breaks diplomatic relations with Cuba, warns Americans to beware of "military-industrial complex." CIA-backed Bay of Pigs invasion fails to overthrow Castro regime in Cuba (Apr. 17). Commander Alan B. Shephard, Jr., U.S. Navy, first American in space on *Mercury* rocket (May 5). Soviet construction of Berlin Wall creates temporary crisis (Aug. 13). Pres. Kennedy creates Peace Corps and Alliance for Progress. American families advised to build nuclear fallout shelters. "Freedom Rides" civil rights protests broken up by riots in Anniston and Birmingham, Ala. American Medical Association reports link between smoking and heart disease. National Council of Churches endorses birth control for families.

1962 Lt. Col. John H. Glenn, Jr., first American to orbit Earth. Stock market has worst day since 1929 (May 28). Pres. Kennedy convinces steel companies to rescind price increases. U.S. conducts first successful test of sea-launched long-range ballistic missile with nuclear warhead. Pres. Kennedy sends U.S. marshals to protect James H. Meredith, a black student at University of Mississippi. U.S. extends $100 million emergency loan to the UN. Threat of nuclear war during Cuban Missile Crisis averted when Soviet Union agrees to withdraw missiles from Cuba (Oct. 22–28). Rachel Carson's *Silent Spring* draws attention to environmental crisis. U.S. Military Assistance Command set up in South Vietnam.

1963 Pres. Kennedy proposes Medicare program. U.S., Great Britain, and Soviet Union conclude Nuclear Test–Ban Treaty outlawing atmospheric testing (July 25). "Hot line" between Washington and Moscow put in place. Civil rights movement reaches climax with mass demonstrations in Birmingham, Ala., and epic March on Washington, where Martin Luther King, Jr., delivers his "I Have a Dream" speech (Aug. 28). Pres. Kennedy assassinated in Dallas, Tex., by Lee Harvey Oswald (Nov. 22), who is murdered by Jack Ruby (Nov. 24). Joseph Valachi testifies before Congress about extent of organized crime in U.S. Arnold Palmer first pro golfer to earn over $100,000 in one year.

1964 Pres. Lyndon B. Johnson, taking up Pres. Kennedy's cause, calls for "War on Poverty." Supreme Court orders states to redraw congressional boundaries to ensure fair representation. Alaska declared disaster area after major earthquake rocks Anchorage (Mar. 28). Mississippi "Freedom Summer" begins with murder of three civil rights workers (June 22). Pres. Johnson pushes landmark Civil Rights and Economic Opportunity acts through Congress. After alleged North Vietnamese attack on U.S. Navy destroyers, Congress passes Tonkin Gulf Resolution, giving Pres. Johnson free hand in Vietnam (Aug. 7). Warren Commission reports there was no conspiracy to assassinate Pres. Kennedy (Sept. 27). Martin Luther King, Jr., wins Nobel Peace Prize. Verrazano Narrows Bridge, the longest suspension bridge in world, opened in New York.

1965 Pres. Johnson calls for "Great Society." Black nationalist Malcolm X assassinated in New York City (Feb. 21). Pres. Johnson orders U.S. Marines into South Vietnam (Mar. 8) and into Santo Domingo (Apr. 28). U.S. troops authorized to undertake offensive operations in South Vietnam (June 8). Martin Luther King, Jr., leads civil rights marches from Selma to Montgomery, Ala., and in white neighborhoods of Chicago. Congress approves Medicare (July 30) and Voting Rights Act (Aug. 6). Watts Riot in Los Angeles leaves 34 dead and over $200 million in damage (Aug. 11–16), accelerating wave of ghetto riots. Tornadoes sweep Midwest, killing 271 and injuring 5,000. East Coast power blackout affects over 30 million Americans and Canadians (Nov. 9–10).

1966 East Coast blizzard results in 165 deaths (Jan. 29–31). Pres. Johnson orders first B-52 strategic bombing raids on North Vietnam (Apr. 12). Supreme Court rules police must advise suspects of their rights (June 13). Cesar Chavez leads United Farm Workers strike and boycott against California grape growers. Stokeley Carmichael of Student Non-Violent Coordinating Committee demands "Black Power." Congress enacts safety standards for automobiles. Edward W. Brooke of Massachusetts is first black senator since Reconstruction. National Football League and American Football League agree to play Super Bowl championship game. Number of blacks voting in South nearly doubles in one year. U.S. troops in Vietnam increase from 215,000 to over 400,000.

1967 The 500th U.S. plane shot down over North Vietnam (Apr. 4). Hundreds of thousands of antiwar protesters march on Washington (Apr. 15 and Oct. 21–22). Pres. Johnson announces U.S. troop level will reach 525,000 by end of 1968. Worst race riot in U.S. history erupts in Detroit, Mich. (July 23), leaving 43 dead, while riot in Newark, N.J. (July 12), kills another 26. Sen. Eugene McCarthy of Minnesota announces antiwar candidacy for president (Nov. 30). U.S. agrees to refrain from placing nuclear weapons in space and joins General Agreement on Tariffs and Trade (GATT). Albert DeSalvo, the "Boston Strangler," sentenced to life in prison. Stalin's daughter Svetlana Aliluyeva defects to U.S. Thurgood Marshall becomes first black justice on Supreme Court.

1968 North Korea seizes USS *Pueblo,* holding 82 crewmen hostage (Jan. 23). North Vietnam and Viet Cong launch massive Tet Offensive (Jan. 30). Pres. Johnson makes surprise announcement that he will not seek reelection (Mar. 31). Martin Luther King, Jr., murdered by James Earl Ray in Memphis, Tenn. (Apr. 4). Student protesters take over Columbia University (Apr. 23). Washington-Hanoi peace talks begin in Paris (May 10). After winning California primary, Sen. Robert F. Kennedy of New York murdered by Sirhan Sirhan in Los Angeles (June 5). U.S. signs Nuclear Non-Proliferation Treaty. Democratic Convention in Chicago marred by riots and police violence against antiwar demonstrators. Shirley Chisholm of New York is first black woman elected to Congress. *Apollo 8* completes first moon orbit.

1969 Oil spill off Santa Barbara, Calif., draws attention to need for environmental protection (Feb. 5). Pres. Richard Nixon asks Congress to fund Anti-Ballistic Missile program (ABM) as "safeguard" for strategic defense. U.S. losses in Vietnam exceed losses in Korean War. U.S. troop withdrawals from Vietnam begin (July 8). Sen. Edward M. Kennedy of Massachusetts drives off bridge at Chappaquiddick, Mass., killing Mary Jo Kopechne (July 18). After $25 billion spent on U.S. space program, Neil Armstrong and Buzz Aldrin of *Apollo 11* are first men to walk on moon (July 20). Hurricane Camille claims over 300 victims in South. Trial of Chicago Eight (later Chicago Seven, after Bobby Seale tried separately) begins. Woodstock music festival near Bethel, N.Y., draws 400,000 young fans (Aug. 15–18). Vietnam Moratorium and "March against Death" antiwar demonstrations draw hundreds of thousands to Washington. U.S. and the USSR begin Strategic Arms Limitation Talks (SALT) in Helsinki, Finland.

1970 Pres. Nixon calls for "Vietnamization" to decrease U.S. involvement in war. U.S. bombing of North Vietnam escalates dramatically; nationwide protests break out when U.S. invades Cambodia (Apr. 29). Four students killed and nine wounded by National Guard units at Kent State University in Ohio (May 4). Lt. William L. Calley court-martialed for massacre of 102 civilians in My Lai, South Vietnam (Nov. 12). Supreme Court upholds new 18-year-old voting age (Dec. 21). Congress passes Water Quality Improvement Act, Air Quality Control Act, and Occupational Safety and Health Act.

U.S. troops in Vietnam down to 340,000 at year's end. U.S. population tops 200 million.

1971 Pres. Nixon proposes federal revenue sharing with states. Charles Manson and three women followers convicted for Tate-LaBianca murders in Los Angeles (Jan. 25). Major earthquake rocks southern California, killing 64 and injuring over 1,000 (Feb. 9). U.S. Ping-Pong team visits China, relaxing Cold War tensions. Supreme Court approves busing to achieve school integration. Indian occupation of Alcatraz Island in San Francisco Bay comes to end. Prison riot in Attica, N.Y., kills 43 inmates and guards. *New York Times* begins publishing "Pentagon Papers," top-secret history of Vietnam War (June 13). U.S. devalues dollar (Dec. 18). U.S. troops in Vietnam reach 139,000; U.S. air attacks are heaviest since 1968. Billie Jean King first woman athlete to earn over $100,000 in one year.

1972 Nixon first president to visit China (Feb. 21–28) and Soviet Union (May 22–30). Airlines begin screening passengers to prevent hijackings. Congress passes Equal Rights Amendment and submits it to states for ratification. Gov. George Wallace of Alabama shot and seriously wounded while campaigning for president in Laurel, Md. (May 15). Five men arrested for breaking into Democratic National Committee headquarters at Watergate complex in Washington, D.C. (June 17). Federal grand jury indicts five burglars and two former White House aides in Watergate trial (Sept. 15). Pres. Nixon angers farmers with "Great Grain Robbery," a secret deal to sell wheat at discount to Soviet Union. National security adviser Henry Kissinger announces "peace is at hand" in Vietnam in time for Pres. Nixon to carry 49 states in election. U.S. troops in Vietnam fall to 69,000 as Nixon orders resumption of heavy bombing of North Vietnam (Dec. 18).

1973 Supreme Court disallows state restrictions on abortions *(Roe* v. *Wade).* U.S. signs Paris peace accords ending Vietnam War (Jan. 27). Trial of Watergate burglars reveals conspiracy to conceal White House involvement. Top presidential aides H.R. Haldeman, John Ehrlichman, John Dean, and Atty. Gen. Richard Kleindienst resign amid charges of White House cover-up (Apr. 30). Sen. Sam Ervin of North Carolina chairs Senate investigation of Watergate scandal on national television (May 17–Nov. 15). Vice Pres. Spiro Agnew resigns after threat of indictment for tax evasion (Oct. 10). Gasoline prices skyrocket after Arab nations embargo oil exports to U.S. in retaliation for U.S. aid to Israel in Yom Kippur War (Oct. 17). Pres. Nixon fires Watergate Special Prosecutor Archibald Cox and others in "Saturday Night Massacre" (Oct. 20). Pres. Nixon turns over first White House tapes, which include mysterious 18½-minute gap (Nov. 26). Gerald R. Ford of Michigan sworn in as first vice president chosen under 25th Amendment (Dec. 6).

1974 Arab oil embargo of U.S. lifted (Mar. 18). Supreme Court rules that Pres. Nixon must submit all White House tapes to Special Prosecutor Leon Jaworski (July 24). House Judiciary Committee votes three articles of impeachment (July 24–30). Pres. Nixon releases transcripts of tapes that show he ordered cover-up (Aug. 5). Citing "political" difficulties, Pres. Nixon resigns (Aug. 8), elevating Vice Pres. Ford to presidency (Aug. 9). Pres. Ford shocks nation by pardoning Nixon for all crimes committed in office (Sept. 8). Democrats make major gains in midterm elections. Pres. Ford meets with Soviet premier Leonid Brezhnev in Vladivostock to approve SALT treaty (Nov. 23–24). FBI and CIA efforts to disrupt civil rights and antiwar movements in 1960s revealed. Newspaper heiress Patty Hearst kidnapped by Symbionese Liberation Army, which extorts $2 million food giveaway for needy.

1975 Nixon aides convicted of obstructing justice in Watergate investigation (Jan. 1). Senate committee chaired by Frank Church begins investigation into illegal CIA and FBI activities. Last Americans evacuate Saigon as South Vietnam falls to North Vietnamese invasion (Apr. 30). Cambodia seizes USS *Mayaguez* (May 12), and Pres. Ford orders rescue operation (May 14). *Apollo-Soyuz,* joint Soviet-American space mission, achieves linkup in space (July 17). Lynette "Squeaky" Fromme and Sarah Jane Moore attempt to assassinate Pres. Ford in separate California incidents (Sept. 5 and 22). Congress votes to admit women to army, navy, and air force academies. Democrats in House of Representatives dismantle seniority system. Church Committee discovers CIA helped overthrow Salvador Allende of Chile and plotted to assassinate Fidel Castro of Cuba.

1976 Congress repeatedly overrides Pres. Ford's vetoes of bills providing for jobs, health, education, and welfare programs. Supreme Court upholds death penalty (July 3). Bicentennial of U.S. celebrated coast to coast. Congressman Wayne Hays of Ohio, chairman of House Ways and Means Committee, resigns over sex scandal. Sec. of Agriculture Earl Butz forced to resign for telling racist joke. NASA's *Viking I* and *Viking II* space probes land on Mars and transmit scientific data, along with color photographs, back to Earth. "Legionnaire's Disease" breaks out at American Legion convention in Philadelphia, eventually claiming 29 victims. Patty Hearst convicted of armed robbery in California. Hundreds of West Point cadets found to have cheated on exams.

1977 Pres. Carter pardons Vietnam War draft evaders, threatens to reduce foreign aid to countries violating human rights, calls for "moral equivalent of war" in energy conservation, and signs Panama Canal treaty (Sept. 7). U.S. declares 200-mi. sovereignty zone in Atlantic and Pacific Oceans to exclude foreign fishing vessels. Power blackout sets off arson and looting spree in New York City (July 13–14). Oil begins flowing through Alaska pipeline. Severe drought leads to water rationing on West Coast. ABC's miniseries "Roots" draws 130 million viewers.

1978 Pres. Carter postpones production of neutron bomb. California voters approve Proposition 13, reducing property taxes and setting off nationwide "taxpayers' revolt." Supreme Court gives limited approval to affirmative action programs but disallows quotas for college admissions (June 28). In private talks with Anwar Sadat and Menachem Begin, Pres. Carter mediates peace between Egypt and Israel with landmark Camp David Accords (Sept. 17). Nearly 1,000 American followers of the Rev. Jim Jones commit mass suicide in Jonestown, Guyana, after cult members murder Congressman Leo Ryan of California. Federal loan guarantees rescue New York City from financial crisis.

1979 U.S. resumes diplomatic relations with China (Jan 1). Worst nuclear accident in U.S. history takes place at Three Mile Island power plant near Harrisburg, Pa., releasing giant clouds of radioactive steam (Mar. 28). Pres. Carter and Premier Brezhnev sign SALT II treaty in Vienna (June 18). Shah of Iran and Anastasio Somoza of Nicaragua, both U.S.-supported dictators, flee revolutions in their countries. Iranian militants seize U.S. embassy in Tehran, taking 66 American hostages and demanding return of shah from U.S. (Nov. 4). Iranians release 13 American hostages, all blacks or women. Pres. Carter deports illegal Iranian students, freezes Iranian assets, and bars oil imports from Iran. Pope John Paul II visits U.S. Inflation reaches highest level in 33 years as Organization of Petroleum Exporting Countries (OPEC) doubles price of oil.

1980 Canadian embassy officials help six Americans escape from Iran (Jan. 29). In response to Soviet invasion of Afghanistan, Pres. Carter embargoes grain and high-tech exports to Soviet Union, approves arms sales to China, and secures U.S. boycott of Olympics in Moscow. Congress grants Pres. Carter's request for Crude Oil Windfall Profits Tax and for resumption of Selective Service draft registration. Pres. Carter's secret rescue mission for American hostages in Iran fails when U.S. Navy helicopter crashes in desert, killing eight servicemen (Apr. 24). Race riot breaks out in Miami, protesting police brutality (May 17). Mt. St. Helens erupts in Washington State, killing 26 people and causing $2.7 billion in damage (May 18). Banking and trucking industries deregulated. FBI's "Abscam" operation implicates over 30 public officials, including a senator and seven congressmen, for accepting bribes. Republicans capture control of Senate for only second time in 50 years.

1981 Minutes after Pres. Ronald Reagan is sworn in, Iran releases 52 American hostages after 444 days in captivity. Pres. Reagan shot by John Hinckley in Washington, D.C. (Mar. 30); undergoes surgery and makes full recovery. *Columbia* completes first successful space shuttle mission (Apr. 12–14). Federal air-traffic controllers go on strike and lose jobs when Pres. Reagan fires all 13,000 of them. Senate votes 99 to 0 to confirm Sandra Day O'Connor as first woman justice of Supreme Court. Pres. Reagan lifts grain embargo against Soviet Union but imposes new sanctions after Poland declares martial law. Congress accepts Pres. Reagan's plans for tax cuts, lower domestic spending, and major defense buildup.

1982 Ending 13-year antitrust suit, American Telephone and Telegraph agrees to surrender control of local Bell System phone companies in return for expansion into new business pursuits (Jan. 8). Pres. Reagan calls for "New Federalism," transferring programs to state and local control. Half a million Americans demonstrate in New York City in favor of nuclear freeze (June 12). Congress rejects nuclear freeze (Aug. 5). Unemployment exceeds 10 percent for first time since Great Depression, and federal budget deficit exceeds $100 billion a year for first time ever. After a decade, Equal Rights Amendment fails, falling three states short of ratification.

1983 Inflation slows as oil prices decline sharply. Congress admits internment of Japanese-Americans during World War II was unjust and agrees to bail out Social Security system. Sally Ride, aboard space shuttle *Challenger*, is first American woman astronaut. Pres. Reagan strongly condemns Soviet Union for shooting down Korean airliner with 269 people aboard (Sept. 1). U.S. Marines join multinational peacekeeping force in Beirut, Lebanon, where Muslim terrorists kill 240 of them in suicide bombing (Oct. 23). U.S. invades Grenada to overthrow Cuban-backed regime (Oct. 25). Pres. Reagan calls for large-scale funding of Strategic Defense Initiative, or "Star Wars."

1984 Reagan recovery under way as unemployment falls, inflation rate declines, economic growth accelerates, and U.S. dollar soars on international markets. Pres. Reagan orders U.S. Marines out of Lebanon (Feb. 7). Congress censures Pres. Reagan for misusing funds to mine Nicaraguan harbors. Rep. Geraldine Ferraro, Democrat of New York, is first woman to receive major party nomination for vice president. Soviet bloc countries boycott Los Angeles Olympics. The Rev. Jesse Jackson mounts first major challenge by black candidate for major party nomination. Pres. Reagan wins landslide reelection over Democrat Walter Mondale.

1985 Pres. Reagan calls for more tax and budget cuts to sustain economic growth (Feb. 4–6). Despite worldwide protests from Jewish organizations, Pres. Reagan visits West Germany to deliver address at Bitburg cemetery, where Nazi SS troops are buried (May 5). Muslim terrorists hijack TWA airliner (June 14), kill one American hostage, then release rest in Beirut (June 30). Pres. Reagan and Soviet premier Mikhail Gorbachev hold their first summit meeting in Geneva (Nov. 19–21). Pres. Reagan signs Gramm-Rudman Act, requiring automatic spending cuts if Congress cannot reduce burgeoning federal deficit. Plane crash in Gander, Newfoundland, kills 248 U.S. troops coming home for Christmas (Dec. 12).

1986 Space shuttle *Challenger* explodes in midair over Florida, killing six astronauts and civilian passenger (Jan. 28); investigations reveal NASA relaxed safety regulations to speed up launch date. U.S. Navy repels attack by Libyan forces during maneuvers in Gulf of Sidra (Mar. 24). Pres. Reagan blames Libya for death of two Americans in terrorist bombing of West Berlin disco, then orders retaliatory air raids on Tripoli and Benghazi (Apr. 14). Second Reagan-Gorbachev summit in Reykjavík, Iceland, reaches impasse over arms control and "Star Wars" (Oct. 12). Congress approves sweeping revision of U.S. tax structure. Democrats regain control of Senate. Pres. Reagan denies trading arms for hostages as Iran-Contra scandal breaks (Nov. 19). Wall Street financier Ivan Boesky fined $100 million for illegal insider-trading on stock market.

1987 Pres. Reagan submits first trillion-dollar U.S. budget to Congress as national debt mounts steadily. Stock market closes above 2,000 for first time. Tower Commission inquiry into Iran-Contra affair criticizes White House staff and Pres. Reagan's "management style," prompting Chief of Staff Donald Regan to resign. After Pres. Reagan orders U.S. Navy into Persian Gulf to escort Kuwaiti oil tankers, an Iraqi warplane accidentally attacks USS *Stark*, killing 37 sailors (May 17). Congressional hearings on Iran-Contra affair bestow fame on former White House aide Lt. Col. Oliver North. Stock market crashes 508 points in one day, an all-time record, jolting markets around world (Oct. 16). Third Reagan-Gorbachev summit in Washington, D.C., produces agreement to dismantle medium-range missiles in Europe (Dec. 8).

1988 Vice Pres. Bush denies involvement in Iran-Contra scandal. Congress rejects Pres. Reagan's request for aid to Contras. After Iran lays mines in Persian Gulf, U.S. Navy warships and planes destroy two Iranian oil platforms and repel Iranian counterattacks (Apr. 18–19). USS *Vincennes* accidentally shoots down Iranian passenger plane, killing 290 people (July 3). Summer drought afflicts North America; fires burn four million acres of forest. Atty. Gen. Edwin Meese resigns amid accusations of financial misdealings. George Bush becomes first sitting vice president elected president since 1836. Terrorist bomb aboard Pan Am Flight 103 kills all 259 aboard, mostly Americans, and 11 on the ground in Lockerbie, Scotland (Dec. 21). Drexel Burnham Lambert agrees to pay record $650 million penalty for securities fraud (Dec. 21). Kohlberg Kravis Roberts acquires RJR Nabisco for $25 billion, largest leveraged buyout in history.

1989 *Exxon Valdez* supertanker spills over 11 million gallons of oil off Alaska coast (Mar. 24). Abortion rights rally brings 500,000 marchers to Washington, D.C. (Apr. 9). HUD scandal reveals fraud, mismanagement, and influence peddling under Reagan administration. Top Democrats Jim Wright, Speaker of the House, and Tony Coelho, majority whip, resign from House over ethics violations. Supreme Court upholds right to burn U.S. flag and approves state limits on abortion. Pres. Bush signs $300 billion savings and loan bailout (Aug. 9). Severe earthquake, second worst in U.S. history, inflicts $6 billion damage and leaves 62 dead in San Francisco Bay Area (Oct. 17). L. Douglas Wilder of Virginia is first black elected governor. After Panama declares "state of war" with U.S., Pres. Bush orders invasion by 24,000 U.S. troops to overthrow Noriega regime and install U.S.-backed popularly elected government (Dec. 20).

1990 After Iraq's invasion of Kuwait (Aug. 2), U.S. launches Operation Desert Shield: more than 200,000 U.S. troops move into Saudi Arabia, and the navy blockades all oil exports from Iraq and all imports except food. Bush and Gorbachev meet twice: U.S. agrees to provide some economic aid, grants USSR most-favored-nation trade status, and secures some arms reductions and agreement that Iraq must withdraw from Kuwait. John Poindexter, national security adviser to Pres. Reagan, convicted in Iran-Contra scandal. Pres. Bush breaks campaign pledge of "no new taxes." A major flaw in the $1.5 billion Hubble Space Telescope is discovered shortly after its deployment. Wall Street firm Drexel Burnham Lambert defaults on $100 million in loans, and Michael Milken, head of "junk bond" department, is fined $600 million and sentenced to jail. Three New York teenagers are convicted of raping and beating a Central Park jogger, but they are acquitted of attempted murder.

1991 U.S. sends 400,000 troops, 1,500 aircraft, and 65 warships to the Persian Gulf to drive Iraq's armed forces from Kuwait (Jan. 17). They drop 89,000 tons of explosives on Iraqi positions. The ground war begins six weeks later and lasts only 100 hours (Feb. 23–27). Only 144 Americans are killed in the war. Cease-fire proves to be premature, however, as Pres. Saddam Hussein retains power. Bush and Gorbachev sign first nuclear arms reduction treaty (July 31), but Soviet Union's government and economy continue to crumble throughout the year. U.S. provides aid and establishes diplomatic relations with former Soviet republics Estonia, Latvia, and Lithuania. Unemployment rate rises to highest level in a decade. Interest rates are cut to lowest levels in 20 years. Senate's confirmation of Clarence Thomas as the second African-American to sit on the Supreme Court is delayed by Anita Hill's luridly detailed charges (Oct. 6) of sexual harassment 10 years earlier. Chemical Bank and Manufacturers Hanover Trust announce largest bank merger in U.S. history ($135 bil. in assets). U.S. regulators seize Bank of Credit and Commerce International (BCCI) on charges of fraud and money-laundering worldwide. Oliver North and John Poindexter are exonerated in connection with the Iran-Contra scandal. Four white Los Angeles policemen indicted for videotaped beating of black motorist Rodney King (Mar. 3).

1992 The Americans with Disabilities Act, the most sweeping antidiscrimination legislation since the Civil Rights Act of 1964 takes effect

(Jan. 26), guaranteeing the disabled equal access to businesses. President Bush and Russian president Boris Yeltsin issue joint statement officially ending the Cold War (Feb. 1). Pres. Bush and German chancellor Helmut Kohl unveil plan for seven leading industrial nations to give Russia $24 billion in aid (Apr. 1). For second time in three years, half a million people march on Washington in support of abortion rights (Apr. 5). Riots erupt in South Central Los Angeles minutes after an all-white jury acquits four L.A. police officers on charges of beating Rodney King (Apr. 29–May 4). More than 50 people are killed, 2,000 injured, and over 7,000 arrested. Estimated cost of the damage: $1 billion. The 27th Amendment to the Constitution is adopted, prohibiting Congress from voting itself a pay raise "until an election of Representatives shall have intervened" (May 18). Salomon Brothers investment house agrees to pay $290 million fine for submitting phony bids in U.S. Treasuries auctions (May 20). At first-ever Earth summit (June 3–17), U.S. is lone industrial nation not to sign biodiversity treaty on preservation of plant, animal, and microbial species. Billionaire populist Ross Perot enters the presidential race as a third-party candidate. Supreme Court rules (5–4) that state laws cannot ban racial, religious, or sexual insults as "hate speech" or "bias crimes" (June 22). Supreme Court rules (7–2) that people can sue cigarette makers for damages in the event of death or illness from smoking (June 24). Federal Reserve cuts discount rate to 3 percent, its lowest rate since 1963, after unemployment skyrockets to 7.8 percent, its highest level since 1983 (July 2). In effort to limit nuclear proliferation, Pres. Bush announces United States will end production of weapons-grade plutonium and uranium (July 13). Bill Clinton wins the Democratic nomination (July 16). Hurricane Andrew rips through South Florida (Aug. 24) and Louisiana (Aug. 26), destroying the city of Homestead, Fla., killing at least 32, causing more than $1 billion in damage, and leaving half a million homeless or without water or power. Pres. Bush pledges federal aid to pay virtually all costs of rebuilding. Congress overrides Pres. Bush's veto of legislation regulating the cable TV industry, the first time in 36 tries it is able to override a Bush veto (Oct. 5). Bill Clinton defeats George Bush and Ross Perot to become the 42nd president of the United States; a record 104 million Americans vote (Nov. 3). Pres. Bush commits at least 28,000 U.S. troops to protect the delivery of relief supplies to war- and famine-torn Somalia (Dec. 3). IBM announces it will cut 25,000 more jobs in 1993 in the wake of $6 billion losses, the biggest loss ever for an American corporation (Dec. 15). Weeks before leaving office, Pres. Bush pardons six Reagan administration officials, including former secretary of defense Caspar W. Weinberger, for their involvement in the Iran-Contra scandal (Dec. 24). U.S. and Russia announce nuclear arms reduction treaty that would lower each country's nuclear arsenal to 1960s levels of 3,500 and 3,000 respectively (Dec. 29).

1993 In the first attempt ever to eliminate an entire category of weapons, more than 120 nations, including the U.S. and Russia, sign an agreement to ban production, stockpiling, and use of all chemical weapons and to destroy them all within 10 years (Jan. 13). William Jefferson Clinton is officially sworn in as the 42nd president of the United States. In his inaugural speech, he tells Americans to assume greater responsibility for their country's future, declaring: "There is nothing wrong with America that cannot be cured by what is right with America (Jan. 20)." In his first official act as president, Clinton announces he will reverse the military's longstanding ban on homosexuals in the armed services. The Joint Chiefs of Staff criticize the move and declare their intention to fight it (Jan. 21). Hillary Rodham Clinton becomes the first First Lady to have an office in the West Wing (or business side) of the White House. Pres. Clinton designates her to chair a committee to overhaul the nation's health-care system (Jan. 25). Sears Roebuck and Co. announces it will close 113 stores, eliminate 50,000 jobs, and cease publication of the Sears Catalog after 97 years (Jan. 25). Congress passes the family leave bill guaranteeing workers up to 12 weeks of unpaid leave for medical emergencies. Pres. Clinton immediately signs this bill that Bush had twice vetoed (Feb. 4). Pres. Clinton says the deficit is much greater than even the government's own estimates. As a result, he must ask for tax increases, the brunt of which will be borne by those earning over $100,000 a year (Feb 15). Without warning, a powerful car bomb rips through the underground parking garage of one of the twin towers of New York's World Trade Center, killing seven, injuring about 1,000, and causing the evacuation of more than 50,000 workers (Feb. 26). A bloody gunfight erupts near Waco, Tex., when more than 100 agents from the Federal Bureau of Alcohol, Tobacco and Firearms storm the compound of religious cult leader David Koresh to arrest him on a weapons charge. Four agents are killed and at least 15 injured before they retreat. The Bureau sends 400 law-enforcement agents to patrol the compound, beginning a month-long siege (Feb. 28). An antiabortion protester shoots and kills Dr. David Gunn, who performed abortions at a Pensacola, Fla., clinic (Mar. 10). "The worst storm of the century" according to the National Weather Service pelts the mid-Atlantic and Northeast regions with as much as 40 inches of snow, killing at least 104 people, cutting off power to three million homes, and forcing eight states to declare states of emergency (Mar. 13). The Senate passes the "motor voter" allowing people to register to vote when they obtain a driver's license or apply for disability benefits (Mar. 27). The U.S. Centers for Disease Control announces that more than one in five Americans is infected with a sexually transmitted disease (Mar. 31). Federal agents end their 51-day standoff with cult leader David Koresh and send tanks in to assault the cult's Waco, Tex., compound. Koresh orders his followers to set the buildings on fire, resulting in a conflagration that kills Koresh and 86 followers, including 17 children (Apr. 19). The Supreme Court rules (9–0) that public school systems must permit religious groups to use their buildings after-hours if they allow community groups to do so (June 7). Federal and local law enforcement officials raid a suspected bomb factory in New York City in a dramatic attempt to smash a large, highly organized terrorist group allegedly planning to bomb the UN and federal office buildings, as well as the Lincoln and Holland Tunnels, and to assassinate the UN Secretary General, Sen. Alfonse D'Amato, and others. Eight suspects are arrested, all said to be Muslim extremists, several with links to those arrested in connection with the World Trade Center bombing (June 24). The Supreme Court rules (5–4) that legislative districts drawn to increase black representation can violate the constitutional rights of white voters. The worst flooding in 100 years swells rivers in nine states throughout the Midwest, taking 50 lives and leaving 70,000 people homeless. The floods cut off fresh water and electricity supplies for more than 250,000 people in Iowa (July 11) and overflows the 29-foot-high levee in Jefferson City, Mo. (July 19). Congress narrowly passes Pres. Clinton's five-year economic package, which combines tax increases on energy and business with spending cuts in hopes of reducing the federal deficit by $500 bil. (38%) over four years. All 175 Republicans in the House vote against it, and the Senate is split 50–50, leaving Vice Pres. Al Gore to cast the deciding vote well after midnight (Aug. 5–6). Pres. Clinton presents his health-care plan guaranteeing coverage to all Americans either via HMOs, health insurance, or a combination of both. The program would remain largely employment-based, with even small employers being forced to provide health plans (Sept. 22). At least 12 U.S. soldiers are killed and 78 wounded when Somali gunmen shoot down two helicopters during UN military operations in Mogadishu. Pres. Clinton orders thousands of new U.S. troops to Somalia (Oct. 3–6) and sets a six-month deadline for the withdrawal of all U.S. forces. The Centers for Disease Control reports that AIDS is now the leading killer among men aged 25–44 (Oct. 30). In a surprise victory for Pres. Clinton, the House approves the North American Free Trade Agreement, ending tariffs on goods traded between the United States, Mexico, and Canada (Nov. 17). Pres. Clinton signs the Brady bill, requiring gun purchasers to wait five days before taking possession, to give sellers and law enforcement officials time to check the buyers' backgrounds for criminal records or mental instability. The United States and Europe agree on the terms of the General Agreement on Tariffs and Trade (GATT), reducing tariffs substantially on trade in more industries in more countries than any other pact in history. The Fox network outbids CBS for the rights to broadcast National Football Conference games each Sunday for the next four years. A congressional study reveals the United States deliberately released large amounts of radiation into the environment during the 1940s and '50s in an attempt to create radioactive weapons. The study contradicts government claims made at the time that the radioactive particles falling to earth from open-air tests of atomic bombs posed little or no risk to civilians (Dec. 15). The Pentagon rules that gays and lesbians may now serve in the military, but may not openly engage in homosexual behavior or proclaim their sexual orientation. Space shuttle astronauts succeed in restoring full vision to the $1.6 billion Hubble Space Telescope.

1994 Federated Department Stores acquires rival R.H. Macy & Company, creating the largest department store chain in America. Figure skater Nancy Kerrigan is clubbed across the knees by a man later revealed to be connected to rival skater Tonya Harding. Ironically, both skaters end up on the U.S. Olympic team. In the Olympic competition, watched by nearly half of all American televisions, Kerrigan places second; Harding breaks a shoelace and finishes eighth. A violent earthquake measuring 6.6 on the Richter scale rips through Los Angeles. Because the quake occurs so early in the morning, few people are killed. Pres. Clinton asks Congress to appropriate $6.6 billion in emergency financing (Jan. 17). Iran-Contra prosecutor, Lawrence E. Walsh, releases his final report on the incident, finding no credible evidence that Pres. Reagan or Vice Pres. Bush broke the law (Jan. 18). Pres. Clinton ends the 19-year-long trade embargo on Vietnam (Feb. 3). Viacom pays $9.7 billion to acquire Paramount Communications, creating the world's second-largest media conglomerate after Time-Warner. A federally financed study finds that the drug AZT drastically reduces transmission of the HIV virus from infected mothers to their newborn babies. Federal prosecutors accuse former CIA agent Aldrich H. Ames of being a double agent for the KGB and compromising some of the most closely guarded U.S. intelligence secrets (Feb. 22). The Senate falls four votes short of passing a balanced budget amendment. All four of the men on trial for the World Trade Center bombing are found guilty of all 38 charges against them and are each sentenced to 240 years in prison. The Supreme Court unanimously rules that parody is exempt from copyright law (Mar. 7). The Dow Corning Corporation, Bristol-Myers Squibb Company, and the Baxter-Healthcare Corporation agree to pay $3.7 billion over 30 years to up to 25,000 women injured by silicone breast implants. Rodney King wins $3.8 mil. in damages in compensation for his 1991 beating by the L.A. police. John Wayne Gacy, the nation's worst serial killer ever, is executed in Illinois (May 10). The French manufacturer of the abortion pill RU-486 donates the U.S. patent rights to the Population Council, making it available to the American public by 1996 (May 18). A federal grand jury indicts Rep. Dan Rostenkowski (D-Ill.) on 17 criminal charges, including abusing the congressional payroll (May 31). Los Angeles police charge former football star O.J. Simpson with two counts of murder in the June 12 stabbing deaths of his ex-wife and her friend. Simpson leads police on a bizarre 60-mile low-speed car chase (televised live on all major networks) before surrendering to police (June 17). The dollar dips below 100 Japanese yen, a post–World War II low (June 21). Pres. Clinton replaces Chief of Staff Thomas McLarty with budget director Leon Panetta (June 27). Employees of United Airlines acquire an ownership (55%) stake in the company. The Census Bureau reports that the number of children living with an unwed parent soared by 70 percent from 1983 to 1993. Comet Shoemaker-Levy 9 crashes into Jupiter, creating a spectacular firestorm as large as Earth when the fragments enter the Jovian atmosphere (July 19). A doctor and his volunteer security escort are murdered outside a Pensacola, Fla., clinic by an antiabortion activist (July 29). Major league baseball players begin the longest strike in professional sports history, resulting in the cancellation of the World Series for the first time ever (Aug. 11). Pres. Clinton signs the crime bill, outlawing semiautomatic weapons and increasing the number of police. The Lockheed Corp. and Martin Marietta Corp. announce a $10 billion merger that will make it the nation's largest military contractor. A lone pilot crashes his plane into the White House as Secret Service officials stand by powerless to stop him. The pilot is killed instantly, though no one at the White House is injured (Sept. 12). The National Hockey League, claiming poverty, locks out its players. Agriculture Sec. Mike Espy resigns after months of scrutiny of his ethical conduct (Oct. 3). Director Steven Spielberg joins forces with entertainment executives David Geffen and Jeffrey Katzenberg to form their own movie studio. The Centers for Disease Control reports that the homicide rate for teenage boys rose 154 percent between 1985 and 1991. The Bureau of Justice Statistics announces that the number of inmates in state and federal prisons topped one million, giving the United States the highest incarceration rate in the world. Former Navy Lieutenant Paula A. Coughlin wins a total of $6.7 million in damages from the Las Vegas Hilton, where she was sexually assaulted at the infamous 1991 Tailhook Association convention. A 26-year-old Colorado man empties a clip of bullets from a Chinese-made semiautomatic rifle into the north side of the White House. No one is injured; two civilians wrestle the gunman to the ground (Oct. 29). In midterm elections, Republicans take control of both houses of Congress for the first time in 40 years (Nov. 8). Pres. Clinton says he is open to a constitutional amendment to allow school prayer. House Speaker designate Newt Gingrich says the 104th Congress will work 20-hour days, seven days a week, if necessary, to implement the Contract with America within the first 100 days of the new legislature.

For a chronology of United States and world events from November 1994 to October 1995, see Part I: "The Year in Review."

Biographies of U.S. Presidents

1. George Washington (1789–1797)

Born in Westmoreland County, Virginia, on Feb. 22, 1732, the first president, with a love for the land, trained as a surveyor in his teens. At age 16 he went to live with his brother Lawrence, who built Mount Vernon. Lawrence died only four years later, leaving his property to George, who went on to become one of Virginia's foremost landowners, ultimately acquiring more than 100,000 acres in Virginia and what is now West Virginia. In 1753 Washington joined the French and Indian War as an officer in the Virginia militia and fought bravely if poorly. The war provided Washington with the beginnings of his anti-British sentiments, exposing him to the arrogance of his British commanders. Upon returning to plantation life, and marrying Martha Custis, in 1759, Washington's resentment of the British was further fueled by their commercial restrictions. With the passage of the Stamp Act of 1765, Washington joined opposition to imperial rule in the Virginia House of Burgesses, becoming ever more active in resisting the British. He went as a delegate to the Continental Congress, which chose him to command the Continental Army when war with Britain broke out in 1775. Washington proved an uncommonly resourceful general, keeping his ragtag army together through years of defeat, retreat, and hard winters to outlast the British and finally prevail at Yorktown in 1781. Here, as in all his life, Washington earned respect for his judgment, dignity, and bearing. Retiring to Mount Vernon after the war, the general quashed suggestions that he assume military dictatorship of the fledgling republic, not wanting to subvert the very principles for which the Americans had fought. But because of his belief in a strong central government, Washington felt compelled to return to public life to salvage his country from the chaotic Articles of Confederation. In 1787 he presided over the Constitutional Convention in Philadelphia, which framed the presidency with him in mind, the only president ever elected unanimously in the electoral college (twice).

Washington's renowned judgment equaled the task of setting presidential precedent, for, as he wrote, "It is devoutly wished on my part, that these precedents may be fixed on true principles." His first act as president was to urge adoption of the Bill of Rights. Other notable achievements included national unity, quelling the Whiskey Rebellion, bolstering the treasury with a national bank, settling Jay's Treaty of commerce with Britain, and maintaining neutrality in the French Revolution. Washington successfully implemented executive power and quieted fears and suspicions of executive tyranny. But he regretted the rivalry between Thomas Jefferson and Alexander Hamilton, which led to the birth of political parties in his own cabinet; Washington feared that allegiance to "factions" would someday eclipse the guiding light of patriotism. After refusing a third term in 1796, Washington in his Farewell Address warned against party spirit, sectionalism, and "entangling alliances" with other nations. He died on Dec. 14, 1799, "first in war, first in peace, and first in the hearts of his countrymen," as his friend Henry Lee eulogized him.

2. John Adams
(1797–1801)

A fifth-generation American directly descended from a *Mayflower* passenger, John Adams was born on Oct. 30, 1735, in Braintree, Massachusetts. At Harvard Adams considered the ministry but turned to law. He joined his cousin Sam Adams as an early opponent of the Stamp Act of 1765, organizing the Sons of Liberty and defending Americans accused of smuggling. Yet he also defended the British soldiers brought to trial for the Boston Massacre in 1770. In the Revolution, Adams persuaded the Continental Congress to commission George Washington as commander in chief, declare independence, and put stars and stripes on the flag. He wrote the Massachusetts state constitution in 1779 and negotiated peace with Britain in 1782. The first vice president, Adams called that position the "most insignificant office that ever the invention of man contrived or his imagination conceived."

Elected president as a Federalist in 1796, Adams retained Washington's cabinet, but Alexander Hamilton turned the party against him for refusing to make war on France. Adams built up the navy and kept the peace, but disaffecting the Federalists and signing the Alien and Sedition Acts (1798) politically weakened "His Rotundity." Adams lost the 1800 election to the increasingly popular Thomas Jefferson. The first president to reside in the White House, Adams lived to be 90, able to see his son John Quincy Adams elected the sixth president in 1824. John Adams died on the same day that Thomas Jefferson did: July 4, 1826, the 50th anniversary of the Declaration of Independence they both signed.

3. Thomas Jefferson
(1801–1809)

Thomas Jefferson was born on Apr. 13, 1743, in Albemarle County, Virginia, son of a self-made Virginian who died when Jefferson was 14. Jefferson graduated from William and Mary in 1762, began practicing law in 1767, and joined the Virginia House of Burgesses in 1769. With his pen Jefferson sharply criticized British rule, winning a place on Virginia's Committee of Correspondence to keep in touch with patriots in other colonies. His writings amassed great respect, earning him the right, as a delegate to the Continental Congress in 1776, to draft the Declaration of Independence. He then returned to Virginia as wartime governor, narrowly escaping capture when British troops destroyed his home. Congress sent Jefferson to Europe in 1784; he was minister to France during the Constitutional Convention and the early French Revolution, an event that affected him profoundly. As secretary of state under Washington, Jefferson's faith in democracy and states' rights clashed repeatedly with Alexander Hamilton's pursuit of central executive power. Jefferson resigned in 1793 and led opposition to the Federalists, whom Jefferson called "monarchists in principle." As vice president after 1796, Jefferson speeded the Federalists' downfall by secretly authoring the Kentucky Resolutions, critical of the Alien and Sedition Acts.

The House of Representatives chose Jefferson (ironically, with Hamilton's support) over Aaron Burr, whose electoral votes for president equaled his in 1800. "We are all Republicans—we are all Federalists," appealed Jefferson in his inaugural address, easing the transfer of power. In his first term, Jefferson slashed the budget, lowered taxes, reduced the national debt, and sent marines to fight Barbary pirates. Despite some concern over his constitutional authority to make the acquisition, Jefferson's greatest feat was the Louisiana Purchase from France in 1803, which doubled the size of the United States. "The less said about the constitutional difficulties, the better," wrote Jefferson, sending Lewis and Clark to explore the new lands. In his second term, Jefferson's unpopular Embargo Act (1807) was an attempt to avoid war with Britain or France, but it ruined American merchants. Retiring to Monticello in 1809, Jefferson busied himself with inventions and designing the University of Virginia. He died on the 50th anniversary of the Declaration of Independence, July 4, 1826. His amazingly broad interests spanned music, science, architecture, agronomy, and the classics, as well as politics and government.

4. James Madison
(1809–1817)

James Madison was born to a wealthy family on Mar. 16, 1751, in Port Conway, Virginia. A Princeton graduate, Madison attended the first Virginia state convention in 1776, drafting a bill that guaranteed religious liberty. As the youngest member of the Continental Congress in 1780, he led the movement to revise the Articles of Confederation. At the Constitutional Convention in Philadelphia in 1787, Madison's Virginia Plan became the pivot of discussion. Madison, dubbed the Father of the Constitution, tirelessly directed debate and applied his political wisdom. His voluminous notes provide the best record of the convention. Madison helped ratify the Constitution by coauthoring *The Federalist* (1787–88) with John Jay and Alexander Hamilton. A four-term congressman, Madison drafted the Bill of Rights and cofounded the Democratic-Republican party. In 1794 he married a young and ebullient widow, Dolley Payne Todd, an especially popular first lady. Madison led the opposition to the Federalists' Alien and Sedition Acts with the Virginia Resolutions, arguing the acts were unconstitutional attacks on liberty. Jefferson chose Madison as his secretary of state and later as his successor. Madison easily won the election of 1808. Britain and France preyed on American shipping throughout Madison's first term. Pushed by war hawks in Congress, Madison asked for a declaration of war to defend American rights against British outrages. Reelected despite numerous American defeats in the War of 1812, Madison barely escaped Washington as the British burned the White House. Yet he persisted in "Mr. Madison's War" until the Peace of Ghent (1814) and belated victory at New Orleans (1815) vindicated him. War expenses forced Madison to recharter the national bank and raise the tariff, contrary to his Jeffersonian principles. But by 1817 Madison could retire confident of secure independence, surging nationalism, and the total collapse of his Federalist opponents who had opposed the war. He died on June 28, 1836, having outlived all the founding fathers. Madison's presidency pales beside his greatest contributions—the Constitution and the Bill of Rights.

5. James Monroe
(1817–1825)

The last Revolutionary hero and member of the "Virginia Dynasty" to become president, James Monroe was born on Apr. 28, 1758, in Westmoreland County, Virginia. He left the College of William and Mary to answer the call to arms in 1775. Wounded at Trenton, Monroe fought courageously and rose to lieutenant colonel under Gen. Washington. He learned law as an aide to Thomas Jefferson, who helped Monroe into Congress and the Senate. Much diplomatic experience followed Monroe's appointment as minister to France in 1794. Governor of Virginia from 1799 to 1802, Monroe returned to Europe to negotiate the Louisiana Purchase and later served in Britain and Spain. James Madison appointed him secretary of state in 1811 and secretary of war in 1814. Chosen to succeed Madison, Monroe won the 1816 election and presided over the Era of Good Feeling, a period marked by minimal sectional or partisan discord. Monroe bought Florida from Spain in 1819, and his popularity survived the Panic of 1819 as well as rancorous debates over the admission of Missouri as a slave state. Monroe toured the nation to jubilant crowds, winning reelection with all but one electoral vote in 1820. John Quincy Adams, his secretary of state, suggested Monroe proclaim American opposition to European encroachment in the Western Hemisphere, which he did in 1823; decades later this became known as the Monroe Doctrine. After retiring, Monroe became a regent of the University of Virginia (1826) and a member of the Virginia constitutional convention of 1829. Because of lack of attention over the years, his private affairs had suffered greatly, and Monroe discovered he was lapsing into bankruptcy. He sold his plantation and died all but penniless on Independence Day, July 4, 1831.

6. John Quincy Adams
(1825–1829)

The only president's son to become president, John Quincy Adams was born on July 11, 1767, in Braintree, Massachusetts. A true child of the Revolution, Adams watched the Battle of Bunker Hill while holding his mother's hand, and he spent his teens in Europe with his father, John Adams, on diplomatic missions for the new nation. He entered Harvard in 1785, already an experienced diplomat fluent in seven languages. After a brief career as a Boston lawyer, Adams was minister to Holland in 1794 and to Prussia in 1797. As a Federalist, Adams was elected to the Senate in 1803, but after supporting Thomas Jefferson, he had to resign. James Madison made Adams minister to Russia in 1809, in time to witness Napoleon's invasion. Then Adams helped negotiate the Peace of Ghent (1814) before serving as ambassador to England, the second of three Adams generations to hold that post. James Monroe recalled Adams from Europe—where he had spent most of his life—to appoint him secretary of state in 1817, and in that post, Adams purchased Florida from Spain, patched relations with Britain, and conceived the Monroe Doctrine.

Running for president in 1824, Adams was beaten by Andrew Jackson in both popular and electoral votes; but with Henry Clay's support, the House of Representatives made Adams president. No one ever became president with less than Adams's 31 percent of the vote, yet he refused to conciliate his foes or even act like a politician. Adams posed above politics and made no effort to deal with Congress or use patronage. Consequently, elaborate plans for internal improvements and national academies came to naught. Adams, like his father, could not win a second term, as Jackson gained revenge at the polls in 1828. Massachusetts rescued Adams from despair by sending him to Congress in 1830, and "Old Man Eloquent" remained a powerful antislavery leader until he collapsed on the floor of the House at age 80; he died in the Speaker's Room on Feb. 23, 1848. John Quincy Adams, who considered himself a failure as president, worked for the first 11 presidents and numbers among the most important architects of early American foreign policy.

7. Andrew Jackson
(1829–1837)

Born to Scotch-Irish immigrants in Waxhaw, South Carolina, on Mar. 15, 1767, Andrew Jackson was the first first-generation American to become president, as well as the first president from the western frontier and the first of seven to be born in a log cabin. Orphaned at 15, he was by then already a Revolutionary veteran, a former prisoner of war, and scarred by the saber of a British officer whose boots he refused to clean. Jackson read law and made his way to the Tennessee frontier, marrying Rachel Donelson Robards in 1791. She neglected to divorce her first husband, but Jackson challenged to a duel anyone who questioned his marriage, once even killing a man on the field of honor. Jackson's frontier law practice prospered, and Tennessee elected him its first congressman in 1796. He served only briefly in the Senate; Washington so disgusted the rough-hewn Jackson that he resigned. Back in Tennessee, Jackson became a respected judge and honorary major general of the militia. In the War of 1812, Jackson led troops to victory at the Battle of New Orleans (1815), his men routing British invaders twice their number.

"Old Hickory" was now a national icon, reentering the Senate in 1823 and running for president as a hero above party. Jackson won more popular and electoral votes than anyone in 1824 but lost when the election was thrown into the House and Henry Clay supported John Quincy Adams. Vowing revenge against the politicians, Jackson swept to victory in 1828 as the "people's choice" reform candidate. Jackson's wife died on the eve of his inauguration. As president, Jackson aggrandized the power of his office on behalf of the common man by expanding suffrage, rotating officeholders (the "spoils system"), and economizing in government. Under Jackson the federal government completely paid off the national debt. Jackson vetoed federal road-building and banking—yet he asserted federal authority by ordering troops to South Carolina in the Nullification Crisis of 1832–33. The Whig party arose in opposition to "King Andrew I," especially to his high-handed veto of the national bank, but voters endorsed Jackson's war on privilege by reelecting him in 1832. In his second term, Jackson seized land from the Native Americans, ignoring the Supreme Court, and he recognized Texas in hopes of taking more land from Mexico. He became the first president to ride a train (1833) and to survive an assassination attempt (1835). After placing his friend Martin Van Buren in the White House, Jackson retired to the Hermitage, his plantation in Tennessee. He remained quite influential behind the scenes, persuading the Democrats to discard Van Buren and nominate James K. Polk in 1844. Andrew Jackson finally succumbed to dropsy and old wounds on June 8, 1845.

8. Martin Van Buren
(1837–1841)

The first president to have played no part in the Revolution, Martin Van Buren was born to a Dutch family in Kinderhook, New York, on Dec. 5, 1782. Apprenticed to a lawyer at 14, Van Buren took to law and politics—so well, in fact, that he came to be called the Little Magician. By 1821 staunch party loyalty elevated him to the Senate, where Van Buren led northern supporters of Andrew Jackson and guided his victory in 1828. Brief service as New York governor ended when Jackson appointed him secretary of state in 1829. Van Buren helped build the Democratic party, and Jackson made him vice president in 1832. As Jackson's heir apparent, Van Buren won the 1836 election, but two months after he took office, the Panic of 1837 launched a severe depression that spoiled his presidency. "Martin Van Ruin" responded by creating the independent treasury system, but his lack of popularity was beyond repair. He made enemies in the North by protecting slavery and in the South by refusing to annex Texas. Though the self-made son of an innkeeper, Van Buren was cast by his opponents as an aristocrat; William Henry Harrison's "Hard Cider" campaign of 1840 (touting that Van Buren sipped champagne while Harrison preferred hard cider) washed him out of office. In 1844 Van Buren lost the Democratic nomination when Jackson abandoned him over the Texas issue. But in 1848 Van Buren guaranteed a Democratic defeat by founding the Free Soil party and running for president, which split the decisive New York vote. Van Buren died a Unionist on July 24, 1862, the only president whose life touched both the Revolution and the Civil War.

9. William Henry Harrison
(1841)

Son of a signatory of the Declaration of Independence and grandfather of a president, William Henry Harrison was born in Charles City County, Virginia, on Feb. 9, 1773. Campaign legend held that his birthplace was a log cabin, but in fact it was a plantation mansion. Harrison left medical school to join the army and fight Native Americans in the Northwest in 1791. After an illustrious military career, he served in Congress (1816–19), the U.S. Senate (1825–28), and as ambassador to Colombia (1828–29) before falling victim to Andrew Jackson's spoils system. Harrison fit Whig designs of defeating Jacksonians with a war hero of their own and received the Whig nomination to face Martin Van Buren in 1840. Harrison's campaign sidestepped issues to cast him as a plain frontiersman who guzzled hard cider while Van Buren sipped champagne. In the first modern election full of hoopla and hype, "Tippecanoe and Tyler Too"—the Whig slogan—linked Harrison's most famous victory with his obscure running mate. A huge turnout gave Harrison the victory at age 67, the oldest president before Ronald Reagan. Harrison delivered a record 8,500-word inaugural address hatless and coatless on a drizzly winter day. He caught a cold that never left and succumbed to pneumonia on Apr. 4, 1841, the first president to die in the White House—where he lived for only 31 days. His grandson, Benjamin Harrison, was the 23rd president.

10. John Tyler
(1841–1845)

The first vice president to become president by succession, the first president to see impeachment proposed against him, and the only president to change parties in office, John Tyler was born on Mar. 29, 1790, in Charles City County, Virginia. He was a Virginia legislator, congressman, senator, and governor before the

Whigs chose him as William Henry Harrison's running mate in 1840. Though a strict constructionist and states' rights advocate, Tyler earned the Whigs' favor by opposing Andrew Jackson. But as president after Harrison's death, "His Accidency" earned their ire by vetoing, in mid-1842, two tariff bills vital to the Whig party. Eventually, his cabinet resigned and his party expelled him. Outraged members of Congress called for his impeachment. On July 10, 1842, John Minor Botts, a Whig representative from Richmond, Va., proposed the appointment of a special committee to investigate Tyler's conduct in office with an eye toward impeachment. The proposal was defeated on Jan. 10, 1843, by a vote of 127 to 83. This was the first time presidential impeachment proceedings were introduced in Congress. Tyler concluded the Webster-Ashburton Treaty (1842), which adjusted the northeastern boundary of the United States, and the Texas annexation (1845), but without popular or partisan support, he was powerless and decided against running for reelection. A veto on his last day in office became the first ever to be overridden. Tyler died on Jan. 18, 1862, awaiting his seat in the Confederate Congress.

11. James Knox Polk
(1845–1849)

The first dark-horse president, James Knox Polk was born in Mecklenburg County, North Carolina, on Nov. 2, 1795. A star orator in Tennessee politics, Polk idolized Andrew Jackson. "Young Hickory" took Jackson's old seat in Congress in 1825 and was reelected seven times. Polk was Speaker of the House from 1835 to 1839 and governor of Tennessee until 1841. He lost two bids for reelection, and his political career seemed over when the Democrats nominated him for president in 1844. Polk's name had not even appeared on the first seven ballots, but the deadlocked convention latched onto Polk as a proexpansion dark horse. In the election he defeated Henry Clay by 1.5 percent of the vote on a platform that ignored slavery. From his inaugural address onward, Polk pursued expansion in the West. In 1846, he bluffed the British into believing the United States would go to war over Oregon, extracting a treaty for it. When Mexico attacked U.S. troops in disputed Texas territory, Polk called it an invasion and got a declaration of war. The ensuing Mexican War (1846–48) won California and the Southwest for the United States in the Treaty of Guadalupe-Hidalgo. Polk declined a second term, having fulfilled the nation's "Manifest Destiny" to span the continent. The last strong president before Abraham Lincoln, Polk added a million square miles to the United States. But the issue of slavery in the new territories split the Democrats and soon the whole country. "The presidency is not a bed of roses," complained Polk, who left the White House totally exhausted and died three months later, on June 15, 1849.

12. Zachary Taylor
(1849–1850)

Zachary Taylor, the first president to have no previous political experience, was born on Nov. 24, 1784, in Montebello, Virginia. His father was a colonel in the Revolutionary War, and Taylor—along with four brothers—served as a professional soldier for nearly 40 years. After distinguished service against the British and Native Americans, Gen. Taylor's finest hour came during the Mexican War, when he captured Monterrey and smashed Gen. Santa Ana's much larger army at the Battle of Buena Vista (1847). Though Taylor had never held office or even voted, the Whigs eagerly nominated "Old Rough and Ready" for president in 1848; Taylor, like William Henry Harrison, was an apolitical war hero above the slavery controversy. He won the election when the new Free Soil party siphoned off Democratic votes, but Taylor took office with Congress in chaos over the admission of California as a free state. Taylor opposed the Compromise of 1850 and probably would have vetoed it, but he died suddenly of acute indigestion on July 9, 1850. (A long, hot Fourth of July at Washington Monument ceremonies had no doubt contributed to his weakened state.) Backers of the compromise rejoiced that Taylor's death saved the Union. Taylor was both the last of eight slave owners and the last Whig to be elected president.

13. Millard Fillmore
(1850–1853)

Born in a log cabin on Jan. 7, 1800, Millard Fillmore was the son of a poor farmer in Locke Township, New York. Apprenticed to a cloth maker in his youth, Fillmore struggled for an education and got a job teaching even though he never attended college. Clerking for a judge taught Fillmore enough law to join the bar at age 23, and he became a prosperous New York attorney. Fillmore entered politics as an Anti-Mason and was a four-term congressman when the Whigs made him Zachary Taylor's vice president in 1848. Dignified good looks were Fillmore's main political asset; he was quite unprepared for the presidency when Taylor died suddenly in 1850. Fillmore delayed civil war another decade by signing the Compromise of 1850, but he lost the nomination in 1852 when the Whigs turned to Gen. Winfield Scott, yet another genial war hero and their last candidate. In 1856 Fillmore ran again for president as candidate of the American, or "Know-Nothing," party. Fillmore hoped to unite the country behind anti-Catholicism and nativism, submerging the slavery issue, but he carried only Maryland. Though a Unionist in the Civil War, Fillmore denounced Abraham Lincoln and remained sharply critical of Republicans until his death on Mar. 8, 1874.

14. Franklin Pierce
(1853–1857)

Son of a Revolutionary War hero, Franklin Pierce was born in Hillsboro, New Hampshire, on Nov. 23, 1804—the first president born in the 19th century. A leader of Jacksonian Democrats in Congress in the 1830s, Pierce had been absent from national politics for a decade when the deadlocked Democratic convention nominated him for president on the 49th ballot in 1852. A dark horse candidate, Pierce won enough southern votes to defeat Gen. Winfield Scott, his Mexican War commander, becoming the youngest president as of that date. Pierce greatly hastened the coming of the Civil War by signing the Kansas-Nebraska Act (1854), which repealed the Missouri Compromise and reopened the dangerous issue of slavery expansion. He continually appeased the South by backing proslavery ruffians in "Bleeding Kansas," encouraging slavery expansionists who coveted Cuba, and buying the land known as the Gadsen Purchase from Mexico for a southern railroad. As a result Pierce's party lost elections to Republicans who charged that "slave power" controlled the White House. In 1856 Pierce became the only elected president to be denied his own party's renomination. During the Civil War, Pierce criticized the Emancipation Proclamation and was nearly lynched by angry New Englanders. He died a forgotten, depressed alcoholic, in Concord, New Hampshire, on Oct. 8, 1869, the only president from New Hampshire.

15. James Buchanan
(1857–1861)

Considered one of the worst presidents because of his lack of good judgment and moral courage, and also the only bachelor president, James Buchanan was born in Mercersburg, Pennsylvania, on Apr. 23, 1791. A lawyer and veteran of the War of 1812, Buchanan compiled more than 40 years of public service as legislator and diplomat. The Democrats nominated Buchanan in 1856 largely because he was in England during the Kansas-Nebraska debate and thus remained untainted by either side of the issue. Millard Fillmore's "Know-Nothing" candidacy helped Buchanan defeat John C. Frémont, the first Republican candidate for president. Buchanan favored "popular sovereignty" over slavery in the territories and was the last of the Doughfaces, or northern politicians submissive to the South. Few Americans shared Buchanan's faith that the Supreme Court's *Dred Scott* decision (1857) would end conflict over slavery expansion "speedily and finally." When it did not, Buchanan tried to close the issue himself by urging that Kansas be admitted as a slave state—an even worse miscalculation. Democrats deserted him, and Republicans won the House in 1858, but Buchanan's vetoes and southern votes in the Senate stalemated the government. He inadvertently helped Abraham Lincoln win in 1860 by refusing to conciliate his own party. The secession crisis paralyzed Buchanan, who denied both the southern right to secede and the federal government's right to do anything about it; he was relieved to hand Lincoln the reins. Buchanan died on June 1, 1868. On the day before, he predicted that "history will vindicate my memory," but historians continue mainly to denigrate him.

16. Abraham Lincoln
(1861–1865)

A largely unpopular president until he was assassinated (the first assassinated president), Abraham Lincoln was born in a log cabin in Hodgenville, Kentucky, on Feb. 12, 1809. He accumulated barely a year's total education while growing up, though he did learn to write and developed a fondness for reading. Family moves took him to Indiana and then to Illinois by the time he was 21. At age 19 Lincoln had worked his way down the Mississippi and came away appalled at slavery. He served in the Black Hawk War (1832) before losing an election for the state legislature. A failed storekeeper, Lincoln worked odd jobs while he taught himself law, sometimes walking 20 miles to borrow books. He finally made the state legislature in 1834 as a Whig, and in 1842 married Mary Todd, having canceled their engagement once previously.

Elected to Congress in 1846, Lincoln denounced James K. Polk for precipitating the Mexican War. He returned to his Springfield, Ill., law practice after only one term. But the repeal of the Missouri Compromise shocked Lincoln back into politics, and he helped organize the Illinois Republicans. An unsuccessful candidate for the Senate in 1858, Lincoln drew national attention in debates with Stephen A. Douglas, the nation's leading Democrat. Lincoln was rewarded with his party's nomination for president in 1860, the least objectionable candidate among several more prominent Republicans. He defeated three opponents in the election, though his name did not even appear on the ballot in the South. As Southern states left the Union, Lincoln preached conciliation and promised no harm to slavery—but he vowed to crush secession and forced the issue at Ft. Sumter. After early reverses in the Civil War, Lincoln decided slavery had to be abolished altogether to restore the Union, and he issued the Emancipation Proclamation (1862). Lincoln's management of the war was thwarted by incompetent generals, feuding politicians, and his own inexperience, which matched that of his troops. Yet, like them, Lincoln learned on the job, settling on Ulysses S. Grant as his top general by 1864. The powers of the presidency expanded dramatically under Lincoln, who stretched the Constitution on behalf of the war effort. Lincoln defeated Gen. George McClellan for reelection in 1864, vowing to "bind up the nation's wounds." Before he had the chance, Lincoln was shot on Good Friday, five days after the war's end, by John Wilkes Booth, an arch-Confederate. Lincoln died the next morning, on Apr. 15, 1865. His martyrdom spurred the vengefulness of Reconstruction, ironically against Lincoln's own wishes. Millions of Americans lined the 1,700-mile route of Lincoln's funeral train, their mournful cries resounding all the way back to Illinois. Lincoln's prestige has grown with time, until many have come to regard him as the greatest president.

17. Andrew Johnson
(1865–1869)

The only president ever impeached, Andrew Johnson was born in Raleigh, North Carolina, on Dec. 29, 1808, the son of a poor laborer. No president could claim humbler origins: Johnson's father died when he was three, his mother worked as a washerwoman, and he never attended a day of school in his life. As a teenager he ran away to Tennessee, opened a successful tailor's shop, and got elected mayor of Greeneville by age 21. A fiery Democratic stump speaker, Johnson's attacks on Whigs and rich planters won him a seat in the state legislature in 1835 and in Congress in 1843, made him governor in 1853, and took him to the Senate in 1857. Alone among 22 southern senators, Johnson stayed loyal to the Union in 1861, though a mob of Virginians nearly lynched him for it. Lincoln appointed Johnson military governor of Tennessee, and he was nominated for vice president on the "National Union" ticket in 1864. Suddenly made president by Lincoln's assassination, Johnson vowed to carry on Lincoln's policy of leniency toward the South, but radical Republican opposition and his own coarse ineptitude led to serious clashes with Congress. Johnson vetoed 29 bills and was overridden 15 times, more than any other president to that time. A former slave owner, Johnson resisted Republican efforts to aid the freedmen. His only victory was the unpopular purchase of Alaska in 1867. Congress systematically stripped him of power until Johnson fought back by removing his disloyal secretary of war, Edwin M. Stanton. Impeached in the House for defying the Tenure of Office Act, Johnson was tried in the Senate and acquitted by a single vote on May 26, 1868. Few presidents were so stymied in office. Tennessee helped vindicate Johnson by making him the only former president elected to the Senate, but he died a few months later, on July 31, 1875.

18. Ulysses S. Grant
(1869–1877)

A better general than president, Ulysses Simpson Grant was born in Point Pleasant, Ohio, on Apr. 27, 1822. Having barely passed West Point's height requirement for entrance, Grant attended the academy and graduated in the middle of his class in 1843. Fifty of Grant's classmates fought with or against him as Civil War generals. He served under Gen. Zachary Taylor in the Mexican War before marrying his sweetheart, Julia Dent, in 1848. Assigned to isolated posts after 1852, Grant grew bored away from his family and reportedly turned to heavy drinking. Finally resigning from the army in 1854, he went to Missouri, only to fail in farming and real estate. When the Civil War began, Grant was working in his younger brother's leather shop in Galena, Ill. He received a commission and rose rapidly to brigadier general. U.S. Grant acquired the nickname Unconditional Surrender for his string of western victories, notably at Vicksburg and Chattanooga in 1863. Once Abraham Lincoln made him supreme commander in 1864, Grant opened a relentless offensive that quickly ended the war. He personally accepted Gen. Robert E. Lee's surrender at Appomattox in 1865. After feuding with Andrew Johnson, Grant joined the Republicans and was elected president in 1868. Grant pressed radical Reconstruction in the South with mixed results. Corruption—notably the Jay Gould (1869), Crédit Mobilier (1872), and Whiskey Ring (1875) scandals—marred Grant's presidency; nevertheless, he easily won reelection in 1872. The Panic of 1873 triggered a deep economic depression that dissuaded Grant from a third term in 1876. Reconsidering in 1880, he sought the Republican nomination again and nearly succeeded. Afterward Grant retired and went bankrupt. To provide for his family, he began writing his memoirs. Developing cancer, Grant valiantly hung on to finish the project, which would earn him some literary fame and his family half a million dollars. He died on July 23, 1885, just four days after completing his autobiography.

19. Rutherford B. Hayes
(1877–1881)

Rutherford Birchard Hayes was born a frail child on Oct. 4, 1822, in Delaware, Ohio, where he was raised by his mother. After attending Harvard Law School, he set up a successful Cincinnati law practice in 1849. Hayes defended fugitive slaves and helped found the Ohio Republicans. In 1852 he married Lucy Ware Webb, the first college graduate first lady. A decorated Civil War veteran, Hayes was wounded five times and promoted to general. From 1868 to 1876 he served as governor of Ohio. Republicans turned to Hayes as a scandal-free hero in 1876 and nominated him for president. He lost the election to Samuel Tilden of the Democrats, but Republicans in Congress disputed enough state vote totals to connive "Rutherfraud" into office with the support of southern Democrats. Hayes's first acts were to appoint an ex-Confederate to his cabinet and to withdraw federal troops from the South. He never overcame the resulting stigma of political bargain, and facing a Democratic Congress, Hayes seemed destined for a weak presidency. Yet he put the nation back on the gold standard, put down railroad strikes, reformed the civil service, and banished liquor from the White House before keeping his promise to serve only one term. Hayes viewed the return of prosperity and Republican majorities in Congress as personal triumphs. He worked quietly for charitable causes until his death on Jan. 17, 1893.

20. James A. Garfield
(1881)

The last log cabin president, James Abram Garfield was born near Orange, Ohio, on Nov. 19, 1831, and like Rutherford B. Hayes, Garfield was raised by his mother. Garfield graduated from Williams College in 1856, became a classics professor, president of Hiram College, a lawyer, and at age 30 the youngest Union general in the Civil War. Garfield left the battlefield in 1864 to enter Congress, where he remained until the Republicans nominated him for president in 1880, a dark-horse compromise between Grant and James G. Blaine. Garfield defeated Gen. Winfield Scott Hancock of the Democrats by 0.1 percent of the vote in a campaign stressing tariffs. Republicans immediately swarmed to Garfield, demanding patronage for their rival "Stalwart" and "Half-Breed" factions. After only four months in office, Garfield was shot in a train station by Charles J. Guiteau, a disappointed Stalwart office-seeker. Garfield died 80 days later, on Sept. 19, 1881, the second presidential assassination ending the second-shortest presidency. When hordes of Republican hopefuls had besieged the White House begging for jobs, Garfield had exclaimed: "My God! What is there in this place that a man should ever want to get in it?"

21. Chester A. Arthur
(1881–1885)

Chester Alan Arthur was born a preacher's son on Oct. 5, 1829, in Fairfield, Vermont. He grew up in Vermont and in New York to become an ardent abolitionist like his father. A true machine politician, Arthur worked for Republican candidates in New York and enjoyed several patronage jobs during the Civil War. Ulysses S. Grant appointed him collector of the port of New York in 1871, and Arthur prospered there until 1879, when Rutherford B. Hayes removed him in the name of reform. In 1880 "Half-Breed" Republicans nominated Arthur for vice president in a conciliatory gesture to his "Stalwart" faction. "The office of Vice President is a greater honor than I ever dreamed of attaining," he said. But Arthur acceded to the presidency on Sept. 19, 1881, when another Stalwart assassinated James A. Garfield. Perhaps shamed into supporting civil service reform, Arthur signed the Pendleton Act (1883) and rooted out post office graft. Democrats in Congress thwarted the rest of Arthur's initiatives; Republicans, whose calls for spoils Arthur ignored, denied him renomination in 1884. He lost a Senate race in New York and died two years later, on Nov. 18, 1886. Arthur was the last of three presidents in the single year 1881.

22, 24. Grover Cleveland
(1885–1889; 1893–1897)

The only president to serve two nonconsecutive terms, Stephen Grover Cleveland was a minister's son, born in Caldwell, New Jersey, on Mar. 18, 1837. The family moved to New York, where Cleveland's uncle made him a lawyer. He showed scant interest in politics until Buffalo elected him mayor in 1881, and the next year Cleveland became governor. His war on corrupt Tammany Hall made Cleveland the perfect Democratic reform candidate for president in 1884. During the election campaign, backers of James G. Blaine, the Republican candidate, accused Cleveland of fathering an illegitimate child. He admitted it and won anyway—by 0.3 percent of the vote—but not before the Republicans came up with the immortal campaign chant "Ma! Ma! Where's my Pa?/Gone to the White House,/Ha! Ha! Ha!" The first Democratic president after the Civil War, Cleveland pushed for civil service reform and lower tariffs. In the first White House wedding, Cleveland married Frances Folsom in 1886. Cleveland cast over 300 vetoes—more than twice the combined total of all previous presidents. He cut Civil War pensions, seized 81 million acres of unused land from railroads, and signed the Interstate Commerce Act (1887). Defeated in the 1888 election, Cleveland claimed there was "no happier man in the United States"; yet four years later he won a rematch with Benjamin Harrison. Back in the White House, Cleveland underwent a secret operation to remove his cancerous upper jaw. His tight-money policies did nothing to help the depression after the Panic of 1893. Cleveland sent federal troops to break up the Pullman strike (1894) and supported William McKinley, a Republican, for president in 1896. "I have tried so hard to do right," Cleveland said on his deathbed on June 24, 1908.

23. Benjamin Harrison
(1889–1893)

Benjamin Harrison was born on Aug. 20, 1833, at the North Bend, Ohio, farm of his grandfather William Henry Harrison, the ninth president. He took up the law in Indiana before joining the Union Army in 1862. Harrison finished the Civil War a brigadier general and returned to Indiana, where he was a prominent Republican, defeated for governor in 1876 but elected senator in 1881. A colorless compromise candidate for president, Harrison won the 1888 election despite receiving fewer popular votes than Grover Cleveland. Harrison bowed to the "Billion Dollar Congress" of free-spending Republicans who escalated Civil War pensions, transportation subsidies, naval construction, and spoils patronage. The McKinley Tariff, the Sherman Anti-Trust Act, the Sherman Silver Purchase Act (all 1890), and Secretary of State James G. Blaine's vigorous foreign policy were hallmarks of Harrison's administration, which oversaw the admission of six new states. Democrats won back Congress in 1890 and the White House in 1892, when Harrison lost to Cleveland in their rematch. A legal expert, Harrison taught at Stanford University and defended Venezuela in a boundary dispute with Britain before his death, on Mar. 13, 1901. Harrison referred to the White House as "my jail."

25. William McKinley
(1897–1901)

The last Civil War veteran to become president, William McKinley was born in Niles, Ohio, on Jan. 29, 1843, son of an iron founder. A college dropout, McKinley was a post office clerk when the Civil War began. He volunteered as a private and mustered out as a 22-year-old major. McKinley studied law and was elected to Congress in 1876. A longtime Republican floor leader, he authored the record-high McKinley Tariff of 1890, before losing his seat that same year. Ohio millionaire Marcus Hanna, McKinley's political manager, engineered two governor's terms for him and funded McKinley's run for the presidency in 1896. William Jennings Bryan opposed him on a free-silver platform, but McKinley's dignified front porch campaign stressed sound money, tariffs, and the "full dinner pail." He won the election with the first popular majority since Grant's reelection. Strongly probusiness, McKinley raised the tariff still higher and reluctantly led the country into the Spanish-American War (1898). By acquiring the Philippines and other islands, the country became a world power under McKinley, who went on to proclaim the open-door policy in China. McKinley defeated Bryan by an even larger margin in 1900 and was enjoying great popularity when anarchist Leon Czolgosz shot him in Buffalo, N.Y. McKinley died two weeks later, on Sept. 14, 1901.

26. Theodore Roosevelt
(1901–1909)

Theodore Roosevelt was born in New York City on Oct. 27, 1858, the only president born there. A small, sickly child plagued by asthma, Roosevelt overcame a pampered youth to live the "strenuous life": he boxed, hiked, hunted, rode horses, and climbed the Matterhorn. After graduating Phi Beta Kappa from Harvard in 1880, he attended Columbia Law School and became the youngest member of New York's legislature. Rich men of his day did not consider politics a suitable avocation, but Roosevelt desperately wanted "to be of the governing class." His first wife, Alice Hathaway Lee, died on the same day his mother died in 1884. Roosevelt wrote books and ran a cattle ranch in North Dakota until he married Edith Kermit Carow in 1886 and they moved to Oyster Bay, N.Y. During the Spanish-American War, Roosevelt left a job at the Navy Department in 1898 to lead the Rough Riders volunteer regiment in Cuba, achieving glory in the Battle of San Juan Hill. Elected governor of New York immediately upon returning home, Roosevelt soon thereafter was named William McKinley's vice-presidential running mate, in 1900. Roosevelt learned of McKinley's death while on a mountain-climbing expedition.

The youngest president at 42, "T.R." promised a Square Deal to close the gap between capital and labor. He mounted well-publicized campaigns against big business and successfully arbitrated major strikes. "Teddy's" popularity soared when he humbled billionaire J.P. Morgan in the Northern Securities case, and a record plurality reelected him in 1904. Roosevelt signed progressive laws to regulate railroads, inspect food and drugs, and create more than 150 million acres of national parks and forests. No less vigorous in foreign policy, Roosevelt's corollary to the Monroe Doctrine asserted the country would intervene to prevent European involvement in Latin America. For helping to end the Russo-Japanese War, Roosevelt became the first American to win the Nobel Prize, but he considered the Panama Canal his greatest achievement. Roosevelt kept his pledge not to seek a third term in 1908—but in 1912 he ran against his chosen successor, William Howard Taft. Denied his party's nomination, Roosevelt survived an assassination attempt and won more than four million votes as the Progressive, or Bull Moose, candidate. During World War I, Roosevelt bitterly denounced the neutrality policy of Woodrow Wilson, who then denied Roosevelt's request to lead troops in France. Roosevelt's four sons fought there; Quentin, the youngest, was killed in action. While laying plans for another run at the White House, Roosevelt died suddenly of a cardiac embolism on Jan. 6, 1919. "No president has ever enjoyed himself as much as I have enjoyed myself," he said.

27. William Howard Taft
(1909–1913)

By far the largest president at over 330 pounds, William Howard Taft was born in Cincinnati, Ohio, on Sept. 15, 1857. He graduated from Yale in 1878, then followed his father into law and Republican politics: "I always had my plate right side up when offices were falling," Taft wrote. William McKinley sent him to govern the Philippines in 1900, and Theodore Roosevelt appointed him secretary of war in 1904. Taft traveled around the world as Roosevelt's personal emissary, becoming T.R.'s chosen successor in 1908. As president, Taft tried to carry on Roosevelt's policies, but he wrecked the Republican party by alienating progressives from conservative "Stand-Patters" over tariff and conservation issues. Taft initiated the income tax and pursued antitrust suits against big business—but generally he sided with wealthy interests. An infuriated Roosevelt challenged Taft unsuccessfully for the Republican nomination in 1912, then outpolled him in the election, giving Woodrow Wilson the victory. With eight electoral votes, Taft suffered the worst-ever defeat for an incumbent president. But the better part of his career lay ahead: Taft, always more comfortable as a jurist, taught law at Yale until he was appointed chief justice of the United States in 1921. He served with distinction, alternating a liberal nationalism in economic affairs with political and social conservatism. Taft died on Mar. 8, 1930. Never nostalgic for the White House, Taft once said, "I don't remember that I ever was president."

28. Woodrow Wilson
(1913–1921)

Born on Dec. 28, 1856, in Staunton, Virginia, the son of a Presbyterian minister, Thomas Woodrow Wilson grew up in Virginia, Georgia, South Carolina, and North Carolina—the first southern president since Andrew Jackson. Probably dyslexic, Wilson was slow to read; yet he became the most highly educated president. Graduated from Princeton in 1879, Wilson studied law before taking a Ph.D. in political science at Johns Hopkins in 1886. He taught at Bryn Mawr and Wesleyan University before Princeton appointed him professor in 1890. Wilson attracted the attention of Democratic bosses after he was elected Princeton's president in 1902, and they persuaded him to run for New Jersey governor in 1910. A strong progressive, Wilson won easily—and then turned on party bosses by sponsoring antimachine reforms. In 1912 the Democrats nominated Wilson for president on the 46th ballot, and he won, with Theodore Roosevelt and William Howard Taft splitting the Republican vote.

Wilson's expert knowledge of government and strong party leadership pushed the Underwood Tariff, the Federal Reserve Act, the Federal Trade Commission, and the Clayton Antitrust Act through Congress by 1914. Restoring competition to the monopoly-plagued economy was the goal of Wilson's "New Freedom," until war in Europe made neutrality his top priority. German attacks on Allied ships carrying Americans strained Wilson's commitment, but he was narrowly reelected in 1916 on the slogan "He Kept Us Out of the War." After Germany spurned Wilson's mediation and resumed attacks on Allied shipping, Congress declared war at Wilson's behest in April 1917. World War I would "make the world safe for democracy," Wilson vowed, and he issued "Fourteen Points" for a just peace. After the armistice in November 1918, Wilson became the first president to visit Europe, when he attended the Paris peace conference that produced the Versailles Treaty. Wilson's dream of "peace without vengeance" was frustrated at Versailles, where he compromised away his Fourteen Points to obtain the League of Nations for collective security. In July 1919, Wilson returned home to face hostile Republicans in the Senate, where his treaty languished. On a nationwide speaking tour, Wilson collapsed from exhaustion in Colorado and suffered a paralytic stroke in October 1919. Wilson, all but incapacitated, refused to compromise as the Senate rejected the Versailles Treaty. Wilson's second wife, Edith Bolling Galt, whom he married in 1915, shielded the disabled president from the press and politicians until the end of his term in 1921. Woodrow Wilson died in his sleep on Feb. 3, 1924, frustrated by his own country's refusal to join the League of Nations.

29. Warren G. Harding
(1921–1923)

The first president born after the Civil War, Warren Gamaliel Harding was born in Blooming Grove, Ohio, which earlier had been named Corsica, on Nov. 2, 1865. He taught, studied law, and sold insurance before following his father into the newspaper business. Marriage to Florence DeWolfe, a wealthy widow, in 1891 helped finance Harding's paper, the *Marion Star.* A staunch Republican, Harding's probusiness editorials got him elected state senator and lieutenant governor. Although defeated for governor in 1910, Harding was elected senator four years later. Republicans turned to him in 1920 as a compromise candidate for president, the "best of the second-raters"; his good looks were expected to win over women first-time voters. Elected by an unprecedented 61 percent majority, Harding promised a return to "normalcy" for Americans tired of war and Woodrow Wilson. Harding's administration featured higher tariffs, lower taxes, and immigration restriction—but perhaps most notably, pervasive corruption and incompetence by Harding's crooked appointees. Harding was disturbed by the dishonesty of "my God-damn friends," two of whom committed suicide to avoid prosecution. While visiting San Francisco, Harding died suddenly of an embolism on Aug. 2, 1923. Scandals involving secret love affairs, official graft, and the vast Teapot Dome swindle erupted soon thereafter. Mrs. Harding zealously tracked down Harding's letters and destroyed them, leaving him the most enigmatic president, and certainly one of the worst.

30. Calvin Coolidge
(1923–1929)

The only president to share the nation's birthday, John Calvin Coolidge was born in Plymouth, Vermont, on July 4, 1872. Descended from a long line of New Englanders, he graduated from Amherst in 1895, practiced law in Massachusetts, and entered Republican politics in 1899. Coolidge rose slowly through a succession of state offices until he was elected governor of Massachusetts in 1918. Acclaimed for crushing the Boston police strike in 1919, Coolidge became the unexpected Republican vice-presidential nominee in 1920. After Warren G. Harding's death while still in office, Coolidge's own father swore him in as the new president. "Silent Cal" was the butt of jokes for his laconic utterances, but his minimalist approach to government fit the public mood, and he restored respectability to the White House, tainted by Harding's corrupt appointees and all-night poker parties. Instead of the whiskey that once flowed freely there, ice water in paper cups was served to visitors. Coolidge, untouched by leftover scandals, won the election in his own right in 1924. Pronouncing that the "business of America is business," he ushered in the heady years of Coolidge Prosperity, as the stock market soared higher and higher. Coolidge ignored foreign affairs and made frugality his trademark, slashing the budget at the expense of farmers and veterans, even driving out a White House cook who could not abide Coolidge's cost cutting. "It's a pretty good idea to get out when they still want you," Coolidge said, surprising the nation at the peak of his success by declining to run again in 1928. A popular president, Coolidge was safely out of politics when the Great Depression arrived. He died on Jan. 5, 1933, on the eve of the New Deal.

31. Herbert Hoover
(1929–1933)

Born in West Branch, Iowa, on Aug. 10, 1874, Herbert Clark Hoover was the first president from west of the Mississippi. Orphaned at eight and raised by Quaker relatives in Iowa and Oregon, Hoover joined the first graduating class of Stanford University in 1895. He became a world-famous mining engineer and a multimillionaire by age 40. In World War I, Hoover helped rescue Americans stranded in Europe, distributed food supplies to occupied Belgium, and convinced the nation to save food ("Hooverize") for the war effort. Hoover was Woodrow Wilson's economic adviser at Versailles, and he organized relief for famine-struck Russia during the revolution. Joining the Republicans in 1919, Hoover earned prominence as the secretary of commerce in the 1920s and was elected president in 1928—the only electoral victory of his life. He promised a "chicken in every pot," but a few months later, the Wall Street crash brought on the Great Depression. Paralyzed by his conservative instincts, Hoover could not halt the spread of bank failures, bankruptcy, unemployment, and despair. Government should not get involved, he believed, and public relief would ruin American morals—so Hoover called for a balanced budget while promising the return of prosperity. He sent tanks to disperse veterans begging for pensions, and shantytowns across the country were dubbed Hoovervilles. Massively defeated by Franklin D. Roosevelt in 1932, Hoover called the New Deal "socialistic, collectivistic, fascistic and communistic." For decades Americans blamed Hoover for the depression and criticized his hard-hearted refusal to help the needy. Hoover lived another 31 years, the longest postpresidential lifespan, and he salvaged his reputation with more relief work after World War II. In retirement Hoover chaired two bipartisan commissions on government reorganization, issuing many important recommendations for federal reform. Boulder Dam on the Colorado River was renamed to honor Hoover before he died, at age 90, on Oct. 20, 1964.

32. Franklin D. Roosevelt
(1933–1945)

The only president elected more than twice, Franklin Delano Roosevelt was born to a wealthy Hyde Park, New York, family on Jan. 30, 1882. He followed his cousin, Theodore Roosevelt, into Harvard and Columbia Law School—but not into the Republican party. F.D.R. was a Democratic state senator, assistant secretary of the navy, and nominee for vice president in 1920. Paralyzed by polio in 1921, Roosevelt learned to walk with braces and canes. As governor of New York after 1928, he pioneered unemployment relief in the Great Depression, earning him the Democratic nomination for president in 1932. Herbert Hoover, brooding and baffled by the depression, posed little challenge to the beaming, magnetic Roosevelt, who won the election by 23 million to 16 million votes. F.D.R. promised vague but bold experimentation ("above all, try something"), and as he took office in the worst inaugural crisis since Abraham Lincoln's, he assured Americans they had "nothing to fear but fear itself." F.D.R.'s first 100 days set a breakneck pace as compliant congressmen approved his New Deal for relief and recovery. Major landmarks were the National Industrial Recovery Act, the Agricultural Adjustment Act, the Tennessee Valley Authority, the Works Progress Administration, the National Labor Relations Act (Wagner Act), and the Social Security Act (1933–35). Though often contradictory and ineffective, the New Deal established the federal government's responsibility for protecting farmers, workers, and the unemployed while actively regulating the economy to prevent another crash. F.D.R.'s high-profile "fireside chats," public works projects, and Social Security programs overcame despair and restored public confidence in the economy and government.

Reelected by a huge margin in 1936, Roosevelt proved incapable of ending the depression, as he ran afoul of the "nine old men" on the Supreme Court. Almost as many Americans called Roosevelt a Communist as praised him for rescuing the common man. Despite alienating many voters with his court-packing plan and "soak the rich" taxes, F.D.R. won an unprecedented third term in 1940. As war loomed in Europe, F.D.R. used his mastery of public opinion to lead Americans away from isolation, helping Britain with the destroyers-for-bases deal (1940) and Lend-Lease Act (1941) even before Pearl Harbor. World War II then occupied F.D.R.'s full attention as he shelved the New Deal and orchestrated the mammoth war effort. Roosevelt crisscrossed the globe to meet with Allied leaders and kept close personal control of diplomacy and grand strategy. He rallied a powerful sense of national purpose in the war, winning his fourth election in 1944. Together with Winston Churchill and Josef Stalin, F.D.R. planned a postwar peace of UN cooperation. Just after the Yalta Conference, Roosevelt died suddenly of a cerebral hemorrhage on Apr. 12, 1945, days before the war's end. His wife of 40 years, Eleanor Roosevelt, easily the most influential first lady, led her husband's campaign on behalf of disadvantaged Americans and continued it long after his death.

33. Harry S Truman
(1945–1953)

A plain midwestern farmer and World War I artilleryman, Harry S Truman (the *S* does not stand for a middle name) was born on May 8, 1884, in Lamar, Missouri. After his Kansas City haberdashery failed, Truman entered politics as a Democrat in the 1920s, and the local Pendergast machine arranged his election to the Senate as a New Dealer in 1934. National attention came to Truman when he headed a congressional committee investigating government waste during World War II. When Franklin D. Roosevelt needed a new vice president in 1944, he chose Truman. After only a few weeks in office, Truman had the presidency thrust upon him by Roosevelt's sudden death in April 1945. "Pray for me boys," he told his first press conference. Utterly unprepared, Truman did not even know about the atomic bomb project, but he vowed to carry on Roosevelt's policies. Truman proved a remarkably capable chief executive, educating himself in foreign affairs and dispatching crucial decisions rapidly. In his first four months, Truman approved the United Nations, accepted the German surrender, met with Allied leaders at Potsdam, and ordered atomic bombs dropped on Japan. As the Cold War commenced, Truman talked tough with the Soviets, accusing them of breaking agreements and intimidating helpless neighbors. In 1947 he proclaimed the Truman Doctrine, promising U.S. aid to threatened countries, and the Marshall Plan to aid European recovery and contain communism. The next year Truman ordered the Berlin airlift when the Soviets cut off West Berlin, and he promised to help Third World countries with the Point Four program. No less assertive at home, Truman made progress on civil rights, subdued restive unions, and prevented the Republican-controlled Congress from dismantling the New Deal—a specter that he effectively raised to win surprise reelection in 1948. Truman committed the country to the NATO alliance in 1949 and sent troops to South Korea when Communist armies invaded in 1950. But as Congress rejected Truman's ambitious Fair Deal domestic program and the Korean War bogged down, Truman's last years were barren. He had more vetoes overridden than all presidents but Andrew Johnson, and his poll ratings were lower than all but Jimmy Carter's. Truman, who initially raised fears of subversion with his loyalty program, could not quell the Red Scare that swept his party from power in 1952, as Republicans hammered away on the theme that Democrats were "soft on communism." Truman was convinced that he saved the world from communism, prevented World War III, and could have won another term if he chose to run in 1952. "He did his damndest" was the only eulogy Harry Truman desired on his death, on Dec. 26, 1972. Out of favor when he left office, Truman has gained rising respect since his death.

34. Dwight D. Eisenhower (1953–1961)

The last war hero president, Dwight David Eisenhower was born in Denison, Texas, on Oct. 14, 1890, and grew up poor in Kansas. A military history buff, Eisenhower graduated with the 1915 class of West Point that produced 59 generals. He married Mamie Doud, his wife of 52 years, and spent World War I as a tank-training instructor. Eisenhower, only a major at age 40, rose rapidly during World War II, promoted past 350 senior officers to become commander of U.S. forces in Europe in 1942. By the end of 1944, he was the first U.S. five-star general and Supreme Allied Commander, taking the German surrender in May 1945. By that point a global celebrity, Eisenhower was army chief of staff until 1948, when he resigned to become president of Columbia University. Harry S Truman named him to command NATO forces in 1950, but two years later Eisenhower retired again to take the Republican nomination and run for president against Adlai E. Stevenson.

"Ike" became perhaps the most popular president in U.S. history, though many questioned his lax work habits, detached management style, and baffling speeches. Prominent millionaires in Eisenhower's cabinet and archconservatives such as Sec. of State John Foster Dulles seemed to have free rein, and Eisenhower acquiesced in Sen. Joe McCarthy's wild charges of subversion. His administration stockpiled atomic weapons and promised "massive retaliation" against Soviet aggression—yet did nothing when the Red Army rolled into Hungary in 1956. Eisenhower did end the Korean War, concluded several alliance agreements, and cut the defense budget. The "Eisenhower Doctrine" promised U.S. aid to Middle Eastern countries fighting communism. When Britain, France, and Israel invaded the Suez Canal in 1956, Eisenhower led UN condemnation and forced them to withdraw, though he sent U.S. Marines into Lebanon two years later. He began heavy U.S. involvement in Vietnam by backing the French and then the puppet Diem regime. At home Eisenhower promised to scale back the government—yet he expanded Social Security; created the Department of Health, Education, and Welfare; and spent billions on public housing and freeways. He pointedly stressed religious devotion. The Supreme Court's *Brown* decision, which Eisenhower deeply regretted, inaugurated the civil rights movement. Eisenhower defeated Stevenson again in 1956, but Soviet domination of space, revolution in Cuba, embarrassment over the Soviets' shooting down of a U.S. spy plane, and his own ill health marred his second term. Eisenhower reluctantly sent paratroopers to enforce desegregation in Little Rock, Ark., in 1957. Democrats controlled Congress for all but two years of Eisenhower's presidency, and they called for more active leadership when he ended his term as the oldest president before Ronald Reagan. In retirement Eisenhower approved of U.S. intervention in Vietnam and counseled presidents until his death, on Mar. 28, 1969.

35. John F. Kennedy (1961–1963)

The youngest man elected president, the only Roman Catholic, and the first born in the 20th century, John Fitzgerald Kennedy was born in Brookline, Massachusetts, on May 29, 1917, to a family of Irish politicos. His father, Joseph P. Kennedy, was ambassador to England and one of the richest men in America. Kennedy attended Dexter and Choate Academies, the London School of Economics, and Princeton before graduating from Harvard in 1940. A patrol boat commander in World War II, Kennedy was decorated for bravery in saving the lives of wounded crew members. Kennedy's father arranged his election to Congress, where he served three undistinguished terms before entering the Senate in 1952. After 1953, the year he married wealthy socialite Jacqueline Bouvier, Kennedy's health deteriorated from Addison's disease and agonizing back ailments. He won the Pulitzer Prize for *Profiles in Courage* (1957), a study of principled politicians supposedly written from his hospital bed. Kennedy positioned himself for a presidential run by lambasting Republicans for insufficient anticommunism and "vigor." In 1960, Kennedy prevailed over three prominent opponents for the Democratic nomination, then scraped past Richard M. Nixon in the election by 118,000 votes out of 69 million cast. The campaign featured the first televised presidential debates, capitalizing on Kennedy's exceptional poise and polish.

In accepting the Democratic nomination, Kennedy had pledged a New Frontier, but his social programs languished in Congress. Undaunted, Kennedy plunged into foreign affairs, his primary interest. Just after taking office, he approved the disastrous Bay of Pigs invasion, and a year later he terrified the world by confronting the Soviets over the presence of their missiles in Cuba. He visited the Berlin Wall and expressed solidarity with Germans under the Russian gun. Kennedy's bellicosity eventually subsided as he set up the Washington-Moscow hotline and signed the Nuclear Test Ban Treaty (1963). Thousands of U.S. troops went to Vietnam as Kennedy escalated the commitment to containing communism. Kennedy vastly increased spending for defense and space programs, vowing to put a man on the Moon. He also engineered a $10 billion tax cut that eventually brought prosperity and increased revenues. As racial unrest spread, Kennedy cautiously supported the civil rights movement, introducing sweeping legislation that would not pass in his lifetime—nor would his plans for aid to education and medical care for the elderly reach fruition before his death. Gearing up for reelection, Kennedy embarked on a speaking tour across the South, where he was least popular. In a Dallas, Tex., motorcade on Nov. 22, 1963, he was fatally shot. Kennedy's alleged assassin, Lee Harvey Oswald, a left-wing ex-marine, was in turn murdered by Jack Ruby two days later. While doubts persisted that Oswald acted alone, Kennedy's martyrdom helped realize his legislative legacy, and subsequent revelation of his many peccadilloes have not tarnished the "Kennedy myth."

36. Lyndon B. Johnson (1963–1969)

The eighth vice president to succeed by death of a president, Lyndon Baines Johnson was born on his father's Texas ranch near Stonewall on Aug. 27, 1908. He worked his way through Southwest Texas State Teachers College, taught briefly, then took a job in Washington—where he would live for all but two years until he left the White House. Government fascinated Johnson, and he reveled in making connections, marrying heiress Claudia Alta "Lady Bird" Taylor after a two-month courtship in 1934. An ardent New Dealer, Johnson won election to Congress as a Democrat in 1937. Reelected three times without opposition, Johnson became the first congressman to volunteer for combat in World War II, winning a Silver Star before returning to Washington. In 1948, on his second try, "Landslide Lyndon" was elected to the Senate by just 87 votes. Hard work and Texas oil money made Johnson the youngest Senate majority leader by 1955. A huge and hearty man, Johnson's powers of persuasion were legendary, but he failed in his bid for the Democratic nomination for president in 1960. Johnson accepted John F. Kennedy's offer of the vice presidency and campaigned hard in the South to aid their narrow victory. Made president a thousand days later by the tragedy in Dallas, Johnson vowed to continue Kennedy's programs, pushing them through Congress with surprising ease. Notable were the Civil Rights Act outlawing segregation and the Equal Opportunity Act, which declared "war on poverty." After less than a year in office, Johnson defeated Barry Goldwater by the biggest plurality in history.

Now president in his own right, Johnson unveiled plans for a Great Society free from poverty and discrimination and passed the Education Act, Medical Care Act, and the Voting Rights Act in 1965. But Johnson came to grief in Vietnam, where he broke his 1964 campaign promise not to send "American boys to fight Asian wars." Earlier administrations committed the U.S. to defending South Vietnam, but Johnson intervened massively to prove American credibility to allies and enemies alike. No doubt he also feared resurgent McCarthyism if another nation were "lost" to communism. Following the Tonkin Gulf incident (1964), Johnson steadily expended American power and lives in Vietnam, but victory, or a means to achieve it, never came within reach—despite the presence of over half a million U.S. troops by 1968. Johnson's presidency unraveled as American losses mounted, antiwar protests grew strident, race riots exploded in inner cities across the nation, and the government developed a credibility gap. Virtually a prisoner of the White House, Johnson faced a war he could neither win nor leave behind and a nation more deeply divided than at any time since the Civil War. In March 1968

Johnson effectively resigned by announcing he would not seek another term. He retired to his sprawling Texas ranch and stayed out of politics until his death, on Jan. 22, 1973. Johnson left a domestic reform legacy second only to the New Deal; but he squandered it in Vietnam by raising expectations he could not meet at home and abroad. The day after he died, diplomats signed the Paris peace agreement, formally ending the war.

37. Richard M. Nixon
(1969–1974)

The only president to resign from office, Richard Milhous Nixon was born in Yorba Linda, California, to a poor Quaker family on Jan. 9, 1913. A graduate of Whittier College and Duke University Law School, Nixon married Thelma "Pat" Ryan in 1940, saw noncombat service in World War II, and rode into Congress on the Republican wave of 1946. He gained fame in the anti-Communist trial of Alger Hiss before entering the Senate in 1950. Dwight D. Eisenhower made Nixon his running mate in 1952, but Nixon was nearly forced to resign for accepting questionable contributions. He appealed for national exoneration in the televised "Checkers" speech. A well-traveled vice president, Nixon almost lost his life to hostile Latin American mobs in 1958, and he waged an impromptu debate in Moscow with Soviet premier Nikita Khrushchev in 1959. Eisenhower's obvious successor in 1960, Nixon narrowly lost the election to John F. Kennedy, and when he lost a California gubernatorial race in 1962, Nixon's career seemed over. Yet he practiced law in New York until the Republicans nominated him again in 1968. To a nation riven by the Vietnam War, Nixon promised "law and order," appealing to calm and unity against a background of riots, assassinations, and protest. Nixon defeated Hubert H. Humphrey with the smallest victor's share of the vote since 1912.

Vowing to "bring us together," Nixon tried to thwart the bureaucracy and Democrats in Congress by centralizing executive power. To control inflation, he ordered wage-price controls and devalued the dollar for the first time since the depression. Seeking "peace with honor" in Vietnam, Nixon built up the South Vietnamese army and withdrew U.S. troops—while massively escalating bombing of North Vietnam. Antiwar protests reached fever pitch when the United States invaded Cambodia in 1970. Nixon responded with appeals to the "silent majority," attacks on press freedom, and clandestine harassment of administration critics. High points of his first administration were the *Apollo* moon landing in 1969, Nixon's path-breaking visit to China in 1972, and the first Strategic Arms Limitation Treaty with the Soviet Union. Twelve days after announcing "peace is at hand" in Vietnam, Nixon was reelected by a landslide, carrying an unprecedented 49 states. During the campaign five burglars were arrested in the Democratic party headquarters, and by early 1973, they were linked to the White House. The ensuing "Watergate" scandal exposed the Nixon administration's rampant corruption, illegality, and deceit. Nixon himself downplayed the scandal as mere politics, but when his aides resigned in disgrace, Nixon's role in ordering an illegal cover-up came to light in the press, courts, and congressional investigations. Nixon evaded taxes, accepted illicit campaign contributions, ordered secret bombings, and harassed opponents with executive agencies, wiretaps, and break-ins. Vice Pres. Spiro T. Agnew resigned in October 1973 for accepting bribes, but Nixon hung on to power, claiming, "I am not a crook," as the House began impeachment proceedings. Subpoenas and Supreme Court orders forced Nixon to release tapes of his White House conversations authorizing the Watergate cover-up. Ultimately, he resigned to avoid impeachment for obstruction of justice, abuse of power, and contempt of Congress. Claiming to have lost his "political base," Nixon announced his resignation on national television on Aug. 9, 1974. He never admitted wrongdoing, though he later conceded errors of judgment. Saved by a blanket pardon from Gerald R. Ford, his second vice president and successor as president, Nixon retired to his California mansion, later moving to New York and then New Jersey. He dedicated the remainder of his life to unsullying his name, while becoming a valued foreign policy adviser to Presidents Reagan, Bush, and Clinton, until his death at the age of 81 in 1994.

38. Gerald R. Ford
(1974–1977)

The only vice president and president never elected to either office, Gerald Rudolph Ford was born in Omaha, Nebraska, on July 14, 1913. An Eagle Scout, he grew up in Michigan and attended the University of Michigan on a football scholarship, playing on the national championship teams of 1932 and 1933. After graduating in 1935, Ford coached football and boxing at Yale while attending law school. In the navy he earned 10 battle stars in the Pacific during World War II. Ford ran for Congress in 1948 as a Republican, marrying divorcée Betty Bloomer during the campaign, which he won. Thereafter he would be reelected 12 times, never by less than 60 percent of the vote. In Congress Ford's solid conservative record elevated him to House Republican minority leader by 1965. For supporting Richard M. Nixon in Congress, Ford was rewarded with the vice presidency in December 1973, replacing Spiro T. Agnew under the 25th Amendment. "I do not think the public would stand for it," Ford said at his confirmation hearings, when asked if he would ever pardon Nixon. For eight months Ford stayed loyal to Nixon, until his resignation made Ford the new president on Aug. 9, 1974. Ford announced "our long national nightmare is over," but a month later he shocked the nation by giving Nixon a blanket pardon. Ford denied any deal had been made, but his public standing never recovered. He struggled with huge Democratic majorities in Congress to stem soaring inflation and unemployment, casting 66 vetoes in all. Congress refused Ford's request for aid to South Vietnam and intervention in the Angolan civil war. In the *Mayaguez* incident, Ford sent the marines to rescue 39 Americans captured by Cambodia.

Breaking a 1973 pledge, Ford decided to seek reelection, and while campaigning, he survived two assassination attempts by California women. Ford was far behind Jimmy Carter in the polls, but he carried four more states than Carter in the election—which Ford lost by 57 electoral votes. It was the first defeat of an incumbent president since Herbert Hoover's.

39. Jimmy Carter
(1977–1981)

James Earl Carter, the first deep-southerner elected president in 128 years, was born in Plains, Georgia, on Oct. 1, 1924. He grew up on a farm with no plumbing or electricity but realized his dream of attending the U.S. Naval Academy. Carter graduated in 1946 and married Rosalynn Smith. He joined the submarine fleet and studied nuclear physics, leaving the navy in 1953 to run the family peanut business. He was elected to the Georgia state senate in 1962. Defeated for governor in 1966, Carter campaigned constantly for the next four years, winning on his second try in 1970. Carter reorganized the government and hired more blacks, declaring that the "time for racial discrimination is over." A month before leaving office in 1974, Carter was the first Democrat to announce his candidacy for president in 1976, again campaigning constantly. "Jimmy Who?" burst into headlines by winning narrow pluralities over nine rivals in early primaries. Carter's grinning, homespun style and earnest vows of honesty ("I will never lie to you") struck a chord with voters after Watergate. Carter won the nomination and defeated incumbent Gerald R. Ford by 2 percent of the vote. Lack of Washington connections helped his candidacy but not his presidency, for Carter never shook his image as the provincial amateur. Democratic majorities in Congress ignored Carter's pleas for tax reform and a long-range energy policy. Transportation deregulation, environmental protection, and new departments of energy and education were Carter's main domestic achievements.

But as federal spending mounted and oil prices doubled, most Americans blamed Carter for runaway inflation. His 20 percent approval rating in August 1979 was the lowest ever recorded in opinion polls. In foreign affairs Carter obtained a Panama Canal treaty, normalized relations with China, and mediated the Camp David peace accords between Israel and Egypt. He moved toward closer relations with the Soviet Union, signing the SALT II treaty in 1979, but the Soviet invasion of Afghanistan led Carter to embargo grain sales to the USSR and to order a boycott of the 1980 Moscow Olympics. The Carter Doctrine announced the United States would defend the Persian Gulf, where ironically, Carter soon met his downfall in the Iran hostage crisis. Early public support for Carter's restraint gradually withered under the glare of relentless media coverage that kept tensions high throughout 1980. Carter himself became a hostage of Iran, trapped in the White House as Edward Kennedy nearly deprived him of the Democratic nomination. In April 1980, Carter approved a military rescue mission, its tragic failure reinforcing his image of incompetence and weakness, which Republican candidate Ronald Reagan flayed. Reagan won the election in a landslide. Carter left the White House thoroughly discredited, his informal style ridiculed as inappropriate, his platitudes betraying lack of vision, his appeals for support seen as poor leadership. Yet Carter was a hardworking president wrecked by a hostile press, extortionate oil exporters, and forces beyond his control.

40. Ronald Reagan (1981–1989)

Ronald Wilson Reagan was born in Tampico, Illinois, on Feb. 6, 1911. He excelled at acting and campus politics in high school and at Eureka College. Reagan was a radio sports announcer when he made his first movie in 1937. Over 50 more films would follow in Reagan's prolific Hollywood career. In 1940 he married actress Jane Wyman, who divorced him in 1948. During World War II, Reagan made training films, and after the war he was president of the Screen Actors Guild. Then a Democrat, Reagan assailed Communists in Hollywood. He married Nancy Davis, another actress, in 1952. As his movie career waned, Reagan hosted television shows and espoused conservative causes, switching to the Republican party in 1960. Reagan made a dramatic speech at the end of the 1964 campaign, and despite his total lack of experience he was elected governor of California in 1966 by a million votes. As governor, Reagan broke all promises by raising taxes, increasing spending, and expanding the state government—yet he easily won reelection in 1970. He made a stab at the Republican presidential nomination in 1968, then bided his time until 1976, when he almost wrested the nomination from Gerald R. Ford. In 1980 he finally won the Republican nomination, and he swept past Jimmy Carter in the crushing "Reagan Revolution" of 1980, carrying 44 states and making huge Republican gains in Congress.

"Reaganomics" promised to cut taxes and social spending while vastly increasing the defense budget and somehow balancing the budget. Congress was unmoved until Mar. 20, 1981, when a crazed youth named John Hinckley shot Reagan twice in the chest. Reagan's good humor and rapid recovery charmed Americans—especially the press, which had questioned his age and health. Reagan then prevailed over Congress to pass mammoth tax cuts. The national debt began its meteoric rise under Reagan as defense spending outweighed cuts in social programs. By 1986 the U.S. had become a net borrower for the first time since World War I, but falling oil prices slowed inflation and rekindled economic growth, for which Reagan took credit. Calling the Soviet Union an "evil empire," Reagan built up the armed forces, deployed U.S. nuclear missiles in Europe, and began the Strategic Defense Initiative. He sent U.S. Marines to Lebanon, where 240 of them died in a terrorist attack. To halt the spread of communism, Reagan ordered the invasion of Grenada and isolated the Sandinista government of Nicaragua. Reelected by another landslide in 1984, with the economy booming and his public esteem high, Reagan seemed headed for an even more successful second term. He ordered bombing raids on Libya and met with Soviet leader Mikhail Gorbachev, eventually producing historic arms control agreements. But in 1987 Reagan's invincible popularity finally succumbed to the Iran-Contra scandal: White House staff secretly sold arms to Iran in hopes of freeing American hostages held in Lebanon, using the profits illegally to fund Contra fighters in Nicaragua. Many top Reagan aides had to resign, but more damaging was the president's apparent loss of control over his own administration.

By 1988 Reagan was reduced to "lame duck" status, and bestowed his mantle on Vice Pres. George Bush. He left office with the highest approval rating of any departing president since Franklin Roosevelt. In retirement Reagan was knighted by Queen Elizabeth and traveled around the globe, accepting $2 million from a Japanese media company for a pair of 20-minute speeches. As the Iran-Contra trials continued in 1990, Reagan was ordered to testify under oath on videotape. Questioned at length about his role in the scandal, Reagan responded 130 times with "I don't recall" or "I don't remember."

41. George Bush (1989–1993)

The first sitting vice president elected president in over 150 years, George Herbert Walker Bush was born in Milton, Massachusetts, on June 12, 1924. His father was Prescott Sheldon Bush, Wall Street banker and U.S. senator from Connecticut from 1952 to 1963. As a navy pilot during World War II, Bush was shot down over the Pacific and rescued at sea. After the war, he married Barbara Pierce, a Smith College student, on Jan. 6, 1945, and graduated Phi Beta Kappa in economics from Yale in 1948. Bush spurned an offer from his father's Wall Street firm in order to pursue a career in the Texas oil fields that eventually made him a millionaire in his own right. He entered politics in the early 1960s.

Running on a conservative anti-Communist and anti–civil rights platform, Bush won the Republican nomination for Senate in 1964 and again in 1970, but lost the general election both times. In between, he was elected to Congress from a wealthy suburban Houston district, the only elected office he had held until he won the vice-presidency in 1980. Presidents Richard Nixon and Gerald Ford rewarded the Republican party loyalist with appointed offices, including U.S. ambassador to the United Nations (1971), chairman of the Republican National Committee (1973), chief of the U.S. Liaison Office in China (1974), and director of the CIA (1976). After losing the Republican presidential nomination to Ronald Reagan in 1980, Bush accepted Reagan's offer to join him on the winning ticket.

One of the only members of Reagan's staff to emerge unscathed by the Iran-Contra affair, Bush bested Robert Dole for the Republican nomination in 1988. With Reagan's endorsement, Bush defeated Massachusetts governor Michael S. Dukakis, renewing the Reagan pledge of "no new taxes" and vowing to uphold the Reagan legacy of less government, strong defense, and family values. He declared war on "this scourge" of drugs by creating an office of National Drug Control Policy within the White House. Bush's first official act was to proclaim January 20 as the "National Day of Prayer."

Bush suffered early criticism for lack of leadership. For months, many key administration posts went unfilled, and the Senate rejected John Tower as Bush's nominee for defense secretary. But Bush struck back with major initiatives, including major arms control proposals and two summit meetings with Soviet premier Mikhail Gorbachev. In December 1989, Bush ordered the invasion of Panama to protect U.S. citizens and overthrow the regime of Gen. Manuel Noriega.

As one eastern bloc country after another opted for democracy in 1989 and 1990, Bush enjoyed the highest public approval rating of any postwar president. This popularity gave him the political leverage to renege on his campaign pledge of "no new taxes." His popularity rose to record levels when he ordered Operation Desert Storm to liberate Kuwait from Iraqi occupation. As time passed, however, it became apparent that Bush had given the cease-fire order much too early, allowing Saddam Hussein to retain power in Iraq.

Throughout 1991, as the Soviet Union was crumbling, Bush acted quickly and decisively to support those republics seeking independence, and to provide food and medical supplies where needed. He and Gorbachev declared an end to the arms race by signing the first nuclear arms reduction pact in July. He also won high praise for his administration's determination to launch serious Mideast peace talks, which began in October of 1991. He was seriously criticized, however, for granting China most-favored-nation trade status in the wake of the Tiananmen Square massacre and continued repressive government action.

Bush had less success on the domestic front. By the spring of 1992, his approval rating had dipped below 40 percent, reflecting the deepening economic recession that drove unemployment levels to their highest level in a decade. Bush was challenged first in the primaries and then in the general election by opponents who made the economy the central issue of their campaigns. Bush survived a vicious attack from the right wing of his party (in the person of political commentator Patrick Buchanan) to win the Republican nomination. But unable to get the economy on course, Bush lost to Bill Clinton in a three-way race that saw independent candidate Ross Perot capture nearly 20 percent of the vote. It marked only the 10th time in history that an incumbent president had been unseated.

42. Bill Clinton (1993–)

The youngest president since John F. Kennedy and the first Democrat in 12 years, William Jefferson Clinton was born in the tiny town of Hope, Arkansas, on Aug. 19, 1946. His father, William Jefferson Blythe 3rd was killed in an automobile accident before his son was born, leaving his wife, Virginia, to raise their son alone. Four years later, she married Roger Clinton, who legally adopted Bill, and moved the family to nearby Hot Springs, Ark. After graduating from Georgetown University, Clinton went to Oxford University on a Rhodes scholarship and then to Yale Law School, where he met Hillary Rodham, whom he married two years after they both graduated in 1973.

Clinton tasted political defeat early, first as the Texas director of George McGovern's 1972 presidential campaign, then in his own candidacy for a U.S. congressional seat from Arkansas' third district. He had better luck as Arkansas director of Jimmy Carter's successful presidential campaign in 1976, the same year in which Clinton was elected state attorney general. Two years later, he won 59 percent of the vote in a five-man field to become the nation's youngest governor since Harold Stassen was elected in Minnesota 40 years earlier. In 1980 he became the nation's youngest ex-governor, a victim of the nationwide Republican landslide that ushered Ronald Reagan into the White House. Clinton won the governor's mansion back in 1982 and launched a controversial educational reform program that returned him to office in 1984 and 1988.

His first experience in the national spotlight came when he was chosen to give the nominating speech for Michael S. Dukakis at the 1988 Democratic National Convention. But the speech was nearly his political death knell: at 33 minutes long, it was devoid of inspiration or charisma and inspired cheers only when he announced he was about to conclude. So expectations were understandably low when Clinton joined a large field of candidates for the 1992 Democratic nomination for president. Clinton emerged as a shaky front-runner among the six hopefuls, but his campaign was nearly derailed twice: first, when a woman named Gennifer Flowers claimed Clinton had had an extramarital affair with her; second, when it was revealed that Clinton had tried to pull strings to dodge the draft. But as the candidate with the most money, the most flattering press coverage, and the only one with a clearly articulated campaign strategy—creating more jobs—Clinton was able to stay in the race the longest, fending off his last remaining rival, former California governor Jerry Brown, months before the Democratic National Convention.

In a three-way race that saw billionaire populist Ross Perot enter, withdraw, and then reenter the field as an independent candidate, Clinton garnered 366 of the 538 electoral votes, despite winning only 43 percent of the popular vote. Incumbent George Bush captured 37 percent, and Perot 19 percent, of the record 104 million votes cast in 1992.

Clinton entered office hoping that a Democratic president and a Democratic Congress could untangle the gridlock that had paralyzed Washington for the previous 12 years. But it was not to be. His first act as president, a pledge to end the ban on lesbians and gay men in the armed forces, met with heavy resistance from top military leaders. His economic stimulus package fell to defeat in the face of a remarkable Republican filibuster in the Senate. Even his cabinet appointments were scrutinized to the point that his first two attorney general designates, Zöe Baird and Kimba Wood, had to remove their names from consideration because they had failed to pay social security taxes for their nannies.

The young president's second 100 days proved more fruitful. Remembering the people who elected him, Clinton reversed some of the policies of the Reagan-Bush administrations of the previous 12 years: He signed the family leave bill, lifted the restrictions on abortion counseling at federally funded clinics, and supported the UN-sanctioned biodiversity treaty. Some last-minute arm-twisting and compromises allowed him to get his budget through Congress and laid the groundwork for passage of the North American Free Trade Agreement, which removed many trade barriers between the United States, Canada, and Mexico.

Clinton had even greater success on the foreign policy front, especially in regard to assuring the stability of Russia's government as it tried to maintain power in the midst of a coup and parliamentary chaos. In the Middle East, Clinton's secretary of state, Warren Christopher, negotiated a historic peace treaty between Israel and the PLO that recognized Palestinian self-rule in Gaza and part of the West Bank. Clinton's handling of the escalating conflict in Bosnia (placing the issue in the hands of the UN), allowed him to avoid engagement while placing the responsibility for inaction squarely on the European nations. Even his vacillating policy on the military junta in Haiti ultimately allowed for the peaceful return in 1994 of the country's democratically elected leader, Jean-Bertrand Aristide. And his brinkmanship with North Korea resulted in Pyongyang's agreement to dismantle nuclear reactors that could be used to produce ammunition for nuclear weapons.

On the domestic front, however, Clinton found little support for his programs. Despite bipartisan agreement that the nation's health system was in dire need of restructuring, all Clinton's attempts to do so met with harsh criticism. A complex, poorly presented plan (devised by a committee headed by First Lady Hillary Rodham Clinton) called for guaranteed health coverage to all Americans, regardless of a preexisting condition or an inability to pay. But its health purchasing cooperatives promised a huge government bureaucracy that the plan's opponents claimed would make a trip to the doctor resemble a trip to the post office. Senators and congressmen, Democrats and Republicans alike, responded by trotting out their own plans; in the end, of more than five competing bills, none were passed. With Clinton reeling from this defeat, his bill to reform campaign finance was killed by a simple Republican filibuster. And only a last-minute emergency campaign saved a crime bill that would put more police on the streets while prohibiting several categories of semiautomatic weapons.

Clinton's approval ratings continued to lag throughout 1993 and 1994. Several top administration officials were forced to resign, including Deputy Treasury Sec. Roger Altman and Agriculture Sec. Mike Espy, under clouds of corruption. Others, including Housing Sec. Henry Cisneros and Commerce Sec. Ron Brown, were also named in scandals with investigations pending. In November 1993, Democrats lost several key state and local elections, including the governorships of New Jersey and Washington and the mayoralty of New York City.

But the most severe setback came in the 1994 midterm elections, when voters opted overwhelmingly to replace Democrats with Republicans on all levels of government. On the national and state levels, no incumbent Republican lost a bid for reelection, while several Democrats, House Speaker Tom Foley foremost among them, were unseated by political novices. The GOP won control of both houses of Congress for the first time in more than 40 years, and House Speaker Newt Gingrich moved to center stage, proclaiming a Republican revolution. Clinton stood by, barely raising a contrary voice or a veto threat, as the House raced through the provisions of the Contract with America. Instead, he looked for ways to compromise with the new Republican leadership, suggesting he would approve of a constitutional amendment permitting school prayer.

With their newly won power, Congressional Republicans in 1995 opened hearings on the Clintons' controversial investment in a land deal known as Whitewater, and on the 1994 Waco, Tex., massacre of David Koresh and his Branch Davidian cult followers, in the hope of embarrassing the president and keeping him on the defensive. And as the war in Bosnia heated up, the Republicans challenged the president to take a stronger role in the conflict, even though most Americans disapproved of increased U.S. involvement.

As he prepared to run for a second term, Clinton in 1995 hired new political advisers, paid for advertising to counter some Republican policies, and sought to take a centrist position on most of the important issues, including abortion rights, welfare reform, and affirmative action. Perhaps the most contentious issue, however, between the compromising president and the aggressive new Republican majority in Congress, was the federal budget. In their drive to wipe out the $4.5 trillion deficit *and* provide $245 billion in tax cuts in a mere seven years, Republicans in both houses threatened to cut and slash at virtually every government spending program except Defense and Social Security. By contrast, Clinton's budget proposed eliminating the deficit over a 10-year period, reducing the middle class tax cut, and making less deep cuts into spending on Medicare, day care, housing, job training, education, and enforcement of environmental regulations. The "train wreck" of a budget fight threatened to shut down the federal government in September of 1995 before the new fiscal year began on October 1. (For further details, see Part I: "The Year in Review.")

> ***"When I was a boy, I was told that anybody could become President; I'm beginning to believe it."***
> —Clarence Darrow

THE PRESIDENTS

All 41 U.S. presidents (counting Grover Cleveland once) have been native-born white, Christian males between the ages of 41 (Teddy Roosevelt's age when he took office) and 77 (Reagan's age when he left).

Origins

The most common ancestries of presidents are English (18) and Scotch-Irish (7). Virginia is the leading birthplace of presidents (8), followed by Ohio (7), Massachusetts (4), and New York (4). New York, however, is the leading state of residence for successful presidential candidates (8), followed by Ohio (6), and Virginia (5).

Religion

Although all 41 have been Christians, only one (Kennedy) was not a protestant; 11 presidents (including George Bush) were Episcopalians, 7 were Presbyterians, and 4 were Unitarians. Only three presidents (Jefferson, Lincoln, and A. Johnson) claimed no religious affiliation.

Age

The average age for presidents upon taking office is 56, but only eight were under age 50: T. Roosevelt (41), Kennedy (43), Clinton (46), Grant (46), Cleveland (47), Pierce (48), Garfield (49), and Polk (49). The oldest presidents at inauguration were Reagan (69), Harrison (68), Buchanan (65), Taylor (64), and Bush (64).

Education

Andrew Johnson was the president with the least formal education (his wife taught him to read, and he never went to any school); Wilson was the only one to earn a Ph.D. Only 12 presidents were not college graduates, but only one of these (Truman) held office in the 20th century. Harvard has graduated the most presidents (5), followed by Yale, Princeton, West Point, and William and Mary, each of which graduated two.

Profession

More than half of the 41 presidents have been lawyers, though only three of the last 10 (Clinton, Nixon, and Ford) were lawyers. Four presidents were former soldiers, three were businessmen, and two were planters. Andrew Johnson was a tailor before becoming president, Harding was a publisher, and Herbert Hoover was an engineer.

Political affiliation

Since the creation of the Republican party in 1856, the GOP has won 21 of the 35 presidential elections. Only 10 of the 27 presidents elected during that period have been Democrats.

Marriage and family

Buchanan was the only president who never married, Reagan the only one ever divorced. Cleveland and Wilson were both married in the White House. Only six presidents had no children: Washington, Madison, Jackson, Polk, Buchanan, and Harding (although recent evidence indicated he fathered an illegitimate child while president). Grover Cleveland is the only president to admit he had an illegitimate child. Tyler had 15 children, Harrison 10, Hayes 8, and Garfield 7. Four presidents had six children, and four (including Bush) had five.

Salaries

The first 17 presidents earned an annual salary of $25,000. In the "Salary Grab" Act of 1873, Congress doubled the president's salary to $50,000 while raising its own pay by 50 percent just before the beginning of the depression of the 1870s. The president's salary was raised to $75,000 in 1909, and again in 1949 to $100,000 (plus $50,000 in expense allowances). The last raise came in 1969, when the president's salary was doubled to $200,000 plus the same $50,000 expense allowance. (By comparison, the chief justice of the Supreme Court earned only $4,000 in 1789, $13,000 in 1909, and $62,500 in 1969.)

Ex-presidents

Between Bill Clinton's inauguration in January 1993 and Richard Nixon's death in April 1994, there were five living ex-presidents at one time, the most since 1861–62, when Martin Van Buren, John Tyler, Millard Fillmore, Franklin Pierce, and James Buchanan were all alive for the first year of Abraham Lincoln's presidency. The only other times there have been as many as four ex-presidents alive were in 1825–26 (John Adams, Thomas Jefferson, James Madison, and James Monroe), 1857–61 (when Buchanan was in office), 1989–93 (when Bush was in office), and 1994–present. There were no living ex-presidents from 1799–1801, 1875–77, 1908–1909, and 1973–74.

These days, most ex-presidents sell their memoirs for a million dollars and then retire to the golf course. But three presidents returned to federal office after their tenure. John Quincy Adams became known as "Old Man Eloquent" during his 18 years as a Massachusetts congressman after his presidency. Voters in Tennessee in 1874 elected Andrew Johnson to the Senate, the very same body that had narrowly voted against impeaching him from the presidency six years earlier. (He died less than a year into his term.) And William Howard Taft went on to a career as Chief Justice of the Supreme Court that was far more distinguished than his unremarkable tenure as president.

Vice presidents

Fourteen of the 45 men who have been vice president eventually went on to become president. Of these, four succeeded the president they served by winning the following election (a fifth, Richard Nixon, became president eight years after his term as vice president ended). Nine vice presidents took office after the death or resignation of the president they served; of these, only Theodore Roosevelt, Coolidge, Truman, and Johnson later won reelection in their own right.

Died in office

One in five U.S. presidents has died while in office. Half of them (Lincoln, Garfield, McKinley, and Kennedy) were assassinated, while the other half (W.H. Harrison, Taylor, Harding, and F.D. Roosevelt) died of natural causes.

Presidential Elections, 1789–1992

1789 and 1792

George Washington of Virginia ran unopposed for president in 1789 and 1792. He received 69 and 132 electoral votes, respectively, in those years. John Adams of Massachusetts was elected vice president in both years, receiving 34 and 77 electoral votes, respectively.

1796

Party	Candidate	Popular vote	Percent	Electoral vote
Federalist	John Adams (Mass.)	N.A.	N.A.	71
	and Thomas Pinckney (S.C.)	N.A.	N.A.	59
Democratic-Republican	Thomas Jefferson (Va.)	N.A.	N.A.	68
	and Aaron Burr (N.Y.)	N.A.	N.A.	30

Key Issues Washington set a precedent by refusing to run for a third term. Though the founders hoped to avoid parties, factions developed around Hamilton and Jefferson during Washington's first term. Hamilton's Federalists supported a strong central government that would play a major role in the national economy and represent the commercial interests of the North. Jefferson's Republicans advocated states' rights and the agrarian interests of the South. **Regional Influences** Though led by Hamilton, the Federalists nominated the more moderate Adams. Jefferson's strength in the South was balanced by Adams's power in the North. Eleven Federalist electors in New Hampshire failed to vote for Pinckney, their party's vice-presidential nominee, giving the position to Jefferson.

1800

Party	Candidate	Popular vote	Percent	Electoral vote
Democratic-Republican	Thomas Jefferson (Va.)	N.A.	N.A.	73
	and Aaron Burr (N.Y.)	N.A.	N.A.	73
Federalist	John Adams (Mass.)	N.A.	N.A.	65
	and Charles C. Pinckney (S.C.)	N.A.	N.A.	64
Federalist	John Jay (N.Y.)	N.A.	N.A.	1

Key Issues Adams divided the Federalists by keeping the United States out of war with France over seizures of American ships. In the meantime the Republicans under Jefferson organized nationally. They accused the Federalists of aristocratic and monarchial leanings, citing large taxes levied to maintain a standing army and navy, the Alien and Sedition Acts seeking to silence the administration's critics, and suppression of the Whiskey Rebellion. **Regional Influences** The Republicans again carried the South but also won New York through the efforts of vice-presidential nominee Burr. The election was thrown into the House when Jefferson and Burr received an equal number of electoral votes. With Hamilton's support, Jefferson won the election in the Federalist-dominated House.

1804

Party	Candidate	Popular vote	Percent	Electoral vote
Democratic-Republican	Thomas Jefferson (Va.)	N.A.	N.A.	162
	and George Clinton (N.Y.)	N.A.	N.A.	162
Federalist	Charles C. Pinckney (S.C.)	N.A.	N.A.	14
	and Rufus King (N.Y.)	N.A.	N.A.	14

Key Issues In 1804 Vice Pres. Burr, a northern Republican, joined with a group of northeastern Federalists in a plot to unite New York and New England in a separate nation. The plot was exposed, discrediting the Federalists. Jefferson, already popular for his personal qualities as well as the Louisiana Purchase, swept to an easy victory. **Regional Influences** Jefferson lost only three states and even swept all of New England with the exception of Connecticut.

1808

Party	Candidate	Popular vote	Percent	Electoral vote
Democratic-Republican	James Madison (Va.)	N.A.	N.A.	122
	and George Clinton (N.Y.)	N.A.	N.A.	113
Federalist	Charles C. Pinckney (S.C.)	N.A.	N.A.	47
	and Rufus King (N.Y.)	N.A.	N.A.	47

Note: Clinton received six electoral votes for president. Madison and James Monroe of Virginia both received three electoral votes for vice president.

Key Issues Jefferson refused to run for a third term. Madison, his chosen successor, easily won the Republican nomination and the presidency. **Regional Influences** Pinckney and the Federalists regained most of the New England votes lost four years earlier and increased their strength in Congress as a result of commercial opposition to the embargo imposed by Jefferson on the export of American goods to warring European nations.

1812

Party	Candidate	Popular vote	Percent	Electoral vote
Democratic-Republican	James Madison (Va.)	N.A.	N.A.	128
	and Elbridge Gerry (Mass.)	N.A.	N.A.	131
Federalist	DeWitt Clinton (N.Y.)	N.A.	N.A.	89
	and Jared Ingersoll (Pa.)	N.A.	N.A.	86

Key Issues The election was a referendum on Madison's bid for a declaration of war against Great Britain in response to Britain's attempts to block the sale of southern raw materials in European markets. **Regional Influences** Commercial interests in the Northeast were opposed to war with Great Britain. The original 13 states split evenly, favoring Madison 90–89. New England, except Vermont, voted for Clinton, as did most Middle Atlantic states. The South and western states voted unanimously for Madison and thus for war.

1816

Party	Candidate	Popular vote	Percent	Electoral vote
Democratic-Republican	James Monroe (Va.)	N.A.	N.A.	183
	and D.D. Tompkins (N.Y.)	N.A.	N.A.	183
Federalist	Rufus King (N.Y.)	N.A.	N.A.	34
	and John E. Howard (Md.)	N.A.	N.A.	22

Key Issues The postwar period was a time of national and economic growth that saw widespread internal improvements despite opposition from Federalists. **Regional Influences** Monroe's landslide victory seemed to validate Madison's nationalistic program, which called for a stronger standing army, a protective tariff, uniform currency, and a nationwide system of roads and canals, including the Cumberland Road. The Federalists won only three states, all in New England.

1820

Party	Candidate	Popular vote	Percent	Electoral vote
Democratic-Republican	James Monroe (Va.)	N.A.	N.A.	231
	and D.D. Tompkins (N.Y.)	N.A.	N.A.	218
Democratic-Republican	John Q. Adams (Mass.)	N.A.	N.A.	1

Key Issues The election was held at the height of the Era of Good Feelings, though sectional differences over slavery earlier in the year led to the Missouri Compromise. The Federalists ceased to exist as a party by the time of the election and failed to run a candidate against Monroe. **Regional Influences** Monroe ran unopposed for reelection. One elector from New Hampshire voted for Adams so that only Washington would hold the honor of being elected to the presidency by a unanimous vote.

1824

Party	Candidate	Popular vote	Percent	Electoral vote
Democratic-Republican	John Q. Adams (Mass.)	113,122	30.92	84
Democratic-Republican	Andrew Jackson (Tenn.)	151,271	41.34	99
Democratic-Republican	William H. Crawford (Ga.)	40,876	11.17	41
Democratic-Republican	Henry Clay (Ky.)	47,531	12.99	37
Other		13,053	3.57	—
	Total vote	365,833		
	Jackson plurality	38,149		

Key Issues Personalities dominated an election in which all four candidates ran as Democratic-Republicans. John C. Calhoun of South Carolina ran unopposed for vice president. **Regional Influences** Each candidate represented his region: Adams the commercial Northeast, Crawford the cotton South, Clay and Jackson the agrarian West. Jackson won a clear plurality of the popular vote, and was the only candidate with support outside his home region. But no candidate won a majority of the electoral vote and the election was decided in the House, where Speaker Clay's support gave the victory to Adams.

1828

Party	Candidate	Popular vote	Percent	Electoral vote
Democratic-Republican	Andrew Jackson (Tenn.)	642,553	55.97	178
	and John C. Calhoun (S.C.)			171
National-Republican	John Q. Adams (Mass.)	500,987	43.63	83
	and Richard Rush (Pa.)			83
Other		4,568	0.40	—
	Total vote	1,148,018		
	Jackson plurality	141,656		

Key Issues Personalities again overshadowed issues. The Jackson campaign catered to popular prejudices, portraying the contest as one between democracy and aristocracy. The Jackson coalition was a forerunner of the modern Democratic party and reestablished two-party politics in the country. **Regional Influences** Jackson won the South and West easily and appealed to discontented laborers in the North. Adams carried only New England, New Jersey, Maryland, and Delaware.

1832

Party	Candidate	Popular vote	Percent	Electoral vote
Democrat	Andrew Jackson (Tenn.)	701,780	54.23	219
	and Martin Van Buren (N.Y.)			189
National-Republican	Henry Clay (Ky.)	484,205	37.42	49
	and John Sergeant (Pa.)			49
Anti-Masonic	William Wirt (Md.)	100,715	7.78	7
	and Amos Ellmaker (Pa.)			7
Independent	John Floyd (Va.)	N.A.	N.A.	11
	and Henry Lee (Mass.)			11
Other		7,273	0.56	—
	Total vote	1,293,973		
	Jackson plurality	217,575		

Key Issues The Anti-Masons, the first third-party in American politics, began in opposition to secret societies and privileged groups but were at heart an anti-Jackson party. All three parties held national conventions to select a presidential nominee. While Jackson's opposition to the Bank of the United States was made an issue by the two major parties, the election was more a referendum on Jackson himself. **Regional Influences** Anti-Masonic strength was concentrated in rural sections of New England and the Middle Atlantic states where National-Republicans and Anti-Masons supported the same ticket. With the forces against him divided, Jackson won easily. Clay won only half of the New England states, Wirt won only Vermont. Jackson captured Maine and New Hampshire. In South Carolina, where electors still were chosen by the legislature, nullificationists cast their ballots for Floyd.

1836

Party	Candidate	Popular vote	Percent	Electoral vote
Democrat	Martin Van Buren (N.Y.)	764,716	50.83	170
	and Richard M. Johnson (Ky.)			147
Whig	William Henry Harrison (Ohio)	550,816	36.63	73
Whig	Hugh L. White (Tenn.)	146,107	9.72	26
Whig	Daniel Webster (Mass.)	41,201	2.74	14
	Willie P. Mangum (N.C.)	N.A.	N.A.	11
Other		1,234	0.08	—
	Total vote	1,503,534		
	Van Buren plurality	213,360		

Key Issues Jackson's heavy-handed tactics, especially his battle against the national bank, led the National-Republicans to rename themselves Whigs, after the 18th-century British party that tried to lessen the power of the Crown. But lacking effective national leadership, the anti-Jackson forces could not agree on one candidate and ran three regional candidates. **Regional Influences** Whig strategy was to throw the election into the House, where they could unite around a single candidate. Webster was to win New England, Harrison the West, and White the South. But Van Buren, forced on the Democrats by Jackson, picked up enough states throughout the nation to win by a slim majority. Johnson fell one electoral vote short of a majority for vice president and was selected by the Senate.

1840

Party	Candidate	Popular vote	Percent	Electoral vote
Whig	William Henry Harrison (Ohio)	1,275,390	52.88	234
	and John Tyler (Va.)			
Democrat	Martin Van Buren (N.Y.)	1,128,854	46.81	60
Liberty	James G. Birney (N.Y.)	6,797	0.28	—
Other		767	0.03	—
	Total vote	2,411,808		
	Harrison plurality	146,536		

Key Issues With the country still reeling from the Panic of 1837, the Democrats were on the defensive. The Whigs rallied around Harrison and turned the tables on Jackson's party. Harrison, despite his wealthy origins, was portrayed as the "log-cabin, hard-cider candidate" opposing the allegedly aristocratic Van Buren. The Democrats left the selection of a vice-presidential candidate to each state. **Regional Influences** Van Buren won only seven states, just one outside of the South or West. Harrison was long associated with the West, and Tyler was a conservative southerner and friend of Henry Clay. For the first time, active two-party politics was established across the nation.

1844

Party	Candidate	Popular vote	Percent	Electoral vote
Democrat	James K. Polk (Tenn.)	1,339,494	49.54	170
	and George M. Dallas (Pa.)			
Whig	Henry Clay (Ky.)	1,300,004	48.08	105
	and Theodore Frelinghuysen (N.J.)			
Abolitionist	James G. Birney (N.Y.)	62,103	2.30	—
Other		2,058	0.08	—
	Total vote	2,703,659		
	Polk plurality	39,490		

Key Issues Manifest Destiny was the central issue because of the pending annexation of Texas. Opponents of slavery led the Senate to reject a treaty between Texas and the Tyler administration that would have preserved slavery in Texas and made the state a U.S. territory. Clay and Van Buren tried to ignore the Texas issue. But Polk snatched the Democratic nomination with his clear advocacy of annexation of Texas and general territorial expansion. **Regional Influences** Expansionism was immensely popular, especially in the South and West. Support for Manifest Destiny more than made up for antislavery sentiment elsewhere, and Polk won a narrow plurality but a clear victory.

1848

Party	Candidate	Popular vote	Percent	Electoral vote
Whig	Zachary Taylor (La.) and Millard Fillmore (N.Y.)	1,361,393	47.28	163
Democrat	Lewis Cass (Mich.) and William O. Butler (Ky.)	1,223,460	42.49	127
Free Soil	Martin Van Buren (N.Y.) and Charles Francis Adams (Mass.)	291,501	10.12	—
Other		2,830	0.10	—
	Total vote	2,879,184		
	Taylor plurality	137,933		

Key Issues The Wilmot Proviso forbidding the extension of slavery dominated the election. But both major parties evaded the issue. Slavery foes banded together to form the Free Soil party, which drew enough popular support away from the Democrats to throw the election to Old Rough and Ready, Zachary Taylor, a slaveholder. **Regional Influences** Both major parties balanced their tickets with a northerner and southerner. Free Soilers were mostly northern Democrats, antislavery Whigs and abolitionists. Free Soil strength in New York gave the state and the election to the Whigs.

1852

Party	Candidate	Popular vote	Percent	Electoral vote
Democrat	Franklin Pierce (N.H.) and William R.D. King (Ala.)	1,607,510	50.84	254
Whig	Winfield Scott (Va.) and William A. Graham (N.C.)	1,386,942	43.87	42
Free Soil	John P. Hale (N.H.) and George Washington Julian (Ind.)	155,210	4.91	—
Other		12,168	0.38	—
	Total vote	3,161,830		
	Pierce plurality	220,568		

Key Issues The election was a referendum on the Compromise of 1850, in which Congress voted to admit California as a free state, create the territories of New Mexico and Utah with no restriction on slavery, abolish the slave trade in the District of Columbia, purchase disputed land from Texas on behalf of New Mexico, and toughen the Fugitive Slave Act. The Democrats strongly endorsed the Compromise, but the bitterly divided Whigs only vaguely accepted it. **Regional Influences** The Democrats won a resounding electoral victory, capturing 27 states to the four taken by the Whigs: Massachusetts, Vermont, Kentucky, and Tennessee. Free Soilers returned to the Democrats and the Whigs never again were a political force in a nation that believed the slave question was behind it.

1856

Party	Candidate	Popular vote	Percent	Electoral vote
Democrat	James Buchanan (Pa.) and John C. Breckinridge (Ky.)	1,836,072	45.28	174
Republican	John C. Frémont (Calif.) and William L. Dayton (N.J.)	1,342,345	33.11	114
Whig	Millard Fillmore (N.Y.) and Andrew J. Donelson (Tenn.)	873,053	21.53	8
Other		3,177	0.08	—
	Total vote	4,054,647		
	Buchanan plurality	493,727		

Key Issues The Democrats firmly endorsed "popular sovereignty," even though it led to great turmoil in the territory of Kansas. But they chose as their nominee Buchanan, largely because he had been out of the country and was untainted by the "Bleeding Kansas" battle, which pitted supporters and foes of slavery trying to organize the territory into a slave or free state. The Republicans, a new party of northern Whigs and Democrats committed to the containment of slavery, ran Frémont, a popular general and explorer. **Regional Influences** Frémont carried all but five of the free states. But Buchanan won all of the South in addition to the five northern states and was elected. Fillmore, supported by the "Know-Nothings" and Whig remnants, won only Maryland but strongly challenged the Democrats in the South.

1860

Party	Candidate	Popular vote	Percent	Electoral vote
Republican	Abraham Lincoln (Ill.) and Hannibal Hamlin (Maine)	1,865,908	39.82	180
Democrat	Stephen A. Douglas (Ill.) and Herschel V. Johnson (Ga.)	1,380,202	29.46	12
Democrat	John C. Breckinridge (Ky.) and Joseph Lane (Oreg.)	848,019	18.09	72
Constitutional Union	John Bell (Tenn.) and Edward Everett (Mass.)	590,901	12.61	39
Other		531	0.01	—
	Total vote	4,685,561		
	Lincoln plurality	485,706		

Key Issues Sectional differences over slavery came to a head in 1860. The Democrats could not agree on a candidate and split into northern and southern factions. The northern faction backed Douglas and popular sovereignty, the southern faction Breckinridge and federal protection of slavery in the territories. The Republicans, virtually all northerners, were a protariff, nationalistic party that opposed the extension of slavery but did not seek to overturn it where it already existed. Bell, the candidate of Whigs and Know-Nothings who backed Fillmore in 1856, ran for the Constitutional Union, a compromise party expressing support for preservation of the Union. **Regional Influences** In effect there were two separate contests in 1860: Lincoln versus Douglas in the North, Breckinridge versus Bell in the South. Free states outnumbered slave states and cast half again as many electoral votes. Lincoln won every northern state except New Jersey and, though not even on the ballot in 10 southern states, was elected president. Breckinridge captured 11 of the 15 southern states. The four southern states won by Douglas and Bell were in the upper South.

1864

Party	Candidate	Popular vote	Percent	Electoral vote
Republican	Abraham Lincoln (Ill.) and Andrew Johnson (Tenn.)	2,218,388	55.02	212
Democrat	George B. McClellan (N.Y.) and George H. Pendleton (Ohio)	1,812,807	44.96	21
	Total vote	4,031,887		
	Lincoln plurality	405,581		

Key Issues Lincoln's renomination was not assured. Radical Republicans thought he was not aggressive enough in his conduct of the war or plans for the eventual peace, but moderation ultimately prevailed. The Republicans ran as the Union party and nominated Johnson, a pro-Union Democrat, for vice president. The Democrats ran a peace campaign, calling the war a failure. But McClellan, a popular general, broke with his party's platform and denied the war was a failure, denouncing members of his party who seemed to advocate peace at any price. He opposed emancipation as a goal of the war. **Regional Influences** Military victories around election time helped the embattled incumbent. Lincoln won a convincing popular and electoral victory with the support of middle-class professionals, farmers, laborers, and the strongly pro-Union voters who voted for Bell four years earlier. McClellan was strongest in areas carried by Breckinridge four years before. Eleven Confederate states did not participate in the election.

1868

Party	Candidate	Popular vote	Percent	Electoral vote
Republican	Ulysses S. Grant (Ohio) and Schuyler Colfax (Ind.)	3,013,650	52.66	214
Democrat	Horatio S. Seymour (N.Y.) and Francis P. Blair (Mo.)	2,708,744	47.34	80
Other		46	—	—
	Total vote	5,722,440		
	Grant plurality	304,906		

Key Issues The Republicans waved the "bloody shirt" of the war and ran on their program of Radical Reconstruction. While calling for Negro suffrage in the South, the Republicans asserted it was a matter for individual northern states to decide for themselves. Democrats ran against Reconstruction, declaring that the question of Negro suffrage should be decided by individual southern states as well. **Regional Influences** Despite Grant's popularity, the Republicans were just able to win the election. Seymour carried only eight states. Without black votes in the South, Grant would not have received a majority of the popular vote. The votes of the "unreconstructed" states of Mississippi, Texas, and Virginia were not counted.

1872

Party	Candidate	Popular vote	Percent	Electoral vote
Republican	Ulysses S. Grant (Ohio) and Henry Wilson (Mass.)	3,598,235	55.63	286
Liberal Republican/Democrat	Horace Greeley (N.Y.) and Benjamin Gratz Brown (Mo.)	2,834,761	43.83	66
Straight Democrat	Charles O'Conor (N.Y.)	18,602	—	—
Other		16,081	—	—
	Total vote	6,467,679		
	Grant plurality	763,474		

Key Issues Liberal Republicans broke with Grant over corruption in his administration, high tariffs, and continued Radical Reconstruction. They nominated Greeley, editor of the *New York Tribune*. The Democrats endorsed Greeley and the Liberal platform. But the great scandals of the Grant administration were not yet revealed, and the Republicans again waved the bloody shirt to victory. **Regional Influences** Greeley carried only two states in the lower South and four border states. He died shortly after the election (Nov. 29, 1872) and his electoral votes went to other candidates: Thomas Hendricks, Indiana, 42; Benjamin Gratz Brown, Missouri, 18; Charles J. Jenkins, Georgia, 2; and David Davis, Illinois, 1.

1876

Party	Candidate	Popular vote	Percent	Electoral vote
Republican	Rutherford B. Hayes (Ohio) and William A. Wheeler (N.Y.)	4,034,311	47.95	185
Democrat	Samuel J. Tilden (N.Y.) and Thomas A. Hendricks (Ind.)	4,288,546	50.97	184
Greenback	Peter Cooper (N.Y.)	75,973	0.90	—
Other		14,271	0.17	—
	Total vote	8,413,101		
	Tilden plurality	254,235		

Key Issues The Republicans were in trouble as 1876 approached, due to rampant corruption in the Grant administration and the economic depression that followed the Panic of 1873. Hayes, a three-term Ohio governor known for his unassailable integrity, was nominated to run against Tilden, a New York reform governor whose reputation was made in opposition to the Tweed political machine. Both men espoused conservative economics. Cooper and the Greenbacks advocated currency expansion. **Regional Influences** As election day approached, Tilden could count on winning all of the South except for the three states still controlled by Republican carpetbaggers: South Carolina, Louisiana, and Florida. He seemed assured of victory when those states appeared to vote for him, along with several northern states, including New York and New Jersey. But Republicans claimed South Carolina, Louisiana, and Florida for Hayes, arguing that thousands of blacks who would have voted for Hayes were barred from voting there. Election boards in those Republican-controlled states gave Hayes the needed majority, and thus the election. In the uproar that followed, Congress set up an Election Commission to validate the returns. The commission voted strictly along party lines, eight to seven, to give the election to Hayes. Despite charges that Republicans stole the election, Hayes was later inaugurated peaceably after he let it be known that as president he would end military reconstruction by withdrawing federal troops from the South and would restore "efficient local government" there.

1880

Party	Candidate	Popular vote	Percent	Electoral vote
Republican	James A. Garfield (Ohio) and Chester A. Arthur (N.Y.)	4,461,158	48.27	214
Democrat	Winfield S. Hancock (Pa.) and William H. English (Ind.)	4,444,260	48.25	155
Greenback	James B. Weaver (Iowa) and Benjamin J. Chambers (Tex.)	305,997	3.32	—
Other		14,005	0.15	—
	Total vote	9,210,420		
	Garfield plurality	16,898		

Key Issues With the war and Reconstruction behind, no major issues arose over which the major parties disagreed. The Democrats, the party of secession 20 year earlier, nominated Gen. Hancock to help combat the stigma of treason. Garfield made a protectionist tariff central to his campaign. **Regional Influences** The balance between Republican strength in the Midwest and West and Democratic strength in the South resulted in a plurality of less than 17,000 for Garfield out of more than nine million votes cast. Four months into his term, Garfield was shot by a disappointed office-seeker.

1884

Party	Candidate	Popular vote	Percent	Electoral vote
Democrat	Grover Cleveland (N.Y.) and Thomas A. Hendricks (Ind.)	4,874,621	48.50	219
Republican	James G. Blaine (Maine) and John A. Logan (Ill.)	4,848,936	48.25	182
Greenback	Benjamin F. Butler (Mass.)	175,096	1.74	—
Prohibitionist	John P. St. John (Kans.)	147,482	1.47	—
Other		3,619	0.04	
	Total votes	10,049,754		
	Cleveland plurality	25,685		

Key Issues The private lives and morals of the candidates were the focus of a campaign notable for mudslinging. Blaine was accused of accepting bribes from a railroad company for whom he obtained a federal grant, and Republicans taunted Cleveland for fathering a son out of wedlock. Still, Cleveland, known for his independence and integrity in public life, attracted the votes of many liberal Republicans and reformers unable to stomach Blaine, a Radical Republican leader. **Regional Influences** Cleveland carried all of the southern states as well as the key swing states of Indiana, New Jersey, Connecticut, and New York, becoming the first Democrat elected president since the Civil War. Cleveland carried his home state of New York and its 36 electoral votes by less than 1,200 votes.

1888

Party	Candidate	Popular vote	Percent	Electoral vote
Republican	Benjamin Harrison (Ind.) and Levi P. Morton (N.Y.)	5,443,892	47.82	233
Democrat	Grover Cleveland (N.Y.) and Allen G. Thurman (Ohio)	5,534,488	48.62	168
Prohibitionist	Clinton B. Fisk (N.J.)	249,813	2.19	—
Union Labor	Alson J. Streeter (Ill.)	146,602	1.29	—
Other		8,519	0.07	—
	Total vote	11,383,320		
	Cleveland plurality	90,596		

Key Issues Cleveland made tariff reform central to his administration, while the Republicans campaigned to maintain high wages by keeping a high tariff on imported goods. **Regional Influences** Despite the emphasis on the tariff, Cleveland still carried manufacturing states such as New Jersey and Connecticut as well as most of the South. But though Cleveland won the popular vote, Harrison carried the protariff swing states of Indiana and New York by slight margins to win the election in the electoral college in one of the most corrupt campaigns in history.

1892

Party	Candidate	Popular vote	Percent	Electoral vote
Democrat	Grover Cleveland (N.Y.) and Adlai E. Stevenson (Ill.)	5,551,883	46.05	277
Republican	Benjamin Harrison (Ind.) and Whitelaw Reid (N.Y.)	5,179,244	42.96	145
Populist	James B. Weaver (Iowa) and James G. Field (Va.)	1,024,280	8.50	22
Prohibitionist	John Bidwell (Calif.)	270,770	2.25	—
Other		29,920	0.25	—
	Total votes	12,056,097		
	Cleveland plurality	372,639		

Key Issues Cleveland and Harrison again fought over the tariff, which the Republicans drastically raised in 1890. Both men were out of touch with the growing agrarian and populist discontent. Weaver, campaigning for free silver, became the first third-party candidate to gain electoral votes since the war. **Regional Influences** Cleveland improved on his 1884 and 1888 showings to win the most decisive presidential victory in 20 years. He carried the swing states of New York, New Jersey, Connecticut, and Indiana as well as traditionally Republican Illinois, California, and Wisconsin.

1896

Party	Candidate	Popular vote	Percent	Electoral vote
Republican	William McKinley (Ohio) and Garret A. Hobart (N.J.)	7,108,480	51.01	271
Democrat/Populist	William J. Bryan (Nebr.)	6,511,495	46.73	176
	and Democrat Arthur Sewall (Maine)			149
	and Populist Thomas E. Watson (Ga.)			
National Democrat	John M. Palmer (Ill.)	133,435	0.96	—
Prohibition	Joshua Levering (Md.)	125,072	0.90	—
Other		57,256	0.41	—
	Total vote	13,935,738		
	McKinley plurality	596,985		

Key Issues The Democrats abandoned the conservatism of Cleveland by nominating Bryan and adopted key elements of the Populist program, especially the call for free silver. The protariff and progold Republicans led by McKinley and Mark Hanna outspent the Democrats by almost 12 to 1, but Bryan amassed more votes than any victorious candidate before him. **Regional Influences** Bryan did not appeal to labor, and carried no state north of Virginia or east of Missouri. His hold on the agricultural South and West was broken by Republican victories in key states.

1900

Party	Candidate	Popular vote	Percent	Electoral vote
Republican	William McKinley (Ohio) and Theodore Roosevelt (N.Y.)	7,218,039	51.67	292
Democrat	William J. Bryan (Nebr.) and Adlai E. Stevenson (Ill.)	6,358,345	45.51	155
Prohibition	John C. Woolley (Ill.)	209,004	1.50	—
Social Democrat	Eugene V. Debs (Ind.)	86,935	0.62	—
Other		98,147	0.70	—
	Total vote	13,970,470		
	McKinley plurality	859,694		

Key Issues Imperialism in the Philippines joined free silver and the tariff as the key issues in a replay of the 1896 election. Bryan tried to unite the silver interests in the West and South with supporters of the gold standard in a coalition against imperialism, which the Democratic platform called the "paramount issue" of the campaign. But voters did not desert McKinley in a time of prosperity. **Regional Influences** Bryan carried only the solid South and four silver states in the West and was defeated in the silver states of Kansas, South Dakota, Utah, and Wyoming as well as his home state of Nebraska. Both houses of Congress were led by significant Republican majorities.

1904

Party	Candidate	Popular vote	Percent	Electoral vote
Republican	Theodore Roosevelt (N.Y.) and Charles W. Fairbanks (Ind.)	7,626,593	56.41	336
Democrat	Alton B. Parker (N.Y.) and Henry G. Davis (W. Va.)	5,082,898	37.60	140
Socialist	Eugene V. Debs (Ind.)	402,489	2.98	—
Prohibition	Silas C. Swallow (Pa.)	258,596	1.91	—
Other		148,388	1.10	—
	Total votes	13,518,964		
	Roosevelt plurality	2,543,695		

Key Issues Roosevelt stole the mantle of reform from the Democrats with his campaigns against the "malefactors of great wealth." The Democrats turned to the right by nominating the lackluster Parker, a judge with close ties to Wall Street. Parker turned his back on Bryan Democrats by renouncing free silver. **Regional Influences** Roosevelt won a landslide victory based largely on his own personality and popularity. The Democrats won only 13 states, none outside the South.

1908

Party	Candidate	Popular vote	Percent	Electoral vote
Republican	William H. Taft (Ohio) and James S. Sherman (N.Y.)	7,662,258	51.58	321
Democrat	William J. Bryan (Nebr.) and John W. Kern (Ind.)	6,406,801	43.05	162
Socialist	Eugene V. Debs (Ind.)	420,380	2.82	—
Prohibition	Eugene W. Chafin (Ill.)	252,821	1.70	—
Other		126,474	0.85	—
	Total vote	14,882,734		
	Taft plurality	1,269,457		

Key Issues The immensely popular Roosevelt declined to run. Taft, his secretary of war and handpicked successor, debated Bryan over who was better qualified to complete TR's progressive program. Bryan abandoned silver and courted labor but ran a lackluster, losing campaign. **Regional Influences** Bryan again carried the South. But the appeal of Roosevelt's reform programs helped the Republicans do well in the West, and Taft's background as a Yale graduate and federal jurist enabled him to carry the East as well.

1912

Party	Candidate	Popular vote	Percent	Electoral vote
Democrat	Woodrow Wilson (N.J.) and Thomas Marshall (Ind.)	6,293,152	41.84	435
Progressive	Theodore Roosevelt (N.Y.) and Hiram Johnson (Calif.)	4,119,207	27.39	88
Republican	William H. Taft (Ohio) and James S. Sherman (N.Y.)	3,486,333	23.18	8
Socialist	Eugene V. Debs (Ind.)	900,369	5.99	—
Other		241,902	1.61	—
	Total vote	15,040,963		
	Wilson plurality	2,173,945		

Key Issues Taft's conservatism and political ineptitude led Roosevelt to challenge him within the party from the left. Unable to wrest the nomination from Taft, Roosevelt ran a third-party campaign. The election boiled down to a contest between Roosevelt and Wilson and their respective conceptions of progressivism. Roosevelt's "New Nationalism" called for strong federal regulations to control the trusts and big businesses. Wilson's "New Freedom" sought instead to revive competition through vigorous application of antitrust laws. The Progressives advocated a broad array of social reforms to be implemented by the federal government, while the Democrats emphasized the primacy of the states in such matters. **Regional Influences** Though he amassed fewer votes than did Bryan in 1908, Wilson took advantage of the split in the Republican ranks to win a decisive plurality of the vote. He did best in traditional Democratic states but was able to win most traditionally Republican states as well. Roosevelt won only six states, including California, which he carried by fewer than 200 votes. Taft carried Utah and Vermont. The Democrats also won control of both houses of Congress, their best overall performance since the Civil War.

> ***"He kept us out of the war."***
>
> **—Wilson campaign slogan**

1916

Party	Candidate	Popular vote	Percent	Electoral vote
Democrat	Woodrow Wilson (N.J.) and Thomas Marshall (Ind.)	9,126,300	49.24	277
Republican	Charles Evans Hughes (N.Y.) and Charles W. Fairbanks (Ind.)	8,546,789	46.11	254
Socialist	Allen L. Benson (N.Y.)	589,924	3.18	—
Prohibitionist	James F. Hanly (Ind.)	221,030	1.19	—
Other		50,979	0.28	—
	Total vote	18,535,022		
	Wilson plurality	579,511		

Key Issues The campaign was a referendum on Wilson's first term: his program of domestic reform and his policy toward the war in Europe. He ran a peace campaign with the slogan "He Kept Us Out of the War" and attracted the votes of many Bull Moosers. Voters who felt Wilson was either too harsh or too lenient toward Germany tended to vote Republican. Irish-American and German-American extremists, virulently opposed to aiding Great Britain, embarrassed Hughes with their vocal support. A coalition of labor, farmers, reformers, and intellectuals won the election for Wilson. **Regional Influences** Hughes, a former reform governor of New York who left the Supreme Court to challenge Wilson, carried all of the East except New Hampshire and all of the Old Northwest, except Ohio. But the South was again solid for the Democrats as was every state west of the Mississippi except Minnesota, Iowa, South Dakota, and Oregon, which Wilson lost by close margins. The electoral vote was the closest since 1876.

1920

Party	Candidate	Popular vote	Percent	Electoral vote
Republican	Warren G. Harding (Ohio) and Calvin Coolidge (Mass.)	16,133,314	60.30	404
Democrat	James M. Cox (Ohio) and Franklin D. Roosevelt (N.Y.)	9,140,884	34.17	127
Socialist	Eugene V. Debs (Ind.)	913,664	3.42	—
Farmer-Labor	Parley P. Christensen (Utah)	264,540	0.99	—
Other		301,384	1.13	—
	Total vote	26,753,786		
	Harding plurality	6,992,430		

Key Issues The voters turned against Wilsonian progressivism and internationalism by electing Harding, a vacuous party hack who promised a "return to normalcy" after the turbulent years of domestic reform and world war. The undistinguished Cox ran in support of the League of Nations and little else. **Regional Influences** Harding carried every state outside of the South, except Tennessee. The Republicans added to their majorities in both houses of Congress, regained in 1918.

1924

Party	Candidate	Popular vote	Percent	Electoral vote
Republican	Calvin Coolidge (Mass.) and Charles G. Dawes (Ohio)	15,717,553	54.00	382
Democrat	John W. Davis (N.Y.) and Charles W. Bryan (Nebr.)	8,386,169	28.84	136
Progressive Socialist	Robert M. LaFollette (Wis.) and Burton K. Wheeler (Mont.)	4,814,050	16.56	13
Other		158,187	0.55	—
	Total vote	29,075,959		
	Coolidge plurality	7,331,384		

Key Issues The country "kept cool with Coolidge," since the Democrats could not overcome prosperity or themselves. Davis, a conservative Wall Street lawyer, was a compromise nominee selected by a bitterly divided party after 103 ballots. Reformers, laborers, and farmers flocked to the LaFollette candidacy. **Regional Influences** All 12 of the Democratic states were from the South. LaFollette's 13 electoral votes came from his home state of Wisconsin.

1928

Party	Candidate	Popular vote	Percent	Electoral vote
Republican	Herbert C. Hoover (Calif.) and Charles E. Curtis (Kans.)	21,411,911	58.20	444
Democrat	Alfred E. Smith (N.Y.) and Joseph T. Robinson (Ark.)	15,000,185	40.77	87
Socialist	Norman Thomas (N.Y.)	266,453	0.72	—
Workers'	William Z. Foster (Ill.)	48,170	0.13	—
Other		63,565	0.17	—
	Total vote	36,790,364		
	Hoover plurality	6,411,806		

Key Issues Booze, bigotry, Tammany, and prosperity did in the Democrats. Rural America would not vote for an anti-Prohibition, big-city, Catholic machine-politician, despite Smith's success as governor of New York, especially while the Republicans could convincingly cite the success of their economic leadership. **Regional Influences** The solid South was shattered as Hoover Democrats gave Republicans the states of Virginia, North Carolina, Tennessee, Florida, and Texas for the first time since Reconstruction. Smith lost his own state and every western and border state. But Smith set the stage for the New Deal coalition: with the votes of urban ethnics, he carried the nation's 12 largest cities, all of which had been won by the Republicans four years earlier. The Democrats also won votes in the traditionally Republican West among farmers uncertain about prosperity.

1932

Party	Candidate	Popular vote	Percent	Electoral vote
Democrat	Franklin D. Roosevelt (N.Y.) and John Nance Garner (Tex.)	22,825,016	57.42	472
Republican	Herbert C. Hoover (Calif.) and Charles E. Curtis (Kans.)	15,758,397	39.64	59
Socialist	Norman Thomas (N.Y.)	883,990	2.22	—
Communist	William Z. Foster (Ill.)	102,221	0.26	—
Other		179,758	0.45	—
	Total vote	39,749,382		
	Roosevelt plurality	7,066,619		

Key Issues The Democrats won by blaming the Republicans for the Great Depression. Roosevelt, the first presidential nominee of a major party to address his nominating convention, pledged to help the "forgotten man at the bottom of the economic pyramid." In a vague and contradictory platform, the Democrats promised to balance the federal budget by drastically reducing expenses and vowed to spend federal dollars to attack the nation's economic woes. **Regional Influences** Roosevelt lost only six states—Maine, New Hampshire, Vermont, Connecticut, Delaware, and Pennsylvania—carrying all of the agricultural West and South, improving on Smith's margins of victory in the nation's big cities.

1936

Party	Candidate	Popular vote	Percent	Electoral vote
Democrat	Franklin D. Roosevelt (N.Y.) and John Nance Garner (Tex.)	27,747,636	60.79	523
Republican	Alfred M. Landon (Kans.) and Frank Knox (Ill.)	16,679,543	36.54	8
Union	William Lemke (N.Dak.)	892,492	1.96	—
Socialist	Norman Thomas (N.Y.)	187,785	0.41	—
Other		134,847	0.30	—
	Total vote	45,642,303		
	Roosevelt plurality	11,068,093		

Key Issues The great public appeal of the New Deal was confirmed in the most one-sided election since 1820 and sweeping victories for the Democrats in Congress. The populist forces of the late Huey Long coalesced around Lemke but failed to gather widespread support. **Regional Influences** Roosevelt carried every state except Maine and Vermont, and every large city. The middle class, farmers in the West and South, big-city ethnics, laborers, and reform intellectuals flocked to the Democrats. Northern blacks also began to vote heavily Democratic for the first time.

1940

Party	Candidate	Popular vote	Percent	Electoral vote
Democrat	Franklin D. Roosevelt (N.Y.) and Henry A. Wallace (Iowa)	27,263,448	54.70	449
Republican	Wendell L. Willkie (Ind.) and Charles L. McNary (Ore.)	22,336,260	44.82	82
Socialist	Norman Thomas (N.Y.)	116,827	0.23	—
Prohibitionist	Roger W. Babson (Mass.)	58,685	0.12	—
Other		65,223	0.13	—
	Total vote	49,840,443		
	Roosevelt plurality	4,927,188		

Key Issues With war raging in Europe, the electorate turned its attention to foreign affairs. The Democrats broke with tradition and renominated FDR for a third term. The Republicans turned to businessman and political neophyte Willkie, a charismatic former Democrat. Willkie's internationalism and the pledge of both candidates to keep the country out of the war minimized the role of foreign policy in the campaign. **Regional Influences** Willkie carried only 10 states, mostly in the Midwest. But Roosevelt's percentage of the popular vote was markedly down from 1936.

1944

Party	Candidate	Popular vote	Percent	Electoral vote
Democrat	Franklin D. Roosevelt (N.Y.) and Harry S Truman (Mo.)	25,611,936	53.39	432
Republican	Thomas E. Dewey (N.Y.) and John W. Bricker (Ohio)	22,013,372	45.89	99
Socialist	Norman Thomas (N.Y.)	79,100	0.16	—
Prohibitionist	Claude A. Watson (Calif.)	74,733	0.16	—
Other		195,778	0.41	—
	Total vote	47,974,819		
	Roosevelt plurality	3,598,564		

Key Issues Both candidates expressed support for New Deal social legislation and an international organization to maintain peace after the war. Big-city bosses and southern conservatives, with FDR's private support, ousted Henry Wallace from the ticket in favor of Truman. **Regional Influences** Roosevelt won 36 states, and the Democrats improved their control over Congress and the nation's statehouses. The Republicans won only a handful of western and New England states.

1948

Party	Candidate	Popular vote	Percent	Electoral vote
Democrat	Harry S Truman (Mo.) and Alben W. Barkley (Ky.)	24,105,587	49.51	303
Republican	Thomas E. Dewey (N.Y.) and Earl Warren (Calif.)	21,970,017	45.12	189
States' Rights	Strom Thurmond (S.C.) and Fielding L. Wright (Miss.)	1,169,134	2.40	39
Progressive	Henry A. Wallace (Iowa) and Glen H. Taylor (Idaho)	1,157,057	2.38	—
Other		290,647	0.60	—
	Total vote	48,692,442		
	Truman plurality	2,135,570		

Key Issues The Republicans were sure of victory after 16 years of Democratic rule and the desertion of the Democrats by conservative Dixiecrats and the ultraliberal Wallace faction. But Dewey's dour personality and Truman's intense whistle-stop campaign against the "do-nothing, good-for-nothing" Republican 80th Congress resulted in one of the biggest upsets in presidential history. **Regional Influences** Dewey captured all of the Middle Atlantic and New England states, except Massachusetts and Connecticut, along with the Dakotas, Nebraska, Kansas, and Oregon. Thurmond won South Carolina, Mississippi, Alabama, and Louisiana.

1952

Party	Candidate	Popular vote	Percent	Electoral vote
Republican	Dwight D. Eisenhower (Kans.) and Richard M. Nixon (Calif.)	33,936,137	55.13	442
Democrat	Adlai E. Stevenson (Ill.) and John J. Sparkman (Ala.)	27,314,649	44.38	89
Progressive	Vincent W. Hallinan (Calif.)	140,416	0.23	—
Prohibition	Stuart Hamblen (Calif.)	73,413	0.12	—
Other		86,503	0.14	—
	Total vote	61,551,118		
	Eisenhower plurality	6,621,485		

Key Issues Eisenhower swept to victory after uniting the internationalist and isolationist factions of the Republican party. He promised to kick out alleged crooks and Communists in Washington, wage a more aggressive fight against Communists worldwide, and "go to Korea," implying that he had a plan to end the war there. **Regional Influences** Stevenson appealed to northern liberals and southern states' rights Democrats, but carried only nine states in the South. The Republicans also won slight majorities in Congress and were in control of the national government for the first time in 20 years.

1956

Party	Candidate	Popular vote	Percent	Electoral vote
Republican	Dwight D. Eisenhower (Kans.) and Richard M. Nixon (Calif.)	35,585,247	57.37	457
Democrat	Adlai E. Stevenson (Ill.) and Estes Kefauver (Tenn.)	26,030,172	41.97	73
Constitution/States' Rights	T. Coleman Andrews (Va.)	108,055	0.17	—
Socialist-Labor	Eric Hass (N.Y.)	44,300	0.07	—
Other		257,600	0.42	1
	Total vote	62,025,372		
	Eisenhower plurality	9,555,073		

Key Issues Eisenhower won an easy victory in a rematch of the 1952 election. His popularity did not translate into victories for his party elsewhere, as Democrats increased their control of Congress—regained in 1954—and their hold on the nation's governorships. **Regional Influences** Winning even more handsomely than he did in 1952, Eisenhower lost only seven southern states.

1960

Party	Candidate	Popular vote	Percent	Electoral vote
Democrat	John F. Kennedy (Mass.) and Lyndon B. Johnson (Tex.)	34,221,344	49.72	303
Republican	Richard M. Nixon (Calif.) and Henry Cabot Lodge (Mass.)	34,106,671	49.55	219
Socialist-Labor	Eric Hass (N.Y.)	47,522	0.07	—
Other		337,175	0.48	15
Unpledged		116,248	0.17	—
	Total vote	68,828,960		
	Kennedy plurality	114,673		

Key Issues Kennedy called for the government to play a larger role in stimulating the national economy in order to fund domestic social programs as well as to sustain a defense buildup and keep ahead militarily of the USSR. The election was the first in which there were nationally televised debates between the two candidates. Kennedy's slick television performance played a role in his narrow triumph. **Regional Influences** The Democrats won a thin victory by narrowly defeating the Republicans in the Middle Atlantic states, the Deep South, Illinois, and Texas. Nixon carried most of the Midwest, border, and western states. The conservative Democrat senator Harry F. Byrd of Virginia received 15 electoral votes, including all eight of Mississippi's, six of Alabama's 11, and one of Oklahoma's eight.

1964

Party	Candidate	Popular vote	Percent	Electoral vote
Democrat	Lyndon B. Johnson (Tex.) and Hubert H. Humphrey (Minn.)	43,126,584	61.05	486
Republican	Barry M. Goldwater (Ariz.) and William E. Miller (N.Y.)	27,177,838	38.47	52
Socialist-Labor	Eric Hass (N.Y.)	45,187	0.06	—
Socialist Workers	Clifton DeBerry (N.Y.)	32,701	0.05	—
Other		258,794	0.37	—
	Total vote	70,641,104		
	Johnson plurality	15,948,746		

Key Issues Johnson ran for election in his own right on the basis of his "Great Society" domestic programs. The reactionary Goldwater campaigned against the New Deal and for the bombing of North Vietnam. **Regional Influences** Johnson won all but six states—Goldwater's home state of Arizona and five states in the Deep South—in the biggest popular and electoral landslide since 1936. Forty new northern Democrats were elected to the House on LBJ's coattails.

1968

Party	Candidate	Popular vote	Percent	Electoral vote
Republican	Richard M. Nixon (Calif.) and Spiro T. Agnew (Md.)	31,785,148	43.42	301
Democrat	Hubert H. Humphrey (Minn.) and Edmund S. Muskie (Maine)	31,274,503	42.72	191
American Independent	George C. Wallace (Ala.) and Curtis LeMay (Ohio)	9,901,151	13.53	46
Socialist-Labor	Henning A. Blomen (Mass.)	52,591	0.07	—
Other		189,977	0.20	—
	Total vote	73,203,370		
	Nixon plurality	510,645		

Key Issues With the country divided over Vietnam, Humphrey failed to emerge from the shadow of the unpopular Johnson, while the previously hawkish Nixon pledged to end the war. Wallace attacked desegregation, "pointy-headed" intellectuals, the administration's timidity in Vietnam, and federal encroachment on states' rights. **Regional Influences** Barely more than 500,000 votes separated Nixon and Humphrey, but the Republican edge in the Electoral College was comfortable, and the combined anti-Democratic vote was a repudiation of the Johnson-Humphrey administration. Humphrey's strength was in the eastern seaboard states. Wallace won five states in the Deep South.

1972

Party	Candidate	Popular vote	Percent	Electoral vote
Republican	Richard M. Nixon (Calif.) and Spiro T. Agnew (Md.)	47,170,179	60.69	520
Democrat	George S. McGovern (S.Dak.) and R. Sargent Shriver (Md.)	29,171,791	37.53	17
American Independent	John G. Schmitz (Calif.)	1,090,673	1.40	—
People's	Benjamin Spock	78,751	0.10	—
Other		216,196	0.28	(1)
	Total vote	77,727,590		
	Nixon plurality	17,998,388		

Key Issues Seeking to convert Wallace Democrats, Nixon pursued a "Southern strategy" of denouncing busing, the welfare state, the media, and intellectuals. McGovern was unable to overcome Republican charges that he was the candidate of "acid, abortion, and amnesty." **Regional Influences** The GOP gained southern Democratic votes when an assassination attempt knocked Wallace out of the race. Nixon lost only Massachusetts and the District of Columbia.

1. The Libertarian slate (John Hospers/Theodore Nathan) received 1 electoral vote from a Republican elector in Virginia.

1976

Party	Candidate	Popular vote	Percent	Electoral vote
Democrat	Jimmy Carter (Ga.) and Walter F. Mondale (Minn.)	40,830,763	50.06	297
Republican	Gerald R. Ford (Mich.) and Robert Dole (Kans.)	39,147,793	48.00	240[1]
Independent	Eugene J. McCarthy (Minn.)	756,691	0.93	—
Libertarian	Roger MacBride (Va.)	173,011	0.21	—
Other		647,631	0.79	—
	Total vote	81,555,889		
	Carter plurality	1,682,970		

Key Issues In the wake of Watergate, Carter ran a moralistic campaign as a political outsider. He vowed to lead a "government that is as good and honest and decent . . . as filled with love as are the American people." **Regional Influences** Despite an unimpressive campaign filled with miscues, Ford nearly overcame a huge early deficit in the polls. But Carter's background as a southern moderate enabled him to eke out a victory through wins in a combination of northern, southern, and border states.

1. Ronald Reagan received one electoral vote from an elector in Washington.

1980

Party	Candidate	Popular vote	Percent	Electoral vote
Republican	Ronald Reagan (Calif.) and George Bush (Tex.)	43,901,812	50.75	489
Democrat	Jimmy Carter (Ga.) and Walter F. Mondale (Minn.)	35,483,820	41.02	49
Independent	John B. Anderson (Ill.) and Patrick J. Lucey (Wis.)	5,719,722	6.61	—
Libertarian	Edward E. Clark (Calif.)	921,188	1.06	—
Other		486,754	0.56	—
	Total vote	86,513,296		
	Reagan plurality	8,417,992		

Key Issues Inflation, an energy shortage, the taking of American hostages by Iran, and a strong primary challenge from Edward Kennedy of Massachusetts weakened Carter. Reagan, promising to get government "off the backs of the American people," pledged to cut taxes, increase defense spending, and balance the federal budget. Anderson, a Republican, ran as an independent to the left of both Carter and Reagan. **Regional Influences** Reagan swept to a landslide win in the Electoral College, with Carter carrying only six states and the District of Columbia.

1984

Party	Candidate	Popular vote	Percent	Electoral vote
Republican	Ronald Reagan (Calif.) and George Bush (Tex.)	54,450,603	58.78	525
Democrat	Walter F. Mondale (Minn.) and Geraldine Ferraro (N.Y.)	37,573,671	40.56	13
Libertarian	David Bergland (Calif.)	227,949	0.25	—
Other		570,343	0.61	—
	Total vote	92,628,458		
	Reagan plurality	16,876,932		

Key Issues The economy was flying after emerging in late 1983 from the worst economic downturn since the Great Depression. Reagan, whose commercials proclaimed it was "morning in America," ridiculed Mondale as an old-fashioned "tax-and-spend, gloom-and-doom" Democrat. Controversy over her husband's finances blunted Ferraro's appeal as the first woman on a major party ticket. **Regional Influences** Mondale carried only his home state of Minnesota and the District of Columbia, while Reagan won the greatest electoral victory in American history and the fifth-highest share of the popular vote.

"Great men are not chosen president, firstly, because great men are rare in politics; secondly, because the method of choice does not bring them to the top; thirdly, because they are not, in quiet times, absolutely necessary."

—English jurist, historian, and diplomat James Bryce, *The American Commonwealth* (1888)

1988

Party	Candidate	Popular vote	Percent	Electoral vote
Republican	George Bush (Tex.) and Dan Quayle (Ind.)	48,881,011	53.37	426
Democrat	Michael S. Dukakis (Mass.) and Lloyd Bentsen (Tex.)	41,828,350	45.67	111[1]
Libertarian	Ron Paul (Tex.)	431,499	0.47	—
New Alliance	Leonora Fulani (N.Y.)	218,159	0.24	—
Other		226,852	0.25	—
	Total vote	91,585,871		
	Bush plurality	7,052,661		

Key Issues Trailing Dukakis by 17 points in early summer, Bush made an issue of his opponent's "liberalism," depicting the Massachusetts governor as soft on crime. Bush made a household name out of Willie Horton, a black Massachusetts prison inmate who raped a woman while on a prison furlough. Bush also called Dukakis a card-carrying member of the American Civil Liberties Union and said that he didn't share the same values as the American people. Dukakis's failure to respond to those charges and to shed the "liberal" label until late in the campaign ultimately doomed his candidacy, despite Bush's links to the Iran-Contra scandal and to Panama's drug-running leader, Gen. Manuel Noriega. **Regional Influences** Dukakis won the District of Columbia and only 10 states: Washington, Oregon, Hawaii, New York, Minnesota, Wisconsin, Iowa, West Virginia, Rhode Island, and his home state of Massachusetts. Bush easily captured the formerly Democratic "solid South."

1. Bentsen received one electoral vote for president.

1992

Party	Candidate	Popular vote	Percent	Electoral vote
Democrat	Bill Clinton (Ark.) and Al Gore (Tenn.)	44,908,233	42.95	370
Republican	George Bush (Tex.) and Dan Quayle (Ind.)	39,102,282	37.40	168
Independent	Ross Perot (Tex.) and James Stockdale (Calif.)	19,721,433	18.86	—
Libertarian	Andre Marrou	291,612	0.28	—
Populist/ America First	James "Bo" Gritz	98,918	0.09	—
New Alliance	Lenora Fulani	73,248	0.07	—
U.S. Taxpayers	Howard Phillips	42,960	0.04	—
Natural Law	John Hagelin	37,137	0.04	—
Independent	Ron Daniels	27,396	0.03	—
Independent	Lyndon LaRouche	25,863	0.02	—
Socialist Workers	James Mac Warren	22,883	0.02	—
Independent	Drew Bradford	4,749	—	—
Grassroots	Jack Herer	3,875	—	—
Workers League	Helen Halyard	3,050	—	—
Socialist	John Quinn Brisben	2,909	—	—
Independent	John Yiamouyiannis	2,199	—	—
Independent	Delbert Ehlers	1,149	—	—
Apathy	Jim Boren	956	—	—
Prohibition	Earl Dodge	935	—	—
Third Party	Eugene Hem	405	—	—
Looking Back Group	Isabelle Masters	327	—	—
American	Robert J. Smith	292	—	—
Workers World	Gloria Estelle La Riva	181	—	—
Other[1]		179,744	0.17	—
	Total vote	104,552,736		
	Clinton plurality	5,805,951		

Note: Party designations may vary from one state to another. 1. Other includes write-in and none of the above (Nevada). **Sources:** Congressional Quarterly, Inc., *Presidential Elections since 1789* (1983); Federal Election Commission, Press Office (Jan. 14, 1993).

ELECTION ISSUES

Voter Turnout in the 1992 Election

Voter turnout skyrocketed to record levels in 1992 thanks in large part to the Independent presidential bid by Ross Perot. More than 104 million Americans cast ballots in the 1992 presidential race, up nearly 13 million from the 91 million Americans who voted in 1988. Perot's candidacy was responsible for all of this increase and more, as he attracted more than 19 million voters, a large portion of whom had become disaffected from the two traditional parties. The percentage of the voting age population casting ballots, which had plummeted to a 64-year low in 1988, rebounded to over 55 percent in 1992, the highest level in 20 years. And more than three-quarters of registered voters went to the polls in 1992, up five percent from the previous election.

Voter turnout was higher in every state in 1992 than four years earlier, but Perot was not entirely responsible for the increase. Turnout in seven southern states (Alabama, Arkansas, Georgia, North Carolina, South Carolina, Tennessee, and Virginia) as well as Nevada and the District of Columbia increased by more than the number of votes Perot received, meaning that more voters cast Republican and Democratic ballots in 1992 than in 1988. For example, in Georgia, 2.3 million voters went to the polls, up more than 500,000 from the 1.8 million who cast ballots in 1988. But only 309,000 of the additional voters chose Perot, meaning that an additional 201,796 voters picked from the two traditional parties. Overall, the Perot vote exceeded the increase in voter turnout, suggesting that Perot attracted votes that otherwise might have gone to Bill Clinton or George Bush.

The biggest increases came in the biggest states, especially Florida and California, where turnout increased by more than a million voters each. Perot's home state of Texas (also the sometime home of Republican candidate George Bush) reported an increase of 726,608. The biggest percentage increases came in Nevada (up 44.6%), Alaska (29.1%), and Georgia (28.2%). Turnout in Bill Clinton's home state of Arkansas increased by a mere 14.8 percent, or only slightly higher than the national average of 14.0 percent.

The 1992 numbers mark only the second time in 32 years that voter turnout has increased (the other time was in 1984, when 53.1% of the voting-age population voted, compared to 52.6% in 1980). In every other election since 1960, turnout has dropped, sometimes precipitously. The 3 percent decline between 1984 and 1988 was the third largest since 1920. Only the Dewey-Truman race of 1948 and the Nixon-McGovern race of 1972 had bigger drop-offs from the previous election. Additionally, voter turnout figures for the 1972 race were exaggerated by the enfranchisement of voters in the low-voting 18–20 age range.

1992 ELECTION RETURNS BY STATE

		(Republican) George Bush/ Dan Quayle		(Democrat) Bill Clinton/ Albert Gore, Jr.		(Independent) Ross Perot/ James Stockdale	
State	Electoral votes	Popular vote	Percent	Popular vote	Percent	Popular vote	Percent
Alabama	9	804,283	48%	690,080	41%	183,109	11%
Alaska	3	102,000	41	78,294	32	73,481	27
Arizona	8	572,086	39	543,050	37	353,741	24
Arkansas	6	337,324	36	505,823	54	99,132	11
California	54	3,630,575	32	5,121,325	47	2,296,006	21
Colorado	8	562,850	36	629,681	40	366,010	23
Connecticut	8	578,313	36	682,318	42	348,771	22
Delaware	3	20,698	9	192,619	86	9,681	4
District of Columbia	3	102,313	36	126,054	44	59,213	21
Florida	25	2,171,781	41	2,071,651	39	1,052,481	20
Georgia	13	995,252	43	1,008,966	44	309,657	13
Hawaii	4	136,822	37	179,310	49	53,003	14
Idaho	4	202,645	43	137,013	29	130,395	28
Illinois	22	1,734,096	35	2,453,350	48	840,515	17
Indiana	12	989,375	43	848,420	37	455,934	20
Iowa	7	504,891	38	586,353	44	253,468	19
Kansas	6	449,951	39	390,434	34	312,358	27
Kentucky	8	617,178	42	665,104	45	203,944	14
Louisiana	9	733,386	42	815,971	46	211,478	12
Maine	4	206,504	31	263,420	39	206,820	30
Maryland	10	707,094	36	988,571	50	281,414	14
Massachusetts	12	805,039	29	1,318,639	48	630,731	23
Michigan	18	1,554,940	37	1,871,182	44	824,813	19
Minnesota	10	747,841	32	1,020,997	44	562,506	24
Mississippi	7	487,793	50	400,258	41	85,626	9
Missouri	11	811,159	34	1,053,873	44	518,741	22
Montana	3	144,207	36	154,507	38	107,225	26
Nebraska	5	343,678	47	216,864	30	174,104	24
Nevada	4	175,828	35	189,148	38	132,580	27
New Hampshire	4	202,484	38	209,040	39	121,337	23
New Jersey	15	1,356,865	41	1,436,206	43	521,829	16
New Mexico	5	212,824	38	261,617	46	91,895	16
New York	33	2,346,649	34	3,444,450	50	1,090,721	16
North Carolina	14	1,134,661	44	1,114,042	43	357,864	14
North Dakota	3	136,244	44	99,168	32	71,084	23
Ohio	21	1,894,248	39	1,984,919	40	1,036,403	21
Oklahoma	8	592,929	43	473,066	34	319,878	23
Oregon	7	475,757	32	621,314	43	354,091	25
Pennsylvania	23	1,791,841	36	2,239,164	45	902,667	18
Rhode Island	4	131,601	29	213,299	48	105,045	23
South Carolina	8	577,507	48	479,514	40	119,257	12
South Dakota	3	136,718	41	124,888	37	73,295	22
Tennessee	11	841,300	43	933,521	47	199,968	10
Texas	32	2,496,071	40	2,281,815	37	1,354,781	22
Utah	5	322,632	45	183,429	26	203,400	29
Vermont	3	88,122	31	133,592	46	65,991	23
Virginia	13	1,150,517	45	1,038,650	41	348,639	14
Washington	11	731,234	32	993,037	44	541,780	24
West Virginia	5	241,974	36	331,001	49	108,829	16
Wisconsin	11	930,855	37	1,041,066	41	544,479	22
Wyoming	3	79,347	40	68,160	34	51,263	26

Maine, Minnesota, and Montana ranked highest in voter turnout in 1992, with more than 70 percent of eligible voters casting ballots in each of those states. Hawaii ranked lowest in voter turnout, with only 41.94 percent of its voting-age population going to the polls. This may be explained by the fact that the winner had already been determined by the time many Hawaiians reached their polling places. But voters in Alaska were not so deterred: 65.44 percent of voting-age Alaskans cast ballots.

The Federal Election Campaign Act

In 1971 Congress passed the Federal Election Campaign Act to deal with various aspects of campaign financing. The law was amended and strengthened in 1974 and 1976, and the Federal Election Commission (FEC) was established to administer the law, which affects candidates for the U.S. House of Representatives, the U.S. Senate, and the presidency, as well as the political committees that support them. The act requires disclosure of sources and uses of funds for federal elections, provides public financing for presidential elections, and sets limits on campaign contributions. The specific requirements of each of these three parts of the act are detailed below.

Public disclosure Candidates for federal office and the political committees that support them must register and file periodic disclosures of their campaign finance activities with the clerk of the House, the secretary of the Senate, or the FEC. These reports are available to the public within 48 hours of their disclosure. A candidate is defined as one who has raised or spent more than $5,000 in any given year in campaigning for federal office. A political committee is defined as a club, committee, association, or organization that receives contributions or makes expenditures of more than $1,000 to a federal candidate in any calendar year. In recent years they have come to be called PACs, for Political Action Committee.

Public financing Public financing is provided for eligible presidential candidates in primary and general elections, and for national party committees for the nominating conventions. Financing is given in the form of matching payments to primary candidates, public grants to nominees in the general elections, and public grants to the national party committees for the conventions. The money for public financing is raised by the Presidential Election Campaign Fund, which collects one dollar from the tax payment of every taxpayer who checks off this box on his or her federal income-tax return.

Contribution limits and prohibitions In federal elections the act prohibits contributions from the treasuries of national banks, corporations, and labor organizations; contributions from government contractors; contributions from foreign nationals (green card holders); cash contributions in excess of $100 per person; contributions supplied by one person in the name of another person.

Additionally, the act sets contribution limits as shown in the accompanying table.

CAMPAIGN CONTRIBUTION LIMITS FOR INDIVIDUALS AND PACS

	Contributor		
Recipient	**Individual contributor**	**Multi-candidate committee**	**Other political committee**
Each candidate or candidate committee[1]	$ 1,000	$ 5,000	$ 1,000
National party committee[1]	20,000	15,000	20,000
Other political committee[2]	5,000	5,000	5,000
Total per calendar year	**$25,000**	**no limit**	**no limit**

1. Per election year. 2. Per calendar year. **Source:** Federal Election Commission.

The Electoral College

The Electoral College is the body of electors chosen by all of the states that ultimately is responsible for selecting the president of the United States. The Constitution's framers did not want the nation's chief executive chosen by either the national legislature or the people directly. Instead they set up what came to be known as the Electoral College under Article II, section 1, of the Constitution to provide for indirect election of the president: "Each State shall appoint, in such manner as the legislature thereof may direct, a number of Electors, equal to the whole number of Senators and Representatives to which the State may be entitled in the Congress; but no Senator or Representative, or person holding an office of trust or profit under the United States, shall be appointed an Elector."

Electors were supposed to be distinguished, enlightened citizens who would cast a disinterested vote for president. From the start, though, electors have been instruments of partisan passions. At first most state legislatures were responsible for choosing electors. By 1828, however, all states except South Carolina allowed electors to be chosen by direct popular election. (In South Carolina the legislature continued to select electors until the Civil War.) When electors began being selected by popular vote, parties presented slates of candidates for presidential electors who were tacitly pledged to support the party's nominees for president and vice president. This is how the practice began of states voting as a unit. Subsequently, many states passed laws requiring their electors to vote as a bloc. Where it is not required by law, it is customary for all of a state's electors to vote for the candidate receiving a plurality of the popular vote in that state. The names of the candidates for electors may or may not appear on the ballot alongside the names of the candidates to whom they are pledged. Voters really vote for presidential electors, though, even when they seem to be casting a ballot for a presidential candidate.

The presidential electors chosen by the voters in November meet in their state capitals on the first Monday after the second Wednesday in December to cast their vote for president and vice president. The results of this balloting are sent to the president of the U.S. Senate, the directors of the U.S. General Services Administration, the state's secretary of state, and to the judge of the federal district court of the district in which the electors gathered. Sealed state ballots are opened and counted at a joint session of Congress on Jan. 6 following the election year.

Originally, electors voted for two individuals for president on a single ballot. The winner of a majority of the vote was elected president; the runner-up, vice president. The framers fully expected there to be many elections in which no candidate would gain a majority of the vote, and the president would have to be selected by the House of Representatives, where each state delegation would cast a single vote. But in 1789 and 1792, every elector voted for George Washington. In both years John Adams was the runner-up and thus vice president.

Problems inherent in this system became apparent once Washington no longer was a candidate. In 1796 Adams and Thomas Jefferson finished first and second in the balloting and were elected president and vice president, respectively, despite their being fierce foes. By 1800 two formal parties had evolved that nominated candidates specifically for president and vice president. A Federalist elector purposely failed to vote for the party's vice-presidential nominee, Thomas Pinckney, in order to assure a potential majority for John Adams. But overzealous Republican electors all voted for both Jefferson and the party's vice-presidential nominee, Aaron Burr. Both men received the same majority of the electoral vote, and the election had to be decided by the House, where Jefferson won. This led to adoption of the 12th Amendment to the Constitution, implemented in 1804, which required that electors cast separate ballots for president and vice president. If no candidate achieves a majority of the electoral vote for vice president, the position is determined by the Senate, with each senator casting a single ballot. This has happened only once, when the Senate selected Richard M. Johnson after he fell one electoral vote short of a majority for vice president in 1836.

Currently, 270 votes are needed to reach a majority in the Electoral College. There have been two elections in which no candidate received a majority of the electoral vote—in 1824 and in 1876, when disputed results in several states prevented either Rutherford B. Hayes or Samuel J. Tilden from achieving a majority. (John Quincy Adams and Hayes won those contests, respectively.) A candidate also can be elected president despite losing the popular vote. This occurred, again in 1824 and 1876, when the House selected Adams and Hayes, though they lost the popular vote to Andrew Jackson and Tilden, respectively, and in 1888, when Benjamin Harrison was elected over Grover Cleveland despite receiving a minority of the popular vote.

> ***"An honest politician is one who when he is bought will stay bought."***
> —Simon Cameron

Political Officeholders

THE VICE PRESIDENCY

The vice president is a member of the executive branch (to which he is elected with the president) and of the legislative branch, in which he serves as president of the Senate (see the Constitution, Article I, section 3). Unlike the office of president, that of vice president has sometimes been left vacant after the death of the vice president or the latter's assumption of higher office on the death of the president. Until adoption of the 25th Amendment to the Constitution in 1967, there was no provision to fill a vacancy in the vice presidency. Under the amendment the president must name a vice president when the office is vacant, and the nominee must pass a majority vote of approval in both houses of Congress. Gerald Ford, Richard Nixon's choice to replace Spiro Agnew after the latter's resignation in 1973, was the first vice president to gain the office under the amendment. While the 25th Amendment does not supersede the presidential order of succession, it decreases the likelihood of the office's ever falling to the Speaker of the House or a sitting cabinet member.

PRESIDENTIAL ORDER OF SUCCESSION

Article II of the Constitution gives to Congress the power to determine the presidential order of succession should both the president and vice president die, become incapacitated, or be disqualified from office. The present law, passed in 1947, puts the Speaker of the House first in line to the presidency, followed by the president pro tempore of the Senate. The order of succession then goes through the members of the cabinet, in the order in which the executive departments were established: (1) Secretary of State, (2) Secretary of the Treasury, (3) Secretary of Defense, (4) Attorney General, (5) Secretary of the Interior, (6) Secretary of Agriculture, (7) Secretary of Commerce, (8) Secretary of Labor, (9) Secretary of Health and Human Services, (10) Secretary of Housing and Urban Development, (11) Secretary of Transportation, (12) Secretary of Energy, (13) Secretary of Education, (14) Secretary of Veterans Affairs.

Until the 1970 legislation removing the postmaster general from the cabinet and establishing an independent postal service, the postmaster general was fifth in line to the presidency. The heads of new departments are automatically added to the line of succession as the new departments are created.

A cabinet member must be a U.S. citizen and at least 35 years old in order to become acting president. If a cabinet member next in line to fill a presidential vacancy is not yet 35, the presidency passes to the next cabinet member in the order of succession.

VICE PRESIDENTS OF THE UNITED STATES, 1789–1995

Name	Party	Tenure	State, birth–death
1. John Adams	Fed.	1789–97	Mass., 1735–1826
2. Thomas Jefferson	D-R	1797–1801	Va., 1743–1826
3. Aaron Burr	D-R	1801–05	N.Y., 1756–1836
4. George Clinton	D-R	1805–13†	N.Y., 1739–1812
5. Elbridge Gerry	D-R	1813–17†	Mass., 1744–1814
6. Daniel D. Tompkins	D-R	1817–25	N.Y., 1774–1825
7. John C. Calhoun	D-R	1825–33[1]	S.C., 1782–1850
8. Martin Van Buren	D	1833–37	N.Y., 1782–1862
9. Richard M. Johnson	D	1837–41[2]	Ky., 1780–1850
10. John Tyler	Whig	1841[3]	Va., 1790–1862
11. George M. Dallas	D	1845–49	Pa., 1792–1864
12. Millard Fillmore	Whig	1849–50[4]	N.Y., 1800–74
13. William R. King	D	1853–57†	Ala., 1786–1853
14. John C. Breckenridge	D	1857–61	Ky., 1821–75
15. Hannibal Hamlin	R	1861–65	Maine, 1809–91
16. Andrew Johnson	D	1865[5]	Tenn., 1808–75
17. Schuyler Colfax	R	1869–73	Ind., 1823–85
18. Henry Wilson	R	1873–77†	Mass., 1812–75
19. William A. Wheeler	R	1877–81	N.Y., 1819–87
20. Chester A. Arthur	R	1881[6]	N.Y., 1829–86
21. Thomas A. Hendricks	D	1885†	Ind., 1819–85
22. Levi P. Morton	R	1889–93	N.Y., 1824–1920
23. Adlai E. Stevenson	D	1893–97	Ill., 1835–1914
24. Garret A. Hobart	R	1897–1901†	N.J., 1844–99
25. Theodore Roosevelt	R	1901[7]	N.Y., 1858–1919
26. Charles W. Fairbanks	R	1905–09	Ind., 1852–1918
27. James S. Sherman	R	1909–13†	N.Y., 1855–1912
28. Thomas R. Marshall	D	1913–21	Ind., 1854–1925
29. Calvin Coolidge	R	1921–23[8]	Mass., 1872–1933
30. Charles G. Dawes	R	1925–29	Ill., 1865–1951
31. Charles Curtis	R	1929–33	Kans., 1860–1936
32. John Nance Garner	D	1933–41	Tex., 1868–1967
33. Henry A. Wallace	D	1941–45	Iowa, 1888–1965
34. Harry S Truman	D	1945[9]	Mo., 1884–1972
35. Alben W. Barkley	D	1949–53	Ky., 1877–1956
36. Richard M. Nixon	R	1953–61	Calif., 1913–94
37. Lyndon B. Johnson	D	1961–63[10]	Tex., 1908–73
38. Hubert H. Humphrey	D	1965–69	Minn., 1911–78
39. Spiro T. Agnew	R	1969–73[11]	Md., 1918–
40. Gerald R. Ford	R	1973–74[12]	Mich., 1913–
41. Nelson A. Rockefeller	R	1974–77[13]	N.Y., 1908–79
42. Walter F. Mondale	D	1977–81	Minn., 1928–
43. George Bush	R	1981–89	Tex., 1924–
44. J. Danforth Quayle	R	1989–93	Ind., 1947–
45. Albert Gore, Jr.	D	1993–	Tenn., 1948–

Notes: Fed. = Federalist. D = Democrat. D-R = Democratic-Republican. R = Republican. † = Died in office. 1. Resigned to become senator from South Carolina (1832–43). 2. Voted in by Senate after no candidate for vice president gained a majority in the Electoral College. 3. Became president after William Henry Harrison's death. 4. Became president after Zachary Taylor's death. 5. Nominated by Republicans to run with Abraham Lincoln on the Union ticket; became president after Lincoln's assassination. 6. Became president after James Garfield's assassination. 7. Became president after William McKinley's assassination. 8. Became president after Warren Harding's death. 9. Became president after Franklin D. Roosevelt's death. 10. Became president after John F. Kennedy's assassination. 11. Resigned while under investigation for receiving kickbacks as governor of Maryland. 12. First vice president named under terms of the 25th Amendment; assumed presidency after Richard Nixon resigned. 13. Named vice president by Ford.

SPEAKERS OF THE U.S. HOUSE OF REPRESENTATIVES, 1789–1995

Name	Party	State	Tenure
1. Frederick A.C. Muhlenberg	D-R	Pa.	1789–91
2. Jonathan Trumbull	Fed.	Conn.	1791–93
3. Frederick A.C. Muhlenberg	D-R	Pa.	1793–95
4. Jonathan Dayton	Fed.	N.J.	1795–97
5. George Dent	Fed.	Md.	1797–99
6. Theodore Sedgwick	Fed.	Mass.	1799–1801
7. Nathaniel Macon	D-R	N.C.	1801–07
8. Joseph B. Varnum	D-R	Mass.	1807–11
9. Henry Clay	D-R	Ky.	1811–14
10. Langdon Cheves	D-R	S.C.	1814–15
11. Henry Clay	D-R	Ky.	1815–20
12. John W. Taylor	D-R	N.Y.	1820–21
13. Philip Barbour	D-R	Va.	1821–23
14. Henry Clay	D-R	Ky.	1822–24
15. John W. Taylor	D-R	N.Y.	1825–27
16. Andrew Stevenson	D	Va.	1827–34
17. John Bell	D	Tenn.	1834–35
18. James K. Polk	D	Tenn.	1835–39
19. Robert M.T. Hunter	Whig	Va.	1839–41
20. John White	Whig	Ky.	1841–43
21. John W. Jones	D	Va.	1843–45
22. John W. Davis	D	Ind.	1845–47
23. Robert C. Winthrop	Whig	Mass.	1847–49
24. Howell Cobb	D	Ga.	1849–51
25. Linn Boyd	D	Ky.	1851–55
26. Nathaniel Banks	R	Mass.	1855–57
27. James L. Orr	D	S.C.	1857–59
28. William Pennington	Whig	N.J.	1859–61
29. Galusha A. Grow	R	Pa.	1861–63
30. Schuyler Colfax	R	Ind.	1863–69
31. James G. Blaine	R	Maine	1869–75
32. Michael C. Kerr	D	Ind.	1875–76
33. Samuel J. Randall	D	Pa.	1876–81
34. J. Warren Keifer	R	Ohio	1881–83
35. John G. Carlisle	D	Ky.	1883–89
36. Thomas B. Reed	R	Maine	1889–91
37. Charles F. Crisp	D	Ga.	1891–95
38. Thomas B. Reed	R	Maine	1895–99
39. David B. Henderson	R	Iowa	1899–1903
40. Joseph G. Cannon	R	Ill.	1903–11
41. Champ Clark	D	Mo.	1911–19
42. Frederick H. Gillett	R	Mass.	1919–25
43. Nicholas Longworth	R	Ohio	1925–31
44. John N. Garner	D	Tex.	1931–33
45. Henry T. Rainey	D	Ill.	1933–34
46. Joseph W. Byrns	D	Tenn.	1935–36
47. William B. Bankhead	D	Ala.	1936–39
48. Sam Rayburn	D	Tex.	1940–46
49. Joseph W. Martin, Jr.	R	Mass.	1947–49
50. Sam Rayburn	D	Tex.	1949–52
51. Joseph W. Martin, Jr.	R	Mass.	1953–54
52. Sam Rayburn	D	Tex.	1955–61
53. John W. McCormack	D	Mass.	1962–71
54. Carl B. Albert	D	Okla.	1971–76
55. Thomas P. O'Neill, Jr.	D	Mass.	1977–87
56. James C. Wright, Jr.	D	Tex.	1987–89
57. Thomas S. Foley	D	Wash.	1989–95
58. Newt Gingrich	R	Ga.	1995–

Note: D = Democrat, D-R = Democratic-Republican, Fed. = Federalist, R = Republican.

CABINET MEMBERS, 1789–1995

Washington Administration (1789–97)

Secretary of State	Thomas Jefferson	1789–93
	Edmund Randolph	1794–95
	Timothy Pickering	1795–97
Secretary of Treasury	Alexander Hamilton	1789–95
	Oliver Wolcott	1795–97
Secretary of War	Henry Knox	1789–94
	Timothy Pickering	1795–96
	James McHenry	1796–97
Attorney General	Edmund Randolph	1789–93
	William Bradford	1794–95
	Charles Lee	1795–97
Postmaster General	Samuel Osgood	1789–91
	Timothy Pickering	1791–94
	Joseph Habersham	1795–97

John Adams Administration (1797–1801)

Secretary of State	Timothy Pickering	1797–1800
	John Marshall	1800–01
Secretary of Treasury	Oliver Wolcott	1797–1800
	Samuel Dexter	1800–01
Secretary of War	James McHenry	1797–1800
	Samuel Dexter	1800–01
Attorney General	Charles Lee	1797–1801
Postmaster General	Joseph Habersham	1797–1801
Secretary of Navy	Benjamin Stoddert	1798–1801

Jefferson Administration (1801–09)

Secretary of State	James Madison	1801–09
Secretary of Treasury	Samuel Dexter	1801
	Albert Gallatin	1801–09
Secretary of War	Henry Dearborn	1801–09
Attorney General	Levi Lincoln	1801–05
	Robert Smith	1805
	John Breckinridge	1805–06
	Caesar Rodney	1807–09
Postmaster General	Joseph Habersham	1801
	Gideon Granger	1801–09
Secretary of Navy	Robert Smith	1801–09

Madison Administration (1809–17)

Secretary of State	Robert Smith	1809–11
	James Monroe	1811–17
Secretary of Treasury	Albert Gallatin	1809–13
	George Campbell	1814
	Alexander Dallas	1814–16
	William Crawford	1816–17
Secretary of War	William Eustis	1809–12
	John Armstrong	1813–14
	James Monroe	1814–15
	William Crawford	1815–17
Attorney General	Caesar Rodney	1809–11
	William Pinckney	1811–14
	Richard Rush	1814–17
Postmaster General	Gideon Granger	1809–14
	Return Meigs	1814–17
Secretary of Navy	Paul Hamilton	1809–13
	William Jones	1813–14
	Benjamin Crowninshield	1814–17

Monroe Administration (1817–25)

Secretary of State	John Quincy Adams	1817–25
Secretary of Treasury	William Crawford	1817–25
Secretary of War	George Graham	1817
	John C. Calhoun	1817–25
Attorney General	Richard Rush	1817
	William Wirt	1817–25
Postmaster General	Return Meigs	1817–23
	John McLean	1823–25
Secretary of Navy	Benjamin Crowninshield	1817–18
	Smith Thompson	1818–23
	Samuel Southard	1823–25

John Quincy Adams Administration (1825–29)

Secretary of State	Henry Clay	1825–29
Secretary of Treasury	Richard Rush	1825–29
Secretary of War	James Barbour	1825–28
	Peter Porter	1828–29
Attorney General	William Wirt	1825–29
Postmaster General	John McLean	1825–29
Secretary of Navy	Samuel Southard	1825–29

Jackson Administration (1829–37)

Secretary of State	Martin Van Buren	1829–31
	Edward Livingston	1831–33
	Louis McLane	1833–34
	John Forsyth	1834–37
Secretary of Treasury	Samuel Ingham	1829–31
	Louis McLane	1831–33
	William Duane	1833
	Roger B. Taney	1833–34
	Levi Woodbury	1834–37
Secretary of War	John H. Eaton	1829–31
	Lewis Cass	1831–37
	Benjamin Butler	1837
Attorney General	John M. Berrien	1829–31
	Roger B. Taney	1831–33
	Benjamin Butler	1833–37
Postmaster General	William Barry	1829–35
	Amos Kendall	1835–37
Secretary of Navy	John Branch	1829–31
	Levi Woodbury	1831–34
	Mahlon Dickerson	1834–37

Van Buren Administration (1837–41)

Secretary of State	John Forsyth	1837–41
Secretary of Treasury	Levi Woodbury	1837–41
Secretary of War	Joel Poinsett	1837–41
Attorney General	Benjamin Butler	1837–38
	Felix Grundy	1838–40
	Henry D. Gilpin	1840–41
Postmaster General	Amos Kendal	1837–40
	John M. Niles	1840–41
Secretary of Navy	Mahlon Dickerson	1837–38
	James Paulding	1838–41

William Harrison Administration (1841)

Secretary of State	Daniel Webster	1841
Secretary of Treasury	Thomas Ewing	1841
Secretary of War	John Bell	1841
Attorney General	John J. Crittenden	1841
Postmaster General	Francis Granger	1841
Secretary of Navy	George Badger	1841

Tyler Administration (1841–45)

Secretary of State	Daniel Webster	1841–43
	Hugh S. Legaré	1843
	Abel P. Upshur	1843–44
	John C. Calhoun	1844–45
Secretary of Treasury	Thomas Ewing	1841
	Walter Forward	1841–43
	John C. Spencer	1843–44
	George Bibb	1844–45
Secretary of War	John Bell	1841
	John C Spencer	1841–43
	James M. Porter	1843–44
	William Wilkins	1844–45
Attorney General	John J. Crittenden	1841
	Hugh S. Legaré	1841–43
	John Nelson	1843–45
Postmaster General	Francis Granger	1841
	Charles Wickliffe	1841
Secretary of Navy	George Badger	1841
	Abel P. Upshur	1841
	David Henshaw	1843–44
	Thomas Gilmer	1844
	John Y. Mason	1844–45

Polk Administration (1845–49)

Secretary of State	James Buchanan	1845–49
Secretary of Treasury	Robert J. Walker	1845–49
Secretary of War	William L. Marcy	1845–49
Attorney General	John Y. Mason	1845–46
	Nathan Clifford	1846–48
	Isaac Toucey	1848–49
Postmaster General	Cave Johnson	1845–49
Secretary of Navy	George Bancroft	1845–46
	John Y. Mason	1846–49

Tylor Administration (1849–50)

Secretary of State	John M. Clayton	1849–50
Secretary of Treasury	William Meredith	1849–50
Secretary of War	George Crawford	1849–50
Attorney General	Reverdy Johnson	1849–50
Postmaster General	Jacob Collamer	1849–50
Secretary of Navy	William Preston	1849–50
Secretary of Interior	Thomas Ewing	1849–50

Filmore Administration (1850–53)

Secretary of State	Daniel Webster	1850–52
	Edward Evert	1852–53
Secretary of Treasury	Thomas Crowin	1850–53
Secretary of War	Charle Conrad	1850–53
Attorney General	John J. Crittenden	1850–53
Postmaster General	Nathan Hall	1850–52
	Sam D. Hubbard	1852–53
Secretary of Navy	William A. Grahm	1850–52
	John P. Kennedy	1852–53
Secretary of Interior	Thomas McKennan	1850
	Alexander Stuart	1850–53

Pierce Administration (1853–57)

Secretary of State	William L. Marcy	1853–57
Secretary of Treasury	James Guthrie	1853–57
Secretary of War	Jefferson Davis	1853–57
Attorney General	Caleb Cushing	1853–57
Postmaster General	James Campbell	1853–57
Secretary of Navy	James C. Dobbin	1853–57
Secretary of Interior	Robert McClelland	1853–57

Buchanan Administration (1857–61)

Secretary of State	Lewis Cass	1857–60
	Jeremiah S. Black	1860–61
Secretary of Treasury	Howel Cobb	1857–60
	Philip Thomas	1860–61
	John A. Dix	1861
Secretary of War	John B. Floyd	1857–61
	Joseph Holt	1861
Attorney General	Jeremiah S. Black	1857–60
	Edwin M. Stanton	1860–61
Postmaster General	Aaron W. Brown	1857–59
	Joseph Holt	1859–61
	Horatio King	1861
Secretary of Navy	Isaac Toucey	1857–61
Secretary of Interior	Jacob Thompson	1857–61

Lincoln Administration (1861–65)

Secretary of State	William H. Seward	1861–65
Secretary of Treasury	Salmon P. Chase	1861–64
	William P. Fessenden	1864–65
	Hugh McCulloch	1865
Secretary of War	Simon Cameron	1861–62
	Edwin M. Stanton	1862–65
Attorney General	Edward Bates	1861–64
	James Speed	1864–65
Postmaster General	Horatio King	1861
	Montgomery Blair	1861–64
	William Dennison	1864–65
Secretary of Navy	Gideon Welles	1861–65
Secretary of Interior	Caleb B. Smith	1861–63
	John P. Usher	1863–65

Andrew Johnson Administration (1865–69)

Secretary of State	William H. Seward	1865–69
Secretary of Treasury	Hugh McCulloch	1865–69
Secretary of War	Edwin M. Stanton	1865–67
	Ulysses S. Grant	1867–68
	John M. Schofield	1868–69
Attorney General	James Speed	1865–66
	Henry Stanbery	1866–68
	William M. Evarts	1868–69
Postmaster General	William Dennison	1865–66
	Alexander Randall	1866–69
Secretary of Navy	Gideon Welles	1865–69
Secretary of Interior	John P. Usher	1865
	James Harlan	1865–66
	Orville H. Browning	1866–69

Grant Administration (1869–77)

Secretary of State	Elihu B. Washburne	1869
	Hamilton Fish	1869–77
Secretary of Treasury	George S. Boutwell	1869–73
	William Richardson	1873–74
	Benjamin Bristow	1874–76
	Lot M. Morrill	1876–77
Secretary of War	John A. Rawlins	1869
	William T. Sherman	1869
	William W. Belknap	1869–76
	Alphonso Taft	1876
	James D. Cameron	1876–77
Attorney General	Ebenezer Hoar	1869–70
	Amos T. Ackerman	1870–71
	G.H. Williams	1871–75
	Edwards Pierrepont	1875–76
	Alphonso Taft	1876–77

Grant Administration (cont'd)

Postmaster General	John A. J. Creswell	1869–74
	James W. Marshall	1874
	Marshall Jewell	1874–76
	James N. Tyner	1876–77
Secretary of Navy	Adolph E. Borie	1869
	George M. Robeson	1869–77
Secretary of Interior	Jacob D. Cox	1869–70
	Columbus Delano	1870–75
	Zachariah Chandler	1875–77

Hayes Administration (1877–81)

Secretary of State	William M. Evarts	1877–81
Secretary of Treasury	John Sherman	1877–81
Secretary of War	George W. McCrary	1877–79
	Alex Ramsey	1879–81
Attorney General	Charles Devens	1877–81
Postmaster General	David M. Key	1877–80
	Horace Maynard	1880–81
Secretary of Navy	Richard W. Thompson	1877–80
	Nathan Goff, Jr.	1881
Secretary of Interior	Carl Schurz	1877–81

Garfield Administration (1881)

Secretary of State	James G. Blaine	1881
Secretary of Treasury	William Windom	1881
Secretary of War	Robert T. Lincoln	1881
Attorney General	Wayne MacVeagh	1881
Postmaster General	Thomas L. James	1881
Secretary of Navy	William H. Hunt	1881
Secretary of Interior	Samuel J. Kirkwood	1881

Arthur Administration (1881–85)

Secretary of State	James G. Blaine	1881
	F.T. Frelinghuysen	1881–85
Secretary of Treasury	William Windom	1881
	Charles J. Folger	1881–84
	Walter Q. Gresham	1884
	Hugh McCulloch	1884–85
Secretary of War	Robert T. Lincoln	1881–85
Attorney General	Wayne MacVeagh	1881
	Benjamin H. Brewster	1881–85
	Thomas L. James	1881
Postmaster General	Timothy O. Howe	1881–83
	Walter Q. Gresham	1883–84
	Frank Hatton	1884–85
Secretary of Navy	William H. Hunt	1881–82
	William E. Chandler	1882–85
Secretary of Interior	Samuel J. Kirkwood	1881–82
	Henry M. Teller	1882–85

Cleveland Administration (1885–89)

Secretary of State	Thomas F. Bayard	1885–89
Secretary of Treasury	Daniel Manning	1885–87
	Charles S. Fairchild	1887–89
Secretary of War	William C. Endicott	1885–89
Attorney General	Augustus H. Garland	1885–89
Postmaster General	William F. Vilas	1885–88
	Don M. Dickinson	1888–89
Secretary of Navy	William C. Whitney	1885–89
Secretary of Interior	Lucius Q.C. Lamar	1885–88
	William F. Vilas	1888–89
Secretary of Agriculture	Norman J. Colman	1889

Benjamin Harrison Administration (1889–93)

Secretary of State	James G. Blaine	1889–92
	John W. Foster	1892–93
Secretary of Treasury	William Windom	1889–91
	Charles Foster	1891–93
Secretary of War	Redfield Proctor	1889–91
	Stephen B. Elkins	1891–93
Attorney General	William H. H. Miller	1889–93
Postmaster General	John Wanamaker	1889–93
Secretary of Navy	Benjamin F. Tracy	1889–93
Secretary of Interior	John W. Noble	1889–93
Secretary of Agriculture	Jeremiah M. Rusk	1889–93

Cleveland Administration (1893–97)

Secretary of State	Walter Q. Gresham	1893–95
	Richard Olney	1895–97
Secretary of Treasury	John G. Carlisle	1893–97
Secretary of War	Daniel S. Lamont	1893–97
Attorney General	Richard Olney	1893–95
	James Harmon	1895–97
Postmaster General	Wilson S. Bissell	1893–95
	William L. Wilson	1895–97
Secretary of Navy	Hilary A. Herbert	1893–97
Secretary of Interior	Hoke Smith	1893–96
	David R. Francis	1896–97
Secretary of Agriculture	Julius S. Morton	1893–97

McKinley Administration (1897–1901)

Secretary of State	John Sherman	1897–98
	William R. Day	1898
	John Hay	1898–1901
Secretary of Treasury	Lyman J. Gage	1897–1901
Secretary of War	Russell A. Alger	1897–99
	Elihu Root	1899–1901
Attorney General	Joseph McKenna	1897–98
	John W. Griggs	1898–1901
	Philander C. Knox	1901
Postmaster General	James A. Gary	1897–98
	Charles E. Smith	1898–1901
Secretary of Navy	John D. Long	1897–1901
Secretary of Interior	Cornelius N. Bliss	1897–99
	Ethan A. Hitchcock	1899–1901
Secretary of Agriculture	James Wilson	1897–1901

Theodore Roosevelt Administration (1901–09)

Secretary of State	John Hay	1901–05
	Elihu Root	1905–09
	Robert Bacon	1909
Secretary of Treasury	Lyman J. Gage	1901–02
	Leslie M. Shaw	1902–07
	George B. Cortelyou	1907–09
Secretary of War	Elihu Root	1901–04
	William H. Taft	1904–08
	Luke E. Wright	1908–09
Attorney General	Philander C. Knox	1901–04
	William H. Moody	1904–06
	Charles J. Bonaparte	1906–09
Postmaster General	Charles E. Smith	1901–02
	Henry C. Payne	1902–04
	Robert J. Wynne	1904–05
	George B. Cortelyou	1905–07
	George von L. Meyer	1907–09
Secretary of Navy	John D. Long	1901–02
	William H. Moody	1902–04
	Paul Morton	1904–05

Theodore Roosevelt Administration (cont'd)

	Charles J. Bonaparte	1905–06
	Victor H. Metcalf	1906–08
	Truman H. Newberry	1908–09
Secretary of Interior	Ethan A. Hitchcock	1901–07
	James R. Garfield	1907–09
Secretary of Agriculture	James Wilson	1901–09
Secretary of Labor and Commerce	George B. Cortelyou	1903–04
	Victor H. Metcalf	1904–06
	Oscar S. Straus	1906–09

Taft Administration (1909–13)

Secretary of State	Philander C. Knox	1909–13
Secretary of Treasury	Franklin MacVeagh	1909–13
Secretary of War	Jacob M. Dickinson	1909–11
	Henry L. Stimson	1911–13
Attorney General	George W. Wickersham	1909–13
Postmaster General	Frank H. Hitchcock	1909–13
Secretary of Navy	George von L. Meyer	1909–13
Secretary of Interior	Richard A. Ballinger	1909–11
	Walter Fisher	1911–13
Secretary of Agriculture	James Wilson	1909–13
Secretary of Labor and Commerce	Charles Nagel	1909–13

Wilson Administration (1913–21)

Secretary of State	William J. Bryan	1913–15
	Robert Lansing	1915–20
	Bainbridge Colby	1920–21
Secretary of Treasury	William G. McAdoo	1913–18
	Carter Glass	1918–20
	David F. Houston	1920–21
Secretary of War	Lindley M. Garrison	1913–16
	Newton D. Baker	1916–21
Attorney General	James C. McReynolds	1913–14
	Thomas W. Gregory	1914–19
	A. Mitchell Palmer	1919–21
Postmaster General	Albert S. Burleson	1913–21
Secretary of Navy	Josephus Daniels	1913–21
Secretary of Interior	Franklin K. Lane	1913–20
	John B. Payne	1920–21
Secretary of Agriculture	David F. Houston	1913–20
	Edwin T. Meredith	1920–21
Secretary of Commerce	William C. Redfield	1913–19
	Joshua W. Alexander	1919
Secretary of Labor	William B. Wilson	1913–21

Harding Administration (1921–23)

Secretary of State	Charles E. Hughes	1921–23
Secretary of Treasury	Andrew Mellon	1921–23
Secretary of War	John W. Weeks	1921–23
Attorney General	Harry M. Daugherty	1921–23
Postmaster General	Will H. Hays	1921–22
	Hubert Work	1922–23
	Harry S. New	1923
Secretary of Navy	Edwin Denby	1921–23
Secretary of Interior	Albert B. Fall	1921–23
	Hubert Work	1923
Secretary of Agriculture	Henry C. Wallace	1921–23
Secretary of Commerce	Herbert C. Hoover	1921–23
Secretary of Labor	James J. Davis	1921–23

Coolidge Administration (1923–29)

Secretary of State	Charles E. Hughes	1923–25
	Frank B. Kellogg	1925–29

Coolidge Administration (cont'd)

Secretary of Treasury	Andrew Mellon	1923–29
Secretary of War	John W. Weeks	1923–25
	Dwight F. Davis	1925–29
Attorney General	Henry M. Daugherty	1923–24
	Harlan F. Stone	1924–25
	John G. Sargent	1925–29
Postmaster General	Harry S. New	1923–29
Secretary of Navy	Edwin Denby	1923–24
	Curtis D. Wilbur	1924–29
Secretary of Interior	Hubert Work	1923–28
	Roy O. West	1928–29
Secretary of Agriculture	Henry C. Wallace	1923–24
	Howard M. Gore	1924–25
	William M. Jardine	1925–29
Secretary of Commerce	Herbert C. Hoover	1923–28
	William F. Whiting	1928–29
Secretary of Labor	James J. Davis	1923–29

Hoover Administration (1929–33)

Secretary of State	Henry L. Stimson	1929–33
Secretary of Treasury	Andrew Mellon	1929–32
	Ogden L. Mills	1932–33
Secretary of War	James W. Good	1929
	Patrick J. Hurley	1929–33
Attorney General	William D. Mitchell	1929–33
Postmaster General	Walter F. Brown	1929–33
Secretary of Navy	Charles F. Adams	1929–33
Secretary of Interior	Ray L. Wilbur	1929–33
Secretary of Agriculture	Arthur M. Hyde	1929–33
Secretary of Commerce	Robert P. Lamont	1929–32
	Roy D. Chapin	1932–33
Secretary of Labor	James J. Davis	1929–30
	William N. Doak	1930–33

Franklin D. Roosevelt Administration (1933–45)

Secretary of State	Cordell Hull	1933–44
	Edward R. Stettinius, Jr.	1944–45
Secretary of Treasury	William H. Woodin	1933–34
	Henry Morgenthau, Jr.	1934–45
Secretary of War	George H. Dern	1933–36
	Henry A. Woodring	1936–40
	Henry L. Stimson	1940–45
Attorney General	Homer S. Cummings	1933–39
	Frank Murphy	1939–40
	Robert H. Jackson	1940–41
	Francis Biddle	1941–45
Postmaster General	James A. Farley	1933–40
	Frank C. Walker	1940–45
Secretary of Navy	Claude A. Swanson	1933–40
	Charles Edison	1940
	Frank Knox	1940–44
	James V. Forrestal	1944–45
Secretary of Interior	Harold L. Ickes	1933–45
Secretary of Agriculture	Henry A. Wallace	1933–40
	Claude R. Wickard	1940–45
Secretary of Commerce	Daniel C. Roper	1933–39
	Harry L. Hopkins	1939–40
	Jesse Jones	1940–45
	Henry A. Wallace	1945
Secretary of Labor	Frances Perkins	1933–45

Truman Administration (1945–53)

Secretary of State	Edward R. Stettinius, Jr.	1945

Truman Administration (cont'd)

	James F. Byrnes	1945–47
	George C. Marshall	1947–49
	Dean G. Acheson	1949–53
Secretary of Treasury	Fred M. Vinson	1945–46
	John W. Snyder	1946–53
Secretary of War[1]	Robert P. Patterson	1945–47
	Kenneth C. Royall	1947
Attorney General	Tom C. Clark	1945–49
	J. Howard McGrath	1949–52
	James P. McGranery	1952–53
Postmaster General	Frank C. Walker	1945
	Robert E. Hannegan	1945–47
	Jesse M. Donaldson	1947–53
Secretary of Navy[1]	James V. Forrestal	1945–47
Secretary of Interior	Harold L. Ickes	1945–46
	Julius A. Krug	1946–49
	Oscar L. Chapman	1949–53
Secretary of Agriculture	Clinton P. Anderson	1945–48
	Charles F. Brannan	1948–53
Secretary of Commerce	Henry A. Wallace	1945–46
	W. Averell Harriman	1946–48
	Charles W. Sawyer	1948–53
Secretary of Labor	Lewis B. Schwellenbach	1945–48
	Maurice J. Tobin	1948–53
Secretary of Defense[1]	James V. Forrestal	1947–49
	Louis A. Johnson	1949–50
	George C. Marshall	1950–51
	Robert A. Lovett	1951–53

1. On July 26, 1947, the Dept. of War and the Dept. of the Navy were consolidated under the Dept. of Defense, which replaced the War Dept. in order of precedence.

Eisenhower Administration (1953–61)

Secretary of State	John Foster Dulles	1953–59
	Christian A. Herter	1959–61
Secretary of Treasury	George M. Humphrey	1953–57
	Robert B. Anderson	1957–61
Secretary of Defense	Charles E. Wilson	1953–57
	Neil H. McElroy	1957–59
	Thomas S. Gates, Jr.	1959–61
Attorney General	Herbert Brownell, Jr.	1953–58
	William P. Rogers	1958–61
Postmaster General	Arthur E. Summerfield	1953–61
Secretary of Interior	Douglas McKay	1953–56
	Fred A. Seaton	1956–61
Secretary of Agriculture	Ezra T. Benson	1953–61
Secretary of Commerce	Sinclair Weeks	1953–58
	Lewis L. Strauss[1]	1958–59
	Frederick H. Mueller	1959–61
Secretary of Labor	Martin P. Durkin	1953
	James P. Mitchell	1953–61
Secretary of Health, Education, and Welfare	Oveta Culp Hobby	1953–55
	Marion B. Folsom	1955–58
	Arthur S. Flemming	1958–61

1. Apppointed Oct. 1958 but not confirmed.

Kennedy Administration (1961–63)

Secretary of State	Dean Rusk	1961–63
Secretary of Treasury	C. Douglas Dillon	1961–63
Secretary of Defense	Robert S. McNamara	1961–63
Attorney General	Robert F. Kennedy	1961–63
Postmaster General	J. Edward Day	1961–63
	John A. Gronouski	1963
Secretary of Interior	Stewart L. Udall	1961–63
Secretary of Agriculture	Orville L. Freeman	1961–63

Kennedy Administration (cont'd)

Secretary of Commerce	Luther H. Hodges	1961–63
Secretary of Labor	Arthur J. Goldberg	1961–62
	W. Willard Wirtz	1962–63
Secretary of Health, Education, and Welfare	Abraham A. Ribicoff	1961–62
	Anthony J. Celebrezze	1962–63

Lyndon Johnson Administration (1963–69)

Secretary of State	Dean Rusk	1963–69
Secretary of Treasury	C. Douglas Dillon	1963–65
	Henry H. Fowler	1965–69
Secretary of Defense	Robert S. McNamara	1963–68
	Clark Clifford	1968–69
Attorney General	Robert F. Kennedy	1963–64
	Nicholas Katzenbach	1965–66
	Ramsey Clark	1967–69
Postmaster General	John A. Gronouski	1963–65
	Lawrence F. O'Brien	1965–68
	Marvin Watson	1968–69
Secretary of Interior	Stewart L. Udall	1963–69
Secretary of Agriculture	Orville L. Freeman	1963–69
Secretary of Commerce	Luther H. Hodges	1963–64
	John T. Connor	1964–67
	Alexander B. Trowbridge	1967–68
	Cyrus R. Smith	1968–69
Secretary of Labor	W. Willard Wirtz	1963–69
Secretary of Health, Education, and Welfare	Anthony J. Celebrezze	1963–65
	John W. Gardner	1965–68
	Wilbur J. Cohen	1968–69
Secretary of Housing and Urban Development	Robert C. Weaver	1966–69
	Robert C. Wood	1969
Secretary of Transportation	Alan S. Boyd	1967–69

Nixon Administration (1969–74)

Secretary of State	William P. Rogers	1969–73
	Henry A. Kissinger	1973–74
Secretary of Treasury	David M. Kennedy	1969–70
	John B. Connally	1971–72
	George P. Shultz	1972–74
	William E. Simon	1974
Secretary of Defense	Melvin R. Laird	1969–73
	Elliot L. Richardson	1973
	James R. Schlesinger	1973–74
Attorney General	John N. Mitchell	1969–72
	Richard G. Kleindienst	1972–73
	Elliot L. Richardson	1973
	William B. Saxbe	1973–74
Postmaster General	Winton M. Blount	1969–71
Secretary of Interior	Walter J. Hickel	1969–70
	Rogers Morton	1971–74
Secretary of Agriculture	Clifford M. Hardin	1969–71
	Earl L. Butz	1971–74
Secretary of Commerce	Maurice H. Stans	1969–72
	Peter G. Peterson	1972–73
	Frederick B. Dent	1973–74
Secretary of Labor	George P. Shultz	1969–70
	James D. Hodgson	1970–73
	Peter J. Brennan	1973–74
Secretary of Health, Education, and Welfare	Robert H. Finch	1969–70
	Elliot L. Richardson	1970–73
	Caspar W. Weinberger	1973–74
Secretary of Housing and Urban Development	George Romney	1969–73
	James T. Lynn	1973–74
Secretary of Transportation	John A. Volpe	1969–73
	Claude S. Brinegar	1973–74

Ford Administration (1974–77)

Secretary of State	Henry A. Kissinger	1974–77
Secretary of Treasury	William E. Simon	1974–77
Secretary of Defense	James R. Schlesinger	1974–75
	Donald Rumsfeld	1975–77
Attorney General	William Saxbe	1974–75
	Edward Levi	1975–77
Secretary of Interior	Rogers Morton	1974–75
	Stanley K. Hathaway	1975
	Thomas Kleppe	1975–77
Secretary of Agriculture	Earl L. Butz	1974–76
	John A. Knebel	1976–77
Secretary of Commerce	Frederick B. Dent	1974–75
	Rogers Morton	1975–76
	Elliot L. Richardson	1976–77
Secretary of Labor	Peter J. Brennan	1974–75
	John T. Dunlop	1975–76
	W.J. Usery	1976–77
Secretary of Health, Education, and Welfare	Caspar Weinberger	1974–75
	Forrest D. Mathews	1975–77
Secretary of Housing and Urban Development	James T. Lynn	1974–75
	Carla A. Hills	1975–77
Secretary of Transportation	Claude S. Brinegar	1974–75
	William T. Coleman	1975–77

Carter Administration (1977–81)

Secretary of State	Cyrus R. Vance	1977–80
	Edmund Muskie	1980–81
Secretary of Treasury	W. Michael Blumenthal	1977–79
	G. William Miller	1979–81
Secretary of Defense	Harold Brown	1977–81
Attorney General	Griffin Bell	1977–79
	Benjamin R. Civiletti	1979–81
Secretary of Interior	Cecil D. Andrus	1977–81
Secretary of Agriculture	Robert Bergland	1977–81
Secretary of Commerce	Juanita M. Kreps	1977–79
	Philip M. Klutznick	1979–81
Secretary of Labor	F. Ray Marshall	1977–81
Secretary of Health, Education, and Welfare[1]	Joseph A. Califano	1977–79
	Patricia R. Harris	1979
Secretary of Health and Human Services[1]	Patricia R. Harris	1979–81
Secretary of Housing and Urban Development	Patricia R. Harris	1977–79
	Moon Landrieu	1979–81
Secretary of Transportation	Brock Adams	1977–79
	Neil E. Goldschmidt	1979–81
Secretary of Energy	James R. Schlesinger	1977–79
	Charles W. Duncan	1979–81
Secretary of Education[1]	Shirley M. Hufstedler	1979–81

1. The Dept. of Health, Education, and Welfare was redesignated the Dept. of Health and Human Services by the Department of Education Organization Act, effective May 4, 1980.

Reagan Administration (1981–89)

Secretary of State	Alexander M. Haig	1981–82
	George P. Shultz	1982–89
Secretary of Treasury	Donald Regan	1981–85
	James A. Baker III	1985–88
	Nicholas F. Brady	1988–89
Secretary of Defense	Caspar Weinberger	1981–87
	Frank Carlucci	1987–89
Attorney General	William F. Smith	1981–85
	Edwin A. Meese III	1985–88
	Richard L. Thornburgh	1988–89
Secretary of Interior	James Watt	1981–83
	William P. Clark, Jr.	1983–85
	Donald P. Hodel	1985–89
Secretary of Agriculture	John Block	1981–86

Reagan Administration (cont'd)

	Richard E. Lyng	1986–89
Secretary of Commerce	Malcolm Baldrige	1981–87
	C. William Verity, Jr.	1987–89
Secretary of Labor	Raymond Donovan	1981–85
	William E. Brock	1985–87
	Ann McLaughlin	1987–89
Secretary of Health and Human Services	Richard Schweiker	1981–83
	Margaret Heckler	1983–85
	Otis R. Bowen	1985–89
Secretary of Housing and Urban Development	Samuel Pierce	1981–89
Secretary of Transportation	Drew Lewis	1981–83
	Elizabeth Hanford Dole	1983–87
	James H. Burnley	1987–89
Secretary of Energy	James Edwards	1981–82
	Donald P. Hodel	1982–85
	John S. Herrington	1985–89
Secretary of Education	Terrel H. Bell	1981–85
	William J. Bennett	1985–88
	Lauro D. Cavazos	1988–89

Bush Administration (1989–93)

Secretary of State	James A. Baker III	1989–92
	Lawrence Eagleburger	1992–93
Secretary of Treasury	Nicholas F. Brady	1989–93
Secretary of Defense	Richard B. Cheney	1989–93
Attorney General	Richard L. Thornburgh	1989–91
	William P. Barr	1991–93
Secretary of Interior	Manuel Lujan	1989–93
Secretary of Agriculture	Clayton K. Yeutter	1989–91
	Edward Madigan	1991–93
Secretary of Commerce	Robert A. Mosbacher	1989–91
	Barbara Franklin	1991–93
Secretary of Labor	Elizabeth Hanford Dole	1989–90
	Lynn Martin	1990–93
Secretary of Health and Human Services	Louis W. Sullivan	1989–93
Secretary of Housing and Urban Development	Jack F. Kemp	1989–93
Secretary of Transportation	Samuel K. Skinner	1989–91
	Andrew Card	1991–93
Secretary of Energy	James D. Watkins	1989–93
Secretary of Education	Lauro D. Cavazos	1989–90
	Lamar Alexander	1990–93
Secretary of Veterans' Affairs	Edward J. Derwinski	1989–92
	Anthony J. Principi	1992–93

Clinton Administration (1993–)

Secretary of State	Warren M. Christopher	1993–
Secretary of Treasury	Lloyd Bentsen	1993–94
	Robert Rubin	1994–
Secretary of Defense	Les Aspin	1993–94
	William J. Perry	1994–
Attorney General	Janet Reno	1993–
Secretary of Interior	Bruce Babbitt	1993–
Secretary of Agriculture	Mike Espy	1993–94
	Dan Glickman	1995–
Secretary of Commerce	Ronald H. Brown	1993–
Secretary of Labor	Robert B. Reich	1993–
Secretary of Health and Human Services	Donna E. Shalala	1993–
Secretary of Housing and Urban Development	Henry G. Cisneros	1993–
Secretary of Transportation	Federico Peña	1993–
Secretary of Energy	Hazel O'Leary	1993–
Secretary of Education	Richard W. Riley	1993–
Secretary of Veterans' Affairs	Jesse Brown	1993–

EXECUTIVE OFFICE OF THE WHITE HOUSE, 1995

A number of executive orders in 1939 transferred various government agencies to the Executive Office of the President and established the divisions of the Executive Office and defined their functions. Since then, presidents have used executive orders, reorganization plans, and legislative initiatives to reorganize the Executive Office to make its composition compatible with the goals of their administrations. The following list shows the key personnel in Pres. Clinton's Executive Office.

The White House Office:

Chief of Staff	Leon Panetta
Chair, Council of Economic Advisors	Joseph E. Stiglitz
Administrator, Environmental Protection Agency	Carol Browner
Director, Office of Management and Budget	Alice M. Rivlin
Ambassador to the United Nations	Madeleine Albright
United States Trade Representative	Mickey Kantor
Director, Office of National Drug Control Policy	Lee Brown

Senior Policy Advisers:

Office of Science and Technology Policy	John H. Gibbons
National Security Council	Anthony Lake
Domestic Policy Council	Carol Rasco

Source: The White House, Office of the Cabinet Secretary.

The U.S. Supreme Court

IMPORTANT SUPREME COURT DECISIONS

***Marbury* v. *Madison* (1803)** The Court struck down a law "repugnant to the constitution" for the first time and set the precedent for judicial review of acts of Congress. In a politically ingenious ruling on the Judiciary Act of 1789, Chief Justice John Marshall asserted the Supreme Court's power "to say what the law is," while avoiding a confrontation with Pres. Thomas Jefferson. Not until the *Dred Scott* case of 1857 would another federal law be ruled unconstitutional.

***Fletcher* v. *Peck* (1810)** The Court ruled that Georgia could not deprive land speculators of their title, even though the previous owners had obtained the land from the state through fraud and bribery. Arising from the infamous Yazoo land frauds of 1795, this decision followed the Constitution's obligation of contracts clause and was the first time the Court invalidated a state law.

***Dartmouth College* v. *Woodward* (1819)** The Court encouraged business investment with this decision by treating corporate charters as fully protected contracts. Not even the state legislatures that originally granted them could tamper with charters to private corporations, unless they retained the power to do so. Dartmouth College remained a private institution despite New Hampshire's attempt to take it over. This decision, which opened the way for abuse of corporate privileges, would later be modified in the *Charles River Bridge* v. *Warren Bridge* (1837) and *Munn* v. *Illinois* (1877) cases.

***McCulloch* v. *Maryland* (1819)** "Broad," as opposed to "strict," construction of the Constitution received high-court approval in Chief Justice John Marshall's opinion upholding the constitutionality of the national bank against a Maryland challenge. This ruling enhanced federal governmental authority by liberally interpreting the power of Congress to make laws "necessary and proper" for its specified powers. At a time when states were trying to tax the Bank of the United States out of existence, this decision also forbade such state interference with the federal government. "The power to tax," Marshall wrote, "involves the power to destroy."

***Cohens* v. *Virginia* (1821)** With this ruling, the Court reiterated its power to hear appeals from state courts, and affirmed the national supremacy of federal judicial power. Virginia's conviction of the Cohens for selling lottery tickets in violation of state law was upheld, but so too was the Cohens' right to appeal to the Court, which Virginia had challenged. Critics of judicial "consolidationalism" were reminded of the Court's comprehensive powers as the ultimate appellate court for all Americans.

CHIEF JUSTICES OF THE UNITED STATES, 1789–1995

Chief Justice	Tenure[1]	Appointed by
John Jay	1789–95	George Washington
John Rutledge[2,3]	1795	George Washington
Oliver Ellsworth	1796–1800	George Washington
John Marshall[4]	1801–35	John Adams
Roger B. Taney	1836–64	Andrew Jackson
Salmon P. Chase	1864–73	Abraham Lincoln
Morrison R. Waite	1874–88	Ulysses S. Grant
Melville W. Fuller	1888–1910	Grover Cleveland
Edward D. White	1910–21	William Howard Taft
William Howard Taft[5]	1921–30	Warren G. Harding
Charles Evans Hughes[2]	1930–41	Herbert Hoover
Harlan F. Stone[2]	1941–46	Franklin D. Roosevelt
Fred M. Vinson	1946–53	Harry S Truman
Earl Warren	1953–69	Dwight D. Eisenhower
Warren E. Burger	1969–87	Richard M. Nixon
William H. Rehnquist[2]	1987–	Ronald Reagan

1. Dates are for tenure as chief justice. For complete tenure on Supreme Court, see "Supreme Court Justices." 2. Served as associate justice prior to appointment as chief justice. 3. Served one term, but appointment not confirmed by Senate. 4. Longest tenure as chief justice. 5. Formerly served as 27th president of the United States.

***Gibbons* v. *Ogden* (1824)** In a dispute arising from a New York ferry monopoly, the Court ruled that states could not restrain interstate commerce in any way, and that congressional power to regulate interstate commerce "does not stop at the jurisdictional lines of the several states." The decision helped prevent interstate trade wars, quite common under the Articles of Confederation, from breaking out under the Constitution. Chief Justice Marshall's opinion also confirmed the broad potential power of the Constitution's commerce clause.

***Charles River Bridge* v. *Warren Bridge* (1837)** A key decision for economic development, this case arose when state-chartered proprietors of a Boston toll bridge objected that a new state-chartered bridge across the Charles River would put them out of business. Chief Justice Roger B. Taney, in his first constitutional ruling, held that state charters implied no vested rights and that ambiguities must be construed in favor of the public, who would benefit from the new toll-free bridge. This decision balanced private property rights against the public welfare.

***Dred Scott* v. *Sanford* (1857)** Dred Scott, a Missouri slave, sued for his liberty after his owner took him into free territory. The Court ruled that Congress could not bar slavery in the territories. Scott remained a slave because the Missouri Compromise of 1820, prohibiting slavery from part of the Louisiana Purchase, violated the Fifth Amendment by depriving slave owners of their right to enjoy property without due process of law. Scott himself could not even sue, for he was held to be property, not a citizen. This decision sharpened sectional conflict by sweeping away legal barriers to the expansion of slavery.

***Ex Parte Milligan* (1866)** Pres. Abraham Lincoln's suspension of some civil liberties during the Civil War was attacked in this decision, which upheld the right of habeas corpus. The Court ruled that the president could not hold military tribunals in areas remote from battle and where civil courts were open and functioning. Milligan's conviction by such a Civil War tribunal in Indianapolis, Indiana, was overturned. The Constitution, admonished the Court, applies "at all times, and under all circumstances."

***Slaughter-House Cases* (1873)** In its first ruling on the 14th Amendment, the Court held that Louisiana's grant of a butcher monopoly did not violate the privileges and immunities of competitors, nor deny them equal protection of the laws, nor deprive them of property without due process. Only a few rights deriving from "federal citizenship" were subject to federal protection, while states still protected most civil and property rights. Federal protection of civil rights, even for former slaves, was very narrowly interpreted in this ruling. But this decision broadly upheld business regulation by states until *Santa Clara Co.* v. *Southern Pacific Railroad Co.* (1886) applied the 14th Amendment to defense of corporate property rights.

JUSTICES OF THE U.S. SUPREME COURT, 1789–1995

Name	Tenure	Appointed by
Baldwin, Henry	1830–44	Andrew Jackson
Barbour, Philip P.	1836–41	Andrew Jackson
Black, Hugo L.	1937–71	Franklin D. Roosevelt
Blackmun, Harry A.	1970–94	Richard M. Nixon
Blair, John	1789–96	George Washington
Blatchford, Samuel	1882–93	Chester A. Arthur
Bradley, Joseph P.	1870–92	Ulysses S. Grant
Brandeis, Louis D.	1916–39	Woodrow Wilson
Brennan, William J., Jr.	1956–90	Dwight D. Eisenhower
Brewer, David J.	1889–1910	Benjamin Harrison
Breyer, Stephen G.	1994–	Bill Clinton
Brown, Henry B.	1890–1906	Benjamin Harrison
Burger, Warren E.[1]	1969–87	Richard M. Nixon
Burton, Harold H.	1945–58	Harry S Truman
Butler, Pierce	1922–39	Warren G. Harding
Byrnes, James F.	1941–42	Franklin D. Roosevelt
Campbell, John A.	1853–61	Franklin Pierce
Cardozo, Benjamin N.	1932–38	Herbert Hoover
Catron, John	1837–65	Martin Van Buren
Chase, Salmon P.[1]	1864–73	Abraham Lincoln
Chase, Samuel	1796–1811	George Washington
Clark, Tom C.	1949–67	Harry S Truman
Clarke, John H.	1916–22	Woodrow Wilson
Clifford, Nathan	1858–81	James J. Buchanan
Curtis, Benjamin R.	1851–57	Millard Fillmore
Cushing, William	1789–1810	George Washington
Daniel, Peter V.	1841–60	Martin Van Buren
Davis, David	1862–77	Abraham Lincoln
Day, William R.	1903–22	Theodore Roosevelt
Douglas, William O.[2]	1939–75	Franklin D. Roosevelt
Duval, Gabriel	1811–36	James Madison
Ellsworth, Oliver[1]	1796–1800	George Washington
Field, Stephen J.	1863–97	Abraham Lincoln
Fortas, Abe	1965–69	Lyndon B. Johnson
Frankfurter, Felix	1939–62	Franklin D. Roosevelt
Fuller, Melville W.[1]	1888–1910	Grover Cleveland
Ginsburg, Ruth Bader	1993–	Bill Clinton
Goldberg, Arthur J.	1962–65	John F. Kennedy
Gray, Horace	1881–1902	Chester A. Arthur
Grier, Robert C.	1846–70	James K. Polk
Harlan, John Marshall	1877–1911	Rutherford B. Hayes
Harlan, John Marshall[3]	1955–71	Dwight D. Eisenhower
Harrison, Robert H.	1789–90	George Washington
Holmes, Oliver Wendell	1902–32	Theodore Roosevelt
Hughes, Charles Evans[1,4]	1910–16	William Howard Taft
Hughes, Charles Evans[1,4]	1930–41	Herbert Hoover
Hunt, Ward	1872–82	Ulysses S. Grant
Iredell, James	1790–99	George Washington
Jackson, Howell E.	1893–95	Benjamin Harrison
Jackson, Robert H.	1941–54	Franklin D. Roosevelt
Jay, John[1]	1789–95	George Washington
Johnson, Thomas	1791–93	George Washington
Johnson, William	1804–34	Thomas Jefferson
Kennedy, Anthony M.	1987–	Ronald Reagan
Lamar, Joseph R.	1911–16	William Howard Taft
Lamar, Lucius Q. C.	1888–93	Grover Cleveland
Livingston, H. Brockholst	1806–23	Thomas Jefferson
Lurton, Horace H.	1910–14	William Howard Taft
Marshall, John[1]	1801–35	John Adams
Marshall, Thurgood	1967–91	Lyndon B. Johnson
Matthews, Stanley	1881–89	James A. Garfield
McKenna, Joseph	1898–1925	William McKinley
McKinley, John	1837–52	Martin Van Buren
McLean, John	1829–61	Andrew Jackson
McReynolds, James C.	1914–41	Woodrow Wilson
Miller, Samuel F.	1862–90	Abraham Lincoln
Minton, Sherman	1949–56	Harry S Truman
Moody, William H.	1906–10	Theodore Roosevelt
Moore, Alfred	1799–1804	John Adams
Murphy, Frank	1940–49	Franklin D. Roosevelt
Nelson, Samuel	1845–72	John Tyler
O'Connor, Sandra Day	1981–	Ronald Reagan
Paterson, William	1793–1806	George Washington
Peckham, Rufus W.	1895–1910	Grover Cleveland
Pitney, Mahlon	1912–22	William Howard Taft
Powell, Lewis F., Jr.	1972–87	Richard M. Nixon
Reed, Stanley F.	1938–57	Franklin D. Roosevelt
Rehnquist, William H.[1]	1972–	Richard M. Nixon
Roberts, Owen J.	1930–45	Herbert Hoover
Rutledge, John[1]	1789–91	George Washington
Rutledge, John[1]	1795	George Washington
Rutledge, Wiley B.	1943–49	Franklin D. Roosevelt
Sanford, Edward T.	1923–30	Warren G. Harding
Scalia, Antonin	1986–	Ronald Reagan
Shiras, George	1892–1903	Benjamin Harrison
Souter, David H.	1990–	George Bush
Stevens, John Paul	1975–	Gerald R. Ford
Stewart, Potter	1959–81	Dwight D. Eisenhower
Stone, Harlan F.[1]	1925–46	Calvin Coolidge
Story, Joseph	1811–45	James Madison
Strong, William	1870–80	Ulysses S. Grant
Sutherland, George	1922–38	Warren G. Harding
Swayne, Noah H.	1862–81	Abraham Lincoln
Taft, William Howard[1,5]	1921–30	Warren Harding
Taney, Roger B.[1]	1836–64	Andrew Jackson
Thomas, Clarence	1991–	George Bush
Thompson, Smith	1823–43	James Monroe
Todd, Thomas	1807–26	Thomas Jefferson
Trimble, Robert	1826–28	John Quincy Adams
Van Devanter, Willis	1910–37	William Howard Taft
Vinson, Fred M.[1]	1946–53	Harry S Truman
Waite, Morrison R.[1]	1874–88	Ulysses S. Grant
Warren, Earl[1]	1953–69	Dwight D. Eisenhower
Washington, Bushrod	1798–1829	John Adams
Wayne, James M.	1835–67	Andrew Jackson
White, Byron R.	1962–93	John F. Kennedy
White, Edward D.[1]	1894–1921	Grover Cleveland
Whittaker, Charles E.	1957–62	Dwight D. Eisenhower
Wilson, James	1789–98	George Washington
Woodbury, Levi	1845–51	James K. Polk
Woods, William B.	1880–87	Rutherford B. Hayes

Note: As of Aug. 31, 1991. Dates reflect complete tenure on the Supreme Court, including tenure as chief justice. 1. Served as chief justice. See "Chief Justices of the United States." 2. Longest-serving justice. 3. The two Harlans were grandfather and grandson. 4. Stepped down as associate justice to run for president in 1916; later appointed chief justice. 5. Formerly served as 27th president of the United States.

***Munn* v. *Illinois* (1877)** This decision, in one of the "Granger Cases," enabled states to regulate private property in the public interest when the public had an interest in that property. The Court held that Illinois laws setting maximum rates for grain storage did not violate the 14th Amendment's ban on deprivation of property without due process of law and did not restrain interstate commerce. But for the next half-century, the Court imposed the burden of proof on the states for their regulatory laws.

***Civil Rights Cases* (1883)** Racial equality was postponed 80 years by this decision, which struck down the Civil Rights Act of 1875 and allowed for private segregation. The 14th Amendment's guarantee of equal protection, the Court ruled, applied against state action—but not against private individuals, whose discrimination unaided by the states was beyond federal control. Segregation of public facilities was approved soon afterward in *Plessy* v. *Ferguson* (1896).

***United States* v. *E.C. Knight Co.* (1895)** The first ruling on the Sherman Antitrust Act of 1890, this decision curtailed federal regulation of monopolies by placing national manufacturers beyond the reach of the Constitution's commerce clause. Only the actual interstate commerce of monopolies, not their production activities, was subject to federal control. The Court's distinction between production and commerce impeded federal regulation of manufacturing until *National Labor Relations Board* v. *Jones & Laughlin Steel Corp.* (1937).

***Plessy* v. *Ferguson* (1896)** The "separate but equal" doctrine supporting public segregation by law received the Court's approval in this ruling, which originated with segregated railroad cars in Louisiana. The Court held that as long as equal accommodations were provided, segregation was not discrimination and did not deprive blacks of equal protection of the laws under the 14th Amendment. This decision was overturned in *Brown* v. *Board of Education* (1954).

***Lochner* v. *New York* (1905)** This decision struck down a New York law placing limits on maximum working hours for bakers. The law violated the 14th Amendment by restricting individual "freedom of contract" to buy and sell labor and was an excessive use of state police power, the Court held. The ruling was soon modified in *Muller* v. *Oregon* (1908), which approved state-regulated limits on women's labor after the Court utilized sociological and economic data to consider the health and morals of women workers.

***Standard Oil Co. of New Jersey* v. *United States* (1911)** Federal efforts to break up monopolies under the Sherman Antitrust Act had to follow the "rule of reason," according to this ruling. Only those combinations in restraint of trade that were contrary to the public interest, and therefore unreasonable, were illegal. Although the Taft administration's prosecution of Standard Oil was upheld, breaking up one of the nation's leading monopolies, further antitrust suits were impaired by this decision, which facilitated the 1920s' merger movement.

Schenk v. United States (1919) The Court unanimously held that World War I limits on freedom of speech did not violate the First Amendment—if the speech in question represented a "clear and present danger." That famous doctrine of Justice Oliver Wendell Holmes, which approved the arrest of a draft resister for handing out pamphlets to soldiers in wartime, became an important standard for interpreting the First Amendment. But in subsequent cases of this period, the Court added that the mere "bad tendency" of speech to cause danger could be grounds for censorship.

Schechter Poultry Corp. v. United States (1935) At the height of its assault on the New Deal, the Court struck down the National Industrial Recovery Act in the famous "Sick Chicken Case." The NIRA was found to delegate excessive legislative regulatory powers to the executive without constitutional authority, and to regulate commerce within states in violation of the commerce clause. Schechter's kosher chicken supply house in New York did not have to abide by the NIRA's rigid industry codes, the Court ruled.

National Labor Relations Board v. Jones & Laughlin Steel Corp. (1937) Under pressure from public opinion and Pres. Franklin D. Roosevelt, the Court made an abrupt about-face and began approving New Deal legislation. In this case, laws protecting unions and barring "unfair labor practices" were upheld by the "stream of commerce" doctrine, holding that employers who sold their goods and obtained their raw materials through interstate commerce were subject to federal regulation. This ruling overturned *United States* v. *E.C. Knight Co.* (1895) and became the basis for the modern, expansive understanding of commerce power.

West Virginia Board of Education v. Barnette (1943) The Court reversed its earlier ruling in *Minersville School District* v. *Gobitis* (1940), which had required Jehovah's Witnesses to salute the flag in school. In this case, also brought against a Jehovah's Witness, the Court recognized that refusing to salute the flag did not violate anyone's rights, and that the First Amendment protected the "right of silence" as well as freedom of speech.

Korematsu v. United States (1944) Pres. Franklin D. Roosevelt's Executive Order No. 9066, which approved the West Coast evacuation and internment of 120,000 Japanese-Americans during World War II, was upheld on the grounds of "military necessity" in this ruling. The Court was reluctant to interfere with executive authority in time of national emergency. But in *Ex parte Endo* (1944), the Court held that persons of proven loyalty should not be interned. In August 1988 Congress made a formal apology to former internees and appropriated $1.25 billion in compensation for the 60,000 survivors.

Dennis v. United States (1951) At the height of the postwar "Red Scare," the Court upheld the conviction of 11 American Communist leaders under the Smith Act of 1940, which made it a crime to belong to organizations teaching or advocating the violent overthrow of the government. The "clear and present danger" doctrine could be disregarded, the Court held, if "the gravity of the 'evil,' discounted by its improbability, justifies such invasion of free speech as is necessary to avoid the evil." Over 100 Communists were indicted as a result, effectively destroying the Communist party as a political force.

Youngstown Sheet and Tube Co. v. Sawyer (1952) During the Korean War, when Pres. Harry S Truman seized steel plants to keep them operating despite a strike, the Court held that his action was an unconstitutional usurpation of legislative authority. Only an act of Congress, not the president's inherent executive powers or military powers as commander in chief, could justify such a sizable confiscation of property, despite the wartime emergency.

Brown v. Board of Education of Topeka (1954) Chief Justice Earl Warren led the Court unanimously to decide that segregated schools violated the equal protection clause of the 14th Amendment. The "separate but equal" doctrine of *Plessy* v. *Ferguson* (1896) was overruled after a series of cases dating back to *Missouri ex. rel. Gaines* v. *Canada* (1938) had already limited it. "Separate educational facilities are inherently unequal," held the Court. Efforts to desegregate southern schools after the *Brown* decision met with massive resistance for many years.

Baker v. Carr (1962) Overrepresentation of rural districts in state legislatures, which effectively disfranchised millions of voters, led the Court to abandon its traditional noninterference in drawing legislative boundaries. Tennessee citizens deprived of full representation by "arbitrary and capricious" malapportionment were denied equal protection under the 14th Amendment, ruled the Court. All states eventually reapportioned their legislatures in conformance with the "one man, one vote" doctrine of *Reynolds* v. *Sims* (1964).

Gideon v. Wainwright (1963) Reversing an earlier ruling in *Betts* v. *Brady* (1942), the Court held that the Sixth Amendment guaranteed access to qualified counsel, which was "fundamental to a fair trial." Gideon was entitled to a retrial because Florida failed to provide him with an attorney. After this decision, states were required to furnish public defenders for indigent defendants in felony cases. In *Argersinger* v. *Hamlin* (1972), the ruling was extended to all cases that might result in imprisonment.

Heart of Atlanta Motel, Inc. v. United States (1964) The Court upheld Title II of the Civil Rights Act of 1964, outlawing private discrimination in public accommodations, as a legitimate exertion of federal power over interstate commerce. Congress had "ample power" to forbid racial discrimination in facilities that affected commerce by serving interstate travelers. The Heart of Atlanta Motel was located on two interstate highways, so the Court could sidestep the *Civil Rights Cases* (1883) protection of private discrimination to overrule it.

Griswold v. Connecticut (1965) In striking down an 1879 Connecticut law against the use of contraceptives, the Court established a "right to privacy" that was implied by, though not specifically enumerated in the First, Third, Fourth, Fifth, Ninth, and 14th Amendments. The case is most notable for laying the groundwork for other legal challenges invoking this new-found unenumerated constitutional right to privacy. Foremost among them is the 1973 *Roe* v. *Wade* decision allowing women to choose abortion.

South Carolina v. Katzenbach (1966) Federal intervention on behalf of voting rights was upheld in this decision. South Carolina sued the attorney general, contending that the 1965 Voting Rights Act encroached on the reserved powers of the states, treated the states unequally, and violated separation of powers. Chief Justice Warren ruled that the 15th Amendment gave Congress broad powers to "use any rational means to effectuate the constitutional prohibition of racial discrimination in voting." After this decision blacks registered and voted in massive numbers in the South.

Miranda v. Arizona (1966) Expanding on *Gideon* v. *Wainwright* (1963) and *Escobedo* v. *Illinois* (1964), the Court set forth stringent interrogation procedures for criminal suspects, to protect their Fifth Amendment freedom from self-incrimination. Miranda's confession to kidnapping and rape was obtained without counsel and without his having been advised of his right to silence, so it was ruled inadmissable as evidence. This decision obliged police to advise suspects of their rights upon taking them into custody.

New York Times Co. v. United States (1971) When the *New York Times* and the *Washington Post* published the top-secret "Pentagon Papers" in 1971, revealing government duplicity in the Vietnam War, the Nixon administration obtained an injunction against the *Times* on grounds of national security. But in a brief *per curiam* opinion, the Court observed that in this case the government had not met the "heavy burden of showing justification" for "prior restraint" on freedom of the press.

Roe v. Wade (1973) In a controversial ruling, the Court held that state laws restricting abortion were an unconstitutional invasion of a woman's right to privacy. Only in the last trimester of pregnancy, when the fetus achieved viability outside the womb, might states regulate abortion—except when the life or health of the mother was at stake. Feelings ran high on both sides in the aftermath of this decision. In *Planned Parenthood of Central Missouri* v. *Danforth* (1976), the Court added further that wives did not need their husbands' consent to obtain abortions.

United States v. Nixon (1974) In a unanimous ruling, the Court held that the secret White House recordings of Pres. Richard

M. Nixon's conversations with aides were subject to subpoena in the Watergate cover-up trial. Nixon's claim to "executive privilege" was rejected as invalid because military and national security issues were not at stake, and Chief Justice Warren Burger cited *Marbury* v. *Madison* (1803) to assert the Court's primacy in constitutional issues. Once the tapes were released, documenting Nixon's obstruction of justice, the president resigned to avoid impeachment.

***University of California Regents* v. *Bakke* (1978)** Twice refused admission to medical school, Bakke sued the University of California for giving "affirmative action" preference to less-qualified black applicants. In an ambiguous 5–4 ruling, the Court agreed that Bakke's right to equal protection was denied, that he should be admitted, and that affirmative action quotas should be discarded. But at the same time, the Court recognized race as a "factor" in admissions and hiring decisions. Affirmative action could continue as long as rigid quotas did not constitute, in effect, "reverse discrimination."

***Immigration and Naturalization Service* v. *Chadha* (1983)** The legislative veto, contained in hundreds of federal statutes since 1932, was disallowed in this decision. Congress exceeded its constitutional powers when it blocked the attorney general's suspension of a deportation order for Jagdish Rai Chadha, a Kenyan student who overstayed his visa. The Court held that the Immigration and Nationality Act's legislative veto provision violated the constitutional separation of powers. Chief Justice Warren Burger recognized that Congress would prefer to delegate authority to the executive branch and reserve the right to veto administrative regulations, but "we have not found a better way to preserve freedom" than the separation of powers.

***Bowers* v. *Hardwick* (1986)** In a controversial 5–4 decision applauded by fundamentalists but protested by gay activists, the Court ruled that the constitutional right to privacy does not protect homosexual relations, even between consenting adults in their own homes. Georgia's law against oral and anal sex, passed in 1816, could be applied to homosexuals—though the Court declined to rule on whether heterosexuals might also be prosecuted. The decision raised fears of bedroom patrols and sexual surveillance, despite the constitutional right to privacy in intimate personal matters established in cases dating back to the 1920s. Justice Byron White ruled that "none of the rights announced in those cases bears any resemblance to the claimed constitutional right of homosexuals to engage in acts of sodomy."

THE FEDERAL GOVERNMENT

In their desire to create a government based on an elaborate system of "checks and balances," the Founding Fathers divided the sources of power into three separate and distinct branches of government—the legislative, the judicial, and the executive. The fundamental purpose, organization, and workings of these three branches are set down in the first three articles of the Constitution. Despite the passing of more than two centuries, the creation of dozens of departments, agencies, and commissions, the ongoing employment of two million civilian workers, and the creation of a standing peacetime military force of over two million, this structure remains essentially unchanged.

Below is a list of every major body within the federal government. Each entry mentions the date the entity was founded and summarizes its official function. (The primary source of this information is the National Archives and Record Administration, Office of the Federal Register, *United States Government Manual 1994–95*.)

The Legislative Branch

Architect of the Capitol U.S. Capitol Building, Washington, DC 20515. (202) 228–1793. First architect appointed in 1793 by president. Permanent authority for care of Capitol established by act of Aug. 15, 1876. Responsible for care and maintenance of Capitol building and grounds, Library of Congress buildings, and U.S. Supreme Court building. Operates Senate and House restaurants. Maintains, operates, and cares for House and Senate office buildings. Plans future construction, renovation, reconstruction, and alterations to existing buildings.

U.S. Botanic Garden Director's Office: 245 First St. SW, Washington, DC 20024. (202) 225–8333. Conservatory: Maryland Ave.–First to Second Sts. SW, Washington, DC 20024. (202) 225–6646. Nursery: Poplar Point, 700 Howard Rd. SE, Anacostia, DC 20020. (202) 225–6420. Created in 1820. Collects, cultivates, and grows vegetable and plant matter of U.S. and other countries for exhibition and display. Provides study materials on vegetable and plant matter for students, botanists, horticulturists, floriculturists, and garden clubs.

General Accounting Office (GAO) 441 G St. NW, Washington, DC 20548. (202) 512–3000. Created in 1921 by Budget and Accounting Act. Provides legal, accounting, auditing, and claims-settlement services for Congress. Facilitates more efficient and effective government operations.

Government Printing Office (GPO) North Capitol and H Sts. NW, Washington, DC 20401. (202) 512–0000. Created June 23, 1860, by Congressional Joint Resolution 25. Provides printing and binding services for Congress and departments and establishments of federal government. Furnishes blank paper, ink, and supplies to all agencies. Prepares and distributes catalogs and publications.

Library of Congress 101 Independence Ave. SE, Washington, DC 20540. (202) 707–5000. Created by law of Apr. 24, 1800. Librarian appointed by president. Buys books necessary for use by Congress and/or other governmental agencies. National library of U.S. develops and maintains national book classification systems such as Library of Congress and Dewey Decimal systems. Maintains and publishes *The National Union Catalogs.*

Office of Technology Assessment (OTA) 600 Pennsylvania Ave. SE, Washington, DC 20510. (202) 224–8996. Created by Technology Assessment Act of 1972. Provides objective analyses and evaluations of scientific and technological public-policy issues.

Congressional Budget Office (CBO) Second and D Sts. SW, Washington, DC 20515. (202) 226–2621. Created by Congressional Budget Act of 1974. Provides Congress with basic budget data. Analyzes and evaluates alternative fiscal and budgetary policy options and programs and makes recommendations to Congress. Publishes annual report on budget.

U.S. Tax Court 400 Second St. NW, Washington, DC 20217. (202) 606–8751. Created under Article I of Constitution. Independent judicial body in legislative branch. Tries and adjudicates controversies involving deficiencies or overpayments of income, estate, and gift taxes.

HOW A BILL BECOMES LAW

Usually bills are raised in any of the various committees of the Senate or House of Representatives. If the bill is supported by a majority of the committee, it is brought to the floor of the house in which it originated and voted on. If it gains majority support in the full Senate or House, the other house of Congress votes on it. If the bill is passed in both the Senate and House, it is sent to the president, who may either sign it, veto it, or not act on it.

If the president signs it or refuses to act within 10 days and the Congress is still in session, the bill becomes law. If the president vetoes it, it is returned to the Senate and the House for another vote; a two-thirds majority in each house is then required to overturn the veto. However, if the president refuses to act on a bill and Congress adjourns before the end of the 10-day period, the legislation is dead. This is known as a pocket veto.

Occasionally bills are raised on the floor of the Senate or the House, in which case the first step of committee voting is avoided and the legislation process begins with the full Senate or House vote. All other processes remain the same.

THE 104TH CONGRESS OF THE UNITED STATES

The House of Representatives is composed of 435 members. The number representing each state is determined by population every ten years; every state is entitled to at least one representative. Members are elected by popular vote for two-year terms, all terms running for the same period. In addition to state representatives, there are delegates from the District of Columbia, American Samoa, Guam, and the Virgin Islands (also elected for two years), and a resident commissioner from Puerto Rico (elected for four years). Delegates and the resident commissioner may take part in floor debates, but they have no vote.

The Senate is composed of 100 members, two from each state, elected to terms of six years. Senators are divided into three classes, and a new class is elected every two years.

The accompanying table shows ratings for each senator according to three prominent political groups of differing viewpoints. The Americans for Democratic Action (ADA), a liberal group founded in 1947, rates members of Congress on a wide variety of issues, but they stand basically for slowing defense spending, preventing violations of civil rights, and for government activity to end inequality. The American Conservative Union (ACU) rates members for their votes on budgetary, social, and foreign-policy issues from a conservative perspective. The American Security Council's rating, called the National Security Index (NSI), has been measuring congressional votes on defense since 1965; a high rating indicates support for developing large weapons systems and support of the peace-through-strength approach to foreign policy.

THE 104TH CONGRESS OF THE UNITED STATES

The Senate
The Capitol
Washington, D.C. 20510
(202) 224–3121

Senate Offices

President	Albert Gore, Jr. (D)
Majority leader	Robert Dole (R)
Majority whip	Trent Lott (R)
Minority leader	Thomas A. Daschle (D)
Minority whip	Wendell Ford (D)

The House of Representatives
The Capitol
Washington, D.C. 20515
(202) 224–3121

House Offices

Speaker	Newt Gingrich (R)
Majority leader	Dick Armey (R)
Majority whip	Tom DeLay (R)
Minority leader	Richard Gephardt (D)
Minority whip	David Bonior (D)

THE 104TH CONGRESS: U.S. SENATE

State	Senator	ADA[1]	ACU[2]	NSI[3]
Alabama	Howell Heflin (D)	55	28	100
	Richard C. Shelby (R)	30	55	100
Alaska	Ted Stevens (R)	25	77	100
	Frank H. Murkowski (R)	10	96	100
Arizona	John McCain (R)	10	96	100
	Jon Kyl (R)	N.A.	N.A.	N.A.
Arkansas	Dale Bumpers (D)	80	4	20
	David Pryor (D)	80	4	20
California	Dianne Feinstein (D)	70	0	40
	Barbara Boxer (D)	95	8	0
Colorado	Hank Brown (R)	30	92	90
	Ben Nighthorse Campbell (R)	55	25	56
Connecticut	Christopher J. Dodd (D)	80	0	10
	Joseph I. Lieberman (D)	65	8	70
Delaware	William V. Roth, Jr. (R)	35	68	90
	Joseph R. Biden, Jr. (D)	80	0	10
Florida	Bob Graham (D)	75	8	90
	Connie Mack (R)	10	96	100
Georgia	Sam Nunn (D)	50	33	100
	Paul Coverdell (R)	5	100	100
Hawaii	Daniel K. Inouye (D)	75	0	43
	Daniel K. Akaka (D)	85	0	30
Idaho	Larry E. Craig (R)	0	100	100
	Dirk Kempthorne (R)	0	100	100
Illinois	Paul Simon (D)	95	4	10
	Carol Moseley-Braun (D)	85	4	10
Indiana	Richard G. Lugar (R)	10	76	100
	Dan Coats (R)	5	92	100
Iowa	Chuck Grassley (R)	15	92	80
	Tom Harkin (D)	100	0	0
Kansas	Robert Dole (R)	0	0	100
	Nancy Landon Kassebaum (R)	45	48	90
Kentucky	Wendell H. Ford (D)	60	24	60
	Mitch McConnell (R)	5	92	90
Louisiana	J. Bennett Johnston (D)	55	22	50
	John B. Breaux (D)	55	17	50
Maine	William S. Cohen (R)	40	45	100
	Olympia Snowe (R)	N.A.	N.A.	N.A.
Maryland	Paul S. Sarbanes (D)	95	0	0
	Barbara A. Mikulski (D)	85	0	10
Massachusetts	Edward M. Kennedy (D)	90	0	10
	John F. Kerry (D)	95	0	10
Michigan	Carl Levin (D)	90	0	0
	Spencer Abraham (R)	N.A.	N.A.	N.A.
Minnesota	Paul Wellstone (DFL)	100	4	0
	Rod Grams (IR)	N.A.	N.A.	N.A.
Mississippi	Thad Cochran (R)	10	92	100
	Trent Lott (R)	5	100	100
Missouri	Christopher S. Bond (R)	20	83	100
	John Ashcroft (R)	N.A.	N.A.	N.A.
Montana	Max Baucus (D)	85	0	30
	Conrad R. Burns (R)	0	92	100
Nebraska	J. James Exon (D)	65	25	80
	J. Robert Kerrey (D)	80	24	30
Nevada	Harry Reid (D)	85	4	30
	Richard H. Bryan (D)	75	12	70
New Hampshire	Bob Smith (R)	5	100	100
	Judd Gregg (R)	15	79	100
New Jersey	Bill Bradley (D)	85	4	0
	Frank R. Lautenberg (D)	95	4	10
New Mexico	Peter V. Domenici (R)	25	84	90
	Jeff Bingaman (D)	60	16	60
New York	Daniel Patrick Moynihan (D)	100	0	0
	Alfonse D'Amato (R)	20	92	90
North Carolina	Jesse Helms (R)	0	100	100
	Lauch Faircloth (R)	5	100	100
North Dakota	Kent Conrad (D)	85	12	30
	Byron L. Dorgan (D)	85	8	20
Ohio	John Glenn (D)	80	4	70
	Mike DeWine (R)	N.A.	N.A.	N.A.
Oklahoma	Don Nickles (R)	60	100	100
	James Inhofe (R)	N.A.	N.A.	N.A.
Oregon	Mark O. Hatfield (R)	80	29	20
	Bob Packwood (R)	50	67	90
Pennsylvania	Arlen Specter (R)	55	46	100
	Rick Santorum (R)	N.A.	N.A.	N.A.
Rhode Island	Claiborne Pell (D)	95	0	0
	John H. Chafee (R)	65	30	70
South Carolina	Strom Thurmond (R)	5	96	100
	Ernest F. Hollings (D)	50	22	40
South Dakota	Larry Pressler (R)	0	96	90
	Thomas A. Daschle (D)	80	4	20
Tennessee	Bill Frist (R)	N.A.	N.A.	N.A.
	Fred Thompson (R)	N.A.	N.A.	N.A.
Texas	Phil Gramm (R)	5	100	100
	Kay Bailey Hutchison (R)	10	96	100
Utah	Orrin G. Hatch (R)	5	100	100
	Robert F. Bennett (R)	5	100	100
Vermont	Patrick J. Leahy (D)	95	0	10
	James M. Jeffords (R)	85	12	50
Virginia	John W. Warner (R)	20	80	100
	Charles S. Robb (D)	60	12	90
Washington	Slade Gorton (R)	30	80	100
	Patty Murray (D)	90	0	0
West Virginia	Robert C. Byrd (D)	75	40	50
	John D. Rockefeller IV (D)	95	0	20
Wisconsin	Herb H. Kohl (D)	90	12	20
	Russell D. Feingold (D)	100	4	0
Wyoming	Alan K. Simpson (R)	15	88	100
	Craig Thomas (R)	N.A.	N.A.	N.A.

Note: D = Democrat; DFL = Democratic-Farmer-Labor (Minn.); IR = Independent Republican (Minn.); R = Republican. 1. Americans for Democratic Action: based on 20 Senate votes in 1994. 2. American Conservative Union: based on 25 Senate votes in 1994. 3. National Security Index of the American Security Council: based on 10 Senate votes in 1994. **Source:** Americans for Democratic Action; The American Conservative Union; American Security Council; Clerk of the U.S. House of Representatives.

THE 104TH CONGRESS: U.S. HOUSE OF REPRESENTATIVES

State/ Dist.	City	Representative	ADA[1]	ACU[2]	NSI[3]
	Alabama				
1st	Mobile	H.L. "Sonny" Callahan (R)	5	100	100
2nd	Montgomery	Terry Everett (R)	0	100	100
3rd	Anniston	Glen Browder (D)	25	62	100
4th	Jasper	Tom Bevill (D)	35	50	90
5th	Huntsville	Robert E. Cramer, Jr. (D)	40	38	90
6th	Birmingham	Spencer Bachus III (R)	15	95	100
7th	Tuscaloosa	Earl Hilliard (D)	80	29	20
	Alaska				
1st	At-large	Don Young (R)	10	100	100
	Arizona				
1st	Tempe	Matt Salmon (R)	N.A.	N.A.	N.A.
2nd	Phoenix	Ed Pastor (D)	80	14	20
3rd	Flagstaff	Bob Stump (R)	0	100	100
4th	Scottsdale	John Shadegg (R)	N.A.	N.A.	N.A.
5th	Tucson	Jim Kolbe (R)	15	80	100
6th	Mesa	J.D. Hayworth (R)	N.A.	N.A.	N.A.
	Arkansas				
1st	Jonesboro	Blanche Lambert (D)	60	10	40
2nd	Little Rock	Ray Thornton (D)	75	19	70
3rd	Fort Smith	Tim Hutchinson (R)	5	95	100
4th	Pine Bluff	Jay Dickey (R)	0	95	100
	California				
1st	Fairfield	Frank Riggs (R)	N.A.	N.A.	N.A.
2nd	Chico	Wally Herger (R)	5	100	100
3rd	Sacramento	Vic Fazio (D)	75	14	50
4th	Roseville	John T. Doolittle (R)	5	100	100
5th	Sacramento	Robert T. Matsui (D)	75	11	50
6th	Marin County	Lynn Woolsey (D)	100	0	0
7th	Richmond	George Miller (D)	90	0	0
8th	San Francisco	Nancy Pelosi (D)	90	0	0
9th	Oakland	Ron Dellums (D)	100	5	0
10th	Walnut Creek	Bill Baker (R)	0	100	100
11th	Stockton	Richard W. Pombo (R)	5	100	100
12th	San Mateo	Tom Lantos (D)	70	24	40
13th	Hayward	Fortney H. "Pete" Stark (D)	95	0	0
14th	Palo Alto	Anna G. Eshoo (D)	95	0	20
15th	Sunnyvale	Norman Y. Mineta (D)	90	10	40
16th	San Jose	Zoe Lofgren (D)	N.A.	N.A.	N.A.
17th	Monterey	Sam Farr (D)	90	0	13
18th	Modesto	Gary A.Condit (D)	45	38	50
19th	Fresno	George Radanovich (R)	N.A.	N.A.	N.A.
20th	Fresno	Calvin M. Dooley (D)	55	22	22
21st	Bakersfield	William M. Thomas (R)	10	84	90
22nd	Santa Barbara	Andrea H. Seastrand (R)	N.A.	N.A.	N.A.
23rd	Simi Valley	Elton Gallegly (R)	10	95	100
24th	Thousand Oaks	Anthony C. Beilenson (D)	95	0	20
25th	Santa Clarita	Howard "Buck" McKeon (R)	5	95	100
26th	Van Nuys	Howard L. Berman (D)	90	0	20
27th	Pasadena	Carlos J. Moorhead (R)	0	100	100
28th	Claremont	David Dreier (R)	5	100	100
29th	Hollywood	Henry Waxman (D)	90	0	10
30th	Boyle Heights	Xavier Becerra (D)	100	0	0
31st	Alhambra	Matthew G. Martinez (D)	70	15	44
32nd	Culver City	Julian C. Dixon (D)	75	10	40
33rd	East Los Angeles	Lucille Roybal-Allard (D)	100	0	20
34th	La Puente	Esteban Edward Torres (D)	75	10	20
35th	Watts	Maxine Waters (D)	100	10	10
36th	Rolling Hills	Jane Harman (D)	N.A.	N.A.	N.A.
37th	Compton	Walter Tucker (D)	90	11	20
38th	Long Beach	Steve Horn (R)	30	57	70
39th	Fullerton	Ed Royce (R)	10	95	90
40th	Redlands	Jerry Lewis (R)	0	88	100
41st	Ontario	Jay Kim (R)	5	95	90
42nd	San Bernardino	George Brown (D)	80	10	20
43rd	Riverside	Ken Calvert (R)	5	90	100
44th	Moreno Valley	Sonny Bono (R)	N.A.	N.A.	N.A.
45th	Huntington Beach	Dana Rohrabacher (R)	10	86	70
46th	Anaheim	Robert K. Dornan (R)	0	100	100
47th	Irvine	C. Christopher Cox (R)	0	100	100
48th	San Clemente	Ronald C. Packard (R)	0	95	100
49th	San Diego	Brian Bilbray (R)	N.A.	N.A.	N.A.
50th	Chula Vista	Bob Filner (D)	100	0	10
51st	Escondido	Randall "Duke" Cunningham (R)	15	95	100
52nd	El Cajon	Duncan L. Hunter (R)	0	100	100
	Colorado				
1st	Denver	Patricia Schroeder (D)	100	5	0
2nd	Boulder	David E. Skaggs (D)	80	10	40
3rd	Pueblo	Scott McInnis (R)	15	81	100
4th	Greeley	Wayne Allard (R)	5	95	80
5th	Colorado Springs	Joel Hefley (R)	0	100	100
6th	Lakewood	Dan Schaefer (R)	10	90	100

State/ Dist.	City	Representative	ADA[1]	ACU[2]	NSI[3]
	Connecticut				
1st	Hartford	Barbara B. Kennelly (D)	85	10	30
2nd	New London	Samuel Gejdenson (D)	80	10	30
3rd	New Haven	Rosa L. DeLauro (D)	90	5	30
4th	Stamford	Christopher Shays (R)	55	38	30
5th	Waterbury	Gary A. Franks (R)	20	70	100
6th	New Britain	Nancy L. Johnson (R)	30	52	80
	Delaware				
1st	At-large	Michael N. Castle (R)	20	67	100
	Florida				
1st	Pensacola	Joe Scarborough (R)	N.A.	N.A.	N.A.
2nd	Tallahassee	Douglas "Pete" Peterson (D)	50	38	70
3rd	Jacksonville	Corrine Brown (D)	85	24	60
4th	Jacksonville	Tillie K. Fowler (R)	N.A.	N.A.	N.A.
5th	Gainesville	Karen L.Thurman (D)	65	19	40
6th	Ocala	Clifford B. Stearns (R)	0	100	100
7th	New Smyrna Beach	John L. Mica (R)	10	95	100
8th	Orlando	Bill McCollum (R)	0	95	100
9th	Clearwater	Michael Bilirakis (R)	20	86	90
10th	St. Petersburg	C.W. (Bill) Young (R)	25	81	100
11th	Tampa	Sam Gibbons (D)	70	16	40
12th	Dade City	Charles T. Canady (R)	5	90	100
13th	Sarasota	Dan Miller (R)	20	90	100
14th	Fort Myers	Porter J. Goss (R)	10	86	100
15th	Vero Beach	Dave Weldon (R)	N.A.	N.A.	N.A.
16th	West Palm Beach	Mark Adam Foley (R)	N.A.	N.A.	N.A.
17th	Miami	Carrie P. Meek (D)	95	10	50
18th	South Beach	Ileana Ros-Lehtinen (R)	25	65	90
19th	Boca Raton	Harry A. Johnston (D)	90	5	20
20th	Key Largo	Peter Deutsch (D)	60	19	40
21st	Hialeah	Lincoln Diaz-Balart (R)	25	71	90
22nd	Fort Lauderdale	E. Clay Shaw, Jr. (R)	15	74	100
23rd	Fort Lauderdale	Alcee L. Hastings (D)	80	7	25
	Georgia				
1st	Savannah	Jack Kingston (R)	5	100	90
2nd	Albany	Sanford D. Bishop (D)	75	25	56
3rd	Jonesboro	Michael Collins (R)	0	95	100
4th	Buckhead	John Linder (R)	0	95	100
5th	Atlanta	John Lewis (D)	100	5	0
6th	Marietta	Newt Gingrich (R)	5	100	100
7th	Rome	Bob Barr (R)	35	38	90
8th	Macon	Saxby Chambliss (R)	N.A.	N.A.	N.A.
9th	LaFayette	Nathan Deal (D)	15	67	80
10th	Athens	Charlie Norwood (R)	N.A.	N.A.	N.A.
11th	Augusta	Cynthia McKinney (D)	100	0	0
	Hawaii				
1st	Honolulu	Neil Abercrombie (D)	100	0	0
2nd	Outer Islands	Patsy T. Mink (D)	100	0	0
	Idaho				
1st	Boise	Helen Chenoweth (R)	N.A.	N.A.	N.A.
2nd	Pocatello	Michael D. Crapo (R)	5	90	100
	Illinois				
1st	Chicago, south side	Bobby L. Rush (D)	100	5	0
2nd	Lake Calumet	Mel Reynolds (D)	85	0	11
3rd	Oak Lawn	William O. Lipinski (D)	45	38	40
4th	Chicago	Luis Gutierrez (D)	90	0	0
5th	Chicago	Michael Flanagan (R)	N.A.	N.A.	N.A.
6th	Des Plaines	Henry J. Hyde (R)	5	90	100
7th	Chicago, loop	Cardiss Collins (D)	95	6	0
8th	Schaumburg	Philip Crane (R)	5	100	90
9th	Evanston	Sidney R. Yates (D)	100	0	0
10th	Waukegan	John E. Porter (R)	30	52	80
11th	Joliet	Jerry Weller (R)	N.A.	N.A.	N.A.
12th	Belleville	Jerry F. Costello (D)	50	38	50
13th	Oak Brook	Harris W. Fawell (R)	25	81	100
14th	Batavia	J. Dennis Hastert (R)	5	95	100
15th	Bloomington	Thomas W. Ewing (R)	10	90	100
16th	Rockford	Donald Manzullo (R)	5	95	90
17th	Moline	Lane Evans (D)	100	0	0
18th	Peoria	Ray LaHood (R)	N.A.	N.A.	N.A.
19th	Decatur	Glenn Poshard (D)	55	38	50
20th	Springfield	Richard J. Durbin (D)	95	0	10
	Indiana				
1st	Gary	Peter J. Visclosky (D)	75	19	60
2nd	Muncie	David McIntosh (R)	N.A.	N.A.	N.A.
3rd	South Bend	Tim Roemer (D)	65	14	40
4th	Fort Wayne	Mark Souder (R)	N.A.	N.A.	N.A.
5th	Kokomo	Steve Buyer (R)	0	100	100
6th	Indianapolis	Dan Burton (R)	0	100	100
7th	Terre Haute	John Myers (R)	5	100	90
8th	Evansville	John Hostettler (R)	N.A.	N.A.	N.A.
9th	Bloomington	Lee H. Hamilton (D)	60	38	70
10th	Indianapolis	Andrew Jacobs, Jr. (D)	85	30	11

State/ Dist.	City	Representative	ADA[1]	ACU[2]	NSI[3]
	Iowa				
1st	Cedar Rapids	Jim Leach (R)	40	33	40
2nd	Waterloo	Jim Nussle (R)	25	70	40
3rd	Ames	Jim Ross Lightfoot (R)	5	95	80
4th	Des Moines	Greg Ganske (R)	N.A.	N.A.	N.A.
5th	Sioux City	Tom Latham (R)	N.A.	N.A.	N.A.
	Kansas				
1st	Dodge City	Pat Roberts (R)	0	100	100
2nd	Topeka	Sam Brownback (R)	N.A.	N.A.	N.A.
3rd	Kansas City	Jan Meyers (R)	30	57	100
4th	Wichita	Todd Tiahrt (R)	N.A.	N.A.	N.A.
	Kentucky				
1st	Paducah	Edward Whitfield (R)	N.A.	N.A.	N.A.
2nd	Owensboro	Ron Lewis (R)	0	86	100
3rd	Louisville	Mike Ward (D)	N.A.	N.A.	N.A.
4th	Covington	Jim Bunning (R)	5	95	100
5th	Somerset	Harold Rogers (R)	15	89	90
6th	Lexington	Scotty Baesler (D)	45	33	70
	Louisiana				
1st	Metairie	Robert L. Livingston, Jr. (R)	0	95	100
2nd	New Orleans	William J. Jefferson (D)	90	15	33
3rd	Houma	W.J. "Billy" Tauzin (D)	15	76	90
4th	Baton Rouge	Cleo Fields (D)	90	5	10
5th	Shreveport	Jim McCrery (R)	5	90	100
6th	Alexandria	Richard H. Baker (R)	0	100	100
7th	Lafayette	James A. Hayes (D)	20	83	90
	Maine				
1st	Portland	James Longley (R)	N.A.	N.A.	N.A.
2nd	Bangor	John Baldacci (D)	N.A.	N.A.	N.A.
	Maryland				
1st	Annapolis	Wayne Gilchrest (R)	30	62	80
2nd	Towson	Robert Ehrlich, Jr. (R)	N.A.	N.A.	N.A.
3rd	Baltimore	Benjamin L. Cardin (D)	75	10	30
4th	Landover	Albert R. Wynn (D)	95	0	0
5th	Bowie	Steny H. Hoyer (D)	70	24	70
6th	Hagerstown	Roscoe G. Bartlett (R)	0	100	100
7th	Baltimore	Kweisi Mfume (D)	95	0	0
8th	Rockville	Constance Morella (R)	70	29	40
	Massachusetts				
1st	Pittsfield	John Olver (D)	100	0	0
2nd	Springfield	Richard E. Neal (D)	95	0	20
3rd	Worcester	Peter Blute (R)	20	67	80
4th	Brookline	Barney Frank (D)	100	0	0
5th	Lowell	Martin Meehan (D)	85	16	20
6th	Salem	Peter Torkildsen (R)	15	67	90
7th	Lexington	Edward J. Markey (D)	85	0	0
8th	Cambridge	Joseph P. Kennedy II (D)	90	5	0
9th	Boston	John Joseph Moakley (D)	95	0	0
10th	Quincy	Gerry E. Studds (D)	95	0	10
	Michigan				
1st	Upper Peninsula	Bart Stupak (D)	70	24	40
2nd	Muskegon	Peter Hoekstra (R)	20	86	100
3rd	Grand Rapids	Vernon Ehlers (R)	25	81	100
4th	Houghton Lake	David Camp (R)	20	95	90
5th	Saginaw	James Barcia (D)	50	43	50
6th	Kalamazoo	Fred Upton (R)	35	67	60
7th	Jackson	Nick Smith (R)	5	95	100
8th	Lansing	Dick Chrysler (R)	N.A.	N.A.	N.A.
9th	Flint	Dale Kildee (D)	90	5	20
10th	Port Huron	David E. Bonior (D)	95	5	20
11th	Bloomfield Hills	Joseph Knollenberg (R)	0	100	100
12th	Sterling Heights	Sander M. Levin (D)	85	5	40
13th	Ann Arbor	Lynn Rivers (D)	N.A.	N.A.	N.A.
14th	Detroit	John Conyers, Jr. (D)	100	5	0
15th	Detroit	Barbara-Rose Collins (D)	100	0	0
16th	Dearborn	John D. Dingell (D)	70	15	56
	Minnesota				
1st	Rochester	Gil Gutknecht (IR)	N.A.	N.A.	N.A.
2nd	Willmar	David Minge (DFL)	N.A.	N.A.	N.A.
3rd	Bloomington	Jim Ramstad (IR)	30	62	80
4th	St. Paul	Bruce F. Vento (DFL)	100	0	0
5th	Minneapolis	Martin Olav Sabo (DFL)	95	10	30
6th	Stillwater	William Luther (DFL)	N.A.	N.A.	N.A.
7th	St. Cloud	Colin C. Peterson (DFL)	45	52	10
8th	Duluth	James L. Oberstar (DFL)	80	15	0
	Mississippi				
1st	Oxford	Roger F. Wicker (R)	N.A.	N.A.	N.A.
2nd	Vicksburg	Bennie G. Thompson (D)	80	20	22
3rd	Meridian	G.V. "Sonny" Montgomery (D)	35	57	100
4th	Jackson	Mike Parker (D)	20	67	90
5th	Pascagoula	Gene Taylor (D)	15	67	100
	Missouri				
1st	St. Louis	William B. Clay (D)	85	14	20
2nd	Kirkwood	Jim Talent (R)	5	95	100
3rd	St. Louis	Richard A. Gephardt (D)	80	5	100
4th	Jefferson City	Ike Skelton (D)	35	62	40
5th	Kansas City	Karen McCarthey (D)	N.A.	N.A.	N.A.
6th	St. Joseph	Pat Danner (D)	70	29	30
7th	Springfield	Mel Hancock (R)	10	95	100
8th	Cape Girardeau	Bill Emerson (R)	0	100	100
9th	Hannibal	Harold L. Volkmer (D)	50	48	60
	Montana				
1st	At-large	Pat Williams (D)	75	19	20
	Nebraska				
1st	Lincoln	Douglas K. Bereuter (R)	15	71	90
2nd	Omaha	Jon Christensen (R)	N.A.	N.A.	N.A.
3rd	Grand Island	Bill Barrett (R)	5	95	100
	Nevada				
1st	Las Vegas	John Ensign (R)	N.A.	N.A.	N.A.
2nd	Reno	Barbara F. Vucanovich (R)	0	100	100
	New Hampshire				
1st	Manchester	William H. Zeliff, Jr. (R)	5	86	100
2nd	Concord	Charles Bass (R)	N.A.	N.A.	N.A.
	New Jersey				
1st	Camden	Robert E. Andrews (D)	45	26	80
2nd	Atlantic City	Frank LoBiondo (R)	N.A.	N.A.	N.A.
3rd	Cherry Hill	Jim Saxton (R)	15	67	90
4th	Trenton	Chris Smith (R)	30	70	100
5th	Ridgewood	Marge Roukema (R)	35	50	40
6th	New Brunswick	Frank Pallone, Jr. (D)	70	14	40
7th	Union	Bob Franks (R)	25	62	80
8th	Paterson	Bill Martini (R)	N.A.	N.A.	N.A.
9th	Hackensack	Robert G. Torricelli (D)	65	6	33
10th	Newark	Donald M. Payne (D)	95	10	0
11th	Morristown	Rodney Frelinghuysen (R)	N.A.	N.A.	N.A.
12th	Princeton	Dick Zimmer (R)	25	57	60
13th	Jersey City	Robert Menendez (D)	90	5	22
	New Mexico				
1st	Albuquerque	Steven Schiff (R)	15	80	100
2nd	Picacho	Joseph R. Skeen (R)	0	95	90
3rd	Santa Fe	Bill Richardson (D)	55	26	56
	New York				
1st	Centereach	Michael P. Forbes (R)	N.A.	N.A.	N.A.
2nd	Babylon	Rick Lazio (R)	20	57	90
3rd	Westbury	Peter T. King (R)	5	81	100
4th	Garden City	Dan Frisa (R)	N.A.	N.A.	N.A.
5th	Queens	Gary L. Ackerman (D)	90	0	30
6th	Jamaica	Floyd H. Flake (D)	95	0	10
7th	Flushing	Thomas J. Manton (D)	70	15	44
8th	Manhattan, west side	Jerrold Nadler (D)	100	5	0
9th	Brooklyn	Charles E. Schumer (D)	90	5	20
10th	Brooklyn Heights	Edolphus Towns (D)	85	0	0
11th	Flatbush	Major R. Owens (D)	90	0	0
12th	Brooklyn	Nydia M. Velázquez (D)	100	0	0
13th	Staten Island	Susan Molinari (R)	20	71	90
14th	Manhattan, east side	Carolyn B. Maloney (D)	100	0	20
15th	Harlem	Charles B. Rangel (D)	95	5	0
16th	Bronx	José E. Serrano (D)	95	0	0
17th	Yonkers	Eliot L. Engel (D)	100	0	10
18th	White Plains	Nita M. Lowey (D)	85	10	30
19th	Poughkeepsie	Sue W. Kelly (R)	N.A.	N.A.	N.A.
20th	Newburgh	Benjamin A. Gilman (R)	35	52	80
21st	Albany	Michael R. McNulty (D)	55	42	40
22nd	Saratoga Springs	Gerald B.H. Solomon (R)	0	95	100
23rd	Utica	Sherwood L. Boehlert (R)	50	38	70
24th	Watertown	John M. McHugh (R)	10	90	100
25th	Syracuse	James T. Walsh (R)	20	67	90
26th	Kingston	Maurice D. Hinchey (D)	95	5	0
27th	Seneca Falls	Bill Paxon (R)	0	10	100
28th	Rochester	Louise McIntosh Slaughter (D)	95	0	10
29th	Niagara Falls	John J. LaFalce (D)	80	15	40
30th	Buffalo	Jack Quinn (R)	30	76	100
31st	Corning	Amo Houghton (R)	20	68	100
	North Carolina				
1st	Greenville	Eva M. Clayton (D)	100	0	0
2nd	Durham	David Funderburk (R)	N.A.	N.A.	N.A.
3rd	Outer Banks	Walter B. Jones, Jr. (R)	N.A.	N.A.	N.A.
4th	Raleigh	Fred Heineman (R)	N.A.	N.A.	N.A.
5th	Winston-Salem	Richard Burr (R)	N.A.	N.A.	N.A.
6th	Greensboro	Howard Coble (R)	5	95	60
7th	Wilmington	Charlie Rose (D)	75	14	56
8th	Salisbury	W.G. "Bill" Hefner (D)	65	19	60
9th	Charlotte	Sue Myrick (R)	N.A.	N.A.	N.A.
10th	Hickory	Cass Ballenger (R)	5	90	100
11th	Asheville	Charles H. Taylor (R)	5	100	100
12th	Charlotte	Melvin L. Watt (D)	100	10	0
	North Dakota				
1st	At-large	Earl Pomeroy (D)	65	14	50
	Ohio				
1st	Cincinnati	Steve Chabot (R)	N.A.	N.A.	N.A.
2nd	Indian Hill	Rob Portman (R)	10	86	90
3rd	Dayton	Tony P. Hall (D)	85	19	50

State/ Dist.	City	Representative	ADA[1]	ACU[2]	NSI[3]
4th	Lima	Michael Oxley (R)	0	95	100
5th	Sandusky	Paul E. Gillmor (R)	15	86	100
6th	Portsmouth	Frank A. Cremeans (R)	N.A.	N.A.	N.A.
7th	Marysville	David L. Hobson (R)	20	67	100
8th	Hamilton	John A. Boehner (R)	5	100	100
9th	Toledo	Marcy Kaptur (D)	60	20	60
10th	Cleveland	Martin R. Hoke (R)	15	80	80
11th	Shaker Heights	Louis Stokes (D)	100	10	11
12th	Columbus	John R. Kasich (R)	10	76	100
13th	Oberlin	Sherrod Brown (D)	75	14	10
14th	Akron	Thomas C. Sawyer (D)	90	5	30
15th	Columbus	Debra Pryce (R)	15	67	100
16th	Canton	Ralph S. Regula (R)	15	86	100
17th	Youngstown	James A. Traficant, Jr. (D)	65	33	40
18th	Steubenville	Robert W. Ney (R)	N.A.	N.A.	N.A.
19th	Ashtabula	Steven C. LaTourette (R)	N.A.	N.A.	N.A.
	Oklahoma				
1st	Tulsa	Steve Largent (R)	N.A.	N.A.	N.A.
2nd	Muskogee	Tom A. Coburn (R)	N.A.	N.A.	N.A.
3rd	Marietta	Bill K. Brewster (D)	30	60	70
4th	Norman	J.C. Watts (R)	N.A.	N.A.	N.A.
5th	Oklahoma City	Ernest J. Istook (R)	5	98	100
6th	Cheyenne	Frank D. Lucas (R)	0	100	71
	Oregon				
1st	Portland	Elizabeth Furse (D)	95	5	0
2nd	Medford	Wes Cooley (R)	N.A.	N.A.	N.A.
3rd	Portland	Ron Wyden (D)	80	0	0
4th	Eugene	Peter A. DeFazio (D)	70	29	0
5th	Salem	Jim Bunn (R)	N.A.	N.A.	N.A.
	Pennsylvania				
1st	Philadelphia	Thomas M. Foglietta (D)	95	0	0
2nd	West Philadelphia	Chaka Fattah (D)	N.A.	N.A.	N.A.
3rd	NE Philadelphia	Robert A. Borski (D)	65	29	50
4th	Beaver	Ron Klink (D)	50	43	50
5th	State College	William F. Clinger, Jr. (R)	15	95	100
6th	Reading	Tim Holden (D)	45	43	60
7th	Swarthmore	Curt Weldon (R)	10	74	100
8th	Bucks County	James C. Greenwood (R)	20	70	100
9th	Altoona	Bud Shuster (R)	0	100	100
10th	Scranton	Joseph McDade (R)	20	83	90
11th	Wilkes-Barre	Paul E. Kanjorski (D)	55	29	30
12th	Johnstown	John P. Murtha (D)	50	38	90
13th	Villanova	Jon D. Fox (R)	N.A.	N.A.	N.A.
14th	Pittsburgh	William J. Coyne (D)	100	0	0
15th	Allentown	Paul McHale (D)	45	24	70
16th	Lancaster	Robert S. Walker (R)	0	100	100
17th	Harrisburg	George W. Gekas (R)	10	95	90
18th	McKeesport	Michael F. Doyle (D)	N.A.	N.A.	N.A.
19th	York	William F. Goodling (R)	10	90	90
20th	Washington	Frank Mascara (D)	N.A.	N.A.	N.A.
21st	Erie	Philip English (R)	N.A.	N.A.	N.A.
	Rhode Island				
1st	Providence	Patrick J. Kennedy (D)	N.A.	N.A.	N.A.
2nd	Warwick	Jack Reed (D)	85	5	30
	South Carolina				
1st	Charleston	Mark Sanford (R)	N.A.	N.A.	N.A.
2nd	Columbia	Floyd Spence (R)	5	95	100
3rd	Aiken	Lindsey O. Graham (R)	N.A.	N.A.	N.A.
4th	Spartanburg	Bob Inglis (R)	5	100	100
5th	Rock Hill	John M. Spratt, Jr. (D)	65	24	70
6th	Florence	James E. Clyburn (D)	75	15	20
	South Dakota				
1st	At-large	Tim Johnson (D)	55	24	30
	Tennessee				
1st	Kingsport	James H. Quillen (R)	5	95	80
2nd	Knoxville	John J. Duncan, Jr. (R)	20	76	50
3rd	Chattanooga	Zach Wamp (R)	N.A.	N.A.	N.A.
4th	Shelbyville	Van Hilleary (R)	N.A.	N.A.	N.A.
5th	Nasvhille	Bob Clement (D)	35	35	60
6th	Murfreesboro	Bart Gordon (D)	55	24	70
7th	Memphis	Ed Bryant (R)	N.A.	N.A.	N.A.
8th	Jackson	John S. Tanner (D)	30	67	90
9th	Memphis	Harold E. Ford (D)	75	0	0
	Texas				
1st	Texarkana	Jim Chapman (D)	45	45	80

State/ Dist.	City	Representative	ADA[1]	ACU[2]	NSI[3]
2nd	Lufkin	Charles Wilson (D)	55	53	90
3rd	North Dallas	Sam Johnson (R)	0	100	100
4th	Tyler	Ralph M. Hall (D)	10	95	90
5th	Dallas	John Bryant (D)	80	5	11
6th	Waxahachie	Joe Barton (R)	0	100	100
7th	Houston	Bill Archer (R)	0	100	100
8th	College Station	Jack M. Fields (R)	0	100	100
9th	Beaumont	Steve Stockman (R)	N.A.	N.A.	N.A.
10th	Austin	Lloyd Doggett (D)	N.A.	N.A.	N.A.
11th	Waco	Chet Edwards (D)	45	38	90
12th	Fort Worth	Pete Geren (D)	15	67	100
13th	Amarillo	William M. Thornberry (R)	N.A.	N.A.	N.A.
14th	Victoria	Greg Laughlin (D)	50	60	90
15th	McAllen	E. "Kika" de la Garza (D)	50	45	90
16th	El Paso	Ronald D. Coleman (D)	80	19	70
17th	Abilene	Charles W. Stenholm (D)	5	90	90
18th	Houston	Sheila Jackson-Lee (D)	N.A.	N.A.	N.A.
19th	Lubbock	Larry Combest (R)	0	100	90
20th	San Antonio	Henry B. Gonzalez (D)	75	15	50
21st	Midland	Lamar Smith (R)	5	95	100
22nd	Brazoria	Tom DeLay (R)	0	100	100
23rd	Laredo	Henry Bonilla (R)	0	95	90
24th	Arlington	Martin Frost (D)	55	25	70
25th	Pasadena	Ken Bentsen (D)	N.A.	N.A.	N.A.
26th	Irving	Dick Armey (R)	0	100	100
27th	Corpus Christi	Solomon P. Ortiz (D)	45	48	80
28th	San Antonio	Frank Tejeda (D)	50	43	80
29th	Houston	Gene Green (D)	80	16	30
30th	Dallas	Eddie Bernice Johnson (D)	85	19	40
	Utah				
1st	Ogden	James Hansen (R)	0	95	100
2nd	Salt Lake City	Enid G.Waldholtz	N.A	N.A.	N.A.
3rd	Provo	Bill Orton (D)	25	79	60
	Vermont				
1st	At-large	Bernard Sanders (I)	100	0	0
	Virginia				
1st	Newport News	Herbert H. Bateman (R)	10	90	100
2nd	Virginia Beach	Owen B. Pickett (D)	35	48	80
3rd	Norfolk	Robert C. Scott (D)	80	24	40
4th	Portsmouth	Norman Sisisky (D)	35	48	90
5th	Charlottesville	Lewis F. Payne (D)	25	57	90
6th	Roanoke	Bob Goodlatte (R)	10	90	90
7th	Richmond	Thomas J. Bliley, Jr. (R)	0	100	100
8th	Alexandria	James P. Moran (D)	55	29	40
9th	Blacksburg	Rick Boucher (D)	65	30	50
10th	Arlington	Frank R. Wolf (R)	0	86	100
11th	Fairfax	Thomas M. Davis III (R)	N.A.	N.A.	N.A.
	Washington				
1st	Redmond	Rick White (R)	N.A.	N.A.	N.A.
2nd	Everett	Jack Metcalf (R)	N.A.	N.A.	N.A.
3rd	Olympia	Linda Smith(R)	N.A.	N.A.	N.A.
4th	Yakima	Doc Hastings (R)	N.A.	N.A.	N.A.
5th	Spokane	George Nethercutt (R)	N.A.	N.A.	N.A.
6th	Tacoma	Norman D. Dicks (D)	65	14	60
7th	Seattle	James A. McDermott (D)	95	5	0
8th	Bellevue	Jennifer Dunn (R)	5	86	100
9th	Renton	Randy Tate (R)	N.A.	N.A.	N.A.
	West Virginia				
1st	Wheeling	Alan B. Mollohan (D)	60	38	80
2nd	Charleston	Robert E. Wise, Jr. (D)	75	30	56
3rd	Huntington	Nick Joe Rahall II (D)	75	24	30
	Wisconsin				
1st	Kenosha	Mark Neumann (R)	N.A.	N.A.	N.A.
2nd	Madison	Scott Klug (R)	45	43	60
3rd	Eau Claire	Steve Gunderson (R)	10	81	70
4th	Milwaukee	Gerald D. Kleczka (D)	85	5	20
5th	Wauwatosa	Tom Barrett (D)	90	0	20
6th	Oshkosh	Thomas Petri (R)	25	76	60
7th	Wausau	David R. Obey (D)	80	10	20
8th	Green Bay	Toby Roth (R)	15	81	40
9th	Sheboygan	F. James Sensenbrenner, Jr. (R)	20	76	50
	Wyoming				
1st	At-large	Barbara Cubin (R)	N.A.	N.A.	N.A.

NONVOTING REPRESENTATIVES

American Samoa	Delegate Eni F.H. Faleomavaega (D)	**Puerto Rico**	Resident Commissioner Carlos A. Romero-Barceló (D)
Guam Delegate	Robert A. Underwood (D)		
District of Columbia	Delegate Eleanor Holmes Norton (D)	**Virgin Islands**	Delegate Victor O. Frazer (I)

Note: D = Democrat; DFL = Democratic-Farmer-Labor (Minn.); I = Independent; IR = Independent Republican (Minn.); R = Republican. 1. Americans for Democratic Action: based on 20 House votes in 1994. 2. American Conservative Union: based on 21 House votes in 1994. 3. National Security Index of the American Security Council: based on 10 House votes in 1994. **Source:** Americans for Democratic Action; The American Conservative Union; American Security Council; Clerk of the U.S. House of Representatives.

The Judicial Branch

SUPREME COURT OF THE UNITED STATES

United States Supreme Court Building; 1 First St. NE; Washington, DC 20543. (202) 479–3000. Created by Judiciary Act of Sept. 24, 1789, in accordance with Article III, Section 1 of Constitution. Composed of chief justice and a number of associate justices to be fixed by Congress. Justices (including the chief justice) are chosen by president with advice and consent of Senate and have lifetime tenure. Court terms begin first Monday of October and usually last until end of June. The Court hears approximately 150 cases a year, though in recent years it has heard fewer and fewer.

Jurisdiction of Supreme Court is outlined by Constitution in Article III, Section 2. In general, Supreme Court has original jurisdiction in cases in which a state or an ambassador is party; it has appellate jurisdiction in other federal cases involving the various states or in which the United States is party.

THE SUPREME COURT, 1995

Name	Appointed by	Born	State	Law school
William H. Rehnquist	Nixon, 1972 (justice) Reagan, 1986 (chief justice)	1924	Arizona	Stanford
John Paul Stevens	Ford, 1975	1920	Illinois	Northwestern
Sandra Day O'Connor	Reagan, 1981	1930	Arizona	Stanford
Antonin Scalia	Reagan, 1986	1936	Virginia	Harvard
Anthony M. Kennedy	Reagan, 1987	1936	California	Harvard
David H. Souter	Bush, 1990	1939	New Hampshire	Harvard
Clarence Thomas	Bush, 1991	1948	Georgia	Yale
Ruth Bader Ginsburg	Clinton, 1993	1933	New York	Columbia
Stephen G. Breyer	Clinton, 1994	1945	Illinois	Yale

HOW A CASE GETS TO THE SUPREME COURT

In both civil and criminal law, the United States Supreme Court is the ultimate court of appeal. All other remedies must be exhausted before petitioning the Court for appeal or review of a lower court decision. Cases originating in state courts can be appealed to the Court directly from state supreme courts; cases originating in federal court must go through the United States District Court and the United States Court of Appeals first. The Constitution limits the Court to original jurisdiction only in cases involving the United States or citizens of different states or foreign ambassadors or a state against a state. The Court itself decides whether to hear a case or let a decision stand. When the Court accepts a case, it grants a *writ of appeal*—or more often, a *writ of certiorari*—which announces the Court's intention to review a decision. Very rarely, the Court grants a *writ of certification* in response to a lower court's direct request for the Court's opinion. But in all cases, the Court will decline to review decisions lacking a "substantial federal question" at issue, which is what happens to the vast majority of cases brought before it. Yet the mounting backlog of cases awaiting the Court's attention periodically raises calls for easing the Court's workload by changing its review and appeal procedures, or even by adding another layer of appellate courts.

LOWER COURTS

U.S. Courts of Appeals

These intermediate appellate courts were created by act of Mar. 3, 1891, to relieve Supreme Court of having to reconsider all trials originally decided by federal courts. Decisions of these courts are final except when law provides for direct review by Supreme Court. Each of the 50 states is assigned to one of 12 judicial circuits that compose the court of appeals system.

District of Columbia Circuit
Circuit Justice William H. Rehnquist
Circuit Judges Harry T. Edwards (chief judge), Patricia M. Wald, Laurence H. Silberman, James L. Buckley, Stephen F. Williams, Douglas H. Ginsburg, David B. Sentelle, Karen LeCraft Henderson, A. Raymond Randolph, Judith W. Rogers

First Circuit Districts of Maine, Massachusetts, New Hampshire, Puerto Rico, and Rhode Island
Circuit Justice David H. Souter
Circuit Judges Juan R. Torruella (chief judge), Bruce M. Selya, Conrad K. Cyr, Michael Boudin, Norman H. Stahl

Second Circuit Districts of Connecticut, New York, and Vermont
Circuit Justice Clarence Thomas
Circuit Judges Jon O. Newman, (chief judge), Amalya Lyle Kearse, Ralph K. Winter, Jr., Roger J. Miner, Frank X. Altimari, J. Daniel Mahoney, John M. Walker, Jr., Joseph M. McLaughlin, Dennis G. Jacobs, Pierre N. Leval, Guido Calabresi, Jose A. Cabranes

Third Circuit Districts of Delaware, New Jersey, Pennsylvania, and the Virgin Islands
Circuit Justice David H. Souter
Circuit Judges Dolores K. Sloviter (chief judge), Edward R. Becker, Walter K. Stapleton, Carol Los Mansmann, Morton I. Greenberg, William D. Hutchinson, Anthony J. Scirica, Robert E. Cowen, Richard L. Nygaard, Samuel A. Alito, Jr., Jane R. Roth, Timothy K. Lewis, Theodore A. McKee

Fourth Circuit Districts of Maryland, North Carolina, South Carolina, Virginia, and West Virginia
Circuit Justice William H. Rehnquist
Circuit Judges Sam J. Ervin III (chief judge), Donald Stuart Russell, H. Emory Widener, Jr., Kenneth K. Hall, Francis D. Murnaghan, Jr., J. Harvie Wilkinson III, William W. Wilkins, Jr., Paul V. Niemeyer, Clyde H. Hamilton, J. Michael Luttig, Karen J. Williams, M. Blane Michael, Diana Gribbon Motz

Fifth Circuit Districts of Louisiana, Mississippi, and Texas
Circuit Justice Antonin Scalia
Circuit Judges Henry A. Politz (chief judge), Carolyn Dineen King, William L. Garwood, E. Grady Jolly, Patrick E. Higginbotham, W. Eugene Davis, Edith Hollan Jones, Jerry E. Smith, John M. Duhe, Jr., Rhesa H. Barksdale, Jacques L. Wiener, Jr., Emilio M. Garza, Harold R. DeMoss, Jr., Fortunato P. Benavides, Carl E. Stewart, Robert M. Parker

Sixth Circuit Districts of Kentucky, Michigan, Ohio, and Tennessee
Circuit Justice John Paul Stevens
Circuit Judges Gilbert S. Merritt (chief judge), Damon J. Keith, Cornelia G. Kennedy, Boyce F. Martin, Jr., Nathaniel R. Jones, H. Ted Milburn, David A. Nelson, James L. Ryan, Danny J. Boggs, Alan E. Norris, Richard F. Suhrheinrich, Eugene E. Siler, Jr., Alice M. Batchelder, Martha Craig Daughtrey

Seventh Circuit Districts of Illinois, Indiana, and Wisconsin
Circuit Justice John Paul Stevens
Circuit Judges Richard A. Posner (chief judge), Walter J. Cummings, William J. Bauer, John L. Coffey, Joel M. Flaum, Frank H. Easterbrook, Kenneth F. Ripple, Daniel A. Manion, Michael S. Kanne, Ilana Diamond Rovner

Eighth Circuit Districts of Arkansas, Iowa, Minnesota, Missouri, Nebraska, North Dakota, and South Dakota

Circuit Justice Stephen G. Breyer
Circuit Judges Richard S. Arnold (chief judge), Theodore McMillian, George G. Fagg, Pasco M. Bowman II, Roger L. Wollman, Frank J. Magill, C. Arlen Beam, James B. Loken, David R. Hansen, Morris S. Arnold

Ninth Circuit Districts of Alaska, Arizona, California, Guam, Hawaii, Idaho, Montana, Nevada, Northern Mariana Islands, Oregon, and Washington
Circuit Justice Sandra Day O'Connor
Circuit Judges J. Clifford Wallace (chief judge), James R. Browning, Procter Hug, Jr., Mary M. Schroeder, Betty B. Fletcher, Jerome Farris, Harry Pregerson, Cecil F. Poole, Dorothy W. Nelson, William C. Canby, Jr., William A. Norris, Stephen Reinhardt, Robert R. Beezer, Cynthia H. Hall, Charles E. Wiggins, Melvin Brunetti, Alex Kozinski, John T. Noonan, Jr., David R. Thompson, Diarmuid F. O'Scannlain, Edward Leavy, Stephen S. Trott, Ferdinand F. Fernandez, Pamela A. Rymer, Thomas G. Nelson, Andrew J. Kleinfeld

Tenth Circuit Districts of Colorado, Kansas, New Mexico, Oklahoma, Utah, and Wyoming
Circuit Justice Ruth Bader Ginsburg
Circuit Judges Stephanie K. Seymour (chief judge), John P. Moore, Stephen H. Anderson, Deanell R. Tacha, Bobby R. Baldock, Wade Brorby, David M. Ebel, Paul J. Kelly, Jr., Robert H. Henry

Eleventh Circuit Districts of Alabama, Florida, and Georgia
Circuit Justice Anthony M. Kennedy
Circuit Judges Gerald B. Tjoflat (chief judge), Phyllis A. Kravitch, Joseph W. Hatchett, R. Lanier Anderson III, J.L. Edmondson, Emmet R. Cox, Stanley F. Birch, Jr., Joel F. Dubina, Susan H. Black, Edward E. Carnes, Rosemary Barkett

U.S. Court of Appeals for the Federal Circuit
Circuit Justice William H. Rehnquist
Circuit Judges Glenn L. Archer, Jr. (chief judge), Helen W. Nies, Giles S. Rich, Pauline Newman, H. Robert Mayer, Paul R. Michel, S. Jay Plager, Alan D. Lourie, Raymond C. Clevenger III, Randall R. Rader, Alvin A. Schall

U.S. District Courts These are trial courts of general federal jurisdiction. There are 89 courts, including at least one in each state and the District of Columbia. Each has from 2 to 27 federal district judgeships. Overall, there are 541 permanent district judges in the 50 states, 15 in the District of Columbia, and 7 in Puerto Rico. Usually one judge is required to decide a case, but in some cases it is required that three judges be called together to compose the court.

Territorial Courts Estab. pursuant to Article IV, Section 3 of the Constitution. In Guam and the Virgin Islands these have jurisdiction not only over the subjects described in the judicial article of the Constitution but also over many local matters that, within the states, are decided by state courts.

CASES BEFORE U.S. SUPREME COURT, U.S. COURTS OF APPEALS, AND U.S. DISTRICT COURTS, 1970–94

Status	1970	1975	1980	1985	1990	1993	1994
U.S. Supreme Court[1]							
Total cases on docket	4,212	4,761	5,144	5,158	6,316	7,786	N.A.
Cases argued	151	179	154	171	125	99	N.A.
Number of signed opinions	109	138	123	146	112	84	N.A.
U.S. Courts of Appeals[2]							
Cases commenced	11,662	16,658	23,200	33,360	40,898	49,770	48,815
Cases terminated	10,699	16,000	20,887	31,387	38,520	47,466	48,546
Cases disposed of[3]	6,139	9,077	10,607	16,369	21,006	25,567	26,475
Median months to final disposition[4]	8.2	7.4	8.9	10.3	10.1	10.4	10.5
U.S. District Courts[2]							
Civil cases commenced[5]	87,300	117,300	168,800	273,700	217,900	228,600	236,000
Trials[5,6]	8,000	8,700	10,100	12,300	9,200	7,900	7,900
Percent reaching trial	10.0%	8.4%	6.5%	4.7%	4.3%	3.5%	3.4%
Criminal cases commenced[5,7]	38,100	41,000	28,000	38,500	46,500	45,700	44,900
Defendants disposed of	36,400	49,200	36,600	47,400	56,500	59,500	61,200
Not convicted	8,200	11,800	8,000	8,800	9,800	9,200	10,000
Convicted	28,200	37,400	28,600	38,500	46,700	50,400	51,100

1. Statutory term of court begins first Monday in October. 2. For year ending June 30. 3. Terminated on the merits after hearing or submission. Beginning 1975, data not comparable with earlier years due to changes in criteria. 4. Prior to 1985, the figure is from filing of complete record to final disposition; beginning 1985, figure is from filing notice of appeal to final disposition. 5. Figures rounded in source. 6. A trial is defined as a contested proceeding (other than a hearing on a motion) before either court or jury in which evidence is introduced and final judgment sought. 7. Excludes transfers. **Sources:** Office of the Clerk, Supreme Court of the United States, unpublished data; Administrative Office of the U.S. Courts, *Annual Report of the Director.*

Judicial Panel on Multidistrict Legislation Created Apr. 29, 1968, this body of seven judges is authorized to temporarily transfer civil actions pending in different districts and involving common questions of fact to a single district for coordinated or consolidated pretrial proceedings.

Special Courts

The power to create special courts is vested in Congress in part by Article III of the Constitution and in part by Supreme Court decree. Appeals from these special courts may be taken to the U.S. Court of Appeals for the Federal Circuit.

Temporary Emergency Court of Appeals Estab. by Economic Stabilization Act Amendments of 1971. Has exclusive jurisdiction over all appeals from district courts arising from economic stabilization and energy conservation laws.

U.S. Claims Court Estab. Oct. 1, 1982, to replace the Court of Claims. Composed of 16 judges appointed for 15-year terms by president with advice and consent of Senate. President designates chief judge; has jurisdiction over monetary claims against the United States based on the Constitution or acts of Congress.

U.S. Court of International Trade Estab. June 10, 1890, as Board of United States General Appraisers. Has jurisdiction over civil actions against the U.S. involving federal laws governing imports.

U.S. Court of Military Appeals Estab. May 5, 1950. Serves as final court of appeal to review court-martial convictions for all the armed services. Subject only to certiorari review by the Supreme Court in a limited number of cases.

U.S. Court of Veterans Appeals Estab. Nov. 18, 1988. Exclusive jurisdiction to review decisions of the Board of Veterans Appeal.

OTHER JUDICIAL AGENCIES

Administrative Office of the U.S. Courts Thurgood Marshall Federal Judiciary Building, One Columbus Circle NE, Washington, DC 20002. (202) 273-1000. Created by act of Aug. 7, 1939. Its areas of primary concern are administering courts, supervising probation office, and overseeing administration of bankruptcy courts, magistrate offices, and public defender's offices.

Federal Judicial Center Thurgood Marshall Federal Judiciary Building, One Columbus Circle NE, Washington, DC 20002. (202) 273-4153. Created by act of Dec. 20, 1967. Conducts research, develops improvement of personnel and data systems, and recommends improvements in administration and management.

U.S. Sentencing Commission Suite 2-500 South Lobby, One Columbus Circle NE, Washington, DC 20002. (202) 273-4500. Created by Sentencing Reform Act of 1984. Develops sentencing policies and practices for the Federal criminal justice system.

The Executive Branch

EXECUTIVE OFFICE OF THE PRESIDENT

White House Office 1600 Pennsylvania Ave. NW, Washington, DC 20500. (202) 456-1111. Serves president in performance of duties incident to his office. Maintains communication with Congress, individual members of Congress, heads of executive agencies, media, and public.

Council of Economic Advisers Old Executive Office Building, Washington, DC 20500. (202) 395-5084. Created by Employment Act of 1946. Council's three members—appointed by president—analyze the various segments of the economy, appraise and assess existing economic programs, recommend new economic programs, and assist in preparation of president's economic reports to Congress.

Council on Environmental Quality 722 Jackson Place NW, Washington, DC 20503. (202) 395-5754. Created by National Environmental Policy Act of 1969. Recommends national policies to improve quality of environment. Analyzes environmental changes and trends. Assesses and evaluates existing environmental programs. Assists president in compiling annual environmental quality report to Congress.

National Critical Materials Council 810 7th St. NW, Washington, DC 20241. (202) 501-3737. Estab. by National Critical Materials Act of 1984. Advises president on policies related to maintaining sufficient supplies of strategic minerals and materials for national security, economic well-being, and industrial productivity.

National Security Council (NSC) Old Executive Office Building, Washington, DC 20506. (202) 456-7430. Created by National Security Act of 1947. Chaired by president. Members include vice president and secretaries of state and defense. Chairman of Joint Chiefs of Staff is statutory military adviser; CIA director is intelligence adviser. Advises president on integration of domestic, foreign, and military policies relating to national security.

Office of Administration 725 17th St., Washington, DC 20503. (202) 395-6963. Created Dec. 12, 1977, by Reorganization Plan No. 1. Provides administrative services to all units within executive office except those in direct support of president.

Office of Management and Budget (OMB) Executive Office Building, Washington, DC 20503. (202) 395-3080. Created July 1, 1970, by Reorganization Plan No. 2 of 1970. Assists president in reviewing and assessing efficiency of structure and management of executive branch. Expands interagency cooperation. Assists president in preparing government's budget and fiscal program. Supervises, controls, and administers budget. Coordinates departmental advice and makes recommendations to president based on this advice. Plans, conducts, and promotes evaluation efforts to help president assess program objectives, performance, and efficiency. Keeps president informed of work planned and performed by the various government agencies.

Office of National Drug Control Policy Executive Office of the President, Washington, DC 20500. (202) 395-6700. Estab. by National Narcotics Leadership Act of 1988, effective Jan. 29, 1989. Coordinates federal, state, and local efforts to control illegal drug abuse and devises national strategies to ensure that national antidrug activities are carried out effectively.

The Cabinet

The president is the administrative head of the executive branch of the federal government. A creation of custom and tradition dating back to George Washington's administration, the cabinet functions at the pleasure of the president. Its purpose is to advise the president on any subject on which he requests information. The cabinet is composed of the heads of the 14 executive departments and certain other executive officials to whom the president accords cabinet rank. In addition, the Office of Management and Budget and the Office of the U.S. Trade Representative have cabinet rank in the Clinton administration. The vice president also participates regularly in cabinet meetings.

President, **Bill Clinton**
Vice President, **Albert Gore, Jr.**

Department	Cabinet officer
State	Warren M. Christopher
Treasury	Robert E. Rubin
Defense	William J. Perry
Justice	Janet Reno
Interior	Bruce Babbitt
Agriculture	Dan Glickman
Commerce	Ronald H. Brown
Labor	Robert B. Reich
Health and Human Services	Donna E. Shalala
Housing and Urban Development	Henry G. Cisneros
Transportation	Federico Peña
Energy	Hazel O'Leary
Education	Richard W. Riley
Veterans Affairs	Jesse Brown
Chief of Staff	Leon E. Panetta
Environmental Protection Agency	Carol Browner, administrator
Council of Economic Advisors	Joseph E. Stiglitz, chair
Office of Management and Budget	Alice M. Rivlin, director
Ambassador to the United Nations	Madeleine K. Albright
U.S. Trade Representative	Mickey Kantor

Office of Science and Technology Policy Old Executive Office Building, Washington, DC 20500. (202) 456-7116. Created May 11, 1976, by National Science and Technology Policy, Organization, and Priorities Act of 1976. Serves as source of scientific, engineering, and technological analysis and expertise for president with respect to public policy in areas of economy, national security, health, foreign relations, and environment. Appraises sale, quality, and effectiveness of U.S. efforts in science and technology.

Office of the U.S. Trade Representative 600 17th St. NW, Washington, DC 20506. (202) 395-3230. Created as Office of the Special Representative for Trade Negotiations by Executive Order 11075 of Jan. 15, 1963. Congress made it agency of executive office under Trade Act of 1974. Administers trade agreements program of Tariff Act of 1930, Trade Expansion Act of 1962, and Trade Act of 1974. Sets and administers overall trade policy. Representative is chief representative of U.S. for all activities of General Agreement on Tariffs and Trade (GATT) and at discussions, meetings, and negotiations in most conferences in which trade and commodity are issues.

Office of the Vice President of the United States Old Executive Office Building, Washington, DC 20501. (202) 456-2326. Vice president participates in cabinet meetings and is, by statute, a member of National Security Council and board of regents of the Smithsonian Institution; serves as president of Senate; empowered to succeed to presidency pursuant to Article II and the 20th and 25th amendments to the Constitution.

EXECUTIVE DEPARTMENTS

Department of Agriculture (USDA) 14th St. and Independence Ave. SW, Washington, DC 20250. (202) 447-2791. Created by act of May 15, 1862. Works to improve farms and farm income, expand foreign markets for U.S. agriculture, and curb poverty, hunger, and malnutrition. Helps maintain natural resources such as soil, water, and forests. Maintains food quality standards through inspection and grading. Among the most important of its services are the following:

Agricultural Marketing Service Estab. Apr. 2, 1972. Administers standardization, grading, and classing of more than 600 agricultural commodities. Provides inspection, market news, and research, promotion, and regulatory programs.

Agricultural Stabilization and Conservation Service Estab. June 5, 1961. Administers commodity and related land-use programs designed for voluntary production adjustment, resource protection, and price, market, and farm income stabilization.

Commodity Credit Corporation Estab. July 1, 1948 (first organized 1933). Stabilizes, supports, and protects farm income and prices; assists in maintaining balanced and adequate supplies of agricultural commodities and their products, and facilitates orderly distribution of commodities.

Extension Service Created 1914. As part of Cooperative Extension System—with land-grant universities, Tuskegee University, and 3,150 local county offices—links research, science, and technology to farmers' needs. Assists in science and technology transfer; mitigation of natural disasters and catastrophes.

Farmers Home Administration (FHA) Estab. by Consolidated Farm and Rural Development Act of 1921. Provides loans for farm and home ownership, natural resource conservation, farm improvement, and other needs for those unable to get credit from other sources at reasonable rates and terms.

Forest Service Created Feb. 1, 1905. Provides sustained flow of renewable resources to meet current and future needs. Manages 156 national forests, 19 national grasslands, 15 land utilization projects on 191 million acres in 44 states, the Virgin Islands, and Puerto Rico. Some 32 million acres are set aside as wilderness, and 175,000 acres as primitive areas where timber will not be harvested.

Rural Development Administration Estab. Dec. 31, 1991. Helps rural communities become more economically competitive through technical assistance and credit programs for rural community facilities, water and waste systems, and business and industry.

Rural Electrification Administration Estab. May 11, 1935, by executive order. Credit agency that helps obtain financing through loans, loan guarantees, or other assistance for construction, expansion, or improvement; has provided 1,000 rural electric and 1,000 rural telephone utilities in 47 states and in U.S. territories.

Soil Conservation Service Estab. 1935. Develops and implements soil and water conservation programs. Assists in agricultural pollution control, environmental improvement, and rural community development.

Department of Commerce 14th St. between Constitution Ave. and E St. NW, Washington, DC 20230. (202) 482–2000. Created Feb. 14, 1903, as part of Department of Commerce and Labor. Redesignated Department of Commerce by act of Mar. 4, 1913. Promotes international trade, economic growth, and technological advancement through encouragement of competitive free-enterprise system, prevention of unfair trade, granting of patents, economic promotion of domestic development, research in telecommunications, promotion of tourism, and assistance in growth of minority businesses. Department is divided into 12 operating units.

Bureau of the Census Estab. Mar. 6, 1902, by act of Congress. Collects, tabulates, and publishes census statistics about America, its people, and its economy. Statistics are used by Congress, president, and public to aid development and evaluation of public policy. Population and housing censuses are performed every 10 years. Censuses of agriculture, state and local governments, manufacturers, mineral industries, distributive trades, and construction and transportation industries are performed every five years. Special censuses are performed on demand from state and local governments.

Bureau of Economic Analysis (BEA) Estab. Dec. 1, 1953, by secretary of commerce. Prepares diagnoses of health of economy through compilation and assessment of economic indicators.

Bureau of Export Administration (BXA) Estab. Oct. 1, 1987, by secretary of commerce. Licenses exporters, advises on matters of economic export regulations, and enforces U.S. export control laws.

Economic Development Administration (EDA) Estab. by Public Works and Economic Development Act of 1965. Promotes new jobs, protects existing jobs, and stimulates job growth in areas where unemployment is high or incomes are low. Programs are carried out through sponsorship of industrial parks, water and sewer lines, and airport developments; loan guarantees to industrial and commercial firms; planning grants to states, cities, districts, and Indian reservations; technical assistance for existing firms; planning grants; and emergency aid to communities to avoid long-term economic deterioration.

International Trade Administration (ITA) Estab. Jan. 2, 1980. Promotes world trade and strengthens U.S. position in relation to world trade and investment.

Minority Business Development Agency (MBDA) Estab. Nov. 1, 1979. Promotes minority business. Ensures effective, equitable, and competitive participation by minority business in free enterprise system.

National Oceanic and Atmospheric Administration (NOAA) Estab. Oct. 3, 1970. Investigates and maps oceans of world. Discovers, utilizes, and conserves living resources of oceans. Monitors and predicts conditions of atmosphere, sun, and oceans; warns against deterioration of these conditions arising from natural and man-made events and circumstances. Provides weather reports and forecasts. Forecasts floods, hurricanes, and other weather-related natural disasters.

National Technical Information Service (NTIS) Clearinghouse for sale of government-sponsored research, development, and engineering reports. Its library exceeds 1.5 million titles.

National Telecommunications and Information Administration (NTIA) Estab. Mar. 27, 1978. Fosters development and use of telecommunication and information services.

Patent and Trademark Office (PTO) Estab. by Congress in Article I, Section 8 of Constitution. Promotes incentives to invent and make inventions public through granting of exclusive patents. Issues more than 75,000 patents and 55,000 trademarks every year. Patents are of three kinds: design, plant, and utility.

Technology Administration Estab. by Congress in 1988 and includes the Office of Technology, National Technical Information Service, and the National Institute of Standards and Technology. Works with U.S. industries to promote competitiveness and to maximize the impact of technology on economic growth.

United States Travel and Tourism Administration (USTTA) Estab. 1981 by National Tourism Policy Act of 1981. Ensures fullest utilization of U.S. tourism resources. Expands tourism where possible. Stimulates demand abroad for tourism in U.S.

Department of Defense (DOD) The Pentagon, Washington, DC 20301–1155. (703) 545–6700. Created by National Security Act Amendments of 1949. Provides necessary military forces to deter war and protect security of the country. Advises president on matters of war and military security. Includes 14 defense agencies, various field organizations, five colleges, four institutes, and two universities, as well as other offices in addition to those listed below. (See also "The National Defense.")

Organization of the Joint Chiefs of Staff Consists of chairman of Joint Chiefs of Staff; chief of staff of U.S. Army; chief of naval operations; chief of staff of U.S. Air Force; and commandant of Marine Corps. Advises and assists president and secretary of defense on most military issues. Assists president and secretary of defense in planning, direction, and allocation of strategic resources. Compares strengths and capabilities of American forces with those of potential adversaries.

Department of the Air Force Estab. Sept. 18, 1947, by National Security Act of 1947. Works in conjunction with other armed forces to protect peace and security of the U.S. Focuses on air missions and protecting American interests from invasion by air.

Department of the Army U.S. Army estab. June 14, 1775, by Continental Congress. Dept. of the Army estab. 1947 by National Security Act of 1947. Organizes, trains, and equips active and reserve forces to protect peace, security, welfare, and defense of U.S. Works in conjunction with other armed forces. Its mission focuses on land operations and maneuvers.

Department of the Navy U.S. Navy estab. Oct. 13, 1775, by Continental Congress. Dept. of the Navy estab. by act of Apr. 30, 1798. Protects U.S. from attack by sea. Encompasses Marine Corps. Maintains freedom of the seas. Seizes or defends naval bases. Supports and works together with other armed forces.

Department of Education 400 Maryland Ave. SW, Washington, DC 20202. (202) 708–5366. Created Oct. 17, 1979, by Department of Education Organization Act. Establishes policy for, administers, and coordinates almost all federal assistance to education. Department's budget includes funding for the following corporations:

American Printing House for the Blind Distributes Braille books, books on tape, and educational aids for the blind.

Gallaudet University Provides college education for deaf who need special facilities. Encourages further education and study by its students.

Howard University Has special responsibility for admission and education of black students.

National Institute for Literacy A joint effort of

the Secretaries of Education, Labor, and Health and Human Services, the institute is designed to enhance the national effort to eliminate illiteracy by the year 2000 by creating a national network.

National Technical Institute for the Deaf (NTID) (Rochester Institute of Technology) Educates large numbers of deaf students within university designed for hearing students. Helps deaf students adapt to and join mainstream American hearing society.

Department of Energy (DOE) 1000 Independence Ave. SW, Washington, DC 20585. (202) 586–5000. Created Oct. 1, 1977, by Department of Energy Organization Act. Coordinates and administrates energy functions of federal government, including research and development of energy technology, marketing federal power, energy conservation, nuclear weapons, and energy regulation.

Department of Health and Human Services (HHS) 200 Independence Ave. SW, Washington, DC 20201. (202) 619–0257. Created Apr. 11, 1953, as Department of Health, Education, and Welfare. Redesignated Department of Health and Human Services Oct. 17, 1979, by Department of Education Organization Act. Advises president in formulation of public policy regarding health, welfare, and income and security programs. Department is divided into the following operating administrations.

Administration on Aging Estab. by Older Americans Act of 1965. Advises secretary on the characteristics, circumstances, and needs of older people. Develops policies, plans, and programs designed to promote their welfare.

Administration for Children and Families Created Apr. 15, 1991. Advises secretary on programs and administrations ranging from combating developmental disabilities to finding deadbeat dads to providing support for Native American and Alaskan families.

Public Health Service (PHS) Estab. July 16, 1946, by Federal Security Agency Reorganization Plan II of 1946. Administers national social insurance program known as Social Security. (See also "Key Government Functions.")

Substances Abuse and Mental Health Services Administration Disseminates accurate and up-to-date information on and provides leadership in the prevention and treatment of addictive and mental disorders.

Health Care Financing Administration (HCFA) Estab. Mar. 8, 1977. Oversees Medicare and Medicaid Health Insurance and grant programs. (See also "Key Government Functions.")

Social Security Administration (SSA) Estab. July 16, 1946, by Federal Security Agency Reorganization Plan II of 1946. Administers national social insurance program known as Social Security. (See also "Key Government Functions.")

Department of Housing and Urban Development (HUD) 451 Seventh St. SW, Washington, DC 20410. (202) 708–1422. Created Nov. 9, 1965, by Department of Housing and Urban Development Act. Administers mortgage programs to help families become home owners. Fosters construction of new housing and renovation of existing rental housing. Provides aid for low-income families who cannot afford their rent. Enacts programs to prevent housing discrimination. Encourages strong private-sector housing industry. Department's program areas are considered neither bureaus nor administrations. They include Community Planning and Development, Fair Housing and Equal Opportunity Housing, Public and Indian Housing, Government National Mortgage Association, and Policy Development and Research. The field operations of HUD are carried out through a series of regional and field offices. Regional offices are located in Boston, New York, Philadelphia, Atlanta, Chicago, Fort Worth, Kansas City, Denver, San Francisco, and Seattle.

Department of the Interior 1849 C St. NW, Washington, DC 20240. (202) 208–3171. Created by act of Mar. 3, 1849. Principal U.S. conservation agency. Directs use and conservation of public lands and natural resources; administers over 500 million acres of federal land and has trust responsibilities for approximately 50 million acres, mostly Indian reservations. Prescribes use of land and water resources, fish and wildlife, national parks and historic places, and mineral resources; aids in preservation of American Indian reservation communities.

United States Fish and Wildlife Service Conserves and protects fish and wildlife and their habitats. Assesses environmental impact of pesticides, thermal pollution, hydroelectric dams, and nuclear power sites.

National Park Service Estab. by act of Aug. 25, 1916. Administers, protects, and maintains diverse system of national parks, monuments, historic areas, and recreation areas and encourages understanding of the historic value of these sites through lectures, tours, exhibits, and films. Operates campgrounds, concessions, and transportation services.

National Biological Survey Estab. in 1993 in order to gather, analyze, and distribute information about America's biological systems and their benefits to society. Provides support in making decisions regarding America's ecosystems.

Bureau of Mines Estab. July 1, 1910, by Organic Act of May 16, 1910. Ensures that U.S. has enough nonfuel minerals for security. Attempts to replace imported minerals with domestic ones. Seeks to suppress pollution, increase mine safety, and encourage recycling.

U.S. Geological Survey Estab. by act of Mar. 3, 1879. Identifies and classifies land, water, energy, and mineral resources. Investigates potential hazards such as earthquakes and volcanoes. Conducts topographic mapping.

Office of Surface Mining Reclamation and Enforcement (OSMRE) Estab. by Surface Mining Control and Reclamation Act of 1977. Protects society from adverse effects of coal mining. Ensures continuing surface coal mining without permanent damage to land and water resources.

Bureau of Indian Affairs Estab. 1824 as part of Department of War. Transferred to Department of Interior in 1849. Trains American Indian and Alaska native peoples to manage their own affairs under trust relationship to federal government. Facilitates public and private aid to advancement of these peoples.

Minerals Management Service (MMS) Estab. Jan. 19, 1982, by Secretarial Order No. 3071. Assesses nature, extent, value, and recoverability of leasable minerals on outer continental shelf. Collects royalties on use of these minerals.

Bureau of Land Management (BLM) Estab. July 16, 1946, by consolidation of the General Land Office and the Grazing Service. Manages 270 million acres of public lands primarily in Far West and in Alaska. Resources in these lands include timber, oil, gas, hard minerals, and wildlife habitats.

Bureau of Reclamation Estab. 1902 as Reclamation Service, within U.S. Geological Survey, by Reclamation Act of 1902. Renamed Bureau of Reclamation in 1923. Provides year-round water and irrigation supply for towns, farms, and industries in western states. Generates hydroelectric power, regulates rivers and flood control, and enhances fish and wildlife habitats.

Department of Justice Constitution Avenue and 10th St. NW, Washington, DC 20530. (202) 514–2000. Created by act of June 22, 1870. Enforces the law in the public interest. Ensures fair competition in free enterprise system; enforces drug, immigration, and naturalization laws; aids in law enforcement, crime prevention, crime detection, and prosecution and rehabilitation of criminals. Conducts all Supreme Court suits in which U.S. is party or is concerned. Advises president on legal matters. Encompassed in department's authority are seven bureaus.

Federal Bureau of Investigation (FBI) Estab. 1908. Principal investigative bureau of Justice Department. Investigates violations of federal law. Areas of primary concern are organized crime (including drug trafficking), terrorism, white-collar crime, and foreign counterintelligence. Gathers and reports facts, locates witnesses, and compiles evidence in federal cases.

Bureau of Prisons Imprisons and rehabilitates criminals convicted of federal crimes and sentenced to serve time in federal prison.

United States Marshals Service Provides security and support to federal court system. Apprehends federal fugitives. Ensures safety of federal witnesses. Executes court orders and arrest warrants. Maintains custody, manages, and sells property seized from criminals.

International Criminal Police Organization (INTERPOL) Estab. in 1923. Promotes international cooperation in prevention and suppression of international crime.

Immigration and Naturalization Service (INS) Estab. by act of Mar. 3, 1891. Controls immigration into U.S. by facilitating entry to qualified persons and denying admission to unqualified aliens. Deports illegal aliens already in U.S. Encourages and facilitates naturalization and citizenship.

Drug Enforcement Administration (DEA) Estab. July 1973. Investigates interstate drug-trafficking.

Enforces government regulations regarding manufacture, distribution, sale, and dispensing of controlled substances; manages national narcotics intelligence system; performs research, training, and information exchange to foster drug traffic prevention and control.

Office of Justice Programs (OJP) Estab. by Justice Assistance Act of 1984. Fosters cooperation and coordination among the various arms of criminal justice system to create more effective justice.

Department of Labor 200 Constitution Ave. NW, Washington, DC 20210. (202) 219–5000. Created by act of Mar. 4, 1913. Improves welfare and working conditions of wage earners. Guarantees minimum wages and overtime pay as well as unemployment insurance and workers' compensation. Prevents employment discrimination. Protects pension rights. Provides for job training programs. Strengthens collective bargaining. Helps workers find jobs. Pays special attention to labor-related needs of minority workers, old and young, women, and disabled people.

Employment and Training Administration (ETA) Provides employment security through unemployment insurance, worker dislocation programs, and federal-state employment service system. Trains or retrains and finds employment for disadvantaged workers through Job Training Partnership Act (JTPA).

Office of the American Workplace Estab. 1993 and designed to promote workplace programs that encourage competitiveness and better relations between labor and management.

Pension and Welfare Benefits Administration (PWBA) Estab. Sept. 2, 1974, by Employment Retirement Income Security Act of 1974. Requires private pension and welfare plan administrators to give participants summaries of pension and welfare plans. Keeps summaries on file. Regulates financial operations of pension and welfare plans.

Employment Standards Administration Administers and directs programs dealing with minimum wage and overtime requirements, wages for government-sponsored work, affirmative action, and workers' compensation.

Occupational Safety and Health Administration (OSHA) Estab. 1970 by Occupational Safety and Health Act. Promotes safety and health standards in workplace. Issues regulations, conducts investigations, issues citations, and proposes penalties for violations of health standards and regulations.

Mine Safety and Health Administration (MSHA) Estab. 1977 by Federal Mine Safety and Health Amendments Act of 1977. Responsible for all mine safety and health regulations. Issues regulations, investigates violations, assesses penalties for noncompliance, and in coordination with Department of Health and Human Services, improves mine safety and health research.

Bureau of Labor Statistics (BLS) Data-gathering agency. Collects, processes, interprets, and distributes data involving employment, unemployment, wages, family income and expenditures, workers' compensation, industrial relations, productivity, and technological change.

Veterans' Employment and Training Service (VETS) Maximizes training and employment opportunities for veterans and disabled. Ensures that legislation involving veterans is carried out by local public employment services and by private enterprise.

Department of State 2201 C St. NW, Washington, DC 20520. (202) 647–4000. Created by act of July 27, 1789, as Department of Foreign Affairs. Renamed Department of State by act of Sept. 15, 1789. Advises president on foreign policy. Formulates and executes policy to protect and defend American interests overseas. Negotiates treaties and agreements with foreign countries.

United States Mission to the United Nations Represents U.S. at UN. Carries out U.S. foreign policy as it relates to UN.

Foreign Service Maintains relations with more than 140 nations around world. Reports to State Department on developments relating to safety and welfare of U.S., its citizens, and their interests. Ambassadors to each country are personal representatives of the president and have full responsibility for carrying out U.S. foreign policy within the country. Ambassadors negotiate agreements between host country and U.S., explain and administer U.S. foreign policy, and maintain relations with government and public of host country.

Department of Transportation (DOT) 400 Seventh St. SW, Washington, DC 20590. (202) 366–4000. Created by act of Oct. 15, 1966. Establishes nation's comprehensive transportation policy. The following umbrella administrations are responsible for highway planning, development, and construction; urban mass transit; railroads; aviation; and the safety of waterways, ports, highways, and oil and gas pipelines. Decisions made in conjunction with state and local authorities have strong bearing on land planning, energy conservation, and resource utilization policies.

United States Coast Guard Estab. by act of Jan. 28, 1915. Included in Dept. of Transportation Apr. 1, 1967. Coast Guard is at all times a branch of armed forces and a service with Dept. of Transportation except when operating as part of navy during war. Primary maritime law enforcement agency for U.S. Suppresses drug smuggling and trafficking. Licenses marine vessels. Administers and inspects violations of safety standards for design, construction, equipment, and maintenance of commercial marine vessels and offshore structures in U.S. waters. Provides search and rescue functions for saving lives and property in U.S. waters. Provides flood relief and removes hazards to navigation. Enforces rules ensuring safe and orderly navigation through ports, waterways, and bridges. Operates ice-breaking vessels to facilitate marine transportation. Provides military and reserve training.

Federal Aviation Administration (FAA) Estab. 1958 by Federal Aviation Act. Included in Dept. of Transportation in 1967 by Dept. of Transportation Act. Regulates air commerce in effort to promote safety and secure national defense interests. Directs use of navigable U.S. airspace. Promotes and encourages civil aeronautics. Installs and operates air-navigation facilities. Develops and operates system of air traffic control for both civil and military aircraft. Regulates aircraft noise and other environmental effects of civil aviation.

Federal Highway Administration (FHWA) Included in Dept. of Transportation in 1967 by Dept. of Transportation Act. Promotes highway safety. Provides aid for construction and maintenance of state and federal highway systems. Facilitates and provides aid for safety improvements to state and federal highway systems. Helps states formulate agreed-upon size and weight regulations for trucks and commercial traffic. Administers highway planning and beautification programs.

Federal Railroad Administration (FRA) Estab. 1966 by section 3(e)(1) of Dept. of Transportation Act of 1966. Administers and enforces railroad safety regulations such as track maintenance, inspection and equipment standards, and operating practices. Maintains research and development programs and Transportation Test Center to foster further safety and efficiency of rail travel.

National Highway Traffic Safety Administration Estab. 1970 by Highway Safety Act of 1970. Promotes highway safety through various programs. These include enforcing a uniform and nationwide speed limit, administering laws to prevent odometer tampering, issuing theft prevention standards, setting average fuel-economy and air-pollution standards for motor vehicles, and enforcing inspection standards. Research and development programs are aimed at reducing number of highway collisions, reducing severity of injuries and economic loss involved in highway accidents, and reducing fatalities resulting from highway crashes.

Federal Transit Administration Estab. July 1, 1968, by Reorganization Plan No. 2 of 1968, Section 3. Improves equipment and methods used in urban mass transit. Encourages planning of cost-effective mass transit systems. Provides economic and technical assistance for mass transit programs. Encourages private sector involvement in local mass-transit systems.

Maritime Administration (MARAD) Estab. May 24, 1950, by Reorganization Plan No. 21 of 1950. Included in Dept. of Transportation Aug. 6, 1981, by Maritime Act of 1981. Constructs or supervises construction of U.S.-flag merchant ships for federal government. Generates business for U.S. ships. Develops ports and facilities for maritime transport. Promotes domestic shipping. Provides economic and technical aid to private shipbuilding. Regulates sales of ships.

Saint Lawrence Seaway Development Corporation Estab. by act of May 13, 1954. Owns, develops, maintains, and operates St. Lawrence Seaway between Montreal and Lake Erie within territorial limits of U.S. Provides safe and efficient waterway for maritime commerce. Charges user tolls and encourages traffic. Operates in coordination with Canadian owners, St. Lawrence Seaway Authority of Canada.

Research and Special Programs Administration (RSPA) Estab. Sept. 23, 1977; reorganized 1985. Its six umbrella organizations regulate transportation of hazardous materials; enforce safety standards for pipeline transportation of liquid and gaseous materials involved in or affecting interstate commerce; maintain information and research offices devoted to transportation, safety, and economics of aviation; and prepare emergency transportation programs.

Bureau of Transportation Statistics Estab. by Transportation Efficiency Act of 1991. Compiles, analyzes, and publishes transportation statistics. Develops guidelines to improve credibility and effectiveness of Transportation Department statistics.

Department of the Treasury 1500 Pennsylvania Ave. NW, Washington, DC 20220. (202) 622–2000. Created by act of Sept. 2, 1789. Formulates and recommends economic, financial, tax, and fiscal policies. Acts as financial agent for U.S. government. Manufactures coins and currency. Department is divided into 12 bureaus, offices, and administrations.

Bureau of Alcohol, Tobacco and Firearms Estab. July 1, 1972, by Treasury Dept. Order No. 221. Enforces and administers laws regulating production, use, distribution, and sale of alcohol and tobacco products, firearms, and explosives. Bureau's objectives are to eliminate illegal trafficking, possession, and use of firearms and explosives, to suppress illegal alcohol and tobacco trafficking, and to ensure safety of storage facilities for explosives.

Office of the Comptroller of the Currency Estab. by act of Feb. 25, 1863. Issues and executes laws regulating national banks. Inspects, examines, and issues official approvals of national banks, their operations, and their financial soundness.

United States Customs Service Estab. Mar. 3, 1927, as Bureau of Customs. Redesignated Customs Service Apr. 4, 1973, by Treasury Dept. Order 165–23. Collects revenue from imports. Enforces customs treaties. Assesses and collects customs duties, excise taxes, fees, and penalties on imported merchandise. Seizes contraband including narcotics and illegal drugs. Processes people, mail, carriers, and cargo in and out of U.S. Apprehends violators of U.S. customs regulations and related laws including copyright, patent, and trademark, and import quotas. Suppresses traffic of illegal narcotics, pornography, counterfeit monetary instruments, and quarantined animals, plants, and foods.

Bureau of Engraving and Printing Estab. by act of July 11, 1862. Designs, prints, and finishes Federal Reserve notes, U.S. postage stamps, identification cards, and Treasury securities. Inhibits counterfeiting of these documents.

Federal Law Enforcement Training Center Estab. Mar. 2, 1970, by Treasury Dept. Order 217. Teaches basic law-enforcement skills to police and investigators. Also teaches courses in white-collar crime, computer crime, law enforcement photography, contract fraud, and marine law enforcement.

Financial Management Service Manages money of federal government. Improves cash management, credit management, and debt collection and payment programs. Invests social security and other trust funds. Serves as government's central accounting system. Publishes daily, monthly, and quarterly reports of government's financial operations and status.

Internal Revenue Service (IRS) Estab. by act of July 1, 1862. Administers and enforces internal revenue laws except those relating to alcohol, tobacco, firearms, and explosives. Determines, assesses, and collects federal tax revenues from public. Encourages, assesses, and enforces compliance with tax laws.

United States Mint Mint of the United States estab. by act of Apr. 2, 1792. Bureau of the Mint estab. Feb. 12, 1873. Renamed United States Mint Jan. 9, 1984, by Secretarial Order. Manufactures and distributes coins for circulation through Federal Reserve Banks. Mints foreign coins. Processes gold and silver bullion. Manufactures national medals, proof coin sets, and commemorative coins for sale to public.

Bureau of the Public Debt Estab. June 30, 1940, by Reorganization Act of 1939. Manages public debt. Offers public-debt securities. Audits retired securities and interest coupons. Maintains accounting control over public-debt receipts and expenditures, securities, and interest costs. Adjudicates claims of lost, stolen, or destroyed securities.

United States Savings Bonds Division Estab. Dec. 26, 1945, by Treasury Order. Promotes sale and retention of U.S. Savings Bonds. Encourages support and understanding of Savings Bonds program.

United States Secret Service Protects president and vice president (and president-elect and vice president-elect) of U.S. and their families. Protects former presidents and their wives until their death. Protects distinguished foreign visitors and U.S. officials abroad at direction of president. Detects and apprehends counterfeiters. Suppresses forgery of government securities and documents. Provides security at White House complex, vice president's residence, and various foreign diplomatic missions or embassies as directed by president.

Office of Thrift Supervision (OTS) 1700 G St. NW, Washington, DC 20552. (202) 906–6913. Estab. by the Financial Institutions Reform, Recovery and Enforcement Act, Aug. 9, 1989. Established by Congress as part of a reorganization of the thrift regulatory structure, the OTS has authority to charter federal thrift institutions, and to serve as the primary regulator of the approximately 2,600 federal and state chartered thrifts belonging to the Savings Association Insurance Fund (SAIF).

Department of Veterans Affairs 810 Vermont Ave. NW, Washington, DC 20420. (202) 273–4900. Estab. by Department of Veterans Affairs Act of 1988; predecessor Veterans Administration created 1930. Administers benefit programs for veterans and their families, including military-related death or disability compensation, pensions, education and rehabilitation, home loan guaranty, and medical care programs.

Veterans Health Services and Research Administration Provides hospital, nursing home, and domiciliary care and outpatient care to eligible veterans. Operates 171 medical centers, 35 domiciliaries, 340 outpatient clinics, 127 nursing home care units, and 196 Vietnam Veteran Outreach Centers.

Veterans Benefit Administration Has responsibility for claims for disability compensation and pension, specially adapted housing and automobiles, special clothing allowances, and emergency officers' retirement pay, survivors' claims for death compensation, dependency and indemnity compensation, burial and plot allowance claims, and reimbursement for headstones.

National Cemetery System Provides services and monuments for graves of veterans, their spouses, and eligible dependents in 112 national, state, and private veterans' cemeteries and aid to states for establishment and improvement of veterans' cemeteries. Cemeteries are designated national shrines.

INDEPENDENT ESTABLISHMENTS, CORPORATIONS, AND QUASI-OFFICIAL AGENCIES

Administrative Conference of the United States 2120 L Street NW, Washington, DC 20037. (202) 254–7020. Created in 1964 by Administrative Conference Act. Develops improvements in federal administration of government programs. Agency heads meet with lawyers, university professors, and other experts to exchange ideas, share experiences and judgments, and conduct studies at this forum.

African Development Foundation 1400 Eye St. NW, Washington, DC 20005. (202) 673–3916. Created in 1984 by African Development Foundation Act. Nonprofit government corporation. Through grants, loans, and loan guarantees, aids self-help efforts by poor people in African countries. Fosters stronger bonds between Africa and United States. Stimulates and assists expansion and development by Africans in their respective nations.

AMTRAK (National Railroad Passenger Corporation) 60 Massachusetts Ave. NE, Washington, DC 20002. (202) 906–3000. Created by Rail Passenger Service Act of 1970. Develops, operates, and improves intercity rail passenger service to create national rail transportation system. Operates 210 trains per day, serving over 500 stations on 24,000 miles of track.

Central Intelligence Agency (CIA) Washington, DC 20505. (703) 482–1100. Created by National Security Act of 1947. Under direction of president and National Security Council. Advises NSC on intelligence matters of national security. Collects, evaluates, and disseminates intelligence information relating to national security and to drug production and trafficking. Collects, produces, and disseminates counterintelligence and foreign intelligence here (in conjunction with FBI) and abroad. Conducts special activities as directed by president. Protects security of its activities, information, and personnel by necessary and appropriate means.

Commission on Civil Rights (CCR) 624 9th St. NW., Washington DC 20425. (202) 376–8177; for deaf and hearing impaired (202) 376–8116. Created by Civil Rights Act of 1957. Holds public hearings and collects and studies information on discrimination or denial of equal protection based on race, color, religion, sex, age, disability, or national origin. Studies in particular fair enforcement of civil rights laws and guarantee of voting rights and equal opportunity in education, employment, and housing.

Commodity Futures Trading Commission (CFTC) 2033 K St. NW, Washington, DC 20581. (202) 254–6387. Created May 14, 1973, by Commodity Futures Act of 1973. Regulates trading on the 11 U.S. futures exchanges. Regulates activities of commodity exchange members, public brokerage houses, commodity trading advisers, and other related employees. Ensures fair futures trading. Protects rights of customers and financial integrity of marketplace.

Consumer Product Safety Commission (CPSC) East-West Towers, 4330 East-West Highway, Bethesda, Md 20814. (301) 504–0580. Created May 14, 1973, by Consumer Product Safety Act. Protects public from unreasonable risk of injury from consumer products. Develops, enforces, and evaluates safety standards for consumer products.

Defense Nuclear Facilities Safety Board Suite 700, 625 Indiana Ave. NW, Washington, DC 20004. (202) 208–6400. Created Sept. 29, 1988, by Atomic Energy Act of 1954 as amended. Reviews and evaluates content and implementation of standards relating to design, construction, operation, and decommissioning of defense nuclear facilities of the Dept. of Energy.

Environmental Protection Agency (EPA) 401 M St. SW, Washington, DC 20460. (202) 260–2090. Created Dec. 2, 1970, by Reorganization Plan No. 3 of 1970. Protects and enhances environment. Controls and reduces pollution of air and water. Regulates solid-waste disposal and use of pesticides, radiation, and toxic substances.

Equal Employment Opportunity Commission (EEOC) 1801 L St. NW, Washington, DC 20507. (202) 663–4900; (800) 669-EEOC. Created July 2, 1965, by Title VII of Civil Rights Act of 1964. Protects against discrimination based on race, color, handicap, religion, sex, age, and national origin in hiring, promoting, firing, wages, testing, training, apprenticeship, and all other terms and conditions of employment.

Export-Import Bank of the United States 811 Vermont Ave. NW, Washington, DC 20571. (202) 566–8990. Created Feb. 2, 1934, by Executive Order 6581. Facilitates and aids exports of U.S. goods and services through loans, loan guarantees, and insurance to exporters and private banks.

Farm Credit Administration 1501 Farm Credit Drive, McLean, VA 22102–5090. (703) 883–4056. Created by Farm Credit Act of 1971. Regulates and examines programs, banks, associations, and organizations of the Farm Credit System, which provides credit to farmers, ranchers, producers of farm products, rural home owners, and associations and organizations of farmers, ranchers, and farm-equipment producers.

Federal Communications Commission (FCC) 1919 M Street NW, Washington, DC 20554. (202) 632–7000. Created by Communications Act of 1934. Regulates interstate and foreign communications by radio, television, wire, and cable. Oversees development of broadcast services and rapid and efficient provision of telephone and telegraph services nationwide.

Federal Deposit Insurance Corporation (FDIC) 550 17th St. NW, Washington, DC 20429. (202) 393–8400. Created June 16, 1933, by Federal Reserve Act. Protects money supply by insuring deposits in and reviewing operations of state-chartered banks that are not members of Federal Reserve System. Assumed responsibility for insuring savings and loan institutions formerly insured by defunct Federal Savings and Loan Insurance Corp. (FSLIC) in 1989.

Federal Election Commission (FEC) 999 E St. NW, Washington, DC 20463. (202) 219–3420; (800) 424–9530. Created by Federal Election Campaign Act of 1971. Provides public funding for presidential elections. Ensures public disclosure of campaign finance activities. Administers and enforces contribution and spending limits for federal elections. (See also "U.S. Presidential Elections.")

Federal Emergency Management Agency (FEMA) 500 C St. SW, Washington, DC 20472. (202) 646–4600. Created Mar. 31, 1979, by Reorganization Plan No. 3 of 1978. Provides single point of accountability for all federal emergency preparedness, mitigation, and response activities. Facilitates most efficient use of resources in cases of natural or man-made emergencies.

Federal Housing Finance Board 1777 F St. NW, Washington, DC 20006. (202) 408–2500. Created Aug. 9, 1989, by Financial Institutions Reform, Recovery, and Enforcement Act of 1989. Succeeds Federal Home Loan Bank Board; administers and enforces Federal Home Loan Bank Act as amended.

Federal Labor Relations Authority (FLRA) 607 14th St. NW, Washington, DC 20424. (202) 482–6550. Created Jan. 1, 1979, by Reorganization Plan No. 2 of 1978. Protects rights of federal employees to organize, bargain collectively, and participate in labor organizations. Oversees rights and obligations of federal employees and labor organizations that represent them.

Federal Maritime Commission 800 North Capitol St. NW, Washington, DC 20573–0001. (202) 523–5707. Created Aug. 12, 1961, by Reorganization Plan No. 7 of 1961. Regulates foreign and domestic maritime offshore commerce. Keeps U.S. international trade open and fair to all nations. Protects against unauthorized activity in U.S. waterborne commerce.

Federal Mediation and Conciliation Service 2100 K St. NW, Washington, DC 20427. (202) 653–5290. Created in 1947 by Labor Management Relations Act. Promotes development of stable labor-management relations. Prevents or minimizes work stoppages by helping to settle disputes and by advocating collective bargaining, mediation, and arbitration.

Federal Mine Safety and Health Review Commission 1730 K St. NW, Washington, DC 20006. (202) 653–5625. Estab. by Federal Mine Safety and Health Amendments Act of 1977. Quasi-judicial agency that decides cases brought by Mine Safety and Health Board, mine operators, and miners.

Federal Reserve System Board of Governors of Federal Reserve System. 20th St. and Constitution Ave. NW, Washington, DC 20551. (202) 452–3000. Created Dec. 23, 1913, by Federal Reserve Act. Central bank of U.S. Administers and creates national credit and monetary policy. Regulates money supply. Maintains soundness of banking industry.

Federal Retirement Thrift Investment Board 1250 H Street NW, Washington, DC 20005. (202) 942–1600. Created by Federal Employees' Retirement System Act of 1986. Administers Thrift Savings Plan for federal employees.

Federal Trade Commission (FTC) Pennsylvania Ave. at Sixth St. NW, Washington, DC 20580. (202) 326–2222. Created in 1914 by Federal Trade Commission Act and Clayton Act. Maintains free and fair competition in free enterprise system. Breaks up monopolies. Seeks to prevent corruption, restraints on trade, and unfair trade practices.

General Services Administration (GSA) General Service Building, 18th and F Sts. NW, Washington, DC 20405, (202) 708–5082; (202) 501–0705. Created July 1, 1949, by Federal Property and Administrative Services Act of 1949. Establishes policy for and manages government property and records, construction of buildings, distribution of supplies, and other government services. Its services are divided among four service agencies.

Information Resources Management Services (IRMS) Coordinates and manages government's information distribution systems and programs. Facilitates use of automated data processing and telecommunications equipment, improves federal records and information, and manages and operates Federal Information Centers.

Federal Supply Service (FSS) Contracts and distributes supplies, services, and property to federal agencies worldwide.

Public Buildings Service (PBS) Oversees design, building, appraisal, repair, operation, and maintenance of most federally controlled buildings.

Federal Property Resources Service (FPRS) Utilizes and disposes of government-owned real estate. Acquires, sells, and manages National Defense Stockpile of strategic and critical materials.

Inter-American Foundation 901 North Stuart St., Arlington, VA 22203. (703) 841–3800. Created by Congress in 1969. Supports social and economic development in Latin America and Caribbean. Makes grants to self-help organizations for the poor.

Interstate Commerce Commission (ICC) 12th St. and Constitution Ave. NW, Washington, DC 20423. (202) 927–7119. Created by act of Feb. 4,

1887. Regulates interstate transportation involved in commerce. Certifies interstate carriers. Ensures fair rates and services to public.

Legal Services Corporation 750 First St. NE, Washington, DC 20002. (202) 336–8800. Created by Legal Services Corporation Act of 1974. Makes legal assistance for noncriminal proceedings available to those who would otherwise be unable to afford it.

Merit Systems Protection Board (MSPB) 1120 Vermont Ave. NW, Washington, DC 20419 (202) 653–7124. Created Jan. 1, 1979, to succeed United States Civil Service Commission (estab. Jan. 16, 1883). Oversees personnel practices of government. Hears and decides charges of wrongdoing and orders corrective and disciplinary action against agencies when necessary. (See also "Office of Special Counsel.")

National Aeronautics and Space Administration (NASA) 300 E Street SW, Washington, DC 20546. (202) 358–1000. Created by National Aeronautics and Space Act of 1958. Develops, constructs, tests, and operates vehicles for in-flight research within and outside Earth's atmosphere. Disseminates information about space exploration and agency's activities.

National Archives and Records Administration (NARA) Seventh St. and Pennsylvania Ave. NW, Washington, DC 20408. (202) 501–5400. Created by act of Oct. 19, 1984. Establishes policy for managing records of U.S. government and making them available to public. Maintains 11 regional archives and 14 federal records centers, as well as 11 presidential libraries or collections.

National Capital Planning Commission (NCPC) Suite 301, 801 Pennsylvania Ave. NW, Washington, DC 20576. (202) 724–0174. Created by National Capital Planning Act of 1952. Coordinates planning and development activities in National Capital region, which includes Washington DC, Montgomery and Prince Georges Counties in Maryland, and Fairfax, Loudon, Prince William, and Arlington Counties in Virginia.

National Credit Union Administration (NCUA) 1775 Duke St., Alexandria, VA 22314–3428. (703) 518–6300. Created by act of Mar. 10, 1970. Charters, insures, supervises, and examines federal credit unions. Administers National Credit Union Share Insurance Fund. Supplies emergency loans to credit unions through Central Liquidity Facility. Credit unions are financial cooperatives that encourage thrift and provide credit at reasonable rates to their members.

National Foundation on the Arts and the Humanities 1100 Pennsylvania Ave. NW, Washington, DC 20506. (202) 682–5400. Created by National Foundation on the Arts and the Humanities Act of 1965. Its three divisions encourage and support national progress in humanities and arts. *National Endowment for the Arts (NEA)* (202) 682–5400. Fosters professional excellence in arts. Creates climate for arts to flourish and be appreciated, experienced, and enjoyed by the public. *National Endowment for the Humanities (NEH)* (202) 606–8438. Independent grant-making agency supports research, education, and public programs in humanities. *Institute of Museum Services (IMS)* (202) 606–8536. Independent grant-making agency assists museums in maintaining, increasing, and improving services to the public.

National Labor Relations Board (NLRB) 1099 14th Street NW, Washington, DC 20570. (202) 273–1000. Created by National Labor Relations Act of 1935 (also known as Wagner Act). Administers federal labor law. Safeguards employees' rights to organize, conducts elections to determine whether workers want unions as their bargaining representative, and prevents or remedies unfair labor practices.

National Mediation Board 1301 K Street NW, Suite 250 East, Washington, DC 20572. (202) 523–5920. Created June 21, 1934, by amendment to Railway Labor Act. Resolves and investigates representation disputes in railroad and airline industries that could interrupt flow of commerce and endanger national economy. These disputes include grievances over wages, hours, and working conditions. Supervises representation disputes in the two industries.

National Railroad Passenger Corporation See "AMTRAK."

National Science Foundation (NSF) 4201 Wilson Blvd., Arlington, VA 22230. (703) 306–1234. Created by National Science Foundation Act of 1950. Promotes progress of science and engineering through support of research and education programs. Educational programs are designed to facilitate increased understanding of science and engineering and to ensure adequate supply of scientists for country's needs.

National Transportation Safety Board (NTSB) 490 L'Enfant Plaza SW, Washington, DC 20594. (202) 382–6600. Created Apr. 1, 1975, by Independent Safety Board Act of 1974. Ensures safe operation of all types of transportation in U.S. Investigates accidents, conducts studies, and makes policy recommendations to government agencies, transportation industry, and others on ways to implement and improve safety measures and programs.

Nuclear Regulatory Commission (NRC) Washington, DC 20555. (301) 492–7000. Created by Energy Reorganization Act of 1974. Licenses and regulates uses of civilian nuclear energy to protect public health and environment. Sets licensing regulations, issues licenses for, and inspects construction, ownership, and operation of nuclear reactors and other nuclear materials.

Occupational Safety and Health Review Commission (OSHRC) 1120 20th Street NW, Washington, DC 20036. (202) 606–5100. Created by Occupational Safety and Health Act of 1970. Adjudicates disputes forwarded by Department of Labor over results of safety and health inspections performed by Occupational Safety and Health Administration (OSHA). Serves as court of both first and last resort for health and safety violations in workplace.

Office of Government Ethics Suite 500, 1201 New York Ave. NW, Washington, DC 20005–3917. (202) 523–5757. Created Oct. 1, 1989, by Ethics in Government Act of 1978, as amended. Provides overall direction for executive branch policies to prevent conflicts of interest on the part of officers and employees of all executive agencies.

Office of Personnel Management (OPM) 1900 E St. NW, Washington, DC 20415. (202) 606–1800. Created Jan. 1, 1979, by Reorganization Plan No. 2 of 1978. Recruits, examines, trains, and promotes people for government jobs, regardless of race, religion, sex, political influence, and other nonmerit factors. Provides direct benefits to employees and to retired employees and their survivors.

Office of Special Counsel Suite 300, 1730 M Street NW, Washington, DC 20036. (202) 653–7188; (800) 872–9855. Estab. Jan. 1, 1979. Investigates allegations of certain activities prohibited by civil service laws, rules, or regulations before the Merit Systems Protection Board. Protects whistleblowers from reprisals from their employers or former employers for reporting statutory violations.

Panama Canal Commission 1825 Eye St. NW, Suite 1050, Washington, DC 20006. (202) 634–6441. Created by Panama Canal Act of 1979. Operates, maintains, and improves the Panama Canal to provide safe and economical transit for world shipping. Will perform these functions until expiration of Panama Canal Treaty of 1979 on Dec. 31, 1999, when Republic of Panama will assume full responsibility for canal.

Peace Corps 1990 K St. NW, Washington, DC 20526. (202) 606–3886; (800) 424–8580. Created by Peace Corps Act of 1961. Promotes world peace and friendship. Helps people of other countries develop manpower. Promotes understanding of American people by people abroad and vice versa. Special emphasis placed on helping poorest areas of countries served by the Peace Corps.

Pennsylvania Avenue Development Corporation (PADC) Suite 1220 North, 1331 Pennsylvania Ave. NW, Washington, DC 20004–1703. (202) 724–9091. Created by act of Oct. 27, 1972. Guides and oversees development and revitalization of Pennsylvania Avenue between White House and Capitol and adjacent blocks north of the avenue.

Pension Benefit Guaranty Corporation (PBGC) 1200 K St. NW, Washington, DC 20005. (202) 326–4000. Created Sept. 2, 1974, by Title IV of Employee Retirement Income Security Act of 1974. Guarantees payment of nonforfeitable pension benefits in covered private-sector defined benefit pension plans.

Postal Rate Commission 1333 H St. NW, Washington, DC 20268–0001. (202) 789–6800. Created Aug. 12, 1970, by Postal Reorganization Act. Recommends changes in postal rates, fees, services, programs, studies, and mail classification schedules. Hears complaints about postal rates, services, and fees.

Railroad Retirement Board 844 N. Rush St., Chicago, IL 60611. (312) 751–4776. Created by Railroad Retirement Act of 1935. Administers retirement-survivor and unemployment-sickness benefit programs for railroad workers and their families under Railroad Retirement and Railroad Unemployment Insurance Acts.

Resolution Trust Corporation (RTC) 801 17th St. NW, Washington, DC 20434. (202) 416–6900. Estab. by the Financial Institutions Reform, Recovery and Enforcement Act, Aug. 9, 1989. The RTC is a federally chartered corporation the sole purpose of which is to contain, manage, and resolve failed savings associations acquired from the defunct Federal Savings and Loan Insurance Corporation (FSLIC)—or new insolvencies acquired from the Office of Thrift Supervision (OTS)—and to recover funds through the management and ultimate sale of the institutions' assets.

Securities and Exchange Commission (SEC) 450 Fifth St. NW, Washington, DC 20549. (202) 272–3100. Created July 2, 1934, by Securities Exchange Act of 1934. Provides fullest possible disclosure to the public of securities sales, operations, and registrations. Protects public against malpractice in securities and financial markets.

Selective Service System National Headquarters, Arlington, VA 22209–2425. (703) 235–2555. Created June 24, 1948, by Military Selective Service Act. Requires registration, and maintains list of males age 18–26 eligible to serve in armed forces in case of national security emergency.

Small Business Administration (SBA) 409 Third St. SW, Washington, DC 20416. (202) 205–6533; (800) 827–5722. Created by Small Business Act of 1953. Aids, counsels, makes loans to, and protects interests of small businesses; ensures that they receive fair amount of government purchases and contracts and sales of government property.

Smithsonian Institution 1000 Jefferson Drive SW, Washington, DC 20560. (202) 357–1300; (202) 357–1729 (hearing impaired). Created by act of Aug. 10, 1846. Performs fundamental research; publishes results of studies, explorations, and investigations; preserves for study and research more than 100 million items of scientific, cultural, and historical interest. Maintains exhibits representative of arts, American history, technology, aeronautics, and natural history. Many institutions and museums are under direction of Smithsonian. Most prominent are Arthur M. Sackler Gallery (Cambridge, Mass.), Cooper-Hewitt Museum of Design (New York City), National Air and Space Museum, National Zoological Park, Smithsonian Astrophysical Laboratories, National Gallery of Art, and John F. Kennedy Center for the Performing Arts (Washington, DC).

State Justice Institute Suite 600, 1650 King St., Alexandria, VA 22314. (703) 684–6100. Created by State Justice Institute Act of 1984. Directs and ensures protection of fair and effective judicial system, fosters cooperation with federal judiciary, and disseminates information regarding state judicial systems.

Tennessee Valley Authority (TVA) 400 West Summit Hill Dr., Knoxville, TN 37902–2003. (615) 632–2101. 1 Massachusetts Ave. NW, Washington, DC 20444–0001. (202) 898–2999. Created by act of May 18, 1933. Government-owned corporation. Conducts resource development programs for advancement of growth in Tennessee Valley region. Controls floods, develops navigation, produces electric power, develops fertilizer, improves recreation, and develops forestry and wildlife.

Thrift Depositor Protection Oversight Board 808 17th St. NW, Washington, DC 20232. (202) 416–2650. Formerly the Oversight Board, estab. by the Federal Home Bank Act amendments of Aug. 9, 1989. Responsible for general oversight of the Resolution Trust Corporation (RTC) and the Resolution Funding Corporation (REFCORP). Develops and establishes strategies, policies, and goals for the RTC's activities; also reviews the RTC's performance relative to approved budget plans pursuant to the terms of the Financial Institutions Reform, Recovery and Enforcement Act.

Trade and Development Agency Room 309, State Annex 16, Washington, DC 20523–1602. (703) 875–4357. Estab. July 1, 1980, as component of International Development Cooperation Agency. Made an independent agency Oct. 28, 1992, by Jobs Through Export Act of 1992. Promotes economic development in, and the export of U.S. goods to, developing and middle-income countries.

United States Arms Control and Disarmament Agency (ACDA) 320 21st St. NW, Washington, DC 20451. (202) 647–8677. Created by act of Sept. 26, 1961. Formulates and implements arms control and disarmament policies to promote security and foreign relations. Prepares and participates in negotiations on strategic arms limitations, mutual force reductions in central Europe, chemical weapons, worldwide arms trade, and other issues.

United States Information Agency (USIA) 301 Fourth St. SW, Washington, DC 20547. (202) 619–4700. Created by United States Information and Educational Exchange Act of 1948 and Mutual Educational and Cultural Exchange Act of 1961. Oversees and administers overseas information and cultural programs, including Voice of America and Fulbright scholarship program. Strengthens foreign understanding of American society and tries to obtain support abroad for U.S. foreign policies. Advises president and National Security Council on worldwide opinion of U.S. policies.

United States Institute of Peace 1550 M St. NW, Washington, DC 20005–1708. (202) 457–1700. Created by act of Oct. 19, 1984. Develops and disseminates knowledge about peaceful resolution of international conflicts. Provides grants to other institutions promoting peace through development and dissemination of information.

United States International Development Cooperation Agency (IDCA) 320 21st St. NW, Washington, DC 20523–0001. (202) 647–1850. Created Oct. 1, 1979, by Reorganization Plan No. 2 of 1979. Plans, sets, and coordinates policy relevant to international economic issues affecting developing countries. Ensures that development goals are considered in all executive-branch policies regarding trade, financing and monetary affairs, technology, and other economic issues. It is divided into two umbrella agencies.

Agency for International Development (AID) Carries out economic assistance and self-help programs for people in developing countries. Improves human and natural resources, quality of life, and political and economic stability.

Overseas Private Investment Corporation (OPIC) Facilitates, fosters, and encourages U.S. investments in more than 100 foreign countries that both reap profits for investors and help social and economic development of the countries.

United States International Trade Commission 500 E St. SW, Washington, DC 20436. (202) 205–2000. Created by act of Sept. 8, 1916. Furnishes studies, reports, and recommendations regarding international trade and tariffs to president, Congress, and other government agencies. Conducts investigations, public hearings, and research projects pertaining to U.S. international economic policies.

United States Postal Service 475 L'Enfant Plaza SW, Washington, DC 20260–0010. (202) 268–2000. Created Aug. 12, 1970, by Postal Reorganization Act. Provides mail-processing and delivery service to individuals and businesses in U.S. Protects mail from loss or theft and apprehends violators of postal laws.

SOME INTERNET ADDRESSES IN THE EXECUTIVE BRANCH

Countless information is available over the Internet from hundreds of federal agencies. These are the Internet addresses of just a few government departments. Each address may have dozens of subdirectories from which to select information.

Agency	Location and address	
The White House	World Wide Web	http://www.whitehouse.gov/
Dept. of Agriculture	World Wide Web	http://web.fie.com/web/fed/agr
Dept. of Commerce	World Wide Web	http://www.doc.gov/
Dept. of Defense	World Wide Web	http://www.whitehouse.gov/White House/Cabinet/html/ Department of Defense.html
Dept. of Education	World Wide Web	http://www.ed.gov/
	Gopher	gopher.ed.gov
Dept. of Energy	World Wide Web	http://apollo.osti.gov/home.html
Dept. of Health and Human Services	World Wide Web	http://www.os.dhhs.gov/
	Gopher	gopher.os.dhhs.gov
Dept. of HUD	World Wide Web	http://web.fie.com/web/fed/hud
Dept. of the Interior	World Wide Web	http://info.er.usgs.gov/doi/doi.html
Dept. of Justice	Gopher	justice2.usdoj.gov
Dept. of Transportation	World Wide Web	http://www.dot.gov
	Gopher	depository.dot.gov
Dept. of the Treasury	World Wide Web	http://www.ustreas.gov
Dept. of Veterans Affairs	World Wide Web	http://www.va.gov

Federal Employees and Budget

FEDERAL JOBS AND SALARIES

As of Mar. 31, 1994, there were 1,951,507 full-time nonpostal federal civilian employees. Nearly 97 percent of the federal civilian work force was employed in the United States; 14,029 (0.7%) worked in U.S. territories, and 47,965 (2.4%) worked in foreign countries. The majority of government employees worked in metropolitan statistical areas, led by the Washington, D.C., MSA, with 305,537, or 15.7 percent of the total.

Four executive departments accounted for nearly 70 percent of the federal civilian work force. The Department of Defense employed 851,178 civilians (43.6% of the total), Veterans Affairs (218,079 or 11.2%), the Treasury (162,345 or 8.3%), and Health and Human Services (116,701 or 6.0%).

Federal government civilian employees are paid according to a number of different systems: the General Schedule (GS), Federal Wage Systems, and other acts and administratively determined systems. Overall, the average salary for full-time civilian government employees was $39,129, a 4.8 percent increase from the previous year. Employees under the General Schedule on average earned more than those on Federal Wage Systems ($39,070 to $31,299), but not as much as employees covered by other acts and administrative determinations, who averaged $51,996. Average salaries by major geographic areas were: United States, $39,214; Washington, D.C., area, $48,962; foreign countries, $38,366; and U.S. territories, $31,019.

White-collar Employees

General Schedule General Schedule employment declined to 1,479,010 in 1994, a drop of 44,412 workers, or 2.7 percent from the previous year. There are 15 grades broadly defined in terms of responsibility, difficulty, and qualifications; within each grade there are 10 steps. Within-grade advancement occurs on a fixed schedule, though employees demonstrating "high quality performance" can receive "quality step increases." In all, General Schedule employees make up more than three-quarters of all civilians employed by the government.

Foreign Service and Veterans Affairs Foreign Service Personnel and Officers pay systems covered 12,112 employees with an average salary of $53,892. Department of Veterans Affairs pay systems covered 7,492 physicians and dentists with an average salary of $85,266; 176 podiatrists and optometrists ($73,485); 33,551 nurses ($44,760); and 1,012 physicians' assistants ($49,723).

Executive Schedule (EX) and Senior Executive Service (ES) The Executive Schedule (EX) covers top officials in the executive branch above the SL level. Broadly speaking, the five Executive Schedule levels include the following job titles: level I, cabinet members; level II, deputy secretaries of major departments; level III, presidential advisers, chief administrators of major independent agencies, and under secretaries; level IV, assistant secretaries, deputy under secretaries, and general counsels in executive departments; and level V, deputy assistant secretaries, administrators, commissioners, and directors. EX employment nearly doubled, from 225 in 1993 to 410 in 1994; average salaries dropped slightly from $120,649 to $119,561. The Senior Executive Service (ES) covers most managerial and policy positions in the executive branch that do not require Senate confirmation. In 1994, there were 7,822 employees covered by ES; salaries averaged $110,668.

Special rates The government has difficulty recruiting and retaining qualified personnel in certain occupations and for certain locations with higher competitive salaries. To alleviate this problem, the Office of Personnel Management has the authority to establish special rates for certain white-collar positions. The number of white-collar employees receiving special-rate salaries varies from year to year, but is close to 200,000.

Blue-collar Employees

As of Mar. 31, 1994, the federal government employed 289,525 workers (14.8% of the civilian government work force) in blue-collar (trades and labor) occupations. Most of these (282,645 or 97.6%) were employed in the United States, and 14,615, or 5.0 percent, worked in and around the Washington, D.C., metro area. Another 6,880 were employed by the U.S. government overseas. The Department of Defense employed 223,985, or 77.4 percent of all blue-collar government workers.

Blue-collar pay rates are governed by federal Wage Systems and determined on a prevailing rate basis by pay locality. The worldwide average salary for the blue-collar work force in 1994 was $31,299, up from $30,268 the year before. Salaries were higher in the United States (where they averaged $31,424) and lowest in foreign countries, (where they averaged just $24,676). Blue-collar salaries averaged $30,862 in the Washington, D.C., metropolitan area, but only $26,641 in U.S. territories and possessions.

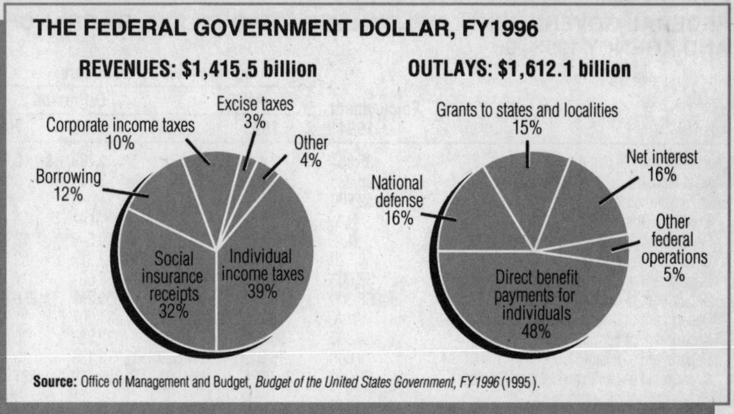

Source: Office of Management and Budget, *Budget of the United States Government, FY1996* (1995).

FEDERAL GOVERNMENT PAY SYSTEMS, 1994

Grade	Employees	Mean salary
General schedule		
GS-1	370	$13,038
GS-2	2,443	14,880
GS-3	25,764	17,003
GS-4	97,627	19,597
GS-5	166,176	22,133
GS-6	108,556	24,804
GS-7	140,609	27,274
GS-8	41,034	30,892
GS-9	145,110	32,973
GS-10	16,090	37,700
GS-11	210,657	39,952
GS-12	239,332	48,051
GS-13	159,427	58,230
GS-14	85,490	69,539
GS-15	40,325	83,925
Total	**1,479,010**	**$39,070**
Senior Level (SL)	**384**	**$79,931–115,700[1]**
Executive schedule		
Level I	25	$148,400
Level II	252	133,600
Level III	84	123,100
Level IV	32	115,700
Level V	17	108,200
Total	**410**	**$119,561**

Note: As of March 31. 1. Mean salary not available. Salary range shown. **Source:** U.S. Office of Personnel Management, *Pay Structure of the Federal Civil Service 1994* (1995).

FEDERAL GOVERNMENT EMPLOYMENT AND OUTLAYS, BY BRANCH AND AGENCY, 1993–96

Agency	Employment 1994[1]	Outlays (millions of dollars) Actual 1993	Actual 1994	Estimated 1995	Estimated 1996
Legislative branch	35,357	$ 2,406	$ 2,561	$ 2,793	$ 2,957
Judicial branch	28,035	2,628	2,677	3,101	3,336
Executive branch:[2]	2,052,700	—	—	—	—
Executive Office of the President	N.A.	194	229	192	191
Funds appropriated to the president	N.A.	11,534	10,511	10,860	10,779
Department of Agriculture	109,800	63,144	60,753	62,313	62,276
Department of Commerce	36,000	2,798	2,915	3,601	4,109
Department of Defense[3] (military functions)	868,300	278,574	268,635	260,269	250,045
Department of Defense (civil functions)	N.A.	29,266	30,407	31,207	31,934
Department of Education	4,800	30,290	24,699	32,888	30,651
Department of Energy	19,800	16,942	17,839	16,135	15,758
Department of Health and Human Services (except Social Security)	62,900	253,835	278,901	301,439	331,437
Department of Housing and Urban Development	13,100	25,181	25,845	26,854	26,276
Department of the Interior	76,300	6,784	6,900	7,329	7,340
Department of Justice	95,300	10,170	10,005	11,821	13,525
Department of Labor	117,500	44,651	37,047	31,942	35,853
Department of State	25,200	5,377	5,718	6,272	5,547
Department of Transportation	66,400	34,457	37,228	37,992	37,337
Department of the Treasury	157,300	298,804	307,577	351,816	386,082
Department of Veterans Affairs	227,700	35,487	37,401	38,231	37,951
Environmental Protection Agency	17,600	5,930	5,855	6,274	6,609
General Services Administration	19,500	743	334	1,131	639
National Aeronautics and Space Administration (NASA)	23,900	14,305	13,695	14,241	14,127
Office of Personnel Management	5,300	36,794	38,596	40,308	42,795
Small Business Administration	6,300	785	779	703	437
Social Security Administration (off-budget)	64,500	298,349	313,881	331,289	349,364
Other independent agencies	129,300	-11,428	10,356	7,934	13,702
Totals[5,6]	**2,116,092**	**$1,408,675**	**$1,460,914**	**$1,538,920**	**$1,612,128**

Note: Outlays are the measure of government spending—payments to liquidate obligations (other than the repayment of debt), net of cash, and offsetting collections. Outlays are generally recorded on a cash basis, but also include many cash-equivalent transactions and interest accrued on public issues of the public debt. 1. Employment figures exclude developmental positions under the Worker-Trainee Opportunity Program; participants in the Cooperative Education Program; disadvantaged summer and part-time workers under such Office of Personnel Management programs as Summer Aids, stay-in-school, and junior fellowship; and certain statutory exemptions. Figures for executive branch rounded at source. 2. Civilian employment. 3. By law (10 U.S.C. Chapter 4, section 140b) the Department of Defense is exempt from full-time equivalent employment controls. Data shown are estimated. 4. The Social Security Administration became a separate agency in 1995. Employment figures do not include 500 exempt full-time equivalents. 5. Employment totals do not include FDIC or U.S. Postal Service. 6. Outlay totals do not account for undistributed offsetting receipts. **Source:** Office of Management and Budget, *Budget of the United States Government FY1996* (1995).

GOVERNMENT EMPLOYMENT AND POPULATION, 1961–94

Fiscal year	Federal executive branch[1] ('000s)	State and local goverments ('000s)	All governmental units ('000s)	Federal civilian as percent of all governmental units	Federal civilian employment per 1,000 population
1961[2]	2,407	6,295	11,246	21.4%	13.3
1965	2,496	7,683	12,898	19.4	12.8
1970[2]	2,944	5,673	11,758	25.0	14.4
1975	2,848	12,114	17,174	16.6	13.2
1980[2]	2,821	13,542	18,507	15.2	12.3
1985	2,964	13,827	19,037	15.6	12.4
1990[2]	3,067	15,628	20,862	14.7	12.2
1991[2]	3,048	15,436	20,589	14.8	12.0
1992	3,020	15,676	20,608	14.7	11.8
1993	2,946	15,902	20,658	14.3	11.4
1994	2,908	16,171	20,793	14.0	11.2

1. Covers total year-end civilian employment of full-time permanent, temporary, part-time, and intermittent employees in the executive branch, including the Postal Service, and beginning in 1970, includes various disadvantaged worker-trainee programs. 2. Includes temporary employees in the decennial census. **Source:** Office of Management and Budget, *Budget of the United States Government, FY1996* (1995).

SALARIES OF FEDERAL OFFICIALS

Branch/Official	Salary
Executive branch	
President	$200,000
Expense allowance	50,000
Travel allowance	100,000
Vice president	171,500
Expense allowance	10,000
Legislative branch	
Senate:[1]	
President pro tempore, majority and minority leaders	$148,400
Expense allowance, each	10,000
Senators	133,600
Expense allowance for majority and minority leaders, each	10,000
Expense allowance for majority and minority whips, each	5,000
Expense allowance for chairmen of majority and minority conference committees, each	3,000
House of Representatives:[1]	
Speaker of the House	171,500
Expense allowance	25,000
Minority and majority leaders	148,400
Expense allowance, each	10,000
Representatives	133,600
Expense allowance for majority and minority whips, each	5,000
Judicial branch	
Chief Justice	$171,500
Associate justices	164,100
Circuit judges	141,700
District and other judges	133,600
Bankruptcy judges and magistrates	123,000

1. Expenses listed are over and above personnel, expense, and transportation allowances given to all members of Congress, the amount of which is based on the population of the senator or representative's district and the distance between his or her home state and Washington, D.C. **Source:** Executive Office of the White House; U.S. Congress; U.S. Supreme Court; Administrative Office of the U.S. Courts.

U.S. FEDERAL EMPLOYMENT, 1992–94

Description	1992	1993	1994
Executive branch civilian employment[1]	2,226,778	2,156,790	2,085,438
U.S. Postal Service[2]	792,049	790,340	822,754
Military personnel on active duty[3]	1,847,600	1,744,337	1,647,964
Department of Defense	1,808,131	1,705,103	1,610,490
Department of Transportation (Coast Guard)	39,469	39,234	37,474
Total executive branch employment	**4,866,427**	**4,691,467**	**4,556,156**
Legislative branch	38,509	38,258	35,357
Judicial branch	27,987	28,120	28,035
Total federal employment	**4,932,923**	**4,757,845**	**4,619,548**

1. Excludes Postal Service employees. 2. Includes Postal Rate Commission. 3. Excludes reserve components. **Source:** Office of Management and Budget, *Budget of the United States Government, FY1996* (1995).

GLOSSARY OF FEDERAL BUDGET TERMS

Budget deficit/surplus A budget deficit occurs when government *outlays* exceed government *receipts;* a surplus occurs when receipts exceed outlays. The budget deficit in 1992 was a record $290.4 billion. The last year in which a budget surplus was recorded was 1969 ($3.2 billion).

Fiscal year The federal government's fiscal year begins Oct. 1 and ends Sept. 30 of the next calendar year.

Intergovernmental expenditure/revenue Amounts paid to or received from other governments either in the form of shared revenues and grants-in-aid, reimbursements for performance of general government activities or for specific services such as care of prisoners for the paying government, or in lieu of taxes.

Off-budget/on-budget On-budget totals reflect the transactions of all federal government entities except those excluded from the budget totals by law, the two Social Security *trust funds* (old-age and survivors insurance and the federal disability insurance trust funds), and the Postal Service fund. Off-budget totals reflect the transactions of government entities excluded from the on-budget totals by law.

Offsetting collections Collections from the public that result from business-type or market-oriented activities and collections; one example is the proceeds from the sale of postage stamps.

Outlays Budget outlays are expenditures and net lending of funds under *budget authority* during the fiscal year. They constitute the spending side of the budget.

Receipts Budget receipts constitute the income side of the budget and are composed almost entirely of taxes or other compulsory payments to the government.

Trust fund In the federal budget, a trust fund means only that the law requires that funds must be accounted for separately and used only for specified purposes. The largest trust funds are those for civil service and military retirement, Social Security, Medicare, and unemployment insurance. These are financed by Social Security taxes and contributions and payments from the general fund. There are also major trust funds for transportation and bank deposit insurance which are financed by *user charges*.

User charges Charges for services rendered, collected in the form of taxes, such as highway excise taxes to fund the highway trust fund.

THE FEDERAL GOVERNMENT: EMPLOYEES AND BUDGET, 1901–95

		Budget (millions)		
Year	Number of employees[1]	Receipts	Outlays	Surplus or deficit (–)
1901	239,476	$ 588	$ 525	$ 63
1910	388,708	676	694	–18
1920	655,265	6,649	6,358	291
1930	601,319	4,058	3,320	738
1940	1,042,420	6,548	9,468	–2,920
1945	3,816,310	45,159	92,712	–47,553
1950	1,960,708	39,443	42,562	–3,119
1960	2,398,704	92,492	92,191	301
1970	2,984,574	192,807	195,649	–2,842
1980	2,875,866	517,112	590,947	–73,835
1985	3,001,000	734,057	946,391	–212,334
1990	3,128,267	1,031,321	1,252,705	–221,384
1991	3,112,145	1,054,272	1,323,441	–269,169
1992	3,131,274	1,090,453	1,380,856	–290,403
1993	3,012,839	1,153,535	1,408,675	–255,140
1994	2,971,584	1,257,745	1,460,914	–203,169
1995[2]	N.A.	1,346,414	1,538,920	–192,506

1. Paid civilians only. 2. Projected. **Source:** U.S. Bureau of the Census, *Statistical History of the U.S.* (1976); Office of Management and Budget, *Budget of the United States Government FY1996* (1995).

FEDERAL GOVERNMENTAL RECEIPTS BY SOURCE, 1980–96 (billions of dollars)

	Actual			Estimated		
Source	1980	1985	1990	1994	1995	1996
Individual income taxes	$244.1	$334.5	$466.9	$543.1	$588.5	$623.4
Corporation income taxes[1]	64.6	61.3	93.5	140.4	150.9	157.4
Social insurance taxes and contributions	157.8	265.1	380.0	461.5	484.4	509.3
On-budget	(45.6)	(79.0)	(98.4)	(126.4)	(133.2)	(139.0)
Off-budget	(113.2)	(186.2)	(281.7)	(335.0)	(351.3)	(370.4)
Excise taxes	24.3	36.0	35.3	55.2	57.6	57.2
Other[2]	25.3	37.0	55.5	57.6	65.1	68.1
Total	**$517.1**	**$734.1**	**$1,031.3**	**$1,257.7**	**$1,346.5**	**$1,415.5**
On-budget	(403.9)	(547.9)	(749.7)	(922.7)	(995.2)	(1,045.1)
Off-budget	(113.2)	(186.2)	(281.7)	(335.0)	(351.3)	(370.4)

1. Beginning in 1990 includes trust fund receipts for the hazardous substance superfund. 2. Includes estate and gift taxes, customs duties and fees, federal reserve deposits, and other. **Source:** Office of Management and Budget, *Budget of the U.S. Government FY1996* (1995).

OUTLAYS BY BUDGET ENFORCEMENT ACT CATEGORY, 1970–95 (billions of dollars)

Category	1970	1980	1985	1990	1994	1995[1]
Total outlays	**$195.6**	**$590.9**	**$946.4**	**$1,252.7**	**$1,460.9**	**$1,538.9**
Discretionary outlays	124.6	276.5	416.2	501.7	545.6	553.8
National defense	81,9	134.6	253.1	300.1	282.2	272.1
International	4.0	12.8	17.4	19.1	20.8	22.1
Domestic	38.7	129.1	145.7	182.5	242.6	259.6
Mandatory outlays	56.7	261.9	400.7	566.8	712.4	750.9
Social Security	29.6	117.1	186.4	246.5	316.9	333.7
Deposit insurance	–0.5	–0.4	–2.2	58.1	–7.6	–12.3
Means-tested entitlements[2]	10.1	45.0	62.2	94.1	170.4	184.5
Other	26.1	120.3	187.0	204.7	270.5	286.3
Undistributed offsetting receipts[3]	–8.6	–19.9	–32.7	–36.7	–37.8	–41.4
Net interest	14.4	52.5	129.5	184.2	203.0	234.2

1. Estimate. 2. Includes Medicaid, food stamps, family support assistance (AFDC), supplemental security income (SSI), child nutrition programs, earned income tax credits, and veterans' pensions. 3. Includes asset sales. **Source:** Office of Management and Budget, *Budget of the United States Government, FY1996* (1995).

THE CONGRESSIONAL BUDGET PROCESS

On or before	Action to be completed
First Monday in February	President submits his budget. Congressional committees have six weeks to submit views and estimates to budget committees.
February 15	Congressional Budget Office submits report to budget committees.
April 1	Senate Budget Committee reports concurrent resolution[1] on the budget.
April 15	Congress completes action on concurrent resolution[1] on the budget.
May 15	Annual appropriation bills may be considered in the House.
June 10	House Appropriations Committee reports last annual appropriations bill.
June 15	Congress completes action on reconciliation legislation.
June 30	House completes action on annual appropriation bills.
October 1	Fiscal year begins.

1. A concurrent resolution sets levels for new budget authority and outlays, direct loan obligations, primary loan guarantee commitments, the amount by which federal revenues should be increased or decreased, the budget surplus or dificit, the public debt, and so on. **Source:** Committee on Ways and Means, U.S. House of Representatives, *Overview of Entitlement Programs, 1992 Green Book* (1992).

BUDGET OUTLAYS AND PERCENT DISTRIBUTION, BY FUNCTION, 1975–94 (millions of dollars)

Function	1975	1980	1985	1990	1993	1994
National defense	**$86,509**	**$133,995**	**$252,748**	**$299,331**	**$291,086**	**$281,563**
As percentage of total	26.0%	22.7%	26.7%	23.9%	20.7%	19.3%
Human resources	**$173,245**	**$313,374**	**$471,822**	**$619,329**	**$827,535**	**$869,418**
As percentage of total	52.1%	53.0%	49.9%	49.4%	58.7%	59.5%
Education, training, employment, and social services	$16,022	$ 31,843	$ 29,342	$ 38,755	$ 50,012	$ 46,307
Health	12,930	23,169	33,542	57,716	99,415	107,122
Medicare	12,875	32,090	65,822	98,102	130,552	144,747
Income security	50,160	86,540	128,200	147,022	207,250	214,036
Social Security	64,658	118,547	188,623	248,623	304,585	319,565
Veterans benefits and services	16,599	21,185	26,292	29,112	35,720	37,642
Physical resources	**$35,449**	**$65,985**	**$56,789**	**$125,546**	**$45,890**	**$69,749**
As percentage of total	10.7%	11.2%	6.0%	10.0%	3.3%	4.8%
Energy	$ 2,916	$10,156	$ 5,685	$ 3,341	$ 4,319	$ 5,219
Natural resources and environment	7,346	13,858	13,357	17,080	20,239	21,064
Commerce and housing credit	9,947	9,390	4,229	67,142	–22,719	–5,122
Transportation	10,918	21,329	25,838	29,485	35,004	38,134
Community and regional development	4,322	11,252	7,680	8,498	9,052	10,454
Net interest	**$23,244**	**$52,538**	**$129,504**	**$184,221**	**$198,811**	**$202,957**
As percentage of total	7.0%	8.9%	13.7%	14.7%	14.1%	13.9%
Other functions	**$27,487**	**$44,996**	**$68,227**	**$60,893**	**$82,733**	**$74,998**
As percentage of total	8.3%	7.6%	7.2%	4.9%	5.8%	5.1%
International affairs	$ 7,097	$12,714	$16,176	$13,764	$17,248	$17,083
General science, space, and technology	3,991	5,832	8,627	14,444	17,030	16,227
Agriculture	3,036	8,839	25,565	11,958	20,490	15,121
Administration of justice	2,955	4,584	6,270	9,993	14,955	15,256
General government	10,408	13,028	11,588	10,734	13,009	11,312
Total[1]	**$332,332**	**$590,947**	**$946,391**	**$1,252,705**	**$1,408,675**	**$1,460,914**

1. Includes undistributed offsetting receipts not shown separately. **Source:** Office of Management and Budget, *Budget of the United States Government, FY1996* (1995).

SUMMARY OF FEDERAL GOVERNMENT FINANCES, 1987/88–1991/92

Item	Amount 1987–88 (millions)	Amount 1991–92 (millions)	Per capita 1991–92[1]
REVENUES			
Revenue, total	**$1,012,343**	**$1,259,383**	**$4,937.25**
General revenue	692,555	854,821	3,351.21
General revenue from own sources	689,696	851,390	3,337.76
Taxes	562,600	659,041	2,583.68
Income	495,376	578,735	2,261.01
Individual	401,181	476,485	1,867.92
Corporation	94,195	100,270	393.10
Sales, gross receipts, and customs	52,604	63,684	249.66
Customs duties	19,317	17,480	66.53
Motor fuel	12,876	19,885	77.88
Alcoholic beverages	5,830	7,907	31.00
Public utilities	5,701	7,259	28.43
Air transportation	3,146	4,300	16.86
Telephone	2,555	2,953	11.58
Tobacco products	4,523	5,190	20.35
Other sales and gross receipts taxes	7,357	5,989	28.48
Oil windfall profit tax	2,418	—	—
Motor fuel vehicles, chassis, and body	1,156	928	3.54
Tires, inner tubes, and tread rubber	319	284	1.11
Other categories not shown	3,464	5,070	19.83
Other taxes	14,620	18,024	70.66
Death and gift	7,594	11,143	43.68
All other	7,026	6,681	26.98

Item	Amount 1987–88 (millions)	Amount 1991–92 (millions)	Per capita 1991–92[1]
Charges and miscellaneous general revenue	$127,096	$192,349	$ 754.08
Current charges	80,081	89,482	350.80
Postal receipts	33,986	45,158	177.04
National defense and international relations	7,191	6,677	34.02
Natural resources	25,336	15,528	60.86
Commodity Credit Corporation—sale of agricultural products	12,583	937	3.67
Tennessee Valley Authority	5,020	5,685	21.82
Department of Interior—energy sales	2,140	1,021	4.00
Mineral ore and product sales	653	573	2.25
Timber sales	680	861	3.38
All other resource charges	4,260	6,571	25.76
Other current charges	13,568	20,499	80.36
Sale of property	5,089	3,723	14.80
Interest earnings	15,166	10,397	40.76
Other miscellaneous general revenue	26,760	88,747	347.92
Federal Reserve System—earnings	17,163	19,158	75.11
Continental shelf lands—lease and royalty revenues	3,548	3,150	12.35
Other	6,049	43,701	171.32
Insurance trust revenue	319,788	404,562	1,588.03
Social Security and Medicare insurance (OASDHI)	310,023	394,268	1,545.68
Employee retirement	4,444	4,658	18.26
Railroad retirement	4,423	4,608	18.07
Veterans' life insurance	703	894	3.50
Unemployment compensation	195	134	0.53

Item	Amount 1987–88 (millions)	Amount 1991–92 (millions)	Per capita 1991–92[1]
EXPENDITURES			
Expenditure, total	**$1,214,812**	**$1,524,589**	**$5,976.99**
Expenditure, by function:			
General expenditure	878,523	1,067,220	4,183.90
Intergovernmental expenditure	118,906	183,324	718.70
Education[2]	19,531	26,821	105.16
Elementary and secondary education	3,886	4,985	19.54
School breakfast and lunch	3,408	4,262	16.71
Federally affected area assistance	691	743	2.91
Public welfare[2]	51,253	94,760	371.49
Medical assistance	31,785	54,464	213.52
Maintenance assistance	11,377	11,929	46.77
Low income energy assistance	2,532	3,556	13.94
Health and hospitals[2]	5,412	7,625	29.89
Special supplemental food programs—WIC programs	1,932	2,387	9.36
National Institutes of Health	825	986	3.87
Highways	14,065	15,490	60.73
Natural resources, parks and recreations	2,218	2,517	9.87
Housing and community development	11,436	16,405	64.31
Other[2]	14,963	19,708	77.25
Urban mass transportation	3,263	3,855	15.11
Contribution to District of Columbia	550	671	2.63
Direct expenditure	759,617	883,896	3,485.20
Selected federal programs:			
National defense and international relations[2]	329,993	351,684	1,376.73
Military functions	306,474	335,849	1,316.65
Economic assistance	6,169	7,996	31.35
Atomic energy	8,081	10,970	43.01
Foreign affairs, n.e.c.	4,012	4,808	18.95
Food for freedom	1,060	1,553	8.09
Military assistance	4,009	—	—
Postal service	33,892	44,890	178.99
Space research and technology	8,866	13,550	53.12
Education service:			
Education	14,277	22,186	88.78
Veterans' education benefits	561	1,423	5.56
Other	13,716	20,713	81.20
Libraries	275	478	1.87
Social service and income maintenance:			
Public welfare	28,656	47,722	187.09
Hospitals	8,045	10,435	40.91
Public hospitals	7,379	10,081	39.52
Veterans	6,524	8,676	34.01
Other public hospitals	855	1,405	5.51
Other hospitals	666	351	1.39

Item	Amount 1987–88 (millions)	Amount 1991–92 (millions)	Per capita 1991–92[1]
Health	$ 8,804	$ 9,619	$ 37.71
Social insurance administration	4,313	5,455	21.39
Veterans' services	18,340	20,320	79.68
Transportation:			
Highways	377	813	3.19
Air transportation	4,186	5,871	23.02
Water transport and terminals	2,112	2,721	10.67
Public safety:			
Police protection	4,657	6,703	26.28
Correction	1,168	2,411	9.45
Environment and housing:			
Natural resources, parks and recreation	81,481	53,485	209.68
Soil, water, mineral, and electric energy resources[2]	16,142	17,814	69.84
Energy programs	5,586	5,216	20.45
Tennessee Valley Authority	4,608	3,867	15.12
Army Corps of Engineers	1,660	452	1.77
Soil Conservation Service	725	911	3.18
Stabilization of farm prices and income[2]	46,151	19,665	77.09
Commodity Credit Corporation	44,440	12,227	47.93
Farm credit programs	14,418	5,383	21.10
Forestry	2,362	2,493	9.77
Other agricultural resources	1,685	2,233	8.75
Other natural resources[2]	2,123	3,913	15.34
National Oceanographic and Atmospheric Administration (NOAA)	1,214	1,412	5.54
Housing and community development	11,969	15,482	60.70
Government administration:			
Financial administration	6,865	10,762	42.19
Judicial and legal	2,639	4,415	17.31
Other government administration	1,187	1,668	6.54
Interest on general debt	158,119	199,713	782.95
General expenditure, n.e.c.	29,396	53,583	209.99
Insurance trust expenditure	336,289	454,730	1,782.71
Social Security and Medicare insurance (OASDHI)	299,475	410,855	1,610.70
Employee retirement	28,371	33,987	133.24
Railroad retirement	6,343	7,401	29.01
Veterans' life insurance	1,987	2,401	9.41
Unemployment compensation	113	86	0.34
DEBT			
Gross debt outstanding at end of fiscal year	2,614,581	4,082,871	16,006.36
Public debt	2,602,183	3,865,303	14,369.34
Federal agency debt	12,398	17,751	69.59
Held by federal government	550,649	1,016,453	3,987.87
Other debt outstanding	2,063,932	3,066,418	12,021.78

Note: n.e.c. = not elsewhere classified. Detail may not add to total due to rounding. Figures are preliminary. 1. Per capita figures are calculated on the basis of amounts rounded to the nearest thousand. 2. Includes amounts not shown in detail. **Source:** U.S. Bureau of the Census, *Government Finances 1991–92* (1995).

KEY GOVERNMENT FUNCTIONS

National Defense

Throughout history, the primary goal of every central government has been the protection of its citizens from hostile attacks of foreign enemies. In 1993, the United States spent nearly $270 billion to keep 1.7 million people in active military service and to maintain the greatest arsenal of weapons ever known.

Since the end of World War II, a large percentage of people and matériel has been committed to regions around the world that the government has determined are vital to U.S. interests. Between 1961 and 1980, the defense budget averaged around $200 billion annually (in 1982 constant dollars)—even during the Vietnam War. In 1981, however, the Reagan administration began a massive defense buildup that swelled successive defense budgets to unprecedented numbers and in the process helped to quadruple the annual federal deficit in less than five years.

Partly in response to the nation's budget deficit, and partly thanks to the end of the Cold War, politicians of all stripes are looking at the defense budget as the likeliest place to make savings, the outstanding question being how much. Nevertheless, the United States remains committed to maintaining active duty and reserve forces sufficient for quick and effective response to crises around the world.

The defense establishment The Department of Defense (DOD) is a cabinet-level organization responsible for providing the military forces needed to deter war and protect the security of the United States. The major elements of these forces are the Army, Navy, Air Force, and Marine Corps. Under the president, who is also the commander-in-chief, the secretary of defense exercises direction, authority, and control over the Department of Defense, which includes the three military departments, the Joint Chiefs of Staff and Joint Staff, 10 unified and specified commands, the DOD inspector general, 13 defense agencies, and seven DOD field activities.

The four armed services are subordinate to the military departments, which are responsible for recruiting, training, and equipping their forces. The Marine Corps is the second armed service in the Department of the Navy. (A fifth armed service, the U.S. Coast Guard, reports to the Department of Transportation in peacetime and to the Department of the Navy in wartime.)

The earliest precursor to the Department of Defense was the War Department, established by Congress in 1789; a separate Navy Department was created in 1798. These were merged under the National Security Act of 1947 and subsequent amendments. By 1949 the secretary of defense was established as the principal assistant to the president on defense matters in charge of the Department of Defense.

Chain of command Operational command of U.S. combat forces is assigned to the nation's unified and specified commands. The chain of command runs from the president to the secretary of defense, through the Joint Chiefs of Staff to the commanders-in-chief of the unified and specified commands. (The four service secretaries are not part of this chain of command.) A *unified command* is composed of forces from two or more services, has a broad and continuing mission, and is normally organized on a geographical basis. The eight unified commands are: U.S. European Command, U.S. Pacific Command, U.S. Atlantic Command, U.S. Southern Command, U.S. Central Command, U.S. Space Command, U.S. Special Operations Command, and U.S. Transportation Command. A *specified command* also has a broad and continuing mission but is organized on a functional basis and is normally made up of forces from a single service. The two specified commands are the Strategic Air Command (SAC) and the Forces Command.

U.S. Army

In peacetime, the primary mission of the continental U.S. armies is to train reserves and national guard, plan for mobilization, and coordinate domestic emergency relief efforts. The largest unit is a numbered *army*, such as the Fifth Army. (In time of war, two or three armies may be brought under a single command in an *army group*.) An *army* comprises two or more corps plus a headquarters (HQ) unit; a *corps* is made up of two to five divisions and an HQ.

There are 18 active and 10 reserve divisions in the U.S. Army combat forces. The *division* is a self-sufficient force, typically consisting of three brigades (each comprising three to five battalions) and various combat support elements. A *brigade* is made up of two or more regiments or battalions; a *regiment*, of subordinate units such as battalions, companies, or squadrons; a *battalion*, of four or more companies; a *company* of several platoons; and a *platoon* of four squads. A *squad* consists of about 10 soldiers.

CHAIRMEN OF THE JOINT CHIEFS OF STAFF, 1949–95

General of the Army Omar N. Bradley, USA, 1949–53
Adm. Arthur W. Radford, USN, 1953–57
Gen. Nathan F. Twining, USAF, 1957–60
Gen. Lyman L. Lemnitzer, USA, 1960–62
Gen. Maxwell D. Taylor, USA, 1962–64
Gen. Earle G. Wheeler, USA, 1964–70
Adm. Thomas H. Moorer, USN, 1970–74
Gen. George S. Brown, USAF, 1974–78
Gen. David C. Jones, USAF, 1978–82
Gen. John W. Vessey, Jr., USA, 1982–85
Adm. William J. Crowe, USN, 1985–89
Gen. Colin L. Powell, USA, 1989–93
Gen. John Shalikashvili, USA, 1993–present

Source: U.S. Dept. of Defense, *Defense 93* (1993).

U.S. Marine Corps

Marine Corps organization emphasizes the close integration of airground operations for service with the U.S. fleet and for the conduct of land operations essential to the prosecution of a naval campaign. All marines serve "at the pleasure of the president," and the Corps's mission includes "performing such other duties as the president may direct."

The smallest tactical unit of Marine Corps infantry is the *fire team*, which consists of four marines. A *squad* is made up of three fire teams, and there are three squads to a *platoon*, three platoons to a *company*, three companies to a *battalion*, three battalions to a *regiment*, three regiments to a *brigade*, and three brigades to a *division*.

These components are organized into three basic organizational structures called *Marine air-ground task forces*, or MAGTFs. The largest—about 47,500 personnel—is the *Marine Expeditionary Force* (MEF), which consists of a Marine air wing (330 planes), a Marine division, and a force service support group. The *Marine Expeditionary Brigade* (MEB) consists of a Marine air group (150 planes), a regimental landing group, and a brigade service support group—about 15,000 personnel. The smallest and most responsive Marine force, the *Marine Expeditionary Unit* (MEU) consists of about 2,500 personnel and is made up of a helicopter squadron, a battalion landing team, and a unit service support group. MEUs are sea-based, can be airlifted, and are equipped and trained to be self-sustaining in the field for up to 30 days. There are currently three MEFs, six MEBs, and five MEUs.

U.S. Navy

The ships of the U.S. Navy are organized into the Pacific Fleet, the Atlantic Fleet, and U.S. Naval Forces Europe. These are composed of numbered fleets which consist of *carrier battle groups*, *amphibious ready groups*, and one or more *underway replenishment groups*. Smaller subdivisions of naval forces are the *flotilla*, consisting of two or more squadrons; a *squadron*, of two or more divisions; and a *division*, normally made up of four ships.

A naval *task force* designates a collection of ships under a single command designed to accomplish a particular tactical or strategic purpose. An *amphibious squadron* consists of amphibious assault ships, amphibious transport docks, dock landing ships, and tank landing ships and transports troops and equipment necessary for an assault landing from the sea.

U.S. Coast Guard

The Coast Guard is a branch of the armed forces of the United States at all times. What distinguishes it from the other services is that it is part of the Department of Transportation—not Defense—except during wartime, or at the direction of the president, when it operates as part of the navy. A successor to the

MAJOR NAVAL OPERATING FORCES

Name	Headquarters
Pacific Fleet	Pearl Harbor, Hawaii
Third Fleet	San Diego, Calif.
Seventh Fleet	Yokosuka, Japan
Atlantic Fleet	Norfolk, Va.
Second Fleet	Norfolk, Va.
U.S. Naval Forces Europe	London, England
Sixth Fleet	Gaeta, Italy
Military Sealift Command	Washington, D.C.
Naval Reserve Force	New Orleans, La.
Mine Warfare Command	Ingleside, Tex.
Operational and Test Evaluation Force	Norfolk, Va.
Naval Forces Southern Command	Rodman, Panama
Naval Forces Central Command	Pearl Harbor, Hawaii
Middle East Force	Bahrain
Naval Special Warfare Command	Coronado, Calif.

Source: U.S. Dept. of Defense, *Defense 94* (1994).

Revenue Marine established in 1790, its primary function is to enforce federal maritime law. In 1990 the Coast Guard's budget was $3.2 billion, and the active duty force consisted of 37,690 personnel.

U.S. Air Force

The air force is organized into a number of commands. Within commands concerned with the strategic or tactical operation of aircraft, the primary subdivisions are indicated by the term *air force* prefaced by a number, such as the Eighth Air Force. Such an air force is composed of wings; a *wing* consists of two or more groups or squadrons; a *group* of two or more squadrons; and a *squadron* of two or more flights. A *flight* is the basic tactical unit and consists of four or more planes.

Nuclear Forces

Nuclear forces are classified as either strategic or nonstrategic. A strategic weapon is a nuclear-armed missile of intermediate or intercontinental range (usually more than 5,500 km or 3,300 mi.) capable of attacking large target areas in another country. The strategic triad—a cornerstone of post–World War II U.S. defense—is composed of land-based missile forces, including intercontinental ballistic missiles (ICBMs); submarine-launched ballistic missiles (SLBMs); and manned aircraft of the strategic bomber force. Nonstrategic nuclear weapons are shorter-range weapons that can be deployed on the battlefield and include sea-launched cruise missiles, artillery-fired atomic projectiles, and dual-capable (conventional and nuclear) aircraft.

Special Operations Forces (SOF)

A unified command whose elements are drawn from the four major services, the special operations forces are designated to achieve military objectives of a limited and specific nature.

MAJOR U.S. ARMY FORCES

Unit	Headquarters
Forces Command	**Ft. McPherson, Ga.**
First U.S. Army	Ft. Meade, Md.
Second U.S. Army	Ft. Gillem, Ga.
Third U.S. Army	Ft. McPherson, Ga.
Fifth U.S. Army	Ft. Sam Houston, Tex.
Sixth U.S. Army	San Francisco, Calif.
I Corps	Ft. Lewis, Wash.
III Corps, "Phantom Corps"	Ft. Hood, Tex.
1st infantry division (mech.), "The Big Red One"	Ft. Riley, Kans.
4th infantry division (mech.), "The Ivy Division"	Ft. Carson, Colo.
1st cavalry division	Ft. Hood, Tex.
2nd armored division	Ft. Hood, Tex.
III Corps Artillery	Ft. Sill, Okla.
13th corps support command	Ft. Hood, Tex.
XVIII Airborne Corps	Ft. Bragg, N.C.
24th infantry division (mech.), "Victory"	Ft. Stewart, Ga.
82nd airborne division, "All American"	Ft. Bragg, N.C.
101st airborne division (air assault), "Screaming Eagles"	Ft. Campbell, Ky.
XVIII Airborne Corps Artillery	Ft. Bragg, N.C.
1st corps support command	Ft. Bragg, N.C.
National Training Center	Ft. Irwin, Calif.
U.S. Army Europe (7th Army)	**Heidelberg, Germany**
V Corps	Frankfurt, Germany
3rd infantry division (mech.), "Marne"	Würzburg, Germany
1st armored division, "Old Ironsides"	Bad Kreuznach, Germany
32nd Army air defense command	Darmstadt, Germany
1st personnel command	Schwetzingen, Germany
3rd corps support command	Wiesbaden, Germany
21st theater army area command	Kaiserslautern, Germany
Seventh Army training command	Grafenwöhr, Germany
U.S. Army Pacific	**Ft. Shafter, Hawaii**
U.S. Army, Japan/IX Corps	Camp Zama, Japan
U.S. Army, Alaska	Ft. Wainwright, Alaska
25th infantry division (light), "Tropic Lightning"	Schofield Barracks, Hawaii
8th Army	**Seoul, South Korea**
2nd infantry division, "Indianhead"	Ouijonbu, South Korea
19th theater army area command	Taegu, South Korea
U.S. Army South	**Ft. Clayton, Panama**
3rd special operations support command (airborne)	Ft. Clayton, Panama
Army Matériel Command	**Alexandria, Va.**
Army Special Operations Command	**Ft. Bragg, N.C.**
Army Training and Doctrine Command	**Ft. Monroe, Va.**
Army Intelligence and Security Command	**Ft. Belvoir, Va.**
Information Systems Command	**Ft. Huachuca, Ariz.**
Criminal Investigation Command	**Falls Church, Va.**
Corps of Engineers	**Washington, D.C.**
Medical Command	**Ft. Sam Houston, Tex.**
National Guard divisions:	
28th infantry division, "Keystone"	Harrisburg, Pa.
29th infantry division (light), "Blue and Grey"	Ft. Belvoir, Va.
34th infantry division	St. Paul, Minn.
35th infantry division (mech.), "Santa Fe"	Ft. Leavenworth, Kans.
38th infantry division, "Cyclone"	Indianapolis, Ind.
40th infantry division (mech.), "Sunshine"	Los Alamitos, Calif.
42nd infantry division, "Rainbow"	Troy, N.Y.
49th armored division, "Lone Star"	Austin, Tex.

Source: U.S. Army Force Command, *Army* magazine, October 1995.

MAJOR COAST GUARD COMMANDS

Name	Headquarters
Coast Guard Headquarters	Washington, D.C.
Atlantic Area	New York, N.Y.
1st District	Boston, Mass.
2nd District	St. Louis, Mo.
5th District	Portsmouth, Va.
7th District	Miami, Fla.
8th District	New Orleans, La.
9th District	Cleveland, Ohio
Pacific Area	Alameda, Calif.
11th District	Long Beach, Calif.
13th District	Seattle, Wash.
14th District	Honolulu, Hawaii
17th District	Juneau, Alaska

Source: U.S. Coast Guard.

MAJOR MARINE CORPS COMMANDS

Name	Headquarters
Fleet Marine Force, Atlantic	Camp Lejeune, N.C.
Fleet Marine Force, Pacific	Camp H.M. Smith, Hawaii
Marine Corps Combat Development Command	Quantico, Va.
Marine Corps Systems Command	Quantico, Va.
I Marine Expeditionary Force	Camp Pendleton, Calif.
II Marine Expeditionary Force	Camp Lejeune, N.C.
III Marine Expeditionary Force	Camp Butler, Okinawa, Japan
Marine Corps Air Ground Combat Center	Twentynine Palms, Calif.

Source: U.S. Dept. of Defense, *Defense 94* (1994).

Among the various elements of the SOF are: *Army* special forces; Rangers; psychological operations, civil affairs, and special operations aviation units; *Navy* SEAL (sea-air-land) teams and special boat units; and *Air Force* 23rd Air Force special operations force.

Reserve Forces

The reserve forces constitute the initial and primary augmentation of active forces in any emergency requiring rapid expansion of those forces. The objective of the Department of Defense's "total force policy" is to achieve the most cost-effective mix of active duty, reserve, and contract personnel consistent with the requirements of peacetime deployments and responsiveness to war.

There are seven reserve components: Army National Guard, Army Reserve, Naval Reserve, Marine Corps Reserve, Air National Guard, Air Force Reserve, and Coast Guard Reserve. All National Guard and reserve personnel are assigned to one of three categories: Ready Reserve, Standby Reserve, or Retired Reserve. All National Guard members are in the Ready Reserve. The Ready Reserve consists of the Selected Reserve, Individual Ready Reserve, and Inactive National Guard. Some reservists are organized in units, others train as individuals. All are subject to orders for active duty in time of war or national emergency.

In addition, members of the Selected Reserve may be ordered to active duty under implementation of the presidential call-up authority. The president can activate up to 200,000 members of the Selected Reserve involuntarily, for operational missions of not more than 90 days, without declaring a national emergency.

DEFENSE ESTABLISHMENT EMPLOYEES, 1993

Branch	Active duty[1]	Guard and reserve[1]	Civilian employees[1]
Army	572,423	1,131,670	295,032
Navy	509,950	302,387	285,934[2]
Marine Corps	178,379	111,604	—
Air Force	444,351	321,243	201,991
Total DOD	**1,705,103**	**1,866,904**	**935,875**
Coast Guard[3]	37,926	8,000	6,169

1. As of Sept. 30, 1993. 2. Includes Marine Corps civilian personnel. 3. As of May 31, 1993. **Source:** U.S. Dept. of Defense, *Defense 94* (1994).

STRATEGIC OFFENSIVE FORCES

Land-based missile forces

B-1 bomber bases: McConnell AFB, Kans.; Grand Forks AFB, N.Dak.; Ellsworth AFB, S.Dak.; Dyess AFB, Tex.

B-2 bomber base: Whiteman AFB, Mo.

B-52 bomber bases:[1] Eaker AFB, Ark.; Castle AFB, Calif; Barksdale AFB, La.; Loring AFB, Me.; K.I. Sawyer AFB, Mich.; Wurtsmith AFB, Mich.; Griffiss AFB, N.Y.; Minot AFB, N.Dak.; Carswell AFB, Tex.; Fairchild AFB, Wash.

Minuteman bases: Malmstrom AFB, Mont.; Whiteman AFB, Mo.; Ellsworth AFB, S.Dak.; Grand Forks AFB, N.Dak.; Minot AFB, N.Dak.

Peacekeeper base: Francis E. Warren AFB, Wyo.

Strategic submarine forces[2]

SSBN[3] bases: Kings Bay, Ga.; Charleston, S.C.; Bangor, Wash.

1. The B-52 squadrons at Loring AFB and Barksdale AFB are assigned a conventional bomber role. 2. Includes 31 nuclear-armed submarines. 3. SSBN = ballistic missile submarine, nuclear-powered. **Source:** U.S. Dept. of Defense, *Annual Report to the President and the Congress.*

MAJOR AIR FORCE UNITS

Name	Headquarters/Location
Air Combat Command	Langley AFB, Hampton, Va.
1st Air Force	Tyndall AFB, Panama City, Fla.
8th Air Force	Barksdale AFB, Bossier City, La.
9th Air Force	Shaw AFB, Sumter, S.C.
12th Air Force	Davis-Monthan AFB, Tucson, Ariz.
Air Education and Training Command	Randolph AFB, San Antonio, Tex.
2nd Air Force	Keesler AFB, Biloxi, Miss.
19th Air Force	Randolph AFB, San Antonio, Tex.
59th Medical Wing	Maxwell AFB, Montgomery, Ala.
Air Force Matériel Command	Wright-Patterson AFB, Dayton, Ohio
Air Force Space Command	Peterson AFB, Colorado Springs, Colo.
14th Air Force	Vandenberg AFB, Lompoc, Calif.
20th Air Force	F.E. Warren AFB, Cheyenne, Wyo.
Air Force Space Warfare Center	Falcon AFB, Colorado Springs, Colo.
Air Force Special Operations Command	Hurlburt Field, Fort Walton Beach, Fla.
Air Mobility Command	Scott AFB, Belleville, Ill.
15th Air Force	Travis AFB, Fairfield, Calif.
21st Air Force	McGuire AFB, Trenton, N.J.
Air Mobility Warfare Center	Fort Dix, N.J.
Tanker Airlift Control Center	Scott AFB, Belleville, Ill.
Pacific Air Forces	Hickam AFB, Honolulu, Hawaii
5th Air Force	Yokota AFB, Tokyo, Japan
7th Air Force	Osan AB, Osan, South Korea
11th Air Force	Elmendorf AFB, Anchorage, Alaska
13th Air Force	Andersen AFB, Yigo, Guam
U.S. Air Forces, Europe	Ramstein AB, Ramstein, Germany
3rd Air Force	RAF Mildenhall, Cambridge, England
16th Air Force	Aviano AB, Venice, Italy
17th Air Force	Sembach AB, Kaiserslautern, Germany

Note: AB = air base; AFB = air force base; RAF = Royal Air Force (UK). **Source:** Air Force Association, *1993 USAF Almanac* (1995).

GUARD AND RESERVE FORCES, 1994

Status	Army National Guard	Army Reserve	Naval Reserve	Marine Corps Reserve	Air National Guard	Air Force Reserve	Total DoD	Coast Guard Reserve
Selected Reserve								
Officers	45,650	53,457	26,040	3,810	14,005	15,581	158,543	1,209
Enlisted	360,103	203,381	93,085	36,618	100,465	61,574	855,226	6,536
Total	405,753	256,838	119,125	40,428	114,470	77,155	1,013,769	7,745
Individual Ready Reserve/Inactive National Guard								
Officers	603	70,110	19,301	5,347	—	18,554	113,915	565
Enlisted	6,070	371,889	153,449	63,204	—	88,093	682,705	8,704
Total	6,673	441,999	172,750	68,551	—	106,647	796,620	9,269
Total Ready Reserve								
Officers	46,253	123,567	45,341	9,157	14,005	34,135	272,458	1,774
Enlisted	366,173	575,270	246,534	99,822	100,465	149,667	1,537,931	15,240
Total	412,426	698,837	291,875	108,979	114,470	183,802	1,810,389	17,014
Standby Reserve								
Officers	—	722	6,058	240	—	9,593	16,613	504
Enlisted	—	1,171	8,984	39	—	1,056	11,250	128
Total	—	1,893	15,042	279	—	10,649	27,863	632

Note: As of Apr. 30. **Source:** U.S. Dept. of Defense, *Defense 94* (1994).

TOP 10 DEFENSE CONTRACTORS, 1994

Company	Awards (millions)
1. McDonnell Douglas Corp.	$7,539
2. Lockheed Corporation	6,911
3. Martin Marietta Corp.	4,727
4. General Motors Corp.	4,076
5. Raytheon	3,233
6. United Technologies Corp.	3,083
7. Northrop Corporation	3,004
8. General Dynamics Corp.	2,147
9. Loral Corp.	1,729
10. Grumman Corp.	1,705

Source: U.S. Dept. of Defense, *Defense 94* (1994).

MILITARY PERSONNEL ON ACTIVE DUTY: SELECTED YEARS 1801–1994

Year/War	Total[1]
1801	7,108
1810	11,554
WAR OF 1812	
1813	25,152
1814	46,858
1815	40,885
1820	15,113
1830	11,942
1840	21,616
MEXICAN WAR	
1846	39,165
1847	57,761
1848	60,308
1850	20,824
1860	27,958
CIVIL WAR	
1861	217,112
1862	673,124
1863	960,061
1864	1,031,724
1865	1,062,848
1870	50,348
1880	37,894
1890	38,666
SPANISH-AMERICAN WAR	
1898	235,785
1900	139,344
1915	174,112
WORLD WAR I	
1917	643,833
1918	2,897,167
1919	1,172,602
1920	343,302
1930	255,648
1940	458,365
1941	1,801,101
WORLD WAR II	
1942	3,858,791
1943	9,044,745
1944	11,451,719
1945	12,123,455
1946	3,030,088
1950	1,460,261
KOREAN CONFLICT	
1951	3,249,455
1952	3,635,912
1953	3,555,067
1960	2,476,435
VIETNAM CONFLICT	
1966	3,094,058
1967	3,376,880
1968	3,547,902
1969	3,460,162
1970	3,066,294
1975	2,128,000[2]
1980	2,051,000
1985	2,151,000
1986	2,169,000
1987	2,174,000
1988	2,138,200
1989	2,130,200
1990	2,043,700
1991	1,992,800
1992	1,793,400
1993	1,710,700
1994	1,705,103

1. Excludes the Coast Guard. 2. Figures rounded in source. **Source:** U.S. Bureau of the Census, *Statistical History of the U.S.* (1976) and *Statistical Abstract of the United States, 1995* (1995).

U.S. SERVICE AND CASUALTIES IN MAJOR WARS AND CONFLICTS

Division of service	Number serving	Battle deaths	Other deaths	Wounds not mortal
Revolutionary War (1775–83)				
Army	N.A.	4,044	N.A.	6,004
Navy	N.A.	342	N.A.	114
Marines	N.A.	49	N.A.	70
Total	N.A.	4,435	N.A.	6,188
War of 1812 (1812–15)				
Army	N.A.	1,950	N.A.	4,000
Navy	N.A.	265	N.A.	439
Marines	N.A.	45	N.A.	66
Total	286,730	2,260	N.A.	4,505
Mexican War (1846–48)				
Army	N.A.	1,721	11,550	4,102
Navy	N.A.	1	N.A.	3
Marines	N.A.	11	N.A.	47
Total	78,718	1,733	11,550	4,152
Civil War (1861–65)[1]				
Army	2,128,948	138,154	221,374	280,040
Navy	84,415[2]	2,112	2,411	1,710
Marines	—	148	312	131
Total	2,213,363	140,414	224,097	281,881
Spanish-American War (1898)				
Army	280,564	369	2,061	1,594
Navy	22,875	10	0	47
Marines	3,321	6	0	21
Total	306,760	385	2,061	1,662
World War I (1917–1918)				
Army	4,057,101	50,510	55,868	193,663
Navy	599,051	431	6,856	819
Marines	78,839	2,461	390	9,520
Total	4,734,991	53,402	63,114	204,002
World War II (1941–46)				
Army	11,260,000	234,874	83,400	565,861
Navy	4,183,466	36,950	25,664	37,778
Marines	669,100	19,733	4,778	67,207
Total	16,112,556	291,557	113,842	670,846
Korean Conflict (1950–53)				
Army	2,834,000	27,709	N.A.	77,596
Navy	1,177,000	468	939	1,576
Marines	424,000	4,267	1,261	23,744
Air Force	1,285,000	1,302	243	368
Total	5,720,000	33,746	N.A.	103,284
Vietnam Conflict (1964–73)				
Army	4,368,000	30,905	7,275	96,802
Navy	1,842,000	1,631	925	4,178
Marines	794,000	13,081	1,754	51,392
Air Force	1,740,000	1,738	842	931
Total	8,744,000	47,355	10,796	153,303
Operation Desert Storm (1990–91)[3]				
Army	246,682	98	105	N.A.
Navy	98,652	6	8	N.A.
Marines	71,254	24	26	N.A.
Air Force	50,751	20	6	N.A.
Total	467,159	148	145	467

Note: N.A. = not available. Prior to World War I, dates are approximate. Actual period covered for World War I: Apr. 6, 1917–Nov. 11, 1918; World War II: Dec. 7, 1941–Dec. 31, 1946; Korea: June 25, 1950–July 27, 1953; Vietnam: Aug. 4, 1964–Jan. 27, 1973. 1. Union forces only; authoritative statistics for Confederate forces not available. Estimates of the number who served range from 600,000 to 1.5 million. *The Final Report of the Provost Marshal General, 1863–1866* indicated 133,821 Confederate deaths (74,524 battle and 59,297 other) based upon incomplete returns. In addition, an estimated 26,000–31,000 Confederate prisoners died in prisons. 2. Includes Navy and Marines. 3. Deployment figures changed continuously throughout the operation and have since, and have depended on, among other things, the timely reporting and posting of data. **Source:** U.S. Dept. of Defense, *Defense 91* (1991).

FEDERAL BUDGET OUTLAYS FOR NATIONAL DEFENSE FUNCTIONS, 1970–95

(billions of dollars)

Function	1970	1980	1985	1990	1991	1993	1994[1]	1995[1]
Military personnel	$29.0	$40.9	$67.8	$78.9	$84.2	$76.0	$70.8	$70.5
Percent of defense budget	35.5%	30.5%	26.8%	26.9%	28.9%	28.4%	28.4%	28.0%
Operations and maintenance[2]	$21.6	$44.9	$72.4	$88.3	$117.2	$89.2	$88.0	$92.9
Procurement	21.6	29.0	70.4	81.3	71.7	52.8	44.5	43.3
Research, development, test, and evaluation	7.2	13.1	27.1	36.4	36.2	38.0	34.8	36.2
Military construction	1.2	2.5	4.3	5.1	5.2	4.6	6.0	5.0
Family housing	0.6	1.7	2.6	3.1	3.3	3.9	3.5	3.3
Other[3]	–1.1	–1.1	0.6	–0.3	–41.6	3.0	1.5	0.9
Total outlays	**$81.7**	**$134.0**	**$252.7**	**$293.6**	**$276.2**	**$267.4**	**$249.0**	**$252.2**
Annual percent change[4]	10.1%	15.2%	11.1%	1.4%	–5.9%	–3.2%	–6.9%	–1.3%

1. Estimate. 2. In 1991–92, abrupt increases in budget authority, especially operations and maintenance, were due to the incremental costs of Operation Desert Shield/Storm. 3. Includes revolving and management funds, trust funds, special foreign currency programs, allowances, and offsetting receipts. 4. Change from immediate prior year; except for 1970 (change from 1965) and 1993 (change from 1991). **Source:** U.S. Dept. of Defense, *Defense 94* (1994).

WOMEN IN UNIFORM, 1994

Service	Number	Percent
Officers		
Army	11,049	12.7%
Navy	7,996	12.5
Marine Corps	616	3.4
Air Force	12,181	15.0
Total	**31,842**	**12.7**
Enlisted		
Army	60,170	12.9%
Navy	44,019	10.6
Marine Corps	7,046	4.5
Air Force	53,829	15.4
Total	**165,064**	**11.9**

Note: As of Apr. 30, 1994. **Source:** U.S. Dept. of Defense, *Defense 94* (1994).

MINORITIES IN UNIFORM, 1994

Service	Black Americans Number	Black Americans Percent	Hispanic Americans Number	Hispanic Americans Percent	Other[1] Number	Other[1] Percent	Total Number	Total Percent
Officers								
Army	9,816	11.3%	2,403	2.8%	3,508	4.0%	15,727	18.1%
Navy	3,100	4.9	1,782	2.8	2,110	3.3	6,992	11.0
Marine Corps	989	5.4	593	3.2	427	2.3	2,009	11.0
Air Force	4,594	5.6	1,609	2.0	2,801	3.4	9,004	11.1
Total	18,499	7.4	6,387	2.6	8,846	3.5	33,732	13.5
Enlisted								
Army	142,787	30.5%	24,193	5.2%	26,532	5.7%	193,512	41.3%
Navy	73,675	17.8	29,662	7.2	24,948	6.0	128,285	31.0
Marine Corps	27,277	17.5	13,881	8.9	5,583	3.6	46,741	30.0
Air Force	58,527	16.8	13,484	3.9	11,534	3.3	83,545	24.0
Total	302,266	21.8	81,220	5.9	68,597	4.9	452,083	32.6

Note: As of Apr. 30, 1994. 1. Includes Native Americans, Alaskan Natives, and Pacific Islanders. **Source:** U.S. Dept. of Defense, *Defense 94* (1994).

ACTIVE DUTY, MONTHLY BASIC PAY TABLE

Pay grade	Rank	Years of service: 2	10	20	26
Commissioned officers					
0-10	General, Admiral	$7,223.70	$7,501.20	$9,051.00	$9,614.70
0-9	Lt. General, Vice-Admiral	6,346.50	6,646.50	7,916.70	8,482.80
0-8	Maj. General, Rear Admiral	5,769.60	6,346.50	7,501.20	7,686.00
0-7	Brig. General, Commodore	4,971.00	5,495.80	6,783.00	6,783.00
0-6	Colonel, Captain	3,790.20	4,038.60	5,193.90	5,959.50
0-5	Lt. Colonel, Commander	3,239.70	3,463.80	4,698.60	4,862.70
0-4	Major, Lt. Commander	2,832.00	3,212.70	4,065.60	4,065.60
0-3	Captain, Lieutenant	2,416.50	3,102.30	3,516.30	3,516.30
0-2	1st Lieutenant, Lt. (J.G.)	2,058.00	2,608.80	2,608.80	2,608.80
0-1	2nd Lieutenant, Ensign	1,703.10	2,058.00	2,058.00	2,058.00
Warrant officers					
W-5	Chief Warrant Officer	N.A.	N.A.	$3,757.80	$4,182.00
W-4	Chief Warrant Officer	$2,362.50	$2,748.30	3,375.90	3,760.80
W-3	Chief Warrant Officer	2,170.80	2,526.30	2,969.70	3,185.10
W-2	Chief Warrant Officer	1,896.30	2,253.30	2,664.60	2,772.00
W-1	Warrant Officer	1,674.30	2,058.00	2,472.90	2,472.90
Enlisted personnel					
E-9	Sgt. Major, Master C.P.O.	N.A.	$2,561.70	$2,855.70	$3,297.90
E-8	Master Sgt., Senior C.P.O.	N.A.	2,209.80	2,502.90	2,945.10
E-7	Sgt. 1st Class, Chief Petty Officer	$1,619.10	1,913.70	2,208.30	2,649.90
E-6	Staff Sgt., Petty Officer, 1st Class	1,406.40	1,701.90	1,934.10	1,934.10
E-5	Sergeant, Petty Officer, 2nd Class	1,232.40	1,554.90	1,641.60	1,641.60
E-4	Corporal, Petty Officer, 3rd Class	1,115.40	1,322.40	1,322.40	1,322.40
E-3	Private 1st Class, Seaman	1,049.70	1,134.60	1,134.60	1,134.60
E-2	Private, Seaman	957.60	957.60	957.60	957.60
E-1	Recruit, Seaman Recruit	854.40	854.40	854.40	854.40

Note: Effective Jan. 1, 1995. N.A. = not applicable. **Source:** U.S. Dept. of Defense.

U.S. ARMED FORCES WORLDWIDE, 1993

Location	Army	Navy	Marine Corps	Air Force	Total DoD
United States[1]					
Continental U.S.	396,747	256,841	134,104	339,550	1,127,242
Alaska	9,548	1,676	50	10,741	22,015
Hawaii	18,831	11,272	8,147	4,708	42,958
Guam	56	4,813	66	2,489	7,424
Puerto Rico	284	3,272	146	37	3,739
Transients	10,636	11,367	6,711	9,813	38,527
Afloat	—	154,387	436	—	154,823
Total[2]	436,392	443,661	149,660	367,370	1,397,083
Europe					
Belgium	1,192	103	33	480	1,808
Germany	87,030	313	144	17,767	105,254
Greece	18	227	73	489	807
Greenland	—	—	—	131	131
Iceland	1	1,718	91	1,068	2,878
Italy	3,166	4,945	159	2,063	10,333
Netherlands	569	19	13	1,625	2,226
Norway	32	36	20	108	196
Portugal	32	172	8	1,108	1,320
Spain	17	3,190	136	477	3,820
Turkey	342	25	19	3,663	4,049
United Kingdom	305	1,892	242	13,661	16,100
Afloat	—	14,985	1,983	—	16,968
Total[2]	92,766	27,663	3,122	42,698	166,249
East Asia and Pacific					
Australia	11	52	12	264	339
Japan	1,961	7,247	21,520	15,403	46,131
Philippines	N.A.	N.A.	N.A.	N.A.	N.A.
South Korea	25,316	315	59	9,140	34,830
Thailand	45	11	18	32	106
Afloat	—	15,281	1,869	—	17,150
Total[2]	27,392	23,113	23,591	24,926	99,022
Africa, Near East, and South Asia					
Bahrain	11	343	16	9	379
Diego Garcia	7	1,109	93	24	1,233
Egypt	493	33	34	45	605
Saudi Arabia	655	51	56	188	950
Afloat	—	7,803	—	—	7,803
Total[2]	1,448	9,369	346	327	11,490
Other Western Hemisphere					
Bermuda	1	521	5	—	527
Canada	17	417	11	102	547
Cuba (Guantanamo)	—	1,751	436	2	2,189
Honduras	626	2	13	55	696
Panama	7,550	513	187	2,292	10,542
Afloat	—	2,526	172	—	2,698
Total[2]	8,318	5,867	1,059	2,514	17,758
Worldwide					
Ashore	572,423	314,761	173,919	444,351	1,505,454
Afloat	—	195,189	4,460	—	199,649
Total	572,423	509,950	178,379	444,351	1,705,103

Note: Includes countries and regional areas where 100 or more U.S. military members are assigned. 1. Includes territories and special locations. 2. Regional totals include countries with less than 100 assigned U.S. military members. **Source:** U.S. Dept. of Defense, *Defense 94* (1994).

MAJOR WEAPON SYSTEMS AND COMBAT FORCES, 1980–94

Weapon or force	1980	1984	1990	1993	1994[1]
Strategic forces					
Land-based ICBMs[2]					
Minuteman	1,000	1,000	950	737	617
Peacekeeper	0	0	50	50	50
Strategic bombers (PAA)					
B-52G/H[3]	241	241	154	84	84
B-1B	0	0	90	84	84
Fleet Ballistic Missile Launchers (SLBMs)					
Poseidon (C-3 and C-4)[4]	336	384	368	96	48
Trident (C-4 and D-5)	—	72	216	312	336
Strategic Defense Interceptors (PAA/squadrons)					
Active	127/7	90/5	18/1	0/0	0/0
Reserve	166/10	162/10	216/12	216/12	150/10
General purpose forces					
Active land forces					
Army divisions	16	16	18	14	12
Marine Corps divisions	3	3	3	3	3
Army separate brigades[5]	8	8	8	7	7
Army Special Forces groups	2	4	5	5	5
Army Ranger regiments	0	0	1	1	1
Active tactical air forces (PAA/squadrons)					
Air Force attack and fighter aircraft	1,608/74	1,734/77	1,722/76	1,212/56	963/50
Conventional bombers (B-52G)	0	0	33	33	19
Navy attack and fighter aircraft	696/60	616/63	622/57	610/56	590/50
Marine Corps attack and fighter aircraft	329/25	256/24	334/24	330/23	332/23
Naval forces					
Strategic forces ships	48	41	39	24	18
Battle forces ships	384	425	412	342	312
Support forces ships	41	46	65	51	41
Reserve forces ships	6	12	31	18	16
Total battle forces deployable	479	524	547	435	387
Surface combatants/mine warfare ships	44	24	16	15	—
Support ships	8	9	3	2	9
Total other forces	52	33	19	17	9
Airlift and sealift forces					
Intertheater airlift (PAA)					
C-5	70	70	109	109	109
C-141	234	234	234	214	214
KC-10	0	25	57	57	57
Intratheater airlift (PAA)					
C-130	482	520	460	406	382
Sealift ships[6]					
Tankers, active	21	21	28	20	18
Cargo, active	23	30	40	40	52
Ready Reserve Force (RRF)	24	51	96	97	99
National Defense Reserve Fleet (NDRF)[7]	0	0	121	59	59

Note: PAA = primary aircraft authorized. 1. Estimate as of September 1993. 2. Number on-line. 3. Does not include conventional B-52 force. 4. C-3 missiles were removed from Poseidon submarines in September of 1992. 5. Does not include roundout brigades; does include the Eskimo scout group and the armored cavalry regiments. 6. Includes fast sealift ships, afloat prepositioned force ships, and common user (charter) ships. 7. Beginning in FY88, specific NDRF ships were designated militarily useful ships. **Source:** U.S. Dept. of Defense, *Defense 94* (1994).

DEPARTMENT OF DEFENSE CONTRACT AWARDS, PAYROLL, AND CIVILIAN AND MILITARY PERSONNEL, BY STATE, 1993

State	Payroll[1] ('000s)	Contract awards[2] ('000s)	Personnel	
			Military	Civilian[3]
Alabama	$ 2,320,128	$ 1,744,313	17,607	25,004
Alaska	1,197,331	554,331	22,015	4,772
Arizona	1,563,659	2,593,378	20,650	9,258
Arkansas	682,747	329,160	6,188	4,336
California	14,157,530	22,951,965	169,464	109,556
Colorado	2,209,849	2,615,661	37,997	13,898
Connecticut	623,405	2,894,638	5,463	4,530
Delaware	274,612	135,601	4,436	1,738
District of Columbia	1,353,315	1,691,559	13,902	16,320
Florida	6,338,015	6,485,989	66,150	30,935
Georgia	4,202,383	4,017,518	60,930	34,989
Hawaii	2,378,723	631,021	42,958	17,341
Idaho	315,040	67,484	4,842	1,588
Illinois	1,866,173	1,359,421	25,066	17,287
Indiana	1,155,632	1,761,204	4,571	15,466
Iowa	214,712	363,500	411	1,565
Kansas	1,177,340	658,655	21,137	6,462
Kentucky	1,844,417	847,091	33,692	13,097
Lousiana	1,346,236	1,554,603	20,695	8,744
Maine	641,968	1,109,861	4,243	7,945
Maryland	3,334,465	3,992,356	31,759	38,623
Massachusetts	1,005,809	5,935,650	6,843	10,543
Michigan	883,908	1,335,901	4,662	9,859
Minnesota	377,396	1,497,124	848	2,842
Mississippi	1,167,446	1,575,387	12,566	10,804
Missouri	1,512,651	5,605,884	15,425	17,179
Montana	252,708	79,195	4,739	1,222
Nebraska	625,659	302,064	9,869	3,690
Nevada	600,541	235,849	8,267	2,088
New Hampshire	231,077	396,064	344	1,372
New Jersey	1,732,979	2,600,831	9,497	23,015
New Mexico	1,065,569	809,746	15,664	8,513
New York	1,891,845	4,641,425	23,452	16,427
North Carolina	4,102,689	1,212,482	92,711	16,894
North Dakota	333,442	172,044	9,854	1,770
Ohio	2,248,803	3,445,640	10,537	34,400
Oklahoma	1,967,108	633,792	27,681	20,187
Oregon	451,468	161,835	957	2,850
Pennsylvania	2,634,261	2,968,230	4,905	42,921
Rhode Island	446,392	389,693	3,719	4,103
South Carolina	2,582,590	729,552	39,102	15,843
South Dakota	261,100	96,106	5,431	1,265
Tennessee	1,057,697	937,326	7,935	6,949
Texas	6,919,548	9,010,273	102,210	55,882
Utah	1,022,935	542,372	5,764	17,510
Vermont	82,260	62,735	137	646
Virginia	11,698,489	7,482,748	92,152	102,211
Washington	3,331,597	1,890,677	36,121	27,018
West Virginia	216,089	132,193	514	1,655
Wisconsin	427,971	845,488	844	3,322
Wyoming	180,440	57,804	3,705	1,000
Undistributed	N.A.	N.A.	28,040	N.A.
Total U.S.	**$100,510,147**	**$114,145,419**	**1,198,671**	**847,434**

Note: For year ending Sept. 30. 1. Payroll estimates cover active duty military and direct hire civilian personnel, including Army Corps of Engineers. 2. Military awards for supplies, services, and construction; expenditures relating to awards may extend over several years. Net value of contracts of over $25,000 for work in each state; the state in which the prime contractor is located is not necessarily the state in which the subcontracted work is done. 3. Civilian employees represent direct-line civilian employees. **Source:** U.S. Dept. of Defense, *Defense 94* (1994).

Social Insurance Programs

In order to provide a safety net for disadvantaged, elderly, and disabled persons, the federal government administers a range of social insurance and social assistance programs, including Medicare, unemployment insurance, workers' compensation, and temporary disability insurance. Also included are an array of "income support programs" such as supplemental security income (SSI), aid to families with dependent children (AFDC), Medicaid, food stamps, low-income home-energy assistance, public housing, special nutritional programs, and general assistance. Three additional programs provide for veterans, public employees, and railroad employees.

Social insurance programs were not developed all at once to fulfill a specific agenda of national need. Rather, they are a hodgepodge of legislation passed (and often altered) over the years to meet the needs of particular groups of citizens at particular times. In what the government calls social insurance programs, certain risks—injury, disability, unemployment, old age, and death—are lumped together. "Premiums," usually in the form of a payroll tax, are paid by employees and/or their employers. The benefit is paid, regardless of other financial resources (other than earnings), when one of those "risks" occurs.

Social Security

The Great Depression proved that traditional support systems—the family, private charities, and local government—failed in nationwide economic hard times. Many old people had exhausted their savings and were destitute; during the depression less than 10 percent of the aged left estates large enough to be probated. This led to the enactment of one of the most comprehensive pieces of legislation ever passed by Congress, the Social Security Act.

Signed into law by Franklin Roosevelt on Aug. 14, 1935, the Social Security Act established two social insurance programs: a federal system of old-age benefits for retired workers in commerce and industry, and a federal-state system of unemployment insurance. The law also provided for federal matching grants-in-aid to states to help them assist the needy aged, blind persons, and children. Today, in the words of former Social Security Commissioner Dorcas R. Hardy, it is the "most complex government program that God and Congress ever created."

The first payments of monthly benefits were made in 1940; since then, $2.9 trillion in cash benefits have been paid. Major changes in the scope of Social Security were made in 1956, when the program was broadened through the addition of disability insurance; in 1965, through the addition of Medicare and Medicaid; in 1970, when the "black lung" program was developed to provide benefits to coal miners who suffer from black lung disease; in 1972, when Congress authorized cost-of-living increases; and in 1974, when Social Security insurance was taken over by the Social Security Administration. In 1983, amendments provided for the taxing of up to one-half of benefits for certain upper-income beneficiaries.

Workers and their employers each contribute an equal amount to the Social Security program to pay for retirement, disability, and Medicare benefits. The amount deducted from paychecks increased steadily from 1983 until 1990, when it leveled off at 7.65% on earnings up to $51,300. (The cap on earnings can be adjusted for inflation; in 1994 it was $60,600.) Employers must contribute the same amount. Self-employed workers, who are both employee and employer, pay both shares, or a total of 15.3%.

Old-age, survivors and disability insurance (OASDI) This program's basic principles are that benefits are related to earnings in covered work, benefits are paid regardless of income from savings, pensions, etc., and universal compulsory coverage is to assure a base of economic security. Monthly benefits are payable at age 65 to workers who are eligible, and lump sum payments are made to the estates of workers who die before reaching 65. The addition of disability insurance in 1956 and hospital insurance in 1965 broadened the program's scope, and in 1972 Congress authorized provisions for cost-of-living increases. The 1983 amendments improved the program's financial footing with

APPROXIMATE MONTHLY RETIREMENT, DISABILITY, AND SURVIVOR BENEFITS

Worker's age, 1995	Worker's family	Insured worker's earnings, 1994: $20,000	$30,000	$40,000	$50,000	$60,600 or more
	Retirement benefits[1]					
45	Retired worker only	$ 775	$1,039	$1,178	$1,302	$1,418
	Worker and spouse[2]	1,162	1,558	1,767	1,953	2,127
55	Retired worker only	770	1,033	1,163	1,253	1,325
	Worker and spouse[2]	1,155	1,549	1,744	1,879	1,987
65	Retired worker only	761	1,014	1,111	1,166	1,199
	Worker and spouse[2]	1,141	1,521	1,666	1,749	1,798
	Disability benefits[3]					
25	Disabled worker only	$ 771	$1,033	$1,174	$1,297	$1,409
	Disabled, with dependents[4]	1,156	1,549	1,762	1,946	2,113
35	Disabled worker only	768	1,028	1,171	1,293	1,383
	Disabled, with dependents[4]	1,152	1,542	1,757	1,940	2,075
45	Disabled worker only	767	1,027	1,170	1,271	1,329
	Disabled, with dependents[4]	1,151	1,541	1,756	1,906	1,993
55	Disabled worker only	767	1,027	1,143	1,211	1,251
	Disabled, with dependents[4]	1,150	1,540	1,715	1,817	1,876
64	Disabled worker only	764	1,017	1,117	1,171	1,203
	Disabled, with dependents[4]	1,147	1,526	1,675	1,757	1,805
	Survivor benefits[5]					
35	Spouse and 1 child[6]	$1,152	$1,542	$1,758	$1,940	$2,088
	Spouse and 2 children[7]	1,426	1,800	2,051	2,264	2,435
	1 child only	576	771	879	970	1,044
	Spouse at age 60[8]	549	735	838	925	995
45	Spouse and 1 child[6]	1,150	1,540	1,750	1,914	2,006
	Spouse and 2 children[7]	1,423	1,797	2,049	2,235	2,342
	1 child only	575	770	875	957	1,003
	Spouse at age 60	548	734	837	913	957
55	Spouse and 1 child[6]	1,150	1,540	1,714	1,816	1,876
	Spouse and 2 children[7]	1,422	1,797	2,001	2,120	2,189
	1 child only	575	770	857	908	938
	Spouse at age 60	548	734	817	866	894

Note: Assumes steady earnings; actual benefits depend on the pattern of past and future earnings. 1. If worker retires at normal retirement age with steady lifetime earnings. 2. Spouse is assumed to be the same age as the worker. Spouse may qualify for a higher retirement benefit based on his or her own work record. 3. For workers with steady earnings and disabled in 1994. 4. Includes spouse and child, the maximum family benefit. 5. For workers with steady earnings who died in 1995. 6. Benefits are the same for two children if no parent survives or if the surviving parent has substantial earnings. 7. Equals maximum family benefit. 8. Figures for 1994 only. Spouses turning 60 in the future would receive higher benefits. **Source:** Social Security Administration, *Understanding Social Security* (1995).

tax rate increases, permanent increases in self-employment tax rates, and taxing up to one half of benefits for certain upper-income beneficiaries: single retirees with adjusted gross income (AGI) above $25,000 and married couples with AGI above $32,000.

Eligibility Insured status: A worker must have a specific amount of work-covered employment (about 97% of all jobs today are covered by the program, compared with 55% in 1939). Persons reaching age 62 in 1991 or later will need credit for 10 years of work in covered jobs to qualify for retirement benefits. If a worker dies before achieving fully insured status, survivor benefits may be paid to his or her spouse.

Annual earnings test Monthly benefits are paid to a worker and to his or her family members and survivors only when they do not have substantial earnings from work. In 1995, retirees under 65 were permitted to earn up to $8,160. Retirees age 65 to 69 could earn $11,280 in income before their benefits were reduced. Retirees over age 70 receive benefits regardless of income.

For beneficiaries under age 65 who have earnings in excess of these amounts, $1 of benefits is lost for each $2 of earnings; for beneficiaries age 65–69, the reduction rate is $1 for every $3 of earnings in excess of the exempt amount.

Disability requirement For monthly benefits, the impairment must prohibit the individual from engaging in any kind of substantial gainful work (up to $500 a month). Work is encouraged by referrals to state vocational rehabilitation agencies, and the individual is allowed a trial period of work during which benefits continue.

Benefit amounts A worker's Social Security benefit is based on his or her average "covered" earning computed over the period of time he or she could have been expected to work. Workers become eligible for benefits at age 62. However, a worker who retires at 62 receives as little as 80 percent of the full amount that would have been payable at age 65. The normal retirement age will be increased gradually from 65 to 67, beginning in 2000. See the accompanying table for approximate monthly benefits for retired, disabled, and survivor recipients.

The OASDI programs are financed from taxes collected on earnings in covered jobs from employees and employers, which are deposited in two separate trust funds. The money received by the trust funds can be used only to pay OASDI benefits and operating expenses.

Medicare The Social Security Amendments of 1965 established two contributory health insurance programs designed to provide assistance for medical expenses for the aged and disabled. The first is a compulsory program of hospital insurance (HI) which provides basic protection against the costs of inpatient hospital services and related post-hospital care, including home health services, part-time nursing care, and physical therapy. Persons reaching age 65 without qualifying for HI may voluntarily enroll by paying a monthly premium.

The second health program is supplementary medical insurance (SMI) coverage, a voluntary program in which enrolled individuals pay a monthly premium ($46.10 in 1995). The program's

OASDI BENEFICIARIES AND BENEFIT PAYMENTS, 1994

Type of beneficiaries	Number ('000s)	Percent of all beneficiaries	Average monthly benefit
Retired workers	26,493	61.2%	$699
Wives and husbands of retired workers	3,038	7.0	360
Children of retired workers	446	1.0	311
Surviving children	1,901	4.4	457
Widowed mothers and fathers	276	0.6	457
Widows and widowers	5,054	11.7	659
Disabled widow(er)s	167	0.4	449
Disabled workers	4,067	9.4	662
Wives and husbands of disabled workers	268	0.6	160
Children of disabled workers	1,396	3.2	178
Total monthly beneficiaries[1]	**143,109**	**100.0%**	**$629**

Note: OASDI = old-age, survivors and disability insurance. 1. Includes small numbers of uninsured persons over the age of 72 not shown separately. Individual components do not add up to total because of independent rounding. **Source:** Social Security Administration, *Fact Sheet on the OASDI Program,* 1995.

SOCIAL SERVICE PROGRAMS

Information about social service programs can be obtained from the following government agencies:

Aid to Families with Dependent Children (AFDC) Administration on Children, Youth, and Families, U.S. Dept. of Health and Human Services.

Black lung program Office of Workers Compensation Progs., U.S. Dept. of Labor.

Food stamps Food and Nutrition Service, U.S. Dept. of Agriculture.

Head Start Administration on Children, Youth and Families, U.S. Dept. of Health and Human Services.

Housing subsidies Special Needs Assistance Progs., U.S. Dept. of Housing and Urban Development; Farmers Home Admin.

Medicaid Health Care Financing Admin., U.S. Dept. of Health and Human Services.

Medicare (HI) Health Care Financing Admin., U.S. Dept. of Health and Human Services.

Social Security (OASDI) Social Security Admin., U.S. Dept. of Health and Human Services.

Special nutrition programs Food and Nutrition Service, U.S. Dept. of Agriculture.

Supplemental Security Income (SSI) Social Security Admin., U.S. Dept. of Health and Human Services.

Temporary disability insurance Employment and Training Admin., U.S. Dept. of Labor.

Unemployment insurance Office of Workers Compensation Progs., U.S. Dept. of Labor.

Veterans' benefits U.S. Dept. of Veterans Affairs.

Note: For additional information see Part II: "Executive Departments."

MEDICARE: RECIPIENTS AND BENEFITS, 1975–94 (numbers in thousands)

Category	1975	1980	1985	1990	1992	1993[1]	1994[1]
Enrollees with hospital insurance (HI)							
Total enrolled	23,842	27,539	30,067	33,071	34,369	35,463	36,148
Aged	21,795	24,571	27,123	29,801	30,808	31,630	32,054
Disabled	2,047	2,968	2,944	3,270	3,561	3,833	4,094
Total beneficiaries	5,362	6,664	6,840	6,750	7,445	7,625	7,825
Aged	4,906	5,943	6,168	6,070	6,710	6,820	6,960
Disabled	456	721	672	680	735	805	865
Average annual benefit	$327	$863	$1,587	$1,987	$2,345	$2,553	$2,807
Aged	326	853	1,563	1,971	2,324	2,539	2,800
Disabled	345	948	1,806	2,139	2,861	2,665	2,861
Enrollees with supplementary medical insurance (SMI)							
Total enrolled	23,339	27,120	29,721	32,333	33,634	34,365	35,010
Aged	21,504	24,422	27,049	29,426	30,471	30,982	31,354
Disabled	1,835	2,698	2,672	2,907	3,163	3,383	3,656
Total beneficiaries	12,108	17,703	22,132	26,004	28,125	28,766	29,713
Aged	11,311	16,034	20,199	23,820	25,603	25,994	26,682
Disabled	797	1,669	1,933	2,184	2,522	2,772	3,031
Average annual benefit	$161	$374	$733	$1,282	$1,445	$1,525	$1,621
Aged	153	347	705	1,250	1,403	1,474	1,593
Disabled	259	615	1,021	1,602	1,847	1,994	1,863

1. Estimate. **Source:** Social Security Administration, publ. in U.S. House of Representatives, Committee on Ways and Means, *Overview of Entitlement Programs, 1994 Green Book* (1994).

MEDICAID RECIPIENTS AND EXPENDITURES, 1975–94

Year	Aged	Blind	Disabled	Dependent children under 21	Adults in families with dependent children	Other	Total
				Recipients ('000s)			
1975	3,615	109	2,355	9,598	4,529	1,800	22,207
1981	3,367	86	2,993	9,581	5,187	1,364	21,980
1985	3,061	80	2,937	9,757	5,518	1,214	21,814
1990	3,202	83	3,635	11,220	6,010	1,105	25,255
1992	3,742	84	4,378	15,104	6,954	664	30,926
1994	4,040	87	5,373	17,189	7,582	580	35,056
				Payments (millions of constant 1992 dollars[1])			
1975	$11,723	$250	$ 8,210	$ 5,880	$ 5,547	$1,323	$32,931
1981	15,584	242	14,603	5,508	5,908	867	42,710
1985	18,466	326	17,296	5,782	6,217	1,045	49,135
1990	23,229	469	25,887	9,828	9,277	1,135	70,048
1992	29,078	530	33,326	14,491	12,185	1,032	90,814
1994	33,385	648	41,583	17,306	13,581	1,254	107,982
				Payments per capita (constant 1992 dollars[1])			
1975	$3,241	$2,287	$3,486	$613	$1,224	$ 734	$1,496
1981	4,628	2,801	4,880	575	1,338	636	1,944
1985	6,033	4,066	5,890	592	1,127	862	2,252
1990	7,254	5,629	7,123	876	1,543	1,147	2,773
1992	7,770	6,298	7,612	959	1,752	1,814	2,936
1994	8,243	7,450	7,739	1,006	1,791	2,162	3,080

Note: A small number of recipients are in more than one category. 1. Except 1994, which are current dollars. **Source:** Health Care Financing Administration, *Statistical Report on Medical Care* (1995).

coverage includes physician's and surgeon's services, outpatient services and laboratory tests, ambulance services, surgical dressings, home health services, and comprehensive outpatient services.

As with OASDI, hospital insurance is financed by a tax on earnings: of the 7.65 percent tax on earnings (FICA) deducted from employee paychecks, 1.65 percent is for hospital insurance and the 6.2 percent is for OASDI.

Effectiveness of Social Security According to the government, the Social Security system has achieved its basic goal of helping elderly people maintain a basic standard of living. It has dramatically reduced the poverty rate for the elderly from 35% in 1959 to 12.2% in 1992. The benefits are the primary source of cash income for most elderly Americans, providing 53% of total income for all retirees age 65 and over. For 23% of the elderly, it constitutes 90% or more of total income. And for 14% of the elderly, Social Security is the only source of income. For all people receiving Social Security—not just the elderly—the payouts lifted 17.3 million out of poverty, reducing the number of poor to 36.9 million in 1992. Means-tested cash and in-kind transfers reduce the poverty count by an additional 7.0 million individuals.

Future of Social Security Originally funded on a "pay-as-you-go" basis, the system was overhauled in 1988 to keep it fiscally sound into the future. In 1988 the program's funds were running down because of an interval in the 1970s when prices outpaced wages and cost-of-living adjustments were not being offset by increased payments into the funds. To bolster the funds and protect today's young generation from large tax hikes when the baby-boom generation retires, the government ordered incremental increases in the Social Security tax rate. The program quickly began building reserves because there were millions more workers paying into the system than there were retirees and others receiving benefits. Projections indicate annual surpluses reaching $500 million a day or close to $200 billion a year by the start of the next century. Only well into the next century, when the baby boomers retire, do forecasts show the surpluses diminishing. However, the Hospital Insurance Fund (Medicare) will start to run a deficit because of the aging population by the year 2000 unless it receives additional funding. Estimates are that the "nest egg" for retirement benefits will have disappeared by 2050, eaten away by baby boomers who will have started to retire in 2010.

Other Programs

Unemployment compensation The Social Security Act provided an inducement to states to enact unemployment insurance laws. The Department of Labor oversees the system, but each state, as well as the District of Columbia, Puerto Rico, and the Virgin Islands, administers its own program. Covered employers are charged a tax of 6.2 percent on the first $7,000 of each worker's covered wages annually. Nationwide, about 109 million workers—98 percent of all wage and salary workers, or 90 percent of all employed persons—were covered in 1993.

Eligibility Workers must be ready, able, and willing to work and must be registered for work at a state public employment office. A worker's benefit is based on his or her employment in covered work over a prior performance period. No state can deny benefit to a claimant if he or she refuses to accept a new job under substandard labor conditions or where he or she would be required to join a company union.

In 1993, there were 7.8 million beneficiaries, down significantly from the 9.6 million people claiming unemployment benefits in 1992 and the 10.6 million in 1991. Their average weekly benefit was $173 and the average duration of benefit was 15.6 weeks, making the average total benefit $2,699. The weekly benefit varies from state to state, but the general formula is designed to compensate for between 50% and 70% of average weekly pretax wage, up to a state-determined minimum. All but two states provide a statutory maximum of 26 weeks of benefits in a benefit year—the maximum in Massachusetts and Washington is 30 weeks. Minimum benefits, ranging from $5 in Hawaii to $73 in Washington, are provided in every state. Maximum benefits range from $133 in Puerto Rico to $487 in Massachusetts.

Workers' compensation Social insurance began in the United States with workers' compensation. A law covering federal civilian employees engaged in hazardous jobs was enacted in 1908; the first state compensation law to be held constitutional was enacted in 1911. These laws made industry responsible for the compensation of workers (or their survivors) injured or killed while on the job. A worker incurring an occupational injury is compensated regardless of fault or blame in the accident. A separate federal program enacted in 1969 protects coal miners (see "Black lung program" below).

Coverage and benefits Workers' compensation is almost exclusively financed by employers on the principle that the cost of work-related accidents is part of the expense of production. Employers can use private insurance companies or can qualify as self-insurers. Workers' compensation covered nearly 94 million workers in 1991, or 87.0% of employed wage and salary workers. The most usual exempted workers are domestic, agricultural, and casual laborers. The cash benefit for temporary total disability, permanent, total or partial disability, or death of a breadwinner is usually about 66.7% of weekly earnings at the time of the accident. Most state laws pay temporary disability benefits for as long as the disability lasts and the condition has not been stabilized to the point where no further improvement can result from medical treatment. Total benefit payments under workers' compensation programs in 1991, including medical care and hospitalization, topped $42 billion, an increase of 10.3% over 1990.

Permanent partial disability Compensation for specific, or "schedule," injuries (for clearly measurable matters) is generally subject to different (usually lower) dollar maximums and is determined without regard to loss of earning power. Compensation for "nonschedule" injuries (injuries to head, back, nervous system) is the difference between wages before and after impairment.

Death benefits Compensation is related to earnings and is graduated by the number of dependents.

Medical benefits are furnished without limit as to time or amount for accidental injuries.

Black lung program Established by the Federal Coal Mine Health and Safety Act of 1969, this provides monthly cash benefits to coal miners who are totally disabled because of black lung disease (pneumoconiosis) and to survivors of miners who die from this disease. Benefits, paid mostly out of a trust fund financed by an excise tax on coal, totaled $1.4 billion in 1991. That's a 25 percent decrease from the peak year of 1980. Older beneficiaries continue to die in greater numbers than new claimants enter the program. At the end of 1992, 316,886 disabled workers, dependents, and survivors were receiving cash benefits.

Temporary disability insurance provides coverage against the risk of lost wages due to short-term nonoccupational disability. The Federal Unemployment Tax Act permits states where employees make contributions under the unemployment insurance program to use some or all of those contributions for disability benefits. It is estimated that about two-thirds of the nation's wage and salary earners have some protection through various voluntary and governmental group arrangements. In general the benefit amount for a week is intended to replace at least half the weekly wage loss for a maximum of 26 to 39 weeks per year.

Income Support Programs

To be eligible for these programs, a person must have income and assets below a certain level and often must meet other eligibility criteria. Today Supplemental Security Income (SSI) and Aid to Families with Dependent Children (AFDC) are the two major cash assistance programs. A number of other programs, including Medicaid and food stamps, provide benefits for special needs and purposes.

Poverty income guidelines The poverty income guidelines are used to determine whether a person or family is eligible for assistance under a particular federal program. The poverty threshold is established each year by increasing the previous year's threshold by the change in the Consumer Price Index. The original poverty threshold was devised in the 1960s and was equal to three times the amount of money needed to buy the cheapest "nutritionally adequate" diet as dictated by the Department of Agriculture.

SUPPLEMENTAL SECURITY INSURANCE BENEFICIARIES AND BENEFITS, 1993

Type of payment	Total	Aged	Blind	Disabled
Number of beneficiaries				
Federal SSI payments	5,561,334	1,321,959	78,499	4,160,876
Federal SSI only	3,406,549	792,980	44,084	2,569,485
Federal SSI and state supplementation	2,154,785	528,979	34,415	1,591,391
State supplementation	2,501,056	680,551	41,801	1,778,704
State supplementation only	346,271	151,572	7,386	187,313
Total	**5,907,605**	**1,473,531**	**85,885[1]**	**4,348,189[2]**
Average monthly amount				
Federal SSI payments	$316.83	$202.34	$310.84	$353.32
State supplementation	109.91	115.31	157.48	106.73
Total	**$344.80**	**$234.73**	**$360.76**	**$381.76**

Note: As of September. 1. Includes approximately 21,609 persons age 65 or older. 2. Includes approximately 614,782 persons aged 65 or older. **Source:** Social Security Administration, publ. in U.S. House of Representatives, Committee on Ways and Means, *Overview of Entitlement Programs, 1994 Green Book* (1994).

SOCIAL INSURANCE PROGRAMS: BENEFICIARIES AND PAYMENTS, 1994

Program	Beneficiaries ('000s)	Benefits (billions)
OASDI	43,109	$325.2
Medicare	36,893	159.3
Medicaid	35,056	108.0
Food stamps	22,206	27.0
AFDC	14,226	22.8
SSI	6,295	26.5

Note: OASDI = old-age, survivors, and disability insurance; AFDC = aid to families with dependent children; SSI = supplemental security insurance. **Source:** Social Security Administration; Administration on Children and Families; Health Care Financing Administration.

Programs for Special Groups

Veterans' benefits The tradition of veterans' benefits dates to the 18th century when the Continental Congress provided disability pensions for veterans of the Revolutionary War. Today, the Department of Veterans Affairs (DVA) offers a wide range of services and benefits to eligible veterans, their dependents, and their survivors. In 1994, federal outlays for veterans' benefits and services were $34.7 billion.

While the veteran population as a whole is decreasing in numbers, from about 29.5 million in 1975 to 26.8 million in 1992—the number of veterans age 65 or older is increasing rapidly, from about 2.2 million in 1975 to about 8.0 million in 1992. The use and cost of medical care are expected to grow more rapidly over the next several years than those of other veterans' benefits and services. Compensation and pension caseloads are decreasing steadily due to beneficiary deaths, terminations for excess incomes, and age limitation for dependents. The number of trainees under the Montgomery GI bill will increase as more veterans become eligible.

VETERANS' BENEFITS AND SERVICES: EXPENDITURES AND RECIPIENTS, 1975–94

Fiscal year	Compensation and pensions	Readjustment, education, job training	Medical programs	Housing loans
Outlays (millions)				
1975	$ 7,860	$4,593	$ 3,665	([1])
1980	11,688	2,342	6,515	([1])
1985	14,714	1,059	9,547	([1])
1990	15,241	278	12,134	([1])
1991	16,961	427	12,889	([1])
1992	17,296	783	14,091	([1])
1993	17,758	826	14,812	([1])
1994	17,221	1,964	15,531	([1])
Recipients ('000s)				
1975	4,855	2,804	1,985	290
1980	4,646	1,232	2,671	297
1985	4,005	491	2,963	179
1990	3,614	329	3,018	196
1991	3,546	275	2,963	181
1992	3,462	318	2,927	266
1993	3,397	362	2,800	383
1994	2,900	756	2,765	500

1. No dollar figures for housing loans are provided because these are revolving funds and are not comparable to program expenditures in the other columns. **Source:** U.S. Dept. of Veterans Affairs.

Service-connected compensation is paid to veterans who have incurred injuries or illness while in service. The amounts of the monthly payments are determined by disability ratings. Death compensation or dependency and indemnity compensation is paid to survivors of veterans who died as a result of service-connected causes. In 1994, 2.5 million veterans or their survivors received $14.1 billion in compensation payments.

Veterans pensions are means-tested benefits paid to war veterans who have become permanently and totally disabled from non-service-connected causes, and to survivors of war veterans. Benefits are based on family size, and the pensions provide a floor of income. The basic benefit before subtracting other income sources is $10,240 for a veteran with one dependent ($7,818 for a veteran living alone). A surviving spouse with no children could receive two-thirds of the basic benefit amount given a single veteran. About 388,000 people received $3.2 billion in veterans' pension payments in 1994.

Medical programs The DVA operates 172 hospital centers, 128 nursing homes, 37 domiciliaries, and 353 outpatient clinics. In 1994 the DVA's nationwide health system received 2.8 million applicants for care, almost all of whom received outpatient care; 500,000 were treated as inpatients. In 1994, DVA medical programs cost the federal government $15.5 billion.

The DVA extends free priority care to service-connected disabled veterans, to veterans in special categories, and to needy non-service-connected veterans.

Housing and loan programs The DVA made 500,000 guaranteed loans for housing for veterans in 1994. The maximum guaranty is as follows: 50 percent of the loan amount for loans of $45,000 or less; $22,500 for loans between $45,001 and $56,250; the lesser of $36,000 or 40% of the loan for loans between $56,251 and $144,000; and the lesser of $46,000 or 25 percent of the loan for loans in excess of $144,000.

Other veterans' programs In 1994, the DVA spent $1.96 billion for a variety of education and training programs for eligible veterans and military personnel. The largest program is the Montgomery GI bill, which provides educational assistance. Contributions are required, and veterans can receive a basic educational benefit of up to $400 per month for 36 months while in an educational program.

The veterans' job training act program provides payments to defray training costs of employers who hire certain veterans of the Korean conflict or Vietnam era who have been unemployed for long periods of time.

Supplemental Security Income (SSI)

In 1974, Congress replaced the federal-state programs for needy aged (over 65 years old), blind, and disabled people with a single federal Supplementary Security Income program. Monthly cash payments are made to eligible persons whose "countable" income (in 1994) is less than $5,592 for individuals receiving only Social Security, or $11,724 for individuals with only wage income. (For married couples, the figures are $8,268 and $17,076 respectively.) Individual assets are limited to $2,000 for an individual and $3,000 for a couple. The qualifying standards for disability benefits are the same as those used for the Social Security disability insurance program. In 1994, the regular federal SSI benefit was $446 for eligible individuals and $669 for eligible couples. To encourage SSI recipients to work, $65 of earned income in any month is excluded from countable income. In 1993, 6.0 million persons were receiving federal SSI payments totaling $24.0 billion, or an average of $317 per month. In addition, states have the option of supplementing federal SSI under their own programs or in programs administered by the federal government. More than 2.5 million persons received state supplements in 1993; the average payment was $110.

Medicaid

Enacted jointly with Medicare in 1965, Medicaid provides federal matching funds to states to help pay the cost of medical care and services for low-income persons. Payments are made to suppliers of the care and service. To be eligible for matching funds, a state Medicaid program must cover all persons who receive assistance under AFDC. (Most SSI recipients are also covered.) In 1994, 35 million aged, blind, disabled, or poor persons with families received Medicaid benefits at a total cost to state and federal governments of $108 billion. Medicaid may also pay the premiums for supplementary medical insurance and the deductible and coinsurance cost of hospital insurance. Medicaid also covers some medical services that Medicare does not.

Aid to Families with Dependent Children

The Social Security Act of 1935 included a provision authorizing a federal-state program to help needy families with children. To qualify for grants, the states must comply with federal guidelines. States may choose whom they will assist, how the assistance will be given, and how much it will be. The states compute "needs standards," taking into account allowances for food, clothing, shelter, utilities, and other necessities. A family's need is theoretically equal to the difference between the amount of the "needs standard" and the family's income. However, states are not required to provide the full amount of the difference. For a family to qualify, children generally have to be under the age of 18. Since 1990, states have been required to implement a Job Opportunities and Basic Skills (JOBS) training program designed to prevent children from repeating the cycle of welfare dependency. Enrollment is mandatory for all able-bodied recipients, and the program must include an educational component.

Food stamps

By providing eligible applicants with coupons to buy food, this program enables families in need to purchase a nutritionally adequate diet. In general, a household is considered eligible if it has less than $2,000 in liquid assets, or if 30 percent of its countable cash income is insufficient to purchase an adequate low-cost diet, as defined by the U.S. Department of Agriculture (USDA) "Thrifty Food Plan." The Food Stamp Act of 1964 set eligibility requirements for food stamp program participants and provides coupons through state and local agencies that are used to buy food in approved retail stores. States delegate varying degrees of authority to counties and cities, but the federal government finances 100 percent of the state-issued food benefits and part of the state's administrative costs.

The federal government spent $22.0 billion to distribute food stamps to a total of 27.0 million people in 1994; each participant received an average of $68 in monthly coupons.

Special nutrition programs

The USDA administers a number of programs designed to help safeguard the health and well-being of the nation's children by assisting the states in providing adequate meals to all children at a moderate cost. The programs include the National School Lunch Program, the School Breakfast Program, the Summer Food Service Program, the Child Care Food Program, the Special Milk Program, and the Special Supplemental Food Program for Women, Infants, and Children (WIC) Program. The nutrition program for the elderly requires no income test, but preference is given to those with the greatest need.

Housing subsidies

The federal government has traditionally provided housing aid directly to lower-income households in the form of rental and mortgage-interest subsidies. The primary purposes are to improve housing quality and to reduce housing costs for lower-income households.

Most housing aid is targeted to very-low-income renters through two basic types of rental assistance programs. Project-based aid is typically tied to projects specifically produced for

AFDC BENEFICIARIES AND BENEFITS, 1970–94

Year	Average monthly beneficiaries ('000s)			Average monthly benefit	Total benefits
	Families	Recipients	Children		
1970	1,909	7,429	5,494	$178	$ 4,082
1975	3,269	11,067	7,821	208	8,153
1980	3,574	10,597	7,220	269	11,540
1985	3,692	10,813	7,165	329	14,580
1990	3,974	11,460	7,755	389	18,539
1991	4,375	12,595	8,515	388	20,356
1992	4,769	13,625	9,225	389	22,240
1993	4,981	14,144	9,539	373	22,286
1994	5,046	14,226	9,590	376	22,796

Note: AFDC = Aid to Families with Dependent Children. **Source:** Administration for Children and Families, unpublished data.

U.S. WEIGHTED AVERAGE POVERTY THRESHOLDS, 1960–93

	Maximum yearly income						
Year	1 person	2 people	3 people	4 people	5 people	6 people	7 people
1960	$1,490	$1,924	$ 2,359	$ 3,022	$ 3,560	$ 4,002	$ 4,921[1]
1965	1,582	2,048	2,514	3,223	3,797	4,264	5,248[1]
1970	1,954	2,525	3,099	3,968	4,680	5,260	6,468[1]
1975	2,724	3,506	4,293	5,500	6,499	7,316	9,022[1]
1980	4,190	5,363	6,565	8,414	9,966	11,269	12,761
1985	5,469	6,998	8,573	10,989	13,007	14,696	16,656
1990	6,652	8,509	10,419	13,359	15,792	17,839	20,241
1991	6,932	8,865	10,860	13,924	16,456	18,587	21,058
1992	7,143	9,137	11,186	14,335	16,592	19,137	21,594
1993	7,363	9,414	11,522	14,763	17,449	19,718	22,383

1. Seven people or more. **Source:** U.S. Bureau of the Census, *Statisticial Abstract, 1995.*

FEDERAL FOOD ASSISTANCE PROGRAMS, 1970–93

Program	1970	1980	1990	1993
Participants (millions)				
Food stamps	4.3	21.1	20.1	27.0
National school lunch program[1]	22.4	26.6	24.1	24.9
School breakfast[2]	0.5	3.6	4.1	5.4
Women-infants-children	—	1.9	4.5	5.9
Child and adult care[3]	0.1	0.7	1.5	2.0
Summer feeding[4]	0.2	1.9	1.7	2.1
Nutrition program for the elderly[5]	—	166	246	245
Federal cost (millions)				
Food stamps	$4,624	$8,721	$14,187	$22,006
National school lunch program[1]	300	2,279	3,214	4,081
School breakfast[2]	11	288	596	869
Women-infants-children	—	584	1,637	2,115
Child and adult care[3]	6	207	720	1,082
Summer feeding[4]	2	104	145	195
Nutrition program for the elderly	—	75	142	145

1. Data are for month in which most pupils participated nationwide. Covers public and private elementary and secondary schools and residential child care institutions. Costs do not include the value of USDA-donated commodities. 2. September through May average lunches or breakfasts served, divided by the ratio of average daily attendance to enrollment. 3. Provides year-round subsidies to feed preschool children in child care centers and family day care programs. Certain care centers serving disabled or elderly adults also receive meal subsidies. 4. Provides free meals to poor children in summer months. Number of participants is July average daily attendance at participating institutions. 5. Number of meals served. **Source:** U.S. Dept. of Agriculture, *Annual Historical Review of Food and Nutrition Service Programs* (annual), and unpublished data.

HEAD START PARTICIPATION AND FUNDING, 1966–95

Year	Enrollment	Budget authority (millions)
1966	733,000	$ 198.9
1970	477,400	325.7
1975	349,000	403.9
1980	376,300	735.0
1985	452,080	1,075.0
1990	548,470	1,552.0[1]
1991	583,471	1,951.8
1992	621,078	2,201.8
1993	713,903	2,776.3
1994	750,000[2]	3,326.0
1995	752,000[2]	3,534.4

Note: Since 1982, only full-year services have been provided. 1. After sequestration. 2. Estimated. **Source:** U.S. Dept of Health and Human Services, Administration for Children and Families, unpublished data, 1995.

lower-income households through new construction or substantial renovation. Almost all project-based aid is provided through production-oriented programs, including the public-housing program, the section 8 new construction and substantial rehabilitation program, and the section 236 mortgage-interest-subsidy program (all administered by the Department of Housing and Urban Development), and the section 515 mortgage-interest-subsidy program administered by the Farmers Home Administration.

Household-based subsidies permit renters to choose from standard housing units in the existing private housing stock. Rental assistance programs generally reduce tenants' rent payments to 30 percent of their income, with the government paying the balance of the contract rents.

The federal government also assists some lower- and moderate-income householders in becoming home owners by making long-term commitments to reduce their mortgage interest. These generally reduce mortgage payments, property taxes, and insurance costs to a fixed percentage of income, ranging from 20 percent to 28 percent.

The total number of households receiving assistance has increased substantially, from 3.2 million at the beginning of fiscal year 1977 to 5.8 million at the beginning of 1994. The number of households receiving rental subsidies increased from 2.1 million to 5.0 million, while the number of home owners receiving assistance in a given year has declined steadily, from an all-time high of 1.2 million in 1983 to fewer than 800,000 in 1994. Total outlays for housing aid rose from $2.9 billion in 1977 to $21.8 billion in 1994, while per unit outlays rose from $1,160 to $4,540 over the same period.

Housing for the homeless HUD funding for homeless programs is made available to state and local governments, Indian tribes, and nonprofit organizations. In 1991, $234.5 million was appropriated for homeless programs. The specific programs are the Emergency Shelter Grants (ESG) Program, the Supportive Housing Demonstration Program, Shelter-Plus-Care Homeless Rental Housing Assistance, and the HUD-Owned Single Property Disposition Program.

Head Start Head Start provides a wide range of services to children of low-income families (and their families) up to the age of five. Its goals are to improve the social competence, learning skills, and health and nutrition status of low-income children so that they can begin school on an equal footing with their more advantaged peers. The services include cognitive and language development, medical, dental, and mental health services (including screening and immunizations), and nutritional and social services. Parental involvement is extensive, through both volunteer participation and employment of parents as Head Start staff.

At least 90% of Head Start children come from families with incomes at or below the poverty line, and at least 10% of enrollment slots in each state must be available to disabled children. Since 1990, though, at least 13% of the slots have gone to disabled children. Head Start provides services to about 750,000 children annually, at a total federal cost of $3.5 billion. Approximately 55% of Head Start children came from families receiving AFDC benefits. Since 1980, the children served by Head Start have grown younger, less black, and more Hispanic. Five-year-olds made up 21% of the Head Start population in 1980; in 1993 they constituted only 6%. Meanwhile, four-year-olds increased from 55% to 64%.

SOCIAL SECURITY AND YOU

While Social Security benefits are automatic for all people who hold a Social Security card and who are eligible for programs, the Social Security Administration (SSA) recommends that workers check the agency's records of their earnings every three to five years. If their records are not accurate—the SSA says that 1 percent of eligible wages are not credited to workers' records—your benefits could be lower than you deserve.

To find out what your earnings are, pick up a Personal Earnings and Benefit Estimate Statement (Pebes). This, as well as free booklets detailing eligibility requirements and benefit payments, is available at any of the more than 1,300 local SSA offices nationwide; or call 1-800-234-5SSA.

Internal Revenue Service

Founded in 1862, the Internal Revenue Service (IRS) is the office of the Department of the Treasury charged with collecting federal taxes. The Constitution empowers Congress to levy excise taxes and—in emergencies—to raise direct taxes. Congress's right to levy taxes on the income of individuals and corporations was contested throughout the 19th century, but that authority was written into the Constitution with the passage of the 16th Amendment in 1913. Today, the source of most of the federal government's revenues is the individual income tax, corporate income tax, excise taxes, estate taxes, and gift taxes. The IRS is responsible for these taxes as well as for collecting employee and employer payments for social insurance and retirement insurance (see "Social Insurance Programs"); since 1986, taxes on alcohol, tobacco, firearms, and explosives have been collected by the Bureau of Alcohol, Tobacco, and Firearms.

In 1993, the IRS processed 207.4 million tax returns totaling $1,176.7 trillion. Individual returns made up 55 percent of the number of returns, and net revenues from individual income taxes comprised 47 percent of total revenues.

Principal Deductions

Personal exemptions Taxpayers are allowed to claim personal exemptions for the taxpayer and each dependent claimed in filing income tax. Congress determines the amount (since 1990, pegged to the inflation rate) allowable for deductions on personal and other exemptions.

Interest expenses As of 1991, there is no longer a deduction allowed for personal interest expenses (such as those accrued on credit cards), though there was in prior years. Nonbusiness interest expense falls into four categories: consumer interest (on loans used for personal reasons, such as auto loans, school loans, and insurance: mortgage interest; investment interest; and passive activity interest.

Medical expenses Although almost all medical expenses are deductible, it is difficult to take a deduction because your combined expenses for the year must total 7.5 percent of your adjusted gross income. So, for someone with an adjusted gross income of $25,000, medical expenses would have to exceed $1,875.

Examination and Enforcement

Over 83 percent of all taxpayers pay their taxes voluntarily; but to ensure that appropriate taxes are paid, and to locate delinquent taxpayers, the IRS has a number of examination and enforcement procedures. The most broad-reaching of the IRS's examination systems is the matching document program, formally known as the Information Returns Program (IRP). This matches third-party information on wages, interest, dividends, and certain deductions with the amounts reported by taxpayers on their returns, and identifies people who are reported to have received income but did not file returns. When information does not agree with filed documents, taxpayers are asked to explain the discrepancy. In 1993 the IRS received 1.04 billion information returns. They identified 2.72 million people who underreported their earnings, and 1.57 million people who failed to file taxes altogether. The additional taxes and penalties assessed totaled $3.7 billion.

In 1993, the IRS examined 1,058,966 individual returns, or 0.92 percent of all individual federal returns filed. Of these, 986,816 (or 93 percent of returns audited) resulted in additional taxes and penalties worth $5.7 billion, or over $5,700 per person. However, some 72,150 lucky taxpayers came away from audits with refunds totaling just under half a billion dollars, or an average of $5,934 per refund.

INTERNAL REVENUE PERSONNEL SUMMARY, 1993

Location and type	Employees
Location	
National office	9,482
Regional offices	101,198
Service, total	**110,680**
Type	
Data processing operations	35,292
Collection	18,161
Taxpayer service	7,743
Examination	27,842
Employee plans/exempt organizations	2,361
Appeals	2,660
Tax fraud	4,562
Executive direction	193
Management services	1,671
Resources management	5,022
Counsel	3,041
Inspection	1,442
International	690

Note: At close of year. **Source:** Internal Revenue Service, *Annual Report 1993* (1994).

INTERNAL REVENUE COLLECTIONS BY PRINCIPAL SOURCES, 1961–93 (thousands of dollars)

Year	Total internal revenue collections	Corporate income and profits tax	Individual income tax	Employment taxes	Estate and gift taxes	Excise taxes
1961	$ 94,401,086	$ 21,764,940	$ 46,153,001	$ 12,502,451	$ 1,916,392	$12,064,302
1965	114,434,634	26,131,334	53,660,683	17,104,306	2,745,532	14,792,779
1970	195,722,096	35,036,983	103,651,585	37,449,188	3,680,076	15,904,264
1975	293,822,726	45,746,660	156,399,437	70,140,809	4,688,079	16,847,741
1980	519,375,273	72,379,610	287,547,782	128,330,480	6,498,381	24,619,021
1985	742,871,541	77,412,769	396,659,558	225,214,568	6,579,703	37,004,944
1990	1,056,365,652	110,016,539	540,228,408	367,219,321	11,761,939	27,139,445
1991	1,086,851,401	113,598,569	546,876,876	384,451,220	11,473,141	30,451,596
1992	1,120,799,558	117,950,796	557,723,156	400,080,904	11,479,116	33,565,587
1993	1,176,685,625	131,547,509	585,774,159	411,510,516	12,890,965	34,962,476

Source: Internal Revenue Service, *Annual Report 1993* (1994).

INTERNAL REVENUE COLLECTIONS, 1993 (thousands of dollars)

Type of return	Gross collections	Refunds[1]	Net collections: Amount	Net collections: Percent of total
Corporation income taxes	$131,547,509	$14,459,853	$117,087,657	10.8%
Individual income taxes[2]	585,774,159	75,099,513	510,674,646	47.1
Employment taxes, total	411,510,516	646,717	410,863,799	37.9
OASDHI[4]	401,687,644	530,730	401,156,934	37.0
Railroad retirement	4,261,551	3,719	4,257,832	0.4
Unemployment insurance	5,561,301	112,268	5,449,033	0.5
Estate and gift taxes	12,890,965	334,594	12,556,371	1.2
Excise taxes	34,962,476	896,540	34,065,936	3.1
Grand total	**$1,176,685,625**	**$91,437,217**	**$1,085,248,408**	**100.0%**

Note: Detail may not add to totals due to rounding. 1. Does not include interest paid on refunds. 2. Includes Presidential Election Campaign Fund contributions of $27,643,464 in fiscal year 1993. 3. Refunds of forms 1040, 1040A, 1040PC, and 1040EZ, including withheld taxes minus FICA. 4. Old-age, survivor's, disability, and hospital insurance; includes federal insurance and self-employment insurance contributions not shown separately. **Source**: Internal Revenue Service, *Annual Report 1993* (1994).

The IRS also examined 79,873 corporate returns, or 3.1 percent of all returns filed. These resulted in additional taxes and penalties of $14.7 billion—an average of $184,465 per return examined. A total of 6,590 corporations received refunds totaling $1.1 billion, or $181,580 per refund. The IRS's most sophisticated program is the Coordinated Examination Program, which reviews the returns of the 1,500 largest corporate taxpayers. The program reviewed more than 1,800 corporations with earnings of $250 million or more, resulting in additional taxes and penalties worth nearly $11 billion.

TAX FREEDOM DAY, 1929–95

To gauge the extent of the total tax burden on individual taxpayers, experts have devised a formula to calculate how much a person has to work to pay all his or her obligations to the state. Suppose you began paying your taxes for the year on January 1 and spent no money until these were paid off. The day you finished paying these taxes and started paying for food, rent, schools, and other necessities is called tax freedom day. In 1929, the beginning of the Great Depression, tax freedom day fell on Feb. 9; in 1995, it was May 6. The tax increases passed in the 1993 federal budget were responsible for pushing tax freedom back three days.

Looked at another way, while you would have spent 52 minutes out of each eight-hour day to earn enough money for a day's worth of taxes in 1929, you now spend 2 hours and 45 minutes. In other words, you spend 3.10 times more of your annual income on taxes now than you would have 60 years ago. To put the size of this bite in perspective, Americans today spend more time working to pay taxes than they do to feed (51 minutes), clothe (21 minutes), and house (1 hour and 21 minutes) their families combined.

		Tax bite in the eight-hour day		
Year	**Tax Freedom Day**	**Total**	**Federal**	**State/ Local**
1929	Feb. 9	0:52	0:19	0:33
1940[1]	Mar. 8	1:29	0:45	0:44
1950	Apr. 3	2:02	1:30	0:32
1960[1]	Apr. 16	2:20	1:40	0:40
1970	Apr. 26	2:32	1:40	0:52
1980[1]	May 1	2:40	1:48	0:52
1990	May 3	2:41	1:45	0:56
1991	May 3	2:41	1:45	0:56
1992[1]	May 2	2:41	1:43	0:58
1993	May 3	2:41	1:43	0:58
1994	May 6	2:46	1:49	0:57
1995	May 6	2:46	1:49	0:57

1. Leap year makes Tax Freedom Day appear a calendar day earlier. **Source:** Tax Foundation (Washington, D.C.), *Special Report: Tax Freedom Day* (1995).

A FLAT TAX?

"How much money did you make last year? Mail it in."

—Simplified tax form suggested by Stanton Delaplane

INTERNATIONAL TAX BURDEN COMPARSIONS, 1992

		Percentage distribution by source					
Country	**Total taxes as percentage of income**	**Personal income taxes**	**Corporate income taxes**	**Social Security taxes**	**Sales and VAT taxes**	**Property taxes**	**Tax Freedom Day**
U.S.	33.4%	34.9%	7.3%	29.8%	16.8%	11.2%	May 2
Japan	33.9	26.9	20.0	30.1	13.5	9.3	May 4
Britain	40.2	28.5	8.9	17.8	32.7	8.2	May 27
Canada	43.8	40.7	5.5	15.3	27.3	9.5	June 9
Germany	44.9	27.1	4.3	39.1	26.7	2.8	June 13
France	49.1	13.5	4.5	43.8	27.1	5.8	June 28

Source: Tax Foundation (Washington, D.C.), *Special Report: Tax Freedom Day* (1994).

RETURNS FILED AND EXAMINED, AND ADDITIONAL TAXES AND PENALTIES, 1993

Type of return	**Total filed 1993[1]**	**Total returns examined**	**Percent examined**	**Additional taxes and penalties (thousands)[2]**	**Average tax and penalty per return[3]**
All returns, total	153,453,600	1,300,230	0.85%	$23,080,361	—
Individual, total	114,718,900	1,058,966	0.92	5,653,094	$ 13,547
1040A, TPI under $25,000	42,846,900	315,469	0.74	923,444	6,778
Non 1040A, TPI under $25,000	18,983,500	125,697	0.66	332,917	6,168
TPI $25,000–$50,000	27,478,100	159,070	0.58	494,225	8,023
TPI $50,000–$100,000	14,422,600	127,484	0.88	469,763	8,864
TPI $100,000 and over	3,399,600	136,908	4.03	1,725,394	28,128
Schedule C—TGR under $25,000	2,314,400	51,934	2.24	159,564	3,988
Schedule C—TGR $25,000–$100,000	2,868,300	69,253	2.41	455,335	9,748
Schedule C—TGR $100,000 and over	1,578,700	61,768	3.91	972,900	21,018
Schedule F—TGR under $100,000	564,900	5,980	1.06	12,295	4,551
Schedule F—TGR $100,000 and over	261,900	5,403	2.06	107,257	34,138
Corporation, total	2,620,900	79,873	3.05	14,733,808	58,436
Under $250,000	235,000	4,653	1.98	422,838	37,582
$250,000–$500,000	1,670,700	22,257	1.33	401,081	18,558
$500,000–$1 million	445,300	17,532	3.94	260,988	15,029
$1 million–$5 million	176,700	16,514	9.35	385,223	23,650
$5 million–$10 million	25,400	4,837	19.04	295,632	63,048
$10 million–$50 million	28,400	6,621	23.31	560,074	86,250
$50 million–$100 million	7,200	1,840	25.56	317,571	148,160
$100 million–$250 million	6,000	1,869	31.15	819,880	319,315
$250 million and over[4]	6,200	3,231	52.11	10,917,585	1,007,521
Form 1120F	20,000	519	2.60	352,935	554,554
Fiduciary	2,888,100	6,030	0.21	101,476	18,537
Estate, total	70,000	11,829	16.90	1,050,473	90,208
Gross estate under $1 million	40,500	3,815	9.42	126,708	33,848
Gross estate $1 million–$5 million	27,100	6,740	24.87	306,431	46,015
Gross estate $5 million and over	2,400	1,274	53.08	617,335	489,168
Gift	170,500	2,120	1.24	202,009	93,834
Employment	28,739,200	68,595	0.24	696,145	8,100
Excise	832,000	43,447	5.22	417,156	7,206
Windfall profit	—	383	—	185,402	1,342,193
Miscellaneous taxable[5]	—	556	—	40,798	51,091
Partnership	1,608,700	9,850	0.61	—	—
S-Corporation	1,805,300	18,466	1.02	—	—
Miscellaneous nontaxable	—	115	—	—	—

Note: TPI = total personal income. TGR = total gross receipts. Totals may not add due to rounding. 1. Calendar year. 2. Recommended. 3. Includes only returns reviewed by revenue agents. Additional taxes and penalties were recovered through reviews of individual returns by tax auditors and service centers. 4. Includes 1,800 returns examined under the Coordinated Enforcement Program, which examines large corporations. These examinations produced an average of $5.3 million in additional taxes and penalties, half the total amount collected in this category. 5. Includes taxable small business corporations (1120S). **Source:** Internal Revenue Service, *Annual Report 1993* (1994).

TAX RATE SCHEDULES

Taxable income	What you pay	Taxable Income	What you pay
SINGLE INDIVIDUALS		**MARRIED INDIVIDUALS FILING JOINTLY, OR QUALIFYING WIDOW(ER)**	
$0.00–$22,100	15.0% of sum over $0.00	$0.00–$36,900	15.0% of sum over $0.00
$22,100–$53,500	$3,315 + 28.0% of sum over $22,100	$36,900–$89,150	$5,535.00 + 28.0% of sum over $36,900
$53,500–$115,000	$12,107 + 31.0% of sum over $53,500	$89,150–$140,000	$20,165.00 + 31.0% of sum over $89,150
$115,000–$250,000	$31,172 + 36.0% of sum over $115,000	$140,000–$250,000	$35,928.50 + 36.0% of sum over $140,000
over $250,000	$79,772 + 39.6% of sum over $250,000	over $250,000	$75,528.50 + 39.6% of sum over $250,000
HEADS OF HOUSEHOLDS		**MARRIED, FILING SEPARATE RETURNS**	
$0.00–$28,750	15.0% of sum over $0.00	$0.00–$18,450	15.0% of sum over $0.00
$28,750–$76,400	$4,312.50 + 28.0% of sum over $28,750	$18,450–$44,575	$2,767.50 + 28.0% of sum over $18,450
$76,400–$127,500	$17,024.50 + 31.0% of sum over $76,400	$44,575–$70,000	$10,082.50 + 31.0% of sum over $44,575
$127,500–$250,000	$33,385.00 + 36.0% of sum over $127,500	$70,000–$125,000	$17,964.25 + 36.0% of sum over $70,000
over $250,000	$77,485.00 + 39.6% of sum over $250,000	over $125,000	$37,764.25 + 39.6% of sum over $125,000

Source: Internal Revenue Service, 1994.

TAX RETURNS PROCESSED, 1990–93

Type of return	Number of returns 1990	1991	1992	1993
Individual income tax (Form 1040 series)	112,492	114,058	114,999	114,155
Estimated tax (Form 1040ES)	38,188	38,386	37,321	41,201
Fiduciary (Form 1041 series)	2,702	2,765	2,885	2,970
Fiduciary estimated tax (Form 1041ES)	651	612	614	706
Partnership (Form 1065)	1,741	1,671	1,604	1,583
Corporate income tax (Forms 1120 series, 1066)	4,311	4,354	4,472	4,593
Estate tax (Forms 706, 706NA)	59	64	67	73
Gift tax (Form 709)	146	155	168	211
Employment taxes (Forms 94X series, CT-1, 1042)	28,914	28,516	28,664	28,879
Exempt organizations (Forms 990 series, 4720, 5227)	484	513	531	543
Employee plans (Form 5500 series)	1,016	1,117	1,160	1,206
Excise taxes (Forms 720, 730, 2290, 11C)	840	809	811	860
Supplemental documents (1040X, 2688, 4868, 7004, 1041A)	10,170	10,694	10,780	10,443
Total tax returns	**201,715**	**203,713**	**204,075**	**207,423**

Source: Internal Revenue Service, *Annual Report 1993* (1994).

INTERNAL REVENUE COLLECTIONS, COSTS, AND TAX PER CAPITA, 1960–93

Fiscal year	Collections	Cost of collecting $100	Tax per capita
1960	$ 91,774,802,823	$0.40	$ 507.97
1965	114,434,633,721	0.52	588.95
1970	195,722,096,497	0.45	955.31
1975	293,822,725,772	0.54	1,375.84
1980	519,375,273,361	0.44	2,275.66[1]
1985	742,871,541,283	0.48	3,098.99[1]
1986	782,251,812,225	0.49	3,232.51[1]
1987	886,290,589,996	0.49	3,627.22[1]
1988	935,106,594,000	0.54	3,796.17[1]
1989	1,013,322,133,000	0.51	4,062.84[1]
1990	1,056,365,651,631	0.52	4,222.00[1]
1991	1,086,851,401,315	0.56	4,288.53[1]
1992	1,120,799,558,292	0.58	4,374.58
1993	1,176,685,625,083	0.60	4,543.33

Note: 1. Tax Per Capita figures have been revised to agree with the Census Bureau's adjusted data on population. **Source**: Internal Revenue Service, *Annual Report 1993* (1994).

AVERAGE ITEMIZED DEDUCTIONS BY ADJUSTED GROSS INCOME, 1993

Adjusted gross income ranges	Average deduction for: Taxes	Gifts	Interest	Total[1]	Deductions as percentage of income[2]
$30,000–$40,000	$ 2,772	$ 1,384	$ 5,503	$ 9,659	27.6%
$40,000–$50,000	3,322	1,541	5,738	10,601	23.6
$50,000–$75,000	4,442	1,739	6,618	12,799	19.0
$75,000–$100,000	6,220	2,319	8,282	16,821	19.2
$100,000–$200,000	10,035	3,427	11,389	24,851	16.6
$200,000–$500,000	22,655	8,207	17,772	48,634	13.9
$500,000–$1 million	52,462	20,635	27,605	100,702	13.4
$1 million or more	173,490	108,883	60,427	342,800	N.A.

1. Does not include deductions for medical expenses not shown separately. Very few medical expenses are deductible. 2. Percentages calculated by *Universal Almanac* using the median income of the range shown. **Source:** Research Institute of America, 1995.

"That the power to tax involves the power to destroy; that the power to destroy may defeat and render useless the power to create . . . are propositions not to be denied."

—Chief Justice John Marshall, *McCulloch* v. *Maryland* (1819)

U.S. Postal Service

At first glance the most compelling facts about today's Postal Service are the sheer size and scope of the operation. With over 700,000 employees moving more than 170 billion pieces of mail annually, or more than 40 percent of the world's total, this is surely one of the most vital services the government performs for business and the citizenry alike. What most people don't realize is that it's done at a cost to the consumer significantly less than in any other industrial nation, and that for first-class mail the on-time delivery rate is still over 95 percent for local mail and 90 percent for cross-country.

First established by the Continental Congress in 1775, the Postal Service was made part of the federal system in the Constitution and the office of postmaster general established in George Washington's very first cabinet. In 1969, however, in response to vociferous complaints of mismanagement, waste, unreliable service, and staggering financial losses, the Nixon administration reorganized the service as an independent establishment within the executive branch. The Postal Service Act of 1969 removed the postmaster general from the cabinet and created a self-supporting postal corporation owned by the federal government and vested power in an 11-member board of governors, nine of whom are appointed by the president with the consent of the Senate; these in turn appoint the postmaster general, who serves as the CEO of the postal service; the 11th member of the board is chosen by the other 10 and serves as deputy postmaster general.

Finally, the 1969 law established an independent Postal Rate Commission of five members, appointed by the president, to recommend postal rates and classifications for adoption by the Board of Governors. Under this agreement, the Postal Service turned a profit five times in the early 1980s. But since 1987, the Postal Service has operated at a loss every year except 1989, when it posted a profit of $61 million. Total losses for 1994 were $913.6 million. A hike in the price of stamps, like the one that occurred on Jan. 1, 1995, usually returns the Postal Service to profitability—at least for one year. Since 1982, the Postal Service has relied exclusively on postage and fees for its operations. It receives no taxpayer revenues.

Although complaints about slow and inattentive service are legend, the majority of people report happiness with their dealings with the Postal Service. A 1994 customer satisfaction poll found that 85 percent of households nationwide rated their experiences with the Postal Service as "excellent," "good," or "very good." Moreover, despite the advent of overnight delivery services, couriers, messengers, and fax machines, the total volume of mail has increased steadily since 1989. The Postal Service delivers more mail in a single day than Federal Express delivers all year. In 1994, total mail volume reached a new record of 177 billion pieces.

POSTAL ABBREVIATIONS FOR STATES AND TERRITORIES

State	Postal abbrev.	State	Postal abbrev.
Alabama	AL	New Hampshire	NH
Alaska	AK	New Jersey	NJ
Arizona	AZ	New Mexico	NM
Arkansas	AR	New York	NY
California	CA	North Carolina	NC
Colorado	CO	North Dakota	ND
Connecticut	CT	Ohio	OH
Delaware	DE	Oklahoma	OK
District of Columbia	DC	Oregon	OR
Florida	FL	Pennsylvania	PA
Georgia	GA	Rhode Island	RI
Hawaii	HI	South Carolina	SC
Idaho	ID	South Dakota	SD
Illinois	IL	Tennessee	TN
Indiana	IN	Texas	TX
Iowa	IA	Utah	UT
Kansas	KS	Vermont	VT
Kentucky	KY	Virginia	VA
Louisiana	LA	Washington	WA
Maine	ME	West Virginia	WV
Maryland	MD	Wisconsin	WI
Massachusetts	MA	Wyoming	WY
Michigan	MI	American Samoa	AS
Minnesota	MN	Canal Zone	CZ
Mississippi	MS	Guam	GU
Missouri	MO	Northern Mariana Islands	CM
Montana	MT	Puerto Rico	PR
Nebraska	NE	Trust Territory of the Pacific	TT
Nevada	NV	Virgin Islands	VI

POSTAL SERVICE EMPLOYEES AND OFFICES, 1990–94

Category	1990	1993	1994
Employees			
Headquarters (Washington, D.C.)	2,291	1,762	1,701
Field support units	5,691	4,157	4,117
Inspection services (field)	4,259	4,181	4,308
Area offices	N.A.	1,062	1,262
Postmasters	26,995	25,304	26,803
Supervisors, managers	43,458	31,936	34,616
Professional, administrative, technical personnel	9,793	10,306	10,924
Clerks	290,380	257,147	265,294
Nurses	286	224	181
Mailhandlers	51,123	51,078	54,859
City delivery carriers	236,081	211,893	229,138
Motor vehicle operators	7,308	7,199	7,577
Rural delivery carriers and substitutes on vacant routes	42,252	44,456	45,049
Special delivery messengers	2,012	1,571	1,574
Building and equipment maintenance personnel	33,323	35,444	36,767
Vehicle maintenance personnel	4,874	4,576	4,689
Total career employees[1]	760,668	691,723	728,944
Noncareer employees	26,829	25,889	25,674
Offices, stations, and branches			
Post offices	28,959	28,728	28,657
Stations and branches	11,108	10,664	10,715
Classified stations and branches	5,008	4,692	5,682
Contract stations and branches	4,397	4,367	3,424
Community post offices	1,703	1,605	1,609
Total offices, branches, and stations	**40,067**	**39,392**	**39,372**

1. 1995 figure includes 85 employees of discontinued operations not shown separately. **Source:** U.S. Postal Service, *Postal Facts* (1995).

VOLUME OF MAIL HANDLED, 1993–94

Service	Millions of pieces 1993	1994	Percent change
First-class[1]	92,169.4	94,376.1	2.4%
Presort letters and cards	34,051.5	33,360.4	6.8
Priority mail	664.4	768.3	15.6
Express mail	52.4	56.2	7.3
Mailgrams	7.2	5.3	–25.8
Second-class[1]	10,306.1	10,227.7	–0.8
Nonprofit	2,296.3	2,268.7	–1.2
Third-class[1]	65,773.2	69,400.1	5.5
Carrier,-route presort (regular rate)	27,803.9	29,811.2	7.2
Nonprofit	11,957.7	11,895.7	–0.5
Fourth-class[1]	743.8	870.6	–17.0
Parcel post	186.8	223.9	19.8
Bound printed matter	353.6	520.1	18.8
Special rate	164.8	190.9	15.8
Library rate	38.7	35.8	–7.5
U.S. Postal Service	543.7	448.0	–17.6
Total mail	**171,220.0**	**177,100.0**	**3.4%**

1. Includes other mail not shown separately. **Source:** U.S. Postal Service, *Comprehensive Statement on Postal Operations 1994* (1995).

The price of a first-class letter is 80 cents in Japan, 64 cents in Germany, and 32 cents in the U.S.

DOMESTIC POSTAGE RATES

First-class Mail

Weight	Rate	Weight	Rate
1 oz.	$0.32	7 oz.	$1.70
2 oz.	0.55	8 oz.	1.93
3 oz.	0.78	9 oz.	2.16
4 oz.	1.01	10 oz.	2.39
5 oz.	1.24	11 oz.	2.62
6 oz.	1.47		

Note: Letters up to 2.5 oz. with Zip + 4 Codes are priced 1.5 cents less than regular letters. Bar-coded mail is discounted by an additional 1 cent. For letters more than 11 oz. use priority mail.

Postcards Single postcard = $0.20. Postcards cannot exceed 4.25" × 6", nor be smaller than 3.5" × 5".

Priority mail Priority mail is a zone-based domestic service providing two-day delivery between all major business centers in the United States. The rates for packages up to 5 lbs. are as follows, regardless of the zone to which they are going:

Weight	Rate	Weight	Rate
Up to 2 lbs.	$3.00	4 lbs.	$5.00
3 lbs.	4.00	5 lbs.	6.00

For packages weighing more than 5 lbs., different rates apply depending on weight and the zone, from $6.90 for a 6-lb. package to Zone 1 to a maximum of $77.20 for a 70-lb. package.

Express mail is an overnight delivery service available every day of the year for items up to 70 lbs. in weight and 108 in. in combined length and girth. The post office will pick up packages to be sent by express mail for a $4.95 fee. Call 1-800-222-1811.

Weight	Rate
Up to 8 oz.	$10.25
8 oz.–2 lb.	$12.05
2 lb.–70 lb.	$14.20–$98.95
Pickup fee	$4.95

Second-class mail Regular and preferred second-class rates are available only to newspapers and periodicals that have been authorized second-class mail privileges. The general public can mail newspapers and periodicals only by first-, third-, or fourth-class mail, express mail, or priority mail.

Third-class rates are for circulars, books, catalogs, and other printed matter; merchandise, seeds, cuttings, bulbs, roots, scions, and plants, weighing less than 16 oz. Bulk rates are also available.

Weight (up to)	Rate	Weight (up to)	Rate
1 oz.	$0.32	7 oz.	$1.70
2 oz.	0.55	8 oz.	1.93
3 oz.	0.78	10 oz.	2.39
4 oz.	1.01	11 oz.	2.62
5 oz.	1.24	13 oz.	2.90
6 oz.	1.47	16 oz.	2.95

Fourth-class mail (parcel post) Parcel post is a zone-based class of mail for sending merchandise; written communications having the nature of current and personal correspondence are not permitted. The maximum rate is $39.03 for a 70 lb. package sent to Zone 8.

Source: U.S. Postal Service, "Ratefold," Jan. 1, 1995.

INTERNATIONAL POSTAL RATES

Type/Weight	Canada	Mexico	All other countries
First-class letters:			
0.5 oz.	$0.46	$0.40	$0.60
1 oz.	0.52	0.46	1.00
1.5 oz.	0.64	0.66	1.40
2 oz.	0.72	0.86	1.80
Postcards	0.40	0.35	0.50
Aerogrammes	0.50	0.50	0.50

Source: U.S. Postal Service, Postal Bulletin, June 22, 1995.

ZIP CODES

As of September 1994, there were 43,263 separate ZIP Codes designated by the U.S. Postal Service. The number of ZIP Codes increases by about 250 each year. While the assignment of ZIP Codes seems random, the system is a logical one. ZIP Codes are five-digit or nine-digit (ZIP + 4) codes that identify areas within the United States and its territories for purposes of simplifying delivery of the U.S. mail. The USPS divides the United States into ten geographical areas each consisting of three or more states and/or territories. Key post offices with each area are designated sectional centers. The first number in a ZIP Code indicates its geographical area, and the first three digits stand for either a sectional center or a large city. The last two digits stand for either a particular post office or a postal delivery area. To find the ZIP Code for any city in America, call your local post office and ask them to look it up in the National ZIP Code Directory.

ZIP Code beginning	States
0 – – – –	Connecticut, Maine, Massachusetts, New Hampshire, New Jersey, Puerto Rico, Rhode Island, Vermont, Virgin Islands
1 – – – –	Delaware, New York, Pennsylvania
2 – – – –	District of Columbia, Maryland, North Carolina, South Carolina, Virginia, West Virginia
3 – – – –	Alabama, Florida, Georgia, Mississippi, Tennessee
4 – – – –	Indiana, Kentucky, Michigan, Ohio
5 – – – –	Iowa, Minnesota, Montana, North Dakota, South Dakota, Wisconsin
6 – – – –	Illinois, Kansas, Missouri, Nebraska
7 – – – –	Arkansas, Louisiana, Oklahoma, Texas
8 – – – –	Arizona, Colorado, Idaho, Nevada, New Mexico, Utah, Wyoming
9 – – – –	Alaska, American Samoa, California, Federated States of Micronesia, Guam, Hawaii, Marshall Islands, Northern Mariana Islands, Oregon, Palau, Wake, Washington

POSTAGE STAMPS

The first stamps issued by the precursor to the U.S. Postal Service were a 5-cent Benjamin Franklin (the nation's first postmaster general) and a 10-cent George Washington, both in 1847. Today, there are three main categories of stamps. **Definitive issues** are generally two-color and printed in quantities of hundreds of millions over several years. The Postal Service is committed to always having a definitive flag issue in circulation in the standard first-class (32-cent in 1995) denomination. All stamps supporting third-class mailing rates are definitive issues. These include fractional rate stamps in series such as the Great American and Transportation series used by large companies for sending mass mailings.
Commemorative issues generally celebrate historic events or personalities and are more elaborate in their design and printing. They are issued in quantities of about 150 million over the course of three months, during which they can be purchased at all post offices. (They are available for up to one year at philatelic windows in main post offices.)
Airmail issues (for overseas mail) are printed for longer than commemorative issues, although modest demand results in smaller quantities being printed.

Recognizing that the local post office isn't always the most convenient place to buy stamps, the Postal Service has begun increasing the ways in which people may purchase stamps. *Stamps by Mail,* begun almost 20 years ago, has tripled its sales in the past four years, generating more than $65 million in revenue in 1993. The *Stamps on Consignment* program allows consumers to purchase stamps at more than 27,000 local businesses nationwide, including drugstores and supermarkets, contributing $600 million to Postal Service coffers. *Stamps by Phone* lets people buy stamps using a telephone and a credit card (and was responsible for $5 million in revenues). And *Stamps by ATM* lets people get stamps whenever they go to the cash machine.

STATES, TERRITORIES, AND POSSESSIONS

This section, a compilation of history and statistics about the 50 United States, the District of Columbia, and U.S. territories and possessions, includes a brief history of each state and territory; its official motto and other emblems; a summary of geographic, demographic, and economic facts; and a list of prominent natives, places, and dates.

Statistical sources include the U.S. Census Bureau's 1990 decennial census and *The Statistical Abstract* (annual); the Council of State Governments' *Book of the States* and *State Elective Officials and the Legislatures;* and the Bureau of Economic Analysis's *Survey of Current Business.*

The headings for demographic statistics in the paragraphs on People and Language conform to U.S. Census Bureau usage, except "Indian" is used as a short form for American Indian, Eskimo, and Aleut, and "Asian" is used for Asian and Pacific Islander. Note that Hispanics may be of any race.

The Fifty States

Alabama

The memory of the Native American presence is particularly strong in Alabama. Trade with the Northeast via the Ohio River valley began during the Burial Mound Period (1000 B.C.–A.D. 700) and continued until European contact. Meso-American influence is evident in the agrarian Mississippian culture that followed. Pressured by white settlers in the early 19th century, the Creeks warred against the U.S. government until defeated by Gen. Andrew Jackson.

The cradle of the Confederacy during the Civil War, Alabama was center stage in the civil rights movement of the 1950s and 1960s. Although cotton is still a major crop, the northern part of the state around Birmingham is an important industrial area with abundant coal, iron ore, limestone, and electricity from the TVA. Increasingly urban—70 percent of the population lived in rural areas 50 years ago, compared with less than 40 percent today—Alabama's economy is progressing slowly. It still ranks near last in taxes and most services.

NAME Probably after Alabama tribe. NICKNAMES Yellowhammer State, Heart of Dixie. CAPITAL Montgomery. ENTERED UNION Dec. 14, 1819 (22nd). MOTTO "We dare defend our rights."

Emblems BIRD Yellowhammer. DANCE Square dance. GAME BIRD Wild turkey. FISH Tarpon. FOSSIL *Basilosaurus oetoides.* MINERAL Hematite. NUT Pecan. SONG "Alabama." STONE Marble. TREE Southern (longleaf) pine.

Land TOTAL AREA 51,705 sq. mi. (29th), incl. 938 sq. mi. inland water. BORDERS Tenn., Ga., Fla., Gulf of Mexico, Miss. RIVERS Alabama, Chattahoochee, Mobile, Tennessee, Tennessee-Tombigbee Waterway, Tensaw, Tombigbee. LAKES Guntersville, Pickwick, Wheeler, Wilson (all formed by Tennessee Valley Authority [TVA]); Dannelly Res., Martin, Lewis Smith, Weiss. MOUNTAINS Cumberland, Lookout, Raccoon, Sand.

Elected officials Gov. Fob James, Jr. (R, term exp. 1999). Lt. Gov. Don Siegelman (D). Sec. State Jim Bennett (D). Atty. Gen. Jeff Sessions (R).

People (1994) 4,218,792 (22nd). RACE/NATIONAL ORIGIN (1990): White 73.6%. Black 25.3%. Indian 0.4%. Asian 0.5%. Other 0.1%. Hispanic 0.6%.

Cities (1990) Birmingham 265,968. Mobile 196,278. Montgomery 187,106. Huntsville 159,789. Tuscaloosa 77,759. Dothan 53,589. Decatur 48,761. Gadsden 42,523. Hoover 39,788. Florence 36,426.

Business GROSS STATE PRODUCT (GSP, 1992) $78.14 bil. (24th). SECTORS OF GSP: Farms 1.87%; agricultural services, forestry, and fisheries 0.41%; mining 2.11%; construction 3.83%; manufacturing 22.83%; transportation and public utilities 9.96%; wholesale trade 5.94%; retail trade 9.19%; finance, insurance, and real estate 13.27%; services 15.30%; federal government 4.70%; federal military 1.48%; state and local government 9.10%. *FORTUNE* 500 COMPANIES (1994): 1: Bruno's.

Famous natives Hank Aaron, baseball player. Tallulah Bankhead, actress. William B. Bankhead, politician. Hugo L. Black, jurist. Wernher von Braun (b. Germany), rocket scientist. Nat "King" Cole, singer. Red Eagle (William Weatherfield), Creek leader. W.C. Handy, musician. Frank M. Johnson, Jr., jurist. Helen Keller, author. Coretta Scott (Mrs. Martin Luther) King, reformer. Harper Lee, author. Joe Louis, boxer. Jesse Owens, runner. Leroy Robert "Satchel" Paige, baseball player. Walker Percy, author. George Wallace, politician. Hank Williams, singer.

Noteworthy places Alabama Deep Sea Fishing Rodeo, Dauphin Island. Alabama Space and Rocket Center, U.S. Space Camp, Huntsville. Battleship USS *Alabama*, Mobile. Birmingham Museum of Art. First White House of the Confederacy, Montgomery. Horseshoe Bend Natl. Military Park. Mound State Monument Archaeological Museum, Moundville. Museum of Natural History, Univ. Alabama, Tuscaloosa. Point Clear (resort). Russell Cave Natl. Monument. Tuskegee Institute.

Memorable events Humans first inhabit Russell Cave c. 6000 B.C. Temple Mound culture flourishes around Moundville, A.D. 1200–1500. First Europeans in Mobile Bay 1519. Hernando de Soto's battle with Tuscaloosa possibly bloodiest encounter ever between Europeans and Native Americans in United States 1540. Spanish at Mobile Bay 1599. Pierre Le Moyne, sieur d'Iberville, establishes first permanent colony at Mobile 1711. Treaty of Paris gives Mobile to Britain 1763. U.S. control recognized 1783. Chickasaws, Choctaws, and Cherokees cede lands to United States 1805. First Baptist Church established 1808. Gen. Andrew Jackson defeats Creek Indian Confederacy at Horseshoe Bend 1814. Cotton principal cash crop 1820s. Beginning of coal and iron mining and steel manufacturing 1850s.

POPULATION OF THE STATES, 1990

State	Population 1990	Rank	Change 1980–90 Number	Change 1980–90 Percent
United States	**248,709,873**	**—**	**22,165,068**	**9.8%**
Alabama	4,040,587	22	146,699	3.8
Alaska	550,043	49	148,192	36.9
Arizona	3,665,228	24	947,013	34.8
Arkansas	2,350,725	33	64,290	2.8
California	29,760,021	1	6,092,119	25.7
Colorado	3,294,394	26	404,430	14.0
Connecticut	3,287,116	27	179,540	5.8
Delaware	666,168	46	71,830	12.1
District of Columbia[1]	606,900	—	–31,433	–4.9
Florida	12,937,926	4	3,191,602	32.7
Georgia	6,478,216	11	1,015,111	18.6
Hawaii	1,108,229	41	143,538	14.9
Idaho	1,006,749	42	62,814	6.7
Illinois	11,430,602	6	4,084	0.0
Indiana	5,544,159	14	53,935	1.0
Iowa	2,776,755	30	–137,053	–4.7
Kansas	2,477,574	32	113,895	4.8
Kentucky	3,685,296	23	24,519	0.7
Louisiana	4,219,973	21	14,073	0.3
Maine	1,227,928	38	103,268	9.2
Maryland	4,781,468	19	564,493	13.4
Massachusetts	6,016,425	13	279,388	4.9
Michigan	9,295,297	8	33,219	0.4
Minnesota	4,375,099	20	299,129	7.3
Mississippi	2,573,216	31	52,578	2.1
Missouri	5,117,073	15	200,387	4.1
Montana	799,065	44	12,375	1.6
Nebraska	1,578,385	36	8,560	0.5
Nevada	1,201,833	39	401,340	50.1
New Hampshire	1,109,252	40	188,642	20.5
New Jersey	7,730,188	9	365,365	5.0
New Mexico	1,515,069	37	212,175	16.3
New York	17,990,455	2	432,383	2.5
North Carolina	6,628,637	10	746,871	12.7
North Dakota	638,800	47	–13,917	–2.1
Ohio	10,847,115	7	49,485	0.5
Oklahoma	3,145,585	28	120,295	4.0
Oregon	2,842,321	29	209,216	7.9
Pennsylvania	11,881,643	5	17,748	0.1
Rhode Island	1,003,464	43	56,310	5.9
South Carolina	3,486,703	25	364,883	11.7
South Dakota	696,004	45	5,236	0.8
Tennessee	4,877,185	17	286,065	6.2
Texas	16,986,510	3	2,757,319	19.4
Utah	1,722,850	35	261,813	17.9
Vermont	562,758	48	51,302	10.0
Virginia	6,187,358	12	840,540	15.7
Washington	4,866,692	18	734,536	17.8
West Virginia	1,793,477	34	–156,167	–8.0
Wisconsin	4,891,769	16	186,002	4.0
Wyoming	453,588	50	–15,969	–3.4

1. If the District of Columbia were included with the states it would have ranked 48th in 1990 and 47th in 1980. **Source**: U.S. Bureau of the Census release, 1991.

Alabama secedes from Union; first capital of Confederate States of America at Montgomery 1861. Battle of Mobile Bay 1864. Readmitted to Union 1868. Booker T. Washington founds Tuskegee Institute 1881. Destruction of cotton crops by boll weevils leads to diversification of rural economy 1915. Tennessee Valley Authority enacted by Congress 1933. Montgomery bus boycott 1955. Freedom march from Selma to Montgomery 1965.
Tourist information 1–800–ALABAMA or 1–205–242–4169.

Alaska

One-fifth the size of the entire lower 48 states, Alaska is a vast, geographically varied wilderness. The coast from the Bering Sea to the Arctic was originally inhabited by Eskimos and Aleuts, while inland and to the south were Athapascans and people of the Northwest Indian culture. Russian fur traders in the 1740s were the first Europeans to recognize the region's commercial potential, and the Russian Orthodox faith is still found in the old territorial capital of Sitka (New Archangel).

Russia sold Alaska to the United States in 1867 for $7.2 million—2 cents an acre—and Alaska experienced successive booms in furs, fishing, whaling, and gold. Discovery of oil on the North Slope near Prudhoe Bay in 1968 and completion of an 800-mile trans-Alaska pipeline a decade later made oil production the centerpiece of the state's economy in the 1980s. But in 1989 oil production at Prudhoe Bay declined for the first time. In anticipation of the end of the oil boom, government and industry officials are looking at ways to diversify the state's economy. One possibility, additional exploration at Arctic National Wildlife Refuge, was endangered when the *Exxon Valdez* struck a reef outward-bound from Valdez, spilling 10 million gallons of oil into Prince William Sound on Mar. 24, 1989. However, as the public memory of the disaster recedes and the Persian Gulf oil supplies are threatened by regional insecurity, the refuge is once again being considered.

NAME From Aleut *alaska* and Eskimo *alakshak*, both meaning "mainland." NICKNAME None. CAPITAL Juneau. ENTERED UNION Jan. 3, 1959 (49th). MOTTO "North to the future."
Emblems BIRD Willow ptarmigan. FISH King salmon. FLOWER Forget-me-not. GEM Jade. MARINE MAMMAL Bowhead whale. MINERAL Gold. SONG "Alaska's Flag." SPORT Mushing (dog-team racing). TREE Sitka spruce.
Land TOTAL AREA 591,004 sq. mi. (1st), incl. 20,171 sq. mi. inland water. BORDERS Arctic Ocean (Chukchi Sea, Beaufort Sea), Yukon, British Columbia, Pacific Ocean, and Bering Strait. RIVERS Colville, Porcupine, Noatak, Yukon, Susitna, Copper, Kobuk, Koyukuk, Kuskokwim, Tanana. MOUNTAINS Alaska Range (Mt. McKinley 20,320 ft., highest in North America), Aleutian Range, Brooks Range, Kuskokwim, St. Elias. OTHER NOTABLE FEATURES Aleutian Islands, Alexander Archipelago, Kodiak Island, Nunivak Island, Point Barrow (71°23'N), Pribilof Islands, Seward Peninsula, St. Lawrence Island.
Elected officials Gov. Tony Knowles (D, term exp. 1999). Lt. Gov. Fran Ulmer (D). Atty. Gen. Bruce Botelho (D).
People (1994) 606,276 (48th). RACE/NATIONAL ORIGIN (1990): White 75.5%. Black 4.1%. Indian 15.6%. Asian 3.6%. Other 1.2%. Hispanic 3.2%.
Cities (1990) Anchorage 226,338. Fairbanks 30,843. Juneau 26,751. Sitka 8,588. Ketchikan 8,263. Kodiak 6,365. Kenai 6,327. Bethel 4,674. Valdez 4,068. Wasilla 4,028.
Business GROSS STATE PRODUCT (GSP, 1992) $25.96 bil. (41st). SECTORS OF GSP: Farms 0.07%; agricultural services, forestry, and fisheries 1.84%; mining 36.24%; construction 3.23%; manufacturing 4.07%; transportation and public utilities 12.49%; wholesale trade 1.82%; retail trade 4.69%; finance, insurance, and real estate 13.48%; services 8.21%; federal government 3.11%; federal military 3.02%; state and local government 7.72%. *FORTUNE* 500 COMPANIES (1994): 0.
Famous natives Aleksandr Baranov (b. Russia), first governor of Russian America. Vitus Bering (b. Denmark), explorer. Ernest Gruening (b. N.Y.), governor. Carl Ben Eielson, bush pilot. Walter Hickel (b. Kans.), governor.
Noteworthy places Aniakchak Natl. Monument. Cape Krusenstern Natl. Monument. Denali Natl. Park (formerly Mt. McKinley Natl. Park). Gates of the Arctic Natl. Park. Glacier Bay Natl. Park. Katmai Natl. Park (Valley of Ten Thousand Smokes). Kenai Fjords Natl. Park. Klondike Gold Rush Natl. Hist. Park. Kobuk Valley Natl. Park. Lake Clark Natl. Park. Little Diomede Island—2.5 mi. from Big Diomede Island (Russia). Sitka Natl. Hist. Park. St. Michael's Cathedral, Sitka. Wrangell–St. Elias Natl. Park.
Memorable events Earliest migration from Asia to Americas across Bering Sea land bridge, c. 15,000 years ago. Alaska inhabited by Tlingits, Tinnehs, Aleuts, and Eskimos. Peter the Great sponsors expedition to find land opposite Siberia 1728. Bering expedition lands near Mt. Elias; begins Pacific Northwest fur trade with Europe and Asia 1741. Russians establish first European settlement at Three Saints Bay 1784. Russian-American Company chartered 1799. Baranov's massacre of Tlingits at Sitka 1802. Gold discovered at Stikine Creek (1861), Juneau (1880), Fortymile Creek (1886), Nome (1898), Fairbanks (1903). Russians sell Alaska to U.S. for $7.2 million 1867. First salmon cannery established 1878. Japanese occupy Agattu, Attu, and Kiska Islands 1942–43. Alaskans vote for statehood 1946. Statehood 1959. Earthquake destroys Anchorage, Northwest Panhandle, and Cook Inlet; tsunami wipes out Valdez; coast sinks 32 ft. at Kodiak and Seward and rises 16 ft. at Cordova 1964. Oil discovered on North Slope 1968. Alaska Native Claims Settlement Act gives Alaska's Native Americans 44 million acres for native landholdings 1971. Completion of 789-mi. pipeline to Valdez 1977. Population growth of 32.8% highest in United States 1980–86. *Exxon Valdez* spills 10 million gallons of oil into Prince William Sound off Valdez—worst oil spill in U.S history 1989.
Tourist information 1–907–465–2010.

Arizona

The Hopi village of Oraibi is the oldest continuously inhabited town in the United States, and today vast tracts of Arizona are reserved for Apaches, Hopis, Navajos, Papagos, and other Native Americans. Last of the 48 conterminous states admitted to the Union, Arizona was sparsely settled until the advent of airconditioning in the postwar years made it habitable and a poplar destination for retirees. More recently, there has been a boom in manufacturing and light industry, and in the 1980s population growth was among the highest in the nation. Mexican-Americans are an especially important political force.

As in most southwestern states, water scarcity is a major problem. Arizona draws 2.8 million acre-feet of water from the Colorado River, whose water it shares with five other states and Mexico. The Central Arizona Project (CAP), a 330-mile, $3.5 billion pipeline to Phoenix and Tucson, is under construction.

NAME Probably from the Pima or Papago for "place of small springs." NICKNAME Grand Canyon State. CAPITAL Phoenix. ENTERED UNION Feb. 14, 1912 (48th). MOTTO *Ditat deus* (God enriches).
Emblems BIRD Cactus wren. FLOWER Blossom of the saguaro cactus. GEMSTONE Turquoise. OFFICIAL NECK WEAR Bola tie. SONGS "Arizona March Song," "Arizona." TREE Palo verde.
Land TOTAL AREA 114,000 sq. mi. (6th), incl. 492 sq. mi. inland water. BORDERS Utah, Colo., N.Mex., Sonora, Baja California Norte, Calif., Nev. RIVERS Colorado, Gila, Little Colorado, Salt, Zuni. LAKES Havasu, Mead, Mohave, Powell, Roosevelt, San Carlos. MOUNTAINS Black, Gila, Hualapai, Mohawk, San Francisco Peaks (Humphreys Peak 12,633 ft.). OTHER NOTABLE FEATURES Grand Canyon, Kaibab Plateau, Painted Desert, Petrified Forest, Sonoran Desert.
Elected officials Gov. Fife Symington (R, term exp. 1999). Sec. State Jane Dee Hull (R). Atty. Gen. Grant Woods (R).
People (1994) 4,075,052 (23rd). RACE/NATIONAL ORIGIN (1990): White 80.8%. Black 3.0%. Indian 5.6%. Asian 1.5%. Other 9.1%. Hispanic 18.8%.
Cities (1990) Phoenix 983,403. Tucson 405,390. Mesa 288,091. Glendale 148,134. Tempe 141,865. Scottsdale 130,069. Chandler 90,533. Yuma 54,923. Peoria 50,618. Flagstaff 45,857.
Business GROSS STATE PRODUCT (GSP, 1992) $74.06 bil. (26th). SECTORS OF GSP: Farms 1.53%; agricultural services, forestry, and fisheries 0.64%; mining 1.37%; construction 5.19%; manufacturing 14.09%; transportation and public utilities 8.85%; wholesale trade 5.42%; retail trade 11.38%; finance, insurance, and real estate 17.38%; services 20.01%; federal government 2.66%; federal military 1.33%; state and local government 10.16%. *FORTUNE* 500 COMPANIES (1994): 3: Dial, Phelps Dodge, Microage.

Famous natives Bruce Babbitt, politician. Cesar Chavez, labor leader. Cochise, Apache chief. Andrew Ellicott Douglass (b. Vt.), dendrochronologist. Wyatt Earp (b. Ill.), lawman. Barry Goldwater, politician. Goyathlay (Geronimo), Apache chieftain. Carl T. Hayden, congressman. Eusebio Kino (b. Italy), missionary. Sandra Day O'Connor, jurist. William H. Rehnquist, jurist. Linda Ronstadt, singer. Morris Udall, politician.
Noteworthy places Canyon de Chelly Natl. Monument. Casa Grande Ruins Natl. Monument. Chiricahua Natl. Monument. Ft. Bowie. Grand Canyon Natl. Park. Heard Museum, Phoenix. London Bridge, Lake Havasu City. Montezuma Castle Natl. Monument. Navajo Natl. Monument. Organ Pipe Cactus Natl. Monument. Painted Desert. Petrified Forest Natl. Park. Pipe Spring Natl. Monument. Saguaro Natl. Monument. Sunset Crater Natl. Monument. Taliesin West, near Scottsdale. Tonto Natl. Monument. Tumacacori Natl. Monument. Tuzigoot Natl. Monument. Walnut Canyon Natl. Monument. Wupatki Natl. Monument.
Memorable events Apaches and Navajos absorb Pueblos c. A.D. 1000. Alvar Núñez Cabeza de Vaca, first Spanish explorer 1536. Marcos de Niza 1539. Ruled as part of New Spain 1598–1821. First missionaries among Hopis 1638. Tubac first European settlement 1752. Tucson founded 1776. Apaches wipe out settlements under Mexican control, except Tucson 1821. Northern part ceded to United States following Mexican War 1848. Area south of Gila River to United States after Gadsden Purchase 1853. Territory 1863. Southern Pacific Railroad reaches Tucson 1880. Apaches subjugated 1886. Congress refuses to grant statehood 1906. Roosevelt Dam and Reservoir built on Salt River 1911. Native Americans given right to vote 1948. Glen Canyon Dam built on Colorado River 1964. Population growth of 22.1 percent highest in continental United States 1980–86.
Tourist information 1–800–842–8257 or 1–602–542–3618.

Arkansas

First inhabited by bluff dwellers 10,000 years ago, the Boston and Ouachita Mountains of western Arkansas are the only mountains between the Appalachians and the Rockies. By the time of the Hernando de Soto expedition of 1541, Arkansas was inhabited by a variety of peoples: the agrarian Quapaws to the south, the Caddo to the west and south, the Osage to the north, and the Chickasaw and Choctaw in the northeast. The Arkansas Post, the first permanent settlement in the Mississippi valley, became the pillar of the French claim to the region of what became the Louisiana Purchase.

Not fully part of the deep south, and cut off geographically from the Midwest, Arkansas has developed slowly. Although cotton was a mainstay of the economy and Arkansas joined the Confederacy during the Civil War, it was the first southern state to have integrated public colleges after World War II, a fact overshadowed by Gov. Orville Faubus's resistance to the integration of the Little Rock public schools. In recent years, Arkansas has attracted manufacturing and industry, but has one of the highest rural populations and ranks low in services, income, and education attainment.

NAME For term for Quapaw tribe given by other Indians. NICKNAME Land of Opportunity. CAPITAL Little Rock. ENTERED UNION June 15, 1836 (25th). MOTTO *Regnat populus* (Let the people rule).
Emblems BIRD Mockingbird. FLOWER Apple blossom. GEM Diamond. SONG "Arkansas." TREE Pine.
Land TOTAL AREA 53,187 sq. mi. (27th), incl. 1,109 sq. mi. inland water. BORDERS Mo., Tenn., Miss., La., Tex., Okla. RIVERS Arkansas, Mississippi, Ouachita, Red, St. Francis, White. LAKES Beaver, Bull Shoals, Chicot, Dardanelle, Greers Ferry, Greeson, Norfolk, Ouachita. OTHER NOTABLE FEATURES Ozark Mts.
Elected officials Gov. Jim Guy Tucker (D, term exp. 1997). Lt. Gov. Mike Huckabee (R). Sec. State Sharon Priest (D). Atty. Gen. Winston Bryant (D).
People (1994) 2,452,671 (33rd). RACE/NATIONAL ORIGIN (1990): White 82.7%. Black 15.9%. Indian 0.5%. Asian 0.5%. Other 0.3%. Hispanic 0.8%.
Cities (1990) Little Rock 175,795. Fort Smith 72,798. North Little Rock 61,741. Pine Bluff 57,140. Jonesboro 46,535. Fayetteville 42,099. Hot Springs 32,462. Springdale 29,941. Jacksonville 29,101. West Memphis 28,259.
Business GROSS STATE PRODUCT (GSP, 1992) $43.99 bil. (33rd). SECTORS OF GSP: Farms 4.53%; agricultural services, forestry, and fisheries 0.56%; mining 1.05%; construction 3.73%; manufacturing 24.73%; transportation and public utilities 11.52%; wholesale trade 5.37%; retail trade 10.13%; finance, insurance, and real estate 13.40%; services 13.96%; federal government 2.10%; federal military 1.09%; state and local government 7.84%. *FORTUNE* 500 COMPANIES (1994): 5: Wal-Mart Stores, Dillard Department Stores, Tyson Foods, Beverly Enterprises, Alltel.
Famous natives Maya Angelou, author. Linda Bloodworth-Thomason, television producer/director. Glen Campbell, singer. Hattie W. Caraway, first woman senator. Johnny Cash, singer. Eldridge Cleaver, author. Bill Clinton, U.S. president. William Fulbright (b. Mo.), politician. Alan Ladd, actor. Douglas MacArthur, general. Dick Powell, actor. Brooks Robinson, baseball player. Winthrop Rockefeller (b. N.Y.), politician/philanthropist. Edward Durrell Stone, architect. C. Vann Woodward, historian.
Noteworthy places Arkansas Post Natl. Monument (first permanent French settlement in lower Mississippi valley). Buffalo Natl. River. Crater of Diamonds State Park, Murfreesboro. Eureka Springs. Ft. Smith Natl. Hist. Site. Hot Springs Natl. Park. Pea Ridge Natl. Military Park.
Memorable events Bluff-dwellers present c. A.D. 500, followed by mound-building cultures. Hernando de Soto explores for Spain 1541. Jacques Marquette and Louis Jolliet explore for France 1673. René-Robert de La Salle meets Quapaws 1682. Henri de Tonti founds Arkansas Post on Arkansas River 1686. Ceded from France to Spain 1782; to France 1800; to United States 1803. Territory 1819. Admitted to Union as slave state, under terms of 1820 Missouri Compromise, 1836. Secedes from Union 1861. Fall of Little Rock to Union army 1863. Readmitted to Union 1868. Bauxite discovered 1887. Oil production begins 1920s. Federal troops called to Little Rock to ensure high school desegregation 1957. McClellan-Kerr Arkansas River Navigation system links Arkansas and Oklahoma to Mississippi River system 1971.
Tourist information 1–800–643–8383 or 1–800–828–8974.

California

Before the arrival of Europeans, no area of comparable size in North America was home to a greater variety of languages and cultures than what is now California, and today the state's population is more diverse than any other. Some demographers expect that within 50 years more than 40 percent of California's population will be of Hispanic origin, a larger proportion than at any time since before the Gold Rush of 1849. But the trend toward a two-tiered society is also increasing, with Caucasians and Asians on top and African-Americans and Hispanics on the bottom.

The largest state by population since the 1960s, California gained seven additional representatives in Congress as a result of the 1990 census, for a total of 52. This factor, as well as plans to hold its presidential primary before that of most other states, will make California more of a bellwether in national affairs than ever. Moreover, by some estimates California is the sixth largest economic power in the world.

Despite these attractions, and the state's rugged terrain and dramatic vistas, California has problems. The state's position as a leader in agriculture masks an alarming lack of water. It already draws off 4.4 million acre-feet from the Colorado River, mostly for irrigating the Imperial Valley—a desert when settlers crossed it 150 years ago. Almost the entire flow of the San Joaquin River is similarly diverted for the Central Valley. This inefficient use of water leaves less and less for consumption by people, whose numbers have leaped from 15 million in 1960 to 29.7 million in 1990.

Of more immediate concern is the threat of earthquakes. California has already suffered eight major earthquakes in this century. The 1906 quake destroyed San Francisco, and the Loma Prieta earthquake on Oct. 17, 1989—the second most powerful in U.S. history—killed 67 people, left 48,000 people homeless, and resulted in $10 billion in property damage. Like surfers waiting for the perfect wave, scientists are still bracing for "the big one."

NAME Probably from mythical island in García Ordoñez de Montalvo's 16th-century romance, *The Deeds of Esplandián*. NICKNAME Golden State. CAPITAL Sacramento. ENTERED UNION Sept. 9, 1850 (31st). MOTTO "Eureka" (I have found it).

Emblems ANIMAL California grizzly bear (extinct). BIRD California valley quail. FISH California golden trout. FLOWER Golden poppy. FOSSIL California saber-toothed cat. GEMSTONE Benitoite. INSECT California dog-face butterfly. MARINE MAMMAL California gray whale. MINERAL Gold. REPTILE California desert tortoise. ROCK Serpentine. SONG "I Love You, California." TREE California redwood.

Land TOTAL AREA 158,706 sq. mi. (3rd), incl. 2,407 sq. mi. inland water. BORDERS Oreg., Nev., Ariz., Baja California Norte, Pacific Ocean. RIVERS American, Colorado, Colorado River Aqueduct, Eel, Friant-Kern Canal, Klamath, Russian, Sacramento, Salinas, San Joaquin. LAKES Clear, Goose, Honey, Mono, Owens, Salton Sea, Shasta, Tahoe. MOUNTAINS Coast Ranges, Klamath, Lassen Peak, Sierra Nevada (Mt. Whitney 14,494 ft.). OTHER NOTABLE FEATURES Catalina Islands, Death Valley (282 ft. below sea level), San Francisco Bay, San Joaquin Valley.

Elected officials Gov. Pete Wilson (R, term exp. 1999). Lt. Gov. Gray Davis (D). Sec. State Bill Jones (R). Atty. Gen. Daniel E. Lungren (R).

People (1994) 31,430,697 (1st). RACE/NATIONAL ORIGIN (1990): White 69.0%. Black 7.4%. Indian 0.8%. Asian 9.6%. Other 13.2%. Hispanic 25.8%.

Cities (1990) Los Angeles 3,485,398. San Diego 1,110,549. San Jose 782,248. San Francisco 723,959. Long Beach 429,433. Oakland 372,242. Sacramento 369,365. Fresno 354,202. Santa Ana 293,742. Anaheim 266,406.

Business GROSS STATE PRODUCT (GSP, 1992) $787.90 bil. (1st). SECTORS OF GSP: Farms 1.49%; agricultural services, forestry, and fisheries 0.72%; mining 0.72%; construction 4.83%; manufacturing 15.62%; transportation and public utilities 7.45%; wholesale trade 6.46%; retail trade 9.63%; finance, insurance, and real estate 20.34%; services 21.14%; federal government 1.92%; federal military 1.55%; state and local government 8.12%. *FORTUNE* 500 COMPANIES (1994): 51: including Chevron, Hewlett-Packard, BankAmerica Corp., Atlantic Richfield, Safeway, Lockheed, McKesson, Intel, Rockwell International, Pacific Gas & Electric, Walt Disney, Apple Computer, Unocal, Northrop Grumman, Wells Fargo & Co., Times Mirror, Dole Food, Gap, Mattel, Southern Pacific Railway, Avery Dennison, American President, Food 4 Less Supermarkets.

Famous natives Ansel Adams, photographer. Dave Brubeck, musician. Luther Burbank (b. Mass.), horticulturist. John Cage, composer. Joe DiMaggio, baseball player. Robert Frost, poet. Ernest and Julio Gallo (b. Italy), vintners. Pancho Gonzales, tennis player. Samuel Ichiye Hayakawa, politician/educator. William Randolph Hearst, publisher. Steve Jobs, computer scientist. Billie Jean King, tennis player. Allen Lockheed, aviator. Jack London, author. Paul Masson (b. France), vintner. Marilyn Monroe, actress. John Muir (b. Scotland), naturalist. Richard M. Nixon, U.S. president. John Northrop, aviator. Adlai Stevenson, politician. John Steinbeck, author. Levi Strauss (b. Germany), clothier. Edward Teller (b. Hungary), nuclear physicist. Shirley Temple, actress. Earl Warren, politician/jurist.

Noteworthy places Big Sur, Monterey. Cabrillo Natl. Monument. California Academy of Sciences, San Francisco. California Palace of the Legion of Honor, San Francisco. Channel Islands Natl. Park. Devils Postpile Natl. Monument. Death Valley Natl. Monument. Disneyland. Fine Arts Museum of San Francisco. Fishermen's Wharf, San Francisco. Hollywood. Huntington Library and Botanical Gardens, San Marino. J. Paul Getty Museum, Malibu. Joshua Tree Natl. Monument. Kings Canyon Natl. Park. Lassen Volcanic Natl. Park. Lava Beds Natl. Monument. Los Angeles Co. Museum of Art. Muir Woods Natl. Monument. Mt. Palomar Observatory. Natl. Maritime Museum, San Francisco. Natural History Museum, Los Angeles. Natural History Museum of San Diego. Norton Simon Museum of Art at Pasadena. Pinnacles Natl. Monument. Redwood Natl. Park. Rosicrucian Egyptian Museum, San José. San Diego Museum of Art. San Diego Museum of Man. San Diego Zoo. San Francisco Museum of Modern Art. Sequoia Natl. Park. Southwest Museum (Casa de Adobe), Los Angeles. Yosemite Natl. Park.

Memorable events João Rodrigues Cabrilho lands at San Diego Bay 1542. Francis Drake lands north of San Francisco Bay 1579. Junípero Serra founds missions at San Diego (1769), Monterey (1770), San Luis Obispo (1772), and San Juan Capistrano (1776). California declares allegiance to independent Mexico 1821. First wagon train from Missouri 1841. Gold discovered north of Los Angeles 1842. California declares itself independent republic 1846. Gold found at John Sutter's mill; nine days later, by Treaty of Guadalupe Hidalgo, Mexico cedes California to United States 1848. Announcement of gold discovery brings 80,000 'Forty-niners. Gold rush peaks 1852. Transcontinental telegraph completed 1861. Transcontinental railway completed 1869. U.S. Congress enacts Chinese Exclusion Act, prohibiting immigration of Chinese laborers 1882, 1892, and 1902; Act repealed 1943. San Francisco earthquake kills 452, destroys 28,000 buildings 1906. Webb Alien Land Law prohibits Japanese from holding land 1913. Los Angeles has one car for every three people, twice national average, 1925. Dust Bowl immigrants 1930. Hollywood produces bulk of movies for U.S. theaters, which number more than banks 1940. Most populous state 1963. Proposition 13 limits property tax 1978. Loma Prieta earthquake registers 7.1 on Richter scale—second most powerful in U.S. history; 67 dead, 48,000 homeless, and $10 billion in property damage 1989.

Tourist information 1–800–862–2543 or 1–916–322–2881.

Colorado

The native peoples of Colorado were the Plains Indians (Arapaho and Cheyenne) to the east and the Great Basin Indians (Utes) to the west. This pre-Columbian division of the land is reflected today in Colorado's economy, which is a mix of agriculture and technology in the east and mining and ski tourism in the mountains. Despite a lack of natural sources of water on the Plains, sugar-beet processing has for years been a staple of the agricultural sector. During the oil price shocks of the 1970s, shale-oil production on the Western Slope created a boom comparable to Colorado's silver and lead boom in the late 19th century. Colorado's love of the outdoors is increasingly in conflict with its tradition of unhindered growth. Colorado's cities east of the Rockies sprawl without effective plans for land use. While a state of great natural beauty, it must cope with a high altitude that almost doubles the effect of auto emissions. Economic development means in large part resource extraction and requires more and more water, whose limited supply poses a great question for the future.

NAME Spanish for the color red. NICKNAME Centennial State. CAPITAL Denver. ENTERED UNION Aug. 1, 1876 (38th). MOTTO *Nil sine numine* (Nothing without providence).

Emblems ANIMAL Rocky Mountain bighorn sheep. BIRD Lark bunting. FLOWER Rocky Mountain Columbine. GEM Aquamarine. SONG "Where the Columbines Grow." TREE Colorado blue spruce.

Land TOTAL AREA 104,091 sq. mi. (8th), incl. 496 sq. mi. inland water. BORDERS Wyo., Nebr., Kans., Okla., N.Mex., Ariz., Utah. RIVERS Arkansas, Colorado, Green, Platte, Rio Grande. LAKES Blue Mesa, Dillon, Granby. MOUNTAINS Front Range, Laramie, Sangre de Cristo, San Juan, Sawatch Range (Mt. Elbert 14,443 ft.).

Elected officials Gov. Roy Romer (D, term exp. 1999). Lt. Gov. Gail Schoettler (D). Sec. State Vicki Buckley (R). Atty. Gen. Gale Norton (R).

People (1994) 3,655,647 (26th). RACE/NATIONAL ORIGIN (1990): White 88.2%. Black 4.0%. Indian 0.8%. Asian 1.8%. Other 5.1%. Hispanic 12.9%.

Cities (1990) Denver 467,610. Colorado Springs 281,140. Aurora 222,103. Lakewood 126,481. Pueblo 98,640. Arvada 89,235. Fort Collins 87,758. Boulder 83,312. Westminster 74,625. Greeley 60,536.

Business GROSS STATE PRODUCT (GSP, 1992) $82.46 bil. (23rd). SECTORS OF GSP: Farms 1.96%; agricultural services, forestry, and fisheries 0.49%; mining 2.10%; construction 3.97%; manufacturing 13.53%; transportation and public utilities 9.99%; wholesale trade 6.39%; retail trade 10.36%; finance, insurance, and real estate 16.87%; services 20.41%; federal government 3.33%; federal military 1.70%; state and local government 8.91%. *FORTUNE* 500 COMPANIES (1994): 4: US West, Tele-Communications, Cyprus Amax Minerals, Manville.

Famous natives Charlie Bent (b. Va.), trapper. "Unsinkable" Molly Brown, *Titanic* survivor. Scott Carpenter, astronaut. Lon Chaney, actor. Jack Dempsey, boxer. Mamie Eisenhower, first lady. Douglas Fairbanks, actor. Anne Parrish, novelist. Lowell Thomas, journalist. Byron R. White, jurist. Paul Whiteman, conductor.

Noteworthy places Black Canyon of the Gunnison Natl. Monument. Buffalo Bill grave site, Evergreen. Central City Opera House. Colorado Springs Fine Arts Center. Denver Art Museum.

Denver Mint. Denver Museum of Natural History. Dinosaur Natl. Monument. Florissant Fossil Beds Natl. Monument. Garden of the Gods, Colorado Springs. Great Sand Dunes Natl. Monument. Hovenweep Natl. Monument. Mesa Verde Natl. Park. Molly Brown House, Denver. Pikes Peak. Red Rocks Amphitheater. Rocky Mountain Natl. Park, Aspen. U.S. Air Force Academy, Colorado Springs. U.S. Olympic Headquarters, Colorado Springs. Yucca House Natl. Monument.
Memorable events Pueblos build cliff dwellings near Mesa Verde through 1200s. Arapahos and Cheyennes settle area after 13th century. France abandons claims 1763. Juan de Uribarri explores area 1786. Spain restores area to France 1801. To United States as part of Louisiana Purchase 1803. Zebulon Pike explores for United States 1806. Kit Carson and other scouts explore and trade with Native Americans 1810s–20s. Native Americans form alliance at Brent's Fork 1840. John Frémont's explorations 1842–53. Present territorial limits after Mexican War 1848. First permanent settlement at San Luis 1851. Gold found west of Denver—"Pike's Peak or Bust"—1858. Mineral springs bring first tourists 1861. Homestead Act encourages farming 1862. U.S. Army kills 400 Cheyenne at Sand Creek Massacre 1864; Utes and Cheyennes fight white settlement through 1870s. John Wesley Powell and nine others navigate Colorado River from the Green River branch in Wyoming to the end of Grand Canyon in Arizona 1869. Railroad link to Denver 1870. Silver and lead discoveries 1875. Uranium discovered near Grand Junction 1946. U.S. Air Force Academy founded Denver 1954; to Colorado Springs 1958. Shale oil boom on Western Slope 1974 and 1979. Accumulation of nuclear waste threatens suspension of operations at Rocky Flats 1988.
Tourist information 1–800–433–2656 or 1–303–592–5510.

Connecticut

Called the "arsenal of the nation" during the Revolution, Connecticut today leads the 50 states in defense-contract dollars per capita, although population ebb and flow continue to test its manufacturing wealth. Hartford has been the insurance capital of the world since before 1800, and Connecticut's quarries provided much of the red sandstone that became known as "brownstone" after it lined New York City streets.

With conditions favorable for affluent business, Connecticut has the highest per capita income in the country. However, it faced severe budget deficits in 1991; this forced passage of a state income tax after a prolonged budget crisis. The disparities in wealth between the very rich suburbs and the decaying industrial cities were highlighted by the city of Bridgeport's bankruptcy filing in June 1991. Although located in one of the country's wealthiest counties, Bridgeport's 180,000 mostly lower-middle-class inhabitants shoulder all the costs for county-wide health and criminal justice services themselves, in a pattern repeated statewide.

NAME From Mahican word meaning "beside the long tidal river." NICKNAMES Constitution State, Nutmeg State. CAPITAL Hartford. ENTERED UNION Jan. 9, 1788 (5th). MOTTO *Qui transtulit sustinet* (He who transplanted still sustains).
Emblems ANIMAL Sperm whale. BIRD American robin. FLOWER Mountain laurel. HERO Nathan Hale. INSECT European praying mantis. MINERAL Garnet. SHIP USS *Nautilus*. SONG "Yankee Doodle." TREE White oak.
Land TOTAL AREA 5,018 sq. mi. (48th), incl. 146 sq. mi. inland water. BORDERS Mass., R.I., Long Island Sound, N.Y. RIVERS Connecticut, Housatonic, Mianus, Naugatuck, Thames. LAKES Bantam, Barkhamstead, Candlewood, Waramaug. OTHER NOTABLE FEATURES Berkshire Hills, Long Island Sound.
Elected officials Gov. John G. Rowland (R, term exp. 1999). Lt. Gov. M. Jodi Rell (R). Sec. State Miles Rapoport (D). Atty. Gen. Richard Blumenthal (D).
People (1994) 3,275,251 (27th). RACE/NATIONAL ORIGIN (1990): White 87.0%. Black 8.3%. Indian 0.2%. Asian 1.5%. Other 2.9%. Hispanic 6.5%.
Cities (1990) Bridgeport 141,686. Hartford 139,739. New Haven 130,474. Waterbury 108,961. Stamford 108,056. Norwalk 78,331. New Britain 75,491. Danbury 65,585. Bristol 60,640. Meriden 59,479.
Business GROSS STATE PRODUCT (GSP, 1992) $98.87 bil. (21st). SECTORS OF GSP: Farms 0.36%; agricultural services, forestry, and fisheries 0.40%; mining 0.08%; construction 4.29%; manufacturing 20.52%; transportation and public utilities 7.34%; wholesale trade 6.93%; retail trade 9.35%; finance, insurance, and real estate 22.50%; services 19.29%; federal government 1.26%; federal military 0.73%; state and local government 6.97%. *FORTUNE* 500 COMPANIES (1994): 23: including General Electric, United Technologies, GTE, XEROX, Aetna Life & Casualty, American Brands, Tosco, Champion International, Dun & Bradstreet, Union Carbide, Pitney Bowes, Caldor, Stanley Works, Shawmut National Corp., Phoenix Home Life Mutual Insurance.
Famous natives Benedict Arnold, traitor. P.T. Barnum, showman. Lyman Beecher, theologian. John Brown, abolitionist. Samuel Colt, inventor. Jonathan Edwards, theologian. Charles Goodyear, inventor. Nathan Hale, patriot. Katharine Hepburn, actress. Charles Ives, composer. J.P. Morgan, financier. Ralph Nader, consumer advocate. Frederick Law Olmsted, landscape architect. Harriet Beecher Stowe, author. John Trumbell, artist. Noah Webster, lexicographer. Eli Whitney, inventor.
Noteworthy places Charles Ives Center, Danbury. Eugene O'Neill Memorial Theater Center, Waterford. Gilette Castle. Housatonic State Park. Mark Twain House, Hartford. Mystic Marinelife Aquarium. Mystic Seaport. Norwalk Maritime Center. U.S. Coast Guard Academy. USS *Nautilus*, New London. Wadsworth Atheneum, Hartford. Whitney Museum of Modern Art, Stamford. Yale Center for British Art, New Haven. Yale University, New Haven.
Memorable events Adriaen Block claims for Dutch 1614. First English settlement in Windsor 1633. Royal charter of 1662 hidden in Charter Oak 1687. *Hartford Courant*, oldest continuously published newspaper in U.S., first published 1764. Samuel Colt develops six-shooter 1835. Horace Wells uses first anesthesia 1844. Elias Howe invents sewing machine 1845. U.S. Coast Guard Academy founded New London 1876. First woman governor elected in her own right, Ella T. Grasso 1974.
Tourist information 1–800–CT–BOUND or 1–203–258–4355.

Delaware

The du Pont family has enjoyed a political and economic prominence in Delaware unmatched in the history of the other 49 states. Seven generations ago E.I. du Pont de Nemours and Co. was founded as a gunpowder mill, then grew into a monopoly, and in the wake of World War I diversified into today's giant, with interests in banking, media, and real estate. Only half the size of Los Angeles County, Delaware was called the corporate state by Ralph Nader's "raiders" in 1973. Its liberal incorporation laws have led more than half the *Fortune* 500 companies to incorporate there. It was one of the few states to prosper even during the recession of the early 1980s.

NAME For Thomas West, Lord De La Warre, colonial governor of Virginia. NICKNAMES First State, Diamond State. CAPITAL Dover. ENTERED UNION Dec. 7, 1787 (1st). MOTTO "Liberty and Independence."
Emblems BIRD Blue hen chicken. FISH Weakfish. FLOWER Peach blossom. INSECT Ladybug. ROCK Sillimanite. SONG "Our Delaware." TREE American holly.
Land TOTAL AREA 2,044 sq. mi. (49th), incl. 112 sq. mi. inland water. BORDERS Pa., N.J., Atlantic Ocean, Md. RIVERS Chesapeake and Delaware Canal, Delaware, Nanticoke.
Elected officials Gov. Tom Carper (D, term exp. 1997). Lt. Gov. Ruth Ann Miner (D). Sec. State Edward Freel. Atty. Gen. M. Jane Brady (R).
People (1994) 706,351 (46th). RACE/NATIONAL ORIGIN (1990): White 80.3%. Black 16.9%. Indian 0.3%. Asian 1.4%. Other 1.1%. Hispanic 2.4%.
Cities (1990) Wilmington 71,529. Dover 27,630. Newark 25,098. Milford 6,040. Elsmere 5,935. Seaford 5,689. Smyrna 5,231. New Castle 4,837. Middletown 3,834. Georgetown 3,732.
Business GROSS STATE PRODUCT (GSP, 1992) $23.67 bil. (44th). SECTORS OF GSP: Farms 1.31%; agricultural services, forestry, and fisheries 0.28%; mining 0.03%; construction 4.72%; manufacturing 24.53%; transportation and public utilities 5.95%; wholesale trade 3.90%; retail trade 6.67%; finance, insurance, and real estate 30.12%; services 13.51%; federal government 1.50%; federal military 0.94%; state and local government 6.53%. *FORTUNE* 500 COMPANIES (1994): 3: E.I. du Pont de Nemours, Columbia Gas System, Hercules.
Famous natives Valerie Bertinelli, actress. John Dickinson (b. Md.), Penman of the Revolution. Eleuthère I. du Pont, manufacturer. Pierre S.

("Pete") du Pont, politician. Morgan Edwards, founder of Brown University (R.I.). Thomas Macdonough, navy officer. Howard Pyle, illustrator. Edward R. Squibb, physician/manufacturer. Christopher Ward, historian.

Noteworthy places Brandywine Zoo, Wilmington. Delaware Art Museum, Wilmington. Delaware State Museum, Dover. Dover Downs International Speedway. Grand Opera House, Wilmington. Hagley Museum, Wilmington. Rehoboth Beach.

Memorable events Dutch arrive 1631. Swedes establish first permanent settlement at Wilmington 1638. Captured by Dutch 1655. To England 1664. Part of territory granted to William Penn 1682. Breaks off from Pennsylvania; first to ratify Constitution 1787. E.I. du Pont de Nemours Co. founded 1802. Railroad connects Wilmington to Philadelphia and Baltimore 1838. Though slave state, sides with Union during Civil War 1861–65. Delaware last state to abolish whipping post (last used 1952) 1972.

Tourist information 1–800–441–8846 or 1–800–282–8667 (in Del.).

District of Columbia

Chosen as the site for the nation's capital by George Washington, Washington, D.C., was carved out of land ceded by Maryland and Virginia. Although under federal jurisdiction, the District has petitioned for statehood as New Columbia. In 1961 Congress enacted the 23rd Amendment granting citizens of D.C. the right to vote in presidential elections for the first time, and 10 years later gave the District a nonvoting delegate to the House of Representatives. The District's largest employer is the federal government, and printing is the largest industry. Pres. John F. Kennedy called it a city of "Southern efficiency and Northern charm," but since his time, the city has become a leading patron of the arts. The problems of any large city are made worse by the city's largely transient population of government workers. The city, as the seat of the U.S. government, is a mecca for tourists from around the world, and more than 17 million people visit it each year.

NAME After Christopher Columbus; Columbia was commonly used for the United States before 1800. NICKNAME None. CAPITAL Washington. BECAME CAPITAL Dec. 1, 1800. MOTTO *Justitia omnibus* (Justice for all).

Emblems BIRD Wood thrush. FLOWER American beauty rose. TREE Scarlet oak.

Land TOTAL AREA 69 sq. mi., incl. 6 sq. mi. inland water. BORDERS Md., Va. RIVERS Anacostia, Potomac.

Elected official Mayor Marion Barry (D, term exp. 1999).

People (1994) 570,175. RACE/NATIONAL ORIGIN (1990): White 29.6%. Black 65.8%. Indian 0.2%. Asian 1.8%. Other 2.5%. Hispanic 5.4%.

Business GROSS STATE PRODUCT (GSP, 1992) $40.44 bil. (34th). SECTORS OF GSP: Farms 0.00%; agricultural services, forestry, and fisheries 0.03%; mining 0.02%; construction 1.70%; manufacturing 3.53%; transportation and public utilities 5.86%; wholesale trade 1.70%; retail trade 4.23%; finance, insurance, and real estate 12.95%; services 33.28%; federal government 29.43%; federal military 2.32%; state and local government 4.95%. *FORTUNE* 500 COMPANIES (1994): 5: Federal National Mortgage Association, MCI Communications, Marriott International, Student Loan Marketing Association, GEICO.

Famous natives Edward Albee, playwright. Carl Bernstein, journalist. John Foster Dulles, politician. Duke Ellington, composer. J. Edgar Hoover, FBI director. Marjorie Kinnan Rawlings, novelist. John Philip Sousa, composer.

Noteworthy places The Capitol. Chesapeake & Ohio Canal Natl. Hist. Park. Corcoran Gallery of Art. Dumbarton Oaks. Folger Shakespeare Library. Freer Gallery of Art. Hirshhorn Museum. Jefferson Memorial. Kennedy Center. Library of Congress. Lincoln Memorial. Natl. Air and Space Museum. Natl. Gallery of Art. Natl. Museum of African Art. Natl. Museum of American Art. Natl. Museum of American History. Natl. Museum of Natural History. Natl. Portrait Gallery. Naval Observatory. Navy Memorial Museum. Renwick Gallery. Smithsonian Institution. Vietnam Veterans Memorial. Washington Monument. Washington Zoo. White House. Woodrow Wilson House.

Memorable events Originally part of Maryland. Congress approves plan to secure land for seat of federal government, no more than 10 miles square, on land in Virginia and Maryland 1787. George Washington commissions Pierre Charles l'Enfant to lay out city 1791. Government moves 1800. British sail up the Potomac and burn capital 1814. Virginia reclaims its half of District 1846. Pres. Abraham Lincoln assassinated 1865. Coxey's Army marches on Washington 1894. The Bonus army—17,000 veterans—marches on Washington 1932. Led by Martin Luther King, Jr., 200,000 march for civil rights 1963. One hundred thousand protest Vietnam War 1971. Democratic party headquarters at Watergate burglarized by men linked to Pres. Richard M. Nixon's reelection effort 1972. Congress grants limited self-rule; mayor and city council elected 1975. Mayor Marion Barry convicted on drug charge 1991.

Tourist information 1–202–789–7000.

Florida

A vast network of swamps, rivers, and lakes, much of Florida is barely above sea level. Florida is home to Disney World, Cypress Gardens, the wealth-laden resort of Palm Beach, the *National Enquirer*, and the Okefenokee Swamp, and the pleasant climate and proximity to the Caribbean and Latin America have attracted large populations of the elderly and immigrants, as well as millions of tourists. One of the fastest-growing states, Florida has been plagued by drug trafficking, racial disturbances, and environmental damage to such wildlife as the crocodile, alligator, and the Florida panther.

NAME By Juan Ponce de León for Pascua Florida (Easter festival of the flowers). NICKNAME Sunshine State. CAPITAL Tallahassee. ENTERED UNION Mar. 3, 1845 (27th). MOTTO "In God We Trust." POET LAUREATE Dr. Edmund Skellings.

Emblems ANIMAL Florida panther. BEVERAGE Orange juice. BIRD Mockingbird. FLOWER Orange blossom. FRESHWATER FISH Florida largemouth bass. GEM Moonstone. MARINE MAMMALS Dolphin, manatee. SALTWATER FISH Atlantic sailfish. SHELL Horse conch. SONG "Old Folks at Home" ("Swanee River"). STONE Agatized coral. TREE Sabal palmetto palm.

Land TOTAL AREA 58,664 sq. mi. (22nd), incl. 4,511 sq. mi. inland water. BORDERS Ga., Atlantic Ocean, Gulf of Mexico, Ala. RIVERS Apalachicola, Caloosahatchee, Indian, Kissimmee, Perdido, St. Johns, St. Mary's, Suwanee, Withlacoochee. LAKES Apopka, George, Okeechobee, Seminole. OTHER NOTABLE FEATURES Everglades, Florida Keys, Okefenokee Swamp.

Elected officials Gov. Lawton Chiles (D, term exp. 1999). Lt. Gov. Buddy MacKay (D). Sec. State Sandra Mortham (R). Atty. Gen. Robert A. Butterworth (D).

People (1994) 13,952,714 (4th). RACE/NATIONAL ORIGIN (1990): White 83.1%. Black 13.6%. Indian 0.3%. Asian 1.2%. Other 1.8%. Hispanic 12.2%.

Cities (1990) Jacksonville 672,971. Miami 358,548. Tampa 280,015. St. Petersburg 238,629. Hialeah 188,004. Orlando 164,693. Ft. Lauderdale 149,377. Tallahassee 124,773. Hollywood 121,697. Clearwater 98,784.

Business GROSS STATE PRODUCT (GSP, 1992) $268.61 bil. (5th). SECTORS OF GSP: Farms 1.55%; agricultural services, forestry, and fisheries 0.78%; mining 0.33%; construction 5.33%; manufacturing 9.40%; transportation and public utilities 9.08%; wholesale trade 6.84%; retail trade 11.93%; finance, insurance, and real estate 19.13%; services 22.72%; federal government 1.99%; federal military 1.81%; state and local government 9.11%. *FORTUNE* 500 COMPANIES (1994): 12: Winn-Dixie Stores, Publix Super Markets, W.R. Grace, FPL Group, Ryder System, Eckerd, Office Depot, Harris, Barnett Banks, Florida Progress, Knight-Ridder, Tech Data.

Famous natives Mary Bethune, educator/reformer. Faye Dunaway, actress. Zora Neale Hurston, writer. James Weldon Johnson, lawyer/novelist. Osceola, Seminole chief. Sidney Poitier, actor. A. Philip Randolph, labor leader. Edmund Kirby Smith, Confederate general. Joseph Warren "Vinegar Joe" Stillwell, army officer. Ben Vereen, actor/singer.

Noteworthy places Biscayne Natl. Park. Castillo de San Marcos, St. Augustine. Everglades Natl. Park. Florida State Museum, Gainesville. Ft. Jefferson Natl. Monument. Ft. Matanzas Natl. Monument. Kennedy Space Center, Cape Canaveral. Ringling Museum, Sarasota. St. Augustine. Walt Disney World/EPCOT Center, Orlando.

Memorable events Juan Ponce de León claims Florida for Spain 1513. French stake claim for Florida 1562; build Ft. Caroline 1564. Pedro Menéndez de Avilés founds St. Augustine, first permanent European settlement in U.S. 1565. Spain cedes Florida to United States 1819.

Seminole War 1835–42. State secedes from Union 1861. Readmitted 1868. Carl Fisher begins to develop Miami Beach as resort 1912. Florida's first paper mill opens, expanding forest industry 1931. More than 100,000 Cuban refugees enter United States, most through Florida, during Mariel boat lift 1980. Army Corps of Engineers announce plans to let Kissimmee River, canalized in 1971, return to natural course to Lake Okeechobee; the largest back-to-nature project ever undertaken in U.S. 1990.
Tourist information 1–904–487–1462.

Georgia

The largest state east of the Mississippi River, Georgia is diverse in its terrain, embracing the woods of the Blue Ridge Mountains to the north and the alligators of the Okefenokee Swamp in the south. Though two-thirds of the population are urban dwellers, Georgia's farms rank first in poultry production and are leading producers of pecans, cattle, hogs, and peanuts. Up from a past of slavery and separate-but-equal facilities, in the early 1970s Atlanta elected Andrew Young the first black member of the U.S. Congress and Maynard Jackson the first black mayor from the South since Reconstruction. Today divisions linger in Georgia, the cities favoring a progressive stance and the rural areas clinging to some of the ways of the Old South.

NAME For King George II of England 1732. NICKNAMES Empire State of the South, Peach State. CAPITAL Atlanta. ENTERED UNION Jan. 2, 1788 (4th). MOTTO "Wisdom, justice, moderation."
Emblems BIRD Brown thrasher. FISH Largemouth bass. FLOWER Cherokee rose. FOSSIL Shark tooth. GEM Quartz. INSECT Honeybee. SONGS "Georgia," "Georgia on My Mind." TREE Live oak. WILDFLOWER Azalea.
Land TOTAL AREA 58,910 sq. mi. (21st), incl. 854 sq. mi. inland water. BORDERS Tenn., N.C., S.C., Atlantic Ocean, Fla., Ala. RIVERS Altamaha, Apalachicola, Chattahoochee, Flint, Ocmulgee, Oconee, Savannah, Suwanee. LAKES Clark Hill, Harding, Hartwell, Seminole, Sidney Lanier, Sinclair, Walter F. George, West Point Lake. OTHER NOTABLE FEATURES Blue Ridge Mountains (Mt. Enotah 4,784 ft.), Okefenokee Swamp.
Elected officials Gov. Zell Miller (D, term exp. 1999). Lt. Gov. Pierre Howard (D). Sec. State Max Cleland (D). Atty. Gen. Michael J. Bowers (D).
People (1994) 7,055,336 (11th). RACE/NATIONAL ORIGIN (1990): White 71.0%. Black 27.0%. Indian 0.2%. Asian 1.2%. Other 0.7%. Hispanic 1.7%.
Cities (1990) Atlanta 394,017. Columbus 179,278. Savannah 137,560. Macon 106,612. Albany 78,122. Roswell 47,923. Athens 45,734. Augusta 44,639. Marietta 44,129. Warner Robins 43,726.
Business GROSS STATE PRODUCT (GSP, 1992) $153.53 bil. (13th). SECTORS OF GSP: Farms 1.34%; agricultural services, forestry, and fisheries 0.37%; mining 0.57%; construction 4.70%; manufacturing 18.98%; transportation and public utilities 10.44%; wholesale trade 9.15%; retail trade 9.64%; finance, insurance, and real estate 15.52%; services 16.78%; federal government 2.69%; federal military 1.49%; state and local government 8.33%. *FORTUNE* 500 COMPANIES (1994): 15: United Parcel Service, Bellsouth, Coca-Cola, Georgia-Pacific, Home Depot, Delta Air Lines, Southern, AFLAC, Coca-Cola Enterprises, Genuine Parts, Suntrust Banks, Turner Broadcasting, Shaw Industries, Alumax, First Financial Management.
Famous natives James Brown, singer. Erskine Caldwell, author. James Earl ("Jimmy") Carter, U.S. president. Ray Charles, musician. Ty Cobb, baseball player. James Dickey, poet. Martin Luther King, Jr., minister/reformer. Sidney Lanier, author. Little Richard, musician. Carson McCullers, author. Alexander McGillivray, Creek chief. Margaret Mitchell, author. Elijah Muhammad, religious leader. Flannery O'Connor, author. Burt Reynolds, actor. Jackie Robinson, baseball player. Tomochichi, Yamacraw chief. Joanne Woodward, actress.
Noteworthy places Chickamauga and Chattanooga Natl. Military Park. Confederate Memorial, Stone Mountain. Ft. Frederica Natl. Monument. Ft. Pulaski Natl. Monument. High Museum of Art, Atlanta. Martin Luther King Natl. Hist. Site, Atlanta. Ocmulgee Natl. Monument. Okefenokee Swamp. Savannah Historic District.
Memorable events Hernando de Soto explores region 1540. Cotton gin invented 1793. Georgia expels Cherokee Indian tribes on Trail of Tears 1832–38. Secedes from Union 1860. Gen. William T. Sherman's 60,000 troops cut 60-mi. swath in their "march to the sea" 1864. Formula for Coca-Cola developed by chemist in search of cure for hangover 1886. Cyclone kills 1,000 in Charleston, South Carolina, and Savannah 1893. Franklin D. Roosevelt dies at the Little White House, Warm Springs 1945. First state to give vote to 18-year-olds 1948. Emory University designated to receive $100-million philanthropic gift from Robert W. Woodruff 1979. Dept. of Justice rules that state's process for electing superior court judges violates 1965 Voting Rights Act 1990.
Tourist information 1–800–VISIT–GA or 1–404–656–3590.

Hawaii

What the air conditioner did for the Sunbelt, the jetliner has done for Hawaii. Because of the jet, Hawaii is a possible vacation spot for millions and welcomes 20 times the air travelers of 25 years ago. Thousands of miles from both California and mainland Asia, Hawaii was originally peopled by Polynesian seafarers around A.D. 500 and has the richest ethnic mix of any state, with the lowest percentage of whites and highest percentages of Asians. It was partly fear of this diversity that stalled its statehood. A link between the United States and Asia, Hawaii is the center of U.S. defense in the Pacific and is home to 100,000 veterans, three-quarters of them veterans of Vietnam. Hawaii produces large quantities of pineapples and sugarcane, and efforts are under way to harness thermal electric power from Mauna Loa volcano.

NAME Of unknown origin, perhaps from Hawaii Loa, traditional discoverer of islands, or from Hawaiki, the traditional Polynesian homeland. NICKNAMES Aloha State, Paradise of the Pacific. CAPITAL Honolulu. (21°19'N, 157°52'W). ENTERED UNION Aug. 21, 1959 (50th). MOTTO *Ua mau ke ea o ka aina i ke pono* (The life of the land is perpetuated in righteousness).
Emblems BIRD Nene (Hawaiian goose). FISH Humuhumunukunukuapuaa. FLOWER Pua aloalo (hibiscus). SONG "Hawaii Ponoi." TREE Kukui (candlenut).
Land TOTAL AREA 6,470 sq. mi. (47th), incl. 45 sq. mi. inland water. Surrounded by Pacific Ocean. RIVERS Kaukonahua Stream, Wailuku Stream. LAKES Halulu, Kolekole, Salt Lake, Waiia Res. OTHER NOTABLE FEATURES Pearl Harbor. Hualalai, Kilauea, Mauna Kea (13,796 ft.), and Mauna Loa volcanoes. MAIN ISLANDS Hawaii, Kauai, Maui, Molokai, Oahu.
Elected officials Gov. Benjamin J. Cayetano (D, term exp. 1999). Lt. Gov./Sec. State Mazie Hirono (D). Atty. Gen. Margery Bronster.
People (1994) 1,178,564 (40th). RACE/NATIONAL ORIGIN (1990): White 33.4%. Black 2.5%. Indian 0.5%. Asian 61.8%. Other 1.9%. Hispanic 7.3%.
Cities (1990) Honolulu 365,272. Hilo 37,808. Kailua 36,818. Kaneohe 35,448. Waipahu 31,435. Pearl City 30,993. Waimatu 29,967. Mililani Town 29,359. Schofield Barracks 19,597. Wahiawa 17,386.
Business GROSS STATE PRODUCT (GSP, 1992) $33.20 bil. (38th). SECTORS OF GSP: Farms 1.26%; agricultural services, forestry, and fisheries 0.43%; mining 0.05%; construction 6.81%; manufacturing 3.83%; transportation and public utilities 9.85%; wholesale trade 4.15%; retail trade 11.47%; finance, insurance, and real estate 19.43%; services 22.50%; federal government 4.77%; federal military 7.30%; state and local government 8.16%. *FORTUNE* 500 COMPANIES (1994): 0.
Famous natives Bernice P. Bishop, philanthropist. Sanford B. Dole, statehood advocate. Charlotte (b. Ohio) and Luther Halsey Gulick, Camp Fire Girls founders. Don Ho, singer. Daniel J. Inouye, politician. Duke Kahanamoku, swimmer. Victoria Kaiulani, last heiress presumptive to Hawaiian throne. Kamehameha I, king. Kamehameha III, king. Liliuokalani, queen. Bette Midler, singer.
Noteworthy places Bernice P. Bishop Museum, Honolulu. Diamond Head. Haleakala Natl. Park, Maui. Hawaii Volcanoes Natl. Park (Kilauea and Mauna Loa), Hawaii. Iolani Palace, Honolulu. Kaloko-Honokohau Natl. Hist. Park, Molokai. Natl. Cemetery of the Pacific and USS *Arizona* Memorial. Polynesian Cultural Center, Laiea. Pu'uhonua o Honaunau Natl. Hist. Park, Hawaii.
Memorable events Polynesians first arrive sixth century. Second wave of Polynesians arrive 10th century. Captain James Cook first European to visit islands 1778; killed on Hawaii 1779. Sugar production begins 1835. Land reform

ends feudal system 1848. Monarchy rule ends in revolution 1893. Becomes U.S. Territory 1900. Japanese attack Pearl Harbor 1941. Statehood 1959.
Tourist information 1–808–923–1811.

Idaho

Idaho is 25 percent Mormon, and the Latter-day Saints here have their greatest influence outside Utah. The northern panhandle, where people tend to look west to Washington, and the south, where Mormons look to Utah, are connected by a single highway. The health of Boise's economy, with its large share of home-grown industrial success, unites the two other areas. Home to some of the most isolated and rugged country in the United States, Idaho's diversified economy has traditionally been based on lumber, potatoes, and mining. In the 1980s these were augmented by a number of small high-tech industries fleeing the high cost of business in California.

NAME Means "gem of the mountains." NICKNAME Gem State. CAPITAL Boise. ENTERED UNION July 3, 1890 (43rd). MOTTO *Esto perpetua* (May it last forever).
Emblems BIRD Mountain bluebird. FLOWER Syringa. GEM Star garnet. HORSE Appaloosa. SONG "Here We Have Idaho." TREE Western white pine.
Land TOTAL AREA 83,564 sq. mi. (13th), incl. 1,152 sq. mi. inland water. BORDERS British Columbia, Mont., Wyo., Utah, Nev., Oreg., Wash. RIVERS Bear, Clearwater, Payette, Salmon, Snake. LAKES American Falls Res., Coeur d'Alene, Pend Oreille. MOUNTAINS Bitterroot Range, Centennial, Clearwater, Salmon River, Sawtooth Range (Castle Peak 11,820 ft.), Wasatch Range. OTHER NOTABLE FEATURES Grand Canyon of the Snake River.
Elected officials Gov. Phil Batt (R, term exp. 1999). Lt. Gov. C.L. "Butch" Otter (R). Sec. State Pete T. Cenarrusa (R). Atty. Gen. Alan G. Lance (R).
People (1994) 1,133,034 (42nd): RACE/NATIONAL ORIGIN (1990): White 94.4%. Black 0.3%. Indian 1.4%. Asian 0.9%. Other 3.0%. Hispanic 5.3%.
Cities (1990) Boise 125,738. Pocatello 46,080. Idaho Falls 43,929. Nampa 28,365. Lewiston 28,082. Twin Falls 27,591. Coeur d'Alene 24,563. Moscow 18,519. Caldwell 18,400. Rexburg 14,302.
Business GROSS STATE PRODUCT (GSP, 1992) $20.86 bil. (46th). SECTORS OF GSP: Farms 8.71%; agricultural services, forestry, and fisheries 1.05%; mining 1.08%; construction 4.70%; manufacturing 15.93%; transportation and public utilities 8.18%; wholesale trade 5.32%; retail trade 9.79%; finance, insurance, and real estate 18.61%; services 14.71%; federal government 2.50%; federal military 1.16%; state and local government 8.24%. *FORTUNE* 500 COMPANIES (1994): 3: Albertson's, Boise Cascade, Morrison Knudsen.
Famous natives Joseph, Nez Percé chief. Ezra Taft Benson, politician. Gutzon Borglum, sculptor. Frank Church, politician. Ezra Pound, poet. Harmon Killebrew, baseball player. Jerry Kramer, football player. Sacagawea (Bird Woman), Shoshone interpreter. Lana Turner, actress.
Noteworthy places Craters of the Moons Natl. Monument. Hell's Canyon Natl. Recreation Area. Nez Percé Natl. Hist. Park. Sawtooth Natl. Recreation Area. Sun Valley ski resort. Yellowstone Natl. Park.
Memorable events Lewis and Clark expedition 1805. Becomes part of United States when Idaho Treaty concluded with Britain 1846. Gold Rush 1860. Nez Percé War 1877. Statehood 1890. World's first breeder reactor built at Idaho Falls, 1951. Snake River opened to navigation, linking Lewiston to Pacific Ocean at Astoria, Oregon, 1975. New Teton River Dam collapses as it is being filled for first time; 10 dead, $400 million in damage 1976.
Tourist information 1–800–635–7820 or 1–208–334–2470.

Illinois

The Illinois economy is enormously productive and diverse. While Chicago is a leader in world finance and trade, the southern part of the state has rich farmlands (the state is second to Iowa in corn and soybean exports) and mineral deposits (both coal and gas—there are especially rich coal deposits in the southeast region around Cairo, known as Little Egypt). Manufacturing centers around Chicago, Rockford—the state's second-largest city—and Springfield, the capital. Chicago is also a major transportation hub with extensive rail networks, an international port serving ships from both the Atlantic and Gulf of Mexico, and the largest airport in the country. Another leading industry in Illinois is political patronage, infecting both the Chicago-based Democrats and the downstate Republicans. Reform of the system, which boasted 12,000 patronage positions for the governor and cabinet officials in the 1970s, seems a remote possibility and would take the bite out of the state's tradition of muckraking journalism.

NAME Corruption of *iliniwek* ("tribe of the superior men"), natives of region at time of earliest French explorations. NICKNAME Prairie State. CAPITAL Springfield. ENTERED UNION Dec. 3, 1818 (21st). MOTTO "State sovereignty—national unity." SLOGAN "Land of Lincoln."
Emblems ANIMAL White-tailed deer. BIRD Cardinal. FLOWER Violet. INSECT Monarch butterfly. MINERAL Fluorite. SONG "Illinois." TREE White oak.
Land TOTAL AREA 56,345 sq. mi. (24th), incl. 700 sq. mi. inland water. BORDERS Wis., Lake Michigan, Ind., Ky., Mo., Iowa. RIVERS Fox, Illinois, Illinois Waterway, Kankakee, Kaskaskia, Mississippi, Ohio, Rock, Vermillion, Wabash. LAKES Carlyle, Crab Orchard. OTHER NOTABLE FEATURES Charles Mound (1,235 ft.), Little Egypt.
Elected officials Gov. Jim Edgar (R, term exp. 1999). Lt. Gov. Bob Kustra (R). Sec. State George H. Ryan (R). Atty. Gen. Jim Ryan.
People (1994) 11,751,774 (6th). RACE/NATIONAL ORIGIN (1990): White 78.3%. Black 14.8%. Indian 0.2%. Asian 2.5%. Other 4.2%. Hispanic 7.9%.
Cities (1990) Chicago 2,783,726. Rockford 139,426. Peoria 113,504. Springfield 105,227. Aurora 99,581. Naperville 85,351. Decatur 83,885. Elgin 77,010. Joliet 76,836. Arlington Heights Village 75,460.
Business GROSS STATE PRODUCT (GSP, 1992) $294.45 bil. (4th). SECTORS OF GSP: Farms 1.23%; agricultural services, forestry, and fisheries 0.36%; mining 0.60%; construction 4.50%; manufacturing 19.47%; transportation and public utilities 9.32%; wholesale trade 8.17%; retail trade 8.82%; finance, insurance, and real estate 18.54%; services 19.55%; federal government 1.83%; federal military 0.60%; state and local government 7.02%. *FORTUNE* 500 COMPANIES (1994): 40: including Sears Roebuck, State Farm Group, Amoco, Motorola, Sara Lee, Caterpillar, UAL, Ameritech, Archer Daniels Midland, WMX Technologies, Walgreen, Deere, McDonald's, Quaker Oats, Stone Container, Navistar International, First Chicago Corp., R.R. Donnelley & Sons, Spiegel, Brunswick, Fruit of the Loom.
Famous natives Jane Addams, reformer (Nobel Peace Prize, 1930). Ernie Banks, baseball player. Saul Bellow, author (Nobel Prize, 1976). Harry A. Blackmun, jurist. Ray Bradbury, author. Gwendolyn Brooks, poet. William Jennings Bryan, politician. Edgar Rice Burroughs, novelist. St. Frances Xavier Cabrini (b. Italy). Clarence Darrow, lawyer. Miles Davis, musician. John Dos Passos, novelist. Enrico Fermi (b. Italy), nuclear physicist (Nobel Prize, 1938). Robert Louis "Bob" Fosse, choreographer. Milton Friedman, economist (Nobel Prize, 1976). Benny Goodman, musician. Ernest Hemingway, novelist. Charlton Heston, actor. William Holden, actor. Vachel Lindsay, poet. Archibald MacLeish, poet. Ludwig Mies van der Rohe (b. Germany), architect. Charles W. Post, cereal manufacturer. Ronald Reagan, U.S. president. Carl Sandburg, poet. Albert G. Spalding, merchant. John Paul Stevens, jurist. Gloria Swanson, actress.
Noteworthy places Art Institute of Chicago. Crab Orchard Wildlife Refuge. Dickson Mounds Museum, Lewistown. Field Museum of Natural History, Chicago. Ft. Chartres. Ft. Kaskaskia. Ft. Massac. Frank Lloyd Wright Historic District, Oak Park. Illinois State Museum, Springfield. Lincoln Home Natl. Hist. Park, Springfield. Mormon Settlement, Nauvoo. Morton Arboretum, Lisle. Museum of Science and Industry, Chicago. Shawnee Natl. Forest. Starved Rock State Park.
Memorable events French missionary explorers Jacques Marquette and Louis Jolliet in Illinois 1673. Cahokia first European settlement 1699. Territory to England after French and Indian War 1763. Chicago founded by Jean-Baptiste Point du Sable 1779. Illinois and Michigan Canal links Lake Michigan and Mississippi River 1848. Lincoln-Douglas Debates at Springfield 1860. Half of Chicago destroyed by great fire 1871. Terrorist bombing leaves nine dead and 130 wounded in Haymarket affair, Chicago 1886. Columbia Exposition, Chicago 1893. First successful

nuclear chain reaction created at University of Chicago 1942. Riots at Democratic National Convention in Chicago 1968. Sears Tower, world's tallest building (1,454 ft.), completed in Chicago 1973.

Tourist information 1-800-223-0121 or 1-312-280-5740.

Indiana

Indiana is strong in both farms and manufacturing. Its southern half has large coal deposits and produces most of the limestone quarried in the United States. To the north the fertile land helps make Indiana one of the primary farm-belt states. Indiana is also very much a part of the industrial Midwest, where unemployment is always a threat, especially in the heavily industrial areas of Gary and Indianapolis (the latter of which has developed into a center for high-tech industries through the 1980s and 1990s). These geographic divisions have parallels in the political history of the state, which during the Civil War was Union in the north and Confederate in the south. In 1966 the state's patronage politics were upset by reapportionment, and urban counties increased representation.

NAME For the land of Indians by early settlers, who found many distinct tribes living in region. NICKNAME Hoosier State. CAPITAL Indianapolis. ENTERED UNION Dec. 11, 1816 (19th). MOTTO "The Crossroads of America."

Emblems BIRD Cardinal. FLOWER Peony. POEM "Indiana." SONG "On the Banks of the Wabash, Far Away." STONE Indiana limestone. TREE Tulip tree.

Land TOTAL AREA 36,185 sq. mi. (38th), incl. 253 sq. mi. inland water. BORDERS Lake Michigan, Mich., Ohio, Ky., Ill. RIVERS Kankakee, Ohio, Tippecanoe, Wabash, White, Whitewater. LAKES Freeman, Shafer.

Elected officials Gov. Evan Bayh (D, term exp. 1997). Lt. Gov. Frank L. O'Bannon (D). Sec. State Sue Ann Gilroy (R). Atty. Gen. Pamela Fanning Carter (D).

People (1994) 5,752,073 (14th). RACE/NATIONAL ORIGIN (1990): White 90.6%. Black 7.8% Indian 0.2%. Asian 0.7%. Other 0.7%. Hispanic 1.8%.

Cities (1990) Indianapolis 741,952. Fort Wayne 173,072. Evansville 126,272. Gary 116,646. South Bend 105,511. Hammond 84,236. Muncie 71,035. Bloomington 60,633. Anderson 59,459. Terre Haute 57,483.

Business GROSS STATE PRODUCT (GSP, 1992) $121.65 bil. (15th). SECTORS OF GSP: Farms 1.90%; agricultural services, forestry, and fisheries 0.34%; mining 0.67%; construction 4.29%; manufacturing 29.79%; transportation and public utilities 9.32%; wholesale trade 5.62%; retail trade 9.96%; finance, insurance, and real estate 14.09%; services 14.34%; federal government 1.83%; federal military 0.40%; state and local government 7.46%. *FORTUNE* 500 COMPANIES (1994): 6: Eli Lilly, Lincoln National, Cummins Engine, Bindley Western, Associated Insurance, Ball.

Famous natives Larry Bird, basketball player. Hoagy Carmichael, composer. Eugene V. Debs, politician/organizer. Theodore Dreiser, author. Benjamin Harrison, U.S. president. Jimmy Hoffa, union leader. Michael Jackson, singer. David Letterman, comedian. Carole Lombard, actress. Cole Porter, composer. Ernie Pyle, journalist. Knute Rockne (b. Norway), football player. Paul Samuelson, economist (Nobel Prize, 1960). Booth Tarkington, author. Kurt Vonnegut, author. Wendell L. Willkie, politician. Wilbur Wright, aviation pioneer.

Noteworthy places Ernie Pyle birthplace, Dana. George Rogers Clark Natl. Hist. Park, Vincennes. Benjamin Harrison home, Indianapolis. Hoosier Natl. Forest. Indiana Dunes Natl. Lakeshore. Indianapolis Motor Speedway and Museum. Indianapolis Museum of Art. New Harmony village. Old state capital, Corydon. Wilbur Wright State Memorial, Millville. Wyandotte Cave. Tippecanoe sites.

Memorable events Mound Builders present c. A.D. 1000. René-Robert Cavelier de La Salle explores for French 1679–87. French near Vincennes from c. 1700. French cede territory to British 1763. Gen. Ambrose Clark captures Ft. Vincennes 1779. Territory ceded to U.S. 1783; included in Northwest Territory 1787. Miamis defeat U.S. twice in 1790. Gen. Anthony Wayne defeats Miamis at Battle of Fallen Timbers 1794. Territory included in Indiana Territory 1800. Gen. William Henry Harrison defeats Tecumseh's Indian Confederation at Tippecanoe 1811. Statehood 1816. Studebaker wagon company founded in South Bend 1852. U.S. Steel establishes mill at company-built town of Gary 1906. First Indianapolis 500 run 1911. Only a dozen car companies producing cars, down from a pre–World War I peak of 375, 1920. Studebaker, last Indiana-based car manufacturer, closes 1963.

Tourist information 1-800-289-6646 or 1-317-232-8860.

Iowa

Iowa lies between the two great rivers of the central United States, the Mississippi and the Missouri, with a quarter of the nation's richest and deepest topsoil. Iowa's farmers lead the country in the production of corn, and Iowa is also a big producer of hogs, cattle, and other livestock. With about 75 percent of Iowans employed in agriculture-related industries and 90 percent of the land farmed, Iowa is deeply affected by natural disasters such as the 1988 drought. Yet more than 120 *Fortune* 500 companies have production facilities in this farm state. Industrial production has risen since World War II, though in the early 1980s many workers were laid off in the Mississippi River cities of Dubuque and Davenport. Iowans send abroad a quarter of the food they produce. As a result, this traditionally Republican state is better attuned to world developments than one might initially suspect.

NAME For Iowa tribe. NICKNAME Hawkeye State. CAPITAL Des Moines. ENTERED UNION Dec. 28, 1846 (29th). MOTTO "Our liberties we prize and our rights we will maintain."

Emblems BIRD Eastern goldfinch. FLOWER Wild rose. SONG "The Song of Iowa." STONE Geode. TREE Oak.

Land TOTAL AREA 56,275 sq. mi. (25th), incl. 310 sq. mi. inland water. BORDERS Minn., Wis., Ill., Mo., Nebr., S.Dak. RIVERS Big Sioux, Des Moines, Mississippi, Missouri. LAKES Okoboji, Rathburn Res., Red Rock, Saylorville Res., Spirit, Storm. OTHER NOTABLE FEATURES Ocheyedan Mound (1,675 ft.).

Elected officials Gov. Terry E. Branstad (R, term exp. 1999). Lt. Gov. Joy C. Corning (R). Sec. State Paul Danny Pate (D). Atty. Gen. Tom Miller (D).

People (1994) 2,829,252 (30th). RACE/NATIONAL ORIGIN (1990): White 96.6%. Black 1.7%. Indian 0.3%. Asian 0.9%. Other 0.5%. Hispanic 1.2%.

Cities (1990) Des Moines 193,187. Cedar Rapids 108,751. Davenport 95,333. Sioux City 80,505. Waterloo 66,467. Iowa City 59,738. Dubuque 57,546. Council Bluffs 54,315. Ames 47,198. Cedar Falls 34,298.

Business GROSS STATE PRODUCT (GSP, 1992) $59.46 bil. (30th). SECTORS OF GSP: Farms 7.99%; agricultural services, forestry, and fisheries 0.68%; mining 0.17%; construction 3.14%; manufacturing 23.19%; transportation and public utilities 8.12%; wholesale trade 6.49%; retail trade 8.60%; finance, insurance, and real estate 15.69%; services 14.67%; federal government 2.11%; federal military 0.28%; state and local government 9.01%. *FORTUNE* 500 COMPANIES (1994): 2: Principal Mutual Life Insurance, Maytag.

Famous natives Norman E. Borlaug, agronomist (Nobel Peace Prize, 1970). William F. "Buffalo Bill" Cody, scout/showman. George Gallup, pollster. Josiah B. Grinnell (b. Vt.), abolitionist. Herbert Hoover, U.S. president. Harry L. Hopkins, politician. John L. Lewis, labor leader. John R. Mott, religious leader. Billy Sunday, baseball player/evangelist. John Wayne, actor. Meredith Wilson, composer. Grant Wood, painter.

Noteworthy places Amana Colonies. Davenport Art Gallery. Des Moines Art Center. Effigy Mounds Natl. Monument, Marquette. Ft. Dodge Hist. Museum. Herbert Hoover birthplace and library, West Branch. Natl. Rivers Hall of Fame, Dubuque. Putnam Museum, Davenport.

Memorable events Mound Builders present c. A.D. 1000. Jacques Marquette and Louis Jolliet claim land for France 1673. Part of Louisiana Purchase 1803. Part of Missouri Territory 1812–21. Black Hawk Wars 1832, 1834–37. First permanent settlement at Dubuque 1833. Organized as Iowa Territory (incl. parts of Minnesota, North Dakota, and South Dakota) 1838. Statehood 1846. Capital moved from Iowa City to Des Moines 1857. Fifty percent of Iowa's farms foreclosed during depression 1929–35. Urban population exceeds rural for first time 1960. Population loss of 2.2 percent greater than any other state 1980–86.

Tourist information 1-800-345-IOWA.

Kansas

Kansas burst on the American scene as the territory called Bleeding Kansas, seething with conflict over slavery. Victorious New England abolitionists imprinted the state with the Puritan ethic. They were early supporters of prohibition, partly to discourage foreign newcomers. Kansas suffered enormously during the Great Depression and "Dust Bowl" days of the 1930s but rebounded strongly during the war. Wichita's aircraft industries, vital to the war effort, helped the Kansas economy to remain strong in the postwar years as family farming declined dramatically. Today Kansas remains a primary producer of wheat, cattle, and other agricultural products. Its manufacturing base still includes extensive aircraft industries, and it leads the states in the production of helium. The geographic center of the continental United States is near Lebanon.

NAME For Kansa or Kaw, "people of the south wind." NICKNAME Sunflower State. CAPITAL Topeka. ENTERED UNION Jan. 29, 1861 (34th). MOTTO *Ad astra per aspera* (To the stars through adversity).

Emblems ANIMAL American buffalo. BIRD Western meadowlark. FLOWER Wild native sunflower. MARCH "The Kansas March." SONG "Home on the Range." TREE Cottonwood.

Land TOTAL AREA 82,277 sq. mi. (14th), incl. 499 sq. mi. inland water. BORDERS Nebr., Mo., Okla., Colo. RIVERS Arkansas, Kansas, Missouri, Republican, Saline, Smoky Hill, Solomon. LAKES Kanapolis, Malvern, Perry, Pomona, Tuttle Creek, Waconda. OTHER NOTABLE FEATURES Flint Hills.

Elected officials Gov. Bill Graves (R, term exp. 1999). Lt. Gov. Sheila Frahm (R). Sec. State Ron Thornburgh (R). Atty. Gen. Carla J. Stovall (R).

People (1994) 2,554,047 (32nd). RACE/NATIONAL ORIGIN (1980): White 90.1%. Black 5.8%. Indian 0.9%. Asian 1.3%. Other 2.0%. Hispanic 3.8%.

Cities (1990) Wichita 304,011. Kansas City 149,767. Topeka 119,883. Overland Park 111,790. Lawrence 65,608. Olathe 63,352. Salina 42,303. Hutchinson 39,308. Leavenworth 38,495. Shawnee 37,993.

Business GROSS STATE PRODUCT (GSP, 1992) $56.16 bil. (31st). SECTORS OF GSP: Farms 4.11%; agricultural services, forestry, and fisheries 0.44%; mining 1.89%; construction 3.53%; manufacturing 19.18%; transportation and public utilities 11.19%; wholesale trade 7.08%; retail trade 9.25%; finance, insurance, and real estate 14.87%; services 15.59%; federal government 2.45%; federal military 1.65%; state and local government 8.76%. *FORTUNE* 500 COMPANIES (1994): 2: Sprint, Yellow.

Famous natives "Buffalo Bill" Cody. Walter Chrysler, carmaker. Robert Dole, politician. Amelia Earhart, aviator. Dwight David Eisenhower (b. Tex.), general/U.S. president. Dennis Hopper, actor. William Inge, playwright. Nancy Landon Kassebaum, politician. Alf Landon, politician. Edgar Lee Masters, poet. James Naismith, inventor of basketball. Carry Nation (b. Ky.), prohibitionist. Charlie ("Bird") Parker, musician. Damon Runyon, writer. Gale Sayers, football player. William Allen White, the Sage of Emporia, editor.

Noteworthy places Agricultural Hall of Fame, Kansas City. Dodge City. Eisenhower Center, Abilene. Ft. Larned. Ft. Leavenworth. Ft. Riley. Ft. Scott. John Brown's Cabin, Osawatomie. Kansas Cosmosphere and Space Discovery Center, Hutchinson. Kansas State Historical Society Museum, Topeka. Wichita Art Museum.

Memorable events First major expedition to region under Francisco Vásquez de Coronado 1540–41. La Salle claims territory including Kansas for France 1682. Part of Louisiana Purchase 1803. Area visited by Meriwether Lewis and George Rogers Clark (1803), Zebulon Pike (1806), and Stephen H. Long (1819). Santa Fe Trail crosses Kansas 1821. Fts. Leavenworth (1827), Scott (1842), and Riley (1853) established to protect pioneers on Santa Fe and Oregon trails. Organized as Territory by Kansas-Nebraska Act 1854, which repealed Missouri Compromise of 1820. "Bleeding Kansas" scene of free vs. slave rivalry 1854–56. Statehood 1861. Introduction of winter wheat makes Kansas leading U.S. wheat producer 1870. Airplane manufacturing starts in Wichita 1919. World-famous Menninger Foundation for mental health founded 1919. "Dust Bowl" drought drives thousands of farmers off the land, especially in western Kansas, 1934–35. Murder of Clutter family by Richard E. Hickock and Perry E. Smith at Holcomb (later the subject of Truman Capote's *In Cold Blood*)1959.

Tourist information 1–800–2KANSAS (252–6727).

Kentucky, Commonwealth of

First pioneered by English immigrants in the mid-17th century, Kentucky's golden age as a choice frontier destination in the early 1800s was brought to an end by the Civil War. During the Civil War, the Bluegrass gentry supported the Confederacy, while the Appalachian backwoods men enlisted in the Union Army. Many took advantage of their uniforms to settle old accounts, and the social order was often threatened before the turn of the century. Though the state is known today for its bourbon and horse breeding, many Kentuckians make their living from the land as tobacco farmers or coal miners. The Appalachian part of the state in the east delivers about 20 percent of the nation's coal, but its economic problems remain acute, despite vast expenditures during the "war on poverty."

NAME Corruption of Iroquois *kenta-ke* (meadowland) or Wyandot *kah-ten-tah-teh* (land of tomorrow). NICKNAME Bluegrass State. CAPITAL Frankfort. ENTERED UNION June 1, 1792 (15th). MOTTO "United we stand, divided we fall."

Emblems BIRD Cardinal. COLORS Blue and gold. FISH Bass. FLOWER Goldenrod. SONG "My Old Kentucky Home." TREE Kentucky coffee tree. WILD ANIMAL Gray squirrel.

Land TOTAL AREA 40,409 sq. mi. (37th), incl. 740 sq. mi. inland water. BORDERS Ind., Ohio, W.Va., Va., Tenn., Mo., Ill. RIVERS Cumberland, Kentucky, Licking, Ohio, Tennessee. LAKES Barkley, Barren River Res., Dewey, Grayson Res., Laurel Res., Nolin Res., Rough Res. MOUNTAINS Appalachian (Black Mt. 4,145 ft.), Cumberland. OTHER NOTABLE FEATURES Tennessee Valley.

Elected officials Gov. Brereton C. Jones (D, term exp. 1995). Lt. Gov. Paul Patton (D). Sec. State Bob Baggage (D). Atty. Gen. Chris Gorman (D).

People (1994) 3,826,794 (24th). RACE/NATIONAL ORIGIN (1990): White 92.0%. Black 7.1%. Indian 0.2%. Asian 0.5%. Other 0.2%. Hispanic 0.6%.

Cities (1990) Louisville 269,063. Lexington-Fayette 225,366. Owensboro 53,549. Covington 43,264. Bowling Green 40,641. Hopkinsville 29,809. Paducah 27,256. Frankfort 25,968. Henderson 25,945. Ashland 23,622.

Business GROSS STATE PRODUCT (GSP, 1992) $75.56 bil. (25th). SECTORS OF GSP: Farms 2.93%; agricultural services, forestry, and fisheries 0.44%; mining 4.02%; construction 3.83%; manufacturing 24.98%; transportation and public utilities 9.12%; wholesale trade 5.18%; retail trade 9.60%; finance, insurance, and real estate 12.29%; services 12.22%; federal government 3.19%; federal military 1.55%; state and local government 7.65%. *FORTUNE* 500 COMPANIES (1994): 3: Ashland, Humana, Providian.

Famous natives Muhammad Ali, boxer. Alben W. Barkley, politician. Daniel Boone (b. Pa.), frontiersman. Louis D. Brandeis, jurist. Kit Carson, frontiersman. Henry Clay, politician. Jefferson Davis, president of Confederate States of America. D.W. Griffith, director. John Marshall Harlan, jurist. Abraham Lincoln, U.S. president. Col. Harland Sanders, entrepreneur. Frederick M. Vinson, jurist. Robert Penn Warren, author.

Noteworthy places Abraham Lincoln birthplace, Hodgenville. Churchill Downs, Louisville. George S. Patton, Jr., Military Museum, Fort Knox. J.B. Speed Art Museum, Louisville. Land Between the Lakes Natl. Rec. Area. Mammoth Cave Natl. Park. My Old Kentucky Home, Bardstown. Old Ft. Harrod State Park.

Memorable events English enter territory through Cumberland Gap 1750. Territory included in area ceded by French 1763. Daniel Boone leads expeditions into region 1769. First settlement Harrodsburg 1774. Daniel Boone blazes Wilderness Trail through Cumberland Gap, establishes Ft. Boonesborough 1775. Organized as a county of Virginia 1776. British support Indian resistance ("Dark and Bloody Wars") until George Rogers Clark captures British forts in Indiana and Illinois 1778. Included as part of United States after Revolution 1783. Virginia approves separate statehood, achieved 1792. First steamboat reaches Louisville from New Orleans 1815. Invaded by Confederate armies 1862. Kentucky Derby first run at Louisville 1875. State has highest per capita income of southern states 1900; ranks last among all 48 states in per capita income 1940. Farm population decreases by 76 percent, and total number of farms by 53 percent, 1945–80.

Tourist information 1–800–225–TRIP or 1–800–255–PARK.

Louisiana

European influences and ethnic diversity distinguish Louisiana from the rest of the nation. When Louisiana entered the Union in 1812, it brought with it a French legal system and a bilingualism that still survive. African-Americans, Cajuns, and Creoles have all contributed to its distinctive music and cuisine. The state has rich farmland, more oil and gas reserves than any other state but Texas, and in New Orleans an international port that serves the most extensive river system in North America (see also "Transportation").

The "devil's bargain" with the petrochemical industry struck by charismatic populist governor Huey Long (assassinated in 1935) brought needed jobs to the state. But the environmental impact of 100 loosely regulated petrochemical plants on the Mississippi River between New Orleans and Baton Rouge is being assessed only now. The state's reliance on the petroleum industry was felt when a downturn in oil prices in the 1980s led to massive unemployment—15 percent in 1987; in addition, 200,000 people left the state. Another burden from the Long days is the state's property tax—the lowest rate in the nation. With only meager revenues, government has invested little in infrastructure or education, and the state had the highest high school dropout rate in the nation in 1989.

Economic diversification is under way. The Red River should be cleared for commercial navigation as far as Shreveport by 1992, which will make the lumber and farming in the northwest part of the state more profitable. In 1987, 19.3 million tourists, almost 400,000 from abroad, spent almost $4 billion in "the sportsman's paradise," and in an effort to attract foreign tourists, the state allows foreign visitors a rebate on the state sales tax.

NAME For King Louis XIV. NICKNAME Pelican State. CAPITAL Baton Rouge. ENTERED UNION Apr. 30, 1812 (18th). MOTTO "Union, justice, confidence."

Emblems BIRD Eastern brown pelican. COLORS Gold, white, and blue. CRUSTACEAN Crawfish. DOG Catahoula leopard. FLOWER Magnolia. FOSSIL Petrified palmwood. GEM Agate. INSECT Honeybee. SONGS "Give Me Louisiana," "You Are My Sunshine." TREE Bald cypress.

Land TOTAL AREA 47,751 sq. mi. (31st), incl. 3,230 sq. mi. inland water. BORDERS Ark., Miss., Gulf of Mexico, Tex. RIVERS Atchafalaya, Mississippi, Ouachita, Pearl, Red, Sabine. LAKES Bistineau, Borgne, Caddo, Catahoula, Grand, Maurepas, Pontchartrain, Salvador, White. OTHER NOTABLE FEATURES Bayou Barataria, Bayou Bodcau, Bayou D'Arbonne, Driskill Mt. (535 ft.).

Elected officials Gov. Edwin W. Edwards (D, term exp. 1996). Lt. Gov. Melinda Schwegmann (D). Sec. State W. Fox McKeithen (R). Atty. Gen. Richard Ieuyob (D).

People (1994) 4,315,085 (21st). RACE/NATIONAL ORIGIN (1990): White 67.3%. Black 30.8%. Indian 0.4%. Asian 1.0%. Other 0.5%. Hispanic 2.2%.

Cities (1990) New Orleans 496,938. Baton Rouge 219,531. Shreveport 198,525. Lafayette 94,440. Kenner 72,033. Lake Charles 70,580. Monroe 54,909. Bossier City 52,721. Alexandria 49,188. New Iberia 31,828.

Business GROSS STATE PRODUCT (GSP, 1992) $96.24 bil. (22nd). SECTORS OF GSP: Farms 1.05%; agricultural services, forestry, and fisheries 0.31%; mining 15.35%; construction 3.73%; manufacturing 18.81%; transportation and public utilities 10.17%; wholesale trade 4.90%; retail trade 7.91%; finance, insurance, and real estate 13.89%; services 14.19%; federal government 1.45%; federal military 1.20%; state and local government 7.05%. *FORTUNE* 500 COMPANIES (1994): 1: Entergy.

Famous natives Louis "Satchmo" Armstrong, jazz musician. Pierre Beauregard, Confederate general. Braxton Bragg, Confederate general. Truman Capote, author. Clyde Cessna, aviator. Michael DeBakey, surgeon. Fats Domino, singer. Lillian Hellman, author. Mahalia Jackson, singer. Jean Baptiste Le Moyne, sieur de Bienville (b. Canada), founded New Orleans. Jerry Lee Lewis, singer. Huey P. Long, senator. Ferdinand Joseph La Menthe "Jelly Roll" Morton, musician. Leonidas K. Polk, clergyman/Confederate general. Henry Miller Shreve (b. N.J.), riverboat captain. Edward D. White, Jr., jurist.

Noteworthy places Avery Island. Cabildo, New Orleans. French Quarter, New Orleans. Garden District, New Orleans. Hodges Gardens, Natchitoches. Jean Lafitte Natl. Hist. Park, Chalmette. Kent House Museum, Alexandria. Longfellow-Evangeline State Commemorative Area, St. Martinsville. Louisiana Maritime Museum, Baton Rouge. New Orleans Museum of Art.

Memorable events Area first visited by Alonso Alvarez de Piñeda 1519. Claimed by René-Robert Cavelier de La Salle for France 1682. New Orleans founded 1718. French crown colony 1731. Four thousand Acadians (Cajuns) from Nova Scotia forcibly transported by British to Louisiana and settled in Bayou Teche 1755. Lands west of Mississippi given to Spain for help in French and Indian War 1763. Lands east of Mississippi ceded to Britain 1763. Same lands retroceded to France 1800. Jefferson negotiates Louisiana Purchase; United States acquires 885,000 sq. mi. for $15 million 1803. Statehood 1812. Andrew Jackson beats British at Battle of New Orleans 1815. State secedes 1861. Surrenders to Union forces 1862. Readmitted to Union 1868. Petroleum discovered 1901. Huey "The Kingfish" Long elected to Senate 1928; assassinated 1935. Racial designation law of 1970 repealed 1983.

Tourist information 1–800–33–GUMBO or 1–504–342–8119.

Maine

Down-Easters—the original Puritans as well as the later French Canadians—are distinct from the New Englanders of Maine's economically more vital sister states. Their land, especially the coast, is rugged, and the living everywhere is hard. Maine touches only one other state, and it has an end-of-the-line feel to it. Lumbering, fishing, and potato farming were the traditional industries. More than half of the state is still unorganized territory largely owned by paper companies. In the 18th century, canneries, textiles, and shoe factories developed. Recently Maine's economy has combined light industry and tourism that is moving it into the mainstream. The modern Maine entrepreneur, often an out-of-stater, seeks an economy based on small industries and more in keeping with Maine's independent temperament.

NAME Either for Maine in France or to distinguish mainland from islands in Gulf of Maine. NICKNAME Pine Tree State. CAPITAL Augusta. ENTERED UNION Mar. 15, 1820 (23rd). MOTTO *Dirigo* (I direct).

Emblems ANIMAL Moose. BIRD Chickadee. FISH Landlocked salmon. FLOWER White pinecone and tassel. INSECT Honeybee. MINERAL Tourmaline. SONG "State of Maine Song." TREE Eastern white pine.

Land TOTAL AREA 33,265 sq. mi. (39th), incl. 2,270 sq. mi. inland water. BORDERS Quebec, New Brunswick, Atlantic Ocean, N.H. RIVERS Alagash, Androscoggin, Aroostock, Kennebec, Machias, Penobscot, Piscataqua, Salmon Falls, St. John. LAKES Chamberlain, Chesuncook, Grand, Moosehead, Rangeley, Sebago. OTHER NOTABLE FEATURES Longfellow Mts. (Mt. Katahadin 5,268 ft.), Mt. Desert Island, Penobscot Bay.

Elected officials Gov. Angus S. King, Jr. (I, term exp. 1999). Sec. State G. William Diamond (D). Atty. Gen. Andrew Ketterer (D).

People (1994) 1,240,209 (39th). RACE/NATIONAL ORIGIN (1990): White 98.4%. Black 0.4%. Indian 0.5%. Asian 0.5%. Other 0.1%. Hispanic 0.6%.

Cities (1990) Portland 64,358. Lewiston 39,757. Bangor 33,181. Auburn 24,309. South Portland 23,163. Augusta 21,325. Biddeford 20,710. Waterville 17,173. Westbrook 16,121. Saco 15,181.

Business GROSS STATE PRODUCT (GSP, 1992) $24.08 bil. (43rd). SECTORS OF GSP: Farms 1.37%; agricultural services, forestry, and fisheries 1.25%; mining 0.30%; construction 5.79%; manufacturing 19.06%; transportation and public utilities 7.35%; wholesale trade 5.82%; retail trade 11.41%; finance, insurance, and real estate 16.93%; services 17.46%; federal government 3.25%; federal military 1.70%; state and local government 8.60%. *FORTUNE* 500 COMPANIES (1994): 2: Unum, Hannaford Brothers.

Famous natives Cyrus H.K. Curtis, publisher. Hannibal Hamlin, politician. Sarah Orne Jewett, novelist. Henry Wadsworth Longfellow, poet. Sir Hiram and Hudson Maxim, inventors. Edna St. Vincent Millay, poet. Edmund S. Muskie, politician. John Knowles Paine, composer. Kenneth Roberts, novelist. Edward Arlington Robinson, poet. Nelson Rockefeller, politician. Marguerite Yourcenar (b. France), author.

Noteworthy places Acadia Natl. Park, Mt. Desert Island. Allagash Natl. Wilderness Waterway. Boothbay Railway Museum. Campobello Longfellow House, Portland. Maine Maritime Museum, Bath. Portland Art Museum Roosevelt-Campobello Intl. Park, Campobello Island. St. Croix Island Natl. Monument.

Memorable events Vikings explore coast c. A.D. 1000. Bartholomew Gosnold sails along coast 1602. French settlers at St. Croix River 1604. Included in grant to Plymouth Company 1606. Monhegan Island and Saco settled 1622. Annexed to Massachusetts Colony 1652. French attack northern territory intermittently through 1713. Statehood 1820. Border with Canada settled 1842. First state prohibition law enacted 1851. Penobscot and Passamaquoddy tribes file claim against state for $300 million compensation for land seized in violation of 1790 Indian Non-Intercourse Act, 1972; settled for $81.5 million 1980. First state to allow inheritance taxes to be paid with works of art 1979.
Tourist information 1–207–623–0363.

Maryland

Maryland wraps like a fishhook from the Atlantic Ocean around the fish-rich Chesapeake Bay and into the Cumberland Mountains in the northwest. Baltimore—full of urban problems but newly redeveloped with urban homesteading and shopsteading—holds the center. The suburbs of Baltimore and Washington seem far removed from the Delmarva (DELaware, MARyland, VirginiA) peninsula with its watermen hanging on to an older way of life. Terrain, cultures, and history are a border state's mix of North and South. Founded as a haven for Catholics, Maryland's population is still 20 percent Catholic.

NAME For Henrietta Maria, queen consort of Charles I. NICKNAMES Old Line State, Free State. CAPITAL Annapolis. ENTERED UNION Apr. 28, 1788 (7th). MOTTO *Fatti maschii, parole femine* (Manly deeds, womanly words).
Emblems BIRD Baltimore oriole. DOG Chesapeake Bay retriever. FISH Rockfish. FLOWER Black-eyed Susan. FOSSIL *Ecphora quadricostata* (extinct snail). INSECT Baltimore checkerspot butterfly. SONG "Maryland, My Maryland." SPORT Jousting. TREE White oak.
Land TOTAL AREA 10,460 sq. mi. (42nd), incl. 623 sq. mi. inland water. BORDERS Pa., Del., Atlantic Ocean, Va., D.C., W.Va. RIVERS Chester, Choptank, Nanticoke, Patapsco, Patuxent, Pocomoke, Potomac, Susquehanna. OTHER NOTABLE FEATURES Allegheny Mts., Blue Ridge Mts., Chesapeake Bay.
Elected officials Gov. Parris Glendening (D, term exp. 1999). Lt. Gov. Kathleen Kennedy Townsend (D). Sec. State John Willis (D). Atty. Gen. Joseph Curran, Jr. (D).
People (1994) 5,006,265 (19th). RACE/NATIONAL ORIGIN (1990): White 71.0%. Black 24.9%. Indian 0.3%. Asian 2.9%. Other 0.9%. Hispanic 2.6%.
Cities (1990) Baltimore 736,014. Rockville 44,835. Frederick 40,148. Gaithersburg 39,542. Bowie 37,589. Hagerstown 35,445. Annapolis 33,187. Cumberland 23,706. College Park 21,927. Greenbelt 21,096.
Business GROSS STATE PRODUCT (GSP, 1992) $116.17 bil. (16th). SECTORS OF GSP: Farms 0.68%; agricultural services, forestry, and fisheries 0.48%; mining 0.13%; construction 7.21%; manufacturing 10.41%; transportation and public utilities 8.28%; wholesale trade 5.97%; retail trade 10.32%; finance, insurance, and real estate 18.36%; services 21.58%; federal government 6.56%; federal military 1.52%; state and local government 8.52%. *FORTUNE* 500 COMPANIES (1994): 6: Martin Marietta, Black & Decker, Giant Food, USF&G, Baltimore Gas & Electric, Hechinger.
Famous natives Russell Baker, journalist. Benjamin Banneker, surveyor. Eubie Blake, pianist. Rachel Carson, biologist/author. Stephen Decatur, navy officer. Frederick Douglass, abolitionist. Billie Holiday, singer. Johns Hopkins, financier/philanthropist. Francis Scott Key, lawyer/poet. Thurgood Marshall, jurist. H.L. Mencken, writer. Charles Willson Peale, artist. William Pinckney, statesman. James Rouse, urban planner. Babe Ruth, baseball player. Upton Sinclair, author. Roger B. Taney, jurist. Harriet Tubman, abolitionist. John Waters, filmmaker.
Noteworthy places Aberdeen Proving Ground. Antietam Natl. Battlefield, Sharpsburg. Assateague Island Natl. Seashore. Natl. Aquarium in Baltimore. Baltimore Museum of Art. Baltimore Museum of Industry. Calvert Marine Museum, Solomons. Chesapeake & Ohio Canal Natl. Hist. Park. Chesapeake Bay Maritime Museum, St. Michaels. Ft. McHenry Natl. Monument, Baltimore. Harpers Ferry Natl. Hist. Park. Liberty ship *John W. Brown,* Baltimore. St. Marys City. State House, Annapolis. U.S. Naval Academy, Annapolis. USS *Constellation*, Baltimore. Walters Art Gallery, Baltimore.
Memorable events John Smith explores area 1608. William Claiborne sets up trading post on Kent Island 1631. Land granted to Cecilius Calvert, Lord Baltimore, 1632. Leonard Calvert and 200 Roman Catholic settlers land on Blakistone Island 1634. Mason Dixon Line establishes northern boundary of state 1763–67; later identified as boundary between slave and nonslave states. Francis Scott Key composes "The Star Spangled Banner" after British fail to take Ft. McHenry 1814. U.S. Naval Academy founded Annapolis 1845. State under federal military control during Civil War 1861–65. First state to adopt income tax 1938. Alabama Gov. George C. Wallace shot in Laurel while campaigning in Democratic presidential primary 1972.
Tourist information 1–410–333–6611.

Massachusetts, Commonwealth of

Massachusetts is rich in the history of the early American republic. The Boston Tea Party, the "shot heard 'round the world" from Lexington and Concord, and the Battle of Bunker Hill are American folklore. So is the feast of Thanksgiving, first celebrated by the Puritans at Plymouth. Fishing, trade, textiles, and leather industries were the backbone of Massachusetts's 19th-century economy. Today Boston's Route 128 is the East Coast's counterpart to California's Silicon Valley, with some of the nation's most advanced computer and electronic research and manufacturing. The state's "economic miracle" of the 1980s is over, and Massachusetts endured a severe downturn in the recession of the early 1990s. In late 1989 its Standard & Poor's credit rating was downgraded to BBB—the lowest ranking of any state.

A staple of the Massachusetts scene is education, in which the state is a national leader. Boston alone boasts such institutions as Harvard University (founded 1636), M.I.T., Northeastern, Brandeis, Boston University, Boston College, Wellesley, and Tufts. To the west are the University of Massachusetts, Amherst, Williams, Smith, and Mt. Holyoke.

NAME For Massachuset tribe, whose name means "at or about the great hill." NICKNAME Bay State. CAPITAL Boston. ENTERED UNION Feb. 6, 1788 (6th). MOTTO *Ense petit placidam sub libertate quietem* (By the sword we seek peace, but peace only under liberty).
Emblems BEVERAGE Cranberry juice. BIRD Chickadee. BUILDING & MONUMENT STONE Granite. DOG Boston terrier. EXPLORER ROCK Dighton Rock. FISH Cod. FLOWER Mayflower. FOLK SONG "Massachusetts." GEM Rhodonite. HEROINE Deborah Samson. HISTORICAL ROCK Plymouth Rock. HORSE Morgan. INSECT Ladybug. MARINE MAMMAL Right whale. MINERAL Babingtonite. POEM "Blue Hills of Massachusetts." ROCK Roxbury pudding stone. SONG "All Hail to Massachusetts." STONE Granite. TREE American elm.
Land TOTAL AREA 8,284 sq. mi. (45th), incl. 460 sq. mi. inland water. BORDERS Vt., N.H., Atlantic Ocean, R.I., Conn., N.Y. RIVERS Cape Cod Canal, Connecticut, Merrimack, Taunton. OTHER NOTABLE FEATURES Buzzard's Bay, Cape Ann, Cape Cod, Cape Cod Bay, Connecticut Valley, Elizabeth Islands, Martha's Vineyard, Monomoy Island, Nantucket Island.
Elected officials Gov. William Weld (R, term exp. 1999). Lt. Gov. Argeo Paul Cellucci (R). Sec. State William Francis Galvin (D). Atty. Gen. L. Scott Harshbarger (D).
People (1994) 6,041,123 (13th). RACE/NATIONAL ORIGIN (1990): White 89.8%. Black 5.0%. Indian 0.2%. Asian 2.4%. Other 2.6%. Hispanic 4.8%.
Cities (1990) Boston 574,283. Worcester 169,759. Springfield 156,983. Lowell 103,439. New Bedford 99,922. Cambridge 95,802. Brockton 92,788. Fall River 92,703. Quincy 84,985. Newton 82,585.
Business GROSS STATE PRODUCT (GSP, 1992) $161.97 bil. (10th). SECTORS OF GSP: Farms 0.21%; agricultural services, forestry, and fisheries 0.49%; mining 0.05%; construction 4.01%; manufacturing 18.34%; transportation and public utilities 6.72%; wholesale trade 7.10%; retail trade 8.76%; finance, insurance, and real estate 20.43%; services 24.47%; federal government 1.52%; federal military 0.43%; state and local government 7.47%. *FORTUNE* 500 COMPANIES (1994): 17: Digital Equipment, Raytheon, Liberty Mutual Insurance Group, Gillette, John Hancock Mutual Life Insurance, Massachusetts Mutual Life Insurance, Bank of Boston Corp., TJX, Stop & Shop, Waban, Harcourt General, Reebok, Allmerica Financial, EG&G, Polaroid, New England Electric Systems, New England Mutual Life Insurance.

Famous natives John Adams, U.S. president. John Quincy Adams, U.S. president. Samuel Adams, patriot. Horatio Alger, clergyman/author. Susan B. Anthony, suffragette. Clara Barton, nurse. Leonard Bernstein, composer. George Herbert Walker Bush, U.S. president. John "Johnny Appleseed" Chapman, pioneer. Richard Cardinal Cushing, prelate. Bette Davis, actress. Emily Dickinson, poet. Ralph Waldo Emerson, author. Marshall Field, merchant. R. Buckminster Fuller, inventor/engineer. John Hancock, patriot. Oliver Wendell Holmes, jurist. Winslow Homer, painter, John F. Kennedy, U.S. president. Jack Kerouac, author. Cotton Mather, theologian. Samuel Eliot Morison, historian. Samuel Morse, inventor. Thomas P. "Tip" O'Neill, congressman. Edgar Allan Poe, poet/author. Paul Revere, patriot/silversmith. Louis Sullivan, architect. Henry David Thoreau, author.

Noteworthy places Addison Gallery of American Art, Andover. Arnold Arboretum, Boston. Arthur M. Sackler Museum, Cambridge. Berkshires Museum, Pittsfield. Boston Museum of Fine Arts. Boston Natl. Hist. Park (incl. Bunker Hill, Charlestown Navy Yard, Old North Church). Busch-Reisinger Museum, Cambridge. Cape Cod Natl. Seashore. Clark Art Institute, Williamsburg. Fogg Art Museum, Boston. Gardner Art Museum, Boston. Lowell Natl. Hist. Park. Minute Man Natl. Hist. Park, Lexington and Concord. Nantucket Hist. Society. Old Sturbridge. Peabody Museum, Salem. Plimoth Plantation, Plymouth. Shaker Village. Tanglewood Music Festival, Lenox. USS *Constitution* ("Old Ironsides"), Charlestown. Walden Pond. Woods Hole Oceanographic Institute. Worcester Art Museum.

Memorable events Pilgrims land at Plymouth 1620. First Thanksgiving celebrated 1621. Harvard College founded 1636. Region acquires province of Maine 1652. Colonists battle Wampanoags in King Philip's War 1655–56. Boston Massacre 1770. Boston Tea Party protests taxation 1773. Battles at Lexington, Concord, and Bunker Hill 1775. Shays's Rebellion 1785–86. Maine becomes a separate state 1820. Massachusetts receives influx of Irish immigrants fleeing famine 1845. Textile workers' strike at Lawrence brings International Workers of the World (IWW) to prominence in East 1912. Cape Cod Canal completed 1914. International protest follows trial and execution of anarchists Nicola Sacco and Bartolomeo Vanzetti for robbery and murder 1920; names cleared by governor's proclamation 1970. Eleven robbers steal $2.7 million from Brink's North Terminal Garage 1950. Martha's Vineyard and Nantucket symbolically vote to secede from state 1973.

Tourist information 1–617–727–3201 or 1–617–536–4100 (Greater Boston).

Michigan

The automobile is the single commodity with which Michigan is most identified, and it is the home of the big three automakers, General Motors, Ford, and Chrysler. More than 50 percent of Michiganders live in the southeastern corner of the state, where the car industry flourishes. In the Upper Peninsula, across the Straits of Mackinac, lumber and copper have been the principal commodities from the 19th century, and the northern part of the Lower Peninsula boasts rich farmland. Michigan's boundaries include parts of four of the five Great Lakes, and it has more coastline than any state except Alaska. Michigan has had an outstanding reputation in higher education, and the University of Michigan at Ann Arbor and Michigan State are helping to foster the state's high-tech industries. But the state's heavy reliance on auto manufacturing makes it vulnerable to economic downturns, as well as the general contraction of the American industry. The state's unemployment rate was 8.2 percent in early 1992 and was expected to remain high for the foreseeable future.

NAME From Fox *mesikami*, "large lake." NICKNAMES Wolverine State, Lake State. CAPITAL Lansing. ENTERED UNION Jan. 26, 1837 (26th). MOTTO *Si quaeris peninsulam amoenam circumspice* (If you are looking for a beautiful peninsula, look around you).

Emblems BIRD Robin. FISH Trout. FLOWER Apple blossom. GEM Chlorastrolite. INSECT Dragonfly. SONG "Michigan, My Michigan." STONE Petoskey stone. TREE White pine.

Land TOTAL AREA 58,527 sq. mi. (23rd), incl. 1,573 sq. mi. inland water. BORDERS Lake Superior, Ontario, Lake Huron, Lake Erie, Ohio, Ind., Lake Michigan, Wis. RIVERS Brule, Detroit, Kalamazoo, Menominee, Montreal, Muskegon, St. Joseph, St. Mary's. LAKES Burt, Higgins, Houghton, Huron, Manistique, Michigan, Mullett, St. Clair, Superior. OTHER NOTABLE FEATURES Isle Royale, Mt. Curwood (1,980 ft.), Saginaw Bay, Traverse Bay, Whitefish Bay.

Elected officials Gov. John Engler (R, term exp. 1999). Lt. Gov. Connie Binsfeld (R). Sec. State Candace Miller (R). Atty. Gen. Frank J. Kelley (D).

People (1994) 9,496,147 (8th). RACE/NATIONAL ORIGIN (1990): White 83.4%. Black 13.9%. Indian 0.6%. Asian 1.1%. Other 0.9%. Hispanic 2.2%.

Cities (1990) Detroit 1,027,974. Grand Rapids 189,126. Warren 144,864. Flint 140,761. Lansing 127,321. Sterling Heights 117,810. Ann Arbor 109,592. Livonia 100,850. Dearborn 89,286. Westland 84,724.

Business GROSS STATE PRODUCT (GSP, 1992) $204.42 bil. (9th). SECTORS OF GSP: Farms 1.01%; agricultural services, forestry, and fisheries 0.32%; mining 0.61%; construction 3.83%; manufacturing 27.13%; transportation and public utilities 7.36%; wholesale trade 6.39%; retail trade 9.33%; finance, insurance, and real estate 15.75%; services 17.51%; federal government 1.21%; federal military 0.31%; state and local government 9.21%. *FORTUNE* 500 COMPANIES (1994): 16: General Motors, Ford Motor, Chrysler, K mart, Dow Chemical, Whirlpool, Kellogg, Masco, CMS Energy, Upjohn, Detroit Edison, NBD Bancorp, Lear Seating, Comerica, Kelly Services, Dow Corning.

Famous natives Ralph J. Bunche, statesman (Nobel Peace Prize, 1950). Paul de Kruif, bacteriologist. Thomas Dewey, politician. Herbert H. Dow (b. Canada), chemical manufacturer. Edna Ferber, author. Henry Ford, industrialist. Edgar Guest, journalist/poet. Robert Ingersoll, industrialist. Will Kellogg, businessman/philanthropist. Charles A. Lindbergh, aviator. Antoine de La Mothe, sieur de Cadillac (b. France), founded Detroit. Pontiac, Ottawa chief. William Upjohn, drug manufacturer.

Noteworthy places Detroit Historical Society. Detroit Institute of Arts. Dossin Great Lakes Museum, Detroit. Great Lakes Indian Interpretive Museum, Detroit. Greenfield Village, Dearborn. Historic Ft. Wayne, Detroit. Isle Royale Natl. Park. Mackinac Island. Pictured Rocks Natl. Lakeshore, Lake Superior. Sleeping Bear Dunes Natl. Lakeshore, Lake Superior.

Memorable events French explorers in region 1634. Jacques Marquette settles Sault Ste. Marie 1668. Detroit founded as French military post 1701. Region ceded to England 1763; to United States 1783. Included in Northwest Territory but British maintain control until 1796. Michigan Territory 1805. First steamboat on Great Lakes reaches Detroit 1818. Statehood 1837. First state to outlaw capital punishment 1846. Republican party organized at Jackson 1854. Canals at Sault Ste. Marie link Lakes Superior and Huron 1855. Ransom E. Olds and Henry Ford, working independently, develop gas-powered car 1896. United Auto Workers first to use sit-down strike successfully in contract negotiations 1935. Race riot, one of the worst in U.S. history, leaves 43 dead and $200 million in damages in Detroit 1967. Congress authorizes $1.5 billion in federal loan guarantees to bail out Chrysler Corporation 1979.

Tourist information 1–800–543–2937 or 1–517–373–0670.

Minnesota

A land of at least 10,000 lakes, Minnesota is a magnet for outdoorsmen, canoers, and fishermen. It is also home to the largest Scandinavian populations in the United States. Originally exploited for its wealth of lumber and iron—the Mesabi Range still produces 60 percent of the nation's iron ore—Minnesota also has highly developed agribusinesses (especially dairy products), manufacturing, and transportation industries. Minneapolis and St. Paul are at the north end of the Mississippi River system, and Duluth at the westernmost point of Lake Superior is the largest U.S. inland port. Both self-sufficient and politically liberal, Minnesota has one of the best state school systems.

NAME From the Sioux *minisota*, "sky-tinted waters." NICKNAMES North Star State, Gopher State. CAPITAL St. Paul. ENTERED UNION May 11, 1858 (32nd). MOTTO *L'étoile du nord* (Star of the north).

Emblems BIRD Common loon. DRINK Milk. FISH Walleye. FLOWER Pink and white lady's slipper. GEM Lake Superior agate. GRAIN Wild rice. MUSHROOM Morel, or sponge mushroom. SONG "Hail, Minnesota!" TREE Red pine.

Land TOTAL AREA 84,402 sq. mi. (12th), incl. 4,854 sq. mi. inland water. BORDERS Manitoba, Ontario, Lake Superior, Wis., Iowa, S.Dak., N.Dak. RIVERS Minnesota, Mississippi, Red River of the North, St. Croix. LAKES Itasca, Lake of the Woods, Leech, Mille Lacs, Red, Winnibigoshish. OTHER NOTABLE FEATURES Mesabi Range.

Elected officials Gov. Arne Carlson (R, term exp. 1999). Lt. Gov. Joanne Benson (R). Sec. State Joan Anderson Growe (D). Atty. Gen. Hubert H. Humphrey III (D).

People (1994) 4,567,267 (20th). RACE/NATIONAL ORIGIN (1990): White 94.4%. Black 2.2%. Indian 1.1%. Asian 1.8%. Other 0.5%. Hispanic 1.2%.

Cities (1990) Minneapolis 368,383. St. Paul 272,235. Bloomington 86,335. Duluth 85,493. Rochester 70,745. Brooklyn Park 56,381. Coon Rapids 52,978. Burnsville 51,288. Plymouth 50,889. St. Cloud 48,812.

Business GROSS STATE PRODUCT (GSP, 1992) $110.28 bil. (18th). SECTORS OF GSP: Farms 3.71%; agricultural services, forestry, and fisheries 0.40%; mining 0.60%; construction 4.28%; manufacturing 21.75%; transportation and public utilities 8.08%; wholesale trade 7.43%; retail trade 9.18%; finance, insurance, and real estate 16.67%; services 17.20%; federal government 1.96%; federal military 0.26%; state and local government 8.48%. *FORTUNE* 500 COMPANIES (1994): 16: Dayton Hudson, Supervalu, Minnesota Mining and Manufacturing (3M), Northwest Airlines, General Mills, Honeywell, Norwest Corp., St. Paul Cos. United Healthcare, Hormel Foods, Best Buy, Nash Finch, Northern States Power, First Bank System, International Multifoods, Lutheran Brotherhood.

Famous natives Warren Burger, jurist. Bob Dylan, musician. F. Scott Fitzgerald, novelist. Judy Garland, actress. J. Paul Getty, businessman. Garrison Keillor, humorist. Sinclair Lewis, author (Nobel Prize, 1930). Paul Manship, sculptor. William and Charles Mayo, surgeons. Eugene McCarthy, politician. Walter F. Mondale, politician. Charles Schulz, cartoonist. Richard W. Sears, merchant.

Noteworthy places Boundary Waters Canoe Area. Grand Portage Natl. Monument. International Falls. Lake Itasca State Park (headwaters of Mississippi). Mayo Clinic, Rochester. Minneapolis Institute of Arts. Minnehaha Falls, Minneapolis. Minnesota Zoo, Apple Valley. Pipestone Natl. Monument. Tyrone Guthrie Theater, Minneapolis. Voyageurs Natl. Park. Walker Art Center, Minneapolis.

Memorable events Pierre Esprit Radisson and Médard Chouart des Groselliers visit area 1654–60. René-Robert de La Salle and Louis Hennepin explore upper Mississippi 1680. Daniel Greysolon, sieur Duluth, claims region for France 1679. Area east of Mississippi to Britain 1763; to United States 1783. Western region of state as part of Louisiana Purchase 1803. Britain cedes northern strip to United States 1818. Ft. Snelling built 1820. Northern border settled by Ashburton Treaty 1842. Minnesota Territory created 1849. Statehood 1858. Sioux driven from state after uprising led by Chief Little Crow 1862. Iron ore deposits discovered in Mesabi Range 1890. Democratic party merges with Farmer-Labor party 1944.

Tourist information 1–800–657–3700 or 1–612–296–5029.

Mississippi

Mississippi's rank as the poorest state in the nation can be traced to the Civil War. Before the Civil War, Mississippi was the fifth-wealthiest state in the nation. The war cost the state 30,000 men. Plantation owners who survived the war were virtually bankrupted by the emancipation of the slaves, and Union troops under Sherman and others left widespread destruction in their wake. The increasingly harsh race laws passed around 1900 also cost the state in the emigration of almost half a million (75% blacks, 25% whites) in the 1940s. Compounding all this was the fact that until World War II, Mississippi had virtually no urban center such as Jackson to attract or sustain major industry. In race relations particularly, Mississippi has made vast improvements, and there have been substantial gains in education and the attraction of out-of-state companies, especially light industry.

NAME From Ojibwa *misi sipi*, "great river." NICKNAME Magnolia State. CAPITAL Jackson. ENTERED UNION Dec. 10, 1817 (20th). MOTTO *Virtute et armis* (By virtue and arms).

Emblems BEVERAGE Milk. BIRD Mockingbird. FISH Largemouth or black bass. FLOWER Magnolia. FOSSIL Prehistoric whale. INSECT Honeybee. MAMMAL White-tailed deer. SONG "Go, Mississippi." STONE Petrified wood. TREE Magnolia. WATERFOWL Wood duck. WATER MAMMAL Porpoise.

Land TOTAL AREA 47,689 sq. mi. (32nd), incl. 456 sq. mi. inland water. BORDERS Tenn., Ala., Gulf of Mexico, La., Ark. RIVERS Big Black, Mississippi, Pearl, Tennessee, Yazoo. LAKES Arkabutla, Grenada, Ross Barnett Res., Sardis. OTHER NOTABLE FEATURES Pontotoc Ridge.

Elected officials Gov. Kirk Fordice (D, term exp. 1996). Lt. Gov. Eddie Briggs (D). Sec. State Dick Molpus (D); Atty. Gen. Mike Moore (D).

People (1994) 2,669,111 (31st). RACE/NATIONAL ORIGIN (1990): White 63.5%. Black 35.6%. Indian 0.3%. Asian 0.5%. Other 0.1%. Hispanic 0.6%.

Cities (1990) Jackson 196,637. Biloxi 46,319. Greenville 45,226. Hattiesburg 41,882. Meridian 41,036. Gulfport 40,775. Tupelo 30,685. Pascagoula 25,899. Columbus 23,799. Clinton 21,847.

Business GROSS STATE PRODUCT (GSP, 1992) $44.30 bil. (32nd). SECTORS OF GSP: Farms 2.80%; agricultural services, forestry, and fisheries 0.49%; mining 2.29%; construction 3.28%; manufacturing 24.27%; transportation and public utilities 11.98%; wholesale trade 5.08%; retail trade 10.00%; finance, insurance, and real estate 13.86%; services 12.29%; federal government 2.68%; federal military 1.85%; state and local government 9.13%. *FORTUNE* 500 COMPANIES (1994): 1: LDDS Communications.

Famous natives Medgar Evers, reformer. William Faulkner, novelist. Shelby Foote, historian. Jim Henson, puppeteer. B.B. King, musician. Elvis Presley, singer. Leontyne Price, opera singer. John C. Stennis, politician. Conway Twitty, singer. Muddy Waters, musician. Eudora Welty, novelist. Ben Ames Williams, novelist. Tennessee Williams, playwright. Richard Wright, author.

Noteworthy places Delta Blues Museum, Clarksdale. Natchez Trace Natl. Parkway. Seafood Industry Museum, Biloxi. Tupelo Natl. Battlefield. Vicksburg Natl. Military Park.

Memorable events Hernando de Soto's expedition travels through Mississippi 1540–41. René-Robert Cavelier de La Salle claims Mississippi valley for France 1682. Pierre Le Moyne, sieur d'Iberville builds Ft. Maurepas on Biloxi Bay 1699. Natchez (Ft. Rosalie) established 1716. France cedes territory to Britain 1763. Mississippi Territory (including presentday Alabama) created 1798. Statehood (Natchez first capital) 1817. Secedes from Union; Jefferson Davis becomes president of Confederacy 1861. Siege of Vicksburg 1863. Petroleum discovered 1939. Gov. Ross R. Barnett found guilty of contempt in preventing desegregation of University of Mississippi; James H. Meredith first black enrolled at University of Mississippi 1962. Civil rights leader Medgar Evers assassinated in Jackson and buried in Arlington National Cemetery 1963. White civil rights workers James Cheney, Andrew Goodman, and Michael Schwerner killed 1964.

Tourist information 1–800–647–2290 or 1–601–359–3297.

Missouri

Missouri is remarkable for the number and variety of its neighbors—southern states (Arkansas, Kentucky, and Tennessee), midwestern states (Illinois and Iowa), and Plains states (Oklahoma, Nebraska, and Kansas). For Missouri, geography was destiny. Still one of the country's most important inland ports, St. Louis was founded at the confluence of the Missouri and Mississippi Rivers and became the gateway to the West; and Independence (now part of metropolitan Kansas City) got its start provisioning wagons for the Oregon and Santa Fe trails. The Pony Express from St. Joseph to Sacramento began in 1860, and the first attempt at airmail service was tried in St. Louis in 1911. While farming and livestock are still important to the state's economy, manufacturing and services are now the biggest sectors.

NAME From Iliniwek *missouri*, "owner of big canoes." NICKNAME Show-Me State. CAPITAL Jefferson City. ENTERED UNION Aug. 10, 1821 (24th). MOTTO *Salus populi suprema lex esto* (The welfare of the people shall be the supreme law).

Emblems BIRD Bluebird. FLOWER Hawthorne. INSECT Honeybee. MINERAL Galena. ROCK Mozarkite. SONG "Missouri Waltz." TREE Dogwood.

Land TOTAL AREA 69,697 sq. mi. (19th), incl. 752 sq. mi. inland water. BORDERS Iowa, Ill., Ky., Tenn., Ark., Okla., Kans., Nebr. RIVERS Des Moines, Mississippi, Missouri, Osage, St. Francis.

LAKES Bull Shoals, Clearwater, Lake of the Ozarks, Lake of the Woods, Tablerock, Wappapella. OTHER NOTABLE FEATURES Ozark Mts. (Taum Sauk Mt. 1,772 ft.).
Elected officials Gov. Mel Carnahan (D, term exp. 1997). Lt. Gov. Roger B. Wilson (D). Sec. State Rebecca Cook (D). Atty. Gen. Jeremiah W. Nixon (D).
People (1994) 5,277,640 (16th). RACE/NATIONAL ORIGIN (1990): White 87.7%. Black 10.7%. Indian 0.4%. Asian 0.8%. Other 0.4%. Hispanic 1.2%.
Cities (1990) Kansas City 435,146. St. Louis 396,685. Springfield 140,494. Independence 112,301. St. Joseph 71,852. Columbia 69,101. St. Charles 54,555. Florissant 51,206. Lee's Summit 46,418. St. Peters 45,779.
Business GROSS STATE PRODUCT (GSP, 1992) $111.60 bil. (17th). SECTORS OF GSP: Farms 1.77%; agricultural services, forestry, and fisheries 0.39%; mining 0.35%; construction 4.13%; manufacturing 21.13%; transportation and public utilities 10.84%; wholesale trade 6.99%; retail trade 10.05%; finance, insurance, and real estate 15.37%; services 18.41%; federal government 2.72%; federal military 0.67%; state and local government 7.15%. *FORTUNE* 500 COMPANIES (1994): 12: McDonnell Douglas, May Department Stores, Anheuser-Busch, Emerson Electric, Monsanto, Ralston Purina, Farmland Industries, Trans World Airlines, Jefferson Smurfit, Payless Cashways, Graybar Electric, Boatmen's Bancshares.
Famous natives Thomas Hart Benton, painter. Yogi Berra, baseball player. George Caleb Bingham (b. Va.), painter. Omar Bradley, general. Adophus Busch (b. Germany), brewer. George Washington Carver, botanist. Walter Cronkite, journalist. Walt Disney, film producer. T.S. Eliot, poet. Walker Evans, photographer. Langston Hughes, poet. Jesse James, outlaw. Marianne Moore, poet. Reinhold Niebuhr, theologian. J.C. Penney, businessman. John J. "Black Jack" Pershing, soldier. Joseph Pulitzer (b. Hungary), publisher. Ginger Rogers, dancer. Casey Stengel, baseball player. Virgil Thompson, composer. Harry S Truman, U.S. president. Mark Twain, writer. Tom Watson, golfer. Shelley Winters, actress.
Noteworthy places Churchill Memorial, St. Aldermanbury Church, Fulton. Gateway Arch, St. Louis. George Washington Carver Natl. Monument, Diamond. Harry S Truman Library, Independence. Mark Twain Area, Hannibal. Nelson-Atkins Museum of Art, Kansas City. Pony Express Museum, St. Joseph. St. Louis Art Museum. Wilson's Creek Natl. Battlefield.
Memorable events French miners and hunters settle at Ste. Genevieve 1735. Pierre Laclade settles St. Louis 1765. New Madrid earthquakes (8.6 on Richter scale) rock buildings as far away as Baltimore 1811–12. Statehood 1821. Missouri legislature split over secession: minority party adopts secession ordinance; Missouri admitted to Confederacy; majority party remains loyal to Union 1861. Jesse James killed by fellow gang member at St. Joseph 1882. Lake of the Ozarks formed after completion of Bagnell Dam on Osage River 1931. Winston Churchill delivers "iron curtain" speech at Fulton 1952. Gateway Arch, 630 ft. high, opened at St. Louis 1964. St. Louis population declines 47 percent 1950–80.
Tourist information 1-800-877-1234 or 1-314-751-4133.

Montana

Mountains account for only the western two-fifths of the state, where copper mining, lumbering, and tourism are the chief industries. The eastern portion of the state is part of the Great Plains. There the "Big Sky Country" is devoted to agriculture and especially ranching. For many years Montana was in the grip of the Anaconda Copper Mining Company, which virtually owned the state government and took most of the company's profits out of the state. After Anaconda's demise in the 1970s, Montana developed some of the most stringent environmental laws in the West. Although the copper mining damage is done, these laws will have a beneficial impact on the southeastern corner of the state, which is now being exploited for its enormous reserves of low-sulphur coal.

NAME From Spanish *montaña*, "mountainous." NICKNAMES Treasure State, Big Sky Country. CAPITAL Helena. ENTERED UNION Nov. 8, 1889 (41st). MOTTO *Oro y plata* (Gold and silver).
Emblems BIRD Western meadowlark. FISH Black-spotted cutthroat trout. FLOWER Bitterroot. GEMS Yogo sapphire, Montana agate. GRASS Bluebunch wheatgrass. SONG "Montana." STATE BALLAD "Montana Melody." TREE Ponderosa pine.
Land TOTAL AREA 147,046 sq. mi. (4th), incl. 1,658 sq. mi. inland water. BORDERS British Columbia, Alberta, Saskatchewan, N.Dak., S.Dak., Wyo., Idaho. RIVERS Kootenai, Milk, Missouri, Musselshell, Powder, Yellowstone. LAKES Bighorn, Canyon Ferry, Elwell, Flathead, Ft. Peck. MOUNTAINS Absaroka Range, Beartooth Range (Granite Peak 12,799 ft.), Big Belt, Bitterroot Range, Centennial, Crazy, Lewis Range, Little Belt. OTHER NOTABLE FEATURES Continental Divide, Missoula Valley.
Elected officials Gov. Marc Racicot (R, term exp. 1997). Lt. Gov. Dennis Rehberg (R). Sec. State Mike Cooney (D). Atty. Gen. Joe Mazurek (D).
People (1994) 856,047 (44th). RACE/NATIONAL ORIGIN (1990): White 92.7%. Black 0.3%. Indian 6.0%. Asian 0.5%. Other 0.5%. Hispanic 1.5%.
Cities (1990) Billings 81,151. Great Falls 55,097. Missoula 42,918. Butte–Silver Bow 33,941. Helena 24,569. Bozeman 22,660. Kalispell 11,917. Anaconda–Deer Lodge Co. 10,278. Havre 10,201. Miles City 8,461.
Business GROSS STATE PRODUCT (GSP, 1992) $15.23 bil. (47th). SECTORS OF GSP: Farms 5.53%; agricultural services, forestry, and fisheries 0.66%; mining 6.47%; construction 3.63%; manufacturing 8.41%; transportation and public utilities 12.97%; wholesale trade 5.52%; retail trade 9.68%; finance, insurance, and real estate 16.23%; services 16.71%; federal government 3.65%; federal military 1.36%; state and local government 9.18%. *FORTUNE* 500 COMPANIES (1994): 0.
Famous natives Gary Cooper, actor. Marcus Daly (b. Ireland), mine owner. Chet Huntley, journalist. Myrna Loy, actress. Mike Mansfield (b. N.Y.), politician/diplomat. Jeannette Rankin, politician/reformer. Charles M. Russell, artist.
Noteworthy places Big Hole Natl. Battlefield. Bob Marshall Wilderness. Charles M. Russell Museum, Great Falls. Custer Battlefield Natl. Monument. Ft. Union Trading Post Natl. Hist. Site. Lewis and Clark Caverns State Park. Museum of the Plains Indian, Browning. Natl. Bison Range. Waterton-Glacier International Peace Park. World Museum of Mining, Butte. Yellowstone Natl. Park.
Memorable events French explorers and trappers visit region 1740s. Large part of state in Louisiana Purchase 1803. Lewis and Clark expedition 1805–6. Ft. Benton first permanent settlement 1846. Western part of state included in Washington Territory 1853 and 1859; eastern part in Nebraska (1854) and Dakota (1861) territories. Gold discovered at Bannack (1862) and Alder Gulch (1863). Organized as Montana Territory 1864. Dakota and Cheyenne defeat U.S. troops under Gen. William Armstrong Custer at Battle of Little Bighorn 1876. Under Chief Joseph, Nez Percé beat U.S. Army at Big Hole Basin 1877. Marcus Daly discovers copper near Butte 1880s. Statehood 1889. Homesteaders enter state 1909. Ft. Peck Dam completed 1940. Anaconda Copper Mining, dominant in Montana industry and politics since 1915, closes mining operations at Butte 1983. Elizabeth Prophet (Guru Ma) convinces 3,000 disciples of the Church Universal and Triumphant to await nuclear cataclysm in underground shelters in Paradise Valley while state bureaucrats worried over sewage facilities 1990.
Tourist information 1-800-541-1447, 1-800-548-3390, or 1-406-444-2654.

Nebraska

Although set aside as Indian territory in 1834 and made off-limits to white settlement, thousands of whites crossed the region along the Independence, Mormon, and Oregon trails. Eventually Congress opened the land to settlement, which accelerated after the Homestead Act of 1862 and the coming of the railroads. The newcomers took up ranching and farming under hard conditions. The winter of 1886–87 killed thousands of cattle and drove many large-scale ranchers into bankruptcy, while the dust bowl of the 1930s spurred a mass exodus. Significant industry did not develop until World War II, when many war-related industries and army airfields moved to the center of the country. Among the leading agricultural states, especially in the production of corn for grain and livestock, Nebraska has a farming industry that accounted for almost 11 percent of its gross state product in 1989 and nearly 10 percent of the workforce. A state constitutional amendment passed in 1982 prevents the sale of farmlands and ranch lands to anyone other than a Nebraska family farm corporation.

NAME From Oto *nebrathka*, "flat water." NICKNAME Cornhusker State. CAPITAL Lincoln. ENTERED UNION Mar. 1, 1867 (37th). MOTTO "Equality before the law."

Emblems BIRD Western meadowlark. FLOWER Goldenrod. FOSSIL Mammoth. GEM Blue agate. GRASS Little blue stem. INSECT Honeybee. MAMMAL White-tailed deer. ROCK Prairie agate. SOIL Soils of the Holdrege series. SONG "Beautiful Nebraska." TREE Western cottonwood.

Land TOTAL AREA 77,355 sq. mi. (15th), incl. 711 sq. mi. inland water. BORDERS S.Dak., Iowa, Mo., Kans., Colo., Wyo. RIVERS Missouri, North Platte, Republican, South Platte. LAKES Harlan Co. Res., Lewis and Clark Lake. OTHER NOTABLE FEATURES Pine Ridge, Sand Hills.

Elected officials Gov. Ben Nelson (D, term exp. 1999). Lt. Gov. Kim Robak (D). Sec. State Scott Moore (R). Atty. Gen. Don Stenberg (R).

People (1994) 1,622,858 (37th). RACE/NATIONAL ORIGIN (1990): White 93.8%. Black 3.6%. Indian 0.8%. Asian 0.8%. Other 1.0%. Hispanic 2.3%.

Cities (1990) Omaha 335,795. Lincoln 191,972. Grand Island 39,386. Bellevue 30,982. Kearney 24,396. Fremont 23,680. Hastings 22,837. North Platte 22,605. Norfolk 21,476. Columbus 19,480.

Business GROSS STATE PRODUCT (GSP, 1992) $37.21 bil. (35th). SECTORS OF GSP: Farms 9.70%; agricultural services, forestry, and fisheries 0.61%; mining 0.22%; construction 3.21%; manufacturing 13.50%; transportation and public utilities 10.43%; wholesale trade 7.67%; retail trade 8.62%; finance, insurance, and real estate 16.01%; services 15.43%; federal government 2.94%; federal military 1.65%; state and local government 10.01%. *FORTUNE* 500 COMPANIES (1994): 5: Conagra, IBP, Mutual of Omaha Insurance, Berkshire Hathaway, Peter Kiewit Sons.

Famous natives Fred Astaire, dancer. Marlon Brando, actor. Willa Cather (b. Va.), author. Loren Eiseley, anthropologist. The Rev. Edward J. Flanagan (b. Ireland), reformer. Henry Fonda, actor. Gerald Ford, U.S. president. Rollin Kirby, cartoonist. Melvin Laird, politician. Harold Lloyd, actor. Mahpiua Luta (Red Cloud), Oglala Sioux chief. Malcolm X, religious leader. Roscoe Pound, educator.

Noteworthy places Agate Fossil Beds Natl. Monument. Arbor Lodge State Park, Nebraska City. Boys Town, Omaha. Buffalo Bill Ranch State Hist. Park. Chimney Rock Hist. Site. Homestead Natl. Monument, Beatrice. Oregon Trail. Pioneer Village, Minden. Scotts Bluff Natl. Monument. Stuhr Museum of the Prairie Pioneer, Grand Island.

Memorable events Acquired as part of Louisiana Purchase 1803. Separate territory created by Kansas-Nebraska Act 1854. Size reduced after creation of Colorado and Dakota Territories 1861. Statehood 1867. To encourage tree planting, becomes first state to observe Arbor Day 1872. Adopts unicameral legislature 1937. Oil discovered 1939. Population peaks at 1,605,000 1984–85.

Tourist information 1–800–228–4307.

Nevada

Set in the Great Basin desert, Nevada is one of the most barren places in North America, and the state receives less rainfall than any other. First explored by Europeans in 1776, it was 75 years before anyone thought of establishing a town in the area, and it did not last a decade. Miners came to Nevada early, but the discovery of the Comstock Lode in 1859 brought thousands. To add free-state congressional votes, Nevada was hustled into the Union in 1864, three years before its boundaries were settled. The Comstock Lode was depleted by the 1870s, and it took more gold and silver strikes in the early 1900s, as well as the discovery of copper, to get the economy rolling again. The mainstay of the economy since World War II has been the gambling industry, which generates virtually half of all tax revenues; Las Vegas alone can accommodate as many as 150,000 conventioneers and tourists at one time.

NAME From Spanish, meaning "snow-covered sierra." NICKNAMES Sagebrush State, Silver State. CAPITAL Carson City. ENTERED UNION Oct. 31, 1864 (36th). MOTTO "All for our country."

Emblems ANIMAL Desert bighorn sheep. BIRD Mountain bluebird. FLOWER Sagebrush. FOSSIL Icthyosaur. GRASS Indian ricegrass. METAL Silver. SONG "Home Means Nevada." TREE Singleleaf piñon.

Land TOTAL AREA 110,561 sq. mi. (7th), incl. 667 sq. mi. inland water. BORDERS Oreg., Idaho, Utah, Ariz., Calif. RIVERS Colorado, Humboldt. LAKES Pyramid, Walker, Winnemucca. OTHER NOTABLE FEATURES Black Rock Desert, Carson Sink, Humboldt Salt Marsh, Mojave Desert.

Elected officials Gov. Robert J. Miller (D, term exp. 1999). Lt. Gov. Loni Hammargren (R). Sec. State Dean Heller (R). Atty. Gen. Frankie Sue Del Papa (D).

People (1994) 1,457,028 (38th). RACE/NATIONAL ORIGIN (1990): White 84.3%. Black 6.6%. Indian 1.6%. Asian 3.2%. Other 4.4%. Hispanic 10.4%.

Cities (1990) Las Vegas 258,295. Reno 133,850. Henderson 64,942. Sparks 53,367. North Las Vegas 47,707. Carson City 40,443. Elko 14,736. Boulder City 12,567. Fallon 6,438. Winnemucca 6,134.

Business GROSS STATE PRODUCT (GSP, 1992) $36.82 bil. (36th). SECTORS OF GSP: Farms 0.54%; agricultural services, forestry, and fisheries 0.38%; mining 6.29%; construction 6.64%; manufacturing 3.83%; transportation and public utilities 9.35%; wholesale trade 4.22%; retail trade 9.38%; finance, insurance, and real estate 15.82%; services 33.60%; federal government 1.83%; federal military 1.04%; state and local government 7.08%. *FORTUNE* 500 COMPANIES (1994): 0.

Famous natives Walter Van Tilburg Clark (b. Maine), author. Sarah Winnemucca Hopkins, interpreter/teacher. John William MacKay, miner. William Morris Stewart (b. N.Y.), lawyer/senator.

Noteworthy places Death Valley Natl. Monument. Lehman Caves Natl. Monument. Valley of the Fire State Park, Overton.

Memorable events Francisco Tomás Garcés explores area 1775–76. Jedediah Smith, trader, crosses region 1826–27. Old Spanish Trail (1830) and California Trail (1833) cross region. John Frémont explores area 1843–45. To United States after Mexican War 1846. Genoa, first settlement in Nevada, founded as Mormon Station 1849. Gold of Comstock Lode discovered 1859. Organized as separate territory 1861. Statehood 1864. Nevada legalizes gambling 1931. Hoover Dam built on Colorado River 1935. Nuclear tests begun at Yucca Flats 1951. Population grows more than 550 percent 1950–88.

Tourist information 1–800–NEVADA8.

New Hampshire

New Hampshire has a disproportionate influence on presidential elections because by state law its primary must fall at least one week before any other state's (though Iowa's caucuses can come earlier). Through independence the mainstays of the economy were fishing, trade, and farming. Boston proved more suitable for trade, and New Hampshire's stubborn land was outproduced by the more fertile valleys to the south and west. The state's economy receded until the beginning of the Industrial Revolution, when there was tremendous growth in textile-producing mill towns in the Merrimack River Valley. The mills began to close after World War I, and the economy faltered again. Improvement came as high-tech firms from Boston sought refuge in New Hampshire's favorable tax climate, but the state's economy was pummeled by the severe New England recession in the early 1990s.

NAME For English county of Hampshire. NICKNAME Granite State. CAPITAL Concord. ENTERED UNION June 21, 1788 (9th). MOTTO "Live free or die."

Emblems AMPHIBEAN Spotted newt. BIRD Purple finch. FLOWER Purple lilac. GEM Smoke quartz. INSECT Ladybug. MINERAL Beryl. SONG "Old New Hampshire." TREE White birch.

Land TOTAL AREA 9,279 sq. mi. (44th), incl. 286 sq. mi. inland water. BORDERS Quebec, Maine, Atlantic Ocean, Mass., Vt. RIVERS Connecticut, Merrimack, Piscataqua, Saco, Salmon Falls. LAKES First Connecticut, Francis, Newfound, Ossipee, Sunapee, Winnipesaukee. OTHER NOTABLE FEATURES Isles of Shoals, White Mts. (Mt. Washington 6,288 ft., highest peak in Northeast).

Elected officials Gov. Steve Merrill (R, term exp. 1999). Sec. State William M. Gardner (D). Atty. Gen. Jeffrey Howard (R).

People (1994) 1,136,820 (41st). RACE/NATIONAL ORIGIN (1990): White 98.0%. Black 0.6%. Indian 0.2%. Asian 0.8%. Other 0.3%. Hispanic 1.0%.

Cities (1990) Manchester 99,567. Nashua 79,662. Concord 36,006. Rochester 26,630. Dover 25,042. Portsmouth 22,925. Keene 22,430. Laconia 15,743. Claremont 13,902. Lebanon 12,183.

Business GROSS STATE PRODUCT (GSP, 1992) $25.52 bil. (42nd). SECTORS OF GSP: Farms 0.44%; agricultural services, forestry, and fisheries 0.47%; mining 0.13%; construction 5.37%;

manufacturing 22.32%; transportation and public utilities 5.96%; wholesale trade 5.66%; retail trade 10.48%; finance, insurance, and real estate 19.89%; services 19.97%; federal government 1.48%; federal military 0.51%; state and local government 7.33%. *FORTUNE* 500 COMPANIES (1994): 1: Tyco International.

Famous natives Salmon P. Chase, jurist. Ralph Adams Cram, architect. Mary Baker Eddy, founder, Church of Christ, Scientist. Daniel Chester French, sculptor. Horace Greeley, journalist. Sarah Buell Hale, author. Franklin Pierce, U.S. president. Augustus Saint-Gaudens (b. Ireland), sculptor. Alan Shepard, astronaut. Daniel Webster, politician. Eleazar Wheelock (b. Conn.), Dartmouth founder.

Noteworthy places Currier Gallery of Art, Manchester. The Flume (gorge). Franconia Notch. Isles of Shoals. Lake Winnipesaukee. Mt. Washington. Shaker Village, Canterbury. St. Gaudens Natl. Hist. Site. Strawberry Banke. White Mountains Natl. Forest.

Memorable events Martin Pring sails along coast 1603. Champlain explores area 1604. John Smith visits Isles of Shoals 1614. Included in king's grant to John Mason and Sir Ferdinando Gorges 1622. First settlers at Little Harbor, near Portsmouth 1623. Made separate royal province 1679, though under Massachusetts governor 1699–1741. Rogers's Rangers halt Indian raids 1759. New Hampshire patriots seize British fort at Portsmouth and drive out Royal governor 1775. Province relinquishes claims to New Connecticut (Vermont) 1782. First textile mill built 1803. Treaty of Portsmouth ends Sino-Russian War 1905. Bretton Woods conference leads to establishment of International Monetary Fund 1944. First state to adopt lottery to support public education 1963.

Tourist information 1–603–271–2666.

New Jersey

With the entire state population classified as living in metro areas, New Jersey is the most densely populated state, 15 times the national average. The image survives of New Jersey as a chemical-industrial wasteland south of New York Harbor. Pharmaceuticals and chemicals are in fact New Jersey's leading products, but the next most important industry is tourism, because of the money tourists spend at the gaming tables of Atlantic City. What earns New Jersey its nickname, the Garden State, is its extensive small-scale agriculture, which produces tomatoes, dairy products, asparagus, blueberries, corn, and poultry.

New Jersey lies on a plain between Philadelphia and New York City, two larger neighbors that have overshadowed New Jersey on the national scene since colonial days. Yet during the Revolution, more than 100 battles were fought on New Jersey soil, and today the overwhelming majority of containerized shipping in the Port of New York and New Jersey is shipped from New Jersey terminals. Per capita income is always among the top five in the nation.

NAME After English Channel Island of Jersey. NICKNAME Garden State. CAPITAL Trenton. ENTERED UNION Dec. 18, 1787 (3rd). MOTTO "Liberty and prosperity."

Emblems ANIMAL Horse. BIRD Eastern goldfinch. FLOWER Violet. INSECT Honeybee. MEMORIAL TREE Dogwood. TREE Red oak.

Land TOTAL AREA 7,787 sq. mi. (46th), incl. 319 sq. mi. inland water. BORDERS N.Y., Atlantic Ocean, Del., Pa. RIVERS Delaware, Hackensack, Hudson, Passaic. LAKES Greenwood, Hopatcong, Round Valley Res., Spruce Run. OTHER NOTABLE FEATURES Delaware Water Gap, Kittatinny Mts., Palisades, Pine Barrens, Ramapo Mts.

Elected officials Gov. Christine Todd Whitman (R, term exp. 1998). Sec. State Lana Hooks (R). Atty. Gen. Debra Poritz (R).

People (1994) 7,903,925 (9th). RACE/NATIONAL ORIGIN (1990): White 79.3%. Black 13.4%. Indian 0.2%. Asian 3.5%. Other 3.6%. Hispanic 9.6%.

Cities (1990) Newark 275,221. Jersey City 228,537. Paterson 140,891. Elizabeth 110,002. Edison CDP 88,680. Trenton 88,675. Camden 87,492. East Orange 73,552. Clifton 71,742. Cherry Hill 69,319.

Business GROSS STATE PRODUCT (GSP, 1992) $223.14 bil. (8th). SECTORS OF GSP: Farms 0.22%; agricultural services, forestry, and fisheries 0.33%; mining 0.06%; construction 4.65%; manufacturing 17.86%; transportation and public utilities 9.26%; wholesale trade 8.65%; retail trade 8.35%; finance, insurance, and real estate 20.00%; services 20.65%; federal government 1.62%; federal military 0.37%; state and local government 7.97%. *FORTUNE* 500 COMPANIES (1994): 24: including Prudential Insurance of America, Johnson & Johnson, Merck, AlliedSignal, Great Atlantic & Pacific Tea, American Home Products, Toys "R" Us, CPC International, Supermarkets General Holdings, Campbell Soup, Warner-Lambert, Chubb, Ingersoll-Rand, American Standard, Becton Dickinson, First Fidelity Bancorp.

Famous natives Count Basie, jazz musician. William J. Brennan, jurist. Aaron Burr, politician. Grover Cleveland, U.S. president. James Fenimore Cooper, novelist/historian. Stephen Crane, author. Albert Einstein (b. Germany), nuclear physicist. Waldo Frank, author. Joyce Kilmer, poet. Jerry Lewis, actor. Jack Nicholson, actor. Zebulon Pike, explorer. Molly Pitcher, revolutionary war heroine. Paul Robeson, actor/singer. Walter Schirra, astronaut. Frank Sinatra, singer. Alfred Stieglitz, photographer. Meryl Streep, actress. Aaron Montgomery Ward, merchant. William Carlos Williams, poet.

Noteworthy places Cape May Historic District. Edison Natl. Hist. Site, West Orange. Lakehurst Naval Air Station. Liberty State Park, Jersey City. Morristown Natl. Hist. Park. Newark Museum. Palisades Interstate Park. Pine Barrens wilderness area. Princeton University. Walt Whitman House, Camden.

Memorable eventsGiovanni de Verrazano explores 1524. Hudson explores up Hudson River 1609. Dutch settlers establish Ft. Nassau 1623. New Jersey taken over by British and organized as colony under Sir George Carteret 1665. Major battles of Revolution at Trenton (1776), Princeton (1777), and Monmouth (1778). Women given vote at Elizabethtown 1800. Voting rights restricted to men 1807. Adopts state constitution 1844. Passenger ship *Morro Castle* burns off Asbury Park; 134 die 1934. Dirigible *Hindenburg* explodes while mooring at Lakehurst; 36 die 1937. New Jersey Turnpike linking New York City and Philadelphia opens 1952. Five days of race riots in Newark leave 26 dead 1967. Gambling legalized in Atlantic City 1978. State enacts strictest gun legislation in United States 1990.

Tourist information 1–800–JERSEY7 or 1–609–989–7888.

New Mexico

The development problem of the western states is shared by New Mexico, which of all states has the smallest percentage of its area covered by water. Rich in other resources, it is the uranium capital of the world. The state mineral tax brings in 28 percent of state revenues, some of which goes into permanent endowments. Distribution of wealth in New Mexico remains uneven, but Hispanics, who tend to register as Democrats, vote in roughly the same ways as Anglos. A higher percentage of Native Americans lives in New Mexico than in any other state. Today mining is a major industry, manufacturing is growing, and service industry jobs are expanding rapidly, to the point where they are projected to account for nearly one in every three New Mexico jobs by 2000. Despite the enormous governmental investment in research at Los Alamos, where the atom bomb was born, the highly classified nature of this work limits the development of related industry.

NAME By Spanish explorers after Mexico. NICKNAME Land of Enchantment. CAPITAL Santa Fe. ENTERED UNION Jan. 6, 1912 (47th). MOTTO *Crescit eundo* (It grows as it goes).

Emblems ANIMAL Black bear. BIRD Roadrunner (chaparral bird). FISH Cutthroat trout. FLOWER Yucca. FOSSIL *Coelphysis* dinosaur. GEM Turquoise. SONGS "O, Fair New Mexico," "Así es Nuevo Mejico." TREE Piñon. VEGETABLES Frijole, chili.

Land TOTAL AREA 121,593 sq. mi. (5th), incl. 258 sq. mi. inland water. BORDERS Colo., Okla., Tex., Chihuahua, Ariz. RIVERS Gila, Pecos, Rio Grande, Zuni. LAKES Conchas Res., Eagle Nest, Elephant Butte Res., Navajo Res., Ute Res. MOUNTAINS Chuska, Guadalupe, Sacramento, San Andres, Sangre de Cristo. OTHER NOTABLE FEATURES Carlsbad Caverns, Continental Divide, Staked Plain.

Elected officials Gov. Gary Johnson (R, term exp. 1999). Lt. Gov. Walter Bradley (R). Sec. State Stephanie Gonzales (D). Atty. Gen. Tom Udall (D).

People (1994) 1,653,521 (36th). RACE/NATIONAL ORIGIN (1990): White 75.6%. Black 2.0%. Indian 8.9%. Asian 0.9%. Other 12.6%. Hispanic 38.2%.

Cities (1990) Albuquerque 384,736. Las Cruces 62,126. Santa Fe 55,859. Roswell 44,654. Farmington 33,997. Rio Rancho 32,505. Clovis 30,954.

Hobbs 29,115. Alamogordo 27,596. Carlsbad 24,952.

Business Gross state product (GSP, 1992) $31.86 bil. (39th). Sectors of GSP: Farms 2.08%; agricultural services, forestry, and fisheries 0.38%; mining 10.59%; construction 4.08%; manufacturing 6.83%; transportation and public utilities 10.75%; wholesale trade 4.25%; retail trade 9.92%; finance, insurance, and real estate 14.46%; services 18.60%; federal government 4.56%; federal military 2.01%; state and local government 11.47%. *Fortune* 500 companies (1994): 0.

Famous natives William "Billy the Kid" Bonney (b. N.Y.), outlaw. Peter Hurd, artist. Archbishop Jean Baptiste Lamy (b. France), missionary. Georgia O'Keeffe (b. Wis.), artist. Popé, Tewa Pueblo chief.

Noteworthy places Aztec Ruins Natl. Monument. Bandelier Natl. Monument. Capulin Mt. Natl. Monument. Carlsbad Caverns Natl. Park. Chaco Culture Natl. Hist. Park. El Morro Natl. Monument. Ft. Union Natl. Monument. Gila Cliff Dwellings Natl. Monument. Museum of New Mexico, Santa Fe. Pecos Mission. Salinas Mission. Santa Fe Opera. Wheelwright Museum of the American Indian, Santa Fe. White Sands Natl. Monument.

Memorable events Marcos de Niza enters Zuni country 1539. Juan de Oñate establishes first Spanish settlement on Rio Grande near Española 1598. Santa Fe founded; becomes capital of New Mexico 1710. Santa Fe Trail from Independence, Missouri, completed; Mexico secedes from Spain 1821. Manuel Armijo suppresses revolt against Mexican rule (1837); defeats invasion from Republic of Texas (1841). Land annexed by United States after Mexican-American War 1848. Organized as territory with Arizona and part of Colorado 1850. Lincoln County War pits cattlemen against merchants 1878–81. Statehood; 17 killed in raid by Pancho Villa 1912. Los Alamos selected as first research and development facility for nuclear weapons 1942. First atom bomb exploded at Alamogordo Air Base 1945.

Tourist information 1–800–545–2040 or 1–505–827–7400.

New York

New York's greatest and most inviting asset has always been its strategic location and long arteries into the hinterland. New York Bay is one of the great natural harbors of the world, and the broad Hudson River is one of the most fortunately placed. After the opening of the Erie Canal between the Hudson and Lake Erie in 1825, New York City became the trading center for the Midwest as well as the Hudson Valley and the Atlantic Coast. Buffalo also experienced a boom, becoming a major Great Lakes industrial port. New York is still the first state in number of manufacturing establishments and employees. Wall Street alone employs half a million people.

Although New York's population grew by nearly half a million people between 1980 and 1990, its relatively slow rate of growth resulted in a loss of three congressional seats—an indication of the change in the state's political clout. As its place among the 50 states has fallen by some measures, New York City's worldwide importance in business, culture, and communications has risen.

Name For Duke of York, later James II, of England. Nickname Empire State. Capital Albany. Entered Union July 26, 1788 (11th). Motto *Excelsior* (Higher).

Emblems Animal Beaver. Beverage Milk. Bird Bluebird. Fish Brook or speckled trout. Flower Rose. Fossil Prehistoric crab *(Eurypterus remipes)*. Fruit Apple. Gem Garnet. Song "I Love New York." Tree Sugar maple.

Land Total area 49,108 sq. mi. (30th), incl. 1,731 sq. mi. inland water. Borders Lake Ontario, Ontario, Quebec, Vt., Mass., Conn., Atlantic Ocean, N.J., Pa., Lake Erie. Rivers Allegheny, Delaware, Genesee, Hudson, Mohawk, New York State Barge Canal, Niagara, St. Lawrence, Susquehanna. Lakes Cayuga, Champlain, Chautauqua, Erie, George, Oneida, Ontario, Seneca. Mountains Adirondack (Mt. Marcy 5,344 ft.), Allegheny, Berkshire Hills, Catskill, Kittatinny, Ramapo. Other notable features Hudson Valley, Mohawk Valley, Niagara Falls, Palisades, Thousand Islands.

Elected officials Gov. George Pataki (D, term exp. 1999). Lt. Gov. Betsy McCaughey (R). Sec. State Alexander F. Treadwell (R). Atty. Gen. Dennis Vacco (R).

People (1994) 18,169,051 (3rd). Race/national origin (1990): White 74.4%. Black 15.9%. Indian 0.3%. Asian 3.9%. Other 5.5%. Hispanic 12.3%.

Cities (1990) New York 7,322,564. Buffalo 328,123. Rochester 231,636. Yonkers 188,082. Syracuse 163,860. Albany 101,082. Utica 68,637. New Rochelle 67,265. Mount Vernon 67,153. Schenectady 65,566.

Business Gross state product (GSP, 1992) $497.56 bil. (2nd) Sectors of GSP: Farms 0.37%; agricultural services, forestry, and fisheries 0.22%; mining 0.11%; construction 3.93%; manufacturing 14.29%; transportation and public utilities 8.58%; wholesale trade 6.99%; retail trade 7.79%; finance, insurance, and real estate 23.93%; services 22.43%; federal government 1.42%; federal military 0.31%; state and local government 9.63%. *Fortune* 500 companies (1994): 65: including AT&T, International Business Machines, Philip Morris, Texaco, Citicorp, Pepsico, ITT, American International Group, Metropolitan Life Insurance, Travelers Inc., Merrill Lynch, Eastman Kodak, American Express, RJR Nabisco Holdings, Woolworth, Pfizer, Viacom, Colgate-Palmolive, Capital Cities/ABC, Corning, Avon Products, CBS, Reader's Digest Assn., New York Times.

Famous natives Woody Allen, director. John Jacob Astor (b. Germany), merchant. Humphrey Bogart, actor. George Burns, actor. Aaron Copland, composer. Agnes De Mille, choreographer. George Eastman, camera inventor. Millard Fillmore, U.S. president. Lou Gehrig, baseball player. George Gershwin, composer. Julia Ward Howe, reformer. Washington Irving, author. Henry James, author. Vince Lombardi, football coach. Groucho Marx, comedian. Herman Melville, author. Ogden Nash, poet/humorist. Eugene O'Neill, playwright. Otetiani "Red Jacket," Seneca chief. Channing E. Phillips, minister/reformer. John D. Rockefeller, industrialist. Norman Rockwell, illustrator. Richard Rodgers, composer. Franklin Delano Roosevelt, U.S. president. Theodore Roosevelt, U.S. president. Jonas Salk, physician. Elizabeth Ann Seton, first American saint. Elizabeth Cady Stanton, suffragette. James Johnson Sweeney, art critic. Martin Van Buren, U.S. president. Mae West, actress. E.B. White, author. Walt Whitman, poet.

Noteworthy places Albright-Knox Gallery of American Art, Buffalo. American Merchant Marine Museum, Kings Point. Baseball Hall of Fame, Cooperstown. Bear Mt. State Park. Buffalo Museum of Science. Corning Glass Center, Corning. Erie Canal Museum, Syracuse. Farmers' Museum, Cooperstown. Fenimore House, Cooperstown. Franklin D. Roosevelt Natl. Hist. Site, Hyde Park. Ft. Stanwix Natl. Monument, Rome. Ft. Ticonderoga. Hudson Valley. Mohawk Valley. Niagara Falls. Palisades Interstate Park. Saratoga Natl. Hist. Park. Vanderbilt Museum, Hyde Park. U.S. Military Academy, West Point. Women's Rights Natl. Hist. Park, Seneca Falls. New York City American Academy of Arts & Sciences. American Museum of Natural History. Bronx Zoo. Brooklyn Botanical Garden. Brooklyn Museum. Cathedral of St. John the Divine. Cooper-Hewitt Museum. Federal Hall. Fraunces Tavern. Frick Collection. Guggenheim Museum. Hispanic Society of America. Jewish Museum. Lincoln Center for the Performing Arts. Metropolitan Museum of Art. Museum of Modern Art. Museum of the American Indian. N.Y. Public Library. N.Y. Stock Exchange. Rockefeller Center. South Street Seaport Museum. Statue of Liberty. United Nations.

Memorable events Giovanni de Verrazano sails into New York Bay 1524. Samuel de Champlain sails down the St. Lawrence River 1603. Henry Hudson sails up Hudson River 1609. Dutch establish Ft. Orange (Albany) 1614. Peter Minuit buys Manhattan Island and founds colony of New Amsterdam 1625. British take New Amsterdam and name it New York 1664. Ethan Allen takes Ft. Ticonderoga 1775. George Washington inaugurated president New York City 1789. U.S. Military Academy founded West Point 1802. Erie Canal opened 1825. Statue of Liberty dedicated 1886. New York City includes Manhattan, Bronx, Queens, Brooklyn, and Staten Island 1898. Pres. William McKinley assassinated in Buffalo 1901. UN headquarters established at New York City 1945. St. Lawrence Seaway opened 1959.

Tourist information 1–800–225–5697 or 1–518–474–4116.

North Carolina

At the time of the Revolution, tobacco and rice plantations dominated the economy of the eastern part of the state, which in turn dominated the legislature. Next to last to ratify the

Constitution, North Carolina was the last southern state to secede from the Union. The Civil War cost North Carolina dearly; reconstruction was short-lived, and blacks were effectively disenfranchised again by the turn of the century. Since World War II, the state has grown increasingly prosperous, especially in the "academic triangle" that encloses the University of North Carolina at Chapel Hill, Duke, and North Carolina State. The traditional industries of textiles, furniture, and tobacco still lead, partly because of diversification within them. North Carolina benefits from the general Sunbelt boom and from an influx of foreign capital, has a relatively low unemployment rate (5.7% in December 1991), maintains a healthy manufacturing sector, and appeared to be poised for steady economic growth in the 1990s.

NAME For King Charles I (Carolus is Latin for Charles). NICKNAMES Tarheel State, Old North State. CAPITAL Raleigh. ENTERED UNION Nov. 21, 1789 (12th). MOTTO *Esse quam videri* (To be rather than to seem).

Emblems BIRD Cardinal. FISH Channel bass. FLOWER Dogwood. INSECT Honeybee. PRECIOUS STONE Emerald. REPTILE Eastern box turtle. ROCK Granite. SHELL Scotch bonnet. SONG "The Old North State." TREE Pine.

Land TOTAL AREA 52, 669 sq. mi. (28th), incl. 3,826 sq. mi. inland water. BORDERS Va., Atlantic Ocean, S.C., Ga., Tenn. RIVERS Albemarle, Pee Dee, Roanoke, Yadkin. LAKES Buggs Island, High Rock, Mattamuskeet, Norman, Waccamaw. MOUNTAINS Black, Blue Ridge, Great Smoky, Unaka. OTHER NOTABLE FEATURES Great Dismal Swamp, Outer Banks, Pamlico Sound.

Elected officials Gov. James B. Hunt (D, term exp. 1997). Lt. Gov. Dennis A. Wicker (D). Sec. State Rufus L. Edmisten (D). Atty. Gen. Mike Easley (D).

People (1994) 7,069,836 (10th). RACE/NATIONAL ORIGIN (1990): White 75.6%. Black 22.0%. Indian 1.2%. Asian 0.8%. Other 0.5%. Hispanic 1.2%.

Cities (1990) Charlotte 395,934. Raleigh 207,951. Greensboro 183,521. Winston-Salem 143,485. Durham 136,611. Fayetteville 75,695. High Point 69,496. Asheville 61,607. Wilmington 55,530. Gastonia 54,732.

Business GROSS STATE PRODUCT (GSP, 1992) $159.64 bil. (11th). SECTORS OF GSP: Farms 2.02%; agricultural services, forestry, and fisheries 0.46%; mining 0.32%; construction 4.15%; manufacturing 30.83%; transportation and public utilities 7.86%; wholesale trade 6.10%; retail trade 9.63%; finance, insurance, and real estate 13.17%; services 13.47%; federal government 1.58%; federal military 2.16%; state and local government 8.27%. *FORTUNE* 500 COMPANIES (1994): 7: Nationsbank Corp., First Union Corp., Lowe's, Duke Power, Nucor, Wachovia Corp., Carolina Power & Light.

Famous natives Virginia Dare, first English colonist born in North America (1587). Benjamin Newton Duke and James Buchanan Duke, industrialists/philanthropists. Richard J. Gatling, inventor. Billy Graham, minister. O. Henry, writer. Jesse Jackson, minister/reformer. Andrew Johnson, U.S. president. William Rufus King, politician. Meadowlark Lemon, athlete. Dolley Madison, first lady. Thelonius Monk, musician. Edward R. Murrow, journalist. James Knox Polk, U.S. president. Moses Waddell, Confederate general.

Noteworthy places Bennett Place. Blue Ridge Natl. Parkway. Cape Hatteras and Cape Lookout Natl. Seashore. Carl Sandburg home, Hendersonville. Ft. Raleigh. Great Smoky Mountains Natl. Hist. Park. Guilford Courthouse Natl. Military Park. Mint Museum, Charlotte. Moores Creek Natl. Battlefield. North Carolina Maritime Museum, Beaufort. North Carolina Museum of Art, Raleigh. Roanoke Island. Wright Brothers Natl. Memorial, Kitty Hawk.

Memorable events Part of Carolina grant given to eight noblemen by Charles II 1663. Culpeper's Rebellion in reaction to unfair tax collection policies 1677. Tuscarora lose war against European immigrants 1713. Proprietors sell rights to Crown; becomes royal province 1729. Mecklenburg Declaration (1775), forerunner of Declaration of Independence. Becomes first colony to sanction explicitly declaration of independence from Britain in April 1776. Gen. Charles Cornwallis wins Battle of Guilford Courthouse, but British lose control of colony 1781. Ratifies Constitution 1789. Gives up claims to western territories, now part of Tennessee 1790. Establishes first state university system in United States 1829. Cherokees driven out of North Carolina to Oklahoma 1838. Secedes 1861. Readmitted to Union 1868. American Tobacco Company founded 1890. Wright brothers launch first successful airplane at Kitty Hawk 1903. Confrontation between Ku Klux Klan and anti-Klan demonstrators leaves five dead; 12 Klansmen charged with first-degree murder 1979.

Tourist information 1–800–VISITNC or 1–919–733–4171.

North Dakota

The first permanent settlers in North Dakota were Scots-Canadians who settled at Pembina on the Red River near the Canadian border, and who traded primarily with Winnipeg and St. Paul. The arrival of the Northern Pacific Railway in 1872 created a surge of huge farms, many of which were wiped out by drought and harsh winters in the 1880s. There followed a huge influx of Norwegians and Germans whose influence is still very apparent today. North Dakota's economy is heavily agricultural and leads the nation in production of wheat. Farming is centered in the fertile Red River of the North Valley, with livestock throughout the rest of the state. In recent years this has been augmented by mining—North Dakota has the greatest lignite coal reserves of any state in the United States and some natural gas reserves.

NAME For northern section of Dakota territory; *dakota* is Sioux word for "allies." NICKNAMES Sioux State, Peace Garden State, Flickertail State. CAPITAL Bismarck. ENTERED UNION Nov. 2, 1889 (39th). MOTTO "Liberty and union, now and forever, one and inseparable."

Emblems BEVERAGE Milk. BIRD Western meadowlark. FISH Northern pike. FLOWER Wild prairie rose. GRASS Western wheatgrass. MARCH "Spirit of North Dakota." SONG "North Dakota Hymn." STONE Teredo petrified wood. TREE American elm.

Land TOTAL AREA 70,703 sq. mi. (17th), incl. 1,403 sq. mi. inland water. BORDERS Saskatchewan, Manitoba, Minn., S.Dak., Mont. RIVERS Missouri, Red River of the North. LAKES Ashtabula, Devils, Oahe, Sakakawea. OTHER NOTABLE FEATURES Geographical center of North America, Missouri Plateau, Red River Valley, Rolling Drift Prairie.

Elected officials Gov. Edward Schafer (R, term exp. 1997). Lt. Gov. Rosemarie Myrdal (R). Sec. State Alvin A. Jaeger (R). Atty. Gen. Heidi Heitkamp (D).

People (1994) 637,988 (47th). RACE/NATIONAL ORIGIN (1990): White 94.6%. Black 0.6%. Indian 4.1%. Asian 0.5%. Other 0.3%. Hispanic 0.7%.

Cities (1990) Fargo 74,111. Grand Forks 49,425. Bismarck 49,256. Minot 34,544. Dickinson 16,097. Jamestown 15,571. Mandan 15,177. Williston 13,131. West Fargo 12,287. Wahpeton 8,751.

Business GROSS STATE PRODUCT (GSP, 1992) $13.06 bil. (50th). SECTORS OF GSP: Farms 9.85%; agricultural services, forestry, and fisheries 0.54%; mining 7.29%; construction 3.33%; manufacturing 6.65%; transportation and public utilities 9.75%; wholesale trade 7.70%; retail trade 9.34%; finance, insurance, and real estate 17.25%; services 14.69%; federal government 2.61%; federal military 2.86%; state and local government 8.19%. *FORTUNE* 500 COMPANIES (1994): 0.

Famous natives Angie Dickinson, actress. John Bernard Flannagan, sculptor. Louis L'Amour, novelist. Peggy Lee, singer. Eric Sevareid, broadcaster. Vihjalmur Stefansson (b. Canada), ethnologist. Lawrence Welk, entertainer.

Noteworthy places Ft. Abraham Lincoln State Park. Ft. Union Trading Post Natl. Hist. Site. International Peace Garden. Knife River Indian Villages Natl. Hist. Site. Theodore Roosevelt Natl. Park, the Badlands.

Memorable events Pierre Gaultier de Varennes, sieur de Vérendrye first European to visit area 1738. United States acquires half of territory in Louisiana Purchase 1803. Meriwether Lewis and George Rogers Clark expedition builds Ft. Mandan 1804–5. First permanent settlement at Pembina 1812. Britain cedes western half of state to United States. 1818. Missouri River steamboats reach territory 1838. First railroad arrives 1873. Statehood 1889. First state to hold presidential primary 1912. Garrison Dam completed, forming Lake Sakakawea; gambling (blackjack) legalized 1981.

Tourist information 1–800–435–5663, or 1–701–224–2525.

Ohio

The first settlements in Ohio were Marietta, in 1788, and Cincinnati in 1789, on the Ohio River, but significant migration into the state didn't occur until after the War of 1812. Shipping flourished in the 1820s and 1830s thanks to a network of canals connecting the Ohio and Lake Erie. Since 1959 the St. Lawrence Seaway has helped keep Ohio among the top five exporting states. Heavy industry also flourished in the northern cities that had access to coal and iron ore from the Lake Superior region. The 1870s saw the development of a manufacturing base that later became an integral part of the automotive industry. Although Ohio's economy has traditionally been well balanced between agriculture, industry, mining, and trade, the recession of the early 1980s weakened manufacturing, triggered flight from the industrial cities, and saw a dramatic shift to a service economy.

NAME From Iroquois *oheo*, "beautiful." NICKNAME Buckeye State. CAPITAL Columbus. ENTERED UNION Mar. 1, 1803 (17th). MOTTO "With God, all things are possible."

Emblems BEVERAGE Tomato juice. BIRD Cardinal. FLOWER Scarlet carnation. GEM Ohio flint. INSECT Ladybug. SONG "Beautiful Ohio." TREE Buckeye.

Land TOTAL AREA 41,330 sq. mi. (35th), incl. 326 sq. mi. inland water. BORDERS Mich., Lake Erie, Pa., W.Va., Ky., Ind. RIVERS Cuyahoga, Maumee, Miami, Muskingum, Ohio, Sandusky, Scioto. LAKES Berlin Res., Dillon Res., Erie, Mosquito Res., St. Mary's.

Elected officials Gov. George Voinovich (R, term exp. 1999). Lt. Gov. Nancy Hollister (R). Sec. State Bob Taft (R). Atty. Gen. Betty Montgomery (R).

People (1994) 11,102,198 (7th). RACE/NATIONAL ORIGIN (1990): White 87.8%. Black 10.6%. Indian 0.2%. Asian 0.8%. Other 0.5%. Hispanic 1.3%.

Cities (1990) Columbus 632,910. Cleveland 505,616. Cincinnati 364,040. Toledo 332,943. Akron 223,019. Dayton 182,044. Youngstown 95,732. Parma 87,876. Canton 84,161. Lorain 71,245.

Business GROSS STATE PRODUCT (GSP, 1992) $241.60 bil. (7th). SECTORS OF GSP: Farms 0.96%; agricultural services, forestry, and fisheries 0.31%; mining 0.62%; construction 4.00%; manufacturing 27.43%; transportation and public utilities 8.37%; wholesale trade 6.40%; retail trade 9.52%; finance, insurance, and real estate 15.29%; services 17.18%; federal government 1.77%; federal military 0.39%; state and local government 7.76%. *FORTUNE* 500 COMPANIES (1994): 30: including Procter & Gamble, Kroger, Goodyear Tire & Rubber, Nationwide Insurance Enterprise, TRW, Federated Department Stores, Banc One Corp., Limited, Dana, Borden, Mead, Roadway Services, Chiquita Brands Intl., Owens-Corning Fiberglas, Sherwin Williams, Revco D.S., Ohio Edison.

Famous natives Sherwood Anderson, writer. Neil Armstrong, astronaut. George Bellows, artist. Ambrose Bierce, author. George Armstrong Custer, army officer. Paul Laurence Dunbar, poet. Thomas A. Edison, inventor. James A. Garfield, U.S. president. John Glenn, astronaut/politician. Ulysses S. Grant, U.S. president/general. Zane Grey, author. Warren G. Harding, U.S. president. Benjamin Harrison, U.S. president. Rutherford B. Hayes, U.S. president. Bob Hope, entertainer. William McKinley, U.S. president. Annie Oakley, markswoman. Ransom Eli Olds, carmaker. Eddie Rickenbacker, pilot. William Sherman, army officer. William Howard Taft, U.S. president/chief justice. Art Tatum, pianist. Tecumseh, Shawnee chief. James Thurber, humorist. Orville Wright, airplane inventor.

Noteworthy places Air Force Museum, Dayton. Cleveland Museum of Art. Cleveland Museum of Natural History. Columbus Museum of Art. Great Lakes Historical Society Museum, Vermilion. Mound City Group Natl. Monument, Chillicothe. Neil Armstrong Air and Space Museum, Wapakoneta. Ohio River Museum, Marietta. Pro Football Hall of Fame, Canton. Toledo Museum of Art.

Memorable events Hopewell Mound-Builders present throughout state prior to arrival of Miamis, Shawnees, Wyandots, and Delawares. Conflicting claims by France, Virginia, Connecticut, and New York 1609–1786. René-Roger Cavelier de La Salle visits region 1669–70. To Britain 1763. To United States after 1783. Becomes part of Northwest Territory 1787. First settlement at Marietta 1788. Gen. "Mad" Anthony Wayne beats Tecumseh at Battle of Fallen Timbers 1794. Enters Union 1803. Harrison beats Tecumseh at Battle of Tippecanoe 1811. Oliver Hazard Perry beats British fleet at Battle of Put-in-Bay 1813. Ohio and Erie Canal completed 1832. Dayton flood kills 400 in Miami River valley; damage put at $100 million 1913. Carl B. Stokes elected mayor of Cleveland, first black mayor of major U.S. city 1967. Four students protesting Vietnam War killed by National Guard at Kent State University 1970.

Tourist information 1–800–BUCKEYE.

Oklahoma

French trappers entered the region of Oklahoma in the 1700s. In 1830 the land was designated the Indian Country, set aside for members of the Cherokees, Chickasaw, Choctaw, Creek, and Seminole deported from the southeast by the Indian Removal Act of 1830. These "Five Civilized Tribes," among others, fared well until the Civil War. They supported the Confederacy (some were actually slave-holders), and in 1868 Col. George Armstrong Custer led a massacre of Cheyenne at the Battle of the Washita. Twenty years later the government abrogated its treaty commitments and opened the territory to settlement. Today the state has a distinctly southern character. The region bordering the Red River is known as "Little Dixie," and as many as two-thirds of all Oklahomans consider themselves born-again Christians.

Oklahoma has a diversified economy. The state led the country in oil and gas production through the 1920s. Agriculture was hit heavily by the dust bowl of the 1930s, and thousands of "Okies" fled west. While agriculture and petroleum are still vital to the economy, manufacturing is increasingly important. The state is crossed by two of the country's longest rivers. The Arkansas links Catoosa (near Tulsa) to the Gulf of Mexico and the Mississippi River system; but the Red River is not navigable in Oklahoma, and dissolved salts make it useless for agriculture, industry, or residential purposes.

NAME From Choctaw *okla humma*, "land of the red people." NICKNAME Sooner State. CAPITAL Oklahoma City. ENTERED UNION Nov. 16, 1907 (46th). MOTTO *Labor omnia vincit* (Work overcomes all obstacles).

Emblems ANIMAL American buffalo. BIRD Scissor-tailed flycatcher. COLORS Green and white. FISH White bass. FLORAL EMBLEM Mistletoe. GRASS Indian grass. POEM "Howdy Folks." REPTILE Collared lizard (mountain boomer). SONG "Oklahoma!" STONE Barite rose (rose rock). TREE Redbud. WALTZ "Oklahoma Wind."

Land TOTAL AREA 69,956 sq. mi. (18th), incl. 1,301 sq. mi. inland water. BORDERS Kans., Mo., Ark., Tex., N.Mex., Colo. RIVERS Arkansas, Canadian, Cimarron, Red. LAKES Canton, Lake o' the Cherokees, Oologah, Texoma. OTHER NOTABLE FEATURES Ouachita Mts., Ozark Plateau, Staked Plain, Wichita Mts.

Elected officials Gov. Frank Keating (R, term exp. 1999). Lt. Gov. Mary Fallin (R). Sec. State Tom Cole (R). Atty. Gen. Drew Edmondson (R).

People (1994) 3,258,069 (28th). RACE/NATIONAL ORIGIN (1990): White 82.1%. Black 7.4%. Indian 8.0%. Asian 1.1%. Other 1.3%. Hispanic 2.7%.

Cities (1990) Oklahoma City 444,719. Tulsa 367,302. Lawton 80,561. Norman 80,071. Broken Arrow 58,043. Edmond 52,315. Midwest City 52,267. Enid 45,309. Moore 40,318. Muskogee 37,708.

Business GROSS STATE PRODUCT (GSP, 1992) $60.19 bil. (29th). SECTORS OF GSP: Farms 3.12%; agricultural services, forestry, and fisheries 0.35%; mining 7.54%; construction 2.89%; manufacturing 15.65%; transportation and public utilities 9.86%; wholesale trade 5.83%; retail trade 9.99%; finance, insurance, and real estate 14.80%; services 15.55%; federal government 3.56%; federal military 1.71%; state and local government 9.16%. *FORTUNE* 500 COMPANIES (1994): 5: Fleming, Phillips Petroleum, Kerr-McGee, Mapco, Williams.

Famous natives Ralph Ellison, author. Woody Guthrie, reformer/musician. Patrick J. Hurley, diplomat. Karl Jansky, electrical engineer. Mickey Mantle, baseball player. Wiley Post, aviator. Tony Randall, actor. Oral Roberts, evangelist. Will Rogers, humorist. Maria Tallchief, ballerina. Jim Thorpe, athlete.

Noteworthy places American Indian Hall of Fame, Anadarko. Chisholm Trail Museum, Kingfisher. Ft. Gibson Stockade, Muskogee. Natl. Cowboy Hall of Fame, Oklahoma City. Ouachita Natl. Forest. Pioneer Woman Museum, Ponca City. Will Rogers Memorial, Claremore.

Memorable events Francisco Vásquez de Coronado expedition in territory 1541. Except for panhandle, becomes part of Louisiana Purchase 1803. Region made Indian Territory (not organized) in 1830 and becomes home of "Five Civilized Tribes"—Cherokee, Choctaw, Chickasaw, Creek, and Seminole—after they left the southeast on Trail of Tears 1828–46. United States acquires panhandle with annexation of Texas 1845.

Territory opened to homesteaders 1889. Commercial oil well at Bartlesville 1897. Indian Territory and Oklahoma Territory merged and granted statehood 1907. Gov. John C. Walton impeached after declaring martial law to quell violence 1923. McClellan-Kerr Arkansas River Navigation system links Oklahoma to Mississippi, making Catoosa (Tulsa) major inland port 1971.
Tourist information 1–800–652–6552 or 1–405–521–2409.

Oregon

Although the Lewis and Clark expedition reached the mouth of the Columbia River in 1805, interest in the area was kindled by the Hudson's Bay Company and later by Jason Lee, a Methodist minister who settled near Salem in 1834. After the decline of the fur trade, lumbering became the most important industry in Oregon. Though lumbering and related industries are still leading employers—the state is the leading grower of Christmas trees—Oregon has benefited from the arrival of smaller computer and electronics firms leaving California in search of a more favorable business climate. Traditionally progressive, it is one of the most active states in the environmental protection movement. Only one-third of the population is affiliated with an organized religion.

NAME Unknown origin, first applied to Columbia River. NICKNAME Beaver State. CAPITAL Salem. ENTERED UNION Feb. 14, 1859 (33rd). MOTTO "The Union." POET LAUREATE William E. Stafford.
Emblems ANIMAL Beaver. BIRD Western meadowlark. DANCE Square dance. FISH Chinook salmon. FLOWER Oregon grape. INSECT Swallowtail butterfly. SONG "Oregon, My Oregon." STONE Thunderegg. TREE Douglas fir.
Land TOTAL AREA 97,073 sq. mi. (10th), incl. 889 sq. mi. inland water. BORDERS Wash., Idaho, Nev., Calif., Pacific Ocean. RIVERS Columbia, Snake, Willamette. MOUNTAINS Cascade Range, Coast Range, Klamath. OTHER NOTABLE FEATURES Willamette Valley.
Elected officials Gov. John Kitzhaber (D, term exp. 1999). Sec. State Phil Keisling (D). Atty. Gen. Theodore R. Kulongoski (D).
People (1994) 3,086,188 (29th). RACE/NATIONAL ORIGIN (1990): White 92.8%. Black 1.6%. Indian 1.4%. Asian 2.4%. Other 1.8%. Hispanic 4.0%.
Cities (1990) Portland 437,319. Eugene 112,669. Salem 107,786. Gresham 68,235. Beaverton 53,310. Medford 46,951. Corvallis 44,757. Springfield 44,683. Hillsboro 37,520. Lake Oswego 30,576.
Business GROSS STATE PRODUCT (GSP, 1992) $62.72 bil. (28th). SECTORS OF GSP: Farms 2.88%; agricultural services, forestry, and fisheries 1.10%; mining 0.15%; construction 4.14%; manufacturing 19.53%; transportation and public utilities 9.35%; wholesale trade 7.42%; retail trade 9.43%; Finance, insurance, and real estate 16.13%; services 17.49%; federal government 2.90%; federal military 0.35%; state and local government 9.12%. *FORTUNE* 500 COMPANIES (1994): 6: Nike, Pacificorp, Thrifty Payless Holdings, Fred Meyer, Louisiana-Pacific, Willamette Industries.
Famous natives In-mut-too-yah-lat-lat (Joseph), Nez Percé chief. Edwin Markham, poet. Dr. John McLoughlin, fur trader, "Father of Oregon." Linus Pauling, chemist. John Reed, author. William Simon U'Ren (b. Wis.), lawyer/reformer.
Noteworthy places Bonneville Dam, Columbia River. Columbia River Gorge. Columbia River Museum, Astoria. Crater Lakes Natl. Park. Ft. Clatsop Natl. Monument. Hells Canyon. High Desert Museum, Bend. John Day Fossil Beds Natl. Monument. Mt. Hood. Oregon Caves Natl. Monument. Oregon Dunes Natl. Recreation Area. Point Perpetua. Timberline Lodge.
Memorable events Sir Francis Drake turns away from fogbound coast of Pacific Northwest 1578. Capt. James Cook visits 1778. Mouth of Columbia River explored by Capt. Robert Gray, who claims region for U.S. 1792. Meriwether Lewis and George Rogers Clark expedition arrives at mouth of Columbia 1805. Claims to Oregon Territory, from California border to Alaska and east to Montana and Wyoming, relinquished by Spain (1819), Russia (1825), and Britain (1846). First settlers arrive Willamette Valley 1843. Organized as territory 1848. Statehood 1859. Railroad arrives 1883. Bonneville Dam completed 1937. Following severe rain and snow that claim 40 lives, Oregon declared disaster area 1964. First state to enact "bottle law" 1972. Snake River opened to navigation, linking Astoria to Lewiston, Idaho 1975.
Tourist information 1–800–547–7842.

Pennsylvania, Commonwealth of

William Penn and his Quakers encouraged settlement and religious tolerance, and Pennsylvania was the first state to abolish slavery. In the late colonial period, Philadelphia was the cultural capital of the colonies. The first Continental Congress convened there in 1774, and it was for a decade the U.S. capital. With access to both the Great Lakes and to the Atlantic, Pennsylvanians took a lead in opening up the Midwest. Its resources include large coal deposits—which contribute to its iron-making capabilities—lumber, textiles, and leather. Leadership in these sectors lasted well into the 20th century, when Pennsylvania lost ground to Sunbelt states. As in many states, there has been growth in tourist and service industries, though machinery production and trade continue to expand significantly.

NAME For Adm. William Penn, father of William Penn, founder of commonwealth. NICKNAME Keystone State. CAPITAL Harrisburg. ENTERED UNION Dec. 12, 1787 (2nd). MOTTO "Virtue, liberty and independence."
Emblems ANIMAL White-tailed deer. BEAUTIFICATION AND CONSERVATION PLANT Penngift crown vetch. BEVERAGE Milk. BIRD Ruffed grouse. DOG Great dane. FISH Brook trout. FLOWER Mountain laurel. INSECT Firefly. SONG "Pennsylvania." TREE Hemlock.
Land TOTAL AREA 45,308 sq. mi. (33rd), incl. 420 sq. mi. inland water. BORDERS N.Y., N.J., Del., Md., W.Va., Ohio, Lake Erie. RIVERS Allegheny, Delaware, Juniata, Monongahela, Ohio, Schuylkill, Susquehanna. LAKES Allegheny Res., Erie, Pymatuning Res., Shenango Res. MOUNTAINS Allegheny, Kittatinny, Laurel Hills, Pocono.
Elected officials Gov. Tom Ridge (R, term exp. 1999). Lt. Gov. Mark Schwieker (R). Sec. State Robert N. Grant (D). Atty. Gen. Ernest D. Preate, Jr. (R).
People (1994) 12,052,367 (5th). RACE/NATIONAL ORIGIN (1990): White 88.5%. Black 9.2%. Indian 0.1%. Asian 1.2%. Other 1.0%. Hispanic 2.0%.
Cities (1990) Philadelphia 1,585,577. Pittsburgh 369,879. Erie 108,718. Allentown 105,090. Scranton 81,805. Reading 78,380. Bethlehem 71,428. Lancaster 55,551. Harrisburg 52,376. Altoona 51,881.
Business GROSS STATE PRODUCT (GSP, 1992) $266.97 bil. (6th). SECTORS OF GSP: Farms 0.85%; agricultural services, forestry, and fisheries 0.37%; mining 0.75%; construction 4.63%; manufacturing 20.41%; transportation and public utilities 9.36%; wholesale trade 6.16%; retail trade 9.14%; finance, insurance, and real estate 17.83%; services 20.55%; federal government 2.50%; federal military 0.42%; state and local government 7.08%. *FORTUNE* 500 COMPANIES (1994): 33: including Cigna, USX, Bell Atlantic, ALCOA, Westinghouse Electric, Union-Pacific, Alco Standard, Sun, UNISYS, H.J. Heinz, PPG Industries, Bethlehem Steel, Scott Paper, Rite Aid, Mellon Bank Corp., Conrail, Hershey Foods, U.S. Healthcare, York International.
Famous natives Louisa May Alcott, author. Maxwell Anderson, playwright. James Buchanan, U.S. president. Alexander Calder, sculptor. Andrew Carnegie (b. Scotland), industrialist/philanthropist. Mary Cassatt, painter. Wilt Chamberlain, basketball player. Bill Cosby, comedian/philanthropist. Stephen Foster, songwriter. Benjamin Franklin (b. Mass.), inventor/statesman. Robert Fulton, inventor. Milton S. Hershey, chocolatier. George C. Marshall, statesman. Andrew W. Mellon, financier/philanthropist. Robert E. Peary, explorer. Betsy Ross, patriot. Andy Warhol, artist. Johnny Weismuller, swimmer/actor. Benjamin West, painter.
Noteworthy places Academy of Natural Sciences, Philadelphia. Carnegie Institute, Pittsburgh. Delaware Water Gap Natl. Recreation Area. Ft. Necessity Natl. Battlefield. Franklin Institute, Philadelphia. Gettysburg Battlefield. Hugh Moore Hist. Park and Museums, Easton. Independence Natl. Hist. Park, Philadelphia. Liberty Bell, Carpenters Hall, Philadelphia. Pennsylvania Academy of Fine Arts, Philadelphia. Pennsylvania Dutch Country. Philadelphia Museum of Art. Pine Creek Gorge. Valley Forge Natl. Hist. Park.
Memorable events Cornelis Jacobssen sails into Delaware Bay 1614. Swedes settle at Tinicum Island 1643. Charles II grants proprietary charter to William Penn 1681. First U.S. hospital established, in Philadelphia, 1751. Mason-Dixon Line establishes southern boundary of state 1763–67—later, boundary between slave and nonslave states. Declaration of Independence (1776) and Constitution (1787) signed in

Philadelphia. Becomes first state to abolish slavery 1780. Bank of North America becomes first bank chartered in United States 1781. Philadelphia capital of United States 1790–1800. First iron furnace in United States 1792. First oil well in the world driven near Titusville 1859. Battle of Gettysburg turning point in Civil War; Lincoln's Gettysburg Address 1863. Centennial Exhibition at Philadelphia 1876. Johnstown flood—worst in U.S. history—kills 2,200 people 1889. Pinkerton detectives kill 12 strikers at Homestead steel works near Pittsburgh 1892. Twenty coal miners killed during strike for eight-hour day and other concessions 1897. More than 500 injured during three-day race riot in Philadelphia 1964. Partial meltdown at Three Mile Island forces closure of nuclear reactor 1979. Storage tank spills 713,000 gallons diesel fuel into Monongahela River, disrupting water supplies in Pennsylvania, West Virginia, and Ohio 1988.

Tourist information 1-800-VISITPA.

Rhode Island and Providence Plantations

Giovanni de Verrazano was the first European to record visiting the area of Narragansett Bay, the prominent inlet that almost splits the eastern third of the state from the rest. The first settlers were followers of Roger Williams, who left the restrictive religious atmosphere of the Puritan Massachusetts Bay Colony to found Providence in 1636. Rhode Island is the site of the first U.S. Baptist church, at Providence, and at Newport the first Quaker meetinghouse and the first synagogue. It was the last of the 13 original colonies to ratify the Constitution, the centralized federalism of which many Rhode Islanders objected to. The development of 19th-century Rhode Island was influenced by immigration and the Industrial Revolution; the state's leading manufactures are still silver, jewelry, and textiles.

NAME For Rhode Island in Narragansett Bay, named in turn for Mediterranean island of Rhodes. NICKNAMES Ocean State, Little Rhody. CAPITAL Providence. ENTERED UNION May 29, 1790 (13th). MOTTO "Hope."

Emblems BIRD Rhode Island red. FLOWER Violet. MINERAL Bowenite. ROCK Cumberlandite. SONG "Rhode Island." TREE Red maple.

Land TOTAL AREA 1,212 sq. mi. (50th), incl. 157 sq. mi. inland water. BORDERS Mass., Atlantic Ocean, Conn. RIVERS Blackstone, Pawcatuck, Providence, Sakonnet. OTHER NOTABLE FEATURES Block Island, Narragansett Bay, Rhode Island (Aquidneck Island).

Elected officials Gov. Lincoln Almond (R, term exp. 1999). Lt. Gov. Robert A. Weygand (D). Sec. State James Langevine (D). Atty. Gen. Jeffrey B. Pine (R).

People (1994) 996,757 (43rd). RACE/NATIONAL ORIGIN (1990): White 91.4%. Black 3.9%. Indian 0.4%. Asian 1.8%. Other 2.5%. Hispanic 4.6%.

Cities (1990) Providence 160,728. Warwick 85,427. Cranston 76,060. Pawtucket 72,644. East Providence 50,380. Woonsocket 43,877. Newport 28,227. Central Falls 17,637.

Business GROSS STATE PRODUCT (GSP, 1992) $21.58 bil. (45th). SECTORS OF GSP: Farms 0.27%; agricultural services, forestry, and fisheries 0.70%; mining 0.04%; construction 4.46%; manufacturing 20.97%; transportation and public utilities 5.80%; wholesale trade 5.27%; retail trade 9.49%; finance, insurance, and real estate 21.04%; services 20.54%; federal government 1.87%; federal military 1.85%; state and local government 7.71%. *FORTUNE* 500 COMPANIES (1994): 3: Textron, Fleet Financial Group, Hasbro.

Famous natives George M. Cohan, actor/producer. Nathanael Greene, army officer. Metacomet (King Philip), Wampanoag chief. Oliver H. Perry and Matthew C. Perry, naval officers. Gilbert Stuart, portraitist.

Noteworthy places John Carter Brown Library, Providence. First Baptist church in North America (1638), Providence. Ft. Adams State Park, Newport. Nathanael Greene homestead, Coventry. Hoffenreffer Museum of Anthropology, Bristol. Museum of Art of the Rhode Island School of Design, Providence. Naval War College Museum, Newport. Newport mansions. Museum of Yachting, Newport. Tennis Hall of Fame, Newport. Trouro Synagogue (1763, oldest extant in North America), Newport.

Memorable events Roger Williams, expelled from Massachusetts Bay Colony, settles in Providence 1636. Other religious exiles settle in Portsmouth (1638), Newport (1639), and Warwick (1642). King Philip's War 1675–76. First Quaker meetinghouse in North America founded 1699. First colony to renounce allegiance to Britain 1776. Last colony to ratify Constitution 1790. Dorr's Rebellion achieves liberalization of state constitution, which had remained unchanged since 1663, 1842. America's Cup race held in Newport for first time 1930. Newport Bridge across Narragansett Bay completed 1969. *Australia II* first non–United States boat to win America's Cup in 132 years 1983.

Tourist information 1-800-556-2484 or 1-401-277-2601.

South Carolina

South Carolina's early economy was based on rice—its plantations worked by slaves—though tobacco later played a major role. As was true in North Carolina, many settlers made their way into the back country where they eked out a living as tenant farmers. During the Revolution, Ft. Charlotte was the first British installation to fall to Colonial troops, and at the outbreak of the Civil War, Ft. Sumter was the first Union installation to fall to Confederate forces. While agriculture remained a staple of the state's economy through the close of the 19th century, textile manufacture took over in the early 20th century. The postwar era has seen the rapid expansion of the chemical and paper industries, as well as large-scale development of the Atlantic Coast ports of Charleston, Georgetown, and Port Royal. In September 1989, Hurricane Hugo took 24 lives and caused $6 billion in property damage. According to some officials, relief efforts were hampered by widespread illiteracy, a crisis worsened by—or due to—the doubling of the high school dropout rate between 1986 and 1990.

NAME For King Charles II (Carolus is Latin for Charles). NICKNAME Palmetto State. CAPITAL Columbia. ENTERED UNION May 23, 1788 (8th). MOTTO *Animis opibusque parati* (Prepared in mind and deed); *Dum spiro spero* (While I breathe I hope). POET LAUREATE Helen von Kolnitz Hyer.

Emblems ANIMAL White-tailed deer. BEVERAGE Milk. BIRD Carolina wren. DANCE Shag. DOG Boykin spaniel. FISH Striped bass. FLOWER Yellow jessamine. FRUIT Peach. SHELL Lettered olive. SONG "Carolina." STONE Blue granite. TREE Palmetto. WILD GAME BIRD Wild turkey.

Land TOTAL AREA 31,113 sq. mi. (40th), incl. 910 sq. mi. inland water. BORDERS N.C., Atlantic Ocean, Ga. RIVERS Congaree, Edisto, Pee Dee, Savannah, Tugalos, Wateree. LAKES Greenwood, Hartwell, Keowee, Marion, Murray, Santee Res., Wylie. OTHER NOTABLE FEATURES Blue Ridge Mts., Congaree Swamp, Sea Islands.

Elected officials Gov. David Beasley (R, term exp. 1999). Lt. Gov. Bob Peeler (R). Sec. State Jim Miles (R). Atty. Gen. Charlie Condon (R).

People (1994) 3,663,984 (25th). RACE/NATIONAL ORIGIN (1990): White 69.0%. Black 29.8%. Indian 0.2%. Asian 0.6%. Other 0.3%. Hispanic 0.9%.

Cities (1990) Columbia 98,052. Charleston 80,414. North Charleston 70,218. Greenville 58,282. Spartanburg 43,467. Sumter 41,943. Rock Hill 41,643. Mount Pleasant Town 30,108. Florence 29,813. Anderson 26,184.

Business GROSS STATE PRODUCT (GSP, 1992) $69.81 bil. (27th). SECTORS OF GSP: Farms 0.88%; agricultural services, forestry, and fisheries 0.43%; mining 0.24%; construction 5.75%; manufacturing 25.31%; transportation and public utilities 8.80%; wholesale trade 4.90%; retail trade 10.53%; finance, insurance, and real estate 13.21%; services 14.15%; federal government 2.44%; federal military 3.51%; state and local government 9.86%. *FORTUNE* 500 COMPANIES (1994): 2: Flagstar, Sonoco Products.

Famous natives James F. Byrnes, politician/jurist. John C. Calhoun, politician. Dizzy Gillespie, musician. Althea Gibson, athlete. DuBose Heyward, author. Andrew Jackson, U.S. president. Eartha Kitt, singer. James Longstreet, army officer. Francis Marion, army officer/politician. Charles C. Pinckney and Thomas Pinckney, diplomats. Edward Rutledge and John Rutledge, politicians. Strom Thurmond, politician.

Noteworthy places Charleston Museum (1773, oldest in United States). Congaree Swamp Natl. Monument. Cowpens Natl. Battlefield. Ft. Moultrie, Ft. Johnson, and Ft. Sumter Natl. Monument, Charleston. Hilton Head Island. Kings Mountain Natl. Military Park. Ninety-Six Natl. Hist. Site, Greenwood. Patriots Point Maritime Museum, Charleston. Sea Islands. Spoleto Music Festival, Charleston.

Memorable events Spanish visit 1521. French Huguenots at Port Royal 1562. Included in

Carolina grant by Charles II 1663. Charleston founded 1680. Becomes royal province 1729. Ratifies Constitution 1787. *Best Friend of Charleston*, first American steam locomotive built for passenger use 1833. First state to secede from Union Dec. 20, 1860. Confederate forces attack Ft. Sumter Apr. 12, 1861. Secession repealed 1865. Readmitted to Union 1868. Cyclone kills 1,000 in Savannah, Georgia, and Charleston 1893. Savannah River nuclear plant begins production near Aiken 1951; closed for safety reasons 1988.

Tourist information 1–803–734–0122.

South Dakota

The United States did not organize the Dakota Territory until 1861, and even then interest in the region was scant until gold was discovered in 1874. The majority of those who remained after the gold rush turned to cattle ranching, which was a mainstay of the economy through the first half of the 20th century. A manufacturing base was developed after four major dams were built on the Missouri River in the 1930s. They provided hydroelectric power and increased irrigation along the Missouri, which cuts the state in half. Concerned especially over the abrogation of 19th-century treaties, the American Indian Movement (AIM) took over the courthouse at Wounded Knee for 10 weeks in 1973. While U.S. courts have found in favor of the Sioux in several cases concerning the earlier treaties, many maintain that the settlements are insufficient, and the disparity in living conditions between whites and Native Americans remains pronounced.

NAME For southern section of Dakota territory; *dakota* is Sioux word for "allies." NICKNAMES Coyote State, Sunshine State. CAPITAL Pierre. ENTERED UNION Nov. 2, 1889 (40th). MOTTO "Under God the people rule."

Emblems ANIMAL Coyote. BIRD Chinese ring-necked pheasant. FISH Walleye. FLOWER Pasque flower. GEM Fairburn agate. GRASS Western wheatgrass. INSECT Honeybee. MINERAL Rose quartz. SONG "Hail, South Dakota." TREE Black Hills spruce.

Land TOTAL AREA 77,116 sq. mi. (16th), incl. 1,164 sq. mi. inland water. BORDERS N.Dak., Minn., Iowa, Nebr., Wyo., Mont. RIVERS Cheyenne, James, Missouri, Moreau, White. LAKES Belle Fourche Res., Big Stone, Traverse. OTHER NOTABLE FEATURES Badlands, Black Hills (Harney Peak 7,242 ft.).

Elected officials Gov. Bill Janklow (R, term exp. 1999). Lt. Gov. Carol Hillard (R). Sec. State Joyce Hazeltine (R). Atty. Gen. Mark Barnett (R).

People (1994) 721,164 (45th). RACE/NATIONAL ORIGIN (1990): White 91.6%. Black 0.5%. Indian 7.3%. Asian 0.4%. Other 0.2%. Hispanic 0.8%.

Cities (1990) Sioux Falls 100,814. Rapid City 54,523. Aberdeen 24,927. Watertown 17,592. Brookings 16,270. Mitchell 13,798. Pierre 12,906. Yankton 12,703. Huron 12,448. Vermillion 10,034.

Business GROSS STATE PRODUCT (GSP, 1992) $15.13 bil. (48th). SECTORS OF GSP: Farms 13.41%; agricultural services, forestry, and fisheries 0.61%; mining 1.43%; construction 3.40%; manufacturing 8.80%; transportation and public utilities 7.93%; wholesale trade 6.03%; retail trade 9.90%; finance, insurance, and real estate 21.20%; services 14.30%; federal government 3.69%; federal military 1.90%; state and local government 7.40%. *FORTUNE* 500 COMPANIES (1994): 1: Gateway 2000.

Famous natives Tom Brokaw, journalist. Martha "Calamity" Jane Burk (b. Mo.) frontierswoman. Alvin Hansen, economist. Hubert H. Humphrey, politician. Ernest O. Lawrence, physicist (Nobel Prize, 1939). George McGovern, politician. Tasunko-witko (Crazy Horse), Oglala Sioux chief. Tatanka Iyotake (Sitting Bull), Sioux chief.

Noteworthy places Badlands Natl. Park. Crazy Horse State Memorial, Custer. Custer State Park. Ft. Sisseton. Geographical center of the United States. Jewel Cave Natl. Monument. Mount Rushmore Natl. Memorial. Wind Cave Natl. Park.

Memorable events French visit region 1742–43. Region to United States in Louisiana Purchase 1803. Ft. Pierre first permanent settlement 1817. Part of Dakota Territory 1861. Gold discovered in Black Hills 1874. Divided from North Dakota; statehood 1889. U.S. troops massacre Sioux at Battle of Wounded Knee 1890.

Tourist information 1–800–843–1930 or 1–800–952–2217.

Tennessee

At first claimed by Virginia and later by North Carolina, Tennessee had its first great pioneer in Daniel Boone, who traversed the region in the 1760s. Political attitudes in the 18th century were shaped by the land, with the cotton and tobacco growers in the fertile western part of the state favoring slavery and the backwoods people of the eastern hills opposed to it. The Cherokees were removed to Oklahoma by the federal government in the 1830s. The state was captured by Union troops in 1862 and put under the governorship of Andrew Johnson, later a U.S. president.

Its economy was radically altered in the 1930s and 1940s by the creation of the Tennessee Valley Authority, which provided abundant energy for industry, and to a lesser extent by the location of the government's first uranium enrichment facility at Oak Ridge during World War II. The state's leading industries are textiles, food processing, and chemicals, and there is considerable lead and coal mining in the east.

NAME For Tenase, principal village of Cherokees. NICKNAME Volunteer State. CAPITAL Nashville. ENTERED UNION June 1, 1796 (16th). MOTTO "Agriculture and commerce." SLOGAN "Tennessee—America at its best." POET LAUREATE Richard M. ("Pek") Gunn.

Emblems ANIMAL Raccoon. BIRD Mockingbird. FOLK DANCE Square dance. CULTIVATED FLOWER Iris. GEM Tennessee pearl. INSECTS Ladybug, firefly. POEM "Oh Tennessee, My Tennessee." PUBLIC SCHOOL SONG "My Tennessee." ROCK Limestone agate. SONGS "When It's Iris Time in Tennessee," "The Tennessee Waltz," "My Homeland, Tennessee," "Rocky Top." TREE Tulip poplar. WILDFLOWER Passion flower.

Land TOTAL AREA 42,144 sq. mi. (34th), incl. 989 sq. mi. inland water. BORDERS Ky., Va., N.C., Ga., Ala., Miss., Ark., Mo. RIVERS Clinch, Cumberland, Mississippi, Tennessee. LAKES Boone, Center Hill, Cherokee, Dale Hollow, Douglass, J. Percy Priest, Watauga. OTHER NOTABLE FEATURES Cumberland Mts., Great Smoky Mts., Tennessee Valley, Unaka Mts.

Elected officials Gov. Don Sundquist (R, term exp. 1999). Lt. Gov. John Wilder (D). Sec. State Riley Darnell (D). Atty Gen. Charles Burson (D).

People (1994) 5,175,240 (17th). RACE/NATIONAL ORIGIN (1990): White 83.0%. Black 16.0%. Indian 0.2%. Asian 0.7%. Other 0.2%. Hispanic 0.7%.

Cities (1990) Memphis 610,337. Nashville–Davidson (CC) 510,784. Knoxville 165,121. Chattanooga 152,466. Clarksville 75,494. Johnson City 49,381. Jackson 48,949. Murfreesboro 44,922. Kingsport 36,365. Germantown 32,893.

Business GROSS STATE PRODUCT (GSP, 1992) $108.89 bil. (20th). SECTORS OF GSP: Farms 1.22%; agricultural services, forestry, and fisheries 0.36%; mining 0.38%; construction 3.91%; manufacturing 23.26%; transportation and public utilities 7.45%; wholesale trade 7.08%; retail trade 11.34%; finance, insurance, and real estate 14.41%; services 17.74%; federal government 4.43%; federal military 0.71%; state and local government 7.68%. *FORTUNE* 500 COMPANIES (1994): 6: Columbia/HCA Healthcare, Federal Express, Eastman Chemical, Service Merchandise, HealthTrust, Provident Life & Accident Insurance.

Famous natives James Agee, author. Davy Crockett, frontiersman. David Farragut, naval officer. Aretha Franklin, singer. Cordell Hull, statesman (Nobel Peace Prize, 1945). Dolly Parton, singer. Sikawyi (Sequoya), Cherokee scholar. Alvin York, soldier.

Noteworthy places American Museum of Science and Energy, Oak Ridge. Andrew Johnson Natl. Hist. Site, Greenville. Chickamauga and Chattanooga Natl. Military Park. Cumberland Natl. Hist. Park. Ft. Donelson Natl. Military Park. Grand Ole Opry, Nashville. Great Smoky Mountains Natl. Park. The Hermitage (Andrew Jackson home), Nashville. Lookout Mountain, Chattanooga. The Parthenon, Nashville. Shiloh Natl. Military Park, Pittsburg Landing. Stones River Natl. Battlefield, Murfreesboro.

Memorable events De Soto expedition passes through region 1540. French claim territory as part of Louisiana; English claim territory as part of Carolina grant 1663. French claim given up after French and Indian War 1763. State of Franklin established in what is now eastern Tennessee 1784–87. Organized as Territory South of the Ohio 1790. Statehood 1796. Secedes from Union 1861. Battles of Shiloh (1862), Chattanooga (1863), Stones River (1863), and Nashville (1864). Readmitted to Union 1866. Clarence Darrow defends John T. Scopes for violating ban on teaching evolution in public schools; loses case 1925. Congress creates Tennessee Valley Authority 1933. First operational nuclear

reactor at Oak Ridge 1943. Martin Luther King assassinated at Memphis 1968.
Tourist information 1–615–741–2158.

Texas

The land that is Texas today was originally part of Spain's holdings in Mexico. After Mexico won independence, the new government invited U.S. citizens to settle there. After many clashes between the Mexican and Anglo cultures, Texas broke away and for 10 years was an independent country before becoming a state in 1845. Modern Texas was made by oil, discovered at Spindletop in 1901, and the state's economy has been tied to the oil market ever since. After World War II, the Texas economy soared, bringing both prosperity and an unprecedented population boom. With the oil glut of the early 1980s, growth came to a halt, causing a drastic realignment of economic priorities. Unemployment jumped more than 20 percent between 1980 and 1988, and remained higher than the national average in 1990, a year that saw many bank failures. The economy has been forced to diversify; currently the petroleum industry accounts for only 7 percent of state revenues, down from 25 percent a decade before. Texas has enormous resources ranging from cotton, cattle, and timber to aerospace, computers, and electronics. The largest of the 48 conterminous states, Texas's image as a state of wide-open spaces is understandable, but fully 80 percent of its people live in metropolitan areas, and Dallas, Houston, and San Antonio are among the nation's 10 largest cities. Twenty-five percent of the population is Hispanic, and the majority of those are Mexican-American.

NAME From Caddo *tavshas*, "friends." NICKNAME Lone Star State. CAPITAL Austin. ENTERED UNION Dec. 29, 1845 (28th). MOTTO "Friendship."
Emblems BIRD Mockingbird. DISH Chili. FLOWER Bluebonnet. GEM Topaz. GRASS Sideoats grama. SONGS "Texas, Our Texas," "The Eyes of Texas." STONE Palmwood. TREE Pecan.
Land TOTAL AREA 266,807 sq. mi. (2nd), incl. 4,790 sq. mi. inland water. BORDERS Okla., Ark., La., Gulf of Mexico, Tamaulipas, Coahuila, Chihuahua, N.Mex. RIVERS Brazos, Colorado, Natchez, Red, Rio Grande, Sabine, Trinity. LAKES Sam Rayburn Res., Texoma, Toledo Bend Res. OTHER NOTABLE FEATURES Balcomes Escarpment, Diablo Sierra, Edwards Plateau, Guadalupe Mts., Staked Plain, Stockton Plateau.
Elected officials Gov. George Walker Bush (R, term exp. 1999). Lt. Gov. Bob Bullock (D). Sec. State Antonio Garza (R). Atty. Gen. Dan Morales (D).
People (1994) 18,378,185 (2nd). RACE/NATIONAL ORIGIN (1990): White 75.2%. Black 11.9%. Indian 0.4%. Asian 1.9%. Other 10.6%. Hispanic 25.5%.
Cities (1990) Houston 1,630,553. Dallas 1,006,877. San Antonio 935,933. El Paso 515,342. Austin 465,622. Ft. Worth 447,619. Arlington 261,721. Corpus Christi 257,453. Lubbock 186,206. Garland 180,650.
Business GROSS STATE PRODUCT (GSP, 1992) $416.87 bil. (3rd). SECTORS OF GSP: Farms 1.41%; agricultural services, forestry, and fisheries 0.38%; mining 7.77%; construction 3.71%; manufacturing 17.57%; transportation and public utilities 10.14%; wholesale trade 6.68%; retail trade 9.38%; finance, insurance, and real estate 15.39%; services 16.72%; federal government 2.05%; federal military 1.15%; state and local government 7.85%. *FORTUNE* 500 COMPANIES (1994): 36: including Exxon, J.C. Penney, AMR, Tenneco, SBC Communications, SYSCO, Compaq Computer, Texas Instruments, Coastal, Enron, Kimberly-Clark, Continental Airlines, Burlington Northern, Tandy, Browning-Ferris Industries, Dell Computer, Centex, Southwest Airlines, Pennzoil.
Famous natives Stephen Austin (b. Va.), pioneer. James "Jim" Bowie (b. Ky.), army officer. Carol Burnett, comedian. J. Frank Dobie, folklorist. Dwight D. Eisenhower, U.S. president/general. Samuel Houston (b. Va.), president Republic of Texas/governor state of Texas. Howard Hughes, industrialist/aviator. Lyndon Baines Johnson, U.S. president. Janis Joplin, singer. Barbara Jordan, politician. Audie Murphy, soldier/actor. Chester Nimitz, navy officer. Katherine Anne Porter, author. Samuel T. Rayburn, politician. Mildred "Babe" Didrikson Zaharias, athlete.
Noteworthy places The Alamo, San Antonio. Alibates Flint Quarries Natl. Monument. Big Bend Natl. Park. Ft. Davis. Galveston Historical Foundation. Guadalupe Mountains Natl. Park. Houston Museum of Fine Arts. Lyndon B. Johnson Natl. Hist. Park, Johnson City. Lyndon B. Johnson Space Center, Houston. Old Stone Ft., Nacogdoches. Padre Island Natl. Seashore. San Antonio Missions Natl. Hist. Park. Texas Ranger Museum, Waco.
Memorable events Alonso Alvarez de Piñeda sails along coast 1519. Estevanico blazes trail through West Texas 1539. Spanish establish settlement at Ysleta near El Paso 1682. René-Robert Cavelier de La Salle attempts to found colony on Matagorda Bay, establishing claim to region for France 1685. Effective Spanish occupation 1715. United States acquires French claim to region with Louisiana Purchase 1803. United States relinquishes claim to Spain 1819. Americans move into region in early 19th century. Mexico, of which Texas is a province, wins independence from Spain 1821. Declaration of Independence from Mexico; Santa Anna victor at Battle of the Alamo; Sam Houston victor at Battle of San Jacinto; founding of Republic of Texas 1836. Texas granted statehood by United States 1845. Secedes from Union 1861; readmitted 1870. Hurricane kills 6,000 at Galveston 1900. NASA Space Center opens at Houston 1962. Pres. Kennedy assassinated at Dallas 1963.
Tourist information 1–800–888–8TEX.

Utah

In the middle of the Great Basin between the Rocky Mountains and the Sierra Nevada, Utah was an arid and uninviting region. After Joseph Smith, the founder of the Church of Jesus Christ of Latter-day Saints (Mormons), was shot in Illinois, Brigham Young led his people west, ultimately to the Salt Lake Valley in 1847. The chief obstacle to statehood was polygamy, which the church eventually renounced. There was an influx of non-Mormons after the discovery of silver in 1863, but Mormons still comprise two-thirds of the state's population, and the state remains conservative in outlook. Although the federal government is a major employer, government policy has lately been challenged by increased concern over the issues of chemical weapons testing, the MX missile, and disposal of nuclear waste from the Rocky Mountain Arsenal in neighboring Colorado.

NAME For Ute Indians. NICKNAMES Beehive State, Mormon State. CAPITAL Salt Lake City. ENTERED UNION Jan. 4, 1896 (45th). MOTTO "Industry."
Emblems ANIMAL Elk. BIRD Seagull. EMBLEM Beehive. FISH Rainbow trout. FLOWER Sego lily. GEM Topaz. SONG "Utah, We Love Thee." TREE Blue spruce.
Land TOTAL AREA 84,899 sq. mi. (11th), incl. 2,826 sq. mi. inland water. BORDERS Idaho, Wyo., Colo., Ariz., Nev. RIVERS Bear, Colorado, Green, Sevier. LAKES Bear, Great Salt, Utah. MOUNTAINS La Sal, Uinta (Kings Peak 13,528 ft.), Wasatch Range. OTHER NOTABLE FEATURES Great Salt Lake Desert (Bonneville Salt Flats), Kaibab Plateau.
Elected officials Gov. Mike Leavitt (R, term exp. 1997). Lt. Gov. Orlene Walker (R). Atty. Gen. Jan Graham (D).
People (1994) 1,907,936 (34th). RACE/NATIONAL ORIGIN (1990): White 93.8%. Black 0.7%. Indian 1.4%. Asian 1.9%. Other 2.2%. Hispanic 4.9%.
Cities (1990) Salt Lake City 159,936. West Valley City 86,976. Provo 86,835. Sandy 75,058. Orem 67,561. Ogden 63,909. Taylorsville-Bennion 52,351. West Jordan 42,892. Layton 41,784. Bountiful 36,659.
Business GROSS STATE PRODUCT (GSP, 1992) $35.59 bil. (37th). SECTORS OF GSP: Farms 1.40%; agricultural services, forestry, and fisheries 0.24%; mining 4.33%; construction 3.71%; manufacturing 15.22%; transportation and public utilities 10.48%; wholesale trade 6.20%; retail trade 9.35%; finance, insurance, and real estate 15.02%; services 18.32%; federal government 4.95%; federal military 0.99%; state and local government 9.79%. *FORTUNE* 500 COMPANIES (1994): 2: American Stores, Smith's Food & Drug Centers.
Famous natives Maude Adams, actress. John Moses Browning, inventor. Philo Farnsworth, engineer. Merlin Olsen, football player/actor. Ivy Baker Priest, U.S. treasurer. Brigham Young (b. Vt.), religious leader. Loretta Young, actress.
Noteworthy places Arches Natl. Park. Bryce Canyon Natl. Park. Canyonlands Natl. Park. Capitol Reef Natl. Park. Cedar Breaks Natl. Monument. Dinosaur Natl. Monument. Flaming Gorge Dam Natl. Monument. Great Salt Lake. Lake Powell Natl. Monument. Monument Valley. Mormon Tabernacle, Salt Lake City. Natural Bridges Natl. Monument. Promontory Point. Rainbow Bridge Natl. Monument. Temple Square, Salt Lake City. Timpanogas Cave Natl. Monument. Zion Natl. Park.

Memorable events First visited probably by explorers from Coronado expedition 1540. Silvestre Vélez de Escalante and Francisco Atanasio Dominguez explore for Spain 1776. James Bridger discovers Great Salt Lake 1824. Led by Brigham Young, Mormons reach Great Salt Lake 1847. United States acquires Utah region from Mexico 1848. Mormons organize state of Deseret 1849; Congress refuses to recognize and instead organizes Territory of Utah 1850. Silver discovered at Little Cottonwood Canyon 1868. First transcontinental railroad completed with driving of golden spike at Promontory Point 1869. Mormon church renounces polygamy 1890, paving way to statehood 1896. Uranium discovered near Moab 1952.
Tourist information 1–801–538–1030.

Vermont

Originally claimed by both New Hampshire and New York, Vermont's independence was asserted by Ethan Allen. His Green Mountain Boys rid the state of New Yorkers in 1770, fought well against the British in the Revolution, and declared the independent republic of New Connecticut in 1777. Allen was eventually overthrown, and Vermont joined the Union in 1791.

Vermont traditionally has strong ties to Canada, and there was an influx of French-Canadians as Vermont began to develop its manufacturing base in the mid-19th century. Vermont's politics have always been characterized by tolerance and progressivism. As New Connecticut, it abolished slavery and allowed universal male suffrage. More recently, Bernard Sanders, Socialist mayor of Burlington from 1981 to 1989, was elected to Congress in 1990, where he serves as an Independent. Vermont's environmental concerns focus on acid rain and the degree to which development (especially by the tourist industry) should infringe on the state's remaining unspoiled land.

NAME From French *vert mont*, "green mountain." NICKNAME Green Mountain State. CAPITAL Montpelier. ENTERED UNION Mar. 4, 1791 (14th). MOTTO "Freedom and unity."
Emblems ANIMAL Morgan horse. BEVERAGE Milk. BIRD Hermit thrush. COLD-WATER FISH Brook trout. FLOWER Red clover. INSECT Honeybee. SONG "Hail, Vermont!" TREE Sugar maple. WARM-WATER FISH Walleye pike.
Land TOTAL AREA 9,614 sq. mi. (43rd), incl. 341 sq. mi. inland water. BORDERS Quebec, N.H., Mass., N.Y. RIVERS Connecticut, Lamoille, Otter Creek, Poultney, White, Winooski. LAKES Bomoseen, Champlain, Memphremagog, Willoughby. OTHER NOTABLE FEATURES Grand Isle, Green Mts. (Mt. Mansfield 4,393 ft.), Taconic Mts.
Elected officials Gov. Howard Dean (D, term exp. 1999). Lt. Gov. Barbara W. Snelling (R). Sec. State Jim Milne (R). Atty. Gen. Jeffrey L. Amestoy (R).
People (1994) 580,209 (49th). RACE/NATIONAL ORIGIN (1990): White 98.6%. Black 0.2%. Indian 0.1%. Asian 0.2%. Other 0.2%. Hispanic 0.5%.
Cities (1990) Burlington 37,712. Rutland 18,436. South Burlington 10,679. Barre 9,824. Essex Junction 7,033. Montpelier 8,241. St. Albans 7,308. Winooski 6,318. Newport 4,756. Bellows Falls 3,456.
Business GROSS STATE PRODUCT (GSP, 1992) $11.84 bil. (51st). SECTORS OF GSP: Farms 2.19%; agricultural services, forestry, and fisheries 0.65%; mining 0.28%; construction 5.56%; manufacturing 19.57%; transportation and public utilities 8.04%; wholesale trade 5.42%; retail trade 10.57%; finance, insurance, and real estate 17.97%; services 18.77%; federal government 2.12%; federal military 0.43%; state and local government 8.44%. *FORTUNE* 500 COMPANIES (1994): 0.
Famous natives Ethan Allen (b. Conn.), army officer. Chester A. Arthur, U.S. president. Calvin Coolidge, U.S. president. John Deere, industrialist. George Dewey, naval officer. John Dewey, philosopher. Stephen Douglas, politician. James Fisk, financier. Rudy Vallee, singer.
Noteworthy places Bennington Battleground/Monument. Calvin Coolidge Homestead, Plymouth. Maple Grove Maple Museum, Rock of Ages Tourist Center, Graniteville. Shelburne Museum. St. Johnsbury. Vermont Marble Exhibit, Proctor.
Memorable events Samuel de Champlain explores for France 1609. First French settlement at Ste. Anne 1666. First English settlers build Ft. Drummer near Brattleboro 1724. Bennington settled 1761. Ethan Allen organizes Green Mountain Boys 1764. Green Mountain Boys capture Ft. Ticonderoga and Ft. Crown Point 1775. Gen. John Stark defeats British general John Burgoyne near Bennington; constitution abolishes slavery and grants universal male suffrage 1777. Claims to area relinquished by Massachusetts (1781), New Hampshire (1782), and New York (1790). First state admitted after original 13 1791. MacDonough defeats British Lake Champlain fleet 1814. Canal between Hudson River and Lake Champlain gives Vermont direct access to port of New York 1823. Confederate soldiers steal $400,000 from St. Albans bank 1864. Blue law repealed, allowing stores to open on Sundays 1982.
Tourist information 1–802–828–3236 or 1–800–VERMONT.

Virginia, Commonwealth of

The first successful English settlement in America was at Jamestown in 1607. The differences between the Virginia colonists and those of Massachusetts were pronounced, and the commercial southern planter class shared little of their New England counterparts' religious zeal. Virginia bred its own strain of independence, and it was the fiery Patrick Henry who heralded the American Revolution with the cry "Give me liberty or give me death." Seven of the first 12 presidents were from Virginia. With an economy very dependent on labor-intensive tobacco in the mid-19th century, Virginia seceded from the Union over the slavery issue, despite the misgivings of many, including Robert E. Lee. After the war Virginia developed an increasingly diversified industrial and manufacturing base that survives today, with food products, tobacco, and chemicals leading the way. Despite the dramatic decline of the American merchant marine, Virginia's shipbuilding industry in Newport News flourished in the 1980s, thanks to the Pentagon's commitment to a 600-ship navy. Norfolk is also one of the country's leading commercial ports.

NAME For Elizabeth I, called Virgin Queen. NICKNAMES Old Dominion, Mother of Presidents, Mother of States. CAPITAL Richmond. ENTERED UNION June 25, 1788 (10th). MOTTO *Sic semper tyrannis* (Thus always to tyrants).
Emblems BEVERAGE Milk. BIRD Cardinal. DOG Foxhound. FLOWER Dogwood. SHELL Oyster. SONG "Carry Me Back to Old Virginia." TREE Dogwood.
Land TOTAL AREA 40,767 sq. mi. (36th), incl. 1,063 sq. mi. inland water. BORDERS Md., D.C., Atlantic Ocean, N.C., Tenn., Ky., W.Va. RIVERS James, Potomac, Rappahannock, Roanoke, Shenandoah, York. LAKES Buggs Island, Claytor, Gaston, Leesville. MOUNTAINS Allegheny, Blue Ridge, Cumberland, Unaka. OTHER NOTABLE FEATURES Great Dismal Swamp, Shenandoah Valley.
Elected officials Gov. George Allen, Jr. (R, term exp. 1998). Lt. Gov. Donald S. Beyer, Jr. (D). Sec. of State Betty Davis Beamer (R). Atty. Gen. James Gilmore (R).
People (1994) 6,551,522 (12th). RACE/NATIONAL ORIGIN (1990): White 77.4%. Black 18.8%. Indian 0.2%. Asian 2.6%. Other 0.9%. Hispanic 2.6%.
Cities (1990) Virginia Beach 393,069. Norfolk 261,229. Richmond 203,056. Newport News 170,045. Chesapeake 151,976. Hampton 133,793. Alexandria 111,183. Portsmouth 103,907. Roanoke 96,397. Lynchburg 66,049.
Business GROSS STATE PRODUCT (GSP, 1992) $153.81 bil. (12th). SECTORS OF GSP: Farms 0.85%; agricultural services, forestry, and fisheries 0.38%; mining 0.75%; construction 5.33%; manufacturing 16.23%; transportation and public utilities 8.51%; wholesale trade 5.31%; retail trade 9.31%; finance, insurance, and real estate 15.91%; services 18.28%; federal government 5.93%; federal military 5.30%; state and local government 7.90%. *FORTUNE* 500 COMPANIES (1994): 13: Mobil, CSX, USAir Group, Federal Home Loan Mortgage, Reynolds Metals, James River Corp. of Va., Norfolk Southern, Dominion Resources, Circuit City Stores, Gannett, General Dynamics, Universal, Owens & Minor.
Famous natives Richard E. Byrd, explorer/aviator. William Clark, explorer. Jerry Falwell, evangelist. William Henry Harrison, U.S. president. Patrick Henry, Revolutionary patriot. Thomas Jefferson, U.S. president. Joseph E. Johnston, Confederate general. John Paul Jones (b. Scotland), navy officer. Robert E. Lee, Confederate general. Meriwether Lewis, explorer. James Madison, U.S. president. John Marshall, jurist. Cyrus Hall McCormick, inventor. James Monroe, U.S. president. Walter Reed, doctor. Pat Robertson, evangelist/politician. Bill ("Bojangles") Robinson, dancer. George C. Scott, actor. Thomas Sumter, army officer. Zachary Taylor, U.S. president. John Tyler, U.S. president.

Booker T. Washington, educator. George Washington, U.S. president. Woodrow Wilson, U.S. president.

Noteworthy places Appomattox Courthouse Natl. Hist. Park. Arlington Natl. Cemetery. Booker T. Washington Natl. Monument, Roanoke. Colonial Natl. Hist. Park (incl. Jamestown, Yorktown, and Williamsburg). Fredericksburg and Spotsylvania Natl. Military Park. George Washington birthplace, Frederick Co. Harpers Ferry Natl. Hist. Site. The Mariners' Museum, Newport News. Monticello, Charlottesville. Mount Vernon. Petersburg Natl. Battlefield. Robert E. Lee Memorial, Lexington. Shenandoah Natl. Park. Virginia Beach. Virginia Museum of Fine Arts. Wolf Trap Farm for the Performing Arts, Reston.

Memorable events John Smith founds Jamestown, first permanent settlement in North America, 1607. John Rolfe marries Pocahontas, daughter of Powhatan, leader of so-called Powhatan Confederacy 1614. First English women arrive at Jamestown; House of Burgesses established 1619. Northampton Declaration first resistance to taxation without representation 1653. College of William and Mary founded 1693. First state to establish Committee of Correspondence 1773. American Revolution ends with Charles Cornwallis's surrender to George Washington at Yorktown 1781. Nat Turner's slave revolt 1831. State secedes from Union 1861. Civil War ends with Robert E. Lee's surrender to Ulysses S. Grant at Appomattox Courthouse 1865. Readmitted to Union 1870. Norfolk Naval Base founded 1917. John D. Rockefeller, Jr., undertakes restoration of Colonial Williamsburg 1926. E. Claiborne Robins donates $50 million to University of Richmond 1969.

Tourist information 1–800–VISITVA or 1–804–786–4484.

Washington

The northwest corner of the continental United States was originally the locus of a rich Native American culture noted today primarily for its ornately carved canoes and totem poles. In 1792, Boston merchant Capt. Robert Gray began a trade in sea otter pelts, but the first permanent settlers in the region did not establish themselves for almost 50 years. Agriculture and lumbering were, and remain, mainstays of the state's economy—the farming regions in the east, rich in dairy products, fruit and wheat, and the lumber industry in the western part of the state rely heavily on exports to the Far East. This geographic split reflects the weather patterns: eastern Washington rarely gets more than 10 inches of rain in a year, while on the Pacific Coast it rains almost every day.

Since World War I, Puget Sound has been a center of heavy industry and shipbuilding, and 60 percent of the population is concentrated in the region. Boeing maintains one of the country's largest airplane-manufacturing plants in the Seattle-Tacoma area. The industrial work force was open to progressive and sometimes radical unionism, and the International Workers of the World (Wobblies) had their national headquarters at Seattle. Before statehood the territorial government pioneered women's suffrage, but Congress declared the women's right to vote unconstitutional.

NAME For George Washington. NICKNAME Evergreen State. CAPITAL Olympia. ENTERED UNION Nov. 11, 1889 (42nd). MOTTO *Alki* (By and by).

Emblems BIRD Willow goldfinch. FISH Steelhead trout. FLOWER Western rhododendron. GEM Petrified wood. SONG "Washington, My Home." TREE Western hemlock.

Land TOTAL AREA 68,138 sq. mi. (20th), incl. 1,627 sq. mi. inland water. BORDERS British Columbia, Idaho, Oreg., Pacific Ocean. RIVERS Chehalis, Columbia, Pend Oreille, Snake, Yakima. LAKES Baker, Bank, Chelan, Franklin D. Roosevelt, Ross, Rufus Woods. MOUNTAINS Cascade Range, Coast Range, Kettle River Range, Olympic. OTHER NOTABLE FEATURES Puget Sound, San Juan Islands, Strait of Juan de Fuca.

Elected officials Gov. Mike Lowry (D, term exp. 1997). Lt. Gov. Joel Pritchard (R). Sec. State Ralph Munro (R). Atty. Gen. Christine Gregoire (D).

People (1994) 5,343,090 (15th). RACE/NATIONAL ORIGIN (1990): White 88.5%. Black 3.1%. Indian 1.7%. Asian 4.3%. Other 2.4%. Hispanic 4.4%.

Cities (1990) Seattle 516,259. Spokane 177,196. Tacoma 176,664. Bellevue 86,874. Everett 69,961. Yakima 54,827. Bellingham 52,179. Vancouver 46,380. Kennewick 42,155. Renton 41,668.

Business GROSS STATE PRODUCT (GSP, 1992) $127.58 bil. (14th). SECTORS OF GSP: Farms 2.06%; agricultural services, forestry, and fisheries 1.20%; mining 0.28%; construction 4.90%; manufacturing 19.11%; transportation and public utilities 7.81%; wholesale trade 7.13%; retail trade 10.28%; finance, insurance, and real estate 16.54%; services 16.51%; federal government 3.15%; federal military 1.96%; state and local government 9.06%. *FORTUNE* 500 COMPANIES (1994): 7: Boeing, Price/Costco, Weyerhauser, Microsoft, Paccar, Nordstrom, Safeco.

Famous natives Harry L. "Bing" Crosby, singer. Merce Cunningham, choreographer. Jimi Hendrix, guitarist. Henry M. "Scoop" Jackson, politician. Robert Joffrey, choreographer. Marcus Whitman (b. N.Y.), missionary/pioneer.

Noteworthy places Klondike Gold Rush Natl. Hist. Park, Seattle. Mount Rainier Natl. Park. Mount Saint Helens Natl. Monument. North Cascades Natl. Park. Olympic Natl. Park. San Juan Islands Natl. Hist. Park. Seattle Art Museum.

Memorable events Sir Francis Drake skirts coast of Pacific Northwest 1579. Juan de Fuca sails into straits now bearing his name. Bruno de Heceta lands at Hoh River 1775. Capt. James Cook arrives 1778. Capt. Robert Gray discovers mouth of Columbia River, which he names for his ship; George Vancouver explores Puget Sound 1792. Lewis and Clark expedition winters at Columbia River 1805. Marcus Whitman, Protestant Mission Board, settles near Walla Walla 1836. Territorial status 1853. Northern Pacific railroad reaches Puget Sound 1883. Alaska-Yukon-Pacific Exposition at Seattle 1909. Grand Coulee Dam, largest concrete hydroelectric dam in United States, completed 1941. Hanford Works atomic energy plant opens 1943. Upholding treaty provisions from Washington's days as a territory, a decision awards Native Americans half the catch of Northwest salmon and steelhead 1974. Mt. Saint Helens erupts, killing 60 1980. Washington Public Power Supply System (known as "whoops") defaults on $8.25 billion bond issue 1983. Reports linking growth-enhancing chemical Alar to cancer generate $140 million loss for Washington's apple growers 1988.

Tourist information 1–800–544–1800.

West Virginia

When Virginia seceded in 1861, its western counties reorganized and in 1863 were admitted to the Union as a separate state. Despite the rugged terrain, through which transportation has always been difficult, farming remained the backbone of the economy until the close of the 19th century, when coal mining and other extractive industries developed. After World War II, the manufacturing base developed to include steel and chemical manufacturing. The Monongahela, Kanahwa, and Little Kanahwa Rivers are all navigable tributaries of the Ohio River, which forms West Virginia's western border, but the state's internal transportation needs have not been met. Even with vast natural resources, West Virginia has long been one of the poorest states in the union. Population losses since the 1950s have been pronounced, and the 8 percent loss between 1980 and 1990 was the highest in the country. There is low participation in the work force by women, and educational achievements are well below the national average.

NAME for western part of Virginia. NICKNAME Mountain State. CAPITAL Charleston. ENTERED UNION June 20, 1863 (35th). MOTTO *Montani semper liberi* (Mountaineers are always free).

Emblems ANIMAL Black bear. BIRD Cardinal. COLORS Old gold and blue. FISH Brook trout. FLOWER *Rhododendron maximum* (big laurel). FRUIT Apple. SONGS "The West Virginia Hills," "West Virginia, My Home Sweet Home," "This Is My West Virginia." TREE Sugar maple.

Land TOTAL AREA 24,231 sq. mi. (41st), incl. 112 sq. mi. inland water. BORDERS Ohio, Pa., Md., Va., Ky. RIVERS Big Sandy, Guayandotte, Kanahwa, Little Kanahwa, Monongahela, Ohio, Potomac. LAKES Summersville Dam. MOUNTAINS Allegheny, Blue Ridge, Cumberland.

Elected officials Gov. Gaston Caperton (D, term exp. 1997). Sec. State Ken Hechler (D). Atty. Gen. Darrell McGraw (D).

People (1994) 1,822,021 (35th). RACE/NATIONAL ORIGIN (1990): White 96.2%. Black 3.1%. Indian 0.1%. Asian 0.4%. Other 0.1%. Hispanic 0.5%.

Cities (1990) Charleston 57,287. Huntington 54,844. Wheeling 34,882. Parkersburg 33,862. Morgantown 25,879. Weirton 22,124. Fairmont 20,210. Beckley 18,296. Clarksburg 18,059. Martinsburg 14,073.

Business GROSS STATE PRODUCT (GSP, 1992) $30.70 bil. (40th). SECTORS OF GSP: Farms 0.86%; agricultural services, forestry, and fisheries 0.27%; mining 11.79%; construction 4.01%; manufacturing 16.77%; transportation and public utilities 12.99%; wholesale trade 4.95%; retail trade 8.99%; finance, insurance, and real estate 13.64%; services 14.15%; federal government 2.14%; federal military 0.36%; state and local government 9.08%. *FORTUNE* 500 COMPANIES (1994): 0.

Famous natives Newton D. Baker, politician. Pearl Buck, novelist (Nobel Prize, 1938). John W. Davis, politician. Dwight Whitney Morrow, lawyer/diplomat. Michael Owens, manufacturer. Walter Reuther, labor leader. Cyrus Vance, statesman. Charles "Chuck" Yeager, pilot.

Noteworthy places Cass Scenic Railroad. Harpers Ferry Natl. Hist. Park. Monongahela Natl. Forest. New River Gorge Bridge. Science and Cultural Center, Charleston.

Memorable events First permanent settlement by Morgan Morgan at Mill Creek 1731. Coal discovered on Coal River 1742. Wheeling Convention repudiates act of secession; forms new state of Kanahwa 1861. Enters Union as West Virginia 1863. Population peaks at 2.5 million 1950. Unemployment jumps 8.6 percent to 18.0 percent, highest in nation, 1980–83.

Tourist information 1-800-CALLWVA.

Wisconsin

The indigenous people of the region had a largely agricultural economy, but the fur trade drew Europeans into the region. Native resistance to white settlement was strong and not overcome until the Black Hawk Wars of 1832. In the early 19th century, German, Scandinavian, and Dutch farmers immigrated to the region in large numbers. Many social welfare policies now common to the nation as a whole—including aid to dependent children, workmen's compensation, and old-age assistance—were pioneered in Wisconsin. Although manufacturing accounts for the lion's share of Wisconsin's profits, agriculture is extremely important, and the state is the nation's leading producer of dairy products. There are major shipping facilities at Superior, Green Bay, and Milwaukee.

NAME From Ojibwa *wishkonsing*, "place of the bearer." NICKNAME Badger State. CAPITAL Madison. ENTERED UNION May 29, 1848 (30th). MOTTO "Forward."

Emblems ANIMAL Badger. BIRD Robin. DOMESTIC ANIMAL Dairy cow. FISH Muskellunge. FLOWER Wood violet. INSECT Honeybee. MINERAL Galena. ROCK Red granite. SOIL Antigo silt loam. SONG "Oh, Wisconsin!" SYMBOL OF PEACE Mourning dove. TREE Sugar maple. WILDLIFE ANIMAL White-tailed deer.

Land TOTAL AREA 56,153 sq. mi. (26th), incl. 1,727 sq. mi. inland water. BORDERS Minn., Lake Superior, Mich., Lake Michigan, Ill., Iowa. RIVERS Black, Chippewa, Menominee, Mississippi, St. Croix, Wisconsin. LAKES Chippewa, Du Bay, Mendota, Michigan, Superior, Winnebago. OTHER NOTABLE FEATURES Apostle Islands, Door Peninsula, Green Bay.

Elected officials Gov. Tommy G. Thompson (R, term exp. 1999). Lt. Gov. Scott McCallum (R). Sec. State Douglas LaFollette (D). Atty. Gen. James Doyle (D).

People (1994) 5,081,658 (18th). RACE/NATIONAL ORIGIN (1990): White 92.2%. Black 5.0%. Indian 0.8%. Asian 1.1%. Other 0.9%. Hispanic 1.9%.

Cities (1990) Milwaukee 628,088. Madison 191,262. Green Bay 96,466. Racine 84,298. Kenosha 80,352. Appleton 65,695. West Allis 63,221. Waukesha 56,958. Eau Claire 56,856. Oshkosh 55,006.

Business GROSS STATE PRODUCT (GSP, 1992) $109.52 bil. (19th). SECTORS OF GSP: Farms 3.23%; agricultural services, forestry, and fisheries 0.47%; mining 0.14%; construction 3.93%; manufacturing 28.24%; transportation and public utilities 7.64%; wholesale trade 5.95%; retail trade 8.80%; finance, insurance, and real estate 16.13%; services 15.39%; federal government 1.50%; federal military 0.26%; state and local government 8.32%. *FORTUNE* 500 COMPANIES (1994): 5: Northwestern Mutual Life Insurance, Johnson Controls, Manpower, Aid Association for Lutherans, Roundy's.

Famous natives King Camp Gillette, inventor/businessman. Harry Houdini (b. Hungary), magician. Robert La Follette, politician. Liberace (Wladziu Valentino), pianist. Alfred Lunt, actor. Joseph R. McCarthy, politician. Spencer Tracy, actor. Thorstein Veblen, economist. Orson Welles, director. Laura Ingalls Wilder, novelist. Thornton Wilder, author. Frank Lloyd Wright, architect.

Noteworthy places Apostle Island Natl. Lakeshore. Chequamegon Natl. Forest. Circus World Museum, Baraboo. Door County Peninsula. Ice Age Natl. Scientific Reserve. Manitowoc Maritime Museum. Milwaukee Art Museum. Milwaukee Public Museum. Nicolet Natl. Forest. Old Wade House and Carriage Museum, Greenbush. Old World Wisconsin, Eagle. Villa Louis, Prairie du Chien. Wisconsin Dells.

Memorable events Jean Nicolet lands at Green Bay 1634. French establish mission and trading post near Ashland 1634. British take control of region 1763. Land ceded to United States 1787, but U.S. control not established until after War of 1812. Becomes independent territory 1836. Statehood 1848. More than 800 die in forest fire near Peshtigo 1871. First hydroelectric plant completed at Appleton 1882. Ringling Brothers circus formed at Baraboo 1884. First state to enact income tax 1911.

Tourist information 1-800-372-2737, 1-800-432-8747, 1-608-266-2161.

Wyoming

Tens of thousands of migrants traveled through the region of Wyoming along the Oregon Trail, which was pioneered in 1812–13, but few settled the land until Ft. Laramie was built in 1834. Territorial status came in 1869. Wyoming was the first state to give the vote to women, and in 1925 Nellie Tayloe Ross became the first woman governor following the death of her husband. Cattle ranching is the traditional mainstay of the economy. The state ranks second in uranium output and has 35 percent of the country's deposits. In the last 20 years, petroleum and coal production have become increasingly important. Wyoming is best known for its natural wonders. Yellowstone National Park—the site of Old Faithful—is the oldest and largest national park in the country. Following a decade-long mining boom in the 1970s and 1980s, Wyoming's population declined, and it has fallen behind even Alaska in total population.

NAME From Delaware *maugh-wau-wa-ma*, "large plains" or "mountains and valleys alternating." NICKNAME Equality State. CAPITAL Cheyenne. ENTERED UNION July 10, 1890 (44th). MOTTO "Equal rights."

Emblems BIRD Meadowlark. FLOWER Indian paintbrush. GEM Jade. SONG "Wyoming." TREE Cottonwood.

Land TOTAL AREA 97,809 sq. mi. (9th), incl. 820 sq. mi. inland water. BORDERS Mont., S.Dak., Nebr., Colo., Utah, Idaho. RIVERS Bighorn, Green, North Platte, Powder, Snake, Yellowstone. LAKES Bighorn, Yellowstone. MOUNTAINS Absaroka, Bighorn, Black Hills, Laramie, Owl Creek, Teton Range, Wind River Range, Wyoming Range.

Elected officials Gov. Jim Geringer (R, term exp. 1999). Sec. State Diana Ohman (R). Atty. Gen. Joseph B. Meyer (D).

People (1994) 475,981 (50th). RACE/NATIONAL ORIGIN (1990): White 94.2%. Black 0.8%. Indian 2.1%. Asian 0.6%. Other 2.3%. Hispanic 5.7%.

Cities (1990) Cheyenne 50,008. Casper 46,742. Laramie 26,687. Rock Springs 19,050. Gillette 17,635. Sheridan 13,900. Green River 12,711. Evanston 10,903. Rawlins 9,380. Riverton 9,202.

Business GROSS STATE PRODUCT (GSP, 1992) $13.19 bil. (49th). SECTORS OF GSP: Farms 2.31%; agricultural services, forestry, and fisheries 0.37%; mining 30.02%; construction 3.34%; manufacturing 4.15%; transportation and public utilities 17.41%; wholesale trade 2.81%; retail trade 6.94%; finance, insurance, and real estate 11.93%; services 8.65%; federal government 2.24%; federal military 1.02%; state and local government 8.83%. *FORTUNE* 500 COMPANIES (1994): 0.

Famous natives James Bridger (b. Va.), pioneer. Jackson Pollock, painter. Nellie Tayloe Ross (b. Mo.), politician.

Noteworthy places Buffalo Bill Museum, Cody. Devil's Tower Natl. Monument. Ft. Bridger State Park. Ft. Laramie Natl. Hist. Site. Fossil Butte Natl. Monument. Grand Teton Natl. Park. Natl. Elk Refuge. Yellowstone Natl. Park (Old Faithful).

Memorable events Part of Louisiana Territory claimed for France 1682. Pierre Gaultier de Varennes, sieur de Vérendrye explores region for France 1743. Region to United States with Louisiana Purchase 1803. John Colter crosses area of Yellowstone 1807–8. Part of region under joint Anglo-American occupation 1818–46. Indian Wars follow massacre of army detachments 1854 and 1866. Wyoming Territory organized 1868. Women's suffrage adopted permanently (first instance in United States); Union Pacific railroad crosses state 1869. Yellowstone, world's

first national park, opens 1872. White mob kills 28 Chinese miners and burns Chinatown in Rock Springs 1885. Statehood 1890. Nellie Tayloe Ross first woman governor 1925. First Intercontinental Ballistic Missile (ICBM) base opens near Cheyenne 1951. Fires consume 1.6 million acres of land in and around Yellowstone Park 1988—the worst fire to hit the nation's (and the world's) oldest national park—but the land has undergone intense rejuvenation.
Tourist information 1-800-CALLWYO.

U.S. Territories and Possessions

Today the United States administers a number of overseas territories and commonwealth states under a variety of circumstances. The provisions of the Northwest Ordinance of 1787 established the system under which U.S. territories can achieve statehood. In order to elect a territorial legislature and send a nonvoting delegate to Congress, a territory must contain 5,000 inhabitants of voting age; it is eligible for statehood when the population numbers 60,000.

In 1947, the United Nations created the Trust Territory of the Pacific Islands—comprised of what are known today as the Federated States of Micronesia (FSM), the Republic of the Marshall Islands, the Commonwealth of the Northern Mariana Islands (CNMI), and the Republic of Palau. Micronesia and the Marshall Islands both declared their independence in 1986, the same year that the Northern Mariana Islands and the United States approved a convenant to establish a Commonwealth. CNMI residents are subject to U.S. laws (except those regarding customs, minimum wages, immigration, and taxation) and are, as a rule, U.S. citizens. Palau became the last territory to leave the trust in October 1994, when it declared its independence. Under the terms of a compact, the United States will provide $517 million in aid over 15 years in return for the right to establish military bases on Palau and operate nuclear warships in Palau's territorial waters for the next 50 years.

American Samoa came under U.S. control in 1889, and Guam and Puerto Rico were ceded to the United States by Spain after the Spanish-American War in 1899. American Samoa is an unorganized, unincorporated territory with its own government, but under the plenary authority of the Department of the Interior. Guam is an unincorporated, organized territory. And Puerto Rico is a commonwealth of the United States, rejecting statehood most recently in 1994. The Virgin Islands of the United States (USVI) is an unincorporated, organized territory. American Samoa, Guam, and the USVI have nonvoting representatives in Congress, and Puerto Rico is represented by a nonvoting resident commissioner. Residents of American Samoa are U.S. nationals; those of Guam, Puerto Rico, and the USVI are U.S. citizens.

In addition to these territories, the United States has a number of possessions whose population is too small to make local government practicable, or which are uninhabited altogether.

American Samoa

Territory of American Samoa

Geography Location: seven islands (Tutuila, Ta'u, Olosega, Ofu, Aunun, Rose, Swain's) in southern central Pacific Ocean; Pago Pago 14°17'S, 170°41'W. **Boundaries:** Hawaii about 2,300 mi. (3,700 km) to NNE, Cook Islands to E, Tonga to SW, Western Samoa to W. **Total land area:** 76.1 sq. mi. (199 sq km). **Coastline:** 72 mi. (116 km). **Comparative area:** slightly larger than Washington, D.C. **Land use:** 10% arable land; 5% permanent crops; 0% meadows and pastures; 75% forest and woodland; 10% other. **Major cities:** (1990 census) Pago Pago (capital; Ma'oputasi Co.) 10,640.

People Population: 55,223 (July 1994 est.). Nationality: noun—American Samoan(s); adjective—American Samoan. **Ethnic groups:** 89% Samoan (Polynesian), 2% Caucasian, 4% Tongan, 5% other. **Languages:** Samoan (closely related to Hawaiian and other Polynesian languages) and English; most people are bilingual. **Religions:** 50% Christian Congregationalist, 20% Roman Catholic, 30% mostly Protestant denominations and other.

Government Type: unincorporated and unorganized territory of U.S. **Constitution:** ratified 1966, in effect 1967. **National holiday:** Flag Day, Apr. 17 (1900). **Heads of government:** A.P. Lutali, governor (since Jan. 1993). **Structure:** executive—governor is popularly elected to four-year term and exercises authority under direction of U.S. Secretary of Interior; legislative—bicameral legislature (Fono) with 18-member Senate chosen by county councils to serve four-year terms and House of Representatives with 20 members popularly elected to serve two-year terms, plus a nonvoting delegate from Swain's Island; judicial—high court with chief justice and associate justices appointed by U.S. Secretary of Interior.

Economy Monetary unit: U.S. dollar. **Budget:** (1990) ***income:*** $51.2 mil.; ***expend.:*** $59.9 mil. **GNP:** $128 mil., $2,600 per capita (1991). **Chief crops:** bananas, coconuts, vegetables, taro, breadfruit, yams, copra, pineapples, papayas. **Natural resources:** pumice and pumicite. **Major industries:** tuna canneries (largely dependent on foreign supplies of raw tuna), meat canning, handicrafts, dairy farming, tourism. **Labor force:** 14,400 (1990 est.). **Exports:** $306 mil. (f.o.b., 1989); 93% canned tuna. **Imports:** $360 mil. (c.i.f., 1989); 56% materials for canneries, 8% food, 7% petroleum, 6% machinery and parts. **Major trading partners:** ***exports:*** 99.6% U.S.; ***imports:*** 62% U.S., 11% Australia, 9% Japan, 7% New Zealand, 4% Fiji, 7% other.

American Samoa consists of seven islands between 14° and 15° south, and 168° and 171° west. First peopled by Polynesians in the first millennium B.C., the islands had as their first European visitor Louis Antoine de Bougainville, who visited in 1768 and called them the "Islands of the Navigators," in recognition of the islanders' seamanship. American whalers and missionaries began arriving in the 1830s, and the United States secured trading privileges by treaty in 1878. In 1889 the United States, Britain, and Germany established tripartite control of the islands. After 10 years of warring among the islanders, the British withdrew their claim, and Germany and the United States divided responsibility for the islands along longitude 171° west. The high chiefs of Tutuila ceded the islands of Tutuila and Aunun to the United States in 1900, and the high chiefs of the Manu'a islands ceded those of Ta'u, Ofu, Olosega, and Rose in 1904. Swain's Island became part of American Samoa in 1925.

Administered by the U.S. Department of the Interior since 1904, American Samoa is an unincorporated and unorganized territory, with its own government but under the plenary authority of the Department of the Interior. There is no congressional intent to grant statehood to the island. American Samoans will reconsider their relationship with the United States in 1994. The people have their own constitution and elect their own governor and representatives to the Fono; but the justices of the high court are appointed by the secretary of the interior. The population is more than 80 percent rural.

Baker and Howland Islands

About 1,600 miles (2,575 km) southwest of Hawaii and 1,000 miles west of Jarvis Island are Baker Island (0°14'N, 176°28'W) and Howland Island (0°48'N, 176°38'W, 40 mi. north of Baker). Discovered in 1842, the two coral atolls were worked for guano until about 1890. Great Britain claimed them in 1889, but the United States made them territories in 1935 and sent colonists to them. With an area of about one square mile each, neither is inhabited today. Both are unincorporated territories administered by the U.S. Fish and Wildlife Service as part of the National Wildlife Refuge.

Guam

Territory of Guam

Geography Location: southernmost and largest of Mariana Islands in western North Pacific Ocean; Agaña 13°28'N, 144°45'E. **Boundaries:** Tokyo, Japan, about 1,350 mi. (2,170 km) to N; Honolulu, Hawaii 3,300 mi. (5,955 km) to ENE; Federated States of Micronesia to S, Philippines to W across Philippine Sea. **Total land area:** 209 sq. mi. (541 sq km). **Coastline:** 78 mi. (125.5 km). **Comparative area:** slightly more than three times size of Washington, D.C. **Land use:** 11% arable land; 11% permanent crops; 15% meadows and pastures; 18% forest and woodland; 45% other. **Major cities:** Agaña (capital).

People Population: 149,620 (July 1994 est.). **Nationality:** noun—Guamanian(s); adjective—Guamanian. **Ethnic groups:** 47% Chamorro, 25% Filipino, 10% Caucasian, 18% Chinese, Japanese, Korean, other. **Languages:** English, Chamorro, and Japanese. **Religions:** 98% Roman Catholic, 2% other.

Government Type: organized, unincorporated territory of U.S. **Constitution:** Organic Act of Aug. 1, 1950. **National holiday:** Guam Discovery Day, first Monday in March. **Heads of government:** Joseph F. Ada, governor (since 1986). **Structure:** executive—governor elected to four-year term; legislative—Senate has 21 members elected for two-year terms; judicial—U.S. District Court, Guam Superior Court.

Economy Monetary unit: U.S. dollar. **Budget:** (1991 est.) ***income:*** $525 mil.; ***expend.:*** $395 mil. **GNP:** $2.0 bil., $14,000 per capita (1991 est.). **Chief crops:** fruits, vegetables, eggs, copra; relatively undeveloped with most food imported. **Livestock:** poultry, pigs. **Natural resources:** fishing (largely undeveloped), tourism (especially from Japan). **Major industries:** U.S. military, tourism, petroleum refining. **Labor force:** 46,930 (1990); 40% government, 60% other. **Exports:** $34 mil. (f.o.b., 1984); mostly transshipments of refined petroleum products, construction materials, fish, food and beverage products. **Imports:** $493 mil. (c.i.f., 1984); petroleum and petroleum products; food, manufactured goods. **Major trading partners:** ***exports:*** 63% Palau, 25% U.S., 12% other; ***imports:*** 23% U.S., 19% Japan, 58% other.

Guam was inhabited by Chamorros from the Malay Peninsula as early as 1500 B.C.; the first European to stop at Guam was Ferdinand Magellan in 1521. Spanish colonization began with the arrival of Jesuit missionaries in 1668. By 1700 pestilence and insurrection had reduced the Chamorro population from 50,000 to about 2,000. Guam was ceded to the United States in 1899. In 1941 it was occupied by Japan—the only inhabited U.S. territory to be seized by enemy forces during World War II—and was retaken by the Americans in 1944. (Congress designated 1,960 acres as the War in the Pacific National Historic Park in 1978.) In 1950 it received its first nonmilitary administration in more than 200 years. Though Guam is unincorporated, the congressionally approved Guam Organic Act provides for a republican form of government with executive, legislative, and judicial branches. The Guam Commonwealth Act has been approved by plebiscite and is awaiting congressional ratification. Although Chamorros represent a significant portion of the population, Guam is a multiethnic state.

Jarvis Island, Kingman Reef, and Palmyra Atoll

Jarvis Island (0°23'S, 160°02'W; about 1,300 mi. (2,090 km) S of Hawaii), Kingman Reef (6° 24'N, 162°22'W; about 995 mi. (1,600 km) SSW of Hawaii), and Palmyra Atoll (5°52'N, 162° 05'W; about 995 mi. (1,600 km) SSW of Hawaii) are in the Line Island group. Discovered in 1798, Kingman Reef (0.4 sq. mi.; 1 sq km) was annexed by the United States in 1922 and used as an aviation station during the 1930s. Discovered in 1802, Palmyra Atoll consists of about 50 islets with a combined area of four square miles. It was annexed by the kingdom of Hawaii in 1862, by Great Britain in 1889, and claimed by the United States in 1912. Privately owned, it is administered by the Department of the Navy, as is Kingman Reef. Jarvis Island (1.8 sq. mi.; 4.5 sq km) was claimed by the United States in 1857, annexed by Great Britain in 1889, and reclaimed by the United States in 1935. Its rich guano deposits were worked by U.S. and British companies in the late 19th century.

Johnston Atoll

Geography Location: Johnston Island (16° 45'N, 169°32'W) and three uninhabited islands in central Pacific Ocean. **Boundaries:** Honolulu, Hawaii, about 825 mi. (1,330 km) to ENE; Marshall Islands to SW. **Total land area:** 1.1 sq. mi. (2.8 sq km). **Coastline:** 6.21 mi. (10 km). **Comparative area:** about 4.7 times size of the Mall in Washington, D.C. **Land use:** 0% arable land; 0% permanent crops; 0% meadows and pastures; 0% forest and woodland; 100% other. **Major cities:** none.

People Population: 1,400 (1993), all U.S. government personnel and contractors.

Government Type: unincorporated territory of U.S.

Johnston Atoll (16°45'N, 169°32'W) includes Johnston, Hikina, and Akan Islands, with a total area of 1.1 square miles. Claimed by the United States in 1858, Johnston Atoll is manned and administered by the Defense Nuclear Agency (DNA), and managed jointly as a National Wildlife Refuge by the DNA and the Fish and Wildlife Service.

Midway Islands

Geography Location: Sand Island and Eastern Island in northern Pacific Ocean; 28°15'N, 177°25'W. **Boundaries:** Honolulu about 1,460 mi. (2,350 km) to SE, Marshall Islands to SW. **Total land area:** 2.0 sq. mi. (5.2 sq km). **Coastline:** 9.3 mi. (15 km). **Comparative area:** about nine times size of the Mall in Washington, D.C. **Land use:** 0% arable land; 0% permanent crops; 0% meadows and pastures; 0% forest and woodland; 100% other. **Major cities:** none.

People Population: 453 U.S. military personnel (1992). **Nationality:** noun—Midway Islander(s); adjective—Midway Island. **Languages:** English. **Religions:** Christianity.

Government Type: unincorporated territory of U.S.

Economy Monetary unit: U.S. dollar. **Major industries:** support of U.S. naval air facility.

Midway (28°13'N, 177°26'W) consists of Midway Atoll, Eastern Island, and Sand Island. Although they are part of the Leeward Islands—the westernmost islands of the Hawaiian chain—they are not part of the state of Hawaii. They were the site of the Battle of Midway, June 1942, a turning point in the Pacific theater of World War II. Today they are administered by the Department of the Navy, which maintains a naval air station there. The navy and the Fish and Wildlife Service jointly manage the islands as a National Wildlife Refuge.

Navassa

Located in the Caribbean between the islands of Jamaica and Haiti and 100 mi. (160 km) south of the U.S. naval base at Guantánamo, Cuba. Navassa was claimed by the United States in 1856. It is uninhabited except for a lighthouse under U.S. Coast Guard administration. The island is about 2 sq. mi. (5.2 sq km).

Northern Mariana Islands

Commonwealth of the Northern Mariana Islands

Geography Location: nine major islands (incl. Saipan, Rota, Tinian) in western central Pacific Ocean; Saipan 15°13'N, 145°44'E. **Boundaries:** Japan to N; Honolulu, Hawaii, about 3,500 mi. (5,635 km) to E; Guam to SW; Philippines to W across Philippine Sea. **Total land area:** 293 sq. mi. (759 sq km). **Coastline:** undetermined. **Comparative area:** slightly more than 2.5 times size of Washington, D.C. **Land use:** 5% arable land; N.A.% permanent crops; 19% meadows and pastures; N.A.% forest and woodland; N.A.% other. **Major cities:** (1990 census) Saipan (capital) 38,896.

People Population: 49,799 (July 1994 est.). **Nationality:** undetermined. **Ethnic groups:** Chamorro majority, Carolinians, other Micronesians; Spanish, German, Japanese admixtures. **Languages:** English, Chamorro, Carolinian. **Religions:** Christian with Roman Catholic majority; some traditional beliefs.

Government Type: commonwealth. **Constitution:** Covenant Agreement effective Nov. 3, 1986. **National holiday:** Commonwealth Day, Jan. 8. **Heads of government:** Lorenzo I. DeLeon Guerrero, governor (since Jan. 1990). **Structure:** executive—governor elected by popular vote; legislative—bicameral legislature (nine-member Senate elected for four-year term, 15-member House of Representatives elected for two-year term); judiciary—U.S. District Court, Commonwealth Trial Court, Commonwealth Appeals Court.

Economy Monetary unit: U.S. dollar. **Budget:** (1992) ***income:*** $147 mil.; ***expend.:*** $127.7 mil. **GNP:** $541 mil., $11,500 per capita (1992). **Chief crops:** coconuts, coffee, fruit, vegetables. **Livestock:** cattle, pigs. **Natural resources:** arable land, fish. **Major industries:** tourism, construction, light industry, handicrafts. **Labor force:** 7,476 total indigenous labor force, 2,699 unemployed, 21,188 foreign workers (1990). **Exports:** $263.4 mil. (f.o.b., 1991); manufactured goods, garments, bread, pastries, concrete blocks, light iron works. **Imports:** $392.4 mil. (c.i.f., 1991); food, construction equipment, materials. **Major trading partners:** N.A.

Running north from the island of Guam across a 600-mile-long archipelago in the Pacific Island group known as Micronesia, the islands of the Northern Marianas (CNMI) were originally settled by Pacific argonauts as early as 1500 B.C. Ferdinand Magellan landed at Saipan in 1521, introducing Western culture to the region. The Spanish took control of the archipelago in 1565 and ruled until 1898, when Germany took over the islands. After World War I, the League of Nations mandated the Marianas to Japan, which developed extensive sugar-processing works on Saipan. Allied forces took the Marianas in 1944.

In 1947 the islands were included in the UN Trust Territory of the Pacific and placed under U.S. administration. In 1976 the CNMI adopted its own constitution. A mutually approved Covenant to Establish a Commonwealth was implemented by the Marianas and the United States in 1986. The Northern Marianas are subject to provisions of U.S. law, except regarding customs, minimum wages, immigration, and taxation. The people are, as a rule, U.S. citizens.

The CNMI benefits substantially from U.S. assistance. A seven-year agreement to end in 1992 allocates $288 million for development, government operations, and other programs, and the CNMI is also eligible for other federal programs provided to the 50 states. Tourism—which has registered a yearly increase of 7.5 percent since 1980—accounts for approximately 37 percent of the island's gross product. The government is the largest employer.

Puerto Rico

Commonwealth of Puerto Rico

Geography **Location:** large island of Puerto Rico, together with Vieques, Culebra, and many smaller islands, in northeastern Caribbean Sea; San Juan 18°29'N, 66°08'W. **Boundaries:** Atlantic Ocean to N, Virgin Islands to E, Caribbean Sea to S, Dominican Republic 50 mi. (80 km) to W. **Total land area:** 3,459 sq. mi. (8,959 sq km). **Coastline:** 311 mi. (501 km). **Comparative area:** slightly less than three times size of Rhode Island. **Land use:** 8% arable land; 9% permanent crops; 41% meadows and pastures; 20% forest and woodland; 22% other. **Major cities:** (1990 census) San Juan (capital) 437,745; Bayamón 220,262; Ponce 187,749; Carolina 177,806; Caguas 133,447.

People **Population:** 3,801,977 (July 1994 est.). **Nationality:** noun—Puerto Rican(s); adjective—Puerto Rican. **Ethnic groups:** almost entirely Hispanic. **Languages:** Spanish (official), English. **Religions:** mostly Christian, 85% Roman Catholic, 15% Protestant and other.

Government **Type:** commonwealth associated with U.S. **Constitution:** effective July 25, 1952. **National holiday:** Constitution Day, July 25. **Heads of government:** Pedro Rosello, governor, since Jan. 1993. **Structure:** executive—governor elected by direct vote to four-year term; legislative—bicameral legislature (Senate with 27 members, House of Representatives with 53 members, all elected by popular vote to four-year terms); judiciary—Supreme Court appointed by governor.

Economy **Monetary unit:** U.S. dollar. **Budget:** (1989) ***income:*** $5.8 bil.; ***expend.:*** $5.8 bil. **GNP:** $26.8 bil., $7,100 per capita (1992 est.). **Chief crops:** sugarcane, coffee, pineapples, plantains, bananas (imports a large share of food needs). **Livestock:** cattle, chickens. **Natural resources:** copper, nickel; potential for crude oil. **Major industries:** manufacturing of pharmaceuticals, electronics, apparel, food products, instruments, tourism. **Labor force:** 1,170,000 (1992); 20% government, 17% trade, 14% manufacturing, 5% construction, 5% communications and transportation, 39% other. **Exports:** $21.8 bil. (1992); pharmaceuticals, electronics, apparel, canned tuna, rum. **Imports:** $14.8 bil. (1992); chemicals, clothing, food, fish, petroleum products. **Major trading partners:** (1990) ***exports:*** 88.3% U.S.; ***imports:*** 68.8% U.S.

Initially peopled by the Igneri and Taíno tribes, Puerto Rico's first European visitor was Christopher Columbus, who landed on the island in 1493. In 1508, Juan Ponce de Léon led the first settlers to San Juan, and by 1514 the Taíno population had dropped from an estimated 30,000 to 4,000. In the 17th and 18th centuries, Puerto Rico was invaded by both English and Danish forces, and though San Juan was captured or burned several times, the Spanish maintained their control of the island.

The Spanish constitution granted Puerto Ricans citizenship in 1812, but a revolution was put down in 1868. Spain granted Puerto Rico self-government in 1897, but this was repealed when sovereignty was transferred to the United States after the Spanish-American War. Despite early attempts to Americanize Puerto Rico, including an effort to make English the official language and granting citizenship in 1917, the Popular Democratic party, founded in 1938, brought about a change in political status from that of a U.S. colony to an autonomous commonwealth in 1952.

Governed under the Puerto Rican Federal Relations Act and a constitution modeled on that of the United States, Puerto Rico is nonetheless an autonomous political entity in voluntary association with the United States. Despite dramatic increases in industrial development since the 1950s, Puerto Rico suffered from net outward migration until 1988.

Puerto Ricans remain almost equally divided between those who favor statehood and those who favor maintaining commonwealth status, with those seeking independence constituting a vocal but small minority. In the most recent balloting on the issue, held Nov. 14, 1993 48 percent of Puerto Ricans voted to remain a commonwealth, compared to 46 percent supporting statehood, and 4 percent preferring independence.

Virgin Islands

Virgin Islands of the United States

Geography **Location:** three main inhabited islands (St. Croix, St. Thomas, and St. John) and about 50 smaller islands, mostly uninhabited, in northeastern Caribbean Sea; Charlotte Amalie 18°22'N, 64°56'W. **Boundaries:** British Virgin Islands to N, Netherlands Antilles to E, Caribbean Sea to S, Puerto Rico about 40 mi. (64 km) to W. **Total land area:** 136 sq. mi. (352 sq km). **Coastline:** 117 mi. (188 km). **Comparative area:** slightly less than twice size of Washington, D.C. **Land use:** 15% arable land; 6% permanent crops; 26% meadows and pastures; 6% forest and woodland; 47% other. **Major cities:** (1990 census) Charlotte Amalie (capital) 12,331; Christiansted 2,555; Frederiksted 1,064.

People **Population:** 97,564 (July 1994 est.). **Nationality:** noun—Virgin Islander(s); adjective—Virgin Islander. **Ethnic groups:** 74% West Indian (45% born in Virgin Islands, 29% born elsewhere in West Indies), 13% U.S. mainland, 5% Puerto Rican, 8% other; 80% black, 15% white, 5% other; 14% of Hispanic origin. **Languages:** English (official), Spanish, Creole. **Religions:** 42% Baptist, 34% Roman Catholic, 17% Episcopalian, 7% other.

Government **Type:** organized, unincorporated territory of U.S. **Constitution:** Revised Organic Act of July 22, 1954, serves as constitution. **National holiday:** Transfer Day (from Denmark to U.S.), Mar. 31. **Heads of government:** Alexander Farrelly, governor (since Jan. 1987). **Structure:** executive—governor elected to four-year term; legislative—unicameral legislature (senate with 15 members elected to two-year terms); judiciary—two U.S. district courts.

Economy **Monetary unit:** U.S. dollar. **Budget:** (1992) ***income:*** $364.4 mil.; ***expend.:*** $364.4 mil. **GDP:** $1.2 bil., $11,000 per capita. **Chief crops:** truck gardens, food crops, fruit, sorghum. **Livestock:** Senepol cattle. **Natural resources:** sun, sand, sea, surf. **Major industries:** tourism, petroleum refining, watch assembly, rum distilling, construction, pharmaceuticals, textiles, electronics. **Labor force:** 45,000 (1988). **Exports:** $2.8 bil. (f.o.b., 1990); mostly refined petroleum products. **Imports:** $3.3 bil. (c.i.f., 1990); crude oil, foodstuffs, consumer goods, building materials. **Major trading partners:** ***exports:*** U.S., Puerto Rico; ***imports:*** U.S., Puerto Rico.

The Virgin Islands of the United States (USVI) consist of more than 50 islands located about 40 miles east of Puerto Rico and about 1,730 miles east-southeast of Miami. Excavations have revealed evidence of human habitation in the Virgin Islands (both British and U.S.) from as early as A.D. 100. By 1493, when Christopher Columbus landed on the islands—which he named the Virgin Islands for the virgin martyr St. Ursula—they were inhabited by Carib Indians who were driven out by the Spanish in 1555.

In 1672 St. Thomas was settled by the Danish West India Company. The Danes laid claim to St. John in 1683 and purchased St. Croix from the French in 1773. The United States purchased the Virgin Islands from Denmark for $25 million in 1917, making them a territory under the jurisdiction of the navy. U.S. citizenship was granted in 1927, and the Department of the Interior assumed administration of the islands in 1931. The first governor elected by popular vote was installed in 1970, and an independent constitution was voted down by the electorate in 1979.

The primary industry is tourism, which accounts for 70 percent of GDP and employs 70 percent of the workforce. International business and financial services are increasingly important. The world's largest petroleum refinery is at St. Croix.

Wake Islands

Geography Location: three islands (Wake, Wilkes, and Peale) in western Pacific Ocean; Wake 19°18'N, 166°36'E. **Boundaries:** Honolulu 2,300 mi. (3,700 km) to E, Marshall Islands to S, Guam about 1,280 mi. (2,060 km) to W. **Total land area:** 2.5 sq. mi. (6.5 sq km). **Coastline:** 12 mi. (19.3 km). **Comparative area:** about 11 times size of the Mall in Washington, D.C. **Land use:** 0% arable land; 0% permanent crops; 0% meadows and pastures; 0% forest and woodland; 100% other. **Major cities:** none.

People Population: 302 (July 1994); no indigenous inhabitants; temporary population consists of U.S. Air Force personnel and about 225 U.S. and Thai contractors.

Government Type: unincorporated territory of U.S., administered by U.S. Air Force.

The Wake Island group was first discovered by British captain William Wake in 1796. It was charted by Capt. Charles Wilkes's surveying expedition, which was accompanied by a naturalist named Peale. Annexed by the United States in 1898, Wake became a civil aviation station in the 1930s and was captured by the Japanese shortly after Pearl Harbor. It was retaken in 1944. Formerly an important commercial aviation base, it is now used only by U.S. military and some commercial cargo planes.

State Government Finances

REVENUES AND EXPENDITURES

Revenues Revenue of state governments from all sources in 1993 was $804.8 billion, an 8% increase over the year before. Taxes accounted for 43.9%, or $353.3 billion of the total state general revenue, also up 8% from 1992. More than 27% of state revenues came from the federal government. Sales taxes and gross receipts accounted for 26.7% and individual income taxes for 17.2% of general revenue. Charges were responsible for 8.8% of state revenues.

Expenditures State government expenditures in 1993 totaled $743.1 billion, an increase of 6% from the amount spent in 1992. State general expenditures amounted to $646.2 billion, 5.6% more than in 1992. The leading expenditure categories, by function, were education services (34%), public welfare programs (26%), and health and hospitals (8%).

COMPOSITION OF STATE LEGISLATURES, 1994

	Senate			House		
State or other jurisdiction	**Democrats**	**Republicans**	**Total**	**Democrats**	**Republicans**	**Total**
Alabama	27	8	35	82	23	105
Alaska	10	10	20	20	18	40[1]
Arizona	12	18	30	25	35	60
Arkansas	30	5	35	88	11	100[2]
California	22	16	40[3]	47	33	80
Colorado	16	19	35	31	34	65
Connecticut	19	17	36	86	65	151
Delaware	15	6	21	18	23	41
Florida	20	20	40	71	49	120
Georgia	39	17	56	128	52	180
Hawaii	22	3	25	47	4	51
Idaho	12	23	35	20	50	70
Illinois	27	32	59	67	51	118
Indiana	22	28	50	55	45	100
Iowa	27	23	50	49	51	100
Kansas	13	27	40	59	66	125
Kentucky	24	14	38	71	29	100
Louisiana	33	6	39	88	16	105[2]
Maine	20	15	35	91	60	151
Maryland	38	9	47	117	24	141
Massachusetts	31	9	40	122	35	160[2,4]
Michigan	16	22	38	55	55	110
Minnesota	45[5]	22[6]	67	85[5]	49[6]	134
Mississippi	39	13	52	96	24	122
Missouri	20	14	34	98	65	163
Montana	30	20	50	47	53	100
Nebraska	Nonpartisan		49	Unicameral		
Nevada	10	11	21	27	12	42[7]
New Hampshire	11	13	24	138	254	400[7,8]
New Jersey	16	24	40	27	53	80
New Mexico	27	15	42	52	18	70
New York	26	35	61	100	50	150
North Carolina	39	11	50	78	42	120
North Dakota	25	24	49	33	65	98
Ohio	13	20	33	53	46	99
Oklahoma	37	11	48	68	33	101
Oregon	16	14	30	28	32	60
Pennsylvania	24	26	50	105	98	203
Rhode Island	39	11	50	85	15	100
South Carolina	30	16	46	73	50	124[2]
South Dakota	20	15	35	28	42	70
Tennessee	19	14	33	63	36	99
Texas	18	13	31	92	58	150
Utah	18	11	29	26	49	75
Vermont	14	16	30	87	57	150[9]
Virginia	22	18	40	52	47	100[2]
Washington	28	21	49	65	33	98
West Virginia	32	2	34	79	21	100
Wisconsin	16	17	33[1]	52	47	99
Wyoming	10	20	30	19	41	60
All states	1,139	794	1,984[10]	3,193	2,219	5,440[11]
Dist. of Columbia[12]	12	0	13[2]	Unicameral		
American Samoa	Nonpartisan		18	Nonpartisan		21
Guam	14	7	21	Unicameral		
Northern Mariana Islands	3	6	9	6	10	18[3]
Puerto Rico	8[13]	20[14]	29[15]	15[13]	37[14]	53[15]
U.S. Virgin Islands	8	4	15[16]	Unicameral		

Note: As of April 1994. 1. Includes one Independent and one Alaskan Independent. 2. Includes one Independent. 3. Includes two Independents. 4. Includes two vacancies. 5. Democrat-Farmer-Labor. 6. Independent-Republican. 7. Includes three vacancies. 8. Includes one Independent and four Libertarians. 9. Includes four Independents and two Progressives. 10. includes 49 nonpartisans (from Nebraska) and two Independents. 11. Includes 20 third-party legislators and eight vacancies. 12. Council of the District of Columbia. 13. Popular Democratic party. 14. New Progressive party. 15. Includes one Puerto Rican Independent party. 16. Includes two Independents and one Independent Citizens Movement. **Source:** Council of State Governments, *State Elective Officials and the Legislatures, 1994–95* (1994).

SALARIES OF MAJOR STATE ADMINISTRATIVE OFFICIALS, 1995

State	Governor	Lieutenant governor	Secretary of state	Attorney general
Alabama	$ 81,151	$ (1)	$ 57,204	$ 90,475
Alaska	81,648	76,188	(2)	86,760
Arizona	75,000	(3)	47,735	76,440
Arkansas	60,000	29,000	37,500	50,000
California	114,286[4]	90,000	90,000	102,000
Colorado	60,000	48,500	48,500	60,000
Connecticut	78,000	55,000	49,999	60,000
Delaware	95,000	38,400	80,700	88,900
Florida	97,850	93,728	96,861	96,490
Georgia	94,390	61,647	75,811	77,536
Hawaii	94,780	90,041	(2)	85,302
Idaho	75,000	20,000	62,500	67,500
Illinois	103,097	72,775	90,968	90,968
Indiana	77,200[4]	64,000	46,000	59,200
Iowa	76,700	60,000	60,000	73,600
Kansas	76,476	71,642	59,112	68,328
Kentucky	81,647	69,412	67,378	69,412
Louisiana	73,440	63,372	60,169	60,169
Maine	69,992	(5)	49,587	66,123
Maryland	120,000	100,000	70,000	100,000
Massachusetts	75,000	60,000	85,000	62,500
Michigan	112,025[4]	84,315	109,000	109,000
Minnesota	109,053	59,981	59,981	85,194
Mississippi	75,600	40,800	59,400	68,400
Missouri	91,615	55,286	73,450	79,505
Montana	55,850	40,310	37,525	50,646
Nebraska	65,000	47,000	52,000	64,500
Nevada	90,000	20,000	62,000	85,000
New Hampshire	82,325[4]	(5)	50,955	73,492
New Jersey	85,000	(5)	100,225	100,225
New Mexico	90,000	65,500	65,000	72,500
New York	130,000[4]	110,000	90,832	110,000
North Carolina	93,777	77,289	77,289	77,289
North Dakota	68,280	56,112	51,744	58,416
Ohio	110,250	57,011	81,445	85,517
Oklahoma	70,000	40,000	42,500	55,000
Oregon	80,000	(5)	61,500	66,000
Pennsylvania	105,000	83,000	72,000	84,000
Rhode Island	69,900	52,000	52,000	55,000
South Carolina	103,998	44,737	90,203	90,203
South Dakota	72,475	9,889[6]	49,224	61,556
Tennessee	85,000	(5)	80,700	100,200
Texas	99,122	99,122	76,976	79,247
Utah	77,250	60,000	(2)	65,000
Vermont	80,724	33,654	50,793	61,027
Virginia	110,000	32,000	73,023	97,500
Washington	121,000[4]	62,700	64,300	92,000
West Virginia	72,000	(5)	43,200	50,400
Wisconsin	92,823	49,673	45,088	82,706
Wyoming	70,000	(3)	55,000	71,298

1. Receives $12 per day (seven days a week), $50 per session day, and $3,780 per month in expenses. 2. Functions of secretary of state are the responsibility of the lieutenant governor. 3. Functions of lieutenant governor are the responsibility of the secretary of state. 4. Official salary; governor accepts less or returns part of salary. 5. No lieutenant governor. Speaker or president of the Senate next in line of succession to the governorship. 6. Annual salary for duties as presiding officer of the Senate. **Source:** Council of State Governments, *The Book of the States* (1994–95).

STATE GOVERNMENT INDIVIDUAL INCOME TAXES, 1994

State	Taxable income rate range	Taxable income brackets: Lowest: amount under	Taxable income brackets: Highest: amount over	Federal income tax deductible[1]
Alabama[2]	2.0–5.0%	$ 500	$ 3,000	Yes
Arizona	3.25–6.9	10,000	150,000	No
Arkansas	1.0–7.0	3,000	25,000	No
California[3]	1.0–11.0	4,722	214,929	No
Colorado	5% of modified federal taxable income			No
Connecticut	4.5	Flat rate on income over $12,000		N.A.
Delaware[2, 4]	3.2–7.7	2,000	40,000	No
District of Columbia	6.0–9.5	10,000	20,000	No
Georgia	1.0–6.0	750	7,000	No
Hawaii	2.0–10.0	1,500	20,500	No
Idaho	2.0–8.2	1,000	20,000	No
Illinois	3.0	Flat rate on income over $1,000		No
Indiana[2]	3.4	Flat rate on income over $1,000		No
Iowa[3, 5]	0.4–9.98	1,060	47,700	Yes
Kansas	4.4–7.75	20,000	30,000	No
Kentucky[2]	2.0–6.0	3,000	8,000	No
Louisiana	2.0–6.0	10,000	50,000	Yes
Maine[3]	2.0–8.5	4,150	16,500	No
Maryland[2, 6]	2.0–6.0	1,000	100,000	No
Massachusetts[7]	5.95–12.0	Flat rate		No
Michigan[2]	4.4	Flat rate on income over $1,500		No
Minnesota	6.0–8.5	15,230	50,030	No
Mississippi	3.0–5.0	5,000	10,000	No
Missouri[2]	1.5–6.0	1,000	9,000	Yes[8]
Montana[3]	2.0–11.0	1,800	62,700	Yes
Nebraska[3]	2.62–6.99	2,000	46,750	No
New Hampshire	Limited income tax[9]			
New Jersey[10]	1.9–6.65	20,000	75,000	No
New Mexico	1.7–8.5	5,500	41,600	No
New York[2, 11]	4.0–7.875	5,500	13,000	No
North Carolina	6.0–7.75	12,750	60,000	No
North Dakota	14% of federal income tax liability			Yes
Ohio[2]	0.743–7.5	5,000	200,000	No
Oklahoma[12]	0.5–7.0	1,000	9,950	Yes
Oregon[3, 13]	5.0–9.0	2,050	5,150	Yes
Pennsylvania[2]	2.8	Flat rate		No
Rhode Island	27.5% of federal income tax liability			No
South Carolina[3]	2.5–7.0	2,190	10,950	No
Tennessee[14]	Limited income tax			
Utah	2.55–7.2	750	3,750	50%
Vermont	25% of federal income tax liability			No
Virginia	2.0–5.75	3,000	17,000	No
West Virginia	3.0–6.5	10,000	60,000	No
Wisconsin	4.9–6.93	7,500	15,000	No

Note: Alaska, Florida, Nevada, South Dakota, Texas, Washington, and Wyoming have no state income tax. 1. A state provision that allows the taxpayer to deduct fully the federal income tax payment reduces the effective marginal tax rate for persons in the highest state and federal tax brackets by approximately one-third the nominal tax rate—the deduction is a lesser benefit to other taxpayers. 2. States in which one or more local governments levy a local income tax. 3. Indexed by an inflation factor. 4. No tax on income under $2,000. 5. Tax may not reduce after-tax income of taxpayer below $9,000 (single) or $13,500 (all other filers). 6. All counties have a local income tax surcharge of at least 20% of the state tax liabilty; in most counties the surcharge is 50%. 7. A 12% (flat rate) tax is imposed on net capital gains, interest, and dividends of residents, and Massachusetts business income of nonresidents. 8. Federal income tax deduction limited to $5,000 per return ($10,000 married). 9. There is a 5% tax on dividend and interest income in excess of $1,200 ($2,400 married). 10. No tax on income under $7,500. 11. A supplemental tax is imposed on taxpayers with adjusted gross incomes over $100,000. 12. For individuals deducting federal income tax, rates range from 0.5% of the first $1,000 to 10% on income over $16,000 (single taxpayers). 13. Federal tax deduction limited to $3,000. 14. Interest and dividends (except for savings account interest) are taxed at 6%. **Source:** Advisory Commission on Intergovernmental Relations, *Significant Features of Fiscal Federalism* (1995).

STATES RANKED ACCORDING TO SELECTED TAX AMOUNTS, 1992

			Per capita tax amounts (dollars)					
State	Total tax collections ('000s)	Rank	Total sales tax	Rank	General sales tax	Rank	Individual income tax	Rank
Alabama	$ 4,217,916	25	$1,019.81	42	$ 269.71	43	$298.31	37
Alaska	1,590,198	41	2,709.03	1	(X)	46	(X)	44
Arizona	4,826,755	22	1,259.59	25	544.96	7	323.69	36
Arkansas	2,746,079	32	1,144.68	32	430.40	18	354.36	32
California	46,128,169	1	1,494.42	10	483.52	13	551.71	10
Colorado	3,520,866	29	1,014.66	43	263.29	44	464.54	19
Connecticut	6,060,190	19	1,847.06	4	637.04	4	568.64	9
Delaware	1,341,005	43	1,946.31	3	(X)	46	722.19	5
Florida	14,504,207	5	1,075.34	41	617.29	6	(X)	44
Georgia	7,266,981	15	1,076.43	40	398.07	25	456.48	20
Hawaii	2,709,518	33	2,335.79	2	1,116.14	1	781.88	3
Idaho	1,401,585	42	1,313.58	21	411.60	21	501.86	14
Illinois	13,463,435	6	1,157.55	31	364.68	32	393.98	25
Indiana	6,476,135	18	1,143.79	33	490.84	10	389.00	29
Iowa	3,601,571	28	1,280.79	24	359.26	34	501.75	15
Kansas	2,801,692	31	1,110.46	35	379.77	29	330.46	35
Kentucky	5,080,971	21	1,353.12	16	364.01	33	447.01	21
Louisiana	4,250,245	24	991.43	44	295.94	41	202.35	39
Maine	1,664,359	40	1,347.66	17	464.31	14	478.94	16
Maryland	6,502,494	17	1,324.88	19	321.88	38	592.39	8
Massachusetts	9,903,246	10	1,651.09	7	329.89	37	889.79	1
Michigan	11,279,170	9	1,195.21	28	388.42	27	343.49	33
Minnesota	7,449,787	13	1,662.90	5	488.99	11	669.44	6
Mississippi	2,494,392	34	954.24	47	452.32	15	168.16	41
Missouri	5,131,360	20	988.13	45	369.09	31	355.09	31
Montana	1,034,876	45	1,255.92	26	(X)	46	390.22	28
Nebraska	1,889,877	38	1,176.76	30	412.93	20	406.37	23
Nevada	1,823,376	39	1,374.06	14	672.74	2	(X)	44
New Hampshire	829,144	46	746.30	50	(X)	46	31.47	42
New Jersey	12,802,662	7	1,643.68	9	519.87	8	526.63	11
New Mexico	2,242,712	36	1,418.54	12	621.49	5	281.66	38
New York	30,113,133	2	1,661.96	6	331.45	36	823.08	2
North Carolina	9,009,742	11	1,316.64	20	317.26	39	523.60	12
North Dakota	754,555	48	1,186.41	29	403.43	23	187.89	40
Ohio	12,114,788	8	1,099.74	37	340.55	35	400.06	24
Oklahoma	3,882,148	27	1,208.64	27	302.41	40	379.26	30
Oregon	3,313,496	30	1,113.03	34	(X)	46	746.15	4
Pennsylvania	16,269,988	4	1,354.82	15	374.70	30	390.47	27
Rhode Island	1,307,111	44	1,300.61	22	387.05	28	476.08	18
South Carolina	3,935,500	26	1,092.28	39	403.00	24	391.59	26
South Dakota	565,032	50	794.70	49	406.93	22	(X)	44
Tennessee	4,525,662	23	900.81	48	500.56	9	18.58	43
Texas	17,030,546	3	964.58	46	485.72	12	(X)	44
Utah	1,987,793	37	1,096.41	38	442.60	16	430.99	22
Vermont	763,391	47	1,339.28	18	275.49	42	476.19	17
Virginia	7,025,345	16	1,101.67	36	246.32	45	520.82	13
Washington	8,476,932	12	1,650.49	8	979.67	2	(X)	44
West Virginia	2,351,858	35	1,297.93	23	439.78	17	338.09	34
Wisconsin	7,389,207	14	1,475.78	11	424.87	19	627.56	7
Wyoming	645,929	49	1,386.11	13	391.73	26	(X)	44

Note: (X) = state collects no tax for that item. **Source**: U.S. Bureau of the Census, *State Government Tax Collections, 1992* (1993).

STATE EXCISES ON GENERAL SALES, CIGARETTES, AND MOTOR FUEL, 1992

State	General sales and gross receipts			Cigarettes (cents per package)	Gasoline (cents per gallon)
	Percentage rate	Food exempt[1]	Drugs exempt[2]		
Alabama	4.0%[3]	No	Yes	16.5¢	16¢
Alaska	(X)	(X)	(X)	29	8
Arizona	5.0[3]	Yes	Yes	18	18
Arkansas	4.5[3]	No	Yes	22	18.5
California	6.0[3]	Yes	Yes	35	16
Colorado	3.0[3]	Yes	Yes	20	22
Connecticut	6.0	Yes	Yes	45	26
Delaware	(X)	(X)	(X)	24	19
District of Columbia	6.0	Yes	Yes	50	18
Florida	6.0[3]	Yes	Yes	33.9	4
Georgia	4.0[3]	No	Yes	12	7.5[4]
Hawaii	4.0	No	Yes	([5])	16[6]
Idaho	5.0	No	Yes	18	21
Illinois	6.25[3]	No[7]	No[7]	30	19
Indiana	5.0	Yes	Yes	15.5	15
Iowa	5.0[3]	Yes	Yes	36	20
Kansas	4.9[3]	No	Yes	24	18
Kentucky	6.0	Yes	Yes	3	15
Louisiana	4.0	No[8]	Yes	20	20
Maine	6.0	Yes	Yes	37	19
Maryland	5.0	Yes	Yes	36	23.5
Massachusetts	5.0	Yes	Yes	26	21
Michigan	4.0	Yes	Yes	25	15
Minnesota	6.0[3]	Yes	Yes	48	20
Mississippi	7.0	No	Yes	18	18
Missouri	4.225[3]	No	Yes	13	13
Montana	(X)	(X)	(X)	19.25¢	20¢
Nebraska	5.0%[3]	Yes	Yes	27	23.7
Nevada	6.5[3]	Yes	Yes	35	18.75
New Hampshire	(X)	(X)	(X)	25	18
New Jersey	6.0	Yes	Yes	40	10.5
New Mexico	5.0[3]	No	No	15	16
New York	4.0[3]	Yes	Yes	39	8
North Carolina	4.0[3]	No	Yes	5	22.3
North Dakota	5.0	Yes	Yes	29	17
Ohio	5.0[3]	Yes	Yes	18	21
Oklahoma	4.5[3]	No	Yes	23	17
Oregon	(X)	(X)	(X)	28	22
Pennsylvania	6.0	Yes	Yes	31	12
Rhode Island	7.0	Yes	Yes	37	23
South Carolina	5.0[3]	No	Yes	7	16
South Dakota	4.0[3]	No	Yes	23	18
Tennessee	6.0[3]	No	Yes	13	20
Texas	6.25[3]	Yes	Yes	41	20
Utah	5.0[3]	No	Yes	23	19
Vermont	5.0	Yes	Yes	18	15
Virginia	3.5[3]	No	Yes	2.5	17.5
Washington	6.5[3]	Yes	Yes	34	23
West Virginia	6.0	No	Yes	17	15.5
Wisconsin	5.0[3]	Yes	Yes	38	22.2
Wyoming	3.0[3]	No	Yes	12	9

Note: X = no tax levied. 1. Reflects status as of end of fiscal year for sale of most food products for consumption off premises; federal statute prohibits states from taxing food purchased with USDA food stamps. 2. Reflects status as of end of fiscal year. 3. State authorizes state collection of combined state and local sales taxes in those jurisdictions which approve supplemental local sales taxes under state enabling legislation. 4. An additional tax is levied at the rate of 3% of the retail sales price of the motor fuel, less the current 7.5 cents per gallon tax. This tax is levied, collected, and administered in the same manner as the sales and use tax. 5. Rate is 40% of wholesale price. 6. Combined state and county rates are: Hawaii, 24.8 cents; Honolulu, 32.5 cents; Kauai, 26 cents; and Maui, 25 cents. 7. Subject to a 1% state tax, effective Jan. 1, 1990. In addition, these items may be subject to a 1% local tax. 8. Subject to a 2% state tax until July 1, 1994. **Source:** U.S. Bureau of the Census, *State Government Tax Collections, 1992* (1994).

SUMMARY OF STATE GOVERNMENT FINANCES, 1993

Item	Amount (thousands)
TOTAL REVENUES	**$804,494,781**
General Revenue	653,135,160
Intergovernmental revenue	188,630,461
Taxes	353,327,654
Sales and gross receipts	174,218,430
Individual income	112,555,495
Corporation net income	24,207,888
Other taxes	42,345,841
Current charges	57,381,219
Miscellaneous general revenue	53,795,826
Utility revenue	3,675,192
Liquor stores revenue	3,070,460
Insurance trust revenue	144,613,969
TOTAL EXPENDITURES	**$742,936,130**
Intergovernmental expenditure	213,936,862
Direct expenditure	528,999,268
Current operation	345,397,445
Capital outlay	49,775,877
Insurance benefits and repayments	87,050,267
Assistance and subsidies	21,975,671
Interest on debt	24,800,008
Exhibit: Salaries and wages	115,283,209

Item	Amount (thousands)
General expenditure	$646,087,617
Intergovernmental expenditure	213,936,862
Direct expenditure	432,150,755
General expenditure, by function:	
Education	221,341,950
Public welfare	168,421,272
Hospitals	27,434,629
Health	25,766,959
Highways	51,268,395
Police protection	5,600,358
Correction	20,689,729
Natural resources	11,212,480
Parks and recreation	3,006,496
Governmental administration	22,452,869
Interest on general debt	23,989,656
Other and unallocable	61,189,961
Utility expenditure	7,239,731
Liquor stores expenditure	2,550,636
Insurance trust expenditure	87,050,267
Debt at end of fiscal year	**$387,679,640**
Cash and security holdings	**$1,120,649,019**

Source: U.S. Bureau of the Census, *State Government Finances in 1993* (1995).

CITIES AND COUNTIES IN THE U.S.

Included here is basic information about population change, cost of living, and government finances in major U.S. cities, metropolitan statistical areas, and counties. In addition there are brief descriptions and statistics for each of the 50 largest cities—from Albuquerque to Washington, D.C. Statistical sources include the U.S. Census Bureau's 1990 decennial census, *City Government Finances, County Government Finances,* and the *Statistical Abstract of the United States* (all annual publications).

FORMS OF LOCAL GOVERNMENT

In addition to the one federal and 50 state governments, the Bureau of the Census recognizes five basic types of organized local government. In addition to these, which are authorized in state constitutions and statutes, some local governments operate under "home-rule charters," the form and organization of which are specified by locally approved charters rather than by general or special state law. The number of local governments and officials continues to skyrocket, even as the size of the federal bureaucracy shrinks. In 1992, there were a total of 85,006 state and local governments and 510,497 elected officials, compared with 83,236 and 497,155 five years earlier.

Counties County governments are established to provide general government, and include those governments designated as boroughs in Alaska, parishes in Louisiana, and counties in the other states. In 1992 there were 3,043 county governments; the most common forms are:

Council-commission A county government without a chief executive but with an elected governing body that shares administrative responsibility with officials elected or appointed to specific positions.

Council-administrator A county government with an elected governing body responsible for overall policy, and an appointed administrator (sometimes called a county manager, county commissioner, or county judge) responsible for administration. The powers of the administrator under this form of government may vary widely.

Council-elected executive A county government with an elected governing body and an elected chief executive—sometimes called a president or a chairperson of the board. The powers of the executive under this form of government may vary widely.

Municipalities Municipal governments are established to provide general government for a specific concentration of population in a defined area and include those governments designated as cities, villages, boroughs (except in Alaska), and towns (except in the six New England states, Minnesota, New York, and Wisconsin). In 1992 there were 19,279 municipal governments; the most common forms are:

Mayor-council A municipal government with an elected mayor and an elected council or other governing body. In some mayor-council municipalities, the mayor is the chief executive, with broad powers. In some other mayor-council cities, the mayor has limited powers.

Council-manager A municipal government with an elected council or other governing body responsible for overall policy, and an appointed manager responsible for administration. The council may select a chairperson from among their own number who may be designated as the mayor.

Commission A municipal government with an elected board of commissioners responsible for overall policy. Each commissioner is responsible for administration of one or more departments of the municipal government. The board may select a chairperson from among their own number who may be designated as the mayor.

Towns Township governments are established to provide general government for areas defined without regard to population concentration and include those governments designated as towns in Connecticut, Maine (including organized plantations), Massachusetts, Minnesota, New Hampshire (including organized locations), New York, Rhode Island, Vermont, and Wisconsin, and townships in other states. In 1992 there were 16,556 township governments; the most common forms are:

Town meeting A township government in which an annual meeting of resident voters makes basic policy. An elected board (often called "a board of selectmen" or "township supervisors") is responsible for day-to-day administration of the township.

Representative town meeting A township government in which a town meeting composed of elected representatives of the resident voters makes basic policy. This form of government is usually found in more populous towns or townships. An elected board (often called "a board of selectmen" or "township supervisors") is responsible for day-to-day administration of the township.

School districts School district governments are organized local entities providing public elementary, secondary, and/or higher education which, under state law, have sufficient administrative and fiscal autonomy to qualify as separate governments. Excludes "dependent public school systems" of county, township, or state governments. In 1992 there were 14,422 school district governments.

Special district governments All organized local entities other than the four categories listed above, authorized by state law to provide only one or a limited number of designated functions, and with sufficient administrative and fiscal autonomy to qualify as separate governments; known by a variety of titles, including districts, authorities, boards, commissions, etc., as specified in the state legislation. In 1992 there were 31,355 special district governments.

Source: U.S. Bureau of the Census, *1992 Census of Governments: Popularly Elected Officials* (1995).

GOVERNMENT EXPENDITURES IN THE 50 LARGEST CITIES

City	Total expenditures (millions)
New York City	$42,499
Los Angeles	3,577
Chicago	3,887
Houston	1,758
Philadelphia	3,723
San Diego	1,311
Detroit	2,131
Dallas	1,620
Phoenix	1,091
San Antonio	1,501
San Jose	760
Baltimore	1,687
Indianapolis	954
San Francisco	3,024
Jacksonville	1,686
Columbus	729
Milwaukee	684
Memphis	1,762
Washington, D.C.	5,036
Boston	1,781
Seattle	1,173
El Paso	359
Cleveland	803
New Orleans	773
Nashville	1,525
Denver	1,649
Austin	1,113
Fort Worth	523
Oklahoma City	417
Portland	581
Kansas City	662
Long Beach	737
Tucson	436
St. Louis	603
Charlotte	566
Atlanta	767
Virginia Beach	716
Albuquerque	546
Oakland	554
Pittsburgh	429
Sacramento	399
Minneapolis	795
Tulsa	491
Honolulu	1,101
Cincinnati	659
Miami	359
Fresno	303
Omaha	222
Toledo	258
Buffalo	774

Note: Figures for 1992, latest year available. **Source:** U.S. Bureau of the Census, *City Government Finances in 1992* (1994).

Fifty Largest Cities

Albuquerque, New Mexico

Seventy million years ago, earthquakes and volcanoes pushed the land that is now Albuquerque above the sea, forming the Rio Grande Valley and a ring of mountain ranges. Even today the 10,000-foot-high Sandia Mountains are rising slowly, and the Rio Grande Valley continues gradually to deepen. During the Ice Age, Sandia Man roamed the area hunting mastodon and buffalo, and some 3,000 years ago the Anasazi built stone and adobe cities, which still stand. The 1530s marked the arrival of Spanish conquistadors and missionaries.

Founded as a Spanish villa in 1706, when 35 families moved to the land along the Rio Grande, Albuquerque was named by Don Francisco Cuervo y Valdez in honor of the duke of Albuquerque, King Phillip's viceroy of New Spain. Indian raids arrested the villa's expansion, and 100 years after its founding its population numbered a mere 2,200. Benefiting from their proximity to the Santa Fe Trail, the people farmed; raised cattle; marketed adobe, for building and wool; and ran trading posts, military supply depots, saloons, hotels, and mercantile businesses. The introduction of the railroad in 1880 spurred Albuquerque's growth, and the 1940 population of 35,000 has since grown more than tenfold.

Albuquerque occupies a central position along the Rio Grande Research Corridor, which stretches from Los Alamos to Las Cruces, and is home to the University of New Mexico and such major high-tech installations as Sandia National Laboratories, GTE Communications Systems, Unisys, and General Electric. Albuquerque's cultural and historic attractions include the Albuquerque Museum, the Indian Pueblo Cultural Center, the Maxwell Museum of Anthropology, the National Atomic Museum, the Spanish History Museum, and Petroglyph National Monument.

Population 384,736 (1990). Rank: 38. Race/national origin: Black 3.0%; Hispanic 34.5%; Asian 1.7%; American Indian 3.0%. Pop. density: 3,025/sq. mi. (1,167/sq km).

Location 35°05'N, 106°47'W. County: Bernalillo.

Terrain and climate Elev.: 5,300 ft. Area: 127.2 sq. mi. (329.4 sq km). Avg. daily min. temp.: Jan.: 22.3°F/–5.3°C; avg. daily max.: July: 92.8°F/33.7°C. Avg. annual rainfall: 8.12"; snowfall: 11"; clear days: 71; precipitation days: 135.

Government Form: mayor and council. Mayor: Martin Chavez. Election: Nov. 1997. Municipal tel. number: (505) 768–3000.

Visitor info.: (505) 243–3696.

Atlanta, Georgia

Atlanta, the capital and largest city of Georgia, lies at the base of the Blue Ridge Mountains near the Chattahoochee River. First settled in 1836, the area became the terminus for the Georgia Railroad in 1845 and took the name Atlanta. The population grew to 15,000 by 1861, and during the Civil War Atlanta became a strategic Confederate depot and collection point for recruits, establishing it as one of the most important cities of the Confederacy and making it a vital objective during Gen. William Tecumseh Sherman's infamous march to the sea in 1864. After two months of bitter battle, Sherman took the city on Sept. 1. After the war the ravaged city was rebuilt, and it became the state capital in 1878.

The chief commercial, industrial, insurance, telecommunications, and distributing center of the Southeast, Atlanta includes among its wide cross-section of industries railroad shops, large printing and publishing operations, automobile assembly plants, telecommunications equipment manufacturing, and numerous factories producing items ranging from foods and beverages to furniture.

An important educational and cultural center, the city boasts more than 20 institutions of higher learning, including Georgia Tech, Emory University, and Oglethorpe University, and is the site of the Atlanta Historical Society Library and exhibition, the Cyclorama (a three-dimension painting re-creating the battle of Atlanta during the Civil War), the Atlanta Science and Technology Museum, High Museum of Art, and the Fernbank Science Center, featuring the nation's third-largest planetarium. Atlanta will be the host city for the 1996 Summer Olympics.

Population 394,017 (1990). Rank: 36. Race/national origin: Black 67.1%; Hispanic 1.9%; Asian 0.9%; American Indian 0.1%. Pop. density: 3,003/sq. mi. (1,160/sq km).

Location 33°50'N, 84°24'W. Counties: DeKalb, Fulton.

Terrain and climate Elev.: 1,034 ft. Area: 131.2 sq. mi. (339.80 sq km). Avg. daily min. temp.: Jan.: 32.6°F/0.3°C; avg. daily max.: July: 87.9°F/31°C. Avg. annual rainfall: 48.61"; snowfall: 2"; clear days: 108; precipitation days: 116.

Government Form: mayor and council. Mayor: William Craig Campbell. Election: Nov. 1997. Municipal tel. number: (404) 521–6600.

Visitor info: 1–800–ATLNOWS or (404) 222–6688.

Austin, Texas

Austin, the capital of Texas, lies about 80 miles northeast of San Antonio on the banks of the Colorado River. First inhabited by nomadic Indian tribes, the area had as its first permanent European settler Jacob Harrell, in 1835, who, with the three families who joined him a few years later, established the town of Waterloo. In 1838 it was chosen as the site of the Texas Republic's capital and was renamed Austin after Stephen F. Austin, who brought the first Anglo settlers to Texas in the 1820s. After 1845, when Texas gained admission into the Union, Austin began to flourish, and by 1930 it had grown into a major regional center with a population of 75,000.

Austin was originally a business and distribution center serving the farmers of the Blackland Prairies to the east; its farmers now produce cotton, maize, corn, livestock, and poultry. Traditional industries such as meat packing, canning, and furniture manufacturing have been outstripped by the high-tech companies that have helped to nearly double the population since 1970. The University of Texas, founded in 1881 in Austin, boasts the highest endowment of any U.S. university—a legacy of the Texas oil fields. As the university developed into a first-class institution feeding the city's cultural and economic life, and with the influx of electronics and computer companies, Austin has prospered into a metropolis of national, even worldwide, scope.

Population 465,622 (1990). Rank: 27. Race/national origin: Black 12.4%; Hispanic 23.0%; Asian 3.0%; American Indian 0.4%. Pop. density: 2,007/sq. mi. (775/sq km).

Location 30°20'N, 97°45'W. Counties: Travis, Williamson.

Terrain and climate Elev.: 570 ft. Area: 232 sq. mi. (600.9 sq km). Avg. daily min. temp.: Jan.: 38.8°F/3.8°C; avg. daily max.: July: 95.4°F/35.2°C. Avg. annual rainfall: 31.50"; snowfall: 1"; clear days: 115; precipitation days: 82.

Government Form: council and manager. Mayor: Bruce Todd. Election: May 1997. Municipal tel. number: (512) 499–2000.

Visitor info.: 1–800–888–8287 or (512) 478–0098.

Baltimore, Maryland

One of America's most active seaports since Colonial days and chartered in 1729 as a major conduit of tobacco exportation, Baltimore was named after the founder of the colony of Maryland, George Calvert, Lord Baltimore. By the time of the Revolutionary War, it earned fame as an important commercial and maritime center, and ships sailing from Baltimore plied their trade with northern Europe, the Mediterranean, and the Caribbean. Chartered as a city in 1797, Baltimore saw its commercial activity surge with the burgeoning of its iron and copper industries, its proximity to the nation's capital, and the arrival of the Baltimore and Ohio Railroad, which developed links to the Midwest. However, the deep, divisive passions of the Civil War stunted growth, and it was years before the city recovered.

A fire in 1904 destroyed almost every building in the downtown area, providing impetus for needed revitalization. The two world wars renewed demands for Baltimore's port facilities and fostered development of a solid heavy-industrial base. But following World War II, the city's infrastructure aged and decayed. Today Baltimore remains a large port and industrial city with one of the largest steel plants in the world (Bethlehem Steel's Sparrow Point works). Much of the city has been rebuilt through urban renewal efforts, including the nationally acclaimed Inner Harbor Project near the downtown area and the new Oriole Park at Camden Yards. The population seems to have stabilized after a loss of almost 20 percent in the 1960s.

Among the city's historic sites is Fort McHenry, where Francis Scott Key wrote "The Star-Spangled Banner." Baltimore is home to St. Mary's Seminary and University (1791), Johns Hopkins University (1876), and the University of Baltimore (1925), among other noted institutions of higher learning.

Population 736,014 (1990). Rank: 13. Race/national origin: Black 59.2%; Hispanic 1.0%; Asian 1.1%; American Indian 0.3%. Pop. density: 9,166/sq. mi. (3,539/sq km).
Location 39°18'N, 76°37'W. County: independent city within Baltimore County.
Terrain and climate Elev.: 155 ft. Area: 80.3 sq. mi. (208 sq km). Avg. daily min. temp.: Jan.: 24.3°F/–4.2°C; avg. daily max.: July: 87.1°F/30.6°C. Avg. annual rainfall: 43.39"; snowfall: 22"; clear days: 106; precipitation days: 112.
Government Form: mayor and council. Mayor: Kurt L. Schmoke. Election: Nov. 1995. Municipal tel. number: (301) 396–3100.
Visitor info.: 1–800–282–6632.

Boston, Massachusetts

Named for the English port from which many Puritan immigrants came to America, Boston was first settled in 1630 under the leadership of John Winthrop. As the capital of the Massachusetts Bay Colony, it quickly became the cultural and mercantile capital of the New England colonies. Bostonians never wholly embraced British authority, and they provided the earliest challenges to British rule in their reaction to the Stamp Act (1765) and through the Boston Tea Party (1773). The colonists killed in the Boston Massacre (1770) were the first to fall in the years immediately preceding the American Revolution.

With the end of the Revolution, Boston merchants found themselves shut out of English ports by prohibitive tariffs, and in their quest for new markets for American goods opened American trade to the Orient and India. In the 19th century, Boston benefited early from the Industrial Revolution and from several waves of immigration, particularly blacks from the southern states, and Irish and Italians from Europe.

Although Boston's preeminence in trade and industry did not survive the 19th century, the city continues to be a major center for banking and financial services. Since World War II, its suburbs have flourished as centers of research and development and of the computer industry—Route 128 is the East Coast's answer to California's "Silicon Valley"—spurring investment in downtown Boston. However, the recession of the early 1990s hit Boston and all of New England severely. As the gateway to New England and the birthplace of the Revolution, Boston is also a center for tourism.

Perhaps most important to its identity is Boston's wealth of diverse educational, cultural, and religious institutions. Harvard (across the Charles River in Cambridge, 1636) is the country's oldest college, and Roxbury Latin (1645) the country's oldest privately endowed secondary school. Today Boston embraces more than 20 colleges and universities, as well as some of the finest cultural institutions in the country, including the American Academy of Arts and Sciences (1780), the Massachusetts Historical Society (1791), the Boston Athenaeum (1807), the Boston Public Library (the nation's first, 1854), the Boston Museum of Fine Arts (1870), and the Boston Symphony (1881). The *Boston Globe* is one of the nation's oldest and most distinguished daily and Sunday newspapers.
Population 574,283 (1990). Rank: 20. Race/national origin: Black 25.6%; Hispanic 10.8%; Asian 5.3%; American Indian 0.3%. Pop. density: 12,167/sq. mi. (4,700/sq km).
Location 42°20'N, 71°05'W. County: Suffolk.
Terrain and climate Elev.: 10 ft. Area: 47.2 sq. mi. (122.2 sq km). Avg. daily min. temp.: Jan.: 22.8°F/–5.1°C; avg. daily max.: July: 81.8°F/27.6°C. Avg. annual rainfall: 43.81"; snowfall: 42"; clear days: 99; precipitation days: 128.
Government Form: mayor and council. Mayor: Thomas M. Menino. Election: Nov. 1997. Municipal tel. number: (617) 725–4000.
Visitor info.: 1–800–888–5515 or (617) 536–4100.

Buffalo, New York

Bordering Lake Erie and located on the Niagara River where the Peace Bridge connects the United States to Canada, Buffalo, the second-largest city in New York State, offers a wide variety of commercial activity. An international inland port via the St. Lawrence Seaway and the Erie Canal, one of the busiest railroad systems in the country, and its position as the western terminus for the New York State Thruway, all make Buffalo an important transportation center. While the city's manufacturing base declined from 32 percent of total commerce in 1971 to 19 percent in 1987, the emergence of service businesses and financial organizations, particularly banks, has bolstered the local economy. The proximity to Niagara Falls lures thousands of tourists to the city every year.

The Erie Canal made Buffalo a strategic gateway to the West. The town dates back to the 1700s when the Holland Land Company acquired tracts of land in western New York, and after a plan was drawn up in 1800, the residents chose the name Buffalo, probably after the Indians' mispronunciation of the French *beau fleuve* (beautiful river)—the Niagara. After completion of the Erie Canal in 1825, the city evolved into a heavy manufacturing center, the biggest ship-to-rail grain-transfer point in the country, and in 1832 the "Queen City of the Great Lakes" was incorporated.

Buffalo was home to Presidents Millard Fillmore and Grover Cleveland, the latter of whom served as its mayor for one year. The Wilcox Mansion, where Theodore Roosevelt was sworn in after the assassination of William McKinley, stands as a national historic site.
Population 328,123 (1990). Rank: 50. Race/national origin: Black 30.7%; Hispanic 4.9%; Asian 1.0%; American Indian 0.8%. Pop. density: 7,850/sq. mi. (3,030/sq km).
Location 42°55'N, 78°50'W. County: Erie.
Terrain and climate Elev.: 706 ft. Area: 41.8 sq. mi. (108.3 sq km). Avg. daily min. temp.: Jan.: 17°F/–8°C; avg. daily max.: July: 80.2°F/ 26.7°C. Avg. annual rainfall: 37.52"; snowfall: 90"; clear days: 55; precipitation days: 168.
Government Form: mayor and council. Mayor: Anthony Masiello. Election: Nov. 1997. Municipal tel. number: (716) 851–4200.
Visitor info.: 1–800–BUFFALO or (716) 852–0511.

Charlotte, North Carolina

An area of lush green foothills lying at the southernmost tip of the Carolina Piedmont, Charlotte has long been a crossroads city and an important distribution point for the surrounding farmlands. About 250 years ago, Scottish and Irish settlers retracing old Catawba Indian trading routes established a settlement where the paths crossed, and in 1762 it was named Charlotte, after the new bride of King George III. Remembering Gen. Cornwallis's reference to Charlotte as a "hornet's nest" while his army briefly occupied it during the American Revolution, the city adopted the symbol as its emblem. The discovery of a 17-pound gold nugget in 1799 triggered a gold rush, and although the mines dotting the landscape boosted business, the California gold rush in the mid-1800s lured away prospectors, putting Charlotte on its future course as a top cotton producer. A leading city of the Confederacy in the Civil War, Charlotte hosted the last full meeting of the Confederate cabinet in 1865.

Recently, the city's economy has diversified to include the production of chemicals, foodstuffs, machinery, metals, and textiles. The city has matured into a major center of world trade and technology, with more than 160 multinational companies engaging in such businesses as microelectronics, insurance, machining, and biomedical supplies. Located equidistant from the northeastern, midwestern, and southern Florida markets, with an inland port of entry for goods and a foreign trade zone where items may be held without duty, Charlotte remains a key distribution conduit. A midsize city at the heart of a rapidly expanding metropolitan region, Charlotte ranks as the nation's fifth-largest urban area with a population of more than five million living within a 100-mile radius of the city. The Charlotte Motor Speedway, and the Charlotte Hornets, one of the expansion teams added to the NBA in 1988, are sources of civic pride.
Population 395,934 (1990). Rank: 35. Race/national origin: Black 31.8%; Hispanic 1.4%; Asian 1.8%; American Indian 0.4%. Pop. density: 2,603/sq. mi. (1,005/sqkm).
Location 35°16'N, 80°46'W. County: Mecklenburg.
Terrain and climate Elev.: 665 ft. Area: 152.1 sq. mi. (393.9 sq km). Avg. daily min. temp.: Jan.: 31°F/–0.56°C; avg. daily max.: July: 88°F/31.1°C. Avg. annual rainfall: 43.16"; snowfall: 6"; clear days: 111; precipitation days: 111.
Government Form: council-mayor and manager. Mayor: Richard Vinroot. Election: Nov. 1995. Municipal tel. number: (704) 336–2241.
Visitor info.: (704) 331–2700 or 1–800–231–4636.

Chicago, Illinois

Chicago extends roughly 26 miles along the southwestern shoreline of Lake Michigan. The city has historically been a major transportation hub and gateway to the Great Plains and continues to be one today, with major air, rail, and highway hubs. Nineteen trunk-line railroad routes converge at Chicago, linking it with every major U.S. and Canadian city. The city has three major airports, including O'Hare, the busiest in the nation. It is also a hub for major interstate highways running east-west and north-south.

Historically, Chicago's rise parallels the westward expansion of the American republic. Chicago was first settled in 1779, when Jean Baptiste Point de Sable built a house on the site. In 1803 federal troops built a stockade named Fort Dearborn, but by 1830 only 12 families had settled in the area. In the 1830s, however, the population grew rapidly as Americans spread westward, and the city of Chicago was incorporated in 1837 with a population of 4,170. Chicago then began to grow into a bustling Great Lakes port, connected to the Mississippi via a system of rivers and canals.

Chicago has maintained its strategic importance despite changes in transportation technology and remains today a prosperous city. Over the years Chicago has been noted as a hotbed of labor reform, the center of violent organized-crime gang wars during the Prohibition era, and a prime example of the good and the bad of American city machine-politics. Despite its checkered past, however, it has grown into the wealthiest and most vibrant city in the Midwest. Chicago ranks first among American cities in the number of employed chemists and second in engineers. It has grown into a financial center with three of the nation's four largest futures exchanges and the world's largest listed-stock-options exchange. The city's financial district and much of the downtown area were shut down on Apr. 13, 1992, when the Chicago River burst into an aged underground tunnel system, flooding many buildings and disrupting business.

Major attractions include the Museum of Science and Industry, the Field Museum of Natural History, the Chicago Historical Society, the Lincoln Park Zoo, the Chicago Lyric Opera Company, the Chicago Symphony Orchestra, and the Chicago Art Institute. Downtown Chicago currently has three of the five tallest man-made structures in the world—the Sears Tower (110 stories, 1,454 ft. high), the Amoco building (1,136 ft.), and the John Hancock building (1,127 ft.). It is also home to the world's tallest apartment complex, the 70-story Lake Point Tower, and the world's largest commercial building, the Merchandise Mart.

Population 2,783,726 (1990). Rank: 3. Race/national origin: Black 39.1%; Hispanic 19.6%; Asian 3.7%; American Indian 0.3%. Pop. density: 12,204/sq. mi. (4,712/sq km).

Location 41°53'N, 87°40'W. County: Cook.

Terrain and climate Elev.: 623 ft. Area: 228.1 sq. mi. (590.8 sq km). Avg. daily min. temp.: Jan.: 13.6°F/–10.2°C; avg. daily max.: July: 83.3°F/ 28.5° Avg. annual rainfall: 33.34"; snowfall: 40"; clear days: 94; precipitation days: 123.

Government Form: mayor and council. Mayor: Richard M. Daley. Election: Apr. 1999. Municipal tel. number: (312) 744–4000.

Visitor info.: (312) 744–2400.

Cincinnati, Ohio

Cincinnati's origins can be traced to 1789, when the U.S. government set up Fort Washington in the town of Losantiville to quell Indian attacks. A year later, the burgeoning city was renamed Cincinnati, after the Society of the Cincinnati, an organization of Revolutionary War veterans. Settlement of the city increased after the Battle of Fallen Timbers (1794) put down Miami resistance to European-settler control of the region.

In 1811 the *New Orleans*, the first steamboat on the western rivers, arrived from Pittsburgh, and thereafter Cincinnati became a major inland port. The city's commercial status was consolidated in the 1840s after the opening of the Miami and Erie Canal, which joined the Ohio River at Cincinnati with Lake Erie at Toledo, and the arrival of the first railroads in 1843. Large numbers of German immigrants gave the city a European flavor. By mid-century Cincinnati had reached its zenith as a commercial and manufacturing center, well deserving of Longfellow's epithet, "Queen City of the West." Cincinnati continued to prosper after the Civil War, though it was beset by problems ranging from perennial flooding to extensive government corruption. By 1910 its population had reached 360,000, about what it is today.

Cincinnati continues to be a hub of transportation and industry, particularly strong in the manufacture of transportation equipment and industrial machinery, food and beverage production, steel, and printing. It is one of the nation's largest inland coal ports and a regional center for wholesaling, retailing, insurance, and finance.

Among its many colleges and universities are the University of Cincinnati, Cincinnati Technical College, the Athenaeum of Ohio, Hebrew Union College-Jewish Institute of Religion (founded in 1875 and the oldest rabbinic college in the U.S.), and Cincinnati Bible Seminary. It is the home of the William Howard Taft birthplace, the Harriet Beecher Stowe House State Memorial, Tyler-Davidson Fountain, and the Cincinnati Zoo, the second-oldest zoo in the country.

Population 364,040 (1990). Rank: 45. Race/national origin: Black 37.9%; Hispanic 0.7%; Asian 1.1%; American Indian 0.2%. Pop. density: 4,667/sq. mi. (1,802/sq km).

Location 39°10'N, 84°26'W. County: Hamilton.

Terrain and climate Elev.: 540 ft. Area: 78 sq. mi. (202 sq km). Avg. daily min. temp.: Jan.: 20.4°F/–6.4°C; avg. daily max.: July: 85.8°F/ 29.8°C. Avg. annual rainfall: 40.10"; snowfall: 19"; clear days: 80; precipitation days: 131.

Government Form: council and manager. Mayor: Roxanne Qualles. Election: Nov. 1995. Municipal tel. number: (513) 352–3000.

Visitor info.: 1–800–CINCYUSA or (513) 621–2142.

Cleveland, Ohio

The heart of the largest metropolitan area in Ohio, Cleveland was founded in 1795 and named after Moses Cleaveland, a surveyor with the Connecticut Land Company, which administered the state of Connecticut's lingering claim on 3.5 million acres of what is now Ohio (the Western Reserve). A frontier village at the mouth of the Cuyahoga River on Lake Erie, Cleveland was transformed into the business and manufacturing center of northern Ohio by the opening of the Erie Canal in 1825, and the Ohio and Erie Canal, which linked Cleveland with Portsmouth on the Ohio River. When the Soo Locks opened Lake Superior to trade with the Lower Lakes in 1855, Cleveland became a major shipping center for ore, lumber, copper, coal, and farm produce.

During the Civil War, the city's iron ore and coal deposits were mined for steel production, and commercial activity increased to meet the Union's increased demands for heavy machinery, railroad equipment, and ships. In the postwar years, Cleveland's mills and factories expanded even further to satisfy the increased needs of new cities and farms springing up in the wake of westward migration.

Although heavy manufacturing employs 22.5 percent of the city's workforce (more than the national average), the national trend toward a service economy has had a severe impact on the local economy. Nonetheless, heavy industry is a cornerstone of the city's economy, with many large industrial companies located there. In addition, there are many medical and industrial research firms, most notably the world-famous Cleveland Clinic and NASA's Lewis Research Center.

Cleveland's industrial strength manifests itself in its flourishing cultural institutions, including Case Western Reserve University (a merger of Western Reserve University and Case Institute of Technology); the Cleveland Play House, the nation's oldest repertory theater; the world-famous Cleveland Orchestra; the Cleveland Museum of Natural History; Western Reserve Historical Society; the Cleveland Health Museum; Allen Memorial Medical Library; the Cleveland Zoo; the Cleveland Institute of Art; the Cleveland Institute of Music; and the Karamu Center for interracial cultural events.

Population 505,616 (1990). Rank: 24. Race/national origin: Black 46.6%; Hispanic 4.6%; Asian 1.0%; American Indian 0.3%. Pop. density: 6,400/sq. mi. (2,471/sq km).

Location 41°28'N, 81°43'W. County: Cuyahoga.

Terrain and climate Elev.: 805 ft. Area: 79 sq. mi. (204.6 sq km). Avg. daily min. temp.: Jan.: 18.5°F/–7.5°C; avg. daily max.: July: 81.7°F/ 27.6°C. Avg. annual rainfall: 35.40"; snowfall: 54"; clear days: 70; precipitation days: 156.

Government Form: mayor and council. Mayor: Michael R. White. Election: Nov. 1997. Municipal tel. number: (216) 664–2000.

Visitor info.: 1–800–321–1004 or (216) 621–4110.

Columbus, Ohio

The Ohio legislature designated a site along the banks of the Scioto River in the center of the state as the capital in 1812 and named it Columbus in honor of the famous explorer of the New World. From the first, the city exploited its status as the seat of government and its prime location in the middle of the nation's growing network of roads, canals, and highways. Incorporated in 1834, Columbus became a thriving hub of agricultural trade.

Between 1850 and 1900, its population grew from 17,800 to more than 100,000. Because of the many carriage factories, in the 19th century Columbus was known as the Buggy Capital of the World. Five railroads passed through the city, so banks soon began to spring up, making Columbus a financial center for the surrounding farm counties.

As in the 19th century, Columbus's modern economy is built on government, agriculture, local finance, and education. In 1950, to counter the trend of suburbanization, the city developed a policy of annexation of surrounding communities. Because it is less reliant on heavy industry than other Midwestern cities, it has weathered the decline of the rust belt better than most, remaining a bustling metropolis. In the 1980s the city realized the creation of more than $780 million in new development and 97,550 new jobs.

Ohio State University, one of the nation's large state universities, opened as the Ohio Agricultural and Mechanical College in 1870, and the city today has a rich academic community that includes the Ohio Dominican College (whose origins date to 1868), the Columbus College of Art and Design, and the Ohio Institute of Technology. Business leaders and politicians have joined in an effort to make the city a center for the arts, refurbishing three theaters and building a complex of three more.

Population 632,910 (1990). Rank: 16. Race/national origin: Black 22.6%; Hispanic 1.1%; Asian 2.4%; American Indian 0.2%. Pop. density: 3,388/sq. mi. (1,308/sq km).

Location 39°57'N, 83°01'W. Counties: Fairfield, Franklin.

Terrain and climate Elev.: 833 ft. Area: 186.8 sq. mi. (483.8 sq km). Avg. daily min. temp.: Jan.: 19.4°F/–7°C; avg. daily max.: July: 84.4°F/29.1°C. Avg. annual rainfall: 36.97"; snowfall: 28"; clear days: 75; precipitation days: 136.

Government Form: mayor and council. Mayor: Gregory S. Lashutka. Election: Nov. 1995. Municipal tel. number: (614) 645–7671.

Visitor info.: 1–800–354–2657 or (614) 221–6623.

Dallas, Texas

First settled in 1841 by John Neely Bryan, a Tennessee trader and lawyer, Dallas stretches about 30 miles east of Fort Worth on the Trinity River. Named in 1846 after James K. Polk's vice president, George Mifflin Dallas, it was chartered as a city in 1871. Though it grew substantially with the arrival of railroads in 1872, the population numbered a mere 92,000 in 1910.

Located in the heart of the northern Texas oil belt, Dallas today has a diverse economic base, which, in addition to oil and natural gas, includes production of brick clay and the raw materials for Portland cement, and cotton, grains, fruits, beef, dairy cattle, hogs, sheep, and poultry from surrounding farms. Dallas is one of the largest inland cotton markets, and a leading distributor of farm goods and machinery. Key manufacturing industries include aerospace, electronics, transportation equipment, machinery, food and related products, and apparel. Among its leading high-tech employers are Texas Instruments, Electronic Data Systems, and E Systems Inc.

Some of Dallas's distinguished universities are Southern Methodist, Southwestern Medical School of the University of Texas, Dallas Theological Seminary and Graduate School of Theology, and the Baylor University Schools of Dentistry and Nursing. The Dallas Symphony Orchestra, Dallas Theater Center, Dallas Civic Opera, Dallas Historical Society Museum in the Texas Hall of State, and the Dallas Garden Center contribute to the city's rich cultural life. Fair Park, the site of the annual State Fair of Texas, remains the most widely attended state fair in the country.

Population 1,006,877 (1990). Rank: 8. Race/national origin: Black 29.5%; Hispanic 20.9%; Asian 2.2%; American Indian 0.5%. Pop. density: 3,038/sq. mi. (1,173/sq km).

Location 32°50'N, 96°50'W. Counties: Collin, Dallas, Denton, Kaufman, Rockwall.

Terrain and climate Elev.: 596 ft. Area: 331.4 sq. mi. (858.3 sq km). Avg. daily min. temp.: Jan.: 33.9°F/1°C; avg. daily max.: July: 97.8°F/36.5°C. Avg. annual rainfall: 34.16"; snowfall: 3"; clear days: 138; precipitation days: 79.

Government Form: council and manager. Mayor: Ronald Kirk. Election: May 1999. Municipal tel. number: (214) 670–3011.

Visitor info.: 1–800–CDALLAS or (214) 746–6677.

Denver, Colorado

Denver was born during the great "Pike's Peak or Bust" gold rush of 1859, when small flakes of placer gold were found where the South Platte River meets Cherry Creek. In its first few years, the city survived a flood, several major fires, Indian attacks, and an invasion by Confederate soldiers during the Civil War. With the discovery of more gold in the Rocky Mountains, Denver became a boom town. Saloons, gambling halls, and wagon trains lined the mud-filled streets, and just about every outlaw, desperado, and lawman in the West made at least one visit to the city. The turn of the century brought respectability, and the wealth of the mountains was poured into parks, fountains, tree-lined streets, and elaborate mansions.

In 1993, the expansion Colorado Rockies baseball team drew more than four million fans to a converted football stadium. And in 1995, after countless setbacks stemming from problems with its automated baggage system, the much-heralded Denver International Airport finally opened its doors, thus completing the final chapter of a vastly overbudgeted boondoggle.

Denver's population is among the youngest in the nation. The youthful flavor of the city is very evident; Denver leads the nation in movie attendance and has more sporting goods stores per resident than any other city in the world. The city's 205 parks are so active that a speed limit was recently instituted—for bicycles.

Population 467,610 (1990). Rank: 26. Race/national origin: Black 12.8%; Hispanic 23.0%; Asian 2.4%; American Indian 1.2%. Pop. density: 4,378/sq. mi. (1,691/sq km).

Location 39°45'N, 105°00'W. County: Denver.

Terrain and climate Elev.: 5,280 ft. Area: 106.8 sq. mi. (276.6 sq km). Avg. daily min. temp.: Jan.: 15.9°F/–8.9°C; avg. daily max: July: 88°F/31°C. Avg. annual rainfall: 15.31"; snowfall: 60"; clear days: 115; precipitation days: 88.

Government Form: mayor and council. Mayor: Wellington E. Webb. Election: June 1999. Municipal tel. number: (303) 640–2721.

Visitor Info.: 1–800–888–1990 or (303) 892–1112.

Detroit, Michigan

Founded in 1701 by Antoine de La Mothe, sieur de Cadillac, Detroit lies on the Detroit River between Lake Erie and Lake Huron. Named Fort Pontchartrain-du-Détroit (of the strait), the oldest permanent settlement on the Great Lakes flourished as a trading post for trappers, under French control (to 1760), then British (to 1796), and then American.

The first steamboat reached Detroit from Buffalo in 1818, but it was the easy access to Eastern markets via the Erie Canal in 1825 that allowed Detroit to exploit the abundant natural resources in the Michigan peninsula and fostered its emergence as a modern industrial giant in the post–Civil War years. Tenth among cities in the value of its manufactures by 1899, Detroit's main exports included iron ore, copper, lead, salt, and fish. The development of the automotive industry, which eventually became centered in Detroit, propelled Detroit to number three by the 1920s. While Detroit is the home of General Motors, Chrysler, and Ford, recently the automotive industry has been as much a curse as a blessing, for every setback to any of the "Big Three" is felt throughout the Motor City.

Despite the fact that it remains third in industrial manufacturing in the country, Detroit has been plagued by urban decline. The relatively low standard of living among the predominantly black inhabitants ignited riots in the 1940s and 1960s, and the city's crime rate is today among the highest in the nation. However, it was Detroit blacks who gave rise to one of the most sensational expressions of popular culture in the 1960s. Founded in 1960, the Tamla Motown label propelled the Jackson 5, the Supremes, and Stevie Wonder—among others—to world renown, and in the process created the largest black-owned business in the country.

The city's rich and diverse cultural institutions include the Detroit Institute of Arts, which houses one of the largest collections of American art in the world, in addition to extensive European holdings; the Detroit Symphony; the Cranbrook Academy of Art; and the 1,000-acre Belle Isle Park, situated on an island in the Detroit River and including beaches, a yacht basin, a zoo, an aquarium, and a botanical garden.

Population 1,027,974 (1990). Rank: 7. Race/national origin: Black 75.7%; Hispanic 2.8%;

Asian 0.8%; American Indian 0.4%. Pop. density: 7,581/sq. mi. (2,927/sq km).
Location 42°23'N, 83°05'W. County: Wayne.
Terrain and climate Elev.: 581 ft. Area: 135.6 sq. mi. (351.2 sq km). Avg. daily min. temp.: Jan.: 16.1°F/–8.8°C; avg. daily max.: July: 83.1°F/28.3°C. Avg. annual rainfall: 30.97"; snowfall: 39"; clear days: 75; precipitation days: 133.
Government Form: mayor and council. Mayor: Dennis Archer. Election: Nov. 1997. Municipal tel. number: (313) 224–3270.
Visitor info.: 1-800–DETROIT or (313) 259–4333.

El Paso, Texas

The largest Texas city bordering Mexico, El Paso sits in the western part of the state on the northern bank of the Rio Grande across from Juarez. A major port of entry, with the biggest commercial and manufacturing base in the area, the city encompasses a region of mines, oil fields, livestock ranches, and farms (principal crops: pecans, fruit, cotton, alfalfa, onions, lettuce, chilies). Important industries include metals smelting and refining, oil and gas refining, textiles, meat packing, and food processing. The city is also home to the University of Texas at El Paso.

In 1536 Alvar Núñez Cabeza de Vaca crossed the Rio Grande, becoming the first European to step foot in the area, but settlement did not follow until 1659, with the establishment of both El Paso del Norte on the southern bank of the Rio Grande, and the Mission of Guadalupe. In 1682 settlers from New Mexico founded Yselta, an area within the current city limits of El Paso, but permanent settlement did not begin until the arrival of Juan Maria Ponce de Léon in 1827. Incorporated as a city in 1873, El Paso grew into a major industrial center with the introduction of the railroads in 1881.

El Paso's access to sources of cheap labor complemented its mining, refining, and agricultural activities and helped build the city's manufacturing base. In recent years, however, the movement of manufacturing back to Mexico, where labor costs are far less, has created serious concern for that portion of the economy.

El Paso's proximity to Juarez, Mexico, makes it a vibrant tourist haven, and its pleasant climate, combined with its position on the immigration route from Latin America, have made El Paso one of the fastest-growing cities in the country. El Paso also has the highest percentage of citizens with Hispanic ancestry of any American city.
Population 515,342 (1990). Rank: 22. Race/national origin: Black 3.4%; Hispanic 69.0%; Asian 1.2%; American Indian 0.4%. Pop. density: 2,150/sq. mi. (830/sq km).
Location 31°50'N, 106°30'W. County: El Paso.
Terrain and climate Elev.: 3,700 ft. Area: 239.7 sq. mi. (620.8 sq km). Avg. daily min. temp.: Jan.: 30.4°F/–0.8°C; avg. daily max.: July: 95.3°F/35.1°C. Avg. annual rainfall: 7.82"; snowfall: 5"; clear days: 194; precipitation days: 45.
Government Form: mayor and council. Mayor: Larry Francis. Election: Apr. 1999. Municipal tel. number: (915) 541–4145.
Visitor info.: 1-800–351–6024 or (915) 534–0653.

Fort Worth, Texas

Named in 1849 after Gen. William J. Worth, commander of the U.S. Army in Texas, Fort Worth originally served to protect settlers from Indian attacks. It grew slowly, mainly as a stopover on the cattle drives along the Chisholm Trail, until the Texas and Pacific Railroad reached the city in 1871. Stockyards sprang up, making Fort Worth a conduit of cattle shipping, and with the building of a grain elevator it developed into a milling center as well. By the turn of the century, it had also emerged as a successful meat-packing market. Oil was discovered in 1917, bringing prosperity and transforming the city into a major refining center with a dozen operating facilities. The two world wars introduced military installations (particularly airfields) to the area. Fort Worth is the sixth-largest city in Texas, boasting three of the state's finest art museums and a network of parks with total acreage second only to Chicago's. In 1990 it was announced that Fort Worth would become the first city outside of Washington, D.C., where paper money is printed.
Population 447,619 (1990). Rank: 28. Race/national origin: Black 22.0%; Hispanic 19.5%; Asian 2.0%; American Indian 0.4%. Pop. density: 1,732/sq. mi. (668/sq km).
Location 32°45'N, 97°25'W. County: Tarrant.
Terrain and climate Elev.: 670 ft. Area: 258.5 sq. mi. (670.3 sq km). Avg. daily min. temp.: Jan.: 33.9°F/1°C; avg. daily max.: July: 97.8°F/36.5°C. Avg. annual rainfall: 29.45"; snowfall: 1.4"; clear days: 137; precipitation days: 78.
Government Form: council and manager. Mayor: Kay Granger. Election: May 1999. Municipal tel. number: (817) 871–8900.
Visitor info.: 1-800–433–5747 or (817) 336–8791.

Fresno, California

Fresno grew up around a train station established in 1872 for what became the Southern Pacific Railway. The city was incorporated in 1874. With the introduction of irrigation to the fertile San Joaquin Valley in the 1880s, the small city thrived at the center of a healthy agricultural economy. Today Fresno County is the number one producer of agricultural products in the nation—and the world—and averages more than $2 billion a year in the production and processing of 200 commercial crops, including grapes (for wine and raisins), melon, alfalfa, barley, grains, cattle, sheep, and poultry.

Fresno's population grew 63 percent between 1980 and 1990, and in the 1980s it was the ninth-fastest-growing city in the United States and by far the fastest growing of the nation's 50 largest cities.

Located in central California, Fresno—the name is Spanish for ash tree—is a gateway to the Sierra Nevadas, and it is less than 90 minutes from three national parks—Kings Canyon (55 miles), Sequoia (85 miles), and Yosemite (92 miles). Among the attractions to be found within the city limits are the Fresno Art Museum, the Fresno Zoo, the Kearney Mansion Museum (restored home of Theo Kearney, "Raisin King of California"), the Fresno Metropolitan Museum, and the Discovery Center. There are also 10 colleges and universities, including a campus of California State University and Fresno City College.
Population 354,202 (1990). Rank: 47. Race/national origin: Black 8.3%; Hispanic 29.9%; Asian 12.5%; American Indian 1.1%. Population density: 3,564/sq. mi. (1,378/sq km).
Location 36°47'N, 119°50'W. County: Fresno.
Terrain and climate Elev. 328 ft. Area: 99.4 sq. mi. (257 sq km). Avg. daily min. temp. Jan.: 37.4°/3°C; avg. daily max. July: 98.7°F/37°C. Avg. annual rainfall: 10"; snowfall 0"; clear days: 200; precipitation days: 44.
Government Form: council manager. Mayor: Jim Patterson. Election: May 1997. Municipal tel.: (209) 233–1561.
Visitor info.: (209) 233–0836 or 1-800–788–0836.

Honolulu, Hawaii

Discovered by Europeans in 1794, Honolulu, meaning "sheltered harbor," has attracted droves of visitors ever since. Situated on Oahu Island, it benefits from a large bay fully protected by coral reefs and its large port facilities. Because of its hospitable climate—it is the southernmost city in the United States—the beaches of Waikiki, its majestic mountains, and exotic locale, Honolulu's major industry is tourism; several million visitors come annually, mainly from the U.S. mainland and the Far East, particularly from Japan.

The defense industry is the second mainstay of Honolulu's economy; the United States has long maintained major installations around the island, including the naval base at Pearl Harbor, Hickam Air Force Base, and the U.S. Army's Schofield Barracks and Fort Shafter. Honolulu also serves as the center for Hawaii's export crops—sugar, pineapple, and molasses—and is the principal port for the import of much of the island state's necessities.
Population 365,272 (1990). Rank: 44. Race/national origin: Black 1.3%; Hispanic 4.6%; Asian 70.5%; American Indian 0.3%. Pop. density: 14,438/sq. mi. (5,575/sq km).
Location 21°19'N, 157°52'W. County: Honolulu.
Terrain and climate Elev.: 15 ft. Area: 25.3 sq. mi. (65.52 sq km). Avg. daily min. temp.: Jan.: 65.3°F/18.5°C; avg. daily max.: July: 87.1°F/30.6°C. Avg. annual rainfall: 23.47"; snowfall: 0"; clear days: 90; precipitation days: 102.
Government Form: mayor and council. Mayor: Frank F. Fasi. Election: Nov. 1996. Municipal tel. number: (808) 523–4385.
Visitor info.: (808) 923–1811.

Houston, Texas

On Aug. 30, 1836, brothers August C. and John K. Allen founded this city, naming it after Sam Houston, the first president of the Republic of Texas. The Allens paid just over $1.40 per share for 6,642 acres of land near the headwaters of Buffalo Bayou about 50 miles inland from the Gulf of Mexico. Houston's proximity to Stephen Austin's central Texas colonies gave it great potential as a marketing and distribution site. Incorporated in 1837, the city served as capital of the Republic of Texas until 1840. When the first railroad in Texas began operating out of Houston in 1853, the city developed into a major agricultural center, while the discovery of oil in southeast Texas at Spindletop in 1901 and the opening of the man-made Houston Ship Channel in 1914 stimulated petroleum refining and metal fabricating. During World War II, petrochemical production began on a large scale, and with the building of NASA's $761 million complex in the early 1960s (now known as the Johnson Space Center), Houston took center stage as the main player in manned spacecraft.

A major corporate and international business center—16 *Fortune* 500 companies are based there—present-day Houston has successfully limited its dependence on the energy economy. It ranks third nationally in number of trade offices, fifth in foreign consulates, and sixth in international air passengers. With more than half the Port of Houston's cargo in foreign trade in 1987, Houston ranked second among U.S. ports in foreign tonnage.

The presence of the Texas Medical Center also makes Houston a vital U.S. center for the practice and progress of modern high-tech medicine. The center's 39 institutions occupy in excess of 550 acres, and as of 1992 employed over 51,000 workers; Houston's total health services employment exceeded 100,000

Population 1,630,553 (1990). Rank: 4. Race/national origin: Black 28.1%; Hispanic 27.6%; Asian 4.1%; American Indian 0.3%. Pop. density: 2,847/sq. mi. (1,099/sq km).

Location 29°50'N, 95°20'W. Counties: Fort Bend, Harris, Montgomery.

Terrain and climate Elev.: 49 ft. Area: 572.7 sq. mi. (1,483.3 sq km). Avg. daily min. temp.: Jan.: 40.8°F/4.8°C; avg. daily max.: July: 93.6°F/34.2°C. Avg. annual rainfall: 44.77"; snowfall: 0"; clear days, 94; precipitation days: 107.

Government Form: mayor and council. Mayor: Robert C. Lanier. Election: Nov. 1997. Municipal tel. number: (713) 247–1000.

Visitor info.: (713) 523–5050 or 1–800–231–7799.

Indianapolis, Indiana

Indianapolis, the capital of Indiana and a major commercial center in the country's heartland, is intersected by more highways than any other city in the nation, earning it the name the Crossroads of America. Fifty percent of America's population is within a day's drive of the city, a geographic asset that makes it a focal point of transportation and manufacturing.

The Euro-American settlement, established in 1820 where Fall Creek meets the White River, was chosen as the location of Indiana's capital in 1825. The state government created jobs triggering an expanding population that further swelled with the routing of the National Road (U.S. 40) in 1830. Development mushroomed in 1839 with the building of the Central Canal on the White River, providing a vital transportation link and the necessary waterpower to run factories, sawmills, and paper mills. Maintenance of the canal, however, proved impossible, and the town declined until the introduction of the railroad. By 1853 railroad lines fed into Indianapolis from every corner of the nation, and at one point nearly 200 trains passed through daily. At the turn of the century, Indianapolis had emerged as a sophisticated city with sidewalks and streetcars. The city's economy prospered during early stages of the automotive industry, producing more than 50 types of cars—including the Dusenberg, the Marmon, and the Stutz—before Detroit gained ascendancy.

Having survived the decline in heavy industry and the flight of the affluent to the suburbs, Indianapolis remains a hub of manufacturing and transportation, with a bustling wheat, soybean, and livestock market. Key industries include electronics, metal fabrication, pharmaceuticals, and transportation equipment. Downtown Indianapolis has enjoyed a renaissance with the construction of a convention center, the Hoosier Dome, Market Square Arena, and the refurbishment of Union Station. The city has also built a number of amateur sports arenas and in 1987 hosted the Pan Am Games. But the city's premier attraction remains the Indianapolis 500, the annual Memorial Day weekend race first held in 1911.

Population 741,952 (1990). Rank: 12. Race/national origin: Black 22.6%; Hispanic 1.1%; Asian 0.9%; American Indian 0.2%. Pop. density: 2,109/sq. mi. (814/sq km).

Location 39°42'N, 86°10'W. County: Marion.

Terrain and climate Elev.: 808 ft. Area: 352 sq. mi. (911.7 sq km). Avg. daily min. temp.: Jan.: 17.8°F/–7.8°C; avg. daily max.: July: 85.2°F/29.5°C. Avg. annual rainfall: 39.12"; snowfall: 21"; clear days: 90; precipitation days: 122.

Government Form: mayor and council. Mayor: Stephen Goldsmith. Election: Nov. 1995. Municipal tel. number: (317) 327–4622.

Visitor info.: (317) 237–5200 or 1–800–323–4639.

Jacksonville, Florida

The first Europeans to visit the area were French Huguenots, who in 1564 established a colony at Fort Caroline on the Saint Johns River in northeast Florida. The Spanish destroyed the fort in the following year. Permanent settlement began in 1816, and in 1822 Jacksonville was laid out and named for then Maj. Gen. Andrew Jackson, who had led the U.S. campaign to take Florida from the Spanish. Growth was slow until after the Civil War, but by 1960 the population was more than 200,000. In 1968 the population jumped to more than 500,000 when it was consolidated with Duval County, and Jacksonville became the largest city by area in the nation.

Presently Florida's largest city, Jacksonville is a major regional center for commerce, industry, finance, and medicine. After years of improvements on its harbor, 25 miles west from the mouth of the Saint Johns, it has grown into a major port of entry and is the primary distribution center for the region. Jacksonville has also emerged as a leading resort with extensive recreational and convention facilities. Among its amenities are the Haydon Burns Library, Cummer Gallery of Art, Jacksonville Art Museum, Jacksonville Zoological Park, Saint Johns River Park, and Fort Caroline National Memorial, site of the first European colony in Florida. Among its leading educational institutions are Jacksonville University and the University of Northern Florida.

Population 672,971 (1990). Rank: 15. Race/national origin: Black 25.2%; Hispanic 2.6%; Asian 1.9%; American Indian 0.3%. Pop. density: 801/sq. mi. (342/sq km).

Location 30°15'N, 81°38'W. County: Duval.

Terrain and climate Elev.: 31 ft. Area: 840 sq. mi. (1,967.6 sq km). Avg. daily min. temp.: Jan.: 41.7°F/°C; avg. daily max.: July: 90.7°F/29.5°C. Avg. annual rainfall: 52.77"; snowfall: 0"; clear days: 98; precipitation days: 116.

Government Form: mayor and council. Mayor: John A. Delaney. Election: May 1999. Municipal tel. number: (904) 630–1776.

Visitor info.: 1–800–733–2668 or (904) 353–9736.

Kansas City, Missouri

Kansas City's Euro-American beginnings were as a trading outpost established by the French fur trader François Chouteau in 1821. In 1833 the town of Westport was founded nearby, and in 1850 the City of Kansas received its first charter. (Its name was changed to Kansas City in 1889.)

Situated at the confluence of the Kansas and Missouri Rivers, Kansas City prospered early on as a river port and as the terminus of the Santa Fe and Oregon Trails. With the arrival of the railroad in 1866, Kansas City's status as a major commercial hub was assured. Thanks to its central location and the development of excellent and diversified transportation and storage facilities, Kansas City is one of the nation's key markets for agricultural and livestock products, as well as for the distribution of heavy agricultural machinery. The Kansas City Board of Trade is one of the largest grain and commodities trading markets in the world. Other major industries are greeting card publishing, telecommunications, and high-tech manufacturing, especially instrument-landing systems for airplanes. Kansas City is also home to the 10th Federal Reserve Bank.

An early oasis of culture in the midst of an unsettled (by Euro-Americans), "untamed" prairie (the city once boasted two opera houses), Kansas City remains a mecca of the arts, with such cultural offerings as the Kansas City Art Institute, the Nelson-Atkins Museum of Art, the Kansas City Symphony, the Lyric Opera, and the Missouri Repertory Theatre. The city's beginnings are preserved in the Lone Jack Civil War Museum and in Missouri Town 1855, and it is the site of the annual American Royal Livestock, Horse Show, and Rodeo. Among its institutes of higher learning are Rockhurst College (1916), the University of Missouri–Kansas City, and the DeVry Institute of Technology.

Population 435,146 (1990). Rank: 31. Race/national origin: Black 29.6%; Hispanic 3.9%; Asian 1.2%; American Indian 0.5%. Pop. density: 1,375/sq. mi. (531/sq km).

Location 39°07'N, 94°38'W. Counties: Cass, Clay, Jackson, Platte.

Terrain and climate Elev.: 744 ft. Area: 316.4 sq. mi. (819.5 sq km). Avg. daily min. temp.: Jan.: 17.2°F/–8.2°C; avg. daily max.: July: 88.5°F/ 31.3°C. Avg. annual rainfall: 29.27"; snowfall: 5.9"; clear days: 132; precipitation days: 97.
Government Form: council and manager. Mayor: Emanuel Cleaver. Election: Apr. 1999. Municipal tel. number: (816) 274–2000.
Visitor info.: 1–800–767–7700 or (816) 221–5242.

Long Beach, California

Originally the site of an Indian trading camp, by the end of the 18th century the area that is now Long Beach was part of the Spanish Ranchos Los Alamitos and Cerritos. In 1882 William E. Willmore began development of the land as a resort (which he named for himself). When first incorporated in 1888, it was named Long Beach after its 8.5 miles of Pacific beachfront. Content to remain a resort community, Long Beach had its fortunes rewritten in 1921 when extensive petroleum deposits were first discovered at Signal Hill. Today industry is a major presence in Long Beach—especially ship repair, transportation, oil refining, and marine research; in addition the navy maintains a large base with dry dock facilities.

Among its cultural and recreational attractions are Long Beach's own Museum of Art; the Terrace Theater, home of the Long Beach Symphony Orchestra; and the Long Beach Community Playhouse. Popular tourist attractions include Los Cerritos, a Spanish adobe house dating to 1844; the magnificent ocean liner *Queen Mary*, which today serves as a floating maritime museum, convention center, and hotel; and the *Spruce Goose*, Howard Hughes's unflyable plane of gigantic proportions. Long Beach is also the site of a Formula 1 Grand Prix every spring. Disneyland is in nearby Anaheim.
Population 429,433 (1990). Rank: 32. Race/ national origin: Black 13.7%; Hispanic 23.6%; Asian 13.6%; American Indian 0.6%. Pop. density: 8,623/sq. mi. (3,329/sq km).
Location 33°46'N, 118°10'W. County: Los Angeles.
Terrain and climate Elev.: 35 ft. Area: 49.8 sq. mi. (129 sq km). Avg. daily min. temp.: Jan.: 44.3°F/ 6.8°C; avg. daily max.: July: 83°F/ 28.3°C. Avg. annual rainfall: 12"; snowfall: 0"; clear days, 143; precipitation days: 35.
Government Form: council and manager. Mayor: Beverly O'Neill (I). Election: June 1998. Municipal tel. number: (310) 590–6101.
Visitor info.: 1–800–262–7838 or (310) 436–3645.

Los Angeles, California

In pre-Spanish days, the area of Los Angeles was inhabited by approximately 4,000 Indian peoples, representing some 30 different groups. The Uto-Aztecan village of Yang-na, with a population of 300, was located in what is now downtown Los Angeles, in the vicinity of Alameda and Commercial Streets. In October 1542 João Rodrigues Cabrilho, a Portuguese explorer in the employ of Spain, became the first European to set foot on Los Angeles soil, but 200 years passed before a land expedition under the command of Gaspar de Portola crossed the territory on the way from Monterey to San Diego in 1769.

The establishment of the Mission of San Gabriel (destined to become the largest of the Franciscan missions) followed, and in 1781 Spanish governor Felipe Neve founded the city of El Pueblo de Nuestra Señora de los Angeles de Porciuncula (The Village of Our Lady of the Angels) as part of a plan to colonize California. Spanish rule continued until 1822, when Spain relinquished her holdings in western America, prompting California to pledge her allegiance to the Mexican empire. With the Treaty of Guadalupe Hidalgo (1848), the United States acquired all of California from Mexico, and in 1850 Los Angeles was incorporated as a city. Introduction of the Southern Pacific Railroad in 1876 sparked a 12-year land boom, promoting the city's growth. By 1892 Los Angeles thrived as a center of oil production, and in 1899 work began on the largest man-made deep-water facility in the world. It had emerged as the motion picture capital of the world by 1910. Industry accelerated in the 1920s, and today L.A. ranks as one of the three great industrial cities in the country.

A thriving metropolis, Los Angeles boasts one of the finest highway systems in the world, handling over 4.9 million cars registered in the Los Angeles metropolitan area—1.6 cars per household, the highest ratio in the world. Three transcontinental railway systems terminate in L.A., 37 certified air carriers fly to all parts of the world, its harbors have 46 miles of waterfront, and the city has the largest trucking center in the West. L.A. remains the world's movie mecca, teeming with studios, stars, and the starstruck.

Los Angelinos live with daily problems of smog, traffic jams, spectacular traffic accidents, and the ever-present threats of mud slides, fires, floods, high winds, and earthquakes. But the year-round sunshine and the abundance of beaches and mountain areas, all within an easy drive, tend to ameliorate one's anxiety. The city was shaken in 1992 by three days of rioting and looting that broke out Apr. 29, after a jury acquitted police officers of criminal wrongdoing in the videotaped beating of motorist Rodney King.
Population 3,485,398 (1990). Rank: 2. Race/ national origin: Black 14.0%; Hispanic 39.9%; Asian 9.8%; American Indian 0.5%. Pop. density: 7,481/sq. mi. (2,888/sq km).
Location 34°00'N, 118°10'W. County: Los Angeles.
Terrain and climate Elev.: 104 ft. Area: 465.9 sq. mi. (1,206.7 sq km). Avg. daily min. temp.: Jan.: 47.3°F/8.5°C; avg. daily max.: July: 75.3°F/24°C. Avg. annual rainfall: 14.85"; snowfall: 0"; clear days: 143; precipitation days: 35.
Government Form: mayor and council. Mayor: Richard Riordan. Election: June 1997. Municipal tel. number: (213) 485–2121.
Visitor info.: (213) 624–7300.

Memphis, Tennessee

The first settlers in the area of Memphis arrived on the bluffs overlooking the Mississippi River more than a thousand years ago. The Chickasaw forcibly displaced these people—about whom little is known, including their name—and lived there for eight centuries until 1838, when the U.S. government scattered the entire tribe to Oklahoma and parts farther west so that Euro-Americans could develop the land. The Spanish explorer Hernando de Soto first set eyes on the bluffs in 1541. Other explorers passed through over the next century, and in 1739 the French built Fort Assumption. The French, Spanish, and Chickasaw fought over the land for the balance of the 18th century until it became a part of the United States in 1797. The area's original American owners, Gen. James Winchester, Judge John Overton, and Gen. Andrew Jackson (who later sold his share and went on to become president), established the town in 1819 and named it Memphis, after the ancient Egyptian city on the Nile.

River boatmen gave young Memphis a reputation for brawls and bawdiness, while mosquitoes gave it a history of yellow fever epidemics, which in the 1880s claimed more than half the city's population and jeopardized its charter. A sewage system, the first of its kind, finally helped conquer the epidemic. Between the river traffic and cotton crops, the city prospered, attracting Irish and German immigrants, and by the 20th century was on its way to becoming the unofficial capital of the mid-South. Elvis Presley, who expanded on the city's rhythm and blues tradition to become the world's first rock 'n' roll idol, remains the city's single most enduring contribution to popular culture.

In 1991, the Lorraine Motel, where civil rights leader Dr. Martin Luther King, Jr., was assassinated in 1968, was opened as the National Civil Rights Museum.
Population 610,337 (1990). Rank: 18. Race/ national origin: Black 54.8%; Hispanic 0.7%; Asian 0.8%; American Indian 0.2%. Pop. density: 2,311/sq. mi. (892/sq km).
Location 35°07'N, 90°00'W. County: Shelby.
Terrain and climate Elev.: 307 ft. Area: 264.1 sq. mi. (684 sq km). Avg. daily min. temp.: Jan.: 30.9°F/–0.6°C; avg. daily max.: July: 91.5°F/ 33°C. Avg. annual rainfall: 51.57"; snowfall: 6"; clear days: 118; precipitation days: 106.
Government Form: mayor and council. Mayor: Dr. W. W. Herenton. Election: Nov. 1995. Municipal tel. number: (901) 576–6000.
Visitor info.: (901) 543–5300.

Miami, Florida

Miami, the most southerly major city in the continental United States, sits about 2 degrees north of the Tropic of Cancer, a location that has made it a long-standing resort haven. Miami in the 1980s also thrived as a major hub of commerce and as a population center for Latin American immigrants, particularly those arriving from Cuba, whose ambition and business acumen contributed to the city's prosperity. While tourists still generate over 60 percent of the area's economic activity, many other areas of enterprise, such as construction, light industry, and agriculture (limes, tomatoes, avocados, mangoes, and beans) have flourished.

Miami (whose name is thought to derive from the Indian *mayami*, meaning "big water"), dates back to the 16th century when Native Americans occupied the southern part of Florida. Fort Dallas, built near the mouth of the Miami River in 1836 as a base of war against the Seminoles, became the first permanent Euro-American settlement. The building of the Florida East Coast Railroad, coinciding with Miami's incorporation as a city in 1896 (population 343), offered ready access to the area. Resort hotels quickly cropped up, and Miami, along with the rest of Florida, enjoyed great success. In 1926 a severe hurricane submerged much of its land under water, abruptly ending Miami's prosperity, but the city managed to grow steadily by draining and developing swampland. After World War II, new resorts rose up, and Miami thrived. In 1991, Major League Baseball awarded the city one of two expansion team franchises.

The relative success of the large influx of Hispanics—especially Cubans—since the 1960s is a source of ill feelings, especially to many in the black community, and the city has been wracked by rioting in recent years.

Population 358,548 (1990). Rank: 46. Race/national origin: Black 27.4%; Hispanic 62.5%; Asian 0.6%; American Indian 0.2%. Pop. density: 10,453/sq. mi. (4,038/sq km).

Location 25°45'N, 80°15'W. County: Dade.

Terrain and climate Elev.: 12 ft. Area: 34.3 sq. mi. (88.8 sq km). Avg. daily min. temp.: Jan.: 59.2°F/15.1°C; avg. daily max.: July: 88.7°F/31.5°C. Avg. annual rainfall: 57.55"; snowfall: 0"; clear days: 76; precipitation days: 129.

Government Form: council and manager. Mayor: Stephen Clark. Election: Nov. 1997. Municipal tel. number: (305) 250–5300.

Visitor info.: 1-800–933–8448 or (305) 539–3000.

Milwaukee, Wisconsin

During the 1670s the French explorers Jacques Marquette and Louis Jolliet were the first Europeans to visit the site of present-day Milwaukee, an area on the western shore of Lake Michigan at the confluence of the Menomonee and Kinnickinnic Rivers. In 1795 Jacques Vicau of the North West Company established a trading post, and in 1818 Solomon Laurent Juneau, the first permanent Euro-American settler, founded Milwaukee (from the Indian term *millioke*, meaning "beautiful land"). From the 1840s on, large numbers of German immigrants came to the city, making up more than 60 percent of the 1850 population; today an estimated one-third of the city's residents are of German descent.

A flourishing agricultural center, Milwaukee had by the Civil War become the largest wheat market in the world. Its industrial base expanded after the war, and by 1940 the city ranked fourth in manufacturing among U.S. cities. Still one of the most vigorous producers of durable goods—especially automotive parts, construction and road-building equipment, diesel and gasoline engines, tractors, and outboard motors—Milwaukee has also emerged as a major meat-packing center. Reflecting its German heritage, the city developed a successful brewing industry, with two of the largest beer-producing companies in the country—Schlitz and Pabst. A major Great Lakes and, since the opening of the St. Lawrence Seaway, international port, Milwaukee handles 12 international steamship lines.

Population 628,088 (1990). Rank: 17. Race/national origin: Black 30.5%; Hispanic 6.3%; Asian 1.9%; American Indian 0.9%. Pop. density: 6,556/sq. mi. (2,532/sq km).

Location 43°09'N, 87°58'W. County: Milwaukee.

Terrain and climate Elev.: 581 ft. Area: 95.8 sq. mi. (248.1 sq km). Avg. daily min. temp.: Jan.: 11.3°F/–11.5°C; avg. daily max.: July: 79.8°F/26.5°C. Avg. annual rainfall: 30.94"; snowfall: 45"; clear days: 96; precipitation days: 122.

Government Form: mayor and council. Mayor: John O. Norquist. Election: Apr. 1996. Municipal tel. number: (414) 278–3200.

Visitor info.: (800) 231–0903.

Minneapolis, Minnesota

Despite its arctic winters, Minneapolis is one of the most desirable cities in the United States. It sits astride the Mississippi River, near the headwaters of the Minnesota River, about 350 miles northwest of Chicago. While it is the largest commercial metropolis in the north between Milwaukee and Seattle, no single industry dominates, although many large computer and electronics companies make Minneapolis their home. A regional banking center and the site of the Federal Reserve Bank for the Ninth District, Minneapolis has the world's largest cash grain exchange and the world's four largest wheat-flour–milling companies, and provides the upper Midwest with truck, barge, and air transport.

In 1682 Father Louis Hennepin, the French priest who explored the Mississippi, was the first European to set eyes on the Falls of St. Anthony, the future site of Minneapolis. Unsettled until Fort Snelling was built in 1819 to protect fur traders from the Sioux and Chippewa, the town of St. Anthony began growing up on one side of the Mississippi and a second settlement on the other. The two were consolidated in 1872; the new name was a hybrid of the Indian word *minne*, meaning "water," and the Greek word for "city," *polis*. Minneapolis blossomed on the basis of its flour and lumber milling. By century's end, the forests to the north had been depleted, but flour milling continues as a thriving industry to this day.

Long considered a center of progressive political and social thinking, Minneapolis is a mecca of education and culture. It is the site of the main campus of the University of Minnesota, the Minnesota Orchestra, and the Minneapolis Institute of the Arts. A haven for outdoor enthusiasts, the park system numbers 153 parks encompassing 6,000 acres, and with 10 percent of its surface covered by water, Minneapolis has 12 lakes within its city limits.

Population 368,383 (1990). Rank: 42. Race/national origin: Black 13.0%; Hispanic 2.1%; Asian 4.3%; American Indian 3.3%. Pop. density: 6,686/sq. mi. (2,582/sq km).

Location 44°58'N, 93°20'W. County: Hennepin.

Terrain and climate Elev.: 828 ft. Area: 55.1 sq. mi. (142.7 sq km). Avg. daily min. temp.: Jan.: 2.4°F/–16.4°C; avg. daily max.: July: 83.4°F/28.5°C. Avg. annual rainfall: 26.36"; snowfall: 46"; clear days: 100; precipitation days: 113.

Government Form: mayor and council. Mayor: Sharon Belton. Election: Nov. 1997. Municipal tel. number: (612) 673–2100.

Visitor info.: 1–800–445–7412 or (612) 348-4313.

Nashville, Tennessee

In the winter of 1779–80, settlers from North Carolina, led by James Robertson, arrived at a place on the Cumberland River called Big Salt Lick, and built forts on both sides of the river, one of which they named Nashborough, after Gen. Francis Nash of the Revolutionary Army. Adopting the name Nashville in 1784, the settlement was chartered as a city in 1806, became state capital in 1843, and prospered until the Civil War as the northern terminus of the Natchez Trace, a 500-mile road to Natchez, Mississippi. The site of one of the war's last major battles in December 1864, the city underwent a long period of rebuilding, and by the end of the century the population reached 81,000. The city continued to grow, doubling in population by World War II, and has experienced even greater expansion since that time.

While best known as a major center of both the recording and music-publishing industries—it refers to itself as Music City, U.S.A.—Nashville enjoys a widely diversified economic foundation and serves as a distribution and marketing point for the upper southern region of the country. Several religious organizations and their publishing operations are headquartered here, and the city is home to more than a dozen institutions of higher learning, including Vanderbilt University, Fisk University, and Tennessee State University. With a growing base of manufacturing, particularly in the automotive sector, and with the insurance and banking industries solidly entrenched, Nashville leaders project a prosperous future. Nashville, as home of the Grand Ole Opry, has also developed into a regional tourist and convention attraction. A full-scale replica of the Greek temple the Parthenon is a noted site.

Population 510,784 (1990). Rank: 23. Race/national origin: Black 24.3%; Hispanic 0.9%; Asian 1.4%; American Indian 0.2%. Pop. density: 1,065 sq. mi. (411/sq km).

Location 36°12'N, 86°46'W. County: Davidson.

Terrain and climate Elev.: 605 ft. Area: 479.5 sq. mi. (1,241.9 sq km). Avg. daily min. temp.: Jan.: 27.8°F/–2.3°C; avg. daily max.: July: 89.8°F/32.1°C. Avg. annual rainfall: 48.49"; snowfall: 10.7"; clear days: 103; precipitation days: 119.

Government Form: mayor and council. Mayor: Phil Bredesen. Election: Aug. 1995. Municipal tel. number: (615) 862–6000.

Visitor info.: (615) 259–4755.

New Orleans, Louisiana

Founded in 1718 by Jean Baptiste le Moyne and named Ville d'Orléans after the regent of France, the city of New Orleans is one of the nation's most distinctive cities. Situated only 110 miles from the mouth of the Mississippi River, it has long been a major international port (it ranks second in the nation today), and thanks to overlapping waves of French, Spanish, African-American, and Anglo-American immigrants, it has one of the most richly textured cultures of any city in North America. It is geographically distinct, too, in that much of it is below sea level; the almost constant threat of flooding is mitigated by an intricate network of canals and levees.

After half a century under French rule, New Orleans became the capital of Spanish Louisiana in 1763. It was briefly under French rule again (1800–1803) before being acquired by the United States as part of the Louisiana Purchase. Although Louisiana was admitted as a state in 1815, New Orleans continues to reflect its Spanish and French heritage in its architecture, cuisine, and its flamboyant Mardi Gras celebration at the beginning of Lent. African-American traditions are strong here, too, and Dixieland jazz—long heralded as a uniquely American music—is a fusion of African and European styles.

In addition to being a major port for the export of cotton, rice, petroleum products, iron, steel, and corn and the import of sugar, bananas, coffee, bauxite, and molasses, New Orleans is a major center for offshore drilling in the Gulf of Mexico. In recent years its industrial sector, with an emphasis on aerospace research and technology, petroleum refinement, and shipbuilding, has been strong.

A major tourist attraction in its own right, the city includes among its special points of interest St. Louis Cathedral, the French Market, Preservation Hall and Dixieland Hall, and the Presbytère—all in the French Quarter—the celebrated residential architecture of the Garden District, the New Orleans Museum of Art, the Confederate Museum, and Audubon Park Zoo. Among its educational institutions are Tulane University, Sophie Newcomb College, and Dillard University.

Population 496,938 (1990). Rank: 25. Race/national origin: Black 61.9%; Hispanic 3.5%; Asian 1.9%; American Indian 0.2%. Pop. density: 2,492/sq. mi. (962/sq km).

Location 30°00'N, 90°05'W. Parish: Orleans.

Terrain and climate Elev.: 30 ft. Area: 199.4 sq. mi. (516.4 sq km). Avg. daily min. temp.: Jan.: 43°F/6.1°C; avg. daily max.: July: 90.7°F/32.6°C. Avg. annual rainfall: 59.74"; snowfall: 0.2"; clear days: 109; precipitation days: 113.

Government Form: mayor and council. Mayor: Marc H. Morial. Election: May 1998. Municipal tel. number: (504) 565–6000.

Visitor info.: (504) 566–5011.

New York City, New York

Even before the arrival of Europeans in North America, the waters that today make New York one of the world's foremost ports—and the foremost city in the United States—were the scene of lively trade between the predominant Algonquian tribes in the region. The city's modern history dates to 1524, when the Florentine explorer Giovanni de Verrazano sailed into New York Bay. In 1609 Henry Hudson, an English navigator sailing for the Dutch East India Company, explored the river that bears his name today. In 1625 Peter Minuit's Dutch West India Company purchased Manhattan and established Nieuw Amsterdam, which quickly became a profitable trading post. Dutch settlers soon expanded beyond the original colony, settling Breukelen, Nieuw Harlem, Bronx, and Staaten Eylandt. Taken by the British in 1664 (the Dutch briefly regained control in 1673–74), and renamed for the duke of York, the town continued to prosper.

As resentment of British authority grew, New York became a seat of colonial discontent, participating in actions against the Stamp Act (1763) and tea tax (1773). But after the Battle of Long Island and Washington's retreat in August 1776, the British held New York through the end of the war. Yet Washington was inaugurated president at Federal Hall (today the site of the second Federal Reserve Bank) on Wall Street, and in 1789–90 New York was the nation's capital.

Industry and trade expanded dramatically after the opening of the Erie Canal from Troy (150 miles up the Hudson River) and Buffalo (350 miles west of Troy) gave New York direct access to raw materials and markets of the Great Lakes states. In the mid-19th century, New York became the country's primary port of immigration, and many of the millions of immigrants who came to America carved out distinctly ethnic neighborhoods throughout the city in a patchwork that survives to the present.

In 1898 an act of the state legislature created "Greater New York," and today New York's population is greater than that of Los Angeles and Chicago (the second- and third-largest cities in the country) combined. Even if they were separate cities, four of New York boroughs would rank in the top 10—Brooklyn fourth (2.3 million), Queens fifth (1.9 million), Manhattan eighth (1.5 million), and the Bronx ninth (1.2 million).

New York's attractions are almost innumerable—enough to draw over 17 million visitors per year—but they include 150 museums, 400 art galleries, 38 Broadway theaters, and scores of concert halls, clubs, and dance halls. In addition there are 780 landmark buildings, 50 landmark interiors, and 51 historic districts. (A list of attractions can be found under "New York State.") The city leads the nation in the arts, fashion, advertising, banking and financial services, publishing, broadcasting, and certain of the service industries; it is the home of the UN General Assembly; and there are 87 colleges and universities, including Columbia University, New York University, Long Island University, Brooklyn College, St. Johns University, the Pratt Institute of Technology, the Juilliard School, and the School of Visual Arts. Manufactured goods include apparel, chemicals, metal products, and printing.

Population 7,322,564 (1990). Rank: 1. Race/national origin: Black 28.7%; Hispanic 24.4%; Asian 7.0%; American Indian 0.4%. Pop. density: 24,287/sq. mi. (9,377/sq km).

Location 40°45'N, 74°00'W. Counties: Bronx, Kings, New York, Queens, Richmond.

Terrain and climate Elev.: 87 ft. Area: 301.5 sq. mi. (780.9 sq km). Avg. daily min. temp.: Jan.: 25.6°F/-3.5°C; avg. daily max.: July: 85.3°F/29.6°C. Avg. annual rainfall: 44.12"; snowfall: 29"; clear days: 107; precipitation days, 121.

Government Form: mayor and council. Mayor: Rudolph Giuliani. Election: Nov. 1997. Municipal tel. number: (212) 788–3000.

Visitor info.: (212) 397–8222.

Oakland, California

The first Euro-American to settle present-day Oakland was Dom Luis Maria Peralta, in 1820, who established the 44,000-acre settlement called Rancho San Antonio in 1820. Its first real growth began with the establishment of ferry service to San Francisco in 1852, though the ferry was dramatically superceded by Oakland's selection as the western terminus of the first transcontinental railroad in 1869. The city remained in the economic shadow of its more sophisticated neighbor across the bay until the San Francisco earthquake of 1906 drove 100,000–150,000 people to Oakland for shelter. An estimated 65,000 of these are thought to have settled there permanently, providing an impetus for Oakland's long period of growth as an international port and industrial center.

A major commercial and cultural center with a container port ranked 10th in the world, Oakland is also the major northern hub of the California freeway system, which is integrated with the Bay Area Rapid Transit (BART) system. It has also become the premier biotechnology center in the region, and regional and international headquarters for firms in finance, medicine, telecommunications, international trade, and heavy industry are located there.

Long a primarily industrial urban center, Oakland has pumped hundreds of millions of dollars into development of its downtown area and the Jack London waterfront—named for the author who spent his youth on the Oakland docks. More artists reside in Oakland than anywhere else in the country with the exception of New York's Greenwich Village. Oakland embraces a racially and culturally diverse populace, and a 1980 University of Wisconsin study found it the most integrated city in the nation. Oakland sustained heavy damage in an Oct. 17, 1989, earthquake rated at 7.1 on the Richter scale. Two years later, almost to the day, the worst fire in California history leveled more than 1,000 buildings in the Oakland hills, killing 14 people. In all, the fire ravaged over 1,800 acres at a cost of roughly $1.5 billion.

Population 372,242 (1990). Rank: 39. Race/national origin: Black 43.9%; Hispanic 13.9%; Asian 14.8%; American Indian 0.6%. Pop. density: 6,906/sq. mi. (2,666/sq km).

Location 37°50'N, 122°18'W. County: Alameda.

Terrain and climate Elev.: 42 ft. Area: 53.9 sq. mi. (139.6 sq km). Avg. daily min. temp.: Jan.: 43.4°F/6.3°C; avg. daily max.: July: 70.6°F/29.6°C. Avg. annual rainfall: 18.03"; snowfall: N.A.; clear days: N.A.; precipitation days: N.A.

Government Form: council and manager. Mayor: Elihu M. Harris. Election: Nov. 1998. Municipal tel. number: (510) 238–3611.

Visitor info.: 1–800–262-5526 or (510) 839–9000.

Oklahoma City, Oklahoma

Oklahoma City sprang up during the Great Land Rush of 1889 and, by presidential proclamation, opened for Euro-American settlement officially on Apr. 22 of that year. At day's end approximately 10,000 settlers had moved in—the greatest one-day nonannexation population increase in the history of cities. Oklahoma became a state in 1907 and Oklahoma City its capital in 1910, by which time the population had swelled to about 64,000. Since then, it has become Oklahoma's largest city, its leading commercial center, and home to the National Cowboy Hall of Fame.

Oklahoma City's economy, based on oil and livestock, thrives on petroleum production, meat processing, and the breeding of stocker and feeder cattle. The city hosts a flourishing printing and publishing industry and manufactures a diversity of products, including automobiles, electronics equipment, computers, communications switches, and oil well supplies. As a vital banking center serving the central and western regions of the state, Oklahoma City is home to a Federal Reserve branch bank. On a somewhat less positive note, Oklahoma City reportedly sparked the "go-go" banking syndrome that characterized the 1970s oil boom, when Penn Square Bank's ill-advised oil patch loans nearly devastated the U.S. banking system.

Population 444,719 (1990). Rank: 29. Race/national origin: Black 16.0%; Hispanic 5.0%; Asian 2.4%; American Indian 4.2%. Pop. density: 736/sq. mi. (284/sq km).

Location 35°25'N, 97°30'W. Counties: Canadian, Cleveland, McClain, Oklahoma.

Terrain and climate Elev.: 1,304 ft. Area: 604 sq. mi. (1,564.4 sq km). Avg. daily min. temp.: Jan.: 25.2°F/–3.7°C; avg. daily max.: July: 93.5°F/34.1°C. Avg. annual rainfall: 30.89"; snowfall: 9"; clear days: 141; precipitation days: 81.

Government Form: council and manager. Mayor: Ronald J. Norick. Election: Apr. 1998. Municipal tel. number: (405) 297–2424.

Visitor info.: 1–800–225–5652 or (405) 521–2409.

Omaha, Nebraska

Permanent settlement in what is now Omaha began with a fur-trading post established shortly after the Lewis and Clark expedition passed through the area in 1804. In 1820 the U.S. government built Ft. Atkinson, and the surrounding community became a major stop on both the Mormon and the Lewis and Clark Trails, and was incorporated as a city in 1854. After strong lobbying by citizens of Council Bluffs, Iowa, just across the Missouri River to the east, Omaha (the name means "above all others on the stream") became the eastern terminus of the Union-Pacific transcontinental railroad, the country's first railroad, in 1869. Within six years the population grew to 39,000, and by the turn of the century had passed the 100,000 mark.

As a major transportation hub of the Midwest—Omaha today boasts seven major railroads, and the recently expanded Port of Omaha services a dozen barge lines—the city became a major distribution center for meat and grain, living up to its motto, "We Feed the World." Its major food products include pasta, potato chips, coffee, pancake mixes, frozen dinners, and Omaha steaks. With *Fortune* 500 manufacturing operations and a healthy publishing industry (roughly one out of every four manufacturers is either a publisher or printer), Omaha's diversified economy also has strong roots in insurance, communications, and sophisticated medical facilities, centered at the medical schools of Creighton University and the University of Nebraska.

Among its performing arts institutions are the Omaha Symphony, Opera/Omaha, the Omaha Ballet, the Orpheum Theater, and the Omaha Community Playhouse. Museums and historic sites include the Boys Town Hall of Fame, the Henry Doorly Zoo and Aquarium, the Great Plains Black Museum, the historic ships USS *Hazard* and USS *Marlin*, and the Old Market, a mixed-use National Historic District on the Missouri River.

Population 335,795 (1990). Rank: 48. Race/national origin: Black 13.1%; Hispanic 3.1%; Asian 1.0%; American Indian 0.7%. Pop. density: 3,382/sq. mi. (1,306/sq km).

Location 41°15'N, 95°55'W. County: Douglas.

Terrain and climate Elev.: 982 ft. Area: 99.3 sq. mi. (257.2 sq km). Avg. daily min. temp.: Jan.: 10.2°F/–12.1°C; avg. daily max.: July: 88.5°F/31.3°C. Avg. annual rainfall: 30.34"; snowfall: 32"; clear days: 113; precipitation days: 99.

Government Form: mayor and council. Mayor: Hal Daub. Election: May 1997. Municipal tel. number: (402) 444–5000.

Visitor info.: 1–800–332–1819 or (402) 444–4600.

Philadelphia, Pennsylvania

In 1632 a small contingent of Swedes and Finns came to the land where the Schuylkill River meets the Delaware and founded New Sweden. In 1655 Peter Stuyvesant seized New Sweden for the Dutch, inciting conflict with the British until the Dutch relinquished their rights to the territory in 1673. Nine years later William Penn established a town between the Schuylkill and the Delaware Rivers, naming it Philadelphia, the "city of brotherly love," and in two years it evolved into an active settlement of about 2,500 people, most of them Quakers.

In the mid-1700s, Benjamin Franklin began shaping the destiny of Philadelphia by presiding over the founding of the University of Pennsylvania (America's first university), Pennsylvania Hospital, and a fire insurance company (both also firsts). Under his guidance Philadelphia became the premier Colonial city for the arts and the home of many famous educators, scientists, mathematicians, authors, and painters. In addition a total of 17 libraries were founded at this time. The meeting place of the Continental Congress and the site of the signing of the Declaration of Independence, Philadelphia was the nation's capital from 1790 to 1800, the year the federal government moved permanently to Washington, D.C.

Throughout the 19th century, the influx first of Irish and German, then Jewish, Italian, Polish, and Slavic immigrants from Europe, and blacks from the South, helped build the city's industrial base. Today Philadelphia ranks second among U.S. cities in oil refining; other principal industries are electrical machinery, automobile and truck bodies, petrochemicals, metalworking, and scientific instruments.

Population 1,585,577 (1990). Rank: 5. Race/national origin: Black 39.9%; Hispanic 5.6%; Asian 2.7%; American Indian 0.2%. Pop. density: 11,659/sq. mi. (4,502/sq km).

Location 40°00'N, 75°10'W. County: Philadelphia.

Terrain and climate Elev.: 28 ft. Area: 136 sq. mi. (352.2 sq km). Avg. daily min. temp.: Jan.: 23.8°F/–4.5°C; avg. daily max.: July: 86.1°F/30°C. Avg. annual rainfall: 41.42"; snowfall: 20"; clear days: 92; precipitation days: 116.

Government Form: mayor and council. Mayor: Edward G. Rendell. Election: Nov. 1995. Municipal tel. number: (215) 686–1776.

Visitor info.: (215) 636–1666.

Phoenix, Arizona

Phoenix, the capital of Arizona and its largest city, sits in the Salt River Valley in a former desert that has become a prosperous agricultural area because of a network of irrigated dams located northeast of the city. Long a resort area owing to its mild climate, Phoenix has recently emerged as a lively commercial and agricultural center as well. A prospering high-tech haven attracting businesses engaged in electronics, communications, and research and development, the city also has a strong manufacturing base, which includes airport parts, electronic equipment, agricultural chemicals, radios, air conditioners, and leather goods. Among its agricultural products are lettuce, melons, vegetables, grapefruit, oranges, lemons, and olives.

While Phoenix benefits from modern irrigation efforts, the Hohokam Indian people dug the area's first irrigation ditches in the third century B.C. and developed an extensive network of canals during their culture's decline in A.D. 1400. The area was not resettled until 1864, when a hay camp was established to supply Camp McDowell 30 miles away. Jack Weilling and "Lord Darrell" Dupa rebuilt the old Indian irrigation ditches in 1867 and named the site Phoenix, after the mythical bird that rose from its own ashes. The settlement grew as a trading post, was incorporated as a city in 1881, and became capital of the territory in 1889 and state capital when Arizona was admitted to the Union in 1912.

With the westward exodus from the snowbelt states, and the perfecting of air conditioning to make the summer heat bearable, the small 1950s resort city of 106,818 people has since swelled almost ninefold. In the 1980s alone, Phoenix's population grew 24.5 percent from 789,704 to just under a million.

Population 983,403 (1990). Rank: 9. Race/national origin: Black 5.2%; Hispanic 20.0%; Asian 1.7%; American Indian 1.9%. Pop. density: 2,622/sq. mi. (1,012/sq km).

Location 33°30'N, 112°04'W. County: Maricopa.

Terrain and climate Elev.: 1,117 ft. Area: 375 sq. mi. (971.3 sq km). Avg. daily min. temp.: Jan.: 44.4°F/6.8°C; avg. daily max.: July: 107.5°F/41°C. Avg. annual rainfall: 7.11"; snowfall: 0"; clear days: 214; precipitation days: 34.

Government Form: Mayor and council. Mayor: Thelda Williams. Election: Nov. 1995. Municipal tel. number: (602) 262–6011.
Visitor info.: (602) 254–6500.

Pittsburgh, Pennsylvania

Long one of the leading urban industrial areas in the country, Pittsburgh sits at the confluence of the Allegheny and Monongahela Rivers, which join to form the Ohio River. In 1754 the British chose the site for its access to this extensive river network (which today reaches to the Gulf of Mexico, the Great Lakes, and up the Missouri River) and began building Fort Pitt, named for Prime Minister William Pitt. Pittsburgh is also situated in the midst of extensive deposits of oil, coal, and natural gas; the production of steel and iron began in the 1790s. In the 19th century, Pittsburgh was one of the nation's largest producers of steel and iron, and in 1881 its industrial workers formed the American Federation of Labor.

After the boom years of the 1940s and 1950s, the city's fortunes began to shrivel with the decline of heavy industry, a dwindling population, and high unemployment in the 1980s. Yet with 40 miles of riverfront, Pittsburgh remains the country's largest inland port, and is still a leader in the manufacture of petrochemicals and glass products, as well as the home of more than 150 industrial research companies.

Moreover, Pittsburgh's industrial past has left a rich cultural legacy, which contributed to its ranking in the mid-1980s as number one in the country by *Places Rated Almanac.* Its cultural institutions include Phipps Conservatory, Buhl Planetarium, Carnegie Institute, Carnegie Music Hall, and Carnegie Museum of Natural History (the latter three named for the Scots-born industrialist and philanthropist Andrew Carnegie), as well as the Pittsburgh Symphony Orchestra, the Pittsburgh Public Theater, and Pittsburgh Dance Theater. Its universities include the University of Pittsburgh, Pittsburgh Theological Seminary, Duquesne University, and Carnegie-Mellon University.

Population 369,879 (1990). Rank: 40. Race/national origin: Black 25.8%; Hispanic 0.9%; Asian 1.6%; American Indian 0.2%. Pop. density: 6,677/sq. mi. (2,578/sq km).
Location 40°25'N, 79°55'W. County: Allegheny.
Terrain and climate Elev.: 1,223 ft. Area: 55.4 sq. mi. (143.5 sq km). Avg. daily min. temp.: Jan.: 19.2°F/–7.1°C; avg. daily max.: July: 86.1°F/30°C. Avg. annual rainfall: 36.29"; snowfall: 45"; clear days: 59; precipitation days: 152.
Government Form: mayor and council. Mayor: Tom Murphy. Election: Nov. 1997. Municipal tel. number: (412) 255–2626.
Visitor info.: 1–800–366–0093 or (412) 281–7711.

Portland, Oregon

Portland's renowned beauty is a result of its unique natural setting, which offers a view of the Cascade Mountains and Mt. Hood to the east, Mt. Adams to the northeast, and Mt. St. Helens and Mt. Rainier to the north. Eleven bridges span the Willamette River, which divides the city into east and west sections.

Indian traders traveling between Oregon City and Vancouver carved out an acre of land by the Willamette River 12 miles north of Oregon City, which became known as The Clearing. In 1884 William Overton claimed the 640 acres surrounding the area, which he then sold to Asa Lovejoy and Francis W. Pettygrove, who set out to build a city. Winning a coin toss, Pettygrove named the city-to-be after his hometown in Maine.

As a vital port of entry (the coast's only freshwater port) with a large inland harbor, Portland is a leader in the shipping of lumber, flour, and grain and has blossomed into Oregon's largest city. Main industries also include paper and pulp, mining, high-tech equipment, and aerospace. Portland enjoys an active arts community, and its residents partake of the beaches and ski slopes within easy driving distance.

Population 437,319 (1990). Rank: 30. Race/national origin: Black 7.7%; Hispanic 3.2%; Asian 5.3%; American Indian 1.2%. Pop. density: 3,839/sq. mi. (1,482/sq km).
Location 45°35'N, 122°40'W. Counties: Clackamas, Multnomah, Washington.
Terrain and climate Elev.: 39 ft. Area: 113.9 sq. mi. (295 sq km). Avg. daily min. temp.: Jan.: 33.5°F/0.8°C; avg. daily max.: July: 79.5°F/26.3°C. Avg. annual rainfall: 37.39"; snowfall: 7"; clear days: 69; precipitation days: 152.
Government Form: commission. Mayor: Vera Katz. Election: Nov. 1996. Municipal tel. number: (503) 823–4000.
Visitor info.: (503) 222–2223.

Sacramento, California

The capital of California and its seventh-largest city, Sacramento sits 75 miles northeast of San Francisco at the confluence of the American and Sacramento Rivers. A wholesale and retail center for the surrounding rich farmland, the city includes among its main commercial enterprises food processing and canning and one of the world's largest almond-shelling plants.

Receiving a land grant from the Mexican government in 1839, Swiss-American John Augustus Sutter founded a colony called New Helvetia, and when Fort Sutter was constructed in 1844, it became one of California's chief trading posts. Established soon after the discovery of gold in 1848, Sacramento grew to 7,000 residents by 1850, became state capital in 1854, and in 1863 was incorporated as a city.

The "Gateway to the Goldfields," "Old Sacramento" became a pivotal point of commerce in the 1860s, connected to the mining towns by the American River and transporting produce from the farms and orchards lining the banks of the Sacramento River. Sailors stopping in San Francisco visited Sacramento to replenish their stocks of fresh produce and to entertain themselves in the saloons and gambling halls. The wealthy lived in great mansions by the river, and cobblestone streets, gaslights, and wood sidewalks imbued the town with a touch of civility. Today's Sacramento, appreciated for its subtle, quiet charms, embraces 120 parks; hiking and biking trails along the American River Parkway; a large collection of art galleries; two symphony orchestras; ballet, theater and opera companies; and a number of jazz clubs and coffeehouses.

Population 369,365 (1990). Rank: 41. Race/national origin: Black 15.3%; Hispanic 16.2%; Asian 15.0%; American Indian 1.2%. Pop. density: 3,796/sq. mi. (1,466/sq km).
Location 38°33'N, 121°30'W. County: Sacramento.
Terrain and climate Elev.: 25 ft. Area: 97.3 sq. mi. (252 sq km). Avg. daily min. temp.: Jan.: 37.9°F/3.2°C; avg. daily max.: July: 93.3°F/34°C. Avg. annual rainfall: 17.87"; snowfall: 0.1"; clear days: 193; precipitation days: 57.
Government Form: council and manager. Mayor: Joe Serna, Jr. Election: June 1996. Municipal tel. number: (916) 264–5704.
Visitor info.: (916) 264–7777.

St. Louis, Missouri

St. Louis is one of the nation's major centers of transportation, manufacturing, commerce, and education. With abundant water and electric power, with a workforce of over a million people in the metropolitan area, and in an area rich in mineral resources, St. Louis ranks as one of the top 10 industrial areas in the country. It is also one of the nation's busiest river ports, the third-largest rail center, and the eighth-largest trucking center, and has the sixth-busiest airport. Aircraft, automobiles, printing, beer, and chemicals are among the principal products. The metropolitan area boasts five universities, 23 colleges, and seven junior colleges. St. Louis University, the oldest university west of the Mississippi, founded in 1818, and Washington University are world famous for their medical schools and research programs and their Nobel Prize winners.

For the 40 years after its founding in 1764 by Pierre Laclade, St. Louis was a French settlement and trading post, outfitting fur trading expeditions up the Missouri River. With the Louisiana Purchase in 1803, St. Louis came under American control. The city was incorporated in 1823 with a population of almost 5,000 people. The first steamboat docked at St. Louis in 1817, and steamboats then became a vital part of the city's growth. Fueled by settlers from the east and especially Irish and German immigrants attracted by the prosperity of the river trade, the city's population grew rapidly. In 1870 St. Louis had a population of 311,000, and it was the country's third-largest city after New York and Philadelphia. The population grew to a peak of 856,800 in 1950, but the post–World War II flight to the suburbs hit St. Louis hard, reducing its population by almost half.

The downtown St. Louis area has many landmarks and historic buildings. The Old Cathedral, completed in 1834, and the Old Courthouse, where the Dred Scott case was first tried, have been preserved as part of the Jefferson National Expansion Memorial. Atop the famous Gateway Arch, the observation room provides a panoramic view of St. Louis. Kiel Auditorium contains a 3,500-seat opera house and a 10,000-seat convention hall. Forest Park, site of the 1904 Louisiana

Purchase Exposition (also known as the St. Louis World's Fair), comprises the St. Louis Zoo, McDonnell Planetarium, and the Jewel Box, an all-glass floral display house. St. Louis is also the home of the Missouri Botanical Gardens, which features the Climatron—a geodesic dome with rare orchids and other tropical plants—and the nation's largest Japanese garden. The St. Louis Symphony (founded in 1880) is the country's second oldest and is housed in Powell Symphony Hall.

Population 396,685 (1990). Rank: 34. Race/national origin: Black 47.5%; Hispanic 1.3%; Asian 0.9%; American Indian 0.2%. Pop. density: 6,461/sq. mi. (2,495/sq. km).

Location 38°40'N, 90°12'W. County: independent city.

Terrain and climate Elev.: 564 ft. Area: 61.4 sq. mi. (159 sq km). Avg. daily min. temp.: Jan.: 19.9°F/–6.7°C; avg. daily max.: July: 89°F/31°C. Avg. annual rainfall: 33.91"; snowfall: 18"; clear days: 105; precipitation days: 108.

Government Form: mayor and council. Mayor: Freeman Bosley. Election: Apr. 1997. Municipal tel. number: (314) 622–3201.

Visitor info.: 1–800–247–9791 or (314) 421–1023.

San Antonio, Texas

San Antonio, the third-largest city in Texas, lies in the state's south-central region at the edge of the Gulf Coastal Plain 140 miles from the Gulf of Mexico. Its economy thrives on agriculture, livestock, and the activity of wholesale traders who dominate the commerce of southwestern Texas and northern Mexico, and it is a regional leader in the emerging area of biotechnology. Adding further stimulus to the economy are five major military installations—Fort Sam Houston, Randolph Air Force Base, Kelly Air Force Base, Lackland Air Force Base, and Brooks Air Force Base. The military contributes $3 billion to the area's economy.

The founding of the mission of San Antonio de Valero (later known as the Alamo) and the Presidio of San Antonio in 1718 represented the area's first permanent Euro-American settlement. When 56 settlers from the Canary Islands joined the original coterie of ranchers, missionaries, and soldiers, they formed the first municipal organization in Texas, called the villa of San Fernando de Bexar, which became a city in 1809. They remained under Mexican rule until the battle of San Jacinto in 1836. With the influx of American pioneers and German immigrants following Texas statehood, the population grew to more than 96,000 by 1910, and has since increased nearly tenfold.

Today San Antonio is a popular haven for vacationers, with over 10 million visitors per year. San Antonio's attractions include the Alamo and its four sister missions; the Riverwalk along the San Antonio River; Breckenridge Park, home of one of America's largest zoos; Sea World of Texas; La Villita; the Tower of the Americas; and the Spanish Governor's Palace.

Population 935,933 (1990). Rank: 10. Race/national origin: Black 7.0%; Hispanic 55.6%; Asian 1.1%; American Indian 0.4%. Pop. density: 3,074/sq. mi. (1,187/sq km).

Location 29°30'N, 98°30'W. County: Bexar.

Terrain and climate Elev.: 701 ft. Area: 304.5 sq. mi. (788.7 sq km). Avg. daily min. temp.: Jan.: 39°F/3.8°C; avg. daily max.: July: 96.3°F/35.7°C. Avg. annual rainfall: 29.13"; snowfall: 0.5"; clear days: 110; precipitation days: 81.

Government Form: council and manager. Mayor: Bill Thornton. Election: May 1997. Municipal tel. number: (210) 299–7235.

Visitor info.: 1–800–447–3372 or (210) 270–8748.

San Diego, California

Sixty years after João Rodrigues Cabrilho first sailed into San Diego Bay, Sebastian Vizcaino embarked from Spain with three ships to explore the coast of California, and in November 1602 anchored on the lee of what is now known as Point Loma. When he finished charting the bay two days later, he changed its original name, San Miguel, to San Diego, in honor of San Diego de Alcalal de Henares. In 1769 Father Junipero Serra established California's first mission, the Mission San Diego de Alcala.

Compared to its sister cities to the north—Los Angeles and San Francisco—San Diego developed slowly, despite its large and hospitable harbor. In 1887 the city became the southern terminus for the Santa Fe Railroad, but floods soon washed out the tracks and track beds, and the railroad was rebuilt to terminate in L.A. This, along with L.A.'s man-made harbor, put San Diego at an almost insurmountable disadvantage. With its industrial development stunted, San Diego welcomed the establishment of a U.S. Navy base during World War I; since then, about a quarter of the navy's seagoing vessels and roughly 20 percent of the marine corps's forces have located there. Jonas Salk's work on polio and the emergence of the University of California at San Diego has earned the city the reputation as a premier biomedical research center, luring billions of dollars in development and research grants.

San Diego, a picturesque city with many tourist attractions, enjoys abundant sunshine, enticing both residents and visitors to its 70 beaches and the parks, resorts, and health spas lining its great bay. Coronado Island is a popular attraction. Balboa Park, host to international expositions in 1915 and 1935, contains the San Diego Zoo, one of the finest in the nation. The pleasure boats berthed at the city's numerous yacht clubs offer a curious contrast to the naval warships moored nearby. San Diego was the site of the 1992 America's Cup yacht races.

Population 1,110,549 (1990). Rank: 6. Race/national origin: Black 9.4%; Hispanic 20.7%; Asian 11.8%; American Indian 0.6%. Pop. density: 3,376/sq. mi. (1,303/sq km).

Location 32°43'N, 117°10'W. County: San Diego.

Terrain and climate Elev.: 13 ft. Area: 329 sq. mi. (852.1 sq km). Avg. daily min. temp.: Jan.: 48.4°F/9.1°C; avg. daily max.: July: 75.6°F/ 24.2°C. Avg. annual rainfall: 9.32"; snowfall: 0"; clear days: 150; precipitation days: 41.

Government Form: council and manager. Mayor: Susan Golding. Election: Nov. 1996. Municipal tel. number: (619) 236–5555.

Visitor info.: (619) 236–1212.

San Francisco, California

Located near the Golden Gate, the strait between San Francisco Bay and the Pacific Ocean, fog-bound San Francisco hid from some of the greatest European navigators to explore the West Coast. João Rodrigues Cabrilho discovered the Farallon Islands just off the coast in 1542, and Sir Francis Drake landed a few miles north of the Golden Gate in 1579. Yet it was another 200 years before Don Gasper de Portola sailed into the bay, followed six years later by Don Juan Manuel Ayala, who established a town and mission.

Neither the Spanish nor (after 1821) the Mexican governments were very keen on capitalizing on San Francisco's temperate and strategic location, and when Capt. John Montgomery raised the American flag there on July 9, 1846, the community consisted of only 840 people. The discovery of gold at Sutter's Mill in 1848, and the gold rush of 1849—which brought 40,000 of the hopeful to California, most by ship—catapulted San Francisco onto the world map, and the following year it was incorporated as a city.

San Francisco continued to prosper as a major transportation and industrial center, but in 1906 an earthquake registering 8.6 on the Richter scale claimed 452 lives, 28,000 buildings, and losses totaling approximately $350 million. San Francisco rose from the ashes to become a thriving, multifaceted, cosmopolitan city and one of the country's leaders in world trade. Another major earthquake, measuring 7.1 on the Richter scale, struck on Oct. 17, 1989, causing extensive damage and 67 deaths in the region.

San Francisco is now a port of call for more than 40 steamship lines, which import approximately $25 billion worth of goods from more than 300 ports around the world. A major international financial center, it is the headquarters of three of the nation's largest banks, the 12th Federal Reserve District, and the Pacific Stock Exchange. There are also more than 650 insurance companies, and the city is a haven for venture capitalists and entrepreneurs: More than 90 percent of its businesses have fewer than 25 employees. Several U.S. military installations are based in the area.

Well known for its spirit of individualism, San Francisco was a haven for the beat movement of the 1950s, and the capital of the 1960s hippie movement was the Haight-Ashbury district. The city's more traditional arts institutions include the San Francisco Ballet, the San Francisco Opera, the San Francisco Symphony, and the American Conservatory Theater. Among its leading educational institutions are the University of San Francisco, the Heald Institute of Technology, the University of California, the San Francisco Art Institute, the San Francisco Conservatory of Music, and the San Francisco College of Mortuary Science. Among its many

museums are the National Maritime Historic Park, the Fine Arts Museum, and the California Palace of the Legion of Honor. Other attractions include its historic cable cars (first used in 1873), Chinatown, and Fisherman's Wharf.
Population 723,959 (1990). Rank: 14. Race/national origin: Black 10.9%; Hispanic 13.9%; Asian 29.1%; American Indian 0.5%. Pop. density: 15,603/sq. mi. (6,023/sq km).
Location 37°47'N, 122°30'W. County: San Francisco.
Terrain and climate Elev.: 155 ft. Area: 46.4 sq. mi. (120.2 sq km). Avg. daily min. temp.: Jan.: 41.5°F/5.2°C; avg. daily max.: July: 71°F/21°C. Avg. annual rainfall: 19.71"; snowfall: 0"; clear days: 162; precipitation days: 67.
Government Form: mayor and council. Mayor: Frank M. Jordan. Election: Nov. 1995. Municipal tel. number: (415) 554–6141.
Visitor info: (415) 974–6900.

San Jose, California

Located at the southern end of San Francisco Bay, about 45 miles south of San Francisco, San Jose was the first nonreligious European community founded in California. Pueblo de San Jose de Guadalupe was settled in 1777 by enterprising farmers who sought to make themselves and the region independent of Mexico and the Spanish-mission network for their supplies. Fruit and olive trees, hides, tallow, livestock, grain, and lively retail activity all contributed to San Jose's early prosperity, and it was the first state capital (1849–52).

San Jose remained an agricultural center until World War II, when industry and technology began to expand. The rapid growth of innovative industry over the last 20 years, taking its lead from research and development begun at nearby Stanford University in the 1930s, changed the area dramatically. With the revolution in high technology, Santa Clara County became known as Silicon Valley, excelling in the production of information systems, personal computers, and peripherals, and fostering a burgeoning semiconductor industry. At the same time, financial services, real estate, construction, and retail industries all flourished.

More than 2,600 high-tech companies employing 250,000 people are located in San Jose, and one-third of the labor force works in manufacturing, a very high proportion in postindustrial America. Santa Clara County has the highest median family income in California, and according to a 1987 survey of buying power by *Sales and Marketing* magazine, the San Jose metropolitan area is third in the nation in median household "effective buying power." The same survey ranks it second in California and fifth in the nation, in manufacturing as measured by value of shipments—$30.5 billion in 1986.
Population 782,248 (1990). Rank: 11. Race/national origin: Black 4.7%; Hispanic 26.6%; Asian 19.5%; American Indian 0.7%. Pop. density: 4,623/sq. mi. (1,785/sq km).
Location 37°20'N, 121°53'W. County: Santa Clara.
Terrain and climate Elev.: 65 ft. Area: 169.2 sq. mi. (438.2 sq km). Avg. daily min. temp.: Jan.: 41.1°F/5°C; avg. daily max.: July: 81.5°F/27.5°C. Avg. annual rainfall: 13.86"; snowfall: 0"; clear days: N.A.; precipitation days: N.A.
Government Form: council and manager. Mayor: Susan Hammer. Election: Nov. 1998. Municipal tel. number: (408) 277–4237.
Visitor info: 1–800–SAN JOSE or (408) 295–9600.

Seattle, Washington

Located on the protected waters of Puget Sound, Seattle was the first Euro-American settlement established in the Pacific Northwest north of the Columbia River. Starting out at Alki Point in 1851, the settlers moved to what is now known as Pioneer Square. Befriended by the Suquamish chief Sealth (Seattle is a loose approximation of his name), the people turned to lumber harvesting and log milling, which formed the backbone of the city's economy.

With the completion of the Great Northern Railway in 1893 and with the Alaska gold rush of 1897, when Seattle became the "Gateway to the Klondike," the city was transformed into a metropolis of merchants and entrepreneurs. Even as gold fever abated, and despite a devastating fire in 1899, the city prospered as a major port to the Orient and as an industrial center. In 1909 Seattle was the site of the Alaska-Yukon-Pacific Exposition. The completion of the Panama Canal in 1914 brought even more business to the already bustling port. Two years later a small company began building two-seater biplanes, marking the start of Seattle's enduring link with the aerospace industry. In time the little company became Boeing, the world's largest producer of commercial planes, employing more than 100,000 people in the Seattle area.

Endowed with spectacular natural beauty, with the broad expanse of Puget Sound before it and the snow-capped peaks of the Cascade Mountains and Mt. Rainier visible to the south and east, the Seattle area offers a wide variety of outdoor activities, from skiing and hiking to fishing and boating. A second international exposition, the Seattle World's Fair in 1962, helped establish the city's reputation as a center of technology, trade, industry, and tourism. The leading cultural programs are put on by the Seattle Symphony Orchestra, the Seattle Opera Association, and the Seattle Repertory Theater. Other attractions include the Seattle Art Museum, Pioneer Square, Pike Place Market, the historic ships on Lake Union, and Woodland Park and Zoo, as well as the many events at the 74-acre Seattle Center, whose buildings and parklike grounds and fountains are legacies of the World's Fair. Among the 20 universities and colleges in the area are the University of Washington and Seattle Pacific University.
Population 516,259 (1990). Rank: 21. Race/national origin: Black 10.1%; Hispanic 3.6%; Asian 11.8%; American Indian 1.4%. Pop. density: 6,175/sq. mi. (2,385/sq km).
Location 47°41'N, 122°15'W. County: King.
Terrain and climate Elev.: 450 ft. Area: 83.6 sq. mi. (216.5 sq km). Avg. daily min. temp.: Jan.: 34.3°F/1.2°C; avg. daily max.: July: 75.2°F/24°C. Avg. annual rainfall: 38.85"; snowfall: 15"; clear days: 57; precipitation days: 160.
Government Form: mayor and council. Mayor: Norman B. Rice. Election: Nov. 1997. Municipal tel. number: (206) 684–4000.
Visitor info: (206) 461–5840.

Toledo, Ohio

Toledo's origins can be traced to late 18th-century speculators who purchased tracts of land on either side of the Maumee River near its mouth, at the western end of Lake Erie. Although the smaller upriver towns of Perrysburg and Maumee were settled earlier, the twin towns of Port Lawrence and Vistula, laid out in 1832, were right on the lake. When it was found that steamers could navigate the river, the newer towns merged, adopting an anonymous suggestion to name itself for the city in Spain.

Toledo's early history and prosperity were tied to plans for the Miami and Erie Canal, which when completed in 1845 linked the Ohio River and Lake Erie. The border between Ohio (statehood, 1803) and Michigan (1837) was ill-defined. In the Toledo War (1835–36), Michigan held that Toledo was theirs. But Toledans opted for Ohio, figuring that Ohio would not finance a canal to the benefit of another state. (In exchange Michigan received the Upper Peninsula and admission to the Union.)

Though the canal was only moderately successful, Toledo benefited from the railroads that superceded it, and by the Civil War it was a major rail center. Toledo is a major shipper of coal, grain, iron ore, and general cargo. The city's manufactures include automotive components, plastics, and glass. In 1887, Edward Libbey relocated his New England Glass Company in Toledo, and Toledo's nickname is "Glass Capital of the World." Although Toledo was the hardest-hit area of Ohio in the recession of the early 1990s, it has developed a base of new businesses, especially medical research companies drawn by the Medical College of Ohio's development of the Health Technology Park.

Toledo's cultural attractions include the Toledo Opera, Toledo Symphony Orchestra, Toledo Ballet, and the Toledo Repertoire Theatre. In addition there is the excellent Toledo Museum of Art as well as the Glass Apple, which exhibits glass pieces by local and international artists. Toledo's major educational institutions include the University of Toledo, Bowling Green State University, and the Medical College of Ohio.
Population 332,943 (1990). Rank: 49. Race/national origin: Black 19.7%; Hispanic 4.0%; Asian 1.0%; American Indian 0.3%. Pop. density: 3,954/sq. mi. (1,527/sq km).
Location 41°37'N, 83°33'W. County: Lucas.
Terrain and climate Elev.: 692 ft. Area: 84.2 sq. mi. (218.1 sq km). Avg. daily min. temp.: Jan.: 15.5°F/–9.1°C; avg. daily max.: July: 83.4°F/28.5°C. Avg. annual rainfall: 31.77"; snowfall: 37"; clear days: 71; precipitation days: 136.
Government Form: city manager. Mayor: Carty Finkbeiner. Election: Nov. 1997. Municipal tel. number: (419) 245–1010.
Visitor info: 1–800–243–4667.

Tucson, Arizona

The first European to travel through the area that is now Tucson was the Jesuit missionary Eusebio Kino in 1692. In 1700 the mission of San Xavier del Bac was established among the Papago Indians nearby. It was not until 1776, however, that the Spanish established a permanent settlement, taking its name from the Papago *Stjukshon* (or *Chuk Shon*), meaning "village of the dark spring at the foot of the mountain." Tucson remained under Spanish and Mexican control until it was acquired by the U.S. government as part of the Gadsden Purchase in 1853. During the Civil War it was under Confederate control, but from 1867 to 1877 it was the territorial capital.

Despite the arrival of the Southern Pacific railroad in 1880 and the discovery of extensive copper deposits in southern Arizona, neither Tucson's location nor its natural resources much stimulated its economy. It was best known as a winter and health resort and as a commercial hub for the surrounding agricultural and mining industries. In 1950 the population was only 45,500.

The last 40 years have seen a dramatic change. One of the many beneficiaries of the exodus from the industrial states to the Sunbelt, Tucson has seen its population grow almost tenfold in that period, and in the last decade, Tucson added 20,000 manufacturing jobs. Surrounded by a wealth of natural beauty, the city is still appealing to retirees and tourists, as is reflected in the many golf courses, ranches, and resorts in and around Tucson. It is surrounded by four mountain ranges: the Rincon, Santa Catalina, Tucson, and Santa Rita. Other natural wonders include Sabino Canyon (which has the only year-round stream in the region), the Saguaro National Monument (a preserve for Saguaro cacti), and Tucson Mountain Park, site of the Arizona-Sonora Desert Museum. The University of Arizona is located in Tucson, and the Davis-Mothan Air Force Base and Kitts Peak Observatory are nearby.

Population 405,390 (1990). Rank: 33. Race/national origin: Black 4.3%; Hispanic 29.3%; Asian 2.2%; American Indian 1.6%. Pop. density: 3,243/sq. mi. (1,248/sq km).

Location 32°14'N, 110°59'W. County: Pima.

Terrain and climate Elev.: 2,584 ft. Area: 125 sq. mi. (324.8 sq km). Avg. daily min. temp.: Jan.: 38.1°F/3.3°C; avg. daily max.: July: 98.5°F/3.3°C. Avg. annual rainfall: 11.14"; snowfall: 2"; clear days: 198; precipitation days: 50.

Government Form: council and manager. Mayor: George Miller. Election: Nov. 1995. Municipal tel. number: (602) 791-4201.

Visitor info: 1-800-638-8350 or (602) 624-1817.

Tulsa, Oklahoma

Tulsa was first settled by Indian nations forced out of the South Atlantic states by the Indian Removal Act of 1830. The name they chose for their new home was Tulsey Town, a corruption of *Tullahassee*, meaning "Old Town." The name Tulsa was made official with the establishment of a post office in 1879. In 1900, Tulsa's population numbered less than 2,000, but the discovery of extensive oil fields at the turn of the century, beginning with the Glenn Pool and Red Fork strikes, started Tulsa on its way from a small Indian settlement to a sizable metropolis. By 1907 its population had increased to 7,298, and by 1920 it was 10 times that. Soon Tulsa was "Oil Capital of the World."

While still heavily involved in the oil and gas industry—it remains the home of about 500 oil-related companies—modern Tulsa is a far more diverse city than its oil patch origins. Among Tulsa's top employers are regional, national, and international firms involved in aviation and aerospace, energy, computer technology, insurance, telecommunications, health care, and electronic equipment. The Port of Catoosa, which opened in 1971 after completion of the 445-mile Arkansas-Mississippi Waterway, is a major inland port, providing Tulsa with a direct link to the Mississippi River system and the Gulf of Mexico.

While growing in business, Tulsa has preserved the cultural heritage of its early oil barons and workers as well as that of its original Indian settlers. Thomas Gilcrease, a Creek Indian, became a millionaire with the Glenn Pool oil strike, and founded the Thomas Gilcrease Institute of American History and Art, devoted to American Indian heritage. The Tulsa Opera Company was founded in the early 1900s, and along with the city's philharmonic, ballet, and theaters, it gives Tulsa just cause to lay claim to being the cultural capital of Oklahoma. Tulsans also honor their roots through rodeos and regional music festivals. In addition, representatives of the state's 65 Indian tribes gather in Tulsa each summer for their annual powwow. Among Tulsa's eight colleges and universities are the University of Tulsa, Oral Roberts University, and University Center at Tulsa, a consortium of Langston University, Northeastern State University, Oklahoma State University, and the University of Oklahoma.

Population 367,302 (1990). Rank: 43. Race/national origin: Black 13.6%; Hispanic 2.6%; Asian 1.4%; American Indian 4.7%. Pop. density: 1,974/sq. mi. (762/sq km).

Location 36°10'N, 96°00'W. Counties: Osage, Tulsa.

Terrain and climate Elev.: 676 ft. Area: 186.1 sq. mi. (482 sq km). Avg. daily min. temp.: Jan.: 24.8°F/-4°C; avg. daily max.: July: 93.9°F/34.3°C. Avg. annual rainfall: 38.77"; snowfall: 9"; clear days: 127; precipitation days: 90.

Government Form: commission. Mayor: Susan Savage. Election: Apr. 1998. Municipal tel. number: (918) 596-7411.

Visitor info: (918) 585-1201.

Virginia Beach, Virginia

Throughout much of its history—which dates to the landing of the Jamestown colonists at Point Henry in 1607—Virginia Beach was overshadowed by its northern neighbor, Norfolk, which with its magnificent harbor was long the home of many shipping and naval enterprises at the mouth of Chesapeake Bay. But Virginia Beach has seen remarkable change in the last two decades.

In 1970 Virginia Beach's population was 172,000, only slightly more than half that of Norfolk. By 1990 it had grown 128 percent, to 393,000, and it is one of fastest-growing of the country's 50 largest cities. Local initiative accounts for most of this growth; in the same period, Norfolk's population fell 11 percent. A dominant presence is the U.S. Navy, which has three bases—Oceana Naval Air Station, Little Creek Naval Amphibious Base, and the Dam Neck Fleet Training Center—and which, together with the U.S. Army's Fort Story, employs 36,000 military and civilian personnel.

With 38 miles of Atlantic shoreline, 28 miles of public beaches, and the Seashore State Park—2,700 acres of shady upland woods, cypress swamps, and Spanish moss—the city continues to depend on tourism as a major factor in its economy and attracts 2.5 million visitors a year. The city's main industries, which include marine and engineering services, construction, communications, and electronics, occupy 10 industrial/business parks, including four built by the Virginia Beach Development Authority.

Among Virginia Beach's outstanding historic and recreational attractions are the Virginia Marine Science Museum; the Adam Thoroughgood House (c. 1680, one of the oldest brick houses in North America); the Old Cape Henry Lighthouse, authorized by the first Congress in 1790; and the statue of Adm. Compte de Grasse, whose defeat of the British at the Battle of the Virginia Capes brought about the defeat of Gen. Cornwallis at Yorktown and the end of the American Revolution in 1781.

Population 393,069 (1990). Rank: 37. Race/national origin: Black 13.9%; Hispanic 3.1%; Asian 4.3%; American Indian 0.4%. Pop. density: 1,740/sq. mi. (672/sq km).

Location 36°54'N, 75°58'W. County: independent city.

Terrain and climate Elev.: 12 ft. Area: 225.9 sq. mi. (585.1 sq km). Avg. daily min. temp.: Jan.: 31.7°F/-0.1°C; avg. daily max.: July: 86.9°F/30.5°C. Avg. annual rainfall: 45.22"; snowfall: 7"; clear days: 110; precipitation days: 115.

Government Form: council and manager. Mayor: Meyera E. Oberndorf. Election: May 1996. Municipal tel. number: (804) 427-4581.

Visitor info: 1-800-VA-BEACH (822-3224).

Washington, D.C.

(For description, see District of Columbia entry in "States, Territories, and Possessions.")

Population 606,900 (1990). Rank: 19. Race/national origin: Black 65.8%; Hispanic 5.4%; Asian 1.8%; American Indian 0.2%. Pop. density: 9,679/sq. mi. (3,737/sq km).

Location 38°52'N, 77°00'W. County: independent city.

Terrain and climate Elev.: 30 ft. Area: 62.7 sq. mi. (162.4 sq km). Avg. daily min. temp.: Jan.: 27.5°F/-2.5°C; avg. daily max.: July: 87.9°F/31°C. Avg. annual rainfall: 39"; snowfall: 16"; clear days: 101; precipitation days: 111.

Government Form: mayor and council. Mayor: Marion Barry. Election: Nov. 1998. Municipal tel. number: (202) 727-6600.

Visitor info: (202) 789-7000.

Cities in America

Since 1960 the growth of the urban population has occurred primarily in cities of under 250,000. In that year there were five cities of a million or more people; in 1990 there were eight. Over the same time period, the number of cities of between 500,000 and one million inhabitants remained unchanged at 16, while the number of cities of 250,000 to 500,000 inhabitants grew 33 percent, from 30 to 40.

The 1990 census recorded 29 new cities joining the rank of those with populations over 100,000. Eighteen were in California, four in Texas, two in Arizona, and one each in Florida, Kansas, Massachusetts, Oregon, and South Dakota. Two of the California cities over 100,000, Santa Clarita in Los Angeles County and Moreno Valley in Riverside County, were not incorporated cities in 1980.

Five cities fell from the ranks of 100,000+ cities since 1980: Columbia, S.C.; Davenport, Iowa; Pueblo, Colo.; Roanoke, Va.; and Youngstown, Ohio.

MAJOR U.S. CITIES: POPULATION, POPULATION CHANGE, POPULATION DENSITY, AND LAND AREA, 1970–90

	Population						
	Population ('000s)			Rank	Percent change	Per sq. mi.	Land area (sq. mi.)
City	1970	1980	1990	1990	1980–90	1990	1990
Abilene, Tex.	90	98	107	180	8.5%	1,035	103.1
Akron, Ohio	275	237	223	71	–6.0	3,586	62.2
Albany, N.Y.	116	102	100	196	–1.7	4,674	21.4
Albuquerque, N.Mex.	245	332	385	38	15.5	2,909	132.2
Alexandria, Va.	111	103	111	164	7.7	7,267	15.3
Allentown, Pa.	110	104	105	183	1.5	5,949	17.7
Amarillo, Tex.	127	149	158	110	5.6	1,793	87.9
Anaheim, Calif.	166	219	266	59	21.4	6,014	44.3
Anchorage, Alaska	48	174	226	69	29.8	133	1,697.7
Ann Arbor, Mich.	100	108	110	170	1.5	4,231	25.9
Arlington, Tex.	90	160	262	61	63.5	2,814	93.0
Atlanta, Ga.	495	425	394	36	–7.3	2,990	131.8
Aurora, Colo.	75	159	222	72	40.1	1,676	132.5
Austin, Tex.	254	346	466	27	34.6	2,138	217.8
Bakersfield, Calif.	70	106	175	97	65.5	1,904	91.8
Baltimore, Md.	905	787	736	12	–6.4	9,108	80.8
Baton Rouge, La.	166	220	220	73	–0.4	2,969	74.0
Beaumont, Tex.	118	118	114	155	–3.2	1,427	80.1
Berkeley, Calif.	114	103	103	190	–0.6	9,783	10.5
Birmingham, Ala.	301	284	266	60	–6.5	1,791	148.5
Boise City, Idaho	75	102	126	145	23.0	2,726	46.1
Boston, Mass.	641	563	574	20	2.0	11,860	48.4
Bridgeport, Conn.	157	143	142	123	–0.6	8,855	16.0
Buffalo, N.Y.	463	358	328	50	–8.3	8,083	40.6
Cedar Rapids, Iowa	111	110	109	173	–1.3	2,033	53.5
Charlotte, N.C.	241	315	396	35	25.5	2,272	174.3
Chattanooga, Tenn.	120	170	152	113	–10.0	1,288	118.4
Chesapeake, Va.	90	114	152	114	32.8	446	340.7
Chicago, Ill.	3,369	3,005	2,784	3	–7.4	12,251	227.2
Chula Vista, Calif.	68	84	135	131	61.0	4,661	29.0
Cincinnati, Ohio	454	385	364	45	–5.5	4,717	77.2
Cleveland, Ohio	751	574	506	23	–11.9	6,565	77.0
Colorado Springs, Colo.	136	215	281	54	30.7	1,535	183.2
Columbus, S.C.	114	101	103	188	2.2	884	117.1
Columbus, Ga.[1]	155	169	179	93	5.5	827	216.1
Columbus, Ohio	540	565	633	16	12.0	3,315	190.9
Concord, Calif.	85	104	111	163	7.3	3,773	29.5
Corpus Christi, Tex.	205	232	257	64	10.9	1,907	135.0
Dallas, Tex.	844	905	1,008	8	11.4	2,943	342.4
Dayton, Ohio	243	194	182	89	–5.9	3,310	55.0
Denver, Colo.	515	493	468	26	–5.1	3,051	153.3
Des Moines, Iowa	201	191	193	80	1.1	2,567	75.3
Detroit, Mich.	1,514	1,203	1,028	7	–14.6	7,410	138.7
Durham, N.C.	95	101	137	130	35.1	1,972	69.3
Elizabeth, N.J.	113	106	110	168	3.6	8,929	12.3
El Monte, Calif.	70	79	106	181	33.5	11,175	9.5
El Paso, Tex.	322	425	515	22	21.2	2,100	245.4
Erie, Pa.	129	119	109	175	–8.7	4,944	22.0
Escondido, Calif.	37	64	109	176	68.8%	3,048	35.6
Eugene, Oreg.	79	106	113	159	6.6	2,962	38.0
Evansville, Ind.	139	130	126	144	–3.2	3,102	40.7
Flint, Mich.	193	160	141	125	–11.8	4,161	33.8
Fort Lauderdale, Fla.	140	153	149	116	–2.6	4,753	31.4
Fort Wayne, Ind.	178	172	173	99	0.4	2,762	62.7
Fort Worth, Tex.	393	385	448	28	16.2	1,592	281.1
Fremont, Calif.	101	132	173	98	31.4	2,250	77.0
Fresno, Calif.	166	217	354	47	62.9	3,573	99.1
Fullerton, Calif.	86	102	114	156	11.6	5,160	22.1
Garden Grove, Calif.	121	123	143	120	16.0	7,974	17.9
Garland, Tex.	81	139	181	91	30.1	3,150	57.4
Gary, Ind.	175	152	117	154	–23.2	2,322	50.2
Glendale, Ariz.	36	97	148	117	52.4	2,837	52.2
Glendale, Calif.	133	139	180	92	29.5	5,882	30.6
Grand Rapids, Mich.	198	182	189	83	4.0	4,273	44.3
Greensboro, N.C.	144	156	184	88	18.2	2,304	79.8
Hampton, Va.	121	123	134	133	9.1	2,583	51.8
Hartford, Conn.	158	136	140	128	2.5	8,077	17.3
Hayward, Calif.	93	94	111	162	19.0	2,560	43.5
Hialeah, Fla.	102	145	188	85	29.4	9,772	19.2
Hollywood, Fla.	107	121	122	148	0.3	4,464	27.3
Honolulu, Hawaii[2]	325	365	377	39	3.3	4,400	85.7
Houston, Tex.	1,234	1,595	1,631	4	2.2	3,021	539.9
Huntington Beach, Calif.	116	171	182	90	6.5	6,871	26.4
Huntsville, Ala.	139	143	160	109	12.2	973	164.4
Independence, Mo.	112	112	112	160	0.5	1,436	78.2
Indianapolis, Ind.[1]	737	701	731	13	4.3	2,022	361.7
Inglewood, Calif.	90	94	110	169	16.4	11,952	9.2
Irvine, Calif.	(3)	62	110	167	77.6	2,607	42.3
Irving, Tex.	97	110	155	112	41.0	2,293	67.6
Jackson, Miss.	154	203	197	78	–3.1	1,804	109.0
Jacksonville, Fla.[1]	504	541	635	15	17.9	837	758.7
Jersey City, N.J.	260	224	229	67	2.2	15,337	14.9
Kansas City, Kans.	168	161	150	115	–7.1	1,390	107.8
Kansas City, Mo.	507	448	435	31	–2.9	1,397	311.5
Knoxville, Tenn.	175	175	165	102	–5.7	2,135	77.2
Lakewood, Colo.	93	114	126	143	11.1	3,100	40.8
Lansing, Mich.	131	130	127	142	–2.4	3,755	33.9
Laredo, Tex.	69	91	123	147	34.4	3,739	32.9
Las Vegas, Nev.	126	165	258	63	56.8	3,100	83.3
Lexington-Fayette, Ky.[1]	108	204	225	70	10.4	792	284.5
Lincoln, Nebr.	150	172	192	81	11.7	3,033	63.3
Little Rock, Ark.	132	159	176	96	10.5	1,709	102.9
Livonia, Mich.	110	105	101	193	–3.8	2,823	35.7
Long Beach, Calif.	359	361	429	32	18.8	8,586	50.0
Los Angeles, Calif.	2,812	2,969	3,485	2	17.4	7,426	469.3
Louisville, Ky.	362	299	270	58	–9.8	4,341	62.1

City	Population ('000s) 1970	Population ('000s) 1980	Population ('000s) 1990	Rank 1990	Percent change 1980–90	Per sq. mi. 1990	Land area (sq. mi.) 1990
Lowell, Mass.	94	92	103	189	11.9%	7,506	13.8
Lubbock, Tex.	149	174	186	87	6.8	1,789	104.1
Macon, Ga.	122	117	107	179	–8.2	2,241	47.9
Madison, Wis.	172	171	191	82	11.8	3,300	57.8
Memphis, Tenn.	624	646	610	18	–5.5	2,384	256.0
Mesa, Ariz.	63	152	288	53	89.0	2,653	108.6
Mesquite, Tex.	55	67	101	191	51.3	2,369	42.8
Miami, Fla.	335	347	359	46	3.5	10,074	35.6
Milwaukee, Wis.	717	636	628	17	–1.3	6,537	96.1
Minneapolis, Minn.	434	371	368	43	–0.7	6,706	54.9
Mobile, Ala.	190	200	196	79	–2.1	1,663	118.0
Modesto, Calif.	62	107	165	103	54.0	5,458	30.2
Montgomery, Ala.	133	178	188	86	5.4	1,389	135.0
Moreno Valley, Calif.	(3)	(3)	119	151	N.A.	2,418	49.1
Nashville–Davidson, Tenn.[1]	426	456	488	25	6.9	1,032	473.3
Newark, N.J.	382	329	275	56	–16.4	11,554	23.8
New Haven, Conn.	138	126	130	138	3.5	6,922	18.9
New Orleans, La.	593	558	497	24	–10.9	2,751	180.7
Newport News, Va.	138	145	171	100	18.3	2,510	68.3
New York, N.Y.	7,896	7,072	7,323	1	3.5	23,701	309.0
Norfolk, Va.	308	267	261	62	–2.2	4,856	53.8
Oakland, Calif.	362	339	372	40	9.7	6,640	56.1
Oceanside, Calif.	40	77	128	140	67.1	3,164	40.5
Oklahoma City, Okla.	368	404	445	29	10.1	731	608.2
Omaha, Nebr.	347	314	336	48	7.0	3,336	100.7
Ontario, Calif.	64	89	133	134	49.9	3,624	36.8
Orange, Calif.	77	91	111	166	21.0	4,741	23.3
Orlando, Fla.	99	128	165	104	28.4	2,448	67.3
Overland Park, Kans.	78	82	112	161	36.7	2,007	55.7
Oxnard, Calif.	71	108	143	121	31.8	5,843	24.4
Pasadena, Calif.	113	118	132	137	11.4	5,724	23.0
Pasadena, Tex.	90	113	119	150	6.1	2,726	43.8
Paterson, N.J.	145	138	141	124	2.1	16,693	8.4
Peoria, Ill.	127	124	114	157	–8.6	2,776	40.9
Philadelphia, Pa.	1,949	1,688	1,586	5	–6.1	11,734	135.1
Phoenix, Ariz.	584	790	983	9	24.5	2,342	419.9
Pittsburgh, Pa.	520	424	370	41	–12.8	6,649	55.6
Plano, Tex.	18	72	128	141	76.8	1,929	66.3
Pomona, Calif.	87	93	132	136	42.0	5,770	22.8
Portland, Oreg.	380	368	437	30	18.8	3,508	124.7
Portsmouth, Va.	111	105	104	186	–0.6	3,139	33.1
Providence, R.I.	179	157	161	107	2.5	8,707	18.5
Raleigh, N.C.	123	150	211	74	40.4	2,395	88.1
Rancho Cucamonga, Calif.	(3)	55	101	192	83.5	2,682	37.8
Reno, Nev.	73	101	134	132	32.8	2,328	57.5
Richmond, Va.	249	219	203	76	–7.5	3,374	60.1
Riverside, Calif.	140	171	227	68	32.8	2,916	77.7
Rochester, N.Y.	295	242	230	66	–4.7	6,435	35.8
Rockford, Ill.	147	140	140	127	0.2	3,110	45.0
Sacramento, Calif.	257	276	369	42	34.0	3,836	96.3
Salem, Oreg.	69	89	108	178	21.0%	2,595	41.5
St. Louis, Mo.	622	453	397	34	–12.4	6,405	61.9
St. Paul, Minn.	310	270	272	57	0.7	5,157	52.8
St. Petersburg, Fla.	216	239	240	65	0.7	4,059	59.2
Salinas, Calif.	59	80	109	174	35.2	5,839	18.6
Salt Lake City, Utah	176	163	160	108	–1.9	1,467	109.0
San Antonio, Tex.	654	786	936	10	19.1	2,810	333.0
San Bernardino, Calif.	107	119	164	105	38.2	2,980	55.1
San Diego, Calif.	697	876	1,111	6	26.8	3,428	324.0
San Francisco, Calif.	716	679	724	14	6.6	15,502	46.7
San Jose, Calif.	460	629	782	11	24.3	4,568	171.3
Santa Ana, Calif.	156	204	294	52	44.0	10,842	27.1
Santa Clarita, Calif.	(3)	(3)	111	165	N.A.	2,733	40.5
Santa Rosa, Calif.	50	83	113	158	37.1	3,362	33.7
Savannah, Ga.	118	142	138	129	–2.6	2,204	62.6
Scottsdale, Ariz.	68	89	130	139	46.8	706	184.4
Seattle, Wash.	531	494	516	21	4.5	6,154	83.9
Shreveport, La.	182	206	199	77	–4.1	2,013	98.6
Simi Valley, Calif.	60	78	100	195	29.3	3,034	33.0
Sioux Falls, S.Dak.	72	81	101	194	24.0	2,236	45.1
South Bend, Ind.	126	110	106	182	–3.8	2,897	36.4
Spokane, Wash.	171	171	177	94	3.4	3,169	55.9
Springfield, Ill.	92	100	105	184	5.2	2,474	42.5
Springfield, Mass.	164	152	157	111	3.1	4,890	32.1
Springfield, Mo.	120	133	140	126	5.5	2,068	68.0
Stamford, Conn.	109	102	108	177	5.5	2,865	37.7
Sterling Heights, Mich.	61	109	118	152	8.1	3,215	36.6
Stockton, Calif.	110	150	211	75	42.3	4,013	52.6
Sunnyvale, Calif.	96	107	117	153	10.0	5,353	21.9
Syracuse, N.Y.	197	170	164	106	–3.7	6,528	25.1
Tacoma, Wash.	154	159	177	95	11.5	3,677	48.1
Tallahassee, Fla.	73	82	125	146	53.0	1,972	63.3
Tampa, Fla.	278	272	280	55	3.1	2,577	108.7
Tempe, Ariz.	64	107	142	122	32.7	3,590	39.5
Thousand Oaks, Calif.	36	77	104	185	35.4	2,104	49.6
Toledo, Ohio	383	355	333	49	–6.1	4,132	80.6
Topeka, Kans.	125	119	120	149	1.0	2,173	55.2
Torrance, Calif.	135	130	133	135	2.5	6,487	20.5
Tucson, Ariz.	263	331	405	33	22.6	2,594	156.3
Tulsa, Okla.	330	361	367	44	1.8	2,001	183.5
Vallejo, Calif.	72	80	109	171	36.0	3,613	30.2
Virginia Beach, Va.	172	262	393	37	49.9	1,583	248.3
Waco, Tex.	95	101	104	187	2.3	1,367	75.8
Warren, Mich.	179	161	145	118	–10.1	4,226	34.3
Washington, D.C.	757	638	607	19	–4.9	9,883	61.4
Waterbury, Conn.	108	103	109	172	5.5	3,815	28.6
Wichita, Kans.	277	280	304	51	8.6	2,640	115.1
Winston-Salem, N.C.	134	132	143	119	8.8	2,018	71.1
Worcester, Mass.	177	162	170	101	4.9	4,520	37.6
Yonkers, N.Y.	204	195	188	84	–3.7	10,403	18.1

Note: Cities over 100,000 population. N.A. = not available. 1. Represents the portion of a consolidated city not within one or more separately incorporated areas. 2. Data represent the census designated place of Honolulu, as delineated by the State of Hawaii. 3. Not incorporated. **Source:** U.S. Bureau of the Census, *Statistical Abstract of the United States 1990* (1990), and release (1991).

RESIDENT POPULATION OF U.S. CITIES BY RACE AND HISPANIC ORIGIN, 1990

City	Total population ('000s)	Percent distribution: Black	His-panic[1]	Asian or Pacific Islander	American Indian
Abilene, Tex.	107	7.0%	15.5%	1.3%	0.4%
Akron, Ohio	223	24.5	0.7	1.2	0.3
Albuquerque, N.Mex.	385	3.0	34.5	1.7	3.0
Alexandria, Va.	111	21.9	9.7	4.2	0.3
Allentown, Pa.	105	5.0	11.7	1.3	0.2
Amarillo, Tex.	158	6.0	14.7	1.9	0.8
Anaheim, Calif.	266	2.5	31.4	9.4	0.5
Anchorage, Alaska	226	6.4	4.1	4.8	6.4
Ann Arbor, Mich.	110	9.0	2.6	7.7	0.4
Arlington, Va.	171	10.5	13.5	6.8	0.3
Arlington, Tex.	262	8.4	8.9	3.9	0.5
Atlanta, Ga.	394	67.1	1.9	0.9	0.1
Aurora, Colo.	222	11.4	6.6	3.8	0.6
Austin, Tex.	466	12.4	23.0	3.0	0.4
Bakersfield, Calif.	175	9.4	20.5	3.6	1.1
Baltimore, Md.	736	59.2	1.0	1.1	0.3
Baton Rouge, La.	220	43.9	1.6	1.7	0.1
Beaumont, Tex.	114	41.3	4.3	1.7	0.2
Birmingham, Ala.	266	63.3	(Z)	0.6	0.1
Boise City, Idaho	126	0.6	2.7	1.6	0.6
Boston, Mass.	574	25.6	10.8	5.3	0.3
Bridgeport, Conn.	142	26.6	26.5	2.3	0.3
Buffalo, N.Y.	328	30.7	4.9	1.0	0.8
Cedar Rapids, Iowa	109	2.9	1.1	1.0	0.2
Charlotte, N.C.	396	31.8	1.4	1.8	0.4
Chattanooga, Tenn.	152	33.7	0.6	1.0	0.2
Chesapeake, Va.	152	27.4	1.3	1.2	0.3
Chicago, Ill.	2,784	39.1	19.6	3.7	0.3
Chula Vista, Calif.	135	4.6	37.3	8.9	0.6
Cincinnati, Ohio	364	37.9	0.7	1.1	0.2
Citrus Heights, Calif.	107	2.3	6.9	3.3	1.1
Cleveland, Ohio	506	46.6	4.6	1.0	0.3
Colorado Springs, Colo.	281	7.0	9.1	2.4	0.8
Columbus, Ga.	179	38.1	3.0	1.4	0.3
Columbus, Ohio	633	22.6	1.1	2.4	0.2
Concord, Calif.	111	2.4	11.5	8.7	0.7
Corpus Christi, Tex.	257	4.8	50.4	0.9	0.4
Dallas, Tex.	1,007	29.5	20.9	2.2	0.5
Dayton, Ohio	182	40.4	0.7	0.6	0.2
Denver, Colo.	468	12.8	23.0	2.4	1.2
Des Moines, Iowa	193	7.1	2.4	2.4	0.4
Detroit, Mich.	1,028	75.7	2.8	0.8	0.4
Durham, N.C.	137	45.7	1.2	2.0	0.2
East Los Angeles, Calif.	126	1.4	94.7	1.3	0.4
Elizabeth, N.J.	110	19.8	39.1	2.7	0.3
El Monte, Calif.	106	1.0	72.5	11.8	0.6
El Paso, Tex.	515	3.4	69.0	1.2	0.4
Erie, Pa.	109	12.0	2.4	0.5	0.2
Escondido, Calif.	109	1.5	23.4	3.7	0.8
Eugene, Oreg.	113	1.3	2.7	3.5	0.9
Evansville, Ind.	126	9.5	0.6	0.6	0.2
Flint, Mich.	141	47.9	2.9	0.5	0.7
Fort Lauderdale, Fla.	149	28.1	7.2	0.9	0.2
Fort Wayne, Ind.	173	16.7	2.7	1.0	0.3
Fort Worth, Tex.	448	22.0	19.5	2.0	0.4
Fremont, Calif.	173	3.8	13.3	19.4	0.7
Fresno, Calif.	354	8.3	29.9	12.5	1.1
Fullerton, Calif.	114	2.2	21.3	12.2	0.5
Garden Grove, Calif.	143	1.5	23.5	20.5	0.6
Garland, Tex.	181	8.9	11.6	4.5	0.5
Gary, Ind.	117	80.6%	5.7%	0.2%	0.2%
Glendale, Ariz.	148	3.0	15.5	2.1	0.9
Glendale, Calif.	180	1.3	21.0	14.1	0.3
Grand Rapids, Mich.	189	18.5	5.0	1.1	0.8
Greensboro, N.C.	184	33.9	1.0	1.4	0.5
Hampton, Va.	134	38.9	2.0	1.7	0.3
Hartford, Conn.	140	38.9	31.6	1.4	0.3
Hayward, Calif.	111	9.8	23.9	15.5	1.0
Hialeah, Fla.	188	1.9	87.6	0.5	0.1
Hollywood, Fla.	122	8.5	11.9	1.3	0.2
Honolulu, Hawaii	365	1.3	4.6	70.5	0.3
Houston, Tex.	1,631	28.1	27.6	4.1	0.3
Huntington Beach, Calif.	182	0.9	11.2	8.3	0.6
Huntsville, Ala.	160	24.4	1.2	2.1	0.5
Independence, Mo.	112	1.4	2.0	1.0	0.6
Indianapolis, Ind.	731	22.6	1.1	0.9	0.2
Inglewood, Calif.	110	51.9	38.5	2.5	0.4
Irvine, Calif.	110	1.8	6.3	18.1	0.2
Irving, Tex.	155	7.5	16.3	4.6	0.6
Jackson, Miss.	197	55.7	0.4	0.5	0.1
Jacksonville, Fla.	635	25.2	2.6	1.9	0.3
Jersey City, N.J.	229	29.7	24.2	11.4	0.3
Kansas City, Kans.	150	29.3	7.1	1.2	0.7
Kansas City, Mo.	435	29.6	3.9	1.2	0.5
Knoxville, Tenn.	165	15.8	0.7	1.0	0.2
Lakewood, Colo.	126	1.0	9.1	1.9	0.7
Lansing, Mich.	127	18.6	7.9	1.8	1.0
Laredo, Tex.	123	0.1	93.9	0.4	0.2
Las Vegas, Nev.	258	11.4	12.5	3.6	0.9
Lexington-Fayette, Ky.	225	13.4	1.1	1.6	0.2
Lincoln, Nebr.	192	2.4	2.0	1.7	0.6
Little Rock, Ark.	176	34.0	0.8	0.9	0.3
Long Beach, Calif.	429	13.7	23.6	13.6	0.6
Los Angeles, Calif.	3,485	14.0	39.9	9.8	0.5
Louisville, Ky.	269	29.7	0.7	0.7	0.2
Lubbock, Tex.	186	8.6	22.5	1.4	0.3
Macon, Ga.	107	52.2	0.6	0.4	0.1
Madison, Wis.	191	4.2	2.0	3.9	0.4
Memphis, Tenn.	610	54.8	0.7	0.8	0.2
Mesa, Ariz.	288	1.9	10.9	1.5	1.0
Metairie, La.	149	4.9	6.2	1.8	0.2
Miami, Fla.	359	27.4	62.5	0.6	0.2
Milwaukee, Wis.	628	30.5	6.3	1.9	0.9
Minneapolis, Minn.	368	13.0	2.1	4.3	3.3
Mobile, Ala.	196	38.9	1.0	1.0	0.2
Modesto, Calif.	165	2.7	16.3	7.9	1.0
Montgomery, Ala.	187	42.3	0.8	0.7	0.2
Moreno Valley, Calif.	119	13.8	22.9	6.6	0.7
Nashville-Davidson, Tenn.	488	24.3	0.9	1.4	0.2
Newark, N.J.	275	58.5	26.1	1.2	0.2
New Haven, Conn.	130	36.1	13.2	2.4	0.3
New Orleans, La.	497	61.9	3.5	1.9	0.2
Newport News, Va.	170	33.6	2.8	2.3	0.3
New York, N.Y.	7,323	28.7	24.4	7.0	0.4
Bronx Borough	1,204	37.3	43.5	3.0	0.5
Brooklyn Borough	2,301	37.9	20.1	4.8	0.3
Manhattan Borough	1,488	22.0	26.0	7.4	0.4
Queens Borough	1,952	21.7	19.5	12.2	0.4
Staten Island Borough	379	8.1	8.0	4.5	0.2
Norfolk, Va.	261	39.1	2.9	2.6	0.4

City	Total population ('000s)	Black	Hispanic[1]	Asian or Pacific Islander	American Indian
		Percent distribution			
Oakland, Calif.	372	43.9%	13.9%	14.8%	0.6%
Oceanside, Calif.	128	7.9	22.6	6.1	0.7
Oklahoma City, Okla.	445	16.0	5.0	2.4	4.2
Omaha, Nebr.	336	13.1	3.1	1.0	0.7
Ontario, Calif.	133	7.3	41.7	3.9	0.7
Orange, Calif.	111	1.4	22.8	7.9	0.5
Orlando, Fla.	165	26.9	8.7	1.6	0.3
Overland Park, Kans.	112	1.8	2.0	1.9	0.3
Oxnard, Calif.	142	5.2	54.4	8.6	0.8
Paradise, Nev.	125	4.9	10.5	4.0	0.6
Pasadena, Calif.	132	19.0	27.3	8.1	0.4
Pasadena, Tex.	119	1.0	28.8	1.6	0.5
Paterson, N.J.	141	36.0	41.0	1.4	0.3
Peoria, Ill.	114	20.9	1.6	1.7	0.2
Philadelphia, Pa.	1,586	39.9	5.6	2.7	0.2
Phoenix, Ariz.	983	5.2	20.0	1.7	1.9
Pittsburgh, Pa.	370	25.8	0.9	1.6	0.2
Plano, Tex.	129	4.1	6.2	4.0	0.3
Pomona, Calif.	132	14.4	51.3	6.7	0.6
Portland, Oreg.	437	7.7	3.2	5.3	1.2
Providence, R.I.	161	14.8	15.5	5.9	0.9
Raleigh, N.C.	208	27.6	1.4	2.5	0.3
Reno, Nev.	134	2.9	11.1	4.9	1.4
Richmond, Va.	203	55.2	0.9	0.9	0.2
Riverside, Calif.	227	7.4	26.0	5.2	0.8
Rochester, N.Y.	232	31.5	8.7	1.8	0.5
Rockford, Ill.	139	15.0	4.2	1.5	0.3
Sacramento, Calif.	369	15.3	16.2	15.0	1.2
St. Louis, Mo.	397	47.5	1.3	0.9	0.2
St. Paul, Minn.	272	7.4	4.2	7.1	1.4
St. Petersburg, Fla.	239	19.6	2.6	1.7	0.2
Salem, Oreg.	108	1.5	6.1	2.4	1.6
Salinas, Calif.	109	3.0	50.6	8.1	0.9
Salt Lake City, Utah	160	1.7	9.7	4.7	1.6
San Antonio, Tex.	936	7.0	55.6	1.1	0.4
San Bernardino, Calif.	164	16.0	34.6	4.0	1.0
San Diego, Calif.	1,111	9.4	20.7	11.8	0.6
San Francisco, Calif.	724	10.9%	13.9%	29.1%	0.5%
San Jose, Calif.	782	4.7	26.6	19.5	0.7
Santa Ana, Calif.	294	2.6	65.2	9.7	0.5
Santa Clarita, Calif.	111	1.5	13.4	4.2	0.6
Santa Rosa, Calif.	113	1.8	9.5	3.4	1.2
Savannah, Ga.	138	51.3	1.4	1.1	0.2
Scottsdale, Ariz.	130	0.8	4.8	1.2	0.6
Seattle, Wash.	516	10.1	3.6	11.8	1.4
Shreveport, La.	199	44.8	1.1	0.5	0.2
South Bend, Ind.	106	20.9	3.4	0.9	0.4
Spokane, Wash.	177	1.9	2.1	2.1	2.0
Springfield, Ill.	105	13.0	0.8	1.0	0.2
Springfield, Mass.	157	19.2	16.9	1.0	0.2
Springfield, Mo.	140	2.5	1.0	0.9	0.7
Stamford, Conn.	108	17.8	9.8	2.6	0.1
Sterling Heights, Mich.	118	0.4	1.1	2.9	0.2
Stockton, Calif.	211	9.6	25.0	22.8	1.0
Sunnyvale, Calif.	117	3.4	13.2	19.3	0.5
Syracuse, N.Y.	164	20.3	2.9	2.2	1.3
Tacoma, Wash.	177	11.4	3.8	6.9	2.0
Tallahassee, Fla.	125	29.1	3.0	1.8	0.2
Tampa, Fla.	280	25.0	15.0	1.4	0.3
Tempe, Ariz.	142	3.2	10.9	4.1	1.3
Toledo, Ohio	333	19.7	4.0	1.0	0.3
Topeka, Kans.	120	10.6	5.8	0.8	1.3
Torrance, Calif.	133	1.5	10.1	21.9	0.4
Tucson, Ariz.	405	4.3	29.3	2.2	1.6
Tulsa, Okla.	367	13.6	2.6	1.4	4.7
Vallejo, Calif.	109	21.2	10.8	23.0	0.7
Virginia Beach, Va.	393	13.9	3.1	4.3	0.4
Warren, Mich.	145	0.7	1.1	1.3	0.5
Washington, D.C.	607	65.8	5.4	1.8	0.2
Waterbury, Conn.	109	13.0	13.4	0.7	0.3
Wichita, Kans.	304	11.3	5.0	2.6	1.2
Winston-Salem, N.C.	143	39.3	0.9	0.8	0.2
Worcester, Mass.	170	4.5	9.6	2.8	0.3
Yonkers, N.Y.	188	14.1	16.7	3.0	0.2

Note: Cities with populations over 105,000 as of April 1, 1990. Z = Less than .05 percent. 1. Hispanic persons may be of any race. **Source:** U.S. Bureau of the Census, Press Release, 1992.

CITIES, BY POPULATION SIZE, 1960–90

Population size	Number of cities				Population (millions)				Percent of total			
	1960	1970	1980	1990	1960	1970	1980	1990	1960	1970	1980	1990
Total	18,088	18,666	19,097	19,290	115.9	131.9	140.3	152.9	100.0%	100.0%	100.0%	100.0%
1 million or more	5	6	6	8	17.5	18.8	17.5	20.0	15.1	14.2	12.5	13.0
500,000–1 million	16	20	16	15	11.1	13.0	10.9	10.1	9.6	9.8	7.8	6.6
250,000–500,000	30	30	33	41	10.8	10.5	11.8	14.2	9.3	7.9	8.4	9.3
100,000–250,000	79	97	114	131	11.4	13.9	16.6	19.1	9.8	10.5	11.8	12.5
50,000–100,000	180	232	250	309	12.5	16.2	17.6	21.2	10.8	12.2	12.3	13.9
25,000–50,000	366	455	526	567	12.7	15.7	18.4	20.0	11.0	11.9	13.1	13.0
10,000–25,000	978	1,127	1,260	1,290	15.1	17.6	19.8	20.3	13.1	13.3	14.1	13.3
Under 10,000	16,434	16,699	16,892	16,929	24.9	26.4	28.0	28.2	21.5	20.0	20.0	18.4

Note: Population totals may not add due to independent rounding. **Source**: U.S. Bureau of the Census, *Statistical Abstract of the United States 1994* (1994).

POPULATION OF THE 50 LARGEST CITIES, 1950–90

City	1950	1960	1970[1]	1980[1]	1990
New York, N.Y.	7,891,957	7,781,984	7,896,000	7,072,000	7,322,564
Los Angeles, Calif.	1,970,358	2,479,015	2,812,000	2,969,000	3,485,398
Chicago, Ill.	3,620,962	3,550,404	3,369,000	3,005,000	2,783,726
Houston, Tex.	596,163	938,219	1,234,000	1,595,000	1,630,672
Philadelphia, Pa.	2,071,605	2,002,512	1,949,000	1,688,000	1,585,577
San Diego, Calif.	334,387	573,224	697,000	876,000	1,110,549
Detroit, Mich.	1,849,568	1,670,144	1,514,000	1,203,000	1,027,974
Dallas, Tex.	434,462	679,684	844,000	905,000	1,006,831
Phoenix, Ariz.	([2])	439,170	584,000	790,000	983,403
San Antonio, Tex.	408,442	587,718	654,000	786,000	935,927
San Jose, Calif.	([2])	([2])	460,000	629,000	782,225
Indianapolis, Ind.	427,173	476,258	737,000	701,000	741,952
Baltimore, Md.	949,708	939,024	905,000	787,000	736,014
San Francisco, Calif.	775,357	742,855	716,000	679,000	723,959
Jacksonville, Fla.	204,517	([2])	504,000	541,000	635,230
Columbus, Ohio	375,901	471,316	540,000	565,000	632,958
Milwaukee, Wis.	637,392	741,324	717,000	636,000	628,088
Memphis, Tenn.	396,000	497,524	624,000	646,000	610,337
Washington, D.C.	802,178	763,956	757,000	638,000	606,900
Boston, Mass.	801,444	697,197	641,000	563,000	574,283
Seattle, Wash.	467,591	557,087	531,000	494,000	516,259
El Paso, Tex.	([2])	276,687	322,000	425,000	515,342
Nashville, Tenn.	([2])	([2])	426,000	456,000	510,784
Cleveland, Ohio	914,808	876,050	751,000	574,000	505,616
New Orleans, La.	570,445	627,525	593,000	558,000	496,938
Denver, Colo.	415,786	493,887	515,000	493,000	467,610
Austin, Tex.	([2])	([2])	254,000	346,000	465,577
Fort Worth, Tex.	278,778	356,268	393,000	385,000	447,619
Oklahoma City, Okla.	243,504	324,253	368,000	404,000	444,730
Portland, Oreg.	373,628	372,676	380,000	368,000	437,398
Kansas City, Mo.	456,622	475,539	507,000	448,000	435,141
Long Beach, Calif.	250,767	344,168	359,000	361,000	429,433
Tucson, Ariz.	([2])	([2])	263,000	331,000	405,390
St. Louis, Mo.	856,796	750,026	622,000	453,000	396,685
Charlotte, N.C.	([2])	([2])	241,000	315,000	396,003
Atlanta, Ga.	332,314	487,455	495,000	425,000	394,017
Virginia Beach, Va.	([2])	([2])	172,000	262,000	393,069
Albuquerque, N.Mex.	([2])	([2])	245,000	332,000	384,736
Oakland, Calif.	384,575	367,548	362,000	339,000	372,242
Pittsburgh, Pa.	676,806	604,332	520,000	424,000	369,879
Sacramento, Calif.	([2])	([2])	257,000	276,000	369,365
Minneapolis, Minn.	521,718	482,872	434,000	371,000	368,383
Tulsa, Okla.	([2])	261,685	330,000	361,000	367,193
Honolulu, Hawaii	248,034	294,194	325,000	365,000	365,272
Cincinnati, Ohio	503,998	502,550	454,000	385,000	364,040
Miami, Fla.	249,276	291,688	335,000	347,000	358,548
Fresno, Calif.	([2])	([2])	166,000	217,000	354,202
Omaha, Neb.	251,117	301,598	347,000	314,000	335,795
Toledo, Ohio	303,616	318,003	383,000	355,000	332,943
Buffalo, N.Y.	580,132	532,759	463,000	358,000	328,123

Note: Cities ranked by 1990 population. 1. Figure rounded at source. 2. City was not one of 50 largest for year. **Source**: U.S. Bureau of the Census, *Current Population Reports.*

POPULATION CHANGE IN THE 50 LARGEST U.S. CITIES, RANKED BY PERCENTAGE CHANGE, 1980–90

Rank/City	Population		Change 1980–90		Rank
	1980	1990	Number	Percent	1990
1. Fresno, Calif.	217,491	354,202	136,711	62.9%	47
2. Virginia Beach, Va.	262,199	393,069	130,870	49.9	37
3. Austin, Tex.	345,890	465,622	119,732	34.6	27
4. Sacramento, Calif.	275,741	369,365	93,624	34.0	41
5. San Diego, Calif.	875,538	1,110,549	235,011	26.8	6
6. Charlotte, N.C.	315,474	395,934	80,460	25.5	35
7. Phoenix, Ariz.	789,704	983,403	193,699	24.5	9
8. San Jose, Calif.	629,400	782,248	152,848	24.3	11
9. Tucson, Ariz.	330,537	405,390	74,853	22.6	33
10. El Paso, Tex.	425,259	515,342	90,083	21.2	22
11. San Antonio, Tex.	785,940	935,933	149,993	19.1	10
12. Portland, Oreg.	368,148	437,319	69,171	18.8	30
13. Long Beach, Calif.	361,498	429,433	67,935	18.8	32
14. Jacksonville, Fla.	571,003	672,971	101,968	17.9	15
15. Los Angeles, Calif.	2,968,528	3,485,398	516,870	17.4	2
16. Fort Worth, Tex.	385,164	447,619	62,455	16.2	28
17. Albuquerque, N.Mex.	332,920	384,736	51,816	15.6	38
18. Columbus, Ohio	565,021	632,910	67,889	12.0	16
19. Dallas, Tex.	904,599	1,006,877	102,278	11.3	8
20. Oklahoma City, Okla.	404,014	444,719	40,705	10.1	29
21. Oakland, Calif.	339,337	372,242	32,905	9.7	39
22. Omaha, Nebr.	313,939	335,795	21,856	7.0	48
23. Nashville-Davidson, Tenn.	477,811	510,784	32,973	6.9	23
24. San Francisco, Calif.	678,974	723,959	44,985	6.6	14
25. Seattle, Wash.	493,846	516,259	22,413	4.5	21
26. Indianapolis, Ind.	711,539	741,952	30,413	4.3%	12
27. New York, N.Y.	7,071,639	7,322,564	250,925	3.5	1
28. Miami, Fla.	346,681	358,548	11,867	3.4	46
29. Houston, Tex.	1,595,138	1,630,553	35,415	2.2	4
30. Boston, Mass.	562,994	574,283	11,289	2.0	20
31. Tulsa, Okla.	360,919	367,302	6,383	1.8	43
32. Honolulu, Hawaii	365,048	365,272	224	0.1	44
33. Minneapolis, Minn.	370,951	368,383	–2,568	–0.7	42
34. Milwaukee, Wis.	636,297	628,088	–8,209	–1.3	17
35. Kansas City, Mo.	448,028	435,146	–12,882	–2.9	31
36. Washington, D.C.	638,432	606,900	–31,532	–4.9	19
37. Denver, Colo.	492,686	467,610	–25,076	–5.1	26
38. Memphis, Tenn.	646,174	610,337	–35,837	–5.5	18
39. Cincinnati, Ohio	385,409	364,040	–21,369	–5.5	45
40. Philadelphia, Pa.	1,688,210	1,585,577	–102,633	–6.1	5
41. Toledo, Ohio	354,635	332,943	–21,692	–6.1	49
42. Baltimore, Md.	786,741	736,014	–50,727	–6.4	13
43. Atlanta, Ga.	425,022	394,017	–31,005	–7.3	36
44. Chicago, Ill.	3,005,072	2,783,726	–221,346	–7.4	3
45. Buffalo, N.Y.	357,870	328,123	–29,747	–8.3	50
46. New Orleans, La.	557,927	496,938	–60,989	–10.9	25
47. Cleveland, Ohio	573,822	505,616	–68,206	–11.9	24
48. St. Louis, Mo.	452,801	396,685	–56,116	–12.4	34
49. Pittsburgh, Pa.	423,959	369,879	–54,080	–12.8	40
50. Detroit, Mich.	1,203,368	1,027,974	–175,394	–14.6	7

Source: U.S. Bureau of the Census release, 1991.

25 FASTEST-GROWING MAJOR CITIES IN THE U.S., 1980–90

Rank/City	Population 1980	Population 1990	Percent change	Rank 1980	Rank 1990
1. Mesa, Ariz.	152,404	288,091	89.0%	102	53
2. Rancho Cucamonga, Calif.	55,250	101,409	83.5	N.A.	191
3. Plano, Tex.	72,331	128,713	77.9	N.A.	140
4. Irvine, Calif.	62,134	110,330	77.6	N.A.	167
5. Escondido, Calif.	64,355	108,635	68.8	N.A.	176
6. Oceanside, Calif.	76,698	128,398	67.4	N.A.	141
7. Bakersfield, Calif.	105,611	174,820	65.5	152	97
8. Arlington, Tex.	160,113	261,721	63.5	94	61
9. Fresno, Calif.	217,491	354,202	62.9	65	47
10. Chula Vista, Calif.	83,927	135,163	61.0	N.A.	131
11. Las Vegas, Nev.	164,674	258,295	56.9	89	63
12. Modesto, Calif.	106,963	164,730	54.0	147	103
13. Tallahassee, Fla.	81,548	124,773	53.0	N.A.	146
14. Glendale, Ariz.	97,172	148,134	52.4%	N.A.	117
15. Mesquite, Tex.	67,053	101,484	51.3	N.A.	190
16. Ontario, Calif.	88,820	133,179	49.9	N.A.	134
17. Virginia Beach, Va.	262,199	393,069	49.9	56	37
18. Scottsdale, Ariz.	88,622	130,069	46.8	N.A.	139
19. Santa Ana, Calif.	204,023	293,742	44.0	69	52
20. Stockton, Calif.	148,283	210,943	42.3	107	74
21. Pomona, Calif.	92,742	131,723	42.0	N.A.	136
22. Irving, Tex.	109,943	155,037	41.0	142	112
23. Aurora, Colo.	158,588	222,103	40.1	97	72
24. Raleigh, N.C.	150,255	207,951	38.4	105	75
25. San Bernardino, Calif.	118,794	164,164	38.2	131	105

Note: Cities over 100,000 population. N.A. = not available. **Source:** U.S. Bureau of the Census release (1991).

25 MAJOR U.S. CITIES WITH LARGEST DECLINES IN POPULATION, 1980–90

Rank/City	Population 1980	Population 1990	Percent change	Rank 1980	Rank 1990
1. Gary, Ind.	151,968	116,646	–23.2%	104	154
2. Newark, N.J.	329,248	275,221	–16.4	46	56
3. Detroit, Mich.	1,203,368	1,027,974	–14.6	6	7
4. Pittsburgh, Pa.	423,959	369,879	–12.8	30	40
5. St. Louis, Mo.	452,801	396,685	–12.4	26	34
6. Cleveland, Ohio	573,822	505,616	–11.9	18	24
7. Flint, Mich.	159,611	140,761	–11.8	95	125
8. New Orleans, La.	557,927	496,938	–10.9	22	25
9. Warren, Mich.	161,134	144,864	–10.1	93	118
10. Chattanooga, Tenn.	169,514	152,466	–10.1	88	113
11. Louisville, Ky.	298,694	269,063	–9.9	49	58
12. Macon, Ga.	116,896	106,612	–8.8	135	180
13. Erie, Pa.	119,123	108,718	–8.7	130	175
14. Peoria, Ill.	124,160	113,504	–8.6%	126	157
15. Buffalo, N.Y.	357,870	328,123	–8.3	39	50
16. Richmond, Va.	219,214	203,056	–7.4	64	76
17. Chicago, Ill.	3,005,072	2,783,726	–7.4	2	3
18. Atlanta, Ga.	425,022	394,017	–7.3	29	36
19. Kansas City, Kans.	161,148	149,767	–7.1	92	115
20. Birmingham, Ala.	284,413	265,968	–6.5	50	60
21. Baltimore, Md.	786,741	736,014	–6.4	10	13
22. Toledo, Ohio	354,635	332,943	–6.1	40	49
23. Philadelphia, Pa.	1,688,210	1,585,577	–6.1	4	5
24. Akron, Ohio	237,177	223,019	–6.0	59	71
25. Dayton, Ohio	193,536	182,044	–5.9	73	89

Note: Cities over 100,000 population. **Source**: U.S. Bureau of the Census release (1991).

City Finances

REVENUES AND EXPENDITURES

General revenues Municipalities in the U.S. received nearly $210.5 billion in revenues in 1990–91. More than one-fifth of this revenue came from other governments. State governments contributed $34.9 billion, the federal government $7.6 billion, and local governments $3.7 billion. The single largest source of income was from property taxes, which contributed $37.7 billion to city coffers, representing 17.9% of all city revenues. Sales and income taxes were responsible for another $29.2 billion, or 13.9%, while utilities (gas, transit, water, and electric) contributed $34.2 billion, or 16.2%.

General expenditures Cities in 1990–91 spent nearly $211.5 billion, up 6.4% from the previous fiscal year. More than $147.6 billion of this total went toward current operation. Education services accounted for $22.4 billion, or 13.6%, of all general expenditures, while $33.2 billion (20.2%) went toward public safety. Transportation accounted for $22.9 billion (14.0%), with highways responsible for most of the expenditures.

20 BEST-PAID U.S. MAYORS, 1995

Rank/Mayor	City	Salary
1. Richard M. Daley	Chicago	$175,000
2. Robert Lanier	Houston	133,552
3. Rudolph Giuliani	New York	130,000
4. Frank Jordan	San Francisco	129,356
5. Richard Riordan	Los Angeles	117,876[1]
6. Dennis Archer	Detroit	117,000
7. Sharpe James	Newark, N.J.	110,455
8. Thomas Menino	Boston	110,000
9. Dick A. Greco	Tampa, Fla.	110,000
10. Edward Rendell	Philadelphia	110,000
11. Willie W. Herenton	Memphis	$108,000
12. S.J. Schulman	White Plains, N.Y.	107,500
13. Norman Rice	Seattle	105,850
14. John O. Norquist	Milwaukee	102,543
15. Terence Zaleski	Yonkers, N.Y.	102,000
16. Edward Austin	Jacksonville, Fla.	100,613
17. Bill Campbell	Atlanta	100,000
18. Jeremy Harris	Honolulu	100,000
19. David J. Fischer	St. Petersburg, Fla.	100,000
20. Joseph P. Riley, Jr.	Charleston, S.C.	98,699

1. Official salary. Riordan accepts only $1 of the mayoral salary. **Source:** U.S. Conference of Mayors.

SUMMARY OF CITY GOVERNMENT FINANCES, 1990–91

Item	Amount 1990–91 (millions)	Percent distribution 1990–91	Percent change over 1989–90
REVENUES			
Revenue, total	**$210,498**	**—**	**4.0%**
General revenue	164,319	100.0%	3.8
Intergovernmental revenue	46,260	28.2	2.1
From state governments	34,901	21.2	1.9
General local government support	9,236	5.6	5.5
From federal government	7,615	4.6	0.9
From local governments	3,744	2.3	6.4
General revenue from own sources	118,059	71.8	4.5
Taxes	72,213	43.9	5.0
Property	37,654	22.9	7.5
General sales	11,738	7.1	0.8
Selective sales	7,866	4.8	4.3
Income	9,595	5.8	5.1
Other	5,359	3.3	–1.6
Charges and miscellaneous	45,846	27.9	3.7
Current charges	27,221	16.6	7.7
Sewerage	9,308	5.7	9.8
Hospitals	4,035	2.5	2.7
Interest earnings	11,355	6.9	–3.3
Special assessments	904	0.6	–12.5
Sale of property	528	0.3	–31.3
Other and unallocable	5,838	3.6	8.2
Utility revenue	34,216	100.0	3.7
Electric power	17,926	52.4	3.5
Water supply	12,067	35.3	4.2
Transit system	1,924	5.6	8.9
Gas supply	2,299	6.7	–1.5
Liquor store revenue	270	—	–1.8
Insurance trust revenue	11,693	100.0	8.0
Employee retirement	11,620	99.4	8.0
Unemployment compensation[1]	74	0.6	4.2
EXPENDITURES			
Expenditure, total	**$211,506**	**100.0%**	**6.4%**
Expenditure by function:			
General expenditure	164,226	100.0	6.8
Intergovernmental expenditure	4,869	3.0	–0.4
Direct general expenditure	159,357	97.0	7.1
Capital outlay	26,842	16.3	9.7
Other	132,515	80.7	6.6
Education services:			
Education	18,793	11.4	8.2
Libraries	2,119	1.3	9.3
Social services and income maintenance:			
Public welfare	8,941	5.4	13.3
Cash assistance payments	2,549	1.6	15.2
Medical vendor payments	386	0.2	0.5
Other	6,006	3.7	13.4
Hospitals	7,049	4.3	7.1
Own	$ 6,441	3.9%	6.9%
Other	608	0.4	9.2
Health	2,769	1.7	8.2
Transportation:			
Highways	12,627	7.7	4.3
Air transportation	2,970	1.8	3.2
Parking facilities	622	0.4	6.9
Water transport	485	0.3	–10.4
Transit subsidies	973	0.6	–10.7
Public safety:			
Police protection	19,388	11.8	6.6
Fire protection	10,045	6.1	5.9
Correction	2,252	1.4	–1.3
Protective inspection and regulation	1,569	1.0	5.4
Environment and housing:			
Sewerage	11,316	6.9	6.3
Solid waste management	6,287	3.8	7.9
Parks and recreation	8,450	5.1	11.4
Housing and community development	8,286	5.0	8.2
Natural resources	227	0.1	24.7
Government administration:			
Financial administration	3,907	2.4	0.3
Judicial and legal	2,291	1.4	7.0
General public buildings	1,947	1.2	10.2
Other	3,904	2.4	24.6
Interest on general debt	11,370	6.9	0.5
General expenditure not elsewhere classified	15,639	9.5	7.2
Utility expenditure	39,478	100.0	3.4
Electric power	17,656	44.7	0.9
Water supply	14,229	36.0	4.8
Transit system	5,375	13.6	10.7
Gas supply	2,218	5.6	–2.0
Liquor store expenditure	250	—	—
Insurance trust expenditure	7,552	100.0	13.2
Employee retirement	7,433	98.4	12.8
Unemployment compensation[1]	119	1.6	54.5
Exhibit: Salaries and wages	72,108	34.1	7.7
INDEBTEDNESS AND DEBT TRANSACTIONS			
Debt outstanding at end of fiscal year	**$226,554**	**100.0%**	**6.4%**
Long-term debt outstanding	220,591	97.4	6.3
Short-term debt outstanding	5,963	2.6	9.8
Long-term debt issued	30,166	100.0	7.8
Long-term debt retired	16,245	100.0	–9.6
CASH AND SECURITY HOLDINGS			
Total, end of fiscal year	**$259,725**	**100.0%**	**4.7%**
Employment retirement	104,395	40.2	5.6
Unemployment compensation[1]	43	—	–46.2
Other	155,287	59.8	4.1

1. Washington, D.C., only. **Source:** U.S. Bureau of the Census, *City Government Finances in 1990–91*, (1993).

TAX BURDENS IN MAJOR U.S. CITIES

Tax rates differ widely not only from state to state and city to city, but also from one income level to another. Any tax system in which the percentage of taxes paid rises with the income level is said to be *progressive*. A system where the percentage tax burden is the same at all income levels is said to be *proportional*. And a system in which the percentage of taxes paid decreases as income rises is said to be *regressive*. Because progressivity is measured as the ratio of one tax rate to another, progressivity does not necessarily reflect the actual tax burden.

TAX BURDEN BY INCOME LEVEL IN SELECTED CITIES, 1993

City	$25,000		$50,000		$75,000		$100,000		Progres-sivity index
	Percent[1]	Amount	Percent[1]	Amount	Percent[1]	Amount	Percent[1]	Amount	
Albuquerque, N.Mex.	6.7%	$1,681	7.5%	$3,758	8.5%	$ 6.365	9.0%	$ 9,002	0.747
Anchorage, Alaska	3.3	819	3.0	1,514	3.1	2,293	2.9	2,858	1.146
Atlanta, Ga.	10.3	2,565	10.1	5,046	11.6	8,675	10.9	10,933	0.939
Baltimore, Md.	11.0	2,478	11.0	5,522	11.5	8,606	11.3	11,307	0.972
Billings, Mont.	6.4	1,606	8.0	4,024	8.9	6,665	9.3	9,314	0.690
Birmingham, Ala.	6.4	1,591	8.8	4,396	9.2	6,895	8.9	8,934	0.712
Boise City, Idaho	6.8	1,693	8.1	4,042	9.5	7,162	10.2	10,169	0.666
Boston, Mass.	11.7	2,931	11.3	5,638	12.2	9,168	12.1	12,115	0.968
Bridgeport, Conn.	14.4	3,602	15.3	7,657	18.2	13,635	17.8	17,831	0.808
Burlington, Vt.	7.3	1,813	7.9	3,937	9.1	6,812	9.6	9,634	0.753
Charleston, W.Va.	7.9	1,968	8.0	4,001	9.5	7,090	9.8	9,814	0.802
Charlotte, N.C.	8.7	2,168	9.2	4,601	10.1	7,602	10.1	10,091	0.859
Cheyenne, Wyo.	4.5	1,122	3.7	1,867	4.4	3,286	4.2	4,171	1.076
Chicago, Ill.	10.9	2,717	11.0	5,521	11.2	8,391	10.9	10,919	0.995
Columbia, S.C.	8.0	2,011	9.6	4,787	11.0	8,218	10.8	10,824	0.743
Columbus, Ohio	10.9	2,729	9.2	4,622	12.3	9,222	12.4	12,364	0.883
Denver, Colo.	8.1	2,021	8.6	4,301	9.1	6,789	9.0	8,992	0.899
Des Moines, Iowa	8.7	2,164	9.3	4,673	10.3	7,731	10.3	10,341	0.837
Detroit, Mich.	12.0	2,988	12.3	6,133	12.7	9,556	12.5	12,537	0.953
Fargo, N.Dak.	7.0	1,759	6.8	3,411	7.4	5,558	7.5	7,518	0.936
Honolulu, Hawaii	7.8	1,943	8.9	4,453	10.0	7,513	10.2	10,181	0.763
Houston, Tex.	6.4	1,610	5.8	2,916	6.1	4,547	5.8	5,759	1.119
Indianapolis, Ind.	8.6	2,161	7.9	3,965	8.9	6,650	8.5	8,548	1.011
Jackson, Miss.	7.5	1,881	7.7	3,853	9.6	7,163	10.5	10,469	0.719
Jacksonville, Fla.	4.5	1,136	4.9	2,438	5.4	4,049	5.3	5,298	0.858
Kansas City, Mo.	9.1	2,277	8.9	4,462	9.6	7,201	9.4	9,446	0.964
Las Vegas, Nev.	5.6	1,393	4.9	2,436	5.2	3,891	4.9	4,873	1.143
Little Rock, Ark.	8.0	1,995	8.9	4,428	9.7	7,304	9.8	9,756	0.818
Los Angeles, Calif.	6.6	1,640	7.6	3,780	9.7	7,304	10.7	10,717	0.612
Louisville, Ky.	10.7	2,671	10.8	5,417	11.5	8,612	11.4	11,413	0.936
Manchester, N.H.	9.9	2,478	9.3	4,645	9.6	7,168	9.0	9,010	1.100
Memphis, Tenn.	6.3	1,581	5.2	2,619	5.5	4,097	5.2	5,192	1.218
Milwaukee, Wis.	12.5	3,115	13.3	6,659	13.6	10,173	13.3	13,267	0.939
Minneapolis, Minn.	7.3	1,833	8.9	4,465	10.3	7,722	10.4	10,415	0.704
New Orleans, La.	4.2	1,061	6.2	3,086	7.5	5,652	8.0	7,966	0.533
New York, N.Y.	10.9	2,721	13.5	6,731	15.0	11,226	15.4	15,446	0.705
Newark, N.J.	13.6	3,395	13.4	6,694	14.2	10,639	14.4	14,424	0.942
Oklahoma City, Okla.	7.3	1,836	7.4	3,700	8.5	6,353	8.8	8,838	0.831
Omaha, Nebr.	10.2	2,546	9.9	4,946	10.9	8,169	11.2	11,158	0.912
Philadelphia, Pa.	12.8	3,201	12.4	6,181	12.7	9,390	12.3	12,283	1.042
Phoenix, Ariz.	9.4	2,343	8.0	4,021	9.1	6,833	9.5	9,460	0.991
Portland, Me.	12.3	3,085	12.3	6,158	14.4	10,793	14.5	14,471	0.853
Portland, Oreg.	8.1	2,013	7.0	3,491	10.6	7,971	10.4	10,379	0.776
Providence, R.I.	11.2	2,800	10.8	5,417	12.3	9,245	12.5	12,472	0.898
Salt Lake City, Utah	7.8	1,950	9.0	4,491	9.8	7,337	9.7	9,673	0.807
Seattle, Wash.	7.4	1,853	6.5	3,227	6.9	5,165	6.5	6,520	1.137
Sioux Falls, S.Dak.	9.2	2,291	7.9	3,934	8.4	6,328	8.0	8,004	1.145
Virginia Beach, Va.	9.1	2,270	9.1	4,530	10.2	7,657	10.0	10,034	0.905
Washington, D.C.	8.4	2,099	9.5	4,737	10.6	7,939	10.9	10,913	0.770
Wichita, Kans.	7.8	1,941	7.6	3,804	9.3	6,977	9.5	9,459	0.821
Wilmington, Del.	8.0	1,997	9.3	4,664	10.1	7,582	10.2	10,200	0.783
Fifty-one-city average[2]	**8.6%**	**$2,153**	**8.9%**	**$4,427**	**9.9%**	**$7,419**	**9.9%**	**$9,916**	**0.869**

Note: Tax burdens computed for a family of four. The four major taxes compared are the individual income tax, real property taxes on residential property, general sales and use taxes, and various automobile taxes, including the gasoline tax, registration fees, excise taxes, and personal property taxes. 1. Percentage of income. 2. Average of the largest city in each state plus the District of Columbia. **Source:** Government of the District of Columbia, Dept. of Finance and Revenues, *Tax Rates and Tax Burdens in the District of Columbia: A Nationwide Comparison* (1994).

Tax Progressivity

Several factors contribute to the progressivity of a tax system. A graduated individual income tax rate combined with exemptions and credits to lessen the regressiveness of the property tax will increase the progressivity of a tax system. Progressivity can be lessened by lack of an individual income tax as well as by reliance on regressive taxes such as the sales tax and certain automobile taxes. The upper and lower income levels chosen for comparison also affect progressiveness.

The accompanying table shows the percentage tax burden at various income levels in the five most and least progressive cities in the table "Tax Burdens by Income Level." (The 51-city average is 0.869.)

TAX PROGRESSIVITY IN SELECTED CITIES, 1993

Most progressive		Least progressive	
City	**Index**	**City**	**Index**
New Orleans, La.	0.533	Memphis, Tenn.	1.218
Los Angeles, Calif.	0.612	Anchorage, Alaska	1.146
Boise City, Idaho	0.666	Sioux Falls, S.Dak.	1.145
Billings, Mont.	0.690	Las Vegas, Nev.	1.143
Minneapolis, Minn.	0.704	Seattle, Wash.	1.137
Average progressivity[1]	**0.869**		

Note: An index coefficient of less than 1.000 indicates a progressive tax system; an index coefficient of greater than one indicates a regressive tax system. A proportional system is indicated by a coefficient of 1.000. 1. The average of the largest city in each state plus the District of Columbia. **Source:** Government of the District of Columbia, Dept. of Finance and Revenues, *Tax Rates and Tax Burdens in the District of Columbia: A Nationwide Comparison* (1994).

THE COST OF LIVING INDEX

The cost of living index, compiled by the American Chamber of Commerce Researchers Association, measures relative price levels for consumer goods and services. The nationwide average equals 100 and each area's index is read as a percentage of the nationwide average. So, Philadelphia is significantly above the national average in every category, while Tulsa is below the average in all but one category. The index reflects differentials for a mid-manager standard of living by its weighting structure. Housing costs, for example, are more heavily weighted than they would be if the index were structured to reflect average costs for a clerical worker, or for all urban consumers. Tax burdens are not included in the cost of living index.

THE COST OF LIVING INDEX IN SELECTED U.S. CITIES, 1994

Urban area	Composite index (100%)	Grocery items (16%)	Housing (28%)	Utilities (8%)	Transportation (10%)	Health care (5%)	Misc. goods & services (33%)
Albuquerque, N.Mex.	103.4	97.7	108.5	96.7	101.3	113.5	102.3
Atlanta, Ga.	97.2	100.3	88.0	109.9	98.6	108.6	98.1
Austin, Tex.	95.5	93.3	88.7	92.7	103.4	100.9	100.0
Baltimore, Md.	103.1	103.5	107.2	98.1	106.5	103.0	99.6
Boston, Mass.	137.7	123.1	171.0	191.8	118.3	139.8	108.3
Charlotte, N.C.	98.7	97.4	97.7	99.1	95.7	110.2	98.9
Cincinnati, Ohio	101.0	95.6	99.5	103.3	104.3	95.5	104.4
Cleveland, Ohio	104.3	97.2	106.1	131.0	104.5	105.6	99.4
Columbus, Ohio	104.3	101.8	97.6	131.6	108.1	96.4	105.1
Dallas, Tex.	101.9	99.2	93.5	124.4	105.1	108.3	102.7
Denver, Colo.	104.5	100.0	116.3	92.7	106.1	124.0	95.5
El Paso, Tex.	94.2	93.8	84.3	91.9	110.7	93.4	99.0
Fresno, Calif.	107.7	104.5	110.2	101.2	117.8	122.1	103.3
Fort Worth, Tex.	93.7	100.0	80.1	110.4	100.5	101.6	94.7
Houston, Tex.	97.0	95.7	90.8	99.8	108.1	104.2	98.0
Indianapolis, Ind.	94.7	93.9	92.9	93.1	93.9	96.9	96.8
Jacksonville, Fla.	94.9	98.3	81.3	99.4	109.3	104.8	98.0
Kansas City, Mo.	95.0	97.0	90.0	104.1	90.6	101.0	96.1
Las Vegas, Nev.	109.0	101.7	115.2	96.4	120.2	116.8	105.9
Little Rock, Ark.	87.2	91.2	76.1	124.0	97.1	78.4	84.6
Los Angeles–Long Beach, Calif.	123.9	114.3	148.3	82.1	110.6	142.1	118.4
Miami, Fla.	107.8	101.4	104.0	120.5	114.1	120.2	107.1
Memphis, Tenn.	96.1	101.8	88.4	91.2	106.2	99.4	97.6
Minneapolis, Minn.	101.5	99.2	96.4	89.4	106.2	126.2	104.0
Nashville, Tenn.	90.7	96.9	83.3	89.2	92.0	81.5	95.7
New Orleans, La.	95.8	94.9	90.5	125.6	103.4	94.7	91.6
New York, N.Y.	228.3	150.3	439.5	145.3	132.1	205.3	137.6
Oklahoma City, Okla.	92.9	93.5	79.6	106.9	94.0	96.9	99.5
Omaha, Nebr.	92.1	95.8	88.0	96.6	103.0	89.0	90.3
Orlando, Fla.	98.5	96.9	89.1	109.8	97.8	111.5	102.2
Philadelphia, Pa.	127.8	120.6	143.5	184.3	115.4	106.4	111.5
Phoenix, Ariz.	101.2	105.0	94.2	102.3	110.6	109.5	101.1
Portland, Oreg.	109.7	99.9	124.2	77.4	110.3	127.3	106.7
St. Louis, Mo.	97.8	102.6	93.5	105.9	93.6	109.3	96.1
Salt Lake City, Utah	108.0	99.8	134.2	92.7	100.4	104.5	96.1
San Antonio, Tex.	94.9	93.8	90.7	80.5	108.9	96.3	98.3
San Diego, Calif.	122.3	112.2	163.7	74.1	127.9	125.1	101.8
Tampa, Fla.	94.9	97.1	94.6	100.3	96.5	103.6	90.7
Toledo, Ohio	98.8	97.1	90.9	118.9	107.1	94.7	100.0
Tucson, Ariz.	99.7	99.6	100.0	100.6	93.4	106.8	99.6
Tulsa, Okla.	91.0	92.3	83.5	92.6	81.9	96.8	97.7
Washington, D.C.	132.4	116.6	182.1	107.3	135.9	122.5	104.9

Note: Percentage figures in parentheses show relative weight of component indexes used in calculating composite cost of living index. Figures are for fourth quarter, 1994. **Source:** American Chamber of Commerce Researchers Association, *Cost of Living Index: Comparative Data for 302 Urban Areas, Fourth Quarter 1994* (1994).

Metropolitan Statistical Areas (MSAs)

For statistical purposes, the Office of Management and Budget (OMB) divides the population of the United States into metropolitan and nonmetropolitan populations. The OMB distinguishes between metropolitan statistical areas (MSAs), consolidated metropolitan statistical areas (CMSAs), primary metropolitan statistical areas (PMSAs), and in the Northeast, New England county metropolitan areas (NECMAs).

An MSA is either one city of 50,000 or more inhabitants, or an urbanized area (as defined by the Census Bureau) of at least 50,000 inhabitants and a total MSA population of at least 100,000 (in New England, 75,000). An MSA includes the county in which the central city is located plus any adjacent counties in which at least 50 percent of the population lives in the urbanized area. Within metropolitan complexes of one million or more population, separate component areas—PMSAs—are defined if specified criteria are met; and any area containing PMSAs is designated a CMSA. Although the 283 metropolitan areas of the United States make up only about 16 percent of the country's land area, they are home to 77.5 percent of all Americans.

According to the 1990 census, the U.S. population living in all metropolitan areas totaled 192,725,741, an increase of just over 20 million

METROPOLITAN AREAS, BY POPULATION SIZE, 1990

Size of metropolitan area	Number of areas	Population (millions)
All metropolitan areas	**284**	**192.7**
Over 5 million	5	52.8
2.5 to 5 million	9	31.7
1 to 2.5 million	25	40.2
500,000 to 1 million	34	24.9
250,000 to 500,000	61	21.5
100,000 to 250,000	125	19.4
Under 100,000	25	2.1

Source: U.S. Bureau of the Census, *1990 Census Profile* (September 1991).

(11.6%) since 1980. The same areas grew 10.6 percent in the 1970s. The population living outside metropolitan areas totaled only 55,984,132 people, increasing by only about 2.1 million (3.9%) since 1980.

The 1990 census indicated that there were 39 metropolitan areas of at least one million population; these areas have a combined population of 124.8 million people, or 50.2 percent of the national total. By contrast, the 1950 census showed only 14 metropolitan areas of this size, and their combined population of about 45 million people amounted to less than 30 percent of the total U.S. population.

POPULATION OF U.S. METROPOLITAN AREAS BY RACE AND HISPANIC ORIGIN, 1990

Rank/Metropolitan area	Total	White	Black	American Indian	Asian or Pacific Islander	Other race	Hispanic origin[1]
1. New York–Northern New Jersey–Long Island, N.Y.–N.J.–Conn. CMSA	18,087,251	12,699,119	3,289,465	46,191	873,213	1,179,263	2,777,951
New York, N.Y. PMSA	8,546,846	4,826,081	2,250,026	29,711	556,399	884,629	1,889,662
Nassau–Suffolk, N.Y. PMSA	2,609,212	2,305,434	193,967	4,636	62,399	42,776	165,238
Newark, N.J. PMSA	1,824,321	1,279,952	422,802	3,144	52,898	65,525	188,299
Bergen–Passaic, N.J. PMSA	1,278,440	1,043,437	106,108	2,221	66,743	59,931	147,868
Middlesex–Somerset–Hunterdon, N.J. PMSA	1,019,835	865,158	70,670	1,420	56,804	25,783	71,695
Monmouth–Ocean, N.J. PMSA	986,327	895,986	59,264	1,327	19,098	10,652	36,357
Jersey City, N.J. PMSA	553,099	380,612	79,770	1,460	36,777	54,480	183,465
Bridgeport–Milford, Conn. PMSA	443,722	371,493	45,826	806	6,577	19,020	44,741
Orange County, N.Y. PMSA	307,647	273,600	22,223	824	3,549	7,451	21,535
Stamford, Conn. PMSA	202,557	171,834	20,767	203	5,570	4,183	13,732
Danbury, Conn. PMSA	187,867	175,780	5,398	301	4,355	2,033	7,136
Norwalk, Conn. PMSA	127,378	109,752	12,644	138	2,044	2,800	8,223
2. Los Angeles–Anaheim–Riverside, Calif. CMSA	14,531,529	9,388,957	1,229,809	87,487	1,339,048	2,486,228	4,779,118
Los Angeles–Long Beach, Calif. PMSA	8,863,164	5,035,103	992,974	45,508	954,485	1,835,094	3,351,242
Riverside–San Bernardino, Calif. PMSA	2,588,793	1,930,095	178,525	24,905	100,792	354,476	686,096
Anaheim–Santa Ana, Calif. PMSA	2,410,556	1,894,593	42,681	12,165	249,192	211,925	564,828
Oxnard–Ventura, Calif. PMSA	669,016	529,166	15,629	4,909	34,579	84,733	176,952
3. Chicago–Gary–Lake County, Ill.–Ind.–Wis. CMSA	8,065,633	5,772,110	1,547,725	15,758	256,050	473,990	893,422
Chicago, Ill. PMSA	6,069,974	4,098,747	1,332,919	11,550	229,492	397,266	734,827
Gary–Hammond, Ind. PMSA	604,526	460,532	117,142	1,108	3,716	22,028	48,384
Lake County, Ill. PMSA	516,418	450,666	34,771	1,198	12,588	17,195	38,570
Joliet, Ill. PMSA	389,650	335,284	38,382	737	4,887	10,360	20,721
Aurora–Elgin, Ill. PMSA	356,884	307,694	19,216	693	4,698	24,583	45,340
Kenosha, Wis. PMSA	128,181	119,187	5,295	472	669	2,558	5,580
4. San Francisco–Oakland–San Jose, Calif. CMSA	6,253,311	4,334,064	537,753	40,847	926,961	413,686	970,403
Oakland, Calif. PMSA	2,082,914	1,372,818	303,826	14,230	269,566	122,474	273,087
San Francisco, Calif. PMSA	1,603,678	1,058,796	122,494	7,232	329,599	85,557	233,274
San Jose, Calif. PMSA	1,497,577	1,032,190	56,211	9,269	261,466	138,441	314,564
Vallejo–Fairfield–Napa, Calif. PMSA	451,186	325,761	47,043	3,898	47,044	27,440	61,458
Santa Rosa–Petaluma, Calif. PMSA	388,222	351,650	5,547	4,397	10,774	15,854	41,223
Santa Cruz, Calif. PMSA	229,734	192,849	2,632	1,821	8,512	23,920	46,797
5. Philadelphia–Wilmington–Trenton, Pa.–N.J.–Del.–Md. CMSA	5,899,345	4,540,541	1,100,347	11,307	123,458	123,692	225,868
Philadelphia, Pa.–N.J. PMSA	4,856,881	3,717,175	929,907	8,335	104,595	96,869	173,980
Wilmington, Del.–N.J.–Md. PMSA	578,587	477,243	85,641	1,128	7,737	6,838	13,875
Trenton, N.J. PMSA	325,824	244,656	61,481	533	9,992	9,162	19,665
Vineland–Millville–Bridgeton, N.J. PMSA	138,053	101,467	23,318	1,311	1,134	10,823	18,348
6. Detroit–Ann Arbor, Mich. CMSA	4,665,236	3,569,087	975,199	17,961	69,454	33,535	90,947
Detroit, Mich. PMSA	4,382,299	3,332,697	943,479	16,885	57,730	31,508	85,216
Ann Arbor, Mich. PMSA	282,937	236,390	31,720	1,076	11,724	2,027	5,731
7. Boston–Lawrence–Salem, Mass.–N.H. CMSA	4,171,643	3,708,228	239,059	7,542	121,405	95,409	193,199
Boston, Mass. PMSA	2,870,669	2,499,859	209,970	5,250	95,044	60,546	128,883
Lawrence–Haverhill, Mass.–N.H. PMSA	393,516	359,052	7,363	857	5,146	21,098	36,300
Lowell, Mass.–N.H. PMSA	273,067	248,937	3,598	388	14,251	5,893	12,193
Salem–Gloucester, Mass. PMSA	264,356	257,396	2,448	305	2,347	1,860	5,506
Brockton, Mass. PMSA	189,478	168,133	13,770	445	2,158	4,972	7,044
Nashua, N.H. PMSA	180,557	174,851	1,910	297	2,459	1,040	3,273
8. Washington, D.C.–Md.–Va. MSA	3,923,574	2,577,933	1,041,934	11,036	202,437	90,234	224,786
9. Dallas–Fort Worth, Tex. CMSA	3,885,415	2,924,673	554,616	18,972	97,578	289,576	518,917
Dallas, Tex. PMSA	2,553,362	1,854,577	410,766	12,635	67,195	208,189	368,884
Fort Worth–Arlington, Tex. PMSA	1,332,053	1,070,096	143,850	6,337	30,383	81,387	150,033

Rank/Metropolitan area	Total	White	Black	American Indian	Asian or Pacific Islander	Other race	Hispanic origin[1]
10. Houston–Galveston–Brazoria, Tex. CMSA	3,711,043	2,507,455	665,378	11,029	132,131	395,050	772,295
Houston, Tex. PMSA	3,301,937	2,188,370	611,243	9,465	126,601	366,258	707,536
Galveston–Texas City, Tex. PMSA	217,399	164,210	38,154	752	3,569	10,714	30,962
Brazoria, Tex. PMSA	191,707	154,875	15,981	812	1,961	18,078	33,797
11. Miami–Fort Lauderdale, Fla. CMSA	3,192,582	2,438,598	591,440	5,700	43,437	113,407	1,061,846
Miami–Hialeah, Fla. PMSA	1,937,094	1,413,015	397,993	3,066	26,307	96,713	953,407
Fort Lauderdale–Hollywood–Pompano Beach, Fla. PMSA	1,255,488	1,025,583	193,447	2,634	17,130	16,694	108,439
12. Atlanta, Ga. MSA	2,833,511	2,020,017	736,153	5,532	51,486	20,323	57,169
13. Cleveland–Akron–Lorain, Ohio CMSA	2,759,823	2,261,217	441,940	5,133	28,187	23,346	52,997
Cleveland, Ohio PMSA	1,831,122	1,435,768	355,619	3,038	20,528	16,169	33,921
Akron, Ohio PMSA	657,575	583,900	65,091	1,357	6,180	1,047	3,815
Lorain–Elyria, Ohio PMSA	271,126	241,549	21,230	738	1,479	6,130	15,261
14. Seattle–Tacoma, Wash. CMSA	2,559,164	2,211,710	123,266	32,071	164,286	27,831	75,555
Seattle, Wash. PMSA	1,972,961	1,713,068	81,056	23,727	135,251	19,859	54,993
Tacoma, Wash. PMSA	586,203	498,642	42,210	8,344	29,035	7,972	20,562
15. San Diego, Calif. MSA	2,498,016	1,672,256	159,306	20,066	198,311	248,077	510,781
16. Minneapolis–St. Paul, Minn.–Wis. MSA	2,464,124	2,270,360	89,710	23,956	65,204	14,894	37,448
17. St. Louis, Mo.–Ill. MSA	2,444,099	1,985,500	423,182	4,947	23,686	6,784	26,014
18. Baltimore, Md. MSA	2,382,172	1,709,309	616,065	6,444	42,634	7,720	30,160
19. Pittsburgh–Beaver Valley, Pa. CMSA	2,242,798	2,041,897	178,857	2,257	16,174	3,613	12,852
Pittsburgh, Pa. PMSA	2,056,705	1,867,138	168,382	2,054	15,797	3,334	11,728
Beaver County, Pa. PMSA	186,093	174,759	10,475	203	377	279	1,124
20. Phoenix, Ariz. MSA	2,122,101	1,799,420	74,257	38,017	36,294	174,113	345,498
21. Tampa–St. Petersburg–Clearwater, Fla. MSA	2,067,959	1,827,492	185,503	5,467	23,055	26,442	139,248
22. Denver–Boulder, Colo. CMSA	1,848,319	1,599,734	97,755	13,884	42,642	94,304	226,200
Denver, Colo. PMSA	1,622,980	1,389,544	95,796	12,571	37,134	87,935	211,005
Boulder–Longmont, Colo. PMSA	225,339	210,190	1,959	1,313	5,508	6,369	15,195
23. Cincinnati–Hamilton, Ohio–Ky.–Ind. CMSA	1,744,124	1,521,061	203,607	2,457	14,260	2,739	9,376
Cincinnati, Ohio–Ky.–Ind. PMSA	1,452,645	1,246,169	190,473	2,078	11,601	2,324	7,909
Hamilton–Middleton, Ohio PMSA	291,479	274,892	13,134	379	2,659	415	1,467
24. Milwaukee–Racine, Wis. CMSA	1,607,183	1,335,470	214,182	8,522	19,786	29,223	60,340
Milwaukee, Wis. PMSA	1,432,149	1,183,372	197,183	8,001	18,782	24,811	51,306
Racine, Wis. PMSA	175,034	152,098	16,999	521	1,004	4,412	9,034
25. Kansas City, Mo.–Kans. MSA	1,566,280	1,320,564	200,508	7,631	17,444	20,133	45,227
26. Sacramento, Calif. MSA	1,481,102	1,170,505	101,940	17,021	114,520	77,116	172,374
27. Portland–Vancouver, Oreg.–Wash. CMSA	1,477,895	1,350,155	41,671	13,603	52,030	20,436	49,921
Portland, Oreg. PMSA	1,239,842	1,124,963	38,695	11,307	46,360	18,517	44,049
Vancouver, Wash. PMSA	238,053	225,192	2,976	2,296	5,670	1,919	5,872
28. Norfolk–Virginia Beach–Newport News, Va. MSA	1,396,107	947,160	398,093	4,679	35,205	10,970	32,329
29. Columbus, Ohio MSA	1,377,419	1,184,770	164,602	2,880	21,059	4,108	11,363
30. San Antonio, Tex. MSA	1,302,099	978,505	88,778	4,648	16,058	214,110	620,290
31. Indianapolis, Ind. MSA	1,249,822	1,061,142	172,326	2,510	10,081	3,763	11,084
32. New Orleans, La. MSA	1,238,816	770,406	430,470	3,615	21,380	12,945	53,226
33. Buffalo–Niagara Falls, N.Y. CMSA	1,189,288	1,037,211	121,956	7,611	11,026	11,484	24,347
Buffalo, N.Y. PMSA	968,532	831,903	109,852	5,600	10,220	10,957	22,249
Niagara Falls, N.Y. PMSA	220,756	205,308	12,104	2,011	806	527	2,098
34. Charlotte–Gastonia–Rock Hill, N.C.–S.C. PMSA	1,162,093	911,904	231,654	4,107	11,304	3,124	10,671
35. Providence–Pawtucket–Fall River, R.I.–Mass. CMSA	1,141,510	1,055,370	37,106	3,782	20,050	25,202	47,467
Providence, R.I. PMSA	654,854	590,671	30,526	3,079	14,522	16,056	31,453
Pawtucket–Woonsocket–Attleboro, R.I.–Mass. PMSA	329,384	310,677	5,494	535	3,987	8,691	13,949
Fall River, Mass.–R.I. PMSA	157,272	154,022	1,086	168	1,541	455	2,065
36. Hartford–New Britain–Middletown, Conn. CMSA	1,085,837	933,568	94,925	1,826	15,845	39,673	75,627
Hartford, Conn. PMSA	767,841	641,345	81,550	1,365	12,201	31,380	58,362
New Britain, Conn. PMSA	148,188	132,519	6,574	190	1,937	6,968	13,387
Middletown, Conn. PMSA	90,320	82,829	5,454	143	1,163	731	2,059
Bristol, Conn. PMSA	79,488	76,875	1,347	128	544	594	1,819
37. Orlando, Fla. MSA	1,072,748	888,913	133,308	3,199	20,474	26,854	96,418
38. Salt Lake City–Ogden, Utah MSA	1,072,227	1,000,082	10,464	8,337	25,598	27,746	61,964
39. Rochester, N.Y. MSA	1,002,410	875,886	93,819	2,870	13,978	15,857	31,238
40. Nashville, Tenn. MSA	985,026	818,424	152,349	2,121	10,012	2,120	7,665
41. Memphis, Tenn.–Ariz.–Miss. MSA	981,747	570,511	399,011	1,791	8,178	2,256	7,986
42. Oklahoma City, Okla. MSA	958,839	777,589	101,082	45,720	17,742	16,706	34,152
43. Louisville, Ky.–Ind. MSA	953,662	818,898	124,761	1,576	5,640	1,787	5,765
44. Dayton–Springfield, Ohio MSA	951,270	811,393	126,238	1,915	9,278	2,446	7,254

Rank/Metropolitan area	Total	White	Black	American Indian	Asian or Pacific Islander	Other race	Hispanic origin[1]
45. Greensboro–Winston-Salem–High Point, N.C. MSA	942,091	747,835	182,284	3,196	6,381	2,395	7,096
46. Birmingham, Ala. MSA	907,810	655,609	245,726	1,506	4,014	955	3,989
47. Jacksonville, Fla. MSA	906,727	701,911	181,265	2,587	15,362	5,602	22,479
48. Albany–Schenectady–Troy N.Y. MSA	874,304	815,315	41,112	1,560	10,789	5,528	15,840
49. Richmond–Petersburg, Va. MSA	865,640	595,714	252,340	2,705	11,864	3,017	9,327
50. West Palm Beach–Boca Raton–Delray Beach, Fla. MSA	863,518	732,231	107,705	1,211	9,020	13,351	66,613
51. Honolulu, Hawaii MSA	836,231	264,372	25,875	3,532	526,459	15,993	56,884
52. Austin, Tex. MSA	781,572	600,023	72,254	2,827	18,770	87,698	159,942
53. Las Vegas, Nev. MSA	741,459	602,658	70,738	6,416	26,043	35,604	82,904
54. Raleigh–Durham, N.C. MSA	735,480	533,056	183,447	1,933	13,834	3,210	9,019
55. Scranton–Wilkes-Barre, Pa. MSA	734,175	720,692	7,660	580	3,827	1,416	5,640
56. Tulsa, Okla. MSA	708,954	590,612	58,186	48,196	6,563	5,397	14,534
57. Grand Rapids, Mich. MSA	688,399	623,787	41,311	3,394	7,831	12,076	22,631
58. Allentown–Bethlehem–Easton, Pa.–N.J. MSA	686,688	649,890	13,466	688	7,293	15,351	28,885
59. Fresno, Calif. MSA	667,490	422,839	33,423	7,119	57,239	146,870	236,634
60. Tucson, Ariz. MSA	666,880	524,976	20,795	20,330	11,964	88,815	163,262
61. Syracuse, N.Y. MSA	659,864	605,924	39,095	3,948	7,740	3,157	8,926
62. Greenville-Spartanburg, S.C. MSA	640,861	522,632	111,334	959	4,617	1,319	5,120
63. Omaha, Nebr.–Iowa MSA	618,262	550,758	51,426	3,159	6,374	6,545	16,371
64. Toledo, Ohio MSA	614,128	526,555	69,717	1,423	6,146	10,287	20,382
65. Knoxville, Tenn. MSA	604,816	561,535	36,400	1,505	4,540	836	3,232
66. El Paso, Tex. MSA	591,610	452,512	22,110	2,590	6,485	107,913	411,619
67. Harrisburg–Lebanon–Carlisle, Pa. MSA	587,986	536,738	39,472	737	6,251	4,788	10,239
68. Bakersfield, Calif. MSA	543,477	378,479	30,131	7,026	16,541	111,300	151,995
69. New Haven–Meriden, Conn. MSA	530,180	441,831	64,220	947	8,430	14,752	32,907
70. Springfield, Mass. MSA	529,519	457,749	35,081	864	5,397	30,428	47,635
71. Baton Rouge, La. MSA	528,264	363,692	156,509	902	5,657	1,504	7,532
72. Little Rock–North Little Rock, Ark. MSA	513,117	404,808	101,862	1,870	3,347	1,230	4,164
73. Charleston, S.C. MSA	506,875	343,776	153,227	1,613	6,113	2,146	7,512
74. Youngstown–Warren, Ohio MSA	492,619	432,024	54,902	785	1,958	2,950	7,400
75. Wichita, Kans. MSA	485,270	423,784	36,979	5,160	9,109	10,238	19,793
76. Stockton, Calif. MSA	480,628	353,169	27,094	5,085	59,690	35,590	112,673
77. Albuquerque, N. Mex. MSA	480,577	369,445	13,199	16,296	7,386	74,251	178,310
78. Mobile, Ala. MSA	476,923	339,418	130,512	2,570	3,619	804	4,186
79. Columbia, S.C. MSA	453,331	307,454	137,906	1,013	4,820	2,138	5,949
80. Worcester, Mass. MSA	436,905	408,123	9,553	891	7,967	10,371	20,009
81. Johnson City–Kingsport–Bristol, Tenn.–Va. MSA	436,047	424,751	8,925	766	1,247	358	1,690
82. Chattanooga, Tenn.–Ga. MSA	433,210	370,586	58,218	891	2,825	690	2,539
83. Lansing–East Lansing, Mich. MSA	432,674	381,371	31,365	2,655	8,320	8,963	16,963
84. Flint, Mich. MSA	430,459	336,651	84,257	3,132	2,902	3,517	8,877
85. Lancaster, Pa. MSA	422,822	397,815	10,038	484	4,652	9,833	15,639
86. York, Pa. MSA	417,848	399,694	11,911	501	2,471	3,271	6,381
87. Lakeland–Winter Haven, Fla. MSA	405,382	341,952	54,385	1,158	2,486	5,401	16,600
88. Saginaw–Bay City–Midland, Mich. MSA	399,320	346,643	38,810	1,975	2,504	9,388	17,715
89. Melbourne–Titusville–Palm Bay, Fla. MSA	398,978	358,391	31,417	1,369	5,379	2,422	12,261
90. Colorado Springs, Colo. MSA	397,014	341,400	28,593	3,242	9,841	13,938	34,473
91. Augusta, Ga.–S.C. MSA	396,809	264,801	123,482	941	5,438	2,147	5,620
92. Jackson, Miss. MSA	395,396	224,999	167,899	346	1,754	398	1,944
93. Canton, Ohio MSA	394,106	365,675	25,187	1,015	1,558	671	2,854
94. Des Moines, Iowa MSA	392,928	368,386	14,952	1,015	6,218	2,357	6,614
95. McAllen–Edinburg–Mission, Tex. MSA	383,545	286,858	806	668	1,088	94,125	326,972
96. Daytona Beach, Fla. MSA	370,712	328,530	33,455	915	2,739	5,073	14,840
97. Modesto, Calif. MSA	370,522	297,315	6,450	4,039	19,223	43,495	80,897
98. Santa Barbara–Santa Maria–Lompoc, Calif. MSA	369,608	285,461	10,402	3,351	16,429	53,965	98,199
99. Madison, Wis. MSA	367,085	344,617	10,511	1,201	8,666	2,090	5,744
100. Fort Wayne, Ind. MSA	363,811	326,568	30,380	1,056	2,769	3,038	6,628
101. Spokane, Wash. MSA	361,364	341,874	5,105	5,539	6,569	2,277	6,994
102. Beaumont–Port Arthur, Tex. MSA	361,226	264,365	84,665	890	5,687	5,619	15,241
103. Salinas–Seaside–Monterey, Calif. MSA	355,660	227,008	22,849	3,017	27,856	74,930	119,570
104. Davenport–Rock Island–Moline, Iowa–Ill. MSA	350,861	322,805	19,115	902	2,502	5,537	13,134
105. Corpus Christi, Tex. MSA	349,894	265,002	13,659	1,394	2,646	67,193	181,860
106. Lexington–Fayette, Ky. MSA	348,428	305,725	37,212	561	4,037	893	3,117
107. Pensacola, Fla. MSA	344,406	277,620	55,893	3,347	6,021	1,525	6,236
108. Peoria, Ill. MSA	339,172	309,325	25,142	587	2,759	1,359	3,642

Rank/Metropolitan area	Total	White	Black	American Indian	Asian or Pacific Islander	Other race	Hispanic origin[1]
109. Reading, Pa. MSA	336,523	314,561	10,003	333	2,746	8,880	17,174
110. Fort Myers–Cape Coral, Fla. MSA	335,113	306,200	22,184	672	1,894	4,163	15,094
111. Shreveport, La. MSA	334,341	213,610	116,892	863	2,023	951	4,394
112. Atlantic City, N.J. MSA	319,416	260,185	44,398	778	5,389	8,666	17,972
113. Utica–Rome, N.Y. MSA	316,633	297,746	13,849	613	2,314	2,111	6,174
114. Appleton–Oshkosh–Neenah, Wis. MSA	315,121	306,775	932	2,796	3,805	813	2,280
115. Huntington–Ashland, W.Va.–Ky.–Ohio MSA	312,529	304,244	6,751	372	937	225	1,274
116. Visalia–Tulare–Porterville, Calif. MSA	311,921	204,835	4,618	3,992	13,319	85,157	120,893
117. Montgomery, Ala. MSA	292,517	184,414	105,196	622	1,782	503	2,124
118. Rockford, Ill. MSA	283,719	251,783	23,383	697	3,136	4,720	9,836
119. Eugene–Springfield, Oreg. MSA	282,912	269,798	2,107	3,207	5,557	2,243	6,852
120. Macon–Warner–Robins, Ga. MSA	281,103	180,383	97,294	571	1,941	914	2,832
121. Evansville, Ind.–Ky. MSA	278,990	260,832	16,115	477	1,237	329	1,321
122. Salem, Oreg. MSA	278,024	255,212	2,332	4,041	4,746	11,693	21,027
123. Sarasota, Fla. MSA	277,776	262,836	12,073	483	1,430	954	5,882
124. Erie, Pa. MSA	275,572	257,879	14,304	438	1,411	1,540	3,364
125. Fayetteville, N.C. MSA	274,566	170,069	87,496	4,425	5,769	6,807	13,298
126. New London–Norwich, Conn.–R.I. MSA	266,819	245,933	12,077	1,433	3,549	3,827	8,517
127. Binghamton, N.Y. MSA	264,497	254,447	4,647	450	3,990	963	2,845
128. Provo–Orem, Utah MSA	263,590	253,596	374	1,913	3,958	3,749	8,488
129. Brownsville–Harlington, Tex. MSA	260,120	214,424	825	413	750	43,708	212,995
130. Poughkeepsie, N.Y. MSA	259,462	229,194	21,788	374	5,826	2,280	9,765
131. Killeen–Temple, Tex. MSA	255,301	181,144	49,687	1,405	7,201	15,864	31,238
132. Reno, Nev. MSA	254,667	225,095	5,680	4,921	9,824	9,147	22,959
133. Fort Pierce, Fla. MSA	251,071	214,278	30,709	526	1,565	3,993	10,680
134. Charleston, W.Va. MSA	250,454	234,518	13,919	292	1,450	275	1,042
135. South Bend–Mishawaka, Ind. MSA	247,052	216,984	24,190	846	2,507	2,525	5,201
136. Columbus, Ga.–Ala. MSA	243,072	144,326	91,484	765	3,107	3,390	7,388
137. Savannah, Ga. MSA	242,622	152,513	86,228	515	2,412	954	2,951
138. Johnstown, Pa. MSA	241,247	236,459	3,836	152	527	273	1,216
139. Springfield, Mo. MSA	240,593	233,186	3,784	1,471	1,600	552	1,991
140. Duluth, Minn.–Wis. MSA	239,971	232,507	1,276	4,487	1,342	359	1,153
141. Huntsville, Ala. MSA	238,912	184,197	48,116	1,601	4,232	766	2,984
142. Tallahassee, Fla. MSA	233,598	158,398	70,227	568	2,788	1,617	5,679
143. Anchorage, Alaska MSA	226,338	182,736	14,544	14,569	10,910	3,579	9,258
144. Roanoke, Va. MSA	224,477	194,645	27,602	281	1,602	347	1,359
145. Portsmouth–Dover–Rochester, N.H.–Maine MSA	223,578	218,216	2,285	414	2,136	527	1,994
146. Kalamazoo, Mich. MSA	223,411	197,427	19,879	1,017	3,168	1,920	3,950
147. Lubbock, Tex. MSA	222,636	176,037	17,154	686	2,722	26,037	51,011
148. Hickory–Morganton, N.C. MSA	221,700	201,558	17,540	417	1,673	512	1,449
149. Waterbury, Conn. MSA	221,629	196,680	15,414	538	1,576	7,421	16,384
150. Portland, Maine MSA	215,281	211,376	1,188	562	1,867	208	1,257
151. Lincoln, Nebr. MSA	213,641	202,663	4,659	1,207	3,367	1,745	3,938
152. Bradenton, Fla. MSA	211,707	190,328	16,400	501	1,227	3,251	9,424
153. Lafayette, La. MSA	208,740	154,146	51,378	440	1,915	861	3,115
154. Boise City, Idaho MSA	205,775	198,888	958	1,382	2,887	1,660	5,556
155. Gainesville, Fla. MSA	204,111	158,479	38,982	443	4,656	1,551	7,205
156. Biloxi–Gulfport, Miss. MSA	197,125	156,255	35,055	595	4,495	725	3,488
157. Ocala, Fla. MSA	194,833	167,094	24,844	638	945	1,312	5,860
158. Green Bay, Wis. MSA	194,594	186,621	1,012	3,869	2,522	570	1,525
159. St. Cloud, Minn. MSA	190,921	188,080	738	637	1,171	295	910
160. Bremerton, Wash. MSA	189,731	171,063	5,107	3,211	8,282	2,068	6,169
161. Springfield, Ill. MSA	189,550	173,114	14,373	319	1,391	353	1,311
162. Waco, Tex. MSA	189,123	146,100	29,520	563	1,384	11,556	23,643
163. Yakima, Wash. MSA	188,823	139,514	1,938	8,405	1,922	37,044	45,114
164. Amarillo, Tex. MSA	187,547	158,517	9,788	1,355	3,216	14,671	25,390
165. Fort Collins–Loveland, Colo. MSA	186,136	175,971	1,114	1,063	2,777	5,211	12,227
166. Houma–Thibodaux, La. MSA	182,842	147,453	26,735	6,814	1,370	470	2,625
167. Chico, Calif. MSA	182,120	165,200	2,361	3,241	5,170	6,148	13,606
168. Merced, Calif. MSA	178,403	120,280	8,523	1,516	15,128	32,956	58,107
169. Fort Smith, Ark.–Okla. MSA	175,911	155,580	6,831	9,054	3,755	691	2,120
170. New Bedford, Mass. MSA	175,641	161,018	4,623	504	841	8,655	7,347
171. Asheville, N.C. MSA	174,821	158,979	14,336	486	765	255	1,173
172. Champaign–Urbana–Rantoul, Ill. MSA	173,025	146,506	16,559	331	8,033	1,596	3,485

Rank/Metropolitan area	Total	White	Black	American Indian	Asian or Pacific Islander	Other race	Hispanic origin[1]
173. Clarksville–Hopkinsville, Tenn.–Ky. MSA	169,439	128,583	34,801	688	2,712	2,655	5,567
174. Cedar Rapids, Iowa MSA	168,767	163,164	3,334	363	1,401	505	1,591
175. Lake Charles, La. MSA	168,134	128,181	38,445	387	590	531	1,847
176. Longview–Marshall, Tex. MSA	162,431	122,270	35,975	670	635	2,881	3,053
177. Benton Harbor, Mich. MSA	161,378	133,259	24,872	685	1,487	1,075	2,683
178. Olympia, Wash. MSA	161,238	148,221	2,864	2,498	6,101	1,554	4,873
179. Topeka, Kans. MSA	160,976	141,189	13,365	1,836	1,179	3,407	7,785
180. Wheeling, W.Va.–Ohio MSA	159,301	155,313	3,196	145	546	101	569
181. Muskegon, Mich. MSA	158,983	133,931	21,617	1,338	555	1,542	3,623
182. Athens, Ga. MSA	156,267	124,076	29,003	257	2,352	579	2,011
183. Elkhart–Goshen, Ind. MSA	156,198	146,505	7,106	453	997	1,137	2,932
184. Lima, Ohio MSA	154,340	140,402	12,379	252	749	558	1,483
185. Fargo–Moorhead, N.Dak.–Minn. MSA	153,296	149,004	446	1,497	1,396	953	1,879
186. Naples, Fla. MSA	152,099	139,073	6,986	428	584	5,028	20,734
187. Tyler, Tex. MSA	151,309	113,676	31,572	520	638	4,903	8,986
188. Tuscaloosa, Ala. MSA	150,522	109,398	39,377	253	1,264	230	948
189. Richland–Kennewick–Pasco, Wash. MSA	150,033	129,749	2,395	1,124	3,115	13,650	19,940
190. Jacksonville, N.C. MSA	149,838	111,939	29,808	939	2,994	4,158	8,035
191. Jackson, Mich. MSA	149,756	135,557	11,983	655	653	908	2,303
192. Parkersburg–Marietta, W.Va.–Ohio MSA	149,169	146,698	1,567	242	520	142	479
193. Manchester, N.H. MSA	147,809	144,159	1,133	278	1,442	797	2,415
194. Redding, Calif. MSA	147,036	137,977	1,081	3,954	2,684	1,340	5,652
195. Waterloo–Cedar Falls, Iowa MSA	146,611	136,236	8,584	237	1,137	417	984
196. Medford, Oreg. MSA	146,389	140,188	340	1,863	1,429	2,569	5,949
197. Anderson, S.C. MSA	145,196	120,384	24,151	173	340	148	559
198. Fort Walton Beach, Fla. MSA	143,776	125,191	13,007	776	3,658	1,144	4,427
199. Steubenville–Weirton, Ohio–W.Va. MSA	142,523	136,078	5,591	237	439	178	710
200. Lynchburg, Va. MSA	142,199	110,847	30,079	277	743	253	923
201. Monroe, La. MSA	142,191	96,870	44,096	239	740	246	1,194
202. Jamestown–Dunkirk, N.Y. MSA	141,895	136,311	2,405	558	545	2,076	4,055
203. Janesville–Beloit, Wis. MSA	139,510	130,803	6,638	369	985	715	1,754
204. Eau Claire, Wis. MSA	137,543	134,056	269	617	2,400	204	611
205. Battle Creek, Mich. MSA	135,982	118,737	14,383	696	1,068	1,098	2,583
206. Las Cruces, N.Mex. MSA	135,510	123,434	2,172	1,009	1,164	7,731	76,448
207. Joplin, Mo. MSA	134,910	130,093	1,327	2,452	751	287	1,150
208. Laredo, Tex. MSA	133,239	93,657	156	201	484	38,741	125,069
209. Greeley, Colo. MSA	131,821	117,247	567	785	1,133	12,089	27,502
210. Decatur, Ala. MSA	131,556	113,685	14,879	2,434	389	169	686
210. Alexandria, La. MSA	131,556	92,989	36,805	564	908	290	1,526
212. Burlington, Vt. MSA	131,439	128,580	814	299	1,465	281	1,171
213. Florence, Ala. MSA	131,327	114,380	16,263	302	289	93	500
214. Charlottesville, Va. MSA	131,107	109,049	18,895	148	2,623	392	1,384
215. Dothan, Ala. MSA	130,964	100,878	27,801	526	1,201	558	1,679
216. Terre Haute, Ind. MSA	130,812	122,933	6,029	338	1,176	336	1,063
217. Anderson, Ind. MSA	130,669	119,734	9,870	299	415	351	885
218. Lafayette–West Lafayette, Ind. MSA	130,598	122,013	2,660	320	4,821	784	2,078
219. Altoona, Pa. MSA	130,542	128,840	1,073	118	380	131	431
220. Bloomington–Normal, Ill. MSA	129,180	121,057	5,563	203	1,624	733	1,671
221. Bellingham, Wash. MSA	127,780	119,229	650	4,014	2,363	1,524	3,718
222. Panama City, Fla. MSA	126,994	109,570	13,713	949	2,229	533	2,256
223. Mansfield, Ohio MSA	126,137	115,078	9,981	223	578	277	903
224. Sioux Falls, S.Dak. MSA	123,809	120,454	754	1,680	714	207	648
225. State College, Pa. MSA	123,786	116,552	2,801	179	3,841	413	1,350
226. Pueblo, Colo. MSA	123,051	104,304	2,253	991	729	14,774	44,090
227. Yuba City, Calif. MSA	122,643	95,062	3,478	2,616	10,996	10,491	17,320
228. Wichita Falls, Tex. MSA	122,378	102,427	11,221	903	1,851	5,976	10,555
229. Bryan–College Station, Tex. MSA	121,862	94,866	13,672	274	4,313	8,737	16,713
230. Hagerstown, Md. MSA	121,393	112,828	7,245	241	793	286	905
231. Sharon, Pa. MSA	121,003	114,479	5,882	115	393	134	506
232. Wilmington, N.C. MSA	120,284	94,895	24,097	435	616	241	924
233. Texarkana, Tex.–Ark. MSA	120,132	92,342	26,423	560	405	402	1,644
234. Muncie, Ind. MSA	119,659	111,232	7,167	274	641	345	853
235. Abilene, Tex. MSA	119,655	100,237	7,547	450	1,449	9,972	17,511
236. Odessa, Tex. MSA	118,934	91,309	5,557	647	662	20,759	37,315

Rank/Metropolitan area	Total	White	Black	American Indian	Asian or Pacific Islander	Other race	Hispanic origin[1]
237. Williamsport, Pa. MSA	118,710	115,040	2,816	219	469	166	641
238. Glens Falls, N.Y. MSA	118,539	115,157	2,352	214	392	424	1,789
239. Decatur, Ill. MSA	117,206	102,197	14,135	157	506	211	540
240. Santa Fe, N.Mex. MSA	117,043	96,454	711	2,948	941	15,989	50,947
241. Anniston, Ala. MSA	116,034	92,873	21,578	296	869	418	1,282
242. Wausau, Wis. MSA	115,400	112,189	89	490	2,499	133	470
243. Pascagoula, Miss. MSA	115,243	90,114	23,581	254	1,115	179	1,060
244. Sioux City, Iowa–Nebr. MSA	115,018	107,579	1,953	1,999	1,624	1,863	3,728
245. Florence, S.C. MSA	114,344	69,501	44,276	145	307	115	508
246. Billings, Mont. MSA	113,419	107,921	511	3,235	612	1,140	3,158
247. Fayetteville–Springdale, Ark. MSA	113,409	108,743	1,676	1,486	1,043	461	1,526
248. Albany, Ga. MSA	112,561	60,041	51,522	281	498	219	928
249. Columbia, Mo. MSA	112,379	100,055	8,377	394	3,129	424	1,226
250. Lawton, Okla. MSA	111,486	79,666	19,908	5,153	3,065	3,694	6,923
251. Bloomington, Ind. MSA	108,978	102,752	2,835	216	2,713	462	1,367
252. Danville, Va. MSA	108,711	73,817	34,350	117	325	102	515
253. Burlington, N.C. MSA	108,213	86,373	20,822	303	487	228	736
254. Yuma, Ariz. MSA	106,895	80,702	3,056	1,429	1,393	20,315	43,388
255. Midland, Tex. MSA	106,611	86,977	8,281	414	888	10,051	22,780
256. Rochester, Minn. MSA	106,470	101,880	788	295	3,237	270	970
257. Sheboygan, Wis. MSA	103,877	100,389	430	357	2,061	640	1,688
258. Fitchburg–Leominster, Mass. MSA	102,797	95,540	2,356	196	1,789	2,916	7,312
259. Cumberland, Md.–W.Va. MSA	101,643	98,821	2,270	71	391	90	420
260. Gadsden, Ala. MSA	99,840	85,274	13,799	250	419	98	331
261. San Angelo, Tex. MSA	98,458	79,533	4,136	373	998	13,418	25,501
262. La Crosse, Wis. MSA	97,904	94,319	438	340	2,667	140	640
263. Kokomo, Ind. MSA	96,946	91,410	4,408	246	508	374	1,178
264. Kankakee, Ill. MSA	96,255	80,194	14,399	150	644	868	1,946
265. Iowa City, Iowa MSA	96,119	89,649	1,979	176	3,837	478	1,435
266. Elmira, N.Y. MSA	95,195	88,370	5,245	211	690	679	1,441
267. Sherman–Denison, Tex. MSA	95,021	85,553	6,565	1,046	412	1,445	2,795
268. Bangor, Maine MSA	88,745	86,328	467	1,008	798	144	509
269. Lewiston–Auburn, Maine MSA	88,141	86,799	443	197	514	188	559
270. Owensboro, Ky. MSA	87,189	83,168	3,619	101	229	72	312
271. Dubuque, Iowa MSA	86,403	85,367	354	77	437	168	437
272. Pine Bluff, Ariz. MSA	85,487	47,878	36,877	227	352	153	427
273. Bismarck, N.Dak. MSA	83,831	81,306	79	2,016	286	144	435
274. St. Joseph, Mo. MSA	83,083	79,378	2,635	273	266	531	1,709
275. Lawrence, Kans. MSA	81,798	72,885	3,324	2,161	2,581	847	2,138
276. Rapid City, S.Dak. MSA	81,343	72,769	1,288	5,835	933	518	1,777
277. Pittsfield, Mass. MSA	79,250	76,597	1,702	142	548	261	770
278. Jackson, Tenn. MSA	77,982	53,423	24,170	66	253	70	376
279. Great Falls, Mont. MSA	77,691	72,345	1,061	3,072	792	421	1,398
280. Victoria, Tex. MSA	74,361	59,251	4,906	208	257	9,739	25,372
281. Cheyenne, Wyo. MSA	73,142	66,280	2,218	528	821	3,295	7,310
282. Grand Forks, N.Dak. MSA	70,683	66,766	1,446	1,244	881	346	1,053
283. Casper, Wyo. MSA	61,226	59,323	458	404	280	761	2,252
284. Enid, Okla. MSA	56,735	52,403	2,020	1,234	587	491	1,086

1. Hispanic persons may be of any race. **Source:** U.S. Bureau of the Census, Press Release 1992.

POPULATION OF METROPOLITAN STATISTICAL AREAS, 1980–90

Metropolitan statistical area	1980	1990	Change 1980–90		CMSA/MSA rank	
			Number	Percent	1980	1990
Abilene, Tex. MSA	110,932	119,655	8,723	7.9%	235	235
Albany, Ga. MSA	112,394	112,561	167	0.1	232	248
Albany–Schenectady–Troy, N.Y. MSA	824,729	861,424	36,695	4.4	46	48
Albuquerque, N.Mex. MSA	485,429	589,131	103,702	21.4	80	77
Alexandria, La. MSA	135,282	131,556	–3,726	–2.8	196	210
Allentown–Bethlehem, Pa.–N.J. MSA	551,052	595,081	44,029	8.0	54	58
Altoona, Pa. MSA	136,621	130,542	–6,079	–4.4	195	219
Amarillo, Tex. MSA	173,699	187,547	13,848	8.0%	157	164
Anchorage, Alaska MSA	174,431	226,338	51,907	29.8	156	143
Anderson, Ind. MSA	139,336	130,669	–8,667	–6.2	189	217
Anderson, S.C. MSA	133,235	145,196	11,961	9.0	199	197
Anniston, Ala. MSA	119,761	116,034	–3,727	–3.1	218	241
Appleton–Oshkosh–Neenah, Wis. MSA	291,369	315,121	23,752	8.2	107	114
Asheville, N.C. MSA	177,761	191,774	14,013	7.9	171	171

Metropolitan statistical area	1980	1990	Change 1980–90 Number	Change 1980–90 Percent	CMSA/MSA rank 1980	CMSA/MSA rank 1990
Athens, Ga. MSA	104,672	126,262	21,590	20.6%	204	182
Atlanta, Ga. MSA	2,233,229	2,959,950	726,721	32.5	16	12
Atlantic City, N.J. MSA	276,385	319,416	43,031	15.6	113	112
Augusta, Ga.–S.C. MSA	344,905	395,065	50,160	14.5	95	91
Austin, Tex. MSA	585,051	846,227	261,176	44.6	63	52
Bakersfield, Calif. MSA	403,089	543,477	140,388	34.8	84	68
Baltimore, Md. MSA	2,199,497	2,382,172	182,675	8.3	15	18
Bangor, Maine MSA	86,079	91,629	5,550	6.4	270	268
Baton Rouge, La. MSA	444,083	470,050	25,967	5.8	69	71
Battle Creek, Mich. MSA	141,579	135,982	–5,597	–4.0	186	205
Beaumont–Port Arthur, Tex. MSA	373,211	361,226	–11,985	–3.2	88	102
Bellingham, Wash. MSA	106,701	127,780	21,079	19.8	242	221
Benton Harbor, Mich. MSA	171,276	161,378	–9,898	–5.8	161	177
Billings, Mont. MSA	108,035	113,419	5,384	5.0	240	246
Biloxi–Gulfport–Pascagoula, Miss. MSA	300,176	312,368	12,192	4.1	153	156
Binghamton, N.Y. MSA	263,460	264,497	1,037	0.4	123	127
Birmingham, Ala. MSA	815,333	840,140	24,807	3.0	42	46
Bismarck, N.Dak. MSA	79,988	83,831	3,843	4.8	275	273
Bloomington, Ind. MSA	98,787	108,978	10,191	10.3	253	251
Bloomington–Normal, Ill. MSA	119,149	129,180	10,031	8.4	219	220
Boise City, Idaho MSA	256,881	295,851	38,970	15.2	158	154
Boston–Brockton–Nashua, Mass.–N.H.–Maine–Conn. CMSA	5,121,673	5,455,403	333,730	6.5	7	7
Boston, Mass.–N.H.–Maine–Conn. PMSA	4,762,629	5,050,761	288,132	6.0	N.A.	N.A.
Brockton, Mass. PMSA	224,902	236,409	11,507	5.1	N.A.	N.A.
Lawrence–Haverhill, Mass.–N.H. PMSA	339,090	393,516	54,426	16.1	N.A.	N.A.
Lowell, Mass.–N.H. PMSA	243,142	273,067	29,925	12.3	N.A.	N.A.
Nashua, N.H. PMSA	134,142	168,233	34,091	25.4	N.A.	N.A.
Salem–Gloucester, Mass. PMSA	258,231	264,356	6,125	2.4	N.A.	N.A.
Bradenton, Fla. MSA	148,445	211,707	63,262	42.6	181	152
Bremerton, Wash. MSA	147,152	189,731	42,579	28.9	182	160
Brownsville–Harlingen, Tex. MSA	209,727	260,120	50,393	24.0	138	129
Bryan–College Station, Tex. MSA	93,588	121,862	28,274	30.2	259	229
Buffalo–Niagara Falls, N.Y. CMSA	1,242,826	1,189,288	–53,538	–4.3	29	33
Buffalo, N.Y. PMSA	1,015,472	968,532	–46,940	–4.6	N.A.	N.A.
Niagara Falls, N.Y. PMSA	227,354	220,756	–6,598	–2.9	N.A.	N.A.
Burlington, N.C. MSA	99,319	108,213	8,894	9.0	251	253
Burlington, Vt. MSA	133,117	151,506	18,389	13.8	225	212
Canton, Ohio MSA	404,421	394,106	–10,315	–2.6	83	93
Casper, Wyo. MSA	71,856	61,226	–10,630	–14.8	278	283
Cedar Rapids, Iowa MSA	169,775	168,767	–1,008	–0.6	163	174
Champaign–Urbana–Rantoul, Ill. MSA	168,392	173,025	4,633	2.8	164	172
Charleston, S.C. MSA	430,346	506,875	76,529	17.8	77	73
Charleston, W.Va. MSA	269,595	250,454	–19,141	–7.1	118	134
Charlotte–Gastonia–Rock Hill, N.C.–S.C. MSA	971,447	1,162,093	190,646	19.6	36	34
Charlottesville, Va. MSA	113,568	131,107	17,539	15.4	226	214
Chattanooga, Tenn.–Ga. MSA	393,422	399,487	6,065	1.5	78	82
Cheyenne, Wyo. MSA	68,649	73,142	4,493	6.5	281	281
Chicago–Gary–Kenosha, Ill.–Ind.–Wis. CMSA	8,114,844	8,239,820	124,976	1.5	3	3
Aurora–Elgin, Ill. PMSA	315,607	356,884	41,277	13.1	N.A.	N.A.
Chicago, Ill. PMSA	7,246,048	7,410,858	164,810	2.3	N.A.	N.A.
Gary–Hammond, Ind. PMSA	642,733	604,526	–38,207	–5.9	N.A.	N.A.
Joliet, Ill. PMSA	355,042	389,650	34,608	9.7	N.A.	N.A.
Kenosha, Wis. PMSA	123,137	128,181	5,044	4.1	N.A.	N.A.
Lake County, Ill. PMSA	440,388	516,418	76,030	17.3	N.A.	N.A.
Chico, Calif. MSA	143,851	182,120	38,269	26.6	185	167
Cincinnati–Hamilton, Ohio–Ky.–Ind. CMSA	1,726,430	1,817,571	91,141	5.3	20	23
Cincinnati, Ohio–Ky.–Ind. PMSA	1,467,643	1,526,092	58,449	4.0	N.A.	N.A.
Hamilton–Middletown, Ohio PMSA	258,787	291,479	32,692	12.6	N.A.	N.A.

Metropolitan statistical area	1980	1990	Change 1980–90 Number	Change 1980–90 Percent	CMSA/MSA rank 1980	CMSA/MSA rank 1990
Clarksville–Hopkinsville, Tenn.–Ky. MSA	150,220	169,439	19,219	12.8%	179	173
Cleveland–Akron, Ohio CMSA	2,938,277	2,859,644	–78,633	–2.7	11	13
Akron, Ohio PMSA	660,328	657,575	–2,753	–0.4	N.A.	N.A.
Cleveland–Lorain–Elyria, Ohio PMSA	2,277,949	2,202,069	–75,880	–3.3	N.A.	N.A.
Colorado Springs, Colo. MSA	309,424	397,014	87,590	28.3	105	90
Columbia, Mo. MSA	100,376	112,379	12,003	12.0	250	249
Columbia, S.C. MSA	409,953	453,331	43,478	10.6	82	79
Columbus, Ga.–Ala. MSA	254,660	260,860	6,200	2.4	131	136
Columbus, Ohio MSA	1,214,291	1,345,450	131,159	10.8	28	29
Corpus Christi, Tex. MSA	326,228	349,894	23,666	7.3	99	105
Cumberland, Md.–W.Va. MSA	107,782	101,643	–6,139	–5.7	241	259
Dallas–Fort Worth, Tex. CMSA	3,046,136	4,037,282	991,146	32.5	10	9
Dallas, Tex. PMSA	2,055,284	2,676,248	620,964	30.2	N.A.	N.A.
Fort Worth–Arlington, Tex. PMSA	990,852	1,361,034	370,182	37.4	N.A.	N.A.
Danville, Va. MSA	111,789	108,711	–3,078	–2.8	233	252
Davenport–Rock Island–Moline, Iowa–Ill. MSA	384,749	350,861	–33,888	–8.8	86	104
Dayton–Springfield, Ohio MSA	942,083	951,270	9,187	1.0	39	44
Daytona Beach, Fla. MSA	269,675	399,413	129,738	48.1	124	96
Decatur, Ala. MSA	120,401	131,556	11,155	9.3	217	211
Decatur, Ill. MSA	131,375	117,206	–14,169	–10.8	210	239
Denver–Boulder–Greeley, Colo. CMSA	1,741,899	1,980,140	238,241	13.7	21	22
Boulder–Longmont, Colo. PMSA	189,625	225,339	35,714	18.8	N.A.	N.A.
Denver, Colo. PMSA	1,428,836	1,622,980	194,144	13.6	N.A.	N.A.
Des Moines, Iowa MSA	367,561	392,928	25,367	6.9	89	94
Detroit–Ann Arbor–Flint, Mich. CMSA	5,293,161	5,187,171	–105,990	–2.0	6	6
Ann Arbor, Mich. PMSA	454,977	490,058	35,081	7.7	N.A.	N.A.
Detroit, Mich. PMSA	4,387,735	4,266,654	–121,081	–2.8	N.A.	N.A.
Dothan, Ala. MSA	122,453	130,964	8,511	7.0	214	215
Dubuque, Iowa MSA	93,745	86,403	–7,342	–7.8	258	271
Duluth–Superior, Minn.–Wis. MSA	266,650	239,971	–26,679	–10.0	119	140
Eau Claire, Wis. MSA	130,932	137,543	6,611	5.0	203	204
El Paso, Tex. MSA	479,899	591,610	111,711	23.3	70	66
Elkhart–Goshen, Ind. MSA	137,330	156,198	18,868	13.7	193	183
Elmira, N.Y. MSA	97,656	95,195	–2,461	–2.5	255	266
Enid, Okla. MSA	62,820	56,735	–6,085	–9.7	284	284
Erie, Pa. MSA	279,780	275,572	–4,208	–1.5	111	124
Eugene–Springfield, Oreg. MSA	275,226	282,912	7,686	2.8	115	119
Evansville–Henderson, Ind.–Ky. MSA	276,252	278,990	2,738	1.0	114	121
Fargo–Moorhead, N.Dak.–Minn. MSA	137,574	153,296	15,722	11.4	191	185
Fayetteville, N.C. MSA	247,160	274,566	27,406	11.1	127	125
Fayetteville–Springdale–Rogers, Ark. MSA	178,609	210,908	32,299	18.1	249	247
Fitchburg–Leominster, Mass. MSA	94,018	102,797	8,779	9.3	257	258
Flint, Mich. MSA	450,449	430,459	–19,990	–4.4	73	84
Florence, Ala. MSA	135,065	131,327	–3,738	–2.8	197	213
Florence, S.C. MSA	110,163	114,344	4,181	3.8	236	245
Fort Collins–Loveland, Colo. MSA	149,184	186,136	36,952	24.8	180	165
Fort Myers–Cape Coral, Fla. MSA	205,266	335,113	129,847	63.3	140	110
Fort Pierce–Port St. Lucie, Fla. MSA	151,196	251,071	99,875	66.1	178	133
Fort Smith, Ark.–Okla. MSA	162,813	175,911	13,098	8.0	169	169
Fort Walton Beach, Fla. MSA	109,920	143,776	33,856	30.8	237	198
Fort Wayne, Ind. MSA	444,772	456,281	11,509	2.6	93	100
Fresno, Calif. MSA	577,737	755,580	177,843	30.8	67	59
Gadsden, Ala. MSA	103,057	99,840	–3,217	–3.1	245	260
Gainesville, Fla. MSA	151,369	181,596	30,227	20.0	160	155
Glens Falls, N.Y. MSA	109,649	118,539	8,890	8.1	238	238
Grand Forks, N.Dak.–Minn. MSA	100,944	103,181	2,237	2.2	283	282
Grand Rapids–Muskegon–Holland, Mich. MSA	840,824	937,891	97,067	11.5	56	57
Great Falls, Mont. MSA	80,696	77,691	–3,005	–3.7	274	279
Greeley, Colo. MSA	123,438	131,821	8,383	6.8	212	209

Metropolitan statistical area	1980	1990	Change 1980–90 Number	Change 1980–90 Percent	CMSA/MSA rank 1980	CMSA/MSA rank 1990
Green Bay, Wis. MSA	175,280	194,594	19,314	11.0%	155	158
Greensboro–Winston-Salem–High Point, N.C. MSA	950,763	1,050,304	99,541	10.5	44	45
Greenville-Spartanburg–Anderson, S.C. MSA	744,428	830,563	86,135	11.6	59	62
Hagerstown, Md. MSA	113,086	121,393	8,307	7.3	227	230
Harrisburg–Lebanon–Carlisle, Pa. MSA	556,242	587,986	31,744	5.7	62	67
Hartford, Conn. MSA	1,080,710	1,157,585	76,875	7.1	35	36
Bristol, Conn. PMSA	73,762	79,488	5,726	7.8	N.A.	N.A.
Hartford, Conn. PMSA	715,923	767,841	51,918	7.3	N.A.	N.A.
Middletown, Conn. PMSA	81,582	90,320	8,738	10.7	N.A.	N.A.
New Britain, Conn. PMSA	142,241	148,188	5,947	4.2	N.A.	N.A.
Hickory–Morganton, N.C. MSA	270,457	292,409	21,952	8.1	142	148
Honolulu, Hawaii MSA	762,565	836,231	73,666	9.7	47	51
Houma–Thibodaux, La. MSA	176,876	182,842	5,966	3.4	154	166
Houston–Galveston–Brazoria, Tex. CMSA	3,118,480	3,731,131	612,651	19.6	9	10
Brazoria, Tex. PMSA	169,587	191,707	22,120	13.0	N.A.	N.A.
Galveston–Texas City, Tex. PMSA	195,738	217,399	21,661	11.1	N.A.	N.A.
Houston, Tex. PMSA	2,753,155	3,322,025	568,870	20.7	N.A.	N.A.
Huntington–Ashland, W.Va.–Ky.–Ohio MSA	311,350	288,189	–23,161	–7.4	97	115
Huntsville, Ala. MSA	242,971	293,047	50,076	20.6	144	141
Indianapolis, Ind. MSA	1,305,911	1,380,491	74,580	5.7	30	31
Iowa City, Iowa MSA	81,717	96,119	14,402	17.6	273	265
Jackson, Mich. MSA	151,495	149,756	–1,739	–1.1	177	191
Jackson, Miss. MSA	362,038	395,396	33,358	9.2	92	92
Jackson, Tenn. MSA	74,548	77,982	3,436	4.6	277	278
Jacksonville, Fla. MSA	722,252	906,727	184,475	25.5	50	47
Jacksonville, N.C. MSA	112,784	149,838	37,054	32.9	229	190
Jamestown–Dunkirk, N.Y. MSA	146,925	141,895	–5,030	–3.4	183	202
Janesville–Beloit, Wis. MSA	139,420	139,510	90	0.1	188	203
Johnson City–Kingsport–Bristol, Tenn.–Va. MSA	433,638	436,047	2,409	0.6	76	81
Johnstown, Pa. MSA	264,506	241,247	–23,259	–8.8	121	138
Joplin, Mo. MSA	127,513	134,910	7,397	5.8	209	207
Kalamazoo–Battle Creek, Mich. MSA	420,771	429,453	8,682	2.1	136	146
Kankakee, Ill. MSA	102,926	96,255	–6,671	–6.5	246	264
Kansas City, Mo.–Kans. MSA	1,449,380	1,582,875	133,495	9.2	25	25
Killeen–Temple, Tex. MSA	214,587	255,301	40,714	19.0	135	131
Knoxville, Tenn. MSA	546,488	585,960	39,472	7.2	60	65
Kokomo, Ind. MSA	103,715	96,946	–6,769	–6.5	243	263
La Crosse, Wis.–Minn. MSA	109,438	116,401	6,963	6.4	262	262
Lafayette, La. MSA	330,786	344,953	14,167	4.3	150	153
Lafayette, Ind. MSA	153,247	161,572	8,325	5.4	215	218
Lake Charles, La. MSA	167,223	168,134	911	0.5	165	175
Lakeland–Winter Haven, Fla. MSA	321,652	405,382	83,730	26.0	101	87
Lancaster, Pa. MSA	362,346	422,822	60,476	16.7	91	85
Lansing–East Lansing, Mich. MSA	419,750	432,674	12,924	3.1	81	83
Laredo, Tex. MSA	99,258	133,239	33,981	34.2	252	208
Las Cruces, N.Mex. MSA	96,340	135,510	39,170	40.7	256	206
Las Vegas, Nev.–Ariz. MSA	528,000	852,737	324,737	61.5	72	53
Lawrence, Kans. MSA	67,640	81,798	14,158	20.9	282	275
Lawton, Okla. MSA	112,456	111,486	–970	–0.9	231	250
Lewiston–Auburn, Maine MSA	89,265	93,679	4,414	4.9	268	269
Lexington, Ky. MSA	370,900	405,936	35,036	9.4	103	106
Lima, Ohio MSA	154,795	154,340	–455	–0.3	175	184
Lincoln, Nebr. MSA	192,884	213,641	20,757	10.8	147	151
Little Rock–North Little Rock, Ark. MSA	474,463	513,117	38,654	8.1	71	72
Longview–Marshall, Tex. MSA	180,355	193,801	13,446	7.5	176	176
Los Angeles–Riverside–Orange County, Calif. CMSA	11,497,548	14,531,529	3,033,981	26.4	2	2
Anaheim–Santa Ana, Calif. PMSA	1,932,921	2,410,556	477,635	24.7%	N.A.	N.A.
Los Angeles–Long Beach, Calif. PMSA	7,477,238	8,863,164	1,385,926	18.5	N.A.	N.A.
Riverside–San Bernardino, Calif. PMSA	1,558,215	2,588,793	1,030,578	66.1	N.A.	N.A.
Ventura, Calif. PMSA	529,174	669,016	139,842	26.4	N.A.	N.A.
Louisville, Ky.–Ind. MSA	953,520	948,829	–4,691	–0.5	38	43
Lubbock, Tex. MSA	211,651	222,636	10,985	5.2	137	147
Lynchburg, Va. MSA	182,207	193,928	11,721	6.4	187	200
Macon, Ga. MSA	272,945	290,909	17,964	6.6	122	120
Madison, Wis. MSA	323,545	367,085	43,540	13.5	100	99
Manchester, N.H. MSA	129,305	147,809	18,504	14.3	205	193
Mansfield, Ohio MSA	181,280	174,007	–7,273	–4.0	202	223
McAllen–Edinburg–Mission, Tex. MSA	283,323	383,545	100,222	35.4	110	95
Medford–Ashland, Oreg. MSA	132,456	146,389	13,933	10.5	200	196
Melbourne–Titusville–Palm Bay, Fla. MSA	272,959	398,978	126,019	46.2	116	89
Memphis, Tenn.–Ark.–Miss. MSA	938,777	1,007,306	68,529	7.3	40	41
Merced, Calif. MSA	134,558	178,403	43,845	32.6	198	168
Miami–Fort Lauderdale, Fla. CMSA	2,643,766	3,192,582	548,816	20.8	12	11
Fort Lauderdale–Hollywood–Pompano Beach, Fla. PMSA	1,018,257	1,255,488	237,231	23.3	N.A.	N.A.
Miami, Fla. PMSA	1,625,509	1,937,094	311,585	19.2	N.A.	N.A.
Midland, Tex. MSA	82,636	106,611	23,975	29.0	272	255
Milwaukee–Racine, Wis. CMSA	1,570,152	1,607,183	37,031	2.4	23	24
Milwaukee–Waukesha, Wis. PMSA	1,397,020	1,432,149	35,129	2.5	N.A.	N.A.
Racine, Wis. PMSA	173,132	175,034	1,902	1.1	N.A.	N.A.
Minneapolis–St. Paul, Minn.–Wis. MSA	2,198,190	2,538,834	340,644	15.5	17	16
Mobile, Ala. MSA	443,536	476,923	33,387	7.5	74	78
Modesto, Calif. MSA	265,900	370,522	104,622	39.3	120	97
Monroe, La. MSA	139,241	142,191	2,950	2.1	190	201
Montgomery, Ala. MSA	272,687	292,517	19,830	7.3	117	117
Muncie, Ind. MSA	128,587	119,659	–8,928	–6.9	206	234
Muskegon, Mich. MSA	157,589	158,983	1,394	0.9	173	181
Naples, Fla. MSA	85,971	152,099	66,128	76.9	266	186
Nashville, Tenn. MSA	850,505	985,026	134,521	15.8	45	40
New Bedford, Mass. MSA	166,699	175,641	8,942	5.4	166	170
New Haven–Meriden, Conn. MSA	500,642	530,180	29,718	5.9	68	69
New London–Norwich, Conn.–R.I. MSA	272,900	290,734	17,834	6.5	125	126
New Orleans, La. MSA	1,304,212	1,285,270	–18,942	–1.5	27	32
New York–Newark, N.Y.–N.J.–Pa. PMSA	16,448,157	16,937,653	489,496	3.0	1	1
Bergen–Passaic, N.J. PMSA	1,292,970	1,278,440	–14,530	–1.1	N.A.	N.A.
Bridgeport–Milford, Conn. PMSA	438,557	443,722	5,165	1.2	N.A.	N.A.
Danbury, Conn. PMSA	170,369	187,867	17,498	10.3	N.A.	N.A.
Jersey City, N.J. PMSA	556,972	553,099	–3,873	–0.7	N.A.	N.A.
Middlesex–Somerset–Hunterdon, N.J. PMSA	886,383	1,019,835	133,452	15.1	N.A.	N.A.
Monmouth–Ocean, N.J. PMSA	849,211	986,327	137,116	16.1	N.A.	N.A.
Nassau–Suffolk, N.Y. PMSA	2,605,813	2,609,212	3,399	0.1	N.A.	N.A.
New York, N.Y. PMSA	8,274,961	8,546,846	271,885	3.3	N.A.	N.A.
Newark, N.J. PMSA	1,879,147	1,824,321	–54,826	–2.9	N.A.	N.A.
Norwalk, Conn. PMSA	126,692	127,378	686	0.5	N.A.	N.A.
Orange County, N.Y. PMSA	259,603	307,647	48,044	18.5	N.A.	N.A.
Stamford–Norwalk, Conn. PMSA	325,546	329,935	4,389	1.3	N.A.	N.A.
Norfolk–Virginia Beach–Newport News, Va.–N.C. MSA	1,200,998	1,443,244	242,246	20.2	31	28
Ocala, Fla. MSA	122,488	194,833	72,345	59.1	213	157
Odessa–Midland, Tex. MSA	198,010	225,545	27,535	13.9	224	236
Oklahoma City, Okla. MSA	860,969	958,839	97,870	11.4	43	42
Olympia, Wash. MSA	124,264	161,238	36,974	29.8	211	178
Omaha, Nebr.–Iowa MSA	605,419	639,580	34,161	5.6	57	63
Orlando, Fla. MSA	804,774	1,224,852	420,078	52.2	51	37
Owensboro, Ky. MSA	85,949	87,189	1,240	1.4	267	270

Metropolitan statistical area	1980	1990	Change 1980–90 Number	Change 1980–90 Percent	CMSA/MSA rank 1980	CMSA/MSA rank 1990
Panama City, Fla. MSA	97,740	126,994	29,254	29.9%	254	222
Parkersburg–Marietta, W.Va.–Ohio MSA	157,893	149,169	–8,724	–5.5	172	192
Pascagoula, Miss. MSA	118,015	115,243	–2,772	–2.3	221	243
Pensacola, Fla. MSA	289,782	344,406	54,624	18.9	109	107
Peoria–Pekin, Ill. MSA	365,864	339,172	–26,692	–7.3	90	108
Philadelphia–Wilmington–Atlantic City, Pa.–N.J.–Del.–Md. CMSA	5,649,031	5,892,937	243,906	4.3	4	5
Philadelphia, Pa.–N.J. PMSA	4,781,235	4,922,175	140,940	2.9	N.A.	N.A.
Vineland–Millville–Bridgeton, N.J. PMSA	132,866	138,053	5,187	3.9	N.A.	N.A.
Trenton, N.J. PMSA	307,863	325,824	17,961	5.8	N.A.	N.A.
Wilmington–Newark, Del.–Md. PMSA	458,545	513,293	54,748	11.9	N.A.	N.A.
Phoenix–Mesa, Ariz. MSA	1,600,093	2,238,480	638,387	39.9	24	20
Pine Bluff, Ark. MSA	90,718	85,487	–5,231	–5.8	263	272
Pittsburgh, Pa. MSA	2,571,223	2,394,811	–176,412	–6.9	13	19
Beaver County, Pa. PMSA	204,441	186,093	–18,348	–9.0	N.A.	N.A.
Pittsburgh, Pa. PMSA	2,218,870	2,056,705	–162,165	–7.3	N.A.	N.A.
Pittsfield, Mass. MSA	93,871	88,695	–5,176	–5.5	271	277
Portland, Maine MSA	198,277	221,095	22,818	11.5	145	150
Portland–Salem, Oreg.–Wash. CMSA	1,583,518	1,793,476	209,958	13.3	N.A.	N.A.
Portland–Vancouver, Oreg.–Wash. PMSA	1,333,623	1,515,452	181,829	13.6	26	27
Portland, Oreg. PMSA	1,105,750	1,239,842	134,092	12.1	N.A.	N.A.
Vancouver, Wash. PMSA	192,227	238,053	45,826	23.8	N.A.	N.A.
Portsmouth–Dover–Rochester, N.H.–Maine MSA	190,938	223,578	32,640	17.1	148	145
Poughkeepsie, N.Y MSA	245,055	259,462	14,407	5.9	129	130
Providence–Fall River–Warwick, R.I.–Mass. MSA	1,076,557	1,134,350	57,793	5.4	33	35
Fall River, Mass.–R.I. PMSA	157,222	157,272	50	0.0	N.A.	N.A.
Pawtucket–Woonsocket–Attleboro, R.I.–Mass. PMSA	307,403	329,384	21,981	7.2	N.A.	N.A.
Providence, R.I. PMSA	618,514	654,854	36,340	5.9	N.A.	N.A.
Provo–Orem, Utah MSA	218,106	263,590	45,484	20.9	134	128
Pueblo, Colo. MSA	125,972	123,051	–2,921	–2.3	210	226
Raleigh–Durham–Chapel Hill, N.C. MSA	664,788	855,545	190,757	28.7	61	54
Rapid City, S.Dak. MSA	70,361	81,343	10,982	15.6	279	276
Reading, Pa. MSA	312,509	336,523	24,014	7.7	104	109
Redding, Calif. MSA	115,613	147,036	31,423	27.2	223	194
Reno, Nev. MSA	193,623	254,667	61,044	31.5	146	132
Richland–Kennewick–Pasco, Wash. MSA	144,469	150,033	5,564	3.9	184	189
Richmond–Petersburg, Va. MSA	761,311	865,640	104,329	13.7	48	49
Roanoke, Va. MSA	220,393	224,477	4,084	1.9	133	144
Rochester, Minn. MSA	92,006	106,470	14,464	15.7	261	256
Rochester, N.Y. MSA	1,030,630	1,062,470	31,840	3.1	37	39
Rockford, Ill. MSA	325,852	329,676	3,824	1.2	112	118
Sacramento–Yolo, Calif. CMSA	1,099,814	1,481,102	381,288	34.7	32	26
Saginaw–Bay City–Midland, Mich. MSA	421,518	399,320	–22,198	–5.3	79	88
Salem, Oreg. PMSA	249,895	278,024	28,129	11.3	126	122
Salinas, Calif. MSA	290,444	355,660	65,216	22.5	108	103
Salt Lake City–Ogden, Utah MSA	910,222	1,072,227	162,005	17.8	41	38
San Angelo, Tex. MSA	84,784	98,458	13,674	16.1	269	261
San Antonio, Tex. MSA	1,088,881	1,324,749	235,868	21.7	34	30
San Diego, Calif. MSA	1,861,846	2,498,016	636,170	34.2	19	15
San Francisco–Oakland–San Jose, Calif. CMSA	5,367,900	6,253,311	885,411	16.5	5	4
Oakland, Calif. PMSA	1,761,710	2,082,914	321,204	18.2	N.A.	N.A.
San Francisco, Calif. PMSA	1,488,895	1,603,678	114,783	7.7	N.A.	N.A.
San Jose, Calif. PMSA	1,295,071	1,497,577	202,506	15.6	N.A.	N.A.
Santa Cruz–Watsonville, Calif. PMSA	188,141	229,734	41,593	22.1	N.A.	N.A.
Santa Rosa, Calif. PMSA	299,681	388,222	88,541	29.5	N.A.	N.A.
Vallejo–Fairfield–Napa, Calif. PMSA	334,402	451,186	116,784	34.9	N.A.	N.A

Metropolitan statistical area	1980	1990	Change 1980–90 Number	Change 1980–90 Percent	CMSA/MSA rank 1980	CMSA/MSA rank 1990
Santa Barbara–Santa Maria–Lompoc, Calif. PMSA	298,694	369,608	70,914	23.7%	106	98
Santa Fe, N.Mex. MSA	93,118	117,043	23,925	25.7	260	240
Sarasota–Bradenton, Fla. MSA	350,696	489,483	138,787	39.6	143	123
Savannah, Ga. MSA	230,728	258,060	27,332	11.8	132	137
Scranton–Wilkes-Barre–Hazleton, Pa. MSA	659,387	638,466	–20,921	–3.2	49	55
Seattle–Tacoma–Bremerton, Wash. CMSA	2,408,749	2,970,328	561,579	23.3	18	14
Seattle–Bellevue–Everett, Wash. PMSA	1,651,666	2,033,156	381,490	23.1	N.A.	N.A.
Tacoma, Wash. PMSA	485,667	586,203	100,536	20.7	N.A.	N.A.
Sharon, Pa. MSA	128,299	121,003	–7,296	–5.7	208	231
Sheboygan, Wis. MSA	100,935	103,877	2,942	2.9	248	257
Sherman–Denison, Tex. MSA	89,796	95,021	5,225	5.8	264	267
Shreveport–Bossier City, La. MSA	376,789	376,330	–459	—	98	111
Sioux City, Iowa–Nebr. MSA	117,457	115,018	–2,439	–2.1	222	244
Sioux Falls, S.Dak. MSA	123,377	139,236	15,859	12.9	239	224
South Bend, Ind. MSA	241,617	247,052	5,435	2.2	130	135
Spokane, Wash. MSA	341,835	361,364	19,529	5.7	96	101
Springfield, Ill. MSA	187,770	189,550	1,780	0.9	151	161
Springfield, Mass. MSA	569,777	587,884	18,107	3.2	66	70
Springfield, Mo. MSA	228,118	264,346	36,228	15.9	139	139
St. Cloud, Minn. MSA	133,348	148,976	15,628	11.7	168	159
St. Joseph, Mo. MSA	101,868	97,715	–4,153	–4.1	265	274
St. Louis, Mo.–Ill. MSA	2,414,061	2,492,525	78,464	3.3	14	17
State College, Pa. MSA	112,760	123,786	11,026	9.8	230	225
Steubenville–Weirton, Ohio–W.Va. MSA	163,734	142,523	–21,211	–13.0	167	199
Stockton–Lodi, Calif. MSA	347,342	480,628	133,286	38.4	94	76
Syracuse, N.Y. MSA	722,865	742,177	19,312	2.7	53	61
Tallahassee, Fla. MSA	190,329	233,598	43,269	22.7	149	142
Tampa–St. Petersburg–Clearwater, Fla. MSA	1,613,600	2,067,959	454,359	28.2	22	21
Terre Haute, Ind. MSA	155,476	147,585	–7,891	–5.1	194	216
Texarkana, Tex.–Texarkana, Ark. MSA	113,067	120,132	7,065	6.2	228	233
Toledo, Ohio MSA	616,864	614,128	–2,736	–0.4	55	64
Topeka, Kans. MSA	154,916	160,976	6,060	3.9	174	179
Tucson, Ariz. MSA	531,443	666,880	135,437	25.5	64	60
Tulsa, Okla. MSA	657,173	708,954	51,781	7.9	52	56
Tuscaloosa, Ala. MSA	137,541	150,522	12,981	9.4	192	188
Tyler, Tex. MSA	128,366	151,309	22,943	17.9	207	187
Utica–Rome, N.Y. MSA	320,180	316,633	–3,547	–1.1	102	113
Victoria, Tex. MSA	68,807	74,361	5,554	8.1	280	280
Visalia–Tulare–Porterville, Calif. MSA	245,738	311,921	66,183	26.9	128	116
Waco, Tex. MSA	170,755	189,123	18,368	10.8	162	162
Washington, D.C.–Md.–Va.–W.Va. PMSA	3,477,972	4,223,485	745,513	21.4	8	8
Waterbury, Conn. MSA	190,812	205,811	14,999	7.9	141	149
Waterloo–Cedar Falls, Iowa MSA	137,961	123,798	–14,163	–10.3	170	195
Wausau, Wis. MSA	111,270	115,400	4,130	3.7	234	242
West Palm Beach–Boca Raton, Fla. MSA	576,758	863,518	286,760	49.7	58	50
Wheeling, W.Va.–Ohio MSA	185,566	159,301	–26,265	–14.2	152	180
Wichita Falls, Tex. MSA	128,348	130,351	2,003	1.6	216	228
Wichita, Kans. MSA	442,401	485,270	42,869	9.7	75	75
Williamsport, Pa. MSA	118,416	118,710	294	0.2	220	237
Wilmington, N.C. MSA	103,471	120,284	16,813	16.2	244	232
Worcester, Mass. MSA	402,918	436,905	33,987	8.4	85	80
Yakima, Wash. MSA	172,508	188,823	16,315	9.5	159	163
York, Pa. MSA	312,963	339,574	26,611	8.5	87	86
Youngstown–Warren, Ohio MSA	644,922	600,895	–44,027	–6.8	65	74
Yuba City, Calif. MSA	101,979	122,643	20,664	20.3	247	227
Yuma, Ariz. MSA	76,205	106,895	30,690	40.3	276	254

Note: CMSA = consolidated metropolitan statistical area; MSA = metropolitan statistical area; PMSA = primary metropolitan statistical area; N.A. = not applicable. **Source:** U.S. Bureau of the Census release, 1991.

TOP 25 METROPOLITAN STATISTICAL AREAS BY POPULATION, 1980–90

Metropolitan statistical area	Population 1980	Population 1990	Change 1980–90 Number	Change 1980–90 Percent
1. New York–Northern New Jersey–Long Island, N.Y.–N.J.–Conn. CMSA	17,539,532	18,087,251	547,719	3.1%
2. Los Angeles–Anaheim–Riverside, Calif. CMSA	11,497,549	14,531,529	3,033,980	26.4
3. Chicago–Gary–Lake County, Ill.–Ind.–Wis. CMSA	7,937,290	8,065,633	128,343	1.6
4. San Francisco–Oakland–San Jose, Calif. CMSA	5,367,900	6,253,311	885,411	16.5
5. Philadelphia–Wilmington–Trenton, Pa.–N.J.–Del.–Md. CMSA	5,680,509	5,899,345	218,836	3.9
6. Detroit–Ann Arbor, Mich. CMSA	4,752,764	4,665,236	–87,528	–1.8
7. Boston–Lawrence–Salem, Mass.–N.H. CMSA	3,971,792	4,171,643	199,851	5.0
8. Washington, D.C.–Md.–Va. MSA	3,250,921	3,923,574	672,653	20.7
9. Dallas–Fort Worth, Tex. CMSA	2,930,568	3,885,415	954,847	32.6
10. Houston–Galveston–Brazoria, Tex. CMSA	3,099,942	3,711,043	611,101	19.7
11. Miami–Fort Lauderdale, Fla. CMSA	2,643,766	3,192,592	548,816	20.8
12. Atlanta, Ga. MSA	2,138,136	2,833,511	695,375	32.5%
13. Cleveland–Akron–Lorain, Ohio CMSA	2,834,062	2,759,823	–74,239	–2.6
14. Seattle–Tacoma, Wash. CMSA	2,093,285	2,559,164	465,879	22.3
15. San Diego, Calif. MSA	1,861,846	2,498,016	636,170	34.2
16. Minneapolis–St. Paul, Minn.–Wis. MSA	2,137,133	2,464,124	326,991	15.3
17. St. Louis, Mo.–Ill. MSA	2,376,968	2,444,099	67,131	2.8
18. Baltimore, Md. MSA	2,199,497	2,382,172	182,675	8.3
19. Pittsburgh–Beaver Valley, Pa. CMSA	2,423,311	2,242,798	–180,513	–7.4
20. Phoenix, Ariz. MSA	1,509,175	2,122,101	612,926	40.6
21. Tampa–St. Petersburg–Clearwater, Fla. MSA	1,613,600	2,067,959	454,359	28.2
22. Denver–Boulder, Colo.	1,618,461	1,848,319	229,858	14.2
23. Cincinnati–Hamilton, Ohio–Ky.–Ind. CMSA	1,660,257	1,744,124	83,867	5.1
24. Milwaukee–Racine, Wis. CMSA	1,570,152	1,607,183	37,031	2.4
25. Kansas City, Mo.–Kans. MSA	1,433,464	1,566,280	132,816	9.3

Note: CMSA = consolidated metropolitan statistical area; MSA = metropolitan statistical area. **Source:** U.S. Bureau of the Census release, 1991.

25 FASTEST-GROWING MSAs, 1980–90

Metropolitan statistical area	Population 1980	Population 1990	Change 1980–90 Number	Change 1980–90 Percent
1. Naples, Fla. MSA	85,971	152,099	66,128	76.9%
2. Fort Pierce, Fla. MSA	151,196	251,071	99,875	66.1
3. Fort Myers–Cape Coral, Fla. MSA	205,266	335,113	129,847	63.3
4. Las Vegas, Nev. MSA	463,087	741,459	278,372	60.1
5. Ocala, Fla. MSA	122,488	194,833	72,345	59.1
6. Orlando, Fla. MSA	699,904	1,072,748	372,844	53.3
7. West Palm Beach–Boca Raton–Delray Beach, Fla. MSA	576,758	863,518	286,760	49.7
8. Melbourne–Titusville–Palm Bay, Fla. MSA	272,959	398,978	126,019	46.2
9. Austin, Tex. MSA	536,688	781,572	244,884	45.6
10. Daytona Beach, Fla. MSA	258,762	370,712	111,950	43.3
11. Bradenton, Fla. MSA	148,445	211,707	63,262	42.6
12. Las Cruces, N.Mex. MSA	96,340	135,510	39,170	40.7
13. Phoenix, Ariz. MSA	1,509,175	2,122,101	612,926	40.6
14. Yuma, Ariz MSA	76,205	106,895	30,690	40.3
15. Modesto, Calif. MSA	265,900	370,522	104,622	39.3
16. Stockton, Calif. MSA	347,342	480,628	133,286	38.4
17. Sarasota, Fla. MSA	202,251	277,776	75,525	37.3
18. McAllen–Edinburg–Mission, Tex. MSA	283,323	383,545	100,222	35.4
19. Bakersfield, Calif. MSA	403,089	543,477	140,388	34.8
20. Sacramento, Calif. MSA	1,099,814	1,481,102	381,288	34.7
21. San Diego, Calif. MSA	1,861,846	2,498,016	636,170	34.2
22. Laredo, Tex. MSA	99,258	133,239	33,981	34.2
23. Jacksonville, N.C. MSA	112,784	149,838	37,054	32.9
24. Dallas–Fort Worth, Tex. CMSA	2,930,568	3,885,415	954,847	32.6
25. Merced, Calif. MSA	134,558	178,403	43,845	32.6

Note: CMSA = consolidated metropolitan statistical area; MSA = metropolitan statistical area. **Source:** U.S. Bureau of the Census release, 1991.

25 FASTEST-DECLINING MSAs, 1980–90

Metropolitan statistical area	Population 1980	Population 1990	Change 1980- Number	Change 1980- Percent
1. Casper, Wyo. MSA	71,856	61,226	–10,630	–14.8%
2. Wheeling, W.Va.–Ohio MSA	185,566	159,031	–26,265	–14.2
3. Steubenville–Weirton, Ohio–W.Va. MSA	163,734	142,523	–21,211	–13.0
4. Decatur, Ill. MSA	131,375	117,206	–14,169	–10.8
5. Duluth, Minn.–Wis. MSA	266,650	239,971	–26,679	–10.0
6. Waterloo–Cedar Falls, Iowa MSA	162,781	146,611	–16,170	–9.9
7. Enid, Okla. MSA	62,820	56,735	–6,085	–9.7
8. Davenport–Rock Island–Moline, Iowa–Ill. MSA	384,749	350,861	–33,888	–8.8
9. Johnstown, Pa. MSA	264,506	241,247	–23,259	–8.8
10. Dubuque, Iowa MSA	93,745	86,403	–7,342	–7.8
11. Pittsburgh–Beaver Valley, Pa. CMSA	2,423,311	2,242,798	–180,513	–7.4
12. Youngstown–Warren, Ohio MSA	531,350	492,619	–38,731	–7.3
13. Peoria, Ill. MSA	365,864	339,172	–26,692	–7.3
14. Huntington–Ashland, W.Va.–Ky.–Ohio MSA	336,410	312,529	–23,881	–7.1
15. Charleston, W.Va. MSA	269,595	250,454	–19,141	–7.1
16. Muncie, Ind. MSA	128,587	119,659	–8,928	–6.9
17. Kokomo, Ind. MSA	103,715	96,946	–6,769	–6.5
18. Kankakee, Ill. MSA	102,926	96,255	–6,671	–6.5
19. Anderson, Ind. MSA	139,336	130,669	–8,667	–6.2
20. Benton Harbor, Mich. MSA	171,276	161,378	–9,898	–5.8
21. Pine Bluff, Ark. MSA	90,718	85,487	–5,231	–5.8
22. Sharon, Pa. MSA	128,299	121,003	–7,296	–5.7
23. Cumberland, Md.–W.Va.	107,782	101,643	–6,139	–5.7
24. Parkersburg–Marietta, W.Va.–Ohio MSA	157,893	149,169	–8,724	–5.5
25. St. Joseph, Mo. MSA	87,888	83,803	–4,805	–5.5

Note: CMSA = consolidated metropolitan statistical area; MSA = metropolitan statistical area. **Source:** U.S. Bureau of the Census release, 1991.

Counties in America

In 1990 there were 3,141 counties in the United States. While 50 percent of Americans live in cities, almost every American lives in a county. Counties were originally the creation of state governments, which saw them as the local arm of state authority, with special responsibility for rural areas. Counties were intended more for the administrative convenience of the state than to meet the immediate needs of county residents and were not designed to have the intimate relationship with or understanding of the needs of localities theoretically characteristic of municipalities. But most states have loosened the reins on county governments in recent years, giving them more authority to meet the needs of population centers that have pushed beyond municipal limits. (Note that in Louisiana, counties are called parishes, and in Alaska they are known as boroughs. The five boroughs of New York City are counties.)

County Government Finances

Expenditures County governments spent $144.2 billion on revenues of $142.1 billion in fiscal year 1990–91. Among the major programs

THE 50 LARGEST U.S. COUNTIES, 1990

Rank/County	Population 1990	Population 1980	Change 1980–90 Number	Change 1980–90 Percent	Pop. Rank 1980
1. Los Angeles County, Calif.	8,863,164	7,477,238	1,385,926	18.5%	1
2. Cook County, Ill.	5,105,067	5,253,628	−148,561	−2.8	2
3. Harris County, Tex.	2,818,199	2,409,547	408,652	17.0	3
4. San Diego County, Calif.	2,498,016	1,861,846	636,170	34.2	8
5. Orange County, Calif.	2,410,556	1,932,921	477,635	24.7	6
6. Kings County, N.Y.	2,300,664	2,231,028	69,636	3.1	5
7. Maricopa County, Ariz.	2,122,101	1,509,175	612,926	40.6	12
8. Wayne County, Mich.	2,111,687	2,337,843	−226,156	−9.7	4
9. Queens County, N.Y.	1,951,598	1,891,325	60,273	3.2	7
10. Dade County, Fla.	1,937,094	1,625,509	311,585	19.2	10
11. Dallas County, Tex.	1,852,810	1,556,419	296,391	19.0	11
12. Philadelphia County, Pa.	1,585,577	1,688,210	−102,633	−6.1	9
13. King County, Wash.	1,507,319	1,269,898	237,421	18.7	20
14. Santa Clara County, Calif.	1,497,577	1,295,071	202,506	15.6	18
15. New York County, N.Y.	1,487,536	1,428,285	59,251	4.1	15
16. San Bernardino County, Calif.	1,418,380	895,016	523,364	58.5	30
17. Cuyahoga County, Ohio	1,412,140	1,498,400	−86,260	−5.8	13
18. Middlesex County, Mass.	1,398,468	1,367,034	31,434	2.3	16
19. Allegheny County, Pa.	1,336,449	1,450,195	−113,746	−7.8	14
20. Suffolk County, N.Y.	1,321,864	1,284,231	37,633	2.9	19
21. Nassau County, N.Y.	1,287,348	1,321,582	−34,234	−2.6	17
22. Alameda County, Calif.	1,279,182	1,105,379	173,803	15.7	22
23. Broward County, Fla.	1,255,488	1,018,257	237,231	23.3	23
24. Bronx County, N.Y.	1,203,789	1,168,972	34,817	3.0	21
25. Bexar County, Tex.	1,185,394	988,971	196,423	19.9	26
26. Riverside County, Calif.	1,170,413	663,199	507,214	76.5	52
27. Tarrant County, Tex.	1,170,103	860,880	309,223	35.9	34
28. Oakland County, Mich.	1,083,592	1,011,793	71,799	7.1	25
29. Sacramento County, Calif.	1,041,219	783,381	257,838	32.9	40
30. Hennepin County, Minn.	1,032,431	941,411	91,020	9.7	29
31. St. Louis County, Mo.	993,529	974,180	19,349	2.0	27
32. Erie County, N.Y.	968,532	1,015,472	−46,940	−4.6	24
33. Franklin County, Ohio	961,437	869,126	92,311	10.6	32
34. Milwaukee County, Wis.	959,275	964,988	−5,713	−0.6	28
35. Westchester County, N.Y.	874,866	866,599	8,267	1.0	33
36. Hamilton County, Ohio	866,228	873,203	−6,975	−0.8	31
37. Palm Beach County, Fla.	863,518	576,758	286,760	49.7	70
38. Hartford County, Conn.	851,783	807,766	44,017	5.4	37
39. Pinellas County, Fla.	851,659	728,531	123,128	16.9	45
40. Honolulu County, Hawaii	836,231	762,565	73,666	9.7	43
41. Hillsborough County, Fla.	834,054	646,939	187,115	28.9	57
42. Fairfield County, Conn.	827,645	807,143	20,502	2.5	38
43. Shelby County, Tenn.	826,330	777,113	49,217	6.3	41
44. Bergen County, N.J.	825,380	845,385	−20,005	−2.4	36
45. Fairfax County, Va.	818,584	595,754	222,830	37.4	66
46. New Haven County, Conn.	804,219	761,325	42,894	5.6	44
47. Contra Costa County, Calif.	803,732	656,331	147,401	22.5	54
48. Marion County, Ind.	797,159	765,233	31,926	4.2	42
49. DuPage County, Ill.	781,666	658,858	122,808	18.6	53
50. Essex County, N.J.	778,206	851,304	−73,098	−8.6	35

Source: U.S. Bureau of the Census Press Release, 1991.

counties spent their money on were public welfare, education, health, and transportation. Counties also have responsibilities involving law enforcement, jails and detention facilities, electoral and judicial administration, public record-keeping, tax assessment and collection, issuance of licenses, building and upkeep of roads and highways, and programs to promote agriculture and rural areas, public health, and welfare. Many counties also run community colleges.

Revenues The primary source of funds for counties in 1990–91 was intergovernmental aid: monies received from other governments mostly in the form of grants or shared revenues. Intergovernmental aid accounted for $49.9 billion, or 35.9% of all county revenues. The second-largest source of county funds was property taxes, which made up $38.6 billion, or 27.2% of the total. Sales, income, and other taxes contributed 9.5% to county coffers.

Most of the intergovernmental aid received by counties was contributed by state governments, which accounted for $44.5 billion, or 89% of all intergovernmental aid. In 1986 the Reagan administration ended the Federal General Revenue Sharing program, established in 1972 to distribute funds directly to county governments to meet locally identified needs. The end of federal revenue sharing and cutbacks in other federal programs aiding local governments

SUMMARY OF COUNTY GOVERNMENT FINANCES, 1990–91

Item	Amount 1990–91 (millions)	Percent distribution 1990–91	Percent change over 1989–90
REVENUES			
Revenue, total	**$142,107**	**—**	**6.9%**
General revenue	137,223	100.0%	7.3
Intergovernmental revenue	49,863	36.3	8.2
From state governments	44,535	32.5	7.7
General local government support	4,991	3.6	5.5
From federal government	3,058	2.2	10.0
From local governments	2,271	1.7	16.6
General revenue from own sources	87,360	63.7	6.8
Taxes	52,154	38.0	7.0
Property	38,610	28.1	8.1
General sales	7,950	5.8	4.7
Selective sales	1,750	1.3	10.5
Income	1,513	1.1	3.3
Other	2,330	1.7	–2.3
Charges and miscellaneous	35,206	25.7	6.5
Current charges	21,889	16.0	9.1
Sewerage	1,256	0.9	7.8
Hospitals	9,691	7.1	6.5
Education	1,100	0.8	11.9
Interest earnings	8,959	6.5	–1.0
Special assessments	696	0.5	4.5
Sale of property	141	0.1	2.2
Other and unallocable	3,523	2.6	11.6
Utility revenue	1,613	100.0	8.5
Electric power	130	8.1	21.5
Water supply	1,323	82.0	8.1
Transit system	147	9.1	4.3
Gas supply	14	0.9	—
Liquor store revenue	287	—	11.2
Employment retirement	2,984	—	–10.0
EXPENDITURES			
Expenditure, total	**$144,203**	**100.0%**	**9.1%**
Expenditure by function:			
General expenditure	139,267	100.0	9.1
Intergovernmental expenditure	6,224	4.5	–3.5
Direct general expenditure	133,043	95.5	9.8
Capital outlay	15,332	11.0	13.8
Other	117,711	84.5	9.3
Education services:			
Education	19,821	14.2	7.8
Libraries	1,304	0.9	11.3
Social services and income maintenance:			
Public welfare	20,171	14.5	11.4
Cash assistance payments	9,016	6.5	11.3
Medical vendor payments	863	0.6	12.8
Other	10,291	7.4	11.3
Hospitals	$14,164	10.2%	8.8%
Own	13,568	9.7	9.3
Other	597	0.4	–0.7
Health	9,362	6.7	6.5
Transportation:			
Highways	10,246	7.4	8.8
Air transportation	1,606	1.2	31.9
Parking facilities	69	—	19.0
Water transport and terminals	79	0.1	–18.6
Transit subsidies	610	0.4	–7.9
Public safety:			
Police protection	7,382	5.3	10.3
Fire protection	1,822	1.3	10.6
Correction	7,447	5.3	13.0
Protective inspection and regulation	441	0.3	6.5
Environment and housing:			
Sewerage	2,404	1.7	13.6
Solid waste management	2,386	1.7	18.5
Parks and recreation	2,830	2.0	13.8
Housing and community development	1,214	0.9	13.8
Natural resources	1,371	1.0	4.3
Government administration:			
Financial administration	3,613	2.6	7.4
Judicial and legal	7,052	5.1	9.8
General public buildings	2,317	1.7	6.2
Other	2,896	2.1	6.2
Interest on general debt	8,223	5.9	3.1
General expenditure not elsewhere classified	10,435	7.5	7.9
Utility expenditure	3,012	100.0	6.6
Electric power	136	4.5	3.0
Water supply	2,055	68.2	3.6
Transit system	808	26.8	16.3
Gas supply	13	0.4	–13.3
Liquor store expenditure	250	—	11.6
Employee retirement	1,673	—	9.0
Exhibit: Salaries and wages	50,992	35.4	8.9
INDEBTEDNESS AND DEBT TRANSACTIONS			
Debt outstanding at end of fiscal year	**$121,755**	**100.0%**	**4.9%**
Long-term debt outstanding	117,041	96.1	3.7
Short-term debt outstanding	4,714	3.9	46.6
Long-term debt issued	11,589	100.0	–11.8
Long-term debt retired	8,470	100.0	–1.9
CASH AND SECURITY HOLDINGS			
Total, end of fiscal year	**$138,217**	**100.0%**	**2.3%**
Employment retirement	30,821	22.3	8.5
Other	107,395	77.7	0.6

Source: U.S. Bureau of the Census, *County Government Finances in 1991* (1992).

have forced state governments to find new sources of funds for local governments to continue providing needed services. This has been done mostly through increases in direct financial assistance to the counties by the states and by the states granting counties more authority to raise local taxes.

According to a study by the National Association of Counties, 39% of the country's 443 counties with populations greater than 100,000 faced budget deficits in 1991. The average budget shortfall was $8.3 mil. with the worst hit being Philadelphia Co. ($219 million), New York Co. (Manhattan: $100 mil.), and bordering Washington, D.C., Maryland's Montgomery Co. ($85 million), and Prince Georges Co. ($80 million). The worst-hit states were California, where 74% of all counties reported a deficit, Maryland (73%), New York (73%), Virginia (61%), North Carolina (44%), and Ohio (28%).

From 1972 to 1986, local governments received annual payments of as much as $6.8 billion from the federal government through the General Revenue Sharing program. Of this, approximately 30% was allocated to counties. As a consequence of fiscal federalism—a cornerstone of "Reaganomics"—general revenue sharing was eliminated in 1986. This resulted in a drop in federal assistance as a percentage of total county revenues of 73% between 1980 and 1986. This coincided with rapid population growth in the counties and the necessity for developing costly infrastructure and services such as public health and safety, coupled with a number of unfunded states and federal mandates.

While state aid to counties increased 15.5% over the period 1978–86, revenues from their own sources increased 52%. Most of this increase came from real property tax, both from increased tax revenues as property values went up and from hikes in property tax rates.

HEALTH AND MEDICINE

MILESTONES IN THE HISTORY OF MEDICINE

B.C.

c. 2700 Chinese emperor Shen Nung develops principles of herbal medicine and acupuncture.

c. 1700 The Code of Hammurabi, king of Babylon, comprises regulations concerning physicians, including what they may treat and what their fees should be.

c. 1500 The Ebers Papyrus describes many remedies used in Ancient Egypt to treat dental ailments.

c. 400 Hippocrates of Cos (Greek: c. 460–c. 377), teacher and medical practitioner known as Father of Medicine, writes Hippocratic Oath, which sets ethical standards still followed by physicians throughout the world.

c. 300 Herophilus (Greek: c. 355–280) pioneers dissection of human body and founds first school of anatomy.

A.D.

c. 20 Aulus Cornelius Celsus (Roman: first cent.) writes first-known medical textbook.

c. 100 Romans develop a public medical service and appoint physicians to provide medical help to poor.

c. 180 Galen (Greek: c. 130–c. 201) writes *Methodus Medando*, which summarizes medical knowledge of ancient times. Galen's views on human physiology and disease would influence medical thought for more than 1,500 years.

c. 450 Susruta (Indian) notes relationship of malaria to mosquitoes and of bubonic plague to rats.

c. 900 Rhazes (Persian: c. 865–923/35) is first to describe smallpox and establish criteria for diagnosing and treating it.

1030 Ibn Sina (Avicenna; Persian: 980–1037) publishes *Canon of Medicine*, which becomes leading medical encyclopedia for centuries.

c. 1270–80 Spectacles are introduced by Venetian glassmakers.

1403 Venice imposes world's first quarantine of infected areas as safeguard against Black Death (bubonic plague).

1530 First book devoted to dentistry published anonymously in Germany.

1543 Andreas Vesalius (Flemish: 1514–64) publishes first accurate anatomy text and establishes foundations of modern anatomy.

1597 Gasparo Tapliacossi (Italian) publishes first textbook of plastic surgery and revives operation of rhinoplasty (nose surgery).

1601 Sir James Lancaster (English: c. 1554–1618) writes that lemon juice helps prevent scurvy.

1628 William Harvey (English: 1578–1657) describes functions of the heart and how blood circulates throughout the body.

1658 Jan Swammerdam (Dutch: 1637–80) discerns red blood cells.

1670 Thomas Willis (English: 1621–75) rediscovers connection between sugar in urine and diabetes (known in antiquity by Greeks, Chinese, and Indians).

1751 Pennsylvania Hospital, first general hospital in U.S., founded in Philadelphia by Quakers.

1761 Leopold Auenbrugger von Auenbrugg (Austrian: 1722–1809) discovers that fluid in chest cavity and other health problems can be detected by tapping gently on the chest.
Giovanni B. Morgagni (Italian: 1682–1771) establishes modern pathological anatomy with publication of *On the Seats and Causes of Disease*.

1796 Edward Jenner (English: 1749–1823) develops smallpox vaccine from cowpox serum.

1816 René T.H. Laënnec (French: 1781–1826) invents stethoscope and introduces practice of auscultation (monitoring sounds made by internal organs).

1818 James Blundel (English) performs first successful human blood transfusion.

1831 Samuel Guthrie (American: 1782–1848) discovers chloroform.

1833 William Beaumont (American: 1785–1853) provides first clear insight into nature of gastric digestion.

1839 Horace Hayden (American: 1769–1844) and Chapin Harris (1806–60) found world's first dental school, Baltimore College of Dental Surgery.

1842 Crawford Long (American: 1815–78) removes tumor from patient inhaling ether—first known operation under general anesthesia; publishes his findings in 1849, three years after William Morton (American: 1819–68) demonstrates effectiveness of ether as anesthetic.

1850 Hermann Helmholtz (German: 1821–94) invents ophthalmoscope, instrument used to examine interior of the eye.

1855 Manuel Garcia (Spanish: 1805–1906) invents modern laryngoscope, device used to inspect the throat, especially the larynx and vocal cords.

1863 International Red Cross established at Geneva, Switzerland.

1865 Joseph Lister (English: 1827–1912) revolutionizes surgery when he introduces use of disinfectants to reduce infection.
Louis Pasteur (French: 1822–95) shows that spoilage of wine can be prevented by partial heat-sterilization; process, called pasteurization, soon applied to milk and other foods.

1866 Sir Thomas C. Allbutt (English: 1836–1925) invents clinical thermometer.

1868 Carl Wunderlich (German: 1815–77) establishes that fever is a symptom, not a disease, and introduces use of thermometer for taking body temperature.

1876 Robert Koch (German: 1843–1910) demonstrates that anthrax is caused by rod-shaped bacterium—the first time a microorganism is proved cause of a disease.

1881 Pasteur produces vaccine that successfully prevents anthrax—first disease prevented by vaccine.

1890 Emil von Behring (German: 1854–1917) and Shibasaburo Kitasato (Japanese: 1852–1931) independently discover antitoxins.

1892 Dmitri Ivanovski (Russian: 1864–1920) discovers filterable viruses (viruses tiny enough to pass through fine filters previously believed to trap all living organisms).

1893 Felix Hofmann (German) develops a process for production of acetylsalicylic acid, the form of aspirin used today.

1895 Wilhelm Röntgen (German: 1845–1923) discovers X rays, which soon leads to their use as diagnostic tools for medicine and surgery.

1900 Sigmund Freud (Austrian: 1856–1955), founder of psychoanalysis, publishes *The Interpretation of Dreams*.
Karl Landsteiner (Austrian-American: 1868–1943) discovers three blood groups, later named A, B, and O; fourth group, to be named AB, discovered in 1902.
Walter Reed (American: 1851–1902) establishes that yellow fever virus is transmitted by mosquitoes.

1901 Jokichi Takamine (Japanese-American: 1854–1922) isolates adrenaline, first hormone to be isolated.

1902 Eugene Opie (American) establishes that diabetes results from destruction of specific portions of pancreatic tissue—the islets of Langerhans.

1905 Albert Einhorn (American) synthesizes procaine (novocaine), which becomes the most widely used dental anesthetic.

1906 August von Wassermann (German: 1866–1925) develops blood test for syphilis.

1910 Marie Curie (French: 1867–1934) isolates pure radium metal, which came to be used to treat cancer.

1913 Elmer McCollum (American: 1879–1967) and Marguerite Davis discover fat-soluble factor in butterfat, later named vitamin A.
Béla Schick (Hungarian-American: 1877–1967) perfects test for determining susceptibility to diphtheria.

1915 Death certificates come into general use in U.S.
Margaret Sanger (American: 1883–1966) founds the National Birth Control League, which in 1942 becomes Planned Parenthood.

1918 Francis Benedict (American: 1870–1957) devises basal metabolism test for measuring rate at which metabolism (total of all chemical reactions) occurs in the body.

1921 Sir Frederick G. Banting (Canadian: 1891–1941) and Charles H. Best (1899–1978) extract insulin from the pancreas.

1928 Sir Alexander Fleming (Scottish: 1881–1955) discovers penicillin, a substance in green mold *Penicillium notatum* that destroys certain bacteria.

1929 Hans Berger (German: 1873–1941) publishes his results of the first electroencephalograms of humans.

1935 Gerhard Domagk (German: 1895–1964) announces discovery of protosil (sulfonamide–crysoidin), the first useful sulfa drug.

1937 First blood bank is established, at Cook County Hospital in Chicago. Alton Ochsner (American: 1896–1981) and Michael De Bakey (1908–) suggest that cigarette smoking is cause of lung cancer.

1944 Willem Kolff (Dutch-American: 1911–) develops first kidney dialysis machine.
Oswald Avery (Canadian: 1877–1955), Colin MacLeod, and Maclyn McCarty prove that DNA (deoxyribonucleic acid) is blueprint of heredity that determines how an organism develops.
First eye bank, Eye-Bank for Sight Restoration, founded in New York.
Albert Schatz (American: 1921–) and Selman Waksman (American: 1888–1973) isolate streptomycin, an antibiotic effective against bacterium that causes tuberculosis.

1945 Alfred Blalock (American: 1899–1964) introduces first operation to enable blue, or cyanotic, babies to survive (cyanosis, caused by poor circulatory flow or other problems, results in diminished oxygen in blood, causing bluish discoloration of the skin).

1947 Eugene Payne (American) uses chloromycetin, developed by Parke-Davis researchers, to treat typhus patients; first use of "broad-spectrum" antibiotic.

1948 Philip S. Hench (American: 1896–1965) and Edward C. Kendall (1886–1972) synthesize cortisone and use it to treat arthritis victims.

1952 Jonas Salk (American: 1914–95) develops first vaccine against polio.

1953 John H. Gibbon, Jr. (American: 1903–) uses heart-lung machine he invented in successful open-heart operation.

1954 Surgeons led by Joseph Murray (American) perform first successful kidney transplant.
E. Cuyler Hammond (American: 1912–86) and Daniel Horn (American) present dramatic evidence of dangers in smoking.

1957 Alick Isaacs (Scottish: 1921–67) and Jean Lindenmann (English) discover interferon, a protein that interferes with viral reproduction.

1958 Wilson Greatbatch (American) invents the implantable artificial pacemaker.

1961 Scientists at Bell Laboratories (Americans) announce first continuously operating laser, a tool having many surgical uses.

1963 Thomas Starzl (American: 1926–) performs first human liver transplant operation.

1964 James Hardy (American: 1918–) performs first human lung transplant.

1965 Medicare and Medicaid are established, guaranteeing medical insurance coverage for the aged and the poor.

1966 Paul Parkman and Harry Myer (Americans) develop vaccine for rubella (German measles).
Insulin synthesized independently by Michael Katsoyannis (American) and scientists in the People's Republic of China—first hormone to be synthesized.

1967 Christiaan Barnard (South African: 1922–) performs world's first heart transplant.
Rene Favaloro (Argentinian) performs first successful coronary bypass operation.
First modern hospice founded in London.

1969 Denton Cooley (American: 1920–) implants first temporary artificial heart in human being.

1972 Computerized axial tomography (CAT scan) is introduced in Great Britain.

1975 First cases of what comes to be known as Lyme disease are reported in Lyme, Connecticut.

1976 First recognized outbreak of "Legionnaires' disease" occurs at American Legion convention in Philadelphia.
First known outbreak of Ebola virus occurs in Ebola region of Zaire.

1977 Scientists at Genentech Corporation (Americans) induce bacteria to make human-brain hormone somatostatin—first human chemical produced by recombinant-DNA techniques.

1978 First "test-tube baby" (person conceived outside human body) is born, in England.

1981 Scientists identify previously unknown disease, acquired immune deficiency syndrome (AIDS).
Surgeons at University of California at San Francisco perform first successful operation on a fetus.

1982 William DeVries (American) performs first complete replacement of human heart with artificial heart on Dr. Barney B. Clark at University of Utah.

1984 First baby produced from frozen embryo is born, in Melbourne, Australia.
Luc Montagnier (French) discovers virus believed to cause AIDS.

1990 R. Michael Blaese, W. French Anderson, and Kenneth W. Culver (Americans) develop procedure to infuse genetically engineered blood cells for treatment of immune system disorder—first gene therapy used in a human.

1993 The U.S. Environmental Protection Agency concludes that environmental tobacco smoke ("secondhand smoke") is a lung carcinogen and causes serious respiratory problems for infants and young children.

HEALTH CARE EXPENDITURES

Health care costs continue to increase much faster than the general inflation rate. However, there has been a significant slowing of growth since 1990. In 1990, national health care expenditures increased 11.6 percent over 1989, while the gross domestic product (GDP) grew 5.6 percent. In 1993, health care spending increased 7.8 percent over 1992, while the GDP increased 5.4 percent. The nation spent $884.2 billion on health care in 1993—a record 13.9 percent of GDP.

For 1994, health care expenditures were expected to be close to $1 trillion.

A variety of factors contribute to the rising costs of health care, including:

1. Use of sophisticated, expensive medical equipment.
2. Excessive and arguably unnecessary procedures, including duplication of tests and use of technologies that yield similar results.
3. Increasing elderly population, which use medical care more intensely than younger people.
4. Increasing number of accidents and crimes that require emergency medical services.
5. Labor intensiveness and rapid earnings growth for health care professionals and executives.
6. Malpractice insurance.
7. Administrative waste.
8. Fraud.

The United States spends more than any other developed nation on health care relative to its economy. The nation's 1993 health expenditures amounted to an estimated average of $3,300 per person, up from $2,685 in 1990. Close to 90 percent of these moneys were for personal health care; the remainder went to research, construction, program administration, the net cost of private health insurance, and public health activities.

Hospital Care

Hospital care has long claimed the biggest share of health care dollars—and the percentage has grown. In 1950 hospital care accounted for 30.4 percent of personal health care costs. By 1980, the percentage had zoomed to 46.7 percent. More recently it declined—to 41.7 percent in 1993—as hospitals contained costs with shorter hospital stays and increased treatment on an outpatient basis.

Costs vary markedly depending on the care required and the locale. For example, according to the Health Insurance Association of America, surgical costs of a hysterectomy averaged $4,165 in New York City in 1989, as compared to $1,885 in Atlanta; a triple coronary bypass averaged $5,624 in Philadelphia versus $4,425 in Dallas.

Nursing-Home Care

The number of skilled nursing facilities increased rapidly during the 1960s, decreased during the early 1970s, and has been increasing ever since, reaching 11,436 by the beginning of 1994. Over 1.7 million persons were estimated to have received care in skilled nursing facilities and other intermediate care facilities covered by Medicare during 1994.

People who reach age 65 have a 44 percent chance of spending some time in a nursing home before they die. The cost for such care is high: Medicare payments to nonhospital-based skilled nursing facilities averaged $103 per day, or $3,316 per admission in 1992.

THE BOOMING COST OF HOSPITAL CARE, BY STATE, 1980–93

State	Average daily room charge			Average cost per day[1]			Average cost per stay[1]		
	1980	1985	1990	1980	1985	1993	1980	1985	1993
U.S. total	**$127**	**$212**	**$297**	**$245**	**$460**	**$881**	**$1,851**	**$3,245**	**$6,132**
Alabama	96	161	210	209	389	775	1,459	2,653	5,229
Alaska	189	295	407	408	693	1,136	2,276	3,742	7,594
Arizona	106	191	300	290	591	1,091	2,013	3,547	5,528
Arkansas	86	140	170	185	381	678	1,172	2,292	4,585
California	161	281	453	362	654	1,221	2,395	4,050	6,918
Colorado	124	211	321	247	486	961	1,760	3,221	6,212
Connecticut	127	206	456	271	502	1,058	2,039	3,610	7,478
Delaware	125	214	385	238	474	1,028	1,937	3,357	7,307
Dist. of Columbia	170	274	325	358	612	1,201	3,189	4,962	8,594
Florida	109	181	271	247	494	940	1,803	3,381	6,169
Georgia	92	150	191	218	386	775	1,380	2,501	5,554
Hawaii	127	231	348	245	420	823	1,868	3,522	7,633
Idaho	110	197	259	208	373	659	1,251	2,402	4,635
Illinois	144	248	300	277	498	912	2,183	3,607	6,318
Indiana	107	184	258	214	446	898	1,620	2,942	5,677
Iowa	107	179	221	199	359	612	1,465	2,735	4,980
Kansas	104	183	256	207	401	666	1,592	2,954	5,108
Kentucky	92	175	242	189	367	703	1,268	2,323	4,749
Louisiana	89	154	203	233	475	875	1,492	2,842	5,781
Maine	124	208	335	217	394	738	1,707	2,870	5,543
Maryland	119	186	266	251	443	889	2,136	3,237	5,632
Massachusetts	151	229	351	294	500	1,036	2,578	4,194	6,843
Michigan	151	267	337	267	507	902	2,087	3,666	6,147
Minnesota	105	187	282	203	369	652	1,818	3,302	5,867
Mississippi	67	113	167	174	319	555	1,178	2,037	4,053
Missouri	107	185	268	230	457	863	1,848	3,383	6,161
Montana	113	201	318	160	312	481	1,321	2,658	4,953
Nebraska	100	155	209	194	347	626	1,526	2,892	6,024
Nevada	125	243	251	343	677	900	2,201	3,953	6,796
New Hampshire	125	200	304	203	422	976	1,432	2,644	6,964
New Jersey	146	183	273	212	400	829	1,850	2,914	6,540
New Mexico	115	193	254	263	501	1,046	1,549	2,837	5,600
New York	157	228	339	257	419	784	2,469	3,930	7,716
North Carolina	87	139	220	187	356	763	1,397	2,416	5,571
North Dakota	93	173	230	177	322	507	1,528	2,918	5,403
Ohio	139	228	308	241	493	940	1,907	3,428	5,923
Oklahoma	101	162	220	239	455	797	1,527	2,814	5,093
Oregon	133	225	338	277	549	1,053	1,671	2,879	5,309
Pennsylvania	132	255	375	234	468	861	1,947	3,412	6,564
Rhode Island	138	206	342	260	447	885	2,162	3,432	5,672
South Carolina	80	145	212	186	358	838	1,367	2,508	5,955
South Dakota	96	161	208	189	282	506	1,265	2,442	5,052
Tennessee	91	140	182	204	397	859	1,427	2,709	5,798
Texas	91	159	223	226	461	1,010	1,491	2,799	6,021
Utah	112	173	353	271	556	1,081	1,462	2,799	5,314
Vermont	116	209	378	183	343	676	1,472	2,705	5,241
Virginia	101	165	220	211	399	830	1,647	2,862	5,504
Washington	125	229	334	262	546	1,143	1,502	3,062	5,792
West Virginia	110	166	223	195	399	701	1,393	2,520	4,712
Wisconsin	104	166	222	218	392	744	1,765	2,974	5,348
Wyoming	98	173	234	242	367	537	1,189	2,357	4,706

1. These are costs to the hospital. **Sources:** Health Insurance Association of America, *Source Book of Health Insurance Data* (annual), and *Survey of Semi-Private Room Charges* (semiannual); American Hospital Association, *Hospital Statistics* (annual).

Americans spent $1 billion on nursing-home care in 1960, $4.9 billion in 1970, $20.5 billion in 1980, and $54.8 billion in 1990. By 1993, the figure had reached $69.6 billion. Out-of-pocket payments, including personal savings and social security benefits, covered approximately 33 percent of this cost; Medicare and Medicaid covered most of the remaining costs.

Paying for Health Care

Medical care is generally paid for in one of three ways:

1. By patients; according to the U.S. Dept. of Health and Human Services, an estimated 20.1 percent of the nation's personal health care costs in 1993 were paid directly by patients.

2. By an insurance plan; 33.0 percent of personal health care expenditures are financed by private insurers. A survey of 2,097 employers found that their average cost of health benefits in 1994 was $3,741, a 1.1 percent decline from 1993. The decline, which reversed a decade-long trend of increases, was attributed to several causes, including a requirement that workers pay a larger share of health care costs out of their own pockets; a tendency of businesses to replace full-time positions that included benefits with part-time and temporary positions that lack paid benefits; and a move away from traditional insurers and into managed care programs.

3. As a public charge, which means that the government—and, ultimately, the taxpayer—pays the bill; an estimated 43.1 percent of personal health care costs are paid for by federal, state, and local governments. In some instances the percentage is even greater. For example, injuries caused by firearms cost an estimated $429 million annually in hospital expenses alone. According to a University of California study published in 1988, 85.6 percent of this is borne by taxpayers. The cost would top $1 billion if expenses such as ambulance services, doctors' fees, follow-up care, and rehabilitation were included.

Health insurance Americans spend more than 3 percent of their disposable income for health insurance premiums. There are five basic types of insurance:

1. Hospital expense insurance—pays costs of hospital room, X rays, medicines, etc.

2. Surgical expense insurance—pays costs of an operation.

3. Medical expense insurance—pays for visits to a physician's office.

4. Major medical expense insurance—pays costs associated with extended sickness or injury.

5. Disability income insurance—pays a benefit when the person is unable to work because of illness or injury.

Federal insurance plans Two government health programs, Medicare and Medicaid, finance one-third of U.S. personal health care costs. (The remaining federal health spending covers military and veterans' health care.)

Medicare is a federal health insurance plan for people age 65 and older and for severely disabled people under age 65. Medicaid is a health care program for poor people. It is funded jointly by federal and state agencies. (See also Part II: "Social Insurance Programs.")

Managed care providers A managed health care plan provides comprehensive health care coverage to enrolled members on a prepaid basis; that is, insurance and health care delivery are integrated within one system. The objective is to control costs, assure access to effective treatments, and eliminate inappropriate and duplicative services.

The oldest managed care providers are health maintenance organizations (HMOs), which started in the 1940s. They either employ physicians in clinics or hospitallike buildings, or contract with hundreds or even thousands of physicians who practice in their private offices. Between 1976 and the end of 1992 the number of HMOs increased from 174 to 544 and enrollment rose from 6 million to 41.4 million. This represented 16.1 percent of the total population and 18.8 percent of insured individuals. HMO enrollment was projected to grow to about 56 million—about 25 percent of the U.S. population—by the end of 1995.

HEALTH EXPENDITURES AS A PERCENTAGE OF GNP FOR SELECTED COUNTRIES, 1960–92

Nation	1960	1970	1980	1992[1]
United States	5.3%	7.4%	9.2%	13.6%
Canada	5.5	7.1	7.4	10.3
France	4.2	5.8	7.6	9.4
Switzerland	3.3	5.2	7.3	9.3
Australia	4.9	5.7	7.3	8.8
Germany	4.8	5.9	8.4	8.7
Netherlands	3.9	6.0	8.0	8.6
Italy	3.6	5.2	6.9	8.5
Sweden	4.7	7.2	9.4	7.9
New Zealand	4.3	5.2	7.2	7.7
United Kingdom	3.9	4.5	5.8	7.1
Spain	1.5	3.7	5.6	7.0
Japan	3.0	4.6	6.6	6.9
Greece	2.9	4.0	4.3	5.4

1. Preliminary data. **Source:** U.S. Dept. of Health and Human Services, National Center for Health Statistics, *Health United States, 1994* (1995).

HEALTH CARE SPENDING, BY CATEGORY, 1993

Category	Amount (billions)	Percent
Hospital care	$326.6	36.9%
Physicians' services	171.2	19.4
Dentists' services	37.4	4.2
Other professional services	51.2	5.8
Drugs, other aids and supplies	87.6	9.9
Nursing-home care	69.6	7.9
Home health care	20.8	2.4
Other personal health care	18.2	2.1
Administration and net cost of private health insurance	48.0	5.4
Government public health activities	24.7	2.8
Research	14.4	1.6
Construction	14.6	1.6
Total	**$884.2**	**100.0%**

Source: U.S. Dept. of Health and Human Services, Health Care Financing Administration, *Health Care Financing Review* (Fall 1994).

NATIONAL EXPENDITURES FOR HEALTH CARE, 1960–93

Category	1960	1965	1970	1975	1980	1985	1990	1993
Amount in billions of dollars								
Total expenditures	$27.1	$41.6	$74.3	$132.9	$251.1	$434.5	$696.6	$884.2
Private	20.5	31.3	46.6	77.8	145.8	259.4	410.0	496.4
Public	6.7	10.3	27.7	55.1	105.3	175.1	286.5	387.8
Federal	2.9	4.8	17.8	36.4	72.0	123.3	195.8	280.6
State and local	3.7	5.5	9.9	18.7	33.3	51.8	90.7	107.3
Per capita amount								
Total expenditures	$143	$204	$346	$592	$1,068	$1,761	$2,686	$3,299
Private	108	154	217	346	620	1,051	1,581	1,852
Public	35	50	129	245	448	709	1,105	1,447
Federal	15	24	83	162	306	500	755	1,047
State and local	20	27	46	83	142	210	350	400
Percent distribution								
Total expenditures	100.0%	100.0%	100.0%	100.0%	100.0%	100.0%	100.0%	100.0%
Private	75.5	75.3	62.7	58.5	58.1	59.7	58.9	56.1
Public	24.5	24.7	37.3	41.5	41.9	40.3	41.1	43.9
Federal	10.7	11.6	24.0	27.4	28.7	28.4	28.1	31.7
State and local	13.8	13.2	13.4	14.1	13.3	11.9	13.0	12.1
Percent of GDP								
National health expenditures	5.3%	5.9%	7.4%	8.3%	9.3%	10.8%	12.6%	13.9%

Note: Figures may not add to totals because of rounding. **Source:** U.S. Dept. of Health and Human Services, Health Care Financing Administration.

HOSPITAL FACILITIES AND THEIR USE, 1946–93

Year	Number of hospitals	Number of beds ('000s)	Admissions ('000s)	Occupancy rate	Outpatient visits ('000s)
1946	6,125	1,436	15,675	79.5%	N.A.
1950	6,788	1,456	18,483	86.0	N.A.
1955	6,956	1,604	21,073	85.0	N.A.
1960	6,876	1,658	25,027	84.6	N.A.
1965	7,123	1,704	28,812	82.3	125,793
1970	7,123	1,616	31,759	80.3	181,370
1975	7,156	1,466	36,157	76.7	254,844
1980	6,965	1,365	38,892	77.7	262,951
1985	6,872	1,318	36,304	69.0	282,140
1990	6,649	1,213	33,774	69.5	368,184
1993	6,467	1,163	33,201	67.3	435,619

Note: N.A. = not available. **Source:** American Hospital Association, *Hospital Statistics* (annual).

UNINSURED ADULTS, 1993

Category	Men	Women
Total	**17.5%**	**15.2%**
Age		
18–24	29.7	23.5
25–34	21.5	16.5
35–44	13.5	13.2
45–54	10.7	11.9
55–64	9.7	10.6
Race/Ethnicity		
White[1]	14.5	12.6
Black[1]	22.7	20.0
Hispanic	36.5	31.3
Annual household income		
Under $10,000	43.8	36.8
$10,000–$19,999	38.2	29.3
$20,000–$34,999	16.5	12.4
$35,000 or more	6.4	4.2
Education level		
Less than high school	37.2	33.1
High school	21.1	17.0
Some college	15.7	12.9
College graduate	7.7	6.8

Note: Weighted percentage of people age 18 to 64 who were uninsured at the time of interview. 1. Non-Hispanic. **Source:** U.S. Dept. of Health and Human Services, Centers for Disease Control and Prevention, 1993 Behavioral Risk Factor Surveillance System.

HMO patients generally must use their HMO's physicians in order to be reimbursed. Preferred provider organizations (PPOs), a modified version of HMOs, permit enrollees to use nonplan providers (physicians and hospitals). However, patients who use services outside their PPO must pay a financial penalty.

The uninsured An ever-growing number of Americans have no health insurance. A study based on 1994 Census Bureau data concluded that 41 million Americans—16.1 percent of the population—had no health insurance in 1993.

The probability of being uninsured varied by place of residence, earnings, and the size of the company for which a person worked. The states with the lowest number of uninsured residents under age 65 in 1993 were Hawaii (6.9%), Minnesota (9.0%), and Massachusetts (10.1%); those with the highest percentage of uninsured were Louisiana (25.6%), New Mexico (23.8%), and Texas (23.4%). The higher a person's income and the larger the company for which he or she worked, the greater the probability of having health insurance.

SURGERY

Increases in the number of surgical operations during recent years have been accompanied by dramatic changes in the rates of some procedures. An example is the incidence of cesarean sections—surgical incisions through the abdomen and uterus for removal of a baby, performed when normal vaginal delivery is deemed hazardous for the mother or child. Cesareans accounted for 22.8 percent of all live births in 1993. This was the lowest rate since 1985 (22.7%) but approximately four times the rate in 1970 (5.5%) and among the highest rates for developed nations. According to a 1993 report from the Centers for Disease Control and Prevention, 349,000 of the 1991 cesareans were unnecessary, costing the nation more than $1 billion.

The frequency of certain procedures varies according to age, but, surprisingly, there may also be variations from one geographical region to another. For example, the 1993 cesarean rate was highest in the South—25.9 for every 100 births—and lowest in the West (19.3).

Eliminating the Need for Exploratory Surgery

Technological advances continually create new milestones in the art of medicine. Nowhere is this more apparent—or welcome—than in the diagnosis of people's health. Thanks to sophisticated electronics and other tools, physicians can obtain highly detailed views of internal organs without surgery. This often can be done on an outpatient basis, thereby lowering costs and avoiding risks associated with exploratory surgery. Furthermore, the techniques enable physicians to detect cancers and other problems in their earliest stages, allowing them to take preventive action that will decrease chances of severe damage or death. Modern imaging techniques include the following:

CAT Computerized Axial Tomography—Uses X rays to take pictures, or tomograms, of the patient's body. The pictures are reconstructed by a computer to produce a crisp, 3-D image. CAT

MOST COMMON SURGICAL PROCEDURES, 1980–92

	Procedures ('000s)			Procedures per 1,000 population		
Sex and procedure	**1980**	**1990**	**1992**	**1980**	**1990**	**1992**
Males, all ages[1]	**8,505**	**8,538**	**8,646**	**78.1**	**68.8**	**68.4**
Cardiac catheterization	228	620	636	2.2	5.2	5.1
Coronary bypass	108	286	347	1.0	2.4	2.8
Prostatectomy	335	364	353	3.1	2.8	2.7
Reduction of fracture (excluding skull, nose, and jaw)	325	300	311	2.9	2.4	2.4
Spinal disc operations	118	248	254	1.1	2.0	1.9
Operations on muscles, tendons, fascia, and bursa	210	175	168	1.9	1.4	1.3
Females, all ages[1]	**15,989**	**14,513**	**14,607**	**126.1**	**100.3**	**99.1**
Procedures to assist delivery	2,391	2,491	2,441	18.4	17.3	16.9
Cesarean section	619	945	921	4.8	6.6	6.4
Repair of lacerations due to giving birth	355	795	790	2.8	5.5	5.5
Hysterectomy	649	591	580	5.2	4.3	4.2
Removal of one or both ovaries	483	476	464	3.9	3.4	3.4
Destruction or closing off of fallopian tubes	641	419	380	4.9	2.9	2.6
Diagnostic dilation and curettage of uterus	923	109	87	7.3	0.8	0.6

Note: Data are for inpatients discharged from nonfederal, short-stay hospitals, based on a sample of hospital records. Beginning in 1989, the definition of some procedures was revised, thus causing a discontinuity in the trends for the totals. 1. Includes procedures not listed. Rates are age adjusted. **Source:** U.S. Dept. of Health and Human Services, National Center for Health Statistics, *Health United States 1993* (1994).

scans are particularly helpful in locating tumors, including ones deep in the brain.

DSA Digital Subtraction Angiography—An iodine-containing substance that is opaque to X rays is injected into blood vessels. Before-and-after X-ray images create a sharp picture of the vessels and the flow of blood.

ESA Electrocortical Spectral Analysis—A grid of electrodes implanted on the surface of a brain measures brain activity and produces images of the flow of thought from one part of the brain to another. ESA enables doctors to pin down the source of trouble and assess the risk of removing brain tissue around the source.

MRI Magnetic Resonance Imaging—Uses a combination of a strong magnetic field and radio waves to measure the distribution and chemical bonds of the protons in the body's hydrogen atoms. A computer translates measurements into 3-D images. MRI is frequently used to view the brain and other soft tissues.

PET Positron-Emission Tomography—Small amounts of positron-emitting isotopes are injected into the blood to study the flow of blood and its distribution to heart muscles or other tissues.

SPECT Single Photo Emission Computer Tomography—Uses radioisotopes to measure blood flow in small vessels. SPECT is particularly well suited to imaging the brain and is used to study such disorders as epilepsy, schizophrenia, Parkinson's disease, and strokes.

Thermographic imaging Data on the body's heat gathered by an infrared camera is converted by a computer into a temperature map, which is useful in detecting cancers and studying blood flow into limbs.

Ultrasound imaging, or sonography High-frequency sound waves are beamed at the body's organs. The echoes that bounce back are translated into computer images. Because it doesn't use X rays, sonography is recommended for use on pregnant women. It also is well suited for examining the gall bladder, liver, heart, and prostate gland.

Organ Transplantation

Transplant surgery is more successful than ever, thanks to improved surgical techniques, a better understanding of the body's immune system, and the development of drugs that combat rejection of implanted organs. Kidney transplants, for instance, enjoy a high rate of success and are much less expensive—and much more convenient—than maintaining a patient on dialysis. Unfortunately, a scarcity of donor organs keeps thousands of patients waiting, sometimes in vain.

In addition to organs, tissues—cornea, bone, and skin—can be transplanted. In fact, corneal transplants are the most frequently performed transplant surgery. According to the Eye Bank Association, there were 43,743 such operations in 1994, with a success rate averaging better than 90 percent. As with organs, the need for tissues frequently exceeds the supply.

There are 69 organ procurement programs in the United States. Many have toll-free telephone numbers. The United Network for Organ Sharing (UNOS) operates the national waiting list (1-800-24-DONOR).

To perform transplants, hospitals must be licensed. According to UNOS, 278 medical institutions operated organ transplant programs as of May 1995. These can be separated into organ-specific programs, including:

248—kidney transplants
165—heart transplants
117—liver transplants
116—pancreas transplants
92—heart-lung transplants
85—lung transplants
19—intestine transplants

NUMBER AND SURVIVAL RATES OF TRANSPLANT OPERATIONS

Organ	Year first performed	Number (1994)	Survival rates[1] Graft	Patient
Heart	1967	2,340	78.3%	78.3%
Heart-lung	1981	71	51.2	51.2
Kidney[2]	1954	10,622	—	—
Cadaver	—	7,642	74.5	90.4
Living donor	—	2,980	87.7	95.9
Liver	1963	3,650	63.6	74.9
Lung	1963	720	59.7	59.7
Pancreas[2]	1966	102	66.9	85.5

1. Two-year survival rates for operations performed between Oct. 1, 1987, and Dec. 31, 1992. 2. In addition, 746 kidney-pancreas transplants were performed. **Source:** United Network for Organ Sharing.

REPORTED ABORTIONS, 1972–92

Category	1972	1980	1990	1992[1]
Number of abortions				
Reported abortions	586,760	1,297,606	1,429,577	1,359,145
Number per 1,000 live births	180	359	345	335
Percent of total				
Race				
White	77.0%	69.9%	64.8%	62.9%
Black[2]	23.0	30.1	31.8	33.3
Marital Status				
Married	29.7%	23.1%	21.7%	20.7%
Unmarried	70.3	76.9	78.3	79.3
Age				
Under 20	32.6%	29.2%	22.4%	20.1%
20–24	32.5	35.5	33.2	34.6
25 or older	34.9	35.3	44.4	45.3
Weeks of gestation				
Up to 8	34.0%	51.7%	51.6%	52.6%
9–10	30.7	26.2	25.3	24.6
11–12	17.5	12.2	11.7	11.6
13–15	8.4	5.1	6.4	5.9
16–20	8.2	3.9	4.0	4.1
21 or more	1.2	0.9	1.0	1.2

1. Preliminary. 2. Data for 1972 and 1980 include other nonwhite groups. **Source:** U.S. Dept. of Health and Human Services, Centers for Disease Control and Prevention, *Morbidity and Mortality Weekly Report* (Dec. 23, 1994).

Abortion

The deliberate termination of a pregnancy before the fetus is capable of living outside the womb has generally been legal in the United States since 1973, when the Supreme Court ruled (in *Roe* v. *Wade*) that abortion cannot be prohibited during the first three months of pregnancy. From 1973 through 1980, the ratio of abortions to live births increased significantly. Since then, the ratio has declined slightly.

According to a 1994 report from the Centers for Disease Control and Prevention (CDC), women who obtained abortions in 1992 were predominantly 24 years of age or younger, white, unmarried, and had no live-born children. More than half of the abortions were performed during the first eight weeks of gestation; 88.8 percent were performed in the first 12 weeks. Curettage was the primary abortion procedure, accounting for 98.9 percent of all abortions.

The rate of abortion among American women is greater than among women in many other industrialized nations. Based on data provided to the CDC, the abortion rate—the number of abortions per 1,000 women age 15 to 44—remained stable at 23 to 24 from 1980 through 1992.

DISEASE

Five of the most common categories of disease are:

1. Hereditary diseases—transferred from parent to child by genes. Examples: hemophilia, Down's syndrome, cystic fibrosis, sickle cell anemia.

2. Deficiency diseases—caused by lack of vitamins or other essential nutrients. Examples: scurvy, pellagra.

3. Infectious diseases—caused by viruses, bacteria, fungi, and other organisms and transferred from person to person. Examples: common cold, influenza, chicken pox, measles.

4. Diseases caused by chemical and physical agents such as radiation, smoke, drugs, and poisons. Examples: allergies, asbestosis, byssinosis, lead poisoning.

5. Degenerative diseases—resulting from natural aging processes. In some cases, cancer and high blood pressure are degenerative diseases.

Heart Disease

Cardiovascular diseases (diseases of the heart and blood vessels) are America's number one killer. About one in four Americans—some 59 million people—suffer some form of cardiovascular disease. During 1992 these diseases claimed 925,079 lives. This represented 42.5 percent of all deaths.

Death rates vary according to age, sex, race, even geographical location. Rates increase with age and are about 77 percent higher among men than among women. For both sexes, death rates are significantly higher among blacks than among whites, though the disparity has narrowed in the past 25 years.

HEART DISEASE DEATH RATES, 1960–91 (per 100,000 population)

Age	1960[1]	1970	1980	1991
All ages				
Age adjusted	286.2	253.6	202.2	148.2
Crude	369.0	362.0	336.0	285.9
Under 1 year	6.6	13.1	22.8	17.6
1–4 years	1.3	1.7	2.6	2.2
5–14 years	1.3	0.8	0.9	0.8
15–24 years	4.0	3.0	2.9	2.7
25–34 years	15.6	11.4	8.3	8.0
35–44 years	74.6	66.7	44.6	31.6
45–54 years	271.8	238.4	180.2	118.0
55–64 years	737.9	652.3	494.1	357.0
65–74 years	1,740.5	1,558.2	1,218.6	872.0
75–84 years	4,089.4	3,683.8	2,993.1	2,219.1
85 and older	9,317.8	7,891.3	7,777.1	6,613.4

1. Includes deaths of nonresidents of the U.S. **Source:** U.S. Dept. of Health and Human Services, National Center for Health Statistics, *Health United States, 1993* (1994).

REPORTED CASES OF COMMON INFECTIOUS DISEASES, 1950–94

Disease	1950	1960	1970	1980	1990	1994[1]
Aseptic meningitis	N.A.	1,593	6,480	8,028	11,852	8,050
Brucellosis (undulant fever)	3,510	751	213	183	85	95
Cholera	N.A.	N.A.	N.A.	9	6	47
Diphtheria	5,796	918	435	3	4	1
Encephalitis	1,135	2,341	1,950	1,402	1,446	781
Legionnellosis	N.A.	N.A.	N.A.	N.A.	1,370	1,535
Leprosy (Hansen's disease)	44	54	129	223	198	111
Malaria	2,184	72	3,051	2,062	1,292	1,065
Meningococcal infections	3,788	2,259	2,505	2,840	2,451	2,638
Mumps	N.A.	N.A.	104,953	8,576	5,292	1,322
Pertussis (whooping cough)	120,718	14,809	4,249	1,730	4,570	3,590
Plague[2]	N.A.	2	13	18	2	14
Poliomyelitis	33,300	3,190	33	9	7	1
Rabies, in animals	7,901	3,567	3,224	6,421	4,826	7,347
Rabies, in humans	18	2	3	0	1	5
Rubella (German measles)	N.A.	N.A.	56,552	3,904	1,125	209
Tetanus	486	368	148	95	64	29
Toxic shock syndrome	N.A.	N.A.	N.A.	N.A.	322	183
Trichinosis	327	160	109	131	129	35
Tuberculosis	N.A.	55,494	37,137	27,749	25,701	22,152
Tularemia[3]	927	390	172	234	152	85
Typhoid fever	2,484	816	346	510	552	410
Typhus fever, tick-borne	464	204	380	1,163	654	441
Venereal disease						
Gonorrhea	286,746	258,933	600,072	1,004,029	690,169	400,592
Syphilis[4]	23,939	16,145	21,982	27,204	50,223	20,183

1. Incomplete due to late reporting. 2. Plague: disease caused by the bite of fleas infected with the bacterium *Yersinia pestis.* 3. Tularemia: disease caused by the bacterium *Pasturella tularensis,* transmitted to humans by insects or direct contact with infected animals. 4. Primary and secondary syphilis cases. **Source:** U.S. Dept. of Health and Human Services, Centers for Disease Control and Prevention, *Morbidity and Mortality Weekly Report,* Oct. 21, 1994, and Jan. 6, 1995.

CARDIOVASCULAR OPERATIONS IN THE U.S., 1992

	Sex		Age			
Operation	Male	Female	Under 15	15–44	45–64	65 plus
Total procedures	**2,630,000**	**1,794,000**	**152,000**	**501,000**	**1,544,000**	**2,226,000**
Cardiac catheterization[1]	675,000	409,000	17,000	103,000	453,000	510,000
Bypass	347,000	122,000	—	16,000	200,000	252,000
Angioplasty	262,000	136,000	—	30,000	177,000	192,000
Pacemaker	61,000	52,000	—	—	19,000	91,000
Endarterectomy	56,000	35,000	—	—	24,000	67,000
Valve replacement	35,000	28,000	—	8,000	17,000	38,000
Open heart surgery[2]	382,000	150,000	—	24,000	217,000	290,000

Note: Estimated figures. 1. Does not include outpatient and other nonhospitalized procedures. 2. Includes valves, bypass, and "other" open heart procedures. **Source:** American Heart Association, *Heart and Stroke Facts: 1995 Statistical Supplement* (1995).

Hawaii has the lowest death rate from cardiovascular disease (149.2 per 100,000 population in 1991), followed by Utah, Colorado, New Mexico, and Alaska. Mississippi has the highest death rate (265.3), followed by Louisiana, the District of Columbia, West Virginia, and South Carolina.

The good news is that death rates from cardiovascular disease have declined dramatically. In 1950 the death rate was 424.2 per 100,000 population; by 1991 it had dropped to 186.0. This is due in part to improved drug treatments and other medical advancements. Another factor has been improved personal health habits: people have stopped smoking, lowered the fat content of their diets, and taken other steps that reduce the risks of cardiovascular disease.

Heart attacks A heart attack occurs when the blood supply to the heart muscles is blocked. An uncomfortable pressure, fullness, squeezing, or pain in the center of the chest that lasts for two minutes or more may be a sign of a heart attack. Sweating, dizziness, nausea, fainting, or shortness of breath may also occur. Some 1,500,000 people suffer heart attacks annually. One-third of these people do not survive. Of the survivors, 20 percent of the women and 16 percent of the men will have a second heart attack within four years.

Strokes and bypass surgery Each year, approximately 500,000 Americans—72 percent of them over age 65—suffer a stroke; of these, almost 145,000 die within a year. A stroke occurs when the blood supply to the brain is blocked, usually by a clot. The primary signal of a stroke is a sudden, temporary weakness or numbness of the face, arm, or leg on one side of the body. Other signals include temporary loss of speech, difficulty in speaking or understanding speech, temporary vision problems (particularly in one eye), unsteadiness, or unexplained dizziness.

The American Heart Association estimates that 468,000 bypass operations were performed on 309,000 patients in 1992, more than triple the number performed in 1980; 74 percent of the 1992 operations were performed on men. In this operation a blood vessel from elsewhere in the body is used to reroute blood around a blocked coronary artery. The purpose: to reduce the person's risk of a stroke. While bypass operations have resulted in improved survival rates and better quality of life for many people, some research has found that a large percentage of these operations are unnecessary or inappropriate; in such cases, patients treated nonsurgically do equally well.

Cancer

The nation's second leading cause of death is a group of diseases characterized by the unrestrained growth of cells. It afflicts people of all ages and races, and it varies greatly in cause, symptoms, response to treatment, and possibility of cure.

Overall, cancer incidence and mortality rates have increased steadily. In part this is due to an increasingly aging population. Also, some cancers, particularly lung cancer, have a long latency period, developing after years of exposure to tobacco smoke or other cancer-causing agents.

A U.S. male has a 1 in 2 probability of developing invasive cancer at some time during his life; a female, 1 in 3. The incidence of cancer varies from state to state. According to the American Cancer Society, the highest cancer death rates for 1987–91 occurred in the District of Columbia (227 cancer deaths per 100,000 population), Delaware (196), Louisiana (193), and Maryland (192). The states with the lowest cancer death rates were Utah (125), Hawaii (137), New Mexico (146), and Colorado (148).

Cancer survival rates According to the American Cancer Society, more than eight million Americans are alive who have a history of cancer, five million of them with diagnosis made five or more years ago. Chances of surviving cancer have steadily improved. In the 1930s, fewer than two out of 10 American cancer patients survived at least five years after diagnosis. In contrast, four out of 10 who get cancer this year will be alive five years after diagnosis.

Survival depends on many factors. Two of the most important are the site of the tumor and how much the cancer has spread before treatment is begun. The American Cancer Society estimated that of people diagnosed with cancers of the breast, tongue, mouth, colon, rectum, cervix, prostate, testis, and melanoma (skin cancer) during 1995, about 100,000 more would survive if their cancers had been detected in a localized stage and treated promptly. In addition, the society estimates that 170,000 lives would be lost in 1995 to cancer because of tobacco use.

Cancer death rates Since 1950, cancer death rates have declined 60 percent for children. Slighter declines have occurred among adults under age 55, while death rates for older adults have increased somewhat. The pattern also varies according to sex and race. For white males, the age-adjusted rate rose from 130.9 cancer deaths per 100,000 population in 1950 to 157.6 in 1992. The rise was much greater for black males, from 126.1 to 241.0. For white females, the rate fell from 119.4 to 110.0, while for black females it rose from 131.9 to 135.8.

The American Cancer Society estimated that 547,000 Americans would die of cancer in 1995—nearly 1,500 people a day. Lung cancer is the leading cause of cancer deaths, killing an estimated 95,400 men and 62,000 women in 1995. Among women, breast cancer is the second most common killer, though if detected early and treated properly, it has a very high cure rate. Among men, prostate cancer causes the second greatest number of deaths. It, too, has a high survival rate if discovered while still localized within the general region of the prostate.

Cancer warning signs Early detection is the key in fighting cancer. See your doctor if one of the following symptoms lasts longer than two weeks.

1. Unusual bleeding or discharge.
2. A sore that does not heal.
3. A change in a wart or mole.

CANCER DEATH RATES, 1950–91
(per 100,000 population)

Age	1950[1]	1960[1]	1970	1980	1991
All ages					
Age adjusted	125.3	125.8	129.8	132.8	134.5
Crude	139.8	149.2	162.8	183.9	204.1
Under 1 year	8.7	7.2	4.7	3.2	1.9
1–4 years	11.7	10.9	7.5	4.5	3.5
5–14 years	6.7	6.8	6.0	4.3	3.1
15–24 years	8.6	8.3	8.3	6.3	5.0
25–34 years	20.0	19.5	16.5	13.7	12.4
35–44 years	62.7	59.7	59.5	48.6	43.1
45–54 years	175.1	177.0	182.5	180.0	155.1
55–64 years	392.9	396.8	423.0	436.1	448.4
65–74 years	692.5	713.9	751.2	817.9	871.6
75–84 years	1,153.3	1,127.4	1,169.2	1,232.3	1,351.6
85 and older	1,451.0	1,450.0	1,320.7	1,594.6	1,773.9

1. Includes deaths of nonresidents of the U.S. **Source**: U.S. Dept. of Health and Human Services, National Center for Health Statistics, *Health United States, 1993* (1994).

ESTIMATED NEW CANCER CASES AND CANCER DEATHS, BY SITE AND SEX, 1995

	New cases			Deaths		
Site	Total	Male	Female	Total	Male	Female
Skin[1]	34,100	18,700	15,400	7,200	4,500	2,700
Oral	28,150	18,800	9,350	8,370	5,480	2,890
Lung, bronchus, and other respiratory	186,300	108,400	77,900	162,950	99,470	63,480
Breast	183,400	1,400	182,000	46,240	240	46,000
Esophagus	12,100	8,800	3,300	10,900	8,200	2,700
Stomach	22,800	14,000	8,800	14,700	8,800	5,900
Liver and bile passages	18,500	9,800	8,700	14,200	7,700	6,500
Pancreas	24,000	11,000	13,000	27,000	13,200	13,800
Small intestine	4,600	2,400	2,200	1,120	590	530
Colon and rectum	138,200	70,700	67,500	55,300	27,200	28,100
Other digestive plus unspecified digestive	2,800	1,300	1,500	1,110	440	670
Urinary (bladder, kidney, etc.)	79,300	54,400	24,900	22,900	14,600	8,300
Leukemias	25,700	14,700	11,000	20,400	11,100	9,300
Other blood plus lymph tissues	71,200	41,100	30,100	34,450	18,120	16,330
Bone	2,070	1,100	970	1,280	750	530
Connective tissue	6,000	3,300	2,700	3,600	1,800	1,800
Endocrine glands	15,380	3,900	11,480	1,780	760	1,020
Eye	1,870	1,000	870	240	130	110
Brain and central nervous system	17,200	9,700	7,500	13,300	7,300	6,000
Ovary	26,600	—	26,600	14,500	—	14,500
Uterus	48,600	—	48,600	10,700	—	10,700
Other genital, female	5,700	—	5,700	1,200	—	1,200
Prostate	244,000	244,000	—	40,400	40,400	—
Testis	7,100	7,100	—	370	370	—
Other genital, male	1,100	1,100	—	210	210	—
All other plus unspecified sites	45,230	30,300	14,930	32,580	17,640	14,940

Note: Figures for invasive cancer only. In addition, about 120,000 new cases in situ are diagnosed each year, with carcinoma in situ of the uterine cervix accounting for about 65,000 of that number. 1. Melanoma only; about 2,100 nonmelanoma skin cancer deaths will occur in 1995. **Source:** American Cancer Society, *Cancer Facts & Figures—1995* (1995).

5-YEAR SURVIVAL RATES FOR CANCER, BY RACE AND SITE, 1960–90

Cancer site	1960–63	1970–73	1983–90
	Whites		
All sites	**39%**	**43%**	**56%**
Bladder	53	61	81
Breast (females)	63	68	82
Cervix	58	64	70
Colon	43	49	61
Leukemia	14	22	40
Liver	2	3	7
Lung and bronchus	8	10	14
Ovary	32	36	42
Pancreas	1	2	3
Prostate	50	63	81
Rectum	38	45	58
Stomach	11	13	18
Thyroid	83	86	95
	Blacks		
All sites	**27%**	**31%**	**40%**
Bladder	24	36	60
Breast (females)	46	51	66
Cervix	47	61	56
Colon	34	37	50
Leukemia	N.A.	N.A.	31
Liver	N.A.	N.A.	4
Lung and bronchus	5	7	11
Ovary	32	32	38
Pancreas	1	2	5
Prostate	35	55	66
Rectum	27	30	49
Stomach	8	13	19
Thyroid	N.A.	N.A.	90

Note: Rates are an average of cases diagnosed in years shown. **Source:** U.S. Dept. of Health and Human Services, National Cancer Institute; published in American Cancer Society, *Cancer Facts and Figures—1995* (1995).

4. A lump or thickening in the breast or elsewhere.
5. A change in bowel or bladder habits.
6. Nagging cough or hoarseness.
7. Indigestion or difficulty in swallowing.

AIDS

The epidemic of acquired immune deficiency syndrome (AIDS) continues to spread, and "will be an integral part of the human condition for a very long time," said Dr. Peter Piot, head of the United Nations HIV/AIDS program. By the end of 1994, according to the Centers of Disease Control and Prevention (CDC), the disease had been diagnosed in 441,528 people in the United States and its territories; of these, 270,870 had died. Yet this devastating disease was unknown until 1981.

AIDS is caused by the human immunodeficiency virus (HIV), which is spread through contact with infected body fluids such as blood and semen. Infected people may harbor the virus within their bodies for several years or even longer before developing any symptoms. Though symptomless, they can still infect others. The CDC estimates that approximately one million persons in the United States are infected with HIV.

The illness suppresses the body's immune system, making patients very susceptible to deadly "opportunistic diseases" that strike when body defenses are down. Among these are Kaposi's Sarcoma, a rare form of skin cancer, and pneumocystis, a parasitic lung infection.

In 1992 the CDC revised its definition of AIDS, effective Jan. 1, 1993, to include additional indicator diseases and HIV-infected people with CD4 cell counts below 200 per cubic millimeter (healthy individuals have 800 to 1,700 CD4 cells per cubic millimeter). As a result, the number of reported AIDS cases rose sharply. More than 106,000 new cases were reported in 1993 and about 81,000 in 1994, as contrasted to approximately 47,000 cases in 1992 (under the pre-1993 definition).

Although AIDS apparently is fatal, a small group of people seem to be able to suppress reproduction of HIV, and thus remain symptom-free for many years. There also have been reports of HIV-positive infants who fought off the infection. No cure for the disease has yet been developed, but researchers are testing experimental vaccines that may prove successful in preventing infection. Numerous drugs to combat AIDS also are being tested, and several are being used to suppress the AIDS virus and combat the infections that afflict AIDS patients. Only azidothymidine (AZT) has thus far been demonstrated to extend life. (See also "World Health" for information about AIDS worldwide.)

AIDS patients In the United States, homosexual and bisexual males make up approximately 53 percent of all adult and adolescent AIDS patients. The other major group afflicted with AIDS is intravenous drug abusers—both men and women—who constitute 25 percent of the total. An additional 7 percent of the cases are among men who both have sex with men and inject drugs. New infections have been increasing at a higher rate among drug users than among homosexuals.

AIDS CASES AND DEATHS IN THE UNITED STATES, 1981–94

Year	Cases diagnosed	Cases diagnosed to date	Known deaths	Known deaths to date
Pre-1981	96	96	31	31
1981	317	413	128	159
1982	1,173	1,586	460	619
1983	3,096	4,682	1,500	2,119
1984	6,245	10,927	3,486	5,605
1985	11,834	22,761	6,948	12,553
1986	19,149	41,910	12,040	24,593
1987	28,768	70,678	16,305	40,898
1988	35,626	106,304	21,013	61,911
1989	42,496	148,798	27,631	89,542
1990	47,778	196,576	31,269	120,811
1991	57,905	254,481	36,165	156,976
1992	74,724	329,205	39,307	196,283
1993	71,213	400,418	41,920	238,203
1994	41,110	441,528	32,330	270,533[1]

Note: Delays in reporting cases and deaths substantially impact data, particularly for recent years. 1. In addition, through 1994 there were 337 people known to have died but whose dates of death are unknown. **Source:** U.S. Dept. of Health and Human Services, Centers for Disease Control and Prevention, *HIV/AIDS Surveillance Report, 1994.*

AIDS IN THE CITIES, 1994

City	Number of cases
New York, N.Y.	71,934
Los Angeles, Calif.	27,247
San Francisco, Calif.	20,750
Miami, Fla.	14,050
Washington, D.C.	12,527
Chicago. Ill.	12,489
Houston, Tex.	11,414
Newark, N.J.	10,096
Philadelphia, Pa.	9,897
Atlanta, Ga.	8,858
Boston, Mass.	8,252
Dallas, Tex.	7,444
Ft. Lauderdale, Fla.	6,979
Baltimore, Md.	6,915
San Diego, Calif.	6,284
Oakland, Calif.	5,326
Tampa–St. Petersburg, Fla.	4,845
Detroit, Mich.	4,358
Seattle, Wash.	4,312
Jersey City, N.J.	4,047
Nassau–Suffolk, N.Y.	3,938
West Palm Beach, Fla.	3,930
Riverside–San Bernardino, Calif.	3,900
New Orleans, La.	3,867
Denver, Colo.	3,723
Orange County, Calif.	3,523

Note: Provisional data. **Source:** U.S. Dept. of Health and Human Services, Centers for Disease Control and Prevention, *HIV/AIDS Surveillance Report, 1994.*

ADULTS AND ADOLESCENTS WITH AIDS, 1981–94

	Males		Females		Total	
Exposure category	Cases	Percent	Cases	Percent	Cases	Percent
Homosexual/Bisexual males	228,954	61%	—	—	228,954	53%
Intravenous (IV) drug abusers	81,491	22	27,902	48%	109,393	25
Homosexual male and IV drug abusers	28,521	8	—	—	28,521	7
Heterosexual contact	10,641	3	21,021	36	31,663	7
Blood transfusion, blood components, or tissue	4,047	1	2,819	5	6,866	2
Hemophilia/Coagulation disorder	3,545	1	97	—	3,642	1
Other/Undetermined[1]	19,690	5	6,589	11	26,280	6
Total[2, 3]	**376,889**	**100%**	**58,428**	**100%**	**435,319**	**100%**

Note: Provisional data. Cases with more than one risk factor other than the combinations listed are tabulated only in the category listed first. 1. Includes patients whose mode of exposure to HIV is unknown; also includes four people who developed AIDS within the health-care setting. 2. Category totals may be more than 100% due to rounding. 3. Includes two persons whose sex is unknown. **Source:** U.S. Dept. of Health and Human Services, Centers for Disease Control and Prevention, *HIV/AIDS Surveillance Report, 1994.*

CHILDREN WITH AIDS, 1981–94

	1990		1994		Cumulative 1981–94	
Exposure category	Total	Percent	Total	Percent	Total	Percent
Mother with/at risk of AIDS[1]	693	88%	933	92%	5,541	89%
Blood transfusion, blood components, or tissue	38	5	28	3	357	6
Hemophilia/Coagulation disorder	31	4	12	1	221	4
Undetermined[2]	26	3	44	4	90	1
Total	**788**	**100%**	**1,017**	**100%**	**6,209**	**100%**

Note: Provisional data. Includes all patients under 13 years of age at time of diagnosis. Cases with more than one risk factor other than the combinations listed are tabulated only in the category listed first. 1. Data suggest transmission from an infected mother to her fetus or infant during the perinatal period. 2. Includes patients on whom risk information is incomplete and patients still under investigation. **Source:** U.S. Dept. of Health and Human Services. Centers for Disease Control and Prevention, *HIV/AIDS Surveillance Report, 1994.*

Cases are not limited to these high-risk groups. Anyone may become infected by having sex with someone who is infected with the HIV virus. Babies of infected women may be born with the disease because it can be transmitted from the mother to the baby before or during birth. Also, prior to blood screening that began in 1985, some hemophiliacs and other people were infected when they received blood contaminated with the HIV virus.

The overwhelming majority of AIDS cases are found in large cities and metropolitan areas. Through 1994, metropolitan areas with 500,000 or more population accounted for 374,533 of the 441,528 reported AIDS cases.

Heterosexuals and AIDS Cases of AIDS attributed to heterosexual contacts represent 7 percent of the total number of U.S. cases. Despite the comparatively low percentage, the disease is spreading faster among heterosexuals than among any other group. Heterosexuals most at risk are those with venereal disease and multiple sex partners. A 1989 study of patients at two clinics in Baltimore found that heterosexuals who had syphilis were seven to nine times more likely to have AIDS than other patients at the clinic. (Sores caused by syphilis and other venereal diseases are believed to make it easier for AIDS viruses to enter the body.) A 1992 report showed that 19 percent of American high school students have had four or more sex partners, thus putting themselves at high risk for AIDS.

Of the adult and adolescent AIDS cases reported during 1994, only 4 percent of all AIDS cases in men were attributed to heterosexual contact. Almost all of these cases occurred either among men born in countries where transmission is predominantly heterosexual or among men who had had sex with female intravenous drug users. In contrast, 38 percent of all AIDS cases among women have been attributed to heterosexual contact; the majority resulted from sex with male intravenous drug users.

Many women infected with the AIDS virus give birth to babies that are also infected. By the end of 1994, there were 5,541 reported cases of AIDS transmission from mothers to newborns.

Sexually Transmitted Diseases

The most common sexually transmitted diseases (STDs) include genital warts, herpes, chlamydia, gonorrhea, and syphilis. STDs have been around since the beginning of recorded history, and while the prevalence of some have declined, rates for others have exploded. Today, millions of people suffer from STDs. The ubiquity of these diseases can be attributed in part to the fact that more people have been engaging in sex, and with more than one partner.

Many STDs have similar symptoms. Some have no symptoms at all; unrecognized infection is "highly prevalent" among adolescents and young adults, many of whom are asymptomatic, noted the Centers for Disease Control and Prevention (CDC). The following may indicate the presence of an STD: vaginal or penile discharge; inflammation, itching, or pain in the genital or anal area; pain during intercourse; burning during urination; sores, blisters, bumps, or rashes; fever or swollen glands; lower abdominal or testicular pain.

Immediate, proper treatment is urged for all STDs. Failure to do so can have serious consequences, resulting in infertility, blindness, cancer, and death. Children born to women afflicted with STDs may suffer brain damage and other disorders.

State health departments are required to report cases of syphilis and gonorrhea to the CDC. In addition, the CDC estimates that there are one million new cases of genital warts and 250,000 to 500,000 new cases of genital herpes annually. Chlamydia, a disease caused by the bacterium *Chlamydia trachomatis*, is perhaps the fastest-spreading STD in the country today; the CDC estimates that some four million new infections occur anually.

Viral Hepatitis: A Major Cause of Liver Disease

One of today's most serious health problems caused by viruses is viral hepatitis, a sometimes-fatal disease that attacks the liver. Several viruses are responsible, but in the United States 97 percent of acute cases and 83 percent of chronic cases are accounted for by hepatitis viruses A, B, C, D, and E.

Of particular concern is hepatitis B, which is generally transmitted via contact with the blood of an infected person during sex, during birth, or through contaminated needles and syringes. People at high risk are intravenous drug users who share needles, homosexual men, and heterosexuals with multiple partners.

According to the Centers of Disease Control and Prevention (CDC), there are an estimated 200,000 new infections of hepatitis B annually. Some of those infected become chronic carriers. An estimated one million Americans are believed to be chronic carriers, capable of transmitting the virus to other people. Furthermore, chronic carriers are at high risk of developing cirrhosis or liver cancer; each year in the United States, about 1,000 hepatitis B patients die of these illnesses.

Worldwide, there are an estimated 300 million carriers of hepatitis B, and some one million deaths each year. The toll is particularly high in developing countries, where the virus often is passed from mothers to their newborn infants. The CDC and medical associations now recommend that all newborns be vaccinated against hepatitis B.

In 1995, the United States licensed the first vaccine to prevent hepatitis A, which is spread primarily by fecal contamination of food and water and through person-to-person contact. The CDC estimates that the virus infects 150,000 Americans each year.

Resurgence of Old Diseases

In recent years there have been widespread outbreaks of infectious diseases once thought to be under control.

Tuberculosis By the late 1970s, public health experts were predicting that this chronic bacterial disease would be almost completely eliminated in the United States by the end of the century. Beginning in 1988, however, the number of cases increased annually, reaching 26,673 new cases in 1992; by 1994, new cases had declined to 22,152. The resurgence resulted primarily from underfinanced and inadequate tuberculosis-control programs and from the fact that people weakened by the AIDS virus are very susceptible to tuberculosis. Other high-risk groups include drug users, alcoholics, the homeless, and people living in crowded conditions. Complicating the situation has been the emergence of strains of tuberculosis that are resistant to multiple medications. According to the World Health Organization (WHO), tuberculosis is the "world's most neglected health crisis." Some 1.9 billion people are infected with tuberculosis worldwide, and the disease kills an estimated 3 million people annually. A tuberculosis vaccine, known as BCG, has been injected in an estimated 3 billion people worldwide but is used infrequently in the United States.

Measles cases jumped to a 10-year high in the United States during 1990, with 27,786 cases, including 89 deaths, reported to the Centers for Disease Control and Prevention (CDC). Reported cases then declined dramatically to 277 in 1993, thanks to intensive immunization programs. But measles was on the rise again in 1994, with

CHILDHOOD VACCINES: RECOMMENDED IMMUNIZATION SCHEDULE

Age	Vaccines
Birth	Hepatitis B
2 months	Hepatitis B; polio; diphtheria, tetanus, pertussis (DTP); Haemophilus B (Hib)
4 months	Polio, DTP, Hib
6 months	Hepatitis B, polio, DTP, Hib
12–15 months	DTP; Hib; measles, mumps, rubella (MMR); chicken pox
4–6 years	Polio, DTP, MMR
11–12 years	Diphtheria, tetanus

Note: It generally takes several doses of each vaccine for full protection. In some cases, there is a range of acceptable ages for vaccination; for example, the third dose of hepatitis B vaccine may be given between 6 and 18 months of age. For additional information, contact your physician or call the CDC at 800-232-2500. **Sources:** American Academy of Pediatrics; American Academy of Family Physicians; and U.S. Dept. of Health and Human Services, Centers for Disease Control and Prevention.

895 reported cases. According to WHO, about 49 million people are infected worldwide, and the disease kills about 1.5 million people annually.

Malaria is caused by a parasite transmitted by the anopheles mosquito. The number of infected people rose steadily during the 1980s and early 1990s, in part because developing equatorial countries have encouraged development in swampy, anopheles-infected regions. As many as 300 million people are infected worldwide, and more than two million people die annually from the disease. Almost all of the approximately 1,100 Americans who contract malaria each year get the disease while traveling abroad.

Cholera is caused by a bacterium that is spread principally through food and drinking water contaminated with human feces. The disease is associated with poverty and is most prevalent in places that lack clean water supplies and hygienic sewage-disposal systems. In 1991 a cholera epidemic broke out in Peru—the first major outbreak of cholera in the Western Hemisphere in the 20th century. By September 1994 a total of 1,041,422 cases and 9,643 deaths had been reported throughout Central and South America. Meanwhile, a new strain of cholera was spreading across south Asia; attacks from older strains do not produce lasting immunity to this new strain. Cholera epidemics also occur regularly in crowded refugee camps. In 1994, for example, an estimated 20,000 to 30,000 Rowandan refugees in Zaire died from cholera. A total of 103 cases of cholera were reported in the United States for 1992—more than in any year since the CDC began cholera surveillance in 1961. U.S cases were significantly lower in 1993 (18) and 1994 (47); almost all of these cases were associated with foreign travel.

Emerging Diseases

The emergence of exotic new diseases and new strains of ancient scourges have erased the hope that modern medicine might soon end the threat of infectious diseases. Lyme disease, Legionnaire's disease, toxic shock syndrome, AIDS, and pulmonary hantavirus syndrome are among the diseases that were unknown a few decades ago but that now are serious medical problems. Various factors account for this development, including the evolution of drug-resistant germs, rapid and extensive international travel, overcrowding among human populations, and climate changes.

A 1992 report from the National Academy of Sciences warned that additional new diseases will emerge, "although it is impossible to perdict their individual emergence in time and place." In 1994 the Centers for Disease Control and Prevention launched a global network that will provide public health officials and physicians with early warnings of new diseases, resurgent diseases, and diseases migrating from other countries.

DEATH

Approximately 2,268,000 deaths occurred in the United States in 1993, about 91,000 more deaths than in the previous year. The death rate of 8.8 per 1,000 population was 3 percent higher than the rate of 8.5 for 1992.

Males experience greater number of deaths and higher death rates than females, with black males having significantly higher numbers and rates than white males. Age-adjusted death rates (which take into account changes and variations in the age composition of the population) for 1993 were: white females, 366.1 deaths per 100,000 population; black females, 583.1; white males, 631.2; and black males, 1,051.1.

DEATHS AND DEATH RATES, 1993

Age	Total deaths	Rate per 100,000 population: Both sexes	Male	Female
All ages	**2,268,000**	**879.3**	**927.2**	**833.7**
Under 1 year	33,300	848.7	965.1	727.2
1–4 years	7,020	44.5	49.0	39.7
5–14 years	8,740	23.6	27.4	19.6
15–24 years	35,190	97.6	144.1	49.2
25–34 years	59,740	142.6	211.4	73.7
35–44 years	95,920	234.9	327.9	143.5
45–54 years	133,180	464.6	602.7	332.6
55–64 years	241,980	1,156.6	1,480.1	864.4
65–74 years	490,500	2,629.8	3,414.8	2,008.9
75–84 years	638,630	5,930.4	7,719.5	4,825.6
85 and older	522,980	15,523.3	18,099.4	14,511.6
Not stated	780	—	—	—

Note: Provisional data, estimated from a 10 percent sample of deaths. **Source:** U.S. Dept. of Health and Human Services, National Center for Health Statistics. *Monthly Vital Statistics Report* (Oct. 11, 1994).

LEADING CAUSES OF DEATH, 1970–93

Cause of death	Deaths in 1993	Death rate per 100,000: 1970	1980	1993
All causes	**2,268,000**	**945.3**	**878.3**	**879.3**
Heart diseases	739,860	362.0	336.0	286.9
Cancer	530,870	162.8	183.9	205.8
Cerebrovascular diseases	149,740	101.9	75.1	58.1
Pulmonary diseases	101,090	15.2	24.7	39.2
Accidents	88,630	56.4	46.7	34.4
Pneumonia and influenza	81,730	30.9	24.1	31.7
Diabetes mellitus	55,110	18.9	15.4	21.4
AIDS	38,500	—	—	14.9
Suicide	31,230	11.6	11.9	12.1
Homicide and legal intervention	25,470	8.3	10.7	9.9
Liver disease and cirrhosis	24,730	15.5	13.5	9.6
Kidney diseases	23,500	4.4	7.4	9.1
Septicemia	20,420	1.7	4.2	7.9
Atherosclerosis	17,090	15.6	13.0	6.6
Perinatal-related conditions	15,820	21.3	10.1	6.1

Source: U.S. Dept. of Health and Human Services, National Center for Health Statistics, *Monthly Vital Statistics Report*, Oct. 11, 1994.

ESTIMATED NUMBER OF DEATHS AND DEATH RATES, BY SEX AND RACE, 1940–93

Year	Total	All races: Male	All races: Female	Whites: Male	Whites: Female	Blacks: Male	Blacks: Female
Deaths							
1940	1,417,269	791,003	626,266	690,901	540,322	95,517	83,226
1950	1,452,454	827,749	624,705	731,366	544,719	92,004	77,602
1960	1,711,982	975,648	736,334	860,857	644,478	107,701	88,309
1970	1,921,031	1,078,478	842,553	942,437	739,659	127,540	98,107
1980	1,989,841	1,075,078	914,763	933,878	804,729	130,138	102,997
1985	2,086,440	1,097,758	988,682	950,455	868,599	133,610	110,597
1990	2,162,000	1,121,850	1,040,430	966,270	911,930	139,320	116,440
1993	2,268,000	1,167,360	1,100,600	993,800	956,880	153,250	128,180
Death rates (per 100,000 population)							
1940	1,076.4	1,197.4	954.6	1,162.2	919.4	N.A.	N.A.
1950	963.8	1,106.1	823.5	1,089.5	803.3	N.A.	N.A.
1960	954.7	1,104.5	809.2	1,098.5	800.9	1,181.7	905.0
1970	945.3	1,090.3	807.8	1,086.7	812.6	1,186.6	829.2
1980	878.3	976.9	785.3	983.3	806.1	1,034.1	733.3
1985	873.9	945.0	806.6	960.0	837.1	976.8	727.7
1990	861.9	917.2	809.3	937.2	847.9	941.5	711.0
1993	879.3	927.2	833.7	943.9	874.0	1,004.7	757.8

Note: Death rates are based on population estimates prepared by the U.S. Bureau of the Census. **Source:** U.S. Dept. of Health and Human Services, National Center for Health Statistics, *Monthly Vital Statistics Report*, Oct. 11, 1994.

CHANGES IN LEADING CAUSES OF DEATH IN U.S., 1900–1993

Cause of death	Death rate (per 100,000 population)
1900: All causes	**1,719.1**
Pneumonia and influenza	202.2
Tuberculosis	194.4
Diarrhea, enteritis, and ulceration of the intestines	142.7
1920: All causes	**1,298.9**
Pneumonia and influenza	207.3
Heart disease	159.6
Tuberculosis	113.1
1940: All causes	**1,074.1**
Heart disease	291.3
Cancer	120.0
Cerebrovascular disease	90.8
1960: All causes	**954.7**
Heart disease	369.0
Cancer	149.2
Cerebrovascular disease	108.0
1980: All causes	**878.3**
Heart disease	336.0
Cancer	183.9
Cerebrovascular disease	75.1
1990: All causes	**863.8**
Heart disease	289.5
Cancer	203.3
Cerebrovascular disease	57.9
1993: All causes	**879.3**
Heart disease	286.9
Cancer	205.8
Cerebrovascular disease	58.1

Source: U.S. Dept. of Health and Human Services, National Center for Health Statistics, *Monthly Vital Statistics Report*, Oct. 11, 1994.

Causes of Death

For the purpose of national mortality statistics, every death is attributed to one underlying condition. The 15 leading causes of death in 1993 accounted for 86 percent of all deaths in the United States. The leading causes of death from 1980 through 1993 generally were the same, but the order sometimes varied. The exception was AIDS, which ranked as a cause of death for the first time in 1987.

During the 20th century the leading causes of death have changed significantly. In 1900, infectious diseases took many lives, a fact reflected in the five leading causes of death: (1) pneumonia and influenza, (2) tuberculosis, (3) gastritis, (4) heart disease, and (5) cerebrovascular diseases. Today none of the top five causes of death is an infectious disease.

Suicide

Each year, some 30,000 Americans kill themselves—about one person every 20 minutes. In addition, an estimated 400,000 unsuccessful attempts are made. Although more attempts are made by women, more completed suicides are by men. In 1993, there were 24,990 suicides committed by men and 6,250 committed by women.

SUICIDE IN THE U.S., 1950–93

Age	Total 1993	Rate per 100,000 population 1950	1993
All ages	**31,230**[1]	**11.4**	**12.1**
0–4 years	—	—	—
5–14 years	310	0.2	0.6
15–24 years	4,960	4.5	13.8
25–34 years	6,240	9.1	14.9
35–44 years	5,910	14.3	14.5
45–54 years	4,040	20.9	14.1
55–64 years	2,980	27.0	14.2
65–74 years	3,400	29.3	18.2
75–84 years	2,520	31.1	23.4
85 and older	860	28.8	25.5

Note: Provisional data. 1. Includes 10 people of unknown age. **Source:** U.S. Dept. of Health and Human Services, National Center for Health Statistics, *Monthly Vital Statistics Report*, Oct. 11, 1994.

Particularly troublesome is the suicide rate for people age 15 to 24, which has tripled since 1950. The causes of youth suicide are not yet known, although some evidence suggests that suicide is not as frequently associated with depression in young people as it is in adults. Many young suicide victims had a history of impulsive, aggressive, or antisocial behavior, often complicated by drug abuse. Having a parent who committed suicide also seems to increase a person's vulnerability.

Significant differences in suicide rates exist among the states. For 1992, the highest rates were reported for Nevada (24.6 per 100,000 population), New Mexico (19.2), Montana (18.6), Wyoming (18.1), and Colorado (17.3). The lowest were for the District of Columbia (5.8), New Jersey (6.6), Rhode Island (7.3), New York (8.5), and Massachusetts (8.9).

Most Americans who commit suicide shoot themselves, usually with handguns. Other common methods, in decreasing order of frequency, include drug overdose (primarily drugs prescribed by physicians), cutting and stabbing, jumping from high places, inhaling poisonous gas, hanging, and drowning.

Many experts believe that suicide statistics are grimmer than reported. They contend that numerous suicides are categorized as accidents or other deaths to spare families.

ACCIDENTAL DEATHS IN U.S., 1910–93 (per 1,000 population)

Year	Death rate	Year	Death rate
1910	84.4	1960	52.1
1920	71.2	1970	56.2
1930	80.5	1980	46.5
1940	73.4	1990	36.9
1950	60.3	1993	34.9

Sources: U.S. Dept. of Health and Human Services, National Center for Health Statistics (1910–90); National Safety Council (1993).

ACCIDENTAL DEATHS AND DEATH RATES BY NATION

Nation	Year reported	Accidental deaths	Rate per 100,000 pop.
Australia	1992	4,350	24.9
Austria	1992	3,172	40.2
Bulgaria	1992	3,762	44.1
Canada	1991	8,785	32.2
Costa Rica	1991	899	28.9
Czech Republic	1992	6,077	58.9
Denmark	1992	2,326	45.0
Finland	1992	2,706	53.7
France	1991	32,520	57.0
Germany	1991	29,582	37.0
Greece	1991	3,646	35.7
Hong Kong	1991	868	15.1
Hungary	1992	8,582	83.1
Iceland	1992	71	27.2
Ireland	1991	1,023	29.0
Japan	1992	34,677	28.1
Korea, Republic of	1991	26,308	60.8
Mexico	1991	39,240	45.1
Netherlands	1991	3,586	23.8
New Zealand	1991	1,243	36.8
Norway	1991	1,780	41.8
Poland	1992	21,096	55.0
Portugal	1992	4,478	45.4
Puerto Rico	1991	1,159	32.5
Singapore	1991	487	17.6
Switzerland	1992	3,369	49.0
Trinidad and Tobago	1991	350	28.0
United Kingdom	1992	12,436	21.4
United States	1990	91,983	37.0

Note: Accidental deaths are classified on the basis of a World Health Organization standard. However, differences in reporting among nations affect comparisons. **Source:** World Health Organization.

ACCIDENTS

Every 10 minutes, two people are killed and 350 suffer a disabling injury in accidents in the United States. Accidents are the nation's fifth most common cause of death. But for people between the ages of 1 and 37, accidents are the leading cause of death.

On a positive note, the accident death rate has fallen significantly over the years. In 1992 it was a record-low 32.5 deaths per 100,000 population—a steep decline from the 1912 rate of 82.5. In 1993, according to National Safety Council estimates, the death total was 90,000, a 5 percent increase from the 1992 total; the death rate of 34.9 was the second lowest on record. Accident rates vary significantly from one place to another. National Safety Council estimates indicate that the highest accidental death rates were in Alaska (69.6), New Mexico (61.0), and Mississippi (54.9); the lowest were in Massachusetts (22.8), Connecticut (24.2), and New Jersey (24.9).

TYPES OF ACCIDENTAL DEATHS IN U.S., 1993

Type	Number of deaths	Age group (years) 0–4	5–14	15–24	25–44	45–64	65–74	75+
All accidents	**90,000**	**3,400**	**3,600**	**13,900**	**25,900**	**14,500**	**7,900**	**20,800**
Motor vehicle	42,000	1,000	2,000	10,600	14,200	6,900	2,900	4,400
Falls	13,500	90	80	230	900	1,300	1,500	9,400
Poisoning by solids and liquids[1]	6,500	40	30	280	4,300	1,100	300	450
Drowning	4,800	700	500	900	1,400	800	240	260
Fires and burns	4,000	850	350	200	650	600	500	850
Suffocation	2,900	140	30	30	200	450	550	1,500
Firearms	1,600	40	180	550	450	210	60	110
Poisoning by gases	700	40	30	110	200	140	50	130
All other[2]	14,000	500	400	1,000	3,600	3,000	1,800	3,700

1. Deaths from poisons, drugs, medicines, mushrooms, and shellfish. Excludes poisonings from spoiled foods, salmonella, etc., which are classified as disease deaths. 2. Medical complications, air and water transport, machinery, excessive cold, etc. **Source:** National Safety Council, *Accident Facts* (1994).

LIFE EXPECTANCY AT BIRTH IN U.S., 1920–93

Year[1]	All races Male	All races Female	Whites Male	Whites Female	Others Male	Others Female
1920	53.6	54.6	54.4	55.6	45.5	45.2
1930	58.1	61.6	59.7	63.5	47.3	49.2
1940	60.8	65.2	62.1	66.6	51.5	54.9
1950	65.6	71.1	66.5	72.2	59.1	62.9
1960	66.6	73.1	67.4	74.1	61.1	66.3
1970	67.1	74.7	68.0	75.6	61.3	69.4
1980	70.0	77.4	70.7	78.1	65.3	73.6
1990	71.8	78.8	72.7	79.4	67.0	75.2
1993[2]	72.1	78.9	73.0	79.5	67.4	75.5

1. Data prior to 1960 exclude Alaska and Hawaii. Data prior to 1940 are for death-registration states only. 2. Provisional data. **Source**: U.S. Dept. of Health and Human Services, National Center for Health Statistics, *Monthly Vital Statistics Report*, Oct. 11, 1994.

ESTIMATED NUMBER OF INJURIES IN U.S., SELECTED PRODUCTS, 1993

Product	Estimated injuries	Product	Estimated injuries
Stairs, steps	1,055,355	Trampolines	46,215
Bicycles, accessories	604,066	Crutches, canes, walkers	45,445
Knives	460,625		
Tables	340,184	Razors, shavers	43,691
Chairs	307,066	Hot water	43,250
Nails, screws, tacks	233,627	Chain saws	40,149
Bathtubs, showers	151,852	Shopping carts	37,304
Ladders	141,616	Television	36,457
Drinking glasses	127,232	Contact lenses	33,162
Fences, fence posts	126,980	Pens, pencils	30,683
Carpets, rugs	116,201	Scissors	28,998
Drugs, medications	115,814	Paper money, coins	28,592
Metal containers	105,879	Skateboards	27,718
Bottles, jars	100,536	Refrigerators	27,337
Footwear	94,228	Baby walkers, jumpers	25,457
Lawn mowers	71,598		
Sinks, toilets	63,192	Gasoline	20,092
Wheelchairs	61,133	Pins, needles	19,486
Sleds	55,260	Telephones, accessories	18,899
Hammers	52,882		
Jewelry	51,017	Irons	16,447
Bunk beds	48,311	Pesticides	16,281

Notes: These national estimates are based on injuries treated in hospital emergency rooms participating in the National Electronic Injury Surveillance System. Patients said their injuries were related to the products; this does not necessarily mean the injuries were caused by the products. **Source:** Consumer Product Safety Commission, National Electronic Injury Surveillance System, *NEISS Product Summary Report* (1994).

Approximately 18.2 million disabling injuries occurred in 1993—injuries that disabled people for one or more days.

The costs incurred from accidents totaled an estimated $407.5 billion in 1993—for medical care, wage loss, insurance administration, property damage, fire loss, and so on.

Motor Vehicle Deaths, 1993

Since the nation's first motor vehicle death—reportedly in New York City on September 13, 1899—some 2.9 million people have died in motor vehicle accidents. Over the years, however, the numbers of deaths per 100,000 population and per 100,000 registered vehicles have declined drastically. For example, noted the National Safety Council, there were 3,100 motor vehicle deaths in 1912, when the number of registered vehicles totaled only 950,000. In 1993 there were 42,000 fatalities, but registered vehicles had risen to almost 197 million. Here's how people died in motor vehicle accidents in 1993:

17,900—collisions between two or more motor vehicles
11,900—collisions with guardrails and other fixed objects
6,200—pedestrians struck by motor vehicles
4,500—noncollision accidents
800—collisions with cyclists
600—collisions with railroad trains
100—other types of collisions, usually ones involving animals or animal-drawn vehicles.

Data suggest that safety belts, air bags, bicycle and motorcycle helmets, and child safety seats save thousands of lives each year. In 1992, for example, safety belts saved approximately 5,226 lives; child restraints saved 268 lives—but an estimated 455 lives could have been saved if all children under age five were using mandatory safety seats.

ACCIDENTS BY SITE, 1993

Site	Deaths	Disabling injuries	Cost (billions)
Total[1]	**90,000**	**18,200,000**	**$407.5**
Motor vehicle	42,000	2,000,000	167.3
Home	22,500	6,600,000	86.5
Public[2]	20,000	6,600,000	58.9
Work	9,100	3,200,000	111.9

1. Deaths and injuries for the four separate classes total more than national figures due to rounding and because some deaths and injuries are included in more than one class. For example, 3,500 work deaths involved motor vehicles and are in both the work and motor-vehicle totals. 2. Includes accidents in public places or places used in a public way, and not including motor vehicles. **Source:** National Safety Council, *Accident Facts* (1994).

LIFE EXPECTANCY

Life expectancy figures represent the average number of years that infants are expected to live. Life expectancy has improved steadily over the years, largely due to a decline in deaths during childhood. The development of drugs to combat infectious diseases, plus improved nutrition and better environmental sanitation, have all played major roles in combating early deaths.

In 1993, the average length of life in the United States was 75.5 years—a decline of 0.2 year since 1992 and the first decline since 1980. The decline may reflect higher mortality associated with influenza epidemics in 1993. For whites, the average length of life was 76.3 years, while for blacks it was 69.3, a full seven years shorter than for whites. Homicides, killings in police confrontations, auto accidents, AIDS, tuberculosis, and other categories have had a disproportionate impact on the races in recent years, affecting blacks more than whites.

INFANT MORTALITY

In 1993 there were 33,300 reported deaths of infants age one year or less. The most commonly used index for measuring the risk of dying during the first year of life are infant mortality

U.S. INFANT MORTALITY RATE, 1940–93 (per 1,000 live births)

Year	All races	White	Black
1940	47.0	43.2	72.9
1950	29.2	26.8	43.9
1960	26.0	22.9	44.3
1970	20.0	17.8	32.6
1980	12.6	11.0	21.4
1990	9.2	7.6	18.0
1993	8.5	7.0	17.0

Source: U.S. Dept of Health and Human Services, National Center for Health Statistics, *Monthly Vital Statistics Report*, Oct. 11, 1994.

rates, which are calculated by dividing the number of infant deaths by the number of live births registered for the same period. The 1993 rate of 8.3 infant deaths per 1,000 live births was the lowest ever recorded for the United States; that's 2 percent lower than the previous low of 8.5 recorded in 1992. Preliminary data suggested that in 1994 the rate fell to 7.9.

The rate among white infants is less than half that of black infants: 6.9 infant deaths per 1,000 live births for whites in 1992, versus 16.8 per 1,000 for blacks. The reasons for this discrepancy are not clear, although an important factor is believed to be the quality of medical care received by people of different socioeconomic groups. For example, several studies of infant deaths have shown that adequate prenatal care is strongly associated with higher infant birth weight and survival. Many black mothers, who are far more likely to be poor than white mothers, do not have access to proper prenatal care. Poor nutrition, alcohol and drug abuse, and other social factors also play significant roles.

Disproportionate poverty among minority groups is not the whole story, however. Studies have shown that even black infants born to college-educated mothers had nearly twice the mortality rate of comparable white infants.

The four leading causes of infant deaths in 1992 were congenital anomalies (21.5% of all deaths), sudden infant death syndrome (14.1%), disorders relating to short gestation and low birthweight (11.7%), and respiratory distress syndrome (6.0%).

(See also "World Health" for infant mortality rates in other nations.)

AVERAGE REMAINING LIFE EXPECTANCY IN U.S. (in years)

Age in 1992	All races		White		Other races		Age in 1992	All races		White		Other races	
	M	F	M	F	M	F		M	F	M	F	M	F
At birth	72.3	79.1	73.2	79.8	67.7	75.7	43	32.8	38.0	33.3	38.4	30.0	35.8
1	72.0	78.7	72.8	79.3	67.7	75.7	44	32.0	37.1	32.4	37.5	29.2	34.9
2	71.1	77.8	71.8	78.3	66.8	74.8	45	31.1	36.2	31.5	36.5	28.4	34.0
3	70.1	76.8	70.9	77.3	65.9	73.8	46	30.2	35.3	30.6	35.6	27.6	33.1
4	69.1	75.8	69.9	76.3	64.9	72.9	47	29.4	34.3	29.7	34.7	26.8	32.2
5	68.1	74.8	68.9	75.4	63.9	71.9	48	28.5	33.4	28.8	33.7	26.0	31.4
6	67.2	73.9	67.9	74.4	62.9	70.9	49	27.6	32.5	28.0	32.8	25.3	30.5
7	66.2	72.9	66.9	73.4	62.0	69.9	50	26.8	31.6	27.1	31.9	24.5	29.6
8	65.2	71.9	65.9	72.4	61.0	68.9	51	25.9	30.7	26.3	31.0	23.7	28.8
9	64.2	70.9	65.0	71.4	60.0	68.0	52	25.1	29.8	25.4	30.1	23.0	28.0
10	63.2	69.9	64.0	70.4	59.0	67.0	53	24.3	29.0	24.6	29.2	22.2	27.1
11	62.2	68.9	63.0	69.4	58.0	66.0	54	23.5	28.1	23.7	28.3	21.5	26.3
12	61.2	67.9	62.0	68.4	57.0	65.0	55	22.7	27.2	22.9	27.5	20.8	25.5
13	60.3	66.9	61.0	67.4	56.1	64.0	56	21.9	26.4	22.1	26.6	20.1	24.7
14	59.3	65.9	60.0	66.5	55.1	63.0	57	21.1	25.5	21.3	25.7	19.4	23.9
15	58.3	65.0	59.1	65.5	54.1	62.0	58	20.4	24.7	20.6	24.9	18.8	23.2
16	57.4	64.0	58.1	64.5	53.2	61.1	59	19.6	23.9	19.8	24.1	18.1	22.4
17	56.4	63.0	57.2	63.5	52.3	60.1	60	18.9	23.1	19.1	23.2	17.5	21.7
18	55.5	62.0	56.2	62.5	51.4	59.1	61	18.2	22.3	18.3	22.4	16.8	20.9
19	54.6	61.1	55.3	61.6	50.5	58.1	62	17.5	21.5	17.6	21.6	16.2	20.2
20	53.7	60.1	54.3	60.6	49.6	57.2	63	16.8	20.7	16.9	20.8	15.6	19.5
21	52.7	59.1	53.4	59.6	48.7	56.2	64	16.1	19.9	16.2	20.0	15.0	18.8
22	51.8	58.2	52.5	58.7	47.9	55.3	65	15.4	19.2	15.5	19.3	14.4	18.1
23	50.9	57.2	51.6	57.7	47.0	54.3	66	14.8	18.4	14.9	18.5	13.9	17.4
24	50.0	56.2	50.6	56.7	46.1	53.3	67	14.2	17.7	14.3	17.8	13.3	16.7
25	49.1	55.2	49.7	55.7	45.2	52.4	68	13.5	16.9	13.6	17.0	12.8	16.1
26	48.2	54.3	48.8	54.8	44.4	51.4	69	12.9	16.2	13.0	16.3	12.2	15.4
27	47.2	53.3	47.8	53.8	43.5	50.5	70	12.4	15.5	12.4	15.6	11.7	14.8
28	46.3	52.3	46.9	52.8	42.6	49.5	71	11.8	14.8	11.8	14.9	11.2	14.2
29	45.4	51.4	46.0	51.8	41.8	48.6	72	11.2	14.1	11.3	14.2	10.8	13.6
30	44.5	50.4	45.1	50.9	40.9	47.7	73	10.7	13.5	10.7	13.5	10.3	13.0
31	43.6	49.4	44.1	49.9	40.0	46.7	74	10.1	12.8	10.2	12.9	9.8	12.4
32	42.7	48.5	43.2	48.9	39.2	45.8	75	9.6	12.2	9.6	12.2	9.4	11.8
33	41.8	47.5	42.3	48.0	38.3	44.9	76	9.1	11.6	9.1	11.6	8.9	11.2
34	40.9	46.6	41.4	47.0	37.4	43.9	77	8.6	10.9	8.6	11.0	8.5	10.6
35	40.0	45.6	40.5	46.0	36.6	43.0	78	8.1	10.3	8.1	10.4	8.1	10.0
36	39.1	44.7	39.6	45.1	35.8	42.1	79	7.7	9.7	7.7	9.8	7.6	9.5
37	38.2	43.7	38.7	44.1	34.9	41.2	80	7.2	9.2	7.2	9.2	7.2	8.9
38	37.3	42.8	37.8	43.2	34.1	40.3	81	6.8	8.6	6.8	8.6	6.8	8.4
39	36.4	41.8	36.9	42.2	33.3	39.3	82	6.4	8.1	6.4	8.1	6.4	7.9
40	35.5	40.9	36.0	41.2	32.4	38.4	83	6.0	7.6	6.0	7.6	6.0	7.4
41	34.6	39.9	35.1	40.3	31.6	37.5	84	5.6	7.1	5.6	7.1	5.7	6.9
42	33.7	39.0	34.2	39.3	30.8	36.6	85 and over	5.3	6.6	5.3	6.6	5.4	6.5

Note: Based on an individual's age in 1992. For example, a nonwhite female age 61 in 1992 would be expected to live 20.9 more years, or to about 82 years old. A white male born in 1992 would be expected to live to 73 years of age. **Source:** U.S. Dept. of Health and Human Services, National Center for Health Statistics, unpublished data.

SUBSTANCE ABUSE

Illicit Drugs

A significant portion of the American public continues to use illegal drugs. The 1993 National Household Survey on Drug Abuse found that 11.7 million Americans, or 5.6 percent of people age 12 and older, were users in 1993. The peak year for illicit drug use was 1979, when there were an estimated 24 million users (13.7% of the population). As in the past, the 1993 rate of illicit drug use was highest among 18- to 25-year-olds (13.5%) and lowest for those age 35 and older (2.8%). Marijuana is the most commonly used illicit drug in the United States, followed by cocaine.

Another indicator of drug use is the Drug Abuse Warning Network (DAWN), which collects information on patients seeking hospital emergency room treatment related to their abuse of legal and illicit drugs. Of the estimated 466,900 drug-related emergency room episodes during 1993, 36,300 resulted from recreational drug use, 144,300 from dependence, 184,400 from attempted suicides, and 101,900 from other or unknown motives.

While the precise dimensions of illegal drug use in the United States are unknown, there is no doubt that the effects on society of these drugs are enormous. A study released by the U.S. Department of Health and Human Services in 1990 estimated that drug abuse costs the United States $58.3 billion a year. Of this amount, $42.2 billion (72%) is for nonhealth costs related to crime. Lost productivity accounts for $7.2 billion, treatment for $2.7 billion, and mortality for $3.0 billion.

Marijuana is the most commonly used illegal drug, used by 77 percent of current drug users. It is made from the leaves and flowering tops of the hemp plant, *Cannabis sativa,* which contains psychoactive substances called cannabinoids. The primary psychoactive ingredient in marijuana and hashish (a resin exuded from the flowering tops) is tetrahydrocannabinol, or THC. The amount of each cannabinoid varies markedly from one plant to another depending on climate, soil, and other factors.

Marijuana is typically prepared as a tobacco-like mixture that is smoked in hand-rolled cigarettes or in pipes. It typically produces a "high"—a feeling of well-being, relaxation, and sleepiness. It also interferes with coordination and mental abilities. For instance, it distorts judgment and reaction time, which can be particularly dangerous when a user drives a car. Adverse effects may also include delusions, anxiety, and paranoia.

Possession or sale of marijuana has been illegal in the United States since 1937. Nonetheless, marijuana has legitimate medical uses. A significant body of evidence shows that marijuana combats nausea and weight loss in cancer and AIDS patients. It also helps reduce pressure within the eyes of glaucoma patients. But because the drug is illegal, most patients find it difficult or impossible to obtain. A recent Harvard University survey of 2,500 cancer specialists found that almost 50 percent would prescribe marijuana to control the nausea that often accompanies chemotherapy; 44 percent said they had already recommended marijuana to patients despite the drug's illegality. Still, the U.S. government has resisted pressure to reclassify the drug as one that may be legally prescribed.

Cocaine is made from the leaves of the coca plant, a shrub native to South America. In the late 1800s and early 1900s, before its dangers were recognized, cocaine was used by doctors as an anesthetic because of its effectiveness in depressing nerve endings. It has since been replaced by less toxic, nonaddictive anesthetics.

Cocaine causes a short-lived euphoria (sensation of well-being or elation). It also suppresses appetite, interferes with sleep, and increases heart rate and blood pressure. Even small doses have been linked to heart attacks and cerebral hemorrhages. Repeated usage is required to maintain a "high." Abusers who try to abstain often experience a tremendous craving for the drug—a hallmark of addiction.

Crack is a highly addictive, smokable form of cocaine that appeared in the mid-1980s. Sold in small beige chunks called pellets or rocks, it usually is smoked in a glass pipe. Its effects on the brain are almost immediate, producing a brief but intense high. Within minutes, however, depression sets in, combined with a craving for another "hit." People can become addicted to crack in weeks or even days. Continued use often results in irritability, sleeplessness, delusions, hallucinations, and other psychological damage. It also can cause weight loss and lung and heart damage, leading in some cases to fatal heart attacks. Crack's increased use has been accompanied by rises in deaths, emergency room visits, and crime.

Alcohol

Consumption of alcohol constitutes the nation's most common drug abuse problem. The 1993 National Household Survey on Drug Abuse reported that approximately 103 million people age 12 and older currently used alcohol (defined as any use in the past month). About 11 million Americans were heavy drinkers. Usage exhibited a downward trend since 1985, when there were an estimated 112 million drinkers. Heavy alcohol use changed little since 1985, when there were some 12 million heavy drinkers. In contrast to the pattern for illicit drugs, the higher the level of educational attainment, the more likely the current use of alcohol. In 1993, 64 percent of adults with college degrees were current drinkers, compared with 36 percent of those having less than a high school education.

The economic costs of alcohol abuse were estimated to be $98.6 billion in 1990. This amount included $36.6 billion (37%) for reduced productivity, $33.6 billion for mortality losses, and $10.5 billion for treatment. Alcohol is believed to be implicated in half of all homicides, almost half of all traffic fatalities, and one-third of all suicides. Plus it takes an immeasurable emotional toll on family and other relationships.

DRUG USE BY U.S. HIGH SCHOOL SENIORS, 1975–92

Drug	1975	1980	1985	1990	1992
Alcohol	68.2%	72.0%	65.9%	57.1%	51.3%
Cigarettes	36.7	30.5	30.1	29.4	27.8
Marijuana	27.1	33.7	25.7	14.0	11.9
LSD	2.3	2.3	1.6	1.9	2.0
Cocaine	1.9	5.2	6.7	1.9	1.3
Heroin	0.4	0.2	0.3	0.2	0.3

Note: Drug use during the 30 days preceding the survey. **Source:** University of Michigan, National High School Senior Survey.

U.S. EMERGENCY ROOM DRUG-ABUSE EPISODES, 1988–93

Drug	1988	1990	1993
Total episodes[1]	403,578	371,208	466,897
Alcohol-in-combination	115,671	115,162	145,394
Cocaine	101,578	80,355	123,317
Heroin/Morphine	38,063	33,884	62,965
Acetaminophen	23,320	25,422	34,980
Marijuana/Hashish	19,962	15,706	29,166
Aspirin	22,766	19,188	19,347
Ibuprofen	14,829	16,299	18,169
Methamphetamine	8,992	5,236	10,052
PCP/PCP combinations	12,346	4,408	6,527
LSD	3,836	3,869	3,369

Note: Figures are estimates. 1. Includes both legal and illegal drugs. **Source:** U.S. Dept. of Health and Human Services, National Institute on Drug Abuse, *Preliminary Estimates from the Drug Abuse Warning Network* (December 1994).

LIFETIME EXPERIENCE WITH ILLICIT DRUGS, 1993

Age	Used in lifetime	Used in past year	Used in past month
All ages [1]	37.2%	11.8%	5.6%
12–17	17.9	13.6	6.6
18–25	50.9	26.6	13.5
26–34	61.1	17.4	8.5
35 and older	29.9	6.3	2.8

Note: Includes marijuana, cocaine, heroin, hallucinogens, inhalants, or prescription-type psychotherapeutic drugs (stimulants, sedatives, tranquilizers, and analgesics) for nonmedical purposes. 1. Age 12 and older. **Source:** U.S. Dept. of Health and Human Services, Substance Abuse and Mental Health Services Administration, *Preliminary Estimates from the 1993 National Household Survey on Drug Abuse* (1994).

U.S. ALCOHOL CONSUMPTION, 1940–92 (gallons of ethanol, per capita)

Year	Beer	Wine	Spirits	All beverages
1940	0.73	0.16	0.67	1.56
1950	1.04	0.23	0.77	2.04
1960	0.99	0.22	0.86	2.07
1970	1.14	0.27	1.11	2.52
1980	1.38	0.34	1.04	2.76
1990	1.34	0.33	0.78	2.46
1992	1.29	0.30	0.72	2.31

Note: Based on population age 15 and older prior to 1970 and on population age 14 and older thereafter. **Source:** U.S. Dept of Health and Human Services, National Institute on Alcohol Abuse and Alcoholism, *Surveillance Report #31* (November 1994).

COMMONLY ABUSED DRUGS

Drug	Primary effect	Popular names
Alcohol	Depressant	Drink, booze
Amphetamines	Stimulant	Pep pills, uppers; *methamphetamines:* speed, meth
Amyl or butyl nitrites	Stimulant	Poppers, snappers, rush, locker room
Barbituates	Depressant	Sleeping pills, dolls
Cocaine	Stimulant	Coke, snow, lady; *smokable form:* crack
Heroin	Depressant	Snow, smack; *synthetic heroin:* China white, Persian heroin, gasoline dope; *combined heroin and cocaine:* speedball
D-lysergic acid diethylamide	Hallucinogen	LSD, acid
Marijuana	Hallucinogen/depressant	Pot, grass, joint, cannabis, dope, reefer, herb, weed
MDMA (combination of synthetic mescaline and an amphetamine)	Stimulant/hallucinogen	Ecstasy, love potion
Mescaline	Hallucinogen	Peyote, cactus
Morphine	Depressant	
PCP (phencyclidine)	Hallucinogen	Angel dust
Tranquilizers	Depressants	Downers; *brand names:* Valium, Librium, Darvon, etc.

Consumption According to the National Institute on Alcohol Abuse and Alcoholism (NIAAA), per capita consumption of beer, spirits, and wine grew slightly (1.0%) during the 1950s, rose rapidly (21.3%) during the 1960s, rose moderately (9.1%) in the 1970s, and decreased (12.0%) during the 1980s. In 1990, consumption increased by 1.2% from 1989, but 1991 saw a return to the declines of the 1980s; there was no change from 1991 to 1992. Annual per capita consumption in 1992 was 2.31 gallons of ethanol (pure alcohol), down from 2.46 gallons in 1990. Studies show that men are heavier drinkers than women, and younger people drink more than older people. Consumption was highest in Nevada (4.33 gallons of ethanol per capita), New Hampshire (4.30), and the District of Columbia (4.15). It was lowest in Utah (1.37), West Virginia (1.67), and Kentucky (1.72).

Several factors have contributed to consumption declines, including the general aging of the population, increased state and federal taxes on alcoholic beverages, stricter penalties for drinking and driving, and the formation of minority advocacy groups to counter industry efforts to target minority populations.

Health consequences Alcohol is toxic, or poisonous. In addition to myriad social consequences, excessive alcohol intake affects many organs of the body. Primary problems include:

1. Liver damage. Drinking increases the chance of "alcoholic hepatitis," characterized by inflammation and destruction of liver cells. Heavy drinkers also run the risk of developing cirrhosis, a disease in which fibrous tissue and nodules replace normal tissue, interferring with liver functions.

2. Nervous system damage. In addition to mental deterioration and behavioral problems, heavy drinking may cause permanent brain damage.

3. Cancer. Heavy drinking increases the risk of developing various cancers, particularly those of the liver, mouth, and esophagus.

4. Fetal damage. When a pregnant woman takes a drink, she is sharing that drink with her unborn child, creating the risk that the child will be born with fetal alcohol syndrome, a disorder characterized by physical and mental defects. Because even low alcohol usage can result in damage to the fetus, pregnant women are advised to abstain completely from alcohol from time of conception until they have finished nursing.

Identifying alcoholism The following were among 33 statements used in a national survey of alcohol use and alcohol-related problems conducted by NIAAA. Survey participants responded "true" or "false" to each statement. A person who answers "true" to at least one statement may be an alcohol abuser or an alcoholic.

I have often taken a drink the first thing when I get up in the morning.

I deliberately tried to cut down or quit drinking but was unable to do so.

Once I started drinking it was difficult for me to stop before I became completely intoxicated.

I have had a quick drink when no one was looking.

I have skipped a number of regular meals while drinking.

I have awakened the next day not being able to remember some of the things I had done while drinking.

I have lost a job, or nearly lost one, because of my drinking.

My drinking contributed to getting hurt in an accident (in a car or elsewhere).

A physician suggested I cut down on drinking.

I have stayed away from work or gone to work late because of a hangover.

Tobacco

Smoking is the single most preventable cause of death in our society. Each year, an estimated 419,000 people die in the United States as a result of smoking. Government agencies and independent economists estimate that smoking costs the nation as much as $100 billion a year—for lost productivity, medical bills, insurance premiums, heating and cooling expenses, maintenance, and cleaning costs. For medical care alone, smoking-attributable costs in 1993 were estimated at $50 billion.

The percentage of adults who smoke decreased dramatically after 1964, the year the U.S. surgeon general first warned about the link between smoking and health problems such as cancer and heart disease. At that time, 40 percent of the adult population were smokers; by 1992 the figure had fallen to 26 percent (48 million people). Per capita cigarette consumption dropped to 2,640—the lowest since 1942. The increased cost of cigarettes, a growing number of smoking restrictions in public places, and decreasing social acceptability of smoking also played roles in the decline.

The adult smoking population has remained static since 1990; teenage smoking has increased, and is a primary barrier to reducing smoking prevalence. Surveys indicate that more than 90 percent of adults who are regular smokers began smoking while they were teenagers. Both sexes are equally likely to smoke, but male adolescents are significantly more likely than females to use smokeless tobacco. White adolescents are more likely to use all forms of tobacco than are blacks and Hispanics. In 1995, David A. Kessler, commissioner of Food and Drugs, called smoking "a pediatric disease," and outlined a comprehensive program to combat the problem.

HEAVY ALCOHOL USERS IN U.S., 1993

	Age of user				
	12–17	18–25	26–34	35 and older	Total, all ages
Total	**280,000**	**2,899,000**	**2,668,000**	**5,060,000**	**10,907,000**
Sex					
Male	222,000	2,327,000	2,258,000	4,491,000	9,298,000
Female	58,000	572,000	410,000	569,000	1,609,000
Race					
White	191,000	2,467,000	2,147,000	4,084,000	8,889,000
Black	11,000	142,000	253,000	574,000	979,000
Hispanic	56,000	271,000	254,000	366,000	946,000
Other	(1)	20,000	15,000	(1)	94,000
Region					
Northeast	38,000	734,000	684,000	990,000	2,447,000
North Central	93,000	665,000	564,000	1,660,000	2,982,000
South	67,000	942,000	854,000	1,289,000	3,152,000
West	81,000	560,000	566,000	1,121,000	2,327,000

Notes: Preliminary data. Heavy alcohol users are defined as drinking five or more drinks per occasion on five or more days in the past month. 1. Low precision; no estimate reported. **Source:** U.S. Dept. of Health and Human Services, Substance Abuse and Mental Health Services Administration, *Preliminary Estimates from the 1993 National Household Survey on Drug Abuse* (1994).

ADULT CIGARETTE SMOKERS IN THE U.S., 1993

Category	Men	Women	Total
Total	**27.7%**	**22.5%**	**25.0%**
Age (years)			
18–24	28.8	22.9	25.8
25–44	31.1	27.3	29.2
45–64	29.2	23.0	26.0
65 and older	13.5	10.5	11.8
Race			
White	27.0	24.0	25.4
Black	32.4	21.0	26.0
Hispanic	28.3	12.7	20.4
Education[1]			
9 to 11 years	42.1	32.3	36.8
12 years	32.0	26.9	29.2
13 to 15 years	28.4	22.1	25.0
16 years or more	14.8	11.9	13.5

1. Age 25 and older. **Source:** U.S. Dept. of Health and Human Services, Centers for Disease Control and Prevention, *Morbidity and Mortality Weekly Report* (Dec. 23, 1994).

U.S. CIGARETTE CONSUMPTION 1900–1994

Year	Total cigarettes (billions)	Cigarettes per capita[1]
1900	2.5	54
1910	8.6	151
1920	44.6	665
1930	119.3	1,485
1940	181.9	1,976
1950	369.8	3,552
1960	484.4	4,171
1970	536.5	3,985
1980	631.5	3,849
1990	525.0	2,817
1994[2]	480.0	2,493

1. Among persons age 18 and older. 2. Estimated data. **Source:** U.S. Dept. of Health and Human Services, Centers for Disease Control and Prevention, *Morbidity and Mortality Weekly Report* (Nov. 18, 1994).

Health effects The major effects of smoking include:

- Shortened life span. Each year, over 400,000 Americans—and 2.5 million people worldwide—die prematurely as a result of smoking.
- Cancer of the lungs, mouth, esophagus, stomach, bladder, kidney, pancreas, and cervix. Smoking is responsible for 30 percent of all cancer deaths in the United States each year, including 87 percent of lung cancer deaths.
- Cardiovascular disease, including heart attack, stroke, aneurysm, and peripheral vascular disease. Smoking weakens the heart's ability to pump blood, promotes clot formation, and damages the inner lining of blood vessels.
- Pulmonary illness, including emphysema, pneumonia, and chronic bronchitis. Annually, more than 80,000 Americans die from noncancerous chronic lung diseases linked to smoking.
- Spontaneous abortions. Women who smoke during pregnancy are 10 times more likely to miscarry than are nonsmokers.
- Underweight, sickly babies. Each year, the deaths of more than 2,000 children under a year old are attributed to the mothers' smoking while pregnant. Infants of smokers have a 50 percent higher risk of developing Sudden Infant Death Syndrome (SIDS) and are 74 percent more likely to be of low birth weight than are infants born to mothers who do not smoke. An infant exposed to *any* cigarette smoke is 3.5 times more likely to die of SIDS than an infant not exposed to smoke.
- Environmental smoking risks. Nonsmokers who are exposed to the tobacco smoke of other people are at increased risk for various diseases. So-called "secondhand smoke" is responsible for approximately 3,000 lung cancer deaths annually among nonsmokers and 150,000 to 300,000 cases of lower respiratory tract infections such as bronchitis and pneumonia in children up to 18 months old.

It's never too late to quit The risk of disease and premature death declines when a person stops smoking, regardless of age. For example, a study of people with clogged heart arteries found that over six years the death rate of older people who continued to smoke was 70 percent higher than the rate of people who had quit shortly before the study began.

AGRICULTURE

In the United States during the colonial period and the early years of the Republic, agriculture, while vital (involving 95% of the population), remained relatively small-scale and in economic terms primitive, with the exception of large plantations in the South devoted to cotton, tobacco, and rice. The Civil War brought higher food prices and increased mechanization throughout the farming industry. It also led to federal legislation aimed at encouraging farming; the Homestead Act of 1862 and the Morrill Land Grant College Act were especially important.

FARMS—NUMBER AND ACREAGE, BY STATE, 1980–94

State	Farms 1980	Farms 1994	Acreage (millions) 1980	Acreage (millions) 1994	Acreage per farm 1980	Acreage per farm 1994
Alabama	59,000	46,000	12	10	207	217
Alaska	(Z)	1,000	2	1	3,378	1,788
Arizona	8,000	8,000	38	36	5,080	4,557
Arkansas	59,000	44,000	17	15	280	350
California	81,000	76,000	34	30	417	388
Colorado	27,000	25,000	36	33	1,358	1,292
Connecticut	4,000	4,000	(Z)	(Z)	117	108
Delaware	4,000	3,000	1	1	186	220
Florida	39,000	39,000	11	10	344	264
Georgia	59,000	43,000	15	12	254	281
Hawaii	4,000	4,000	2	2	458	389
Idaho	24,000	21,000	15	14	623	659
Illinois	107,000	77,000	29	28	269	368
Indiana	87,000	63,000	17	16	193	254
Iowa	119,000	100,000	34	33	284	332
Kansas	75,000	65,000	48	48	644	735
Kentucky	102,000	89,000	15	14	143	158
Louisiana	37,000	28,000	10	8	273	300
Maine	8,000	7,000	2	1	195	201
Maryland	18,000	15,000	3	2	157	152
Massachusetts	6,000	6,000	1	1	116	102
Michigan	65,000	52,000	11	11	175	206
Minnesota	104,000	85,000	30	30	291	349
Mississippi	55,000	39,000	15	13	265	326
Missouri	120,000	104,000	31	30	261	288
Montana	24,000	23,000	62	60	2,601	2,584
Nebraska	65,000	55,000	48	47	734	856
Nevada	3,000	2,000	9	9	3,100	3,708
New Hampshire	3,000	3,000	1	(Z)	160	180
New Jersey	9,000	9,000	1	1	109	101
New Mexico	14,000	14,000	47	44	3,467	3,274
New York	47,000	37,000	9	8	200	216
North Carolina	93,000	58,000	12	9	126	160
North Dakota	40,000	32,000	42	40	1,043	1,263
Ohio	95,000	75,000	16	15	171	203
Oklahoma	72,000	70,000	35	34	481	486
Oregon	35,000	38,000	18	18	517	467
Pennsylvania	62,000	51,000	9	8	145	153
Rhode Island	1,000	1,000	(Z)	(Z)	87	87
South Carolina	34,000	24,000	6	5	188	213
South Dakota	39,000	34,000	45	44	1,169	1,300
Tennessee	96,000	84,000	14	12	142	146
Texas	196,000	185,000	138	129	705	699
Utah	14,000	13,000	12	11	919	854
Vermont	8,000	6,000	2	1	226	230
Virginia	58,000	43,000	10	9	169	200
Washington	38,000	36,000	16	16	429	445
West Virginia	22,000	20,000	4	4	191	185
Wisconsin	93,000	78,000	19	17	200	217
Wyoming	9,000	9,000	35	35	3,846	3,772
U.S. total	**2,440,000**	**2,040,000**	**1,039**	**975**	**426**	**478**

Note: Z = fewer than 500,000 acres. **Source:** U.S. Dept. of Agriculture, *Farm Numbers and Land in Farms* (July 1995).

The decision to build a transcontinental rail system—undertaken by private enterprise abetted by government grants—opened up large areas of the Great Plains to farming, and the railroad companies recruited immigrants to buy and farm the land the government had given the companies.

In the early 20th century, machinery gradually replaced animal power. In 1910, for example, U.S. farms used 24.2 million horses and mules and only about a thousand tractors; by 1959 the figures had changed to 4.7 million tractors and only 3.2 million draft animals. World War I stimulated agriculture, but the stimulus led to overproduction, which, with the coming of peace, depressed prices and land values. This decline both contributed to and was intensified by the Great Depression, one of the most paralyzing aspects of which was a near total cessation of world agricultural trade. The plight of farmers during the 1930s prompted considerable government remedies, including various forms of credit, price supports, rural electrification, and serious efforts at soil conservation. World War II again gave impetus to agriculture.

After the war, new machinery, new chemicals, and hybrid crops, more resistant to weather and biological enemies, significantly increased crop yields. By the end of the 1940s, the United States had become the world's largest single producer of wheat, corn, and soybeans. One byproduct of this success was the creation of huge surpluses. U.S. agriculture proved a potent force in the world economy and in foreign policy, and in 1954, Public Law 480 provided for the export of surplus grains to poorer nations both to prevent starvation and stimulate economic development, and to alleviate the pressures on the domestic agriculture sector caused by the surpluses.

Research into developing ever hardier strains of food crops and livestock continues. Yet the number of American farms has declined as small units lose out to huge agribusinesses owned by corporations with assets that smaller farmers cannot match. Between 1980 and 1994, the number of farms fell from 2.4 million to 2.0 million (a decline of 16%), while average acreage per farm rose from 426 to 478 (an increase of 12%). Overall, the total land area devoted to farming dropped from 1,039,000 acres to 975,000, a decline of 6 percent. Because agribusinesses are much less labor intensive, the total farm population has also declined precipitously. This diminishing opportunity for farm work has accelerated internal migration from country to city.

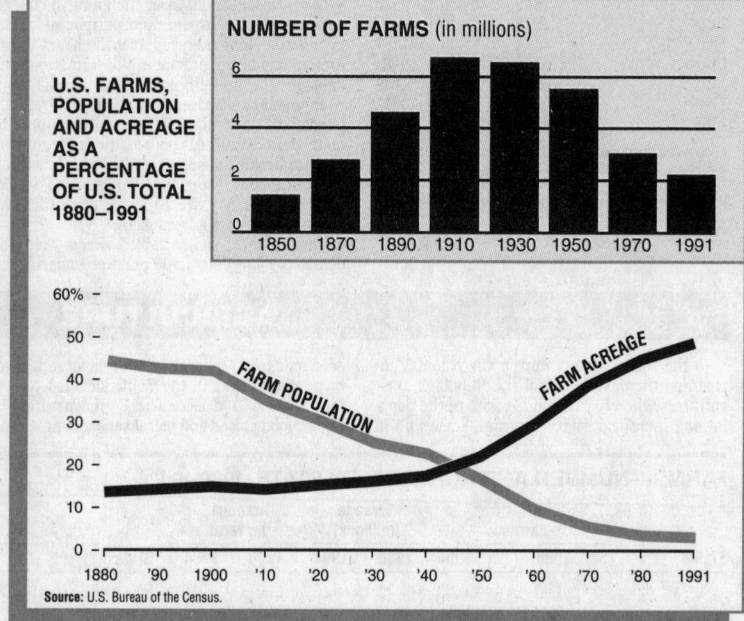

Source: U.S. Bureau of the Census.

U.S. FARMS, ACREAGE, AND POPULATION, 1850–1994

		Acreage			Population	
Year	Farms ('000s)	Total ('000s)	Per farm	Percent of U.S.	Total ('000s)	Percent of U.S.
1850	1,449	293,561	203	15.6%	—	—
1860	2,044	407,213	199	21.4	—	—
1870	2,660	407,735	153	21.4	—	—
1880	4,009	536,082	134	28.2	21,973	43.8%
1890	4,565	623,219	137	32.7	24,771	42.3
1900	5,740	841,202	147	37.0	29,835	41.9
1910	6,366	881,431	139	38.8	32,077	34.9
1920	6,454	958,677	149	42.2	31,974	30.1
1930	6,295	990,112	157	43.6	30,529	24.9
1940	6,102	1,065,114	175	46.8	30,547	23.2
1950	5,388	1,161,420	216	51.1	23,048	15.3
1960	3,962	1,176,946	297	49.5[1]	15,635	8.7
1970	2,954	1,102,769	373	47.0[2]	9,712	4.8
1980	2,440	1,039,000[3]	426	44.8	6,051	2.7
1985	2,293	1,012,000[3]	441	N.A.	N.A.	N.A.
1990	2,140	987,000[3]	461	42.7	4,801	1.9
1991	2,105	983,000[3]	467	42.5	4,591	1.9
1992	2,094	980,000[3]	468	N.A.	N.A.	N.A.
1993	2,064	978,000[3]	474	N.A.	N.A.	N.A.
1994	2,040	975,000[3]	478	N.A.	N.A.	N.A.

1. Figure for 1959. 2. Figure for 1969. 3. Figure rounded in source. **Source:** U.S. Bureau of the Census, *Statistical History of the United States* (1970); *Statistical Abstract of the United States 1995* (1995).

FARM OPERATORS—TENURE AND CHARACTERISTICS, 1987–92

Characteristic	1987	1992
Total operators	**2,088**	**1,925**
Race and sex		
White	2,043	1,882
Black	23	19
American Indian, Eskimo, and Aleut	7	8
Asian or Pacific Islander	8	8
Hispanic origin[1]	17	21
Female	132	145
Age		
Under 25 years old	36	28
25–34 years old	243	179
35–44 years old	411	382
45–54 years old	455	429
55–64 years old	496	430
65 years old and over	447	478
Average age (in years)	52.0	53.3

Characteristic	1987	1992
Ownership		
Full owner	1,239	1,112
Part owner	609	597
Tenant	240	217
Principal occupation		
Farming	1,138	1,053
Other	950	872
Years on present farm		
2 or less	114	95
3–4 years	135	133
5–9 years	304	259
10 years or more	1,163	1,113
Days worked off farm		
None	844	802
Fewer than 100 days	200	165
100 to 199 days	178	162
200 days or more	737	666

Note: Excludes not reported. 1. People of Hispanic origin may be of any race. **Source:** U.S. Bureau of the Census, *Statistical Abstract of the United States, 1994.*

THE MEDIA

The Print Media

NEWSPAPERS

The mutual distrust between government and the media dates back to the very first American newspaper in 1690, when a three-page publication called *Publick Occurrences, Both Foreign and Domestick* was suppressed by the government after one issue. A number of newspapers sprang up during the pre–Revolutionary War period, and by 1775 the colonies, with a population of 2.5 million people, were served by 48 weekly newspapers, small in both size and circulation. The first daily, the *Pennsylvania Evening Post and Daily Advertiser,* was not published until 1783. By 1800 there were 20 daily newspapers and more than 1,000 small-town and frontier weeklies. Most of the dailies, filled with political

NEWSPAPERS—NUMBER AND CIRCULATION, 1900–1994

	Total		Morning		Evening		Sunday	
Year	Number of papers	Daily circulation ('000s)	Number of papers	Daily circulation ('000s)	Number of papers	Daily circulation ('000s)	Number of papers	Daily circulation ('000s)
1900	2,226	15,102	—	—	—	—	—	—
1915	2,580	28,777	—	—	—	—	571	16,480
1920	2,042	27,791	437	—	1,605	—	522	17,084
1930	1,942	39,589	388	—	1,554	—	521	26,413
1940	1,878	41,132	380	16,114	1,498	25,018	525	32,371
1950	1,772	53,829	322	21,266	1,450	32,563	549	46,582
1960	1,763	58,882	312	24,029	1,459	34,853	563	47,699
1970	1,748	62,108	334	25,934	1,429	36,174	586	49,217
1975	1,756	60,655	339	25,490	1,436	36,165	639	51,096
1980	1,745	62,202	387	29,414	1,388	32,787	735	54,672
1985	1,676	62,766	482	36,362	1,220	26,405	798	58,826
1990	1,611	62,324	559	41,308	1,084	21,015	863	62,634
1993	1,552	59,593	607	42,690	966	16,904	888	62,591
1994[1]	1,538	59,025	611	42,826	947	16,198	889	62,412

Note: All-day newspapers are listed in both morning and evening columns, but are counted only once in the total. There were 20 such papers in 1994. 1. Preliminary. **Source:** Newspaper Association of America, *Facts About Newspapers, 1995.*

TOP 100 U.S. DAILY NEWSPAPERS, BY CIRCULATION, 1994

Rank	Newspaper	Average daily paid circulation
1.	Wall Street Journal	1,780,422
2.	USA Today	1,465,926
3.	New York Times	1,114,905
4.	Los Angeles Times	1,062,202
5.	Washington Post	810,675
6.	New York Daily News	753,024
7.	Long Island/New York Newsday	693,556
8.	Chicago Tribune	678,081
9.	Detroit Free Press	544,606
10.	San Francisco Chronicle	518,094
11.	Chicago Sun-Times	509,548
12.	Dallas Morning News	506,545
13.	Boston Globe	491,480
14.	Philadelphia Inquirer	478,999
15.	Newark Star Ledger	455,919
16.	Houston Chronicle	409,340
17.	Minneapolis Star Tribune	407,504
18.	Cleveland Plain Dealer	405,318
19.	New York Post	394,692
20.	Miami Herald	393,791
21.	San Diego Union-Tribune	372,466
22.	Arizona Republic (Phoenix)	362,199
23.	Detroit News	355,970
24.	St. Petersburg Times	354,164
25.	Orange County Register	350,887
26.	Denver Rocky Mountain News	344,585
27.	Portland Oregonian	334,744
28.	St. Louis Post Dispatch	333,968
29.	Boston Herald	309,935
30.	Atlanta Constitution	309,906
31.	Buffalo News	296,820
32.	Kansas City Star	290,650
33.	Denver Post	287,213
34.	San Jose Mercury-News	283,590
35.	Houston Post	281,628
36.	Sacramento Bee	257,696
37.	Orlando Sentinel	270,970
38.	New Orleans Times-Picayune	267,938
39.	Fort Lauderdale Sun-Sentinel	263,256
40.	Tampa Tribune	264,400
41.	Columbus Dispatch	260,355
42.	Baltimore Sun	248,520
43.	Pittsburgh Post-Gazette	248,183
44.	Louisville Courier-Journal	239,595
45.	Fort Worth Star-Telegram	237,031
46.	Charlotte Observer	236,579
47.	Omaha World-Herald	233,035
48.	San Antonio Express-News	232,037
49.	Indianapolis Star	231,423
50.	Seattle Times	230,286
51.	Hartford Courant	226,533
52.	Milwaukee Journal	214,243
53.	Richmond Va. Times-Dispatch	211,227
54.	St. Paul Pioneer Press	207,802
55.	Oklahoma City Oklahoman	207,759
56.	Los Angeles Daily News	207,011
57.	Seattle Post-Intelligencer	203,679
58.	Cincinnati Enquirer	203,118
59.	Philadelphia Daily News	196,239
60.	Providence Journal-Bulletin	190,876
61.	Memphis Commercial Appeal	185,834
62.	Des Moines Register	184,591
63.	Jacksonville Times-Union	181,841
64.	Los Angeles Investor's Business Daily	176,740
65.	Austin American-Statesman	176,696
66.	Milwaukee Sentinel	175,330
67.	Little Rock Democrat-Gazette	174,883
68.	West Palm Beach Post	172,744
69.	Tulsa World	170,208
70.	Norfolk Virginian-Pilot	165,940
71.	Asbury Park (N.J.) Press	163,282
72.	Dayton Daily News	162,039
73.	Riverside (Calif.) Press-Enterprise	161,659
74.	Birmingham News	159,823
75.	Hackensack (N.J.) Record	159,545
76.	Akron Beacon Journal	155,812
77.	Fresno Bee	150,438
78.	Toledo Blade	149,750
79.	Raleigh News & Observer	148,618
80.	Grand Rapids Press	147,530
81.	Nashville Tennessean	144,331
82.	Rochester (N.Y.) Democrat & Chronicle	143,392
83.	Atlanta Journal	140,473
84.	Las Vegas Review-Journal	137,153
85.	Allentown (Pa.) Morning Call	136,645
86.	Columbia (S.C.) State	130,649
87.	Tacoma Morning News Tribune	128,932
88.	Wilmington News Journal	125,742
89.	Salt Lake City Tribune	125,037
90.	Chicago Dalily Herald	124,595
91.	Spokane Spokesman-Review	121,909
92.	Knoxville News-Sentinel	119,388
93.	Long Beach Press-Telegram	117,742
94.	Albuquerque Journal	114,807
95.	Sarasota Herald Tribune	114,250
96.	Lexington Herald-Leader	113,818
97.	Roanoke Times and World-News	113,502
98.	Worcester Telegram & Gazette	112,121
99.	San Francisco Examiner	112,051
100.	Wichita Eagle	111,827

Source: *Editor & Publisher Yearbook, 1995.*

TOP 100 U.S. MAGAZINES, BY CIRCULATION, 1994

Rank	Magazine	Combined circulation	Percent change 1993–94
1.	NRTA/AARP Bulletin	21,875,436	–0.95%
2.	Modern Maturity	21,716,727	–2.29
3.	Reader's Digest	15,126,664	–5.83
4.	TV Guide	14,037,062	–0.61
5.	National Geographic Magazine	9,203,079	–2.00
6.	Better Homes and Gardens	7,613,661	0.17
7.	Good Housekeeping	5,223,935	1.19
8.	Ladies' Home Journal	5,048,081	–2.05
9.	Family Circle	5,005,301	–2.13
10.	Woman's Day	4,724,500	–2.76
11.	McCall's	4,611,848	0.14
12.	Time	4,063,146	–0.99
13.	Prevention	3,427,803	6.43
14.	AAA World	3,425,655	0.75
15.	People Weekly	3,424,858	–0.63
16.	Redbook	3,401,775	1.68
17.	Playboy	3,401,264	1.73
18.	Sports Illustrated	3,252,641	–3.10
19.	Newsweek	3,158,617	0.08
20.	National Enquirer	3,066,032	–9.91
21.	The American Legion Magazine	2,945,123	1.99
22.	Star	2,752,280	–6.95
23.	Cosmopolitan	2,527,928	–3.79
24.	Southern Living	2,472,689	4.39
25.	U.S. News & World Report	2,240,710	–1.78
26.	Smithsonian	2,214,509	0.09
27.	Motorland	2,194,221	3.00
28.	Glamour	2,181,316	–5.36
29.	Home & Away	2,146,295	3.22
30.	NEA Today	2,115,968	0.91
31.	V.F.W. Magazine	2,038,216	–1.65
32.	Field & Stream	5,004,087	–0.19
33.	Money	1,982,123	–5.61
34.	Seventeen	1,978,155	1.94
35.	Ebony	1,937,095	0.26
36.	YM	1,933,775	13.26
37.	Country Living	1,932,840	–2.12
38.	Parents Magazine	1,852,517	4.50
39.	Popular Science	1,808,140	–0.42
40.	Popular Mechanics	1,636,210	–1.25
41.	Life	1,596,862	–1.74
42.	Outdoor Life	1,503,257	0.04
43.	Sunset, the Magazine of Western Living	1,498,417	3.95
44.	Golf Digest	1,465,494	0.27
45.	Soap Opera Digest	1,422,958	–0.64
46.	The Elks Magazine	1,305,156	–3.04
47.	Penthouse	1,304,719	8.57
48.	Mademoiselle	1,304,059	7.80
49.	New Woman	1,301,859	–0.95
50.	'Teen	1,280,148	9.34
51.	Golf Magazine	1,269,642	3.94%
52.	Men's Health	1,258,493	36.99
53.	Cooking Light	1,248,939	11.53
54.	Boy's Life	1,242,594	–1.77
55.	First For Women	1,236,019	–2.66
56.	Rolling Stone	1,221,417	–1.22
57.	Consumers Digest	1,208,643	–3.62
58.	Self	1,201,395	–6.88
59.	Bon Appetit	1,187,437	–8.30
60.	Vogue	1,181,313	–5.50
61.	Us	1,177,395	6.07
62.	Woman's World	1,167,314	–4.08
63.	Vanity Fair	1,130,993	–2.31
64.	Car and Driver	1,125,119	6.61
65.	Sesame Street Magazine	1,117,074	–5.96
66.	Entertainment Weekly	1,115,024	4.59
67.	Kiplinger's Personal Finance Magazine	1,095,652	–0.30
68.	PC Magazine	1,051,381	1.12
69.	The Family Handyman	1,041,098	0.07
70.	Scouting	1,037,291	0.29
71.	Weight Watchers Magazine	1,031,177	–0.42
72.	House Beautiful	1,023,697	1.41
73.	Globe	1,021,929	2.49
74.	Country Home	1,018,362	–3.22
75.	Home Mechanix	1,009,347	–1.53
76.	Discover	1,008,916	–2.19
77.	Home	1,005,751	–3.66
78.	Country America	1,001,089	–2.01
79.	Endless Vacation	975,869	5.00
80.	Disney Adventures	961,992	13.67
81.	AAA Going Places	953,194	6.14
82.	PC World	951,849	3.99
83.	Motor Trend	951,650	2.01
84.	Essence	950,634	3.56
85.	Martha Stewart Living	948,838	27.24
86.	Jet	948,254	–2.59
87.	Travel & Leisure	927,790	–8.22
88.	Mature Outlook	921,384	–7.38
89.	Health	916,952	–4.59
90.	Gourmet	912,342	0.67
91.	Condé Nast Traveler	909,092	4.91
92.	Victoria	907,034	–0.60
93.	Elle	905,498	–2.05
94.	PC/Computing	900,165	2.05
95.	Architectural Digest	881,232	–11.93
96.	Business Week (North America)	880,357	–0.38
97.	Nation's Business	861,620	0.03
98.	Parenting Magazine	856,019	6.27
99.	Midwest Living	852,704	3.31
100.	The New Yorker	830,307	2.69
Total, top 100		**253,224,488**	**–0.72%**

Note: Leading Audit Bureau of Circulation (ABC) magazines by average paid combined circulation per issue, second six months of 1993. **Source:** Magazine Publishers of America, 1995.

and business news, were expensive and aimed at educated, affluent readers. The first of the mass-circulation dailies, known as the penny press, was the *New York Sun*, started in 1833 and sold for the bargain price of one cent. The *Sun*, with its crime stories and soft features, marked a dramatic change in newspaper coverage.

The next major change in newspapers came in the era during and after the Civil War. Dramatic technological improvements such as the

TOP 50 MAGAZINES, RANKED BY ADVERTISING REVENUES, 1994

Rank	Magazine	Revenues	Percent change 1992–93
1.	People Weekly	$405,712,515	10.4%
2.	TV Guide	391,726,593	21.6
3.	Sports Illustrated	385,254,202	27.6
4.	Time	372,044,007	8.1
5.	Newsweek	278,948,289	7.0
6.	Business Week	233,798,642	7.5
7.	U.S. News & World Report	221,148,254	9.4
8.	Better Homes and Gardens	220,966,386	17.1
9.	Good Housekeeping	218,604,695	5.6
10.	Forbes	189,219,133	8.9
11.	Family Circle	178,725,375	9.5
12.	Woman's Day	167,273,807	14.3
13.	Fortune	163,605,389	9.6
14.	Cosmopolitan	147,986,564	5.1
15.	Ladies' Home Journal	138,762,981	8.6
16.	Reader's Digest	134,286,773	2.2
17.	McCall's	114,360,315	11.6
18.	Vogue	110,967,075	–1.0
19.	Money	104,154,013	5.8
20.	Redbook	100,404,104	6.2
21.	Glamour	98,321,208	–3.6
22.	Southern Living	96,516,245	10.1
23.	Rolling Stone	83,214,849	16.4
24.	Golf Digest	82,744,019	–1.9
25.	Car and Driver	82,412,969	36.8
26.	The New Yorker	77,438,810	9.7
27.	Entertainment Weekly	69,983,140	43.4
28.	Bride's	69,793,046	16.9
29.	Country Living	67,848,805	4.5
30.	Parents Magazine	62,336,883	–8.4
31.	Elle	60,118,245	11.3
32.	Inc.	59,506,871	7.3
33.	Golf Magazine	55,133,202	14.2
34.	Harper's Bazaar	54,653,035	–4.6
35.	Road & Track	54,218,425	35.2
36.	Vanity Fair	53,498,707	–6.7
37.	Modern Bride	53,374,628	5.6
38.	Modern Maturity	53,249,371	2.0
39.	Self	50,395,944	12.0
40.	Gentlemen's Quarterly	49,517,255	4.8
41.	Sunset	49,397,888	–5.0
42.	Travel & Leisure	48,426,465	–5.4
43.	House Beautiful	48,106,877	12.5
44.	Seventeen	47,859,918	19.4
45.	National Geographic	47,718,960	2.0
46.	Playboy	45,871,253	–0.4
47.	New York Magazine	43,181,902	–0.5
48.	Parenting	42,805,528	22.9
49.	Gourmet	41,048,930	13.0
50.	Condé Nast Traveler	40,557,759	10.4
	Magazine supplements		
1.	Parade	$447,649,714	9.0%
2.	USA Weekend	218,095,370	19.4
3.	The New York Times	110,655,805	0.0
4.	The Los Angeles Times	33,604,626	–14.4

Source: Magazine Publishers of America, *Publishers Information Bureau Publications Ranked by Revenue, January–December 1994* (1995).

transatlantic cable, the telephone, the electric light bulb, typewriters, web-fed presses, and the typesetting machine made possible cheap, mass-circulation newspapers. By 1900 the number of daily newspapers had jumped to 2,226. Over the next half-century, the number of newspapers steadily declined while readership increased, owing in part to the popularity of Sunday editions.

Newspapers today. In 1994, 1,538 daily newspapers were published in the United States—947 afternoon publications and 611 morning papers. (There were 20 papers printed all day in 1994; they are counted as both morning and evening papers, but are counted only once in the total.) The number of newspapers have been slowly declining for decades, in part because of radio and television, but also because in the fight for readers and advertising, competing papers have battled until a single winner emerged. Fewer than 50 cities have competing newspapers today, a major change from the turn of the century when most major cities had more than two newspapers. By contrast, 17 cities have competing newspapers only by virtue of a joint operating agreement that combines all of the two papers' operations except for their editorial staffs, which remain independent (in some cases fiercely) of each other.

Daily circulation for all newspapers dropped for the seventh consecutive year in 1994 to just over 59 million. Evening newspapers were responsible for all of the dropoff, even counteracting a 136,802 increase in circulation by morning papers. Circulation of Sunday editions dropped slightly to 62 million. Despite the dropoff in circulation, the American Newspaper Association reported that the number of people who read a newspaper actually increased, from 114.7 million per day in 1993 to 115.4 million (61.5% of the population) in 1994. That suggests an increase in the number of people reading the paper over somebody else's shoulder: Newspapers in 1994 had an average of 2.34 readers per copy.

The vast majority of newspapers have circulations of less than 50,000; 126 have circulations between 50,000 and 100,000; and 129 have a daily circulation of more than 100,000. The top seven newspaper companies—Gannett, Knight-Ridder, Newhouse, Times Mirror, the New York Times Co., Dow Jones & Co., and Thomson Newspapers—account for more than a third of all newspaper circulation.

MAGAZINES

Consumer magazines range from the very specialized *(Fly Fisherman)* to general interest *(People)* and are sold either by subscription or through retail outlets (supermarkets, newsstands, etc.). The Audit Bureau of Circulations (ABC) monitors the sales of about 500 of the most popular consumer magazines. While single-copy sales of ABC magazines have decreased steadily since 1978, subscriptions have increased about 50 percent during the same period, more than offsetting the single-copy decline. Trade publications are magazines with a narrow focus in a particular area of business (e.g., trucking, restaurants, computers). There are about 3,700 trade publications; they are sold either by subscription or distributed free.

Almost all magazines make money through revenues from both circulation and advertising. The most financially successful magazines are not necessarily the largest sellers, the difference being in the advertising fees they are able to obtain. *Fortune*, for example, is in the top 15 of all magazines in revenues but does not even make the top-100 list in circulation.

BOOKS

NUMBER AND VALUE OF U.S. BOOKS SOLD, 1987–94 (in millions)

Type of publication and market area	Publishers' units 1987	Publishers' units 1994	Consumer expenditures 1987	Consumer expenditures 1994
Type of publication				
Trade	600.2	836.2	$ 4,453.0	$ 9,161.5
Adult trade	373.5	510.0	3,398.6	7,155.1
Juvenile trade	226.7	326.2	1,054.4	2,006.4
Religious	135.5	151.0	1,104.0	1,690.1
Professional	135.9	161.7	2,349.7	3,867.0
Book clubs	123.6	118.7	659.8	849.5
Mail order publications	132.6	98.8	678.6	575.5
Mass market paperback	441.4	520.2	1,411.1	2,156.5
University press	14.7	17.8	199.2	377.4
Elementary and high school	216.2	220.2	1,632.8	2,074.0
College	129.6	148.5	1,802.6	2,536.0
Subscription reference	1.1	1.2	380.5	511.0
All books	**1,930.8**	**2,274.4**	**$14,671.3**	**$23,798.5**
Hardbound total[1]	642.1	753.1	8,267.0	13,378.7
Paperbound total[1]	1,155.0	1,421.3	5,345.2	9,333.3
Market area				
Domestic (total)	1,803.9	2,126.9	$14,671.0	$23,798.5
General retailers	864.4	1,122.4	6,116.9	11,455.6
Colleges	229.5	268.9	2,635.6	4,061.1
Libraries and institutions	80.7	96.3	1,252.2	2,011.8
Schools and school libraries	235.5	245.9	1,945.6	2,556.5
Direct to consumers	298.9	283.9	2,476.6	3,320.0
Other	95.0	109.5	244.1	393.5
Export	127.1	147.5	N.A.	N.A.
Total	**1,931.0**	**2,274.4**	**$14,671.0**	**$23,798.5**

Note: Includes all titles released by publishers in the United States, and imports that appear under the imprint of American publishers. Multivolume sets such as encyclopedias are counted as one unit. N.A. = not applicable. 1. Does not include mail order or subscription reference publications. **Source:** Book Industry Study Group, Inc., *Book Industry Trends*, annual (1995), reprinted by permission.

NEW BOOKS AND EDITIONS PUBLISHED, BY SUBJECT, 1980–93

Subject	1980	1990	1992	1993
Agriculture	461	514	565	558
Art	1,691	1,262	1,392	1,540
Biography	1,891	1,957	2,007	2,071
Business	1,185	1,191	1,367	1,442
Education	1,011	1,039	1,184	1,247
Fiction	2,835	5,764	5,690	5,419
General works	1,643	1,760	2,153	1,870
History	2,220	2,248	2,322	2,317
Home economics	879	758	826	881
Juvenile	2,859	5,172	5,144	5,469
Language	529	649	617	699
Law	1,102	896	1,063	1,143
Literature	1,686	2,049	2,227	2,169
Medicine	3,292	3,014	3,234	3,094
Music	357	289	346	377
Philosophy/psychology	1,429	1,688	1,806	1,764
Poetry and drama	1,179	874	899	1,004
Religion	2,055	2,285	2,540	2,633
Science	3,109	2,742	2,729	2,678
Sociology, economics	7,152	7,042	7,432	7,502
Sports, recreation	971	978	1,113	1,146
Technology	2,337	2,092	2,152	2,247
Travel	504	495	468	487
Total	**42,377**	**46,748**	**49,276**	**49,757**

Note: Comprises new books (published for the first time) and new editions (with changes in text or format). Excludes government publications, books sold only by subscription, dissertations, periodicals, quarterlies, and pamphlets under 49 pages. **Source:** R.R. Bowker Co., New York, N.Y., *Publishers Weekly*, Mar. 20, 1995 (copyright by Reed Publishing, 1994, used with permission).

BESTSELLERS IN AMERICA, 1960–94

Year	Fiction
1960	*Advise and Consent*, Allen Drury
1961	*The Agony and the Ecstasy*, Irving Stone
1962	*Ship of Fools*, Katherine Anne Porter
1963	*The Shoes of the Fisherman*, Morris L. West
1964	*The Spy Who Came in From the Cold*, John LeCarré
1965	*The Source*, James A. Michener
1966	*Valley of the Dolls*, Jacqueline Susann
1967	*The Arrangement*, Elia Kazan
1968	*Airport*, Arthur Hailey
1969	*Portnoy's Complaint*, Philip Roth
1970	*Love Story*, Erich Segal
1971	*Wheels*, Arthur Hailey
1972	*Jonathan Livingston Seagull*, Richard Bach
1973	*Jonathan Livingston Seagull*, Richard Bach
1974	*Centennial*, James A. Michener
1975	*Ragtime*, E. L. Doctorow
1976	*Trinity*, Leon Uris
1977	*The Silmarillion*, J.R.R. Tolkien
1978	*Chesapeake*, James A. Michener
1979	*The Matarese Circle*, Robert Ludlum
1980	*The Covenant*, James Michener
1981	*Noble House*, James Clavell
1982	*E.T. The Extra-Terrestrial Storybook*, William Kotzwinkle
1983	*Return of the Jedi Storybook*, Joan D. Vinge
1984	*The Talisman*, Stephen King, Peter Straub
1985	*The Mammoth Hunters*, Jean M. Auel
1986	*It*, Stephen King
1987	*The Tommyknockers*, Stephen King
1988	*The Cardinal of the Kremlin*, Tom Clancy
1989	*Clear and Present Danger*, Tom Clancy
1990	*The Plains of Passage*, Jean Auel
1991	*Scarlett*, Alexandra Ripley
1992	*Dolores Claiborne*, Stephen King
1993	*The Bridges of Madison County*, Robert James Waller
1994	*The Chamber*, John Grisham

Year	Nonfiction
1960	*Folk Medicine*, D.C. Jarvis
1961	*The New English Bible: The New Testament*
1962	*Calories Don't Count*, Dr. Herman Taller
1963	*Happiness Is a Warm Puppy*, Charles M. Schulz
1964	*Four Days*, American Heritage
1965	*How To Be a Jewish Mother*, Dan Greenburg
1966	*How to Avoid Probate*, Norman F. Dacey
1967	*Death of a President*, William Manchester
1968	*Better Homes and Gardens New Cook Book*
1969	*American Heritage Dictionary of the English Language*, ed. William Morris
1970	*Everything You Wanted to Know About Sex but Were Afraid to Ask*, David Reuben, M.D.
1971	*The Sensuous Man*, "M."
1972	*The Living Bible*, Kenneth Taylor
1973	*The Living Bible*, Kenneth Taylor
1974	*The Total Woman*, Marabel Morgan
1975	*Angels: God's Secret Agents*, Billy Graham
1976	*The Final Days*, Bob Woodward, Carl Bernstein
1977	*Roots*, Alex Haley
1978	*If Life is a Bowl of Cherries—What Am I Doing in the Pits?* Erma Bombeck
1979	*Aunt Erma's Cope Book*, Erma Bombeck
1980	*Crisis Investing*, Douglas R. Casey
1981	*The Beverly Hills Diet*, Judy Mazel
1982	*Jane Fonda's Workout Book*, Jane Fonda
1983	*In Search of Excellence*, Thomas J. Peters, Robert H. Waterman, Jr.
1984	*Iacocca: An Autobiography*, Lee Iacocca with William Novak
1985	*Iacocca: An Autobiography*, Lee Iacocca with William Novak
1986	*Fatherhood*, Bill Cosby
1987	*Time Flies*, Bill Cosby
1988	*The Eight-Week Cholesterol Diet*, Robert Kowalski
1989	*All I Really Need to Know I Learned in Kindergarten*, Robert Fulghum
1990	*A Life on the Road*, Charles Kuralt
1991	*Me: Stories of My Life*, Katharine Hepburn
1992	*The Way Things Ought to Be*, Rush Limbaugh
1993	*See, I Told You So*, Rush Limbaugh
1994	*In the Kitchen with Rosie*, Rosie Daley

Sources: Alice Payne Hackett, *70 Years of Best Sellers*; *Publishers Weekly*.

The Electronic Media

TOP 50 U.S. TV SHOWS, BY RATING

Rank/Program	Date	Network	Rating
1. *M*A*S*H* Special* (last episode)	2/28/83	CBS	60.2%
2. *Dallas* (Who shot J.R.?)	11/21/80	CBS	53.3
3. *Roots*, part 8	1/30/77	ABC	51.1
4. Super Bowl XVI (San Francisco/Cincinnati)	1/24/82	CBS	49.1
5. Super Bowl XVII (Washington/Miami)	1/30/83	NBC	48.6
6. XVII Winter Olympics(Figure skating first round)	2/23/94	CBS	48.5
7. Super Bowl XX (Chicago/New England)	1/26/86	NBC	48.3
8. *Gone with the Wind*, pt. 1	11/7/76	NBC	47.7
9. *Gone with the Wind*, pt. 2	11/8/76	NBC	47.4
10. Super Bowl XII (Dallas/Denver)	1/15/78	CBS	47.2
11. Super Bowl XIII (Pittsburgh/Dallas)	1/21/79	NBC	47.1
12. *Bob Hope Christmas Show*	1/15/70	NBC	46.6
13. Super Bowl XVIII (L.A. Raiders/Washington)	1/22/84	CBS	46.4
13. Super Bowl XIX (San Francisco/Miami)	1/20/85	ABC	46.4
15. Super Bowl XIV (Pittsburgh/L.A. Rams)	1/20/80	CBS	46.3
16. *ABC Theater "The Day After"*	1/20/83	ABC	46.0
17. *The Fugitive*	8/29/77	ABC	45.9
17. *Roots*, part 6	1/28/67	ABC	45.9
19. Super Bowl XXI (N.Y. Giants/Denver)	1/25/87	CBS	45.8
20. *Roots*, part 5	1/27/77	ABC	45.7
21. Super Bowl XXVIII (Dallas/Buffalo)	1/29/94	NBC	45.5
21. *Cheers* (last episode)	5/20/93	NBC	45.5
23. *The Ed Sullivan Show*	2/9/64	CBS	45.3
24. Super Bowl XXVII (Dallas/Buffalo)	1/31/93	NBC	45.1
25. *Bob Hope Christmas Show*	1/14/71	NBC	45.0
26. *Roots*, part 3	1/25/77	ABC	44.8%
27. Super Bowl XI (Oakland/Minnesota)	1/9/77	NBC	44.4
27. Super Bowl XV (Oakland/Philadelphia)	1/25/81	NBC	44.4
29. Super Bowl VI (Dallas/Miami)	1/16/72	CBS	44.2
30. *Roots*, part 2	1/24/77	ABC	44.1
30. XVII Winter Olympics (Figure skating finals)	2/25/94	CBS	44.1
32. *The Beverly Hillbillies*	1/8/64	CBS	44.0
33. *The Ed Sullivan Show* (with the Beatles)	2/16/64	CBS	43.8
33. *Roots*, part 4	1/26/77	ABC	43.8
35. Super Bowl XXIII (San Francisco/Cincinnati)	1/22/89	NBC	43.5
36. Academy Awards	4/7/70	ABC	43.4
37. *The Thorn Birds*, part 3	3/29/83	ABC	43.2
38. *The Thorn Birds*, part 4	3/30/83	ABC	43.1
39. NFC Championship game (San Francisco/Dallas)	1/10/82	CBS	42.9
40. *The Beverly Hillbillies*	1/15/64	CBS	42.8
41. Super Bowl VII (Miami/Washington)	1/14/73	NBC	42.7
42. *The Thorn Birds*, part 2	3/28/83	ABC	42.5
43. *The Beverly Hillbillies*	2/26/64	CBS	42.4
43. Super Bowl IX (Pittsburgh/Minnesota)	1/12/75	NBC	42.4
45. *Cinderella*	2/22/65	CBS	42.3
45. *Love Story* (Sunday night movie)	10/1/72	ABC	42.3
45. *Airport* (Movie Special)	11/11/73	ABC	42.3
45. Super Bowl X (Pittsburgh/Dallas)	1/18/76	CBS	42.3
45. *Roots*, part 7	1/29/77	ABC	42.3
50. *The Beverly Hillbillies*	3/25/64	CBS	42.2

Note: As of May 20, 1993. Does not include programs broadcast on more than one network (e.g., the Apollo moon landing) or programs under minutes scheduled duration. **Source:** Nielsen Media Research.

TELEVISION

Few people today doubt the pervasiveness of television's influence on America. Once a symbol of luxury, the color television has found its way into almost every home in America, and a great majority of American households have two or more televisions. At least one of these televisions was on in each household for 7 hours and 51 minutes in 1993, nearly two hours more than in 1971, when the average was just over 6 hours, and 19 minutes more than in 1992. Women over the age of 18 watched longest: they averaged 5 hours and 11 minutes per day, compared with 4 hours and 25 minutes for men over 18. Children age 2–17 watched more than 3 hours of TV each day. With that kind of use, it's not surprising to find that TV sales continue to be brisk. More than 33 million televisions (including color, black and white, stereo, and projection TVs) are sold each year.

LONGEST-RUNNING NATIONAL NETWORK SERIES OF ALL TIME

Program	Number of seasons	Years[1]
Walt Disney	33	1954–90
60 Minutes	27	1968–
The Ed Sullivan Show	24	1948–71
Gunsmoke	20	1955–75
The Red Skelton Show	20	1951–71
Meet the Press	18	1947–65
What's My Line?	18	1950–67
I've Got a Secret	17	1952–76
Lassie	17	1954–71
The Lawrence Welk Show	17	1955–71

Note: Includes prime-time (6–11 p.m.) shows only; sports broadcasts and movie series are not included. 1. These dates reflect the first and last broadcasts of each show. Programs did not necessarily run continuously throughout this period. **Source:** Baseline II, Inc., 1995.

TOP 10 TV SHOWS, 1994–95

Rank/Program	Network	Average rating[1]	Average share[2]
1. *Seinfeld*	NBC	20.5	31
2. *E.R.*	NBC	20.0	33
3. *Home Improvement*	ABC	19.9	29
4. *Grace Under Fire*	ABC	18.9	29
5. *NFL Monday Night Football*	ABC	17.8	30
6. *60 Minutes*	CBS	17.1	28
7. *NYPD Blue*	ABC	16.5	27
8. *Friends*	NBC	16.1	25
9. *Roseanne*	ABC	15.6	24
9. *Murder, She Wrote*	CBS	15.6	24

Note: For the period from September 19, 1994, to April 16, 1995. 1. The percentage of all TV households tuned to a particular program. 2. The percentage of households using TVs at a given time tuned to a particular program. **Source:** Nielsen Media Research.

MOST POPULAR TV SHOWS, BY DECADE

These charts are based on a show's average rating throughout each decade, and are thus an indication of both popularity and longevity.

Decade and program	Network	Average rating
1950–59		
1. *Arthur Godfrey's Talent Scouts*	CBS	32.9%
2. *I Love Lucy*	CBS	31.6
3. *You Bet Your Life*	NBC	30.1
4. *Dragnet*	NBC	24.6
5. *The Jack Benny Show*	CBS	22.3
6. *A. Godfrey and Friends*	CBS	19.5
7. *Gunsmoke*	CBS	15.6
8. *The Red Skelton Show*	NBC	15.2
9. *December Bride*	CBS	13.8
10. *I've Got a Secret*	CBS	12.9
1960–69		
1. *Bonanza*	NBC	29.6%
2. *The Red Skelton Show*	CBS	26.4
3. *The Andy Griffith Show*	CBS	22.4
4. *The Beverly Hillbillies*	CBS	21.9
5. *The Ed Sullivan Show*	CBS	21.7
6. *The Lucy Show/Here's Lucy*	CBS	21.3
7. *The Jackie Gleason Show*	CBS	16.5
8. *Bewitched*	ABC	14.8
9. *Gomer Pyle*	CBS	13.4
10. *Candid Camera*	CBS	11.2
1970–79		
1. *All in the Family*	CBS	23.1%
2. *M*A*S*H*	CBS	17.6
3. *Hawaii Five-O*	CBS	16.5
4. *Happy Days*	ABC	15.9
5. *The Waltons*	CBS	14.0
6. *The Mary Tyler Moore Show*	CBS	13.7
7. *Sanford & Son*	NBC	13.4
8. *One Day at a Time*	CBS	11.4
9. *Three's Company*	ABC	10.8
10. *60 Minutes*	CBS	10.0
1980–89		
1. *60 Minutes*	CBS	23.5%
2. *Dallas*	CBS	21.0
3. *The Cosby Show*	NBC	16.9
4. *Dynasty*	ABC	14.5
5. *Knots Landing*	CBS	14.2
6. *Cheers*	NBC	14.0
7. *Magnum, P.I.*	CBS	13.7
8. *Murder, She Wrote*	CBS	12.9
9. *Who's the Boss?*	ABC	12.2
10. *Family Ties*	NBC	11.8
1990–93		
1. *60 Minutes*	CBS	21.3%
2. *Roseanne*	ABC	19.7
3. *Cheers*	NBC	18.4
4. *Murphy Brown*	CBS	17.8
5. *Murder, She Wrote*	CBS	17.0
6. *NFL Monday Night Football*	ABC	16.9%
7. *Coach*	ABC	16.7
8. *Full House*	ABC	16.3
9. *Unsolved Mysteries*	NBC	15.8
10. *CBS Sunday Night Movie*	CBS	15.6

Source: Baseline II, Inc.; basic data, Nielsen Media Research.

CABLE TELEVISION

Cable television was originally designed as a means of improving TV reception in some rural areas. In the 1960s, operators realized that viewers were willing to pay for commercial-free programming, but their efforts to capitalize on the idea were hampered by stringent Federal Communications Commission restrictions. Not until 1975, when RCA put its first communications satellite into operation, did the industry really bloom. Under the name Home Box Office, the company started to transmit programming that could be received by independent operators around the country and then relayed to subscribers at minimal cost. With the dismissal of most of the FCC's regulations by a federal court in 1977, the door was opened for the development of what is now a multibillion-dollar industry.

As the accompanying table demonstrates, cable has changed the television broadcasting landscape, drawing away as much as one-fourth of the total television viewing audiences. But while the number of cable channels and subscribers both continue to increase, the extraordinary growth sustained during the 1980s, when cable viewership more than tripled, will never again be replicated. The number of cable subscribers is currently increasing by about 1.5 million per year. And although the number of cable channels continues to climb inexorably toward the fabled 500-channel level, less than 13 percent of all cable systems carry more than 54 channels.

TOP 5 PAY-CABLE SERVICES, 1994

Rank/Network	Subscribers	Content
1. Home Box Office	19,200,000	Movies, variety, sports, documentaries
2. The Disney Channel	12,600,000	Movies, cartoons
3. Showtime/The Movie Channel	11,900,000	Movies, variety, comedy, specials
4. Spice	11,000,000	Adult movies
5. Cinemax	7,800,000	Movies, comedy, music specials

Source: National Cable Television Association, *Cable TV Developments* (April 1995).

BASIC AND PAY CABLE TV SYSTEMS AND SUBSCRIBERS, 1952–95

		Basic cable		Pay cable	
Year	Number of systems	Subscribers	Percent of U.S. TV households	Subscribers	Percent of households with cable
1952	70	14,000	0.1%	N.A.	N.A.
1955	400	150,000	0.5	N.A.	N.A.
1960	640	650,000	1.4	N.A.	N.A.
1965	1,325	1,300,000	2.3	N.A.	N.A.
1970	2,490	3,900,000	6.7	N.A.	N.A.
1975	3,506	9,196,690	13.2	469,000	23.6%
1980	4,225	17,671,490	22.6	9,144,000	50.6
1985	6,600	39,872,520	46.2	30,596,000	83.5
1990	9,575	54,871,330	59.0	41,505,000	80.2
1991	10,704	55,786,390	60.6	39,900,000	74.7
1992	11,035	57,211,600	61.5	40,700,000	73.7
1993	11,108	58,834,440	62.5	41,500,000	72.6
1994	11,214	60,495,090	63.4	43,510,000	74.0
1995[1]	11,351	61,025,350	64.0	43,730,000	71.7

1. Preliminary. **Source:** National Cable Television Association, *Cable TV Developments* (April 1995).

TOP 10 CABLE TELEVISION NETWORKS, 1994

Rank/Network	Subscribers (millions)	Number of systems	Launch date	Content
1. ESPN	64.9	26,700	1979	Sports events and sports news
2. Cable News Network (CNN)	64.7	11,593	1980	24-hour news, special-interest reports
3. TBS	64.4	11,668	1976	Movies, sports, original, and syndicated shows
4. The Nashville Network (TNN)	63.6	13,639	1983	Country music, family entertainment
5. USA Network	63.0	12,500	1980	Sports, family entertainment
5. The Discovery Channel	63.0	10,036	1985	Nonfiction, nature, science
5. TNT (Turner Network Television)	63.0	9,840	1988	Vintage movies, sports, original films
8. C-SPAN	61.7	5,162	1979	Public affairs, live congressional coverage
9. The Family Channel	61.4	10,555	1977	Family-oriented, religious programs
10. Arts and Entertainment Network (A&E)	60.0	9,500	1984	Original biographies, mysteries, and specials

1. Preliminary. **Source: National Cable Television Association,** *Cable TV Developments* (April 1995).

VIEWING SHARES OF FREE AND CABLE TELEVISION NETWORKS, 1983–94

Year	Broadcast network affiliates	Independent TV stations[1]	Public TV stations	Basic cable Networks[2]	Pay cable services
1983–84	69%	19%	3%	9%	5%
1985–86	66	18	3	11	5
1987–88	61	20	4	15	7
1989–90	55	20	3	21	6
1990–91	53	21	3	24	6
1992–93	53	21	4	25	5
1993–94	52	21	4	26	5

Note: For all television viewing Monday-Sunday, 24 hours a day. Due to multiset use and independent roundings, totals add up to more than 100. 1. Includes the FOX network. 2. For broadcast years 1983–84 through 1985–86, superstation shares are divided between independent stations and basic cable networks. Since 1986–87, TBS has been counted in the basic cable network category. **Source:** A.C. Nielsen Television Index, *Cable TV Facts* (1995).

RADIO

According to statistics compiled by the Radio Advertising Bureau, 98 percent of all U.S. households have at least one radio. Of Americans over age 12, 95.3 percent listen to radio for an average of 3 hours and 20 minutes each workday. There are a total of 576.5 million radios in the United States, 26 percent more than in 1980, distributed as follows: 367.4 million are in homes, 142.8 million in cars, 43.7 million in trucks, vans, and RVs, and 22.6 million in the workplace.

U.S. RADIO STATIONS, BY PRIMARY FORMAT, 1990–94

Format	1990	1993	1994
Total commercial stations	**9,444**	**9,890**	**10,057**
Country	2,452	2,612	2,642
Adult contemporary	2,135	1,895	1,784
Religion (teaching and music)	745	915	1,028
News, talk, business, sports	405	841	926
Oldies	659	734	721
Rock (album, modern, classic)	419	643	714
Top 40	824	441	470
Adult standards	383	421	435
Spanish and other ethnic	342	421	358
Urban, black, urban adult contemporary	294	321	328
Easy listening	240	116	106
Variety	97	68	63
Jazz and new age	68	45	44
Classical, fine arts	52	45	43
Preteen	3	13	19
Comedy	1	0	1
Off air	210	345	369
Changing formats or not available	116	14	6
Total noncommercial stations	**1,636**	**1,849**	**1,917**
Total all stations	**11,080**	**11,739**	**11,974**

Note: As of September of each year. **Source:** M Street Corporation, 1994.

U.S. RADIO STATIONS AND RADIO SALES, 1946–94

Year	Radio stations on air[1]	Unit sales to dealers ('000s)[2]
1946	961	N.A.
1950	2,773	N.A.
1955	3,211	7,327
1960	4,133	18.031
1965	5,249	31,689
1970	6,760	34,049
1975	7,744	25,276
1980	8,566	28,104
1985	10,359	21,575
1990	10,819	21,585
1992	11,312	21,553
1993	11,608	20,140
1994	11,080	18,350[3]

1. Includes AM and FM, commercial and noncommercial. 2. Includes table, clock, and portable—but not auto—radios. 3. Estimate. **Source:** M Street Corporation, 1994; Electronic Industries Association, *Consumer Electronics, U.S. Sales* (1995).

CONSUMER ELECTRONICS: SALES AND PENETRATION IN U.S. HOMES, 1990–95

Product	Sales (thousands of units) 1990	1995[1]	Percent of U.S. homes 1990	1995
Radio	21,585	17,670	99%	98%
Television set	29,576	39,890	98	98
Color television set	20,384	25,600	96	97
VCR[2]	11,986	17,700	68	85
Audio system	1,557	1,100	92	82
Telephone answering device	13,560	20,050	31	54
Cordless telephone	10,148	18,000	25	52
Color TV with stereo sound	6,655	12,160	19	47
Compact disc player	9,155	30,390	19	44
Home computer	5,500	7,650	23	33
Compact audio system	2,447	5,550	N.A.	29
Camcorder	2,962	3,340	10	20
Cellular telephone[3]	1,888	5,000	N.A.	20
Projection television	351	790	6	10
Fax machine	350	2,780	N.A.	6
TV/VCR combination	424	2,680	N.A.	5
Satellite dish	330	330	3	N.A.
Laserdisc player	168	280	N.A.	1

N.A. = not available. 1. Estimate. 2. Includes mono and stereo decks, but not machines that play but do not record. Does not include TV/VCR combinations. 3. Reflects both consumer and business purchases. **Source:** Consumer Electronics U.S. Sales, © 1995 Electronic Industries Association. Reprinted by permission.

THE RECORDING INDUSTRY

In less than 10 years, the compact disc has gone from technological breakthrough to the music format of choice among most consumers. Fewer than 100,000 CDs were sold in 1983, the first year they were available, but the format quickly overtook LPs by 1988, and topped cassette sales in 1992. The recording industry's willingness to support the new technology—discs can be sold for about twice the price of albums and cassettes—by releasing a large amount of music on disc has no doubt played a large part in the CD's growth.

The sales of different types of music are in almost as constant a flux as the music types themselves. Rock and roll records constituted more than 40 percent of all records sold in 1989 before falling to 30.2 percent in 1993. But in 1994, rock sales jumped back up to 35.1 percent. Rock's gain came at the expense of rap and country, which fell from 9.2 to 7.9 and 18.7 to 16.3, respectively.

Teenagers (adults aged 15–19) are still the single largest group of consumers of recorded music as a percentage of total dollar value sales—they purchased 16.8 percent of all albums in 1994—but they do not dominate the market the way they did as recently as 1989, when they made 22.9 percent of all music purchases. Meanwhile, adults over the age of 30 are picking up the slack. They represented 47.3 percent of all music purchases in 1994, compared with just 35.0 percent in 1989. The total U.S. dollar value of all music sold has nearly doubled in the past five years, from $6.58 billion in 1989 to $12.07 billion in 1993.

SALES OF RECORDED MUSIC, BY GENRE AND AGE GROUP, 1990–94

Characteristic	1990	1991	1992	1993	1994
Genre					
Rock	31.6%	34.8%	31.6%	30.2%	35.1%
Country	9.6	12.8	17.4	18.7	16.3
Pop	13.7	12.1	11.5	11.9	10.3
Urban contemporary	11.6	9.9	9.8	10.6	9.6
Rap	8.5	10.0	8.6	9.2	7.9
Classical	3.1	3.2	3.7	3.3	3.7
Jazz	4.8	4.0	3.8	3.1	3.0
Other[1]	11.3	11.3	11.4	10.9	11.8
Age group					
10–14	7.6%	8.2%	8.6%	8.6%	7.9%
15–19	18.3	18.1	18.2	16.7	16.8
20–24	16.5	17.9	16.1	15.1	15.4
25–29	14.6	14.5	13.8	13.2	12.6
30–34	13.2	12.5	12.2	11.9	11.8
35–39	10.2	9.8	10.9	11.1	11.5
40–44	7.8	6.7	7.4	8.5	7.9
45+	11.8	12.5	12.9	14.8	16.1

Note: Figures represent a percentage of that year's total U.S. dollar sales. 1. Includes gospel, sound tracks, children's music, and other categories not shown separately. Totals may not add to 100 percent due to "Don't Know/No Answer" responses. **Source:** Recording Industry Association of America, *1994 Consumer Profile* (1995).

VIDEO

BEST-SELLING PRERECORDED VIDEOS OF ALL TIME

Rank/Title	Distributor	Units sold (millions)
1. *Beauty and the Beast*	Buena Vista	24.5
2. *101 Dalmatians*	Buena Vista	15.8
3. *Fantasia*	Buena Vista	14.1
4. *Batman*	Warner	13.5
5. *E.T.—The Extra-Terrestrial*	MCA	13.0
5. *Pinocchio*	Buena Vista	13.0
7. *Bambi*	Buena Vista	10.5
8. *Home Alone*	Fox Video	10.3
9. *The Little Mermaid*	Buena Vista	9.8
10. *Jungle Book*	Buena Vista	9.3

Note: As of June 1, 1993. **Source:** *Video Store* magazine (1993).

BEST-SELLING PRERECORDED VIDEOS, 1994

Rank/Title	Distributor	Units sold (millions)
1. Snow White	Buena Vista/Disney	27.0
2. Jurassic Park	MCA/Universal	21.5
3. Mrs. Doubtfire	Fox Video	12.0
4. The Fox and the Hound	Buena Vista/Disney	11.5
5. The Flintstones	MCA/Universal	9.1
6. Speed	Fox Video	8.2
7. The Return of Jafar	Buena Vista/Disney	7.5
8. Beethoven's 2nd	MCA/Universal	5.2
9. The Fugitive	Warner	5.1
10. D2: The Mighty Ducks	Buena Vista/Disney	4.2
11. Ace Ventura: Pet Detective	Warner	4.1
12. The Nightmare Before Christmas	Buena Vista/Disney	3.9
13. Thumbelina	Warner	3.0
14. The Secret Garden	Warner	2.5
15. Black Beauty	Warner	2.5
16. We're Back: A Dinosaur's Story	MCA/Universal	2.1
17. Batman: Mask of the Phantasm	Warner	2.0
18. An Affair to Remember	Fox Video	2.0
19. The Polar Bear King	Hemdale	1.9
20. Princess and the Goblin	Hemdale	1.1

Source: *Video Store Magazine/Video Week*, "Tape Track" (1995).

FILM

MOST POPULAR FILMS, BY DECADE

Title	Year	Director	Rental (millions)
Pre-1930			
The Birth of a Nation	1915	D.W. Griffith	$10.0
The Big Parade	1925	K. Vidor	5.5
The Singing Fool	1928	L. Bacon	4.0
1930–39			
Gone with the Wind	1939	V. Fleming	$77.6
Snow White and the Seven Dwarfs	1937	(Animated)	62.8
King Kong	1933	M. Cooper	5.0
The Wizard of Oz	1939	V. Fleming	4.5
San Francisco	1936	W.S. Van Dyke	4.0
1940–49[1]			
Cinderella	1949	(Animated)	$38.5
Pinocchio	1940	(Animated)	32.9
Song of the South	1946	H. Foster/ W. Jackson	29.2
Fantasia	1940	(Animated)	28.5
Bambi	1942	(Animated)	28.4
1950–59			
The Ten Commandments	1956	C.B. DeMille	$43.0
Lady and the Tramp	1955	(Animated)	40.2
Ben Hur	1959	W. Wyler	36.7
Around the World in 80 Days	1956	M. Anderson	23.1
Sleeping Beauty	1959	(Animated)	21.5
1960–69			
The Sound of Music	1965	R. Wise	$79.98
Doctor Zhivago	1965	D. Lean	60.96
Butch Cassidy and the Sundance Kid	1969	G.R. Hill	45.95
Mary Poppins	1964	R. Stevenson	45.00
The Graduate	1968	M. Nichols	44.09
1970–79			
Star Wars	1977	G. Lucas	$193.77
Jaws	1975	S. Spielberg	129.55
Grease	1978	R. Kleiser	96.30
The Exorcist	1973	W. Friedkin	89.00
The Godfather	1972	F.F. Coppola	86.30
Superman	1978	R. Donner	82.80
Close Encounters of the Third Kind	1977	S. Spielberg	82.75
The Sting	1973	G.R. Hill	78.21
Saturday Night Fever	1977	J. Badham	74.10
National Lampoon's Animal House	1978	J. Landis	70.83
1980–89			
E.T.—The Extra-Terrestrial	1982	S. Spielberg	$228.17
Return of the Jedi	1983	R. Marquand	168.19
Batman	1989	T. Burton	150.50
The Empire Strikes Back	1980	J. Kershner	141.67
Ghostbusters	1984	I. Reitman	132.72
Raiders of the Lost Ark	1981	S. Spielberg	115.60
Indiana Jones and the Last Crusade	1989	S. Spielberg	115.50
Indiana Jones and the Temple of Doom	1984	S. Spielberg	109.00
Beverly Hills Cop	1984	M. Brest	108.00
Back to the Future	1985	R. Zemeckis	105.50
1990–93			
Jurassic Park	1993	S. Spielberg	$205.00
Home Alone	1990	C. Columbus	140.10
Terminator 2	1991	J. Cameron	112.50
Home Alone 2: Lost in New York	1992	C. Columbus	103.38
Batman Returns	1992	T. Burton	100.10
Mrs. Doubtfire	1993	C. Columbus	98.33
Ghost	1990	J. Zucker	98.20
The Fugitive	1993	A. Davis	92.60
Robin Hood: Prince of Thieves	1991	K. Reynolds	86.00
Aladdin	1992	J. Musker/ R. Clements	82.54

Note: Film rentals are the portion of a film's box-office receipts paid by theater owners to the film's distribution company for renting the film. Figures include the U.S. and Canada through February 13, 1994. 1. All films listed for this decade were made by Disney studios and have been rereleased on a regular basis ever since. Their dominance on this chart is partly due to the fact that they are "continually" generating revenue. **Source:** *Variety*.

U.S. FILM BOX-OFFICE RECEIPTS, THEATERS, ADMISSIONS, AND ADMISSION CHARGES, 1926–94

Year	Box office receipts (millions)	Theaters: Indoor	Theaters: Drive-in	Admissions ('000s)	Average admission charge
1926	$ 720.0	N.A.	N.A.	2,600,000	N.A.
1930	732.0	N.A.	N.A.	4,680,000	N.A.
1935	566.0	N.A.	N.A.	3,900,000	$0.24
1940	735.0	N.A.	N.A.	4,160,000	0.24
1945	1,450.0	N.A.	N.A.	4,680,000	0.35
1950	1,376.0	N.A.	N.A.	3,120,000	0.53
1955	1,326.0	N.A.	N.A.	3,392,000	0.50
1960	951.0	N.A.	N.A.	2,080,000	0.69
1965	927.0	N.A.	N.A.	2,288,000	1.01
1970[1]	1,162.0	10,335	3,720	920,400	1.55
1975	2,115.0	11,402	3,628	988,000	2.05
1980	2,748.5	14,029	3,561	1,021,500	2.69
1985	3,749.4	18,327	2,820	1,056,100	3.55
1990[2]	5,021.8	22,774	915	1,188,600	4.23
1992	4,871.0	24,233	872	1,173,200	4.15
1993	5,154.2	24,887	850	1,244,000	4.14
1994	5,396.2	25,701	885	1,291,700	4.18

1. Theater figures are for 1971. 2. Beginning in 1990, admission totals and average prices are supplied by the National Association of Theater Owners and are not strictly comparable with data from previous years, which are based on the U.S. Department of Commerce's Consumer Price Index. **Source:** U.S. Dept. of Commerce; *Film Daily Yearbook*; Motion Picture Association of America, *1994 U.S. Economic Review* (1995).

15 TOP-GROSSING FEATURE FILMS, 1994

Rank/Title	Distributor	Domestic box-office gross (millions)
1. *The Lion King*	Buena Vista	$298.88
2. *Forrest Gump*	Paramount	298.10
3. *True Lies*	20th Century Fox	146.26
4. *The Santa Clause*	Buena Vista	134.56
5. *The Flintstones*	Universal	130.52
6. *Clear and Present Danger*	Paramount	121.72
7. *Speed*	20th Century Fox	121.25
8. *The Mask*	New Line	118.64
9. *Mrs. Doubtfire*	20th Century Fox	107.43
10. *Maverick*	Warner Bros.	101.63
11. *Interview with the Vampire*	Warner Bros.	100.01
12. *The Client*	Warner Bros.	92.12
13. *Schindler's List*	Universal	91.08
14. *Philadelphia*	Sony	76.88
15. *Ace Ventura: Pet Detective*	Warner Bros.	72.22

Note: As of Jan. 1, 1995. Figures represent total receipts from all North American ticket sales during the calendar year 1994 only. **Source:** *Variety*, Jan. 30–Feb. 5, 1995.

THE INFORMATION SUPERHIGHWAY

During the 1990s, new forms of electronic media have emerged from the ever-increasing presence of the personal computer in the home and office. In 1994, 5.6 million new personal computers were purchased for home use alone. Most of these machines now come equipped with CD-ROM drives and built-in modems allowing ready access to the information superhighway, also known as the Internet. In 1991, the Internet community, the groups of users with computers that are able to talk to each other over telephone lines, consisted of just over a million people, according to most estimates. The number of users has doubled every year since then, reaching somewhere in the vicinity of 25 million people in 1995. No wonder, then, that almost every media outlet, publishing company, perfume manufacturer, and nonprofit organization has rushed to get an address on the Internet, regardless of what they plan to do with it.

So what exactly is this thing called the Internet? Loosely defined, the Internet is a network (actually a network of networks) of computers linked by telephone lines. With the appropriate modems and software, the Internet allows people to communicate with each other directly from their computers. The Defense Department created the Internet in the late 1960s as a faster way for universities and research agencies to share information, and as an emergency means of communications in case more traditional means were cut off.

But the boom in consumer Internet use didn't occur until the 1980s, when the National Science Foundation created equipment that would allow other computer networks to connect to the government's larger network. From there, commercial services such as CompuServe and Prodigy tapped into the ever-growing network and brought a wealth of information to any individual user with a computer, a modem, and the ability to pay a monthly fee.

E-mail The most popular use of this high-speed information link is E-mail, or electronic mail, which allows users to type letters and send them directly to each others' computers. The process, which takes only a few seconds, is similar to faxing a letter, but requires no paper. The cost of this instantaneous communication, now used by more than 30 million people worldwide, is the price of a local phone call.

But because of the wealth of information available on the Internet, most users don't limit themselves simply to E-mail. Topics discussed on bulletin boards (electronic town forums) range from fish to Phish, from feminism to football. Of course there's lots of discussion about *Star Trek.* And everything you always wanted to know about sex, but were afraid to ask for at your local newsstand. Users can also "talk" live to each other in chat rooms, each devoted to one of dozens of topics.

The best source of information, however, is the U.S. government, which up through 1994 published all of its information on plain old paper. But in a cost-cutting measure, the Department of Commerce in 1995 began putting many of its publications on the Internet and ceased printing hard copy versions of them. Literally thousands of government documents (including many of the ones reprinted in this book) can be obtained from scores of government agencies over the Internet.

The World Wide Web (WWW) is another network of information whose popularity is growing at immeasurable rates. Created in 1989 by CERN, the European Particle Physics Lab in Geneva, the Web is fast becoming *the* place to find information for the business, scientific, and computer communities. This spiderweb of links uses a hypertext programming language to transmit information quickly over phone lines. To access this information, users must have a translation program called a browser that converts the programming language into languages understood by humans. Mosaic, developed at the University of Minnesota, was the first widely-used browser; it was recently supplanted, however, by Netscape, which is now used by about 90 percent of Web users.

COMMERCIAL ON-LINE SERVICE PROVIDERS

Although direct access to the Internet is becoming simpler and more popular each day—users at government agencies and most major colleges and universities already have direct Internet links—when most people say they are on the information superhighway, they mean they have on-line access provided by one of the major commercial service providers. The three largest providers are America OnLine, Prodigy, and CompuServe. In addition to their own E-mail, bulletin boards, and chat rooms, these services provide access to government data and other information that is distributed on the Internet free of charge. But they make their money from commercial services like on-line magazines, stock quotes, and direct access to airline reservation computers. The cost of these services is passed on to the consumer in the form of a monthly flat fee plus an hourly usage rate. Descriptions of each of the major on-line services providers follow.

CompuServe (800-848-8199 for enrollment information) is the oldest service and, according to the figures released by each company, still the largest with three million subscribers in more than 150 countries. It charges $9.95 a month for unlimited access to 120 basic services such as stock quotes, travel reservations, and restaurant reviews. The monthly fee includes up to 90 E-mail messages. Extended services, including chat rooms, specialized bulletin boards, and libraries are available for an additional $4.80 per hour.

Prodigy (800-776-3449) charges $9.95 a month for the first five hours. There is no extra charge for specialized services (E-mail use is unlimited), but additional hours cost $2.95. Prodigy is the most commercial of the three. Prodigy was the first service to offer unlimited use of the World Wide Web.

America OnLine (800-827-6364) is the newest of the big three, and the fastest-growing, with 2.5 million subscribers. It's also the most user-friendly, with the most convenient interface (so you can point and click instead of memorizing computerese), and the most aggressively marketed. AOL charges $9.95 a month for five hours and $2.95 for additional hours.

CD-ROMs

CD-ROMs, shorthand for Compact Disk–Read Only Memory, are quickly becoming the information storage and retrieval technology of choice. Approximately the same size as a musical compact disk, CD-ROM disks hold much more information than computer disks, tapes, or other methods because the information on them can only be read, it cannot be manipulated or erased. Thanks to the CD-ROM, the 26-volume *Oxford English Dictionary,* which takes up an entire bookshelf, can be captured on a single disk. Reference books are still the most popular use for the CD-ROM format. They represented 43 percent of all CD-ROMs sold in 1993, followed by games (34%) and educational disks (17%).

15 BEST-SELLING MULTIMEDIA CD-ROM TITLES, 1994

Rank/Title	Distributor
1. Myst	Broderbund
2. Doom II	GT Interactive
3. 5 Ft. 10 Pack Volume I	Sirius
4. Star Wars Rebel Assault	LucasArts
5. 7th Guest	Virgin
6. Microsoft Encarta	Microsoft
7. The Lion King	Origin
8. Print Shop Deluxe CD Ensemble	Broderbund
9. Quicken CD-ROM Deluxe	Intui
10. Corel Gallery	Corel
11. 5 Ft. 10 Pack Volume II	Sirius
12. Microsoft Bookshelf	Microsoft
13. Outpost	Sierra
14. Street Atlas USA	DeLorme
15. Just Grandma and Me	Living Books

Source: PC Data.

CD-ROM SALES, 1991–94

Category	1991	1992	1993	1994[1]
UNITS				
Total[2]	597,000	4,064,000	16,500,000	23,400,000
IBM-PC	434,000	3,488,000	11,900,000	18,000,000
Macintosh	163,000	576,000	4,600,000	5,400,000
Revenues (millions)				
Total	$11.9	$81.5	$324.5	$454.5
Retail[3]	4.4	30.9	153.5	287.0
Bundle[4]	7.5	50.6	171.0	167.5
Disk drives (units)[5]	685,000	1,000,000	3,400,000	N.A.

1. Projected 2. Based on shipments of the 3,500 most popular CD-ROM titles. Does not include small numbers of shipments of less popular titles. 3. Sold directly to consumer. 4. Included in software and applications packages sold with computers. 5. Includes drives sold to dataprocessing markets but not drives sold to consumer platforms and video games. **Source:** Dataquest, *Multimedia Market Trends,* 1994.

RELIGION IN AMERICA

RELIGIOUS AFFILIATION

As of 1992, 160 million Americans claimed affiliation with a religious group. This represents about 63 percent of the population, up from 61 percent (147.5 million) in 1987. The accompanying table shows that 94 percent of the religiously affiliated were members of Christian or quasi-Christian denominations. Non-Christian religions—primarily Judaism and Islam—account for the other 6 percent.

Christians in the United States are members of a bewildering variety of denominations, each independent of the next. The *Yearbook of American and Canadian Churches* lists about 220 Christian denominations, and other sources list more than 1,000. For simplicity's sake the accompanying table groups the denominations into 26 major families with memberships of 100,000 or more. Denominations listed in the same family nearly always share common historical roots and some principal doctrines. They may disagree violently about other doctrines and issues, however. The following are brief descriptions of each of the Christian denominational families and of major non-Christian faiths. (See also Part III: "World Religions.")

CHRISTIANITY

Roman Catholic Church

The Roman Catholic Church is the largest single Christian denomination in the United States. It claims nearly 37 percent of all religiously affiliated people—23 percent of the total population. Worldwide, there are nearly 900 million Roman Catholics (see "World Religion").

Many U.S. Catholics—descendants of immigrants from Ireland, Germany, Poland, Italy, and France—are concentrated in the Northeast and the industrial Midwest. Hispanic-Americans in Florida and the Southwest are also predominantly Catholic.

The church is hierarchically organized. Bishops, who administer church affairs in a given region, are appointed by higher authority. The world leader of the Roman church is the pope, who directs the church from Vatican City in Rome.

Priests are male and in most parts of the church must be and remain unmarried. Orders of nuns and monks provide many educational and charitable services. Many local churches operate parochial elementary schools. Regional bodies and religious orders operate high schools and help administer many seminaries and church-related colleges. In recent years the number of applicants for the priesthood and for religious orders has sharply decreased, even as membership in the church has continued to increase.

Catholic leaders have taken strong stands on many contemporary issues. The National Conference of Catholic Bishops has taken relatively liberal positions on efforts to bring about world peace and economic justice. In areas of personal conduct, the church is more conservative. It leads the campaign to outlaw abortion and opposes artificial means of birth control.

Baptist Churches

The Baptist family of churches is the largest Protestant family in the United States. Baptists trace their theological roots back to radical reformers in Europe in the 1500s, but the number of Baptists in the world was tiny until the 1800s, when Baptist faith and practice became predominant in the American South (both for whites and for blacks). Baptists are still most heavily represented in the southern and border states.

Local Baptist congregations have great independence, determining many of their own policies. At the same time, these churches share many practices. They agree that the rite of baptism should be administered only to those who have reached an age of independent judgment. Consequently, children are baptized no earlier than the age of six or seven, often by total immersion in the baptismal water. A Baptist child is not counted as a member until after baptism, which means that small children are not included in the membership totals reported above.

Most Baptists take a strong stand on the authority of the Bible, and many (though not all) believe that it should be interpreted literally. Baptists have traditionally been strong supporters of separation of church and state. Many Baptist denominations have mounted energetic missionary campaigns to bring the Christian message to people around the world.

The Southern Baptist Convention, a predominantly white church, is the largest Protestant denomination in the United States. The two National Baptist Conventions and the Progressive National Baptist Convention are predominantly black churches. Together they account for the religious affiliation of more blacks than any other family of churches.

Methodist Churches

Methodist churches trace their origins to John Wesley (1703–91), a minister in the Church of England who sought to bring a new sense of warmth and commitment to individuals' religious life. He urged his followers to set aside regular times to study the Bible and pray together. Wesley's opponents laughingly called his followers Methodists because of their discipline and seriousness. Wesley himself remained in the Church of England his whole life, but his followers began to develop independent organizations, both in England and the United States.

On the American frontier, Methodist "circuit riders" traveled from settlement to settlement, preaching and marrying, baptizing and burying members of pioneer families. Methodism grew with astonishing swiftness. By 1820 it was the largest religious family in the United States, and it remained the largest Protestant family until the 1920s.

The United Methodist Church accounts for more than two thirds of the Methodist family's total membership. This denomination is made up of not only traditional Methodists but also several churches of German origin whose beliefs and spirit accorded well with Methodism. The two "African" churches and the Christian Methodist Church are predominantly black churches, and they account for nearly all of the remaining third of the Methodist group.

Lutheran Churches

Lutherans trace their churches back to the German reformer Martin Luther (1483–1546). Luther sought to reform the doctrine and practice of the Roman Christian Church in Europe. He complained about corruption among the clergy and advocated worship in the language of the people rather than in Latin. He also came to favor a married, rather than a celibate, clergy. The Church of Rome considered Luther disloyal and eventually drove him out. He then helped establish independent churches in northern Germany.

Immigrants from Germany and Scandinavia brought the Lutheran faith to North America, concentrating first in Pennsylvania. Later immigrants settled in the upper Midwest. By 1900 scores of small Lutheran church bodies were divided from one another by language, theology, and degree of assimilation into American society. The Evangelical Lutheran Church in America represents a uniting of many of those earlier churches. The Lutheran Church–Missouri Synod, a national church despite its name, is more conservative theologically.

Pentecostal Churches

The Pentecostal churches share a belief that God grants believers special spiritual gifts—especially the experience called "speaking in tongues," a common feature of Pentecostal services.

Pentecostal churches trace their origin to the day of Pentecost, described in the biblical book of Acts, when early Christians received ecstatic or mystical powers. Modern Pentecostalism began in the early 1900s, when members of some Holiness churches received the gift of tongues (see "Holiness Churches").

Pentecostal congregations tend to be small. They may meet in storefronts or in rented quarters on upper floors. Yet the Pentecostal faith, with its immediacy and emotional power, is perhaps the fastest-growing in the nation, attracting thousands of new adherents each year. In addition, Pentecostal beliefs have had an impact on Roman Catholic, Lutheran, Episcopal, and other denominations. These denominations report a growth among adherents of "charismatic renewal," a movement based on spiritual gifts.

The two Churches of God in Christ and the United Pentecostal Church are predominantly black denominations. The Assemblies of God is the largest predominantly white denomination. Many Pentecostal organizations are regional or purely local. Because of this loose organization, there are likely to be thousands of Pentecostal believers not counted here because

RELIGIOUS AFFILIATIONS IN THE UNITED STATES

FAMILY/Denomination	Local congregations	Total clergy	Total membership	Percent of total affiliated
ALL RELIGIOUSLY AFFILIATED	**300,132**	**534,854**	**163,471,391**	**100.0%**
ROMAN CATHOLIC CHURCH	**19,787**	**50,320**	**59,858,042**	**36.6%**
BAPTIST CHURCHES	**95,601**	**119,729**	**36,433,523**	**22.3%**
Southern Baptist Convention	38,682	60,439	15,398,642	
National Baptist Convention, USA, Inc.	33,000	32,832	8,200,000	
American Baptist Churches in the USA	5,796	7,545	1,516,505	
Baptist Bible Fellowship International	3,500	4,500	1,500,000	
National Baptist Convention of America	2,500	N.A.	3,500,000	
National Missionary Baptist Convention of America	N.A.	N.A.	2,500,000	
Progressive National Baptist Convention, Inc.	1,400	1,400	2,500,000	
American Baptist Association	1,705	1,760	250,000	
Baptist Missionary Association of America	1,362	2,745	230,747	
National Association of Free Will Baptists	2,513	2,900	214,577	
Conservative Baptist Association of America	1,084	1,324	200,000	
General Association of Regular Baptist Churches	1,505	N.A.	154,943	
Baptist General Conference	821	1,700	134,658	
Other (6 denominations)	1,733	2,584	133,451	
METHODIST CHURCHES	**53,235**	**56,032**	**14,285,851**	**8.7%**
United Methodist Church	36,771	38,479	8,646,595	
African Methodist Episcopal Church	8,000	6,550	3,500,000	
African Methodist Episcopal Zion Church	3,000	2,686	1,200,000	
Christian Methodist Episcopal Church	2,340	2,650	718,922	
The Wesleyan Church	1,583	3,125	115,368	
Other (7 denominations)	1,541	2,542	104,966	
PENTECOSTAL CHURCHES	**41,165**	**95,530**	**10,281,559**	**6.3%**
Church of God in Christ	15,300	33,593	5,499,875	
Assemblies of God	11,762	31,057	2,271,718	
Church of God (Cleveland, Tenn.)	5,899	5,302	700,517	
Pentecostal Assemblies of the World	1,005	600	500,000	
United Pentecostal Church International	213	7,464	500,000	
International Church of the Foursquare Gospel	1,638	2,537	217,515	
Church of God in Christ, International	300	1,600	200,000	
Pentecostal Church of God	1,174	1,741	102,760	
Other (15 denominations)	3,874	11,636	289,174	
LUTHERAN CHURCHES	**19,153**	**28,911**	**8,350,212**	**5.1%**
Evangelical Lutheran Church in America	11,023	17,455	5,212,785	
Lutheran Church—Missouri Synod	6,134	8,844	2,598,935	
Wisconsin Evangelical Lutheran Synod	1,220	1,641	416,886	
Other (8 denominations)	776	971	121,606	
LATTER-DAY SAINTS CHURCHES	**11,071**	**48,063**	**4,672,850**	**2.9%**
Church of Jesus Christ of Latter-day Saints	10,007	31,059	4,520,000	
Reorganized Church of Jesus Christ of Latter-day Saints	1,001	16,742	150,143	
The Church of Jesus Christ (Bickertonites)	63	262	2,707	
PRESBYTERIAN CHURCHES	**14,306**	**25,077**	**4,273,721**	**2.6%**
Presbyterian Church (USA)	11,501	20,585	3,796,766	
Presbyterian Church in America	1,212	2,217	239,500	
Other (6 denominations)	1,593	2,275	237,455	
CHURCHES OF CHRIST	**22,553**	**23,677**	**3,679,736**	**2.2%**
Churches of Christ	13,013	10,000	1,651,103	
Christian Churches and Churches of Christ	5,579	6,596	1,070,616	
Christian Church (Disciples of Christ)	3,961	7,081	958,017	
EPISCOPAL CHURCH	**7,388**	**15,000**	**2,504,682**	**1.5%**
REFORMED CHURCHES	**7,965**	**13,220**	**2,079,634**	**1.3%**
United Church of Christ	6,225	10,230	1,530,178	
Reformed Church in America	923	1,763	316,553	
Christian Reformed Church in North America	738	1,152	214,545	
Other (3 denominations)	79	75	18,358	
ORTHODOX (EASTERN) CHURCHES	**1,482**	**2,066**	**1,885,346**	**1.2%**
Orthodox Church in America	700	945	600,000	
Armenian Church of America, Diocese of the	72	70	414,000	
Antiochian Orthodox Christian Archdiocese of North America	178	350	350,000	
Coptic Orthodox Church	85	68	180,000	
Armenian Apostolic Church of America	32	27	150,000	
Other (8 denominations)	415	606	191,346	
JEHOVAH'S WITNESSES	**9,985**	**0**	**926,614**	**0.6%**
ADVENTIST CHURCHES	**4,696**	**5,267**	**794,859**	**0.5%**
Seventh-day Adventist Church	4,270	4,684	761,703	
Other (3 denominations)	426	583	33,156	
CHURCH OF CHRIST, SCIENTIST[1]	**2,400**	**N.A.**	**700,000**	**0.4%**
CHURCH OF THE NAZARENE	**5,161**	**9,363**	**591,134**	**0.4%**
INTERNATIONAL COUNCIL OF COMMUNITY CHURCHES	**423**	**616**	**500,000**	**0.3%**
SALVATION ARMY	**1,151**	**5,241**	**446,403**	**0.3%**
CHRISTIAN AND MISSIONARY ALLIANCE	**1,943**	**2,407**	**302,414**	**0.2%**
CHURCHES OF GOD	**3,061**	**4,379**	**267,676**	**0.2%**
Church of God (Anderson, Ind.)	2,314	3,563	216,117	
Other (4 denominations)	747	816	51,559	
MENNONITE CHURCHES (10 denominations)	**2,656**	**7,920**	**249,798**	**0.2%**
EVANGELICAL FREE CHURCH OF AMERICA	**1,202**	**2,233**	**226,391**	**0.1%**
BRETHREN CHURCHES	**1,800**	**2,533**	**218,905**	**0.1%**
Church of the Brethren	1,135	1,229	146,713	
Other (5 denominations)	665	1,304	72,192	
CHRISTIAN CONGREGATION	**1,437**	**1,433**	**112,437**	**0.1%**
FRIENDS (QUAKER) CHURCHES (3 denominations)	**1,074**	**654**	**84,047**	**0.1%**
OTHER CHRISTIAN CHURCHES (35 denominations)	**5,528**	**8,577**	**753,550**	**0.5%**
TOTAL CHRISTIAN CHURCHES	**296,649**	**528,247**	**154,470,621**	**94.4%**
JEWS[2]	**3,416**	**6,500**	**5,981,000**	**3.7%**
MUSLIMS[3]	**N.A.**	**N.A.**	**3,000,000**	**1.8%**
BUDDHIST CHURCHES OF AMERICA[2]	**67**	**107**	**19,441**	**(Z)**

Note: Z = less than 0.1 percent. 1. Estimate. Denomination does not report membership. 2. Figure from 1992. 3. No reliable statistics exist listing the numbers of Muslims in the United States. The 3,000,000 figure is equal to the total number of Muslim immigrants in the United States, although it is believed that the actual number of adherents is about equal to the number of Jews. **Source:** *Yearbook of American and Canadian Churches*, 1995.

their local congregations are not affiliated with a regional or national group.

Reformed Churches

The Reformed churches are those that trace their descent to the French-Swiss reformer John Calvin (1509–64). These churches were especially significant in the early settlement of the present-day United States. The Pilgrims and Puritans who settled in New England established the Congregational church, which is a main component of today's United Church of Christ. New York was settled by the Dutch, who established the present-day Reformed Church in America. Later, immigrants of Scottish and Scotch-Irish descent established a strong Presbyterian church. Presbyterians differed from Congregationalists in matters of church governance but shared many points of theology and practice.

Reformed church buildings are generally simple and sparsely adorned. Similarly, worship in these churches is austere and simple. Reformed churches generally value a well-educated clergy. In the past they helped found Harvard, Yale, and Princeton. Direct ties to these universities have ended, but Reformed organizations still support many colleges.

The Presbyterian Church (USA) is the result of several mergers between smaller Presbyterian churches that had been separated by regional and doctrinal differences. The United Church of Christ includes, in addition to Congregational churches, descendants of German Reformed churches and of the Evangelical and Reformed Church (also of German descent). The Reformed Church in America and the Christian Reformed Church are both of Dutch descent.

Orthodox Churches

The first great schism in the Christian church occurred in A.D. 1054 between the Western church, centered at Rome, and the Eastern church, centered at Constantinople (present-day Istanbul). In 1054 Eastern Christianity was predominant in Greece and the Middle East, and missionaries had already introduced the faith in Russia. The Russian church celebrated its 1,000th anniversary in 1988. Immigrants from these countries brought Orthodox churches to the United States.

The two largest Orthodox churches in the United States today are Greek and Russian, respectively. The next largest represent Armenians and Syrians. Together these four churches have more than 80 percent of the Orthodox membership.

Orthodox churches are organized hierarchically. Archbishops and bishops possess special spiritual authority and administer church affairs. Religious observances tend to be solemn and elaborate. Ancient liturgies in the ancient languages have been carefully preserved. Orthodox clergy are male, and in most churches they are allowed to marry. Because of differences in calculating feast days, Easter and other movable feasts may occur on different dates in the Orthodox Church than in the Western churches.

In the United States, many Orthodox churches have served as cultural centers for immigrants seeking to preserve their own ethnic heritage. At the same time, however, many denominations are active members of ecumenical groups such as the National Council of Churches.

Latter-day Saints (Mormons)

The Church of Jesus Christ of Latter-day Saints, known popularly as the Mormon Church, was "established anew," according to Mormon doctrine, on Apr. 6, 1830, by a 19th-century American prophet named Joseph Smith (1805–44). Smith, who grew up in western New York State, reported direct revelations from God. The Book of Mormon, which Smith translated, tells of a visit by the resurrected Jesus Christ to pre-Columbian America.

Smith assembled a community of believers that settled first in western New York and later in Ohio, Missouri, and Illinois. Wherever it went, it aroused the antagonism of neighboring non-Mormons, in part because Mormons allow men to take more than one wife. Persecution peaked with the murder of Smith himself in 1844.

The next great leader of the church was Brigham Young (1801–77), who led the majority of Mormons westward to settle in the then-uninhabited basin by the Great Salt Lake. There the church grew and prospered. To this day, the majority of religiously affiliated people in Utah are Mormons. There are also many adherents in surrounding states, especially western Colorado and Arizona.

Most of the church's five-million-plus members live in the United States, but the Mormons' legendary missionary work goes on around the globe. Since about 1900, the church has encouraged converts to stay in their own countries and organize congregations there.

The Reorganized Church is the largest of the groups that did not make the trek to the Great Salt Lake. Its headquarters are in Independence, Missouri, which Smith had designated as the site of a great future temple. Members of the Reorganized Church do not consider themselves Mormons.

Christian Churches and Churches of Christ

This family of churches traces its origins to a great religious awakening in 1800 on the Pennsylvania and Kentucky frontiers. Discouraged by sectarian competition among Methodists, Presbyterians, and others, leaders of the revival did not seek to form a denomination but to reestablish a single nondenominational Christian church. In time they became a denomination themselves.

In the 1870s the Churches of Christ and the Christian Church (Disciples) split over questions of using musical instruments in worship and over the issue of centralizing some church functions. The Churches of Christ opposed both instrumental music and national organization. The Disciples allowed instrumental music and established a central missionary board to coordinate mission work. They are ecumenically minded and have a long history of cooperation and discussion with other denominations.

The third group, the Christian churches and Churches of Christ, split from the Disciples in the 1920s and 1930s. They do allow instrumental music but are theologically more conservative than the Disciples.

Episcopal Family of Churches

The Episcopal churches are descendants of the Church of England, which was established as a separate church by King Henry VIII in 1534. Churches descending from the English church make up the worldwide Anglican Communion. The American church takes its name from the word *bishop*, which suggests its hierarchical organization.

In colonial times the Church of England was established in the southern colonies and had some influence in the middle colonies, but it was not welcome in New England, where Reformed churches were predominant. During the American Revolution, most Church of England members and clergy remained loyal to England. Thousands emigrated to Canada. Those who remained were under suspicion, and some were persecuted. The church almost ceased to function.

After the Revolution, a small group of Anglicans loyal to the United States gradually revived the church. It never grew as rapidly as the Methodist and Baptist families, but it did gain considerable influence. Especially in eastern cities, many families of wealth and power were Episcopalian.

The Episcopal Church accommodates a wide spectrum of belief and practice. It is usually considered Protestant and shares much with other Protestant denominations, yet its worship services retain much of pre-Reformation Catholic tradition. One wing of the church retains a strong emphasis on the church's Catholic heritage.

Holiness Churches

The Holiness churches grew from a religious revival in the late 1800s, primarily in Methodist congregations. The originators of the movement objected to the excessive bureaucracy of established denominations and sought to refocus attention on the need for deep personal change. They placed great emphasis on the teachings of Methodism's founder, John Wesley, that those who are saved may aspire to the gift of complete sanctification, or holiness.

Around 1900, groups of especially intense Holiness worshipers began experiencing further "gifts of the Spirit." From these experiences grew the first Pentecostal churches with their emphasis on speaking in tongues. Many who began as adherents of Holiness churches became Pentecostalists. The Holiness churches rejected what they considered the extremism of Pentecostal worship.

Jehovah's Witnesses

Jehovah's Witnesses are a remarkably active and dynamic sect, visible to most from street-corner or door-to-door encounters. They were founded by Charles Taze Russell (1852–1916) in western Pennsylvania in the 1870s. The Witnesses preach a slightly unorthodox form of the Christian message and look intently for the end of the present world. They claim three million members worldwide, of whom about a quarter live in the United States.

Church of Christ, Scientist

Christian Scientists, as adherents are often known, follow the teachings of Mary Baker Eddy (1821–1910), who founded the church in 1879 in Boston and wrote *Science and Health with a Key to the Scriptures*, which remains a major sourcebook for the church. Christian Science asserts that sickness and other adversities exist only in the mind and that disciplined spiritual thinking can correct them. Thus, Christian Scientists refuse most or all medical treatment. Christian Science practitioners help adherents deal with illness but do not serve as clergy. The church operates many reading rooms open to the public.

The Adventist Family of Churches

Adventist churches sprang up in the United States in the 1840s with a wave of concern about prophecies of the end of the world. Adventists anticipate and prepare for the world's end and the second coming of Jesus Christ. The largest Adventist group, the Seventh-day Adventists, is one of the most dynamic religious groups in the world today, claiming a worldwide membership of five million and a growth rate of more than 7 percent annually. As their name suggests, they worship on Saturday rather than Sunday. They operate parochial schools, colleges, medical schools, and hospitals.

The Salvation Army

The Salvation Army is familiar to outsiders through its work among the homeless and the poor and its fund-raising on the streets, especially before Christmas. The church, which originated in England in 1865, is organized in quasi-military style, and many of its members devote their lives to its service.

Roman Rite Churches

The Roman Rite churches are those that have split from the Roman Catholic Church in recent times but have maintained many of its rituals and doctrines. The Polish church was established in Scranton, Pennsylvania, in the 1890s by church leaders of Polish descent. The Old Catholic churches had their origin in Europe after 1870.

Mennonite Churches

Mennonites trace their roots to a small group of Christians after 1530 who sought a reformation even more radical than those advocated by Lutherans and Calvinists. They were called Mennonites after Menno Simons (1469–1561), one of their early leaders. Their most distinctive practice is adult baptism, offered only to those who have made a decision to follow Christ's teachings.

Because they would not swear oaths and would not bear arms in the service of their temporal leaders, Mennonites were severely persecuted. Small bands were scattered to many corners of the world. Some settled in Pennsylvania beginning in the late 1600s. In the 1870s other groups arrived from Russia. Today more than 40 percent of the world's Mennonites live in the United States. The next-largest group (estimated to be 150,000) lives in the Soviet Union. In recent times Mennonites have become well known for their world relief work.

The Amish are groups with Mennonite beliefs who seek to remain quite aloof from the surrounding culture. The Old Order Amish, centered in Pennsylvania, wear "plain" clothing and still drive horses and buggies rather than automobiles.

Churches of the Brethren

The Brethren, founded as a dissenting group in Germany in the early 1700s, immigrated to Pennsylvania in the 1720s to escape persecution. There they have remained. Brethren share many doctrinal points with their neighbors, the Mennonites. They practice adult baptism, refuse to swear oaths, and will not serve as combatants in war. The various Brethren denominations agree in basic theology but differ on less significant matters of interpretation.

Unitarian Universalist Association

Unitarianism was an outgrowth of New England Congregationalism in the late 1700s and early 1800s. Unitarians asserted God's unity and repudiated the doctrine of the Trinity. They also interpreted other Christian beliefs in a liberal, figurative manner. Universalism was a separate movement emphasizing the availability of God's care to all people, not only to a small chosen group. In 1961 Unitarian and Universalist organizations merged.

Friends (Quaker) Churches

Known popularly as Quakers, the Friends were established by the English religious mystic George Fox (1624–91) in the mid-1600s. They were persecuted in England for refusing to take oaths or to serve as combatants in war. Under the protection of William Penn (1644–1718), many settled in Pennsylvania. According to Fox, they were called Quakers because they were admonished to "tremble at the word of the Lord." In Pennsylvania the Quakers set themselves apart, dressing plainly and avoiding worldly amusements. In Philadelphia they became influential business people.

The most distinctive doctrine of the Friends is that of the Inner Light, the spark of God in each individual. Friends have avoided setting up formal church structures, and many groups have no clergy. Friends have organized remarkable world relief and peace organizations, by which they are perhaps best known to outsiders.

Other Christian Churches

Among the other denominations reported by the *Yearbook of American and Canadian Churches*,

CONTRIBUTIONS TO SELECTED U.S. CHURCHES, 1993

Church	Membership	Contributions: Total	Contributions: Per capita
Highest per capita contributions			
Allegheny Wesleyan Methodist Connection	2,043	$ 4,183,730	$2,047.84
Evangelical Mennonite Church	4,228	6,843,942	1,618.72
The Missionary Church	28,408	39,377,092	1,386.13
Independent Fundamental Churches of America	71,672	96,996,899	1,353.34
The Wesleyan Church, USA	115,368	137,770,586	1,194.18
Evangelical Presbyterian Church	56,421	64,036,670	1,134.98
Primitive Methodist Church in the USA	7,360	8,267,662	1,123.32
Presbyterian Church in America	239,500	261,178,991	1,090.52
Evangelical Covenant Church of America	89,511	96,223,815	1,074.99
Mennonite Church	95,634	99,358,651	1,038.95
Lowest per capita contributions			
Apostolic Faith Mission Church of God	15,400	$ 86,300	$ 4.38
Church of Illumination	4,000	206,600	51.65
Albanian Orthodox Diocese of America	1,885	188,100	99.79
The Latvian Evangelical Lutheran Church in America	13,380	3,344,631	249.97
American Baptist Churches in the USA	1,516,505	398,282,631	262.63
National Association of Free Will Baptists	214,577	60,300,000	281.02
Evangelical Lutheran Church in America	5,212,785	1,640,393,973	314.69
Southern Baptist Convention	15,398,642	5,382,456,000	349.54
Lutheran Church Missouri Synod	2,598,935	920,583,347	354.22
Evangelical Lutheran Synod	21,493	8,166,976	379.98
U.S. AVERAGE (52 churches)			**$420.67**

Note: Based on church finance statistics submitted to the Yearbook of American and Canadian Churches. Not all churches report their finances.
Source: *Yearbook of American and Canadian Churches*, 1995.

there is a wide variety of religious belief and practice. Many of the groups are radically congregational, making generalizations risky. Other groups are heterodox offshoots from the Pentecostal family. In many cases they depend on a single strong leader. The smallest denominations listed may actually be a single local congregation that reports as a separate church body.

Among the miscellaneous groups are spiritualist and other "New Age" groups. Some of these mix spiritualism with Christianity; others may not consider themselves Christian in any sense.

The estimated one million adherents of unlisted organizations are primarily members of independent Christian congregations. These may be Baptist, Methodist, Holiness, or Pentecostal in belief or practice; they may be unaffiliated because of disputes with a regional or national body or simply by long-standing tradition. Many such congregations are remote and isolated.

OTHER RELIGIONS

Judaism

Judaism is the largest non-Christian religious family in the United States. As descendants of the Jews of biblical times, Jews worship one God and follow the religious precepts in the Hebrew scriptures, the writings called the Old Testament by Christians. Jews recognize Jesus as a religious teacher but do not acknowledge him as the Messiah or Son of God. Jews still await the coming of the Messiah as foretold by the prophets.

A handful of Jews arrived in North America in the 1600s. In the 1800s, Jews from Germany arrived with other immigrants. Then between 1890 and 1920, several million Jews arrived from eastern Europe, fleeing persecution and hard times in Russia and Poland. In the 1930s and 1940s, Jews reached America as refugees from the Nazi extermination campaigns. The slaughter of some six million Jews by the Germans, called the Holocaust, is one of two central facts of modern Jewish experience. The second is the establishment of Israel as an independent state in 1948. Today more Jews live in Israel than in any other country except the United States.

Jewish organizations report that there are 5.8 million American Jews. Of these, perhaps 3.8 million are religiously affiliated or observant. The remaining two million consider their Judaism to be more ethnic or cultural than religious.

There are three main branches of religious Judaism in the United States today: Orthodox, Reform, and Conservative.

Orthodox Judaism is by far the most rigorous and by far the smallest of the three branches, with an estimated 400,000 adherents. Orthodox Jews may keep entirely separate kitchens for milk and meat, refuse to operate electric and mechanical devices on the Sabbath, and often attend temple services or hold prayer sessions every day. Orthodox services are conducted in Hebrew, and require men and women to pray separately, even when not in temple. Many orthodox communities, especially self-contained communities such as the Hasidic Jews (located mainly in New York), impose strict dress codes, dictating not only the clothes, but also the hairstyles of their members.

Reform Judaism is the least strict branch. It flowered in the United States in the late 1800s, especially among immigrants from Germany. Reform Jews do not generally wear yarmulkes, don't usually observe the kosher dietary laws, and conduct their religious services primarily in English (though most of the prayers are recited in Hebrew). About 1.4 million Jews are affiliated with Reform temples.

Conservative Judaism rose in response to the Reform movement. It sought to preserve more of the ancient observances of the old orthodoxy, but without losing touch with American culture and behavior. As a middle road between Reform and Orthodox Judaism, Conservative Judaism has gained many adherents. About two million Jews are affiliated with Conservative institutions.

Islam

The Islamic faith, whose followers are called Muslims, is the third of the great theistic world religions, along with Judaism and Christianity. Each of these religions worships the same God (for whom the Muslim name is Allah), and each has its holiest places in the Middle East. Jerusalem is a holy city for all three faiths (see "World Religions").

The first sizable group of Muslims arrived in the United States from Lebanon in the early 1900s. Later waves of immigration have brought Pakistanis, Indians, Arabs, and Iranians, among others. Some have been refugees from political or religious persecution. Some came as students and remained. Perhaps one million engage in at least some religious observance during the year. Many of the rest consider themselves loyal supporters of Islam even if they do not participate regularly.

There are about 600 Islamic centers in the United States, many of which include a mosque for worship. The largest concentrations of Muslims are in cities in the Northeast and industrial Midwest. Observances may vary from one center to another, depending on the nationality of its adherents and their length of residence in the United States. In general, recent immigrants are more conservative and follow Islamic ritual and custom more closely.

Buddhist Churches of America

The Buddhist Churches of America is the oldest and largest U.S. Buddhist group. It represents the Jodo Shinshu sect of Buddhism, and many of its members are of Japanese descent.

There are many other Buddhist organizations in the United States and may be as many as 100,000 additional Americans who subscribe to Buddhist tenets.

EDUCATION

The American people's unwavering commitment to public education dates back more than 150 years. Fueled by a demand for literacy from two different creeds, one described in the Bible, the other in the Declaration of Independence, the American system of education grew to be an essential element in our faith that this nation was uniquely the land of opportunity.

Today that belief has evolved into what is called equality of opportunity, and this vital idea has helped to create a school system whose size and scope is unrivaled by any western democracy.

Over 60 million students and nearly 4 million teachers, administrators, and support staff are directly involved in education. The cost of this undertaking is, of course, staggering: nearly $400 billion annually—more than $6,000 per student—or 8 percent of the gross domestic product, virtually all of it for public education. The proportion of GDP spent on education rose rapidly between 1959 and 1965, declined in the 1970s as enrollment in elementary and secondary schools fell, and began rising steadily again in 1984. And while some may complain bitterly about the quality of the results, or about overt waste, mismanagement, and even fraud, no one any longer questions the essential role of education in American life today.

PUBLIC ELEMENTARY AND SECONDARY SCHOOLS

Expenditures on public elementary and secondary schools have been increasing faster than inflation in almost every year since figures were first kept in 1900. The exception was the period between 1978 and 1982, when inflation outpaced increases in expenditures. Total

NUMBER OF SCHOOLS IN THE U.S., 1992–93

Elem. and secondary	Total	Public	Private[1]
Elementary	75,381	59,680	15,701
Secondary	22,462	19,995	2,467
Combined	9,071	2,549	6,522
Other schools	2,277	2,277	N.A.
Total	**111,308**	**84,501**	**26,807**
Colleges and universities	**Total[2]**	**Public**	**Private**
4-year colleges	2,169	600	1,493
2-year colleges	1,469	1,024	179
Total	**3,638**	**1,624**	**2,014**

1. 1990–91: latest year available. 2. Includes proprietary schools not shown separately. **Source:** U.S. Dept. of Education, National Center for Education Statistics, *Digest of Education Statistics, 1994*.

expenditures topped $263 million in 1993–94, and expenditures per student reached a record high of $5,967. Even after adjusting for inflation, this is a 26 percent increase over 1982–83 levels.

HOW THE STATES RANK IN PUBLIC EDUCATION, 1994–95

State	Enrollment	Rank	Expenditures per pupil	Rank	Average teacher salary	Rank
U.S.	43,929,467	—	$5,442	—	$36,933	—
Ala.	733,736	23	4,194	44	31,144	37
Alaska	131,097[1]	46	8,120[1]	4	47,951	2
Ariz.	733,960[1]	22	3,982[1]	46	32,090[1]	29
Ark.	446,024[1]	34	3,795[1]	48	28,409	45
Calif.	5,340,000	1	4,606	37	40,667[1]	10
Colo.	640,522	26	5,101	27	34,571	24
Conn.	507,987	29	8,147	3	51,300	1
Del.	106,813	48	6,591	8	39,076	12
D.C.	80,450	N.A.	7,520	N.A.	42,959	N.A.
Fla.	2,108,968	4	5,185	24	32,588	27
Ga.	1,270,948	9	4,595	38	32,828	26
Hawaii	182,972	42	5,740	15	38,518	14
Idaho	240,448	39	3,976[1]	47	29,783	41
Ill.	1,919,225	5	4,752	33	41,041	8
Ind.	967,739[1]	13	5,158[1]	25	36,516[1]	18
Iowa	498,837	31	5,139	26	31,511	32
Kans.	460,905	33	5,315	22	34,936	22
Ky.	644,726[1]	24	5,007[1]	30	32,257	28
La.	774,415	21	4,525	39	26,574	48
Ma.	212,182	40	6,048	13	31,856	31
Md.	790,935	20	6,212	12	40,636	11
Mass.	890,420[1]	15	6,383[1]	9	42,078[1]	7
Mich.	1,624,043[1]	8	6,240[1]	11	47,412[1]	3
Minn.	826,600	19	5,413[1]	21	37,412	15
Miss.	503,301	30	3,469[1]	49	26,910	47
Mo.	861,532	17	4,502	40	31,217	36
Mont.	164,295	43	5,091	28	28,785	43
Nebr.	285,756	37	5,018[1]	29	30,822	39
Nev.	250,747	38	4,677	36	34,836	23
N.H.	188,930	41	5,845	14	34,974[1]	21
N.J.	1,174,216	10	9,206	1	46,801	5
N.Mex.	302,513	36	4,870	32	28,865	42
N.Y.	2,790,700	3	8,217	2	47,250	4
N.C.	1,146,639	11	4,739	34	31,079	38
N.Dak.	119,288	47	4,459[1]	41	26,327	49
Ohio	1,787,049	6	5,482	20	36,685	17
Okla.	609,800	27	4,042[1]	45	27,971	46
Oreg.	521,000	28	5,710	16	38,700	13
Pa.	1,779,790	7	6,909	5	44,489	6
R.I.	147,490	44	6,729	7	40,729	9
S.C.	641,371	25	4,401	42	30,341	40
S.Dak.	135,494	45	4,693[1]	35	26,017[1]	50
Tenn.	865,729	16	4,208	43	31,270	35
Tex.	3,680,271	2	4,894	31	31,310	33
Utah	471,557	32	3,431	50	28,676	44
Vt.	101,045[1]	49	6,879[1]	6	36,311[1]	19
Va.	1,060,806	12	5,303	23	33,753	25
Wash.	939,333	14	5,563	19	36,120	20
W.Va.	309,888	35	5,565	18	31,923	30
Wis.	856,661	18	6,358	10	37,349[1]	16
Wyo.	100,314	50	5,582	17	31,300	34

1. Data estimated by NEA. **Source:** National Education Association, *Estimates of School Statistics* (1995).

In 1979, a historic shift occurred in the source of money to operate the American public school system. That was the year the state share of revenues rose above the local share for the first time. The federal share for elementary and secondary schools has always been relatively small.

Public elementary and secondary school enrollment declined every year from 1971 to 1984 as the number of young people decreased. That trend evidenced itself in secondary school populations between 1980 and 1990. Since 1990, however, both elementary and secondary school populations are again on the rise, increasing slightly each year. These numbers suggest that baby boomers started a boom of their own, the fruits of which are now starting to reach high school.

REVENUES FOR PUBLIC ELEMENTARY AND SECONDARY SCHOOLS, 1920–92

School year ending	Total revenues (billions)	Source by percent: Federal	State	Local[1]
1920	$ 1.0	0.3%	16.5%	83.2%
1930	2.1	0.4	16.9	82.7
1940	2.3	1.8	30.3	68.0
1950	5.4	2.9	39.8	57.3
1960	14.7	4.4	39.1	56.5
1970	40.3	8.0	39.9	52.1
1975	64.4	9.0	42.2	48.8
1980	96.9	9.8	46.8	43.4
1985	137.3	6.6	48.9	44.4
1986	149.1	6.7	49.4	43.9
1987	158.5	6.4	49.7	43.9
1988	169.6	6.3	49.5	44.1
1989	192.0	6.2	47.8	46.0
1990	207.8	6.1	47.3	46.6
1991	223.3	6.2	47.2	46.7
1992	234.5	6.6	46.4	47.0

1. Includes a relatively small amount from nongovernmental sources (gifts and tuition and transportation fees from patrons). **Source:** U.S. Dept. of Education, National Center for Education Statistics, *Digest of Education Statistics 1994.*

PRIVATE SCHOOLS

The U.S. Department of Education updates its data on private schools less frequently than it does for public institutions. The 1990–91 school year is the latest year for which data is available for private elementary and secondary schools.

Schools and enrollment There were 24,690 private schools engaged in educating 4,673,878 students. Of these schools, 15,636 were

SCHOOL ENROLLMENT, KINDERGARTEN THROUGH UNIVERSITY LEVEL, 1970–95

Type of school	Fall enrollment (millions of students) 1970	1975	1980	1985	1990	1991	1995[1]
Elementary (K–8)							
Public	32.6	30.5	27.7	27.0	29.9	30.5	32.3
Private	4.1	3.7	4.0	4.2	4.1	4.1	4.4
Secondary (9–12)							
Public	13.3	14.3	13.2	12.4	11.3	11.5	12.8
Private	1.3	1.3	1.3	1.4	1.1	1.1	1.3
Higher education							
Public	6.4	8.8	9.5	9.5	10.8	11.3	11.7
Private	2.2	2.4	2.6	2.8	3.0	3.0	3.3
Total	**59.9**	**61.0**	**58.3**	**57.2**	**60.3**	**61.6**	**65.7**

1. Projected. **Source:** U.S. Dept. of Education, National Center for Education Statistics, *Digest of Education Statistics, 1994.*

EDUCATION EXPENDITURES, 1950–94

School year ending	All educational institutions: Total expenditures (millions)	As percentage of GDP	Elementary and secondary schools: Public Total (millions)	Public Per pupil	Private (millions)	Colleges and universities: Public (millions)	Private (millions)
1950	$ 8,911	N.A.	$ 5,838	$ 231	$ 411	$ 1,430	$ 1,233
1960	23,860	4.8%	15,613	440	1,100	3,904	3,244
1970	68,459	7.1	40,683	878	2,500	16,234	9,041
1980	165,627	6.7	95,962	2,290	7,200	41,434	21,031
1985	247,657	6.6	137,000	3,456[1]	12,400	63,705	34,553
1986	269,485	6.7	148,600	3,724[1]	13,200	70,069	37,616
1987	291,974	6.8	160,900	3,995[1]	14,300	74,552	42,222
1988	313,375	6.9	172,699	4,310[1]	15,300	79,859	45,516
1989	346,883	7.1	192,977	4,738	16,400	87,107	50,398
1990	382,062	7.3	212,100	5,158	18,200	97,095	54,668
1991	414,690	7.5	229,430	5,486	19,500	105,631	60,128
1992[2]	438,971	7.7	241,567	5,641	20,200	112,271	64,933
1993[1]	462,700	7.7	253,800	5,830	21,500	118,400	69,000
1994[1]	484,000	7.8	263,500	5,967	21,900	125,300	73,300

Note: N.A. = not available. 1. Estimated. 2.Preliminary. **Source:** U.S. Dept. of Education, National Center for Education Statistics, *Digest of Education Statistics, 1994.*

elementary schools (responsible for educating 2,653,599 students), 2,486 were secondary schools (888,944 students), and 6,569 offered instruction in all 12 grades (1,131,335 students). Most private schools were religiously affiliated. Thirty-five percent, or 8,731 schools, were affiliated with the Catholic church; 11,476 were affiliated with other religious groups. Only 4,483 schools were nonsectarian.

Tuitions Average tuitions for private school students was $2,595 per year. But that average is brought down by the large number of parochial schools offering free or low-cost private education. The average cost of all nonsectarian private schools (elementary and secondary) was $5,727, and more than half of such schools charge at least $5,000 per year in tuition. Average tuition for nonsectarian secondary schools was over $8,000 per year.

Teachers There were 356,285 full-time private school teachers, almost equally divided between elementary and secondary schools. The vast majority of these teachers (274,521) were women, and an even greater number (328,624) were white. The average teacher salary in private schools was $21,673, a fraction of the $33,578 earned by public school teachers. Male teachers earned substantially more than their female counterparts in both public and private schools, but the difference was most pronounced in private schools, where male compensation ($27,196) was 36 percent greater than female salaries ($19,999).

Race and ethnicity Private schools remain almost entirely white enclaves. More than a third (9,885) of all private schools had minority enrollments of less than 5 percent, and another third (7,114) had minority populations below 20 percent, even though the majority of private school students came from central cities.

Student-teacher ratios Students in private schools continue to get more teacher attention than do students in public schools. Pupil-teacher ratios were 16.0–1 in private elementary schools, compared with 18.9–1 in public elementary schools. The difference was even more pronounced on the secondary school level, where private school teachers averaged a mere 11.1 students, while each public school teacher was responsible for 14.8 pupils.

NUMBER OF CATHOLIC SCHOOLS, PUPILS, AND TEACHERS, 1960–95

Category	1960	1970	1980	1990	1993	1994	1995
			Elementary				
Number	10,501	9,362	8,043	7,291	7,174	7,114	6,979
Pupils	4,373,000	3,355,000	2,269,000	1,883,906	1,983,725	1,992,183	1,990,784
Teachers	108,000	112,000	97,000	91,039	109,825	112,199	116,494
Religious	79,000	52,000	25,000	10,837	11,351	10,982	10,564
Lay	29,000	60,000	72,000	80,202	97,769	100,400	105,930
			Secondary				
Number	2,392	1,981	1,516	1,296	1,249	1,231	1,238
Pupils	880,000	1,008,000	837,000	591,533	583,905	584,662	614,571
Teachers	44,000	55,000	49,000	40,159	44,991	45,002	46,599
Religious	33,000	29,000	14,000	6,579	5,594	5,061	6,193
Lay	11,000	26,000	35,000	33,580	37,897	38,345	40,406

Source: National Catholic Education Association.

EDUCATIONAL ATTAINMENT BY STATE, 1994

State	Persons over 25 ('000s)	4 years high school or more	Rank	4 years college or more	Rank
U.S. total	**164,510**	**80.9%**	**—**	**22.2%**	**—**
Alabama	2,646	72.5	50	15.2	48
Alaska	346	90.9	2	24.8	13
Arizona	2,552	84.2	20	19.9	33
Arkansas	1,536	74.5	46	12.4	50
California	19,447	79.1	38	24.7	14
Colorado	2,304	91.1	1	28.5	3
Connecticut	2,144	86.4	9	27.0	6
Delaware	454	83.2	23	21.9	24
District of Columbia	393	79.0	39	36.0	1
Florida	9,250	81.3	30	21.0	29
Georgia	4,429	79.0	40	24.5	16
Hawaii	773	85.4	15	24.3	17
Idaho	673	85.4	16	21.8	25
Illinois	7,441	81.0	31	23.5	21
Indiana	3,506	79.3	37	15.0	49
Iowa	1,756	83.6	22	19.3	38
Kansas	1,553	86.7	7	22.7	23
Kentucky	2,382	73.9	47	16.8	46
Louisiana	2,581	73.7	49	17.0	43
Maine	781	84.3	19	21.2	27
Maryland	3,353	82.6	25	26.0	10
Massachusetts	4,003	85.6	13	30.1	2
Michigan	5,989	83.0	24	19.1	39
Minnesota	2,802	87.7	6	26.3	8
Mississippi	1,568	73.8	48	19.8	36
Missouri	3,340	79.7%	35	21.3%	26
Montana	538	84.9	17	24.3	18
Nebraska	992	87.8	5	21.1	28
Nevada	950	86.6	8	16.9	44
New Hampshire	731	84.8	18	26.2	9
New Jersey	5,240	83.8	21	28.1	4
New Mexico	1,004	79.4	36	24.1	19
New York	11,937	82.0	29	25.1	12
North Carolina	4,484	75.8	42	19.0	40
North Dakota	383	82.3	26	19.9	34
Ohio	7,049	82.1	28	19.8	35
Oklahoma	2,045	80.7	32	20.3	32
Oregon	2,009	85.9	11	24.5	15
Pennsylvania	7,923	80.4	33	19.5	37
Rhode Island	653	75.4	43	23.9	20
South Carolina	2,291	74.9	45	18.0	41
South Dakota	436	82.2	27	17.3	42
Tennessee	3,301	75.1	44	16.2	47
Texas	11,030	77.3	41	20.8	31
Utah	1,000	89.3	3	22.8	22
Vermont	386	86.0	10	27.7	5
Virginia	4,069	80.0	34	26.4	7
Washington	3,379	88.6	4	25.1	11
West Virginia	1,213	71.0	51	11.4	51
Wisconsin	3,180	85.5	14	20.9	30
Wyoming	285	85.7	12	16.8	45

Source: U.S. Bureau of the Census, *Current Population Survey* (1995).

EDUCATIONAL ATTAINMENT OF THE POPULATION, AGE 25 AND OVER, 1994

Characteristic	Number of persons ('000s)	4 or more years of high school	At least some years of college	4 or more years of college
All persons	164,512	80.9%	46.5%	22.2%
Sex				
Male	78,539	81.0	48.8	25.1
Female	85,973	80.7	44.6	19.6
Race				
White	139,760	82.0	47.5	22.9
Black	18,103	72.9	36.7	12.9
Hispanic origin[1]	13,714	53.3	27.2	9.1
Age groups				
25 to 44 years	83,473	87.5	53.7	25.2
45 to 64 years	50,259	81.2	45.9	23.1
65 years or older	30,779	62.4	28.3	12.5
Region				
Northeast	38,652	82.7	46.0	23.1
Midwest	44,462	82.5	45.7	19.1
South	65,958	77.2	44.0	18.4
West	40,915	82.0	52.8	21.9
Residence				
Metropolitan area	128,518	82.3	49.4	24.6
Nonmetropolitan area	35,994	75.9	36.3	13.8

1. People of Hispanic origin may be of any race. **Source:** Bureau of the Census, *Current Population Survey*, unpublished data, 1995.

EDUCATIONAL ATTAINMENT OF POPULATION 25+ YEARS, 1940–94

Year	Both sexes	Male	Female
Completed 4 years of high school or more			
1940	24.5%	22.7%	26.3%
1950	34.3	32.6	36.0
1959	43.7	42.2	45.2
1970	55.2	55.0	55.4
1980	68.6	69.1	68.1
1987	75.6	76.0	75.3
1991	78.4	78.5	78.3
1992	79.4	79.7	79.2
1993	80.2	80.5	80.0
1994	80.9	81.0	80.7
Completed 4 years of college or more			
1940	4.6%	5.5%	3.8%
1950	6.2	7.3	5.2
1959	8.1	10.3	6.0
1970	11.0	14.1	8.2
1980	17.0	20.8	13.5
1987	19.9	23.6	16.5
1991	21.4	24.3	18.8
1992	21.4	24.3	18.6
1993	21.9	24.8	19.2
1994	22.2	25.1	19.6

Source: U.S. Bureau of the Census, *Educational Attainment in the U.S.* (February 1995).

COLLEGE ENTRANCE EXAMINATION SCORES

SATs (Scholastic Aptitude Tests) purportedly measure verbal and mathematical reasoning abilities. These tests are developed and administered by the Educational Testing Service, Princeton, N.J., for the College Board, which is headquartered in New York City. The College Board is a nonprofit organization that provides tests and many other educational services for students, schools, and colleges.

In 1994, some 1,050,386 students took the SATs, scoring an average of 902 points, the same as the year before. (The test is scored on a range from 400 to 1600.) The scores of each ethnic group were not demonstrably different than the year before, but blacks, Hispanics, and Native Americans continue to score about 100 points lower than whites. And though the gap is closing, men continue to outscore women by about 40 points. Moreover, no group has done much to reverse a steep decline that began in 1969, when average scores were 956.

Because males consistently outscore females on these tests, many groups have asserted that the tests are inherently unfair to women students. In fact, a New York court found such a bias in 1989 and disallowed awarding of scholarships based solely on SAT scores. In response to criticisms of racial and gender bias, the College Board rewrote the SAT in 1994 to make it a test of aptitude, rather than of knowledge or test-taking techniques. The new test has fewer multiple choice questions and more open-ended questions that the College Board claims makes the test uncoachable. The leading coaching services disagree, however, and have already tailored their books and courses to help students improve their scores. If the 1994 scores are any example, the new test seems just as biased as the old one.

ACTs are administered by the American College Testing Program, a nonprofit educational organization, which has its national headquarters in Iowa City, Iowa. The ACT composite score is the average of four tests that measure academic abilities in English, mathematics, social studies, and natural sciences. Average ACT scores increased slightly for the second straight year, to 20.8. The average was 20.6 in 1992 and 20.7 in 1993. Average scores for almost all ethnic groups (except Asian-Americans) have also increased gradually over the past several years.

AVERAGE SAT AND ACT SCORES BY GROUP, 1985–94

	SAT					ACT				
	Combined scores				Total test-takers,	Composite scores				Total test-takers,
Groups	1985	1990	1993	1994	class of 1994	1989	1990	1993	1994	class of 1994
American Indian, Alaskan Native	820	825	847	837	8,150	17.5	18.0	18.4	18.5	11,026
Asian-American, Pacific Islander	922	938	950	951	81,097	21.9	21.7	21.7	21.7	26,168
Black	722	737	741	740	102,679	16.6	17.0	17.1	17.0	81,806
Mexican-American	808	809	802	799	35,397	18.1	18.3	18.5	18.4	29,558
Puerto Rican	777	764	776	778	13,036	(1)	(1)	(1)	(1)	(1)
Other Hispanic	N.A.	817	817	818	29,295	19.3	19.3	19.3	19.3	15,119
White	939	933	938	938	662,107	21.3	21.2	21.4	21.4	623,366
Men	936	928	930	926	493,063	21.2	21.0	21.0	20.9	396,953
Women	877	874	877	881	557,323	20.1	20.3	20.5	20.7	494,761
National average[2]	**906**	**900**	**902**	**902**	**1,050,386**	**20.6**	**20.6**	**20.7**	**20.8**	**891,714**

Note: N.A. = not available. 1. Puerto Rican ACT test-takers included with Other Hispanic. 2. Includes students of other ethnicities and students who did not identify their ethnicities. **Source:** The College Board, American College Testing Program.

MOST POPULAR MAJORS AMONG INCOMING FRESHMEN, 1990–94

Major	Percentage 1990	1993	1994
Nursing	4.2%	5.5%	5.4%
Elementary education	5.1	4.9	4.7
Premedicine, predental, preveterinary	3.2	4.0	4.2
Psychology	4.2	4.5	4.1
Accounting	5.3	4.4	4.0
Therapy	2.3	4.9	3.9
Business administration	5.5	4.1	3.7
General biology	1.8	2.9	2.9
Management	4.0	2.9	2.8
Political science	3.0	2.4	2.3
Law enforcement	1.7	2.6	2.1
Secondary education	1.9%	1.9%	2.0%
Electrical engineering	2.5	2.1	1.9
Computer science	1.7	1.6	1.9
Marketing	2.5	1.7	1.8
Mechanical engineering	2.0	1.9	1.7
Arts	2.0	1.7	1.7
Communications	2.3	2.0	1.6
Architecture or urban planning	N.A.	1.3	1.6
English language and literature	1.0	1.4	1.4

Source: Higher Education Research Institute, University of California, Los Angeles, *The American Freshman: National Norms for Fall, 1994.*

HIGHER EDUCATION

The accompanying figures give a startling picture of just how the coming of age of the Baby Boom generation transformed U.S. higher education. In just one decade (the 1960s) the number of undergraduate degrees conferred more than doubled, while the number of doctorates actually tripled. These extraordinary changes were matched in kind by dramatic shifts in what students wanted to study: during the late 1960s, for example, the number of degrees in sociology and psychology jumped by more than 15,000 each in just a few years (1966–70), while interest in business soared during the 1980s. That trend has begun to reverse in the 1990s, as the need for social workers and other health and human service professionals has expanded, while jobs on Wall Street and in business generally have become more scarce.

Between 1980 and 1993, college enrollment increased about 20 percent, from just over 12 million to a record 14.6 million. This increase has come even as the traditional college age population has dropped. Much of this growth was fueled by increases in older students, women and minorities, and part-time students. Enrollment of students aged 25 and older rose 34 percent, while women on campus increased by 17 percent. Minorities, especially Hispanics and Asians, have increased from 15.7 percent of the campus population in 1976 to 21.2 percent in 1992. The percentage of blacks on campus has fluctuated over the past 15 years, but remains about the same as it was in 1976.

AVERAGE COST OF 4-YEAR COLLEGES, 1980–95
(tuition and fees, per year)

Year	Public	Private
1980–81	$ 804	$ 3,617
1981–82	909	4,113
1982–83	1,031	4,639
1983–84	1,148	5,093
1984–85	1,228	5,556
1985–86	1,318	6,121
1986–87	1,414	6,658
1987–88	1,537	7,116
1988–89	1,646	7,722
1989–90	1,781	8,446
1990–91	1,908	9,340
1991–92	2,137	10,017
1992–93	2,334	10,449
1993–94	2,535	11,007
1994–95	2,686	11,709

Source: The College Board.

NUMBER OF DEGREES CONFERRED IN U.S., BY TYPE, 1950–95

Year	All degrees[1]	Bachelor's	First professional[2]	Master's	Doctorate
1949–50	496,661	432,058[3]		58,183	6,420
1959–60	476,704	392,440[3]		74,435	9,829
1969–70	1,065,098	792,317	34,578	208,291	29,912
1979–80	1,330,244	929,417	70,131	298,081	32,615
1984–85	1,373,734	979,477	75,063	286,251	32,943
1985–86	1,383,953	987,823	73,910	288,567	33,653
1986–87	1,386,271	991,264	71,617	289,349	34,041
1987–88	1,397,349	994,829	70,735	299,317	34,870
1988–89	1,435,952	1,018,755	70,856	310,621	35,720
1989–90	1,485,004	1,051,344	70,988	324,301	38,371
1990–91	1,542,948	1,094,538	71,948	337,168	39,294
1991–92	1,604,196	1,136,553	74,146	352,838	40,659
1992–93[4]	1,624,100	1,145,000	73,900	364,000	41,200
1993–94[4]	1,651,000	1,165,000	74,700	370,000	41,300
1994–95[4]	1,671,400	1,178,000	75,100	377,000	41,300

1. Does not include associate of arts (A.A.) or associate of science (A.S.) degrees; more than 400,000 of these have been given each year since 1980. 2. Degrees are: medical doctor, law, dentistry, optometry, podiatry, pharmacy, theology, chiropractic, and veterinary medicine. 3. Prior to 1961, bachelor's and first professional degrees were listed together. 4. Projected. **Source:** U.S. Dept. of Education, National Center for Education Statistics, *Digest of Education Statistics, 1994.*

THE UNITED STATES ECONOMY

GROSS NATIONAL PRODUCT AND GROSS DOMESTIC PRODUCT

The goal of an economic system is to transform resources into final products by business enterprises for consumption by society. This includes manufacturing goods such as cars, bread, furniture, and so on, and providing services such as health care, education, and motion pictures. The most commonly used measures associated with this goal are gross national product (GNP) and gross domestic product (GDP). GNP is the total national output of goods and services valued at market prices. GNP in this broad context measures the output attributable to the factors of production—labor and property—supplied by a country's residents. GNP differs from "national income" mainly in that GNP includes allowances for depreciation and for indirect business taxes (sales and property taxes). GDP is the measure of the output of production attributable to all factors of production (labor and property) physically located within a country. GDP, therefore, excludes net property income from abroad (such as the earnings of U.S. nationals working overseas) that is included in GNP.

The word *final* serves to exclude intermediate goods sold to producers and used to make finished products eventually sold to consumers in the market. Auto parts such as batteries and tires are examples of intermediate goods and are included in GNP or GDP only through the price of a car when it is sold. GNP and GDP, in terms of expenditure categories, comprise purchases of goods and services by consumers and government, gross private domestic investment (or business purchases), and net exports.

The assessment of GNP and GDP in current dollars is referred to as a nominal measure. Nominal measures may be misleading because GNP and GDP can appear to rise as average prices rise with inflation. An alternative method is to evaluate GNP and GDP by measuring the value of goods and services using constant prices for a given year; the government currently uses 1987 as the base year. Assessments based on constant prices are referred to as real measures because they indicate the change in quantity of output produced by the economy.

An important criticism of the GNP as an indicator of progress is that it may not be an accurate assessment of the standard of living an economy provides. Not all goods and services are equally important, for example, but all are counted equally in the GNP. Similarly, many of the characteristics that reflect the quality of life in an economy, such as education levels, the availability of health services, and leisure, may not be captured by GNP measures.

DEFINITIONS OF OUTPUT, INCOME, AND EXPENDITURE TERMS

Capital consumption adjustment Used for corporations, nonfarm sole proprietorships, and partnerships, this is the difference between capital consumption claimed on income tax returns and capital consumption allowances measured at straight-line depreciation, consistent-service lives, and replacement cost. The tax return data are valued at historical costs and reflect changes over time in service lives and depreciation patterns as permitted by tax regulations.

Consumer expenditure Consumer expenditure statistics presented in the accompanying tables are arrived at from the findings of the Consumer Expenditure Survey program, designed to provide a continuous flow of data on the buying habits of American consumers, necessary for future revisions of the Consumer Price Index. One group of 5,000 consumers in 85 urban areas around the country keeps diaries of expenditures on small, frequently purchased items, such as food and beverages, tobacco, housekeeping supplies, nonprescription drugs, and personal care products and services. Another 5,000 consumers are interviewed quarterly for information about large expenditures, such as those for property, automobiles, and major appliances, or about expenditures occurring on a fairly regular basis, such as rent, utilities, and insurance premiums.

Disposable personal income is that income after personal tax and nontax payments; this is the income available to persons for spending and saving. Personal tax and nontax payments are tax payments (except personal contributions for social insurance, net of refunds) by persons that are not chargeable to business expense, and also include certain personal payments to general government that are treated like taxes. Personal taxes include income, estate, gift, and personal property taxes and motor vehicle licenses. Nontax payments include passport fees, fines and penalties, donations, and tuitions and fees paid to schools and hospitals operated mainly by government.

Family income The term *family* refers to a group of two or more persons related by birth, marriage, or adoption who reside together; all such persons are considered members of one family. Family income refers to the sum of all income of the family members.

Gross domestic product (GDP) See "Gross National Product and Gross Domestic Product," above.

Gross national product (GNP) See "Gross National Product and Gross Domestic Product," above.

Gross state product (GSP) is the gross market value of the goods and services attributable to labor and property located in a state. It is the state counterpart of the nation's GDP.

Household income A household includes related family members and all unrelated persons, if any—such as lodgers, foster children, wards, or employees—who share a house, an apartment, or a single room when it is occupied or intended for occupancy as separate living quarters by that household; that is, when the members of the household do not live and eat with any other persons in the structure and there is direct access from the outside or through a common hall. Household income, therefore, is the sum of all income of household members. The "householder" (which replaced the term *head of household* beginning with the 1980 Current Population Survey) is the person in whose name the home is owned or rented. In the case of joint ownership, one person in each household is designated as the householder for statistical purposes.

Inventory valuation adjustment This represents the difference between the book value of inventories used in production and the cost of replacing them.

GROSS DOMESTIC PRODUCT (GDP), BY INDUSTRY, IN CURRENT AND CONSTANT (1987) DOLLARS, 1980–92

	Current dollars				Constant (1987) dollars			
Industry	**1980**	**1985**	**1990**	**1992**	**1980**	**1985**	**1990**	**1992**
Gross Domestic Product (GDP)	**$2,708**	**$4,039**	**$5,546**	**$6,020**	**$3,776**	**$4,280**	**$4,897**	**$4,979**
Private industries	2,370	3,571	4,862	5,256	3,203	3,759	4,324	4,431
Agriculture, forestry, and fisheries	67	84	112	116	63	82	96	110
Farms	56	67	85	86	51	64	72	81
Agricultural services	11	17	27	30	12	18	24	30
Mining	113	131	103	85	80	83	92	89
Construction	129	179	240	222	185	209	210	201
Manufacturing[1]	588	798	1,025	1,063	725	811	929	925
Durable goods[1]	349	472	564	568	424	468	537	534
Lumber and wood products	19	24	31	31	22	25	28	25
Furniture and fixtures	8	14	16	17	12	14	14	15
Stone, clay, and glass products	18	24	25	25	24	25	26	25
Primary metal industries	44	36	44	40	49	35	35	36
Fabricated metal products	45	57	67	70	55	58	60	60
Industrial machinery, except electrical	77	87	109	102	103	78	102	108
Electric and electronic equipment	55	84	86	86	70	83	91	93
Motor vehicles and equipment	27	58	46	57	40	63	49	51
Other transportation equipment	26	48	65	61	38	47	64	54
Instruments and related products	20	27	56	60	24	27	50	50
Misc. manufacturing industries	10	14	19	20	10	14	17	17
Nondurable goods[1]	239	327	461	495	301	342	392	391
Food and kindred products	52	72	97	104	64	75	84	83
Tobacco manufactures	7	11	16	19	20	14	9	8
Textile mill products	15	17	22	24	17	18	21	23
Apparel and other textile products	17	21	25	27	20	21	24	25
Paper and allied products	23	33	46	46	31	36	42	44
Printing and publishing	33	52	72	77	53	59	62	58
Chemicals and allied products	48	67	104	111	58	67	88	88
Petroleum and coal products	24	24	40	43	15	23	26	25
Rubber and misc. plastic products	17	26	35	39	19	26	32	35
Leather and leather products	4	4	4	5	5	4	4	4
Transportation and public utilities	242	378	481	529	336	382	463	495
Transportation	103	136	177	194	120	137	169	184
Railroad transportation	21	22	22	23	19	20	24	26
Local interurban passenger transit	5	7	10	11	9	8	9	9
Trucking and warehousing	40	54	73	78	51	58	69	77
Water transportation	7	8	10	10	9	8	8	8
Transportation by air	18	27	40	46	19	26	40	45
Pipelines, except natural gas	5	6	4	5	5	5	5	5
Transportation services	6	11	17	20	9	12	15	15
Communications	69	113	147	162	94	116	141	154
Telephone and telegraph	62	100	123	135	81	103	121	131
Radio and television broadcasting	7	12	24	28	14	13	20	23
Electric, gas, and sanitary services	70	129	158	173	122	129	153	157
Wholesale trade	192	277	363	394	191	273	320	341
Retail trade	245	391	516	558	320	421	478	487
Finance, insurance, and real estate	418	682	982	1,106	693	776	868	893
Services	377	651	1,040	1,183	609	722	869	890
Private households	6	7	9	10	7	8	9	9
Government and government enterprises	324	482	676	756	509	528	582	584
Federal	115	171	221	248	179	183	193	189
General government	96	140	180	200	139	149	156	152
Government enterprise	19	31	41	48	39	34	37	37
State and local	209	311	455	508	330	345	388	395
General government	194	283	413	462	301	313	353	360
Government enterprise	15	28	42	46	29	32	35	35
Statistical discrepancy	14	–14	8	9	19	–15	7	7

1. Includes items not shown separately. **Sources:** U.S. Bureau of Economic Analysis, *The National Income and Product Accounts of the United States, 1929–82,* and *Survey of Current Business.*

GDP IN CURRENT AND CONSTANT (1987) DOLLARS, 1960–94 (billions of dollars)

Item	1960	1965	1970	1975	1980	1985	1987	1990	1991	1992	1993	1994
Current dollars												
Gross domestic product (GDP)	$513.4	$702.7	$1,010.7	$1,585.9	$2,708.0	$4,038.7	$4,540.0	$5,546.1	$5,724.8	$6,020.2	$6,343.3	$6,738.4
Personal consumption expenditures	332.4	444.6	646.5	1,024.9	1,748.1	2,667.4	3,052.2	3,761.2	3,902.4	4,136.9	4,378.2	4,628.4
Durable goods	43.5	63.5	85.3	134.3	212.5	352.9	403.7	468.2	456.6	492.7	538.0	591.5
Nondurable goods	153.1	191.9	270.4	416.0	682.9	919.4	1,011.1	1,229.2	1,257.8	1,295.5	1,339.2	1,394.3
Services	135.9	189.2	290.8	474.5	852.7	1,395.1	1,637.4	2,063.8	2,188.1	2,348.7	2,501.0	2,642.7
Gross private domestic investment	78.7	118.0	150.3	226.0	467.6	714.5	749.3	808.9	744.8	788.3	882.0	1,032.9
Fixed investment	75.5	108.3	148.1	231.7	477.1	689.9	723.0	802.0	746.6	785.2	866.7	980.7
Nonresidential	49.2	74.1	106.7	169.0	353.8	504.0	497.8	586.7	557.0	561.4	616.1	697.6
Residential	26.3	34.2	41.4	62.7	123.3	185.9	225.2	215.3	189.6	223.8	250.6	283.0
Change in business inventories	3.2	9.7	2.3	–5.7	–9.5	24.6	26.3	6.9	–1.8	3.0	15.4	52.2
Net exports of goods and services	2.4	3.9	1.2	13.6	–14.7	–115.6	–143.1	–71.4	–19.9	–30.3	–65.3	–98.2
Exports	25.3	35.4	57.0	136.3	279.2	302.1	364.0	557.1	601.1	638.1	659.1	718.7
Imports	22.8	31.5	55.8	122.7	293.9	417.6	507.1	628.5	620.9	668.4	724.3	816.9
Government purchases[1]	99.8	136.3	212.7	321.4	507.1	772.3	881.5	1,047.4	1,097.4	1,125.3	1,148.4	1,175.3
Federal	55.3	69.5	100.1	129.4	209.1	344.3	384.9	426.5	445.8	449.0	443.6	437.3
National defense	45.3	51.0	76.8	89.6	142.7	258.6	292.1	314.0	322.8	314.2	302.7	292.3
State and local	44.5	66.8	112.6	192.0	298.0	428.1	496.6	620.9	651.6	676.3	704.7	738.0
Constant (1987) dollars												
Gross domestic product (GDP)	$1,970.8	$2,473.5	$2,873.9	$3,221.7	$3,776.3	$4,279.8	$4,540.0	$4,897.3	$4,867.6	$4,979.3	$5,134.5	$5,344.0
Personal consumption expenditures	1,210.8	1,497.0	1,813.5	2,007.5	2,447.1	2,865.8	3,052.2	3,272.6	3,259.4	3,349.5	3,458.7	3,579.6
Durable goods	115.4	156.2	183.7	226.8	262.7	370.1	403.7	443.1	425.3	452.6	489.9	532.1
Nondurable goods	526.9	616.7	717.2	767.1	860.5	958.7	1,011.1	1,060.7	1,047.7	1,057.7	1,078.5	1,109.5
Services	568.5	724.1	912.5	1,103.6	1,323.9	1,537.0	1,637.4	1,768.8	1,786.3	1,839.1	1,890.3	1,938.1
Gross private domestic investment	290.8	413.0	429.7	437.6	594.4	745.9	749.3	746.8	683.8	725.3	819.9	951.5
Fixed investment	282.7	387.9	423.8	451.5	602.7	723.8	723.0	741.1	684.9	722.9	804.6	903.8
Nonresidential	173.3	250.6	292.0	316.8	437.8	521.8	497.8	546.5	515.4	525.9	591.6	672.4
Residential	109.4	137.3	131.8	134.7	164.8	202.0	225.2	194.5	169.5	196.9	213.0	231.3
Change in business inventories	8.1	25.1	5.9	–13.9	–8.3	22.1	26.3	5.7	–1.1	2.5	15.3	47.8
Net exports of goods and services	–7.6	–6.4	–35.2	23.1	30.7	–145.3	–143.1	–54.7	–19.5	–32.3	–73.9	–110.0
Exports	88.4	118.1	161.3	232.9	320.5	309.2	364.0	510.5	542.6	578.8	602.5	657.0
Imports	96.1	124.5	196.4	209.8	289.9	454.6	507.1	565.1	562.1	611.2	676.3	766.9
Government purchases[1]	476.9	509.9	665.8	663.5	704.2	813.4	881.5	932.6	944.0	936.9	929.8	922.8
Federal	259.0	285.1	315.0	262.7	284.8	355.2	384.9	384.1	386.7	373.5	356.6	337.6
National defense	—	—	—	184.9	194.2	265.6	292.1	283.6	281.4	261.4	243.7	226.7
State and local	217.9	284.8	350.9	400.8	419.4	458.2	496.6	548.5	557.2	563.3	573.1	585.2

1. Purchases of goods and services. **Source:** U.S. Bureau of Economic Analysis, *National Income and Product Accounts of the United States: Volume 1, 1929–59, and Volume 2, 1959–88,* and *Survey of Current Business* (March 1995).

Mean vs. median income Mean (or average) income refers to the sum of all incomes of a group divided by the number of incomes in that group. Median income is the middle income when they are arranged in order of size—that is, there are the same number of incomes above and below the median. For example, consider incomes of $2,000, $3,000, $4,000, $15,000 and $95,000: the mean income is the sum of these divided by five, or $23,800; the median income is $4,000.

Money income This refers to income received (exclusive of certain money receipts such as capital gains) before payments for such things as personal income taxes, Social Security, union dues, and Medicare deductions. Money income does not include income in the form of noncash benefits such as food stamps, health benefits, and subsidized housing; rent-free housing and goods produced and consumed on farms; or the use of business transportation and facilities, full or partial payments by business for retirement programs, medical and educational expenses, and so on. These elements should be considered when comparing income levels. None of the aggregate income concepts (GNP, national income, or personal income) is exactly comparable with money income, although personal income is the closest.

National income, the aggregate of labor and property earnings derived from the current production of goods and services, is the sum of employee compensation, proprietors' income,

PERSONS BELOW POVERTY LEVEL, BY RACE, 1960–93

	Number below poverty level (millions)				Percent below poverty level				Average income cutoffs for family of four at poverty level[3]
Year	All races[1]	White	Black	Hispanic[2]	All races[1]	White	Black	Hispanic[2]	
1960	39.9	28.3	N.A.	N.A.	22.2%	17.8%	N.A.	N.A.	$ 3,022
1970	25.4	17.5	7.5	N.A.	12.6	9.9	33.5%	N.A.	3,968
1975	25.9	17.8	7.5	3.0	12.3	9.7	31.3	26.9%	5,500
1980	29.3	19.7	8.6	3.5	13.0	10.2	32.5	25.7	8,414
1985	33.1	22.9	8.9	5.2	14.0	11.4	31.3	29.0	10,989
1990	33.6	22.3	9.8	6.0	13.5	10.7	31.9	28.1	13,359
1991	35.7	23.7	10.2	6.3	14.2	11.3	32.7	28.7	13,924
1992	38.0	25.3	10.8	7.6	14.8	11.9	33.4	28.7	14,335
1993	39.3	26.2	10.9	8.1	15.1	12.2	33.1	29.6	14,763

1. Includes other races not shown separately. 2. Hispanic persons may be of any race. 3. Prior to 1980, income cutoffs are for nonfarm families only. **Source:** U.S. Bureau of the Census, *Current Population Reports* (series).

rental income, corporate profits, and net interest. It measures the total factor costs of the goods and services produced by the economy. Income is measured before deduction of taxes.

Personal income is the current income received by persons from all sources minus their personal contributions for social insurance. *Persons* include individuals (including owners of unincorporated firms), nonprofit institutions serving individuals, private trust funds, and private noninsured welfare funds. Personal income includes transfers (payments not resulting from current production) from government and business, such as Social Security benefits and public assistance, but excludes transfers among persons. Also included are certain nonmonetary types of income: estimated net rental value to owner-occupants of their homes, the value of services furnished without payment by financial intermediaries, and food and fuel produced and consumed on farms.

Poverty level is an estimate of the income necessary to purchase what society defines as a minimally acceptable standard of living. Families and unrelated individuals are classified as being above or below the poverty level according to their money income as a group and the number of people in the group (e.g., in 1990 a family of four with total money income below $13,359 lived below the poverty level). Classification is based on the poverty index originated by the Social Security Administration in 1964 and revised in 1969 and 1980. The poverty index is based solely on money income and does not reflect the fact that many low-income persons receive noncash benefits such as food stamps, Medicaid, and public housing. The poverty thresholds are updated every year to reflect changes in the Consumer Price Index.

Private domestic investment This consists of (1) nonresidential fixed investment, i.e., firms' purchases of capital goods such as plants and equipment; (2) residential fixed investment (the building of single- and multifamily housing units); and (3) the change in business inventories, which are stocks on hand of raw materials and finished goods.

POVERTY LEVELS BASED ON MONEY INCOME FOR FAMILIES AND UNRELATED INDIVIDUALS, 1993

Size of unit	1993
1 person (unrelated individual)	$ 7,363
Under 65 years	7,518
65 years and over	6,930
2 persons	9,414
Householder under 65 years	9,728
Householder 65 years and over	8,740
3 persons	11,522
4 persons	14,763
5 persons	17,449
6 persons	19,718
7 persons	22,383
8 persons	24,838
9 persons or more	29,529

Note: Weighted averages. **Source:** U.S. Bureau of the Census, *Statistical Abstract 1995* (1995).

NUMBER (AND PERCENT) OF PERSONS AND FAMILIES BELOW POVERTY LEVEL BY STATE, 1990

	Number (and percent) below poverty level					
State	Total population[1]	All families	All families with children under 18	Female householder families	Female householder families with children under 18	Female householder families with children under 5
Ala.	723,614 (18.3%)	158,369 (14.3%)	112,705 (19.5%)	79,510 (40.7%)	67,736 (52.1%)	31,185 (65.6%)
Alaska	47,906 (9.0)	9,198 (6.8)	7,935 (9.1)	4,238 (24.1)	4,050 (28.0)	2,397 (39.0)
Ariz.	564,362 (15.7)	108,662 (11.4)	84,870 (17.5)	43,657 (31.6)	38,910 (40.0)	21,203 (56.4)
Ark.	437,089 (19.1)	97,026 (14.8)	67,822 (20.3)	39,345 (41.2)	34,370 (52.1)	15,937 (66.9)
Calif.	3,627,585 (12.5)	670,685 (9.3)	553,586 (14.2)	304,579 (26.2)	276,033 (36.1)	149,729 (50.3)
Colo.	375,214 (11.7)	73,715 (8.6)	59,396 (12.9)	36,245 (29.9)	33,445 (38.8)	17,519 (57.2)
Conn.	217,347 (6.8)	43,965 (5.0)	35,616 (8.6)	29,634 (21.7)	27,396 (34.0)	15,141 (51.5)
Del.	56,223 (8.7)	10,851 (6.1)	8,300 (9.3)	6,250 (22.3)	5,609 (31.8)	2,878 (45.3)
D.C.	96,278 (16.9)	16,453 (13.3)	12,926 (20.2)	12,164 (25.1)	10,495 (33.0)	5,868 (41.7)
Fla.	1,604,186 (12.7)	319,978 (9.0)	229,558 (14.7)	151,639 (28.4)	133,078 (38.6)	68,852 (53.9)
Ga.	923,085 (14.7)	197,681 (11.5)	150,470 (16.0)	110,893 (34.3)	97,665 (44.3)	48,318 (57.4)
Hawaii	88,408 (8.3)	16,053 (6.0)	12,760 (8.9)	6,937 (19.6)	6,382 (29.8)	3,426 (41.7)
Idaho	130,588 (13.3)	25,767 (9.7)	19,883 (13.9)	9,242 (33.2)	8,528 (42.3)	4,080 (61.2)
Ill.	1,326,731 (11.9)	264,413 (9.0)	210,142 (13.8)	150,913 (30.7)	135,526 (43.2)	70,427 (58.6)
Ind.	573,632 (10.7)	118,225 (7.9)	91,923 (11.9)	62,068 (29.6)	55,810 (39.7)	27,358 (55.8)
Iowa	307,420 (11.5)	62,747 (8.4)	46,469 (12.6)	27,404 (33.5)	25,140 (45.1)	12,828 (64.1)
Kans.	274,623 (11.5)	55,341 (8.3)	41,239 (12.0)	24,327 (30.8)	21,963 (40.0)	11,213 (57.3)
Ky.	681,827 (19.0)	163,206 (16.0)	114,416 (21.4)	60,887 (39.6)	51,519 (51.8)	22,177 (67.7)
La.	967,002 (23.6)	213,030 (19.4)	162,199 (25.7)	114,006 (49.6)	98,525 (60.1)	47,330 (73.4)
Maine	128,466 (10.8)	26,313 (8.0)	19,932 (11.8)	12,745 (29.9)	11,896 (41.6)	6,050 (62.8)
Md.	385, 296 (8.3)	75,313 (6.0)	58,455 (9.0)	47,808 (20.9)	42,170 (29.1)	21,948 (40.1)
Mass.	519, 339 (8.9)	102,748 (6.7)	81,601 (11.1)	64,764 (24.7)	59,636 (39.4)	33,070 (58.0)
Mich.	1,190,698 (13.1)	251,687 (10.2)	204,821 (16.0)	155,142 (35.8)	141,744 (48.1)	76,198 (64.6)
Minn.	435,331 (10.2)	82,888 (7.3)	63,701 (10.8)	39,519 (29.2)	36,613 (40.0)	19,778 (59.1)
Miss.	631,029 (25.2)	137,025 (20.2)	103,009 (27.0)	71,668 (50.6)	62,305 (61.4)	29,066 (72.5)
Mo.	663,075 (13.3)	139,463 (10.1)	102,664 (14.7)	63,941 (31.4)	56,922 (42.0)	28,721 (58.2)
Mont.	124,853 (16.1)	25,691 (12.0)	19,766 (17.6)	10,270 (39.7)	9,407 (49.3)	4,521 (67.1)
Nebr.	170,616 (11.1)	33,509 (8.0)	25,201 (11.7)	14,508 (29.6)	13,292 (39.5)	7,304 (59.9)
Nev.	119, 660 (10.2)	22,599 (7.3)	16,907 (10.8)	10,683 (23.2)	9,774 (31.1)	5,370 (44.7)
N.H.	69,104 (6.4)	12,842 (4.4)	9,299 (6.1)	5,860 (17.6)	5,307 (25.4)	3,017 (44.5)
N.J.	573,152 (7.6)	113,848 (5.6)	88,717 (9.0)	67,594 (20.6)	60,563 (32.8)	29,730 (45.9)
N.Mex.	305,934 (20.6)	65,042 (16.5)	52,252 (23.1)	25,502 (40.9)	22,567 (50.2)	10,760 (62.2)
N.Y.	2,277,296 (13.0)	454,872 (10.0)	360,162 (15.8)	271,681 (30.1)	240,040 (43.4)	124,058 (57.2)
N.C.	829,858 (13.0)	179,906 (9.9)	128,082 (13.9)	93,929 (31.0)	81,111 (41.1)	39,565 (55.9)
N.Dak.	88,276 (14.4)	18,388 (10.9)	13,404 (15.2)	6,527 (38.0)	5,996 (50.4)	3,008 (70.2)
Ohio	1,325,768 (12.5)	283,906 (9.7)	227,253 (15.2)	157,143 (33.7)	141,748 (46.4)	71,552 (63.1)
Okla.	509,854 (16.7)	112,652 (13.0)	82,352 (18.4)	46,243 (38.3)	40,807 (48.3)	19,109 (65.0)
Oreg.	344,867 (12.4)	66,173 (8.7)	50,725 (13.5)	29,786 (30.5)	27,346 (40.0)	14,684 (60.9)
Pa.	1,283,629 (11.1)	259,117 (8.2)	195,435 (13.0)	137,239 (27.9)	119,205 (42.4)	59,427 (58.4)
R.I.	92,670 (9.6)	17,867 (6.8)	14,371 (11.6)	11,061 (26.5)	10,312 (41.7)	5,773 (62.2)
S.C.	517,793 (15.4)	111,173 (11.9)	83,423 (16.6)	61,878 (36.0)	53,668 (45.8)	25,889 (58.4)
S.Dak.	106,305 (15.9)	21,127 (11.6)	15,937 (16.5)	7,739 (38.7)	7,136 (48.8)	3,785 (66.2)
Tenn.	744,941 (15.7)	168,182 (12.4)	117,828 (17.1)	78,055 (34.3)	66,148 (45.2)	30,920 (59.4)
Tex.	3,000,515 (18.1)	617,981 (14.1)	478,367 (19.2)	241,700 (35.4)	208,016 (43.6)	99,997 (57.0)
Utah	192,415 (11.4)	35,443 (8.6)	29,006 (11.5)	14,210 (30.3)	13,234 (38.9)	7,485 (57.1)
Vt.	53,369 (9.9)	10,104 (6.9)	7,968 (10.3)	5,029 (26.9)	4,762 (36.4)	2,425 (53.6)
Va.	611,611 (10.2)	126,897 (7.7)	92,509 (10.9)	66,480 (26.7)	57,485 (36.4)	28,048 (50.3)
Wash.	517,933 (10.9)	100,149 (7.8)	80,799 (12.3)	51,193 (30.1)	47,630 (39.5)	25,006 (57.5)
W.Va.	345,093 (19.7)	80,485 (16.0)	58,277 (23.2)	28,203 (39.8)	23,222 (55.0)	9,495 (71.5)
Wis.	508,545 (10.7)	97,466 (7.6)	79,490 (12.1)	53,139 (31.2)	49,932 (43.3)	26,703 (61.9)
Wyo.	52,453 (11.9)	11,294 (9.3)	8,917 (13.1)	5,024 (36.9)	4,767 (45.4)	2,290 (62.4)

Note: Figures are from 1990 census, which are different from those in the Current Population Survey. 1. Only persons for whom poverty status has been determined. **Source:** Census Bureau, Press Release, 1992.

PERSONAL INCOME PER CAPITA IN CURRENT DOLLARS, BY STATE, 1970–94

State	Personal income 1970	Personal income 1980	Personal income 1990	Personal income 1994[1]	Income rank 1980	Income rank 1994
Alabama	$2,945	$ 7,704	$14,903	$18,010	48	41
Alaska	5,073	13,835	20,881	23,788	1	9
Arizona	3,789	9,172	16,265	19,001	33	38
Arkansas	2,827	7,465	13,784	16,898	50	50
California	4,746	11,603	20,654	22,493	4	15
Colorado	4,025	10,598	18,814	22,333	14	18
Connecticut	5,037	12,112	25,427	29,402	3	2
Delaware	4,587	10,249	19,719	22,828	15	12
District of Columbia	5,250	12,322	24,648	31,136	2	1
Florida	3,943	9,764	18,788	21,677	25	21
Georgia	3,377	8,348	17,123	20,251	39	31
Hawaii	4,944	10,617	20,906	24,057	12	7
Idaho	3,467	8,569	15,301	18,231	37	40
Illinois	4,563	10,837	20,159	23,784	8	10
Indiana	3,771	9,245	16,816	20,378	32	29
Iowa	3,804	9,537	16,684	20,265	27	30
Kansas	3,770	9,941	17,642	20,896	18	24
Kentucky	3,141	8,022	14,747	17,807	44	43
Louisiana	3,071	8,682	14,281	17,651	35	46
Maine	3,405	8,218	17,039	19,663	40	35
Maryland	4,475	10,790	22,090	24,933	9	6
Massachusetts	4,514	10,612	22,247	25,616	13	5
Michigan	4,133	10,165	18,237	22,333	16	17
Minnesota	3,995	10,062	18,779	22,453	17	16
Mississippi	2,597	6,926	12,571	15,838	51	51
Missouri	3,809	9,298	17,409	20,717	30	25
Montana	$3,528	$8,924	$14,741	$17,865	34	42
Nebraska	3,759	9,274	17,379	20,488	31	26
Nevada	4,878	11,421	20,254	24,023	6	8
New Hampshire	3,890	9,788	20,227	23,434	24	11
New Jersey	4,805	11,573	24,182	28,038	5	3
New Mexico	3,145	8,169	14,213	17,106	42	48
New York	4,855	10,721	22,321	25,999	11	4
North Carolina	3,236	7,999	16,275	19,669	45	34
North Dakota	3,129	8,538	15,321	18,546	38	39
Ohio	4,033	9,723	17,548	20,928	26	23
Oklahoma	3,436	9,393	15,119	17,744	29	44
Oregon	3,889	9,866	17,199	20,419	20	28
Pennsylvania	4,042	9,891	18,883	22,324	19	19
Rhode Island	4,050	9,518	19,032	22,251	28	20
South Carolina	3,004	7,589	15,106	17,695	49	45
South Dakota	3,200	8,217	15,630	19,577	41	36
Tennessee	3,151	8,030	15,905	19,482	43	37
Texas	3,629	9,798	16,749	19,857	23	33
Utah	3,297	7,952	14,060	17,043	46	49
Vermont	3,604	8,577	17,442	20,224	36	32
Virginia	3,743	9,827	19,537	22,594	22	14
Washington	4,165	10,725	19,265	22,610	10	13
West Virginia	3,078	7,915	13,967	17,208	47	47
Wisconsin	3,889	9,845	17,398	21,019	21	22
Wyoming	3,797	11,339	16,902	20,436	7	27

1. Preliminary data. **Source:** U.S. Bureau of Economic Analysis, *Survey of Current Business* (May 1995) and unpublished data.

PERSONAL INCOME PER CAPITA FOR SELECTED METROPOLITAN AREAS, 1970–93

Metropolitan statistical area, ranked by 1993 income	1970	1980	1990	1993
United States	$4,047	$ 9,940	$18,635	$20,800
Metropolitan portion	4,304	10,543	19,747	21,994
Nonmetropolitan portion	3,108	7,784	14,333	16,111
Lowest per capita income				
1. McAllen–Edinburg–Mission, Tex.	$1,930	$5,244	$9,012	$10,085
2. Laredo, Tex.	2,204	5,371	8,977	10,757
3. Brownsville–Harlingen, Tex.	2,163	5,693	9,592	11,042
4. El Paso, Tex.	2,962	6,377	11,510	12,790
5. Jacksonville, N.C.	3,088	5,977	10,202	13,168
6. Las Cruces, N.Mex.	2,897	6,632	12,281	13,228
7. Provo–Orem, Utah	2,657	6,244	11,395	13,401
8. Yuma, Ariz.	3,034	7,920	12,096	13,529
9. Sumter, S.C.	2,574	6,356	12,249	13,706
10. Houma, La.	2,832	9,321	12,450	14,192
11. Bryan–College Station, Tex.	2,879	7,001	12,480	14,602
12. Clarksville–Hopkinsville, Tenn.–Ky.	3,012	7,210	12,088	14,657
14. Hattiesburg, Miss.	2,753	7,143	12,749	14,707
15. Lawton, Okla.	3,093	7,231	13,181	14,794
16. Pine Bluff, Ark.	2,781	7,465	13,135	14,890
17. Merced, Calif.	3,736	9,246	14,264	15,082
18. Goldsboro, N.C.	3,022	6,976	13,150	15,261
19. Visalia–Tulare–Porterville, Calif.	3,549	9,176	14,393	15,319
20. Lafayette, La.	2,486	8,819	13,629	15,434
21. Killeen–Temple, Tex.	3,343	7,575	12,894	15,486
22. Monroe, La.	2,731	7,812	13,653	15,586
23. Anniston, Ala.	2,749	7,123	13,575	15,679
24. Cumberland, Md.–W.Va.	3,271	7,932	14,458	15,900
25. Biloxi–Gulfport–Pascagoula, Miss.	3,032	7,529	13,307	15,920
Highest per capita income				
1. San Francisco, Calif.[1]	$6,105	$15,226	$29,672	$32,927
2. West Palm Beach–Boca Raton, Fla.	4,851	12,820	29,103	32,230
3. New Haven–Bridgeport–Stamford–Danbury–Waterbury, Conn.[1]	5,384	12,945	27,791	31,151
4. Bergen–Passaic, N.J.	5,424	13,136	28,174	30,298
5. Trenton, N.J.[1]	4,843	11,965	25,877	29,385
6. Naples, Fla.	5,403	12,298	27,296	29,237
7. Middlesex–Somerset–Hunterdon, N.J.	4,855	12,583	26,106	28,999
8. Newark, N.J.	5,121	12,028	25,433	28,687
9. Nassau–Suffolk, N.Y.	5,224	12,615	26,733	28,630
10. New York, N.Y.	5,383	11,721	24,664	27,975
11. Washington, D.C.–Md.–Va.–W.Va.[1]	5,089	12,487	25,132	27,761
12. San Jose, Calif.[1]	4,869	13,084	24,547	27,360
13. Reno, Nev.	5,272	13,228	23,114	26,671
14. Anchorage, Alaska	5,891	14,933	24,117	26,619
15. Hartford, Conn. (NECMA)	4,875	11,773	24,091	26,147
16. Seattle–Bellevue–Everett, Wash.	4,616	12,369	22,962	26,121
17. Monmouth–Ocean, N.J.	4,409	11,254	23,154	25,805
18. Sarasota–Bradenton, Fla.	4,393	11,501	23,233	25,634
19. Oakland, Calif.	4,906	12,414	23,359	25,621
20. Orange County, Calif.	4,890	13,136	24,287	25,022
21. Honolulu, Hawaii	5,118	11,026	22,009	24,929
22. Boston–Worcester–Lawrence–Lowe, Mass.	4,539	10,766	22,589	24,861
23. Chicago, Ill.	4,985	11,829	22,156	24,857
24. Boulder–Longmont, Colo.	4,241	11,325	21,125	24,612
25. Atlantic–Cape May, N.J.	4,316	11,751	22,559	24,397

Note: Does not include residents and military living abroad. NECMA = New England county metropolitan area. See "Metropolitan Statistical Areas" in index for definitions. 1. Primary Metropolitan Statistical Area. **Source:** Bureau of Economic Analysis, *Survey of Current Business* (May 1995).

PERSONAL INCOME PER CAPITA FOR SELECTED COUNTIES, 1993

Rank/County	Per capita income 1993	Percent of national average
Lowest per capita income		
1. Starr, Tex.	$ 6,306	30.3%
2. Shannon, S.Dak.	7,517	36.1
3. Maverick, Tex.	7,925	38.1
4. Todd, S.Dak.	8,455	40.6
5. Zavala, Tex.	8,658	41.6
6. Zapata, Tex.	9,055	43.5
7. Sioux, N.Dak.	9,272	44.6
8. Elliot, Ky.	9,307	44.7
9. Dimmit, Tex.	9,468	45.5
10. Hudspeth, Tex.	9,526	45.8
11. Owsley, Ky.	9,644	46.4
12. Jefferson, Miss.	9,686	46.6
13. Apache, Ariz.	9,769	47.0
14. Morgan, Ky.	9,957	47.9
15. Presidio, Tex.	9,958	47.9
16. Menifee, Ky.	10,017	48.2
17. Hidalgo, Tex.	10,085	48.5
18. Willacy, Tex.	10,092	48.5
19. McCreary, Ky.	10,165	48.9
20. Cibola, N.Mex.	10,166	48.9
21. Jackson, S.Dak.	10,175	48.9
22. Mora, N.Mex.	10,235	49.2
23. McKinley, N.Mex.	10,256	49.3
24. San Juan, Utah	10,305	49.5
25. Dixie, Fla.	10,334	49.7
Highest per capita income		
1. New York, N.Y.	$52,277	251.3%
2. Sherman, Tex.	42,373	203.7
3. Sully, S.Dak.	39,707	190.9
4. Pitkin, Colo.	39,481	189.8
5. Marin, Calif.	38,310	184.2
6. Fairfield, Conn.	37,642	181.0
7. Somerset, N.J.	36,542	175.7
8. Teton, Wyo.	35,983	173.0
9. Westchester, N.Y.	35,945	172.8
10. Greeley, Kans.	35,594	171.1
11. Esmeralda, Nev.	35,465	170.5
12. Bergen, N.J.	34,658	166.6
13. Morris, N.J.	34,412	165.4
14. Montgomery, Md.	34,299	164.9
15. Arlington, Va.	34,216	164.5
16. Alexandria City, Va.	34,023	163.6
17. Nantucket, Mass.	33,991	163.4
18. Hartley, Tex.	33,863	162.8
19. Hamilton, Kans.	33,459	160.9
20. Nassau, N.Y.	32,966	158.5
21. San Francisco, Calif.	32,777	157.6
22. Montgomery, Pa.	32,753	157.5
23. Hansford, Tex.	32,596	156.7
24. Fairfax–Fairfax City–Falls Church, Va.	32,422	155.9
25. Palm Beach, Fla.	32,230	155.0

1. Combination area consisting of one or two independent cities with populations less than 100,000 combined with an adjacent county. The county name appears first, followed by the city name(s). Separate estimates for the jurisdictions making up the combined areas are not available. **Source:** U.S. Bureau of Economic Analysis, *Survey of Current Business* (May 1995).

PER CAPITA MONEY INCOME, BY RACE AND HISPANIC ORIGIN, 1970–93

	Current dollars				Constant (1993) dollars			
Year	All races	White	Black	Hispanic[1]	All races	White	Black	Hispanic[1]
1970	$ 3,177	$ 3,354	$1,869	N.A.	$11,116	$11,735	$6,539	N.A.
1975	4,818	5,072	2,972	$2,847	12,388	13,041	7,642	$7,320
1980	7,787	8,233	4,804	4,865	13,672	14,455	8,435	8,542
1985	11,013	11,671	6,840	6,613	14,790	15,673	9,186	8,881
1990	14,387	15,265	9,017	8,424	15,906	16,877	9,969	9,313
1991	14,617	15,510	9,170	8,662	15,508	16,455	9,729	9,190
1992	15,033	15,981	9,296	8,874	15,483	16,459	9,574	9,140
1993	15,777	16,800	9,863	8,830	15,777	16,800	9,863	8,830

Note: N.A. = not available. 1. Hispanic persons may be of any race. **Source:** U.S. Bureau of the Census, *Current Population Reports* (series).

MEDIAN MONEY INCOME OF YEAR-ROUND, FULL-TIME CIVILIAN WORKERS, BY SEX AND AGE, 1970–93

	Female				Male			
Age[1]	1970	1980	1990	1993	1970	1980	1990	1993
Total with income	$5,440[2]	$11,591	$20,591	$22,469	$9,184[2]	$19,173	$28,979	$31,077
15–19 years	3,783[3]	6,779	13,944[4]	15,277[4]	3,950[3]	7,753	15,462[4]	15,948[4]
20–24 years	4,928	9,407	N.A.	N.A.	6,655	12,109	N.A.	N.A.
25–34 years	5,923	12,190	20,184	21,949	9,126	17,724	25,355	26,087
35–44 years	5,531	12,239	22,505	25,282	10,258	21,777	32,607	35,233
45–54 years	5,588	12,116	21,938	24,412	9,931	22,323	35,732	39,685
55–64 years	5,468	11,931	20,755	22,587	9,071	21,053	33,169	35,736
65 and over	4,884	12,342	22,957	24,875	6,754	17,307	35,520	37,085

Note: N.A. = not available. 1. Age as of March of following year. 2. 14 years old and over. 3. 14 to 19 years old. 4. Includes 15 to 24 years old. **Source:** U.S. Bureau of the Census, *Current Population Reports* (series), and unpublished data.

NATIONAL INCOME, BY TYPE OF INCOME, 1970–94 (billions of current dollars)

Type of income	1970	1980	1985	1990	1993	1994
National income	**$833.5**	**$2,196.2**	**$3,268.4**	**$4,491.0**	**$5,131.4**	**$5,458.4**
Compensation of employees	618.3	1,644.4	2,382.8	3,297.6	3,780.4	4,004.6
Wages and salaries	551.5	1,376.6	1,986.3	2,745.0	3,100.8	3,279.0
Government and government enterprise	117.1	261.4	373.7	516.0	583.8	602.8
Other	434.3	1,115.2	1,612.6	2,229.0	2,517.0	2,676.2
Supplements to wages and salaries	66.8	267.8	396.5	552.5	679.6	725.6
Employer contributions for social insurance	34.3	127.9	204.7	278.3	324.3	344.6
Other labor income	32.5	139.8	191.8	274.3	355.3	381.0
Proprietors' income[1]	79.9	171.8	259.9	363.3	441.6	473.7
Farm	14.6	11.5	21.5	41.9	37.3	39.5
Nonfarm	65.3	160.3	238.4	321.4	404.3	434.2
Rental income of persons[2]	17.8	13.2	18.7	–14.2	24.1	27.7
Corporate profits[1]	77.5	177.7	280.8	380.6	485.8	542.7
Corporate profits[3]	71.8	197.8	225.3	354.7	456.7	505.0
Profits before tax	78.4	240.9	225.0	365.7	462.4	524.5
Profits tax liability	34.4	84.8	96.5	138.7	173.2	202.5
Profits after tax	44.0	156.1	128.5	227.1	289.2	322.0
Dividends	23.7	59.0	92.4	153.5	191.7	205.2
Undistributed profits	20.3	97.1	36.1	73.6	97.5	116.9
Inventory valuation adjustment	–6.6	–43.0	0.2	–11.0	–6.2	–19.5
Capital consumption adjustment	5.6	–20.2	55.5	25.9	29.5	37.7
Net interest	40.0	191.2	326.2	463.7	399.5	409.7

1. With inventory valuation and capital consumption adjustments. 2. With capital consumption adjustment. 3. With inventory valuation adjustment. **Sources:** U.S. Bureau of Economic Analysis, *National Income and Product Accounts of the United States*, Volume 2, 1959–88, and *Survey of Current Business* (annual).

PERCENT DISTRIBUTION OF NATIONAL INCOME, BY TYPE, 1970–94

Type of income	1970	1980	1985	1990	1993	1994
National income, total	**100.0%**	**100.0%**	**100.0%**	**100.0%**	**100.0%**	**100.0%**
Compensation of employees	74.2	74.9	72.9	73.7	73.4	73.4
Wages and salaries	66.2	62.7	60.8	61.4	60.3	60.1
Supplements to wages, salaries	8.0	12.2	12.1	12.2	13.1	13.3
Proprietors' income[1]	9.6	7.8	7.9	8.2	8.6	8.7
Farm	1.8	0.5	0.6	0.9	0.9	0.7
Nonfarm	7.8	7.3	7.3	7.3	7.7	8.0
Rental income of persons[2]	2.1%	0.6%	0.6%	–0.2%	0.2%	0.5%
Corporate profits[1]	9.2	8.1	8.6	8.1	9.1	9.9
Profits before tax	9.4	11.0	6.9	8.0	8.7	9.6
Profits after tax	5.3	7.1	3.8	4.9	5.4	5.9
Inventory valuation adjustment	–0.8	–2.0	(Z)	–0.3	–0.1	–0.4
Capital consumption adjustment	0.7	–0.9	1.6	0.5	0.5	0.7
Net interest	4.8	8.7	9.6	10.3	8.7	7.5

Note: Z = less than 0.05%. 1. With inventory valuation and capital consumption adjustments. 2. With capital consumption adjustment. **Source:** U.S. Bureau of the Census, based on data from U.S. Bureau of Economic Analysis, *The National Income and Product Accounts of the United States, 1929–82*, and *Survey of Current Business* (annual).

MONEY INCOME OF FAMILIES—MEDIAN FAMILY INCOME BY RACE AND HISPANIC ORIGIN, 1994

	Number ('000s)				Median family income			
Characteristic	**All families[1]**	**White**	**Black**	**Hispanic[2]**	**All families[1]**	**White**	**Black**	**Hispanic[2]**
All families	68,506	57,881	7,993	5,946	$36,959	$39,300	$21,542	$23,654
Type of family								
Married-couple families	53,181	47,452	3,715	4,038	$43,005	$43,675	$35,218	$28,454
Wife in paid labor force	32,194	28,539	2,417	2,121	51,204	51,630	44,805	35,973
Wife not in paid labor force	20,988	18,913	1,298	1,917	30,218	30,878	22,207	20,721
Male householder, wife absent	2,914	2,298	450	410	26,467	28,269	19,476	21,717
Female householder, husband absent	12,411	8,131	3,828	1,498	17,443	20,000	11,909	12,047
Number of earners								
No earners	10,546	8,622	1,574	860	$15,515	$17,656	$6,858	$8,362
One earner	19,301	15,556	2,999	2,044	26,193	28,574	16,571	17,121
Two earners	30,137	26,336	2,620	2,248	47,424	48,332	37,124	32,172
Three earners	6,367	5,486	651	538	57,745	58,651	49,489	40,724
Four or more earners	2,155	1,882	149	256	72,673	73,269	59,678	49,876

Note: Families as of March 1994. 1. Includes other races not shown separately. 2. Hispanic persons may be of any race. **Source:** U.S. Bureau of the Census, *Current Population Reports* (August 1994).

ECONOMIC INDICATORS

All market economies regularly go through cycles of recession—when output declines and unemployment rises—and expansion—when output and employment rise. These "business cycles" are one of the most important factors determining the socioeconomic conditions in any society. Although economists still have very little idea what actually causes recessions and what leads the economy to begin expanding again, they have had some success in predicting business cycles. Economic forecasting is the science of making these predictions. It is especially useful to be able to predict recessions sufficiently far in advance so that governments can take actions to stimulate the economy and reduce the severity of these downturns.

Economic indicators track developments in areas of the economy that are thought to be crucial to the future health of the economy, just as a barometer measures changes in air pressure that are crucial to changes in the weather. The development of economic indicators began around World War I but suffered a setback when the early forecasters failed to predict the Great Depression in 1929. During the depression the government asked a private research group, the National Bureau of Economic Research, to develop a set of measures that would help predict changes in business cycles. The group devised a list of measures based on analyses of previous business cycles. Since then, the list has been revised several times—most recently in March 1989—to reflect changes in the way the economy is structured.

Leading Indicators

There are currently 11 leading economic indicators, representing a broad spectrum of economic activity. These indicators are said to "lead" because their numbers change months in advance of a change in the general level of economic activity. They are as follows:

1. Average length of workweek of production workers in manufacturing.
2. Average weekly state unemployment insurance claims.
3. New orders for consumer goods and materials in 1982 dollars.
4. Vendor performance (percent of companies receiving slower deliveries from suppliers).
5. Contracts and orders for plant and equipment in 1982 dollars.
6. Index of new private housing units authorized by local building permits.
7. Change in manufacturers' unfilled orders of durable goods in 1982 dollars. (See "Note.")

COMPOSITE INDEX OF LEADING, COINCIDENT, AND LAGGING INDICATORS, 1950–95 (1987 = 100)

Year	Leading indicators	Coincident indicators	Lagging indicators
1950	72.7	32.6	54.0
1955	76.7	40.0	66.5
1960	78.7	46.2	79.5
1965	86.5	53.8	82.8
1970	86.7	65.7	96.0
1975	81.2	71.5	99.2
1980	90.1	86.8	100.4
1985	94.7	93.8	98.2
1986	96.6	96.2	100.1
1987	99.0	98.1	100.1
1988	99.4	101.8	101.2
1989	100.9	105.6	102.9
1990	99.5	108.2	104.7
1991	95.0	105.2	104.9
1992	97.5	105.3	99.0
1993	98.9	107.9	96.3
1994	100.5	111.4	96.4
1995	102.5	116.7	100.0

Note: As of January of each year. **Source:** U.S. Dept. of Commerce, unpublished data.

8. Change in sensitive materials prices.

9. Index of stock prices, i.e., of 500 common stocks (Standard and Poor's 500).

10. Money supply-M2 in 1982 dollars. (See "Money and Banking" section.)

11. Index of consumer expectations. (See "Note" below.)

(Note: Numbers 7 and 11 of the above list were added to the index in March 1989, while "change in business and consumer credit outstanding" and "change in manufacturing and trade inventories on hand and on order" were dropped, owing to untimely data availability. In addition the base year of the index was changed from 1972 to 1982.)

This composite of leading economic indicators is published by the U.S. Department of Commerce, Bureau of Economic Analysis. The composite has a noteworthy record: since 1948 it has accurately predicted every downturn and upswing in the economy. One major reason for this success is that many of the indicators represent commitments to economic activity in the coming months. The average lead for the index is 9.5 months at business cycle peaks (indicating the end of a business cycle expansion and the beginning of a recession) and 4.5 months at business cycle troughs (indicating the end of a business cycle recession and the beginning of an expansion).

Coincident and Lagging Indicators

In addition to the leading economic indicators, two other sets of measures are used to track business cycles and the state of the economy. One set includes the coincident indicators, which measure how well the economy is doing at that moment (roughly, within three months of the business cycle turning points). These include the number of employees on nonagricultural payrolls; manufacturing and trade sales in 1982 dollars; index of industrial production; and personal income less transfer payments in 1982 dollars. The second set includes lagging economic indicators. These are the ratio of consumer installment credit outstanding to personal income; commercial and industrial loans outstanding in 1982 dollars; the average prime interest rate charged by banks; the ratio of manufacturing and trade inventories to sales in 1982 dollars; the average duration of unemployment in weeks (inverted); the change in index of labor cost per unit of output in manufacturing; and the change in the Consumer Price Index for services per unit labor costs. At business cycle peaks, the average lag of the index is 4.5 months, and at business cycle troughs 8.5 months. It seems reasonable to wonder what use there is for an indicator that tells you where you have already been. But in fact that is exactly their use: they provide another way of measuring whether turning points in the business cycle truly have occurred.

The government produces a wide variety of economic indicators in addition to those discussed here for use in tracking more specific aspects of the economy, such as labor or capital markets.

PRICES AND INFLATION

Inflation

Inflation is a sustained rise in the general price level in the economy. It affects the level and timing of spending in the economy since it indicates the extent to which income will cover the purchase of a consumer's basket of goods (food, clothes, entertainment, medical services, housing, gasoline, and so on). For example, if a consumer is considering purchasing a television and inflation is high (that is, prices are rising rapidly), he or she will buy the television as soon as possible since savings may not cover the cost a month or a year from now. Inflation is closely watched to determine wage contracts and Social Security benefits that contain cost-of-living adjustment clauses. If wage contracts cover a long period of time and inflation is

CONSUMER PRICE INDEXES FOR SELECTED METROPOLITAN STATISTICAL AREAS, 1994 (1982–84 = 100)

Area	All items	Food and beverages	Food	Housing	Apparel and upkeep	Transportation	Medical care	Entertainment	Fuel and utilities
U.S. city average	**148.2**	**144.9**	**144.3**	**141.8**	**133.4**	**134.3**	**211.0**	**150.1**	**122.8**
Anchorage, Alaska	135.0	131.9	130.5	122.9	128.9	136.9	197.8	166.6	142.1
Atlanta, Ga.	146.7	141.1	142.9	140.1	167.3	123.8	227.0	172.3	132.2
Baltimore, Md.	146.9	149.7	150.3	138.4	135.3	132.8	218.1	154.7	113.1
Boston–Lawrence–Salem, Mass.–N.H.	154.9	150.0	149.8	147.9	146.8	135.0	251.1	163.9	119.9
Buffalo–Niagara Falls, N.Y.	146.8	143.1	143.0	155.9	118.7	120.9	174.5	177.7	127.0
Chicago–Gary–Lake County, Ill.–Ind.–Wis.	148.6	147.0	145.8	144.8	131.0	130.3	213.2	160.0	110.7
Cincinnati–Hamilton, Ohio–Ky.–Ind.	142.4	135.6	134.5	135.2	140.5	129.4	213.8	147.1	117.5
Cleveland–Akron–Lorain, Ohio	144.4	144.4	144.8	142.4	128.8	128.6	195.8	149.4	121.8
Dallas–Ft. Worth, Tex.	141.2	142.2	140.3	129.0	148.2	134.5	205.6	147.1	126.3
Denver–Boulder, Colo.	141.8	134.4	135.5	131.1	96.8	148.4	230.3	145.6	121.3
Detroit–Ann Arbor, Mich.	144.0	138.7	137.8	137.6	136.1	138.6	199.7	145.7	116.8
Honolulu, Hawaii	164.5	153.4	153.2	171.6	118.7	156.4	206.0	142.3	121.3
Houston–Galveston–Brazoria, Tex.	137.9	137.5	136.8	120.4	146.7	132.9	204.6	157.4	107.6
Kansas City, Mo.–Kans.	141.3	140.2	140.1	133.1	123.3	128.1	202.9	160.5	125.7
Los Angeles–Anaheim–Riverside, Calif.	152.3	148.5	146.7	151.0	129.6	140.5	215.2	137.2	143.1
Miami–Ft. Lauderdale, Fla.	143.6	152.7	152.7	135.2	143.5	135.3	188.1	134.4	111.9
Milwaukee, Wis.	147.0	141.5	142.2	148.0	122.5	134.2	201.7	130.2	106.3
Minneapolis–St. Paul, Minn.–Wis.	143.6	149.1	147.0	129.6	148.1	134.2	205.4	151.8	112.5
New Orleans, La.	129.0	123.6	124.8	115.9	185.5	120.7	169.1	134.8	127.7
New York–Northern New Jersey–Long Island, N.Y.–N.J.–Conn.	158.2	151.9	151.6	159.9	126.2	141.8	217.6	154.0	112.4
Philadelphia–Wilmington–Trenton, Pa.–N.J.–Del.–Md.	154.6	142.7	141.3	155.1	105.8	144.0	223.9	160.3	120.5
Pittsburgh–Beaver Valley, Pa.	144.6	140.6	139.2	145.2	133.2	122.3	207.0	153.6	136.1
Portland–Vancouver, Oreg.–Wash.	148.9	135.9	135.2	149.5	123.7	139.6	192.8	157.7	124.3
St. Louis–East St. Louis, Mo.–Ill.	141.3	144.0	143.0	136.7	125.1	129.2	201.7	142.6	119.8
San Diego, Calif.	154.5	147.6	146.8	153.4	141.7	141.8	217.8	157.8	114.7
San Francisco–Oakland–San Jose, Calif.	148.7	148.9	149.0	151.5	115.5	125.7	204.3	164.5	142.8
Seattle–Tacoma, Wash.	147.8	146.9	146.7	147.9	120.9	135.0	199.8	146.7	112.7
Tampa–St. Petersburg–Clearwater, Fla.[1]	126.5	121.9	121.4	121.4	143.6	118.8	172.8	109.9	115.9
Washington, D.C.–Md.–Va.	152.2	144.2	143.7	150.9	141.5	137.0	203.5	155.9	123.5

1. 1987 = 100. **Sources:** U.S. Bureau of Labor Statistics, *Monthly Labor Review* and *CPI Detailed Report* (January issues).

CONSUMER PRICE INDEX (CPI-U), 1947–94 (1982–84 = 100)

Year	CPI	Year	CPI
1947	22.3	1984	103.9
1950	24.1	1985	107.6
1955	26.8	1986	109.6
1960	29.6	1987	113.6
1965	31.5	1988	118.3
1970	38.8	1989	124.0
1975	53.8	1990	130.7
1980	82.4	1991	136.2
1981	90.9	1992	140.3
1982	96.5	1993	144.5
1983	99.6	1994	148.2

Note: Indicates annual averages for all urban consumers. **Source:** U.S. Bureau of the Census, *Current Population Reports* (series).

PRODUCER PRICE INDEXES FOR SELECTED COMMODITIES, 1970–93 (1982 = 100)

Commodity group	1970	1975	1980	1985	1990	1992	1993
All commodities	**38.1**	**58.4**	**89.8**	**103.2**	**116.3**	**117.2**	**118.9**
Farm products and processed foods and feeds	**44.9**	**74.0**	**98.3**	**100.7**	**118.6**	**115.9**	**118.4**
Farm products	45.8	77.0	102.9	95.1	95.1	103.6	107.1
Processed foods and feeds	44.6	72.6	95.9	103.5	103.5	122.1	124.0
Industrial commodities	**35.2**	**54.9**	**88.0**	**103.7**	**115.8**	**174.4**	**119.0**
Textile products and apparel	52.4	67.4	89.7	102.9	114.9	117.8	118.0
Hides, skins, leather, related products	42.0	56.5	94.7	108.9	141.7	140.4	143.7
Fuels, related products, power	15.3	35.4	82.8	91.4	82.2	80.4	80.0
Chemicals and allied products	35.0	62.0	89.0	103.7	123.6	125.9	128.2
Rubber and plastic products	44.9	62.2	90.1	101.9	113.6	115.1	116.0
Lumber and wood products	39.9	62.1	101.5	106.6	129.7	146.6	174.0
Pulp, paper, and allied products	37.5	59.0	86.3	113.3	141.3	145.2	147.3
Metals and metal products	38.7	61.5	95.0	104.4	123.0	119.2	119.2
Machinery and equipment	40.0	57.9	86.0	107.2	120.7	123.4	124.0
Furniture and household durables	51.9	67.5	90.7	107.1	119.1	122.2	123.7
Nonmetallic mineral products	35.3	54.4	88.4	108.6	114.7	117.3	120.0
Transportation equipment	41.9	56.7	82.9	107.9	121.5	130.4	133.7

Source: U.S. Bureau of Labor Statistics, *Producer Price Indexes* (monthly and annual).

rapid, consumers' standard of living will fall in the interim before new contracts can be negotiated. Savings will tend to fall as consumers store their wealth in the form of commodities.

The cause of inflation is often described as "too much money chasing too few goods," brought about by the money supply rising rapidly or production of goods falling behind demand for them. Inflation may be due to (1) cost-push factors—that is, if the cost of inputs such as labor, raw materials, or other intermediate goods rises, the cost of the final product also rises; or (2) demand-pull factors—that is, if the demand for goods and services rises above the full employment level, wages rise as employers compete for labor, and the general price level of goods and services rises.

Consumer Price Index (CPI)

Often referred to as the "cost of living index," the Consumer Price Index is the most commonly used measure of inflation. The index measures the average change in prices relative to an arbitrary base year of a common bundle of goods and services bought by the average consumer on a regular basis. The Bureau of Labor Statistics publishes two CPIs: (1) CPI-U for All Urban Consumers, which includes wage earners and clerical workers; professional, managerial, and technical workers; the self-employed; short-term workers; the unemployed; retirees and others not in the labor force—altogether covering 80 percent of the population—and (2) CPI-W for Urban Wage Earners and Clerical Workers, covering 32 percent of the population. Prices (including direct taxes) are collected from over 57,000 housing units and 19,000 establishments in 85 areas across the country. In calculating the index number, based on 100,000 price quotes a month, larger weights are assigned to goods that represent larger proportions of consumer expenditure. The index costs $26 million a year to produce and requires 40 economists and analysts tracking price changes in 365 categories.

Producer Price Index

The Producer Price Index measures average changes in prices received by producers of all commodities, at all stages of processing, produced in the United States. Prices used in constructing the index are collected from sellers and generally apply to the first significant large-volume commercial transaction for each commodity—i.e., the manufacturer's or other producer's selling price or the selling price on an organized exchange or at a central market. The weights used in the index represent the total net selling value of commodities produced or processed in the country. Values are f.o.b. (free on board) at the production point and are exclusive of excise taxes.

PURCHASING POWER OF THE DOLLAR, 1950–94 (PPI, 1982 = $1.00; CPI, 1982–84 = $1.00)

As indicated below, a 1982 dollar would have bought $4.15 worth of merchandise in 1950, while in 1994 only $0.68 worth of merchandise could be purchased with the same dollar.

Year	Annual average as measured by: Producer prices	Consumer prices
1950	$3.546	$4.151
1955	3.279	3.732
1960	2.994	3.373
1965	2.933	3.166
1970	2.545	2.574
1975	1.718	1.859
1980	1.136	1.215
1985	0.955	0.928
1989	0.880	0.807
1990	0.839	0.766
1991	0.822	0.734
1992	0.812	0.713
1993	0.802	0.692
1994	0.797	0.675

Note: PPI = Producer Price Index; CPI = Consumer Price Index. **Source:** U.S. Bureau of Labor Statistics and U.S. Bureau of Economic Analysis, *Survey of Current Business* (monthly data).

Implicit Price Deflator

The implicit price deflator (also called the GDP deflator) is derived from the ratio of current- to constant-dollar GDP (multiplied by 100) and measures the value of current production in current prices relative to the value of the same goods and services in prices for the base year. For example, in 1994, GDP in current dollars was $6,738.4 billion, and GDP in constant (1987) dollars was $5,344.0 billion. Therefore, the GDP deflator for 1994 was (6,738.4 ÷ 5,344.0) × 100, or 126.1, which is simply a comparison of 1987 and 1994 prices. It is a weighted average of the detailed price indexes used in the deflation of GDP, but the indexes are combined using weights that reflect the composition of GDP in each period. Thus, changes in the implicit price deflator reflect not only changes in prices but also changes in the composition of GDP.

MONEY AND BANKING

Federal Reserve System

The government's interest in monitoring and controlling the banking industry and managing the money supply led to the Federal Reserve Act of 1913. The act created the Federal Reserve System (or the "Fed," as it is popularly known), the nation's central bank. There are 12 regional Fed banks located in major cities throughout the country (Boston, New York, Philadelphia, Cleveland, Richmond, Atlanta, Chicago, St. Louis, Minneapolis, Kansas City, Dallas, and San Francisco). Commercial banks within each region select a majority of the directors who run each regional Fed bank. The president of the United States appoints a board of governors for the whole system, and the board is responsible for coordinating policies across the system. But the regional Feds play an important role in shaping those policies by representing regional interests and decentralizing the decision-making process.

The Fed has three main policy tools for managing the overall economy. First, it controls the *reserve requirements* at all depository institutions. These requirements determine what percentage of a bank's deposits must be held in reserve in the form of either deposits with Federal Reserve banks or vault cash. Raising the reserve requirements reduces the amount of loans available to borrowers and helps slow down the economy.

A more frequently used instrument is *the discount rate*, the interest rate the Federal Reserve banks charge their commercial bank customers to borrow money. The Fed is known as the lender of last resort because of its responsibility to lend to banks in need, and it thus maintains the stability of the banking system. Raising the discount rate generally leads the commercial banks to raise the interest rates they charge their customers. This raises the costs of borrowing in the private sector and slows the economy. (Cutting the discount rate does the reverse and stimulates the economy.)

Most important, the Fed can also control the level of bank reserves through *open market operations;* that is, the direct sale on purchase of Treasury securities and other government debt instruments. When the Fed sells securities, it takes money from the buyer and holds it in its reserves, reducing the money supply; when it buys these instruments, it pays for them by taking money from its reserves, which then goes into circulation, increasing the money supply.

Controlling the money supply through open market operations is certainly the most common and, many would argue, the most important function of the Fed. The money supply shapes interest rates, through the supply and demand of money. Because the Fed is constantly involved in these open market operations (in order to keep the size of the money supply in proportion with a growing economy, for example), adjustments can be made subtly.

In addition, the Federal Reserve regulates banks through the Federal Deposit Insurance Corporation, influences foreign-currency exchange rates through the sale or purchase of foreign currencies, and coordinates international financial policy.

The money supply Money provides a medium of exchange as well as a way to store value, and traditionally, currency (paper money and coins) served that role exclusively. But over time, new financial instruments have developed

FEDERAL RESERVE BANK OF NEW YORK—DISCOUNT RATES, 1976–95

Effective date	Rate per year[1]	Effective date	Rate per year[1]	Effective date	Rate per year[1]	Effective date	Rate per year[1]
Jan. 19, 1976	5.50%	Oct. 8, 1979	12.00%	Aug. 27, 1982	10.00%	Aug. 9, 1988	6.50%
Nov. 22, 1976	5.25	Feb. 15, 1980[2]	13.00	Oct. 12, 1982	9.50	Feb. 24, 1989	7.00
Aug. 31, 1977	5.75	May 30, 1980	12.00	Nov. 22, 1982	9.00	Dec. 19, 1990	6.50
Oct. 26, 1977	6.00	June 13, 1980	11.00	Dec. 15, 1982	8.50	Feb. 1, 1991	6.00
Jan. 9, 1978	6.50	July 28, 1980	10.00	Apr. 9, 1984	9.00	April 30, 1991	5.50
May 11, 1978	7.00	Sept. 26, 1980	11.00	Nov. 21, 1984	8.50	Sept. 13, 1991	5.00
July 3, 1978	7.25	Nov. 17, 1980	12.00	Dec. 24, 1984	8.00	Nov. 6, 1991	4.50
Aug. 21, 1978	7.75	Dec. 5, 1980	13.00	May 20, 1985	7.50	Dec. 20, 1991	3.50
Sept. 22, 1978	8.00	May 5, 1981	14.00	Mar. 7, 1986	7.00	July 2, 1992	3.00
Oct. 16, 1978	8.50	Nov. 2, 1981	13.00	Apr. 21, 1986	6.50	May 17, 1994	3.50
Nov. 1, 1978	9.50	Dec. 4, 1981	12.00	July 11, 1986	6.00	Aug. 16, 1994	4.00
July 20, 1979	10.00	July 20, 1982	11.50	Aug. 21, 1986	5.50	Nov. 15, 1994	4.75
Aug. 17, 1979	10.50	Aug. 2, 1982	11.00	Sept. 4, 1987	6.00	Feb. 1, 1995[3]	5.25
Sept. 19, 1979	11.00	Aug. 16, 1982	10.50				

1. Rates for short-term adjustment credit. 2. Discount rates for 1980 and 1981 do not include the surcharge applied to frequent borrowings by large institutions. The surcharge reached 3% in 1980 and 4% in 1981 and was eliminated in November 1981. 3. In effect as of July 7, 1995. **Source:** Board of Governors of the Federal Reserve System, *Federal Reserve Bulletin* (monthly) and *Annual Statistical Digest.*

THE MONEY SUPPLY: MONEY STOCK AND LIQUID ASSETS, 1970–94 (in billions of dollars)

Item	1970	1975	1980	1985	1990	1994
M1, total	**$214**	**$288**	**$409**	**$620**	**$826**	**$1,148**
Currency[1]	49	73	115	168	247	354
Travelers checks[2]	1	2	4	6	8	8
Demand deposits[3]	165	212	261	267	278	382
Other checkable deposits[4]	(Z)	1	28	180	294	403
M2, total	**$628**	**$1,023**	**$1,629**	**$2,575**	**$3,353**	**$3,613**
M1	214	288	409	620	826	1,148
Nontransaction components in M2[5]	414	736	1,221	1,955	2,527	2,465
Overnight repurchase (RP) agreements and Eurodollars[6]	1	6	29	76	77	117
Money market funds, general-purpose broker/dealer	(Z)	3	62	177	355	390
Money market deposit accounts[7]	261	389	401	815	920	1,144
Commercial banks	99	161	186	457	582	752
Thrift institutions	162	228	215	359	338	392
Small time-deposits[8]	151	338	728	886	1,174	817
Commercial banks	79	142	286	386	611	502
Thrift institutions	72	196	442	499	563	314

Item	1970	1975	1980	1985	1990	1994
M3, total	**$677**	**$1,172**	**$1,989**	**$3,212**	**$4,126**	**$4,302**
M2	628	1,023	1,629	2,575	3,353	3,613
Nontransaction components in M3[5]	49	149	359	637	773	689
Large time-deposits[9]	45	129	260	434	489	361
Commercial banks[10]	44	123	215	282	369	297
Thrift institutions	1	6	45	152	121	64
Term RPs and term Eurodollars[6,11]	4	18	84	139	158	159
Money market funds, institution only	(Z)	(Z)	15	65	135	181
L, total	**$816**	**$1,367**	**$2,326**	**$3,839**	**$4,975**	**$5,283**
M3	677	1,172	1,989	3,212	4,126	4,302
Savings bonds	52	67	72	79	126	180
Short-term Treasury securities[12]	49	68	134	298	332	365
Bankers' acceptances	3	11	32	42	36	10
Commercial paper[13]	34	48	99	207	355	426

Note: As of December of year shown. Adjusted seasonally. Figures may not add up because of independent rounding. Z = less than $500 million. 1. Currency outside U.S. Treasury, Federal Reserve Banks, and the vaults of depository institutions. 2. Outstanding amount of nonbank issuers. 3. At commercial banks and foreign-related institutions. 4. Consists of negotiable order of withdrawal (NOW) and automatic transfer service (ATS) accounts at all depository institutions, credit union share draft balances and demand deposits at thrift institutions. 5. This sum is seasonally adjusted as a whole. 6. Not seasonally adjusted. 7. Data for savings deposits included with money market deposit accounts. 8. Issued in amounts of less than $100,000. Includes retail repurchase agreements. Excludes individual retirement accounts (IRAs) and Keogh accounts. 9. Issued in amounts of $100,000 or more. Excludes those booked at international banking facilities. 10. Excludes those held by money market mutual funds, depository institutions, and foreign banks and official institutions. 11. Excludes those held by depository institutions and money market mutual funds. 12. U.S. Treasury bills and coupons with remaining maturities of less than 12 months held by other than depository institutions, Federal Reserve Banks, money market mutual funds, and foreign entities. 13. Excludes commercial paper held by money market mutual funds. **Sources:** Board of Governors of the Federal Reserve System, *Federal Reserve Bulletin* (monthly), and *Money Stock, Liquid Assets, and Debt Measures, Federal Reserve Statistical Release H.6* (weekly).

that serve at least some of the functions of money; checking accounts serve exactly the same role as currency, and to an extent money-market funds and other instruments can do so as well.

The Fed uses four different measures of the money supply, which include different monetary instruments:

M1 is the original and most commonly reported measure of the money supply, which embraces currency and coins, demand deposits, traveler's checks, and other checkable deposits.

M2 is M1 plus overnight repurchasement agreements, overnight Eurodollars, money-market mutual-fund balances, money-market deposit accounts, and savings and small time-deposits.

M3 is M2 plus money-market mutual-fund balances held by financial institutions, term repurchase agreements and term Eurodollars, and large time-deposits.

L is M3 plus Treasury bills, commercial paper, and other very liquid assets such as savings bonds.

The U.S. Banking System

Commercial banks are the largest financial institutions in the country and are the principal vehicles for exchanging money. The nation's first commercial bank was the Bank of America (now First Pennsylvania Bank), established in Philadelphia in 1782. Commercial banks hold about two-thirds of the nation's money deposits. Savings and loans, the next-largest source of deposits, hold about half as much.

There are approximately 12,000 commercial banks in the country. They may be chartered either by the federal government or by individual states. While banks themselves may not operate across states, they may be owned by holding companies that can operate interstate, if state laws permit.

Commercial banks can make loans to individuals and to commercial operations, establish checking or demand deposits, maintain "trust" departments that make investments for customers, and perform a variety of other functions such as issuing credit cards. Until the deregulation of the 1980s, commercial banks were the only ones permitted to issue checking accounts. Regulations that developed after bank failures in the Great Depression still keep these banks out of the investment business—largely to protect depositors and the solvency of banks from potential effects of bad investments. But deregulation of the banking industry in the 1980s is blurring many of these distinctions. In particular, investment companies are now permitted to issue demand deposits and to compete with banks in other areas as well. (As a result these companies are sometimes referred to as nonbanks.)

Bank failures The failure of a commercial bank is an especially serious problem because of the domino effect it may have on other financial institutions and businesses. Banks, and indeed all depository institutions, ultimately fail when many of their loans go bad and cannot be repaid. But even before that happens, depositors may get nervous about the security of their accounts and withdraw them all at once—a "run on the bank." Because banks loan out deposits and hold in reserve only a small percentage of the value of those deposits, banks experiencing a run would have to call in some of their loans (mainly those already due), putting sudden pressure on many commercial borrowers and causing some to fail. In addition the withdrawal of deposits and of loans reduces the money supply sharply. This process was an important cause of the Great Depression. Following the banking failures during the depression (2,293 banks failed in 1931, and 4,000 banks failed in 1933), the Federal Deposit Insurance Corporation (FDIC) was created in 1933 to protect the accounts of depositors and, more important, to help prevent bank failures. The FDIC charges banks a premium to pay for this coverage. The corporation is designed to prevent runs on banks by insuring deposits and lending to banks to prevent the need to call in loans.

But banks still fail because of bad loans. Between 1945 and 1980, U.S. banks failed at the rate of about six per year. Since then, hundreds of banks have failed each year, and in 1989, 207 failures were recorded. Most of these failures occurred in agricultural states where the failure of farms led to defaults on loans; more than half of all bank failures can be attributed to agriculture loans. Fraud also played an important role, especially in Tennessee, where more than 30 banks have failed since 1982. When a bank fails, the FDIC pays off each depositor (currently, up to $1,000,000 in banks that are members of the Federal Reserve System and in such nonmember banks as join the insurance

FDIC/BIF-INSURED BANKS—NUMBER, BANKING OFFICES, ASSETS, AND DEPOSITS, 1994

Charter class	Banks	Offices	Assets	Deposits
Commercial banks	10,450	55,144	$4,010,664	$2,874,351
National banks	3,075	28,558	2,255,940	1,629,988
State banks (Federal Reserve members)	975	8,390	845,067	533,321
State banks (Non-Federal Reserve members)	6,400	18,196	909,656	711,042
Savings banks	2,152	14,927	1,008,644	737,143
Federal charter	1,187	10,378	713,235	502,388
State charter	965	4,549	295,410	234,755
Under RTC conservatorship	2	56	1,993	1,239
All banks[1]	**12,602**	**70,071**	**$5,019,308**	**$3,611,494**

1. Excludes banks under RTC conservatorship. **Source:** Federal Deposit Insurance Corp., *Statistics on Banking, 1994* (1995).

TOP 25 U.S. COMMERCIAL BANKS, RANKED BY ASSETS AND BY DEPOSITS, 1994

Rank by assets/Bank, city	Assets ('000s)	Deposits ('000s)	Rank by deposits
1. Citibank, NA, New York	$210,487	$141,934	1
2. Bank of America NT&SA, San Francisco	147,670	112,211	2
3. Chemical Bank, New York	135,742	78,271	3
4. Morgan Guaranty Trust Co., New York	124,384	44,570	5
5. Chase Manhattan Bank, NA, New York	94,193	65,557	4
6. Bankers Trust, New York	71,000	26,400	9
7. Wells Fargo Bank, NA, San Francisco	52,216	42,376	6
8. PNC Bank, NA, Pittsburgh	44,625	24,730	14
9. First National Bank, Chicago	42,543	25,738	12
10. NationsBank of Texas, NA, Dallas	39,329	26,099	10
11. Bank of New York	39,287	29,293	7
12. First National Bank, Boston	36,887	24,923	13
13. First Fidelity Bank, NA, Elkton, Md.	33,411	27,055	8
14. Mellon Bank, NA, Pittsburgh	$32,489	$23,332	15
15. Republic National Bank of New York	32,396	19,402	18
16. NBD Bank, NA, Detroit	31,494	20,722	17
17. First Union National Bank of Florida, Jacksonville	31,339	25,909	11
18. NationsBank, NA (Carolinas), Charlotte	31,280	16,582	24
19. Comerica Bank, Detroit	27,044	17,430	22
20. First Interstate Bank of California, Los Angeles	25,251	21,446	16
21. Society National Bank, Cleveland	24,571	17,669	21
22. First Union National Bank of North Carolina, Charlotte	23,082	18,046	19
23. NationsBank of Florida, NA, Tampa	22,918	17,976	20
24. Wachovia Bank of North Carolina, NA, Winston-Salem	22,225	11,166	35
25. CoreStates Bank, NA, Philadelphia	21,889	16,858	23

Note: NA = national association. Federal regulatory report of condition for Dec. 31, 1994, and various state banking departments. With respect to mergers, American Banker follows the bank of charter in determining the surviving bank. **Source:** *American Banker* (Apr. 28, 1995).

fund) and then sells the bank's assets. Sometimes the FDIC arranges for another bank's acquisition of the failed bank by subsidizing the sale. On Dec. 31, 1990, the FDIC made its largest payout—$424.4 million—to depositors of the failed Capital Bank and Trust Co. in Boston.

Thrifts are depository institutions including savings and loans (S&Ls), savings banks, and credit unions. The largest and most important thrifts are the S&Ls, which were created to provide home mortgages for borrowers and long-term savings deposits for individual investors. Until recently, thrifts were prohibited from engaging in riskier loans—including most commercial loans—and issuing checking deposits, and a ceiling was placed on the rate of interest they could pay depositors. Congress lifted the ceiling on interest payments to depositors in 1980 and in 1982 allowed the S&Ls to issue commercial loans and to invest directly in real estate developments. Unwise investment in these areas by many thrifts was a major cause of the savings and loan debacle of the late 1980s and early 1990s.

The Federal Home Loan Bank System was established in 1932 to serve some of the same functions for S&Ls that the Federal Reserve provides for banks. It has now been succeeded by the Office of Thrift Supervision (OTS), which identifies institutions that may be financially distressed or likely to fail. All federally chartered S&Ls are regulated by the system (and must have the word *Federal* in their name). Less than half the thrifts are federally chartered, however; the rest are chartered by states, although most of these have joined the system as well. The FSLIC (Federal Savings and Loan Insurance Corporation) insured deposits at member S&Ls until 1989, when it became insolvent and was dismantled.

The savings and loan crisis The S&Ls came under enormous economic pressure in the 1970s, when interest rates paid by banks and other financial institutions rose well above the rate ceiling for thrifts, and they started losing depositors. Further, they were in a financial bind because their outstanding loans were all in mortgages—long-term, 30-year loans issued at low interest. In part because of this, the thrifts were deregulated, released from many of the restrictions on their activities and allowed to pursue a more diverse market for loans. With this new freedom, however, many S&Ls took on loans that were at a higher level of risk in order to earn a higher rate of return. Some argue that the insurance on deposits provided by the Federal Home Loan Bank encouraged the S&Ls to make loans that were too risky.

Lending institutions fail mainly if a large percentage of their loans go bad and cannot be collected. And mortgage loans fail, not just because buyers cannot make their payments, but also because the collateral (the buildings) may decline in price so that it is less than the value of the loan. Especially in the Southwest, many of the loans for real estate development failed when the oil industry declined in the 1980s, taking local economies with it. S&Ls started to collapse at an alarming rate—517 thrifts closed between 1980 and 1988. With liabilities of $100 billion in excess of assets, the FSLIC ran out of money. Its insurance obligations passed to the FDIC, and the Resolution Trust Corporation (RTC) was formed to dispose of (sell) approximately $400 billion of insolvent thrifts' assets. The government dealt with 205 insolvent S&Ls in 1988 alone by subsidizing their sale to more secure institutions.

As of July 1993, the RTC had resolved 657 institutions, and there were 83 institutions under conservatorship. Under the conservatorship program, the RTC assigns a managing agent and a credit specialist to each participating institution to oversee its operations and ensure that management adheres to RTC policies and procedures and that no fraudulent practices are in evidence. From the program's inception through July 1992, the RTC spent $84.5 billion to bail out S&Ls. Government estimates suggest that it will cost American taxpayers $500 billion over the coming years to bail them out. Some estimates conclude that fraud contributed to more than one-third of these insolvent cases, suggesting that FSLIC monitoring and enforcement of regulations were hopelessly inadequate.

DEPOSIT-TAKING INSTITUTIONS: NUMBER AND PERCENTAGE SHARE OF DEPOSITS, 1994

Type of institution	Number of institutions	Percent share	Deposits[1] (billions)	Percent share
Commercial banks	10,719	56.9%	$2,394.0	85.0%
Savings banks[2]	623	3.3	239.0	8.5
Credit unions[3]	7,498	39.8	182.5	6.5
Total	**18,840**	**100.0%**	**$2,815.5**	**100.0%**

1. Includes deposits gathered both domestically and internationally by U.S. institutions. 2. Includes federal and state-chartered savings institutions. 3. Federally insured credit unions only. **Sources:** Federal Deposit Insurance Corp., *FDIC Data Book* (June 30, 1994); Credit Union National Association (unpublished data).

CONSUMER INSTALLMENT CREDIT OUTSTANDING, 1980–94 (billions of dollars)

Type of credit	1980	1985	1990	1992	1993	1994
Installment credit outstanding	**$298.2**	**$517.7**	**$734.9**	**$731.1**	**$794.3**	**$911.3**
Automobile paper	112.0	210.2	283.1	257.7	282.0	324.5
Revolving[1]	55.1	121.8	223.5	257.3	287.9	337.7
Other	131.1	185.7	228.3	216.1	224.4	249.1

1. Consists mainly of outstanding balances on credit card accounts, but also includes borrowing under check credit and overdraft plans, and unsecured personal lines of credit. **Source:** *Statistical Abstract of the United States, 1995* (1995).

TOP 25 U.S. THRIFTS, RANKED BY ASSETS AND BY DEPOSITS, 1994

Rank by assets/Name, city	Assets ('000s)	Deposits ('000s)	Rank by deposits
1. Home Savings of America, FSB, Irwindale, Calif.[1]	$53,443	$41,068	1
2. Great Western Bank, FSB, Chatsworth, Calif.	39,697	28,750	2
3. World Savings & Loan Assn., Oakland, Calif.	31,027	19,441	3
4. American Savings Bank, FA, Irvine, Calif.	18,552	12,850	4
5. Washington Mutual Savings Bank, Seattle[1]	17,477	9,788	6
6. Glendale Federal Bank, FSB, Calif.[1]	15,687	7,003	11
7. First Nationwide Bank, FSB, Dallas	14,745	9,074	7
8. California Federal Bank, FSB, Los Angeles[1]	14,215	8,430	8
9. Citibank, FSB, San Francisco[2]	13,524	10,305	5
10. Standard Federal Bank, Troy, Mich.	12,077	8,143	9
11. Dime Savings Bank of New York, FSB	10,018	5,788	15
12. Anchor Savings Bank, FSB, Hewlett, N.Y.	9,710	6,813	12
13. Bank United of Texas, FSB, Houston	9,628	4,794	21
14. Household Bank, FSB, Newport Beach, Calif.	$9,487	$7,255	10
15. Guaranty Federal Savings Bank, Dallas	8,759	6,718	13
16. Roosevelt Bank, FSB, Chesterfield, Mo.	8,407	4,927	20
17. First Federal of Michigan, Detroit[1]	8,384	2,724	45
18. Coast Federal Bank, Los Angeles	8,213	5,908	14
19. First Bank, FSB, Fargo, N.Dak.	7,916	5,462	17
20. LaSalle Talman Bank, FSB, Chicago[3]	6,924	5,199	19
21. Greenpoint Savings Bank, Brooklyn, N.Y.	6,778	5,341	18
22. First Federal Savings & Loan Assn., Rochester, N.Y.	6,637	4,036	29
23. Sovereign Bank, FSB, Wyomissing, Pa.	6,564	4,027	30
24. People's Bank, Bridgeport, Conn.	6,501	4,652	22
25. Charter One Bank, FSB, Cleveland	6,116	4,350	24

Note: FSB = federal savings bank; FA = federal association. 1. Consolidated to include thrift subsidiaries. 2. Owned by a commercial banking company. 3. Owned by a foreign bank. **Source:** *American Banker* (May 17, 1995).

Credit unions are employer-sponsored cooperative organizations that provide consumer and mortgage credit to their members. Employers often arrange for payroll-deduction savings plans through the credit union.

Mortgage loans Mortgages are loans backed by buildings—either private dwellings or commercial buildings. Until the 1970s, virtually all mortgages had fixed-interest payments and 30-year terms. With the escalation of interest rates beginning in the late 1970s, however, several alternative arrangements have developed. For example, in order to reduce the interest payments, many borrowers repay their loans in 15 years. Others use a *variable* or *adjustable-rate mortgage* in which the interest rate varies with market rates. Some mortgages that hold payments down in the first few years and then increase them rapidly for the remaining term of the mortgage are known as balloon mortgages.

Financial Instruments

Money instruments **Treasury bills** are securities sold by the U.S. Treasury in denominations of $10,000 that mature at various dates, but all in less than one year. Treasury bills pay an interest rate that is adjusted by the Treasury according to supply and demand. The Treasury bill rate is thought to be the highest risk-free rate of return among all investments.

Federal funds are the reserves the Fed requires depository institutions such as commercial banks to hold on deposit at their regional Federal Reserve Bank as protection against withdrawals. Banks and other depository institutions can loan reserves in excess of those required by the Fed to each other. These Fed Fund loans can provide institutions with large amounts of liquid assets on very short notice, and most loans are for no more than one day.

Commercial paper consists of debt or promissory notes (similar to an I.O.U.) issued by corporations as a way to borrow money in the short-term, generally less than one year. Commercial paper provides an alternative, generally cheaper way of raising money than taking a commercial bank loan. The rate of interest paid on commercial paper is higher than that on Treasury bills because of the greater risk; the risk that even large, secure companies such as IBM will default on their debts is still greater than the risk that the U.S. government will. Commercial paper is one of the most important investments made by money-market accounts.

Certificates of deposit (CDs) Customers who make these deposits at commercial banks or thrift institutions receive a certificate describing the maturity date of the deposit (e.g., a five-year CD). CDs guarantee a rate of return for as long as 10 years into the future. In addition, the fact that they can be purchased at local banks also makes them easy to secure. These factors make them appealing to the general public. The interest paid on CDs is set by the market and is generally the same across large institutions. However, some institutions that are not as strong financially may have to pay a higher rate of return in order to compensate for the greater risk (although still perhaps negligible in an absolute sense) of default.

Money-market accounts Customers pool their money into a fund that then purchases short-term debt such as Treasury bills and commercial paper in order to earn a high rate of return while maintaining liquidity (i.e., being able to convert assets quickly into cash). Customers typically can write checks on their money-market accounts, which are processed through cooperating banks, but checks generally have to be in large denominations—greater than $250—to prevent customers from using them as demand deposit accounts with the high administrative costs associated with them.

Capital instruments **Stock, or equity,** the most important source of capital for firms, represents a claim on the assets or equity of a business as well as on its earnings. The owners of stock are literally the owners of the firm and vote on issues affecting it, most importantly voting to elect the directors who control the firm's management. The claims of stockholders are subordinate to the claims of bondholders. There is also a distinction between preferred stock and common stock; the claims of those holding the former must be paid first. The price of stock depends heavily on expectations about the firm's earnings. Stock prices vary with the state of the economy because the earnings

MONEY-MARKET INTEREST RATES AND MORTGAGE RATES, 1970–94 (percent per year)

Type	1970	1975	1980	1985	1990	1994
Federal funds, effective rate	7.18%	5.82%	13.35%	8.10%	8.10%	4.21%
Commercial paper, 3-month[1,2]	N.A.	6.25	12.61	7.95	8.06	4.66
Prime rate charged by banks	7.91	7.86	15.26	9.93	10.01	7.15
Eurodollar deposits, 3-month	8.52	7.03	14.00	8.27	8.16	4.63
Finance paper, 3-month[2,3]	7.18	6.15	11.49	7.77	7.87	4.53
Bankers' acceptances, 90-day[2,4]	7.31	6.29	12.67	7.91	7.93	4.56
Large negotiable certificates of deposit, 3-month, secondary market	7.56	6.44	13.07	8.05	8.15	4.63
Federal Reserve discount rate[5]	5.50–6.00	6.00–7.75	10.00–13.00	7.50–8.00	6.50–7.00	3.00–4.75
U.S. Government securities:[6]						
3-month Treasury bill	6.39	5.78	11.39	7.47	7.50	4.25
6-month Treasury bill	6.51	6.09	11.32	7.65	7.46	4.64
1-year Treasury bill	6.48	6.28	10.85	7.81	7.35	5.02
Home mortgages (HUD series):[7]						
FHA insured, secondary market[8]	9.03	9.19	13.44	12.24	10.17	8.68
Conventional, new-home[9,10]	8.52	9.10	13.95	12.28	10.08	8.58
Conventional, existing-home[9]	8.56	9.14	13.95	12.29	10.08	8.59

Note: N.A. = not available. 1. Based on daily offering rates of dealers. 2. Yields are quoted on a bank-discount basis, rather than an investment yield basis (which would give a higher figure). 3. Placed directly; averages of daily offering rates quoted by finance companies. 4. Based on representative closing yields. From Jan. 1, 1981, rates of top-rated banks only. 5. Federal Reserve Bank of New York, low and high. The discount rates for 1980 and 1981 do not include the surcharge applied to frequent borrowings by large institutions. The surcharge reached 3% in 1980 and 4% in 1981. Surcharge was eliminated in November 1981. 6. Averages based on daily closing bid yields in secondary market, bank discount basis. 7. HUD = Housing and Urban Development. 8. Averages based on quotations for one day each month as compiled by FHA. 9. Primary market. 10. Average contract rates on new commitments. **Sources:** Except as noted, Board of Governors of the Federal Reserve System, *Federal Reserve Bulletin*, monthly, and *Annual Statistical Digest*.

BOND AND STOCK YIELDS, 1970–94 (percent per year)

Type	1970	1975	1980	1985	1990	1994
U.S. Treasury, constant maturities:[1,2]						
3-year	7.29%	7.49%	11.51%	9.64%	8.26%	6.27%
5-year	7.38	7.77	11.45	10.12	8.37	6.69
10-year	7.35	7.99	11.43	10.62	8.55	7.69
U.S. govt., long-term bonds[2,3]	6.58	6.98	10.81	10.75	8.74	7.41
State and local govt. bonds, Aaa[4]	6.12	6.42	7.86	8.60	6.82	5.77
State and local govt. bonds, Baa[4]	6.75	7.62	9.02	9.58	7.14	6.17
High-graded municipal bonds (Standard & Poor's)[5]	6.51	6.89	8.51	9.18	7.25	N.A.
Municipal (Bond Buyer, 20 bonds)	6.35	7.05	8.59	9.11	7.27	6.18
Corporate Aaa seasoned[4]	8.04	8.83	11.94	11.37	9.32	7.97
Corporate Baa seasoned[4]	9.11	10.61	13.67	12.72	10.36	8.63
Corporate (Moody's)[4,6]	8.51	9.57	12.75	12.05	9.77	8.26
Industrials (49 bonds)[7]	8.26	9.25	12.35	11.80	9.77	8.21
Public utilities (51 bonds)[8]	8.68	9.88	13.15	12.29	9.76	8.30
Stocks (Standard & Poor's):[5]						
Preferred (10 stocks)[9]	7.22	8.36	10.60	10.44	8.96	N.A.
Common: Composite (500 stocks)	3.83	4.31	5.26	4.25	3.61	2.82
Industrials (400 stocks)	3.62	3.96	4.95	3.76	3.16	N.A.

1. Yields on the more actively traded issues adjusted to constant maturities by the U.S. Treasury. 2. Yields are based on closing bid prices quoted by at least five dealers. 3. Averages (to maturity or call) for all outstanding bonds neither due nor callable in less than 10 years, including several very low yielding "flower" bonds. 4. **Source:** Moody's Investors Service, New York, N.Y. 5. **Source:** U.S. Bureau of Economic Analysis, *Survey of Current Business* (monthly). Annual averages of weekly figures. 6. For 1970–85, includes railroad bonds, which were discontinued as part of composite in 1989. 7. Covers 40 bonds for 1970–83, 38 bonds for 1984–86, and 37 bonds for 1987 and 1988. 8. Covers 40 bonds for 1970–88. 9. Yields based on 10 stocks, 4 yields. Issues converted to a price equivalent to $100 par and a 7 percent annual dividend before averaging. **Source:** Except as noted, Board of Governors of the Federal Reserve System, *Federal Reserve Bulletin* (monthly).

prospects of firms vary depending on whether the economy is in an expansion or recession. Unlike debt instruments that come due at a fixed point in the future, stock never comes due; it represents a permanent claim on future earnings, and that is why changes in even the most long-term prospects for a firm will affect the price of its stock.

Treasury bonds, or notes, have longer-term dates of maturity, from one to 10 years, than do Treasury bills. They are sold by the Treasury in denominations of $1,000 and are the principal means of funding government borrowing and the national debt. The interest on these bonds is paid out regularly and is known as coupons. (Historically, owners of the bonds had to send in coupons that were then redeemed for interest payments, hence the phrase *clipping coupons*).

Other government securities Some agencies of the government that are involved in lending are permitted to sell securities in order to raise funds. The most important of these is the Federal National Mortgage Association—FNMA, or "Fanny Mae." It buys and sells mortgages insured by the federal government and stabilizes the market for those mortgages in the process.

Corporate bonds are sold by corporations to dealers called underwriters and then to the public in order to raise long-term funds for investment. Corporate bonds are the alternative to issuing stock for raising funds. Bondholders are not the owners of the corporation the way stockholders are, and one advantage of issuing bonds therefore is that ownership and control over the corporation is not affected. So-called "junk bonds" are a type of corporate bond with very high risk—for example, where there is not enough collateral to back the value of the bonds.

Municipal bonds are issued by state and local governments to raise funds, usually to provide public works and other facilities. The federal government is prohibited by the Constitution from interfering in the ability of state and local governments to raise revenue, so income from municipal bonds is not subject to federal taxes. So-called revenue bonds are paid for by user fees—for example, tolls collected on a parkway are used to pay for the bonds used to build it. General-obligation bonds are paid for through general taxes. Municipal bonds tend to be very safe, although there have been occasions on which some state and local governments have had to take extraordinary actions to avoid default—most notably, New York City in 1975, which received a federal loan and sold new bonds to its municipal employee unions in order to avoid default.

GOVERNMENT DEBT

One of the most debated economic issues is the importance of the government's budget deficit, usually called the national debt. The national debt totaled over $4.3 trillion as of July 1993. The government raises most of its resources through taxes, but it can also raise money by borrowing or by selling bonds (e.g., Treasury bonds and savings bonds)—which increasingly have been purchased by investors outside the country. The bonds raise money now but must be repaid in the future through revenues from taxes. The budget deficit in any year indicates the difference between what the government takes in through taxes and other forms of revenues and what it expends. The deficit therefore suggests how much the government needs to borrow to fill that gap. The total amount of present and past borrowing, plus interest, constitutes the total government debt. In 1993, interest on the public debt amounted to $292.5 billion, or 20.8 percent of federal outlays. This is only partially offset by interest earnings received by trust funds such as the civil service retirement and disability fund, Medicare, and Social Security.

Governments routinely borrow to pay for long-term projects that will benefit the community both immediately and in the future. It can be argued that because much of the benefit from projects such as highways and other public works will be enjoyed by the next generation of taxpayers, the latter should also bear much of the cost. And they can do that by paying off the government debt (paying the premiums on government bonds) through taxes in the future. Controversy arises when the government borrows to pay for its more routine expenditures. One justification for such borrowing is that it can be used to manage business cycles in the economy; in other words, during recessions the government can borrow in order to increase expenditures and expand the economy without raising taxes, which would slow it down.

FEDERAL RECEIPTS, OUTLAYS, AND DEBT, 1977–94 (billions of dollars)

				Gross federal debt (end of period)	
Fiscal year	Total receipts	Total outlays	Deficit	Total	Held by the public
1977	$ 355.6	$ 409.2	$–53.6	$ 709.1	$ 551.8
1978	399.6	458.7	–59.2	780.4	610.9
1979	463.3	503.5	–40.2	833.8	644.6
1980	517.1	590.9	–73.8	914.3	709.8
1981	599.3	678.2	–78.9	1,003.9	785.3
1982	617.8	745.7	–127.9	1,147.0	919.8
1983	600.6	808.3	–207.8	1,381.9	1,131.6
1984	666.5	851.8	–185.3	1,576.7	1,300.5
1985	734.1	946.3	–212.3	1,827.5	1,499.9
1986	769.1	989.8	–220.7	2,129.5	1,736.7
1987	854.1	1,002.1	–148.0	2,354.3	1,888.7
1988	909.0	1,064.1	–155.1	2,614.6	2,050.8
1989	990.8	1,142.8	–152.0	2,881.1	2,189.9
1990	1,031.2	1,251.6	–220.4	3,190.5	2,410.7
1991	1,054.3	1,323.0	–268.7	3,599.0	2,688.1
1992	1,090.5	1,380.9	–290.4	4,002.7	2,998.8
1993	1,153.5	1,408.2	–254.7	4,326.5	3,247.5
1994	1,257.7	1,460.9	–203.2	4,643.7	3,432.2

Source: U.S. Office of Management and Budget, *Budget of the United States Government* (annual) and *Monthly Treasury Statement of Receipts and Outlays of the United States Government.*

When the total amount of government debt becomes large, some economists believe that it damages the economy in a number of ways. First, the fact that the government is selling large amounts of debt means that it is competing for limited investor dollars with private borrowers, driving up the cost of borrowing and making it harder for private-sector businesses to make investments for future growth. Second, the future taxes needed to pay off large amounts of government debt may place a serious drain on the future economy, again diverting resources from investment in the private sector. Politicians are concerned because debt payments must be funded from tax revenues, so they must either raise taxes or reduce government spending in other areas (e.g., in defense and entitlement programs).

PUBLIC DEBT OF, AND INTEREST PAID BY, THE FEDERAL GOVERNMENT, 1940–93

	Public debt			Interest paid	
Year	Total[1] (billions)	Average annual percent change[2]	Per capita[3]	Total (billions)	Percent of federal outlays[4]
1940	$ 43.0	8.4%	$ 325	$ 1.0	10.5%
1945	258.7	43.0	1,849	3.8	4.1
1950	256.1	–0.1	1,688	5.7	13.4
1955	272.8	1.3	1,651	6.4	9.4
1960	284.1	0.9	1,572	9.2	10.0
1965	313.8	2.0	1,613	11.3	9.6
1970	370.1	3.3	1,814	19.3	9.9
1975	533.2	12.4	2,475	32.7	9.8
1980	907.7	9.8	3,985	74.9	12.7
1981	997.9	9.9	4,338	95.6	14.1
1982	1,142.0	14.4	4,913	117.4	15.7
1983	1,377.2	20.6	5,870	128.8	15.9
1984	1,572.3	14.2	6,640	153.8	18.1
1985	1,823.1	16.0	7,616	178.9	18.9
1986	2,125.3	16.6	8,793	187.1	18.9
1987	2,350.3	10.6	9,630	195.4	19.5
1988	2,602.3	10.9	10,556	214.1	20.1
1989	2,857.4	9.8	N.A.	241.0	21.1
1990	3,233.3	13.2	N.A.	264.9	21.2
1991	3,569.3	10.4	N.A.	286.0	21.6
1992	3,972.6	11.3	N.A.	292.3	21.2
1993	4,351.9	9.5	N.A.	292.5	20.8
1994	4,643.7	6.7	N.A.	296.3	20.2

Note: N.A. = not available. For fiscal years ending in year shown. Total public debt is restricted to borrowing by the Treasury and the value of savings bonds at current redemption value. 1. Adjusted to exclude nonmarketable issues to the International Monetary Fund and other international institutions for 1950, 1955, 1960, 1965, and 1970. 2. From preceding year shown; for 1940, change is from 1935. 3. For 1940–75, based on estimated July 1 population; thereafter, based on Oct. 1 resident population; prior to 1960, excludes Alaska and Hawaii. 4. Calculated on total expenditures not reduced by interfund transactions representing interest and certain other payments to Treasury through 1950. Beginning 1955, total budget outlays. **Sources:** Through U.S. fiscal 1980—U.S. Dept. of the Treasury, *Statistical Appendix to the Annual Report of the Secretary of the Treasury on the State of the Finances;* thereafter—U.S. Dept. of the Treasury, *Monthly Statement of the Public Debt of the United States* and *Final Monthly Treasury Statement of Receipts and Outlays of the U.S. Government.*

The debate over debt really turns on how much is "too much." Between 1935 and 1981, the only two significant increases in the deficit occurred during World War II and certain years of the Vietnam War when deficits were about $25 billion; between 1981 and 1989, however, the Reagan administration ran annual deficits averaging $167 billion and increased the nation's total outstanding gross debt from just over $1 trillion to over $2.6 trillion. In 1992, the national debt topped $4 trillion for the first time ever, and the annual deficit was close to $300 billion. The deficit has narrowed to closer to $200 billion per year, but the total debt continues to spiral toward $5 trillion. The interest on that amount alone is greater each year than the annual deficit.

THE LABOR FORCE

Labor Force Participation Rate The labor force (or Labor Force Participation Rate—LFPR) is that proportion of the population that is either employed or actively seeking employment, 66.6 percent in 1990. It represents the supply of labor available for the economy. The LFPR is lower for young people because many are in school, and also for older people because many have retired. It is highest for married men and for women who are heads of households.

Women in the work force One of the most important developments in the labor force has been the sharp increase in the LFPR of women, which has virtually doubled since the early 1960s. With higher levels of education than ever before, most women now opt for careers in the labor force rather than homemaking. Women are having fewer children, are having them later in life—after they have started to establish their careers—and are returning to work sooner after childbirth. Furthermore, women are continuing to make inroads into professions like law and medicine that have previously been dominated by men.

Women have joined the labor force at an astounding rate since 1960. A few highlights of this trend:

- In 1990, 56.7 million women were in the U.S. civilian labor force (57.5% of all women). Of those, 29.8 million were married, 2.7 million separated, and 6.2 million divorced.
- In 1990 over half of all married women (58.4%) were either employed or actively seeking employment, compared to less than one-third (30.5%) in 1960.
- While there has been a smaller percentage increase among separated and divorced women, their LFPRs in 1988 were 60.9% and 75.7%, respectively, compared with 52.1% and 71.5% in 1970 (statistics for 1960 are not available).
- Unemployment rates have dropped from 1960 to 1990 for married and divorced women. In other words, of the women who want to work, a greater percentage can successfully find employment, reflecting the increased acceptance of women's roles in the labor force.
- For married women with children under six years of age, the increase in labor participation during 1960–88 is even more dramatic—it more than tripled, from 18.6% to 57.1%.
- Of all married women, black women with children between the ages of six and 13 had the highest LFPR in 1988—81.4%.
- During the recession of 1982–83, when overall unemployment reached 9.7%, women who were separated and had children under the age of six were particularly hard hit, with an unemployment rate of 27.6%.
- Median weekly earnings for women working full-time (74% of all working women) were $348 (as opposed to $485 for men) per week in 1990, up 2.9% from one year earlier, but still only 70% of men's median weekly earnings. Median weekly earnings for white women were $355, for black women $308, and $280 for Hispanic women.
- The number of firms owned by women increased by 57% from 1982 to 1987; 55.1% of all service businesses are owned by women.

Unemployment rate One of the most closely watched labor force statistics is the unemployment rate, which surged to 7.4 percent in 1992 before dropping back to 6.8 percent in 1993 and 6.1 percent in 1994. Contrary to popular opinion, the unemployment rate is only an indirect measure of the people without jobs. In fact, the unemployment rate measures, as a proportion of the total labor force, those people without jobs who are actively seeking employment (within the last four weeks). So the unemployment rate may rise as new job seekers enter the labor force; every spring, for example, it rises slightly as school graduates enter the labor force and look for jobs. It may also fall as workers retire or otherwise leave the labor force. Further, when the economy is in a prolonged recession, the unemployment rate may actually drop slightly simply because some of the job seekers may give up trying to find a job and withdraw from the labor force.

The unemployment rate over time for the United States is a measure associated with identifying periods of expansion and recession. It reached a peak of 9.6 percent during the 1982–83 recession. The relatively high periods of unemployment beginning in the mid-1970s are in part due to the expansion of the labor force as the Baby Boom generation left school and began looking for work.

Hispanics One of the most interesting developments in the U.S. labor force is the rise of Hispanic workers and firms. They are the fastest-growing population group in the labor force, in large part due to immigration, with Mexicans making up the largest share. By the year 2000, the number of Hispanic workers in the labor force will account for 10 percent of the total labor force. Most of this projected increase can be attributed to the rise in the proportion of Hispanic women working (historically, these women were more likely to stay at home). Overall, however, Hispanic workers earn only 74 percent as much as the average for all workers. They

PERCENT OF FEMALE WORKERS IN SELECTED OCCUPATIONS, 1975–94

Occupation	Women as percent of total employed		
	1975	1985	1994
Airline pilot	—	2.6%	2.6%
Auto mechanic	0.5%	0.6	1.0
Bartender	35.2	47.9	55.1
Bus driver	37.7	49.2	47.0
Cab driver, chauffeur	8.7	10.9	10.3
Carpenter	0.6	1.2	1.0
Child care worker	98.4	96.1	97.3
Computer programmer	25.6	34.3	29.3
Computer systems analyst	14.8	28.0	31.4
Data entry keyer	92.8	90.7	83.8
Data processing equipment repairer	1.8	10.4	18.0
Dentist	1.8	6.5	13.3
Dental assistant	100.0	99.0	96.6
Economist	13.1	34.5	47.4
Editor, reporter	44.6	51.7	48.8
Elementary school teacher	85.4	84.0	85.6
Garage, gas station attendant	4.7	6.8	5.2
Lawyer, judge	7.1	18.2	24.8
Librarian	81.1	87.0	84.1
Mail carrier (Postal Service)	8.7	17.2	34.0
Office machine repairer	1.7	5.7	2.1
Physician	13.0	17.2	22.3
Registered nurse	97.0	95.1	93.8
Social worker	60.8	66.7	69.3
Teachers, college and university	31.1	35.2	42.5
Telephone installer, repairer	4.8	12.8	16.8
Telephone operator	93.3	88.8	88.8
Waiter/waitress	91.1	84.0	78.6
Welder	4.4	4.8	4.4

Note: N.A. = not available. **Source:** U.S. Department of Labor, Bureau of Labor Statistics, *Employment and Earnings* (monthly), January issues.

EFFECTIVE FEDERAL MINIMUM HOURLY WAGE RATES, 1950–95

In effect	Minimum rate for nonfarm workers	Percent of avg. earnings[1]	Minimum rate for farm workers[2]
1950–55	$0.75	54%	N.A.
1956–60	1.00	52	N.A.
1961–62	1.15	50	N.A.
1963–66	1.25	51	N.A.
1967	1.40	50	$1.00
1968–73	1.60	54	1.15
1974	2.00	46	1.60
1975	2.10	45	1.80
1976–77	2.30	46	2.00
1978	2.65	44	2.65
1979	2.90	45	2.90
1980	3.10	44	3.10
1981–88	3.35	43	3.35
1989–90	3.35	32	3.35
1991–95[3]	4.25	38	4.25

Note: N.A. = not applicable. 1. Percent of gross average hourly earnings of production workers in manufacturing. 2. Not included until 1966. 3. In effect as of July 28, 1995. **Source:** U.S. Dept. of Labor.

EMPLOYMENT STATUS OF THE POPULATION BY RACE AND HISPANIC ORIGIN, 1975–94 (numbers in thousands)

		Civilian labor force				
Year	Civilian non-institutional population[1]	Total	Percent of population	Number employed	Employment/population ratio[2]	Percent unemployed
		White				
1975	134,790	82,831	61.5%	76,411	56.7%	7.8%
1980	146,122	93,600	64.1	87,715	60.0	6.3
1985	153,679	99,926	65.0	93,736	61.0	6.2
1990	160,415	107,177	66.8	102,087	63.6	4.7
1991	161,511	107,486	66.6	101,039	62.6	6.0
1992	162,658	108,526	66.7	101,479	62.4	6.5
1993	163,921	109,359	66.7	102,812	62.7	6.0
1994[3]	165,555	111,082	67.1	105,190	63.5	5.3
		Black				
1975	15,751	9,263	58.8%	7,894	50.1%	14.8%
1980	17,824	10,865	61.0	9,313	52.2	14.3
1985	19,664	12,364	62.9	10,501	53.4	15.1
1990	21,300	13,493	63.3	11,966	56.2	11.3
1991	21,615	13,542	62.6	11,863	54.9	12.4
1992	21,958	13,891	63.3	11,933	54.3	14.1
1993	22,329	13,943	62.4	12,146	54.4	12.9
1994[3]	22,879	14,502	63.4	12,835	56.1	11.5
		Hispanic[4]				
1975	N.A.	N.A.	N.A.	N.A.	N.A.	N.A.
1980	9,598	6,146	64.0%	5,527	57.6%	10.1%
1985	11,915	7,698	64.6	6,888	57.8	10.5
1990	14,297	9,576	67.0	8,808	61.6	8.0
1991	14,770	9,762	66.1	8,799	59.6	9.9
1992	15,244	10,131	66.5	8,971	58.9	11.4
1993	15,753	10,377	65.9	9,272	58.9	10.6
1994[3]	18,117	11,975	66.1	10,788	59.5	9.9

Note: N.A. = not available. 1. Age 16 and over. 2. Civilians employed as a percent of the civilian noninstitutional population. 3. Data for 1994 are not directly comparable with data for previous years because of a major redesign of the Current Population Survey questionnair and collection methodology and the introduction of 1990 census-based population controls, adjusted for the estimated undercount. 4. Hispanic persons may be of any race. **Source:** U.S. Bureau of Labor Statistics, *Employment and Earnings* (monthly), January issues.

EMPLOYMENT STATUS OF THE POPULATION BY SEX, 1960–94 (numbers in thousands)

		Civilian labor force				
Year	Civilian non-institutional population[1]	Total	Percent of population	Number employed	Employment/population ratio[2]	Percent unemployed
		Total				
1960	117,245	69,628	59.4%	65,778	56.1%	5.5%
1965	126,513	74,455	58.9	71,088	56.2	4.5
1970	137,085	82,771	60.4	78,678	57.4	4.9
1975	153,153	93,775	61.2	85,846	56.1	8.5
1980	167,745	106,940	63.8	99,303	59.2	7.1
1985	178,206	115,461	64.8	107,150	60.1	7.2
1990	188,049	124,787	66.4	117,914	62.7	5.5
1993	193,550	128,040	66.2	119,306	61.6	6.8
1994[3]	196,814	131,056	66.6	123,060	62.5	6.1
		Male				
1960	55,662	46,388	83.3%	43,904	78.9%	5.4%
1965	59,782	48,255	80.7	46,340	77.5	4.0
1970	64,304	51,228	79.7	48,990	76.2	4.4
1975	72,291	56,299	77.9	51,857	71.7	7.9
1980	79,398	61,453	77.4	57,186	72.0	6.9
1985	84,469	64,411	76.3	59,891	70.9	7.0
1990	89,650	68,234	76.1	64,435	71.9	5.6
1993	92,620	69,633	75.2	64,700	69.9	7.1
1994[3]	94,355	70,817	75.1	66,450	70.4	6.2
		Female				
1960	61,582	23,240	37.7%	21,874	35.5%	5.9%
1965	66,731	26,200	39.3	24,748	37.1	5.5
1970	72,782	31,543	43.3	29,688	40.8	5.9
1975	80,860	37,475	46.3	33,989	42.0	9.3
1980	88,348	45,487	51.5	42,117	47.7	7.4
1985	93,736	51,050	54.5	47,259	50.4	7.4
1990	98,399	56,554	57.5	53,479	54.3	5.4
1993	100,930	58,407	57.9	54,606	54.1	6.5
1994[3]	102,460	60,239	58.8	56,610	55.3	6.0

Note: N.A. = not available. 1. Age 16 and over. 2. Civilians employed as a percent of the civilian noninstitutional population. 3. Data for 1994 are not directly comparable with data for previous years because of a major redesign of the Current Population Survey questionnaire and collection methodology and the introduction of 1990 census-based population controls, adjusted for the estimated undercount. **Source:** U.S. Bureau of Labor Statistics, *Employment and Earnings* (monthly), January issues.

also have a significantly higher unemployment rate, though not as high as the rate for blacks. Both hit all-time highs in 1992 (14.1 for blacks; 11.4 for Hispanics) before retreating in 1993 and 1994.

Productivity measures how much output an economy or organization can generate from a given amount of input. Higher levels of productivity suggest greater efficiency—doing more with the same amount of resources, just as an efficient or economical car goes farther on a gallon of gasoline. Increases in productivity, as the result of better tools or improved methods, provide the main mechanism for increasing output in an economy and ultimately for raising standards of living. Productivity is usually measured in terms of labor—output per worker or per hour of labor—not only because labor is the most important resource but also because it is one of the easiest to measure.

Wages vary not only among the different professions but also between sexes and regions of the country. For example, women in year-round, full-time executive, administrative, and managerial positions have a median yearly income of only 61 percent of the median income for men in the same occupation group. This percentage is higher in the field of laborers, precision production, craft, and repair; but for all major occupation groups reported by the U.S. Bureau of the Census, women receive only a fraction of that received by their male counterparts. This may be due, in part, to the fact that women enter and leave the work force more times throughout their lives than do men and spend a smaller percentage of their lives economically active.

Another factor influencing the discrepancy between men's and women's wages is the concentration of women in occupations that pay less. In 1985, 70 percent of all women were employed in occupations in which 75 percent of employees were women. Five of the top 10 occupations employing women were sales clerk, clerical worker, bookkeeper, cashier, and social worker. The next two most popular were registered nurse and elementary school teacher.

Minimum wage in the nation was first enacted by the state of Massachusetts in 1912, covered only women, and was designed to shorten hours and raise pay in the covered industries. Nationwide a minimum wage was established during the Great Depression, but the amount varied among industries, usually around $0.35 per hour. The minimum wage rose from $3.35 to $4.25 per hour in April 1991, although employers may pay a special subminimum training wage of $3.35 (or 85% of the minimum wage) for a period of 90 days. States may require higher minimum wages, and 10 do so; 6.5 percent of all workers receive wages no higher than the minimum wage.

30 METROPOLITAN AREAS WITH HIGHEST JOB GROWTH, 1994–2015
(in thousands)

Rank/Metropolitan statistical area	Number of jobs 1994	Number of jobs 2015	Change in employment 1994–2015
1. Atlanta, Ga.	2,137.0	3,538.7	1,401.7
2. Washington, D.C.–Md.–Va.	3,034.0	4,348.5	1,314.5
3. Los Angeles–Long Beach Calif.	4,764.2	6,006.1	1,241.8
4. Houston, Tex.	2,085.6	3,297.2	1,211.6
5. Dallas, Tex.	1,928.1	3,102.6	1,174.4
6. Orange County, Calif.	1,499.3	2,491.1	991.8
7. Phoenix, Ariz.	1,384.1	2,359.4	975.3
8. Seattle, Wash.	1,460.9	2,352.5	891.6
9. San Diego, Calif.	1,389.4	2,264.1	874.6
10. Minneapolis–St. Paul, Minn.	1,820.9	2,572.9	752.0
11. Tampa–St. Petersburg–Clearwater, Fla.	1,152.8	1,867.5	714.7
12. Chicago, Ill.	4,446.1	5,158.4	712.3
13. Boston–Worcester–Lawrence–Lowell–Brockton, Mass.–N.H.	3,401.0	4,106.7	705.7
14. Denver, Colo.	1,203.8	1,864.3	660.6
15. Orlando, Fla.	840.7	1,496.7	656.0
16. Riverside–San Bernardino, Calif.	1,045.0	1,647.6	602.5
17. Sacramento, Calif.	761.0	1,302.0	541.0
18. Fort Worth–Arlington, Tex.	802.3	1,293.4	491.1
19. Miami, Fla.	1,155.3	1,634.1	478.8
20. San Jose, Calif.	996.0	1,469.0	473.0
21. Portland–Vancouver, Oreg.–Wash.	999.9	1,468.8	468.9
22. Austin–San Marcos, Tex.	626.8	1,091.1	464.4
23. Fort Lauderdale, Fla.	714.5	1,178.0	463.6
24. Salt Lake City–Ogden, Utah	721.9	1,176.7	454.8
25. Raleigh–Durham–Chapel Hill, N.C.	664.6	1,110.2	445.6
26. Las Vegas, Nev.–Ariz.	594.2	1,034.3	440.1
27. Oakland, Calif.	1,156.4	1,593.9	437.5
28. Philadelphia, Pa.–N.J.	2,602.8	3,019.9	417.1
29. San Antonio, Tex.	780.7	1,179.9	399.2
30. San Francisco, Calif.	1,190.1	1,569.5	379.4
Total 30 MSAs	47,359.6	68,595.1	21235.5
U.S. total	**144,035.7**	**191,743.9**	**47,708.2**

Source: NPA Data Services, Inc., *Regional Economic Growth in the U.S. Projections for 1994–2015* (1995).

10 METROPOLITAN AREAS WITH FASTEST JOB GROWTH, 1994–2015

Rank/Metropolitan statistical area	Number of jobs ('000s) 1994	Number of jobs ('000s) 2015	Annual percent increase 1994–2015
1. Punta Gorda, Fla.	44.1	93.5	3.6%
2. Naples, Fla.	106.0	212.0	3.4
3. Fort Myers–Cape Coral, Fla.	180.1	355.2	3.3
4. Fort Pierce–Port St. Lucie, Fla.	120.1	221.5	3.0
5. Bryan–College Station, Tex.	78.3	143.2	2.9
6. Santa Fe, N.Mex.	92.3	167.1	2.9
7. Olympia, Wash.	94.1	168.9	2.8
8. Orlando, Fla.	840.7	1,496.7	2.8
9. Tallahassee, Fla.	164.4	288.3	2.7
10. Sarasota–Bradenton, Fla.	285.0	499.6	2.7

Source: NPA Data Services, Inc., *Regional Economic Growth in the U.S. Projections for 1994–2015* (1995).

AVERAGE HOURLY AND WEEKLY EARNINGS IN CURRENT AND CONSTANT (1982) DOLLARS, BY PRIVATE INDUSTRY GROUP, 1970–94

While it is true that average hourly and weekly nominal wages (in current dollars) have more than tripled since 1970, the following table illustrates that when inflation is accounted for, real earnings (in constant dollars) have been decreasing steadily over the past two decades. Hourly earnings have declined nearly 8% since 1970, while weekly earnings have dropped 14%. Thus, even though 1994 paychecks have more zeroes on the end, they don't go as far as a 1970 paycheck to cover living expenses.

	Current dollars					Constant (1982)[1] dollars				
Private industry group	**1970**	**1980**	**1985**	**1990**	**1994**	**1970**	**1980**	**1985**	**1990**	**1994**
Average hourly earnings	**$3.23**	**$6.66**	**$8.57**	**$10.01**	**$11.12**	**$8.03**	**$7.78**	**$7.77**	**$7.52**	**$7.40**
Manufacturing	3.35	7.27	9.54	10.83	12.06	8.33	8.49	8.65	8.14	8.02
Mining	3.85	9.17	11.98	13.68	14.89	9.58	10.71	10.86	10.28	9.91
Construction	5.24	9.94	12.32	13.77	14.69	13.03	11.61	11.17	10.35	9.77
Transportation, public utilities	3.85	8.87	11.40	12.97	13.88	9.58	10.36	10.34	9.74	9.23
Wholesale trade	3.43	6.95	9.15	10.79	12.01	8.53	8.12	8.30	8.11	7.99
Retail trade	2.44	4.88	5.94	6.75	7.49	6.07	5.70	5.39	5.07	4.98
Finance, insurance, real estate	3.07	5.79	7.94	9.97	11.83	7.64	6.76	7.20	7.49	7.87
Services	2.81	5.85	7.90	9.83	11.07	6.99	6.83	7.16	7.39	7.37
Average weekly earnings	**$120**	**$235**	**$299**	**$345**	**$385**	**$296**	**$275**	**$271**	**$259**	**$256**
Manufacturing	133	289	386	442	507	332	337	350	332	337
Mining	164	397	520	603	666	409	464	471	453	443
Construction	195	368	464	526	570	486	430	421	395	379
Transportation, public utilities	156	351	450	505	554	388	410	408	379	368
Wholesale trade	137	267	351	411	460	341	312	318	309	306
Retail trade	82	147	175	194	216	205	172	158	146	144
Finance, insurance, real estate	113	210	289	357	424	281	245	262	268	282
Services	97	191	257	319	360	240	223	233	240	239

1. Earnings in current dollars divided by the Consumer Price Index on a 1982 base. **Source:** U.S. Bureau of Labor Statistics, *Employment and Earnings* (monthly).

Unions A labor union is an organization of workers who engage in collective bargaining with employers for higher wages, better working conditions, and increased benefits. In the United States, unions are organized at three levels: (1) labor federations or voluntary associations of national unions, which settle disputes between national unions, lobby for favorable labor legislation, and engage in public relations. There is only one labor foundation in the country—the American Federation of Labor and Congress of Industrial Organizations, or AFL-CIO—to which virtually all union members belong; (2) national unions, which coordinate agreements across local unions and conduct collective bargaining negotiations with industry employers; and (3) local unions, which administer labor contracts, serving individual members, employers, and in some cases, establishments directly. Unions can be divided into two groups: (1) industrial unions, representing workers of a particular firm or industry, such as autoworkers and steelworkers, and (2) craft unions, representing employees with a specific skill, such as pilots and musicians.

Many workers choose not to unionize because of the potential costs involved in membership, such as dues, lost pay during strikes, and possible retribution by employers. Union membership in the nation declined between 1983 and 1990 by one million members (17.7 million to 16.7 million). In 1990, 16.1 percent of the total labor force and 36.5 percent of government employees belonged to unions. This is down from a peak of around 25.4 percent of the total labor force in 1954. Notable examples of membership decline are among steelworkers, garment workers, and oil, chemical, and atomic workers, which each fell by about 50 percent during 1979–90. Virtually all of these losses are due to the loss of jobs in unionized firms. A number of factors may have contributed to this decline, such as changes in technology that displace workers, as in the music industry, and increased factor costs and international competition that make production less economically feasible, as in the steel industry.

WORK STOPPAGES, 1960–94

Year	Number of work stoppages[1]	Workers involved[2] ('000s)	Days idle: Number[3] ('000s)	Days idle: Percent estimated working time[4]
1960	222	896	13,260	0.09%
1965	268	999	15,140	0.10
1970	381	2,468	52,761	0.29
1975	235	965	17,563	0.09
1980	187	795	20,844	0.09
1985	54	324	7,079	0.03
1990	44	185	5,926	0.02
1991	40	392	4,584	0.02
1992	35	364	3,989	0.01
1993	35	182	3,981	0.01
1994	45	322	5,021	0.02

Note: Excludes work stoppages involving fewer than 1,000 workers and lasting less than one day. 1. Beginning in the year indicated. 2. Workers are counted more than once if involved in more than one stoppage during the year. 3. Resulting from all stoppages in effect in a year, including those that began in an earlier year. 4. Agricultural and government employees are included in the total working time; private household, forestry, and fishery employees are excluded. **Source:** U.S. Bureau of Labor Statistics, *Compensation and Conditions* (monthly).

U.S. MEMBERSHIP IN AFL-CIO– AFFILIATED UNIONS, BY SELECTED UNION, 1979–93 (thousands of workers)

Labor organization	1979	1985	1993
Total[1]	**13,621**	**13,109**	**13,299**
Actors and artists	75	100	93
Automobile, aerospace, and agriculture (UAW)	N.A.	974	771
Bakery, confectionery, and tobacco	131	115	99
Boilermakers, iron shipbuilders[2,3]	129	110	58
Bricklayers	106	95	84
Carpenters[2]	626	609	408
Clothing and textile workers (ACTWU)[2]	308	228	143
Communications workers (CWA)	485	524	472
Electrical workers (IBEW)	825	791	710
Electronic, electrical, and salaried[2,4]	243	198	143
Operating engineers	313	330	305
Firefighters	150	142	151
Food and commercial workers (UFCW)[2]	1,123	989	997
Garment workers (ILGWU)	314	210	133
Glass, molders, pottery, and plastics[2]	50	72	73
Government, American Federation (AFGE)	236	199	149
Graphic communications[2]	171	141	95
Hotel employees and restaurant employees	373	327	258
Ironworkers	146	140	91
Laborers	475	383	408
Letter carriers (NALC)	151	186	210
Longshoremen's association	63	65	58
Machinists and aerospace (IAM)[2]	688	520	474
Marine Engineers Beneficial Assn.	23	22	52
Mine workers	N.A.	N.A.	75
Office and professional employees	83	90	89
Oil, chemical, atomic workers (OCAW)	146	108	86
Painters	160	133	106
Paperworkers international	262	232	188
Plumbing and pipefitting	228	226	220
Postal workers	245	232	249
Retail, wholesale, department store	122	106	80
Rubber, cork, linoleum, plastic	158	106	81
Seafarers	84	80	80
Service employees (SEIU)[2,5]	537	688	919
Sheet metal workers	120	108	108
Stage employees, moving picture machine operators	50	50	51
State, county, municipal (AFSCME)[5]	889	997	1,167
Steelworkers	964	572	421
Teachers (AFT)	423	470	574
Teamsters[6]	N.A.	N.A.	1,316
Transit union	94	94	94
Transport workers	85	85	78
Transportation Union, United	121	52	60

Note: Figures represent the labor organizations as constituted in 1989 and reflect past merger activity. Membership figures based on average per capita paid membership to the AFL-CIO for the two-year period ending in June of the year shown and reflect only actively employed members. Labor unions shown had a membership of 70,000 or more in 1989. 1. Includes other AFL-CIO–affiliated unions, not shown separately. 2. Figures reflect mergers with one or more unions since 1979. 3. Includes blacksmiths, forgers, and helpers. 4. Includes machine and furniture workers. 5. Excludes hospital and health care employees, which merged into both unions on June 1, 1989 (membership of 23,000 in 1985 and 58,000 in 1989). 6. Includes chauffeurs, warehousemen, and helpers. **Source:** American Federation of Labor and Congress of Industrial Organizations, *Report of the AFL-CIO Executive Council* (annual).

U.S. BUSINESS

The Office of Management and Budget (OMB) classifies the entire national economy into industries, based on principal product or activity. There are nine industrial divisions, which are further classified into groups and subgroups. For example, "food and kindred products" would fall under "manufacturing," and beneath that, "meat-packing plants." The nine industrial divisions listed in the OMB's Standard Industry Classification (SIC) are agriculture, forestry, and fishing; mining; construction; manufacturing; transportation and public utilities; finance, insurance, and real estate; wholesale trade; retail trade; and services. In 1992, 6.3 million establishments employed 92.8 million workers, with payrolls totaling $2.3 trillion.

Services and Manufacturing

Another way to view the economy is to divide it into manufacturing industries, producing such tangible goods as cars, shoes, and furniture, and services industries, producing such intangible products as entertainment, tourism, and banking. The manufacturing industries are further broken down into those producing durable goods—that is, goods consumed over time, such as cars and houses—and nondurable goods consumed in the short run, such as food and soap. Services have played an increasingly important role in the economy, partly because manufacturing companies increasingly contract for services, such as transportation, accounting, marketing, and communications, previously performed in-house.

The service sector, which includes government, is responsible for approximately three-quarters of U.S. employment, and is expected to account for four of every five jobs by the year 2005.

The strongest service industries in 1994 included data processing, electronic information, health services, and space commerce. The strongest manufacturing industries were machine tools, electronic components and accessories, and surgical appliances. The slowest growing manufacturing industries were aircraft,

10 FASTEST GROWING MANUFACTURING INDUSTRIES, 1993–94

Industry	Percent change, 1993–94
Machine tools, metal cutting types	12.8%
Electronic components and accessories	11.1
Surgical appliances	10.0
Mobile homes	9.4
Automotive parts and accessories	7.7
Surgical and medical instruments	7.0
Lighting fixtures	6.6
Mattresses and bedsprings	6.4
Leather tanning and finishing	6.0
Analytical instruments	6.0

Note: In constant (1987) dollars. **Source:** U.S. Dept. of Commerce, *U.S. Industrial Outlook 1994* (1994).

GROWTH RATES FOR SELECTED SERVICE INDUSTRIES, 1994

Industry	Unit of measure	Rate of growth
Accounting	Receipts	5.6%
Advertising	Receipts	3.8
Banks	Loans	4.0
Cable television	Revenues	9.5
Computer professional services	Revenues	9.6
Credit unions	Loans	7.0
Data processing	Revenues	15.5
Education and training	Expenditures	5.8
Electronic information services	Revenues	14.7
Equipment leasing	Original equipment cost	3.0
Health services	Revenues	12.5
Legal services	Receipts	4.3
Life and health insurance	Premium receipts	6.0
Management consulting	Receipts	6.9
Motion picture theaters	Receipts	3.1
Prerecorded music	Manufacturers' value	13.5
Property–casualty insurance	Net premiums written	4.0
Railroads (class 1)	Revenue ton-miles	2.4
Retail sales, total	Sales	7.0
Apparel and accessories stores	Sales	3.7
General merchandise stores	Sales	14.3
Eating and drinking places	Sales	4.4
Food retailing	Sales	3.1
Savings institutions	Mortgage-related loans	–5.1
Space commerce	Revenues	22.6
Telecommunications services	Revenues	7.7
Travel services	Expenditures	5.8
Trucking	Revenues	5.8
Venture capital	Capital commitments	–6.8
Wholesale sales, total	Sales	4.0

Note: Growth rates are projections for change in value 1993–94. **Source:** U.S. Dept. of Commerce, *U.S. Industrial Outlook, 1994* (1994).

GROWTH RATE ESTIMATES AND PROJECTIONS FOR SELECTED INDUSTRY GROUPS, 1992–94

Industry group	1992	1993	1994
Electronic components	13.4	13.1	11.1
Motor vehicles and parts	4.9	9.6	6.4
Computers	6.1	7.8	5.9
Metal working equipment	0.1	7.4	5.7
Instruments, controls, and medical equipment	4.1	5.0	5.2
Plastics and rubber	1.2	3.6	4.7
Production machinery	–2.8	2.8	3.9
Electrical equipment	–1.2	2.0	3.8
Durable consumer goods	4.6	4.0	3.3
Paper and allied products	1.0	0.5	3.0
Steel mill products	8.4	5.0	2.5
Wood products	4.9	0.2	2.3
Construction	7.3	3.0	1.9
Printing and publishing	–0.8	1.1	1.9
Chemicals	–0.6	–0.1	1.4
Food and beverages	1.0	1.3	1.0
Petroleum refining	1.6	1.0	1.0
Construction materials	3.3	0.4	0.8
Telecommunications and navigation equipment	–2.9	–2.2	–2.6
Aerospace	–0.5	–11.0	–11.0

Note: All data are based on shipments in constant 1987 dollars, except computers (current dollars). **Source:** U.S. Dept. of Commerce, *U.S. Industrial Outlook 1994* (1994).

aircraft parts and engines, search and navigation equipment, and ship building and repairing, all of which declined in 1994.

Financing Business

When an individual or a group of individuals decides to start a new company, they need money to rent or buy office space and equipment and to pay workers. Since there is a time lag between the day a business opens and the day a business sells its first good or service, funds must be borrowed from a bank or other financial institution or from individual investors to meet costs before revenues are generated. Additional funds may be needed throughout the life of the business to finance research and development of a new product or service or for the construction of new factories. Financing can take many forms, from short-term bank loans, commercial paper, or trade credit to long-term stocks and bonds.

Trade credit, the largest category of short-term financing, is an arrangement between a company and its suppliers whereby materials and supplies are delivered to the company with a promise to pay the invoice, plus interest, usually within a specified number of weeks. Commercial bank lending may take the form of a single loan with repayment in a lump sum or in installments over the life of the loan, or it may be a line of credit up to a maximum the bank will allow the company to overdraw on its account. Commercial paper is a promissory note of a well-established firm sold primarily to other business firms, with repayments made in two to six months. The only problem with commercial paper is that its resources are limited to the liquidity that corporations have at any given time for lending to other firms.

Intermediate-term financing (with a time-frame of one to 15 years) may take the form of lease financing, whereby a company rents, rather than buys, the assets it uses; conditional sales contracts, by which equipment is bought over a period of time (the seller continues to have title of ownership until payment is completed); or term loans or business credit supplied by commercial banks and life insurance companies, repaid by amortization payments over the life of the loan (one to 15 years).

The issuance of stocks and bonds constitute the long-term source of finance for firms. Bonds are debt instruments (IOUs issued by a company to the bondholder) that obligate the firm to pay interest at specific times. Alternatively, firms can raise money by issuing preferred and common stocks. Unlike bonds, stocks entitle the holder to share in ownership and profits made by the firm through dividends paid out for the entire period the investor owns the stock. However, if the business has low profits or limited funds, bondholders are paid first, preferred stockholders next, and common stockholders last.

WALL STREET

The U.S. stock market, commonly known as Wall Street, began in the late 18th century as a merchant-organized public auction in stocks and government bonds for the purpose of financing the government and expanding business and trade. At that time brokers handed over securities to auctioneers who sold securities to the highest bidder. Today, while the form of the stock exchange has changed dramatically, the purpose remains the same.

The most commonly cited index of Wall Street's performance is the Dow Jones average (see "Glossary of Financial Terms"). The Dow rose dramatically in the 1980s, passing the 2,000 mark in January 1987 and reaching over 2,700 by August, only to drop by over 500 points on "Black Monday," Oct. 19, 1987, losing over 22 percent of its value in one day (nearly 10 percentage points more than the day of the Great Crash of 1929) and closing around 1,700. Black Monday was precipitated by investors' fear of a falling dollar and increased interest rates in order to attract external funds to finance the enormous U.S. trade deficit ($15.7 billion for the month of August 1987 alone). For corporations and consumers, this translated into increased borrowing costs, lower investment and spending, recession, and a decrease in corporate earnings, culminating in the heavy sales of equities on Oct. 19, 1987.

Since then, the Dow Jones Industrial Average has more than made up the loss, breaking 3,000 in mid-1991 and the 4,000 mark in February 1994.

New York Stock Exchange (NYSE) In 1994, 73.4 billion shares with a value of $2.5 trillion were traded on the New York Stock Exchange. The oldest exchange in the country was formally founded in 1817, when fewer than 100 shares were traded each day.

The American Stock Exchange (AMEX) The American Stock Exchange, located a few blocks from the New York Stock Exchange in New York's financial district, is known as the stock market for the small investor and small companies. The stock issues of organizations that do not meet the listing and size requirements of the NYSE are typically traded there. For years, the AMEX was known as the "New York Curb Exchange" because its trading was conducted on the street outside the office buildings of many brokers. The exchange moved indoors in 1921.

Trading on the AMEX in 1994 was down from the all-time highs set in 1993. Average daily trading volume was 17.9 million shares, down from 18.1 million in 1993. There were 824 companies listed on the AMEX at the end of 1994,

NYSE: SHARES TRADED, 1900–1994 (in thousands)

Year	Daily average	Record High	Record Low
1900	505	1,627	89
1910	601	1,656	111
1920	828	2,008	227
1930	2,959	8,279	1,090
1940	751	3,940	130
1950	1,980	4,859	1,061
1955	2,578	7,717	1,230
1960	3,042	5,303	1,894
1965	6,176	11,434	3,028
1970	11,564	21,345	6,660
1975	18,551	35,158	8,670
1980	44,871	84,297	16,132
1985	109,169	181,027	62,055
1990	156,777	292,364	56,853
1991	178,917	317,362	69,644
1992	202,266	389,036	95,140
1993	264,519	379,483	89,851
1994	291,351	482,754	113,811

Source: New York Stock Exchange, *Fact Book 1994.*

NYSE LISTED STOCKS, 1924–94 (figures in millions)

Year-end	Number of shares	Market value	Average price[1]
1924	433	$ 27,072	$62.45
1945	1,592	73,765	46.33
1950	2,353	93,807	39.86
1960	6,458	306,967	47.53
1970	16,065	636,380	39.61
1975	22,478	85,110	30.48
1980	33,709	1,242,803	36.87
1985	52,427	1,950,332	37.20
1990	90,732	2,819,778	31.08
1991	99,622	3,712,835	37.27
1992	115,839	4,035,100	34.83
1993	131,053	4,540,850	34.10
1994	142,281	4,448,284	31.26

1. This average cannot be used as an index of price trend owing to changes in shares listed caused by new listings, suspensions, stock splits, and stock dividends. **Source:** New York Stock Exchange, *Fact Book 1994.*

NYSE MEMBERSHIP PRICES, 1875–1994

Year	High	Low	Year	High	Low
1875	$ 6,800	$ 4,300	1975	$ 138,000	$ 55,000
1895	20,000	17,000	1980	275,000	175,000
1905	85,000	72,000	1985	480,000	310,000
1915	74,000	38,000	1987[1]	1,150,000	605,000
1925	150,000	99,000	1990	430,000	250,000
1935	140,000	65,000	1991	440,000	345,000
1945	95,000	49,000	1992	600,000	410,000
1955	90,000	80,000	1993	775,000	500,000
1965	250,000	190,000	1994	830,000	760,000
1970	320,000	$130,000			

1. All-time record. **Source:** New York Stock Exchange, *Fact Book 1994.*

44 fewer than the year before. Nearly 4.6 billion shares changed hands on the AMEX in 1994, down only slightly from 1993 totals.

NASDAQ The most heavily traded over-the-counter stocks are exchanged though the NASDAQ National Market System, the second-largest stock market in the United States and the fifth-largest in the world in terms of dollar value of its shares. Founded in 1971, NASDAQ—the National Association of Securities Dealers Automated Quotations—uses computers and high-technology telecommunications to trade—and to monitor the trading of—millions of securities daily.

More than 74.4 billion shares were traded through NASDAQ in 1994, an increase of more than 50 percent since 1992, when 48.5 million shares were traded. The dollar volume of this trading was a whopping $1.45 trillion, making the NASDAQ bigger than the markets of most countries. Only the NYSE and the Tokyo, London, and German exchanges are bigger.

The average number of shares traded daily on NASDAQ in 1994 was 295.1 million, a ninefold increase over the 1981 average of 30.9 million. In 1980, when 19.7 billion shares were traded on the NASDAQ, NYSE, and AMEX markets combined, NASDAQ accounted for 34 percent of the total. Fourteen years later, when 152.3 billion shares were traded on those same markets, the 4,902 companies listed on the NASDAQ accounted for 48.8 percent of the total, an even higher percentage than the 48.2 percent traded on the New York Stock Exchange.

GLOSSARY OF FINANCIAL TERMS

Arbitrage Simultaneous purchase and sale of a commodity or currency in at least two markets where price discrepancies exist. The arbitrageur makes a profit by buying an asset with a low price in one market and selling it in another market where the asset carries a higher price.

Bear/bull A bear is a speculator who expects prices to fall and sells stocks or *bonds* in order to buy them later at a lower price. A bull expects prices to rise and therefore buys now for resale later. Thus, a bearish (bullish) market is one in which prices are generally falling (rising).

Blue chip stock A stock that is considered a safe investment, with a low *yield* and a high price per share, issued by companies that are well known and have a history of good management and increasing profit levels.

Bond A debt obligation requiring the issuer to pay a fixed sum of money annually until maturity (interest payments) and then, at maturity, a fixed sum of money to repay the initial amount borrowed (principal). (See "Corporate bond.")

Capital gain An increase in the market value of an asset above the price originally paid for it, realized when the asset is sold.

Capital loss A decrease in the market value of an asset below the price originally paid for it, realized when the asset is sold.

Common stock/equity A piece of paper that entitles the owner to a share of the *firm*'s profits and a share of the voting power in shareholder elections. In other words, a shareholder is part owner of the firm. If he owns 50 percent of the issued shares of common stock (when no *preferred stock* is issued), he owns 50 percent of the company, and will receive 50 percent of profits paid out in *dividends.* Over 40 million Americans invest in common stocks.

Convertible bond A debt instrument that carries an option for the holder to convert it into a specified amount of company stock.

Corporate bond A debt obligation requiring the corporation to pay a fixed sum of money annually until maturity (interest payments) and then, at maturity, a fixed sum of money to repay the initial amount borrowed (principal). *Bonds* carry no claim to ownership and therefore pay no *dividends,* but payments to bondholders take priority over payments to stockholders.

Debenture A debt *security* that pays a fixed interest rate, issued by a company in order to raise finance for commercial or industrial operations.

Derivative is a contract to buy or sell an asset, such as a security or a commodity, in the future. Examples of derivative products are: futures contracts, put and call options, forward rate agreements, forward commodity agreements, and mortgage backed securities. Derivatives are so called because their value (the contract price) is *derived* from the value of the underlying asset to be bought or sold. Underlying assets include stocks; bonds; commodities; Treasury bills; mortgages; and exchange and interest rates.

Divestiture The sale by a company of a product line, subsidiary, or division. (See section "Mergers and Acquisitions.")

Dividend A payment made to *common* and *preferred stock* holders out of a *firm*'s profits either in the form of cash or additional shares.

Dow Jones Industrial Average Dating back to 1893, this index of 30 *blue chip stocks* in industry traded on the New York Stock Exchange (and determined by the editors of the *Wall Street Journal*) is the most widely cited indicator of how the stock market is doing.

Establishment A physical place of business activity such as a factory, assembly plant, retail store, or warehouse, where goods are made, stored, or processed or where services are performed.

Eurocurrency A currency deposited outside its country of origin for use as a medium of international credit. The Eurocurrency market developed in the late 1950s and constitutes a vast international pool of highly mobile money. Eurocurrencies are used to facilitate international trade and the payment of deficits and for currency speculation.

Firm A business organization that owns and/or operates one or more *establishments.* Also called a company, enterprise, or business venture. Firms can be of three types: (1) sole proprietorships—firms owned directly by one person; (2) partnerships—firms whose ownership is shared by a fixed number of proprietors; and (3) corporations—firms created by a government charter, which grants them greater accessibility to financial capital through the selling of *common* or *preferred stock*, greater accessibility to debt capital through the selling of *bonds*, and limited liability in the event of bankruptcy.

Futures market/forward market A market in which commodities or *securities* are bought and sold at prices fixed now, for delivery at specified future date. Futures are traded on the American Stock Exchange; the Chicago Board of Trade; Chicago Board Options Exchange; Chicago Mercantile Exchange; Chicago Rice and Cotton Exchange; Commodity Exchange, New York (COMEX); Kansas City Board of Trade; MidAmerica Commodity Exchange, Chicago; Minneapolis Grain Exchange; New York Coffee, Sugar, and Coca Exchange (including the Citrus Associates); New York Cotton Exchange; New York Futures Exchange; New York Mercantile Exchange; New York Stock Exchange; Pacific Stock Exchange, Los Angeles and San Francisco; and Philadelphia Stock Exchange.

Greenmail Analogous to blackmail, the practice of purchasing enough shares in a *firm* or trading company to threaten a takeover, thereby forcing the owners to buy them back at a higher rate in order to retain control of the business.

Insider trading Trading in the stock market based on information that has not been made public and that is intended to remain confidential—for example, information that a small company is about to become part of a national corporation. The penalties paid by individuals and corporations for such activities in recent years have reached into the hundreds of millions of dollars.

Junk bond/high yield bond *Bonds* with a *rating* below investment grade—that is, at or below Ba1 (Moody's Investors Service), at or below BB+ (Standard & Poor's), or unrated. Issuers of junk bonds are usually small companies who in the past have been limited to borrowing from banks to raise capital for corporate growth.

NUMBER OF BUSINESS ESTABLISHMENTS WITH EMPLOYEES AND PAYROLL, BY MAJOR GROUP, 1992

Major group	Number of establishments	Number of employees	Annual payroll ('000s)
Total	**6,317,690**	**92,800,870**	**$2,271,962,391**
Agricultural services, forestry, and fishing	**97,245**	**593,518**	**10,040,725**
Agricultural services	93,251	559,574	9,250,618
Forestry	2,138	18,588	340,130
Fishing, hunting, and trapping	1,798	12,553	349,665
Administrative and auxiliary	58	2,803	100,312
Mining	**29,130**	**650,554**	**$25,605,273**
Metal mining	900	50,636	1,918,805
Coal mining	2,730	123,361	4,838,635
Oil and gas extraction	18,875	270,001	9,672,529
Nonmetallic minerals, except fuels	5,390	96,653	3,018,596
Administrative and auxiliary	1,235	109,903	6,156,708
Construction	**588,667**	**4,500,006**	**$122,089,076**
General contractors and operative builders	181,026	1,124,863	29,905,767
Heavy construction contractors	31,601	650,891	22,310,695
Special trade contractors	375,651	2,707,645	69,016,590
Administrative and auxiliary	389	16,607	856,024
Manufacturing	**386,629**	**18,162,480**	**$563,073,835**
Food and kindred products	20,799	1,471,536	36,865,979
Tobacco products	126	38,783	1,568,101
Textile mill products	6,133	623,833	12,912,499
Apparel and other textile products	24,570	987,443	15,437,903
Lumber and wood products	35,881	648,983	14,005,422
Furniture and fixtures	11,568	460,841	10,037,863
Paper and allied products	6,441	624,923	20,597,632
Printing and publishing	66,305	1,492,533	41,774,310
Chemicals and allied products	12,111	859,632	33,226,727
Petroleum and coal products	2,116	121,993	5,493,484
Rubber and misc. plastics products	15,414	870,500	22,746,882
Leather and leather products	2,090	104,635	1,883,520
Stone, clay, and glass products	16,411	474,278	13,350,401
Primary metal industries	6,818	664,576	22,321,850
Fabricated metal products	35,971	1,372,946	39,632,603
Industrial machinery and equipment	55,811	1,790,703	58,966,898
Electric and electronic equipment	17,059	1,433,646	44,728,967
Transportation equipment	11,614	1,657,880	63,460,949
Instruments and related products	11,319	889,535	32,540,819
Miscellaneous manufacturing industries	17,357	373,420	8,765,858
Administrative and auxiliary	10,715	1,199,861	62,755,168
Transportation and other public utilities	**258,500**	**5,517,458**	**$175,450,694**
Local and interurban passenger transit	16,849	331,427	4,969,542
Trucking and warehousing	109,866	1,544,548	39,382,799
Water transportation	8,055	163,314	5,108,419
Transportation by air	11,029	660,304	22,897,178
Pipelines, except natural gas	837	18,326	879,690
Transportation services	48,425	378,067	9,004,476
Communication	39,927	1,309,995	47,422,574
Electric, gas, and sanitary services	20,942	941,449	39,792,257
Administrative and auxiliary	2,570	170,028	5,993,759
Wholesale trade	**492,095**	**6,094,175**	**$190,840,514**
Wholesale trade—durable goods	309,756	3,371,428	107,642,953
Wholesale trade—nondurable goods	176,579	2,379,054	67,843,359
Administrative and auxiliary	5,760	343,693	15,354,202
Retail trade	**1,564,245**	**19,672,221**	**$258,566,355**
Building materials and garden supplies	69,648	685,141	12,166,659
General merchandise stores	36,281	2,058,993	24,414,201
Food stores	190,280	3,089,579	38,759,514
Automotive dealers and service stations	202,771	1,981,665	40,978,490
Apparel and accessory stores	146,615	1,167,816	12,648,286
Furniture and home furnishings stores	113,147	799,704	13,996,768
Eating and drinking places	430,098	6,571,253	54,273,568
Miscellaneous retail	359,164	2,496,399	35,955,232
Administrative and auxiliary	16,241	821,671	25,373,637
Finance, insurance, and real estate	**596,888**	**6,905,698**	**$221,022,396**
Depository institutions	104,526	2,157,509	57,890,934
Nondepository institutions	40,921	456,706	16,042,492
Security and commodity brokers	32,135	425,583	34,112,255
Insurance carriers	52,571	1,569,307	50,835,122
Insurance agents, brokers, and service	114,032	641,875	19,443,560
Real estate	223,995	1,325,795	28,361,416
Holding and other investment offices	27,259	266,334	11,293,821
Administrative and auxiliary	1,449	62,589	3,042,796
Services	**2,217,677**	**30,653,593**	**$703,596,685**
Hotels and other lodging places	53,343	1,501,654	20,163,377
Personal services	198,056	1,232,589	14,920,026
Business services	306,537	5,346,332	110,434,649
Auto repair, services, and garages	167,266	860,971	15,709,347
Miscellaneous repair services	67,999	384,024	8,982,174
Motion pictures	40,694	462,558	9,607,965
Amusement and recreation services	84,268	1,125,023	19,201,871
Health services	464,879	9,726,647	266,722,040
Legal services	153,588	951,908	39,857,204
Educational services	41,613	1,918,707	35,018,080
Social services	139,396	1,954,217	25,700,708
Museums, botanical, zoological gardens	3,815	69,879	1,255,563
Membership organizations	238,165	2,040,059	25,999,402
Engineering and management services	235,303	2,619,303	91,697,749
Miscellaneous services	13,532	75,237	2,752,407
Administrative and auxiliary	9,223	384,485	15,574,123
Unclassified establishments	**86,614**	**51,167**	**$1,676,838**

Note: Excludes most government employees, railroad employees, and self-employed persons. **Source:** U.S. Bureau of the Census, *County Business Patterns 1992* (1994).

Despite the fact that the major ratings services consider junk bonds risky (hence their name), they have a historically low default rate—only 1.5 percent between the mid-1970s and mid-1980s. The junk market grew considerably in the 1980s, and by 1987 accounted for over 25 percent of the value of all *corporate bonds* outstanding.

Leveraged buyout The purchase of a company by one of its employee groups (usually upper management) or a large shareholder with borrowed funds, usually using the company's assets as security for the loans. Leveraged buyouts have been used to combat hostile takeover bids.

Mutual fund A pool of financial assets in which investors may buy shares and derive the benefits or share the losses, depending on the performance of the collective *securities.* Shares are sold publicly and can be redeemed at any time. Funds can consist of stocks, *bonds,* gold, government securities, or other assets, and their names are descriptive of their primary purpose; for example, bonds funds, equity-fund portfolios, income funds, money market–mutual funds, and municipal funds. (See "Money Market Accounts" under "Money and Banking" in the section "The United States Economy.")

Option A contract to buy or sell commodities or *securities* within a given time period at a fixed price. For stocks, this period is usually three months. A contract to sell is a *put option* (or put); to buy, a *call option* (or call); and one to buy or sell is a *double option.* A buyer (seller) will gain if the trading price rises (falls) by more than the cost of entering into the contract. Options are traded on the same exchanges as *futures* contracts.

Over-the-counter (OTC) stock A *security* not listed on a *stock exchange* that is traded between two individuals. The name stems from the 18th-century practice of merchants selling stocks directly to investors over the counter in their own shops, without the use of *stockbrokers* or auctioneers.

Pension fund A scheme whereby private- or public-sector employers, unions, and—as in the case of individual retirement accounts (IRAs) and Keogh plans—individuals contribute to a fund from which money is paid out to the employees, union members, or contributors (or their dependents) upon death, disability, or retirement. Contributions can be based on a percentage of salary or corporate profits; in some cases employees may make voluntary or mandatory contributions to the fund. Pension fund assets are usually held in the form of *securities* or property with a preference for long-term assets.

Preferred stock Similar to *common stock,* except that owners of preferred stock have no voting rights and are paid their *dividends* at a fixed rate, before common-stock holders receive any dividends.

Rating An agency evaluation of the quality of a debt instrument or a company issuing debt. Standard & Poor's and Moody's Investment Service are the two major credit ratings agencies in the United States. The ratings measure the safety of interest and principal payments of bonds. S&P bond ratings are, from most to least secure, AAA, AA, A, BBB, BB, B, CCC, CC, C. Moody's ratings are Aaa, Aa, A, Baa, Ba, B, Caa, Ca, C.

Securities Financial assets (usually long-term), such as equities or stocks and *debentures* or *bonds;* may also refer to shorter-term assets such as U.S. Treasury bills.

Securities and Exchange Commission (SEC) U.S. government agency that regulates the *securities* industry by requiring registration of *stockbrokers,* dealers, and *stock exchanges.* The SEC also reviews the financial position of companies issuing securities for public sale and investigates illegal activities such as *insider trading.*

Standard & Poor's 500 Composite Stock Price Index (S&P 500) A widely used measure of the movement of the U.S. stock market. The S&P 500 was introduced in 1957 and is one of 12 leading economic indicators used by the U.S. Commerce Department. The 500 issues include 400 industrial, 40 utility, 20 transportation, and 40 financial companies—primarily those listed on the New York Stock Exchange (NYSE). The index is considered to be value-weighted because each stock is weighted according to its market value; calculated on a total return basis with *dividends* reinvested.

Stock exchange A market in which *securities* (other than bills and similar short-term instruments) issued by central and local government bodies and public companies are traded (e.g., the New York Stock Exchange, the American Stock Exchange, the London Stock Exchange). Only members of a stock exchange may deal on it, and membership and arrangements for trading are strictly regulated. Stock exchanges in the United States are the American Stock Exchange (New York); Boston Stock Exchange; Cincinnati Stock Exchange; Intermountain Stock Exchange (Salt Lake City); Midwest Stock Exchange (Chicago); New York Stock Exchange; Pacific Stock Exchange (Los Angeles, San Francisco); Philadelphia Stock Exchange; and Spokane Stock Exchange.

Stock market An institution in which stocks and shares are traded, existing in all advanced Western countries. Stock markets enable companies to raise equity or loan capital more easily from the public, since investors can quickly realize their holdings because of the stock exchange share quotation. The principal overseas stock markets are located in Amsterdam, Brussels, Frankfurt, Hong Kong, Johannesburg, London, Milan, Paris, Singapore, Stockholm, Sydney, Tokyo, Toronto, and Zurich.

Stockbroker An individual who acts as an adviser and an agent (working on commission) to buy and sell stocks on behalf of a client on a particular *stock exchange* of which the stockbroker is a member.

Wilshire 5000 Index The broadest measure of the U.S. stock market, containing some 5,000 issues, including all publicly traded U.S. stocks for which daily pricing is available (i.e., includes all AMEX, NYSE, and OTC *stocks*).

Yield The annual return on a *security,* as a percentage of its current market price. A stock's *dividend* yield is the annual dividend divided by its current stock price.

BIG BUSINESS: THE *FORTUNE* 500

Reflecting a fundamental change in the way corporate America views itself and keeps score, the editors of *Fortune* magazine in 1995 restructured the *Fortune* 500 to include service corporations for the first time. For the previous 40 years, the magazine had ranked industrial corporations and service corporations in separate *Fortune* 500s. The industrial listing was the one most people meant when they referred to a *Fortune* 500 company; the Service 500 grew out of a series of lists of the most profitable businesses in the fields of communications, banking, transportation, life insurance, retailing, and utilities. But with giant mega-corporations owning and producing goods and services ranging from publishing companies to sports franchises, and with today's communications technologies spanning both the industrial and service sectors, the old definitions (previously, an industrial corporation had to generate more than 50 percent of its income from manufacturing or mining) no longer applied. Thus the time was right to rank all businesses in the same list.

The overhaul did little to upset the structure at the very top of the *Fortune* 500. General Motors, Ford, and Exxon still placed one, two, and three, while Wal-Mart, AT&T, and Sears Roebuck were the only service companies to crack the top 10. But from there on down, the change is overwhelming. More than half the list now consists of companies that last year would have appeared only on the Service 500. And the requirements for inclusion have grown a lot more formidable. In 1993, a company needed sales of only $614 million to break the *Fortune* 500; in 1994, the 500th-ranked company—Dow Corning—had sales of $2.2 billion.

There are several measures of a corporation's economic health. By profits, Ford, Exxon, and GM again led the way, with each posting profits of more than $4.9 billion. But by returns on revenues, United Healthcare, Microsoft, and Merck were the top companies. United Healthcare's profits were equal to 44 percent of its revenues. It also led the way in terms of returns on assets, with a 47.7 percent rate of return, nearly double that of the second-place company. General Electric topped the list of companies ranked by market value, with $93 billion, followed by Exxon ($83 billion) and AT&T ($82 billion). But Dell Computer proved to be the best single-year investment, with an 81.2 percent return on money invested. Over a 10-year period, United Healthcare (47.4%), Compaq Computer (43.0%), and The Gap (39.0%) were the best investments.

By industry, food and drugstores, pharmaceuticals, and beverages provided the highest one-year return on investment. Over a 10-year period, the best returns came from the computer and data services, food services, and food industries, with each returning more than 20 percent on money invested. Pharmaceuticals provided the highest return on revenues, the highest return on assets, and the highest returns on equity.

FORTUNE 500 LARGEST U.S. CORPORATIONS, 1994

Rank/ Company	Sales (millions)
1. General Motors	$154,951
2. Ford Motor Company	128,439
3. Exxon	101,459
4. Wal-Mart Stores	83,412
5. AT&T	75,094
6. General Electric	64,687
7. IBM	64,052
8. Mobil	59,621
9. Sears Roebuck	54,559
10. Philip Morris	53,776
11. Chrysler	52,224
12. State Farm Group	38,850
13. Prudential Insurance Co.	36,946
14. E.I. du Pont de Nemours	34,968
15. K mart	34,313
16. Texaco	33,768
17. Citicorp	31,650
18. Chevron	31,064
19. Procter & Gamble	30,296
20. Pepsico	28,472
21. Amoco	26,953
22. Hewlett-Packard	24,991
23. ITT	23,767
24. ConAgra	23,512
25. Kroger	22,959
26. American International Group	22,386
27. Metropolitan Life Insurance	22,258
28. Motorola	22,245
29. Boeing	21,924
30. Dayton Hudson	21,311
31. United Technologies	21,197
32. J.C. Penney	21,082
33. Dow Chemical	20,015
34. GTE	19,944
35. United Parcel Service	19,576
36. Federal Natl. Mortgage Assn.	18,572
37. Travelers Inc.	18,465
38. Cigna	18,392
39. American Stores	18,355
40. Merrill Lynch	18,233
41. Xerox	17,837
42. Aetna Life and Casualty	17,525
43. Eastman Kodak	16,862
44. BellSouth	16,844
45. USX	16,799
46. BankAmerica Corp.	16,531
47. Price-Costco	16,481
48. Coca-Cola	16,172
49. AMR	16,137
50. Supervalu	15,937
51. Fleming	15,754
52. Johnson & Johnson	15,734
53. Atlantic Richfield	15,682
54. Safeway	15,627
55. American Express	15,593
56. Sara Lee	15,536
57. RJR Nabisco Holdings	15,366
58. Minnesota Mining & Manufacturing (3M)	15,079
59. Merck	14,970
60. International Paper	14,966
61. Caterpillar	14,328
62. UAL	$13,950
63. Bell Atlantic	13,791
64. Loews	13,515
65. Digital Equipment	13,451
66. MCI Communications	13,338
67. NYNEX	13,307
68. Tenneco	13,222
69. McDonnell Douglas	13,176
70. Lockheed	13,130
71. Nationsbank Corp.	13,126
72. Allied-Signal	12,817
73. Georgia-Pacific	12,738
74. Chemical Banking Corp.	12,685
75. Sprint	12,662
76. Ameritech	12,570
77. Home Depot	12,477
78. McKesson	12,428
79. Phillips Petroleum	12,367
80. Delta Air Lines	12,359
81. Goodyear Tire and Rubber	12,288
82. May Department Stores	12,223
83. IBP	12,075
84. New York Life Insurance	12,067
85. Anheuser-Busch	12,054
86. Bristol-Myers Squibb	11,984
87. J.P. Morgan and Co.	11,915
88. Albertson's	11,895
89. SBC Communications	11,618
90. Intel	11,521
91. US West	11,506
92. Archer Daniels Midland	11,374
93. Melville	11,286
94. Rockwell International	11,205
95. Chase Manhattan Corp.	11,187
96. Nationwide Insurance Enterprise	11,183
97. Columbia/HCA Healthcare	11,132
98. Winn-Dixie Stores	11,082
99. Sysco	10,942
100. Compaq Computer	10,866
101. TIAA	10,551
102. Pacific Gas and Electric	10,447
103. Weyerhaeuser	10,398
104. Aluminum Co. of America	10,392
105. Great Atlantic and Pacific Tea	10,384
106. Texas Instruments	10,315
107. WMX Technologies	10,097
108. Walt Disney	10,055
109. Raytheon	10,013
110. Coastal	10,013
111. Martin Marietta	9,874
112. Textron	9,683
113. CSX	9,608
114. Northwestern Mutual Life	9,581
115. Ashland Oil	9,505
116. Pacific Telesis Group	9,494
117. Occidental Petroleum	9,416
118. Morgan Stanley Group	9,376
119. Baxter International	9,324
120. Walgreen	9,235
121. Lehman Brothers	9,208
122. Westinghouse Electric	9,190
123. Apple Computer	9,189
124. Abbott Laboratories	$9,156
125. Northwest Airlines	9,143
126. TRW	9,087
127. Deere	9,030
128. Liberty Mutual Insurance Group	8,986
129. Enron	8,984
130. American Home Products	8,966
131. Toys "R" Us	8,746
132. Publix Super Markets	8,742
133. Emerson Electric	8,607
134. Fluor	8,556
135. General Mills	8,517
136. Federal Express	8,480
137. American Brands	8,442
138. Marriott International	8,415
139. Scecorp	8,345
140. McDonald's	8,321
141. Federated Department Stores	8,316
142. Southern	8,297
143. Woolworth	8,293
144. Pfizer	8,281
145. Monsanto	8,272
146. Union Pacific	8,140
147. Whirlpool	8,104
148. Principal Mutual Life Insurance	8,007
149. Alco Standard	7,996
150. Banc One Corp.	7,857
151. Sun	7,792
152. Ralston Purina	7,705
153. Viacom	7,637
154. Colgate-Palmolive	7,588
155. Bankers Trust New York Corp.	7,503
156. Bergen Brunswig	7,484
157. CPC International	7,425
158. Unisys	7,400
159. Time Warner	7,396
160. Kimberly-Clark	7,364
161. Limited	7,321
162. Supermarkets General Holdings	7,226
163. Unocal	7,072
164. H.J. Heinz	7,047
165. Eli Lilly	7,001
166. USAir Group	6,997
167. Lincoln National	6,984
168. Federal Home Loan Mortgage	6,923
169. Johnson Controls	6,870
170. Dana	6,740
171. Northrop Grumman	6,711
172. Amerada Hess	6,699
173. Campbell Soup	6,690
174. Farmland Industries	6,678
175. Dean Witter Discover	6,603
176. Kellogg	6,562
177. Borden	6,495
178. Equitable	6,447
179. Warner-Lambert	6,416
180. W.R. Grace	6,381
181. Capital Cities/ABC	6,379
182. Tosco	6,366
183. PPG Industries	6,331
184. Salomon	6,278
185. Unicom	6,278
186. Cooper Industries	$6,258
187. First Union Corp.	6,254
188. Consolidated Edison of N.Y.	6,240
189. United Services Automobile Association	6,181
190. Guardian Life Insurance Co.	6,134
191. AFLAC	6,111
192. Lowe's	6,110
193. Levi Strauss Associates	6,074
194. Gillette	6,070
195. Honeywell	6,057
196. Eaton	6,052
197. Norwest Corp.	6,032
198. Reynolds Metals	6,013
199. Coca-Cola Enterprises	6,011
200. Entergy	5,963
201. Quaker Oats	5,955
202. Public Service Enterprise Group	5,916
203. Cardinal Health	5,790
204. Stone Container	5,749
205. Hallibruton	5,740
206. Dillard Department Stores	5,729
207. Chubb	5,710
208. Continental Airlines	5,670
209. John Hancock Mutual Life Insurance	5,669
210. Texas Utilities	5,664
211. American Electric Power	5,505
212. FPL Group	5,423
213. James River Corp. of Virginia	5,417
214. Foxmeyer Health	5,409
215. KeyCorp	5,373
216. TransAmerica	5,354
217. Navistar International	5,337
218. Mass. Mutual Life Insurance	5,332
219. Dresser Industries	5,331
220. Champion International	5,318
221. Black & Decker	5,248
222. Continental	5,164
223. Aramark	5,162
224. Mead	5,123
225. Tyson Foods	5,110
226. First Chicago Corp.	5,095
227. Merisel	5,019
228. Vons	4,997
229. Burlington Northern	4,995
230. VF	4,972
231. Wells Fargo & Co.	4,965
232. Tandy	4,944
233. Tele-Communications	4,936
234. Dun & Bradstreet	4,896
235. R.R. Donnelley & Sons	4,889
236. Union Carbide	4,865
237. Genuine Parts	4,858
238. American General	4,840
239. Bethlehem Steel	4,819
240. Corning	4,799
241. Cummins Engine	4,737
242. Scott Paper	4,726
243. St. Paul Cos.	4,701
244. Sun Microsystems	4,670
245. Ryder System	4,686

Rank/ Company	Sales (millions)
246. PNC Bank Corp	$4,684
247. Consolidated Freightways	4,680
248. Schering-Plough	4,657
249. Arrow Electronics	4,649
250. Microsoft	4,649
251. Household International	4,603
252. Panhandle Eastern	4,585
253. Norfolk Southern	4,581
254. Roadway Services	4,572
255. Eckerd	4,549
256. Bank of Boston	4,547
257. Litton Industries	4,535
258. LTV	4,529
259. Ingersoll-Rand	4,508
260. Paccar	4,499
261. Inland Steel Industries	4,497
262. Dominion Resources	4,491
263. Duke Power	4,489
264. Masco	4,468
265. American Standard	4,458
266. Crown Cork & Steel	4,452
267. Fleet Financial Group	4,445
268. Rite Aid	4,332
269. Eastman Chemical	4,329
270. Avon Products	4,325
271. Browning-Ferris Industries	4,314
272. Amerisource Distribution	4,302
273. Manpower	4,296
274. Office Depot	4,266
275. Bank of New York Co.	4,251
276. First Interstate Bancorp.	4,246
277. AON	4,157
278. Niagara Mohawk Power	4,152
279. Boise Cascade	4,142
280. Circuit City Stores	4,130
281. FMC	4,051
282. Service Merchandise	4,050
283. Peco Energy	4,041
284. Bindley Western	4,037
285. AMP	4,028
286. Loral	4,009
287. Houston Industries	4,002
288. Mutual of Omaha Insurance	3,982
289. Paine Webber Group	3,964
290. Chiquita Brands International	3,962
291. Mellon Bank Corp.	3,957
292. Nordstrom	3,894
293. Lyondell Petrochemical	3,857
294. Times Mirror	3,856
295. Berkshire Hathaway	3,848
296. TJX	3,843
297. Dole Food	3,842
298. General RE	3,826
299. Gannett	3,824
300. Pitney Bowes	3,823
301. Nike	3,790
302. Stop & Shop	3,789
303. United Healthcare	3,769
304. Conrail	3,733
305. Gap	3,723
306. CBS	3,712
307. General Dynamics	3,702
308. Humana	3,654
309. Owens-Illinois	3,653
310. Waban	3,650
311. General Public Utilities	$3,650
312. Northeast Utilities	3,643
313. Harcourt General	3,640
314. UNUM	3,624
315. Central & South West	3,623
316. CMS Energy	3,619
317. Hershey Foods	3,606
318. Giant Food	3,568
319. Upjohn	3,566
320. Avnet	3,552
321. Safeco	3,552
322. Dial	3,547
323. Rohm & Haas	3,534
324. Flagstar	3,526
325. Detroit Edison	3,519
326. Associated Insurance	3,511
327. Pacificorp	3,506
328. Seagate Technology	3,500
329. Air Products & Chemicals	3,485
330. Dell Computer	3,475
331. Illinois Tool Works	3,461
332. NBD Bancorp	3,461
333. Premark International	3,451
334. National Medical Enterprises	3,443
335. Bear Stearns	3,441
336. Marsh & McLennan	3,435
337. Trans World Airlines	3,408
338. Union Camp	3,396
339. H.F. Ahmanson	3,381
340. Maytag	3,372
341. Kerr-McGee	3,353
342. Owens-Corning Fiberglas	3,351
343. Thrifty-Payless Holdings	3,347
344. Penn Traffic	3,333
345. Harris	3,326
346. Phelps Dodge	3,289
347. Reebok	3,288
348. Allmerica Financial	3,273
349. Tyco International	3,263
350. Suntrust Banks	3,252
351. Jefferson Smurfit	3,233
352. USF&G	3,221
353. Centex	3,214
354. Mattel	3,205
355. Lear Seating	3,148
356. Southern Pacific Rail	3,143
357. Fred Meyer	3,128
358. Intelligent Electronics	3,127
359. Sherwin-Williams	3,100
360. Barnett Banks	3,098
361. Dover	3,085
362. Long Island Lighting	3,067
363. Hormel Foods	3,065
364. Mapco	3,059
365. Student Loan Marketing Assn.	3,057
366. Reliance Group Holdings	3,047
367. Louisiana-Pacific	3,040
368. Consolidated Natural Gas	3,036
369. W.W. Granger	3,023
370. Agway	3,017
371. Spiegel	3,016
372. Willamette Indutries	3,008
373. Best Buy	3,007
374. Great Western Financial Corp.	2,998
375. Peter Kiewit Sons	2,991
376. ServiceMaster	$2,985
377. Beverly Enterprises	2,984
378. Smith's Food & Drug Centers	2,981
379. Nucor	2,976
380. Universal	2,975
381. U.S. Healthcare	2,974
382. Wachovia Corp.	2,970
383. HealthTrust	2,970
384. AllTel	2,962
385. Providian	2,959
386. Santa Fe Pacific	2,955
387. Temple-Inland	2,938
388. Cinergy	2,924
389. National City Corp.	2,905
390. Pacificare Health Systems	2,893
391. Carolina Power & Light	2,877
392. Yellow	2,868
393. Avery Dennison	2,857
394. Morton International	2,850
395. Brunswick	2,836
396. Bruno's	2,835
397. Columbia Gas System	2,833
398. Nash Finch	2,832
399. Hercules	2,821
400. Mercantiie Stores	2,820
401. Transco Energy	2,816
402. Turner Broadcasting	2,809
403. Readers Digest Association	2,806
404. Noram Energy	2,801
405. American President	2,794
406. Shaw Industries	2,788
407. Cyprus Amax Minerals	2,788
408. Baltimore Gas & Electric	2,783
409. Florida Progress	2,772
410. Provident Life	2,762
411. McGraw-Hill	2,761
412. Alumax	2,755
413. Armstrong World Industries	2,753
414. Caldor	2,749
415. Aid Association for Lutherans	2,734
416. Payless Cashways	2,733
417. Pennsylvania Power & Light	2,725
418. Geico	2,716
419. Praxair	2,711
420. Pacific Enterprises	2,702
421. Gateway 2000	2,701
422. Williams	2,673
423. Hasbro	2,670
424. Pittston	2,667
425. Whitman	2,659
426. Olin	2,658
427. Knight-Ridder	2,649
428. Turner Corp.	2,639
429. EG&G	2,633
430. Diamond Shamrock	2,621
431. Westvaco	2,613
432. United States Shoe	2,598
433. Ball	2,595
434. Southwest Airlines	2,592
435. Food 4 Less Supermarkets	2,585
436. Computer Sciences	2,583
437. Parker Hannifin	2,576
438. Cotter	2,574
439. Pennzoil	2,563
440. Manville	2,560
441. Republic New York Corp.	$2,560
442. Becton Dickinson	2,560
443. Comerica	2,559
444. Longs Drug Stres	2,558
445. First Fidelity Bacorp.	2,553
446. Varity	2,521
447. Stanley Works	2,511
448. Baker Hughes	2,505
449. Revco Drug Stores	2,504
450. Morrison Knudsen	2,500
451. Corestates Financial Group	2,497
452. Northern States Power	2,486
453. Grand Union Holdings	2,477
454. Ultramar	2,475
455. FHP International	2,473
456. Automatic Data Processing	2,469
457. Roundy's	2,465
458. Hechinger	2,454
459. Allegheny Power System	2,452
460. Dean Foods	2,431
461. Caremark International	2,426
462. York International	2,422
463. Centerior Energy	2,421
464. Tech Data	2,418
465. Progressive	2,415
466. Owens & Minor	2,396
467. Teledyne	2,391
468. Engelhard	2,386
469. American Medical Holdings	2,382
470. First Bank System	2,375
471. Fleetwood Enterprises	2,369
472. Ohio Edison	2,368
473. AST Research	2,367
474. Conner Peripherals	2,365
475. Graybar Electric	2,364
476. Kelly Services	2,363
477. New York Times	2,358
478. Ace Hardware	2,326
479. Shawmut National Corp.	2,316
480. Polaroid	2,312
481. Health Systems International	2,306
482. Sonoco Products	2,300
483. Fruit of the Loom	2,298
484. National Semiconductor	2,295
485. Boatmen's Bancshares	2,294
486. Hannaford Brothers	2,292
487. USG	2,290
488. Foster Wheeler	2,271
489. Olsten	2,260
490. Phoenix Home Life Insurance	2,254
491. New England Electrical Systems	2,243
492. New England Mutual Life Insurance	2,238
493. Witco	2,235
494. Echlin	2,230
495. International Multifoods	2,225
496. Lutheran Brotherhood	2,223
497. Microage	2,221
498. LDDS Communications	2,221
499. First Financial Management	2,208
500. Dow Corning	2,205

Source: *Fortune* (May 15, 1995); reprinted by permission of Time-Life.

THE TOP *FORTUNE* 1,000 COMPANIES, BY INDUSTRY, 1994

Industry, company (*Fortune* 1,000 rank)

Advertising, marketing
- Interpublic Group (537)
- Omnicom Group (588)
- QVC (687)

Aerospace
- Boeing (29)
- United Technologies (31)
- McDonnell-Douglas (69)

Airlines
- AMR (American) (49)
- UAL (United) (62)
- Delta Air Lines (80)

Apparel
- Levi Strauss Associates (193)
- VF (230)
- Fruit of the Loom (483)

Beverages
- Coca-Cola (48)
- Anheuser-Busch (85)
- Coca-Cola Enterprises (199)

Brokerage
- Merrill Lynch (40)
- Lehman Brothers (122)
- Salomon (184)

Building materials
- Corning (240)
- Owens-Illinois (309)
- Owens-Corning Fiberglas (342)

Chemicals
- E.I. du Pont de Nemours (14)
- Dow Chemical (33)
- Occidental Petroleum (117)
- Monsanto (145)
- W.R. Grace (180)

Commercial banks
- Citicorp (17)
- BankAmerica Corp. (46)
- Nationsbank Corp. (71)
- Chemical Bank Corp. (74)
- J.P. Morgan & Co. (87)

Computer/Data services
- Dun & Bradstreet (234)
- Microsoft (250)
- Computer Sciences (436)

Computers, office equipment
- IBM (7)
- Hewlett-Packard (22)
- Digital Equipment (65)
- Compaq Computer (100)
- Apple Computer (123)

Diversified Financials
- ITT (23)
- FNMA (36)
- American Express (55)

Electric and gas utilities
- Pacific Gas & Electric (102)
- Scecorp (139)
- Southern (142)
- Unicom (185)
- Con Edison of N.Y. (188)

Electronics
- General Electric (6)
- Motorola (28)
- Intel (90)
- Rockwell International (94)
- Texas Instruments (106)

Engineering/Construction
- Fluor (134)
- Halliburton (205)
- Centex (353)

Entertainment
- Walt Disney (108)
- Viacom (153)
- Time Warner (159)

Food
- Philip Morris (10)
- ConAgra (24)
- Sara Lee (56)
- IBP (83)
- Acher Daniels Midland (92)

Food and drugstores
- Kroger (25)
- American Stores (39)
- Safeway (54)
- Albertson's (88)
- Winn-Dixie Stores (98)

Food services
- Pepsico (20)
- McDonald's (140)
- Aramark (223)

Forest and paper products
- International Paper (60)
- Georgia-Pacific (73)
- Weyerhauser (103)
- Kimberly-Clark (160)
- Stone Container (204)

Furniture
- Legget & Platt (566)
- Interco (592)
- Herman Miller (888)

General merchandisers
- Wal-Mart Stores (4)
- Sears Roebuck (9)
- K mart (15)
- Dayton Hudson (30)
- J.C. Penney (32)

Health care
- Columbia/HCA Healthcare (97)
- United Healthcare (303)
- Humana (308)
- National Medical Enterprises (334)
- Beverly Enterprises (377)

Hotels/Casinos/Resorts
- Marriott International (138)
- Bally Entertainment (624)
- Promus (630)

Industrial/Farm equipment
- Caterpillar (61)
- Tenneco (68)
- Deere (127)
- Dresser Industries (219)
- Black & Decker (221)

Insurance (stock)
- American International Group (26)
- Travelers Inc. (37)
- Cigna (38)
- Aetna Life & Casualty (42)
- Lincoln National (167)

Insurance (mutual)
- State Farm Group (12)
- Prudential Insurance (13)
- Metropolitan Life Insurance (27)
- New York Life Insurance (84)
- Nationwide Insurance (96)

Metal products
- Gillette (194)
- Masco (264)
- Crown Cork & Seal (266)

Metals
- Alcoa (104)
- Reynolds Metals (198)
- Bethlehem Steel (239)
- LTV (258)
- Inland Steel Industries (261)

Mining/Crude oil production
- Cyprus Amax Minerals (407)
- Asarco (530)
- Freeport-McMoran (538)

Miscellaneous
- ServiceMaster (376)
- PHH (511)
- H&R Block (615)

Motor vehicles and parts
- General Motors (1)
- Ford Motor (2)
- Chrysler (11)
- TRW (126)
- Johnson Controls (169)

Package/Freight delivery
- United Parcel Service (35)
- Federal Express (136)
- Pittston (424)

Petroleum refining
- Exxon (3)
- Mobil (8)
- Texaco (16)
- Chevron (18)
- Amoco (21)

Pharmaceuticals
- Johnson & Johnson (52)
- Merck (59)
- Bristol-Myers Squibb (86)

Pipelines
- Enron (129)
- Panhandle Eastern (252)
- Transco Energy (401)

Publishing and printing
- R.R. Donnelley (235)
- Times Mirror (294)
- Gannett (299)

Railroads
- CSX (113)
- Union Pacific (146)
- Burlington Northern (229)

Rubber and plastic products
- Goodyear Tire & Rubber (81)
- Premark International (333)
- Rubbermaid (503)

Savings institutions
- H.F. Ahmanson (339)
- Great Western Finance (374)
- Golden West Financial Corporation (553)

Scientific/Photo equipment
- Xerox (41)
- Eastman Kodak (43)
- Minn. Mining & Manufacturing (58)

Soaps and cosmetics
- Procter & Gamble (19)
- Colgate-Palmolive (154)
- Avon Products (270)

Specialist retailers
- Price Costco (47)
- Home Depot (77)
- Melville (93)
- Toys "R" Us (131)
- Woolworth (143)

Telecommunications
- AT&T (5)
- GTE (34)
- BellSouth (44)
- Bell Atlantic (63)
- MCI Communications (66)

Temporary Help
- Manpower (273)
- Kelly Services (476)
- Olsten (489)

Textiles
- Shaw Industries (406)
- Burlington Industries (515)
- Springs Industries (526)

Tobacco
- RJR Nabisco Holdings (57)
- American Brands (137)
- Universal (380)

Transportation equipment
- Brunswick (395)
- Trinity Industries (581)
- Harley-Davidson (642)

Truck leasing
- Ryder System (245)
- Amerco (783)
- Penske Truck Leasing (839)

Trucking
- Consolidated Frgtwys (247)
- Roadway Services (254)
- Yellow (392)

Waste management
- WMX Technologies (107)
- Browning-Ferris Industries (271)
- Ogden (520)

Source: *Fortune* magazine; printed with permission from Time-Life Inc.

TOP 50 FRANCHISES, BY NUMBER OF FRANCHISES, 1993

Rank/Franchise	Business	Franchise fees	Number of franchises
1. 7-Eleven Convenience Stores	Convenience stores	varies	10,604
2. McDonald's	Fast food restaurants	$22,500	9,770
3. Subway	Submarine sandwich restaurants	10,000	8,013
4. Burger King Corp.	Fast food restaurants	40,000	5,903
5. Century 21 Real Estate Corp.	Real estate brokers	up to 28,000	5,891
6. Dairy Queen	Ice cream stores	30,000	5,304
7. Jazzercise Inc.	Dance/exercise classes	325–650	4,948
8. ServiceMaster	Commercial cleaning services	8,700–19,700	4,131
9. Jani-King	Commercial cleaning services	6,500–14,000+	3,793
10. Baskin-Robbins USA Co.	Ice cream stores	0	3,557
11. Chem-Dry	Carpet, upholstery, and drapery cleaning	11,400	3,523
12. Blockbuster Video	Videotape sales and rentals	20,000–55,000	3,389
13. Little Caesar's Pizza	Takeout pizza shops	20,000	3,339
14. Dunkin' Donuts	Donuts and bakery products	40,000	3,162
15. Kentucky Fried Chicken	Fast food fried chicken restaurants	25,000	3,019
16. Wendy's International Inc.	Fast food restaurants	25,000	2,880
17. Snap-on Tools	Professional tools and equipment	3,000	2,821
18. Coverall North America Inc.	Commercial office cleaning	3,250–33,600	2,735
19. Electronic Realty Associates	Real estate services	16,900–18,900	2,713
20. Hardee's	Fast food restaurants	15,000	2,571
21. Choice Hotels International	Hotels, inns, and resorts	15,000–40,000	2,515
22. Arby's Inc.	Roast beef fast food restaurants	25,000–37,500	2,335
23. Midas International Corp.	Auto maintenance centers	20,000	2,208
24. Mail Boxes Etc.	Postal/business/ communication services	24,950	2,106
25. RE/Max International Inc.	Real estate brokers	15,000–25,000	2,013
26. Coldwell Banker Residential Affiliates, Inc.	Residential real estate brokers	$7,500–20,000	1,737
27. Holiday Inn Worldwide	Hotels	varies	1,575
28. Shafiee Corp./RoboClean	Ceiling/air-duct cleaning	5,000–25,000	1,448
29. Fantastic Sam's	Hair salons	25,000–30,000	1,314
30. Decorating Den	Interior decorating services	8,900–23,900	1,296
31. Sonic Drive-In Restaurants	Fast food drive-in restaurants	15,000	1,129
32. CleanNet USA Inc.	Commercial office cleaning	2,950–32,000	1,105
33. Budget Rent A Car	Auto and truck rentals	15,000+	1,058
34. Diet Center	Weight loss programs and products	18,000	1,051
35. Super 8 Motels Inc.	Economy motels	20,000+	1,017
36. Uniglobe Travel	Travel agencies	47,500	989
37. The Medicine Shoppe	Pharmacies	up to 18,000	960
38. Miracle Ear	Hearing aids	25,000+	954
39. Kwik-Kopy Corp.	Printing services	25,000	930
40. Ben Franklin Stores, Inc.	Variety/craft stores	24,000	925
41. Novus Windshield Repair	Windshield repair	11,000	898
42. Minuteman Press International Inc.	Printing centers	32,500	895
43. Meineke Discount Mufflers	Auto maintenance centers	22,500	884
44. One Hour Martinizing Dry Cleaning	Dry cleaning and laundry services	25,000	843
45. Servpro	Carpet, upholstery, and drapery cleaning	18,800	837
46. Sir Speedy Printing Inc.	Printing services	17,500	833
47. Thrifty Rent-A-Car Systems	Vehicle rentals and leasing	8,500+	816
48. O.P.E.N. Cleaning Systems	Office/commercial cleaning	3,000–120,000	816
49. Pip Printing	Business printing services	40,000	801
50. Matco Tools	Automotive tools	0	768

Note: Includes only companies that have a U.S. disclosure document verified by *Entrepreneur* magazine. Does not include franchises owned by the company. **Source:** *Entrepreneur* (January 1994).

SMALL BUSINESS

Small businesses account for 99 percent of the 19 million nonfarm businesses in the United States today. Sole proprietorships make up 13.2 million of these small businesses, while 1.8 million are partnerships and 4 million are corporations. Small businesses employ 55 percent of the private work force, make 44 percent of all sales in America, and produce 38 percent of the nation's gross national product. Since 1978 the number of small businesses has increased 56 percent.

Most Americans—nearly 67 percent—get their first employment experience through small firms. Small businesses lead the way in the creation of new jobs in the American economy. Between 1981 and 1986, small businesses with fewer than 500 employees created 62 percent of the 8.9 million new jobs in the country. Among the fastest-growing small businesses today are eating and drinking establishments, trucking firms, doctors' offices, computer and data services, and amusements and recreation services.

The standards used by the U.S. Small Business Administration to determine whether a business is small vary from industry to industry and are relative within an industry. In manufacturing, a firm with 500 to 1,500 employees is classified a small business. In construction, this classification applies to companies with gross annual receipts between $7 million and $14.7 million. A company in the services and retail industry with gross annual receipts between $2.5 million and $14 million is considered a small business. A wholesaler with as many as 100 employees also will be classified as a small business. Thus a steel mill with 1,200 employees is considered to be a small business right along with a mom-and-pop candy store.

Franchising

Franchising, a century-old tradition, has never been more popular in the United States than it is now. Franchises did more than $260 billion in sales in 1993, a 6% increase over the previous year. Franchised business represented nearly 40 percent of all U.S. retail sales. The Department of Commerce estimates that by the year 2000, franchising will account for more than half of all sales. More than 8 million people work in over half a million franchise outlets around the United States and the world.

ADVERTISING

If they wish to make a profit, both large and small purveyors of consumer products and services must find ways to let their potential customers know about their business. Since the U.S. media (newspapers, radio, television, magazines) also are run as profit-earning enterprises, it seems natural that the two forces would be joined by their common needs. This in fact happened about 150 years ago, when whole pages of newspapers were jammed with the unadorned but paid announcements of everything from patent medicines to clothing and hardware. By 1900 so many large businesses had sprung up (Procter & Gamble and Kellogg's, for example) that nationally distributed magazines (including *Ladies' Home Journal*) became enormously profitable ventures based on the advertising placed by these firms. By 1910 over $1 billion a year was being spent on advertising, which was itself now entrenched as a business of its own with established practices and with dozens of schools specially designed to teach the most persuasive selling techniques.

Throughout the 20th century, advertising expanded along with the economy and it provided

American business with a distinctly American voice that moved the merchandise in an unprecedented manner. Few facts reveal the extraordinary growth of the so-called mass-consumption society as vividly as those dealing with the advertising business. In 1950, as the postwar economy began to heat up, American business spent $5.7 billion to advertise its goods and services; by 1960 that figure would double, and then almost double again by 1970. Between 1970 and 1990, as the Baby Boom generation entered the marketplace and the economy expanded, advertising expenditures grew at a spiraling rate, topping $100 billion in 1986. That rate of growth has not been sustained, but advertising spending continues to reach new heights, nevertheless. Total expenditures on all forms of advertising in 1994 were more than $150 billion.

Nearly 60 percent of all advertising dollars are spent to place ads in newspapers or magazines or to run commercials on radio and television. The biggest advertisers are the nation's

ADVERTISING EXPENDITURES IN THE U. S., 1776–1994

(millions of dollars)

Year	Amount[1]	Year	Amount[1]
1776	$ 0.2	1955	$ 9,150.0
1800	1.0	1960	11,960.0
1820	3.0	1965	15,250.0
1840	7.0	1970	19,550.0
1850	12.0	1975	28,160.0
1860	22.0	1980	54,780.0
1867	40.0	1985	94,750.0
1876	150.0	1986	102,140.0
1880	175.0	1987	109,787.0
1890	300.0	1988	118,050.0
1900	450.0	1989	125,550.0
1909	1,000.0	1990	128,640.0
1915	1,100.0	1991	126,400.0
1940	2,110.0	1992	131,290.0
1945	2,840.0	1993	138,080.0
1950	5,700.0	1994	150,030.0

1. These are estimated figures of the monies spent on placing advertising in all media; the costs of producing the advertising are not included. **Sources:** McCann-Erickson, N.Y.; figures through 1975 were compiled for *Advertising Age* and reprinted July 5, 1976.

TOP 25 U.S.-BASED CONSOLIDATED AD AGENCIES, BY GROSS DOMESTIC INCOME, 1994 (millions of dollars)

U.S. rank/Agency, headquarters	U.S. gross income	U.S. gross billings	U.S. employees	Worldwide gross income	Rank by worldwide gross income
1. Young & Rubicam, New York	$424.0	$3,604.8	1,378	$ 985.5	2
2. DDB Needham Worldwide, New York	407.6	3,306.3	3,426	875.7	5
3. BBDO Worldwide, New York	367.4	3,362.4	2,622	917.7	3
4. J. Walter Thompson, New York	351.7	2,460.4	2,199	915.7	4
5. Grey Advertising, New York	332.1	2,215.0	2,501	749.8	8
6. Saatchi & Saatchi Advertising, New York	329.6	2,637.1	1,801	690.5	9
7. Leo Burnett Co., Chicago	322.1	2,226.3	2,018	677.5	10
8. Lintas Worldwide, New York	307.3	2,049.6	1,820	760.5	7
9. True North Communications, Chicago	306.7	3,055.2	2,361	619.0	11
10. McCann-Erickson Worldwide, New York	274.2	1,828.6	1,725	1,076.1	1
11. D'Arcy Masius Benton & Bowles, New York	273.6	2,690.4	2,561	587.9	12
12. Ogilvy & Mather Worldwide, New York	247.2	2,303.9	1,725	768.7	6
13. Bozell Worldwide, New York	234.4	1,895.0	1,501	299.6	15
14. Bates Worldwide, New York	158.0	1,248.3	1,105	516.7	13
15. Lowe Group, New York	144.7	1,052.1	950	374.4	14
16. TMP Worldwide, New York	117.7	784.8	N.A.	127.1	17
17. Chiat/Day, Venice, Calif.	106.6	820.0	533	122.9	19
18. Campbell Mithun Esty, Minneapolis	106.3	850.6	668	125.1	18
19. DIMAC Direct, Bridgeton, Mo.	99.3	271.4	N.A.	99.3	21
20. N. W. Ayer & Partners, New York	98.8	861.2	N.A.	101.0	20
21. Wells Rich Greene BDDP, New York	95.8	840.6	499	95.8	22
22. Gage Marketing Group, Minneapolis	95.7	638.3	N.A.	95.7	23
23. Ketchum Communications, Pittsburgh	76.7	668.9	N.A.	94.0	24
24. Ross Roy Group, Bloomfield Hills, Mich.	76.2	508.0	N.A.	76.2	25
25. Messner Vetere Berger McNamee Schmetterer, New York	64.1	708.0	310	N.A.	N.A.

Note: N.A. = not available. Includes income from advertising-related subsidiaries and international networks. **Source:** *Advertising Age* (Apr. 10, 1995); reprinted by permission of Crain Communications, Inc.

TOTAL U.S. ADVERTISING VOLUME BY MEDIUM, 1993–94 (millions of dollars)

Medium	1993 Expenditures	1993 Percent share	1994 Expenditures	1994 Percent share	Percent change 1993–94
Newspapers, total	$32,025	23.4%	$34,356	22.9%	7.3%
National	3,620	2.7	3,906	2.6	7.9
Local	28,405	20.7	30,450	20.3	7.2
Magazines, total	7,357	5.3	7,916	5.3	7.6
Weeklies	2,850	2.1	3,140	2.1	10.2
Women's	2,009	1.4	2,106	1.4	4.8
Monthlies	2,498	1.8	2,670	1.8	6.9
Farm publications	243	0.2	262	.02	8.0
Television, total	30,584	22.4	34,167	22.8	11.7
Four TV networks	10,209	7.8	10,942	7.3	7.2
Cable TV networks	1,970	1.3	2,321	1.5	17.8
Syndication	1,576	1.3	1,734	1.2	10.0
Spot (national)	7,800	5.8	8,993	6.0	15.3
Spot (local)	8,435	6.1	9,464	6.3	12.2
Cable (nonnetwork)	594	0.4	713	0.5	20.0
Radio, total	9,457	6.6	10,529	7.0	11.3
Network	458	0.3	463	0.3	1.0
Spot (national)	$ 1,657	1.2%	$ 1,902	1.3%	14.8%
Spot (local)	7,342	5.1	8,164	5.4	11.2
Direct mail	27,266	19.3	29,638	19.7	8.7
Business papers	3,260	2.4	3,358	2.2	3.0
Outdoor, total	1,090	0.8	1,167	.08	7.1
National	605	0.5	648	0.4	7.1
Local	485	0.3	519	0.4	7.1
Yellow Pages, total	9,517	7.1	9,825	6.6	3.2
National	1,230	0.9	1,314	0.9	6.8
Local	8,287	6.2	8,511	5.7	2.7
Miscellaneous, total	17,281	12.5	18,812	12.5	8.9
National	12,759	9.2	13,928	9.3	9.1
Local	4,522	3.3	4,884	3.2	8.0
Total national	80,010	57.9	87,325	58.2	9.1
Total local	58,070	42.1	62,705	41.8	8.0
Grand total	**$138,080**	**100.0%**	**$150,030**	**100.0%**	**8.7%**

Source: *Advertising Age*, May 8, 1995.

largest manufacturers of automobiles, food, soft drinks, tobacco, and beer.

Most advertising dollars are filtered through about 6,000 advertising agencies, who mainly create the ads and buy the space or time from the media. The agency business has undergone a dramatic restructuring recently, as the corporate raider mentality invaded Madison Avenue with a vengeance. Many of the largest agencies, most of them with worldwide connections, have merged to form enormous corporations. The largest advertising organization in the world is the WPP Group, a London-based conglomerate—its U.S. agencies include Ogilvy & Mather and J. Walter Thompson—that had a worldwide gross income of $2.8 billion in 1994.

THE 100 LEADING U.S. ADVERTISERS, 1991–94 (millions of dollars)

1994 Rank/Company (1993 rank)	Total spending 1991	1993	1994
1. Procter and Gamble Co. (1)	$1,166.4	$1,299.9	$1,459.8
2. General Motors Corp. (2)	1,056.5	1,099.3	1,377.5
3. Philip Morris Cos. (3)	1,110.4	999.7	1,311.8
4. Ford Motor Co. (4)	517.7	722.8	892.7
5. Chrysler Corp. (7)	414.8	585.3	750.1
6. AT&T Co. (8)	391.7	481.4	669.5
7. PepsiCo Inc. (5)	542.0	633.1	669.5
8. Sears, Roebuck & Co. (6)	462.3	594.7	656.0
9. Toyota Motor Corp. (9)	442.5	463.5	588.8
10. General Mills (11)	419.1	429.4	493.9
11. Kellogg Co. (12)	381.3	413.9	483.6
12. Walt Disney Co. (15)	257.3	403.7	477.5
13. Johnson & Johnson (16)	371.1	385.9	472.5
14. Time Warner Inc. (18)	311.3	366.9	454.3
15. Nestlé SA (14)	307.6	406.4	452.9
16. McDonald's Corp. (13)	387.4	410.0	425.6
17. General Motors Corp. Local Dealers (25)	123.6	308.4	418.9
18. Unilever PLC (10)	371.4	461.0	407.5
19. May Department Stores Co. (19)	194.0	363.2	376.3
20. Federated Dept. Stores (45)	111.4	178.4	374.7
21. General Motors Corp. Dealers Assoc. (20)	198.0	352.2	369.2
22. News Corp. Ltd. (21)	358.6	350.0	361.0
23. Honda Motor Co. (33)	242.5	253.8	353.2
24. Nissan Motor Co. (23)	212.0	320.4	343.9
25. Grand Metropolitan PLC (28)	326.7	285.1	342.0
26. Sony Corp. (17)	262.8	374.1	330.7
27. American Home Products Corp. (29)	290.6	280.9	308.4
28. MCI Communications Corp. (40)	94.1	199.5	318.8
29. Ford Motor Co. Local Dealers (22)	87.4	342.8	314.2
30. Circuit City Stores Inc. (31)	128.2	262.2	311.3
31. Anheuser-Busch Cos. (24)	327.9	311.9	306.7
32. K mart Corp. (27)	186.5	293.9	287.3
33. Warner-Lambert Co. (32)	224.5	256.6	284.0
34. J.C. Penney Co. Inc. (30)	105.2	264.9	281.2
35. National Amusements Inc. (N.A.)	N.A.	N.A.	278.4
36. RJR Nabisco Holdings Corp. (N.A.)	N.A.	N.A.	$273.6
37. Coca-Cola Co. (44)	$218.8	$187.6	268.9
38. Ford Motor Co. Dealers Assoc. (41)	126.1	192.7	244.9
39. Dayton Hudson Corp. (38)	108.7	210.7	242.4
40. Matsushita Electric Industrial Co. Ltd. (42)	146.1	191.7	227.7
41. Mazda Motor Corp. (47)	157.2	165.6	223.1
42. Hasbro Inc. (34)	161.1	221.8	220.2
43. Toyota Motor Co. Ltd. Local Dealers (36)	68.7	213.2	215.3
44. Mars Inc. (46)	128.2	170.3	200.6
45. American Express Co. (35)	156.2	214.9	194.9
46. Quaker Oats Co. (64)	111.7	115.8	191.6
47. Valassis Communications Inc. (43)	239.6	189.0	178.6
48. Sprint Corp. (50)	N.A.	143.4	176.8
49. Mattel Inc. (52)	63.8	140.4	172.4
50. Bristol-Myers Squibb Co. (57)	184.0	130.4	165.0
51. U.S. Government (49)	123.4	152.8	165.0
52. Sara Lee Corp. (51)	129.5	142.1	162.2
53. Mitsubishi Motors Corp. (90)	77.0	87.0	160.2
54. Chrysler Corp. Local Dealers (48)	43.0	161.9	157.2
55. Roll International Corp. (58)	77.2	128.0	157.0
56. Wendy's International (56)	94.4	131.3	156.4
57. Clorox Co. (53)	127.8	138.8	156.0
58. Ralston Purina Co. (55)	141.6	134.2	149.9
59. Tandy Corp. (65)	79.0	115.3	144.0
60. Nike Inc. (54)	109.5	137.7	137.1
61. Wm. Wrigley, Jr. Co. (61)	111.6	118.8	134.1
62. Bayer Group (92)	55.8	85.5	133.3
63. Campbell Soup Co. (77)	109.5	100.0	129.8
64. Adolph Coors Co. (63)	130.3	116.7	129.8
65. Gillette Co. (82)	93.1	95.0	129.2
66. Wal-Mart Stores (72)	76.7	106.1	129.0
67. SmithKline Beecham PLC (66)	83.3	113.2	124.9
68. Chrysler Corp. Dealer Assn. (69)	90.8	111.8	124.3
69. Joh A. Benckiser (78)	12.7	99.6	121.6
70. Nissan Motor Co. Ltd. Local Dealers (67)	61.1	112.7	117.9
71. International Business Machines Corp. (94)	$ 49.5	$ 83.9	$117.1
72. Broadway Stores Inc. (N.A.)	N.A.	N.A.	116.3
73. Schering-Plough Corp. (62)	95.9	118.2	112.7
74. Visa International (87)	52.1	91.4	119.9
75. Montgomery Ward & Co. Inc. (76)	63.6	101.5	110.9
76. Turner Broadcasting System Inc. (N.A.)	N.A.	N.A.	110.0
77. S.C. Johnson & Sons Inc (68)	93.1	112.2	108.9
78. Kimberly-Clark Corp. (83)	85.4	94.7	107.2
79. Reckitt & Colman PLC (N.A.)	N.A.	N.A.	104.5
80. General Electric Co. (86)	90.8	91.9	101.9
81. Hershey Foods Corp. (81)	74.0	95.2	101.0
82. Dillard Department Stores (79)	26.2	99.1	100.4
83. Toyota Auto Dealers Assn. (75)	73.4	102.5	98.7
84. Volkswagen AG (N.A.)	N.A.	N.A.	95.7
85. Upjohn Co. (93)	69.2	84.8	95.3
86. American Stores Co. (80)	127.0	98.2	94.0
87. United Dairy Industry Assn. (74)	.5	102.7	94.0
88. Bertelsmann AG (N.A.)	N.A.	N.A.	93.5
89. Helene Curtis Industries (70)	91.3	111.7	93.1
90. ConAgra (97)	112.0	82.1	93.0
91. Citicorp (59)	69.2	122.0	92.3
92. Goodyear Tire & Rubber Co. (96)	54.9	83.0	90.7
93. Levi Strauss Associates Inc. (73)	53.8	103.6	89.6
94. Bradford Exchange (88)	77.0	89.1	89.3
95. Delta Air Lines Inc. (N.A.)	N.A.	N.A.	88.5
96. MasterCard International Inc. (N.A.)	N.A.	N.A.	87.2
97. Dr. Pepper/Seven-Up Cos. Inc (98)	N.A.	80.9	86.7
98. Honda Motor Co. Ltd. Local Dealers (84)	37.1	92.3	86.6
99. The Wiz (N.A.)	N.A.	N.A.	86.6
100. BWW AG	N.A.	N.A.	85.5
TOTAL, top 100 companies	**N.A.**	**$23,531.2**	**$26,900.4**

Note: N.A. = not available. **Source:** Competitive Media Reporting, *The Leading Advertisers 1991–1994* (1995).

U.S. ENERGY

Energy is usually measured in millions or larger quantities of British thermal units (Btu). One Btu is approximately equal to the energy released in burning a wooden match. An engine burning 8 gallons of gasoline releases 1 million (10^6) Btu. One quadrillion (10^{15}) Btu is the equivalent of the energy released from an engine burning 8 billion gallons of gasoline.

Historically, three fossil fuels have accounted for the bulk of U.S. energy production, which in 1993 topped 65 quadrillion Btu, the third straight year in which energy production declined. For the first time since 1984, natural gas (both dry and liquid forms) accounted for the largest share of domestic energy production, followed closely by coal and crude oil. Coal dominated domestic production between 1949 and 1951 and again from 1984 until 1992. In all other years, crude oil and natural gas dominated.

The relationship between total energy consumption and real gross domestic product (GDP) is a primary indicator of the energy intensity of the economy. Energy consumption more than doubled between 1949 and 1973 (from 30 quadrillion to 74 quadrillion Btu), increasing at approximately the same rate as GDP. But although energy consumption reached a record high 83.96 quadrillion Btu in 1993, energy consumption per constant (1987) dollar of GDP was only 16,340 Btu, a 29 percent decline since 1970.

A second indicator is per capita consumption. In the 1960s and early 1970s, per capita end-use consumption rose from 212 million Btu in 1960 to a peak of 285 million Btu in 1973. Thereafter, per capita consumption dropped to 225 million Btu in 1983 before rising again to 245 million Btu in 1993.

U.S. ENERGY CONSUMPTION, TOTAL AND PER CAPITA, 1950–93

	Total energy consumption (quadrillion Btu)		Per capita consumption (million Btu)	
Year	Total	End-use[1]	Total	End-use[1]
1950	33.08	29.37	219	194
1955	38.82	34.02	235	206
1960	43.80	37.96	244	212
1965	52.68	44.93	272	232
1970	66.43	54.91	327	270
1975	70.55	56.16	327	261
1980	75.96	58.59	335	259
1985	73.98	55.12	310	231
1990	81.26	59.72	327	240
1991	81.12	59.18	322	235
1992	82.14	60.31	322	236
1993[2]	83.96	63.30	326	245

1. Total energy consumption less losses from generation, transmission, and distribution of electricity, power plant use, and unaccounted-for losses. 2. Preliminary. **Source:** U.S. Dept. of Energy, *Annual Energy Review 1993* (1994).

U.S. ENERGY OVERVIEW, 1993

PRODUCTION 65.81 quadrillion Btu		CONSUMPTION 83.96 quadrillion Btu	
Natural gas[1]	32%	Petroleum products	40%
Coal	31	Natural gas	25
Crude oil[2]	22	Coal	23
Nuclear electric power	10	Nuclear power	8
Hydroelectric power	4	Hydroelectric power	4
Other	0.3	Other	0.2

Note: Preliminary figures. 1. Includes natural gas plant liquids. 2. Includes lease condensate. **Source:** U.S. Dept. of Energy, *Annual Energy Review, 1993* (1994).

U.S. ENERGY OVERVIEW, 1960–93 (quadrillion Btu)

Activity and energy source	1960	1970	1975	1980	1985	1990	1992	1993[1]
PRODUCTION								
Crude oil[2]	14.93	20.40	17.73	18.25	18.99	15.57	15.22	14.48
Natural gas plant liquids	1.46	2.51	2.37	2.25	2.24	2.17	2.36	2.40
Natural gas[3]	12.66	21.67	19.64	19.91	16.98	18.36	18.38	18.98
Coal	10.82	14.61	14.99	18.60	19.33	22.46	21.59	20.49
Nuclear electric power	0.01	0.24	1.90	2.74	4.15	6.16	6.61	6.52
Hydroelectric power	1.61	2.63	3.15	2.90	2.97	2.93	2.50	2.76
Other[4]	(5)	0.02	0.07	0.11	0.21	0.20	0.19	0.18
Total	**41.49**	**62.07**	**59.86**	**64.76**	**64.87**	**67.85**	**66.85**	**65.81**
IMPORTS								
Crude oil[6]	2.20	2.81	8.72	11.19	6.81	12.77	13.25	14.63
Petroleum products[7]	1.80	4.66	4.23	3.46	3.80	4.35	3.71	3.67
Natural gas	0.16	0.85	0.98	1.01	0.95	1.55	2.16	2.29
Other[8]	0.07	0.07	0.19	0.31	0.54	0.32	0.52	0.60
Total	**4.23**	**8.39**	**14.11**	**15.97**	**12.10**	**18.99**	**19.65**	**21.19**
EXPORTS								
Coal	1.02	1.94	1.76	2.42	2.44	2.77	2.68	1.95
Crude oil and petroleum products	0.43	0.55	0.44	1.16	1.66	1.82	2.01	2.11
Other[9]	0.03	0.18	0.16	0.14	0.14	0.31	0.33	0.25
Total	**1.48**	**2.66**	**2.36**	**3.72**	**4.23**	**4.91**	**5.02**	**4.31**
CONSUMPTION								
Petroleum products[10]	19.92	29.52	32.73	34.20	30.92	33.55	33.53	33.77
Natural gas	12.39	21.79	19.95	20.39	17.83	19.30	20.13	20.79
Coal	9.84	12.26	12.66	15.42	17.48	19.10	18.87	19.63
Nuclear power	0.01	0.24	1.90	2.74	4.15	6.16	6.61	6.52
Hydroelectric power[11]	1.66	2.65	3.22	3.12	3.40	2.95	2.79	3.06
Other[12]	(5)	–0.04	0.09	0.08	0.20	0.21	0.22	0.20
Total	**43.80**	**66.43**	**70.55**	**75.96**	**73.98**	**81.26**	**82.14**	**83.96**

Note: Data do not include consumption of wood energy (other than that consumed by electric utilities) which totaled about 2.6 quadrillion Btu in 1984. This table also does not include small quantities of other energy forms for which consistent historical data are not available, such as geothermal, waste, wind, photovoltaic, or solar thermal energy sources except that consumed by electric utilities. Sum of components may not equal due to independent rounding. 1. Preliminary. 2. Includes lease condensate. 3. Dry natural gas. 4. Includes electricity produced from geothermal, wood, waste, wind, photovoltaic, and solar thermal energy sources connected to electric utility distribution systems. 5. Less than .005 quadrillion Btu. 6. Includes imports of crude oil for the Strategic Petroleum Reserve which began in 1977. 7. Includes imports of unfinished oils and natural gas plant liquids. 8. Includes coal, coal coke, and hydroelectric power. 9. Includes natural gas, coal coke, and hydroelectric power. 10. Petroleum products supplied include natural gas plant liquids and crude oil burned as fuel. 11. Includes industrial generation of hydroelectric power and net electricity imports. 12. Includes electricity produced from geothermal wood, waste, wind, photovoltaic, and solar thermal sources connected to electric utility distribution systems, and net imports of coal coke. **Source:** U.S. Dept. of Energy, *Annual Energy Review 1993* (1994).

U.S. FUEL CONSUMPTION, BY TYPE AND END-USE SECTOR, 1950–93

Petroleum (million barrels/day)

Year	Residential and commercial	Industrial	Transportation	Electric utilities	Total
1950	1.07	1.82	3.36	0.21	6.46
1955	1.40	2.39	4.46	0.21	8.46
1960	1.71	2.71	5.14	0.24	9.80
1965	1.91	3.25	6.04	0.32	11.51
1970	2.18	3.81	7.78	0.93	14.70
1975	1.95	4.04	8.95	1.39	16.32
1980	1.52	4.84	9.55	1.15	17.06
1985	1.30	4.10	9.85	0.48	15.73
1990	1.14	4.32	10.97	0.55	16.99
1991	1.14	4.25	10.80	0.52	16.71
1992	1.12	4.55	10.95	0.42	17.03
1993[1]	1.13	4.45	11.16	0.46	17.19

Natural gas (trillion cubic feet/year)

Year	Residential and commercial	Industrial	Transportation	Electric utilities	Total
1950	1.59	3.43	0.13	0.63	5.77
1955	2.75	4.54	0.25	1.15	8.69
1960	4.12	5.77	0.35	1.72	11.97
1965	5.34	7.11	0.50	2.32	15.28
1970	7.24	9.25	0.72	3.93	21.14
1975	7.43	8.36	0.58	3.16	19.54
1980	7.36	8.20	0.63	3.68	19.88
1985	6.86	6.87	0.50	3.04	17.28
1990	7.01	8.25	0.66	2.79	18.72
1991	7.29	8.36	0.60	2.79	19.04
1992	7.49	8.70	0.59	2.77	19.54
1993[1]	7.86	9.03	0.61	2.68	20.18

Coal (million short tons/year)

Year	Residential and commercial	Industrial	Transportation	Electric utilities	Total
1950	114.6	224.6	63.0	91.9	494.1
1955	68.4	217.8	17.0	143.8	447.0
1960	40.9	177.4	3.0	176.7	398.1
1965	25.7	200.8	0.7	244.8	472.0
1970	16.1	186.6	0.3	320.2	523.2
1975	9.4	147.2	(2)	406.0	562.6
1980	6.5	127.0	(3)	569.3	702.7
1985	7.8	116.4	(3)	693.8	818.0
1990	6.7	115.2	(3)	773.5	895.5
1991	6.1	109.3	(3)	772.3	887.6
1992	6.2	106.4	(3)	779.9	892.4
1993[1]	6.7	107.7	(3)	814.0	928.4

1. Preliminary. 2. Less than 0.05 million short tons. 3. Small quantities consumed by transportation sector are included in "industrial" column. **Source:** U.S. Dept. of Energy, *Annual Energy Review 1993* (1994).

A third indicator is energy consumption per household, which declined from 138 million Btu in 1978 to 98 million Btu in 1990. In 1993, energy consumption by all U.S. households totaled more than 9 quadrillion Btu. Energy consumed by households has four primary applications: space heating, air conditioning, water heating, and appliance operation.

Energy consumption is divided among three sectors: residential and commercial, industrial, and transportation. The first two sectors were each responsible for more than 36 percent of total consumption (30.34 and 30.77 quadrillion Btu respectively) in 1993; transportation accounted for less than 27 percent (22.83 quadrillion Btu). That's a remarkably different picture from the 1950s, when industrial consumption was double the consumption levels of the other two sectors. Consumption has increased by about 10 percent in all three sectors since 1985.

FOSSIL FUELS

Petroleum Since 1958 the United States has consumed more energy than it produces; the difference has been met with energy imports. Net imports of energy (primarily petroleum) grew rapidly through 1973, when they totaled 13 quadrillion Btu, or 20% of consumption. Despite the Arab oil embargo of 1973–74 and increases in the price of crude oil, petroleum net imports continued to grow, reaching a peak of nearly 19 quadrillion Btu in 1977. That year, U.S. dependence on petroleum net imports peaked at 47% of consumption. In 1985, petroleum net imports dropped to 9 quadrillion Btu and U.S. dependence on foreign oil fell to 27% of consumption, its lowest level since 1972. But excess world production in 1986 led to declining prices and inhibited domestic oil production, causing U.S. reliance on imports to jump to 33% in 1986, 36% in 1987, and 38% in 1988. The 1990 Iraqi invasion of Kuwait drove the price of oil up to $19.63 a barrel, but by 1993, the price had fallen back to $13.21 a barrel, its lowest annual average in 20 years. Despite the changing oil prices, though, U.S. reliance on foreign oil has remained consistently in the 40% range. Dependence on exports in 1993 was 44%, the highest level in 16 years, primarily because of the low price of foreign oil. Saudi Arabia, Venezuela, and Canada are the United States' primary suppliers of foreign oil; each export more than a million barrels of oil per day to the United States. Mexico and Nigeria each export more than 700,000 barrels per day to the United States.

Natural gas Natural gas is the primary source of energy for space heating in 50 million U.S. households. U.S. natural gas trade was limited to the border countries of Mexico and Canada until shipping natural gas in liquified form emerged as an alternative to pipelines. In 1969, the first shipments of liquified natural gas (LNG) were sent to Japan, and U.S. imports from Algeria began the following year. In 1993, U.S. net imports of natural gas by all routes totaled 2.1 trillion cubic feet (the vast majority from Canada), up 10% from the year before. Imports were responsible for 10.5% of domestic natural gas consumption in 1993, up from 9.8% in 1992.

Coal Since World War II coal has been the major U.S. energy export. Throughout most of the 1960s and 1970s, U.S. exports of coal increased, peaking at 113 million short tons in 1981. Exports dropped to just under 80 million short tons in 1987 before rebounding to 109 million short tons in 1991. In 1993, the continuing weakness of the European economy and ongoing subsidies for domestic European coal caused a dramatic drop in U.S. coal exports to 75 million short tons, its lowest level in 14 years. Exports to almost every country in Europe dropped by 50% or more, while exports to Canada, the largest market for U.S. coal, fell 41%. Canada, Japan, Italy, Belgium/Luxembourg, Brazil, and the Netherlands remain the largest markets for U.S. coal. But they accounted for only 44 million short tons of coal in 1993, compared with 60 million the year before.

Electric utilities are the primary domestic consumers of coal. Their consumption grew from a 17% share in 1949 to an 88% share in 1993. Over the same period, consumption in all other sectors declined, most dramatically in the transportation sector, due primarily to railroads switching from coal to petroleum-driven trains. Transportation sector consumption, which topped 70 million tons in 1949, has totaled fewer than 50,000 short tons every year since 1975. Consumption by the residential and commercial sector has also declined steadily, from a high of 117 million short tons in 1949 to 6.7 million short tons in 1993.

ELECTRICITY

Net generation of electricity by electric utilities topped 2.9 trillion kWh in 1993, up slightly from the year before. Coal continued to fuel most of the generation, accounting for 1.6 trillion kWh, while natural gas contributed 259 billion kWh. Lower petroleum prices contributed to an increase in petroleum-fired generation, from 88 billion kWh in 1991 to 100 billion kWh in 1993. For the same reason, nuclear-based generation declined for the first time in 12 years, from 619 billion kWh in 1992 to 610 billion kWh in 1993. For the 12th straight year, nuclear-based generation reached an all-time high, reaching 619 billion kWh in 1992. Hydroelectric generation totaled 269 billion kWh, up 10 percent from 1992 levels.

GASOLINE AND HEATING OIL RETAIL PRICES, 1950–93 (cents per gallon)

	Motor gasoline[1]				Residential heating oil[2]	
	Leaded regular		Unleaded regular			
Year	Current	Constant[3]	Current	Constant[3]	Current	Constant[3]
1950	26.8¢	132.7¢	N.A.	N.A.	N.A.	N.A.
1955	29.1	127.1	N.A.	N.A.	N.A.	N.A.
1960	31.1	119.6	N.A.	N.A.	15.0¢	57.7¢
1965	31.2	109.9	N.A.	N.A.	16.0	56.3
1970	35.7	101.4	N.A.	N.A.	18.5	52.6
1975	56.7	115.2	N.A.	N.A.	37.7	76.6
1980	119.1	166.1	124.5¢	173.6¢	97.4	135.8
1985	111.5	118.1	120.2	127.3	105.3	111.5
1990	114.9	101.4	116.4	102.7	106.3	93.8
1991	N.A.	N.A.	114.0	96.9	101.9	86.6
1992	N.A.	N.A.	112.7	93.1	93.4	77.1
1993	N.A.	N.A.	110.8	89.2	91.1[4]	73.3[4]

Note: N.A. = not available. 1. Prices are calculated from a sample of stations providing all types of services (i.e., full-, mini-, and self-serve). Geographic coverage: 1949–73, 55 representative cities; 1974–77, 56 urban areas; 1978–92, 85 urban areas. 2. Prices derived by dividing sum of estimated national retail sales for residential heating oil (No. 2 fuel oil) by the estimated volume of retail sales for residential heating. 3. In 1987 dollars, calculated using implicit GDP price deflators. 4. Preliminary. **Source:** U.S. Dept. of Energy, *Annual Energy Review 1993* (1994).

U.S. NET GENERATION OF ELECTRICITY BY UTILITIES, BY ENERGY SOURCE, 1950–93 (billion kilowatt-hours)

Year	Coal	Natural gas	Petroleum[1]	Nuclear power	Hydroelectric power	Geothermal and other[2]	Total
1950	155	45	34	0	96	(3)	329
1955	301	95	37	0	113	(3)	547
1960	403	158	48	1	146	(3)	756
1965	571	222	65	4	194	(3)	1,055
1970	704	373	184	22	248	1	1,532
1975	853	300	289	173	300	3	1,918
1980	1,162	346	246	251	276	6	2,286
1985	1,402	292	100	384	281	11	2,470
1990	1,560	264	117	577	283	11	2,808
1991	1,551	264	111	613	280	10	2,825
1992	1,576	264	89	619	244	10	2,797
1993[4]	1,639	259	100	610	269	10	2,882

1. Includes distillate fuel oil, residual fuel oil (including crude oil burned as fuel), jet fuel, and petroleum coke. 2. Other is wood, waste, photovoltaic, and solar thermal energy used to generate electricity for distribution. 3. Less than 0.5 billion kilowatt-hours. 4. Preliminary. **Source:** U.S. Dept. of Energy, *Annual Energy Review 1993* (1994).

The weighted average real price (based on 1987 dollars) of electricity to all sectors in 1993 was 5.6 cents per kWh, 19 percent below the price in 1960, but the same as in 1992. But although prices of other major energy sources increased significantly during the same period, electricity remained by far the most expensive source of energy on a Btu basis.

NUCLEAR POWER

Between 1980 and 1993 the number of nuclear power plants in operation in the United States grew 55% and net nuclear generation of electricity grew 143%, from 251 billion kilowatt-hours (kWh) in 1980 to 610 billion kWh in 1992. More than three-quarters of the 109 nuclear power plants in the United States are located east of the Mississippi River. One unit (Comanche Peak 2 in Texas) came on-line in 1993, while one other unit (Trojan, in Oregon) shut down. An additional eight units have received construction permits. So while the United States still has the highest number of reactors of any country in the world, the total of 117 units in all stages of planning, construction, or operation in 1992 is well below the total of 236 in 1975. Since then many planned units have been canceled, and no orders for new units have been announced since 1978.

Several factors have contributed to the decline in the number of planned nuclear units. Growth in electricity demand has been slower than expected; longer lead times for licensing and construction coupled with higher financing expenses have increased costs; and rising interest rates and an uncertain economic environment have eroded electric utilities' willingness to commission new plants. Furthermore, nuclear plant operators have been able to increase their generation of electricity without increasing the number of reactors.

A further deterrent has been the increased public opposition to nuclear power plants because of uncertainties concerning their safety and the disposal of spent nuclear fuel. These concerns were heightened in the wake of the accident at Three Mile Island near Harrisburg, Pa., in 1979, and the far more devastating one at Chernobyl in the Soviet Union in 1986.

U.S. NUCLEAR GENERATING UNITS WITH LEAST UNSCHEDULED DOWNTIME

Rank/Unit	Utility	Year of initial operation	Lifetime forced outage rate[1]
1. Point Beach 2	Wisconsin Electric Power	1973	0.6%
2. Vogtle 2	Georgia Power	1989	1.3
3. Monticello	Northern States Power (Minnesota)	1971	1.4
4. Point Beach 1	Wisconsin Electric Power	1970	1.5
5. Kewaunee	Wisconsin Public Service	1973	1.9
6. Byron 1	Commonwealth Edison (Illinois)	1985	2.0
7. Callaway 1	Union Electric (Missouri)	1984	2.1
8. Diablo Canyon	Pacific Gas and Electric (California)	1984	2.2
9. Byron 2	Commonwealth Edison (Illinois)	1987	2.2
10. Haddam Neck	Connecticut Yankee Atomic Power	1967	2.2

1. Unscheduled downtime as a percentage of time since the unit was put in operation. Does not include scheduled downtime for maintenance and refueling. **Source:** U.S. Dept. of Energy, *World Nuclear Outlook 1994* (1994).

U.S. COMMERCIAL NUCLEAR PLANTS IN OPERATION, 1994

As of Jan. 1, 1994, there were 109 operable nuclear reactors in 32 states. This table lists the total number of reactors in each state, the names of individual units, and their locations.

Alabama = 5
Browns Ferry 1, 2, & 3, Decatur
Joseph M. Farley 1 & 2, Dothan
Arizona = 3
Palo Verde 1, 2, & 3, Wintersburg
Arkansas = 2
Arkansas Nuclear 1 & 2, Russellville
California = 4
Diablo Canyon 1 & 2, Avila Beach
San Onofre 2 & 3, San Clemente
Connecticut = 4
Haddam Neck, Haddam Neck
Millstone 1, 2, & 3, Waterford
Florida = 5
Crystal River 3, Red Level
St. Lucie 1 & 2, Ft. Pierce
Turkey Point 3 & 4, Florida City
Georgia = 4
Hatch 1 & 2, Baxley
Vogtle 1 & 2, Waynesboro
Illinois = 13
Braidwood 1 & 2, Braidwood
Byron 1 & 2, Byron
Clinton 1, Clinton
Dresden 2 & 3, Morris
La Salle 1 & 2, Seneca
Quad Cities 1 & 2, Cordova
Zion 1 & 2, Zion
Iowa = 1
Duane Arnold, Palo
Kansas = 1
Wolf Creek, Burlington
Louisiana = 2
River Bend 1, St. Francisville
Waterford 3, Taft
Maine = 1
Maine Yankee, Wicasset
Maryland = 2
Calvert Cliffs 1 & 2, Lusby
Massachusetts = 2
Pilgrim 1, Plymouth
Michigan = 5
Big Rock Point, Charlevoix
Donald C. Cook 1 & 2, Bridgman
Fermi 2, Newport
Palisades, South Haven
Minnesota = 3
Monticello, Monticello
Prairie Island 1 & 2, Red Wing
Mississippi = 1
Grand Gulf 1, Port Gibson
Missouri = 1
Callaway 1, Fulton
Nebraska = 2
Cooper 1, Brownville
Fort Calhoun 1, Fort Calhoun
New Hampshire = 1
Seabrook 1, Seabrook
New Jersey = 4
Hope Creek 1, Salem
Oyster Creek 1, Forked River
Salem 1 & 2, Salem
New York = 6
Indian Point 2 & 3, Buchanan
James A. Fitzpatrick, Scriba
Nine Mile Point 1 & 2, Oswego
Robert E. Ginna, Rochester
North Carolina = 5
Brunswick 1 & 2, Southport
McGuire 1 & 2, Cowens Ford Dam
Shearon Harris 1, New Hill
Ohio = 2
Davis-Besse 1, Oak Harbor
Perry 1, North Perry
Pennsylvania = 9
Beaver Valley 1 & 2, Shippingport
Limerick 1 & 2, Pottstown
Peach Bottom 2 & 3, Lancaster
Susquehanna 1 & 2, Berwick
Three Mile Island 1, Middletown
South Carolina = 7
Catawba 1 & 2, Clover
H.B. Robinson 2, Hartsville
Oconee 1, 2, & 3, Seneca
Summer 1, Jenkinsville
Tennessee = 2
Sequoyah 1 & 2, Daisy
Texas = 4
Comanche Peak 1 & 2, Glen Rose
South Texas 1 & 2, Bay City
Vermont = 1
Vermont Yankee, Vernon
Virginia = 4
North Anna 1 & 2, Mineral
Surry 1 & 2, Surry
Washington = 1
WNP 2, Richland
Wisconsin = 3
Kewaunee, Carlton
Point Beach 1 & 2, Two Creeks

Source: U.S. Dept. of Energy, *World Nuclear Outlook 1994* (1994).

TRANSPORTATION

Americans spend nearly $500 billion for transportation products and services annually. In 1992, the United States recorded 4.2 trillion passenger miles of travel and 3.3 trillion revenue ton-miles of freight traffic. Transportation and transportation-related businesses employ one-tenth of the American work force. As a share of consumer spending, transportation accounts for more than 11 percent of the total.

The government has traditionally played a leading role in the development of the nation's transportation infrastructure. Technological, economic, and demographic changes all help to shape the government's priorities. In the 19th and early 20th centuries, for instance, the nation made enormous direct and indirect contributions to the development of the nation's railroads. Today, the nation's 135,000-mile-long rail network is the largest in the world (the former Soviet Union had a larger network before it dissolved); but in terms of passenger-miles per person carried (50 miles per person per year) the United States doesn't even rank in the top 50, and the government spends vastly more on highways and aviation than on railroad transportation. In 1992, total revenues were $691 billion for highway transportation, $68 billion for aviation, $30 billion for railroads, and $16 billion for mass transit.

Costs

Transportation costs vary dramatically among the primary carrier types, though in all cases, mass transit is much more cost-efficient. Witness: the average revenue per passenger-mile—that is, the revenue generated from carrying one passenger one mile—was between 11 and 13 cents for commuter rail, Amtrak, and intercity bus, and coach seats on airplanes (first-class airline service produced close to 27 cents per passenger mile). By comparison, the average cost of operating a car in 1994 (including variable costs for gas and oil, maintenance and tires, and fixed costs for insurance, registration, depreciation, and finance charges) was 47 cents per mile.

A Nation on the Move

The high price of automobile travel has not hurt America's love affair with the car, however. Of the 4.2 trillion passenger-miles traveled in 1992, 2.8 trillion—or two of every three—were by passenger car, motorcycle, or taxi and another 853 billion (20%) were by truck. Certificated airlines accounted for 366 billion miles, or 9 percent. Intercity buses accounted for 23.7 billion (0.6%), general aviation for 12.2 billion (0.3%) and railroads (not including commuter rail) for 10.7 billion (0.3%) of passenger-miles traveled. The 100,274 vehicles engaged in local mass transit accounted for a total of 40.4 billion (1.0%) passenger miles. The average trip was 815 miles by airplane, 136 miles by intercity bus, 23.0 miles by commuter rail, and 290 miles by Amtrak. Average one-way passenger fares in 1992 were $103.60 by plane, $41.11 by Amtrak, $21.86 by bus, $3.09 by commuter rail, and $0.73 by local mass transit. Fares are double what they were 10 years earlier for all modes of transportation except air. Airfares have risen only 22 percent since 1980, a sure sign that despite all its flaws, airline deregulation has succeeded in making air travel more accessible to all Americans.

PASSENGER MILES AND REVENUE TON-MILES OF FREIGHT, BY MODE OF TRANSPORTATION, 1980–92 (in millions)

Mode of transport	1980	1985	1990	1991	1992
Passenger miles					
Air carrier[1]	200,087	277,836	345,873	338,085	354,764
General aviation, intercity	14,700	12,300	13,000	12,600	12,200
Highway:					
Passenger car and taxi	2,000,872	2,142,961	2,284,908	2,668,380	2,776,062
Intercity bus	27,400	23,800	23,000	23,500	23,700
Commuter rail	6,516	6,534	7,082	7,344	7,342
Amtrak	4,503	4,785	6,041	6,274	6,075
Revenue ton-miles of freight					
Air carrier[1,2]	4,528	5,156	9,064	8,858	9,820
Oil pipeline	588,000	564,000	584,000	579,000	573,000
Class I rail	918,958	876,984	1,033,969	1,038,875	1,066,781
Intercity trucks	555,000	610,000	735,000	758,000	815,000
Water transport:					
Inland waterways and Great Lakes	410,240	392,604	460,000	443,000	454,000
Domestic waterways	631,000	611,000	479,000	469,000	462,000

1. Includes domestic operations, certificated, all services. 2. Includes revenue ton-miles, U.S. and foreign mail, and express, as reported on AIM Form 41. **Source:** U.S. Dept. of Transportation, *National Transportation Statistics 1995* (1995).

NUMBER OF VEHICLES IN THE U.S., 1980–92

Mode of transport	1980	1985	1990	1991	1992
Air carrier, certificated, all services[1]	2,818	3,100	4,727	4,580	4,884
General aviation	211,045	210,654	212,229	198,474	184,433
Motorcycle	5,693,940	5,444,404	4,259,462	4,177,365	4,065,118
Passenger car and taxis[2]	121,601,000	131,864,000	143,453,000	142,956,000	144,213,000
Truck, total	33,666,587	39,196,161	44,712,887	5,936,288	45,504,067
Intercity bus	21,400	20,200	19,491	19,296	N.A.
Local transit, total[3]	70,888	90,334	89,546	91,930	95,763
Motor bus[3]	59,411	64,258	59,714	60,377	61,959
Heavy rail	9,641	9,326	10,419	10,331	10,245
Light rail	1,013	717	913	1,095	1,058
Trolley bus	823	676	832	752	907
Demand response	N.A.	14,490	16,471	17,879	19,566
Other	N.A.	867	1,197	1,496	2,028
Commuter rail	4,500	4,035	4,415	4,370	4,413
Class I rail, total	1,196,208	889,618	677,737	651,833	623,193
Freight cars	1,168,114	867,070	658,902	633,489	605,189
Locomotives	28,094	22,548	18,835	18,344	18,004
Amtrak, total	2,547	2,200	2,301	2,283	2,298
Passenger train cars	2,128	1,818	1,983	1,967	1,962
Locomotives	419	382	318	316	336
Water transport, total	37,149	39,230	36,858	N.A.	36,697
Dry cargo barges and scows	27,426	29,287	27,091	N.A.	26,984
Tankers	4,166	4,252	3,913	N.A.	3,905
Towboats and tugboats	4,693	4,954	5,218	N.A.	5,205
Oceangoing ships[4]	864	737	636	619	603

Note: As of December of year shown. 1. Domestic and international certificated aircraft, all services. 2. Figure rounded in source. 3. Prior to 1984, excludes most rural and smaller transit systems. 4. Vessels 1,000 gross tons and over. **Source:** U.S. Dept. of Transportation, *National Transportation Statistics 1995* (1995).

WORLD MOTOR VEHICLE PRODUCTION, 1992–93

Country	1992 Total	1992 Percent of total	1993 Total	1993 Percent of total	Percent change 1992–93
Argentina	261,943	0.6%	342,350	0.7%	30.7%
Australia	284,408	0.6	479,781	1.0	68.7
Austria	27,970	—	44,719	0.1	59.9
Belgium	298,072	0.6	403,952	0.9	35.5
Brazil	1,071,564	2.3	1,390,261	3.0	29.7
Canada	1,968,497	4.2	2,237,733	4.8	13.6
China	1,080,000	2.3	1,310,000	2.8	21.2
Commonwealth of Independent States	1,530,000	3.2	1,807,000	3.9	18.1
Czechoslovakia	229,058	0.5	234,050	0.5	2.2
France	3,767,800	8.0	3,155,717	6.7	–16.2
Germany	5,193,942	11.0	3,990,650	8.5	–23.2
Hungary	18,000	—	15,710	—	–12.7
India	324,385	0.7	371,630	0.8	14.6
Italy	1,686,487	3.7	1,267,195	2.7	–24.9
Japan	12,499,284	26.4	11,227,545	24.0	–10.2
Korea, South	1,729,696	3.7	2,050,058	4.5	18.5
Malaysia	129,187	0.3	115,00	0.2	–11.0
Mexico	1,083,091	2.3	1,080,274	2.3	–0.3
Netherlands	117,992	0.2	99,192	0.2	–15.2
Poland	230,000	0.5	304,000	0.6	32.2
Spain	2,121,887	4.5	1,767,640	3.8	–16.7
Sweden	356,595	0.8	337,386	0.7	–5.4
Taiwan	N.A.	N.A.	382,900	0.8	N.A.
United Kingdom	1,540,333	3.3	1,568,934	3.3	1.8
United States	9,701,502	20.5	10,864,203	23.2	12.0
Yugoslavia	125,641	0.3	8,313	—	–93.4
Total	**47,377,334**	**100.0%**	**48,856,193**	**100.0%**	**–1.1%**

Note: N.A. = not available. Includes passenger vehicles, trucks, and buses. Percentages calculated by *The Universal Almanac.* **Source:** American Automobile Manufacturers Association, *AAMA Motor Vehicle Facts & Figures '94* (1994).

U.S. MASS TRANSIT, 1991

Mode	Passenger trips (millions)	Passenger miles (millions)	Average length of trip (miles)	Vehicles operated, maximum service
Motor bus	4,825	18,104	3.7	42,940
Heavy rail	2,167	10,488	4.8	8,106
Commuter rail	324	7,383	22.8	3,989
Light rail	183	661	3.6	811
Demand response	42	274	6.5	8,434
All other	193	563	N.A.	1,524
All modes	**7,734**	**37,473**	**4.8**	**65,804**

Source: U.S. Dept. of Transportation, *National Urban Mass Transportation Statistics, 1991 Section 15 Annual Report* (1993).

THE CAR IN AMERICAN LIFE

Almost 90% of America's 93 million households had access to at least one car, van, or light truck in 1989; just over half had two or more. Fifty-seven percent of households had access to shelter (a garage or carport) for their vehicles, and 33% had off-street parking such as a driveway or parking lot. The remaining 10% had to use public streets.

Approximately 88% of all U.S. workers drove to work: 76% drove alone; only 12% were in car pools. (Of the remaining 12%, only 5% used mass transportation, while 6% walked or worked at home, and 1% used bicycles, motorcycles, boats, etc.)

Source: U.S. Bureau of the Census, *Statistical Brief,* "Americans and Their Automobiles" (1992).

WORLD MOTOR VEHICLE PRODUCTION, 1950–93
(in thousands)

Year	United States	Canada	Europe	Japan	Other	World total	U.S. share of total
1950	8,006	388	1,991	32	160	10,577	75.7%
1955	9,204	452	3,741	68	163	13,628	67.5
1960	7,905	398	6,837	482	866	16,488	47.9
1965	11,138	847	9,572	1,876	834	24,267	45.9
1970	8,284	1,160	13,033	5,289	1,637	29,403	28.2
1975	8,987	1,385	13,473	6,942	2,211	32,998	27.2
1980	8,010	1,324	15,445	11,043	2,692	38,514	20.8
1985	11,653	1,933	16,015	12,271	2,939	44,811	26.0
1990	9,783	1,928	18,651	13,487	4,491	48,345	20.2
1992	9,729	1,963	17,244	12,499	6,259	47,694	20.4
1993	10,864	2,238	15,004	11,228	7,522	46,856	23.2

Source: American Automobile Manufacturers Association, *AAMA Motor Vehicle Facts & Figures '94* (1994).

WORLD MOTOR VEHICLE REGISTRATIONS, 1960–92

Year	Cars	Trucks and buses	Total vehicles	Population Per car	Population Per vehicle
1960	98,317,475	28,637,342	126,954,817	29.2	22.6
1965	139,779,540	38,127,320	177,906,860	22.7	17.9
1970	193,515,717	52,851,828	246,367,545	18.4	14.4
1975	260,207,459	67,693,176	327,900,635	14.6	11.6
1980	320,539,030	90,573,495	411,112,525	13.5	10.8
1985	374,727,233	112,816,433	487,543,666	12.6	10.5
1990	444,899,624	138,082,153	582,981,777	12.0	8.9
1991	456,032,819	139,273,829	595,306,648	11.0	8.8
1992	469,942,881	143,587,318	613,530,199	11.0	9.0

Source: American Automobile Manufacturers Association, *AAMA Motor Vehicle Facts and Figures '94* (1994).

U.S. MOTOR VEHICLE FACTORY SALES AND REGISTRATIONS, 1900–1993

Year	Factory sales: Passenger cars	Factory sales: Trucks and buses	Factory sales: Total	Motor vehicle registrations[1]
1900	4,192	—	4,192	8,000
1905	24,250	750	25,000	78,800
1910	181,000	6,000	187,000	468,500
1915	895,930	74,000	969,930	2,490,932
1920	1,905,560	321,789	2,227,349	9,239,161
1925	3,735,171	530,659	4,265,830	19,940,724
1930	2,787,456	575,364	3,362,820	26,531,990
1940	3,717,385	754,901	4,472,286	32,453,233
1945	69,532	655,683	725,215	31,035,420
1950	6,665,863	1,337,193	8,003,056	49,161,691
1955	7,920,186	1,249,106	9,169,292	62,688,792
1960	6,674,796	1,194,475	7,869,271	73,857,768
1965	9,305,561	1,751,805	11,057,366	90,357,667
1970	6,546,817	1,692,440	8,239,257	108,418,197
1975	6,712,852	2,272,160	8,985,012	132,948,709
1980	6,400,026	1,667,283	8,067,309	155,796,219
1985	8,002,259	3,464,327	11,466,586	171,653,675
1990	6,049,749	3,725,205	9,774,954	188,655,462
1992	5,685,299	4,062,002	9,747,301	190,362,228
1993	5,960,327	4,895,224	10,855,551	192,865,000[2]

1. Data exclude military vehicles as well as farm trucks registered at a nominal fee in certain states and restricted to use in the vicinity of owners' farms; in 1991, there were 67,255 such trucks. 2. Estimate. **Source:** American Automobile Manufacturers Association, *AAMA Motor Vehicle Facts & Figures '94* (1994).

TOP SELLING CARS AND LIGHT TRUCKS IN THE U.S., 1992–93

Cars

Make and model, 1992	Units sold	Make and model, 1993	Units sold
1. Ford Taurus	409,751	1. Ford Taurus	360,448
2. Honda Accord	393,477	2. Honda Accord	330,030
3. Toyota Camry	286,602	3. Toyota Camry	299,737
4. Ford Escort	236,622	4. Chevrolet Cavalier	273,617
5. Honda Civic	219,228	5. Ford Escort	269,034
6. Chevrolet Lumina	218,114	6. Honda Civic	255,579
7. Chevrolet Cavalier	212,374	7. Saturn	229,356
8. Pontiac Grand Am	210,332	8. Chevrolet Lumina	219,683
9. Ford Tempo	207,173	9. Ford Tempo	217,644
10. Saturn	196,126	10. Pontiac Grand Am	214,761
11. Toyota Corolla	196,118	11. Toyota Corolla	193,749
12. Chevrolet Beretta/Corsica	166,625	12. Chevrolet Beretta/Corsica	171,794
13. Nissan Sentra	158,909	13. Nissan Sentra	166,961
14. Buick LeSabre	138,409	14. Buick LeSabre	149,299
15. Cadillac DeVille	127,766	15. Oldsmobile Ciera	143,699
16. Oldsmobile Ciera	117,292	16. Nissan Altima	133,879
17. Mercury Sable	116,623	17. Ford Thunderbird	122,415
18. Lincoln Town Car	115,075	18. Mercury Sable	120,977
19. Buick Century	114,273	19. Dodge Shadow	119,262
20. Pontiac Grand Prix	103,517	20. Buick Century	116,034

Light trucks

Make and model, 1992	Units sold	Make and model, 1993	Units sold
1. Ford F-Pickups	470,788	1. Ford F-Pickups	544,396
2. Chevrolet C/K	428,188	2. Chevrolet C/K	513,348
3. Ford Explorer	306,681	3. Ford Ranger	340,184
4. Dodge Caravan	251,921	4. Ford Explorer	302,201
5. Ford Ranger	247,777	5. Dodge Caravan	271,523
6. Plymouth Voyager	201,016	6. Jeep Grand Cherokee	212,564
7. Chevrolet S-10 Pickup	191,982	7. Plymouth Voyager	211,813
8. Toyota Compact Pickup	175,150	8. Ford Aerostar	191,148
9. Ford Aerostar	166,951	9. Chevrolet S-10 Pickup	183,700
10. Chevrolet S-10 Blazer	147,742	10. Toyota Compact Pickup	182,498

Source: American Automobile Manufacturers Association, *AAMA Motor Vehicle Facts & Figures '94* (1994).

U.S. ROADS AND STREETS, 1904–92

	Surfaced mileage ('000s)			Total mileage ('000s)			
Year	State control	County and local control	Total	State control	County and local control	Total	Percent surfaced
1904	0	—	204	—	—	2,351	8.7%
1921	84	363	447	203	2,957	3,160	14.1
1930	227	627	854	324	2,935	3,259	26.2
1935	374	881	1,255	523	2,787	3,310	37.9
1940	449	1,108	1,557	551	2,736	3,287	47.4
1945	482	1,239	1,721	574	2,745	3,319	51.9
1950	542	1,397	1,939	609	2,704	3,313	58.5
1955	610	1,663	2,273	651	2,767	3,418	66.5
1960	660	1,897	2,557	694	2,852	3,546	72.1
1965	701	2,075	2,776	728	2,962	3,690	75.2
1970	748	2,198	2,946	781	2,949	3,730	79.0
1975	763	2,338	3,101	796	3,042	3,838	80.8
1980	753	2,605	3,358	781	3,174	3,955	84.9
1985	612	2,868	3,480	613	3,249	3,862	90.1
1990	619	2,899	3,518	620	3,260	3,880	90.7
1991	620	2,940	3,560	620	3,269	3,889	91.5
1992	619	2,933	3,552	619	3,283	3,902	91.0

Source: American Automobile Manufacturers Association, *AAMA Motor Vehicle Facts and Figures '94* (1994).

U.S. MOTOR VEHICLE REGISTRATIONS BY STATE, 1993

State	Automobiles[1]	Buses	Trucks	Total motor vehicles	Percent change 1992–93	Automobiles per capita
Ala.	2,136,277	8,351	1,245,737	3,390,365	2.6%	0.51
Alaska	310,002	1,916	177,086	489,004	0.6	0.51
Ariz.	2,068,438	4,400	818,751	2,891,589	3.2	0.52
Ark.	986,955	5,612	535,058	1,527,625	1.7	0.40
Calif.	17,300,825	41,423	5,481,464	22,823,712	2.8	0.55
Colo.	2,253,697	5,566	772,825	3,032,088	4.0	0.63
Conn.	2,455,811	8,210	130,348	2,594,369	1.0	0.75
Del.	428,541	2,230	123,779	554,550	1.8	0.60
D.C.	249,844	2,737	11,056	263,637	2.8	0.43
Fla.	8,072,492	38,761	2,058,303	10,169,556	−0.6	0.58
Ga.	3,959,891	14,746	1,657,788	5,632,425	−4.5	0.57
Hawaii	659,365	4,241	99,885	763,491	−1.4	0.56
Idaho	636,250	3,372	383,557	1,023,179	−1.1	0.57
Ill.	6,650,165	15,991	1,404,308	8,070,464	1.1	0.56
Ind.	3,413,908	22,890	1,233,503	4,670,301	3.4	0.59
Iowa	1,947,821	9,044	781,282	2,738,147	1.2	0.69
Kans.	1,264,010	3,754	654,465	1,922,229	0.1	0.50
Ky.[2]	1,713,125	11,831	904,174	2,629,130	−11.9	0.45
La.	2,010,084	19,622	1,136,449	3,166,155	2.3	0.46
Me.	792,731	2,853	232,358	1,027,942	5.1	0.64
Md.	2,956,688	10,899	591,971	3,559,558	−3.5	0.59
Mass.	3,326,871	10,739	499,887	3,837,497	4.8	0.55
Mich.	5,730,607	23,630	1,644,321	7,398,558	1.2	0.60
Minn.	2,905,647	14,728	795,728	3,716,103	6.7	0.64
Miss.	1,526,480	9,050	464,109	1,999,639	2.3	0.57
Mo.	2,857,878	12,080	1,195,728	4,065,686	1.5	0.54
Mont.	554,753	2,894	381,573	939,220	3.6	0.65
Nebr.	942,264	5,794	490,968	1,439,026	6.2	0.58
Nev.	631,592	1,779	303,856	937,227	1.8	0.45
N.H.	742,896	1,725	214,120	958,741	7.3	0.66
N.J.	5,180,485	18,679	441,711	5,640,875	0.9	0.65
N.Mex.	855,920	3,412	561,321	1,420,653	5.1	0.52
N.Y.	8,746,964	40,809	1,374,728	10,162,501	3.9	0.48
N.C.	3,840,995	33,990	1,489,586	5,364,571	1.1	0.55
N.Dak.	397,332	2,320	262,179	661,831	1.0	0.62
Ohio	7,482,837	31,711	1,764,425	9,278,973	2.8	0.67
Okla.	1,758,903	14,043	998,407	2,771,353	1.3	0.54
Oreg.	2,000,645	11,540	611,942	2,624,127	1.6	0.65
Pa.	6,599,468	32,486	1,650,112	8,282,066	1.3	0.54
R.I.	589,198	1,583	104,529	695,310	11.8	0.59
S.C.	1,997,482	14,487	671,742	2,683,711	3.2	0.55
S.Dak.	485,332	2,560	319,792	807,684	12.2	0.67
Tenn.	3,989,183	15,699	958,966	4,963,848	6.9	0.78
Tex.	8,880,679	65,670	4,171,972	13,118,321	2.7	0.48
Utah	839,842	1,187	493,755	1,334,784	6.6	0.45
Vt.	361,515	1,832	119,875	483,222	4.0	0.62
Va.	4,126,394	16,225	1,265,116	5,407,735	3.2	0.63
Wash.	3,122,732	7,442	1,282,824	4,412,998	−1.2	0.59
W.Va.	829,023	3,563	512,809	1,345,395	5.7	0.45
Wis.	2,460,142	11,939	1,342,614	3,814,695	2.1	0.49
Wyo.	283,317	2,387	271,912	557,616	15.5	0.59
Total	**146,314,296**	**654,432**	**47,094,754**	**194,063,482**	**1.9%**	**0.56**

Note: Includes privately owned vehicles and federal, state, and municipal vehicles; does not include vehicles owned by the military services. Farm trucks, registered at a nominal fee and restricted to use on farms, are not included. 1. Includes taxicabs. 2. Figures do not include transfer tags or reregistrations. **Source:** U.S. Dept. of Transportation, *Highway Statistics 1993* (1994).

FUEL EFFICIENCY OF U.S. PASSENGER CARS, 1955–94

		New car, model year basis	
Year	Average U.S. passenger car	Domestic cars	Domestic and imported cars
1955	14.53 mpg	16.0 mpg	16.1 mpg
1960	14.28	15.5	16.1
1965	14.27	15.4	15.9
1970	13.52	14.1	15.2
1975	13.52	15.1	16.2
1980	15.46	22.6	24.3
1985	18.20	26.3	27.6
1990	21.02	26.9	28.0
1991	21.69	27.3	28.3
1992	21.60	27.0	27.8
1993	N.A.	27.8	28.4
1994	N.A.	27.3	28.2

Note: mpg = miles per gallon; calculated on the basis of 55% city and 45% highway miles sales weighted harmonic average. **Source:** U.S. Dept. of Transportation, *National Transportation Statistics Annual Report* (1995).

U.S. RETAIL SALES OF PASSENGER CARS BY SIZE AND COUNTRY OF ORIGIN, 1983–93

Category	1983	1985	1987	1989	1991	1992	1993
By size							
Small	38.8%	37.9%	38.4%	36.6%	33.0%	32.9%	32.8%
Middle	40.6	42.1	42.3	41.9	44.9	44.5	43.3
Large	10.7	9.8	9.1	11.9	8.3	9.2	11.1
Luxury	9.9	10.2	10.2	11.6	13.9	13.4	12.8
By origin							
United States	74.0%	74.3%	68.9%	72.4%	75.1%	76.4%	79.1%
Imports	26.0	25.7	31.1	27.6	24.9	23.6	20.9
Japan	20.9	20.1	21.3	19.4	18.4	17.7	15.6
Germany	3.0	3.8	3.4	2.5	2.4	2.4	2.2
Other countries	2.0	1.7	6.4	5.7	4.2	3.5	3.2

Source: American Automobile Manufacturers Association, *AAMA Motor Vehicle Facts & Figures '94* (1994).

Safety

Automobile accidents are responsible for the overwhelming majority of transportation fatalities in the United States every year. Of the 42,739 transportation-related fatalities in 1993, 93 percent, or 40,115, involved automobiles. Of these, 21,494 were drivers of or passengers in cars, 9,097 were driving or riding in trucks, 814 were bicyclists, and 5,638 were pedestrians. More than three million others are injured in automobile accidents each year. Automobiles are responsible for 99 percent of all transportation injuries. Though much more celebrated than car accidents, plane crashes accounted for only 715 fatalities and 383 injuries in 1993, fewer even than the 800 people who died and the 3,559 who were injured in boating accidents.

Commerce

In 1992, the average freight revenue per ton-mile—that is, the revenue generated from carrying one ton of freight one mile—was 64 cents for an air carrier, 22 cents for a common carrier truck, 3 cents for railroad, 1 cent for oil pipeline, and 0.8 cents for inland waterway carriers. Of the 3.3 trillion ton-miles of freight traveled in 1992, 25% went by truck, 30% by rail, 26% by water, 17% by oil pipeline, and a mere 0.23% by air.

Motor Vehicles

Production of motor vehicles dropped to 46.8 million vehicles in 1993, the third decline in the past four years. U.S. production actually increased, from 9.7 to 10.9 million vehicles, but not enough to offset dropoffs in Europe and Japan. Japan continues to be the world production leader, however, with more than 11 million vehicles each year (24%). That's a vastly different picture than 1950, when the United States made more than 75 percent of the world's automobiles and Japan produced a tiny 1 percent.

RAILROAD NETWORKS AND PASSENGER MILES PER PERSON, SELECTED NATIONS

Country	Railway network (thousands of miles)	Country	Passenger miles per person
Former USSR	148.3	Japan	1,647.0
United States	135.2	Switzerland	913.8
Canada	39.5	East Germany	811.8
India	37.1	Czechoslovakia	771.6
China	31.6	Poland	769.2
Australia	23.6	Former USSR	765.6
France	20.8	France	644.4
Argentina	20.5	Austria	582.6
West Germany	16.4	Denmark	562.2
Poland	14.5	Hungary	543.6

Note: Latest available figures, 1986–88. **Source:** Union Internationale des Chemins de Fer, *Statistiques Internationales des Chemins de Fer.*

COMMUTER AND RAPID RAIL SYSTEMS IN THE U.S., 1993

System	Passenger trips ('000s)	Passenger miles ('000s)	Stations	Route miles	Vehicles operated
Commuter rail					
New York, Long Island RR	92,462.0	1,960,886.2	134	638.2	967
New York, Metro North	59,119.4	1,379,836.1	108	535.4	696
Newark, New Jersey Transit	44,469.9	958,293.9	158	954.0	583
Chicago RTA	29,711.1	608,481.5	126	467.4	421
Chicago & NW Transit	22,380.7	491,350.2	62	309.4	338
Boston, Amtrak/MBTA	21,595.9	402,376.0	101	529.8	291
Philadelphia SEPTA	19,018.7	275,919.9	181	442.8	263
Chicago, Burlington Northern	11,310.0	235,378.6	27	75.0	151
Indiana, NW Indiana CTD	2,531.2	70,811.5	18	138.4	45
Rapid or heavy rail					
New York City TA	1,178,121.5	5,571,179.8	469	492.9	4,954
Washington Metro Area TA	191,428.0	930,027.3	70	162.1	534
Metro Boston TA	190,329.5	578,601.8	53	75.8	378
Chicago TA	135,369.7	823,357.3	145	220.3	856
Philadelphia, SEPTA	94,332.5	422,610.6	76	76.1	304
San Francisco, BART	78,301.8	931,234.9	34	142.0	406
Metro Atlanta RTA	65,005.0	336,388.1	33	80.8	160
New York, PATH	61,814.6	270,393.2	13	28.6	282
Miami/Dade Co. TA	14,817.9	117,329.0	21	42.2	76
Philadelphia, PATCO	11,323.3	98,479.5	13	31.5	102
Baltimore MTA	11,114.2	60,194.7	12	26.6	48
Cleveland RTA	6,563.3	50,181.5	18	38.2	35
New York, Staten Island RT	5,141.0	37,684.2	22	28.6	36
Los Angeles MTA	1,982.7	3,142.5	5	6.0	16

Note: Rapid rail includes subways, elevated trains, and metros. BART = Bay Area Rapid Transit Authority; MBTA = Metropolitan Boston Transit Authority; PATH = Port Authority Trans Hudson; SEPTA = Southeastern Pennsylvania Transit Authority. **Source:** U.S. Dept. of Transportation, *National Transit Database, 1993 Section 15 Annual Report* (1994).

AMTRAK OPERATING STATISTICS, 1985–94

Category	1985	1990	1991	1992	1993	1994
System						
Route miles	24,000	24,000	25,000	25,000	25,000	25,000
Stations	503	516	523	524	535	540
Train miles operated (mil.)	30	33	34	34	35	34
On-time performance						
Systemwide	81%	76%	77%	77%	72%	72%
Short Distance	82	82	82	82	79	78
Long Distance	78	53	59	61	47[1]	49
Ridership						
Passengers (mil.)	20.8	22.2	22.0	21.3	22.1	21.8
Northeast corridor	11.2	11.2	10.9	10.1	10.3	11.7
Short distance	4.5	5.2	5.0	5.3	5.6	4.6
Long distance	5.0	5.8	6.1	5.9	6.2	5.5
Passenger miles (mil.)	4,582	6,057	6,273	6,091	6,199	5,921
Locomotive units						
Operating fleet	291	318	316	336	360	338
Available for service (daily average)	93.2%	84.0%	86.0%	83.0%	84.0%	85.0%
Average age (years)	7	12	13	13	13.2	13.4
New units	0	0	0	20	26	18
Passenger-train cars						
Operating fleet[2]	1,854	1,863	1,786	1,796	1,853	1,852
Average age (years)	14.2	20.0	21.0	21.5	22.6	22.4
Financial						
Revenues (mil.)	$ 825	$1,308	$1,359	$1,325	$1,403	$1,413
Expenses (mil.)	1,600	2,012	2,081	2,037	2,134	2,490

1. This 14% decrease from the previous year was due to the extensive Midwest floods of July 1993. 2. Includes some older or damaged cars awaiting overhaul, conversion to head-end power, or sale. **Source:** Amtrak—National Railroad Passenger Corporation, *1994 Annual Report Appendix* (1995).

U.S. RAILROADS: TRAIN-MILES OPERATED AND ACCIDENT RATES, 1993

Rank/Railroad class and company	Train-miles operated	Accidents per million train miles
CLASS I RAILROADS, TOTAL	**454,138,540**	**3.98**
Amtrak (National Railroad Passenger Corp.)	34,944,913	2.91
Atchison, Topeka and Santa Fe Railway Co.	44,093,275	3.61
Burlington Northern Railroad Co.	72,546,142	5.40
Chicago and North Western Trans.	15,332,861	5.10
Consolidated Rail Corp. (Conrail)	35,498,134	4.17
CSX Transportation	58,827,191	2.62
Denver and Rio Grande Western Railroad	5,760,644	5.73
Grand Trunk Western Railroad Inc.	3,710,170	9.04
Illinois Central Railroad Co.	5,659,428	10.34
Kansas City Southern Railway Co.	4,346,892	5.91
Norfolk Southern Corp.	45,990,741	2.23
St. Louis Southwestern Railway Co.	8,669,268	3.24
Soo Line Railroad Co.	8,557,854	8.90
Southern Pacific Transportation Co.	31,438,335	4.67
Union Pacific Railroad Co.	78,762,692	5.40
GROUP II RAILROADS	**30,376,319**	**6.92**
OTHER RAILROADS	**13,918,011**	**12.22**
Total, all railroads	**498,432,870**	**4.54**

Note: Group II Railroads are those with an annual accumulation of over 400,000 employee hours worked. **Source:** U.S. Dept. of Transportation, *Accident/Incident Bulletin, No. 162, Calendar Year 1993* (1994).

WORLD'S 50 BUSIEST AIRPORTS, 1994

TOTAL PASSENGERS

Rank/Airport		Rank/Airport	
1. Chicago O'Hare Intl.	66,466,269	26. Houston Intercontinental	22,526,299
2. Hartsfield Atlanta Intl.	54,093,051	27. Orlando Intl.	22,392,412
3. Dallas/Ft. Worth Intl.	52,601,125	28. Changi, Singapore	21,644,677
4. Heathrow Airport, London	51,717,918	29. Gatwick, London	21,212,117
5. Los Angeles Intl.	51,050,275	30. Bangkok Intl.	21,009,259
6. Tokyo-Haneda Intl.	42,245,667	31. Sea-Tac Intl., Seattle/Tacoma	20,972,819
7. Frankfurt/Main, Germany	35,122,528	32. Lester B. Pearson Intl., Toronto	20,863,922
8. San Francisco Intl.	34,643,095	33. Charlotte/Douglas Intl.	20,751,628
9. Stapleton Intl., Denver	33,133,428	34. La Guardia, New York	20,730,467
10. Miami Intl.	30,203,269	35. Osaka Intl., Japan	20,366,293
11. Charles de Gaulle, Paris	29,630,222	36. Fiumicino, Rome	20,316,058
12. J.F. Kennedy Intl., New York	28,806,638	37. Pittsburg Intl.	19,490,709
13. Newark Intl.	28,020,482	38. Mexico City Intl.	18,889,256
14. Kimpo Intl., Seoul	27,333,241	39. Barajas, Madrid	18,427,086
15. McCarran Intl., Las Vegas	26,850,486	40. Salt Lake City Intl.	17,564,149
16. Detroit Metropolitan Wayne Co.	26,800,951	41. Kingsford Smith, Sydney	17,483,193
17. Orly, Paris	26,617,556	42. Philadelphia Intl.	17,274,871
18. Hong Kong Intl.	25,948,789	43. Washington, D.C., National	15,517,470
19. Sky Harbor Intl., Phoenix	25,626,132	44. Chitose, Sapporo, Japan	15,093,583
20. Logan Intl., Boston	25,195,005	45. Manchester, UK	14,814,299
21. Minneapolis–St. Paul Intl.	24,471,944	46. Zurich, Switzerland	14,506,865
22. New Tokyo Intl.–Narita	23,745,240	47. Fukuoko Intl., Japan	14,475,617
23. Schiphol, Amsterdam	23,559,456	48. Palma de Mallorca, Spain	14,142,035
24. Lambert–St. Louis Intl.	23,362,671	49. Dusseldorf, Germany	14,003,365
25. Honolulu Intl.	22,995,976	50. Copenhagen Intl.	13,955,178

TOTAL CARGO (metric tons)

Rank/Airport		Rank/Airport	
1. Memphis Intl., Tennessee	1,653,270	28. Logan Intl., Boston	417,600
2. New Tokyo Intl.–Narita	1,605,313	29. Sea-Tac Intl., Seattle/Tacoma	415,141
3. Los Angeles Intl.	1,545,025	30. Eldorado, Bogota, Colombia	400,197
4. J.F. Kennedy Intl., N.Y.	1,449,724	31. Brussels Airport	395,189
5. Frankfurt/Main, Germany	1,401,942	32. Osaka Intl., Japan	392,420
6. Standiford, Louisville, Ky.	1,347,815	33. Stapleton Intl., Denver	381,157
7. Miami Intl.	1,332,799	34. Guarulhos Intl., São Paulo, Brazil	379,083
8. Hong Kong Intl.	1,320,206	35. Minneapolis–St. Paul Intl.	377,533
9. Chicago O'Hare Intl.	1,255,844	36. Toledo Express	364,899
10. Heathrow Airport, London	1,047,761	37. Ontario Intl., Ontario, California	344,579
11. Kimpo Intl., Seoul	1,029,166	38. Zurich, Switzerland	337,376
12. Changi, Singapore	1,026,703	39. Detroit Metropolitan Wayne Co.	328,518
13. Charles de Gaulle, Paris	882,488	40. Orly, Paris	313,455
14. Schiphol, Amsterdam	874,701	41. Cophenhagen Intl.	302,091
15. Newark Intl.	861,681	42. B Aquino Intl., Manila	301,207
16. Hartsfield Atlanta Intl.	805,599	43. Fiumicino, Rome	297,486
17. Anchorage Intl.	736,533	44. Houston Intercontinental	283,739
18. Dallas/Ft. Worth Intl.	724,494	45. Dulles Intl., Washington, D.C.	276,561
19. San Francisco Intl.	687,502	46. Subang–Kuala Lumpur Intl., Malaysia	274,732
20. Dayton Intl., Ohio	622,009	47. Cologne–Bonn, Germany	264,292
21. Chiang Kai Shek Intl., Taipei	613,530	48. Luis Muñoz Marin, San Juan, Puerto Rico	260,253
22. Tokyo-Haneda Intl.	603,207	49. Dubai Intl., United Arab Emirates	258,158
23. Bangkok Intl.	590,308	50. Soekarno Hatta Intl., Jakarta, Indonesia	256,401
24. Indianapolis Intl., Indiana	540,277		
25. Oakland Intl.	497,203		
26. Philadelphia Intl.	485,898		
27. Honolulu Intl., Hawaii	429,523		

Source: Airports Association Council International, *Worldwide Airport Traffic Report—Calendar Year 1994* (1995).

Aviation

With more than 65 million people passing through its security detectors each year, Chicago's O'Hare International is the busiest airport in the world. But the airport that handles the most cargo (1.7 million tons) each year is Tennessee's Memphis International, thanks in large part to the fact that it is the primary hub for Federal Express, which logged more than 4.4 billion freight ton-miles of cargo in 1994. United Airlines and American Airlines, both with major hubs in Chicago, again finished 1 and 2 in number of revenue passenger miles in 1994, but Delta topped them both in terms of total number of passengers. More than 88 million people flew Delta in 1994, compared with 81 million for American and 74 million for United. An obvious effect of deregulation of the airline industry has been the growth of the biggest airlines and the winnowing of smaller carriers from the market. The four largest airlines, American, United, Delta, and USAir, flew more passengers than all other carriers combined. A second tier of national and regional airlines (Northwest, Southwest, Continental, TWA, America West, and Alaska) compete for passengers not well served by the bigger carriers. None of the rest of the top 25 airlines—primarily commuter and short hop companies—carried more than six million passengers in 1994.

TOP 25 U.S. AIRLINES, 1994

Rank/Airline	Passengers ('000s)	Revenue passenger miles ('000s)[1]	Rank
1. Delta	88,922	86,298,231	3
2. American	81,082	98,735,550	2
3. United	74,070	107,968,110	1
4. USAir	59,494	37,940,181	5
5. Northwest	45,496	57,851,349	4
6. Southwest	44,238	19,789,354	8
7. Continental	39,947	37,509,894	6
8. Trans World	20,880	24,692,395	7
9. America West	15,629	12,198,973	9
10. Alaska	8,885	7,529,006	10
11. Aloha	5,032	675,796	25
12. Hawaiian	4,576	2,860,837	13
13. Simmons	4,517	946,698	21
14. Horizon Air	3,481	733,398	24
15. Morris	3,393	1,831,640	16
16. Reno	3,370	1,622,087	17
17. Atlantic Southeast	3,120	781,035	23
18. Continental Micronesia	2,281	4,097,771	11
19. Markair	2,094	1,999,646	15
20. ValuJet	1,968	938,574	22
21. Trans States	1,700	N.A.	—
22. American Trans Air	1,686	3,017,313	12
23. Business Express	1,640	N.A.	—
24. Air Wisconsin	1,603	N.A.	—
25. Executive Airlines	1,274	N.A.	—

Note: Carriers certificated under section 401, Federal Aviation Act. 1. One paying passenger traveling one mile generates one revenue passenger mile. **Source:** Air Transport Association of America, *Air Transport 1995: The Annual Report of the U.S. Scheduled Airline Industry* (1995).

TOP 25 U.S. CARGO AIRLINES, 1994

Rank/Airline	Freight ton-miles ('000s)[1]
1. Federal Express	4,410,736
2. United Parcel Service	2,921,871
3. Northwest	2,015,865
4. American	1,616,901
5. United	1,594,121
6. Delta	1,079,225
7. Continental	427,917
8. Trans World	341,129
9. Evergreen	298,981
10. Southern Air	224,841
11. DHL Airways	214,146
12. Challenge Air Cargo	154,086
13. Tower	145,518
14. Polar Air	134,663
15. USAir	128,692
16. Arrow	95,187
17. Continental Micronesia	65,361
18. Alaska	56,314
19. America West	44,388
20. Fine Airlines	42,170
21. Atlas Air	41,546
22. American International	33,443
23. Hawaiian	29,135
24. Amerijet	28,114
25. Southwest	27,185

Note: Carriers certificated under Section 401, Federal Aviation Act. 1. One ton of freight traveling one mile generates one freight-ton mile. **Source:** Air Transport Association of America, *Air Transport 1995: The Annual Report of the U.S. Scheduled Airline Industry* (1995).

TOP 25 DOMESTIC AIRLINE ROUTES, 1994

Rank	Metropolitan areas		Passengers
1.	New York	Los Angeles	2,821,910
2.	New York	Chicago	2,664,240
3.	New York	Boston	2,511,250
4.	New York	Miami	2,474,220
5.	Honolulu	Kahului, Maui	2,316,680
6.	New York	Washington	2,247,840
7.	Dallas/Fort Worth	Houston	2,224,240
8.	Los Angeles	San Francisco	2,164,500
9.	New York	San Francisco	1,926,970
10.	New York	Orlando	1,883,570
11.	New York	Ft. Lauderdale	1,753,460
12.	New York	Atlanta	1,716,300
13.	New York	San Juan	1,657,460
14.	Los Angeles	Las Vegas	1,601,880
15.	Chicago	Detroit	1,365,900
16.	Honolulu	Lihue, Kauai	1,323,120
17.	Los Angeles	Phoenix	1,322,930
18.	New York	West Palm Beach	1,289,270
19.	Los Angeles	Honolulu	1,255,820
20.	Los Angeles	Oakland	1,216,900
21.	Honolulu	Kona, Hawaii	1,158,500
22.	Chicago	Los Angeles	1,132,240
23.	Boston	Washington	1,100,120
24.	Honolulu	Hilo, Hawaii	1,082,210
25.	San Francisco	San Diego	1,049,700

Note: For twelve months ended December 1993. Passengers inbound plus outbound. Includes all commercial airports in a metropolitan area. Does not include connecting passengers. **Source:** Air Transport Association of America, *Air Transport 1995: The Annual Report of the U.S. Scheduled Airline Industry* (1995).

U.S. AIR TRAVEL ARRIVALS FROM AND DEPARTURES TO FOREIGN COUNTRIES, 1980–93 (thousands of passengers)

Country	Arrivals from 1980	Arrivals from 1993	Departures to 1980	Departures to 1993
Australia	227	591	245	588
Bahamas	1,123	1,370	1,006	1,046
Barbados	135	208	126	207
Belgium	242	408	231	372
Bermuda	497	436	467	247
Brazil	300	711	291	696
China/Taiwan	113	606	90	616
Colombia	315	389	299	353
Denmark	267	285	254	272
Dominican Republic	468	1,027	443	949
France	689	1,877	635	1,759
Germany[1]	1,175	2,922	1,178	2,788
Grand Cayman	121	185	112	244
Greece	208	165	190	150
Haiti	133	200	124	180
Hong Kong	228	511	152	477
Ireland	220	582	212	324
Israel	189	293	186	317
Italy	537	903	495	878
Jamaica	429	982	382	887
Japan	1,624	4,999	1,602	4,757
Korea, South	234	1,070	186	961
Mexico	2,886	4,778	2,886	4,371
Netherlands	427	1,297	409	1,150
Netherlands Antilles	327	360	282	347
Panama Republic	150	201	142	194
Philippines	194	318	160	249
Spain	312	600	273	576
Switzerland	312	603	306	593
United Kingdom	2,973	6,006	2,840	5,682
Venezuela	533	653	518	641
U.S. carrier	10,031	21,940	9,369	20,232
Foreign carrier	10,231	19,618	9,886	18,022
Total passengers	**20,262**	**41,558**	**19,256**	**38,254**

Note: Covers passengers on international commercial flights arriving at or departing from U.S. airports. Excludes traffic between U.S. and Canada, border crossers, crewmen, and military personnel but includes travelers between U.S. ports in the 50 states, territories, and possessions. 1. Data for 1980 refer to the former West Germany before reunification. **Source:** U.S. Dept. of Transportation, *National Transportation Statistics 1995*.

CRIME AND PUNISHMENT

National crime statistics are maintained by the Federal Bureau of Investigation (FBI) and the Bureau of Justice Statistics (BJS), two divisions of the Department of Justice, using very different methodologies. The FBI data is compiled from monthly law enforcement reports of homicide, forcible rape, robbery and aggravated assault (collectively known as violent crimes), and burglary, larceny-theft, motor vehicle theft, and arson (property crimes). The Bureau of Justice Statistics uses data collected by U.S. Census Bureau personnel in face-to-face interviews about crime with about 100,000 people in 49,000 households. The interviewers ask people about their experience with rape, personal robbery, aggravated and simple assault (violent crimes), household burglary, personal and household theft, and motor vehicle theft (property crimes). It does not measure homicide or commercial crimes (such as burglaries of stores), but it does ask whether and why people report each type of crime to law enforcement authorities.

Each method has its flaws. Because the FBI statistics measure only crimes reported to law enforcement authorities, they do not necessarily reflect the number and rates of crimes actually committed. For various reasons, especially in the case of rape, people don't always report crime to the police. (Only 53 percent of all rapes or attempted rapes reported to Census Bureau interviewers between 1987 and 1991 were reported to law enforcement authorities.) The Bureau of Justice Statistics Survey extrapolates data from a sampling of people to provide information about the entire country as a whole. These statistics, published annually in the National Crime Victimization Survey, are vulnerable to criticism that the sample is not representative of the entire population (called a sampling variation or a margin of error). Its failure to keep data on homicide and commercial crime is another obvious shortcoming.

The data from each agency are not strictly comparable, though when used together, they provide a much broader picture of crime trends. Unfortunately, politicans often use the set of statistics that best fits their purpose. For example, the FBI data shows that the rate of violent crime has increased by more than 20 percent since 1988 alone. But the BJS data shows that the rate of violent crime has remained about the same for the past 20 years. Completing the picture is the fact that BJS statistics show that reporting of crime has increased by about 20 percent since 1973. Knowing the approach and the fallacies of each methodology allows the user to find the truth hidden in both sets of statistics: that people are reporting crime in much greater numbers than they used to, even though the crime rate isn't changing.

REPORTED CRIME

The United States is the most violent industrialized democracy in the world, as measured by the number of crimes reported to the FBI by state and local law enforcement agencies. In 1993, there were 24,530 murders reported to police in the United States, about one every 21 minutes. This was a 3% increase over the year before. Guns were the weapon of choice, accounting for 70% of all murders in 1993, up from 59% in 1986 and 1987. Handguns alone accounted for more than half of all murders. By comparison, the next most common weapon category, knives or cutting instruments, accounted for only 13% of murders in 1993, down from 20% in 1987.

Among youthful victims, the numbers of homicides resulting from the use of firearms is even more pronounced and demonstrate the ease with which teenagers and young adults are able to obtain guns. In 1990, 82% of homicides among teenagers 15–19 years of age were associated with firearms (91% and 77% among black and white males, respectively); at 20–24 years of age, 76% of homicides were from firearms (87% and 71%); and at 25–34 years of age, 69% of homicides (75% and 72%) were caused by firearms. Proportions of female homicides due to firearms were lower for both races.

Despite all the attention paid to murder, the violent crime increasing the fastest is aggravated assault, which has jumped 65.6% since 1984. By comparison, the number of murders has increased only 31.2% over the same period. And even though the overall number of property crimes has increased only 15.2% since 1984, the number of motor vehicle thefts has increased a whopping 51.2% over that period. The number of all serious crimes reported to police (violent crimes plus property crimes) has increased 19.0% since 1984.

Raw numbers of crime do not necessarily tell the whole story. A more accurate picture of how safe our streets are is the crime rate per 100,000 inhabitants, which takes into account population growth. In 1993, there were 5,483 total serious crimes per 100,000 inhabitants, an increase of only 9.0% since 1984, and a *decrease* of 4.5% since 1980. There were 746.1 violent crimes for every 100,000 people in 1993, a 38.4% increase over 1984. Aggravated assault (440.1 per 100,000; up 51.7%) and robbery (255.8 per 100,000; up 24.5%) made up the lion's share of the rate and increase in violent crimes. Property crimes totaled 4,736.9 per 100,000 inhabitants in 1993, an increase of only 5.4% since 1984. Larceny and theft constitute the majority of property crimes, but the biggest increase in the rate was in motor vehicle theft, which jumped 38.5% since 1984.

The biggest states, of course, had the most crimes. But the rate of crime (a much better measure of how likely you are to be a victim) was greatest in Florida (8,351.0 serious crimes

SERIOUS CRIME IN THE U.S., 1975–93

Crime	1975	1980	1985	1990	1992	1993	Percent change, 1989–93
Number of offenses reported to police							
Violent crime	**1,039,710**	**1,344,520**	**1,328,800**	**1,820,130**	**1,932,270**	**1,924,190**	**16.9%**
Murder	20,510	23,040	18,980	23,440	23,760	24,530	14.1
Forcible rape	56,090	82,990	88,670	102,560	109,060	104,810	10.9
Robbery	470,500	565,840	497,870	639,270	672,480	659,760	14.1
Aggravated assault	492,620	672,650	723,250	1,054,860	1,126,970	1,135,100	19.3
Property crime	**10,252,700**	**12,063,700**	**11,102,600**	**12,655,500**	**12,505,900**	**12,216,700**	**–3.1%**
Burglary	3,265,300	3,795,200	3,073,300	3,073,900	2,979,900	2,834,800	–10.5
Larceny/Theft	5,977,700	7,136,900	6,926,400	7,945,700	7,915,200	7,820,900	–0.7
Motor vehicle theft	1,009,600	1,131,700	1,102,900	1,635,900	1,610,800	1,561,000	–0.2
Total serious crimes	**11,292,400**	**13,408,300**	**12,431,400**	**14,475,600**	**14,438,200**	**14,141,000**	**–0.8%**
Rate per 100,000 inhabitants							
Violent crime	**487.8**	**596.6**	**556.6**	**731.8**	**757.5**	**746.1**	**12.5%**
Murder	9.6	10.2	7.9	9.4	9.3	9.5	9.2
Forcible rape	26.3	36.8	37.1	41.2	42.8	40.6	6.6
Robbery	220.8	251.1	208.5	257.0	263.6	255.8	9.8
Aggravated assault	231.1	298.5	302.9	424.1	441.8	440.1	14.8
Property crime	**4,810.7**	**5,353.3**	**4,650.5**	**5,088.5**	**4,902.7**	**4,736.9**	**–6.7%**
Burglary	1,532.1	1,684.1	1,287.3	1,235.9	1,168.2	1,099.2	–13.9
Larceny/Theft	2,804.8	3,167.0	2,901.2	3,194.8	3,103.0	3,032.4	–4.4
Motor vehicle theft	473.7	502.2	462.0	657.8	631.5	605.3	–4.0
Total serious crimes	**5,298.5**	**5,950.0**	**5,207.1**	**5,820.3**	**5,660.2**	**5,482.9**	**–4.5%**

Note: Totals may not add up due to independent rounding. **Source:** Federal Bureau of Investigation, *Uniform Crime Reports: Crime in the United States 1993* (1994).

SERIOUS CRIME PER 100,000 POPULATION, BY STATE, 1993

		Violent crime				Property crime		
State	All serious crime	Murder	Forcible rape	Robbery	Aggravated assault	Burglary	Larceny/ Theft	Motor vehicle theft
Ala.	4,878.8	11.6	35.1	159.5	574.3	1,088.6	2,672.0	337.8
Alaska	5,567.9	9.0	83.8	122.4	545.6	816.9	3,539.4	450.9
Ariz.	7,431.7	8.6	37.8	162.9	505.7	1,465.5	4,387.4	863.8
Ark.	4,810.7	10.2	42.4	124.9	415.8	1,099.3	2,795.7	322.5
Calif.	6,456.9	13.1	37.7	405.1	621.8	1,327.0	3,029.1	1,023.0
Colo.	5,526.8	5.8	45.8	116.7	399.0	1,009.8	3,499.4	450.3
Conn.	4,650.4	6.3	24.4	196.7	228.7	978.1	2,620.6	595.5
D.C.	11,761.1	78.5	56.1	1,229.6	1,557.6	1,995.5	5,449.0	1,394.8
Del.	4,872.1	5.0	77.0	186.7	417.1	892.0	2,979.0	315.3
Fla.	8,351.0	8.9	53.8	357.6	785.7	1,835.4	4,413.9	895.7
Ga.	6,193.0	11.4	35.4	248.0	428.3	1,307.3	3,568.7	593.8
Hawaii	6,277.0	3.8	33.6	103.6	120.1	1,135.7	4,429.4	450.8
Idaho	3,845.1	2.9	35.3	16.9	226.7	668.8	2,711.1	183.4
Ill.[1]	5,617.9	11.4	34.6	381.2	532.6	1,015.5	3,084.0	558.7
Ind.	4,465.1	7.5	39.1	119.8	322.6	852.0	2,695.9	428.1
Iowa	3,846.4	2.3	24.4	53.9	244.8	730.7	2,599.4	190.8
Kans.[1]	4,975.3	6.4	40.1	123.6	326.3	1,132.2	3,024.0	322.7
Ky.	3,259.7	6.6	34.3	90.4	331.4	740.1	1,840.7	216.2
La.	6,846.6	20.3	42.3	283.6	715.4	1,368.3	3,802.9	613.7
Me.	3,153.9	1.6	26.6	21.3	76.3	719.0	2,174.7	134.4
Md.	6,106.5	12.7	44.0	434.7	506.4	1,132.8	3,292.5	683.4
Mass.	4,893.9	3.9	33.4	175.7	592.0	1,001.7	2,271.3	816.1
Mich.[2]	5,452.5	9.8	71.1	238.5	472.1	982.7	3,063.2	615.0
Minn.[2]	4,386.2	3.4	35.2	112.7	175.8	844.5	2,872.0	342.6
Miss.	4,481.3	13.5	42.6	139.3	238.4	1,285.8	2,363.5	335.1
Mo.	5,095.4	11.3	36.2	241.8	455.2	1,025.5	2,777.8	547.7
Mont.	4,790.0	3.0	27.9	32.4	114.2	714.2	3,652.1	246.2
Nebr.	4,117.1	3.9	27.8	55.4	252.0	663.5	2,912.9	201.6
Nev.	6,180.1	10.4	60.9	340.1	463.9	1,245.0	3,321.6	738.3
N.H.	2,905.0	2.0	44.4	27.3	64.1	515.1	2,058.0	194.0
N.J.	4,800.8	5.3	28.1	296.0	297.5	974.0	2,486.1	714.0
N.Mex.	6,266.1	8.0	52.1	138.4	731.1	1,421.2	3,510.1	405.1
N.Y.	5,551.3	13.3	27.5	561.2	471.5	998.6	2,644.2	835.0
N.C.	5,652.3	11.3	34.3	192.4	441.3	1,515.8	3,168.8	288.5
N.D.	2,820.3	1.7	23.5	8.3	48.7	373.2	2,216.2	148.7
Ohio	4,485.3	6.0	49.1	192.7	256.3	878.1	2,667.7	435.3
Okla.	5,294.3	8.4	49.3	121.8	455.3	1,235.0	2,943.7	480.7
Oreg.	5,765.6	4.6	51.3	129.6	317.6	1,024.8	3,656.9	580.7
Pa.	3,271.4	6.8	26.5	179.0	205.1	582.0	1,831.7	440.2
R.I.	4,499.0	3.9	28.6	101.1	268.1	1,040.9	2,410.0	646.3
S.C.	5,903.4	10.3	52.3	187.3	773.4	1,309.2	3,226.8	344.0
S.Dak.	2,958.2	3.4	44.5	15.0	145.6	549.2	2,086.0	114.5
Tenn.	5,239.5	10.2	49.9	220.1	485.5	1,182.6	2,700.2	591.0
Tex.	6,439.1	11.9	55.0	224.4	470.8	1,297.3	3,687.3	692.3
Utah	5,237.4	3.1	44.6	58.6	194.7	790.8	3,903.4	242.2
Vt.	3,972.4	3.6	39.8	9.0	61.8	874.3	2,851.2	132.6
Va.	4,115.5	8.3	32.1	142.0	189.8	667.7	2,790.1	285.5
Wash.	5,952.3	5.2	64.4	137.1	307.9	1,067.2	3,914.4	456.1
W.Va.	2,532.6	6.9	20.1	43.0	138.5	599.1	1,563.5	161.5
Wis.	4,054.1	4.4	25.2	113.4	121.4	663.0	2,762.0	364.7
Wyo.	4,163.0	3.4	34.3	17.2	231.3	643.2	3,078.7	154.9
U.S.	**5,482.9**	**9.5**	**40.6**	**255.8**	**440.1**	**1,099.2**	**3,032.4**	**605.3**

Note: Offense totals are based on reporting agencies and estimated for unreported areas. 1. Complete data not available for the states of Illinois and Kansas. Some data are estimated. 2. Forcible rape data by the state-level Uniform Crime Reporting Program administered by the Michigan State Police and the Minnesota Department of Public Safety were not in accordance with national crime reporting guidelines. Forcible rape totals were estimated using the national rate of forcible rapes when grouped by like agencies. **Source:** Federal Bureau of Investigation, *Uniform Crime Reports: Crime in the United States 1993* (1994).

SERIOUS CRIME PER 100,000 POPULATION, BY METROPOLITAN STATISTICAL AREA, 1993

		Violent crime				
City	All serious crime	Murder	Forcible rape	Robbery	Aggravated assault	Property crimes
Albuquerque	7,547.8	9.1	60.0	259.0	945.5	6,274.2
Atlanta	7,594.5	12.2	42.4	369.1	500.1	6,670.6
Austin	7,584.5	6.0	54.6	190.3	277.3	7,056.3
Baltimore	7,275.4	17.2	49.7	636.2	653.0	5,919.3
Boston[2]	4,844.6	4.3	31.3	202.5	539.0	4,067.6
Buffalo	5,283.8	7.3	37.0	293.0	417.4	4,529.1
Charlotte	7,277.0	16.6	46.7	343.0	798.2	6,072.6
Cincinnati	4,833.6	3.8	53.5	202.1	314.3	4,260.1
Columbus	6,012.8	8.3	63.3	318.1	292.5	5,330.5
Dallas	7,290.9	14.6	59.0	326.4	546.3	6,344.5
Denver	6,090.8	7.5	45.5	186.5	492.2	5,359.0
Detroit	N.A.	15.8	N.A.	400.2	564.5	5,408.6
El Paso	7,827.7	8.6	53.1	254.2	715.2	6,796.7
Fort Lauderdale	8,904.1	7.9	40.4	366.5	590.6	7,898.7
Fort Worth	6,880.9	11.7	64.1	264.0	484.8	6,056.3
Fresno	8,099.6	16.9	52.2	427.7	587.8	7,015.0
Honolulu	6,442.9	3.5	32.7	123.9	125.5	6,157.3
Houston	N.A.	15.9	68.2	N.A.	N.A.	5,337.0
Jacksonville	8,598.0	15.1	85.3	406.0	913.5	7,178.1
Los Angeles–Long Beach	7,049.6	21.3	40.3	721.6	899.3	5,367.1
Memphis	7,408.6	21.9	85.8	548.9	452.7	6,299.3
Miami	13,500.4	18.1	53.0	913.3	1,151.8	11,364.2
Milwaukee	5,355.8	11.4	35.4	301.1	134.2	4,873.6
Minneapolis	N.A.	4.4	N.A.	184.3	235.7	4,830.6
Nashville[2]	7,331.8	10.3	74.0	292.9	721.4	6,233.1
New Orleans[2]	8,511.7	37.7	52.3	558.9	663.8	7,199.1
New York	7,532.9	23.2	34.8	1,047.7	759.9	5,667.3
Oakland	7,329.6	14.4	43.0	453.1	627.0	6,192.1
Oklahoma City	7,692.7	10.4	73.9	203.8	540.1	6,864.4
Philadelphia	4,355.3	12.0	31.0	327.2	292.0	3,693.1
Phoenix	7,787.9	9.6	36.8	205.1	555.3	6,981.1
Pittsburgh	3,111.2	5.3	27.2	167.2	193.7	2,717.8
Portland, Oreg.	6,244.5	5.7	56.6	196.1	453.4	5,532.8
Sacramento	7,038.4	11.1	38.4	296.2	469.9	6,232.9
San Antonio	8,450.9	18.6	48.9	232.9	329.3	7,821.3
San Diego	6,160.5	9.3	30.6	285.2	548.7	5,286.8
San Francisco	6,697.5	10.1	34.0	593.8	450.2	5,609.4
San Jose	4,640.3	4.0	38.2	116.7	365.8	4,115.6
Seattle	6,588.1	5.3	69.8	191.4	303.3	6,018.3
Toledo	6,222.5	7.9	68.0	276.0	245.3	5,625.3
Tucson	9,219.9	9.2	60.2	152.9	531.9	8,465.7
Tulsa	5,484.1	8.5	57.1	170.0	565.4	4,683.0
Washington, D.C.	5,462.4	15.8	33.4	324.0	398.2	4,691.0

1. Data do not include arson. 2. Forcible rape data by the state-level Uniform Crime Reporting Program administered by the Michigan State Police and the Minnesota Department of Public Safety were not in accordance with national crime reporting guidelines. Forcible rape totals were estimated using the national rate of forcible rapes when grouped by like agencies. **Source:** Federal Bureau of Investigation, *Uniform Crime Reports: Crime in the United States 1993* (1994).

per 100,000 residents), Arizona (7,431.7), and Louisiana (6,846.6). All three of these states have the reputation of being tough on crime, and all three have the death penalty—Florida does so with zeal—yet these measures have apparently had little impact on crime. Meanwhile, New York, supposedly one of the most dangerous states, was just slightly above the national average of 5,482.9. The most dangerous place to live, however, was the nation's capital, with a whopping 11,761.1 serious crimes per 100,000 residents, more than double the national average. No wonder crime always ranks high on politicians' lists of priorities. By metropolitan area, Miami (13,500.4), Tucson (9,219.9) and Fort Lauderdale (8,904.1) topped the list of dangerous cities, followed by Jacksonville, New Orleans, and San Antonio. New York City placed 14th.

CRIME VICTIMS

Victimization statistics are compiled by the Bureau of Justice Statistics based on interviews with a sampling of people about their personal experience with crime. (The BJS does not ask about or keep statistics on homicides.) Unlike the number of crimes reported, the number of victimizations is not going up. In fact, for some types of crime, victimization levels are declining. The number of violent crimes (not counting murder), for example, was statistically the same in 1992 as it was in 1991 and 1981. And the number of personal thefts and household crimes are both *down* more than 20 percent since 1981.

As the accompanying table shows, the victims of most kinds of crime are most likely to be black, young, poor, urban, and except for rape and domestic violence, male. People with family incomes of less than $7,500 were almost twice as likely as anybody else to be victimized by crime, especially violent crime. In fact, the poorer a person is, the more likely he or she is to be the victim of a crime. Blacks were nearly three times as likely to be the victim of robbery as whites, and almost twice as likely to be the victim of aggravated assault. And while senior citizens often feel most vulnerable to crime, it is teenagers who are most likely to be victimized by all kinds of crime. Children between the ages of 12 and 15 are nearly 16 times as likely to be the victims of violent crime as people over the age of 65.

Rape

The traditional picture of rape as a crime perpetrated by an armed assailant in a dark alleyway continues to be eroded by statistics. More than half the victims of rape or attempted rape between 1987 and 1991 knew their attacker, and 43 percent were raped in or near their own home, according to data gathered from interviews conducted by the Bureau of Justice Statistic's National Crime Victimization Survey. The majority of rapes took place at night, regardless of whether the victim knew her attacker. Rapists who did not know their victims were much more likely (27% to 17%) to be armed than rapists known by their victims; victims were much more likely (64% to 50%) to report the crime to the police if their assailant was armed. Slightly more than half of all rape victims reported the crime to the police, regardless of whether they knew their attacker. The majority of victims (especially those raped by a stranger) cited a desire to punish the offender as the most important reason for reporting the crime. Women who did not report their rapes to police said they considered it a private matter (28%) or because they were afraid of a reprisal from their assailant (17%). An indication of the shame rape victims continue to feel is the fact that 40 percent of women who did not report their rape to the police refused to explain why they did not turn in their assailants.

All statistics regarding rape must be read with the understanding that many women still

VICTIMIZATION LEVELS FOR SELECTED CRIMES, 1975–92

		Victimizations ('000s)		
Year	Total	Violent crimes[1]	Personal theft	Household crimes
1975	39,266	5,573	16,294	17,400
1980	40,252	6,130	15,300	18,821
1981	41,454	6,582	15,863	19,009
1985	34,864	5,823	13,474	15,568
1986	34,118	5,515	13,235	15,368
1987	35,336	5,796	13,575	15,966
1988	35,796	5,910	14,056	15,830
1989	35,818	5,861	13,829	16,128
1990	34,404	6,009	12,975	15,419
1991	35,497	6,587	12,885	16,025
1992	33,649	6,621	12,211	14,817

1. Does not include murder. **Source:** Bureau of Justice Statistics Bulletin, *Criminal Victimization 1992* (1993).

VICTIMIZATION RATES, BY SEX, AGE, RACE, INCOME, AND RESIDENCE, 1993

In 1979, the Bureau of Justice Statistics began a decade-long redesign of the National Crime Victimization Survey to make it more accurate at measuring crime, especially crimes that people don't report to police or even to Justice Department interviewers. The data in the following table are from the first survey to use the new data collection methods. Therefore, 1993 statistics are not directly comparable with those from previous years.

		Crimes of violence[1]			
Characteristic	All crimes	Total	Rape/ Sexual assault	Robbery	Assault
By sex					
Male	63.3	61.0	0.4	8.5	52.1
Female	45.2	42.6	4.0	4.0	34.5
By age					
12–15	125.3	120.8	4.5	13.6	102.6
16–19	120.7	117.0	7.2	11.7	98.1
20–24	97.7	93.6	5.7	10.5	77.4
25–34	61.2	58.8	2.4	7.4	49.1
35–49	44.9	43.0	1.6	5.1	36.2
50–64	18.3	17.1	0.2[3]	3.0	13.9
65+	7.9	5.6	0.3[3]	1.3	4.1
By race					
White	51.8	49.8	2.3	5.1	42.4
Black	72.6	67.0	2.7	13.0	51.3
Hispanic[2]	62.5	59.1	2.1	10.8	46.2
Family income					
Less than $7,500	93.5	89.5	5.5	12.2	71.8
$ 7,500–$ 9,999	59.4	57.5	2.7	8.9	45.9
$10,000–$14,999	53.5	50.5	2.5	5.9	42.2
$15,000–$24,999	51.9	50.2	2.3	4.7	43.3
$25,000–$29,999	51.5	49.2	1.9	5.0	42.3
$30,000–$49,999	47.6	45.9	1.1	4.6	40.2
$50,000 or more	40.9	38.2	1.9	4.2	32.1
By residence					
Central city	73.8	69.2	3.4	10.9	54.8
Suburban	47.8	46.0	1.7	5.1	39.3
Rural	43.4	42.1	2.2	3.0	36.9

Note: Rates per 1,000 people ages 12 or older. 1. The National Crime Victimization Survey cannot measure murder because it is impossible to question the victim. 2. Persons of Hispanic origin may be of any race. 3. Estimate based on small sample. **Source:** Bureau of Justice Statistics Bulletin, *Criminal Victimization 1993* (1995).

CHARACTERISTICS OF RAPE INCIDENTS, 1987–91

	Percent of rape victimizations		
		Victim-offender relationship	
Characteristic	Total	Non-stranger	Stranger
TOTAL	**100%**	**55%**	**44%**
Place of occurrence			
At or near own home	43%	52%	25%
At or near friend's home	16	21	8
At commercial establishment or school	6	9	4
Public parking area or garage	5	4	8
Open area or public area	18	5	43
Not ascertained	12	9	12
Time of occurrence			
6 A.M.–noon	16%	15%	18%
Noon–6 P.M.	16	18	14
6 P.M.–midnight	37	38	32
Midnight–6 A.M.	31	25	34
Offender had weapon	**21%**	**17%**	**29%**
Victim took self-protective action	**85%**	**85%**	**85%**
Self-protective action helped	61	58	68
Self-protective action made situation worse	17	16	20
Victim sustained injuries other than rape injury	**47%**	**43%**	**60%**
Victim reported incident to police	**53%**	**53%**	**55%**

Note: Rape incidents include completed rape and attempted rape as reported by victims to Census Bureau interviewers. **Source:** Bureau of Justice Statistics, *Violence Against Women* (January 1994).

MURDER VICTIMS, BY TYPE OF WEAPON USED, 1987–93

Weapon	1987	1990	1992	1993
Total firearms	10,612	13,035	15,489	16,189
Handguns	7,847	10,099	12,580	13,252
Rifles	776	746	706	754
Shotguns	1,101	1,245	1,111	1,059
Other guns	16	25	42	38
Firearms not stated	872	920	1,050	1,086
Knives or cutting instruments	3,643	3,526	3,296	2,957
Blunt objects[1]	1,045	1,085	1,040	1,024
Personal weapons[2]	1,165	1,119	1,131	1,164
Poison	34	11	13	9
Explosives	12	13	19	26
Fire	200	288	203	217
Narcotics	24	29	24	22
Drowning	51	36	29	23
Strangulation	360	312	314	329
Asphyxiation	115	96	115	113
Other weapons not stated	702	723	1,043	1,198
Total	**17,963**	**20,273**	**22,716**	**23,271**

1. Clubs, hammers, and so on. 2. Hands, fists, feet, and so on. **Source:** Federal Bureau of Investigation, *Uniform Crime Reports 1993: Crime in the United States* (1994).

MURDER VICTIM/OFFENDER RELATIONSHIPS BY RACE AND SEX, 1993

	Race of victim			Sex of victim	
Category	White	Black	Other/ Unknown	Male	Female
Race of offender					
White	4,686	304	72	3,469	1,582
Black	849	5,393	57	4,869	1,413
Other/Unknown	113	85	162	246	91
Sex of offender					
Male	5,057	4,985	237	7,487	2,765
Female	536	730	30	1,004	290

Note: Data based on 11,721 single victim/single offender incidents. Does not include 146 incidents for which the sex of the offender and/or victim is unknown. **Source:** Federal Bureau of Investigation, *Uniform Crime Reports: Crime in the United States 1993* (1994).

VALUE OF PROPERTY STOLEN, BY TYPE, 1993

	Value of property		
Type of property	Stolen ('000s)	Recovered ('000s)	Percent recovered
Clothing and furs	$ 328,787	$ 47,445	14.4%
Consumable goods	103,112	10,026	9.7
Currency, notes, etc.	886,252	42,394	4.8
Firearms	113,969	11,849	10.4
Household goods	223,149	12,327	5.5
Jewelry and precious metals	1,145,813	55,386	4.8
Livestock	36,549	4,534	12.4
Miscellaneous	2,438,705	201,006	8.2
Motor vehicles	6,682,729	4,125,665	61.7
Office equipment	327,563	22,414	6.8
Television, stereos, etc.	1,017,950	45,095	4.4
Total[1]	**$13,304,578**	**$4,578,141**	**34.4%**

Note: Based on a survey of 11,748 law enforcement agencies representing 216,355,000 inhabitants. Complete data not available for the states of Kansas and Illinois. 1. All totals and percentages calculated before rounding. **Source:** Federal Bureau of Investigation, *Uniform Crime Reports 1993: Crime in the United States* (1994).

don't report rape, not even to survey interviewers. Therefore, the numbers of rape (and percentage that go unreported to police) are most likely higher than those published by the BJS, though the exact amount of the undercount is impossible to ascertain.

Value of Stolen Property

While the taxpayer cost of fighting crime can be easily calculated, the emotional cost to victims and their families, and the overall burden to society, is inestimable. The most immediate cost is to the crime victim in value of property or goods stolen. In 1993, this amounted to $13.3 bil., of which only $5.2 bil., or 34.4%, was recovered. Motor vehicles represented more than half the value of all property stolen and 90% of the value of all property recovered. A surprising 61.7% of all cars stolen are recovered, though not necessarily in the same condition as when they were stolen. By comparison, only 4.8% of stolen jewelry or precious metals and 12.4% of stolen livestock are ever recovered.

LAW ENFORCEMENT

The nation's collective response to perceptions of increasing crime continues to be building more prisons and hiring more police. As of October 1993, there were 553,773 sworn police officers in the United States and an additional 212,353 civilians employed in police departments. This translates into 2.3 police for every 1,000 residents. In cities with more than 250,000 residents, the ratio was even higher: they averaged 3.6 police per 1,000 residents. The number of law enforcement employees per 1,000 inhabitants was highest in suburban and rural counties (3.6 and 3.9, respectively), but that was due primarily to a large number of civilian employees in those police departments. Suburban and rural police departments employed roughly two civilians for every three sworn officers, while big cities employed close to four officers for each civilian. By sex, nine out of every 10 sworn officers in almost every police department is male, but civilian police employees are overwhelmingly female (as many as 75% in some departments).

Arrests

Nationwide, law enforcement agencies made an estimated 11.8 million arrests in 1993 for all criminal infractions except traffic violations. This represents a rate of 5,490 arrests per 100,000 population. In cities with populations of 250,000 or more, the arrest rate was 7,103 per 100,000; it was 4,009 per 100,000 for suburban counties and 3,989 per 100,000 for rural counties. The greatest number of arrests were for driving under the influence of drugs or alcohol (1.2 million), larceny or theft (1.3 million), simple assault (1.0 million), and drug abuse (1.0 million).

Because the number of agencies reporting arrests each year to the FBI varies, the total number of arrests each year are not strictly comparable. But when the number of agencies is held constant, the arrest rate has increased 18.4 percent since 1984, with arrests for violent crime increasing 49.7 percent.

By age, 6% of all people arrested nationwide in 1993 were under 15; 17% were under 18; 30% were under 21; and 45% were under 25. Of people arrested for crime index offenses, 12% were under the age of 15, 29% were under 18, 43% under 21, and 55% under 25. The under-25 age group was responsible for 47% of all violent crime arrests and 58% of all property crime arrests.

By sex, 81% of all those arrested were males, who accounted for 77% of crime index offense arrests—87% of those for violent crimes, and 74% of those for property crime. Females were most often arrested for larceny/theft. These crimes alone accounted for 18% of all arrests of women, and for 74% of all crime index offense arrests of women.

By race, 67% of all those arrested were white, 31% were black, and 2% were of other races. Whites accounted for 61% of crime index offense arrests, 53% of violent crime arrests, and 64% of property crime arrests.

ARRESTS IN THE U.S., 1984–93

Crime	Total arrests 1984	1989	1992	1993	Rate per 100,000 1993
Violent crime	400,877	487,673	616,391	648,416	302.9
Murder	15,126	16,146	18,755	20,285	9.5
Forcible rape	28,565	27,461	31,507	32,523	15.2
Robbery	115,522	123,317	150,600	153,533	71.7
Aggravated assault	241,664	320,749	415,529	442,075	206.5
Property crime	1,431,812	1,600,947	1,738,176	1,774,423	828.8
Burglary	338,737	320,470	341,516	338,238	158.0
Larceny/Theft	981,812	1,102,112	1,214,778	1,251,277	584.4
Motor vehicle theft	96,975	165,317	166,617	168,795	78.8
Arson	14,288	13,048	15,265	16,113	7.5
All serious crimes	1,832,689	2,088,620	2,354,567	2,422,839	1,131.6
Other crimes	6,995,758	7,902,737	8,849,213	9,330,429	N.A.
Total arrests	**8,828,447**	**9,991,357**	**11,203,780**	**11,753,268**	**5,489.8**

Note: Based on a survey of approximately 10,000 law enforcement agencies representing approximately 180,000 inhabitants. The number of agencies surveyed and the populations they represent changes from year to year. **Source:** Federal Bureau of Investigation, *Uniform Crime Reports 1993: Crime in the United States* (1994).

ARRESTS BY RACE, 1993

Offense charged	Total	White Number	White Percent	Black Number	Black Percent	Other[1] Number	Other[1] Percent
All arrests	**11,741,751**	**7,855,287**	**66.9%**	**3,647,174**	**31.1%**	**239,290**	**2.1%**
All serious crimes	**2,419,225**	**1,481,923**	**61.3%**	**883,966**	**36.5%**	**53,336**	**2.2%**
Violent crime	**647,448**	**340,237**	**52.6%**	**296,066**	**45.7%**	**11,145**	**1.8%**
Murder	20,243	8,243	40.7	11,656	57.6	344	1.7
Forcible rape	32,469	18,473	56.9	13,419	41.3	577	1.8
Robbery	153,281	55,893	36.5	95,164	62.1	2,224	1.4
Aggravated assault	441,455	257,628	58.4	175,827	39.8	8,000	1.9
Property crime	**1,771,777**	**1,141,686**	**64.4%**	**587,900**	**33.2%**	**42,191**	**2.4%**
Burglary	337,810	226,857	67.2	104,473	30.9	6,480	1.9
Larceny/Theft	1,249,303	806,511	64.6	411,705	33.0	31,087	2.4
Motor vehicle theft	168,591	96,328	57.1	67,938	40.3	4,325	2.6
Arson	16,073	11,990	74.6	3,784	23.5	299	1.8

Note: Based on a survey of 10,509 law enforcement agencies representing 213,093,000 inhabitants. 1. Includes American Indian, Alaskan Native, Asian, and Pacific Islander. **Source:** Federal Bureau of Investigation, *Uniform Crime Reports 1993: Crime in the United States* (1994).

SENTENCED PRISONERS IN THE U.S., BY SYSTEM AND BY SEX, 1991–93

Category	Number 1991	1992	1993[2]	Percent change 1991–93	Incarceration rate[1] 1991	1992	1993[2]	Percent change 1991–93
Total	**789,609**	**847,271**	**910,462**	**15.3%**	**310**	**329**	**351**	**13.2%**
By system:								
Federal	57,044	65,706	74,398	30.4	22	26	29	31.8
State	732,565	781,565	836,064	14.1	287	303	322	12.2
By sex and race:								
White male	363,600	388,000	N.A.	6.7[3]	352	372	N.A.	5.7[3]
Black male	372,200	401,700	N.A.	7.9[3]	2,523	2,678	N.A.	6.1[3]
White female	20,900	22,100	N.A.	5.7[3]	19	20	N.A.	5.2[3]
Black female	22,200	23,800	N.A.	7.2[3]	135	143	N.A.	5.9[3]

Note: Prisoners sentenced to more than one year in prison. 1. Sentenced prisoners per 100,000 resident population. 2. Preliminary. 3. Percent change 1991–92. **Source:** Bureau of Justice Statistics Bulletin, *Prisoners in 1993* (1994).

CORRECTIONS

The United States has more people in jail (as well as more people in jail per capita) than any other industrialized nation. In 1994 the Bureau of Justice Statistics reported a record 1.5 million inmates in federal and state prisons. The prison population has increased 36.2 percent since 1990, and 219.5 percent since 1980. Convinced that incarceration is the only way to reduce crime, federal and state governments continue to build more and more prisons and to impose mandatory sentences for many drug-related crimes. Since 1980 the number of sentenced inmates per 100,000 residents has risen from 139 to 387.

During 1994 prison populations increased in 16 states by at least 10 percent. Texas reported the largest increase (28.5%), followed by Georgia (20.3%), Nevada (16.0%), Virginia (14.6%), and Wisconsin (14.1%). Three states and the District of Columbia experienced less than 2 percent growth. The District of Columbia had the smallest percentage growth (.9%), followed by Oklahoma (1.4%), South Carolina (1.6%), and Massachusetts (1.6%).

Jails and Prisons

Although the terms tend to be used synonymously, "jails" and "prisons" differ in the types of inmates they house, their locations, their physical size, and their programs. Jails are locally administered facilities that house inmates after arraignment, prisoners serving terms of less than one year, and prisoners who cannot be housed in state prisons due to overcrowding.

Prisons are administered by either state or federal government authority. Typically they hold convicted offenders sentenced to terms of confinement for more than one year. They tend to be located away from dense population centers, and they are usually larger than jails and have more rehabilitation programs.

Prisons and Race

Increasing percentages of state and federal inmates are from racial or ethnic minority groups. Between 1980 and 1993, the latest available data, the percent of sentenced inmates who were black rose from 46.5% to 50.8%. Relative to the number of residents in the United States population, blacks were seven times more likely than whites to have been incarcerated in a state or federal prison. An estimated 1,471 blacks per 100,000 black residents and 207 whites per 100,000 white residents were incarcerated in the nation's prisons on December 31, 1993.

The number of prisoners with sentences of more than a year rose 616,292 between 1980 and 1993 (up 195%). The number of white males grew 163%, the number of black males 217%, the number of white females 327%, and the number of black females 343%. The growth in the number of black male prisoners (304,800) accounted for nearly half of the total increase during the 13-year period.

SPENDING ON INMATES AT LOCAL JAILS, BY STATE, 1983–93

State	Operating costs per inmate 1983	Operating costs per inmate 1993	Number of inmates 1983	Number of inmates 1993	Percent change, 1983–93
U.S. total	**$9,360**	**$14,667**	**223,551**	**459,804**	**106%**
Alabama	5,466	8,297	4,464	7,072	58
Alaska	25,444	N.A.	37	31	N.A.
Arizona	10,258	8,552	2,940	7,231	146
Arkansas	7,345	11,201	1,602	2,846	78
California	7,582	14,134	41,720	69,298	66
Colorado	10,661	19,177	2,747	6,316	130
District of Columbia	10,845	N.A.	2,843	1,687	N.A.
Florida	9,479	17,530	14,668	34,183	133
Georgia	5,384	10,259	10,214	22,663	122
Idaho	7,918	11,676	604	1,485	146
Illinois	6,529	13,766	8,849	14,549	64
Indiana	7,106	10,255	3,599	8,297	131
Iowa	11,861	17,399	839	1,602	91
Kansas	8,681	18,972	1,328	2,797	111
Kentucky	6,197	11,416	3,711	6,813	84
Louisiana	6,040	8,404	8,507	16,208	91
Maine	8,828	21,200	560	704	26
Maryland	9,957	16,812	4,608	9,358	103
Massachusetts	11,883	27,531	3,304	7,878	138
Michigan	10,993	16,451	7,637	12,479	63
Minnesota	12,733	24,238	1,954	3,654	87
Mississippi	5,696	7,014	2,498	4,851	94
Missouri	7,484	14,575	3,783	5,030	33
Montana	$10,464	$13,121	405	680	68%
Nebraska	9,765	15,198	844	1,680	99
Nevada	16,439	23,367	940	2,987	218
New Hampshire	11,749	22,993	475	1,127	137
New Jersey	11,120	17,259	5,971	15,122	153
New Mexico	8,793	13,273	1,346	3,058	127
New York	24,294	29,297	16,154	29,809	85
North Carolina	6,040	12,620	3,496	8,939	156
North Dakota	12,535	17,607	243	361	49
Ohio	10,341	18,152	7,116	11,695	64
Oklahoma	6,655	9,397	2,215	4,102	85
Oregon	9,235	24,345	2,304	3,777	64
Pennsylvania	10,165	16,448	10,170	19,231	89
South Carolina	5,218	8,438	2,690	5,713	112
South Dakota	8,038	13,109	316	623	97
Tennessee	6,465	7,675	6,005	14,375	139
Texas	6,813	9,304	15,224	55,395	264
Utah	8,191	16,129	906	1,895	109
Virginia	8,816	15,872	5,719	14,623	156
Washington	9,947	15,331	3,610	7,435	106
West Virginia	7,275	11,474	1,015	1,771	74
Wisconsin	8,947	15,057	3,030	7,879	160
Wyoming	8,912	20,130	341	495	45

Note: Five states—Connecticut, Delaware, Hawaii, Rhode Island, and Vermont—had integrated jail-prison systems and were excluded from the report. **Source:** Bureau of Justice Statistics, *Jails and Jail Inmates 1993–94* (1995).

JAIL POPULATION, 1983–94

Sex and legal status	1983	1988	1993	1994
	One-day count[1]			
All inmates	**223,551**	**343,569**	**459,804**	**490,442**
Adults	221,815	341,893	455,500	483,717
Male	206,163	311,594	411,500	434,838
Female	15,652	30,299	44,100	48,879
Juveniles[2]	—	—	4,300	6,725
Held as adults	—	—	3,300	5,139
Held as juveniles	1,736	1,676	1,000	1,586
	Average daily population[3]			
All inmates	**227,541**	**336,017**	**466,155**	**479,757**
Adults	225,781	334,566	462,800	—
Male	210,451	306,379	418,200	—
Female	15,330	28,187	44,600	—
Juveniles[2]	1,760	1,451	3,400	—

1. As of June 30. 2. Juveniles are persons defined by state statute as being under a certain age, usually 18, and subject initially to juvenile court authority even if tried as adults. In 1994, the definition was changed to include all persons under age 18. 3. The average daily population is the sum of the number of inmates in a jail each day for a year, divided by 365. **Source:** Bureau of Justice Statistics, *Jails and Jail Inmates 1993–94* (1995).

STATE AND FEDERAL PRISON POPULATIONS, 1980–94

Year	Number of inmates	Annual percent change	Total percent change since 1980
1980	329,821	—	—
1981	369,930	12.2%	12.2%
1982	413,806	11.9	25.5
1983	436,855	5.6	32.5
1984	462,002	5.8	40.1
1985	502,507	8.8	52.4
1986	544,972	8.5	65.2
1987	585,084	7.4	77.4
1988	627,600	7.3	90.3
1989	712,364	13.5	116.0
1990	773,919	8.4	134.6
1991	825,619	6.7	150.3
1992	883,656	7.2	167.9
1993	970,444	7.4	187.7
1994	1,053,738	8.6	219.5

Source: Bureau of Justice Statistics Bulletin, *Prisoners in 1994* (1995).

Hispanics, who may be of any race, are the fastest growing minority group—increasing from 7.7% of all state and federal inmates in 1980 to 14.3% in 1993. During this period, the Hispanic incarceration rate more than tripled—from 163 sentenced prisoners per 100,000 Hispanic residents in 1980 to 529 per 100,000 Hispanic residents in 1993. At year-end 1993 nearly 139,000 Hispanics were in state or federal prisons.

Prison Capacity

The country's 52 prison jurisdictions (the 50 states, the District of Columbia, and the federal prison system) estimate their capacities in one of three ways: by the number of beds a corrections rating authority assigns to it; by the number of prisoners that can be accommodated based on a facility's staff, programs, and services; or by the number of prisoners the facility was built to house. These can result in three widely different estimates of total capacity. Moreover, measures of the relationship between a prison's population and its capacity can be based on the highest or lowest capacity. At the

NUMBER OF PRISONERS EXECUTED, BY SYSTEM, 1930–93 (ranked by executions since 1977)

System	Number executed: Since 1930	Since 1977	In 1993	On death row, 1993[1]	Method of execution
Texas	368	71	17	357	Injection
Florida	202	32	3	324	Electrocution
Virginia	114	22	5	49	Electrocution
Louisiana	154	21	1	45	Injection
Georgia	383	17	2	96	Electrocution
Missouri	73	11	4	80	Gas; injection
Alabama	145	10	0	120	Electrocution
Nevada	34	5	0	65	Injection
North Carolina	268	5	0	99	Gas; injection
Arkansas	122	4	0	33	Electrocution; injection
Mississippi	158	4	0	50	Gas; injection
South Carolina	166	4	0	47	Electrocution
Utah	17	4	0	11	Firing squad; injection
Arizona	41	3	2	112	Gas; injection
Delaware	15	3	2	15	Injection
Oklahoma	63	3	0	122	Injection
California	294	2	1	363	Gas; injection
Indiana	43	2	0	47	Electrocution
Illinois	91	1	0	152	Injection
Washington	48	1	1	10	Hanging; injection
Wyoming	8	1	0	0	Gas; injection
Colorado	47	0	0	3	Gas; injection
Connecticut	21	0	0	5	Electrocution
Federal system	33	0	0	6	Method of state of execution
Idaho	3	0	0	22	Firing squad; injection
Kentucky	103	0	0	30	Electrocution
Maryland	68	0	0	15	Gas
Montana	6	0	0	8	Hanging; injection
Nebraska	4	0	0	11	Electrocution
New Hampshire	1	0	0	0	Hanging; injection
New Jersey	74	0	0	7	Injection
New Mexico	8	0	0	1	Injection
Ohio	172	0	0	129	Electrocution; injection
Oregon	19	0	0	13	Injection
Pennsylvania	152	0	0	169	Injection
South Dakota	1	0	0	2	Injection
Tennessee	93	0	0	98	Electrocution
New York[2]	329	(2)	(2)	(2)	(2)
Kansas[3]	15	(3)	(3)	(3)	(3)
Massachusetts	27	0	No death penalty statute		
Iowa	18	0	No death penalty statute		
Vermont	4	0	No death penalty statute		
Rhode Island	0	0	No death penalty statute		
West Virginia	40	No death penalty statute			
District of Columbia	40	No death penalty statute			
North Dakota	0	No death penalty statute			
Michigan	0	No death penalty statute			
Total U.S.	**4,085**	**226**	**38**	**2,716**	

Note: Alaska, Hawaii, Maine, Minnesota, and Wisconsin have not had death penalty statutes on the books since 1930. 1. As of December 31. 2. Death penalty restored in 1995; no executions yet carried out. 3. Death penalty statute restored in 1994; no executions yet carried out. **Source:** Bureau Justice Statistics Bulletin, *Capital Punishment 1993* (1994).

PRISONERS EXECUTED BY RACE, SELECTED YEARS, 1930–93

Year	Total	White	Black	Other
1930	155	90	65	0
1935	199	119	77	3
1940	124	49	75	0
1945	117	41	75	1
1950	82	40	42	0
1955	76	44	32	0
1960	56	21	35	0
1965	7	6	1	0
1967	2	1	1	0
Total, 1930–67	**3,859**	**1,751**	**2,066**	**42**
1977	1	1	0	0
1980	0	0	0	0
1981	1	1	0	0
1982	2	1	1	0
1983	5	4	1	0
1984	21	13	8	0
1985	18	11	7	0
1986	18	11	7	0
1987	25	13	12	0
1988	11	6	5	0
1989	16	8	8	0
1990	23	16	7	0
1991	14	7	7	0
1992	31	19	11	1
1993	38	23	14	1
Total, 1977–93	**226**	**136**	**88**	**2**
Total, 1930–93	**4,085**	**1,887**	**2,154**	**44**

Note: Executions under civil authority only. Does not include 160 executions carried out under military authority since 1930. There were no executions carried out between 1968 and 1977. **Source:** Bureau of Justice Statistics, *Sourcebook of Criminal Justice Statistics* and *Capital Punishment 1993* (1994).

end of 1993, 41 jurisdictions, including the federal prison system, were operating at 100 percent or more of their lowest rated capacity. The federal system was estimated to be operating at 36 percent over capacity. Taken together, state prisons were estimated to be operating at 118 percent of their highest capacity, and 129 percent of their lowest capacity.

To ease overcrowding in the state prison system, some state prisoners are held in local jails. Overall, 23 jurisdictions reported a total of 50,966 prisoners—or about 5.4 percent of the total state prison population—being held in local jails. Those numbers are up markedly from just a year before, when 38,006 prisoners (4.3%) were held in local jails.

Probation and Parole

When an offender is convicted, the primary sentencing alternatives are incarceration or probation. Once imprisoned, the offender may become eligible for parole, a form of conditional release. The explosion in the prison population has understandably led to a corresponding increase in the number of prisoners released on probation or parole (163 percent since 1980). In 1993, according to the Bureau of Justice Statistics, a total of nearly five million people were under "correctional supervision" in the United States—in jail or prison, on parole or on probation. More than half of this population (2.8 million) were on probation; another 671,000 were on parole. If the entire correctional population comprised a separate state, it would rank 17th in the nation by population, smaller than Wisconsin but slightly larger than Tennessee.

CAPITAL PUNISHMENT

In the period 1930–93, 4,085 executions were carried out under state or federal authority. Overall, the number of prisoners executed each year declined steadily between 1930 and 1968. There were 1,667 executions in the 1930s, 1,284 in the 1940s, 717 in the 1950s, and 191 between 1960 and 1967. There were none between 1968 and 1978—the Supreme Court ruled the death penalty unconstitutional in 1972, and reinstated it in 1976—but between 1977 and 1993, 226 executions were carried out, all but one male. Another 2,716 prisoners were on death row at the end of 1993 (all of whom had been convicted of murder) where they had been waiting for an average of five years and seven months while they exhausted their legal appeals. Prisoners actually executed in 1993 had been on death row for an average of nine years and five months since their most recent conviction. The time elapsed between imposition of the death sentence and execution continues to grow even as the number of prisoners executed increases.

Fifteen states have carried out 100 or more executions since 1930; but as of 1995, 12 states and the District of Columbia did not authorize the death penalty for any crime. In Maine, Minnesota, and Wisconsin, there has been no death penalty statute in force since 1930. Alaska and Hawaii have never had death penalty statutes. The death penalty was either abolished or declared unconstitutional in Michigan (1963), Iowa and West Virginia (1965), the District of Columbia (1973), Rhode Island (1979), Oregon (1981), and Massachusetts (1984). Kansas abolished the death penalty in 1973, but restored it July 1994. New York abolished it in 1984, but Governor George Pataki made it a priority in his campaign—he was elected largely because of his pro-death penalty stance—and restored capital punishment early in 1995. And South Dakota abolished the death penalty in 1915, restored it in 1939, abolished it again 1977, and restored it again 1979.

Race and Capital Punishment

Apart from the broad question of whether it is right for the state to take the life of an individual, the three major issues of concern to those opposed to capital punishment are whether it is a deterrent to crime, whether it violates the Eighth Amendment to the Constitution, prohibiting "cruel and unusual punishment" (the U.S. is the only industrialized democracy in the world that hasn't abolished it), and whether it is used fairly with respect to race.

Historically, blacks have been more likely to be executed than whites in proportion both to the general population and to the prison population. Blacks represent 53% of prisoners executed between 1930 and 1993, as against 46% whites and 1% classified as other. However, since 1977, 60% of all those executed were white, and 39% were black.

Automatic Review

Of the 36 states with capital punishment statutes in 1992, 35 provided for automatic review of all death penalty sentences. Only Arkansas and the federal government lack this provision. While most states authorize automatic review of both the conviction and the sentence, Idaho, Indiana, and Montana require review of the sentence only. Typically, the review is undertaken regardless of the defendant's wishes and is conducted by the state's highest appellate court. If either the conviction or the sentence is vacated, the case may be remanded to the trial court for additional proceedings or for retrial, and the death penalty may be reimposed as a result of retrial or resentencing.

With the number of state and federal appeals available to death row prisoners, it should not come as a surprise that a capital sentence ultimately costs more in lawyer's and court fees than a sentence of life in prison without parole. Only a small percentage of prisoners sentenced to death are actually executed. None of the 282 prisoners sentenced to death in 1993 was executed, though three died of other causes while on death row. Since 1986, a grand total of 23 out of 2,268 prisoners have been executed; 36 have died of other causes, while 152 have had their convictions overturned. Of the total of 4,984 prisoners sentenced to death since 1973, only 226 (5%) have been executed. Although the federal government has made efforts to expedite the use of the death penalty for state prisoners—most notably several Supreme Court decisions limiting prisoners' rights to appeal their sentences—only one federal prisoner has been sentenced to death since 1974. That sentence was handed down in 1991.

GUNS AND GUN CONTROL

The proliferation of guns of all kinds during the late 1980s and thereafter brought about a significant change in the public's attitudes about gun control, an issue once thought too politically charged to address because of the powerful National Rifle Association lobby. But with surveys showing that people are much more worried about crime, especially violent crime, than about the economy or any other single issue, Congress passed two pieces of legislation in 1993–94 designed to halt the inexorable proliferation of firearms on city streets across the country. The Brady bill, which requires gun purchasers to wait five days before taking possession of their weapons (to give sellers and law enforcement officials time to check the buyers' backgrounds for criminal records or mental instability), was signed into law on Nov. 24, 1993. Named for James Brady, Ronald Reagan's chief of staff who was wounded and left paralyzed during the 1981 attack on Pres. Reagan, the bill was the first major gun control legislation passed by Congress since the ban on mail-order rifles in 1968. The Senate had failed to pass this legislation for the previous seven years.

The bigger surprise to people on both sides of the gun control issue was the May 5, 1994, passage of a ban on 19 different kinds of semiautomatic assault weapons. A version of this bill was included in the Senate's anticrime package, but it stood little chance of being passed by the House. But heavy lobbying by Pres. Clinton and Treasury Sec. Lloyd Bentsen, and a last-minute switch by Indiana Democrat Andrew Jacobs, secured passage of the bill by a 216–214 margin. The legislation outlawed weapons that have no other purpose than to kill people quickly without having to take aim.

Although the National Rifle Association suffered two stunning defeats in Congress, diminishing the organization's power to block gun control legislation, the new Republican majority seems intent on repealing both bills.

MANUFACTURE AND IMPORTATION OF FIREARMS IN THE U.S, 1981–91

	Manufactured domestically						Imported			
Year	Pistols	Revolvers	Rifles	Shotguns	Machine guns	Total[1]	Handguns	Rifles	Shotguns	Total
1981	835,167	1,702,062	1,680,945	1,155,567	36,878	5,410,712	305,576	199,559	183,592	688,727
1982	853,444	1,775,179	1,622,890	878,568	27,418	5,157,843	332,556	175,145	157,143	664,844
1983	733,814	1,233,022	1,109,830	959,663	21,453	4,058,466	411,012	228,111	198,771	837,894
1984	752,919	926,790	1,106,761	1,086,077	4,930	3,886,158	341,658	212,679	219,111	773,448
1985	706,542	843,529	1,140,669	769,505	6,092	3,474,866	229,497	270,571	197,417	697,485
1986	692,977	734,650	970,541	641,482	41,482	3,086,429	231,000	269,000	201,000	701,000
1987	963,562	695,270	1,006,100	857,949	3,963	3,530,944	342,113	413,780	307,620	1,063,513
1988	991,011	754,711	1,144,707	928,070	2,239	3,856,696	621,620	282,640	372,008	1,276,268
1989	1,402,660	628,765	1,407,317	935,541	2,387	4,419,527	440,132	293,152	274,497	1,007,781
1990	1,376,399	462,496	1,156,213	848,948	3,809	3,906,197	448,517	203,505	191,787	843,809
1991	1,300,512	456,892	681,536	352,991	2,101	2,810,586	293,231	311,285	116,141	720,657

1. Includes other types of firearms not shown separately. **Source:** Bureau of Alcohol, Tobacco and Firearms, Firearms and Explosives Operations Branch, *ATF Ready Reference 1992* (1992).

THE AMERICAN PEOPLE TODAY

The United States is the third most populous nation in the world, ranking behind only China and India. According to the U.S. Census Bureau, on Mar. 6, 1990, the resident population of the United States reached the 250 million mark, more than three times the 1900 figure of 76 million, about double what it was in 1930, and almost 100 million more than the 1950 total. The Census Bureau predicts that this kind of rapid growth, based mainly as it was on high birth rates and, during the first two decades of the century, extraordinarily high immigration rates, cannot occur during the next century. In fact the underlying shifts in social behavior that will cause dramatic changes in the nature of the population have been in place for 20 years or so, just at the end of a most prolific period of population expansion.

Between 1946 and 1964, just over 75 million babies were born in America, a demographic achievement so noteworthy that those born during this time have their own collective designation, the "Baby Boom generation." During these years the crude birth rate soared to as high as 24 live births (per 1,000 population) in some years, compared to 20 or so in the years before the war; fertility rates, too, reached exceptional levels, ranging from 101 to 121 (per 1,000 women ages 15–44), as compared with an average of about 75 in earlier years. As a result the population grew at an annual rate of between 1.4 percent and 1.8 percent.

Quite remarkably, however, this population burst came to a sudden unexpected halt, so sudden that by 1968 the population growth had sunk to 1 percent, the birth rate to under 18, and fertility rates to about 85, levels that have sunk much farther since. As a result projected population growth over the next few decades is extremely low: 7.1 percent for the 1990s and 5.3 percent for the first decade of the new century. By way of comparison, between 1950 and 1960, the population grew 19 percent.

That period of unparalleled growth has affected many aspects of daily life and will continue to do so for another 50 years. Demographers sometimes refer to the Baby Boomers, somewhat inelegantly perhaps, as the "Pig in the Python" in order to explain how this group has continued to distort the normal contours of the general body of the population. During the fifties their numbers required great capital outlays for new schools and later for expanding colleges and universities. In the seventies they jammed the labor market, causing higher unemployment rates, but helped the economy by increasing consumption and expanding the housing market. After the turn of the century, the Baby Boom generation will begin to enter the retirement years, and even here they will cause a strain on existing structures. What will happen is that the ratio of people working—those born during the 1970s and 1980s, now being called the Baby Bust—to those retired will shrink dramatically. Today that ratio is 5–1, but by 2020 or so, it will be 2.5–1.

If the Baby Boomers and those in much smaller numbers who followed them represent, demographically speaking, the most significant group among the American people, it is the immigrant group that has caused the most interest in recent years. Because their numbers have increased greatly since the 1960s, many see them as the key to preventing future population decline, as current U.S. birth and fertility rates stabilize at a very low level. In recent years immigration has accounted for over 25 percent of the nation's growth. Over the last 20 years, the origins of most immigrants have been Asian and Latin American nations, so the ethnic composition of the American people is clearly going to change and become even more diverse than today.

In the pages that follow, all of these matters are taken up—fertility, race, immigration—to create a statistical portrait of the population both past and present, with a glimpse at the future as well.

The 1990 Census

Article I, section 2 of the U.S. Constitution requires Congress to undertake a census of the population every 10 years for the purpose of apportioning seats in the House of Representatives. Today the decennial census is also used to apportion federal and state funds totaling as much as $100 billion a year, so it is vitally important to local governments and individuals throughout the country. City and county planners and health care administrators, as well as the entire marketing and advertising industries, are strongly dependent on census data for their day-to-day operations. So it's not surprising that the 1990 census, officially taken on Apr. 1, was the largest undertaking of its kind in our history. The first results—state population figures—were released in December 1990, as required by law.

HIGHLIGHTS OF THE CENSUS

Population growth Since the 1980 census, the resident population of the United States increased by 22,164,873, from 226,545,805 to 248,709,873—a growth rate of 9.8 percent, the second lowest in census history. Only the Depression decade of the 1930s was lower (7.3%), while by contrast the Baby Boom era of the 1950s reached a growth rate of 18.5 percent. (Between 1790 and 1910 the rate was never less than 21%.)

Regional growth During the 1980s, the South and the West together accounted for 89 percent of national population growth, about the same as they did in the 1970s. As of 1990 their combined share of the U.S. population was 55.6 percent, up from 52.3 percent in 1980 and 48.0 percent in 1970.

The West had the highest growth rate (22.3%) in the 1980s, a slight decline from the 1970s (23.9%) but still more than twice the national rate. The South's growth rate fell sharply to 13.4 percent from 20.0 percent, but was still significantly higher than the national rate. Growth rates rose in the Northeast (from 0.2% to 3.4%), but fell in the Midwest (from 4.0% to 1.4%).

State population growth For the first time in census history, only three states accounted for over half the national population growth. The combined increases in California (6.1 million), Florida (3.2 million), and Texas (2.8 million) totaled 12.0 million, or 54 percent, of the 22.2 million national population increase.

California continued to grow at record levels during the 1980s, so that by 1990 12.0 percent of all Americans lived there. In addition its numerical growth of 6.1 million and its 26 percent share of national population growth are unprecedented in census history.

The five fastest growing states during the 1980–90 decade were Nevada (50.1% increase), Alaska (36.9%), Arizona (34.8%), Florida (32.7%), and California (25.7%). Over the last 50 years Arizona, Florida, and Nevada have been on every such list while Alaska and California only missed once.

Only two states in the Northeast had growth rates higher than the national average, New Hampshire (20.5%) and Vermont (10.0%); none of the Midwest states did. Four states lost population during the eighties: West Virginia (–8.0%), Iowa (–4.7%), Wyoming (–3.4%), and North Dakota (–2.1%).

Urban and rural population growth Since the 1920 census, more than one-half of all Americans have lived in an urban area, which can be loosely defined as a place of 2,500 or more inhabitants. During the 1980s, the population of urban areas grew by 20 million people, from 167.1 million to 187.1 million, an increase of 12%. By 1990, the proportion of the U.S. population living in urban areas reached 75.2%, up from 73.7% in 1980. California had the highest proportion of urban population, at 92.6%. In comparison, the country's rural population grew by 3.6%, from 59.5 million in 1980 to 61.7 million in 1990. Only 11 states had increased percentages of rural population in the 1980s (see the accompanying table) even though 32 states recorded an increase in the number of rural residents. Vermont had the highest rural percentage of population, 67.8%.

Population growth in metropolitan areas The 1990 census revealed that 77.5% of all U.S. residents (192,725,741) lived in one of the 284 metropolitan areas in the United States, an increase of 11.6%, or more than 20 million. The number of one-million-plus metropolitan areas rose from 35 to 39, and the population in these areas rose to 124.8 million, or 50.2% of the total U.S. population. About 90% of population growth in the 1980s took place in metropolitan areas.

A total of 46 metropolitan areas grew by more than 25% (Florida dominated the list with nine of the 11 top areas). The Los Angeles–Anaheim–Riverside metropolitan area gained about three million people in the 1980s, by far the largest numerical increase of any area (in fact the increase alone was greater than the total population of 272 metropolitan areas).

The population living outside metropolitan areas totaled 55,984,132, an increase of only 2.1 million (3.9%) over the decade.

Congressional representation As a result of population changes between 1980 and 1990 eight states had more representatives and 13 had fewer when the 103rd Congress convened in January 1993.

Congressional seats gained

California	7	Georgia	1
Florida	4	North Carolina	1
Texas	3	Virginia	1
Arizona	1	Washington	1

Congressional seats lost

New York	–3	Kentucky	–1
Illinois	–2	Louisiana	–1
Michigan	–2	Massachusetts	–1
Ohio	–2	Montana	–1
Pennsylvania	–2	New Jersey	–1
Iowa	–1	West Virginia	–1
Kansas	–1		

Race and Hispanic origin Between 1980 and 1990 the number of whites in the U.S. population increased from 188.4 million to 199.7 million, a growth rate of 6.0%, significantly below the 9.8% national rate. Since 1970, the white population of the U.S. has decreased from 87.5% of the total to 80.3%.

The black population increased by 13.2% during the 1980s, from 26.5 million to 29.1 million, and now comprises 12.1% of the total population, up from 11.1% in 1970.

The Hispanic population continued its dramatic growth—53%—during the last census decade, as their numbers increased from 14.6 million in 1980 to 22.4 million in 1990. Hispanics now comprise 9.0% of the U.S. population, up from an estimated 4.5% in 1970, and 6.4% in 1980.

The fastest growing population group in the U.S. is the Census Bureau category Asian or Pacific Islander. With literally millions of Asian immigrants coming to the United States, the number in this category has grown by an extraordinary 108 percent in only one decade, from 3.5 million to 7.3 million. While the Asian or Pacific Islander group made up just under 3 percent of the total U.S. population in 1990, this was about twice what it was in 1980 (1.5%).

All told, 21.6 million Americans said they were born outside the United States. About 45% came from the Western Hemisphere, 22% from Europe, 25% from Asia, and 2% from Africa. Included in this figure were about 1.9 million people born abroad of American parents.

U.S. POPULATION BY STATE, 1790–1990

State	1790	1800	1810	1820	1830	1840	1850	1860	1870
Total U.S.	**3,929,214**	**5,308,483**	**7,239,881**	**9,638,453**	**12,860,702**	**17,063,353**	**23,191,876**	**31,443,321**	**38,558,371**
Alabama	—	1,250	9,046	127,901	309,527	590,756	771,623	964,201	996,992
Alaska	—	—	—	—	—	—	—	—	—
Arizona	—	—	—	—	—	—	—	—	9,658
Arkansas	—	—	1,062	14,273	30,388	97,574	209,897	435,450	484,471
California	—	—	—	—	—	—	92,597	379,994	560,247
Colorado	—	—	—	—	—	—	—	34,277	39,864
Connecticut	237,946	251,002	261,942	275,248	297,675	309,978	370,792	460,147	537,454
Delaware	59,096	64,273	72,674	72,749	76,748	78,085	91,532	112,216	125,015
District of Columbia	—	8,144	15,471	23,336	30,261	33,745	51,687	75,080	131,700
Florida	—	—	—	—	34,730	54,477	87,445	140,424	187,748
Georgia	82,548	162,686	252,433	340,989	516,823	691,392	906,185	1,057,286	1,184,109
Hawaii	—	—	—	—	—	—	—	—	—
Idaho	—	—	—	—	—	—	—	—	14,999
Illinois	—	—	12,282	55,211	157,445	476,183	851,470	1,711,951	2,539,891
Indiana	—	5,641	24,520	147,178	343,031	685,866	988,416	1,350,428	1,680,637
Iowa	—	—	—	—	—	43,112	192,214	674,913	1,194,020
Kansas	—	—	—	—	—	—	—	107,206	364,399
Kentucky	73,677	220,955	406,511	564,317	687,917	779,828	982,405	1,155,684	1,321,011
Louisiana	—	—	76,556	153,407	215,739	352,411	517,762	708,002	726,915
Maine	96,540	151,719	228,705	298,335	399,455	501,793	583,169	628,279	626,915
Maryland	319,728	341,548	380,546	407,350	447,040	470,019	583,034	687,049	780,894
Massachusetts	378,787	422,845	472,040	523,287	610,408	737,699	994,514	1,231,066	1,457,351
Michigan	—	—	4,762	8,896	31,369	212,267	397,654	749,113	1,184,059
Minnesota	—	—	—	—	—	—	6,077	172,023	439,706
Mississippi	—	7,600	31,306	75,448	136,621	375,651	606,526	791,305	827,922
Missouri	—	—	19,783	66,586	140,455	383,702	682,044	1,182,012	1,721,295
Montana	—	—	—	—	—	—	—	—	20,595
Nebraska	—	—	—	—	—	—	—	28,841	122,993
Nevada	—	—	—	—	—	—	—	6,857	42,491
New Hampshire	141,885	183,858	214,460	244,161	269,328	284,574	317,976	326,073	318,300
New Jersey	184,139	211,149	245,562	277,575	320,823	373,306	489,555	672,035	906,096
New Mexico	—	—	—	—	—	—	61,547	93,516	91,874
New York	340,120	589,051	959,049	1,372,812	1,918,608	2,428,921	3,097,394	3,880,735	4,382,759
North Carolina	393,751	478,103	555,500	638,829	737,987	753,419	869,039	992,622	1,071,361
North Dakota	—	—	—	—	—	—	—	—	2,405
Ohio	—	45,365	230,760	581,434	937,903	1,519,467	1,980,329	2,339,511	2,665,260
Oklahoma	—	—	—	—	—	—	—	—	—
Oregon	—	—	—	—	—	—	12,093	52,465	90,923
Pennsylvania	434,373	602,365	810,091	1,049,458	1,348,233	1,724,033	2,311,786	2,906,215	3,521,951
Rhode Island	68,825	69,122	76,931	83,059	97,199	108,830	147,545	174,620	217,353
South Carolina	249,073	345,591	415,115	502,741	581,185	594,398	668,507	703,708	705,606
South Dakota	—	—	—	—	—	—	—	4,837	11,776
Tenneesee	35,691	105,602	261,727	422,832	681,904	829,210	1,002,717	1,109,801	1,258,520
Texas	—	—	—	—	—	—	212,592	604,215	818,579
Utah	—	—	—	—	—	—	11,380	40,273	86,786
Vermont	85,425	154,465	217,895	235,981	280,652	291,948	314,120	315,098	330,551
Virginia[2]	747,610	880,200	974,600	1,065,366	1,211,405	1,239,797	1,421,661	1,596,318	1,225,163
Washington	—	—	—	—	—	—	1,201	11,594	23,955
West Virginia	—	—	—	—	—	—	—	—	442,014
Wisconsin	—	—	—	—	—	30,945	305,391	775,881	1,054,670
Wyoming	—	—	—	—	—	—	—	—	9,118

Note: Excludes military and overseas population. Wherever possible, 1980 state boundaries are used in calculating populations of regions, areas, and figures for West Virginia between 1790 and 1860, even though it did not become a state until 1863. Since the result diminishes Virginia's population by

1880	1890	1900	1910	1920	1930	1940	1950	1960	1970	1980[1]	1990	State
50,189,209	**62,979,766**	**76,212,168**	**92,228,496**	**106,021,537**	**123,202,624**	**132,164,569**	**151,325,798**	**179,323,175**	**203,302,031**	**226,542,203**	**248,709,873**	**Total U.S.**
1,262,505	1,513,401	1,828,697	2,138,093	2,348,174	2,646,248	2,832,961	3,061,743	3,266,740	3,444,354	3,894,025	4,040,587	Alabama
33,426	32,052	63,592	64,356	55,036	59,278	72,524	128,643	226,167	302,583	401,851	550,043	Alaska
40,440	88,243	122,931	204,354	334,162	435,573	499.261	749,587	1,302,161	1,775,399	2,716,546	3,665,228	Arizona
802,525	1,128,211	1,311,564	1,574,449	1,752,204	1,854,482	1,949,387	1,909,511	1,786,272	1,923,322	2,286,357	2,350,725	Arkansas
864,694	1,213,396	1,485,053	2,377,549	3,426,861	5,677,251	6,907,387	10,586,223	15,717,204	19,971,069	23,667,764	29,760,021	California
194,327	413,249	539,700	799,024	939,629	1,035,791	1,123,296	1,325,089	1,753,947	2,209,596	2,889,735	3,294,394	Colorado
622,700	746,258	908,420	1,114,756	1,380,631	1,606,903	1,709,242	2,007,280	2,535,234	3,032,217	3,107,564	3,287,116	Connecticut
146,608	168,493	184,735	202,322	223,003	238,380	266,505	318,085	446,292	548,104	594,338	666,168	Delaware
177,624	230,392	278,718	331,069	437,571	486,869	663,091	802,178	763,956	756,668	638,432	606,900	District of Columbia
269,493	391,422	528,542	752,619	968,470	1,468,211	1,897,414	2,771,305	4,951,560	6,791,418	9,746,961	12,937,926	Florida
1,542,180	1,837,353	2,216,331	2,609,121	2,895,832	2,908,506	3,123,723	3,444,578	3,943,116	4,587,930	5,462,982	6,478,216	Georgia
—	—	154,001	191,874	255,881	368,300	422,770	499,794	632,772	769,913	964,691	1,108,229	Hawaii
32,610	88,548	161,772	325,594	431,866	445,032	524,873	588,637	667,191	713,015	944,127	1,006,749	Idaho
3,077,871	3,826,352	4,821,550	5,638,591	6,485,280	7,630,654	7,897,241	8,712,176	10,081,158	11,110,285	11,427,409	11,430,602	Illinois
1,978,301	2,192,404	2,516,462	2,700,876	2,930,390	3,238,503	3,427,796	3,934,224	4,662,498	5,195,392	5,490,214	5,544,159	Indiana
1,624,615	1,912,297	2,231,853	2,224,771	2,404,021	2,470,939	2,538,268	2,621,073	2,757,537	2,825,368	2,913,808	2,776,755	Iowa
996,096	1,428,108	1,470,495	1,690,949	1,769,257	1,880,999	1,801,028	1,905,299	2,178,611	2,249,071	2,364,236	2,477,574	Kansas
1,648,690	1,858,635	2,147,174	2,289,905	2,416,630	2,614,589	2,845,627	2,944,806	3,038,156	3,220,711	3,660,324	3,685,296	Kentucky
939,946	1,118,588	1,381,625	1,656,388	1,798,509	2,101,593	2,363,880	2,683,516	3,257,022	3,644,637	4,206,116	4,219,973	Louisiana
648,936	661,086	694,466	742,371	768,014	797,423	847,226	913,774	969,265	993,722	1,125,043	1,227,928	Maine
934,943	1,042,390	1,188,044	1,295,346	1,449,661	1,631,526	1,821,244	2,343,001	3,100,689	3,923,897	4,216,933	4,781,468	Maryland
1,783,085	2,238,947	2,805,346	3,366,416	3,852,356	4,249,614	4,316,721	4,690,514	5,148,578	5,689,170	5,737,093	6,016,425	Massachusetts
1,636,937	2,093,890	2,420,982	2,810,173	3,668,412	4,842,325	5,256,106	6,371,766	7,823,194	8,881,826	9,262,044	9,295,297	Michigan
780,773	1,310,283	1,751,394	2,075,708	2,387,125	2,563,953	2,792,300	2,982,483	3,413,864	3,806,103	4,075,970	4,375,099	Minnesota
1,131,597	1,289,600	1,551,270	1,797,114	1,790,618	2,009,821	2,183,796	2,178,914	2,178,141	2,216,994	2,520,770	2,573,216	Mississippi
2,168,380	2,679,185	3,106,665	3,293,335	3,404,055	3,629,367	3,784,664	3,954,653	4,319,813	4,677,623	4,916,762	5,117,073	Missouri
39,159	142,924	243,329	376,053	548,889	537,606	559,456	591,024	674,767	694,409	786,690	799,065	Montana
452,402	1,062,656	1,066,300	1,192,214	1,296,372	1,377,963	1,315,834	1,325,510	1,411,330	1,485,333	1,569,825	1,578,385	Nebraska
62,266	47,355	42,335	81,875	77,407	91,058	110,247	160,083	285,278	488,738	800,508	1,201,833	Nevada
346,991	376,530	411,588	430,572	443,083	465,293	491,524	533,242	606,921	737,681	920,610	1,109,252	New Hampshire
1,131,116	1,444,933	1,883,669	2,537,167	3,155,900	4,041,334	4,160,165	4,835,329	6,066,782	7,171,112	7,365,011	7,730,188	New Jersey
119,565	160,282	195,310	327,301	360,350	423,317	531,818	681,187	951,023	1,017,055	1,303,302	1,515,069	New Mexico
5,082,871	6,003,174	7,268,894	9,113,614	10,385,227	12,588,066	13,479,142	14,830,192	16,782,304	18,241,391	17,558,165	17,990,455	New York
1,399,750	1,617,949	1,893,810	2,206,287	2,559,123	3,170,276	3,571,623	4,061,929	4,556,155	5,084,411	5,880,095	6,628,637	North Carolina
36,909	190,983	319,146	577,056	646,872	680,845	641,935	619,636	632,446	617,792	652,717	638,800	North Dakota
3,198,062	3,672,329	4,157,545	4,767,121	5,759,394	6,646,697	6,907,612	7,946,627	9,706,397	10,657,423	10,797,603	10,847,115	Ohio
—	258,657	790,371	1,657,155	2,028,283	2,396,040	2,336,434	2,233,351	2,328,284	2,559,463	3,025,487	3,145,585	Oklahoma
174,768	317,704	413,536	672,765	783,389	953,786	1,089,684	1,521,341	1,768,687	2,091,533	2,633,156	2,842,321	Oregon
4,282,891	5,258,113	6,302,115	7,665,111	8,720,017	9,631,350	9,900,180	10,498,012	11,319,366	11,800,766	11,864,720	11,881,643	Pennsylvania
276,531	345,506	428,556	542,610	604,397	687,497	713,346	791,896	859,488	949,723	947,154	1,003,464	Rhode Island
995,577	1,151,149	1,340,316	1,515,400	1,683,724	1,738,765	1,899,804	2,117,027	2,382,594	2,590,713	3,120,729	3,486,703	South Carolina
98,268	348,600	401,570	583,888	636,547	692,849	642,961	652,740	680,514	666,257	690,768	696,004	South Dakota
1,542,359	1,767,518	2,020,616	2,184,789	2,337,885	2,616,556	2,915,841	3,291,718	3,567,089	3,926,018	4,591,023	4,877,185	Tennessee
1,591,749	2,235,527	3,048,710	3,896,542	4,663,228	5,824,715	6,414,824	7,711,194	9,579,677	11,198,655	14,225,513	16,986,510	Texas
143,963	210,779	276,749	373,351	449,396	507,847	550,310	688,862	890,627	1,059,273	1,461,037	1,722,850	Utah
332,286	332,422	343,641	355,956	352,428	359,611	359,231	377,747	389,881	444,732	511,456	562,758	Vermont
1,512,565	1,655,980	1,854,184	2,061,612	2,309,187	2,421,851	2,677,773	3,318,680	3,966,949	4,651,448	5,346,797	6,187,358	Virginia
75,116	357,232	518,103	1,141,990	1,356,621	1,563,396	1,736,191	2,378,963	2,853,214	3,413,244	4,132,353	4,866,692	Washington
618,457	762,794	958,800	1,221,119	1,463,701	1,729,205	1,901,974	2,005,552	1,860,421	1,744,237	1,950,186	1,793,477	West Virginia
1,315,497	1,693,330	2,069,042	2,333,860	2,632,067	2,939,006	3,137,587	3,434,575	3,951,777	4,417,821	4,705,642	4,891,769	Wisconsin
20,789	62,555	92,531	145,965	194,402	225,565	250,742	290,529	330,066	332,416	469,557	453,588	Wyoming

territories prior to their statehoods. 1. 1980 figures are revised estimates issued by the Census Bureau in 1987. 2. The figures for Virginia through 1860 are from the 1960 census; in the 1980 summary, the Census Bureau gave separate over 300,000 in 1850 and 1860, a crucial period, we decided to keep the earlier breakdowns. **Sources:** U.S. Bureau of the Census, *1980 Census of Population: U.S. Summary, Number of Inhabitants* (1981), and Release (1990).

U.S. POPULATION, POPULATION DENSITY, AND AREA OF RESIDENCE, 1790–1990

Year	Total population	Percent increase	Pop. per sq. mi.	Percent urban	Percent rural
1790	3,929,214	N.A.	4.5	5.1%	94.9%
1800	5,308,483	35.1%	6.1	6.1	93.9
1810	7,239,881	36.4	4.3	7.3	92.7
1820	9,638,453	33.1	5.5	7.2	92.8
1830	12,866,020	33.5	7.4	8.8	91.2
1840	17,069,453	32.7	9.8	10.8	89.2
1850	23,191,876	35.9	7.9	15.3	84.7
1860	31,443,321	35.6	10.6	19.8	80.2
1870	39,818,449	26.6	13.4	25.7	74.3
1880	50,155,783	26.0	16.9	28.2	71.8
1890	62,947,714	25.5	21.2	35.1	64.9
1900	75,994,575	20.7	25.6	39.6	60.4
1910	91,972,266	21.0	31.0	45.6	54.4
1920	105,710,620	14.9	35.6	51.2	48.8
1930	122,775,046	16.1	41.2	56.1	43.9
1940	131,669,275	7.2	44.2	56.5	43.5
1950	150,697,361	14.5	50.7	64.0	36.0
1960	179,323,175	18.5	50.6	69.9	30.1
1970	203,302,031	13.4	57.4	73.5	26.5
1980	226,545,805	11.4	64.0	73.7	26.3
1990	248,709,873	9.8	70.2[1]	75.2	24.8

1. Estimated. **Sources:** U.S. Bureau of the Census, *The Statistical History of the U.S.* (1976) and *Statistical Abstract of the United States 1992* (1992).

POPULATION GROWTH, BY REGION, 1790–2000 (in thousands)

Year	Northeast	Midwest[1]	South[2]	West
1790	1,968	N.A.	1,961	N.A.
1800	2,636	51	2,622	N.A.
1810	3,487	292	3,461	N.A.
1820	4,360	859	4,419	N.A.
1830	5,542	1,610	5,708	N.A.
1840	6,761	3,352	6,951	N.A.
1850	8,627	5,404	8,983	179
1860	10,594	9,097	11,133	619
1870	12,299	12,981	12,288	991
1880	14,507	17,364	16,517	1,801
1890	17,407	22,410	20,028	3,134
1900	21,047	26,333	24,524	4,309
1910	25,869	29,889	29,389	7,082
1920	29,662	34,020	33,126	9,214
1930	34,427	38,594	37,858	12,324
1940	35,977	40,143	41,666	14,379
1950	39,478	44,461	47,197	20,190
1960	44,678	51,619	54,973	28,053
1970	49,041	56,572	62,795	34,804
1980	49,135	58,866	75,372	43,172
1990	50,809	59,669	85,446	52,786
2000[3]	51,800	59,600	96,900	59,400

1. Called North Central prior to 1980. 2. Includes black slave population through 1860. 3. Projections. **Sources:** U.S. Bureau of the Census, *The Statistical History of the U.S.* (1976) and *Statistical Abstract of the United States 1991* (1991).

ESTIMATES OF THE RESIDENT POPULATION OF STATES, APRIL 1990–JULY 1994

State	Population ('000s) 1990 census	Population ('000s) July 1, 1994	Change 1990–94 Number	Change 1990–94 Percent
U.S. Total	**248,710**	**260,341**	**11,631**	**4.7%**
Alabama	4,041	4,219	178	4.4
Alaska	550	606	56	10.2
Arizona	3,665	4,075	410	11.2
Arkansas	2,351	2,453	102	4.3
California	29,760	31,431	1,671	5.6
Colorado	3,294	3,656	362	11.0
Connecticut	3,287	3,275	–12	–0.4
Delaware	666	706	40	6.0
Dist. of Columbia	607	570	–37	–6.1
Florida	12,938	13,953	1,015	7.8
Georgia	6,478	7,055	577	8.9
Hawaii	1,108	1,179	71	6.3
Idaho	1,007	1,133	126	12.5
Illinois	11,431	11,752	321	2.8
Indiana	5,544	5,752	208	3.8
Iowa	2,777	2,829	52	1.9
Kansas	2,478	2,554	76	3.1
Kentucky	3,687	3,827	140	3.8
Louisiana	4,220	4,315	95	2.2
Maine	1,228	1,240	12	1.0
Maryland	4,781	5,006	225	4.7
Massachusetts	6,016	6,041	25	0.4
Michigan	9,295	9,496	201	2.2
Minnesota	4,375	4,567	192	4.4
Mississippi	2,575	2,669	96	3.6
Missouri	5,117	5,278	161	3.1
Montana	799	856	57	7.1
Nebraska	1,578	1,623	45	2.8
Nevada	1,202	1,457	255	21.2
New Hampshire	1,109	1,137	28	2.5
New Jersey	7,730	7,904	174	1.0
New Mexico	1,515	1,654	139	9.1
New York	17,990	18,169	179	2.2
North Carolina	6,632	7,070	437	6.6
North Dakota	639	638	–1	–0.1
Ohio	10,847	11,102	255	2.4
Oklahoma	3,146	3,258	112	3.6
Oregon	2,842	3,086	244	8.6
Pennsylvania	11,882	12,052	170	1.4
Rhode Island	1,003	997	–6	–0.7
South Carolina	3,487	3,664	177	5.1
South Dakota	696	721	25	3.6
Tennessee	4,877	5,175	298	6.1
Texas	16,987	18,378	1,391	8.2
Utah	1,723	1,908	185	10.7
Vermont	563	580	17	3.1
Virginia	6,189	6,552	362	5.9
Washington	4,867	5,343	476	9.8
West Virginia	1,793	1,822	29	1.6
Wisconsin	4,892	5,082	190	3.9
Wyoming	454	476	22	4.9

Note: Includes armed forces residing in each state. **Source:** U.S. Bureau of the Census, *Census and You*, Dec. 28, 1994.

THE ACCURACY OF THE CENSUS

According to the Census Bureau's own estimates, the 1990 census missed between 4.3 million and 6.3 million persons, an undercount of 1.7% to 2.5%. (In 1980, the estimate was three million persons, or 1.2%.) The postcensus survey, based on a sampling of 165,000 households and released in April 1991, indicated that the total population was between 252.9 million and 254.9 million, not the 248.7 million who were actually counted. Moreover, the most severe cases of undercounting were found in large cities and among minority groups.

Despite the fact that the postcensus survey was instituted because several cities (including New York and Los Angeles) had filed lawsuits against the Census Bureau in 1987, Secretary of Commerce Robert A. Mosbacher refused to adjust the census counts. After taking advice from demographers both in and out of the Census Bureau—who reportedly split evenly on the question—he came to the conclusion that an adjustment would improve the figures for the nation as a whole and for 29 of the 50 states but not for the localities where the majority of Americans live. Most Democrats and the leaders of every major city denounced the decision as politically motivated.

U.S. POPULATION ABROAD BY SELECTED COUNTRY, 1994

Country	Resident U.S. citizens ('000s)	Country	Resident U.S. citizens ('000s)
Argentina	13	Italy	104
Australia	62	Jerusalem	43
Canada	296	Mexico	539
Costa Rica	23	Netherlands	19
Dominican Republic	97	Panama	36
Egypt	17	Portugal	28
France	59	Saudi Arabia	40
Germany	354	South Korea	30
Greece	32	Spain	79
Hong Kong	24	Switzerland	27
Ireland	46	United Kingdom	259
Israel	112	Venezuela	24

Source: U.S. Bureau of the Census, *Statistical Abstract of the United States 1994* (1994), from unpublished data of the U.S. Dept. of State.

U.S. RESIDENT POPULATION AND POPULATION CHANGE, BY STATE, 1980–90

State	1980 Population	1980 Rank	1990 Population	1990 Rank	Number change	Percent change
United States	**226,545,805**	**—**	**248,709,873**	**—**	**22,165,068**	**9.8%**
Alabama	3,893,888	(22)	4,040,587	(22)	146,699	3.8
Alaska	401,851	(50)	550,043	(49)	148,192	36.9
Arizona	2,718,215	(29)	3,665,228	(24)	947,013	34.8
Arkansas	2,286,435	(33)	2,350,725	(33)	64,290	2.8
California	23,667,902	(1)	29,760,021	(1)	6,092,119	25.7
Colorado	2,889,964	(28)	3,294,394	(26)	404,430	14.0
Connecticut	3,107,576	(25)	3,287,116	(27)	179,540	5.8
Delaware	594,338	(47)	666,168	(46)	71,830	12.1
District of Columbia[1]	638,333	—	606,900	—	–31,433	–4.9
Florida	9,746,324	(7)	12,937,926	(4)	3,191,602	32.7
Georgia	5,463,105	(13)	6,478,216	(11)	1,015,111	18.6
Hawaii	964,691	(39)	1,108,229	(41)	143,538	14.9
Idaho	943,935	(41)	1,006,749	(42)	62,814	6.7
Illinois	11,426,518	(5)	11,430,602	(6)	4,084	0.0
Indiana	5,490,224	(12)	5,544,159	(14)	53,935	1.0
Iowa	2,913,808	(27)	2,776,755	(30)	–137,053	–4.7
Kansas	2,363,679	(32)	2,477,574	(32)	113,895	4.8
Kentucky	3,660,777	(23)	3,685,296	(23)	24,519	0.7
Louisiana	4,205,900	(19)	4,219,973	(21)	14,073	0.3
Maine	1,124,660	(38)	1,227,928	(38)	103,268	9.2
Maryland	4,216,975	(18)	4,781,468	(19)	564,493	13.4
Massachusetts	5,737,037	(11)	6,016,425	(13)	279,388	4.9
Michigan	9,262,078	(8)	9,295,297	(8)	33,219	0.4
Minnesota	4,075,970	(21)	4,375,099	(20)	299,129	7.3
Mississippi	2,520,638	(31)	2,573,216	(31)	52,578	2.1
Missouri	4,916,686	(15)	5,117,073	(15)	200,387	4.1%
Montana	786,690	(44)	799,065	(44)	12,375	1.6
Nebraska	1,569,825	(35)	1,578,385	(36)	8,560	0.5
Nevada	800,493	(43)	1,201,833	(39)	401,340	50.1
New Hampshire	920,610	(42)	1,109,252	(40)	188,642	20.5
New Jersey	7,364,823	(9)	7,730,188	(9)	365,365	5.0
New Mexico	1,302,894	(37)	1,515,069	(37)	212,175	16.3
New York	17,558,072	(2)	17,990,455	(2)	432,383	2.5
North Carolina	5,881,766	(10)	6,628,637	(10)	746,871	12.7
North Dakota	652,717	(46)	638,800	(47)	–13,917	–2.1
Ohio	10,797,630	(6)	10,847,115	(7)	49,485	0.5
Oklahoma	3,025,290	(26)	3,145,585	(28)	120,295	4.0
Oregon	2,633,105	(30)	2,842,321	(29)	209,216	7.9
Pennsylvania	11,863,895	(4)	11,881,643	(5)	17,748	0.1
Rhode Island	947,154	(40)	1,003,464	(43)	56,310	5.9
South Carolina	3,121,820	(24)	3,486,703	(25)	364,883	11.7
South Dakota	690,768	(45)	696,004	(45)	5,236	0.8
Tennessee	4,591,120	(17)	4,877,185	(17)	286,065	6.2
Texas	14,229,191	(3)	16,986,510	(3)	2,757,319	19.4
Utah	1,461,037	(36)	1,722,850	(35)	261,813	17.9
Vermont	511,456	(48)	562,758	(48)	51,302	10.0
Virginia	5,346,818	(14)	6,187,358	(12)	840,540	15.7
Washington	4,132,156	(20)	4,866,692	(18)	734,536	17.8
West Virginia	1,949,644	(34)	1,793,477	(34)	–156,167	–8.0
Wisconsin	4,705,767	(16)	4,891,769	(16)	186,002	4.0
Wyoming	469,557	(49)	453,588	(50)	–15,969	–3.4

1. If the District of Columbia were included with the states it would have ranked 48th in 1990 and 47th in 1980. **Source:** U.S. Bureau of the Census release, 1991.

STATE URBAN AND RURAL PERCENTAGE OF LAND AREA AND POPULATION, 1980–90

State	Land area 1990			Population 1980		Population 1990	
	Sq. miles	Urban	Rural	Urban	Rural	Urban	Rural
U.S. total	**3,536,278**	**2.5%**	**97.5%**	**73.7%**	**26.3%**	**75.2%**	**24.8%**
Alabama	50,750.2	5.3	94.7	60.0	40.0	60.4	39.6
Alaska	570,373.5	0.1	99.9	64.5	35.5	67.5	32.5
Arizona	113,642.2	1.8	98.2	83.8	16.2	87.5	12.5
Arkansas	52,075.3	2.3	97.7	51.6	48.4	53.5	46.5
California	155,973.2	5.2	94.8	91.3	8.7	92.6	7.4
Colorado	103,728.8	1.3	98.7	80.6	19.4	82.4	17.6
Connecticut	4,845.4	25.9	74.1	78.8	21.2	79.1	20.9
Delaware	1,954.6	10.7	89.3	70.7	29.3	73.0	27.0
Dist. of Columbia	61.4	100.0	0.0	100.0	0.0	100.0	0.0
Florida	53,937.2	9.5	90.5	84.3	15.7	84.8	15.2
Georgia	57,918.7	4.9	95.1	62.3	37.7	63.2	36.8
Hawaii	6,423.4	10.0	90.0	86.5	13.5	89.0	11.0
Idaho	82,751.0	0.4	99.6	54.0	46.0	57.4	42.6
Illinois	55,593.3	5.5	94.5	83.0	17.0	84.6	15.4
Indiana	35,870.1	5.0	95.0	64.2	35.8	64.9	35.1
Iowa	55,874.9	2.0	98.0	58.6	41.4	60.6	39.4
Kansas	81,823.0	1.1	98.9	66.7	33.3	69.1	30.9
Kentucky	39,732.3	2.7	97.3	50.8	49.2	51.8	48.2
Louisiana	43,566.1	3.7	96.3	68.6	31.4	68.1	31.9
Maine	30,864.5	2.3	97.7	47.5	52.5	44.6	55.4
Maryland	9,774.6	16.1	83.9	80.3	19.7	81.3	18.7
Massachusetts	7,838.0	27.4	72.6	83.8	16.2	84.3	15.7
Michigan	56,809.2	4.7	95.3	70.7	29.3	70.5	29.5
Minnesota	79,616.5	2.3	97.7	66.8	33.2	69.9	30.1
Mississippi	46,913.7	2.4	97.6	47.3	52.7	47.1	52.9
Missouri	68,898.1	2.7%	97.3%	68.1%	31.9%	68.7%	31.3%
Montana	145,556.3	0.2	99.8	52.9	47.1	52.5	47.5
Nebraska	76,877.7	0.5	99.5	62.7	37.3	66.1	33.9
Nevada	109,805.5	0.9	99.1	85.3	14.7	88.3	11.7
New Hampshire	8,969.4	5.7	94.3	52.2	47.8	51.0	49.0
New Jersey	7,418.8	32.7	67.3	89.0	11.0	89.4	10.6
New Mexico	121,364.5	0.7	99.3	72.2	27.8	73.0	27.0
New York	47,223.8	7.2	92.8	84.6	15.4	84.3	15.7
North Carolina	48,718.1	4.6	95.4	48.0	52.0	50.4	49.6
North Dakota	68,994.3	0.2	99.8	48.8	51.2	53.3	46.7
Ohio	40,952.6	8.8	91.2	73.3	26.7	74.1	25.9
Oklahoma	68,678.5	2.7	97.3	67.3	32.7	67.7	32.3
Oregon	96,002.5	0.9	99.1	67.9	32.1	70.5	29.5
Pennsylvania	44,819.6	6.7	93.3	69.3	30.7	68.9	31.1
Rhode Island	1,045.0	28.5	71.5	87.0	13.0	86.0	14.0
South Carolina	30,111.1	4.7	95.3	54.1	45.9	54.6	45.4
South Dakota	75,896.0	0.3	99.7	46.4	53.6	50.0	50.0
Tennessee	41,219.5	5.7	94.3	60.4	39.6	60.9	39.1
Texas	261,914.3	2.9	97.1	79.6	20.4	80.3	19.7
Utah	82,168.1	0.9	99.1	84.4	15.6	87.0	13.0
Vermont	9,249.3	1.5	98.5	33.8	66.2	32.2	67.8
Virginia	39,597.8	5.5	94.5	66.0	34.0	69.4	30.6
Washington	66,581.2	2.7	97.3	73.6	26.4	76.4	23.6
West Virginia	24,086.6	1.6	98.4	36.2	63.8	36.1	63.9
Wisconsin	54,313.7	2.9	97.1	64.2	35.8	65.7	34.3
Wyoming	97,104.6	0.2	99.8	62.8	37.2	65.0	35.0

Source: U.S Bureau of the Census press release (December 1991).

The Population by Race and Hispanic Origin

It is important to note that the Census Bureau's classification of the population by race, in its words, "reflects common usage, not an attempt to define biological stock." Only since 1960, however, have the Census Bureau's race figures been based on self-identification.

The people of the United States are predominantly white, accounting for an estimated 80.3 percent of the total population in 1990. This dominance has been true since colonial days, although even then the indigenous peoples and the African slaves were significant racial minorities. In fact, as slave labor became essential to the Southern economy, so many slaves were brought here that just before the Civil War blacks constituted 15 percent of the population.

After the war, however, the proportion of whites rapidly increased as millions of immigrants from northern Europe settled throughout the country. The relentless movement of the population westward deprived the Native Americans of their lands and—with the assistance of several bloody wars—helped to reduce their numbers in 1900 to a small fraction (less than 100,000 perhaps) of what they were estimated to have been only a century before.

The black population, with 9–10 percent of the total, remained the only significant minority group until the 1960s, when a surge of new immigrants from Puerto Rico, Mexico, and Cuba made the Hispanic presence felt in very short order. So rapid and strong an impression did these groups make that the Census Bureau created a new population category, "Hispanic Origin"; since some Hispanics are black, some white, and still others Indian, this designation has nothing to do with race.

During the 1970s and 1980s, the arrival of several million Asians again caused a noticeable change in the composition of the population. The 1990 census was the first one to include a separate category for Asians and Pacific Islanders; in previous years they had been included, together with American Indians, Aleuts, and Eskimos, in the "Other Races" grouping.

RESIDENT POPULATION OF THE STATES BY RACE AND HISPANIC ORIGIN, 1990

State	Total	White	Black	American Indian, Eskimo, or Aleut	Asian or Pacific Islander	Other	Hispanic origin[1]
United States	**248,709,873**	**199,686,070**	**29,986,060**	**1,959,234**	**7,273,662**	**9,804,847**	**22,354,059**
Alabama	4,040,587	2,975,797	1,020,705	16,506	21,797	5,782	24,629
Alaska	550,043	415,492	22,451	85,698	19,728	6,674	17,803
Arizona	3,665,228	2,963,186	110,524	203,527	55,206	332,785	688,338
Arkansas	2,350,725	1,944,744	373,912	12,773	12,530	6,766	19,876
California	29,760,021	20,524,327	2,208,801	242,164	2,845,659	3,939,070	7,687,938
Colorado	3,294,394	2,905,474	133,146	27,776	59,862	168,136	424,302
Connecticut	3,287,116	2,859,353	274,269	6,654	50,698	96,142	213,116
Delaware	666,168	535,094	112,460	2,019	9,057	7,538	15,820
Dist. of Columbia	606,900	179,667	399,604	1,466	11,214	14,949	32,710
Florida	12,937,926	10,749,285	1,759,534	36,355	154,302	238,470	1,574,143
Georgia	6,478,216	4,600,148	1,746,565	13,348	75,781	42,374	108,922
Hawaii	1,108,229	369,616	27,195	5,099	685,236	21,083	81,390
Idaho	1,006,749	950,451	3,370	13,780	9,365	29,783	52,927
Illinois	11,430,602	8,952,978	1,694,273	21,836	285,311	476,204	904,446
Indiana	5,544,159	5,020,700	432,092	12,720	37,617	41,030	98,788
Iowa	2,776,755	2,683,090	48,090	7,349	25,476	12,750	32,647
Kansas	2,477,574	2,231,986	143,076	21,965	31,750	48,797	93,670
Kentucky	3,685,296	3,391,832	262,907	5,769	17,812	6,976	21,984
Louisiana	4,219,973	2,839,138	1,299,281	18,541	41,099	21,914	93,044
Maine	1,227,928	1,208,360	5,138	5,998	6,683	1,749	6,829
Maryland	4,781,468	3,393,964	1,189,899	12,972	139,719	44,914	125,102
Massachusetts	6,016,425	5,405,374	300,130	12,241	143,392	155,288	287,549
Michigan	9,295,297	7,756,086	1,291,706	55,638	104,983	86,884	201,596
Minnesota	4,375,099	4,130,395	94,944	49,909	77,886	21,965	53,884
Mississippi	2,573,216	1,633,461	915,057	8,525	13,016	3,157	15,931
Missouri	5,117,073	4,486,228	548,208	19,835	41,277	21,525	61,702
Montana	799,065	741,111	2,381	47,679	4,259	3,635	12,174
Nebraska	1,578,385	1,480,558	57,404	12,410	12,422	15,591	36,969
Nevada	1,201,833	1,012,695	78,771	19,637	38,127	52,603	124,419
New Hampshire	1,109,252	1,087,433	7,198	2,134	9,343	3,144	11,333
New Jersey	7,730,188	6,130,465	1,036,825	14,970	272,521	275,407	739,861
New Mexico	1,515,069	1,146,028	30,210	134,355	14,124	190,352	579,224
New York	17,990,455	13,385,255	2,859,055	62,651	693,760	989,734	2,214,026
North Carolina	6,628,637	5,008,491	1,456,323	80,155	52,166	31,502	76,726
North Dakota	638,800	604,142	3,524	25,917	3,462	1,755	4,665
Ohio	10,847,115	9,521,756	1,154,826	20,358	91,179	58,996	139,696
Oklahoma	3,145,585	2,583,512	233,801	252,240	33,563	42,289	86,160
Oregon	2,842,321	2,636,787	46,178	38,496	69,269	51,591	112,707
Pennsylvania	11,881,643	10,520,201	1,089,795	14,733	137,438	119,476	232,262
Rhode Island	1,003,464	917,375	38,861	4,071	18,325	24,832	45,752
South Carolina	3,486,703	2,406,974	1,039,884	8,246	22,382	9,217	30,551
South Dakota	696,004	637,515	3,258	50,575	3,123	1,533	5,252
Tennessee	4,877,185	4,048,068	778,035	10,039	31,839	9,204	32,741
Texas	16,986,510	12,774,762	2,021,632	65,877	319,459	1,804,780	4,339,905
Utah	1,722,850	1,615,845	11,576	24,283	33,371	37,775	84,597
Vermont	562,758	555,088	1,951	1,696	3,215	808	3,661
Virginia	6,187,358	4,791,739	1,162,994	15,282	159,053	58,290	160,288
Washington	4,866,692	4,308,937	149,801	81,483	210,958	115,513	214,570
West Virginia	1,793,477	1,725,523	56,295	2,458	7,459	1,742	8,489
Wisconsin	4,891,769	4,512,523	244,539	39,387	53,583	41,737	93,194
Wyoming	453,588	427,061	3,606	9,479	2,806	10,636	25,751

1. Persons of Hispanic origin may be of any race. **Source:** U.S. Bureau of the Census release, 1991.

THE BLACK POPULATION

Ever since the Founding Fathers reached their famous "compromise" declaring a slave the equivalent of three-fifths of a person, the black population has had a less-than-equal standing in relation to the majority of Americans. Over the last two centuries, the struggle for equality, even in a nation pledged to that ideal, has proven long, hard, and in many cases, intractable, as many contemporary facts and figures in this book make evident. From higher infant mortality rates and poverty rates to lower life expectancy and family income levels, the black population continues to suffer the effects of two centuries of slavery and one of institutionalized segregation.

In 1992, the black population numbered 31.6 million, an estimated 12.4 percent of all Americans, by far the nation's largest minority group. Since 1980, the black population has grown by 18.6 percent, double the rate of growth for whites (9.3%). The Census Bureau projections indicate that this trend will continue throughout the 1990s. So too will the age differences between the races. In 1991, the median age for blacks was 28.0, or close to six years below the

BLACK POPULATION OF METROPOLITAN AREAS, 1980–90

Rank/Metropolitan area	1980	1990	Number change	Percent change
1. New York–Northern New Jersey–Long Island, N.Y.–N.J.–Conn. CMSA	2,825,102	3,289,465	464,363	16.4%
2. Chicago–Gary–Lake County, Ill.–Ind.–Wis. CMSA	1,557,287	1,547,725	–9,562	–0.6
3. Los Angeles–Anaheim–Riverside, Calif. CMSA	1,059,124	1,229,809	170,685	16.1
4. Philadelphia–Wilmington–Trenton, Pa.–N.J.–Del.–Md. CMSA	1,032,882	1,100,347	67,465	6.5
5. Washington, D.C.–Md.–Va. MSA	870,657	1,041,934	171,277	19.7
6. Detroit–Ann Arbor, Mich. CMSA	921,168	975,199	54,031	5.9
7. Atlanta, Ga. MSA	525,676	736,153	210,477	40.0
8. Houston–Galveston–Brazoria, Tex. CMSA	564,838	665,378	100,540	17.8
9. Baltimore, Md. MSA	560,952	616,065	55,113	9.8
10. Miami–Fort Lauderdale, Fla. CMSA	394,042	591,440	197,398	50.1
11. Dallas–Fort Worth, Tex. CMSA	419,030	554,616	135,586	32.4
12. San Francisco–Oakland, San Jose, Calif. CMSA	468,477	537,753	69,276	14.8
13. Cleveland–Akron–Lorain, Ohio CMSA	425,861	441,940	16,079	3.8
14. New Orleans, La. MSA	409,076	430,470	21,394	5.2
15. St. Louis, Mo.–Ill. MSA	407,918	423,182	15,264	3.7
16. Memphis, Tenn–Ark.–Miss. MSA	364,253	399,011	34,758	9.5
17. Norfolk–Virginia Beach–Newport News, Va. MSA	326,102	398,093	71,991	22.1
18. Richmond–Petersburg, Va. MSA	221,456	252,340	30,884	13.9
19. Birmingham, Ala. MSA	240,271	245,726	5,455	2.3
20. Boston–Lawrence–Salem, Mass.–N.H. MSA	176,265	239,059	62,794	35.6
21. Charlotte–Gastonia–Rock Hill, N.C.–S.C. MSA	194,056	231,654	37,598	19.4
22. Milwaukee–Racine, Wis. CMSA	164,571	214,182	49,611	30.1
23. Cincinnati–Hamilton, Ohio–Ky.–Ind. CMSA	185,728	203,607	17,879	9.6
24. Kansas City, Mo.–Kans. MSA	180,161	200,508	20,347	11.3%
25. Tampa–St. Petersburg–Clearwater, Fla. MSA	148,465	185,503	37,038	24.9
26. Raleigh–Durham, N.C. MSA	146,624	183,447	36,823	25.1
27. Greensboro–Winston-Salem–High Point, N.C. MSA	162,134	182,284	20,150	12.4
28. Jacksonville, Fla. MSA	156,025	181,265	25,240	16.2
29. Pittsburgh–Beaver Valley, Pa. CMSA	181,644	178,857	–2,787	–1.5
30. Indianapolis, Ind. MSA	157,254	172,326	15,072	9.6
31. Jackson, Miss. MSA	149,457	167,899	18,442	12.3
32. Columbus, Ohio MSA	137,287	164,602	27,315	19.9
33. San Diego, Calif. MSA	104,452	159,306	54,854	52.5
34. Baton Rouge, La. MSA	137,581	156,509	18,928	13.8
35. Charleston, S.C. MSA	133,478	153,227	19,749	14.8
36. Nashville, Tenn. MSA	137,348	152,349	15,001	10.9
37. Columbia, S.C. MSA	117,906	137,906	20,000	17.0
38. Orlando, Fla. MSA	90,595	133,308	42,713	47.1
39. Mobile, Ala. MSA	126,835	130,512	3,677	2.9
40. Dayton–Springfield, Ohio MSA	118,294	126,238	7,944	6.7
41. Louisville, Ky.–Ind. MSA	120,610	124,761	4,151	3.4
42. Augusta, Ga.–S.C. MSA	106,729	123,482	16,753	15.7
43. Seattle–Tacoma, Wash. CMSA	87,976	123,266	35,290	40.1
44. Buffalo–Niagara Falls, N.Y. CMSA	113,975	121,956	7,981	7.0
45. Shreveport, La. MSA	110,478	116,892	6,414	5.8
46. Greenville–Spartanburg, S.C. MSA	97,561	111,334	13,773	14.1
47. West Palm Beach–Boca Raton–Delray Beach, Fla. MSA	77,576	107,705	30,129	38.8
48. Montgomery, Ala. MSA	94,494	105,196	10,702	11.3
49. Sacramento, Calif. MSA	61,594	101,940	40,346	65.5
50. Little Rock–North Little Rock, Ark. MSA	90,783	101,862	11,079	12.2

Source: U.S. Bureau of the Census release, 1991.

BLACK POPULATION OF THE U.S. BY REGION AND PERCENT OF TOTAL POPULATION, 1985–2010 (in thousands)

Region	1985 Number	1985 Percent	1990 Number	1990 Percent	2000[1] Number	2000[1] Percent	2010[1] Number	2010[1] Percent
Northeast	4,848	9.9%	5,613	11.0%	6,363	12.3%	6,941	13.2%
Midwest	5,337	9.1	5,716	9.6	6,542	11.0	7,013	11.9
South	14,048	18.6	15,829	18.5	18,546	19.1	20,630	19.7
West	2,262	5.2	2,262	5.4	3,555	6.0	4,126	6.3
Total U.S.	**26,495**	**11.7**	**29,986**	**12.1**	**35,006**	**13.1**	**38,710**	**13.7**

1. Projections. **Source:** U.S. Bureau of the Census, *1990 Census Profile (Number 2), Race and Hispanic Origin* (1991); *Projections of the Population of States By Age, Sex, and Race: 1988 to 2010* (1989).

white population's median age of 33.9. Other indications of the youthful nature of the black population are the proportion over 65 (only 8%, compared with 13% for whites) and the percentage under 18 (33% to 25%).

Most black people (52.4%) continue to live in the South, where they made up 18.8% of the population in 1992. Blacks constituted 12.0% of the population in the Northeast, 9.9% in the Midwest, and just 5.5% in the West in 1992. The majority of blacks (56.3%) lived in central cities of metropolitan areas, more than twice the percentage of whites (25.7%). The ratios for the suburbs were just the opposite: 50.7% of whites live in suburban areas, compared to 26.7% of blacks.

Significant differences between the races also exist in other demographic categories, most notably in the high divorce rates for blacks and the related numbers of married-couple families and households run by women. Between 1970 and 1991, the percentage of black families headed by a female with no husband present jumped from 28.0% to 45.9%. Meanwhile, the percentage of black married-couple families declined from 68.3% in 1970 to 47.8% in 1991.

BLACK POPULATION OF THE U.S., 1790–1995

Year	Number ('000s)	Percent of total pop.	Year	Number ('000s)	Percent of total pop.
1790	757	19.3%	1950	15,042	10.0%
1800	1,002	18.9	1960[1]	18,872	10.5
1850	3,639	15.7	1970	22,581	11.1
1860	4,442	14.1	1980	26,683	11.8
1870	4,880	12.7	1985	28,994	12.1
1880	6,581	13.1	1990	30,486	12.3
1890	7,489	11.9	1991	31,111	12.3
1900	8,834	11.6	1992	31,659	12.4
1910	9,828	10.7	1993	32,180	12.5
1920	10,463	9.9	1994	32,672	12.5
1930	11,891	9.7	1995	33,117	12.6
1940	12,866	9.8			

1. Includes Alaska and Hawaii for first time. **Source:** U.S. Bureau of the Census release, 1995, and *Statistical Abstract of the United States* (annual).

(See also "The United States Economy" for information about black employment, income, wealth, and poverty.)

10 STATES WITH HIGHEST PERCENTAGE OF BLACK POPULATION, 1990

Rank/State	Total population	Black population	Percent black
1. Mississippi	2,573,216	915,057	35.6%
2. Louisiana	4,219,973	1,299,281	30.8
3. South Carolina	3,486,703	1,039,884	29.8
4. Georgia	6,478,216	1,746,565	27.0
5. Alabama	4,040,587	1,020,705	25.3
6. Maryland	4,781,468	1,189,899	24.9
7. North Carolina	6,628,637	1,456,323	22.0
8. Virginia	6,187,358	1,162,994	18.8
9. Delaware	666,168	112,460	16.9
10. Tennessee	4,877,185	778,035	16.0

Source: U.S. Bureau of the Census release, 1991.

10 STATES WITH THE LARGEST BLACK POPULATION, 1990

Rank/State	Black population	Percent of total population
1. New York	2,859,055	15.9%
2. California	2,208,801	7.4
3. Texas	2,021,632	11.9
4. Florida	1,759,534	13.6
5. Georgia	1,746,565	27.0
6. Illinois	1,694,273	14.8
7. North Carolina	1,456,323	22.0
8. Louisiana	1,299,281	30.8
9. Michigan	1,291,706	13.9
10. Maryland	1,189,899	24.9

Source: U.S. Bureau of the Census release, 1991.

TWENTY U.S. CITIES WITH LARGEST BLACK POPULATIONS, 1990

Black rank	Overall rank	City	Total pop. ('000s)	Black pop. ('000s)	Percent black
1	1	New York, N.Y.	7,322.6	2,102.5	29%
2	3	Chicago, Ill.	2,783.7	1,087.7	39
3	7	Detroit, Mich.	1,028.0	777.9	76
4	5	Philadelphia, Pa.	1,585.6	631.9	40
5	2	Los Angeles, Calif.	3,485.4	487.7	14
6	4	Houston, Tex.	1,630.6	458.0	28
7	13	Baltimore, Md.	736.0	435.8	59
8	19	Washington, D.C.	606.9	399.6	66
9	18	Memphis, Tenn.	610.3	334.7	55
10	25	New Orleans, La.	496.9	307.7	62
11	8	Dallas, Tex.	1,006.9	297.0	30
12	36	Atlanta, Ga.	394.0	264.3	67
13	24	Cleveland, Ohio	505.6	235.4	47
14	17	Milwaukee, Wis.	628.1	191.3	31
15	34	St. Louis, Mo.	396.7	188.4	48
16	60	Birmingham, Ala.	266.0	168.3	63
17	12	Indianapolis, Ind.	742.0	165.6	22
18	15	Jacksonville, Fla.	673.0	163.9	24
19	39	Oakland, Calif.	372.2	163.3	44
20	56	Newark, N.J.	275.2	160.9	59

Source: Populations Reference Bureau, *African Americans in the 1990s* (1991), based on unpublished data from 1990 census.

THE HISPANIC POPULATION

The Hispanic population is one of the fastest growing segments of the U.S. population. Between 1980 and 1991, the number of Hispanics grew by 7.8 million, or 47 percent, close to five times the rate of the population in general (9.8%). All told, Hispanics numbered 21.1 million in 1991, according to the Census Bureau.

A look at earlier population statistics reveals a pattern of tremendous growth among U.S. Hispanics. In 1970, there were approximately nine million Hispanics in the United States. By 1980 the number had increased to 14.6 million, and by 1987 it had reached 18.8 million. Prior to 1970, Census Bureau surveys were conducted differently from the way they are now. Spanish surnamed Americans and people who were born or whose parents were born in a Hispanic country were identified, but non–Spanish-surnamed Hispanics and third- or fourth-generation Hispanics were not. Therefore, government data on Hispanics compiled before 1970 are highly inaccurate.

The rapid growth of the Hispanic population is due to immigration and a higher fertility rate than that of the non-Hispanic population. According to the National Center for Health Statistics, between 1983 and 1985 the birth rate among Hispanic women rose 11%, as compared to 3% for non-Hispanics. In 1985, Hispanic births accounted for 17% of all births in the United States, although Hispanics only comprised about 7% of the population.

Within the next 20 years the Hispanic population will become the largest minority in the United States, surpassing blacks, who currently outnumber Hispanics by about eight million, or 42 percent. The number of Hispanics is likely to exceed 30 million by the year 2000 and is expected to overtake the non-Hispanic black population by 2010. Hispanics will number 39 million in 2010, according to Census Bureau projections, compared to 38 million blacks.

Geographical distribution Over half of all U.S. Hispanics (53.8%) live in California or Texas. In 1990, 7.7 million (25.8%) of the residents of California and 4.3 million (25.5%) of the residents of Texas were Hispanic. The great majority of the Hispanics in these two states are of Mexican origin. New York, with 2.2 million (12.3%), is the state with the third-largest number of Hispanics, the majority of whom are Puerto Rican. Florida, where 2.2 million (12.2%) Hispanics reside, has the fourth-largest Hispanic population; the majority are of Cuban background. Florida had the highest growth rate (83%) since 1980, with Texas second at 45 percent.

As the accompanying table demonstrates, the growth of the Hispanic population in metropolitan areas reflects the high concentration of Hispanics in Texas and California. Since 1980 the Los Angeles area has witnessed a 73.4 percent increase, adding over two million Hispanics, and Dallas–Fort Worth has more than doubled its Hispanic population (109%) with an increase of 271,000.

STATES WITH LARGEST HISPANIC POPULATIONS, 1990

State	Hispanics (millions)	Percent of U.S. Hispanics	Percent of state's population
California	7.7	34.4%	25.8%
Texas	4.3	19.4	25.5
New York	2.2	9.9	12.3
Florida	1.6	7.0	12.2
Illinois	0.9	4.0	7.9
Arizona	0.7	3.1	18.8
New Jersey	0.7	3.3	9.6
New Mexico	0.6	2.6	38.2
Colorado	0.4	1.9	12.9

Source: U.S. Bureau of the Census release, 1991.

Who is Hispanic? Broadly understood, the term Hispanic refers to people of Spanish or Spanish-American origin. American Hispanics are of diverse backgrounds. The majority trace their roots to Mexico, Puerto Rico, or Cuba; however, every Spanish-speaking country is represented in the U.S. Hispanic population. (People of Brazilian origin are not included because Brazil is a Portuguese-speaking country.) In recent years extreme poverty and upheaval have led political Salvadorans and other Central Americans to emigrate to the United States in increasing numbers.

Contrary to popular opinion, Spanish-speaking countries are not culturally homogeneous but varied and complex, incorporating Spanish and other European influences as well as Indian and African traits. In the Caribbean area, Panama, and the coasts of Venezuela, Colombia, Ecuador, and sections of Peru, African culture has left a strong legacy. In Mexico, most of Central America, and the Andean countries, diverse Indian cultures have had a major impact. Latin American society varies greatly according to social class, and vast differences exist between urban and rural areas. Since American Hispanics come from different countries and social backgrounds, they do not compose a uniform, cohesive population group.

U.S. Hispanics are of many races, since every race is represented in Spanish America. In some areas intermingling has made it impossible to distinguish one race from another, but in others, races are clearly defined. In Argentina, for example, there is a white majority of 99.6 percent—mostly of Italian, German, or English extraction. Cuba, the Dominican Republic, Panama, Venezuela, and the coastal areas of Colombia, Ecuador, and Peru all have significant black populations. In Bolivia about one half of the population is Indian and a third is mestizo (of mixed white and Indian ancestry). Both Peru and Cuba have concentrations of persons of Chinese ancestry, and Peru has a growing Japanese population. About 63 percent of U.S. Hispanics trace their roots to Mexico, where about 55 percent of the population is mestizo, 30 percent Indian, and 15 percent white.

HISPANIC POPULATION OF METROPOLITAN AREAS, 1980–90

Rank/Metropolitan area	1980	1990	Number change	Percent change
1. Los Angeles–Anaheim–Riverside, Calif. CMSA	2,755,914	4,779,118	2,023,204	73.4%
2. New York–Northern New Jersey–Long Island, N.Y.–N.J.–Conn. CMSA	2,050,998	2,777,951	726,953	35.4
3. Miami–Fort Lauderdale, Fla. CMSA	621,309	1,061,846	440,537	70.9
4. San Francisco–Oakland, San Jose, Calif. CMSA	660,190	970,403	310,213	47.0
5. Chicago–Gary–Lake County, Ill.–Ind.–Wis. CMSA	632,443	893,422	260,979	41.3
6. Houston–Galveston–Brazoria, Tex. CMSA	448,460	772,295	323,835	72.2
7. San Antonio, Tex. MSA	481,511	620,290	138,779	28.8
8. Dallas–Fort Worth, Tex. CMSA	247,823	518,917	271,094	109.4
9. San Diego, Calif. MSA	275,177	510,781	235,604	85.6
10. El Paso, Tex. MSA	297,001	411,619	114,618	38.6
11. Phoenix, Ariz. MSA	199,003	345,498	146,495	73.6
12. McAllen–Edinburg–Mission, Tex. MSA	230,212	326,972	96,760	42.0
13. Fresno, Calif. MSA	150,790	236,634	85,844	56.9%
14. Denver–Boulder, Colo. CMSA	173,687	226,200	52,513	30.2
15. Philadelphia–Wilmington–Trenton, Pa.–N.J.–Del.–Md. CMSA	147,902	225,868	77,966	52.7
16. Washington, D.C.–Md.–Va. MSA	94,968	224,786	129,818	136.7
17. Brownsville–Harlingen, Tex. MSA	161,654	212,995	51,341	31.8
18. Boston–Lawrence–Salem, Mass.–N.H. CMSA	92,463	193,199	100,736	108.9
19. Corpus Christi, Tex. MSA	158,119	181,860	23,741	15.0
20. Albuquerque, N.Mex. MSA	154,620	178,310	23,690	15.3
21. Sacramento, Calif. MSA	105,665	172,374	66,709	63.1
22. Tucson, Ariz. MSA	111,418	163,262	51,844	46.5
23. Austin, Tex. MSA	94,367	159,942	65,575	69.5
24. Bakersfield, Calif. MSA	87,026	151,995	64,969	74.7
25. Tampa–St. Petersburg–Clearwater, Fla. MSA	80,265	139,248	58,983	73.5

Source: U.S. Bureau of the Census release, 1991.

Despite their diversity there are many factors that unite the Hispanic peoples, among them language, religion, customs, and attitudes toward self, family, and society. In the United States, these factors vary in importance according to the degree to which an individual has assimilated into the mainstream. For example, although language has traditionally been an important unifying factor, large numbers of second-generation Hispanics are English-dominant. About 85 percent of U.S. Hispanics speak English. Although the Spanish language continues to exert a strong emotional pull among U.S. Hispanics, it is difficult to assess to what extent Spanish will remain a unifying force among future generations.

Origins of U.S. Hispanics The majority of U.S. Hispanics are of Mexican origin. Mexicans and Mexican-Americans comprise 62.6 percent of the total U.S. Hispanic population. The number of people of Mexican background living in the United States grew from about 8.4 million in 1980 to 13.4 million in 1991.

About 2.3 million, or 11.1 percent, of U.S. Hispanics are Puerto Rican. These figures do not include Puerto Ricans living in Puerto Rico, a U.S. territory for which a separate census report is issued. In recent years, the flow of Puerto Ricans to U.S. cities has been reversed, with more Puerto Ricans emigrating from the mainland to the island than the other way around.

As recently as 1981, the numbers of Central Americans living in the United States were so small that the Census Bureau lumped them together with "other" Hispanics, rather than counting them as a separate category. But beginning in 1982, the U.S. Central American population had increased so significantly that the Census Bureau created a new category: Central and South American. Today, this is still one of the fastest-growing segments of the Hispanic (and the U.S.) population, nearly doubling in number since it was first counted in 1982. The Census Bureau's 1990 figures counted more than 2.8 million Americans of Central or South American origin. They comprise 13.8 percent of the total U.S. Hispanic population.

SELECTED CHARACTERISTICS OF PERSONS OF HISPANIC AND NON-HISPANIC ORIGINS IN THE U.S., 1993

			Hispanic origin				
Characteristic	Total non-Hispanic origin	Total Hispanic origin	Mexican	Puerto Rican	Cuban	Central and South American	Other
Number ('000s)[1]	231,490	22,752	14,628	2,402	1,071	3,052	1,598
Percent of total	N.A.	100.0%	64.3%	10.6%	4.7%	13.4%	7.0%
Median age	34.4	26.7	24.6	26.9	43.6	28.6	32.5
Percent male	48.7%	50.1%	50.5%	47.5%	49.1%	51.1%	48.4%
Marital status[2]							
Never married	26.0%	32.8%	33.1%	35.7%	23.1%	34.5%	29.8%
Married	58.3	56.3	57.1	20.2	61.3	57.1	53.6
Widowed	7.2	4.1	3.6	4.6	7.7	3.3	5.4
Divorced	8.6	6.8	6.1	9.6	8.0	5.1	11.1
Type of household							
Number of households ('000s)[1]	89,765	6,626	3,869	841	405	937	574
Married-couple families	55.1%	55.4%	60.0%	41.4%	57.9%	54.4%	45.5%
Male householder, no wife present	2.9	6.1	6.9	4.8	4.3	5.9	4.3
Female householder, no husband present	11.9	18.7	16.1	31.4	13.9	19.8	19.1
Nonfamily households	30.0	19.7	17.0	22.4	23.8	19.8	31.1
Size of household							
Average number of persons	2.57	3.41	3.78	2.85	2.65	3.25	2.78
One person	25.2%	15.0%	13.0%	18.8%	21.0%	12.2%	23.9%
Two persons	33.1	22.3	19.6	25.9	31.7	22.0	28.8
Three persons	17.4	19.5	18.6	20.3	22.1	21.9	18.9
Four persons	15.2	19.4	19.1	21.2	16.5	22.4	16.5
Five persons	6.2	12.1	13.5	9.4	6.2	13.8	7.9
Six persons	2.0	6.2	8.1	2.8	1.6	5.3	3.2
Seven or more persons	1.0	5.4	8.1	1.5	0.8	2.3	0.8

1. Estimate. 2. Age 15 and over. **Source:** U.S. Bureau of the Census, Current Population Reports, *The Hispanic Population in the U.S., March 1993* (1994).

Most Central American immigrants are from Nicaragua and El Salvador, although a significant number are from Guatemala. Statistical data on Salvadorans is uncertain, since the 1980 census did not break the Central American category down according to country or origin and since many Salvadorans arrived here illegally after 1980 and do not figure in any subsequent census update. During the latter part of the 1980s, large numbers of Nicaraguans entered the country as political refugees. In Miami, where between 150 and 200 Central American immigrants arrive every week, Central Americans comprise nearly 17 percent of the entire Hispanic population; in 1970, they comprised less than 1 percent. There are an estimated 250,000 Nicaraguans presently living in the United States.

Cubans and Cuban-Americans make up 4.9 percent of the total number of Hispanics in the United States. Large numbers of Cubans arrived in 1961 during the Cuban airlift and again in 1980 during the Mariel boat lift. Between 1980 and 1991, the number of Americans of Cuban origin increased from 800,000 to over a million. Since 1985 the Cuban population has shown little fluctuation or perhaps a very slight decrease.

The remaining 8.4 percent of the U.S. Hispanic population is of "Other Spanish" origin. This group grew from approximately 1.2 million in 1982 to 1.6 million in 1991.

RESIDENT POPULATION DISTRIBUTION FOR THE U.S., BY RACE AND HISPANIC ORIGIN, 1980–90

	1980		1990		Change	
Race/Hispanic origin[1]	Number	Percent	Number	Percent	Number	Percent
Total population	**226,545,805**	**100.0%**	**248,709,873**	**100.0%**	**22,164,068**	**9.8%**
White	188,371,622	83.1	199,686,070	80.3	11,314,448	6.0
Black	26,495,025	11.7	29,986,060	12.1	3,491,035	13.2
American Indian, Eskimo, or Aleut	1,420,400	0.6	1,959,234	0.8	538,834	37.9
Asian or Pacific Islander	3,500,439	1.5	7,273,662	2.9	3,773,223	107.8
Other race	6,758,319	3.0	9,804,847	3.9	3,046,528	45.1
Hispanic origin	14,608,673	6.4	22,354,059	9.0	7,745,386	53.0

1. Persons of Hispanic origin may be of any race. **Source**: U.S. Bureau of the Census release, 1991.

THE ASIAN AND PACIFIC ISLANDER POPULATION

In 1970 the Census Bureau counted about 1.5 million Asians and Pacific Islanders living in the United States. By the 1980 census, that figure had more than doubled to 3.5 million, thanks in large part to the more than 400,000 Southeast Asian refugees who came to America during 1975–80 under the Refugee Resettlement Program. Between 1980 and 1989, 2.4 million more Asian immigrants entered the United States, resulting in a 1990 census count of 7,273,662 Asians and Pacific Islanders, or a 107.8 percent increase over 1980. In 1990 this group represented 2.9 percent of the total U.S. population, as compared to 1.5 percent a decade earlier.

ASIAN POPULATION OF THE U.S., 1980–90

	1980 Census		1990 Census			
Group	Number	Percent	Number	Percent	Number change	Percent change
Asian Indian	361,531	0.2%	815,447	0.3%	453,916	125.6%
Chinese	806,040	0.4	1,645,472	0.7	839,432	104.1
Filipino	774,652	0.3	1,406,770	0.6	632,118	81.6
Guamanian	32,158	0.0	49,345	0.0	17,187	53.4
Hawaiian	166,814	0.1	211,014	0.1	44,200	26.5
Japanese	700,974	0.3	847,562	0.3	146,588	20.9
Korean	354,593	0.2	798,849	0.3	444,256	125.3
Samoan	41,948	0.0	62,964	0.0	21,016	50.1
Vietnamese	261,729	0.1	614,547	0.2	352,818	134.8
Other Asian or Pacific Islander	N.A.	N.A.	821,692	0.3	N.A.	N.A.
Total Asian or Pacific Islander	**3,500,439[1]**	**1.5**	**7,273,662**	**2.9**	**3,773,223**	**107.8**

Note: N.A. = not available from 1980 tabulations. 1. Figures for 1980 are not strictly comparable with those for 1990. The total for 1980 includes only the nine specific groups listed. **Source:** U.S. Bureau of the Census release, 1991.

ASIAN AND PACIFIC ISLANDER POPULATION OF METROPOLITAN AREAS, 1980–90

Rank/Metropolitan area	1980	1990	Number change	Percent change
1. Los Angeles–Anaheim–Riverside, Calif. CMSA	561,876	1,339,048	777,172	138.3%
2. San Francisco–Oakland–San Jose, Calif. CMSA	454,647	926,961	472,314	103.9
3. New York–Northern New Jersey–Long Island, N.Y.–N.J.–Conn. CMSA	370,731	873,213	502,482	135.5
4. Honolulu, Hawaii MSA	456,465	526,459	69,994	15.3
5. Chicago–Gary–Lake County, Ill.–Ind.–Wis. CMSA	144,626	256,050	111,424	77.0%
6. Washington, D.C.–Md.–Va. MSA	83,008	202,437	119,429	143.9
7. San Diego, Calif. MSA	89,861	198,311	108,450	120.7
8. Seattle–Tacoma, Wash. CMSA	78,255	164,286	86,031	109.9
9. Houston–Galveston–Brazoria, Tex. CMSA	53,056	132,131	79,075	149.0
10. Philadelphia–Wilmington–Trenton, Pa.–N.J.–Del.–Md. CMSA	53,291	123,458	70,167	131.7

Source: U.S. Bureau of the Census release, 1991.

THE AMERICAN INDIAN, ESKIMO, AND ALEUT POPULATION

Revised figures from the 1990 census report 1,959,234 American Indians, including 85,698 Alaska Natives (Eskimos and Aleuts), living in the United States. This represents a significant increase since the 1960 census, when only 524,000 (42,500 Alaska Natives) were counted. About 46 percent of American Indians live in the West, 29.7 percent in the South, 17.8 percent in the Midwest, and only 6.5 percent in the Northeast. According to the 1990 census, four states had over 100,000 Native Americans: Oklahoma (252,089), California (236,078), Arizona (203,009), and New Mexico (134,097).

The 1990 census reported that only 437,431 members of the American Indian, Eskimo, and Aleut populations lived inside federally "identified areas." These areas include reservations that the federal government recognizes as territory in which American Indian tribes have jurisdiction (state reservations are lands held in trust by state governments for the use and benefit of a given tribe), and "trust lands" that are held in trust by the federal government but that consist of property associated with a particular tribe or reservation. The overall population of these areas was 808,163, with Native Americans making up only 54.1 percent of the total.

The federal government's Bureau of Indian Affairs recognizes 503 distinct Native American communities, including numerous Alaska Native villages; 278 reservations, where about

POPULATION OF SELECTED RESERVATIONS AND TRUST LANDS, 1990

Rank/Reservation or Trust Land	Total population	American Indian, Eskimo, or Aleut: Population	American Indian, Eskimo, or Aleut: Percent of total
1. Navajo and Trust Lands, Ariz.–N.Mex.–Utah	148,451	143,405	96.6%
2. Pine Ridge and Trust Lands, Nebr.–S.Dak.	12,215	11,182	91.5
3. Fort Apache, Ariz.	10,394	9,825	94.5
4. Gila River, Ariz.	9,540	9,116	95.6
5. Papago, Ariz.	8,730	8,480	97.1
6. Rosebud and Trust Lands, S.Dak.	9,696	8,043	83.0
7. San Carlos, Ariz.	7,294	7,110	97.5
8. Zuni Pueblo, Ariz.–N.Mex.	7,412	7,073	95.4
9. Hopi and Trust Lands, Ariz.	7,360	7,061	95.9
10. Blackfeet, Mont.	8,549	7,025	82.2
11. Turtle Mountain and Trust Lands, N.Dak.–S.Dak.	7,106	6,772	95.3
12. Yakima and Trust Lands, Wash.	27,668	6,307	22.8
13. Osage, Okla.[1]	41,645	6,161	14.8
14. Fort Peck, Mont.	10,595	5,782	54.6%
15. Wind River, Wyo.	21,851	5,676	26.0
16. Eastern Cherokee, N.C.	6,527	5,388	82.5
17. Flathead, Mont.	21,259	5,130	24.1
18. Cheyenne River, S.Dak.	7,743	5,100	65.9
19. Standing Rock, N.Dak.–S.Dak.	7,956	4,870	61.2
20. Crow and Trust Lands, Mont.	6,370	4,724	74.2
21. Mississippi Choctaw and Trust Lands, Miss.	4,073	3,932	96.5
22. Colville, Wash.	6,957	3,788	54.4
23. Laguna Pueblo and Trust Lands, N.Mex.	3,731	3,634	97.4
24. Red Lake, Minn.	3,699	3,602	97.4
25. Northern Cheyenne and Trust Lands, Mont.–S.Dak.	3,923	3,542	90.3

Note: Ranked by total American Indian, Eskimo, or Aleut population. 1. The Osage Reservation is coextensive with Osage County. **Source:** U.S. Bureau of the Census release, 1991.

25 percent of the population (340,000) still resides; and the so-called historic areas of Oklahoma, former reservations whose boundaries were legally established during the 1900–1907 period (9% of the total population, or 116,000, lived there in 1980).

The 1990 census is expected to show many changes in the Native American situation. One that has been written about only slightly may have more profound effects than expected. Throughout the country Native Americans have begun to recognize the economic and political potential of their vast, untapped wealth in land and minerals. Native American property within U.S. boundaries, including original treaty lands and land won in legal battles, currently amounts to 53 million acres, about 2.5 percent of total U.S. acreage. At 16 million acres, the Navajo nation alone is about the size of West Virginia.

These lands include some of the most beautiful areas in the country, as well as some of the most valuable. Sixty percent of the U.S. uranium resources, a third of the strippable coal west of the Mississippi, a third of the U.S. reserves of low-sulphur coal, 15 percent of the total U.S. coal reserves, and 15 percent of the total U.S. natural gas reserves are under Native American lands.

For many reasons—including legal complexities, federal bureaucracy, fragile tribal governments—the vast majority of Native American communities have yet to translate this raw wealth into better lives for themselves. A few enterprising native groups, however, have made enormous economic strides, among them a Choctaw group in Mississippi, whose auto parts assembly plants and other enterprises make them the state's 15th-largest employer; the Warm Springs tribe of Oregon, who control a substantial fishing industry, a major resort, and a hydroelectric plant; and the Passamaquoddy and Penobscot tribes of Maine, who have parlayed a 1980 land claims settlement into more than $100 million in business investments and land holdings.

While it is too soon to tell just what kind of impact the ventures will have on the well-being of these tribes, it clearly cannot be measured in financial terms alone. For the first time in centuries, the destiny of some Native Americans is actually in their own hands, and that is the true revolution in their status.

The U.S. Population by Age and Sex

Population by Age

With birth rates and fertility rates declining rapidly since 1965, it should come as no surprise that the average age of the U.S. population has been increasing almost as quickly. It will continue to rise for the foreseeable future, in part because of the aging of the Baby Boom generation.

During the Baby Boom years of the 1950s and 1960s, the median age of the population actually declined, the only time it has done so. Since then, however, the steady decline in the percentage of young people, especially those under 18 years of age (from 34.1% in 1970, to 25.6% in 1990), combined with the increase of those between 25 and 44 (they were 23.6% of the population in 1970, but 32.6% in 1990), has driven the median age from 28 in 1970 to 33 in 1990. A five-year increase in 20 years is unprecedented in U.S. history, but what's more remarkable is that we will most likely duplicate that feat over the next 20 years.

The other major factor in the so-called "graying of America" is the increased life expectancy for older people. The Census Bureau estimates that 31.7 million Americans (12.3% of the population) were over the age of 65 in 1990; this represents a 24.1 percent increase since 1980 and a 1,000 percent increase since 1900. There were seven million people 80 or older in 1990, three million 85 or older, nearly a million 90 or older, and 36,000 people over the age of 100. By the year 2000 the bureau projects there will be 34.9 million people over the age of 65, an increase of 10.2 percent. Over the first decade of the 21st century the over-65 population will grow at about the same rate—between 10 percent and 12 percent—but in the decades of the 2010s and 2020s the projected increases jump to 31.2 percent and 25.6 percent, as the members of the Baby Boom generation finally become senior citizens. In the year 2030, 21 percent of the population, or 65 million Americans, will

GROWTH OF THE POPULATION AGE 65 AND OVER, BY NUMBER AND PERCENT, 1900–2050

Year	Population 65 and over ('000s)	Percent increase by decade	Percent of population 65 and over
1900	3,099	N.A.	4.1%
1910	3,986	28.6%	4.3
1920	4,929	23.7	4.7
1930	6,705	36.0	5.5
1940	9,031	34.7	6.9
1950	12,397	37.3	8.1
1960	16,675	34.5	9.2
1970	20,107	20.6	9.8
1980	25,549	27.1	11.3
1990	31,224	22.2	12.5
2000	35,322	13.1	12.8
2010	40,104	13.5	13.3
2020	53,348	33.0	16.4
2030	70,175	44.4	20.1
2040	77,014	9.7	20.7
2050	80,109	4.0	20.4

Note: Figures for 2000 through 2050 are Census Bureau projections based on their "most likely" series of estimates. **Source:** U.S. Bureau of the Census, *Population Projections of the U.S by Age, Sex, Race, and Hispanic Origin, 1993–2050* (1994).

CHARACTERISTICS OF THE POPULATION OVER AGE 65, 1994

Characteristic	Male	Female
Total (millions)	12.7	18.0
White	11.5	16.1
Black	1.0	1.5
Percent distribution		
Marital status:	4.7%	4.3%
Single	77.2	42.8
Married	75.1	41.0
Spouse absent	2.1	1.8
Widowed	13.1	46.9
Divorced	5.0	6.0
Family status:		
In families[1]	81.3%	57.8%
Nonfamily householders	17.1	41.1
Secondary individuals	1.6	1.1
Living arrangements:		
Living in household	99.9%	99.8%
Living alone	16.0	40.2
Spouse present	75.1	41.0
Living with someone else	8.8	18.6
Not in household	0.1	0.2
Labor force participation:		
Employed	16.2%	8.8%
Unemployed	0.7	0.4
Not in labor force	83.1	90.8
Percent below poverty level	7.9%	15.2%

1. Excludes those living in unrelated subfamilies. **Source:** U.S. Bureau of the Census, *Statistical Abstract of the United States 1995* (1995).

U.S. POPULATION BY SEX: TOTALS AND RATIO OF MALES TO FEMALES, 1920–93

Year	Male ('000s)	Female ('000s)	Males per 100 females: All ages	14–24	25–44	65+
1920	53,900	51,810	104.0	97.3	105.1	101.3
1930	62,137	60,638	102.5	98.4	101.8	100.5
1940	66,062	65,608	100.7	98.9	98.5	95.5
1950	74,833	75,864	98.6	98.2	96.4	89.6
1960	88,331	90,992	97.1	98.7	95.7	82.8
1970	98,926	104,309	94.8	98.7	95.5	72.1
1980	110,053	116,493	94.5	101.9	97.4	67.6
1990	122,049	127,875	95.1	104.6	98.9	67.2
1991	123,421	129,257	95.2	104.7	99.0	67.5
1992	124,493	130,589	95.3	104.6	99.2	67.8
1993	127,076	133,265	95.4	104.4	99.1	68.5

Source: U.S. Bureau of the Census, *Statistical Abstract of the United States*, 1995.

RESIDENT POPULATION OF STATES, BY AGE, 1994 (in thousands)

State	Resident population	Under 5 years	5 to 17 years	18 to 24 years	25 to 44 years	45 to 64 years	65 years and over	Median age
United States	**260,341**	**19,727**	**48,291**	**25,263**	**83,013**	**50,888**	**33,158**	**34.0**
Alabama	4,219	302	778	446	1,278	862	552	34.3
Alaska	606	56	136	61	215	110	28	30.9
Arizona	4,075	344	795	392	1,245	753	546	33.1
Arkansas	2,453	172	468	247	700	503	362	34.9
California	31,431	2,833	5,844	3,085	10,724	5,598	3,346	32.2
Colorado	3,656	270	700	344	1,235	739	367	34.1
Connecticut	3,275	231	557	281	1,069	672	465	35.6
Delaware	706	51	124	68	234	139	89	34.2
District of Columbia	570	43	76	58	206	111	77	34.5
Florida	13,953	962	2,300	1,174	4,146	2,799	2,571	37.1
Georgia	7,055	549	1,344	729	2,368	1,357	710	32.7
Hawaii	1,179	95	209	116	385	231	142	34.2
Idaho	1,133	87	252	120	325	217	132	32.6
Illinois	11,752	915	2,168	1,128	3,764	2,295	1,481	34.0
Indiana	5,752	407	1,066	591	1,797	1,157	735	34.3
Iowa	2,829	188	541	274	827	563	437	35.4
Kansas	2,554	184	506	247	782	480	354	34.1
Kentucky	3,827	261	709	400	1,181	787	489	34.5
Louisiana	4,315	337	898	458	1,305	823	494	32.4
Maine	1,240	78	228	115	393	253	173	35.7
Maryland	5,006	379	884	441	1,736	1,006	559	34.2
Massachusetts	6,041	423	1,001	566	2,030	1,172	849	34.8
Michigan	9,496	701	1,824	932	2,996	1,863	1,180	34.0
Minnesota	4,567	327	914	416	1,479	860	572	33.9
Mississippi	2,669	207	549	304	772	506	332	32.4
Missouri	5,278	376	1,003	498	1,608	1,048	745	34.7
Montana	856	59	179	80	247	178	114	35.4
Nebraska	1,623	116	326	158	485	309	230	34.3
Nevada	1,457	115	261	124	488	305	165	34.2
New Hampshire	1,137	80	212	100	393	217	136	34.4
New Jersey	7,904	579	1,352	688	2,566	1,642	1,078	35.5
New Mexico	1,654	140	358	162	499	314	181	32.4
New York	18,169	1,382	3,129	1,702	5,863	3,700	2,393	34.6
North Carolina	7,070	510	1,246	733	2,263	1,434	885	34.2
North Dakota	638	43	129	66	189	118	94	34.2
Ohio	11,102	784	2,070	1,079	3,446	2,232	1,491	34.7
Oklahoma	3,258	237	643	328	948	659	443	34.3
Oregon	3,086	209	574	278	968	635	422	35.8
Pennsylvania	12,052	799	2,099	1,105	3,666	2,465	1,919	36.3
Rhode Island	997	71	169	97	318	187	155	35.0
South Carolina	3,664	274	678	394	1,152	731	435	33.5
South Dakota	721	54	154	70	205	131	106	33.6
Tennessee	5,175	366	931	518	1,621	1,081	658	34.7
Texas	18,378	1,559	3,742	1,919	5,905	3,385	1,868	31.9
Utah	1,908	181	491	232	544	291	168	26.7
Vermont	580	38	108	57	190	117	70	35.0
Virginia	6,552	469	1,134	670	2,232	1,321	725	33.9
Washington	5,343	394	1,014	492	1,774	1,051	618	34.3
West Virginia	1,822	108	321	190	521	402	280	37.0
Wisconsin	5,082	350	997	483	1,587	982	683	34.3
Wyoming	476	33	104	49	142	95	53	33.9

Note: Includes armed forces residing in each state. **Source:** Census Bureau, Press Release, Mar. 1, 1995.

be 65 years old or older. That's only 40 years from now, a demographic stone's throw away. By comparison, bear in mind that 40 years ago, in 1950, the over-65 population totaled 7 percent of all Americans and numbered nine million.

Population by Sex

In 1993, according to the Census Bureau, there were 38 million men and 45 million women who had never married or who were currently widowed or divorced, a ratio of 84 unmarried men per 100 unmarried women. The popular interpretation of these figures—that there is a shortage of eligible men—fails to consider that women are more likely to live longer (and so be counted among the widowed) and less likely to remarry after a divorce. In fact, the seven million surplus of women can be entirely attributed to the fact that widows over the age of 65 outnumber widowers over 65. But during the peak marrying ages, unmarried men actually outnumber unmarried women: among persons under age 25 there were 111 unmarried men for every 100 unmarried women; in the 25-to-29 age group, there were 127 men for every 100 women; and men 30–34 outnumber women 122 to 100. It's not until the 40-to-44 age group that the reversal begins; and among the 65-and-over age group there is a dramatic change, with only 29 unmarried men for every 100 unmarried women.

NUMBER OF PERSONS AND PERCENT OF TOTAL POPULATION, BY AGE GROUP, 1960–2020 (numbers in thousands)

Age in years	1960 ('000s)	1960 Percent	1970 ('000s)	1970 Percent	1980 ('000s)	1980 Percent	1990 ('000s)	1990 Percent	2000 ('000s)	2000 Percent	2010 ('000s)	2010 Percent	2020 ('000s)	2020 Percent
Under 5	20,341	11.3%	17,166	8.4%	16,458	7.2%	18,408	7.4%	16,898	6.3%	16,899	6.0%	17,095	5.8%
5–13	32,965	18.2	36,672	17.9	31,095	13.7	32,393	12.9	33,483	12.5	31,001	11.0	31,697	10.8
14–17	11,219	6.2	15,924	7.8	16,142	7.1	13,237	5.3	15,332	5.7	14,746	5.2	14,074	4.8
18–24	16,128	8.9	24,712	12.1	30,350	13.3	26,140	10.4	25,231	9.4	27,155	9.6	25,018	8.5
25–34	22,919	12.7	25,323	12.3	37,626	16.5	43,925	17.5	37,149	13.8	37,572	13.3	39,100	13.3
35–44	24,221	13.4	23,150	11.3	25,868	11.4	37,897	15.1	43,911	16.4	37,202	13.2	37,591	12.8
45–64	36,203	20.0	41,999	20.5	44,515	19.5	46,851	18.7	61,381	22.9	78,637	27.8	77,722	26.4
65+	16,675	9.2	20,107	9.8	25,704	11.3	31,559	12.6	34,882	13.0	39,362	13.9	52,067	17.7
85+	940	0.5	1,430	0.7	2,269	1.0	3,254	1.3	4,622	1.7	6,115	2.2	6,651	2.3
100+	3	—	5	—	15	—	56	—	100	—	171	0.1	266	0.1
Total U.S. pop.		**180,671**		**205,052**		**227,757**		**250,410**		**268,266**		**282,575**		**294,364**
Median age		**29.4**		**27.9**		**30.0**		**33.0**		**36.4**		**38.9**		**40.2**

Note: Figures for 1990 and after are the projections the Census Bureau calls the "middle" or "most likely" series. **Sources:** U.S. Bureau of the Census, *Projections of the Population of the U.S. by Age, Sex, and Race 1988 to 2040* (1989) and *Statistical Abstract of the United States 1989* (1989).

Vital Statistics: Births, Deaths, Marriages, Divorces

The National Center for Health Statistics does a month-by-month tracking of four sets of numbers which both it and the Census Bureau refer to as "vital": births, deaths, marriages, and divorces.

Births An estimated 3.98 million babies were born in the United States in 1994, 1.5 percent less than the provisional number reported in 1993. This represents the third straight year that the number of total births has declined since the post–Baby Boom high of 4.2 million in 1990. The crude birth rate—the number of live births per 1,000 total population—also decreased for the third straight year, to 15.3, its lowest level in more than 15 years. The increase in births and the birth rate in the late 1980s was attributable to the number of Baby Boom–era women entering their child-bearing years and to women having children later in life. The decrease since then can be blamed in large part on the recession of the early 1990s.

Deaths A record 2.28 million people died in 1994. The death rate of 8.8 per 1,000 population (the same as in 1993) was significantly higher than in previous years, but not nearly as high as the 14.7 recorded in 1910. (For infant mortality figures and for more specific information about death rates by cause see the section "Health and Medicine.")

In 1994 there were 1,693,000 more births than deaths; this figure is called the *natural increase,* meaning the growth in population without immigration (which has accounted for another 600,000 people per year in recent years).

Marriages An estimated 2.36 million couples married during 1994, a slight increase over 1993 levels; the rate per 100,000 people rose slightly to 9.1 after falling to 9.0 in 1993, its lowest rate since the 1960s. In addition to getting married in fewer numbers, people are quite clearly getting married at a later age. In 1960, for example, about 40% of all 19-year-old women were married, but by 1990 only 11% were. Also in 1960, about 92% of all women were married before they reached age 30, but by 1990 only 81% were. Moreover, between 1970 and 1990, the proportion of 30-to-34-year-olds who had never married almost tripled, rising from 6% to 16% for women, and from 9% to 27% for men; for those age 35 to 39, the proportion of never married doubled over the two decades, from 5% to 10% for women and from 7% to 15% for men.

BIRTHS AND DEATHS IN THE U.S., 1910–94 (in thousands)

Year	Live births	Birth rate[1]	Deaths[2]	Death rate[1]
1910	2,777	30.1	N.A.	14.7
1920	2,950	27.7	N.A.	13.0
1930	2,618	21.3	N.A.	11.3
1935	2,377	18.7	1,393	10.9
1940	2,559	19.4	1,417	10.8
1945	2,858	20.4	1,402	10.6
1950	3,632	24.1	1,452	9.6
1955	4,097	25.0	1,529	9.3
1960	4,258	23.7	1,712	9.5
1965	3,760	19.5	1,828	9.4
1970	3,731	18.4	1,921	9.5
1975	3,144	14.6	1,893	8.8
1980	3,612	15.9	1,990	8.8
1981	3,629	15.8	1,978	8.6
1982	3,681	15.9	1,975	8.5
1983	3,639	15.5	2,019	8.6
1984	3,669	15.5	2,039	8.6
1985	3,761	15.8	2,086	8.8
1986	3,757	15.6	2,105	8.8
1987	3,829	15.7	2,127	8.8
1988	3,910	16.0	2,171	8.9
1989	4,041	16.4	2,150	8.7
1990	4,158	16.7	2,148	8.6
1991	4,111	16.3	2,170	8.6
1992	4,084	16.0	2,177	8.5
1993	4,039	15.7	2,268	8.8
1994	3,979	15.3	2,286	8.8

1. Per 1,000 total population. 2. Excludes fetal deaths. **Sources:** U.S. Bureau of the Census, *The Statistical History of the U.S.* (1976); U.S. National Center for Health Statistics, *Vital Statistics of the United States 1987* (1988) and *Monthly Vital Statistics Report* (June 13, 1995).

MARRIAGES AND DIVORCES IN THE U.S., 1920–94 (in thousands)

Year	Marriages	Rate per 1,000 of population	Divorces	Rate per 1,000 of population
1920	1,274	12.0	171	1.6
1925	1,188	10.3	175	1.5
1930	1,127	9.2	196	1.6
1935	1,327	10.4	218	1.7
1940	1,596	12.1	264	2.0
1945	1,613	12.2	485	3.5
1950	1,667	11.1	385	2.6
1955	1,531	9.3	377	2.3
1960	1,523	8.5	393	2.2
1965	1,800	9.3	479	2.5
1970	2,163	10.6	708	3.5
1975	2,153	10.0	1,036	4.8
1980	2,390	10.0	1,036	4.8
1981	2,422	10.6	1,213	5.3
1982	2,456	10.6	1,170	5.0
1983	2,446	10.5	1,158	4.9
1984	2,477	10.5	1,169	5.0
1985	2,413	10.1	1,190	5.0
1986	2,400	10.0	1,159	4.8
1987	2,421	9.9	1,166	4.8
1988	2,389	9.7	1,167	4.8
1989	2,404	9.7	1,163	4.7
1990	2,448	9.8	1,175	4.7
1991	2,371	9.4	1,187	4.7
1992	2,362	9.3	1,215	4.8
1993	2,334	9.0	1,187	4.6
1994	2,362	9.1	1,191	4.6

Source: U.S. Bureau of the Census, *The Statistical History of the U.S.* (1976); U.S. National Center for Health Statistics, *Vital Statistics of the United States* (annual) and *Monthly Vital Statistics Report* (June 13, 1995).

MEDIAN AGE AT FIRST MARRIAGE, BY SEX, 1890–1993

Year	Male	Female	Year	Male	Female
1890	26.1	22.0	1980	24.7	22.0
1900	25.9	21.9	1985	25.5	23.3
1910	25.1	21.6	1988	25.9	23.6
1920	24.6	21.2	1989	26.2	23.8
1930	24.3	21.3	1990	26.1	23.9
1940	24.3	21.5	1991	26.3	24.1
1950	22.8	20.3	1992	26.5	24.4
1960	22.8	20.3	1993	26.5	24.5
1970	23.2	20.8			

Sources: U.S. Bureau of the Census, *The Statistical History of the U.S.* (1976) and *Marital Status and Living Arrangements: March 1993* (1994).

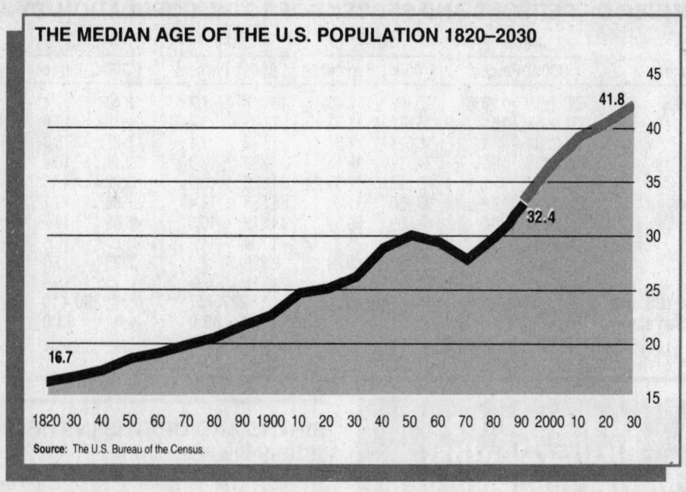

Source: The U.S. Bureau of the Census.

DIVORCED PERSONS PER 1,000 MARRIED PERSONS, BY SEX AND RACE, 1960–93

Sex/Race	1960	1970	1980	1990	1993
Both sexes					
All races	35	47	100	142	154
White	33	44	92	133	144
Black	62	83	203	282	296
Hispanic[1]	N.A.	61	98	129	136
Male					
All races	28	35	79	118	125
White	27	32	74	112	119
Black	45	62	149	208	216
Hispanic	N.A.	40	64	103	114
Female					
All races	42	60	120	166	182
White	38	56	110	153	170
Black	78	104	258	358	378
Hispanic	N.A.	81	132	155	157

Note: Per 1,000 married persons with spouse present. 1. Persons of Hispanic origin may be of any race. **Source:** U.S. Bureau of the Census, *Marital Status and Living Arrangements: March 1993* (1994).

MARITAL STATUS, BY RACE AND HISPANIC ORIGIN, 1970–93

Race and marital status	1970 Number ('000s)	1970 Percent	1980 Number ('000s)	1980 Percent	1993 Number ('000s)	1993 Percent
All races	132,507	100.0%	159,528	100.0%	187,135	100.0%
Married	94,999	71.7	104,564	65.5	114,538	61.2
Unmarried	37,508	28.3	54,964	34.5	72,597	38.8
Never married	21,443	16.2	32,342	20.3	42,258	22.6
Widowed	11,784	8.9	12,734	8.0	13,681	7.3
Divorced	4,282	3.2	9,886	6.2	16,658	8.9
White	118,179	100.0%	139,480	100.0%	158,729	100.0%
Married	85,784	72.6	93,800	67.2	100,917	63.6
Unmarried	32,395	27.4	45,681	32.8	57,813	36.4
Never married	18,444	15.6	26,405	18.9	32,385	20.4
Widowed	10,280	8.7	10,938	7.8	11,464	7.2
Divorced	3,671	3.1	8,338	6.0	13,963	8.8
Black	12,972	100.0%	16,638	100.0%	21,317	100.0%
Married	8,310	64.1	8,545	51.4	9,242	43.4
Unmarried	4,662	35.9	8,093	48.6	12,075	56.6
Never married	2,668	20.6	5,070	30.5	8,006	37.6
Widowed	1,427	11.0	1,627	9.8	1,827	8.6
Divorced	567	4.4	1,396	8.4	2,242	10.5
Hispanic[1]	5,066	100.0%	7,888	100.0%	14,913	100.0%
Married	3,637	71.8	5,176	65.6	9,008	60.4
Unmarried	1,429	28.2	2,711	34.4	5,905	39.6
Never married	943	18.6	1,901	24.1	4,159	27.9
Widowed	286	5.6	350	4.4	652	4.4
Divorced	200	3.9	460	5.8	1,095	7.3

Note: Only those people 18 years old and over are included. 1. Hispanic persons may be of any race. **Source:** U.S. Bureau of the Census, *Marital Status and Living Arrangements: March 1993* (1994).

Divorces An estimated 1.2 million divorces were granted in 1994. The divorce rate per 1,000 population, however, held steady at 4.6 percent, its lowest rate in 20 years. The divorce rate peaked in 1979 at 5.3 per 1,000 population. (In that year the divorce rate per 1,000 married women reached 22.8, up from 9.2 in 1960.) While the divorce rate has stabilized, the ratio of divorced persons to married persons (with spouse present) has skyrocketed. Between 1970 and 1993, the proportion more than tripled, from 47 divorced per 1,000 married to 154 per 1,000. For blacks, the rise was even greater, going from 83 per 1,000 to 296 per 1,000 in the same period.

In 1988, the most recent year for which final divorce statistics (as opposed to estimates) are available, divorce rates were highest for teenage wives (56.3 per 1,000), about twice the rate of wives 30 to 34.

Divorce is generally more prevalent among the young. In 1988, 53 percent of men and 50 percent of women divorcing were under 25, figures that reflect the early demise of a sizable portion of all marriages: over one-third of all divorces in 1988 were for couples married less than five years, and almost two thirds for couples married less than 10 years.

In 1993, there were 16.7 million currently divorced persons in the United States, 8.4% of the total adult population. There are more divorced women (9.9 million) than men (6.8 million) because women are less likely to remarry.

MARITAL STATUS OF THE POPULATION BY SEX AND AGE, 1993 (in thousands)

Age	Total number	Single, never married	Married, spouse present	Married, spouse absent[1]	Widowed	Divorced
			MALE			
18–19	3,263	3,162	84	12	—	6
20–24	8,786	7,113	1,483	92	7	91
25–29	9,767	4,727	4,327	268	11	435
30–34	11,089	3,333	6,534	385	15	822
35–39	10,606	2,085	6,893	407	33	1,189
40–44	9,298	1,008	6,756	335	51	1,148
45–54	13,847	951	10,670	483	142	1,602
55–64	10,205	670	7,884	367	380	904
65–74	8,114	389	6,316	186	765	458
75–84	3,925	157	2,826	79	759	104
85+	792	23	426	19	305	20
Total 18+	**89,693**	**23,618**	**54,198**	**2,631**	**2,468**	**6,778**

Age	Total number	Single, never married	Married, spouse present	Married, spouse absent[1]	Widowed	Divorced
			FEMALE			
18–19	3,244	2,918	282	30	—	14
20–24	9,016	6,019	2,529	267	7	194
25–29	9,836	3,258	5,271	494	25	789
30–34	11,171	2,153	7,251	509	58	1,200
35–39	10,861	1,362	7,465	545	121	1,367
40–44	9,577	867	6,571	494	181	1,465
45–54	14,655	798	10,191	569	648	2,448
55–64	11,042	469	7,269	360	1,594	1,349
65–74	10,249	376	5,359	178	3,607	728
75–84	5,992	297	1,777	102	3,548	269
85+	1,798	122	182	13	1,424	57
Total 18+	**97,442**	**18,640**	**54,148**	**3,560**	**11,213**	**9,880**

Source: U.S. Bureau of the Census, *Marital Status and Living Arrangements: March 1993* (1994).

PERCENT OF POPULATION NEVER MARRIED, BY AGE AND SEX, 1960–93

Age	1960	1970	1980	1990	1993
			MEN		
Total: 15 and over	**23.2%**	**28.1%**	**29.6%**	**29.9%**	**30.3%**
15–17	98.8	99.4	99.4	99.8	99.9
18	94.6	95.1	97.4	98.5	96.9[1]
19	87.1	89.9	90.9	95.3	([1])
20–24	53.1	54.7	68.8	79.3	81.0
25–29	20.8	19.1	33.1	45.2	48.4
30–34	11.9	9.4	15.9	27.0	30.1
35–39	8.8	7.2	7.8	14.7	19.7
40–44	7.3	6.3	7.1	10.5	10.8
45–54	7.4	7.5	6.1	6.3	6.9
55–64	8.0	7.8	5.3	5.8	6.6
65 and over	7.7	7.5	4.9	4.2	4.4
			WOMEN		
Total: 15 and over	**17.3%**	**22.1%**	**22.5%**	**22.8%**	**23.0%**
15–17	93.2	97.3	97.0	98.5	98.7
18	75.6	82.0	88.0	92.0	89.9[1]
19	59.7	68.8	77.6	88.7	([1])
20–24	28.4	35.8	50.2	62.8	66.8
25–29	10.5	10.5	20.9	31.1	33.1
30–34	6.9	6.2	9.5	16.4	19.3
35–39	6.1	5.4	6.2	10.4	12.5
40–44	6.1	4.9	4.8	8.0	9.0
45–54	7.0	4.9	4.7	5.0	5.4
55–64	8.0	6.8	4.5	3.9	4.3
65 and over	8.5	7.7	5.9	4.9	4.4

1. Population aged 18–19 included under 18. **Source:** U.S. Bureau of the Census, *Marital Status and Living Arrangements: March 1993* (1994).

BLACK-WHITE MARRIED COUPLES IN THE U.S., 1970–94 (in thousands)

Year	Total married couples	Total black-white	Husband black, wife white	Wife black, husband white
1970	44,597	65	41	24
1980	49,714	167	122	45
1990	53,227	231	158	73
1992	53,512	246	163	83
1993	54,199	242	182	60
1994	54,251	296	196	100

Source: U.S. Bureau of the Census, *Statistical Abstract of the United States*, 1995.

UNMARRIED COUPLE HOUSEHOLDS, 1960–93 (in thousands)

Characteristic	Total	Without children under 15	With children under 15
1960	439	242	197
1970	523	327	196
1980	1,589	1,159	431
1990	2,856	1,966	891
1991	3,039	2,077	982
1992	3,308	2,187	1,121
1993	3,510	2,274	1,236

Note: Figures may not add to total due to rounding. **Source:** U.S. Bureau of the Census, *Marital Status and Living Arrangements: March 1993* (1994).

"Marriage is a great institution, but I'm not ready for an institution."

—Mae West (1893–1980)

WOMEN AND CHILDBEARING: CURRENT TRENDS

According to the Census Bureau's Current Population Survey, there were 60.1 million women in the United States between the ages of 15 and 44 in 1994; 3.9 million of them reported giving birth in the preceding 12 months, resulting in an estimated fertility rate of 64.7 births per 1,000 women ages 15 to 44. These figures have not fluctuated a great deal over the last decade, despite the increased number of women of childbearing age in the population.

Minorities Significantly higher fertility rates were reported among minorities: 99.2 per 1,000 Hispanic women, and 66.5 for black women, as compared to 64.0 for white women. Hispanic women ages 15 to 44 represented only 11% of all women of childbearing age in the United States, but they accounted for 16.6 percent of all births in 1994.

Women over 29 The Census Bureau noted again, as it had in previous reports, that a significant number of women in their thirties were having children or were planning to. The birth rate per 1,000 women ages 30–34 was a record 90.4 in 1994, compared with 80.4 just four years earlier. Equally surprising is the birth rate for women ages 35–39, which was 36.0 in 1994, 60 percent higher than in 1976. And the birth rate per women ages 40–44 has increased from 6.5 to 8.7 over the same period.

Pregnancies of unmarried women The Census Bureau reported that the number of children born to unmarried women continues to skyrocket, especially among black women. Two out of every three black children born in 1992 were to unmarried mothers (up from 56.7% in 1990) according the Census Bureau, nearly four times the rate for white women, and double the rate for Hispanic women. Just over a million unmarried women ages 15–44 gave birth in 1994; they represented 25.9% of all women who gave birth. The number of unmarried teenagers (ages 15–19) giving birth also increased, from 229,000 in 1990 to 288,000 in 1994. Nearly three-quarters of all teenage births were out of wedlock; the rates were 66.0% for whites, 65.7% for Hispanics, and 89.7% for black teenagers (down from a whopping 93.8% just two years earlier).

FERTILITY RATES OF AMERICAN WOMEN

Population experts predict future trends in population growth by studying many factors, including the crude birth rate (see "Vital Statistics") and two significant fertility rates. The *general fertility rate,* as defined by the Census Bureau, measures the ratio of live births to the total number of women ages 18 to 44. (In 1990 the Census Bureau began reporting based on women ages 15 to 44, thereby lowering the fertility rate but more accurately measuring the increasing number of teenage pregnancies.)

The *total fertility rate,* as used by the National Center for Health Statistics, is the number of births 1,000 women ages 10 to 50 would have in their lifetimes if at each year of age they experienced the birth rates occurring to women of that age in the specified calendar year. The total fertility rate is sometimes defined in the popular media as the number of likely births one woman will have in her lifetime.

The total fertility rate is most helpful in measuring long-term trends, especially in determining whether or not the nation is sustaining a level of reproduction necessary for maintaining current population levels. That level, generally regarded as 2,100 per 1,000 women, has not been achieved in the United States since 1971. Since 1987 the figure has been moving upward, reflecting both the large number of women in their thirties who are having babies and the fact that women are having more babies.

BABY BOOM AND BUST: 1940–90
(Births per 1,000 U.S. women aged 15-44)

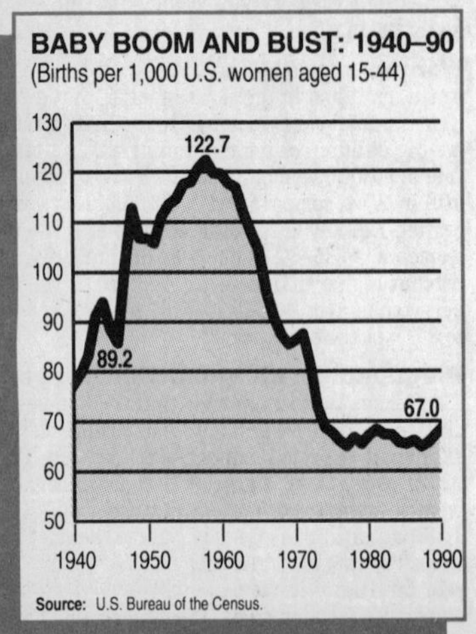

Source: U.S. Bureau of the Census.

FERTILITY RATES OF U.S. WOMEN, 1930–94

Year	General fertility rate[1]	Total fertility rate	Year	General fertility rate[1]	Total fertility rate	Year	General fertility rate[1]	Total fertility rate	Year	General fertility rate[1]	Total fertility rate
1930	89.2	2,600	1947	113.3	3,274	1963	108.5	3,333	1979	67.2	1,808
1931	84.6	2,467	1948	107.3	3,109	1964	105.0	3,208	1980	68.4	1,840
1932	81.7	2,383	1949	107.1	3,110	1965	96.6	2,928	1981	67.4	1,815
1933	76.3	2,235	1950	106.2	3,091	1966	91.3	2,736	1982	67.3	1,829
1934	78.5	2,294	1951	111.4	3,267	1967	87.6	2,573	1983	65.8	1,803
1935	77.2	2,250	1952	113.8	3,355	1968	85.7	2,477	1984	65.4	1,806
1936	75.8	2,207	1953	115.0	3,418	1969	86.5	2,465	1985	66.2	1,843
1937	77.1	2,236	1954	117.9	3,537	1970	87.9	2,480	1986	64.9	1,836
1938	79.1	2,288	1955	118.3	3,574	1971	81.6	2,267	1987	65.7	1,871
1939	77.6	2,238	1956	121.0	3,682	1972	73.1	2,010	1988	67.3	1,932
1940	79.9	2,301	1957	122.7	3,760	1973	68.8	1,879	1989	68.0	2,014
1941	83.4	2,399	1958	120.0	3,693	1974	67.8	1,835	1990	67.0	2,081
1942	91.5	2,628	1959	119.9	3,705	1975	66.0	1,774	1991	69.6	2,073
1943	94.3	2,718	1960	118.0	3,654	1976	65.0	1,738	1992	69.2	2,054[2]
1944	88.8	2,568	1961	117.2	3,629	1977	66.8	1,790	1993	68.3	2,074[2]
1945	85.9	2,491	1962	112.2	3,474	1978	65.5	1,760	1994	67.1	N.A.
1946	101.9	2,943									

1. Figures through 1989 are based on all women ages 18 to 44; figures after 1989 include all women 15–44. 2. Estimate. **Sources:** *The Fertility of American Women: 1994* (1995); U.S. National Center for Health Statistics, *Vital Statistics* (annual).

NUMBER AND RATE OF LIVE BIRTHS, DEATHS, AND MARRIAGES BY MONTH IN U.S., 1994

	Births		Deaths		Marriages	
Month	Number	Rate per 1,000 population	Number	Rate per 1,000 population	Number	Rate per 1,000 population
January	325,000	16.0	224,000	10.2	107,000	4.9
February	294,000	14.8	204,000	10.3	156,000	8.0
March	350,000	15.9	199,000	9.0	147,000	6.8
April	302,000	14.1	182,000	8.5	175,000	8.3
May	329,000	14.9	186,000	8.4	232,000	10.5
June	319,000	14.9	176,000	8.2	262,000	12.2
July	346,000	15.6	184,000	8.3	222,000	10.0
August	392,000	17.7	190,000	8.6	262,000	11.8
September	329,000	15.3	178,000	8.3	224,000	10.4
October	340,000	15.3	190,000	8.6	232,000	10.5
November	313,000	14.5	182,000	8.5	171,000	7.9
December	314,000	14.1	190,000	8.5	173,000	7.8

Note: Figures are provisional. **Source:** U.S. National Center for Health Statistics, *Monthly Vital Statistics Report* (June 13, 1995).

WOMEN AND CHILDBEARING IN THE U.S., BY AGE, 1976–94

Characteristic	1976	1980	1990	1994
Total number of women, 18–44 years old[1]	41,618	45,652	58,381	60,088
Percent of childless women				
All women 18–44 years old[1]	35.0%	36.7%	41.6%	42.0%
18–24 years[2]	69.0	70.0	77.7	77.9
25–29 years	30.8	36.8	42.1	43.6
30–34 years	15.6	19.8	25.7	26.3
35–39 years	10.5	12.1	17.7	19.6
40–44 years	10.2	10.1	16.0	17.5

Characteristic	1976	1980	1990	1994
Births per 1,000 women				
All women 18–44 years old[1]	67.2	71.1	67.0	64.7
18–24 years[2]	93.2	96.6	78.0	73.7
25–29 years	104.8	114.8	112.1	107.7
30–34 years	56.4	60.0	80.4	90.4
35–39 years	22.6	26.9	37.3	36.0
40–44 years	6.5	9.9	8.6	9.6

1. Figures for 1990 and 1994 include women 15–44 years old. 2. Figures for 1990 and 1994 include women 15–24 years old. **Source:** U.S. Bureau of the Census, *Fertility of American Women: 1994* (1995).

Households and Families

Since the very first census in 1790, the federal government has not only attempted to count every individual, it has also tried to determine where those individuals live and with whom. While the definition of *household* has changed somewhat over the years, it has remained a central element in understanding the basic structure of American society. Since 1970 the size and composition of the household unit has revealed the extent of social change more clearly than any other measure.

Households

Virtually all Americans are part of a household. As of March 1993, the Census Bureau determined that 253.5 million persons—out of a total population of 258 million—belonged to some form of household unit (the remainder were in institutions or other kinds of group living arrangements). According to the official Census Bureau definition, a household consists of "all persons who occupy a housing unit. A house, an apartment or other group of rooms, or a single room is regarded as a housing unit when it is occupied or intended for occupancy as separate living quarters; that is, when the occupants do not live and eat with any other persons in the structure, and there is direct access from the outside or through a common hall."

There are two major categories of households identified by the Census Bureau: family and nonfamily. A family or family household requires the presence of at least two persons, the householder (i.e., the person in whose name the housing unit is owned or rented) and one or more additional family members related to the householder through birth, adoption, or marriage. A nonfamily household consists of a householder who either lives alone or exclusively with persons who are not related to the householder. Since 1970 the rapid growth of nonfamily households has led to a continuous increase in the number of households and a fall in the average number of persons in each.

As of March 1993, there were 96.4 million households in the United States, the largest number ever, with an average of 2.63 persons in each. This continues a trend begun during the 1970s, when the number of households increased by more than 20% and over 17.3 million units, nearly double the growth of the 1940s and 1950s and over 60% more than the relatively explosive 1960s. The most significant change helping to ignite this surge was the unprecedented increase in the number of nonfamily households, which grew by 77.7% in the 1970s and 28.4% during the 1980s.

Several factors help to account for this change, including the rapid rise in the divorce rate, as well as an increase in the number of young single people living on their own and deciding to postpone marriage. In 1993, some 24 million

FAMILY HOUSEHOLDS BY TYPE, RACE, AND HISPANIC ORIGIN OF HOUSEHOLDER, 1970–93

Type of family	1970 Number ('000s)	1970 Percent	1980 Number ('000s)	1980 Percent	1993 Number ('000s)	1993 Percent	Average annual percent change 1970–1980	1980–1990	1990–1993
ALL RACES									
Family households	51,456	100.0%	59,550	100.0%	68,144	100.0%	1.5%	1.0%	1.0%
Married-couple families	44,728	86.9	49,112	82.5	53,171	78.0	0.9	0.6	0.5
Male householder[1]	1,228	2.4	1,733	2.9	3,026	4.4	3.4	5.1	1.6
Female householder[1]	5,500	10.7	8,705	14.6	11,947	17.5	4.6	2.2	3.1
WHITE									
Family households	46,165	100.0%	52,243	100.0%	57,858	100.0%	1.2%	0.8%	0.7%
Married-couple families	41,029	88.9	44,751	85.7	47,601	82.3	0.9	0.5	0.4
Male householder[1]	1,038	2.2	1,441	2.8	2,409	4.2	3.3	4.7	1.5
Female householder[1]	4,099	8.9	6,052	11.6	7,848	13.6	3.9	1.9	2.4
BLACK									
Family households	4,856	100.0%	6,184	100.0%	7,888	100.0%	2.4%	1.9%	1.8%
Married-couple families	3,317	68.3	3,433	55.5	3,748	47.5	0.3	0.9	—
Male householder[1]	181	3.7	256	4.1	406	5.8	3.5	5.6	1.0
Female householder[1]	1,358	28.0	2,495	40.3	3,680	46.7	6.1	2.7	3.9
ASIAN OR PACIFIC ISLANDER[2]									
Family households	N.A.	N.A.	818	100.0%	1,662	100.0%	N.A.	6.3%	2.7%
Married-couple families	N.A.	N.A.	691	84.5	1,335	80.3	N.A.	6.0	2.0
Male householder[1]	N.A.	N.A.	39	4.8	95	5.7	N.A.	7.9	3.3
Female householder[1]	N.A.	N.A.	88	10.8	232	14.0	N.A.	7.6	7.0
HISPANIC[3]									
Family households	2,004	100.0%	3,029	100.0%	5,318	100.0%	4.1%	4.3%	3.1%
Married-couple families	1,615	80.6	2,282	75.3	3,674	69.1	3.5	3.6	2.6
Male householder[1]	82	4.1	138	4.6	407	7.7	5.2	7.9	7.1
Female householder[1]	307	15.3	610	20.1	1,238	23.3	6.9	5.5	3.5

Note: N.A. = not available. 1. No spouse present. 2. 1980 data for Asian or Pacific Islander from 1980 Census of Population, Vol. 1, Table 141. 3. Persons of Hispanic origin may be of any race. 1970 Hispanic data from 1970 Census of Population, Vol. II, 4A, Table 6. **Source:** U.S. Bureau of the Census, *Household and Family Characteristics: March 1993* (1994).

HOUSEHOLDS AND FAMILIES: GROWTH AND CHANGE, 1960–93
(in thousands)

Type of unit	1960	1970	1980	1990	1993	Percent change 1970–80	1980–90
All households	**52,799**	**63,401**	**80,776**	**93,347**	**96,391**	**27.4%**	**15.5%**
Average size	3.33	3.14	2.76	2.63	2.63	—	—
Family households	44,905	51,456	59,550	66,090	68,144	15.7	10.9
Married couple	39,254	44,728	49,112	52,317	53,171	9.8	6.6
Male householder[1]	1,228	1,228	1,733	2,884	3,026	41.1	66.4
Female householder[1]	4,422	5,500	8,705	10,890	11,947	58.3	25.1
Nonfamily households	7,895	11,945	21,226	27,257	28,247	77.7	28.4
Male householder	2,716	4,063	8,807	11,606	12,254	116.8	31.8
Female householder	5,179	7,882	12,419	15,651	15,993	57.6	26.0
One person	6,896	10,851	18,296	22,999	23,642	68.6	25.7
Families	**45,111**	**51,586**	**59,550**	**66,090**	**68,144**	**15.4%**	**11.0%**
Average size	3.67	3.58	3.29	3.17	3.16	—	—
Married couple	39,329	44,755	49,112	52,317	53,171	9.7	6.5
Male householder[1]	1,275	1,239	1,733	2,884	3,026	39.9	66.4
Female householder[1]	4,507	5,591	8,705	10,890	11,947	55.7	25.1
Unrelated subfamilies	**207**	**130**	**360**	**534**	**708**	**176.9%**	**48.3%**
Married couple	75	27	20	68	83	N.A.[2]	N.A.[2]
Father-child[1]	47	11	36	45	68	N.A.[2]	N.A.[2]
Mother-child[1]	85	91	304	421	557	234.1	38.5
Related subfamilies	**1,514**	**1,150**	**1,150**	**2,403**	**2,671**	**0%**	**109.0%**
Married couple	871	617	582	871	945	–5.7	49.7
Father-child[1]	115	48	54	153	170	N.A.[2]	183.0
Mother-child[1]	528	484	512	1,378	1,556	5.8	169.1

1. No spouse present. 2. Not shown; base less than 75,000. **Sources:** U.S. Bureau of the Census, *Household and Family Characteristics: March 1993* (1994) and *The Statistical History of the U.S.* (1976).

people, or one in 10, lived alone; they represented 84% of all nonfamily households and 69% of the total nonfamily population. The most recent Census Bureau figures indicate, however, that the trend is abating: the number of people living alone grew by 5.2% each year during the 1970s and 2.3% in the 1980s, but only a total of 2.8% between 1990 and 1993.

An additional 2.6 million unmarried-couple households make up the largest proportion of the remaining number; while they comprise only 5% of the 54.4 million couples in the United States who maintain their own households, their sudden appearance on the American social landscape during the 1970s—they increased by about 120% during that decade—made them the subject of widespread media coverage. As currently defined by the Census Bureau, an unmarried-couple household is two persons of the opposite sex who share living quarters; although a close personal relationship is implied, other types—including tenancy—are included. No more than two unrelated adults are present in an unmarried-couple household, although children under age 15 may be present.

Despite all the attention given to the growth of nonfamily households, the fact remains that the overwhelming majority of Americans—215 million in 1993—live in some kind of family situation. This is not to say that the size and structure of the family hasn't undergone major revamping in recent decades, but rather to emphasize its inherent strength as the basic social unit despite the presence of powerful forces for change.

Families

In 1993 there were 68.1 million families in the United States; 78% (53.2 million) were married couples, and 33 million had children of their own under age 18. But since 1970, significant changes in the basic structure of the American family have taken place. Average family size, for example, declined dramatically from 3.58 in 1970 to 3.16 in 1993, and the percentage of families without children rose from 44.1% to 51.2%.

More importantly, perhaps, the proportion of married-couple families declined from 86.9% of all family households in 1970 to 78.0% in 1993, while the number of family households headed by females with no husbands present rose from 5.5 million, or 10.7%, of all family households in 1970, to 11.9 million, or 17.5%, in 1993. (Among black families, that figure was 46.7%, up from 28.0% in 1970.)

A related development, recently turned into a political issue by those advocating "family values," has been the rising number of single-parent situations. Among all 33 million family groups with children in 1993, more than 25% were single-parent situations, up from only 13% in 1970. In 1993, 85% of those one-parent families were maintained by the mother, down from 90% in 1970.

Another important, though less vital, sign of change is the growth in the number of so-called *subfamilies*. These are families who live in a

ONE-PARENT FAMILY GROUPS BY RACE, HISPANIC ORIGIN, AND MARITAL STATUS OF HOUSEHOLDER, 1970–93

Type of family	1970 Number ('000s)	1970 Percent	1980 Number ('000s)	1980 Percent	1993 Number ('000s)	1993 Percent	Average annual percent change 1970–1980	1980–1990	1990–1993
ALL RACES									
One-parent family groups	3,808	100.0%	6,920	100.0%	10,901	100.0%	6.0%	3.4%	3.7%
Maintained by mother	3,415	89.7	6,230	90.0	9,339	85.7	6.0	3.0	3.5
Never married	248	6.5	1,063	15.4	3,448	31.6	14.6	9.6	7.2
Spouse absent	1,377	36.2	1,743	25.2	1,974	18.1	2.4	0.5	2.4
Separated	962	25.3	1,483	21.4	1,670	15.3	4.3	0.5	2.3
Divorced	1,109	29.1	2,721	39.3	3,497	32.1	9.0	1.6	3.0
Widowed	682	17.9	703	10.2	420	3.9	0.3	–1.7	–11.5
Maintained by father	393	10.3	690	10.0	1,562	14.3	5.6	6.7	4.8
Never married	22	0.6	63	0.9	510	4.7	(1)	(1)	13.0
Spouse absent[2]	247	6.5	181	2.6	288	2.6	–3.1	1.8	9.4
Divorced	N.A.	N.A.	340	4.9	683	6.3	N.A.	7.2	–0.8
Widowed	124	3.3	107	1.5	80	0.7	–1.5	–1.8	–3.6
WHITE									
One-parent family groups	2,638	100.0%	4,664	100.0%	7,167	100.0%	5.7%	3.1%	3.8%
Maintained by mother	2,330	88.3	4,122	88.4	5,901	82.3	5.7	2.5	3.5
Never married	73	2.8	379	8.1	1,478	20.6	16.5	11.0	8.7
Spouse absent	796	30.2	1,033	22.1	1,288	18.0	2.6	1.5	2.2
Separated	477	18.1	840	18.0	1,091	15.2	5.7	1.9	2.4
Divorced	930	35.3	2,201	47.2	2,825	39.4	8.6	1.5	3.4
Widowed	531	20.1	511	11.0	311	4.3	–0.4	–2.2	–9.3
Maintained by father	307	11.6	542	11.6	1,265	17.7	5.7	6.9	5.3
Never married	18	0.7	32	0.7	356	5.0	(1)	(1)	11.4
Spouse absent[2]	196	7.4	141	3.0	239	3.3	–3.3	1.8	11.6
Divorced	N.A.	N.A.	288	6.2	606	8.5	N.A.	7.2	0.8
Widowed	93	3.5	82	1.8	64	0.9	–1.3	–2.3	(1)
BLACK									
One-parent family groups	1,148	100.0%	2,114	100.0%	3,377	100.0%	6.1%	3.8%	3.1%
Maintained by mother	1,063	92.6	1,984	93.9	3,135	92.8	6.2	3.7	3.1
Never married	173	15.1	665	31.5	1,871	55.4	13.5	8.6	5.8
Spouse absent	570	49.7	667	31.6	611	18.1	1.6	–1.6	2.3
Separated	479	41.7	616	29.1	532	15.8	2.5	–2.0	1.9
Divorced	172	15.0	477	22.6	562	16.6	10.2	1.9	–0.7
Widowed	148	12.9	174	8.2	91	2.7	1.6	–1.9	–15.3
Maintained by father	85	7.4	129	6.1	242	7.2	4.2	5.4	3.0
Never married	4	0.3	30	1.4	130	3.8	(1)	(1)	(1)
Spouse absent[2]	50	4.4	37	1.8	38	1.1	(1)	(1)	(1)
Divorced	N.A.	N.A.	43	2.0	61	1.8	N.A.	(1)	–14.1
Widowed	30	2.6	19	0.9	13	0.4	(1)	(1)	(1)
HISPANIC[3]									
One-parent family groups	N.A.	N.A.	568	100.0%	1,344	100.0%	N.A.	7.0%	5.5%
Maintained by mother	N.A.	N.A.	526	92.6	1,157	86.1	N.A.	6.5	4.8
Never married	N.A.	N.A.	120	21.1	476	35.4	N.A.	11.0	9.2
Spouse absent	N.A.	N.A.	199	35.0	318	23.7	N.A.	4.6	0.4
Separated	N.A.	N.A.	170	29.9	252	18.8	N.A.	3.8	0.4
Divorced	N.A.	N.A.	162	28.5	304	22.6	N.A.	5.0	4.5
Widowed	N.A.	N.A.	46	8.1	58	4.3	N.A.	(1)	(1)
Maintained by father	N.A.	N.A.	42	7.4	187	13.9	N.A.	(1)	10.1
Never married	N.A.	N.A.	7	1.2	88	6.5	N.A.	(1)	(1)
Spouse absent[2]	N.A.	N.A.	13	2.3	40	3.0	N.A.	(1)	(1)
Divorced	N.A.	N.A.	13	2.3	46	3.4	N.A.	(1)	(1)
Widowed	N.A.	N.A.	8	1.4	14	1.0	N.A.	(1)	(1)

Note: Family groups comprise family households, related subfamilies, and unrelated subfamilies. N.A. = not available. 1. Base less than 75,000. 2. Data for 1970 include divorced fathers. 3. Persons of Hispanic origin may be of any race. **Source:** U.S. Bureau of the Census, *Household and Family Characteristics, March 1993* (1994).

household and are either related or not related to the householder; the Census Bureau describes a *related subfamily* as a married couple with or without children, or one parent with one or more single (never married) children under 18, living in a household and related to the person who maintains the household. Related subfamilies have more than doubled since 1980 and now stand at 2.7 million; almost all of them are made up of mothers with children. They are not counted in the total number of families.

An *unrelated subfamily* is a group of two persons or more who are related to each other by birth, marriage, or adoption, but who are not related to the householder. Unrelated subfamilies numbered 708,000 in 1993, up 97% since 1980 and up 33% just since the 1990 Census.

FAMILIES: NUMBER, AVERAGE SIZE, AND PERCENT DISTRIBUTION, BY NUMBER OF CHILDREN, 1970–94

Year	No. of families ('000s)	Avg. size of family	Percent distribution by number of own children under 18: None	1	2	3	4 or more
1970	51,586	3.58	44.1%	18.2%	17.4%	10.6%	9.8%
1975	55,712	3.42	46.0	19.7	18.0	9.3	6.9
1980	59,550	3.29	47.9	20.9	19.3	7.8	4.1
1985	62,706	3.23	50.4	20.9	18.6	7.2	3.0
1988	65,133	3.17	51.0	21.0	18.2	7.0	2.8
1990	66,090	3.17	51.1	20.5	18.5	7.0	2.8
1991	66,322	3.18	51.0[1]	20.0[1]	19.0[1]	10.0[2]	(2)
1992	67,173	3.17	53.0[1]	18.0[1]	19.0[1]	10.0[2]	(2)
1993	68,144	3.17	51.2	20.1	18.8	9.9	(2)
1994	68,490	3.20	50.3	20.2	19.1	7.6	2.8

1. Figure rounded in source. 2. From 1991–93 the Census Bureau changed the "4 or more" category to "3 or more." **Source:** U.S. Bureau of the Census, *Statistical Abstract*, 1995.

NUMBER OF U.S. HOUSEHOLDS AND AVERAGE NUMBER OF PERSONS PER HOUSEHOLD, 1940–93

Year	Number of households ('000s)	Average number per household: All ages	Under 18 yrs.	18 yrs. and older
1940	34,949	3.67	1.14	2.53
1950	43,544	3.37	1.06	2.31
1955	47,874	3.33	1.14	2.19
1960	52,799[1]	3.33	1.21	2.12
1965	57,436	3.29	1.21	2.09
1970	63,401	3.14	1.09	2.05
1975	71,120	2.94	0.93	2.01
1980	80,776	2.76	0.79	1.97
1985	86,789	2.69	0.72	1.97
1990	93,347	2.63	0.69	1.94
1991	94,312	2.63	0.69	1.94
1992	95,669	2.62	0.69	1.93
1993	96,391	2.63	0.70	1.94

1. Alaska and Hawaii included for first time. **Sources:** U.S. Bureau of the Census, *The Statistical History of the U.S.* (1976) and *Household and Family Characteristics: March 1993* (1994).

LIVING ARRANGEMENTS OF CHILDREN UNDER 18, BY RACE, 1970–93 (in thousands)

Living arrangement	1970 Number	1970 Percent	1980 Number	1980 Percent	1993 Number	1993 Percent
All children						
Children under 18	69,162	100.0%	63,427	100.0%	66,893	100.0%
Living with:						
Two parents	58,939	85.2%	48,624	76.7%	47,181	70.5%
One parent	8,199	11.9	12,466	19.7	17,872	26.7
Mother only	7,452	10.8	11,406	18.0	15,586	23.3
Father only	748	1.1	1,060	1.7	2,286	3.4
Other relatives	1,547	2.2	1,949	3.1	1,443	2.2
Nonrelatives only	477	0.7	388	0.6	398	0.6
White children						
Children under 18	58,790	100.0%	52,242	100.0%	53,075	100.0%
Living with:						
Two parents	52,624	89.5%	43,200	82.7%	40,996	77.2%
One parent	5,109	8.7	7,901	15.1	11,110	20.9
Mother only	4,581	7.8	7,059	13.5	9,256	17.4
Father only	528	0.9	842	1.6	1,854	3.5
Other relatives	696	1.2	887	1.7	726	1.4
Nonrelatives only	362	0.6	254	0.5	243	0.5
Black children						
Children under 18	9,422	100.0%	9,375	100.0%	10,660	100.0%
Living with:						
Two parents	5,508	58.5%	3,956	42.2%	3,796	35.6%
One parent	2,996	31.8	4,297	45.8	6,079	57.0
Mother only	2,783	29.5	4,117	43.9	5,757	54.0
Father only	213	2.3	180	1.9	322	3.0
Other relatives	820	8.7	999	10.7	657	6.2
Nonrelatives only	97	1.0	123	1.3	127	1.2
Hispanic children						
Children under 18	4,006	100.0%	5,459	100.0%	7,776	100.0%
Living with:						
Two parents	3,111	77.7%	4,116	75.4%	5,017	64.5%
One parent	N.A.	N.A.	1,152	21.1	2,472	31.8
Mother only	N.A.	N.A.	1,069	19.6	2,176	28.0
Father only	N.A.	N.A.	83	1.5	296	3.8
Other relatives	N.A.	N.A.	183	3.4	228	2.9
Nonrelatives only	N.A.	N.A.	8	0.1	58	0.7

Note: N.A. = not available. Hispanic children may be of any race. Excludes persons under 18 years who were maintaining households or family groups and spouses. **Source:** U.S. Bureau of the Census, *Marital Status and Living Arrangements: March 1993* (1994).

Living Arrangements of Children and Young Adults

Among the social changes that have taken place over the last 20 years, two of the most revealing are with whom children live and how soon young people get to live on their own. Since 1970, the number of children under 18 living with only one parent has more than doubled both in number and as a percentage of all children under 18. In 1993, close to 27% lived with only one parent, as compared to just under 12% in 1970. This increase reflects the soaring divorce rate of the period. Especially affected were black children, of whom 57% lived with only one parent.

Inflation, soaring housing costs, stagnant wage rates, and postponement of marriage have helped to keep young adults of both sexes living at home with their parents for an increasingly long period. In 1992, 30% of unmarried persons 25–29 lived with their parents, as did 18% of unmarried people between the ages of 35 and 39. By contrast, 97% of married people maintained their own household. This tendency was true even among young marrieds: Of the 4.5 million married couples between the ages of 20 and 24, 66% lived independent of their parents or other relatives.

LIVING WITH GRANDPARENTS

In 1993, the Census Bureau found that 5.0% of the nation's 67 million children under age 18 lived in the home of their grandparents. Nearly half lived there with their mothers, 6.8% with their fathers, 141% with both parents, and 30.2% lived in grandparents' home with neither parent present.

Source: U.S. Bureau of the Census, *Marital Status and Living Arrangements: March 1993* (1994).

Housing

According to the U.S. Bureau of the Census, *Current Housing Reports*, there were 106.6 million housing units in the United States in 1993, the latest year for which data were available. Of these units:

- 94.7 million (88.8%) were occupied.
- 61.3 million (57.5%) were occupied by homeowners.
- 33.4 million (31.3%) were occupied by renters.
- 8.8 million (8.3%) were vacant (the rental vacancy rate was 7.3%).
- 3.0 million (2.8%) were seasonal dwellings only.

Housing units The American ideal of the intact nuclear family may be somewhat tarnished in these days of high divorce rates and growing single-parent households, but U.S. housing patterns still reflect traditional values. About 70 million—or two of every three—homes were single-unit structures, according to the Census Bureau's 1993 *American Housing Survey*. Mobile homes or trailers, numbering more than seven million, are not included in those totals. Almost 30 million units were in multiple dwellings, ranging from two- to four-family houses (10.1%) to large apartment buildings with more than 50 units (3.8%). Cooperatives and condominiums, totaling more than 5.6 million, are counted separately since they may include any number of dwellings.

Size of housing units The median number of rooms per house in 1993 was 5.3, and the vast majority of homes (79.7 million, or 74.8%) had between four and seven rooms. Most houses had two (31.9%) or three (38.6%) bedrooms and one full bathroom (47.8%).

The median size of all single, detached one-family houses (including mobile homes) was 1,677 square feet; for those that were owner-occupied the figure was 1,805 square feet; about 19 percent (13.4 million) had more than 2,500 square feet, and 16 percent (11.3 million) had less than 1,000 square feet. The biggest houses are also the newest: in recent years the size of new privately owned one-family houses has skyrocketed from an average of 1,500 square feet in 1970 to 1,947 square feet in 1993.

Growth of housing In 1993, the median age of all housing structures in the United States was only 28 years (1965). Only 10.3 million units built before 1919 were still in use. This reflects the extraordinary growth of the housing industry during the 1970s and 1980s, when 40.6 million of the 106.6 million extant units were built. By comparison, only 19.7 million of the housing units still in use were built between 1920 and 1950.

Home ownership Of the 61.2 million owner-occupied housing units listed by the Census Bureau in 1993, just under 90% (54.9 million) were owned by whites, 8% (4.8 million) by blacks, and 5% (2.8 million) by Hispanics. Two out of every three white householders owned the unit where they lived. Among black households, the percentage was 43.0%; it was 42.1% for Hispanic households. Home ownership rates were 64.6% overall, down from the 65.6% recorded in 1980, but up slightly from 1991. The decline in home ownership rates during the 1980s—the first decline since the 1930s—was due in large part to an increasing number of non-married-couple family households and skyrocketing home prices, which prevented married couples under the age of 50 from buying a home. Home ownership rates for owners over the age of 65 actually increased slightly during the 1980s and stood at 77.1% in 1993. One in every four home owners (or 16 million) was over the age of 65 in 1993; only five million seniors were renters.

Married-couple families own most of the homes in the United States. In 1993, over 39.7 million (65%) of the 61.3 million owner-occupied units belonged to nuclear families with no nonrelatives; one-person households accounted for 11.3 million. Among these households, the majority (7.5 million) were headed by women.

HOUSING UNITS 1993, BY TYPE AND YEAR BUILT

Characteristic	Units ('000s)	Percent of units
Units in structure		
Single, detached	64,283	60.2%
Single, attached	6,079	5.7
Mobile home or trailer	10,732	10.1
2 to 4	5,521	5.2
5 to 9	5,025	4.7
10 to 19	3,826	3.6
20 to 49	4,072	3.8
50 or more	7,072	6.6
Total units	**106,611**	**100.0%**
Year built		
1919 or earlier	10,252	9.6%
1920–29	5,677	5.3
1930–39	6,747	6.3
1940–49	8,529	8.0
1950–59	13,633	12.8
1960–69	16,070	15.1
1970–74	11,559	10.8
1975–79	11,915	11.2
1980–84	8,143	7.6
1985–89	8,951	8.4
1990–94	5,134	4.8

Median year built: 1965

Note: Figures may not add to totals due to rounding. **Source:** U.S. Bureau of the Census, *1993 American Housing Survey* (1995).

Housing costs In 1994, the average sales price of a new one-family house jumped from $147,700 to an all-time high of $154,500. That's more than double the 1980 median price of $76,400, and three times the average price paid in 1977 ($54,200). Median prices were higher in the Northeast and in metropolitan areas throughout the country, and were lowest in the South. San Diego continued to be the most expensive place to buy a home: the 1993 median sale price there of $225,000 was $33,600 higher than the median price in New York City and $85,200 higher than Los Angeles.

According to an annual survey by the Chicago Title Insurance Company, the median price paid by first-time home-buyers was $125,000 in 1994; for buyers who previously owned a home, the median price was $163,500. Relatively low real estate prices continued to attract first-time buyers to the housing market: they made up 47.1 percent of all home sales, down only slightly from an all-time high of 47.7 percent in 1992. Average monthly mortgage payments for all homeowners rose $13 from $1,015 in 1993 to $1,028 in 1994. These payments represented 31.4 percent of owners' incomes, down from 31.5 percent the year before. Payments were higher among repeat buyers, but first-time buyers paid a larger percentage of their incomes towards their mortgages. The conventional, fixed-rate mortgage, in which the consumer locks into a monthly payment for the life of the loan, is still the most popular method of financing, attracting 63 percent of mortgage buyers. But as interest rates increased during 1994, so did the popularity of adjustable, or variable rate mortgages. These types of mortgages, in which the monthly payment rises and falls based on the prevailing national interest rates, usually feature lower interest rates (as much as 3 percent points lower) for the first several years and higher rates toward the end of the loan. Adjustable rate mortgages were responsible for 30.3 percent of all mortgages, compared with just 16.3 percent in 1991. First-time buyers (32.7%) were more likely to opt for adjustable rate mortgages than were repeat buyers (28.7%), who were more likely to want to lock into a rate. The average mortgage length was 28.7 years for first-time home buyers, 27.3 years for repeat buyers. The average down payment for all buyers was 20.2% of the purchase price; it was 13.7% for first-time buyers and 26.1% for repeat buyers. About 80 percent of all new homes are mortgaged, but only 58 percent of all owner-occupied homes, including condominiums, still had mortgages in 1993 (7.9% had two or more). The remaining 39.9 percent (most of them elderly) owned their homes "free and clear" of any bank or mortgage.

HOME OWNER AND RENTAL VACANCY RATES FOR THE 61 LARGEST METROPOLITAN AREAS, 1986–94

	Home owner vacancy				Rental vacancy			
Metropolitan area	**1986**	**1990**	**1993**	**1994**	**1986**	**1990**	**1993**	**1994**
All metropolitan areas (avg.)	**1.5%**	**1.7%**	**1.4%**	**1.5%**	**7.2%**	**7.1%**	**7.5%**	**7.3%**
Albany–Schenectady–Troy, N.Y.	0.1	0.7	1.2	1.7	4.8	7.2	6.1	10.3
Anaheim–Santa Ana, Calif.	0.8	1.4	1.8	2.8	2.5	4.8	8.6	9.6
Atlanta, Ga.	1.7	2.6	1.8	1.9	6.3	11.6	9.3	4.3
Baltimore, Md.	0.7	0.9	2.2	1.8	6.7	5.2	8.5	8.3
Bergen–Passaic, N.J.	0.9	1.5	1.0	0.9	3.6	6.6	5.5	2.8
Birmingham, Ala.	1.6	2.8	1.3	1.3	5.2	5.2	6.6	5.8
Boston, Mass.	0.7	0.9	0.8	1.2	4.6	6.0	6.5	5.6
Buffalo, N.Y.	0.1	1.0	1.1	1.3	3.5	3.4	5.4	8.4
Charlotte–Gastonia–Rock Hill, N.C.–S.C.	1.7	1.6	1.4	1.1	6.5	5.9	5.6	6.4
Chicago, Ill.	0.7	0.8	1.1	1.5	6.8	6.6	7.3	8.0
Cincinnati, Ohio–Ky.–Ind.	0.9	1.3	0.9	0.8	6.6	6.3	7.0	7.4
Cleveland, Ohio	1.3	1.0	0.7	1.3	5.3	7.8	9.4	6.7
Columbus, Ohio	1.9	1.1	1.5	0.9	6.7	5.0	7.1	5.7
Dallas, Tex.	2.1	2.1	1.7	2.6	17.2	12.3	10.6	9.4
Dayton–Springfield, Ohio	1.4	0.9	2.2	2.0	5.3	5.0	7.4	4.8
Denver, Colo.	2.4	2.6	1.2	1.0	8.4	8.9	4.6	4.6
Detroit, Mich.	0.5	1.0	0.8	1.0	5.0	7.6	9.6	10.0
Ft. Lauderdale–Hollywood–Pompano Beach, Fla.	2.1	2.3	3.2	1.6	9.8	8.0	6.4	8.5
Ft. Worth–Arlington, Tex.	2.0	4.6	2.6	1.5	16.1	8.9	9.0	8.2
Greensboro–Winston-Salem–High Point, N.C.	0.7	1.9	1.3	0.8	7.8	7.9	6.3	8.5
Hartford, Conn.	0.2	2.9	0.7	2.1	3.7	11.2	8.8	6.9
Honolulu, Hawaii	0.9	0.7	1.3	1.9	5.0	3.8	3.9	6.9
Houston, Tex.	3.7	2.1	2.0	0.9	18.0	9.6	11.8	8.2
Indianapolis, Ind.	3.4	1.3	2.2	1.5	7.1	6.1	9.7	7.6
Jacksonville, Fla.	1.9	2.6	2.9	2.5	11.1	9.5	8.3	5.8
Kansas City, Mo.–Kans.	1.1	1.4	0.6	0.7	12.5	9.9	13.1	11.8
Los Angeles–Long Beach, Calif.	1.0	1.6	1.4	1.7	3.5	6.2	9.5	8.7
Louisville, Ky.–Ind.	1.4	1.0	1.3	1.3	15.9	7.5	15.2	7.8
Memphis, Tenn.–Ark.–Miss.	1.4	1.7	0.8	1.3	5.9	10.2	7.4	9.3
Miami–Hialeah, Fla.	3.3	2.7	1.0	1.5	8.5	6.3	3.5	5.7
Middlesex–Somerset–Hunterton, N.J.	0.5%	1.7%	2.2%	0.9%	2.9%	5.2%	7.5%	4.6%
Milwaukee, Wis.	1.8	0.9	1.4	1.1	3.1	3.6	5.4	5.7
Minneapolis–St. Paul, Minn.–Wis.	0.9	1.3	1.1	1.8	3.9	6.5	5.2	3.5
Monmouth–Ocean, N.J.	0.4	2.9	1.3	1.3	3.2	8.3	6.7	6.3
Nashville, Tenn.	0.9	2.4	0.7	0.5	5.3	11.3	4.9	4.0
Nassau–Suffolk, N.Y.	0.5	1.1	0.7	1.1	3.9	6.5	5.5	4.3
New Orleans, La.	2.3	2.5	1.7	1.3	12.8	13.8	6.6	9.4
New York, N.Y.	2.1	3.3	2.7	3.2	2.5	4.7	4.9	5.1
Newark, N.J.	0.8	1.2	0.7	1.5	4.3	4.1	8.7	9.3
Norfolk–Virginia Beach–Newport News, Va.	1.1	2.3	1.7	2.1	7.5	9.2	10.5	12.7
Oakland, Calif.	1.1	1.5	1.1	1.5	5.9	6.3	4.5	10.7
Oklahoma City, Okla.	6.3	2.7	2.2	1.4	21.1	22.6	21.2	11.5
Orlando, Fla.	2.2	1.9	2.9	1.7	12.2	10.1	10.8	9.2
Philadelphia, Pa.–N.J.	1.5	1.4	1.1	1.2	4.5	9.6	12.4	12.0
Phoenix, Ariz.	2.2	2.2	1.4	1.1	13.2	10.3	7.3	6.0
Pittsburgh, Pa.	1.8	1.1	1.2	1.2	10.1	8.3	5.1	5.6
Portland, Oreg.	1.9	0.4	0.1	0.5	5.3	3.3	6.6	4.7
Providence–Fall River–Pawtucket, R.I.–Mass.	0.5	1.5	1.6	1.5	4.3	9.4	8.8	8.4
Richmond–Petersburg, Va.	0.8	2.1	1.3	1.6	8.3	5.3	10.0	6.8
Rochester, N.Y.	0.5	1.4	0.9	1.6	4.3	5.6	7.7	6.2
Sacramento, Calif.	1.4	1.1	0.8	1.1	10.2	7.4	10.6	10.0
Salt Lake City–Ogden, Utah	1.7	1.8	0.4	0.6	10.6	7.8	2.7	2.1
San Antonio, Tex.	1.8	3.3	0.4	0.7	13.9	11.7	3.4	5.8
San Bernardino–Riverside, Calif.	1.1	3.2	2.6	3.2	7.5	9.9	10.3	8.1
San Diego, Calif.	1.3	2.8	2.4	2.6	5.4	6.9	7.8	6.5
San Francisco, Calif.	1.2	3.0	1.9	1.7	4.6	4.2	5.9	3.8
San Jose, Calif.	1.4	1.4	0.8	1.4	4.6	4.6	7.3	4.3
Seattle, Wash.	1.1	0.5	0.9	0.6	3.1	3.1	6.2	8.1
St. Louis, Mo.–Ill.	0.8	2.0	2.4	1.3	6.6	10.7	7.8	9.4
Tampa–St. Petersburg–Clearwater, Fla.	2.3	2.4	3.5	3.1	14.7	10.4	9.1	8.3
Washington, D.C.–Md.–Va.	1.0	2.2	2.5	2.5	3.7	6.7	8.0	6.6

Source: U.S. Bureau of the Census, Current Housing Reports, *Housing Vacancies and Home Ownership, Annual Statistics: 1994* (1995).

AVERAGE SALES PRICES OF NEW ONE-FAMILY HOUSES, BY REGION, 1965–94 (in current dollars)

Year	United States	Northeast	Midwest	South	West
1965	$21,500	$22,900	$22,800	$18,900	$23,200
1970	26,600	32,800	28,000	24,000	26,900
1975	42,600	47,000	43,400	39,600	44,300
1980	76,400	80,300	74,400	69,100	89,400
1985	100,800	121,900	95,400	88,900	111,800
1988	138,300	179,300	123,700	114,800	155,700
1990	149,800	190,500	133,000	123,500	180,600
1991	147,200	188,800	134,500	123,000	176,400
1992	144,100	194,900	136,400	126,900	157,800
1993	147,700	183,600	143,100	133,600	161,900
1994	154,500	200,500	152,700	136,800	168,900

Source: U.S. Bureau of the Census, *New One-Family Houses Sold, 1995.*

MEDIAN SALES PRICES OF NEW ONE-FAMILY HOUSES IN SELECTED METROPOLITAN AREAS, 1987–93 (in thousands)

Metropolitan area	1987	1992	1993
Atlanta, Ga.	$ 94.6	$101.6	$118.2
Baltimore, Md.	113.6	152.5	161.4
Chicago, Ill.	147.2	200.7	159.5
Dallas–Fort Worth, Tex.	89.5	121.3	123.0
Denver, Colo.	111.0	148.9	174.6
Houston, Tex.	95.9	111.6	114.2
Kansas City, Mo.	75.2	87.5	99.3
Las Vegas, Nev.	91.2	118.1	121.7
Los Angeles–Anaheim–Riverside, Calif.	133.6	135.1	139.8
Miami–Ft. Lauderdale, Fla.	91.7	122.0	131.5
Minneapolis–St. Paul, Minn.	99.6	133.5	155.6
New York–New Jersey–Long Island, N.Y.–N.J.–Conn.	$195.1	$194.2	$191.4
Phoenix, Ariz.	98.4	114.8	113.9
St. Louis, Mo.	96.1	129.1	144.5
San Antonio, Tex.	87.3	96.3	117.9
San Diego, Calif.	156.9	234.4	225.0
Seattle–Tacoma, Wash.	114.7	167.8	159.7
Tampa–St. Petersburg–Clearwater, Fla.	85.2	109.6	113.7
Washington, D.C.–Md.–Va.	135.6	185.1	196.5
West Palm Beach–Boca Raton–Delray Beach, Fla.	105.3	144.9	158.4

Note: Figures are for houses sold. **Source:** U.S. Bureau of the Census, *Characteristics of New Housing, 1993* (1994).

FAIR MARKET RENTS FOR EXISTING HOUSING FOR SELECTED METROPOLITAN AREAS, 1995 (projected)

Metropolitan area	1 Bed-room	2 Bed-rooms	3 Bed-rooms
Anaheim–Santa Ana, Calif.[1]	$751	$ 883	$1,104
Atlanta, Ga.	521	606	807
Austin, Tex.	477	636	883
Baltimore, Md.	506	617	815
Boston, Mass.	643	804	1,005
Chicago, Ill.	602	716	895
Charlotte, N.C.	459	516	681
Cincinnati, Ohio	372	495	665
Cleveland, Ohio	418	517	658
Columbus, Ohio	385	493	626
Dallas, Tex.	454	583	806
Denver, Colo.	435	580	805
Detroit, Mich.	476	574	718
El Paso, Tex.	414	491	682
Fort Lauderdale–Hollywood–Pompano Beach, Fla.	581	717	997
Fort Worth, Tex.	411	534	743
Fresno, Calif.	433	516	717
Honolulu, Hawaii	943	1,109	1,498
Houston, Tex.	439	570	793
Indianapolis, Ind.	433	522	652
Jacksonville, Fla.	437	527	697
Kansas City, Mo.–Kans.	408	489	677
Las Vegas, Nev.	551	656	911
Los Angeles–Long Beach, Calif.	695	880	1,188
Memphis, Tenn.	392	462	642
Miami–Hialeah, Fla.	613	766	1,050
Milwaukee, Wis.	451	566	708
Minneapolis–St. Paul, Minn.–Wis.	483	615	834
Nashville, Tenn.	422	520	708
New Orleans, La.	390	488	664
New York, N.Y.[2]	740	840	1,052
Oklahoma City, Okla.	331	430	598
Philadelphia, Pa.–N.J.	565	697	872
Phoenix, Ariz.	416	522	725
Pittsburgh, Pa.	389	469	588
Portland, Oreg.	444	548	762
Sacramento, Calif.	505	631	878
San Antonio, Tex.	404	523	728
San Diego, Calif.	553	691	960
San Francisco, Calif.	808	1,022	1,401
San Jose, Calif.	793	979	1,342
Seattle, Wash.	528	668	929
St. Louis, Mo.–Ill.	367	476	619
Tampa–St. Petersburg–Clearwater, Fla.	452	559	743
Tucson, Ariz.	399	531	739
Tulsa, Okla.	372	485	676
Washington, D.C.–Md.–Va.	725	851	1,158
West Palm Beach–Boca Raton–Delray Beach, Fla.	581	718	955

Note: Except where indicated figures are projections for 1995 made in 1994. 1. 1994 figures. 2. Figures include areas outside Manhattan. **Source:** U.S. Dept. of Housing and Urban Development, Office of the Federal Housing Commissioner, as recorded in *The Federal Register*, Sept. 28, 1994.

MEDIAN SALES PRICE OF EXISTING SINGLE-FAMILY HOMES FOR SELECTED METROPOLITAN AREAS, 1985–95

Metropolitan statistical area	1985	1990	1993	1994	1995[1]
Atlanta, Ga.	$ 66,200[2]	$ 86,400	$ 91,800	$ 93,600	$ 94,400
Baltimore, Md.	72,600	105,900	115,700	115,400	109,500
Boston, Mass.	134,200	174,100	173,200	179,300	176,500
Chicago, Ill.	81,100	116,800	142,000	144,100	143,300
Cincinnati, Ohio	60,200	79,800	91,400	96,500	94,600
Cleveland, Ohio	64,400	80,600	95,000	98,500	93,200
Dallas, Tex.	94,000	89,500	94,500	95,000	90,600
Denver, Colo.	84,300	86,400	104,700	116,800	120,800
Detroit, Mich.	51,700	76,700	86,000	87,000	90,500
Houston, Tex.	78,600	70,700	80,900	80,500	77,200
Kansas City, Mo.–Kans.	61,400	74,100	83,600	87,100	88,500
Los Angeles–Long Beach, Calif.	125,200	212,100	213,100	191,600	177,100
Miami–Hialeah, Fla.	80,500	89,300	98,800	103,200	102,600
Milwaukee, Wis.	67,500	84,400	104,100	109,000	108,800
Minneapolis–St. Paul, Minn.	75,200	88,700	98,200	101,500	103,700
New York City area, N.Y.	134,000	174,900	173,200	173,200	167,200
Philadelphia, Pa.	74,000	108,700	118,000	119,500	113,400
Phoenix, Ariz.	74,800	84,000	89,100	91,400	91,600
Pittsburgh, Pa.	N.A.	70,100	82,200	80,700	77,200
St. Louis, Mo.	65,700	76,700	84,800	85,000	83,300
San Diego, Calif.	107,400	183,200	176,900	176,000	172,100
San Francisco Bay Area, Calif.	145,100	259,300	254,400	255,600	244,500
Seattle–Tacoma, Wash.	N.A.	142,000	150,200	155,900	155,100
Tampa–St. Petersburg–Clearwater, Fla.	58,400	71,400	75,000	76,200	72,200
Washington, D.C.–Md.–Va.	97,100	150,500	158,300	157,900	150,100
U.S. average	**N.A.**	**N.A.**	**$106,800**	**$109,800**	**$107,700**

1. First quarter only. 2. Figure is for 1984. **Source:** National Association of Realtors, *Home Sales* (May 1995).

HOME OWNERSHIP RATES IN THE U.S., BY AGE AND FAMILY STATUS, 1982–94

Age of householder	1982	1988	1993	1994
All households	64.8%	63.8%	64.0%	64.0%
Less than 25 years	19.3	15.8	14.8	14.9
25–29	38.6	35.9	33.6	34.1
30–34	57.1	53.2	50.8	50.6
35–39	67.6	63.6	61.8	61.2
40–44	73.0	70.7	68.6	68.2
45–49	76.0	74.4	73.7	73.8
50–54	78.8	77.1	77.2	76.8
55–59	80.0	79.3	78.9	78.4
60–64	80.1	79.8	80.9	80.1
65 years and over	74.4	75.6	77.3	77.4
Married-couple families	78.5	78.9	78.7	78.8
Less than 25 years	32.6	29.1	26.4	27.1
Less than 35 years	58.2	58.0	55.7	55.8
35–44	82.0	80.5	79.3	79.1
45–54	87.4	86.8	86.3	86.6
55–64	89.5	89.7	90.3	89.6
65 years and over	86.6	88.8	90.2	90.4
Non-married-couple households				
Male householder	59.3%	56.1%	53.7%	52.8%
Less than 25 years	21.6	17.6	18.8	21.6
Less than 35 years	35.8	31.8	31.5	32.9
35–44	62.3	60.0	56.1	52.0
45–54	72.2	66.8	65.6	64.9
55–64	77.7	77.0	73.3	69.5
65 years and over	75.3	80.0	82.8	83.5

Age of householder	1982	1988	1993	1994
Female householder	47.1%	45.3%	43.9%	44.2%
Less than 25 years	8.9	8.4	8.7	8.6
Less than 35 years	20.9	18.5	16.8	16.6
35–44	48.3	44.7	42.2	42.0
45–54	61.7	57.5	59.8	59.7
55–64	68.7	69.0	68.8	69.7
65 years and over	75.1	78.3	78.7	79.9
One-person households	45.6	46.3	49.8	49.8
Male householder	38.0	39.9	42.8	43.1
Less than 25 years	13.9	13.6	14.0	12.7
Less than 35 years	23.7	24.0	24.8	25.2
35–44	37.6	39.0	39.8	39.5
45–54	39.5	44.4	48.3	48.3
55–64	49.1	49.6	53.9	53.0
65 years and over	58.6	60.1	64.1	63.7
Female householder	51.2	51.8	54.6	54.5
Less than 25 years	7.5	9.5	8.3	6.2
Less than 35 years	15.1	17.8	18.8	18.6
35–44	37.0	38.1	41.8	42.0
45–54	49.1	52.1	55.6	55.0
55–64	62.4	62.7	64.3	63.5
65 years and over	62.2	62.0	64.5	64.6

Note: Rate is the percentage of householders who were home owners. **Source:** U.S. Bureau of the Census, *Housing Vacancies and Homeownership, Annual Statistics: 1994* (1995).

The Homeless

Although homeless people have become a common sight in almost every community, their plight is always surrounded by some kind of controversy, one that is fueled by a wide range of opinions, some based on fact and others on stereotypes. The often shrill debate about just who the homeless are and what can or should be done for them has been hampered by a lack of reliable information on everything from the causes of homelessness to the actual number of people living on the streets or in shelters.

The number of homeless Estimates of the total number vary depending on the group doing the counting. The total ranges from about 50,000 (the U.S. Department of Housing and Urban Development) to three million (homeless advocacy groups).

A 1989 study by the National Alliance to End Homelessness calculated that on a given night there are about 735,000 homeless in the United States, and that during the course of the year between 1.3 and two million people will be homeless for one or more nights. Another study, released in 1989 by the Urban Institute, concluded that there were about 600,000 Americans living in shelters or on the streets on a given night.

The first comprehensive federal effort to count the homeless was done as part of the 1990 census count. The Census Bureau hired approximately 22,000 people who, armed with flashlights and survey questionnaires, attempted to locate every homeless person they could find between 6 P.M. and 4 A.M. on Mar. 20–21. They visited 11,000 shelters and 24,000 street sites and reported a total of 228,621 homeless persons—178,828 in emergency shelters and 49,793 at "preidentified street locations." Among the states, California (48,887) and New York (43,204) ranked first and second; the next two, Florida and Pennsylvania, were far behind with 10,299 and 9,549 respectively. Among the major cities none came remotely close to New York's 33,830.

No one, not even the Census Bureau, believes that nearly all the homeless were counted. In fact, census officials claim they never believed they could count all the homeless but that a strong effort was needed to help estimate the total population of the country. Despite this disclaimer, every advocacy group for the homeless feared the low count would be used to lower the amount of federal funding currently allocated.

Who are the homeless? While a 1991 study of 28 major cities by the U.S. Conference of Mayors did not give a figure for the total number of homeless, the study did pinpoint a number of characteristics. Contrary to common belief, not all homeless are single men. The number of middle-age men has been shrinking, while families with young children are the fastest-growing group. And the demographics of the homeless differ dramatically from city to city.

The composition of the cities' homeless population, on average, was 50% single men; 35% members of families; 12% single women; and 3% runaway and so-called throwaway youth (children rejected by parents). Children—both in families and runaways—account for about 24% of the population; persons considered mentally ill account for about 29%; substance abusers account for 40%; 7% have AIDS or HIV-related illness. The survey also found that 18% of homeless people are employed in full- or part-time jobs; 25% are veterans.

Another study found that the average age of single homeless men and women was between 34 and 37, which is much lower than found in previous decades. Homeless adults are likely to have never been married. They also usually don't have strong family ties.

The Institute of Medicine (part of the National Academy of Sciences) looked at a number of surveys and found that minorities comprised the largest number of homeless in major cities like New York, Detroit, Chicago, Baltimore and St. Louis. Whites accounted for the highest percentage in Milwaukee, Phoenix, Portland, and the state of Ohio.

Cities in which single men accounted for 60 percent or more of the homeless population included Charleston, Hartford, Minneapolis, Nashville, Phoenix, St. Paul, Salt Lake City, and San Diego. Cities where single men accounted for 30 percent or less of the population included Kansas City (Mo.), New York, Norfolk, and Trenton.

Unaccompanied youths—runaways and throwaways—account for 10 percent or more of the population in Los Angeles and San Francisco.

ESTIMATES OF THE HOMELESS POPULATION IN SELECTED U.S. CITIES, 1990

Rank/City	Total	Number in shelters	Number visible on street
1. New York	33,830	23,383	10,447
2. Los Angeles	7,706	4,597	3,109
3. Chicago	6,764	5,180	1,584
4. San Francisco	5,569	4,003	1,566
5. San Diego	4,947	2,846	2,101
6. Washington, D.C.	4,813	4,682	131
7. Philadelphia	4,485	3,416	1,069
8. Newark	2,816	1,974	842
9. Seattle	2,539	2,170	360
10. Atlanta	2,491	2,431	60
11. Boston	2,463	2,245	218
12. Houston	1,931	1,780	151
13. Phoenix	1,786	1,710	276
14. Portland	1,702	1,553	149
15. Sacramento	1,552	1,287	265
16. Baltimore	1,531	1,144	387
17. Dallas	1,493	1,200	293
18. Denver	1,269	1,169	100
19. Oklahoma City	1,250	1,016	234
20. Minneapolis	1,080	1,052	28

Source: U.S. Bureau of the Census release, 1991.

Thirty percent or more of the homeless were considered severely mentally ill in Boston, Charleston, Cleveland, Los Angeles, Nashville, Philadelphia, Phoenix, San Francisco, and Trenton. A survey funded by the Robert Wood Johnson Foundation estimated that a third of homeless adults are mentally ill.

Forty percent or more of the homeless were considered to be substance abusers in Cleveland, Minneapolis, Nashville, New Orleans, Philadelphia, Seattle, and Trenton.

Homeless families Families with children account for more than half the homeless population in Chicago, Kansas City (Mo.), New York, Norfolk, San Antonio, and Trenton. They account for 20 percent or less in Boston, Hartford, Nashville, Portland, St. Paul, San Francisco, and San Juan. Among homeless families, 28 percent were headed by two parents; the rest by single parents, usually a woman with two to three children under the age of five. A 1988 U.S. Education Department survey estimated that there were 220,000 homeless school-age children. Of those children, more than 65,000 do not attend school regularly.

Causes of homelessness Every city surveyed by the Conference of Mayors cited lack of affordable housing for low-income people as the main cause of homelessness. Other causes frequently cited were unemployment, mental illness, substance abuse, poverty, teen pregnancy, and domestic violence.

A 1988 Institute of Medicine review of data on the causes of homelessness found three patterns: temporary, episodic, and chronic. In the first category fell people displaced from their homes by natural and man-made disasters, like hurricanes and fires. Once a low-income or poor person or family is temporarily homeless, it often becomes difficult to resettle in permanent housing because of other problems like loss of possessions, family breakup, and substance abuse. Episodically homeless people are frequently welfare recipients who run out of funds halfway into the month, as well as runaway or throwaway youths who move in and out of family situations. They are also abused wives and children who may move in with relatives or friends from time to time. The chronically homeless—who live on the streets for long periods of time—are more likely to suffer from substance abuse and mental illness than members of the other groups.

The institute study also found that there appears to be a direct correlation between the reduced availability of low-cost housing and the increased number of homeless. The number of low-cost housing units has decreased, because as many as half a million are lost annually through conversion, abandonment, fire, or demolition. Moreover, since 1980 the federal government has reduced its subsidies for the construction and maintenance of such units by 60 percent. According to the institute, approximately 2.5 million low-cost units have been lost since 1980.

The institute also pointed to the jump in the number of poor Americans, about 10 million over the last decade, as a reason for the growing number of homeless.

The institute also noted that in several studies there was general agreement that deinstitutionalization from large mental facilities contributed to the increased number of homeless in the 1980s. They cited the lack of local community mental health services, such as group homes, as one of the primary reasons mentally ill people end up homeless.

Federal funding The various federal government programs to assist the homeless are grouped under the Stewart B. McKinney Homeless Assistance Act, which became law in July 1987. The act includes nearly 20 different provisions for emergency shelter, food, health care, mental health care, housing, educational programs, job training, and other community services. Federal agencies providing services include HUD, Health and Human Resources, the Federal Emergency Management Agency, and the Labor, Education, and Veterans' departments. Although the bill authorized $634 million in payments in fiscal 1989, Congress appropriated only $388 million. Pres. George Bush's proposed 1990 budget included full funding for the McKinney program at $676 million. Congress has appropriated $1.1 billion total for McKinney Act programs. However, states and cities still pick up the major part of the bill for caring for the homeless. New York City, for example, budgeted $475 million to help the homeless in fiscal 1989.

Immigration

Over the last two centuries, the mingling of peoples from all parts of the world has been a vital element in the formation of the United States, both as a land of opportunity and in its emergence as a world power. In one relatively brief period, between 1880 and 1920, the massive influx of more than 20 million European immigrants provided the inexhaustible and indefatigable labor supply necessary to transform the nation from an agricultural society to an industrialized one with unparalleled rapidity.

Over the next 40 years, however, the flow of immigration was reduced dramatically by a governmental decision to close the doors to most foreign groups. Motivated at first by a disconcerting kind of nativism, anti-immigration sentiments were later bolstered by the Great Depression and the need to provide work for those already living here. World War II and the subsequent national readjustment limited immigration for several decades.

Since 1960 a steadily increasing number of immigrants—both legal and illegal—has had a very noticeable impact on both the size and ethnic composition of the American population. The startling upsurge in the number of Asian and Hispanic immigrants during the 1970s and 1980s has been caused by a variety of factors, from wars and political upheaval to the mundane fact of geographical proximity in the case of Mexico. Currently, over half a million new legal immigrants are arriving annually, and well over half are from those two ethnic backgrounds.

While immigration is higher today than in the recent past, it is hard to predict what the future holds. Many demographers argue that if the immigration rate falls much below current levels, the effect on American population growth could be severe. With the dramatic decline in its birth rates and fertility rates, the United States might very well begin to experience negative population growth by the year 2030; by 2020, immigration will most likely add more population than natural increase will. According to the Office of Population Research at Princeton University, the United States will need 464,000 immigrants each year over the next century just to keep total population in 2100 at the same size as in 1980.

Eligibility

Prior to 1875 anyone from any foreign country could enter the United States freely and take up permanent residence here. Over the next 60 years, however, Congress passed laws restricting immigration on the basis of morality (no prostitutes or convicts), race (the Chinese Exclusion Act of 1882 was the first), and national origin (immigrants from Southern and Central Europe as well as Asia were severely limited during the 1920s). In 1952 Congress passed the Immigration and Nationality Act, which reaffirmed national origin as the central criterion for eligibility and established a preferential system for skilled workers and for relatives of U.S. citizens.

For many years the United States restricted the total number of immigrants to 270,000 each year. However, the number of exceptions to this limit was far greater even than the 270,000 limit. An average of more than 700,000 immigrants legally entered the United States. each year during the 1980s (not counting illegal aliens naturalized under provisions of the 1986 Immigration Reform and Control Act).

In 1992, the 270,000 limit was replaced with a sliding cap that is less restrictive than previous immigration laws. The 1990 Immigration Act limits the total number of immigrants to 700,000 from 1992 to 1995, and to 675,000 thereafter. The act increases the number of openings for immigrants with valuable employment skills from 54,000 to 140,000 each year, and reserves 55,000 openings each year for immigrants from underrepresented countries. In addition, the new law introduces a sliding scale for admitting family-sponsored immigrants. As in previous years, there is no limit to the number of immediate family members admitted each year. However, beginning in 1992, the number of immediate family members admitted in the previous year is subtracted from 465,000 (or

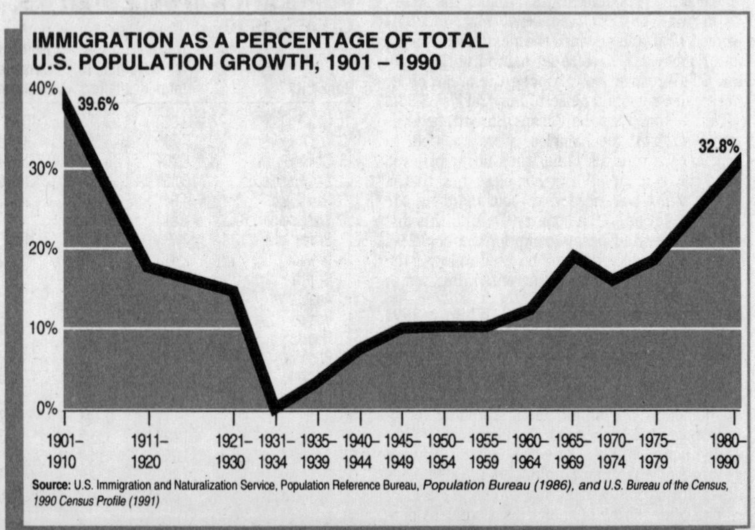

Source: U.S. Immigration and Naturalization Service, Population Reference Bureau, *Population Bureau (1986), and U.S. Bureau of the Census, 1990 Census Profile (1991)*

from 480,000 beginning in 1995) to determine the number of family-sponsored immigrants eligible for admission. The family-sponsored limit may not go below 226,000 in any year, however.

The 1990 Act also abolished one of the most odious provisions of the McCarran-Walter Act, a 1952 immigration law that prohibited communists from even visiting the United States. The law had prevented, among others, Nobel Prize–winning author Gabriel García Marquez from speaking in America.

PERCENT OF IMMIGRANTS ADMITTED BY REGION, 1955–93

Region	1955 –64	1965 –74	1975 –84	1985 –90	1991 –93
Europe	50.2%	29.8%	13.4%	9.4%	11.8%
Asia	7.7	22.4	43.3	37.6	29.0
Africa	0.7	1.5	2.4	2.7	2.5
Oceania	0.4	0.7	0.8	0.6	0.4
North America[1]	36.0	39.6	33.6	43.3	51.2
Caribbean	7.1	18.0	15.1	13.7	9.1
Central Am.	2.5	2.6	3.7	6.3	6.1
Other No. Am.[1]	26.4	19.0	14.8	23.3	19.7
South America	5.1	6.0	6.6	6.4	5.1

Note: Data are for fiscal years. 1. Includes more than two million illegal immigrants from Mexico granted permanent legal residence under the 1986 Immigration Reform and Control Act. **Source:** U.S. Dept. of Justice, *1993 Statistical Yearbook of the Immigration and Naturalization Service* (1994).

FIVE STATES WITH HIGHEST PERCENTAGE OF FOREIGN-BORN POPULATION, 1990

State	Foreign-born population	Foreign-born population as a percentage of total population	Percent of total population entering U.S., 1980–90
California	6,458,825	21.7%	10.9%
New York	2,851,861	15.8	6.6
Hawaii	162,704	14.7	6.0
Florida	1,662,601	12.8	5.1
New Jersey	966,610	12.5	5.0

Source: U.S. Bureau of the Census, series of press releases from 1990 census (1992).

IMMIGRATION AS A PERCENTAGE OF TOTAL POPULATION GROWTH, 1901–90

Period	Percent	Period	Percent
1901–10	39.6%	1950–54	10.6%
1911–20	17.7	1955–59	10.7
1921–30	15.0	1960–64	12.5
1930–34	–0.1	1965–69	19.7
1935–39	3.2	1971–80	19.4
1940–44	7.4	1981–90	32.8
1945–49	10.2		

Sources: U.S. Immigration and Naturalization Service, Population Reference Bureau, *Population Bulletin*, "Immigration to the U.S.: The Unfinished Story" (1986), U.S. Bureau of the Census, *1990 Census Profile* (1991).

FOREIGN-BORN POPULATION BY PLACE OF BIRTH, 1990

Place of birth	Number	Percent
All Foreign-born persons	**21,631,601**	**100.0%**
Europe	**4,812,117**	**22.2%**
Austria	94,398	0.4
Belgium	41,111	0.2
Czechoslovakia	90,042	0.4
Denmark	37,657	0.2
Estonia	9,251	—
Finland	23,547	0.1
France	162,934	0.8
Germany	1,163,004	5.4
Greece	189,267	0.9
Hungary	112,419	0.5
Ireland	177,420	0.8
Italy	639,518	3.0
Latvia	26,380	0.1
Lithuania	30,344	0.1
Netherlands	104,216	0.5
Norway	46,240	0.2
Poland	397,014	1.8
Portugal	218,525	1.0
Romania	92,627	0.4
Spain	103,518	0.5
Sweden	57,166	0.3
Switzerland	43,991	0.2
United Kingdom	764,627	3.5
Yugoslavia	144,563	0.7
Other Europe	42,338	0.2
Soviet Union	**336,889**	**1.6%**
Asia	**5,412,127**	**25.0%**
Afghanistan	28,988	0.1
Cambodia	119,581	0.6
China	543,208	2.5
Hong Kong	152,263	0.7
India	463,132	2.1
Indonesia	50,388	0.2
Iran	216,963	1.0
Iraq	45,936	0.2
Israel	97,006	0.4
Japan	421,921	2.0
Jordan	33,019	0.2
Korea, South	663,465	3.1
Laos	172,925	0.8
Lebanon	91,037	0.4
Malaysia	34,906	0.2
Myanmar	20,441	0.1
Pakistan	93,663	0.4
Philippines	997,745	4.6
Saudi Arabia	17,312	0.1
Syria	37,654	0.2
Taiwan	253,719	1.2
Thailand	119,862	0.6
Turkey	65,244	0.3
Vietnam	556,311	2.6
Other Asia	115,438	0.5
North America	**8,524,594**	**39.4%**
Canada	870,850	4.0
Caribbean	1,986,835	9.2
Antigua and Barbuda	12,452	0.1
Bahamas	24,341	0.1
Barbados	44,311	0.2
Cuba	750,609	3.5
Dominican Republic	356,971	1.7
Grenada	18,183	0.1
Haiti	229,108	1.1
Jamaica	343,458	1.6
Trinidad and Tobago	119,221	0.6
Other Caribbean	88,181	0.4
Central America	5,650,374	26.1
Belize	31,222	0.1
Costa Rica	48,264	0.2
El Salvador	472,885	2.2
Guatemala	232,977	1.1
Honduras	114,603	0.5
Mexico	4,447,439	20.6
Nicaragua	171,950	0.8
Panama	124,695	0.6
Other Central America	6,339	—
Other North America	16,535	0.1
South America	**1,107,000**	**5.1%**
Argentina	97,422	0.5
Bolivia	33,637	0.2
Brazil	94,023	0.4
Chile	61,212	0.3
Colombia	303,918	1.4
Ecuador	147,867	0.7
Guyana	122,554	0.6
Peru	152,315	0.7
Uruguay	21,628	0.1
Venezuela	51,571	0.2
Other South America	20,853	0.1
Africa	**400,691**	**1.9%**
Cape Verde	14,821	0.1
Egypt	68,662	0.3
Ethiopia	37,422	0.2
Ghana	21,714	0.1
Kenya	15,871	0.1
Morocco	21,529	0.1
Nigeria	58,052	0.3
Senegal	2,369	—
South Africa	38,163	0.2
Other Africa	122,088	0.6
Oceania	**122,137**	**0.6%**
Australia	52,469	0.2
Fiji	16,269	0.1
New Zealand	18,039	0.1
Tonga	11,040	0.1
Western Samoa	12,638	0.1
Other Oceania	11,682	0.1
Not reported	**916,046**	**4.2%**

Note: The foreign-born population includes 1,864,285 persons who were born abroad of American parents. **Source**: U.S. Bureau of the Census, 1990 Census special tabulations (1992).

FOREIGN-BORN POPULATION BY STATE, 1990

State	Population	Foreign-born	Entered U.S., 1980–90
Alabama	4,040,587	43,533	17,696
Alaska	550,043	24,814	10,813
Arizona	3,665,228	278,205	117,497
Arkansas	2,350,725	24,867	10,446
California	29,760,021	6,458,825	3,255,660
Colorado	3,294,394	142,434	57,039
Connecticut	3,287,116	279,383	89,533
Delaware	666,168	22,275	7,377
District of Columbia	606,900	58,887	33,892
Florida	12,937,926	1,662,601	659,618
Georgia	6,478,216	173,126	90,063
Hawaii	1,108,229	162,704	66,652
Idaho	1,006,749	28,905	13,027
Illinois	11,430,602	952,272	371,137
Indiana	5,544,159	94,263	30,509
Iowa	2,776,755	43,316	19,278
Kansas	2,477,574	62,840	30,891
Kentucky	3,685,296	34,119	13,789
Louisiana	4,219,973	87,407	34,789
Maine	1,227,928	36,296	7,069
Maryland	4,781,468	313,494	147,953
Massachusetts	6,016,425	573,733	223,147
Michigan	9,295,297	355,393	93,598
Minnesota	4,375,099	113,039	51,491
Mississippi	2,573,216	20,383	8,206
Missouri	5,117,073	83,633	29,575
Montana	799,065	13,779	3,327
Nebraska	1,578,385	28,198	10,492
Nevada	1,201,833	104,828	47,706
New Hampshire	1,109,252	41,193	10,159
New Jersey	7,730,188	966,610	384,515
New Mexico	1,515,069	80,514	31,102
New York	17,990,455	2,851,861	1,189,865
North Carolina	6,628,637	115,077	52,090
North Dakota	638,800	9,388	2,917
Ohio	10,847,115	259,673	70,639
Oklahoma	3,145,585	65,489	29,828
Oregon	2,842,321	139,307	60,839
Pennsylvania	11,881,643	369,316	116,233
Rhode Island	1,003,464	95,088	35,079
South Carolina	3,486,703	49,964	18,139
South Dakota	696,004	7,731	2,487
Tennessee	4,877,185	59,114	25,657
Texas	16,986,510	1,524,436	717,697
Utah	1,722,850	58,600	25,912
Vermont	562,758	17,544	3,387
Virginia	6,187,358	311,809	158,517
Washington	4,866,692	322,144	128,643
West Virginia	1,793,477	15,712	4,276
Wisconsin	4,891,769	121,547	40,952
Wyoming	453,588	7,647	2,424

Source: U.S. Bureau of the Census, series of press releases from 1990 census (1992).

ESTIMATED NUMBER OF U.S. IMMIGRANTS, BY REGION AND SELECTED COUNTRY OF LAST RESIDENCE, 1820–1993

Region/Country	Total 1820–1993	1993
Europe	**37,566,702**	**165,711**
Austria	1,837,232[1]	1,880
Belgium	212,990	776
Czechoslovakia[2]	148,092	792
Denmark	372,572	762
France	800,016	3,959
Germany	7,117,192	9,965
Greece	711,461	2,460
Hungary	1,670,777[1]	1,034
Ireland	4,755,172	13,396
Italy	5,419,285	3,899
Netherlands	378,764	1,542
Norway	803,281[3]	713
Poland	675,221	27,288
Portugal	510,686	2,075
Romania	221,051	4,517
Spain	291,643	1,791
Sweden	1,288,763[3]	1,540
Switzerland	363,008	1,263
Former USSR	3,572,281	59,949
United Kingdom	5,178,264	20,422
Yugoslavia[4]	144,595	2,781
Other Europe	188,025	2,907
Asia	**7,051,564**	**345,425**
China[5]	1,025,700	57,775
Hong Kong	348,953	14,026
India	571,917	38,653
Iran	202,681	8,908
Israel	153,810	5,216
Japan	487,252	7,673
Korea	703,732	17,320
Philippines	1,222,287	63,406
Turkey	422,483	3,487
Vietnam	536,190	31,894
Other Asia	1,376,559	97,067
North America	**9,478,377**	**150,540**
Canada	4,360,955	23,898
Mexico	5,117,422	126,642
Caribbean	**3,035,898**	**98,185**
Cuba	782,050	12,976
Dominican Republic	638,970	45,464
Haiti	302,458	9,899
Jamaica	487,518	16,761
Other Caribbean	824,902	13,085
Central America	**1,046,963**	**58,666**
El Salvador	374,461	26,794
Other Central America	672,502	31,872
South America	**1,440,413**	**54,077**
Argentina	142,404	2,972
Colombia	340,107	12,597
Ecuador	180,451	7,400
Other South America	777,451	31,108
Other America	**110,147**	**8**
Africa	**417,926**	**25,532**
Oceania	**223,821**	**6,144**
Not specified	**267,639**	**4**
All countries	**60,699,450**	**904,292**

Note: Because of changes in boundaries and government, figures for many countries, especially those in Asia, are not available for all years or were not reported separately for all years, and are therefore not strictly comparable throughout. Data for many countries are included with countries to which they belonged prior to World War I. 1. Data for Austria and Hungary not reported separately for all years. Total does not include 846,076 immigrants whose country of last residence is listed as Austria-Hungary. 2. Data for 1993 includes both Czech and Slovak republics. 3. Data for Norway and Sweden not reported separately for all years. Total does not include 60,255 immigrants whose country of last residence is listed as Norway-Sweden. 4. Since 1922, includes immigrants from the Serb, Croat, and Slovene Kingdom. 5. Beginning in 1957, China includes Taiwan. **Source:** U.S. Dept. of Justice, *1993 Statistical Yearbook of the Immigration and Naturalization Service* (1994).

TOP 20 METROPOLITAN AREAS OF INTENDED RESIDENCE FOR U.S. IMMIGRANTS, 1992–93

Metropolitan area	Immigrants 1992	Immigrants 1993
New York, N.Y.	127,875	128,434
Los Angeles-Long Beach, Calif.	129,266	106,703
Chicago, Ill.	37,236	44,121
Miami-Hialeah, Fla.	31,627	30,464
Washington D.C.-Md.-Va.	27,387	27,427
Orange County, Calif.	34,417	24,921
Houston, Tex.	27,067	22,634
San Francisco, Calif.	21,276	21,054
Boston-Lawrence-Lowell, Mass.	18,259	20,414
San Jose, Calif.	23,537	19,473
San Diego, Calif.	20,936	16,931
Oakland, Calif.	17,187	16,087
Newark, N.J.	13,734	13,551
Bergen-Passaic, N.J.	12,405	12,931
Philadelphia, Pa.-N.J.	11,882	12,842
Nassau-Suffolk, N.Y.	11,415	11,601
Seattle-Bellevue-Everett, Wash.	9,855	11,509
Riverside-San Bernardino, Calif.	16,535	11,187
Dallas, Tex.	12,312	10,959
Detroit, Mich.	N.A.	9,816
Other MSAs	290,200	138,241
Non-MSAs	65,594	44,861
Unknown	411	242
Total	**973,977**	**904,292**

1. Under the Immigration Reform and Control Act (IRCA) of 1986, illegal aliens with temporary resident status became eligible for permanent legal residence. **Source:** U.S. Dept. of Justice, *1993 Statistical Yearbook of the Immigration and Naturalization Service* (1994).

TOP 20 COUNTRIES OF BIRTH FOR U.S. IMMIGRANTS, AND MAJOR CATEGORIES OF ADMISSION, 1993

Country of birth	Total immigrants[1]	Percent	Category of admission: Relative preferences	Occupational preferences	Immediate relatives	Refugees and asylees	IRCA legalization[2]
All countries	**904,292**	**100.0%**	**226,776**	**147,012**	**255,059**	**127,343**	**24,278**
Mexico	126,561	14.0	33,044	3,710	31,525	29	17,534
China, mainland	65,578	7.3	12,603	38,509	12,052	1,153	26
Philippines	63,457	7.0	16,143	11,882	32,225	122	268
Vietnam	59,614	6.6	5,692	118	6,241	30,249	1
Dominican Republic	45,420	5.0	26,741	427	16,493	18	534
India	40,121	4.4	16,381	10,439	10,827	103	100
Poland[3]	27,846	3.1	6,572	1,674	3,405	731	117
El Salvador	26,818	3.0	12,818	3,833	3,554	811	1,301
United Kingdom	18,783	2.1	1,604	6,801	7,561	7	71
Ukraine	18,316	2.0	54	207	814	16,977	—
Korea	18,026	2.0	5,254	5,243	7,091	1	77
Jamaica	17,241	1.9	9,121	1,043	6,293	3	272
Canada	17,156	1.9	1,729	7,854	6,338	8	75
Iran	14,841	1.6	2,056	2,876	4,817	3,875	141
Taiwan	14,329	1.6	4,564	6,912	2,652	1	20
Cuba	13,666	1.5	1,327	23	653	11,603	16
Ireland[3]	13,590	1.5	205	370	709	—	15
Colombia	12,819	1.4	4,333	1,294	5,949	63	307
Russia	12,079	1.3	95	910	1,804	8,965	—
Guatemala	11,870	1.3	6,282	1,808	2,228	210	601

1. Total includes Amerasians, Soviet, and Indochinese parolees, foreign government officials, special immigrants, and admissions from nonpreference "underrepresented countries," suspension of deportation, and private law. 2. Under the Immigration Reform and Control Act (IRCA) of 1986, illegal aliens with temporary resident status became eligible for permanent legal residence. 3. Includes more than 12,000 immigrants admitted under Diversity Transition. **Source:** U.S. Dept. of Justice, *1993 Statistical Yearbook of the Immigration and Naturalization Service* (1994).

U.S. IMMIGRATION RATE BY DECADE, 1820–1993

Period	Total number ('000s)	Rate per 1,000 U.S. pop.	Period	Total number ('000s)	Rate per 1,000 U.S. pop.
1820–30	152	1.2	1911–20	5,736	5.7
1831–40	599	3.9	1921–30	4,107	3.5
1841–50	1,713	8.4	1931–40	528	0.4
1851–60	2,598	9.3	1941–50	1,035	0.7
1861–70	2,315	6.4	1951–60	2,515	1.5
1871–80	2,812	6.2	1961–70	3,322	1.7
1881–90	5,247	9.2	1971–80	4,493	2.1
1891–1900	3,688	5.3	1981–90	7,338	2.9
1901–10	8,795	10.4	1991–93[1]	3,705	1.4

1. Includes more than two million aliens adjusting under the legalization provisions of the Immigration Reform and Control Act of 1986. **Source:** U.S. Immigration and Naturalization Service, *1993 Statistical Yearbook* (1994).

THE STATUE OF LIBERTY

The Statue of Liberty Enlightening the World was conceived and designed by Frédéric-Auguste Bartholdi (with Gustave Eiffel's help) and given to the United States by the French government in honor of the centennial of American independence in 1876. Funded by subscriptions from the French people, it was dedicated by Pres. Grover Cleveland in 1886 and became a national monument in 1924.

Measuring 151 feet (46 m) to the top of her torch, Miss Liberty still stands guard over the entrance to New York harbor, the inscription on her base a poignant reminder of the vision Americans once had of their country:

> ". . . Give me your tired, your poor
> Your huddled masses yearning to breathe free,
> The wretched refuse of your teeming shore.
> Send these, the homeless, tempest-tost to me,
> I lift my lamp beside the golden door!"

—Emma Lazarus, "The New Colossus"

IMMIGRATION TO THE U.S. IN THE 1980s and 1990s

More immigrants to the United States came from Mexico than from the next 14 countries combined between 1991 and 1993. Of course, the vast majority of Mexican immigrants in 1989–91 were already living illegally in the United States and were granted permanent legal residence under the 1986 Immigration Reform and Control Act. The following table lists the 15 nations that sent the most legal immigrants to the United States between 1991 and 1993 and the number each country sent to the United States during the 1980s. Approximately two-thirds of Mexico's total consists of illegal immigrants granted permanent legal residence under the 1986 Immigration Reform and Control Act.

Country	1981–90	1991–93
Mexico	1,655,843	1,288,693
Philippines	548,764	195,634
Dominican Republic	252,035	128,834
Former USSR	57,677	128,675
India	250,786	116,201
China (mainland and Taiwan)	346,747	111,324
El Salvador	213,539	99,794
Vietnam	280,782	77,913
Poland	83,232	68,885
Haiti	138,379	67,701
Canada	156,938	65,370
Korea	333,746	61,484
United Kingdom	159,173	59,114
Jamaica	208,148	58,018
Hong Kong	98,215	46,723

Source: U.S. Dept. of Justice, *1993 Statistical Yearbook of the Immigration and Naturalization Service* (1994).

NATIONS SENDING LARGEST PERCENTAGE OF TOTAL U.S. IMMIGRANTS, 1820–1993

Country	Number	Percent
Total	**60,699,450**	**100.0%**
Germany	7,117,192	11.7
Italy	5,419,285	8.9
United Kingdom	5,178,264	8.5
Mexico	5,117,422	8.4
Ireland	4,755,172	7.8
Canada	4,360,955	7.2
Austria-Hungary[1]	4,354,085	7.1
Former USSR	3,572,281	5.9
Norway-Sweden[2]	2,152,299	3.5
Philippines	1,222,287	2.0

1. Austria and Hungary not counted separately for all years. Includes 1,837,232 immigrants from Austria, 1,670,777 immigrants from Hungary, and 846,076 immigrants from Austria-Hungary. 2. Norway and Sweden not counted separately for all years. Includes 803,281 immigrants from Norway, 1,288,763 from Sweden, and 60,255 from Norway-Sweden. **Source:** U.S. Immigration and Naturalization Service, *1993 Statistical Yearbook* (1994).

Sex in America

Pollsters scrutinize every angle of American life, including what goes on behind closed bedroom doors. The research ranges from the statistical—like the survey done by the National Center for Health Statistics—to the anecdotal, such as reader polls taken by popular magazines. Here's a summary of the two most serious studies, one conducted by the federal government, the other by a leading university.

Women and Sex

The National Survey of Family Growth is conducted periodically by the National Center for Health Statistics, with a national sample of women ages 15 to 44 years old. The most recent report, issued in July 1990, used data compiled in 1988. Questions concerned marriage and sexual activity. Some findings from the report:

- Nearly 75 percent of women ages 15 to 44 have had nonmarital intercourse.
- Almost 68 percent of women who have never married are sexually experienced.
- 75 percent of all married women had premarital intercourse.
- 40 percent of women have had their first intercourse by age 18 and 60 percent by age 20. Women in their early 20s began having intercourse earlier than women who are presently in their early 30s.

An earlier survey found that patterns of first intercourse were affected by educational level and family lifestyle. College-educated women were likely to begin having intercourse later (and to marry later) than high-school dropouts. Women who came from single-parent families were more likely to begin having intercourse (and to marry) at earlier ages than women who had lived with both parents.

Among women who had intercourse in the three months before the National Survey of Family Growth interview, more than two-thirds reported having intercourse once a week or more, and over two-fifths said they had intercourse at least several times a week. Women ages 25 to 29 were more likely than either older or younger women to have intercourse several times a week. The data suggest a pattern in which intercourse becomes more frequent as age increases, reaches a peak in the mid to late 20s, and then declines.

Sex Partners and Frequency of Intercourse

The National Opinion Research Center (NORC) at the University of Chicago periodically conducts a study of the sexual behavior of adults. The center interviews a nationwide representative sample of about 1,500 adults to collect data on a wide range of topics dealing with sex, including frequency of intercourse, number of sexual partners, and whether people have paid for or been paid for sex. In 1993, the center interviewed 1,476 people about their sexual habits over the past year. Some of the survey's primary findings:

Sex partners Almost 90 percent of adults were either monogamous or abstained from sex entirely. Women were more likely to have been celibate over the previous 12 months, but they were almost as likely as men to have had two or more sexual partners. Slightly over 5 percent of men and women claimed two partners, while 3.7 percent of men and 1 percent of women claimed three partners. A small percentage (two men and two women out of the 1,476 people surveyed) claimed 11 or more partners in a year. Over a lifetime, the average American adult will have had 7.14 sex partners since age 18.

FREQUENCY OF SEXUAL INTERCOURSE IN PAST 12 MONTHS, BY SEX, AGE, AND MARITAL STATUS, 1993

	Frequency of intercourse						
Category	0 times	1–2 times	Once a month	2–3 times a month	Weekly	2–3 times a week	4+ times a week
All men and women	**17.5%**	**6.3%**	**12.3%**	**16.2%**	**20.6%**	**19.8%**	**7.1%**
All men	**13.1%**	**7.3%**	**11.7%**	**18.2%**	**21.5%**	**21.0%**	**7.1%**
By age							
18–29	16.0	7.1	11.7	11.7	14.6	26.3	12.5
30–44	4.8	5.0	10.4	16.7	28.9	27.4	6.7
45–60	7.7	7.4	11.1	29.9	25.5	14.4	4.1
61+	36.8	13.2	15.8	14.7	7.9	7.4	4.2
By marital status							
Never married	23.7	11.7	15.7	8.8	9.5	21.9	8.8
Married	6.6	5.6	10.0	22.4	27.7	22.0	5.7
Widowed	63.3	10.0	—	10.0	—	16.7	—
Divorced/separated	18.3	7.9	16.7	15.1	14.3	14.3	13.5
All women	**21.1%**	**5.5%**	**12.6%**	**14.7%**	**19.9%**	**18.9%**	**7.2%**
By age							
18–29	12.9	3.4	8.6	14.4	20.1	25.3	15.2
30-44	5.1	4.9	12.5	18.1	24.2	26.9	8.4
45–60	15.3	9.1	14.7	17.8	24.4	15.9	2.8
61+	65.0	5.0	15.0	5.3	7.3	1.3	1.0
By marital status							
Never married	26.8	5.9	13.4	12.6	16.7	16.0	8.6
Married	6.2	5.8	14.8	17.0	25.9	22.8	7.6
Widowed	86.6	—	3.8	7.6	1.3	0.6	—
Divorced/separated	27.4	7.8	10.0	12.8	13.2	19.6	9.1

Note: Dash (—) indicates zero. **Source:** National Opinion Research Center (NORC), *General Society Survey* (1993).

ADULTS REPORTING NUMBER OF SEXUAL PARTNERS IN THE PAST 12 MONTHS BY SEX, AGE, AND MARITAL STATUS, 1993

	Number of partners in past year						
Category	0	1	2	3	4	5–10	11+
All men and women	**17.4%**	**72.0%**	**5.6%**	**2.1%**	**1.4%**	**1.3%**	**0.3%**
All men	**12.7%**	**73.6%**	**5.6%**	**3.7%**	**2.1%**	**2.0%**	**0.3%**
By age							
18–29	16.7	55.5	11.4	8.5	4.3	2.8	0.7
30–44	6.4	81.5	3.8	3.8	2.1	2.1	0.2
45–60	8.9	82.1	5.4	0.7	1.4	1.4	—
61+	28.0	68.4	2.1	0.5	—	1.0	—
By marital status							
Never married	26.7	40.6	9.6	11.4	6.8	3.9	1.1
Married	5.2	91.8	1.4	0.5	0.3	0.9	—
Widowed	63.3	23.3	13.3	—	—	—	—
Divorced/separated	16.8	45.6	21.6	7.2	4.0	4.8	—
All women	**21.0%**	**70.7%**	**5.5%**	**1.0%**	**0.9%**	**0.7%**	**0.3%**
By age							
18–29	12.8	66.2	12.2	3.4	2.3	2.6	0.6
30-44	5.8	85.3	6.4	0.6	1.2	0.4	0.4
45–60	14.7	82.7	2.6	—	—	—	—
61+	63.9	36.1	—	—	—	—	—
By marital status							
Never married	26.9	51.3	13.7	1.8	2.6	3.0	0.7
Married	6.7	91.7	1.6	—	—	—	—
Widowed	85.4	13.9	—	—	—	—	—
Divorced/separated	27.0	48.2	15.3	4.5	3.2	1.4	0.5

Note: Dash (—) indicates zero. **Source:** National Opinion Research Center (NORC), *General Society Survey* (1993).

Abstinence According to the NORC survey, 12.7 percent of men and 20.9 percent of women claimed no sex partners in 1993, down significantly from 14.6 percent and 26.7 percent respectively in 1988. Abstinence was up among men and women ages 18 to 29—almost twice as many men and women in this age group claimed no sex partner in 1993 as in 1988—but down dramatically among men and women 45–60 (from 16.4% to 8.9% among men; from 28.5% to 14.7% among women). By age, the oldest adults were most likely not to have had sex in the past year, with women over 60 more than twice as likely as men over 60 to be abstinent. This most likely reflects the large number of widows in this age group. All told, exactly half of adults over 60—28.0 percent of men and 63.9 percent of women—did not have sex in 1993. The next largest group of abstainers was men under 29, 16.7 percent of whom had no sex partners in 1993.

Marital fidelity About 21% of men and 13% of women admitted to having sex with someone other than their spouse. Close to one third of married men 45–60 admitted to having extramarital sex, more than double the percentage of women in this age group. And men over 60 were nearly three times as likely (18.2% to 7.1%) as women over 60 to have strayed from their mates. Fidelity rates for men and women under the age of 45 are about equal. Not surprisingly, 46.6 percent of divorced or separated men and 32.1 percent of divorced or separated women had partners other than their spouses. Only 16.8 percent of currently married men and 8.7 percent of currently married women admitted to having had an affair.

Frequency of sexual intercourse Americans have sex about once a week on average. Approximately one fifth of adults have sex weekly, another fifth two or three times a week, and another fifth have sex just two or three times a month. The remaining two-fifths are split between those who have no sex at all (13.1%), those who have sex once or twice a year (7.3%), those who copulate once or twice a month (11.7%), and the active 7.1% who have sex four or more times a week. Men and women ages 30 to 44 were most likely to have sex more than once a week, followed by men (26.3%) and women (25.3%) ages 18 to 29. Women 18 to 29 were most likely to engage in intercourse four or more times a week, more so (by 15.2% to 12.5%) even than their male counterparts in the same age group.

Sex for money In 1993, the NORC survey asked respondents for the first time whether they had ever paid for or been paid to have sex. A surprising 17.0 percent of men admitted to doing so, while only 1.6 percent of women claimed to fit this category. The survey did not distinguish between those who paid for sex and those who received money for performing sexual acts. Divorced or separated men of all ages (33.1%) and widowers (29.4%) were most likely to have engaged in sex for money. By age group, men 45–60 (23.8%) and men over 60 (19.9%) were most likely to have paid for sex. Among women, the largest group to engage in sex for money were widows, 5.2 percent of whom paid for or were paid to have sex.

Teenage Sex

More and more teenagers are having sex at an earlier age today than in years past. According to a survey by Alan Gutttmacher Institute, 73% of 18-year-old boys in 1988 said they had had intercourse, up from just 64% only three years earlier. In 1970, only 55% of 18-year-old boys had ever had intercourse. For women, the figures are even more striking. Only 35% of 18-year-old girls in 1970 said they had ever had sex, but by 1988, fully 56% were sexually experienced. And although the number of very young teenagers (13- and 14-year-olds) having sex remains very low, sexual activity continues to increase among teenagers of all ages. In 1987, for example, 21% of 16-year-old girls said they had had intercourse, compared with 9% in 1972 and 8% in 1960. Among boys, 41% of 16-year-olds had had sex in 1987, compared with 30% respectively in 1972 (1960 figures are not available for boys).

Not surprisingly, the number of teenage pregnancies are also on the rise. Between 1972 and 1990, the teenage pregnancy rate (the number of pregnancies per 1,000 women age 15–19) jumped from 95 to 117. But this pregnancy rate ignores the fact that many more teenagers are having sex (and therefore more likely to become pregnant). A better measure of how often teenage sex results in pregnancy is the sexually active pregnancy rate, which measures the number of pregnancies per 1,000 sexually active women ages 15–19. Except for a brief period from 1976–80, that rate has declined steadily, from 254 in 1972 to 207 in 1990. In all, 12% of teenage women become pregnant every year (21% of sexually active women), totaling over a million pregnancies annually. According to the Guttmacher Institute survey, 85 percent of these pregnancies are unintended, even though teenagers' use of contraception is not significantly different than contraceptive use by older people, according to the Guttmacher survey.

Between 1972 and 1984, the percentage of teenage pregnancies ending in birth declined dramatically from 76 percent to 54 percent, evidencing the growing availability of abortion services following the Supreme Court's 1973 *Roe* v. *Wade* decision legalizing abortion. But since 1984, more teenage women have taken their pregnancies to term: 60 percent in 1990. Meanwhile, abortion rates have declined from 95 per 1,000 women age 15–19 in 1980 to 72 per 1,000 women in 1990. This too is attributable to statutory changes: only three states (and the District of Columbia) specifically allow a minor to obtain an abortion without permission from her parents, whereas 21 states have enacted laws requiring teenagers to notify or obtain the consent of one (and in some cases both) parents before having an abortion. Race, ethnicity, and income also play a large role in whether a pregnant teenager selects birth or adoption. Nearly 60 percent of white teenagers (and close to three-quarters of higher-income girls) choose abortion compared with less than half of black and Hispanic adolescents. The number of teenagers who give their babies up for adoption is very small.

AGE AT WHICH TEENAGERS BECOME SEXUALLY ACTIVE

Percent of teenagers who have had sex

	Boys		Girls		
Age	1972	1987	1960	1972	1987
13	11%	9%	1%	0%	2%
14	15	13	2	1	5
15	20	27	3	4	10
16	30	41	8	9	21
17	41	52	16	20	36
18	55	64	27	35	52
19	67	75	46	53	66
20	74	80	61	68	76

Source: Alan Guttmacher Institute, *Teens and Sex*, 1994.

Should Abortion Be Legal?

Many surveys of American public opinion have been done on this controversial issue. The National Opinion Research Center has been asking the same questions about abortion since 1965. Its results show that a majority of Americans (ranging from 75% to 90%) consistently support legalized abortion when a woman's health is seriously endangered, when the woman has been raped, or when the baby is likely to be born with serious birth defects. However, when the woman wants an abortion because she is unmarried or does not want more children for emotional or financial reasons, the surveys have found that less than half of all Americans think legal abortion should be available.

The famous Gallup Poll has also been asking questions about abortion for a long period of time. Although opinions about abortion remained relatively constant between 1975 and 1988, the number of people who believe abortion should be legal under any circumstance has increased dramatically since then, while there has been a steady decrease in those who think abortion should be outlawed altogether.

Position on abortion	1975	1980	1990	1992
Legal, any circumstances	21%	25%	31%	31%
Legal, certain circumstances	54	53	53	53
Illegal, all circumstances	22	18	12	14

Gallup also polled Americans on their opinions about *Roe* v. *Wade*, the 1973 Supreme Court case upholding women's rights to abortion. By a 2–1 ratio, Americans opposed attempts to overturn this landmark decision. The poll was taken before the Court's 1992 *Casey* decision, which upheld *Roe* v. *Wade*, but allowed states to place restrictions on women's rights to choose abortion.

Birth Control

According to the National Center for Health Statistics, in 1988 there were 57.9 million women of reproductive age (15–44) in the U.S.; approximately 35 million or 60.3 percent were using some form of contraception. Of the 23 million (39.7% of women aged 15–44) not using contraception:

- 16% (3.8 million) were at risk for unintended pregnancy.

The other 19.2 million women were not at risk because:

- 35% never had intercourse.
- 19% had not had intercourse in the last three months.
- 15% were pregnant or postpartum.
- 14% were noncontraceptively sterile.
- 12% were seeking pregnancy.
- 4% were nonsurgically sterile.

Sterilization has become the leading form of birth control for married couples, more than doubling from 16% in 1973 to 36% in 1988. Most of this increase was in female sterilization. In 1988, 23.4% of married women were sterilized (compared with 9% in 1973) and 13% of married men (up from 8% in 1973). Use of the pill has declined sharply among married women from a high of 25% in 1973 to 15% in 1988. The pill is still the first choice among single women, however, with 25% choosing this method. One reason for the difference is that many physicians discourage use of the pill after age 35, so a sizable number of married women with children turn to sterilization after years on the birth control pill. Condoms are the second most common birth control method for single women, doubling from 4% in 1982 to 8% in 1988, followed by diaphragms. Increased use of condoms is probably related to prevention of sexually transmitted diseases.

Homosexuality in the U.S.

With gay rights and AIDS both becoming such political footballs in the past decade, statistics regarding the number of homosexuals in the United States have become easily manipulated for political purposes. For many years, the conventional wisdom, based on the 1948 Alfred Kinsey Report, was that about one in 10 men was homosexual. That number seemed high to most people in 1948, and may have been influenced by Dr. Kinsey's inclusion in his sample population of a disproportionate number of prison inmates, a group much more likely to engage in homosexual activity.

On the other hand, many people may be reluctant to admit their homosexual orientation, even in a survey, for fear of discrimination. Equally problematic is the definition of just what is a homosexual: does it reflect behavior, desire, a single sexual experience, self-identification, or some combination of all of these?

A 1994 study by the University of Chicago attempted to put all these questions in perspective. In a survey of 3,432 Americans between the ages of 18 and 59, researchers found that 10.1% of men and 8.6% of women reported at least one homosexual experience or desire. But in a reflection of how much lesbians and gay men continue to be persecuted, only 2.8% of men and 1.4% of women identified themselves as homosexual or bisexual. As might be expected, gay populations were much larger in big cities and much smaller in rural areas.

METHODS OF CONTRACEPTION, BY AGE, RACE, AND MARITAL STATUS OF U.S. WOMEN, 1988

Age, race, and marital status	Women ('000s)	Using any method	Female sterilization	Male sterilization	Pill	IUD	Diaphragm	Condom	Other methods
All women	57,900	60.3%	27.5%	11.7%	30.7%	2.0%	5.7%	14.6%	7.7%
By age									
15–24	18,592	45.7%	3.6%	1.3%	64.9%	0.2%	2.7%	20.8%	6.5%
25–34	21,726	66.3	25.0	10.2	32.6	2.1	7.3	13.7	9.1
35–44	17,582	68.3	47.6	20.8	4.3	3.1	6.0	11.2	6.9
By race									
White	47,077	61.8%	26.1%	13.6%	29.8%	1.8%	6.2%	14.9%	7.5%
Black	7,679	56.7	38.1	0.9	38.0	3.1	1.9	10.3	7.8
By marital status									
Never married	21,058	41.9%	6.4%	1.8%	59.0%	1.3%	4.9%	19.6%	7.0%
Currently married	29,147	74.3	31.4	17.3	20.4	2.0	6.2	14.3	8.4
Formerly married	7,695	57.6	50.7	3.6	25.3	3.6	5.3	5.9	5.7

Source: U.S. Dept. of Health and Human Services, *Advance Data from Vital and Health Statistics of the National Center for Health Statistics* (Mar. 20, 1990).

HOMOSEXUALITY IN THE U.S.

Item	Men	Women
Total reporting same-sex experience or desire	**10.1%**	**8.6%**
Identified self as homosexual or bisexual	2.8	1.4
Had same-sex intercourse sex at least once since puberty	5.3	3.5
Felt desire for same-sex intercourse sex	7.7	7.5
BY LOCATION		
12 largest cities	10.2%	2.1%
Next 88 largest cities	4.0	2.0
Suburbs of 12 largest cities	2.7	1.2
Rural	1.0	0.6
BY EDUCATION		
College graduate	3.5%	2.5%
Some college	3.0	1.1
High school graduate	1.4	0.8
Less than high school	3.1	0.9

Note: Individual items do not add up to total reporting same-sex experience or desire because some individuals responded to more than one category. **Source:** *The Social Organization of Sexuality*, University of Chicago Press, 1994.

Associations, Clubs, and Fraternities

There are more than 20,000 formally organized associations in the United States today, surely proof enough that we remain a nation of joiners. These groups range in size from a few dozen members to those with millions (the famous American Association of Retired Persons has 32 million, making it by far the largest association in the world). A large number of associations are tightly-knit professional or business groups that set standards and provide information for specific fields; many others are service organizations to the sick and needy, and others are well-known groups whose major aim is socializing among people who share the same interests or backgrounds.

Many associations can be very helpful to writers and researchers, as well as to interested citizens seeking information on a particular topic. For this reason, we have organized the list by subject area.

Amateur Athletics

Amateur Athletic Union of the United States 3400 W. 86th St., P.O. Box 68207, Indianapolis, Ind. 46268. (317) 872–2900. **Sponsors** AAU/USA Junior Olympics. **Est.** 1888. **Members** 60 regional groups.

American Bowling Congress 5301 S. 76th St., Greendale, Wis. 53129. (414) 421–6400. **Est.** 1895. **Teams** 1,300,000. **Members** 3,400,000.

American Running and Fitness Association 9310 Old Georgetown Rd., Bethesda, Md. 20814. (301) 897–0197. Promotes running and other aerobic activities. **Est.** 1968. **Members** 20,000.

Little League Baseball P.O. Box 3485, Williamsport, Pa. 17701. (717) 326–1921. **Est.** 1939. **Members** 2,500,000.

National Collegiate Athletic Association (NCAA) 6201 College Blvd., Overland Park, Kans. 66211. (913) 339–1906. Universities, colleges, and allied educational athletics associations; administers intercollegiate athletics. **Est.** 1906. **Members** 1,020.

National Junior College Athletic Association P.O. Box 7305, Colorado Springs, Colo. 80933. (719) 590–9788. Promotes junior college athletics on all levels. **Est.** 1938. **Members** 1,053.

National Wheelchair Athletic Association 3595 E. Fountain Blvd., Ste. L-10, Colorado Springs, Colo. 80910. (719) 574–1150. Men and women who compete in various amateur sports events in wheelchairs. **Est.** 1958. **Members** 2,000.

Road Runners Club of America 629 S. Washington St., Alexandria, Va. 22314. (703) 836–0558. Promotes noncompetition long-distance running. **Est.** 1958. **Members** 115,000.

U.S.A. Amateur Boxing Federation 1750 E. Boulder St., Colorado Springs, Colo. 80909. (719) 578–4506. Boxers, judges, trainers; promotes amateur boxing. **Est.** 1887. **Members** 30,000.

Young American Bowling Alliance 5301 S. 76th St., Greendale, Wis. 53129. (414) 421–4700. Bowlers under age 21. **Est.** 1982. **Members** 700,000.

Animal Rights

American Kennel Club 51 Madison Ave., New York, N.Y. 10010. (212) 696–8200. Maintains stud book registry with pedigree records of more than 36 million dogs; approves breeding standards and governs shows and trials. **Est.** 1884. **Members** 465 clubs.

American Society for the Prevention of Cruelty to Animals (ASPCA) 441 E. 92nd St., New York, N.Y. 10128. (212) 876–7700. **Est.** 1866. **Members** 350,000.

Animal Protection Institute of America P.O. Box 22505, Sacramento, Calif. 95822. (916) 731–5521. Promotes humane treatment of animals. **Est.** 1968. **Members** 150,000.

Animal Rights Network 3201 Elliot Street, Baltimore, Md. 21224. (410) 675–4566. Fosters cooperation and unity within animal rights/welfare movement. **Est.** 1979. **Members** Nonmembership.

Animal Welfare Institute P.O. Box 3650, Georgetown Sta., Washington, D.C. 20007. (202) 337–2332. Promotes humane treatment of animals. **Est.** 1951. **Members** 8,000.

Friends of Animals P.O. Box 1244, Norwalk, Conn. 06856. (203) 866–5223. Works to reduce number of stray animals by educating pet owners to prevent the birth of unwanted pets. **Est.** 1957. **Members** 120,000.

Humane Society of the United States 2100 L. St. NW, Washington, D.C. 20037. (202) 452–1100. **Est.** 1954. **Members** 1,000,000.

International Society for Animal Rights 421 S. State St., Clarks Summit, Pa. 18411. (717) 586–2200. Promotes animal rights through education and legislation. **Est.** 1959. **Members** 38,000.

National Anti-Vivisection Society 53 W. Jackson, Ste. 1552, Chicago, Ill. 60604. (312) 427–6065. Educational programs to acquaint public with animal vivisection. **Est.** 1929. **Members** 54,000.

Arms and Guns

Center to Prevent Handgun Violence 1225 Eye St. NW, Ste. 1100, Washington, D.C. 20005. (202) 289–7319. **Est.** 1983. **Members** Nonmembership.

Citizens Committee for the Right to Keep and Bear Arms 12500 N.E. 10th Pl., Bellevue, Wash. 98005. (206) 454–4911. Citizens interested in defending the Second Amendment. **Est.** 1971. **Members** 450,000.

Handgun Control, Inc. 1225 Eye St. NW, Ste. 1100, Washington, D.C. 20005. (202) 898–0792. Public citizens' lobby for regulations on civilian possession of handguns. **Est.** 1974. **Members** 250,000.

National Rifle Association (NRA) 1600 Rhode Island Ave. NW, Washington, D.C. 20036. (202) 828–6000. Promotes right of Americans to own guns. **Est.** 1871. **Members** 3,000,000.

Arts, Film, Music, and TV

Academy of Motion Picture Arts and Sciences 8949 Wilshire Blvd., Beverly Hills, Calif. 90211. (310) 247–3000. Motion picture producers, actors, and technicians who vote and present Oscar Awards. **Est.** 1927. **Members** 5,210.

Academy of Television Arts and Sciences 3500 W. Olive Ave., Ste. 700, Burbank, Calif. 91505. (818) 953–7575. Advances the arts and sciences of television and fosters creative leadership in television industry. **Est.** 1948. **Members** 6,500.

Actor's Equity Association 165 W. 46 St., New York, N.Y. 10036. (212) 869–8530. Represents professional actors and stage managers; makes awards and grants to organizations or charities in support of theater and members. **Est.** 1913. **Members** 39,000.

Actors' Fund of America 1501 Broadway, Ste. 518, New York, N.Y. 10036. (212) 221–7300. Charitable organization to aid aged, sick, and needy members of entertainment profession. **Est.** 1882. **Members** 6,000.

American Academy and Institute of Arts and Letters 633 W. 155 St., New York, N.Y. 10032. (212) 368–5900. Artists, writers, and composers qualified by notable achievement in their fields. **Est.** 1898. **Members** 250.

American Academy of Arts and Sciences Norton's Woods, 136 Irving St., Cambridge, Mass. 02138. (617) 492–8800. Honorary society and interdisciplinary studies center. **Est.** 1780. **Members** 2,800.

American Council for the Arts 1285 Ave. of the Americas, 3rd floor, Area M, New York, N.Y. 10019. (212) 245–4510. Research, publications, advocacy, and discussion on issues affecting art. **Est.** 1960. **Members** 2500.

American Federation of Arts 41 E. 65 St., New York, N.Y. 10021. (212) 998–7700. Individuals interested in fostering art appreciation in the U.S. **Est.** 1909. **Members** 600.

American Federation of Musicians of the United States and Canada Paramount Bldg., 1501 Broadway, Ste. 600, New York, N.Y. 10036. (212) 869–1330. Affiliated with AFL-CIO Musicians Union. **Est.** 1896. **Members** 200,000.

American Federation of Television and Radio Artists 260 Madison Ave., New York, N.Y. 10016. Tel. (212) 532–0800. Affiliated with the AFL-CIO Performing Arts Union. **Est.** 1937. **Members** 67,000.

American Symphony Orchestra League 777 14th St. NW, Washington, D.C. 20005. (202) 628–0099. Research on symphony orchestra operations and development. **Est.** 1942. **Members** 5,330.

American Watercolor Society 47 Fifth Ave., New York, N.Y. 10003. (212) 206–8986. Members devoted to advancement of watercolor painting. **Est.** 1866. **Members** 2,300.

Country Music Association P.O. Box 22299, 1 Music Circle S., Nashville, Tenn. 37203. (615) 244–2840. Promotes and publicizes country music. **Est.** 1958. **Members** 7,000.

Directors Guild of America 7950 Sunset Blvd., Los Angeles, Calif. 90046. (213) 289–2000. Independent. Negotiates agreements for members; bestows awards. Formed by merger of Screen Directors Guild of America (1936) and Radio and Television Directors Guild (1946). **Est.** 1959. **Members** 9,000.
National Association of Broadcasters 1771 N St. NW, Washington, D.C. 20036. (202) 429–5300. **Est.** 1922. **Members** 7,500.
Satellite Broadcasting and Communications Assoc. 225 Reinekers Ln., Ste. 600, Alexandria, Va. 22314. (703) 549–6690. **Est.** 1986. **Members** 500.
Screen Actors Guild 7065 Hollywood Blvd., Hollywood, Calif. 90028. (213) 465–4600. **Est.** 1933. **Members** 75,000.
Shakespeare Association of America Southern Methodist Univ., Dept. of English, Admin. Offices, Dallas, Tex. 75275. (615) 322–2541. Scholars and teachers of Shakespeare. **Est.** 1972. **Members** 800.
Songwriters Guild of America 276 5th Ave., New York, N.Y. 10001. (212) 686–6820. Helps professional songwriters, negotiates with music publishers. **Est.** 1931. **Members** 4,000.
Theatre Guild 226 W. 47 St., New York, N.Y. 10036. (212) 869–5470. Theatrical producing organization which promotes and encourages artistic excellence. **Est.** 1919. **Members** 105,000.

Business

American Federation of Small Businesses 407 S. Dearborn St., Chicago, Ill. 60605. (312) 427–0207. Helps self-employed professionals with information. **Est.** 1963. **Members** 25,000.
Chamber of Commerce of the United States 1615 H Street NW, Washington, D.C. 20062. (202) 659–6000. Works to advance human progress through an economic, political, and social system based on individual freedom and initiative. **Est.** 1912. **Members** N.A.
Council of Better Business Bureaus 4200 Wilson Blvd., Ste. 800, Arlington, Va. 22203. (703) 276–0100. Serves as national voice for business in the consumer field; promotes consumer education. **Est.** 1970. **Members** 700.
Future Business Leaders of America Phi Beta Lambda, P.O. Box 17417 Dulles, Washington, D.C. 20041. (703) 860–3334. **Est.** 1942. **Members** 275,000.
National Federation of Business and Professional Women's Clubs, Inc., of the U.S.A. 2012 Massachusetts Ave. NW, Washington, D.C. 20036. (202) 293–1100. Promotes full and equal participation of working women in work force. **Est.** 1919. **Members** 125,000.
National Small Business Assn. 1155 15th St. NW, Ste. 710, Washington, D.C. 20005. (202) 293–8830. Fosters development of independent small business. **Est.** 1986. **Members** 50,000.
Toastmasters International P.O. Box 9052, Mission Viejo, Calif. 92690. (714) 858–8255. Promotes improvement of communication and leadership skills. **Est.** 1924. **Members** 160,000.

Camping

American Alpine Club 113 E. 90 St., New York, N.Y. 10128. (212) 722–1628. Members have made mountain ascents. Conducts scientific studies and explorations. **Est.** 1902. **Members** 1,600.
American Camping Association 5000 State Rd., 67N, Martinsville, Ind. 46151. (317) 342–8456. People interested in organized camping. **Est.** 1910. **Members** 5,500.
American Hiking Society P.O. Box 20160, Washington, D.C. 20041-2160. (703) 385–3252. Educates public in appreciation of walking and use of foot trails; promotes hikers' interests. **Est.** 1977. **Members** 4,500.
Appalachian Mountain Club 5 Joy St., Boston, Mass. 02108. (617) 523–0636. Promotes knowledge and enjoyment of the outdoors throughout northeastern U.S. **Est.** 1876. **Members** 37,000.
Appalachian Trail Conference P.O. Box 807, Harpers Ferry, W.Va. 25425. (304) 535–6331. Trail and hiking clubs and individuals interested in walking. **Est.** 1925. **Members** 24,000.
Explorers Club 46 E. 70 St., New York, N.Y. 10021. (212) 628–8383. Promotes exploration and disseminates information about scientific exploration. **Est.** 1904. **Members** 3,200.
National Campers and Hikers Association 4808 Transit Rd., Bldg. 2, Depew, N.Y. 14043. (716) 668–6242. Family campers and hikers interested in outdoor activities and conservation. **Est.** 1949. **Members** 120,000.
National Camping Association 353 W. 56 St., New York, N.Y. 10019. (212) 246–0052. Cooperative organization of camp owners and directors. **Est.** 1947. **Members** 18,900.

Child Welfare and Domestic Violence

Batterers Anonymous 1269 N.E. St., San Bernardino, Calif. 92405. (714) 355–1100. Self-help program designed to rehabilitate men abusive toward women. **Est.** 1980. **Members** N.A.
Child Welfare League of America 440 1st St. NW, Ste. 310, Washington, D.C. 20001. (202) 638–2952. Seeks to improve care and services for deprived, dependent, or neglected children and their families. **Est.** 1920. **Members** 567.
Children's Defense Fund 25 E St. NW, Washington, D.C. 20001. (202) 628–8787. **Est.** 1973. **Staff** 95.
La Leche League International 9616 Minneapolis Ave., P.O. Box 1209, Franklin Park, Ill. 60131. (708) 455–7730. Women interested in breast-feeding of infants. **Est.** 1956. **Members** 40,000.
National Black Child Development Institute 1463 Rhode Island Ave. NW, Washington, D.C. 20005. (202) 387–1281. Seeks to ensure that black children and youth develop to their fullest potential. **Est.** 1970. **Members** 3,250.
National Coalition Against Domestic Violence P.O. Box 18749, Denver, Colo. 80218. (303) 839–1852. Provides information and referrals. **Est.** 1978. **Members** 1,200.
National Committee For Prevention of Child Abuse 332 S. Michigan Ave., Ste. 1600, Chicago, Ill. 60604. (312) 663–3520. Seeks to stimulate public awareness about child abuse. **Est.** 1972. **Members** N.A.
National Council on Child Abuse and Family Violence 1155 Connecticut Ave. NW, Ste. 300, Washington, D.C. 20036. (202) 429–6695. To provide assistance to persons who are victims of abuse and violence. **Est.** 1984. **Members** N.A.
Parents Anonymous 6733 S. Sepulveda, Ste. 270, Los Angeles, Calif. 90045. (213) 410–9732. Rehabilitates child abusers and ensures physical and emotional well-being of their children. **Est.** 1970. **Members** Nonmembership.
Parents United P.O. Box 952, San Jose, Calif. 95108. (408) 453–7616. Assists families affected by child abuse. **Est.** 1972. **Members** 10,000.
Parents without Partners 8087 Colesville Rd., Silver Springs, Md. 20910. (301) 588–9354. Helps single parents in raising their children. **Est.** 1957. **Members** 145,000.
Roberta Jo Society Box 916, Circleville, Ohio 43113. (616) 474–5020. Missing children agency named for Roberta Jo Steely, and founded by her father. Serves as clearinghouse for parents of missing children. **Est.** 1979. **Members** 144,000.
Society for Young Victims Spooner Bldg., 54 Broadway, Newport, R.I. 02840. (401) 847–5083. Assists families in search for and recovery of missing children. **Est.** 1975. **Members** 4,000.

Children and Young People

Alpha Phi Omega 14901 E. 42nd St., Independence, Mo. 64055 (816) 373–8667. Fraternity of former Boy Scouts. **Est.** 1925. **Members** 200,000.
Boy Scouts of America 1325 Walnut Hill Lane, Irving, Tex. 75015. (214) 580–2000. Promotes character development, citizenship training, and mental and physical fitness of boys and young adults ages 6–20. **Est.** 1910. **Members** 5,363,593.
Boys Clubs of America 771 First Ave., New York, N.Y. 10017. (212) 351–5900. Promotes health, social, educational, and vocational pursuits to urban boys ages 6–18. **Est.** 1906. **Members** 1,285,000.
Camp Fire Boys and Girls 4601 Madison Ave., Kansas City, Mo. 64112. (816) 756–1950. Helps girls and boys realize their full potential; small group focus. **Est.** 1910. **Members** 600,000.
4-H Program, Extension Service, U.S. Dept. of Agriculture Washington, D.C. 20250. (202) 447–5853. Encourages character development and good citizenship in young people ages 9–19 through head, heart, hands, and health. **Est.** 1900. **Members** 5,145,548.
Girl Scouts of the U.S.A. 420 5th Ave., New York, N.Y. 10018. (212) 852–8000. "To help girls (ages 5–17) develop as happy, resourceful individuals." **Est.** 1912. **Members** 3,165,802.
Girls Clubs of America 30 E. 33rd St., New York, N.Y. 10016. (212) 689–3700. Career guidance, sports, health, sex education, self-awareness, and the arts. **Est.** 1945. **Members** 250,000.
Pioneer Clubs Box 788, 27 W. 130 St., Charles Rd, Wheaton, Ill. 60189. (708) 293–1600. Religious group of clubs in over 2,800 churches of some 70 Christian denominations, for children 4–18. **Est.** 1939. **Members** 120,000.

Computers

Accountants Computer Users Technical Exchange 6081 E. 82nd St., Ste. 110, Indianapolis, Ind. 46250. (317) 845–8702. **Est.** 1965. **Members** 450.

American Association for Artificial Intelligence 445 Burgess Dr., Menlo Park, Calif. 94025. (415) 328–3123. **Est.** 1979. **Members** 17,000.

American Society for Information Science 8720 Georgia Ave., Ste. 501, Silver Springs, Md. 20910. (301) 495–0900. **Est.** 1937. **Members** 4,000.

Association for Computer Educators c/o Dr. Ben Bauman, College of Business, James Madison Univ., Harrisonburg, Va. 22807. (703) 568–6189. Promotes knowledge and use of computers in educational institutions. **Est.** 1960. **Members** 1,000.

Association for Computing Machinery 11 West 42nd St., New York, N.Y. 10036. (212) 869–7440. Professional association offering technical and nontechnical computing information to public. **Est.** 1947. **Members** 75,000.

Association for Systems Management 1433 W. Bagley Rd., Cleveland, Ohio 44138. (216) 243–6900. **Est.** 1947. **Members** 8,300.

Data Entry Management Association 101 Merritt 7, 5th Fl., Corporate Park, Norwalk, Conn. 06851. (203) 846–3777. **Est.** 1976. **Members** 1,600.

Data Processing Management Association 505 Busse Highway, Park Ridge, Ill. 60068. (708) 825–8124. **Est.** 1951. **Members** 40,000.

EDP Auditors Association 455 E. Kehoe Blvd., Ste. 106, Carol Stream, Ill. 60188. (718) 682–1200. **Est.** 1969. **Members** 10,000.

IEEE Computer Society 1730 Massachusetts Ave. NW, Washington, D.C. 20036. (202) 371–0101. Professional association promoting technical interactions through programs and activities in all aspects of computing. **Est.** 1951. **Members** 100,000.

Independent Computer Consultants Association 933 Gardenview Office Parkway, St. Louis, Mo. 63141. (314) 997–4633. **Est.** 1976. **Members** 1,900.

Information Industry Association 555 New Jersey Ave. NW, Ste. 800, Washington, D.C. 20001. (202) 639–8262. Trade association representing companies that create, store, manage, or distribute information either electronically or traditionally. **Est.** 1968. **Members** 800.

National Apple Works User Group P.O. Box 87453, Canton, Mich. 48187. (313) 454–1115. Technical support group. **Est.** 1986. **Members** 16,000.

National Association of Desktop Publishers 1260 Boylston St., Boston, Mass. 02205. (617) 426–2885. **Est.** 1986. **Members** 10,000.

National Computer Association 1485 E. Fremont Circle S., Littleton, Colo. 80122. (303) 797–3559. A computer users group serving primarily users of small vendor's products. **Est.** 1980. **Members** N.A.

National Computer Graphics Association 2722 Merrilee Dr., Ste. 200, Fairfax, Va. 22031. (703) 698–9600. **Est.** 1979. **Members** 6,000.

Software Publishers Association 1730 M St. NW, Ste. 700, Washington, D.C. 20036. (202) 452–1600. **Est.** 1984. **Members** 660.

Women in Information Processing Lock Box 39173, Washington, D.C. 20016. (202) 328–6161. **Est.** 1979. **Members** 4,827.

Consumer Advocacy

American Council on Consumer Interests 240 Stanley Hall, Univ. of Missouri, Columbia, Mo. 65211. (314) 882–3817. Researchers, teachers, counselors, and others involved in consumer protection. **Est.** 1953. **Members** 1,750.

Fairness and Accuracy in Reporting 130 W. 25th St., New York, N.Y. 10001. (212) 633–6700. Focuses attention on improving the media. **Est.** 1986. **Members** Nonmembership.

National Coalition against Censorship 2 W. 64th St., New York, N.Y. 10023. (212) 724–1500. **Est.** 1974. **Members** N.A.

National Safety Council 1121 Spring Lake Dr., Itasca, Ill. 60143. (708) 285–1121. Voluntary nongovernmental organization for the exchange of safety and health ideas. Safety Training Institute offers background courses. **Est.** 1913. **Members** 12,000.

Disabled

Alexander Graham Bell Association for the Deaf 3417 Volta Pl. NW, Washington, D.C. 20007. (202) 337–5220. Assists schools and agencies working for better educational facilities for deaf children. **Est.** 1890. **Members** 7,000.

American Council of the Blind 1155 15th St. NW, Ste. 720, Washington, D.C. 20005. (202) 393–3666. National clearinghouse for information on blindness. **Est.** 1961. **Members** 17,000.

American Foundation for the Blind 15 W. 16th St., New York, N.Y. 10011. (212) 620–2000. Provides services and programs to help the blind and visually impaired achieve independence in society. **Est.** 1921. **Members** Nonmembership.

Association for Retarded Citizens of the U.S. P.O. Box 6109, Arlington, Tex. 76005. (817) 640–0204. Promotes research, public understanding, and legislation for the mentally retarded and their families. **Est.** 1950. **Members** 160,000.

Disabled American Veterans P.O. Box 14301, Cincinnati, Ohio 45250. (606) 441–7300. 2,700 local groups. **Est.** 1920. **Members** 1,100,000.

Guide Dog Foundation for the Blind 371 E. Jericho Turnpike, Smithtown, N.Y. 11787. (516) 265–2121. Works to provide independence and mobility for qualified blind applicants by presenting them with trained guide dogs free of charge. **Est.** 1946. **Members** 450.

Information Center for Individuals with Disabilities Ft. Point Place, 27–43 Wormwood St., Boston, Mass. 02110. (617) 727–5540. Assists individuals with disabilities in finding resources and agencies that promote a more independent lifestyle. **Est.** 1977. **Members** N.A.

March of Dimes Birth Defects Foundation 1275 Mamaroneck Ave., White Plains, N.Y. 10605. (914) 428–7100. Offers public and professional health education and community action programs to improve maternal and newborn health. **Est.** 1938. **Members** N.A.

National Association of the Physically Handicapped Bethesda Scarlet Oaks, No. 117, 440 Lafayette Ave., Cincinnati, Ohio 45220. (513) 961–8040. Promotes social, economic, and physical welfare of physically handicapped. **Est.** 1958. **Members** 850.

National Association of the Deaf 814 Thayer Ave., Silver Spring, Md. 20910. (301) 587–1788. Protects civil rights of the deaf; promotes legislation and programs that benefit the deaf. **Est.** 1880. **Members** 20,000.

National Federation of the Blind 1800 Johnson St., Baltimore, Md. 21230. (301) 659–9314. Seeks complete equality for and integration of the blind into society; monitors legislation. **Est.** 1940. **Members** 651 (representing 50,000 blind people).

National Society for Shut-ins P.O. Box 1392, Reading, Pa. 19603. (215) 374–2930. Promotes emotional and spiritual well-being and self-worth in individuals confined to their homes or institutions due to age, sickness, handicap, or imprisonment. **Est.** 1970. **Members** N.A.

National Society to Prevent Blindness 500 E. Remington Rd., Schaumburg, Ill. 60173. (708) 843–2020. Promotes and supports glaucoma screening programs, preschool vision tests, and industrial eye safety. **Est.** 1908. **Members** 150.

National Stuttering Project 4601 Irving St., San Francisco, Calif. 94122. (415) 566–5324. Self-help organization of people who stutter and speech pathologists. **Est.** 1977. **Members** 4,000.

Research to Prevent Blindness 598 Madison Ave., New York, N.Y. 10022. (212) 752–4333. **Est.** 1960. **Members** N.A.

United Cerebral Palsy Associations 1522 K St. NW, Ste. 1112, Washington, D.C. 20005. (202) 842–1266. **Est.** 1948. **Members** N.A.

Disease and Illness

(See also DISABLED and MEDICAL)

Alzheimer's Association 919 N. Michigan Ave., Ste. 1000, Chicago, Ill. 60611. (312) 335–8700. **Est.** 1980. **Members** 30,000.

American Cancer Society 1599 Clifton Rd. NE, Atlanta, Ga. 30329. (404) 320–3333. **Est.** 1913. **Members** N.A.

American Diabetes Association National Center, P.O. Box 25757, 1660 Duke St., Alexandria, Va. 22314. (703) 549–1500. **Est.** 1940. **Members** 280,000.

American Parkinson's Disease Association (Neurological Disorders), 60 Bay St., Ste. 401, Staten Island, N.Y. 10301. (212) 981–8001. **Est.** 1961. **Members** N.A.

Autism Society of America 8601 Georgia Ave., Ste. 503, Silver Springs, Md. 20910. (301) 565–0433. **Est.** 1965. **Members** 7,500.

Huntington's Disease Society of America 140 W. 22 St., 6th Fl., New York, N.Y. 10011. (212) 242–1968. **Est.** 1986. **Members** 37,000.

Leukemia Society of America 600 Third Ave., New York, N.Y. 10016. (212) 573–8484. **Est.** 1949. **Members** 1,800.

Muscular Dystrophy Association 810 Seventh Ave., New York, N.Y. 10019. (212) 586–0808. **Est.** 1950. **Members** N.A.

National Down Syndrome Society 666 Broadway, New York, N.Y. 10012. (212) 460–9330. **Est.** 1979. **Members** N.A.

National Multiple Sclerosis Society 205 E. 42 St., New York, N.Y. 10017. (212) 986–3240. **Est.** 1946. **Members** 470,000.

National Reye's Syndrome Foundation 426 N. Lewis, Bryan, Ohio 43506. (419) 636–2679. **Est.** 1974. **Members** 10,000.

National Sudden Infant Death Syndrome Foundation 10500 Little Patuxent Pkwy, No. 420, Columbia, Md. 21044. (301) 964–8000. **Est.** 1962. **Members** N.A.

Parkinson's Disease Foundation William Black Medical Research Bldg., Columbia Presbyterian Medical Center, 650 W. 168 St., New York, N.Y. 10032. (212) 923–4700. **Est.** 1957. **Members** 57,000.

Skin Cancer Foundation 245 Fifth Ave., Ste. 2402, New York, N.Y. 10016. (212) 725–5176. **Est.** 1977. **Members** N.A.

Education

American Council on Education One Dupont Circle NW, Ste. 800, Washington, D.C. 20036. (202) 939–9300. Colleges, universities, and educational organizations. **Est.** 1918. **Members** 1,853.

American Forum: Education in a Global Age 45 John St., Ste. 1200, New York, N.Y. 10038. (212) 732–8606. Prepares American students (K–12) for international cooperation. **Est.** 1987. **Members** Nonmembership.

American Historical Association 400 A St. SE, Washington, D.C. 20003. (202) 544–2422. **Est.** 1884. **Members** 13,000.

American Library Association 50 E. Huron St., Chicago, Ill. 60611. (312) 944–6780. Librarians and others interested in promoting and improving library services. **Est.** 1876. **Members** 50,500.

American Montessori Society 150 Fifth Ave., Ste. 203, New York, N.Y. 10011. (212) 924–3209. Association for promotion of Dr. Maria Montessori's approach to early learning. **Est.** 1960. **Members** 12,000.

Association of American Colleges 1818 R St. NW, Washington, D.C. 20009. (201) 387–3760. Grants and aid offered to colleges and universities committed to academic excellence. Research and consultative services. **Est.** 1915. **Members** 620.

Association of American Universities 1 Dupont Circle, Ste. 730, Washington, D.C. 20036. (202) 466–5030. Association of executive heads of universities. **Est.** 1900. **Members** 59.

Association for Childhood Education International 11141 Georgia Ave., Ste. 200, Wheaton, Md. 20902. (301) 942–2443. **Est.** 1931. **Members** 15,000.

The College Board 45 Columbus Ave., New York, N.Y. 10023. (212) 713–8000. Testing and placement service for high school and college students; provides assistance in guidance, admissions, and financial aid. **Est.** 1900. **Members** 2,700.

Council for Sex Information and Education 444 Lincoln Blvd., Ste. 107, Venice, Calif. 90291. **Est.** 1977. **Members** N.A.

Educators for Social Responsibility 23 Garden St., Cambridge, Mass. 02138. (617) 492–1764. Educators and parents helping students to become aware of their social responsibilities in the nuclear age. **Est.** 1981. **Members** 20,000.

Global Education Associates 475 Riverside Dr., Ste. 456, New York, N.Y. 10115. (212) 870–3290. Sponsors workshops and conferences to challenge international competition over weapons, money, and scarce natural resources. **Est.** 1973. **Members** 7,000.

International Studies Association David M. Kennedy Center, Brigham Young Univ., 216 HRCB, Provo, Utah 84602. (801) 378–5459. Academics, government officials, and others involved in international affairs and cross-cultural studies. **Est.** 1959. **Members** 2,100.

Junior Achievement 1 Education Way, Colorado Springs, Colo. 80906. (719) 540–8000. Business professionals and educators; teaches students about how business system works. **Est.** 1919. **Members** 1,200,000.

Literacy Volunteers of America 5795 Widewaters Parkway, Syracuse, N.Y. 13214. (315) 445–8000. 240 local groups train and aid individuals and organizations to tutor adults in basic reading and conversational English. **Est.** 1962. **Members** 80,000.

Modern Language Association of America 10 Astor Pl., 5th Floor, New York, N.Y. 10003. (212) 475–9500. **Est.** 1883. **Members** 32,000.

National Catholic Educational Association 1077 30th St. NW, Ste. 100, Washington, D.C. 20007. (202) 337–6232. **Est.** 1904. **Members** 20,000.

National Council for the Social Studies 3501 Newark St. NW, Washington, D.C. 20016. (202) 966–7840. **Est.** 1921. **Members** 25,000.

National Council of Teachers of English 1111 Kenyon Rd., Urbana, Ill. 61801. (217) 328–3870. **Est.** 1911. **Members** 120,000.

National Education Association 1201 16th St. NW, Washington, D.C. 20036. (202) 833–4000. Professional organization and union educators. **Est.** 1857. **Members** 2,000,800.

National Geographic Society 17th and M Sts. NW, Washington, D.C. 20036. (202) 857–7000. **Est.** 1888. **Members** 10,500,000.

National PTA-National Congress of Parents and Teachers 700 N. Rush St., Chicago, Ill. 60611. (312) 787–0977. **Est.** 1897. **Members** 6,100,000.

National School Boards Association 1680 Duke St., Alexandria, Va. 22314. (703) 838–6722. Group of state Virgin Islands school boards; disseminates educational information. **Est.** 1940. **Members** 52.

National Science Teachers Association 1742 Connecticut Ave. NW, Washington, D.C. 20009. (202) 328–5800. **Est.** 1895. **Members** 63,000.

United Negro College Fund 500 E. 62nd St., New York, N.Y. 10021. (212) 326–1118. Service and fund-raising agency for private and accredited black colleges and universities. **Est.** 1944. **Members** 43.

Environment

Greenpeace USA 1436 U St. NW, Washington, D.C. 20009. (202) 462–1177. Conducts nonviolent direct action against environmental destruction. **Est.** 1971. **Members** 1,500,000.

International Union for the Conservation of Nature and Natural Resources (IUCN) World Conservation Center, Avenue du Mont-Blanc, CH-1196 Gland, Switzerland Tel. N.A. Alliance of conservation authorities, government departments, and independent organizations. **Est.** 1948. **Members** 500.

National Audubon Society 950 Third Ave., New York, N.Y. 10022. (212) 832–3200. 500 local groups interested in ecology and conservation of natural resources, emphasizing wildlife and their habitats. **Est.** 1905. **Members** 600,000.

National Wildlife Federation 1400 16th St. NW, Washington, D.C. 20036. (202) 797–6800. **Est.** 1936. **Members** 5,000,000.

Natural Resources Defense Council (NRDC) 40 W. 20th St., New York, N.Y. 10011. (212) 727–2700. Works for legislative change by drafting laws and public education. **Est.** 1970. **Members** 158,000.

The Nature Conservancy 1815 N. Lynn St., Arlington, Va. 22209. (703) 841–5300. Protects endangered species and habitats through land acquisition. **Est.** 1917. **Members** 550,000.

Sierra Club 730 Polk St., San Francisco, Calif. 94109. (415) 776–2211. Undertakes scientific studies concerning the protection of the world's ecosystems. **Est.** 1892. **Members** 565,000.

United Nations Environment Programme (UNEP) New York Liaison Office, 2 United Nations Plaza, Room 812, New York, N.Y. 10017. (212) 963–8139. UN coordinating body on the environment. **Est.** 1972. **Members** Nonmembership.

Wilderness Society 900 17th St. NW, Washington, D.C. 20006. (202) 833–2300. Focus is on issues involving federal public lands, including national parks and wildlife preserves. **Est.** 1935. **Members** 390,000.

World Wildlife Fund 1250 24th St. NW, Washington, D.C. 20037. (202) 293–4800. **Est.** 1961. **Members** 1,000,000.

Ethnic and Racial Groups

African-American Institute 833 United Nations Plaza, New York, N.Y. 10017. (212) 949–5666. Works to further development in Africa, improve African-American understanding, and inform Americans about Africa. **Est.** 1953. **Members** Nonmembership.

American Jewish Congress 15 E. 84th St., New York, N.Y. 10028. (212) 879–4500. American Jews opposed to racism and committed to the unity, security, dignity, and creative survival of Jews in Israel and elsewhere. **Est.** 1918. **Members** 50,000.

American Oriental Society Univ. of Michigan, Harlan Hatcher Library, Rm. 111E, Ann Arbor, Mich. 48109. (313) 747–4760. Promotes research in Oriental languages, history, and civilizations. **Est.** 1842. **Members** 1,400.

Asia Society 725 Park Ave., New York, N.Y. 10021. (212) 288–6400. Promotes American understanding of Asia and its place in the international community. **Est.** 1956. **Members** 5,600.

Association on American Indian Affairs 95 Madison Ave., New York, N.Y. 10016. (212) 689–8720. Provides legal and technical assistance to Indian tribes throughout the U.S. **Est.** 1923. **Members** 40,000.

Association of the Sons of Poland 591 Summit Ave., Rm. 205, Jersey City, N.J. 07306. (201) 653–1163. Fraternal benefit life insurance society for men and women of Polish birth or ancestry. **Est.** 1903. **Members** 10,000.

Congress of Racial Equality (CORE) 1457 Flatbush Ave., Brooklyn, N.Y. 11210. (718) 434–3580. Persons of African ancestry; promotes right of blacks to govern themselves in those areas which are demographically and geographically defined as theirs. **Est.** 1942. **Members** N.A.

Hispanic Institute in the United States 612 W. 116th St., New York, N.Y. 10027. (212) 280–4187. Provides research programs; offers lectures and concerts. **Est.** 1920. **Members** 189.

Hispanic Society of America 613 W. 155th St., New York, N.Y. 10032. (212) 926–2234. People who have made distinguished contributions in Hispanic art, literature, history, and culture. **Est.** 1904. **Members** 400.

Indian Rights Association 1601 Market St., Philadelphia, Pa. 19103. (215) 665–4523. Promotes welfare and legal and human rights of Native Americans. **Est.** 1882. **Members** 1,000.

Irish American Cultural Institute 2115 Summit Ave., Box 5026, College of St. Thomas, St. Paul, Minn. 55105. (612) 962–6040. Works to stimulate creativity in Irish arts and sciences; sponsors international exchange of academics in Irish arts and sciences. **Est.** 1962. **Members** N.A.

Italian Historical Society of America 111 Columbia Heights, Brooklyn, N.Y. 11201. (718) 852–2929. Perpetuates Italian heritage in America and gathers historical data on Italian-Americans. **Est.** 1949. **Members** 1,900.

Japan Foundation 142 W. 57th St., New York, N.Y. 10019. (212) 949–6360. Promotes international cultural and educational exchange programs. **Est.** 1972. **Members** N.A.

Japan Society 333 E. 47th St., New York, N.Y. 10017. (212) 832–1155. Americans and Japanese individuals, institutions, and corporations representing the business, professional, and academic worlds. **Est.** 1907. **Members** 8,000.

Japanese American Citizens League 1765 Sutter St., San Francisco, Calif. 94115. (415) 921–5225. Works to defend civil and human rights of all peoples, particularly Japanese-Americans; seeks to preserve cultural and ethnic heritage of Japanese-Americans. **Est.** 1929. **Members** 28,000.

National Association for the Advancement of Colored People (NAACP) 4805 Mt. Hope Dr., Baltimore, Md. 21215. (312) 481–4100. Promotes equal rights and elimination of racial discrimination in housing, employment, voting, schools, courts, transportation, prisons, recreation, and business enterprises. **Est.** 1909. **Members** 400,000.

National Association of Arab Americans 2033 M St. NW, Ste. 300, Washington, D.C. 20036. (202) 467–4800. Encourages and promotes friendship between U.S. and Arab peoples through political, social, cultural, and educational activities. **Est.** 1972. **Members** N.A.

National Black United Fund 50 Park Pl., Ste. 1538, Newark, N.J. 07102. (201) 643–5122. Solicits funds to support projects in education, health, human services, economic development, social justice, arts and culture, and emergency needs of black communities nationwide. **Est.** 1972. **Members** 30.

National Urban League 500 E. 62nd St., New York, N.Y. 10021. (212) 310–9000. Aims to eliminate racial segregation and discrimination in the United States and to achieve parity for blacks and other minorities in American life. **Est.** 1910. **Members** 50,000.

Society of the Friendly Sons of St. Patrick in the City of New York 80 Wall St., Rm. 712, New York, N.Y. 10005. (212) 269–1770. Men of Irish descent in New York area; conducts charitable activities. **Est.** 1784. **Members** 1,500.

Sons of Norway 1455 W. Lake St., Minneapolis, Minn. 55408. (612) 827–3611. Promotes preservation of Norwegian cultural heritage with language and crafts classes and camps; produces motion pictures, filmstrips, and multimedia programs on Norwegian folk culture and fine arts. **Est.** 1895. **Members** 90,000.

Ukrainian National Association 30 Montgomery St., 3rd Fl., Jersey City, N.J. 07303. (201) 451–2200. Fraternal benefit life insurance society for people of Ukrainian and Slavic ancestry. **Est.** 1894. **Members** 75,000.

Fraternities, Sororities, and Honor Societies

Alpha Chi Box 773, Harding Univ., Searcy, Ark. 72143. (501) 268–3121. Honor society for college students in top 10 percent of their class; scholarships and fellowships. **Est.** 1922. **Members** 180,440.

Alpha Delta Kappa 1615 W. 92nd St., Kansas City, Mo. 64114. (816) 363–5525. Educational society. **Est.** 1947. **Members** 58,000.

Alpha Epsilon Delta Garrett Hall, Univ. of Virginia, Charlottesville, Va. 22904. (804) 924–7520. Pre-med society. **Est.** 1926. **Members** 88,600.

Alpha Epsilon Phi 6100 Channingway Blvd., Ste. 302, Columbus, Ohio 43213. (614) 866–6814. **Est.** 1909. **Members** 50,000.

Alpha Lambda Delta P.O. Box 1576, Muncie, Ind. 47308. (317) 282–5620. Honor society; awards 14 fellowships annually to members for professional or graduate studies. **Est.** 1924. **Members** 380,000.

Alpha Omicron Pi 9025 Overlook Blvd., Brentwood, Tenn. 37027. (615) 370–0920. **Est.** 1897. **Members** 90,000.

Alpha Zeta P.O. Box 595, Lafayette, Ind. 47902. (317) 742–2538. Maintains Alpha Zeta Foundation and National AZ Foundation of America which provide financial and professional support for agriculture students. **Est.** 1897. **Members** 95,000.

Beta Beta Beta P.O. Box 670, Madison, N.J. 07940. (201) 377–8407. Organization for biology students. **Est.** 1922. **Members** 116,000.

Beta Gamma Sigma 605 Old Ballas Rd., Ste. 200, St. Louis, Mo. 63141. (314) 432–5650. Organization for business students. **Est.** 1913. **Members** 280,000.

Beta Phi Mu School of Library and Info. Sci., University of Pittsburgh, Pittsburgh, Pa. 15260. (412) 624–9435. Professional honor society of librarians. **Est.** 1948. **Members** 23,000.

Beta Sigma Phi 1800 W. 91st Pl., Kansas City, Mo. 64114. (816) 444–6800. Social and cultural organization for women over 18. **Est.** 1931. **Members** 250,000.

Chi Omega 3111 Carew Tower, 441 Vine St., Cincinnati, Ohio 45202. (513) 421–7005. Social organization. **Est.** 1895. **Members** 195,000.

Delta Delta Delta 2313 Brookhollow Plaza Dr., P.O. Box 5987, Arlington, Tex. 76005. (817) 640–8001. Social organization. **Est.** 1888. **Members** 152,000.

Delta Gamma 3250 Riverside Dr., Columbus, Ohio 43221. (614) 481–8169. Social organization. **Est.** 1873. **Members** 140,000.

Kappa Alpha Theta 8740 Founders Rd., Indianapolis, Ind. 46268. (317) 876–1870. Social organization. **Est.** 1870. **Members** 126,000.

Kappa Kappa Gamma 530 E. Town St., Box 2079, Columbus, Ohio 43216. (614) 228–6515. Social organization. **Est.** 1870. **Members** 150,000.

Kappa Sigma P.O. Box 5066, Charlottesville, Va. 22905. (804) 295–3193. Social organization. **Est.** 1869. **Members** 175,000.

Lambda Chi Alpha 8741 Founders Rd., Indianapolis, Ind. 46268. (317) 872–8000. Social organization with scholarship program, awards, hall of fame, museum, and educational and leadership conclaves. **Est.** 1909. **Members** 195,000.

National Beta Club P.O. Box 730, Spartanburg, S.C. 29304. (803) 583–4553. Service organization. **Est.** 1933. **Members** 200,000.

National Honor Society 1904 Association Dr., Reston, Va. 22091. (703) 860–0200. Organization for secondary school students. **Est.** 1921. **Members** 5,000,000.

National Junior Honor Society 1904 Association Dr., Reston, Va. 22091. (703) 860–0200. Organization for middle and junior high school students. **Est.** 1929. **Members** 215,000.

Phi Alpha Theta 2333 Liberty St., Allentown, Pa. 18104. (215) 433–4140. Organization for history students. **Est.** 1921. **Members** 166,071.

Phi Beta Kappa 1811 Q St. NW, Washington, D.C. 20009. (202) 265–3808. Honorary society for liberal arts and sciences. **Est.** 1776. **Members** 425,000.

Phi Delta Theta 2 S. Campus Ave., Oxford, Ohio 45056. (513) 523–6345. Social organization. **Est.** 1848. **Members** 180,000.

Phi Kappa Phi P.O. Box 16000, Louisiana State Univ., Baton Rouge, La. 70893. (504) 388–4917. Honor society; awards first-year graduate fellowship and other awards. **Est.** 1897. **Members** 500,000.

Pi Beta Phi 7730 Carondelet, Ste. 333, St. Louis, Mo. 63105. (314) 727–7338. Social organization. **Est.** 1867. **Members** 164,639.

Pi Gamma Mu 1717 Ames St., Winfield, Kans. 67156. (316) 221–3128. Social sciences honor society. Presents awards; sponsors graduate scholarships. **Est.** 1924. **Members** 165,000.

Pi Sigma Alpha 4000 Albemarle St. NW, #310, Washington, D.C. 20016. (202) 362–5342. Political science organization. **Est.** 1920. **Members** 98,000.

Psi Chi 201 Frazier Ave., Ste. F, Chattanooga, Tenn. 37405. (615) 756–2044. National honor society in psychology. **Est.** 1929. **Members** 200,000.

Sigma Alpha Epsilon P.O. Box 1856, Evanston, Ill. 60204. (708) 475–1856. Social organization. **Est.** 1856. **Members** 212,213.

Sigma Chi Corporation 1714 Hinman Ave., Evanston, Ill. 60204. (708) 869–3655. Social

fraternity; maintains grants and awards, placement service, museum, biographical archives, and 4,000-volume library. **Est.** 1855. **Members** 203,000.
Sigma Delta Pi P.O. Box 55125, Riverside, Calif. 92517. (714) 684–4340. Spanish organizations. **Est.** 1919. **Members** 90,000.
Sigma Nu P.O. Box 1869, Lexington, Va. 24450. (703) 463–2164. Social organization. **Est.** 1869. **Members** 150,000.
Sigma Phi Epsilon 310 S. Boulevard, P.O. 1901, Richmond, Va. 23215. (804) 353–1901. Social organization; maintains Sigma Phi Epsilon Educational Foundation and National Housing Corp. Awards Outstanding College Senior, Outstanding News Reporter, and Outstanding Alumni, and 10 student members. **Est.** 1901. **Members** 165,000.
Sigma Theta Tau International 550 W. North St., Indianapolis, Ind. 46202. (317) 634–8171. Nursing organization. **Est.** 1922. **Members** 150,000.
Sigma Xi 99 Alexander Dr., P.O. Box 13975, Research Triangle Park, N.C. 27709. (919) 549–4691. Scientific research society for men and women in natural sciences. **Est.** 1886. **Members** N.A.
Tau Beta Pi Association P.O. Box 8840, Univ. Station, Knoxville, Tenn. 37996. (615) 546–4578. Engineering organization. **Est.** 1885. **Members** 340,000.

Gay Rights and AIDS Organizations

ACT UP (AIDS Coalition to Unleash Power) 135 W. 29th St., New York, N.Y. 10001. (212) 564–2437. Dedicated to direct action to end the AIDS crisis. **Est.** 1987. **Members** 150 chapters worldwide.
Gay Men's Health Crisis (GMHC) 129 W. 20th St., New York, N.Y. 10011. (212) 807-6664. Professionals and volunteers in service to AIDS victims and their families. **Est.** 1982. **Members** N.A.
Lambda Legal Defense Fund 666 Broadway, New York, N.Y. 10012. (212) 995–8585. Fights for legal rights of gays, lesbians, and people with AIDS and HIV. **Est.** 1973. **Members** 16,000.
Lesbian Feminist Liberation Gay Community Center, 208 W. 13th St., New York, N.Y. 10011. (212) 620–7310. Promotes lesbian and women's rights. **Est.** 1973. **Members** 20.
National Gay and Lesbian Task Force 1517 U St. NW, Washington, D.C. 20009. (202) 332–6483. Dedicated to the elimination of prejudice based on their sexual orientation. **Est.** 1973. **Members** 18,000.
People with AIDS Coalition 31 W. 26th St., New York, N.Y. 10010. (212) 532–0290. Local support group. **Est.** 1985. **Members** Nonmembership.
San Francisco AIDS Foundation P.O. Box 6182, San Francisco, Calif. 94101. (415) 864–5855. AIDS prevention through education and social service programs for AIDS victims. **Est.** 1982. **Members** Nonmembership.

Hobbies

Academy of Model Aeronautics 1810 Samuel Morse Dr., Reston, Va. 22090. (703) 435–0750. **Est.** 1936. **Members** 170,000.
American Birding Association P.O. Box 6599, Colorado Springs, Colo. 80934. (719) 634–7736. **Est.** 1969. **Members** 7,000.
American Contract Bridge League 2990 Airways Blvd., Memphis, Tenn. 38116. (901) 332–5586. **Est.** 1927. **Members** 190,000.
American Darts Organization 13841 Eastbrook Ave., Bellflower, Calif. 90706. (213) 925–1205. **Est.** 1976. **Members** 100,000.
American Federation of Astrologers P.O. Box 22040, Tempe, Ariz. 85282. (602) 838–1751. **Est.** 1938. **Members** N.A.
American Motorcyclist Association P.O. Box 6114, Westerville, Ohio 43081. (614) 891–2425. **Est.** 1924. **Members** 140,000.
American Numismatics Association 818 Cascade Ave., Colorado Springs, Colo. 80903. (719) 632–2646. **Est.** 1891. **Members** 35,000.
American Philatelic Society P.O. Box 8000, 100 Oakwood Ave., State College, Pa. 16803. (814) 237–3803. **Est.** 1886. **Members** 56,000.
American Radio Relay League 225 Main St., Newington, Conn. 06111. (203) 666–1541. Ham radio operators. **Est.** 1914. **Members** 159,000.
Antique Automobile Club of America 501 W. Governor Rd., Hershey, Pa. 17033. (717) 534–1910. **Est.** 1935. **Members** 53,000.
Boat Owners Association of the United States 880 S. Pickett St., Alexandria, Va. 22304. (703) 823–9550. Consumer service organization. **Est.** 1966. **Members** 330,000.
Gold Prospectors Association of America P.O. Box 507, Bonsall, Calif. 92003. (619) 728–6620. **Est.** 1965. **Members** 84,000.
Les Amis du Vin 2302 Perkins Pl., Silver Spring, Md. 20910. (301) 588–0980. Wine lovers association. **Est.** 1965. **Members** 81,000.
National Association of Watch and Clock Collectors 514 Poplar St., Columbia, Pa. 17512. (717) 684–8261. **Est.** 1943. **Members** 31,500.
National Model Railroad Association 4121 Cromwell Rd., Chattanooga, Tenn. 37421. (615) 892–2846. **Est.** 1935. **Members** 24,000.
Photographic Society of America 3000 United Founders Blvd., Ste. 103, Oklahoma City, Okla. 73112. **Est.** 1934. **Members** 11,000.
United States Chess Federation 186 Rte. 9W, New Windsor, N.Y. 12553. (914) 562–8350. **Est.** 1939. **Members** 58,000.

Homeless

National Alliance to End Homelessness (formerly Nat'l Citizens Committee for Food and Shelter) 1518 K St. NW, Ste. 206, Washington, D.C.. 20005. (202) 638–1526. Works with public and private sector to develop solutions to the problem of America's homeless. **Est.** 1983. **Members** Nonmembership.
National Coalition for the Homeless 1621 K St. NW, Ste. 1004, Washington, D.C. 20006. (202) 775–1322. Legal assistance for the homeless and clearinghouse for information. **Est.** 1982. **Members** 9,000.

Humanitarian Aid

American Red Cross 17th and D Sts. NW, Washington, D.C. 20006. (202) 737–8300. Emergency aid for natural disasters, blood centers. **Est.** 1881. **Members** N.A.
Amnesty International of the U.S.A. 322 Eighth Ave., New York, N.Y. 10001. (212) 807–8400. Human rights activists; opposes torture, tries to help political prisoners. **Est.** 1966. **Members** 400,000.
Bread for the World 802 Rhode Island Ave. NE, Washington, D.C. 20018. (202) 269–0200. Financial aid to poor countries, investment, and trade. **Est.** 1973. **Members** 40,000.
CARE 660 First Ave., New York, N.Y. 10016. (212) 686–3110. Helps foreign governments with water supply, feeding centers, clinics, schools, agricultural development, and conservation. **Est.** 1945. **Members** N.A.
Catholic Charities, USA 1731 King St., Ste. 200, Alexandria, Va. 22314. (703) 549–1390. Consultation and information services; helps with housing, unemployment, and other social problems. **Est.** 1910. **Members** 4,000.
Christian Children's Fund P.O. Box 26511, Richmond, Va. 23261. Assistance to needy children in foreign countries. **Est.** 1938. **Members** 4,633.
Covenant House 346 W. 17th Street, New York, N.Y. 10011. (212) 727–4000. Extensive aid and support for runaway and homeless children. **Est.** 1972. **Members** N.A.
Food for the Hungry, Inc. P.O. Box E, Scottsdale, Ariz. 85252. (602) 998–3100. Food distribution, shelter, water development, animal husbandry, and vegetable growing. **Est.** 1971. **Members** N.A.
The Hunger Project 1 Madison Ave., 8A, New York, N.Y. 10010. (212) 532–4255. **Est.** 1977. **Members** N.A.
International League for Human Rights 432 Park Ave. South, Rm. 1103, New York, N.Y. 10016. (212) 684–1221. Fights racial discrimination, slavery, genocide, and apartheid. **Est.** 1942. **Members** N.A.
National Coalition to Abolish the Death Penalty 1325 G St. NW, Lower Level B, Washington, D.C. 20005. (202) 347–2411. Seeks to abolish death penalty in U.S. **Est.** 1976. **Members** 115.
National Easter Seal Society 230 W. Monroe, Chicago, Ill. 60606. (312) 726–6200. Provides rehabilitation services for handicapped. **Est.** 1919. **Members** 165.
National Execution Alert Network c/o National Coalition to Abolish the Death Penalty, 1325 G St. NW, Lower Level B, Washington, D.C. 20005. (202) 347–2411. Seeks abolition of capital punishment. **Est.** 1979. **Members** 500.
Oxfam America 115 Broadway, Boston, Mass. 02116. (617) 428–1211. Funds self-help programs in foreign countries; emphasis on economic and food programs. **Est.** 1970. **Members** Nonmembership.
Salvation Army 615 Slaters Lane, P.O. Box 269, Alexandria, Va. 22313. (703) 684–5500. International charity; religious and social welfare activities. **Est.** 1880. **Members** 434,002.
Save the Children Federation 54 Wilton Rd., Westport, Conn. 06880. (203) 221–4000. **Est.** 1932. **Members** Nonmembership.
Second Harvest, the National Food Bank Network 116 S. Michigan Ave., Ste. 4, Chicago, Ill. 60603. (312) 263–2303. Provides food to local charities; training and technical information. **Est.** 1979. **Members** 185.

United Jewish Appeal 99 Park Ave., New York, N.Y. 10016. (212) 818–9100. Aid for Jews in Israel and 33 other countries. **Est.** 1939. **Members** N.A.

World Jewish Congress 501 Madison Ave., 17th Floor, New York, N.Y. 10022. (212) 755–5770. Supports protection of human rights regardless of race or religion. **Est.** 1936. **Members** 33.

Legal

American Bar Association 750 N. Lake Shore Dr., Chicago, Ill. 60611. (312) 988–5000. Research, educational projects, and seminars for improvement of the legal profession. **Est.** 1878. **Members** 360,000.

National Association of Women Lawyers 750 N. Lake Shore Dr., Chicago, Ill. 60611. (312) 988–6186. **Est.** 1911. **Members** 1,200.

National Conference of Black Lawyers 126 W. 119th St., New York, N.Y. 10026. (212) 864–4000. Legal service to black and poor communities. **Est.** 1968. **Members** 1,000.

National Lawyers Guild 55 6th Ave., New York, N.Y. 10003. (212) 966–5000. Commitment to the right of political dissent. **Est.** 1937. **Members** 9,000.

National Legal Aid and Defender Association 1625 K St. NW, 8th Fl., Washington, D.C. 20006. (202) 452–0620. Offers technical advice and services to local organizations offering legal services to the poor; information clearinghouse for legal aid and defender services. **Est.** 1911. **Members** 2,800.

Phi Alpha Delta 10722 White Oak Ave, Granada Hills, Calif. 91344. (818) 360–1941. Professional law fraternity. **Est.** 1902. **Members** 130,000.

Phi Delta Phi International Legal Fraternity 1750 N St. NW, Washington, D.C. 20036. (202) 628–0148. Professional law fraternity; awards, student loans, and placement service. **Est.** 1869. **Members** 141,000.

Medical

(See also DISEASE and DISABLED)

American Academy of Allergy and Immunology 611 E. Wells St., Milwaukee, Wis. 53202. (414) 272–6071. Professional society of physicians. **Est.** 1943. **Members** 4,100.

American Chiropractic Association 1701 Clarendon Blvd., Arlington, Va. 22209. (202) 276–8800. **Est.** 1930. **Members** 20,000.

American Dental Association 211 E. Chicago Ave., Chicago, Ill. 60611. (312) 440–2500. **Est.** 1859. **Members** 140,000.

American Heart Association 7272 Greenville Ave., Dallas, Tex. 75231. (214) 373–6300. Physicians, scientists, and lay persons in support of research and education. **Est.** 1924. **Members** 200,000.

American Hospital Association 840 N. Lake Shore Dr., Chicago, Ill. 60611. (312) 280–6000. Hospitals, health care institutions, and other groups. **Est.** 1898. **Members** 54,500.

American Institute of Nutrition 9650 Rockville Pike, Bethesda, Md. 20814. (301) 530–7050. **Est.** 1928. **Members** 2,770.

American Lung Association 1740 Broadway, New York, N.Y. 10019. (212) 315–8700. Association of physicians, nurses, and laymen interested in the prevention and control of lung disease. **Est.** 1904. **Members** 9,500.

American Medical Association 515 N. State St., Chicago, Ill. 60610. (312) 644–5000. **Est.** 1847. **Members** 271,000.

American Nurses' Association 2420 Pershing Rd., Kansas City, Mo. 64108. (816) 474–5720. Represents registered nurses. Sponsors American Nurses Foundation for Research. Presents awards. **Est.** 1896. **Members** 200,000.

American Physicians Association of Computer Medicine 10 N. Main St., Pittsford, N.Y. 14534. (716) 586–8159. Encourages the use of computers in medicine; seeks to inform physicians about computer application in patient care, education, and research. **Est.** 1984. **Members** 350.

American Public Health Association 1015 15th St. NW, Washington, D.C. 20005. (202) 789–5600. Protects and promotes personal, mental, and environmental health. **Est.** 1872. **Members** 31,500.

International Chiropractors Association 1110 N. Glebe Rd., Ste. 1000, Arlington, Va. 22201. (703) 528–5000. **Est.** 1926. **Members** 8,000.

National Amputation Foundation 12–45 150th St., Whitestone, N.Y. 11357. (718) 767–0596. Veterans with service-connected amputation, helping all amputees including non-vets. **Est.** 1919. **Members** 5,200.

National Association for Hearing and Speech Action 10801 Rockville Pike, Rockville, Md. 20852. (301) 897–8682. **Est.** 1919.

National Hearing Aid Society 20361 Middlebelt Rd., Livonia, Mich. 48152. (313) 478–2610. **Est.** 1951. **Members** 4,000.

National League for Nursing 350 Hudson St., New York, N.Y. 10014. (212) 989–9393. Assesses nursing needs, improves organized nursing services and education, and fosters collaboration between nursing and other health and community services. **Est.** 1952. **Members** 19,800.

National Medical Association 1012 Tenth St. NW, Washington, D.C. 20001. (202) 347–1895. **Est.** 1895. **Members** 14,500.

National Mental Health Association 1021 Prince St., Alexandria, Va. 22314. (703) 684–7222. Consumer advocacy organization devoted to the fight against mental illness and advancement of mental health. **Est.** 1909. **Members** N.A.

Politics and Government

American Civil Liberties Union (ACLU) 132 W. 43rd St., New York, N.Y. 10036. (212) 944–9800. Champions rights guaranteed by Constitution and Bill of Rights. **Est.** 1920. **Members** 275,000.

American Conservative Union 38 Ivy St. SE, Washington, D.C. 20003. (202) 546–6555. Provides education in political activities, media bias, foreign, military, and domestic economic policy, the arts, professions, and science. **Est.** 1964. **Members** 100,000.

American Political Science Association 1527 New Hampshire Ave. NW, Washington, D.C. 20036. (202) 483–2512. Encourages the impartial study and promotes the development of the art and science of government. **Est.** 1903. **Members** 12,000.

American Security Council Washington Communications Center, Boston, Va. 22713. (703) 547–1776. Advocates strong national defense; supports research and information center on national security; rates members of congress on key votes about defense. **Est.** 1955. **Members** 325,700.

Americans for Democratic Action 1511 K St. NW, Ste. 941, Washington, D.C. 20005. (202) 638–6447. Formulates liberal domestic and foreign policies. **Est.** 1947. **Members** 85,000.

Americas Society 680 Park Ave., New York, N.Y. 10021. (212) 249–8950. Promotes greater understanding and cooperation among peoples of the American republics for advancement of common interests. **Est.** 1982. **Members** 830.

Common Cause 2030 M St. NW, Washington, D.C. 20036. (202) 833–1200. Devoted to making government at the national and state levels more open and accountable to citizens and to improving government performance. **Est.** 1970. **Members** 265,000.

Eagle Forum Box 618, Alton, Ill. 62002. (618) 462–5415. Conservative pro-family advocacy group; opposes Equal Rights Amendment (ERA). **Est.** 1975. **Members** 80,000.

Foreign Policy Association 729 Seventh Ave., New York, N.Y. 10019. (212) 764–4050. Encourages citizen expression of opinion on foreign policy issues through conferences and the media. **Est.** 1918. **Members** N.A.

Heritage Foundation 214 Massachusetts Ave. NE, Washington, D.C. 20002. (202) 546–4400. Dedicated to principles of free enterprise; publications disseminate basic tenets of limited government. **Est.** 1973. **Members** N.A.

John Birch Society P.O. Box 8040, Appleton, Wis. 54913. (414) 749–3780. Right-wing education group; promotes "less government"; urges withdrawal from United Nations. **Est.** 1958. **Members** N.A..

League of Conservation Voters 1150 Connecticut NW, Ste. 201, Washington, D.C. 20002. (202) 785–8683. Supports environmentalist candidates. **Est.** 1970. **Members** 100,000.

National Taxpayers Union 325 Pennsylvania Ave. SE, Washington, D.C. 20003. (202) 543–1300. Lobbies to reduce government spending, cut taxes, and protect rights of taxpayers. **Est.** 1969. **Members** 200,000.

United Nations Association U.S.A. 485 5th Avenue, 2nd Floor, New York, N.Y. 10017. (212) 697–3232. Carries out research and public programs in the United Nations. **Est.** 1964. **Members** 25,000.

U.S. Conference of Mayors 1620 Eye St. NW, Washington, D.C. 20006. (202) 293–7330. **Founded** 1932. **Members** 600.

Population

Alternatives to Abortion International 1213½ S. James Rd., Columbus, Ohio 43227. (614) 239–9433. Offers assistance to women contemplating abortion. **Est.** 1971. **Members** 500.

American Pro Life Council (Right-to-Life) 1612 S. Prospect, Park Ridge, Ill. 60068. (708) 692–2183. Antiabortion activities; lobbies for Human Life Amendment to U.S. Constitution. **Est.** 1980. **Members** 50,000.

Birthright, U.S.A. 686 N. Broad St., Woodbury, N.J. 08096. (609) 848–1819. Interdenominational private groups; helps pregnant women find alternatives to abortion. **Est.** 1968. **U.S. Chapters** 540.

Center for Development and Population Activities 1717 Massachusetts Ave. NW, #202, Washington, D.C. 20036. (202) 667–1142. Provides training, technical assistance, and support to development and population professionals in Third World countries. **Est.** 1975. **Members** N.A.

Family Planning International Assistance 810 Seventh Ave., New York, N.Y. 10019. (212) 541–7800. Financial and technical assistance to family planning organizations in developing countries. **Est.** 1971. **Members** N.A.

National Abortion Federation 1436 U St. NW, Ste. 103, Washington, D.C. 20009. (202) 667–5881. Seeks to unite abortion service providers into a professional community dedicated to excellent health care and upgrading abortion facilities. **Est.** 1977. **Members** 300.

National Abortion Rights Action League (NARAL) 1101 14th St. NW, Washington, D.C. 20005. (202) 408–4600. Advocates support of 1973 Supreme Court decision on abortion. **Est.** 1969. **Members** 400,000.

National Right to Life Committee 419 Seventh St. NW, Ste. 500, Washington, D.C. 20004. (202) 626–8800. For protection of all human life, young or old; antiabortion programs and counseling about adoption methods. **Est.** 1973. **Members** N.A.

Physicians for Choice c/o Planned Parenthood Federation of America, 810 Seventh Ave., New York, N.Y. 10019. (212) 541–7800. Promotes right of women to decide about abortion. **Est.** 1981. **Members** 5,000.

Planned Parenthood Federation of America 810 Seventh Ave., New York, N.Y. 10019. (212) 541–7800. Dissemination of literature and advice on birth control and family planning. **Est.** 1916. **Members** N.A.

Population Association of America 1722 N St. NW, Washington, D.C. 20036. (202) 429–0891. Professional society interested in scientific demography. **Est.** 1931. **Members** 2,700.

Population Council One Dag Hammarskjold Pl., New York, N.Y. 10017. (212) 644–1300. Scientific group dedicated to development and improvement of contraceptive methods. **Est.** 1952. **Members** N.A.

Psychology and Therapy

American Group Psychotherapy Association 25 E. 21st St., 6th Fl., New York, N.Y. 10010. (212) 477–2677. Professional group. **Est.** 1942. **Members** 3,500.

American Psychiatric Association 1400 K St. NW, Washington, D.C. 20005. (202) 682–6000. Assists in formulating programs to meet mental health needs. **Est.** 1844. **Members** 36,000.

American Psychoanalytic Association 309 E. 49th St., New York, N.Y. 10022. (212) 752–0450. Develops standards for the training of psychoanalysts. **Est.** 1911. **Members** 3,025.

National Academy of Counselors and Family Therapists 55 Morris Ave., Springfield, N.J. 07081. (201) 379–7496. Promotes strong family life through family counseling, education, and legislation. **Est.** 1972. **Members** 800.

National Alliance for the Mentally Ill 2101 Wilson Blvd., Ste. 302, Arlington, Va. 22201. (703) 524–7600. Alliance of self-help/advocacy groups to provide emotional support and practical guidance to families of the mentally ill; monitors treatment, rehabilitation, and support services. **Est.** 1979. **Members** 130,000.

National Council on Family Relations 3989 Central Ave. NE, Ste. 550, Minneapolis, Minn. 55421. (612) 781–9331. Interprofessional group of family life workers, to act together in marriage and family relationships. **Est.** 1938. **Members** 3,900.

National Psychological Association for Psychoanalysis 150 W. 13th St., New York, N.Y. 10011. (212) 924–7440. Professional society; conducts training programs to obtain certification in psychoanalysis. **Est.** 1946. **Members** 342.

Religious

American Academy of Religion c/o James B. Wiggins, Dept. of Religion, 501 Hall of Languages, Syracuse Univ., Syracuse, N.Y. 13244. (315) 443–4019. Encourages scholarship in teaching religion; research grants, placement services, statistics, and speaker's bureau. **Est.** 1909. **Members** 5,500.

American Atheists P.O. Box 140195, Austin, Tex. 78714. (512) 458–1244. Advocates separation of state and church, taxation of church real estate and income. **Est.** 1958. **Members** 100,000.

American Bible Society 1865 Broadway, New York, N.Y. 10023. (212) 408–1200. Translates, publishes, and distributes Bibles internationally; Over 90 religious denominations. **Est.** 1816. **Members** 500,000.

Anglican Society c/o St Andrews Episcopal Church, 2067 Fifth Ave., New York, N.Y. 10035. (212) 534–0896. Promotes Anglican Catholic faith and practices in accordance with principles of the Book of Common Prayer. **Est.** 1932. **Members** 500.

Association of Theological Schools 42 E. National Rd., P.O. Box 130, Vandalia, Ohio 45377. (513) 898–4654. Represents nondenominational, interdenominational, and denominational seminaries and theological colleges in U.S. and Canada. **Est.** 1918. **Members** 205.

B'nai B'rith International 1640 Rhode Island Ave. NW, Washington, D.C. 20036. (202) 857–6600. Offers religious and cultural programs for Jewish teenagers; presents awards for humanitarian services. **Est.** 1843. **Members** 500,000.

Congress of National Black Churches 600 New Hampshire Ave. NW, Ste. 650, Washington, D.C. 20037. (202) 333–3060. Promotes economic development, family and social support, housing, education, and foreign relations in black communities through religious education and evangelism. **Est.** 1978. **Members** 6.

Council of Jewish Federations 730 Broadway, New York, N.Y. 10003. (212) 475–5000. Raises funds for local, national, and overseas Jewish needs. **Est.** 1932. **Members** 200.

Gideons International 2900 Lebanon Rd., Nashville, Tenn. 37214. (615) 883–8533. Distributes Bibles to individuals, hotels, hospitals, schools and institutions in 137 countries "to win others for the Lord Jesus Christ." **Est.** 1899. **Members** 100,000.

Hadassah the Women's Zionist Organization of America 50 W. 58th St., New York, N.Y. 10019. (212) 355–7900. Provides "basic Jewish education" and conducts community services in U.S. and Israel. **Est.** 1912. **Members** 385,000.

International Society for Krishna Consciousness 1030 Grand Ave., San Diego, Calif. 92109. (619) 272–8334. Dedicated to teaching self-realization and Krishna consciousness; yoga basic to teachings. **Est.** 1966. **Members** N.A.

Knights of Columbus 1 Columbus Plaza, New Haven, Conn. 06507. (203) 722–2130. Fraternal society of Catholic men. **Est.** 1882. **Members** 1,495,251.

Mennonite Central Committee 21 S. 12th St., Akron, Pa. 17501. (717) 859–1151. Works to promote economic development in 45 countries. **Est.** 1920. **Members** 37.

National Conference of Christians and Jews 71 Fifth Ave., Ste. 1100, New York, N.Y. 10003. (212) 206–0006. Promotes understanding and cooperation among all religions. **Est.** 1928. **Members** N.A.

National Council of Jewish Women 53 W. 23rd St., New York, N.Y. 10010. (212) 645–4048. Sponsors education, social action, and community service programs for youth, elderly, and women. **Est.** 1893. **Members** 100,000.

National Spiritual Assembly of the Baha'is of the U.S. 536 Sheridan Rd., Wilmette, Ill. 60091. (708) 869–9039. **Est.** 1927. **Members** 9.

Presbyterian Historical Society 425 Lombard St., Philadelphia, Pa. 19147. (215) 627–1852. Preserves written history of American Presbyterianism; library, archives, and publications. **Est.** 1852. **Members** 1,100.

Southern Christian Leadership Conference 334 Auburn Ave. NE, Atlanta, Ga. 30312. (404) 522–1420. Advocates nonviolence for ending racial injustice. **Est.** 1957. **Members** N.A.

Unitarian Universalist Association 25 Beacon St., Boston, Mass. 02108. (617) 742–2100. **Est.** 1986. **Members** N.A.

U.S. Conference for the World Council of Churches 475 Riverside Dr., Rm. 915, New York, N.Y. 10115. (212) 870–2533. Interprets program of the World Council of Churches in U.S. **Est.** 1948. **Members** 28.

Science

American Association for the Advancement of Science 1333 H St. NW, Washington, D.C. 20005. (202) 326–6400. Helps scientists and science in the promotion of human welfare. **Est.** 1848. **Members** N.A.

Federation of American Scientists 307 Massachusetts Ave. NE, Washington, D.C. 20002. (202) 546–3300. Acts on public issues that affect science or require scientific expertise. **Est.** 1946. **Members** 5,000.

National Research Council—National Academy of Sciences 2101 Constitution Ave. NW,

Washington, D.C. 20418. (202) 334–2000. Advises federal government. **Est.** 1916. **Members** 9,500.

Scientists' Institute for Public Information 355 Lexington Ave., 16th Fl., New York, N.Y. 10017. (212) 661–9110. Disseminates scientific data on social issues. **Est.** 1963. **Members** N.A.

Senior Citizens

American Association of Retired Persons 601 E St. NW, Washington, D.C. 20049. (202) 434–2277. Provides services and advice for older people. **Est.** 1958. **Members** 32,000,000.

Gray Panthers 1424 16th St. NW, Ste. 602, Washington, D.C. 20036. (202) 387–3111. Works against age discrimination. **Est.** 1970. **Members** 6,000.

International Senior Citizens Association 1102 S. Crenshaw Blvd., Los Angeles, Calif. 90019. (213) 857–6434. Provides coordination of international organizations promoting interests and needs of senior citizens worldwide. **Est.** 1963. **Members** 500.

Service and Fraternal Organizations

Associations of Junior League 660 First Ave., New York, N.Y. 10016. (212) 683–1515. Women between 18 and 45 who promote voluntarism. **Est.** 1921. **Members** 180,000.

Benevolent and Protective Order of Elks of the U.S.A. 2750 Lake View Ave., Chicago, Ill. 60614. (312) 477–2750. Men's fraternal and benevolent society. **Est.** 1868. **Members** 1,500,000.

Big Brothers/Big Sisters of America 230 N. 13th St., Philadelphia, Pa. 19107. (215) 567–7000. To provide a child from a single parent home with an adult friend who can provide regular guidance, understanding, and acceptance. **Est.** 1977. **Members** 485 agencies.

Independent Order of Odd Fellows Sovereign Grand Lodge, 422 N. Trade St., Winston-Salem, N.C. 27101. (919) 725–5955. Fraternal society. **Est.** 1819. **Members** 523,370.

Kiwanis International 3636 Woodview Trace, Indianapolis, Ind. 46268. (317) 875–8755. Local clubs of business and professional people in 71 countries. Provides assistance to the young and elderly, develops community facilities and supports programs to eliminate crime. **Est.** 1915. **Members** 325,000.

Lions Clubs International 300 22nd St., Oak Brook, Ill. 60521. (708) 571–546. Business and professional men in 162 countries; provides community service; promotes international relations. **Est.** 1917. **Members** 1,368,000.

Loyal Order of the Moose Mooseheart, Ill. 60539. (708) 859–2000. Fraternal society for men. **Est.** 1888. **Members** 1,804,000.

National Grange 1616 H St. NW, Washington, D.C. 20006. (202) 628–3507. Fraternal and service organization for rural families. **Est.** 1867. **Members** 365,000.

National Society of the Daughters of the American Revolution 1776 D St. NW, Washington, D.C. 20006. (202) 628–1776. Female descendants of Revolutionary War patriots. Conducts historical and educational activities through historical research, an Americana museum and documentary collections. Maintains two schools and supports others. Bestows medals and awards. **Est.** 1890. **Members** 204,000.

Order of the Eastern Star, General Grand Chapter 1618 New Hampshire Ave. NW, Washington, D.C. 20009. (202) 667–4737. Master masons and their female relatives dedicated to serving the needy; awards scholarships for religious training. **Est.** 1876. **Members** 2,087,063.

Rotary International 1 Rotary Center, 1560 Sherman Ave., Evanston, Ill. 60201. (708) 866–3000. Business and professional executives; promote community work and high ethical business standards in 160 countries. **Est.** 1905. **Members** 1,077,211.

Shriners (Imperial Council of the Ancient Arabic Order of the Nobles of the Mystic Shrine for North America) P.O. Box 31356, Tampa, Fla. 33631. (813) 281–0300. Fraternal and charitable organization; maintains 22 hospitals for crippled and burned children. **Est.** 1872. **Members** 775,000.

Telephone Pioneers of America 22 Cortlandt St., Room 2588, New York, N.Y. 10007. (212) 393–2955. Fellowship and service activities for active and retired telephone employees with 18+ years service. **Est.** 1911. **Members** 805,000.

United Service Organization (USO) 601 Indiana Ave. NW, Washington, D.C. 20004. (202) 783–8121. Operates service facilities and outreach programs to serve the social, welfare, and recreational needs of U.S. service personnel and their families. **Est.** 1941. **Members** Nonmembership.

Veterans of Foreign Wars of the U.S.A. (VFW) V.F.W. Memorial Building, 200 Maryland Ave. NE, Washington, D.C. 20002. **Tel.** N.A. **Est.** 1899. **Members** 2,095,204.

Substance Abuse and Addiction

Al-Anon Family Group Headquarters P.O. Box 862, Midtown Station, New York, N.Y. 10018. (212) 302–7240. Group for relatives and friends of alcoholics. **Est.** 1951. **Members** N.A.

Alcoholics Anonymous (AA) World Services 475 Riverside Dr., New York, N.Y. 10025. (212) 870–3400. Organization for alcoholics trying to stop drinking. **Est.** 1935. **Members** 1,793,834.

Drugs Anonymous P.O. Box 473, Ansonia Station, New York, N.Y. 10023. (212) 874–0700. Support group for people addicted to drugs; sponsors Drug-Anon Family Program. **Est.** 1975. **Members** N.A.

Families in Action National Drug Information Center 2296 Henderson Mill Rd., Ste. 204, Atlanta, Ga. 30345. (404) 934–6364. Drug information clearinghouse for parents and other adults. **Est.** 1977. **Members** 5,000.

Gamblers Anonymous 3255 Wilshire Blvd., #610, Los Angeles, Calif. 90010. (213) 386–8789. Helps compulsive gamblers. **Est.** 1957. **Members** N.A.

Group Against Smokers' Pollution (GASP) P.O. Box 632, College Park, Md. 20740. (301) 459–4791. **Est.** 1971. **Members** 10,000.

Partnership for a Drug-Free America 666 Third Ave., New York, N.Y. 10017. (212) 922–1560. Advertising, production, and communications industries working creatively for drug abuse prevention. **Est.** 1986. **Members** 2,500.

Mothers Against Drunk Driving (MADD) 511 E. John Carpenter Fwy., No. 700, Irving, Tex. 75062. (214) 744–6233. Promotes reform of drunk driving problem through education, legislation, and research. **Est.** 1980. **Members** 2,800,000.

Narcotics Anonymous P.O. Box 9999, Van Nuys, Calif. 91409. (818) 780–3951. International organization for recovering addicts. **Est.** 1953. **Local groups** 18,000.

National Association for Children of Alcoholics 31582 Coast Hwy., Ste. B, South Laguna, Calif. 92677. (714) 499–3889. **Est.** 1983. **Members** 8,500.

National Commission on Accreditation of Alcoholism and Drug Abuse Counselor Credentialing Bodies Ad Care, 107 Lincoln St., Worcester, Mass. 01605. (617) 799–9000. Develops standards for drug and alcohol abuse counselors. **Est.** 1974. **Members** 70.

National Council on Alcoholism and Drug Dependence 12 W. 21st St., New York, N.Y. 10010. (212) 206–6770. Tries to prevent and control alcoholism through public and private means. **Est.** 1944. **Local groups** 184.

National Parents' Resource Institute for Drug Education 50 Hurt Plaza, Ste. 210, Atlanta, Ga. 30303. (404) 577–4500. Parents, teachers, and others against drug abuse through education and research; sponsors International Drug Conference. **Est.** 1977. **Members** N.A.

National Woman's Christian Temperance Union 1730 Chicago Ave., Evanston, Ill. 60201. (708) 864–1396. Educates American youth against harmful effects of alcohol, narcotics, and tobacco. **Est.** 1874. **Members** 50,000.

Overeaters Anonymous P.O. Box 92870, Los Angeles, Calif. 90009. (213) 542–8363. **Est.** 1960. **Local groups** 10,200.

Students Against Driving Drunk (SADD) P.O. Box 800, Marlboro, Mass. 01752. (508) 481–3568. **Est.** 1981. **Members** 26,000 local groups, 50 state groups.

Telecommunications

American Electronics Association 5201 Great American Parkway, Santa Clara, Calif. 95054. (408) 987–4200. Trade association. **Est.** 1943. **Members** 3,500.

Electronic Industries Association Pennsylvania Ave. NW, Ste. 1100, Washington, D.C. 20006. (202) 457–4900. Trade association. **Est.** 1924. **Members** 1,200.

International Communications Association 12750 Merit Dr., Ste. 710, LB-89, Dallas, Tex. 75251. (214) 233–3889. Trade association for voice, data, and image telecommunications industries. **Est.** 1948. **Members** 740.

North American Telecommunications Association 2000 M St. NW, Ste. 550, Washington, D.C. 20036. (202) 296–9800. Trade association for telecommunications and computer industries. **Est.** 1970. **Members** 650.

Society of Manufacturing Engineers One SME Dr., P.O. Box 930, Dearborn, Mich. 48121. (313) 271–1500. **Est.** 1932. **Members** 80,000.

Tele-Communications Association 858 S. Oak Park Rd., Ste. 102, Covina, Calif. 91724. (818) 967–9411. Professional association; sponsors conferences and educational programs. **Est.** 1961. **Members** 2,400.

Telecommunications Industry Assoc. 2001 Pennsylvania Ave. NW, Ste. 800, Washington, D.C. 20006. (202) 457-4912. Professional association for telecommunications industry. **Est.** 1988. **Members** 600.

Travel and Student Exchange

AFS-Intercultural Programs 313 W. 43rd St., New York, N.Y. 10017. (212) 949-4242. High school student exchange program. **Est.** 1914. **Members** 100,000.

American Automobile Association 1000 AAA Drive, Heathrow, Fla. 32746. (407) 444-7000. Provides travel services, emergency road service, and insurance. **Est.** 1902. **Members** 31,000,000.

American Society of Travel Agents 1101 King St., Alexandria, Va. 22314. (703) 739-2782. Professional organization. **Est.** 1931. **Members** 22,000.

American Youth Hostels (AYH) P.O. Box 37613, Washington, D.C. 20013. (202) 783-6161. Maintains 275 hostels in U.S. **Est.** 1934. **Members** 130,000.

Council of International Educational Exchange 205 E. 42nd St., New York, N.Y. 10017. (212) 661-1414. Provides voluntary service opportunities for students from U.S. and abroad. **Est.** 1947. **Members** 205.

International Christian Youth Exchange (U.S. Committee) 134 W. 26th St., New York, N.Y. 10001. (212) 206-7307. International exchange programs for youths ages 16-24. **Est.** 1949. **Members** N.A.

National Council for International Visitors 1420 K St. NW, Ste. 800, Washington, D.C. 20005. (202) 842-1414. Encourages exchange and training programs; informational services. **Est.** 1961. **Members** N.A.

Travel Industry Association of America 2 Lafayette Center, 1133 21st St. NW, Washington, D.C. 20036. (202) 293-1433. Stimulates domestic and international travel through promotion and legislation,. **Est.** 1969. **Members** 1,700.

INTEREXCHANGE (formerly U.S. Student Travel Service) 356 W. 34th St., No. 306, New York, N.Y. 10001. (212) 947-9533. International travel service for students including jobs, language study, and special interest tours. **Est.** 1968. **Members** N.A.

Veterans and Armed Services

American Legion 700 N. Pennsylvania St., Indianapolis, Ind. 46204. (317) 635-8411. 16,000 local groups of honorably discharged wartime veterans. **Est.** 1919. **Members** 3,000,000.

American Veterans of World War II, Korea and Vietnam (AMVETS) 4647 Forbes Blvd., Lanham, Md. 20706. (301) 459-9600. **Est.** 1944. **Members** 200,000.

Women

American Association of University Women 1111 16 St. NW, Washington, D.C. 20036. (202) 785-7700. Lobbies for women's issues. **Est.** 1881. **Members** 140,000.

National Council of Negro Women 1211 Connecticut Ave. NW, Ste. 702, Washington, D.C. 20036. (202) 659-0006. Promotes black women's leadership in business, community, and politics; maintains Bethune Museum and Archives for Women's Rights. **Est.** 1935. **Members** 40,000.

National Organization for Women (NOW) 1000 16th St. NW, Ste. 700, Washington, D.C. 20006. (202) 331-0066. Works to end sex bias, for passage of Equal Rights Amendment, and for greater representation of women in elective politics. **Est.** 1966. **Members** 250,000.

Women Against Pornography 321 W. 47th St., New York, N.Y. 10036. (212) 307-5055. **Est.** 1979. **Members** 10,000.

Writing and Journalism

American Booksellers Association 137 W. 25th St., New York, N.Y. 10001. (212) 463-8450. **Est.** 1900. **Members** 5,500.

American Society of Journalists and Authors 1501 Broadway, Ste. 1907, New York, N.Y. 10036. (212) 997-0947. Helps nonfiction writers; promotes a code of ethics for writers. **Est.** 1948. **Members** 790.

American Society of Magazine Editors 575 Lexington Ave., New York, N.Y. 10022. (212) 752-0055. **Est.** 1963. **Members** 700.

Authors Guild 234 W. 44th St., New York, N.Y. 10036, (212) 398-0838. Professional book and magazine writers. **Est.** 1912. **Members** 6,500.

Authors League of America 234 W. 44th St., New York, N.Y. 10036. (212) 391-9198. Professional organization of authors of books, articles, and plays. **Est.** 1912. **Members** 14,700.

Fairness and Accuracy in Reporting (FAIR) 130 W. 25th St., New York, N.Y. 10001. (212) 633-6700. **Est.** 1986. **Members** N.A.

Magazine Publishers Association 575 Lexington Ave., New York, N.Y. 10022. (212) 752-0055. **Est.** 1919. **Members** 215.

Mystery Writers of America 17 E. 47 St., 6th Fl., New York, N.Y. 10017. (212) 888-8171. Professional and unpublished writers, agents, and publishers. **Est.** 1945. **Members** 2,400.

National Association of Science Writers P.O. Box 294, Greenlawn, N.Y. 11740. (516) 757-5664. Interprets science news for public; presents awards. **Est.** 1934. **Members** 1,630.

National Coalition Against Censorship 2 W. 64th Street, New York, N.Y. 10023. (212) 724-1500. **Est.** 1974. **Members** 42 non-profit organizations.

National Federation of Press Women 1105 Main St., Box 99, Blue Springs, Mo. 64013. (816) 229-1666. **Est.** 1937. **Members** 5,000.

National Press Club National Press Bldg., 529 14th St. NW, Washington, D.C. 20045. (202) 662-7500. Journalists from all media engaged in cultural and recreational activities. **Est.** 1908. **Members** 4,600.

National Writers Union 13 Astor Pl., 7th Fl., New York, N.Y. 10003. (212) 254-0279. Bargaining and other services for independent writers not represented by other unions. **Est.** 1983. **Members** 3,000.

Quill and Scroll Society School of Journalism, Univ. of Iowa, Iowa City, Iowa 52242. (319) 335-5795. Honors high school journalism students; provides information to professionals; and grants annual scholarships. **Est.** 1926. **Members** 1,000,000.

Science Fiction Writers of America P.O. Box 4236, West Columbia, S.C. 29171. **Tel.** N.A. Encourages public interest in science fiction; sponsors conferences and lectures. **Est.** 1965. **Members** 1,100.

Society of Professional Journalists 16 S. Jackson, Greencastle, Ind. 46135. (317) 653-3333. Runs seminars; offers internships; sponsors awards program. **Est.** 1909. **Members** 19,000.

Songwriters Guild of America 276 Fifth Ave., New York, N.Y. 10001. (212) 686-6820. Represents songwriters in negotiations with music publishers. **Est.** 1931. **Members** 4,000.

World Science Fiction Society P.O. Box 8442, Van Nuys, Calif. 91409. (818) 366-3827. National and regional meetings for professional and amateur writers; presents annual awards. **Est.** 1939. **Members** 10,000.

Writers Guild of America, East 555 W. 57th St., New York, N.Y. 10019. (212) 767-7800. Labor union for writers in fields of motion picture, TV, and radio. **Est.** 1954. **Members** 3,000.

Writers Guild of America, West 8955 Beverly Blvd., Los Angeles, Calif. 90048. (213) 550-1000. Labor union for writers in fields of motion picture, TV, and radio. **Est.** 1954. **Members** 6,600.

PART III THE WORLD

WORLD GEOGRAPHY

GLOSSARY OF GEOGRAPHICAL WORDS AND TERMS

(*Note:* See also Part IV: "Earth Sciences, Composition of the Earth.")

Altitude How high a place or a thing is, usually measured from sea level or from the surface of the land.
Archipelago A cluster of islands.
Arctic Circle An imaginary line drawn along approximately latitude 66½°N. The climate north of the Arctic Circle is very cold, and relatively few people live there.
Atoll A coral reef that partially or completely surrounds a lagoon.
Basin A portion of land that is lower than the surrounding area. Basins are created when vertical movement causes the Earth's crust to warp. Also, the area drained by a river and its tributaries.
Bay Part of an ocean, sea, or other body of water that extends inland. Bays are generally smaller than gulfs.
Bight A bay formed by a bend in the coastline.
Caldera A huge crater formed when the top of a volcano collapses or is exploded away.
Canyon A narrow, deep valley with steep sides. Many canyons have a river on their floor.
Continent A large unbroken land mass, distinguished from an island or peninsula. The seven continents are North America, South America, Europe, Asia, Africa, Australia, and Antarctica, though Europe and Asia are a continuous land mass divided along the spine of the Ural Mountains running south from the Arctic Ocean.
Continental drift theory The theory, proposed in 1915 by Alfred Wegener, that all of the continents used to be joined in one supercontinent, Pangaea. Some 200 million years ago, Pangaea began to break up, and the continents "drifted" through the oceans to their present locations. The continental drift theory has now largely been replaced by the plate tectonics theory.
Continental shelf The edge of a continent covered by shallow ocean water, up to about 100 fathoms (600 feet), beyond which is the continental slope, which descends to the deep-sea plain, about 13,000–20,000 feet (4,000–6,000 m).
Cove A small and sheltered bay or inlet. Also, a small valley in a mountain.
Crater The bowl-shaped depression at the top of a volcano. Also, the depression made when a meteorite hits the Earth. (See *Caldera.*)
Delta A triangular-shaped piece of land formed by sediment at the mouth of a river.
Desert (See "The Great Deserts.")
Dune A hill or ridge of sand that has been deposited by wind.
Equator An imaginary line that circles the Earth halfway between the Poles. The equator is at latitude 0°.
Equinox The two times during the year (on or about Mar. 21 and Sept. 23) when the sun's rays strike the equator vertically. At equinox, day and night are the same length everywhere in the world. (See *Solstice.*)
Erosion The gradual wearing away of the surface of the land. For example, soil is eroded by wind and water; rock is eroded by freezing and thawing.
Estuary A valley at the mouth of a river where fresh water and sea water mix. Estuaries are created either when the land sinks or when the sea level rises and are generally shaped like a funnel.
Fjord A long, narrow inlet of the ocean with steeply sloping sides.
Floodplain Flat, low-lying land along either side of a river that is subject to flooding.
Geyser A jet of hot water or steam periodically thrown up by a hot spring.
Glacier A large mass of slowly moving ice. Glaciers are formed on land when snow is compacted and recrystallizes.
Gorge An especially narrow and steep-walled canyon.
Gulf Part of an ocean or sea that extends inland. Gulfs are generally larger than bays.
Hemisphere One-half of the Earth's surface, whether divided latitudinally or longitudinally. For example, the Northern Hemisphere lies north of the equator, the Southern Hemisphere south of the equator. By convention, the Eastern Hemisphere consists of the continents of Europe, Asia, and Africa; the Western Hemisphere, of North America and South America.

WORLD AREA AND POPULATION BY SELECTED REGION

Region	Area: Square miles	Area: Square kilometers	Area: Percent of world total	Population (1992): Total ('000s)	Population (1992): Percent of total	Population (1992): Per square mile	Population (1992): Per square kilometer
World total[1]	**57,308,757**	**148,429,000**	**100.0%**	**5,420,391**	**100.0%**	**94.6**	**36.5**
Africa	11,687,188	30,269,680	20.4	654,600	12.1	56.0	21.6
Antarctica	5,100,023	13,209,000	8.9	(2)	(2)	(2)	(2)
Asia	17,176,102	44,485,900	30.0	3,317,800	61.2	193.2	74.6
Australia	3,035,651	7,862,300	5.2	17,800	0.3	5.8	2.3
Europe	4,065,945	10,530,750	7.1	684,400	12.6	168.3	65.0
North America	9,357,294	24,235,280	16.3	435,800	8.1	46.5	17.9
South America	6,880,638	17,820,770	8.9	299,900	5.5	43.6	16.8

1. Land only. 2. Antarctica has no indigenous population. **Source:** *National Geographic Atlas of the World* (1992).

THE CONTINENTS: HIGHEST AND LOWEST ELEVATIONS

Continent	Highest point	Location	Distance above sea level: Feet	Distance above sea level: Meters	Lowest point	Location	Distance below sea level: Feet	Distance below sea level: Meters
Asia	Mt. Everest	Nepal-China	29,028	8,848	Dead Sea	Israel, Jordan	1,312	400
S. America	Mt. Aconcagua	Argentina	22,834	6,960	Valdes Peninsula	Argentina	131	40
N. America	Mt. McKinley	U.S. (Alaska)	20,320	6,194	Death Valley	U.S. (California)	282	86
Africa	Mt. Kilimanjaro	Tanzania	19,340	5,895	Lake Assal	Djibouti	512	156
Europe	Mt. Elbrus	Russia	18,510	5,642	Caspian Sea	Russia, Kazakhstan	92	28
Antarctica	Vinson Massif	Ellsworth Mts.	16,066	4,897	Ice covered	—	8,327	2,538
Australia	Mt. Kosciusko	New South Wales	7,310	2,228	Lake Eyre	South Australia	52	16

Source: *National Geographic Atlas of the World* (1992).

OCEANS OF THE WORLD

Name	Area ('000s) Sq. mi.	Area ('000s) Sq km	Maximum depth Feet	Maximum depth Meters
Atlantic Ocean:	**31,830**	**82,440**	**30,246**	**9,219**
with marginal seas	41,100	106,460	—	—
Arctic Ocean	5,400	14,090	17,881	5,450
Caribbean Sea	1,063	2,754	25,197	7,680
Mediterranean Sea	967	2,505	16,470	5,020
Norwegian Sea	597	1,547	13,189	4,020
Gulf of Mexico	596	1,544	14,370	4,380
Hudson Bay	475	1,230	850	259
Greenland Sea	465	1,205	15,899	4,846
North Sea	222	575	2,170	659
Black Sea	178	461	7,360	2,237
Baltic Sea	163	422	1,440	437
Pacific Ocean:	**63,800**	**165,250**	**36,200**	**11,034**
with marginal seas	69,370	179,680	—	—
South China Sea	1,331	3,447	18,241	5,560
Sea of Okhotsk	610	1,580	11,063	3,372
Bering Sea	876	2,270	13,750	4,191
Sea of Japan	389	1,007	12,280	3,733
East China Sea	290	752	9,126	2,782
Yellow Sea	161	417	300	91
Indian Ocean:	**28,360**	**73,440**	**24,442**	**7,450**
with marginal seas	28,930	74,920	—	—
Arabian Sea	1,492	3,863	19,029	5,800
Bay of Bengal	839	2,172	17,251	5,258
Red Sea	169	438	7,370	2,240

Source: International Hydrographic Organization.

THE WORLD'S LARGEST ISLANDS

Island	Location	Flags	Area Sq. mi.	Area Sq km
Greenland	N. Atlantic Ocean	Denmark	840,000	2,175,600
New Guinea	S. Pacific Ocean	Indonesia, Papua New Guinea	306,000	792,540
Borneo	S. Pacific Ocean	Indonesia, Malaysia, Brunei	280,100	725,459
Madagascar	Indian Ocean	Madagascar	226,658	587,044
Baffin	Arctic Ocean	Canada	195,928	507,454
Sumatra	Indian Ocean, S. Pacific Ocean	Indonesia	165,000	427,350
Honshu	N. Pacific Ocean	Japan	87,805	227,415
Great Britain	N. Atlantic Ocean	United Kingdom	84,200	218,078
Victoria	Arctic Ocean	Canada	83,896	217,291
Ellesmere	Arctic Ocean	Canada	75,767	196,237
Celebes	Pacific Ocean	Indonesia	69,000	178,710
South Island	S. Pacific Ocean	New Zealand	58,305	151,010
Java	Indian Ocean, S. Pacific Ocean	Indonesia	48,900	126,651
Cuba	Caribbean Sea	Cuba	44,218	114,525
North Island	S. Pacific Ocean	New Zealand	44,035	114,051
Newfoundland	N. Atlantic Ocean	Canada	42,030	108,858
Luzon	N. Pacific Ocean	Philippines	40,880	105,879
Iceland	N. Atlantic Ocean	Iceland	39,769	103,002
Mindanao	N. Pacific Ocean	Philippines	36,775	95,247
Novaya Zemlya	Arctic Ocean	Russia	35,000	90,650
Ireland	N. Atlantic Ocean	Ireland, UK	32,599	84,431
Hokkaido	S. Pacific Ocean	Japan	30,144	78,073
Hispaniola	Caribbean Sea	Haiti, Dominican Republic	29,530	76,483
Sakhalin	N. Pacific Ocean	Russia	29,500	76,405
Banks	Arctic Ocean	Canada	27,033	70,015
Tasmania	S. Pacific Ocean	Australia	26,178	67,801
Sri Lanka	Indian Ocean	Sri Lanka	25,332	65,610
Devon	Arctic Ocean	Canada	21,331	55,247

Source: National Geographic Society.

Inlet An indentation in the shore of a sea, an ocean, or the bank of a river. Also, a narrow waterway that connects a lagoon to a larger body of water or that passes between two peninsulas.

Island A landmass completely surrounded by water.

Isthmus A narrow strip of land that connects two larger land masses.

Lagoon A shallow pool or pond completely, or almost completely, separated from the sea.

Lake A body of water, often of considerable size, surrounded by land.

Latitude and longitude Latitude is the angle (measured in degrees, minutes, and seconds) between a point on the Earth's surface north or south of the equator, the center of the Earth, and the equator (0°0'0" latitude). Longitude is the angle between a point on the Earth's surface, the center of the Earth, and the prime meridian (0°0'0" longitude). There are 90 degrees of latitude between the equator and each of the poles (shown on a globe as parallel horizontal lines). There are 360 degrees of longitude (shown as vertical lines) divided into 180° east and west of the prime meridian (180°E and 180°W are thus the same). Since 1884 Greenwich, England (near London), has been universally recognized as the point through which the prime meridian passes. A degree (°) is 1/360 of a circle, a minute (') 1/60 of a degree, and a second (") 1/60 of a minute.

Lava Magma that reaches the surface of the Earth and from which most of the gases have escaped. (See *Volcano.*)

Leeward The direction or side sheltered from the wind. (See *Windward.*)

Lithosphere The outer layer of the Earth composed of rock; about 50 miles thick.

Magma Molten rock that lies deep within the Earth. In a volcanic eruption, magma bursts through the outer surface of the Earth's crust. (See *Lava, Volcano.*)

Mountain Land that rises above its surroundings. Mountains are higher than hills. Older mountain ranges, like the Appalachians, are rounded because they are old and worn down; younger ranges, like the Andes or the Himalayas, have jagged peaks because they are still rising.

North Pole The northernmost point on the Earth, or the northern axis on which the Earth spins. The North Pole, at latitude 90°N, lies in the middle of the Arctic Circle.

Ocean (See "Oceans of the World.")

Peninsula A portion of land almost entirely surrounded by water.

Plain A large portion of level or rolling land that is treeless.

Plate tectonics theory The theory, first proposed in 1968, that the lithosphere is made up of some 20 sections, each of which consists of continental and ocean crust. The plates shift, moving continents, changing the size and shape of

MAJOR RIVERS OF THE WORLD, BY LENGTH

River	Length: Miles	Length: Km	Source	Outflow
Nile	4,145	6,673	Tributaries of Lake Victoria, E. Africa	Mediterranean Sea
Amazon	4,000	6,440	Andes Mts., Peru	Atlantic Ocean
Mississippi–Missouri	3,740[1]	6,021[1]	Confluence of Jefferson, Madison, and Galatin Rivers, Montana	Gulf of Mexico
Changjiang (Yangtze)	3,720	5,989	Kunlun Mts., China	China Sea
Yenisei–Angara	3,650[2]	5,877[2]	Lake Baikal, Russia	Kara Sea (Arctic)
Amur–Argun	3,590[2]	5,780[2]	Khingan Mts., China	Sea of Japan
Ob–Irtysh	3,360[2]	5,410[2]	Altai Mts., China	Gulf of Ob (Arctic)
Plata–Parana	3,030[2]	4,878[2]	Confluence of Paranaiba and Grande Rivers, Brazil	Atlantic Ocean
Huang He (Yellow)	2,903	4,674	Kunlun Mts., China	Yellow Sea
Congo (Zaire)	2,900	4,669	Confluence of Luapula and Lualaba Rivers, Zaire	Atlantic Ocean
Lena	2,730	4,395	Baikal Mts., Russia	Laptev Sea (Arctic)
MacKenzie	2,635[2]	4,242[2]	Headwaters of Finlay Rivers, British Columbia	Beaufort Sea (Arctic)
Mekong	2,600	4,186	T'ang-ku-la Mts.; Tibet	South China Sea
Niger	2,600	4,186	Guinea	Atlantic Ocean
Missouri	2,533	4,078	Confluence of Jefferson, Madison, and Galatin Rivers, Montana	Mississippi River
Mississippi	2,348[3]	3,780[3]	Lake Itasca, Minnesota	Gulf of Mexico
Murray–Darling	2,330	3,751	Great Dividing Range, Australia	Indian Ocean
Volga	2,290	3,687	Valdai Hills, Russia	Caspian Sea
Madeira	2,013	3,241	Confluence of Mamore and Beni Rivers, Bolivia/Brazil	Amazon River
Sao Francisco	1,988	3,201	Minas Gerais State, Brazil	Atlantic Ocean
Yukon	1,979	3,186	Confluence of Lewes and Pelly Rivers, Yukon Terr.	Bering Sea
Rio Grande	1,885	3,035	San Juan Mts., Colorado	Gulf of Mexico
Purus	1,860	2,995	Andes Mts., Peru	Amazon River
Tunguska, Lower	1,860	2,995	North of Lake Baikal, Russia	Yenesei River
Indus	1,800	2,898	Himalayas, Tibet	Arabian Sea
Danube	1,776	2,859	Confluence of Breg and Brigach Rivers, Germany	Black Sea
Brahmaputra	1,770	2,850	Himalayas, Tibet (China)	Ganges River
Salween	1,750	2,818	Tibetan Plateau, Tibet	Bay of Bengal
Para–Tocantins	1,710[2]	2,753[2]	Goias State, Brazil	Atlantic Ocean
Zambezi	1,700	2,737	Zambia	Indian Ocean
Paraguay	1,610	2,592	Mato Grosso State, Brazil	Parana River
Nelson–Saskatchewan	1,600	2,576	Rocky Mts., Canada	Hudson Bay
Amu Darya	1,578	2,541	Pamir Mts., Uzbekistan/Turkmenistan	Aral Sea
Ural	1,575	2,536	Ural Mts., Russia	Caspian Sea
Ganges	1,560	2,512	Himalayas, India	Bay of Bengal
Euphrates	1,510	2,431	Confluence of Murat Nehri and Kara Su Rivers, Turkey	Shatt-al-Arab
Arkansas	1,450	2,335	Colorado	Mississippi River
Colorado	1,450	2,335	Colorado	Gulf of California
Dnieper	1,420	2,286	Valdai Hills, Russia	Black Sea
Atchafalaya–Red	1,400	2,254	New Mexico	Gulf of Mexico
Syr Darya	1,370	2,206	Tien Shan, China/Kyrghyzstan	Aral Sea
Kasai	1,338	2,154	Angola	Congo (Zaire) River
Kolyma	1,320	2,130	Kolyma Mts., Russia	Arctic Ocean
Irrawaddy	1,300	2,093	Confluence of Mali and Nmai Rivers, Myanmar	Bay of Bengal
Ohio–Allegheny	1,300	2,093	Pennsylvania	Mississippi River
Orange	1,300	2,093	Lesotho	Atlantic Ocean
Orinoco	1,280	2,060	Sierra Parima Mts., Venezuela	Atlantic Ocean
Columbia	1,243	2,001	Columbia L., British Columbia	Pacific Ocean
Tigris	1,180	1,900	Turkey	Shatt-al-Arab
Rhine	820	1,320	Confluence of Hinterrhein and Vorderrhein Rivers, Switzerland	North Sea
St. Lawrence	800	1,288	L. Ontario	Gulf of St. Lawrence

1. From the mouth of the Mississippi up the Missouri to the Red Rock River in Montana. 2. Includes the length of tributaries that are part of the main trunk stream. 3. From the mouth of the Mississippi up to its source in Minnesota. **Source:** U.S. Dept. of Commerce, National Oceanic and Atmospheric Admin., *Principal Rivers and Lakes of the World* (1982).

oceans, causing earthquakes, and creating volcanos and mountains. The plate tectonics theory has largely replaced the continental drift theory.
Plateau A portion of land, generally large and with a level surface, that is sharply elevated above the surrounding land. Plateaus are created when vertical movement causes the Earth's crust to warp.
Pond A small body of water surrounded by land.
Prairie Level or rolling land generally covered with grasses, with few trees.
River A large stream.
Sahel The Arabic word for "shore," the Sahel is a dry region separating the Sahara desert from tropical West and Central Africa running from Senegal to the Sudan. The meager rainfall (4–8 in. per year) supports limited crops and grazing.
Savanna A portion of land in the tropics or subtropics with only scattered trees but whose grasses can survive with scant rainfall.
Sea A large body of salt water, generally considered smaller than an ocean.
Solstice The time when the sun's rays strike vertically the Tropic of Cancer or the Tropic of Capricorn. At solstice the daylight hours reach their maximum or minimum. In the Northern Hemisphere, the summer solstice occurs on or about June 22; that is the "longest day of the year" and signals the beginning of summer. The winter solstice occurs on or about Dec. 22; that is the "shortest day of the year" and signals the beginning of winter. In the Southern Hemisphere, the longest and shortest days of

MAJOR NATURAL LAKES OF THE WORLD

Lake	Surface area		Location	Maximum depth		Elevation	
	Sq. mi.	Sq km		Feet	Meters	Feet	Meters
Caspian Sea[1]	143,240	370,992	Russia, Kazakhstan, Azerbaijan, Turkmenistan, Iran	3,363	1,025	–92	–28
Superior	31,700	82,103	Ontario, Can.; Mich., Wis., Minn.	1,333	406	600	183
Victoria	26,820	69,464	Uganda, Kenya, Tanzania	279	85	3,720	1,134
Aral Sea[1]	24,904	64,501	Uzbekistan, Kazakhstan	220	67	174	53
Huron	23,000	59,570	Ontario, Can.; Mich.	750	229	576	176
Michigan	22,300	57,757	Mich., Ind., Ill., Wis.	923	281	579	176
Tanganyika	12,350	31,987	Burundi, Tanzania, Zambia, Zaire	4,800	1,463	2,543	775
Baikal	12,160	31,494	Russia	5,315	1,620	1,493	455
Great Bear	12,028	31,153	Northwest Terr., Can.	1,356	413	512	156
Nyasa (Malawi)	11,150	28,879	Tanzania, Mozambique, Malawi	2,280	695	1,550	472
Great Slave	11,030	28,568	Northwest Terr., Can.	2,015	614	513	156
Erie	9,910	25,667	Ontario, Can.; N.Y., Pa., Ohio, Mich.	210	64	570	174
Winnipeg	9,417	24,390	Manitoba, Can.	92	28	713	217
Ontario	7,540	19,529	Ontario, Can.; N.Y.	802	244	245	75
Balkhash[1]	7,115[2]	18,428[2]	Kazakhstan	87	27	1,115	340
Ladoga	6,835	17,703	Russia	755	230	13	4
Chad	6,300	16,317	Chad, Nigeria, Niger	36	11	787	240
Maracaibo[3]	5,200	13,468	Venezuela	115	35	sea level	sea level
Patos[3]	3,920	10,153	Brazil	15	5	(4)	(4)
Onega	3,720	9,635	Russia	394	120	108	33
Titicaca	3,200	8,288	Bolivia, Peru	990	302	12,500	3,810
Nicaragua	3,150	8,159	Nicaragua	230	70	102	31
Mai-Ndombe	3,100[2]	8,029[2]	Zaire	36	11	1,116	340
Athabasca	3,064	7,936	Saskatchewan, Alberta, Can.	407	124	700	213
Eyre[1]	2,970[2]	7,692[2]	Australia	4	1	–52	–16
Reindeer	2,568	6,651	Saskatchewan, Manitoba, Can.	720	219	1,106	337
Tonle Sap	2,500[2]	6,475[2]	Cambodia	39	12	(4)	(4)
Rudolf[1]	2,473	6,405	Kenya, Ethiopia	240	73	1,401	427
Issyk-Kul[1]	2,355	6,099	Kyrghyzstan	2,303	702	5,279	1,609
Torrens[1]	2,230[2]	5,776[2]	Australia	0.5	0.2	92	28
Albert	2,160	5,594	Uganda, Zaire	168	51	2,030	619
Vanern	2,156	5,581	Sweden	325	99	144	44
Nettilling	2,140	5,543	Baffin Is., Can.	(4)	(4)	95	29
Winnipegosis	2,075	5,374	Manitoba, Can.	39	12	830	253
Bangweulu	1,930	4,999	Zambia	16	5	3,500	1,067
Nipigon	1,872	4,848	Ontario, Can.	541	165	1,050	320
Gairdner[1]	1,840[2]	4,763[2]	Australia	0.5	0.2	112	34
Urmia[1]	1,815[2]	4,701[2]	Iran	49	15	4,180	1,274
Manitoba	1,800	4,662	Manitoba, Can.	92	28	813	248
Kyoga	1,710	4,429	Uganda	26	8	3,400	1,036
Khanka	1,700	4,403	China, Russia	33	10	226	69
Lake of the Woods	1,695	4,390	Minn.; Ontario, Manitoba, Can.	69	21	1,060	323
Great Salt[1]	1,680	4,351	Utah	48	15	4,200	1,280
Mweru	1,680	4,351	Zambia, Zaire	10	3	3,008	917
Peipus	1,660	4,299	Estonia, Russia	41	12	98	30
Koko Nor (Tsing Hai)	1,650	4,274	China	125	38	10,515	3,205
Dubawnt	1,600	4,144	Northwest Terr., Can.	(4)	(4)	774	236
Tung-t'ing Hu	1,430[2]	3,704[2]	China	(4)	(4)	36	11
Van Golu[1]	1,420	3,678	Turkey	82	25	5,643	1,720
Tana	1,390	3,600	Ethiopia	30	9	6,003	1,830

1. Saltwater. A lake is a body of water surrounded by land; the Caspian Sea is thus a lake. It was called a sea by the Romans because of its salty water. 2. Subject to large seasonal variation in surface area. 3. Lagoon. 4. No information available. **Source:** U.S. National Oceanic and Atmospheric Administration, *Principal Rivers and Lakes of the World* (1982).

the year occur on Dec. 22 and June 22, respectively. (See *Equinox.*)

Sound A body of water that separates an island from the mainland, or that connects two oceans, seas, or other bodies of water. Sounds are generally long and narrow.

South Pole The southernmost point on the Earth, or the southern axis on which the Earth spins. The South Pole, at latitude 90°S, lies in the middle of the Antarctic Circle.

Steppe A portion of land with little rainfall, extreme temperature variations, and drought-resistant vegetation.

Strait A narrow body of water that connects two large bodies of water.

Stream Any body of running water that flows on or under the surface of the Earth. Brooks and creeks are small streams; rivers are large streams.

Swamp A portion of wet, waterlogged, or flooded land.

Tide The rise and fall of the surface of the ocean and of bays, gulfs, and other bodies of water connected to the ocean. Tides are caused by the gravitational pull of the moon, which passes over the same meridian of the Earth about once every 24 hours and 50 minutes. The length of time between successive high (or low) tides is about 12 hours and 25 minutes.

Tributary A stream or river that flows into a larger stream or river.

Tropic of Cancer Latitude 23½°N, which marks the northernmost limit of the sun's vertical rays. The area between the Tropic of Cancer and the Tropic of Capricorn is known as the "tropics." (See *Equinox.*)

Tropic of Capricorn Latitude 23½°S, which marks the southernmost limit of the sun's vertical rays.

Tundra An area of treeless plain near or above the Arctic Circle. Tundra subsoil is permanently frozen, but the soil thaws enough to support the growth of mosses, lichens, and some small flowering shrubs.

Valley A long and sometimes narrow depression on the surface of the Earth, usually between two mountain ridges or ranges.

Volcano A mountain formed by lava and/or other materials that have burst forth from deep within the Earth. (See *Caldera, Lava, Magma.*)

Windward The direction or side facing the wind.

OCEANS OF THE WORLD

The water of the world's oceans covers more than 70 percent of the world's surface. While for many years the so-called World Ocean was divided into five parts—the Pacific, Atlantic, Indian, Arctic, and Antarctic—scientists today commonly recognize only the first three as separate and distinct oceans. The Arctic and Antarctic, as well as other large bodies of water such as the Caribbean Sea, the Gulf of Mexico, Hudson Bay, the Mediterranean and Black Seas, and the South China Sea are termed marginal seas. The International Hydrographic Organization identifies 66 seas, gulfs, bays, bights, straits, channels, and passages, many of which are further subdivided. For instance, the Mediterranean Sea is divided into western and eastern basins, and the western basin is subdivided into the Strait of Gibraltar, the Balearic Sea, Ligurian Sea, Tyrrhenian Sea, Ionian Sea, Adriatic Sea, and Aegean Sea. The accompanying table gives the area and maximum depths of the world's three major oceans and selected marginal seas.

THE WORLD'S HIGHEST MOUNTAIN PEAKS

Mountain peak	Range	Location	Height Feet	Height Meters
Everest	Himalayas	Nepal–China	29,028	8,848
K2 (Godwin Austen)	Karakoram	Kashmir	28,250	8,611
Kanchenjunga	Himalayas	Nepal–India	28,208	8,598
Lhotse I	Himalayas	Nepal–China	27,923	8,511
Makalu I	Himalayas	Nepal–China	27,824	8,481
Lhotse II	Himalayas	Nepal–China	27,560	8,400
Dhaulagiri	Himalayas	Nepal	26,810	8,172
Manaslu I	Himalayas	Nepal	26,760	8,156
Cho Oyu	Himalayas	Nepal–China	26,750	8,153
Nanga Parbat	Himalayas	Kashmir	26,660	8,126
Annapurna	Himalayas	Nepal	26,504	8,078
Gasherbrum	Karakoram	Kashmir	26,470	8,068
Broad	Karakoram	Kashmir	26,400	8,047
Gosainthan	Himalayas	China	26,287	8,012
Annapurna II	Himalayas	Nepal	26,041	7,937
Gyachung Kang	Himalayas	Nepal–China	25,910	7,897
Disteghil Sar	Karakoram	Kashmir	25,858	7,882
Himalchuli	Himalayas	Nepal	25,801	7,864
Nuptse	Himalayas	Nepal–China	25,726	7,841
Masherbrum	Karakoram	Kashmir	25,660	7,821
Nanda Devi	Himalayas	India	25,645	7,817
Rakaposhi	Karakoram	Kashmir	25,550	7,788
Kanjut Sar	Karakoram	Kashmir	25,461	7,761
Kamet	Himalayas	India–China	25,447	7,756
Namcha Barwa	Himalayas	China	25,445	7,756
Kua-la-man-ta-t'a (Gurla Mandhata)	Himalayas	China	25,355	7,728
Wu-lu-k'o-mu-shih (Ulugh Muztagh)	Kunlun	China	25,340	7,724
Kung-ko-erh (Kungur)	Mu-ssu-t'a-ko-a-t'e (Muztagh Ata)	China	25,325	7,719
Tirich Mir	Hindu Kush	Pakistan	25,230	7,690
Saser Kangri	Karakoram	Kashmir	25,172	7,672
Makalu II	Himalayas	Nepal–China	25,120	7,657
Minya Konka (Gonggashan)	Daxue Shan	China	24,900	7,590
Kula Kangri	Himalayas	Bhutan–China	24,784	7,554
Chang-tzu	Himalayas	Nepal–China	24,780	7,553
Mu-ssu-t'a-ko-a-t'e (Muztagh Ata)	Mu-ssu-t'a-ko-a-t'e (Muztagh Ata)	China	24,757	7,546
Skyang Kangri	Himalayas	Kashmir	24,750	7,544
Communism Peak	Pamirs	Tajikistan	24,590	7,495
Jongsong Peak	Himalayas	Nepal–India	24,472	7,459
Pobeda Peak	Tien Shan	Kyrghyzstan–China	24,406	7,439
Sia Kangri	Himalayas	Kashmir	24,350	7,422
Haramosh Peak	Karakoram	Kashmir	24,270	7,397
Istoro Nal	Hindu Kush	Pakistan	24,240	7,388
Tent Peak	Himalayas	Nepal–India	24,165	7,365
Chomo Lhari	Himalayas	Bhutan–China	24,040	7,327
Chamlang	Himalayas	Nepal	24,012	7,319
Kabru	Himalayas	Nepal–India	24,002	7,316
Alung Gangri	Himalayas	China	24,000	7,315
Baltoro Kangri	Himalayas	Kashmir	23,990	7,312
Muztagh Ata	Kunlun	China	23,890	7,282
Mana	Himalayas	India	23,860	7,273
Baruntse	Himalayas	Nepal	23,688	7,220
Nepal Peak	Himalayas	Nepal–India	23,500	7,163
Amne Machin	Kunlun	China	23,490	7,160
Gauri Sankar	Himalayas	Nepal–China	23,440	7,145
Badrinath	Himalayas	India	23,420	7,138
Nunkun	Himalayas	Kashmir	23,410	7,135
Lenin Peak	Pamirs	Tajikistan	23,405	7,134
Pyramid	Himalayas	Nepal–India	23,400	7,132
Api	Himalayas	Nepal	23,399	7,132
Pauhunri	Himalayas	India–China	23,385	7,128
Trisul	Himalayas	India	23,360	7,120
Korzhenevski Peak	Pamirs	Tajikistan	23,310	7,105
Kangto	Himalayas	India–China	23,260	7,090
Nyainqentanglha	Nyainqentanglha Shan	China	23,255	7,088
Trisuli	Himalayas	India	23,210	7,074
Dunagiri	Himalayas	India	23,184	7,066
Revolution Peak	Pamirs	Tajikistan	22,880	6,974
Aconcagua	Andes	Argentina	22,834	6,960
Ojos del Salado	Andes	Argentina–Chile	22,572	6,880
Bonete	Andes	Argentina	22,546	6,872
Tupungato	Andes	Argentina–Chile	22,310	6,800
Moscow Peak	Pamirs	Tajikistan	22,260	6,785
Pissis	Andes	Argentina	22,241	6,779
Mercedario	Andes	Argentina	22,211	6,770
Huascaran	Andes	Peru	22,205	6,768
Llullaillaco	Andes	Argentina–Chile	22,057	6,723
El Libertador	Andes	Argentina	22,047	6,720
Cachi	Andes	Argentina	22,047	6,720
Kailas	Himalayas	China	22,027	6,714
Incahuasi	Andes	Argentina–Chile	21,720	6,620
Yerupaja	Andes	Peru	21,709	6,617
Kurumda	Pamirs	Tajikistan	21,686	6,610
Galan	Andes	Argentina	21,654	6,600
El Muerto	Andes	Argentina–Chile	21,457	6,540
Sajama	Andes	Bolivia	21,391	6,520
Nacimiento	Andes	Argentina	21,302	6,493
Illimani	Andes	Bolivia	21,201	6,462
Coropuna	Andes	Peru	21,083	6,426
Laudo	Andes	Argentina	20,997	6,400
Ancohuma	Andes	Bolivia	20,958	6,388
Ausangate	Andes	Peru	20,945	6,384
Toro	Andes	Argentina–Chile	20,932	6,380
Illampu	Andes	Bolivia	20,873	6,362
Tres Cruces	Andes	Argentina–Chile	20,853	6,356
Huandoy	Andes	Peru	20,852	6,356
Parinacota	Andes	Bolivia–Chile	20,768	6,330
Tortolas	Andes	Argentina–Chile	20,745	6,323
Ampato	Andes	Peru	20,702	6,310
El Condor	Andes	Argentina	20,669	6,300
Salcantay	Andes	Peru	20,574	6,271
Chimborazo	Andes	Ecuador	20,561	6,267
Huancarhuas	Andes	Peru	20,531	6,258
Famatina[1]	Andes	Argentina	20,505	6,250
Pumasillo	Andes	Peru	20,492	6,246
Solo	Andes	Argentina	20,492	6,246
Polleras	Andes	Argentina	20,456	6,235
Pular	Andes	Chile	20,423	6,225
Chani	Andes	Argentina	20,341	6,200
McKinley	Alaska	U.S. (Alaska)	20,320	6,194
Aucanquilcha	Andes	Chile	20,295	6,186
Juncal	Andes	Argentina–Chile	20,276	6,180
Negro	Andes	Argentina	20,184	6,152
Quela	Andes	Argentina	20,128	6,135
Condoriri	Andes	Bolivia	20,095	6,125
Palermo	Andes	Argentina	20,079	6,120
Solimana	Andes	Peru	20,068	6,117
San Juan	Andes	Argentina–Chile	20,049	6,111
(Sierra) Nevada	Andes	Argentina–Chile	20,023	6,103
Antofalla	Andes	Argentina	20,013	6,100
Marmolejo	Andes	Argentina–Chile	20,013	6,100

Note: Mountains over 20,000 feet. 1. Formerly General Manuel Belgrano. **Source:** National Geographic Society.

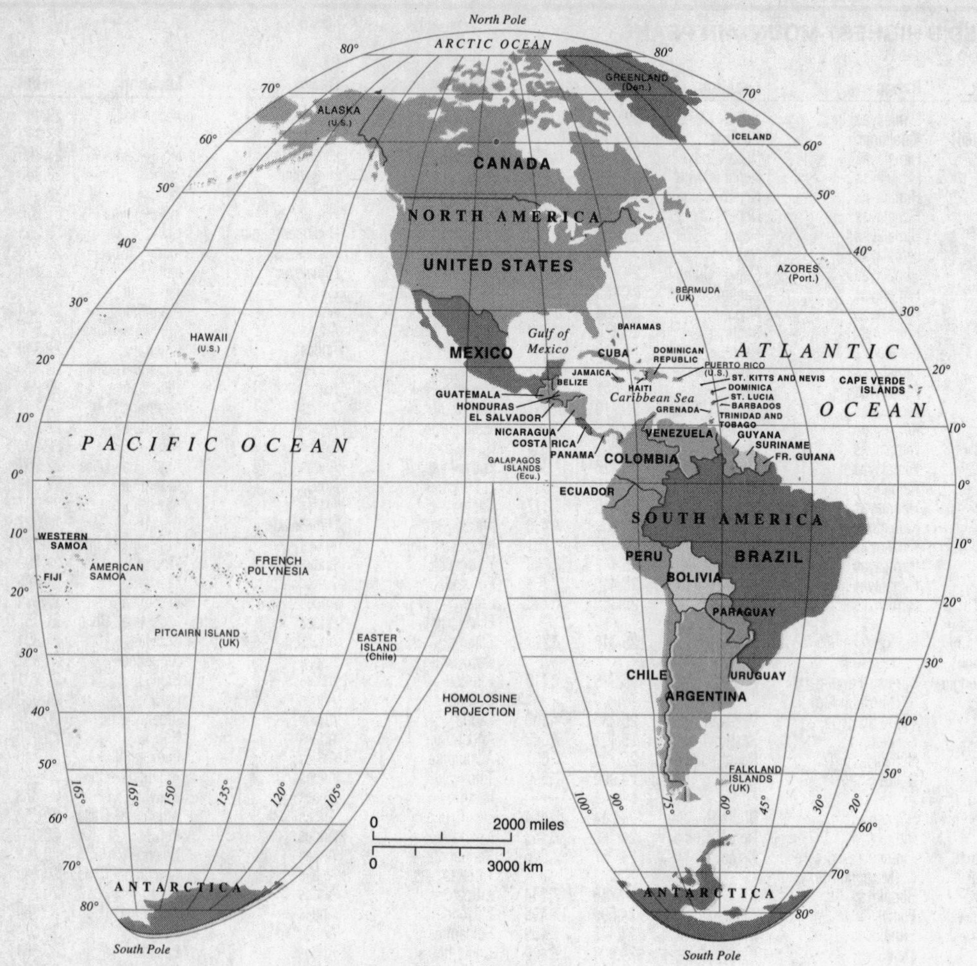

THE WORLD: WESTERN HEMISPHERE

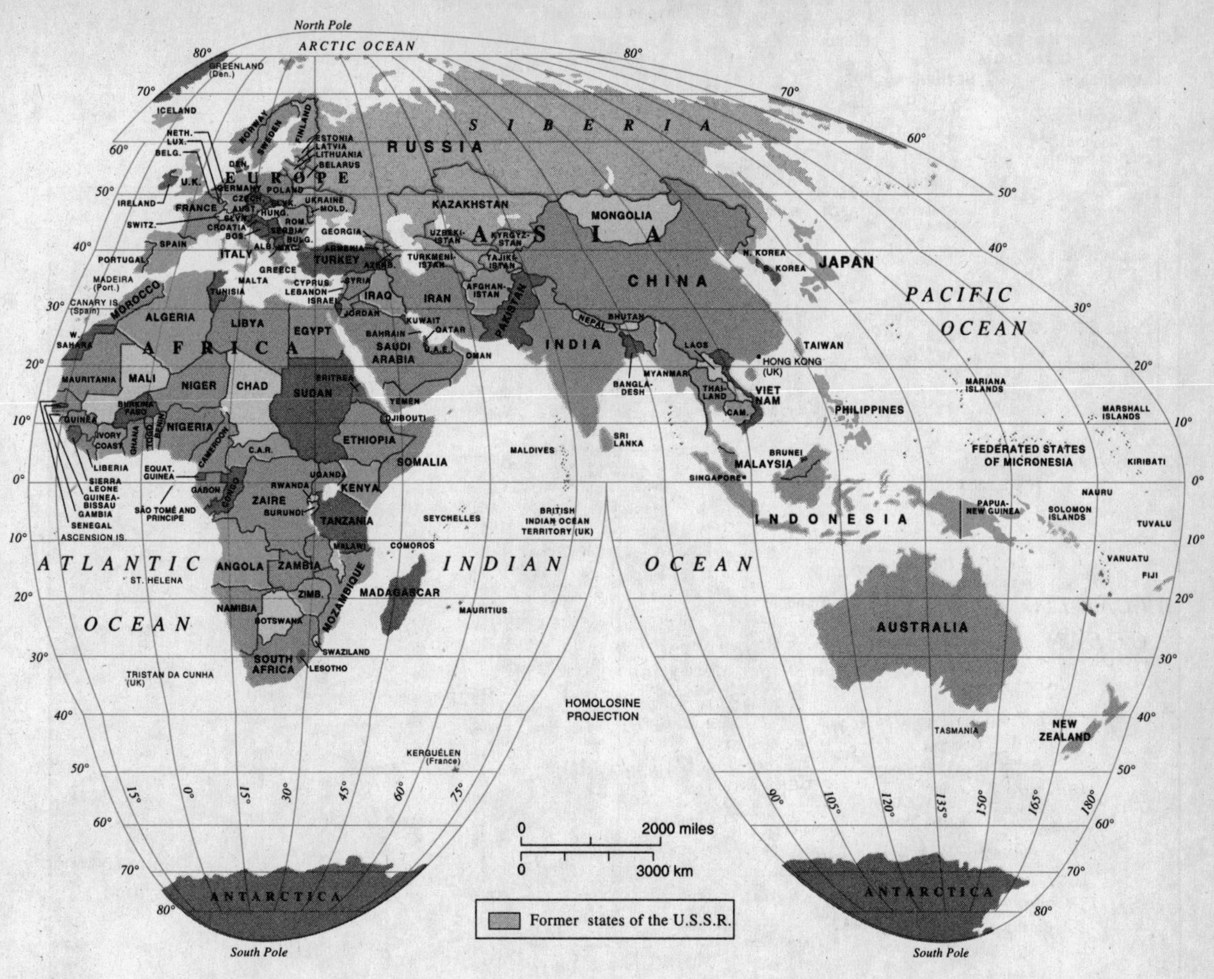

THE WORLD: EASTERN HEMISPHERE

DENMARK
SWEDEN
LITHUANIA
Liverpool
North Sea
Copenhagen
Baltic Sea
UNITED KINGDOM
Hamburg
RUSSIA
Gdansk
Birmingham
NETHERLANDS
Elbe
Vistula
Amsterdam
Berlin
Oder
London
Warsaw
English Channel
Antwerp
GERMANY
Lodz
Channel Islands
Brussels
Dusseldorf
Köln
Leipzig
BELGIUM
Bonn
Dresden
POLAND
Seine
LUXEMBOURG
Luxembourg
Frankfurt
Prague
Paris
CZECH REPUBLIC
Krakow
Nantes
Strasbourg
Rhine
Danube
SLOVAKIA
Yonne
Loire
LIECHTENSTEIN
Munich
Bratislava
Zürich
Vienna
FRANCE
SWITZERLAND
Vaduz
AUSTRIA
Debrecen
Bern
Graz
Budapest
Lyon
Geneva
Bordeaux
SLOVENIA
HUNGARY
Rhône
Milan
ITALY
Trieste
Ljubljana
Zagreb
ROMANIA
Venice
CROATIA
YUGO.
ARCTIC OCEAN
Kara Sea
70°
Novaya Zemlaya
Barents Sea
0
500 miles
750 km
North Cape
Arctic Circle
Reykjavik
ICELAND
Murmansk
30°
60°
Prime Meridian
White Sea
URAL MOUNTAINS
Archangel
Norwegian Sea
FAEROE ISLANDS (Den.)
Gulf of Bothnia
ATLANTIC OCEAN
Trondheim
FINLAND
Ekaterinburg
Shetland Islands
L. Oneza
Orkney Islands
NORWAY
Tammerfors
Bergen
SWEDEN
L. Ladoga
Oslo
Helsinki
St. Petersburg
20°
Tallinn
Gulf of Finland
Stockholm
ESTONIA
Volga River
North Sea
Glasgow
Göteborg
Nizhny Novgorod
Belfast
Edinburgh
Ålborg
LATVIA
Baltic Sea
Riga
Moscow
IRELAND
DENMARK
Dublin
UNITED KINGDOM
LITHUANIA
Cork
Copenhagen
50°
Vilnius
RUSSIA
Hamburg
Minsk
Birmingham
Gdansk
BELARUS
NETHERLANDS
Amsterdam
KAZAKHSTAN
London
Warsaw
Berlin
Channel Islands (U.K.)
GERMANY
Kiev
Kharkov
Brussels
BELGIUM
POLAND
Brest
Prague
LUXEMBOURG
Dnepropetrovsk
Paris
Danube
CZECH REP.
UKRAINE
Dnieper River
Nantes
SLOVAKIA
Munich
Bratislava
LIECHT.
Vienna
HUNGARY
MOLDOVA
Sea of Azov
Bay of Biscay
SWITZERLAND
Bern
AUSTRIA
Budapest
Kishinev
Caspian Sea
Lyon
Ljubljana
SLOVENIA
Odessa
Venice
ROMANIA
Bilbao
FRANCE
Zagreb
Milan
Trieste
Belgrade
Bucharest
Porto
Douro
Ebro
Marseilles
BOSNIA HERZ.
Constanta
Black Sea
GEORGIA
Tbilisi
Baku
40°
CROATIA
PORTUGAL
ANDORRA
MONACO
SAN MARINO
Sarajevo
YUGOSLAVIA
Varna
ARMENIA
Andorra
Danube River
BULGARIA
Yerevan
Lisbon
Madrid
Corsica
Rome
Adriatic Sea
Sofia
Barcelona
VATICAN CITY
Skopje
AZERBAIJAN
Tagus
Istanbul
SPAIN
ITALY
MACEDONIA
IRAN
Tiranë
Ankara
L. Van
10°
Seville
Palma
Naples
ALBANIA
Thessaloniki
Bursa
Balearic Islands
Sardinia
Tyrrhenian Sea
Aegean Sea
TURKEY
GIBRALTAR (UK)
Strait of Gibraltar
Palermo
Ionian Sea
Patras
Izmir
Adana
Athens
Sicily
Nicosia
SYRIA
MOROCCO
MALTA
GREECE
Crete
ALGERIA
Valletta
LEBANON
IRAQ
TRIMETRIC PROJECTION
TUNISIA
Mediterranean
Sea
CYPRUS
ISRAEL
0°
10°
20°
30°
40°

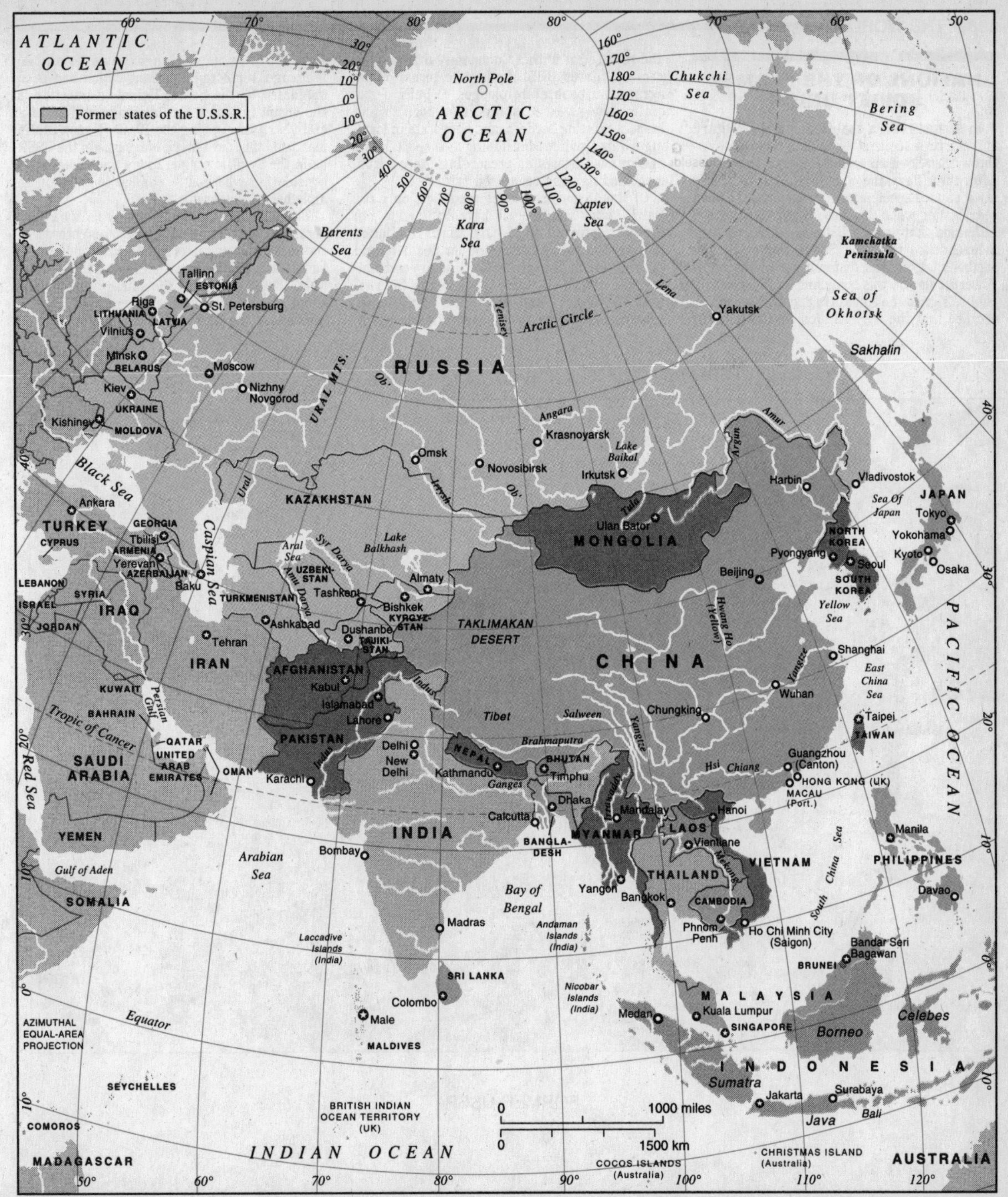
ATLANTIC OCEAN
Former states of the U.S.S.R.
North Pole
ARCTIC OCEAN
Chukchi Sea
Bering Sea
Barents Sea
Kara Sea
Laptev Sea
Kamchatka Peninsula
Sea of Okhotsk
Sakhalin
Lena
Yakutsk
Yenisey
Arctic Circle
Tallinn
ESTONIA
Riga
LATVIA
LITHUANIA
St. Petersburg
Vilnius
Minsk
BELARUS
Moscow
Nizhny Novgorod
URAL MTS.
RUSSIA
Ob'
Kiev
UKRAINE
Kishinev
MOLDOVA
Angara
Krasnoyarsk
Lake Baikal
Irkutsk
Amur
Argun
Omsk
Novosibirsk
Irtysh
Harbin
Vladivostok
JAPAN
Sea Of Japan
Tokyo
Yokohama
Kyoto
Osaka
Black Sea
Ankara
TURKEY
CYPRUS
GEORGIA
Tbilisi
ARMENIA
Yerevan
AZERBAIJAN
Baku
Caspian Sea
Ural
KAZAKHSTAN
Tula
Ulan Bator
MONGOLIA
Aral Sea
Syr Darya
Lake Balkhash
UZBEKISTAN
Amu Darya
Almaty
Tashkent
Bishkek
KYRGYZSTAN
TURKMENISTAN
Ashkabad
Dushanbe
TAJIKISTAN
TAKLIMAKAN DESERT
NORTH KOREA
Pyongyang
Seoul
SOUTH KOREA
Beijing
Hwang Ho (Yellow)
Yellow Sea
LEBANON
SYRIA
ISRAEL
IRAQ
JORDAN
Tehran
IRAN
AFGHANISTAN
Kabul
Islamabad
Lahore
Indus
CHINA
Shanghai
East China Sea
Yangtze
Wuhan
PACIFIC OCEAN
KUWAIT
Persian Gulf
BAHRAIN
Tropic of Cancer
QATAR
UNITED ARAB EMIRATES
OMAN
SAUDI ARABIA
Red Sea
PAKISTAN
Karachi
Delhi
New Delhi
NEPAL
Kathmandu
Ganges
Tibet
Salween
Brahmaputra
BHUTAN
Timphu
Chungking
Taipei
TAIWAN
Hsi Chiang
Guangzhou (Canton)
HONG KONG (UK)
MACAU (Port.)
Dhaka
Calcutta
BANGLADESH
Irrawaddy
Mandalay
MYANMAR
Hanoi
LAOS
Vientiane
Mekong
VIETNAM
South China Sea
Manila
PHILIPPINES
YEMEN
Gulf of Aden
SOMALIA
Arabian Sea
Bombay
INDIA
Bay of Bengal
Yangon
Bangkok
THAILAND
CAMBODIA
Phnom Penh
Ho Chi Minh City (Saigon)
Davao
Madras
Laccadive Islands (India)
Andaman Islands (India)
Bandar Seri Bagawan
BRUNEI
SRI LANKA
Colombo
Nicobar Islands (India)
MALAYSIA
Kuala Lumpur
Medan
SINGAPORE
Celebes
Borneo
Equator
Male
MALDIVES
AZIMUTHAL EQUAL-AREA PROJECTION
INDONESIA
Sumatra
Jakarta
Surabaya
Java
Bali
SEYCHELLES
BRITISH INDIAN OCEAN TERRITORY (UK)
0 1000 miles
0 1500 km
COMOROS
INDIAN OCEAN
CHRISTMAS ISLAND (Australia)
COCOS ISLANDS (Australia)
MADAGASCAR
AUSTRALIA

ASIA

NATIONS OF THE FORMER SOVIET UNION

In August 1991, a coalition of KGB, military, and party leaders attempted a coup to overthrow then-Soviet president Mikhail Gorbachev. After three days, the coup failed, but the disarray it caused accelerated a demise that began a year earlier, when the three Baltic Republics—Lithuania, Latvia, and Estonia—declared their independence from the Soviet Union. By December of 1991, the dismantling of the once-powerful empire was complete, as 11 former republics signed the Alma-Ata declaration, which decreed that the Soviet Union ceased to exist, and replaced it with a Commonwealth of Independent States (CIS). Under the terms of the agreement, each state pledged to build democratic, law-governed states, to recognize and respect existing borders, and cooperate in forming foreign policy, developing transport links, and in such issues as preserving the environment and fighting organized crime.

Of the 15 former Soviet republics, only the Baltic states and Georgia have declined to join the CIS. However, all 15 have joined the United Nations and the Organization for Security and Cooperation in Europe (OSCE) and are completing the formal procedures to join the International Monetary Fund (IMF) and World Bank. A major change for each country is the establishment of its native language as its official language, replacing Russian, which had been mandated by the Soviet Union. In question is the script in which the language will be officially written. During the 1940s, Joseph Stalin mandated that most major languages in the USSR be in the Cyrillic script. Today, each country is considering whether to change to the Roman alphabet or the Arabic script.

The map below shows the new national borders. Economic and demographic, and other statistics as well as histories of each country can be found in the section "Nations of the World." **Note:** The spelling of the name of each new country is as officially registered by the government at the United Nations.

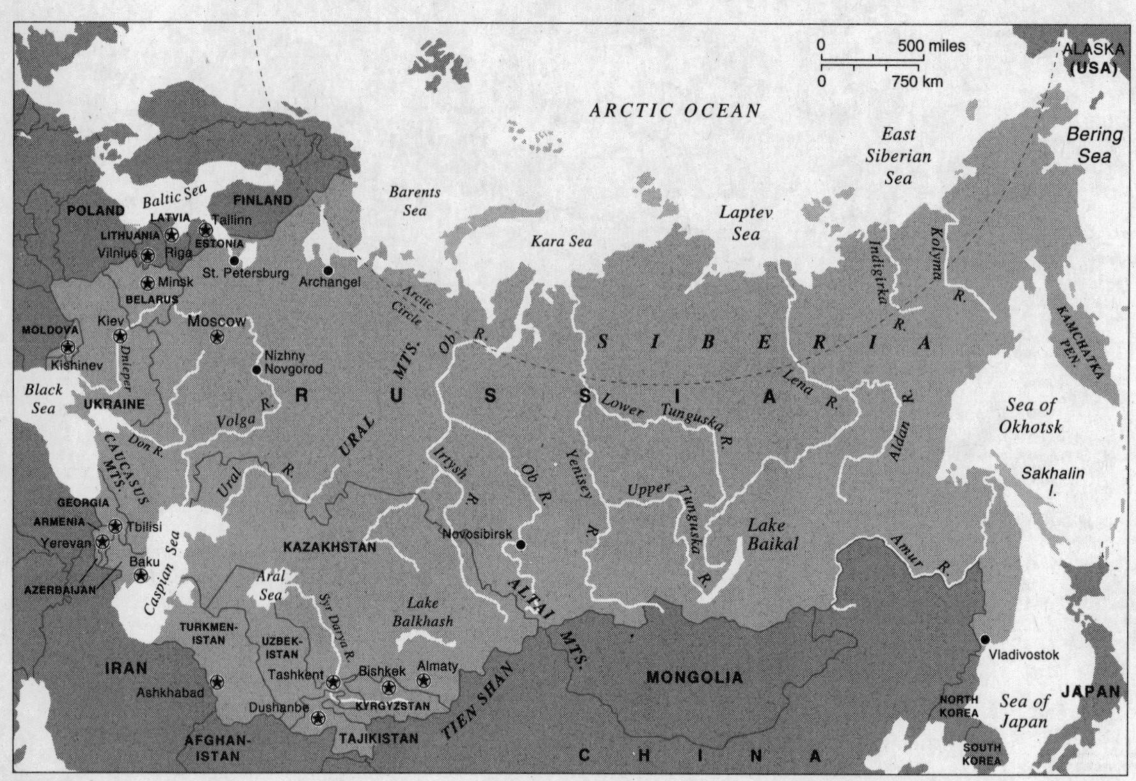

FORMER USSR

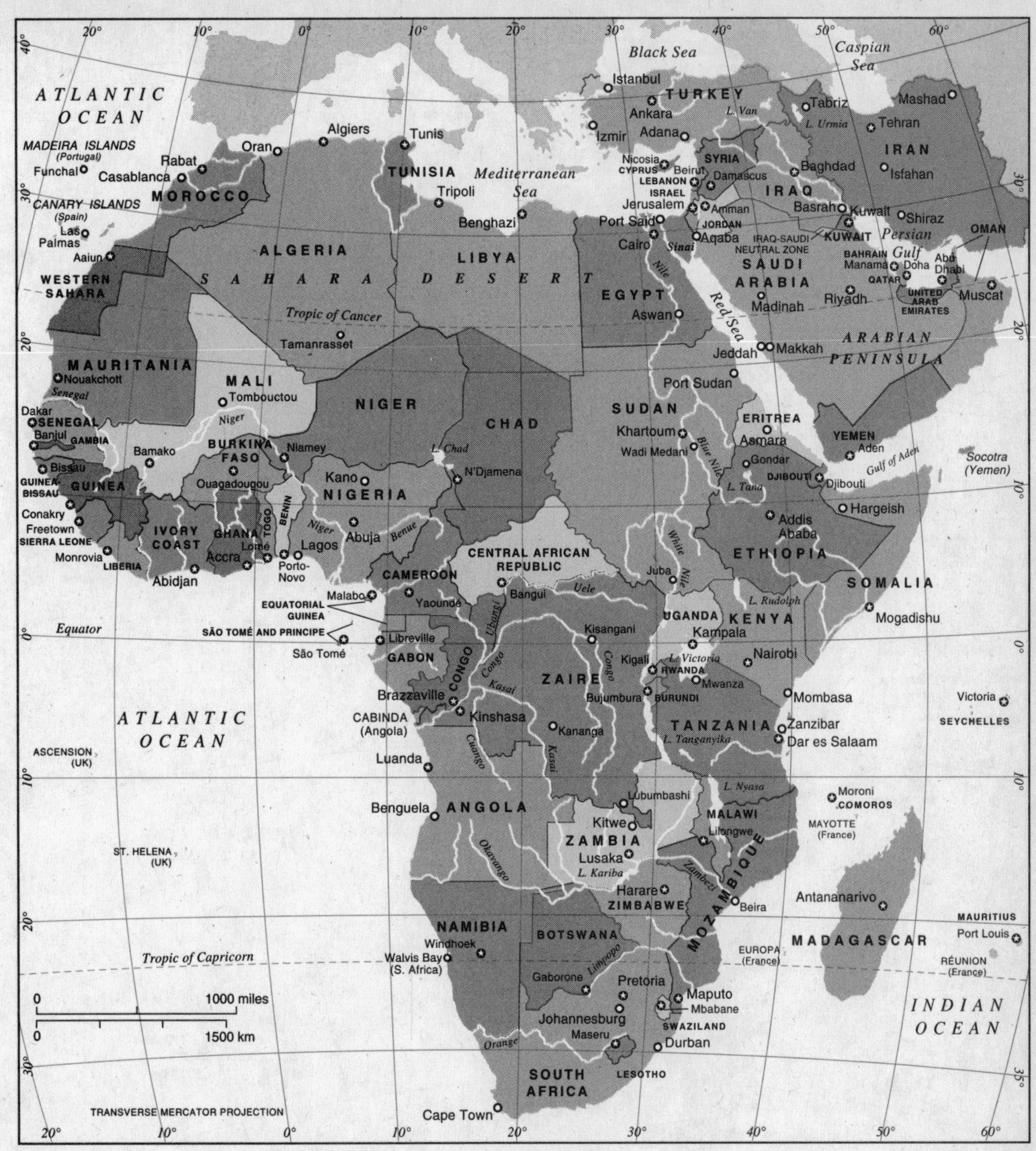

AFRICA AND MIDDLE EAST

Caribbean Sea
NICARAGUA
COSTA RICA
PANAMA
Panama Canal
NETHERLANDS ANTILLES (Neth.)
GRENADA
ST. VINCENT
TRINIDAD AND TOBAGO
Barranquilla
Maracaibo
Caracas
Orinoco
VENEZUELA
Georgetown
GUYANA
Paramaribo
SURINAME
Cayenne
FRENCH GUIANA (France)
ATLANTIC OCEAN
Medellín
Bogotá
Cali
COLOMBIA
Equator
Quito
ECUADOR
Guayaquil
Iquitos
Manaus
Amazon
Belém
Xingu
Fortaleza
PERU
BRAZIL
Recife
São Francisco
Callao
Lima
Cuzco
Salvador
PACIFIC OCEAN
Lake Titicaca
La Paz
Arequipa
Brasília
BOLIVIA
Sucre
Iquique
PARAGUAY
Concepcíon
Rio de Janeiro
São Paulo
Tropic of Capricorn
Asunción
SAN FÉLIX (Chile)
Paraná
Uruguay
Salto
Rosario
URUGUAY
ISLAS DE JUAN FERNANDEZ (Chile)
Valparaíso
Santiago
Montevideo
Buenos Aires
Río de la Plata
ATLANTIC OCEAN
Mar del Plata
CHILE
ARGENTINA
0 500 miles
0 750 km
FALKLAND ISLANDS (UK)
Stanley
Punta Arenas
Cape Horn
AZIMUTHAL PROJECTION
SOUTH GEORGIA ISLANDS (UK)
80°
70°
60°
50°
40°
10°
0°
20°
30°
100°
90°

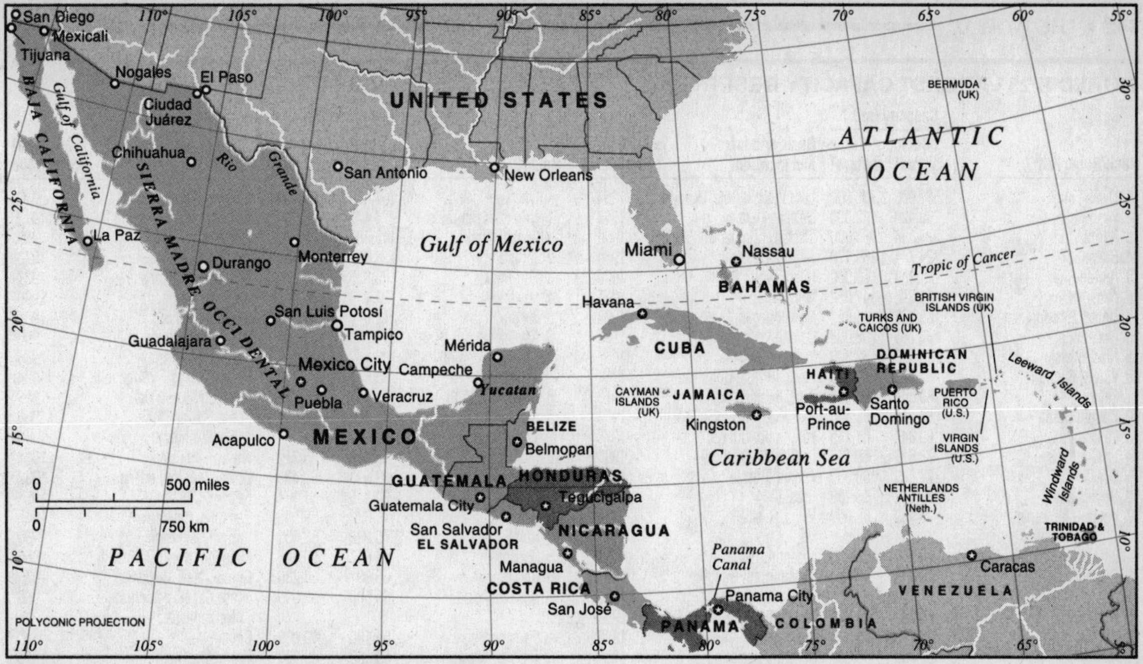

San Diego
Mexicali
Tijuana
Nogales
El Paso
Ciudad Juárez
BAJA CALIFORNIA
Gulf of California
Chihuahua
Rio Grande
SIERRA MADRE OCCIDENTAL
UNITED STATES
San Antonio
New Orleans
ATLANTIC OCEAN
BERMUDA (UK)
La Paz
Durango
Monterrey
Gulf of Mexico
Miami
Nassau
Tropic of Cancer
BAHAMAS
San Luis Potosí
Tampico
Havana
BRITISH VIRGIN ISLANDS (UK)
TURKS AND CAICOS (UK)
Guadalajara
Mérida
CUBA
DOMINICAN REPUBLIC
HAITI
Leeward Islands
Mexico City
Campeche
Puebla
Veracruz
Yucatan
CAYMAN ISLANDS (UK)
JAMAICA
Port-au-Prince
Santo Domingo
PUERTO RICO (U.S.)
Kingston
VIRGIN ISLANDS (U.S.)
Acapulco
MEXICO
BELIZE
Belmopan
Caribbean Sea
Windward Islands
GUATEMALA
HONDURAS
Guatemala City
Tegucigalpa
NETHERLANDS ANTILLES (Neth.)
0 500 miles
0 750 km
San Salvador
EL SALVADOR
NICARAGUA
TRINIDAD & TOBAGO
PACIFIC OCEAN
Managua
Panama Canal
Caracas
COSTA RICA
San José
Panama City
VENEZUELA
PANAMA
COLOMBIA
POLYCONIC PROJECTION

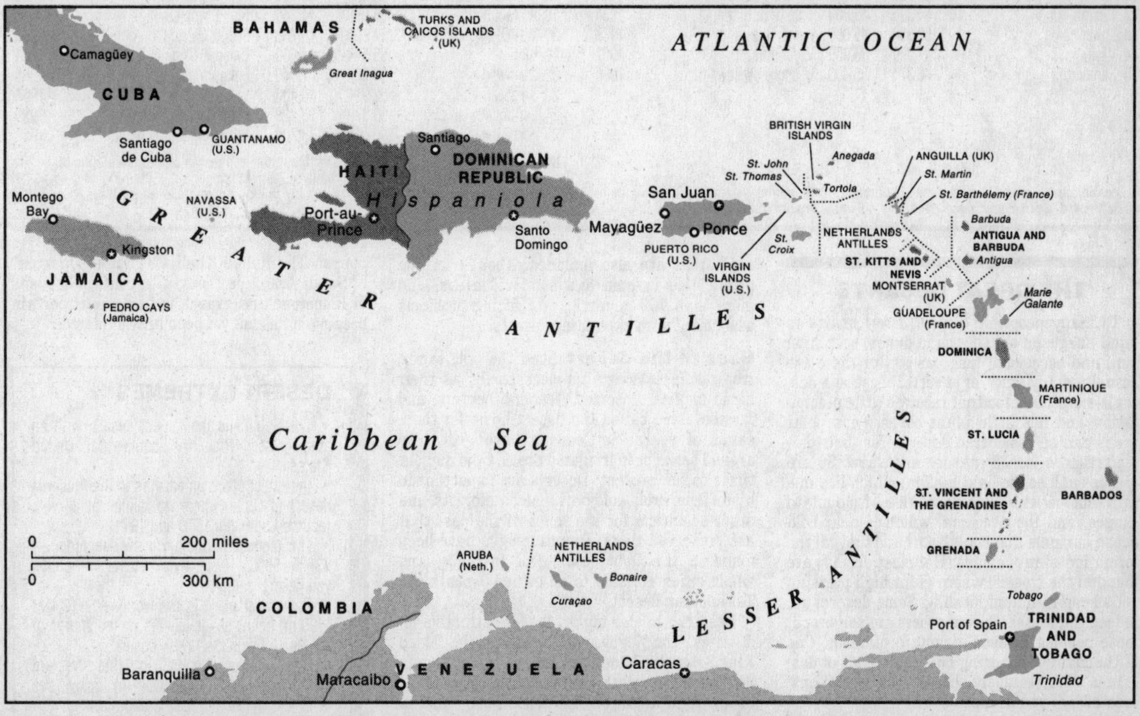

BAHAMAS
TURKS AND CAICOS ISLANDS (UK)
ATLANTIC OCEAN
Camagüey
Great Inagua
CUBA
Santiago de Cuba
GUANTANAMO (U.S.)
Santiago
DOMINICAN REPUBLIC
BRITISH VIRGIN ISLANDS
Anegada
ANGUILLA (UK)
St. John
St. Thomas
Tortola
St. Martin
St. Barthélemy (France)
HAITI
Hispaniola
Montego Bay
NAVASSA (U.S.)
GREATER ANTILLES
Port-au-Prince
Santo Domingo
San Juan
Mayagüez
Ponce
PUERTO RICO (U.S.)
St. Croix
VIRGIN ISLANDS (U.S.)
NETHERLANDS ANTILLES
Barbuda
ANTIGUA AND BARBUDA
Antigua
ST. KITTS AND NEVIS
MONTSERRAT (UK)
Kingston
JAMAICA
PEDRO CAYS (Jamaica)
GUADELOUPE (France)
Marie Galante
DOMINICA
MARTINIQUE (France)
Caribbean Sea
ST. LUCIA
ST. VINCENT AND THE GRENADINES
BARBADOS
0 200 miles
0 300 km
ARUBA (Neth.)
NETHERLANDS ANTILLES
Bonaire
Curaçao
GRENADA
Tobago
COLOMBIA
LESSER ANTILLES
Port of Spain
TRINIDAD AND TOBAGO
Trinidad
Baranquilla
Maracaibo
VENEZUELA
Caracas

WORLD'S 25 LARGEST CAPACITY RESERVOIRS

Rank/Reservoir	Capacity (mil.) Cubic yards[1]	Cubic meters[1]	River or basin, and location	Year (to be) completed
1. Owen Falls[2]	3,537,000	2,700,000	Lake Victoria/Nile, Uganda	1954
2. Kakhovskaya	238,420	182,000	Dnieper, Ukraine	1955
3. Kariba	236,586	180,600	Zambezi, Zimbabwe/Zambia	1959
4. Bratsk	221,744	169,270	Angara, Russia	1964
5. Aswan High	221,259	168,900	Nile, Egypt	1970
6. Akosombo	185,826	141,852	Volta, Ghana	1965
7. Daniel Johnson	185,826	141,852	Manicouagan, Quebec	1968
8. Guri	180,780	138,000	Caroni, Venezuela	1986
9. Krasnoyarsk	96,023	73,300	Yenesei, Russia	1967
10. W.A.C. Bennett	92,105	70,309	Peace, British Columbia	1967
11. Zeya	89,604	68,400	Zeya, Russia	1978
12. Cabora Bassa	82,530	63,000	Zambezi, Mozambique	1974
13. La Grande 2	80,847	61,715	La Grande, Quebec	1978
14. La Grande 3	78,626	60,020	La Grande, Quebec	1981
15. Ust-Ilim	77,683	59,300	Angara, Russia	1977
16. Boguchany	76,242	58,200	Russia	1989
17. Volga—V.I. Lenin (Kuibyshev)	75,980	58,000	Volga, Russia	1955
—Serra da Mesa (Sao Felix)[3]	70,740	54,000	Tocantins, Brazil	(1993)
18. Caniapiscau	70,478	53,800	Caniapiscau, Quebec, Canada	1981
19. Bukhtarma	65,238	49,800	Irtysh, Russia	1960
20. Atatürk	63,797	48,700	Euphrates, Turkey	1990
21. Irkutsk	60,260	46,000	Angara, Russia	1956
22. Tucurui	56,330	45,800	Tocantins, Brazil	1984
23. Lower Kama	58,858	45,000	Kama, Russia	1987
24. Vilyui	47,029	35,900	Vilyui, Russia	1967
25. Sanmenxia	46,374	35,400	Huanghe (Yellow), China	1960

1. One cubic meter equals 1.31 cubic yards. 2. Includes a natural lake. 3. Uncompleted reservoirs are not officially ranked. **Source:** *International Water Power & Dam Construction Handbook 1993* (1993).

WORLD'S 25 LARGEST VOLUME DAMS

Rank/Dam	Volume ('000s) Cubic yards[1]	Cubic meters[1]	River or basin, and location	Year (to be) completed
—Syncrude Tailings[2]	707,400	540,000	Alberta, Canada	UC
1. New Cornelia Tailings	274,445	209,500	Ten Mile Wash, Arizona	1973
—Kambaratinsk[2]	146,982	112,200	Naryn, Kyrghyzstan	UC
2. Tarbela	138,297	106,000	Indus, Pakistan	1976
3. Fort Peck	125,825	96,050	Missouri, Montana	1937
4. Lower Usuma	121,830	93,000	Usuma, Nigeria	1990
5. Tucurui	111,612	85,200	Tocantins, Brazil	1984
6. Atatürk	111,350	84,500	Euphrates, Turkey	1990
7. Guri (Raul Leoni)	102,142	77,971	Caroni, Venezuela	1986
—Yaycretá[2]	88,687	67,700	Parana, Paraguay/Argentina	(1994)
8. Oahe	87,137	66,517	Missouri, South Dakota	1958
9. Gardiner	85,726	65,400	South Saskatchewan, Saskatchewan	1968
10. Mangla	85,646	65,379	Jhelum, Pakistan	1967
11. Afsluitdijk	83,093	63,430	Zuider Zee, Netherlands	1932
12. Oroville	80,125	61,164	Feather, California	1968
13. San Luis	78,022	59,559	San Luis, California	1967
14. Nurek	75,980	58,000	Vakhsh, Tajikistan	1980
15. Garrison	66,607	50,845	Missouri, North Dakota	1956
16. Cochiti	65,801	50,230	Grande, New Mexico	1975
17. Öosterschelde	65,500	50,000	Vense Gat Öosterschelde, Netherlands	1986
— Xiaolangdi[2]	64,190	49,000	China	UC
18. Tabqua (Thawra)	60,260	46,000	Euphrates, Syria	1976
19. Aswan, High	58,033	44,300	Nile, Egypt	1970
20. W.A.C. Bennett	57,290	43,733	Peace, Canada	1967
21. Kiev	55,544	42,400	Dnieper, Ukraine	1964
22. Dantiwada	53,762	41,040	Banas, India	1965
23. Saratov	52,924	40,400	Volga, Russia	1967
24. Earthquake Lake	50,079	38,228	Madison, Montana	1959
25. Fort Randall	50,042	38,200	Missouri, South Dakota	1952

Note: Volume refers to amount of material (earth, concrete, etc.) used in construction of dam. UC = under construction. Tailings dams are formed from waste ore (tailings) from mining. 1. One cubic meter equals 1.31 cubic yards. 2. Uncompleted dams are not officially ranked. **Source:** *International Water Power & Dam Construction Handbook 1993* (1993).

THE GREAT DESERTS

To many people, the word *desert* brings to mind images of shifting sand dunes, scorching sun, and occasional lush oases. But there are actually many kinds of deserts, because a desert is simply an area that receives little precipitation and has little plant cover. Thus polar areas can be considered deserts, for their precipitation is locked into ice and snow. So are places such as the Taklimakan, which lies in a rain shadow on the leeward side of mountain ranges, and the Atacama, which is near cold ocean currents that cool the air and prevent the formation of rain clouds. But most deserts are found in the tropics, where giant high-pressure cells keep rain from forming. Some deserts are indeed flat and sandy, but others are solid rock, loose pebbles, or even mountain plateaus. One of the many fascinating characteristics of deserts is their strangely shaped rock formations, created by wind-whipped sand.

Altogether, arid lands cover about a fifth of the Earth's total land surface—a third, if semiarid areas are also included. About a billion people live in arid and semiarid areas, and more than 100 countries are facing problems associated with expanding deserts.

Uses of the desert Even the hot, sandy, tropical deserts are not necessarily, as their name implies, deserted. Traders, herders, and farmers have called the desert home for thousands of years. Settlements have grown up around oases or in irrigated areas, from ancient times to the present. Deserts are important to historians, archaeologists, paleontologists, and other scientists for the relics of the past that are preserved there. Dinosaur eggs have been found in the Gobi desert, for instance, and whole cities are said to lie buried beneath the Taklimakan desert.

Deserts are also important for extractive industries. The Negev was the site of the fabled King Solomon's Mines. In the 19th century, borax was mined in Death Valley. Petroleum is found in the Sahara (Arabic for "wilderness") and in the deserts of the Arabian peninsula. The Atacama is famed for its deposits of nitrate and copper. The Rub al-Khali, or "Empty Quarter," of Saudi Arabia is thought to contain deposits of limestone and gravel, but no one is certain because it has not yet been fully explored.

DESERT EXTREMES

- The Sahara is the largest desert, with an area greater than the continental United States.
- The driest place on earth is in the Atacama desert of Chile, where no rainfall at all was recorded between 1570 and 1971.
- The highest temperature ever recorded—136°F (58°C)—was at Al-Aziziya, in the Libyan desert.
- The lowest point in the world—1,312 feet (400 m) below sea level—is on the shores of the Dead Sea in the Negev desert.
- The lowest point in the Western Hemisphere—282 feet (86 m) below sea level—is in Death Valley, California.

GREAT DESERTS OF THE WORLD

Desert	Location	Approximate size Sq. mi.	Sq km
An Nafud[1]	N Saudi Arabia	40,000	103,600
Atacama	N Chile	70,000	181,300
Black Rock	NW Nevada	1,000	2,600
Chihuahuan	Texas, New Mexico, Arizona; Mexico	140,000	362,600
Dasht-e-Kavir	Central Iran	300 x 100	485 x 160
Dasht-e-Lut	E Iran	20,000	51,800
Death Valley	E California, SW Nevada	3,000	7,800
Gibson[2]	W Australia	120,000	310,800
Gobi	Mongolia; China	500,000	1,295,000
Great Sandy[2]	NW Australia	150,000	338,500
Great Victoria[2]	SW Australia	150,000	338,500
Kalahari	S Africa	225,000	582,800
Kara Kum (Turkestan)	Turkmenistan	120,000	310,800
Kyzyl Kum	Uzbekistan	100,000	259,000
Libyan[3]	Libya; SW Egypt; Sudan	450,000	1,165,500
Mojave	S California, W Arizona	15,000	38,900
Namib	Namibia	800[4]	1,290[4]
Negev	S Israel	4,700	12,200
Nubian[3]	NE Sudan	100,000	259,000
Painted Desert	N Arizona	200[5]	320[5]
Rub al-Khali ("Empty Quarter")[1]	S Saudi Arabia	250,000	647,500
Sahara	N Africa	3,500,000	9,065,000
Simpson[2]	Central Australia	40,000	103,600
Sonoran	SW Arizona, SE California; NW Mexico	70,000	181,300
Syrian[1]	N Saudi Arabia; E Jordan; S Syria; W Iraq	100,000	259,000
Taklimakan	Xinjiang Uygur Autonomous Region, China	140,000	362,600
Thar (Great Indian)	NW India; Pakistan	100,000	259,000

1. Part of Great Arabian desert. 2. Part of Great Australian desert. 3. Part of Sahara desert. 4. Length; width varies from 30–100 mi. (48–160 km). 5. Length; width varies from 15–30 mi. (24–48 km).

THE POLAR REGIONS

Antarctica

Geography Location: centered on the South Pole and situated almost entirely within the Antarctic Circle at 66½°S. **Boundaries:** None. Bordered by South Atlantic, Indian, and South Pacific Oceans. **Total land area:** about 5,404,000 sq. mi. (14,000,000 sq km). **Coastline:** 11,165 mi. (17,968 km). **Comparative area:** twice the size of Australia. **Land use:** 98% continental ice sheet; 2% barren rock. **Natural resources:** None presently exploited. Iron ore, chromium, copper, gold, nickel, platinum, and other minerals, as well as coal and hydrocarbons have been found in small uncommercial qualities. **Temperature:** Varies with location and altitude. East Antarctica is coldest; Antarctic peninsula in the west is mildest; mean annual temperature of the interior regions is –57°C (–71°F); mean temperatures at the coastal McMurdo station range from –28°C (–18°F) in August to –3°C (27°F) in January. **Daylight/Darkness:** six months of continuous daylight from mid-September to mid-March; six months of continuous darkness from mid-March to mid-September. **Major cities:** none.

The land Some 200 million years ago Antarctica was joined to South America, Africa, India, and Australia as one large continent. Geological changes caused the breakup into separate continents. Studies indicate that Antarctica once had a tropical environment, but that its present ice form is at least 20 million years old. Approximately 98 percent of the continent is covered by ice; contains about 90 percent of the world's ice and 70 percent of the fresh water. Elevations average from 6,600 to 13,200 ft. (2,000–4,000 m); mountain ranges up to 16,500 ft. (5,500 m) high. Ice-free coastal areas include parts of southern Victoria Land, Wilkes Land, and Ross Island. The Antarctic ice sheet averages 7,090 ft. (2,160 m) in depth and is 15,670 ft. (4,776 m) deep at its thickest point. Altitude at the South Pole is about 9,800 ft. (3,000 m).

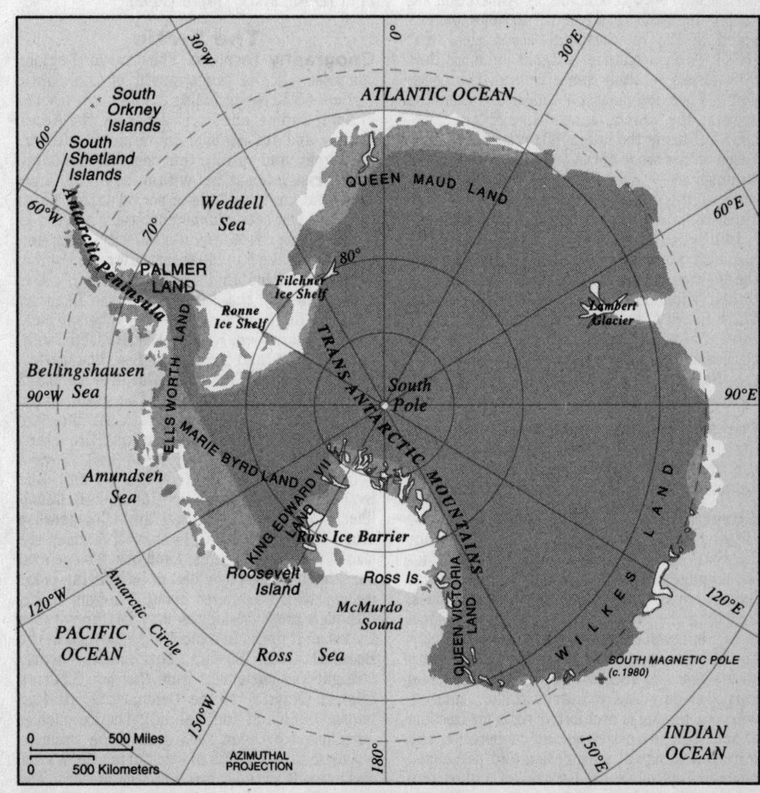

ANTARCTICA

Land/sea life Land life includes bacteria, lichens, mosses, two kinds of flowering plants in the ice-free areas, penguins, and some flying birds. Sea life includes several types of seals and whales, many of which were hunted to near extinction but are now protected by international conventions.

Exploration British captain James Cook circumnavigated the continent without sighting land in 1772–75. U.S. captain John Davis made the first known landing on the continent on Feb. 7, 1821. In 1908 the United Kingdom became the first nation to claim a "slice" of the continent, subsequently followed by claims from New Zealand (1923), France (1924), Australia (1933), Norway (1939), Chile (1940), and Argentina (1943). The United States and Russia have never claimed any Antarctica territory. Claims made by other nations are not recognized by other countries or the UN.

In 1911 Capt. Robert F. Scott and Roald Amundsen of Norway began a "race to the pole." Amundsen's party arrived at the South Pole on Dec. 14, 1911, while Scott located the pole on Jan. 18, 1912.

Scientific research The greatest scientific study ever conducted in Antarctica occurred in 1957–58 when 67 nations participated in the International Geophysical Year (IGY). Twelve countries established more than 50 stations to study the effects of the continent's huge ice mass on global weather, the oceans, the aurora australis, and the ionosphere. During the late 1980s research was focused on the study of the ozone depletion in the stratosphere—called the ozone hole—which allows high levels of potentially harmful ultraviolet radiation to reach the Earth's surface.

In 1993, 18 different countries maintained 42 research stations year-round. Argentina and the former Soviet Union each had six, the United Kingdom maintained five, Australia, Chile, South Africa, and the United States kept three, China and Japan each had two, and Brazil, Finland, France, Germany, India, South Korea, New Zealand, Poland, and Uruguay each had one.

People **Population:** No indigenous inhabitants. Staffing of research stations varies seasonally; summer (January) pop.: approximately 4,415; winter (July) pop.: approximately 1,046.

Government **Antarctica Treaty:** Signed in 1959 by the 12 IGY nations (in force as of June 23, 1961), it establishes a legal framework for the management of Antarctica. The treaty was renewed in 1991 in Madrid, where 24 countries, including the United States, signed a protocol to ban mineral and oil exploration for 50 years and to provide wildlife protection. The treaty states that the area is to be used for peaceful purposes only and military activity such as weapons testing is prohibited; calls for freedom of scientific investigation and cooperation and a free exchange of information and personnel; nuclear explosions or disposal of radioactive wastes is forbidden; and treaty-state observers have free access, including aerial observation, to any area and may inspect all stations, installations, and equipment.

At the Treaty's 17th meeting in November 1992, there were 26 consultative (voting) members and 15 acceding (nonvoting) members. The 26 consultative members include the seven countries that claim part of Antarctica as national territory (Argentina, Australia, Chile, France, New Zealand, Norway, and the United Kingdom), as well as 15 nonclaimant nations. The claimant nations all signed the Antarctica Treaty in 1959; the 15 nonclaimant nations (followed by the year they signed the treaty) are Belgium (1959), Brazil (1983), China (1985), Ecuador (1990), Finland (1989), Germany (1981), India (1983), Italy (1987), Japan (1959), South Korea (1989), Netherlands (1990), Peru (1989), Poland (1977), South Africa (1959), Spain (1988), Sweden (1988), Uruguay (1985), the United States (1959), and Russia (1959). The nonvoting members (and their year of accession) are Austria (1987), Bulgaria (1978), Canada (1988), Colombia (1988), Cuba (1984), Czechoslovakia (1962), Denmark (1965), Greece (1987), Guatemala (1991), Hungary (1984), North Korea (1987), Papua New Guinea (1981), Romania (1971), Switzerland (1990), and Ukraine (1992).

The Arctic

Geography **Location:** The Arctic Regions comprise all the lands north of the Arctic Circle—66°30'N—including the northern reaches of Asia, Europe, and North America, the Arctic Ocean, and its islands. In terms of climate, geography, and culture this demarcation is relatively insignificant, but within the Arctic Circle there is at least one 24-hour period during which the sun never sets (summer solstice), and one in which it never rises (winter solstice). The Arctic Ocean is the fourth largest after the Pacific, Atlantic, and Indian; its primary marginal seas are Baffin Bay, the Barents Sea, the Beaufort Sea, the Chukchi Sea, the East Siberian Sea, the Greenland Sea, Hudson Bay, Hudson Strait, the Kara Sea, and the Laptev Sea. **Boundaries:** None. **Total area:** The Arctic Ocean is 5,430,505 sq. mi. (14,056,000 sq km). The main island groups are the Canadian Arctic Archipelago (550,000 sq. mi.; 1,424,483 sq km), Greenland (840,000 sq. mi.; 2,175,590 sq km), Novaya Zemlya (31,000 sq. mi.; 80,290 sq km), and Svalbard (24,000 sq. mi.; 62,160 sq km). **Coastline:** 17,525 sq. mi. (45,389 km). **Comparative area:** The Arctic Ocean is about 1.5 times the size of the United States. **Land use:** The central surface is covered by a perennial drifting polar ice cap which averages about 3 meters thick, although pressure ridges may be three times that size. It drifts in a clockwise pattern in the Beaufort Gyral Stream, but exhibits nearly straight-line movement from the New Siberian Islands (Russia) to the Denmark Strait (between Greenland and Iceland). The ice pack is surrounded by open seas during the summer, but more than doubles in size during the winter and extends to the encircling land masses. The ocean floor is about 50 percent continental shelf (the highest percentage of any ocean) with the remainder a central basin interrupted by three submarine ridges (the Alpha Cordillera, Nansen Cordillera, and Lomonsov Ridge). The maximum depth is 15,305 ft. (4,665 m) in the Fram Basin. **Natural resources:** In the Arctic Ocean there are sand and gravel aggregates, placer deposits, polymetallic nodules, oil and gas fields, fish, and marine mammals (seals and whales). **Climate:** The dominant fact of life is the frigid conditions: persistent cold and relatively modest annual temperature ranges; winters characterized by continuous darkness, cold and stable weather conditions, and clear skies; summers characterized by continuous daylight, damp and foggy weather, and weak cyclones with rain or snow. Between 60°N and 75°N there is seasonal freezing, while north of 75°N there is permanent ice. In North America, temperatures during the colder months average –25°F (–31°C), while Siberia is somewhat colder at –35°F (–37°C). **Environment:** Endangered marine species include walruses and whales; ice islands occasionally break away from northern Ellesmere Island; icebergs calved from western Greenland and extreme northeastern Canada; maximum snow cover in March or April is about 20–50 cm over the frozen ocean and lasts about 10 months; permafrost in islands; virtually ice-locked from October to June; fragile ecosystem slow to change and slow to recover from disruptions or damage. **Major cities:** none.

People **Population:** Ethnologists distinguish three native cultural areas—the Western Arctic, including Eskimo peoples (from the east coast of Greenland to Alaska) and Aleuts; Paleo-Siberian, including the Chukchi and Eskimo of Eastern Asia; and Eurasian Arctic, including some Chukchi, Yakut, Nenets, and Lapps. Today, however, the vast majority of the people living and working within the Arctic Circle are nonnative people in industry or scientific enterprises.

Government Governments with territory north of the Arctic Circle are Canada, the United States, Russia, Finland, Sweden, Norway, and Denmark (Greenland). Svalbard is the focus of a maritime boundary dispute between Norway and Russia.

Economy While there is a fair amount of economic activity in the continental portions of the Arctic—principally extractive industries in Siberia, northern Canada, and Alaska's North Slope—conditions in the numerous Arctic islands all but prevent significant development there. Norwegian and Russian miners extract about 1 million tons of coal per year from mines on Svalbard, and in Greenland there are large deposits of cryolite, lead, and other minerals, but only lead can be mined economically. Economic activity in the Arctic Ocean is limited to the exploitation of natural resources including crude oil, natural gas, fishing, and sealing.

Communications **Ports:** Churchill (Canada), Murmansk (Russia), Prudhoe Bay (U.S.). **Telecommunications:** No submarine cables. **Transportation:** There is a sparse network of air, ocean, river, and land routes. The Arctic provides the shortest marine link between the extremes of eastern and western Russia. The two major waterways are the Northwest Passage, in North America, and the Northern Sea Route, in Asia, but ships are subject to superstructure icing from October to May. The United States and Russia operate floating research stations. Access to the Arctic Ocean from the Pacific Ocean is through the Bering Strait; from the Atlantic, through the Davis Strait (between Canada and Greenland), the Denmark Strait (between Greenland and Iceland), or the Norwegian Sea (between Iceland and Norway).

TIME ZONES AND AREA CODES FOR SELECTED NATIONS AND TERRITORIES

Country	Hours from EST	Country code	City codes
Afghanistan	+9.5	Direct dialing not available	
Albania	+6	355	Durres 52, Elbassan 545, Tirana 42
Algeria	+6	213	Adrar 7, Ain Defla 3, Bejaia 5, Guerrar 9
American Samoa	–6	684	Not required
Andorra	+6	376	
Angola	+6	244	Luanda 2, other areas not required
Argentina	+2	54	Buenos Aires 1, Córdoba 51, Rosario 41
Armenia	+8	374	All points 885
Aruba	+1	297	All points 8
Ascension Island	+5	247	Not required
Australia[1]	+15	61	Adelaide 8, Brisbane 7, Canberra 6, Melbourne 3, Perth 9, Sydney 2
Austria	+6	43	Graz 316, Innsbruck 512, Linz 70, Salzburg 662, Vienna 1
Azerbaijan	+8	994	Baku 8922, Sumgait 89264, Tashkent 3712
Bahrain	+8	973	Not required
Bangladesh	+11	880	Chittagong 31, Dhaka 2, Khulna 41
Belarus	+8	375	Minsk 0172, Mahilou 0222
Belgium	+6	32	Antwerp 3, Brussels 2, Ghent 91, Liège 41
Belize	–1	501	Belize City 2, Belmopan 8, Orange Walk 3
Benin	+6	229	Not required
Bhutan	+10.5	975	Not required
Bolivia	+1	591	La Paz 2, Santa Cruz de la Sierra 33, Sucre 64, Cochabamba 42
Bosnia/Herzegovina	+6	387	Mostar 88, Sarajevo 71, Zenica 72
Botswana	+7	267	Francistown 21
Brazil[2]	+2	55	Belo Horizonte 31, Brasília 61, Rio de Janeiro 21, São Paulo 11, Salvador 71
Brunei	+13	673	Bandar Seri Begawan 2, Kuala Belait 3
Bulgaria	+7	359	Plovdiv 32, Sofia 2, Varna 52
Burkina Faso	+5	226	Not required
Burundi	+7	257	Not required
Cambodia	+12	855	Phnom Penh 23
Cameroon	+6	237	Not required
Canada	Similar to U.S.		*See* "Area Codes of the United States, Canada, and the Caribbean" in Part II, U.S. Geography
Cape Verde Islands	+4	238	Not required
Central African Republic	+6	236	Not required
Chad	+6	235	N'Djamena 51, Moundou 69
Chile	+1	56	Concepción 41, Gran Santiago 2, Valparaíso 32, Viña del Mar 32
China (PRC)	+12	86	Beijing 1, Fuzhou 591, Ghuangzhou (Canton) 20, Shanghai 21
Christmas Island	+12	61	Christmas 4
Cocos Islands	+12	61	Cocos 3
Colombia	0	57	Barranquilla 58, Bogotá 1, Cali 23, Cartagena 53, Medellín 4
Comoros	+9	269	Not required
Congo	+6	242	Not required
Cook Islands	–5	682	Not required
Costa Rica	–1	506	Not required
Croatia	+6	385	Dubrovnik 50, Rijeka 51, Split 58, Zagreb 41
Cuba	0	53	Havana 7, Santiago 226
Cyprus[3]	+7	357	Larnaca 4, Limassol 5, Nicosia 2
Czech Republic	+6	42	Brno 5, Prague 2, Ostrava 69
Denmark	+6	45	Not required
Djibouti	+8	253	Not required

Country	Hours from EST	Country code	City codes
Ecuador	0	593	Cuenca 7, Guayaquil 4, Machala 7, Quito 2
Egypt	+7	20	Alexandria 3, Cairo 2, Mansoura 50
El Salvador	–1	503	Not required
Equatorial Guinea	+6	240	Bata 8, Malabo 9
Eritrea	+8	291	Asmara 4, Makale 3, Massawa 4
Estonia	+7	372	Tallinn 2, Tartu 34
Ethiopia	+8	251	Addis Ababa 1, Awasa 6, Dire Dawa 5
Faeroe Islands	+5	298	Not required
Falkland Islands	+1	500	Not required
Fiji	+17	679	Not required
Finland	+7	358	Helsinki 0, Tampere 31, Turku 21
France[4]	+6	33	Lyon 7, Marseilles 91, Nice 93, Paris 1
French Antilles	+1	596	Not required
French Guiana	+2	594	Not required
French Polynesia[5]	–5	689	Not required
Gabon	+6	241	Not required
Gambia	+5	220	Not required
Georgia	+8	7	Sukhumi 88122, Tbilisi 883
Germany	+6	49	Berlin 30, Bonn 228, Cologne 221, Frankfurt 69, Hamburg 40, Leipzig 341, Munich 89
Ghana	+5	233	Accra 21, Kumasi 51
Gibraltar	+6	350	Not required
Greece	+7	30	Athens 1, Piraeus 1, Thessaloniki 31
Greenland	+2	299	Godthåb 2
Guadeloupe	+1	590	Not required
Guam	+15	671	Not required
Guatemala	–1	502	Guatemala City 2; all other cities 9
Guinea	+5	224	Conakry 4
Guinea-Bissau	+5	245	Not required
Guyana	+2	592	Georgetown 2, New Amsterdam 3
Haiti	0	509	Not required
Honduras	–1	504	Not required
Hong Kong	+13	852	Not required
Hungary	+6	36	Budapest 1, Debrecen 52, Miskole 46
Iceland	+5	354	Akureyri 6, Keflavík 2, Reykjavík 1
India	+10.5	91	Bombay 22, Calcutta 33, Hyderabad 842, Madras 44, New Delhi 11
Indonesia[6]	+12	62	Jakarta 21, Medan 61, Surabaya 31, Bandung 22
Iran	+8.5	98	Esfahan 31, Mashad 51, Tehran 21
Iraq	+8	964	Baghdad 1, Basra 40, Mosul 60
Ireland	+5	353	Cork 21, Dublin 1, Galway 91, Limerick 61
Israel	+7	972	Haifa 4, Jerusalem 2, Tel Aviv 3
Italy	+6	39	Florence 55, Genoa 10, Milan 2, Naples 81, Rome 6, Turin 11
Ivory Coast	+5	225	Not required
Japan	+14	81	Kyoto 75, Nagoya 52, Osaka 6, Sapporo 11, Tokyo 3, Yokohama 45
Jordan	+7	962	Amman 6, Irbid 2, Salt 5, Zagra 9
Kazakhstan	+11	7	Almaty 3272, Petropavlovsk 315
Kenya	+8	254	Mombasa 11, Nairobi 2, Nakuru 37
Kiribati	+17	686	Not required
Korea, North	+14	850	Pyonyang 2
Korea, South	+14	82	Inchon 32, Kwangju 62, Pusan 51, Seoul 2, Taegu 53
Kuwait	+8	965	Not required
Kyrgyzstan	+11	7	Bishkek 3312, Osh 33222

Country	Hours from EST	Country code	City codes
Laos	+12	856	Vientiane 21, other areas not required
Latvia	+7	371	Daugav'pils 54, Liepaja 34, Riga 0132
Lebanon	+7	961	Beirut 1, Juniyah 9, Tarabulus (Tripoli) 6, Zahleh 8
Lesotho	+7	266	Not required
Liberia	+5	231	Not required
Libya	+6	218	Benghazi 61, Misurata 51, Tripoli 21
Liechtenstein	+6	41	All points 75
Lithuania	+7	370	Kaunas 7, Klaipeda 61, Vilnius 2
Luxembourg	+6	352	Not required
Macau	+13	853	Not required
Macedonia	+6	389	Skopje 91, Bitola 97
Madagascar	+8	261	Antananarivo 2, Fianarantsoa 7
Malawi	+7	265	Blantyre, Lilongwe: Not required
Malaysia[7]	+13	60	Ipoh 5, Johore Bahru 7, Kuala Lumpur 3
Maldives	+10	960	Not required
Mali	+5	223	Not required
Malta	+6	356	Not required
Marshall Islands	+17	692	Ebeye 871, Majuro 9
Mauritania	+5	222	Not required
Mauritius	+9	230	Not required
Mayotte Island	+8	269	All points 6
Mexico[8]	–1	52	Acapulco 74, Guadalajara 36, Mexico City 5, Monterrey 83, Puebla 22, Tijuana 66
Micronesia	+16	691	Kosrae 370, Ponape 320, Truk 330, Yap 350
Moldova	+8	373	Bendery 32, Kishinev 2
Monaco	+6	33	All points 93
Mongolia	+13	976	Ulan Bator 1
Morocco	+4	212	Casablanca 2, Rabat 7, Marrakech 4, Tangiers 99
Mozambique	+7	258	Maputo 1
Myanmar	+11.5	95	Bassein 42, Mandalay 2, Yangon 1
Namibia	+7	264	Windhoek 61
Nauru	+17	674	Not required
Nepal	+10.5	977	Kathmandu 1, Gorkha 64
Netherlands	+6	31	Amsterdam 20, Rotterdam 10, The Hague 70
Netherlands Antilles	+1	599	Bonaire 7, Curaçao 9, St. Maarten 5
New Caledonia	+16	687	Not required
New Zealand	+17	64	Auckland 9, Christchurch 3, Wellington 4
Nicaragua	–1	505	Granada 55, León 311, Managua 2
Niger Republic	+6	227	Not required
Nigeria	+6	234	Lagos 1
Niue	–6	683	Not required
Norfolk Island	+16.5	672	Not required
Northern Mariana Islands	+15	670	Rota Is. 532, Saipan 2348, Tinian Is. 433
Norway	+6	47	Bergen 55, Oslo 25, Trondheim 73
Oman	+9	968	Not required
Pakistan	+10	92	Islamabad 51, Karachi 21, Lahore 42
Palau	+14	680	Not required
Panama	0	507	Not required
Papua New Guinea	+15	675	Not required
Paraguay	+2	595	Asunción 21, Pedro Juan Caballero 36
Peru	0	51	Arequipa 54, Callao 14, Lima 14, Trujillo 44
Philippines	+13	63	Cebu City 32, Davao City 82, Iloilo 33, Manila 2
Poland	+6	48	Krakow 12, Gdansk 58, Lódź 42, Warsaw 22
Portugal	+5	351	Coimbra 39, Lisbon 1, Porto 2, Setubal 65
Qatar	+8	974	Not required
Reunion Island	+9	262	Not required
Romania	+7	40	Braşov 92, Bucharest 1, Iasi 98, Timisoara 96
Russia[9]	+8	7	Moscow 095, St. Petersburg 812
Rwanda	+7	250	Not required
Saint Helena	+5	290	Not required
Saint Pierre and Miquelon	+2	508	Not required
San Marino	+6	378	All points 549
Sao Tomé	+5	239	Not required
Saudi Arabia	+8	966	Jeddah 2, Mecca 2, Riyadh 1, Medina 4
Senegal	+5	221	Not required
Seychelles	+9	248	Not required
Sierra Leone	+5	232	Freetown 22; other areas not required
Singapore	+13	65	Not required
Slovakia	+6	42	Bratislava 7, Presov 91
Slovenia	+6	386	Llubljana 61, Maribor 62
Solomon Islands	+16	677	Not required
Somalia	+8	Direct dialing not available	
South Africa	+7	27	Cape Town 21, Durban 31, Johannesburg 11
Spain	+6	34	Barcelona 3, Madrid 1, Seville 5, Valencia 6
Sri Lanka	+10.5	94	Colombo 1
Sudan	+7	Direct dialing not available	
Suriname	+2	597	Not required
Swaziland	+7	268	Not required
Sweden	+6	46	Göteburg 31, Malmö 40, Stockholm 8
Switzerland	+6	41	Basel 61, Berne 31, Geneva 22, Zurich 1
Syria	+8	963	Aleppo 21, Damascus 11, Homs 31
Taiwan	+13	886	Kaohsiung 7, Taichung 89, Taipei 2
Tajikistan	+11	7	Dushanbe 3772
Tanzania	+8	255	Dar es Salaam 51, Mwanza 68, Tanga 53
Thailand	+12	66	Bangkok 2, Chon Buri 39, Chiang Mai 54
Togo	+5	228	Not required
Tonga	+18	676	Not required
Tunisia	+6	216	Bizeria 2, Kef 8, Tunis 1
Turkey	+7	90	Adana 71, Ankara 4, Istanbul 1, Izmir 51
Turkmenistan	+10	7	Ashkhabad 3632, Chardzou 378
Tuvalu	+17	688	Not required
Uganda	+8	256	Jinja 43, Kampala 41
Ukraine	+8	380	Kharkov 572, Kiev 44
United Arab Emirates	+9	971	Abu Dhabi 2, Dubai 4, Sharjah 6
United Kingdom	+5	44	Belfast 1232, Birmingham 121, Glasgow 141, Manchester 161, London: inner 171, outer 181, Sheffield 114
Uruguay	+2	598	Montevideo 2, Paysandú 722
Uzbekistan	+11	7	Karish 37522, Samarkand 3662, Tashkent 3712
Vanuatu	+16	678	Not required
Vatican City	+6	39	All points 6
Venezuela	+1	58	Caracas 2, Maracaibo 61, Valencia 41
Vietnam	+12	84	Hanoi 4, Ho Chi Minh City 8
Wallis and Futuma Islands	+17	681	Not required
Western Samoa	–6	685	Not required
Yemen	+8	967	Ta'lz 4; elsewhere 00 for operator assistance
Yugoslavia	+6	381	Belgrade 11, Novi Sad 21
Zaire	+6	243	Kinshasa 12, Lubumbashi 222
Zambia	+7	260	Kitwe 2, Lusaka 1, Ndola 2
Zimbabwe	+7	263	Bulawayo 9, Harare 4, Mutare 20

Note: Area codes for cities in the U.S., Canada, and the Caribbean can be found in Part II, "U.S. Geography." 1. More than one time zone; difference based on Sydney. 2. More than one time zone; difference based on Rio de Janeiro. 3. Turkish-occupied Cyprus uses the country code for Turkey (90), plus Famagusta 536, Kyrenia 581. 4. All codes in Paris are 1 + 8 digits beginning with 3, 4, or 6. 5. More than one time zone; difference based on Tahiti. 6. More than one time zone; difference based on Jakarta. 7. More than one time zone; difference based on Kuala Lumpur. 8. More than one time zone; difference based on Mexico City. International code applies for calls made from international direct dial areas. From other areas, to call Mexico City dial 90 + 5; consult operator for other calls. 9. More than one time zone; difference based on Moscow. **Source:** AT&T, *International Dialing Guide* (1993).

THE 50 TALLEST BUILDINGS IN THE WORLD

Rank/Building	City	Year built	Stories	Height Meters	Height Feet
1. Petronas Tower 1	Kuala Lumpur	UC96	88	450	1,476
2. Petronas Tower 2	Kuala Lumpur	UC96	88	450	1,476
3. Sears Tower	Chicago	1974	110	443	1,454
4. Jin Mao Building	Shanghai	UC98	88	421	1,379
5. World Trade Center, North	New York	1972	110	417	1,368
6. World Trade Center, South	New York	1973	110	415	1,362
7. Empire State Building	New York	1931	102	381	1,250
8. Central Plaza	Hong Kong	1992	78	374	1,227
9. Bank of China Tower	Hong Kong	1989	70	369	1,209
10. Tuntex and Chien-Tai Tower	Kaoshiung	UC97	85	348	1,140
11. Amoco	Chicago	1973	80	346	1,136
12. John Hancock Center	Chicago	1969	100	344	1,127
13. Sky Central Plaza	Guangzhou	UC96	80	322	1,056
14. Baiyoke Tower II	Bangkok	UC97	90	320	1,050
15. Chrysler Building	New York	1930	77	319	1,046
16. Shenzhen Avic Plaza Building	Shenzhen	UC97	63	313	1,025
17. NationsBank Plaza	Atlanta	1992	55	312	1,023
18. First Interstate World Center	Los Angeles	1989	75	310	1,018
19. Texas Commerce Tower	Houston	1982	75	305	1,000
20. Ryugyong Hotel	Pyongyang	UC95	105	300	984
21. Two Prudential Plaza	Chicago	1990	64	298	978
22. First Interstate Bank Plaza	Houston	1983	71	296	972
23. Landmark Tower	Yokohama	1993	70	296	971
24. 311 South Wacker Drive	Chicago	1990	65	292	959
25. Jubilee Street/Queen's Road Central	Hong Kong	UC97	69	292	958
26. First Canadian Place	Toronto	1975	72	290	952
27. American International Building	New York	1932	66	290	950
28. One Liberty Place	Philadelphia	1987	61	287	945
29. Columbia Seafirst Center	Seattle	1985	76	287	943
30. 40 Wall Street	New York	1930	70	283	927
31. Nations Bank Plaza	Dallas	1985	72	281	921
32. Overseas Union Bank Plaza	Singapore	1986	66	280	919
33. United Overseas Bank Plaza	Singapore	1992	66	280	919
34. Republic Plaza	Singapore	1995	66	280	919
35. Citicorp Center	New York	1977	59	279	915
36. Scotia Plaza	Toronto	1989	68	275	902
37. Transco Tower	Houston	1983	64	275	901
38. Society Center	Cleveland	1991	57	271	888
39. AT&T Corporate Center	Chicago	1989	60	270	885
40. 900 North Michigan	Chicago	1989	66	265	871
41. NationsBank Corporate Center	Charlotte	1992	60	265	871
42. One Peachtree Center	Atlanta	1992	60	264	867
43. Canada Trust Tower	Toronto	1990	51	263	863
44. Water Tower Place	Chicago	1976	74	262	859
45. First Interstate Tower	Los Angeles	1974	62	262	858
46. Transamerica Pyramid	San Francisco	1972	48	260	853
47. GE Rockefeller Center	New York	1933	70	259	850
48. One First National Plaza	Chicago	1969	60	259	850
49. Commerzbank Tower	Frankfurt	UC97	60	259	850
50. Two Liberty Place	Philadelphia	1990	58	258	848

Note: Height is measured from sidewalk level of main entrance to structural top of building. Television and radio antennas and flag poles are not included. UC = under construction, followed by expected completion date. **Source:** Council on High Buildings and Urban Habitat, Lehigh University (1995).

CLIMATE AND WEATHER

CLIMATES OF THE WORLD

Knowing the similarities and differences between climates in various parts of the world helps us understand many things about our planet: why people live where they do; how they make their living; the problems and potentials of their land. Climates are very complex, however, and no climatic classification is ideal. The most commonly used classification was developed more than 50 years ago by a German climatologist, Wladimir Koppen. The Koppen system uses temperature and precipitation as the major criteria for grouping climates. Boundaries between climatic zones are determined by the limits of where certain plants grow.

The five major climatic zones are known by the capital letters **A**, **B**, **C**, **D**, and **E**; each major zone has subzones. High-altitude areas are sometimes shown with the letter **H** because their climates are so complex that small maps cannot show all the detail. (In the text that follows, **R** stands for the annual rainfall in centimeters; **T** is the average annual temperature in degrees Celsius.)

A Humid tropical climates The average temperature of every month is 64°F (18°C) or higher. There is no winter.

Af *Rain forest.* The driest month has at least 2.4 inches (6 cm) of rain. The Amazon basin is an example of an **Af** climate.

Am *Monsoon.* Similar to **Af**, but with a short dry season. The amount of rainfall in the driest

> *"Everybody talks about the weather, but nobody does anything about it."*
>
> —Mark Twain

WEATHER EXTREMES

Hottest: Dalol Danakil Depression, Ethiopia. Average annual temperature: 35°C/95°F.

Coldest: Plateau Station, Antarctica. Average annual temperature: –56.7°C/–71.7°F.

Wettest: Mawsynram, Assam, India. Average annual rainfall: 11.873 m, 38.925 ft.

Driest: Atacama desert, Chile. Average annual rainfall: too small to measure.

Source: *National Geographic Atlas of the World* (1992).

CLIMATE OF SELECTED U.S. CITIES

The first line following each city lists the normal daily high temperatures for each month (in degrees Fahrenheit); the second line lists the normal monthly precipitation (rain, snow, and melted ice); the third line lists the average monthly snowfall and ice pellets.

City	Jan.	Feb.	Mar.	Apr.	May	June	July	Aug.	Sept.	Oct.	Nov.	Dec.
Atlanta, Ga.	51°	55°	63°	73°	81°	87°	89°	89°	83°	74°	63°	55°
	4.9"	4.4"	5.9"	4.4"	4.0"	3.4"	4.7"	3.4"	3.2"	2.5"	3.4"	4.2"
	0.9"	0.5"	0.4"	T	—	—	—	—	—	—	—	0.2"
Baltimore, Md.	41°	44°	53°	65°	74°	83°	87°	86°	79°	68°	56°	45°
	3.0"	3.0"	3.7"	3.4"	3.4"	3.8"	3.9"	4.6"	3.5"	3.1"	3.1"	3.4"
	6.0"	6.4"	3.5"	0.1"	T	—	T	—	—	—	1.0"	3.5"
Boston, Mass.	36°	38°	45°	57°	67°	77°	82°	80°	72°	63°	52°	40°
	4.0"	3.7"	4.1"	3.7"	3.5"	2.9"	2.7"	3.7"	3.4"	3.4"	4.2"	4.5"
	12.0"	11.2"	7.4"	0.9"	—	—	—	—	—	—	1.3"	7.4"
Charlotte, N.C.	50°	54°	62°	72°	79°	85°	88°	88°	82°	72°	62°	53°
	3.8"	3.8"	4.8"	3.3"	3.6"	3.6"	3.9"	3.8"	3.6"	2.7"	2.9"	3.4"
	2.1"	1.7"	1.2"	—	—	—	—	—	—	—	0.1"	0.5"
Chicago, Ill.	29°	34°	44°	59°	70°	79°	83°	82°	76°	64°	48°	35°
	1.6"	1.3"	2.6"	3.7"	3.2"	4.1"	3.6"	3.5"	3.4"	2.3"	2.1"	2.1"
	10.5"	8.1"	6.8"	1.7"	0.1"	T	T	T	T	0.4"	1.9"	8.5"
Cleveland, Ohio	33°	35°	45°	58°	69°	78°	82°	80°	74°	63°	49°	38°
	2.5"	2.2"	3.0"	3.3"	3.3"	3.5"	3.4"	3.4"	2.9"	2.5"	2.8"	2.8"
	12.6"	11.8"	10.3"	2.3"	0.1"	—	—	—	T	0.6"	5.1"	11.8"
Columbus, Ohio	35°	38°	49°	62°	73°	81°	84°	83°	77°	65°	51°	39°
	2.8"	2.2"	3.2"	3.4"	3.8"	4.0"	4.0"	3.7"	2.8"	1.9"	2.6"	2.6"
	8.3"	6.1"	4.4"	0.9"	—	T	—	—	T	—	2.3"	5.5"
Dallas–Fort Worth, Tex.	54°	59°	67°	77°	84°	93°	98°	97°	90°	80°	66°	58°
	1.7"	1.9"	2.4"	3.6"	4.3"	2.6"	2.0"	1.8"	3.3"	2.5"	1.8"	1.7"
	1.2"	1.0"	0.2"	T	T	—	—	—	—	—	0.1"	0.2"
Denver, Colo.	43°	47°	51°	61°	71°	82°	88°	86°	78°	67°	52°	46°
	0.5"	0.7"	1.2"	1.8"	2.5"	1.6"	1.9"	1.5"	1.2"	1.0"	0.8"	0.6"
	8.3"	7.3"	12.7"	9.0"	1.6"	—	T	T	1.6"	3.7"	8.8"	7.4"
Detroit, Mich.	31°	34°	43°	58°	69°	79°	83°	82°	74°	63°	48°	35°
	1.9"	1.7"	2.5"	3.2"	2.8"	3.4"	3.1"	3.2"	2.3"	2.1"	2.3"	2.5"
	10.2"	8.9"	6.7"	1.6"	T	—	—	—	T	0.2"	3.0"	10.4"
El Paso, Tex.	58°	63°	70°	79°	87°	96°	95°	93°	88°	79°	66°	58°
	0.4"	0.5"	0.3"	0.2"	0.2"	0.6"	1.6"	1.2"	1.4"	0.7"	0.3"	0.4"
	1.4"	0.8"	0.4"	0.3"	T	T	T	—	—	—	1.0"	1.7"
Honolulu, Hawaii	80°	80°	81°	83°	85°	86°	87°	88°	88°	87°	84°	81°
	3.8"	2.7"	3.5"	1.5"	1.2"	0.5"	0.5"	0.6"	0.6"	1.9"	3.2"	3.4"
	—	—	—	—	—	—	—	—	—	—	—	—
Houston, Tex.	62°	66°	72°	79°	85°	91°	94°	93°	89°	82°	72°	65°
	3.2"	3.3"	2.7"	4.2"	4.7"	4.1"	3.3"	3.7"	4.9"	3.7"	3.4"	3.7"
	0.2"	0.2"	—	—	T	T	—	—	—	—	T	—
Indianapolis, Ind.	34°	39°	49°	63°	73°	82°	85°	84°	78°	66°	51°	39°
	2.7"	2.5"	3.6"	3.7"	3.7"	4.0"	4.3"	3.5"	2.7"	2.5"	3.0"	3.0"
	6.1"	5.6"	3.4"	0.5"	—	T	—	T	—	0.2"	1.8"	4.9"
Jacksonville, Fla.	65°	67°	73°	80°	85°	89°	91°	90°	87°	80°	72°	66°
	3.1"	3.5"	3.7"	3.3"	4.9"	5.4"	6.5"	7.2"	7.3"	3.4"	1.9"	2.6"
	T	—	—	—	—	—	T	—	—	—	—	—
Kansas City, Mo.	35°	41°	51°	65°	75°	83°	89°	87°	79°	68°	52°	40°
	1.1"	1.2"	2.4"	3.2"	4.4"	4.7"	4.4"	3.6"	4.1"	3.1"	1.6"	1.4"
	5.7"	4.3"	3.6"	0.8"	T	T	T	—	T	—	1.1"	4.4"
Las Vegas, Nev.	56°	62°	68°	77°	87°	99°	105°	102°	95°	82°	66°	57°
	0.5"	0.5"	0.4"	0.2"	0.2"	0.1"	0.5"	0.5"	0.3"	0.3"	0.4"	0.3"
	1.0"	0.1"	—	T	—	—	—	T	—	T	0.1"	0.1"
Los Angeles, Calif.	67°	69°	69°	71°	73°	78°	84°	84°	83°	79°	73°	68°
	3.7"	3.0"	2.4"	1.2"	0.2"	0.0"	0.0"	0.1"	0.3"	0.2"	1.9"	2.0"
	—	T	—	—	—	—	—	—	—	—	—	T
Memphis, Tenn.	48°	53°	61°	73°	81°	88°	92°	90°	84°	75°	61°	52°
	4.6"	4.3"	5.4"	5.8"	5.1"	3.6"	4.0"	3.7"	3.6"	2.4"	4.2"	4.9"
	2.4"	1.4"	0.9"	T	T	—	—	—	—	T	0.1"	0.7"
Miami, Fla.	75°	76°	79°	82°	85°	87°	89°	89°	88°	84°	80°	76°
	2.1"	2.1"	1.9"	3.1"	6.5"	9.2"	6.0"	7.0"	8.1"	7.1"	2.7"	1.9"
	—	—	—	—	—	—	—	—	—	—	—	—
Milwaukee, Wis.	26°	30°	39°	54°	65°	75°	80°	78°	71°	60°	45°	32°
	1.6"	1.3"	2.6"	3.4"	2.7"	3.6"	3.5"	3.1"	2.9"	2.3"	2.0"	2.0"
	12.8"	9.6"	8.6"	1.7"	0.1"	T	T	T	T	0.3"	2.9"	10.6"
Minneapolis–St. Paul, Minn.	20°	26°	38°	56°	69°	79°	83°	81°	71°	60°	41°	27°
	0.8"	0.9"	1.7"	2.1"	3.2"	4.1"	3.5"	3.6"	2.5"	1.9"	1.3"	0.9"
	9.7"	8.5"	10.8"	2.9"	0.1"	T	—	T	—	0.5"	7.9"	9.4"
New Orleans, La.	62°	65°	71°	79°	85°	90°	91°	90°	87°	79°	70°	64°
	5.0"	5.2"	4.7"	4.5"	5.1"	4.6"	6.7"	6.0"	5.9"	2.7"	4.1"	5.3"
	—	0.1"	T	T	T	—	—	—	—	—	T	0.1"
New York, N.Y.	38°	40°	49°	61°	72°	80°	85°	84°	76°	66°	54°	42°
	3.2"	3.1"	4.2"	3.8"	3.8"	3.2"	3.8"	4.0"	3.7"	3.4"	4.1"	3.8"
	7.6"	8.4"	4.9"	0.9"	T	—	T	—	—	—	0.9"	5.4"
Oklahoma City, Okla.	47°	52°	61°	72°	79°	88°	94°	93°	85°	74°	60°	51°
	1.0"	1.3"	2.1"	2.9"	5.5"	3.9"	3.0"	2.4"	3.4"	2.7"	1.5"	1.2"
	3.1"	2.5"	1.4"	—	T	T	—	—	T	T	0.5"	1.8"
Philadelphia, Pa.	39°	41°	51°	63°	73°	82°	86°	85°	78°	67°	55°	43°
	3.2"	2.8"	3.9"	3.5"	3.2"	3.9"	3.9"	4.1"	3.4"	2.8"	3.3"	3.5"
	6.5"	6.3"	3.6"	0.3"	T	—	—	—	—	—	0.7"	3.5"
Phoenix, Ariz.	65°	70°	75°	83°	92°	102°	105°	102°	98°	88°	74°	66°
	0.7"	0.6"	0.8"	0.3"	0.1"	0.2"	0.7"	1.0"	0.6"	0.6"	0.5"	0.8"
	T	—	T	T	T	—	—	—	—	T	—	—
Pittsburgh, Pa.	34°	37°	48°	61°	71°	79°	83°	81°	75°	63°	50°	38°
	2.9"	2.4"	3.6"	3.3"	3.5"	3.3"	3.8"	3.3"	2.8"	2.5"	2.3"	2.6"
	11.5"	9.1"	8.0"	1.7"	0.1"	T	T	—	T	0.2"	3.3"	8.2"
St. Louis, Mo.	38°	43°	53°	67°	76°	85°	89°	87°	81°	69°	54°	43°
	1.7"	2.1"	3.3"	3.6"	3.5"	3.7"	3.6"	2.6"	2.7"	2.3"	2.5"	2.2"
	5.3"	4.4"	4.3"	0.4"	T	T	—	—	—	T	1.4"	3.9"
San Antonio, Tex.	62°	66°	74°	80°	86°	92°	95°	95°	89°	82°	71°	65°
	1.6"	1.9"	1.3"	2.7"	3.7"	3.0"	1.9"	2.7"	3.8"	2.9"	2.3"	1.4"
	0.5"	0.2"	T	T	T	T	—	—	—	—	—	—
San Diego, Calif.	65°	66°	66°	68°	69°	71°	76°	78°	77°	75°	70°	66°
	2.1"	1.4"	1.6"	0.8"	0.2"	0.1"	0.0"	0.1"	0.2"	0.3"	1.1"	1.4"
	T	—	T	—	—	—	—	—	—	—	T	T
San Francisco, Calif.	57°	61°	62°	63°	65°	68°	69°	70°	73°	70°	63°	57°
	4.5"	2.8"	2.6"	1.5"	0.4"	0.2"	0.0"	0.1"	0.2"	1.1"	2.5"	3.5"
	T	T	T	—	—	—	—	—	—	—	—	T
Seattle, Wash.	45°	50°	53°	58°	65°	69°	75°	74°	69°	60°	51°	47°
	5.9"	4.2"	3.7"	2.5"	1.7"	1.5"	0.9"	1.4"	2.0"	3.4"	5.4"	6.3"
	3.1"	0.9"	0.7"	—	T	—	—	—	—	T	0.7"	1.9"
Washington, D.C.	43°	46°	55°	67°	76°	84°	88°	86°	80°	69°	57°	47°
	2.8"	2.6"	3.5"	2.9"	3.5"	3.4"	3.9"	4.4"	3.2"	2.9"	2.8"	3.2"
	5.4"	5.3"	2.0"	—	T	—	T	T	—	—	0.9"	3.1"

Note: — = no precipitation; T = trace. **Source:** U.S. Department of Commerce, National Oceanic and Atmospheric Administration, *Comparative Climatic Data for the United States through 1992* (1993).

month is less than 2.4 inches (6 cm), but equal to or greater than 10 (R/25). The southwestern coast of India is an example of an **Am** climate.

Aw *Savanna.* There is a well-defined dry season in the winter. The amount of rainfall in the driest month is less than 10 (R/25). The Brazilian highlands are a large area with an **Aw** climate.

As (Rare) There is a well-defined dry season in the summer.

B Dry climates Annual rainfall is less than annual potential evaporation. The boundary between dry areas and humid areas is R < 2T + 28 when at least 70 percent of the rainfall occurs in the warmer six months; R < 2T when at least 70 percent of the rainfall occurs in the cooler six months; or R < 2T + 14 when neither half of the year receives at least 70 percent of the total annual rainfall.

BS *Steppe.* The boundary between steppe and desert is half of the dry/humid boundary. Steppes border many of the world's large deserts.

BSh *Low-latitude steppe.* The average annual temperature is at least 64°F (18°C).

BSk *Mid-latitude steppe.* The average annual temperature is less than 64°F (18°C).

BW *Desert.* The boundary between desert and steppe is half of the dry/humid boundary. The Sahara desert is the largest area with a **BW** climate.

BWh *Low-latitude desert.* The average annual temperature is at least 64°F (18°C).

BWk *Mid-latitude desert.* The average annual temperature is less than 64°F (18°C).

C Subtropical climates The average temperature of the coldest month is between 64°F (18°C) and 27°F (–3°C). These are mainly humid mid-latitude areas with mild winters. The principal natural vegetation is broad-leaved forest.

Cw (Rare) The wettest month occurs in summer and has at least 10 times as much rainfall as the driest month in winter. **Cw** zones are mainly areas of evergreen forest in mountainous **Aw** zones.

Cs *Dry summer.* The wettest month occurs in winter and has at least three times as much rainfall as the driest month in summer. Less than 1.5 inches (4 cm) of rain falls during the driest summer month.

Csa *Warm, dry summer.* The average temperature of the warmest month is more than 72°F (22°C), and for at least four months the average temperature is more than 50°F (10°C). Italy and other Mediterranean countries have a **Csa** climate.

Csb *Cool, dry summer.* In no month is the average temperature more than 72°F (22°C), but for at least four months the average temperature is more than 50°F (10°C). **Csb** climates are found near San Francisco, Calif.; on the coast near Santiago, Chile; and in Portugal.

Cf *Humid summer.* Areas that cannot meet the criteria for **Cw** and **Cs**.

Cfa *Humid, warm summer.* The average temperature of the warmest month is more than 72°F (22°C), and for at least four months the average temperature is more than 50°F (10°C). Much of the eastern United States is in a **Cfa** zone.

Cfb *Marine west coast.* In no month is the average temperature more than 72°F (22°C), but for at least four months the average temperature is

CLIMATE OF SELECTED WORLD CITIES

Average highest and lowest temperatures for selected months in degrees Fahrenheit. Precipitation is the average monthly amount in inches of rainfall equivalent.

	January			April			July			October		
	Temp.		Avg.	Temp.		Avg.	Temp.		Avg.	Temp.		Avg.
City	**Max.**	**Min.**	**precip.**	**Max.**	**Min.**	**precip.**	**Max.**	**Min.**	**precip.**	**Max.**	**Min.**	**precip.**
Accra, Ghana	87°	73°	0.6"	88°	76°	3.2"	81°	73°	1.8"	85°	74°	2.5"
Amsterdam, Netherlands	40	34	2.0	52	43	1.6	69	59	2.6	56	48	2.8
Athens, Greece	54	42	2.2	67	52	0.8	90	72	0.2	74	60	1.7
Auckland, New Zealand	73	60	3.1	67	56	3.8	56	46	5.7	63	52	4.0
Baghdad, Iraq	60	39	0.9	85	57	0.5	110	76	trace	92	61	0.1
Bangkok, Thailand	89	67	0.2	95	78	2.3	90	76	6.9	88	76	9.9
Beirut, Lebanon	62	51	7.5	72	58	2.2	87	73	trace	81	69	2.0
Berlin, Germany	35	26	1.9	55	38	1.7	74	55	3.1	55	41	1.7
Bogotá, Colombia	67	48	2.3	67	51	5.8	64	50	2.0	66	50	6.3
Bombay, India	88	62	0.1	93	74	trace	88	75	24.3	93	73	2.5
Budapest, Hungary	35	26	1.5	62	44	2.0	82	61	2.0	61	45	2.1
Buenos Aires, Argentina	85	63	3.1	72	53	3.5	57	42	2.2	69	50	3.4
Cairo, Egypt	65	47	0.2	83	57	0.1	96	70	0.0	86	65	trace
Calcutta, India	80	55	0.4	97	76	1.7	90	79	12.8	89	74	4.5
Cape Town, South Africa	78	60	0.6	72	53	1.9	63	45	3.5	70	52	1.2
Caracas, Venezuela	75	56	0.9	81	60	1.3	78	61	4.3	79	61	4.3
Casablanca, Morocco	63	45	2.1	69	52	1.4	79	65	0.0	76	58	1.5
Copenhagen, Denmark	36	29	1.6	50	37	1.7	72	55	2.2	53	42	2.1
Dakha, Bangladesh	77	56	0.3	92	74	5.4	89	79	13.0	88	75	5.3
Dakar, Senegal	79	64	trace	81	65	trace	88	76	3.5	89	76	1.5
Dublin, Ireland	47	35	2.7	54	38	1.9	67	51	2.8	57	43	2.7
Geneva, Switzerland	39	29	1.9	58	41	2.5	77	58	2.9	58	44	3.8
Hanoi, Vietnam	68	58	0.8	80	70	3.6	92	79	11.9	84	72	3.5
Hong Kong	64	56	1.3	75	67	5.4	87	78	15.0	81	73	4.5
Istanbul, Turkey	45	36	3.7	61	45	1.9	81	65	1.7	67	54	3.8
Jakarta, Indonesia	84	74	11.8	87	75	5.8	87	73	2.5	87	74	4.4
Jerusalem, Israel	55	41	5.1	73	50	0.9	87	63	0.0	81	59	0.3
Kabul, Afghanistan	36	18	1.3	66	43	3.3	92	61	0.1	73	42	0.4
Karachi, Pakistan	77	55	0.5	90	73	0.1	91	81	3.2	91	72	0.1
Kinshasa, Zaire	87	70	5.3	89	71	7.7	81	64	0.1	88	70	4.7
Lagos, Nigeria	88	74	1.1	89	77	5.9	83	74	11.0	85	74	8.1
Lima, Peru	82	66	0.1	80	63	trace	67	57	0.3	71	58	0.1
Lisbon, Portugal	56	46	3.3	64	52	2.4	79	63	0.2	69	57	3.1
London, United Kingdom	44	35	2.0	56	40	1.8	73	55	2.0	58	44	2.3
Madrid, Spain	47	33	1.1	64	44	1.7	87	62	0.4	66	48	1.9
Manila, Philippines	86	69	0.9	93	73	1.3	88	75	17.0	88	74	7.6
Melbourne, Australia	78	57	1.9	68	51	2.3	56	42	1.9	67	48	2.6
Mexico City, Mexico	66	42	0.2	78	52	0.7	74	54	4.5	70	50	1.6
Montreal, Canada	21	6	3.8	50	33	2.6	78	61	3.7	54	40	3.4
Moscow, Russia	21	9	1.5	47	31	1.9	76	55	3.0	46	34	2.7
Nairobi, Kenya	77	54	1.5	75	58	8.3	69	51	0.6	76	55	2.1
New Delhi, India	71	43	0.9	97	68	0.3	95	80	7.1	93	64	0.4
Osaka, Japan	47	32	1.7	65	47	5.2	87	73	5.9	72	55	5.1
Oslo, Norway	30	20	1.7	50	34	1.6	73	56	2.9	49	37	2.9
Paris, France	42	32	1.5	60	41	1.7	76	55	2.1	59	44	2.2
Prague, Czechoslovakia	34	25	0.9	55	40	1.5	74	58	2.6	54	44	1.2
Rio de Janiero, Brazil	84	73	4.9	80	69	4.2	75	63	1.6	77	66	3.1
Riyadh, Saudi Arabia	70	46	0.1	89	64	1.0	107	78	0.0	94	61	0.0
Rome, Italy	54	39	3.3	68	46	2.0	88	64	0.4	73	53	4.3
Santiago, Chile	85	53	0.1	74	45	0.5	59	37	3.0	72	45	0.6
São Paulo, Brazil	77	63	8.8	73	59	2.2	66	53	1.5	68	57	4.6
Seoul, South Korea	32	15	1.2	62	41	3.0	84	70	14.8	67	45	1.6
Shanghai, China	47	32	1.9	67	49	3.6	91	75	5.8	75	56	2.9
Singapore	86	73	9.9	88	75	7.4	88	75	6.7	87	74	8.2
Stockholm, Sweden	31	23	1.5	45	32	1.5	70	55	2.8	48	39	2.1
St. Petersburg, Russia	23	12	1.0	45	31	1.0	71	57	2.5	45	37	1.8
Sydney, Australia	78	65	3.5	71	58	5.3	60	46	4.6	71	56	2.8
Tahiti, French Polynesia	89	72	13.2	89	72	6.8	86	68	2.6	87	70	3.4
Taipei, Taiwan	66	53	3.8	77	64	5.3	92	76	8.8	80	68	5.5
Tehran, Iran	45	27	1.8	71	49	1.4	99	72	0.1	76	53	0.3
Tokyo, Japan	47	29	1.9	63	46	5.3	83	70	5.6	69	55	8.2
Toronto, Canada	30	16	2.7	50	34	2.5	79	59	3.0	56	40	2.4
Vienna, Austria	34	26	1.5	57	41	2.0	75	59	3.0	55	44	2.0
Warsaw, Poland	30	21	1.2	54	38	1.5	75	56	3.0	54	41	1.7

Source: U.S. Dept. of Commerce, *Climates of the World* (1991).

BEAUFORT WIND SCALE

In 1806, Adm. Sir Francis Beaufort devised a scale for recording wind force at sea based on the effect of the wind on a full-rigged ship of war. In 1838 this scale was adopted by the British Admiralty, and in 1874 it was adopted for international use. It is now the chief scale for specifying the force of the wind and is used in all parts of the world, both on land and sea. Originally there were no specific wind speeds corresponding to various force numbers on the Beaufort scale. Since 1946, wind speed has been determined according to measurements made by an anemometer (a device for measuring wind) at 10 m (30 ft.) above the ground.

Force	Description of wind	Mean wind speed in knots[1]	Specification for use on land and at sea
Force 0	Calm	Less than 1	Calm, smoke rises vertically. Sea like a mirror.
Force 1	Light air	1–3	Direction of wind shown by smoke drift, but not by wind vanes. Ripples with appearance of scales are formed, but without foam crests.
Force 2	Light breeze	4–6	Wind felt on face; leaves rustle; ordinary vane moved by wind. Small wavelets, still short but more pronounced; crests have a glassy appearance and do not break.
Force 3	Gentle breeze	7–10	Leaves and small twigs in constant motion; wind extends light flag. Large wavelets; crests begin to break; foam of glassy appearance; perhaps scattered white horses.
Force 4	Moderate breeze	11–16	Raises dust and loose paper; small branches are moved. Small waves becoming longer; fairly frequent white horses.
Force 5	Fresh breeze	17–21	Small trees in leaf begin to sway; crested wavelets form on inland waters. Moderate waves, taking a more pronounced long form; many white horses are formed (chance of some spray).
Force 6	Strong breeze	22–27	Large branches in motion; whistling heard in telegraph wires; umbrellas used with difficulty. Large waves begin to form; the white foam crests are more extensive everywhere (probably some spray).
Force 7	Moderate gale, near gale	28–33	Whole trees in motion; inconvenience felt when walking against wind. Sea heaps up and white foam from breaking waves begins to be blown in streaks along the direction of the wind.
Force 8	Fresh gale, gale	34–40	Breaks twigs off trees; generally impedes progress. Moderately high waves of greater length; edges of crests begin to break into spindrift; foam is blown in well-marked streaks.
Force 9	Strong gale	41–47	Slight structural damage occurs (chimney pots and slate removed). High waves; dense streaks of foam; crests of waves begin to topple, tumble, and roll over.
Force 10	Whole gale, storm	48–55	Seldom experienced inland; trees uprooted; considerable structural damage occurs. Very high waves with long overhanging crests; the resulting foam, in great patches, is blown in dense white streaks; the sea takes a white appearance; the tumbling of the sea becomes heavy and shocklike; visibility affected.
Force 11	Storm, violent storm	56–63	Very rarely experienced; accompanied by widespread damage. Exceptionally high waves at sea (medium-sized ships might be lost to view behind the waves); the sea is completely covered with white patches of foam; visibility affected.
Force 12+	Hurricane[2]	64 and above	The air is filled with foam and spray; sea completely white with driving spray; visibility very seriously affected.

1. Nautical miles-per-hour; one nautical mile = 1.151 statute miles. 2. Force 13: 72–80 knots; force 14: 81–89; force 15: 90–99; force 16: 100–108; force 17: 109–118. **Sources:** Smithsonian Institution, *Smithsonian Meteorological Tables* (1966); Hydrographer of the Navy (UK), *Ocean Passages for the World* (1977).

more than 50°F (10°C). Great Britain, New Zealand, and the west coast of Alaska are all examples of **Cfb** climates.

D Continental climates The average temperature of the warmest month is more than 50°F (10°C), and the average temperature of the coldest month is 27°F (–3°C) or below. Forests are the principal natural vegetation.

Dfa *Humid, warm summer.* All seasons have some precipitation. The average temperature of the warmest month is more than 72°F (22°C), and for at least four months the average temperature is more than 50°F (10°C). The northern Great Plains of the United States have a **Dfa** climate.

Dwa *Humid, warm summer.* The wettest month occurs in summer and has at least 10 times as much rainfall as the driest month in winter. The average temperature of the warmest month is more than 72°F (22°C), and for at least four months the average temperature is more than 50°F (10°C). The land around the northern part of the Yellow Sea has a **Dwa** climate.

Dfb *Humid, cool summer.* All seasons have some precipitation. In no month is the average temperature more than 72°F (22°C), but for at least four months the average temperature is more than 50°F (10°C). A large **Dfb** area stretches from eastern Europe into Asia.

Dwb *Humid, cool summer.* The wettest month occurs in summer and has at least 10 times as much rainfall as the driest month in winter. In no month is the average temperature more than 72°F (22°C), but for at least four months the average temperature is more than 50°F (10°C). Much of the area between Manchuria and the Sea of Okhotsk has a **Dwb** climate.

Dfc *Subpolar.* All seasons have some precipitation. For one to three months, the average temperature is 50°F (10°C) or more. A huge **Dfc** area is in Siberia and adjacent parts of the Soviet Union.

E Polar climates The average temperature of the warmest month is less than 50°F (10°C). There is no summer, and no trees grow.

ET *Tundra.* The average temperature of the warmest month is less than 50°F (10°C) but more than 32°F (0°C). Vast areas of northern North America, Europe, and Asia lie in the **ET** climate zone.

EF *Ice cap.* The average temperature of the warmest eight months is 32°F (0°C) or less. The **EF** climate is found at the North and South poles and in interior Greenland.

GLOSSARY OF WEATHER WORDS

Air mass A large body of air that, at a given elevation, has about the same temperature and humidity throughout.

Barometric pressure The weight of a column of air at a particular place is determined by measuring the height of a column of mercury under a vacuum. The instrument for making such a measurement is called a barometer. At sea level the standard barometric pressure measured this way is 29.92 inches (76 cm). In the International

TORNADOES, FLOODS, AND TROPICAL CYCLONES IN THE U.S., 1980–93

Item	1980	1985	1986	1987	1989	1990	1991	1992	1993
Tornadoes, number	866	684	764	656	856	1,133	1,132	1,303	N.A.
Lives lost, total	28	94	15	59	49	53	39	39	N.A.
Most in a single tornado	5	18	3	30	21	29	13	10	N.A.
Floods: lives lost	97	304	80	82	81	147	63	87	N.A.
Property loss (millions)	$1,500	$3,000	$4,000	$1,490	$415	$2,058	$1,416	$800	N.A.
North Atlantic tropical storms and hurricanes:									
Number reaching U.S. coast	2	11	6	7	11	14	8	6	8
Hurricanes only	1	6	2	1	3	0	1	1	1
Lives lost in U.S.	2	30	9	0	56	13	15	24	3
Property loss (millions)[1]	N.A.	$4,457	$18	$8	$7,840	$57	$1,500	$25,000	$35

Note: A tornado is a violent, rotating column of air descending from a cumulonimbus cloud in the form of a tubular or funnel-shaped cloud, usually characterized by movements along a narrow path and wind speeds from 100 to 300 miles per hour; also known as a twister or waterspout. Tropical cyclones have maximum winds of 39 to 73 miles per hour; hurricanes have maximum winds of 74 miles per hour or higher. The increase in number of tornadoes is due in large part to improved detection and documentation. N.A. = not available. 1. In constant (1990) dollars. **Source:** U.S. Bureau of Census, *Statistical Abstract of the United States* (annual).

System, air pressure is measured in bars or in kiloPascals. A bar is slightly less than the standard air pressure at sea level, and a kiloPascal is one-hundredth of a bar. At any location, however, barometric pressure is affected by changes in temperature, humidity, or elevation. When the "barometer is falling," the air pressure is decreasing, often a sign of a storm.

Climate General weather conditions over a long period of time.

Cold front The place where cold air that is advancing meets warm air that is retreating before it. This kind of weather not only lowers temperature as it passes but also causes high winds and may cause thunderstorms.

Cyclone A region of low atmospheric pressure (see "Depression"). Severe cyclones are known as hurricanes, tropical cyclones, and typhoons.

Degree-days A degree-day is one degree of deviation of the daily mean temperature from a given norm, usually 65°F. Cooling degree-days are the number of degrees Fahrenheit by which the mean temperature exceeds 65°F, while heating degree-days are the number of degrees the mean temperature is below 65°F. During a year, keeping track of the total number of degree-days (adding the ones for each day) is used to keep track of cooling or heating needs. For example, oil companies use heating degree-days to estimate how much oil their customers have used and when they might need a refill.

Depression Any region of low air pressure. In temperate regions over land, the typical depression is a *low*. The often more powerful depression occurring over tropical waters is called a *tropical depression*. If the air pressure in a tropical depression continues to fall, it becomes a tropical storm or, lower still, a *hurricane*.

Dew point The temperature at which dew (drops of water) begins to form as air cools. Air can hold only a certain amount of water vapor at a given temperature. When the temperature falls, excess water vapor must turn into a liquid.

El Niño A change in the circulation and temperature of the waters off the west coast of South America that occurs every few years. Water that is normally cold is replaced by warmer water, disrupting the local environment in many ways (e.g., moving fish away from the surface, which results in less food for water fowl, and causing rain in normally dry regions). Because El Niño is linked to other weather systems, a strong El Niño can affect weather worldwide.

Front The boundary between two different air masses.

High An air mass characterized hy higher-than-normal air pressure; usually this is a fair-weather system. Some highs are typically found in the same place each year, such as one that occurs over Bermuda in most summers.

Hurricane A huge tropical rainstorm with winds that swirl rapidly around a calm, dry, central "eye." To be classified a hurricane, a tropical storm must have wind speeds of more than 74 mph (119 km/hour). The average hurricane is 375 miles (600 km) in diameter and extends up 40,000 feet (12,000 m) above the surface of the ocean. The eye averages 12.5 miles (20 km) in diameter. When a hurricane hits land, its fierce winds and floods can do great damage. On average five hurricanes each year threaten the eastern and southern United States.

Jet stream A strong river or two of high winds in the upper atmosphere (but below the stratosphere) that travels from west to east at between 75 and 150 mph (120–240 km/hour), most often in the middle latitudes. Discovered by American bomber pilots in World War II, it is now known to have significant effects on weather.

Low An air mass characterized by lower-than-normal air pressure; usually this is the heart of a storm system. Some lows are found in the same region most of the year, such as the low in the Pacific just off the coast of Alaska.

Mean temperature Technically, this should be the average of all temperatures during the day; sometimes it is the average of 24 temperatures taken once each hour; but most often the mean temperature is simply the average of the high and low for the day.

Monsoon A wind system in which the prevailing direction of the wind reverses itself from season to season. Southeast Asia is the most typical monsoon region. The summer (southwest) monsoon, characterized by hot, moist air and heavy rains, last from April to September. The winter (northeast) monsoon lasts from October to March and is characterized by cool, dry air.

Occluded front When a cold front overtakes a warm front, the denser cold air flows under the less dense warm air.

Prevailing winds Throughout the world, winds follow regular patterns. In some places winds are so light and infrequent as to scarcely exist, such as in the doldrums along the equator and in the horse latitudes near latitude 30° north and south. In other places the winds tend to come from a particular direction and are called prevailing winds.

Rain shadow An area on the leeward side of a mountain range that receives little rainfall.

COSTLIEST HURRICANES IN U.S. HISTORY

Hurricane (year)	Damages (millions)[1]	Deaths
Andrew (1992)	$20,000[2]	28
Hugo (1989)	7,000	504
Betsy (1965)	6,320	74
Agnes (1972)	6,280	118
Camille (1969)	5,130	256
Diane (1955)	4,120	400
New England (1938)	3,520	600
Frederic (1979)	3,430	31
Alicia (1983)	2,340	17
Carol (1954)	2,320	68

1. In constant (1989) dollars. 2. Estimate. **Source:** University of Calorado Natural Hazards Center, Federal Emergency Management Agency.

Relative humidity The amount of moisture (water vapor) in the air compared with the total amount it can hold expressed as a percent. Warm air can hold more water vapor than cold air, so a relative humidity of 75 percent on a warm summer day is moister than a relative humidity of 75 percent on a cool winter day. However, because evaporation is greater on warm days, the relative humidity in summer is generally higher than in winter.

Secondary cold front A cold front that sometimes forms behind another cold front and that is often even colder than the first front.

Secondary depression A low that forms to the south or east of a low that is a storm center.

Squall line A line of instability that often precedes a cold front, marked by wind gusts and often by heavy rain.

Stationary front A front that stays in the same place.

Storm surge The rise in water levels in the ocean or a large lake that comes from a combination of wind and low pressure during a storm, especially pronounced during a hurricane.

DETERMINING THE WIND-CHILL FACTOR

Sometimes called a wind-chill index, this is a measure of the cooling power of air movement and low temperature on the human body. Because heat passes directly from a warm body to the cooler air surrounding it—a process known as convection—wind produces a continuing source of cooler air and a chilling effect that is equivalent to a lower temperature. The effect of wind on a warm day is pleasant, but as temperatures approach freezing, wind chill is not only unpleasant but can be dangerous. As the table below shows, a temperature of 5°F combined with a breeze of 10 mph produces a wind-chill temperature of –15°F—a temperature at which frostbite occurs much sooner than at 5°F. Wind speeds above 45 mph have little additional cooling effect.

Wind	Actual temperature																	Wind
speed	35°F	30°F	25°F	20°F	15°F	10°F	5°F	0°F	–5°F	–10°F	–15°F	–20°F	–25°F	–30°F	–35°F	–40°F	–45°F	speed
5 mph	33°	27°	21°	16°	12°	7°	0°	–5°	–10°	–15°	–21°	–26°	–31°	–36°	–42°	–47°	–52°	5 mph
10 mph	22	16	10	3	–3	–9	–15	–22	–27	–34	–40	–46	–52	–58	–64	–71	–77	10 mph
15 mph	16	9	2	–5	–11	–18	–25	–31	–38	–45	–51	–58	–65	–72	–78	–85	–92	15 mph
20 mph	12	4	–3	–10	–17	–24	–31	–39	–46	–53	–60	–67	–74	–81	–88	–95	–102	20 mph
25 mph	8	1	–7	–15	–22	–29	–36	–44	–51	–59	–66	–74	–81	–88	–96	–103	–110	25 mph
30 mph	6	–2	–10	–18	–25	–33	–41	–49	–56	–64	–71	–79	–86	–93	–101	–109	–116	30 mph
35 mph	4	–4	–12	–20	–27	–35	–43	–52	–58	–67	–74	–82	–89	–97	–105	–113	–120	35 mph
40 mph	3	–5	–13	–21	–29	–37	–45	–53	–60	–69	–76	–84	–92	–100	–107	–115	–123	40 mph
45 mph	2	–6	–14	–22	–30	–38	–46	–54	–62	–70	–78	–85	–93	–102	–109	–117	–125	45 mph

Temperature-humidity index A number derived from a formula relating temperature and humidity to discomfort. When it is 75, many are uncomfortable, while at 80 or above, almost everyone is uncomfortable. Temperatures are less comfortable at high humidities because cooling by sweating is less efficient.

Tornado A small and short-lived but very severe windstorm. Tornadoes are whirling columns of air that reach down from a cloud, and they often accompany thunderstorms, rain, and hail. With wind speeds up to 300 mph (480 km/hr) tornadoes can do tremendous damage. The diameter of the average tornado is between 500 and 2,000 feet (150–600m). The average tornado moves along the ground at 28 mph (45 km/hr) and has a "path" that is 16 miles (26 km) long. In the United States some 750 tornadoes are reported every year, most frequently between April and June.

Tropical storm A storm that forms over the ocean in the tropics and often moves onto land, where it loses strength. Technically, a storm is designated a tropical storm only when winds are between 39 and 73 miles per hour. If winds become greater, a tropical storm becomes a hurricane.

Trough A low that is long, rather than nearly circular.

Typhoon A hurricane formed in the western Pacific Ocean.

Warm front The boundary of a moving warm-air mass.

Weather The condition of the atmosphere—temperature, rain, and wind, for example—in a particular place. A climate is defined by weather conditions over a long period of time.

Wind Any current of air, measured on land in miles per hour and at sea in knots. The direction of a given wind is determined from the point of the compass from which it blows (e.g., northeast, south). In various regions of the world, names are given to seasonal winds of particular quality. Among these are the *bora*, a cold, usually dry north/northeast wind along the eastern Adriatic; *brickfielder*, a hot north wind of southeastern Australia; *buran*, a cold, violent north/northeast wind of Siberia and central Asia, common in winter; *chinook*, a dry winter or spring wind that blows down the eastern slopes of the Rocky Mountains, often warm enough to melt the snow; *harmattan*, a hot, dry north wind in West Africa that cools as it evaporates the moist air of the coast; *mistral*, a cold, strong north/northwest wind of the western Mediterranean, with a surface strength of 60 km/hour, frequent in winter; *pampero*, a sudden, cold south or west wind in Argentina and Uruguay, frequent in summer; *Santa Ana*, a hot, dry wind that blows from the north or east in southern California; *sirocco*, a hot south wind of North Africa and southern Italy; *southerly burster*, a cold, violent south wind of southeastern Australia; *williwaw*, a violent squall that blows in the Strait of Magellan (South America); and *zonda*, a hot, dry north wind of Argentina and Uruguay.

WORLD POPULATION

In 1995 total world population was 5.7 billion according to United Nations estimates. Of this total, 1.2 billion people were in the developed countries and 4.5 billion were in the developing nations. Asia, with the world's largest land mass, had the world's largest regional population, 3.458 billion. Africa had 728.1 million and Northern America had 292.8 million people. The most populous nation was China with 1.222 billion people, followed by India with 935.7 million. The United States ranked fourth with a population of 263.5 million.

In 1960 Europe was the most densely populated region in the world, with virtually all of its major countries exceeding 200 persons per square mile. Only a few small island nations or city-states had a population density that high. Most developing regions had well under 100 persons per square mile.

By 1991, according to the U.S. Bureau of the Census, population density in Asia had far surpassed that in Europe. Although other regional averages were still lower, four out of every 10 developing countries had reached a density of over 200 persons per square mile. Not counting city-states, Bangladesh had the world's highest density with 2,255 persons per square mile, followed by South Korea with 1,138 per square mile and Japan with 814. China, while having the largest total population, had a population density of 320 persons per square mile. The United States had 71 people per square mile.

As many as 70 million people, mostly from developing countries, are working (legally or illegally) in other countries. Over one million people emigrate permanently to other countries and close to another million seek asylum each year. During the 1980s eight million legal immigrants settled in the United States, Canada, and Australia.

THE WORLD'S LARGEST URBAN AREAS, RANKED BY 1990 ESTIMATED POPULATION (in millions)

The following chart is arranged according to urban areas that had populations of more than three million in 1990. An urban area is a central city, or several cities, and the surrounding urbanized areas, also called a metropolitan area.

Urban area	Country	1950	1970	1990	2000[1]
1. Mexico City	Mexico	3.1	9.4	20.2	25.6
2. Tokyo	Japan	6.7	14.9	18.1	19.0
3. São Paulo	Brazil	2.4	8.1	17.4	22.1
4. New York	United States	12.3	16.2	16.2	16.8
5. Shanghai	China	5.3	11.2	13.4	17.0
6. Los Angeles	United States	4.0	8.4	11.9	13.9
7. Calcutta	India	4.4	6.9	11.8	15.7
8. Buenos Aires	Argentina	5.0	8.4	11.5	12.9
9. Bombay	India	2.9	5.8	11.2	15.4
10. Seoul	South Korea	1.0	5.3	11.0	12.7
11. Beijing	China	3.9	8.1	10.8	14.0
12. Rio de Janeiro	Brazil	2.9	7.0	10.7	12.5
13. Tianjin	China	2.4	5.2	9.4	12.7
14. Jakarta	Indonesia	2.0	3.9	9.3	13.7
15. Cairo	Egypt	2.4	5.3	9.0	11.8
16. Moscow	Russia	4.8	7.1	8.8	9.0
17. Delhi	India	1.4	3.5	8.8	13.2
18. Metro Manila	Philippines	1.5	3.5	8.5	11.8
19. Osaka	Japan	3.8	7.6	8.5	8.6
20. Paris	France	5.4	8.3	8.5	8.6
21. Karachi	Pakistan	1.0	3.1	7.7	11.7
22. Lagos	Nigeria	0.3	2.0	7.7	12.9
23. London	United Kingdom	8.7	8.6	7.4	13.9
24. Bangkok	Thailand	1.4	3.1	7.2	10.3
25. Chicago	United States	4.9	6.7	7.0	7.3
26. Teheran	Iran	1.0	3.3	6.8	8.5
27. Istanbul	Turkey	1.1	2.8	6.7	9.5
28. Dhaka	Bangladesh	0.4	1.5	6.6	12.2
29. Lima	Peru	1.0	2.9	6.2	8.2
30. Madras	India	1.4	3.0	5.7	7.8
31. Hong Kong	Hong Kong	1.7	3.4	5.4	6.1
32. Milan	Italy	3.6	5.5	5.3	5.4
33. Madrid	Spain	1.6	3.4	5.2	5.9
34. St. Petersburg	Russia	2.6	4.0	5.1	5.4
35. Bangalore	India	0.8	1.6	5.0	8.2
36. Bogotá	Colombia	0.6	2.4	4.9	6.4
37. Shenyang	China	2.1	3.5	4.8	6.3
38. Philadelphia	United States	2.9	4.0.	4.3	4.5
39. Caracas	Venezuela	0.7	2.0	4.1	5.2
40. Baghdad	Iraq	0.6	2.0	4.0	5.1
41. Lahore	Pakistan	0.8	2.0	4.1	6.0
42. Wuhan	China	1.2	2.7	3.9	5.3
43. Alexandria	Egypt	1.0	2.0	3.7	5.1
44. Detroit	United States	2.8	4.0	3.7	3.7
45. Guangzhou	China	1.3	3.0	3.7	4.8
46. San Francisco	United States	2.0	3.0	3.7	4.1
47. Ahmedabad	India	0.9	1.7	3.6	5.3
48. Belo Horizonte	Brazil	0.4	1.6	3.6	4.7
49. Naples	Italy	2.8	3.6	3.6	3.6
50. Hyderabad	India	1.1	1.7	3.5	5.0
51. Kinshasa	Zaire	0.2	1.4	3.5	5.5
52. Toronto	Canada	1.0	2.8	3.5	3.9
53. Athens	Greece	1.8	2.5	3.4	3.8
54. Barcelona	Spain	1.6	2.7	3.4	3.7
55. Dallas	United States	0.9	2.0	3.4	4.4
56. Katowice	Poland	1.7	2.8	3.4	3.7
57. Sydney	Australia	1.7	2.7	3.4	3.7
58. Yangon	Myanmar	0.7	1.4	3.3	4.7
59. Casablanca	Morocco	0.7	1.5	3.2	4.6
60. Guadalajara	Mexico	0.4	1.5	3.2	4.1
61. Ho Chi Minh City	Vietnam	0.9	2.0	3.2	4.1
62. Chongqing	China	1.7	2.3	3.1	4.2
63. Porto Alegre	Brazil	0.4	1.5	3.1	3.9
64. Rome	Italy	1.6	2.9	3.1	3.1
65. Algiers	Algeria	0.4	1.3	3.0	4.5
66. Chengou	China	0.7	1.8	3.0	4.1
67. Harbin	China	1.0	2.1	3.0	3.9
68. Houston	United States	0.7	1.7	3.0	3.6
69. Monterrey	Mexico	0.4	1.2	3.0	3.9
70. Montreal	Canada	1.3	2.4	3.0	3.1
71. Taipei	China	0.6	1.8	3.0	4.2

1. Projected figures. **Source:** United Nations Department of International Economic and Social Affairs, *World Urbanization Projections 1990* (1991).

PERCENTAGE DISTRIBUTION OF THE WORLD'S POPULATION, BY MAJOR AREA, 1950–2050

Area	1950	1990	2050
Developed countries	29.9%	20.5%	12.4%
Europe	15.6	9.4	4.9
Northern America	6.6	5.2	3.3
Oceania	0.5	0.5	0.4
USSR[1]	7.2	5.4	3.8
Developing countries	70.1	79.5	87.6
Africa	8.8	12.1	22.6
Latin America	6.6	8.5	9.2
China	22.1	21.5	15.2
India	14.2	16.1	17.0
Other Asia	18.4	21.2	23.7

1. Republics of former Soviet Union. **Source**: United Nations Department of International Economic and Social Affairs, *Long-range World Population Projections, 1950–2150* (1992).

ESTIMATED AND PROJECTED POPULATION OF MAJOR WORLD AREAS, 1950–2050 (in millions)

Area	1950	1990	2000	2025	2050
World	**2,518**	**5,292**	**6,261**	**8,504**	**10,019**
Developed	752	1,089	1,143	1,237	1,233
Europe	393	498	510	515	486
Northern America	166	276	295	332	326
Oceania	13	26	30	38	41
USSR[1]	180	289	308	352	380
Developing	1,766	4,203	5,118	7,267	8,786
Africa	222	642	867	1,597	2,265
Latin America	166	448	538	757	922
China	555	1,139	1,299	1,513	1,521
India	358	853	1,042	1,442	1,699
Other Asia	465	1,121	1,372	1,958	2,379

1. Republics of former Soviet Union. **Source**: United Nations Department of International Economic and Social Affairs, *Long-Range World Population Projections, 1950–2150* (1992).

GLOSSARY OF DEMOGRAPHIC TERMS

Birth rate The average annual number of births during a year per 1,000 population at midyear; also known as crude birth rate.

Contraception Deliberate use of methods to prevent conception or pregnancy; also known as family planning.

Death rate The average annual number of deaths during a year per 1,000 population at midyear; also known as crude death rate.

Demography The statistical study of the characteristics of human populations including size and density, growth, distribution, migration, and vital statistics, and the effect of these factors on social and economic conditions.

Developed country The UN describes developed countries as industrialized nations that have a high gross national product (GNP), high per capita GNP, and advanced science and technology. Approximately 45 countries, including those in Europe, North America, Japan, Australia, and New Zealand are considered developed.

Developing country The United Nations describes developing countries as nations that have a low GNP, generally poorer people, an economy based on agricultural production, and a lack of advanced technologies. Approximately 125 countries, including those in Africa, the Near East, Latin America and the Caribbean, and Asia (except Japan) and Oceania (except Australia and New Zealand), are considered developing.

Growth rate The average annual percent change in the population, resulting from a surplus (or deficit) of births over deaths and the balance of migrants entering and leaving a country. The rate may be positive or negative; also known as population growth rate or average annual rate of growth.

Infant mortality rate The number of deaths to infants under one year of age in a given year per 1,000 live births occuring in the same year.

Projections Data on population and vital rates derived for future years based on statistics from population censuses, vital registration systems, or sample surveys pertaining to the recent past; and on assumptions about future trends.

Vital events Births and deaths.

Vital rates Birth rates and death rates.

POPULATION INDICATORS BY REGION AND NATION

Region/Country	Population estimate ('000s) 1995	Population estimate ('000s) 2025	Birth rate per 1,000 1990–95	Death rate per 1,000 1990–95	Life expectancy 1990–95	Percent urban 1995	Fertility rate per woman 1995
World total	**5,716,400**	**8,294,300**	**26**	**9**	**65**	**45%**	**3.0**
More developed regions	1,166,600	1,238,400	14	10	75	75	1.7
Less developed regions	4,549,800	7,055,900	29	9	62	38	3.4
Least developed countries	575,400	1,162,300				22	5.6
AFRICA	**728,100**	**1,495,800**	**43**	**14**	**53**	**34**	**5.6**
Eastern Africa	**227,100**	**494,600**	**48**	**16**	**49**	**22**	**6.2**
Burundi	6,400	13,500	46	17	48	8	6.5
Eritrea	3,500	7,000				17	5.6
Ethiopia	55,100	126,900	49	18	47	13	6.8
Kenya	28,300	63,400	44	10	59	28	6.0
Madagascar	14,800	34,400	45	13	55	27	5.9
Malawi	11,100	22,300	54	21	44	14	6.9
Mauritius	1,100	1,500	18	7	70	41	2.3
Mozambique	16,000	35,100	45	18	47	34	6.3
Rwanda	8,000	15,800	52	18	46	6	6.3
Somalia	9,300	21,300	50	19	47	26	6.8
Tanzania	29,700	62,900	48	15	51	24	5.7
Uganda	21,300	48,100	51	21	42	13	7.1
Zambia	9,500	19,100	46	18	44	43	5.7
Zimbabwe	11,300	19,600	41	11	56	32	4.8
Middle Africa	**82,300**	**189,100**	**46**	**15**	**51**	**33**	**6.2**
Angola	11,100	26,600	51	19	46	32	6.9
Cameroon	13,200	29,200	41	12	56	45	5.5
Central African Republic	3,300	6,400	44	18	47	39	5.5
Chad	6,400	12,900	44	18	48	21	5.7
Congo	2,600	5,700	45	15	52	59	6.0
Gabon	1,300	2,700	43	16	54	50	5.5
Zaire	43,900	104,600	47	15	52	29	6.5
Northern Africa	**160,600**	**268,600**	**34**	**9**	**61**	**46**	**4.0**
Algeria	27,900	45,500	34	7	66	56	3.6
Egypt	62,900	97,300	31	9	62	45	3.7
Libya	5,400	12,900	42	8	63	86	6.2
Morocco	27,000	40,700	32	8	63	48	3.4
Sudan	28,100	58,400	42	14	52	25	5.6
Tunisia	8,900	13,300	27	6	68	57	3.0
Southern Africa	**47,400**	**82,800**	**32**	**9**	**63**	**48**	**4.1**
Botswana	1,500	3,000	38	9	61	28	4.7
Lesotho	2,100	4,200	34	10	61	23	5.0
Namibia	1,500	3,000	43	11	59	37%	5.0
South Africa	41,500	71,000	31	9	63	51	4.0
Western Africa	**210,700**	**460,600**	**46**	**15**	**51**	**37**	**6.3**
Benin	5,400	12,300	49	18	46	31	6.9
Burkina Faso	10,300	21,700	47	18	48	27	6.3
Ghana	17,500	38,000	42	12	56	36	5.8
Guinea	6,700	15,100	51	20	45	30	6.8
Guinea-Bissau	1,100	2,000	43	21	44	22	5.6
Ivory Coast	14,300	36,800	50	15	52	44	7.1
Liberia	3,000	7,200	47	14	55	45	6.6
Mali	10,800	24,600	51	19	46	27	6.9
Mauritania	2,300	4,400	46	18	48	54	5.2
Niger	9,200	22,400	51	19	47	17	7.3
Nigeria	111,700	238,400	45	14	53	39	6.2
Senegal	8,300	16,900	43	16	49	42	5.8
Sierra Leone	4,500	8,700	48	22	43	36	6.3
Togo	4,100	9,400	45	13	55	31	6.3
LATIN AMERICA	**482,000**	**709,800**	**26**	**7**	**68**	**74**	**3.0**
Caribbean	**35,800**	**49,600**	**24**	**8**	**69**	**62**	**2.7**
Cuba	11,100	12,700	17	7	76	76	1.8
Dominican Republic	7,800	11,200	28	6	68	65	2.9
Haiti	7,200	13,100	35	12	57	32	4.7
Jamaica	2,400	3,300	22	6	74	54	2.2
Puerto Rico	3,700	4,600	18	7	75	73	2.1
Trinidad and Tobago	1,300	1,800	23	6	71	72	2.3
Central America	**126,400**	**197,500**	**30**	**6**	**69**	**68**	**3.3**
Belize	200	400	—	—	—	47	3.9
Costa Rica	3,400	5,600	26	4	76	50	3.1
El Salvador	5,800	9,700	33	7	66	45	3.8
Guatemala	10,600	21,700	39	8	65	42	5.1
Honduras	5,700	10,700	37	7	66	44	4.6
Mexico	93,700	136,600	28	5	70	75	3.0
Nicaragua	4,400	9,100	40	7	67	63	4.8
Panama	2,600	3,800	25	5	73	53	2.8
South America	**319,800**	**462,700**	**24**	**7**	**67**	**78**	**2.9**
Argentina	34,600	46,100	20	9	71	88	2.7
Bolivia	7,400	13,100	34	9	61	61	4.6

Region/Country	Population estimate ('000s) 1995	Population estimate ('000s) 2025	Birth rate per 1,000 1990–95	Death rate per 1,000 1990–95	Life expectancy 1990–95	Percent urban 1995	Fertility rate per woman 1995
Brazil	161,800	230,300	23	7	66	78%	2.8
Chile	14,300	19,800	23	6	72	84	2.5
Colombia	35,100	49,400	24	6	69	73	2.6
Ecuador	11,500	17,800	30	7	67	58	3.3
Paraguay	5,000	9,000	33	6	67	53	4.1
Peru	23,800	36,700	8	65	71	72	3.3
Uruguay	3,200	3,700	17	10	72	90	2.3
Venezuela	21,800	34,800	26	5	70	93	3.1
NORTHERN AMERICA	**292,800**	**369,600**	**16**	**9**	**76**	**76**	**2.0**
Canada	29,500	38,300	14	8	77	77	1.9
United States	263,300	331,200	16	9	76	76	2.1
ASIA	**3,458,000**	**4,960,000**	**26**	**8**	**65**	**35**	**3.0**
Eastern Asia	**1,424,200**	**1,745,800**	**20**	**7**	**72**	**37**	**1.9**
China	1,221,500	1,526,100	21	7	71	30	2.0
Hong Kong	5,900	5,900	13	6	78	95	1.2
Japan	125,100	121,600	11	7	79	78	1.5
Korea, North	23,900	33,400	24	5	71	61	2.3
Korea, South	45,000	54,400	16	6	71	81	1.8
Mongolia	2,400	3,800	34	8	64	61	3.4
South-eastern Asia	**484,300**	**713,400**	**28**	**8**	**63**	**34**	**3.2**
Cambodia	10,300	19,700	39	14	51	21	5.1
Indonesia	197,600	275,600	27	8	63	35	2.8
Laos	4,900	9,700	45	15	51	22	6.4
Malaysia	20,100	31,600	29	5	71	54	3.4
Myanmar	46,500	75,600	33	11	58	26	4.0
Philippines	67,600	104,500	30	7	65	54	3.8
Singapore	2,800	3,400	16	6	74	100	1.7
Thailand	58,800	73,600	21	6	69	20	2.1
Vietnam	74,500	118,200	29	9	64	21	3.7
South Central Asia	**1,381,200**	**2,196,300**	**32**	**10**	**59**	**29**	**3.9**
Afghanistan	20,100	45,300	53	22	43	20	6.6
Bangladesh	120,400	196,100	38	14	53	18	4.1
Bhutan	1,600	3,100	40	17	48	6	5.7
India	935,700	1,392,100	29	10	60	27	3.6
Iran	67,300	123,500	40	7	67	59	4.8
Nepal	21,900	40,700	37	13	54	14	5.2
Pakistan	140,500	284,800	41	10	59	35	5.9
Sri Lanka	18,400	25,000	21	6	72	22	2.4
Western Asia	**168,400**	**304,600**	**34**	**7**	**66**	**66**	**4.3**
Iraq	20,400	42,700	39	7	66	75	5.5
Israel	5,600	7,800	21	7	77	91	2.8
Jordan	5,400	12,000	40	5	68	72	5.4
Kuwait	1,500	2,800	28	2	75	97	3.0
Lebanon	3,000	4,400	27	7	69	87	2.9
Oman	2,200	6,100	40	5	70	13	6.9
Saudi Arabia	17,900	42,700	36	5	69	80	6.2
Syria	14,700	33,500	42	6	67	52	5.6
Turkey	61,900	90,900	28	7	67	69	3.2
United Arab Emirates	1,900	3,000	21	4	71	84	4.1
Yemen	14,500	33,700	48	14	53	34	7.4
EUROPE	**727,000**	**718,200**	**13**	**11**	**75**	**74**	**1.6**
Eastern Europe	**308,700**	**299,400**	**14**	**11**	**71**	**70**	**1.6**
Bulgaria	8,800	7,800	13	12	72	71	1.5
Czech Republic	10,300	10,600	—	—	—	65%	1.8
Hungary	10,100	9,400	12	14	70	65	1.7
Poland	38,400	41,500	14	10	72	65	1.9
Romania	22,800	21,700	16	11	70	55	1.5
Slovakia	5,400	6,000	—	—	—	59	1.9
Northern Europe	**93,500**	**98,600**	**14**	**11**	**76**	**84**	**1.9**
Denmark	5,200	5,100	12	12	76	85	1.7
Estonia	1,500	1,400	14	12	71	73	1.6
Finland	5,100	5,400	13	10	76	63	1.9
Ireland	3,600	3,900	14	9	75	58	2.1
Latvia	2,600	2,300	14	12	71	73	1.6
Lithuania	3,700	3,800	15	10	73	72	1.8
Norway	4,300	4,700	15	11	77	73	2.0
Sweden	8,800	9,800	14	11	78	83	2.1
United Kingdom	58,300	61,500	14	11	76	90	1.8
Southern Europe	**143,900**	**139,300**	**11**	**10**	**76**	**65**	**1.4**
Albania	3,400	4,700	23	5	73	37	2.8
Bosnia and Herzegovina	3,500	4,500	—	—	—	49	1.6
Croatia	4,500	4,200	—	—	—	64	1.7
Greece	10,500	9,900	10	10	78	65	1.4
Italy	57,200	52,300	10	10	77	67	1.3
Macedonia	2,200	2,600				60	2.0
Portugal	9,800	9,700	12	10	75	36	1.6
Slovenia	1,900	1,800				64	1.5
Spain	39,600	37,600	11	9	78	76	1.2
Yugoslavia	10,800	11,500	—	—	—	57	2.0
Western Europe	**180,800**	**180,900**	**12**	**11**	**76**	**81**	**1.5**
Austria	8,000	8,300	12	11	76	56	1.6
Belgium	10,100	10,400	12	11	76	97	1.6
France	58,000	61,200	13	10	77	73	1.7
Germany	81,600	76,400	11	11	76	87	1.3
Netherlands	15,500	16,300	14	9	77	89	1.6
Switzerland	7,200	7,800	13	10	78	61	1.6
OCEANIA	**28,500**	**41,000**	**19**	**8**	**73**	**70**	**2.5**
Australia–New Zealand	**21,700**	**29,000**	**15**	**8**	**77**	**85**	**1.9**
Australia	18,100	24,700	15	8	77	85	1.9
Melanesia	5,800	10,100	32	9	59	21	4.5
New Zealand	3,600	4,400	17	8	76	86	2.1
Papua New Guinea	4,300	7,500	33	11	56	16	4.8
Countries of the former USSR with economies in transition							
Armenia	3,600	4,700	23	6	71	69	2.5
Azerbaijan	7,600	10,100	27	7	70	56	2.4
Belarus	10,100	9,900	16	10	72	71	1.7
Georgia	5,500	6,100	18	9	72	59	2.1
Kazakhstan	17,100	21,700	24	8	69	60	2.4
Kyrgyzstan	4,700	7,100	31	7	68	39	3.5
Moldova	4,400	5,100	21	10	68	52	2.1
Russian Federation	147,000	138,500	16	11	70	76	1.5
Tajikistan	6,100	11,800	40	7	70	32	4.7
Turkmenistan	4,100	6,700	36	8	65	45	3.8
Ukraine	51,400	48,700	14	12	71	70	1.6
Uzbekistan	22,800	37,700	—	—	—	41	3.7

Note: Totals may not add because of rounding numbers. Data for small countries or areas, generally those with population of 200,000 or less in 1990, are not given in this table. **Source:** United Nations Populations Fund (UNFPA), *The State of World Population 1995* (1995) and *The State of World Population 1994* (1994).

WORLD POPULATION TRENDS

World population reached 5.72 billion in mid-1995 according to United Nations estimates. The UN projects that world population will reach six billion in 1998, 8.5 billion by 2025, and 10 billion by 2050. Approximately 97 million people will be added each year until 2000, the equivalent of the current United States every two and a half years. Nearly all of this population growth will be in Africa, Asia, and Latin America. Over half will be in Africa and south Asia.

People living in industrialized nations constitute about 20 percent of world population, but will contribute less than 2 percent of world population increase from 1990 to the 22nd century. Ninety-eight percent of future world population growth will take place in Africa, Asia, and Latin America. From 1990 to 1995, the average growth rate is estimated at 0.5 percent in the developed areas and 2.1 percent growth rate in developing nations.

After increasing by 45 percent between 1950 and 1990, the population of the developed countries is projected to increase by only a further 13 percent between 1990 and 2050 and then decline by 3 percent into the 22nd century.

The ultimate population for Europe is projected to be smaller than its current size of 498 million. It is expected to decrease to 486 million in 2050 and continue to decline even further thereafter. North America is projected to increase from 276 million persons in 1990 to 360 million in 2025 and then continually decline into the 22nd century. The population of the former USSR nations and Oceania are projected to increase continually: the USSR nations from 1990 levels of 289 million to 344 million in 2025, and Oceania from 26 million to 41 million in the same period.

Africa has been and will continue to be the fastest growing region. In 1950 Africa had 222 million people, 8.8 percent of the world total. By 1990 the population was 642 million, 12.1 percent of the world total, and it is projected to reach 867 million in 2000, 1.582 billion in 2025, and 2.265 billion in 2050. By 2050 Africa will contain 23 percent of the world's people.

Latin America's population increased from 166 million in 1950 to 448 million in 1990 and is projected to reach 538 million in 2000 and 701.1 million in 2025. In 1950 India contained 14.2 percent of the world's population, 358 million persons. By 1990 the number had increased to 853 million, or 16.1 percent. India's population is projected to reach 1.042 billion in 2000 and 1.393 billion in 2025 and will surpass China's population around 2050, when it reaches 1.699 billion compared to China's anticipated 1.521 billion people.

The population of China doubled between 1950 and 1990, a trend similar to that of other Asian nations. It had a population of 1.139 billion in 1990, 21.5 percent of the world total. China's population is projected to peak in 2035 at 1.54 billion, an increase of 35 percent from 1990. It is projected to decline thereafter.

As the South grows more youthful, the North grows older. In 1990, developed countries had only 23 percent of the world's population but 44 percent of the people over 60 years old. In 2025 half the population of western Europe will be over 45.

The labor force in North America will not increase between now and 2025 except through immigration. In Central America it will increase by 50.5 million. Western Europe's labor force will fall by 14.5 million; North Africa's will increase by 56.6 million.

WORLD BIRTHS, DEATHS, AND POPULATION GROWTH, 1994

Characteristic	World	Developed	Developing
Population	5,642,151,000	1,240,354,000	4,401,797,000
Births	139,324,000	16,944,000	122,380,000
Deaths	52,514,000	11,715,000	40,799,000
Natural increase	86,810,000	5,229,000	81,582,000
Births per 1,000 population	25	14	28
Deaths per 1,000 population	9	9	9
Growth rate (percent)	1.5%	0.4%	1.9%

Source: U.S. Bureau of the Census, *World Population Profile: 1994* (1994).

WORLD BIRTHS, DEATHS, AND POPULATION GROWTH, per time unit, projected to July 13, 1995, at 3:52:33 P.M. EST

The U.S. Census Bureau has a Home Page on Internet that contains a "POPClock." This real-time population chart ticks global population changes as you view the screen.

Time unit	Births	Deaths	Natural increase
Year	139,667,270	52,889,287	86,777,983
Month	11,638,939	4,407,441	7,231,499
Day	382,650	144,902	237,748
Hour	15,944	6,038	9,906
Minute	266	101	165
Second	4.4	1.7	2.8

Note: Figures may not add to totals due to rounding. **Source:** U.S. Bureau of the Census, *International Programs Center 1995* (1995): http://www.census.gov/cgi-bin/popclockw

THREE MORE PEOPLE EACH SECOND

Every two seconds, nine babies are born and three people die. The net increase of three people each second results in a growth in world population of 10,600 per hour, 254,000 per day, 1.8 million per week, 7.7 million per month, and 93 million per year. Eighty-seven million of the annual increase occurs in developing countries, six million in developed countries.

By the year 2000, annual growth will increase to 94 million, and by 2020 it will be 98 million. In 2020, 98 percent of the increase will be in developing countries.

Source: U.S. Bureau of the Census, *World Population Profile: 1989* (1989).

WHERE IN THE WORLD DO THEY LIVE?

According to the U.S. Bureau of the Census, 75 of each 100 persons in the world today live in only 22 countries. The other 25 live in any of the remaining 184 countries. Note that 37 people out of every 100 live in China and India.

Of every 100 people in the world in 1991:

21 live in China (mainland)
16 live in India
5 live in the former Soviet Union
5 live in the United States
4 live in Indonesia
3 live in Brazil
2 live in Bangladesh
2 live in Japan
2 live in Mexico
2 live in Nigeria
2 live in Pakistan
1 lives in Egypt
1 lives in Ethiopia
1 lives in France
1 lives in Germany
1 lives in Iran
1 lives in Italy
1 lives in the Philippines
1 lives in Thailand
1 lives in Turkey
1 lives in the United Kingdom
1 lives in Vietnam

Source: U.S. Bureau of the Census, *World Population Profile 1991* (1991).

COUNTRIES WITH DECLINING POPULATION ESTIMATES, 1995–2025

Country	1995	2025	Decrease	Country	1995	2025	Decrease
Russian Federation	147,000,000	138,000,000	8,500,000	Greece	10,500,000	9,900,000	600,000
Germany	81,600,000	76,400,000	5,200,000	Croatia	4,500,000	4,200,000	300,000
Italy	57,200,000	52,300,000	4,900,000	Latvia	2,600,000	2,300,000	300,000
Ukraine	51,400,000	48,700,000	2,700,000	Belarus	10,100,000	9,900,000	200,000
Spain	39,600,000	37,600,000	2,000,000	Denmark	5,200,000	5,100,000	100,000
Romania	22,800,000	21,700,000	1,100,000	Estonia	1,500,000	1,400,000	100,000
Bulgaria	8,800,000	7,800,000	1,000,000	Portugal	9,800,000	9,700,000	100,000
Hungary	10,100,000	9,400,000	700,000	Slovenia	1,900,000	1,800,000	100,000

Source: United Nations Population Fund (UNFPA), *The State of World Population 1995* (1995).

URBANIZATION

According to the United Nations, in 1995, 45 percent of the world's population resided in urban areas. Seventy-five percent of these live in the more developed regions and 37 percent of those in the less developed regions. By 2005, half of the world's population will live in urban areas. By 2025, over three fifths of the world population will be urban.

Between 1985 and 1990, the population of Mexico City surpassed that of Tokyo/Yokohama and became the largest urban area in the world. The United Nations estimates that Mexico City had 20.2 million inhabitants in 1990, exceeding the populations of Tokyo with 18.1 million, São Paulo with 17.4 million, and New York with 16.2 million.

The 10 largest urban areas changed considerably during the past 20 years and are projected to change again during the next decade. From 1970 to 1990 London, Paris, and Beijing fell from the top 10 list and were replaced by Calcutta, Bombay, and Seoul.

Mexico City is projected to retain its first place as the world's most populous city in 2000 with a population of 25.6 million, and São Paulo is projected to be the second largest urban area, reaching 22.1 million. The projections indicate that Buenos Aires and Seoul will fall to the 12th and 15th places, respectively, in 2000. They are expected to be replaced by Beijing and Jakarta. Hence, it is projected that by the year 2000, six of the 10 largest urban areas of the world will be from Asia—Tokyo, Japan; Shanghai and Beijing, China; Calcutta and Bombay, India; and Jakarta, Indonesia. Two of the 10 will be from Latin America—Mexico City, Mexico, and São Paulo, Brazil. The other two will be from North America—New York and Los Angeles, United States.

In 1950 only New York and London had more than eight million inhabitants. By 1970, there were eight new urban areas with eight million or more inhabitants. Three, Tokyo, Los Angeles, and Paris, were in the developed regions and five in the developing regions. Of the latter five, three were in Latin America: Mexico City, Mexico; São Paulo, Brazil; and Buenos Aires, Argentina. Two were in China: Shanghai and Beijing.

NATIONS WITH HIGHEST AND LOWEST FERTILITY RATES, 1995 ESTIMATES

HIGHEST FERTILITY RATES				LOWEST FERTILITY RATES			
Country	Fertility rate per woman	Country	Fertility rate per woman	Country	Fertility rate per woman	Country	Fertility rate per woman
Yemen	7.4	Ethiopia	6.8	Hong Kong	1.2	Slovenia	1.5
Niger	7.3	Guinea	6.8	Spain	1.2	Austria	1.6
Ivory Coast	7.1	Somalia	6.8	Italy	1.3	Belgium	1.6
Uganda	7.1	Afghanistan	6.6	Germany	1.3	Estonia	1.6
Angola	6.9	Liberia	6.6	Greece	1.5	Latvia	1.6
Benin	6.9	Burundi	6.5	Bulgaria	1.5	Netherlands	1.6
Mali	6.9	Zaire	6.5	Japan	1.5	Portugal	1.6
Malawi	6.9	Laos	6.4	Romania	1.5	Switzerland	1.6
Oman	6.9			Russia	1.5	Ukraine	1.6

Source: United Nations Fund for Population Activities (UNFPA), *The State of World Population 1995* (1995).

According to the latest United Nations estimates, 20 urban areas have now reached eight million or more people. By the year 2000, it is projected that the eight million mark will be attained by 28 urban areas, most of which will be in developing countries.

FERTILITY RATES

Across the world, women are having fewer children now than 20 years ago. In developed regions fertility rates dropped from an average of 2.6 births per woman in 1970 to 1.7 births in 1990. Births in developing regions dropped from an average of five to seven births per woman to three to six births. Projections by the United Nations Population Fund (UNFPA) anticipate a total world fertility rate of 3.3 in 1990–95. Of this total, developed nations are expected to have 1.7 births per woman and developing regions 3.7 births per woman.

Replacement-level fertility represents the point at which each couple has only the number of births required to replace themselves in the population, usually taken as 2.1 births per woman. Most countries of Europe and North America have fertility rates at or below that level. Around the end of the present decade or soon thereafter, negative growth rates (i.e., decreasing populations) are expected in Austria, Finland, Italy, and Switzerland.

The United Nations reports growing evidence that a broad-based fertility decline may have begun in sub-Saharan Africa and south-central Asian countries where fertility levels have for decades remained very high and constant. Rwanda, long having the highest fertility rate in the world, is now in 20th place. From 1980–85 to 1995 Rwanda's fertility rate has decreased from 8.1 to 6.3. During the same period Tanzania has dropped from 6.7 to 5.7 births per woman and Namibia has declined from 5.8 to 5.0. Recent evidence shows new fertility reductions in Zambia, Zimbabwe, South Africa, and Gambia and declines are continuing in Kenya, Madagascar, and Botswana.

In Iran, fertility is estimated to have declined from 6.8 children per woman in 1980–85 to 5.0 currently. Declines are continuing in Bangladesh, from 6.2 in 1980–85 to 4.4 in 1995, India from 4.5 to 3.7, and Nepal from 6.3 to 5.4.

China, Thailand, and Mexico made the greatest fertility-rate reductions from 1970 to 1995. China's fertility rate went from 6.0 to 2.1, Thailand's from 6.1 to 2.2, and Mexico's from 6.7 to 3.0. (See the table "Population Indicators by Region and Nation" for fertility rates for other countries.)

THE INTERNATIONAL ECONOMY

This section contains basic facts and statistics relating to the two most important elements of the international economy: finance and trade. Issues of world trade, including the creation of new trading blocs around the world, have taken center stage in recent years, so a description of the General Agreement on Tariffs and Trade (GATT), and a detailed discussion of the emergence of the European Union (EU) are provided. Finally, key economic indicators for 200 nations are presented mainly for comparative purposes.

Generally speaking, most contemporary analyses and future projections about the global economy begin with the assumption that the nations of the world are divided into two basic categories, developed and developing. While no precise definitions of these terms have ever been established, they are used to differentiate the few wealthy industrialized nations from the many poor countries trying to emerge from agricultural-based economies that are incapable of generating high income levels. In 1993, according to the World Bank, 4.7 billion of the world's 5.5 billion people lived in countries where the GNP per capita was less than $4,320, while only 834 million lived in countries where it was higher. But in fact the disparity between rich and poor nations is even more dramatic since, as the accompanying table shows, three-fifths of the world's people (3.1 billion) live in countries where GNP per capita is less than $380. These include China and India, the most highly populated nations, as well as most of Africa and Southeast Asia. The wealthiest nations are located mainly in Western Europe and North America, with only Japan, Australia, and New Zealand representing the Pacific region. The wealthiest nations are at the center of the international economy and are responsible for promoting trade among the peoples of the world, for helping to finance development in the poorer countries, and for maintaining a stable economic world.

These activities are directed mainly by the largest economic powers, loosely joined in the so-called *"Group of Seven"* or G-7: Canada, France, Germany, Italy, Japan, United Kingdom, and the United States. These nations produce about 75 percent of the world's total output of goods and services. The leaders of the G-7 countries meet once a year to discuss international economic policy in what has become a well-publicized media event. In recent years their activities have centered mainly on trade policy issues related to GATT (a.k.a. the WTO; see below).

Another important group of developed nations bound together for economic purposes is the 24-member Organization for Economic Cooperation and Development (OECD) which monitors trends, publishes a large number of surveys, and provides a forum for the development of fair and coherent economic policies.

INTERNATIONAL TRADE

International trade takes place because no single country can produce efficiently all of the commodities it needs, and some nations enjoy an advantage in producing certain kinds of products, either because of a comparative wealth of resources (capital, labor, natural resources) or more efficient production techniques. Even an economy with the most efficient technology has a limit on its resources, however, and rather than using them to produce all kinds of products, it concentrates its resources on what it makes most efficiently. It then trades those goods for other commodities, importing those it produces least efficiently. As a result, all countries are better off; specialization results in the expansion of the total supply of goods, and the cost of acquiring them falls accordingly.

Efficiency can be measured by output per hour of production. The comparative output-per-hour measure shows how slow the increase in U.S. productivity has been relative to its competitors. While U.S. productivity more than doubled since 1960, productivity tripled in most of Europe and rose more than eightfold in Japan. In part these improvements in other countries reflect their low starting points, especially in Japan and West Germany, where their economies were recovering from the devastation of World War II. However, productivity has risen by nearly the same rate in the United States, Japan, and Europe since 1982.

Just which commodities a country will export and import depends on the relative prices of the factors used in production. A country such as India has abundant labor and low wages. It therefore exports labor-intensive products, such as garments. A country such as Canada, which has abundant natural resources, specializes in agriculture and raw materials. Countries such as Canada and India then import goods for which the factors of production are in relatively short supply.

The relative price of labor depends in part on the labor force participation rate, which has been rising owing largely to women leaving homemaking for the work force. Unemployment is also on the rise, especially in the United States, Canada, and Great Britain, where economic activity has taken a downturn. The ability of the Japanese and Swedish economies to keep unemployment rates low, even in the middle of the recession, is certainly impressive and represents the commitment and active efforts of their governments to that goal.

Of course, there are political reasons why countries do not completely specialize their production. No country, for example, wants to import all of its military equipment for fear that supplies would be cut off in the event of international conflict. Similarly, even inefficient producers, such as farmers in Japan where land is scarce and expensive, may have political power that forces their governments to subsidize them.

10 LARGEST U.S MERCHANDISE IMPORTS AND EXPORTS, 1987–93 (millions of dollars)

Rank, 1993/Product group	Volume 1987	1991	1992	1993
EXPORTS				
1. Electric machinery and parts	$16,670	$34,359	$37,424	$43,178
2. Road vehicles	21,370	33,369	37,946	41,178
3. Transportation equipment	17,917	36,989	38,613	33,394
4. Office and ADP machines	19,945	29,434	30,983	31,348
5. Miscellaneous manufactured articles	10,303	21,134	23,283	24,282
6. Industrial machinery and parts	8,573	17,523	18,876	20,126
7. Power-generating machinery	10,311	17,397	18,454	19,676
8. Special industrial machinery	9,676	17,069	17,245	18,338
9. Professional/scientific/control instruments	8,381	14,056	14,944	15,844
10. Telecom and sound-reproduction equipment	5,656	10,863	12,327	14,237
Total, top ten exports	**$130,940**[1]	**$232,192**	**$250,095**	**$261,598**

Rank, 1993/Product group	Volume 1987	1991	1992	1993
IMPORTS				
1. Road vehicles	$72,585	$70,631	$75,252	$83,332
2. Electric machinery and parts	23,747	35,103	39,729	46,752
3. Office and ADP machines	18,318	30,064	36,393	43,182
4. Apppare/clothing/accessories	20,495	26,206	31,242	33,787
5. Miscellaneous manufactured articles	19,467	24,850	28,541	31,783
6. Telecom and sound-reproduction equipment	20,797	23,469	25,819	27,302
7. Power-generating machinery	10,650	14,230	15,910	17,163
8. Industrial machinery and parts	11,403	14,422	15,522	17,084
9. Special industrial machinery	11,233	10,914	11,826	13,546
10. Nonmetallic mineral manufactures	8,853	9,693	10,170	11,558
Total, top ten imports	**$217,548**	**$259,583**	**$290,403**	**$325,489**

1. Includes other categories not shown separately. **Source:** U.S. Dept. of Commerce, International Trade Administration, *U.S. Foreign Trade Highlights 1993* (1994).

U.S. MERCHANDISE TRADE PARTNERS, 1994 (millions of dollars)

Country	Exports	Imports	Net balance
Belgium and Luxembourg	$ 11,079	$ 8,464	$ 2,615
France	13,610	16,674	–3,064
Germany	18,744	31,677	–12,933
Italy	7,007	14,785	–7,778
Netherlands	13,321	6,004	7,317
United Kingdom	25,972	24,861	1,111
Canada	114,869	131,115	–16,246
Japan	51,817	119,135	–67,318
Australia	9,586	3,202	6,384
Brazil	7,914	8,683	–769
Mexico	50,741	50,053	688
Venezuela	3,960	8,370	–4,410
China	9,242	38,787	–29,545
Hong Kong	11,417	9,695	1,722
South Korea	16,988	19,605	–2,617
Singapore	12,168	15,357	–3,189
Taiwan	16,116	26,706	–10,590
TOTAL[1]	**$502,485**	**$668,584**	**–$166,099**

1. Includes other countries not shown separately. **Source:** U.S. Dept. of Commerce, *Survey of Current Business*, June 1995.

FOREIGN EXCHANGE RATES: CURRENCY UNITS PER DOLLAR

Country/Currency	1975	1980	1985	1990	1993	1994
Australia/dollar	0.77	0.88	1.43	1.28	1.47	1.37
Austria/schilling	17.40	12.90	20.70	11.30	11.60	11.40
Belgium/franc	36.70	29.20	59.30	33.40	34.60	33.40
Canada/dollar	1.02	1.17	1.37	1.17	1.29	1.37
Denmark/krone	5.74	5.63	10.60	6.19	6.49	6.36
Finland/markka	3.67	3.72	6.20	3.83	5.73	5.23
France/franc	4.28	4.22	8.98	5.45	5.67	5.55
Germany/deutsche mark	2.46	1.82	2.94	1.62	1.66	1.62
Greece/drachma	32.30	42.60	138.10	158.50	229.30	242.60
Hong Kong/dollar	4.94	4.98	7.79	7.79	7.74	7.73
India/rupee	8.38	7.86	12.40	17.50	30.50	31.40
Ireland/pound	0.45	0.49	0.94	0.60	0.68	0.67
Israel/new shekel	0.64	5.12	1.18	2.02	2.83	3.01
Italy/lira	652.40	855.10	1,909.00	1,198.00	1,573.00	1,611.00
Japan/yen	296.70	225.70	238.50	145.00	111.10	102.20
Luxembourg/franc	36.80	29.20	59.40	33.40	34.60	33.50
Mexico/peso	12.50	23.00	256.90	2,813.00	3,116.00	3,375.00
Netherlands/guilder	2.52	1.99	3.32	1.82	1.86	1.82
New Zealand/dollar	0.82	1.03	2.01	1.68	1.85	1.69
Norway/krone	5.21	4.94	8.59	6.25	7.10	7.06
Pakistan/rupee	9.90	9.90	15.90	21.70	28.10	30.60
Portugal/escudo	25.50	50.10	172.10	142.70	161.10	165.90
Singapore/dollar	2.37	2.14	2.20	1.81	1.62	1.53
South Korea/won	484.00	607.40	870.00	707.80	802.70	803.40
Spain/peseta	57.40	71.60	170.00	102.00	127.50	133.90
Sri Lanka/rupee	7.05	16.50	27.20	40.10	48.30	49.40
Sweden/krona	4.14	4.23	8.60	5.92	7.80	7.72
Switzerland/franc	2.58	1.68	2.46	1.39	1.48	1.37
Taiwan/dollar	38.00	36.00	39.90	26.90	26.40	26.50
United Kingdom/pound	0.45	0.43	0.77	0.56	0.67	0.65

Note: Averages of certified noon buying rates in New York for cable transfers. **Source:** *Federal Reserve Bulletin*, monthly.

Tariffs, quotas, GATT, and WTO One way to protect a country's own producers, especially where they are inefficient compared with the international competition, is with import tariffs—taxes on goods that are produced abroad. Import tariffs raise the price of imports relative to domestic alternatives and discourage demand for the former. If one country is the sole importer or even the main importer of another's exports, it is possible that an import tariff will simply force the exporter to cut its selling price (in order to keep the price to consumers—including the tariff—from rising sharply and cutting off demand). In this case, the exporter pays virtually the whole cost of the tariff. If, on the other hand, the importer badly needs the import and there are few substitutes, raising the tariff simply raises the costs to one's own consumers. Critics of U.S. trade policy point out that because Japan is now virtually the sole supplier of many consumer electronic products in the United States, tariffs against those products simply raise their prices and fuel U.S. inflation. Import quotas attempt to achieve a restriction on imports without the price rises associated with tariffs, by setting direct limits on the number of items imported. Perhaps the most important import quota in recent years was when Japan agreed in the 1980s to abide by a limit on the number of cars it exported to the United States. As a result, Japanese automakers are now exporting larger, more expensive cars, and 18 percent of the U.S. auto market now goes to Japanese cars.

So-called "trade wars" start when one country imposes a tariff on imports from a second country, and the latter responds with tariffs of its own against the first country. The arguments presented above about the benefits of trade have led to efforts to restrict the use of tariffs and maintain free trade. The General Agreement on Tariffs and Trade (GATT) is an agreement among 125 countries (together accounting for more than 85 percent of world trade) to apply all reductions in tariffs and other measures to liberalize trade achieved between member countries. After its creation in 1948, GATT regulated most of the world's trade. GATT was created specifically as an agreement, rather than as a treaty, so that its provisions needed approval only of a simple majority of the U.S. Congress. A treaty would require a two-thirds majority to approve GATT decisions.

At their October 1993 meeting, GATT's members agreed to the most comprehensive trade-liberalizing accord in history. The agreement, officially called the Uruguay Round's Final Act, because it completed negotiations originally begun at GATT's 1986 meeting in Punta del Este, Uruguay, was expected to add about $270 billion to the world economy. It was officially signed in April 1994 in Morocco, and took effect July 1, 1995, giving signatory countries a year and a half to approve it. Under the terms of the treaty, GATT agreements will be administered by the new World Trade Organization (WTO), a new agency with stronger powers to mediate trade disputes among the signatories. The WTO has 125 members, including the United States, which joined in January 1995 despite fears that it gave too much power over U.S. affairs to an outside agency.

Dumping Sometimes exporters sell commodities abroad at prices below those they charge for the same item in their home market. This situation is known as dumping. It may occur sporadically because of overproduction for home markets; the excess is then sold abroad cheaply, or "dumped." It also may occur more regularly because of government subsidies to maintain production in the face of declining demand in the home country (e.g., to maintain jobs). Finally, it may be part of an anticompetitive strategy to crush the domestic competition in one's foreign markets and then to raise prices once competitors have been eliminated. Consumers may benefit from dumping in the short run, but it may also do long-term damage to domestic producers.

Trends in U.S. exports The top U.S. merchandise exports account for about one third of the total, and high-technology exports (computers, electronic components, radiological apparatus, electrical apparatus) account for about 60 percent of total exports. Exports of agriculture will probably never reach the growth levels of the 1970s, since the green revolution and trading policies, particularly of the European Union, have created worldwide food surpluses that are not likely to be eliminated soon.

INTERNATIONAL FINANCE

Because countries have their own currencies, trade between them also involves exchanging or trading currencies. In order for Americans to buy Japanese cars, for example, dollars must first be converted to Japanese yen in order to pay for them. The exchange rate between currencies represents the ratio at which they can be exchanged or the price of one currency in terms of the other. For example, if the exchange rate between the British pound and the U.S. dollar is $1.50/£, then one British pound can be purchased for $1.50.

The exchange rate for most world currencies is determined by the market. Some Eastern bloc countries can maintain fixed exchange rates because by law all sales take place through the government. The exchange rate of a currency rises, or appreciates, when the demand for it rises and/or the supply falls. This may happen because foreign buyers want to buy more of its goods or because consumers within the country decide to buy fewer imports. It may also happen because the country reduces its money supply. Finally, the central banks of countries can manipulate their exchange rates slightly by buying and selling their own and other currencies (see "The Federal Reserve"). The dollar has depreciated during the 1990s due to declining U.S. interest rates and economic growth rates lower than in other countries, notably Germany and Japan, which have made the dollar a less attractive currency in which to invest.

The gold standard Before World War I, exchange rates for world currencies were fixed, artificially, by tying them to a certain amount of gold—$32, for example, might equal one ounce of gold. Central banks would then buy and sell gold in order to equalize supply and demand for the currencies and maintain the fixed exchange rates. For this reason the central banks maintained enormous gold stockpiles, such as the United States had at Fort Knox. People therefore referred to currencies as being "backed by gold." Long-term changes in trading relationships and in the demand for various currencies eventually made the fixed exchange rates of the gold standard impossible to support. In 1944, the Bretton Woods agreement established the U.S. dollar as the world standard, but the United States still backed its dollars with gold and used gold to settle its debts. After 1973 the United States abandoned that role, and most of the world's exchange rates were set by market forces.

Balance of payments The balance of payments accounts are the list of transactions between a country and the rest of the world. This account comprises three parts: the current account—a record of exports and imports of goods (e.g., oil, clothing), services (e.g., tourism), net investment income, and unilateral transfers (the trade balance includes the export and import of goods alone); the capital account—a record of exports and imports of assets such as bank loans and corporate stock purchases; and the official-reserves accounts—a record of a country's sales and purchases of official reserve assets at the central bank.

Trade balance When a country imports goods from another country worth more than the value of its exports to that country, there is said to be a deficit in the balance of trade between the countries. Changes in exchange rates tend to equalize the supply and demand for currencies and the balance of trade; in the case above, the exchange rate for the first country's currency should fall relative to the second country's, reducing imports by making them more expensive and encouraging exports by making them cheaper. But this equalization may take a long time to occur (consumers and producers in the two countries must change their behavior). And central banks may want to slow the pace at which exchange rates adjust to slow the effects on trading sectors within their economies.

WORLD'S 50 LARGEST BANKS, RANKED BY ASSETS, 1994

Rank/Company	Country	Assets (millions)	Rank/Company	Country	Assets (millions)
1. Sanwa Bank	Japan	$588,349	26. Citicorp	United States	$249,049
2. Dai-Ichi Kangyo Bank	Japan	587,773	27. Barclays Bank	U.K.	248,606
3. Fuji Bank	Japan	577,107	28. National Westminster Bank	U.K.	244,753
4. Sumitomo Bank	Japan	571,942	29. Compangnie Financiiere de Paribas	France	242,146
5. Sakura Bank	Japan	565,381	30. Westdeutsche Landesbank Girozentrale	Germany	237,292
6. Mitsubishi Bank	Japan	553,515	31. Toyo Trust & Banking Co.	Japan	236,612
7. Norinchukin Bank	Japan	500,434	32. Union Bank of Switzerland	Switzerland	226,966
8. Industrial Bank of Japan	Japan	437,853	33. Commerzbank	Germany	220,478
9. Mitsubishi Trust & Banking Corp.	Japan	394,001	34. BankAmerica Corp.	United States	214,406
10. Long-Term Credit Bank of Japan	Japan	375,515	35. Bayerische Vereinsbank	Germany	204,214
11. Deutsche Bank	Germany	367,883	36. Shoko Chukin Bank	Japan	186,800
12. Sumitomo Trust & Banking Co.	Japan	355,984	37. Nippon Credit Bank	Japan	183,862
13. Tokai Bank	Japan	351,637	38. Bayerische Hypotheken-und Wechsel-Bank	Germany	177,354
14. Mitsui Trust & Banking Co.	Japan	331,209	39. Credit Suisse	Switzerland	176,910
15. Credit Agricole Mutuel	France	328,054	40. Zenshinren Bank	Japan	175,190
16. Credit Lyonnais	France	327,806	41. Bayerische Landesbank Girozentrale	Germany	171,640
17. Asahi Bank	Japan	317,472	42. Chemical Bank	United States	170,319
18. HSBC Holdings	U.K.	314,368	43. NationsBank Corp.	United States	168,920
19. Daiwa Bank	Japan	304,716	44. Swiss Bank Corp.	Switzerland	162,128
20. ABN-AMRO Bank	Netherlands	290,666	45. Banbkgesellschaft Berlin	Germany	158,769
21. Societe Generale	France	277,923	46. Deutsche Genossenschaftsbank	Germany	158,065
22. Bank of Tokyo	Japan	274,075	47. Rabobank Nederland	Netherlands	154,992
23. Yasuda Trust & Banking Co.	Japan	271,580	48. Bank of Yokohama	Japan	154,331
24. Banque Nationale de Paris	France	271,561	49. Istituto Bancario San Paolo di Torino	Italy	153,711
25. Dresdner Bank	Germany	258,079	50. Abbey National	U.K.	147,138

Source: *American Banker* (1995).

The balance of trade indicates something about how an economy is changing and, ultimately, about its competitiveness vis-à-vis other countries. A rising balance-of-trade deficit indicates that an economy is not able to sell its goods abroad, and that consumers are favoring imports over domestically produced goods.

International lending: The World Bank and the IMF As a part of the Bretton Woods Conference in 1944, the 42 countries represented created two important international financial institutions: the International Monetary Fund (IMF) and the International Bank for Reconstruction and Development (IBRD), commonly known as the World Bank. Each of the 151 IMF members contributes resources to the fund; financial contributions and voting rights are proportional to the size of their international payments. (The United States, Japan, West Germany, France, the United Kingdom, Belgium, the Netherlands, and Canada are the largest members.) The IMF makes loans to member countries having difficulty paying foreign debts and establishes many of the guidelines through which international financial transactions take place. The IBRD, together with its affiliates the International Development Association (IDA) and the International Finance Corporation (IFC), makes longer-term loans to developing countries to promote economic growth and development. Funds for the World Bank are raised by subscription from its

HOURLY COMPENSATION COSTS IN U.S. DOLLARS FOR PRODUCTION WORKERS, SELECTED COUNTRIES, 1975–94

Country	1975	1980	1985	1990	1993	1994
Austria	$4.51	$ 8.87	$ 7.58	$17.75	$20.37	$21.73
Australia	5.62	8.47	8.20	13.07	12.49	13.66
Belgium	6.41	13.11	8.97	19.22	21.62	22.97
Brazil	0.87	1.38	1.12	2.64	N.A.	N.A.
Canada	5.98	8.67	10.98	15.94	16.33	15.68
Denmark	6.28	10.83	8.13	17.96	19.11	20.44
Finland	4.61	8.24	8.16	21.03	16.56	18.89
France	4.52	8.94	7.52	15.23	16.23	17.04
Germany[1]	6.35	12.33	9.60	22.15	25.70	27.31
Greece	1.69	3.73	3.66	6.71	6.94	N.A.
Hong Kong	0.76	1.51	1.73	3.20	4.29	4.80
Ireland	3.03	5.95	5.92	11.76	12.16	N.A.
Israel	2.25	3.79	4.06	8.55	8.82	9.14
Italy	4.67	8.15	7.63	17.74	16.00	16.16
Japan	3.00	5.52	6.34	12.80	19.01	21.42
Korea, South	$0.32	$ 0.96	$ 1.23	$ 3.71	$ 5.51	$ 6.25
Luxembourg	6.35	11.98	7.72	16.37	18.49	N.A.
Mexico	1.44	2.21	1.59	1.64	2.56	2.61
Netherlands	6.58	12.06	8.75	18.29	19.95	20.91
New Zealand	3.21	5.33	4.47	8.33	8.01	8.93
Norway	6.77	11.59	10.37	21.47	20.21	20.91
Portugal	1.58	2.06	1.53	3.77	4.50	4.57
Singapore	0.84	1.49	2.47	3.78	5.25	6.29
Spain	2.53	5.89	4.66	11.33	11.50	11.45
Sri Lanka	0.28	0.22	0.28	0.35	0.42	N.A.
Sweden	7.18	12.51	9.66	20.93	17.70	18.81
Switzerland	6.09	11.09	9.66	20.86	22.63	24.83
Taiwan	0.40	1.00	1.50	3.95	5.22	5.55
United Kingdom	3.37	7.56	6.27	12.71	12.76	13.62
United States	6.36	9.87	13.01	14.91	16.73	17.10

Note: Hourly compensation includes wages, premiums, bonuses, vacation, holidays and other leave, insurance, and benefit plans. N.A. = not available. 1. Prior to 1991, data for Germany were for West Germany. **Source:** U.S. Bureau of Labor Statistics, *International Comparisons of Hourly Compensation Costs for Production Workers in Manufacturing, 1994* (May 1995).

THE WORLD'S MOST SEVERELY INDEBTED COUNTRIES, 1985–93

Country	Total external debt (millions)			Debt as a percent of GNP		
	1985	1990	1993	1985	1990	1993
Albania	N.A.	$ 349	$ 755	N.A.	N.A.	N.A.
Algeria	$ 18,242	27,637	25,757	31.9%	48.2%	57.4%
Angola	2,497	8,042	9,655	46.4	84.1	N.A.
Argentina	50,946	62,233	74,473	61.1	46.0	29.6
Bolivia	4,805	4,278	4,213	176.6	100.5	79.7
Brazil	106,121	116,417	132,749	50.3	24.9	24.0
Bulgaria	3,852	10,871	12,250	22.0	57.0	124.9
Burundi	455	907	1,063	40.3	80.6	109.8
Cameroon	2,940	5,982	6,601	38.5	56.6	71.8
Central African Republic	347	716	904.3	50.0	56.0	74.7
Congo	3,028	4,931	5,071	156.8	197.8	248.6
Ecuador	8,703	12,109	14,110	77.4	122.7	101.9
Egypt	42,136	40,455	40,626	134.2	127.9	104.8
Equatorial Guinea	132	241	268.0	175.2	190.9	180.9
Ethiopia	2,013	3,780	4,729	42.4	63.6	116.2
Ghana	2,226	3,799	4,590	50.3	62.1	76.9
Guinea-Bissau	308	606	691	197.4	243.6	292.0
Guyana	1,485	1,915	1,938	383.2	760.1	647.2
Honduras	2,729	3,714	3,865	78.5	135.6	125.6
Ivory Coast	9,641	16,622	N.A.	151.4	195.9	N.A.
Jamaica	4,068	4,663	4,279	237.6	128.3	121.4
Jordan	4,168	7,276	6,972	85.0	205.9	142.9
Kenya	4,111	7,126	6,994	69.6	88.1	135.2
Laos	620	1,768	1,986	26.2	203.7	149.1
Liberia	$ 1,244	$ 1,849	$ 1,926	62.7%	N.A.	N.A.
Madagascar	2,723	4,236	4,594	99.8	145.0%	142.6%
Mali	1,468	2,472	2,650	120.0	101.2	100.5
Mauritania	1,483	2,143	2,203	235.1	223.1	245.1
Mexico	96,867	106,026	118,028	55.2	44.9	35.5
Morocco	16,528	23,532	21,430	136.6	94.3	81.7
Mozambique	2,714	4,770	5,263	82.9	380.7	419.2
Myanmar	3,091	4,673	5,478	45.5	19.1	N.A.
Nicaragua	5,821	10,692	10,445	220.4	807.8	762.0
Niger	1,208	1,820	1,704	86.6	75.0	78.6
Nigeria	19,550	34,538	32,531	25.1	107.3	100.7
Peru	12,884	20,068	20,328	86.2	68.2	51.6
Poland	33,336	49,336	45,306	48.7	83.8	52.7
Rwanda	367	736	910	21.4	33.2	63.4
São Tomé and Príncipe	63	153	254	188.1	330.2	711.6
Sierra Léone	723	1,155	1,388	57.1	149.5	218.8
Somalia	1,639	2,370	2,501	198.1	283.9	N.A.
Sudan	9,127	15,303	16,560	93.1	175.3	N.A.
Syria	10,819	17,068	19,975	66.4	125.5	N.A.
Tanzania	3,750	6,119	7,522	54.6	256.8	N.A.
Uganda	1,239	2,669	3,056	51.5	96.4	77.0
Zaire	6,171	10,270	11,280	93.1	N.A.	N.A.
Zambia	4,576	7,242	6,788	173.6	240.8	231.9

Note: N.A. = not available. **Source:** The World Bank, *World Debt Tables, External Finance for Developing Countries,* 1994–95.

THE *FORTUNE* 100 WORLD'S LARGEST INDUSTRIAL CORPORATIONS, 1994

1994 Rank/Company/Country	Sales (millions of U.S. dollars)
1. Mitsubishi, Japan	$175,836
2. Mitsui, Japan	171,490
3. Itochu, Japan	167,825
4. Sumitomo, Japan	162,476
5. General Motors, U.S.	154,951
6. Marubeni, Japan	150,187
7. Ford Motor Company, U.S.	128,439
8. Exxon, U.S.	101,459
9. Nissho Iwai, Japan	100,876
10. Royal Dutch/Shell Group, Britain/Netherlands	94,881
11. Toyota Motor, Japan	88,159
12. Wal-Mart Stores, U.S.	83,412
13. Hitachi, Japan	76,431
14. Nippon Life Insurance, Japan	75,350
15. AT&T, U.S.	75,094
16. Nippon Telegraph & Telephone, Japan	70,844
17. Matsushita Electric Industrial, Japan	69,947
18. Tomen, Japan	69,902
19. General Electric, U.S.	64,687
20. Daimler-Benz, Germany	64,169
21. International Business Machines, U.S.	64,052
22. Mobil, U.S.	59,621
23. Nissan Motor, Japan	58,732
24. Nichimen, Japan	56,203
25. Kanematsu, Japan	55,856
26. Dai-Ichi Mutual Life Insurance, Japan	54,900
27. Sears Roebuck, U.S.	54,825
28. Philip Morris, U.S.	53,776
29. Chrysler, U.S.	52,224
30. Siemens, Germany	51,055
31. British Petroleum, Britain	50,737
32. Tokyo Electric Power, Japan	50,359
33. U.S. Postal Service	49,383
34. Volkswagen, Germany	$49,350
35. Sumitomo Life Insurance, Japan	49,063
36. Toshiba, Japan	48,228
37. Unilever, Britain/Netherlands	45,451
38. IRI, Italy	45,389
39. Nestlé, Switzerland	41,626
40. Deutsche Telekom, Germany	41,071
41. Fiat, Italy	40,851
42. Allianz Holding, Germany	40,415
43. Sony, Japan	40,101
44. Veba Group, Germany	40,071
45. Honda Motor, Japan	39,927
46. Elf Aquitaine, France	39,459
47. State Farm Group, U.S.	38,850
48. NEC, Japan	37,946
49. Prudential Insurance Co. of America, U.S.	36,946
50. Öesterreichische Post, Austria	36,766
51. Meiji Mutual Life Insurance, Japan	36,344
52. Daewoo, South Korea	35,707
53. E.I. du Pont de Nemours, U.S.	34,968
54. Union Des Assur. de Paris, France	34,597
55. Mitsubishi Motors, Japan	34,370
56. K mart, U.S.	34,313
57. Texaco, U.S.	33,768
58. Philips Electronics, Netherlands	33,517
59. Électricité de France, France	33,467
60. Deutsche Bank, Germany	33,069
61. Fujitsu, Japan	32,795
62. Mitsubishi Electric, Japan	32,726
63. ENI, Italy	32,566
64. Renault, France	32,188
65. Daiei, Japan	32,062
66. Citicorp, U.S.	31,650
67. Industrial Bank of Japan, Japan	31,072
68. Chevron, U.S.	$31,064
69. Hoechst, Germany	30,604
70. Procter & Gamble, U.S.	30,296
71. Alcatel Alsthom, France	30,224
72. Peugeot, France	30,112
73. Fuji Bank, Japan	30,103
74. Mitsubishi Bank, Japan	29,991
75. Abb Asea Brown Boveri, Switzerland	29,718
76. Sumitomo Bank, Japan	29,621
77. Nippon Steel, Japan	29,004
78. Sanwa Bank, Japan	28,799
79. Mitsubishi Heavy Industries, Japan	28,676
80. Ito-Yokado, Japan	28,632
81. RWE Group, Germany	28,628
82. Pepsico, U.S.	28,472
83. Pemex, Mexico	28,195
84. CIE Générale des Eaux, France	28,153
85. Crédit Agricole, France	27,753
86. Amoco, U.S.	26,953
87. BASF, Germany	26,928
88. ING Group, Netherlands	26,926
89. Bayer, Germany	26,771
90. Asahi Mutual Life Insurance, Japan	26,506
91. Dai-Ichi Kangyo Bank, Japan	26,500
92. Crédit Lyonnais, France	26,388
93. Sakura Bank, Japan	26,069
94. BMW, Germany	25,973
95. France Télécom, France	25,706
96. Kansai Electric Power, Japan	25,585
97. Hewlett-Packard, U.S.	24,991
98. Total, France	24,653
99. East Japan Railway, Japan	24,643
100. Long-Term Credit Bank of Japan, Japan	24,605

Source: *Fortune*, Aug. 7, 1995.

members among Western industrialized countries. In recent years, however, there has been a reversal of the flow of funds between developed and developing countries, due to a drastic reduction in new lending and the large debt service payments. Developing countries are usually characterized by low average real per capita income, low life expectancy and literacy rates, high rates of population growth, a high proportion of the labor force in primary activities such as agriculture and mining, and low growth rates of per capita income.

International debt of developing economies, an issue that has been front-page news since the debt crisis in 1982 when Mexico suspended all loan repayments, now tops $1.3 trillion. Reducing this enormous debt is important to the United States for a number of reasons. Beyond philanthropic considerations, the United States relies on a number of developing countries as trading partners and thus buyers of U.S. goods. If these economies are strapped with large loan repayments, there will be less money for investment (unless new money is printed—fueling inflation and further destabilizing the economy), economic activity will likely slow, and demand for imports will fall, thereby reducing employment in the United States, something the United States cannot afford considering its slowing domestic demand. Decreased exports to Latin America since 1982 resulted in the loss of 340,000 U.S. jobs.

THE EUROPEAN UNION (EU)

Ever since the Marshall Plan saved Europe from economic collapse at the end of World War II, European leaders have looked to the creation of a single European superpower—"Europe without frontiers"—to restore economic prosperity to the continent's 350 million people. Encouraged by the success of the 1944 Benelux (Belgium, the Netherlands, and Luxembourg) customs union, European leaders have long hoped that economic integration will avoid duplication and inefficiencies, increase economic competition, and eliminate gluts and shortages in different industries in the separate countries. Variously named the European Economic Community (EEC), the Common Market, the European Community (EC), and now the European Union (EU), this increased economic cooperation among European powers has done much in 50 years to achieve economic prosperity, but the goal of a Europe without borders still remains a long way off.

The first attempt at economic cooperation was proposed in 1950, when French foreign minister Robert Schuman suggested that France's and West Germany's coal and steel industries submit to a supranational (not intergovernmental) "high authority." The idea so excited German chancellor Konrad Adenauer that he announced his country's willingness to negotiate with France the very night Schuman announced his plan. Within a year, the two countries, joined by Italy and the Benelux countries, had hammered out a treaty establishing the European Coal and Steel Community (ECSC), effective July 1, 1952.

Great Britain, fearing loss of sovereignty, refused to join the union. As a result, it missed out on the benefits the treaty afforded. Real coal prices dropped for residents of the six countries as import and export duties were dropped. And even though high production costs prevented rapid growth in the amount of coal mined, distribution of coal supplies improved, as customers were able to buy from the nearest ECSC mine, rather than from far-off national mines. The success in the steel and iron ore industry was even greater. French production of iron ore increased 50 percent between 1952 and 1958; sales to other ECSC countries increased by two-thirds. Steel production among treaty countries also grew 50 percent, while trade in steel grew two and a half times.

Hoping to achieve the same success in other industries, "The Six" nations negotiated another set of treaties in March of 1957 (the Treaty of Rome), creating the European Economic Community (the EEC or the Common Market), and the European Atomic Energy Community (Euratom). The EEC was designed for a trio of purposes: to reduce and eventually abolish all tariffs among its members; to establish a single external tariff system for the Community; and to foster the free movement not only of goods but of labor and capital as well. Euratom was intended for the common development of peaceful uses of atomic energy and to establish a nuclear energy industry on a European scale. Denmark, Ireland, and the UK joined Euratom, the ECSC, and the EEC in 1973; Greece joined in 1981, and Portugal and Spain joined in 1986.

The 1958 election of Charles de Gaulle as president of the new (Fifth) French Republic had a powerful effect upon the communities. That same year, the United Kingdom suggested expanding the EEC into an Atlantic free-trade area, but France exercised its veto. In response Britain fostered in 1959 the European Free Trade Association (EFTA) whose members, besides Britain, were the three Scandinavian nations, Portugal, Austria, and Switzerland. A free-trade association, however, was not a common market since it established no common external tariff, leaving its members free to maintain their own tariffs with respect to nonmembers.

Then began the second stage in the EC's development. In 1961, Britain sought entry into the Common Market, but de Gaulle, fearing American influence and objecting to the special terms that Britain sought for the Commonwealth countries, exercised France's veto in 1963. He then pushed for agricultural integration, a thorny issue since each of the Six had its own system of protectionist duties, agricultural subsidies, and crop controls. The huge German market beckoned for France's farm surpluses, but Germany hesitated to sacrifice its own farmers in return for cheaper food.

A serious crisis impended, a crisis averted by the Dutch ("Mansholt") proposals to integrate agricultural policies by 1970: a common market with common prices, duties upon imports into the Community and subsidies for exporters, and a fair living standard for farmers. This Common Agricultural Policy, adopted in 1962, has meant protection for farmers through managed (higher-than-market) prices, overproduction (especially of butter and wine), and direction not by the market but by Brussels' so-called "Eurocrats."

The third stage came with the formation, by the Brussels Treaty of 1965 (often called the "Second Treaty of Rome"), of the EC—a merger of the EEC, the ECSC, and Euratom into one, with a four-part structure: commission, council, parliament, and court. The Commission replaced the High Authority of the ECSC and the separate commissions of the EEC and Euratom; its members, appointed by the separate governments but forbidden by treaty to take instructions from the governments that named them, formed the civil service of the EC, carrying out policy but also proposing laws for the Community. The Council of Ministers represented the member governments of the Community and enacted legislation proposed by the Commission. The European Parliament (whose first elections were held in 1979) was not a legislature but a body elected by the citizens of the countries of the EC with power to review and debate and advise concerning proposed legislation, somewhat like the old Senate of Rome; but it had final power over the budget of the EC. Finally, the Court of Justice was empowered to interpret the Treaties and issue rulings binding not only the Commission and Council but upon member governments as well.

It was this "refounded" EC that the United Kingdom was at last permitted to join in 1973 (after another Gaullist veto in 1967). As in its earlier attempts, the United Kingdom was accompanied by Ireland, Denmark, and Norway. (Norwegian voters subsequently rejected by referendum the terms of the treaty, so that the Six became the Nine.) The Community was further enlarged subsequently by the accession of Greece in 1981 and Spain and Portugal in 1986.

In 1979, the European Monetary System (EMS) was founded. It consisted of four main components: a European Currency Unit *(ecu)*, credit facilities, transfer arrangements, and exchange-rate stabilization mechanisms. The United Kingdom, and later Greece (in 1981), declined to participate in the EMS.

THE EUROPEAN UNION

Members		Current applicants	
1957	Belgium France Germany Italy Luxembourg Netherlands	**1987**	Turkey
		1990	Cyprus Malta
		1992	Poland Czech Republic Slovakia Hungary Romania Bulgaria
1973	Denmark Ireland United Kingdom		
1981	Greece		
1986	Portugal Spain		
1995	Austria Finland Sweden		

1992 and the Maastricht Treaty As late as 1986, the full vision of the Treaty of Rome had not yet been realized, and "Europe without frontiers" still remained just a slogan. Seeking to bring its promise to fruition, Commission president Jacques Delors set forth the Single European Act of 1986, which set 1992 as the target date for a single economic market without barriers to the free movement of goods, services, capital, and labor. But a decade later, the meaning of this compendium of nearly 300 rules and directives remains unclear. The fundamental difference as to its meaning concerns the extent to which "harmonization" among the members of the Community will be the result of Commission directives or the result of market forces. More precisely, what will be the mix of the two?

Each of the member states relies upon a Value Added Tax (a hidden sales tax) for revenue; but rates vary widely. Without Commission directives, business should shift to the low-tax states, imperiling the revenue, and the social services therefore, of the high-tax states. On the other hand, Commission directives establishing a permissible range of rates would represent the Community's setting tax rates for the member states, a serious diminution of national sovereignty. Similar difficult questions have arisen for myriad areas of economic life: wage differences; varying safety laws; banking regulations and taxes on investment income; the existence of certain import quotas—and perhaps hundreds more.

Even as 1992 has come and gone, all of these actual and potential areas of dispute continue to cast an air of uncertainty upon a single European economic nation. Since the more serious disputes will almost certainly be referred to the Community's Court of Justice, the Court is expected to play a crucial role in establishing a body of "case law" through precedents and may thereby grow to be a major force among the four institutions of the Community.

With the Maastricht Treaty of December 1991, the EC seemed to have reached a crucial fourth stage of development, for it set in motion the creation of a European Economic and Monetary Union (EMU) with two chief aspects: the transformation of the 1979 *ecu* from an abstract unit of account to a functioning unit of currency that would cross shop counters from Edinburgh to Seville and a unified system of central banking for the EC. Together these were designed to change the EC from a free-trade market bloc of sovereign states into a giant financial and capital market called Europe.

The treaty envisioned a three-stage (1991, 1994, 1997) creation of the EMU. During the first two stages the 12 members of the EC were to adopt converging policies in four areas: inflation rates, interest rates, currency exchange rates, and "fiscal position" (the last requiring that budget deficits be less than 3 percent of gross domestic product and that the governments' ratios of debt to GDP be 60 percent or less). Meanwhile, during the second stage, central bank financing of government spending would be eliminated and the EC's Committee of Central Bank Governors would be replaced by a European Monetary Institute (EMI) to coordinate the 12 countries' monetary policies, oversee the clearing system for the *ecu*, prepare for the issuance of *ecu* bank notes, and in general organize its own abolition in stage three.

In the third stage, the EMI was to be replaced with the European Central Bank with the task of proposing and carrying out the EC's monetary policies. With an Exchange Rate Mechanism (ERM) allowing currency exchange rates to fluctuate no more than 2.25 percent (6% for Spain and Portugal) the *ecu* would be introduced as Europe's actual circulating currency and the EMU would commence—by Jan. 1, 1999, at the latest. By itself, the EMU would have been an event of immense political significance. But in addition, the Maastricht Treaty provided, though more vaguely, for a closer political union of the EC through common defense and foreign policies.

The collapse of the single currency

The June 1992 referendum of Danish voters seemed to bring the whole scheme to naught, for the treaty requires unanimity and, narrowly but clearly, the Danes voted to reject it. Shaken Community leaders, meeting in Edinburgh's Holyrood Palace in December, agreed to a compromise of an odd sort: declaring the Maastricht Treaty unchanged, the Community issued a "legally binding decision" permitting Denmark to ratify while retaining the right to opt out of treaty provisions concerning a single currency, common defense measures, immigration and judicial policies, and the concept of a common European citizenship which would allow foreigners to vote in national elections. In addition, the Community issued a separate declaration of "subsidiarity" to allay misgivings and worries about national identities being swallowed up in "Eurocracy": that the Community may act only in areas beyond the capacity of its members. With this "à la carte" sort of membership permitted, Danish voters on May 18, 1993, reversed their rejection of the previous June, voting (56.8% to 43.2%) to accept the treaty.

Denmark was not the only country reluctant to agree to the single currency. British prime minister John Major won concessions to the treaty permitting Britain to opt out of the common currency. Then in the summer of 1993, an exchange rate furor fueled by recession and high German interest rates resulting from the high cost of reunification plunged the French franc to the lowest value allowed by the Exchange Rate Mechanism. Faced with the prospect of French withdrawal from the pact, finance ministers and the leaders of the central banks held an emergency meeting in Brussels, where they scuttled the ERM, allowing exchange rates to rise and fall by as much as 15 percent. The decision, which effectively ended plans for a single European currency, restored to each country the flexibility needed to respond to its particular economic circumstances. Almost immediately, order and calm returned to the currency markets, while the value of the French franc sank by more than 2 percent. In 1995 the plans for monetary union were put off until 2003.

But even without a common currency, the "single market" without internal customs and without passport checks that began Jan. 1, 1993, is transforming Europe as industries and families hunt for bargains across national borders, knitting transnational regional economic ties, leveling tax and interest rates—all without abolishing any national traits at all. A change in EC agricultural policy in May of 1992 brought about a sharp reduction in farm subsidies and lowered agricultural production ceilings in response to criticisms by the United States and other agricultural exporters such as Argentina and Brazil. Economists estimate the savings to EC consumers alone at $25 billion.

European Union (EU) On Nov. 1, 1993, Germany became the 12th and final member formally to ratify the Maastricht Treaty on European Union, and the plan, which was to have gone into effect 11 months earlier, finally took hold. The name for the economic agreement among the 12 countries was changed from the European Community to the European Union.

But even at the formal ratification date, the countries seemed anything but united. Leaders from the 12 countries haggled over where to locate the European Central Bank (which still hopes some day to issue a common European currency) and 10 other pan-European agencies. In the end, they agreed to place the Bank in Frankfurt, home of Germany's Bundesbank. Europol, an international police force devoted to combating organized crime and drug smuggling, was located in The Hague; the European environmental agency was slated for Copenhagen; and Madrid got both the Trademark Office and the Workplace Health and Safety Agency. London, which had sought to be the site of the Central Bank despite its opposition to the single currency, became the home of the Medicine Evaluation Agency, which registers pharmaceuticals.

Moreover, on Feb. 1, 1994, the 12 EU nations failed for the fourth time to meet the terms of the "Schengen Accord" on open borders, and did not even set a new target date. And at the June summit on Corfu, Britain refused to go along with the other 11 countries in backing Belgian premier Jean-Luc Dehaene to succeed the EU's chief executive Jacques Delors. Only a month later were all 12 countries able to agree on Jacques Santer, premier of Luxembourg, to preside over the European Commission.

Nevertheless, the desire for European unity seems unweakened. In March 1994, the EU agreed to expand its membership from 12 to 16, accepting Austria, Finland, Norway, and Sweden as full members effective Jan. 1, 1995. (At the end of 1994, however, voters in Norway soundly defeated the idea of joining the EU.) The EU offered aid totaling $4 billion over four years to ease the transition, especially for farmers.

And the EU does not lack for suitors. Six states of east-central Europe—Poland, Slovakia, the Czech Republic, Hungary, Romania, and Bulgaria—have been invited to apply, though it is not likely they will join before the year 2000. Cyprus, Malta, and Turkey are knocking at the door.

Whatever may come of monetary union, the EU can expect to be broadened before its union is deepened. And de Gaulle's dream of "Europe from the Atlantic to the Urals" may be realized.

Structure of EU

The Commission is composed of 20 commissioners appointed by member governments, and approved by the European Parliament. The five largest countries, France, Germany, Italy, Spain, and the United Kingdom, appoint two commissioners each. The EU treaties direct Commission members to act independently of their governments and represent the entire community's interests. The Commission supervises implementation of EU treaties, initiates and implements EU policy, transacts negotiations with nonmember states, and manages EU funds. The Commission can be forced to resign by two-thirds majority vote of the European Parliament. The Commission headquarters are in Brussels. The president, who is appointed by the Council of Ministers, serves a two-year term.

The Council of Ministers consists of the foreign ministers of the 15 member governments and is the chief decision-making body of the EU, passing legislation on the major issues affecting all members. Votes are by majority. The Council meets in Brussels (usually three times a year), and its presidency alternates among the member countries for six-month terms.

The European Parliament The 626 deputies of the European Parliament are elected directly by the citizens of the individual countries. The Parliament oversees the EU budget and passes on Commission proposals to the Council of Ministers. The Parliament also passes on new applications to the EU, and, as of 1995, formally approves the membership of the Commission. Deputies are elected to five-year terms and meet monthly in Strasbourg.

The Court of Justice is the court of last resort for the EU, interpreting EU treaties and legislation and hearing complaints about member-government violations. The Court also resolves differences between EU legislation and national laws. The 15 judges and five advocates-general are appointed by the member governments and serve six-year terms. Decisions are made by simple majority but announced unanimously. The court is located in Luxembourg.

The Economic and Social Committee is composed of 220 members representing employers' organizations, trade unions, and "special interests" (small businesses, consumers, agriculturalists, and professions). Through consultation, the Committee presents its views to the Council of Ministers and the EU Commission.

WORLD ECONOMIC INDICATORS, 1993

Country	GNP: 1993 (millions of U.S. dollars)	GNP: Average inflation rate 1985–93	GNP per capita: (in U.S. dollars) 1993	GNP per capita: Real growth rate 1980–91	GNP per capita: Real growth rate 1985–93	Agriculture's share in GDP: 1970	Agriculture's share in GDP: 1993	Primary school enrollment 1991	Illiteracy rate 1990
Afghanistan	—	—	$ <695	—	—	—	N.A.	—	71%
Albania	$ 1,167	15.0%	340	—	–7.0%	—	40%	—	—
Algeria	44,347	20.0	1,650	–0.8%	–2.2	10%	15	88%	43
Andorra	—	—	>8,626	—	—	—	—	—	—
Angola	—	5.9	696–2,785	—	–0.9	45	—	—	58
Antigua and Barbuda	425	4.8	6,390	3.8	2.4	—	4	—	—
Argentina	244,013	398.0	7,290	–1.5	1.4	13	6	—	5
Armenia[2]	2,471	71.3	660	2.1[3]	–11.7	N.A.	48	—	—
Australia	309,967	4.6	17,510	1.2	1.1	6	3	98	<5[1]
Austria	183,530	3.2	23,120	2.1	2.1	7	2	91	<5[1]
Azerbaijan[2]	5,424	75.5	730	0.4[3]	–9.4	N.A.	22	—	—
Bahamas	3,059	2.5	11,500	1.3	–02	—	N.A.	—	—
Bahrain	4,283	0.3	7,870	–3.8	–1.0	—	1	86	23
Bangladesh	25,882	7.2	220	1.9	1.8	55	33	69	65
Barbados	1,620	3.1	6,240	1.3	–0.4	11	N.A.	90	—
Belarus[2]	29,290	81.2	2,840	3.3[3]	–0.2	N.A.	21	—	—
Belgium	213,435	3.1	21,210	2.1	2.4	4	2	95	<5[1]
Belize	499	3.5	2,440	2.5	5.7	—	19	—	—
Benin	2,189	1.4	420	–1.1	–1.1	49	37	45	77
Bhutan	253	8.8	170	6.8	4.5	—	41	—	62
Bolivia	5,472	23.1	770	–2.0	1.4	17	N.A.	81	23
Botswana	3,630	12.7	2,590	5.8	5.7	33	5	98	26
Brazil	471,978	822.8	3,020	0.4	–0.6	12	11	86	19
Brunei	—	—	>8,626	—	—	—	3	89	—
Bulgaria	9,773	35.5	1,160	1.7	–2.8	—	13	82	<5[1]
Burkina Faso	2,928	1.7	300	1.3	0.0	44	N.A.	29	82
Burundi	1,102	4.7	180	1.4	0.6	71	54	51	50
Cambodia	—	—	<695	—	—	—	47	—	65
Cameroon	9,663	–0.6	770	–0.9	–7.3	31	22	76	46
Canada	574,884	3.3	20,670	2.1	0.4	—	N.A.	98	<5[1]
Cape Verde	347	8.1	870	2.2	2.1	—	13	95	60+[1]
Central African Republic	1,263	1.4	390	–1.5	–3.0	35	50	56	62
Chad	1,248	–0.2	200	3.8	0.5	43	44	38	70
Chile	42,454	18.9	3,070	1.7	6.1	7	N.A.	87	7
China	581,109	8.1	490	7.8	6.5	35	21	97	27
Colombia	50,119	25.6	1,400	1.2	2.3	25	16	74	13
Comoros	272	2.6	520	–1.0	–2.2	—	39	—	—
Congo	2,318	–2.1	920	–0.2	–1.9	18	11	—	43
Costa Rica	7,041	18.4	2,160	1.0	2.6	23	15	87	7
Cuba	—	—	696–2,785	—	—	—	—	97	6
Cyprus	7,539	4.1	10,380	4.9	5.2	—	6	100	—
Czechoslovakia	28,192	11.0	2,730	0.4	–2.0	—	6	—	<5[1]
Denmark	137,610	3.2	26,510	2.1	1.1	—	4	96	<5[1]
Djibouti	448	4.4	780	—	—	—	3	37	—
Dominica	193	4.5	2,680	4.7	4.8	—	26	—	—
Dominican Republic	8,039	31.2	1,080	–0.2	0.3	20	18	—	17
Ecuador	13,217	49.0	1,170	–0.3	0.8	24	12	—	14
Egypt	36,679	16.9	660	2.0	0.7	29	16	—	52
El Salvador	7,233	16.9	1,320	–0.3	1.2	28	9	71	27
Equatorial Guinea	161	–0.4	360	3.4[3]	1.5	—	47	—	50
Estonia[2]	4,703	50.1	3,040	2.1[3]	–5.2	N.A.	10	—	—
Ethiopia[4]	—	4.6	100	–1.6	–1.8	56	48	28	20–39[1]
Fiji	1,626	5.4	2,140	0.0	2.5	29	18	100	15
Finland	96,220	4.4	18,970	2.5	–0.3	—	5	—	<5[1]
France	1,289,235	3.0	22,360	1.8	1.8	—	3	100	<5[1]
Gabon	5,004	0.3	4,050	–4.2	–1.7	17	8	—	39
Gambia	372	11.2	360	–0.1	1.0	33	27	52	73
Georgia[2]	3,071	116.4	560	2.2	–16.4	N.A.	70	—	—
Germany	1,902,995	3.2	23,560	2.2	1.9	3	1	89	<5[1]

Country	GNP: 1993 (millions of U.S. dollars)	GNP: Average inflation rate 1985–93	GNP per capita: (in U.S. dollars) 1993	GNP per capita: Real growth rate 1980–91	GNP per capita: Real growth rate 1985–93	Agriculture's share in GDP: 1970	Agriculture's share in GDP: 1993	Primary school enrollment 1991	Illiteracy rate 1990
Ghana	$ 7,036	29.4%	$ 430	−0.3%	1.3%	47%	47%	—	40%
Greece	76,698	16.0	7,390	1.2	1.3	18	18	93%	7
Grenada	219	4.1	2,410	5.3[3]	4.1	—	14	—	—
Guatemala	11,092	20.1	1,110	−1.8	0.8	—	25	—	45
Guinea	3,170	20.2	510	—	1.3	—	24	26	76
Guinea-Bissau	233	70.4	220	1.3	1.6	47	44	45	64
Guyana	285	53.5	350	−4.2	0.6	19	30	—	4
Haiti	—	7.7	<695	−2.4	−3.4	—	—	26	47
Honduras	3,220	11.7	580	−0.7	0.0	32	20	93	27
Hungary	34,254	19.2	3,330	0.7	0.0	18	6	86	<5[1]
Iceland	6,236	14.7	23,620	1.3	0.1	—	12	—	<5[1]
India	262,810	9.7	290	3.3	3.0	47	31	—	52
Indonesia	136,991	8.6	730	3.9	4.8	45	19	98	23
Iran	—	21.9	—	−1.1	−0.7	19	23	98	46
Iraq	—	—	696–2,785	—	—	17	—	94	40
Ireland	44,906	2.0	12,580	2.2	4.8	—	8	91	<5[1]
Israel	72,662	19.1	13,760	1.8	2.3	—	N.A.	—	5
Italy	1,134,980	6.5	19,620	2.1	1.9	8	3	—	3
Ivory Coast	N.A.	N.A.	N.A.	−3.4	N.A.	40	N.A.	N.A.	46
Jamaica	3,362	26.9	1,390	−0.3	3.1	7	8	100	2
Japan	3,926,668	1.4	31,450	3.7	3.6	6	2	100	<5[1]
Jordan[5]	4,893	7.0	1,190	−3.3[3]	−5.9	10	8	91	20
Kazakhstan[2]	26,490	91.9	1,540	0.9[3]	−4.6	N.A.	29	—	—
Kenya	6,743	10.6	270	0.3	0.3	33	29	—	31
Kiribati	54	5.1	710	0.5[3]	−1.3	—	24	—	—
Korea, North	—	—	696–2,785	—	—	—	—	—	—
Korea, South	338,062	6.9	7,670	8.8	8.1	26	7	100	<5[1]
Kuwait	34,120	—	23,350	—	0.8	0	0	82	27
Kyrgyzstan	3,752	73.2	830	2.1[3]	−2.1	N.A.	43	—	—
Laos	1,295	26.9	290	1.2[3]	2.1	—	51	59	56
Latvia	5,257	60.5	2,030	2.8[3]	−4.5	N.A.	15	—	—
Lebanon	—	—	696–2,785	—	—	9	—	—	20
Lesotho	1,254	14.6	660	0.0	0.8	35	10	70	26
Liberia	—	—	<695	—	—	24	—	—	61
Libya	—	—	2,786–8,625	—	—	2	N.A.	—	36
Liechtenstein	N.A.	N.A.	N.A.	N.A.	N.A.	N.A.	N.A.	N.A.	N.A.
Lithuania	4,891	84.6	1,310	2.5[3]	−6.4	N.A.	21	—	—
Luxembourg	14,233	3.3	35,850	3.8	2.7	4	1	85	<5[1]
Madagascar	3,039	15.1	240	−2.4	−1.7	30	34	64	20
Malawi	2,034	17.8	220	0.1	0.4	44	38	48	59
Malaysia	60,061	3.1	3,160	2.9	5.7	29	16	—	22
Maldives	194	—	820	6.7	—	—	20	—	—
Mali	2,744	0.5	300	−0.1	−4.3	61	42	15	68
Malta	—	2.7	2,786–8,625	3.8	—	7	N.A.	99	16
Marshall Islands	—	—	696–2,785	—	—	N.A.	—	87	—
Mauritania	1,087	7.4	510	−1.8	−0.1	29	27	—	66
Mauritius	3,309	9.0	2,980	6.1	5.8	16	10	89	17
Mexico	324,951	45.1	3,750	−0.5	0.9	12	8	100	13
Micronesia	—	—	696–2,785	N.A.	—	N.A.	—	—	N.A.
Moldova[2]	5,160	90.2	1,180	1.8[3]	−5.4	N.A.	33	—	—
Monaco	N.A.	N.A.	N.A.	N.A.	N.A.	N.A.	N.A.	N.A.	N.A.
Mongolia	943	34.4	400	—	−0.3	—	28	—	—
Morocco	27,645	5.5	1,030	1.6	0.9	20	14	57	51
Mozambique	1,375	54.3	80	−3.6	1.9	—	33	44	67
Myanmar	—	26.7	<695	—	—	38	63	—	19
Namibia	2,594	10.0	1,660	−1.5	2.3	—	11	81	—
Nepal	3,174	10.4	160	2.1	1.8	67	49	61	74
Netherlands	316,404	1.3	20,710	1.5	2.0	6	4	95	<5[1]
New Zealand	44,674	5.9	12,900	0.2	0.2	—	N.A.	100	<5[1]
Nicaragua	1,421	1,836.2	360	−4.6	−6.2	25	30	78	—
Niger	2,313	−1.3	270	−4.1	−2.1	65	39	25	72
Nigeria	32,988	29.3	310	−1.7	3.2	40	36	—	49

Country	GNP 1993 (millions of U.S. dollars)	GNP Average inflation rate 1985–93	GNP per capita (in U.S. dollars) 1993	GNP per capita Real growth rate 1980–91	GNP per capita Real growth rate 1985–93	Agriculture's share in GDP 1970	Agriculture's share in GDP 1993	Primary school enrollment 1991	Illiteracy rate 1990
Norway	$113,527	3.5%	$ 26,340	2.2%	0.5%	6%	3%	99%	<5%[1]
Oman	9,631	0.6	5,600	4.5[3]	1.2	16	3	82	—
Pakistan	53,250	8.4	430	3.2	1.5	37	25	—	65
Panama	6,621	1.3	2,580	−1.8	−0.7	15	10	91	12
Papua–New Guinea	4,637	4.1	1,120	−0.7	1.1	37	26	72	48
Paraguay	6,995	27.2	1,500	−0.8	1.3	32	24	97	10
Peru	34,030	615.6	1,490	−2.6	−3.5	19	N.A.	95	15
Philippines	54,609	10.0	830	−1.2	1.6	30	22	97	10
Poland	87,315	112.8	2,270	0.5	−1.8	—	7	96	<5[1]
Portugal	77,749	13.0	7,890	2.7	4.7	—	N.A.	97	15
Qatar	7,871	—	15,140	−10.9[3]	−0.7	—	N.A.	88	24
Romania	25,427	49.4	1,120	−0.1	−6.5	—	23	—	—
Russian Federation[2]	348,413	91.4	2,350	1.3[3]	−5.0	N.A.	11	—	—
Rwanda	1,499	2.4	200	−2.6	−3.5	62	41	67	50
Saint Kitts and Nevis	185	5.8	4,470	5.8	5.2	—	6	—	—
Saint Lucia	480	3.5	3,040	2.9[3]	4.3	—	11	—	—
Saint Vincent	233	3.8	2,130	5.2	4.6	—	18	—	—
São Tomé and Príncipe	41	32.8	330	−3.5	−1.8	37	N.A.	—	20–39[1]
Saudi Arabia	—	2.5	—	−4.2[3]	−0.9	6	6	62	38
Senegal	5,867	1.7	730	0.0	−0.3	24	19	48	62
Seychelles	444	4.1	6,370	2.5[3]	4.0	—	4	—	—
Sierra Leone	647	72.3	140	−1.3	−0.6	28	38	—	79
Singapore	55,372	3.5	19,310	4.9	6.1	2	0	100	14
Solomon Islands	261	11.2	750	3.5	2.5	—	N.A.	—	—
Somalia	—	75.4	<695	—	−2.3	59	N.A.	—	76
South Africa	118,057	13.8	2,900	0.9[3]	−1.5	8	4	—	—
Spain	533,986	6.8	13,650	2.9	3.1	—	4	100	5
Sri Lanka	10,658	11.2	600	2.5	2.6	28	25	100	12
Sudan	—	55.3	<695	−2.4[3]	−0.2	43	34	—	73
Suriname	488	20.5	1,210	−4.5[3]	2.2	7	14	100	5
Swaziland	933	11.3	1,050	3.1[3]	3.8	33	13	88	32
Sweden	216,294	6.3	24,830	1.7	0.1	—	2	100	<5[1]
Switzerland	254,066	3.8	36,410	1.6	0.7	—	N.A.	91	<5[1]
Syria	—	22.1	696–2,785	−2.1[3]	−2.1	20	30	99	36
Taiwan	N.A.	N.A.	N.A.	N.A.	N.A.	N.A.	N.A.	N.A.	N.A.
Tajikistan[2]	2,686	33.0	470	−0.1[3]	−7.8	N.A.	33	—	—
Tanzania[6]	2,521	23.4	100	−1.1	1.4	41	43	50	—
Thailand	120,235	5.1	2,040	5.9	8.4	26	12	—	7
Togo	1,325	2.3	330	−1.7	−3.4	34	49	76	57
Tonga	150	10.4	1,610	1.5[3]	1.5	—	—	—	—
Trinidad and Tobago	4,776	5.9	3,730	−5.2	−2.7	5	2	90	40
Tunisia	15,332	6.6	1,780	1.2	2.2	20	16	97	35
Turkey	126,330	56.2	2,120	2.9	3.0	30	15	100	19
Turkmenistan[2]	—	46.0	—	0.7[3]	−1.6	N.A.	32	—	—
Uganda	3,486	79.3	190	3.3	1.9	54	56	—	52
Ukraine[2]	99,677	103.0	1,910	2.3[3]	−3.9	—	31	—	—
United Arab Emirates	38,720	—	22,470	−5.8[3]	0.5	—	2	100	—
United Kingdom	1,042,700	5.7	17,970	2.6	1.3	—	2	97	<5[1]
United States	6,387,686	3.5	24,750	2.1	1.2	3	N.A.	98	<5[1]
Uruguay	12,314	76.2	3,910	−0.4	3.0	13	9	91	4
Uzbekistan[2]	21,100	65.0	960	0.8[3]	−1.6	N.A.	36	—	—
Vanuatu	198	6.3	1,230	−0.2[3]	0.2	—	N.A.	—	—
Venezuela	58,916	35.2	2,840	−1.5	1.0	6	5	91	8
Vietnam	11,997	118.7	170	—	4.8	—	2.9	—	12
Western Samoa	159	10.6	980	5.1[3]	−0.1	—	40	—	—
Yemen	—	—	<695	—	—	52	21	—	62
Yugoslavia[7]	—	—	696–2,785	−1.4[3]	—	18	—	—	7[3]
Zaire	—	—	<695	−1.6[3]	−0.8	16	N.A.	58	28
Zambia	3,152	89.0	370	−2.9[3]	1.8	11	29	81	27
Zimbabwe	5,756	20.5	540	0.2	−1.1	15	18	—	33

N.A. = not available. 1. Estimated. 2. Data for republics of the former Soviet Union are still preliminary. 3. Figure for year(s) other than those specified. 4. Includes Eritrea. 5. Data for GNP cover the East Bank only. 6. Data for GNP and GNP per capita cover mainland Tanzania only. 7. Data refer to the former Socialist Federal Republic of Yugoslavia. **Source:** The World Bank, *The World Bank Atlas, 1994* (1995).

COUNTRIES WITH HIGHEST GNP PER CAPITA, 1993

Country	GNP per capita (in U.S. dollars)	Country	GNP per capita (in U.S. dollars)
Switzerland	$36,410	Netherlands	$20,710
Luxembourg	35,850	Canada	20,670
Japan	31,450	Italy	19,620
Denmark	26,510	Singapore	19,310
Norway	26,340	Finland	18,970
Sweden	24,830	United Kingdom	17,970
United States	24,750	Australia	17,510
Iceland	23,620	Qatar	15,140
Germany	23,560	Israel	13,760
Kuwait	23,350	Spain	13,650
Austria	23,120	New Zealand	12,900
United Arab Emirates	22,470	Ireland	12,580
France	22,360	Bahamas	11,500
Belgium	21,210	Cyprus	10,380

Note: Rankings based on countries reporting GNP and GNP per capita to the World Bank. Does not include countries for which GNP and GNP per capita have been estimated. 1. Includes Eritrea. 2. Mainland only. **Source**: The World Bank, *The World Bank Atlas 1994* (1995).

COUNTRIES WITH LOWEST GNP PER CAPITA, 1993

Country	GNP per capita (in U.S. dollars)	Country	GNP per capita (in U.S. dollars)
Mozambique	$ 80	Kenya	$270
Ethiopia[1]	100	Niger	270
Tanzania[2]	100	India	290
Sierra Leone	140	Laos	290
Nepal	160	Burkina Faso	300
Bhutan	170	Mali	300
Vietnam	170	Nigeria	310
Burundi	180	São Tomé and Príncipe	330
Uganda	190	Togo	330
Chad	200	Albania	340
Rwanda	200	Guyana	350
Bangladesh	220	Equatorial Guinea	360
Guinea-Bissau	220	Gambia	360
Malawi	220	Nicaragua	360
Madagascar	240		

Note: Rankings based on countries reporting GNP and GNP per capita to the World Bank. Does not include countries for which GNP and GNP per capita have been estimated. 1. Includes Eritrea. 2. Mainland only. **Source:** The World Bank, *The World Bank Atlas 1994* (1995).

WORLD HEALTH

The World Health Organization (WHO), a specialized agency of the United Nations, is the global intergovernmental directing and coordinating authority for international health work. WHO was created in 1948, and since 1977 its motto has been "Health for All by the Year 2000." This global health strategy focuses on supporting governments in improving education on current health problems, proper food supply and nutrition, safe water and sanitation, maternal and child health, immunization against major infectious diseases, prevention and control of local diseases, and provision of essential pharmaceuticals. Headquartered in Geneva, Switzerland, WHO gathers health statistics, sets international health standards, provides assistance to individual countries when invited, and issues publications.

This section examines major global health issues, including cardiovascular disease, cancer, tobacco smoking, childhood immunization, maternal deaths, and HIV/AIDS. Also included is a table listing the latest official number of AIDS cases for every country of the world. Another table shows life expectancy, calorie supply, infant mortality rates, health expenditure, and access to safe water and sanitation for every country. Most of the information is from the World Health Organization. (For information on the United States, see the section "Health and Medicine" in Part II.)

CARDIOVASCULAR DISEASES

According to the World Health Organization, heart attacks and strokes kill about 12 million people each year, and millions more are disabled. Cardiovascular diseases (CVDs) account for about one quarter of all deaths worldwide, more than any other disease. In the Western industrialized nations, CVDs cause about one half of all deaths. In developing countries, CVDs cause about 16 percent of all current deaths, and WHO expects this number to increase to 30 percent by the year 2000.

In the 1970s and 1980s many developed countries had a decrease in cardiovascular mortality, but some experienced increases. Bulgaria and Poland, for example, had a 10 percent increase in cardiovascular-related deaths over the last two decades. The highest decreases in CVD mortality were in Australia, Canada, the United States, and Japan; several other Western countries had at least a 10 percent decrease in mortality over this same time period. Some nations, including Greece, Hungary, Norway, and Yugoslavia, had stable CVD death rates.

Coronary heart disease (CHD) is linked to lifestyle. The CHD mortality rates vary by a factor of 10 across industrialized countries,

CAUSES OF DEATH WORLDWIDE, 1990

Main cause of death	Estimated number	Rate per 100,000
Infectious and parasitic diseases	17,499,000	331
Circulatory system diseases[1]	11,931,000	225
Malignant neoplasms	5,121,000	97
External causes[2]	3,466,000	65
Perinatal causes	3,116,000	59
Chronic obstructive pulmonary diseases	2,888,000	55
Maternal causes	504,000	10
Other and unknown causes[3]	5,413,000	102
All causes	49,936,000	944

1. Includes heart diseases, cerebrovascular diseases, other diseases of the circulatory system, etc. 2. Includes accidents, suicide, etc. 3. Includes AIDS, diabetes, diseases of the digestive system, genitourinary diseases, ill-defined causes including senility, etc. **Source**: World Health Organization, *Global Health Situation and Projections* (1992).

COMPARATIVE DEATH RATES FOR SELECTED NATIONS, 1994 AND 2000 (projected)

Selected developed nations	1994	2000
Australia	7.4	7.4
Canada	7.4	7.7
France	9.3	9.3
Germany	10.9	10.5
Italy	9.7	10.0
Japan	7.3	8.3
Russia	11.3	11.2
Spain	8.8	9.2
United Kingdom	10.8	10.3
United States	8.7	8.8
Selected developing nations	**1994**	**2000**
China	7.4	7.0
India	10.3	9.1
Indonesia	8.6	8.1
Korea, South	6.2	6.4
Nigeria	12.4	10.1
Peru	7.0	6.3
Tanzania	19.4	22.4
Uganda	23.7	26.3
Vietnam	7.8	7.0
Zaire	16.7	15.5

Note: Death rate is the crude rate, the number of deaths per 1,000 persons based on midyear population. **Source:** U.S. Bureau of the Census, International Data Base.

being lowest in Japan and highest in Finland, England, and Wales. In the United States, death rates for coronary heart disease declined by more than 40 percent between 1970 and 1987 for those between the ages of 35 and 74. (As a result, cancer became the leading cause of death in this age group in 1987.) The U.S. rate for coronary heart disease is six times higher than that in Japan. However, Japanese who live in the U.S. have a rate between the low level of Japanese residents and the high level of white Americans. This suggests that lifestyle plays a greater role in CHD than ethnic background.

Hypertension is the most common cardiovascular disorder: global estimates suggest that 8 to 18 percent of adults have blood pressures of 160/95 mmHg and above. In developing countries, hypertension accounts for up to 40 percent of cardiac cases admitted to hospitals; strokes account for up to 10 percent.

A heart ailment caused by Chagas disease, a parasitic illness, currently affects about 17 million people in Latin America and poses as a potential threat to the United States because of immigration.

Rheumatic fever and rheumatic heart disease, though preventable, affect large numbers of people in poor communities. In developing countries they account for more than 30 percent of cardiac cases admitted to hospitals.

CANCER

The World Health Organization estimates that in 1990 about nine million people developed cancer, more than 20 million suffered from the disease, and 5.1 million died. Before the year 2000, over 60 million people will die of cancer, and over 80 million will die of cancer in the first decade of the next century.

WHO reports that in 1985, 4.9 million people died of cancer worldwide, and projects that in 2015 there will be 9.1 million deaths, an increase of 86 percent. Of the total cancer deaths in 1985, 2.2 million were in developed countries, and WHO estimates that 2.6 million in these countries will die of the disease in 2015, an increase of 18 percent. In 1985 developing countries had 2.7 million cancer deaths, and 6.5 million deaths are projected for 2015, an increase of 141 percent.

WHO expects people in developing countries to have an additional 1.5 million cases of lung cancer, of which 90 percent will be incurable, as a result of increased cigarette smoking.

(See also "Health and Medicine" in Part II.)

SMOKING: A GLOBAL HEALTH PROBLEM

Worldwide, about half of adult men and 10 percent of adult women smoke. In industrialized countries, 30 to 40 percent of men and women smoke, while in the developing nations only 2 to 10 percent of the smokers are women, but 40 to 60 percent of the men smoke. Smoking is increasing at a rate of 2 percent a year, mostly in developing countries.

Half the global increase in tobacco use from 1976 to 1986 occurred in China. Today, more than 250 million people (mostly men) in China smoke 1.5 trillion cigarettes a year. China produces about half the world's tobacco and nearly one-quarter of the world's cigarettes, and has an open-door policy to foreign tobacco corporations. Given current trends, 50 million Chinese children alive today will eventually die from tobacco-related diseases.

The World Health Organization estimates that tobacco will kill about three million people a year in the 1990s, two million in the developed countries, and at least one million in the developing countries. This figure is currently projected to increase by five times over the next 50 years, so that by 2040 cigarette smoking will kill a total of some 12.5 million people annually, primarily in the developing nations. Add in rates for chronic diseases associated with smoking, which are at least 10 times higher than for nonsmokers, and total deaths from smoking-related causes are enormous.

Measures to discourage smoking, adopted mostly in Western countries in the last 20 years, have resulted in a 10 to 30 percent decline in cigarette use. Yet in Eastern Europe and the former Soviet Union, where smoking has not been discouraged, consumption actually increased 20 to 30 percent over the same time period. In the developing world, India has passed laws to reduce tobacco consumption, and Nigeria has banned smoking in public.

One of the major reasons for the massive expansion of cigarette smoking in developing countries is aggressive advertising campaigns by American cigarette companies coupled with U.S. government pressures to allow cigarette sales into these countries. The U.S. government has threatened trade sanctions against Japan, Taiwan, South Korea, and other countries unless U.S. tobacco products are accepted and cigarette advertising permitted. In 1990, for the first time, Philip Morris sold more cigarettes outside the United States than within.

(See also "Health and Medicine" in Part II.)

CHILDHOOD DEATHS

The World Health Organization estimates that in 1990 about 13.1 million children under the age of five died. Of this total, 9.4 million were less than one year old and 3.7 million were one to four years of age.

Overall, the global infant mortality rate is estimated at 66 per 1,000 live births, with rates of 14 per 1,000 in developed countries and 75 per 1,000 in developing countries. Infant and child deaths constitute about 26 percent of the total number of deaths occurring in the world.

At least one-third of all deaths of children under five years of age take place in the first month of life, most frequently within the first week. These infant deaths are usually the result of the poor health and nutrition of the mother.

In the developed world, injuries from accidents have replaced infectious diseases as the greatest health hazard for children.

LEADING CAUSES OF CHILDHOOD DEATHS, 1990

(birth to four years of age)

Cause	Estimated number of deaths	Percent of total
World total	**12,900,000**	**100.0%**
Acute respiratory infections (mostly pneumonia)	3,560,000	27.6
Diarrhea (alone)	3,000,000	23.3
Birth asphyxia	860,000	6.7
Malaria	800,000	6.2
Neonatal tetanus	560,000	4.3
ARI—measles	480,000	3.7
Congenital anomalies	450,000	3.5
Birth trauma	430,000	3.3
Prematurity	430,000	3.3

Source: World Health Organization, *Global Health Situation and Projections* (1992).

CHILDHOOD IMMUNIZATION

In 1991 UNICEF and the World Health Organization certified that 80 percent of all the world's one-year-olds were immunized against the six deadly childhood diseases—diphtheria, whooping cough, measles, tuberculosis, polio, and tetanus—thereby effectively stopping the spread of these diseases. An estimated 3.2 million infants in the developing world are now saved from measles, neonatal tetanus, and pertussis, and 445,000 infants will avoid being paralyzed by polio. The World Health Organization announced the eradication of smallpox from all peoples on Earth in 1980.

In 1974 WHO established a major immunization program to protect children against the six diseases named above. It was estimated that five million children were dying each year from these diseases. Most of these deaths and disabilities were in developing countries where less than 5 percent of the children were being immunized in the critical first year of life.

The WHO immunization program has been reducing infant and child deaths. For example, in 1985 an estimated two million children died from measles. By 1990 immunization reduced the deaths to 880,000. Deaths from whooping cough declined from 600,000 to 360,000 in the same time period. Polio vaccines are reducing this dreaded disease; WHO and UNICEF anticipate that polio will be eradicated by 1995.

On the other hand, relatively little progress has been made in reducing mortality from the acute respiratory infections (primarily pneumonia) and the group of perinatal conditions.

CURRENT WORLD HEALTH INDICATORS, BY NATION

Country	Life expectancy at birth (years)		Daily calorie supply	Infant mortality per 1,000 births[1]	Population with access to		
	1970	1992	1989	1992	Health services 1985–91	Safe water 1988–91	Sanitation 1988–91
Afghanistan	37	43	—	162	48%	21%	—
Albania[2]	67	73	—	28	—	97	100%
Algeria	53	66	2,866	61	90	70	60
Angola	37	46	1,807	125	30	34	18
Antigua & Barbuda	67	74	—	20	100	100	100
Argentina	67	71	3,113	29	—	—	89
Armenia[2]	—	72	—	21	—	—	—
Australia	71	77	3,216	7	327	—	—
Austria[2]	70	77	3,495	8	—	100	100
Azerbaijan	—	71	—	32	—	—	—
Bahamas	65	70	—	25	100	100	100
Bahrain	62	70	—	30	100	100	100
Bangladesh	45	53	2,021	101	60	—	32
Barbados	69	75	—	10	100	100	100
Belarus[2]	—	71	—	15	—	—	—
Belgium[2]	71	76	—	8	—	100	100
Belize	—	69	—	41	95	75	48
Benin	44	51	2,305	110	30	54	42
Bhutan	42	48	—	129	70	31	9
Bolivia	46	60	1,916	82	63	52	35
Botswana	50	68	2,375	35	89	60	42
Brazil	59	66	2,751	57	—	86	78
Brunei	—	74	—	7	96	95	95
Bulgaria[2]	70	71	—	17	—	99	100
Burkina Faso	40	48	2,288	132	60	71	12
Burundi	45	48	1,932	106	80	56	48
Cambodia	42	51	2,166	116	53	37	15
Cameroon	49	56	2,217	61	41	54	78
Canada	73	78	3,482	7	207	100	—
Cape Verde	56	68	—	40	—	72	17
Central African Rep.	42	47	2,036	105	30	12	21
Chad	38	47	1,743	122	30	—	—
Chile	62	72	2,581	17	97	88	88
China	59	71	2,639	38	90	83	97
Colombia	59	69	2,598	37	100	93	63
Comoros	48	56	—	87	82	75	83
Congo	51	51	2,590	114	—	21	—
Costa Rica	67	76	2,808	14	97	92	97
Croatia[2]	—	73	—	12	—	—	—
Cuba	70	76	—	11	100	98	92
Cyprus	71	77	—	10	95	100	100
Czech Republic[2]	69	73	3,632	12	—	100	100
Denmark[2]	73	76	3,628	8	—	100	99
Djibouti	40	49	—	111	99	86	59
Dominica	—	72	—	18	100	96	99
Dominican Rep.	59	68	2,359	53	100	67	60
Ecuador	58	67	2,531	53	88	54	48
Egypt	51	62	3,336	57	99	88	51
El Salvador	58	66	2,317	46	60	47	58
Equatorial Guinea	40	48	—	116	—	32	37
Estonia[2]	—	70	—	13	—	—	—
Ethiopia	43	49	1,667	168	46	28	16
Fiji	64	72	—	23	100	79	75
Finland[2]	70	76	3,253	6	—	95	100
France[2]	72	77	3,465	7	—	100	100
Gabon	44	54	2,383	92	90	68	—
Gambia	36	45	—	132	90	77	44
Georgia[2]	—	73	—	17	—	—	—
Germany[2]	71	76	3,443	7	—	100	93
Ghana	49	55	2,248	81	60%	54%	42%
Greece[2]	72	78	3,825	10	—	98	98
Guatemala	53	65	2,235	58	50	60	60
Guinea	36	44	2,132	133	40	64	24
Guinea-Bissau	36	39	—	147	80	39	25
Guyana	65	65	—	48	96	64	90
Haiti	48	55	2,013	93	50	39	27
Honduras	53	66	2,247	49	66	78	67
Hungary[2]	70	70	3,644	16	—	98	100
Iceland[2]	74	78	—	6	—	100	100
India	48	60	2,229	88	—	—	15
Indonesia	47	60	2,750	72	80	51	44
Iran	55	65	3,181	65	87	61	51
Iraq	55	64	2,887	58	99	91	70
Ireland[2]	71	75	3,778	8	—	100	100
Israel[2]	71	77	—	9	—	100	99
Italy[2]	72	78	3,504	8	—	100	100
Ivory Coast	—	52	2,577	94	45	70	35
Jamaica	67	74	2,609	15	90	100	90
Japan	72	79	2,956	5	—	—	—
Jordan	55	70	2,634	47	97	99	76
Kazakhstan	—	69	—	31	—	—	—
Kenya	50	59	2,163	66	77	50	43
Kiribati	—	56	—	60	—	—	—
Korea, North	—	71	—	24	100	—	—
Korea, South	60	71	—	13	100	92	100
Kuwait	66	75	3,195	14	100	100	98
Kyrgyzstan	—	66	—	40	—	—	—
Laos	40	51	—	97	67	37	24
Latvia[2]	—	69	—	16	—	—	—
Lebanon	64	66	—	34	95	98	81
Lesotho	49	57	2,299	79	80	48	25
Liberia	47	55	2,382	131	39	54	15
Libya	52	63	3,324	68	100	93	95
Lithuania[2]	—	70	—	14	—	—	—
Luxembourg[2]	70	76	—	9	—	100	100
Macedonia[2]	—	72	—	29	—	—	—
Madagascar	45	51	2,158	113	65	20	5
Malawi	40	44	2,139	142	80	53	—
Malaysia	62	71	2,774	14	90	72	94
Mali	40	48	2,314	159	35	41	23
Malta[2]	70	76	—	10	—	100	100
Mauritania	39	48	2,685	117	40	70	23
Mauritius	62	70	2,887	18	100	100	98
Mexico	62	70	3,052	35	90	77	55
Micronesia	—	71	—	25	—	—	—
Moldova[2]	—	68	—	23	—	—	—
Monaco[2]	—	63	—	63	—	—	—
Mongolia	60	64	2,479	60	100	79	73
Morocco	52	63	—	63	63	73	57
Mozambique	41	47	1,680	147	39	24	24
Myanmar	51	60	2,440	72	48	31	36
Namibia	48	58	1,946	70	70	52	15
Nepal	42	54	2,077	99	—	42	8
Netherlands[2]	74	77	3,151	7	—	100	100
New Zealand	72	76	3,362	9	—	100	—
Nicaragua	54	67	2,265	53	—	54	52
Niger	38	46	2,308	123	30	55	10
Nigeria	44	52	2,312	84	72	50	15

Country	Life expectancy at birth (years) 1970	1992	Daily calorie supply 1989	Infant mortality per 1,000 births[1] 1992	Population with access to: Health services 1985–91	Safe water 1988–91	Sanitation 1988–91
Norway[2]	74	77	3,326	8	—	100%	100%
Oman	45	70	—	30	87%	79	44
Pakistan	48	59	—	95	90	56	24
Panama	66	73	2,539	21	80	84	92
Papua New Guinea	47	56	2,403	54	97	32	56
Paraguay	65	67	2,757	47	—	36	60
Peru	54	65	2,186	52	95	56	59
Philippines	57	65	2,375	40	75	82	69
Poland[2]	70	71	—	15	—	89	100
Portugal[2]	—	74	—	11	—	92	96
Qatar	61	71	—	26	100	89	97
Romania[2]	69	70	3,155	27	—	95	98
Russia[2]	—	69	—	20	—	—	—
Rwanda	48	46	1,971	110	80	66	58
St. Kitts & Nevis	—	71	—	34	100	100	98
St. Lucia	62	72	—	17	100	—	—
St. Vincent & the Grenadines	63	71	—	20	80	89	100
São Tomé & Príncipe	—	68	—	65	—	—	—
Saudi Arabia	52	69	2,874	31	98	93	82
Senegal	43	48	2,369	80	40	47	54
Seychelles	—	71	—	16	99	99	65
Sierra Leone	34	43	1,799	143	37	50	62
Singapore	68	75	3,198	6	100	100	96
Slovakia[2]	—	72	—	12	—	—	—
Slovenia[2]	—	73	—	10	—	—	—
Solomon Islands	40	65	—	44	80	60	—
Somalia	—	49	1,906	127	27	60	17
South Africa	53	63	—	53	—	—	—
Spain[2]	72	77	3,572	8	—	100	100
Sri Lanka	64	72	2,277	18	90	71	60
Sudan	—	52	1,974	99	60%	45%	70%
Suriname	64	69	—	37	91	89	52
Swaziland	46	57	—	108	55	35	40
Sweden[2]	75	78	2,960	6	—	100	100
Switzerland[2]	73	78	3,562	7	—	100	100
Syria	56	67	—	39	99	73	83
Tajikistan	—	69	—	49	—	—	—
Tanzania	45	51	2,206	115	80	51	66
Thailand	58	69	2,316	26	70	76	74
Togo	45	54	2,214	85	60	59	21
Tonga	—	68	—	21	—	—	—
Trinadad & Tobago	66	71	2,853	18	99	97	99
Tunisia	54	68	—	41	91	99	96
Turkey[2]	57	67	3,236	56	—	92	—
Turkmenistan	—	66	—	55	—	—	—
Uganda	47	46	2,153	118	70	15	31
Ukraine[2]	—	70	—	18	—	—	—
United Arab Emirates	61	72	—	22	100	100	94
United Kingdom[2]	72	76	3,149	7	—	100	100
United States	71	76	3,671	9	536	100	—
Uruguay	—	74	2,653	20	90	85	—
Uzbekistan	—	69	—	44	—	—	—
Vanuatu	—	65	—	65	82	74	46
Venezuela	65	70	2,582	33	—	90	94
Vietnam	—	67	2,233	36	90	27	18
Western Samoa	—	66	—	45	100	83	94
Yemen	42	53	—	106	30	—	68
Yugoslavia[2]	68	72	3,634	28	—	83	63
Zaire	45	52	1,991	91	40	33	25
Zambia	47	48	2,077	108	74	48	43
Zimbabwe	51	60	2,299	47	83	36	42

Note: Not every nation reports in all categories, and some do not report any information at all. Nonreporting nations do not appear in the table. 1. Rate for children under 5 per 1,000 live births. 2. For Israel and all countries in Europe, Health Services data is from 1987–90, Safe Water and Sanitation Access data are from 1988–90. **Sources:** The World Bank, *World Bank Atlas 1994* (1993); United Nations Development Programme, *Human Development Report 1994* (1994); World Health Organization, *World Health Statistics Annual 1991* (1992).

MATERNAL DEATHS WORLDWIDE

Approximately half a million women around the world die each year from pregnancy-related causes, according to the World Health Organization. In parts of some developing countries, the chance of a woman dying this way is 100 times greater than in industrialized countries.

Fully 99 percent of maternal deaths occur in developing countries, with an estimated 25,000 in Latin America, 169,000 in Africa, and 311,000 in Asia and Oceania.

The five major causes of maternal death are hemorrhage, infection, unsafe abortion, hypertension, and obstructed labor. WHO reports that maternal deaths are not only due to a lack of hospital facilities but are also the result of the social, cultural, and economic environment. Women do not have adequate family planning materials and services so that they have unwanted pregnancies and bear too many children, or they have children when they are too young or too old, or have children too close together.

INFANT MORTALITY RATES BY REGION, 1994

Region	Infant mortality rate (per 1,000 live births)
World	**65**
Developed regions	15
Developing regions	72
Sub-Saharan Africa	95
Asia	68
Near East and North Africa	60
Latin America and Caribbean	43
North America	8
Europe	9
Former USSR	34

Source: U.S. Bureau of the Census, *World Population Profile: 1994* (1994).

WHO estimates that about 52 percent of births in the developing world are attended by a trained health practitioner, and that less than half of the births take place in a health institution. The highest proportion of births attended by a trained attendant in the developing world

GLOBAL SEX FACTS

According to the World Health Organization, sexual intercourse occurs more than 100 million times a day around the world. As a result, approximately 910,000 conceptions take place, as well as 350,000 cases of sexually transmitted diseases.

WHO estimates that 1,440 women die each day (an average of one a minute) because of complications during pregnancy or childbirth. About 150,000 unwanted pregnancies end each day in abortion.

The number of people using contraception in Third World countries has increased sharply in recent years, rising from 31 million in the 1960–65 period to 381 million during 1985–90. Women in developing countries had, on average, 6.1 children in the years 1965–70, but that figure declined to 3.9 children in 1985–90.

Source: World Health Organization, *Reproductive Health, a Key to a Brighter Future* (1992).

NATIONS WITH HIGHEST AND LOWEST INFANT MORTALITY RATES, 1994

Nation	Infant mortality rate[1]	Nation	Infant mortality rate[1]
Highest infant mortality		**Lowest infant mortality**	
Afghanistan	156	Iceland	4
Western Sahara	152	Japan	4
Angola	145	Finland	5
Sierra Leone	142	Liechtenstein	5
Malawi	141	Hong Kong	6
Guinea	139	Netherlands	6
Central African Rep.	137	Norway	6
Chad	132	San Marino	6
Mozambique	129	Singapore	6
Somalia	126	Sweden	6
Gambia	124	Taiwan	6
Bhutan	121	Austria	7
Guinea-Bissau	120	Australia	7
Rwanda	119	Belgium	7
Burkina Faso	118	Canada	7
Burundi	114	Denmark	7
Liberia	113	France	7
Yemen	113	Germany	7
Uganda	112	Ireland	7
Cambodia	111	Luxembourg	7
Congo	111	Monaco	7
Djibouti	111	Spain	7
Niger	111	United Kingdom	7
Zaire	111	Andorra	8
Benin	110	Aruba	8
Tanzania	110	Italy	8
		Malta	8
		Réunion	8
		Slovenia	8
		United States	8

1. Per 1,000 live births. **Source:** U.S. Bureau of the Census, *World Population Profile: 1994* (1994).

NUMBER OF REPORTED AIDS CASES, BY REGION, 1983–95

Region	1983	1986	1989	1992	Cumulative total 1995[1]
Total	**3,671**	**28,853**	**107,699**	**161,863**	**1,169,811**
Africa	17	3,357	40,637	56,299	418,051
Americas	3,345	21,256	53,040	84,918	580,129
Asia	8	81	269	1,207	23,912
Europe	295	3,915	13,073	18,628	141,275
Oceania	6	254	680	811	6,444

1. Total as of June 30, 1995. **Source**: World Health Organization, Global Programme on AIDS, *The Current Situation of the HIV/AIDS Pandemic* (July 3, 1995).

AIDS FACTS WORLDWIDE, 1995

19,500,000	people estimated to have been infected with HIV since pandemic began
18,000,000	adults have been infected with HIV
1,500,000	children have been infected with HIV
14–15,000,000	adults are estimated to be alive now and infected with HIV
1,169,811	AIDS cases reported to WHO in mid-1995
4,500,000	estimated AIDS cases since pandemic began
6,000	people are infected with HIV each day
50%	of HIV infections to date have been in 15–24 year olds
80–90%	of HIV-infected children are in sub-Saharan Africa
80%	of HIV infections and AIDS cases are in developing countries
90%	of newly infected adults acquire HIV from heterosexual intercourse
30–40 million	people are expected to have HIV by 2000

Source: World Health Organization, Global Programme on AIDS, *The Current Situation of HIV/AIDS Pandemic* (July 3, 1995).

ESTIMATED HIV INFECTIONS IN ADULTS, BY CONTINENT OR REGION, 1995

Continent/Region	Estimated HIV infections
Sub-Saharan Africa	11,000,000+
South and Southeast Asia	3,500,000+
Latin America and the Caribbean	2,000,000
North America	1,100,000+
Western Europe	600,000+
North Africa and Middle East	150,000
Eastern Europe and Central Asia	50,000+
East Asia and Pacific	50,000
Australasia	25,000+

Note: As of June 30, 1995. **Source:** World Health Organization, Global Programme on AIDS, *The Current Global Situation of the HIV/AIDS Pandemic* (July 3, 1995).

AIDS CASES BY CONTINENT OR REGION

	Reported	Estimated
Total cases:	**1,169,811**	**4,500,000**
Percent of total:		
United States	38.0%	9%
Africa	35.5	70
Americas	12.0	9
Europe	12.0	4
Asia	2.0	6
Oceania	0.5	1

Source: World Health Organization, Global Programme on AIDS, *The Current Situation of HIV/AIDS Pandemic* (July 3, 1995).

is in East Asia, where coverage levels are uniformly high in all countries except in the rural areas of South Korea.

According to WHO, if all women who said they want no more children were actually able to stop childbearing, the number of births would be reduced by an average of 35 percent (4.4 million) in Latin America, 33 percent (24.4 million) in Asia, and 17 percent (4 million) in Africa. Maternal mortality would fall by even higher proportions, since the pregnancies that would be averted would tend to be the high-parity/high-risk pregnancies and the unwanted pregnancies that so often lead to unsafe abortions.

AIDS WORLDWIDE

According to the World Health Organization (WHO), in mid-1995 around 19.5 million people, including 1.5 million children, have been infected with HIV (human immunodeficiency virus), the causative agent for AIDS, since the pandemic began in the late 1970s to early 1980s. WHO estimates that during 1994 around 2.5 million people were newly infected with HIV. There are approximately 6,000 new HIV infections each day. Half of all infections to date have been in 15- to 24-year-olds.

The actual number of reported cases is far less than these estimates because many people who have AIDS are not aware of it and most people don't report their infection to medical authorities. By mid-1995 WHO had received reports of 1,169,811 cases of AIDS (acquired immunodeficiency syndrome) since the disease was first reported in the United States in 1981. However, because of underreporting WHO believes that over 4.5 million individuals infected with HIV have developed AIDS since the disease was first recorded. People with HIV are likely to contract AIDS within 10 years. Given present trends, 30 to 40 million people will contract the HIV virus by the year 2000.

The major route of transmission is sexual intercourse, whether heterosexual or homosexual. Transmission also occurs through HIV-infected blood, blood products, or transplanted organs or tissues, for example, by direct blood transfusion or through the use of improperly sterilized needles and syringes that have been in contact with contaminated blood. Also, HIV can be transmitted from an HIV-infected woman to her fetus or infant before, during, or shortly after birth.

In mid-1995, 80 percent of all people infected with HIV were in developing countries. By the year 2000, this number is expected to increase to 90 percent. In the developing world, two thirds of all estimated AIDS cases are thought to have occurred in sub-Saharan Africa, where one in 40 adults is already infected. In certain cities in Africa, one in every three people is HIV-positive. HIV infection rates have been spiraling in South and Southeast Asia as well. To date more than three million people in this part of the world have been infected with HIV; in Thailand, 1 in 50 adults is infected.

WHO estimates that there were 14 to 15 million living adults infected with HIV in mid-1995: 8.5 million in Africa, 3 million in South and South-East Asia, 750,000+ in the United States/Canada, 450,000 in Western Europe, 100,000+ in North Africa and the Middle East, 50,000+ in Eastern Europe and Central Asia, 50,000 in East Asia and the Pacific, and 20,000 in Australasia.

Because the disease primarily affected gay men (and intravenous drug users) at first, for many years men made up the majority of people infected with AIDS. But because women are biologically more susceptible to acquiring HIV infection through heterosexual intercourse than are men, women are now contracting the disease at the same rates as men. In Uganda, women make up more than 60 percent of people with HIV.

(For more detailed information on AIDS in the United States, see "Health and Medicine" in Part II.)

NATIONS WITH THE LARGEST NUMBER OF REPORTED AIDS CASES, 1995

Nation	Cases	Nation	Cases
United States	441,528	Zimbabwe	38,552
Brazil	62,314	Malawi	37,673
Kenya	56,573	France	35,773
Uganda	46,120	Spain	31,221
Tanzania	45,968	Zambia	29,734

Note: As of June 30, 1995. **Source:** World Health Organization, Global Programme on AIDS. *The Current Situation of the HIV/AIDS Pandemic* (July 3, 1995).

WOMEN AND AIDS

According to the World Health Organization, women throughout the world are now becoming infected with the virus that causes AIDS about as often as men; by the year 2000, most new infections will be in women. Speaking at the 1992 international conference on AIDS in July, Dr. Michael Merson, head of WHO's global program on AIDS, said that since Jan. 1, "Close to half of the one million newly infected adults have been women," As a result of this increase in infection rates among women, the number of children born with HIV, the virus that causes AIDS, has also risen; in addition, tens of thousands of infants, even if they escape infection, are fated to become orphans when their mothers die from AIDS.

"The disease is now everywhere," Dr. Merson said, "and we want to get home the point that the AIDS epidemic is becoming heterosexual everywhere."

AIDS CASES BY NATION AND TERRITORY, 1995

Region/ Country/Territory	Cumulative cases
AFRICA	**415,595**
Algeria	217
Angola	895
Benin	856
Burkina Faso	3,722
Botswana	3,110
Burundi	7,024
Cameroon	5,375
Central African Republic	3,730[1]
Cape Verde	92
Chad	3,457
Congo	7,773
Comoros	5
Equatorial Guinea	74
Eritrea	1,539
Ethiopia	18,042
Gabon	881
Gambia	340
Ghana	15,006
Guinea-Bissau	707
Guinea	1,548
Ivory Coast	25,236
Kenya	56,573
Lesotho	515
Liberia	191
Madagascar	18
Mali	2,594
Malawi	37,673
Mauritius	27
Mauritania	59
Mozambique	1,815
Namibia	5,101
Nigeria	1,591
Niger	1,691
Réunion	65[1]
Rwanda	10,706
Senegal	1,297
Seychelles	6
Sierra Leone	155
South Africa	3,849
São Tomé and Príncipe	13
Swaziland	413
Tanzania	45,968
Togo	5,109
Uganda	46,120
Zaire	26,131
Zambia	29,734
Zimbabwe	38,552
THE AMERICAS	**580,129**
Anguilla	5
Antigua and Barbuda	40
Argentina	6,187
Bahamas	1,711
Barbados	537
Belize	100
Bermuda	267
Bolivia	97
Brazil	62,314
Canada	11,192
Cayman Islands	18
Chile	1,016
Colombia	5,577
Costa Rica	760
Cuba	364
Dominica	31
Dominican Republic	2,589
Ecuador	491
El Salvador	1,096
French Guiana	359[2]
Grenada	63
Guadeloupe	370
Guatemala	594
Guyana	602
Haiti	4,967[1]
Honduras	4,283
Jamaica	1,029
Martinique	266
Mexico	22,055
Montserrat	7
Netherland Antilles	168
Nicaragua	101
Panama	864
Paraguay	84
Peru	1,176
Saint Lucia	69
Saint Vincent	66
Saint Kitts and Nevis	46
Suriname	189
Trinidad and Tobago	1,742
Uruguay	587
United States	441,528
Venezuela	4,475
EASTERN MEDITERRANEAN	**3,171**
Afghanistan	0[1]
Bahrain	20
Cyprus	41
Djibouti	712
Egypt	113
Iran	114
Iraq	38
Jordan	38
Kuwait	15
Lebanon	83
Libya	15
Morocco	265
Oman	51
Pakistan	46
Qatar	112
Saudi Arabia	106
Somalia	13[3]
Sudan	1,129
Syria	30
Tunisia	209
United Arab Emirates	8
Yemen	13
EUROPE	**141,768**
Albania	0
Armenia	2
Austria	1,333
Azerbaijan	1
Belgium	1,872
Belarus	12
Bulgaria	34
Croatia	83
Czech Republic	63
Denmark	1,662
Germany	12,808
Estonia	4
Finland	199
France	35,773
Georgia	2
Greece	1,045
Hungary	180
Iceland	35
Ireland	463
Israel	316
Italy	27,511
Kazakhstan	5
Kyrgyzstan	0
Lithuania	5
Luxembourg	95
Latvia	9
Malta	34
Moldova	4
Monaco	35
Netherlands	3,488
Norway	447
Poland	289
Portugal	2,413
Romania	3,119
Russian Federation	173
San Marino	1
Spain	31,221
Slovak Republic	12
Slovenia	40
Sweden	1,170
Switzerland	4,465
Tajikistan	0
Turkmenistan	1
Turkey	164
Ukraine	36
United Kingdom	10,693
Uzbekistan	2
Yugoslavia[4]	449
SOUTHEAST ASIA	**20,758**
Bangladesh	1
Bhutan	0
India	1,036
Indonesia	67
North Korea	0
Maldives	2
Myanmar	475
Mongolia	0
Nepal	35
Sri Lanka	47
Thailand	19,095
WESTERN PACIFIC	**8,390**
American Samoa	0
Australia	5,737
Brunei Darussalam	3
Cambodia	13
China	65
Fiji	7
French Polynesia	45
Guam	30
Hong Kong	142
Japan	924
Kiribati	0
South Korea	32
Laos	10
Malaysia	200
Macao	8
Marshall Islands	2
Micronesia	2
Nauru	0
New Caledonia	43
New Zealand	473
Papua New Guinea	91
Philippines	136
Samoa	1
Singapore	123
Solomon Islands	0
Tonga	5
Tuvalu	0
Vanuatu	0
Vietnam	228

1. 1992 figure. 2. 1990 figure. 3. 1991 figure. 4. Refers to states/areas of the former Socialist Republic of Yugoslavia not otherwise listed separately. **Source**: World Health Organization, Global Programme on AIDS, *The Current Global Situation of the HIV/AIDS Pandemic* (July 3, 1995).

WORLD ENERGY

The world's primary energy sources in 1993 were crude oil and natural gas liquids, natural gas, coal, and electricity from hydroelectric and nuclear power. Energy is measured in British thermal units (Btu) in order to compare the energy produced by different sources. Energy production and consumption worldwide increased drastically during the 1980s, but both have remained fairly constant at about 345 quadrillion (10^{15}) Btu since 1990. Crude oil and natural gas liquids accounted for 39.7% of total output, coal 25.1%, dry natural gas 21.8%, hydroelectric power for 6.8%, and nuclear power 6.4%. The most notable change in consumption since 1990 has been a 4 percent increase in natural gas use, at the expense of coal consumption.

Crude oil World production of crude oil and natural gas liquids topped 60 million barrels per day in 1993, about the same as the previous year's consumption. The United States, Russia, and Saudi Arabia together accounted for 36.3 percent of world crude oil production, or nearly 22 million barrels of oil per day. Iran, which has doubled its production since 1980, was responsible for an additional 6.0 percent. Oil production reached an all-time high of over 62 million barrels per day in 1979, declined during the early 1980s, and began increasing again in 1987. Ironically, the biggest producers are suffering the biggest declines in production, while production is increasing in the Middle East, Africa, Central and South America, and the Far East.

Meanwhile, petroleum consumption continues to increase—from 58.7 million barrels per day in 1983 to 66.7 million barrels a day in 1993. As in previous years, the United States in 1993 was responsible for fully one fourth of that consumption level, or more than 17 million barrels per day. That's higher than the combined consumption of all the countries in Central Ameriça, South America, and Western Europe. No other single country consumes even half that much oil. Japan, the next-largest consumer, uses only 5.4 million barrels per day.

Natural gas liquids Production of natural gas liquids worldwide rose 31 percent from 1985 to 1993. The United States accounted for one third of the world's natural gas plant liquids production in 1993. Consumption of natural gas liquids is included in petroleum consumption figures.

Dry natural gas World production of dry natural gas increased 22% between 1985 and 1993. Russia accounted for 29% and the United States for 24% of world production in 1993. The United States was responsible for 27% of world consumption while Russia accounted for 21%.

Coal World coal production decreased for the third straight year in 1993, to 4.9 billion short tons, the same level as in 1985. China continues to lead the world in production, with more than 1.2 billion short tons per year. The United States, which had been the world leader until 1987,

WORLD ENERGY PRODUCTION BY REGION, 1980–93

Region	1980	1985	1990	1991	1992	1993[1]
Crude oil *(thousand barrels/day)*	**59,599**	**53,981**	**60,566**	**60,207**	**60,213**	**60,640**
North America	11,968	13,187	11,461	11,644	11,446	11,198
Central and South America	3,647	3,602	4,318	4,535	4,621	4,787
Western Europe	2,531	3,847	4,125	4,326	4,676	4,792
Eastern Europe and former USSR	12,038	11,909	11,216	10,191	8,727	7,905
Middle East	18,442	10,307	16,545	16,130	17,373	18,446
Africa	6,125	5,371	6,432	6,721	6,755	6,778
Far East and Oceania	4,848	5,758	6,468	6,660	6,614	6,736
Dry Natural Gas *(trillion cubic ft.)*	**53.19**	**62.17**	**73.71**	**74.83**	**74.53**	**76.01**
North America	23.17	20.45	22.66	22.75	23.29	24.13
Central and South America	1.20	1.76	2.12	2.12	1.97	2.12
Western Europe	7.32	7.22	7.19	7.83	7.89	8.33
Eastern Europe and former USSR	17.04	24.50	30.13	29.85	28.42	27.73
Middle East	1.33	2.38	3.71	3.83	4.13	4.52
Africa	0.69	1.86	2.46	2.69	2.77	2.83
Far East and Oceania	2.44	4.00	5.44	5.76	6.06	6.35
Coal *(million short tons)*	**4,196.13**	**4,869.40**	**5,336.44**	**5,020.25**	**4,996.07**	**4,885.27**
North America	877.37	955.77	1,109.0	1,079.7	1,075.6	1,028.0
Central and South America	16.66	21.31	32.98	38.05	35.82	37.15
Western Europe	845.33	928.34	845.24	747.58	683.20	619.51
Eastern Europe and former USSR	1,282.36	1,331.37	1,337.12	1,119.12	1,082.81	998.50
Middle East	0.99	1.38	1.43	1.54	1.65	1.82
Africa	137.91	197.48	201.37	205.56	205.25	210.54
Far East and Oceania	1,035.51	1,433.75	1,809.32	1,828.75	1,911.75	1,989.80
Hydroelectric power *(billion kWh)*	**1,735.2**	**1,973.1**	**2,159.3**	**2,193.0**	**2,182.4**	**2,264.1**
North America	546.9	611.1	599.2	604.9	575.9	607.3
Central and South America	199.3	285.7	363.5	383.0	388.7	392.1
Western Europe	431.7	453.2	452.9	450.0	477.7	495.4
Eastern Europe and former USSR	211.3	230.7	253.9	259.3	253.8	259.5
Middle East	9.6	9.5	12.2	12.6	14.8	15.4
Africa	60.2	46.7	53.5	53.3	52.9	53.1
Far East and Oceania	276.2	336.4	424.2	429.9	418.7	441.3
Nuclear power *(billion kWh)*	**684.4**	**1,425.7**	**1,894.0**	**1,990.4**	**2,004.9**	**2,080.0**
North America	287.0	440.8	647.7	696.7	698.5	703.6
Central and South America	2.2	8.4	9.0	9.1	8.4	7.7
Western Europe	219.2	572.5	707.4	731.9	744.2	777.4
Eastern Europe and former USSR	83.2	200.3	251.4	249.5	245.6	254.6
Middle East	N.A.	N.A.	N.A.	N.A.	N.A.	N.A.
Africa	0.0	5.5	8.5	9.2	9.4	7.3
Far East and Oceania	92.7	198.2	270.1	294.0	298.8	329.3

1. Preliminary. **Source:** Energy Information Administration, *International Energy Annual, 1993.*

WORLD PRIMARY ENERGY PRODUCTION BY SOURCE, 1980–93 (quadrillion Btu)

Source	1980	1985	1990	1991	1992	1993[1]
Petroleum	133.22	121.21	136.35	135.93	136.46	137.35
Natural gas	52.65	61.38	72.91	73.99	73.80	75.34
Coal	74.48	85.77	94.97	90.43	88.62	86.67
Hydroelectric power	18.05	20.56	22.46	22.80	22.67	23.51
Nuclear electric power	7.58	15.37	20.30	21.27	21.30	22.10
Geothermal, solar, and wind electric power	0.40	0.60	0.75	0.77	0.79	0.79
Total, all sources	**286.38**	**304.89**	**347.74**	**345.19**	**343.64**	**345.76**

1. Preliminary. **Source:** Energy Information Administration, *International Energy Annual 1993.*

TOP 10 PRODUCERS OF PRIMARY ENERGY, BY SOURCE, 1993

Crude oil[1]	(thousand barrels per day)	Dry natural gas	(trillion cubic feet)
1. Saudi Arabia	8,198	1. Russia	21.80
2. Russia	6,890	2. United States	18.24
3. United States	6,847	3. Canada	4.96
4. Iran	3,650	4. Netherlands	3.11
5. China	2,911	5. United Kingdom	2.31
6. Mexico	2,671	6. Turkmenistan	2.13
7. Venezuela	2,450	7. Algeria	1.98
8. Norway	2,264	8. Indonesia	1.85
9. United Arab Emirates	2,191	9. Uzbekistan	1.58
10. Nigeria	2,050	10. Saudi Arabia	1.27

Natural gas plant liquids[2]	(thousand barrels per day)	Coal[3]	(million short tons)
1. United States	1,736	1. China	1,293
2. Saudi Arabia	704	2. United States	945
3. Canada	503	3. Russia	336
4. Mexico	457	4. Germany	315
5. Russia	220	5. India	291
6. United Kingdom	169	6. Australia	246
7. United Arab Emirates	160	7. Poland	214
8. Algeria	145	8. South Africa	201
9. Venezuela	113	9. Ukraine	128
10. Norway	100	10. Kazakhstan	123

Hydro-electric power[4,5]	(billion kWh)	Nuclear electric power[5]	(billion kWh)
1. Canada	319.1	1. United States	610.3
2. United States	268.2	2. France	350.2
3. Brazil	225.0	3. Japan	234.0
4. Russia	173.4	4. Germany	145.8
5. China	143.1	5. Russia	116.9
6. Norway	117.8	6. Canada	88.6
7. Japan	90.4	7. United Kingdom	81.0
8. Sweden	75.5	8. Ukraine	75.2
9. India	68.0	9. Sweden	58.7
10. France	63.4	10. South Korea	55.2

Note: Preliminary. 1. Includes lease condensate. 2. Does not include China, for which data are unavailable. 3. Includes anthracite, sub-anthracite, bituminous, subbituminous, lignite, and brown coal. 4. Net generation; data consist of both utility and nonutility sources. Excludes generation from pumped storage. 5. Net generation; excludes energy consumed by the generating unit. **Source:** U.S. Dept. of Energy, *International Energy Annual 1993.*

WORLD ENERGY CONSUMPTION BY REGION, 1980–93

Region	1980	1985	1990	1991	1992	1993[1]
Petroleum *(thousand barrels/day)*	**63,067**	**60,098**	**66,155**	**66,715**	**66,574**	**66,715**
North America	20,204	18,701	20,410	20,136	20,509	20,747
Central and South America	3,573	3,185	3,595	3,654	3,741	3,885
Western Europe	14,322	12,385	13,246	13,660	13,813	13,796
Eastern Europe and former USSR	10,707	10,461	9,725	9,431	7,847	6,812
Middle East	2,058	2,854	3,465	3,400	3,397	3,489
Africa	1,471	1,826	2,100	2,153	2,176	2,170
Far East and Oceania	10,729	10,686	13,614	14,283	15,091	15,817
Dry Natural Gas *(trillion cubic ft.)*	**52.93**	**62.06**	**73.05**	**74.54**	**74.28**	**75.51**
North America	22.67	20.40	22.08	22.48	23.13	24.05
Central and South America	1.22	1.75	2.12	2.12	1.97	2.12
Western Europe	8.56	9.34	10.48	11.39	11.26	11.74
Eastern Europe and former USSR	15.86	23.11	27.81	27.53	26.17	25.24
Middle East	1.48	2.27	3.59	3.60	4.01	4.31
Africa	0.61	1.07	1.35	1.52	1.48	1.54
Far East and Oceania	2.53	4.12	5.61	5.90	6.25	6.52
Coal *(million short tons)*	**4,152.22**	**4,883.31**	**5,252.73**	**4,987.89**	**4,967.26**	**4,911.95**
North America	752.09	873.87	957.19	949.54	956.76	985.59
Central and South America	24.17	27.97	33.74	35.77	31.71	31.50
Western Europe	961.91	1,058.04	1,000.80	923.01	859.46	768.00
Eastern Europe and former USSR	1,235.12	1,292.11	1,292.02	1,077.73	1,028.97	951.83
Middle East	1.07	4.85	6.66	6.97	8.29	8.38
Africa	112.37	151.11	156.96	155.96	155.19	157.19
Far East and Oceania	1,066.49	1,475.37	1,805.38	1,838.89	1,926.89	2,009.46
Hydroelectric power *(billion kWh)*	**1,756.2**	**2,014.1**	**2,161.3**	**2,215.2**	**2,210.8**	**2,292.6**
North America	567.9	652.0	601.2	627.2	604.3	635.8
Central and South America	199.3	285.7	363.5	383.0	388.7	392.1
Western Europe	431.7	453.2	452.9	450.0	477.7	495.4
Eastern Europe and former USSR	211.3	230.7	253.9	259.3	253.8	259.5
Middle East	9.6	9.5	12.2	12.6	14.8	15.4
Africa	60.2	46.7	53.5	53.3	52.9	53.1
Far East and Oceania	276.2	336.4	424.2	429.9	418.7	441.3
Nuclear power *(billion kWh)*	**684.3**	**1,425.7**	**1,894.0**	**1,990.4**	**2,004.9**	**2,080.0**
North America	287.0	440.8	647.7	696.7	698.5	703.6
Central and South America	2.2	8.4	9.0	9.1	8.4	7.7
Western Europe	219.2	572.5	707.4	731.9	744.2	777.4
Eastern Europe and former USSR	83.2	200.3	251.4	249.5	245.6	254.6
Middle East	N.A.	N.A.	N.A.	N.A.	N.A.	N.A.
Africa	0.0	5.5	8.5	9.2	9.4	7.3
Far East and Oceania	92.7	198.2	270.1	294.0	298.8	329.3

1. Preliminary. **Source:** Energy Information Administration, *International Energy Annual, 1993.*

WORLD PRIMARY ENERGY CONSUMPTION BY SOURCE, 1980–93 (quadrillion Btu)

Source	1980	1985	1990	1991	1992	1993[1]
Petroleum	130.92	123.14	135.39	136.55	136.25	136.17
Natural gas	52.58	61.42	72.48	73.99	73.84	75.15
Coal	73.19	86.39	93.35	89.71	88.71	87.60
Hydroelectric power	18.26	20.99	22.48	23.03	22.97	23.81
Nuclear electric power	7.58	15.37	20.30	21.27	21.30	22.10
Geothermal, solar, and wind electric power	0.37	0.59	0.76	0.78	0.82	0.80
Total, all sources	**282.62**	**307.48**	**344.72**	**345.10**	**343.59**	**345.33**

Note: Totals may not add up due to independent rounding. 1. Preliminary. **Source:** Energy Information Administration, *International Energy Annual, 1993.*

produced just under a billion short tons. Together, the United States and China account for close to half the world's coal production. They also account for the bulk of coal consumption. China consumed 1.3 billion short tons (26% of world consumption) and the United States consumed 926 million short tons (19%).

Hydroelectric power Generation of hydroelectric power worldwide rose 15 percent between 1985 and 1993 to an all-time high of 2.2 trillion kilowatthours (kWh). Canada (319 billion kWh), the United States (268 billion kWh), and Brazil (225 billion kWh) produced 37 percent of the worldwide total. They were also the three biggest users of hydroelectric power, making up 37 percent of world consumption.

Nuclear electric power World generation of nuclear electric power increased more than 45 percent between 1985 and 1993. The U.S., with 109 operable reactors, was the leading producer of nuclear electric power, followed by France (57 reactors) and Japan (48 reactors).

WORLD CRUDE OIL PRODUCTION, 1960–93 (million barrels per day)

Country	1960	1970	1975	1980	1985	1990	1993[1]
Organization of Petroleum Exporting Countries (OPEC)[2]							
Indonesia	0.41	0.85	1.31	1.58	1.33	1.46	1.51
Iran	1.07	3.83	5.35	1.66	2.25	3.09	3.65
Iraq	0.97	1.55	2.26	2.51	1.43	2.04	0.51
Nigeria	0.02	1.08	1.78	2.06	1.50	1.81	2.05
Saudi Arabia[3]	1.31	3.80	7.08	9.90	3.39	6.41	8.20
Venezuela	2.85	3.71	2.35	2.17	1.68	2.14	2.38
Other OPEC	2.06	8.59	6.87	6.91	4.79	6.52	7.39
Total OPEC	**8.69**	**23.41**	**26.99**	**26.78**	**16.35**	**23.47**	**25.68**
Non-OPEC countries							
Canada	0.52	1.26	1.43	1.44	1.47	1.55	1.67
China	0.10	0.60	1.49	2.11	2.51	2.77	2.92
Mexico	0.27	0.49	0.71	1.94	2.75	2.55	2.66
United Kingdom	(4)	(4)	0.01	1.62	2.53	1.82	1.91
United States	7.04	9.64	8.38	8.60	8.97	7.36	6.84
Russia[5]	2.91	6.99	9.52	11.71	11.59	10.88	8.35
Other non-OPEC	1.42	3.50	4.14	5.20	7.54	10.07	11.89
Total world	**20.96**	**45.89**	**52.83**	**59.60**	**53.98**	**60.47**	**60.06**

1. Preliminary. 2. In addition to those listed separately, current OPEC members are: Algeria, Ecuador, Gabon, Kuwait, Libya, Qatar, and United Arab Emirates. 3. Includes about one half of the production in the Neutral Zone between Kuwait and Saudi Arabia. 4. Less than 5,000 barrels per day. 5. Figures for Russia before 1993 refer to the former USSR. **Source:** U.S. Dept. of Energy, *Annual Energy Review 1993* (1994).

WORLD NUCLEAR POWER GENERATION, BY REGION AND COUNTRY, 1980–93 (billion kilowatt-hours)

Region and country	1980	1985	1990	1993[1]	Operable reactors[2]
North America	287.0	440.8	647.7	703.6	132
Canada	35.9	57.1	68.8	88.6	22
Mexico	0.0	0.0	2.0	4.7	1
United States	251.1	383.7	576.9	610.3	109
Central and South America	2.2	8.4	9.0	7.7	3
Argentina	2.2	5.4	7.0	7.3	2
Brazil	0.0	2.9	1.9	0.4	1
Western Europe	207.4	572.5	707.4	777.4	153
Belgium	11.9	32.7	40.6	39.5	7
Finland	6.6	18.0	18.1	18.9	4
France	63.4	211.2	297.7	350.2	57
Germany[3]	55.0	138.6	145.1	145.8	21
Italy	2.1	6.6	0.0	0.0	0
Netherlands	4.0	3.7	3.3	3.8	2
Slovenia[4]	0.0	4.0	4.4	3.8	1
Spain	5.2	28.0	51.9	53.7	9
Sweden	25.3	55.8	65.2	58.7	12
Switzerland	12.9	20.1	22.4	22.2	5
United Kingdom	32.3	53.8	58.7	81.0	35
Eastern Europe	90.7	200.3	251.4	254.6	65
Bulgaria	5.9	12.4	13.5	13.3	6
Commonwealth of Independent States[5]	69.3	170.0	201.3	N.A.	45
Kazakhstan	(5)	(5)	(5)	0.4	1
Russia	(5)	(5)	(5)	116.9	29
Ukraine	(5)	(5)	(5)	75.2	15
Former Czechoslovakia	4.3	11.9	23.4	N.A.	N.A.
Czech Republic	N.A.	N.A.	N.A.	12.5	4
Hungary	0.0	6.1	13.1	13.1	4
Lithuania	(5)	(5)	(5)	12.3	2
Slovakia	N.A.	N.A.	N.A.	11.0	4
Middle East	0.0	0.0	0.0	0.0	0
Africa	0.0	5.5	8.5	7.3	2
South Africa	0.0	5.5	8.5	7.3	2
Far East and Oceania	92.6	198.2	270.1	329.3	75
China	N.A.	N.A.	N.A.	2.5	2
India	2.7	4.7	5.6	5.9	9
Japan	78.7	149.7	182.3	234.0	48
Korea, South	3.3	15.8	50.2	55.2	9
Pakistan	0.1	0.3	0.4	0.4	1
Taiwan	7.8	27.8	31.6	31.3	6
World total	**684.4**	**1,425.7**	**1,894.0**	**2,080.0**	**430**

Note: Net generation; does not include energy consumed by the generating unit. Sum of components may not equal total due to independent rounding. 1. Preliminary. 2. As of Dec. 31, 1993. 3. Includes both the former East Germany and West Germany. 4. Data before 1991 refer to the former Yugoslavia. 5. Total for Kazakhstan, Russia, and Ukraine. Generation figures for republics of former USSR before 1993 are included under Commonwealth of Independent States. **Source:** U.S. Dept. of Energy, *International Energy Annual 1993* and *World Nuclear Outlook 1994* (1994).

LEADING SUPPLIERS OF U.S. OIL

The United States imports about half of the oil it consumes, or more than 8 million barrels of petroleum per day. More than 4 million barrels come from OPEC nations; the other 4 million come from Canada, Mexico, and other countries.

Country	U.S. imports, 1993[1] (barrels/day)	Country	U.S. imports, 1993[1] (barrels/day)
Saudi Arabia	1,408,000	Virgin Islands/ Puerto Rico	283,000
Venezuela	1,285,000		
Canada	1,175,000	Algeria	229,000
Mexico	919,000	Indonesia	81,000
Nigeria	738,000	Total OPEC countries	4,331,000
United Kingdom	340,000	**Total, all imports**	**8,526,000**

1. Preliminary figures. **Source:** Energy Information Administration, *Annual Energy Review*, 1993.

THE STRATEGIC PETROLEUM RESERVE

In an attempt to minimize the wild fluctuations in prices caused by the Arab oil embargoes of the 1970s, the United States in 1977 created the Strategic Petroleum Reserve, which permitted the storage of 580 million barrels of oil. The reserve proved useful in preventing additional oil price hikes during the Iraqi invasion of Kuwait in 1990.

The reserve can also be used as an emergency supply of oil in case of a complete oil embargo. In 1985, the reserve held enough oil to provide a normal level of petroleum to the United States for 115 days in the absence of any other petroleum imports. Since then, the measure has declined to 78 days, because U.S. energy consumption as well as its reliance on foreign imports have both increased.

LANGUAGES OF THE WORLD

The function of language is to enable people to communicate ideas to one another, primarily through audible speech, and secondarily through written words. The number of languages, to say nothing of dialects, is impossible to compute specifically, but estimates put the number at between 4,000 and 10,000 worldwide. Dialects are variations within languages. Estimates of the number of dialects in the world vary from about 20,000 to more than 50,000. There is some disagreement regarding what represents a dialect and what represents a language. Generally, most linguists would accept "the criterion of mutual intelligibility" and decide that two varieties—for example, the "King's English" and "Brooklynese"—are dialects of the same language if their speakers can understand each other. The number of writing systems used to transcribe these languages is considerably less, because not all spoken languages have a written form.

In order to simplify their study of the world's languages, linguists group languages (in groups, families, phyla, complexes, dialects, and so on) according to various similarities of vocabulary, grammar, and other features. A language that has no known relationship to any other is called a language isolate. The accompanying list shows the primary language families and languages, and the regions or countries where they are most commonly found.

LANGUAGE FAMILIES AND LANGUAGES

Afro-Asiatic *Berber* (Cen. Sahara). *Chadic* inc. Hausa (W. Cen. Africa). *Cushitic* (Ethiopia, Somalia). *Semitic* inc. Amharic, Arabic, Hebrew, Maltese, Tigrinya (N. Africa, E. Africa, Mideast, Malta).

Australian aboriginal langs. (Australia).

Austro-Asiatic **Mon-Khmer** inc. Khmer, Viet-Muong (Cambodia, Malaysia, Thailand, Vietnam). **Munda** (India). **Nicobarese** (Nicobar Is.).

Austronesian **Western Malayo-Polynesian** inc. Javanese, Malay, Achinese, Batak, Minangkabau, Sundanese, Madurese, Balinese, Iban, Ngadju, Macasserese, Buginese, Malagasay (Madagascar, Indonesia, S. Asia, Papua New Guinea, Philippines). **Oceanic** inc. Samoan, Tongan, Fijian, Tahitian, Hawaiian, Maori (Oceania). *S. Halmahera-W. New Guinea* langs. *Central Malayo-Polynesian* langs. *Formosan* langs. *Chamic* langs. (S.E. Asia).

Dravidian inc. Tamil, Malayalam, Kannada, Telugu (S. India, Pakistan, Nepal, Sri Lanka, Maldives).

Eurasiatic stock: **Altaic** *Turkic* inc. Turkish, Azerbaijani, Kazakh, Kirghiz, Tatar, Turkmen, Uighur, Uzbek (Turkey, Cyprus, Uzbekistan, Iran, China). *Mongolian* inc. Buryat, Mongolian (Mongolia, China). *Tungusic* inc. Manchu (China). Some linguists also include Japanese and Korean, though these may be language isolates. **Uralic** inc. Hungarian, Finnish, Estonian, Lappish, and *Samoyedic* langs. (N.E. Europe, N. Asia).

Indo-European *Armenian*. *Celtic* langs. (N.W. Europe). *Germanic* inc. Dutch, English, German, Scandinavian langs., Yiddish (N. Europe, N. America, Caribbean, S. Africa). *Greek*. *Italic* inc. Latin. *Romance* inc. French, Italian, Portuguese, Romanian, Spanish (Europe, Latin America, N. America). *Slavonic* inc. Bulgarian, Czech, Polish, Russian, Serbo-Croat, Slovak (E. Europe, Soviet Asia). *Indo-Aryan* inc. Bengali, Gujarati, Hindi, Punjabi, Sanskrit, Urdu (Pakistan, India, Bangladesh). *Iranian* inc. Baluchi, Farsi, Kurdish, Pashto (Turkey, Iraq, Iran, Afghanistan, Pakistan, Soviet Asia).

Indo-Pacific *Papuan* langs., *Tasmanian* langs. (Papua, Tasmania).

Khoisan inc. !Khung (S.W. Africa, Tanzania).

Meso-American Indian: **Mayan** inc. Quich, Yucatec, Cakchiquel, Mam, Kekchi, Tzotzil, Tzeltal, Chol, Huastec, (Guatemala, Mexico, Belize, Honduras). **Misumalpan** inc. Mosquito (Nicaragua, El Salvador). **Mixtecan** inc. Mixtec (Mexico). **Oto-Pamean** inc. Otomian, Mazahua (Mexico). **Popolocan** inc. Mazatec (Mexico). **Totonacan** inc. Totonac (Mexico). **Uto-Aztecan** inc. Aztec (Mexico, U.S.). **Zapotecan** inc. Zapotec (Mexico).

Niger-Kordofanian group: **Niger-Congo** *West Atlantic* inc. Fulani, Serer, Wolof, Dyola (W. Africa). *Mande* inc. Malinke, Mende (W. Africa). *Gur (Voltaic)* inc. Mossi. *Kwa* inc. Yoruba, Akan, Ibo (coastal W. Africa). *Adamawa-Eastern* inc. Sango, Baya (Cen. Africa). *Benue-Congo* inc. Bantu langs. Fang, Kongo, Luba, Luganda, Rwanda, Shona, Sotho, Swahili, Xhosa, Zulu. (S. Cen. Africa). **Kordofanian** langs. (Sudan).

Nilo-Saharan inc. *Chari-Nile* langs., Fur, Koma, Songhai (Cen. Africa).

North American: **Na-Dené** inc. Navajo (U.S.).

Sino-Tibetan **Baric** langs. (India). **Bodish-Himalyish** Tibetan (Himalayas). **Burmese-Lolo** Burmese, Naga, Kachin (Burma, S.E. Asia, Bangladesh, Himalayas). **Chinese** Mandarin, Wu, Xiang, Kan, Hakka, Yue, Min (China, S.E. Asia, Indonesia).

South American Indian: **Quechumaran** inc. Quechua, Aymara, (Bolivia, Peru). **Tupian** inc. Guaraní Tupi (Paraguay, Brazil, Bolivia).

Tai inc. Thai (Thailand, China).

Language isolates inc. Ainu (N. Japan). Basque (N. Spain, S.W. France). Georgian (Caucasus Mts.).

PRINCIPAL LANGUAGES OF THE WORLD

Exact data on language use are notoriously difficult to compile. National censuses are conducted at different intervals, and not all include questions about language. When they do, they can refer either to the language spoken in the home (the language one speaks best), or to the language spoken most often, or to all the languages one might speak. Even without uniform and precise data, about half the world's population speak one of a dozen or so languages, and the general geography of the most widely used languages is fairly clear.

Chinese is the mother tongue of more than one billion people. Although the spoken dialects of Chinese are not mutually intelligible, they share the same writing system *(hanzi)* and two people can speak different dialects and still be able to read each other's writing. This is possible because *hanzi* uses symbols to represent objects and ideas, not sounds.

The principal dialect is *Mandarin*, based on the dialect spoken in northern China around Beijing, and is the official language of China, Taiwan, and Singapore. The mother tongue of some 500–825 million people, its use is expected to grow rapidly because it is now being taught in all Chinese schools. The other principal dialects are *Cantonese* (or *Yue*), spoken in southern China and Hong Kong (where it is an official language); *Wu*, spoken in Shanghai and nearby provinces in eastern China; *Min*, found in southeastern China, Taiwan, and Malaysia; and *Xiang*, *Kan*, and *Hakka*, all spoken in southeastern China and Taiwan.

English, although it is the mother tongue of only 300–450 million people, is spoken by perhaps as many as one-third of the world's people. From the island kingdom of England, it spread throughout the British Empire to the Americas, Africa, India, and throughout the Pacific. Today, English is an official language in 87 nations and territories. The main concentrations of English speakers are found in the United States, Great Britain, India, Nigeria, Canada, Australia, and Ireland.

Hindi is spoken by more than 250–300 million people. One of India's two official languages (with English), Hindi also has significant numbers of speakers in Trinidad, Guyana, South Africa, Mauritius, and other countries. Hindi and Urdu (see below) have a common spoken form, Hindustani; but as literary languages, they remain distinct, Hindi being written in Devanagari script, Urdu in Perso-Arabic.

Arabic is the mother tongue of at least 165 million people. In addition to its being an official language in 18 countries in North Africa and the Middle East, it is also the language of the Koran—and thus, for Muslims, of God—

and it is the second language of many Indians, Indonesians, Iranians, and other inhabitants of largely Muslim nations.

Russian is spoken by 250–300 million people. Although it was the official language of the USSR, according to a 1979 census only 59 percent of the population claimed it as a mother tongue. There are large numbers of nonnative Russian speakers throughout the former territories of the Soviet Union as well as in Eastern Europe.

Malay variants and dialects of Malay are used as an official language in Indonesia (where it is known as *Bahasa Indonesia*), Malaysia *(Bahasa Malaysia)*, and Singapore and Brunei *(Bahasa Melayu)*. Although this represents a population of more than 180 million people, it is not the mother tongue of a majority in any of these countries. The most widely spoken single language is Javanese, spoken by more than 70 million Indonesians.

Bengali is spoken by more than 150 million people in Bangladesh, where it is the official language and the mother tongue of almost the whole country, and in the Indian state of West Bengal.

Spanish is spoken by 125–320 million people worldwide, and is the official language of 20 nations, territories, and colonies, including Spain and former Spanish colonies of the Americas. It is also the first language of many immigrants from these countries to the United States.

French is spoken by 100–150 million people. Though there are fewer native speakers of French than of other major languages, its significance lies in the fact that it is the official language of 37 countries, colonies, and territories in Europe, Africa, the Americas, and the Pacific.

Japanese is the mother tongue of virtually all Japanese, more than 125 million people, almost all of whom live in Japan; there are significant minorities in the United States and Brazil. Modern Japanese employs four writing systems, *kanji* (adapted from the Chinese *hanzi*) *hiragana*, *katakana*, and *romaji*.

Portuguese is spoken by 100–170 million people, the majority of whom live in Brazil. It is the official language there, in Portugal, and in six other countries (most in Southern Africa).

German is spoken by 90–150 million people. It is an official language of six European countries—Germany, Austria, Switzerland, Luxembourg, Liechtenstein, and Belgium—and is spoken by significant minorities, especially in Eastern Europe, Latin America, the United States, and elsewhere.

Urdu is spoken by more than 50–90 million people in Pakistan (where it is the official but by no means most widely spoken language), and India, where there are more than 40 million speakers. (See "Hindi" above.)

WORLD RELIGIONS

In 1985, of an estimated 4.8 billion people on Earth, about four out of five were identified as adherents of a religion. The remainder were either nonreligious (agnostic) or atheistic (actively opposed to theistic religion). This section describes the major religions of the world, their basic tenets, scriptures, schools and sects, and their history. (Additional detail may be found in the section "Religion in America.") The primary source of information in this section is *The World Christian Encyclopedia.*

CHRISTIANITY

Founder Jesus Christ, who is seen by most Christians as the Son of God. The Julian and Gregorian calendars are dated from the traditional year of his birth. Scholars today believe he was actually born about 3 B.C. and died about A.D. 30. Jesus was born and raised a Jew, and became a rabbi, or teacher. According to Christian scripture, he was the Messiah awaited by the Jewish people. He took up preaching and healing at the age of 30. Three years later he was sentenced to death in Jerusalem and was executed by crucifixion. The scriptures further report that he soon rose from the dead.

Scripture The Bible consists of the Old Testament, a collection of books originally written in Hebrew (which are also the holy books of Judaism), and the New Testament, writings in Greek about the life and teachings of Jesus and his early followers.

Beliefs Orthodox belief is in one God as revealed in three persons—God the Father (the Creator), God the Son (Jesus Christ, the Redeemer), and God the Holy Spirit (the Sanctifier). Christians believe that Jesus restored a right relationship between God and human beings through his death by crucifixion and his resurrection from the dead.

Practice Most Christian denominations observe the rite of baptism, administered to children and to newly converted members, and the Eucharist, or Communion, in which members partake of bread and wine in commemoration of Jesus Christ.

Christians are organized into congregations and gather for worship in churches. Most denominations have designated Sunday (the day Jesus rose from the dead) as the day for special observance and worship. A few have designated Saturday, the Jewish Sabbath, instead.

In most Christian denominations, men and women observe monogamy, and divorce is forbidden or discouraged. There are many different standards of personal conduct, ranging from the ascetic to the celebratory.

Schools and sects There are two historic divisions in Christianity. In A.D. 1054 the Eastern (or Orthodox) church and Western (or Roman) church separated. Then, in the 1500s, reformers including Martin Luther and John Calvin broke from the Roman church to form a number of separate denominations that together are called Protestant. The Orthodox churches remain dominant in Greece, the Soviet Union, and in parts of eastern Europe. The Roman church (known today as the Roman Catholic or simply the Catholic church) predominates in southern Europe and Latin America. Protestant churches predominate in northern Europe (including Great Britain), North America, and Australia. Both Catholic and Protestant churches have conducted industrious mission programs in Africa and Asia and share influence in those regions. In addition to the three main groups are many small denominations and sects that do not fit comfortably into any of the three main groups.

History At the time of his death, Jesus had only a small handful of followers. Within a century, however, they had spread the new teaching to much of the Roman Empire. There were small communities of worshipers in the cities of Greece, Asia Minor, and Palestine and in

WORLD RELIGIONS

Group	Adherents	Percent of world pop.
Major World Religions		
Christianity	1,548,500,000	32.4%
Islam	817,000,000	17.1
Hinduism	647,500,000	13.5
Buddhism	295,600,000	6.2
Judaism	17,800,000	0.4
Total	3,326,400,000	69.6%
Other Broad Religious Groupings		
Chinese folk religions	188,000,000	3.9%
New Asian religions	106,400,000	2.2
Tribal religions	91,200,000	1.9
Total	385,600,000	8.0%
Regional and Smaller Religious Groups		
Sikhism	16,100,000	0.34%
Shamanism	12,200,000	0.26
Spiritism	6,700,000	0.14
Confucianism	5,200,000	0.11
Bahaism	4,400,000	0.09
Jainism	3,300,000	0.07
Shintoism	3,200,000	0.07
Parsiism (Zoroastrianism)	500,000	0.01
Total	51,600,000	1.1%
Unaffiliated		
Nonreligious	805,900,000	16.9%
Atheist	210,500,000	4.4
Total	1,026,400,000	21.3%
Total	**4,781,200,000**	**100.0%**

CHRISTIANS, BY SECT AND REGION

Region	Roman Catholic	Orthodox	Protestants and others[1]	Crypto-Christians[2]	Total	Percent of all Christians
Europe	251,100,000	35,800,000	115,700,000	18,300,000	420,900,000	27.2%
Latin America	369,100,000	400,000	21,500,000	1,200,000	392,200,000	25.3
Africa	89,700,000	22,000,000	118,100,000	6,500,000	236,300,000	15.3
North America	86,500,000	5,800,000	134,900,000	0	227,200,000	14.7
South Asia	72,800,000	3,200,000	30,800,000	19,100,000	125,900,000	8.1
Former USSR[3]	3,900,000	63,000,000	4,500,000	30,800,000	102,200,000	6.6
East Asia	3,600,000	100,000	16,400,000	2,200,000	22,300,000	1.4
Oceania	7,400,000	500,000	13,600,000	0	21,500,000	1.4
Total	**884,100,000**	**130,800,000**	**455,500,000**	**78,100,000**	**1,548,500,000**	**100.0%**

1. Includes some Christian groups not traditionally classified as Protestant. 2. People who identify themselves as Christian but who (often for reasons of personal safety or prudence) are not included in membership lists of any Christian organization. 3. Republics of former Soviet Union.

Rome itself. Christians were persecuted cruelly by the Roman state and in many places were driven underground. By A.D. 300, however, Christians had attained some influence. In 313 the emperor Constantine decreed toleration for Christianity and reportedly was baptized on his deathbed. By the end of the century, Christianity was the official religion of the empire.

This marked the beginning of a newly militant phase. Missionaries were sent to the far reaches of Europe to establish churches. Christianity gradually triumphed throughout Europe, from Ireland to the plains of Poland.

During the Middle Ages, the Eastern and Western churches divided. The Western church was a major preserver and extender of learning at home. Abroad it sought to dislodge, in a series of Crusades, the Muslim Turks who had control of the Holy Land.

A long period of religious strife began with the Reformation after 1517. Brutal religious wars convulsed Europe, causing untold suffering. At the same time, European exploration and conquests were spreading Christianity to the Americas and to Asia. Roman Catholics and Protestants proselytized wherever they predominated.

From the mid-1800s to the mid-1900s, the Western churches (Catholic and Protestant) carried out energetic missionary programs to Africa and East Asia. Although they failed in their aim to Christianize the world, they did contribute to the growth of vigorous and independent churches in Africa and Asia. Today there are more Christians in Africa than in North America.

Geography and numbers Although Christianity began in the Middle East, the lands of its origin are now dominated by Judaism and Islam. Yet it has spread quite literally to every continent of the world and claims more than 1.5 billion adherents—about one person in every three in the world population. The accompanying table shows adherents by world region.

Christianity is the predominant religion in Europe, North and South America, and Oceania (Australia, New Zealand, and the Pacific Islands). It is also a major force in sub-Saharan Africa and in parts of South Asia. It is least significant in the Middle East and East Asia.

ISLAM

Founder Muhammad, who is seen as a special prophet of the one God. Muhammad was born about A.D. 570 at Mecca (now in western Saudi Arabia) and died in 632 in the nearby city of Medina.

Scripture The Koran (original language: Arabic). Muslims believe the Koran to be the word of the one God, spoken to Muhammad by angels.

Beliefs Muhammad began preaching about A.D. 610 and established Islam as a powerful new force before his death in 632. His teachings were based in part on those of Judaism and Christianity. In agreement with these, Muhammad recognized one God. He acknowledged Hebrew history and its religious teachers and recognized Jesus as a prophet. However, Muhammad's was a distinct new revelation. His teachings are contained in the Islamic holy book, the Koran.

Practice A Muslim has five main religious duties:

1. To profess faith in a statement that may be translated, "There is only one God and Muhammad is his prophet."
2. To pray five times each day, facing Mecca. In Islamic countries criers in tall minarets call the times of prayer.
3. To give alms for the support of the faith and of the poor.
4. To observe a solemn fast during Ramadan, the ninth month in the Islamic calendar.
5. To make, at least once in a lifetime, a pilgrimage to Mecca.

Devout Muslims maintain strict rules of conduct. Women are expected to dress modestly, even to cover their faces in public. Sale and consumption of alcohol is forbidden. As in orthodox Judaism, eating pork is forbidden. Muslim places of worship are called mosques. The principal weekly worship is on Friday at midday.

Schools and sects The largest division in Islam is between the Sunnites (often called orthodox Muslims), and the Shiites, who have about 20 million members (less than 3 percent of all Muslims). Most Shiites live in Iran and Iraq; the two Muslim countries recently were involved in a bitter and protracted war against each other. The original cause of the break between Sunnites and Shiites was disagreement about the transferal of power from Muhammad to his descendants. Today Shiites follow somewhat different rituals than those of the Sunnites and recognize additional holy days and holy places (mainly in Iraq and Iran).

History From its earliest days, Islam was a militant faith. During the first 100 years, the leaders established an empire that stretched from Spain to India. In 732 a Muslim army aiming to conquer Europe was defeated at Tours, in central France, but Muslims were not overthrown in Spain until 1492.

Muslim leaders often allowed practice of other religions in their territories, but eventually many people in the conquered lands became Muslims. The empire broke into smaller units as leaders fought against each other. During the Middle Ages, Christian Europe mounted several attacks on Islamic states, seeking to free the Christian holy lands. These were known as the Crusades. The Europeans had brief successes, but the Middle East remained predominantly Muslim.

In 1453 the Ottoman Turks conquered the important Christian capital of Constantinople. Eventually the city's name was changed to Istanbul. The Turks pushed north and westward into Europe but were finally defeated near Vienna, Austria, in 1683.

From 1700 to the mid-1900s, many Islamic nations fell under the control of European powers. Europeans brought modern technology and business and, for the most part, a strong prejudice against Islamic laws and ways.

In Muslim countries after World War II, modernist politicians (with strong support from the West) fought many battles against Muslim traditionalists. Beginning in the 1970s, traditionalists, often appealing to the national pride of their people, began a powerful counteroffensive. Muslim traditionalists overthrew the shah of Iran, a major ally of the United States.

Geography and numbers With an estimated 800 million adherents, Islam is the second largest of the major world religions after

ADHERENTS OF MAJOR WORLD RELIGIONS, BY REGION (in thousands)

Region	Christianity Adherents	Christianity Percent	Islam Adherents	Islam Percent	Hinduism Adherents	Hinduism Percent	Buddhism Adherents	Buddhism Percent	Judaism Adherents	Judaism Percent
Africa	236,300	15.3%	215,800	26.4%	1,300	0.2%	(Z)	(Z)	300	1.7%
Asia, East	22,300	1.4	22,300	2.7	(Z)	(Z)	143,400	48.5%	(Z)	(Z)
Asia, South[1]	125,900	8.1	534,900	65.5	644,000	99.5	150,900	51.0	3,900	21.9
Europe	420,300	27.2	9,200	1.1	600	0.1	200	0.1	1,500	8.4
Latin America	392,200	25.3	600	0.1	600	0.1	500	0.2	1,000	5.6
North America	227,200	14.7	2,600	0.3	700	0.1	200	0.1	7,900	44.4
Oceania	21,500	1.4	100	(Z)	300	(Z)	(Z)	(Z)	100	0.6
Former USSR[2]	102,200	6.6	31,500	3.9	(Z)	(Z)	400	0.1	3,100	17.4
Total	**1,548,500**	**100.0%**	**817,000**	**100.0%**	**647,500**	**100.0%**	**295,600**	**100.0%**	**17,800**	**100.0%**

Note: Z = less than 100,000 or 0.1%. 1. Includes Middle East. 2. Republics of former Soviet Union. **Source**: *The World Christian Encyclopedia* (1985).

Christianity. The center of Islam is the Arabian peninsula, where the new faith was established. Mecca and Medina in Saudi Arabia are its holiest places. Predominantly Islamic countries stretch from Morocco in the west to Indonesia in the Far East; these include Egypt, Iran, Pakistan, Bangladesh, and Indonesia. Saudi Arabia and other oil-producing states of the Arabian peninsula are also influential. Muslims are an important minority in sub-Saharan Africa and the Soviet Union.

HINDUISM

Founder No single teacher founded Hinduism. Its origins are lost in the mists of time. Some elements date to 3000 B.C. Other elements may have been brought by Aryan peoples who invaded India about 1500 B.C. Hinduism has gone through many stages and changed its form many times.

Scripture Many writings are considered part of Hindu scriptures. They include four Vedas, among the oldest religious writings known to humankind; two long epic poems, the *Ramayana* and the *Mahabharata;* and the *Bhagavadgita,* a philosophical part of the *Mahabharata.* Indian holy books include ancient prayers and hymns, instructions for religious rituals, philosophy, and elaborate stories about gods and humans. They were first written down in Sanskrit, an ancient language still learned by devoted Hindus.

Beliefs Hinduism is polytheistic, recognizing not just a handful of gods, but thousands of gods. Among the more important are Brahma, the creator; Vishnu, who preserves the world and may appear as the Hindu hero Krishna; and Siva, the god of destruction. Many Hindus are devoted to Siva's wife, who is known by several names. As Uma, she is a protector and goddess of motherhood. As Kali or Durga, she is a destroyer. Many Hindu deities have mixed powers—they are both good and bad, creative and destructive.

Hindus have a deep respect for all living things—even insects. The holiest animal is the cow. In India cattle roam freely, and killing them for their meat is considered a grave offense. From this respect for life grew the philosophy of Mahatma Gandhi, the hero of Indian independence in the mid-1900s. Gandhi's life and writings inspired people in many parts of the world.

Hindus believe in reincarnation. They believe that when a person dies, his or her soul lives on and appears in a new body. If the person has done good things, the soul may appear in an individual at a higher level of existence. An evil person's soul might reappear in the body of a lowly animal.

One of the schools of Hindu philosophy is called yoga. A student of yoga learns bodily and mental exercises to help create readiness for meditation. Yoga has become popular in Western countries, often as a nonreligious discipline to enhance physical and emotional health.

Practice Hindu devotion is largely an individual and family matter. Hindus do not form congregations that meet regularly for worship. Many homes have a shrine to honor particularly important gods.

Hindu temples are buildings devoted to a particular god or group of gods. Many Hindus believe that a statue in a temple is the god himself. Priests at a temple may bathe and dress the statue each day and bring it food. A Hindu priest may serve at a particular temple and be devoted to a particular god. Once or twice a year, a temple may celebrate a holy day in honor of its god. Thousands or even millions may come to see or participate in the festival and to give honor to the god. Some of the most famous temples are on the banks of the Ganges and other rivers in India.

Traditional Hinduism observed caste, the division of people into rigid groups by occupation and social standing. The four traditional castes are (1) Brahmans—priestly leaders and their families, (2) Kshatriyas—princes and soldiers, (3) Vaisyas—merchants and landowners, and (4) Sudras—farmers and workers. In addition there was a large group of outcasts—people with no caste and no standing. Known as untouchables, they were ignored and mistreated until modern times. In 1950 the government of India outlawed the caste system. Still, many Hindus prefer to mix primarily with members of their own caste.

Schools and sects Through its long history, Hinduism has seen many sects. Tantrism, which grew up after A.D. 600, emphasized special rituals as a means of enlightenment. They used mystical diagrams (mandalas) and chants (mantras) in their search. Bhakti, a sect begun after A.D. 1300, emphasized the primacy of love for a deity and used love between humans as an illustration. This sect rejected caste, ritual, and creeds, emphasizing the need for sincerity. Today sects that have melded elements of Hinduism, Christianity, and Islam are seeking converts in India. One of these so-called new religions may develop into a new and distinct world religion.

History From its prehistoric beginnings, Hinduism developed into the first great world religion, extending its influence through the Indian subcontinent and many surrounding regions—especially Sri Lanka, Burma, and parts of Indonesia.

With the rise of Buddhism after 600 B.C., however, Hinduism sank gradually into eclipse. Buddhism dominated India and soon spread through most of the rest of Asia, where it remained a dominant force until recent times. In India, Hinduism gradually regained its primary position. Similarly, after A.D. 650 Islam swept into India from the west. It gained many converts at the expense of Hinduism. Again Hinduism gradually regained its earlier dominance. (Islam remained dominant in the northwestern and northeastern extremities of the subcontinent—now Pakistan and Bangladesh.)

Hinduism has had great influence on distant parts of the world. The founders of Buddhism, Jainism, and Sikhism were all Hindus. The influence of Hinduism in modern times has been mostly indirect. Traditional Hinduism is not a proselytizing religion, and its deep ties to India make it difficult to transport. Still, Hindu doctrines and disciplines promoting meditation have become well known by many in Western countries.

Geography and numbers Hinduism is the traditional religion of India. Its almost 650 million adherents make it the third-largest religious group in the world after Christianity and Islam. Nearly all practicing Hindus in the world live in India itself or in neighboring South Asia. Outside Asia, Hinduism flourishes mainly in expatriate communities of Indians.

BUDDHISM

Founder Siddhartha Gautama (c. 563–483 B.C.), who came to be known as Buddha. According to Buddhist scriptures, Siddhartha Gautama was born into a princely family on the Indian subcontinent (in the present-day country of Nepal). At the age of 29, he had a series of visions that persuaded him to leave his wife and young son. He wandered for some years seeking enlightenment. One day, while sitting under a bo tree in a village, he gained enlightenment. Soon his followers called him Enlightened One, or Buddha. For the rest of his life (he lived to be perhaps 80 years old), Buddha wandered through northern India teaching.

Scripture The Tripitika, or "three baskets," is a collection of sayings and rules for conduct collected by Buddha's early followers. Nearly all Buddhists reverence the Tripitika, although many treasure other works as well.

Beliefs Buddhists share with Hinduism a belief in the cycle of reincarnation. When a person's body dies, the soul is reborn in another person or animal. Buddha believed there was a way to end this cycle of death and rebirth. He taught that a person should seek a state of detachment from worldly things and desires. Achieving this state, called nirvana, could bring contentment and would be the end of the reincarnation cycle for the soul.

Buddha rejected extreme asceticism and extreme self-indulgence. He recommended a Middle Way. The Buddhist discipline is summarized in the Eightfold Path, which consists of right knowledge, right thought, right action, right livelihood, right effort, right mindfulness, right concentration, and right speech.

Practice From early times Buddhists established orders of monks. The monks withdraw from the everyday world and live austere lives of meditation. They live on alms contributed by lay Buddhists. Although many monks devote their lives to their orders, others may spend a year or two as monks before taking up responsibility as laymen. Early monks served as missionaries, carrying the tenets of Buddhism through all of Asia.

Collective rituals play a smaller part in the life of a Buddhist than in the lives of Jews, Christians, or Muslims. Buddhist temples are primarily for individual meditation.

Schools and sects The most significant division in Buddhism is between the Therevada and Mahayana schools. Therevada Buddhism, which remains most influential in Sri Lanka, Burma, Thailand, and Cambodia, is most traditional in seeking to concentrate on the life and teachings of Gautama. Mahayana Buddhism, which became predominant in China and Japan, offers a more liberal interpretation of Buddhist teachings. It reveres other enlightened teachers, or Buddhas, and emphasizes the importance of each person's seeking to become a bodhisattva, one who seeks Buddhahood through compassion and action as well as contemplation.

A more recent school, Zen, has received particular attention in the Western world. This "meditation" school began in the A.D. 700s. One branch emphasizes mental meditation, finding wisdom in the paradoxical statements (koans) of earlier Zen masters. A second branch emphasizes physical discipline as an aid to true meditation.

History The original teachings of Buddhism were spoken and written in Pali, a language of India. Therevada Buddhists still study Buddhist writings in this language. Therevada missionaries carried Buddhism eastward to the rest of South Asia.

Between 200 B.C. and A.D. 200, Mahayana Buddhism spread widely in China. Chinese missionaries carried the teachings to Korea and Japan. The flowering of Buddhism in China provided a second center for the religion, one in which language and practice differed.

After A.D. 700, in a remarkable shift, Buddhism began to lose its influence in India. Islamic conquests claimed many converts, and Hinduism (having absorbed some Buddhist thinking) reawakened. By 1000, Buddhism was virtually nonexistent in India, but it continued to prosper among India's neighbors to the east.

Geography and numbers Although Buddhism originated in India, today the vast majority of Buddhists are outside India in neighboring countries to the east and in East Asia. Recent estimates are that 300 million people adhere to Buddhist beliefs and practices. Many of these may also observe rituals in other religions, such as folk religion (in China) or Shinto (in Japan).

JUDAISM

Founder Judaism was not founded by a single religious leader. It developed among wandering Semitic tribes who came to be known variously as Hebrews, Israelites, and eventually, Jews. The traditional patriarch of the Jewish people is Abraham, to whom God promised a land of plenty. The lawgiver, some centuries later, was Moses, who received God's commandments at Mount Sinai. The Jewish nation reached its height of power under the kings David and Solomon. The latter built an elaborate and beautiful temple at Jerusalem.

Scripture The Jewish scriptures, originally written and still often read and studied in Hebrew, are the same books Christians call the Old Testament. The first five books, known to Jews as the Torah, have special significance. These books tell of the Covenant God made with the Jewish people and outline the laws (including the Ten Commandments) by which they were to live. The remaining books provide additional history, the exhortations of the prophets, hymns and songs for worship (especially the Psalms), and other poetry and wisdom writings.

Beliefs The early Jews, in contrast to neighboring peoples, worshiped one God, whom they recognized as the Creator of all things and the God of all. Among God's characteristics were both judgment and mercy. His Covenant with the Jews promised them his care and protection; they were to follow his laws. During the time of the prophets, when the Jewish states had declined, the prophets told of the coming of a leader anointed by God—the Messiah. Jews still await the coming of the Messiah.

Practice Jews worship in synagogues, often modest places of worship for a small congregation. Saturday, the seventh day of the week, is the Sabbath, a special day of rest and worship. Worship consists of readings from the scriptures, the chanting or singing of psalms or other songs of praise, and prayer.

Schools and sects There are three main branches of modern Judaism. Orthodox Judaism is the most conservative branch, observing laws concerning clean and unclean foods, purification, and other ancient rituals. One part of orthodoxy is the Hasidim, fundamentalist sects that grew up in eastern Europe in the 1700s and 1800s.

Reform Judaism, strong in the United States, is the most liberal of the three main branches. Reform Jews seek to follow the spirit of Judaism and are free to disregard part of the ancient rules of conduct and ritual. Reform places of worship are called temples. Some temples resemble Christian churches in their design and in their observances, which may include, for example, music from a pipe organ and choir.

Conservative Judaism seeks a middle road between Orthodox and Reform. It is the most recent of the three branches and is strong in the United States.

History After wealth and influence during the reigns of David and Solomon (c. 1000 B.C.), the Jewish state was divided by dynastic feuds into a northern and a southern kingdom. Both kingdoms eventually fell victim to neighboring peoples. In 587 the southern kingdom (Judah) was overrun by the Babylonians, and many Jews were taken as slaves to Babylon. Solomon's Temple at Jerusalem was destroyed. Fifty years later the Jews were freed, and they rebuilt the temple. In the 100s B.C., the whole region was conquered by Rome. The Jews mounted a revolt against Rome in A.D. 66. This resulted in Roman reprisals, including the destruction of the second temple in A.D. 70. Jews were dispersed in all directions and were to have no land of their own for nearly 1,900 years.

Judaism and the Jewish people survived in many parts of the world. Some lived in Palestine, some in Babylon. Many moved to Europe—

especially to Spain, France, Germany, Poland, and western Russia.

Christians of Europe often persecuted the Jews. They passed laws against Jews owning land or engaging in certain businesses. Sometimes mobs of angry people destroyed Jewish settlements and killed the inhabitants. In the 1930s Adolf Hitler and his Nazi party blamed Jews for Germany's defeats and sufferings. He planned to exterminate all the Jews in Europe and succeeded in killing an estimated six million. This event is known as the Holocaust.

Even before the Holocaust, Jewish leaders had begun a campaign for the establishment of a Jewish state in the Middle East. After World War II, they received the support of Britain and the United States, and a new country called Israel was carved from Palestine. Since Israel's beginning in 1948, it has often been attacked and harassed by its neighbors, who are Muslim and never agreed to the new state.

Geography and numbers The largest number of Jews live in North America, to which they emigrated in large numbers between 1880 and 1920. They are concentrated in and near large cities, especially New York. The Jews in South Asia are nearly all residents of Israel. Jews in the former Soviet Union have been harassed in recent years, and many are seeking to emigrate to Israel or the United States.

NONRELIGIOUS AND ATHEISTS

Region	Nonreligious	Atheist	Total	Percent
East Asia	618,900,000	123,400,000	742,300,000	73.0%
Former USSR[1]	83,100,000	60,600,000	143,700,000	14.1
Europe	49,400,000	17,400,000	66,800,000	6.6
South Asia	18,400,000	5,100,000	23,500,000	2.3
North America	19,000,000	1,000,000	20,000,000	2.0
Latin America	12,900,000	2,400,000	15,300,000	1.5
Oceania	2,900,000	500,000	3,400,000	0.3
Africa	1,300,000	100,000	1,400,000	0.1
Total	**805,900,000**	**210,500,000**	**1,016,400,000**	**100.0%**

1. Republics of former Soviet Union.

OTHER RELIGIONS

According to scholars who helped assemble *The World Christian Encyclopedia,* three types of religion (in addition to those listed above) claim tens of millions of adherents in the world. These they call Chinese Folk Religion, New Religions, and Tribal Religions. In addition there are many smaller religious groups, some of which have had influence far beyond their present numbers.

Chinese folk religion, estimated to be a primary faith for about 180 million people (about 20 percent of China's population), consists of a blend of ancient ancestor worship with some elements of Buddhism, Confucianism, and Taoism. Confucius, a great Chinese philosopher and teacher, lived in the sixth century B.C. He taught respect for family and ruler. Taoism is a philosophy or religion based on the teachings of Lao-tzu, another great teacher of Confucian times. Chinese folk religion is also followed by many in scattered Chinese settlements in other parts of the world.

New religions are those that have grown up in the past century, principally in Asia. A new religion typically blends elements of (a) local religious tradition and practice; (b) Hinduism, Buddhism, or Islam; and (c) modern Western thought. Whether any of these new religions will develop a truly international following remains to be seen. But together they account for an estimated 100 million adherents, mainly in such Asian countries as Indonesia, the Philippines, and Japan.

Tribal religions are animistic religions practiced by isolated peoples, primarily in Africa and South Asia.

The more important smaller groups are the following:

Sikhism and **Jainism** are developments from certain strands of Hinduism. There are an estimated 16 million Sikhs and more than three million Jains, predominantly in India.

Confucianism is based on the teachings of Confucius, a Chinese teacher of the 500s B.C. Confucianism has had a powerful influence on Chinese history and philosophy. An estimated five million people in East Asia consider themselves Confucianists.

Baha'i is an independent religion that teaches that the revealed religions of the world are in agreement and that each of the prophet-founders of the religions revealed the will of God for a particular time and place in history. The Baha'i faith began in 1844 in Iran. Its prophet-founder is Baha'Ullah, meaning "glory of God." The Baha'i faith has an estimated five million adherents worldwide. Its headquarters are in Haifa, Israel. A major U.S. temple in Wilmette, Ill., attracts many visitors.

Parsees, a people who emigrated centuries ago from Persia (Iran) to India, follow the teachings of the Persian prophet Zoroaster, who lived in the 500s B.C. They are a prosperous sect centered in Bombay, marrying only among themselves and seeking no converts. Estimates of their number range from 200,000 to 500,000.

NONRELIGIOUS AND ATHEISTS

According to *The World Christian Encyclopedia,* more than a billion of the world's people consider themselves nonreligious (agnostic about religious claims) or atheistic (actively opposed to religion). Nearly three-quarters of these people live in East Asia, where they are a majority of the population of China. Nonreligious persons and atheists also make up a majority of people in the Soviet Union.

If the estimates of non- and antireligious peoples are correct, these peoples make up the largest religious bloc in the world after Christianity.

WORLD RELIGIONS: A BRIEF CHRONOLOGY

B.C.

c. 3000 Earliest elements of Hinduism develop in India.

c. 2500 Egyptian pyramids at Giza completed.

c. 1500 Aryan peoples invade India; bring additional elements of Hinduism.

c. 1290 Moses leads Israelites out of Egypt.

1010–922 Reigns of Hebrew kings David and Solomon. A great temple built at Jerusalem.

740 Hebrew prophet Isaiah flourishes.

628 Traditional birth date of Zoroaster, religious teacher in Persia. Followers today are Parsees in India.

604 Traditional birth date of Chinese teacher Lao-tzu, a founder of Taoism.

587 Babylonians destroy Hebrew temple at Jerusalem and take many Hebrews as slaves. Fifty years later, Hebrews are freed; begin to rebuild temple.

560 Birth of Siddhartha Gautama in northern India; later known as Buddha. Dies c. 480. His teachings, on which Buddhism is based, gain many followers in India; later spread to Southeast Asia.

551 Birth of Chinese teacher Confucius. Dies c. 479.

200 Mahayana Buddhism begins to spread in China and Japan.

100s Jewish lands conquered by Roman Empire.

3 Birth of Jesus Christ; Western calendar dated from supposed year of his birth.

A.D.

30 Death and resurrection of Jesus Christ. By 100, Christians are in many parts of present-day Greece, Turkey, Syria, Lebanon, Israel, Egypt, despite active persecution by Romans.

66–70 Jewish revolt against Romans ends in destruction of second temple and scattering of Jews in all directions.

175 Apostles' Creed, a brief statement of Christian beliefs, formulated.

303–12 In final organized program of persecution, Romans kill estimated 500,000 Christians.

313 The emperor Constantine decrees toleration for Christianity in Roman Empire. In 325 he calls synod of Nicaea, which formulates Nicene Creed. By end of 300s, Christianity is official religion of empire.

354 Birth of St. Augustine, influential Christian teacher, in North Africa. Dies 430.

451 Council of Chalcedon (fourth ecumenical council) formulates long-held Christian understanding of Christ, the union in one person of two distinct natures, human and divine.

570 Muhammad, founder of Islam, born at Mecca (now in Saudi Arabia). Dies in 632 in nearby city of Medina.

600+ Tantrism, a Hindu school, grows up, emphasizing special rituals as means of enlightenment; uses mystical diagrams (mandalas) and chants (mantras).

650+ Islam sweeps into India; gains many converts.

700+ Development in China of Zen, a school of Buddhism, which has received particular attention in the modern Western world.

732 A Muslim army aiming to conquer Europe defeated by Franks at Tours in central France.

800 Roman Empire revived in the West with the coronation of Charlemagne as emperor on Christmas Day, in St. Peter's in Rome.

988 Christianity reaches Russia through missionaries from eastern churches.

1054 Eastern (or Orthodox) and Western (or Roman) churches go separate ways after disputes about doctrine and authority.

1096 Christians in Europe go on first Crusade to take Holy Land from Muslims. Seven other major Crusades pursued between 1100 and 1300. Christian warriors temporarily occupy Jerusalem and other cities but soon lose them again to Muslims.

1216 Pope Innocent III approves formation of Franciscans and Dominicans.

1227 Birth of Thomas Aquinas, great Christian theologian, in Italy.

1300+ Bhakti, a Hindu sect, develops, emphasizing primacy of love for a deity and using love between humans as illustration; rejects caste, ritual, and creeds and emphasizes need for sincerity.

1309 The papacy moves from Rome to Avignon, France, where it remains until 1377 ("The Babylonian captivity of the Church").

1377 English theologian and religious reformer John Wycliffe accused of heresy by Pope Gregory XI for attacks on worldliness of the church.

1378–1417 The Great Western Schism, during which first two, then three, claimants sought recognition as pope.

1415 Excommunication and execution of Czech religious leader Jan Hus, who protested sale of indulgences and other papal excesses, sets off Hussite Wars, which end with Compactata of Prague (1436).

1453 Ottoman Turks (Muslims) conquer capital of Eastern Roman Empire, Constantinople. Eventually, city's name changed to Istanbul. Turks push westward into Europe.

1469 Birth of Nanak, founder of Sikhism, in Punjab region of India.

1492 Muslims overthrown in Spain; Spanish Inquisition begins.

1517 Martin Luther, a German priest, posts 95 theses on cathedral door, questioning church teachings. Luther refuses to recant; is excommunicated from Catholic church. With cooperation of north German princes, he forms new Protestant churches. This begins Reformation, which ultimately divides European Christianity into two warring camps.

1534 King Henry VIII of England denies power of pope over church in England and establishes Church of England responsible to monarch. New church gradually adopts Protestant beliefs but maintains many practices of earlier Catholic era.

1536 John Calvin, a young French scholar, publishes *Institutes of the Christian Religion,* and becomes second major leader of Protestant Christianity, helping to create Presbyterian and other Reformed churches.

1540 Ignatius Loyola, a Spaniard, establishes the Jesuits (Society of Jesus) with papal approval. This order becomes powerful instrument of Catholic church in disputes with Protestants, in missionary efforts around world, and in education.

1545–63 Council of Trent makes major reforms in Catholic church and defines disagreements with Protestants. Its work begins Catholic Reformation, or Counter-Reformation.

1588 Defeat of Philip II's (Catholic) Spanish Armada by Elizabeth I's (Protestant) English navy.

1598 In the Edict of Nantes, Henry IV proclaims "peaceful coexistence" of Catholics and Calvinists in France. Revoked in 1685 by Louis XIV.

1618–48 Thirty Years War, caused in part by Protestant-Catholic hatreds, decimates central Europe. Calvinist leaders in England overthrow monarchy and execute king in civil war (1642–49). Monarchy is restored in 1660.

1620 Pilgrims, a small group of English Calvinists, establish colony at Plymouth in North America to escape persecution in England. They are first of thousands of Calvinists to settle in present-day New England.

1683 Muslim Turks defeated near Vienna, Austria, in their last attempt to establish foothold in western Europe.

1734 The Great Awakening, a religious revival, sweeps New England, begun by prominent Massachusetts preacher Jonathan Edwards. English evangelist George Whitefield tours American colonies beginning in 1738, preaching to outdoor gatherings.

1738 Christian conversion experienced by brothers John and Charles Wesley in England. They begin evangelical activities, leading to development of independent Methodist church.

1792 Second Awakening sweeps new United States, lasting more than 20 years. Revivals in Kentucky in 1800 result in formation of new denominations, ancestors of Disciples of Christ, Churches of Christ, and Christian churches.

1830 American Joseph Smith has religious visions that lead him to organize the Church of Jesus Christ of the Latter-day Saints (Mormons). Movement grows rapidly but generates intense opposition. Smith murdered by anti-Mormons in 1844.

1844 Baha'i established in Iran.

1869–79 Vatican Council I, convened by Pope Pius IX, declares that teachings of pope in matters of faith and morals are infallible.

1875 Mary Baker Eddy publishes *Science and Health with Key to the Scriptures* in Boston; it becomes basis of Church of Christ, Scientist.

1900 First documented modern Pentecostal experience—worshipers speak in unknown tongues during prayer meeting in Kansas. Within 20 years, Pentecostal churches form major new Christian denomination.

1938–45 German government carries out destruction of estimated six million European Jews. This event known as the Holocaust.

1947 UN approves creation of the new state of Israel in Middle East for settlement by Jews.

1948 World Council of Churches established at huge assembly in Amsterdam. This ecumenical organization supported by many Protestant, Anglican, and Orthodox denominations. Headquarters are in Geneva, Switzerland.

1962–65 Vatican Council II, convened by Pope John XXIII, announces many liberalizing changes in Roman Catholic liturgy and practice; supports cautious involvement in ecumenical discussions with other Christians.

1978 Karol Josef Wojtyla, archbishop of Krakow, Poland, elected to papacy as John Paul II, the first non-Italian pope since Hadrian VI in 1523.

1981 Pope John Paul II is shot in an assassination attempt by a Turkish gunman in St. Peter's Square.

1988 For the first time, a woman is elected to a bishopric in U.S. Episcopal church.

1991 Religious freedom granted in USSR.

NATIONS OF THE WORLD

The following section presents major facts about all the nations of the world, including statistics on each nation's geography, people, government, economy, membership in major international organizations, and written text describing highlights of the country's history.

The commonly used name for each country is listed first, followed by the formal name. A list of colonial and other former names is found in the following section, "Territories of the World." Geographical descriptions are listed in both miles and kilometers, and the latitude and longitude of most islands are given.

Organizations to which a nation is a party are abbreviated under the category "Intl. Orgs." (For more about these, see "The United Nations" and "International Organizations.")

Sources of information include the Central Intelligence Agency of the United States, the United Nations, the U.S. Bureau of the Census, and the U.S. Department of State. Names of heads of government are from the United Nations official protocol office and are valid as of July 1995.

Afghanistan

Islamic State of Afghanistan

Geography Location: landlocked country in southwestern Asia. **Boundaries:** Turkmenistan to NW, Tajikistan to N, China to NE, Pakistan to E and S, Iran to W. **Total land area:** 250,000 sq. mi. (647,500 sq km). **Coastline:** none. **Comparative area:** slightly smaller than Texas. **Land use:** 12% arable land; negl. % permanent crops; 46% meadows and pastures; 3% forest and woodland; 39% other; includes negl. % irrigated. **Major cities:** (1982 est.) Kabul (capital) 1,036,407; Qandahar 191,345; Herat 150,497; Mazar-i-Sharif 110,367; Jalalabad 57,824.

People Population: 16,903,400 (1994 est.). **Nationality:** noun—Afghan(s); adjective—Afghan. **Ethnic groups:** 38% Pashtun, 25% Tajik, 19% Hazara, 6% Uzbek. **Languages:** 50% Afghan Persian (Dari), 35% Pashtu, 11% Turkic langs. (primarily Uzbek and Turkmen), 4% minor langs. (30, primarily Baluchi and Pashai); much bilingualism. **Religions:** 84% Sunni Muslim, 15% Shia Muslim, 1% other.

Government Type: Islamic. **Independence:** Aug. 1919 (from UK). **Constitution:** newly drafted constitution is awaiting ratification. **National holiday:** Apr. 28. **Heads of government:** Burhanuddin Rabbani, president and chairman of Leadership Council (since Jan. 1993), Gulbaddin Hekmatyar, prime minister (since May 1993). **Structure:** executive—president, Leadership Council (prominent commanders from various factions that were fighting in the Afghani war); legislative—being restructured; judicial—being restructured.

Economy Monetary unit: afghani. **Budget:** (1989 est.) ***income:*** N.A.; ***expend.:*** N.A. **GDP:** N.A. **Chief crops:** subsistence farming and animal husbandry; wheat, fruits, nuts, karakul pelts, wool; illegal producer of opium poppy and cannabis for international drug trade. **Livestock:** sheep, cattle, goats, asses, horses. **Natural resources:** natural gas, crude oil, coal, copper, talc. **Major industries:** small-scale production of textiles, soap, furniture, shoes, fertilizer, and cement for domestic use; handwoven carpets for export; extractive industries (oil and copper). **Labor force:** 4.98 mil. (1980 est.); 67.8% agriculture and animal husbandry, 10.7% services and other, 10.2% industry; (1986) current figures unavailable because of fighting. **Exports:** $243 mil. (f.o.b., 1991); 55% natural gas, 24% fruits and nuts, handwoven carpets, wool, cotton. **Imports:** $737 mil. (c.i.f., 1991); food supplies, petroleum products. **Major trading partners: *exports:*** former USSR, Pakistan; ***imports:*** former USSR, Pakistan.

Intl. Orgs. Colombo Plan, FAO, G-77, IAEA, IBRD, ICAO, IDA, IFAD, IFC, ILO, IMF, INTELSAT, ITU, NAM, UN, UNESCO, UPU, WHO, WMO.

Mountainous and landlocked, Afghanistan has been a crossroads of trans-Asian trade and conquest since antiquity. A part of the Persian Empire, Bactria was conquered by Alexander the Great, and became independent in the third century B.C. before falling to the Parthians in the next century. In the seventh century A.D., a flourishing Buddhist civilization there fell to Islamic conquests. Genghis Khan overthrew the 11th-century empire of Mahmud of Gazni in the early 13th century, and Afghanistan was the center of Tamerlane's empire in the late 14th century. Thereafter, the region was divided among various tribes and petty kingdoms.

Modern Afghan history began with the establishment of a united emirate by Ahmed Shah Durrani in 1747. In the 19th century, Russia and Great Britain contested domination of Afghanistan. The British Afghan Wars of 1838–42 and 1878–80 left Afghanistan unconquered but within Britain's sphere of influence. Afghanistan achieved full independence from Britain in 1919 under Amanullah Khan, who proclaimed himself king in 1926. Modern reforms were instituted by Amanullah and his successors Mohammed Nadir Shah (1929–33) and Mohammed Zahir Shah (1933–73).

The monarchy fell to a military coup in 1973, and Mohammed Daud Khan established a republic. In 1978 pro-Soviet leftists took power in a coup, and, ostensibly at the government's invitation, Soviet troops invaded Afghanistan in December 1979 to put down widespread popular revolts against Communist rule. In the ensuing civil war, the government's forces and their Soviet allies (with an eventual troop strength of more than 100,000) controlled the cities and main transportation routes, but guerrilla forces contested the countryside. In 1988 the Soviet Union began a withdrawal of its troops, completed by February 1989. The rebel factions failed to achieve a united front and the pro-Soviet government confounded predictions that it would fall soon after the Soviet departure.

The government finally fell on Apr. 15, 1992, and rebel troops entered Kabul. A respected religious leader, Sibghatullah Mujaddidi, was named interim president, with the backing of a coalition of forces dominated by rebel commanders Abdul Rashid Dostam and Ahmad Shah Masoud. However, Gulbaddin Hekmatyar, leader of the fundamentalist Hizbe Islami faction, declined to join the ruling coalition. Fighting broke out in and around Kabul between coalition forces and Hekmatyar's troops.

On June 28 Mujaddidi turned over his power to the Leadership Council, which then elected Burhanuddin Rabbani as president. Fighting for control of Kabul continued between forces loyal to the Rabbani government and those backing Hekmatyar. Other factions later joined the fighting, and Kabul was subjected to continual rocket attacks in late 1992 and into the spring of 1993. Hekmatyar was named prime minister in an attempt to make peace. Fighting broke out again in early 1994 with Rabbani's followers getting the upper hand in June after fierce battles in Kabul.

By early 1995, the UN had brokered a scheme uniting the nine major factions in a council to which Rabbani would turn over power. But it was no sooner arranged than it was undone by the emergence of a new force: a fundamentalist Islamic militia called the Taliban, 20,000 strong and composed of students from the Islamic schools, who proved strong enough to drive Hekmatyar's forces from his camp south of Kabul and gain control of 10 of Afghanistan's 30 provinces. They have refused to take part in the council, seeking instead an Islamic Republic.

Albania

Republic of Albania

Geography Location: southeastern Europe. **Boundaries:** Yugoslavia to N, Macedonia to E, Greece to S, and Adriatic and Ionian Seas (parts of Mediterranean Sea) to W. **Total land area:** 11,100 sq. mi. (28,750 sq km). **Coastline:** 225 mi. (362 km). **Comparative area:** slightly larger than Maryland. **Land use:** 21% arable land; 4% permanent crops; 15% meadows and pastures; 38% forest and woodland; 22% other; includes 1% irrigated. **Major cities:** (1990 est.) Tiranë (Tirana; capital) 244,200; Durrës (Durazzo) 85,400; Elbasan 83,300; Shkodër (Scutari) 81,900; Vlorë (Vlonë or Valona) 73,800.

People Population: 3,374,085 (1994 est.). **Nationality:** noun—Albanian(s); adjective—Albanian. **Ethnic groups:** 95% Albanian, 3% Greek, 2% Vlach, Gypsy, Serb, and Bulgarian (1989 est.). **Languages:** Albanian (Tosk is official dialect), Greek. **Religions:** Albania claims to be world's first atheist state; all churches and mosques were closed in 1967 and religious observances prohibited; pre-1967 estimates of religious affiliation—70% Muslim, 20% Greek Orthodox, 10% Roman Catholic.

Government Type: democratic. **Independence:** Nov. 28, 1912 (from Turkey). **Constitution:** being drafted. **National holiday:** Liberation Day, Nov. 29. **Heads of government:** Dr. Sali Berisha, president (since Apr. 1992); Aleksander Meksi, prime minister (since Apr. 1992). **Structure:** executive—president, vice president, prime minister, Council of Ministers; legislative—unicameral People's Assembly, 140 seats; judicial—Supreme Court.

Economy Monetary unit: lek. **Budget:** (1993 est.) ***income:*** $1.1 bil.; ***expend.:*** $1.4 bil. **GDP:** $3.3 bil., $1,100 per capita. **Chief crops:** vegetables, wheat, potatoes, tobacco, sugar beets, cotton, corn. **Livestock:** sheep, goats, cattle, pigs, asses. **Natural resources:** crude oil, natural gas, coal, chromium, copper. **Major industries:** food processing, textiles and clothing, lumber. **Labor force:** 1.5 mil. (1987); about 60% agriculture, 40% industry and commerce (1986). **Exports:** $70 mil. (f.o.b., 1992); asphalt, metals and metallic ores, electricity, oil, vegetables, fruits, tobacco. **Imports:** $524 mil. (f.o.b., 1992); machinery, consumer goods, grains. **Major trading partners:** ***exports:*** Italy, Greece, Czechoslovakia, Germany, Poland, Romania, Bulgaria, Hungary, Macedonia. ***imports:*** Italy, Czechoslovakia, Romania, Germany, Poland, Hungary, Bulgaria, Greece.

Intl. Orgs. FAO, IAEA, IMF, ITU, OSCE, UN, UNESCO, UPU, WHO, WMO.

The city of Epidamnus (Durrës) was colonized by Greeks from Corinth and Corcyra in 625 B.C. Later the Roman province of Illyricum, Albania was a much-coveted area after the fall of Rome and was in turn ruled by Byzantines, Normans, Venetians, Slavs, and the kings of Naples. Under the leadership of Skanderbeg (1405–68), Albania repulsed repeated Turkish invasions. But Albania was part of the Ottoman Empire from 1478 until 1912. Ottoman rule succeeded in converting most of the populace to Islam (with Catholic minorities in the north and Greek Orthodox in the south) but did not destroy the Albanian sense of national identity, based on ties of tribe, clan, and family.

Independence came in 1912 as a result of the First Balkan War, when Austria-Hungary and Italy fostered the creation of an Albanian state. Occupied by its sponsors during World War I, Albania emerged from the war in a state of near-anarchy. With Yugoslav support, a tribal chief, Ahmed Zogu, became president of the republic in 1924; he proclaimed himself King Zog I in 1928.

In 1939 Italy invaded and annexed Albania. During World War II, partisan resistance was dominated by Communist forces under the leadership of Enver Hoxha. In 1944 Hoxha seized control of the government. A socialist republic was established in 1946: foreigners were expelled and their assets nationalized; churches were closed; agriculture and industry were collectivized. Albania under Hoxha became one of the world's most thoroughly totalitarian states.

A doctrinaire Stalinist, Hoxha broke with Nikita Khruschev's Soviet Union in 1961 and became a client state of China. But with liberalization in China after 1977, Hoxha broke that link as well. Albania became almost totally isolated from world affairs.

Hoxha died in April 1985 and was succeeded as president and first secretary of the Albanian Communist party by Ramiz Alia. In 1990, Alia began to ease curbs on religion, tourism, and foreign investment, and to expand foreign trade. In December 1990, he allowed the formation of the opposition Democratic party. The first elections to the National Assembly were held too early, in the spring of 1991, before the awareness spread that the old regime was collapsing, so that the government party was able to carry the countryside and form a government in coalition with the new Democratic party which had carried the towns. But the March 1992 elections completed the rout of the Communists, the Democrats winning 92 of the 140 seats. When Alia resigned in April, heart surgeon Sali Berisha was elected president and appointed archaeologist Alexander Meksi as prime minister. By the end of the year, factions were already forming, with Gramoz Pashko's Democratic Alliance protesting against President Berisha's "autocratic rule."

Meanwhile, the end of communism seemed to mean not so much democracy as anarchy, with food riots in the cities and armed brigandage in the country, while industry functioned at about 5 percent of its already-low capacity. EC and UN grants helped pay for needed imports, but more important was Italian assistance to the Albanian police forces. By early 1993 zones of law and order were being established, churches were reopening, 90 percent of farming had been privatized, and trials of the old Hoxha functionaries had begun, the first being that of the dictator's 71-year-old widow, who was sentenced to nine years in January 1993. Yet a new constitution for Albania, proposed by Pres. Berisha, met defeat in a November 1994 referendum of Albanian voters, 54 percent to 42 percent.

Algeria

Democratic and Popular Republic of Algeria

Geography Location: northern coast of Africa. **Boundaries:** Mediterranean Sea to N, Tunisia and Libya to E, Mali and Niger to S, Morocco, Western Sahara, Mauritania to W. **Total land area:** 919,591 sq. mi. (2,381,740 sq km). **Coastline:** 620 mi. (998 km). **Comparative area:** slightly less than 3.5 times size of Texas. **Land use:** 3% arable land; negl. % permanent crops; 13% meadows and pastures; 2% forest and woodland; 82% other; includes negl. % irrigated. **Major cities:** (1984 est.) Algiers (capital) 1,721,607; Oran 663,504; Constantine 448,578; Annaba 348,322; Blida 191,314.

People Population: 27,895,068 (1994 est.). **Nationality:** noun—Algerian(s); adjective—Algerian. **Ethnic groups:** 99% Arab-Berber, less than 1% European. **Languages:** Arabic (official), French, Berber dialects. **Religions:** 99% Sunni Muslim (state religion), 1% Christian and Jewish.

Government Type: republic. **Independence:** July 5, 1962 (from France). **Constitution:** Nov. 19, 1976, effective Nov. 22, 1976. **National holiday:** Anniversary of the Revolution, Nov. 1. **Heads of government:** Liamine Zeroual, head of state (since Feb. 1994); Mokdad Sifi, prime minister (since Apr. 1994). **Structure:** executive; unicameral legislature (National People's Assembly); judiciary.

Economy Monetary unit: Algerian dinar. **Budget:** (1993 est.) ***income:*** $14.4 bil.; ***expend.:*** $14.6 bil. **GDP:** $89 bil., $3,300 per capita. **Chief crops:** wheat, barley, oats, grapes, olives. **Livestock:** chickens, sheep, goats, cattle, horses. **Natural resources:** crude oil, natural gas, iron ore, phosphates, uranium. **Major industries:** petroleum, light industries, natural gas, mining. **Labor force:** 6.2 mil. (1992 est.); 29.5% government, 22% agriculture, 16.2% construction and public works, 13.6% industry, 13.5% commerce and services, 5.2% transportation and communication (1989). **Exports:** $11.4 bil. (f.o.b., 1992 est.); 97% petroleum and natural gas. **Imports:** $9 bil. (f.o.b., 1993 est.); 39.7% capital goods, 21.7% food, 11.8% consumer goods. **Major trading partners:** ***exports:*** Germany, Spain, Italy, France, U.S.; ***imports:*** 25% France, 8% Italy, 8% Germany, 6% U.S.

Intl. Orgs. Arab League, FAO, G-77, IAEA, IBRD, ICAO, IDA, IFAD, ILO, IMF, IMO, INTELSAT, INTERPOL, ITU, NAM, OAU, OPEC, UN, UNESCO, UPU, WHO, WIPO, WMO.

From around 3000 B.C. nomadic ancestors of the Berbers inhabited Algeria, as the expanding Sahara desert displaced prehistoric grasslands and forests. The Phoenicians established trading centers in the Mediterranean coastal plain around 1200 B.C. Those centers were taken over by the Romans beginning around 200 B.C. With Roman support the Berber chief Masinissa formed the kingdom of Numidia in what is now northern Algeria. From 46 B.C. to about A.D. 640, the area was controlled successively by the Romans, Germanic Vandal tribes, and the Byzantine Empire.

In the eighth century A.D., the Islamic conquests spread Arab culture to Numidia. Most of the Berbers converted to Islam. The blend of Berber and Arab culture in Algeria gave rise to a flourishing and rich Islamic civilization in the coastal plain, while Tuareg and other nomadic peoples controlled the sparsely inhabited interior.

Around 1500 the Christian kingdom of Spain captured Algiers and other coastal cities. In 1518 Barbarossa, a Turkish sea captain, captured Algiers and drove the Spanish out. In so doing, he joined Algeria to the expanding Turkish Ottoman Empire. Piracy became a key source of income for the Ottoman cities of Algeria. In the early 1800s, France, along with England and the United States, began military operations to suppress piracy in the Mediterranean. In 1830 France invaded Algeria, putting an end to Ottoman rule and establishing their own administration. Algeria was ruled as part of France itself. Many French settlers *(colons)* migrated to Algeria. Both they and the native Algerians were considered citizens of France, but the colons were granted substantial political and economic advantages over the indigenous population.

In 1847 a rebellion led by Abd-al-Qadir, a powerful Muslim leader, was suppressed by the French, but the spirit of Algerian nationalism remained alive. In 1848, in the wake of the rebellion, all of Algeria was conquered by the French and legally confirmed as an integral part of France. During World War II, many Algerians joined the Free French, hoping that their display of loyalty would be rewarded with greater self-rule after the war. Those hopes were disappointed, as French administration was resumed in 1945.

In 1954 the Front de Liberation Nationale (FLN) began a guerrilla war against the French in Algeria. They were opposed by French police and military forces and by the Secret Army Organization (OAS), an underground movement of colons who favored continued French rule. As the FLN gained strength, by 1958 French premier Charles de Gaulle established a policy designed to prepare Algeria for self-rule.

Algerian independence was proclaimed on July 3, 1962; a million colons fled to France. A power struggle within the new Algerian government was resolved when Ahmed Ben Bella became the country's first premier in 1963. In 1965 Ben Bella was deposed by Col. Houari Boumidienne, who ruled as the head of a military government. In 1967 Algeria declared war on Israel, broke with the West, and established close relations with the USSR. Since the early 1970s, relations with the West, and particularly with France, have improved, but Algeria remains a member of the hard-line anti-Israel block of the Arab League.

Algeria's economic mainstay is petroleum. Despite attempts at industrialization (steel, textiles, fertilizer, plastics, light manufacturing), the economy is plagued by instability and high unemployment.

The first free, multiparty elections since independence were held on June 12, 1990. The Islamic Salvation Front, which advocates turning Algeria into an Islamic Republic, won overwhelming control of provincial and local assemblies. At the end of 1991 it won 188 seats in Parliament out of 231 up for election and seemed poised to win control of the government when the army interceded to keep the old power structure in place. On June 19, 1992, Pres. Mohammed Boudiaf was assassinated, presumably by Islamic fundamentalists.

Since 1992 the military's High Security Council, knowing the Islamic parties would win any free election, has repeatedly postponed a return to democracy. In January 1994 the High Security Council replaced the collective presidency of the High State Council with Gen. Lamine Zeroual. The death toll since January 1992, in what has become more and more obviously a civil war, is estimated to be as high as 30,000.

Andorra

Principality of Andorra

Geography **Location:** Pyrenees Mountains, southwestern Europe. **Boundaries:** France to N and E, Spain to S and W. **Total land area:** 174 sq. mi. (450 sq km). **Coastline:** none. **Comparative area:** slightly more than 2.5 times size of Washington, D.C. **Land use:** 2% arable land; 0% permanent crops; 56% meadows and pastures; 22% forest and woodland; 20% other. **Major cities:** (1989) Andorra la Vella (capital) 19,566.

People **Population:** 63,930 (1994 est.). **Nationality:** noun—Andorran(s); adjective—Andorran. **Ethnic groups:** Catalan stock; 61% Spanish, 30% Andorran, 6% French, 3% other. **Languages:** Catalan (official); many also speak some French and Castilian. **Religions:** virtually all Roman Catholic.

Government **Type:** unique co-principality under formal sovereignty of president of France and Spanish bishop of Seo de Urgel, who are represented locally by officials called verguers. **Independence:** N.A. **Constitution:** March 1993. **National holiday:** N.A. **Heads of government:** French co-prince François Mitterrand, president of France (since 1981) and Spanish Episcopal co-prince Msgr. Joan Marti Alanís, bishop of Seo de Urgel, Spain (since 1971); Don Marc Forne Molne, prime minister (since Dec. 1994). **Structure:** legislative—General Council of the Valleys (28 members); executive—syndic (manager) and deputy subsyndic chosen by General Council; judiciary—chosen by co-princes, who appoint two civil judges, judge of appeals, and two battles (court prosecutors); final appeal to Supreme Court of Andorra at Perpignan, France, or to Ecclesiastical Court of bishop of Seo de Urgel, Spain.

Economy **Monetary unit:** French franc and Spanish peseta. **Budget:** N.A. **GDP:** $760 mil., $14,000 per capita (1992 est.). **Chief crops:** sheep raising; small quantities of tobacco, rye, wheat, barley, oats, and some vegetables. **Livestock:** N.A. **Natural resources:** hydropower, mineral water, timber, iron ore, lead. **Major industries:** tourism (particularly skiing), sheep, timber, tobacco, smuggling, banking. **Labor force:** largely shepherds and farmers. **Exports:** $30 mil. (f.o.b., 1993 est.). **Imports:** N.A. **Major trading partners:** France, Spain.

Intl. Orgs. UN, UNESCO.

Set high in the Pyrenees, the tiny state of Andorra has been both a medieval relic and a modern capitalist land. Since 1278 Andorra has owed feudal allegiance to two co-rulers, the bishop of Seo de Urgel in Spain and, now, the president of France. Until 1993, Andorra had no constitution, so the exact rights of the co-rulers remained vague. Foreign affairs were handled by France.

Andorra has no customs department and no registration or regulation of businesses. Its traditional economic mainstay had been the "transshipment of goods" (i.e., smuggling) between France and Spain. Andorra attracts tourists drawn by bargain shopping, and it is a banking center. These activities have fueled a seemingly endless economic boom in the postwar period. However, Spain's 1986 entry into the EC led Andorra to seek a customs union with the EC. The March 1990 treaty was Andorra's first in over 700 years. In the same year, the co-princes introduced Andorra's first penal code and a sales tax, soon followed by the adoption of the EC's external tariff. In March 1993 voters—of whom there are only 9,123—adopted a modern constitution that will reduce the power of the co-princes and establish a government of three branches that will have authority to tax and to make foreign policy.

Angola

People's Republic of Angola

Geography **Location:** southwestern Africa. **Boundaries:** Zaire to N and NE, Zambia to E, Namibia to S, South Atlantic Ocean to W; Cabinda district separated from rest of country by Congo to N, Zaire to S. **Total land area:** 481,352 sq. mi. (1,246,700 sq km). **Coastline:** 994 mi. (1,600 km). **Comparative area:** slightly less than twice size of Texas. **Land use:** 2% arable land; negl. % permanent crops; 23% meadows and pastures; 43% forest and woodland; 32% other. **Major cities:** Luanda (capital) 1,200,000 (1982 est.); Huambo (Nova Lisboa) 61,885; Lobito 59,258; Benguela 40,996; Lubango (São da Bandeira) 31,674 (1970 census).

People **Population:** 9,803,576 (1994 est.). **Nationality:** noun—Angolan(s); adjective—Angolan. **Ethnic groups:** 37% Ovimbundu, 25% Kimbundu, 13% Bakongo, 2% Mestiço, 1% European, 22% other. **Languages:** Portuguese (official), various Bantu dialects. **Religions:** 38% Roman Catholic, 47% indigenous beliefs, 15% Protestant.

Government **Type:** multiparty democracy. **Independence:** Nov. 11, 1975 (from Portugal). **Constitution:** Nov. 11, 1975. **National holiday:** Independence Day, Nov. 11. **Heads of government:** José Eduardo dos Santos, president (since Sept. 1979); Marcolino Moco, prime minister (since Dec. 1982). **Structure:** legislative—National People's Assembly; official party is supreme political institution.

Economy **Monetary unit:** kwanza. **Budget:** (1992 est.) ***income:*** $928 mil.; ***expend.:*** $2.5 bil. **GDP:** $5.7 bil. (1993 est.), $600 per capita. **Chief crops:** cash crops—coffee, sisal, corn, cotton, sugar; food crops—cassava, corn, vegetables, plantains, bananas, and other local foodstuffs; disruptions caused by civil war require food imports. **Livestock:** cattle, goats, pigs, sheep. **Natural resources:** petroleum, diamonds, iron ore, phosphates, copper. **Major industries:** petroleum, mining (phosphate rock, diamonds), fish processing. **Labor force:** 2.8 mil. (1985 est.); 85% agriculture, 15% industry. **Exports:** $3 bil. (f.o.b., 1993 est.); oil, coffee, diamonds, sisal, fish and fish products. **Imports:** $1.6 bil. (f.o.b., 1992 est.); capital equipment (machinery, electrical equipment), food, vehicles and spare parts, textiles and clothing, medicines; substantial military deliveries. **Major trading partners:** U.S., Portugal, Brazil, France, Spain.

Intl. Orgs. FAO, G-77, ICAO, IFAD, ILO, IMO, INTELSAT, NAM, OAU, IMF, UN, UNESCO, UPU, WHO, WMO.

Bantu peoples have occupied Angola for at least 2,000 years. Portuguese explorers searching for a sea route to India founded Luanda (1575) and Benguela (1617). Portugal, at first in alliance with the north Angolan kingdom of Bakongo, engaged in an extensive trade of slaves to Brazil—3 million in 300 years.

In the late 19th century, Angola was organized as a Portuguese colony, sometimes called Portuguese West Africa. Portuguese settlers dominated local government, trade, and small-scale industry in addition to organizing plantation-style cultivation of cotton, palm oil, bananas, and coffee. A railroad was built to transport exports of metal from the Katanga region of the Belgian Congo (now Zaire) to the coast.

By the 1950s non-Portuguese Angolans began to agitate for independence. The National Front spearheaded the liberation movement. Guerrilla warfare began in 1961, with several feuding factions fighting the Portuguese. Following the Portuguese revolution of 1974, factional warfare intensified and most Portuguese settlers fled the country, leaving it seriously lacking in trained administrative and commercial personnel. Independence came on Nov. 11, 1975.

Civil war between the National Front, the Popular Movement for the Liberation of Angola (MPLA), and the National Union for the Total Independence of Angola (UNITA) led, in 1976, to the victory of the MPLA, which organized a Marxist state with Soviet backing and Cuban technical support including 37,000 soldiers. Large portions of the country remained in the hands of UNITA, which continued the civil war with Chinese and American support through the 1980s.

Direct clashes between Angolan and South African troops occurred during the 1980s, as Angola gave shelter to SWAPO guerrilla forces seeking independence for Namibia. Cuban troops withdrew from Angola between January 1989 and May 1991, and a cease-fire between the government and UNITA was also concluded in May 1991. While agreeing to recognize the dos Santos government in the interim, UNITA called for elections to be held by September 1992, Angola's first since 1975.

In the elections, José Eduardo dos Santos defeated Jonas Savimbi 51 percent to 39 percent, and in the 223-seat legislature, the MPLA beat UNITA by 58 percent to 33 percent. Savimbi's refusal to honor the results, in which 90 percent of the electorate voted, led to renewed fighting. By September 1993, an estimated 50,000 people had died in the 17-year-old civil war, and the government lost control of several cities, including the oil-refining center of Soyo; there were also millions of refugees and about 1.5 million people at risk of starvation.

Sporadic but often intense fighting continued in 1994 even as peace talks were being held in Lusaka, Zambia. A series of successful government offensives in the latter part of 1994 preceded the dramatic signing on Nov. 20 of a peace treaty between the government and UNITA. Unlike the failed treaties of 1989 and 1991, the current agreement guarantees UNITA some share in government at both national and local levels while assimilating its forces into the Angolan army. A large (7,000) UN peacekeeping force was approved unanimously by the General Assembly in February.

Antigua and Barbuda

Geography Location: eastern Caribbean Sea approximately 300 mi. (480 km) SE of Puerto Rico. Antigua 17°06'N, 61°50'W; Barbuda 17°38'N, 61°48'W. **Boundaries:** Atlantic Ocean to N and E, Caribbean Sea to S and W. **Total land area:** 170 sq. mi. (440 sq km). **Coastline:** 95 mi. (153 km). **Comparative area:** slightly less than 2.5 times size of Washington, D.C. **Land use:** 18% arable land; 0% permanent crops; 7% meadows and pastures; 16% forest and woodland; 59% other; includes N.A. % irrigated. **Major cities:** (1986 est.) St. John's (capital) 36,000.

People Population: 64,762 (1994 est.). **Nationality:** noun—Antiguan(s); adjective—Antiguan. **Ethnic groups:** almost entirely of black African origin; some of British, Portuguese, Lebanese, and Syrian origin. **Languages:** English (official), local dialects. **Religions:** Anglican (predominant), other Protestant sects, some Roman Catholic.

Government Type: independent state recognizing Elizabeth II as chief of state. **Independence:** Nov. 1, 1981 (from UK). **Constitution:** Nov. 1, 1981. **National holiday:** Nov. 1. **Heads of government:** Dr. James B. Carlisle, governor-general (since June 1993); Lester B. Bird, prime minister (since Mar. 1994). **Structure:** executive—prime minister and cabinet; bicameral legislature—17-member popularly elected House of Representatives and 17-member Senate; judiciary—court of appeals.

Economy Monetary unit: East Caribbean (EC) dollar. **Budget:** (1991 est.) ***income:*** $105 mil.; ***expend.:*** $161 mil. **GDP:** $368.5 mil., $5,800 per capita (1993 est.). **Chief crops:** cotton (main crop), sugar. **Livestock:** cattle, sheep, goats, pigs. **Natural resources:** negl.; pleasant climate fosters tourism. **Major industries:** tourism, construction, light manufacturing (clothing, alcohol, household appliances). **Labor force:** 30,000 (1983); 82% commerce and services, 11% agriculture, 7% industry; 20% unemployment (1983). **Exports:** $54.7 mil. (f.o.b., 1992); 48% petroleum products, 23% manufactures, 4% food and live animals, 4% machinery and transportation equipment. **Imports:** $260.9 mil. (c.i.f., 1992); food and live animals, machinery and transport equipment, manufactures, chemicals. **Major trading partners:** ***exports:*** 26% OECS, 15% Barbados, 4% Guyana, 3% U.S., 2% Trinidad and Tobago; ***imports:*** 27% U.S., 16% UK, 3% OECS, 50% other.

Intl. Orgs. Commonwealth, FAO, G-77, IBRD, ICAO, ILO, IMF, OAS, UN, UNESCO, WHO, WMO.

Columbus visited and claimed Antigua for Spain in 1493. It was settled by the British in 1632, who grew tobacco, and later sugar. The island's economy was hobbled by abolition of slavery in 1834, a succession of natural disasters in the 1840s, and the closing of the Royal Dockyard in 1854. Today, tourism is a mainstay of the economy. Residents of Barbuda have been intent on severing political relations between the two islands as a result of cultural and political differences with Antiguans.

Argentina

Argentine Republic

Geography Location: southern South America. **Boundaries:** Bolivia, Paraguay, Brazil to N.; Uruguay, South Atlantic Ocean to E.; Chile to W. **Total land area:** 1,068,298 sq. mi. (2,766,890 sq km) (figures exclude Falkland Islands and Antarctic territory claimed by Argentina). **Coastline:** 3,099 mi. (4,986 km). **Comparative area:** slightly less than three-tenths the size of the United States. **Land use:** 9% arable land; 4% permanent crops; 52% meadows and pastures; 22% forest and woodland; 13% other; includes 1% irrigated. **Major cities:** (1991 census) Buenos Aires (capital) 12,960,976; Córdoba 1,148,305; La Matanza 1,111,811; Rosario 894,645; Morón 641,541.

People Population: 33,912,994 (1994 est.). **Nationality:** noun—Argentine(s); adjective—Argentine. **Ethnic groups:** 85% white, 15% mestizo, Indian, and other nonwhite groups. **Languages:** Spanish (official), English, Italian, German, French. **Religions:** 90% nominally Roman Catholic (less than 20% practicing), 2% Protestant, 2% Jewish, 6% other.

Government Type: republic. **Independence:** July 9, 1816 (from Spain). **Constitution:** May 1, 1853. **National holiday:** Independence Day, May 25. **Head of government:** Carlos Saúl Menem, president (since July 1989). **Structure:** executive (president, vice president, cabinet); legislative (National Congress—Senate, Chamber of Deputies); national judiciary.

Economy Monetary unit: austral. **Budget:** (1992 est.) ***income:*** $33.1 bil.; ***expend.:*** $35.8 bil. **GDP:** $185 bil. (1993 est.), $5,500 per capita. **Chief crops:** cereals, oilseed, livestock products; major world exporter of temperate-zone foodstuffs. **Livestock:** cattle, sheep, pigs, horses, goats. **Natural resources:** fertile plains of the pampas, lead, zinc, copper. **Major industries:** food processing (especially meat packing), motor vehicles, consumer durables. **Labor force:** 10.9 mil. (1985 est.); 57% services, 31% industry, 12% agriculture; 6.5% unemployment (1988 est.). **Exports:** $12.7 bil. (f.o.b., 1993 est.); meat, wheat, corn, oilseed, hides. **Imports:** $16 bil. (c.i.f., 1993 est.); machinery and equipment, chemicals, metals, fuel, lubricants. **Major trading partners:** ***exports:*** 12% U.S., Italy, Brazil, Japan;

imports: 22% U.S., Brazil, Germany, Bolivia, Japan, Italy, Netherlands.

Intl. Orgs. FAO, G-77, IAEA, IBRD, ICAO, IDA, IFAD, IFC, ILO, IMF, IMO, INTELSAT, INTERPOL, ITU, NAM, OAS, UN, UNESCO, UPU, WHO, WMO, WTO.

The indigenous nomads of the area around the river La Plata resisted Spanish intrusion, which began with the first founding of Buenos Aires by Pedro de Mendoza in 1536. Argentina was part of Spain's Viceroyalty of Peru until reforms in the Bourbon dynasty and a need to defend against Portuguese encroachment from Brazil led to the formation of the Viceroyalty of La Plata, including Argentina, Bolivia, Paraguay, and Uruguay, in 1776. Following the relaxation of trade restrictions two years later, Buenos Aires grew from a small town to a city of 50,000 by 1800. A provisional junta of the Provinces of Río de la Plata was established in 1810 after the Napoleonic occupation of Spain, and in 1816 the United Provinces of the Río de la Plata declared their independence.

After independence the question of political relations among the United Provinces was settled by a federalist solution in which the provinces dissolved into a number of practically independent republics. In 1824, a constituent assembly created the office of president, first held by Bernardino Rivadavia. However, the failure to ratify a workable constitution caused Rivadavia to resign.

Juan Manuel de Rosas became governor of Buenos Aires in 1829 and presided over the construction of a federal agreement between the provinces in 1831. Rosas governed Buenos Aires with an iron hand until his expulsion in 1852. The other provinces formed the Argentine Federation, based on a federal constitution of 1853, but Buenos Aires refused to join. Buenos Aires and the Argentine Federation entered into war between 1859 and 1861; they reached an agreement on the inclusion of Buenos Aires in the Argentine Republic in 1862.

Argentina joined Brazil and Uruguay in a war (1865–70) against Paraguay. During the latter part of the 1870s, the government took the initiative against the indigenous populations of Patagonia and Tierra del Fuego, which were partitioned with Chile. Immigration from Europe, especially Spain and Italy, resulted in enormous growth from the mid-19th century. In 1869, there were 2 million inhabitants; by 1914, 8 million; by 1955, 19 million; and by 1990, 32 million. Prior to World War II, Argentina was acutely Eurocentric, with an eye to British finance and French culture; this has changed since.

The Argentine military, led by Lt. Gen. José F. Uriburu, ousted the civilian government of the Radical party in 1930 with the intention of following the European model of politics. In 1946 Juan Domingo Perón won the presidential election and constructed a populist political alliance that included workers, industrialists, and the armed forces. The Perón-inspired populist ideology of *justicialismo* included extension of the franchise to women and redistribution of income to workers and the poor. The activities of Perón's charismatic wife, Eva, bolstered *justicialismo* through her effort to distribute goods to the poor through the Social Aid Foundation.

Tied in with Perón's populist strategy was his policy of nationalist economic development, whereby state-led development was financed through extraction of capital from the old export-agricultural elite and politically supported through populism. The Perón government incurred great expense to gain control over foreign-owned economic infrastructure, including railway systems, telephone companies, and dock facilities. A number of events led to Perón's downfall in 1955. The market for Argentine goods deteriorated after World War II. As Perón shifted his strategy to encourage foreign investment and impose economic austerity, repression against the political opposition grew. The death of Eva Perón in 1952 robbed Perón of an important political resource, and when the government challenged the Catholic church on a number of issues, the military ousted Perón.

After a brief period of military rule, in which an attempt was made to roll back "Perónismo," Arturo Frondizi of the "Intransigent" faction of the Radical party won the presidency and assumed office in 1958. In the following years, the military repeatedly attempted to keep the Perónistas from returning to power. In 1962 the military forced Frondizi to annul Perónist victories in provincial elections and removed him from office. Pres. Arturo Illia was ousted from office in 1966 for the same reason: his failure to tame Perón's followers.

A military bureaucratic authoritarian regime led by a series of Argentine officers was established during 1966–73. Extreme violence by factions on the Left and Right led the military to accept Perón's return to the presidency in 1973. Perón died the following year, and his third wife, Isabel, replaced him in office; she was unable to retain power, and the military removed her in 1976 in the midst of economic and political upheaval.

Determined to deal with what they saw as a leftist threat, the military again opted for a bureaucratic authoritarian solution. As part of this "solution," the armed forces launched what was later called the "dirty war" against leftists, during which up to 20,000 people disappeared and were never heard from again. The authoritarian government collapsed after the ill-starred 1982 Falkland/Malvinas Islands War against Britain led to the resignation of the junta and the holding of elections. Raúl Alfonsín, of the Radical Union party, was elected president in the wake of these events in 1983. In 1989, he was succeeded by Carlos Saúl Menem, who agreed to take office early, in the midst of a severe economic crisis during which inflation reached 3,000 percent and foreign debt $58 billion.

Menem encouraged free enterprise and good relations with the United States. Government controls on foreign investment and trade were relaxed, and the government sold off many state enterprises. In 1993 Argentina's 11-year debt crisis officially ended, and by 1995 inflation was down to 4 percent. Economic hardships caused by Menem's reforms probably led to the Perónists' relatively poor showing (38%) in elections (Apr. 1994) to the Constituent Assembly, but they appeared to have enough votes to influence the rewriting of the 141-year-old constitution.

In early 1995 the government unveiled its austerity plan to fight the budget deficit and its financial plan to cushion the shocks of Mexico's devaluation. In May, Menem was reelected with just under 50 percent of the vote, while his party carried majorities in both houses of the legislature and won control of more than half of Argentina's provincial governments.

Armenia

Republic of Armenia

Geography **Location:** southwest Transcaucasia between Europe and Asia. **Boundaries:** Georgia to N, Azerbaijan to E, Iran to S, Turkey to W. Nakhichevan Autonomous Republic, an Azerbaijan territory, is an enclave within Armenian territory. **Total land area:** 11,506 sq. mi. (29,800 sq km). **Coastline:** none. **Comparative area:** slightly larger than Maryland. **Land use:** 18% cropland; 23% permanent pasture; 12% forest and woodland; 47% other (mostly urban). **Major cities:** (1990 est.) Yerevan (capital) 1,202,000; Kumayri (formerly Leninakan) 123,000; Kirovakan 76,000.

People **Population:** 3,521,517 (1994 est.). **Nationality:** noun—Armenian(s); adjective—Armenian. **Ethnic groups:** 93% Armenian, 1.7% Kurd, 1.5% Russian. **Languages:** Armenian (official), sole member of a distinct Indo-European language group written in Armenian script; Russian, Kurdish, Azerbaijani. **Religions:** Christianity—Armenian Apostolic, Russian Orthodox, Protestant; Islam.

Government **Type:** republic. **Independence:** Sept. 23, 1991 (from USSR). **Constitution:** being drafted. **National holiday:** Sept. 21. **Heads of government:** Levon Ter-Petrossian, president (since Nov. 1991); Hrant Bagratian, prime minister, vice president, and chairman of Council of Ministers (since Feb. 1993). **Structure:** executive—president, vice president, Council of Ministers; legislative—Supreme Council (260 deputies); judicial—Supreme Court.

Economy **Monetary unit:** teram. **Budget:** N.A. ***income:*** N.A.; ***expend:*** N.A. **GDP:** $7.1 bil., $2,040 per capita. **Chief crops:** wine grapes, tobacco, vegetables, melons. **Livestock:** chickens, sheep, cattle, pigs. **Natural resources:** N.A. **Major industries:** nonferrous metallurgy, electrical equipment, instruments, machinery, computers. **Labor force:** 1.578 mil. (1992). **Exports:** $31 mil. outside the former USSR (f.o.b., 1993); machinery, transport equipment, ferrous and nonferrous metals, chemicals. **Imports:** $87 mil. outside the former USSR (c.i.f., 1993); machinery, energy, consumer goods. **Major trading partners:** N.A.

Intl. Orgs. CIS, IMF, OSCE, UN, UNCTAD, UNESCO, WHO, World Bank.

Armenia, a small landlocked country just south of the great Caucasus mountain range, is but a fragment of ancient Armenia, one of the world's oldest civilizations dating back to the sixth century B.C. In about A.D. 300, Armenia adopted Christianity, which today is still an important component of Armenian national identity. Because Armenia forms part of a land bridge between the Black and the Caspian Seas, and between Turks and Slavs, it has long been overrun and controlled by the Byzantine, Arab, Ottoman, Mongol, and Russian Empires. In 1236 the Tatar and Mongol invasion spelled the end of Armenia as a separate state. In 1639, after the conclusion of a major war between Turkey and Iran, the territory of Armenia was partitioned. By the end of the 17th century, czarist Russia was also involved in Armenia, and in 1828 eastern Armenia was ceded to the Russian empire by the Treaty of Turkmenchai.

During the First World War, those Armenians living in the western part of the country under Ottoman rule were increasingly subjected to persecution by the Turks. In April 1915, the Turks forcibly removed the Armenians from the border area, during which more than a million of them either starved or were killed. In 1918, an Armenian republic emerged as the Russian empire collapsed, but this entity was short-lived, as Turkey, Russia, and later Britain fought for control. Finally, the Soviet Red Army moved into the territory and on Nov. 29, 1920, declared it a Soviet republic. Armenia was made part of the Transcaucasian Soviet Federal Socialist Republic of the USSR in 1922, and in 1936, it became one of the Soviet Union's constituent union republics.

Armenian Christians have been subjected to many years of persecution by its various invaders, which caused great numbers of Armenians to live in diaspora throughout the world but especially in the United States and Europe, and which played an important role in developing the modern Armenian identity. In one sense, Armenia is fortunate, for it has the help of the large diaspora community to help it through the difficult times it is experiencing now. Armenia's most pressing issue is the war over Nagorno-Karabakh, the Armenian Christian enclave of Muslim Azerbaijan, and this crisis is hindering the functioning of the economy. Fighting broke out in 1988, with 180,000 ethnic Armenians in Azerbaijan demanding their homeland become part of Armenia. That same year, Armenia was rocked by severe earthquakes that killed thousands, and supplies from both the Soviet Union and the West were blocked by Azeris fighting the Armenians in Nagorno-Karabakh.

Fighting in the region continued even as both nations declared their independence from the Soviet Union (Armenia on Sept. 23, 1991; Azerbaijan a month later). In October 1991, Lovon Ter-Petrossian was elected president, and independent Armenia once again came into being. On Dec. 21, 1991, Armenia was one of 11 former USSR republics that signed the Alma-Ata Declaration that created the Commonwealth of Independent States. Since independence, however, Armenia's economy has remained stagnant while the government and the people remain committed to the war over Nagorno-Karabakh.

Australia

Commonwealth of Australia

Geography Location: continent of Australia, between Indian and Pacific Oceans. **Boundaries:** nearest neighbor is Papua New Guinea, to N. **Total land area:** 2,967,897 sq. mi. (7,686,850 sq km). **Coastline:** 16,010 mi. (25,760 km). **Comparative area:** slightly smaller than U.S. **Land use:** 6% arable land; negl. % permanent crops; 58% meadows and pastures; 14% forest and woodland; 22% other; includes negl. % irrigated. **Major cities:** (1993 est.) Canberra (capital) 325,400; Sydney 3,719,000; Melbourne 3,187,500; Brisbane 1,421,700; Perth 1,221,300.

People Population: 18,077,419 (1994 est.). **Nationality:** noun—Australian(s); adjective—Australian. **Ethnic groups:** 95% Caucasian, 4% Asian, 1% aboriginal and other. **Languages:** English, native langs. **Religions:** 26.1% Anglican, 26.0% Roman Catholic, 24.3% other Christian.

Government Type: federal parliamentary state recognizing Elizabeth II as sovereign or head of state. **Independence:** Jan. 1, 1901 (from federation of UK colonies). **Constitution:** July 9, 1900; effective Jan. 1, 1901. **National holiday:** Australia Day, Jan. 26. **Heads of government:** William G. Hayden, governor general (since Feb. 1989); Paul Keating, prime minister (since Dec. 1991). **Structure:** prime minister and cabinet responsible to House; bicameral legislature (Federal Parliament—Senate and House of Representatives); independent judiciary.

Economy Monetary unit: Australian dollar. **Budget:** (1993) ***income:*** $71.9 bil.; ***expend.:*** $83.1 bil. **GDP:** $339.7 bil. (1993), $19,100 per capita. **Chief crops:** large areas devoted to grazing; 60% of area used for crops is planted in wheat; major products—wool, lamb, beef, wheat, fruits; self-sufficient in food. **Livestock:** sheep, cattle, pigs. **Natural resources:** bauxite, coal, iron ore, copper, tin. **Major industries:** mining, industrial and transportation equipment, food processing. **Labor force:** 8.63 mil. (1991); 33.8% finance and services, 22.3% public and community services, 20.1% wholesale and retail trade, 16.2% manufacturing and industry, 6.9% unemployment rate (1988). **Exports:** $44 bil. (f.o.b., 1992); wheat, barley, beef, lamb, dairy products. **Imports:** $43.6 bil. (f.o.b., 1992); manufactured raw materials, capital equipment, consumer goods. **Major trading partners:** ***exports:*** 23% U.S., 18% Japan, 6% New Zealand, 4% S. Korea, 4% Singapore; ***imports:*** 24% U.S., 19% Japan, 7% Germany, 6% UK, 4% New Zealand.

Intl. Orgs. Colombo Plan, Commonwealth, FAO, IAEA, IBRD, ICAO, IDA, IFAD, IFC, ILO, IMF, IMO, INTELSAT, INTERPOL, ITU, OECD, UN, UNESCO, UPU, WHO, WIPO, WMO, WTO.

The continent-nation of Australia is distinguished by its geographical isolation and by the unique flora and fauna which that isolation has fostered. The ancestors of today's aborigines arrived from Southeast Asia as much as 40,000 years ago. Thereafter, aborigine culture evolved in isolation except for some contact between the peoples of the northern coast and New Guinea. Australia was first sighted by Europeans at the beginning of the 17th century. In the 18th century, it was visited by the Dutch, who named it New Holland. The eastern coast was systematically explored in 1770 by Capt. James Cook, who claimed it for Great Britain.

British settlement began in 1788, with the landing of about 700 convicts near Sydney. Australia remained a penal colony during the first half of the 19th century, during which time the continent was explored and separate colonies were established. Aboriginal populations were displaced and in some areas (most notably the island Tasmania) they were totally exterminated. Discovery of gold in Victoria in 1851 created a gold rush that greatly accelerated immigration. By the end of the 19th century, the three mainstays of the Australian economy—livestock (beef and sheep), mining, and wheat growing—were firmly established.

In 1901, a commonwealth was established consisting of a confederation of the various states except for the Northern Territory, which was added in 1911. The British Crown is represented by an appointed governor-general; the national government is a parliamentary system, but much local authority resides in the separate states. Comprehensive social welfare legislation was passed by the state and national governments soon after the commonwealth's formation. The population is highly educated and enjoys a generally high standard of living, but most aborigines are detribalized and live in considerable poverty.

Australian troops fought with distinction in both world wars. A Japanese threat to Australia in 1942 was averted by Allied victory in the Battle of the Coral Sea. Australia and the United States are firm allies, and Australian troops joined U.S. forces in Korea, Vietnam, and the Persian Gulf War. Australia administers several external island groups and claims territory in Antarctica. (See "Territories of the World.")

The abandonment of discriminatory immigration practices in 1973 led to a new wave of immigration, particularly from Asia. In the process Australian economic ties to Asia and the Pacific Rim have expanded considerably. New exploitation of mineral resources has in many cases been accomplished with Japanese investment or with long-term export contracts to Japan. Australia has undergone considerable industrial development in the past two decades. However, once the richest nation in the world in per capita GNP, it is no longer even in the top 10.

After ten years in office, Prime Minister Bob Hawke was ousted as Labour party leader (and

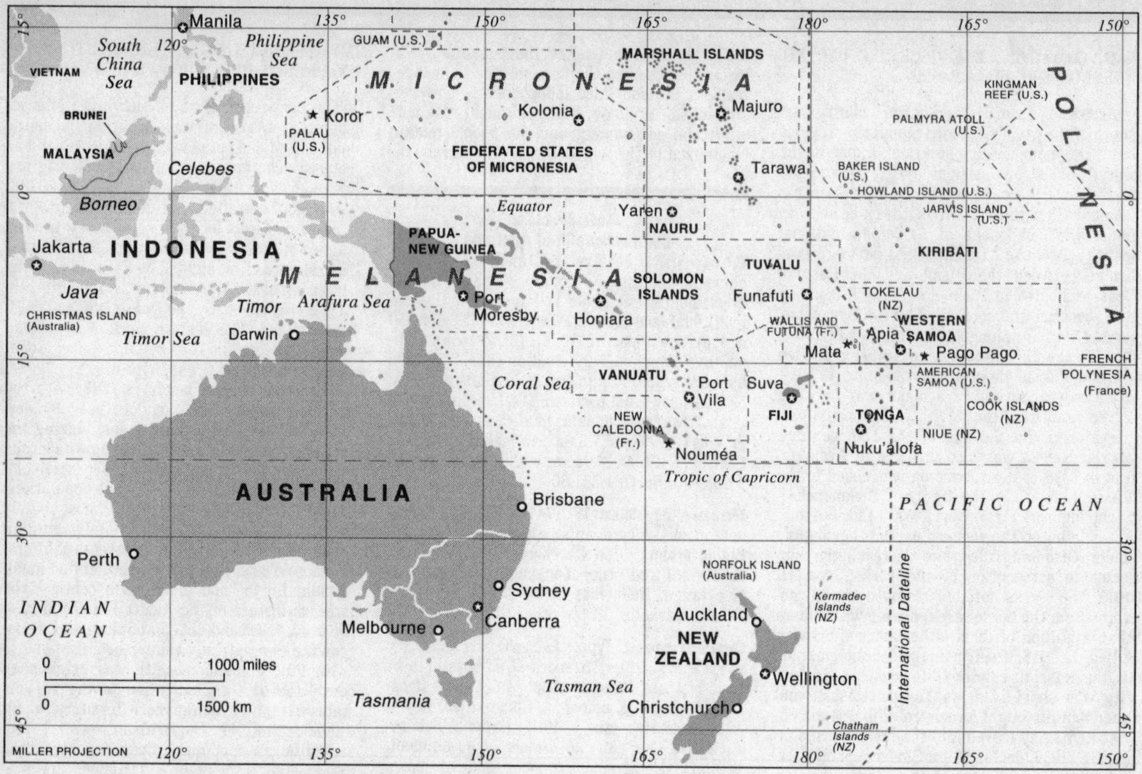

Manila
South China Sea
120°
135°
150°
165°
180°
165°
150°
15°
0°
30°
45°
Philippine Sea
GUAM (U.S.)
MARSHALL ISLANDS
VIETNAM
PHILIPPINES
MICRONESIA
KINGMAN REEF (U.S.)
POLYNESIA
BRUNEI
Koror
PALAU (U.S.)
Kolonia
Majuro
PALMYRA ATOLL (U.S.)
MALAYSIA
Celebes
FEDERATED STATES OF MICRONESIA
Tarawa
BAKER ISLAND (U.S.)
HOWLAND ISLAND (U.S.)
Borneo
Equator
Yaren
NAURU
JARVIS ISLAND (U.S.)
Jakarta
INDONESIA
PAPUA-NEW GUINEA
KIRIBATI
MELANESIA
SOLOMON ISLANDS
TUVALU
Java
Timor
Arafura Sea
Port Moresby
Honiara
Funafuti
TOKELAU (NZ)
CHRISTMAS ISLAND (Australia)
WALLIS AND FUTUNA (Fr.)
WESTERN SAMOA
Apia
Timor Sea
Darwin
Mata
Pago Pago
AMERICAN SAMOA (U.S.)
FRENCH POLYNESIA (France)
Coral Sea
VANUATU
Port Vila
Suva
FIJI
COOK ISLANDS (NZ)
NEW CALEDONIA (Fr.)
Nouméa
TONGA
Nuku'alofa
NIUE (NZ)
Tropic of Capricorn
AUSTRALIA
Brisbane
PACIFIC OCEAN
Perth
NORFOLK ISLAND (Australia)
Kermadec Islands (NZ)
International Dateline
Sydney
INDIAN OCEAN
Canberra
Auckland
Melbourne
NEW ZEALAND
Wellington
0
1000 miles
0
1500 km
Tasman Sea
Tasmania
Christchurch
Chatham Islands (NZ)
MILLER PROJECTION

INDONESIA
Arafura Sea
Darwin
Gulf of Carpentaria
Great Barrier Reef
Coral Sea
Timor Sea
NORTHERN TERRITORY
Great Sandy Desert
AUSTRALIA
Great Dividing Range
Hamersley Range
Gibson Desert
Alice Springs
QUEENSLAND
Great Artesian Basin
WESTERN AUSTRALIA
SOUTH AUSTRALIA
Lake Eyre
Brisbane
Great Victoria Desert
Nullarbor Plain
Lake Gairdner
Lake Torrens
Darling R.
Perth
Great Australian Bight
NEW SOUTH WALES
Adelaide
Murray R.
Sydney
INDIAN OCEAN
Canberra
VICTORIA
Melbourne
Bass Strait
Tasman Sea
0
400 miles
0
600 km
LAMBERT'S AZIMUTHAL EQUAL-AREA PROJECTION
TASMANIA
Hobart

PACIFIC OCEAN
NORTH ISLAND
Auckland
Hamilton
Tasman Sea
Palmerston North
Nelson
Wellington
SOUTH ISLAND
SOUTHERN ALPS
Christchurch
NEW ZEALAND
Dunedin
Invercargill
0
200 miles
0
300 km

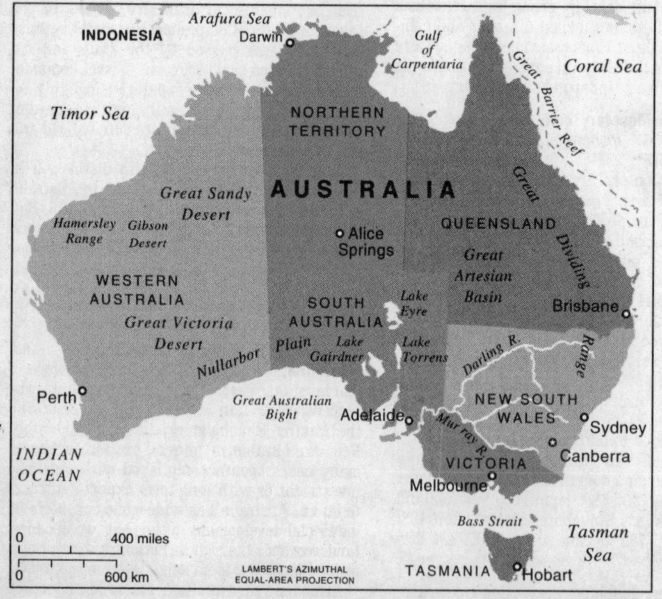

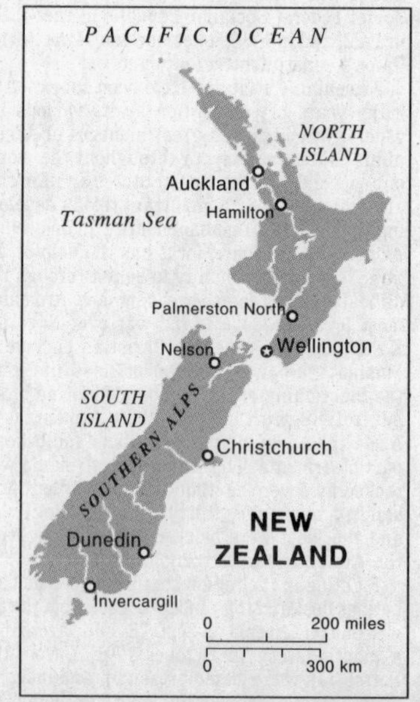

hence as prime minister) in December 1991. He was replaced by Paul Keating. In the March 1993 elections, the Keating Labour government was convincingly reelected despite the persistent economic slump. By early 1995, however, polls showed both the Labour party and Prime Minister Keating at 34 percent.

Austria

Republic of Austria

Geography Location: landlocked country in central Europe. **Boundaries:** Germany and Czech Republic to N, Hungary and Slovak Republic to E, Slovenia and Italy to S, Switzerland and Liechtenstein to W. **Total land area:** 32,377 sq. mi. (83,855 sq km). **Coastline:** none. **Comparative area:** between South Carolina and Maine. **Land use:** 17% arable land; 1% permanent crops; 24% meadows and pastures; 39% forest and woodland; 19% other; includes negl. % irrigated. **Major cities:** (1991 census) Vienna (capital) 1,533,176; Graz 232,155; Linz 202,855; Salzburg 143,971; Innsbruck 114,996.

People Population: 7,954,974 (1994 est.). **Nationality:** noun—Austrian(s); adjective—Austrian. **Ethnic groups:** 99.4% German, 0.3% Croatian, 0.2% Slovene, 0.1% other. **Languages:** German. **Religions:** 85% Roman Catholic, 6% Protestant, 9% none or other.

Government Type: federal republic. **Constitution:** 1920; revised 1929; reinstated Dec. 1945. **National holiday:** Oct. 26. **Heads of government:** Thomas Klestil, president (since July 1992); Franz Vranitzky, chancellor (since June 1986). **Structure:** bicameral legislature (Federal Assembly—Federal Council, National Council); directly elected president whose functions are largely representational; independent federal judiciary.

Economy Monetary unit: schilling. **Budget:** (1993) ***income:*** $52.2 bil.; ***expend.:*** $60.3 bil. **GDP:** $134.4 bil., $17,000 per capita (1993). **Chief crops:** forest products, cereals, potatoes, sugar beets; 84% self-sufficient. **Livestock:** chickens, pigs, cattle, turkeys, sheep. **Natural resources:** iron ore, crude oil, timber, magnesite, aluminum. **Major industries:** foods, iron, steel, machinery. **Labor force:** 3.47 mil. (1989); foreign laborers number 177,840, about 6% of the labor force; 56.4% services, 35.4% industry and crafts; 5.4% unemployment (1988); estimated 200,000 Austrians are employed in other European countries; foreign laborers in Austria number 138,700, about 4.3% of labor force (1984). **Exports:** $39.9 bil. (f.o.b., 1993); machinery, equipment, iron, steel, lumber. **Imports:** $48.5 bil. (f.o.b., 1993); petroleum, foodstuffs, machinery, equipment, vehicles. **Major trading partners: *exports:*** 65.8% EU (39% Germany), 9.1% EFTA, 9% Eastern Europe/former USSR, 2.8% U.S., 1.7% Japan, (1991); ***imports:*** 67.8% EU (43.0% Germany), 6.9% EFTA, 6.0% Eastern Europe/former USSR, 4.8% Japan, 3.9% U.S. (1991).

Intl. Orgs. EFTA, FAO, IAEA, IBRD, ICAO, IDA, IFAD, IFC, ILO, IMF, IMO, INTELSAT, INTERPOL, ITU, OECD, OSCE, UN, UNESCO, UPU, WHO, WIPO, WMO, WTO.

The Celtic tribes in what is now Austria were conquered by Rome under Emperor Augustus. After the fall of Rome, it was overrun by Huns, Lombards, Ostrogoths, and Bavarians. In 788 it was incorporated into the empire of Charlemagne. From the ninth to the 13th century, its territory was divided among a variety of feudal domains. In the late 13th century, Austria was reunited under Rudolph I of Habsburg, whose dynasty became synonymous with Austrian history for the next seven centuries. Rudolph's successors steadily enlarged their domain by conquest and marital diplomacy until, by the reign of Charles V (1500–1558), they ruled not only the Holy Roman Empire, encompassing most of central Europe, but also Spain, the Netherlands, and all of Spain's colonial possessions.

After the reign of Charles V, the Habsburg Empire was split into two branches, one governing Spain, the other the Holy Roman Empire. Habsburg power in Germany declined after the Thirty Years' War (1618–48) but was affirmed in the Danube valley after the defeat of the Turkish siege of Vienna in 1683 and the subsequent reconquest of Hungary from the Turks. The marriage of Maria Teresa to Francis of Lorraine gave rise to the House of Habsburg-Lorraine in 1745. In 1804 the Austrian empire was founded, and two years later, the defunct Holy Roman Empire was abolished. The Ausgleich ("compromise") of 1867 transformed the empire into the Dual Monarchy of Austria-Hungary.

In 1914 the assassination of Archduke Franz Ferdinand, the heir to the Austrian throne, led to the outbreak of World War I, which resulted in a wholesale redrawing of national boundaries in Central Europe. Austria emerged as a small Alpine republic, with about 12 percent of the territory of the old Dual Monarchy. The new republic faced a severe postwar economic crisis, as well as a political stalemate between the Christian Social party and the Social Democratic party, each with the support of about half of the electorate, and each with its own paramilitary organization.

In 1933, as Hitler's National Socialists rose to power in Germany, Austrian Chancellor Engelbert Dollfuss, leader of the Christian Social party, instituted rule by decree and began building a corporate state modeled on Italian fascism. His attempt to disarm the Social Democratic militia led to civil war. The government triumphed, but Dollfuss was assassinated in an attempted coup by Austrian Nazis in July 1934. Hitler finally forced Austrian union with Germany (the Anschluss) in 1938, after which Austria was considered a part of Greater Germany.

Conquered by American and Soviet troops early in 1945, Austria, after World War II, was divided into French, British, American, and Russian zones of occupation, but the occupying powers permitted the formation of a unified national government. A coalition government was formed in November 1945 and recognized by the Western powers in 1946. The occupation ended in 1955 with the signing of the Austrian State Treaty. The four powers withdrew their forces, and Austria pledged itself to a policy of permanent neutrality, with no foreign military alliances or military bases on Austrian territory.

The coalition government continued to 1966, when the People's party under Josef Klaus gained a parliamentary majority. In 1970 the Socialist party under Bruno Kreisky came to power. Socialist dominance continued until 1983, when the Socialists had to form a coalition with the right-wing Freedom party in order to stay in power. Kreisky resigned and was succeeded by Fred Sinowatz.

Since 1987 the "Grand Coalition" of Socialist and People's party ministers has governed Austria under Socialist chancellor Franz Vranitzky. The government has taken cautious steps toward privatizing state-owned enterprises, dramatically cut both corporate and personal taxes, and begun an active role in promoting regional trade with the newly independent states of east-central Europe. Tensions arising from the combination of increasing unemployment and growing immigration of "economic refugees" from eastern Europe and from Asia and Africa has led to some recent worrisome results: amending of Austria's asylum law, consideration of immigration quotas, and the growing electoral strength of the right-wing Freedom party. That growth continued in the October 1994 elections as the Freedom party captured 42 seats, an increase of nine since the 1990 vote.

The Austrian economy, decimated after World War I, has flourished in the post–World War II period under a mild form of socialism and with a boost from the American Marshall Plan. Tourism, a highly developed manufacturing sector, and substantial petroleum reserves have contributed to the country's prosperity. Entering the EU on Jan. 1, 1995, Austria's financial condition was sound enough for immediate entry into the EU's exchange-rate mechanism and common agricultural policy; Austria also joined the Schengen Group, a border-free zone within the EU. More significantly, Austria joined NATO's "Partnership for Peace," a first step away from the neutrality followed since 1955.

Azerbaijan

Republic of Azerbaijan

Geography Location: southern Transcaucasia between Europe and Asia. **Boundaries:** Georgia to NW, Russian Federation to N, Caspian Sea to E, Iran to S, Armenia to SW. Nakhichevan Autonomous Republic (ASSR) is part of Azerbaijan although it is inside Armenian territory. **Total land area:** 33,436 sq. mi. (86,600 sq km). **Coastline:** Caspian Sea. **Comparative area:** about the size of Maine. **Land use:** 16% cropland; 11% forest and woodland; 25% permanent pasture; 48% other. **Major cities:** (1990 est.) Baku (capital) 1,149,000; Gyanja (formerly Kirovabad) 281,000; Sumgait 235,000.

People **Population:** 7,684,456 (1994 est.). **Nationality:** noun—Azerbaijani(s) or Azeri(s); adjective—Azerbaijani. **Ethnic groups:** 82.7% Azerbaijani, 5.6% Armenian, 5.6% Russian, Lezhi, Avar, Ukranian, Tatar, Jewish. **Languages:** Azerbaijani (official), written in Cyrillic script since 1939; Russian, ethnic languages. **Religions:** Muslim—70% Shiite, 30% Sunni; Russian Orthodox, Armenian Apostolic.

Government **Type:** republic. **Independence:** Aug. 30, 1991 (from USSR). **Constitution:** being drafted. **National holiday:** May 28, Independence Day. **Heads of Government:** Heydar Aliyev, president (since Oct. 1993); Suret Husseinov, prime minister (since Aug. 1993). **Structure:** executive—president, vice president, Council of Ministers; legislative—Peoples' National Assembly (50 deputies); judicial—Supreme Court.

Economy **Monetary unit:** manat (since Aug. 1992) and ruble. **Budget:** N.A. ***income:*** N.A.; ***expend.:*** N.A. **GNP:** $15.5 bil. (1993 est.), $2,040 per capita. **Chief crops:** cotton, tea, tobacco, wheat, fruit. **Livestock:** sheep, pigs, cattle. **Natural resources:** petroleum, natural gas, iron ore. **Major industries:** chemical processing, construction, machine building. **Labor force:** 2,789,000 (1990). **Exports:** $355 mil. outside the former USSR (f.o.b., 1993); oil, gas, chemicals, oil-field equipment, textiles, cotton. **Imports:** $240 mil. outside the former USSR (c.i.f., 1993); machinery and parts, consumer durables, foodstuffs, textiles. **Major trading partners:** mostly CIS and European countries.

Intl. Orgs. IMF, OSCE, UN, UNCTAD, World Bank.

The territory of present-day Azerbaijan has been inhabited since Paleolithic times. The name Azerbaijan is derived (via Arabic and Turkish) from Atropates (a vassal of Alexander III of Macedonia), who founded an independent state here in the fourth century B.C. The population of Azerbaijan is approximately seven million, but nearly seven million additional Azeris with the same language and faith live across the border in Iran.

For much of its history, the territory of Azerbaijan, home to an indigenous nomadic people, has been occupied by Persians, Muslim Arabs, Turkic tribes from Mongolia, Ottoman Turks, Mongols, and in the 18th century, Russians. The capital city of Baku was an important outlet on the Volga River–Caspian Sea route; under Peter the Great, the Russians occupied Baku and Derbent, and for a while controlled the Caspian Sea. Command of this territory shifted between Ottomans, Persians, and Russians in the 18th and 19th centuries, with the Russians ultimately establishing military rule by 1828 with the Treaty of Turkmenchai. This treaty ceded the southern half of the country to Persia and the northern half to Russia.

Under the Russians, Azerbaijan became an industrial center and eventually a major oil producer. In 1883 the Russians finished building the Transcaucasian Railway, which linked Baku with the Black Sea coast and central Russia and made Baku one of the most important industrial hubs in the Russian empire. Baku became a revolutionary center around the turn of the century. In 1918 an independent republic was formed, but in 1920 it was overthrown by the Soviet Red Army, and in April 1920 the Azerbaijan Soviet Socialist Republic (SSR) was proclaimed. Two years later, it was joined with the Armenian and Georgian SSRs to form the Transcaucasian Soviet Federal Socialist Republic; in 1936, however, the three again became separate union republics.

While a Soviet republic, the country was industrialized, its agriculture collectivized, and religious persecution was severe.

In January 1990, a series of attacks on Communist party buildings and against Armenians in Azerbaijan precipitated a brutal Soviet Army intervention to restore order. A state of emergency was declared, and the first secretary of the Communist party was fired and replaced by Ayaz Mutalibov. He was elected to the presidency in September 1991. On Oct. 18, 1991, Azerbaijan's Supreme Soviet declared the country's independence. The government of Azerbaijan was one of the few former republics to support the idea of maintaining the USSR and on Dec. 21, 1991, joined 10 other former republics in forming the Commonwealth of Independent States.

After the dissolution of the USSR, Soviet power was diminished in Azerbaijan, and the most important issue became the contested region of Nagorno-Karabakh, which is largely populated with ethnic Armenians but lies within Azerbaijani territory. The conflict over this region began several years before the breakup of the Soviet Union, in February 1988, when the local council of Nagorno-Karabakh unsuccessfully petitioned the Armenian and Azerbaijani Supreme Soviets to transfer the region to Armenia. Since then thousands of people have been killed and wounded over this issue.

After independence, Azerbaijan had problems consolidating its own political future. In early 1992, Pres. Mutalibov was forced from office, and in June Abulfaz Elchibey was elected president. He was driven out by armed rebels after the fighting in Nagorno-Karabakh turned decisively in Armenia's favor. He was replaced by Heydar Aliyev, a former Communist party boss, in 1993. Despite continuance of the Armenian secessionist movement, the government of Pres. Aliyev was able to conclude (Sept. 1994) a $7.4 billion deal with western companies to develop Caspian Sea oil fields and to survive two coup attempts.

Bahamas

Commonwealth of the Bahamas

Geography **Location:** nearly 700 islands in an archipelago that extends 590 mi. (950 km) SE–NW between Florida and Haiti. Nassau 25°05'N, 77°20'W. **Boundaries:** western Atlantic Ocean to N, E, S, and W. **Total land area:** 5,382 sq. mi. (13,940 sq km). **Coastline:** 2,200 mi. (3,542 km). **Comparative area:** slightly larger than Connecticut. **Land use:** 1% arable land; negl. % permanent crops; negl. % meadows and pastures; 32% forest and woodland; 67% other; includes N.A. % irrigated. **Major cities:** (1990) Nassau (capital) 191,542.

People **Population:** 273,055 (1994 est.). **Nationality:** noun—Bahamian(s); adjective—Bahamian. **Ethnic groups:** 85% black, 15% white. **Languages:** English, some Creole among Haitian immigrants. **Religions:** 32% Baptist, 20% Anglican, 19% Roman Catholic; smaller groups of other Protestants, Greek Orthodox, and Jews.

Government **Type:** independent commonwealth recognizing Elizabeth II as chief of state. **Independence:** July 10, 1973 (from UK). **Constitution:** July 10, 1973. **National holiday:** Independence Day, July 10. **Heads of government:** Sir Orville Turnquest, governor-general (since Jan. 1995); Hubert A. Ingraham, prime minister (since Aug. 1992). **Structure:** executive (prime minister and cabinet); bicameral legislature (Parliament—16-member appointed Senate, 49-member elected House of Assembly); judiciary.

Economy **Monetary unit:** Bahamian dollar. **Budget:** (1992) ***income:*** $628.5 mil.; ***expend.:*** $574 mil. **GDP:** $4.4 bil., $16,500 per capita (1993 est.). **Chief crops:** vegetables, tomatoes, pineapples, bananas, citrus fruits; food importer. **Livestock:** sheep, pigs, goats, cattle. **Natural resources:** salt, argonite, timber. **Major industries:** banking, tourism, cement. **Labor force:** 127,400 (1989); 30% government, 25% hotels and restaurants, 10% business services; 30% unemployment (1986). **Exports:** $310 mil. (f.o.b., 1992 est.); pharmaceuticals, cement, rum, crawfish. **Imports:** $1.2 bil. (f.o.b., 1992); foodstuffs, manufactured goods, mineral fuels. **Major trading partners:** ***exports:*** 41% U.S., 30% Norway, 4% Denmark; ***imports:*** 35% U.S., 21% Nigeria, 13% Japan, 11% Angola.

Intl. Orgs. Commonwealth, FAO, G-77, IBRD, ICAO, ILO, IMF, IMO, INTERPOL, ITU, NAM, OAS, UN, UNESCO, UPU, WHO, WIPO, WMO, WTO.

Christopher Columbus made his first landfall in the Americas in the Bahamas Oct. 12, 1492. Though the Spanish never settled the islands, they enslaved and removed to Hispaniola 40,000 of the indigenous Arawaks by 1508. Their shallow seas *(baja mar)* made the islands a haven for pirates in the 17th century—as well as during the Civil War, Prohibition, and for drug smugglers today.

British colonization of the Bahamas began in 1629 and continued slowly over the next two centuries, though it got a big boost from loyalists and their slaves—freed in 1834—during the American Revolution. High unemployment continues to be a problem, but Parliament has relaxed restrictions on offshore banking to stem the flight of international capital prompted by allegations of government corruption and involvement in drug trafficking. In 1992 the government of Prime Minister Lynden Pindling was defeated after 25 years in office, largely because of corruption charges.

Bahrain

State of Bahrain

Geography **Location:** group of 35 islands in western Persian Gulf. Manama 26°17'N, 50°33'E. **Boundaries:** Saudi Arabia about 15 mi. (24 km) to W and Qatar about 17 mi. (28 km) to SE. **Total land area:** 239 sq. mi. (620 sq km). **Coastline:** 161 mi. (259 km). **Comparative area:** slightly less than 3.5 times size of Washington, D.C. **Land use:** 2% arable land; 2% permanent crops; 6% meadows and pastures; 0% forest and woodland; 90% other; includes negl. % irrigated. **Major cities:** (1990 est.) Manama (capital) 138,784; Muharraq Town 75,906.

People **Population:** 585,683 (1994 est.). **Nationality:** noun—Bahraini(s); adjective—Bahraini. **Ethnic groups:** 63% Bahraini, 13% Asian, 10% other Arab, 8% Iranian, 6% other. **Languages:** Arabic (official), Farsi, Urdu; English widely spoken. **Religions:** 70% Shia Muslim, 30% Sunni Muslim.

Government **Type:** traditional monarchy. **Independence:** Aug. 15, 1971 (from UK). **Constitution:** May 26, 1973 (effective Dec. 1973). **National holiday:** Dec. 16. **Heads of government:** Isa bin Salman al-Khalifa, amir (since Nov. 1961); Khalifa bin Sulman al-Khalifa, prime minister (since Jan. 1970). **Structure:** amir rules with help of cabinet led by prime minister; amir dissolved National Assembly (Aug. 1975) and suspended constitutional provision for election of assembly; independent judiciary.

Economy **Monetary unit:** Bahrain dinar. **Budget:** (1992) ***income:*** $1.2 bil.; ***expend.:*** $1.6 bil. **GDP:** $6.8 bil., $12,000 per capita (1993 est.). **Chief crops:** not self-sufficient in food production; produces some fruits and vegetables; engages in dairy and poultry farming and in shrimping and fishing. **Livestock:** goats, sheep, cattle. **Natural resources:** oil, associated and nonassociated natural gas, fish. **Major industries:** petroleum processing and refining, aluminum smelting and fabrication. **Labor force:** 140,000 (1982); 85% industry and commerce (note: 42% of labor force is Bahraini). **Exports:** $3.5 bil. (f.o.b. 1993 est.); 80% petroleum, 7% aluminum. **Imports:** $3.7 bil. (f.o.b., 1993 est.); 59% nonoil, 41% crude oil. **Major trading partners:** ***exports:*** U.S., UAE, Japan, India, Pakistan; ***imports:*** UK, Saudi Arabia, U.S., Japan, UK.

Intl. Orgs. Arab League, FAO, G-77, IBRD, ICAO, ILO, IMF, IMO, INTERPOL, NAM, UN, UNESCO, UPU, WHO, WTO.

Bahrain has been an entrepôt of trade between Arabia and India since the second millenium B.C. The Portuguese fortified Bahrain in the 16th century but were driven out by the Persian shah Abbas I early in the 17th century. At the end of the 18th century, it became an Arab sheikhdom within the Ottoman Empire.

Bahrain entered into treaty relations with Great Britain in 1820 and became a British protectorate in 1861. After British forces withdrew from the gulf, the nation became an independent emirate, in August 1971, under Amir Isa bin Sulman al-Khalifa, who came to the throne in 1961. Today the U.S. maintains a large military base here that served as naval headquarters during the Persian Gulf War.

Oil reserves—first discovered in 1932—were largely depleted by the mid-1970s. The economy now has diversified to include oil refining, aluminum smelting, international banking, and shipping services. Bahrain has close relations with Saudi Arabia; a causeway permits direct-road communication between the two countries.

In June 1995 social and political unrest caused by uneven distribution of wealth and a repressive government erupted into serious rioting.

Bangladesh

People's Republic of Bangladesh

Geography **Location:** southern Asia. **Boundaries:** India to N, E, and W; Myanmar to E, Bay of Bengal to S. **Total land area:** 55,598 sq. mi. (144,000 sq km). **Coastline:** 360 mi. (580 km). **Comparative area:** between Arkansas and Wisconsin. **Land use:** 67% arable land; 2% permanent crops; 4% meadows and pastures; 16% forest and woodland; 11% other; includes 14% irrigated. **Major cities:** (1991 census) Dhaka (formerly Dacca) (capital) 3,637,892; Chittagong 1,566,070; Khulna 601,051; Rajshahi 324,532; Barisal 180,014.

People **Population:** 125,149,469 (1994 est.). **Nationality:** noun—Bangladeshi(s); adjective—Bangladesh. **Ethnic groups:** 98% Bengali, 250,000 Biharis, less than 1 mil. tribals. **Languages:** Bangla (official); English widely used. **Religions:** 83% Muslim, 16% Hindu, less than 1% Buddhist, Christian, and other.

Government **Type:** republic. **Independence:** Dec. 16, 1971 (from Pakistan). **Constitution:** Nov. 4, 1972, effective Dec. 16, 1972, suspended following coup of Mar. 24, 1982, restored Nov. 10, 1986; amended Mar. 1991. **National holiday:** National Day, Mar. 26; Victory Day, Dec. 16. **Heads of government:** Abdur Rahman Biswas, president (since Oct. 1991); Ms. Begum Khaleda Zia, prime minister (since Mar. 1991). **Structure:** presidential system of government, 330-member unicameral legislature (Parliament), and independent judiciary; president has substantial control over judiciary; Parliament dissolved on Dec. 6, 1987.

Economy **Monetary unit:** taka. Budget: (1992) ***income:*** $2.25 bil.; ***expend.:*** $3.7 bil. **GDP:** $122 bil., $1,000 per capita (1993 est.). **Chief crops:** large-scale subsistence farming, heavily dependent on monsoon rain; main crops are jute, tea, and rice; grain, cotton, and oilseed shortages. **Livestock:** chickens, ducks, cattle, goats, buffalo. **Natural resources:** natural gas, uranium, arable land, timber. **Major industries:** jute manufactures, food processing, cotton textiles. **Labor force:** 50.1 mil. (1989); extensive export of labor to Saudi Arabia, UAE, Oman, and Kuwait; 74% agriculture, 15% services, 11% industry and commerce, unemployment 30% (est.). **Exports:** $2.1 bil. (FY93); jute, shrimp, manufacturing, leather, tea. **Imports:** $3.5 bil. (FY93); food, petroleum and other energy, nonfood consumer goods, semiprocessed goods. **Major trading partners:** ***exports:*** 39% Western Europe, 28% U.S.; ***imports:*** 17% Western Europe, 10% Japan, 5% U.S.

Intl. Orgs. Colombo Plan, Commonwealth, FAO, G-77, IAEA, IBRD, ICAO, IDA, IFAD, IFC, ILO, IMF, IMO, INTELSAT, INTERPOL, ITU, NAM, UN, UNCTAD, UNESCO, UPU, WHO, WMO, WTO.

Located on the alluvial plain of the Ganges River northeast of India, Bengal was ruled by Buddhist kings from the eighth to 12th centuries. Conquered by Muslim invaders around 1200, many inhabitants converted to Islam and Bengal became part of the Moghul Empire in the 16th century. The British East India Company established a settlement in 1642, and by 1750 all of Bengal was under British rule. The formerly diverse agricultural economy became dominated by export crops of opium and jute, while rice continued to be grown in the fertile delta. The region's trade flowed through the British-built city of Calcutta.

With Indian independence in 1947, Bengal was partitioned along religious lines, Hindu West Bengal (including Calcutta) remaining with India and Muslim East Bengal becoming the eastern province of Pakistan. In the elections of 1971, the Bengali Awami League gained control of Pakistan's National Assembly. Seating of the new National Assembly was postponed, and riots broke out in East Pakistan. Troops from West Pakistan were sent to quell the riots on May 25; the following day East Pakistan declared its independence as Bangladesh. Civil war followed; 10 million refugees fled to India. Following Indian intervention, Pakistan acknowledged Bangladesh's independence on Dec. 15.

Politics in Bangladesh have been dominated by coups and a series of military governments; the first president, Sheik Mujibur Rahman, was assassinated in 1974. Opposition unrest in December 1990 forced the resignation of Hussain Mohammad Ershad, president since a 1982 military coup. In national elections in February 1991, the Bangladesh Nationalist party (BNP) of Begum Khaleda Zia, widow of former president Ziaur Rahman (assassinated in 1981), won 138 of 330 parliamentary seats. The BNP promotes an Islamic state, free enterprise, and privatization. In September 1991 the constitution was amended to put the prime minister in charge of the government and make the presidency a largely ceremonial post.

A secessionist guerrilla movement in the Chittagong Hill tracts was defused in 1989 after 15 years of warfare when the government granted the region greater local autonomy.

Plagued by overpopulation, a decline in the world market for jute, and frequent catastrophic floods—one in 1975 killed an estimated 500,000 people, and another in 1991 approximately 130,000—Bangladesh remains one of the world's poorest countries and depends heavily on foreign aid.

Opposition to Prime Minister Zia led, in December 1994, to the resignation, en masse, of almost 150 opposition members of Parliament, eliciting a promise that she would resign prior to the general elections scheduled for 1996. Islamic leaders demanding an "Islamic Republic" are the major opposition.

Barbados

Geography **Location:** easternmost of Caribbean islands, about 200 mi. (320 km) NE of Trinidad. Bridgetown 13°06'N, 59°36'W. **Boundaries:** Atlantic Ocean. **Total land area:** 166 sq. mi. (430 sq km). **Coastline:** 60 mi. (97 km). **Comparative area:** slightly less than 2.5 times size of Washington, D.C. **Land use:** 77% arable land; 0% permanent crops; 9% meadows and pastures; 0% forest and woodland; 14% other; includes N.A. % irrigated. **Major cities:** (1980 census) Bridgetown (capital) 7,466.

People **Population:** 255,827 (1994 est.). **Nationality:** noun—Barbadian(s); adjective—Barbadian. **Ethnic groups:** 80% African, 16% mixed, 4% European. **Languages:** English. **Religions:** 70% Anglican, 9% Methodist, 4% Roman Catholic, 17% other, including Moravian.

Government **Type:** independent sovereign state within commonwealth recognizing Elizabeth II as chief of state. **Independence:** Nov. 30, 1966 (from UK). **Constitution:** Nov. 30, 1966. **National holiday:** Independence Day, Nov. 30. **Heads of government:** Dame Ruth Nita Barrow, governor-general (since June 1990); Owen Arthur, prime minister (since Sept. 1994). **Structure:** cabinet headed by prime minister; bicameral legislature (Parliament—21-member appointed Senate and 27-member elected House of Assembly).

Economy **Monetary unit:** Barbados dollar. **Budget:** (1992–93) ***income:*** $547 mil.; ***expend.:*** $620 mil. **GDP:** $2.2 bil., $8,700 per capita (1993 est.). **Chief crops:** sugarcane, subsistence foods. **Livestock:** sheep, pigs, goats, cattle. **Natural resources:** crude oil, fishing, natural gas. **Major industries:** tourism, sugar, light manufacturing. **Labor force:** 120,900 (1991); 37% services and government, 22% commerce, 22% manufacturing and construction. **Exports:** $158 mil. (f.o.b., 1992); sugar and molasses, rum, electrical components, clothing. **Imports:** $465 mil. (f.o.b., 1992); foodstuffs, consumer durables, machinery, fuels. **Major trading partners:** ***exports:*** 31% Caribbean countries, 16% U.S., 13% UK. ***imports:*** 34% U.S., 16% Caribbean countries, 11% UK, 6% Canada.

Intl. Orgs. Commonwealth, FAO, G-77, IBRD, ICAO, IFAD, IFC, ILO, IMF, IMO, INELSAT, INTERPOL, ITU, NAM, OAS, UN, UNESCO, UPU, WHO, WMO, WTO.

Barbados is the only Caribbean island not to have changed hands prior to independence. Although the Spanish removed virtually all the indigenous Arawaks of Barbados by the mid-1500s, the island was not claimed until the British arrived in the 1620s. Tobacco, cotton, and sugarcane—harvested with slave labor until 1833—were mainstays of the economy. The 1966 constitution mandates the promotion of economic equality among Barbadians, and the country was fairly prosperous relative to other Caribbean states until recently, when declining tourism and record-low sugar production have had serious adverse effects.

Belarus

Republic of Belarus

Geography **Location:** northeastern Europe. **Boundaries:** Lithuania and Latvia to N, Russian Federation to NE and E, Ukraine to S, Poland to W, Lithuania and Latvia to NW. **Total land area:** 80,154 sq. mi. (207,600 sq km). **Coastline:** none. **Comparative area:** slightly smaller than Kansas. **Land use:** 30% cropland; 16% permanent pasture; 33% forest and woodland; 21% other. **Major cities:** (1990 est.) Minsk (capital) 1,613,000; Gomel (Homel) 506,000; Mahilou (Mogilev) 363,000; Vitebsk 356,000; Grodno 277,000.

People **Population:** 10,404,862 (1994 est.). **Nationality:** noun—Belarussian(s); adjective—Belarussian. **Ethnic groups:** 79.4% Belarussian, 11.9% Russian, 4.2% Polish, 2.4% Ukrainian, 1.4% Jewish. **Languages:** Belarussian (official), Eastern Slavonic language written in Cyrillic script; Russian, Polish. **Religions:** Christianity—Roman Catholic and Eastern Orthodox; Islam; Judaism.

Government **Type:** republic. **Independence:** Aug. 25, 1991 (from USSR). **Constitution:** being drafted. **National holiday:** July 27, Independence Day. **Heads of government:** Alyksandr Lukashenka, president (since July 1994); Mikhail Chygir, prime minister (since July 1994). **Structure:** executive—chairman of Supreme Soviet and de facto president, Council of Ministers; legislative—Supreme Soviet (360 deputies); judicial—Supreme Court.

Economy **Monetary unit:** rubel. **Budget:** N.A. ***income:*** N.A.; ***expend.:*** N.A. **GNP:** $61 bil., $5,890 per capita (1993 est.). **Chief crops:** potatoes, rye, wheat, barley, oats. **Livestock:** chickens, cattle, pigs, sheep, goats. **Natural resources:** petroleum, coal, peat, natural gas. **Major industries:** machine building, metalworking, cars, heavy-duty vehicles, textiles. **Labor force:** 4.8 mil. (1992). **Exports:** $710 mil. outside the former USSR (f.o.b., 1993); machinery, transport equipment, chemicals, foodstuffs. **Imports:** $743 mil. outside the former USSR (c.i.f., 1993); machinery, chemicals, textiles. **Major trading partners:** Russia, Ukraine, Poland.

Intl. Orgs. CIS, IMF, OSCE, UN, UNESCO, WHO, World Bank.

Belarus, also known as White Russia or Byelorussia, has been inhabited since the seventh century. In the 13th and 14th centuries, present-day Belarus became part of the Grand Duchy of Lithuania, which then became part of Poland in the 16th century. Between 1772 and 1795, Poland was partitioned, which resulted in Belarus becoming part of the Russian empire. After the Bolshevik revolution in 1917, Soviet troops came to Minsk, but they were forced to withdraw in the face of approaching German troops. The Treaty of Brest-Litovsk in March 1918 ceded to Germany most of the territory of Belarus. The same year, an independent Belarussian Democratic Republic was founded, but it had little real power. Once the Germans left, the Soviets easily retook Belarus, and on Jan. 1, 1919, the Belarussian Soviet Socialist Republic (SSR) was proclaimed.

This did not end the divisions of the traditional Belarussian lands. In February 1919 they were merged within the Soviet Union with Lithuania, but the Poles launched an attack in April of the same year and took both Lithuania and Belarus. In 1920 the Belarussian SSR was re-formed, but it included only the eastern portion of historical Belarussian lands. The Treaty of Riga in March 1921 granted the western territories of Belarus to Poland and the eastern portion to the Russian Federation. In 1924 and 1925 the eastern regions were returned to the Belarussian SSR.

After the Soviets invaded Poland in 1939, the lands that Belarus had lost in 1921 were returned to it. Between 1941 and 1945, the Germans occupied the Belarussian lands, and more than a million lost their lives, including most of the large Jewish population. After the war, the Belarussian SSR was restored with all of its historic lands, and Belarus was finally unified. However, when Stalin redrew the Soviet Union's internal borders, he included Belarus's traditional capital of Vilnius in Lithuania, Belarus's neighbor to the west.

Under Soviet rule, Belarus turned from a mainly agricultural to an industrial land. Large numbers of Belarussians fiercely fought Stalin's collectivization plan in the 1930s, and thousands were killed or deported. Both Stalin's purges of the 1930s and World War II, which devastated both its agriculture and industry, inflicted great losses on Belarus. After the war, Soviet policy in Belarus concentrated on rebuilding its economy and encouraging Russian immigration into the republic. Russian replaced Belarussian as the official language, which was an old issue that had initiated the purge of Belarussian intellectuals and nationalists in the 1930s.

The Belarussian SSR was one of the more prosperous and stable of the union republics, so Mikhail Gorbachev's policy of glasnost, or openness, in the 1980s was relatively slow to have an impact. In 1987, however, two big issues had come to the fore in the Belarussian SSR: the status of the Belarussian language and the ecological dangers of Chernobyl, the famous nuclear reactor that had exploded in nearby Ukraine in 1986, but which dropped almost three-quarters of its fallout on southeastern Belarus. In voicing these concerns, the Belarussians formed several new, non-Communist parties that challenged the traditional authority of the ruling Communist party. In January 1990, largely due to these new forces, Belarussian became the official language over Russian. On July 27, 1990, again due to the new political pressures, Belarus declared its sovereignty from the USSR.

Belarus was one of the strongest supporters of maintaining a union of republics, both in political circles and among the population. (Over 80% of the population favored the union in March 1991.) The Belarussian leadership did not oppose the August coup in Moscow, and as a result, the Communist party was suspended after the coup failed, and a centrist politician, Stanislau Shushkevich, took over as interim head of state. In September 1991, the name of the country was officially changed to Belarus. On Dec. 8, 1991, Belarus, Ukraine, and the Russian Federation hosted the talks leading to the Minsk Agreement, which created the Commonwealth of Independent States (CIS). On Dec. 21, 1991, 11 other former Soviet republics joined the commonwealth by signing the Alma-Ata Declaration.

Although at first Belarus viewed CIS as a temporary expedient, Parliament's election of Mechislav Grib as its chairman and president (Jan. 1994) and the popular election of Aleksandr Lukashenko as president indicate a noticeable shift toward closer economic and even political ties to Russia.

Belgium

Kingdom of Belgium

Geography **Location:** northwestern Europe. **Boundaries:** Netherlands to N, Luxembourg and Germany to E, France to S, and North Sea to W. **Total land area:** 11,780 sq. mi. (30,510 sq km). **Coastline:** 40 mi. (64 km). **Comparative area:** slightly larger than Maryland. **Land use:** 24% arable land; 1% permanent crops; 20% meadows and pastures; 21% forest and woodland; 34% other; includes negl. % irrigated. **Major cities:** (1993) Bruxelles (Brussels—capital) 949,070; Antwerpen (Anvers, Antwerp) 462,880; Gent (Gand, Ghent) 228,490; Charleroi 206,898; Liège (Luik) 195,389.

People **Population:** 10,062,836 (1994 est.). **Nationality:** noun—Belgian(s); adjective—Belgian. **Ethnic groups:** 55% Fleming, 33% Walloon, 12% mixed or other. **Languages:** 56% Flemish (Dutch), 32% French, 1% German; 11% legally bilingual; divided along ethnic lines. **Religions:** 75% Roman Catholic; remainder Protestant or other.

Government **Type:** constitutional monarchy. **Independence:** Oct. 4, 1830 (from Netherlands). **Constitution:** Feb. 7, 1831; last revised Aug. 8–9, 1980. **National holiday:** National Day, July 21. **Heads of government:** Albert II, king (since Aug. 1993); Jean-Luc Dehaene (since Mar. 6, 1992). **Structure:** executive branch consists of king and cabinet; cabinet responsible to bicameral parliament (Senate and Chamber of Representatives); independent judiciary; coalition governments are usual.

Economy **Monetary unit:** Belgian franc. **Budget:** (1989) ***income:*** $97.8 bil.; ***expend.:*** $109.3 bil. **GDP:** $177.5 bil., $17,700 per capita (1993). **Chief crops:** grains, sugar beets, flax, potatoes, other vegetables; livestock production predominates. **Livestock:** pigs, cattle, sheep, horses, goats. **Natural resources:** coal, natural gas. **Major industries:** engineering, metal products, processed food, beverages, chemicals. **Labor force:** 4.2 mil. (1988); 69% services, 28% industry; 8.5% unemployment. **Exports:** (Belgium-Luxembourg Economic Union) $117 bil. (f.o.b., 1992); iron, steel, transportation equipment, tractors, diamonds. **Imports:** (Belgium-Luxembourg Economic Union) $120 bil. (c.i.f., 1992); fuels, grains, chemicals. **Major trading partners:** (Belgium-Luxembourg Economic Union, 1989) ***exports:*** 75% EU, 4% U.S., 1% Communist countries; ***imports:*** 72% EU, 5% U.S., 4% oil-exporting developing countries, 2% Communist countries.

Intl. Orgs. EU, FAO, IAEA, IBRD, ICAO, IDA, IFAD, IFC, ILO, IMF, IMO, INTELSAT, INTERPOL, ITU, NATO, OECD, OSCE, UN, UNESCO, UPU, WHO, WIPO, WMO, WTO.

The country now known as Belgium was, during the Middle Ages, part of the powerful duchy of Burgundy. By marriage and diplomacy, the "Low Countries" became part of the Habsburg Empire in 1482 (see "Austria"). In a struggle lasting from the late 16th century to the Treaty of Westphalia in 1648, the northern part of that region (Netherlands) became independent, but the southern portion remained part of the Habsburg Empire—under the Spanish branch until 1715, then under the Austrian branch until the French Revolution. The Congress of Vienna attached the lands to an enlarged Kingdom of the Netherlands in 1815.

In 1830 the Belgians revolted against the Dutch, and in 1831 the Treaty of London recognized an independent Kingdom of Belgium. Throughout the 19th century, its unity was precarious, as the country was bitterly divided politically between Catholic and Liberal parties, and ethnically between Dutch-speaking Flemings and French-speaking Walloons.

In 1885 Belgium became a colonial power in Africa with Leopold II's establishment of the Congo Free State (later the Belgian Congo), which gained independence in 1960 as Zaire.

Belgium was a major battleground during World War I. Its boundaries were reestablished in 1919 by the Treaty of Versailles. When German troops of Hitler's Third Reich overran Belgium in May 1940, King Leopold III quickly signed an armistice, hoping to placate Hitler and avert further fighting. But the Belgian government fled to England, repudiated the armistice, and joined the Allies. The Germans controlled Belgium until the liberation of Brussels in September 1944.

Belgium made a swift postwar recovery. But the political atmosphere was poisoned by the issue of what to do about wartime collaborators up to and including the king. A referendum in 1950 narrowly approved Leopold III's return to the throne, but he was persuaded to abdicate in 1951 in favor of his son, Baudouin I. Belgium became a founding member of the United Nations, the Benelux Pact, NATO, and the EC (Brussels is the seat of the European Parliament).

Belgium has a flourishing economy with a highly modernized industrial sector complemented by tourism and agriculture. The issue of language dominates politics; since the 1960s, Belgium has devolved into a de facto confederation of Flemish-, French-, and German-speaking regions, with Brussels a multilingual region unto itself. The country's complex coalition politics are dominated by three major parties: Christian People's, Socialist, and Liberal, each split into separate Walloon and Flemish parties.

In the May 1995 election, the first under the new decentralized constitution of 1993, the Christian Democrat–Socialist coalition government retained a majority in the Chamber of Representatives.

Belize

Geography **Location:** northeastern coast of Central America. **Boundaries:** Mexico to N, Caribbean Sea to E, Guatemala to S and W. **Total land area:** 8,865 sq. mi. (22,960 sq km). **Coastline:** 240 mi. (386 km). **Comparative area:** between Massachusetts and New Hampshire. **Land use:** 2% arable land; negl. % permanent crops; 2% meadows and pastures; 44% forest and woodland; 52% other; includes negl. % irrigated. **Major cities:** (1993 est.) Belmopan (capital) 3,852; Belize City 47,723; Orange Walk 11,922; San Ignacio 9,702; Corozal 7,644.

People **Population:** 208,949 (1994 est.). **Nationality:** noun—Belizean(s); adjective—Belizean. **Ethnic groups:** 44% mestizo, 30% Creole, 11% Maya, 7.6% Garifuna. **Languages:** English (official), Spanish, Maya, Garifuna (Carib). **Religions:** 60% Roman Catholic, 40% Protestant (Anglican, Seventh-Day Adventist, Methodist, Baptist, Jehovah's Witnesses, Mennonite).

Government **Type:** parliamentary. **Independence:** Sept. 21, 1981 (from UK). **Constitution:** Sept. 21, 1981. **National holiday:** N.A. **Heads of government:** Sir Colville Norbert Young, governor-general (since Nov. 1993); Manuel Esquivel, prime minister (since July 1993). **Structure:** cabinet; bicameral legislature (National Assembly—electoral redistricting in Oct. 1984 expanded House of Representatives from 18 to 28 seats; eight-member appointed Senate; either house may choose its speaker or president, respectively, from outside its membership); judiciary.

Economy **Monetary unit:** Belizean dollar. **Budget:** (1991 est.) ***income:*** $126.8 mil.; ***expend.:*** $123.1 mil. **GDP:** $550 mil., $2,700 per capita (1993 est.). **Chief crops:** sugarcane, citrus fruits, corn, molasses, rice, beans, bananas; net importer of food; illegal producer of cannabis for international drug trade. **Livestock:** cattle, pigs, horses, mules, sheep, goats. **Natural resources:** arable land potential, timber, fish. **Major industries:** sugar refining, clothing, timber, and forest products. **Labor force:** 51,500 (1985); 30% agriculture, 16% services, 15.4% government, 11.2% commerce; shortage of skilled labor and all types of technical personnel; over 14% unemployment. **Exports:** $116 mil. (f.o.b.,

1992); sugar, garments, seafood, molasses, citrus. **Imports:** $273 mil. (c.i.f., 1992 est.); machinery and transportation equipment, food, manufactured goods, fuels, chemicals. **Major trading partners:** (1987) ***exports:*** 47% U.S., UK, Trinidad and Tobago, Canada; ***imports:*** 55% U.S., UK, Netherlands Antilles, Mexico.

Intl. Orgs. Commonwealth, FAO, G-77, IBRD, IDA, IFAD, IFC, ILO, IMF, ITU, UN, UNESCO, UPU, WHO, WTO.

During the 1700s, Spain held sovereignty over Belize but never attempted to settle it. The British gradually did settle there, however, and in 1862, British Honduras, as it was called, became a Crown colony. Although Britain granted Belize independence in 1981, Guatemala claimed sovereignty over the area until 1992, when it finally recognized Belize's independence. But as British defense forces withdrew in 1994, Guatemala reasserted its old claims.

Benin

Republic of Benin

Geography **Location:** western coast of Africa. **Boundaries:** Burkina Faso and Niger to N, Nigeria to E, Gulf of Guinea to S, Togo to W. **Total land area:** 43,483 sq. mi. (112,620 sq km). **Coastline:** 75 mi. (121 km). **Comparative area:** between Tennessee and Pennsylvania. **Land use:** 12% arable land; 4% permanent crops; 4% meadows and pastures; 35% forest and woodland; 45% other; includes negl. % irrigated. **Major cities:** (1981 est.) Porto-Novo (capital) 144,000; Cotonou 383,250.

People **Population:** 5,341,710 (1994 est.). **Nationality:** noun—Beninese (sing., pl.); adjective—Beninese. **Ethnic groups:** 99% African (Fon, Adja, Yoruba, Bariba); 5,500 Europeans. **Languages:** French (official); Fon and Yoruba in south; six major tribal languages in north. **Religions:** 70% indigenous beliefs, 15% Muslim, 15% Christian.

Government **Type:** Multiparty system since Apr. 4, 1991. **Independence:** Aug. 1, 1960 (from France). **Constitution:** Dec. 2, 1990. **National holiday:** Aug. 1. **Head of government:** Nicéphore Soglo, president (since Apr. 1991). **Structure:** executive—president, cabinet; legislative—unicameral National Assembly; judicial—Supreme Court.

Economy **Monetary unit:** Communauté Financière Africaine (CFA) franc. **Budget:** (1990) ***income:*** $218 mil.; ***expend.:*** $355 mil. **GDP:** $6.2 bil., $1,200 per capita (1993 est.). **Chief crops:** cash crops—palm oil, peanuts, cotton, coffee, shea nuts, tobacco; food crops—corn, cassava, yams, rice, sorghum, millet. **Livestock:** sheep, goats, cattle, pigs, horses. **Natural resources:** small offshore oil deposits, limestone, marble, timber. **Major industries:** palm oil and palm kernel oil processing, textiles, beverages. **Labor force:** 1.9 mil. (1987); 60% agriculture, 2% industrial sector, remainder employed in transport, commerce, and public services; 49% of population of working age. **Exports:** $328.8 mil. (f.o.b., 1991 est.); palm products, cotton, crude oil, cocoa. **Imports:** $482.3 mil. (f.o.b., 1991 est.); foodstuffs, beverages, tobacco, petroleum products. **Major trading partners:** ***exports:*** 36% Germany, 16% France, 14% Spain, 8% Italy, 7% UK; ***imports:*** 34% France, 10% Netherlands, 7% Japan, 6% Italy, 5% U.S.

Intl. Orgs. FAO, G-77, IBRD, ICAO, IDA, IFAD, ILO, IMF, IMO, INTERPOL, ITU, NAM, UN, UNESCO, UPU, WHO, WIPO, WMO, WTO.

Although the early history of Benin is sketchy, a number of kingdoms had appeared in the region by the 11th century, and it was a center of wealth and power by the 1300s. In the 16th century, the Allada kingdom was founded in the south. In 1625, three brothers divided their power between Allada, Adjatché (Porto Novo), and Abomey. Under Ouegbadja (r. 1645–85) the latter, known as Dahomey, predominated. Much of its wealth derived from contact with Europeans, and especially the slave trade, which continued until 1885.

European contact began with the arrival of the Portuguese in 1485. Although traders and missionaries were established at Ouidah and Porto Novo in the 1500s, European influence remained slight. Dahomey expansion continued well into the 19th century. A commercial treaty with the French was signed in 1842, and relations between Dahomeyans and Europeans soon worsened. Outright hostilities began under Behanzin (r. 1858–89), who was defeated by the French, and in 1893 the French assimilated Abomey, Allada, and Porto Novo into the colony of Dahomey.

Independence from French rule came in 1960, followed by more than a decade of coups until Mathieu Kerekou came to power in 1972. Kerekou established a Marxist regime, nationalizing large private businesses and abolishing opposition parties. By 1989, the economy was a shambles and most trade was conducted on the black market.

In December, there were demonstrations calling for Kerekou's resignation. The government abandoned Marxism and former World Bank official Nicéphore Soglo was named prime minister. A new constitution was approved in a referendum in November 1990, and legislative elections were held in February 1991. In March, Soglo defeated Kerekou for the presidency and has appealed to the western nations for a "Marshall Plan" for Africa.

Bhutan

Kingdom of Bhutan

Geography **Location:** Himalaya Mountains in southern Asia. **Boundaries:** China to N and W, India to S and E. **Total land area:** 18,147 sq. mi. (47,000 sq km). **Coastline:** none. **Comparative area:** between Maryland and West Virginia. **Land use:** 2% arable land; negl. % permanent crops; 5% meadows and pastures; 70% forest and woodland; 23% other. **Major cities:** (1990 est.) Timphu (capital) 27,000.

People **Population:** 716,380 (1994 est.). **Nationality:** noun—Bhutanese (sing., pl.); adjective—Bhutanese. **Ethnic groups:** 60% Bhote, 25% ethnic Nepalese, 15% indigenous or migrant tribes. **Languages:** Dzongkha (official), various Tibetan dialects, various Nepalese dialects. **Religions:** 75% Lamaistic Buddhism, 25% Indian- and Nepalese-influenced Hinduism.

Government **Type:** monarchy; special treaty relationship with India. **Independence:** Aug. 8, 1949 (from India). **Constitution:** no written constitution or bill of rights. **National holiday:** Dec. 17. **Head of government:** Jigme Singye Wangchuk, king (since July 1972). **Structure:** appointed ministers; 150-member indirectly elected National Assembly consisting of 110 village elders or heads of family, 10 monastic representatives, and 30 senior government administrators.

Economy **Monetary unit:** ngultrums and rupees are legal tender. **Budget:** (1991 est.) ***income:*** $100 mil.; ***expend.:*** $112 mil. **GDP:** $500 mil., $700 per capita (1993 est.). **Chief crops:** rice, corn, barley, wheat, potatoes. **Livestock:** cattle, poultry, pigs, sheep, yaks. **Natural resources:** timber, hydropower, gypsum, calcium carbide. **Major industries:** cement, chemical products, mining. **Labor force:** (1983) 95% agriculture, 1% industry and commerce, massive lack of skilled labor. **Exports:** $66 mil. (f.o.b., FY93); cardamom, gypsum, timber, handicrafts. **Imports:** $125 mil. (c.i.f., FY93 est.); fuels and lubricants, grain, machinery and parts, vehicles. **Major trading partner:** India (93% of exports, 67% of imports).

Intl. Orgs. Colombo Plan, FAO, G-77, IBRD, IDA, IFAD, IMF, NAM, UN, UNESCO, UPU, WHO.

A Tibetan-style Lamaistic Buddhist theocracy was established in this Himalayan enclave in the 16th century. The region came under the domination of the British raj in India in 1865, and Britain established a protectorate in 1910. A 1949 treaty with India granted independence to Bhutan. The present Druk Gyalpo, or Precious Ruler of the Dragon People, is the fourth in a dynasty dating from 1907. During the early years of his reign, he introduced reforms into this feudal, medieval country by broadening educational opportunities and compelling Buddhist monks to take up social work outside their monasteries.

Since 1988, however, King Wangchuk, who rules through a rubber-stamp National Assembly, has introduced a series of laws aimed at driving out Nepalese and Indian settlers even if their families have resided in Bhutan for decades. More than 70,000 refugees have been registered by the UN high commissioner for refugees since 1991, and the numbers continue to grow. A "Gorkha Liberation Movement" has recently carried out raids in Bhutan from sanctuaries in India and Nepal.

Bolivia

Republic of Bolivia

Geography **Location:** landlocked country in central South America. **Boundaries:** Brazil to N and E, Paraguay and Argentina to S, Chile and Peru to W. **Total land area:** 424,162 sq. mi. (1,098,580 sq km). **Coastline:** none. **Comparative area:** between Texas and Alaska. **Land use:** 3% arable land; negl. % permanent crops; 25% meadows and pastures; 52% forest and woodland; 20% other; includes negl. % irrigated. **Major cities:** (1992 est.) La Paz (administrative capital) 1,115,403; Sucre (legal capital and seat of judiciary) 130,952; Santa Cruz de la Sierra 694,616; Cochabamba 404,102; Oruro 183,194.

People Population: 7,719,445 (1994 est.). **Nationality:** noun—Bolivian(s); adjective—Bolivian. **Ethnic groups:** 30% Quechua, 25% Aymara, 25–30% mixed, 5–15% European. **Languages:** Spanish, Quechua, and Aymara (all official). **Religions:** 95% Roman Catholic; active Protestant minority, especially Methodist.

Government Type: republic. **Independence:** Aug, 6, 1825 (from Spain). **Constitution:** Feb. 2, 1967. **National holiday:** Independence Day, Aug. 6. **Head of government:** Gonzalo Sanchez de Lozada, president (since Aug. 1993). **Structure:** executive; bicameral legislature (National Congress—Senate and Chamber of Deputies); Congress began meeting again in Oct. 1982; judiciary.

Economy Monetary unit: boliviano. **Budget:** (1993 est.) ***income:*** $3.19 bil.; ***expend.:*** $3.19 bil. **GDP:** $15.8 bil., $2,100 per capita (1993 est.). **Chief crops:** potatoes, corn, rice, sugarcane, yucca, bananas, coffee; imports significant quantities of wheat; illegal producer of coca for international drug trade. **Livestock:** sheep, cattle, goats, pigs, asses. **Natural resources:** tin, natural gas, crude oil, zinc, tungsten. **Major industries:** mining, smelting, petroleum refining. **Labor force:** 1.7 mil. (1983); 50% agriculture, 26% services and utilities, 10% manufacturing, 10% other; 11% unemployment (1988). **Exports:** $752 mil. (f.o.b., 1993 est.); 45% metals, 32% natural gas, coffee, soybeans, sugar. **Imports:** $1.17 bil. (c.i.f., 1993 est.); food, petroleum, consumer goods, capital goods. **Major trading partners:** ***exports:*** 15% U.S., Argentina. ***imports:*** 22% U.S.

Intl. Orgs. FAO, G-77, IAEA, IBRD, ICAO, IDA, IFAD, IFC, ILO, IMF, INTELSAT, INTERPOL, ITU, NAM, OAS, UN, UNESCO, UPU, WHO, WMO.

The Incan Empire conquered the region that is now Bolivia in the 13th century. The Spanish discovered the fabulous silver deposits of the region and established their presence in the area in the cities of Sucre (1538) and Potosí (1545). From the early colonial period on, Bolivia—then called Upper Peru and part of the Viceroyalty of Peru—depended heavily on the export of minerals. The exploitation of tin and later oil and natural gas has had an important economic and political impact on the country's development.

In 1776, Upper Peru was transferred to the new Viceroyalty of La Plata centered in Buenos Aires. Upper Peru began agitating for independence in 1809, but it was not until liberation by Símon Bolívar (for whom the country was renamed) in 1825 that Bolivia became the last Spanish possession in South America to achieve independence. During 1836–39, Peru formed a brief union with Bolivia, until Chile broke up the confederation.

Bolivia has lost much of its original territory to its neighbors. The dictator Mariano Melgarejo sold large chunks of territory from 1865 to 1871. After the War of the Pacific (1879–84), Bolivia lost its access to the sea. And in the 1932–35 Chaco War with Paraguay, Bolivia lost more territory in the east.

Bolivia has suffered from Indian/non-Indian racial and cultural divisions, and political rivalry between the elites from the Potosí region and those from La Paz and Santa Cruz. Conservatives of the silver-mining southern region of Potosí controlled the government until their ouster in 1898 by the Liberal tin interests of the La Paz region, who presided over a period of stable republican politics that lasted until the Great Depression and the Chaco War.

One of the results of the Chaco War was the fragmentation of the Bolivian military into competing factions as the factions took sides in the struggle for power between conservative landowners and middle-class reformers; this caused political instability until the Bolivian National Revolution in 1952. In 1941 the National Revolutionary Movement (MNR) was formed with the aim of transferring control of the country from conservative landowning elites to the middle sectors. The leadership of the movement found itself outpaced by revolts sponsored by workers and peasants; the MNR incorporated these elements into its program. When the 1952 revolution brought the MNR to power, its leadership, which included the future four-time president Victor Paz Estenssoro, embarked on a reformist political program. The military overthrew the MNR in 1964, and civilian rule was not restored until 1982. Paz Estenssoro was again elected to the presidency in 1985. Jaime Paz Zamora, leader of the Movement of the Revolutionary Left, gained the presidency in 1989.

In elections held in June 1993, MNR candidate Gonzalo Sanchez de Lozada won the presidential election. An advocate of free-market economic reform, as planning minister (1986–88) he reduced the country's hyperinflation rate from 25,000 percent to 15 percent. Recent economic growth has been helped by increased privatization and gas exports. In January 1995 Bolivia sought membership in the newly-formed Southern Common Market (of Argentina, Brazil, Paraguay, and Uraguay). But opposition to free-market reforms brought a general strike by the leftist Bolivian Workers' Confederation and further strikes and unrest in 1995, which led to the government's declaration (April) of a state of siege, suspending civil liberties.

Bosnia and Herzegovina

See Part I: "Major News Stories of the Year."

Botswana

Republic of Botswana

Geography Location: landlocked country in southern Africa. **Boundaries:** Namibia to N and W, Zimbabwe to NE, South Africa to SE and S. **Total land area:** 231,803 sq. mi. (600,370 sq km). **Coastline:** none. **Comparative area:** about size of Texas. **Land use:** 2% arable land; 0% permanent crops; 75% meadows and pastures; 2% forest and woodland; 21% other; includes negl. % irrigated. **Major cities:** (1989 est.) Gaborone (capital) 110,973; Francistown 49,396; Selebi-Phikwe 46,490; Molepolole 29,212; Serowe 28,267.

People Population: 1,359,352 (1994 est.). **Nationality:** noun and adjective—Motswana (sing.), Batswana (pl.). **Ethnic groups:** 95% Batswana; 4% Kalanga, Basarwa, and Kgalagadi; 1% white. **Languages:** English (official), Setswana. **Religions:** 50% Christian, 50% indigenous beliefs.

Government Type: parliamentary republic. **Independence:** Sept. 30, 1966 (from UK). **Constitution:** Mar. 1965, effective Sept. 30, 1966. **National holiday:** Botswana Day, Sept. 30. **Head of government:** Sir Ketumile Masire, head of state (since July 1980). **Structure:** executive—president appoints and presides over cabinet; legislative—bicameral legislature (National Assembly with 34 popularly elected members and four members elected by the 34 representatives; House of Chiefs with deliberative powers only); judiciary—local courts administer customary law; high court and subordinate courts have criminal jurisdiction; court of appeal.

Economy Monetary unit: pula. **Budget:** (1994 est.) ***income:*** $1.7 bil.; ***expend.:*** $1.99 bil. **GDP:** $6 bil., $4,500 per capita (1993 est.). **Chief crops:** corn, sorghum, millet, cowpeas; heavy dependence on imported food. **Livestock:** cattle, goats, sheep, donkeys, horses. **Natural resources:** diamonds, copper, nickel, salt, soda ash. **Major industries:** livestock processing; mining of diamonds, copper, nickel, coal, salt, soda ash, potash; tourism. **Labor force:** 400,000; 163,000 formal-sector employees (1988 est.); most others engaged in cattle raising and subsistence agriculture; 40,000 formal-sector employees spend at least six to nine months per year as wage earners in South Africa (1980); 25% unemployment (1987). **Exports:** $1.6 bil. (f.o.b., 1991); 88% diamonds, 5% copper and nickel, 4% meat, cattle, and animal products. **Imports:** $1.7 bil. (c.i.f., 1991); foodstuffs, vehicles, textiles, petroleum products. **Major trading partners:** Switzerland, U.S., UK, other EU-associated members of Southern African Customs Union.

Intl. Orgs. Commonwealth, FAO, G-77, GATT (de facto), IBRD, ICAO, IDA, IFAD, IFC, ILO, IMF, INTERPOL, ITU, NAM, UN, UNESCO, UPU, WHO, WMO.

Botswana, occupying a high and relatively arid tableland in southern Africa, was traditionally occupied by diverse groups of farmers, pastoralists, and hunter-gatherers. European missionaries arrived from South Africa in the early 19th century. In the late 19th century, native peoples resisted the encroachment of Afrikaners from the Transvaal; in response the British government established a protectorate in what was then called Bechuanaland in 1886. The southern part of the protectorate was organized as a Crown Colony and ultimately passed under the control of South Africa. During the 20th century, the territory remaining in the protectorate saw a steady evolution of local rule.

In 1920 two advisory councils were established to represent the interests of native and European inhabitants. In 1934 British authorities promulgated regulations establishing the powers and jurisdictions of native chiefs and the functions of native councils and courts. Local fiscal powers were established soon thereafter. In 1951 a joint (native-European) advisory council was set up, and 10 years later an elected legislature met under the provisions of a constitution promulgated on May 2, 1961.

In 1963–64 the British government accepted Botswanan proposals for self-government. A new capital was established at Gaborone in February 1965; a new constitution came into effect in the following month, and Botswana became fully independent on Sept. 30, 1966. Since independence, Botswana has been a multiparty, multiracial democracy that has remained untouched by the political turmoil affecting most of its neighbors.

Botswana is also one of the most prosperous countries in Africa. It is the world's largest producer of diamonds; revenues from diamond exports have been wisely managed, leading to significant budgetary surpluses in recent years. Gold and soda ash are also mined. Tourism, bolstered by Botswana's large herds of big game, is the country's major nonmining industry. About 75 percent of the population is engaged in agriculture and herding; Botswana is one of Africa's largest exporters of meat and animal products.

Brazil

Federative Republic of Brazil

Geography **Location:** central and northeastern South America. **Boundaries:** Colombia, Venezuela, Guyana, Suriname, French Guiana to N; Atlantic Ocean to E; Uruguay, Argentina, Paraguay to S; Peru, Bolivia to W. **Total land area:** 3,286,475 sq. mi. (8,511,965 sq km). **Coastline:** 4,652 mi. (7,491 km). **Comparative area:** slightly smaller than U.S. **Land use:** 7% arable land; 1% permanent crops; 19% meadows and pastures; 67% forest and woodland; 6% other; includes negl. % irrigated. **Major cities:** (1991 est.) Brasília (capital) 1,841,028; São Paulo 9,700,111; Rio de Janeiro 6,011,181; Belo Horizonte 2,339,039; Salvador 2,075,392.

People **Population:** 158,739,257 (1994 est.). **Nationality:** noun—Brazilian(s); adjective—Brazilian. **Ethnic groups:** Portuguese, Italian, German, Japanese, black, Amerindian; 55% white, 38% mixed, 6% black, 1% other. **Languages:** Portuguese (official), Spanish, English, French. **Religions:** 90% Roman Catholic (nominal).

Government **Type:** federal republic; democratically elected president since 1985. **Independence:** Sept. 7, 1822 (from Portugal). **Constitution:** Oct. 5, 1988. **National holiday:** Independence Day, Sept. 7. **Head of government:** Fernando Henrique Cardoso, president (since Jan. 1995). **Structure:** strong executive with broad powers; bicameral legislature (National Congress) with growing powers, composed of Senate and Chamber of Deputies; 11-member Supreme Court.

Economy **Monetary unit:** novo cruzado. **Budget:** (1993 est.) ***income:*** $113 bil.; ***expend.:*** $109 bil. **GDP:** $785 bil., $5,000 per capita (1993 est.). **Chief crops:** coffee, rice, corn, sugarcane, cocoa, soybeans; nearly self-sufficient except for wheat. **Livestock:** cattle, pigs, sheep, goats, horses, mules, asses. **Natural resources:** iron ore, manganese, bauxite, nickel, uranium. **Major industries:** textiles and other consumer goods, shoes, chemicals. **Labor force:** 57 mil. (1989 est.); 42% services, 31% agriculture, 27% industry; 2% unemployment (1989). **Exports:** $38.8 bil. (f.o.b., 1993); coffee, metallurgical products, chemical products, foodstuffs, iron ore. **Imports:** $25.7 bil. (f.o.b., 1993); crude oil, capital goods, chemical products, foodstuffs, coal. **Major trading partners:** (1991) ***exports:*** 32.3% EU, 20.3% U.S., 11.6% Latin America, 9% Japan; ***imports:*** 23.5% U.S., 21.8% EU, 18.8% Latin America, 12.4% Middle East, 6% Japan.

Intl. Orgs. FAO, G-77, GATT, IAEA, IBRD, ICAO, IDA, IFAD, IFC, ILO, IMF, IMO, INTELSAT, ITU, OAS, UN, UNESCO, UPU, WHO, WIPO, WMO.

The Portuguese arrived on the coast of what would become Brazil with the expedition of Pedro Alvares Cabral in 1500 and found an indigenous population of semisedentary and nonsedentary cultures. Many of the semisedentary Indians spoke the Tupian language and shared similar cultural features. The Tupians quickly formed economic relationships with the first Europeans, who were interested in the valuable dyewood that was so abundant in Brazil.

The transition of Indian-European economic relations from barter to slavery was given momentum by the introduction of sugar export agriculture, a trend that began in the region in the 1540s. The 1560s saw epidemics of smallpox and measles in the coastal areas, which greatly reduced the indigenous population. Although the European sugar growers initially favored the use of indigenous peoples over imported African slave labor (owing to the lower price of Indian slaves), the shortage of labor resulting from the epidemics led to increasing use of African slave labor by the Portuguese.

The Portuguese vied with other European powers for control of Brazilian territory, and in 1630 the Dutch briefly seized the northeastern sugar-growing area. Brazil's southern regions were underpopulated during the early colonial period, and Portuguese activity was largely limited to cattle raising. With the discovery of gold (1690s) and diamonds (1729), European interest in and settlement of the Minas Gerais area in the southeast quickened.

In 1808, the Portuguese royal court escaped Napoleon's armies with the help of the British fleet, and the prince regent, Dom João VI, sought refuge in Brazil and made it the seat of the Portuguese empire. Dom João returned to a Portugal liberated from Napoleonic occupation in 1821, leaving his son Dom Pedro behind as prince regent. In 1822, defying orders to return to Portugal and opposed to the imminent reversion of Brazil to colonial status, Dom Pedro declared Brazil's independence and was crowned emperor. In 1825 an agreement mediated by the British led to Portuguese recognition of Brazil as a separate kingdom.

The early years of independence were rocky. Dom Pedro became increasingly estranged from his people and began losing control of the Brazilian political situation owing to a continuing series of landowner revolts and to the loss of a war with the United Provinces of Rio de la Plata over what would become Uruguay. In 1831 Dom Pedro abdicated in favor of his five-year-old son, Dom Pedro II; a regency governed Brazil until his accession to the throne in 1840.

The Brazilian empire found itself continually involved in the wars and internal politics of Uruguay, Argentina, and Paraguay in the 1850s and 1860s. The bloody five-year war with Paraguay that began in 1865 resulted in Paraguay's eventual defeat, but the process of the war had important consequences for the future of Brazil: the expansion of the military in numbers and power, the fragmentation of the political party system, and the undermining of the legitimacy of slavery. Slavery was abolished in 1888, and the following year, a military coup overthrew the emperor.

The "Old Republic," which lasted from 1889 to 1930, was a federal system in which much of the political control in Brazilian society was relegated to state-based political networks with local bosses. The presidency was assigned in a de facto rotation system called the "politics of the governors," in which the president's office was controlled by the most important state power networks. The world depression of 1929 hit the Brazilian agricultural export economy hard, and in 1930 the military overthrew the elected president; Getúlio Vargas, a politician from the state of Rio Grande do Sul, took over the presidency.

Vargas proceeded to centralize power in the presidency, diminishing states' rights dramatically. Civil unrest allowed Vargas to declare a state of siege with military backing, and in 1937 he declared the establishment of the Estado Novo, a state wherein Vargas had absolute power, in imitation of Portuguese and Italian regimes of the period. The military ousted Vargas in 1945, ushering in the period of the "Second Republic." Vargas again won reelection in 1950 but committed suicide in 1954. Juscelino Kubitschek, elected president in 1955, sought to develop the country and led the way for construction of the new capital of Brasília in the previously undeveloped interior.

His successor, Jânio da Silva Quadros, resigned in 1961 after only seven months in office, and the presidency passed to populist Vice Pres. João Goulart. The populist mobilization of peasants and workers endorsed by the Goulart government led to his overthrow by the military in 1964.

The Brazilian military governed the country until 1985. Military rule was not maintained in the form of a dictatorship; rather, the military ruled as a more or less cohesive institution. The succession of generals and their technocratic allies attempted to develop the country through a pattern of state-led growth from which civilian politics were excluded. The tendency for the military to become institutionally divided through its involvement in political governance combined with social groups' increasing demands to be included in the political process led to the transition toward civilian leadership in Brazil.

In 1985, Tancredo Neves, a civilian, was elected president, but he died before taking office. José Sarney, the vice presidential candidate, became Brazil's first civilian president since 1964.

Promising to revitalize the economy with a free-market revolution, less government, and more growth, conservative Fernando Collor de Mello became president in 1990. The military's share of the budget was reduced from 6 percent to 2.2 percent, and some companies were privatized, but inflation and debt still strained the economy.

The 1988 murder of environmental activist Chico Mendes focused world attention on the rapidly accelerating deforestation of the Amazon River basin. Pres. Collor campaigned actively to halt the destruction in Amazonia—including protecting the Stone Age Yanomami Indians—and in June 1992 Rio De Janeiro was the site of a UN-sponsored conference on development and the environment.

Pres. Collor lost the confidence of the legislature and the people as evidence mounted that he stole or misappropriated over $20 million, and he resigned in December 1992. His successor, Vice Pres. Itamar Franco, has worked to privatize government industries and halt rampant inflation, but a new corruption scandal involving at least 18 members of the legislature halted most government activity in 1994.

In presidential elections held in October 1994, former finance minister Fernando Henrique Cardoso ran on an anti-inflation platform and won a landslide victory over his nearest challenger.

Brunei

Negara Brunei Darussalam

Geography Location: southeastern Asia, Kalimantan (Borneo) island. Bandar Seri Begawan 4°56'N, 114°58'E. **Boundaries:** surrounded on landward side by Sarawak, state, of Malaysia; South China Sea to N. **Total land area:** 2,228 sq. mi. (5,770 sq km). **Coastline:** 100 mi. (161 km). **Comparative area:** slightly larger than Delaware. **Land use:** 1% arable land; 1% permanent crops; 1% meadows and pastures; 79% forest and woodland; 18% other; includes negl. % irrigated. **Major cities:** Bandar Seri Begawan (formerly Brunei Town) (capital) 50,500 (1986 est.); Seria, Kuala Belait, Tutong.

People Population: 284,653 (1994 est.). **Nationality:** noun—Bruneian(s); adjective—Bruneian. **Ethnic groups:** 64% Malay, 20% Chinese, 16% other. **Languages:** Malay (official), English, Chinese. **Religions:** 60% Muslim (official), 32% Buddhist and indigenous beliefs, 8% Christian.

Government Type: constitutional sultanate. **Independence:** Jan. 1, 1984 (from UK). **Constitution:** Sept. 29, 1959 (some provisions suspended since Dec. 1962, others since independence). **National holiday:** National Day, Feb. 23. **Head of government:** Sir Hassanal Bolkiah, sultan and prime minister (since Aug. 1968). **Structure:** chief of state is sultan (advised by appointed privy council), who appoints executive council and legislative council.

Economy Monetary unit: brunei dollar. **Budget:** (1989) ***income:*** $1.3 bil.; ***expend.:*** $1.5 bil. **GDP:** $2.5 bil., $9,000 per capita (1991 est.). **Chief crops:** rice, pepper. **Livestock:** pigs, buffalo, cattle, goats. **Natural resources:** crude oil, natural oil, natural gas, timber. **Major industries:** crude petroleum, liquefied natural gas, construction. **Labor force:** 89,000 (1986; includes members of army); 50.4% production of oil and natural gas, construction; 47.6% trade, services, and other; 2.0% agriculture, forestry, and fishing. **Exports:** $2.3 bil. (f.o.b., 1992 est.); 98–99% crude oil, liquefied natural gas, petroleum products. **Imports:** $2 bil. (c.i.f., 1992 est.); includes machinery and transport equipment, manufactured goods, beverages, tobacco; most consumer goods and food imported. **Major trading partners:** (1990) ***exports:*** 53% Japan, 12% UK, 9% South Korea, 7% Thailand, 5% Singapore; ***imports:*** 36% Singapore, 26% UK, 9% U.S., 7% Switzerland, 5% Japan.

Intl. Orgs. ASEAN, ICAO, IMO, INTERPOL, ITU, UN, UPU, WHO, WMO, WTO.

The Islamic sultanate of Brunei became dominant in northern Borneo in the 16th century but declined in power after the 17th century under pressure from the Dutch and other foreign powers. An Anglo-Dutch agreement of 1824 assigned North Borneo to Great Britain's sphere of influence in Asia. In 1841 a British adventurer, James Brooke, aided the sultan of Brunei in putting down a rebellion and was rewarded by being given the province of Sarawak, comprising more than half of the sultanate's area. Britain established a protectorate over Sabah, the eastern portion of Brunei, in 1881. That left the sultan with a tiny realm on the Brunei River, which was ultimately placed under British protection in 1888. The discovery of Southeast Asia's richest oilfield in Brunei and its offshore waters made the sultanate an enclave of tremendous wealth from the late 1920s onward.

Following Japanese occupation during World War II, British rule resumed in North Borneo. Sarawak and Sabah became part of Malaysia in 1963. Brunei was granted independence from Great Britain on Dec. 1, 1984. The sultan of Brunei, an absolute monarch, rules from the world's largest royal palace in Bandar Seri Begawan, the nation's capital. The economy is centered almost entirely on petroleum and international banking and investments.

Bulgaria

Republic of Bulgaria

Geography Location: southeastern Europe. **Boundaries:** Romania to N, Black Sea to E, Turkey and Greece to S, Macedonia and Yugoslavia to W. **Total land area:** 42,822 sq. mi. (110,910 sq km). **Coastline:** 220 mi. (354 km). **Comparative area:** between Tennessee and Pennsylvania. **Land use:** 34% arable land; 3% permanent crops; 18% meadows and pastures; 35% forest and woodland; 10% other; includes 11% irrigated. **Major cities:** (1992 est.) Sofia (capital) 1,114,476; Plovdiv 341,374; Varna 308,601; Burges 195,986; Ruse 170,203.

People Population: 8,799,986 (1994 est.). **Nationality:** noun—Bulgarian(s); adjective—Bulgarian. **Ethnic groups:** 85.3% Bulgarian, 8.5% Turk, 2.6% Gypsy, 2.5% Macedonian, 0.3% Armenian, 0.2% Russian, 0.6% other. **Languages:** Bulgarian; secondary languages closely correspond to ethnic breakdown. **Religions:** religious background of population is 85% Bulgarian Orthodox, 13% Muslim, 0.8% Jewish, 0.7% Roman Catholic, 0.5% Protestant, Gregorian-Armenian, and other.

Government Type: emerging democracy. **Independence:** Sept. 22, 1908 (from Ottoman Empire). **Constitution:** July 13, 1991. **National holiday:** National Liberation Day, Mar. 3. **Heads of government:** Zheliu Zhelev, president (since Aug. 1990); Zhan Videnov, prime minister (since Jan. 1995). **Structure:** executive branch—president elected by the people, 15 ministers; legislative—240 popularly elected members; judiciary—Supreme Court, Court of Appeals, regional courts.

Economy Monetary unit: lev. **Budget:** (1991 est.) ***income:*** $14 bil.; ***expend:*** $17.4 bil. **GNP:** $33.9 bil., $3,800 per capita (1993 est.). **Chief crops:** grain, tobacco, fruits, vegetables, cheese, sunflower seeds; mainly self-sufficient. **Livestock:** poultry, sheep, pigs, goats, horses. **Natural resources:** bauxite, copper, lead, zinc, coal. **Major industries:** food processing, machine and metal building, electronics. **Labor force:** 4.3 mil. (1987); 33% industry, 20% agriculture, 47% other; N.A. unemployment. **Exports:** $3.5 bil. (f.o.b., 1991); 30.6% machinery and equipment; 24% agricultural products; 22.2% manufactured consumer goods; 10.5% fuels, minerals, raw materials, metals; 12.7% other. **Imports:** $2.8 bil. (f.o.b., 1991); 58.7% fuels, minerals, raw materials; 15.8% machinery and equipment; 15.2% agricultural products; 4.4% manufactured consumer goods; 5.9% other. **Major trading partners:** ***exports:*** 57.7% former CEMA countries, 26.3% developed countries; ***imports:*** 51% former CEMA countries, 32.8% developed countries.

Intl. Orgs. FAO, IAEA, ICAO, ILO, IMO, ITU, OSCE, UN, UNESCO, UPU, WHO, WIPO, WMO.

Turkic Bulgars arrived at the west shore of the Black Sea in the seventh century, mingling with the indigenous Slavic population. The Bulgars accepted Eastern Orthodox Christianity in the ninth century and were conquered and incorporated into the Byzantine Empire by Basil II in the late 10th century. With the decline of Byzantium, Bulgaria became an independent kingdom, but it was conquered by the Ottoman Turks in 1396 and remained part of the Ottoman Empire for the next 500 years.

In the Treaty of San Stefano, ending the Russo-Turkish War in 1878, a Bulgarian state was promised that was to stretch from the Adriatic to the Black Sea. But the Great Powers would not permit so large a Russian client state, and instead the Berlin Conference of 1878 sanctioned a much smaller Bulgarian state, under a German dynasty with the Ottoman sultan as nominal overlord. Bulgaria gained full independence in 1908.

The Balkan Wars of 1912 and 1913 led to a reduction of Bulgarian territory, and after World War I, Bulgaria, which had been allied with the Central Powers, lost its Aegean coastline to Greece. A series of weak parliamentary governments under King Boris III (r. 1918–43) ended when the king established a personal dictatorship in 1935. Bulgaria joined the Axis powers in 1941 and declared war against the Western powers but not against Russia. Under occupation by its German allies, Bulgaria once again expanded to the Aegean during the war.

Russian troops entered Bulgaria in 1944 and organized a Communist government. The boy-king Simeon II remained on the throne until 1946, when the monarchy was abolished by a popular referendum. The People's Republic of Bulgaria was established in 1947.

Until the end of World War II, Bulgaria was a peasant society, with 80 percent of the population engaged in agriculture; industrial development was rudimentary. The People's Republic established a planned economy on the Soviet model; Russian credits and trade agreements permitted a rapid industrialization focused on machinery and equipment for export.

In 1954 Todor Zhivkov became first secretary of the Bulgarian Communist party. He served as premier in the 1960s and president from 1971 to 1990.

In the 1960s Zhivkov promoted decentralization and responsiveness to market forces, but with the 1968 Russian invasion of Czechoslovakia, he returned the economy to central planning, collective farming, and giant state-industrial enterprises. In October 1985 Zhivkov met with Gorbachev and reforms based on Gorbachev's "self-management" policies were instituted.

Democratic reform began with Zhivkov's sudden resignation in November 1989. There followed a year of popular unrest and political turmoil with a succession of changes in the ruling hierarchy, culminating in the election of Zheliu Zhelev of the reform Union of Democratic Forces as president (Bulgaria's first non-Communist leader in 40 years), and the appointment in 1990 of political independent Dimitar Popov as premier of a coalition government dominated by the Socialist (formerly Communist) party.

Elections in October 1991 ended the Socialist grip on power, as the Union of Democratic Forces won 110 of the Parliament's 240 seats and formed a government under lawyer and novelist Philip Dimitrov. But in mid-1992 the government was bankrupt, inflation was 30 percent, and unemployment was 40 percent. By October, Dimitrov's government was ousted by Parliament. After a two-month search, Lyuben Berov, an economic adviser to Zhelev, was finally chosen. The Berov government was replaced by a caretaker regime (Oct. 1994) until the December elections, in which the Socialists (the renamed Communists) carried an absolute majority of 125 members in the Parliament of 240; the Union of Democratic Forces won only 68 seats. Bulgaria thus followed the lead of Poland, Hungary, and Lithuania in restoring the Communists to power, here under Zhan Videnov as premier.

Burkina Faso

Geography Location: landlocked country in western Africa. **Boundaries:** Mali to N and W, Niger to E, Benin, Togo, Ghana, Ivory Coast to S. **Total land area:** 105,869 sq. mi. (274,200 sq km). **Coastline:** none. **Comparative area:** between Colorado and Nevada. **Land use:** 10% arable land; negl. % permanent crops; 37% meadows and pastures; 26% forest and woodland; 27% other; includes negl. % irrigated. **Major cities:** (1985 census) Ouagadougou (capital) 441,514; Bobo-Dioulasso 228,668; Koudougou 51,926; Ouahigouya 38,902; Banfora 35,319.

People Population: 10,134,661 (1994 est.). **Nationality:** noun—Burkinabe (sing., pl.); adjective—Burkinabe. **Ethnic groups:** Mossi (about 2.5 mil.), Gurunsi, Senufo, Lobi, Bobo, Mande, Fulani. **Languages:** French (official); tribal languages spoken by 90% of population. **Religions:** 65% indigenous beliefs, 25% Muslim, 10% Christian (mainly Roman Catholic).

Government Type: military; established by coup on Aug. 4, 1983. **Independence:** Aug. 5, 1960 (from France). **Constitution:** June 1991; Constitution of Nov. 1977 was abolished following coup of Nov. 25, 1980. **National holiday:** Independence Day, Aug. 4. **Heads of government:** Blaise Compaore, president (since Dec. 1991); M. Marc Christian Roch Kobore, prime minister (since Mar. 1994). **Structure:** executive—president; military council of unknown number; 21-member military and civilian cabinet; judiciary.

Economy Monetary unit: Communauté Financière Africaine (CFA) franc. **Budget:** (1991) ***income:*** $483 mil.; ***expend.:*** $548 mil. **GDP:** $7 bil., $700 per capita (1993 est.). **Chief crops:** cash crops—peanuts, shea nuts, sesame, cotton; food crops—sorghum, millet, corn, rice; food shortages. **Livestock:** cattle, goats, sheep, pigs, asses. **Natural resources:** manganese, limestone, marble; small deposits of gold, antimony, copper, nickel, bauxite. **Major industries:** agricultural processing plants; brewery, cement, and brick plants. **Labor force:** 3.3 mil. (1984); 82% agriculture, 13% industry, 5% other; 20% of male labor force migrates annually to neighboring countries for seasonal employment; 30,000 are wage earners; 44% of population of working age. **Exports:** $300 mil. (f.o.b., 1992); livestock, oilseeds, gold, cotton. **Imports:** $685 mil. (f.o.b., 1992); machinery, grain, dairy products, petroleum. **Major trading partners:** ***exports:*** (1985) 45% EU (30% France), 15% Taiwan, 15% Ivory Coast; ***imports:*** 51% EU (23% France), 25% Africa, 6% U.S.

Intl. Orgs. FAO, G-77, IBRD, ICAO, IDA, IFAD, IFC, ILO, IMF, INTELSAT, INTERPOL, ITU, NAM, UN, UNESCO, UPU, WHO, WIPO, WMO, WTO.

The Mossi empire dominated the area of what is now Burkina Faso, a landlocked nation in western Africa with few natural resources and poor agricultural conditions, from as early as the 11th century. They ruled the region, often resisting Muslim invaders, until modern times.

The region was hardly visited by Europeans before the 1880s, but by 1896 the French had captured the Mossi capital city of Ouagadougou and established a protectorate over the area. The French created Upper Volta in 1919, naming it for the upper basin of the Volta River. Upper Volta became a self-governing state with the French Overseas Community in 1958 and gained independence Aug. 5, 1960.

After a brief period of military rule, the nation ratified a new constitution on June 14, 1970, and made a peaceful transition to civilian rule based on the French model. In 1980 the constitution was overthrown and a military government was set up. There was another coup on Aug. 4, 1983, and a government was established patterned after the Libyan government of Muammar al-Qaddafi. On Aug. 14, 1984, Upper Volta officially changed its name to Burkina Faso.

Two attempted coups against the government of Capt. Blaise Compaore, in September and December 1989, were put down and the leaders executed. In 1992, as president, Compaore convened a National Reconciliation Forum followed by legislative elections that resulted in a new prime minister. In 1994 the World Bank reported significant economic progress in this desperately poor country.

Burundi

Republic of Burundi

Geography Location: landlocked country on northeastern shore of Lake Tanganyika in central Africa. **Boundaries:** Rwanda to N, Tanzania to E and S, Zaire to W. **Total land area:** 10,745 sq. mi. (27,830 sq km). **Coastline:** none. **Comparative area:** slightly larger than Maryland. **Land use:** 43% arable land; 8% permanent crops; 35% meadows and pastures; 2% forest and woodland; 12% other; includes negl. % irrigated.

Major cities: Bujumbura (capital) 215,243 (1987 est.); Gitega 15,943 (1978).

People Population: 6,124,747 (1994 est.). **Nationality:** noun—Burundian(s); adjective—Burundi. **Ethnic groups:** 85% Hutu (Bantu), 14% Tutsi (Hamitic), 1% Twa (Pygmy); 70,000 refugees, mostly Rwandans and Zairians; 3,000 Europeans and 2,000 South Asians. **Languages:** Kirundi and French (both official), Swahili (along Lake Tanganyika and in Bujumbura area). **Religions:** 67% Christian (62% Roman Catholic, 5% Protestant), 32% indigenous beliefs, 1% Muslim.

Government Type: republic. **Independence:** July 1, 1962 (from UN trusteeship under Belgian administration). **Constitution:** Nov. 20, 1981; on taking power Maj. Pierre Buyoya suspended constitution and formed Military Council for National Redemption. **National holiday:** Independence Day, July 1. **Heads of government:** M. Sylvestre Ntibantunganya, president (since Apr. 1994); Antoine Nduwayo, prime minister (since Mar. 1995). **Structure:** executive—president and cabinet; legislature—National Assembly reestablished in 1982; judiciary.

Economy Monetary unit: Burundi franc. **Budget:** (1991 est.) ***income:*** $318 mil.; ***expend.:*** $326 mil. **GDP:** $4.4 bil., $700 per capita (1993 est.). **Chief crops:** cash crops—coffee, cotton, tea; food crops—manioc, yams, peas, corn, sorghum. **Livestock:** goats, cattle, sheep, pigs. **Natural resources:** nickel, uranium, rare earth oxide, peat, cobalt. **Major industries:** light consumer goods such as blankets, shoes, soap; assembly of imports; public works construction. **Labor force:** 1.9 mil. (1983); 93% agriculture, 7% other. **Exports:** $40.8 mil. (f.o.b., 1992 est.); 87% coffee; tea, cotton, hides, skins. **Imports:** $188 mil. (c.i.f., 1992 est.); 31% capital goods, 15% petroleum products, foodstuffs. **Major trading partners:** ***exports:*** 83% EU, 5% U.S., 2% Asia; ***imports:*** 57% EU, 23% Asia, 3% U.S.

Intl. Orgs. FAO, G-77, IBRD, ICAO, IDA, IFAD, IFC, ILO, IMF, INTERPOL, ITU, NAM, UN, UNESCO, UPU, WHO, WIPO, WMO, WTO.

Burundi's population is divided between two ethnic groups, the majority Hutu and the minority, but politically powerful, Tutsi. The Hutu were the original settlers of the country and practiced agriculture; the cattle-herding Tutsi arrived several hundred years ago and established a form of feudal overlordship over the Hutu. The traditional government was monarchical, with a king *(mwami)* chosen from among a group of aristocratic families *(ganwa).*

European exploration of Burundi began in 1858, and the territory was incorporated into German East Africa in 1899. Following World War I, the League of Nations in 1923 awarded Burundi, along with neighboring Rwanda, to Belgium as a mandated territory. Belgian rule over the Territory of Ruanda-Urundi, as it was then called, continued under a UN trusteeship after World War II.

Burundi became independent on July 1, 1962, as a constitutional monarchy under the traditional mwami. The country rapidly lapsed into political chaos. In 1966, with the backing of the army, Capt. Michel Micombero overthrew the monarchy and proclaimed a republic. A Hutu rebellion in 1972 against Tutsi political domination left 10,000 Tutsi dead; Tutsi reprisals in 1972–73 resulted in the slaughter of 150,000 Hutu. The Micombero government was overthrown in a bloodless coup, and on Nov. 1, 1976, Lt. Col. Jean-Baptiste Bagaza took control of the government.

Bagaza was overthrown in September 1987, and his successor, Maj. Pierre Buyoya, proclaimed a policy of nonalignment in foreign affairs, seeking closer links with the West, while maintaining relations with Libya and the eastern bloc. Domestically, the government pledged to eradicate Bagaza's record of persecution of the Catholic church (62% of Burundians are Catholic) and to seek ethnic reconciliation between Hutu and Tutsi. The latter policy was threatened, however, by renewed outbreaks of ethnic violence in 1988. Buyoya led the country to its first free presidential elections in June 1993. Melchior Ndadaye, a Hutu, defeated Buyoya by a wide margin.

But in October 1993 the ethnic violence returned, when the Tutsi-dominated military seized control of the government and assassinated Ndadaye. In the ensuing months, the military massacred more than 100,000 civilians, even as opposition to the military regime mounted. Another Hutu, Cyprien Ntaryamira, was elected president in January of 1994, but he too was assassinated along with Rwandan president Juvénal Habyarimana when a plane carrying both of them was shot down by rocket-fire outside the Rwandan capital of Kigali. It was believed to be the work of the Rwandan military, which is also dominated by Tutsis. In September 1994 the National Assembly elected M. Sylvestre Ntibantunganya (a Hutu) as president. The October attempt to form an ethnically balanced government under a Tutsi premier came to naught when in December the Tutsi Union for National Progress resigned from the cabinet. Another makeshift government was formed in February under Tutsi Antoine Nduwayo.

Burundi continues to be ravaged by ethnic warfare between Tutsis and Hutus. Millions of Burundians have been left homeless and/or forced into exile by this most recent round of ethnic strife. Grave escalation of ethnic violence in March 1995 drove 50,000 Hutu from the capital. The flight of Hutu from Burundi was joined by Rwandan refugees, overwhelming neighboring Zaire and Tanzania. (For further developments, see Part I: "Major News Stories of the Year.")

Cambodia

State of Cambodia

Geography Location: on Indochinese peninsula in Southeast Asia. **Boundaries:** Thailand to W and N, Laos to N, Gulf of Thailand to S, Vietnam to E. **Total land area:** 69,900 sq. mi. (181,040 sq km). **Coastline:** 275 mi. (443 km). **Comparative area:** between Missouri and Oklahoma. **Land use:** 16% arable land; 1% permanent crops; 3% meadows and pastures; 76% forest and woodland; 4% other; includes 1% irrigated. **Major cities:** (1991 est.) Phnom Penh (capital) 900,000.

People Population: 10,264,628 (1994 est.). **Nationality:** noun—Cambodian(s); adjective—Cambodian. **Ethnic groups:** 90% Khmer (Cambodian), 5% Vietnamese, 1% Chinese, 5% other minorities. **Languages:** Khmer (official), French. **Religions:** 95% Theravada Buddhism, 5% other.

Government Type: none; under transitional UN management. **Constitution:** none; to be drafted by newly elected government after May 1993. **Heads of government:** Prince Norodom Sihanouk, president of 11 member Supreme National Council (since Sept. 1993); Sdech Krom Luong Norodom Ranariddh, prime minister (since Sept. 1993). **Structure:** The Paris Agreement of Oct. 23, 1991, established the procedures for the United Nations to take over management of the government and set up free elections for April/May 1993. The transition to UN management is progressive. On Mar. 15, 1992, the United Nations Transitional Authority in Cambodia (UNTAC) was deployed. On July 2, 1992, the civil administration component entered its active phase. The UN is managing five areas: foreign affairs, national defense, finance, information, and public security.

Economy Monetary unit: riel. **Budget:** ***income:*** $350 mil. (1993 est.); ***expend.:*** $350 mil. **GDP:** $6 bil., $600 per capita (1993 est.). **Chief crops:** mainly subsistence farming except for rubber plantations; main crops—rice, rubber, corn; food shortages—rice, meat, vegetables, dairy products, sugar, flour. **Livestock:** cattle, pigs, buffalo, horses. **Natural resources:** timber, gemstones, some iron ore, manganese, phosphates, hydropower potential. **Major industries:** rice milling, fishing, wood and wood products. **Labor force:** 2.5–3 mil.; 80% agriculture (1988 est.). **Exports:** $70 mil. (f.o.b., 1992 est.); natural rubber, rice, pepper, wood. **Imports:** $360 mil. (c.i.f, 1992 est.); international food aid, fuels, consumer goods. **Major trading partners:** Vietnam, Eastern Europe, Japan, India.

Intl. Orgs. Colombo Plan, FAO, G-77, IAEA, IBRD, ICAO, IDA, ILO, IMF, IMO, INTERPOL, ITU, NAM, UN, UNESCO, UPU, WHO, WMO.

The dominant power in Indochina from the Eighth through the 13th centuries, the Khmer Empire encompassed present-day Cambodia and much of western Thailand, southern Laos, and central and southern Vietnam. It built magnificent Buddhist temple cities at Angkor Wat and Angkor Thon. From the 14th century onward, the Khmer Empire came under increasing pressure from the expansionist Vietnamese state of Annam, which absorbed the territories east of the Mekong River. In the 18th century, the kingdom of Siam (Thailand) annexed three western provinces of the Khmer Empire. The remaining Khmer territory became the French protectorate of Cambodia in 1863, and a French colony as part of the Union of Indochina in

1887. In 1907 France forced Siam to return some territory to Cambodia.

During World War II, Cambodia was occupied by Japan from 1942 to 1945, when French control was restored. After the French defeat in Indochina, Cambodia became independent in 1953 under Prince Norodom Sihanouk, who had ascended the throne in 1941. In 1960 Sihanouk was named head of state under a constitutional monarchy. Shaken by the Vietnam War in the 1960s, Cambodia broke relations with the United States in 1965 because of South Vietnamese incursions across the border. In 1969 relations were restored when Sihanouk charged North Vietnam with arming the Khmer Rouge Cambodian Communist rebels. In the same year, American planes began secret bombing raids in Cambodia. In 1970 Sihanouk was ousted by a coup led by pro-U.S. Gen. Lon Nol; the monarchy was abolished, and Prince Sihanouk went into exile.

In April 1975 the Khmer Rouge, led by Pol Pot, captured the capital, Phnom Penh, and established a new government, the Kampuchean People's Republic. In an ensuing reign of terror, an estimated 3 million people died and hundreds of thousands more fled to refugee camps in Thailand. In 1978, Vietnamese troops invaded, capturing Phnom Penh on Jan. 7, 1979, and installing a new government led by Heng Samrin. The Kampuchean People's Republic continued to be recognized as the legal government of Cambodia in the United Nations and by most non-Soviet-bloc nations. A coalition dominated by the Khmer Rouge resisted the Vietnamese takeover, but by 1985 almost all of the country was under Vietnamese control.

Most Vietnamese troops withdrew in 1989, and Prince Sihanouk emerged as the leader of a coalition of antigovernment forces. Starting in late 1988 conferences including representatives from all Cambodian factions were held to forge a political settlement to end the 20-year-old civil war.

A peace agreement was signed on Oct. 23, 1991, providing for a cease-fire under UN supervision, the disarmament of all military factions, and the formation of a coalition government. Over the next half year slow progress was made in clearing mines, disarming factional troops, and resettling refugees; armed Khmer Rouge forces remained a threat to the peace settlement.

Despite bloody efforts by Khmer Rouge forces to disrupt the planned election, Cambodians went to the polls in large numbers on May 23, 1993. The Royalist party emerged with about 42 percent of the vote, ousting Premier Hun Sen's Cambodian People's party. Hun Sen agreed to take part in a coalition cabinet as "second premier," with Sihanouk's son, Prince Ranariddh, as "first premier." Sihanouk took the title "king." In January 1994, the united government went on the offensive and captured the Khmer Rouge stronghold and financial base of Pailin, driving 3,000 troops and 20,000 civilians into Thailand. Sihanouk negotiated $0.7 billion in international loans for rebuilding the devastated country. Surviving a coup attempt in July 1994, the government continued on the offensive against the Khmer Rouge, capturing their base at Phnom Voar in late October.

Cameroon

Republic of Cameroon

Geography **Location:** western coast of central Africa. **Boundaries:** Nigeria to NW, Chad to NE, Central African Republic to E, Congo to SE, Gabon, Equatorial Guinea to S, Gulf of Guinea to W. **Total land area:** 183,568 sq. mi. (475,440 sq km). **Coastline:** 250 mi. (402 km). **Comparative area:** slightly larger than California. **Land use:** 13% arable land; 2% permanent crops; 18% meadows and pastures; 54% forest and woodland; 13% other; includes negl. % irrigated. **Major cities:** (1986 est.) Yaoundé (capital) 653,670; Douala 1,029,731; Nkongsamba (and environs) 123,149; Maroua (and environs) 103,653.

People **Population:** 13,132,191 (1994 est.). **Nationality:** noun—Cameroonian(s); adjective—Cameroonian. **Ethnic groups:** 31% Cameroon Highlanders, 19% Equatorial Bantu, 11% Kirdi, 10% Fulani, 8% Northwestern Bantu, 7% Eastern Nigritic, 13% other African; less than 1% non-African; over 200 ethnic groups of widely differing background. **Languages:** English and French (both official); 24 major African language groups. **Religions:** 51% indigenous beliefs, 33% Christian, 16% Muslim.

Government **Type:** republic; multiparty presidential regime. **Independence:** Jan. 1, 1960 (from UN trusteeship under French administration). **Constitution:** May 20, 1972. **National holiday:** National Day, May 20. **Heads of government:** Paul Biya, president (since Nov. 1982); Achidi Simon Achu, prime minister (since Nov. 1992). **Structure:** executive—president; legislative—National Assembly; judiciary—Supreme Court has power of judicial review when questions of constitutionality are referred to it by president.

Economy **Monetary unit:** Communauté Financière Africaine (CFA) franc. **Budget:** (1989) ***income:*** $1.7 bil.; ***expend.:*** $2.4 bil. **GDP:** $19.1 bil., $1,500 per capita (1993 est.). **Chief crops:** coffee, cocoa, timber, cotton, rubber. **Livestock:** poultry, cattle, goats, sheep, pigs. **Natural resources:** crude oil, bauxite, iron ore, timber, hydropower potential. **Major industries:** crude oil production, small aluminum plant, food processing. **Labor force:** (1983) 74.4% agriculture, 11.4% industry and transport, 14.2% other services; 50% of population of working age (1985). **Exports:** $1.8 bil. (f.o.b., 1991); 56% petroleum products, cocoa, coffee, timber. **Imports:** $1.2 bil. (c.i.f., 1991); machines and electrical equipment, chemical products, consumer goods, transport equipment. **Major trading partners:** ***exports:*** 50% EU, 3% U.S. ***imports:*** 42% France, 9% Germany, 7% Japan, 4% U.S.

Intl. Orgs. FAO, G-77, IAEA, IBRD, ICAO, IDA, IFAD, IFC, ILO, IMF, IMO, INTEL SAT, INTERPOL, ITU, NAM, UN, UNESCO, UPU, WHO, WIPO, WMO, WTO.

Cameroon was settled by the Sao people about 1,000 years ago. In later times others, including the Bamileke, Bassa, Douala, and Fulani, migrated into the region. Portuguese trading stations were established along the coast beginning in the 15th century, and between 1500 and the early 19th century, the population was severely depleted by the slave trade in the hands of various European nations. European rivalries for domination in Cameroon were settled temporarily in 1884 when Germany established a protectorate.

British and French troops invaded German Cameroon during World War I, and following the war the League of Nations divided the protectorate into two mandated territories—French in the eastern sector and British in the west. French Cameroon rejected the Vichy government in World War II and became an important African base for Charles de Gaulle's Free French. In 1946 British and French rule in western and eastern Cameroon was reaffirmed under UN trusteeships.

In 1958 the French trusteeship was abolished, and the Republic of Cameroon became independent on Jan. 1, 1960. In February 1961 a UN-supervised plebiscite was held in British Cameroon, allowing the people of that region to choose between union with Nigeria and union with the Republic of Cameroon. The northern two-thirds of the British territory elected union with Nigeria; the southern portion joined the Republic of Cameroon on Oct. 1, 1961, to form the Federal Republic of Cameroon. In 1972 the federal structure was abolished by a national referendum, and the United Republic of Cameroon was established. In 1984 the nation's name reverted to the Republic of Cameroon.

During the federal period, Cameroon had a multiparty political system, with party divisions coinciding with the old distinctions between west and east Cameroon. In 1966 all political parties were amalgamated to form the Cameroon National Union, which, with various changes in name, has dominated the political life of Cameroon ever since. In 1980 Pres. Ahidjo, the long-time political leader of Cameroon, was elected without opposition to a fifth five-year term in office. He resigned in 1982 and was replaced by Prime Minister Paul Biya, who was reelected in his own right in 1984. He instituted political reforms whereby multiple candidates ran for office within the structure of the country's single-party system. In 1992 he was elected president in the nation's first multiparty elections. His closest rival was put under house arrest.

The economy of Cameroon is based primarily on agriculture. The country is self-sufficient in food and exports coffee, cocoa, rubber, cotton, palm oil, and timber. Oil is the principal export, however, accounting for 60 percent of export earnings. Overreliance on oil export earnings in the 1970s led to the growth of government bureaucracy, corruption, and excessive spending; the fall in oil prices in the 1980s thus led to economic turmoil and dislocation. These negative effects were cushioned to some extent by the health of the agricultural sector of the economy; austerity measures in the 1980s have allowed the government to begin to adjust to an era of shrinking petroleum revenues.

Canada

Geography **Location:** northern North America (excluding Alaska and Greenland); second-largest country in the world. **Boundaries:** Arctic Ocean to N, Greenland to NE across Baffin Bay, Atlantic Ocean to E, United States to S, Pacific Ocean and Alaska to W. **Total land area:** 3,851,794 sq. mi. (9,976,140 sq km). **Coastline:** 151,492 mi. (243,791 km). **Comparative area:** slightly larger than U.S. **Land use:** 5% arable land; negl. % permanent crops; 3% meadows and pastures; 35% forest and woodland; 57% other; includes negl. % irrigated. **Major cities:** (1991 census) Ottawa (capital) 912,100; Toronto 3,863,105; Montréal 3,091,115; Vancouver 1,584,115; Edmonton 832,155.

People **Population:** 28,113,997 (1994 est.). **Nationality:** noun—Canadian(s); adjective—Canadian. **Ethnic groups:** 40% British Isles origin, 27% French origin, 20% other European, 1.5% indigenous Indian or Eskimo. **Languages:** English, French. **Religions:** 46% Roman Catholic, 16% United Church, 10% Anglican.

Government **Type:** federal state recognizing Elizabeth II as sovereign. **Independence:** July 1, 1867 (from UK). **Constitution:** amended British North America Act of 1867 transferred power and rights to Canada, Apr. 17, 1982; charter of rights and unwritten customs. **National holiday:** Canada Day, July 1. **Heads of government:** Jean Chrétien, prime minister (since Nov. 1993); Ramon John Hnatyshyn, governor-general (since Jan. 1990). **Structure:** executive—cabinet collectively responsible to House of Commons and headed by prime minister; legislative—282-seat Parliament with queen represented by governor-general, Senate, and House of Commons; judiciary—judges appointed by governor-general with Supreme Court as highest tribunal.

Economy **Monetary unit:** Canadian dollar. **Budget:** (1993 est.) ***income:*** $92.3 bil.; ***expend.:*** $123.0 bil. **GDP:** $617.7 bil., $22,200 per capita (1993). **Chief crops:** grain (principally wheat), feedgrains, oilseeds, tobacco. **Livestock:** cattle, pigs, sheep. **Natural resources:** nickel, zinc, copper, gold, lead. **Major industries:** processed and unprocessed minerals, food products, wood and paper products. **Labor force:** 13.38 mil.; 75% services, 14% manufacturing; 7.8% unemployment. **Exports:** $133.9 bil. (f.o.b., 1993); newsprint, wood pulp, timber, grain, crude petroleum. **Imports:** $125.3 bil. (c.i.f., 1993); processed foods, beverages, crude petroleum, chemicals, industrial machinery. **Major trading partners:** ***exports:*** U.S., Japan, UK, Germany, other EU, former USSR; ***imports:*** U.S., Japan, UK, Germany, other EU, Taiwan, S. Korea, Mexico.

Intl. Orgs. Colombo Plan, Commonwealth, FAO, IAEA, IBRD, ICAO, IDA, IFAD, IFC, ILO, IMF, IMO, INTELSAT, INTERPOL, ITU, NATO, OAS, OECD, OSCE, UNESCO, UPU, WHO, WIPO, WMO, WTO.

Canada is geographically the second-largest country in the world, but most of its territory is very sparsely settled. The vast majority of the country's 26 million people live in a narrow band along the border with the United States. Despite a long tradition of national independence, Canada's history has been dominated by relations with Great Britain, the United States, and, to a lesser extent, France.

Canada's earliest inhabitants arrived via the Bering land bridge from Asia around 15,000 years ago and diversified to form the various Inuit (Eskimo), Northwest Indian, Plains Indian, and forest Indian cultures that still contribute significantly to Canada's national identity. The earliest-known European settlers of Canada were Vikings, who established a short-lived colony in Newfoundland around A.D. 1000. British, French, and other European explorers made numerous voyages to Canada during the 16th century, stimulated by Canada's rich resources of fish, forest products, and furs.

The first permanent European settlement in Canada was the French trading station at Quebec, founded by Samuel de Champlain in 1608. Fur traders rapidly spread into the interior along the St. Lawrence River and the Great Lakes; European diseases, particularly smallpox, decimated Native American populations as the explorers advanced. In 1663 New France was organized as a French Crown Colony, and royal governors replaced private commercial interests in governing Quebec.

The Hudson Bay Company was chartered by the British Crown in 1670, inaugurating a long period of commercial and territorial rivalry in Canada between Britain and France. In general, France sought to expand New France northward and westward, while Britain sought to expand its domination southward and westward from Hudson Bay. French and British interests clashed directly along the Atlantic coast, where both British and French settlements were established. Local and regional wars between the French and the British were endemic in Canada throughout the 17th and 18th centuries; each side enlisted Native American allies. These wars were often inconclusive, but in Queen Anne's War (1702–13), Britain gained a significant advantage by winning control of Acadia and Newfoundland, and by driving the French from Hudson Bay.

The French and Indian Wars of 1756–63, a North American extension of Europe's Seven Years' War, proved to be the decisive turning point in the Anglo-French rivalry in Canada. Prior to the outbreak of full-scale war, in 1755 the British deported some 7,000–10,000 French settlers from Acadia, in Nova Scotia, to the West Indies; many later settled in Louisiana. When war broke out in Europe in 1756, Britain employed its superior sea power to cut New France off from Europe and captured Quebec in the Battle of the Plains of Abraham in 1759. Montreal capitulated in 1760, leaving Britain in control of New France.

Faced with the difficult problem of governing New France's large and rapidly growing French population (which far outnumbered the English-speaking population of Canada), the British in 1774 passed the Quebec Act, which recognized the territory's legal code and manorial system of land tenure, and granted legal status to the Roman Catholic church. The act also extended Canadian territory south to the Ohio River, which enraged the inhabitants of the 13 American colonies and helped fuel the American Revolution.

During the American Revolution, nearly 40,000 loyalists fled to Canada from the rebellious colonies, establishing English-speaking settlements in New Brunswick and in western Quebec. Friction between English- and French-speaking Canadians led the British in 1791 to divide Canada (west of the Atlantic maritime provinces) into two provinces, Upper Canada and Lower Canada. Each was granted a legislature; that of Upper Canada was based on British institutions, while that of Lower Canada retained the French forms established by the Quebec Act of 1774.

During the War of 1812 between Great Britain and the United States, Canada became a battleground; Toronto was captured and pillaged by the Americans in 1813. Many Americans hoped to expand the territory of the United States at the expense of Canada, or even to entice Canada into a continental American union, but Canadians, whether English- or French-speaking, showed no enthusiasm for joining the United States. A small British garrison, with the support of Native American irregular forces, kept the Americans at bay. The Convention of 1818 established the border between Canada and the United States at latitude 49° north, as far west as the Rocky Mountains, and provided for joint U.S.-British control of Oregon (i.e., the entire Columbia River basin).

Following the War of 1812, British authorities actively encouraged British immigration to Canada, and between 1815 and 1855, one million Britons answered the call. This immigration radically altered the ethnic balance of Canada, making French-speaking Canadians a minority population for the first time. The francophones of Lower Canada, hemmed in on all sides by English speakers, rose in rebellion under the leadership of the Parti Patriote in 1837–38. In response, Lord Durham recommended in 1839 that Canada be united under a single government, and the Union of Canada was enacted in 1841. This move did not, however, quell the growing nationalism of French Canadians.

Oregon became an issue in the American presidential election of 1844, with the United States claiming the entire Columbia River basin north to 54°40' ("fifty-four forty or fight"). War threatened but diplomacy triumphed; in 1846 the boundary at 49° was extended westward to the Pacific Ocean. Gold was discovered in British Columbia in 1856, leading to a gold

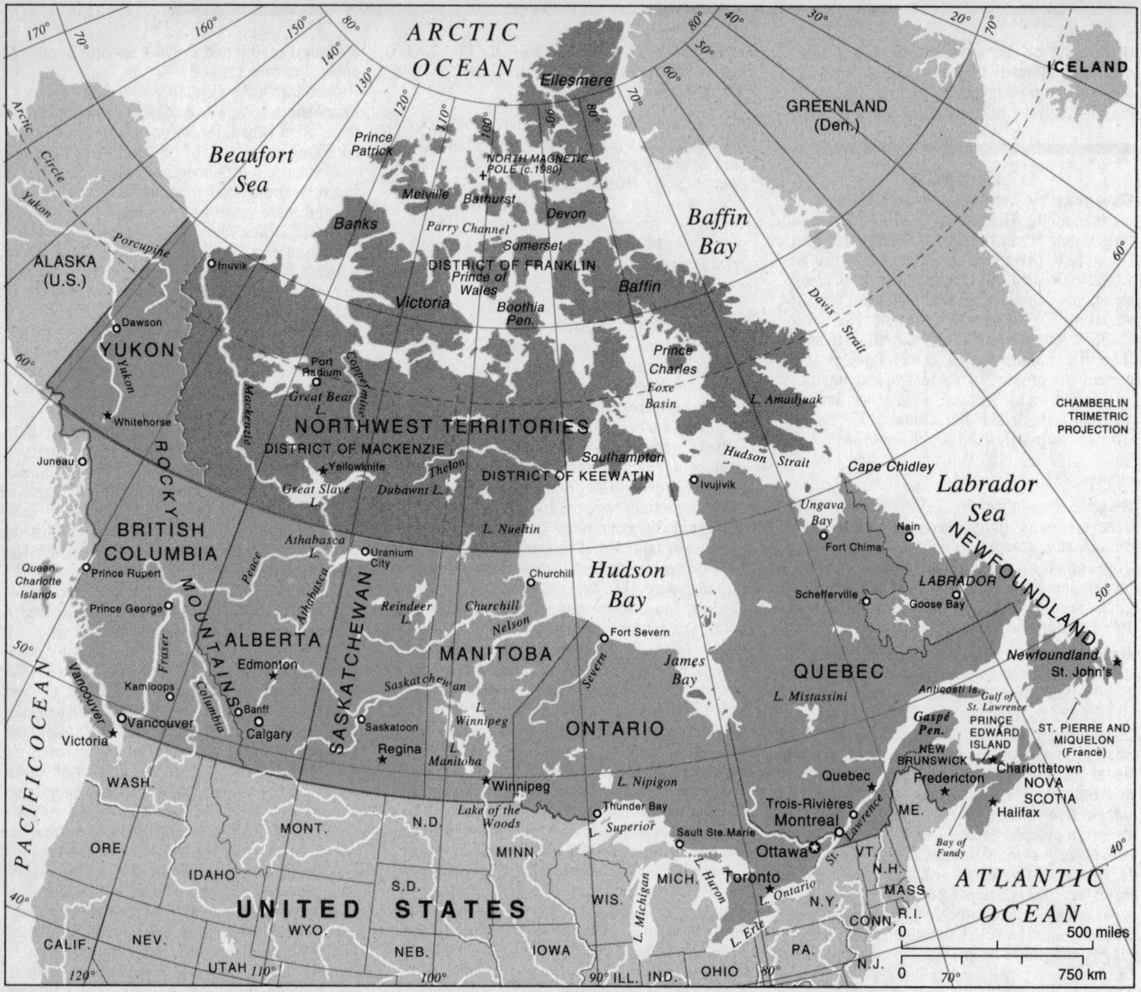

ARCTIC OCEAN
ICELAND
GREENLAND (Den.)
Ellesmere
Beaufort Sea
Prince Patrick
NORTH MAGNETIC POLE (c.1980)
Melville
Bathurst
Devon
Banks
Parry Channel
Somerset
Baffin Bay
DISTRICT OF FRANKLIN
Prince of Wales
Victoria
Boothia Pen.
Baffin
Davis Strait
Arctic Circle
Yukon
Porcupine
ALASKA (U.S.)
Inuvik
Dawson
YUKON
Port Radium
Coppermine
Great Bear L.
Mackenzie
Prince Charles
Foxe Basin
L. Amadjuak
CHAMBERLIN TRIMETRIC PROJECTION
Whitehorse
NORTHWEST TERRITORIES
DISTRICT OF MACKENZIE
Southampton
Hudson Strait
Juneau
Yellowknife
Thelon
DISTRICT OF KEEWATIN
Cape Chidley
Labrador Sea
Great Slave L.
Dubawnt L.
Ivujivik
Ungava Bay
ROCKY MOUNTAINS
BRITISH COLUMBIA
L. Nueltin
Nain
NEWFOUNDLAND
Athabasca L.
Uranium City
Fort Chimo
Queen Charlotte Islands
Prince Rupert
Peace
Athabasca
SASKATCHEWAN
Churchill
Hudson Bay
LABRADOR
Schefferville
Goose Bay
Prince George
Reindeer L.
Churchill
Nelson
Fort Severn
Newfoundland
St. John's
ALBERTA
MANITOBA
James Bay
QUEBEC
Fraser
Edmonton
Saskatchewan
Severn
L. Mistassini
Kamloops
Columbia
Anticosti Is.
Gulf of St. Lawrence
Vancouver
Banff
Calgary
Saskatoon
L. Winnipeg
ONTARIO
Gaspé Pen.
PRINCE EDWARD ISLAND
ST. PIERRE AND MIQUELON (France)
Victoria
Regina
L. Manitoba
NEW BRUNSWICK
Charlottetown
Fredericton
NOVA SCOTIA
WASH.
Winnipeg
L. Nipigon
Quebec
Halifax
Trois-Rivières
Montreal
Thunder Bay
ME.
Lake of the Woods
MONT.
N.D.
L. Superior
Sault Ste.Marie
St. Lawrence
PACIFIC OCEAN
ORE.
MINN.
Ottawa
Bay of Fundy
VT.
IDAHO
S.D.
MICH.
L. Huron
Toronto
N.H.
ATLANTIC OCEAN
L. Ontario
MASS.
UNITED STATES
WIS.
L. Michigan
N.Y.
R.I.
CONN.
CALIF.
NEV.
WYO.
NEB.
IOWA
L. Erie
PA.
N.J.
UTAH
ILL.
IND.
OHIO
0 500 miles
0 750 km

ONTARIO
Gouin Res.
L. St. Jean
Chicoutimi
Gaspé Peninsula
Anticosti Is.
Gulf of St. Lawrence
Sault Ste.Marie
QUEBEC
Saguenay
Rimouski
Sudbury
Magdalen
North Bay
Quebec
NEW BRUNSWICK
PRINCE EDWARD ISLAND
Georgian Bay
L. Huron
Ottawa
Trois-Rivières
St. Lawrence
Montreal
Moncton
Sydney
Ottawa
Sherbrooke
Charlottetown
Cape Breton Island
Fredericton
MICH.
Toronto
Kingston
ME.
St. John
NOVA SCOTIA
Kitchener
Sarnia
Hamilton
L. Ontario
VT.
Bay of Fundy
Detroit
London
Windsor
Niagara Falls
Portland
Yarmouth
Halifax
L. Erie
N.Y.
N.H.
ATLANTIC OCEAN

CANADA

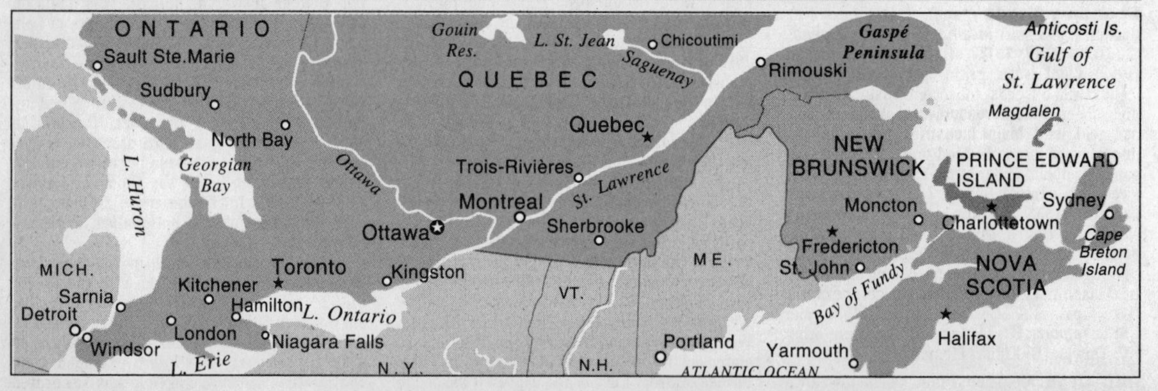

rush and a substantial increase in the population of western Canada.

Growing trade between Canada and the United States from the 1840s onward, and the development of a continental system of railroads in both Canada and the United States in the 1850s, led to a relative decline in British influence in Canada. The American Civil War had the indirect effect of prompting Canadians to seek self-government in a federal union. Previously, there had been little contact between the Canadas (Upper and Lower) and the maritime provinces, while the vast territories of the west were still privately administered by the Hudson Bay Company. A federal union was forged in a series of conferences beginning in 1864, and the federation of Quebec, Ontario, Nova Scotia, and New Brunswick was recognized by the British North America Act of July 1, 1867.

The Dominion of Canada thus established in 1867 became a self-governing entity within the British Empire; Sir J.A. Macdonald became Canada's first prime minister (1867–73). The dominion rapidly expanded. In 1869 it purchased the western territories of the Hudson Bay Company, and in 1870, in response to a rebellion of French-speaking Métis in Manitoba, Manitoba was granted provincial status within the federation. In 1871 the union of British Columbia with Canada was secured with the promise of a transcontinental railway within 10 years; the Canadian Pacific Railway was completed in 1885. Prince Edward Island joined the federation in 1873, but neighboring Newfoundland remained a British colony outside the Canadian federation until 1949.

A second francophone rebellion broke out in Manitoba in 1885. Its leader, Louis Riel, was executed and became a symbol of French Canadian grievances against the English-speaking majority. Wilfred Laurier became Canada's first francophone prime minister in 1896, but he was unable to achieve a solution to the problem of the rights of Catholics and French-speakers outside Quebec. Legislation restricting those rights had already been enacted in Manitoba in 1890.

The Klondike Gold Rush of 1897–98 brought Canada to worldwide attention and indirectly helped promote the settlement of rich agricultural lands in the Canadian west. Immigrants to the prairie region came not only from eastern Canada, but also from Europe, notably Germany, Scandinavia, and the Ukraine. Japanese farmers and Chinese railroad and mining workers settled west of the Rockies, further increasing Canada's ethnic diversity, though Asian immigrants were denied citizenship through discriminatory legislation. Alberta and Saskatchewan were granted provincial status in 1905; the Yukon Territory and the Northwest Territories continued to be governed by controllers appointed by the federal government and patrolled by the famous Royal Canadian Mounted Police.

Urbanization and industrialization were stimulated in the early 20th century by the exploitation of extensive mineral resources in western Canada and in northern Quebec, and by the development of hydroelectric projects and transportation facilities throughout the country. The long-lived Laurier government fell in 1911, when his proposal for free trade with the United States evoked widespread fears that Canada's nascent industries would suffer without protective tariffs.

Laurier's Conservative successor, Robert Borden, sent Canadian volunteer troops to fight in World War I in 1914 and, over the objections of most French Canadian leaders, bolstered Canada's war efforts in Europe through national conscription in 1917. The distinguished performance of Canada's armed forces in the war bought the country renewed international respect and appreciation.

Borden's wartime English-speaking Conservative-Liberal coalition collapsed in 1921. He was succeeded by the Liberal leader William L. Mackenzie King, who was to be Canada's prime minister for over 20 years (1921–30, 1935–48). Mackenzie King faced a challenge from the Progressive party, based in the agricultural plains provinces, but he managed to outwit and neutralize the Progressive leadership; the party disappeared as a political force after the mid-1920s. Mackenzie King skillfully managed the economic prosperity of the 1920s, which saw the establishment in Canada of branch plants of many American industrial firms.

The Statute of Westminster, which created the British Commonwealth in 1931, had the effect of granting full self-government to Canada within the Commonwealth.

Canada's federal structure was ill-equipped to manage the economic collapse of the 1930s, which brought both industrial depression and a drought-induced agricultural crisis. Efforts to deal with unemployment, land foreclosures, and other economic ills fell almost entirely to the provincial governments, which were not up to the task. The growth of private cooperative movements brought some relief to the maritime provinces and the plains provinces, while interest grew in constitutional reform to strengthen the federal government.

Canada's recovery from the Great Depression was stimulated primarily by the advent of World War II, which Canada entered in 1939. Although the war years brought price controls, rationing, and other emergency measures, the overall effect of the war was to strengthen all sectors of Canada's economy and to enhance Canada's international status as a leading military and industrial power. A Liberal electoral victory of 1945 gave Mackenzie King a renewed mandate for the postwar era.

The two decades following the war saw the gradual expansion of federal financial responsibility for national welfare measures, including pensions, unemployment insurance, and comprehensive medical care, though the administration of such programs remained a provincial matter. These developments coincided with an increase in urbanization and industrialization in the major centers of Vancouver, Toronto, and Montreal. Formal "equalization payments" were enacted in the 1950s to reduce economic disparities between rich and poor provinces. The early stages of these developments played a part in persuading Newfoundland to join the federation as Canada's 10th province in 1949.

A landslide Conservative victory in 1958 brought John Diefenbaker to the prime ministership, but the Conservatives proved unable to offer a coherent political program and were ousted in the elections of 1963, which returned the Liberals to power. Canadian politics since the 1960s have been marked by increasing regionalization; the Liberal party is based largely in the east, while the New Democratic party, organized in 1961, has little support east of Ontario. The Conservatives offer a broad but insecure national alternative. Regional politics revolve in part around the different responses of agricultural and industrial provinces to the political and economic impact of the American colossus to the south.

The language issue has continued to divide Canada politically and ideologically. The rise of an aggressive Quebecois nationalism in the 1960s led directly to the Liberal prime ministership of Pierre Trudeau, a Quebecois known as a supporter of a strong federal constitution. Trudeau's efforts toward conciliation and for constitutional guarantees for Quebec within a strong federal structure proved unavailing, however. In 1970 he invoked the War Measures Act to send troops to Quebec to put down a wave of separatist terrorism, leaving the province subdued but sullen.

The 1976 electoral victory in Quebec of the Parti Québécois under René Lévesque provoked fears that Quebec would secede from Canada. Lévesque's plan for a separate "sovereignty-association" status for Quebec was rejected by a popular referendum in 1980, but only because of Trudeau's pledge to seek full autonomy for Canada in order to secure constitutional protection for Quebec's special interests.

In November 1981, Canada's provincial governments reached agreement on proposals for constitutional change. The result was the passage by the British Parliament of the Canada Act, which came into effect on Apr. 17, 1982, granting full independence and constitutional autonomy to Canada and severing its last colonial ties to the British government. Canada's new 1982 Constitution more clearly delineated the powers of the federal and provincial governments, provided for Supreme Court review of legislation, and included a Charter of Rights to protect civil liberties.

A national recession in the late 1970s and early 1980s led to the fall of Trudeau's Liberal government and to the election of the Conservative party leader Brian Mulroney (also a native of Quebec) as prime minister in 1984. The Mulroney government encouraged foreign investment and privatization as a means of revitalizing Canada's economy.

The Meech Lake Agreement, containing a number of articles clarifying the 1982 Constitution, was worked out between Mulroney and Quebec's Liberal premier Robert Bourassa, along with the leaders of Canada's nine other provinces, and signed on June 23, 1987. In general, its provisions enhanced the power of the provinces; a key provision gave constitutional protection to Quebec's efforts to remain a "distinct society," linguistically and culturally French. The aggressive measures of the Quebec government to eradicate the use of English in the public affairs of the province provoked a backlash against bilingualism. The Meech Lake Agreement failed to become law when the legislatures of Newfoundland and Manitoba declined to ratify it by the June 23, 1990, deadline. Canada was plunged into the most serious constitutional crisis in its history.

The most significant achievement of the Mulroney government was the negotiation and passage, in 1988–89, of a free-trade agreement with the United States, to be implemented in stages during the 1990s. The issues of free trade and Quebec's possible secession remained very much alive throughout 1992. A preliminary agreement to restructure the federal government and give more power to the 10 provincial governments met initial opposition in Quebec, and was decisively defeated in a national referendum, leaving the nation to deal once again with the awkward status quo.

Faced with a drastic decline in his popularity, Prime Minister Mulroney resigned in February. In June the Progressive Conservative party convention chose Kim Campbell to lead the government, the first woman to do so in the country's history. In the general election, however, the Conservatives were routed by Jean Chrétien and the Liberals, who gained nearly 100 seats in the House of Commons. The new government announced plans in early 1995 to cut the budget deficit through higher taxes and spending cuts and to privatize Canadian National Railways.

Cape Verde

Republic of Cape Verde

Geography **Location:** archipelago of 15 islands in Atlantic Ocean, off northern Africa. Praia 14°54'N, 23°31'W. **Boundaries:** Senegal about 300 mi. (500 km) to E. **Total land area:** 1,556 sq. mi. (4,030 sq km). **Coastline:** 600 mi. (965 km). **Comparative area:** slightly larger than Rhode Island. **Land use:** 9% arable land; negl. % permanent crops; 6% meadows and pastures; negl. % forest and woodland; 85% other; includes 1% irrigated. **Major cities:** (1990 census) Cidade de Praia (capital) 62,000.

People **Population:** 423,120 (1994 est.). **Nationality:** noun—Cape Verdean(s); adjective—Cape Verdean. **Ethnic groups:** 71% Creole (mulatto), 28% African, 1% European. **Languages:** Portuguese and Crioulo (blend of Portuguese and West African). **Religions:** Roman Catholicism fused with indigenous beliefs.

Government **Type:** republic. **Independence:** July 5, 1975 (from Portugal). **Constitution:** Sept. 7, 1980, amended Feb. 12, 1981. **National holiday:** Independence Day, July 5. **Heads of government:** Antonio M. Monteiro, president (since Feb. 1991); Dr. Carlos Alberto de Carvalho Veiga, prime minister (since Feb. 1991). **Structure:** executive—president; legislative—56-member National People's Assembly.

Economy **Monetary unit:** escudo. **Budget:** (1990 est.) ***income:*** $104 mil. (1991 est.); ***expend.:*** $133 mil. (1991 est.). **GDP:** $415 mil., $1,070 per capita (1991). **Chief crops:** bananas, coffee, sugarcane, corn, beans. **Livestock:** goats, pigs, cattle, asses. **Natural resources:** salt, basalt rock, pozzolana, limestone, kaolin, fish. **Major industries:** salt mining. **Labor force:** 57% agriculture, 29% services, 14% industry (1981); 50% of population of working age (1983). **Exports:** $6 mil. (f.o.b., 1990); fish, bananas, salt, flour. **Imports:** $145 mil. (c.i.f., 1990); petroleum, foodstuffs, consumer goods, industrial products. **Major trading partners:** ***exports:*** Portugal, Angola, Algeria, Belgium/Luxembourg, Italy; ***imports:*** Portugal, Netherlands, Spain, France, U.S., Germany.

Intl. Orgs. FAO, G-77, IBRD, ICAO, IDA, IFAD, ILO, IMF, IMO, ITU, NAM, UN, UNESCO, UPU, WHO, WMO.

In 1462 the Portuguese founded the first European city in the tropics at Ribeira Grande on Santiago, one of the 15 islands that compose the Republic of Cape Verde. Located 385 miles off the west coast of Africa, the Cape Verde Islands prospered during the slave trade in the 16th century and later served as supply stations on sea routes and trading lanes. The rise of whaling in the 19th century led to contact with the United States, as American ships recruited crews from the islands. The United States set up an American consulate, headquarters for the U.S. Navy African Squadron, and a transatlantic cable station in the islands.

Portugal changed the status of the archipelago from colony to overseas province in 1951; five years later, citizens of Cape Verde and Portuguese Guinea organized the African Party for the Independence of Guinea-Bissau and Cape Verde (PAIGC) to petition Portugal to improve living conditions. Beginning as a clandestine organization, the PAIGC became an overt political movement on the islands after the 1974 revolution in Portugal. An agreement between the PAIGC and Portugal, providing for a transitional government in Cape Verde, paved the way for full independence in 1975.

In 1980 the PAIGC became the PAICV, which remained the "supreme expression" of Cape Verdeans' political will until the opposition party, Movement for Democracy, won a parliamentary majority in the nation's first multiparty elections in January 1991. The new government has instituted free market reforms, including privitization of industries.

Central African Republic

Geography **Location:** landlocked country in central Africa. **Boundaries:** Chad to N, Sudan to E, Zaire, Congo to S, Cameroon to W. **Total land area:** 240,533 sq. mi. (622,980 sq km). **Coastline:** none. **Comparative area:** slightly smaller than Texas. **Land use:** 3% arable land; negl. % permanent crops; 5% meadows and pastures; 64% forest and woodland; 28% other. **Major cities:** (1988 est.) Bangui (capital) 427,435; Berbérati 82,492; Bouar 95,193.

People **Population:** 3,142,182 (1994 est.). **Nationality:** noun—Central African(s); adjective—Central African. **Ethnic groups:** 34% Baya, 27% Banda, 21% Mandija, 10% Sara, 4% Mboum, 4% M'Baka; 6,500 Europeans, of which 3,600 are French. **Languages:** French (official), Sangho (lingua franca and national language), Arabic, Hunsa, Swahili. **Religions:** 25% Protestant, 25% Roman Catholic, 24% indigenous beliefs, 15% Muslim, 11% other; indigenous beliefs and practices strongly influence Christian majority.

Government **Type:** republic. **Independence:** Aug. 13, 1960 (from France). **Constitution:** Nov. 21, 1986. **National holiday:** Independence Day, Aug. 13. **Heads of government:** Ange Félixe Patasse, head of state (since Oct. 1993); Jean-Luc Mandaba, prime minister (since Sept. 1993). **Structure:** executive—chief of state; legislative—parliament, includes National Assembly and Social and Economic Council; judiciary.

Economy **Monetary unit:** Communauté Financière Africaine (CFA) franc. **Budget:** (1990 est.) ***income:*** $175 mil.; ***expend.:*** $312 mil. **GDP:** $2.5 bil., $800 per capita (1993 est.). **Chief crops:** cash crops—cotton, coffee, peanuts, sesame, tobacco; food crops—manioc, corn, millet, sorghum, peanuts. **Livestock:** cattle, goats, pigs, sheep. **Natural resources:** diamonds, uranium, timber, gold, oil. **Major industries:** sawmills, breweries, diamond mining. **Labor force:** 775,413 (1986 est.); 85.0% agriculture, 8.9% commerce and services, 6.1% other. **Exports:** $123.5 mil. (f.o.b., 1992); diamonds, cotton, coffee, timber, tobacco. **Imports:** $165.1 mil. (f.o.b., 1992); food, textiles, petroleum products, machinery, electrical equipment, motor vehicles. **Major trading partners:** ***exports:*** France, Belgium, Japan, U.S.; ***imports:*** France, other EU countries, Japan, Algeria, Yugoslavia.

Intl. Orgs. FAO, G-77, IBRD, ICAO, IDA, IFAD, ILO, IMF, INTELSAT, INTERPOL, ITU, NAM, UN, UNESCO, UPU, WHO, WIPO, WMO, WTO.

A landlocked country in Africa's central region, the Central African Republic is one of the least-developed countries in the world. Most of its people are farmers, and the nation has little manufacturing, few reliable roads, and no railroad. Europeans first came to the area in the early 1800s in their search for slaves, but it was not until 1889 that the French established an outpost as the current capital city of Bangui. The region was organized as the territory of Ubangi-Shari five years later. In 1910 Ubangi-Shari was incorporated into French Equitorial Africa along with what are now the countries of Chad, the Congo, and Gabon.

The country was granted internal self-government by the French under its present name in 1958 and became a member of the French Overseas Community. Independence was achieved on Aug. 13, 1960. The first prime minister, Barthelemy Boganda, was killed in an airplane crash in 1959 and was succeeded by his nephew, David Dacko. Dacko was elected to a seven-year term in January 1964, but an army coup in 1966 overthrew his government. The head of the army, Jean-Bedel Bokassa, was installed as president. Named president for life in 1972, in 1976 Bokassa declared himself emperor and changed the name of the country to the Central African Empire.

Dacko returned to power in 1979, however, and Bokassa went into exile in France. The name of the country was changed back to the Central African Republic. A multiparty political system was reinstated in March 1981, but army officers threw Dacko out of office once again six months later and banned all political parties. Though the military was again in control, the government put Bokassa on trial for a variety of crimes after his return in 1986, and he was sentenced to life in prison. Opposition parties were legalized in 1991 and elections were held in 1993. Bokassa was released shortly thereafter.

Chad

Republic of Chad

Geography **Location:** landlocked country in north central Africa. **Boundaries:** Libya to N, Sudan to E, Central African Republic to S, Cameroon, Nigeria to SE, Niger to W. **Total land area:** 495,753 sq. mi. (1,284,000 sq km). **Coastline:** none. **Comparative area:** between Texas and Alaska. **Land use:** 2% arable land; negl. % permanent crops; 36% meadows and pastures; 11% forest and woodland; 51% other; includes negl. % irrigated. **Major cities:** (1988 est.) N'Djamena (capital) 594,000; Sarh 113,400; Moundou 102,000; Abéché 83,000.

People **Population:** 5,466,771 (1994 est.). **Nationality:** noun—Chadian(s); adjective—Chadian. **Ethnic groups:** 200 distinct ethnic groups, most of whom are Muslims (Arabs, Toubou, Fulbe, Kotoko, Hausa, Kanembou, Baguirmi, Boulala, and Maba) in north and center and non-Muslims (Sara, Ngambaye, Mbake, Goulaye, Moudang, Moussei, Massa) in south; some 15,000 nonindigenous, of whom 1,000 are French. **Languages:** French and Arabic (both official); Sara and Sango in south; more than 100 different languages and dialects. **Religions:** 44% Muslim, 33% Christian, 23% indigenous beliefs.

Government **Type:** republic. **Independence:** Aug. 11, 1960 (from France). **Constitution:** Apr. 14, 1962 (currently suspended); National Charter, promulgated March 1991, serves as basis for government. **National holiday:** Independence Day, Aug. 11. **Heads of government:** Idriss Deby, president (since Dec. 1990); Koibla Djimasta, prime minister (since Apr. 1995). **Structure:** executive—president; Council of Ministers; National Consultative Council; judiciary—court of appeal.

Economy **Monetary unit:** Communauté Financière Africaine (CFA) franc. **Budget:** (1991 est.) ***income:*** $115 mil.; ***expend.:*** $412 mil., **GDP:** $2.7 bil., $500 per capita, (1993 est.). **Chief crops:** cash crops—cotton, gum arabic, peanuts, fish; food crops—millet, sorghum, rice, sweet potatoes, yams, cassava, dates. **Livestock:** goats, sheep, cattle, asses, camels. **Natural resources:** small quantities of crude oil (unexploited but exploitation beginning), uranium, natron (sodium carbonate), kaolin, fish (Lake Chad). **Major industries:** cotton textile mills, slaughterhouses, brewery, natron. **Labor force:** 85% agriculture—unpaid subsistence farming, herding and fishing, 15% other. **Exports:** $193.9 mil. (f.o.b., 1991); 48% cotton, 35% cattle, 5% textiles, fish. **Imports:** $294.1 mil. (f.o.b., 1991 est.); 39% machinery and transport equipment, 20% industrial goods, 13% petroleum products, 9% foodstuffs. **Major trading partners:** ***exports:*** France, Nigeria, Cameroon; ***imports:*** U.S., France, Nigeria, Cameroon.

Intl. Orgs. EU (associate), FAO, G-77, IBRD, ICAO, IDA, IFAD, ILO, IMF, INTELSAT, INTERPOL, ITU, NAM, UN, UNESCO, UPU, WHO, WIPO, WMO, WTO.

The Sao and other ancient peoples built centers of civilization near Lake Chad that flourished for many centuries until they were displaced by the medieval kingdoms of Kanem-Bornu, Baguirmi, and Ouaddai. From about 1400 onward, Chad became a meeting ground between the Muslim cultures of the Sahara and the Sahel and the black African societies of the tropics. Between 1500 and 1800, Arab slave raiders were active around Lake Chad, supplying slaves for European traders on Africa's west coast.

French military forces reached Chad from West Africa in 1891 and fought a series of battles over the next two decades with the Arab rulers of the region. A French governorship of Chad was established in 1905 (based in Brazzaville, the Congo), but the country was not brought entirely under French control until 1914. Chad was incorporated into the federation of French Equatorial Africa in 1910 and was organized as a colony within the federation in 1920.

French Equatorial Africa was dissolved in 1959, and Chad became an autonomous member of the French Community. Full independence followed on Aug. 11, 1960; François Tombalbage became Chad's first president. In 1965 the Muslim northern and eastern parts of the country rebelled against the southern-led government; despite the aid of French troops, the government was unable to suppress the rebellion, and civil war became endemic.

Tombalbage was overthrown in 1975 in a military coup led by another southerner, Gen. Felix Malloum. Efforts to broaden the composition of the national government broke down, and in 1979 Prime Minister Hissein Habre broke with the government and led northern forces against the national army. A cease-fire was negotiated under international auspices, and a National Unity Transitional Government (GUNT) was installed in November 1979, but civil war broke out again in March 1980. Pres. Goukouni Oueddei sought Libyan aid in restoring order; a contingent of 7,000 Libyan troops occupied the country until 1981. They were replaced by an international peacekeeping force organized by the Organization of African Unity.

Civil war broke out again in February 1982, and in June, northern forces occupied the capital. A new republican government under the presidency of Hissein Habre was proclaimed on June 7. OAU forces withdrew, and Habre's government soon controlled all of the country except for a few northern areas held by GUNT. In 1983 GUNT launched a counterattack and regained some territory with the aid of Libyan forces. French and Zairian troops were sent to aid Habre's forces. In September 1984 France and Libya agreed to the withdrawal of all foreign forces from Chad, but Libyan forces remained. GUNT forces controlled the country north of the 16th parallel; Libyan forces occupied the Aozou Strip, along the border, with the apparent intention of annexing it to Libya.

Between 1984 and 1986 Habre persuaded most Chadean dissident forces to rejoin the national government, and in November 1986 he launched a campaign to recapture the north. The Chadean forces won a series of victories in 1987, and in May 1988 Libya's Col. Qaddafi declared an end to the 20-year war with Chad, but did not relinquish Libya's claim to the Aozou Strip. The dispute is still before the International Court of Justice.

In November 1990, forces led by renegade Gen. Idriss Deby launched attacks from Sudan and ousted Pres. Habre. Deby, who favors multiparty democracy, proclaimed a provisional government and suspended the constitution. A national charter calling for a new constitution and elections to be held within 30 months came into force in March 1991. Deby has functioned as president since then, suppressing two attempted coups in 1992, and legalizing opposition parties.

Chad, largely arid and lacking natural resources, is overwhelmingly an agricultural and pastoral country; the national economy remains at the subsistence level with only rudimentary industrial development. The country is precariously self-sufficient in food; principal exports are cotton and livestock.

Chile

Republic of Chile

Geography **Location:** South Pacific coast of South America. **Boundaries:** Peru, Bolivia to N, Argentina to E, Pacific Ocean to W. **Total land area:** 292,259 sq. mi. (756,950 sq km). **Coastline:** 3,999 mi. (6,435 km). **Comparative area:** slightly larger than Texas. **Land use:** 7% arable land; negl. % permanent crops; 16% meadows and pastures; 21% forest and woodland; 56% other; includes 2% irrigated. **Major cities:** (1993) Gran Santiago (capital) 4,628,320; Viña del Mar 319,440; Concepción 318,140; Valparaíso 301,677; Temuco 262,624.

People **Population:** 13,950,557 (1994 est.). **Nationality:** noun—Chilean(s); adjective—Chilean.

Ethnic groups: 95% European and European-Indian, 3% Indian, 2% other. **Languages:** Spanish. **Religions:** 89% Roman Catholic, 11% Protestant, small Jewish population.

Government Type: republic. **Independence:** Sept. 18, 1810 (from Spain). **Constitution:** Sept. 11, 1980, effective Mar. 11, 1981; modified by public referendum on July 31, 1989. **National holiday:** Independence Day, Sept. 18. **Head of government:** Eduardo Frei Ruiz-Tagle, president (since Mar. 1994). **Structure:** Executive branch headed by president and cabinet of 20 ministers; legislature consists of Senate of elected and appointed members (47 in June 1990), and Chamber of Deputies, fixed at 102 members; Judicial branch consists of Supreme Court, Courts of Appeals and lower-level tribunals. New Congress first met on Mar. 11, 1990.

Economy Monetary unit: Chilean peso. **Budget:** (1993) ***income:*** $10.9 bil.; ***expend.:*** $10.9 bil. **GDP:** $96 bil., $7,000 per capita (1993 est.). **Chief crops:** wheat, potatoes, corn, sugar beets, onions, beans, fruit; net agricultural importer. **Livestock:** sheep, cattle, pigs, goats, horses. **Natural resources:** copper, timber, iron ore, nitrates, precious metals. **Major industries:** copper, other minerals, foodstuffs, fish processing. **Labor force:** 4.728 mil. (1990); 38.6% services (including 12% government), 31.3% industry and commerce, 15.9% agriculture, forestry, fishing; 7.1% unemployment (1988 est.). **Exports:** $10 bil. (f.o.b., 1992); 48% copper, 33% industrial products, molybdenum, iron ore, wood pulp, fishmeal. **Imports:** $9.2 bil. (f.o.b., 1992); petroleum, wheat, capital goods, spare parts, raw materials. **Major trading partners:** ***exports:*** 32% EU, 18% U.S., 18% Japan, 5% Brazil; ***imports:*** 21% U.S., 18% EU, 9% Brazil, 8% Japan.

Intl. Orgs. FAO, G-77, IAEA, IBRD, ICAO, IDA, IFAD, IFC, ILO, IMF, IMO, INTELSAT, INTERPOL, ITU, OAS, UN, UNESCO, UPU, WHO, WIPO, WMO, WTO.

Before the arrival of Europeans in the mid-1530s, indigenous habitation of the territory that would become Chile included the Araucanian population in the south and peoples under the influence of the Inca Empire in the north.

The Spanish founded the cities of Valparaíso in 1536, Santiago in 1541, and Concepción in 1550. Chile was under the authority of the Viceroyalty of Peru, established in 1544. Between 1810 and 1818, fortunes of the Chilean independence movement ebbed and flowed, culminating in the victory of Bernardo O'Higgins and the separatist forces in 1817. Independence was finally achieved in 1818.

From 1818 to 1833, Chile underwent a period of political instability, the roots of which can be traced to power struggles among elite Chilean families. In 1833 a strong presidential-dominant constitution was written under the influence of leading political figure Diego Portales that set the form of government in Chile until 1891. Chile expanded its territory at the expense of Peru and Bolivia, first in a war with the Peruvian-Bolivian Confederation (1836–39) and later as a result of the War of the Pacific (1879–83).

A civil war was fought in 1890–91 between forces of the president, José Balmaceda, and the Chilean Congress over the issue of the limits of presidential authority. The defeat of the presidential forces led to the establishment of a congressional-dominant parliamentary system. The checks on policy initiative resulting from the parliamentary system left government deadlocked in the face of mounting social and political problems arising at the turn of the century. The occurrence of a number of bloody strike actions crystallized political debate around social issues such as better wages and working conditions. The immobilized parliamentary system was unable to respond to these problems. In 1925, when Congress failed to allocate funds for military pay, the forces overthrew the parliamentary government.

A new constitution was drawn up that same year that moved governmental structure toward presidential dominance. Nevertheless, political instability continued until 1933, when the new constitution was implemented. The Chilean balance of political power from 1958 until 1973 remained almost equally divided among parties representing the right, the center, and the left of the political spectrum. In order to prevent an electoral victory for the leftist parties, forces on the right allied themselves with the centrist Christian Democrats in the 1964 election, and this resulted in the victory of Christian Democratic presidential candidate Eduardo Frei Montalva.

The program of the Christian Democrats, based on ideology and political strategy, included an ambitious agrarian reform and attempts to organize Chile's urban poor. It was believed that these stances would benefit the Christian Democrats at the polls in the 1970 presidential election. As in 1958, the 1970 election fielded three presidential candidates who represented the political right, center, and left. The candidate of the leftist Popular Unity coalition, Dr. Salvador Allende Gossens, won with 36.3 percent of the vote, and the Congress recognized Dr. Allende's victory after a bitter debate.

The Allende government nationalized the foreign-owned copper industry, but the resulting international boycott of Chilean copper imposed in retaliation for this action left Chile unable to market her copper. Other nationalizations by the government included the coal and steel industries and 60 percent of private banking. The Popular Unity government found itself unable to control peasant seizures of land and factory takeovers by workers. The copper embargo, land and factory seizures, government subsidies to the poor for basic goods, and runaway inflation resulted in a deterioration of the national economy that particularly affected the middle classes. Members of Congress from the center and right had hoped to gain enough seats in the 1973 congressional elections to impeach Allende, but instead the Popular Unity made impressive electoral gains, just as it had in the municipal elections of 1971. As political struggle intensified, the president resorted to inclusion of military officers in the government in order to bolster the legitimacy of the Popular Unity administration in the eyes of political opponents.

On Sept. 11, 1973, segments of the military led by commanders of three of Chile's four armed forces took control of the government, killing Allende in the process. Gen. Augusto Pinochet Ugarte emerged from the junta as the new president. The junta announced the arrest of some 13,000 persons, many of whom then lost their lives in a wave of brutal repression. (Mass graves were discovered in the desert in 1990, and in 1991 a commission reported that between 1973 and 1990, 2,279 people were killed, more than 2,000 by the government.) In March 1974 the dictatorship published its Declaration of Principles, the essential elements of which included a laissez-faire economic orientation, anti-Marxism, and nationalism.

A new constitution was approved by plebiscite in 1980. The two-phase evolution of Chile's political structure included an authoritarian "transitional period" between 1980 and 1989 and implementation of a new political structure thereafter. The constitution created a presidential system with very extensive executive powers and a "guardian" role for the military.

In an October 1988 plebiscite, Chileans rejected continuation of Pinochet rule and called for an end to the dictatorship. On Dec. 14, 1989, Patricio Aylwin Azocar of the Christian Democratic party (one of a 17-party alliance) was elected president with over 55 percent of the vote; he took office in March 1990, thereby ending 17 years of military dictatorship. He was succeeded by Eduardo Frei Ruiz-Tagle in March 1994.

In recent years, Chile's economy has expanded, exports have increased, and it has succeeded in lowering its large external debt. Although exports are still dominated by the copper industry—more than 40 percent—other minerals and manufactures are gaining in importance.

China

People's Republic of China

Geography Location: covers vast area of eastern Asia. **Boundaries:** Russia, Mongolia to N; N. Korea to NE; Pacific Ocean to E; India, Nepal, Bhutan, Myanmar, Laos, and Vietnam to S; Afghanistan and Pakistan to W., Kazakhstan, Kyrgyzstan, and Tajikistan to NW. **Total land area:** 3,705,392 sq. mi. (9,596,960 sq km). **Coastline:** 9,112 mi. (14,500 km). **Comparative area:** between U.S. and Canada. **Land use:** 10% arable land; negl. % permanent crops; 31% meadows and pastures; 14% forest and woodland; 45% other; includes 5% irrigated. **Major cities:** (1990 est.) Beijing (capital) 7,000,000; Shanghai 7,830,000; Tianjin 5,770,000; Shenyang 4,540,000; Wuhan 3,750,000.

People Population: 1,190,431,106 (1994 est.). **Nationality:** noun—Chinese (sing., pl.); adjective—Chinese. **Ethnic groups:** 93.3% Han Chinese, 6.7% Zhuang, Uygur, Hui, Yi, Tibetan, Miao,

Manchu, Mongol, Buyi, Korean, and numerous lesser nationalities. **Languages:** Standard Chinese (Putonghua) or Mandarin (based on the Beijing dialect); also Yue (Cantonese), Wu (Shanghainese), Minbei (Fuzhou), Minnan (Hokkien-Taiwanese), Xiang, Gan, Hakka dialects, and minority langs. (see "Ethnic groups" above). **Religions:** officially atheist, but traditionally pragmatic and eclectic; most important elements of religion are Confucianism, Taoism, and Buddhism; about 2–3% Muslim, 1% Christian.

Government Type: Communist state; real authority lies with Communist party's politburo; National People's Congress, in theory the highest organ of government, usually ratifies party's programs; State Council actually directs government. **Constitution:** Dec. 4, 1982. **National holiday:** National Day, Oct. 1. **Heads of government:** Jiang Zemin, president (since Mar. 1993); Rong Yiren, vice president; Li Peng, prime minister. **Structure:** control is exercised by Chinese Communist party, through State Council, which supervises ministries, commissions, and bureaus; all are technically under Standing Committee of National People's Congress.

Economy Monetary unit: yuan. **Budget:** $15.6 bil. deficit (1993); ***income:*** N.A.; ***expend.:*** N.A. **GDP:** $2.61 trillion, $2,200 per capita (1993 est.). **Chief crops:** rice, wheat, corn, other grains, oilseed; mainly subsistence agriculture. **Livestock:** pigs, sheep, cattle and buffalo, goats, horses. **Natural resources:** coal, iron ore, crude oil, mercury, tin; world's largest hydropower potential. **Major industries:** iron, steel, coal. **Labor force:** 567.4 mil. (1990 est.); 61.1% agriculture and forestry, 25.2% industry and commerce; **Exports:** $92 bil. (f.o.b., 1993); textiles, garments, telecommunications, recording equipment, petroleum. **Imports:** $104 bil. (c.i.f., 1993); rolled steel, motor vehicles, textile machinery, oil products. **Major trading partners:** (1989) ***exports:*** Hong Kong, Japan, U.S., Singapore; ***imports:*** Hong Kong, Japan, U.S., Germany.

Intl. Orgs. FAO, IAEA, IBRD, ICAO, IDA, IFAD, IFC, ILO, IMF, IMO, INTELSAT, ITU, UN, UNESCO, UPU, WHO, WIPO, WMO.

China is one of the world's oldest civilizations. Dynastic rule in the North China Plain began around 2000 B.C. The unifying Qin (221 B.C.) and Han (206 B.C.) dynasties greatly expanded the territory of the empire and established the basic pattern of imperial bureaucratic government that would endure until the beginning of the 20th century. Major dynasties during that period include the Han (206 B.C.–A.D. 220), Tang (618–907), Song (960–1279), Yuan or Mongol (1279–1368), Ming (1368–1644), and Qing (1644–1911).

By the late 18th century, the Qing dynasty faced increasingly dangerous problems of explosive population growth, bureaucratic stagnation, and trade pressure from the West. Opium—introduced by Great Britain to balance its trade in tea, silk, porcelain, and other goods—created severe social problems. Western demands for free trade resulted in the Opium War (1839–42), in which China was humiliatingly defeated by the British. The treaties of Nanjing (1842) and Tianjin (1858) opened China to Western merchants and missionaries and created foreign-ruled enclaves on Chinese soil. At the same time, the Taiping Rebellion and other popular uprisings led to the deaths of at least 20 million Chinese between 1850 and 1870.

Such reform efforts as the Self-Strengthening Movement (1870s) and the 1898 Reform Movement proved inadequate to the task of strengthening and modernizing China's dynastic government. Japan, modernizing rapidly after the Meiji Restoration of 1868, joined the race for commercial access to China, decisively winning the Sino-Japanese War of 1894–95. The antiforeign Boxer Uprising of 1900 was put down by a joint foreign military force, dealing a mortal blow to Qing rule. On Oct. 10, 1911, the dynasty fell to a coalition of forces led by the veteran revolutionary nationalist Sun Yat-sen.

China's first attempt at republican government, under Pres. Yuan Shikai and subsequent presidents, quickly degenerated into factionalism and warlord control in the provinces. In 1915 Japan successfully demanded further concessions, provoking public outcries. When news reached China on May 4, 1919, that the Treaty of Versailles granted Japan all of Germany's former concessions in China, students rioted throughout the country, demanding reforms and modernization (the May Fourth Movement). Sun Yat-sen's Nationalist party (Kuomintang, or KMT) and the Chinese Communist party (CCP, founded in 1921 by Mao Zedong) joined forces in 1922 in an attempt to create a second republican revolution.

Sun Yat-sen died in 1925. His successor, Chiang Kai-shek, consolidated KMT forces in Guangzhou and mounted the Northern Expedition (1927–29) to defeat or co-opt the various provincial warlords and reunify the country. In the course of this successful effort, Chiang turned on his Communist allies. A series of failed Communist uprisings and KMT anti-Communist extermination campaigns between 1927 and 1934 nearly wiped out the CCP. Remnants of the party broke out of encirclement in Jiangxi Province in 1934 and undertook the 6,000-mile Long March to a secure base in Yan'an, Shanxi Province. There, under Mao, Zhou Enlai, and Zhu De, the CCP recovered its strength. In the Xi'an Incident of December 1936, Chiang was kidnapped by mutinous KMT allies and forced at gunpoint to agree to forming a United Front with the CCP against Japan.

Meanwhile Japan continued its penetration of China, with the assassination of Manchurian warlord and KMT ally Jiang Zuolin in 1928, the invasion of Manchuria on Sept. 18, 1931, and the establishment of the puppet state of Manchuguo in 1934. On July 7, 1937, fighting erupted between Japanese and Chinese troops near Beijing. The Japanese rapidly moved south to the Yangtse Valley, bombing and capturing Shanghai. The Nationalist capital at Nanjing fell in November 1937, amid widespread atrocities against civilians. The KMT army and government retreated to a wartime capital at Chongqing. The remainder of World War II in China was largely a stalemate, with Japan occupying most of the country. KMT-held areas opposed the Japanese with conventional forces (supported, after 1941, by the Americans), while the Communists harassed the Japanese with guerrilla tactics.

At the end of World War II, American forces ensured that the KMT would receive Japan's surrender throughout most of China, giving the Nationalists a commanding position while U.S. general George Marshall attempted to mediate the creation of a KMT-CCP coalition government. That effort failed, and civil war broke out. The KMT advantage was dissipated by ruinous inflation, corruption, mismanagement, and military ineffectiveness. At the end of 1947, with the Communist forces making continual advances, the United States pulled out of China. After losing several major battles throughout 1948–49, KMT forces retreated to Taiwan; in Beijing, Mao Zedong proclaimed the establishment of the People's Republic of China (PRC) on Oct. 1, 1949.

With American backing, the Republic of China established a temporary capital at Taipei (see "Taiwan") and continued to claim sovereignty over all of China, retaining China's seat in the United Nations. The PRC was quickly granted diplomatic recognition by Soviet bloc nations and some Western nations, notably Great Britain, but was effectively isolated in most international affairs by American support for Nationalist China. Chinese troops entered the Korean War in November 1950, as UN forces approached the Sino-Korean border at the Yalu River. This direct confrontation between China and the United States forestalled any possibility of normal contacts for more than two decades thereafter, as U.S.-Chinese relations were held in the grip of the Cold War.

Within China the CCP rapidly consolidated its control of the country and began the task of rebuilding the nation after decades of internal and external warfare. Priority was given to land reform. Land was confiscated from landlords and returned to peasant ownership; landlords and other "class enemies" were tried and condemned by People's Courts set up under party auspices. Under the first five-year plan, announced in 1953, peasants were urged to set up rural cooperatives, while industrial recovery began with Soviet assistance. Artists, writers, and intellectuals were ordered to devote themselves to the service of the party and the nation. In 1956 Mao announced a policy of "let a hundred flowers bloom, let a hundred schools of thought contend," inviting criticism of the party and government. He was shocked by the vigor of the criticism thus produced; many critics were sent to labor camps in the ensuing Anti-Rightist Campaign of 1957.

Angered by the arrogance of Soviet advisers and by Soviet refusal to share nuclear weapons technology with China, Mao broke with the Soviet Union and expelled all Soviet personnel in 1958. At the same time, he announced the policy of the Great Leap Forward, under which China was to make rapid progress on all fronts without outside aid. Huge rural communes took the place of peasant smallholdings and cooperatives, and agriculture was placed under the direction of centralized planning. In industry, labor and enthusiasm were expected to make up for a shortage of capital and technical expertise. The Great Leap was a catastrophic failure, causing widespread famine and social dislocation, as Mao admitted in a forced self-criticism in 1960. Mao temporarily withdrew into the background as a group of party pragmatists led by Liu Shaoqi assumed power in the early 1960s.

In foreign affairs Chinese shelling of the Nationalist-held offshore islands of Quemoy and Matsu in 1958 led to a crisis in the Taiwan Straits, patrolled by the U.S. Seventh Fleet to prevent a recurrence of China's civil war. A rebellion in Tibet in 1959 was suppressed with much bloodshed, and the dalai lama fled to India. Chinese troop movements into Tibet contributed to the outbreak in 1960 of a border war with India. Throughout the 1960s China worried about being drawn into the Vietnam War.

In late 1965 Mao made a bid to return to full power. His vehicle was the Great Proletarian Cultural Revolution, formally launched in 1966. Shock troops of teenage Red Guards were used to attack the entrenched party bureaucracy; Liu Shaoqi was placed under house arrest, and other prominent officials, including Deng Xiaoping, were exiled to rural areas. By 1968 internal disorder was so great that the military intervened to restore control in many areas. Most established organs of power were replaced under the Cultural Revolution by Revolutionary Committees; intellectuals, technical workers, and bureaucrats were severely persecuted. In 1971 Mao's second-in-command, Marshal Lin Biao, staged an abortive coup and died while attempting to flee the country. With Mao increasingly old and ill, most of his power was exercised by his wife, Jiang Qing, and her associates. Her rival, Premier Zhou Enlai, attempted to maintain orderly government functions in the face of this turmoil.

The 1968 Soviet invasion of Czechoslovakia convinced Mao that the USSR was potentially a greater threat to China than America, and he quietly encouraged the growth of better relations with the United States. With tacit American approval, the PRC replaced the Republic of China (Taiwan) in the UN on Oct. 25, 1971. During Feb. 21–28, 1972, U.S. president Richard Nixon visited China. The Shanghai Communiqué, issued at the end of that visit, clarified the positions of both sides and paved the way for the resumption of U.S.-China relations short of formal diplomatic recognition.

Zhou Enlai died in January 1976, and Deng Xiaoping became acting premier. In April 1976 a rally in Beijing commemorating Zhou's birthday was dispersed by police on orders from Jiang Qing, and a riot ensued. Deng was dismissed from office. But when Mao died on Sept. 9, 1976, Deng reemerged as China's paramount leader, behind the new acting premier and acting party chairman, figurehead Hua Guofeng. Jiang Qing and three associates were arrested along with many of their allies. Labeled the Gang of Four, Jiang Qing's clique was blamed for all the ills of the Cultural Revolution; they were tried and convicted for crimes against the state in 1981.

China's post-Mao transformation took a decisive turn in 1978, with the announcement of the policy of the Four Modernizations (agriculture, industry, science and technology, and defense). Foreign investment and technology transfer were encouraged, and thousands of students were sent to study abroad. For a few months in the winter of 1978–79, the authorities tolerated the public posting of written critiques of the government ("Democracy Wall"). Deng consolidated power in his own hands, still acting behind the scenes; Hua Guofeng was dismissed from office, while Deng's allies Hu Yaobang and Zhao Ziyang were promoted to leadership of the party and government in 1982.

On Jan. 1, 1979, China and the United States entered into formal diplomatic relations; the United States rescinded its recognition of the Republic of China as China's legal government but maintained separate nongovernmental relations with the ROC under the Taiwan Relations Act. China's relations with Vietnam deteriorated in 1978 following Vietnam's invasion of Cambodia. In February 1979, China attempted, with little success, to "teach Vietnam a lesson" in a brief but violent border war. A conflict with Great Britain was resolved in 1984 as both sides agreed that Hong Kong would be returned to Chinese sovereignty, but with considerable local autonomy, in 1997. Relations with the Soviet Union remained strained, China insisting that no improvement could come before the USSR reduced its troop concentrations on the Sino-Soviet border, withdrew from Afghanistan, and pressured Vietnam into withdrawing from Cambodia. China's overall foreign-policy stance in the post-Mao era has been low-key and nonconfrontational.

In the 1980s, China achieved spectacular improvements in agricultural production through dismantling rural communes and returning land to individual peasant holdings under long-term leases. Small-scale private enterprise has been encouraged in both rural and urban areas. Reform in industry and in the centrally controlled price structure has been harder to achieve and has led to such side effects as inflation and increased corruption. Within the overall context of reform, factions of relatively more conservative and reformist leaders have coexisted uneasily. A conservative drive against "spiritual pollution" in 1986 was quickly blunted by Deng, but in January 1987, the reformist party-secretary Hu Yaobang was ousted after student demonstrations calling for more democracy. The CCP 12th Party Congress in October 1987 forced the retirement of some older conservatives, named the reformist Zhao Ziyang as party secretary, and elevated the conservative pragmatist Li Peng as premier.

In April 1989 student demonstrators in Beijing mourning the death of Hu Yaobang launched a general movement for greater democracy. Demonstrators began a hunger strike and disrupted a summit visit by Soviet president Gorbachev. Martial law was proclaimed in May as demonstrations spread to other cities. Troops opened fire in Tienanmen Square on June 3–4, killing hundreds of demonstrators. In the aftermath, Zhao Ziyang was replaced as party secretary by Jiang Zemin, thousands of protesters and suspected dissidents were arrested (and an unknown number executed), and hard-liners in the government took firm control of the country.

World opinion was outraged by the Tienanmen incident; the United States and many other countries instituted sanctions against China, tourism plummeted, and the economy went into general decline. International trade gradually resumed during 1989–90, and the United States renewed China's most-favored-nation status in June 1990 after several hundred dissidents were released from prison.

China strove to put Tienanmen Square behind it by holding speedy trials of those charged in connection with demonstrations. The government also made overtures to the former USSR, and from its permanent seat on the UN Security Council supported coalition efforts against Iraq in the Persian Gulf conflict.

Economic sanctions were lifted by Western governments in 1991. China continued to pursue its economic reform policies while repressing all signs of political dissent. While national politics, dominated by an aging leadership, seemed torpid and adrift, the private-sector economy continued to grow vigorously.

In 1992–93 runaway growth made China's economy the world's fourth-largest by some standards of measurement. This resulted in higher wages and increased consumer spending, but also widening income disparities, increased corruption, smuggling, theft, etc. Official government figures put 1994 growth at 12 percent, inflation at 24 percent.

1992–93 was a difficult time in the evolving status of Hong Kong, as China vehemently rejected political reforms proposed by Hong Kong's new governor-general, Christopher Patten. On the other hand, China and Taiwan held their first-ever official direct talks in Singapore in April 1993, which resulted in several agreements concerning travel and telephone service. A brief "tariff war" with the United States in February 1995 over pirated music- and videotapes ended with Chinese agreement to thwart the piracies, a sign of the growing importance to China of its exports to the United States.

Colombia

Republic of Colombia

Geography **Location:** northwestern coast of South America. **Boundaries:** Caribbean Sea to N, Venezuela, Brazil to E, Peru, Ecuador to S, Panama, Pacific Ocean to W. **Total land area:** 439,734 sq. mi. (1,138,910 sq km). **Coastline:** 1,992 mi. (3,208 km). **Comparative area:** between

Texas and Alaska. **Land use:** 4% arable land; 2% permanent crops; 29% meadows and pastures; 49% forest and woodland; 16% other; includes negl. % irrigated. **Major cities:** (1993 est.) Bogotá (capital) 5,025,989; Cali 1,655,699; Medellín 1,594,967; Cartagena 707,092.

People Population: 35,577,556 (1994 est.). **Nationality:** noun—Colombian(s); adjective—Colombian. **Ethnic groups:** 58% mestizo, 20% white, 14% mulatto, 4% black, 4% other. **Languages:** Spanish. **Religions:** 95% Roman Catholic.

Government Type: republic; executive branch dominates government structure. **Independence:** July 20, 1810 (from Spain). **Constitution:** Aug. 4, 1886, with amendments codified in 1946 and 1968. **National holiday:** Independence Day, July 20. **Head of government:** Ernesto Samper Pizano, president (since Aug. 1994). **Structure:** president; bicameral legislature (Congress—Senate, House of Representatives); judiciary.

Economy Monetary unit: Colombian peso. **Budget:** (1993 est.) ***income:*** $11 bil.; ***expend.:*** $12 bil. **GDP:** $51 bil., $1,500 per capita (1992 est.). **Chief crops:** coffee, rice, corn, sugarcane, plantains, cotton, tobacco, bananas; illegal producer of coca and cannabis for international drug trade. **Livestock:** cattle, sheep, pigs, horses, goats. **Natural resources:** crude oil, natural gas, coal, iron ore, nickel. **Major industries:** textiles, food processing, oil. **Labor force:** 12 mil. (1990); 53% services, 26% agriculture, 21% industry (1981); 12% unemployment (1987). **Exports:** $6.9 bil. (f.o.b., 1992 est.); 30% coffee, 24% petroleum, coal, bananas, fresh cut flowers. **Imports:** $5.5 bil. (c.i.f., 1992 est.); industrial equipment, transportation equipment, foodstuffs, chemicals. **Imports:** $6.7 bil. (c.i.f., 1992 est.); transportation and industrial equipment, consumer goods, chemicals, paper products. **Major trading partners:** ***exports:*** 44% U.S., 21% EU, 5% Japan, 4% Netherlands, 3% Sweden; ***imports:*** 36% U.S., 16% EU, 4% Brazil, 3% Venezuela, 3% Japan.

Intl. Orgs. AO, G-77, IAEA, IBRD, ICAO, IDA, IFAD, IFC, ILO, IMF, IMO, INTELSAT, INTERPOL, ITU, NAM, OAS, UN, UNESCO, UPU, WHO, WIPO, WMO, WTO.

The territory that is now Colombia was home to various sedentary and semisedentary cultures prior to the arrival of Europeans. The Chibcha population of the Andean region might have numbered about one million prior to European contact. Portions of the area that make up modern Colombia fell under the authority of the Inca Empire.

In 1538 the colony of New Granada was established with its capital at Bogotá, and for most of the period up until 1740, the area was within the jurisdiction of the Viceroyalty of Peru. In that year a new viceroyalty was established that included modern-day Colombia, Ecuador, Panama, and Venezuela. During the wars of independence against Spain, forces under Simón Bolívar were victorious over the royalists at the Battle of Boyacá in 1819, and the region gained its independence in 1821.

Colombian territory was a part of the federation of Gran Colombia until the collapse of the federal arrangement in 1830. Thereafter, the country—called New Granada—remained a separate political entity (which included the area of Panama). By the 1850s a federal system had been adopted for the country. But this arrangement rapidly disintegrated, and the practically semisovereign states were involved in a constant struggle with the central government for autonomy. The effort to define the political structure was largely resolved with the constitution of 1886, which ended federalist regional autonomy and made Colombia a unitary republic.

Colombian political struggle since the 1850s had been characterized by a rivalry between two groups that coalesced into the Liberal and Conservative parties. During much of the 19th century, the Liberal-Conservative ideological battle was influenced to a great extent by the definition of the role of the Roman Catholic church in political and social life. The 1887–88 Concordat gave the church "official protection," while the state was given authority over public education. The settlement left a central position for the church in Colombian society that was not substantially altered by the Concordat of 1942.

The Liberal-Conservative struggle led to at least six civil wars, which often ended in interparty compromise. A struggle in 1854 involved the issue of the future direction of the country's economic development and was followed by a settlement among elites. The Liberal-Conservative war of 1860–63 led to a Liberal victory and a period of Liberal political hegemony that lasted until 1886. The period of Conservative rule from 1886 until 1930 was punctuated by the "War of a Thousand Days" (1899–1902), in which the Conservatives defeated the Liberals. In 1903 the Colombian government rejected a U.S. offer for construction of a canal in Panama. As a result Panama (backed by the U.S.) revolted against the Colombian government, ending in the separation of Panama from Colombia.

The world depression of 1929 seriously disrupted both the economy and the politics of Colombia. The loss of popularity of the ruling Conservatives due to both the overall economic collapse and their increasingly brutal repression of the labor movement led to a Liberal victory in 1930. A new civil war between peasants loyal to the two parties also broke out that year. By 1934 Liberal president Alfonso López Pumarejo had inaugurated his "Revolution on the March" program of socioeconomic reform.

During the 1946 presidential election, Conservatives won the presidency with a minority of the overall vote, defeating a split Liberal party. Armed conflict originally instigated by the two party elites erupted. This marked the beginning of *La Violencia* (1948–57) during which more than 200,000 people died. In the summer of 1957, leaders of the Liberal and Conservative parties reached an agreement on constitutional reform in an attempt to end the violence. The agreement, known as the National Front, was to be in force for 16 years and included provisions for regular alternation of the presidency between the parties, as well as an accord on equal staffing of all political positions by both parties. The Liberal and Conservative parties agreed they alone would monopolize the arena of legitimate political competition for the 16-year period. The agreement held up until 1968 constitutional revisions allowed for other organized political groups to be officially recognized.

The emergence of terrorist and paramilitary groups on both the right and left—some with ties to the drug trade—in the 1960s and 1970s weakened the two-party power-sharing monopoly. In March 1990, one of the most notorious left-wing groups, M-19, elected to lay down its arms and enter the political mainstream and immediately captured 19 of 70 seats in a constitutional convention called to rewrite the constitution. Other groups followed suit in 1991.

Colombia has also had to cope with a burgeoning narcotics trade. Throughout the 1980s, narco-terrorists murdered government officials, journalists, and innocent bystanders with impunity. Despite the assassination of four presidential candidates prior to the May 1990 election, the Liberal party's César Gaviria Trujillo won the election campaigning vigorously against the drug traffickers. In 1994 another Liberal party president (Ernesto Samper Pizano) took office pledging to continue the fight against drug traffickers. Samper also promised to invest billions of dollars to improve the infrastructure with money from the newly discovered Cusiana oil field scheduled to be operational in 1996.

Comoros

Federal Islamic Republic of the Comoros

Geography Location: part of archipelago in Mozambique Channel; three main islands, Njazidja, Nzwami, and Mwali (formerly Grande-Comore, Anjouan, and Mohéli). Moroni, Njazidja Is., 11°40'S, 43°16'E. **Boundaries:** between Madagascar and southeast Africa. **Total land area:** 838 sq. mi. (2,170 sq km). **Coastline:** 211 mi. (340 km). **Comparative area:** slightly more than 12 times size of Washington, D.C. **Land use:** 35% arable land; 8% permanent crops; 7% meadows and pastures; 16% forest and woodland; 34% other. **Major cities:** (1980 census) Moroni (capital) 17,267; Mutsamudu 13,000; Fomboni 5,400.

People Population: 530,136 (1994 est.). **Nationality:** noun—Comoran(s); adjective—Comoran. **Ethnic groups:** Antalote, Cafre, Makoa, Oimatsaha, Sakalava. **Languages:** Shaafi Islam (Swahili dialect), Malagasy, French. **Religions:** 86% Sunni Muslim, 14% Roman Catholic.

Government Type: republic. **Independence:** July 6, 1975 (from France). **Constitution:** Oct. 1, 1978, amended Oct. 1982 and Jan. 1985. **National holiday:** Independence Day, July 6. **Heads of government:** Said Mohamed Djohar, head of state; Halifa Houmadi, prime minister (since Oct. 1994). **Structure:** executive—president; legislative—38-member Federal Assembly.

Economy **Monetary unit:** Comoran franc. **Budget:** (1991 est.) ***income:*** $96 mil.; ***expend.:*** $88 mil. **GDP:** $360 mil., $700 per capita (1993 est.). **Chief crops:** cash crops—essential oils for perfumes (mainly ylang-ylang), vanilla, copra, cloves; food crops—rice, manioc, maize, fruits, vegetables. **Livestock:** poultry, cattle, sheep. **Natural resources:** negligible. **Major industries:** perfume distillation. **Labor force:** 140,000 (1982); 80% agriculture, 3% government, 17% other; significant unemployment; 51% of population of working age (1985). **Exports:** $21 mil. (f.o.b., 1992 est.); perfume oils, vanilla, copra, cloves. **Imports:** $60 mil. (f.o.b., 1992 est.); rice and other foodstuffs, cement, fuels, chemicals, textiles. **Major trading partners:** ***exports:*** 53% U.S., 41% France, 4% Africa, 2% Germany; ***imports:*** 62% Europe (22% France), 5% Africa, Pakistan, China.

Intl. Orgs. AFDB, FAO, G-77, IBRD, IDA, IFAD, ILO, IMF, ITU, NAM, UN, UNCTAD, UNESCO, UPU, WHO, WMO.

The Federal Islamic Republic of Comoros is part of an archipelago composed of four prominent islands (the fourth, Mayotte, is a French dependency) and several smaller islands. Numerous groups from Africa, Europe, and Asia invaded the islands over the centuries. Shirazi Arabs introduced Islam to Comoros around the turn of the 16th century, and the French established colonial rule over the archipelago between 1841 and 1912 and developed a plantation-based economy. The islands remained a French territory until 1961 when political autonomy was granted. Comoros gained independence in 1975. (Representatives from the island of Mayotte abstained on the vote for unilateral independence, and it remains under French administration.) Although overthrown by foreign mercenaries in 1975, Pres. Ahmed Abdallah Abderemane returned to power in 1978 and helped establish the country's first constitution. In November 1989 he was assassinated by a small group of rebels who quickly dispersed under pressure from the French government. A new constitution was approved in 1992, and the country's first democratic elections were held in November 1992.

Much of the nation's soil is laden with lava, making it unsuitable for farming, especially on the island of Njazidja (Grand Comore), which is dominated by Mount Kartala, an active volcano. This obstacle to agriculture hinders the growth of Comoros, one of the poorest and least developed nations in the world. Poor transportation links between the islands and a harsh cyclone season add further to the country's problems. But Comoros has invested heavily in its tourism industry.

Congo

Republic of the Congo

Geography **Location:** equatorial country on western coast of Africa. **Boundaries:** Cameroon to NW, Central African Republic to NE, Zaire to E and S, Angolan district of Cabinda to S, Gulf of Guinea to SW, Gabon to W. **Total land area:** 132,046 sq. mi. (342,000 sq km). **Coastline:** 105 mi. (169 km). **Comparative area:** between New Mexico and Montana. **Land use:** 2% arable land; negl. % permanent crops; 29% meadows and pastures; 62% forest and woodland; 7% other. **Major cities:** (1984 census) Brazzaville (capital) 596,200; Pointe-Noire 298,014; Pool 219,329; (1974) Bouenza 135,999; Cuvette 127,558.

People **Population:** 2,446,902 (1994 est.). **Nationality:** noun—Congolese (sing., pl.); adjective—Congolese or Congo. **Ethnic groups:** 75 groups, almost all Bantu—48% Kongo, 20% Sangha, 17% Teke, 12% M'Bochi; about 8,500 Europeans, mostly French. **Languages:** French (official); many African languages with Lingala and Kikongo most widely used. **Religions:** 50% Christian, 42% indigenous beliefs, 2% Muslim.

Government **Type:** republic. **Independence:** Aug. 15, 1960 (from France). **Constitution:** July 8, 1979. Dec. 1990 constitutional amendment legalized multiparty system effective Jan. 1991. **National holiday:** National Day, Aug. 15. **Heads of government:** Pascal Lissouba, president (since Aug. 1992); Jacques Joachim Yhomby-Odango, prime minister (since Jan. 1995). **Structure:** executive—president, prime minister, Council of Ministers (cabinet); legislative—unicameral National People's Assembly; judicial—Supreme Court.

Economy **Monetary unit:** Communauté Financière Africaine (CFA) franc. **Budget:** (1991 est.) ***income:*** $765 mil.; ***expend.:*** $952 mil. **GDP:** $7 bil., $2,900 per capita (1993 est.). **Chief crops:** cash crops—sugarcane, wood, coffee, cocoa beans, palm kernels; food crops—root crops, rice, corn, bananas, manioc. **Livestock:** goats, cattle, sheep, pigs. **Natural resources:** petroleum, timber, potash, lead, zinc. **Major industries:** crude oil, cement, sawmills. **Labor force:** 79,100 (1985); 75% agriculture, 25% commerce, industry, government; 51% of population of working age with 40% economically active; 40,000–60,000 unemployed. **Exports:** $1.1 bil. (f.o.b., 1990); 72% crude petroleum, lumber, plywood, coffee, cocoa. **Imports:** $704 mil. (c.i.f., 1990); foodstuffs, consumer goods, intermediate manufactures, capital equipment. **Major trading partners:** ***exports:*** U.S., France, other EU; ***imports:*** France, Italy, Germany, other EU, U.S.

Intl. Orgs. FAO, G-77, IBRD, ICAO, IDA, IFAD, IFC, ILO, IMF, IMO, INTELSAT, INTERPOL, ITU, NAM, UN, UNESCO, UPU, WHO, WIPO, WMO, WTO.

Beginning around 1,500 years ago, the lower reaches of the Congo River formed the focus of a number of well-organized states. The Kongo and Ndonga flourished south of the river; north of the river, in what is now the Congo, the Loango, Teke, and Bobangi were dominant. Some of these states were weakened beginning in the 16th century by the Portuguese slave trade, although the Loango benefited from the trade through the 19th century.

With the weakening of Portuguese power, the French became the dominant European power in western Africa. In 1883 they established a protectorate over the Teke kingdom, which they renamed Middle Congo. The treaty with the Teke king was concluded by Pierre Savorgnan de Brazza, for whom the capital was—and is—named.

In 1910 the French confederated their protectorates of Gabon, Middle Congo, Ubangi-Shari (later the Central African Republic), and Chad to form French Equatorial Africa. The territory became an important base of Free French activity during World War II, in acknowledgment of which Gen. Charles de Gaulle granted French citizenship to the territory's inhabitants in 1946, and local power was devolved upon advisory assemblies. The Republic of the Congo attained full autonomy upon the dissolution of the confederation of French Equatorial Africa in 1959, and the nation gained full independence on Apr. 15, 1960.

In August 1963 Pres. Fulbert Youlou was driven from office by violent labor unrest; the military took control and then installed a provisional civilian government led by Alphonse Massamba-Debat. He was subsequently elected president for a five-year term.

In 1968 Massamba-Debat was overthrown in a military coup and replaced by Capt. Marien Ngouabi, who in 1969 reorganized the Congo as a People's Republic. Despite its Marxist-Leninist stance, Congo remained strongly linked to France, its main source of trade, aid, and foreign investment. Ngouabi was assassinated in 1977 and replaced by a military committee of the Congolese Labor party led by Gen. Joachim Yhomby-Opango, who resigned and was arrested for treason in 1979. He was succeeded by Denis Sassou-Nguesso, who was reelected to a third five-year term in 1989.

In 1990, Congo began a relatively smooth transition to multiparty democracy. Following mounting calls for liberalization and labor strikes, opposition parties were legalized as of Jan. 1, 1991. Pascal Lissouda was elected president in August 1992, and in December, agronomist Claude Antoine DaCosta was named to head an interim government pending general elections. By 1993, however, ethnic and tribal rivalries led to outbreaks of extreme violence that have persisted into 1994.

The topography of the Congo consists of fertile plains and thick forests. The country is primarily agricultural; palm oil, coffee, cocoa, and tobacco are cultivated for export. The country is rich in minerals, including oil, natural gas, potash, lead, copper, and zinc. Much of the nation's mineral and petroleum earnings has been spent on ill-conceived and unproductive state projects.

Costa Rica

Republic of Costa Rica

Geography **Location:** Central American isthmus. **Boundaries:** Nicaragua to N, Caribbean Sea to E, Panama to S, and Pacific Ocean to W. **Total land area:** 19,730 sq. mi. (51,100 sq km).

Coastline: 801 mi. (1,290 km). **Comparative area**: slightly smaller than West Virginia. **Land use**: 6% arable land; 7% permanent crops; 45% meadows and pastures; 34% forest and woodland; 8% other; includes 1% irrigated. **Major cities**: (1991 est.) San José (capital) 296,625; Alajuela 158,276; Cartago 108,958; Puntarenas 92,360; Heredia 67,387.

People Population: 3,342,152 (1994 est.). **Nationality:** noun—Costa Rican(s); adjective—Costa Rican. **Ethnic groups:** 96% white, 3% black, 1% Indian. **Languages:** Spanish (official), Jamaican dialect of English spoken around Puerto Limón. **Religions:** 95% Roman Catholic.

Government Type: democratic republic. **Independence:** Sept. 15, 1821 (from Spain). **Constitution**: Nov. 9, 1949. **National holiday:** Independence Day, Sept. 18. **Head of government:** José Maria Figueres Olsen, president (since May 1994). **Structure:** executive—president (head of government and chief of state), elected for single four-year term; two vice presidents; legislative—57-delegate unicameral Legislative Assembly elected at four-year intervals (legislator may not serve consecutive terms); judiciary—Supreme Court of Justice (17 magistrates elected by Legislative Assembly at eight-year intervals).

Economy Monetary Unit: colón. **Budget:** (1992 est.) ***income:*** $1.1 bil.; ***expend.:*** $1.34 bil. (1991 est.). **GDP:** $19.3 bil., $5,900 per capita (1993 est.). **Chief crops:** coffee, bananas, sugarcane, rice, corn, cocoa; illegal producer of cannabis for international drug trade. **Livestock:** cattle, pigs, horses. **Natural resources:** hydropower potential. **Major industries:** food processing, textiles, clothing, construction materials. **Labor force:** 868,300 (1985 est.); 35.1% industry and commerce, 27% agriculture, 26.1% government and services, 11.8% other; 6.2% unemployment (1987). **Exports:** $1.9 bil. (f.o.b., 1993); coffee, bananas, textiles, sugar. **Imports:** $2.9 bil. (c.i.f., 1993); petroleum, machinery, consumer durables, chemicals, fertilizer. **Major trading partners:** ***exports:*** 75% U.S., Germany, Guatemala, Netherlands, UK, Japan; ***imports:*** 45% U.S., Japan, Guatemala, Germany.

Intl. Orgs. FAO, G-77, IAEA, IBRD, ICAO, IDA, IFAD, IFC, ILO, IMF, IMO, INTELSAT, INTERPOL, ITU, UN, UNESCO, UPU, WHO, WMO.

Costa Rica was under the jurisdiction of the Spanish colonial kingdom of Guatemala until it broke with Spain in 1821, along with other parts of Central America. With the collapse of the United Provinces of Central America in 1838, Costa Rica became an independent republic, and the country held its first democratic elections in 1889.

An attempt at electoral fraud in 1948 led to a brief civil war, which was won by the National Liberation forces under "Don Pepé" Jose Figueres Ferrer. The Costa Rican army was subsequently abolished.

In the 1980s, under Pres. Oscar Arias Sánchez, Costa Rica vigorously promoted the settlement of civil strife in Nicaragua and El Salvador and he was awarded the 1987 Nobel Peace Prize for his Central American peace plan. Subsequent governments have focused on economic matters and the nation has made strong progress toward solving its economic problems.

In February 1994 Jose Maria Figueres Olsen, son of the legendary "Don Pepé," was elected president of Costa Rica, besting free-market and austerity-minded Miguel Angel Rodriguez.

Croatia

See Part I: "Major News Stories of the Year."

Cuba

Republic of Cuba

Geography Location: largest island in Caribbean Sea, about 100 mi. (160 km) S of Florida. **Boundaries:** North Atlantic Ocean to N, Windward Passage to E, Caribbean Sea to S, Yucatan Channel to W. **Total land area:** 42,803 sq. mi. (110,860 sq km). **Coastline:** 2,319 mi. (3,735 km). **Comparative area:** between Tennessee and Pennsylvania. **Land use:** 23% arable land; 6% permanent crops; 23% meadows and pastures; 17% forest and woodland; 31% other; includes 10% irrigated. **Major cities:** (1993 est.) Havana (capital) 2,175,995; Santiago de Cuba 440,084; Camagüey 293,961; Holguín 242,085; Guantánamo 207,796.

People Population: 11,064,344 (1994 est.). **Nationality:** noun—Cuban(s); adjective—Cuban. **Ethnic groups:** 51% mulatto, 37% white, 11% black, 1% Chinese. **Languages:** Spanish. **Religions:** at least 85% nominally Roman Catholic before Castro assumed power.

Government Type: Communist state. **Independence:** May 20, 1902 (from Spain). **Constitution:** Feb. 24, 1976. **National holiday**: Anniversary of the Revolution, Jan. 1. **Head of government:** Fidel Castro Ruz, prime minister from February 1959, president (since Dec. 1976). **Structure:** executive; legislative (National Assembly of the People's Power); controlled judiciary.

Economy Monetary unit: Cuban peso. **Budget:** (1992 est.) ***income:*** $12.46 bil.; ***expend.:*** $14.45 bil. (1990 est.). **GNP:** $13.7 bil., $1,250 per capita (1993 est.). **Chief crops:** sugar, tobacco, rice, potatoes, tubers, citrus, coffee. **Livestock**: cattle, pigs, horses, sheep. **Natural resources**: cobalt, nickel, iron ore, copper, manganese. **Major industries:** sugar milling, petroleum refining, food and tobacco processing. **Labor force:** 4.6 mil. (1988); 30% services and government, 22% industry, 20% agriculture, 11% commerce; 10% construction, 7% transportation and communications (1988). **Exports:** $1.5 bil. (f.o.b., 1993 est.); sugar, nickel, shellfish, citrus, tobacco, coffee. **Imports:** $1.7 bil. (c.i.f., 1993 est.); capital goods, industrial raw materials, food, petroleum. **Major trading partners:** ***exports:*** 30% Russia, 10% Canada, 9% China, 6% China, 6% Japan, 4% Spain; ***imports:*** 20% Venezuela, 9% China, 9% Spain, 5% Mexico, 5% Italy, 4% Canada, 4% France.

Intl. Orgs. FAO, G-77, IAEA, ICAO, IFAD, ILO, IMO, ITU, NAM, OAS (nonparticipant), UN, UNESCO, UNIDO, UPU, WHO, WIPO, WMO, WTO.

At the time of Christopher Columbus's arrival in 1492, Cuba was home to Arawak, Ciboney, and Guanahatabey Indian people. Cuba served as a launching point for Spanish imperial conquests in the Americas, and the early-19th-century wars of independence that swept the rest of Spanish America did not overthrow the imposing Spanish garrison there. Slavery was abolished in 1886, but Spanish colonialism lingered in Cuba until the 1890s.

Spanish control of the island began to deteriorate in the late 1860s with the beginning of the "Ten Years War" (1868–78), and Cuba finally separated from Spain as a result of the Cuban-U.S.-Spanish war, which ended with the signing of the Treaty of Paris in 1898. Cuba became a U.S. protectorate by virtue of the U.S.-sponsored Platt Amendment (1901) to the new Cuban constitution. The Platt Amendment gave the United States the right to intervene in Cuban affairs, and after the initial occupation of the island, U.S. troops repeatedly invaded and occupied the former Spanish colony.

Corruption and political repression plagued Cuban politics during the first half of the 20th century. Gerardo Machado won election to the presidency in 1925, but he quickly turned his administration of the island into a dictatorship that lasted until his ouster by a progressive coalition of students and labor in 1933. The "revolution" of 1933 installed Ramón Grau San Martín as the new head of the government, but the United States supported Grau's ouster, and army sergeant Fulgencio Batista replaced him. Batista ruled the country either directly or indirectly for the next quarter century.

In 1953 Fidel Castro Ruz lead a failed attack on the Moncada army barracks in Santiago. In December 1956 Fidel and Raúl Castro, Argentine physician Ernesto "Che" Guevara, and 79 others returned to Cuba and waged a guerrilla campaign against the government. Batista's military failed to defeat the guerrillas, and in the wake of increasing demonstrations of public antipathy for his government, the dictator fled the country. The Communist Fidelistas took control Jan. 1, 1959.

By mid-1959, revolutionary tribunals had tried and executed more than 500 political "enemies." The leaders announced an agrarian reform, and by 1960 the nationalization of the economy was in full swing. In 1961 U.S.-Cuban diplomatic relations were severed, and the U.S.-sponsored Bay of Pigs invasion by Cuban exiles failed. In 1962 the Cuban missile crisis brought the world to the brink of nuclear war when U.S. spy planes uncovered Soviet intentions to place nuclear weapons on the island. The Soviets agreed to the withdrawal of missiles in exchange for a U.S. pledge not to invade Cuba.

In its active foreign policy, Cuba has provided technical assistance to a number of left-wing regimes in Africa and Latin America. Between

1975 and 1991 it maintained an extensive military presence in Angola, and it has also supported Communist insurgencies throughout Latin America.

With the collapse of the Soviet Union, Cuba lost huge subsidies, and its economy has been in a downward spiral since 1991. In the summer of 1994, the worsening economy and a growing dissatisfaction with the Castro government fueled a mass migration of Cubans to U.S. shores. More than 20,000 Cuban refugees—aboard boats, homemade rafts, ferries, or anything else that floats—arrived in Florida or were intercepted by Coast Guard ships and taken to safe havens in Panama or Honduras. In September 1994 the United States and Cuba reached an agreement (confirmed in talks in New York in January 1995) for U.S. acceptance annually of 20,000 legal Cuban immigrants in return for Cuban efforts to prevent illegal migration. In February the United States began returning 7,500 Cuban refugees from the "safe havens" in Panama to Guantánamo.

Cyprus

Republic of Cyprus

Geography Location: eastern Mediterranean Sea. Nicosia 35°11'N, 33°23'E. **Boundaries:** 62 mi. (100 km) S of Turkey, Syria to E. **Total land area:** 3,571 sq. mi. (9,250 sq km). **Coastline:** 403 mi. (648 km). **Comparative area:** between Delaware and Connecticut. **Land use:** 40% arable land; 7% permanent crops; 10% meadows and pastures; 18% forest and woodland; 25% other; includes 10% irrigated. **Major cities:** Nicosia (capital) 149,100 (excludes Turkish-occupied portion); Limassol 107,200; Larnaca 48,300 (1982); Famagusta (Gazi Magusa) 39,500 (mid-1974); Phaphos 20,800 (1982).

People Population: 730,084 (1994 est.). **Nationality:** noun—Cypriot(s); adjective—Cypriot. **Ethnic groups:** 78% Greek, 18% Turkish, 4% other. **Languages:** Greek, Turkish, English. **Religions:** 78% Greek Orthodox, 18% Muslim, 4% Maronite, Armenian, Apostolic, and other.

Government Type: republic. **Independence:** Aug. 16, 1960 (from UK). **Constitution:** Aug. 16, 1960; negotiations have been held intermittently to create basis for new or revised constitution to govern the island and relations between Greek and Turkish Cypriots. **National holiday:** Independence Day, Oct. 1. **Heads of government:** Glafcos Clerides, president (since Feb. 1993); Turkish sector—Rauf Denktash, president (since 1975). **Structure:** currently, government of Cyprus has effective authority over only Greek Cypriot community; headed by president of republic and comprising Council of Ministers, House of Representatives, and Supreme Court; Turkish Cypriots declared their own constitution and governing bodies within Turkish Federated State of Cyprus in 1975; state renamed Turkish Republic of Northern Cyprus in 1983.

Economy Monetary unit: Cypriot pound. **Budget:** (1991 est.) ***income:*** $1.7 bil., Greek area; $273 mil., Turkish area; ***expend.:*** $2.2 bil., Greek area; $360 mil., Turkish area. **GDP:** Greek area—$6.7 bil., $11,390 per capita (1992); Turkish area—$550 mil., $3,130 per capita (1992). **Chief crops:** potatoes and other vegetables, grapes, citrus, wheat, carob beans. **Livestock:** chickens, sheep, goats, pigs, cattle. **Natural resources:** copper, pyrites, asbestos, gypsum, timber. **Major industries:** mining (iron pyrites, gypsum, asbestos), manufactures principally for local consumption (beverages, footwear, clothing, cement). **Labor force:** Greek area—285,500 (1992); 42% services, 33% industry, 22% agriculture; 3.4% unemployment; Turkish area—75,000 (1992) 52% services, 26% agriculture, 22% industry. **Exports:** $1.1 bil. (f.o.b., 1993 est.); principal items—food and beverages, including citrus, raisins, potatoes, wine; also, cement, clothing. **Imports:** $3.3 bil. (f.o.b., 1993 est.); 23% consumer goods, 12% petroleum and lubricants, foodstuffs, feed grains, machinery. **Major trading partners:** ***exports:*** 37% Middle East and N. Africa, 27% UK, 11% other EU, 2% U.S.; ***imports:*** 60% EU, 7% Middle East and N. Africa, 4% U.S.

Intl. Orgs. Commonwealth, FAO, G-77, IAEA, IBRD, ICAO, IDA, IFAD, IFC, ILO, IMF, IMO, INTELSAT, INTERPOL, ITU, NAM, OSCE, UN, UNESCO, UPU, WHO, WMO, WTO.

Recent excavations on Cyprus indicate a human presence at least 10,000 years ago. Mycenean (Greek) culture flourished in the second millenium B.C. Phoenicians colonized the island in the 900s, and it remained a major entrepôt for eastern Mediterranean trade. Annexed to Rome in 58 B.C. it was later part of the Byzantine Empire until the English Richard I (Lion Hearted) established a crusader state in A.D. 1191. The Lusignan dynasty ruled until 1489, when Cyprus was annexed by Venice. It was subsequently conquered by the Ottoman Empire in 1571.

In 1878 the Congress of Berlin placed Cyprus under British administration. In 1914 it was annexed outright by Great Britain and was made a British colony in 1925. From 1945 to 1948, the British used Cyprus as a detention area for "illegal" Jewish immigrants to Palestine.

After 1947 the Greek Cypriot community continued its long-standing agitation for union *(enosis)* with Greece, a policy strongly opposed by the Turkish Cypriot community. Communal violence broke out in 1954–55. In 1960 Cyprus was granted full independence under an agreement that forbade either enosis or partition and included guarantees of the rights of both Greeks and Turks. Attempts by the president, Archbishop Makarios, to alter the constitution to favor the Greek majority provoked further communal clashes in 1964, when a UN peacekeeping force was sent to the island. On July 15, 1974, a military coup by officers favoring union with Greece deposed the Makarios government. On July 20 Turkey invaded Cyprus and, after the collapse of cease-fire talks in August, occupied the northern two-fifths of the island. In 1975 the Turkish government announced a de facto partition of Cyprus; the northern territory was proclaimed the Turkish Federated State of Cyprus, under Pres. Rauf Denktash.

Makarios returned as president of the Republic of Cyprus, which was thus reduced in size, and remained in office until his death in 1977. He was succeeded by Spyros Kyprianou. Some 200,000 Greek Cypriots were expelled from the Turkish sector to the Republic; many Turks fled from the Republic to the Turkish sector. With a return of political stability, renewed foreign investment, and a customs union negotiated with the EEC, the Republic's economy has prospered, led by agriculture, light manufacturing, and tourism.

In the Turkish sector, the economy remains stagnant, hampered by the loss of population, wartime damage, and stringent economic controls. The Turkish sector proclaimed its independence as the Turkish Republic of Northern Cyprus in 1983, but the new republic has not gained international recognition.

In March 1995 prospects for a possible federation of the two republics brightened, as Greece dropped its long-standing opposition to an EU-Turkish trade alliance and aid package in return for 1996 opening of negotiations for Cyprus to enter the EU on condition that Greek-Turkish talks on Cypriot unity had made progress.

Czech Republic

Geography Location: Central Europe. **Boundaries:** Poland to N, Slovakia to E, Austria to S, Germany to W. **Total land area:** 30,387 sq. mi. (78,703 sq km). **Coastline:** none. **Comparative area:** about the size of South Carolina. **Land use:** N.A. **Major cities:** (1992 est.) Prague (capital) 1,217,315; Brno 389,999; Ostrava 327,055; Pilsen (Plzeň) 172,318; Olomoue 105,485.

People Population: 10,408,280 (1994 est.). **Nationality:** noun—Czech; adjective—Czech. **Ethnic groups:** 81.3% Czech, 13.2% Moravian, 3% Slovak, Polish, German. **Languages:** Czech (official), Slovak, Polish. **Religions:** Christianity: 39% Roman Catholic, Protestant, Orthodox.

Government Type: republic. **Independence:** Oct. 28, 1918 (from Austro-Hungarian Empire). **Constitution:** Jan. 1, 1993. **National holiday:** Oct. 28. **Heads of government:** Václav Havel, president (since Jan. 1993), Václav Klaus, prime minister (since Jan. 1993). **Structure:** executive—president, prime minister, Council of Ministers; legislative—bicameral parliament (House and Senate); judicial—Supreme Court.

Economy Monetary unit: Czech crown (koruna) (Kc). **Budget:** (1992) ***income:*** $11.9 bil., (1993 est.); ***expend.:*** $11.9 bil. (1993 est.) **GDP:** $75 bil., $7,200 per capita (1993 est.). **Chief crops:** wheat, rye, barley, oats, corn. **Livestock:** cattle, pigs, sheep, and goats. **Natural resources:** coal, lignite, iron ore, crude petroleum. **Major industries:** machines, instruments, chemicals, fibers, textiles, and clothing. **Labor force:** (1990) 5,389,000. **Exports:** $12.6 bil., (f.o.b., 1993 est.); 39.2% machinery and equipment, 8.1% fuels, minerals, metals; 6.2% agricultural and forestry products. **Imports:** $12.4 bil. (f.o.b., 1993 est.); 37.3% machinery and equipment; 22.6% fuels, minerals, metals; 7.0% agricultural and forestry products. **Major trading partners:** (1992) EU countries, Scandinavian countries, former USSR.

Intl. Orgs. FAO, IAEA, IBRD, ICAO, ILO, IMF, IMO, ITU, OSCE, UN, UNCTAD, UNESCO, UNIDO, UPU, WHO, WIPO, WMO, WTO, ZC.

A Moravian empire, Christianized by Cyril and Methodius, existed in the ninth century until destroyed by the Magyars. From the 10th through the 14th century, Bohemia and Moravia, "lands of the crown of St. Vaclav," formed an independent kingdom within the Holy Roman Empire under the Czech Premsylid dynasty. In 1526 the crown lands came under Habsburg rule, a rule that lasted until World War I.

They were the richest crown lands of the Austro-Hungarian Empire. Prosperous agriculture in the central plains and mineral wealth in the hill country were supplemented in the 19th century by industrial development led by urban middle classes, who were largely German and Jewish.

With the crumbling of the Habsburg monarchy during the war, a new multinational state of Czechoslovakia emerged, founded by Eduard Beneŝ and Thomas Masaryk, in which the Czechs (only 45% of the population) ruled over Germans, Slovaks, Magyars, Poles, and Ukranians. Yet it was the most democratic state in Central Europe between the wars.

Following the Munich Pact of September 1938, Hitler annexed the German-speaking regions of the "Sudetenland," and in 1939 he established a "protectorate" over the Czech lands, while Slovakia became a self-governing satellite republic. With the collapse of Hitler's Reich, Czechoslovakia was reestablished (except for the Carpatho-Ukraine, which it was compelled to cede to the USSR) with Beneŝ again as president and a socialist government, independent but pro-Soviet. Three million Germans were expelled, with tens of thousands killed either in mob violence or after hasty trials before "Special People's Courts." In 1948 a Communist coup forced Beneŝ to resign; he was replaced by the Communist leader Klement Gottwald. Jan Masaryk, the foreign minister, committed suicide or was murdered. Purges and persecutions followed.

With Stalin's death in 1953, Gottwald was replaced as party first secretary by Stalinist hard-liner Antonin Novotny, who also became president in 1957. In 1968 Novotny was replaced as first secretary by a Slovak liberal, Alexander Dubcek. Czechoslovakia suddenly was in the vanguard of communist reform. The new regime abolished censorship, denounced Stalin, decentralized economic decision-making, and granted real power to the National Assembly.

The brief "Prague Spring" ended in August 1968, when Warsaw Pact troops invaded. In 1969 Dubcek was replaced by Gustáv Husak. The party was purged, censorship restored, dissent repressed, and the centralized economy restored.

The 1970s brought inflation and economic stagnation but produced no change in policy. The rise of the Solidarity movement in Poland in the early 1980s provoked a backlash of preventive repression in Czechoslovakia, aimed especially at Charter 77, a human-rights organization, and at the Catholic church.

The prodemocracy movement began in earnest in October 1989, inspired by a lack of confidence in Communist rule and by reform movements throughout Eastern Europe. The resignation of Communist leaders throughout December culminated in the parliamentary elections of Václav Havel, a dissident playwright and head of a loose coalition of opposition groups called Civic Forum, as president, and the vindicated Alexander Dubcek as chairman of Parliament.

Despite severe economic difficulties, revelations of state security abuses, environmental pollution, and other problems inherited from the Communist era, Czechoslovakia's "Velvet Revolution" seemed a resounding political and popular success. Soviet troops left by March; and in June Civic Forum and its Slovakian ally, Public Against Violence, won 47% of the vote in parliamentary elections, against 14% for the Communists and 12% for the Christian Democrats. Vaclav Havel was elected president, and Marian Calfa became prime minister.

But Slovak resentment of the Czech majority, heightened by Slovakia's great economic distress in the transition period of austerity and shift to a market economy, led in the spring of 1992 to negotiations arranging a much-reduced federal government, and in September to separate, independent Czech and Slovak republics. With the respective parliaments dividing financial and military assets in a two-to-one ratio to accord with the greater Czech population, an independent Czech Republic came into existence for the first time on January 1, 1993. On February 2 the Czech Parliament (by a surprisingly narrow 109 votes out of 200) elected Havel as president of the republic. (See also "Slovakia.")

Denmark

Kingdom of Denmark

Geography Location: northern Europe. **Boundaries:** Skagerrak channel to N, Baltic Sea to E, Germany to S, North Sea to W. **Total land area:** 16,629 sq. mi. (43,070 sq km). **Coastline:** 2,100 mi. (3,379 km). **Comparative area:** between Maryland and West Virginia. **Land use:** 61% arable land; negl. % permanent crops; 6% meadows and pastures; 12% forest and woodland; 21% other; includes 9% irrigated. **Major cities:** (1994) København (Copenhagen—capital) 1,346,289; Århus (Aarhus) 274,535; Odense 181,824; Alborg (Aalborg) 158,141; Esbjerg 82,593.

People Population: 5,187,821 (1994 est.). **Nationality:** noun—Dane(s); adjective—Danish. **Ethnic groups:** Scandinavian, Eskimo, Faeroese, German. **Languages:** Danish, Faeroese, Greenlandic (Eskimo dialect); small German-speaking minority. **Religions:** 97% Evangelical Lutheran, 2% other Protestant and Roman Catholic, 1% other.

Government Type: constitutional monarchy. **Constitution:** June 5, 1953. **National holiday:** Birthday of the Queen, Apr. 16. **Heads of government:** Margrethe II, queen (since Jan. 1972); Poul Nyrup Rasmussen, prime minister (since Jan. 1993). **Structure:** executive power vested in Crown but exercised by cabinet responsible to Parliament; legislative authority rests jointly with Crown and Parliament (Folketing); Supreme Court, two superior courts, 106 lower courts.

Economy Monetary unit: krone. **Budget:** (1992) ***income:*** $48 bil.; ***expend.:*** $55.7 bil. **GDP:** $95.6 bil., $18,500 per capita (1993). **Chief crops:** highly intensive, specializes in dairying and animal husbandry; main crops—cereals, root crops; food imports—oilseed, grain, animal foodstuffs. **Livestock:** chickens, pigs, cattle, ducks, turkeys. **Natural resources:** crude oil, natural gas, fish, salt, limestone. **Major industries:** food processing, machinery and equipment, textiles, clothing. **Labor force:** 2.55 mil. (1991); 51% services, 34% industry, 8% government, 7% agriculture, forestry, fishing: 9.6% unemployment (1989). **Exports:** $36.7 bil. (f.o.b., 1993); meat and meat products, dairy products, transport equipment, fish. **Imports:** $29.7 bil. (c.i.f., 1993 est,); petroleum, machinery and equipment, chemicals, grain and foodstuffs. **Major trading partners:** ***exports:*** 4.9% U.S., Germany, Norway, Sweden, UK, other EU, Japan; ***imports:*** 5.7% U.S., Germany, Netherlands, Sweden, UK, other EU.

Intl. Orgs. EU, FAO, IAEA, IBRD, ICAO, IDA, IFAD, IFC, ILO, IMF, IMO, INTELSAT, INTERPOL, ITU, NATO, OECD, OSCE, UN, UNESCO, UPU, WHO, WIPO, WMO, WTO.

Scandinavian by history, not geography, Denmark in the 11th century, under its second Christian king, Canute, ruled a great northern empire including Greenland, Iceland, the Faeroe Islands, Great Britain, and Norway. By 1387 Britain was long independent, but Denmark added Sweden and Finland to its domain. Yet it was never a great power. At home its kings never really controlled the nobility, while in foreign affairs it was dominated by the Hansa, the great league of German trading cities.

In the 16th century Denmark had to recognize the independence of Sweden and Finland. In the 19th century it lost Norway (to Sweden in 1814) and Schleswig-Holstein (to Prussia in 1864). In the 20th century Denmark sold the Virgin Islands to the United States in 1914 and had to recognize Iceland's independence in 1944.

In the 19th century, Denmark was transformed from a poor peasant society to one of Europe's richest agricultural nations by means of reforms that established agricultural cooperatives and emphasized intensive specialization in the production of dairy products and pork. These products remain a mainstay of the Danish economy.

Denmark remained neutral during World War I. In 1939 Denmark signed a 10-year nonaggression pact with Germany, but Germany nevertheless invaded Denmark in April 1940; the country surrendered without a fight. In

1941 Denmark's ambassador in Washington transferred defense of Greenland to the United States, and much of Denmark's merchant fleet joined the Allied war effort. Denmark was placed under German martial law in August 1943 and was treated as an enemy nation. Danish resistance succeeded in evacuating 7,000 Jews to neutral Sweden. Denmark was liberated by British troops in May 1945.

Although Denmark was not technically a participant on the Allied side in World War II, it became a UN member in 1946 and a founding member of NATO in 1949. By the latter year, the postwar recovery was complete, with industrial levels exceeding those of the prewar period. High taxes, unemployment, and inflation remained problems, but the economy was aided by the growth of trade with West Germany, which was just beginning its "economic miracle."

In 1953 the king assented to a constitutional reform that abolished the upper house of the legislature, leaving the Folketing as the sole legislative body. Proportional representation meant that it was virtually impossible for any political party to gain a parliamentary majority; Denmark is always governed by coalition regimes. In the postwar period, these normally have been led by the Social Democrats.

In the 1950s Denmark adopted a characteristically Scandinavian program of free enterprise, high taxes, and extensive social welfare systems. A high rate of economic growth, spurred by agricultural exports, continued throughout the 1960s. Denmark joined the EC in 1972. The 1970s brought economic difficulties, as Danish oil exploration in the North Sea yielded disappointing results, and inflation reached double digits annually.

The elections of 1982 installed Denmark's first Conservative government since 1905. A Conservative four-party coalition formed in 1984 remained in office until January 1993 when Prime Minister Schlüter resigned over charges of misleading the Folketing about restrictions on the immigration of Tamil refugees. Social Democrat Poul Nyrup Rasmussen formed a coalition government with only a one-seat majority.

The general revival of the world economy in the 1980s coupled with government austerity measures has led to renewed growth and lowered inflation, with both figures now averaging 3 percent annually. Although as recently as 1986 Danish voters renewed their commitment to the EC, in the June 1992 referendum on the Maastricht Treaty—providing for common defense and foreign policy as well as a common currency and central bank—Denmark said "no." The EU quickly made concessions that guaranteed Denmark's right to opt out of any common EU citizenship, police force, defense policy, or judicial arrangement. In May 1993 Danish voters approved this radically different version of the treaty.

Djibouti

Republic of Djibouti

Geography Location: northeastern Africa. **Boundaries:** Red Sea to N, Gulf of Aden to E, Somalia to SE, Ethiopia to S, W, and NW. **Total land area:** 8,494 sq. mi. (22,000 sq km). **Coastline:** 195 mi. (314 km). **Comparative area:** between Massachusetts and New Hampshire. **Land use:** 0% arable land; 0% permanent crops; 9% meadows and pastures; negl. % forest and woodland; 91% other. **Major cities:** Djibouti (capital) 200,000 (1981); Dikhil, Ali-Sabieh, Tadjourah, Obock.

People Population: 412,599 (1994 est.). **Nationality:** noun—Djiboutian(s); adjective—Djiboutian. **Ethnic groups:** 60% Somali (Issa), 35% Afar, 5% French, Arab, Ethiopian, and Italian. **Languages:** French (official); Arabic, Somali, and Afar widely used. **Religions:** 94% Muslim, 6% Christian.

Government Type: republic. **Independence:** June 27, 1977 (from France). **Constitution:** partial constitution ratified Jan. 1981 by National Assembly. **National holiday:** June 27. **Heads of government:** Hassan Gouled Aptidon, president (since June 1977); Barkat Gourad Hamadou, prime minister (since Sept. 1978). **Structure:** executive; legislative—65-member Parliament (National Assembly); judiciary.

Economy Monetary unit: Djibouti franc. **Budget:** (1990 est.) ***income:*** $170 mil., ***expend.:*** $203 mil. (1991 est.). **GNP:** $500 mil., $1,200 per capita (1993 est.). **Chief crops:** limited commercial crops, including fruits and vegetables. **Livestock:** goats, sheep, camels, cattle, asses. **Natural resources:** geothermal areas. **Major industries:** limited to a few small-scale enterprises, such as dairy products and mineral-water boiling. **Labor force:** small number of semiskilled workers at port; 3,000 railway workers; 52% of population of working age (1983). **Exports:** $158 mil. (f.o.b., 1992 est.); hides and skins and transit of coffee; a large portion consists of reexports to foreign residents of Djibouti. **Imports:** $334 mil. (f.o.b., 1992 est.); foods, machinery, transport equipment, chemicals, petroleum. **Major trading partners:** ***exports:*** 50% Africa, 40% Middle East, 9% W. Europe; ***imports:*** 54% W. Europe, 20% Middle East, 19% Asia.

Intl. Orgs. Arab League, FAO, G-77, IBRD, ICAO, IDA, IFAD, IFC, ILO, IMF, IMO, INTERPOL, ITU, NAM, OAU, UN, UPU, WHO, WMO.

This small, arid region on the Horn of Africa near the southern mouth of the Red Sea became the object of British-French rivalry with the opening of the Suez Canal in 1869. The French sphere of influence, called French Somaliland, was affirmed by agreements with Ethiopia in 1897, 1945, and 1954. In the early 20th century, the French constructed a railroad from Addis Ababa to Djibouti, adding to the colony's strategic value.

French and Italian forces clashed at the border of Ethiopia and French Somaliland with the Italian invasion of Ethiopia in the 1930s. During World War II, the territorial administration at first sided with the Vichy government but in December 1942 established ties with the Free French and the Allies.

The colony was reorganized in 1957 and in 1958 became, by referendum, a French Overseas Territory. In July 1967 its name was changed to the Territory of the Afars and Issas. Growing nationalist sentiment led to a referendum in favor of complete independence. The Republic of Djibouti became independent on June 27, 1977. A new constitution was approved in 1992 and multiparty elections in December resulted in a clean sweep for Popular Rally for Democracy.

Dominica

Commonwealth of Dominica

Geography Location: eastern Caribbean Sea, between Guadeloupe to N and Martinique to S. Roseau 15°18'N, 61°23'W. **Boundaries:** Dominica Passage to N, Atlantic Ocean to E, Martinique Passage to S, Caribbean Sea to W. **Total land area:** 290 sq. mi. (750 sq km). **Coastline:** 92 mi. (148 km). **Comparative area:** slightly more than four times size of Washington, D.C. **Land use:** 9% arable land; 13% permanent crops; 3% meadows and pastures; 41% forest and woodland; 34% other; includes N.A. % irrigated. **Major cities:** (1991 census) Roseau (capital) 20,755.

People Population: 87,696 (1994 est.). **Nationality:** noun—Dominican(s); adjective—Dominican. **Ethnic groups:** mostly black, some Carib-Indians. **Languages:** English (official), French patois widely spoken. **Religions:** 80% Roman Catholic, some Anglican and Methodist.

Government Type: independent state within commonwealth. **Independence:** Nov. 3, 1978 (from UK). **Constitution:** Nov. 3, 1978. **National holiday:** Nov. 3. **Heads of government:** Sir Crispin Anselm Sorhaindo, president (since Oct. 1993); Mary Eugenia Charles, prime minister (since July 1980). **Structure:** executive—cabinet headed by prime minister; legislative—31-member bicameral House of Assembly (one ex-officio member, nine appointed members, and 21 popularly elected members); judicial—magistrate's courts and regional court of appeals.

Economy Monetary unit: East Caribbean (EC) dollar. **Budget:** (1991 est.). ***income:*** $70 mil.; ***expend.:*** $84 mil. **GDP:** $185 mil., $2,100 per capita (1992 est.). **Chief crops:** bananas, coconuts, cocoa, yams, essential oils. **Livestock:** pigs, goats, cattle, sheep. **Natural resources:** timber. **Major industries:** agricultural processing, tourism, soap and other coconut-based products. **Labor force:** 25,000 (1984); 40% agriculture, 32% industry and commerce, 28% services; 15–20% unemployment. **Exports:** $54.6 mil. (1992); bananas, coconuts, lime juice and oil, cocoa, reexports. **Imports:** $97.5 mil. (1992); machinery and equipment, foodstuffs, manufactured articles, cement. **Major trading partners:** ***exports:*** 50% UK, CARICOM countries, U.S., Italy; ***imports:*** 27% U.S., CARICOM countries, UK, Canada.

Intl. Orgs. Commonwealth, FAO, G-77, IBRD, IDA, IFAD, IFC, ILO, IMF, IMO, INTERPOL, OAS, UN, UNESCO, UPU, WHO, WMO.

Pre-Columbian Dominica was a stronghold of Carib Indians, who had expelled the Arawaks in the 14th century, and today it is the only island in the Caribbean with a native Carib population. Dominica was visited by Columbus on his second American voyage; but though frequented by Spanish ships, it was not settled until French missionaries arrived in the 1630s. Carib resistance was so strong that the French and British agreed to consider the island neutral territory, until it passed under British control in 1763.

Later it was administratively joined to the Leeward and then the Windward Islands, and then became part of the West Indies Federation. It entered into political association with the United Kingdom in 1967. In 1978 Dominica gained independence from Britain. Prime Minister Mary Eugenia Charles's Freedom party has held power since 1980 on a program of economic reconstruction. Hurricanes in 1979–80 largely destroyed the island's agriculture. The government has attempted to effect economic diversification policies, including tourism, since the disaster. In 1992 it began a controversial policy of granting citizenship to businessmen, Asians in particular, in exchange for investment in Dominica's economy.

Dominican Republic

Geography Location: eastern Hispaniola, in Caribbean Sea. Santo Domingo 19°30'N, 70°42'W. **Boundaries:** North Atlantic to N, Mona Passage to E, Caribbean Sea to S, Haiti to W. **Total land area:** 18,815 sq. mi. (48,730 sq km). **Coastline:** 800 mi. (1,288 km). **Comparative area:** slightly more than four times size of Washington, D.C. **Land use:** 23% arable land; 7% permanent crops; 43% meadows and pastures; 13% forest and woodland; 14% other; includes 4% irrigated. **Major cities:** (1981) Santo Domingo (capital) 1,313,172; Santiago de los Caballeros 278,638; La Romana 91,571; San Pedro de Macorís 78,562; San Francisco de Macorís 64,906.

People Population: 7,826,075 (1994 est.). **Nationality:** noun—Dominican(s); adjective—Dominican. **Ethnic groups:** 73% mixed, 16% white, 11% black. **Languages:** Spanish. **Religions:** 95% Roman Catholic.

Government Type: republic. **Independence:** Feb. 27, 1844 (from Haiti). **Constitution:** Nov. 28, 1966. **National holiday:** Independence Day, Feb. 27. **Head of government:** Joaquín Balaguer, president (since Aug. 1986). **Structure:** president popularly elected for four-year term; bicameral legislature (National Congress—30-seat Senate and 120-seat Chamber of Deputies elected for four-year terms); Supreme Court.

Economy Monetary unit: Dominican peso. **Budget:** (1992 est.) ***income:*** 1.4 bil.; ***expend.:*** $1.8 bil. **GDP:** $23 bil., $3,000 per capita (1993 est.). **Chief crops:** sugarcane, coffee, rice, cocoa, tobacco, corn. **Livestock:** cattle, pigs, goats, horses, asses, mules, sheep. **Natural resources:** nickel, bauxite, gold, silver. **Major industries:** tourism, sugar processing, ferro-nickel and gold mining. **Labor force:** 2.3–2.6 mil. (1986); 49% agriculture, 33% services, 18% industry. **Exports:** $769 mil. (f.o.b., 1993 est.); sugar, coffee, cocoa, gold, ferro-nickel. **Imports:** $2.2 bil. (c.i.f., 1993 est.); foodstuffs, petroleum, cotton and manufactures, chemicals and pharmaceuticals. **Major trading partners:** ***exports:*** 60% U.S., 19% EU, 8% Puerto Rico; ***imports:*** 50% U.S.

Intl. Orgs. FAO, G-77, IAEA, IBRD, ICAO, IDA, IFAD, IFC, ILO, IMF, IMO, INTELSAT, INTERPOL, ITU, OAS, UN, UNESCO, UPU, WHO, WMO, WTO.

The Dominican Republic takes up the eastern two-thirds of the island of Hispaniola, which it shares with Haiti. Christopher Columbus visited the island in 1492, and Santo Domingo is the oldest continually inhabited European settlement in the Americas, with the oldest cathedral, hospital, and monastery in the Western Hemisphere.

Western Hispaniola (Haiti) was ceded to France in 1697, and the eastern part of the island in 1795. Liberated with the Haitian slave revolts of 1801, it fell under Haitian rule from 1804 to 1808 (when it reverted to Spanish rule), and again from 1822 to 1844. It was again occupied by Spain from 1861 to 1865. Under Ulises Heureux (1882–99), the Dominican Republic enjoyed a period of independence and prosperity. The United States occupied the Dominican Republic between 1916 and 1924. In 1930 Rafael Trujillo set up a dictatorship lasting 31 years. Dominican political strife triggered another U.S. invasion (1965–66) to end the revolution. Reformist party candidate Joaquín Balaguer, president from 1966 to 1978, regained the presidency in 1986, was reelected in 1990, and again (at age 87) in 1994, but only for two years, a compromise arranged in the face of charges of election fraud.

Ecuador

Republic of Ecuador

Geography Location: northwestern South America. **Boundaries:** Colombia to N, Peru to E and S, Pacific Ocean to W. **Total land area:** 109,483 sq. mi. (283,560 sq km); incl. Galapagos Islands, 0°45'S, 90°19'W. **Coastline:** 1,389 mi. (2,237 km). **Comparative area:** between Colorado and Nevada. **Land use:** 6% arable land; 3% permanent crops; 17% meadows and pastures; 51% forest and woodland; 23% other; includes 2% irrigated. **Major cities:** (1990 census) Quito (capital) 1,100,847; Guayaquil 1,508,444; Cuenca 194,981; Machala 144,197; Portoviejo 132,937.

People Population: 10,677,067 (1994 est.). **Nationality:** noun—Ecuadorian(s); adjective—Ecuadorian. **Ethnic groups:** 55% mestizo, 25% Indian, 10% Spanish, 10% black. **Languages:** Spanish (official), Indian languages, especially Quechua. **Religions:** 95% Roman Catholic.

Government Type: republic. **Independence:** May 24, 1822 (from Spain). **Constitution:** Aug. 10, 1979. **National holiday:** Independence Day, Aug. 10. **Head of government:** Sixto Duran Ballen, president (since Aug. 1992). **Structure:** executive; unicameral legislature (Chamber of Representatives); independent judiciary.

Economy Monetary unit: sucre. **Budget:** (1992) ***income:*** $1.9 bil.; ***expend.:*** $1.9 bil. **GDP:** $41.8 bil., $4,000 per capita (1993 est.). **Chief crops:** bananas, coffee, cocoa, sugarcane, corn, potatoes, rice; illegal producer of coca for international drug trade. **Livestock:** pigs, cattle, sheep. **Natural resources:** petroleum, fish, timber. **Major industries:** food processing, textiles, chemicals. **Labor force:** 2.8 mil. (1983); 52% agriculture, 20% services, 13% manufacturing; 8.5% unemployment. **Exports:** $3 bil. (f.o.b., 1992); 47% petroleum, coffee, bananas, cocoa products, shrimp. **Imports:** $2.5 bil. (f.o.b., 1992); transport equipment, vehicles, machinery, chemicals, petroleum. **Major trading partners:** ***exports:*** (1988) 58% U.S., Latin America, Caribbean, EU; ***imports:*** (1987) 28% U.S., Latin America, Caribbean, EU, Japan.

Intl. Orgs. FAO, G-77, IAEA, IBRD, ICAO, IDA, IFAD, IFC, ILO, IMF, IMO, INTELSAT, INTERPOL, ITU, NAM, OAS, OPEC, UN, UNESCO, UPU, WHO, WMO.

The Inca Empire maintained control over the territory that is now Ecuador until the arrival of Spanish conqueror Francisco Pizarro in 1532. The Spanish conquistadores quickly dismantled the indigenous political structure, which had been weakened by a series of wars between the Inca chief Atahualpa and his half brother Huáscar. The Spaniards arrived in the Quito region in 1533 and established the city of Guayaquil shortly thereafter. The administrative center of Spanish rule was originally established through the viceroyalty of Peru in 1544, and an *audiencia* (a regional high court under the nominal authority of the viceroy) was established at Quito in 1563. Administrative control of the region was transferred to Bogotá and the viceroyalty of New Granada in 1718.

The local junta of Quito ousted the audiencia in 1809, but they did not achieve independence for the region until after the military victory of the rebel forces over the royalists at the battle of Pichincha in 1822. Ecuador formed a part of the Confederation of Gran Colombia until the confederation's collapse in 1830. The leader of the forces for independence, Gen. Juan José Flores, removed the country from the Gran Colombian confederation and ruled as dictator until his ouster in 1845. A political rivalry existed between the Liberals of Guayaquil and the Conservatives of Quito, but Conservative dominance of the government lasted until 1895.

During the rule of Conservative president Gabriel García Moreno (1861–75), the Roman Catholic church gained a central place in the political and cultural life of the country. García

Moreno tied citizenship requirements to Catholic religious affiliation, brought in the Jesuits to "purify" the country through a new educational program, and dedicated the country to the Sacred Heart of Jesus. He was assassinated in 1875.

In 1895 the Radical Liberal (anticlerical) party seized power and held it until 1944. José María Velasco Ibarra, who was in and out of power until 1972, dominated the political scene. Political stability within the country had much to do with the state of the economy. The traditional reliance on cacao production was superseded in the 1950s by a "banana boom," and the discovery of large oil deposits by U.S. corporations in the 1960s led to a shift toward reliance on oil revenues by the following decade. A Peruvian invasion in 1941 led to the loss of almost half of Ecuador's national territory; a simmering hostility has remained between the two countries ever since.

Military factions kidnapped Pres. León Febres Cordero in 1987, releasing him in exchange for amnesty for two-time coup leader Lt. Gen. Frank Vargas Pazos. In 1988 Rodrigo Borja, of the Democratic Left party (ID), was elected to the presidency. In 1992 conservative Sixto Durán Ballén, an advocate of free market reforms, won the presidency and immediately moved to eliminate government subsidies and encourage foreign investment.

In 1990, the previously ignored Indian minority emerged as a political force, boycotting the decennial census and staging a series of peaceful demonstrations known simply as "The Uprising." Among their demands were land redistribution, official recognition of Ecuador as a multinational state, Indian control of archaeological sites, funding for bilingual education, research into traditional medicine, and the expulsion of an American evangelical group. In late January 1995 fighting just short of all-out war erupted along a 50-mile segment of the 1,000-mile border with Peru, with Pres. Duran proclaiming a national emergency; a truce was arranged in mid-February, but with neither side yielding any claims.

Stuck between Peru and Colombia (the largest coca leaf grower and largest cocaine refiner in the world, respectively), Ecuador struggles to suppress the drug trade. Heavily dependent on oil, it benefited from oil price increases during the Persian Gulf War, but in 1992 it withdrew from OPEC to protest the organization's policies toward small producers.

Egypt

Arab Republic of Egypt

Geography Location: northeastern Africa and Asia (Sinai peninsula). **Boundaries:** Mediterranean Sea to N, Israel to NE, Red Sea to E, Sudan to S, and Libya to W. **Total land area:** 386,660 sq. mi. (1,001,450 sq km). **Coastline:** 1,523 mi. (2,450 km). **Comparative area:** about 1.4 times size of Texas. **Land use:** 3% arable land; 2% permanent crops; 0% meadows and pastures; negl. % forest and woodland; 95% other; includes 2% irrigated. **Major cities:** (1992 est.) Cairo (capital) 6,800,000; El-Iskandriyah (Alexandria) 3,380,000; Giza 3,700,100; Shoubra el-kheima 834,000; Port Said 460,000.

People Population: 60,765,028 (1994 est.). **Nationality:** noun—Egyptian(s); adjective—Egyptian. **Ethnic groups:** 90% Eastern Hamitic stock, 10% Greek, Italian, Syro-Lebanese. **Languages:** Arabic (official), English and French widely understood by educated classes. **Religions:** (official estimate) 94% Muslim (mostly Sunni), 6% Coptic Christian and other.

Government Type: republic. **Independence:** Feb. 28, 1922 (from UK). **Constitution:** Sept. 11, 1971. **National holiday:** National Day, July 23. **Heads of government:** Mohammed Hosni Mubarak, president (since 1981); Dr. Atef Sidky, prime minister (since Nov. 1986). **Structure:** executive power vested in president, who appoints cabinet; People's Assembly is principal legislative body, with Shura Council having consultative role; independent judiciary administered by minister of justice.

Economy Monetary unit: Egyptian pound. **Budget:** (1992 est.) ***income:*** $16.8 bil.; ***expend.:*** $19.4 bil. **GDP:** $139 bil., $2,400 per capita (1993 est.). **Chief crops:** fodder, maize, wheat, cotton, rice; not self-sufficient in food. **Livestock:** chickens, ducks, buffalo, cattle, goats. **Natural resources:** crude oil, natural gas, iron ore, phosphates, manganese. **Major industries:** textiles, food processing, tourism. **Labor force:** about 15 mil. (1989 est.); 40–45% agriculture, 36% government (local and national), public sector enterprises and armed forces, 20% privately owned service and manufacturing enterprises (1984); shortage of skilled labor; unemployment about 7% (official est.); about 2 million Egyptians work abroad, mostly in Iraq and Gulf Arab states (1988 est.). **Exports:** $3.5 bil. (f.o.b., FY93 est.); raw cotton, crude and refined petroleum, cotton yarn, textiles. **Imports:** $10.5 bil. (c.i.f., FY93 est.); foodstuffs, machinery and equipment, fertilizers, wood products, durable consumer goods. **Major trading partners:** U.S., EU, Japan, Eastern Europe.

Intl. Orgs. Arab League, FAO, G-77, IAEA, IBRD, ICAO, IDA, IFAD, IFC, ILO, IMF, IMO, INTELSAT, INTERPOL, ITU, NAM, OAU, UN, UNESCO, UPU, WHO, WIPO, WMO, WTO.

Civilization began in the fertile valley of the Nile River around 5000 B.C. In about 3200 B.C., King Menes established the first of many dynasties of pharaohs that unified the country from the Nile Delta to Upper Egypt, creating a distinctive ancient civilization of great wealth and cultural brilliance.

The last pharaonic dynasty was overthrown by the Persians in 341 B.C. The Persians in turn were replaced by the Alexandrian and Ptolemaic Greek dynasties and then by the rule of the Roman Empire. Egypt was part of the Byzantine Empire from the third to the seventh centuries A.D., when it was conquered by the Arab Islamic expansion. Arab rule was ended around 1250 when the Mameluke dynasty, of Caucasian origin, established control. The Mamelukes were defeated by the Turks in 1517, and Egypt was incorporated into the Ottoman Empire.

The Suez Canal was built by a French corporation during 1859–69 but was taken over by the British in 1875. This, together with the expansion of the British Empire in East Africa and the Sudan, led to the establishment of de facto British rule in Egypt in 1882, although Egypt remained nominally part of the Ottoman Empire until 1914. A British protectorate in Egypt was established in that year, replaced by a League of Nations Mandate in 1922. The autonomy of the Egyptian monarchy was strengthened in an Anglo-Egyptian treaty of 1936, but Great Britain continued to maintain military forces in Egypt and controlled the Sudan as an Anglo-Egyptian condominium.

Egypt saw heavy fighting between British and Axis forces during World War II. After the war, a nationalist movement gained strength. The 1936 treaty was abrogated by Egypt in 1951. An uprising of the Society of Free Officers on July 23, 1952, forced King Farouk to abdicate. A republic was proclaimed on June 18, 1953. Lt. Col. Gamal Abdel Nasser became premier in 1954 and president in 1956.

British troops were withdrawn from the Suez Canal zone in June 1956. On July 26, 1956, Egypt announced the nationalization of the canal. Israel invaded the Sinai Peninsula at the end of October 1956. France and Great Britain landed forces and bombed Egyptian positions; a cease-fire went into effect under UN supervision on Nov. 17. A UN peacekeeping force patrolled the border between Egypt and Israel from 1957 to 1967.

Increasing Soviet involvement in Egypt was confirmed with its aid to Egypt in the construction of the Aswan High Dam. The dam, completed in 1971, provides both irrigation and hydropower but at the cost of extensive environmental damage.

Egypt and Syria joined together as the United Arab Republic in 1958. Later joined by Yemen, the union was dissolved in 1961.

Egyptian incursions into the Gaza Strip and the Sharm el Sheikh in early June 1967 led to the outbreak of full-scale war with Israel on June 5. The Six-Day War ended on June 10 with Israel in full control of Gaza and the Sinai peninsula to the banks of the Suez Canal. Sporadic fighting between Egyptian and Israeli forces continued throughout 1969–70. The Suez Canal remained closed to shipping until 1975.

Nasser died in 1970 and was succeeded by Vice Pres. Anwar Sadat, who concluded a treaty of friendship with the USSR, but expelled all Soviet troops and advisers in 1972.

On Oct. 6, 1973, Egyptian forces crossed the Suez Canal and attacked Israeli positions in the Sinai (Syrian forces also attacked Israeli positions in the Golan Heights). Israel drove back the attackers, and the Yom Kippur War ended in a cease-fire on Oct. 24.

In 1974 Sadat's government became increasingly friendly to the West, welcoming foreign investment and American aid. In 1974 and 1975 disengagement accords were signed with Israel, providing for the return of the Sinai to Egypt in stages. In November 1977 Sadat visited Jerusalem as a gesture of peace, and a peace treaty between Israel and Egypt was signed (after a series of talks mediated by Pres. Jimmy Carter at Camp David, Maryland) on Mar. 26, 1979. Formal diplomatic relations were established in 1982. As a result of the peace treaty with Israel, Egypt was suspended from the Arab League—it was readmitted in 1989—and attacked by Libyan forces on several occasions along the Egyptian-Libyan border.

Popular unrest fomented by the Muslim Brotherhood in September 1981 led to a military crackdown. Pres. Sadat was assassinated by members of a military conspiracy on Oct. 6, 1981, and was succeeded by Vice Pres. Mohammed Hosni Mubarak. The government has remained on friendly terms with Israel and the United States and has gradually improved relations with the rest of the Arab world. During the Persian Gulf War, it was a staunch member of the anti-Iraq coalition, in return for which the United States forgave $7 billion in debt.

In recent years several Muslim extremist groups such as the Jamaat Islamiya have carried out bombings and assassinations aimed at secular intellectuals, Coptic Christians, and foreigners. One offset has been the crippling of Egypt's vital tourist industry.

El Salvador

Republic of El Salvador

Geography **Location:** Pacific coast of Central America. **Boundaries:** Honduras to N and E, Pacific Ocean to S, Guatemala to W. **Total land area:** 8,124 sq. mi. (21,040 sq km). **Coastline:** 191 mi. (307 km). **Comparative area:** about size of Massachusetts. **Land use:** 27% arable land; 8% permanent crops; 29% meadows and pastures; 6% forest and woodland; 30% other; includes 5% irrigated. **Major cities:** (1992 census) San Salvador (capital) 422,570; Soyapango 251,811; Santa Ana 202,337; San Miguel 182,817; Mejicanos 145,000.

People **Population:** 5,752,511 (1994 est.). **Nationality:** noun—Salvadoran(s); adjective—Salvadoran. **Ethnic groups:** 89% mestizo, 10% Indian, 1% white. **Languages:** Spanish, Nahua (among some Indians). **Religions:** 97% Roman Catholic; activity by Protestant groups throughout country.

Government **Type:** republic. **Independence:** Sept. 15, 1821 (from Spain). **Constitution:** Dec. 20, 1983. **National holiday:** Independence Day, Sept. 15. **Head of government:** Armando Calderon Sol (since June 1994). **Structure:** executive; Legislative Assembly (60 seats); Supreme Court.

Economy **Monetary unit:** Salvadoran colón. **Budget:** (1990 est.) ***income:*** $846 mil.; ***expend.:*** $890 mil. **GDP:** $14.2 bil., $2,500 per capita (1993 est.). **Chief crops:** coffee, cotton, corn, sugar, beans, rice, sorghum, wheat. **Livestock:** cattle, pigs, horses, mules, goats, sheep. **Natural resources:** hydropower and geothermal power, crude oil. **Major industries:** food processing, textiles, clothing. **Labor force:** 1.7 mil. (1982 est.); 40% agriculture, 16% manufacturing, 16% commerce, 13% government; shortage of skilled labor and large pool of unskilled labor, but manpower-training programs improving situation; 30% unemployment (1987 est.). **Exports:** $730 mil. (f.o.b., 1993 est.); 45% coffee, sugar, cotton, shrimp. **Imports:** $1.9 bil. (c.i.f., 1993 est.); petroleum products, consumer goods, foodstuffs, machinery, construction materials. **Major trading partners:** ***exports:*** 33% U.S., Germany, Guatemala, Costa Rica, Japan; ***imports:*** 43% U.S., Guatemala, Venezuela, Mexico, Germany.

Intl. Orgs. FAO, G-77, IAEA, IBRD, ICAO, IDA, IFAD, IFC, ILO, IMF, IMO, INTELSAT, ITU, OAS, UN, UNESCO, UPU, WIPO, WMO.

A number of Indian tribes, of which the Pipil were dominant, originally inhabited the area now called El Salvador. The native population resisted the first attempt at Spanish colonization, begun in 1524, for almost 15 years. In 1821 El Salvador gained its independence from Spain, first as a jurisdiction under the Mexican empire and two years later as a member of the United Provinces of Central America. The Central American Federation collapsed in 1838, and in 1840 El Salvador emerged from a bloody two-year struggle as an independent republic.

The Salvadoran economy came to be dominated by coffee production from the 1860s onward, and a series of laws in the 1880s allowed for concentration of both land ownership and political power in the hands of a coffee oligarchy. In 1931 a reformist president won election, but the military subsequently dismissed him. A revolt ensued (1932) in which 10,000 to 20,000 Salvadorans—mostly peasants—were killed. The apparent result of the massacre, which was called La Matanza, was a period of relative political stability that lasted until the 1970s.

In 1979 a political coup led by a group of junior military officers overthrew Pres. Gen. Carlos Humberto Romero. Owing to the polarization between conservative and reformist political groups, the first two civilian-military juntas resigned as a result of their failure to have their programs implemented by the military. A third government, which included Christian Democrat José Napoleón Duarte, took over on Mar. 5, 1980, on the basis of an armed forces' pledge to carry out an agrarian reform program. In 1980 the coalition of opposition political organizations became the Democratic Revolutionary Front (FDR), and five revolutionary military organizations consolidated under the banner of the Farabundo Marti Front for National Liberation (FMLN). Six social-democratic political leaders were assassinated in November 1980, further cementing the political opposition around the FMLN-FDR coalition. Although the revolutionary opposition called for a "final offensive" to overthrow the political-military structure of rule, this action ultimately failed.

A three-part agrarian reform program was initiated in 1980 in El Salvador, but the central part of the program—to redistribute most of the land involved in export agriculture—was dropped as a result of opposition from the agricultural elite.

In March 1982 elections for a constituent assembly, a majority of seats went to the rightist ARENA coalition. In December 1983 a new constitution went into effect, and in 1984 Christian Democrat José Napoleón Duarte assumed the presidency.

In 1989, Alfredo Cristiani of the conservative Alliance for National Renovation was elected president. On Nov. 11, 1989, FMLN guerrillas launched a new offensive that lasted for several weeks before fading away. The government's failure to prosecute military officers implicated in the murder of six Jesuit priests shortly thereafter jeopardized U.S. military aid, which totaled $6 billion between 1979 and 1992.

In January 1992, the government signed a peace treaty with the FMLN and the 12-year civil war, in which 70,000 people died, officially ended on December 15. The treaty called for the military to cut its forces by almost half (to 31,000 soldiers), and for the FMLN to lay down its arms and become a political party. A UN-sponsored Truth Commission found that 85 percent of all human-rights violations during the war were attributable to the Salvadoran army, security forces, or intelligence-unit death squads. Although the legislature narrowly passed a general amnesty for public officials, military officers, and political party leaders linked to human rights violations in March of 1993, the United States has tried to link further military aid to the dismissal of the worst offenders in the military.

In the March 1994 elections, ARENA's candidate Armando Calderon Sol was elected president (falling just short of an absolute majority, while the FMLN candidate finished second with 26 percent). ARENA also carried half the seats in the National Assembly.

Equatorial Guinea

Republic of Equatorial Guinea

Geography **Location:** mainland territory of Río Muni in western Africa and five inhabited islands: Bioko (3°45'N, 8°50'E), Corisco, Great Elobey, Small Elobey, and Pagalu (Annabon). **Boundaries:** Cameroon to N, Gabon to E and S, Gulf of Guinea to W. **Total land area:** 10,830 sq. mi. (28,050 sq km). **Coastline:** 184 mi. (296 km). **Comparative area:** slightly larger than Maryland. **Land use:** 5% arable land; 4% permanent crops; 4% meadows and pastures; 61% forest and woodland; 26% other. **Major cities:** (1983 census) Malabo (capital) 15,323; Bata 24,100.

People **Population:** 409,550 (1994 est.). **Nationality:** noun—Equatorial Guinean(s); adjective—Equatorial Guinean. **Ethnic groups:** indigenous population of Bioko, primarily Bubi, some Fernandinos; Río Muni, primarily Fang; less than 1,000 Europeans, mostly Spanish. **Languages:** Spanish (official), pidgin English, Fang. **Religions:** nominally Christian, predominantly Roman Catholic, indigenous practices.

Government **Type:** republic. **Independence:** Oct. 12, 1968 (from Spain). **Constitution:** Aug. 15, 1982. **National holiday:** Oct. 12. **Heads of government:** Col. Teodoro Obiang Nguema Mbasogo, president (since Aug. 1979); Don Silvestre Siale Bileka, prime minister (since 1992). **Structure:** executive—president with broad powers, prime minister; unicameral legislature—House of Representatives of the People; free judiciary.

Economy **Monetary unit:** Communauté Financière Africaine (CFA) franc. **Budget:** (1991 est.) ***income:*** $26 mil.; ***expend.:*** $30 mil. **GDP:** $280 mil., $700 per capita (1993 est.); economy destroyed during regime of former Pres. Masie Nguema. **Chief crops:** cash crops—timber and coffee from Río Muni, cocoa from Bioko; food crops—rice, yams, cassava, bananas, oil palm nuts. **Livestock:** sheep, goats, pigs, cattle. **Natural resources:** timber, crude oil, small unexploited deposits of gold, manganese, uranium. **Major industries:** fishing, sawmilling. **Labor force:** (1986) 66% agriculture, 23% services, 11% industry; labor shortages on plantations; 58% of population of working age. **Exports:** $52.8 mil. (f.o.b., 1992); cocoa beans, coffee, timber. **Imports:** $63.6 mil. (c.i.f., 1992); foodstuffs, petroleum, beverages, clothing, machinery. **Major trading partners:** (1987) ***exports:*** 44% Spain, 19% Germany, 12% Italy, 11% Netherlands; ***imports:*** 34% Spain, 16% Italy, 14% France, 8% Netherlands.

Intl. Orgs. FAO, G-77, IBRD, ICAO, IDA, IFAD, ILO, IMF, IMO, INTERPOL, ITU, NAM, UN, UNESCO, UPU, WHO.

Equatorial Guinea consists of the Mbini River basin on the West African coast, and a number of offshore islands, chiefly Bioko and Pagalu (Annobón). Indigenous Pygmies were displaced beginning in the 17th century by migrations of various peoples that now inhabit the coastal region and by the Fang, who comprise 80 percent of the present population.

Bioko was discovered in 1473 by the Portuguese explorer Fernando Po, and until modern times the island bore his name. Portugal controlled the islands and adjacent mainland, exploiting them for the slave trade, until 1778 when the territory was ceded to Spain. Equatorial Guinea remained underdeveloped because of conflicting territorial claims and a lack of Spanish investment. Eventually, however, a plantation system was developed for the cultivation of cocoa, particularly on Bioko, using workers imported from Nigeria.

In 1959 the Spanish territories in the Gulf of Guinea were given status equivalent to a province of Spain. Investment in education, health care facilities, and other social programs, combined with the flourishing plantation economy, made the territory one of the most prosperous and best educated in West Africa. Local autonomy was granted in 1963 and full independence in 1968.

Francisco Macias Nguema was elected Equatorial Guinea's first president in 1968. In 1970 he dissolved all opposition parties and declared a one-party state, and in 1972 proclaimed himself president for life and commenced rule by decree. During the next seven years, a reign of terror resulted in the death or exile of one-third of the country's people. Nigerian workers, along with other foreigners, were expelled from the country in 1976; without their labor and technical skills, the economy was quickly ruined.

Macias Nguema was overthrown in August 1979 in a military coup led by his nephew, Lt. Col. Teodoro Obiang Nguema Mbasogo. Macias Nguema was tried and executed a month later. The Spanish-educated Nguema Mbasogo moved to reduce Soviet influence and to improve relations with Spain. A new constitution was approved in a referendum in August 1982 and again in 1991, the latter calling for a multiparty political system. Nguema Mbasogo, however, retains firm control. Economic prospects have improved with the discovery of oil reserves estimated at over 65 million barrels a year.

Eritrea

State of Eritrea

Geography **Location:** Horn of Africa (central-eastern Africa). **Boundaries:** Sudan to N and W, Red Sea to E, Djibouti and Ethiopia to S. **Total land area:** 46,842 sq. mi. (121,320 sq km). **Coastline:** 680 mi. (1,094 km) on Red Sea. **Comparative area:** about the size of New York. **Land use:** N.A. **Major cities:** (1993 est.) Asmara (capital) 400,000; Asseb, Massawa, Keren.

People **Population:** 3,782,543 (1994 est.). **Nationality:** noun—Eritrean(s); adjective—Eritrean. **Ethnic groups:** Afar, Bilen, Hadareb, Kunama, Nara. **Languages:** Afar, Bilen, Hadareb, Kunama, Nara. **Religions:** Christianity, Islam, some animists.

Government **Type:** transitional government. **Independence:** May 24, 1993 (from Ethiopia). **Constitution:** transitional "constitution" decreed May 1993. **National holiday:** Independence Day, May 24. **Head of government:** Issaias Afwerki, president (since May 1993). **Structure:** executive—president, Council of Ministers; legislative—unicameral (National Assembly); judicial—Supreme Court.

Economy **Monetary unit:** Birr. **Budget:** N.A. ***income:*** N.A. ***expend.*** N.A. **GDP:** $1.7 bil; $500 per capita (1993 est.). **Chief crops:** sorghum, wheat, barley, citrus fruits. **Livestock:** cattle, sheep, goats, camels. **Natural resources:** gold, copper, potash, iron ore. **Major industries:** food processing, beverages, clothing and textiles. **Labor force:** N.A. **Exports:** N.A. **Imports:** N.A. **Major trading partners:** N.A.

Intl. Orgs. OAS, UN, UNCTAD.

In May 1993, after 30 years of fighting, leaders of the Eritrean People's Liberation Front (EPLF) formally declared this small area of north and northeast Ethiopia to be an independent state. Ethiopia, along with the United States, the Sudan, and several other states, quickly recognized the authority of the new transitional government led by Issaias Afwerki, former head of the liberation movement.

During the early 20th century, the region of Eritrea was an outpost of the Italian empire, but it came under British rule during World War II. The British made Eritrea part of Ethiopia when independence was granted in 1952. The secessionist movement began immediately, first against Haile Selassie, then in the 1970s and '80s against the Marxist Mengistu Haile Mariam, who was finally driven from office by other forces in 1991. The new government quickly made peace with the Eritrean rebels, who promised continued access to the sea after independence became a fact.

Estonia

Republic of Estonia

Geography **Location:** northeastern Europe. **Boundaries:** Gulf of Finland to N and NE, Russian Federation to SE, Latvia to SW, Baltic Sea to NW. **Total land area:** 17,413 sq. mi. (45,100 sq km). **Coastline:** Gulf of Finland. **Comparative area:** about twice the size of New Hampshire. **Land use:** 22% cropland; 11% permanent pasture; 31% forest and woodland; 36% other (mostly urban and swampland). **Major cities:** (1994 est.) Tallinn (capital) 442,700; Tartu 105,800; Narva 79,100; Kohtla-Järve 56,600; Pärnu 52,000.

People **Population:** 1,616,882 (1994 est.). **Nationality:** noun—Estonian(s); adjective—Estonian. **Ethnic groups:** 61.5% Estonian, 30.3% Russian, 3.1% Ukrainian, 1.8% Belarussian, 1.1% Finn, Jewish. **Languages:** Estonian (official), closely related to Finnish; Russian, English, German, Finnish. **Religions:** 73% Lutheran, 19% Orthodox (1937).

Government **Type:** republic. **Independence:** On May 8, 1990, Supreme Council (Parliament) voted to restore the first five articles of the 1938 constitution that described Estonia as independent state; Supreme Council declared independence Aug. 20, 1991; recognized by USSR Sept. 6, 1991. **Constitution:** 1938 (on Aug. 7, 1990, Supreme Council nullified 1978 constitution of Estonian SSR); government commission is drafting new constitution. **National holiday:** Feb. 24, Independence Day. **Heads of government:** Lennart Meri, president (since Oct. 1992); Tiit Vähi, prime minister (since Apr. 1995). **Structure:** executive—president, Council of Ministers; legislative—Supreme Council (105 members); judicial—Supreme Court.

Economy **Monetary unit:** Estonian kroon. **Budget:** (1992) ***income:*** $223 mil.; ***expend.:*** $142 mil. **GDP:** $8.8 bil., $5,480 per capita (1993 est.). **Chief crops:** grain, potatoes, vegetables, fruit. **Livestock:** pigs, cattle, sheep, goats. **Natural resources:** oil shale (world's number two producer), phosphorites. **Major industries:** shale oil processing, mineral fertilizers, wood processing, pulp. **Labor force:** 796,000. **Exports:** $765 mil., (f.o.b., 1993); 30% machinery, 17% foodstuffs, 11% chemicals, 9% electric power. **Imports:** $865 mil. (c.i.f.,

1993); 45% machinery, 13% oil, 12% chemicals. **Major trading partners:** former Soviet republics, Finland, Germany.

Intl. Orgs. FAO, IAEA, IMF, OSCE, UN, UNCTAD, World Bank.

Ethnic and linguistic "cousins" of the Finns, the Ests acquired their own independent state only in the 20th century. Previously they had been "colonized" by the Danes (who founded the capital, Tallinn), then in the 13th century by the Teutonic Knights, in the 16th century by the Swedes (who brought the Lutheran Reformation), in the 17th century by the Poles, and in the 18th century by the Russians. Through all these regimes the German element predominated, the "Baltic barons" forming a territorial aristocracy with German burghers ruling the towns. The Ests were restricted to farming, normally as serfs, with serfdom not abolished until 1819.

With that abolition there began a cultural revival with the study of folklore, the collecting of folk songs, the compilation of the national epic, *Kalevipoeg,* published between 1857 and 1861, and the circulation of newspapers in the Estonian language. Political expression of this revived national spirit came with the 1918 Treaty of Brest-Litovsk in which the new Soviet Union recognized the independence of Estonia. By 1920 Estonia was fully independent, under its own constitution adopted on June 15 of that year.

A radical land reform dispossessed German landowners of large estates, which were distributed to peasant owners and tenants. Dangers from extremists of Left (Communists) and Right ("liberators") were averted by the strong presidency of Constantice Päts, but the Hitler-Stalin Pact of 1939 spelled the end of Estonian independence. Allotted to Stalin's sphere of influence, Estonia was forced to accept Soviet garrisons larger than its national army in 1939, and 65,000 Germans were "repatriated" (after 700 years) to the Third Reich. Rigged elections in 1940 led to a government that "requested" incorporation into the USSR, an annexation never recognized by the United States.

There followed nationalization of private property, amalgamation of Estonia's national forces into the Red Army, and a reign of terror against former political leaders and religious and cultural organizations. During and after the war the Estonian people suffered enormous losses through death in battle, murder, flight, and deportation.

Estonia's return to freedom began Mar. 30, 1990, when a freely elected government declared its intention to secede after an unspecified transition period. Violence provoked by Russian "black berets," mass demonstrations, defiance of Gorbachev's economic sanctions and his January 1991 military crackdown, all marked stages toward the Kremlin's recognition in September 1991 of Estonian independence. Estonia, like the other Baltic states, declined to sign the December 1991 Alma-Ata Declaration that created the Commonwealth of Independent States.

Elections were held in September 1992 producing a divided Parliament with the majority headed by a center-right coalition under the leadership of the Fatherland Alliance. In October, Parliament elected Lennart Meri, a nationalist and a devotee of free markets, to the presidency. The election aroused Russia's anger when Estonia effectively disenfranchised 40 percent of the population, mostly Russians, by requiring citizenship since 1940 either for oneself or through ancestors. But a July 1994 Estonian-Russian agreement granting ex-USSR military retirees the right to apply for resident status led to final Russian troop withdrawals at the end of August. Then, in March 1995, Fatherland Alliance took just 5 percent of the parliamentary vote and was replaced by a coalition government headed by the (ex-Communist) Coalition party.

Ethiopia

People's Democratic Republic of Ethiopia

Geography Location: Horn of Africa (central-eastern Africa). **Boundaries:** Eritrea to N, Djibouti and Somalia to E, Kenya to S, Sudan to W. **Total land area:** 435,184 sq. mi. (1,127,127 sq km). **Coastline:** none. **Comparative area:** somewhat smaller than Alaska. **Land use:** 12% arable land; 1% permanent crops; 41% meadows and pastures; 24% forest and woodland; 22% other; includes negl. % irrigated. **Major cities:** (1993 est.) Addis Ababa (New Flower) 2,200,186; Dire Dawa 173,588; Harar 162,645; Gondar 146,777; Nazret 131,585.

People Population: 54,927,108 (1994 est.). **Nationality:** noun—Ethiopian(s); adjective—Ethiopian. **Ethnic groups:** 40% Oromo, 32% Amhara and Tigrean, 9% Sidamo, 6% Shankella. **Languages:** Amharic and English official; 70 different languages. **Religions:** Christianity, Islam.

Government: Transitional government installed July 1991 to write new constitution within two to two-and-a-half years; new democratically elected government will be installed by mid-1994. **Independence:** oldest independent country in Africa and one of oldest in the world—at least 2,000 years. **Constitution:** being drafted. **National holiday:** May 28. **Heads of government:** Meles Zenawi, president (since 1991); Tamirat Layene, prime minister (since 1991). **Structure:** being drafted.

Economy Monetary unit: Ethiopian birr. **Budget:** (1993 est.) ***income:*** N.A.; ***expend.:*** $1.2 bil. **GDP:** $22.7 bil., $400 per capita (1993 est.). **Chief crops:** main crop—coffee; also cereals, pulses, oilseed, meat, hides and skins. **Livestock:** cattle, sheep, goats, asses, horses. **Natural resources:** small reserves of gold, platinum, copper, potash. **Major industries:** cement, textiles, food processing. **Labor force:** 90% agriculture and animal husbandry, 10% government, military, and quasi-government; 51% of population of working age (1985). **Exports:** $189 mil. (f.o.b., FY91); 60% coffee. **Imports:** $472 mil. (c.i.f., FY91); foodstuffs, fuels, capital goods. **Major trading partners:** ***exports:*** EU, Djibouti, Japan, Saudi Arabia, U.S.; ***imports:*** EU, Eastern Europe, Japan, U.S.

Intl. Orgs. FAO, G-77, IAEA, IBRD, ICAO, IDA, IFAD, IFC, ILO, IMF, IMO, INTELSAT, INTERPOL, ITU, NAM, OAU, UN, UNESCO, UPU, WHO, WMO.

Ethiopia played an important role in the Red Sea trade of the classical world and was mentioned by the Greek historian Herodotus in the fifth century B.C. According to legend, the Ethiopian monarchy was founded by Melelik I, son of Israel's King Solomon and the Queen of Sheba (Sab'a, i.e., North Yemen). Coptic Christianity became Ethiopia's dominant religion in the fourth century A.D. Ethiopia successfully resisted Islamic invasions in the seventh century except in areas along the Red Sea coast but was cut off from the rest of the Christian world by the Islamic states of North Africa and the Middle East.

Portugal established forts and trading stations on the Red Sea coast beginning in 1493, strengthening their domination of trade in the Indian Ocean. The Portuguese also sponsored Roman Catholic missionaries but with little success. A century of religious strife ended with the expulsion of all foreign missionaries in the 1630s. Ethiopia successfully resisted an attempted Italian invasion in 1880.

Ethiopia began to emerge into the modern world under Melelik II (r. 1889–1913). A period of instability after his death ended with the accession in 1930 of Haile Selassie. Italy invaded again in 1936 and soon conquered the entire country. Protests by the League of Nations had no effect; Haile Selassie fled to exile in England. The Italians were driven out during World War II by British and Ethiopian forces, and Haile Selassie returned to his throne.

Civil unrest broke out in February 1974, and Haile Selassie was deposed on Sept. 13, 1974. A coalition of urban elites and the armed forces took over, abolishing the monarchy in 1975 and curbing the power of the Coptic church. Land reform was instituted, and a socialist state proclaimed. In 1977–78 a period of "red terror" resulted in the arrest and execution of thousands of the new regime's opponents. A provisional military council, the Dergue, was confirmed in power under the leadership of Col. Mengistu Haile-Mariam.

A military assistance agreement in 1976 between Ethiopia and the USSR ended an earlier military relationship with the United States; American military advisers were expelled. In 1977 Somalia, taking advantage of Ethiopia's shifting military situation, attacked across the Ogaden desert, aiming to restore certain disputed areas of Ethiopia to Somalia. A massive infusion of Soviet arms and Cuban troops expelled the Somalis in March 1978, but border clashes continued thereafter.

After the expulsion of the Italians during World War II, the province of Eritrea, under a UN plan, was to have become autonomous in a federation with Ethiopia. Instead, Eritrea was made a province of the Ethiopian Empire in

1962. A coalition of Marxist and non-Marxist liberation forces—most prominent among them the Eritrean People's Liberation Front (EPLF)—resisted the annexation from the beginning. By the spring of 1991, Eritrean forces had gained control of all of Eritrea, including Ethiopia's only outlets to the sea.

Another rebel group, the Ethiopian People's Revolutionary Democratic Front (EPRDF), sought autonomy for Tigre, a northern region between Ethiopia and Eritrea. In February 1991, the EPRDF launched a major offensive that culminated in Mengistu Haile Mariam's flight in May, a week before scheduled cease-fire talks were to start in London. The talks proceeded quickly under the auspices of the United States, and rebel forces under the leadership of the EPRDF entered Addis Ababa virtually unopposed at the end of May.

Ethiopia faced unparalleled destruction during its civil war and a succession of devastating famines, and securing famine relief from the international community has been a priority of the transitional government that assumed power in May 1991.

Ethiopia is a political shambles with innumerable ethnic parties, and the country's first multiparty elections in June 1992 were so badly handled that the powerful OLF withdrew from the government. The government readily acknowledged Eritrean independence on May 24, and though it faces overwhelming problems in resettling refugees, bringing factions together, and rebuilding the nation's infrastructure, it hosted peace talks on the crises in Somalia and Angola in 1993. In July 1991, a transitional government was installed to draft a new constitution within two to two-and-a-half years.

In June 1994 the EPRDF won 484 of the 547 seats in the Constituent Assembly, which by November had drawn up a constitution for a parliamentary government over nine partially autonomous ethnic regions. The trials of members of Mengistu's Dergue junta for genocide and crimes against humanity began in March 1995; at least 100,000 had died or disappeared under its regime.

Fiji

Republic of Fiji

Geography Location: more than 300 islands (100 inhabited), in South Pacific Ocean. Suva 18°08'S, 178°25'E. **Boundaries:** South Pacific Ocean to N, S, and W; Koro Sea to E; nearest neighbor is Vanuatu, about 600 mi. (1,000 km) to W. **Total land area:** 7,054 sq. mi. (18,270 sq km). **Coastline:** 702 mi. (1,129 km). **Comparative area:** slightly smaller than New Jersey. **Land use:** 8% arable land; 5% permanent crops; 3% meadows and pastures; 65% forest and woodland; 19% other; includes negl. % irrigated. **Major cities:** (1986 census) Suva (capital) 69,665; Lautoka, 29,000.

People Population: 764,382 (1994 est.). **Nationality:** noun—Fijian(s); adjective—Fijian. **Ethnic groups:** 49% Indian; 46% Fijian, 5% European, other Pacific Islanders, overseas Chinese, and others. **Languages:** English (official), Fijian, Hindustani. **Religions:** Fijians are mainly Christian, Indians are Hindu with Muslim minority.

Government Type: republic. **Independence:** Oct. 10, 1970 (from UK). **Constitution:** Oct. 10, 1970 (suspended Oct. 1987). **National holiday:** Fiji Day, Oct. 10. **Heads of government:** Sir Kamisese Mara, head of state (since Jan. 1994); Maj. Gen. Sitiveni Rabuka, prime minister (since Mar. 1994). **Structure:** executive—prime minister and cabinet; judicial—Supreme Court, court of appeal, magistrate's courts.

Economy Monetary unit: Fiji dollar. **Budget:** (1993 est.) ***income:*** $455 mil.; ***expend.:*** $546 mil. **GDP:** $3 bil., $4,000 per capita (1993 est.). **Chief crops:** sugar, copra, ginger, rice; major deficiency, grains. **Livestock:** cattle, goats, horses, pigs. **Natural resources:** timber, fish, gold, copper, offshore oil potential. **Major industries:** sugar, copra, tourism. **Labor force:** 235,000 (1987); 40% paid employees; remainder involved in subsistence agriculture. **Exports:** $417 mil. (f.o.b., 1992); 49% sugar, copra, processed fish, lumber. **Imports:** $517 mil. (c.i.f., 1992 est.); 15% food, petroleum products, 32% machinery and transport, consumer goods. **Major trading partners:** 45% UK, 21% Australia, 6% U.S.; ***imports:*** 6% U.S., New Zealand, Australia, Japan.

Intl. Orgs. Colombo Plan, EU (associate), FAO, G-77, IBRD, ICAO, IDA, IFAD, IFC, ILO, IMF, IMO, INTELSAT, INTERPOL, ITU, UN, UNESCO, UPU, WHO, WIPO, WMO (resigned from Commonwealth Oct. 1986), WTO.

First reported to the West by the Dutch navigator Abel Tasman in 1643, the Fiji Islands were annexed as a British Crown Colony in 1874. Between 1879 and 1916, large numbers of Indian indentured laborers were imported to work on sugar plantations; eventually the original Melanesian inhabitants were outnumbered by persons of Indian descent. Fiji became an independent parliamentary democracy on Oct. 10, 1970, with most land ownership and political power vested in the Fijian minority. A parliamentary election in 1987 brought the Indian party to power; the elected government was ousted in a military coup, and Lt. Col. Sitiveni Rabuka assumed control of the government on May 21, 1987. On June 2, 1992, he was sworn in as prime minister under a new constitution that guarantees a majority of seats for ethnic Fijians in the national legislature. He was reelected as the head of a coalition government in Feb. 1994.

Fiji's economy is based largely on agriculture. Rice, vegetables, and livestock are produced for local consumption; sugar, copra, and ginger are important export crops. Gold and silver mining and limestone quarrying are economically important, as is tourism.

Finland

Republic of Finland

Geography Location: northern Europe. **Boundaries:** Norway to N, Russian Federation to E, Baltic Sea to S, Gulf of Bothnia, Sweden to W. **Total land area:** 130,127 sq. mi. (337,030 sq km). **Coastline:** 700 mi. (1,126 km) excluding islands and coastal indentations. **Comparative area:** between New Mexico and Montana. **Land use:** 8% arable land; 0% permanent crops; negl. % meadows and pastures; 76% forest and woodland; 16% other; includes negl. % irrigated. **Major cities:** (1993 est.) Helsinki (capital) 508,588; Espoo 182,647; Tampere 176,149; Turku 161,103; Vantaa 160,390.

People Population: 5,068,931 (1994 est.). **Nationality:** noun—Finn(s); adjective—Finnish. **Ethnic groups:** Finn, Swede, Lapp, Gypsy. **Languages:** 93.5% Finnish, 6.3% Swedish (both official); small Lapp- and Russian-speaking minorities. **Religions:** 97% Evangelical Lutheran, 1.2% Eastern Orthodox, 1.8% other.

Government Type: republic. **Independence:** Dec. 6, 1917 (from USSR). **Constitution:** July 17, 1919. **National holiday:** Independence Day, Dec. 6. **Heads of government:** Martti Ahtisaari, president (since Mar. 1994); Paavo Tapio Lipponen, prime minister (since Mar. 1995). **Structure:** executive power is vested in president and coalition cabinet responsible to Parliament; legislative authority rests jointly with president and unicameral legislature (Eduskunta); Supreme Court, four superior courts, 193 lower courts.

Economy Monetary unit: markkaa. **Budget:** (1992) ***income:*** $26.8 bil.; ***expend.:*** $40.6 bil. **GDP:** $81.1 bil., $16,100 per capita (1993). **Chief crops:** cereals, sugar beets, potatoes; 85% self-sufficient, but short of food and fodder grains. **Livestock:** poultry, cattle, pigs, reindeer, sheep. **Natural resources:** timber, copper, zinc, iron ore, silver. **Major industries:** metal manufacturing and shipbuilding, forestry and wood processing (pulp, paper), copper refining; shortages—fossil fuels; industrial raw materials (except wood, iron ore); food and fodder grains. **Labor force:** 2.53 mil. (1993 est.); 38.2% services; 22.9% mining and manufacturing; 14.9% commerce; 8.8% agriculture, forestry, and fishing; 3.4% unemployment. **Exports:** $23.4 bil. (f.o.b., 1993); timber, paper and pulp, ships, machinery, clothing, footwear. **Imports:** $18 bil. (c.i.f., 1993 est.); foodstuffs, petroleum and petroleum products, chemicals, transport equipment, iron, steel. **Major trading partners:** ***exports:*** 53.2% EU, 19.5% EFTA, 5.9% U.S., 2.8% Russia, 1.3% Japan; ***imports:*** 47.2% EU, 19% EFTA, 6.1% U.S., 7.1% Russia, 5.5% Japan.

Intl. Orgs. EFTA (associate), FAO, IAEA, IBRD, ICAO, IDA, IFAD, IFC, ILO, IMF, IMO, INTERPOL, ITU, OECD, OSCE, UN, UNESCO, UPU, WHO, WIPO, WMO, WTO.

The Finns originated in the Ural Mountains, and their language is akin to Hungarian and closely similar to Estonian. Migrating from western Siberia to what is now Finland in the eighth century, they drove the indigenous Lapps to northernmost Scandinavia. Finland was conquered and Christianized by the Swedes in the 12th century and in the 16th century became a Swedish grand duchy. Ethnic Swedes make up about 7 percent of the present population. Finland was frequently a battleground in wars between Sweden and Russia; about one-third of the population perished in a war-induced famine in 1696. In 1721 Sweden ceded the province of Viborg to Russia, and all of Finland was taken over by Russia in 1809.

Under the Russians the czars became simultaneously grand dukes of Finland and ruled it as a semiautonomous province. Attempts to "Russify" Finland in the later 19th century provoked great popular resistance. When the Russian empire and then the Russian Republic fell in the 1917 Revolution, Finland lapsed into a fierce civil war between Communists and non-Communists. The "whites" under Baron Gustaf Mannerheim were the victors, and Finland became an independent country for the first time in its history.

In 1939 the USSR attacked the Finnish Republic; Finland's resistance in the "Winter War" was heroic but unavailing. Defeated, it was forced to cede Western Keralia to the USSR. After the German invasion of Russia in 1941, fighting between Finland and Russia resumed; England, but not America, declared war on Finland as a cocombatant with Germany. Russia again defeated Finland in 1944 and obliged the Finns to wage war against the German occupying army in northern Finland; much of the country was devastated.

The terms of the 1944 armistice between Finland and the USSR were very harsh: Finland ceded the Petsamo region to the Soviet Union, and thus was cut off from the Barents Sea; the Porkkala peninsula was leased to the Soviets for 50 years, and reparations amounting to 80 percent of Finland's exports were paid in kind. Soviet pressure forced Finland to reject Marshall Plan aid after World War II, but Finland benefited indirectly from the rapid postwar recovery of the Scandinavian region. The gross national product returned to prewar levels by 1947.

Finland's economy had traditionally been centered on timber and other forest products, including pulp and paper, and on small-scale, highly productive agriculture. In the postwar period, industrial development was emphasized; the production of heavy machinery became the country's leading industry.

In 1948 the Finns signed a mutual defense pact with the USSR, renewed in 1955, 1970, and 1983. Finland's presidents, Juho Paasikivi (1946–56), Urho Kekkonen (1956–81), and Mauno Koivisto (1982–94), although conservative and nationalistic, realized that the country's independence required the avoidance of any appearance of anti-Soviet moves in foreign policy.

With the establishment of good Soviet-Finnish relations, the Porkkala peninsula was returned to Finland in 1956. Finland joined the Nordic Council and the United Nations in 1955. It became an associate member of the European Free Trade Association in 1961 and a full member in 1985, and negotiated a free-trade agreement with the EEC in 1973.

With a strong presidency providing stability despite revolving-door coalition governments in the Eduskunta (parliament), and a prudent foreign policy in the shadow of the USSR, Finland preserved its free economy and civil liberties.

The USSR's collapse struck a heavy blow to Finland's economy; through the 1980s 15–25 percent of Finland's exports had gone to the Soviet Union. Unemployment, recession, and currency devaluation have been constant reminders of these dramatic changes.

In politics the USSR's demise brought a rightward shift, with the first nonsocialist coalition government in 25 years being elected in April 1991 under 37-year-old Esko Aho of the Center party as prime minister. February 1994 saw Finland's first direct election of a president with Social Democrat Martti Ahtisaari carrying 54 percent of the vote. In March, the EU voted to accept Finland as a member in 1995. Prime Minister Aho announced that Finland would join NATO's "partnership for peace" but not as a step to full membership, preferring to maintain Finland's neutrality.

The Finnish electorate and Parliament approved membership in the EU by plebiscite and ratification in late 1994. But years of recession and high unemployment led to the toppling of the Center party government in March 1995 as the Social Democrats emerged as Finland's largest party, with Paavo Lipponen as premier.

France

French Republic

Geography **Location:** western Europe. **Boundaries:** English Channel to N, Belgium, Luxembourg, Germany, Switzerland, Italy to E, Mediterranean Sea, Spain to S, Atlantic Ocean to W. **Total land area:** 176,460 sq. mi. (457,030 sq km). **Coastline:** 2,130 mi. (3,427 km). **Comparative area:** between California and Texas. **Land use:** 32% arable land; 2% permanent crops; 23% meadows and pastures; 27% forest and woodland; 16% other; includes 2% irrigated. **Major cities:** (1990 census) Paris (capital) 2,152,423; Marseille (Marseilles) 800,000; Lyon (Lyons) 415,487; Toulouse 358,688; Nice 342,439.

People **Population:** 57,840,445 (1994 est.). **Nationality:** noun—Frenchman (men), Frenchwoman (women); adjective—French. **Ethnic groups:** Celtic and Latin with Teutonic, Slavic, North African, Indochinese, and Basque minorities. **Languages:** French (100% of population); rapidly declining regional dialects (Provençal, Breton, Alsacian, Corsican, Catalan, Basque, Flemish). **Religions:** 90% Roman Catholic, 2% Protestant, 1% Jewish, 1% Muslim (North African workers), 6% unaffiliated.

Government **Type:** republic, with president whose previously wide powers have been somewhat curtailed by current power-sharing arrangement with prime minister. **Constitution:** Sept. 28, 1958, amended concerning election of president in 1962. **National holiday:** National Day, July 14. **Heads of government:** François Mitterrand, president (since May 1988); Edouard Balladur, prime minister (since Mar. 1993). **Structure:** presidentially appointed prime minister heads Council of Ministers, which is formally responsible to National Assembly; bicameral legislature—National Assembly (577 members), Senate (317 members)—restricted by a delaying action; judiciary independent in principle.

Economy **Monetary unit:** French franc. **Budget:** (1993) ***income:*** $220.5 bil.; ***expend.:*** $249.1 bil. **GDP:** $1.05 trillion, $18,200 per capita (1993). **Chief crops:** cereals, sugarbeets, potatoes, wine grapes (western Europe's foremost producer); self-sufficient for most temperate foodstuffs; agricultural shortages include fats and oils, tropical produce. **Livestock:** cattle, pigs, sheep, goats, horses, asses. **Natural resources:** coal, iron ore, bauxite, fish, timber. **Major industries:** steel, machinery and equipment, textiles and clothing. **Labor force:** 24.17 mil. (1987); 61.5% services, 31.3% industry, 7.3% agriculture; 10.5% unemployment. **Exports:** $270.5 bil. (f.o.b., 1993); machinery and transport equipment, chemicals, foodstuffs, agricultural products, iron and steel products. **Imports:** $250.2 bil. (c.i.f., 1993); crude petroleum, machinery and equipment, agricultural products, chemicals, iron and steel products. **Major trading partners:** ***exports:*** 18.6% Germany, 11% Italy, 11% Spain, 9.1% Belgium-Luxembourg, 8.8% UK, 7.9% Netherlands, 6.4% U.S., 2% Japan, .7% former USSR; ***imports:*** 17.8% Germany, 10.9% Italy, 9.5% U.S., 8.9% Netherlands, 8.8% Spain, 8.5% Belgium-Luxembourg, 7.5% UK, 4.1% Japan, 1.3 former USSR.

Intl. Orgs. EU, FAO, IAEA, IBRD, ICAO, IDA, IFAD, IFC, ILO, IMF, IMO, INTELSAT, INTERPOL, ITU, NATO, OECD, OSCE, UN, UNESCO, UPU, WHO, WIPO, WMO, WTO.

Pre-Roman France, known as Gaul, was populated by Celtic tribes. The Mediterranean coast had been colonized by Phoenician and Greek traders and was conquered by Rome in the second century B.C. The Roman conquest of all of Gaul was carried out by Julius Caesar between 58 and 51 B.C. Gaul became a prosperous and thoroughly Latinized province of the Roman Empire and Christianity was introduced in the first century A.D.

Barbarian invaders including Visigoths, Franks, and Burgundii swept through France in the fifth century. In 486 Clovis, chief of the Franks, unified the country, accepted Christianity, and established the Merovingian dynasty. France was invaded by Muslim Saracens in the seventh century, but in 732 Charles Martel defeated the Saracens. His son, Pepin the Short, overthrew the last Merovingian ruler in 751 and proclaimed himself king. Pepin's son, Charlemagne, greatly expanded his kingdom and was crowned emperor of the West by the pope in 800.

Ninth-century Viking invasions greatly weakened the power of the Carolingians and France broke up into estates, some of them effectively independent countries, ruled by great aristocrats. Among the most important were the dukedoms of Aquitaine and Burgundy and the counties of Flanders, Blois, and Anjou. In 911 the Vikings, who had repeatedly raided the Atlantic coast of France, established the duchy of Normandy.

In 987 the Carolingian dynasty died out in France (although it survived in the Holy Roman Empire) and was replaced by a new line, the Capetians. Steadily expanding in both territory and power from their base in Paris, the Capetians solidified the foundations of the French monarchy. Paris became a great monastic and university city as well as a center of trade and manufacturing. Under the crusader-king Louis IX (St. Louis), France also became an international power.

During the 14th century, the Black Death, peasant rebellions, and the beginning of the Hundred Years' War (1337–1453) with England further weakened the French monarchy. The Norman conquest of England in 1066 had entwined the fortunes of the French and English monarchies, and with the Capetian line in decline, England pursued its claims in France. Henry V of England defeated the French at Agincourt in 1415, and in 1420 Charles IV made Henry heir to the throne of France. Henry's forces were defeated by French armies inspired by Joan of Arc, and in 1429 his claim to the French throne was overturned. In 1435 Burgundy allied itself with France, and in 1453 the English were driven out of France, except for an enclave at Calais.

Louis XI completed the consolidation of France under the French monarchy. France prospered as a center of commerce, industry, agriculture, learning, and culture throughout the 16th century but was disrupted by religious civil wars stemming from the Reformation. The Protestant Henry of Navarre, heir to the throne, was obliged to accept Catholicism before being crowned in 1594; he became founder of the Bourbon monarchy.

The consolidation of power under a highly centralized monarchy continued under Henry's heirs. With a foreign policy shaped by the powerful prime ministers Cardinal Richelieu and Cardinal Mazarin, France under Louis XIII and Louis XIV enhanced its stature in Europe by defeating the Habsburgs in the Thirty Years' War (1618–48). Louis XIV—the Sun King—moved the court from Paris to his new palace at Versailles and presided over the wealthiest and most powerful monarchy in Europe.

Louis XIV's persecution of the Huguenots resulted in a great emigration of Protestants from France. A grand alliance of European states thwarted France's expansionist aims on the continent, but France became a major colonial power in North America, controlling Canada and Louisiana (including most of the Mississippi-Missouri valley), and pursued overseas ventures in Africa and Asia as well.

In the mid-18th century, France was weakened internationally by the expensive and fruitless Wars of the Austrian Succession and the Seven Years' War. Under the Treaty of Paris (1763), France ceded control of Canada to Great Britain. The Enlightenment made France a world center of intellectual activity but also led to the questioning of the political and social bases of the French monarchy. An increasingly wealthy and politically interested but powerless bourgeoisie chafed under the restrictions of an archaic socioeconomic order.

France under Louis XVI supported the American colonies in the Revolutionary War, incurring a large public debt in the process. Combined with unrestrained extravagance on the part of the court and the aristocracy, poverty increased among the rural peasantry and the urban working class, while the bourgeoisie demanded a greater voice in government. These trends came to a head with the storming of the Bastille on July 14, 1789; soon thereafter, the Estates-General took control of the country, and France was in the throes of revolution.

Revolutionary leaders at first allowed Louis XVI to remain on the throne in a limited monarchy, but the king and Marie Antoinette were subsequently tried for treason and executed in 1793. Thousands died during the Reign of Terror which continued until July 1794, ending with the execution of its primary architects, the revolutionary leaders Augustin Robespierre and Georges Danton. The Directory, with five heads of each division of government (1795–99), failed to maintain public order and suffered military reverses in foreign wars in which successive revolutionary governments had been embroiled since 1792. On Nov. 9, 1799, the Directory was overthrown by the Consulate, with Napoleon Bonaparte named first consul.

Napoleon proclaimed himself emperor of France in 1804. He transformed French law through the Code Napoleon and initially expanded the French empire in Europe and the Middle East. Suffering repeated reverses against British naval forces and disastrous losses in his 1812 invasion of Russia, Napoleon was defeated by the British under Wellington at Waterloo in 1815, and the French empire collapsed.

France restored its monarchy in 1815 but not its monarchical absolutism. Charles X, successor to Louis XVIII, was ousted in a coup d'état in 1830 and replaced by the liberal Louis Philippe. The monarchy came to an end in the wave of popular revolt that swept France, along with most of Europe, in 1848; Louis Napoleon (nephew of Bonaparte) became president of the Second Republic. In 1852 he created the Second Empire, ruling as Napoleon III and presiding over a court that set the standards of fashion for the wealthy bourgeois society of 19th-century Europe.

During the 19th century, France again became a major colonial power, acquiring important possessions in North and West Africa and Indochina. It also became a world leader in art, science, and literature and began its slow transformation into a major industrial power. Politically, however, France suffered from endemic weakness. The Second Empire ended disastrously with defeat in the Franco-Prussian War of 1870–71; the Paris Commune, formed during that war, was overthrown with great bloodshed. The Third Republic (1871–1914), despite the glittering pleasures of the Belle Epoque and France's considerable prestige as a world power, was shaken by the Dreyfus Affair of 1894–1906 and ill-served by both its political and military leaders.

France joined with Great Britain and Russia in forming the Triple Entente of 1907, a defensive agreement against the Triple Alliance of Germany, Italy, and the Austro-Hungarian empire. During World War I—in effect a war between these two alliances—France suffered millions of casualties and severe damage in the north. Although its role as a leader of the victorious alliance was confirmed at the Versailles Conference of 1919, France was seriously weakened by the war and played a diminished role as a world power in the postwar era.

France suffered badly in the world depression of the 1930s and could muster neither political nor military energy to offer effective opposition to the rise of Nazi Germany and fascist Italy. France was a participant in the Munich Agreement of 1938, which sealed the fate of central Europe. When World War II broke out in 1939, Hitler initially held off his attack on France, but when it came in May–June 1940, France was swiftly and ignominiously defeated.

During World War II, northern France was under German occupation, while in the south a collaborationist, semifascistic state was organized, with its capital at Vichy. Meanwhile, in London, Gen. Charles de Gaulle rallied the Free French forces, which fought on the Allied side in various campaigns. After the liberation of Paris a "provisional government" of various Resistance groups combined with de Gaulle's supporters drew up a constitution for the Fourth French Republic.

Although it suffered from inherent political weaknesses and often failed to provide stable cabinets, the Fourth Republic presided over postwar recovery, aided by the Marshall Plan; it promoted a mixed socialist–free enterprise economy and instituted social reforms such as women's suffrage and social security. It also led the way toward a united Europe, playing a leading role in the organization of the EEC in 1957. Despite a 20-year alliance with the Soviet Union concluded in 1944, France became a founding member of NATO in 1949.

The Fourth Republic was unable, however, to withstand the strains of the dismantling of France's empire during the postwar wave of decolonization. France's recovery of Indochina in 1945 set off a war of national liberation there that lasted until France withdrew from the colony in 1954. Morocco and Tunisia won their independence in 1956; in Algeria, regarded as part of France itself, France fought on against Front de Liberation Nationale (FLN) rebels.

The Algerian War seriously polarized French public opinion, and, threatened with an army coup, the National Assembly voted in 1958 to grant Pres. Charles de Gaulle emergency powers for six months. De Gaulle outmaneuvered his army backers and negotiated to turn Algeria over to the FLN, a process completed in 1962. Meanwhile he also restored order at home and presided over the drafting of a new constitution that created the Fifth Republic in 1958.

The new constitution created a strong presidency, with powers to name the premier and the Council of Ministers and to preside over their meetings. The legislature was required to give priority to government initiatives and lacked authority over national defense, education, labor, and local government. Under the governments of premiers Michel Debré and Georges Pompidou, the Gaullist regime further advanced modernization of French industry and greatly benefited French agriculture by expanding the Common Market to include agricultural as well as industrial goods.

De Gaulle followed an independent foreign policy, pursuing European integration as well as closer relations with the Communist bloc and the Third World. He blocked British entry into the Common Market; developed an independent nuclear force, refusing to sign nuclear test-ban and nonproliferation treaties; pursued a historic rapprochement with Germany; recognized the People's Republic of China; established a leading French role in the former French colonies of Africa; and withdrew French forces from the NATO military command.

Reelected president in 1965, after a runoff election against the Socialist-Communist alliance candidate François Mitterrand, de Gaulle continued his independent policy until student riots in early 1968 provoked police repression, which led to further popular support for the students, especially in Paris. De Gaulle dissolved the National Assembly and, in an emotional campaign on behalf of national stability, won a large electoral majority. In 1969, however, following minor political reverses, de Gaulle resigned as president.

The elections of June 1969 gave the presidency to former premier Georges Pompidou, who died in office in April 1974. He was succeeded by the Independent Republican Valery Giscard d'Estaing, who served until May 1981. During these years the Gaullist heritage was developed and consolidated. In foreign policy the movement toward European unity continued with the development of the European Parliament and, in a reversal of policy in 1973, French support for British membership in the EEC. The economic shock of the OPEC price rises of 1973–74 led to a decision to stress new industrial ventures in high-technology fields, symbolized by the Anglo-French Concorde supersonic transport.

The 1970s were years of social ferment, with a relaxation of divorce laws and the legalization of contraception advertisements and abortion, and a decline in church membership and attendance. In 1978 disillusionment stemming from inflation and social difficulties under Giscard d'Estaing brought about a leftist electoral victory for the first time under the Fifth Republic.

The Gaullist era came to an end in 1981, when Socialist François Mitterrand defeated Giscard in a presidential election. He immediately dissolved the National Assembly and led his party to an absolute majority. Socialist premier Pierre Mauroy formed a government with four Communist members participating, a government which pursued an aggressive program of nationalization of banks and major industries and reform of local government. Continued economic difficulties led to a loss of popular support for Mitterrand's policies. In the elections of 1986, Jacques Chirac's coalition of Gaullists and Giscardists won an almost absolute majority in the National Assembly, and Chirac became premier—the first time since 1958 that the president and the premier were of opposing parties. An accommodation was worked out in which Mitterrand concentrated on foreign affairs, and Chirac on domestic matters. Mitterrand oversaw a restoration of French military cooperation with NATO and a continuation of Franco-German cooperation, and supported Chad in its war with Libya.

At home Chirac and his party reversed Mitterrand's policy of nationalization of banking and industry, cut taxes, and brought about a significant reduction in the inflation rate. Chirac ran for president against Mitterrand in 1988 but was defeated. Mitterrand's reelection with over 54 percent of the vote carried his Socialist party to a near majority in the assembly, where they constructed a coalition government of the non-Communist Left under Premier Michel Rocard, whose policies were difficult to distinguish from those of the Chirac government. Persistent unemployment at a 9 percent level and the growing appeal of Jean-Marie Le Pen's anti-immigrant National Front brought a cabinet shake-up in May 1991 and the designation of France's first female premier, Edith Cresson.

But the shake-up did nothing to stem voter dissatisfaction with the governing Socialists. Elections to regional councils in March 1992 saw the Socialist vote drop to 18 percent, but not to the benefit of the center-right coalition Union for France, which gained only one-third of the vote. Instead, it was the National Front and the two rival "green" parties—parties outside the old "politics as usual"—that together gained 28 percent of the vote.

Mitterand took a strong position in support of UN intervention in what had been Yugoslavia. He also urged his people to vote for the Maastricht Treaty enlarging the scope of the EC's power, which they did, but by a very narrow margin. But not even the formidable Mitterand could prevent the Socialist rout which was completed in the March 1993 assembly elections: the Rally for France won the most lopsided victory in the history of the Republic, taking 460 of the 577 seats while the left carried only 93. Neither the Greens nor the National Front took even one seat. The new premier, Edouard Balladur, finance minister in Chirac's 1986–88 government, pledged himself to tax and spending cuts and continued dismantling of state enterprises. Rejecting calls for his resignation, Pres. Mitterand reasserted his constitutional prerogatives in defense and foreign policy and vowed to stay on until 1995.

Balladur's government attempted several bold initiatives but met with limited success. In January the Constitutional Council declared financial aid to private schools unconstitutional and in March violent protests forced the government to drop its proposed bill to establish a "youth wage" below the minimum wage. But in January legislation rendered the Bank of France independent of the government.

Mitterand's unprecedented 14-year presidency came to an end in May 1995 as Jacques Chirac won the second round in France's presidential election over Lionel Jospin, 52.6 percent to 47.4 percent. On May 18 he appointed as premier Alain Juppe, a longtime Chirac supporter and foreign minister in the Balladur cabinet. With president and premier of the same party and with the coalition they lead controlling 80 percent of the chamber, the period of "cohabitation" was at a decided end.

Gabon

Gabonese Republic

Geography **Location:** western coast of Africa. **Boundaries:** Equatorial Guinea to NW, Cameroon to N, Congo to E and S, Atlantic Ocean to W. **Total land area:** 103,348 sq. mi. (267,670 sq km). **Coastline:** 550 mi. (885 km). **Comparative area:** slightly smaller than Colorado. **Land use:** 1% arable land; 1% permanent crops; 18% meadows and pastures; 78% forest and woodland; 2% other. **Major cities:** (1988) Libreville (capital) 352,000; Port-Gentil 164,000; Franceville 75,000.

People **Population:** 1,139,006 (1994 est.). **Nationality:** noun—Gabonese (sing., pl.); adjective—Gabonese. **Ethnic groups:** about 40 Bantu groups, including four major tribal groupings (Fang, Eshira, Bapounou, Bateke); about 100,000 expatriate Africans and Europeans, including 27,000 French. **Languages:** French (official), Fang, Myene, Bateke, Bapounou/Eschira, Bandjabi. **Religions:** 55–75% Christian, less than 1% Muslim, remainder indigenous beliefs.

Government **Type:** republic; one-party presidential regime since 1964. **Independence:** Aug. 17, 1960 (from France). **Constitution:** Feb. 21, 1961, revised Apr. 15, 1975. **National holidays:** Renovation Day, Mar. 12; Independence Day, Aug. 17. **Heads of government:** El Hadj Omar Bongo, president (since Dec. 1967); Paulin Obame Nguema, prime minister (since Oct. 1994). **Structure:** power centralized in president, elected by universal suffrage for seven-year term; unicameral legislature—93-member National Assembly, including nine members chosen by Omar Bongo, has limited powers; Constitution amended in 1979 so that assembly deputies will serve five-year terms; independent judiciary.

Economy **Monetary unit:** Communauté Financière Africaine (CFA) franc. **Budget:** (1992 est.) ***income:*** $1.3 bil.; ***expend.:*** $1.5 bil. **GDP:** $5.4 bil., $4,800 per capita (1993 est.). **Chief crops:** cash crops—cocoa, coffee, wood, palm oil, rice; food crops—pineapples, bananas, manioc, peanuts, root crops. **Livestock:** pigs, sheep, goats, cattle. **Natural resources:** crude oil, manganese, uranium, gold, timber, iron ore. **Major industries:** sawmills, petroleum, food, beverages; mining of increasing importance, especially for manganese and uranium.

Labor force: 120,000 (1983); 65% agriculture, 30% industry and commerce; 58% of population of working age. **Exports:** $2.3 bil. (f.o.b., 1992 est.); 70% crude oil, 12% wood, 11% manganese, 6% uranium. **Imports:** $702 mil. (c.i.f., 1992 est.); foodstuffs, chemical products, petroleum products, construction materials, manufactures. **Major trading partners:** ***exports:*** 48% France, 15% U.S., Germany, Japan; ***imports:*** 64% France, 5% U.S., Germany, UK.

Intl. Orgs. FAO, G-77, IAEA, IBRD, ICAO, IDA, IFAD, IFC, ILO, IMF, IMO, INTELSAT, INTERPOL, ITU, NAM, OPEC, UN, UNESCO, UPU, WHO, WIPO, WMO, WTO.

Gabon, an equatorial nation largely covered by dense rain forest, is inhabited by a highly diverse mixture of people who migrated into the region over the course of the past 700 years; the now-dominant Fang arrived during the 19th century. The first Europeans to reach the area were the Portuguese in the 15th century; they were followed by Dutch, French, and British traders in the 16th century. All engaged in the slave trade.

France established an informal protectorate in 1839–41 and set about suppressing the slave trade. In 1849 a group of freed slaves settled near the American mission station at Baraka and renamed the town Libreville. France established a colonial administration in 1903 and in 1910 made it part of French Equatorial Africa. The territory became an important base of Free French activity during World War II, and in 1946 Gen. Charles de Gaulle granted French citizenship to the territory's inhabitants, and local power was devolved upon advisory assemblies. In 1959 French Equatorial Africa was dissolved; Gabon became fully independent on Aug. 17, 1960.

Gabon has remained politically stable under its 1961 constitution. Gabon's first president, Leon M'Ba, was briefly deposed by a military coup in 1964 but quickly reinstated with the aid of French troops. He died in 1967 and was succeeded by the vice president, Omar Bongo. Bongo combined all political parties into the Gabonese Democratic party in 1968, was elected president in his own right in 1975, and was reelected in 1979 and 1986. Despite initial resistance from the government, Gabon has recently made the transition to multiparty democracy, thereby attracting more foreign investment. Bongo's Gabonese Democratic party remains in power.

Gabon is rich in natural resources, including petroleum, manganese, uranium, and timber. Petroleum exports account for 80 percent of foreign earnings. The country was badly hit by the fall in petroleum prices in the early 1980s, and in 1988 foreign creditors agreed to a restructuring of the country's external debt. This pattern of oil boom and bust has continued into the 1990s.

The Gambia

Republic of The Gambia

Geography Location: narrow territory around Gambia River on northwestern coast of Africa. **Boundaries:** Senegal to N, E, and S, Atlantic Ocean to W. **Total land area:** 4,363 sq. mi. (11,300 sq km). **Coastline:** 50 mi. (80 km). **Comparative area:** between Delaware and Connecticut. **Land use:** 16% arable land; 0% permanent crops; 9% meadows and pastures; 20% forest and woodland; 55% other; includes 3% irrigated. **Major cities:** (1983 census) Banjul (capital) 44,188; Serrekunda 68,433; Brikama 19,584; Bakau 19,309; Farafenni 10,168.

People Population: 959,300 (1994 est.). **Nationality:** noun—Gambian(s); adjective—Gambian. **Ethnic groups:** 42% Mandinka, 18% Fula, 16% Wolof, 10% Jola, 9% Serahuli, 1% non-Gambian, 4% other. **Languages:** English (official), Mandinka, Wolof, Fula, and others. **Religions:** 90% Muslim, 9% Christian, 1% indigenous beliefs.

Government Type: republic; on Feb. 1, 1982, The Gambia and Senegal formed a loose confederation named Senegambia that calls for eventual integration of their armed forces and economic cooperation. **Independence:** Feb. 18, 1965 (from UK). **Constitution:** Apr. 24, 1970. **National holiday:** Independence Day, Feb. 18. **Head of government:** Lt. Yahya Jammeh, president (since July 1994). **Structure:** unicameral legislature—43-member Parliament in which four seats are reserved for tribal chiefs, four are government-appointed, 35 are elected for five-year terms; judiciary.

Economy Monetary unit: dalasi. **Budget:** (1991 est.) ***income:*** $94 mil.; ***expend.:*** $80 mil. **GDP:** $740 mil., $800 per capita. (1993 est.). **Chief crops:** peanuts, millet, sorghum, rice, maize. **Livestock:** cattle, goats, sheep, pigs, asses. **Natural resources:** fish. **Major industries:** peanut processing, tourism, beverages. **Labor force:** 400,000 (1986 est.); 75% agriculture, 18.9% industry, commerce, and services; 55% of population of working age. **Exports:** $164 mil. (f.o.b., FY92 est.); peanuts and peanut products, fish, palm kernels. **Imports:** $214 mil. (f.o.b., FY92 est.); textiles, foodstuffs, tobacco, machinery, petroleum products, chemicals. **Major trading partners:** (1989) ***exports:*** 60% Japan, 29% Europe, 5% Africa; ***imports:*** 57% Europe, 25% Asia, 9% former USSR, 6% U.S.

Intl. Orgs. Commonwealth, FAO, G-77, IBRD, ICAO, IDA, IFAD, IFC, IMF, IMO, INTERPOL, ITU, NAM, UN, UNESCO, UPU, WHO, WMO, WTO.

Thirty miles across at its widest point, and 295 miles long, the serpentine republic of The Gambia was gerrymandered into being out of competing French and British colonial interests. Once the westernmost part of the kingdom of Mali, The Gambia was visited by the Portuguese in 1455. In 1588, they sold British traders exclusive rights to the Gambia River, and in 1660 British merchants established a trading fort. England and France struggled for 200 years to gain political and economic control over the territory, but in 1783 the French ceded to Great Britain possession of The Gambia. Its present boundaries were established in 1889 when it became a British Crown Colony. Between 1901 and 1906, legislative councils were established to encourage self-government, and slavery was abolished.

After World War II the country moved quickly toward constitutional government, achieving independence as a constitutional monarchy within the British Commonwealth of Nations in 1965. The Gambia became a republic on Apr. 24, 1970, and it had the same president, Sir Dawda K. Jawara, until 1994.

In 1982, The Gambia and Senegal, which surrounds the country on three sides, established the confederation of Senegambia under which the two countries retained their independence but united their military, monetary systems, and Parliament. Proving ineffective, the confederation was abolished in 1989.

In 1994, Yahya Jammeh, a 29-year-old lieutenant fresh from a military police training course in the United States, led a bloodless coup deposing the government of Pres. Jawara. Jammeh pledged to restore civilian government "as soon as we have set things right." Later that year the United Kingdom, the United States, and the European Union cut off all economic and military aid pending a return to democracy.

Georgia

Republic of Georgia

Geography Location: west and central Transcaucasia between Asia and Europe. **Boundaries:** Russian Federation to N and E, Azerbaijan, Armenia to S, Turkey to SW, Black Sea to W. **Total land area:** 26,911 sq. mi. (69,700 sq km). **Coastline:** Black Sea. **Comparative area:** slightly larger than West Virginia. **Land use:** 11% cropland; 29% permanent pasture; 37% forest and woodland; 23% other (mostly urban). **Major cities:** (1990 est.) Tbilisi (capital) 1,268,000; Kutaisi 236,000; Rustavi 160,000; Batumi 137,000; Sukhumi 122,000.

People Population: 5,681,025 (1994 est.). **Nationality:** noun—Georgian(s); adjective—Georgian. **Ethnic groups:** 68.8% Georgian, 9% Armenian, 7.4% Russian, 5.1% Azerbaijani, 3.2% Ossetian, 1.9% Greek, 1.7% Abkhazian. **Languages:** Georgian (official), a non–Indo-European language written in Georgian script; Russian, ethnic languages. **Religions:** Christianity—Georgian Orthodox; Islam, Judaism.

Government Type: republic. **Independence:** Apr. 9, 1991 (from USSR). **Constitution:** being drafted. **National holiday:** N.A. **Heads of government:** Eduard A. Shevardnadze, president (since 1992); Otar Patsatsia, prime minister. **Structure:** being developed.

Economy Monetary unit: ruble. **Budget:** N.A. ***income:*** N.A.; ***expend.:*** N.A. **GNP:** $7.8 bil., $1,390 per capita (1993 est.). **Chief crops:** grain, fruit, grapes, green tea, vegetables. **Livestock:** chickens, sheep, goats, cattle, pigs. **Natural resources:** manganese, coal. **Major industries:** metallurgy, machine building, construction materials. **Labor force:** 2.763 mil. (1990) **Exports:** N.A.; citrus fruits, tea, machinery, ferrous and nonferrous metals, textiles. **Imports:** N.A.; machinery and parts, fuel, transport equipment, textiles. **Major trading partners:** other former Soviet republics.

Intl. Orgs. IMF, OSCE, UN, UNCTAD, UNESCO, World Bank; applying for membership in other international organizations.

Georgia is a land of rugged natural beauty, and its people are renowned both for their famous war heroes and for their hospitality. Georgia's most famous son was Iosif Djugashvili, otherwise known as Josef Stalin, who was born in the mountain village of Gori in 1879. The name of Georgia derives from the Persian name for the native people, Gorj.

Georgian culture is ancient, for an independent state was first founded in the fourth century B.C. following the conquest of the Persian empire by Alexander III. Christianity became the state religion in the same century. Both the Georgian language and the capital city of Tbilisi date from the fifth century A.D. The Georgian people, whose main occupation was cattle raising and agriculture, began to develop feudal states in the sixth century.

Georgia's subsequent history, however, is one of almost continuous foreign domination. In the 12th century, Georgia gained independence from the Persian empire, but this was short-lived, as it came under the Mongol yoke in 1236. For centuries Georgia was a battleground between Turks and Persians, and the territory was ultimately divided into principalities, some under the control of Persia and some under Turkey. In 1801, the Persian principalities were absorbed into the Russian empire, and by the end of the century the remaining Georgian state under Turkish domination was also annexed to Russia.

Once the Russian empire collapsed in 1917 with the Bolshevik revolution, independent Georgia was once again proclaimed in May 1918. It was dominated by Mensheviks (from the Russian word "minority," as opposed to Bolshevik, meaning "majority"), whose hold on power was short-lived. Although the Soviet Union and Georgia signed a treaty in May 1920 agreeing on their respective borders, the Soviet Red Army led by Sergo Ordzhonikidze (another Georgian, later to serve in Stalin's Politburo) came into Georgia and forcibly incorporated it into the Soviet Union as a Socialist republic in early 1921. In 1922 it was made part of the Transcaucasian Soviet Federal Socialist Republic with Armenia and Azerbaijan, and in 1936 it became one of the USSR's union republics.

The Georgians always have been fiercely nationalistic, even in the face of the USSR's "one Soviet people" policy. Georgian pride was evident from the first demonstrations against "russification" in 1956, and again in 1978 when the rewritten USSR constitution attempted to weaken the status of Georgian language. In November 1988, during Mikhail Gorbachev's policy of "glasnost," or openness, great numbers of Georgians began to call for Georgian sovereignty and secession from the USSR.

Since 1988, this fierce nationalism has plagued Georgian sovereignty. Even as Georgia fought for its independence from the USSR, the autonomous provinces of Abkhazia, Adzharia, and South Ossetia began fighting for independence from Georgia. Tensions continue to run high in Adzharia, where allegiances to Islam frighten many in Christian Georgia, and in South Ossetia, which is struggling to end its association with Georgia and to unite with North Ossetia in the Russian Federation.

But the greatest conflict raged in Abkhazia, the home region of Zviad Gamsakhurdia, who was elected the country's first president in May 1991, but was ousted from office seven months later. Fighting between the Georgian army and troops loyal to Gamsakhurdia continued through 1992 and 1993, with Georgian president Eduard Shevardnadze accusing Russia of aiding the rebels. In late 1993, Shevardnadze submitted his resignation in a successful attempt to force Parliament to give him emergency powers to quell the hostilities. A month later, Georgian and Russian forces seized the final rebel stronghold, setting the stage for a cease-fire (April 4) to end the two-year insurgency. More than 2,000 people were killed in the fighting, including Gamsakhurdia, who in February 1994 was discovered in the independent republic of Chechnya (where he had been living in exile) in a shallow grave with a gunshot wound to the head.

Simultaneously, Georgia began to renew ties with Russia. On February 3, Shevardnadze agreed to a cooperation pact to increase Russia's military influence in his country. And on March 2, over the objections of the opposition National Radical Party, Parliament ratified Georgia's membership in the Commonwealth of Independent States, reuniting it with most of the former Soviet republics.

Germany

Federal Republic of Germany

Geography Location: central Europe. **Boundaries:** Denmark, Baltic Sea to N, Poland, Czech Republic to E, Austria, Switzerland to S, France, Luxembourg, Belgium, Netherlands to W, North Sea to NW. **Total land area:** 137,803 sq. mi. (356,910 sq km). **Coastline:** 1,385 mi. (2,389 km). **Comparative area:** between New Mexico and Montana. **Land use:** 34% arable land; 2% permanent crops; 17% meadows and pastures; 29% forest and woodland; 17% other; includes 1% irrigated. **Major cities:** (1992 est.) Berlin (capital) 3,454,200; Hamburg 1,675,200; München (Munich) 1,241,300; Köln (Cologne) 958,600; Frankfurt 660,800.

People Population: 81,087,506 (1994 est.). **Nationality:** noun—German(s); adjective—German. **Ethnic groups:** predominantly German; small Slavic and Danish minorities. **Languages:** German, Sorbian. **Religions:** 45% Protestant, 37% Roman Catholic, 18% unaffiliated and other.

Government Type: federal republic. **Constitution:** May 23, 1949; provisional constitution known as Basic Law. **National holiday:** Oct. 3. **Heads of government:** Roman Herzog, president (since July 1994); Dr. Helmut Kohl, chancellor (since Oct. 1982). **Structure:** president (titular head of state), bicameral parliament—Bundesrat (Federal Council, upper house), Bundestag (National Assembly, lower house); independent judiciary.

Economy Monetary unit: deutsche mark. **Budget:** (1992) ***income:*** $918 bil.; ***expend.:*** $972 bil. **GDP:** $1.331 trillion, $16,500 per capita (1993). **Chief crops:** wheat, barley, rye, potatoes, sugar beets, fruit. **Livestock:** cattle, pigs, poultry. **Natural resources:** iron, coal, brown coal. **Major industries:** among world's largest producers of iron, steel, coal, cement, chemicals, machinery, vehicles, machine tools, electronics, food and beverages, metal fabrications, brown coal, shipbuilding, machine building, textiles, petroleum refining, and hides and skins. **Labor force:** 36.75 mil. (1987); 41% industry, 6% agriculture, 53% other. **Exports:** $392 bil. (f.o.b., 1993); 86.6% manufactures (includes machines and machine tools, chemicals, motor vehicles, iron and steel products), 4.9% agricultural products, 2.3% raw materials, 1.3% fuels. **Imports:** $374.6 bil. (f.o.b., 1993); 68.5% manufactures, 12% agricultural products, 9.7% fuels, 7.1% raw materials. **Major trading partners:** ***exports:*** 54.3% EU, 17% other Western Europe, 6.4% U.S., 5.6% Eastern Europe, 3.4% OPEC; ***imports:*** 52% EU, 15.2% other Western Europe, 6.6% U.S., 5.5% Eastern Europe, 2.4% OPEC.

Intl. Orgs. EU, FAO, IAEA, IBRD, ICAO, IDA, IFAD, IFC, ILO, IMF, IMO, INTELSAT, INTERPOL, ITU, NATO, OECD, OSCE, UN, UNESCO, UPU, WHO, WIPO, WMO, WTO.

The ancient tribes of Germany resisted Roman conquest with mixed success. German federated troops served in the Roman legions, and Germanic invasions contributed to the fall of Rome. Most of Germany was united within the empire of Charlemagne. Divided among his three sons in 843, the empire's eastern regions became the heart of the Germanies. The Holy Roman Empire, founded in 962, gave some unity to the politically fragmented German territories, but its boundaries included more than Germany, and some Germans remained outside it. But that unity was fragile; the Holy Roman emperor was a feudal overlord rather than a ruler, and hundreds of separate political bodies coexisted within the imperial domain. Along the North Sea and Baltic coasts, the Hanseatic League controlled much of the commerce of northern Europe.

With the Reformation in the 16th century, religious divisions added to Germany's existing political fragmentation and local allegiances. The Thirty Years War (1618–48) resulted in the virtual extinction of the Holy Roman Empire and left Germany without even a shadow of unity.

After the Napoleonic Wars, in which much of Germany was conquered by France, the Congress of Vienna (1814–15) sanctioned the creation of a German League to succeed the Holy Roman Empire. The league consisted of 39 states, including five substantial kingdoms and the German parts of the Austrian empire. Prussia, one of the five kingdoms, had already risen to prominence under Frederick the Great in the 18th century. In a series of wars in the mid-19th century, Prussia conquered the other German states; after defeating France in the Franco-Prussian War of 1870–71, Prussia declared the establishment of the German empire. Under its chancellor, Otto von Bismarck, Germany became a major European power in the late 19th century, with a booming industrial economy, flourishing agriculture, a small colonial empire, and growing military might.

The German empire reached its height under Kaiser Wilhelm II on the eve of World War I. Germany's disastrous defeat in that war was compounded by the harsh terms of the Treaty of Versailles (1919), which stripped Germany of its colonial empire, and returned part of Schleswig to Denmark, Alsace-Lorraine to France, and part of Prussia to Poland.

The Weimar Republic, established in 1919, gradually overcame economic difficulties, including ruinous inflation, to achieve a measure of postwar recovery in the 1920s. The republic was, however, disrupted by labor strife, political fragmentation, and the rise of armed extremist political movements on both left and right. After the onset of the world economic depression in 1929, Adolf Hitler's National Socialist movement gained increasing power, both at the polls and through open thuggery against its opponents. Hitler's appointment as chancellor in 1933 effectively put an end to the Weimar Republic as a functioning democracy.

The onset of World War II in Europe was presaged by Hitler's annexation of Austria and Czechoslovakia in 1938 and precipitated by the German invasion of Poland in 1939. Early military successes gave Germany control of most of Europe, but the eventual victory of the Allied powers in 1945 left the country exhausted and in ruins. Much of the Jewish population of Germany, and of other territories under German control, had been killed during the Holocaust of World War II. German cities were reduced to rubble, and a quarter of the country's homes were uninhabitable. Famine and fuel shortages added to the general misery.

Politically, Germany had essentially ceased to exist in 1945. The Allies divided the country into four zones of occupation, with a similar four-part division of Berlin. As the Cold War rift between the Western powers and the USSR intensified during the late 1940s, so too the division of Germany hardened. In 1948 the USSR imposed a blockade on West Berlin; the city was supplied by a massive airlift from the West for several months. In 1949 two Germanies were created: the German Democratic Republic in the Russian zone in the east, and the Federal Republic of Germany in the Allied zone in the west.

The Federal Republic was largely the creation of one man, Konrad Adenauer. A veteran pre-Hitler politician, he founded the Federation of Christian Democratic Parties (CDU-CSU) in 1945, and as president of the Parliamentary Council formed during the occupation, he virtually wrote the new constitution for West Germany. In the first elections held in the Federal Republic (August 1949), the "bourgeois coalition" led by the CDU-CSU won a parliamentary majority in the Bundestag, and Adenauer became chancellor, a post he held for 14 years. In 1951 the Western powers granted the new state autonomy in foreign affairs, and recognized its full sovereignty in 1954.

Even before the fighting in Germany subsided in 1945, the Soviet Air Force brought Walter Ulbricht, the exiled leader of the German Communist party, back to the USSR's zone of occupation in Germany. Backed by 20 Soviet divisions, Ulbricht and the party commenced the communization of the eastern zone.

After local and state elections embarrassed the Communists, Stalin and Ulbricht forced all other parties into the National Front. With no other electoral lists permitted, voters gave a 99.7 percent approval to the National Front in the first elections to East Germany's "People's Chamber" in 1950.

While Ulbricht attempted to collectivize agriculture and plan industrial development in the eastern zone, the Soviet Union extracted heavy reparations payments, bringing on an acute economic crisis. In June 1953, shortly after Stalin's death, strikes and riots erupted; order was quickly restored. The USSR renounced further reparation payments and declared East Germany a sovereign state.

In foreign affairs Adenauer relied heavily on friendship with the United States and reconciliation with France. He also supported European integration: In 1951 West Germany joined both the Council of Europe and the Coal and Steel Community. West Germany was admitted to NATO in 1955 and in 1957 became one of the six founding members of the EEC.

In domestic affairs the political alliance between Adenauer and Ludwig Erhard led to political stability and the creation of a market-driven economy. With a currency reform program and Marshall Plan aid in place by 1948 under occupation administration, the stage was set for Germany's "economic miracle" of the 1950s. Between 1949 and 1964, industrial production increased by 60 percent and gross national product tripled, while unemployment fell to 1 percent, even as millions of refugees from East Germany were integrated into the West German economy. In the same period, over 8 million houses and apartments were constructed.

In 1963 Erhard succeeded Adenauer as chancellor. Economic growth slowed to an annual 3 percent rate, but West Germany was already one of Europe's strongest economic powers, even providing jobs for hundreds of thousands of "guest workers" from southern Europe and Turkey.

By 1963 East Germany had become the second-largest industrial power in Eastern Europe, and in 1968 it surpassed Czechoslovakia in output. A significant shift of labor to industry reduced the farm population to under 20 percent of total population by 1960. Though farming became mechanized and more productive, it remained relatively inefficient.

Although East Germany enjoyed prestige within the Eastern bloc as an industrial power, the steady stream of emigrants to West Germany told a different story. After a renewed collectivization policy was implemented in 1960, the stream became a flood, and East Germany responded by building the Berlin Wall. The wall was a visible sign of political failure, but it did slow the stream of emigration to a trickle.

Erhard resigned in 1966 when his coalition fell apart over the issue of a planned tax increase. He was succeeded by Kurt Kiesinger, who presided over a historic "great coalition" of Christian Democrats and Social Democrats. Under Willi Brandt (who served as deputy chancellor and foreign minister), the Social Democrats had shifted their orientation from a Marxist party to a reformist, market-oriented stance.

Elections in 1969 produced a majority for the coalition headed by the Social Democrats, a coalition that governed until 1982. Brandt succeeded Kiesinger and pursued an *Ostpolitik* ("opening to the east"), regularizing relations with East Germany, signing a nonagression pact with the USSR, and recognizing the border between East Germany and Poland. But domestically, West Germany suffered serious dislocations from the OPEC oil price increases of the early 1970s; inflation reached almost 8 percent. Revelations that a Brandt aide was an East German spy led to his replacement as chancellor by Helmut Schmidt in 1974.

Schmidt continued Brandt's eastern policy but also pursued improved relations with the West. Economic difficulties persisted, however, and Schmidt's government fell in 1982. The Christian Democrats returned to power under chancellor Helmut Kohl. The general improvement of the world economy in the 1980s led to economic recovery in Germany, boosting Kohl's popularity.

Meanwhile, in East Germany an aging Ulbricht was replaced in May 1971 as party first secretary by Erich Honecker, who also became head of state in 1976. Honecker completed state ownership of all industry in 1972. Industries were grouped into 133 giant monopolies known as Kombinate, each covering one industrial sector and vertically integrated from research to sales.

After Brandt's *Ostpolitik*, the two Germanies grew closer, at least economically. East Germany's trade with West Germany, regarded as "intranational" by Bonn, gave it access to the EC. However, East Germany resisted Mikhail Gorbachev's reform policies in the 1980s, trying to establish itself as a model of old-style communism in Eastern Europe.

In the fall of 1989 tens of thousands of East Germans fled to West Germany through Hungary and Czechoslovakia, triggering a series of dramatic demonstrations and the dismantling of the Berlin Wall in October. Honecker's government collapsed, as did that of his successor, as the momentum for unification became unstoppable. In March 1990 Christian Democrat Lothar de Maizière was elected prime minister on a unification platform.

In July an economic and fiscal union of the Germanies was completed, and in September the victorious wartime allies (the U.S., USSR, UK, and France) agreed to a peace treaty that paved the way for political unification. On October 3, six regions of the former East Germany entered the Federal Republic as member states; eleven days later the Christian Democrats won elections in five of them, the Social Democrats winning one.

In December 1990 all-German elections to the Bundestag were held for the first time in 58 years. The CDU-CSU and the Free Democrats won 398 seats, the Social Democrats 239. Helmut Kohl was sworn in as chancellor Jan. 17, 1991. In June Parliament voted to move the capital to Berlin, but skyrocketing cost may lead to postponement if not repeal after 1994 federal elections.

In the years following unification, euphoria gave way to sober realism; economic restructuring would take many years, since the economy of East Germany proved to be in even worse shape than anyone imagined, with outdated factories, environmental ruin, and a less-than-enthusiastic work force. West Germans have had to pay a higher sales tax and an income tax surcharge as the cost of unification. So although the German economy remains the strongest in Europe, aid to the east is costing much more than anticipated.

Related to these economic woes is the wave of violent attacks by radical nationalists and neo-Nazi gangs upon immigrants and asylum seekers (who number over 2 million). In early 1993 the government banned several violent groups and, in June, amended Germany's liberal asylum law to prevent refugees seeking economic betterment from entering the country.

In the Bundestag elections of October 1994, the Kohl coalition (CDU, CSU, and FD) took 341 seats, maintaining its majority over the opposition, led by the Social Democrats. Kohl was reelected chancellor, for a fourth time.

Ghana

Republic of Ghana

Geography **Location:** western Africa. **Boundaries:** Burkina Faso to N, Togo to E, Gulf of Guinea to S, Ivory Coast to W. **Total land area:** 92,100 sq. mi. (238,540 sq km). **Coastline:** 335 mi. (539 km). Comparative area: slightly smaller than Oregon. **Land use:** 5% arable land; 7% permanent crops; 15% meadows and pastures; 37% forest and woodland; 36% other; includes negl. % irrigated. **Major cities:** (1984 census) Accra (capital) 964,879; Kumasi 348,880; Tamale 136,828; Tema 99,608; Takoradi 61,527.

People **Population:** 17,225,185 (1994 est.). **Nationality:** noun—Ghanaian(s); adjective—Ghanaian. **Ethnic groups:** 99.8% black African (major groups—44% Akan, 16% Moshi-Dagomba, 13% Ewe, 8% Ga), 0.2% European and other. **Languages:** English (official), Akan, Moshi-Dagomba, Ewe, Ga. **Religions:** 38% indigenous beliefs, 30% Muslim, 24% Christian, 8% other.

Government **Type:** presidential parliamentary government scheduled for January 1993. **Independence:** Mar. 6, 1957 (from UK). **Constitution:** Apr. 28, 1992. **National holiday:** Independence Day, Mar. 6. **Head of government:** Flt. Lt. (ret.) Jerry John Rawlings, chairman of PNDC (since Dec. 1981). **Structure:** executive—seven-member Provisional National Defense Council (PNDC); on Jan. 21, 1982, PNDC appointed secretaries to head most ministries.

Economy **Monetary unit:** cedi. **Budget:** (1992 est.) ***income:*** $1 bil.; ***expend.:*** $905 mil. (1991 est.) **GNP:** $25 bil., $1,500 per capita (1993 est.). **Chief crops:** cocoa, coffee, root crops, corn, sorghum, millet, peanuts; not self-sufficient in food production but has that potential; an illegal producer of cannabis for international drug trade. **Livestock:** goats, sheep, cattle, pigs, asses. **Natural resources:** gold, timber, industrial diamonds, bauxite, manganese. **Major industries:** mining, lumbering, light manufacturing. **Labor force:** 3.7 mil. (1983); 54.7% agriculture and fishing, 18.7% industry, 15.2% sales and clerical; 400,000 unemployed; 48% of population of working age. **Exports:** $1 bil. (f.o.b., 1992); 60% cocoa; wood, gold, diamonds, manganese, bauxite, aluminum (aluminum regularly excluded from balance-of-payments data). **Imports:** $1.5 bil. (c.i.f., 1992); textiles and other manufactured goods, food, fuels, transport equipment. **Major trading partners:** ***exports:*** 23% UK, other EU, 12% U.S.; ***imports:*** 23% UK, 11% U.S., Germany, France, Japan, S. Korea.

Intl. Orgs. Commonwealth, FAO, G-77, IAEA, IBRD, ICAO, IDA, IFAD, IFC, ILO, IMF, IMO, INTELSAT, INTERPOL, ITU, NAM, UN, UNESCO, UPU, WHO, WIPO, WMO, WTO.

The connection between modern Ghana and the 10th century Ghana empire of southern Mali is obscure. By the 13th century the Akan around the city of Kumasi were trading gold and other commodities with the Mande to the north. The number of competing states in the region grew rapidly after European contact. The Asante empire began in the early 17th century under Osei Tutu. By 1750 it controlled the northern part of Ghana, and by 1820 it had brought the coastal Fante empire, with its access to the European trade, under its control.

The Portuguese first explored the area, on Africa's west coast, in 1471, naming it the Gold Coast because of its gold deposits and its reserves of "black gold"—slaves. In the 16th and 17th centuries, the British, Danes, and Dutch established slave trading posts there, which is where most American slaves came from. The slave trade ended in the 1850s, and the British gained control of the Gold Coast, making it a protectorate in 1871 and a colony in 1886.

Great Britain gave the colony a new constitution in 1946 under which Africans held a majority of seats in the legislature. Kwame Nkrumah became prime minister of the colony in 1952 and the first prime minister of the nation when it became independent.

At independence, Ghana boasted Africa's largest man-made deep-water port and the most productive gold mine in the world, and it was the second largest producer of industrial diamonds. Nkrumah began to court Communist bloc nations and exert absolute authority. In January 1964 all opposition parties were outlawed. A military council seized power in February 1966 and ousted Nkrumah.

Civilian governments ran the country briefly, but in 1981, Flt. Lt. Jerry Rawlings took power in a coup and has ruled ever since. Ghana suffered severe economic problems throughout the 1970s and 1980s, and many of Ghana's people left for Nigeria to find work. In 1983 Nigeria returned more than one million of these migrant workers, increasing Ghana's economic woes.

After five years of stagnation, Ghana achieved a 6 percent economic growth rate in 1989 under a World Bank restructuring program. But political unrest remained. A new constitution was approved in an April 1992 referendum, and in November Rawlings received 58 percent of the vote. His National Democratic Congress all but swept the legislative elections due to an opposition boycott. Tribal and ethnic rivalries remain a problem, however. In 1994 the northern regions of the country were proclaimed to be in a state of emergency, as struggles between the Konkomba and Manumba peoples left over 100 dead and 150,000 refugees.

Greece

Hellenic Republic

Geography **Location:** southeastern Europe. **Boundaries:** Albania, Macedonia, Bulgaria to N, Turkey to NE, Aegean Sea to E, Mediterranean Sea to S, Ionian Sea to W, Albania to NW; numerous islands surround mainland. **Total land area:** 50,942 sq. mi. (131,940 sq km). **Coastline:** 8,500 mi. (13,676 km). **Comparative area:** slightly larger than New York. **Land use:** 23% arable land; 8% permanent crops; 40% meadows and pastures; 20% forest and woodland; 9% other; includes 7% irrigated. **Major cities:** (1991 census) Athinai (Athens, capital) 772,072; Thessaloniki 383,967; Piraeus 196,389; Patras 153,344; Iraklion 116,178.

People **Population:** 10,564,630 (1994 est.). **Nationality:** noun—Greek(s); adjective—Greek. **Ethnic groups:** 97.7% Greek, 1.3% Turkish, 1.0% Vlach, Slav, Albanian, Pomach (note: Greek government states there are no ethnic divisions in Greece). **Languages:** Greek (official); English and French widely understood. **Religions:** 98% Greek Orthodox, 1.3% Muslim, 0.7% other.

Government **Type:** presidential parliamentary government; monarchy rejected by referendum Dec. 8, 1974. **Constitution:** June 11, 1975. **National holiday:** Independence Day, Mar. 25. **Heads of government:** Constantinos Stephanopoulos, president (since Mar. 1995); Andreas Papandreou, prime minister (since Apr. 1990). **Structure:** executive—president elected by Vouli (Parliament), prime minister, and cabinet; legislative—unicameral legislature (300-member Vouli); judiciary—independent.

Economy **Monetary unit:** Greek drachma. **Budget:** (1992) ***income:*** $28.3 bil.; ***expend.:*** $37.6 bil. **GDP:** $93.2 bil., $8,900 per capita (1993). **Chief crops:** wheat, olives, tobacco, cotton, raisins, fruit; nearly self-sufficient. **Livestock:** chickens, sheep, goats, pigs, cattle. **Natural resources:** bauxite, lignite, magnesite, crude oil, marble. **Major industries:** food and tobacco processing, textiles, chemicals. **Labor force:** 3.97 mil. (1990); 43% services, 27% agriculture, 20% manufacturing and mining; 7.4% unemployment (1986). **Exports:** $6 bil. (f.o.b., 1992); manufactured goods, food, live animals, fuels, lubricants, raw materials. **Imports:** $23.3 bil. (c.i.f., 1992); machinery and transport equipment, light manufactures, fuels, lubricants, foodstuffs, chemicals. **Major trading partners:** ***exports:*** 24% Germany, 18% France, 17% Italy, 11.8% nonoil developing countries, 7.1% U.S., 6.8% UK; ***imports:*** 20% Germany, 14% nonoil developing countries, 14% Italy, 13% oil-exporting countries, 8% France, 4% U.S.

Intl. Orgs. EU, FAO, IAEA, IBRD, ICAO, IDA, IFAD, IFC, ILO, IMF, IMO, INTELSAT, INTERPOL, ITU, NATO, OECD, OSCE, UN, UNESCO, UPU, WHO, WIPO, WMO, WTO.

The Bronze Age and Iron Age cultures of Greece evolved to create the most glorious civilization of the ancient world. During their high point, from the fifth to the third century B.C., the city-states of Greece led the world in art, philosophy, political culture, and science. Greece vied with the Persian Empire for control of Asia Minor and competed with the Phoenicians in maritime commerce in the Mediterranean. Alexander the Great, king of Macedonia, spread Greek civilization widely by conquering much of the Middle East and western Asia, but his empire did not long outlast his death in 323 B.C.

Greece was absorbed into the Roman Empire during the second and first centuries B.C. In the fourth century A.D., with the division of the Roman Empire, Greece became part of the Byzantine (Eastern Roman) Empire. Seven years after the Ottoman Turks captured Constantinople in 1453, they overran Greece and ruled it as part of the Ottoman Empire for 350 years.

Under Ottoman rule, much of the administration of Greece was left in local hands, keeping alive a sense of Greek nationhood and a tradition of Greek leadership, particularly through the clergy of the Greek Orthodox church. Inspired by the French Revolution, a romanticized ideal of the classical past, and the tradition of Greek orthodoxy, in 1821 Greece rebelled against Turkish rule. With the support of England, France, and Russia, Greek independence was won in 1827, although the country included only about half of its present territory.

The Western powers sponsored a monarchical government in Greece, ruled by a German prince. Deposed in a revolt, he was succeeded by King George I, a Danish prince who ruled from 1863 until his assassination in 1913. In the three Balkan Wars of 1912, 1913, and 1914, Greece expanded its borders to reach approximately its present size.

In 1923 a Greek Republic was established, but in 1935 King George II returned to his throne, placing government control in the hands of the patriotic but authoritarian Gen. Ioannis Metaxas. In 1940 Metaxas resisted Italy's attempt to conquer Greece, defeating Mussolini's armies so badly that Hitler sent crack troops to his ally's assistance. The German occupation of Greece was complete by June 1941. The Germans pillaged the country and massacred Jews; their Bulgarian allies colonized Macedonia.

During World War II, resistance grew among both Communist and anti-Communist groups, both beyond the reach of the government-in-exile in London. With the German withdrawal in October 1944, resistance groups battled each other; this led to full-scale civil war by 1946. British, and then American assistance (under the Truman Doctrine), enabled the Greek government to defeat the Communist forces when Stalin refused to intervene.

King George II died in 1947, succeeded by his brother, King Paul I. Political instability—16 governments during 1946–52—prevailed until, under American pressure, the Greeks adopted a new constitution designed to ensure stable government.

Until the postwar period, Greece's economy had been dominated by agriculture and livestock raising. Industry was limited largely to textiles and food processing; shipping was the major service industry. Under policies instituted in 1952 by the government of Marshall Alexandros Papagos, the industrial sector led a period of vigorous economic growth lasting into the 1960s. A market-oriented economy, tariff protection for Greek industry, tight internal security, and close ties with the West formed the mainstays of Greek policy.

Greece joined NATO in 1951, as did Turkey. Conflict over Cyprus divided the two nominal allies, however. The failure of the government of Constantine Karamanlis to resolve the Cyprus situation eroded his popularity, and he was replaced in 1964 by George Papandreou, who governed at the head of a left-center coalition. King Constantine, who succeeded his father in 1963, forced Papandreou to resign in 1964, after he and members of his government were accused of various improprieties. A military coup, led by Col. George Papadopoulos, toppled the government in 1967. A countercoup by King Constantine failed, and the king fled the country.

A military dictatorship ruled from 1967 to 1974. Its failed attempt to intervene in Cyprus in 1974 provoked a Turkish invasion of the island and led to the military regime's collapse. Karamanlis headed the government once again; his party won a large majority in parliamentary elections in November, and a republic was formally established with the promulgation of a new constitution in 1975. Karamanlis's New Democracy party received a renewed but smaller majority in parliamentary elections in 1977.

Greece, an associate member of the EC since 1961, became a full member in 1981. Full military membership in NATO was restored in 1980. In 1981 the Panhellenic Socialist Movement under Andreas Papandreou won a parliamentary majority, renewed in 1984. The left-wing Papandreou government was outspokenly anti-NATO, anti-EC, and anti-American, but its policy was more moderate than its rhetoric, extending even to modest cooperation with Turkey in the Aegean. The Papandreou government was shaken by several pro-Palestinian terrorist incidents in Greece, and by a scandal involving the married Papandreou's relationship with a younger woman.

During 1989–90 Greece struggled through three parliamentary elections in less than a year. In the first two, no major party won a clear victory, leading to weak, short-lived coalition governments. The third, in the spring of 1990, resulted in a slim majority for the New Democracy party (now headed by Prime Minister Constantine Mitsotakis) and the apparent decline of Papandreou's stature as a national leader.

But Papandreou strengthened his grip on power in October 1993, leading his PASOK party to a landslide (47%) victory over the New Democrats (39%), as Greek voters expressed their displeasure with Premier Mitsotakis's deficit-cutting "austerity" policies. Besides promising salary and pension increases and a halt to privatization, Papandreou pledged a hard line in the matter of the former Yugoslavia republic of Macedonia.

Following U.S. recognition of Macedonia on Feb. 9, 1994, Greece broke off consular relations with Macedonia and denied it the use of the Greek port of Salonika through which pass most of Macedonia's imports, including most of its petroleum. The EU, after failing to persuade Greece to drop the trade embargo, sought an injunction from the European Court of Justice on the grounds that member states are prohibited, except for national security reasons, from imposing unilateral trade sanctions. Early in 1995 Greece reluctantly accepted an EU trade pact with Turkey, despite the continuing problem of Cyprus.

Grenada

Geography **Location:** southeastern Caribbean Sea, about 100 mi. (160 km) N of Trinidad. St. George's 12°03'N, 61°45'W. **Boundaries:** Atlantic Ocean to NE, E, and SE.; Caribbean Sea to SW, W, and NW. **Total land area:** 131 sq. mi. (340 sq km). **Coastline:** 75 mi. (121 km). **Comparative area:** about twice size of Washington, D.C. **Land use:** 15% arable land; 26% permanent crops; 3% meadows and pastures; 9% forest and woodland; 47% other; includes N.A. % irrigated. **Major cities:** (1991 census) St. George's (capital) 4,439.

People **Population:** 94,109 (1994). **Nationality:** noun—Grenadian(s); adjective—Grenadian.

Ethnic groups: mainly of black African descent. **Languages:** English (official), some French patois. **Religions:** largely Roman Catholic, some Anglican and other Protestant sects.

Government Type: independent state; recognizes Elizabeth II as chief of state. **Independence:** Feb. 7, 1974 (from UK). **Constitution:** Dec. 19, 1973. **National holiday:** Independence Day, Feb. 7. **Heads of government:** Sir Reginald Oswald Palmer, governor-general (since Aug. 1992); George I. Brizan, prime minister (since Feb. 1995). **Structure:** executive (cabinet led by prime minister); bicameral legislature (15-member elected House of Representatives and 13-member appointed Senate); judiciary (Grenada Supreme Court, composed of High Court of Justice and two-tier court of appeals).

Economy Monetary unit: East Caribbean (EC) dollar. **Budget:** (1992 est.) ***income:*** $78 mil.; ***expend.:*** $51 mil. **GDP:** $250 mil., $3,000 per capita. (1992 est.). **Chief crops:** cocoa, nutmeg, mace, bananas. **Livestock:** sheep, goats, pigs, cattle, asses. **Natural resources:** none. **Major industries:** tourism, fish, beverages. **Labor force:** 36,000 (1985); 31% services, 24% agriculture, 45% other. **Exports:** $19.9 mil. (f.o.b., 1992 est.); 36% nutmeg, 14% bananas, 9% cocoa beans, 8% mace, 5% textiles. **Imports:** $103.2 mil. (f.o.b., 1992 est.); 25% food, 22% manufactured goods, 20% machinery, 10% chemicals, 6% fuel (1989). **Major trading partners:** ***exports:*** 12% U.S., UK, Netherlands, Germany; ***imports:*** 29% U.S., UK, Trinidad and Tobago.

Intl. Orgs. FAO, G-77, IBRD, ICAO, IDA, IFAD, IFC, ILO, IMF, ITU, NAM, OAS, UN, UNESCO, UPU, WHO, WTO.

Dominated in the early 1600s by the warlike Carib Indians, Grenada alternated between French and British possession between 1650 and 1783, when British rule was established.

Independence came in 1974. The leftist New Jewel Movement seized power in a 1979 coup, but its leader, Maurice Bishop, was assassinated during a military coup in 1983. Shortly thereafter, the United States invaded and returned power to the governor-general until 1984. In elections held on Mar. 13, 1990, no party gained a parliamentary majority. Prime Minister Nicholas Braithwaite of the National Democratic Congress party formed a coalition government in April 1990. In 1995 George Brizan succeeded the retiring Braithwaite.

Guatemala
Republic of Guatemala

Geography Location: northern part of Central American isthmus. **Boundaries:** Mexico to N and W, Honduras and Belize to E, El Salvador to S. **Total land area:** 42,042 sq. mi. (108,890 sq km). **Coastline:** 248 mi. (400 km). **Comparative area:** slightly smaller than Tennessee. **Land use:** 12% arable land; 4% permanent crops; 12% meadows and pastures; 40% forest and woodland; 32% other; includes 1% irrigated. **Major cities:** (1994 est.) Guatemala City (capital) 1,150,452; Quezaltenango 100,983; Escuintla 67,958; Mazatenango 42,328; Puerto Barrios 39,267.

People Population: 10,721,387 (1994 est.). **Nationality:** noun—Guatemalan(s); adjective—Guatemalan. **Ethnic groups:** 56% Ladino (mestizo and westernized Indian), 44% Indian. **Languages:** Spanish, but over 40% of population speaks an Indian language as primary tongue (18 Indian dialects, including Quiche, Cakchiquel, Kekchi). **Religions:** predominantly Roman Catholic, some Protestant and traditional Mayan.

Government Type: republic. **Independence:** Sept. 15, 1821 (from Spain). **Constitution:** May 31, 1985, effective Jan. 1986. **National holiday:** Independence Day, Sept. 15. **Head of government:** Ramiro de Leon Carpio, president (since June 1993). **Structure:** traditionally dominant executive; new 100-member congress installed Jan. 14, 1986; power vested in office of president; seven-member (minimum) Supreme Court.

Economy Monetary unit: quetzal. **Budget:** (1992 est.) ***income:*** $604 mil.; ***expend.:*** $808 mil. **GDP:** $31.3 bil., $3,000 per capita (1993 est.). **Chief crops:** coffee, cotton, corn, beans, sugarcane, bananas; illegal producer of opium poppy and cannabis for international drug trade. **Livestock:** cattle, pigs, sheep, horses, goats. **Natural resources:** crude oil, nickel, rare woods, fish, chicle. **Major industries:** sugar, textiles and clothing, furniture. **Labor force:** 2.5 mil. (1985); 57% agriculture, 14% manufacturing, 13% services, 7% commerce; 12% unemployment and underemployment (1987 est.). **Exports:** $1.3 bil. (f.o.b., 1993); 24% coffee, 9% sugar, 8% bananas. **Imports:** $2.6 bil. (c.i.f., 1993); fuel and petroleum products, machinery, grain, fertilizers, motor vehicles. **Major trading partners:** ***exports:*** 36% U.S.; El Salvador, Germany, Costa Rica; ***imports:*** 40% U.S.; Mexico, Japan, Germany, El Salvador.

Intl. Orgs. FAO, G-77, IAEA, IBRD, ICAO, IDA, IFAD, IFC, ILO, IMF, IMO, INTELSAT, INTERPOL, ITU, UN, UNESCO, UPU, WHO, WMO.

Modern Guatemala was the heart of the Maya civilization that began early in the Christian era and flourished from the fourth to the 10th centuries. From the 11th century on there were two major powers, the Cakchiquel and the Quiché. They were overthrown by the Spanish who invaded from the north in 1524.

The captaincy general of Guatemala was the seat of Spanish military authority in Central America until the 19th century. After an earthquake destroyed Antiqua in 1773, the capital was moved to Guatemala City. Despite a lack of economic or commercial prosperity, Guatemala was the center of the United Provinces of Central America after independence was gained from Spain (1821) and Mexico (1823). The United Provinces collapsed after an uprising by Rafael Carrera, and Guatemala became a separate country in 1838.

The Liberal party held power from 1851 to 1944. There was considerable economic development under Manuel Estrada Cabrera (1898–1920) and Jorge Ubico (1931–44), but their regimes were repressive. Juan José Arévalo was elected president in 1945. He was succeeded, with strong Communist support, by Jacobo Arbenz, who was deposed in 1954 by a U.S.-backed coup led by Col. Carlos Castillo Armas. The military has ruled either directly or indirectly since then, although democratic rule resumed officially in 1986.

Antigovernment guerrilla activity, which began in 1960, intensified in the 1980s, and more than 100,000 people, mostly civilians, have died at the hands of the Guatemalan National Revolutionary Union (URNG), the army, and right-wing death squads.

In surprising developments in May 1993, Pres. Jorge Serrano Elías, backed by the military, suspended the Constitution in an effort to crack down on labor and student strikes. Eight days later, in the face of overwhelming popular discontent—including the business community—and international protest, the military replaced Serrano with Atty. Gen. for Human Rights Ramiro de León Carpio. In March 1994 the URNG and the government reached an agreement that sets the stage for an end to the 30-plus-year civil war. But thus far talks held in Mexico have failed to reach agreement on human rights issues. In March 1995, the United States cut off its annual military aid to Guatemala for its failure to prosecute security officials for crimes committed during the civil war.

Guinea
Republic of Guinea

Geography Location: western Africa. **Boundaries:** Guinea-Bissau to NW, Senegal to N, Mali to NE, Ivory Coast to SE, Liberia, Sierra Leone to S, Atlantic Ocean to W. **Total land area:** 94,927 sq. mi. (245,860 sq km). **Coastline:** 199 mi. (320 km). **Comparative area:** between Utah and Oregon. **Land use:** 6% arable land; negl. % permanent crops; 12% meadows and pastures; 42% forest and woodland; 40% other; includes negl. % irrigated. **Major cities:** (1983 est.) Conakry (capital) 656,000.

People Population: 6,391,536 (1994 est.). **Nationality:** noun—Guinean(s); adjective—Guinean. **Ethnic groups:** Fulani, Malinke, Sousou, 15 smaller groups. **Languages:** French (official), tribal languages. **Religions:** 85% Muslim, 10% Christian, 5% indigenous beliefs.

Government Type: republic. **Independence:** Oct. 2, 1958 (from France). **Constitution:** May 14, 1982, suspended after coup of Apr. 3, 1984. **National holiday:** Independence Day, Oct. 2. **Head of government:** Gen. Lansana Conté, president (since Dec. 1984). **Structure:** coup on Apr. 3, 1984, established 17-member Military Committee for National Redressment (CMRN) to determine government policy; highest-ranking CMRN member became president, with other CMRN members assuming most cabinet portfolios.

Economy **Monetary unit:** Guinean franc. **Budget:** (1990 est.) ***income:*** $449 mil.; ***expend.:*** $708 mil. **GDP:** $3.1 bil., $500 per capita (1993 est.). **Chief crops:** cash crops—coffee, bananas, palm products, peanuts, citrus fruits, pineapples; food crops—cassava, rice, millet, corn, sweet potatoes. **Livestock:** cattle, sheep, goats, pigs, asses. **Natural resources:** bauxite, iron ore, diamonds, gold, uranium. **Major industries:** bauxite mining, alumina, diamond mining. **Labor force:** 2.4 mil. (1983); 82% agriculture, 11% industry and commerce; 88,112 civil servants (1987); 52% of population of working age (1985). **Exports:** $622 mil. (f.o.b., 1992 est.); bauxite, alumina, diamonds, coffee, pineapples. **Imports:** $768 mil. (c.i.f., 1992 est.); petroleum products, metals, machinery and transport equipment, foodstuffs, textiles. **Major trading partners:** ***exports:*** 33% U.S., 33% EU, 20% former USSR and Eastern Europe; ***imports:*** 16% U.S., France, Bràzil.

Intl. Orgs. FAO, G-77, IBRD, ICAO, IDA, IFAD, ILO, IMF, IMO, INTELSAT, INTERPOL, ITU, NAM, UN, UNESCO, UPU, WHO, WMO.

Guinea was formed out of the remains of a series of empires that flourished in West Africa between the 10th and 15th centuries. Situated to the southwest of the Sahara desert on the west coast of Africa, Guinea was a crossroads of West African trade long before Europeans arrived.

French merchants began trading in what is now Guinea in the early 17th century. France began acquiring land in the area in the mid-19th century, and in 1845 the territories were organized as a separate colony. The colony received the name French Guinea in 1893.

Most high political posts were held by Europeans until after World War II. In 1946 French Guinea became a territory in the federation of French West Africa. In September 1958 Guinea became the only French colony to reject membership in the Fifth French Republic, resulting in the severance of political ties with France. The territorial assembly proclaimed Guinean independence on Oct. 2, 1958, and a new government headed by Sékou Touré was formed on the same day.

Touré was adamant in his rejection of French colonialism, severing ties with France (1960–63) and soliciting economic and other assistance from the USSR, China, and the United States. Touré remained in power until his death in April 1984. A military government gained power a week after his death. By the end of 1987, relations with France improved, and free-market mechanisms were implemented. Proposals for multiparty democracy, to be phased in over five years, and a free-market economy were announced in late 1989. The government has made a public commitment to multiparty democracy by 1996.

Guinea-Bissau

Republic of Guinea-Bissau

Geography **Location:** northwestern coast of Africa. **Boundaries:** Senegal to N, Guinea to E and S, Atlantic Ocean to W. **Total land area:** 13,946 sq. mi. (36,120 sq km). **Coastline:** 217 mi. (350 km). **Comparative area:** about size of Maryland. **Land use:** 9% arable land; 1% permanent crops; 46% meadows and pastures; 38% forest and woodland; 6% other. **Major cities:** (1979 census) Bissau (capital) 109,214; Bafatá 13,429; Gabú 7,803; Mansoa 5,390; Catió 5,170.

People **Population:** 1,098,231 (1994 est.). **Nationality:** noun—Guinea-Bissauan(s); adjective—Guinea-Bissauan. **Ethnic groups:** about 99% African (30% Balanta, 20% Fula, 14% Manjaca, 13% Mandinga, 7% Papel); less than 1% European and mulatto. **Languages:** Portuguese (official), Criolo, numerous African languages. **Religions:** 65% indigenous beliefs, 30% Muslim, 5% Christian.

Government **Type:** republic; highly centralized one-party regime since Sept. 1974. **Independence:** Sept. 24, 1973 (from Portugal). **Constitution:** May 16, 1984. **National holiday:** Independence Day, Sept. 24. **Head of government:** Gen. João Bernardo Vieira, president (since Nov. 1980); Manuel Saturnino da Costa, prime minister (since Nov. 1994). **Structure:** executive—president and cabinet; legislature—50-member National Popular Assembly, overseen by 15-member Council of State.

Economy **Monetary unit:** Guinea Bissauan pesos. **Budget:** (1991 est.) ***income:*** $33.6 mil.; ***expend.:*** $44.8 mil. **GDP:** $860 mil., $800 per capita (1993 est.). **Chief crops:** rice, palm products, root crops, coconuts, peanuts. **Livestock:** cattle, goats, pigs, sheep. **Natural resources:** unexploited deposits of petroleum, bauxite, phosphates; fish, timber. **Major industries:** agricultural processing, beer, soft drinks. **Labor force:** 2.4 mil. (1983) 90% agriculture; 53% of population of working age. **Exports:** $20.4 mil. (f.o.b., 1991 est.); commodities, alumina, bauxite, diamonds, coffee, pineapples, bananas, palm kernels. **Imports:** $63.5 mil. (c.i.f., 1991 est.); capital equipment, consumer goods, semiprocessed goods, foods, petroleum. **Major trading partners:** ***exports:*** 33% U.S., 33% EU, former USSR and Eastern Europe, Canada; ***imports:*** 16% U.S., France, Brazil.

Intl. Orgs. FAO, G-77, IBRD, ICAO, IDA, IFAD, IFC, ILO, IMF, IMO, ITU, NAM, UN, UNESCO, UPU, WHO, WMO, WTO.

The Portuguese began exploring and trading in what is now Guinea-Bissau in the 15th century and in 1630 began to exert administrative control over the territory. The area became the center of the Portuguese slave trade. When the slave trade declined in the 19th century, the coastal port of Bissau became a major commercial center. Later in the 19th century, the Portuguese began to conquer the interior of the territory and in 1879 consolidated the region into a territory called Portuguese Guinea, which in 1952 became an overseas province of Portugal.

A nationalist movement began in 1956 under the leadership of Amilcar Cabral and the African Party for the Independence of Guinea and Cape Verde (PAIGC). Armed insurrection broke out in 1961. By 1972 the PAIGC exerted influence over much of the country. Civilian rule was established in the territory that it controlled, and elections were held for a national assembly. Cabral was assassinated in 1973, but soon after the PAIGC National Assembly declared the independence of Guinea-Bissau from Portugal. Portugal acknowledged the country's new status on Sept. 24, 1973, after it received U.S. recognition.

The civilian government was overthrown by a military coup in 1980, and the country was run by a Revolutionary Council headed by Brig. Gen. João Bernardo Vieira until a new constitution was adopted in May 1984. Under the new constitution, a new national assembly was selected, and Vieira was elected president in 1984 and 1989. In 1991 the government legalized opposition parties, but presidential elections have been postponed.

Guyana

Co-operative Republic of Guyana

Geography **Location:** northeastern South America. **Boundaries:** North Atlantic Ocean to N, Suriname to E, Brazil to S, Venezuela to W. **Total land area:** 83,000 sq. mi. (214,970 sq km). **Coastline:** 285 mi. (459 km). **Comparative area:** between Kansas and Idaho. **Land use:** 3% arable land; negl. % permanent crops; 6% meadows and pastures; 83% forest and woodland; 8% other; includes 1% irrigated. **Major cities:** (1976 est.) Georgetown (capital) 72,049.

People **Population:** 729,425 (1994 est.). **Nationality:** noun—Guyanese (sing., pl.); adjective—Guyanese. **Ethnic groups:** 51% East Indian, 43% black and mixed, 4% Amerindian, 2% European and Chinese. **Languages:** English, Amerindian dialects. **Religions:** 57% Christian, 33% Hindu, 9% Muslim, 1% other.

Government **Type:** republic within Commonwealth. **Independence:** May 26, 1966 (from UK). **Constitution:** Oct. 6. 1980. **National holiday:** Republic Day, Feb. 23. **Heads of government:** Dr. Cheddi Jagan, president (since Oct. 1992); Samuel Hinds, prime minister (since Oct. 1992). **Structure:** executive—president, who appoints and heads cabinet; unicameral legislature (53-member National Assembly) elected by proportional representation every five years.

Economy **Monetary unit:** Guyanese dollar. **Budget:** (1992 est.) ***income:*** $121 mil.; ***expend.:*** $225 mil. (1990 est.). **GDP:** $1.4 bil., $1,900 per capita (1993 est.). **Chief crops:** sugarcane, rice, other food crops; food shortages—wheat flour, cooking oil, processed meat, dairy products. **Livestock:** pigs, cattle, sheep, goats. **Natural resources:** bauxite, gold, diamonds, hardwood timber, shrimp, fish. **Major industries:** bauxite mining, sugar, rice milling. **Labor force:** 268,000 (1985); public-sector employment amounts to 60–80% of total labor force; 44.5% industry and commerce, 33.8% agriculture, 21.7% services; unemployment and underemployment 30% (1985 est.). **Exports:** $400 mil. (f.o.b., 1993 est.); bauxite, sugar, rice, shrimp, molasses. **Imports:** $520 mil. (c.i.f., 1993 est.); manufactures, machinery, food, petroleum. **Major trading partners:** (1988); ***exports:*** 31% UK, 23% U.S., 7% CARICOM, 6% Canada; ***imports:*** 33% U.S., 10% CARICOM, 9% UK, 2% Canada.

Intl. Orgs. FAO, G-77, IBRD, ICAO, IDA, IFAD, IFC, ILO, IMF, IMO, INTERPOL, ITU, LAES, NAM, OAS, UN, UNESCO, UPU, WHO, WMO, WTO.

Although the region was visited by Europeans in the 15th century, Guyana was only colonized in the early 1600s by the Dutch. Rule in the area was later contested by the French and the British, and it became the colony of British Guiana in 1831. After slavery was abolished, indentured servants from the East Indies were brought to work the land, and their descendants are in the majority today.

The People's National Congress (East Indian) was in power from 1964 to 1992, and socialist policies dominated the political landscape. Most of the country's large companies were nationalized, so despite its having the purest bauxite in the world, some gold, and conditions favorable to agriculture, it remains poor, dependent on foreign aid and remittances from overseas workers for much of its revenue.

In 1992 Cheddi Jagan of the People's Progressive party won the presidency, but attempts to privatize the sugar and bauxite industries have failed.

Haiti

Republic of Haiti

Geography **Location:** western part of Hispaniola in northern Caribbean Sea. Port-au-Prince 18°33'N, 72°20'W. **Boundaries:** North Atlantic Ocean to N, Dominican Republic to E, Caribbean Sea to S, Windward Passage to W. **Total land area:** 10,714 sq. mi. (27,750 sq km). **Coastline:** 1,100 mi. (1,771 km). **Comparative area:** slightly larger than Maryland. **Land use:** 20% arable land; 13% permanent crops; 18% meadows and pastures; 4% forest and woodland; 45% other; includes 3% irrigated. **Major cities:** (1984 est.) Port-au-Prince (capital) 738,342.

People **Population:** 6,491,450 (1994 est.). **Nationality:** noun—Haitian(s); adjective—Haitian. **Ethnic groups:** 95% black, 5% mulatto and European. **Languages:** French (official, but spoken by only 10% of population); all speak Creole. **Religions:** 75–80% Roman Catholic—of which majority also practice voodoo (called vodun)—10% Protestant.

Government **Type:** republic. **Independence:** Jan. 1, 1804 (from France). **Constitution:** Aug. 27, 1983, suspended Feb. 1986; draft constitution approved Mar. 1987. **Heads of government:** The Rev. Jean Bertrand Aristide, president (since Feb. 1991); Robert Malval, prime minister (since Aug. 1993). **Structure:** Consultative Council (45-member civilian advisory body); judiciary appointed by president.

Economy **Monetary unit:** gourde. **Budget:** (1991 est.) ***income:*** $300 mil.; ***expend.:*** $416 mil. **GDP:** $5.2 bil., $800 per capita (1993 est.). **Chief crops:** coffee, sugarcane, rice, corn, sorghum. **Livestock:** cattle, goats, pigs, horses, asses, sheep, mules. **Natural resources:** bauxite. **Major industries:** sugar refining, textiles, flour milling. **Labor force:** 2.3 mil. (1982); 66% agriculture, 25% services, 9% industry; shortage of skilled labor, unskilled labor abundant; significant unemployment. **Exports:** $135 mil. (f.o.b., 1992 est.); 65% light manufactures, 17% coffee, 8% other agriculture. **Imports:** $423 mil. (f.o.b., 1992 est.); 36% machines and manufactures, 21% food and beverages, 12% fats and fuels, 11% petroleum products. **Major trading partners:** ***exports:*** 84% U.S., 4% Italy, 3% France; ***imports:*** 64% U.S., 5% Netherlands Antilles, 5% Japan, 4% France, 3% Germany, 3% Canada.

Intl. Orgs. FAO, G-77, IAEA, IBRD, ICAO, IDA, IFAD, IFC, ILO, IMF, IMO, INTELSAT, INTERPOL, ITU, UN, UNESCO, UPU, WHO, WMO, WTO.

The Arawak island of Haiti was discovered by Christopher Columbus, who renamed it Hispaniola, in December 1492. In the next century the Arawaks were worked to death, murdered, or killed by disease. The western third of the island was harassed by French pirates and was ceded to France in 1697. With a diverse slave-based agricultural economy, the colony accounted for two-thirds of French overseas investment.

A slave revolt in 1791 led to abolition in 1794, and the whole island came under French rule the same year. Toussaint Louverture, an ex-slave, became governor-general in 1801, but he was deposed by the French. In 1803 a black army under Jean-Jacques Dessalines (Emperor Jacques I, 1804–6) and Henry Christophe (Henry I, 1806–20) defeated the French in 1803. Independence was declared in 1804. Under Jean-Pierre Boyer (1820–43), Haiti occupied Santo Domingo (which had been restored to Spain in 1808) from 1822 to 1844.

The next century was marked by political instability and an increased U.S. business and military presence in Haitian affairs. From 1905 to 1947, the United States had direct or indirect control of Haitian finances, and from 1915 to 1934 the country was under U.S. military occupation.

François "Papa Doc" Duvalier took power in 1957 and ruled Haiti with a stern hand. In 1971, he transferred power to his son, Jean-Claude (aka Baby Doc), whose regime was just as authoritarian as his father's. During this period, most of Haiti's wealthy and educated population fled the country, leaving it the poorest and most illiterate nation in the Western Hemisphere. To this day, it remains overwhelmingly dependent on foreign aid.

In 1986, the military ousted Baby Doc, and imposed a succession of short-lived but brutal and incompetent governments. In 1989, Supreme Court Justice Ertha-Pascal Troillot was named interim president, and in 1990, Haiti held its first democratic national elections ever.

The winner of those elections was the Rev. Jean-Bertrand Aristide, a 37-year-old Roman Catholic priest. But seven months into his five-year term, Aristide was overthrown in yet another military coup. He fled to the United States and appealed to the UN and the Organization of American States (OAS). The United States, Canada, and most of Western Europe refused to recognize the military junta and suspended $750 million worth of aid.

Yet despite Haiti's huge dependence on foreign aid, the only effect that this and successive trade embargoes had was to increase hardship among the poorest segments of the population. The military leaders of the junta, propped up by the wealthy, predominantly white, elite that remain in Haiti, began drug trafficking to support their regime and continually defied U.S. and UN requests to allow Aristide's lawful return. As the U.S. demands grew stronger, the military junta stepped up its street patrols and began a campaign of violence against Aristide supporters, killing more than 3,000 by September 1994.

After many months of threats the possibility of a U.S. invasion became a reality and on Oct. 15, 1994, the junta resigned and Aristide was reinstated as president. (For further details, see Part I: "Major News Stories of the Year.")

Holy See

Vatican City

Geography **Location:** entirely within city of Rome, Italy; outside Vatican City, 13 buildings in Rome and Castel Gandolfo (the pope's summer residence) enjoy extraterritorial rights. **Boundaries:** surrounded by Italian territory. **Total land area:** 0.17 sq. mi. (0.44 sq km). **Coastline:** none. **Comparative area:** about seven-tenths size of the Mall in Washington, D.C. **Land use:** 0% arable land; 0% permanent crops; 0% meadows and pastures; 0% forest and woodland; 100% other. **Major cities:** Vatican City (capital).

People **Population:** 821 (1994 est.). **Nationality:** N.A. **Ethnic groups:** primarily Italians, but also many other nationalities. **Languages:** Italian, Latin, various other languages. **Religion:** Roman Catholic.

Government **Type:** monarchical-sacerdotal state, seat of Holy See. **Independence:** Feb. 11, 1929 (from Italy). **Constitution:** Apostolic Constitution of 1967 (effective Mar. 1, 1968). **National holiday:** installation day of Pope John Paul II, Oct. 22. **Heads of government:** John Paul II, supreme pontiff (Karol Wojtylla, elected pope Oct. 16, 1978); Archbishop Angelo Sodano, Pro-Secretary of State of the Holy See. **Structure:** pope possesses full executive, legislative, and judicial powers; he delegates these powers to president of Pontifical Commission, who is subject to pontifical appointment and recall; Secretariat of State and Council of Public Affairs (which handles Vatican diplomacy) and Prefecture of Economic Affairs; College of Cardinals acts as chief papal adviser.

Economy **Monetary unit:** Vatican issues its own coinage called Vatican lira, which is interchangeable with Italian lira. **Budget:** (1993 est.) ***income:*** $86 mil.; ***expend.:*** $178 mil., supported financially by contributions (known as Peter's Pence) from Roman Catholics throughout world; some income derived from sale of Vatican postage stamps and tourist mementos, fees for admission to museums, and sale of publications. **GDP:** N.A. **Chief crops:** N.A. **Livestock:** N.A. **Natural resources:** N.A. **Major industries:** consists of printing and production of small amount of mosaics and staff uniforms; worldwide banking and financial activities. **Labor force:** about 1,500; Vatican City employees are divided into three categories—executives, office workers, and salaried employees. **Exports:** N.A. **Imports:** N.A. **Major trading partners:** N.A.

Intl. Orgs. IAEA, INTELSAT, ITU, UNCTAD, UNHCR, UPU, WIPO; permanent observer status at FAO, IMF, OAS, UN, UNESCO.

The Holy See is the smallest sovereign state in the world both in size and in population. It is a remnant of the "Patrimony of St. Peter," the secular state donated to the popes in the eighth century by Pepin the Short, father of Charlemagne. One of the major political powers on the Italian peninsula throughout the Middle Ages and into modern times, the States of the Church were conquered in 1870 by the new kingdom of Italy, which made Rome its capital.

In 1929 Mussolini's government made peace with the papacy in the Lateran Treaty, which recognized the Holy See as an independent state. The treaty was incorporated into the Italian Constitution of 1947. Under the terms of the treaty, the pope is pledged to perpetual neutrality and may intervene in international affairs as a mediator only upon request.

The pope is the sovereign of the Holy See in his capacity as bishop of Rome, and in that capacity, he accepts the credentials of foreign ambassadors assigned to the Holy See. The United States opened diplomatic relations with the Holy See in 1984, following the repeal of an 1867 law forbidding such relations. Pope John Paul II, a native of Poland, has been a source of spiritual leadership especially for Catholics in Eastern Europe. Since the collapse of communism in Eastern Europe, many countries there have renewed diplomatic relations with the Holy See. In a historic breakthrough the Holy See established diplomatic relations with Israel on Dec. 30, 1993.

As sovereign of the Holy See, the pope is an elected absolute monarch who appoints a Pontifical Council to govern the city on his behalf. The council meets only a few times each year. The economy is based on service industries, including printing; its revenues come from museum fees, philatelic sales, and sales of publications.

Honduras

Republic of Honduras

Geography Location: Central America. **Boundaries:** Caribbean Sea to N, Nicaragua to E, El Salvador, Nicaragua to S, Guatemala, El Salvador to W. **Total land area:** 43,278 sq. mi. (112,090 sq km). **Coastline:** 509 mi. (820 km). **Comparative area:** between Tennessee and Pennsylvania. **Land use:** 14% arable land; 2% permanent crops; 30% meadows and pastures; 34% forest and woodland; 20% other; includes 1% irrigated. **Major cities:** (1992 est.) Tegucigalpa (capital) 718,500; San Pedro Sula 378,300; El Progreso 124,900; Danli 116,000; Choluteca 99,300.

People Population: 5,314,794 (1994 est.). **Nationality:** noun—Honduran(s); adjective—Honduran. **Ethnic groups:** 90% mestizo, 7% Indian, 2% black, 1% white. **Languages:** Spanish, Indian dialects. **Religions:** 97% Roman Catholic, small Protestant minority.

Government Type: republic. **Independence:** Sept. 15, 1821 (from Spain). **Constitution:** Jan. 11, 1982 (effective Jan. 20, 1982). **National holiday:** Independence Day, Sept. 15. **Head of government:** Dr. Carlos Roberto Reina Idiaquez, president (since Jan. 1994). **Structure:** constitution provides for elected president, unicameral legislature (134-member National Congress), and national judicial branch.

Economy Monetary unit: lempira. **Budget:** (1990 est.) ***income:*** $1.4 bil.; ***expend.:*** $1.9 bil. **GDP:** $10 bil., $1,950 per capita (1993 est.). **Chief crops:** bananas, coffee, corn, beans, sugarcane, rice, tobacco. **Livestock:** cattle, pigs, horses, mules. **Natural resources:** timber, gold, silver, copper, lead. **Major industries:** agricultural processing (sugar and coffee), textiles, clothing. **Labor force:** 1.3 mil. (1985); 62% agriculture, 20% services, 9% manufacturing, 3% construction; 13–22% unemployment (1989). **Exports:** $850 mil. (f.o.b., 1993 est.); bananas, shrimp, lobster, coffee, lumber, meat, metals, sugar. **Imports:** $1.1 bil. (c.i.f., 1993 est.); petroleum, chemicals, basic manufactures, machinery and transport equipment. **Major trading partners:** ***exports:*** 65% U.S., 11% Germany; Belgium, Japan, Italy; ***imports:*** 45% U.S., 9% Japan; CACM (Central American Common Market), Venezuela, Mexico.

Intl. Orgs. FAO, G-77, IBRD, ICAO, IDA, IFAD, IFC, ILO, IMF, IMO, INTELSAT, INTERPOL, ITU, UN, UNESCO, UPU, WHO, WMO.

Early in the Christian era, the Mayan civilization extended south to the pre-Columbian city of Copán in what is now northwestern Honduras. The territory was also home to the Lenca Indians and the indigenous people of the Moskitia area.

A silver strike in the 1570s prompted the first major influx of Spanish. The region was also celebrated for its tropical hardwood forests. Although the British controlled the Caribbean coast in the late 1700s, Honduras was a province of the Spanish captaincy of Guatemala. It became a member of the United Provinces of Central America after independence from Spain and Mexico, and an independent republic after the 1838 collapse of the Central American Federation.

Conservatives dominated Honduran politics until the 1870s, when the Liberals came to power and adopted a new constitution that reduced the influence of the church, among other things. Economic development came especially from a number of U.S. firms whose efforts were regarded as exploitative rather than beneficial; in 1912, U.S. president William Taft sent marines to protect U.S. interests.

Political unrest continued until the presidency of Gen. Tuburcio Carías Andino (1932–49), who was followed by a succession of prolabor presidents. In 1963, a coup led by Col. Osvaldo López Arellano deposed the civilian president, and the military ruled almost uninterrupted until 1982. In 1969, the expulsion of thousands of Salvadoran peasants who had immigrated during the 1950s and 1960s led to the Soccer War with El Salvador. An armistice was negotiated by the OAS.

During the 1980s, Honduras was threatened by civil wars in El Salvador and Nicaragua. Honduran territory was used by Nicaraguan Contras, for which Honduras received substantial U.S. military and other aid. Demobilization of the Contras has alleviated tensions between Left and Right within the country, and in Jan. 1994 the new president, Carlos Roberto Reina Idiaquez, took office with the promise of controlling and reducing the power of the military.

Hungary

Republic of Hungary

Geography Location: landlocked country in eastern Europe. **Boundaries:** Slovakia to N, Ukraine to NE, Romania to E, Yugoslavia to SE, Croatia to SW, Slovenia to W, Austria to NW. **Total land area:** 35,919 sq. mi. (93,030 sq km). **Coastline:** none. **Comparative area:** about size of Indiana. **Land use:** 54% arable land; 3% permanent crops; 14% meadows and pastures; 18% forest and woodland; 11% other; includes 2% irrigated. **Major cities:** (1994) Budapest (capital) 1,995,696; Debrecen 217,706; Miskole 189,655; Szeged 178,878; Pécs 172,177.

People Population: 10,319,113 (1994 est.). **Nationality:** noun—Hungarian(s); adjective—Hungarian. **Ethnic groups:** 96.6% Hungarian, 1.6% German, 1.1% Slovak, 0.3% Southern Slav, 0.2% Romanian. **Languages:** 98.2% Hungarian, 1.8% other. **Religions:** 67.5% Roman Catholic, 20.0% Calvinist, 5.0% Lutheran, 7.5% atheist and other.

Government Type: republic. **Constitution:** Aug. 18, 1949; effective Aug. 20, 1949; revised Apr. 19, 1972. **National holiday:** Aug 20. **Heads of government:** Dr. Arpád Göncz, president (since May 1990); Gyula Horn, prime minister (since July 1994). **Structure:** executive—Presidential Council (elected by Parliament); unicameral legislature—National Assembly (elected by direct suffrage); judicial—Supreme Court (elected by Parliament).

Economy Monetary unit: forint. **Budget:** (1993 est.) ***income:*** $10.2 bil.; ***expend.:*** $12.5 bil. **GNP:** $57 bil., $5,500 per capita (1993 est.). **Chief crops:** corn, wheat, potatoes, sugar beets, barley; normally, self-sufficient. **Livestock:** chickens, pigs, sheep, ducks, cattle. **Natural resources:** bauxite, coal, natural gas, fertile soils. **Major industries:** mining, metallurgy, engineering industries. **Labor force:** 5.4 mil. (1991); 43.2% services, trade, government, and other; 18.3% agriculture; N.A. unemployment. **Exports:** $8.9 bil. (f.o.b., 1993 est.); 33% capital goods, 24% foods, 16% consumer goods, 11% fuels and minerals. **Imports:** $12.5 bil. (f.o.b., 1993 est.); 28% machinery and transport equipment, 20% fuels, 16% manufactured consumer goods, 14% chemical products, 6% agriculture. **Major trading partners:** ***exports:*** 70.7% OECD, former CEMA members, LDC; ***imports:*** 71% OECD, former CEMA members, LDC.

Intl. Orgs. FAO, IAEA, IBRD, ICAO, ILO, IMF, IMO, ITU, OSCE, UN, UNESCO, UPU, WHO, WIPO, WMO, WTO.

The Magyars, a tribe of Central Asian horsemen, terrorized Europe in the ninth century A.D. and settled in the Hungarian plain where, under their chieftain Arpad, they displaced earlier Germanic and Slavic settlers and organized a kingdom in 896. The Hungarians converted to Christianity late in the 10th century, and King Stephen (later St. Stephen) received a royal crown from Pope Sylvester II in 1001.

After the Battle of Mohacs in 1526, most of Hungary fell under Ottoman rule. The Turks were driven out in a series of battles with the Habsburg Holy Roman emperors at the end of the 17th century. Thereafter Hungary was part of the Habsburg Empire until 1867, when the Dual Monarchy of Austria-Hungary was organized, making Hungary independent of Austria in all but finance, the military, and foreign affairs.

During the 18th and 19th centuries, Hungary experienced extensive immigration of Romanians from the east and Slovaks from the north; by 1900 Magyars formed only a bare majority of the population. The pre–World War I economy was largely agricultural. Agriculture-related industry (beet sugar factories, breweries, tanneries, textile mills) developed in the late 19th century, along with some heavy industry.

In the dismemberment of Austria-Hungary following the defeat of the Central Powers in World War I, Hungary surrendered extensive territories to Romania, Yugoslavia, and Czechoslovakia. With the Treaty of Trianon ("Bloody Trianon") in 1920, the country lost 70 percent of its territory and 60 percent of its population; one-third of the Magyar people lived on foreign soil.

Short-lived governments—a republic under Michael Karolyi, and a Bolshevist state under Bela Kun—were replaced in 1920 by a new regime, with Adm. Miklós Horthy serving as regent. The Horthy regime was authoritarian but not fascist; its main objective was the recovery of Hungary's lost territories. Hungary established common cause with Germany in 1938 and 1940, recovering some territory from Czechoslovakia and Romania in the bargain, but at the price of participating in Hitler's war with the Soviet Union. Germany occupied Hungary in 1944 and set up a Hungarian Nazi regime. Late in 1944 the Russian army drove out the Germans and set up their own occupation.

The establishment of a full-scale Soviet-satellite regime was relatively slow. A republic was declared in February 1946, and the non-Communist Zoltan Tildy was elected president. Tildy was forced out in 1947, however, and replaced by the Stalinist dictator, Matias Rakosi. After the death of Stalin in 1953, the moderate Imre Nagy became premier and introduced some economic reforms. Nagy was forced out of office in 1955.

Nikita Khrushchev's denunciation of Stalin in 1956, combined with an atmosphere of rising expectations for further reforms in Hungary, led to a popular uprising in October 1956. Nagy, backed by the army, formed a coalition government on Oct. 23, proclaimed Hungary's neutrality, ended censorship, opened the country's borders, and withdrew from the Warsaw Pact. On Nov. 4, Soviet troops launched a massive invasion that soon crushed the rebellion. The Soviet army installed János Kádár as premier; Nagy was executed. About 200,000 Hungarians fled the country, and many more were imprisoned.

After several years of repressive rule, the Kádár regime announced, in 1963, amnesty for participants in the 1956 rebellion. Stalinists were gradually removed from the government, economic reforms emphasizing profit and productivity were introduced, and trade with the West was expanded. Hungary reluctantly took part in the suppression of Czechoslovakia's "Prague Spring" in 1968. In the same year, it announced the New Economic Mechanism (NEM) policy, ending central economic planning and introducing semifree enterprise under bureaucratic control.

After a brief return to central planning in the 1970s, the NEM was reintroduced in 1979 and expanded in 1982, when Hungary joined the World Bank and the IMF. Private ownership of subsidiaries of state-owned enterprises was permitted. In 1987 a pro-Gorbachev premier, Karoly Grosz, took office and in 1988 became head of the Communist party as well.

In May 1989 the boundary with Austria was opened, making Hungary a key escape point for refugees from East Germany and Czechoslovakia. Nagy's reburial the next month was attended by 300,000. By November the Communist party had renounced Marxism and renamed itself, but to no avail.

Free elections were held in March and April of 1990, and the Democratic Forum, led by Jozsef Antall, won a plurality and formed a coalition government with the Smallholders and Christian Democratic parties. Having already achieved substantial perestroika-style economic reforms under communism, Hungary was well-placed to make a rapid transition to free enterprise and was seeking admission to the EC. Sluggish production has, however, reduced tax revenues, resulting in serious deficits and an austerity budget that has increased the sales tax while cutting services.

Hungarian voters signaled just how painful they found the transition in the May 1994 parliamentary elections by electing the Communists (now renamed Socialists) back into office. After gaining only 33 seats in 1990, the Socialists took 209 of the 386 seats, an absolute majority.

Iceland

Republic of Iceland

Geography **Location:** near Arctic Circle in North Atlantic Ocean. Reykyavík 64°09'N, 21°58°W. **Boundaries:** Greenland about 190 mi. (300 km) to NW, Norway about 620 mi. (1,000 km) to E, UK 500 mi. (800 km) to S. **Total land area:** 39,768 sq. mi. (103,000 sq km). **Coastline:** 3,100 mi. (4,988 km). **Comparative area:** slightly smaller than Kentucky. **Land use:** negl. % arable land; 0% permanent crops; 23% meadows and pastures; 1% forest and woodland; 76% other. **Major cities:** (1993 est.) Reykjavík (capital) 101,824.

People **Population:** 263,599 (1994 est.). **Nationality:** noun—Icelander(s); adjective—Icelandic. **Ethnic groups:** homogeneous mixture of descendants of Norwegians and Celts. **Languages:** Icelandic (official). **Religions:** 95% Evangelical Lutheran, 3% other Protestant and Roman Catholic, 2% no affiliation.

Government **Type:** republic. **Independence:** June 7, 1944 (from Denmark). **Constitution:** June 16, 1944; effective June 17, 1944. **National holiday:** Anniversary of the Establishment of the Republic, June 17. **Heads of government:** Mrs. Vigdís Finnbogadottir, president (since July 1980); David Oddsson, prime minister (since Apr. 1991). **Structure:** executive power vested in president but exercised by cabinet responsible to Parliament; legislative authority rests jointly with president and Parliament (Althing); Supreme Court and 29 lower courts.

Economy **Monetary unit:** króna. **Budget:** (1992) ***income:*** $1.8 bil.; ***expend.:*** $1.9 bil. **GDP:** $4.2 bil., $16,000 per capita (1993). **Chief crops:** dairying, hay, potatoes, turnips. **Livestock:** cattle, sheep, horses, pigs, poultry. **Natural resources:** fish, hydroelectric and geothermal power, diatomite. **Major industries:** fish processing, aluminum smelting, ferrosilicon production. **Labor force:** 127,900 (1990); 55.4% commerce, finance, and services; 5.8% agriculture; 14.3% other manufacturing; 7.9% fishing and fish processing; 1.3% unemployment. **Exports:** $1.5 bil. (f.o.b., 1992); fish and fish products, animal products, aluminum, diatomite. **Imports:** $1.5 bil. (c.i.f., 1992); machinery and transport equipment, petroleum, foodstuffs, textiles. **Major trading partners:** ***exports:*** 68% EU (25% UK, 12% Germany), 11% U.S., 8% Japan; ***imports:*** 55% EU (14% Germany, 10% Denmark, 9% UK), 14% Norway, 9% U.S.

Intl. Orgs. EFTA, EU (free-trade agreement pending resolution of fishing limits issue), FAO, IAEA, IBRD, ICAO, IDA, IFC, ILO, IMF, IMO, INTELSAT, INTERPOL, ITU, NATO, OECD, OSCE, UN, UNESCO, UPU, WHO, WMO, WTO.

The volcanic island of Iceland was settled in the ninth century A.D. by Vikings, who established Europe's oldest body of representative government, the Althing, in 930. Christianity was introduced around 1000. In the 13th century, Iceland acknowledged Norwegian rule. In 1380 Denmark, by then in control of all of Scandinavia, conquered Iceland as well. Iceland gained its independence in 1918 but shared a common king, Christian X, with the Danes. During World War II, first British, and then American, troops garrisoned the island; in 1944, with Denmark occupied by the Nazis, Iceland deposed its king and proclaimed itself a republic.

Iceland became a UN member in 1946 and a member of NATO in 1949. Lacking its own armed forces, it grudgingly tolerated the presence of an American air base at Keflavik. The republic developed a Scandinavian-style welfare state, with comprehensive social benefits that have produced one of the world's healthiest and best-educated peoples.

Less than 1 percent of Iceland's territory is arable; the island imports grain and vegetables but is self-sufficient in meat and dairy products. Fishing is the principal industry, accounting for 75 percent of exports and engaging one-seventh of the work force. Between 1958 and 1976, Iceland carried on "cod wars" with the United Kingdom, Norway, and Denmark, involving disputes over Iceland's claim to extensive territorial waters.

Multiparty representation in the Althing has created a trend of government by coalitions or minority cabinets. Politically stable, the republic faces economic problems brought on by high taxes, chronic inflation, and a huge national debt. Iceland maintains close ties with Scandinavia and actively participates in the Nordic Council.

India

Republic of India

Geography Location: Asian subcontinent, with Himalayan mountain range to N. **Boundaries:** Pakistan to NW; China, Bhutan, Nepal to N; Myanmar to NE; Bangladesh to E (surrounded by Indian territory except for short frontier with Myanmar); Bay of Bengal to E; Sri Lanka to SE across Palk Strait; Arabian Sea to W. **Total land area:** 1,269,340 sq. mi. (3,287,590 sq km). **Coastline:** 4,350 mi. (7,000 km). **Comparative area:** slightly more than one-third the size of U.S. **Land use:** 55% arable land; 1% permanent crops; 4% meadows and pastures; 23% forest and woodland; 17% other; includes 13% irrigated. **Major cities:** (1991 census) New Delhi (capital) 7,174,755; Greater Bombay 9,909,547; Calcutta 4,388,262; Madras 3,795,208; Hyderabad 3,005,496.

People Population: 919,903,056 (1994 est.). **Nationality:** noun—Indian(s); adjective—Indian. **Ethnic groups:** 72% Indo-Aryan, 25% Dravidian, 3% Mongoloid and other. **Languages:** Hindi, English, and 14 other official languages; 24 languages spoken by million or more persons each; numerous other languages and dialects; Hindi is national language and primary tongue of 30% of people; English enjoys associate status but is the most important language for national, political, and commercial communication; Hindustani, a variant of Hindi/Urdu, is spoken throughout northern India. **Religions:** 82.6% Hindu, 11.4% Muslim, 2.4% Christian, 2.0% Sikh.

Government Type: federal republic. **Independence:** Aug. 15, 1947 (from UK). **Constitution:** Jan. 26, 1950. **National holiday:** Republic Day, Jan. 26. **Heads of government:** Dr. Shankar Dayal Sharma, president (since July 1992); P.V. Narasimha Rao, prime minister (since June 1991). **Structure:** bicameral parliament—Government Assembly (Rajya Sabha) and People's Assembly (Lok Sabha); relatively independent judiciary.

Economy Monetary unit: rupee. **Budget:** (FY93) ***income:*** $29.6 bil.; ***expend.:*** $45.1 bil. **GNP:** $1.17 trillion, $1,300 per capita (FY94 est.). **Chief crops:** rice, other cereals, pulses, oilseed, cotton; legal producer of opium poppy for pharmaceutical trade but also illegal producer of opium poppy and cannabis for international drug trade. **Livestock:** cattle, goats, buffalo, sheep, pigs. **Natural resources:** coal (4th largest reserves in world), iron ore, manganese, mica, bauxite. **Major industries:** textiles, food processing, steel. **Labor force:** 314.8 mil. (1990); 67% agriculture, more than 10% unemployed and underemployed (1987). **Exports:** $21.4 bil. (f.o.b., 1993); gems and jewelry, engineering goods, clothing, textiles, chemicals, tea, coffee. **Imports:** $22 bil. (c.i.f., 1993); petroleum, capital goods, uncut gems and jewelry, chemicals, iron and steel. **Major trading partners:** ***exports:*** 19% U.S., 8% Germany, 7% Italy (FY93); ***imports:*** 9.8% U.S., 8% Germany, 7.5% (FY93).

Intl. Orgs. Colombo Plan, Commonwealth, FAO, G-77, IAEA, IBRD, ICAO, IDA, IFAD, IFC, ILO, IMF, IMO, INTELSAT, INTERPOL, ITU, NAM, UN, UNESCO, UPU, WHO, WIPO, WMO, WTO.

Indian civilization is one of the oldest in the world. Neolithic agricultural communities had appeared in the Indus River valley by 3000 B.C. and cities at Harappa and Mohenjo-Daro were founded around 2500 B.C. Around 1500 B.C. Indo-Europeans (Aryans) from Central Asia imposed their own religion, culture, and political system on the indigenous population and generated population movements toward southern India.

Indo-European civilization was characterized by caste; everyone was a member of one of four fundamental divisions of society: Brahmins, hereditary priests responsible for higher learning and rituals; Ksatrias, warriors and administrators; Vaisas, merchants; and Sudras, farmers and subjugated peoples. At the bottom were casteless people, known later as untouchables.

By the mid-first millennium B.C., Brahminism had declined into a state of religious formalism. That situation prompted two reformations around 600 B.C., the first of which produced the Jain religion; the second, Buddhism. Jainism remained confined largely to India, while Buddhism eventually influenced most of the cultures of Asia, though it died out in India itself. Buddhism was adopted as a state religion by Asoka, third and greatest emperor of the Mauryan empire (325–184 B.C) under which much of India was united for the first time. Following the collapse of the Mauryan empire, Hinduism evolved out of Buddhism, Brahminism, and other local cults and became the dominant religion of India.

South India in the post-Mauryan period was divided into numerous states, the most prominent of which was Chola, a Tamil kingdom in the southeast that had extensive trade connections throughout the Indian Ocean.

The Gupta dynasty (c. A.D. 320–544), based in the Ganges River valley, established its rule over most of northern India and created what is generally regarded as a golden age of north Indian culture, with flourishing cities and significant achievements in art, literature, and science.

In the seventh century, King Sri Harsha created a short-lived feudal empire that united most of the petty states in the upper Ganges valley, while the Chalyuka dynasty dominated southern India. In the early eighth century, the Indus River valley was invaded by Arabs who introduced Islam to the region. The empire of Sri Harsha fell apart, to be replaced by the numerous petty kingdoms of the Rajputs, while political power became fragmented in the south as well.

The 11th century saw the ascendency of Islam throughout northern India, which came under the shadow of the empire of Mamud of Ghazni, based in Afghanistan. In 1192 the Ghaznavid general Kutb ud-din Aibak defeated a coalition of Rajput states; in 1206 he founded the Sultanate of Delhi, which in the 13th century held off Mongol invasions in northwestern India and brought all of the subcontinent, except for the southernmost states, under its control. While the rulers of the sultanate were Muslims, most of their subjects remained Hindu.

Internal rebellions combined with the sacking of Delhi by Timur Leng (Tamerlane) in 1398 weakened the Sultanate of Delhi. In 1526 Babur, a descendant of Timur Leng, conquered all of northern India and established the Moghul empire. Under Akbar the Great, the empire flourished; Moghul culture gave rise to new styles of architecture, painting, and music.

In the 17th century, the Moghul emperors were threatened by the Hindu Marathas, whose kingdom on the west-central coast rapidly encompassed most of south India. By the late 18th century, Maratha power had spread to the north, and most of the petty kingdoms of the Moghul empire became part of a Maratha confederacy, owing only nominal allegiance to Delhi. By that time all of India was threatened by the expansion of the European powers.

Vasco da Gama had landed at Calicut in 1498, and in 1510 the Portuguese founded a colony at Goa. Dutch traders competed with the Portuguese during the 16th century, and British and French merchants followed in the 17th century. British trading stations were established at Surat (1612), Bombay (1661), and Calcutta (1690). In the mid-18th century, warfare broke out between British and French forces in India, and the French were confined to a few small enclaves. The growing instability of the Moghul empire in the face of Marathan and Rajput revolts and the expansion of the southern kingdom of Mysore encouraged the British to seek further control of Indian territory. Robert Clive's victory at Plassey in 1757 brought Orissa, Bihar, and Bengal under British control; British rule was extended to the upper Ganges in 1775. Victory over the maharaja of Mysore in 1792 paved the way for British control over much of the south.

British parliamentary acts of 1773 and 1784 placed these acquisitions firmly under government control, and in 1803 the Moghul emperor accepted the offer of a protectorate, and British suzerainty in India was assured. After a protracted war, 1812–23, Marathan resistance to British control was broken. The first Anglo-Afghan War, 1838–42, was inconclusive in Afghanistan but led to consolidation of British control of the Punjab.

In 1833 Parliament assumed political control of British interests in South Asia, while private merchants had unrestricted access to the economy. Plantation crops, such as opium and cotton, began to displace subsistence agriculture, which made India more dependent on imported goods.

In 1857 Indian troops in the British colonial forces staged a mutiny in north-central India that lasted 14 months. In 1858 the Moghul empire was dissolved, as was the East India Company. The government of India was made directly subject to the British Crown, which exercised control through a viceroy and through the British Colonial Office. Queen Victoria was crowned empress of India in 1877.

British sovereignty in India—the raj—was a patchwork of direct and indirect rule. In general, coastal areas, major river valleys, and strategic frontier regions were ruled by British authorities, while interior states continued as British protectorates controlled by British advisers to native princes. In 1861 Indians were appointed to advisory councils of the viceroy and provincial governors.

The Indian National Congress was organized in 1885. In the wake of popular demonstrations in 1905, elections were instituted to choose Indian members of the viceroy's legislative council. Separate electorates were created for the Muslim and Hindu communities, formalizing a divisive force in Indian politics and weakening opposition to British rule.

In 1914, with Chinese loss of control in Tibet, India's northern boundary was pushed forward to the McMahon Line, following the highest peaks in the Himalayas. This set the stage for numerous later boundary disputes between China and India, Pakistan, and Burma.

The Government of India Act of 1919 transferred some political power to elected provincial officials but left the appointed British governors firmly in control. In that year Mohandas K. Gandhi organized the first passive-resistance campaigns and was imprisoned. In 1935 the Government of India Act created elected provincial legislatures. In the first elections (1937) the Congress party under Jawaharlal Nehru won control of seven of the 11 provinces. Nehru's goal of a united Indian opposition to British rule was thwarted by Mohammed Ali Jinnah's Moslem League, which demanded the creation of a separate Muslim state.

During World War II, the British military position in South Asia was complicated by calls for Indian independence. An offer of local autonomy, with independence to follow, was spurned by Nehru, and an Indian National army under Subhas Bose fought with the Japanese. Jinnah's call for an independent Pakistan was greatly enhanced by his wholehearted support of the British.

In 1947, the British raj became two independent nations, predominantly Hindu India and predominantly Muslim Pakistan. Despite its considerable stature in the international community at large, India has been troubled by a number of disputes with its neighbors and separatist movements within its own borders. Following independence hundreds of semiautonomous princely states were brought under control of the central government. The French ceded their remaining trading colonies in the 1950s, and Portugal gave up Goa in 1961. In 1962, India warred with China in a still unresolved dispute over their border along Kashmir and Assam. The state of Bhutan was granted independence in 1971, and in 1974 Sikkim was annexed and its monarchy abolished.

India's most intractable disputes have been with Pakistan. Immediately after independence, Hindus in Pakistan and Muslims in India were set upon by the majority populations; hundreds of thousands were killed, and at least 12 million refugees fled over the border in both directions. On Jan. 30, 1948, Gandhi was assassinated by a Hindu extremist who blamed him for partition.

In granting independence, Britain had divided states of Bengal and Punjab between the two countries, but fighting erupted over the status of Jammu and Kashmir, and a cease-fire line negotiated by the UN in 1949 has never been ratified as a formal national boundary. In 1989, separatists in the Indian part of Kashmir began calling for an end to Indian rule, and relations with Pakistan have worsened as India accused its neighbor of providing support for the guerrillas. In 1971, after 10 million refugees poured across its border, India intervened in the Pakistani civil war in an action that prompted an almost immediate cease-fire and the creation of an independent Bangladesh.

India's main separatist movement involves Sikh separatists in the Punjab who seek the formation of an independent state of Khalistan, but who are thought to be supported by Pakistan. The government is also contending with increasingly determined separatist movements in the northeastern states of Assam and its neighbor Nagaland.

The British legacy in India included a sizable national elite, well educated and committed to principles of parliamentary democracy. The English language linked the elites of India's linguistically diverse regions, easing minorities' fears of domination by a Hindi-speaking majority. India's economy had seen some industrial development under the British, but its infrastructure was geared to integration in a colonial empire rather than to independence. Port cities, heavy industry, and plantation agriculture coexisted with widespread rural poverty in subsistence-level villages, and the years following independence saw a massive migration of the rural poor into overburdened cities.

Under Prime Minister Jawaharlal Nehru, India assumed a leadership role in the world movement of nonaligned nations and followed a policy of neutrality in international affairs. The gradual development of good relations between the United States and Pakistan led to correspondingly difficult U.S.-India relations. In August 1971 India signed a 20-year friendship treaty with the Soviet Union.

Nehru died on May 27, 1964, and was succeeded by Lal Bahadur Shastri. Nehru's daughter, Mrs. Indira Gandhi, was named prime minister on Jan. 19, 1966. In 1967 the dominant Congress party faced electoral setbacks; in 1969 it split into "Old" and "New" wings. Mrs. Gandhi's New Congress party won control of the legislature.

Faced with protests and strikes after the New Congress party was convicted of voting irregularities in 1975, Mrs. Gandhi declared a state of emergency in June; censorship was imposed, thousands were arrested for political offenses, and various economic-control measures were adopted. An opposition coalition led by the Janata Dal party won a massive victory in parliamentary elections in 1977. Mrs. Gandhi was driven from office, and the state of emergency was annulled. Mrs. Gandhi's party was returned to power in 1980, and she resumed the prime ministership. After an army attack on the Sikhs' Golden Temple in Amritsar, Gandhi was assassinated by Sikh bodyguards in October 1984. She was succeeded in office by her son, Rajiv, who placed the Punjab under direct control of the federal government.

On Dec. 3, 1984, methyl isocyanate gas leaked from a Union Carbide plant in Bhopal, killing over 2,500 people. The accident prompted a broad inquiry into industrial safety standards in India.

Indian troops, in July 1987, intervened in the growing civil war in Sri Lanka between the government and Tamil separatists. A negotiated truce under Indian auspices broke down, and Indian troops were involved in the conflict until their withdrawal in late 1989.

In November 1989, Rajiv Gandhi's Congress party was voted out of office in general elections after people close to the government were accused of taking kickbacks in a government arms purchase scandal. Gandhi was succeeded by V.P. Singh of the Janata Dal party, whose government collapsed after 11 months over a dispute involving Hindu plans to build a temple on the site of a mosque in Ayodhya. (Hindus contend the mosque was built on the site of Rama's birthplace.) Middle-class Hindus also protested an affirmative action policy to set aside federal government jobs for members of lower castes.

Singh was followed by Chandra Shekhar, whose minority government served only with the backing of the Congress party. After a parliamentary boycott by the Congress party instigated by Rajiv Gandhi, Shekhar quit the government in March 1991, agreeing to stay on as a caretaker until the May election. The election, postponed two weeks following the assassination of Gandhi, was won by the Congress party, and P.V. Narasimha Rao became prime minister.

India has enjoyed significant domestic and international achievements in the 40 years since independence. The nation's territory has been consolidated, and separatist movements in various provinces have been successfully resisted. The federal parliamentary system has proved workable, and the federal government has established its constitutional right to intervene in state affairs under some conditions. India's armed forces are large, well trained, and well equipped, with some nuclear capability. India has maintained watchful, but generally peaceful, relations with two unfriendly neighbors, Pakistan and China, and continues to play a leading role in the nonaligned movement. The Green Revolution of the 1970s has made the country self-sufficient in food for the first time since the 19th century. The country has a large, well-educated middle class and a growing industrial economy.

During 1992 the Rao government attempted to foster economic growth by relaxing the centralized planning and controls on international trade and investment that had long stifled the nation's potential. This policy produced impressive economic gains despite a concurrent rise in corruption-related scandals.

Nevertheless, the nation faces persistent problems, including separatist movements, regional grievances, and communal conflicts. Much of the population (65%) consists of illiterate people living in rural and urban poverty or near-poverty; the benefits of modernization have been unevenly distributed. Corruption is rife in politics and business. Measures to control population growth have been generally unsuccessful.

A rise in Hindu extremist feeling strengthened the hand of the opposition Bharatiya Janata party. On Dec. 6, 1992, a Hindu mob demolished a mosque built several hundred years earlier on a Hindu sacred site in the city of Ayodhya; in the ensuing turmoil, riots broke out in dozens of cities, most notably Bombay, leading to the deaths of hundreds of Muslims at the hands of Hindu attackers. A series of bomb explosions killed hundreds in Bombay on Mar. 12, 1993, while dozens more were killed by an explosion in Calcutta four days later. Further riots followed, amid unsubstantiated accusations that Muslims, aided by Pakistan, were responsible for the explosions.

Meanwhile, separatist rebellions of Sikhs in the Punjab and tribespeople in Assam tended to calm down in 1993, while the Muslim separatist movement in Kashmir grew more violent, with hundreds of deaths at the hands of both the rebels and police and military forces. Talks with Pakistan over Jammu and Kashmir broke off in stalemate in early 1994, followed shortly by a U.S. announcement that it would resume weapons sales to Pakistan in exchange for a halt in production of nuclear weapons materials.

India today is thus in the strange position of being poised for an economic miracle while at the same time descending further into political chaos and communal violence and facing renewed tensions with its chief rival. Although foreign investment continued to grow rapidly, some political discontent was evident in 1994–95 as the Congress party lost many seats in several former strongholds.

Indonesia

Republic of Indonesia

Geography **Location:** archipelago of about 13,700 islands stretching from Malay peninsula to New Guinea between mainland of Southeast Asia and Australia. Jakarta 6°08'S, 106°45'E. **Boundaries:** land borders with Papua New Guinea, to E of Irian Jaya, and with Malaysian states of Sarawak and Sabah in northern Borneo. **Total land area:** 741,097 sq. mi. (1,919,440 sq km). **Coastline:** 34,006 mi. (54,716 km). **Comparative area:** slightly less than three times the size of Texas. **Land use:** 8% arable land; 3% permanent crops; 7% meadows and pastures; 67% forest and woodland; 15% other; includes 3% irrigated. **Major cities:** (1990 census) Jakarta (capital) 8,222,515; Surabaya 2,473,272; Bandung 2,056,915; Medan 1,730,052; Semarang 1,249,230.

People **Population:** 200,409,741 (1994 est.). **Nationality:** noun—Indonesian(s); adjective—Indonesian. **Ethnic groups:** majority of Malay stock comprising 45% Javanese, 14% Sudanese, 7.5% Madurese, 7.5% coastal Malays. **Languages:** Indonesian (modified form of Malay; official); English and Dutch, leading foreign languages; local dialects, most widely spoken of which is Javanese. **Religions:** 88% Muslim, 6% Protestant, 3% Roman Catholic, 2% Hindu.

Government **Type:** republic. **Independence:** Aug. 17, 1945 (from Netherlands). **Constitution:** Aug. 1945, abrogated by Federal Constitution of 1949 and Provisional Constitution of 1950, restored July 5, 1959. **National holiday:** Independence Day, Aug. 17. **Head of government:** Gen. (ret.) Soeharto, president (since Mar. 1968). **Structure:** executive—headed by president who is chief of state and head of cabinet; cabinet selected by president; unicameral legislature (DPR, or House of Representatives) of 500 members (100 appointed, 400 elected); second body (MPR, or People's Consultative Assembly) of 1,000 members includes legislature and 500 other members (chosen by several processes but not directly elected); MPR elects president and vice president and theoretically determines national policy; judicial—Supreme Court is highest court.

Economy **Monetary unit:** Indonesian rupiah. **Budget:** (1991) ***income:*** $32.8 bil.; ***expend.:*** $32.8 bil. **GDP:** $571 bil., $2,900 per capita (1993 est.). **Chief crops:** subsistence food production, and smallholder and plantation production for export; rice, cassava, peanuts, rubber, cocoa; illegal producer of cannabis for international drug trade. **Livestock:** goats, cattle, sheep, pigs, buffalo. **Natural resources:** crude oil, tin, natural gas, nickel, timber. **Major industries:** petroleum, textiles, mining. **Labor force:** 67 mil. (1985 est.); 55% agriculture, 10% manufacturing, 4% construction, 3% transport and communication; 2.9% unemployment. **Exports:** $38.2 bil. (f.o.b., 1993 est.); 40% petroleum and liquefied natural gas, 15% timber, 7% textiles, 5% rubber, 3% coffee. **Imports:** $28.3 bil. (f.o.b., 1993 est.); 39% machinery, 19% chemical products, 16% manufactured goods. **Major trading partners:** (1991) ***exports:*** 37% Japan, 13% Europe, 12% U.S., 8% Singapore; ***imports:*** 25% Japan, 23% Europe, 13% U.S., 5% Singapore.

Intl. Orgs. ASEAN, FAO, G-77, IAEA, IBRD, ICAO, IDA, IFAD, IFC, ILO, IMF, IMO, INTELSAT, INTERPOL, ITU, NAM, OPEC, UN, UNESCO, UPU, WHO, WIPO, WMO, WTO, WTO.

The precolonial East Indies consisted of several Islamic and Hindu kingdoms in the western islands and tribal societies in the easterly ones. The Portuguese established trading posts in the 16th century; by the 17th century, control had largely passed to the Dutch East India Company. With the company's bankruptcy in 1799, the Dutch established direct colonial rule. Several 19th-century anticolonial uprisings, though costly to the Dutch, failed to dislodge them. Nationalist sentiment grew in the early 20th century, organized around Islamic groups, the Indonesian Communist party (PKI, founded 1920), and the Indonesian Nationalist party (PNI, founded 1927). Sukarno, founder of the PNI, achieved prominence as a nationalist leader and was jailed by the Dutch.

The Dutch East Indies fell quickly to the Japanese early in 1942. Some nationalists at first hailed the Japanese as liberators but quickly turned against their harsh occupation. On Aug. 17, 1945, Sukarno proclaimed Indonesia's independence. With British aid, the Dutch returned and tried to reestablish colonial rule; in 1949, threatened with a cutoff of American Marshall Plan aid, they withdrew and acknowledged Indonesia's independent status. Under Sukarno Indonesia took a leading role in international affairs among the nonaligned nations of the Third World.

In 1963 Indonesia gained control of the last Dutch outpost in the Indies, Irian Jaya (western New Guinea). Sukarno then launched a disastrous policy of "confrontation" with Malaysia in North Borneo. Sukarno's politics moved steadily to the left, and Indonesia became hostile to the West and friendly with China. The influence of the PKI grew steadily. On Sept. 30, 1965, the army crushed an attempted coup by the PKI, setting off a popular reaction in which several hundred thousand people were killed as suspected Communists. Sukarno was shunted aside, and power devolved to Gen. Suharto, who became president in 1968. Indonesia played an instrumental role in founding the Association of Southeast Asian Nations (ASEAN) in 1967. The PKI was banned, and Indonesian policy swung sharply in favor of the West and the non-Communist states of Southeast Asia.

The economy grew rapidly, aided by oil revenue, timber exports to Japan, and the Green Revolution in rice agriculture. Foreign investment aided industrial development, which was hampered, however, by domestic content laws and other trade restrictions. A policy of "transmigration" attempted, with mixed success, to move farmers from overcrowded Java and Bali to underdeveloped areas in Sumatra, Borneo, Sulawesi, and Irian Jaya. In 1975 Indonesia invaded the former Portuguese colony of East Timor, which was annexed in 1976. More than 100,000 East Timorese have been killed and the annexation is not recognized internationally. As recently as November 1991, troops fired on a crowd attending a funeral in East Timor, killing an estimated 100 people and provoking international outrage.

In recent years declining oil revenues have been partly offset by the growth of industry and tourism. Pres. Soeharto remains in power, at the head of the Golkar united-front party, but in 1990 the government lifted restrictions on the press and released some political prisoners while taking a strong position against Islamic militants.

Golkar's political grip slipped somewhat in parliamentary elections on June 9, 1992. Soeharto was reelected president for a fifth term in March 1993. Questions about his family's financial dealings remained taboo in the Indonesian press.

Iran

Islamic Republic of Iran

Geography **Location:** western Asia. **Boundaries:** Armenia and Azerbaijan to N, Caspian Sea and Turkmenistan to NE, Pakistan and Afghanistan to E, Persian (Arabian) Gulf and Gulf of Oman to S, and Turkey and Iraq to W. **Total land area:** 636,294 sq. mi. (1,648,000 sq km). **Coastline:** 1,976 mi. (3,180 km). **Comparative area:** slightly larger than Alaska. **Land use:** 8% arable land; negl. % permanent crops; 27% meadows and pastures; 11% forest and woodland; 54% other; includes 2% irrigated. **Major cities:** (1991 census) Tehran (Teheran, capital) 6,475,527; Mashad (Meshed) 1,759,155; Isfahan (Esfahan) 1,127,050; Tabriz 1,088,985; Shiraz 965,117.

People **Population:** 65,615,474 (1994 est.). **Nationality:** noun—Iranian(s); adjective—Iranian. **Ethnic groups:** 63% ethnic Persian, 18% Turkic, 13% other Iranian, 3% Kurdish. **Languages:** Farsi, Turki, Kurdish, Arabic, English, French. **Religions:** 93% Shia Muslim; 5% Sunni Muslim; 2% Zoroastrian, Jewish, Christian, and Baha'i.

Government **Type:** theocratic republic. **Constitution:** Dec. 2–3, 1979. **National holidays:** Shia Islam religious holidays observed nationwide; Victory of the Islamic Revolution, Feb. 11; Islamic Republic Day, April 1. **Head of government:** Ali-Akbar Hahsemi Rafsanjani, president (since Sept. 1989). **Structure:** executive, unicameral legislature (Islamic Consultative Assembly), and judicial branches.

Economy **Monetary unit:** Iranian rial. **Budget:** (1990 est.) ***income:*** N.A.; ***expend.:*** N.A. **GNP:** $303 bil., $4,780 per capita (1993 est.). **Chief crops:** wheat, barley, rice, sugar beets; illegal producer of opium poppy for international drug trade. **Livestock:** sheep, goats, cattle, asses, horses. **Natural resources:** petroleum, natural gas, coal, chromium. **Major industries:** petroleum, petrochemicals, textiles. **Labor force:** 15.4 mil. (1988 est.); 33% agriculture, 21% manufacturing; shortage of skilled labor; 30% unemployment. **Exports:** $15.5 bil. (f.o.b., FY92 est.); 90% petroleum; carpets, fruits, nuts, hides. **Imports:** $23.7 bil. (c.i.f., FY92 est.); machinery, military supplies, metal works, foodstuffs, pharmaceuticals. **Major trading partners:** ***exports:*** Japan, Turkey, Italy, Netherlands, Germany, Spain; **imports:** Germany, Japan, Turkey, UK, Italy.

Intl. Orgs. FAO, G-77, IAEA, IBRD, IDA, IFC, ILO, IMO, INTELSAT, OPEC, UN, UNESCO, UNIDO, WHO, WRPO, WMO, WTO.

In 549 B.C. Cyrus the Great established the Persian empire by uniting Persia and conquered Babylonia. His successors Darius and Xerxes tried unsuccessfully to conquer Greece. Alexander the Great conquered Persia in 333 B.C., but the Persians regained their independence after his death. The Persian Sassanian empire, established in A.D. 226, was the principal eastern rival of the Roman Empire. In 641 the Sassanians were defeated by invading Arabs, and Islam replaced the indigenous Zoroastrian religion. Persia reasserted its national identity—though not its political independence—under Islam and became a major center of Shia Muslim culture. In the early 13th century, Persia was conquered by the Mongols, who ruled the country until 1502.

The brilliant Safavid dynasty (1499–1736) was followed by two centuries of decline. During the 19th century, Persia lost control over Afghanistan and the Caucasus, while internal affairs came increasingly under British and Russian control. In 1907 an Anglo-Russian agreement formally divided Persia into spheres of influence. Following World War I, Persia was recognized as an independent nation, but was virtually a British protectorate. The Soviet Union renounced all claims to Persia in 1921.

In 1921 Reza Khan established a military dictatorship and had himself declared a hereditary monarch, Reza Shah Pahlavi, in 1925. In March 1935, the country's name was formally changed to Iran. In 1941 Great Britain, anxious over access to Iran's rich oil fields, charged Iran with pro-Axis activity, occupied Iran, and forced the abdication of Reza Shah in favor of his son, Mohammad Reza Shah Pahlavi. In 1945 Iran became a charter member of the United Nations, and in 1946–47, the Soviets tentatively backed the creation of the autonomous Republic of Iranian Azerbaijan (in the north) and the Kurdish Republic of Mahabad (between Lake Urmia and Iraq).

Under Mohammed Mossadegh the National Front gained power in 1951. With Mossadegh as premier, Parliament nationalized the oil industry; Britain responded with an economic blockade. The shah was briefly driven from power, but in August 1953, monarchist elements with clandestine British and American support ousted Mossadegh and restored the shah to the throne. The shah pursued a pro-Western policy of modernization and anticommunism and was rewarded with massive military and economic aid. His combination of secular, authoritarian rule and economic and social modernization was popular with the urban business sector but deeply resented by the rural population and the urban poor. Unrestrained use of the secret police to suppress any sign of dissent led to widespread popular disaffection.

Religiously inspired protests resulted in widespread violence in late 1978. A military government was installed by the shah on Nov. 6, with Prime Minister Shahpur Bakhtiar given sweeping powers. The shah went into exile on Jan. 16, 1979. On Jan. 31 Iran's dominant religious leader, Ayatollah Ruhollah Khomeini, returned to Iran from his exile in France. Government forces were routed by Khomeini's supporters, and Bakhtiar's government fell on Feb. 11. Throughout 1979 clashes took place between rival religious factions, between religious parties and secular leftists, and between the urban middle class and the disenfranchised poor. Thousands of people were arrested and executed by the religious militia forces.

On Nov. 4, 1979, militants seized the U.S. embassy in Tehran and held 62 Americans hostage, provoking a long international crisis. An American military raid in April 1980 failed in an attempt to free the hostages. The hostages were finally freed on Jan. 21, 1981, minutes after Ronald Reagan was inaugurated as president of the United States. The following day Iran's president, Abolhassan Bani-Sadr, was dismissed from office, and the Ayatollah Khomeini took over direct executive powers. This was followed by a new wave of executions, with political moderates and non-Islamic religious believers among the principal victims.

On Sept. 22, 1980, a dispute between Iran and Iraq over the Shatt al-Arab waterway flared into open warfare. The war severely crippled Iran. Estimates on casualties range from 450,000 to more than a million dead on both sides, and the war absorbed nearly all Iran's revenue from oil exports, leaving the country nearly bankrupt. The United States was also drawn into the conflict. In 1986, Reagan administration officials attempted to secure the release of hostages in Lebanon by trading arms to the Iranians; and on July 3, 1988, an American ship patrolling in the Persian Gulf accidently shot down an Iranian civilian airliner, killing all aboard.

In September 1988, a UN initiative led to a cease-fire between Iran and Iraq and to the opening of negotiations to find a permanent settlement to the war. Largely isolated from the world community, Iran's domestic priority in the wake of the war is the rebuilding of the nation's economy.

In February 1989, Ayatollah Khomeini pronounced death sentences on Indian-born British author Salman Rushdie and the publishers of his novel *Satanic Verses* because of its alleged insults to Muhammad and Islam. The book was banned in several Muslim countries, and Britain and the EC nations broke diplomatic relations with Iran over the incident.

On June 3, 1989, Ayatollah Khomeini died, but the dire predictions that his death would cause turmoil within the Iranian political hierarchy proved wrong. In September 1989 Ali-Akbar Rafsanjani assumed the presidency and has so far kept the disparate political factions at bay.

Although Iran condemned the presence of Western troops in the Middle East during the Persian Gulf conflict, it abided by UN sanctions against Iraq and grounded Iraqi planes that sought refuge from Allied bombing raids during the war. Yet it was Iran who urged the UN in February 1995 to end sanctions against Iraq, describing them as part of a U.S. plot to divide Arabs.

In elections held Apr. 10, 1992 (the first since the death of Ayatollah Khomeini), supporters of Rafsanjani's moderate economic and foreign policies wrested a parliamentary majority from the radical fundamentalist Islamic factions that had controlled the Iranian Parliament for 13 years. But "moderation" proved an elusive concept, as Rafsanjani's party was subjected to strong pressure from religious extremists. It was perhaps to quiet those extremists that Iran in December 1994 unilaterally named a new spiritual leader for the 100 million Shiites worldwide. In 1993–94 Iran remained mired in economic and political stagnation with some evidence of popular discontent.

Iraq

Republic of Iraq

Geography **Location:** western Asia with narrow outlet to Persian (Arabian) Gulf. **Boundaries:** Turkey to N, Iran to E, Saudi Arabia and Kuwait to S, Syria and Jordan to W. **Total land area:** 168,754 sq. mi. (437,072 sq km). **Coastline:** 36 mi. (58 km). **Comparative area:** slightly larger than California. **Land use:** 12% arable land; 1% permanent crops; 9% meadows and pastures; 3% forest and woodland; 75% other; includes 4% irrigated. **Major cities:** Baghdad (capital) 3,236,000 (1987 census); Basra (Basia) 1,540,000; Mosul 1,220,000; Kirkuk 535,000 (1977 census).

People **Population:** 19,889,666 (1994 est.). **Nationality:** noun—Iraqi(s); adjective—Iraqi. **Ethnic groups:** 75–80% Arab, 15-20% Kurdish, 5% Turkoman, Assyrian, and other. **Languages:** Arabic (official), Kurdish (official in Kurdish areas), Assyrian, Armenian. **Religions:** 97% Muslim (60–65% Shia, 32–37% Sunni), 3% Christian and other.

Government **Type:** republic. **Independence:** Oct. 3, 1932 (from League of Nations mandate under British administration). **Constitution:** Sept. 22, 1968, effective July 16, 1970 (interim constitution). **National holidays:** anniversaries of 1958 and 1968 revolutions celebrated July 14 and 17; various religious holidays. **Heads of government:** Saddam Hussein, president (since July 1979); Ahmed Hussein Khudair, prime minister (since 1994). **Structure:** Ba'ath party of Iraq has been in power since 1968 coup; unicameral legislature (National Assembly).

Economy **Monetary unit:** Iraqi dinar. **Budget:** (1989) ***income:*** N.A.; ***expend.:*** N.A. **GNP:** $38 bil., $2,000 per capita (1993 est.). **Chief crops:** dates, wheat, barley, rice, cotton. **Livestock:** sheep, goats, asses, camels. **Natural resources:** crude oil, natural gas, phosphates, sulphur. **Major industries:** petroleum, textiles, shoes. **Labor force:** 3.5 mil. (1980); 39% services, 33% agriculture, 28% industry, severe labor shortage; about 1 mil. Iraqis work abroad (1987). **Exports:** $10.4 bil. (f.o.b., 1990); crude oil and refined products, dates. **Imports:** $6.6 bil. (c.i.f., 1990); food, manufactures, consumer goods. **Major trading partners:** ***exports:*** U.S., Brazil, Italy, Turkey, France, Japan; ***imports:*** U.S., Germany, Turkey, France, UK.

Intl. Orgs. Arab League, FAO, G-77, IAEA, IBRD, ICAO, IDA, IFAD, IFC, ILO, IMF, IMO, INTELSAT, INTERPOL, ITU, NAM, OPEC, UN, UNESCO, UPU, WHO, WIPO, WMO.

The fertile lands of Mesopotamia, between the Tigris and Euphrates rivers, were the site of one of the world's oldest civilizations. The city-states of Sumer were founded before 3000 B.C. and later became the heart of the Babylonian empire. Babylon became subject to the Assyrian empire after 1350 B.C. and was conquered by the Persians under Cyrus and Darius in the mid-sixth century B.C. Mesopotamia remained under the control of various Persian dynasties for the next 1,000 years.

In the seventh century A.D., the region was rapidly incorporated into the expanding Islamic world. The battle of Basra in 656 decisively established Arab control. In 762 the Caliphate, the center of Islamic rule, was moved from Damascus to the newly founded city of Baghdad, near the ruins of ancient Babylon. Mongol invaders sacked Baghdad in 1258 and destroyed its irrigation works; thereafter the region entered a period of long-term decline. Baghdad fell to the Ottoman Turks in 1534, and Iraq remained a province of the Ottoman Empire until the 20th century.

British troops occupied Iraq in 1915, and Great Britain governed the country under a League of Nations mandate after World War I. A Hashemite monarchy was organized under British protection in 1921. The kingdom of Iraq was granted independence in 1932 but remained closely tied to Great Britain by treaties guaranteeing British interests in petroleum and regional defense. Iraqi oil flowed through British-controlled pipelines traversing Jordan to Haifa (in Israel) and through a French-controlled pipeline traversing Syria to Latakia.

After 1932 several attempted coups by anti-British factions were put down with the aid of British troops. One such coup in April 1941 sought aid from Italy and Germany; British troops landed at Basra in May and restored the pro-British monarchy. Iraq declared war against the Axis powers in 1943. In 1948 Iraq joined the Arab League and participated in the first Arab-Israeli War. Most of Iraq's 85,000 Jews emigrated to Israel after the war ended.

In 1952 a new agreement with Great Britain gave the Iraq Petroleum Company greater control over the country's oil, and a greater share of oil revenues. While remaining part of the Arab League, Iraq in 1955 broke ties with Egypt and also expelled the Soviet ambassador. Iraq signed a mutual defense treaty with Turkey.

A leftist pan-Arab revolutionary coup overthrew the monarchy in 1958 and established a republic, reversing Iraq's former pro-Western stance in international affairs. Oil resources and other industries were nationalized, and large landholdings were broken up. In 1968 a local branch of the international Ba'ath Socialist party came to power and established rule by decree within the republican framework of government. In 1972 the Soviet Union sent arms and advisers to Iraq. In the 1973 Arab-Israeli War, Iraq sent troops to aid Syrian forces on the front lines.

Iranian aid to a long-standing Kurdish rebellion in Iraq's northern mountains strained relations between the two countries. The Kurds were defeated in a bloody campaign in 1975, though the rebellion continued, leading to Iraq's bombing of Kurdish villages in 1979 and other subsequent incidents.

The execution of 21 alleged Communist conspirators in 1978 disrupted relations between Iraq and the USSR. Trade relations with the West were resumed. On July 16, 1979, Gen. Saddam Hussein at-Takriti assumed control of the government and immediately purged leftist elements in the Ba'ath movement.

Several months of intermittent fighting in 1980 between Iraq and Iran for control of the Shatt al-Arab waterway in southern Iraq led to the outbreak of open warfare on Sept. 22, when each country launched bombing attacks on the other's cities. Warfare quickly spread along the entire Iraq-Iran border. The Iran-Iraq War produced eight years of fierce but generally stalemated fighting, with reports of the use of poison gas by both sides. The war spread to the gulf in 1984, as both Iran and Iraq attacked tankers using each other's ports. On June 7, 1981, Israeli war planes destroyed a nuclear reactor near Baghdad, claiming it was capable of producing nuclear weapons.

On May 17, 1987, the USS *Stark*, an American frigate on station in the gulf, was struck by missiles fired by an Iraqi fighter; 37 American sailors were killed. Iraq claimed that the attack was inadvertent and apologized to the U.S. government.

In September 1988, a UN conference led to a cease-fire in the Iran-Iraq War. In the autumn of 1988, refugees in Turkey reported that poison gas had been used against Kurdish villages in northeastern Iraq as the Kurdish rebellion there continued. During 1989–90 Iraq's repressive internal policies and continued arms buildup provoked widespread international criticism. Iraqi agents were caught attempting to smuggle several components of nuclear weapons from the United States and Great Britain.

On Aug. 2, 1990, 120,000 Iraqi troops invaded, occupied, and later annexed neighboring Kuwait. The invasion was met with almost universal disapproval, led by the UN Security Council, and U.S. troops were deployed to Saudi Arabia to defend it against a possible invasion. Total coalition forces in and around Saudi Arabia eventually totalled 500,000 troops from 13 countries.

After a six-week air war that destroyed Iraq's offensive and defensive capabilities, as well as much of the country's infrastructure, Allied ground forces liberated Kuwait and occupied much of southern Iraq in only four days. Emboldened by the proximity of such overwhelming force, Kurdish and Sunni minorities in Iraq began a civil war that was put down with surprising speed and resulted in the displacement of hundreds of thousands of refugees to Turkey and Iran.

During 1992, while the Iraqi people continued to suffer from the war's devastation, Saddam Hussein solidified his hold on the military and remained in total control of the nation. However, UN inspectors discovered his secret plans to build nuclear weapons, and he was forced to destroy the means by which such an arsenal could be built.

Throughout 1992–93 American warplanes provided protection for Kurdish areas in the north and Sunni Muslim areas in the southern marshlands. UN arms inspectors continued to press, not always with complete success, for access to Iraqi weapons plants and military research centers. On June 19, 1993, American cruise missiles destroyed the Baghdad headquarters of Iraq's military intelligence service, in retaliation for a 1992 Iraq-backed plot to assassinate Pres. George Bush.

In November 1994 Iraq formally recognized the sovereignty and territorial integrity of Kuwait. Nonetheless, the UN has retained sanctions against Iraq until two further conditions are met: destroying its stockpiles of weapons of mass destruction and improving its treatment of minorities.

Ireland

Geography **Location:** 26 of 32 counties comprising island of Ireland, in North Atlantic Ocean. Dublin 53°20'N, 6°15'W. **Boundaries:** Northern Ireland (UK) to N, Great Britain 50 mi (80 km) to E. **Total land area:** 27,135 sq. mi. (70,280 sq km). **Coastline:** 900 mi. (1,448 km). **Comparative area:** slightly larger than W. Virginia. **Land use:** 14% arable land; negl. % permanent crops; 71% meadows and pastures; 5% forest and woodland; 10% other. **Major cities:** (1991 census) Dublin (capital) 915,516; Cork 173,694; Limerick 75,436; Galway 50,853; Waterford 41,853.

People **Population:** 3,539,296 (1994 est.). **Nationality:** noun—Irishman (men), Irishwoman (women), Irish (collective pl.); adjective—Irish. **Ethnic groups:** Celtic, with English minority. **Languages:** Irish (Gaelic) and English (official); English widely spoken. **Religions:** 94% Roman Catholic, 4% Anglican, 2% other.

Government **Type:** republic. **Independence:** Dec. 6, 1921 (from UK). **Constitution:** Dec. 29, 1937. **National holiday:** St. Patrick's Day, Mar. 17. **Heads of government:** Mary Robinson, president (since Dec. 1990); John Bruton, prime minister (since Dec. 1994). **Structure:** elected president; bicameral parliament (Seanad, Dail) reflecting proportional and vocational representation; judiciary appointed by president on advice of government.

Economy **Monetary unit:** Irish pound. **Budget:** (1992 est.) ***income:*** $16 bil.; ***expend.:*** $16.6 bil. **GDP:** $46.3 bil., $13,100 per capita (1993). **Chief crops:** turnips, barley, potatoes, sugar beets, wheat; food shortages—grains, fruits, vegetables. **Livestock:** cattle, sheep, pigs. **Natural resources:** zinc, lead, natural gas, crude oil, barite. **Major industries:** food products, brewing, textiles, clothing. **Labor force:** 1.3 mil. (1986); 46.5% services, 21.4% manufacturing and construction, 12.9% agriculture, forestry, fishing; 18.5% unemployment (1988). **Exports:** $28.3 bil. (f.o.b., 1992); live animals, animal products, chemicals, data processing equipment, industrial machinery. **Imports:** $23.3 bil. (c.i.f., 1992); food, animal feed, chemicals, petroleum and petroleum products, machinery, textiles. **Major trading partners:** ***exports:*** 75% EU (34% UK, 11% Germany, 9% France), 9% U.S.; ***imports:*** 66% EU (42% UK, 8% Germany, 4% France), 15% U.S.

Intl. Orgs. EU, FAO, IAEA, IBRD, ICAO, IDA, IFAD, IFC, ILO, IMF, IMO, INTELSAT, INTERPOL, ITU, OECD, OSCE, UN, UNESCO, UPU, WIPO, WMO, WTO.

Ireland, a collection of warring Celtic chieftainships, was converted to Christianity by St. Patrick in the fifth century. Over the next two centuries, Ireland became a great center of monastic Christianity, sending missionaries to Scotland, England, and the Continent. While the Roman Empire decayed, Ireland was a center of peace, culture, and learning. Viking invasions in the ninth and 10th centuries caused substantial damage and overturned the rule of the great monasteries and their secular allies. By the time an Irish monarchy was reestablished by Brian Boru in 1014 and the surviving invaders were integrated into Irish society, Ireland had become an isolated, poor backwater on the periphery of Europe.

Trade gave rise to English commercial interests in Ireland and to Henry II's claim to overlordship of Ireland in the 12th century. Henry VIII declared himself king of Ireland and introduced the Reformation there. Large-scale Scottish immigration to Ulster began during the reign of Elizabeth I. Penal laws were applied, banning Catholics from public life and making the Mass an act of treason. A rebellion in 1641 was crushed by Oliver Cromwell over the course of a decade, ending with a massacre of thousands of Irish at Drogheda. After William of Orange's "Glorious Revolution" of 1688, the Irish supported James II, who was defeated at the Battle of the Boyne in 1690.

Following these events, British economic sanctions destroyed Ireland's flourishing export trade in wool. "Plantations" were established by British and Scottish Presbyterian landlords and farmers on lands seized from Irish Catholics. Much of the native aristocracy fled into exile, and the Gaelic language declined to near extinction.

A separate Irish Parliament, dominated by the Anglo-Irish establishment, was instituted in 1782, but it had little power. In 1798 a popular uprising led by Wolfe Tone, with inspiration and aid from revolutionary France, was put down with great loss of life.

In 1800 Ireland and England were joined by the Act of Union, whereby Ireland was ineffectively represented in the British Parliament. After popular agitation led by Daniel O'Connell, the Catholic Emancipation Act was enacted by Parliament in 1829, though mandatory tithes continued to support the established Anglican church until 1869.

Under absentee landlords, the Irish population had been reduced to a subsistence diet based largely on potatoes. When a potato blight struck the country in the 1840s, disaster ensued. Between 1846 and 1851, one million people starved to death, and 1.6 million emigrated, most of them to America.

In the late 19th century, a home-rule movement under Charles Stewart Parnell won wide popular support. A Home Rule Act finally was passed by Parliament in 1914, but its effect was postponed for the duration of World War I. The Land Purchase Acts of the early 20th century enabled dispossessed peasants to buy land from absentee landlords, creating a rural economic basis for an independent Ireland. The country's economy, based largely on agriculture and pasturage, began to recover. (Industry, principally shipbuilding and textiles, was largely confined to Northern Ireland.)

The postponement of home rule led to the Easter Rebellion of 1916; brutally suppressed, it was followed by the "Troubles," a period of guerrilla warfare lasting to 1920. In that year the Government of Ireland Act established six of Ulster's nine counties as Northern Ireland, an integral part of the United Kingdom but with its own home-rule Parliament. The south's refusal of similar status led to the passage on Dec. 11, 1922, of the Irish Free State Act, by which Ireland became an independent dominion within the British Commonwealth.

The Fine Gael (People of Ireland) party governed until 1932, when Eamon De Valera, as the head of the Fianna Fail (Soldiers of Destiny) party, was elected president, holding that office until 1948. In 1938 the Constitution was revised to sever all connections with the British government except for an "external association" with the British monarchy. The outlawed Irish Republican Army (IRA) pressed for forcible reunification of Ireland and carried out attacks on British interests in both Ireland and Northern Ireland.

Ireland remained neutral during World War II, and its government objected to British military activities in Northern Ireland. But it was generally sympathetic to the Allied war effort, especially after the United States entered the war in 1941.

In 1949 Ireland severed all ties to the British Crown, becoming a fully independent republic. The Fianna Fail, normally the majority party since 1932, won a majority in the republic's first elections, and De Valera became prime minister. In 1954 a coalition government under John Costello took power. De Valera was elected president of the republic in 1959, as a new generation of parliamentary leadership arose.

During the 1950s, Ireland developed a moderate welfare state with the support of both the Fianna Fail and Fine Gael. In the 1960s attention turned to industrial development: zinc and lead mining, and export-oriented production of textiles, ceramics, and machinery. Ireland was admitted to the EC in 1973.

Beginning in the late 1960s, civil rights demonstrations led frequently to civil disorders and an increase in IRA guerrilla activity in the north. While the 1970s were a boom period for the Irish Republic, sectarian violence and terrorism in the north left over 2,500 dead. The 1980s saw the establishment of an Anglo-Irish Intergovernmental Council (1981) and the Hillsborough accords (1985) between the Thatcher government and the Fine Gael–Labour coalition, which gave Ireland a consultative role in Northern Irish disputes.

The government of Charles Haughey, leader of Fianna Fail, elected in 1987, continued to face severe economic problems, including high tax rates, high inflation and unemployment, and in the spring of 1989, Haughey was forced to form a coalition government. After serious losses in the June 1991 local elections and amid charges of corruption, Haughey resigned in January 1992. His successor, Albert Reynolds, faced a deep recession with unemployment rates of about 20 percent. In June 1992 a national vote gave strong support to the EC's Maastricht Treaty.

The Reynolds coalition fell in November 1992. After the election that followed, Reynolds formed a government that was a coalition between Fianna Fail and Labour. In December 1993 Reynolds and UK prime minister John Major announced the "Downing Street Declaration" that Sinn Fein, the political arm of the IRA, would be invited to participate in negotiations concerning the future of Northern Ireland on condition that it call a permanent halt to terrorism and violence. And in January the Reynolds government ended the Irish ban on broadcast appearances by Sinn Fein members. Finally, in September 1994 the IRA announced a cease-fire in its 25-year effort to expel British troops from Northern Ireland.

Preliminary talks among the UK, the Irish Republic, and Sinn Fein began in December but despite apparently large areas of agreement concerning Ulster, public talks remained stymied over opposing demands that the IRA disarm and that Britain withdraw its forces from Ulster. Meanwhile, Ireland's governing coalition fell in November and was replaced by an odd coalition of conservative Fine Gail, trades-union Labour, and Marxist Democratic Left under Prime Minister John Bruton of Fine Gael.

Israel

State of Israel

Geography **Location:** western Asia, on eastern shore of Mediterranean Sea; has outlet to Red Sea via Gulf of Aqaba. **Boundaries:** Lebanon to N, Syria to NE, Jordan to E, Egypt to SW, Mediterranean Sea to W. **Total land area:** 8,019 sq. mi. (20,770 sq km). **Coastline:** 170 mi. (273 km). **Comparative area:** slightly larger than Massachusetts. **Land use:** 17% arable land; 5% permanent crops; 40% meadows and pastures; 6% forest and woodland; 32% other; includes 11% irrigated. **Major cities:** (1992 est.) Jerusalem (capital) 556,500; Tel Aviv–Jaffa 356,900; Haifa 249,800; Holon 162,800; Petach-Tikva 150,900.

People **Population:** 5,050,850 (1994 est.). **Nationality:** noun—Israeli(s); adjective—Israeli. **Ethnic groups:** 83% Jewish, 17% non-Jewish (mostly Arab). **Languages:** Hebrew (official), Arab (official for Arab minority); English most widely used foreign language. **Religions:** 83% Judaism, 13.1% Islam (mostly Sunni Muslim), 2.3% Christian, 1.6% Druze.

Government **Type:** republic. **Independence:** May 14, 1948 (from League of Nations Mandate under British administration). **Constitution:** no formal constitution; some functions of constitution are filled by Declaration of Establishment (1948), the basic laws of the Knesset (legislature)—relating to the Knesset, Israeli lands, the president, government—and Israeli citizenship law. **National holidays:** Israel declared independence on May 14, 1948; because Jewish calendar is lunar, however, holiday varies from year to year; all major Jewish religious holidays are also observed as national holidays. **Heads of government:** Ezer Weizman, president (since May 1993); Yitzhak Rabin, prime minister (since July 1992). **Structure:** president has largely ceremonial functions, except for authority to decide which political leader should try to form ruling coalition following election or fall of previous government; executive power vested in cabinet; unicameral Parliament (Knesset) of 120 members elected under system of proportional representation; legislation provides fundamental laws in absence of written constitution; two distinct court systems (secular and religious).

Economy **Monetary unit:** new shekel. **Budget:** (1993) ***income:*** $33.4 bil.; ***expend.:*** $36.3 bil. **GDP:** $65.7 bil., $13,350 per capita (1993 est.). **Chief crops:** citrus and other fruits, vegetables, cotton, beef, and dairy products. **Livestock:** poultry, cattle, sheep, goats. **Natural resources:** copper, phosphates, bromide, potash, clay. **Major industries:** food processing, diamond cutting and polishing, textiles and clothing. **Labor force:** 1.9 mil. (1992); 29.5% public services; 22.8% industry, mining, and manufacturing; 12.8% commerce; 8% unemployment (1988). **Exports:** $14.1 bil. (f.o.b., 1993 est.); polished diamonds, citrus and other fruits, textiles and clothing, processed foods, fertilizer and chemical products. **Imports:** $20.3 bil. (c.i.f., 1993 est.); military equipment, rough diamonds, oil, chemicals, machinery. **Major trading partners:** ***exports:*** U.S., EU, Japan, Hong Kong, Switzerland; ***imports:*** U.S., EU, Switzerland, Japan, South Africa, Canada.

Intl. Orgs. FAO, IAEA, IBRD, ICAO, IDA, IFAD, IFC, ILO, IMF, IMO, INTELSAT, INTERPOL, ITU, OAS (observer), UN, UNESCO, UPU, WHO, WIPO, WMO, WTO.

In ancient times called the Land of Canaan, the region between the Jordan River and the Mediterranean Sea was one of the earliest sites of agricultural civilization in the Middle East. Hebrew exiles from Egypt arrived c. 1200 B.C.; their kingdom, Eretz Israel, was well established by 1000 B.C., with its capital at Jerusalem. The kingdom expanded under Kings Saul and David, who extended domination over the Philistines, a local seafaring people, and established the norms of Jewish religious worship at the great temple of Jerusalem.

After the reign of King Solomon, the kingdom split into two parts, Israel and Judah. Israel was conquered by the Assyrians in 722 B.C., and Judah by the Babylonians in 586 B.C. A locally autonomous state was reestablished under the Persian empire in the fifth century B.C. And in the fourth century B.C., Alexander the Great conquered the region, beginning a period of Hellenizing influence.

A new Jewish state was established in 141 B.C. after the revolt of the Maccabees against hellenic rule, the state falling to the Roman Empire around 70 B.C. Roman rule was exerted through the puppet kings of the Herodian dynasty. Christianity, a messianic religion centering on the teachings of Jesus of Nazareth, was suppressed in Israel by both the Herodian kings and the Jewish priesthood but spread widely in the eastern Mediterranean in the early first century A.D.

A Jewish rebellion against Rome in A.D. 66 was forcibly suppressed, and the temple at Jerusalem was destroyed by the Romans in A.D. 70. Large numbers of Jews were expelled from Judea, beginning the Jewish Diaspora throughout the Roman world and beyond. A second rebellion of Jews in Israel was quelled in A.D. 132.

The territory of the former kingdoms of Israel and Judah became generally known as Palestine, after the name of its ancient inhabitants, the Philistines.

With the official toleration of Christianity in the Roman Empire under Constantine I (early 4th century), Palestine became a major center of Christian pilgrimage. Politically, Palestine was administered as part of the Byzantine Empire.

Expansion of Islam from Arabia brought Palestine under Islamic rule in 636. Thereafter the region was ruled by the Caliphates of Damascus (661–750) and Baghdad (762–1258). Part of Palestine was captured in 1099 by European Crusaders, who established the short-lived Latin Kingdom of Jerusalem. The region was briefly conquered by the Mongols in 1258; defeat of the Mongols in 1260 at the battle of Ain Jalyut, near Nazareth, prevented a Mongol invasion of Egypt.

Palestine next became part of the Mamluk empire and in turn was incorporated into the Ottoman Empire in 1516. The later Ottoman period was one of administrative decline, although the holy places of Judaism, Christianity, and Islam were maintained by local religious authorities.

The emigration of Jews from Europe to the homeland of Israel began around 1870, under the influence of the Zionist movement. Zionism, traceable in part to the thought of Moses Mendelssohn (1729–86), originally emphasized the need to maintain Jewish identity and religious consciousness as well as to promote Jewish assimilation into European culture. By the time of the First World Zionist Congress, convened in Basel by Theodor Herzl in 1897, emphasis had shifted to the need for a specific Jewish homeland. After 1905, under the leadership of Chaim Weizmann, Jewish emigration to Palestine increased as Weizmann attempted to win Turkish approval for a new state of Israel.

With the collapse of the Ottoman Empire during World War I, Palestine came under British rule in 1917. In that year the British government issued the Balfour Declaration, committing Britain to aiding the establishment of a Jewish homeland in Palestine. After Britain received a League of Nations Mandate to govern Palestine (as well as Transjordan) in 1923, Jewish immigration into Palestine increased significantly. Faced with rising Palestinian Arab opposition to a further increase in Jewish immigration, Britain reinterpreted the Balfour Declaration in greatly restricted terms and attempted to limit the number of Jewish arrivals.

The crisis thus provoked lasted until the outbreak of World War II. During the war the Palestinian Jewish community (then about 500,000) generally supported the British war effort, while some Palestinian Arab leaders translated anti-Zionist sentiments into sympathy for the Axis. In 1946 British authorities refused a recommendation of the Anglo-American Committee of Inquiry that they permit resettlement of 100,000 European Jews in Palestine and that limited further immigration to 2,000 per month. Jewish leaders pressed their cause at the United Nations, while in Palestine, Zionist terrorist organizations waged covert war against the British authorities.

In 1947 a UN Special Committee on Palestine, boycotted by Palestinian Arabs, recommended the partition of Palestine into Jewish and Arab sectors, with Jerusalem to be administered under international control. The United Nations adopted the recommendations on Nov. 29, 1947, and the British began to withdraw their forces, while Palestinian Jews and Arabs prepared for war.

On May 14, 1948, the independent state of Israel was established, with its capital at Tel Aviv. On the same day, troops from the Arab League nations attacked Israel. Fighting and cease-fires alternated throughout 1948; Israel lost control of the Old City of Jerusalem but retained the New City, and elsewhere consolidated its territorial control. Separate armistices between Israel and the Arab nations were concluded in 1949; Jordan retained control of the West Bank, and Egypt occupied Gaza. Large numbers of Palestinian Arab refugees departed for camps in Jordan, Lebanon, and Syria, while equally large numbers of Jews from Arab countries resettled in Israel.

Elections to the Knesset (Parliament) were held in January 1949 and resulted in a coalition government. Chaim Weizmann was elected president, and David Ben-Gurion became prime minister. Laws were enacted to ensure religious control of education and civil law and to affirm the "Right of Return" of all Jews to Israel. The role of labor (organized in the Histadrut) was protected by law, as was the establishment of agricultural collectives (kibbutzim).

Taking advantage of the Suez Crisis between Great Britain, France, and Egypt, Israel invaded Egypt's Sinai Peninsula on Oct. 29, 1956. Israeli forces withdrew under the terms of a UN cease-fire on Nov. 6 but retained control of Gaza. Thereafter an uneasy peace prevailed for 11 years under UN supervision.

Throughout this period Israel's population continued to swell with immigrants from Europe, the United States, and other Western countries, and also from the dwindling Jewish communities of the Arab world. Israel's economy, aided by foreign aid and private remittances, grew rapidly, while foreign military aid and the growth of a substantial domestic armaments industry increased its military preparedness.

On May 19, 1967, UN peacekeeping forces withdrew from the Egypt-Israel border on the insistence of Egypt's president Gamal Abdel Nasser. Egyptian forces then reoccupied Gaza and closed the Gulf of Aqaba to Israeli shipping. In the Six-Day War, June 5–10, Israel recaptured Gaza, occupied the Sinai Peninsula to the Suez Canal, and captured the West Bank and the Old City of Jerusalem from Jordan and the Golan Heights from Syria. Another UN-supervised cease-fire went into effect.

Egypt and Syria, backed by Soviet airlifts, invaded Israel on Yom Kippur, Oct. 6, 1973. Israel, with strong U.S. support, counterattacked, driving back the Syrian forces and crossing the Suez Canal from the Sinai into Egypt. Fighting ceased on Oct. 24, and a disengagement agreement was signed on Jan. 18, 1974. Israeli forces withdrew from the west bank of the Suez Canal and, following further agreements, withdrew in stages from the Sinai Peninsula, completing the withdrawal in 1982.

The government of Prime Minister Golda Meir fell after the Yom Kippur War, and a new coalition took power. A period of domestic and international difficulties followed, with severe inflation in the economy and a marked rise in Palestinian and other terrorist attacks against Israeli targets. Israeli forces repeatedly attacked Palestinian bases in southern Lebanon and aided the Christian militia forces in the Lebanese civil war of 1975–76. On July 3, 1976, Israeli commandos raided the airport at Entebbe, Uganda, to rescue 103 hostages held by Arab and German hijackers.

The 1977 parliamentary elections brought a conservative coalition to power, with Menachem Begin elected prime minister. Egypt's president Anwar Sadat visited Jerusalem in November 1977, and Begin and Sadat met at a conference with U.S. president Jimmy Carter at Camp David in 1979. On Mar. 26, 1979, Egypt and Israel signed a formal peace treaty ending 30 years of war and establishing diplomatic relations between the two nations.

In July 1980 Israel affirmed the transfer of its national capital from Tel Aviv to Jerusalem and the incorporation of the (formerly Jordanian) Old City into Israeli territory. The Israeli government decided in 1980 to promote increased Jewish settlement in the West Bank, provoking protest from Palestinian leaders.

Israeli forces invaded southern Lebanon in March 1978. After a brief occupation, most Israeli forces withdrew and were replaced by a UN peacekeeping force, but Israel continued to cooperate with Lebanese Christian militia forces in anti-Palestinian operations. Israeli forces again reoccupied southern Lebanon for five days in April 1980.

Israeli and Syrian forces clashed briefly in April 1981. On June 7, 1981, Israeli jets destroyed a nuclear reactor near Baghdad, Iraq, that Israel claimed could have been used to manufacture materials for nuclear weapons. Prime Minister Begin was returned to office in a close election on June 30, 1981, and he retired in 1983.

Attacking Palestine Liberation Organization strongholds in Lebanon in May, 1982, Israel mounted a full-scale invasion of Lebanon on June 6. Israeli and Syrian forces fought in Lebanon's Bekaa Valley on June 9 but disengaged after a few days. On June 14 Israeli forces surrounded and shelled Beirut, forcing the PLO to evacuate the city. On Sept. 14 Israeli forces occupied West Beirut, following the assassination of the newly elected Lebanese president, Bashir Gemayel. Lebanese Christian militia, with tacit Israeli permission, entered two Palestinian refugee camps at Sabra and Shatila on Sept. 16 and massacred hundreds of civilians, provoking an international outcry against Israel's occupation of Lebanon. Israeli forces withdrew from Lebanon in June 1985, except for a narrow "security zone" along the border.

Parliamentary elections in 1984 resulted in a stalemate between the conservative Likud party and the Labor party. A grand-coalition government was formed, with power shared by Likud leader Yitzhak Shamir and Labor leader Shimon Peres.

In December 1987, Palestinian residents of Gaza and the West Bank launched a series of violent demonstrations against Israeli authorities. The *intifada*, or uprising, continued into 1991 in a cycle of protest and police reaction that led to the deaths of hundreds of demonstrators and a crisis of Israeli control in the occupied territories. Tensions were exacerbated by the immigration of hundreds of thousands of Soviet Jews to Israel.

Parliamentary elections in November 1988 continued the Likud-Labor stalemate and brought increased power to the minor religious parties. A new grand-coalition government announced in January 1989, with Yitzhak Shamir as prime minister and Shimon Peres as minister of finance, collapsed in mid-March because of disagreements over an American-backed plan for peace talks with the Palestinians. This plunged the country into a crisis, resolved in June 1990 with the formation of a coalition government of Likud and several right-wing religious parties. Shamir managed to survive several no-confidence votes, and his alliance with the religious party Agudat Israel in November solidified his party's power as the Persian Gulf crisis unfolded.

After months of diplomacy spearheaded by U.S. secretary of state James Baker, direct talks between Israel and a (non-PLO) Jordanian-Palestinian join delegation of representatives opened in Washington in December 1991. Despite a promising beginning, the talks broke down in stalemate as Israel refused to compromise over the key issue of new Jewish settlements on the West Bank. In the election of June 23, 1992, the Labor party led by Yitzhak Rabin scored an upset victory over Shamir's Likud coalition government. Rabin disclosed that the Shamir government had pursued a deliberate policy of intransigence in the peace talks in order to allow the accelerated West Bank settlement program to continue unimpeded.

The Palestinian Intifada gained renewed momentum in December 1992 when Israel deported 400 Palestinians to Lebanon on the grounds that they were responsible for acts of violence. Both the United States and the UN opposed the move, which also impeded the Arab-Israeli peace talks, although the two sides continued to meet over the next six months. During July and August, all hopes for a settlement faded when Israel launched a series of air and land attacks on suspected terrorist bases in Lebanon, resulting in severe fighting and many casualties.

The world was stunned only a few weeks later, when on Sept. 13, 1993, Prime Minister Yithak Rabin and PLO leader Yasir Arafat signed an agreement in principle for a peace settlement based on Palestinian recognition of Israel's right to exist, and Israel's acceptance of at least partial self-rule for the Palestinians. By the spring of 1994, several areas in Gaza and the West Bank were under Palestinian control, while on the regional level, many of Israel's hard-line enemies, including Egypt, Jordan, and Syria began to move toward reconciliation.

(For further details, see Part I: "Major News Stories of the Year.")

Italy

Italian Republic

Geography **Location:** peninsula, extending from southern Europe into Mediterranean Sea, with a number of adjacent islands, principally Sicily to SW, and Sardinia to W. **Boundaries:** Switzerland and Austria to N, Slovenia to NE, Adriatic Sea to E, Ionian Sea to SE, Mediterranean Sea to W, France to NW. **Total land area:** 116,305 sq. mi. (301,230 sq km). **Coastline:** 3,105 mi. (4,996 km). **Comparative area:** slightly larger than Arizona. **Land use:** 32% arable land; 10% permanent crops; 17% meadows and pastures; 22% forest and woodland; 19% other; includes 10% irrigated. **Major cities:** (1993) Roma (Rome; capital) 2,687,881; Milano (Milan) 1,334,171; Napoli (Naples) 1,061,583; Torino (Turin) 945,551; Palermo 694,749.

People **Population:** 58,138,394 (1994 est.). **Nationality:** noun—Italian(s); adjective—Italian. **Ethnic groups:** primarily Italian, but includes small clusters of German-, French-, and Slovene-Italians in north and Albanian-Italians in south; Sicilians. **Languages:** Italian; parts of Trentino-Alto Adige region (e.g., Bolzano) are predominantly German-speaking; significant French-speaking minority in Valle d'Aosta region; Slovene-speaking minority in Trieste-Gorizia area. **Religions:** almost 100% nominally Roman Catholic.

Government **Type:** republic. **Independence:** N.A. **Constitution:** Jan. 1, 1948. **National holiday:** Anniversary of the Republic, June 2. **Heads of government:** Oscar Luigi Scalfaro, president (since May 1992); Lamberto Dini, prime minister (since Jan. 1995). **Structure:** executive—president empowered to dissolve Parliament and call national election; commander of armed forces presides over Supreme Defense Council; otherwise, authority to govern invested in Council of Ministers; bicameral legislature—popularly elected Parliament (315-member Senate, 630-member Chamber of Deputies); judiciary—independent.

Economy **Monetary unit:** lire. **Budget:** (1992 est.) ***income:*** $302 bil.; ***expend.:*** $391 bil. **GDP:** $967.6 bil., $16,700 per capita (1993). **Chief crops:** fruits, wine, vegetables, cereals, potatoes, olives; 95% self-sufficient; food shortages—fats, meat, fish, eggs. **Livestock:** sheep, pigs, cattle, goats, horses. **Natural resources:** mercury, potash, marble, sulfur, dwindling natural gas and crude oil reserves. **Major industries:** machinery and transport equipment, iron, steel, chemicals. **Labor force:** 23.98 mil. (1988); 56.7% services, 37.9% industry, 5.4% agriculture. **Exports:** $178.2 bil. (f.o.b., 1992); textiles, clothing, metals, transport equipment, chemicals. **Imports:** $188.5 bil. (f.o.b., 1992); petroleum, industrial machinery, chemicals, metals, food, agricultural products. **Major trading partners:** ***exports:*** 57% EU, 9% U.S., 4% OPEC; ***imports:*** 57% EU, 6% OPEC, 6% U.S.

Intl. Orgs. EU, FAO, IAEA, IBRD, ICAO, IDA, IFAD, IFC, ILO, IMF, IMO, INTELSAT, INTERPOL, ITU, NATO, OAS (observer), OECD, OSCE, UN, UNESCO, UPU, WHO, WIPO, WMO, WTO.

Rome became the major power in Italy around 500 B.C., dominating the Etruscans in the north and Greek settlements in the south. The Roman Republic already dominated most of the Mediterranean and western Europe by the time imperial rule was established under Julius Caesar. The empire was divided between Rome and Byzantium in the fourth century A.D. The Roman Empire in the west was severely weakened by Germanic invasions in the fifth century and thereafter gradually dissolved, so that Italy became a disunited collection of aristocratic holdings and independent cities.

By the 10th century, the city-states, especially in the north, emerged as major powers, rivaling the Papal States of the central peninsula. Venice and Genoa emerged as major maritime powers during the medieval period, while Florence, Siena, and other cities developed into centers of agricultural and commercial wealth, impelling the successive renaissances of the 12th and 15th centuries. With the rise of the Habsburg empire, the monarchical powers of northern Europe vied for power in Italy, and the peninsula's small states became pawns of France, Spain, and Austria.

At the turn of the 19th century, Napoleon created the short-lived Kingdom of Italy as a French satellite, but after his fall, there was a general return to the old pattern, with Austria dominating the north. Metternich in 1815 called Italy a "geographic expression."

The 19th century saw the spread of revolutionary ideals, accompanied by a growing sense of nationalism in both politics and culture. The revolutionary military leader, Giuseppe Garibaldi, and the statesman, Conte Camillo di Cavour, brought about the establishment of the Kingdom of Italy in 1861. The kingdom wrested Venice away from Austria (1866) and absorbed the Papal States in 1870.

Although united territorially, the kingdom was divided by conflict between church and state, north and south, modern urban industry versus semifeudal rural poverty. Parliamentary politics under the constitutional monarchy created a regime that was weak and venal, inspiring little popular support.

Italy joined the Allied powers in World War I, but its minor gains in the Peace of Paris scarcely seemed to justify its wartime suffering and one million dead. Postwar economic dislocation, fear of communism, and political disillusionment abetted the rise of fascism. Benito Mussolini took over the Italian government at the invitation of the king in 1922 and soon acquired dictatorial powers. Papal secular authority in Vatican City was reestablished by the Lateran Agreement of 1929. In the late 1920s and early 1930s, Italy appeared to be a major power, defending Austria from Germany, colonizing Ethiopia, supporting Francisco Franco in the Spanish civil war, and joining in an "axis" with Hitler's Germany.

Mussolini, the senior partner in the fascist axis, soon was eclipsed by Hitler, and Italy was drawn into the disaster of World War II in 1939. Italy annexed Albania and invaded Greece, but that campaign turned into a fiasco from which German troops had to save the Italian army. In 1943 Allied attacks on Italy began; the fascist Grand Council deposed Mussolini, and the king, Victor Emmanuel III, had him arrested. Hitler intervened in September 1943 and began the war in Italy anew, rescuing Mussolini who established another fascist regime in northern Italy, while the legal Italian government in the south switched sides and welcomed Italy's liberation.

The head of the first postwar government was a Christian Democrat, Alcide de Gasperi. The monarchy was abolished by plebiscite in 1946, and the Republic of Italy was established. The north supported the republic, while monarchism retained significant support in the south.

This division reflected a roughly accurate generalization that sees Italy as comprising a progressive commercial and industrial north and a backward agricultural/pastoral south. Despite such industrial giants of the north as Fiat and Pirelli, however, Italy's manufacturing is primarily carried on by medium-size and small firms, while agriculture is characteristic of the whole country. As late as 1956, there were more Italian workers in agriculture than in industry. Agriculture in the north is generally more prosperous than in the south, with its more arid climate and impoverished soil. Italy is a net food importer.

In the first elections under the republic, in 1948, the Christian Democrats benefited from obvious American patronage and a split in the ranks of the Left to win a clear parliamentary majority. Italy accepted Marshall Plan aid and membership in NATO; reintegration into the European mainstream found expression in membership in the Council of Europe and the Coal and Steel Community.

Domestically, reconstruction was the major task, with both industrial and agricultural output severely hampered by social and physical damage from the war; inflation was rampant and basic social services impaired. The Christian Democrats, normally in Center-Right coalitions in the 1950s and Center-Left coalitions in the 1960s, adopted a policy directed at creating a stable currency, a free market, comprehensive social welfare programs, and occasional state intervention in the economy. This created an Italian "economic miracle," with industrial production doubling between 1953 and 1961 and increasing an additional 40 percent by 1966, led by steel, automobiles, machinery, and electrical equipment.

Since the 1970s the Christian Democrats have gradually declined in political influence, normally gaining less than 40 percent of the popular vote while continuing to provide premiers in often short-lived coalition cabinets. Left-wing terrorism became a major national problem. The Christian Democratic leader and former prime minister Aldo Moro was kidnapped and murdered in 1978, and U.S. Brig. Gen./NATO officer James Dozier was kidnapped (and subsequently rescued) in 1981. The government of Bettino Craxi, Italy's first Socialist premier, was severely shaken after it refused to cooperate with the United States in apprehending and trying the hijackers of the *Achille Lauro* in 1985. Craxi resigned in 1987.

Lacking effective political unity, Italy's coalition governments—there have been more than 50 since the war—tended to muddle along in the face of slow economic growth, inflation, and high unemployment. But awareness of Mafia assassinations and revelations of government corruption far beyond even this tolerant people's expectations led to demands for dramatic changes. In April 1993 the electorate overwhelmingly approved reforms that will change the basic elements of Italian political life. The first elections under the reformed system were held in March 1994, and ended half a century of Christian Democrat–led coalition governments. The Christian Democrats, hastily renamed the Italian Popular Party, won only 11 percent of the vote, while the Socialists, normally the second-largest party, fell to 2 percent. What replaced the old guard was not the early favorite Progressive Alliance, which won 213 seats in the 630-seat Chamber of Deputies, but rather the right-wing Alliance for Freedom. It captured 43 percent of the popular vote, gained a majority (366 seats) in the Chamber, and fell a mere six seats short of a majority in the Senate. In May, wealthy publishing executive Silvio Berlusconi was sworn in as prime minister.

But Berlusconi's government lasted only into December. Political disputes with his Northern League coalition partners, union opposition to his austerity budget, and the announcement that magistrates were investigating charges that he had bribed tax officials weakened his hold on the government. On Dec. 22 he resigned, the day after the Northern League left the coalition.

Rather than call new elections, Italy's president asked Lamberto Dini to form a new "non-party" cabinet of businessmen, judges, and professors, a cabinet that won the requisite votes of confidence in the two chambers by Feb. 1. The new government showed surprising staying power, successfully passing its budget (combining tax hikes and spending cuts) in March and negotiating reform of Italy's bloated pension system with leading trade unions in May. In the same month it even began the politically touchy process of investigating the anticrime magistrates for possible violations of civil rights.

Ivory Coast

Republic of Côte d'Ivoire

Geography **Location:** western coast of Africa. **Boundaries:** Mali and Burkina Faso to N, Ghana to E, Gulf of Guinea to S, Liberia and Guinea to W. **Total land area:** 124,502 sq. mi. (322,460 sq km). **Coastline:** 320 mi. (515 km). **Comparative area:** slightly larger than New Mexico. **Land use:** 9% arable land; 4% permanent crops; 9% meadows and pastures; 26% forest and woodland; 52% other; includes negl. % irrigated. **Major cities:** (1979) Yamoussoukro (capital—not recognized by U.S., which recognizes Abidjan); Abidjan 1,423,323; Bouaké 272,640.

People **Population:** 14,295,501 (1994 est.). **Nationality:** noun—Ivorian(s); adjective—Ivorian. **Ethnic groups:** 23% Baoule, 18% Bete, 15% Senoufou, 11% Malinke and Agni; over 60 ethnic groups; 2 million foreign Africans, mostly Burkinabe; about 130,000–330,000 non-Africans (100,000–300,000 Lebanese, 30,000 French). **Languages:** French (official); over 60 African languages and dialects with Dioula most widely spoken. **Religions:** 63% indigenous beliefs, 25% Muslim, 12% Christian.

Government **Type:** republic. **Independence:** Aug. 7, 1960 (from France). **Constitution:** Nov. 3, 1960. **National holiday:** Dec. 7. **Heads of government:** Henri Konan Bedie, president (since Dec. 1993); Daniel Kablan Duncan, prime minister (since Dec. 1993). **Structure:** executive—president has broad powers; unicameral legislature—175-member National Assembly; judiciary.

Economy **Monetary unit:** Communauté Financière Africaine (CFA) franc. **Budget:** (1990 est.) ***income:*** $2.3 bil.; ***expend.:*** $3.6 bil. **GDP:** $21 bil., $1,500 per capita (1993 est.). **Chief crops:** cash crops—coffee, cocoa, wood, bananas, pineapples, palm oil; food crops—corn, millet, yams, rice; other commodities—cotton, rubber, tobacco. **Livestock:** goats, sheep, cattle, pigs. **Natural resources:** crude oil, diamonds, manganese, iron ore, cobalt. **Major industries:** foodstuffs, wood processing, oil refinery. **Labor force:** (1985) over 85% agriculture, forestry, livestock raising; 11% wage earners, nearly half in agriculture and remainder in government, industry, commerce, and professions; 54% of working age. **Exports:** $2.8 bil. (f.o.b., 1990); 30% cocoa, 20% coffee, 11% tropical woods; cotton, bananas. **Imports:** $1.6 bil. (f.o.b., 1990); 50% manufactured goods and semifinished products, 40% consumer goods, 10% raw materials and fuels. **Major trading partners:** ***exports:*** France, Germany, Netherlands, U.S., Belgium. ***imports:*** France, other EU countries, Nigeria, U.S., Japan.

Intl. Orgs. FAO, G-77, IAEA, IBRD, ICAO, IDA, IFAD, IFC, ILO, IMF, IMO, INTELSAT, INTERPOL, ITU, NAM, UN, UNESCO, UPU, WHO, WIPO, WMO, WTO.

The peoples of the Ivory Coast belong to various tribes that had established small and mutually hostile kingdoms prior to the 18th century. The dominant Baule migrated to the Ivory

Coast from Ghana about 200 years ago. European contact began with the Portuguese, who established coastal trading stations in the 15th century. They were followed in rapid succession by the Dutch, British, and finally the French, who landed at Assinie in 1637. Dense tropical forests and a lack of good harbors retarded European exploration.

France established a protectorate over the coastal zone in 1842 and during the remainder of the 19th century expanded its control, by conquest and diplomacy, into the interior. In 1893 the Ivory Coast was organized as a French colony, and in 1904 it was made part of French West Africa.

France's Vichy government controlled French West Africa during World War II and harshly suppressed the region's growing nationalist movements. In 1946 a group of West African leaders, inspired by Félix Houphouet-Boigny, formed the African Democratic Assembly, which later cooperated with the French in the implementation of reforms, including, by 1956, universal suffrage and the formation of locally autonomous assemblies. Complete independence for the Ivory Coast came on Aug. 4, 1960.

Félix Houphouet-Boigny was unanimously elected the first president of the Ivory Coast and has been repeatedly reelected ever since. He played a key role in forming the Organization of African Unity in 1963. Under his presidency, the Ivory Coast has enjoyed both political stability and economic prosperity. The Ivory Coast maintains strong commercial and cultural ties to France and is on good terms with other Western-bloc nations.

In the country's first multiparty elections since independence, Houphouet-Boigny's Democratic party captured 82 percent of the vote against a single opposition candidate, Laurent Gbagbo. In voting for the legislature, the Democrats won 163 of 175 seats.

The government's commitment to liberalization has been marred by continued civil unrest, and Gbagbo and others were jailed in 1992. With the economy strained by depressed prices for coffee and cocoa and the presence of 250,000 refugees from neighboring Liberia, the government has abandoned economic reforms dictated by the IMF and other foreign lenders.

Jamaica

Geography **Location:** northern Caribbean Sea. Kingston 17°58'N, 76°48'W. **Boundaries:** Cuba 87 mi. (145 km) to N. **Total land area:** 4,243 sq. mi. (10,990 sq km). **Coastline:** 635 mi. (1,022 km). **Comparative area:** between Delaware and Connecticut. **Land use:** 19% arable land; 6% permanent crops; 18% meadows and pastures; 28% forest and woodland; 29% other; includes 3% irrigated. **Major cities:** (1982 census) Kingston (capital) 524,638; Spanish Town 89,097; Montego Bay 70,265.

People **Population:** 2,555,064 (1994 est.). **Nationality:** noun—Jamaican(s); adjective—Jamaican. **Ethnic groups:** 76.3% African, 15.1% Afro-European, 3.4% East Indian and Afro-East Indian, 3.2% white, 2% other. **Languages:** English, Creole. **Religions:** predominantly Protestant (including Anglican and Baptist), some Roman Catholic, some spiritualist cults.

Government **Type:** independent state within Commonwealth, recognizing Elizabeth II as head of state. **Independence:** Aug. 6, 1962 (from UK). **Constitution:** Aug. 6, 1962. **National holiday:** Independence Day, first Monday in August. **Heads of government:** Gov. Gen. Howard F.H. Cooke, governor-general (since Aug. 1991); Percival James Patterson, prime minister (since Apr. 1993). **Structure:** cabinet headed by prime minister; bicameral legislature—21-member Senate (13 nominated by prime minister, eight by opposition leader, if any), 60-member elected House of Representatives; judiciary follows British tradition under chief justice.

Economy **Monetary unit:** Jamaican dollar. **Budget:** (1991 est.) ***income:*** $600 mil.; ***expend.:*** $736 mil. **GDP:** $8 bil., $3,200 per capita 1992 est.). **Chief crops:** sugarcane, citrus fruits, bananas, pimientos, coconuts, coffee, cocoa, tobacco; illegal producer of cannabis for international drug trade. **Livestock:** goats, cattle, pigs, asses, mules, horses, sheep. **Natural resources:** bauxite, gypsum, limestone. **Major industries:** tourism, bauxite mining, textiles. **Labor force:** 1,062,100 (1989); 32% agriculture, 28% industry and commerce, 27% services, 13% government; shortage of technical and managerial personnel; 22% unemployment. **Exports:** $1.1 bil. (f.o.b., 1992); alumina, bauxite, sugar, bananas, citrus fruits and fruit products. **Imports:** $1.5 bil. (f.o.b., 1992); petroleum, machinery, transportation and electrical equipment, food, fertilizer. **Major trading partners:** ***exports:*** 39% U.S., UK, Canada, Trinidad and Tobago; ***imports:*** 51% U.S., Venezuela, UK, Japan, Trinidad and Tobago.

Intl. Orgs. Commonwealth, FAO, G-77, IAEA, IBRD, ICAO, IFAD, IFC, ILO, IMF, IMO, INTERPOL, ITU, NAM, OAS, UN, UNESCO, UPU, WHO, WIPO, WMO, WTO.

Christopher Columbus visited Jamaica in 1494, and the Spanish ruled the island—exterminating the native Arawaks in the process—until it fell to British control in 1655. A haven for buccaneers, by the 18th century Jamaica was a major sugar producer and the site of one of the busiest slave markets in the world. Emancipation of the slaves in 1833 and abolition of tariff protection in 1846 contributed strongly to the subsequent downfall of the plantation economy.

In 1962 the island gained its independence. The country has been plagued by racial and class division set within the context of an underdeveloped economy. Michael Manley of the People's National party became prime minister in 1972. He nationalized some industry and established closer ties with Cuba. Edward Seaga's Jamaica Labour party came to power in 1980 and encouraged more private-sector involvement in developing the economy. Though Manley was reelected to office in 1989, he did not reverse this general trend; in 1992 he was succeeded by Percival James Patterson, who led the People's National party to a landslide victory in violence-marred elections in March 1993.

Japan

Geography **Location:** chain of more than 3,000 islands extending 1,300 mi. (2,200 km) NE to SW between Sea of Japan and western Pacific Ocean; southern Japan about 93 mi. (150 km) E of S. Korea; islands of Hokkaido, Honshu, Shikoku, and Kyushu account for 98% of land area. Tokyo 35°40'N, 139°45'E. **Boundaries:** Sea of Okhotsk to N, Pacific Ocean to E, East China Sea to SW, and Sea of Japan to W. **Total land area:** 145,882 sq. mi. (377,835 sq km). **Coastline:** 8,505 mi. (13,685 km). **Comparative area:** slightly larger than Montana. **Land use:** 11% arable land; 2% permanent crops; 2% meadows and pastures; 68% forest and woodland; 17% other; includes 9% irrigated. **Major cities:** (1993) Tokyo (capital) 7,927,084; Yokohama 3,250,584; Osaka 2,495,275; Nagoya 2,095,393; Sapporo 1,704,135.

People **Population:** 125,106,937 (1994 est.). **Nationality:** noun—Japanese (sing., pl.); adjective—Japanese. **Ethnic groups:** 99.4% Japanese, 0.6% other (mostly Korean). **Languages:** Japanese. **Religions:** most Japanese observe both Shinto and Buddhist rites; about 16% belong to other faiths, including 0.8% Christian.

Government **Type:** constitutional monarchy. **Constitution:** May 3, 1947. **National holiday:** Foundation Day, Feb. 11. **Heads of government:** Akihito, emperor (since Jan. 1989); Tomiichi Murayama, prime minister (since June 1994). **Structure:** emperor is symbol of state; executive power is vested in cabinet appointed by prime minister, chosen by lower house of bicameral, elective legislature—Diet (House of Councillors, House of Representatives); judiciary is independent.

Economy **Monetary unit:** yen. **Budget:** (1993) ***income:*** $490 bil.; ***expend.:*** $579 bil. **GNP:** $2.549 trillion, $20,400 per capita (1993). **Chief crops:** land intensively cultivated; rice, sugar, vegetables, fruits; 71% self-sufficient in food (1985); food shortages—wheat, corn, beans. **Livestock:** chickens, pigs, cattle, goats, sheep. **Natural resources:** negl. mineral resources, fish. **Major industries:** metallurgical and engineering industries, electrical and electronic industries, textiles. **Labor force:** 63.3 mil. (1988); 54% trade and services, 33% manufacturing, mining, and construction; **Exports:** $360.9 bil. (f.o.b., 1993); 97% manufactures (including 38% machinery, 17% motor vehicles, 10% consumer electronics). **Imports:** $240.7 bil. (c.i.f., 1993); 42% manufactures, 30% fossil fuels, 15% foodstuffs, 13% nonfuel raw materials. **Major trading partners:** ***exports:*** 31% U.S., 29% Southeast Asia, 21% Western Europe; ***imports:*** 23% Southeast Asia, 23% U.S., 18% Western Europe, 13% Middle East.

Intl. Orgs. FAO, IAEA, IBRD, ICAO, IDA, IFAD, IFC, ILO, IMF, IMO, INTELSAT, INTERPOL, ITU, UN, UNESCO, UPU, WHO, WIPO, WMO, WTO.

Japan's ancient Jomon civilization was displaced by proto-Japanese Yayoi migrants from mainland northeast Asia beginning in the fourth century B.C. In the early Yayoi period, a mounted military aristocracy dominated rice-growing commoners. The shamanic religion of the time was ancestral to Japan's later indigenous religion, Shinto. Yayoi society evolved into the Yamato protostate, c. A.D. 250–500. The Yamato kings were buried in large, elaborate tomb mounds together with haniwa clay sculptures. From the third century A.D., contact with the mainland increased. Korean missionaries introduced Buddhism and Chinese writing in the mid-sixth century. A centralized monarchy developed in the Yamato Plain, central Honshu Island; Prince Shotoku, a great patron of Buddhism, founded the Horyuji and other great temples in the early seventh century.

In 710 the Yamato kings established a permanent capital for the first time, at Nara; the city was modeled on the contemporary Chinese capital. In 785 the court, split by factionalism and dominated by Nara's large and wealthy Buddhist temples, abandoned the capital; in 794 the new capital at Heian (Kyoto) was completed. The ensuing Heian period was one of the most brilliant in Japanese history. A small civil aristocracy, dominated by the Fujiwara family, drew great wealth from provincial estates and created a metropolitan culture of extreme refinement. From the ninth through the 11th centuries, strong Chinese influences were incorporated into Japanese culture.

In the 12th century the power of the Heian court waned as the influence of the provincial military aristocracy (samurai) grew stronger. In 1156 the capital was seized by the Taira family; in 1185 the Taira were overthrown by their rivals, the Minamoto. The Minamoto established a military government under a shogun (generalissimo) at Kamakura; the emperor remained at Kyoto, stripped of all governmental authority. In Kamakura the Minamoto were soon displaced by their former vassals, the Hojo. During the Kamakura period, the Japanese drew away from Chinese influence in art, architecture, literature, and religion in the process of creating a more distinctively Japanese culture. In 1274 and again in 1281, attempted Mongol invasions were repulsed with the aid of timely typhoons (*kamikaze*, "divine winds").

In the course of a failed attempt at imperial restoration, the Kamakura shogunate was overthrown, in the 1330s, by the Ashikaga family, which in 1338 established a new shogunal government at Muromachi, a precinct of Kyoto. The Muromachi period saw the flowering of a new warrior culture, marked by such military virtues as bravery, loyalty, personal honor, and skill with weapons and by adherence to Zen Buddhism and its associated arts (tea ceremony, flower arranging, calligraphy, etc.). With the Onin Wars of the mid-15th century, the Muromachi shogunate lost most of its power, and the country fell into a century of civil war.

The civil wars were brought to an end during the second half of the 16th century by three successive unifiers, Oda Nobunaga, Hideyoshi, and Tokugawa Ieyasu. At the same time, the Jesuit Francis Xavier and his successors established a short-lived Japanese Christian community. Hideyoshi made several attempts (1592–98) to conquer and annex Korea. In 1601 Tokugawa Ieyasu defeated his rivals in the Battle of Sekigahara. He established a shogunal government at Edo (later Tokyo) in 1603; he and his successors formalized the structure of Japanese feudalism, created a rigid class structure, suppressed Christianity, and enforced the isolation of Japan from virtually all outside influence. Some trade with the mainland and a small Dutch trading station at Nagasaki provided Japan's only windows to the outside world for the next 250 years. The Edo period was marked by urbanization and the development of urban culture (Kabuki theater, woodblock prints, etc.) as the merchant class prospered from internal trade.

The Tokugawa shogun's inability to repel the 1854 visit of American commodore Matthew Perry and subsequently to avoid establishing commercial and diplomatic relations with Western nations deeply shocked the samurai class. Patriotic young samurai from Choshu, Satsuma, and other outlying feudal domains began to call for the abolition of the shogunate and the restoration of imperial rule in order to confront the threat of contact with the West. Quickly realizing that isolationism was doomed, the young radicals' program changed from "respect the emperor, expel the barbarians" to "enrich the state, strengthen the military." With the accession of the Meiji emperor in 1868, shogunal government ended.

Under direct imperial rule, feudalism was abolished and a wide-ranging program of military, industrial, commercial, and social modernization was implemented. The Meiji Constitution of 1889 created a constitutional monarchy and a parliamentary system of government. Having avoided domination by Western nations, Japan itself became an imperialist power. Defeating China in the Sino-Japanese War of 1894–95 and Russia in the Russo-Japanese War of 1904–05, Japan gained a dominant position in Manchuria and in Korea, which became a Japanese colony in 1910.

Under the ineffectual Taisho emperor (reigned 1912–26), parliamentary government flourished. Japan sided with the Allied Powers in World War I, and the Treaty of Versailles advanced Japan's international interests, particularly in China. The general prosperity of the 1920s was threatened by the Tokyo earthquake of 1923, by labor strife, and by a stagnant agricultural economy. Militant right-wing nationalism began to play an important role in domestic politics.

During the international economic depression of the early 1930s, right-wing militants gained the upper hand; they assassinated many moderate political figures. Japan invaded Manchuria in 1931 and established the puppet state of Manchuguo in 1934. An attempted military coup in 1936 failed in its immediate objectives but led to the establishment of martial law, under which the Showa emperor (Hirohito; reigned 1926–89) became a pawn of the ultranationalists. An invasion and military takeover of eastern China in 1937 was seen as the first step in the creation of a "Greater East Asian Co-prosperity Sphere," designed to unite Asia under Japanese control.

In 1940 Japan entered the Tripartite Alliance with Italy and Nazi Germany. Japan occupied French Indochina in June 1941, provoking increased Allied resistance to Japanese imperial ambitions. Gen. Hideki Tojo became prime minister in October 1941 and ordered simultaneous preemptive strikes against Pearl Harbor, the Philippines, and Malaya on Dec. 7–8. By mid-1942, Japan controlled most of Southeast Asia and the western Pacific, but American victories at the Battle of the Coral Sea in May 1942 and the Battle of Midway in June 1942 halted further Japanese expansion. Thereafter, Japanese forces were steadily pushed back in "island-hopping" campaigns in the central Pacific and along the western Pacific rim, and by Allied counterattacks in Burma. Air attacks on Japan itself culminated in the nuclear bombing of Hiroshima and Nagasaki in August 1945.

Following Japan's formal surrender on Sept. 2, 1945, an American army in Japan under Gen. Douglas MacArthur took control of the country. A new constitution was promulgated, relegating the emperor to purely symbolic status, renouncing the use of military force, and guaranteeing the civil rights of citizens. The industrial combines that had lent strength to Japan's empire were partially dismantled. An international tribunal tried many wartime leaders as war criminals in 1948. In 1949 considerable authority was returned to the conservative government of Premier Shigeru Yoshida. Japan served as a base for American forces during the Korean War, 1950–53, greatly accelerating Japan's postwar economic recovery. On Apr. 28, 1952, a peace treaty between Japan and the United States went into effect, ending the Occupation. On Mar. 8, 1954, the two nations signed a mutual defense assistance pact.

Japan was admitted to the United Nations in 1956. The success of Japan's postwar recovery was symbolized by the Tokyo Olympic Games of 1964 and Expo '70 at Osaka. Violent student-protest movements in 1968–69 had no clear political goals and no lasting effect. Politically stable under an unbroken succession of Liberal Democratic party governments, Japan emerged as a major and steadily expanding world industrial power.

In general, Japan has shown reluctance to play an international political role consistent with its vast economic power. From the mid-1970s onward, the balance of trade between Japan and the United States has weighed heavily in Japan's favor, leading to strains in U.S.-Japan relations and American charges that Japan engages in unfair trade practices. In a series of conferences of the noncommunist world's seven leading economic powers in the 1980s, Japan has pledged to take various measures to improve foreign access to Japan's domestic economy. In 1986–87 the Japanese yen appreciated markedly against the U.S. dollar. This had relatively little effect on the balance of trade but led to a marked increase in Japanese economic investment in the United States.

Domestically, Japan in the 1980s enjoyed a very high standard of living, marred by the extremely high cost and relatively low quality of housing, and by underinvestment in the public infrastructure. A real estate boom led prices of commercial property in downtown Tokyo to increase as much as 200-fold in the span of a decade.

Politically, Japan has been essentially a one-party state in the postwar period. National politics centers on factions within the ruling Liberal Democratic party (LDP). The government is run by political professionals operating according to a system of consensus. In recent years this system has started to crumble as widespread corruption has been revealed.

Prime Minister Noboru Takeshita was forced to resign in May 1989 as a result of the so-called Recruit Scandal, involving bribery and corruption of senior LDP figures. His successor, Sousuke Uno, lasted only two months before resigning in a scandal over his sexual conduct. Public opinion turned sharply against the LDP, which lost control of the upper house of the Diet in July 1989 elections; the Socialist party, led by Takako Doi, posted significant gains.

Uno's successor, Toshiki Kaifu, expected to be a mere caretaker, emerged as an unexpectedly skillful leader who enhanced Japan's international reputation by offering aid to Eastern Europe and the Soviet Union, and by pledging billions of dollars to support the Persian Gulf War. However, in October 1991 Kaifu was replaced as LDP chairman by a more experienced politician, Kiichi Miyazawa.

Miyazawa's regime was plagued by several political financial scandals and by the near-collapse of the Japanese stock and property markets. Nevertheless, in June 1992 Miyazawa won a significant parliamentary victory with the passage of legislation authorizing the posting abroad of Japanese troops—for the first time since World War II—for peacekeeping missions in noncombat roles.

Ineffectual government countermeasures could not stop the economic slump (1992–93) from threatening the financial health of many of Japan's largest banks, insurance companies, and brokerage houses. Under foreign pressure, the yen was allowed to rise in value, gaining over 15 percent against the dollar in the early months of 1993 and making Japan's exports more expensive abroad. Trade relations between Japan and the United States grew more acrimonious as Japan's trade surplus failed to shrink significantly despite the stronger yen.

Political scandals continued to rock the LDP throughout 1992 and 1993. In August 1992 LDP vice president and "kingmaker" Shin Kanemaru was forced to resign after admitting he had taken bribes. The circle of corruption widened throughout the year, as many top officials admitted ties to organized crime. In June 1993 the LDP lost a legislative vote of no confidence, and politicians left the party in droves, forming a new organization called the Renaissance party. Finally, in parliamentary elections held in July, the LDP was turned out of office for the first time in 38 years.

In the ensuing year, two different coalition governments attempted to rule Japan, both with disastrous results. In April 1994 Morihiro Hosokawa, the leader of a seven-party coalition made up of ex–Liberal Democrats as well as Socialist and Conservatives, abruptly resigned after being linked to yet another series of financial scandals. His successor, Tsutomu Hata, lasted only two months, as the Socialist party left the coalition the same day Hata was elevated to prime minister. The conservative LDP returned to power in June 1994 when it forged an alliance with the Socialist party and elected Socialist candidate Tomiichi Murayama as prime minister.

The unprecedented coalition managed to carry mild political and tax reform bills through the Diet and to survive a "no confidence" vote in June 1995. Japanese attention was directed more to the May 20 nerve gas attack in Tokyo's subway that killed 12 and injured more than 5,000; by May 15 police had arrested Shoko Asahara, leader of the apocalyptic cult Aum Shinrikyo, and 40 others, on charges of murder and attempted murder. (For further details, see Part I: "Major News Stories of the Year.")

Jordan

Hashemite Kingdom of Jordan

Geography Location: western Asia. **Boundaries:** Syria to N, Iraq to NE, Saudi Arabia to SE, Israel to W. **Total land area:** 34,445 sq. mi. (89,213 sq km). **Coastline:** 16 mi. (26 km). **Comparative area:** between Indiana and Kentucky. **Land use:** 4% arable land; 0.5% permanent crops; 1% meadows and pastures; 0.5% forest and woodland; 94% other; includes 0.5% irrigated. **Major cities:** (1991) Amman (capital) 965,000; Zarqa 359,000; Irbid 216,000; Russeita 115,500.

People Population: 3,961,194 (1994 est.). **Nationality:** noun—Jordanian(s); adjective—Jordanian. **Ethnic groups:** 98% Arab, 1% Circassian, 1% Armenian. **Languages:** Arabic (official); English widely understood among upper and middle classes. **Religions:** 95% Sunni Muslim, 5% Christian.

Government Type: constitutional monarchy. **Independence:** May 25, 1946 (from League of Nations Mandate under British administration). **Constitution:** Jan. 8, 1952. **National holiday:** Independence Day, May 25. **Heads of government:** Hussein ibn Talal, king (since Aug. 1952); Sherif Zeid Bin Shaker, prime minister (since Jan. 1995). **Structure:** king holds balance of power; prime minister exercises executive authority in name of king; cabinet appointed by king and responsible to Parliament; bicameral Parliament with House of Representatives, dissolved by king in Feb. 1976 and reconvened Jan. 1984, following national elections; Senate last appointed by king in Jan. 1984; secular court system based on differing legal systems of former Transjordan and Palestine; law western in concept and structure; Sharia (religious) courts for Muslims, and religious community council courts for non-Muslim communities; desert police carry out quasi-judicial functions in desert areas.

Economy Monetary unit: Jordanian dinar. **Budget:** (1992 est.) ***income:*** $1.7 bil.; ***expend.:*** $1.9 bil. **GDP:** $11.5 bil., $3,000 per capita (1993 est.). **Chief crops:** vegetables, fruits, olive oil, wheat; self-sufficient in only a few foodstuffs. **Livestock:** poultry, goats, sheep, cattle, camels. **Natural resources:** phosphates, potash, shale oil. **Major industries:** phosphate mining, petroleum refining, cement. **Labor force:** 600,000 (1992); 20% agriculture, 20% mining and manufacturing. **Exports:** $1.4 bil. (f.o.b., 1993 est.); fruits, vegetables, phosphates, fertilizers. **Imports:** $3.2 bil. (c.i.f., 1993 est.); crude oil, textiles, capital goods, motor vehicles, foodstuffs. **Major trading partners:** ***exports:*** Iraq, Saudi Arabia, India, Kuwait, Japan, China, Yugoslavia, Indonesia; ***imports:*** EC, U.S., Saudi Arabia, Japan, Turkey, Romania, China, Taiwan.

Intl. Orgs. Arab League, FAO, G-77, IAEA, IBRD, ICAO, IDA, IFAD, IFC, ILO, IMF, IMO, INTELSAT, INTERPOL, ITU, NAM, UN, UNESCO, UPU, WHO, WIPO, WMO.

The present territory of the Kingdom of Jordan corresponds to the biblical lands of Edom, Gilead, and Moab. The ancient rock city of Petra was the capital of the Edomite and Nabataean kingdoms. The region was incorporated into the Roman Empire, and later the Latin Kingdom of Jerusalem; it was an important early center of Christianity.

In the 630s Jordan became one of the first areas outside Arabia to fall to the expansion of Islam. It became subject to the Caliphate, located at Damascus and later at Baghdad, and in the 11th century became part of the empire of the Seljuk Turks. The Crusades brought European invaders, but with little lasting impact. The Mongols conquered Jordan in the mid-13th century, and it later passed into the control of the Mamluk sultanate. In 1517 Jordan was incorporated into the Ottoman Empire.

Following the post–World War I breakup of the Ottoman Empire, Jordan came under British control as part of a League of Nations Mandate of Palestine. In 1921 Great Britain sponsored the establishment of a monarchy by Abdullah, son of Hussein ibn Ali, ruler of the Hejaz in Arabia. Britain recognized the independence of the Hashemite Kingdom of Transjordan in 1923; a 1928 treaty gave Britain the unrestricted right to station troops in the kingdom.

Transjordan supported the Allies in World War II and was rewarded with full independence in 1946, though, by treaty, strong military ties to Great Britain were maintained. In 1948 the kingdom joined the Arab League, changed its name to Jordan, and joined other

Arab states in the first Arab-Israeli War. The war resulted in the occupation by Jordanian troops of the West Bank and the Old City of Jerusalem, which were annexed in 1950.

The present ruler, King Hussein I, came to the throne on Aug. 11, 1952. All British military forces were withdrawn from the kingdom in 1957.

Israel recaptured the West Bank and the Old City of Jerusalem in the Six-Day War of 1967, and large numbers of Palestinian refugees fled to Jordan. Jordan played no substantial role in the October 1974 Arab-Israeli War. In 1974 Jordan accepted the decision of an Arab summit conference designating the Palestine Liberation Organization the sole representative of Palestinians in the West Bank. Jordan's role as a front-line opponent of Israel has won it a large annual subvention from Arab oil states; King Hussein's reputation as an Arab moderate has led to significant American economic and military support.

King Hussein strongly opposed the 1979 Camp David Accords and the Egypt-Israeli peace treaty; Jordan broke off diplomatic relations with Egypt in March 1979 but resumed full relations in 1984.

In July 1971 King Hussein, charging the Palestine Liberation Organization with subversion, had forced withdrawal of PLO troops and political headquarters from Jordan. While some hoped that Hussein would represent the Palestinians in talks with Israel, in 1988 the king flatly rejected any such role, implied that the PLO should declare an independent state on the West Bank and in the Gaza Strip, and declared that any future settlement would require direct talks between Israel and the PLO.

The Persian Gulf War had a drastic impact on Jordan's economy. King Hussein actively backed Iraq, thus jeopardizing direct aid from Kuwait and Saudi Arabia. But the historic peace treaty signed with Israel in October 1994 restored Hussein's standing while returning territory taken in the 1967 war.

Kazakhstan

Republic of Kazakhstan

Geography **Location:** central Asia. **Boundaries:** Russian Federation to N and NE, China to SE, Kyrgystan, Uzbekistan, and Turkmenistan to S, Caspian Sea to W. **Total land area:** 1,049,151 sq. mi. (2,717,300 sq km). **Coastline:** 1,441 mi. (2,320 km) on Caspian Sea. **Comparative area:** almost twice the size of Alaska. **Land use:** 13% cropland; 57% permanent pasture; 3% forest and woodland; 27% other (mainly mountain and desert). **Major cities:** (1990) Almaty (formerly Alma-Ata) 1,151,300; Karaganda 613,000; Chimkent 401,000.

People **Population:** 17,267,554 (1994 est.). **Nationality:** noun—Kazakh(s); adjective—Kazakh. **Ethnic groups:** 39.7% Kazakh, 37.8% Russian, 5.8% German, 5.4% Ukrainian, Tatar, Uighur, Korean. **Languages:** Kazakh (official), member of Central Turkic group written in Cyrillic script since 1940; Russian, ethnic languages. **Religions:** Muslim—Sunni; Christian—Eastern Orthodox.

Government **Type:** republic. **Independence:** declared on Dec. 16, 1991 (from USSR). **Constitution:** being drafted. **National holiday:** Dec. 16, Day of the Republic. **Heads of government:** Nursultan A. Nazarbayev, president (since Dec. 1991); Akezhan Magzhan Kazhegeldin, prime minister (since Oct. 1994). **Structure:** executive—president, vice president, Council of Ministers; legislative—Supreme Soviet (360 deputies); judicial—Supreme Court.

Economy **Monetary unit:** tenge. **Budget:** N.A. ***income:*** N.A.; ***expend.:*** N.A. **GDP:** $60.3 bil., $3,510 per capita (1993 est.). **Chief crops:** grains, potatoes, vegetables, sugar beets. **Livestock:** sheep and goats, cattle, pigs. **Natural resources:** coal, iron ore, lead, zinc, copper, petroleum and natural gas. **Major industries:** electric power, rolled ferrous metals, plastics, textiles, food processing. **Labor force:** 8,267,000 (1989). **Exports:** $1.3 bil. outside the former USSR (1993); oil, ferrous and nonferrous metals, chemicals, grain, wool. **Imports:** $358.3 mil. outside the former USSR (1993); machinery and parts, industrial metals. **Major trading partners:** other former Soviet republics, China.

Intl. Orgs. CIS, IMF, OSCE, UN, UNCTAD, UNESCO, World Bank.

Kazakhstan, the largest nation in central Asia, is a land of deserts and plateaus stretching across the rolling tablelands of the Eurasian landmass; approximately 20 percent is mountainous. The Kazakhs are descended from Mongol and Turkic tribes who settled in the area known as Kazakhstan about the 1st century B.C. In the sixth century A.D. the area formed part of the Turkish Khaganate, a loose federation of nomadic tribes, and in the seventh to ninth centuries Islam became established among the settled population. Although the Mongols ruled the area from 1219 to 1447, the Turkish subjects of the Mongol Horde were to play a decisive role in the future of the region.

In the 15th century, the Kazakhs emerged as a distinct people, but by the 17th century, due to internecine fighting, the Kazakhs split into three nomadic federations, known as the Larger, the Middle, and the Lesser Hordes. In the mid-17th century, the Mongols began to invade the region, and the Kazakhs, not being unified enough to repel them, sought protection from the Russians. By the mid-18th century, the Kazakh lands were completely under Russian control. With the freeing of serfs in 1861 in Russia, Kazakhstan experienced its first major influx of Russian and Ukrainian peasants, who were given Kazakh lands. Resentment over this grew until the Kazakhs rebelled against Russian rule in 1916. The Russians brutally repressed the uprising, but not before thousands of Kazakhs and many Russians were killed.

After the 1917 Communist revolution in Russia, a civil war ensued in Kazakhstan, from which the Bolsheviks emerged victorious. The Kazakh territory was incorporated into Russia in 1920, it was granted "autonomous" status in 1925, and in 1936 it formally became one of the USSR's union republics. Kazakhstan benefited from Soviet rule in that it became industrialized, but it also suffered enormously from the USSR's many economic and social programs. In the 1930s, the traditionally nomadic Kazakh people were forcibly settled on collectivized farms, and more than a million died of starvation as a result. In the 1950s, Nikita Khrushchev's failed "Virgin Lands" scheme and the Soviet government's repeated nuclear tests wreaked environmental havoc on Kazakhstan. As a result of years of Soviet economic development programs, the rate of Russian and Ukrainian immigration into Kazakhstan greatly increased. By 1979, 41 percent of Kazakhstan's population was Russian, as opposed to the 36 percent of native Kazakhs.

Under Mikhail Gorbachev's policy of glasnost, or openness, in the 1980s, the corrupt Communist party leader of Kazakhstan and Brezhnev crony Dinmukhamed Kunayev was deposed. He was ultimately replaced by Nursultan Nazarbayev, an ethnic Kazakh, who was elected in April 1990 to the newly formed post of president of Kazakhstan.

Kazakhstan declared its sovereignty in March 1991, and joined the Commonwealth of Independent States in December 1991. Although Kazakhstan held presidential elections in December 1991, Nazarbayev was the only candidate, since his government required opposition candidates to collect 100,000 signatures in a short time. The country's first post-communist parliamentary elections, held Mar. 7, 1994, replaced the 360-member Supreme Soviet with a new body of 177 full-time deputies. However, international observers invited by the president to monitor the elections declare they were marred by the fact that nearly one-fourth of the deputies had to be chosen from a list submitted by the president, and several other candidates were prevented from running. In all, Nazarbayev's supporters garnered close to two-thirds of the seats in Parliament, and limited the opposition to about 30 seats. In March 1995 Nazarbayev, dissatisfied with the slow pace of reform, dissolved Parliament, ruling by decree until new elections are held.

About 1,400 nuclear missiles are still located in Kazakhstan, but the government appears eager to dismantle them under Russian and U.S. auspices.

Kazakhstan's future looks extremely promising because of its enormous untapped reserves of gas and oil (perhaps 25 billion barrels) that have convinced several global corporations to negotiate with the government for rights.

Kenya

Republic of Kenya

Geography **Location:** eastern Africa. **Boundaries:** Sudan to NW, Ethiopia to N, Somalia to E, Indian Ocean to SE, Tanzania to SW, Lake

Victoria, Uganda to W. **Total land area:** 224,962 sq. mi. (582,650 sq km). **Coastline:** 333 mi. (536 km). **Comparative area:** between California and Texas. **Land use:** 3% arable land; 1% permanent crops; 7% meadows and pastures; 4% forest and woodland; 85% other; includes negl. % irrigated. **Major cities:** (1985 est.) Nairobi (capital) 1,162,189; Mombasa 442,369; (1969) Nakuru 47,151; Kisumu 32,431; Thika 18,387.

People Population: 28,240,658 (1994 est.). **Nationality:** noun—Kenyan(s); adjective—Kenyan. **Ethnic groups:** 21% Kikuyu, 14% Luhya, 13% Luo, 11% Kalenjin, 11% Kamba, 6% Kisii, 6% Meru, 1% Asian, European, Arab; 17% other. **Languages:** English and Swahili (both official), indigenous languages. **Religions:** 38% Protestant, 28% Catholic, 26% indigenous beliefs, 6% Muslim, 2% other.

Government Type: republic within Commonwealth. **Independence:** Dec. 12, 1963 (from UK). **Constitution:** Dec. 12, 1963. **National holiday:** Jamhuri Day, Dec. 12. **Head of government:** Daniel T. arap Moi, president (since Oct. 1978). **Structure:** executive—president and cabinet; legislative—unicameral National Assembly of 200 seats, 188 elected by constituencies and 12 appointed by president; judiciary—high court, with chief justice and at least 11 justices, has unlimited original jurisdiction to hear and determine any civil or criminal proceeding; provision for courts of appeal.

Economy Monetary unit: Kenyan shilling. **Budget:** (1990) ***income:*** $2.4 bil.; ***expend.:*** $2.8 bil. **GDP:** $33.2 bil., $1,200 per capita (1993 est.). **Chief crops:** cash crops—coffee, tea, sisal, pyrethrum, cotton; food crops—corn, wheat, sugarcane, rice, cassava; largely self-sufficient in food; an illegal producer of cannabis for international drug trade. **Livestock:** cattle, goats, sheep, camels, pigs. **Natural resources:** gold, limestone, salt barytes, magnesite. **Major industries:** small-scale consumer goods (plastic, furniture, batteries, textiles, soap, cigarettes, flour), agricultural processing, oil refining. **Labor force:** 9.2 mil. (1987); 50% public sector, 18% industry and commerce, 17% agriculture, 13% services; 1.1 mil. wage earners; 45% of population of working age. **Exports:** $1.0 bil. (f.o.b., 1992 est.); 25% tea, 21% coffee, 7% petroleum products (1989). **Imports:** $1.6 bil. (f.o.b., 1992 est.); 29% machinery and transport equipment, 15% petroleum and petroleum products, 7% iron and steel (1989 est.) **Major trading partners:** (1988) ***exports:*** 45% Western Europe, 22% Africa, 10% Far East, 4% U.S., 3% Middle East; ***imports:*** 49% Western Europe, 12% Middle East, 11% Far East, 5% U.S.

Intl. Orgs. Commonwealth, FAO, G-77, IAEA, IBRD, ICAO, IDA, IFAD, IFC, ILO, IMF, IMO, INTELSAT, INTERPOL, ITU, NAM, UN, UNESCO, UPU, WHO, WIPO, WMO, WTO.

Kenya formed part of an ancient network of trade between the Red Sea and the coast of East Africa as early as the fourth century B.C. Persian and Arab trading posts were established on the coast by the eighth century A.D. At about the same time, the indigenous Cushitic people of Kenya had been joined by Bantu and Nilotic immigrants. Swahili, a mixture of Bantu and Arabic, developed as a language of trade throughout the region.

Portuguese explorers reached Kenya in 1498. Portuguese control of the coastal area ended in 1729, when the region came under the control of the sultans of Oman. British adventurers explored Kenya in the late 19th century. In 1885 the Berlin Conference divided East Africa into European spheres of influence. The British East Africa Company established a protectorate over the coastal region in 1890 and extended its control into the interior in 1895. British settlers established farms, mission stations, and towns, and Kenya was given colonial status in 1920.

During World War II, northern Kenya was briefly occupied by troops from the Italian colony of Ethiopia. After the British reasserted control, Africans were granted the right to participate in local government in 1944.

From 1952 to 1959, a state of emergency was declared in Kenya because of the "Mau Mau" rebellion against British colonial rule. In response to local unrest, British authorities widened African participation in government and Africans were elected to the Legislative Council in 1957.

Kenya became independent on Dec. 12, 1963, and in 1964 assumed the status of a republic within the British Commonwealth. Jomo Kenyatta, a member of the dominant Kikuyu population and leader of the main political party, the Kenya African National Union (KANU), was elected Kenya's first president. The minority Kenya African Democratic Union (KADU) voluntarily amalgamated itself with KANU in 1964. A leftist party, the Kenya People's Union (KPU) was organized in 1966, led by Oginga Odinga. In 1969 it was implicated in the assassination of Tom Mboya, a prominent political leader; its leaders were imprisoned and the party dissolved. Since 1969 KANU has been Kenya's sole political party.

Kenyatta died on Aug. 22, 1978, and Vice Pres. Daniel arap Moi succeeded him. In 1982 the constitution was amended to make Kenya a one-party state. Moi was reelected president in 1983 and again in 1988, the latter being the first election conducted without secret ballots. In recent years foreign observers have accused the Moi government of widespread human rights abuses. Riots broke out in several cities in 1991, and sporadic ethnic violence since then has cost thousands of lives.

In 1991, Odinga formed the opposition Forum for the Restoration of Democracy (FORD), in direct defiance of the government. With Western aid conditioned not only on economic reform but political pluralism and an improved human rights record, presidential elections were held in December 1992. The opposition split, and Moi was returned to office for a fourth time. KANU took 96 seats in the national assembly, followed by FORD-Asili (31), FORD-Kenya (31), and the Democratic party (29).

Although Kenya was viewed by many as the success story of postcolonial Africa, by the 1990s overpopulation, widespread government corruption, and economic and industrial inefficiency had taken a heavy toll. Tourism has fallen 25 percent due to the rise in violence, and the economy is further strained by the presence of many refugees from Ethiopia, Somalia, and Sudan.

Early in 1994 the government announced reforms aimed at restoring confidence in the economy, including lifting the restrictions on foreign investment.

Kiribati

Republic of Kiribati

Geography Location: 33 atolls, in three main groups (E to W: Line Is., Phoenix Is., Gilbert Is.) in mid-Pacific Ocean; about 2,400 mi. (3,870 km) E to W and 1,275 mi. (2,050 km) N to S. Tarawa (Gilberts) 1°30'N, 173°00'E. **Boundaries:** surrounded by Pacific Ocean; nearest neighbors are Nauru to W, and Tuvalu and Tokelau to S. **Total land area:** 277 sq. mi. (717 sq km). **Coastline:** 710 mi. (1,143 km). **Comparative area:** about five times size of Washington, D.C. **Land use:** 0% arable land; 51% permanent crops; 0% meadows and pastures; 3% forest and woodland; 46% other. **Major cities:** (1990 census) Tarawa (capital) 25,154.

People Population: 77,853 (1994 est.). **Nationality:** noun—Kiribatian(s); adjective—Kiribati. **Ethnic groups:** Micronesian. **Languages:** English (official), Gilbertese. **Religions:** 48% Roman Catholic, 45% Protestant (Congregational), some Seventh-Day Adventist and Baha'i.

Government Type: republic. **Independence:** July 12, 1979 (from UK). **Constitution:** July 12, 1979. **National holiday:** none. **Head of government:** Ieremia T. Tabai, president (since July 1979). **Structure:** nationally elected president; unicameral legislature—National Assembly (composed of 39 elected members and one nominated representative of Banaban community).

Economy Monetary unit: Australian dollar. **Budget:** (1990 est.) ***income:*** $29.9 mil.; ***expend.:*** $16.3 mil. **GDP:** $36.8 mil., $525 per capita (1990). **Chief crops:** coconuts, copra; subsistence crops of roots and tubers, vegetables, melons, bananas; pigs and chickens; domestic fishing. **Livestock:** chickens, pigs. **Natural resources:** phosphate (production discontinued in 1979). **Major industries:** fishing and handicrafts. **Labor force:** 7,870 economically active (1985 est.). **Exports:** $4.2 mil. (f.o.b., 1992 est.); 55% fish, 42% copra. **Imports:** $33.1 mil. (c.i.f., 1992 est.); foodstuffs, fuel, transportation equipment. **Major trading partners:** (1985) ***exports:*** 20% EU, 12% Marshall Islands, 8% U.S., 4% American Samoa; ***imports:*** 39% Australia, 21% Japan, 6% New Zealand, 6% UK, 3% U.S.

Intl. Orgs. Commonwealth, ICAO, IMF, WHO.

In 1892 the British established a protectorate over the Gilbert Islands, inhabited principally by Micronesians. In 1915 Britain joined the islands administratively with the Polynesian-speaking Ellice Islands to the south to form a British colony, the Gilbert and Ellice Islands (later expanded to include other islands). The Japanese occupied the Gilberts in 1942; in 1943 the Allied forces recaptured them, and Tarawa was the scene of some of the fiercest combat in the Pacific.

In 1971 Britain granted the colony self-rule. The Ellice Islands broke away in 1975, becoming the independent nation of Tuvalu in 1978. On July 12, 1979, the Gilbert Islands became independent as Kiribati. United States claims to portions of the Line and Phoenix islands were settled by a friendship treaty in 1979.

Kiribati's economy is based on subsistence farming and on fishing. Copra exports and the sale of fishing rights (principally to Japan) are the main earners of hard currency. The islands remain heavily dependent on foreign aid, principally from the United Kingdom.

Korea, North

Democratic People's Republic of Korea

Geography **Location:** northern part of Korean peninsula in eastern Asia. **Boundaries:** China to NW, Sea of Japan to E, Republic of Korea to S, Yellow Sea to SW. **Total land area:** 46,541 sq. mi. (120,540 sq km). **Coastline:** 1,551 mi. (2,495 km). **Comparative area:** between Pennsylvania and Mississippi. **Land use:** 18% arable land; 1% permanent crops; negl. % meadows and pastures; 74% forest and woodland; 7% other; includes 9% irrigated. **Major cities:** (1986 est.) Pyongyang (capital) 2,000,000; Hamhung 670,000; Chongjin 530,000; Sinuju 330,000; Kaesong 310,000.

People **Population:** 23,066,573 (1994 est.). **Nationality:** noun—Korean(s); adjective—Korean. **Ethnic groups:** racially homogeneous. **Languages:** Korean. **Religions:** Buddhism and Confucianism; religious activities now almost nonexistent.

Government **Type:** communist state; one-man rule. **Constitution:** adopted 1948, revised Dec. 27, 1972. **National holiday:** Sept. 9. **Heads of government:** Kim Il Jong, president (since Oct. 1994); Kang Song San, prime minister (since Dec. 1992). **Structure:** Supreme People's Assembly theoretically supervises legislative and judicial functions; State Administration Council (cabinet) oversees ministerial operations.

Economy **Monetary unit:** won. **Budget:** (1992) ***income:*** $19.3 bil.; ***expend.:*** $19.3 bil.; **GNP:** $22 bil., $1,000 per capita (1992 est.). **Chief crops:** corn, rice, vegetables; food shortages—meat, fish, cooking oils; production of foodstuffs adequate for domestic needs. **Livestock:** pigs, cattle, sheep, goats, horses. **Natural resources:** coal, lead, tungsten, zinc, graphite. **Major industries:** machine building, military products, electric power, chemicals. **Labor force:** 9.615 mil. (1987); 48% agricultural, 52% nonagricultural; shortage of skilled and unskilled labor. **Exports:** $1.3 bil. (f.o.b., 1992 est.); minerals, metallurgical products, agricultural products, manufactures. **Imports:** $1.9 bil. (f.o.b., 1992 est.); petroleum, machinery and equipment, coking coal, grain. **Major trading partners:** ***exports:*** former USSR, China, Japan, Germany, Hong Kong, Singapore; ***imports:*** former USSR, Japan, China, Germany, Hong Kong, Singapore.

Intl. Orgs. FAO, G-77, IAEA, ICAO, IMF (observer), ITU, NAM, UNCTAD, UNESCO, UPU, WHO, WIPO, WMO; official observer status at UN.

(For pre-1945 history, see "Republic of Korea.")

The Soviet Union's declaration of war against Japan in the waning days of World War II strengthened its position in northeast Asia, and particularly in Korea. After Japan's surrender, Korea was arbitrarily divided into zones of Soviet and American occupation, north and south of latitude 38° north. The Korean Communist party (KCP), founded in 1922, had functioned in exile in the USSR during the Japanese occupation, and KCP workers were quickly moved into the Soviet zone in 1945.

U.S.-Soviet talks aimed at Korean reunification broke down, and in 1948 the establishment of separate regimes in North and South Korea formalized the postwar occupation zones. The Korean Democratic People's Republic was proclaimed on May 1, 1948, and its government was organized in September of that year. It inherited most of the industrial and hydroelectric power infrastructure built during the Japanese colonial period and enjoyed strong Soviet backing.

On June 25, 1950, North Korean troops crossed the 38th parallel in an effort to force the reunification of Korea under a communist regime. UN troops under American leadership came to the defense of the South. (For the Korean War, see "South Korea.") The war was fought to a stalemate, and a truce was signed on July 27, 1953.

North Korea has had a single leader throughout its national history: Kim Il Sung, chairman of the KCP since 1945 and president of the DPRK since 1972. Under Kim Il Sung, North Korea has been a typically Stalinist Soviet nation, concentrating its economic energies on heavy industry and imposing a strictly regimented political and social life on its citizens. Economic development has been strongly supported by aid from the Soviet Union and, to a lesser degree, China. After an impressive program of postwar reconstruction in the 1950s and 1960s, the country fell into economic stagnation.

Relations between North and South Korea have been implacably hostile; the North has made numerous attempts to infiltrate and sabotage the South. In 1983, 17 people, including four South Korean cabinet ministers, were killed in Rangoon, Burma, by a bomb planted by North Korean agents. Since 1985, occasional North-South discussions on such matters as permitting contacts between families divided by the war have produced little result. North Korea originally agreed to cosponsor the 1988 Summer Olympics with South Korea but later boycotted the games. In 1990 the leaders of both countries held three cordial but unproductive meetings.

Much of the goodwill accumulated by these gestures has been greatly harmed by the continuous assertions of the United States and others that North Korea was building, or intended to build, nuclear weapons at a facility the government insists is designed only for peaceful purposes.

In August 1992, China, North Korea's long-term ally and ideological brother, established diplomatic relations with South Korea, leaving North Korea completely isolated. High-level contacts between North and South Korea continued, but reconciliation talks stalled in 1993 as the issue of North Korean nuclear weapons came to the fore. North Korean leaders refused to allow international arms inspectors access to some facilities and withdrew from the Nuclear Non-Proliferation Treaty. North Korea faced international isolation as a result, so it agreed to limited inspections in 1994, only to retreat from that concession shortly thereafter. In June 1994 former U.S. president Jimmy Carter met with Kim Il Sung and arranged for a summit meeting with South Korea and for another with Pres. Clinton to resolve the nuclear weapons issue. Kim Il Sung's sudden death in July prevented immediate progress, but in October an agreement was reached that called for North Korea to dismantle its current nuclear facilities in exchange for two new reactors from which weapons-grade plutonium is hard to extract. Talks, however, continued through early 1995 without a signed treaty.

Korea, South

Republic of Korea

Geography **Location:** southern part of Korean peninsula in eastern Asia. **Boundaries:** North Korea to N, separated by frontier roughly following 38th parallel; Sea of Japan to E, East China Sea to S, and Yellow Sea to W. **Total land area:** 38,023 sq. mi. (98,480 sq km). **Coastline:** 1,500 mi. (2,413 km). **Comparative area:** between Indiana and Kentucky. **Land use:** 21% arable land; 1% permanent crops; 1% meadows and pastures; 67% forest and woodland; 10% other; includes 12% irrigated. **Major cities:** (1991 census est.) Seoul (capital) 10,627,790; Pusan 3,797,566; Taegu 2,228,843; Inchon 1,818,293; Kwangju 1,144,695.

People **Population:** 45,082,880 (1994 est.). **Nationality:** noun—Korean(s); adjective—Korean. **Ethnic groups:** homogeneous; small Chinese minority (about 20,000). **Languages:** Korean; English widely taught in high school. **Religions:** strong Confucian tradition; vigorous Christian minority (28% of total population); Buddhism; pervasive folk religion (shamanism); Chondokyo (religion of the heavenly way), eclectic religion with nationalist overtones founded in 19th century, claiming about 1.5 mil. adherents.

Government **Type:** republic; power centralized in strong executive. **Constitution:** approved by voters on Oct. 27, 1987, effective Feb. 25, 1988; requires direct presidential elections and protects human rights. **National holiday:** Independence Day, Aug. 15. **Heads of government:** Kim Young-Sam, president (since Feb. 1993); Hong-Koo Lee, prime minister (since Dec. 1994). **Structure:** unicameral legislature (National Assembly), judiciary.

Economy Monetary unit: won. **Budget:** (1993) ***income:*** $48.4 bil.; ***expend.:*** $48.4 bil. **GNP:** $242 bil., $9,500 per capita (1993 est.). **Chief crops:** 9 mil. people (22% of population) live in farm households, but agriculture, forestry, and fishing constitute 15% of GNP; main crops—rice, barley, vegetables, legumes. **Livestock:** chickens, pigs, cattle, ducks, rabbits. **Natural resources:** coal (limited), tungsten, graphite, molybdenum. **Major industries:** textiles and clothing, footwear, food processing. **Labor force:** 20 mil. (1991); 52% services and other, 21% agriculture, fishing, and forestry; 3% unemployment. **Exports:** $81 bil. (f.o.b., 1993); textiles and clothing, electronic and electrical equipment, electrical machinery, footwear, steel, automobiles. **Imports:** $78.9 bil. (c.i.f., 1993); machinery, electronics and electronic equipment, oil, steel, transport equipment, textiles. **Major trading partners:** ***exports:*** 30% U.S., 19% Japan; ***imports:*** 27% Japan, 24% U.S.

Intl. Orgs. Colombo Plan, FAO, G-77, IAEA, IBRD, ICAO, IDA, IFAD, IFC, IMF, IMO, INTELSAT, INTERPOL, ITU, UN, UNCTAD, UNDP, UNESCO, UNICEF, UNIDO, UPU, WHO, WIPO, WMO, WTO.

From ancient times Korea has struggled successfully to preserve its national independence. To the native culture—marked by a warrior aristocracy, shamanic religion, and a subject class of rice cultivators—was added, under continuous Chinese influence, a strong adherence to Buddhism and a system of government modeled on Chinese Confucian bureaucratism. The three rival kingdoms of Silla, Paekche, and Koguryo were united, through Chinese intervention, in the seventh century A.D.; unified dynastic rule was maintained thereafter.

The Yi dynasty (1392–1910), under which Korea was known as the Kingdom of Choson, was a staunch tributary ally of China under both the Ming (1368–1644) and Qing (1644–1911) dynasties. A Japanese invasion of Korea in 1592 conquered most of the country but was finally repelled by combined Chinese and Korean forces. From the late 17th century to the 1870s, all non-Chinese foreign influence was rigorously excluded from the country.

Korea's isolation, and its status as a Chinese tributary, ended in 1874, when Japan imposed on it the Treaty of Kangwha, guaranteeing Japanese commercial access and other interests. The Sino-Japanese War of 1894–95 was fought primarily over the status of Korea; following Japan's victory in that war, Korea was made a Japanese protectorate and was annexed as a Japanese colony in 1910. A harsh colonial regime was established with the aim of eradicating Korean culture and incorporating Korea entirely into the Japanese empire.

During the colonial period, Korean resistance to the Japanese regime was violently suppressed, but resistance movements survived in exile—notably the Korean Communist party in the Soviet Union and a republican movement in China. During World War II, tens of thousands of Koreans were conscripted as forced laborers to work in Japan and in Japanese-occupied territories.

Following Japan's surrender, Korea was arbitrarily divided into zones of Soviet and American occupation, north and south of 38° north latitude. The dividing line split Korea economically as well as geographically and politically; Korea's industry and hydroelectric power was concentrated in the north, while the south was primarily agricultural. In contrast to well-laid Soviet plans for installing a Communist government in the north (see "North Korea"), American attempts to reunify the country under a republican regime were inept. By 1948 it had become clear that plans for reunification were hopeless. In May of that year, the Republic of Korea was organized in the south, with Dr. Syngman Rhee as president. The United States withdrew its occupation forces in June 1949.

On June 25, 1950, North Korean troops invaded the south in an apparent attempt to unify the country forcibly under the communist regime. An emergency session of the UN Security Council voted to send troops to Korea; the USSR, having boycotted the session, was unable to exercise its veto on North Korea's behalf. UN troops, dominated by American forces and commanded by Gen. Douglas MacArthur, launched a counterattack in September with a landing at Inchon and swept north, reaching the Chinese border by Nov. 20. On Nov. 26 the tide turned again when Chinese troops entered the war, ostensibly to defend the Chinese border but also to aid their North Korean allies in driving the UN forces south again. Seoul fell once more on Jan. 4, 1951. In February and March another UN counteroffensive drove the combined Chinese and North Korean forces back to the 38th parallel again. Thereafter, the battle lines remained generally stable, although fierce fighting continued at intervals for another two years. On Apr. 11, 1951, Gen. MacArthur was relieved of the Korean command for making unauthorized policy statements and was replaced by Gen. Matthew Ridgway.

Armistice talks began in July 1951 but broke down repeatedly. A truce was signed on July 27, 1953, creating a demilitarized zone along the 38th parallel and establishing a framework for talks on a permanent settlement of the war. Negotiations have continued fruitlessly at the Panmunjom armistice conference headquarters ever since.

Postwar reconstruction, with significant U.S. aid, was overseen by the government of Syngman Rhee. Pres. Rhee resigned in 1960 after a wave of student demonstrations charging him with corruption and undemocratic practices. On May 16, 1961, Gen. Park Chung Hee seized power in a military coup. The military government was given democratic trappings when in 1972 a referendum was passed allowing Gen. Park to run for an unlimited series of six-year presidential terms. Gen. Park was assassinated on Oct. 26, 1979, by the chief of intelligence of the Korean government. In the aftermath of this event, Gen. Chun Doo Hwan rose to power, continuing the military-rule policies of Gen. Park. Gen. Chun's regime was marked by widespread and violent political protest demonstrations.

Despite political repression, South Korea's economy made great strides under Gen. Chun's regime. The traditionally agrarian country was transformed into a modernized, urban, industrial nation. The industrial economy developed a dual structure, dominated by a few conglomerates but also with a very large number of small-scale firms. In 1986 South Korea for the first time achieved a favorable balance-of-payments ratio in foreign trade, and the favorable balance has increased rapidly, led by exports of automobiles, textiles and clothing, and consumer electronic goods.

After weeks of widespread demonstrations in mid-1987, Gen. Chun agreed to allow direct presidential elections to choose his successor. The elections, held in November 1987, were generally regarded as fair; the government candidate, Roh Tae Woo, achieved a plurality over the sharply divided opposition parties. Under Pres. Roh, the political situation has calmed, although student demonstrations have continued, calling for greater efforts for Korean reunification and protesting the presence of large numbers of American troops in the country.

The 1988 Summer Olympics were held in South Korea, bringing widespread, favorable international attention. However, violent student protests continued.

High-level talks between North and South began in 1990, and an agreement in principle was reached that reunification would take place in the near future. South Korea has grown more cautious about reunification, however, after witnessing the tremendous costs West Germany continues to bear in helping East Germany. But South Korea remains one of the strongest economic powers in Asia, and the establishment of diplomatic relations with China in 1992 was a clear signal that it would remain so.

South Korean enthusiasm for reunification waned further in 1993 in the face of North Korean intransigence on the issue of its suspected nuclear weapons facilities, amid fears that the North was becoming more aggressive and confrontational once again.

On Dec. 18, 1992, longtime political opposition leader Kim Young Sam won election as South Korea's first postwar civilian president. Although he was initially able to liberalize some aspects of civil rights in South Korea, the renewed threat of war with North Korea became the overriding preoccupation of the government until late 1994, when an agreement was reached calling for North Korea to dismantle its nuclear facilities in exchange for new reactors, possibly supplied by South Korea.

Kuwait

State of Kuwait

Geography **Location:** northeastern Arabian peninsula. **Boundaries:** Iraq to N, Saudi Arabia to S, Persian Gulf to E. **Total land area:** 6,880 sq. mi. (17,820 sq km). **Coastline:** 310 mi. (499 km). **Comparative area:** between Connecticut and New Jersey. **Land use:** negl. % arable land; 0% permanent crops; 8% meadows and pastures; negl. % forest and woodland; 92% other; includes negl. % irrigated. **Major cities:** (1985 census); Kuwait City (capital) 44,335; Salmiya 153,369; Hawalli 145,126; Faranawiya 68,701; Abraq Kheetan 45,120.

People **Population:** 1,819,322 (1994 est.). **Nationality:** noun—Kuwaiti(s); adjective—Kuwaiti. **Ethnic groups:** 39% Kuwaiti, 39% other Arab, 9% South Asian, 4% Iranian, 9% other. **Languages:** Arabic (official), English widely spoken. **Religions:** 85% Muslim (30% Shi'a, 45% Sunni, 10% other), 15% Christian, Hindu, Parsi, and other.

Government **Type:** nominal constitutional monarchy. **Independence:** June 19, 1961 (from UK). **Constitution:** Nov. 16, 1962 (some provisions suspended since Aug. 29, 1962). **National holiday:** National Day, Feb. 25. **Head of government:** Jaber al-Ahmad al-Jaber al Sabah, amir (since Dec. 1977); Saad Al-Abdulla Al-Salem Al-Sabah, prime minister (since Oct. 1992). **Structure:** executive—Council of Ministers; legislature—National Assembly (suspended since July 1986).

Economy **Monetary unit:** Kuwaiti dinar. **Budget:** (FY93) ***income:*** $9 bil.; ***expend.:*** $13 bil. **GDP:** $25.7 bil., $15,100 per capita (1993 est.). **Chief crops:** virtually none; dependent on imports for food; about 75% of potable water must be distilled or imported. **Livestock:** goats, sheep, cattle, camels. **Natural resources:** petroleum, fish, shrimp, natural gas. **Major industries:** petroleum, petrochemicals, desalination. **Labor force:** 566,000 (1986); 45% services, 20% construction, 12% trade; 70% of labor force is non-Kuwaiti. **Exports:** $10.5 bil. (f.o.b., 1993 est.); 90% oil. **Imports:** $6 bil. (f.o.b., 1993 est.); food, construction material, vehicles and parts, clothing. **Major trading partners:** ***exports:*** Japan, Italy, Germany, U.S.; ***imports:*** Japan, U.S., Germany, UK.

Intl. Orgs. Arab League, FAO, G-77, IAEA, IBRD, ICAO, IDA, IFAD, IFC, ILO, IMF, IMO, INTELSAT, INTERPOL, ITU, NAM, OPEC, UN, UNESCO, UPU, WHO, WMO, WTO.

Kuwait, at the head of the Persian Gulf, was part of the Abbasid empire from the eighth century and was absorbed into the Ottoman Empire in the late 16th century. It was organized as a principality under the al-Sabah dynasty in 1756, but the Ottomans continued to assert sovereignty. Increasing British influence during the 19th century was formalized in 1899, when Kuwait became a British protectorate.

The discovery of oil, first exported from Kuwait after World War II, rapidly made the principality one of the wealthiest in the Middle East. The British protectorate ended in 1961, when Kuwait gained full independence. The great majority of oil field workers in Kuwait are non-Kuwaiti Arabs, including many Palestinians. Oil revenues have made possible a total welfare state for Kuwaiti citizens, who pay no taxes and enjoy a wide range of free social services.

Kuwait allied itself with Iraq in the Iran-Iraq War of 1980–88; Kuwaiti tankers came under heavy attack from Iranian warships in the gulf. In July 1987, Kuwaiti tankers were reflagged with the U.S. flag and placed under escort of American warships in an operation that continued into 1989. Most of Kuwait's territory is barren and sparsely inhabited.

On Aug. 2, 1990, Kuwait was invaded, and later annexed, by Iraq. In February 1991 it was liberated by a coalition of Arab, non-Arab Muslim, and Western nations led by the United States. Much of the country was destroyed or looted by the Iraqis. After its return to power, the ruling al-Sabah family came under strong pressure to institute democratic reforms.

Parliamentary elections were held in October 1992, and opposition candidates won 30 of 50 seats. The sultan then announced a new cabinet with more nonroyal members than ever before.

A brief war-scare flared up in October 1994 as 20,000 Iraqi Republican Guards were moved to the Kuwaiti border, only to retreat in the face of U.S. military opposition. In November, Iraq formally recognized the sovereignty and boundaries of Kuwait.

Kyrgyzstan

Republic of Kyrgyzstan

Geography **Location:** eastern central Asia. **Boundaries:** Kazakhstan to N and NE, China to SE and S, Tajikistan to SW, Uzbekistan to W. **Total land area:** 76,641 sq. mi. (198,500 sq km). **Coastline:** none. **Comparative area:** slightly smaller than South Dakota. **Land use:** 7% cropland; 43% permanent pasture; 3% forest and woodland; 47% other (mostly urban and mountain). **Major cities:** (1990) Bishkek (known as Frunze 1926–91) (capital) 626,900.

People **Population:** 4,698,108 (1994 est.). **Nationality:** noun—Kirghiz (Kyrgyz); adjective—Kirghiz (Kyrgyz). **Ethnic groups:** 52.4% Kirghiz (Kyrgyz), 21.5% Russian, 12.9% Uzbek, 2.5% Ukrainian, 2.4% German, 1.6% Tatar. **Languages:** Kirghiz (official), member of south Turkic language group written in Cyrillic since 1940; 1992 proposal to reintroduce Latin script; 30% Russian, ethnic languages. **Religions:** Muslim—Sunni.

Government **Type:** republic. **Independence:** Aug. 31, 1991 (from USSR). **Constitution:** adopted May 5, 1993. **National holiday:** Independence Day, Aug. 31. **Heads of government:** Askar A. Akayev, president (since Oct. 1991); Apas D. Djumagulov, prime minister (since Dec. 1993). **Structure:** executive—president, vice president, Cabinet of Ministers; legislative—Supreme Soviet; judicial—Supreme Court.

Economy **Monetary unit:** ruble. **Budget:** N.A. ***income:*** N.A. ***expend.:*** N.A. **GDP:** $11.3 bil., $2,440 per capita (1993 est.). **Chief crops:** grain, sugar beet, tobacco, cotton. **Livestock:** sheep and goats, cattle, pigs. **Natural resources:** antimony, mercury, uranium, coal, natural gas, petroleum, lead, zinc. **Major industries:** extraction and processing of its raw materials, including coal, natural gas, petroleum, mining; footwear, textiles. **Labor force:** 1.748 mil. (1990). **Exports:** $100.4 mil. (1993 est.); wool, chemicals, cotton, ferrous and nonferrous metals, shoes. **Imports:** $105.8 mil. (1993 est.); lumber, industrial products, ferrous metals, fuel, machinery. **Major trading partners:** other republics.

Intl. Orgs. CIS, IMF, OSCE, UN, UNCTAD, UNESCO, World Bank.

Kyrgyzstan is largely mountainous, dominated by the massive Tien Shan range in the northeast and the Pamir-Alay range in the southwest. Most of the population lives in one of three major valleys, the Fergana, the Chu, and the Talas, since much of the country is permanently ice-capped and covered with glaciers. The Kyrgyz people are mentioned in early Turkic inscriptions that date back at least to the eighth century A.D.

They were one of the great nomadic tribes of central Asia, who until the 10th century settled around the Upper Yenisei River. With the Mongol invasions of the 13th century, they migrated to the areas of the Tien Shan range in present-day Kyrgyzstan, a territory that has been controlled variously by Mongols, Kalmyks, Manchus, the large tribal empire of the Kokand khanate (or state), and the Russians. In the mid-17th century, the Kyrgyz began to be converted to Islam, but at nearly the same time, the Manchus defeated the Mongols and the Kyrgyz people became Chinese subjects. The Chinese did not interfere with their nomadic life, but in the 19th century they were attacked and came under the control of the khanate of Kokand, during which time Islam was strengthened. In 1868 the khanate became a Russian protectorate and in 1876, the area was merged into the Russian empire as Fergana region. A large Russian influx followed, and many Kyrgyz migrated to China and Afghanistan.

The period immediately following the 1917 Bolshevik revolution was one of great confusion and fighting between the Kyrgyz, the Reds, the Whites, and foreign interventionists. Soviet power was established in 1919, although fighting continued in some parts until 1922. In 1918, Kyrgyzstan was included in the Russian republic's Turkestan Autonomous Soviet Socialist Republic; then, with the National Delimitation of Central Asian Republics in 1924, its name changed to Kara-Kirghiz Autonomous Province (also within the Russian republic). On Dec. 5, 1936, it became a full Soviet Socialist Republic (SSR) of the USSR.

As a Soviet Union republic, advances were made in literacy, education, and public health, although repression of nationalist Kyrgyz was also evident. In the 1920s and 1930s, land reform and collectivization ended the traditional nomadic way of life. Kyrgyz nationalists strongly opposed the changes that Soviet rule brought, but the central government won in the end, and the nationalists were repressed. From the 1930s, ethnic Russians held most of the leading Communist party and government positions in the Kyrgyz SSR.

Mikhail Gorbachev's policy of glasnost, or openness, was responsible for the first public discussion of corruption in government, the emergence of a more liberal Kyrgyz press by 1988, the emergence of nongovernment opposition parties, and, as in other former Union republics, ethnic conflicts. In 1990 disputes over housing and land in the Osh region of the crowded Fergana Valley led to violent confrontations between the Kyrgyz and the republic's Uzbeks. Osh had been incorporated into Kyrgyzstan in 1924, even though the majority population was Uzbek, and at various times the Uzbeks had lobbied for the establishment of an autonomous Uzbek region in Osh. The clashes were bloody and protracted, and hundreds of people were reportedly killed.

In February 1990 traditional Soviet-style elections brought into office many Communist party officials, and in April 1990 the Supreme Soviet elected Absamat Masaliyev, who had been the Kyrgyz republic's Communist party First Secretary. In October 1990, however, largely due to the violence in Osh, Masaliyev did not receive enough Supreme Soviet votes, and the reformer Askar Akayev was elected as president. After the failed coup in Moscow in August 1991, Communist party activities were suspended, although most leaders are still party members. In December 1991 Kyrgyzstan signed the Alma-Ata Declaration that founded the Commonwealth of Independent States.

Beginning in 1992, with the help of the International Monetary Fund, Akayev embarked on a radical economic program that included lowering wages, raising prices, and abolishing customs duties and tariffs with Central Asian neighbors Kazakhstan and Uzbekistan. Although the program initially caused hardship among the people, it has so far proved successful. As a testament to its success (and confounding Akayev's hard-line communist critics in Parliament), in a vote of confidence held Jan. 30, 96.7 percent of voters agreed that Akayev should remain in office until 1996.

Laos

Lao People's Democratic Republic

Geography **Location:** landlocked country in Southeast Asia. **Boundaries:** Myanmar to NW, China to N, Vietnam to E, Cambodia to S, and Thailand to W. **Total land area:** 91,429 sq. mi. (236,800 sq km). **Coastline:** none. **Comparative area:** slightly larger than Utah. **Land use:** 4% arable land; negl. % permanent crops; 3% meadows and pastures; 58% forest and woodland; 35% other; includes 1% irrigated. **Major cities:** (1985 census) Vientiane (capital) 377,409; (1973) Savannaket 50,690; Pakse 44,860; Luang Prabang 44,244; Saya Bury 13,775.

People **Population:** 4,701,654 (1994 est.). **Nationality:** noun—Lao (sing. and pl.); adjective—Laotian or Lao. **Ethnic groups:** 50% Lao, 20% ethnic Thai, 15% Phouteung (Kha), 15% Meo, Hmong, Yao, and other. **Languages:** Lao (official), French, English. **Religions:** 85% Buddhist, 15% animist and other.

Government **Type:** communist state. **Independence:** July 19, 1949 (from France). **Constitution:** draft constitution under discussion since 1976. **National holiday:** Dec. 2. **Heads of government:** Nouhak Phoumsavanh, president (since Nov. 1992); Khamtai Siphandon, prime minister (since Aug. 1991). **Structure:** president; Supreme People's Assembly; cabinet; cabinet is totally Communist but council contains a few nominal neutralists and non-Communists; National Congress of People's Representatives established current government structure in Dec. 1975.

Economy **Monetary unit:** new kip. **Budget:** (1990) ***income:*** $83.0 mil.; ***expend.:*** $188.5 mil. **GDP:** $4.1 bil., $900 per capita (1993 est.). **Chief crops:** rice (overwhelmingly dominant), corn, vegetables, tobacco, coffee; formerly self-sufficient; food shortages (due in part to distribution deficiencies) include rice; illegal producer of opium poppy and cannabis for international drug trade. **Livestock:** pigs, buffalo, cattle, goats, horses. **Natural resources:** tin, timber, gypsum, hydropower potential. **Major industries:** tin mining, timber, electric power. **Labor force:** about 1–1.5 mil.; 85–90% in agriculture, est.; 17% unemployment. **Exports:** $133 mil. (f.o.b., 1992 est.); electricity, wood products, coffee, tin. **Imports:** $266 mil. (c.i.f., 1992 est.); food, fuel oil, consumer goods, manufactures. **Major trading partners:** ***exports:*** Thailand, Malaysia, Vietnam, former USSR, U.S.; ***imports:*** Thailand, former USSR, Japan, France, Vietnam.

Intl. Orgs. Colombo Plan, FAO, G-77, IBRD, ICAO, IDA, IFAD, ILO, IMF, INTERPOL, ITU, NAM, UN, UNCTAD, UNESCO, UPU, WHO, WMO.

Inhabited by the Thai-speaking Lao people in the river valleys and by Hmong and other tribal people in the highlands, Laos historically had little national cohesion and was dominated by its more powerful neighbors, Siam (Thailand) to the west and Vietnam to the east. In 1893 France forced Siam to recognize Laos as a French protectorate; the country was thereafter incorporated into the French Union of Indochina. Laos was occupied by Japan during World War II but saw little major fighting.

In 1946 Laos was united under the Luang Prabang dynasty and was granted local autonomy as a constitutional monarchy in 1949. During the final phases of the Indochina War against French colonialism in 1953–54, Vietnamese Communist (Vietminh) incursions reinforced the position of the Laotian Communist party (Pathet Lao) in Laotian politics. Following the French withdrawal in December 1954, Laos became an independent nation and was admitted to the United Nations in 1955.

The creation of a coalition government under Prince Souvana Phouma in 1962 temporarily resolved a turbulent political situation; an international agreement signed in Geneva that year guaranteed Laos's neutrality. The Pathet Lao withdrew from the coalition in 1964 and renewed its armed uprising against the government, with North Vietnamese support. American planes bombed Vietnamese supply lines along the Ho Chi Minh trail, and American agents recruited Hmong tribesmen as irregular troops to attack Pathet Lao positions. The Pathet Lao nevertheless made steady gains, especially after 1970. In 1973, Prince Souvana Phouma ordered a cease-fire, and in 1975 the Pathet Lao took control of the capital, Vientiane. The Lao People's Democratic Republic was proclaimed on Dec. 3, 1975. Large numbers of Hmong and other tribal people fled to Thailand.

Subsequently, Laos was strongly dominated by Vietnam, which stationed significant numbers of troops in the country. In 1989, in Laos's first election since the communist takeover, a Supreme People's Assembly was elected specifically to approve a new constitution, which it did in 1991; the constitution confirmed the Lao People's Revolutionary party as the sole legal political party. Multistage (but single-party) elections held in Dec. 1992 did little to alter the country's political climate, though observers predicted greater changes in the near future as the Communist old guard began to pass from the scene.

Latvia

Republic of Latvia

Geography **Location:** eastern coast of Baltic Sea in northeastern Europe. **Boundaries:** Baltic Sea to N, Estonia to NE, Russian Federation, Belarus to S, Lithuania to W. **Total land area:** 24,749 sq. mi. (64,100 sq km). **Coastline:** Baltic Sea. **Comparative area:** slightly larger than West Virginia. **Land use:** 27% cropland; 13% permanent pasture; 39% forest and woodland; 21% other (urban and swampland). **Major cities:** (1993 est.) Riga (capital) 874,172; Daugav'pils 124,887; Liepāja 108,256; Jelgava 72,280; Jūrmala 60,091.

People **Population:** 2,749,211 (1994 est.). **Nationality:** noun—Latvian(s); adjective—Latvian. **Ethnic groups:** 51.8% Latvian, 33.8% Russian, 4.5% Belarussian, 3.4% Ukrainian, 2.3% Polish. **Languages:** Latvian (official), an Indo-European language written in Latin script; Russian, ethnic languages. **Religions:** Lutheran, other Protestant, Roman Catholic, Russian Orthodox.

Government **Type:** republic. **Independence:** Aug. 21, 1991 (from USSR); recognized by USSR Sept. 6, 1991. **Constitution:** being drafted. **National holiday:** Nov. 18, Independence Day. **Heads of government:** Guntis Ulmanis, president (since July 1993); Maris Gailis, prime minister (since Sept. 1994). **Structure:** executive—president, Council of Ministers; legislative—Supreme Council (201 deputies); judicial—Supreme Court.

Economy **Monetary unit:** lat. **Budget:** N.A. ***income:*** N.A.; ***expend.:*** N.A. **GNP:** $13.2 bil., $4,810 per capita (1993 est.). **Chief crops:** grain, potatoes, sugar beets, vegetables, fruit. **Livestock:** chickens, pigs, cattle, sheep, goats. **Natural resources:** limited. **Major industries:** machine building, metalworking, chemical processing, petrochemical. **Labor force:** (1990) 1,407,000. **Exports:** $429 mil. from non-FSU countries (f.o.b., 1992); 14% food, 13% railroad cars, 12% chemicals. **Imports:** N.A.; 35% machinery, 13% petroleum products, 9% chemicals. **Major trading partners:** former Soviet republics.

Intl. Orgs. FAO, IAEA, IMF, OSCE, UN, World Bank.

Though the Letts ethnically and linguistically are quite distinct from their northern neighbors the Ests (who are akin rather to the Lithuanians to the south), Latvia's history parallels that of Estonia. German merchants, knights, and missionaries made Latvia a semi-ecclesiastical German colony in the 13th century; in the 16th century Latvia passed under first Swedish, then Lithuanian rule; in the 18th century Peter the Great's Russian empire absorbed the land.

A 19th-century cultural revival, inspired in part by Johann von Herder, a native of Riga, found expression in folkloric societies, archaeological research and the compilation of the epic poem, *Lacplesis*. Brest-Litovsk, the Soviet Union's 1918 peace treaty with Germany, granted Latvia's political independence for the first time in its history.

The constitution of 1922 established a one-house legislature in whose system of proportional representation about 20 different political parties participated. To avoid violence between left and right armed extremists, Prime Minister Karlis Umanlis dissolved the Parliament in May 1934 and ruled as dictator until a new constitution that provided for expanded presidential powers and a second house of the legislature, based on the conception of a corporate state, came into existence in 1938 just before the Hitler-Stalin Pact awarded Latvia to the Russian sphere of interest. Stalin garrisoned troops in Latvia, rigged elections, and incorporated the country as a new union republic of the USSR in 1940.

For 50 years, harsh Soviet rule continued. The bigger cities were Russianized to the extent that Riga no longer had a Latvian majority; the highly educated middle and upper-middle classes were deported throughout Russia. Industrialization brought relative prosperity within the Soviet Union, but the national consciousness was never eradicated.

Mikhail Gorbachev's policy of glasnost, or openness, led to the creation of dissident groups who staged public demonstrations on the anniversaries of the Stalin-Hitler Pact and of the establishment of Latvian independence. After the head of the Latvian Communist party, Boris Pugo (who was to become involved in the failed hard-liner coup in August 1991), was transferred to Moscow, Latvia's Communist party came under the influence of the newly created Latvian Popular Front. With the new political influence of non-Communists, on Sept. 29, 1988, Latvian replaced Russian as the official language.

In March 1990, following Lithuania's example, Latvia announced its intention to secede, survived Gorbachev's January 1991 military crackdown, and after the failed August 1991 coup in Moscow declared independence. Latvia's independence was recognized by the USSR in September 1991. Latvia, like the other Baltic states, declined to sign the Alma-Ata Declaration that created the Commonwealth of Independent States. Tensions between Latvia and Russia increased when Russians were denied voting rights and Russia halted the withdrawal of its troops.

Lebanon

Republic of Lebanon

Geography **Location:** western Asia. **Boundaries:** Syria to N and E, Israel to S, Mediterranean Sea to W. **Total land area:** 4,015 sq. mi. (10,400 sq km). **Coastline:** 140 mi. (225 km). **Comparative area:** between Delaware and Connecticut. **Land use:** 21% arable land; 9% permanent crops; 1% meadows and pastures; 8% forest and woodland; 61% other; includes 7% irrigated. **Major cities:** (1975 est.) Beirut (capital) 1,500,000; Tarabulus (Tripoli) 160,000; Zahleh 45,000; Saida (Sidon) 38,000; Sur (Tyre) 14,000.

People **Population:** 3,620,395 (1994 est.). **Nationality:** noun—Lebanese (sing., pl.); adjective—Lebanese. **Ethnic groups:** 93% Arab, 6% Armenian, 1% other. **Languages:** Arabic and French (both official), Armenian, English. **Religions:** 75% Islam, 25% Christian, negl. Judaism.

Government **Type:** republic. **Independence:** Nov. 22, 1943 (from League of Nations Mandate under French administration). **Constitution:** May 26, 1926 (amended). **National holiday:** Independence Day, Nov. 22. **Heads of government:** M. Elias Hraoui, president (since Nov. 1989); Rafic Al-Hariri, prime minister (since Oct. 1992). **Structure:** power lies with president, who is elected by unicameral legislature (National Assembly); cabinet appointed by president, approved by legislature; independent secular courts on French pattern; religious courts for matters of marriage, divorce, inheritance, etc.; by custom, president is Maronite Christian, prime minister is Sunni Muslim, and president of legislature is Shia Muslim; Parliament seats 108 members, half Christian and half Muslim.

Economy **Monetary unit:** Lebanese pound. **Budget:** (1993 est.) ***income:*** $990 mil.; ***expend.:*** N.A. **GDP:** $6.1 bil., $1,720 per capita (1993 est.). **Chief crops:** fruits, wheat, corn, barley, potatoes; not self-sufficient in food; illegal producer of opium poppy and cannabis for international drug trade. **Livestock:** goats, sheep, cattle, asses, pigs. **Natural resources:** limestone, iron ore, salt; water-surplus state in water-deficit region. **Major industries:** banking, food processing, textiles. **Labor force:** 650,000 (1985); 79% industry, commerce, and services, 11% agriculture, 10% government; 33% unemployment (1987 est.). **Exports:** $925 mil. (f.o.b., 1993 est.); agricultural products, chemicals, textiles, precious and semiprecious metals, and jewelry. **Imports:** $4.1 bil. (c.i.f., 1993 est.). **Major trading partners:** ***exports:*** 16% Saudi Arabia, 8% Switzerland, 6% Jordan, 6% Kuwait, 5% U.S.; ***imports:*** 14% Italy, 12% France, 6% U.S., 5% Turkey, 3% Saudi Arabia.

Intl. Orgs. Arab League, FAO, G-77, IAEA, IBRD, ICAO, IDA, IFAD, IFC, ILO, IMF, IMO, INTELSAT, INTERPOL, ITU, NAM, UN, UNESCO, UPU, WHO, WMO.

The ancient history of Lebanon is essentially coextensive with that of Syria, of which it was long a part. The port cities of Tripoli, Tyre, and Sidon were important centers of the Phoenician empire. The parallel ranges of the Lebanon and Anti-Lebanon mountains, crowned with the country's famous cedar trees, enclose the fertile Bekaa Valley. The coastal cities became strongholds of early Christianity, later fragmented into numerous sects, including Maronites (Syrian Catholic), Roman Catholic, Greek Orthodox, Syrian Orthodox, and others. The mountains of the south became the center of the Druze sect of Islam, while orthodox Sunni Islam dominated in the Bekaa Valley.

Lebanon came under French influence in the late 18th century, as France claimed the role of protector of Syria's Christian community. France intervened in Lebanon in 1841 and again in 1860 when fighting between Maronite and Druze communities led to the massacre of many Christians. Under pressure from France, the Ottoman Empire granted some local autonomy to the Maronites of greater Lebanon.

In the dismemberment of the Ottoman Empire after World War I, France was granted a League of Nations Mandate over the Levant States (Lebanon and Syria), ensuring French control of the Iraq Petroleum Company pipeline from Iraq to Tripoli. In 1926 Lebanon became a self-governing republic under the mandate, but internal unrest and anti-French sentiment continued.

In June 1940 the French administration in Lebanon declared its allegiance to the Vichy government. British and Free French forces occupied Lebanon in June 1941 and declared it an independent republic; but the French retained control, and full independence did not come until Jan. 1, 1944.

Under a National Covenant in 1943, political power in the Lebanese parliament was apportioned among the nation's various communities. The president was always to be a Maronite Christian, the prime minister a Sunni Muslim. This provided a workable formula for power sharing but also ensured that the national government would always be hostage to the considerable power of separate communities and clans.

The years from the end of World War II to the early 1970s were a brief golden age for Lebanon. Beirut developed into a wealthy, cosmopolitan city, the center of Middle Eastern banking and trade, while agriculture and small-scale industry flourished in the rest of the country. A Syrian-backed Muslim uprising in 1958 had no significant impact; U.S. Marines landed in May 1958 to protect American interests and remained until October. By the late 1960s, however, Lebanon's stability was threatened by PLO attacks on Israel from refugee camps in southern Lebanon and by a shift in the country's demographic balance. Muslims had become a majority in Lebanon by the late 1960s and demanded a revision of the National Covenant, while Maronite Christians continued to cling to their position of political dominance.

Throughout the 1970s, Palestinian raids from Lebanon into Israel brought Israeli retaliatory strikes in southern Lebanon. Israeli troops occupied southern Lebanon in 1978 and again in 1980. The Palestinian-Israeli conflict polarized opinion within Lebanon, inflaming nationalist and anti-Western feelings among Lebanon's Sunni Muslims.

Civil war broke out in 1975, with Palestinian and leftist Muslim militias battling militias of the Maronite community, the Christian Phalange party, and other groups. More than 60,000 died, and damage ranged into the billions of dollars. Syrian troops intervened in 1976, battling Palestinian forces in an attempt to restore the status quo. Arab League efforts to negotiate a cease-fire produced an unstable peace at the end of 1976, though Syrian troops remained in Lebanon.

Fighting broke out between Syrian forces and Christian militiamen near Zahle on Apr. 1, 1981. Other groups joined the fighting in a general war of each against all. Israel staged commando raids against Palestinian positions in Tyre and Tulin. Israeli air raids on Beirut caused extensive loss of life and property damage.

Israel invaded Lebanon in a full-scale air and sea assault on June 6, 1982, in an attempt to drive out the PLO. Israeli and Syrian forces came into direct conflict in the Bekaa Valley. Israeli forces surrounded Beirut and began a heavy bombardment of the city. On Aug. 1, Palestinian forces withdrew from Beirut under international supervision. On Sept. 14 newly elected Pres. Bashir Gemayel, a Maronite Christian, was assassinated; Israeli troops occupied the Muslim quarters of West Beirut in response. With tacit Israeli approval, Christian militiamen invaded two refugee camps on Sept. 16 and slaughtered hundreds of Palestinian civilians.

Beirut remained a battle zone in 1983, divided by the "Green Line" into Christian and Muslim sectors. Terrorist bombings were common. The United States, France, Italy, and other Western nations stationed troops in Beirut in an attempt to enforce a cease-fire. Fifty people were killed when a bomb partly destroyed the U.S. embassy on Apr. 18; separate attacks on military installations on Oct. 23 killed 241 U.S. Marines and 58 French soldiers.

Rashid Karami became premier with Syrian support on Apr. 26, 1984. The civil war continued, with fighting among various groups of Christian, Druze, Sunni, Shiite, and Palestinian militias. War between Shiite and Palestinian forces broke out in May 1985. Israeli forces withdrew from most of Lebanon in June, but maintained a "security zone" in the southern part of the country.

Kidnappings of foreign nationals at the hands of various terrorist factions became commonplace in the late 1980s. Premier Karami was assassinated on June 1, 1987, when a bomb destroyed his helicopter.

At an October 1989 Arab League-sponsored meeting, Christian and Muslim leaders agreed on a new national charter. The Taif accord was condemned by Christian militants, led by Gen. Michel Aoun, and Muslim militia leaders. Newly elected Pres. René Mowad, a Syrian-backed Christian, was assassinated on Nov. 22 and succeeded by Elias Hraoui. A revolt by Aoun was put down in October with the help of Syrian forces.

In November 1990, rival Shiite militias—the Syrian-backed Amal and Iranian-backed Party of God—signed an agreement ending three years of fighting. In February 1991 Lebanese troops moved to defend the area for the first time in 13 years and called for Israel to abandon its "security zone" in southern Lebanon.

In addition to leaving 150,000 dead, the civil war severely disrupted the national economy, virtually wiping out the international sector and causing significant damage to the domestic sector.

The government of Christian prime minister Omar Karami collapsed in early May 1992, after riots protesting widespread economic hardship. New elections were held under Syrian supervision during August and September, with Hizbollah and other Islamic fundamentalist parties gaining the most seats in the new parliament, in part because the Christian parties called for an electoral boycott.

In February and March 1994, as Israeli-Hizbollah skirmishes continued in southern Lebanon, the government moved against Lebanese Forces (the Christian political party), arresting some of its leaders and banning the party as well as all "political" broadcasts not government-controlled. In April Lebanon broke diplomatic relations with Iraq and announced the trial of two Iraqi attachés for the murder (allegedly at Saddam Hussein's orders) in Beirut of an Iraqi opposition leader.

Lesotho

Kingdom of Lesotho

Geography **Location:** landlocked country in southern Africa. **Boundaries:** entirely surrounded by South African territory. **Total land area:** 11,718 sq. mi. (30,350 sq km). **Coastline:** none. **Comparative area:** slightly larger than Maryland. **Land use:** 10% arable land; 0% permanent crops; 66% meadows and pastures; 0% forest and woodland; 24% other. **Major cities:** (1976) Maseru (capital) 45,000.

People **Population:** 1,944,493 (1994 est.). **Nationality:** noun—Mosotho (sing.), Basotho (pl.); adjective—Basotho. **Ethnic groups:** 99.7% Sotho; 1,600 Europeans, 800 Asians. **Languages:** Sesotho and English (official); Zulu, Xhosa. **Religions:** 80% Christian, 20% indigenous beliefs.

Government **Type:** constitutional monarchy; independent member of Commonwealth. **Independence:** Oct. 4, 1966 (from UK). **Constitution:** Oct. 4, 1966, suspended Jan. 1970. **National holiday:** Oct. 4. **Heads of government:** Moshoeshoe II, king (since Jan. 1995); Dr. Ntsu Mokhehle, prime minister (since Apr. 1993). **Structure:** executive and legislative authority nominally vested in king; real power rests with Military Council, established after Jan. 1986 coup; 20-member Council of Ministers responsible for administrative duties; judiciary—63 Basotho courts administer customary law, high court and subordinate courts have criminal jurisdiction, court of appeal at Maseru has appellate jurisdiction.

Economy **Monetary unit:** maloti. **Budget:** (1993) ***income:*** $438 mil.; ***expend.:*** $430 mil. **GDP:** $2.8 bil., $1,500 per capita (1993 est.). **Chief crops:** corn, wheat, pulses, sorghum, barley; mostly subsistence farming and livestock. **Livestock:** sheep, goats, cattle, horses, asses. **Natural resources:** some diamonds and other minerals, water, agricultural and grazing land. **Major industries:** tourism. **Labor force:** 689,000 economically active; 86.2% subsistence agriculture; 150,000–250,000 spend from six months to many years as wage earners in South Africa. **Exports:** labor to South Africa (remittances $300 mil. est. in 1985); $109 mil. (f.o.b., 1992); wool, mohair, wheat, cattle, peas. **Imports:** $964 mil. (c.i.f., 1992); mainly corn, building materials, clothing, vehicles, machinery. **Major trading partners:** ***exports:*** 53% South Africa, 30% EU, 13% North and South America; ***imports:*** 95% South Africa, 2% EU.

Intl. Orgs. AfDB, Commonwealth, FAO, G-77, IBRD, ICAO, IDA, IFAD, IFC, ILO, IMF, INTERPOL, ITU, NAM, UN, UNESCO, UPU, WHO, WMO, WTO.

Lesotho, formerly known as Basutoland, is an independent kingdom surrounded entirely by the Republic of South Africa. The area was sparsely populated by Bushmen until the 16th century when refugees from tribal wars in surrounding areas began to move in, an influx that continued through the 19th century. These immigrants eventually coalesced into a fairly homogenous cultural group, the Basothos.

Under King Moshoeshoe, who ruled from 1823 to 1870, several Basotho groups were consolidated. But during his reign much land was lost in a series of wars with South Africa, and Moshoeshoe appealed to Queen Victoria for aid. In 1868 the nation became a British protectorate. Between 1884 and 1959 all executive and legislative authority was in the hands of a British high commissioner. In 1903 a Basotho consultative body was established, and in 1959 a new constitution gave the council power to legislate on internal affairs.

The British began to move the country toward full independence, and on Oct. 4, 1966, Basutoland achieved full independence as the Kingdom of Lesotho. The first elections after independence, held in January 1970, were nullified by the leader of the ruling Basutoland National Party (BNP) when early returns indicated that the party might lose. A state of emergency was declared, the constitution was suspended, and parliament dissolved.

Elections in 1985 were boycotted by opposition parties, and in 1986 the BNP government was ousted in a coup. The nation was run by a military council, which in Feb. 1990 stripped King Moshoeshoe II of his remaining powers. Military rule ended finally in April 1993 when Ntsu Mokhehle was elected prime minister and his Basotholand Congress party (BCP) gained all 243 seats in the legislature.

Liberia

Republic of Liberia

Geography Location: western Africa. **Boundaries:** Sierra Leone, Guinea to N, Ivory Coast to E, Atlantic Ocean to S and W. **Total land area:** 43,000 sq. mi. (111,370 sq km). **Coastline:** 360 mi. (579 km). **Comparative area:** between Indiana and Kentucky. **Land use:** 1% arable land; 3% permanent crops; 2% meadows and pastures; 39% forest and woodland; 55% other; includes negl. % irrigated. **Major cities:** (1984) Monrovia (capital) 421,058.

People Population: 2,972,766 (1994 est.). **Nationality:** noun—Liberian(s); adjective—Liberian. **Ethnic groups:** 95% indigenous peoples, including Kpelle, Bassa, Gio, Kru, Grebo, Mano, Krahn, Gola, Gbandi, Loma, Kissi, Vai, Bella; 5% descendants of repatriated slaves known as Americo-Liberians. **Languages:** 20% English (official); more than 20 languages of Niger-Congo language group. **Religions:** 70% indigenous beliefs, 20% Muslim, 10% Christian.

Government Type: republic. **Independence:** July 26, 1847. **Constitution:** Jan. 6, 1986. **National holiday:** Independence Day, July 26. **Head of government:** David Kpomakpor, president (since Mar. 1994). **Structure:** executive—president, assisted by appointed cabinet; legislative—bicameral legislature; judiciary.

Economy Monetary unit: uses U.S. dollar and Liberian dollar. **Budget:** (1989) ***income:*** $242.1 mil.; ***expend.:*** $435.4 mil. **GDP:** $2.3 bil., $800 per capita (1993 est.). **Chief crops:** rubber, rice, oil palm, cassava, coffee, cocoa; imports rice and wheat. **Livestock:** sheep, goats, pigs, cattle; imports livestock. **Natural resources:** iron ore, timber, diamonds, gold. **Major industries:** rubber processing, food processing, construction materials. **Labor force:** 510,000; 70.5% agriculture, 10.8% services, 4.5% industry and commerce, 14.2% other; 220,000 wage earners; non-Africans hold about 95% of top-level management and engineering jobs; 52% of population of working age. **Exports:** $505 mil. (f.o.b., 1989 est.); 61% iron ore, 20% rubber, 11% timber. **Imports:** $394 mil. (c.i.f., 1989 est.); machinery, transportation equipment, rice, mineral fuels, chemicals, foodstuffs. **Major trading partners: *exports:*** U.S., EU, Netherlands; ***imports:*** U.S., EU, Japan, China, Netherlands.

Intl. Orgs. FAO, G-77, IAEA, IBRD, ICAO, IDA, IFAD, IFC, ILO, IMF, IMO, INTERPOL, ITU, NAM, UN, UNESCO, UPU, WHO, WMO.

Liberia was populated by migrants from the north and east beginning in the 12th century, but it remained relatively isolated from the remainder of West Africa and was not incorporated into any of the region's premodern kingdoms and empires. Portuguese explorers first reached the Liberian coast in 1461 to be followed by other European traders. Until the 19th century, Liberia was largely ignored by the world except for a small-scale coastal trade in slaves and forest products.

In 1816 the U.S. Congress granted a charter to the American Colonization Society, ACS, a private organization dedicated to the African repatriation of freed slaves. The first settlers landed in 1822 at the town that was later to become Monrovia. In 1838 the settlers organized the Commonwealth of Liberia under a governor appointed by the ACS. The commonwealth declared its independence as the Republic of Liberia in 1847 and adopted a constitution modeled after that of the United States. The new government, Africa's first independent republic, was granted diplomatic recognition by Great Britain in 1848, France in 1852, and the United States in 1862.

Bolstered by the moral backing of the United States, Liberia in its first 100 years of independence succeeded, with difficulty, in fending off British and French attempts to encroach on its territory from their neighboring colonies. Although descendants of freed American slaves are a minority in Liberia's ethnically diverse population, they have consistently dominated the country's political life.

William V.S. Tubman was elected president in 1944 and served until his death in 1971, successfully steering Liberia through the post–World War II age of African nationalism and decolonization. He was succeeded by William R. Tolbert, Jr. On Apr. 12, 1980, Tolbert was deposed in a military coup led by Master Sgt. Samuel K. Doe. Doe suspended the constitution and imposed martial law but pledged a new constitution by 1985.

Presidential elections were held on Oct. 15, 1985, under the terms of a provisional constitution that for the first time enacted universal suffrage. Samuel Doe was elected president, and his party won 80 percent of the seats in the national legislature. Despite allegations of fraud that led to a violent but unsuccessful coup attempt in November 1985, the Second Republic, under the new constitution, was inaugurated on Jan. 6, 1986.

On Dec. 24, 1989, about 150 antigovernment guerrillas of the National Patriotic Forces of Liberia (NPFL), led by Charles Taylor, crossed the border from the Ivory Coast. The fighting quickly degenerated into ethnic warfare between the Krahn and Mandingo, in support of the government, and the Gio and Mano, who supported the rebels. In February Prince Johnson split from Taylor's forces and took up fighting both government troops and Taylor. By August there were 5,000 civilians dead, and at least 375,000 refugees had fled to neighboring countries. A peacekeeping force of the Economic Community of West African States (ECOWAS) landed at Monrovia on Aug. 24 to mediate a cease-fire and prepare for free elections. On Sept. 10 Pres. Doe was captured and killed by Prince Johnson, but a cease-fire was not agreed to until Nov. 28, 1990. By some estimates, in 1991 there were as many as 1.3 million displaced persons and refugees.

From 1990 to 1992 Charles Taylor solidified his hold on the country despite the establishment of a government (under Amos Sawyer) in Monrovia by the West African States. By 1993 the government and ECOWAS forces succeeded in containing Taylor's forces. In March 1994 an interim coalition government representing the country's three major factions came into power as peace talks began. Elections were scheduled for November 1995 but factional disputes could cause a delay. An estimated 150,000 have died in this civil war.

Libya

Socialist People's Libyan Arab Jamahiriya

Geography Location: along Mediterranean coast of North Africa. **Boundaries:** Mediterranean Sea to N, Egypt to E, Sudan to SE, Niger, Chad to S, Tunisia, Algeria to W. **Total land area:** 679,359 sq. mi. (1,759,540 sq km). **Coastline:** 1,100 mi. (1,770 km). **Comparative area:** Alaska plus Oregon. **Land use:** 1% arable land; 0% permanent crops; 8% meadows and pastures; 0% forest and woodland; 91% other. **Major cities:** in Jan. 1987, Col. Qaddafi designated Hun, a town 404 mi. (650 km) SE of Tripoli, as administrative capital of country (population N.A.); (1985) Tripoli 858,000; Benghazi 368,000; Misurata 117,000.

People Population: 5,057,392 (1994 est.). **Nationality:** noun—Libyan(s); adjective—Libyan. **Ethnic groups:** 97% Berber and Arab; some Greeks, Maltese, Italians, Egyptians, Pakistanis, Turks, Indians, Tunisians. **Languages:** Arabic, Italian, and English widely understood in major cities. **Religions:** 97% Sunni Muslim.

Government Type: Jamahiriya, or a state of the masses; in theory, governed by populace. **Independence:** Dec. 24, 1951 (from Italy). **Constitution:** Dec. 11, 1969, amended Mar. 2, 1977. **National holidays:** Revolution Day, Sept. 1; British Evacuation Day, Mar. 28; U.S. Evacuation Day, June 16; Declaration of People's Power, Mar. 2. **Head of government:** Col. Muammar al-Qaddafi (no official title; runs country and is treated as chief of state) (since Sept. 1969); Abdulmajid Algaoud, prime minister (since Jan. 1994). **Structure:** officially, paramount political power and authority rests with General People's Congress, which theoretically functions as a parliament with a cabinet called General People's Committee.

Economy **Monetary unit:** Libyan dinar. **Budget:** (1989 est.) ***income:*** $8.1 bil.; ***expend.:*** $9.8 bil. **GNP:** $32 bil., $6,600 per capita (1993 est.). **Chief crops:** wheat, barley, olives, dates, citrus fruits; 75% of food is imported. **Livestock:** chickens, sheep, goats, cattle, camels. **Natural resources:** crude oil, natural gas, gypsum. **Major industries:** petroleum, food processing, textiles. **Labor force:** 1 mil., of which about 280,000 are resident foreigners; 31% industry, 27% services, 24% government, 18% agriculture; **Exports:** $7.7 bil. (f.o.b., 1993 est.); petroleum; **Imports:** $8.26 bil. (f.o.b., 1993 est.). **Major trading partners:** ***exports:*** Italy, former USSR, Germany, Spain, France; ***imports:*** Italy, former Soviet republics, Germany, UK, Japan.

Intl. Orgs. Arab League, FAO, G-77, IAEA, IBRD, ICAO, IDA, IFAD, IFC, ILO, IMF, IMO, INTELSAT, INTERPOL, ITU, NAM, OAU, OPEC, UN, UNESCO, UPU, WHO, WIPO, WMO.

The coastal cities of Libya played an important cultural and commercial role in the Mediterranean in antiquity and were prized possessions of numerous empires. The Libyan coast was successively ruled by Phoenicians, Carthaginians, Berbers, Romans, and Vandals before being incorporated into the Byzantine Empire in the fourth century A.D.; nomadic tribes in the interior were beyond the reach of any government. The Islamic conquests of the seventh and eighth centuries brought Libya into the Muslim world.

Libya was incorporated into the Ottoman Empire shortly after the Ottoman conquest of Egypt in 1517 and was ruled by local Ottoman vassals until 1835 when direct Ottoman government was established. In 1911 Libya was invaded and conquered by Italy. After World War I, local resistance to Italian colonial rule was led by King Idris I, Emir of Cyrenaica. British troops drove Italian and German forces from Libya in 1943. King Idris returned from exile in 1944. Following World War II, most of Libya was ruled as a British protectorate with a smaller portion under French administration.

Libya became an independent constitutional monarchy on Dec. 24, 1951. In 1959 significant oil reserves were discovered, rapidly transforming Libya from one of the poorest states in North Africa to one of the wealthiest.

A military coup on Sept. 1, 1969, led by Col. Muammar al-Qaddafi, deposed the monarchy and declared the establishment of the Libyan Arab Republic. Qaddafi moved rapidly to nationalize foreign assets, expel foreign troops, and close foreign libraries and cultural centers. He also assumed full dictatorial powers under a political system that gives equal weight to Islamic law and his own political philosophy. Popular participation in elections is mandatory, although no government organization outside Qaddafi and his circle of advisers exerts any real authority.

Libya has given strong political and financial aid to various radical Palestinian groups and other enemies of Israel and its supporters, sponsoring terrorist activities throughout Europe and the Middle East in real or putative support of the Palestinian cause. Numerous anti-Qaddafi Libyan exiles were assassinated in Europe. Libya also engaged in sporadic military campaigns against Egypt and the Sudan, and has supported both the government and antigovernment forces in Chad, where it has occupied the northern Aouzou Strip since 1984.

Relations between Libya and the United States were very hostile in the 1980s. On May 6, 1981, the United States closed the Libyan "People's Bureau" (embassy) in Washington, D.C. On Aug. 2, 1981, American jets shot down two attacking Libyan warplanes as U.S. naval forces conducted exercises in the Gulf of Sidra, which Libya claims as national waters. In 1986 the United States imposed economic sanctions on Libya, ordered all Americans to leave the country, and froze Libyan assets in the United States. Another clash in March 1986 ended with the loss of two Libyan ships.

On Apr. 5, 1986, Libyan-sponsored terrorists bombed a nightclub in West Berlin, killing two U.S. soldiers; in response, American bombers attacked Tripoli and Benghazi on Apr. 14 in an apparent attempt to kill Col. Qaddafi himself. In 1990, investigators announced they had linked Libyan agents to the bombing of a Pan Am Jet over Lockerbie, Scotland, in 1988.

Great Britain broke off diplomatic relations with Libya in April 1984 after machine-gun fire from the Libyan "People's Bureau" in London killed a policeman and wounded 10 Libyan exiles demonstrating against Qaddafi's government. In May 1984 an attempted coup against Qaddafi was foiled; this was followed by a purge in which thousands of people were imprisoned or executed.

In January 1989 an international outcry arose when a West German company admitted selling equipment to Libya for a chemical weapons plant. Qaddafi's difficulties with the Western powers continued in 1992, as they demanded he release the suspected terrorists in the Lockerbie bombing. In April the United Nations imposed sanctions on Libya, including a prohibition on sales of military equipment and a ban on all flights in and out of the country.

The Libyan economy depends heavily on petroleum and natural gas. Other industrial activities include gypsum mining and light manufacturing, including textiles and carpets. A narrow strip of fertile land along the coast supports mixed agriculture, and sheep, goats, and camels are raised in the desert interior.

Liechtenstein

Principality of Liechtenstein

Geography **Location:** landlocked country in central Europe. **Boundaries:** Austria to N and E, Switzerland to S and W. **Total land area:** 62 sq. mi. (160 sq km). **Coastline:** none. **Comparative area:** about size of Washington, D.C. **Land use:** 25% arable land; 0% permanent crops; 38% meadows and pastures; 19% forest and woodland; 18% other. **Major cities:** (1992) Väduz (capital) 4,995; Schaan 5,035; Balzers 3,752; Triesen 3,696; Eschen 3,239.

People **Population:** 30,281 (1994 est.). **Nationality:** noun—Liechtensteiner(s); adjective—Liechtenstein. **Ethnic groups:** 95% Alemannic, 5% Italian and other. **Languages:** German (official), Alemannic dialect. **Religions:** 82.7% Roman Catholic, 7.1% Protestant, 10.2% other.

Government **Type:** hereditary constitutional monarchy. **Independence:** N.A. **Constitution:** Oct. 5, 1921. **National holiday:** N.A. **Heads of government:** Hans-Adam II, prince (since Nov. 1989); Mario Frick, prime minister; prince transferred most of his executive powers to his son, Prince Hans Adam, in Aug. 1984. **Structure:** executive—hereditary prince; legislative—unicameral legislature (diet; 15 deputies elected to four-year terms); judiciary—independent.

Economy **Monetary unit:** Swiss franc. **Budget:** (1990); ***income:*** $259 mil.; ***expend.:*** $292 mil. **GDP:** $630 mil., $22,300 per capita. Note: Liechtenstein has prosperous economy based primarily on small-scale light industry and some farming; sale of postage stamps to collectors, estimated at $10 mil. annually, provides 10% of state budget; companies incorporated in Liechtenstein solely for tax purposes provide additional 30% of state budget; low business taxes (maximum tax rate 20%) and easy incorporation rules have induced about 25,000 holding, or so-called letter box, companies to establish nominal offices there; economy is tied closely to that of Switzerland in customs union; no national accounts data available. **Chief crops:** vegetables, corn, wheat, potatoes, grapes. **Livestock:** cattle, pigs, horses, sheep, goats. **Natural resources:** hydroelectric potential. **Major industries:** electronics, metal manufacturing, textiles. **Labor force:** 19,905; 6,885 foreign workers (mostly from Switzerland and Austria); 54.4% industry, trade, and building; 41.6% services; 4% agriculture, fishing, forestry, and horticulture; no unemployment. **Exports:** N.A.; small specialty machinery, dental products, stamps, hardware, pottery. **Imports:** N.A.; machinery, metal goods, textiles, foodstuffs, motor vehicles. **Major trading partners:** ***exports:*** 40% EU, 26% EFTA (19% Switzerland); ***imports:*** N.A.

Intl. Orgs. EFTA, IAEA, INTELSAT, INTERPOL, ITU, OSCE, UN, UNCTAD, UNICEF, UNIDO, UPU, WIPO.

The alpine principality of Liechtenstein, bordered by Austria and Switzerland, is a remnant of the Holy Roman Empire, an ancient constitutional monarchy with a modern industrial economy. The current dynasty was established in 1699; Prince Franz Josef II came to the throne in 1938, yielding his executive powers to his heir apparent, Hans Adam, in 1984.

Liechtenstein was tied to the Austro-Hungarian monarchy until 1918. Since then it has remained in a customs union with Switzerland, which also handles its foreign affairs. The single-chamber diet, the Landtag is elected by universal suffrage, women having won the right to vote in 1984. The relatively conservative Progressive Citizen's party ruled continuously during 1928–70. From 1970 to 1974, and after 1978, the relatively liberal Fatherland Union controlled the government. Currently, the two parties rule in a coalition government. Liechtenstein joined the United Nations in 1990.

The economy, dominated by dairy farming before 1945, has since been radically transformed by industrialization and the development of service industries. Liechtenstein is a corporate haven, with some 25,000 corporations maintaining nominal headquarters there. Foreign workers constitute about 40 percent of the work force.

Lithuania

Republic of Lithuania

Geography **Location:** eastern coast of Baltic Sea in northeastern Europe. **Boundaries:** Latvia to N, Belarus to E and SE, Poland to SW, Russian Federation (Kaliningrad) to W, Baltic Sea to NW. **Total land area:** 25,174 sq. mi. (65,200 sq km). **Coastline:** Baltic Sea. **Comparative area:** slightly larger than West Virginia. **Land use:** 37% cropland; 17% permanent pasture; 24% forest and woodland; 22% other (mostly urban). **Major cities:** (1993 est.) Vilnius (capital) 590,100; Kaunas 429,000; Klaipeda 206,400; Siauliai 147,800; Paievezys 132,000.

People **Population:** 3,848,389 (1994 est.). **Nationality:** noun—Lithuanian(s); adjective—Lithuanian. **Ethnic groups:** 79.6% Lithuanian, 9.4% Russian, 7% Polish, Belarussian, Ukrainian, Jewish. **Languages:** Lithuanian (official), part of Baltic language group that uses Latin alphabet; Russian, Polish, ethnic languages. **Religions:** Christianity—Roman Catholic, Lutheran, Calvinist, modern Protestant denominations; Judaism.

Government **Type:** republic. **Independence:** Mar. 11, 1990 (from USSR); recognized by USSR Sept. 6, 1991. **Constitution:** Nov. 6, 1992. **National holiday:** Feb. 16. **Heads of government:** Algirdas Mykolas Brazauskas, president (since Feb. 1993); Adolfas Slezevicius, prime minister (since Mar. 1993). **Structure:** executive—president, Council of Ministers; legislative—Unicameral Seimas; judicial—Constitutional Court and Supreme Court.

Economy **Monetary unit:** litas. **Budget:** (1992 est.). ***income:*** $258.5 mil.; ***expend.:*** $270.2 mil. **GDP:** $12.4 bil., $3,240 per capita (1993 est.). **Chief crops:** grain, potatoes, sugar beet, vegetables. **Livestock:** pigs, cattle, sheep, goats. **Natural resources:** N.A. **Major industries:** machine building, metalworking, food processing. **Labor force:** 1,836,000 (1990). **Exports:** N.A.; 18% electronics, 16% petroleum products, 10% food, 6% chemicals. **Imports:** N.A.; 24% oil, 14% machinery, 8% chemicals. **Major trading partners:** Russian Federation, Belarus, Ukraine, Germany, Sweden, Denmark, Italy.

Intl. Orgs. IAEA, ILO, IMF, INTERPOL, OSCE, UN, UNCTAD.

Lithuanians and Latvians are closely related peoples whose languages, the only two in the Baltic family of languages, are quite similar. But their histories, at least until 1795, were radically different. Fierce warriors able to stem the German tide during the Middle Ages, the Lithuanians repeatedly defeated the Teutonic knights, defending their independence and retaining their own religion.

In the 14th century, under Grand Duke Gediminas and his sons, Lithuania conquered White Russia (Belarus) and Ukraine and extended the Lithuanian dynasty from the Baltic almost to the Black Sea. The completion of Gediminas's policies came in 1386 when his grandson Jogaila was baptized, married the Polish heiress Jadwiga, and was crowned king of Poland under the title Wladislaw II, thereby creating the Poland-Lithuania Commonwealth. One condition of the union was that Lithuania had to adopt Christianity, which it did in 1387.

With the Third Partition of Poland in 1795, Lithuania was absorbed into Russia. The upper and educated classes took part in Poland's anti-Russian rebellions in 1830 and 1863. After the latter, the Russians required Lithuanians to use the Russian alphabet instead of the Latvian as a move to stop any national renaissance; but after 1883 literature smuggled into the czarist empire from Prussia and secret Lithuanian schools and societies kept alive a national identity based on ethnic, religious, and linguistic grounds rather than on the medieval and Renaissance traditions of political independence.

In January 1921 the victorious allies of World War I formally recognized the new Lithuanian republic that came into being with the Soviet-German Treaty of Brest-Litovsk of March 1918, although a French garrison and administration remained for two more years. The territory of Memel (Klaipeda in Lithuanian), separated from Germany in the Treaty of Versailles, was seized in January 1923 and organized as an autonomous unit of the new republic. The city itself was largely German, but its countryside was Lithuanian and in any case it was Lithuania's only possible outlet to the sea. With the historic capital Vilnius annexed by the new Polish state, the de facto capital became the university city of Kaunas.

Danger from local communists and fascists led the army to dispense with Parliament in December 1926, and an authoritarian regime under Pres. Antana Smetona followed. In 1939 Lithuania, like the other Baltic states, was doomed by the "secret protocols" of the 1939 Nazi-Soviet Pact. In June 1940 a Soviet-approved "people's government" was formed, and after an election in which only pro-Soviet candidates were permitted to run, the Lithuanian Soviet Socialist Republic was proclaimed on July 21, 1940.

Thousands of Lithuanians fled westward, while other thousands disappeared into Siberia. Stalin returned Vilnius (from Poland) and Klaipeda (which Hitler had taken) to Lithuania and fostered industrialization, which elevated living standards above most of the USSR. A high Lithuanian birth rate enabled the country to resist "Russification" more easily than Latvia or Estonia.

Mikhail Gorbachev's policy of glasnost, or openness, spurred the already strong Lithuanian nationalist and dissident movement into action. It began with a public discussion of the "secret protocols" of the 1939 Nazi-Soviet Pact, which had permitted the USSR to annex Lithuania and which the Soviet government long had denied existed. In 1987 the Soviet government tolerated demonstrations in Vilnius, but by February 1988, Soviet troops prevented the Lithuanians from celebrating their 70th year of independence. The Soviet stance resulted in the founding of the new Lithuanian Movement for Reconstruction (Sajudis), which became the main political vehicle for Lithuanian independence from the USSR.

On Mar. 11, 1990, Lithuania formally declared its independence, and in response the Soviets began a 72-day-long economic blockade. On Jan. 13, 1991, the world watched as Soviet paratroopers and tanks attacked the radio and television centers, beginning a standoff between the Soviets and the Lithuanians that lasted until Sept. 6, 1991, when the USSR reluctantly recognized Lithuanian independence.

After independence, Lithuania struggled to break a political deadlock caused by its lack of a constitution. In November 1992 free elections were held. The Democratic Labor party (the renamed Communists) gained 47 percent of the vote and 77 seats in Parliament, while Sajudis gained only 22 percent of the vote and 28 seats. In February 1993 the Democratic Labor candidate, Algirdas Brazauskas, handily won the presidential election with 61 percent of the vote. Direct election of the president was settled in a November constitution.

The last Soviet troops left Lithuania soil Aug. 31, 1993. Both president and premier are pledged to a slower path to a free economy and to better relations with Russia and the other former Soviet states to the east.

Luxembourg

Grand Duchy of Luxembourg

Geography **Location:** landlocked country in western Europe. **Boundaries:** Belgium to N and W, Germany to E, France to S. **Total land area:** 998 sq. mi. (2,586 sq km). **Coastline:** none. **Comparative area:** slightly smaller than Rhode Island. **Land use:** 24% arable land; 1% permanent crops; 20% meadows and pastures; 21% forest and woodland; 34% other. **Major cities:** (1992 est.) Luxembourg-Ville (capital) 75,377; Esch-sur-Alzette 24,012; Differdange 15,699; Dudelange 14,677; Sanem 11,534.

People **Population:** 401,900 (1994 est.). **Nationality:** noun—Luxembourger(s); adjective—Luxembourg. **Ethnic groups:** Celtic base, with

French and German blend; also, guest and worker residents from Portugal, Italy, and European countries. **Languages:** Luxembourgish, German, French. **Religions:** 97% Roman Catholic, 3% Protestant and Jewish.

Government Type: constitutional monarchy. **Independence:** N.A. **Constitution:** Oct. 17, 1868, occasional revisions. **National holiday:** Grand Duke's birthday, June 23. **Heads of government:** Jean de Luxembourg, grand duke (since Nov. 1964); Jean-Claude Juncker, prime minister (since Jan. 1995). **Structure:** parliamentary democracy; seven ministers compose Council of Government, headed by president, which constitutes executive; it is responsible to unicameral legislature (Chamber of Deputies); Council of State, appointed for indefinite term, exercises some powers of an upper house; judicial power exercised by independent courts; coalition governments are usual.

Economy Monetary unit: Luxembourg franc. **Budget:** (1992) ***income***: $3.5 bil.; ***expend.:*** $3.5 bil. **GDP:** $8.7 bil., $22,600 per capita (1993). **Chief crops:** mixed farming, wine. **Livestock:** cattle, horses, pigs, sheep, poultry. **Natural resources:** iron ore (no longer exploited). **Major industries:** banking, iron and steel, food processing. **Labor force:** 177,300 (1988); 48.9% services, 24.7% industry, 13.2% government; one-third of work force is foreign, comprising mostly workers from Portugal, Italy, France, Belgium, and W. Germany; 1.6% unemployment (1987). **Exports:** $6.4 bil. (f.o.b., 1991 est.); iron and steel products, chemicals, rubber products, glass, aluminum. **Imports:** $8.3 bil. (c.i.f., 1991 est.); minerals, metals, foodstuffs, machinery, quality consumer goods. **Major trading partners: *exports:*** 75% EU, 6% U.S.; ***imports:*** 37% Belgium, 37% Germany, 12% France, 2% U.S.

Intl. Orgs. EU, FAO, IAEA, IBRD, ICAO, IDA, IFAD, IFC, ILO, IMF, INTELSAT, INTERPOL, ITU, NATO, OSCE, UN, UNESCO, UPU, WHO, WIPO, WMO, WTO.

One of hundreds of small principalities in the Holy Roman Empire, Luxembourg joined the German league when the empire was abolished in 1806. It shared a monarchy with the Netherlands, but the two countries remained distinct under a single sovereign. In 1831 Luxembourg lost its French-speaking territory to Belgium. The Treaty of London granted sovereignty to Luxembourg in 1867. When King William III died in 1890, different rules of succession severed the dual monarchy; Queen Wilhelmina succeeded him in the Netherlands, while Adolf of Nassau became grand duke of Luxembourg. The nation's full independence dates from that event.

During the 19th century, Luxembourg developed a balanced modern economy, with prosperous small farms being complemented by industry, particularly mining and steel production. As late as 1970, steel accounted for over 25 percent of the nation's GDP and five-eighths of export earnings, although rising international competition has led to a decline since then.

Luxembourg was overrun by Germany during World War I and again in May 1940, in the early stages of World War II. Archduchess Charlotte fled to London and returned with the Allied armed forces in 1944. The constitutional monarchy has enjoyed political stability since the war, with the Christian Social party normally the senior partner in a three-way coalition.

Luxembourg formed a customs union with Belgium in 1921 and joined the Benelux (Belgium, Netherlands, Luxembourg) union even before World War II had ended. A founding member of the United Nations in 1945, Luxembourg abandoned its traditional neutrality in 1948 and joined NATO in 1949. It was a founding member of the EEC under the 1956 Treaty of Rome and is now home to numerous Common Market institutions, including the Secretariat of the European Parliament and the European Investment Bank; international banking accounts for over half of its gross national product. The country's chief problem is a shrinking and aging citizenry, leading to strains on social services and dependence on foreign workers.

Macedonia

See Part I: "Major News Stories of the Year."

Madagascar

Democratic Republic of Madagascar

Geography Location: off southeast Africa in western Indian Ocean. Antananarivo: 18°52'S, 47°30'E. **Boundaries:** about 300 mi. (500 km) E of Mozambique. **Total land area:** 226,656 sq. mi. (587,040 sq km). **Coastline:** 3,000 mi. (4,828 km). **Comparative area:** between California and Texas. **Land use:** 4% arable land; 1% permanent crops; 58% meadows and pastures; 26% forest and woodland; 11% other; includes 1% irrigated. **Major cities:** Antananarivo (capital) 662,585 (1985 est.); Antsirabé 78,941; Toamasina (Tamatave) 77,395; Fianarantsoa 68,054; Mahajanga (Majunga) 65,864 (1975 census).

People Population: 13,427,758 (1994 est.). **Nationality:** noun—Malagasy (sing., pl.); adjective—Malagasy. **Ethnic groups:** highlanders of predominantly Malayo-Indonesian origin (Merina 1,643,000 and related Betsileo 760,000); coastal peoples collectively termed Cotiers, with mixed African, Malayo-Indonesian, and Arab ancestry (Betsimisaraka 941,000; Tsimihety 442,000; Antaisaka 415,000; Sakalava 375,000); 11,000 European French, 5,000 Indians of French nationality, 5,000 Creoles. **Languages:** French and Malagasy (both official). **Religions:** 52% indigenous beliefs, 41% Christian, 7% Muslim.

Government Type: real authority in hands of president, although Supreme Revolutionary Council is theoretically ultimate executive authority. **Independence:** June 26, 1960 (from France). **Constitution:** Dec. 21, 1975. **National holiday:** Independence Day, June 26. **Heads of government:** Albert Zafy, president (since Mar. 1993); Francisque Ravony, prime minister (since Aug. 1993). **Structure:** executive—president, Supreme Revolutionary Council (made up of military and political leaders) assisted by cabinet (Council of Ministers); unicameral legislature—Popular National Assembly; judiciary—courts patterned after French system, High Council of Institutions has power of constitutional review.

Economy Monetary unit: Malagasy franc. **Budget:** (1991) ***income:*** $250 mil; ***expend.:*** $265 mil. **GDP:** $10.4 bil., $800 per capita (1993 est.). **Chief crops:** cash crops—coffee, vanilla, cloves, sugar, tobacco; food crops—rice, cassava, cereals, potatoes, corn. **Livestock:** cattle, pigs, goats, sheep. **Natural resources:** graphite, chromite, coal, bauxite, salt. **Major industries:** agricultural processing (meat canneries, soap factories, brewery, tanneries, sugar refining), light consumer goods industries (textiles, glassware), cement. **Labor force:** 4.9 mil. (1985); 95% nonsalaried family workers engaged in subsistence agriculture; 175,000 wage and salary earners (26% agriculture, 17% domestic service, 15% industry, 14% commerce, 11% construction); 51% of population of working age. **Exports:** $312 mil. (f.o.b., 1991 est.); 45% coffee, 15% vanilla, 11% cloves. **Imports:** $350 mil. (f.o.b., 1992 est.); 30% intermediate manufactures, 28% capital goods, 15% petroleum, 14% consumer goods, 13% food. **Major trading partners: *exports:*** France, Germany, Japan, Italy, U.S.; ***imports:*** France, Germany, UK, other EC, U.S.

Intl. Orgs. FAO, G-77, IAEA, IBRD, ICAO, IDA, IFAD, IFC, ILO, IMF, IMO, INTELSAT, INTERPOL, ITU, NAM, UN, UNESCO, UPU, WHO, WMO, WTO.

The largest island nation, and fourth largest island, in the world, Madagascar was settled by Malayo-Indonesian migrants some 2,000 years ago. Although later waves of African and Arab migrants were absorbed into the population, to a large extent it is still ethnically and culturally Asian. A Portuguese attempt to colonize the island in the 16th century failed, and during the 18th and 19th centuries, a unified kingdom backed by the British ruled the country. Foreign interests—largely British and French—developed extensive coffee plantations, and the French made Madagascar a protectorate in 1885 and a colony in 1896.

During World War II Madagascar sided with the Free French, and French colonial rule was reestablished after the war. The Malagasy Republic was founded as an independent nation on June 26, 1960. A coup in 1972 brought an anti-French and generally anti-Western government to power. Repression and economic stagnation characterized the 1970s.

A coalition government under Guy Razanamasy was formed in late 1991, and a new federal constitution was approved in August 1992. The election of February 1993 resulted in the defeat of Pres. Didier Ratsiraka, the 17-year incumbent, by Albert Zafy, a surgeon.

Madagascar's wildlife—a mixture of African species and others of domestic evolution—makes it of unique scientific interest. In 1990, scientists announced the discovery of the smallest mammal known to science, the dwarf lemur.

Malawi

Republic of Malawi

Geography Location: landlocked country in southern central Africa. **Boundaries:** Tanzania to N, Mozambique to E, S, and SW, Zambia to W; Lake Malawi forms much of eastern boundary. **Total land area:** 45,745 sq. mi. (118,480 sq km). **Coastline:** none. **Comparative area:** slightly larger than Pennsylvania. **Land use:** 25% arable land; negl. % permanent crops; 20% meadows and pastures; 50% forest and woodland; 5% other; includes negl. % irrigated. **Major cities:** Lilongwe (capital) 233,973 (1987 est.); Blantyre 331,558 (1987 census).

People Population: 9,732,409 (1994 est.). **Nationality:** noun—Malawian(s); adjective—Malawian. **Ethnic groups:** Chewa, Nyanja, Tumbuko, Yao, Lomwe, Sena, Tonga, Ngoni, Asian, European. **Languages:** English and Chichewa (both official); Tombuka. **Religions:** 55% Protestant, 20% Roman Catholic, 20% Muslim, indigenous beliefs.

Government Type: one-party state. **Independence:** July 6, 1964 (from UK). **Constitution:** July 6, 1964. **National holiday:** Republic Day, July 6. **Head of government:** Elson Bakili Muluzi, president (since May 1994). **Structure:** executive—strong presidential system with cabinet appointed by president; legislative—unicameral National Assembly of 87 elected and up to 15 nominated members; judiciary—high court with chief justice and at least two justices.

Economy Monetary unit: Malawi kwacha. **Budget:** (1991 est.) ***income:*** $416 mil.; ***expend.:*** $498 mil. **GDP:** $6 bil., $600 per capita (1993 est.). **Chief crops:** cash crops—tobacco, tea, sugar, peanuts, cotton; subsistence crops—corn, sorghum, millet, pulses, root crops; self-sufficient in food production. **Livestock:** cattle, goats, pigs, sheep. **Natural resources:** limestone; unexploited deposits of uranium, coal, bauxite. **Major industries:** agricultural processing (tea, tobacco, sugar), sawmilling, cement. **Labor force:** 428,000 (1986); 52% agriculture, 16% personal services, 9% manufacturing. **Exports:** $413 mil. (f.o.b., 1992); tobacco, tea, sugar, peanuts, cotton. **Imports:** $737 mil. (c.i.f., 1992); manufactured goods, machinery and transport equipment, building and construction materials, fuel, fertilizer. **Major trading partners:** ***exports:*** UK, U.S., South Africa, Zambia; ***imports:*** South Africa, UK, Japan, U.S., Zimbabwe.

Intl. Orgs. Commonwealth, EU (associated member), FAO, G-77, IBRD, ICAO, IDA, IFAD, IFC, ILO, IMF, INTELSAT, INTERPOL, ITU, NAM, UN, UNESCO, UPU, WHO, WIPO, WMO, WTO.

Malawi derives its name from the Maravi, a Bantu people that settled in the region in the 13th century and whose descendants, the Chewas, comprise a significant segment of the current population. In the 1830s, the Ngoni, driven from what is now South Africa by the Zulus, arrived in the area around Lake Nyasa. The arrival of the Scottish missionary David Livingstone in 1859 led to the establishment of the British-controlled Nyasaland Protectorate in 1891. In 1953 Nyasaland formed a federation with Northern and Southern Rhodesia (Zambia and Zimbabwe) and began to organize an independence movement. The fight for independence was led by Dr. H. Kamuzu Banda, an expatriate who assumed the presidency of the Nyasaland African Congress, later the Malawi Congress party, upon his return in 1958. The British granted Nyasaland self-governing status in 1962, and Banda was elected prime minister the following year. Malawi achieved full independence under its present name in 1964.

Banda soon introduced one-party rule and had himself declared president for life in 1971. All dissent was crushed while corruption and nepotism strangled the economy, leaving Malawi's citizens among the poorest in the world.

By 1990 internal unrest and the decline of Banda's popularity (he was now in his 90s) rapidly led to change. In 1992 a series of violent strikes by workers in the two largest cities resulted in more than 35 deaths. The United States, Great Britain, and Germany, hoping to push the Banda government to institute democratic reforms, cut off most of the $500 million they had been giving annually in aid. In June 1993 Malawians voted 2 to 1 to institute a multiparty system and in May 1994 Banda lost his nation's only free election in 30 years to Bakili Muluzi's United Democratic Front (UDF). By January 1995 Banda was under house arrest and charged with murder.

Malaysia

Geography Location: 13 states in Southeast Asia; 11 are in Peninsular Malaysia and two, Sabah and Sarawak, lie about 400 mi. (640 km) across South China Sea on northern coast of island of Borneo (Kalimantan). **Boundaries:** Peninsular Malaysia—Thailand to N, South China Sea to E, Island of Singapore to S across Johor Strait, and Indonesian island of Sumatra to W across Strait of Malacca; Sabah and Sarawak—South China Sea to NW, Sulu Sea to NE, Celebes Sea to E, Indonesia to S; Brunei is enclosed withing Sarawak on coast of South China Sea. **Total land area:** 127,317 sq. mi. (329,750 sq km). **Coastline:** 2,905 mi. (4,675 km). **Comparative area:** between New Mexico and Montana. **Land use:** 3% arable land; 10% permanent crops; negl. % meadows and pastures; 63% forest and woodland; 24% other; includes 1% irrigated. **Major cities:** (1991 census) Kuala Lumpur (capital) 1,145,075; Ipoh 382,633; Johor Baharu 328,646; Melaka (Malacca) 295,999; Petaling Jaya 254,849.

People Population: 19,283,154 (1994 est.). **Nationality:** noun—Malaysian(s); adjective—Malaysian. **Ethnic groups:** 59% Malay and other indigenous, 32% Chinese, 9% Indian. **Languages:** Peninsular Malaysia—Malay (official); English, Chinese dialects, Tamil; Sabah—English, Malay, numerous tribal dialects, Mandarin and Hakka dialects predominate among Chinese; Sarawak—English, Malay, Mandarin, numerous tribal languages. **Religions:** Peninsular Malaysia—Malays nearly all Muslim, Chinese predominantly Buddhist, Indians predominantly Hindu; Sabah—38% Muslim, 17% Christian, 45% other; Sarawak—35% tribal religion, 24% Buddhist and Confucianist, 20% Muslim, 16% Christian, 5% other.

Government Type: Federation of Malaysia formed July 9, 1963; constitutional monarchy nominally headed by paramount ruler (king); bicameral Parliament; Peninsular Malaysian states—hereditary rulers in all but Penang and Melaka, where governors are appointed by Malaysian government, with powers of state governments limited by federal constitution; Sabah—self-governing state, holding 20 seats in House of Representatives, with foreign affairs, defense, internal security, and other powers delegated to federal government; Sarawak—self-governing state, which holds 24 seats in House of Representatives, with foreign affairs, defense, internal security, and other powers delegated to federal government. **Independence:** Aug. 31, 1957 (from UK). **Constitution:** Aug. 31, 1957, amended Sept. 6, 1963, when Federation of Malaya became Federation of Malaysia. **National holiday:** Independence Day, Aug. 31. **Heads of government:** Tuanka Jaafar, king (since Apr. 1994); Dr. Mahathir Mohamad, prime minister (since July 1981). **Structure:** nine state rulers alternate as "king" for five-year terms; locus of executive power vested in prime minister and cabinet, who are responsible to bicameral Parliament (58-member Senate, 177-member House of Representatives); Peninsular Malaysia—executive branches of 11 states vary in detail but are similar in design, with chief minister, appointed by hereditary ruler or governor, heading an executive council (cabinet), which is responsible to elected, unicameral legislature; Sarawak—executive branch headed by governor, appointed by central government, having largely ceremonial role; executive power exercised by chief minister who heads parliamentary cabinet responsible to unicameral legislature; judiciary is part of Malaysian judicial system.

Economy Monetary unit: Malaysian ringgit. **Budget:** (1992 est.) ***income:*** $19.6 bil. ***expend.:*** $18 bil. **GDP:** $141 bil., $7,500 per capita (1993 est.). **Chief crops:** Peninsular Malaysia—natural rubber, palm oil, rice; 10–15% of rice requirements imported; Sabah—mainly subsistence, main crops are rubber, timber, coconut, rice (rice is also food deficit); Sarawak—main crops are rubber, timber, pepper (rice is food deficit). **Livestock:** pigs, cattle, goats, buffalo, sheep. **Natural resources:** tin, crude oil, timber, copper, iron ore. **Major industries:** Peninsular Malaysia—rubber and oil-palm processing and manufacturing, light manufacturing industry, electronics; Sabah—logging, petroleum production; Sarawak—agriculture processing, petroleum production and refining, logging. **Labor force:** 7,258,000 (1991 est.); 34.5% agriculture; trade, hotels, and restaurants; 15.6% manufacturing, 14.9% government. **Exports:** $46.8 bil. (f.o.b., 1993 est.); natural rubber, palm oil, tin, timber, petroleum. **Imports:** $40.4 bil. (f.o.b., 1993 est.). **Major trading partners:** ***exports:*** Japan, Singapore, U.S., former USSR, Australia, EU; ***imports:*** Japan, EU, Singapore, Germany, UK, Thailand, China.

Intl. Orgs. ASEAN, Colombo Plan, Commonwealth, FAO, G-77, IAEA, IBRD, ICAO, IDA, IFC, ILO, IMF, IMO, INTELSAT, INTERPOL, ITU, NAM, UN, UNESCO, UPU, WHO, WMO, WTO.

From ancient times a group of petty principalities in the southern part of the Malay Peninsula, bordering the Strait of Malacca, maintained extensive ties of maritime commerce throughout Southeast Asia. The early Malay states were Hindu, under Indian influence; with the rise of the Kingdom of Malacca in the 15th century, conversion to Islam was widespread. European influence in the Spice Islands began in the 16th century; the Portuguese, initially dominant, gave way to the Dutch, who seized Malacca in 1641.

British influence grew during the 18th century, with the founding of a trading settlement at Penang in 1789. Singapore was founded in 1819, and the Dutch ceded Malacca to Great Britain in 1824. By a series of treaties in the late 19th century, the various Malay states became British protectorates; Britain controlled the entire southern peninsula after 1909. Under British rule, commercial tin mining and the establishment of extensive rubber plantations led to the importation of many Indian and Chinese laborers; eventually ethnic Chinese dominated most of Malaya's domestic economy.

In the 19th century, Great Britain also gained a dominant position in northern Borneo. (Borneo is divided between Brunei, Indonesia, and Malaysia.)

Japan overran Malaya by February 1942. Following World War II, the various Malay states (excluding Singapore) organized into a federation, which replaced the confusing prewar regime of federated and unfederated protectorates. A Communist rebellion disrupted the country throughout the early 1950s. Following the suppression of the Communist movement, elections were held in mid-1955 for a home-rule government. The elections brought the Alliance party of Tungku Abdul Rahman to power, and the Federation of Malaya became independent in 1957.

The nation expanded on Sept. 16, 1963, with the creation of Malaysia, incorporating the Federation of Malaya as well as Singapore and the former British colonies of North Borneo (thereafter called Sabah) and Sarawak. Singapore seceded from Malaysia in 1965 and became an independent nation. Malaysia is a constitutional monarchy with a parliamentary system; monarchs are chosen for five-year terms from among the hereditary rulers of the nine Malay states.

Ethnic concerns dominate Malaysian politics. Muslim Malays have enacted various laws to restrict the economic power and ethnic cohesion of the non-Islamic Chinese and Indian minorities. On Dec. 2, 1989, Malaysia's Communist party signed a cease-fire and lay down its arms after 41 years of conflict along the Malaysia-Thailand border.

By the mid-1980s exports of oil and natural gas had surpassed Malaysia's traditional principal exports of rubber, tin, and other natural-resource-based commodities (palm oil, timber, spices); modernization has created an export-oriented industrial sector producing textiles, electronic equipment, and other manufactured goods.

In recent years the main political preoccupation of Malaysia has been an attempt by Prime Minister Mahathir Mohamad and the ruling UMNO party to curb the powers of Malaysia's traditional sultans.

Maldives

Republic of Maldives

Geography **Location:** chain of more than 1,200 small coral islands (about 220 inhabited), 475 mi. (764 km) from N to S and 80 mi. (207 km) from W to E in Indian Ocean; northernmost atoll about 370 mi. (960 km) southwest of India. Malé 4°00'N, 73°28'E. **Boundaries:** Laccadive Sea to NE, Arabian Sea to N, Indian Ocean to S and W. **Total land area:** 116 sq. mi. (300 sq km). **Coastline:** 400 mi. (644 km). **Comparative area:** about 1.5 times size of Washington, D.C. **Land use:** 10% arable land; 0% permanent crops; 3% meadows and pastures; 3% forest and woodland; 84% other. **Major cities:** (1990) Malé (capital) 56,060.

People **Population:** 252,077 (1994 est.). **Nationality:** noun—Maldivian(s); adjective—Maldivian. **Ethnic groups:** admixtures of Sinhalese, Dravidian, Arab, and black. **Languages:** Divehi (dialect of Sinhala; script derived from Arabic); English spoken by most government officials. **Religions:** Sunni Muslim.

Government **Type:** republic. **Independence:** July 26, 1965 (from UK). **Constitution:** June 4, 1964. **National holidays:** Independence Day, July 26; Republic Day, Nov. 11. **Head of government:** Maumoon Abdul Gayoom, president (since Nov. 1978). **Structure:** elected president, chief executive; popularly elected unicameral national legislature, People's Council (members elected for five-year terms); appointed chief justice responsible for administration of Islamic law.

Economy **Monetary unit:** Maldivian rufiya. **Budget:** (1991 est.) ***income:*** $95 mil.; ***expend.:*** $71 mil. **GDP:** $140 mil., $620 per capita (1991 est.). **Chief crops:** coconut, limited production of millet, corn, pumpkins, sweet potatoes; shortages—rice, sugar, flour. **Livestock:** N.A. **Natural resources:** fish. **Major industries:** fishing, tourism, some coconut processing. **Labor force:** about 66,000; fishing industry employs about 80% of labor force. **Exports:** $56.3 mil. (f.o.b., 1993 est.); 57% fish, 39% clothing. **Imports:** $173.6 mil. (c.i.f., 1993 est.); 47% intermediate and capital goods, 42% consumer goods, 11% petroleum products. **Major trading partners:** ***exports:*** U.S., UK, Sri Lanka; ***imports:*** Singapore, Germany, Sri Lanka, India.

Intl. Orgs. Colombo Plan, Commonwealth (special member), FAO, G-77, IBRD, ICAO, IDA, IFAD, IFC, IMF, IMO, ITU, NAM, UN, UNESCO, UPU, WHO, WMO, WTO.

The small sultanate of the Maldive Islands, with an Islamic population of Sinhalese descent, was made a British protectorate in 1887. The islands' tiny area and poor soil limited development; fishing and fish processing are the main industries, and copra (dried coconut meat for coconut oil) is the only significant crop. The Maldives became an independent nation on July 26, 1965. In 1968 the sultanate was abolished and replaced by a republic. Since independence, tourism has become economically important and now accounts for 10 percent of the gross national product. Protests over the concentration of development on the island of Malé in recent years have led to political unrest in the other islands, while attempts to address the basic needs of those islands have strained the nation's tiny economic base.

The current president, Maumoon Abdul Gayoom, was elected to office in 1978 and subsequently reelected twice. The elections of September 1988 were marked by considerable unrest and demonstrations. An attempted coup against the Gayoom government on Nov. 4, 1988, was put down with the intervention of Indian troops.

Mali

Republic of Mali

Geography **Location:** northwestern Africa. **Boundaries:** Algeria to N, Niger to E, Burkina Faso, Ivory Coast, Guinea to S, Senegal and Mauritania to W. **Total land area:** 478,765 sq. mi. (1,240,000 sq km). **Coastline:** none. **Comparative area:** between Texas and Alaska. **Land use:** 2% arable land; negl. % permanent crops; 25% meadows and pastures; 7% forest and woodland; 66% other; includes negl. % irrigated. **Major cities:** (1976 census) Bamako (capital) 404,000; Ségou 65,000; Mopti 54,000; Sikasso 47,000; Kayes 45,000.

People **Population:** 9,112,950 (1994 est.). **Nationality:** noun—Malian(s); adjective—Malian. **Ethnic groups:** 50% Mande (Bambara, Malinke, Sarakole), 17% Peul, 12% Voltaic, 6% Songhai, 5% Tuareg and Moor. **Languages:** French (official); Bambara spoken by 80% of population. **Religions:** 90% Muslim, 9% indigenous beliefs, 1% Christian.

Government **Type:** republic; single-party constitutional government. **Independence:** Sept. 22, 1960 (from France). **Constitution:** June 2, 1974, effective June 19, 1979. **National holiday:** Independence Day, Sept. 22. **Heads of government:** Alpha Oumar Konare, president (since June 1992); Ihrahim Boubacar Kéita, prime minister (since Feb. 1994). **Structure:** executive—cabinet composed of civilians and army officers; unicameral legislature—National Council; judiciary.

Economy **Monetary unit:** Communauté Financière Africaine (CFA) franc. **Budget:** (1989 est.) ***income:*** $376 mil.; ***expend.:*** N.A. **GDP:** $5.8 bil., $650 per capita (1993 est.). **Chief crops:** millet, sorghum, rice, corn, peanuts; cash crops—peanuts, cotton. **Livestock:** goats, sheep, cattle, asses, camels. **Natural resources:** gold, phosphates, kaolin, salt, limestone, uranium; bauxite, iron ore, manganese, tin, and copper deposits are known but not exploited. **Major industries:** small local consumer goods and processing, construction, phosphate, gold, fishing. **Labor force:** 2,666,000 (1986); 80% agriculture, 19% services; 50% of population of working age (1985). **Exports:** $330 mil. (f.o.b., 1992 est.); livestock, peanuts, dried fish, cotton, skins. **Imports:** $682 mil. (f.o.b., 1992 est.); textiles, vehicles, petroleum products, machinery, sugar, cereals. **Major trading partners:** mostly franc zone and Western Europe.

Intl. Orgs. FAO, G-77, IAEA, IBRD, ICAO, IDA, IFAD, IFC, ILO, IMF, INTELSAT, INTERPOL, ITU, NAM, UN, UNESCO, UPU, WHO, WMO, WTO.

Mali has been a center of West African civilization for over 4,000 years. Iron Age civilizations flourished on the middle reaches of the Niger River from about 200 B.C. The kingdom of Ghana arose about A.D. 750 on the strength of the gold trade with North African Berbers. Ghana was overthrown by the Muslim Almoravids, who ruled only 11 years, though Islam remained a major influence from that time. From 1200 to 1400, the Kingdom of Mali was dominant in the region and was renowned throughout Islam and even in Christian Europe for its wealth and power; when Mansa Musa's retinue stopped in Cairo en route to Mecca, it carried so much gold that the price of gold fell 20 percent. By the end of the 14th century, the Mali empire had been eclipsed by the Songhai (Soyinka) empire, centered on the Niger River cities of Gao and Timbuktu.

The Songhai empire collapsed after Timbuktu was sacked by Moroccans in 1591. It fragmented into a series of smaller states, and power shifted from the desert fringe back to the Niger valley, bringing with it a further spread of Islam.

French exploration of Mali led to conquest in 1896 and the creation of the colony of French Sudan in 1898, governed from Dakar, Senegal. Timbuktu continued to decline in importance, and Bamako became the country's principal urban center.

Malians were granted French citizenship and limited self-rule in 1946. In 1958 the territory became autonomous within the French Overseas Community. In 1959, with French support, the French Sudan and Senegal formed the Federation of Mali, which became independent on June 20, 1960. Senegal seceded from the federation almost immediately, and Mali became an independent republic on Sept. 22, 1960. Modibo Keita was elected the country's first president.

Keita's program of radical control of society and the economy by the central government provoked discontent, and he was overthrown in 1968 by military officers led by Lt. Moussa Traore. Traore's Military Committee of National Liberation ruled until 1979 when it was reorganized under a new constitution as the Malian People's Democratic Union. Traore was ousted in a 1991 coup and a transitional government under a civilian prime minister, Soumana Sacko, set up multiparty elections for June 1992. Alpha Konare was elected president and his Alliance for Democracy in Mali party won 76 of 116 legislative seats. Economic reform and a settlement with ethnic Tuareg to the north are two of the country's most pressing problems.

Mali is primarily agricultural in the south and west, pastoral in the north and east. The livestock sector has been repeatedly devastated by drought and spreading desertification. Mali maintains close ties with France, and the economy remains heavily dependent on foreign assistance.

Malta

Republic of Malta

Geography **Location:** archipelago (largest islands are Malta, Gozo, and Comino) in central Mediterranean. Valletta 35°54'N, 14°32'E. **Boundaries:** Sicily 58 mi. (93 km) to N, Libya 180 mi. (290 km) to S, Tunisia to W. **Total land area:** 124 sq. mi. (320 sq km). **Coastline:** 87 mi. (140 km). **Comparative area:** slightly less than twice size of Washington, D.C. **Land use:** 38% arable land; 3% permanent crops; 0% meadows and pastures; 0% forest and woodland; 59% other; includes 3% irrigated. **Major cities:** (1991 est.) Valletta (capital) 9,183; Birkirkara 21,437; Qormi 19,525, Sliema 13,541.

People **Population:** 366,767 (1994 est.). **Nationality:** noun—Maltese (sing., pl.); adjective—Maltese. **Ethnic groups:** mixture of Arab, Sicilian, Norman, Spanish, Italian, English. **Languages:** Maltese and English. **Religions:** 98% Roman Catholic.

Government **Type:** parliamentary democracy, independent republic within Commonwealth. **Independence:** Sept. 21, 1964 (from UK). **Constitution:** Apr. 26, 1974; effective June 2, 1974. **National holiday:** Freedom Day, Mar. 31. **Heads of government:** Ugo Mifsud Bonnici, president (since Apr. 1994); Eddie Fenech Adami, prime minister (since May 1987). **Structure:** executive—prime minister and cabinet; legislature—65-member House of Representatives; judiciary—independent.

Economy **Monetary unit:** Maltese lire. **Budget:** (1992 est.) ***income:*** $1.2 bil.; ***expend.:*** $1.2 bil. **GDP:** $2.4 bil., $6,600 per capita (1992 est.). **Chief crops:** potatoes, cauliflower, grapes, wheat, barley; adequate supplies of vegetables, milk, and pork products; seasonal or periodic shortages in grain, animal fodder, fruits, other basic foodstuffs; 20% self-sufficient overall. **Livestock:** pigs, cattle, goats, sheep. **Natural resources:** limestone, salt. **Major industries:** tourism, ship repair yard, clothing. **Labor force:** 127,200 (1990); 30% services (except government), 24% manufacturing, 21% government (except job corps); 4.6% registered unemployment. **Exports:** $1.3 bil. (f.o.b., 1992); clothing, textiles, ships, printed matter. **Imports:** $1.93 mil. (f.o.b., 1992); food, petroleum, nonfood raw materials. **Major trading partners:** ***exports:*** 30% Italy, 22% Germany, 11% UK; ***imports:*** 30% Italy, 16% UK, 13% Germany, 4% U.S.

Intl. Orgs. Commonwealth, FAO, G-77, IBRD, ICAO, IFAD, ILO, IMF, IMO, INTERPOL, ITU, NAM, OSCE, UN, UPU, WHO, WIPO, WMO, WTO.

Malta, an ancient crossroads of Mediterranean trade, was ruled successively by Phoenicians, Carthaginians, Greeks, Romans, and Byzantines before being conquered by Islamic Saracens from North Africa in the ninth century. In 1090 the Norman kings of Sicily conquered it and made it a way station for the First Crusade. In 1530 Charles V gave the island to the Knights Hospitalers (the Knights of Malta). The island withstood a siege by the Ottoman Turks in 1565 and fell only to Napoleon in 1798.

The Maltese came under British rule in 1800, and it was annexed in 1814. Limited self-rule was granted under the constitutions of 1921 and 1939. During World War II, Malta suffered devastating air raids by German and Italian forces; the entire population was awarded the George Cross for bravery.

In 1964 Malta was granted independence within the British Commonwealth, with Elizabeth II as its sovereign. Abrogating its mutual defense treaty with Great Britain in 1971, the Maltese government severed all ties to the British Crown, becoming a fully independent republic. British forces withdrew from the island in 1979.

Malta was governed by the leftist, anticlerical, and neutralist Labour party from 1971 to 1987, whose leader, the ardent nationalist Dominic Mintoff, was prime minister from 1971 to 1984. He was succeeded by Mifsud Bonnici. In 1987 the Catholic and pro-Western Nationalist party won a popular electoral majority but not a majority in Parliament. Under the terms of a 1987 constitutional amendment, it was granted sufficient extra seats in Parliament to allow it to organize a government, under Prime Minister Eddie Fenech Adami.

In 1983 the Labour party government passed a law confiscating 75 percent of the wealth of the Catholic church and attempted to ban religiously sponsored schools. Resolution of the church-state issue is the key problem facing the Nationalist government. In foreign affairs it is faced with the need both to maintain good relations with its close neighbor Libya and to pursue improved relations with the West. In early December 1989, Mikhail Gorbachev and Pres. George Bush held a summit meeting aboard U.S. and Soviet naval ships in Valetta harbor.

Following the closing of the British naval base, which had been a principal source of revenue, the government pursued a policy of industrialization, led by textiles, furniture, and paper products. The government has announced its intentions to seek membership in the EU. The port of Marsaxlokk is an important transshipment point for Mediterranean trade.

Marshall Islands

Republic of the Marshall Islands

Geography Location: two groups of islands, the Ratak and Ralik chains, comprising 31 atolls in western Pacific. Majuro 7°09'N, 171°12'E. **Boundaries:** Guam about 1,300 mi. (2,100 km) to NW, Hawaii about 2,000 mi. (3,200 km) to NE, Kiribati to S, Federated States of Micronesia to W. **Total land area:** 70 sq. mi. (181 sq km). **Coastline:** undetermined. **Comparative area:** slightly larger than Washington, D.C. **Land use:** 0% arable land; 60% permanent crops; 0% meadows and pastures; 0% forest and woodland; 40% other. **Major cities:** Majuro (capital—pop. N.A.).

People Population: 54,031 (1994 est.). **Nationality:** noun—Marshallese; adjective—Marshallese. **Ethnic groups:** almost entirely Micronesian. **Languages:** English (official), two major dialects from Malayo-Polynesian family, Japanese. **Religions:** predominantly Christian, mostly Protestant.

Government Type: constitutional government in free association with U.S.; Compact of Free Association entered into force Oct. 21, 1986. **Independence:** Oct. 21, 1986 (from U.S.-administered UN trusteeship). **Constitution:** May 1, 1979. **National holiday:** May 1. **Head of government:** Amata Kabua, president (since 1979). **Structure:** parliamentary-type government with legislative authority vested in 33-member Parliament (Nitijela) and Council of Chiefs (Iroj), a consultative body; Supreme Court, high court.

Economy Monetary unit: U.S. dollar. **Budget:** (1987 est.) ***income:*** $55 mil.; ***expend:*** N.A. **GDP:** $63.0 mil., $1,500 per capita. **Chief crops:** coconuts, cacao, taro, breadfruit, fruits, copra. **Livestock:** pigs, cattle, goats. **Natural resources:** phosphate deposits, marine products, deep seabed minerals. **Major industries:** copra, fish, tourism. **Labor force:** 4,800 (1986); 22% males and 27% females unemployed (1980). **Exports:** $3.9 mil. (f.o.b., 1992 est.); copra, copra oil, agricultural products, handicrafts. **Imports:** $62.9 mil. (c.i.f., 1992 est.); foodstuffs, beverages, building materials. **Major trading partners:** U.S., Japan.

The Marshall Islands, part of the geographic region known as Micronesia, are made up of 31 atolls of the Ratak (Sunrise) and Ralik (Sunset) chains located between 4° and 14°N and 160° and 173°E. Although claimed by Spain in 1592, the islands were left undisturbed by the Spanish empire for 300 years. In 1885, Germany took over the administration on the islands of Jaluit and Ebon. At that time copra (dried coconut meat) trade was the primary industry. Japan assumed control of the Marshalls at the beginning of World War I and held them until 1944, when Allied forces occupied the islands. In 1947 the islands were included in the UN Trust Territory of the Pacific and placed under U.S. administration. In 1946 the U.S. government resettled the inhabitants of Bikini and Enewetak in order to begin nuclear tests, which continued through 1958. Residents began returning to Enewetak in 1980; but the estimated cost of a complete clean-up of Bikini is put at $100 million.

Mauritania

Islamic Republic of Mauritania

Geography Location: northwestern Africa. **Boundaries:** territory of Western Sahara to N, Algeria to NE, Mali to E and S, Senegal to S, Atlantic Ocean to W. **Total land area:** 397,954 sq. mi. (1,030,700 sq km). **Coastline:** 469 mi. (754 km). **Comparative area:** between Texas and Alaska. **Land use:** negl. % arable land; negl. % permanent crops; 38% meadows and pastures; 15% forest and woodland; 47% other; includes negl. % irrigated. **Major cities:** Nouakchott (capital) 350,000 (1984 est.); Nouadhibou (Port Etienne) 21,961; Kaédi 20,848; Zouérate 17,474; Rosso 16,466 (1977 census).

People Population: 2,192,777 (1994 est.). **Nationality:** noun—Mauritanian(s); adjective—Mauritanian. **Ethnic groups:** 40% mixed Moor/black, 30% Moor, 30% black. **Languages:** French (official), Hasaniya Arabic (national), Toucouleur, Fula, Sarakole. **Religions:** nearly 100% Muslim.

Government Type: republic; military first seized power in bloodless coup July 10, 1978; palace coup on Dec. 24, 1984, brought president to power. **Independence:** Nov. 28, 1960 (from France). **Constitution:** May 20, 1961, abrogated after coup of July 10, 1978; provisional constitution published Dec. 17, 1980 but abandoned in 1981; new constitutional charter published Feb. 27, 1985. **National holiday:** Independence Day, Nov. 28. **Heads of government:** Col. Maaouya Ould Sid' Ahmed Taya, president (since Dec. 1984); Sidi Mohamed Ould Boubacar, prime minister (since Apr. 1992). **Structure:** executive—Military Committee for National Salvation rules by decree; national assembly and judiciary suspended pending restoration of civilian rule.

Economy Monetary unit: ouguiya. **Budget:** (1989 est.) ***income:*** $280 mil.; ***expend.:*** $346 mil. **GDP:** $2.2 bil., $1,050 per capita (1992 est.). **Chief crops:** most Mauritanians were nomads or subsistence farmers until drought forced them into cities; cash crop—gum arabic; cereals, vegetables, dates. **Livestock:** sheep, goats, cattle, camels, asses. **Natural resources:** iron ore, gypsum, fish, copper, phosphate. **Major industries:** fishing, fish processing, mining of iron ore and gypsum. **Labor force:** 465,000 (1981 est.); 47% agriculture, 29% services, 14% industry and commerce, 10% government; 45,000 wage earners (1980); considerable unemployment; 53% of population of working age. **Exports:** $432 mil. (f.o.b., 1992 est.); iron ore, processed fish, small amounts of gum arabic and gypsum; also unrecorded but numerically significant cattle exports to Senegal. **Imports:** $413 mil. (c.i.f., 1992 est.); foodstuffs and other consumer goods, petroleum products, capital goods. **Major trading partners:** ***exports:*** 43% EU, 27% Japan, 2% Ivory Coast; ***imports:*** 60% EU, 15% Algeria, 6% China, 3% U.S.

Intl. Orgs. FAO, G-77, IBRD, ICAO, IDA, IFAD, IFC, ILO, IMF, IMO, INTELSAT, INTERPOL, ITU, NAM, UN, UNESCO, UPU, WHO, WIPO, WMO, WTO.

The population of Mauritania is divided between an Arab and Berber majority in the north and various black African peoples in the south and southwest. From the ninth through the 15th centuries, southern Mauritania was part of the kingdoms of, successively, Ghana, Mali, and Sanghay. In the 1050s, a puritanical Muslim sect, the Almoravids, arose in the Tidra Islands, Between 1054 and 1086 they conquered Ghana, Morocco, Western Algeria, and Spain; they were eclipsed in the next century.

Portuguese trade on the Mauritania coast began in the early 15th century; the Portuguese remained dominant until about 1600 when their control was contested by the British, French, and Dutch. France established a protectorate in 1903, and the area was made a French colony in 1920.

In 1958 Mauritania became a self-governing republic within the French Overseas Community. In 1959 Mokhtar Ould Daddah was elected prime minister, and the country became fully independent on Nov. 28, 1960. A new constitution was adopted in 1961, establishing a presidential form of government. The four major political parties were combined into a single party in 1965.

Morocco claimed Mauritania as part of its sphere of influence; after talks about unifying the two countries broke down, Morocco recognized Mauritanian independence in 1970.

Spain relinquished its claim to the Spanish Sahara in 1976. The southern part of that territory was annexed by Mauritania, while the larger northern section was annexed by Morocco. Rebels of the Polisario Front proclaimed the independent state of Western Sahara, and in 1980 Mauritania relinquished its claims to its portion of the Western Sahara, signed a treaty with Polisario, and resumed relations with Algeria, Polisario's chief backer.

In 1978 Ould Daddah was removed from office in a military coup and was replaced as president by Lt. Col. Haidalla. He in turn was overthrown on Dec. 12, 1984, by Chief of Staff Maaouya Ould Sid' Ahmed Taya. Taya normalized relations with Morocco and held regional and local elections in 1986 and 1987 in a first step toward the restoration of democracy.

Border incidents erupted between Mauritania and Senegal in 1989 and Mauritania expelled 40,000 black Senegalese workers. Racial and religious strife has severely hampered the country's economy. Taya introduced multiparty elections in 1991 and a new constitution was approved; Taya and his Democratic and Social Republican party won the presidency and control of the legislature in 1992.

Mauritania maintains close ties to France and is heavily dependent on French aid. Most of the economy depends on livestock, which has been severely depleted in droughts during the past decade. Mineral resources include iron ore and gypsum.

Mauritius

Geography Location: southwestern Indian Ocean. Port Louis 20°09'S, 57°29'E. **Boundaries:** nearest neighbor is Réunion to SW. **Total land area:** 718 sq. mi. (1,860 sq km). **Coastline:** 110 mi. (177 km). **Comparative area:** two-thirds size of Rhode Island. **Land use:** 54% arable land; 4% permanent crops; 4% meadows and pastures; 31% forest and woodland; 7% other; includes 9% irrigated. **Major cities:** (1992 est.) Port Louis (capital) 142,850; Beau Bassin/Rose Hill 94,299; Vacoas-Phoenix 92,072; Curepipe 74,738; Quatre Bornes 71,534.

People Population: 1,116,923 (1994 est.). **Nationality:** noun—Mauritian(s); adjective—Mauritian. **Ethnic groups:** 68% Indo-Mauritian, 27% Creole, 3% Sino-Mauritian, 2% Franco-Mauritian. **Languages:** English (official), Creole, French, Hindi, Urdu, Hakka, Bojpoori. **Religions:** 51% Hindu, 30% Christian (mostly Roman Catholic with a few Anglicans), 17% Muslim.

Government Type: independent state, recognizing Elizabeth II as chief of state. **Independence:** Mar. 12, 1968 (from UK). **Constitution:** Mar. 12, 1968. **National holiday:** Independence Day, Mar. 12. **Heads of government:** Cassam Uteem, president (since July 1992); Anerood Jugnauth, prime minister (since Oct. 1982). **Structure:** executive power exercised by prime minister and 19-member Council of Ministers; unicameral legislature (Legislative Assembly) with 62 members elected by direct suffrage, eight specially elected by so-called best-loser system.

Economy Monetary unit: Mauritian rupee. **Budget:** (1990) ***income:*** $557 mil.; ***expend.:*** $607 mil. **GDP:** $8.6 bil., $7,800 per capita (1993 est.). **Chief crops:** about 90% of cultivated land area planted in sugar; also sugar derivatives, tea, tobacco; most food imported. **Livestock:** cattle, goats, pigs, sheep. **Natural resources:** cultivated land, fish. **Major industries:** food processing (largely sugar milling), textiles, and wearing apparel. **Labor force:** 335,000 (1985); 29% government services, 27% agriculture and fishing, 22% manufacturing, 22% other; 15–20% unemployed; 43% of working age. **Exports:** $1.32 bil. (f.o.b., 1992 est.); 44% textiles, 40% sugar, 10% light manufactures. **Imports:** $1.63 bil. (f.o.b., 1992 est.); 50% manufactured goods, 17% capital equipment, 13% foodstuffs, 8% petroleum products, 7% chemicals. **Major trading partners:** ***exports:*** (EU countries and U.S. have preferential treatment) 77% EU, 15% U.S.; ***imports:*** EU, U.S., South Africa, Japan.

Intl. Orgs. Commonwealth, FAO, G-77, IAEA, IBRD, ICAO, IDA, IFAD, IFC, ILO, IMF, IMO, INTERPOL, ITU, NAM, OAU, UN, UNESCO, UPU, WHO, WIPO, WMO, WTO.

The volcanic island of Mauritius and its seven smaller neighbors lie about 500 miles east of Madagascar and 2,400 miles southwest of India. They were uninhabited when discovered by the Dutch in 1507. Following sporadic Dutch settlement in the 17th century, the French took over in 1721, establishing sugarcane plantations worked by slaves imported from Africa. Mauritius was captured by the British in 1810. Following the abolition of slavery in the British Empire (1834), Indian workers were imported to labor in the cane fields. A majority of the population now is of Indian descent. On Mar. 12, 1968, Mauritius became an independent parliamentary democracy within the British Commonwealth. In 1992 it officially became a republic and the National Assembly elected Cassam Uteem as the country's first president.

The present government is controlled by an alliance of Prime Minister Anerood Jugnauth's Mauritius Socialist Movement and two smaller parties. The country has experienced rapid economic growth in the 1980s, led by exports of woolen knitwear. About 35 percent of the labor force is engaged in manufacturing, principally of clothing and textiles. Sugar remains the most important agricultural crop.

Mexico

United Mexican States

Geography Location: southernmost state in North America. **Boundaries:** U.S. to N, Gulf of Mexico to E, Belize and Guatemala to S, Pacific Ocean to W. **Total land area:** 761,603 sq. mi. (1,972,550 sq km). **Coastline:** 5,798 mi. (9,329 km). **Comparative area:** about 1.25 times size of Alaska. **Land use:** 12% arable land; 1% permanent crops; 39% meadows and pastures; 24% forest and woodland; 24% other; includes 3% irrigated. **Major cities:** (1990 census) Ciudad de México (Mexico City) (capital) 8,236,960; Guadalajara 1,628,617; Netzahualcóyotl 1,259,543; Monterrey 1,064,197; Heróica Puebla de Zaragoza (Puebla) 1,054,921.

People Population: 92,202,199 (1994 est.). **Nationality:** noun—Mexican(s); adjective—Mexican. **Ethnic groups:** 60% mestizo, 30% Amerindian or predominantly Amerindian, 9% white or predominantly white, 1% other. **Languages:** Spanish. **Religions:** 97% nominally Roman Catholic, 3% Protestant.

Government Type: federal republic operating under centralized government. **Independence:** Sept. 16, 1810 (from Spain). **Constitution:** Feb. 5, 1917. **National holiday:** Independence Day, Sept. 16. **Head of government:** Ernesto Zedillo Ponce de León, president (since Dec. 1994). **Structure:** dominant executive; bicameral legislature (National Congress—Senate, Federal Chamber of Deputies); Supreme Court.

Economy Monetary unit: peso. **Budget:** (1992 est.) ***income:*** $58.1 bil.; ***expend.:*** $53 bil. **GDP:** $740 bil., $8,200 per capita (1993 est.). **Chief crops:** corn, cotton, wheat, coffee, sugarcane. **Livestock:** cattle, pigs, goats, sheep, horses. **Natural resources:** crude oil, silver, copper, gold, lead. **Major industries:** food and beverages, tobacco, chemicals. **Labor force:** 26.2 mil. (1990); 31.4% services; 26% agriculture, forestry, hunting, fishing; 13.9% commerce; 12.8% manufacturing; 9.5% construction; 19% unemployment (1988). **Exports:** $50.5 bil. (f.o.b., 1993 est.); crude oil, oil products, coffee, shrimp, engines, cotton. **Imports:** $65.5 bil. (c.i.f., 1993 est.); grain, metal manufactures, agricultural machinery, electrical equipment. **Major trading partners:** ***exports:*** 74% U.S., 8% Japan, 4% EU; ***imports:*** 74% U.S., 11% Japan, 6% EU.

Intl. Orgs. FAO, G-77, IAEA, IBRD, ICAO, IDA, IFAD, IFC, ILO, IMF, IMO, INTELSAT, INTERPOL, ITU, NAM, OAS, UN, UNESCO, UPU, WHO, WIPO, WMO, WTO.

The pre-Columbian history of indigenous Mexican cultures is very rich and includes the high civilizations of the Olmecs, Mayas, Toltecs, and Aztecs, in addition to numerous nomadic cultures. In 1519 Hernán Cortés and several hundred Spanish soldiers entered Tenochtitlán (now Mexico City). A two-year campaign against the Aztecs under Montezuma II ended with the Spanish capture of the city. The Viceroyalty of New Spain—with its center at Mexico City—was proclaimed in 1535. At its height it encompassed the lands from California to Panama, Florida, Spain's Caribbean holdings, and the Philippines.

As was the case with the rest of Spanish America, the movement for independence in New Spain coincided with the weakening of the authority of the Spanish Crown as a result of the Napoleonic takeover of Spain in 1808. In 1810 Miguel Hidalgo led a failed uprising and was executed. Following in Hidalgo's footsteps, José María Morelos led another uprising in the south, and he in turn was captured and put to death. Agustín de Iturbide, leader of the royalist forces, defected to the side of those struggling for independence in 1821. Envisioning independent Mexico as a monarchy, military groups proclaimed Iturbide emperor of Mexico in 1822.

The Mexican empire did not last long, and the Central American counties seceded after Iturbide's ouster by Antonio de Santa Anna in 1823. A republic was declared and Guadalupe Victoria was the first president (1824–29). In 1836, Texas seceded from Mexico in a revolution that cost Santa Anna the presidency. Between 1845 and 1848, Mexico fought the United States over U.S. annexation of Texas, and in 1847 U.S. troops occupied Mexico City. Under the Treaty of Guadalupe Hidalgo (1848), Mexico sold about half its territory—including California, Nevada, Utah, most of Arizona, and parts of New Mexico, Colorado, and Wyoming to the United States—for $15 million.

Santa Anna ruled again, as dictator, from 1853 to 1855, before being toppled by the liberal movement, La Reforma. A new constitution was proclaimed in 1857, but Conservatives declared it void. Following the War of Reform (1858–61), France, Britain, and Spain all claimed compensation for destruction of their nations' property, and in 1862 they landed troops at Veracruz. Britain and Spain withdrew, but Napoleon III attempted to establish a dependent empire in Mexico and installed Archduke Ferdinand Maximilian of Austria on the Mexican throne in 1864. In the face of Mexican resistance and U.S. threats, France ended its Mexican adventure, and in 1867 Maximilian was captured and executed by Liberal forces.

Benito Juárez, who served as provisional president during the War of Reform, was a major force behind the liberal movement called La Reforma, which stressed the promotion of capitalism and the destruction of what were seen as vestiges of feudalism (abolition of *fueros*, traditional corporatist privileges) in Mexico. Juárez won a third presidential term in 1871 but died in office and was succeeded in office by Sebastián Lerdo de Tejada, who was in turn overthrown by Gen. Porfirio Díaz. During the stable dictatorship known as the Porfiriato (1876–1911), Mexico experienced economic growth, though wealthy landowners and the church benefited at the expense of the poor.

The Mexican Revolution began in 1910 after Porfirio Díaz had his electoral opponent, Francisco I. Madero, jailed. In response, Madero formulated his Plan of San Luis Potosí, calling for armed resistance to the dictatorship. Rebellions broke out in the northern state of Chihuahua under the leadership of Pancho Villa and in the southern state of Morelos led by Emiliano Zapata. The two states soon came under rebel control, and in 1911 Díaz left Mexico. Madero was elected president, but his failure to carry through promised reforms resulted in the continuation of the rebellion.

Backed by the U.S., Gen. Victoriano Huerta overthrew Madero in 1913. But the fighting continued, and Huerta lost the support of the U.S. and was forced from office by Zapata, Villa, and Venustiano Carranza, who became president (1914–20). Zapata and Villa continued their resistance, but by 1916 Gen. Alvaro Obregón had driven Villa back to Chihuahua and Zapata's armies had been contained. Carranza called for the election of delegates to a constitutional convention in 1916, and by the following year, the progressive Mexican Constitution of 1917 was in place.

Obregón deposed Carranza in 1920 and served as president until 1924. He was reelected to succeed Plutarco Elías Calles in 1928 but was assassinated before he could take office. In 1929 Calles founded the National Revolutionary party, which became the Institutional Revolutionary party (PRI) in 1946.

Lázaro Cárdenas won the presidency in 1934, sending Calles, the long-time power behind the scene, into exile. This, coupled with Cárdenas's decision to remove himself from politics at the end of his term, greatly stabilized the institutional structure created by the Mexican Revolution. Cárdenas was the last of the "revolutionary" leaders to make good on the promises to labor and the peasantry. He presided over extensive redistribution of land and in 1938 reorganized the ruling party into four constituencies: peasants, labor, the military, and the popular sector (middle class, professionals). Cárdenas also used the national ownership of subsoil rights enshrined in the Mexican constitution to nationalize U.S. oil companies, thus assuring his credentials as a hero of Mexican nationalism.

The political movement of Mexican presidents since Cárdenas has been away from its peasant and labor constituencies toward business and the popular sector, beginning with Miguel Alemán's election in 1946.

The stability of the PRI was seriously challenged in the 1980s as a result of the economic crisis stemming from the severe decline in the price of oil. Mexico borrowed heavily from foreign creditors during the 1970s on the expectation that oil prices would remain high. The debt problem led to cutbacks in government spending, a catastrophic drop in the value of the currency, and capital and human flight out of the country. The political repercussions of this could be seen in the elections of 1988, in which the ruling PRI had its worst showing ever. Although its candidate, Carlos Salinas de Gortari, won the election, the narrow margin was disputed by the opposition Revolutionary Democratic party (PRD) and National Action party (PAN).

Pres. Salinas vigorously pursued economic reform and sought a free-trade agreement with the United States and Canada that resulted in the North American Free Trade Agreement (NAFTA) (1993) which promises to bring more jobs and much-needed increases in capital investment.

The very day NAFTA went into effect, Jan. 2, 1994, a guerrilla group of poor Indians calling themselves the Zapatista Army of National Liberation declared war against the government and began fighting government troops in the southern state of Chiapas. The uprising drew international attention to the plight of Mexican peasants, and cast serious doubt on whether the PRI would be able to retain its 65-year stranglehold on the presidency. That doubt increased when the party's presidential candidate, Luis Donaldo Colosio Murrieta, was assassinated at a campaign stop in Tijuana. The assassination was found to be unrelated to the southern uprising, but it forced the PRI, as it chose a replacement, to select a candidate from the party's modern, reform-minded wing. Over the objections of many of the party's old-time hard-liners, Salinas chose Colosio's campaign manager, Ernesto Zedillo Ponce de León, as the PRI's presidential candidate.

In elections held in August 1994 (and generally seen as free of the fraud that had marred balloting in previous years), Zedillo won with just over 50 percent of the vote, the lowest majority ever by the PRI. Zedillo's presidency began disastrously as the value of the peso collapsed, declining by 40 percent in less than two months. In early 1995 the United States and the IMF offered an enormous aid package in exchange for severe austerity measures by the Mexican government. (For further details, see Part I: "Major News Stories of the Year.")

Micronesia

Federated States of Micronesia

Geography Location: forms (with Palau) archipelago of Caroline Islands, Ponape (6°52'N, 158°15'E), Yap (9°32'N, 138°08'E), Kosrae (5°19'N, 162°59'E), and Truk (7°22'N, 151°54'E), in western Pacific Ocean. **Boundaries:** Guam to NW, Marshall Islands to E, Papua New Guinea to S, Philippines about 497 mi. (800 km) to W. **Total land area:** 271 sq. mi. (702 sq km). **Coastline:** undetermined. **Comparative area:** about four times size of Washington, D.C. **Land use:** N.A. **Major cities:** Kolonia (capital—population N.A.).

People Population: 117,588 (1993 est.). **Nationality:** noun—Micronesian(s); adjective—Micronesian. **Ethnic groups:** nine ethnic Micronesian and Polynesian groups. **Languages:** English (official), Trukese, Pohnpeian, Yapese, Kosrean. **Religions:** predominantly Christian, divided between Roman Catholic and Protestant; also, Assembly of God, Jehovah's Witnesses, Seventh-day Adventists, Latter-day Saints, and Baha'i.

Government Type: constitutional government in free association with U.S.; Compact of Free Association entered into force Nov. 3, 1986. **Independence:** Nov. 3, 1986 (from U.S.-administered UN Trusteeship). **Constitution:** May 10, 1979. **National holiday:** May 10. **Head of government:** Bailey Olter, president (since May 1991). **Structure:** executive—national president and vice president elected from ranks of popularly elected senators; legislative—National Congress (unicameral); judicial—national Supreme Court headed by chief justice.

Economy Monetary unit: U.S. dollar. **Budget:** (1988) ***income:*** $165 mil.; ***expend.:*** $115 mil. **GNP:** $150 mil., $1,500 per capita (1989 est.). **Chief crops:** copra, black pepper, tropical fruits and vegetables, coconuts, cassava, sweet potatoes; mainly subsistence economy. **Livestock:** pigs, chickens. **Natural resources:** forests, marine products, deep seabed minerals. **Major industries:** tourism, craft items from shell, wood, pearl. **Labor force:** undetermined. **Exports:** $2.3 mil. (f.o.b., 1988); copra. **Imports:** $67.7 mil. (c.i.f., 1988). **Major trading partners:** N.A.

Intl. Orgs. IMF, UN, WHO.

The Federated States of Micronesia extend 1,800 miles across an archipelago of the Caroline Islands in the larger island group of Micronesia. Ethnically diverse (there are eight primary languages, not including dialects), the islands are thought to be the first in the Pacific settled by argonauts from the Philippines and Indonesia, about 1500 B.C. Ferdinand Magellan landed in the Marianas in 1521, and Spain claimed sovereignty from 1565 to 1899, when the Caroline Islands were sold to Germany. After World War I, the League of Nations mandated the islands to Japan, which developed agriculture (especially sugarcane), mining, and fishing. After World War II, the islands were included in the UN Trust Territory of the Pacific and placed under U.S. administration. A compact of free association between Micronesia and the United States was signed in 1986, and Micronesia's trust territory status with the UN trusteeship council was officially dissolved in December 1990.

Moldova

Republic of Moldova

Geography Location: southeastern Europe. **Boundaries:** Ukraine to N, E, S, Romania to W. **Total land area:** 13,012 sq. mi. (33,700 sq km). **Coastline:** none. **Comparative area:** about the size of Maine. **Land use:** 53% cropland; 9% permanent pasture; 8% forest and woodland; 30% other (mostly urban). **Major cities:** (1990 est.) Kishinev (Chisinău) (capital) 676,000; Tiraspol 184,000; Beltsy (Balti) 162,000.

People Population: 4,473,033 (1994 est.). **Nationality:** noun—Moldovian(s); adjective—Moldovian. **Ethnic groups:** 64.5% Moldovian, 13.8% Ukrainian, 13% Russian, 3.5% Gagauz, 2% Jewish, 1.5% Bulgarian. **Languages:** Romanian (official), Romance language group now mostly written in Latin alphabet; in 1940 Cyrillic alphabet was introduced and the language was called "Moldavian"; Russian, ethnic languages. **Religions:** Christianity—Eastern Orthodox, Russian Orthodox.

Government Type: republic. **Independence:** declared on Aug. 27, 1991, by Moldovian Parliament and a Grand National Assembly (from USSR). **Constitution:** being drafted. **National holiday:** Aug. 27. **Heads of government:** Mircea Ion Snegur, president (since Sept. 1990); Andrei Sangheli, prime minister (since July 1992). **Structure:** executive—president, Council of Ministers; legislative—Moldovian Parliament (366 deputies); judicial—Supreme Court.

Economy Monetary unit: ruble. **Budget:** N.A. ***income:*** N.A.; ***expend.:*** N.A. **GNP:** $16.3 bil., $3,650 per capita (1993 est.). **Chief crops:** sugarbeet, grain, vegetables, wine grapes, other fruit. **Livestock:** chickens, pigs, sheep, goats, cattle. **Natural resources:** few. **Major industries:** food processing, wine distilleries, tobacco production, textiles, chemicals. **Labor force:** 2,095,000 (1985). **Exports:** $108 mil. outside the former USSR (1992); foodstuffs, wine, tobacco, textiles, footwear. **Imports:** $145 mil. outside the former USSR (1992); oil, gas, coal, steel, machinery, foodstuffs. **Major trading partners:** other former Soviet republics, Romania.

Intl. Orgs. CIS, IMF, OSCE, UN, UNESCO, World Bank.

Historical Moldavia, of which present-day Moldova is only a small portion, encompassed territories that are now in Romania and Ukraine (including southern Bessarabia and northern Bukovina). Moldova is a hilly, fertile land, bounded by two great rivers, the Dniester and the Prut, that flow into the Black Sea. Its climate is very favorable to agriculture.

Moldavia was part of Scythia in the first millennium B.C. and later came under the Roman Empire. Lying on the gateway to Europe, it was invaded successively, but came under the control of Kievan Rus between the 10th and 12th centuries A.D., and in the 13th century it was invaded by the Mongolian empire. In the 16th century, eastern Moldavia, or Bessarabia, came under Turkish control but in 1812 was ceded to the Russian empire. Southern Bessarabia (now in Ukraine) was controlled variously by the Russian empire and by Romania, and in 1878 it again became part of Russia. After the Bolsheviks came to power in 1917 and created the USSR, a Moldavian Autonomous Soviet Socialist Republic (ASSR) was formed on the eastern side of the Dniester River, a territory claimed by Romania but populated by Ukrainians. In June 1940, as a result of the Nazi-Soviet Pact of 1939, Romania was forced to cede Bessarabia and northern Bukovina to the Soviet Union. These lands were made part of the Ukrainian Soviet Socialist Republic (SSR), and the remaining Bessarabian sections were merged with the old Moldavian ASSR to create on Aug. 2, 1940, the Moldavian SSR. Between 1941 and 1944, while Romania and the USSR were at war, Bessarabia again became part of Romania, but in 1944 the Soviets retook the territory and reestablished it as a union republic.

While under Soviet control, Moldavians in the new republic were officially differentiated from their counterparts across the border in Romania. In 1940, the Cyrillic alphabet was imposed on the Romanian language; this official language was called "Moldavian." Contacts between the two countries were discouraged, and the USSR encouraged Russian and Ukrainian immigration to the Moldavian SSR. While a part of the USSR, Moldavia created a diversified economy, which is based on agriculture and food processing, with a small industrial base.

Mikhail Gorbachev's policy of glasnost, or openness, in the late 1980s gave vent to Moldavian complaints about "Russification" and immigration of non-Moldavians. In September 1989, Romanian, now in a Latin script, was restored as the official language. Glasnost also gave birth to new political parties, the largest of which was the Popular Front of Moldavia, which organized protest demonstrations against Soviet power. Disturbances during the 1989 celebration of Soviet Revolution Day in the capital city of Kishinev led to the dismissal of the Slavic Communist party First Secretary, and his replacement by an ethnic Romanian.

The Communist party was banned in Moldova in 1990, and laws to develop the basics of a multiparty system were adopted in September 1991. Moldova officially declared its independence from the USSR on Aug. 27, 1991, and in December, United Front–supported Mircea Snegur was elected president with 98.2% of the votes cast in the elections.

At the time Moldova declared its independence, sentiment was strong for reunification with Romania. So strong, in fact, that ethnic Russians and Ukrainians living in the Trans-Dniester region in eastern Moldova, fearing reunification with Romania, declared an independent Trans-Dniester republic, sparking ethnic violence there. But since then, most activity has focused on reestablishing ties with countries from the former USSR. In December 1991, Moldova singed the Alma-Ata Declaration, joining the other former Soviet republics in the Commonwealth of Independent States. And in the country's first parlimantary elections, held in February of 1994, two nationalist parties captured a combined 15 percent of the vote, while the pro–Russian Socialist party won 25 percent, and the Agrarian Democratic Party, led by former Communists, took 45 percent. Then, in a plebiscite held Mar. 6, 1994, an overwhelming majority (90 percent) of voters rejected reunification with Romania in favor of an independent Moldova. Two-thirds of Moldova's 2.3 million eligible voters cast ballots on the plebiscite. Snegur intended to use the referendum result to entice Trans-Dniester (which had boycotted the parliamentary elections) to rejoin Moldova.

Monaco

Principality of Monaco

Geography Location: tiny enclave on Mediterranean coast of France. **Boundaries:** France to N, E, and W; Mediterranean Sea to S. **Total land area:** 1.21 sq. mi. (1.95 sq km). **Coastline:** 2.6 mi. (4.1 km). **Comparative area:** about three times size of the Mall in Washington, D.C. **Land use:** 0% arable land; 0% permanent crops; 0% meadows and pastures; 0% forest and woodland; 100% other. **Major cities:** Monaco (capital).

People Population: 31,278 (1994 est.). **Nationality:** noun—Monacan(s) or Monegasque(s); adjective—Monacan or Monegasque. **Ethnic groups:** 47% French, 16% Monegasque, 16% Italian, 21% other. **Languages:** French (official), English, Italian, Monegasque. **Religions:** 95% Roman Catholic.

Government Type: constitutional monarchy. **Constitution:** Dec. 17, 1962. **National holiday:** Nov. 19. **Head of government:** Prince Ranier III, chief of state (since Nov. 1949); Paul Dijoud, prime minister (since Dec. 1994). **Structure:** executive—prince, minister of state (senior French civil servant appointed by prince), and Council of Government as cabinet; legislative—prince and National Council of 18 members; judicial—authority delegated by prince to Supreme Tribunal.

Economy Monetary unit: French franc. **Budget:** (1991) ***income:*** $424 mil.; ***expend:*** $376 mil. **GDP:** $475 mil., $16,000 per capita. **Chief crops:** N.A. **Livestock:** N.A. **Natural resources:** none. **Major industries:** pharmaceuticals, food processing, precision instruments. **Labor force:** N.A. **Exports:** N.A. **Imports:** N.A. **Major trading partners:** full customs integration with France, which collects and rebates Monacan trade duties; also participates in EU market system through customs union with France.

Intl. Orgs. IAEA, ICAO, INTELSAT, INTERPOL, ITU, OSCE, UN (permanent observer), UPU, WHO, WIPO.

Known to Phoenicians and Greeks from the beginning of the first millenium B.C., the history of the port of Monaco is coextensive with that of southeastern France for much of its history. A western colony of the great trading city-state of Genoa in the 13th century, Monaco in 1368 became an independent principality under the rule of the Matignon-Grimaldi family. At various times a protectorate of Spain, France, and Sardinia, it was restored to independence in 1861 by the Franco-Monegasque treaty.

In 1911 Monaco became a constitutional monarchy under the Matignon-Grimaldi dynasty. In 1918 France required the principality to conform to its national interests in all respects; by an agreement of 1919, should the dynasty fail to produce a male heir, Monaco would be absorbed into France. However, the family is allowed to adopt an heir if they so choose. The marriage of Prince Ranier III to the U.S film star Grace Kelly produced an heir apparent for this generation. The constitutional monarchy under its "Most Serene Prince" is essentially a one-party state in which the National and Democratic Union won all 18 seats in the National Council in 1968, 1978, 1983, and 1988, though in competition with the Socialist party. In 1993 Monaco became the smallest member nation of the UN.

Despite the fame of the Monte Carlo casino, gambling accounts for only 4 percent of the principality's revenues. The principal industry is tourism, followed by light manufacturing. Monaco also supports a prominent institute of oceanography. Land reclamation projects, impelled by a real estate boom, have added about 20 percent to the nation's territory since World War II.

Mongolia

Mongolian People's Republic

Geography Location: landlocked country in central Asia. **Boundaries:** Russia to N, China to E, S, and W. **Total land area:** 604,247 sq. mi. (1,565,000 sq km). **Coastline:** none. **Comparative area:** slightly larger than Alaska. **Land use:** 1% arable land; 0% permanent crops; 79% meadows and pastures; 10% forest and woodland; 10% other; includes negl. % irrigated. **Major cities:** (1993) Ulan Bator (capital) 619,000; Darhan 66,800; Erdenet 58,200; Choyr, 12,800.

People Population: 2,429,762 (1994 est.). **Nationality:** noun—Mongolian(s) adjective—Mongolian. **Ethnic groups:** 90% Mongol, 4% Kazakh, 2% Chinese; 2% Russian, 2% other. **Languages:** Khalkha Mongol used by over 90% of population; Turkic, Russian, Chinese. **Religions:** predominantly Tibetan Buddhist, about 4% Muslim.

Government Type: communist state. **Independence:** Mar. 13, 1921 (from China). **Constitution:** July 6, 1960. **National holiday:** People's Revolution Day, July 11. **Heads of government:** Punsalmaagiin Ochirbat, president (since Mar. 1990); Puntsagiin Jasrai, prime minister (since July 1992). **Structure:** executive—Council of Ministers; legislative—unicameral Great People's Hural; judicial—court system; Supreme Court elected by Great People's Hural.

Economy Monetary unit: tughrik. **Budget:** (1991) deficit of $67 mil. **GDP:** $2.8 bil., $1,200 per capita (1993 est.). **Chief crops:** livestock raising predominates; wheat, oats, barley. **Livestock:** sheep, goats, cattle, horses, camels. **Natural resources:** coal, copper, molybdenum, tungsten, phosphates. **Major industries:** processing of animal products, building materials, foods and beverages. **Labor force:** primarily agricultural; over half adult population is in labor force, including large percentage of women; shortage of skilled labor. **Exports:** $355 mil. (f.o.b., 1992 est.); livestock, animal products, wool, hides, fluorospar, nonferrous metals. **Imports:** $501 mil. (f.o.b., 1991 est.); machinery and equipment, fuels, food products, industrial consumer goods, chemicals. **Major trading partners: exports:** 75% former USSR, 10% China, 4% Japan; **imports:** 75% former USSR, 5% Austria, 5% China.

Intl. Orgs. FAO, G-77, IAEA, IBRD, ICAO, IDA, IFAD, IFC, ILO, IMF, IMO, ITU, UN, UNESCO, UNIDO, UPU, WHO, WIPO, WMO.

Mongols under Genghis Khan conquered most of Eurasia in the early 13th century. The Mongol empire broke up in the mid-14th century, and Mongolia lapsed into tribal disunion and political insignificance. Chinese rule was established thereafter in Inner Mongolia (ruled directly) and, in 1691, in Outer Mongolia (a province under local rule). With the 1911 Chinese Revolution, Outer Mongolia unsuccessfully proclaimed its independence from China. The nationalist religious leader, the Bogdo Lama, sought Russian support in 1920. Under the revolutionary leaders Sukhe Bataar and Khorloin Choibalsan, a "provisional people's government" again declared independence in 1921. Sukhe Bataar died in 1923; on Nov. 26, 1924, the Mongolian People's Republic (MPR) was established with Soviet sponsorship. The early years of the republic were marked by repeated Stalinist purges of Mongol revolutionary leaders and by disastrous attempts at centralized planning.

Choibalsan emerged as party leader in the late 1930s and was confirmed as premier in 1940. In 1939 combined Soviet and Mongolian armies prevented a Japanese conquest of Mongolia. In 1945 the Republic of China recognized the MPR; recognition was reaffirmed by the People's Republic of China in 1949 but abrogated by the Republic of China (Taiwan) in 1953. In 1948 the first of a new series of five-year plans began to bring industrial and agricultural development to Mongolia, with extensive Soviet aid and support. Choibalsan died in 1952 and was succeeded as premier by Yumjaagiyn Tsedenbal. Following the Sino-Soviet split of 1958, heavy concentrations of Soviet troops and missiles were stationed along the Chinese-Mongolian border. On Oct. 27, 1961, the MPR was admitted to the United Nations; diplomatic relations with various other non-Soviet bloc nations developed gradually thereafter. Tsedenbal was ousted as party chairman and premier in 1984; he was replaced by Zhambyn Batmonh as party chairman and by Dumaagiin Sodnom as premier. The United States and the MPR established diplomatic relations on Jan. 27, 1987.

Following widespread demonstrations calling for human rights, religious freedom, and an end to special privileges for Communist officials, the Communist party voted to give up its constitutional power in March 1990. After the resignation of Pres. Zhambyn Batmonh, the Parliament elected Punsalmaagiin Ochirbat as president; in May he visited Beijing to improve relations and strengthen economic ties; it was the first visit by a Mongolian head of state since 1962. The ex-Communist Mongolian People's Revolutionary party, running on a platform of moderate reform, was returned to power with an overwhelming majority in a national election on June 28, 1992, defeating a coalition of reform parties. Disavowed by the ruling party for his reformist views, Ochirbat was re-elected president on June 6, 1993, at the head of a coalition of opposition parties.

With a young and rapidly growing population, an obsolete industrial base, and a shrinking economy that still depends heavily upon herding and animal products, Mongolia has endured a painful transition to democracy and free markets. Aided by new international loans, the government is pursuing a vigorous program of privatization, currency and banking reform, and the encouragement of foreign investment.

Montenegro

See "Yugoslavia."

Morocco

Kingdom of Morocco

Geography Location: northwestern Africa. **Boundaries:** North Atlantic Ocean to W and NW, Strait of Gibraltar to N, Mediterranean Sea to NE, Algeria to E and SE, Western Sahara to SW. **Total land area:** 172,413 sq. mi. (446,550 sq km). **Coastline:** 1,140 mi. (1,835 km). **Comparative area:** slightly larger than California. **Land use:** 18% arable land; 1% permanent crops; 28% meadows and pastures; 12% forest and woodland; 41% other; includes 1% irrigated. **Major cities:** (1990 est.) Rabat (including Sale; capital) 1,472,000; Casablanca 3,210,000; Marrakech (Marrakesh) 1,517,000; Fès (Fez) 1,012,000; Oujda 962,000.

People Population: 28,558,635 (1993 est.). **Nationality:** noun—Moroccan(s); adjective—Moroccan. **Ethnic groups:** 99.1% Arab-Berber, 0.7% non-Moroccan, 0.2% Jewish. **Languages:** Arabic (official), several Berber dialects; French is language of business, government, diplomacy, and postprimary education. **Religions:** 98.7% Muslim, 1.1% Christian, 0.2% Jewish.

Government Type: constitutional monarchy. **Independence:** Mar. 2, 1956 (from France). **Constitution:** Mar. 10, 1972. **National holiday:** Independence Day, Nov. 18. **Heads of government:** Hassan II, king (since Feb. 1961); Abdellati Filali, prime minister (since June 1994). **Structure:** king has paramount executive powers; Constitution provides for prime minister and ministers named by and responsible to king; unicameral legislature (Representatives) of which two-thirds of members are directly elected and one-third are indirectly elected; judiciary independent of other branches.

Economy Monetary unit: dirham. **Budget:** (1992) ***income:*** $7.5 bil.; ***expend.:*** $7.7 bil. **GDP:** $70.3 bil., $2,500 per capita (1993 est.). **Chief crops:** not self-sufficient in food; cereal farming and livestock raising predominant; barley, wheat, citrus fruit, wine, vegetables; illegal producer of cannabis for international drug trade. **Livestock:** sheep, goats, cattle, asses, mules. **Natural resources:** phosphates, iron ore, manganese, lead, zinc, fish, salt. **Major industries:** phosphate rock mining and processing, food processing, leather goods. **Labor force:** 7.4 mil. (1985); 50% agriculture, 26% services, 15% industry; 15% unemployment (1988). **Exports:** $5.7 bil. (f.o.b., 1992); 30% food and beverages, 23% semiprocessed goods, 21% consumer goods. **Imports:** $8.4 bil. (c.i.f., 1992); 24% capital goods, 22% semiprocessed goods, 16% raw materials, 16% fuel and lubricants. **Major trading partners:** ***exports:*** 58% EU, 7% India, 5% Japan, 5% former USSR, 2% U.S.; ***imports:*** 53% EU, 11% U.S., 4% Canada, 3% Iraq, 3% former USSR, 2% Japan.

Intl. Orgs. Arab League, EU (associate), FAO, G-77, IAEA, IBRD, ICAO, IDA, IFAD, IFC, ILO, IMF, IMO, INTELSAT, INTERPOL, ITU, NAM, UN, UNESCO, UPU, WHO, WIPO, WMO, WTO.

Neolithic inhabitants of Morocco were displaced by Berbers around 1000 B.C. Phoenician and Carthaginian settlements were established along the Mediterranean coast. Morocco came under Roman rule around 40 A.D. and was invaded via Spain by Germanic Vandals in the fifth century. The Islamic invasions of the mid-seventh century established Arab rule in Morocco, and most of the indigenous Berbers converted to Islam. Ethnic tension between Berbers and Arabs has been a basic element of Moroccan politics and society ever since.

In the late eighth century, King Idris ibn Adballah united Berbers and Arabs in a monarchy that lasted for 200 years and made the capital city of Fez one of the major religious and cultural centers of the Islamic world. In the 11th century, the Almoravid dynasty from Mauritania conquered Morocco, western Algeria, and Spain. It was ousted by another Muslin sect, the Almohads, led by Ibn Tumart. After about 1200 the tide of Moorish expansion in the Iberian Peninsula turned; in 1492 Ferdinand and Isabella expelled the last Moors from Grenada.

Naval conflict between Morocco, Spain, and Portugal continued in the western Mediterranean and along the Atlantic coast of northwestern Africa for several centuries more. In the mid-17th century, Morocco was reunited under the present Alawid dynasty. In the early 19th century, American and British forces combatted Moroccan piracy in the Mediterranean, and Spain established colonies in Tangier in the north and along the Atlantic coast between Morocco and Mauritania.

The attempts of Sultan Hassan I (r. 1873–94) to implement reforms to strengthen Morocco's independence were thwarted by European interests. By the early 20th century, France, securely established in Algeria, began exerting increasing control in Morocco. A multipower conference at Algeciras in 1906 affirmed Moroccan independence but upheld the special rights claimed by Spain and France. The Treaty of Fez, signed in 1912 between France and Sultan Abd-al-Hafidn, ended Moroccan independence by granting the country to France and reaffirming a Spanish sphere of influence in the southwest.

Nationalist unrest and tribal uprisings disrupted French administration in Morocco throughout the 1920s and 1930s. Morocco became a battleground during World War II between the Axis-supported Vichy French government and the Free French and their Allied backers. In 1943 Churchill and Roosevelt met at Casablanca to discuss wartime strategy; in the same year, the Istiqlal (Independence) party was founded to fight for independence from the French in the postwar era.

In 1947 Moroccan liberation forces began open warfare against the French. The exiled Sultan Mohammad V was allowed to return, and France promised independence by 1955.

With the withdrawal of French forces, Morocco became independent on Mar. 2, 1956. Tangier (under international administration since 1923) was incorporated into the newly independent state in October 1956, and the Spanish enclave of Ifni was ceded to Morocco in 1969.

A period of instability ensued after 1957 as newly formed political parties vied for power. King Mohammad I died in 1961 and was succeeded by his son, Hassan II. In 1962 an elected parliamentary government took power under the constitutional monarchy. Political unrest and economic difficulties led to the declaration of states of emergency in 1965 and 1970 and a new constitution in 1977.

Spain withdrew from its former territory of Spanish (now Western) Sahara, a phosphate-rich desert territory on Morocco's southern border, in February 1976. On Apr. 14, 1976, Morocco annexed the northern two-thirds of the territory, while Mauritania claimed the remainder. The Polisario Spanish Saharan liberation movement, backed by Algeria and Libya, conducted guerrilla operations against Moroccan and Mauritanian forces. In 1979 Mauritania gave up its claims, and Morocco claimed the entire region.

In April 1987, Morocco completed construction of a 2,000-mile sand wall completely enclosing Western Sahara. Polisario forces, partly cut off from Algerian aid, nevertheless control much of the Western Saharan countryside, while Morocco holds the cities and towns. In May 1987 a Moroccan-Algerian summit was held under the sponsorship of Saudi Arabia, which offered King Hassan $260 million to rebuild Morocco's war-torn economy in return for allowing a self-determination referendum in the Western Sahara. The king refused. By mid-1992 the situation was in effect resolved as Polisario's top leaders accepted an offer of amnesty, leaving the Moroccan government in undisputed possession of the territory.

The Persian Gulf crisis made an already weak economy weaker, and riots during a general strike protesting low wages, economic hardship, and poor job prospects in Fez left 100 dead and hundreds more injured in January 1991. Although Morocco was an active member of the Allied coalition against Iraq, Moroccans also staged huge demonstrations in support of Saddam Hussein in February at the height of the war.

In 1992, demands of Muslim fundamentalist factions for greater political power threatened the stability of King Hassan II's government. In a gesture toward political reform, parliamentary elections were held in June 1993, but the results were not expected to pose any immediate challenge to the monarchy.

Mozambique

Republic of Mozambique

Geography Location: eastern coast of Africa. **Boundaries:** Zambia and Malawi to NW, Tanzania to N, Indian Ocean to E and SE, South Africa and Swaziland to SW, Zimbabwe to W. **Total land area:** 309,494 sq. mi. (801,590 sq km). **Coastline:** 1,535 mi. (2,470 km). **Comparative area:** slightly less than twice size of California. **Land use:** 4% arable land; negl. % permanent crops; 56% meadows and pastures; 20% forest and woodland; 20% other; includes negl. % irrigated. **Major cities:** (1987 est.) Maputo (capital) 1,006,765.

People Population: 17,346,280 (1994 est.). **Nationality:** noun—Mozambican(s); adjective—Mozambican. **Ethnic groups:** Majority from indigenous tribal groups; about 35,000 Euro-Africans, 15,000 Indians, 10,000 Europeans. **Languages:** Portuguese (official), indigenous languages. **Religions:** 60% indigenous beliefs, 30% Christian, 10% Muslim.

Government Type: republic. **Independence:** June 25, 1975 (from Portugal). **Constitution:** Nov. 30, 1990. **National holiday:** Independence Day, June 25. **Heads of government:** Joachím Alberto Chissanó, president (since Nov. 1986); Dr. Pascoal Manuel Mocumbi, prime minister (since Nov. 1994.). **Structure:** unicameral Assembly, Supreme Court.

Economy Monetary unit: meticai. **Budget:** (1992 est.) ***income:*** $252 mil.; ***expend:*** $607 mil. **GDP:** $9.8 bil., $600 per capita (1993 est.). **Chief crops:** cash crops—cotton, cashew nuts, sugar, tea, copra; other crops—corn, wheat, peanuts, potatoes, beans; imports—corn. **Livestock:**

cattle, goats, pigs, sheep, asses. **Natural resources:** coal, natural gas, copper, bauxite, titanium. **Major industries:** food and beverages, chemicals (fertilizer, soap, paints), petroleum. **Labor force:** 95% agriculture, 5% other. **Exports:** $164.4 mil. (f.o.b., 1993 est.); 48% shrimp, 21% cashews, 10% sugar. **Imports:** $1.03 bil. (c.i.f., 1993 est.); food, clothing, farm equipment, petroleum. **Major trading partners:** ***exports:*** U.S., Western Europe, Germany, Japan; ***imports:*** U.S., Western Europe, former USSR.

Intl. Orgs. FAO, G-77, IBRD, ICAO, IFAD, ILO, IMF, IMO, ITU, NAM, UN, UNESCO, UPU, WHO, WMO, WTO.

Mozambique has been inhabited since prehistoric times by a variety of Bantu peoples. Portuguese trading stations were established starting in 1505, and Portugal developed an extensive coastal trade in gold and ivory. Mozambique also served as a way station for Portuguese trade to East Asia.

Despite competition from other European nations, Portugal maintained control of the Mozambique coast. Settlement by sizable numbers of Portuguese immigrants began in the late 19th century. Mozambique was organized as a colony, sometimes called Portuguese East Africa, in 1885; boundaries in the interior were defined in 1891.

Economic development of Mozambique in the 20th century remained almost entirely in Portuguese hands. By the 1950s native peoples began to protest Portuguese rule; a rebellion of the Frelimo (Front for the Liberation of Mozambique) guerrilla movement began in 1961. Rebels controlled most of the northern part of the country by 1964. Fighting continued for another decade.

Following the Portuguese revolution of 1974, Portugal agreed to independence for Mozambique, and many Portuguese settlers returned to Portugal, leaving the country bereft of administrative personnel and infrastructure support. Mozambique became fully independent on June 25, 1975. A Marxist Frelimo government took office, with Samora Michel as the country's first president. The new government formed agricultural collectives and nationalized most private land and industry as well as all social services.

In the late 1970s, fighting broke out between Mozambique and Rhodesia. When Rhodesia achieved independence (and changed its name to Zimbabwe) in 1980, relations between the two governments improved. But a rebel movement, Renamo (Mozambique National Resistance), dedicated to overthrowing the Frelimo government grew stronger during the 1980s.

In 1986, following the death of Samora Michel, Joachím Chissano became president. The Chissano government reintroduced some private small-scale agriculture, loosened ties to the Eastern bloc, and appealed to the West for economic assistance. In 1987 a UN-led relief effort began. In 1989 Mozambique signed a cooperation agreement with South Africa, which cut off its aid to the Renamo insurgents. But fighting continued into 1990.

In November 1990, Mozambique adopted a new constitution widening individual rights and freedoms, including abolition of the death penalty, freedom of the press and speech, and an independent judiciary, as well as establishing multiparty democracy, a presidential regime, and free-market economy. On Oct. 4, 1992, Pres. Chissanó and Renamo leader Afonso Dhlakama signed a cease-fire that ended their civil war; the UN dispatched 7,500 military and civilian personnel to oversee the disarmament and organize elections.

Mozambique's first-ever multiparty elections were held in October 1994. Pres. Chissanó was elected with 53 percent of the vote while his Frelimo party took 129 of the Parliament's 250 seats. (Renamo carried all but nine of the remaining seats.)

Mozambique is rich in agricultural land and mineral resources. Nevertheless, years of communism, drought, and civil war have left the country poor and dependent on foreign aid. In 1992 the worst drought in memory brought the nation to a virtual standstill, as an estimated 1.8 million people became dependent on donations of food from outsiders for survival.

Myanmar

Union of Myanmar

Geography Location: NW region of Southeast Asia. **Boundaries:** China and Laos to NE, Bangladesh, India to NW, Thailand to SE, Andaman Sea to S, and Bay of Bengal to SW. **Total land area:** 261,969 sq. mi. (678,500 sq km). **Coastline:** 1,902 mi. (3,060 km). **Comparative area:** slightly smaller than Texas. **Land use:** 15% arable land; 1% permanent crops; 1% meadows and pastures; 49% forest and woodland; 34% other; includes 2% irrigated. **Major cities:** (1983 census) Yangon (formerly Rangoon) (capital) 2,458,712; Mandalay 532,895; Bassein 335,000; Moulmein 219,991; Akyab 143,000.

People Population: 44,277,014 (1994 est.). **Nationality:** noun—Burmese (sing., pl.); adjective—Burmese. **Ethnic groups:** 68% Burman, 9% Shan, 7% Karen, 4% Raljome, 3% Chinese, 2% Indian, 7% other. **Languages:** Burmese, minority ethnic languages. **Religions:** 85% Buddhist, 15% indigenous beliefs, Muslim, Christian, and other.

Government Type: republic. **Independence:** Jan. 4, 1948 (from UK). **Constitution:** Jan. 3, 1974. **National holiday:** Independence Day, Jan. 4. **Head of government:** Gen. Than Shwe, chairman (since Apr. 1992). **Structure:** Council of State rules through Council of Ministers; National Assembly (Pyithu Hluttaw, or People's Congress) has legislative power.

Economy Monetary unit: kyat. **Budget:** (1992) ***income:*** $8.1 bil.; ***expend.:*** $11.6 bil. **GDP:** $41 bil., $950 per capita (1993 est.). **Chief crops:** paddy, beans, pulses, maize, oilseeds; most rice grown in deltaic land; illegal producer of opium poppy and cannabis for international drug trade. **Livestock:** cattle, pigs, buffalo, goats, sheep. **Natural resources:** crude oil, timber, tin, copper, tungsten. **Major industries:** agricultural processing, textiles and footwear, wood and wood products. **Labor force:** 16 mil. (1992); 65.6% agriculture, 13.7% industry, 9.8% trade, 6.6% government; 10.4% unemployment in urban areas (1986–87). **Exports:** $613.4 mil. (FY94); teak, rice, oilseed, metals, rubber, gems. **Imports:** $1.02 bil. (FY94); machinery, transport equipment, chemicals, food products. **Major trading partners:** ***exports:*** China, India, Thailand, Singapore; ***imports:*** Japan, China, Singapore.

Intl. Orgs. Colombo Plan, FAO, G-77, IAEA, IBRD, ICAO, IDA, IFC, ILO, IMF, IMO, INTERPOL, ITU, UN, UNESCO, UPU, WHO, WMO, WTO.

(Until the summer of 1989 this country was known as Burma.)

Burma, an independent Buddhist monarchy from the 11th century, fell to the Mongol empire in the 13th century, and after the 14th century was a satellite state of China. Anglo-French rivalry over trade left Burma under French influence in the early 19th century, but in a series of three wars (1824–26, 1852, 1885), Great Britain succeeded in bringing all of Burma into the British raj of India. The country became self-governing under a British protectorate in 1937.

Japanese occupation of Burma in early 1942 made the country a major theater of fighting during World War II. The Burma Road, built by the Allies to connect northeastern India with southwestern China, was a key link in bringing supplies to the Chinese Nationalist army during the war.

Burma achieved independence as the Union of Burma on Jan. 4, 1948. Promises of autonomy for ethnic minority regions such as the Shan and Karen States have not been fulfilled, leading to armed separatist movements in those areas ever since. In 1962 a coup led by Gen. Ne Win overthrew the democratic government and established a one-party state under the Burmese Socialist Program party. The party's "Burmese Path to Socialism" resulted in self-imposed international isolation and economic stagnation at home despite the country's potential wealth in agriculture, timber, minerals, and gems.

In July 1988 Ne Win resigned from office in the face of mounting popular demonstrations. A series of short-lived successor governments were unable to restore public order and normal governmental functions; direct military rule was announced in September 1988 as demonstrations continued.

In the general election held on May 27, 1990 (the first multiparty free elections in three decades), the opposition National League for Democracy, led by Aung San Suu Kyi, won a decisive victory, but the results of the election were nullified by the State Law and Order Restoration Council (SLORC), and leaders of the elected government were placed under house arrest. In 1991 the continued political repression in

Myanmar was brought to international attention when Aung San Suu Kyi was awarded the Nobel Peace Prize. This attention helped usher in a period of diminishing repression. A new leader of the ruling military junta, Gen. Than Shwe, has released some political prisoners and a constitutional convention has met sporadically. Peace talks between SLORC and the Karen rebels began in early 1994 and in July 1995, Aung San Suu Kyi was released.

Namibia

Republic of Namibia

Geography **Location:** southwest Africa. **Boundaries:** Angola to N, Botswana to E, South Africa to S, Atlantic Ocean to W. **Total land area:** 318,259 sq. mi. (824,290 sq km). **Coastline:** 925 mi. (1,489 km). **Comparative area:** between Texas and Alaska. **Land use:** 1% arable land; negl. % permanent crops; 64% meadows and pastures; 22% forest and woodland; 13% other; includes negl. % irrigated. **Major cities:** (1988 est.) Windhoek (capital) 114,500.

People **Population:** 1,595,567 (1994 est.). **Nationality:** noun—Namibian(s); adjective—Namibian. **Ethnic groups:** 85.6% black (half of whom are Ovambos), 7.5% white, 6.9% mixed. **Languages:** white population—60% speak Afrikaans, 33% German, and 7% English (all official); several indigenous languages. **Religions:** whites predominantly Christian, nonwhites either Christian or indigenous beliefs.

Government **Type:** republic. **Independence:** Mar. 21, 1990 (from South Africa). **Constitution:** Feb. 16, 1990. **National holiday:** Independence Day, Mar. 21. **Heads of government:** Sam Nujoma, president (since Mar. 1990); Hage G. Geingob, prime minister (since Mar. 1990). **Structure:** Executive Branch—president and cabinet of ministers; Legislative—National Assembly composed of 72 members; Judicial—Supreme Court and regional courts. (Note: President and 72 members of National Assembly elected in Nov. 1989 in Namibia's first free election; election supervised by United Nations.)

Economy **Monetary unit:** South African rand. **Budget:** (1992) ***income:*** $941 mil.; ***expend.:*** $1.05 bil. **GDP:** $2 bil., $1,300 per capita (1992 est.). **Chief crops:** subsistence crops (millet, sorghum, corn, and some wheat) are raised, but most food must be imported. **Livestock:** sheep, cattle, goats, poultry, horses. **Natural resources:** diamonds, copper, uranium, lead, tin. **Major industries:** meat packing, fish processing, dairy products, mining (copper, lead, zinc, diamonds, and uranium). **Labor force:** about 500,000 (1981); 60% agriculture, 19% industry and commerce; 15–17% unemployment. **Exports:** $1.289 bil. (f.o.b., 1992 est.); diamonds, uranium, zinc, copper, meat, processed fish. **Imports:** $1.178 bil. (f.o.b., 1992); foodstuffs, manufactured consumer goods, machinery. **Major trading partners:** ***exports:*** South Africa, Switzerland; ***imports:*** South Africa, Germany, Switzerland, U.S.

Intl. Orgs. FAO, G-77, IAEA, IBRD, ICAO, ILO, IMF, ITU, NAM, UN, UNCTAD, UNESCO, UNHCR, UNIDO, WHO.

The Kalahari desert, on the Namibian plateau, has been inhabited since ancient times by San hunter-gatherers. Various Nama and Bantu peoples migrated into the area more recently. British and Dutch explorers and traders began to penetrate Namibia in the 18th century.

In 1872 Great Britain occupied the area around Walvis Bay and in 1884 annexed it to the Cape Colony. Also in 1884 Germany claimed most of South-West Africa; negotiations between the two powers resulted in German acceptance of Britain's claim of Walvis Bay and British acceptance of Germany's claim to the rest of the coastal region with a sphere of influence in the interior.

During World War I, British troops from South Africa occupied South-West Africa in 1915. In 1920 South Africa received a League of Nations mandate to administer the area. In 1946 when the United Nations succeeded the League, the United Nations proposed that South Africa continue its administration under a UN trusteeship. South Africa refused and annexed South-West Africa.

The proposed UN trusteeship was revoked by the United Nations in 1966. At the same time, the South-West Africa People's Organization (SWAPO), operating from bases in Zambia and Angola, began guerrilla actions against South African troops in the region. In 1968 the United Nations formally renamed the territory Namibia and appointed an 11-nation council to supervise its affairs and devise a plan leading to independence.

In 1971 the International Court of Justice upheld the UN's authority over Namibia and ruled that South Africa's continued occupation of the territory was illegal. In 1975 South Africa convened the Turnhalle Conference, which proposed a plan for Namibian independence based on the racial-separation principles of apartheid. This was rejected by the United Nations, and in 1978 the UN Security Council approved Resolution 435, which called for a general cease-fire to be followed by UN-supervised elections.

In response, South Africa unilaterally held elections in Namibia, which were boycotted by SWAPO and other African organizations and rejected by the United Nations. In 1982 South Africa declared that it would enter into talks about the future of Namibia only after Cuban troops were withdrawn from Angola. In 1983 South Africa launched a major military operation against SWAPO forces in Angola.

In October 1984 Angolan president dos Santos agreed to work out a plan for withdrawal of Cuban troops as part of a settlement in Namibia. In June 1985 South Africa granted limited local authority to a Namibian government made up of a coalition of parties, excluding SWAPO. In 1987 South African troops occupied southern Angola (to aid Angolan rebels), and in early 1988, fighting between South African troops and Namibian rebels in northern Namibia and southern Angola intensified.

A new round of talks on the future of Namibia between South Africa, Cuba, and Angola, mediated by the United States, began in May 1988, and on Dec. 13, 1988, the three parties agreed on a plan for Namibian independence and a pull-out of Cuban troops from Angola.

In January 1989 the Cuban withdrawal from Angola began. On Apr. 1 UN Resolution 435 went into effect in Namibia, and a UN peacekeeping force arrived to supervise the transition to independence. Elections were held in November 1989: SWAPO leader Sam Nujoma won an overwhelming victory, and opposition leaders pledged their support. A Western-style democratic constitution was adopted Feb. 16, 1990, and full independence came on Mar. 21. The first elections under the new constitution were held in December 1994 with SWAPO gaining even stronger control of Parliament.

Most of Namibia consists of a high, semiarid to desert plateau. The country is sparsely inhabited and supports little agriculture; most of the rural population is engaged in raising livestock. Namibia is rich in minerals, including diamonds, copper, lead, and zinc.

Nauru

Republic of Nauru

Geography **Location:** central Pacific Ocean (0°32'S, 166°56'E), about 2,800 mi. (4,500 km) southwest of Hawaii. **Boundaries:** nearest neighbor is Banaba (Ocean Island), in Kiribati, about 185 mi. (300 km) to E. **Total land area:** 8 sq. mi. (21 sq km). **Coastline:** 15 mi. (24 km). **Comparative area:** about one-tenth size of Washington, D.C. **Land use:** 0% arable land; 0% permanent crops; 0% meadows and pastures; 0% forest and woodland; 100% other. **Major cities:** none as such; government offices in Yaren district.

People **Population:** 10,019 (1994 est.). **Nationality:** noun—Nauruan(s) adjective—Nauruan. **Ethnic groups:** 58% Nauruan, 26% other Pacific Islander, 8% Chinese, 8% European. **Languages:** Nauruan, a distinct Pacific Island language (official); English widely understood and spoken and used for most government and commercial purposes. **Religions:** Christian (two-thirds Protestant, one-third Catholic).

Government **Type:** republic. **Independence:** Jan. 31, 1968 (from UN trusteeship under Australia, New Zealand, and UK). **Constitution:** Jan. 29, 1968. **National holiday:** Independence Day, Jan. 31; Constitution Day, May 17; Angram Day, Oct. 26. **Head of government:** Bernard Dowiyogo, president (since Nov. 1992). **Structure:** president elected from and by Parliament for unfixed term; popularly elected 18-member unicameral legislature (Parliament); four-member cabinet to assist president, appointed by him from Parliament members.

Economy **Monetary unit:** Australian dollar. **Budget:** (1986 est.) ***income:*** $69.7 mil.; ***expend.:*** $51.5 mil. **GNP:** over $90 mil., $10,000 per capita (1989). **Chief crops:** negl.; almost completely dependent on imports for food and water. **Livestock:** pigs. **Natural resources:** phosphates. **Major industries:** phosphate mining (about 2 mil. tons per year), financial services, coconuts. **Labor force:** N.A. **Exports:** $93 mil. (1984); phosphates. **Imports:** $73 mil. (1984); food, fuel, manufactures, machinery. **Major trading partners:** ***exports:*** Australia, New Zealand; ***imports:*** Australia, UK, New Zealand, Japan.

Intl. Orgs. Commonwealth (special member), ICAO, INTERPOL, ITU, UPU.

Nauru, formerly known as Pleasant Island, is an isolated island lying west of the Gilbert Islands. It became a German protectorate in 1888. After World War I, Nauru was administered by Australia under a League of Nations mandate. It was occupied by Japan throughout World War II. In 1947 it became a UN Trust Territory administered by Australia, and on Jan. 31, 1968, an independent republic. Nauru has a parliament of 18 members, who elect a prime minister and a cabinet. Most of the island's assets are owned by the state-controlled Nauru Phosphate Corporation and by the Nauru Cooperative Society.

Much of the island is covered by phosphate deposits. Phosphate mining and exports, under leases largely controlled by Australian interests, have given Nauru one of the world's highest per-capita incomes. Currently, national attention is focused on attempts to renegotiate the terms of long-term phosphate export contracts, and on the administration of a national trust fund in preparation for a new era, in the relatively near future, when phosphate deposits will have been exhausted.

Nepal

Kingdom of Nepal

Geography **Location:** central Asia, in Himalayan mountain range. **Boundaries:** China to N, India to E, S, and W. **Total land area:** 54,363 sq. mi. (140,800 sq km). **Coastline:** none. **Comparative area:** between Illinois and Michigan. **Land use:** 17% arable land; negl. % permanent crops; 13% meadows and pastures; 33% forest and woodland; 37% other; includes 2% irrigated. **Major cities:** (1981 census) Kathmandu (capital) 235,160.

People **Population:** 21,041,527 (1994 est.). **Nationality:** noun—Nepalese (sing. and pl.); adjective—Nepalese. **Ethnic groups:** Newars, Indians, Tibetans, Gurungs, Magars, Tamangs, Bhotias, Rais, Limbus, Sherpas, as well as many smaller groups. **Languages:** Nepali (official); 20 languages. divided into numerous dialects. **Religions:** only official Hindu kingdom in world, although no sharp distinction between many Hindu (about 88%) and Buddhist groups; small groups of Muslims and Christians.

Government **Type:** nominally, constitutional monarchy; king exercises autocratic control over multitiered system of government. **Constitution:** Dec. 16, 1962. **National holiday:** Birthday of the king and National Day, Dec. 28. **Heads of government:** Birendra Bir Bikram Shah Dev, king (since Jan. 1972); Man Mohan Adhikari, prime minister (since Nov. 1994). **Structure:** Council of Ministers, appointed by king; Rastriya Panchayat, or National Assembly (140 members serving five-year terms, including 112 directly elected and 28 appointed by king).

Economy **Monetary unit:** Nepalese rupee. **Budget:** (1992) ***income:*** $457 mil.; ***expend.:*** $725 mil. **GDP:** $20.5 bil., $1,000 per capita (1993 est.). **Chief crops:** over 90% of population engaged in agriculture; rice, corn, wheat, sugarcane, oilseeds; illegal producer of cannabis for international drug trade. **Livestock:** cattle, goats, buffalo, sheep, pigs. **Natural resources:** quartz, water, timber, hydroelectric potential, scenic beauty. **Major industries:** small rice, jute, sugar, and oilseed mills; cigarette and brick factories; tourism. **Labor force:** 78.5 mil. (1991 est.); 93% agriculture, 5% services, 2% industry; great lack of skilled labor. **Exports:** $369 mil. (f.o.b., FY93 est.); clothing, carpets, leather goods, grain. **Imports:** $789 mil. (c.i.f., FY93 est.); 20% petroleum products, 11% fertilizer, 10% machinery. **Major trading partners:** (1988) ***exports:*** 38% India, 23% U.S., 6% UK, 9% other Europe; ***imports:*** 36% India, 13% Japan, 4% Europe, 1% U.S.

Intl. Orgs. Colombo Plan, FAO, G-77, IBRD, ICAO, IDA, IFAD, IFC, ILO, IMF, IMO, INTERPOL, ITU, NAM, UN, UNESCO, UPU, WHO, WMO.

The birthplace of Gautama Buddha (c. 600 B.C.), Nepal was for many centuries a collection of petty principalities, inhabited by various Tibeto-Burman peoples who mostly practiced Lamaistic Buddhism. In 1769 the country's three geographical zones—floodplain, foothills, and high mountains—were united under an ascendant group, the Gurkhas, who made Hinduism the country's official religion. Nepal established treaty relations with Great Britain in 1792 and fought a border war with British India in 1814–16, but it was never incorporated into the British Empire.

An armed revolution in 1950 overthrew a government of heriditary rulers that had overthrown the Shah dynasty in the 19th century. King Tribuhavan (a Shah) was restored and tried to introduce democratic reforms, but his son Mahendra dissolved Parliament and introduced a tiered system of town, district, and national councils. Road and air links to India, Pakistan, and Tibet were improved, and Nepal began to emerge from its customary isolation. The successful climb of Mt. Everest by Sir Edmund Hillary and Tenzing Norgay in 1953 focused international attention on Nepal.

Antigovernment demonstrations in the spring of 1990 culminated in the shooting deaths of 63 civilians on Apr. 6, and three days later the king lifted a 30-year ban on political parties. A new constitution establishing multiparty democracy and human rights as essentials of the political system was promulgated Nov. 9. The king remains a constitutional monarch and head of the military, but executive power is vested in the prime minister and his cabinet.

In 1991 elections, organized and won by the Congress party, the Communists won 82 of the 205 seats. But in 1994 elections the Communists won the largest number (86) while the Congress party fell to 76; a new government was formed by Man Mohan Adhikari, who pledged land reform.

In recent years tourism, especially mountaineering and trekking, have increased the country's prosperity but also have created new ecological problems. Additionally, a rapidly increasing population and drastic deforestation have had severe impacts on the country. The economy remains largely in the stage of small-scale agriculture and craft industries.

Netherlands

Kingdom of The Netherlands

Geography **Location:** western Europe. **Boundaries:** North Sea to N and W, Germany to E, Belgium to S. **Total land area:** 14,413 sq. mi. (37,330 sq km). **Coastline:** 280 mi. (451 km). **Comparative area:** 1.3 times size of Maryland. **Land use:** 25% arable land; 1% permanent crops; 34% meadows and pastures; 9% forest and woodland; 31% other; includes 15% irrigated. **Major cities:** (1993) Amsterdam (capital) 719,856; Rotterdam 596,023; The Hague 444,661; Utrecht 234,170; Eindhoven 195,267. The Hague is the seat of government.

People **Population:** 15,367,928 (1994 est.). **Nationality:** noun—Dutchman (men), Dutchwoman (women); adjective—Dutch. **Ethnic groups:** 99% Dutch, 1% Indonesian and other. **Languages:** Dutch (official). **Religions:** 40% Roman Catholic, 31% Protestant, 24% unaffiliated, 5% none.

Government **Type:** constitutional monarchy. **Independence:** N.A. **Constitution:** Feb. 17, 1983. **National holiday:** Queen's Day, Apr. 30. **Heads of government:** Beatrix Wilhelmina Armgard, queen (since Apr. 1980); Wim Kok, prime minister (since Aug. 1994). **Structure:** executive (queen and Cabinet of Ministers), which is responsible to bicameral parliament (States General) consisting of First Chamber (75 indirectly elected members) and Second Chamber (150 directly elected members); independent judiciary; coalition governments are usual.

Economy **Monetary unit:** guilder. **Budget:** (1992 est.) ***income:*** $109.9 bil.; ***expend.:*** $122.1 bil. **GDP:** $262.8 bil., $17,200 per capita (1993). **Chief crops:** horticultural crops, grains, potatoes, sugar beets; food shortages—grains, fats, oils. **Livestock:** chickens, pigs, cattle, sheep, horses, ponies. **Natural recources:** natural gas, crude oil, fertile soil. **Major industries:** agroindustries, metal and engineering products, electrical machinery and equipment. **Labor force:** 5.3 mil. (1986); 50.1% services, 28.2% manufacturing and construction, 15.9% government; 11.1% unemployment (1988). **Exports:** $139 bil. (f.o.b., 1992); agricultural products, processed foods and tobacco, natural gas, chemicals, metal products. **Imports:** $130.3 bil. (f.o.b., 1992); raw materials and semifinished products, consumer goods, transport equipment, crude oil. **Major trading partners:** (1988) ***exports:*** 74.9% EU (28.3% Germany, 14.2% Belgium-Luxembourg, 10.7% France, 10.2% UK), 4.7% U.S., 0.9% Communist countries; ***imports:*** 63.8% EU (26.5% Germany, 23.1% Belgium-Luxembourg, 8.1% UK), 7.9% U.S.

Intl. Orgs. EU, FAO, IAEA, IBRD, ICAO, IDA, IFAD, IFC, ILO, IMF, IMO, INTELSAT, INTERPOL, ITU, NATO, OECD, OSCE, UN, UNESCO, UPU, WHO, WIPO, WMO, WTO.

Historically, the name Netherlands referred to the low-lying areas of the Holy Roman Empire near the mouths of the Rhine, Meuse, and Scheldt rivers. The Habsburg emperor Charles V willed these territories to his son Philip II of Spain in 1555, but by the end of the 16th century, the northern provinces—the Union of Utrecht, formed in 1579 by William the Silent, of the House of Orange—won their independence in a war that was both religious (Calvinist vs. Catholic) and constitutional (aristocratic/patrician vs. foreign monarchy). The independence of the Netherlands was recognized in the Treaty of Westphalia, which ended the Thirty Years' War in 1648.

Dutch prosperity, founded on the woolen trade with England, grew tremendously through trade and seafaring under the 17th-century republic. The Netherlands amassed a world empire, including the Indonesian archipelago, the island of Sri Lanka (then Ceylon), South Africa, Surinam, parts of the West Indies, and the Hudson valley in New Amsterdam (later New York); in addition it monopolized Western trade with Japan after 1637.

The Netherlands were incorporated into the Napoleonic empire. At the Congress of Vienna in 1815, a Dutch monarchy was established, which included Belgium until 1830. Land drainage and reclamation programs maintained the prosperity of the country's small-scale agriculture, while trade and colonial revenues were increasingly supplemented by industrial development in the 19th century. Dutch prosperity and the country's strategic position gave the Netherlands extraordinary influence and prestige in European affairs into the 20th century, despite the country's small size. It remained neutral in World War I.

Germany invaded the Netherlands in May 1940, taking control of the country after five days of fighting. Preparing to incorporate Holland into the Third Reich, Hitler installed a Nazi civilian government that ruled through totalitarian exploitation and cooperated in the persecution of Jews. But Queen Wilhelmina and the Dutch government escaped to England and maintained a government-in-exile throughout the war.

The final stages of fighting on the western front inflicted severe damage on the country, while in Asia the recovery of Indonesia from Japan led immediately to a declaration of independence under Sukarno. Marshall Plan aid was intended to support a domestic postwar recovery; an equal amount was spent by the Dutch government in an attempt to recapture control of Indonesia before that country's independence was recognized in 1949.

Devastated by World War II and the loss of its empire, the country faced a bleak future in the postwar years. Forced to turn its attention to recovery at home, the Netherlands worked through the Benelux (Belgium, Netherlands, Luxembourg) union (founded in 1944) and the Common Market to create another European "economic miracle" between the early 1950s and the 1970s. The older bases of the economy—commerce, maritime industry, dairy farming, and flower farming—were expanded and modernized; Rotterdam was rebuilt to become Europe's most important port. Newer industries, such as chemicals and oil refining, electronics, and steel, relied on the country's highly skilled and productive labor force to turn imported raw materials into finished high-value exports. A huge impoundment project turned the Zuider Zee into a new province, increasing the country's land area by 10 percent.

This postwar prosperity has been based in large part on political stability. A coalition of the Catholic State party and the Labor (formerly Social Democratic) party governed for 10 years under Premier Willem Drees. After 1958 cabinets normally were formed from coalitions headed by three Christian parties (merged in 1980 to form the United Christian Appeal) or by the Liberal party; all pursued essentially the same policies of free enterprise, comprehensive social welfare programs, high taxation, and social liberalism.

Queen Juliana was succeeded in 1980 by Queen Beatrix. From 1982 to 1989 a coalition of Christian Democrats and Liberals provided a cabinet headed by Prime Minister Ruud Lubbers; since 1989 the coalition has been of Christian Democrats and Labor. In 1994 Wim Kok, head of Labor, became prime minister, the first government to exclude the Christian Democrats since World War II.

New Zealand

Geography **Location:** South Pacific Ocean about 1,100 mi. (1,750 km) SE of Australia. **Boundaries:** South Pacific Ocean to N, E, and S; Tasman Sea to W. **Total land area:** 103,738 sq. mi. (268,680 sq km). **Coastline:** 9,406 mi. (15,134 km). **Comparative area:** about size of Colorado. **Land use:** 2% arable land; 0% permanent crops; 53% meadows and pastures; 38% forest and woodland; 7% other; includes 1% irrigated. **Major cities:** (1993 est.) Wellington (capital) 326,900; Auckland 910,200; Christchurch 312,600; Hamilton 151,800; Napier-Hastings 111,200.

People **Population:** 3,388,737 (1994 est.). **Nationality:** noun—New Zealander(s); adjective—New Zealand. **Ethnic groups:** 88% European, 8.9% Maori, 2.9% Pacific Islander, 0.2% other. **Languages:** English and Maori (both official). **Religions:** 81% Christian; 18% none or unspecified; 1% Hindu, Confucian, and other.

Government **Type:** independent state within Commonwealth, recognizing Elizabeth II as head of state. **Independence:** Sept. 26, 1907 (from UK). **Constitution:** no formal, written constitution; consists of various documents, including certain acts of UK and New Zealand parliaments. Constitution Act 1986 brings together "certain provisions of constitutional significance." **National holiday:** Waitangi Day, Feb. 6. **Heads of government:** Dame Catherine Tizard, governor-general (since Dec. 1990); James B. Bolger, prime minister (since Nov. 1990). **Structure:** unicameral legislature (99-member House of Representatives, commonly called Parliament); three-level court system (district courts, High Court; Court of Appeal).

Economy **Monetary Unit:** New Zealand dollar. **Budget:** (1992) ***income:*** N.A.; ***expend.:*** N.A. **GDP:** $53 bil., $15,700 per capita (1993). **Chief crops:** fodder and silage crops, apples and kiwifruit, forestry. **Livestock:** sheep, cattle, goats, pigs, horses, deer. **Natural resources:** natural gas, iron ore, sand, coal, timber. **Major industries:** food processing, wood and paper products, textiles, aluminum smelting, tourism. **Labor force:** 1,486,000 (1993), 72.7% services, 16.5% manufacturing, 10.7% primary production; 8.4% unemployment (1994). **Exports:** $10.3 bil. (FY93); wool, lamb, mutton, beef, fruit, fish. **Imports:** $9.4 bil. (FY93); petroleum, consumer goods, motor vehicles, industrial equipment. **Major trading partners:** ***exports:*** 20% Australia, 16% EU, 15% Japan, 12% U.S., 5% S. Korea; ***imports:*** 22% Australia, 19% U.S., 17% EU, 15% Japan, 3% China.

Intl. Orgs. ANZUS, Australia Group, Colombo Plan, Commonwealth of Nations, FAO, IAEA, IBRD, ICAO, IDA, IFAD, IFC, ILO, IMF, IMO, INTELSAT, INTERPOL, ITU, UN, UNESCO, UPU, WHO, WMO, WTO.

New Zealand was settled by Maori voyagers from Polynesia from about the ninth century A.D. The first European to sight it was the Dutch explorer Abel Tasman, in 1642; he named it, but did not take possession. In 1769, Capt. James Cook visited and claimed it for Britain. The first British missionaries arrived in 1814, and New Zealand became a full-fledged British colony in 1841. By the Treaty of Waitangi in 1840, the Maoris recognized Queen Victoria's protection and agreed to admit British settlers; in return, they were guaranteed possession of their lands. But in a series of bloody wars lasting until 1870, the Maoris were displaced from lands devoted to the expanding British settlements.

As a result of their defeat and of introduced diseases, the Maori population dwindled to about 40,000 by the 1890s. Their numbers have since recovered to over 400,000, and in recent decades, the Maoris have become a cohesive culture and significant political force, directly electing several members of Parliament. In

1985, the Waitangi Tribunal was given wide power to hear Maori claims for repayment for land taken without compensation since the 1840 treaty. Large financial settlements are now being negotiated by the government.

New Zealand was one of the first nations to introduce universal adult suffrage (1893) and to establish a comprehensive welfare state. Legislation beginning in 1898 regulates labor practices, and mandates universal old-age pensions, public sector medical care, and other social services. Since 1907, the country has been an independent member of the British Commonwealth. The crown is represented by a governor-general, while government is drawn from a parliament and headed by a prime minister. Since the 1930s, government has alternated between the National and Labour parties.

New Zealand troops fought on the side of the Allies in both world wars, with UN forces in Korea, and with the United States in Vietnam. In 1951, New Zealand joined Australia and the United States in the ANZUS mutual-defense treaty, but was excluded from it in 1986 after denying port facilities to ships carrying nuclear weapons. New Zealand has also objected strenuously to French testing of nuclear weapons in the South Pacific and pressed for a comprehensive international nuclear test ban treaty.

Upon its election in 1984, the Labour government launched a profound economic restructuring program to transform the country from a protected agrarian economy to an open free-market economy. This program, continued by the National Party, which regained power in 1990, eliminated government subsidies, cut government spending, liberalized imports, deregulated financial markets, reduced tax rates, and deregulated the labor market, largely disempowering the unions. The reforms have resulted in an expanding and competitive economy with low inflation, and, in 1993–94, the first budget surplus in 18 years. The price of this growth, initially, was unemployment, which skyrocketed to over 11 percent, but has since fallen.

New Zealand administers the foreign affairs and defense of several Pacific island dependencies (see "Territories of the World") and the Ross Dependency in Antarctica.

Nicaragua

Republic of Nicaragua

Geography **Location:** Central American isthmus. **Boundaries:** Honduras to N, Caribbean Sea to E, Costa Rica to S, Pacific Ocean to W. **Total land area:** 49,998 sq. mi. (129,494 sq km). **Coastline:** 565 mi. (910 km). **Comparative area:** between Pennsylvania and Mississippi. **Land use:** 9% arable land; 1% permanent crops; 43% meadows and pastures; 35% forest and woodland; 12% other; includes 1% irrigated. **Major cities:** (1983) Managua (capital) 682,111; (1985 est.) León 100,982; Granada 88,636; Masaya 74,946; Chinandega 67,792.

People **Population:** 4,096,589 (1994 est.). **Nationality:** noun—Nicaraguan(s); adjective—Nicaraguan. **Ethnic groups:** 69% mestizo, 17% white, 9% black, 5% Indian. **Languages:** Spanish (official); English- and Indian-speaking minorities on Atlantic coast. **Religions:** 95% Roman Catholic.

Government **Type:** republic. **Independence:** Sept. 28, 1821 (from Spain). **Constitution:** Jan. 1987. **National holidays:** Independence Day, Sept. 15; Anniversary of the Revolution, July 19. **Head of government:** Mrs. Violeta Barrios de Chamorro, president (since Apr. 1990). **Structure:** Executive branch—president and cabinet of ministers; Legislative—National Assembly composed of 92 members; Judicial—Supreme Court and regional courts. (Note: President and 92 members of National Assembly elected in April 1990 in free elections supervised by the United Nations and other international observers.)

Economy **Monetary unit:** córdoba. **Budget:** (1991) ***income:*** $375 mil.; ***expend.:*** $410 mil. **GDP:** $6.4 bil., $1,600 per capita (1993 est.). **Chief crops:** cotton, coffee, sugarcane, rice, corn, beans. **Livestock:** cattle, pigs, horses, mules, sheep, goats. **Natural resources:** gold, silver, copper, tungsten, lead. **Major industries:** food processing, chemicals, metal products. **Labor force:** 1.08 mil. (1987); 44% agriculture, 43% service, 13% industry; 22% unemployment. **Exports:** $228 mil. (f.o.b., 1992); coffee, cotton, sugar, bananas, seafood, meat. **Imports:** $907 mil. (c.i.f., 1992); petroleum, food, chemicals, machinery, clothing. **Major trading partners:** ***exports:*** 75% OECD, 15% former USSR and Eastern Europe; ***imports:*** 30% Latin America, 25% U.S., 20% EU, 10% former USSR and Eastern Europe.

Intl. Orgs. FAO, G-77, IAEA, IBRD, ICAO, IDA, IFAD, IFC, ILO, IMF, IMO, INTELSAT, INTERPOL, ITU, NAM, OAS, UN, UNESCO, UPU, WHO, WMO, WTO.

Nicaragua gained independence from Spain in 1821 and formed a constituent part of the United Provinces of Central America in 1823. With the dissolution of the federation in 1838, Nicaragua became an independent republic. Throughout the territory of the United Provinces, an intra-elite struggle between Liberal and Conservative factions defined the political arena during the early part of the 19th century. Nicaraguan Liberals invited the adventurer William Walker of Tennessee to take their part against their Conservative rivals in 1855. Walker took control of the country in 1856 but was driven out by a combined Central American force the following year.

The Conservatives held power in Nicaragua until 1893, when a planters' revolt brought Liberal José Santos Zelaya to the presidency. Because of Zelaya's intention to pursue an isthmian canal project, the U.S. government intervened in support of a Conservative uprising. The United States sent marines to Nicaragua in 1909, and Zelaya resigned in 1910. The marines occupied the country during 1909–25 and 1926–33.

Refusing to abide by a political settlement between the U.S. government and Nicaraguan Liberal forces in 1927, a Liberal officer, Augusto César Sandino, led a guerrilla war against U.S. occupation forces until 1933. Anastasio Somoza García, head of the Nicaraguan National Guard, had Sandino assassinated in 1934 and took over the presidency in 1937. Somoza and his sons Luis and Anastasio Somoza Debayle controlled Nicaragua until 1979.

A broad coalition of groups led by the Sandinista National Liberation Front (FSLN) overthrew the Somoza dictatorship in 1979. Elections were held in 1984 for the presidency, vice presidency, and a constituent assembly. The Sandinistas won the election for the presidency and vice presidency as well as receiving a working majority in the National Assembly, and a new constitution was promulgated for the country in 1987.

Between 1981 and 1990 the United States actively, but covertly, supported Contra rebels fighting the Sandinista regime in a civil war that cost the country dearly. In 1989, Pres. Daniel Ortega announced elections for early 1990, which he lost in a stunning upset to Violeta Barrios de Chamorro, who headed a 17-party coalition, the United Nicaragua Opposition (UNO). Although the transition has been relatively peaceful, the government faced dissent from former Contras angry at continued Sandinista control of the army and police. In early 1995, however, Gen. Humberto Ortega turned over command of the army, the first peaceful transfer in Nicaragua's history.

Niger

Republic of Niger

Geography **Location:** landlocked country in western Africa. **Boundaries:** Algeria and Libya to N, Chad to E, Nigeria to S, Benin, Burkina Faso to SW, Mali to W. **Total land area:** 489,189 sq. mi. (1,267,000 sq km). **Coastline:** none. **Comparative area:** between Texas and Alaska. **Land use:** 3% arable land; 0% permanent crops; 7% meadows and pastures; 2% forest and woodland; 88% other; includes negl. % irrigated. **Major cities:** Niamey (capital) 225,314; Zinder 75,000 (1981 est.); Marodi 45,852; Tahoua 31,265; Agadez 20,475 (1977).

People **Population:** 8,971,605 (1994 est.). **Nationality:** noun—Nigerien(s); adjective—Nigerien. **Ethnic groups:** 56% Hausa, 22% Djerma, 8.5% Fula, 8% Tuareg, 4.3% Beri Beri (Kanouri); 1.2% Arab, Toubou, and Gourmantche; about 4,000 French expatriates. **Languages:** French (official), Hausa, Djerma. **Religions:** 80% Muslim, 20% indigenous beliefs and Christians.

Government **Type:** republic; military regimes in power since Apr. 1974. **Independence:** Aug. 3, 1960 (from France). **Constitution:** Sept. 24, 1989. **National holiday:** Independence Day, Aug. 3. **Heads of government:** Mahamane Ousmane, president (since Mar. 1993); Hama Amadou, prime minister (since Feb. 1995). **Structure:** executive—president; 93-seat National Assembly.

Economy **Monetary unit:** Communauté Financière Africaine (CFA) franc. **Budget:** (1991 est.) ***income:*** $193 mil.; ***expend.:*** $355 mil. **GDP:** $5.4 bil., $650 per capita (1993 est.). **Chief crops:** cash crops—cowpeas, groundnuts, cotton; food crops—millet, sorghum, rice. **Livestock:** goats, sheep, cattle, asses, camels. **Natural resources:** uranium, coal, iron ore, tin, phosphates. **Major industries:** cement, brick, rice mill. **Labor force:** 2.5 mil. (1982); 90% agriculture; 51% of population of working age. **Exports:** $294 mil. (f.o.b., 1991); uranium, livestock, cowpeas, onions, hides, skins; exports understated because much regional trade not recorded. **Imports:** $346 mil. (c.i.f., 1991); petroleum products, primary materials, machinery, vehicles and parts, electronic equipment. **Major trading partners:** ***exports:*** 65% France, 11% Nigeria; ***imports:*** 26% Germany, 11% Ivory Coast, 5% France, 4% Italy.

Intl. Orgs. FAO, G-77, IAEA, IBRD, ICAO, IDA, IFAD, IFC, ILO, IMF, INTELSAT, INTERPOL, ITU, NAM, UN, UNESCO, UPU, WHO, WIPO, WMO, WTO.

Most of Niger's territory is dominated by the Sahara and the Sahel (the "shore" of the desert), which have spread southward since prehistoric times. Much of the population lives in the narrow fertile belt south of the Niger River. Much of Niger was incorporated during medieval times in large empires centered in neighboring Mali, Chad, and Nigeria.

In the 18th century, Tuaregs migrating from the northern desert began to form tribal confederations in Niger. They united with local Hausa peoples to wage war against the Fulani empire.

In the 19th century, British and German explorers seeking the source of the Niger River explored the region. In the European rivalry that followed, the French, from bases in Mali and Chad, began to dominate Niger by 1900; Niger became a French colony in 1922, administered from Dakar, Senegal.

In 1946 the people of Niger, in common with other peoples in French Africa, were granted French citizenship, and limited self-rule began. This local autonomy was expanded in 1956, and in 1958 Niger became an autonomous state within the French Overseas Community. Full independence followed on Aug. 3, 1960; Niger maintained close ties to France.

Hamani Diori was elected Niger's first president in 1960 and was reelected in 1965 and 1970. He was overthrown in 1974 in a military coup led by Lt. Col. Seyni Kountche, who became Niger's next president. In 1987 Pres. Kountche died and was succeeded by Col. Ali Saibou, who was elected president by the Supreme Military Council. Ratification of a new constitution and National Assembly elections were held in December 1989. Although Niger has been plagued by expanding hostilities with the Tuareg Liberation Front of Air and Azawad, and remains overwhelmingly dependent on foreign aid, the country has been moving toward democracy and a new constitution was approved in late 1992. Mahame Ousmane became president in 1993 and peace has been maintained. Elections in January 1995 gave a small majority in the National Assembly to a coalition opposed to the government.

Nigeria

Federal Republic of Nigeria

Geography **Location:** western coast of Africa. **Boundaries:** Niger to N, Cameroon to E, Gulf of Guinea to S, Benin to W. **Total land area:** 356,668 sq. mi. (923,770 sq km). **Coastline:** 530 mi. (853 km). **Comparative area:** about 1.3 times size of Texas. **Land use:** 31% arable land; 3% permanent crops; 23% meadows and pastures; 15% forest and woodland; 28% other; includes negl. % irrigated. **Major cities:** (1986 est.) Lagos 5,500,000; Ibadan 2,000,000; Kano 1,000,000; Enugu 500,000; Abuja (capital) 379,000.

People **Population:** 98,091,097 (1994 est.). **Nationality:** noun—Nigerian(s); adjective—Nigerian. **Ethnic groups:** 250 tribal groups; Hausa and Fulani in north, Yoruba in southwest, and Ibos in southeast make up 65% of population; 27,000 non-Africans. **Languages:** English (official); Hausa, Yoruba, Ibo, Fulani, and several other languages also widely used. **Religions:** 50% Muslim, 40% Christian, 10% indigenous beliefs.

Government **Type:** military government since Dec. 31, 1983. **Independence:** Oct. 1, 1960 (from UK). **Constitution:** Oct. 1, 1979, amended Feb. 9, 1984. **National holiday:** Independence Day, Oct. 1. **Head of government:** Gen. Sani Abacha, president (since Nov. 1993). **Structure:** Armed Forces Ruling Council; National Council of Ministers and National Council of States; judiciary headed by Supreme Court.

Economy **Monetary unit:** naira. **Budget:** (1992 est.) ***income:*** $9 bil.; ***expend:*** $10.8 bil. **GDP:** $95.1 bil., $1,000 per capita (1993 est.). **Chief crops:** peanuts, cotton, cocoa, rubber, yams; illegal producer of cannabis for international drug trade. **Livestock:** goats, sheep, cattle, pigs, asses. **Natural resources:** crude oil, tin, columbite, iron ore, coal. **Major industries:** mining—crude oil, natural gas, coal, tin, columbite; processing industries—palm oil, peanuts, cotton, rubber, petroleum; manufacturing industries—textiles, cement, building materials, food products, footwear. **Labor force:** $42.8 mil. (1985); 54% agriculture; 19% industry, commerce, and services; 15% government; 49% of population of working age (1985); 7.5% unemployment (1988 est.). **Exports:** $11.9 bil. (f.o.b., 1992); 95% oil, cocoa, palm products, rubber. **Imports:** $8.3 bil. (c.i.f., 1992); consumer goods, capital equipment, chemicals, raw materials. **Major trading partners:** ***exports:*** 51% EU, 32% U.S.; ***imports:*** EU, U.S.

Intl. Orgs. Commonwealth, FAO, G-77, IAEA, IBRD, ICAO, IDA, IFAD, IFC, ILO, IMF, IMO, INTELSAT, INTERPOL, ITU, NAM, OPEC, UN, UNESCO, UPU, WHO, WMO, WTO.

The Nok culture of central Nigeria (500–200 B.C.) was one of the richest and most advanced ancient civilizations in western Africa. Around A.D. 1000, the Muslim Kanem civilization expanded into northern Nigeria; by the 14th century, the amalgamated kingdom of Kanem-Bornu took northern Nigeria as its political center, from which it dominated the Sahel and developed trade routes stretching throughout northern Africa and as far as Europe and the Middle East.

During the 15th and 16th centuries, the Hausa Songhai empire rose to power. It was overthrown by the Fulani Muslim leader Uthman Dan Fodio, who created the Sokoto caliphate.

Southern Nigeria is dominated by the Yoruba, whose Oyo kingdom, centered at Ife, became a major power by A.D. 1000. Oyo gave rise to the Benin civilization, which flourished from the 15th to the 18th centuries and is famous for its brass, bronze, and ivory sculpture.

The Portuguese established trading stations on the Benin coast in the 15th century; initially, trade relations were cordial, and Benin became well-known in Europe as a powerful and advanced kingdom. With the rise of the slave trade (which began with the cooperation of the Benin kings, who brought slaves from the interior), relations became hostile, and Benin declined under European pressure. The Dutch, British, and other Europeans competed strenuously with Portugal for control of the slave trade, and by the 18th century, most of the coastal region of Nigeria was under British control. By the turn of the 19th century, Britain suppressed the slave trade; slaves captured aboard European ships were transported by the British to Freetown in Sierra Leone.

With the slave trade ended, the British traded with Nigerians for agricultural and forest products and commenced exploration of the Niger River. Lagos came under British control in 1851, and in 1861 Nigeria was made a British colony. Despite native resistance the colony was expanded in 1906 to include territory east of the Niger River, which was called the Protectorate of Southern Nigeria, The two areas were administratively joined in 1914.

During the 1920s Britain began to respond to Nigerian demands for local self-rule. In 1946 the colony was divided into three regions, each with an advisory assembly. In 1954 the colony was reorganized as the Nigerian Federation, and the assemblies were given more authority. Sir Akubar Tafawa Balewa became Nigeria's first prime minister.

In 1961 a UN-supervised referendum in British Cameroon led to the joining with Nigeria of the northern part of that territory, while the southern part joined the new nation of Cameroon.

The 1960s were marked by a struggle for political dominance among the major ethnic groups of Nigeria, including the Ibo (or Igbo), Yoruba, Hausa, and Fulani. Attempts to partition the country on tribal lines for administrative purposes provoked controversy, and charges of corruption and fraud in elections held in 1964 and 1965 led to violence and rioting.

In January 1966 civil war broke out when a group of Ibo army officers overthrew the central government and several of the regional governments. Prime Minister Balewa was killed, along with many other political leaders in the northern and western parts of the country. Gen. Johnson Aguiyi-Ironsi, leader of the Ibo forces, took control of the government.

Aguiyi-Ironsi abolished the country's federal structure and set up a strong central government, dominated by the Ibo. Anti-Ibo riots broke out in the north, and many Ibo were massacred. In July 1966 Aguiyi-Ironsi was assassinated by a group of northern army officers. Army Chief of Staff Yakubu Gowon became head of a new military government. The Eastern Region refused to acknowledge Gowon's government.

In 1967 Gowon reapportioned Nigeria into 12 states. The Eastern Region rejected this plan and seceded from Nigeria to form the independent state of Biafra, provoking a civil war that lasted until January 1970, when Biafra was rejoined with Nigeria. An estimated one million Biafrans, mostly Ibos, died from military action or starvation.

The Gowon government tried to aid in the reconstruction of the Eastern Region and to create a harmonious multitribal government. Gowon was overthrown in a coup in 1975. His successor was assassinated in 1976 and succeeded by Lt. Gen. Olusegun Obasanjo. The Obasanjo government increased the number of states from 12 to 19 and promised a return to civilian rule.

Shehu Shagari was elected president in October 1979 and reelected in 1983, but in December 1983 the military again intervened. On Aug. 30, 1985, Maj. Gen. Ibrahim Gbadamosi Babangida came to power.

Despite political difficulties, Nigeria's recovery from the Biafran War was greatly aided in the 1970s by revenues from petroleum exports. Corruption, mismanagement, and overspending of projected petroleum revenues led to a major economic crisis in the early 1980s with the collapse of world crude oil prices. Petroleum export earnings declined from $26 billion in 1980 to $5 billion in 1986. With a high foreign debt, high inflation rate, unemployment, and shortages of basic goods, riots broke out in major population centers.

In addition, in March 1987 religious violence broke out between the Christian south and the Muslim north; numerous churches and mosques were destroyed or vandalized.

The Babangida government in 1987 announced various economic austerity measures and promoted a campaign to lower the birth rate. Despite outbreaks of religious and ethnic violence the government went forward with plans for a new constitution and to restore civilian rule by the end of 1992. Babangida, however, limited the number of political parties to two and dictated both party platforms.

A National Assembly was elected in July 1992, and presidential elections took place the following June. Gen. Babangida annulled the results on the grounds of fraud and corruption. Violence erupted in several areas of the country throughout the following months. In August 1993 Gen. Babangida resigned and his successor, Ernest Shonekan, was ousted in November by Defense Minister Sani Abacha.

Gen. Abacha established a "constitutional conference" in June of 1994 which, by April 1995, had drafted a constitution but dropped its previously targeted January 1996 deadline for its implementation, leaving the decision of timing to the junta's "Provisional Ruling Council."

Norway

Kingdom of Norway

Geography **Location:** western Scandinavian peninsula, northern Europe. **Boundaries:** Norwegian Sea to N and W, Russian Federation, Finland to NE, Sweden to E, North Sea to S and W. **Total land area:** 125,182 sq. mi. (324,220 sq km). **Coastline:** 13,626 mi. (21,925 km)—2,125 mi. (3,419 km) mainland; 1,500 mi. (2,413 km) large islands; 10,002 mi. (16,093 km) long fjords, numerous small islands, and minor indentations. **Comparative area:** slightly larger than New Mexico. **Land use:** 3% arable land; 0% permanent crops; negl. % meadows and pastures; 27% forest and woodland; 70% other; includes negl. % irrigated. **Major cities:** (1993) Oslo (capital) 473,344; Bergen 218,105; Trondheim 140,718; Stavanger 101,463; Kristiansand 67,113.

People **Population:** 4,314,604 (1994). **Nationality:** noun—Norwegian(s); adjective—Norwegian. **Ethnic groups:** Germanic (Nordic, Alpine, Baltic) and racial-cultural minority of 20,000 Lapps. **Languages:** Norwegian (official), small Lapp- and Finnish-speaking minorities. **Religions:** 94% Evangelical Lutheran (state church), 4% other Protestant and Roman Catholic, 2% other.

Government **Type:** constitutional monarchy. **Independence:** Oct. 26, 1905 (from Sweden). **Constitution:** May 17, 1814, and modified in 1884. **National holiday:** Constitution Day, May 17. **Heads of government:** Harald V, king (since Jan. 1991); Mrs. Gro Harlem Brundtland, prime minister (since Nov. 1990). **Structure:** executive power vested in Crown but exercised by cabinet responsible to Parliament; legislative authority rests jointly with Crown and Parliament (Storting-Lagting, upper house; Odelsting, lower house); Supreme Court, five superior courts, 104 lower courts.

Economy (1992) **Monetary unit:** Norwegian krone. **Budget:** ***income:*** $45.3 bil.; ***expend.:*** $51.8 bil. **GDP:** $89.5 bil., $20,800 per capita (1993). **Chief crops:** feed grains, potatoes, fruits, vegetables; 40% self-sufficient; food shortages—food grains, sugar. **Livestock:** sheep, cattle, pigs, goats, horses. **Natural resources:** crude oil, copper, natural gas, pyrites, nickel. **Major industries:** petroleum and gas, food processing, shipbuilding. **Shortages:** most raw materials except timber, petroleum, iron, copper, and ilmenite ore. **Labor force:** 2.13 mil.; 33% services, 17.4% commerce, 17.2% mining and manufacturing; 2.1% unemployment (1987). **Exports:** $32.1 bil. (f.o.b., 1993); 25% petroleum and petroleum products, 11% natural gas, 7% fish, 6% aluminum. **Imports:** $24.8 bil. (c.i.f., 1993); machinery, fuels and lubricants, transport equipment, chemicals, foodstuffs. **Major trading partners:** ***exports:*** 67% EU, 18% Nordic countries, 5% U.S.; ***imports:*** 49% EU, 27% Nordic countries, 9% U.S., 6% Japan.

Intl. Orgs. EFTA, FAO, IAEA, IBRD, ICAO, IDA, IFAD, IFC, ILO, IMF, IMO, INTELSAT, INTERPOL, ITU, NATO, OECD, OSCE, UN, UNESCO, UPU, WHO, WIPO, WMO, WTO.

The Viking age began in 793 with the sack of Lindisfarne in Ireland. By the 10th century, Norse and Danish Vikings had touched in almost every navigable river of Western Europe from Germany to Spain. In addition to coastal raiding, the Norse were beginning the first open-ocean voyages from Europe, sailing direct to Iceland (800 miles) and even to Greenland (2,200 miles), which they colonized in the 10th century.

At the beginning of the 10th century, Harold I united the petty kingdoms of western Scandinavia and extended his realm as far as the Orkney and Shetland islands. Viking nobles fleeing from his conquests consolided the Norse duchy of Normandy in France. Christianity was established under Olaf II at the beginning of the 11th century.

Under Magnus VI (1263–80), medieval Norway reached the height of its power and prosperity. Norwegian independence ended with the accession in 1319 of Magnus VII, who was king of Sweden as well. Under the Kalmar Union of 1397, the three kingdoms of Scandinavia were merged under Danish control; Norway ceased to exist as a nation-state and was governed by the Danes for the following four centuries.

In 1814 Denmark, which had sided with France in the Napoleonic wars, was forced by the victorious powers to cede Norway to Sweden. Under Sweden's military control, but with a growing sense of nationalism, Norway attempted to establish its own monarchy. The attempt failed, but in 1815 Sweden acknowledged the independence of Norway in perpetual union with the Swedish Crown.

Relations between Norway and Sweden remained strained throughout the 19th century. In 1905 the Norwegian legislature, the Storting, declared the union void and deposed Swedish King Oscar II as king of Norway. Sweden acquiesced, and Prince Charles of Denmark was enthroned as king of Norway, ruling as Haakon VII for 52 years.

During the 19th century, large numbers of Norwegians emigrated to North America. A rising tide of cultural nationalism was expressed in the flourishing Norwegian literature and art, as well as in a tradition of Arctic exploration. In the 20th century, industrialization, aided by the development of hydroelectric power, began to supplement Norway's traditional economic mainstays of fishing and seafaring.

Norway remained neutral during World War I and was relatively unaffected by the postwar upheavals. Industrialization led to the rise of the Labor party in 1927.

Norway attempted to remain neutral in World War II as well but was invaded by German troops in April 1940; the country fell after a brief resistance aided by a Franco-British expeditionary force. The king and government fled to London and established a government-in-exile there. The Norwegian merchant marine fleet was also largely transferred to Great Britain and contributed to the Allied cause in the North Atlantic. At home, resistance grew to the collaborationist government of the Fascist leader Vidkun Quisling. As the Nazis retreated in 1945, King Haakon and his government returned home in triumph. Within three years the Norwegian economy had returned to prewar levels.

Elections in 1945 returned a majority Labor government in the Storting. Labor set about establishing a characteristic Scandinavian welfare state, emphasizing privately owned, free-market industry, publicly owned utilities, state planning to ensure ample housing as well as full employment through export-oriented industries, a comprehensive social welfare system, and—to pay for the latter—high taxes.

Norway was a founding member of the United Nations and provided that body with its first secretary-general, Trygve Lie. With the hardening of the Cold War, Norway's foreign policy took on a clear pro-Western stance; Norway joined the NATO alliance in 1949. In 1959 Norway became one of the original members of the European Free Trade Association. Through the 1960s industrial development and exports continued to fuel an economic boom that led to great national prosperity and stability.

The 1970s were the decade of oil and gas, with extensive development of North Sea oil and gas fields at the beginning of the decade. As international energy prices rose, the government's petroleum monopoly, Statoil, seemed to provide an endless source of funds. Because Norway's hydroelectric plants made the country self-sufficient in electric power, almost all of the oil and gas was available for export; by 1981 energy exports amounted to one-third, and by 1985 one-half, of Norway's total exports. The government expanded the welfare state and encouraged large wage increases. Public spending swelled, inflation outpaced wages, and government debt mounted; meanwhile Norway became an economic hostage to OPEC oil prices.

In the 1981 elections, the Conservative party formed a government for the first time since 1928; its austerity policy of holding down government spending while increasing taxes on consumer goods aroused popular opposition, and the government fell in 1986. The new Socialist coalition government faced even greater drops in oil revenues, combined with labor unrest and continued inflation. But in 1987 Norway negotiated the sale of gas to EC countries, and the recovery of energy prices in that year brought a partial return to economic stability and prosperity. With the death of King Olav in January 1991, his son Harald V became the second king of modern Norway, succeeding in June of that year.

In 1993 the government of Prime Minister Brundtland decided to seek admission to the EU, following upon the applications of Sweden and Finland. On Mar. 29, 1994, the EU agreed to admit Norway to membership after long and intricate negotiations limiting Spanish and Portuguese fishing rights in Norwegian waters. But Norweigian voters in a November 1994 referendum rejected EU membership.

Oman

Sultanate of Oman

Geography **Location:** southeastern Arabian peninsula. **Boundaries:** Gulf of Oman to N, Arabian Sea to E and S, Yemen to SW, Saudi Arabia to W, United Arab Emirates to NW; detached portion of Oman lies at tip of Musandam peninsula, on Strait of Hormuz. **Total land area:** 82,031 sq. mi. (212,460 sq km). **Coastline:** 1,299 mi. (2,092 km). **Comparative area:** about size of New Mexico. **Land use:** negl. % arable land; negl. % permanent crops; 5% meadows and pastures; 0% forest and woodland; 95% other; includes negl. % irrigated. **Major cities:** Muscat (capital) 622,506; Al-Batinah 538,763; Al-Sharquia 247,551.

People **Population:** 1,701,470 (1994 est.). **Nationality:** noun—Omani(s); adjective—Omani. **Ethnic groups:** almost entirely Arab, with small Baluchi, Zanzibari, and Indian groups. **Languages:** Arabic (official), English, Baluchi, Urdu, Indian dialects. **Religions:** 75% Ibadhi Muslim, remainder Sunni Muslim, Shia Muslim, some Hindu.

Government **Type:** absolute monarchy; independent, with residual UK influence. **Constitution:** none. **National holiday:** National Days, Nov. 18–19. **Head of government:** Qaboos bin Said, sultan and prime minister (since July 1970). **Structure:** executive—sultan appoints 45-member State Consultative Assembly to advise him; judicial—traditional Islamic judges and nascent civil court system.

Economy **Monetary unit:** rial. **Budget:** (1991) ***income:*** $4.4 bil.; ***expend.:*** $5.2 bil. **GDP:** $16.4 bil., $10,000 per capita (1993 est.). **Chief crops:** based on subsistence farming—fruits, dates, cereals. **Livestock:** cattle, camels. **Natural resources:** crude oil, copper, asbestos, some marble, limestone. **Major industries:** crude oil production and refining, natural gas production, construction. **Labor force:** 430,000; 58% are non-Omani; est. 60% agriculture. **Exports:** $5 bil. (f.o.b., 1993 est.); mostly petroleum; nonoil consist mostly of reexports, processed copper, and some agricultural goods. **Imports:** $3.7 bil. (f.o.b., 1993 est.); machinery, transportation equipment, manufactured goods, food, livestock. **Major trading partners:** ***exports:*** UAE, Japan, South Korea, Singapore, U.S.; ***imports:*** UK, UAE, Japan, U.S.

Intl. Orgs. Arab League, FAO, G-77, IBRD, ICAO, IDA, IFAD, IFC, IMF, IMO, INTELSAT, INTERPOL, ITU, NAM, UN, UNESCO, UPU, WHO, WMO.

Oman occupies the southeastern corner of Arabia. From ancient times an important center of trade in the Persian Gulf and the Indian Ocean, Oman was frequently dominated by Persia prior to the mid-18th century. The principal port, Muscat, was captured by the Portuguese in 1508 and held by them until 1659, when the Ottoman Turks took possession. They were driven out in 1741 by Ahmed ibn Said of Yemen, who consolidated the sultanate of Oman in 1744 and founded the present royal line.

In the early 19th century, Oman was the most powerful state in Arabia, controlling Zanzibar in East Africa, the southern coast of Iran, and much of Baluchistan (between Pakistan and Iran). Zanzibar was separated from Oman in 1856, and the Persian coast and much of Baluchistan was detached from Oman during the latter half of the 19th century. In 1958 Oman's sole remaining Baluchi possession, the city-state of Gwadar, was ceded to Pakistan in return for a monetary settlement.

Growing British influence was consolidated by the formation of a British protectorate in 1891, reconfirmed in 1951. In the 1950s Britain aided the sultanate in putting down rebellions in the desert interior. The British protectorate ended with Britain's withdrawal from the gulf in 1971.

On July 23, 1970, Sultan Said ibn Taimur was overthrown by his son, Sultan Qaboos bin Said, who instituted a national development program and in 1975 defeated a leftist uprising in the western desert.

Petroleum makes up 95 percent of exports. Banking and shipping services are also important. The country is generally barren, with scattered flocks of sheep and camels.

Pakistan

Islamic Republic of Pakistan

Geography **Location:** southern Asia. **Boundaries:** Afghanistan to N, China to far NE, India to E, Arabian Sea to S, and Iran to W. **Total land area:** 310,402 sq. mi. (803,940 sq km). **Coastline:** 650 mi. (1,046 km). **Comparative area:** about twice size of California. **Land use:** 26% arable land; negl. % permanent crops; 6% meadows and pastures; 4% forest and woodland; 64% other; includes 19% irrigated. **Major cities:** (1991 est.) Islamabad (capital) 400,000; Karachi 7,000,000; Lahore 3,500,000; Faisalabad (Lyallpur) 2,000,000; Rawalpindi 800,000.

People **Population:** 128,855,965 (1994 est.). **Nationality:** noun—Pakistani(s); adjective—Pakistani. **Ethnic groups:** Punjabi, Sindhi, Pashtun (Pathan), Baluch, Muhajir (immigrants from India and their descendants). **Languages:** Urdu and English (official); total spoken languages—64% Punjabi, 12% Sindhi, 8% Pashtu, 7% Urdu, 9% Baluchi and other; English is lingua franca of Pakistani elite and most government ministries, however, official policies are promoting its gradual replacement by Urdu. **Religions:** 97% Muslim (77% Sunni, 20% Shi'a); 3% Christian, Hindu, and other.

Government Type: parliamentary with strong executive; federal republic. **Independence:** Aug. 14, 1947 (from UK). **Constitution:** Apr. 10, 1973; suspended July 5, 1977; restored Dec. 30, 1985. **National holiday:** Pakistan Day, Mar. 23. **Heads of government:** Farooq Ahmed Khan Leghari, president (since Nov. 1993); Benazir Bhutto, prime minister (since Oct. 1993). **Structure:** based on English common law but gradually being transformed to correspond to Koranic injunction; former president Mohammad Zia's government established Islamic sharia courts paralleling secular courts and introduced Koranic punishments for some criminal offenses; martial law courts abolished Dec. 30, 1985, and all cases, including those concerning national security, now tried by civilian judiciary under due process safeguards.

Economy Monetary unit: rupee. **Budget:** (1993 est.) ***income:*** $9.4 bil.; ***expend.:*** $10.9 bil. **GNP:** $239 bil., $1,900 per capita (1993 est.). **Chief crops:** wheat, rice, sugarcane, cotton; illegal producer of opium poppy and cannabis for international drug trade. **Livestock:** goats, sheep, cattle, buffalo, asses. **Natural resources:** land, extensive natural gas reserves, limited crude oil, poor quality coal, iron ore. **Major industries:** cotton textiles, food processing. **Labor force:** 28.9 mil. (est.); 54% agriculture, 33% services, 13% mining and manufacturing; extensive export of labor; 3.6% unemployment (1987). **Exports:** $6.8 bil. (f.o.b., 1992); rice, cotton, textiles. **Imports:** $9.1 bil. (f.o.b., 1992); petroleum, petroleum products, machinery, transport equipment, cooking oils. **Major trading partners:** ***exports:*** 31% EU, 11% U.S., 11% Japan; ***imports:*** 26% EU, 15% Japan, 11% U.S.

Intl. Orgs. Colombo Plan, FAO, G-77, IAEA, IBRD, ICAO, IDA, IFAD, IFC, ILO, IMF, IMO, INTELSAT, INTERPOL, ITU, NAM, UN, UNESCO, UPU, WHO, WIPO, WMO, WTO.

Pakistan occupies the heartland of ancient South Asian civilization, in the Indus River valley. Agricultural settlements in that area arose by 3000 B.C., and the great cities at Harappa and Mohenjo-Daro were founded some 500 years later. Indo-European (Aryan) invaders from Central Asia overthrew the ancient civilization around 1500 B.C. and established a new culture that spread throughout Pakistan and northern India. Brahmanism, the religious culture of the early Indo-European invaders, gave rise to Buddhism and Jainism around the sixth century B.C., and evolved into Hinduism in the early centuries A.D. The Indus valley was incorporated into the empire of Alexander the Great, c. 350 B.C., and then into the Mauryan empire of Asoka, which by the third century B.C. controlled all of South Asia except for the southernmost portion of India.

Under various rulers the Indus Valley and the areas to its northwest were a great center of Buddhist culture until the beginning of the eighth century, when the area fell to Muslim Arab invaders. Thereafter, Islam was firmly established throughout the region. But Baluchistan and the Northwest Frontier region became culturally allied to the Persian civilization of Iran and Afghanistan, while Sind and the Punjab were more closely akin to the culture of northern India.

Northern Pakistan was incorporated into the empire of Mahmud of Gazni in the 11th century, and fell to the Mongols in the 13th century. The Indus River became the boundary between the Mongol Inkhanate of Persia and the sultanate of Delhi. The region was conquered by Timur Leng at the end of the 14th century, and after the fall of the Timurid empire was divided between the kingdoms of Sind and Multan, in southern and central Pakistan, and the sultanate of Delhi, in the Punjab. All of Pakistan and northern India was reunited after 1526, when the conquests of Babur established the Mogul empire.

The expansion of British power in India during the 18th century left Pakistan largely untouched; the area was divided among various states, including Sind, the Punjab, Kashmir, and the western reaches of Rajputana. In the first half of the 19th century, British rule extended to the northwest; after the defeat of the Indian Mutiny of 1857, the entire Indus valley came under British rule. Sind and the Punjab were ruled directly by the British, while the native states were ruled as British protectorates.

From the beginning of the 20th century, various nationalist movements arose throughout British India. The Moslem League, under the leadership of Mohammad Ali Jinnah after 1916, advocated greater popular political participation, dominion status for India, and a strong Muslim voice in Indian administration. Muslims and Hindus were allied in the Non-Cooperation movement of the 1920s, but the alliance soon broke down and degenerated into communal frictions. With growing power of the Congress party in Hindu areas and Gandhi's civil disobedience movement in the 1930s, Jinnah's Moslem League charted an increasingly separate course and called for the creation of a separate Muslim state in 1940.

With the British withdrawal from India in 1947, Hindus in the Muslim majority areas of the Indus valley and in East Bengal fled to Hindu northern India, while Muslims in Hindu areas fled in the opposite direction. These massive population movements were accompanied by widespread violence leading to the loss of hundreds of thousands of lives. Jinnah, the father of modern Pakistan, died in 1948. Pakistan, encompassing Sind, the Punjab, Baluchistan, the Northwest Frontier Territories, part of Jammu and Kashmir, and adjacent areas in the west and East Bengal in the east, was granted dominion status within the British Commonwealth in 1947, becoming an independent republic in 1956.

Pakistan joined the Central Treaty Organization and became allied with the West, in contrast to the Soviet-leaning nonalignment of India. In 1958 Gen. Mohammad Ayub Khan seized power in a coup; he was elected president in 1960 and reelected in 1965. Following border clashes with India in 1962, Pakistan entered into friendly relations with China, which also had engaged in border warfare with India. Ayub Khan resigned as president in early 1969 after failing to put down widespread demonstrations in East Pakistan. A new government was formed under Gen. Yahya Khan, and martial law was declared. A parliamentary victory by the East Pakistani Awami League in December 1970 led to civil war and the secession of East Pakistan in 1971 (see "Bangladesh").

India's intervention on behalf of East Bengal had led to war on a western front with Pakistan. On July 3, 1972, India and Pakistan agreed to a mutual withdrawal of troops and entered into negotiations designed to settle border disputes and other outstanding problems. Diplomatic relations between India and Pakistan were resumed in 1976.

The elections of 1970 that had precipitated the civil war also brought Zulfikar Ali Bhutto to the presidency. He remained in office until July 1977, when he was overthrown in a military coup led by Gen. Mohammad Zia ul-Haq. He was convicted of complicity in a 1974 political murder and hanged in April 1979. Under Pres. Zia, Pakistan moved toward the implementation of Islamic law in parallel with the constitutional law of Pakistan's parliamentary system. In 1986 Bhutto's daughter, Benazir Bhutto, returned to Pakistan from exile in Europe to organize opposition parties against Pres. Zia; this movement led to widespread rioting in the months that followed.

On Aug. 17, 1988, Pres. Zia, several senior government officials, and the American ambassador were killed in an airplane crash, the cause of which remains under investigation. Zia's death left the government of Pakistan severely weakened, at least temporarily.

Following the invasion of Afghanistan by Soviet troops in 1979, more than two million Afghan refugees entered Pakistan. The government, with American and Chinese support, gave shelter and substantial assistance to the various Afghan resistance movements.

Benazir Bhutto was elected prime minister in 1988. Her government faced a serious challenge from a violent separatist movement in Sind, and in the spring of 1990 war with India threatened as India accused Pakistan of supporting separatist rebels in Kashmir.

On Aug. 6, 1990, Pres. Isheq Khan dismissed the Bhutto government, accusing her administration of corruption and nepotism. In November Nawaz Sharif became prime minister.

In September 1992 the country was devastated by the worst floods in its recorded history. The heavy loss of life was made worse when officials opened the floodgates of the Mangla Dam without advance warning.

In late 1992 Benazir Bhutto was indicted on corruption charges, and her husband was imprisoned; she in turn vowed to campaign against the Sharif government until she forced a general election. Bhutto and Sharif briefly formed an alliance of convenience in February 1993 to work for a constitutional amendment limiting presidential power, but Sharif then was dismissed as prime minister by Pres. Ghulam Ishaq Khan and arrested on various charges; Balakh Sher Mazari was appointed interim prime minister. But on May 26 the Pakistan supreme court ruled Sharif's dismissal illegal and reinstated him as prime minister.

In October 1993 Benazir Bhutto returned as prime minister after elections in which her Pakistan People's party and its allies took 217 seats in the National Assembly, while Nazar Sharif's Moslem League won 72. Talks in Islamabad with India over the status of Jammu and Kashmir reached stalemate in early January; a month later, 20,000 Pakistani workers went on strike (at Bhutto's request) to rally on the Punjab border in support of Kashmir rebels. At just that time, Bhutto traveled to Sarajevo with Turkish premier Tansu Ciller in a show of support for the Bosnian government. Domestically, Ms. Bhutto tightened her control over the Pakistan People's party by ousting her mother as coleader and having her brother Murtaza arrested.

Pakistan's economy is largely agricultural; wheat, rice, and tobacco are grown in the Indus valley, while pastoralism predominates in the drier areas of the north and west. Urban areas support considerable industry, including textiles, food processing, and manufacturing. Pakistan remains a major recipient of American foreign aid, although recent reports that it has become a haven for Muslim terrorists have aroused some discomfort in the U.S. Congress.

Palau

Republic of Palau

Geography Location: more than 200 islands, in a chain about 400 mi. (650 km) long, in western central Pacific Ocean; Koror 71°21'N, 134°31'E. **Boundaries:** Guam 720 mi. (1,160 km) to NE, Federated States of Micronesia to E, island of New Guinea to S, Philippines 530 mi. (850 km) to NW. **Total land area:** 177 sq. mi. (458 sq km). **Coastline:** 944 mi. (1,519 km). **Comparative area:** slightly more than 2.5 times size of Washington, D.C. **Land use:** N.A.% arable land; N.A.% permanent crops; N.A.% meadows and pastures; N.A.% forest and woodland; N.A.% other. **Major cities:** (1990 census) Koror state 10,501; Koror is the current capital; a new capital is being built at Babelthuap, 20 km northeast.

People Population: 16,071 (1993). **Nationality:** noun—Palauan(s); adjective—Palauan. **Ethnic groups:** composite of Polynesian, Malayan, and Melanesian races. **Languages:** English (official) in all 16 states; Palauan (official) in 13 states; Sonsoralese, Angavr, Japanese, Tobi in one state each. **Religions:** 33% Christian (Catholic, Seventh-day Adventists, Jehovah's Witnesses), Modeknegi (indigenous faith).

Government Type: Republic. **Independence:** Oct. 1, 1994 (from U.S.). **Constitution:** Jan. 11, 1981. **National holiday:** Constitution Day, July 9. **Heads of government:** Kuniwo Nakamure, president (since Jan. 1993). **Structure:** executive—president and vice president popularly elected; legislative—bicameral legislature; judicial—Supreme Court headed by chief justice.

Economy Monetary unit: U.S. dollar. **Budget:** (1986 est.) ***income:*** $60 mil.; ***expend.:*** N.A. **GDP:** $31.6 mil., $2,260 per capita (1986). **Chief crops:** subsistence level production of coconut, copra, cassava, sweet potatoes. **Livestock:** N.A. **Natural resources:** forests, minerals (especially gold), marine products, deep-seabed minerals. **Major industries:** tourism, craft items (shell, wood, pearl), some commercial fishing and agriculture. **Labor force:** N.A. ***Exports:*** $0.5 mil. (f.o.b., 1986). ***Imports:*** $27.2 mil. (c.i.f., 1986). **Major trading partners:** ***exports:*** U.S., Japan; ***imports:*** U.S.

Intl. Orgs. UN.

The first inhabitants of Palau (or Belau) probably arrived from Indonesia and the Philippines about 1500 B.C. The first European to visit the area was Ferdinand Magellan, in 1521. However, it was the British who dominated trade to Palau until 1885, when Pope Leo XIII acknowledged Spain's claims to the Carolines. Spain controlled Palau from 1885 to 1899, when it sold the territory to Germany. The Germans introduced coconut planting and phosphate mining, and introduced sanitary measures that arrested the deadly epidemics of dysentery and influenza, which over 120 years had reduced the population from 40,000 to 4,000.

Japan occupied Palau in 1914, and over the next 30 years increased the mining, agriculture, and fishing industries. In 1938, Palau became a closed military area, and it was the site of heavy fighting during World War II. On July 18, 1947, the United Nations Trusteeship Council placed the Trust Territory of the Pacific Islands, including Palau, under U.S. authority. This trusteeship ended on Oct. 1, 1994, when the Compact of Free Association with the United States (approved by the voters of Palau) went into effect, making Palau an independent country in association with the United States. The United States will continue to provide for Palau's defense and give it $517 million in aid over 15 years (about $190 million of it immediately). In return, the United States has the right to dock military vessels (including nuclear-powered vessels) in the islands for 50 years, and will consult closely on economic and environmental matters.

Panama

Republic of Panama

Geography Location: southern Central America. **Boundaries:** Caribbean Sea to N, Colombia to E, Pacific Ocean to S, Costa Rica to W. **Total land area:** 30,193 sq. mi. (78,200 sq km). **Coastline:** 1,546 mi. (2,490 km). **Comparative area:** slightly smaller than South Carolina. **Land use:** 6% arable land; 2% permanent crops; 15% meadows and pastures; 54% forest and woodland; 23% other; includes negl. % irrigated. **Major cities:** (1992 est.) Panamá (Panama City—capital) 625,150; Colón 137,825; David 99,811.

People Population: 2,630,000 (1994 est.). **Nationality:** noun—Panamanian(s); adjective—Panamanian. **Ethnic groups:** 70% mestizo, 14% West Indian, 10% white, 6% Indian. **Languages:** Spanish (official), 14% speak English as native tongue; many Panamanians bilingual. **Religions:** over 90% Roman Catholic, 6% Protestant.

Government Type: republic. **Independence:** Nov. 3, 1903 (from Colombia); became independent from Spain Nov. 28, 1821. **Constitution:** Oct. 11, 1972, with major reforms adopted in Apr. 1983. **National holiday:** Independence Day, Nov. 3. **Head of government:** Ernesto Perez Balladares, president (since Sept. 1994). **Structure:** Executive branch—president, two vice presidents, cabinet; Legislative—one-house National Assembly of 67 members elected by popular vote; Judicial—Supreme Court and lesser courts.

Economy Monetary unit: balboa. **Budget:** (1992 est.) ***income:*** $1.8 bil.; ***expend.:*** $1.9 bil. **GDP:** $11.6 bil., $4,500 per capita (1993 est.). **Chief crops:** bananas, rice, sugarcane, coffee, corn; self-sufficient in basic foods. **Livestock:** cattle, pigs. **Natural resources:** copper, mahogany forests, shrimp. **Major industries:** manufacturing and construction, petroleum refining, brewing, cement and other construction material. **Labor force:** 921,000 (1992 est.); 27.9% government and community services, 26.2% agriculture, hunting, and fishing, 16% commerce, restaurants, and hotels, 10.5% manufacturing and mining; shortage of skilled labor, but oversupply of unskilled labor; 23% unemployment (1988 est.). **Exports:** $545 mil. (f.o.b., 1993 est.); 40% bananas, 27% shrimp, 4% coffee, sugar, petroleum products. **Imports:** $2.5 bil. (f.o.b., 1993 est.); 16% foodstuffs, 16% crude oil, 9% consumer goods. **Major trading partners:** ***exports:*** 38% U.S., Central America and Caribbean, EU; ***imports:*** 35% U.S., Central America and Caribbean, Mexico, EU, Venezuela.

Intl. Orgs. FAO, G-77, IAEA, IBRD, ICAO, IDA, IFAD, IFC, ILO, IMF, INTELSAT, INTERPOL, ITU, NAM, OAS, UN, UNESCO, UPU, WHO, WMO, WTO.

The Spanish first arrived in what is now Panama in 1501. Vasco Nuñez de Balboa returned in 1510, and Pedro Arias Dávila founded the City of Panama in 1519. Panama became attached to the viceroyalty of New Granada after 1739 and left the Spanish empire with the rest of New Granada in 1821, becoming a part of Gran Colombia. The first canal company proposing the construction of a transisthmian passageway was formed in 1825–26. The completion of a U.S.-financed railway from Colón to Panama City by 1855 enhanced Panama's importance as a transoceanic passage.

Panamanian nationalists waged a "War of a Thousand Days" against the Bogotá government between 1899 and 1902. In 1903 Panama gained independence from Colombia with U.S. complicity. Within a month Panamanian officials accepted an agreement with the United States that created a canal zone under the control of the U.S. government "in perpetuity," and the Panama Canal was completed and opened in 1914.

Panama experienced protectorate status under U.S. control after independence insofar as the United States "guaranteed the independence" of Panama. The United States explicitly upheld its right of unilateral military intervention in Panama when in 1918 it sent troops there without the permission of the Panamanian government. The 1936 Hull-Alvaro Treaty eliminated protectorate status, and the United States dropped its claim to a right of intervention in the cities of Panama and Colón.

In 1968 a power struggle between Pres. Arnulfo Arias and the Panamanian National Guard led to the ouster of the president. A National Guard junta took control of the government, and Col. (later Gen.) Omar Torrijos Herrera became the ruler of the country the following year. In 1972 a new assembly under Torrijos's control offered him the title of Jefe Maximo (chief executive) in addition to drafting a new constitution for the country. Torrijos constructed a populist following through the creation of housing projects, a new labor code, an agrarian reform, and an increase in tax rates imposed on foreign banana-interests.

The Panamanian government and the United States concluded a new canal treaty in 1977, the key provisions of which included integration of the Canal Zone with the rest of Panamanian territory and full Panamanian control of the canal in the year 2000. In 1981 Omar Torrijos died in an air accident.

In 1988 the head of the military and de facto ruler of the country, Gen. Mañuel Noriega, was indicted in the United States on narcotics charges. Gen. Noriega refused to submit to U.S. demands for his resignation. When Panama's Pres. Eric Arturo Delvalle ordered Noriega to resign, the general refused. Pres. Delvalle was forced to go into hiding, and Manuel Solis Palma replaced him in the presidency. The United States responded by freezing Panamanian assets in the United States.

In May 1989 Gen. Noriega annulled election results that showed him losing to Guillermo Endara and assumed the role of dictator. After an unsuccessful coup attempt in October 1989, the United States invaded Panama on Dec. 20, captured Noriega, and brought him to Miami, where he was convicted on narcotics charges. Endara was restored to the presidency and in December 1990 U.S. forces helped put down a rebellion led by Noriega's former chief of the national police.

Endara's government was often accused of corruption but he left power peacefully in 1994. He helped to arrange honest elections that saw U.S.-educated businessman Ernesto Perez Balladares come to power with promises of improving the economy as Panama prepares to take over control of the canal in 1999.

Papua New Guinea

Geography **Location:** eastern section of island of New Guinea and about 600 smaller islands in Bismarck Archipelago (New Britain, New Ireland, and Manus) and northern part of Solomon Islands. Port Moresby 9°30'S, 147°07'E. **Boundaries:** Bismarck Sea to N, Solomon Sea to E, Australia to S, and Indonesia to W. **Total land area:** 178,259 sq. mi. (461,690 sq km). **Coastline:** 3,202 mi. (5,152 km). **Comparative area:** slightly larger than California. **Land use:** negl. % arable land; 1% permanent crops; negl. % meadows and pastures; 71% forest and woodland; 28% other. **Major cities:** (1990 est.) Port Moresby (administrative capital) 173,500.

People **Population:** 4,196,806 (1994 est.). **Nationality:** noun—Papua New Guinean(s); adjective—Papua New Guinean. **Ethnic groups:** predominantly Melanesian and Papuan; some Negrito, Micronesian, and Polynesian. **Languages:** 715 indigenous languages; English spoken by 1–2%, pidgin English widespread, Motu spoken in Papua region. **Religions:** over half of population nominally Christian (490,000 Catholic, 320,000 Lutheran and other Protestant sects); remainder indigenous beliefs.

Government **Type:** independent parliamentary state within Commonwealth recognizing Elizabeth II as head of state. **Independence:** Sept. 16, 1975 (from UN trusteeship under Australian administration). **Constitution:** Sept. 16, 1975. **National holiday:** Independence Day, Sept. 16. **Heads of government:** Wiwa Korowi, governor-general (since Nov. 1991); Julius Chan, prime minister (since Aug. 1994). **Structure:** executive—National Executive Council; legislature—House of Assembly (109 members); judiciary—court system consists of Supreme Court of Papua New Guinea and various inferior courts (district courts, local courts, children's courts, wardens' courts).

Economy **Monetary unit:** kina. **Budget:** (1993 est.) ***income:*** $1.33 bil.; ***expend.:*** $1.49 bil. **GDP:** $8.2 bil., $2,000 per capita (1993 est.). **Chief crops:** copra, cocoa, coffee, rubber, palm oil. **Livestock:** pigs, cattle, goats, chickens, sheep. **Natural resources:** gold, copper, silver, natural gas, timber. **Major industries:** copra crushing, palm-oil processing, plywood processing. **Labor force:** N.A. **Exports:** $1.3 bil. (f.o.b., 1990); gold, copper ore, coffee, copra, palm oil, timber. **Imports:** $1.6 bil. (c.i.f., 1990); machinery and transport equipment, food, fuels, chemicals. **Major trading partners:** ***exports:*** Germany, Japan, Australia, UK, Spain, U.S.; ***imports:*** Australia, Singapore, Japan, U.S., New Zealand.

Intl. Orgs. Commonwealth, FAO, G-77, IBRD, ICAO, IDA, IFAD, IFC, ILO, IMF, IMO, INTELSAT, INTERPOL, ITU, UN, UNESCO, UPU, WHO, WMO, WTO.

The island of New Guinea, the world's second-largest, was settled many thousands of years ago by waves of Papuan and Melanesian migrants who developed large numbers of linguistically diverse and mutually hostile tribes of hunters and small cultivators. In the 19th century, the island was divided between the Dutch (to the west, in what is now the Indonesian province of Irian Jaya), Germany, and the British. The German sector was occupied by Australia in 1914 and administered under a League of Nations mandate after World War I.

Japanese attempts to occupy New Guinea in 1942 met with only partial success. In a series of counteroffensives, the Allies regained control over the entire island by mid-1944.

Beginning in 1949 the former German and British colonies were administered jointly by Australia under a UN mandate. The territories were made self-governing in 1973 and achieved full independence as Papua New Guinea on Sept. 16, 1975. The nation maintains close ties with Australia. Relations are strained with Indonesia, which accuses Papua New Guinea of giving shelter to an Irian Jaya liberation movement.

Papua New Guinea's economy remains largely in the stage of small-scale agriculture. The national economy was badly hurt in 1989 when a vital copper mine on the island of Bougainville was forced to close by separatist guerrillas. But stringent economic measures in response to the Bougainville closing, as well as a boom in gold and oil production, resulted in an 8 percent jump in GDP in 1991, with 17 percent growth predicted for 1992. Nevertheless, fears of crime, violence, and land ownership disputes like the one at Bougainville remain obstacles to foreign investment.

Paraguay

Republic of Paraguay

Geography **Location:** landlocked country in central South America. **Boundaries:** Bolivia to N, Brazil to E, Argentina to S and W. **Total land area:** 157,046 sq. mi. (406,750 sq km). **Coastline:** none. **Comparative area:** about size of California. **Land use:** 20% arable land; 1% permanent crops; 39% meadows and pastures; 35% forest and woodland; 5% other; includes negl. % irrigated. **Major cities:** (1982 census) Asunción (capital) 455,517; Pedro Juan Caballero 37,331; Puerto Presidente Stroessner 36,676; Encarnación 27,632; Villarrica 21,203.

People **Population:** 5,213,772 (1994 est.). **Nationality:** noun—Paraguayan(s); adjective—Paraguayan. **Ethnic groups:** 95% mestizo, 5% white and Indian. **Languages:** Spanish (official), Guaraní. **Religions:** 97% Roman Catholic, Mennonite and other Protestant denominations.

Government **Type:** republic under authoritarian rule. **Independence:** May 14, 1811 (from Spain). **Constitution:** Aug. 25, 1967. **National holiday:** Independence Days, May 14–15. **Head of government:** Juan Carlos Wasmosy, president (since May 1993). **Structure:** president heads executive; bicameral legislature (Senate, Chamber of Deputies); judiciary headed by Supreme Court.

Economy **Monetary unit:** guarani. **Budget:** (1991) ***income:*** $1.2 bil.; ***expend.:*** $1.4 bil. **GDP:** $15.2 bil., $3,000 per capita (1993 est.). **Chief crops:** oilseed, soybeans, cotton, wheat, manioc, sweet potatoes, tobacco, corn, rice, sugarcane; self-sufficient in most foods; illegal producer of cannabis for international drug trade. **Livestock:** cattle, pigs, sheep, horses, goats. **Natural resources:** iron ore, manganese, limestone, hydropower, timber. **Major industries:** meat packing, oilseed crushing, milling. **Labor force:** 1,641,000 (1992 est.); 44% agriculture, 34% industry and commerce, 18% services; 11% unemployment (1988 est.). **Exports:** $728 mil. (f.o.b., 1993 est.); cotton, soybeans, timber, vegetable oils, coffee, tung oil. **Imports:** $1.38 bil. (c.i.f., 1993 est.); 35% capital goods, 20% consumer goods, 19% fuels and lubricants, 16% raw materials, 10% foodstuffs, beverages, tobacco. **Major trading partners:** ***exports:*** 37% EU, 25% Brazil, 10% Argentina, 6% Chile, 6% U.S.; ***imports:*** 30% Brazil, 20% EU, 18% U.S., 8% Argentina, 7% Japan.

Intl. Orgs. FAO, G-77, IAEA, IBRD, ICAO, IDA, IFAD, IFC, ILO, IMF, INTELSAT, INTERPOL, ITU, OAS, UN, UNESCO, UPU, WHO, WMO.

When Europeans arrived in what is now Paraguay in the early 16th century, they encountered various groups of semisedentary and nonsedentary indigenous peoples. The Spanish entered into alliances with the Tupian semisedentary Guaraní against the nomadic Guaycuru Indians in the west of the region. Asunción, founded in 1537, was little more than a Spanish defense outpost against the Portuguese and a trading stopover between the silver mines of Potosí and Buenos Aires.

From early in the 17th century, the Jesuits established an extensive network of missions in the southern portion of the colony, and a rivalry grew between the Jesuits and the elites of Asunción over who would determine the colony's social and economic structure. The isolation of the settlers from the mainstream of Spanish colonial society combined with the lack of valuable resources led to the evolution of a relatively egalitarian social structure in Spanish imperial terms. The political elite of Asunción deposed Spanish authority in 1811, and Paraguayan independence was declared in 1813.

Stable authoritarian rule marked the period from independence until 1870. José Gaspar Rodríguez de Francia was declared ruler for life in 1816 and remained in power until his death in 1840. A period of political turmoil followed the death of Francia but was resolved in the election of Carlos Antonio López in 1844; in 1857 he was named president for life. López chose his son Francisco Solano López to succeed him in office in 1862. Francisco Solano intervened in a Brazilian attempt to control the fate of Uruguay, beginning the Paraguayan War, or the War of the Triple Alliance (Brazil, Argentina, Uruguay) from 1865 to 1870. The war was catastrophic for Paraguay, reducing the population from 450,000 to 220,000; almost the entire male population was killed, and Paraguay lost 60,000 square miles of territory while being saddled with a war debt of 19 million gold pesos ($200,000,000). The Brazilian government later dropped the unrealistic payment demand.

After the war the Colorado and Liberal parties developed, although the real political distinctions were dependent more on individuals and families than political ideology. Colorado-party general Bernardino Caballero, backed by Brazil, was the power behind the scenes of frequent changes in government personnel between 1874 and 1904. The Liberals, backed by Argentina, were in power from 1904 until 1936.

After 18 years of authoritarian military rule, Gen. Alfredo Stroessner, with the backing of Colorado party factions, began his rule in 1954. Stroessner held power until 1989, when Gen. Andrés Rodríguez overthrew him.

Nevertheless, the Colorados maintained their hold on the presidency in hotly contested elections in 1993, when Juan Carlos Wasmosy gained 40 percent of the vote. However, a strong showing by the opposition Authentic Radical Liberal Party (PLRA) and National Encounter prevented a Colorado majority in Congress.

Peru

Republic of Peru

Geography **Location:** western coast of South America. **Boundaries:** Ecuador, Colombia to N, Brazil, Bolivia to E, Chile to S, Pacific Ocean to W. **Total land area:** 496,224 sq. mi. (1,285,220 sq km). **Coastline:** 1,546 mi. (2,414 km). **Comparative area:** slightly smaller than Alaska. **Land use:** 3% arable land; negl. % permanent crops; 21% meadows and pastures; 55% forest and woodland; 21% other; includes 1% irrigated. **Major cities:** (1990 est.) Lima (capital) 6,414,500; Arequipa 634,500; Trujillo 532,000; Callao 515,200; Chiclayo 426,300.

People **Population:** 23,650,671 (1994 est.). **Nationality:** noun—Peruvian(s); adjective—Peruvian. **Ethnic groups:** 45% Indian, 37% mestizo, 15% white, 3% black, Japanese, Chinese, and other. **Languages:** Spanish and Quechua (official), Aymara. **Religions:** predominantly Roman Catholic.

Government **Type:** republic. **Independence:** July 28, 1821 (from Spain). **Constitution:** July 28, 1980; often referred to as 1979 Constitution because constituent assembly met in 1979, but constitution actually took effect following year; reestablished civilian government with popularly elected president and bicameral legislature. **National holiday:** Independence Day, July 28. **Heads of government:** Alberto Fujimori, president (since July 1990); Efrain Goldenberg Schreiber, prime minister (since Apr. 1995). **Structure:** executive; bicameral legislature (Senate, Chamber of Deputies); judicial.

Economy **Monetary unit:** nuevo sol. **Budget:** (1992 est.) ***income:*** $2 bil.; ***expend.:*** $1.7 bil. **GDP:** $70 bil., $3,000 per capita (1993 est.). **Chief crops:** wheat, potatoes, beans, rice, barley, coffee, cotton, sugarcane; imports wheat, meat, lard and oils, rice, corn; illegal producer of coca for international drug trade. **Livestock:** sheep, cattle, pigs, goats, horses. **Natural resources:** copper, silver, gold, petroleum, timber. **Major industries:** mining of metals, petroleum, fishing. **Labor force:** 8 mil. (1992); 44% government and other services, 37% agriculture, 19% industry; 9.5% unemployment. **Exports:** $3.7 bil. (f.o.b., 1993 est.); fish meal, cotton, sugar, coffee, copper. **Imports:** $4.1 bil. (f.o.b., 1993 est.); foodstuffs, machinery, transport equipment, iron and steel semimanufactures, chemicals. **Major trading partners:** ***exports:*** 28% EU, 22% U.S., 13% Japan, 12% Latin America, 2% former USSR; ***imports:*** 32% U.S., 22% Latin America, 17% EU, 6% Switzerland, 3% Japan.

Intl. Orgs. FAO, G-77, IAEA, IBRD, ICAO, IDA, IFAD, IFC, ILO, IMF, IMO, INTELSAT, INTERPOL, ITU, NAM, OAS, UN, UNESCO, UPU, WHO, WMO, WTO.

Peru was the site of the civilization of the Inca empire before the arrival of Europeans. The Incas had extended their control over most of the Andean region by the late 15th century. The civilization was advanced in terms of its ability to provide for the welfare of its subjects and was in possession of sophisticated knowledge in a number of fields, including medicine. By the time of the arrival of the Spanish conqueror Francisco Pizarro in 1532, the empire was already in decline, and a combination of plague and civil war in the decade prior to the appearance of Europeans no doubt made the empire more vulnerable to Spanish conquest. Inca resistance to Spanish domination was not quelled until the execution of Tupac Amarú in 1571. European-borne diseases such as smallpox and measles devastated the Indian population of the region.

Because of the great wealth of precious metals discovered by the Spanish and the adaptability of a sedentary indigenous civilization to the imposition of Spanish imperial control, Peru quickly became a major focal point of Spanish colonialism in the Americas; they founded Lima in 1535. The viceroyalty of Peru, established in 1544, originally served as the political and administrative nerve center of Spanish colonization of South America. For nearly two centuries, Lima was the seat of power and wealth for the whole region. Peru was "liberated" by Simón Bolívar and José de San Martín in 1821 when Bolívar's army defeated the royalist forces at the battles of Junín and Ayacucho.

In the 40 years after independence, the presidency changed hands 35 times, and the country generated at least 15 different constitutions. Only four of the presidents of the period were constitutionally chosen, and the vast majority of the chief executives were military figures. In 1829 Peru tried and failed to annex Ecuador; in the 1830s an attempt at political federation between Peru and Bolivia collapsed with the Chilean invasion of 1839.

A political movement in favor of civilian rule, the Civilistas, began to organize by the 1860s. Chile defeated Peru in the War of the Pacific (1879–83), and Chileans occupied Lima and its port city of Callao for two years. The Peruvian government was deeply in debt after the war, resulting in the loss of ownership of much of Peru's infrastructure and natural resources to foreigners.

Peru experienced a period of civilian leadership between 1895 and 1930. Pres. Augusto B. Leguía (1908–12, 1919–30) extended his rule in an extraconstitutional manner until 1930, when Col. Luis Sánchez Cerro seized power; he ruled until his assassination in 1933. Gen. Oscar Benavides succeeded Cerro and managed to restore confidence in the economy. In 1939 civilian banker Manuel Prado was elected to the presidency, and the military allowed him to complete his term in office, which expired in 1945. During Prado's administration, Peru went to war with Ecuador and was victorious, seizing a great deal of territory.

Víctor Raúl Haya de la Torre founded Peru's most prominent political party, the American Popular Revolutionary Alliance (APRA), in 1924. As initiated, the party put forward an "anti-imperialist" platform aiming at nationalization of land and reconstruction of society in favor of oppressed people. Haya de la Torre was apparently fraudulently deprived of a presidential electoral victory in 1931. The following year Apristas (APRA supporters) seized Trujillo and killed some military personnel. By way of revenge, the army massacred 6,000 Apristas. The result was a continuing enmity between the Peruvian armed forces and the APRA party lasting until the 1980s. Although APRA clearly had majority support from the Peruvian electorate in the intervening period, the party was not allowed to take power directly until 1985.

The Peruvian military, led by Gen. Juan Velasco Alvarado, seized power in 1968 and embarked upon a course of reform that included the nationalization of Standard Oil's International Petroleum Company holdings. The Peruvian military took steps to restructure economic and political power in the country by joining the Andean Pact and undermining the power of the traditional agricultural elite in the country by sponsoring an agrarian reform that mobilized peasant sectors of the population and changed the relations between landlord and peasant. By the late 1970s, however, the military government began to move toward the Right.

The presidency of Peru returned to civilian leadership under Fernando Belaúnde Terry (1980–85). In 1985, for the first time since its founding, the military allowed the APRA presidential candidate, Alan García Pérez, to take office. García promised to spend no more than 10 percent of the country's export earnings on payment of Peru's huge outstanding foreign debt and he was popular during his first years in office. But his public support was undermined by a growing insurgency sponsored by the Sendero Luminoso ("Shining Path") Maoist guerrillas and by runaway inflation.

On June 10, 1990, political novice Alberto Fujimori, the son of Japanese immigrants, defeated the well-known writer Mario Vargas Llosa for the presidency.

Throughout 1991 and 1992, the Shining Path's influence continued to grow, creeping from the rural highlands to more urban centers. The group was responsible for the loss of 25,000 lives and for paralyzing the central government. In a dramatic and surprising move to regain control of the country, Fujimori dissolved the Peruvian legislature in April 1992 and imposed martial law. Fujimori's popularity plummeted as the economy faltered. But on Sept. 12 the police in Lima captured Abimael Guzmán Reynoso, the founder and leader of the Shining Path, and suddenly Fujimori's position was greatly improved.

Since then many groups have protested government violations of civil rights, and the United States and others have linked further aid to an improved human rights record. However, the international lending community is satisfied that Fujimori's policies are bringing the economy under control. Inflation fell from 7,600 percent in 1990 to 57 percent in 1992. The Fujimori government has pursued a free-market policy and has privatized several major state-run organizations, includng the telephone industry. In 1994 the economy grew by 12 percent (highest in the world) and Shining Path rebels were held in check. In April 1995 Fujimori was reelected with 64 percent of the vote and his coalition (Change 90/New Majority) won a majority in Congress.

Philippines

Republic of the Philippines

Geography **Location:** archipelago of some 7,100 islands about 500 mi. (800 km) off southeastern Asia; about 1,100 mi. (2,800 km) from N to S and 650 mi. (1,684 km) from W to E; Luzon in N and Mindanao in S account for 66% of land area. Manila 14°36'N, 120°59'E. **Boundaries:** Luzon Strait to N, Philippine Sea to E, Celebes Sea to S, Sulu Sea to SW, and South China Sea to W. **Total land area:** 115,830 sq. mi. (300,000 sq km). **Coastline:** 22,554 mi. (36,289 km). **Comparative area:** slightly larger than Arizona. **Land use:** 26% arable land; 11% permanent crops; 4% meadows and pastures; 40% forest and woodland; 19% other; includes 5% irrigated. **Major cities:** (1990 census) Manila (capital) 1,598,918; Quezon City 1,666,766; Davao City 849,947; Caloocan City 761,011; Cebu City 610,417.

People **Population:** 69,808,930 (1994 est.). **Nationality:** noun—Filipino(s); adjective—Philippine. **Ethnic groups:** 91.5% Christian Malay, 4% Muslim Malay, 1.5% Chinese, 3% other. **Languages:** Pilipino (based on Tagalog) and English (both official). **Religions:** 83% Roman Catholic, 9% Protestant, 5% Muslim, 3% Buddhist and other.

Government **Type:** republic. **Independence:** July 4, 1946 (from U.S.). **Constitution:** Feb. 2, 1987, effective Feb. 11, 1987. **National holiday:** Independence Day, June 12. **Head of government:** Fidel Ramos, president (since June 1992). **Structure:** constitution provides for presidential form of government with directly elected president and vice president and U.S.-style bicameral legislature (24-seat Senate and 200-member House of Representatives); judicial branch headed by Supreme Court with descending authority in three-tiered system of local, regional trial, and intermediate appellate courts.

Economy **Monetary unit:** peso. **Budget:** (1992 est.) ***income:*** $11.5 bil.; ***expend.:*** $13 bil. **GNP:** $171 bil., $2,500 per capita (1993 est.). **Chief crops:** rice, corn, coconut, sugarcane, bananas; illegal producer of cannabis for international drug trade. **Livestock:** pigs, buffalo, goats, cattle, horses. **Natural resources:** timber, crude oil, nickel, cobalt, silver. **Major industries:** textiles, pharmaceuticals, chemicals. **Labor force:** 24.12 mil. (1989); 47% agriculture, 20% industry and commerce, 13.5% services, 10% government; 11.3% unemployment; much underemployment. **Exports:** $11.1 bil. (f.o.b., 1993 est.); 19% electrical equipment, 16% textiles, 11% minerals and ores, 10% farm products, 10% coconut. **Imports:** $17.1 bil. (f.o.b., 1993 est.); 53% raw materials, 17% capital goods, 17% petroleum products. **Major trading partners:** ***exports:*** 36% U.S., 19% EU, 18% Japan, 9% ESCAP (Economic and Social Commission for Asia and the Pacific), 7% ASEAN; ***imports:*** 25% U.S., 17% Japan, 13% ESCAP, 11% EU, 10% ASEAN, 10% Middle East.

Intl. Orgs. ASEAN, Colombo Plan, FAO, G-77, IAEA, IBRD, ICAO, IDA, IFAD, IFC, ILO, IMF, IMO, INTELSAT, INTERPOL, ITU, UN, UNESCO, UPU, WHO, WIPO, WMO, WTO.

The Philippines were anciently settled by various Malayan peoples in several waves of migration from Southeast Asia. Tribal societies coexisted with petty principalities that had trade links to China, the East Indies, and countries in the Indian Ocean. The Philippines were visited by Magellan (who was killed there) in 1521, and Spanish conquest of the islands began in 1564. The Spanish colonial capital at Manila was founded in 1571 and became a key transit point for trade between Mexico and the Far East. Under Spanish rule a majority of Filipinos became Christian except in the southwestern islands, which remained Muslim. The Spanish period as a whole was marked by a torpid colonial administration and a gradual rise in the power and wealth of the Catholic church.

In the late 19th century, a nationalist movement led by José Rizal gained a wide following. In 1896 an armed uprising began, led by Emilio Aguinaldo. The 1898 victory of Adm. George Dewey at the Battle of Manila Bay during the Spanish-American War led Spain to cede the Philippines to the United States in return for a payment of $20 million. Expecting immediate independence with U.S. support, Aguinaldo declared the islands a republic. When this was not recognized by the United States, Aguinaldo led a new war for independence, which was bloodily suppressed by American troops in a six-year campaign, 1899–1905.

American policy in the Philippines combined military control with a desire to encourage home rule leading to independence. In 1935 the Commonwealth of the Philippines was established, with Manuel Quezon as its first president, beginning what was conceived of as a 10-year period of controlled autonomy leading to full independence on July 4, 1946. In November 1941, Quezon was reelected to the presidency. On Dec. 8, 1941, Japan attacked Manila and destroyed the American bases there. American and Filipino troops, after weeks of fierce fighting, evacuated the islands in March 1942. The battle to recapture the Philippines began with the Battle of Leyte Gulf in October 1944 and was completed by July 1945.

In April 1946, Manuel Roxas was elected president of the Commonwealth. Independence came as scheduled on July 4 of that year, with the United States retaining military bases by treaty and establishing a special economic relationship with the Philippines. The leftist Hukbalahap Rebellion, originally a partisan campaign against the Japanese, caused severe difficulties for the new nation until it was finally defeated in military campaigns led by Ramon Magsaysay who was elected to the presidency in November 1953.

The early years of independence were marked by some economic development, but also great economic inequality. Most land was held by huge estates, and the economy depended primarily on plantation crops (sugar, copra), mining, and timber. Villagers fleeing the rural subsistence economy poured into the cities, leading to huge slums and a climate of urban poverty and violence. Many Filipinos emigrated to America.

In 1966 Ferdinand Marcos was elected president on a reform platform. Overwhelmed in the early 1970s by demonstrations, a new leftist guerrilla movement, and a separatist rebellion by Islamic Moros in Mindinao, Marcos declared martial law on Sept. 21, 1972. On Jan. 17, 1973, Marcos promulgated a new constitution giving unprecedented power to the presidency. His wife, Imelda, began to wield considerable influence, and the climate of unrest, poverty, and corruption worsened throughout the 1970s. Martial law was lifted, however, on Jan. 17, 1981, and Marcos was reelected to a new six-year term as president.

The airport assassination of opposition leader Benigno Aquino on his return to the Philippines on Aug. 21, 1983, led to a new phase in opposition to Marcos's rule. Marcos retained a majority in elections to the National Assembly in 1984, amid widespread reports of electoral fraud. In a bitterly contested presidential election in February 1986, Marcos was officially declared the winner over Corazon Aquino, widow of Benigno Aquino. Mrs. Aquino also declared herself the winner, and her supporters took to the streets in massive anti-Marcos demonstrations. Deserted by key supporters in the military, church, and middle class, Marcos fled the country on Feb. 25, 1986. Mrs. Aquino took office pledging land reform, a new constitution, and a commission to recover the corruptly gained wealth of the Marcos family.

Under Pres. Aquino the situation in the Philippines remained unsettled. Her former ally and vice president, Salvadore Laurel, formed an opposition party. Military and political measures aimed at putting down the Communist insurrection yielded mixed results. The economy of the Philippines continued to be dependent on U.S. and international assistance.

During 1989–90, the Aquino government experienced a steady erosion of power in the face of failure to confront the country's continuing political and economic problems. Sentiment against the continued presence of U.S. military bases (Clark Air Base, Subic Bay Naval Base, and four smaller installations) was strong.

Ferdinand Marcos died in Hawaii in September 1989. In July 1990 Imelda Marcos was acquitted in a New York court of larceny and conspiracy charges stemming from her ownership (with her husband) of several office buildings.

An eruption of Mt. Pinatubo in June 1991 caused massive devastation in central Luzon and destroyed Clark Air Base. In September, the national legislature voted not to renew the leases on American military bases; the United States moved to close the Subic Bay Naval Base.

Aquino declined to run for reelection in 1992. In the May 11 elections, Fidel Ramos won the presidency in a field of strong contenders; Imelda Marcos, who had returned to the Philippines to contest the election, was decisively rejected by the voters. On Jan. 30, 1994, the government announced a cease-fire in the 20-year guerrilla struggle with the Muslim separatist Moro National Liberation Front.

Strong economic growth in 1994 as well as vigorous action against Muslim separatists on Mindanao helped Ramos supporters to increase their power in the House and Senate.

Poland

Republic of Poland

Geography Location: eastern Europe. **Boundaries:** Baltic Sea to N, Russia and Lithuania to NE, Belarus and Ukraine to E, Czech Republic and Slovakia to S, Germany to W. **Total land area:** 120,726 sq. mi. (312,680 sq km). **Coastline:** 305 mi. (491 km). **Comparative area:** between Arizona and New Mexico. **Land use:** 48% arable land; 1% permanent crops; 13% meadows and pastures; 29% forest and woodland; 9% other; includes negl. % irrigated. **Major cities:** (1992 est.) Warszawa (Warsaw, capital) 1,644,500; Lódź 838,400; Krakow (Cracow) 744,800; Wroclaw 640,700; Poznań 582,900.

People Population: 38,654,561 (1994 est.). **Nationality:** noun—Pole(s); adjective—Polish. **Ethnic groups:** 98.7% Polish, 0.6% Ukrainian, 0.5% Byelorussian. **Languages:** Polish. **Religions:** 95% Roman Catholic (about 75% practicing), 5% Uniate, Russian Orthodox, Protestant, and other.

Government Type: republic. **Independence:** N.A. **Constitution:** interim "small" constitution Dec. 1992 while new democratic constitution being drafted. **National holiday:** Constitution Day, May 3. **Heads of government:** Lech Walesa, president (since Dec. 1990); Jozef Olesky, prime minister (since Feb. 1995). **Structure:** Executive branch—president elected by Parliament; Legislative—Parliament (Sejm) has two houses, upper Senate and lower chamber elected by the people in June 1989; Judicial—Supreme Court, Administrative Supreme Court, Courts of Appeals.

Economy Monetary unit: zloti. **Budget:** (1993 est.) ***income:*** $24.3 bil.; ***expend.:*** $27.1 bil. **GNP:** $167.6 bil., $4,400 per capita (1992 est.). **Chief crops:** grain, sugar beets, oilseed, potatoes; exporter of livestock products and sugar; importer of grains; self-sufficient for minimum requirements. **Livestock:** chickens, pigs, cattle, sheep, ducks. **Natural resources:** coal, sulfur, copper, natural gas, silver. **Major industries:** machine building, iron and steel, extractive industries. **Labor force:** 15,609,000 (1991); 37% industry and construction, 29% agriculture, 15% trade, transport, and communications. **Exports:** $13.5 bil. (f.o.b., 1993 est.); 22% machinery, 16% metals, 12% chemicals, 11% fuels and power, 10% food. **Imports:** $15.6 bil. (f.o.b., 1993 est.); 38% machinery and equipment, 20% fuels, minerals, metals, 12% agricultural and forestry products, 9% manufactured consumer goods. **Major trading partners:** ***exports:*** 28% Germany, 11.7% former USSR, 9% UK. ***imports:*** 25.6% former USSR, 17.4% Germany, 5.3% Italy, 5.2% Austria.

Intl. Orgs. FAO, IAEA, ICAO, ILO, IMO, ITU, OSCE, UN, UNESCO, UPU, WHO, WIPO, WMO, WTO.

The Slavic people known as Polonians accepted Christianity in the second half of the 10th century, during the reign of Duke Mieszko, whose close relationship with the papacy prevented the Holy Roman Empire from absorbing Poland. A strong and united Polish kingdom existed under the Piast dynasty until 1370. With that dynasty's extinction, the Anjou king of Hungary succeeded to the throne, followed by his daughter Jadwiga, who in 1386 married the grand duke of Lithuania. Thus was formed the great Commonwealth of Poland-Lithuania.

With the extinction of the Jagellonian line in 1572, the monarchy became elective. With a large nobility, equaling about 10 percent of the population, the monarchy grew weak, and Poland increasingly was subject to foreign intervention. The rise of the expansionist powers of Sweden, Prussia, Russia, and Austria came in part at the expense of the Poles. Jan Sobieski (1624–96), who ruled Poland as John III, saved Vienna from the Turks and briefly revived the Polish monarchy, but Polish royal power ended with his death. In a series of partitions in 1772, 1793, and 1795, Poland was dismembered and finally obliterated as a state.

Napoleon revived a Polish national entity with the Grand Duchy of Warsaw; with Napoleon's fall, the Congress of Vienna re-created a

Kingdom of Poland in 1815, under the rule of the czar of Russia. After 1830 Poland was subjected to systematic Russification.

The fall of Russia in World War I led to Poland's revival. The Lithuanian Socialist Jósef Pilsudski led Poland in war against the new Bolshevik government of Russia until, in the 1921 Treaty of Riga, Poland emerged with its boundaries restored to approximately those after the partition of 1793. It was ethnically about 70 percent Polish, a triumph for Polish nationalism but the end of Pilsudski's dream of a federation of northeastern Europe. Poland also had the largest Jewish population of any country in Europe.

With a strong legislature and a weak president, the new state seemed to Pilsudski too weak for its own defense. He became a virtual dictator in 1926 and ruled until his death in 1935. After his death a weak parliamentary government was controlled by military officers; the tentative revival of republicanism was halted by Hitler's and Stalin's aggression in 1939, yet another partition of Poland.

Like other countries of east-central Europe, Poland was primarily an agricultural country, with grains, sugar beets, and potatoes its principal crops. The postwar republic attempted land reform, with some success; about 750,000 new private farm holdings were created by 1938. Mining—of coal and copper—was the principal traditional industrial activity in the 20th century, supplemented by extraction of natural gas. In the mid-1930s shipbuilding and railroad construction led the way toward a modern economy.

World War II commenced in September 1939, with attacks on Poland by Germany and the Soviet Union. The war brought severe destruction to Poland and the extermination of virtually its entire Jewish population. A government-in-exile was established in London, but the Soviet Union broke relations with it in 1943 when it requested a Red Cross investigation into the murder of 14,000 Polish officers whose bodies were discovered in Katyn Forest. (The Soviet government acknowledged responsibility for the massacre in 1990.) The Soviets established a puppet government in Lublin in 1944. In August the Red Army paused in its western advance on the outskirts of Warsaw, permitting the Nazis to obliterate the Polish Home Army. On Jan. 1, 1945, the USSR recognized the Lublin regime as Poland's provisional government.

By the time of the Allied Powers Conference in Yalta in February 1945, the Red Army was only 40 miles from Berlin and had total control of Poland. The Allies agreed to Stalin's proposal concerning the eastern boundary of Poland (allowing Russia to incorporate the eastern half of the country) and agreed that the government should be constituted from an enlargement of the Lublin regime. At Potsdam in August 1945, it was further agreed that Poland should absorb the eastern portion of Germany. Poland's borders were shifted approximately 200 miles westward from the prewar configuration, becoming once again those of the 10th century. The German population was expelled remorselessly.

The free elections promised in the Yalta Agreement were postponed until 1947, by which time a Communist victory could be assured. In 1948 the Socialists were forcibly merged into the Communist party; in 1949 Premier Boleslaw Bierut requested that Soviet general Konstantin Rokossovski be appointed minister of defense and commander in chief of the Polish army. In the same year, all cultural periodicals and all writers' and artists' associations were taken over by the Communist party.

But there was little collectivization of Polish agriculture or forced industrialization on the Stalinist model. Intellectuals, bolstered by the Catholic church (which deeply resented a 1953 law requiring government approval for appointment of bishops), questioned the regime with some boldness. In 1956 both Bierut and Party Secretary Minc died, and the party refused to reelect Rokossovski to the politburo. Wladislaw Gomulka was elected party chairman in October 1956. As Soviet warships sailed through the Baltic toward Poland, Nikita Khrushchev flew to Poland with a delegation of Soviet generals, where Gomulka assured them that Poland would follow the Soviet lead in foreign policy. Distracted by the crisis in Hungary, the Russians left Gomulka in power and even canceled Poland's debt and allowed the dismantling of agricultural collectives.

For a short time Gomulka permitted cultural and educational freedom, gaining the support of intellectuals and artists. But by 1958 he had reverted to Stalinist form, imposing controls and pursuing a somewhat anti-Semitic Polish nationalism. Gomulka ruled until 1971, when he was replaced as party secretary by Edward Gierek. But moral leadership within Poland had clearly passed to Stefan Cardinal Wyszynski, leader of the increasingly vocal Catholic church; Gierek was forced to improve relations with the church in order to maintain his own credibility as a national leader.

Gierek presided over a decade of increasing unrest, with rising prices and growing discontent. Polish exports of ham and furniture to the West under liberalized terms earned some hard currency but were insufficient to curb the rising national debt. The most significant event in Poland in the 1970s was the election of Karol Wojtyla, bishop of Krakow, as Pope John Paul II in October 1978. His visit to Poland in 1979 set the stage for the extraordinary events of the 1980s.

Gierek's austerity program of February 1980 sent meat prices soaring—60 percent in July alone. Strikes for wage adjustments, especially at the Lenin Shipyards in Gdansk, thrust into a position of national leadership the greatest statesman of postwar Poland, the shipyard worker Lech Walesa. Walesa was elected chairman of the national coordinating committee of independent labor unions, Solidarity. Solidarity demands went far beyond lower prices and higher wages; they included independent labor unions with the right to strike, freedom for political prisoners, and an end to censorship. In September 1980 Gierek resigned as party secretary and was replaced by Stanislaw Kania.

By December, 40 independent trade unions had been formed, and a "rural Solidarity" movement was growing. In February 1981 Soviet Army general Wojciech Jaruzelski was named prime minister, and in October he replaced Kania as party secretary. When in December Solidarity announced plans to hold a referendum on the Jaruzelski regime, martial law was declared; Solidarity leaders were arrested, all its activities were banned, and the right to strike was abolished.

But the government was never able to suppress Solidarity as a popular force, and it was legalized in 1989. In June 1989 elections Solidarity won 99 of 100 Senate seats and 299 of 460 seats in the lower house, although 65 percent of these had been reserved for the Communist party. Jaruzelski was elected president by Parliament and Solidarity leader Tadeusz Mazowiecki became prime minister.

The Communist party voted to disband itself on Jan. 28, 1990, and the Mazowiecki government announced a program of radical economic reform, winning promises of foreign aid and increased investment from Western governments. In June 1990, a commission was appointed to draft a new constitution. Jaruzelski resigned in September, and in presidential elections, Walesa, at the head of Solidarity's labor/Catholic faction, defeated Mazowiecki, representing Solidarity's political/technocrat faction. Mazowiecki resigned and Walesa was sworn in as president on Dec. 22.

The new prime minister, Krzysztof Bielecki, continued the reformist policies of curbing inflation and government spending, fostering foreign investment, and privatizing state enterprises. But the shock therapy, with its higher prices and unemployment (even while creating more than a million new jobs), led to disillusionment among many Poles.

In the first fully free parliamentary elections, held in October 1991, only 42 percent of the voters participated, electing a fragmented 29-party Parliament. Reluctantly, Pres. Walesa named Jan Olszewski as prime minister at the head of a coalition government that commanded only 180 votes in the 460-deputy Sejm. The Olszewski coalition collapsed in June 1992, whereupon Walesa attempted to install his own choice, Waldemar Pawlak, as prime minister. But an equally fragile seven-party coalition (constituting the first parliamentary majority since 1989) instead chose Hanna Suchocka to be Poland's first female prime minister.

Despite high inflation (40%) and high official unemployment (13%), under Poland's "iron lady" the private sector expanded and even the remaining state-owned enterprises responded to market demand, pushing exports from $8 billion in 1988 to $14 billion in 1992. And a bill privatizing 600 companies passed the Polish Parliament in May 1993. By then the private sector was producing 40 percent of all industrial output and employing 50 percent of the work force.

Still, at the end of May 1993, the Suchocka government fell, by one vote, to a Solidarity-sponsored no-confidence measure, in protest against her austerity budget. Pres. Walesa, instead of accepting her resignation, called for new elections. The startling result of the October 1993 elections was the return to power of the Communist party (renamed Democratic Left Alliance), who formed a coalition with the Peasants party. Nevertheless, an austerity budget was passed because the IMF made that a condition for rescheduling Poland's foreign debt.

Portugal

Republic of Portugal

Geography Location: Iberian Peninsula in southwest Europe; also two archipelagos in Atlantic Ocean: Azores (37°29'N, 25°40'W) and Madeira Islands (32°40'N, 16°55'W). **Boundaries:** Spain to N and E, Atlantic Ocean to S and W. **Total land area:** 35,552 sq. mi. (92,080 sq km). **Coastline:** 1,114 mi. (1,793 km). **Comparative area:** between Maine and Indiana. **Land use:** 32% arable land; 6% permanent crops; 6% meadows and pastures; 40% forest and woodland; 16% other; includes 7% irrigated. **Major cities:** (1981 census) Lisboa (Lisbon, capital) 807,937; Porto (Oporto) 327,368; Amadora 95,518; Setubal 77,885; Coimbra 74,616.

People Population: 10,524,210 (1994 est.). **Nationality:** noun—Portuguese (sing., pl.); adjective—Portuguese. **Ethnic groups:** homogeneous Mediterranean stock on mainland, in Azores, and on Madeira Islands; citizens of black African descent who immigrated during decolonization number less than 100,000. **Languages:** Portuguese. **Religions:** 97% Roman Catholic, 1% Protestant, 2% other.

Government Type: republic. **Independence:** Oct. 5, 1910. **Constitution:** Apr. 25, 1976, revised Oct. 1982 and June 1989. **National holiday:** Apr. 25. **Heads of government:** Mário Soàres, president (since Mar. 1986); Anibal Cavaco Silva, prime minister (since Nov. 1985). **Structure:** executive—president and prime minister; legislative—unicameral legislature (popularly elected 250-seat Assembly of the Republic); judiciary—independent.

Economy Monetary unit: escudo. **Budget:** (1991) ***income:*** $27.3 bil.; ***expend.:*** $33.2 bil. **GDP:** $91.5 bil., $8,700 per capita (1993). **Chief crops:** generally underdeveloped; grains, potatoes, olives, grapes for wine; deficit foods—sugar, grain, meat, fish, oilseed. **Livestock:** sheep, pigs, cattle, goats, asses. **Natural resources:** fish, forests (cork), tungsten, iron ore, uranium ore, marble. **Major industries:** textiles, footwear, wood pulp, paper, cork. **Labor force:** 4.6 mil. (1988); 44% services, 34% industry, 22% agriculture; 8% unemployment. **Exports:** $17.5 bil. (f.o.b., 1993 est.); cotton textiles, cork and cork products, canned fish, wine, timber and timber products. **Imports:** $28 bil. (c.i.f., 1993 est.); petroleum, cotton, food grains, industrial machinery, iron and steel. **Major trading partners:** ***exports:*** 72% EU, 13% other developed countries, 6% U.S.; ***imports:*** 67% EU, 15% less developed countries, 13% other developed countries, 4% U.S.

Intl. Orgs. EU, FAO, IAEA, IBRD, ICAO, IFAD, IFC, ILO, IMF, IMO, INTELSAT, INTERPOL, ITU, NATO, OECD, OSCE, UN, UNESCO, UPU, WHO, WIPO, WMO, WTO.

Portugal traces its origins back to the warlike Lusitanian tribes of Roman times. The nation-state originated as a county of the kingdom of Castile, reconquered from the Moors in the 11th century. Portugal won recognition as an independent kingdom in 1143, and conquered Lisbon four years later. In 1267 the Algarve was conquered, and by then Portugal had expanded to its modern boundaries. Except for the period 1580–1640, when it was ruled by the Spanish Habsburgs, the Portuguese dynasty maintained its independence into the 20th century.

Portuguese fishermen had probably frequented the Grand Banks from before the time of Columbus, and the nation's tradition of seafaring gave rise to a world empire in the 15th and 16th centuries. Prince Henry the Navigator (1394–1460) colonized the Azores and the Madeiras and sponsored voyages of exploration along the west coast of Africa. Under his successors, Portugal controlled the west African coast, the shores of the Indian Ocean, and large stretches of southern Asia, as well as, in the Western Hemisphere, Brazil. Yet the rise of the empires of Spain and the Netherlands quickly reduced the Portuguese to second-rank status, leaving only Macao, Goa, and Timor in Asia; Portuguese Guinea (Guinea Bissau), Mozambique, and Angola in Africa; and the great territory of Brazil in Latin America.

In the 19th century, a series of dynastic civil wars weakened the monarchy, allowing Britain to gain control of the country's foreign policy (in addition to the wine trade of Oporto, long in British hands). Brazil declared its independence in 1822.

In 1910 Portugal became the first kingdom in the 20th century to be transformed into a republic. But in the next 15 years, chaos ensued: eight presidents, 44 governments, and a near-collapse of the economy. Finally, the military established a dictatorship, lasting until recent times. In 1928 the military installed a civilian dictator, a professor of economics, Antonio Salazar. A firm believer in law and order, he managed to control the turbulence of political life and made the escudo one of Europe's most stable currencies, yet he could do nothing to alter Portugal's fundamental poverty. Although he ruled through civilian governments, his essential support always came from the army.

Portugal has long been Western Europe's poorest country. As late as 1960, almost half of the country's work force was engaged in agriculture, forestry, and fishing. In the north, agriculture was traditionally carried on in smallholdings; the south was characterized by large estates, remnants of feudal fiefs. Exports were traditionally cork, olive oil, port wine, and fish. Industrialization came late to Portugal, and today manufacturing is mostly carried on by small firms engaged in textile and clothing production and other labor-intensive production.

World War II affected Portugal very little. Salazar deftly managed to remain Britain's ally while keeping his country out of the war as a neutral state. In the postwar period, Portugal accepted Marshall Plan aid and became a member of NATO in 1949. Portugal was a founding member of the European Free Trade Association in 1959 and negotiated a special relationship with the EC in 1972 (when its trading partner and ally, Great Britain, joined that body).

Portugal joined the United Nations in 1955 (having been vetoed until then by the Soviet Union), just in time to become embroiled in the worldwide movement for decolonization. Protesting that Portugal had, not colonies, but "overseas provinces," Salazar refused to bow to the pressure of world opinion. In 1961 India forcibly annexed Goa and other Portuguese enclaves on the subcontinent. In the same year, nationalist revolts broke out in Angola, with Guinea and Mozambique.

The colonial wars of the 1960s placed a terrible strain on Portugal's economy and resulted in severe military losses, and had the unintended effect of spreading Marxist ideas in the armed forces and the universities. And in the end, the colonies gained their independence. Salazar, gravely ill, retired in 1968 and was replaced by Marcelo Caetano. In 1974 Caetano was deposed in a bloodless coup staged by the secret Armed Forces movement. The coup's leader, Antonio de Spinola, after reaching agreements on the independence of most of Portugal's old colonies, resigned as head of government in September 1974. Costa Gomez replaced Spinola, as a Revolutionary Council was instituted. The council survived two coup attempts, one by right-wing soldiers, the other by Communists, and it promulgated a Socialist constitution in 1976. Through a series of unstable governments (16 between 1974 and 1987), the old agrarian estates were expropriated, and banking, insurance, and large industrial concerns were nationalized. The shock of this economic transformation, along with the OPEC price rises, created an economic recession in the 1970s. In addition Portugal had to absorb about a million ethnic Portuguese refugees from the former colonies.

Attempts by center-right coalitions in the 1980s to undo the nationalizations of the 1970s were thwarted by vetoes of the Constitutional Tribunal (successor to the Revolutionary Council), even when the free-market Social Democratic party held an absolute majority in the assembly. Portugal entered the EC on Jan. 1, 1986, pledging to reduce tariffs and end agricultural subsidies over a 10-year transitional period.

In 1987 the Social Democrats, running on an almost Thatcherite platform of spending cuts, privatization of state-owned firms, reversal of agricultural collectivism, and reliance on free enterprise, became the first party since 1974 to win an absolute majority in the legislative assembly. Since then Portugal has had the fastest-growing economy in Europe, averaging 4.5 percent GNP growth per year. Per capita income tripled over the years 1985–92, so that Portugal is no longer the poorest country in the EU. In October 1991 Prime Minister Anibal Cavaco Silva led the Social Democrats to another majority in the assembly, promising four more years of the same. The 1992 sale of the huge state-owned Petroval oil company was a harbinger of a return to free enterprise.

Qatar

State of Qatar

Geography Location: occupies a peninsula, projecting northward from Arabian mainland, into western part of Persian (Arabian) Gulf. **Boundaries:** Persian Gulf to N, E, and W; Saudi Arabia and United Arab Emirates to S. **Total land area:** 4,247 sq. mi. (11,000 sq km). **Coastline:** 350 mi. (563 km). **Comparative area:** between Delaware and Connecticut. **Land use:** negl. % arable land; 0% permanent crops; 5% meadows and pastures; 0% forest and woodland; 95% other. **Major cities:** (1986) Doha (capital) 217,294; Rayyan 91,996; Wakrah 23,682.

People Population: 512,779 (1994 est.). **Nationality:** noun—Qatari(s); adjective—Qatari. **Ethnic groups:** 40% Arab, 18% Pakistani, 18% Indian, 10% Iranian, 14% other. **Languages:** Arabic (official), English commonly used as second language. **Religions:** 95% Muslim.

Government Type: traditional monarchy. **Independence:** Sept. 3, 1971 (from UK). **Constitution:** provisional constitution enacted Apr. 2, 1970. **National holiday:** Independence Day, Sept. 3. **Head of government:** Hamad bin Khalifa al-Thani (since June 1995). **Structure:** executive—amir and Council of Ministers; legislature—State Advisory Council.

Economy Monetary unit: Qatari riyal. **Budget:** (1992 est.) ***income:*** $2.5 bil.; ***expend.:*** $3 bil. **GDP:** $8.8 bil., $17,500 per capita (1993 est.). **Chief crops:** farming and grazing on small scale; commercial fishing increasing in importance; most food imported; rice and dates are staple diet. **Livestock:** sheep, goats, camels, cattle, horses. **Natural resources:** crude oil, natural gas, fish. **Major industries:** crude oil production and refining, fertilizers, petrochemicals. **Labor force:** 104,000 (1983); 85% non-Qatari in private sector. **Exports:** $3.4 bil. (f.o.b., 1993 est.); 90% petroleum products, steel, fertilizers. **Imports:** $1.8 bil. (f.o.b., 1993 est.); excluding military equipment—foodstuffs, beverages, animal and vegetable oils. **Major trading partners:** ***exports:*** 61% Japan, 9% Brazil, 3% UAE, 3% Singapore; ***imports:*** 13% France, 11% UK, 11% Japan, 8% Italy, 9% Germany.

Intl. Orgs. Arab League, FAO, G-77, IBRD, ICAO, IFAD, ILO, IMF, IMO, INTELSAT, INTERPOL, ITU, NAM, OPEC, UN, UNESCO, UPU, WHO, WIPO, WMO, WTO.

The Qatar peninsula was ruled as part of the sheikhdom of Bahrain from the late 18th century until the mid-19th century. An informal British protectorate was established in 1868; the Ottoman Empire also asserted authority over the sheikhs of Qatar from 1872 to 1916. The Ottomans ceded authority to the British in that year, and a formal British protectorate was organized. When British forces withdrew from the Persian Gulf region in 1971, Qatar entered into negotiations with the emirates of the Trucial Coast to join the federation of the United Arab Emirates. When those negotiations broke down, Qatar declared its independence on Sept. 3, 1971. For over 30 years it has been politically stable under one ruler, Sheik Hamad bin Khalifa al-Thani, although he was deposed by his son in a bloodless coup in June 1995.

Qatar's economy is entirely dominated by oil, banking, and shipping services in the port of Doha.

Romania

Geography Location: southeastern Europe. **Boundaries:** Ukraine to N, Moldova to NE, Black Sea to E, Bulgaria to S, Yugoslavia (Serbia) to SW, Hungary to NW. **Total land area:** 91,699 sq. mi. (237,500 sq km). **Coastline:** 140 mi. (225 km). **Comparative area:** between Utah and Oregon. **Land use:** 43% arable land; 3% permanent crops; 19% meadows and pastures; 28% forest and woodland; 7% other; includes 11% irrigated. **Major cities:** (1992 est.) Bucharesti (Bucharest, capital) 2,064,474; Constanta 350,476; Iasi 342,994; Timisoara 334,278; Cluj-Napoca 328,008.

People Population: 23,181,415 (1994 est.). **Nationality:** noun—Romanian(s); adjective—Romanian. **Ethnic groups:** 89% Romanian, 7.8% Hungarian, 1.5% German, 1.6% Ukrainian, Serb, Croat, Russian, Turk, and Gypsy. **Languages:** Romanian, Hungarian, German. **Religions:** 80% Romanian Orthodox, 6% Roman Catholic, 4% Calvinist, Lutheran, Jewish, Baptist.

Government Type: republic. **Independence:** 1881 from Turkey. **Constitution:** Dec. 8, 1991; republic proclaimed Dec. 30, 1947. **National holiday:** National Day, Dec. 1. **Heads of government:** Ion Iliescu, president (since May 1990); Nicolae Vacaroiu, prime minister (since Nov. 1992). **Structure:** Executive branch consists of president and cabinet: legislature is Parliament with upper Senate chamber and lower Chamber of Deputies; judicial branch consists of Supreme Court and Courts of Appeals.

Economy (1991 est.) **Monetary unit:** lei. **Budget:** ***income:*** $19 bil.; ***expend.:*** $20 bil. **GNP:** $63.7 bil., $2,700 per capita (1993 est.). **Chief crops:** corn, wheat, oilseed; consumer and food supplies weak; net exporter. **Livestock:** poultry, sheep, pigs, cattle, horses. **Natural resources:** crude oil, timber, construction materials. **Major industries:** mining, timber, construction materials. **Labor force:** 10.6 mil.; 34% industry, 28% agriculture, 38% other. **Exports:** $4 bil. (f.o.b., 1993); 34.7% machinery and equipment; 24.7% fuels, minerals, and metals; 16.9% manufactured consumer goods; 11.9% agricultural materials and forestry products; 11.6% other. **Imports:** $5.4 bil. (f.o.b., 1993); 51.0% fuels, minerals, and metals, 26.7% machinery and equipment; 11.0% agricultural and forestry products; 4.2% manufactured consumer goods; 7.1% other. **Major trading partners:** (1987) ***exports:*** 27% former USSR, 23% Eastern Europe, 15% EU, 5% U.S., 4% China. ***imports:*** 60% Communist countries, 40% non-Communist countries.

Intl. Orgs. FAO, G-77, IAEA, IBRD, ICAO, IFAD, ILO, IMF, IMO, INTERPOL, ITU, OSCE, UN, UNESCO, UPU, WHO, WIPO, WMO, WTO.

The Roman province of Dacia was sufficiently Latinized to retain the name of Rome long after the legions withdrew in A.D. 27. Overrun by invading Bulgars in the eighth century, the Romanians retained their Latinate language and orthodox Christianity; Romania remained beyond the borders of the Byzantine Empire but was in close contact with it. The country was conquered by the Mongols in the 13th century and formed the independent principalities of Moldavia and Walachia after the Mongols withdrew at the end of that century.

By the 15th century, Moldavia and Walachia had become vassal states of the Ottoman Empire, though with some local autonomy that permitted retention of orthodox Christianity and the creation of a rich local culture. Attempts at national unity against Ottoman rule in 1601 and 1711 failed; in 1861 the provinces united as an autonomous state under the name Romania, within the Ottoman Empire, under Greek administration. Independence came in 1878.

Romania was for centuries the poorest country in Europe. Thoroughly agricultural, it was a land of unfree peasants working the great estates of landowners who were generally wealthy, usually absentee, and often Greek. The peasants not only paid taxes but also were required to perform feudal labor services for the estate owners.

After enlarging itself at Bulgaria's expense in the Second Balkan War (1913), Romania switched sides three times in World War I, joining the Allies just before the war's end. Its reward was a huge expansion in size, doubling its territory with lands taken from Austria, Hungary, Russia, and Bulgaria.

The interwar period was one of political turbulence, marked by violence and assassinations. Twice King Carol II went into exile, leaving his throne to his son Prince Michael; the second time was in 1940, when Russia (in accordance with the Hitler-Stalin pact) reclaimed the territories of Bessarabia and northern Bukovina that it had lost to Romania in 1920, while Hitler required Romania to return about half of Transylvania to Hungary.

During World War II, the pro-Hitler dictator Marshall Ion Antonescu took power, supported by a semifascist "Iron Guard," but when the latter attempted a coup, the military crushed the uprising. Romanian troops participated in Hitler's invasion of Russia in 1941, and the country paid the price in 1944 when Russian troops "liberated" the country, with devastating results. King Michael arrested Antonescu and switched to the Allied side, but to no avail.

The country was quickly transformed into a Soviet satellite through rigged elections in which the communist National Democratic Front replaced the Peasant Alliance in power; a People's Republic was proclaimed on Dec. 30, 1947, and King Michael was forced to abdicate. A peace treaty in 1947 confirmed the loss of Bessarabia to Russia but returned Transylvania to Romania.

Under Russian occupation Romania was a virtual Soviet colony. The occupying armies did not leave until after reparation payments were completed in 1958, leaving the dictator Gheorghe Gheorghiu-Dej in power. Despite Council of Mutual Economic Assistance (COMECON) plans for Romania to become a major food supplier to the Soviet bloc, Gheorghiu-Dej pursued industrialization on the Stalinist model, in the process ruining Romanian agriculture while creating large, labor-intensive, and highly inefficient factories. The result was an economic depression; politically, however, it produced a de facto independence for Romania within the Soviet bloc. Russian troops were forbidden on Romanian soil, and Romania declined to participate in COMECON policies.

With the death of Gheorghiu-Dej in 1965, power passed to Nicolae Ceauşescu. He promulgated a new constitution and instituted a series of purges, lasting to 1968; he became successively party leader in 1965, prime minister in 1967, and president of the republic in 1974. Ceauşescu continued his predecessor's economic policy, deepening the country's misery; he also pursued a policy of "independence" from the USSR, refusing to go along with Soviet policies of de-Stalinization and liberalization.

Romania's "national communism" was expressed in intense and militant nationalism, coupled with severe repression of ethnic minorities, especially Germans and Magyars in Transylvania. Hundreds of ethnically Hungarian villages were bulldozed into oblivion in the name of agricultural collectivization.

Ceauşescu's ambitions included the creation of a family dynasty in the Romanian leadership. In 1979 his wife Elena was named first deputy premier and elevated to the Council of Ministers. Her brothers were given important government positions, Ceauşescu's son, despite his reputation as a decadent playboy, was groomed to replace his father.

Romania's transition from Communist rule was sudden and violent. On Dec. 16–18, 1989, demonstrations in Timisoara calling for Ceauşescu's ouster were put down with brute force by the Securitate (secret police), but they spread and citizens and regular army troops fought pitched battles with Securitate forces in Bucharest. Ceauşescu and his wife fled Bucharest but were captured, tried, and executed by Christmas day. The newly organized Council of National Salvation established a provisional government, consisting primarily of anti-Ceauşescu Communists in league with the Romanian army, with former Communist party official Ion Iliescu as president.

The Communist party was outlawed on Jan. 12, 1990. Despite the Council's domination by former Communists, no effective opposition movement emerged, and in hastily called and rigged elections on May 20, Iliescu was elected president in a landslide and the Council won 233 of 296 seats in the lower house.

In June 1990, many anti-Communist demonstrators were beaten and several killed by troops and armed miners brought to Bucharest by the government, an action that was condemned internationally. Calls for Iliescu's resignation and a purge of Communists from government continued into the fall. Tensions were further aggravated when the government's abrupt move to a market economy resulted in food shortages and sharp price increases.

Continued rioting in 1991 led to the replacement of ex-Communist prime minister Petre Roman by the non-Communist Theodor Stolojan at the head of a "caretaker" coalition in October. Local elections in Februrary 1992 brought strong gains, especially in larger cities, for a 14-party anti-Communist coalition.

More or less free elections in 1992 gave the National Salvation Front 28 percent of the seats in Parliament while the opposition Democratic Convention gained 20 percent; Iliescu defeated the Democratic Convention candidate in the presidential election with 61 percent of the vote. Both Iliescu and the prime minister he named (Nicolae Vacaroiu) were pledged to slowing the transition to a market economy but by 1994 with inflation at over 250 percent (leading to a massive workers' strike in February) the government agreed to IMF's demand for increased privatization and fiscal austerity in order to receive a $700 mil. loan. In 1994 Romania became the first former Soviet satellite to join NATO's "partnership for peace."

Russia

Russian Federation

Geography **Location:** northeastern Europe and northern Asia. **Boundaries:** Baltic Sea, Barents Sea, Kara Sea, East Siberian Sea to N, Bering Sea, Sea of Okhotsk, Sea of Japan to E, China, North Korea, Mongolia, Kazakhstan, Caspian Sea, Azerbaijan, Georgia, Black Sea to S, Ukraine, Belarus to W, Latvia, Estonia, Finland, Norway to NW. **Total land area:** 6,592,745 sq. mi. (17,075,200 sq km). **Coastline:** 26,582 mi. (42,777 km). **Comparative area:** almost twice the size of the United States. **Land use:** N.A. **Major cities:** (1990 est.) Moscow (capital) 8,801,000; St. Petersburg 4,468,000; Novgorod 1,443,000; Novosibirsk 1,443,000; Yekaterinburg 1,367,000; Chelyabins 1,143,000; Irkutsk 626,000; Valdivostok 648,000; Khabarovsk 601,000.

People **Population:** 149,608,953 (1994 est.). **Nationality:** noun—Russian(s); adjective—Russian. **Ethnic groups:** 82.6% Russian, 3.6% Tatar, 2.7% Ukrainian, 1.2% Chuvash, Belarussian, Bashkir, Jewish. **Languages:** Russian (official); ethnic languages. **Religions:** Christianity—Russian Orthodox; Islam, Buddhism, Judaism.

Government **Type:** republic. **Independence:** not formally declared. **Constitution:** being drafted. **National holiday:** June 12, Independence Day, celebrating first presidential election. **Heads of government:** Boris N. Yeltsin, president (since June 1991); Victor S. Chernomyrdin, prime minister (since Dec. 1993). **Structure:** executive—president, vice president, ministers; legislative—Congress of Peoples' Deputies, 1,068 deputies elected Mar. 18, 1990; Supreme Soviet was elected from among the deputies of the Congress on June 9, 1990. It is a bicameral legislature composed of Council of Nationalities and Council of the Republic; judicial—Supreme Court.

Economy **Monetary unit:** ruble. **Budget:** N.A. ***income:*** N.A.; ***expend.:*** N.A. **GNP:** $775.4 bil., $5,190 per capita (1993 est.). **Chief crops:** grain, potatoes, sugar beets, vegetables, sunflowers. **Livestock:** sheep, goats, cattle, pigs. **Natural resources:** coal, petroleum, natural gas, gold, manganese, molybdenum, iron. **Major industries:** extraction and processing raw materials, woven cotton fabrics, woven woolen fabrics, steel pipes. **Labor force:** 75 mil. (1993 est.). **Exports:** $43 bil. (f.o.b., 1993); petroleum and petroleum products, natural gas, wood and wood products, coal, nonferrous metals, chemicals. **Imports:** $27 bil. (f.o.b., 1993); machinery and equipment, chemicals, consumer goods, grain. **Major trading partners:** ***exports:*** Western Europe, Japan, eastern Europe. ***imports:*** Western and eastern Europe, Japan, third-world countries, Cuba.

Intl. Orgs. CIS, IAEA, ICAO, ILO, IMF, IMO, ITU, OSCE, UN, UPU, WHO, WIPO, WMO, World Bank.

Russia is the largest and most powerful of the states to emerge from the former Soviet Union. As the seat of the Soviet empire that existed for over 70 years, the Russians wielded tremendous power both within the USSR and in the international sphere. Almost from their emergence as a separate people, the Russians have extended the boundaries of their country to include a wide variety of non-Russian people. Both the Russian Czars and the Bolsheviks who came to power in 1917 have a long history of expansionist policies, which explains why, even today, an important part of the Russian national identity is that of leader of a large empire.

In the ninth century A.D., Viking traders organized a state, which they called Rus, in the river valleys between the Baltic and the Black Seas, centered on the cities of Kiev and Novgorod. In time the Vikings were absorbed into the native Slavic population; in 998 a Ruthenian prince of Kiev accepted Christianity from Constantinople. In the 13th century, Mongols under Genghis Khan and his descendants conquered most of Russia, and the Mongol Golden Horde maintained its power through the 14th century, exercising loose control over Novgorod and Moscow.

From the mid-19th century, Moscow grew to become the center of a new state that gathered in other cities and territories as Mongol power waned. Ivan III (Ivan the Great, 1440–1505) consolidated the power of Moscow; his marriage to a Byzantine princess led him to regard his empire as a third Rome, heir to the religious tradition of Constantinople. His grandson, Ivan IV (Ivan the Terrible, 1530–84), adopted the title czar (from the Latin *caesar*) when he came to power. He broke the power of the aristocratic boyar class and greatly extended the power of Moscow through military conquest.

Over the next two centuries, Russia carried out a steady program of expansion eastward into Siberia and across the Bering Strait to Alaska, until the empire covered one-sixth of the land surface of the globe. Peter the Great (1672–1725) made Russia a Baltic and Black Sea naval power, brought Russia into the European state system, and instituted a sweeping, if superficial, Westernization of his realm. His new capital at St. Petersburg became one of the most splendid cities in Europe. At the end of the 18th century, Catherine the Great (1729–96) participated with Prussia and Austria in the partitions of Poland, and Russia thereby became a major power in central Europe.

Catherine's grandson Alexander I (1777–1825), member of the grand coalition that defeated Napoleon, was not only czar of Russia but also king of Poland and grand duke of Finland. His troops occupied Paris in 1815. The Russian aristocracy became ardent Francophiles in the 19th century, ignoring growing problems at home. After losing the Crimean War in 1856, Russia began to develop Siberia and the southern territories near the border of Persia. Alaska was sold to the United States in 1867. In a major reform of the agricultural system, serfdom was abolished under Alexander II in 1861, though the newly independent peasantry, organized into agricultural cooperatives, only slowly derived benefits from its freedom. The late 19th century also marked the beginning of modern industrialization in Russia and of extensive development in Siberia, aided by state investment in railroads and mining.

Under the last czar, Nicholas II (1868–1918), Russia was defeated by Japan in a war over Manchuria in 1905. The defeat sparked a naval mutiny and an abortive revolution, which led to the establishment of a constitutional monarchy and other limited political reforms. Further military losses in World War I set the stage for the monarchy's downfall in the revolution of 1917.

The initial revolution of March 1917 brought a relatively moderate socialist (Menshevik) group to power. Its principal leader, Aleksandr Kerensky, organized a republican government and tried to maintain the Russian war effort but failed to gain control of the many contending revolutionary factions of the time. The Germans allowed the radical Bolshevik leader, Vladimir I. Lenin, to return to Russia, where he and his followers organized workers' soviets (councils) hostile to the Menshevik republic. Bolshevik forces occupied Petrograd (St. Petersburg was renamed in 1914) on Nov. 7, 1917 (October in the old Byzantine calendar, hence the name October Revolution), arrested the cabinet, and put in place a Council of People's Commissars, under Lenin's chairmanship. There followed four years of civil war between Bolshevik, Menshevik, and czarist forces, in the course of which Nicholas II and his family were executed by the Bolsheviks in 1918.

Decreeing land to the peasants, worker management in industry, and repudiation of czarist debts, the Bolsheviks won the survival of their regime by withdrawing from World War I. The 1918 Treaty of Brest-Litovsk, which gained peace with Germany, granted freedom to Finland, the Baltic republics, Poland, Ukraine, and Bessarabia. At the conclusion of the civil war (complicated by a war with Poland) in 1921, the Soviet state was established, with Ukraine reabsorbed into the Soviet Union. The Bolshevik victory also resulted in the creation in 1921 of the Mongolian People's Republic as a close Soviet ally.

The early 1920s are now remembered as a "golden age" of Soviet history. Lenin's New Economic Policy (NEP) allowed some role for market forces and private ownership and led to a brief burst of economic growth. Art, literature, and science flourished in an atmosphere of revolutionary enthusiasm and little censorship.

Lenin died on Jan. 21, 1924, and after a power struggle, was succeeded by Josef Stalin. Stalin supported Communist revolutions in China and elsewhere through the Communist International (Comintern) but generally withdrew from foreign engagements in order to concentrate on domestic affairs. Under Lenin, and even more under Stalin, the Communist party established a police state, condemning millions of people to internal exile in the 1920s and consolidating all power in the hands of the state. In 1929 agriculture was forcibly collectivized, leading to the starvation or execution of millions of peasants, while forced industrialization was carried out under a series of five-year plans.

Under the guise of socialist revolution, the Russians continued in much the same manner as their czarist heirs. The Bolsheviks forcibly incorporated most of the territories of the old empire, and once in charge, insisted that Russian be the state language and that Russian Communist party officials run the republics.

On the national level, Stalin's chief rival, Leon Trotsky, was expelled from the USSR in 1929 (and assassinated by Stalinist agents in Mexico in 1940). Stalin's obsession with eliminating all possible rivals for power led to a series of purges which, at their height, saw the summary execution of an estimated seven million of presumed "enemies of the state" and the imprisonment in concentration camps of an estimated 12 million more.

Russia's reemergence as a world power was signaled by the signing in August 1939 of the Hitler-Stalin Pact, a nonaggression treaty through which Stalin aimed to recover territories lost to Russia in 1918. Poland was again partitioned, Bessarabia annexed (as the Moldavian republic), Finland conquered and partitioned, and the Baltic republics absorbed.

When in June 1941 Hitler turned against his ally and invaded Russia, unprepared Russian armies retreated. But Stalin emerged as a national leader in the "Great Patriotic War," restructuring the army and enlisting the support of the Orthodox church and relying on calls to Russian patriotism in rallying the population. In the early winter of 1942, the war changed course as Russia broke the German siege of Stalingrad, and Russian armies began their westward push that would carry them to the Elbe River by April 1945.

By the end of World War II, Stalin had reestablished the old czarist boundaries of Russia, and he had a ring of occupied states along his western boundary and a divided Germany beyond. Over the years 1945–48, he engineered a thorough communization of those occupied states, turning them into Russian satellites. Only Yugoslavia escaped total Russian domination.

Stalin died in March 1953. He was succeeded by a collegial form of party and government leadership, from which Nikita Khrushchev, the party chairman, gradually emerged as the paramount figure. In a secret speech to the party leadership in 1956, Khrushchev denounced Stalin for crimes against the party. He announced a set of new policies designed to bring about rapid modernization and consolidated his power when he became premier in 1958. The Khrushchev years brought a small but steady rise in living standards and a "thaw" in police state methods, the KGB (state security police) being brought under party control.

In foreign policy there was a thaw as well. In 1953 the Soviets agreed to an armistice in Korea and tolerated the formation of a more liberal government in Hungary. In 1955 Russia returned the Porkkala peninsula to Finland and agreed to the Austrian State Treaty, which created an independent and neutral Austria. But the limits of disengagement became clear in 1956 with the ruthless Soviet suppression of the Hungarian uprising. A summit conference between Khrushchev and Eisenhower in 1960 led to a propaganda victory for Russia when an American U-2 spy plane was shot down over Russian territory on May 1. And in 1962 Khrushchev tried to install Soviet missiles in Cuba, a reckless adventure from which he had to back down during the Cuban missile crisis.

While on vacation in 1964, Khrushchev was removed from office and replaced as party secretary by Leonid Brezhnev and as premier by Aleksei Kosygin. His failure to deliver on extravagant promises for domestic economic growth and his recklessness in foreign affairs seem to have been responsible for his downfall. The new leaders embarked on an ambitious program of military (and especially naval) expansion. They also pressed ahead vigorously with a space program that had begun with the triumphant launching of Sputnik I in 1957.

Under Brezhnev and Kosygin the USSR became more aggressive in foreign policy. The severe suppression of Czechoslovakia's "Prague Spring" in 1968 occasioned development of the Brezhnev Doctrine, whereby Russia claimed the right to intervene militarily in any socialist state. Soviet involvement in the Third World grew, with Russia supporting Vietnam against China; Syria and the PLO against Israel; leftist regimes in Angola, Ethiopia, and elsewhere in Africa; and the Sandinistas in Nicaragua. Cuba emerged as the principal Soviet proxy in supplying troops for leftist causes in the Third World. In 1979 Soviet troops moved into Afghanistan, allegedly at the invitation of its Marxist government, and remained bogged down there for a decade. Under American pressure, Brezhnev permitted the emigration of about 130,000 Jews and 40,000 ethnic Germans in the 1970s.

Domestically, the regime grew more oppressive; censorship was tightened and dissidents sentenced to terms in penal mental institutions. Elitism and nepotism created a self-perpetuating and interlocking network of power at the top, while the nation as a whole stagnated.

Brezhnev's death in 1982 brought about a rapid series of leadership transfers. Yuri Andropov, head of the KGB, succeeded Brezhnev as party secretary but died after only 15 months. He was succeeded by Konstantin Chernenko, who died 13 months later. In March 1985 Mikhail Gorbachev became party secretary, ushering in a new era in Soviet history.

Gorbachev first instituted a cautious shake-up of state and party bureaucrats, promoting younger men who were technocrats rather than party professionals. Under the slogan glasnost (openness, candor), censorship was relaxed; by 1988 criticism of not only Stalin but also Brezhnev was permitted, and policy was openly debated in the press. Jamming of broadcasts from the West was ended. By the end of 1990, freedom of the press and of religion had been approved, and private citizens were given limited rights to own small businesses.

Gorbachev's other slogan, perestroika (restructuring), addressed his aim to boost morale and increase economic efficiency by devolving responsibility for economic decisions away from the party and government and toward industrial and agricultural managers. Perestroika raised expectations but not output; the system remained sluggish, inefficient, and burdened with the vested interests of state planners. The nuclear power plant disaster of Chernobyl in April 1986 and a gas pipeline fire that killed hundreds of passengers in passing railroad trains in June 1989 exemplified the industrial mismanagement against which Gorbachev's policies were aimed. During 1989–91 there were strikes by coal miners, and shortages of food and consumer goods worsened.

In foreign policy Gorbachev pursued arms reduction agreements with the United States and withdrew Soviet forces from Afghanistan. His international stature exceeded that of any previous Soviet leader; but his problems at home made him increasingly unpopular among Soviet citizens. Foremost among his problems at home concerned the USSR's various ethnic nationalities. The southern Muslim regions of the USSR were the scene of turmoil since the anti-Russian riots in Kazakhstan in 1986; in 1988 riots broke out in the Christian republic of Armenia over the status of ethnic Armenians in the neighboring Muslim republic of Azerbaijan. Fighting in Armenia and Azerbaijan worsened in 1989–90, leading to a breakdown of government control in some areas. Ethnic warfare between Uzbeks and Turks in Uzbekistan led to numerous deaths, and sporadic violence in other central Asian republics broke out in 1990.

In the northwest, the Baltic republics of Estonia, Latvia, and Lithuania raised their old national flags over their parliaments, enacted laws giving their native languages priority over Russian, and proclaimed the superiority of local republican law over the laws of the Soviet Union. Lithuania proclaimed its independence from the USSR in December 1989, provoking a confrontation with strong international ramifications; Lithuania finally agreed to postpone its independence in 1990 pending negotiations with the Soviet government. Within the USSR itself, the Russian republic elected maverick Boris Yeltsin as president and pressed for greater autonomy; Yeltsin resigned from the Communist party in July 1990.

The total collapse of communist governments in Eastern Europe in 1989–90 added to Gorbachev's problems and led to the dissolution of the Warsaw Pact; the Berlin Wall fell in November 1989; and the Council of Mutual Economic Assistance (COMECON) was dissolved in July 1990. Gorbachev responded by assuming the presidency of the USSR and increasing the powers of that office, and he held off challenges to his leadership in 1990–91. Yet defections from the party by both right- and left-wing groups threw the party's future role in the USSR itself in doubt. Public demonstrations against Gorbachev and the Communist party took place in Moscow and elsewhere as the economy worsened and food supplies dwindled.

In June of 1991, Boris Yeltsin was elected president of the Russian republic in the first direct elections for the post. His stature soared when he rallied opposition to an unsuccessful coup to topple Gorbachev in August. In December 1991 Gorbachev and Yeltsin agreed that the USSR would cease to exist as of Jan. 1, 1992.

In early December 1991, Ukraine, Belarus, and the Russian Federation signed the Minsk Agreement that created the Commonwealth of Independent States, and on Dec. 21, Ukraine and 11 other former union republics officially committed themselves to the union by signing the Alma-Ata Declaration. In February 1992 Russian president Yeltsin agreed to begin dismantling the vast arsenal of Russian nuclear weapons, 80 percent of which are on Russia's territory, the rest being scattered across Ukraine, Belarus, and Kazakhstan. While Belarus has agreed to allow Russia to control the weapons, Kazakhstan and Ukraine have used their weapons as bargaining chips. Another major source of disagreement with Ukraine continues to be the powerful Black Sea fleet in Sevastopol.

Throughout 1993, Pres. Yeltsin took center stage, first signing the historic second Strategic Arms Reduction Treaty (START II) with the United States in January, then in April rallying the people to support a referendum on government elections and to approve his policies, and finally in June calling together a Constitutional Assembly to write a new constitution. As the Russian economy continued to founder, however, Yeltsin became the target of attacks by hard-liners, mainly former Communists. In December 1992, Yeltsin barely survived a series of votes in Parliament that would have severely limited his control.

This struggle came to a violent head on Sept. 21, 1993, when Yeltsin and Parliament effectively threw each other out of office: Yeltsin declared Parliament dissolved and called for new elections to be held in December; Parliament voted to impeach Yeltsin and appointed Vice Pres. Aleksandr V. Rutskoi to replace him. Anti-Yeltsin forces called for a national strike and barricaded themselves inside the Parliament building for two weeks. Anti-Yeltsin rallies escalated into serious violence when 10,000 protesters overwhelmed riot police and broke through government barricades, causing Yeltsin to summon military police. The military's quick response to Yeltsin's call strengthened his command of the Russian government. The leaders of the revolt, Rutskoi and chairman Ruslan I. Khasbulatov, surrendered after tanks fired directly on the Parliament building, and were immediately sent to prison. At least 100 people were killed.

In the aftermath, Yeltsin moved quickly to parlay his victory into even greater political power, by banning several opposition parties, firing powerful opponents, and calling for parliamentary elections to be held Dec. 12, 1993. He announced he would stay in office until his term expired in 1996, and in November 1993 he unveiled the country's first post-Soviet constitution, which centralized power in the executive presidency and limited the powers of the constituent regions. One of these regions, Chechnya, had long threatened secession from Russia and in 1994 its leaders took that action. In December Yeltsin ordered the army to restore government control, but it took months of fighting before Grazny, the rebel capital, fell to Russian troops. (For further details, see Part I: "Major News Stories of the Year.")

Rwanda

Republic of Rwanda

Geography **Location:** landlocked country in central Africa. **Boundaries:** Uganda to N, Tanzania to E, Burundi to S, Zaire to W. **Total land area:** 10,170 sq. mi. (26,340 sq km). **Coastline:** none. **Comparative area:** about size of Maryland. **Land use:** 29% arable land; 11% permanent crops; 18% meadows and pastures; 10% forest and woodland; 32% other; includes negl. % irrigated. **Major cities:** (1978 census) Kigali (capital) 117,749; Butare 21,691; Ruhengeri 16,025; Gisenyi 12,436.

People **Population:** 8,373,963 (1994 est.). **Nationality:** noun—Rwandan(s); adjective—Rwandan. **Ethnic groups:** 90% Hutu, 9% Tutsi, 1% Twa (Pygmy). **Languages:** Kinyarwanda, French (both official); Kiswahili used in commercial centers. **Religions:** 65% Catholic, 9% Protestant, 9% Muslim; indigenous beliefs.

Government Type: republic; presidential system in which military leaders hold key offices. **Independence:** July 1, 1962 (from UN trusteeship under Belgian administration). **Constitution:** Dec. 17, 1978. **National holiday:** National Day, July 1. **Heads of government:** Pasteur Bizimingu, president (since July 1994); Faustin Twagiramungu, prime minister (since July 1994). **Structure:** executive—president, 16-member cabinet; unicameral legislature—National Development Council; judiciary—four senior courts, magistrates.

Economy Monetary unit: Rwanda franc. **Budget:** (1992 est.) ***income:*** $350 mil.; ***expend.:*** N.A. **GNP:** $6.8 bil., $800 per capita (1993 est.). **Chief crops:** cash crops—coffee, tea, pyrethrum; food crops—bananas, cassava; self-sufficiency declining; imports foodstuffs. **Livestock:** goats, cattle, sheep, pigs. **Natural resources:** gold, cassiterite (tin ore), wolframite (tungsten ore), natural gas, hydropower. **Major industries:** mining of cassiterite and wolframite, tin, cement. **Labor force:** 3.6 mil. (1985); 93% agriculture, 7% other. **Exports:** $66.6 mil. (f.o.b., 1992 est.); 85% coffee, tea, tin, cassiterite, wolframite. **Imports:** $259.5 mil. (f.o.b., 1992 est.); textiles, foodstuffs, machines, equipment, capital goods. **Major trading partners:** ***exports:*** Germany, Belgium, Italy, Uganda, UK; ***imports:*** U.S., Belgium, Germany, Kenya, Japan.

Intl. Orgs. FAO, G-77, IBRD, ICAO, IDA, IFAD, IFC, ILO, IMF, INTERPOL, ITU, NAM, UN, UNESCO, UPU, WHO, WMO, WTO.

Tutsi cattle-breeders came to Rwanda, on Africa's east coast, in the late 15th century and slowly conquered the native Hutu farmers. The Tutsi established a monarchy, forcing the Hutus into serfdom. Germans were the first Europeans to arrive in Rwanda and declared it a protectorate in 1899. After World War I Belgium was given a League of Nations mandate over the territory, which became a UN trusteeship after World War II.

Tutsi traditionalists resisted Belgian attempts in the 1950s to institute democratic political institutions. In 1959 the Hutus revolted against the monarchy in a bloody conflict which led to a mass exodus of Tutsis. Two years later the Hutus won a UN-supervised referendum and were granted internal autonomy by Belgium on Jan. 1, 1962. Full independence came on July 1, 1962. Political unrest led to the overthrow of the government in 1973. Maj. Gen. Juvénal Habyarimana dissolved the National Assembly and banned all political activity.

Tutsi refugees in Uganda fought with the army from October 1990, and by 1993 as many as one million people were displaced. A cease-fire and amnesty paved the way for political reform, and a new constitution allowing for multiparty democracy, separation of powers, and presidential term limits went into effect in June 1992. Proposals to merge the armies of the government (Hutu) and the Tutsi Rwandan Patriotic Front were signed in 1993.

But in April 1994, the Hutu presidents of Rwanda and Burundi were both killed when the plane carrying them was shot down by rocket-fire as they were returning from a peace conference in Tanzania aimed at ending the ethnic warfare in both counties. The double assassination renewed the violence, setting off one of the bloodiest civil wars in history. By September 1994, more than a million Rwandans had died in the violence, and close to three million more fled to neighboring Zaire, Uganda, and Tanzania. Cholera outbreaks at refugee camps caused the deaths of thousands more.

On July 18, 1994, the victorious guerrilla army of the Rwandan Patriotic Front established a "new government of national unity." After 35 years of Hutu rule the ancient dominance of the Tutsi over the Hutu returned, although the Tutsi leaders were careful to appoint Hutus to be president and prime minister.

Saint Kitts and Nevis

Federation of Saint Kitts and Nevis

Geography Location: two islands in eastern Caribbean Sea, about 45 mi. (72 km) NW of Antigua. Nevis 17°08'N, 62°37'W; St. Kitts 17°17'N, 62°43'W. **Boundaries:** Caribbean Sea to N, E, S, and W. **Total land area:** 104 sq. mi. (269 sq km). **Coastline:** 84 mi. (135 km). **Comparative area:** slightly more than twice size of Washington, D.C. **Land use:** 22% arable land; 17% permanent crops; 3% meadows and pastures; 17% forest and woodland; 41% other; includes N.A. % irrigated. **Major cities:** (1980 est.) Basseterre (capital) 14,161.

People Population: 40,671 (1994 est.). **Nationality:** noun—Kittsian(s), Nevisian(s); adjective—Kittsian, Nevisian. **Ethnic groups:** mainly of black African descent. **Languages:** English. **Religions:** Anglican, other Protestant sects, Roman Catholic.

Government Type: independent state within Commonwealth, recognizing Elizabeth II as chief of state. **Independence:** Sept. 19, 1983 (from UK). **Constitution:** Sept. 19, 1983. **National holiday:** Independence Day, Sept 19. **Heads of government:** Sir Clement Arrindell, governor-general (since Nov. 1981); Dr. Kennedy Alphonse Simmonds, prime minister (since Feb. 1980). **Structure:** executive (cabinet headed by prime minister); legislative (11-member popularly elected House of Assembly; separate Nevis Island Legislature and Nevis Island Assembly headed by premier).

Economy Monetary unit: East Caribbean (EC) dollar. **Budget:** (1993) ***income:*** $85.7 mil.; ***expend.:*** $85.8 mil. **GDP:** $163 mil., $4,000 per capita (1992). **Chief crops:** sugar on St. Kitts, cotton on Nevis. **Livestock:** sheep, pigs, goats, cattle. **Natural resources:** negl. **Major industries:** sugar processing, tourism, cotton. **Labor force:** 20,000 (1981). **Exports:** $32.4 mil. (f.o.b., 1992); sugar. **Imports:** $100 mil. (f.o.b., 1992); foodstuffs, manufactures, fuel. **Major trading partners:** (1988) ***exports:*** 53% U.S., 22% UK, 5% Trinidad and Tobago. ***imports:*** 36% U.S., 17% UK, 6% Trinidad and Tobago, 3% Canada, 3% Japan.

Intl. Orgs. Commonwealth, FAO, IBRD, G-77, IMF, OAS, UN.

The French settled St. Kitts in 1627; the English settled Nevis in 1628. In 1783 both became British possessions, and the two islands were united in 1882. Britain granted them independence in 1983, and Prime Minister Kennedy Alphonse Simmonds, who pledges national economic diversification, currently heads the government of this twin-island state. Ninety percent of the country's economy is based on sugar exports, thus leaving the welfare of the citizenry dependent on the fluctuating international sugar market. Damage from Hurricane Hugo devastated 1990 sugar yields, and this hardship, combined with labor disputes over the importation of foreign harvest workers, has led to some highly visible political protests.

Saint Lucia

Geography Location: southeastern Caribbean Sea, between Martinique to N and St. Vincent to SW. Castries 14°01'N, 60°59'W. **Boundaries:** St. Lucia Channel to N, Atlantic Ocean to E, St. Vincent Passage to S, Caribbean Sea to W. **Total land area:** 239 sq. mi. (620 sq km). **Coastline:** 98 mi. (158 km). **Comparative area:** about 3.5 times size of Washington, D.C. **Land use:** 8% arable land; 20% permanent crops; 5% meadows and pastures; 13% forest and woodland; 54% other; includes 2% irrigated. **Major cities:** (1992 est.) Castries (capital) 53,883.

People Population: 145,090 (1994 est.). **Nationality:** noun—St. Lucian(s); adjective—St. Lucian. **Ethnic groups:** 90.3% African descent, 5.5% mixed, 3.2% East Indian, 0.8% Caucasian. **Languages:** English (official), French patois. **Religions:** 90% Roman Catholic, 7% Protestant, 3% Church of England.

Government Type: independent state within Commonwealth, recognizing Elizabeth II as chief of state. **Independence:** Feb. 22, 1979 (from UK). **Constitution:** Feb. 22, 1979. **National holiday:** Independence Day, Feb. 22. **Heads of government:** Stanislaus James, governor-general (since Oct. 1988); John Compton, prime minister (since May 1982). **Structure:** executive (cabinet headed by prime minister); bicameral legislature (Senate, House of Representatives).

Economy Monetary unit: East Caribbean (EC) dollar. **Budget:** (1990 est.) ***income:*** $121 mil.; ***expend.:*** $127 mil. **GDP:** $433 mil., $3,000 per capita (1993 est.). **Chief crops:** bananas, coconuts, sugar, cocoa, spices. **Livestock:** sheep, cattle, goats, pigs. **Natural resources:** forests, sandy beaches, minerals (pumice), mineral springs, geothermal potential. **Major industries:** clothing, assembly of electronic components, beverages. **Labor force:** 43,800 (1983 est.); 43.4% agriculture, 38.9% services, 17.7% industry and commerce; 30% unemployment (1984).

Exports: $122.8 mil. (f.o.b., 1992); 54% bananas, 17% clothing, cocoa, vegetables, fruits. **Imports:** $276 mil. (f.o.b., 1992); 22% manufactured goods, 21% machinery and transport equipment, 20% food and live animals. **Major trading partners:** ***exports:*** 55% UK, 21% CARICOM, 18% U.S.; ***imports:*** 33% U.S., 16% UK, 15% CARICOM, 7% Japan.

Intl. Orgs. FAO, G-77, IBRD, ICAO, IDA, IFAD, IFC, ILO, IMF, IMO, NAM, OAS, UN, UNESCO, UPU, WHO, WMO.

In 1650 the French settled St. Lucia, which was ceded to Britain in 1814. A member of the Federation of the West Indies from 1958 to 1962, St. Lucia became internally self-governing in 1967 but was still under Great Britain's protection. In 1979 St. Lucia gained full independence and now enjoys stable competitive politics. Hurricane Allen destroyed many of the country's banana plantations in 1980, and the economy is still recovering from the disaster. The current government of Prime Minister John Compton of the United Workers party has pledged agrarian reform and proposed legalizing gambling to stimulate tourism.

Saint Vincent and the Grenadines

Geography Location: large island of St. Vincent (13°12'N, 61°14'W) and about 50 smaller islands in southeastern Caribbean Sea about 21 mi. (34 km) SW of St. Lucia and 100 mi. (160 km) W of Barbados. **Boundaries:** St. Vincent Passage to N, Atlantic Ocean to E and SE, Caribbean Sea to SW and W. **Total land area:** 131 sq. mi. (340 sq km). **Coastline:** 52 mi. (84 km). **Comparative area:** about twice size of Washington, D.C. **Land use:** 38% arable land; 12% permanent crops; 6% meadows and pastures; 41% forest and woodland; 3% other; includes 3% irrigated. **Major cities:** (1991 census) Kingstown (capital) 15,670.

People Population: 115,437 (1994 est.). **Nationality:** noun—St. Vincentian(s) or Vincentian(s); adjective—St. Vincentian or Vincentian. **Ethnic groups:** mainly of black African descent, remainder mixed, with some white, East Indian, and Carib Indian. **Languages:** English, French patois. **Religions:** Anglican, Methodist, Roman Catholic, Seventh-day Adventist.

Government Type: independent state within Commonwealth, recognizing Elizabeth II as chief of state. **Independence:** Oct. 27, 1979 (from UK). **Constitution:** Oct. 27, 1979. **National holiday:** Independence Day, Oct. 27. **Heads of government:** David Jack, governor-general (since Sept. 1989); James Mitchell, prime minister (since July 1984). **Structure:** bicameral legislature—13-member elected House of Representatives and 6-member appointed Senate; judiciary—Supreme Court.

Economy Monetary unit: East Caribbean (EC) dollar. **Budget:** (1990 est.) ***income:*** $62 mil.; ***expend.:*** $67 mil. **GDP:** $215 mil., $2,000 per capita (1992 est.). **Chief crops:** bananas, arrowroot. **Livestock:** sheep, cattle, pigs, goats. **Natural resources:** negl. **Major industries:** food processing (sugar, flour), cement, furniture. **Labor force:** 67,000 (1984 est.); 35% unemployed (1986). **Exports:** $77.5 mil. (f.o.b., 1992); 45% bananas, eddoes and dasheen (taro), sweet potatoes, spices. **Imports:** $118.6 mil. (f.o.b., 1992); foodstuffs, machinery and equipment, chemicals and fertilizers, minerals and fuels. **Major trading partners:** ***exports:*** 43% UK, 37% CARICOM, 15% U.S.; ***imports:*** 42% U.S., 19% CARICOM, 15% UK.

Intl. Orgs. CARICOM, Commonwealth, FAO, G-77, IBRD, ICAO, IDA, IFAD, IMF, IMO, OAS, UN, UNESCO, UPU, WHO.

Although ceded to Britain in 1763, St. Vincent was inhabited by the fierce Carib Indians, who continued fighting for control of the island until 1796, when they had all been either killed or deported. Just prior to its independence in 1979, St. Vincent and the Grenadines was a self-governing state in association with Great Britain. It is one of the poorest countries in the West Indies. Several natural disasters have plagued the economy, including a 1979 volcanic eruption and two destructive hurricanes in 1980 and 1986. Prime Minister James Mitchell of the New Democratic party currently governs the country.

San Marino

Republic of San Marino

Geography Location: on slopes of Mt. Titano, in the Apennines, within central Italian region of Emilia-Romagna. **Boundaries:** surrounded by Italian territory. **Total land area:** 23 sq. mi. (60 sq km). **Coastline:** none. **Comparative area:** about three-tenths size of Washington, D.C. **Land use:** 17% arable land; 0% permanent crops; 0% meadows and pastures; 0% forest and woodland; 83% other. **Major cities:** (1990 est.) San Marino (capital) 4,185.

People Population: 24,091 (1994 est.). **Nationality:** noun—Sanmarinese (sing., pl.); adjective—Sanmarinese. **Ethnic groups:** N.A. **Languages:** Italian. **Religions:** Roman Catholic.

Government Type: republic. **Independence:** N.A. **Constitution:** Oct. 8, 1600; electoral law of 1926 serves some of functions of constitution. **National holiday:** Anniversary of the Liberation of the Republic, Feb. 5. **Heads of government:** Lonfernini Settimio, president (since Sept. 1995); Dr. Gabriele Gatti, minister of foreign affairs (since July 1986). **Structure:** executive—two captain-regents with six-month terms; actual power wielded by secretary of state for foreign affairs and secretary of state for internal affairs; legislative—Grand and General Council elected by popular vote for five-year terms; Congress of State whose members head administrative departments; judicial—Council of Twelve is supreme judicial body.

Economy Monetary unit: Italian lire. **Budget:** (1991) ***income:*** $275 mil.; ***expend:*** $275 mil. **GDP:** $370 mil., $16,000 per capita (1992 est.). **Chief crops:** wheat, grapes, other grains, fruits, vegetables. **Livestock:** N.A. **Natural resources:** building stones. **Major industries:** wine, olive oil, cement. **Labor force:** about 4,300. **Exports:** trade data included with Italian statistics; commodity trade consisting primarily of exchanging building stone, lime, wood, chestnuts, wheat, and wine for a wide variety of consumer manufactures. **Imports:** see exports. **Major trading partners:** N.A.

Intl. Orgs. IMF, ITU, NAM (observer status), OSCE, UN, UPU, WHO.

The "Most Serene Republic" of San Marino, entirely surrounded by Italy near the city of Rimini, is the oldest republic in the world, with communitarian roots dating to the fourth century A.D. While Piedmont-Sardinia was conquering all of the rest of the Italian peninsula during the period 1860–70, it left San Marino independent; the new kingdom of Italy signed a treaty of friendship and cooperation with the republic in 1862.

Leftist coalitions governed from 1978 through 1986, giving San Marino the only Communist government west of the Soviet bloc. Since 1986 the government has been controlled by a coalition of Communists and Christian Democrats. In 1992 San Marino joined the United Nations.

The economy is balanced between small-scale agriculture (primarily wine grapes and livestock) and industry, including textiles, ceramics, and furniture. Philatelic sales and tourism are important sources of revenue. Lacking extremes of wealth and poverty and with low unemployment, the republic enjoys general prosperity.

São Tomé and Príncipe

Democratic Republic of São Tomé and Príncipe

Geography Location: two main islands, São Tomé (0°19'N, 6°43'E) and Príncipe, and Caroço, Pedras, Tinhosas (off Príncipe), and Rolas (off São Tomé), off west coast of Africa. **Boundaries:** west of Gabon in Gulf of Guinea. **Total land area:** 371 sq. mi. (960 sq km). **Coastline:** 130 mi. (209 km). **Comparative area:** about 5.5 times size of Washington, D.C. **Land use:** 1% arable land; 36% permanent crops; 1% meadows and pastures; 0% forest and woodland; 62% other. **Major cities:** São Tomé (capital).

People Population: 136,780 (1994 est.). **Nationality:** noun—São Toméan(s); adjective—São Toméan. **Ethnic groups:** Mestiço, Angolares (descendants of Angolan slaves), Servicais (contract laborers from Angola, Mozambique, and Cape Verde), Tongas (children of Servicais born on the islands), and Europeans (primarily Portuguese). **Languages:** Portuguese (official). **Religions:** Roman Catholic, Evangelical, Protestant, Seventh-day Adventist.

Government Type: republic. **Independence:** July 12, 1975 (from Portugal). **Constitution:** Nov. 5, 1975, approved Dec. 15, 1982. **National holiday:** Independence Day, July 12. **Heads of government:** Miguel dos Anjos da Cunha Trovoada, president (since Apr. 1991); Dr. Carlos Alberto Monteiro Deas Da Graça, prime minister (since Oct. 1994). **Structure:** executive—president assisted by cabinet of ministers; unicameral legislature—40-member National People's Assembly, elected for five years.

Economy **Monetary unit:** dobra. **Budget:** (1989) ***income:*** $10.2 mil.; ***expend.:*** $36.8 mil. **GDP:** $50 mil., $450 per capita (1990). **Chief crops:** cash crops—cocoa, copra, coconuts, coffee, palm oil, bananas. **Livestock:** goats, pigs, cattle, sheep. **Natural resources:** fish. **Major industries:** small processing factories producing shirts, soap, beer; fish and shrimp processing. **Labor force:** 21,096 (1981); subsistence agriculture and fishing; some unemployment; labor shortages on plantations and for skilled workers; 56% of population of working age (1983). **Exports:** $5.4 mil. (f.o.b., 1992 est.); 90% cocoa, 7% copra, coffee, palm oil. **Imports:** $31.5 mil. (f.o.b., 1992 est.); food products, machinery and electrical equipment, fuels. **Major trading partners:** ***exports:*** Germany, Netherlands, China; ***imports:*** Portugal, Germany, Angola, China.

Intl. Orgs. FAO, G-77, IBRD, ICAO, IDA, IFAD, IFC, ILO, IMF, ITU, NAM, UN, UNESCO, UPU, WHO, WMO.

The islands of São Tomé and Príncipe, located in the Atlantic Ocean 275 and 125 miles, respectively, off the northern coast of Gabon, make up one of Africa's smallest nations. They were uninhabited when first discovered by the Portuguese in 1470 but by the mid-1500s became Africa's foremost exporter of sugar. As the sugar market declined, the islands became a major slave-trading center and producer of coffee and cocoa. By 1908 São Tomé was the world's largest cocoa producer.

Portugal did not abolish slavery until 1876, and abusive labor practices continued until well into the 20th century. In 1953 hundreds of workers were killed in clashes with the Portuguese. Soon after, a small number of São Toméans formed the Movement for the Liberation of São Tomé and Príncipe (MLSTP) with its base in Gabon. But the islands did not gain independence until July 12, 1975.

The MLSTP took over after independence and became the country's only official party. By 1986 the country relied on foreign aid for approximately 41 percent of its gross national product. Although in the past it received military advisers from the former Soviet Union and economic advisers from Cuba, São Tomé and Príncipe has announced a foreign policy based upon nonalignment. Multiparty democracy was introduced in 1991.

Saudi Arabia

Kingdom of Saudi Arabia

Geography **Location:** occupies four-fifths of Arabian peninsula in southwestern Asia. **Boundaries:** Jordan, Iraq, and Kuwait to N, Persian Gulf, Qatar, and United Arab Emirates to E, Oman to SE, Yemen to S and SE, Red Sea to W. **Total land area:** 756,982 sq. mi. (1,960,582 sq km). **Coastline:** 1,559 mi. (2,510 km). **Comparative area:** about size of Texas and Alaska combined. **Land use:** 1% arable land; negl. % permanent crops; 39% meadows and pastures; 1% forest and woodland; 59% other; includes negl. % irrigated. **Major cities:** (1980 est.) Riyadh (capital) 1,250,000; Jeddah 900,000; Makkah (Mecca) 400,000; Ta'If 203,000; Al-Madinah (Medina) 200,000.

People **Population:** 18,196,783 (1994 est.). **Nationality:** noun—Saudi(s); adjective—Saudi or Saudi Arabian. **Ethnic groups:** 90% Arab, 10% Afro-Asian. **Languages:** Arabic. **Religions:** 100% Muslim.

Government **Type:** monarchy. **Constitution:** none; governed according to Sharia or Islamic law. **National holiday:** Sept. 23. **Head of government:** Fahd ibn Abdul-Aziz al-Saud, king (since June 1982). **Structure:** king rules in consultation with royal family and Council of Ministers.

Economy **Monetary unit:** Saudi riyal. **Budget:** (1993 est.) ***income:*** $39 bil.; ***expend.:*** $50 bil. **GDP:** $194 bil., $11,000 per capita (1993 est.). **Chief crops:** dates, grains, livestock; not self-sufficient in food except for wheat. **Livestock:** sheep, goats, cattle, asses, camels. **Natural resources:** crude oil, natural gas, iron ore, gold, copper. **Major industries:** crude oil production, petroleum refining, basic petrochemicals. **Labor force:** 5 mil.; 34% government, 28% industry and oil, 22% services, 16% agriculture; about 60% are foreign workers; 0% unemployment (1987). **Exports:** $42.3 bil. (f.o.b., 1993 est.); 89% petroleum and petroleum products. **Imports:** $26 bil. (f.o.b., 1993 est.); manufactured goods, transport equipment, construction materials, processed food products. **Major trading partners:** ***exports and reexports:*** 22% U.S., 20% Japan, 7% Singapore, 5% France; ***imports:*** 17% UK, 15% U.S., 12% Japan, 8% Germany, 6% France.

Intl. Orgs. Arab League, FAO, G-77, IAEA, IBRD, ICAO, IDA, IFAD, IFC, ILO, IMF, IMO, INTELSAT, INTERPOL, ITU, NAM, OPEC, UN, UNESCO, UPU, WHO, WMO.

In ancient times various cultures flourished in parts of the Arabian peninsula, particularly along the western rim, in cities devoted to trade between the Gulf of Aden and the eastern Mediterranean, and in such agricultural and trading centers as Yemen and Oman. Cultural and political unity was lacking, however, until the rise of Mohammed, the prophet of Islam. In A.D. 622 Mohammed fled from Mecca, the holy city of Arabian paganism, to the nearby city of Medina; the Islamic era dates from that year. Preaching from Medina, Mohammed soon gained converts to Islam throughout Arabia. His army captured Mecca in 630, converting its sacred shrine, the Kaaba, to an Islamic place of worship. By 632, when Mohammed died, all of Arabia was unified under Islamic rule.

In 661 the Caliphate, the ruling body of early Islam, moved from Medina to Damascus. Thereafter Arabia was nominally unified under Islamic rule—but in practice was usually divided among various principalities in the arable areas and trading centers, and under tribal rule in the arid interior. Mecca fell to the Ottoman Empire in 1517, but Ottoman control of Arabia was never complete. The rise of the Wahabi sect of Islam in the 18th century posed a challenge to Ottoman rule. In the 19th century, the Saud family rose to leadership in the Wahabi movement and established a kingdom in Nejd, the central region of Arabia, with a capital at Riyadh.

In 1902 Ibn Saud (1880–1953) consolidated his family's control at Riyadh and in 1912–13 led a new Wahabi revolt against the Ottoman Turks. During World War I, the British aided Ibn Saud's rebellion in the Nejd, along with that of Ibn Saud's rival Hussein ibn Ali in the Hejaz, in the mountains of western Arabia along the coast of the Red Sea. A British protectorate was established in both regions in 1915, and Great Britain maintained a dominant position in Arabia immediately after World War I.

In 1924 Ibn Saud captured Hussein ibn Ali's capital at Mecca, and he proclaimed himself king of Hejaz in 1926 and of Nejd in 1927. Ibn Saud consolidated his control over the following two years, and his kingdom was formally recognized by Great Britain in 1927. The country was renamed Saudi Arabia in 1932.

Saudi Arabia is an absolute monarchy based on Islamic law; it has no written constitution and no parliament. The king exercises sole authority and rules in consultation with a Council of Ministers. Islamic law is enforced; alcohol is prohibited and the public activities of women severely restricted. The Saudi kings have great power within the Islamic world through their control over the holy cities of Mecca and Medina and their administration of the annual Muslim pilgrimages to those cities.

The discovery of oil in eastern Arabia in the early 1930s rapidly transformed Saudi Arabia from an impoverished nation to a center of great wealth. In 1933 an exclusive concession for the exploitation of Saudi Arabian oil was granted to an American-chartered corporation, the Arabian-American Oil Company (Aramco). For many years wealth remained concentrated in the hands of the Saudi clan, and little change was felt in the desert interior, where Bedouin nomads continued to raise sheep and camels. Large numbers of Yemenis, Palestinians, Pakistanis, and other foreign workers are employed in the oil fields.

Saudi Arabia remained neutral during most of World War II but declared war on the Axis powers in March 1945; in the same year, it became a founding member of both the United Nations and the Arab League.

Ibn Saud became a leader of Arab anti-Zionism and contributed a small contingent of troops to the 1948 Arab-Israeli War. That policy was maintained by Ibn Saud's second son and successor, King Faisal, who instituted a policy of providing large annual subsidies to Egypt and other Arab League states following the 1967 Arab-Israeli War. In 1973 King Faisal sent Saudi units to fight in the Arab-Israeli War of that year. He played a leading role in organizing the 1973–74 Arab oil embargo in an effort to force the United States and its allies to take a harder line with Israel.

King Faisal was assassinated by his nephew, Prince Faisal, on Mar. 25, 1975, and was succeeded by King Khalid. Little change in policy resulted. In 1979 Saudi Arabia denounced the Camp David talks and the Egyptian-Israeli peace treaty and led the Arab League effort to ostracize Egypt within the Arab world.

At the same time, Saudi Arabia has consistently opposed leftist and radical movements in the Arab world, sending troops to help put down leftist rebellions in North Yemen and Oman in the 1970s. The Saudi kings have taken a moderate approach toward Arab relations with the West. Following the transfer of Aramco assets to full Saudi Arabian ownership during 1973–76, Saudi Arabia used its leading position within the Organization of Petroleum Exporting Countries (OPEC) to argue for a policy of stable production and prices.

This moderate policy has been rewarded by the willingness of the United States, Great Britain, France, and other Western nations to sell arms—including jet fighters, tanks, and other sophisticated weapons—to Saudi Arabia despite Israeli protests. The multibillion-dollar arms trade has helped to offset the Western oil trade deficit with Saudi Arabia.

Saudi Arabia experienced repeated disturbances in the 1980s. Muslim fundamentalist terrorists seized the Grand Mosque at Mecca on Nov. 20, 1979, provoking a crisis for the Saudi monarchy. On July 31, 1987, Iranian pilgrims rioted in Mecca and were fired upon by Saudi security forces; 402 persons died, including 275 Iranians. Iran's Ayatollah Khomeini denounced the Saudi government and said it was unworthy of being the guardian of Islam's sacred shrines.

A long-time supporter of the Palestine Liberation Organization, the Saudi government gave the PLO $850 million during the 1980s, but ceased when the PLO backed Saddam Hussein's invasion of Kuwait in 1990.

On Aug. 5, 1990, King Fahd granted permission to station U.S. troops in Saudi Arabia to guard against a possible Iraqi attack. The Saudis promised the United States $16.8 billion and Egypt $1.5 billion to defray the costs of their military presence in the Persian Gulf. While little ground fighting took place on Saudi soil, there were missile attacks on Riyadh, Dhahran, and elsewhere, and massive oil spills threatened the operation of crucial desalination plants in the Persian Gulf.

Since the war, Saudi Arabia has played a prominent and pivotal role in the diplomatic efforts of the United States and its allies to reach a permanent accord in the Middle East.

Senegal

Republic of Senegal

Geography Location: northwestern coast of Africa. **Boundaries:** Mauritania to N, Mali to E, Guinea and Guinea-Bissau to S, Atlantic Ocean to W; The Gambia forms narrow enclave extending 200 mi. (320 km) inland from Atlantic coast. **Total land area:** 75,749 sq. mi. (196,190 sq km). **Coastline:** 330 mi. (531 km). **Comparative area:** between North Dakota and South Dakota. **Land use:** 27% arable land; 0% permanent crops; 30% meadows and pastures; 31% forest and woodland; 12% other; includes 1% irrigated. **Major cities:** (1979 est.) Dakar (capital) 850,000; Thiès 120,000; Kaolack 110,000.

People Population: 8,730,508 (1994 est.). **Nationality:** noun—Senegalese (sing., pl.); adjective—Senegalese. **Ethnic groups:** 36% Wolof, 17% Fulani, 17% Serer, 9% Toucouleur, 9% Diola, 9% Mandingo, 1% European and Lebanese. **Languages:** French (official), Wolof, Pulaar, Diola, Mandingo. **Religions:** 92% Muslim, 6% indigenous beliefs, 2% Christian (mostly Roman Catholic).

Government Type: republic under multiparty democratic rule; on Feb. 1, 1982, Senegal and The Gambia formed loose confederation named Senegambia that calls for eventual integration of their armed forces and economic cooperation. **Independence:** Apr. 4, 1960 (from France). **Constitution:** Mar. 3, 1963 (formally signed agreement of confederation with The Gambia Dec. 12, 1981, effective Feb. 1, 1982, as Senegambia). **National holiday:** Independence Day, Apr. 4. **Heads of government:** Abdou Diouf, president (since Jan. 1981); Habib Thiam, prime minister (since Apr. 1991). **Structure:** executive—president; legislative—unicameral 120-member National Assembly, elected for five-year term by universal suffrage; judiciary—Supreme Court, members appointed by president.

Economy Monetary unit: Communauté Financière Africaine (CFA) franc. **Budget:** (1992 est.) ***income:*** $1.2 bil.; ***expend.:*** $1.2 bil. **GDP:** $11.8 bil., $1,400 per capita (1993 est.). **Chief crops:** peanuts (primary cash crop), millet, sorghum, manioc, maize, rice; deficit production of food. **Livestock:** sheep, cattle, goats, asses, horses. **Natural resources:** fish, phosphates, iron ore. **Major industries:** fishing, agricultural processing, phosphate mining. **Labor force:** 2.5 mil. (1985); 77% subsistence agricultural workers; 175,000 wage earners—60% government and parapublic, 40% private sector; 52% of working age. **Exports:** $904 mil. (f.o.b., 1991 est.); 30% manufactures, 27% fish products, 11% peanuts, 11% petroleum products, 10% phosphates. **Imports:** $1.2 bil. (c.i.f., 1991 est.); 30% semimanufactures, 27% food, 17% durable consumer goods, 14% capital goods, 12% petroleum. **Major trading partners:** ***exports:*** France, other EU countries, Ivory Coast, India; ***imports:*** France, other EU countries, Nigeria, Algeria, China, Japan.

Intl. Orgs. FAO, G-77, IAEA, IBRD, ICAO, IDA, IFAD, IFC, ILO, IMF, IMO, INTELSAT, INTERPOL, ITU, NAM, UN, UNESCO, UPU, WHO, WIPO, WMO, WTO.

Inhabited since ancient times, Senegal was dominated in the 13th and 14th centuries by the Mandingo and Jolof empires. Portuguese traders and explorers arrived in Senegal in the early 15th century and later competed with the British, Dutch, and French for domination in Senegal. The French established a trading station at Saint-Louis in 1659 and maintained possession thereafter, except for the British enclave along the Gambia River.

In the early 19th century, the French began a series of campaigns to bring the entire country under their control; the last independent sultanate surrendered in 1893. Senegal became a French colony in 1920, and Dakar became the capital of French West Africa. Senegal became a major contributor of African troops to the French armed forces.

In 1946 a territorial assembly was established, with a limited electorate and advisory powers, which were gradually expanded in subsequent years. With the creation of the French Community of Nations in 1958, Senegal achieved local self-rule within the community.

In 1959, with the encouragement of France, Senegal and French Sudan (now Mali) formed the Federation of Mali, which became fully independent on June 20, 1960. Senegal seceded from the federation on Aug. 20 and declared itself the Republic of Senegal. Leopold Sedar Senghor, one of Africa's leading statesmen, became Senegal's first president.

In 1962 Prime Minister Mamdou Dia attempted a coup against the Senghor government; it failed, and Dia was imprisoned. A new constitution was subsequently adopted, strengthening the power of the presidency. Senghor retired from office in 1981 and was succeeded by Adbou Diouf. He encouraged political pluralism and has presided over a generally stable and democratic government. Diouf was elected in his own right in 1983 and reelected in 1988. Following the 1988 elections, riots broke out over charges of electoral fraud, and a state of emergency was declared.

Diouf, who has taken a lead in African affairs, was reelected for the third time in 1993, but his Socialist party's legislative majority was diminished. Since 1982, Senegal has been troubled by a separatist insurgency fought by the Movement of Democratic Forces of Casamance, a northern region, and despite the creation of a joint commission to study the problem, fighting continues. In 1989, there were border clashes with Mauritania, but full diplomatic relations were restored in 1992. In 1982, Senegal established the confederation of Senegambia with The Gambia, which it surrounds on three sides, but it was dissolved in 1989.

Senegal remains closely tied to France commercially, culturally, and in foreign affairs. Beginning in the mid-1980s, there has been a surge in illegal immigration of Senegalese to the United States.

Senegal's economy is primarily agricultural. Industries include fishing and fish processing (the principal source of export earnings), food processing, light manufacturing, and phosphate mining. Senegalese merchants are active in commercial networks throughout West Africa.

Serbia

See "Yugoslavia."

Seychelles

Republic of Seychelles

Geography Location: more than 90 widely scattered islands in western Indian Ocean about 1,000 mi. (1,600 km) E of Kenya and Tanzania. Victoria (Mahé Is.) 4°37'S, 55°28'E. **Boundaries:** surrounded by Indian Ocean; nearest neighbor is Madagascar about 130 mi. (210 km) S of southernmost island group. **Total land area:** 176 sq. mi. (455 sq km). **Coastline:** 305 mi. (491 km). **Comparative area:** about 2.5 times the size of Washington, D.C. **Land use:** 4% arable land; 18% permanent crops; 0% meadows and pastures; 18% forest and woodland; 60% other. **Major cities:** (1987) Victoria (capital) 24,325 (includes suburbs).

People Population: 72,113 (1994 est.). **Nationality:** noun—Seychellois (sing., pl.); adjective—Seychelles. **Ethnic groups:** Seychellois (mixture of Asians, Africans, Europeans). **Languages:** English, French (official); Creole. **Religions:** 90% Roman Catholic, 8% Anglican, 2% other.

Government Type: republic; member of Commonwealth. **Independence:** June 29, 1976 (from UK). **Constitution:** June 5, 1979. **National holiday:** June 5 and 29. **Head of government:** France Albert René, president (since June 1977). **Structure:** president; Council of Ministers; People's Assembly (25 members—23 elected and two appointed by president for four-year terms).

Economy Monetary unit: Seychelles rupee. **Budget:** (1991 est.) ***income***: $172 mil.; ***expend.***: $181 mil. **GDP:** $407 mil., $5,900 per capita (1992 est.). **Chief crops:** islands depend largely on coconut production and export of copra; cinnamon, vanilla, green leaf tea, and patchouli (used for perfumes) are other cash crops; food crops—small quantities of sweet potatoes, cassava, sugarcane, and bananas; islands not self-sufficient in foodstuffs and bulk of supply must be imported. **Livestock:** pigs, goats, cattle. **Natural resources:** fish, copra, cinnamon trees. **Major industries:** tourism is largest industry; processing of coconut and vanilla, fishing. **Labor force:** formal employment (all sectors)—38.4% government, 30.7% parastatal, 30.8% private; formal employment (by sector)—49.0% industry and commerce, 39.0% services, 11.5% agriculture, forestry, and fishing (1984 est.); 57% of population of working age (1983). **Exports:** $47 mil. (f.o.b., 1992 est.); fish, copra, cinnamon bark; reexports—petroleum products. **Imports:** $186 mil. (c.i.f., 1992 est.); manufactured goods, food, tobacco, beverages, machinery and transport equipment. **Major trading partners:** ***exports***: 63% France, 12% Pakistan, 10% Réunion, 7% UK; ***imports***: 20% UK, 14% France, 13% South Africa, 13% South Yemen, 8% Singapore, 6% Japan.

Intl. Orgs. FAO, G-77, IBRD, ICAO, IFAD, IFC, ILO, IMF, IMO, INTERPOL, NAM, UN, UNESCO, UPU, WHO, WMO.

The Seychelles Islands were occupied by France in the 18th century and seized by Great Britain in 1794. They were administered along with Mauritius until 1903, when the Seychelles became a separate British colony. African and Indian workers were brought in to work in coconut and spice plantations and in guano mining. The present population is of mixed African, Indian, and European descent.

In the post–World War II period, a home-rule government rejected independence as impracticable. At the urging of the Organization of African Unity and the United Nations, the Seychelles declared independence on June 29, 1976. Its first president was ousted in a socialist coup in 1977 led by Prime Minister France Albert René. A new constitution, promulgated in March 1979, formalized one-party Socialist rule. In July 1992 a commission was elected to rewrite the constitution before the end of the year, but the delegates defeated the first results.

Since independence, the economy of the Seychelles has become heavily dependent on the tourist industry, which accounts for 90 percent of the country's foreign exchange earnings. Fishing accounts for 40 percent of exports.

Sierra Leone

Republic of Sierra Leone

Geography Location: west central Africa. **Boundaries:** Guinea to N and E, Liberia to S, Atlantic Ocean to W. **Total land area:** 27,699 sq. mi. (71,740 sq km). **Coastline:** 250 mi. (402 km). **Comparative area:** between West Virginia and South Carolina. **Land use:** 23% arable land; 2% permanent crops; 31% meadows and pastures; 29% forest and woodland; 15% other; includes negl. % irrigated. **Major cities:** Freetown (capital) 469,776 (1985 census); Koidu 80,000; Bo 26,000; Kenema 13,000; Makeni 12,000.

People Population: 4,630,037 (1994 est.). **Nationality:** noun—Sierra Leonean(s); adjective—Sierra Leonean. **Ethnic groups:** over 99% African (30% Temne, 30% Mende, 2% Creole), rest European and Asian. **Languages:** English (official); regular use limited to literate minority; principal languages are Mende in south and Temne in north; Krio is language of resettled ex-slave population of Freetown area and is lingua franca. **Religions:** 30% Muslim, 30% indigenous beliefs, 10% Christian, 30% other or none.

Government Type: republic under presidential regime since Apr. 1971. **Independence:** Apr. 27, 1961 (from UK). **Constitution:** June 14, 1978. **National holiday:** Republic Day, Apr. 19. **Heads of government:** Capt. Valentine Esegragbo Melvine Strasser, president (since May 1992). **Structure:** executive—president; legislature—unicameral Parliament consists of 104 authorized seats, 85 of which are filled by elected representatives of constituencies and 12 by Paramount Chiefs elected by fellow Paramount Chiefs in each district; president authorized to appoint up to seven members; judiciary.

Economy Monetary unit: leone. **Budget:** (1992 est.) ***income:*** $68 mil.; ***expend.:*** $118 mil. **GDP:** $4.5 bil., $1,000 per capita (1993 est.). **Chief crops:** palm kernels, coffee, cocoa, rice, yams; much of cultivated land devoted to subsistence farming; food crops insufficient for domestic consumption. **Livestock:** cattle, sheep, goats, pigs. **Natural resources:** diamonds, titanium ore, bauxite, iron ore, gold, chromite. **Major industries:** mining (diamonds, iron ore, bauxite, rutile), small-scale manufacturing (beverages, textiles, cigarettes, footwear), petroleum refinery. **Labor force:** about 1.5 mil. (1981); 65% agriculture, 19% industry, 16% services; only small minority, some 65,000, earn wages; 55% of population of working age (1985). **Exports:** $149 mil. (f.o.b., FY92); 50% rutile, 17% bauxite, 11% cocoa, 3% diamonds. **Imports:** $131 mil. (c.i.f., FY92); 40% capital goods, 32% foods, 12% petroleum, 7% consumer goods. **Major trading partners:** ***exports:*** U.S., UK, Netherlands, Germany, other Western European countries; ***imports:*** U.S., EU, Japan, China.

Intl. Orgs. Commonwealth, FAO, G-77, IAEA, IBRD, ICAO, IDA, IFAD, IFC, ILO, IMF, IMO, INTERPOL, ITU, NAM, UN, UNESCO, UPU, WHO, WMO, WTO.

Portuguese domination of the Sierra Leone coast began in 1462. English explorers, including Francis Drake, arrived in the late 16th century. Europeans traded for slaves in Sierra Leone, but in 1787 Freetown was founded by the British Sierra Leone Co. as a haven for freed slaves. The settlement was populated by former slaves from Great Britain, North America, and the Caribbean, and later by slaves liberated from slave trading ships by the British navy.

Sierra Leone was reorganized as a British colony in 1808. The ex-slave population, from diverse tribal and national backgrounds, developed an English-speaking Creole culture unique in Africa. Freetown became the center of British colonial administration and trade in West Africa and was the focus of missionary-supported projects in education, health care, and economic development.

The native peoples of Sierra Leone staged numerous rebellions against the British and the Creole elite; resentment focused on the tax system and on the privileges of the English-speaking descendents of ex-slaves.

During the 20th century, home rule developed through an elected advisory legislature. In 1951 a constitutional framework had been developed as the basis of decolonization. Sir Milton Margei became chief minister in 1953, and prime minister in 1961. Full independence came on Apr. 27, 1971. The last ties with the British Crown were cut in 1971, when Sierra Leone became a republic. A referendum in 1978, implemented in 1979, created a one-party state. In 1984 and 1985 student and public employee protests against the government led to riots and the restoration of multiparty elections.

In April 1992, Momoh was ousted in a coup that brought to power Capt. Valentine Strasser and a National Provisional Ruling Council. Despite a wealth of natural resources, Sierra Leone's economy has been burdened by mismanagement and corruption. Since 1990, the government has also participated in the joint West African peacekeeping force in neighboring Liberia, fighting from which has spilled across the border.

A rebel army, the Revolutionary United Front, has been disturbing the peace for several years. An attack on the northern town of Kambia in 1994 resulted in 30,000 refugees.

Singapore

Republic of Singapore

Geography Location: Singapore Island and some 57 islets off southern Malay peninsula (linked by a causeway). **Boundaries:** Johor Strait to N; Pacific Ocean to E; Strait of Malacca to SW, separating Singapore from Indonesian island of Sumatra; and Indian Ocean to W. **Total land area:** 244 sq. mi. (633 sq km). **Coastline:** 120 mi. (193 km). **Comparative area:** about 3.5 times size of Washington, D.C. **Land use:** 4% arable land; 7% permanent crops; 0% meadows and pastures; 5% forest and woodland; 84% other. **Major cities:** Singapore (capital).

People Population: 2,859,142 (1994 est.). **Nationality:** noun—Singaporean(s); adjective—Singapore. **Ethnic groups:** 76.4% Chinese, 14.9% Malay, 6.4% Indian, 2.3% other. **Languages:** Chinese, Malay, Tamil, and English (official); Malay (national). **Religions:** majority of Chinese are Buddhists or atheists; Malays nearly all Muslim; minorities include Christians, Hindus, Sikhs, Taoists, Confucianists.

Government Type: republic. **Independence:** Aug. 9, 1965 (from Malaysia). **Constitution:** June 3, 1959, amended 1965; based on preindependence State of Singapore constitution. **National holiday:** Aug. 9. **Heads of government:** Ong Teng Cheong, president (since Sept. 1993); Goh Chok Tong, prime minister (since Nov. 1990). **Structure:** ceremonial president; executive power exercised by prime minister and cabinet responsible to unicameral legislature (Parliament).

Economy Monetary unit: Singapore dollar. **Budget:** (1993) ***income:*** $11.9 bil.; ***expend.:*** $10.5 bil. **GDP:** $42.4 bil., $15,000 per capita (1993 est.). **Chief crops:** agriculture occupies position of minor importance in economy; self-sufficient in pork, poultry, and eggs; must import much of its other food requirements; major crops—rubber, copra, fruits, vegetables. **Livestock:** N.A. **Natural resources:** negl. **Major industries:** petroleum refining, electronics, oil drilling equipment. **Labor force:** 1.48 mil.; 29% services, 22.4% trade; 3.3% unemployment (1988 est.). **Exports:** $61.5 bil. (f.o.b., 1992); includes transshipments to Malaysia—petroleum products, rubber, electronics, manufactured goods. **Imports:** $66.4 bil. (f.o.b., 1992); includes transshipments to Malaysia—capital equipment, petroleum, chemicals, manufactured goods. **Major trading partners:** ***exports:*** 21% U.S., 14% EU, 13% Malaysia, 9% Japan; ***imports:*** 20% Japan, 16% U.S., 14% Malaysia, 13% EU.

Intl. Orgs. ASEAN, Colombo Plan, Commonwealth, G-77, IAEA, IBRD, ICAO, IFC, ILO, IMF, IMO, INTELSAT, INTERPOL, ITU, NAM, UN, UNESCO, UPU, WHO, WMO, WTO.

Singapore was founded in 1819 by Sir Thomas Stamford Raffles on land ceded to the East India Company by the sultanate of Johore (see "Malaysia"). An Anglo-Dutch treaty turned Singapore over to the British Crown in 1824, and eventually it was administered as part of the Straits Settlements. With its excellent harbor, Singapore quickly eclipsed Penang and Malacca as the dominant port for trade through the Straits of Malacca.

Fortified as a bastion of British defense in Southeast Asia, Singapore was overrun from the rear by Japanese troops in February 1942. The British reoccupied the city of Singapore in September 1945 and reorganized Singapore as a British colony in 1946. On June 5, 1959, Singapore became a self-governing parliamentary democracy within the British Commonwealth. Lee Kwan Yew, head of the People's Action party, became prime minister. On Sept. 16, 1963, Singapore, along with Malaya, Sarawak, and Sabah, formed the Malaysian Federation. Singapore, ethnically Chinese, was uncomfortable within the Malay-dominated federation and seceded after two years, becoming an independent nation on Aug. 9, 1965.

Independent Singapore has enjoyed orderly, if authoritarian, government, steady economic growth, and a high standard of living. Still a major port, its economy now also encompasses international banking, finance, communications, high-technology manufacturing, and tourism. The reporting of financial and political scandals in the international press in the 1980s led to restrictions on the domestic circulation of some foreign periodicals. On Nov. 26, 1990, Lee Kuan Yew, Singapore's only prime minister since independence and the longest serving prime minister in the world, resigned. He was succeeded by Goh Chok Tong, but he remains a force in Singapore's political life.

Slovakia

Slovak Republic

Geography Location: Central Europe. **Boundaries:** Czech Republic and Poland to N, Ukraine to E, Hungary to S, Austria to W. **Total land area:** 18,859 sq. mi. (48,845 sq km). **Coastline:** none. **Comparative area:** about half the size of Indiana. **Land use:** N.A. **Major cities:** (1992 est.) Bratislava (capital) 446,655; Košice 237,336; Nitra 90,866; Prešov 90,069, Banská Bystrica 85,631.

People Population: 5,403,505 (1994 est.). **Nationality:** noun—Slovak(s); adjective—Slovak. **Ethnic groups:** 85.6% Slovak, Hungarian, Polish, Ukrainian, German, Czech. **Languages:** Slovak, Hungarian, Polish. **Religions:** Roman and Greek Catholic, Protestant faiths, Judaism.

Government Type: parliamentary democracy. **Independence:** Jan. 1, 1993 (from Czechoslovakia). **Constitution:** Jan. 1, 1993. **National holiday:** Slovak National Uprising, Aug. 29. **Heads of government:** Michal Kovác, president (since Jan. 1993); Vladimir Mečiar, prime minister (since Dec. 1994). **Structure:** executive—president, prime minister, Council of Ministers; legislative—unicameral (National Council); judicial—Supreme Court.

Economy Monetary unit: Slovak koruna (Sk) (pl. Slovak koruny). **Budget:** (1993 est.) ***income:*** $4.5 bil.; ***expend.:*** $5.2 bil. **GDP:** $31 bil. $5,800 per capita (1993 est.). **Chief crops:** wheat, rye, corn, potatoes, sugar beets. **Livestock:** cattle, pigs, chickens, sheep, goats. **Natural resources:** antimony ore, mercury, iron ore, copper, lead, zinc. **Major industries:** brown coal mining, chemicals, metal working, consumer appliances, fertilizers, plastics, armaments. **Labor force:** 2.5 mil. **Exports:** $5.13 bil (f.o.b., 1993 est.); machinery and transport equipment; chemicals; fuels, minerals and metals; agricultural products. **Imports:** $5.95 bil. (f.o.b., 1993 est.); machinery and transport equipment; fuels and lubricants; manufactured goods; raw materials; chemicals; agricultural products. **Major trading partners:** ***exports:*** Czech Republic, CIS republics, Eastern European countries, Italy, France, UK, U.S.; ***imports:*** Czeck Republic, CIS republics, Germany, Austria, Poland, Switzerland, UK, Italy.

Intl. Orgs. IBRD, ICAO, IDA, IFC, ILO, IMF, ITU, OSCE, UN, UNESCO, UNIDO, UPU, WHO, WIPO, WTO; applying for membership in other international organizations.

Though the Czech and Slovak languages are similar, the two peoples have always been far apart culturally and historically (much like the Letts and Lithuanians). The ninth-century Moravian Empire has been claimed as heritage by both peoples; but with the Magyar invasion of the Pannonian Plain in the 10th century, the Slovaks passed under Hungarian rule for 1,000 years. When in the 19th century a romantic-nationalist revival occurred, the Slovaks, under the leadership of Ludovit Štúr, decided to use their own language in literature (though some of the most prominent writers in the Czech tongue were of Slovak origin, such as the poet Jan Kollár and the historian P.J. Šafarik. Unlike the Czechs, the Slovaks took no part in the revolutions of 1848. They lacked a native aristocracy and bourgeoisie; their national leadership came from wealthy peasants, small-town shopkeepers and, above all, their priests.

In the peacemaking at the end of World War I, as the Austro-Hungarian Empire collapsed, the Czech politicians Beneš and Masaryk claimed to speak for the (nonexistent) Czechoslovak nation. They carried the day despite apparent Slovak loyalty to Hungary and even the opposition of Fr. Hlinka's Slovak Populist party to union with the Czechs. The synthetic "nation" of Czechoslovakia was created, a multinational empire governed by a sort of benevolent democratic dictatorship of the Czechs over the other nations. With the Munich crisis of October 1939, Hitler imposed a federal structure giving Slovakia almost complete autonomy in the renamed Czecho-Slovakia; in the following March, when Hitler obliterated Czech independence, an "independent" Slovakia was formed with Hlinka's successor, Magr Tiso, as president.

But under the circumstances independence was illusory. German protection (against Hungarian revisionism) required complete Slovak accord with Reich foreign policy, including declarations of war on Poland (1939) and on the USSR, the United States, and Great Britain (1941). Domestically, Magr Tiso organized a one-party state with anti-Jewish legislation, half unwilling and half unable to resist the expulsion (and eventual extermination) of 60,000 Jews.

The cement for a restored Czechoslovakia after the war was the Communist tyranny imposed in 1948. But the "Velvet Revolution" in 1989 overturned not only Yalta but also St. Germain and Trianon. While the victory over the Communists was won by an alliance of the Czech Civic Forum and the Slovak Public against Violence, the allies soon fell out. As the Czech premier Václav Klaus pushed for free-market "shock therapy," the Slovak premier Vladimír Meciar defended a slower "Slovak way" to capitalism. Economic differences inflamed by ancient Slovak resentment of the Czech majority led to a much-diminished federal government by the spring of 1992. In the summer the split became the "Velvet Divorce."

In July 1992 Slovak deputies to the federal Parliament blocked the reelection of Václav Havel to the presidency, and the Slovak National Council approved, by a vote of 113 to 24, a declaration of sovereignty. In September the two parliaments agreed to the terms. In accord with a two-to-one ratio of the republics' populations, the military and financial assets of Czechoslovakia were divided. By February even plans for a common currency had gone by the board, with only a customs union linking the two parts of the old state.

On Feb. 15, 1993, the Slovak Parliament elected its first president, Michal Kovác, with Meciar, architect of the divorce, remaining as prime minister. Spiraling inflation and high unemployment coupled with a corruption scandal toppled the Meciar government early in 1994, but a coalition government including many former Communists restored him as prime minister later that year.

Slovenia

See Part I: "Major News Stories of the Year."

Solomon Islands

Geography Location: archipelago in South Pacific E of Papua New Guinea. Honiara (Guadalcanal Is.) 9°28'S, 159°57'E. **Boundaries:** South Pacific Ocean to N, E, and S, Solomon Sea to W; nearest neighbor is Santa Cruz Islands to SE. **Total land area:** 10,985 sq. mi. (28,450 sq km). **Coastline:** 3,302 mi. (5,313 km). **Comparative area:** about size of Maryland. **Land use:** 1% arable land; 1% permanent crops; 1% meadows and pastures; 93% forest and woodland; 4% other. **Major cities:** (1990 est.) Honiara (capital) 35,288.

People Population: 385,811 (1994 est.). **Nationality:** noun—Solomon Islander(s); adjective—Solomon Islander. **Ethnic groups:** 93% Melanesian, 4% Polynesian, 1.5% Micronesian, 0.8% European. **Languages:** 120 indigenous languages; Melanesian pidgin in much of country is lingua franca; English spoken by 1–2% of population. **Religions:** almost all at least nominally Christian; Anglican, Seventh-day Adventist, and Roman Catholic churches dominant.

Government Type: independent parliamentary state within Commonwealth. **Independence:** July 7, 1978 (from UK). **Constitution:** July 7, 1978. **National holiday:** Independence Day, July 7. **Heads of government:** Moses Patakaka, governor-general (since July 1994); Solomon S. Mamaloni, prime minister (since Nov. 1994). **Structure:** executive authority in governor-general; unicameral legislature (38-member National Parliament).

Economy Monetary unit: Solomon Island dollar. **Budget:** (1991 est.) ***income:*** $48 mil.; ***expend.:*** $107 mil. **GDP:** $900 mil., $2,500 per capita (1991 est.). **Chief crops:** copra, cocoa, palm oil, rice, fruits, vegetables. **Livestock:** pigs and cattle. **Natural resources:** fish, forests, gold, bauxite, phosphates. **Major industries:** copra, fish (tuna). **Labor force:** 23,448 economically active (1984); 32.4% agriculture, forestry, and fishing. **Exports:** $84 mil. (f.o.b., 1991); 46% fish, 31% timber, 5% copra, 5% palm oil. **Imports:** $110 mil. (c.i.f., 1991); 30% plant and machinery, 19% fuel, 16% food. **Major trading partners:** (1985) ***exports:*** 51% Japan, 12% UK, 9% Thailand, 8% Netherlands, 2% Australia; ***imports:*** 36% Japan, 23% U.S., 9% Singapore, 9% UK, 9% New Zealand.

Intl. Orgs. Commonwealth, G-77, IBRD, IDA, IFAD, IFC, ILO, IMF, UN, UPU, WHO.

In 1893 Great Britain established a protectorate over the South Solomon Islands, including the large islands of Guadalcanal, San Cristobal, and Malata; the protectorate was extended to the smaller easterly islands of the chain in 1898. In 1900 Germany relinquished to Great Britain its claim to the North Solomons, including Choiseul and Santa Isabel; Bougainville Island was retained by Germany (see "Papua New Guinea"). The major islands were occupied by Japan in 1942 and retaken by the Allies in a series of bloody battles in 1943.

The Solomon Islands were made self-governing in January 1976 and became an independent nation on July 7, 1978. The economy is based on subsistence agriculture and fishing. Some light manufacturing and craft industries have been established in recent years. Copra, cocoa, palm oil, and lumber are the principal exports. The sale of tuna fishing rights in the surrounding waters has given the nation a favorable balance of payments.

Somalia

Somali Democratic Republic

Geography Location: eastern coast of Africa. **Boundaries:** short frontier with Djibouti to NW, Gulf of Aden to N, long coastline on Indian Ocean to E, Kenya to SW, Ethiopia to W. **Total land area:** 246,201 sq. mi. (637,660 sq km). **Coastline:** 1,880 mi. (3,025 km). **Comparative area:** slightly smaller than Texas. **Land use:** 2% arable land; negl. % permanent crops; 46% meadows and pastures; 14% forest and woodland; 38% other; includes 3% irrigated. **Major cities:** (1981 est.) Mogadishu (capital) 500,000; Hargeish 70,000; Kismayu 70,000; Berbera 65,000; Merca 60,000.

People Population: 6,666,873 (1994 est.). **Nationality:** noun—Somali(s); adjective—Somali. **Ethnic groups:** 85% Somali, rest mainly Bantu; 30,000 Arabs, 3,000 Europeans, 800 Asians. **Languages:** Somali (official), Arabic, Italian, English. **Religions:** almost entirely Sunni Muslim.

Government Type: republic. **Independence:** July 1, 1960 (from a merger of British Somaliland, which became independent from UK June 26, 1960, and Italian Somaliland, which became independent from Italian-administered UN trusteeship July 1, 1960, to form Somali Republic). **Constitution:** Aug. 25, 1979, presidential approval Sept. 23, 1979. **National holiday:** Oct. 21. **Heads of government:** Ali Mahdi Moammad, president (since Aug. 1991); Omar Arteh Ghalib, prime minister (since Jan. 1991). **Structure:** president dominates political system; cabinet carries out day-to-day government functions; unicameral legislature (National People's Assembly) exists but has little power.

Economy Monetary unit: Somali shilling. **Budget:** (1989 est.) ***income:*** N.A.; ***expend.:*** N.A. **GDP:** $3.4 bil., $500 per capita (1993 est.). **Chief crops:** mainly a pastoral country, raising livestock; crops—bananas, sugarcane, cotton, cereals. **Livestock:** goats, sheep, camels, cattle, asses. **Natural resources:** uranium, largely unexploited reserves of iron ore, tin, gypsum, bauxite. **Major industries:** a few small industries, including sugar refining, textiles, petroleum refining. **Labor force:** about 2.2 mil. (1985); very few are skilled laborers; 70% pastoral nomads, 30% agricultural, government, traders, fishermen, handicraftsmen, other; 53% of population of working age. **Exports:** $58 mil. (1990 est.); bananas, live animals, fish, hides. **Imports:** $249 mil. (1990 est.); petroleum products, foodstuffs, construction materials. **Major trading partners:** (1985) ***exports:*** 34.6% Saudi Arabia, 19.6% Italy; ***imports:*** 26% Italy, 17% U.S., 12% Saudi Arabia.

Intl. Org. Arab League, FAO, G-77, IBRD, ICAO, IDA, IFAD, IFC, ILO, IMF, IMO, INTELSAT, INTERPOL, ITU, NAM, OAU, UN, UNESCO, UPU, WHO, WMO.

Arab trading settlements in Somalia were established in the seventh century and gradually evolved into independent sultanates. Portuguese traders established settlements and forts along the coast during the 15th and 16th centuries.

In the early 19th century, Great Britain arranged through local treaties to use harbors along the Somali coast and gained control over the northern part of the country by 1840. The border between Somalia and Ethiopia was demarcated by a treaty between Great Britain and Ethiopia in 1897. In 1885 the sultan of Zanzibar granted commercial advantages to Italy, and by further agreements in 1897 and 1908 Italy gained control over southern Somalia.

During the early 20th century, an uprising against British rule was led by Mohamed Abdullah. Abdullah was defeated by the British with help from his local rivals but is now regarded as the father of Somali nationalism.

The Italian invasion of Ethiopia in 1936 gave Italy a dominant position in the Horn of Africa. In the early phases of World War II, Italian troops drove the British from British Somaliland, but a 1940 counterattack led to British occupation of all of Somalia by 1941. After World War II, as discussions of Somalia's future continued, Britain handed over the Ogaden and neighboring territories to Ethiopia.

A UN pact of 1949 created an Italian trusteeship in the former Italian Somaliland. Italy terminated its trusteeship and British Somaliland, a UK protectorate, achieved independence on June 26, 1960. On July 1 the two entities joined to become Somalia.

The new country was plagued by regional clan-based rivalries, with the Somali Youth League emerging as a unifying national force. In 1969 Maj. Gen. Mohamed Siad Barre took control, abolished the National Assembly, established a ruling Supreme Revolutionary Council, instituted a socialist regime, and established relations with the USSR.

In 1972 Somali forces began border raids into Ethiopia's Ogaden region, peopled largely by ethnic Somalis. The Somali army invaded the Ogaden in 1977. The Soviet Union switched its support to Ethiopia, and with Soviet aid and Cuban troops, Ethiopia drove back the Somali invasion. Over a million refugees fled from Ethiopia into Somalia, placing a severe burden on the country's fragile economy. The United States was Somalia's principal source of military and economic aid after 1978.

In May 1988, the Somali National Movement captured a number of cities in the northwest part of the country and held them against the army. In the summer of 1990, the United Somali Congress began a peaceful antigovernment movement around Mogadishu. In December 1990, this flared into a brief but bloody civil war that resulted in the ouster of Pres. Barre on Jan. 26. The Somali National Congress proclaimed a provisional government, but it was not recognized either by the United Somali Movement, which threatened secession, or the Somali Patriotic Movement, which controlled much of central and southern Somalia.

The continued unrest made it difficult to deliver humanitarian aid despite the efforts of Western governments and nongovernment organizations to do so. An estimated 50,000 people were killed between 1988–90.

Despite UN attempts to initiate peace talks, widespread clan and tribal warfare led to a complete breakdown of government authority in 1991–92. A severe drought helped to create over 2 million refugees, and widespread starvation gripped the nation. In addition, relief workers were prevented by chaotic political conditions and warring armed factions from distributing emergency food supplies. An estimated 300,000 people died in 1991–92.

In December 1992, with UN authority, the United States began Operation Restore Hope, in which 28,000 ground troops were deployed to secure distribution of food and other humanitarian aid. Forces from other UN nations accompanied the mission, and in May the United States ceded operational control to a UN peacekeeping force. Although the U.S. presence deterred the factions from further open hostilities, and brought faction leaders to the peace table, UN forces were unable to contain the fighting, and by summer no end to the political power vacuum was in sight. Led by the followers of Gen. Mohammed Farah Aidid, Somali renegades brought death and destruction to the UN mission as they ambushed troops and shot down helicopters. The U.S. withdrew its forces in March 1994. The last UN troops left Mogadishu on Mar. 1, 1995. By the end of March clan warfare had reignited but Somalia disappeared from the world's headlines.

South Africa

Republic of South Africa

Geography **Location:** southern Africa. **Boundaries:** Namibia to NW, Botswana, Zimbabwe to N, Mozambique to NE, Swaziland, Indian Ocean to E, Atlantic Ocean to W; Lesotho entirely surrounded by South African territory. **Total land area:** 471,444 sq. mi. (1,221,040 sq km). **Coastline:** 1,791 mi. (2,881 km). **Comparative area:** between Texas and Alaska. **Land use:** 10% arable land; 1% permanent crops; 65% meadows and pastures; 3% forest and woodland; 21% other; includes 1% irrigated. **Major cities:** (1985 census) Cape Town (legislative capital) 1,911,521; Pretoria (administrative capital) 822,925; Johannesburg 1,609,408; Durban 982,075; Port Elizabeth 651,993.

People **Population:** 43,930,631 (1994 est.). **Nationality:** noun—South African(s); adjective—South African. **Ethnic groups:** 69.9% black, 17.8% white, 2.9% Indian; 9.4% other. **Languages:** Afrikaans, English (official); Zulu, Xhosa, North and South Sotho, Tswana. **Religions:** most whites and about 60% of blacks are Christian; roughly 60% of Indians are Hindu, 20% Muslim.

Government **Type:** republic. **Independence:** May 31, 1910 (from UK). **Constitution:** Sept. 3, 1984. **National holiday:** Republic Day, May 31. **Head of government:** Nelson Roriklahla Mandela, president (since May 1994). **Structure:** executive—president is head of government and chairman of cabinet; tricameral legislature—House of Assembly (whites), House of Representatives (coloreds), and House of Delegates (Indians) elected directly by respective racial electorates; judiciary—courts maintain substantial independence from government influence.

Economy **Monetary unit:** South African rand. **Budget:** (1993 est.) ***income:*** $26.3 bil.; ***expend.:*** $34 bil. **GDP:** $171 bil., $4,000 per capita (1993 est.). **Chief crops:** corn, wheat, sugarcane, tobacco, citrus fruits; self-sufficient in foodstuffs. **Livestock:** sheep, cattle, goats, pigs, horses. **Natural resources:** gold, chromium, antimony, coal, iron ore. **Major industries:** mining (world's largest producer of diamonds, gold, chrome), automobile assembly, metalworking. **Labor force:** 13.4 mil. economically active (1985); 34% services, 30% agriculture, 29% industry and commerce, 7% mining; 19% unemployment (1987). **Exports:** $24.3 bil. (f.o.b., 1993); 40% gold, 33% minerals and metals, 6% food, 3% chemicals. **Imports:** $18.1 bil. (f.o.b., 1993); 32% machinery, 15% chemicals, 11% vehicles and aircraft, textiles, scientific instruments, base metals. **Major trading partners:** ***exports:*** U.S., UK, Germany, Japan, other EU, Hong Kong. ***imports:*** U.S., Germany, Japan, UK, France, Italy, Switzerland.

Intl. Orgs. IAEA, IBRD, IDA, IFC, IMF, INTELSAT, UN, UPU, WHO, WIPO, WMO, WTO.

South Africa was originally inhabited by San and related peoples. Bantu peoples, including the Zulu and Xhosa, migrated to the region beginning around the 15th century and established large native kingdoms.

The Portuguese explorer Bartholomew Diaz discovered and named the Cape of Good Hope in 1488. The Dutch East India Company established a permanent settlement at Cape Town in 1652, which served as a supply and transshipment point for Dutch trade to the East Indies and which attracted Protestant settlers from throughout Western Europe. In a series of wars, the Xhosa people were expelled from the area under Dutch rule.

Great Britain began to dispute Dutch control of the Cape of Good Hope region in the late 18th century. To escape increasing British hegemony, in 1836 many Dutch farmers undertook the Great Trek, a northward migration to lands not under the control of any European power. These Afrikaner pioneers later became known as Boers (farmers). They came into conflict with the Zulu kingdom that, under King Shaka, had recently widened its dominion in the South African interior. The Zulus were defeated at the Battle of Blood River in 1838, but they retained substantial power and territory for another 40 years.

Great Britain formally took control of the Cape Colony in 1841 and annexed Natal in 1843. The other two Afrikaner provinces, the Orange Free State and the Transvaal, remained temporarily free of British control. But when diamonds were discovered in the Orange Free State in 1867 and gold in the Transvaal in 1886, an influx of British miners and entrepreneurs provoked Boer rebellions.

In 1878 the Zulu Kingdom under its last great king, Cetewayo, rebelled against British rule in Natal. British troops attacked Zululand in 1878 and crushed the rebellion in 1879.

The first Anglo-Boer War of 1881–82 led to an inconclusive British victory. A renewed uprising led to the Boer War of 1899–1902, which was fought with great ferocity between British regular troops and Afrikaner guerrilla forces. The eventual British victory led to the establishment of British rule in all of South Africa and to the formation of the Union of South Africa in 1910. The union became a self-governing state within the British Empire in 1934.

South African politics became dominated by friction between British and Afrikaner whites; no effective black participation in government was permitted. The United South African party, led by Jan C. Smuts, advocated cooperation between the two groups and led South Africa to join World War II on the Allied side, over the opposition of the pro-Afrikaner Nationalist party.

After the war the Nationalists prevailed and won control of the government in 1948. Racial politics became the country's paramount concern, and the Nationalists introduced the policy of "apartheid" (separateness), under which racial groups were rigidly defined as white, black, Asian (primarily Indian), and colored (mixed ancestry). Each group was to be kept physically separate and develop its own political institutions within defined areas of residence; mixed neighborhoods, intermarriage, and other relations were prohibited. Blacks, in particular, were restricted by "pass laws" that allowed them only temporary access to white areas for employment.

International condemnation of these policies began almost immediately, as India broke relations with South Africa in 1946 over discrimination against Asians, and South Africa became the focus of mounting protest, UN resolutions, and international sanctions beginning in the 1960s. On May 31, 1961, South Africa gave up its dominion status and became a republic; its application for membership in the British Commonwealth was withdrawn in the face of opposition from the Commonwealth community. The African National Congress (ANC), organized in 1912, was banned by South African authorities. The imprisonment of its leader, Nelson Mandela, provided a focus for black political protest and nationalist aspirations.

Homelands were established under the Promotion of Bantu Self-Government Act of 1959 to further the policy of apartheid by creating separate, but dependent, states for South Africa's blacks. Their form of government was set up in the Black Constitution Act of 1971. The South African government intended that the homelands be regarded as separate nations, but none was ever internationally recognized. The scattered homeland territories comprised only a tiny portion of the total area of South Africa, and tended to include marginal and underdeveloped lands. Residents of the homelands were not considered citizens of South Africa, but rather citizens only of their particular homeland. As such, they could be considered temporary migrant workers and were therefore ineligible for unemployment and other benefits.

An uprising in Soweto in 1976 was put down by South African police and armed forces with the loss of hundreds of lives, providing a further focus of black protest. Pieter Willem Botha was elected president in 1978, pledging to uphold apartheid while seeking solutions to racial problems. In 1983, a majority of white voters approved the adoption of a new constitution that provided for limited power sharing by coloreds and Asians. Blacks, however, continued to be excluded.

In the early 1980s, South African troops intervened in civil wars in Angola and Mozambique and were deployed to counteract growing proindependence rebellions in Namibia. Within South Africa terrorism and uprisings led by the African National Union grew in intensity in 1983–84. A state of emergency was declared in 1985 accompanied by renewed political and economic pressure from abroad. In 1986, Bishop Desmond Tutu, a leading black nationalist, addressed the United Nations and called for renewed sanctions. The Botha government announced an end to the pass laws and promised limited black participation in government. Fighting between black groups in 1986–87 further increased domestic tension.

On May 19, 1986, South African troops conducted raids against ANC bases in Zambia, Zimbabwe, and Botswana. A new national state of emergency was declared in June, as strikes and riots marked the 10th anniversary of the Soweto uprising. The United States announced measures designed to end American investment in South Africa.

In early 1989, in anticipation of elections to be held in September, various proposals were put forward for constitutional reform. Most called for expanded power sharing but still within the context of defined racial groups.

South Africa has the continent's most highly developed economy; it is a fully-developed, capitalist industrial-commercial society with manufacturing, mining, agricultural, service, and other sectors. International sanctions have hampered the economy to a limited extent, but their impact has been lessened by South Africa's status as the world's largest producer of gold, a key source of chromium and other strategic metals, and of gem-quality diamonds.

In July 1989 Pres. Botha had an unprecedented meeting with Nelson Mandela, amid strong suggestions that the white government was seeking an accommodation with the antiapartheid leadership. Botha's successor, F.W. de Klerk, continued that policy.

A series of measures in 1989–90 resulted in the partial dismantling of apartheid, against the vehement opposition of the white right wing, but violence between supporters of the ANC and the Zulu Inkatha movement in Natal led to the declaration of a state of emergency in the province.

Mandela was released from prison in the spring of 1990 and received a rapturous welcome from South Africa's blacks, and later made a triumphant tour of Western Europe and North America. His glory was short-lived, however, as the struggle for supremacy again erupted in murder and violence between Mandela's ANC and Mangosuthu Buthelezi's Inkatha Freedom party throughout the latter part of 1990 and 1991.

At the same time, Pres. de Klerk and Parliament continued to move the nation toward the ending of apartheid by repealing many of the segregation laws that affected hospitals, libraries, schools, and other public institutions for more than 60 years. The government also released other political prisoners and completely repealed the legal foundation for apartheid: the Land Acts of 1913 and 1936, the Group Areas Act, and the Population Registration Act. The United States and other countries began lifting trade sanctions against South Africa in the summer of 1991.

In September 1991, de Klerk, Mandela, and Buthelezi, together with 20 smaller antiapartheid groups, signed an accord to end factional violence. De Klerk proposed a new constitution that would provide universal suffrage and create a two-chamber parliament open to all races. The new constitution abolished the black homelands, consolidating them into one large, multiracial South Africa. In March 1992 a referendum of white voters overwhelmingly approved a government proposal to dismantle all forms of apartheid and to conduct talks with black leaders designed to end white-only rule.

The new constitution was completed in the fall of 1993, and on Nov. 17, 1993, all of the country's major political parties, except for Chief Mangosuthu Buthelezi's Zulu-based Inkatha Freedom party, approved it. The Zulus continued to withhold their support through the spring of 1994, refusing to participate in the country's first-ever multiracial elections in April. As the election approached, violence between Zulus and the Xhosa tribes of the ANC escalated to the point that de Klerk was forced to send government troops into the Zulu homeland to control the raging hostilities. Finally, a week before the election, Buthelezi relented and allowed the Inkatha Freedom party to appear on the election ballots.

Huge numbers of voters turned out to cast ballots. So many, in fact (22.7 million), that the balloting had to be extended from three to four days. In the end, voters overwhelmingly chose the 75-year-old Mandela to guide South Africa for the next five years. In early 1995 a Constituent Assembly was established to draw up a permanent constitution, an 11-member Constitutional Court was sworn in, and a federal budget approved.

Spain

Kingdom of Spain

Geography Location: Iberian Peninsula in southwest Europe; Canary Is. off West Africa (28°07'N, 15°26'W). **Boundaries:** Bay of Biscay and France to N; Mediterranean Sea to E; Morocco 19 mi. (30 km) to S, across Strait of Gibraltar; Portugal to W. **Total land area:** 194,884 sq. mi. (504,750 sq km). **Coastline:** 3,085 mi. (4,964 km). **Comparative area:** between California and Texas. **Land use:** 31% arable land; 10% permanent crops; 21% meadows and pastures; 31% forest and woodland; 7% other; includes 6% irrigated. **Major cities:** (1991 est.) Madrid (capital) 2,984,576; Barcelona 1,653,175; Valencia 777,427; Sevilla (Seville) 683,487; Zaragoza (Saragossa) 614,401.

People **Population:** 39,302,665 (1994 est.). **Nationality:** noun—Spaniard(s); adjective—Spanish. **Ethnic groups:** composite of Mediterranean and Nordic types. **Languages:** Castilian Spanish; second langs. include 17% Catalán, 7% Galician, 2% Basque. **Religions:** 99% Roman Catholic, 1% other.

Government **Type:** parliamentary monarchy. **Independence:** N.A. **Constitution:** Dec. 6, 1978, effective Dec. 29, 1978. **National holiday:** June 24. **Heads of government:** Juan Carlos I, king (since Nov. 1975); Felipe Gonzalez Márquez, prime minister (since Dec. 1982). **Structure:** executive—with acts of king subject to countersignature—prime minister and his ministers responsible to lower house; bicameral legislature—Cortes Generales, consisting of more powerful Congress of Deputies (350 members) and Senate (208 members) with possible addition of one to six members from each new autonomous region; judiciary—independent.

Economy **Monetary unit:** peseta. **Budget:** (1993 est.) ***income:*** $97.7 bil.; ***expend.:*** $128 bil. **GDP:** $498 bil., $12,700 per capita (1993). **Chief crops:** grains, citrus fruits, vegetables, wine grapes; virtually self-sufficient in good crop years. **Livestock:** sheep, pigs, cattle, horses, mules. **Natural resources:** coal, lignite, iron ore, uranium, mercury. **Major industries:** textiles, apparel (including footwear), food and beverages, metals and metal manufacturing. **Labor force:** 14.6 mil. (1988); 44.8% services, 30.9% industry, 15.6% agriculture, 9.1% construction, 8.7% other. **Exports:** $72.8 bil. (f.o.b., 1993); foodstuffs, live animals, wood, footwear, machinery, chemicals. **Imports:** $92.5 bil. (c.i.f., 1993); petroleum, footwear, machinery, chemicals, grain, soybeans, coffee. **Major trading partners:** ***exports:*** 67.8% EU, 9% other developed countries, 6.5% U.S.; ***imports:*** 57% EU, 13% other developed countries, 9% U.S., 3% Middle East.

Intl. Orgs. EU, FAO, IAEA, IBRD, ICAO, IDA, IFAD, IFC, ILO, IMF, IMO, INTELSAT, INTERPOL, ITU, NATO, OAS (observer), OECD, OSCE, UN, UNESCO, UPU, WHO, WIPO, WMO, WTO.

Prehistoric Spain was populated by Iberians, Basques, and Celts. Its Mediterranean ports were frequented by Phoenician traders, and part of the country was incorporated into the empire of Carthage. Spain fell under the Roman Empire around 200 B.C.; Roman rule ended when the Visigoths invaded and took control of the Iberian Peninsula in the fifth century. The Visigoths adopted Christianity but were in turn conquered by Moors from northwest Africa in A.D. 711. The Berber/Arab civilization of the Moors produced the most elegant and cultivated culture in medieval Europe, and was an important conduit for the reintroduction of Greek science into Europe in the 12th century.

The Christian reconquest of the Iberian Peninsula began almost immediately after the Moors had established themselves and proceeded slowly but steadily over a period of 750 years. The consolidation of the region's small, contentious Christian kingdoms came with the marital alliance of Ferdinand of Aragon and Isabella of Castile in 1469. Granada, the last Moorish outpost in Spain, fell to the forces of Ferdinand and Isabella in 1492, just as Columbus, with Isabella's sponsorship, was discovering the lands that were to become Spain's New World empire. Under the Inquisition, begun in 1478, Jews were expelled from Spain in 1492, and Muslims were expelled in 1502.

Under the Habsburg dynasty (1516–1700), Spain reached the zenith of its power and prestige around the year 1600 (despite the 1588 defeat of the Spanish Armada by England), controlling an empire that embraced nearly all of South America (except Brazil), Central America, Mexico, western North America, the Philippines, and smaller territories in Africa and Asia. But Spain's loss of the Netherlands, endless struggles with the French in Europe and the Turks in the Mediterranean, and relentless inflation caused by imports of New World silver—all took their toll. During the 18th century, the Bourbons ruled a declining but still powerful Spain, until Napoleon installed his brother as king in 1808.

After Napoleon's defeat, the Bourbons returned in 1814, but in the 19th century, the loss of the South American colonies, three dynastic wars, and a brief republican interlude after 1868 were all signs of progressive weakness. The crowning blow to Spanish power and prestige was the loss of the Spanish-American War to the United States in 1898, leading to the independence of Cuba and the American takeover of Puerto Rico and the Philippines.

Spain remained neutral in World War I. In 1923 Primo de Rivera established a dictatorship; he was forced out of office by King Alfonso XIII in 1930, but in 1931 the king himself was forced to abdicate. A republic replaced the monarchy. Its volatile mixture of socialism, anticlericalism, and decentralization provoked a right-wing reaction and exacerbated regional separatist tendencies. The government moved to the Right, and in 1934 a miner's strike in Asturia was put down with great bloodshed. A left-wing government was elected in 1936 and deposed in a coup, which led to the terrible Civil War of 1936–39, in which Spain became a battleground for competing world ideologies. The Nationalists, aided by Hitler and Mussolini, defeated the Republicans, aided by Stalin and by leftist volunteers from many countries. Out of the wreckage emerged the dictatorship of the apolitical and intensely patriotic and Catholic general Francisco Franco.

At the time of the Civil War, Spain was still largely an agricultural country, with smallholdings in the north and great estates in the south. Traditional crops included grains, grapes and wine, citrus fruits, olives, and olive oil. In the Basque country, the mining of iron, copper, and lead provided the basis for both exports and a domestic iron and steel industry, which had been the case since the 19th century. In the 20th century, shipbuilding and chemicals were added to the traditional textile industries of the Mediterranean coastal cities. The civil war largely destroyed this industrial base, which was not rebuilt until the 1950s.

Except for a contingent of troops sent to fight with the German invaders of the Soviet Union, Spain remained precariously neutral during World War II; Franco declined to repay Hitler for his support in the Civil War. But wartime Spain, despite its neutrality, could not muster the resources to undertake national reconstruction.

In postwar Europe, the Franco regime seemed like a remnant of the fascism of the 1930s; Stalin's active hostility led the United Nations to treat Spain as an international pariah. Despite foreign disapproval, however, at home Franco represented peace and stability; few Spaniards were willing to risk a return to civil strife by opposing him. Over time the military and Catholic aspects of the regime grew more pronounced, while fascist elements were downplayed. In 1947 the Law of Succession made Spain a monarchy without a king, awaiting the restoration of the throne in the post-Franco era.

In the 1950s the Cold War led to friendlier American relations with Spain and the establishment of American military bases there in 1953. UN membership followed in 1955. Despite some resultant growth in international trade, Spain's economy lagged, with industrialization barely beginning.

In 1958 Franco turned the direction of the economy over to a group of technocrats, mostly neoliberal members of the Opus Dei lay Catholic order. With U.S. economic and military aid, a growing tourist industry, increased foreign investment, and, especially, freer markets, the economy revived. Older industries like iron, steel, and textiles were rejuvenated, while newer ones, such as chemicals, plastics, automobile assembly, and power plants, were created. Agriculture was increasingly mechanized, and it shifted to export-oriented ranching and horticulture.

In 1967 Franco proclaimed the Organic Law, which, while confirming him as head of state, granted some independence to the Cortes (legislature) and permitted heads of families to vote for some of its delegates. This, along with a relaxation of censorship, softened the growing opposition to the regime among students, labor unions, and regional separatists. In 1969 Prince Juan Carlos was named heir apparent to the Spanish throne.

Franco died in 1975 and was duly succeeded by Juan Carlos. With the new prime minister, Adolfo Suarez, the king worked to liberalize the Franco inheritance: Political parties were legalized; the Cortes was transformed into a bicameral legislature, with both houses elected by universal suffrage; the first elections since 1936 were held; and a new constitution was promulgated—all by 1978.

In 1980 Catalonia and the Basque country were granted home rule, following overwhelming victories in home-rule plebiscites. In the Basque lands, however, violent terrorist agitation for complete independence continues.

In February 1981 a right-wing coup attempted to depose the government; armed conspirators entered the Cortes and held the legislators hostage. The coup collapsed in a day when the armed forces declared their loyalty to the king.

Since 1982 the Socialist Workers' party has controlled both houses of the Cortes. Although socialist, the party has abandoned both Marxism and the traditional labor radicalism of prewar Spain; it now resembles, under Prime Minister Filipe Gonzalez Márquez, the mainstream Social Democratic parties of the rest of Western Europe.

Spain joined the Council of Europe in 1977, NATO in 1982, and the EC in 1986. Spain was now a full participant in the affairs of Western Europe and was for a time its rising economic star. GDP grew by an average of almost 5 percent between 1986 and 1990, and business investment by over 10 percent a year. In 1992 the Summer Olympics were held in Barcelona, and the Universal Exposition in Seville.

Economic growth slowed dramatically in 1992–93, but even 22 percent unemployment could not prevent Gonzalez from winning the June 1993 elections. The conservative Popular party made strong gains, however, and several corruption scandals in 1994 severely weakened the Gonzalez government. More serious were indictments of several former members of the Gonzalez government for involvement with the GAL (Antiterrorist Liberation Group), a death squad accused of 26 assasinations of Basque terrorists. The Popular party won 35 percent of the vote, Gonzalez's Socialists 31 percent in 1995 local elections.

Sri Lanka

Democratic Socialist Republic of Sri Lanka

Geography **Location:** Indian Ocean about 50 mi. (80 km) SE of India. Colombo 6°55'N, 79°52'E. **Boundaries:** Palk Strait to N, Bay of Bengal to E, Indian Ocean to S and SW, and Gulf of Mannar to NW. **Total land area:** 25,332 sq. mi. (65,610 sq km). **Coastline:** 833 mi. (1,340 km). **Comparative area:** about size of West Virginia. **Land use:** 16% arable land; 17% permanent crops; 7% meadows and pastures; 37% forest and woodland; 23% other; includes 8% irrigated. **Major cities:** (1990 est.) Colombo (capital) 615,000; Dehiwala-Mount Lavinia 196,000; Moratuwa 170,000.

People **Population:** 18,129,850 (1994 est.). **Nationality:** noun—Sri Lankan(s); adjective—Sri Lankan. **Ethnic groups:** 74% Sinhalese; 18% Tamil; 7% Moor; 1% Burgher, Malay, and Veddah. **Languages:** Sinhala (official); Sinhala and Tamil listed as national languages; Sinhala spoken by about 74% of population, Tamil spoken by about 18%; English commonly used in government and spoken by about 10% of population. **Religions:** 69% Buddhist, 15% Hindu, 8% Christian, 8% Muslim.

Government **Type:** republic. **Independence:** Feb. 4, 1948 (from UK). **Constitution:** Aug. 31, 1978. **National holiday:** Independence Day, May 22. **Heads of government:** Chandrika Bandaranaike Kumaratunga, president (since Nov. 1994); Sirimavo R.D. Bandaranaike, prime minister (since Nov. 1994). **Structure:** 1978 Constitution established strong presidential form of government.

Economy **Monetary unit:** Sri Lankan rupee. **Budget:** (1993) ***income:*** $2.3 bil.; ***expend.:*** $3.6 bil. **GDP:** $53.5 bil., $3,000 per capita (1993 est.). **Chief crops:** rice, coconuts, tea, rubber; agriculture accounts for about 26% of GDP. **Livestock:** cattle, buffalo, goats, pigs, sheep. **Natural resources:** limestone, graphite, mineral sands, gems, phosphates. **Major industries:** processing of rubber, tea, coconuts, and other agricultural commodities; cement, petroleum refinery. **Labor force:** 6.6 mil. (1985 est.); 45.9% agriculture, 13.3% mining and manufacturing, 12.4% trade and transport, 28.4% services and other; extensive underemployment; 19% unemployment (1986 est.). **Exports:** $2.3 bil. (f.o.b., 1992); tea, textiles and garments, petroleum products, coconut, rubber. **Imports:** $3 bil. (c.i.f., 1992); petroleum, machinery and equipment, textiles and textile materials, wheat, transport equipment. **Major trading partners:** ***exports:*** 26% U.S., Germany, Japan, UK, Belgium, Taiwan, Hong Kong, China; ***imports:*** Japan, Saudi Arabia, U.S., India, Singapore, Iran, Taiwan.

Intl. Orgs. Colombo Plan, Commonwealth, FAO, G-77, IAEA, IBRD, ICAO, IDA, IFAD, IFC, ILO, IMF, IMO, INTELSAT, INTERPOL, ITU, NAM, UN, UNESCO, UPU, WHO, WIPO, WMO, WTO.

The ancient Veddah inhabitants of Sri Lanka were conquered by Sinhalese migrants from northern India in the sixth century B.C. The island's spices and precious stones and its position on the trans–Indian Ocean trade routes made it well known in ancient times. Sri Lanka was known to the Greeks as Tabrobane and to the Arabs as Serendip. From the third century A.D., Sri Lanka became a major center of Buddhist culture. Despite numerous invasions from India, the island was usually ruled by native kingdoms, but the invasions added a Tamil community to the premodern population.

The Portuguese conquered the coastal areas after 1505 and also introduced Roman Catholicism. The Dutch displaced the Portugese in 1648; the British expelled the Dutch in 1795. Great Britain was the first foreign power to extend its rule over the entire island, with the defeat of the central kingdom of Kandy in 1833. In that year all of Sri Lanka was incorporated into the British Crown colony of Ceylon. Under British rule, tea and rubber plantations were established in the island's interior, and coconut plantations in coastal areas were consolidated under foreign control.

Ceylon became an independent member of the British Commonwealth on Feb. 4, 1948; the Republic of Sri Lanka was proclaimed on May 22, 1972.

Prime Minister W.R.D. Bandaranaike was assassinated on Sept. 25, 1959. His widow, Sirimavo Bandaranaike, leader of the Freedom party, was elected as his successor. In 1962 her government expropriated the property of foreign oil companies. The conservative United National party won a majority in Parliament in 1965 and agreed to pay compensation for the expropriated assets. In May 1970 Mrs. Bandaranaike was again elected prime minister. Leftists secured the nationalization of foreign plantations in the mid-1970s. Mrs. Bandaranaike's party was ousted by the United National party in 1977. Constitutional reform in 1978 aimed at increasing stability by establishing a presidential form of government. Pres. J.R. Jayawardene was elected on Feb. 4, 1978.

But stability has eluded Sri Lanka because of the long struggle between Tamils and the Sinhalese. The political power acquired by the Tamil (mostly Hindu) middle class under the British was deeply resented by the Sinhalese (Buddhist) majority, which after independence slowly eroded Tamil rights. In 1957 the government proposed a Tamil state in a federal union and gave Tamil the status of a national (but not official) language. The pact was not fully implemented, and in the 1970s extremists began agitating for an independent Tamil state. The Tamils' minority status was reaffirmed in the constitution of 1972, the year the oldest insurgent group, the Liberation Tigers or Tamil Tigers, was founded.

In July 1987 Pres. Jayawardene accepted an offer from India's Prime Minister Rajiv Gandhi to supervise a truce in the Jaffna region under which the government pledged to hold a referendum aimed at granting self-rule to Tamil majority areas in the north and northeast. The plan failed, however; Indian troops became bogged down in battling the rebels, while the planned referendum was disrupted by fighting between separatists who demanded total independence for Tamil areas and more moderate Tamil groups willing to accept self-rule.

At the Sri Lankan government's request, India withdrew its forces in March 1989, and the Tamil Tigers agreed to a cease-fire as the government prepared its plan for Tamil-area autonomy. But this and later cease-fire agreements have all broken down.

In addition to the Tamil insurgency, the government has had to combat the People's Liberation Front (JVP), a nominally Marxist Sinhalese group that opposes any concessions to Tamils and that targets both Tamils and moderate Sinhalese government officials.

The assassinations of both the opposition political leader in April 1993 and the president, Ranasinghe Premadasa, on May 1 left the nation in shock, although peaceful legislative elections were held later in May. Local elections—prevented by the Tamil Tigers since 1988—were held without incident in 1994. After August parliamentary elections in which the People's Alliance ended the 17-year rule of the United National party, new prime minister Chandrika Bandaranaike Kumaratunga won a landslide (62%) victory in the November presidential election, appointing her 78-year-old mother,

Sirimavo Bandaranaike, as the new prime minister—her third term in the post.

Hours after the new president's inauguration, the Tamil Tigers announced a voluntary cease-fire. The truce was formalized in January 1995 negotiations between the rebels and the government. But in April, the Tigers renewed the 12-year-old civil war provoking serious government bomber raids on the northern strongholds of the rebels in May. More than 50,000 people have been killed since 1993.

Sudan

Republic of the Sudan

Geography **Location:** northeastern Africa. **Boundaries:** Egypt to N, Red Sea, Eritrea, and Ethiopia to E, Kenya, Uganda, and Zaire to S, Central African Republic, Chad and Libya to W. **Total land area:** 967,495 sq. mi. (2,505,810 sq km). **Coastline:** 530 mi. (853 km). **Comparative area:** about size of Alaska, Texas, and Nevada combined. **Land use:** 5% arable land; negl. % permanent crops; 24% meadows and pastures; 20% forest and woodland; 51% other; includes 1% irrigated. **Major cities:** (1983 census) Khartoum (capital) 476,218; Omdurman 526,287; Khartoum North 341,146; Port Sudan 206,727; Wadi Medani 141,065.

People **Population:** 29,419,798 (1994 est.). **Nationality:** noun—Sudanese (sing., pl.); adjective—Sudanese. **Ethnic groups:** 52% black, 39% Arab, 6% Beja, 2% foreigners. **Languages:** Arabic (official), Nubian, Ta Bedawie, diverse dialects of Nilotic, Nilo-Hamitic, and Sudanic languages, English; program of Arabization in progress. **Religions:** 70% Sunni Muslim in north, 20% indigenous beliefs, 5% Christian (mostly in south).

Government **Type:** republic. **Independence:** Jan. 1, 1956 (from Egypt and UK). **Constitution:** Apr. 12, 1973, suspended following coup of Apr. 6, 1985; interim constitution Oct. 10, 1985. **National holiday:** Independence Day, Jan. 1. **Head of government:** Lt. Gen. Omer Hassan Ahmed Al Bashir, president (since Jan. 1993). **Structure:** Supreme Council and Civilian Cabinet; regional military governors.

Economy **Monetary unit:** Sudanese pound. **Budget:** (1993 est.) ***income:*** $374.4 mil.; ***expend.:*** $1.2 bil. **GDP:** $21.5 bil., $750 per capita (1993 est.). **Chief crops:** cotton, sorghum, millet, wheat, sesame; not self-sufficient in food production; main cash crops—cotton, sesame, gum arabic, peanuts, sorghum. **Livestock:** cattle, sheep, goats, chickens, camels. **Natural resources:** modest reserves of crude oil, iron ore, copper, chromium ore, zinc. **Major industries:** cotton ginning, textiles, cement. **Labor force:** 6.5 mil. (1983); 80% agriculture, 10% industry and commerce; labor shortages for almost all categories of skilled employment; 52% of population of working age (1985). **Exports:** $350 mil. (f.o.b., FY93); 52% cotton, sesame, gum arabic, peanuts. **Imports:** $1.1 bil. (c.i.f., FY93); foodstuffs, petroleum products, manufactured goods, machinery and equipment, medicines and chemicals. **Major trading partners:** ***exports:*** 46% Western Europe, 14% Saudi Arabia, 9% Eastern Europe, 9% Japan; ***imports:*** 32% Western Europe, 15% Africa and Asia, 13% U.S.

Intl. Orgs. Arab League, FAO, G-77, IAEA, IBRD, ICAO, IDA, IFAD, IFC, ILO, IMF, IMO, INTELSAT, INTERPOL, ITU, NAM, OAU, UN, UNESCO, UPU, WHO, WIPO, WMO.

The northern Sudan, the ancient land of Nubia, was loosely controlled by Egypt in antiquity and incorporated into the Arab world by the Islamic expansion of the seventh century. The southern Sudan was part of tribal black Africa, under no external control but subject to continual raids by slave traders from the north.

Ottoman Egypt conquered the northern Sudan in 1820–21; British influence in Egypt in the 19th century extended into the Sudan as well. In 1881 Muhammed Ahmed ibn Abdalla, a religious leader known as the Mahdi, united northern and north-central Sudan and led a resistance movement against Anglo-Egyptian control. Khartoum, defended by British general Charles George Gordon, fell in 1885, but the Mahdi died soon thereafter, and his revolt came to an end. An Anglo-Egyptian force under Kitchener regained control in 1898; Anglo-Egyptian joint rule was established in the Sudan in 1899.

Great Britain and Egypt granted self-government and self-determination to the Sudan in 1953, and a Sudanese parliament was seated in 1954. Full independence came in 1956. Gen. Ibrahim Abboud took power in a bloodless coup in 1958 but was forced to resign after riots in 1964. In 1969 a new military coup installed a ruling Revolutionary Command Council and instituted a socialist regime. The council's leader, Gen. Muhammed Nimeiri, became prime minister. Disputes between Marxists and non-Marxists, and between arabized northerners and black southerners, led to continual difficulties. An attempted coup was foiled in 1971. In 1972 the Sudan's three black southern provinces were granted local autonomy. Another attempted coup in 1976 was put down by the Nimeiri government, and hundreds of prominent citizens were arrested and executed. The government accused Libya of sponsoring the coup.

In 1983 attempts by the Nimeiri government to institute Islamic law throughout the Sudan led to riots in the south and the imposition of a nationwide state of emergency in 1984. Popular unrest was exacerbated by drought and famine in 1985. On Apr. 6, 1985, Nimeiri was overthrown in a coup led by Gen. Suwar El Dahab. After a brief period of rule by a transitional military council, a civilian cabinet was installed, and free parliamentary elections were held in 1986.

In June 1989 the government was overthrown in a coup led by Lt. Gen. Omar Ahmed al-Bashir. The Bashir government renewed the fight against the southern rebels, and supported the imposition of Islamic law throughout the Sudan. Within three years the civil service, the military, the judiciary, and the educational system were under the control of Muslims. All opposition political parties, newspapers, and trade unions were banned.

In October 1990, the U.S. government stopped aid to the Sudan, citing the Khartoum government's diversion of food and other supplies from the southern provinces to the Muslim north. The Sudan openly supported Iraq in the Persian Gulf War and in January 1991, concerned for the safety of its respresentatives, the UN suspended relief efforts to help the estimated 7.1 million Sudanese threatened by famine.

In the spring of 1992, with the help of Iranian military advisers and the infusion of weapons from China, the government seemed on its way to finally defeating the so-called Sudan People's Liberation Army, led by John Garang. Shortly after driving the rebel force out of the country, the central government established Islamic law in the mostly Christian and animist south. The rebels returned and fierce fighting occurred in early 1994. Peace talks began in March but sporadic fighting continued until March 1995, when, at the behest of former U.S. president Jimmy Carter, Pres. Bashir announced a unilateral cease-fire.

Suriname

Republic of Suriname

Geography **Location:** northeastern coast of South America. **Boundaries:** North Atlantic Ocean to N, French Guiana to E, Brazil to S, Guyana to W. **Total land area:** 63,039 sq. mi. (163,270 sq km). **Coastline:** 240 mi. (386 km). **Comparative area:** between Georgia and Washington. **Land use:** negl. % arable land; negl. % permanent crops; negl. % meadows and pastures; 97% forest and woodland; 3% other; includes negl. % irrigated. **Major cities:** (1980 census) Paramaribo (capital) 67,718.

People **Population:** 422,840 (1994 est.). **Nationality:** noun—Surinamer(s); adjective—Surinamese. **Ethnic groups:** 37% Hindustani (East Indian), 31% Creole (black and mixed), 15.3% Javanese, 10.3% Bush black. **Languages:** Dutch (official), English widely spoken, Sranan Tongo (sometimes called Taki-Taki, the native language of Creoles and much of younger population and lingua franca among others), Hindi Suriname Hindustani, Javanese. **Religions:** 27.4% Hindu, 25.2% Protestant (predominantly Moravian), 22.8% Roman Catholic, 19.6% Muslim.

Government **Type:** in transition from military to civilian rule as of Jan. 1988. **Independence:** Nov. 25, 1975 (from Netherlands). **National holiday:** Independence Day, Nov. 25. **Heads of government:** Runaldo Ronald Venetiaan, president (since Sept. 1991); Jules R. Ajodhia, prime minister (since Oct. 1991). **Structure:** civilian government moving away from military control.

Economy **Monetary unit:** Suriname guilder. **Budget:** (1989) ***income:*** $466 mil.; ***expend.:*** $716 mil. **GDP:** $1.17 bil., $2,800 per capita (1993 est.). **Chief crops:** rice, bananas, palm oil, timber. **Livestock:** cattle, pigs, goats, sheep, horses, mules, asses. **Natural resources:** timber, hydropower potential, fish, shrimp, bauxite.

Major industries: bauxite mining, alumina and aluminum production, lumbering. **Labor force:** 104,000 (1984); 11% agriculture, animal husbandry, fishing; 25–30% unemployment (1987). **Exports:** $290 mil. (f.o.b., 1993 est.); alumina, bauxite, aluminum, agricultural products, wood and wood products. **Imports:** $250 mil. (f.o.b., 1993 est.); capital equipment, petroleum, iron and steel, cotton, flour. **Major trading partners:** (1986) ***exports:*** 28% Netherlands, 11% U.S., 36% Norway, 11% Japan, 10% Brazil, 5% UK; ***imports:*** 41% U.S., 24% Netherlands, 9% Trinidad and Tobago, 4% Brazil.

Intl. Orgs. FAO, G-77, IBRD, ICAO, IFAD, ILO, IMF, IMO, INTERPOL, ITU, NAM, OAS, UN, UNESCO, UPU, WHO, WIPO, WMO, WTO.

In the early 17th century, the Dutch and English settled Suriname, which became a Dutch colony in 1667. Except for brief episodes of British rule, Suriname remained under Dutch control until its independence in 1975, shifting toward authoritarian military rule in 1980. The military created its own political party (the February 25 movement) and banned opposition organizations. The 1988 National Assembly election of Pres. Ramsewak Shankar marked an end to direct military rule, but the restriction of civil liberties continued.

The Shankar government was overthrown in a bloodless coup led by Cmdr. Ivan Graanoogst in 1990, but civilian rule was restored in 1991.

Swaziland

Kingdom of Swaziland

Geography Location: landlocked country in southern Africa. **Boundaries:** South Africa to N, SE, S, and W; Mozambique to E. **Total land area:** 6,703 sq. mi. (17,360 sq km). **Coastline:** none. **Comparative area:** between Connecticut and New Jersey. **Land use:** 8% arable land; negl. % permanent crops; 67% meadows and pastures; 6% forest and woodland; 19% other; includes 2% irrigated. **Major cities:** (1986 census) Mbabane (capital) 38,290; Manzini 18,084.

People Population: 936,369 (1994 est.). **Nationality:** noun—Swazi(s); adjective—Swazi. **Ethnic groups:** 97% African, 3% European. **Languages:** English and siSwati (both official); government business conducted in English. **Religions:** 57% Christian, 43% indigenous beliefs.

Government Type: monarchy; independent member of Commonwealth. **Independence:** Sept. 6, 1968 (from UK). **Constitution:** suspended Apr. 12, 1973; new constitution promulgated Oct. 13, 1978, but not yet formally presented to people. **National holiday:** Somhlolo (Independence) Day, Sept. 6. **Heads of government:** Mswati III, king (since Apr. 1986); Obed M. Dlamini, prime minister (since July 1989). **Structure:** executive—king or queen (with advice of Supreme Council of State), whose assent is required before parliamentary acts become law; king's authority exercised through prime minister and cabinet; legislative—bicameral Parliament (Senate, House of Assembly) formally opened Jan. 1979; 80-member electoral college chose 40 members of lower house and 10 members of upper house; additional 10 members of each house chosen by king; judiciary—part of Ministry of Justice but otherwise independent of executive and legislative branches; cases can be appealed to high court and court of appeal.

Economy Monetary unit: Swazi lilangeni. **Budget:** (1994 est.) ***income:*** $342 mil.; ***expend.:*** $410 mil. **GNP:** $2.3 bil., $2,500 per capita (1993 est.). **Chief crops:** maize, cotton, rice, sugar, citrus fruits. **Livestock:** goats, cattle, sheep, pigs, asses. **Natural resources:** asbestos, coal, clay, tin, hydroelectric power. **Major industries:** mining (coal and asbestos), wood pulp, sugar. **Labor force:** 195,000 (1987); about 92,000 wage earners (many whose employment is off-and-on); 36% agriculture and forestry, 20% community and social services, 14% manufacturing, 9% construction, 21% other; over 60,000 in subsistence agriculture; 24,000–29,000 employed in South Africa. **Exports:** $632 mil. (f.o.b., 1993 est.); sugar, asbestos, wood and forest products, citrus, canned fruits. **Imports:** $734 mil. (c.i.f., 1993 est.); motor vehicles, chemicals, petroleum products, foodstuffs. **Major trading partners:** ***exports:*** 40% South Africa, EU, Canada; ***imports:*** 75% South Africa, Japan, Belgium, UK.

Intl. Orgs. FAO, G-77, IBRD, ICAO, IDA, IFAD, IFC, ILO, IMF, INTERPOL, ITU, NAM, UN, UNESCO, UPU, WHO.

The Kingdom of Swaziland, a landlocked African country, is surrounded on three sides by South Africa and on the fourth by Mozambique. The Swazi are of Bantu origin. They are believed to have migrated in the late 1700s, under their chief Ngwane II, into what is now southeastern Swaziland, finding several different peoples there. Ngwane II and his successors united these tribal clans by the beginning of the 19th century.

Although British and Boer traders began exploring the area in the 1830s, it was not until gold was discovered in the 1880s that settlers began coming in large numbers. They hoodwinked the illiterate Swazi leadership into signing away their rights to the land. The British and Boer governments agreed in 1894 that the Boers would control Swaziland, but power reverted to Great Britain after they defeated the Boers in the Boer War, which ended in 1902. Not until the 1967 did they give Swaziland authority over its internal affairs. Under the British-authored constitution, Swaziland gained its independence in September 1968 as a constitutional monarchy led by King Sobhuza II. He set aside the constitution in 1973 and disbanded the legislature. He ruled the country with the aid of a council of conservative ministers and named a committee to write a new constitution that was supposed to be more in keeping with Swazi traditions. A new legislature was created in 1979. The king died in 1982 and was replaced by his 18-year-old son, who took the name King Mswati III, in 1986.

In 1986 South African forces conducted raids into Swaziland, allegedly in pursuit of African National Congress activists. Swaziland maintains cooperative but cool relations with South Africa and Mozambique.

Sweden

Kingdom of Sweden

Geography Location: Scandinavian peninsula, northwest Europe. **Boundaries:** Norway to NE and W, Finland to NE, Gulf of Bothnia to E, Baltic Sea to E and S, Skagerrak channel to SW. **Total land area:** 173,731 sq. mi. (449,964 sq km). **Coastline:** 2,000 mi. (3,218 km). **Comparative area:** slightly larger than California. **Land use:** 7% arable land; 0% permanent crops; 2% meadows and pastures; 64% forest and woodland; 27% other; includes negl. % irrigated. **Major cities:** (1993 est.) Stockholm (capital) 693,103; Göteburg (Gothenburg) 437,594; Malmö 237,531; Uppsala 178,071; Linköping 128,689.

People Population: 8,778,461 (1994 est.). **Nationality:** noun—Swede(s); adjective—Swedish. **Ethnic groups:** homogeneous white population; small Lappish minority; about 12% foreign-born or first-generation immigrants (Finns, Yugoslavs, Danes, Norwegians, Greeks, Turks). **Languages:** Swedish, small Lapp- and Finnish-speaking minorities; immigrants speak native languages. **Religions:** 93.5% Evangelical Lutheran, 1.0% Roman Catholic, 5.5% other.

Government Type: constitutional monarchy. **Independence:** N.A. **Constitution:** Jan. 1, 1975. **National holidays:** Sweden Day, June 6; King's Birthday, Apr. 30. **Head of government:** Carl XVI Gustaf, king (since Nov. 1973); Ingvar Carlsson, prime minister (since Oct. 1994). **Structure:** executive power vested in cabinet, responsible to Parliament; legislative authority rests with unicameral Parliament (Riksdag); Supreme Court, six superior courts, 108 lower courts.

Economy Monetary unit: Swedish krona. **Budget:** (FY94) ***income:*** $45.1 bil.; ***expend.:*** $73.1 bil. **GDP:** $153.7 bil., $17,600 per capita (1993). **Chief crops:** grain, sugar beets, potatoes; 100% self-sufficient in grains and potatoes, 85% self-sufficient in sugar beets; milk and dairy products account for 37% of farm income. **Livestock:** poultry, pigs, cattle, sheep, goats. **Natural resources:** zinc, iron ore, lead, copper, silver. **Major industries:** iron and steel, precision equipment (bearings, radio and telephone parts, armaments), wood pulp. **Labor force:** 4.55 mil. (1991); 32.8% private services, 30% government services, 22% mining and manufacturing; 1.9% unemployment (1987). **Exports:** $49.7 bil. (f.o.b., 1993 est.); machinery, motor vehicles, paper products, pulp and wood, iron and steel products. **Imports:** $42.3 bil. (c.i.f., 1993 est.); machinery, petroleum and petroleum products, chemicals, motor vehicles, foodstuffs. **Major trading partners:** ***exports:*** 54.4% EU (14.2% Germany, 10% UK, 6.6% Denmark), 8.6% U.S., 8.2% Norway; 5.1% Finland; ***imports:*** 55.3% EU, 8.4% U.S.

Intl. Orgs. EFTA, EU, FAO, IAEA, IBRD, ICAO, IDA, IFAD, IFC, ILO, IMO, INTELSAT, INTERPOL, ITU, OECD, OSCE, UN, UNESCO, UPU, WHO, WIPO, WMO, WTO.

The earliest Swedes, the Svear, conquered and merged with their southern neighbors, the Gotar, by the sixth century. Organized into petty kingdoms, Swedes joined with other Norsemen in the Viking raids of the seventh through 11th centuries; in the 10th century, they began to dominate a trading empire that stretched through Russia to the Black Sea. Christianity was introduced by St. Ansgar in 829 but became fully established only in the 12th century, during the reign of Eric IX, who also conquered Finland. For centuries Sweden warred with its neighbors, Norway and Denmark, for control in the north, and it competed with the German Hanseatic League for control of the Baltic trade.

The Swedish and Norwegian monarchies were merged in 1319 by Magnus VII, and in 1397 Queen Margaret effected the Kalmar Union, which united Sweden, Denmark, and Norway under a single monarchy. Sweden resisted Danish rule, and in 1520 King Christian II responded with the massacre of the Swedish nobility at Stockholm. Sweden then rose against the Danish throne and in 1523 enthroned Gustavus Wasa as Gustavus I, founder of the Swedish monarchy. The Wasa dynasty slowly introduced Lutheran Christianity and in 1604 banned Catholicism.

Sweden became a European champion of Protestantism in the 17th century, intervening against the Habsburgs in the Thirty Years' War. Emerging among the victors after 1648, Sweden successfully waged wars with Denmark and Poland, built a great northern empire, and made the Baltic Sea virtually a Swedish lake. But in the late 17th century and into the 18th, the Russians deprived Sweden of the Baltic's eastern shore and, in 1808, of Finland, while the Prussians drove Sweden from the southern Baltic coast.

The kings of Sweden during the 18th century pursued a pointless despotism that weakened the country politically and socially. Sweden joined the European powers against Napoleon in 1813 and was rewarded with Norway in 1814. In 1905 Norway gained its independence, and Sweden took on its modern boundaries.

Sweden's greatest natural resources are timber, iron ore, and hydroelectric power. The first two were exploited by traditional industries, which supplemented other long-term economic activities such as fishing, maritime trade, and agriculture. All three provided the basis for industrialization in the 19th and 20th centuries, leading to an economic prosperity that was enhanced and protected by political neutrality.

Sweden's neutrality was largely respected by Hitler during World War II. Through the war Sweden continued to be ruled, under King Gustavus V, by a national coalition government lasting until 1945. Sweden's gross national product (GNP) rose by 20 percent during the war years.

The Social Democratic party dominated the Swedish government after 1936, and after 1945 its governance was reestablished, lasting until 1976 under the leadership of Tage Erlander. Sweden, like its Scandinavian neighbors, constructed an economy based on free enterprise, public ownership of utilities, exports, social welfare, and high taxes.

A UN charter member, Sweden accepted Marshall Plan aid and joined the Council of Europe in 1948. Sweden's plan for a Nordic Defense Alliance failed when Norway and Denmark joined NATO (Sweden refused to join the North Atlantic pact), but the political and economic Nordic Council (Sweden, Norway, Denmark, Iceland, and, after 1956, Finland) was formed in 1952–53. This consultative body backed the establishment of SAS as the joint national airline of the first three members; coordination of the welfare programs of member states; and abolition of passport controls and controls on the migration of labor within Scandinavia.

Erlander retired as prime minister in 1969 and was succeeded by Olaf Palme, who pursued a more rigid socialist program than his predecessor. He advocated legislation to make incomes more equal, provoking some labor unrest. When King Gustav VI Adolf died in 1973 the Palme government passed the 1974 Instrument of Government Act, divesting the king of his role as commander in chief of the armed forces and of his right to appoint prime ministers.

Economic growth came to a virtual halt in the 1970s; lacking petroleum and gas resources, Sweden's oil import costs rose 700 percent between 1972 and 1979. Consumer prices rose sharply, and labor unrest grew. The Social Democrats were turned out of office by a conservative coalition in 1976 but returned with a minority cabinet in 1982.

Palme was assassinated in 1986, and he was succeeded by Ingvar Carlsson, whose Social Democratic program focused on a scheme whereby business profits are taxed to fund labor union purchases of sufficient stock to gain labor ownership of private enterprise.

September 1991 elections unseated Carlsson and the Social Democrats, who had ruled Sweden for 53 of the last 59 years. A coalition of four conservative parties under new prime minister Carl Bildt formed a government that pledged to cut taxes (currently 58% of GNP), and phase out some welfare programs.

But in elections held in September 1994, Carlsson returned to power as voters expressed dissatisfaction with inflation, unemployment, and an enormous public debt, all of which spiraled under the Bildt government. The Social Democrats fell 13 votes short of a majority in Parliament, however, forcing them to seek the support of the right-centrist Liberal party in a coalition government. On Jan. 1, 1995, Sweden entered the European Union.

Switzerland

Swiss Confederation

Geography **Location:** landlocked country in central Europe. **Boundaries:** Germany to N, Austria to E, Italy to S, and France to W. **Total land area:** 15,942 sq. mi. (41,290 sq km). **Coastline:** none. **Comparative area:** between Maryland and West Virginia. **Land use:** 10% arable land; 1% permanent crops; 40% meadows and pastures; 26% forest and woodland; 23% other; includes 1% irrigated. **Major cities:** (1992 est.) Berne (Bern, capital) 130,390; Zürich 344,094; Basel (Bâle) 174,976; Genève (Geneva or Genf) 169,503; Lausanne 117,485.

People **Population:** 7,040,119 (1994 est.). **Nationality:** noun—Swiss (sing., pl.); adjective—Swiss. **Ethnic groups:** total population—65% German, 18% French, 10% Italian, 1% Romansh, 5% other; Swiss nationals—74% German, 20% French, 4% Italian, 1% Romansh, 1% other. **Languages:** total population—65% German, 18% French, 12% Italian, 1% Romansh, 4% other; Swiss nationals—74% German, 20% French, 4% Italian, 1% Romansh, 1% other. **Religions:** 49% Catholic, 48% Protestant.

Government **Type:** federal republic. **Independence:** Aug. 1, 1291. **Constitution:** May 29, 1874. **National holiday:** National Day, Aug. 1. **Head of government:** Kaspar Villiger, president (since Jan. 1995). **Structure:** federal council (Bundesrat) has executive authority; bicameral Parliament (National Council, Council of States) has legislative authority; judiciary left chiefly to cantons.

Economy **Monetary unit:** Swiss franc. **Budget:** (1993 est.) ***income:*** $23.7 bil.; ***expend.:*** $26.9 bil. **GDP:** $149.1 bil., $21,300 per capita (1993). **Chief crops:** less than 50% self-sufficient; food shortages—fish, refined sugar, fats and oils (other than butter), grains, eggs, fruits, vegetables, meat; dairy farming predominates. **Livestock:** pigs, cattle, sheep, goats, horses. **Natural resources:** hydropower potential, timber, salt. **Major industries:** machinery, chemicals, watches. **Labor force:** 3.31 mil.; 904,095 foreign workers, mostly Italian (1987); 42% services, 39% industry and crafts, 11% government; 0.7% unemployment (1988 est.). **Exports:** $63 bil. (f.o.b., 1993); machinery and equipment, precision instruments, metal products, foodstuffs. **Imports:** $60.7 bil. (c.i.f., 1993); agricultural products, machinery and transport equipment, chemicals, textiles. **Major trading partners:** ***exports:*** 64% Europe (56% EU, 8% other), 9% U.S., 4% Japan; ***imports:*** 79% Europe (72% EU, 7% other), 5% U.S.

Intl. Orgs. EFTA, FAO, IAEA, ICAO, IFAD, ILO, IMO, INTELSAT, INTERPOL, ITU, OECD, OSCE, UNESCO, UPU, WHO, WIPO, WMO, WTO; permanent observer status at UN.

Switzerland, the Roman province of Helvetia, began to assume its modern form in A.D. 1291, when three independent cantons formed a defensive league against the expansion of Habsburg power. The Swiss League grew to eight cantons in 1353, 13 in 1513, 22 in 1815. The league continues to evolve; it reached its present size of 20 cantons and six half-cantons with the creation of the Canton of Jura in 1979.

The Treaty of Westphalia, which ended the Thirty Years' War in 1648, gave international recognition to the independence of Switzerland from the Holy Roman Empire. Switzerland became a client state of France in the Napoleonic period; the European powers recognized and guaranteed Swiss independence and neutrality at the Congress of Vienna in 1815. Constitutional changes in 1848 and 1874 somewhat increased the power of the central government, but the individual cantons cling stubbornly to their independence within the confederation. This policy has helped ensure stability within a multilingual nation.

The Swiss government consists of an upper house, representing the cantons, and a lower house that is directly elected. No executive can veto, nor court disallow, a bill of the Swiss legislature. Executive power is vested in a seven-member committee chosen by the legislature, with a rotating presidency.

Swiss neutrality is defended by more than simply international guarantees. Switzerland is a highly militarized society; every male is required to serve in the citizen's militia until age 47, keeping an assault rifle and other equipment ready at home. The armed forces are equipped with sophisticated modern weapons, and military spending amounts to 30 percent of the Swiss federal budget.

Landlocked, with little fertile farmland and limited Alpine pastures, lacking both natural resources and a colonial empire, Switzerland was traditionally one of Europe's poorest countries. Until the 19th century, its principal export was soldiers, mercenaries who supplied military services to any European sovereign who could pay for them. (The pope's Swiss Guard is a remnant of this tradition.) With the spread in the late 18th century of the Romantic movement, Europeans learned to appreciate the glamour of Alpine scenery, and a tourist industry was born. It was much expanded in the 20th century with the development of Alpine skiing. Tourism remains a conspicuous, though relatively minor, part of the Swiss economy.

Swiss prosperity came in the 20th century with specialized manufacturing and free trade within the world economy. By 1940 half of the population was engaged in manufacturing, producing products requiring high degrees of skill: processed foods, watches, electrical machinery, engines, fine textiles, and the like.

Neutral in both world wars, Switzerland required no postwar recovery in the 1940s. It capitalized on the restructuring of European politics and economics to expand into the service sector, which now employs half of the work force (while manufacturing has declined to about 40%). Tourism, banking, insurance, and clerical/bureaucratic services to the many international organizations with headquarters in Switzerland help give the nation one of Europe's highest standards of living. Under pressure from the EC and the United States, Switzerland agreed to phase out its famous "Form B" (i.e., secret bank accounts).

In the postwar period, Switzerland has enjoyed both political and economic stability. A cautious approach to economic development led to annual growth rates of over 6 percent in the 1950s and early 1960s, declining to 2 percent in the 1970s; the world economic boom of the 1980s produced higher growth rates. In general the economy has avoided inflation, and the stability of the Swiss franc has been maintained.

Switzerland is a member of the European Free Trade Association and has ties to the EU, although it is not a member. Recent referenda brought overwhelming rejection of UN membership (it currently has observer status), and support for restrictive immigration legislation. The most significant political change in the postwar period has been the gradual extension, canton by canton, of women's right to vote. Almost as startling were the 1989 referendum in which one-third of the voters chose to abolish the Swiss army by the year 2000, and the 1993 approval of casino gambling to fund social security.

Syria

Syrian Arab Republic

Geography Location: western Asia. **Boundaries:** Turkey to N, Iraq to E, Jordan to S, Lebanon and Israel to SW, Mediterranean Sea to W. **Total land area:** 71,498 sq. mi. (185,180 sq km). **Coastline:** 120 mi. (193 km). **Comparative area:** slightly larger than North Dakota. **Land use:** 28% arable land; 3% permanent crops; 46% meadows and pastures; 3% forest and woodland; 20% other; includes 3% irrigated. **Major cities:** (1990 est.) Damascus (capital) 1,378,000; Aleppo 1,355,000; Homs 481,000; Latakia 267,000; Hama 237,000.

People Population: 14,886,672 (1994 est.). **Nationality:** noun—Syrian(s); adjective—Syrian. **Ethnic groups:** 90.3% Arab, 9.7% Kurds, Armenians, and other. **Languages:** Arabic (official), Kurdish, Armenian, Aramaic, Circassian; French and English widely understood. **Religions:** 74% Sunni Muslim; 16% Alawite, Druze, and other Muslim sects; 10% Christian.

Government Type: republic; under left-wing military regime since Mar. 1963. **Independence:** Apr. 17, 1946 (from League of Nations Mandate under French administration). **Constitution:** Mar. 12, 1973. **National holiday:** Independence Day, Apr. 17. **Heads of government:** Lt. Gen. Hafez al-Assad, president (since Mar. 1971); Mahmoud Zoubi, prime minister (since Nov. 1987). **Structure:** executive powers vested in president and Council of Ministers; power rests in unicameral legislature (People's Council); seat of power is Baath party's Regional (Syrian) Command.

Economy Monetary unit: Syrian pound. **Budget:** (1993 est.) ***income:*** $7.13 bil.; ***expend.:*** $9.5 bil. **GDP:** $81.7 bil., $5,700 per capita (1993 est.). **Chief crops:** cotton, wheat, barley, tobacco. **Livestock:** sheep, goats, cattle, asses, horses. **Natural resources:** crude oil, phosphates, chrome and manganese ores, asphalt, iron ore. **Major industries:** textiles, food processing, beverages. **Labor force:** 2.4 mil. (1984); 36% miscellaneous services, 32% agriculture, 32% industry (including construction); majority unskilled; shortage of skilled labor; 5% unemployment (1986). **Exports:** $3.4 bil. (f.o.b., 1993 est.); 40% petroleum, 30% textiles, fruits, vegetables, phosphates. **Imports:** $4.1 bil. (c.i.f., 1993 est.); 21% foodstuffs and beverages, 16% metal and metal products, 14% machinery, textiles. **Major trading partners:** ***exports:*** 42% former USSR and Eastern Europe, 31% EU, 17% Arab countries, 2% U.S./Canada; ***imports:*** 42% EU, 13% former USSR and Eastern Europe, 13% other Europe, 8% U.S./Canada, 6% Arab countries.

Intl. Orgs. Arab League, FAO, G-77, IAEA, IBRD, ICAO, IDA, IFAD, IFC, ILO, IMF, IMO, INTELSAT, INTERPOL, ITU, NAM, UN, UNESCO, UPU, WHO, WMO.

The home of some of the world's most ancient centers of civilization, Syria was successively part of the Hittite, Assyrian, and Persian empires. At various times it was conquered by the Babylonians and the Egyptians. From about 1250 B.C., the coastal cities came under Phoenician rule. Alexander the Great brought Syria into the Hellenic world with his conquests in 332 B.C. After the fall of the Alexandrian empire, Syria came under the domain of the Seleucid empire but was constantly threatened by the Hellenic kingdom of Egypt, based in Alexandria.

In the classical period, Syria embraced a much larger territory than that of the present Syrian nation; it included the entire Levant and parts of present-day Turkey, Iraq, Iran, and Jordan. Greater Syria was conquered by Rome in 63 B.C. Under Roman rule the oasis region of Palmyra grew into a powerful semiautonomous kingdom. With the division of the Roman Empire in the fourth century A.D., Syria became part of the Eastern Roman (Byzantine) Empire. Throughout the Roman and Byzantine periods, the country was an important center of Christianity.

Syria was one of the first areas conquered when Islam began expansion from Arabia; Islamic rule was established by 636. From 661 to 751, Damascus was the center of the Caliphate, the ruling body of the Islamic world. By the late 11th century, the Seljuk Turks had conquered Syria. The large Syrian Christian population welcomed the European Crusaders as liberators from the Turks, but both Christians and Turks were defeated by the Arab general Saladin in the late 12th century. Saladin's rule was followed by that of the Mamluk empire of Egypt. During the Mamluk period, Mongol armies twice invaded Syria, in the mid-13th century and at the turn of the 15th century.

An Ottoman army defeated the Mamluks in Syria in 1516, making Syria part of the Ottoman Empire. In the 18th century, France declared itself the protector of Syria's Christian community against Ottoman abuses. Napoleon invaded Syria in 1799 but withdrew after a brief occupation. In the 1830s Egyptian troops occupied Syria but were forced to withdraw under pressure from the European powers.

Syrian nationalist aspirations emerged as the Ottoman Empire began to crumble before World War I. During the war the British encouraged

Syrians to rebel against Turkish rule. After World War I, France governed both Syria and Lebanon (the Levant States) under a League of Nations mandate. Under French rule, the region was divided into small territorial states along communal lines; Lebanon became independent in 1926. After prolonged negotiations much of Syria was organized into a semiautonomous state in 1930–32.

In June 1940 the French administration in Syria declared its loyalty to the Vichy government. British and Free French forces invaded in June 1941, and an independent Syrian republic was established in September 1941. Separately administered territories were consolidated with the republic over the next two years, and full independence was declared on Jan. 1, 1944; foreign troops did not withdraw, however, until April 1946.

Syria became a founding member of the Arab League and participated in the first Arab-Israeli War in 1948. An armistice with Israel was signed in July 1949. Severe political instability marked the early years of Syrian independence; the government was overthrown by military coups three times in 1949 alone.

Most of Syria's Jews emigrated to Israel before or during 1948, and much of its once-substantial Christian population has emigrated also. Syrian politics remain dominated by communal concerns, however; the Arab majority is divided into Sunni, Shiite, Alawite, and Druze communities.

Syria and Egypt merged as the United Arab Republic in February 1958; Syria seceded from the federation on Sept. 30, 1961. In Mar. 1963 a military coup established the pan-Arab Socialist Baath party in power; all other political parties were abolished. The Baath party leadership is dominated by the minority Alawite community. Pres. Hafez al-Assad took power on Feb. 22, 1971.

In the 1967 Arab-Israeli War (the Six Day War), Israel seized and held the Golan Heights region of Syria, from which Syria had long shelled Israeli communities and military installations. The Golan Heights have since been incorporated into Israeli territory.

Syrian troops aided Palestinian forces fighting government troops in Jordan in September 1970. After the expulsion of Palestinian forces from Jordan in July 1971, Syria broke off relations with Jordan; relations were restored in 1975.

On Oct. 6, 1973, Syrian and Egyptian forces attacked Israel, touching off the third Arab-Israeli War, the Yom Kippur War. A cease-fire took effect on Oct. 24; Syria failed to regain territory lost to Israel in 1967. Following the 1973 war, Syria became a major recipient of economic aid from the Arab oil states and of military equipment from the Soviet Union.

In 1976 Syrian troops entered Lebanon in an attempt to mediate in that nation's civil war and became enmeshed in that conflict. Major fighting between Syrian troops and Lebanese Christian militiamen broke out in April 1981. On June 6, 1982, Israeli troops invaded Lebanon and engaged Syrian troops in a five-day war in the Bekaa Valley. Following serious losses of aircraft and troops, Syria agreed to a cease-fire with Israel on June 11. Syrian troops continue to occupy parts of Lebanon.

An attempted coup, in February 1982, by the Moslem Brotherhood led to serious fighting within Syria, but the rebellion was put down; casualties on both sides were estimated at more than 5,000.

From the time of the 1973 Arab-Israeli War (the Yom Kippur War), Syria consistently adopted a radical stance in Middle Eastern politics, rejecting the 1979 Egyptian-Israeli accord and all other attempts at Arab-Israeli reconciliation. Supporting radical movements within the Palestine Liberation Organization, Syria aided Palestinian militants in driving Yasir Arafat's centrist faction of the PLO from its headquarters in Tripoli in 1983. The Syrian government has been implicated in various acts of international terrorism in support of Palestinian, Libyan, and Iranian causes.

Syria has played a major role in the Lebanese peace process, backing the governments in place since the Taif peace accord and accommodating a peace settlement between rival Shiite militias. Syria also took part in the anti-Iraq coalition in 1990–91, sending 20,000 troops to Saudi Arabia, as well as mobilizing forces on its common border with Iraq. Despite its long-standing enmity toward Israel, the Syrian government in 1994 made serious efforts toward achieving peace in the Middle East, including an offer to normalize relations in exchange for a return of the Golan Heights. Talks continued in early 1995.

Taiwan

Republic of China
(also called Nationalist China, Formosa)

Geography Location: one large and several smaller islands about 100 mi. (160 km) off SE coast of mainland China. Taipei 25°03'N, 121°30'E. **Boundaries:** East China Sea to N, Pacific Ocean to E, Bashi Channel to S, and Formosa Strait to W; separated from mainland by Formosa Strait. **Total land area:** 13,892 sq. mi. (35,980 sq km). **Coastline:** 900 mi. (1,448 km). **Comparative area:** slightly larger than Maryland. **Land use:** 24% arable land; 1% permanent crops; 5% meadows and pastures; 55% forest and woodland; 15% other; includes 14% irrigated. **Major cities:** (1992 est.) Taipei (capital) 2,696,073; Kaohsiung 1,405,909; Taichung 794,960; Tainan 694,630; Panchiao 543,982.

People Population: 21,298,930 (1994 est.). **Nationality:** noun—Chinese (sing., pl.); adjective—Chinese. **Ethnic groups:** 84% Taiwanese, 14% mainland Chinese, 2% aborigine. **Languages:** Mandarin Chinese (official); Taiwanese and Hakka dialects also used. **Religions:** 93% mixture of Buddhist, Confucian, and Taoist; 4.5% Christian, 2.5% other.

Government Type: one-party presidential regime; 1988 political organizations bill permits legal formation of new political parties. **Constitution:** Dec. 25, 1947. **National holiday:** Oct. 10. **Heads of government:** Li Teng-hui, president (since Jan. 1988); Yü Kuo-hua, premier (since June 1984). **Structure:** five independent branches (executive, legislative, judicial, plus traditional Chinese functions of examination and control), dominated by executive branch; president and vice president elected by National Assembly.

Economy Monetary unit: New Taiwan dollar. **Budget:** (1991 est.) ***income:*** $30.3 bil.; ***expend.:*** $30.1 bil. **GDP:** $224 bil., $10,600 per capita (1993 est.). **Chief crops:** rice, sweet potatoes, sugarcane, bananas, pineapples. **Livestock:** chickens, ducks, pigs, geese, turkeys. **Natural resources:** small deposits of coal, natural gas, limestone, marble, and asbestos. **Major industries:** textiles, clothing, chemicals. **Labor force:** 7,880,000 (1986); 41% industry and commerce, 32% services, 20% agriculture; 2% unemployment (1988). **Exports:** $85 bil. (f.o.b., 1993 est.); 19% electrical machinery, 15.6% textiles, 14% general machinery and equipment, 9% communications equipment, 7% basic metals and metal products. **Imports:** $77.1 bil. (c.i.f., 1993 est.); 16% machinery and equipment, 11% chemicals and chemical products, 7% basic metals, 5% crude oil. **Major trading partners:** (1989) ***exports:*** 36% U.S., 17% EU countries, 14% Japan; ***imports:*** 31% Japan, 23% U.S., 9% Saudi Arabia, 17% EU countries.

Intl. Orgs. expelled from UN General Assembly and Security Council, Oct. 25, 1971, and withdrew from other subsidiary organs; expelled from IMF/World Bank group 1980; seeking to join other international organizations.

Nominally part of the Chinese empire since the Song dynasty (960–1279), Taiwan was inhabited only by non-Chinese aboriginals before the 17th century. Around 1600 the Portuguese established a trading station on Taiwan; they named the island Ilha Formosa. In 1620 the Dutch built Fort Zeelandia near present-day Tainan, controlling the island until they were driven out by the Chinese pirate-patriot Koxinga (Zheng Chenggong). Remnants of the overthrown Ming dynasty (1368–1644) held out on the island until 1683, when it came under the sway of the Qing dynasty (1644–1911). Thereafter, substantial numbers of farmers from Fujian Province migrated to the fertile western lowlands of the island, driving the aboriginals into the central mountains. The Qing dynasty administered Taiwan as a semiautonomous subprovince of Fujian Province.

Following China's defeat by Japan in the Sino-Japanese War of 1894–95, Taiwan was ceded to Japan as a colony. The Japanese built roads and railroads to exploit Taiwan's resources of rice, timber, and minerals. In 1945, after Japan's defeat in World War II, Taiwan was returned to Chinese sovereignty.

As the Chinese civil war turned against the Nationalist party of Chiang Kai-shek (see "China"), Nationalist troops began to prepare Taiwan as a base for a retreat from the mainland.

In 1947 Nationalist agents executed several thousand students and others suspected of favoring Taiwan's independence from China. In 1949 approximately two million Nationalist soldiers, government officials, and civilian sympathizers retreated to Taiwan. The relocated Republic of China (ROC) continued to claim to be the legitimate government of all of China, now under Communist control. In addition to Taiwan proper, the Nationalists occupied the P'eng-hu Islands in the Taiwan Straits and the small islands of Quemoy and Matsu just off the coast of Fujian. Recovery of the mainland became a cornerstone of ROC policy, but no serious attempt was made to do so. U.S. policy in the Taiwan Straits was to defend Taiwan against Communist attack but also to keep the two rival governments of China well separated from each other.

A successful program of land reform in the early 1950s led to the creation of surplus capital, which fueled the development of an industrial base on the island. Foreign investment from Japan and the United States, and American military and economic aid, also enhanced economic development. By the early 1970s, the island had developed an export-oriented economy, producing textiles, cement, plastics, assembled electronic appliances, and other manufactured goods.

Chiang Kai-shek, president of the Republic of China since 1928, died in 1975 and was succeeded by his son, Chiang Ching-kuo. Under both father and son, the Nationalist party (Kuomintang, or KMT) controlled both the ROC and the Taiwan Provincial governments; mainland refugees and their descendants (15% of the population) dominated senior government posts and the military officer corps. Native Taiwanese played the leading role in agriculture, industry, and, increasingly, in local and county governments.

In foreign affairs the Republic of China became more and more isolated from the world community. In 1971 China's seat in the United Nations was taken away from the ROC and awarded to the People's Republic of China; international diplomatic recognition of the ROC dwindled steadily thereafter. On Jan. 1, 1979, the United States withdrew its recognition of the ROC and inaugurated mutual diplomatic relations with the People's Republic. Under the Taiwan Relations Act of 1979, nominally nongovernmental relations were maintained between the United States and Taiwan through the American Institute in Taipei and Taiwan's Coordination Council for North American Affairs in Washington, D.C. Similar arrangements elsewhere ensured that Taiwan's trade and other interests would be secured throughout the non-Communist world. Taiwan's economy has continued to be one of the world's most vigorous; Taiwan enjoys a substantial favorable balance of trade with the United States and has foreign-exchange holdings in excess of $75 billion.

In 1986 Pres. Chiang Ching-kuo began a policy of liberalization; in the fall of 1987, he abolished martial law and allowed non-KMT political parties to function legally. Some barriers to travel to and communication with the mainland by ROC citizens were eased, but Taiwan's government continued to rebuff all calls from the mainland for direct contacts and discussions of reunification. Chiang Ching-kuo died in January 1988 and was succeeded by his vice president, Li Teng-hui. In March 1990, Li was overwhelmingly reelected by the National Assembly in the first election for the office.

The ruling KMT maintained its hold on power in legislative elections on Dec. 19, 1992, but the opposition Democratic Progressive party scored a stunning success, tripling its number of legislative seats and bringing the issue of Taiwanese independence to the forefront of the island's political agenda. Meanwhile, factional rivalry deepened in the KMT, with Pres. Li's Wisdom Coalition challenged by the New Kuomintang Alliance of Prime Minister (and former general) Hau Pei-tsun. Hau reluctantly resigned on Feb. 3, 1993, to take responsibility for the electoral fiasco, but his faction, with military backing, continued to pose a threat to Pres. Li's power.

On Apr. 27–29, 1993, Taiwan and the People's Republic of China held their first-ever official talks, in Singapore. Though vague and inconclusive, the talks were deemed a success and both sides pledged further contact.

Tajikistan

Republic of Tajikistan

Geography **Location:** southeast central Asia. **Boundaries:** Kyrgyzstan to NE, China to E, Afghanistan to S and SW, Uzbekistan to NW and N. **Total land area:** 55,251 sq. mi. (143,100 sq km). **Coastline:** none. **Comparative area:** slightly smaller than Wisconsin. **Land use:** 6% cropland; 22% permanent pasture; 5% forest and woodland; 67% other. **Major cities:** (1990 est.) Dushanbe (Stalinabad 1929–61) (capital) 602,000; Khodzhent (formerly Leninabad), 163,000 (1989).

People **Population:** 5,995,469 (1994 est.). **Nationality:** noun—Tajik(s); adjective—Tajik. **Ethnic groups:** 62.3% Tajik, 23.5% Uzbek, 7.6% Russian, 1.4% Tatar. **Languages:** Tajik (official) is closely related to Farsi (Persian) and was written in Cyrillic script since 1940; Arabic script was reinstated in 1989; Russian, ethnic languages. **Religions:** Muslim—Sunni, Isma'ili; Russian Orthodox, Judaism.

Government **Type:** republic. **Independence:** Sept. 9, 1991 (from USSR). **Constitution:** being drafted. **National holiday:** Independence Day, Sept. 9. **Heads of government:** Emomali Rakhmonov; head of state (since Nov. 1994); Jamsheed Karimov (since Dec. 1994). **Structure:** executive—president, vice president, Council of Ministers; legislative—Supreme Soviet; judicial—judicial system.

Economy **Monetary unit:** Russian ruble. **Budget:** (1993 est.). ***income:*** N.A.; ***expend.:*** N.A. **GDP:** $6.9 bil., $1,180 per capita (1993 est.). **Chief crops:** seed cotton, vegetables, fruit, grain, grapes. **Livestock:** sheep, goats, cattle, pigs. **Natural resources:** gold, iron, zinc, lead, mercury, tin, petroleum, natural gas. **Major industries:** mineral processing, textiles, carpet making, food processing. **Labor force:** 1.938 mil. (1990). **Exports:** $263 mil. to outside the FSU countries (1993); aluminum, cotton, fruits, vegetables, oil, textiles. **Imports:** $371 mil. to outside the FSU countries (1993); chemicals, machinery and transport equipment, textiles, foodstuffs. **Major trading partners:** ***exports:*** Russia, Kazakhstan, Ukraine, Uzbekistan. ***imports:*** N.A.

Orgs. CIS, IMF, OSCE, UN, World Bank; applying for membership in other international organizations.

Tajikistan is a mountainous country, with over half of its territory above 10,000 feet. Its mountain ranges are the northern and southern Tian Shan and the Pamirs, where the former Soviet Union's highest points of Lenin Peak and Communism Peak are found. The dense river system and the many fertile valleys make habitation possible in such a mountainous country, although the entire territory is prone to earthquakes.

Tajikistan exemplifies the complexities of central Asia, since, unlike other ethnic groups on the region, the Tajiks were not nomadic but sedentary, and their language was Persian, not Turkic. They are a population that somehow escaped the waves of Turkish influence that swept through central Asia. As early as the eighth century A.D., the Tajiks probably formed a distinctive ethnic group, although they have never been a completely independent people. Despite the formation of several semi-independent states in their history, they have always been a small part of the larger Uzbek lands. In the mid-19th century, the Russian empire expanded southward, and the northern Tajik territories came under Russian rule. At the same time, the tribal state known as the Khanate of Bukhara controlled the southern Tajik territories.

In April 1918 northern Tajikistan came under Soviet control and was included in the Turkestan Autonomous Soviet Socialist Republic (ASSR). Three years later, the Red Army took the other regions that had been ruled by Bukhara. There was local opposition to Soviet rule, and the fighting meant that full Soviet authority over all of the area was not established until 1925. When the USSR created the National Delimitation of the Central Asian Republics in 1924, it founded the Tajik ASSR as part of the Uzbek Soviet Socialist Republic (SSR); on Oct. 16, 1929, it became the Tajik SSR.

The Tajiks were fiercely opposed to the policies of land reform and collectivization, and during the ensuing Soviet repression of the 1930s, almost all native Tajiks were replaced by Russians in leading government and party positions. There have been reports of rising Islamic influence and increasing anti-Russian sentiment and even riots during the 1970s, evidence that the animosity toward the Russians that stemmed with its forced incorporation into the USSR had not abated since the 1920s. Under Soviet rule, there was some economic and social progress, however, living standards in Tajikistan are still among the lowest in the former union. Most people continue to live in rural qishlaqs, or settlements, consisting of 200–700 one-family houses built along an irrigation ditch or a river. The country is a major producer of cotton, and its industries are nonferrous metallurgy, cotton processing, fruit canning, and wine making.

Mikhail Gorbachev's glasnost, or openness, policy resulted in a campaign against corruption, a relaxation of censorship in the press, and increased ethnic tensions over alleged discrimination against Tajiks living in Uzbekistan. In June 1989 there were violent clashes between the two groups on the border between the two republics. There were also riots in February 1990 in Dushanbe, when the suggestion that Armenian refugees would be resettled there spurred the local Tajiks into action. Increased freedom of the press has given rise to a growing interest in Iran and Iranian culture, for even though they are closely related, contact between Iran and the Tajiks was severely limited during the Soviet period.

In large part due to the riots, opposition candidates were barred from the March 1990 elections and the Communist party won 94 percent of the seats. After the failed August 1991 coup in Moscow, the Communist party was banned, and the president was forced to resign over his support of the coup. Since then, there have been several Communist party coups, and the party has been banned and reinstated several times. In the presidential elections in November, former Communist party leader Rakhmon Nabiyev won with 58 percent of the vote. But after a relatively tranquil six months, Islamic fundamentalists, armed allegedly by Iran and Afghanistan, rose up against the Nabiyev regime. Vicious fighting for almost four months led to Nabiyev's resignation at gunpoint and the launching of a fundamentalist government.

In December 1992 the pro-Communist forces launched a successful counterattack in which thousands were killed and perhaps 300,000 displaced. Russian troops remain in Dushanbe and support the new government.

Voters in November 1994 approved by referendum a new (highly presidential) constitution with 90 percent of the vote, and elected as president Emomali Rakhmonov with 60 percent. But the civil war of the current, ex-Communist and Russian-backed government against Islamic rebels continues, despite UN-mediated cease-fires signed in September 1994 and May 1995. (Russian and CIS troops on Tajikistan's border with Afghanistan sent jets and helicopters in April against rebel bases in Afghanistan.)

Tanzania

United Republic of Tanzania

Geography Location: Tanganyika, on eastern coast of Africa, and islands of Zanzibar and Pemba, about 25 mi. (40 km) off Tanganyika coast in Indian Ocean. **Boundaries:** Burundi, Rwanda to NW, Uganda, Kenya to N, Indian Ocean to E, Mozambique, Malawi to S, Zambia to SW, Zaire to W. **Total land area:** 364,900 sq. mi. (945,090 sq km). **Coastline:** 885 mi. (1,424 km). **Comparative area:** slightly larger than twice size of California. **Land use:** 5% arable land; 1% permanent crops; 40% meadows and pastures; 47% forest and woodland; 7% other; includes negl. % irrigated. **Major cities:** (1985 est.) Dar es Salaam (capital) 1,096,000; Mwanza 252,000; Tabora 214,000; Mbeya 194,000; Tanga 172,000.

People Population: 27,985,660 (1994 est.). **Nationality:** noun—Tanzanian(s); adjective—Tanzanian. **Ethnic groups:** mainland—99% native Africans of over 100 groups; 1% Asian, European, and Arab; Zanzibar—almost all Arab. **Languages:** Swahili and English (both official); English primary language of commerce, administration, and higher education; Swahili widely understood and generally used for communication between ethnic groups; first language of most people is one of local languages; primary education generally in Swahili. **Religions:** mainland—33% Christian, 33% Muslim, 33% indigenous beliefs; Zanzibar—almost all Muslim.

Government Type: republic. **Independence:** Tanganyika became independent Dec. 9, 1961 (from UN trusteeship under British administration); Zanzibar became independent Dec. 19, 1963 (from UK); Tanganyika united with Zanzibar Apr. 26, 1964. **Constitution:** Apr. 25, 1977 (Zanzibar has own constitution but remains subject to provisions of union constitution). **National holidays:** Union Day, Apr. 26; Independence Day, Dec. 9. **Heads of government:** Ali Hassan Mwinyi, president (since Nov. 1985); Cleopa David Msuya, prime minister (since Dec. 1994). **Structure:** executive—president has authority on mainland, with government policies subject to validation by party, which is technically superior to government; legislative—National Assembly with 233 members, 72 from Zanzibar, 65 appointed from mainland, and 96 directly elected from mainland; National Assembly dominated by Chama Cha Mapinduzi (Revolutionary party).

Economy Monetary unit: Tanzanian shilling. **Budget:** (1990) ***income:*** $495 mil.; ***expend.:*** $631 mil. **GDP:** $16.7 bil., $600 per capita (1993 est.). **Chief crops:** cotton, coffee, sisal, vegetables, fruits, grain on mainland; cloves and coconuts on Zanzibar. **Livestock:** N.A. **Natural resources:** hydropower potential, tin, phosphates, large unexploited deposits of iron ore and coal, gemstones. **Major industries:** agricultural processing (sugar, beer, cigarettes, sisal twine), diamond mine, oil refinery. **Labor force:** 732,200 wage earners (1986); 90% agriculture, 10% industry and commerce. **Exports:** $418 mil. (f.o.b., 1992 est.); coffee, cotton, sisal, cashew nuts, meat, cloves. **Imports:** $1.51 bil. (c.i.f., 1992 est.); manufactured goods, machinery and transport equipment, cotton piece goods, crude oil, foodstuffs. **Major trading partners:** ***exports:*** Germany, UK, U.S; ***imports:*** Germany, UK, U.S., Iran.

Intl. Orgs. Commonwealth, FAO, G-77, IAEA, IBRD, ICAO, IDA, IFAD, IFC, ILO, IMF, IMO, INTELSAT, INTERPOL, ITU, NAM, UN, UNESCO, UPU, WHO, WMO, WTO.

Tanganyika's indigenous population includes people of diverse ethnic background, including San, Bantu, and Nilotic peoples. It was the site of a number of relatively advanced and well-organized societies.

Zanzibar and the neighboring island of Pemba were a crossroads of trade in East Africa since ancient times. Trade via Zanzibar between the Tanganyika coast and the Middle East dates back to the late Roman Empire, with ivory, gold, and iron the main items of trade. The coast was dominated by various Arab and Persian powers, usually based in Zanzibar, from about the eighth century. Zanzibar and Tanganyika were visited by the Portuguese explorer Vasco da Gama in 1498, and Portugal claimed Zanzibar in 1503 and the entire Tanganyika coast in 1506. The Portuguese established coastal trading stations but did not colonize the interior.

The Portuguese were driven from Zanzibar in 1652 by the sultanate of Oman, which soon expelled them from the mainland as well. Under Omani rule, trade in gold, ivory, and gems was supplemented by a sizable slave trade, and the clove plantations of Zanzibar became commercially important. Under Sultan Seyyid Said, the capital of the sultanate of Oman was transferred to Zanzibar in 1824, and Zanzibar became independent of Oman upon his death in 1856.

Both Germany and Great Britain became active in the region in the 19th century, motivated by trade and, in the British case, by the antislavery movement. Tanganyika was organized as the colony of German East Africa in 1884, while Zanzibar became a British protectorate in 1890. Tanganyika became a secondary battlefield of World War I, with frequent clashes between German and British troops.

Britain assumed control of Tanganyika in 1920 under a League of Nations Mandate and maintained control under a UN trusteeship after 1946. The temperate southern highlands were extensively colonized by British immigrants, and railroads and mines were developed by the British administration.

Elections for a local legislature were held in Zanzibar in July 1957. The island's politics were dominated by a split between Arab and African residents. Zanzibar became independent on Dec. 19, 1963. In January 1964 an African revolt overthrew the sultan of Zanzibar and resulted in the deaths of thousands of Arab residents and the emigration of many more. Political control shifted to the African party and Abeid Karume became president.

Tanganyika became independent in 1961. Julius K. Nyerere was Tanganyika's dominant political figure. Tanzania was formed from the union of Tanganyika and Zanzibar on April 26, 1964, with Zanzibar retaining local autonomy.

The United Republic of Tanzania, under Nyerere's leadership, advocated an "African socialist" form of development and formed close ties with China. Some British settlers left the country, but despite tensions, relations with Great Britain remained important. The Tan-Zan Railroad between Dar es Salaam and Lusaka, Zambia was built with Chinese aid between 1970 and 1975. The ruling parties of Tanganyika and Zanzibar were united in 1977 under Nyerere's leadership.

Political tensions eased and Tanzania adopted a more open political structure in the 1980s. Pres. Ali Hassan Mwinyi has encouraged free-market economic reforms, including encouragement of foreign investment and strengthened ties with Kenya and Uganda (Tanzania invaded the latter in 1979 in an effort to depose Idi Amin). Tanzania's economy has great potential because of the country's extensive natural resources, light industry, and one of Africa's best educational systems; literacy in both English and Swahili is relatively high.

Although only an estimated 20 percent of the population was found to be in favor of political pluralism, in 1992 the Revolutionary party of Tanzania voted in favor of a secular multiparty system, that is one based on neither ethnic nor regional lines. During 1994 the ethnic civil wars in nearby Rwanda and Burundi put an enormous strain on Tanzania's resources as over 700,000 refugees sought safety there. In March 1995 the government closed its border with Burundi.

Thailand

Kingdom of Thailand

Geography Location: extends southward, along isthmus of Kra, to Malay peninsula, in Southeast Asia. **Boundaries:** Myanmar to W and N, Laos to NE, Cambodia and Gulf of Thailand to E, Malaysia to S, Andaman Sea to SW. **Total land area:** 198,456 sq. mi. (514,000 sq km). **Coastline:** 2,001 mi. (3,219 km). **Comparative area:** between California and Texas. **Land use:** 34% arable land; 4% permanent crops; 1% meadows and pastures; 30% forest and woodland; 31% other; includes 7% irrigated. **Major cities:** (1990 census), Bangkok metropolis (capital) 5,876,000; Songkhla 172,604; Chon Buri 115,350; Nakhon Si Thammarat 102,123; Chiang Mai 101,594.

People Population: 59,510,471 (1994 est.). **Nationality:** noun—Thai (sing., pl.); adjective—Thai. **Ethnic groups:** 75% Thai, 14% Chinese, 11% other. **Languages:** Thai; English is secondary language of elite; ethnic and regional dialects. **Religions:** 95.5% Buddhist, 4% Muslim, 0.5% other.

Government Type: constitutional monarchy. **Constitution:** Dec. 22, 1978. **National holiday:** King's Birthday, Dec. 5. **Heads of government:** Bhumibol Adulyadej, king (since June 1946); Chuan Leekpai, prime minister (since Sept. 1992). **Structure:** king is head of state with nominal powers; bicameral legislature (National Assembly—Senate appointed by king, elected House of Representatives); judiciary relatively independent except in important political subversion cases.

Economy Monetary unit: baht. **Budget:** (1993 est.) ***income:*** $21.36 bil. ***expend.:*** $22.4 bil. **GNP:** $323 bil., $5,500 per capita (1993 est.). **Chief crops:** rice, sugar, corn, rubber, manioc; illegal producer of opium poppy and cannabis for international drug trade. **Livestock:** buffalo, cattle, pigs, goats, sheep. **Natural resources:** tin, rubber, natural gas, tungsten, tantalum. **Major industries:** textiles and garments, agricultural processing, beverages; world's second-largest tungsten producer and third-largest tin producer; tourism—largest source of foreign exchange. **Labor force:** 30.87 mil. (1989 est.); 73% agriculture, 11% industry and commerce, 10% services; 6.4% unemployment (1988). **Exports:** $28.4 bil. (f.o.b., 1992); 66% light manufactures, 12% fishery products, 8% rice, 8% tapioca, 6% jewelry. **Imports:** $37.6 bil. (c.i.f., 1992); 23% machinery and parts, 13% petroleum products, 11% chemicals. **Major trading partners:** (1989) ***exports:*** 22% U.S., 17% Japan, 7% Singapore, Netherlands, Germany; ***imports:*** 30% Japan, 11% U.S., 8% Singapore, 5% Germany, Taiwan, S. Korea.

Intl. Orgs. ASEAN, Colombo Plan, FAO, G-77, IAEA, IBRD, ICAO, IDA, IFAD, IFC, ILO, IMF, IMO, INTELSAT, INTERPOL, ITU, UN, UNESCO, UPU, WHO, WMO, WTO.

Ethnic Thai migrating south from China after about A.D. 1000 created a number of petty states in the region, most notably the kingdom of Sukhothai. These came under the influence of Indian civilization from the adjacent states of Burma and the Khmer empire, and Buddhism became established as the dominant religion of the Thai. A unified kingdom of Siam was established c. 1350, with its capital at Ayutthaya. Portuguese and other European traders and missionaries were active in Siam after 1511.

In 1767 Ayutthaya was destroyed in a war with Burma. In 1782 the Chakkri dynasty was established at Bangkok and restored the power of the Thai monarchy. By skillfully playing off the European powers against one another, Kings Mongkut (r. 1851–68) and Chulalongkorn (r. 1868–1910) enabled Siam to be the only Southeast Asian nation to escape European colonization or political domination. In a series of treaties with Great Britain and France, however, King Chulalongkorn was forced to renounce Siam's claims to portions of Malaya, Laos, and Cambodia.

Absolute monarchy ended in 1932, when a military coup forced the granting of a constitution. Japanese troops occupied Siam in December 1941. Siam concluded a nominal alliance with Japan in 1942 and declared war on Great Britain and the United States, while at the same time the monarchy secretly supported a strong anti-Japanese resistance movement. A period of postwar political turmoil ended with the accession in 1950 of King Phumiphon, who instituted a reformist and pro-Western policy. Thai politics since World War II have been democratic but dominated by an oligarchy of military officers and civilians with strong military ties.

During the Vietnam War, Thailand was an important staging area for American forces. U.S. and other foreign investment has contributed to significant industrialization and economic growth. Large numbers of Lao, Vietnamese, and Cambodian refugees have created a significant problem as has the constant political infighting that destabilizes the Thai government. Still, Thailand has emerged as one of Asia's fastest growing economies.

On Dec. 8, 1990, Prime Minister Chatichai Choonhavan resigned amid charges of corruption. Reappointed by the king the next day, Chatichai was overthrown on Feb. 23 by military forces, who invited former diplomat Anand Panyarachun to serve as interim prime minister.

After parliamentary elections in March 1992, Gen. Suchinda Kraprayoon, who held no parliamentary seat, was named prime minister in a government dominated by the military. Mass demonstrations against the Suchinda government, led by former Bangkok governor Chamlong Srimuang, culminated on May 17–18, when troops fired on demonstrators, causing hundreds of fatalities. On May 24, the king intervened; Suchinda resigned and Chamlong agreed to call off the demonstrations. On June 10 Anand Panyarachun was invited to head another transitional government, and Parliament agreed in principle to promulgate a new constitution with a provision that the prime minister must be an elected member of Parliament.

Parliamentary elections in September 1992 gained a majority for a five-party coalition headed by Chuan Leekpai that managed to govern for almost three years, liberalizing financial arrangements, spending heavily on infrastructure, and bringing Thailand to an 8 percent growth rate in 1994. A minor land-reform scandal led the Palang Dharma party, with its 47 seats, to quit the coalition and cause a dissolution of Parliament, with new elections scheduled for July 1995.

Togo

Republic of Togo

Geography Location: western coast of Africa. **Boundaries:** Burkina Faso to N, Benin to E, Gulf of Guinea to S, Ghana to W. **Total land area:** 21,927 sq. mi. (56,790 sq km). **Coastline:** 35 mi. (56 km). **Comparative area:** between Maryland and West Virginia. **Land use:** 25% arable land; 1% permanent crops; 4% meadows and pastures; 28% forest and woodland; 42% other; includes negl. % irrigated. **Major cities:** (1977 est.) Lomé (capital) 229,400; Sokodé 33,500; Palimé 25,500; Atakpamé 21,800; Bassari 17,500.

People Population: 4,255,090 (1994 est.). **Nationality:** noun—Togolese (sing., pl.); adjective—Togolese. **Ethnic groups:** 37 groups; largest are Ewe, Mina, and Kabyè; under 1% European and Syrian-Lebanese. **Languages:** French (both official and language of commerce); Ewe and Mina in south, Dagomba and Kabyè in north. **Religions:** about 70% indigenous beliefs, 20% Christian, 10% Muslim.

Government Type: republic; one-party presidential regime. **Independence:** Apr. 27, 1960 (from UN trusteeship under French administration). **Constitution:** Dec. 30, 1979. **National holiday:** Independence Day, Apr. 27. **Heads of government:** Gen. Gnassingbé Eyadema, president (since 1992); Edem Kodjo, prime minister (since Mar. 1994). **Structure:** executive—president; unicameral legislature—National Assembly; judiciary, including State Security Court, established 1970; constitution provides for elective presidential system and 67-member National Assembly.

Economy Monetary unit: Communauté Financière Africaine (CFA) franc. **Budget:** (1991 est.) ***income:*** $284 mil.; ***expend.:*** $407 mil. **GDP:** $3.3 bil., $800 per capita (1993 est.). **Chief crops:** cash crops—coffee, cocoa, cotton; food crops—yams, cassava, corn, beans, rice. **Livestock:** sheep, goats, pigs, cattle. **Natural resources:** phosphates, limestone, marble. **Major industries:** phosphate mining, agricultural processing, cement, handicrafts, textiles, beverages. **Labor force:** 78% agriculture, 22% industry; about 88,600 wage earners, evenly divided between public and private sectors (1985); 50% of population of working age. **Exports:** $558 mil. (f.o.b., 1991); phosphates, cocoa, coffee, palm kernels. **Imports:** $636 mil. (f.o.b., 1991); food, fuels, durable goods, other intermediate goods, capital goods. **Major trading partners:** (1990) ***exports:*** 40% EU, 16% Africa; ***imports:*** 57% EU, 17% Africa, 5% U.S., 4% Japan.

Intl. Orgs. FAO, G-77, IBRD, ICAO, IDA, IFAD, IFC, ILO, IMF, IMO, INTERPOL, ITU, NAM, UN, UNESCO, UPU, WHO, WIPO, WMO, WTO.

Ewe-speaking peoples began to migrate into what is now Togo, located on Africa's west coast, early in the 14th century. Portuguese explorers arrived in the late 15th century, turning the coast into a point of departure for slaves captured from nearby villages, and between the 1600s and 1800s, the region became known as the "Slave Coast." Germans started to explore and trade in the region in the mid-19th century and declared a protectorate over the area in 1884. After World War I, however, Britain and France divided the nation between them, Britain receiving the western third, France the eastern two-thirds. The League of Nations confirmed this arrangement, giving mandates to British Togoland (later a part of Ghana) and French Togoland.

In 1956 France made French Togo an autonomous republic but retained control of its foreign affairs, defense, and currency; Nicholas Grunitzky was prime minister. The United Nations rejected this plan and in elections in 1958 advocates of complete independence won control of the legislature. On Apr. 27, 1960, French Togo cut its ties with France and became the fully independent Republic of Togo. Sylvanus Olympio became the new nation's first prime minister. Grunitzky went into exile but returned when Olympio was assassinated in January 1963. He led the new government and oversaw the writing of a new constitution allowing more political freedoms.

In 1967 army officers led by Lt. Col. Gnassingbé Eyadema overthrew Grunitzsky, suspended the constitution, and named Eyadema president.

In 1990, Eyadema was forced out by democratic reformers, and Kokou J. Koffigoh was elected prime minister by a national conference in 1991. Eyadema resumed the presidency in 1992, but his refusal to embrace multiparty democracy and Koffigoh's weak leadership led to violence and public calls for the ouster of both men. A new constitution was ratified in September 1992, and in elections held in March 1994, Edem Kodjo took over as prime minister.

Tonga
Kingdom of Tonga

Geography Location: 172 islands in South Pacific Ocean, 36 permanently inhabited. Nuku'alofa 21°09'S, 175°14'W. **Boundaries:** surrounded by South Pacific Ocean; Fiji is about 400 mi. (650 km) to NW and Western Samoa lies N. **Total land area:** 289 sq. mi. (748 sq km). **Coastline:** 260 mi. (419 km). **Comparative area:** about four times size of Washington, D.C. **Land use:** 25% arable land; 55% permanent crops; 6% meadows and pastures; 12% forest and woodland; 2% other. **Major cities:** (1986 census) Nuku'alofa (capital) 28,899; Tongatapu 63,614; Vava'u 15,170; Ha'apai 8,979; 'Eua 4,393.

People Population: 104,778 (1994 est.). **Nationality:** noun—Tongan(s); adjective—Tongan. **Ethnic groups:** Polynesian; about 300 Europeans. **Languages:** Tongan, English. **Religions:** Christian: Free Wesleyan Church claims over 30,000 adherents.

Government Type: constitutional monarchy within Commonwealth. **Independence:** June 4, 1970 (from UK). **Constitution:** Nov. 4, 1875; revised Jan. 1, 1967. **National holidays:** King's Birthday, July 4; Constitution Day, Nov. 4. **Heads of government:** Taufa'ahau Tupou IV, king (since Dec. 1965); Prince Fatafehi Tu'ipelehake, premier (since Dec. 1965). **Structure:** executive—king, cabinet, and privy council; unicameral legislature—28-seat Legislative Assembly consists of king, privy council (composed of eight ministers and governors of Vava'u and Ha'apai), nine representatives of nobles elected by their peers, nine elected representatives of the people elected by the people; king appoints one noble as speaker; judiciary—Supreme Court, magistrate's court, land court.

Economy Monetary unit: Tonga dollar. **Budget:** (1991 est.) ***income:*** $36.4 mil.; ***expend.:*** $68.1 mil. **GDP:** $200 mil., $2,000 per capita (1993 est.). **Chief crops:** dominated by coconut, copra, and banana production; vanilla beans, cocoa, coffee, ginger, black pepper. **Livestock:** poultry, pigs, goats, horses, cattle. **Natural resources:** fish, fertile soil. **Major industries:** tourism, fishing. **Labor force:** 70% engaged in agriculture; 600 engaged in mining. **Exports:** $18.8 mil. (f.o.b., 1992 est.); coconut oil, desiccated coconut, vanilla, copra, bananas. **Imports:** $68.3 mil. (c.i.f., 1992 est.); textiles, food, consumer products, machinery, petroleum. **Major trading partners:** (1987) ***exports:*** 54% New Zealand, 30% Australia, 8% U.S., 5% Fiji; ***imports:*** 39% New Zealand, 25% Australia, 9% Japan, 6% U.S., 5% EU.

Intl. Orgs. Commonwealth, FAO, IFAD, ITU, SPARTECA, SPC, SPF, UNESCO, UPU, WHO.

The Polynesian islands that now compose Tonga were settled some 3,000 years ago. A highly stratified society evolved; the kings of Tonga dominated much of Polynesia by the 13th century. The islands were visited in 1643 by Abel Tasman, and in 1773 by Capt. James Cook, who named them the Friendly Islands. English missionaries arrived in 1797, and the islands came under British political influence. A code of laws was promulgated in 1862, and a constitutional monarchy established in 1875. A series of treaties with Western powers recognized Tonga's independence, but the kingdom became a British protectorate in 1900.

The islands were outside the Japanese perimeter in the Pacific theater of World War II. On June 4, 1970, the British dissolved their protectorate and the Kingdom of Tonga became independent as a member of the British Commonwealth. The present king, Taufa'ahau Tupou IV, came to the throne in 1965.

The Tongan economy is based on subsistence farming and fishing, with some handicraft industries and light manufacturing. Exports include copra, bananas, and vanilla. The tourist industry is developing rapidly. Remittances from Tongans temporarily working abroad (especially in New Zealand) are an important source of income.

Trinidad and Tobago
Republic of Trinidad and Tobago

Geography Location: two islands (Port of Spain, Trinidad Is., 10°38'N, 61°31'W; Tobago Is., 11°11'N, 60°45'W) in southeastern Caribbean Sea, off northeastern South America. **Boundaries:** Caribbean Sea to N and W, Atlantic Ocean to E and S. **Total land area:** 1,981 sq. mi. (5,130 sq km). **Coastline:** 225 mi. (362 km). **Comparative area:** about size of Delaware. **Land use:** 14% arable land; 17% permanent crops; 2% meadows and pastures; 44% forest and woodland; 23% other; includes 4% irrigated. **Major cities:** (1991) Port of Spain (capital) 51,076; San Fernando 30,115; Arima (borough) 29,483.

People Population: 1,328,282 (1994 est.). **Nationality:** noun—Trinidadian(s), Tobagonian(s); adjective—Trinidadian, Tobagonian. **Ethnic groups:** 43% black, 40% East Indian, 14% mixed, 1% white. **Languages:** English (official), Hindi, French, Spanish. **Religions:** 36.2% Roman Catholic, 23% Hindu, 13.1% Protestant, 6% Muslim, 21.7% unknown.

Government Type: parliamentary democracy. **Independence:** Aug. 31, 1962 (from UK). **Constitution:** Aug. 31, 1976. **National holiday:** Independence Day, Aug. 31. **Heads of government:** Noor Mohammed Hassanali, president (since

Mar. 1987); Patrick Manning, prime minister (since Dec. 1991). **Structure:** executive is cabinet led by prime minister; bicameral legislature (36-member elected House of Representatives and 31-member appointed Senate); judiciary headed by chief justice and includes court of appeal, high court, and lower courts.

Economy Monetary unit: Trinidad and Tobago dollar. **Budget:** (1993 est.) ***income:*** $1.6 bil.; ***expend.:*** $1.6 bil. **GDP:** $10.4 bil., $8,000 per capita (1993 est.). **Chief crops:** sugar, cocoa, coffee, rice, citrus, bananas; largely dependent on food imports. **Livestock:** pigs, cattle, goats, sheep, buffalo. **Natural resources:** crude oil, natural gas, asphalt. **Major industries:** petroleum, chemicals, tourism. **Labor force:** 463,900 (1986); 47.9% services (1985 est.), 18.1% construction and utilities, 14.8% manufacturing, mining, and quarrying, 10.9% agriculture; 17% unemployment (1986). **Exports:** $1.4 bil. (f.o.b., 1993); 82% petroleum and petroleum products, 9% steel products, fertilizer, sugar, cocoa (1988). **Imports:** $900 mil. (f.o.b., 1993); 47% raw materials and intermediate goods, 26% capital goods, 26% consumer goods. **Major trading partners:** ***exports:*** 53% U.S., 16% CARICOM, 10% EU, 3% Latin America; ***imports:*** 51% U.S., 10% Latin America, 8% UK, 6% CARICOM, 5% Canada.

Intl. Orgs. Commonwealth, FAO, G-77, IBRD, ICAO, IDA, IFC, ILO, IMF, IMO, INTELSAT, INTERPOL, ITU, NAM, OAS, UN, UNESCO, UPU, WHO, WMO, WTO.

Trinidad was a possession of Spain from 1498 to 1797, when it was surrendered to the British. England took control of Tobago in 1802. Together the two islands achieved independence from the UK in 1962. Prime Minister Arthur Robinson's National Alliance for Reconstruction currently governs the country. Civil and political rights are well respected, and political party competition tends to divide along ethnic (black, East Indian) lines. Agrarian reform designed to create tenable landholdings is a central political issue.

In 1990, militant Muslims seized Prime Minister A.N.R. Robinson and dozens of others in Parliament, paralyzing the government for five days. Peace was restored when the government promised reforms. People's National Movement candidate Carson Charles was elected prime minister in 1991, and in the interest of preserving the peace, he granted the Muslim militants amnesty in 1992.

Tunisia

Republic of Tunisia

Geography Location: northern coast of Africa. **Boundaries:** Mediterranean to N and E, Libya to SE, Algeria to W. **Total land area:** 63,170 sq. mi. (163,610 sq km); includes land and inland waters. **Coastline:** 714 mi. (1,148 km). **Comparative area:** between Georgia and Washington. **Land use:** 20% arable land; 10% permanent crops; 19% meadows and pastures; 4% forest and woodland; 47% other; includes 1% irrigated. **Major cities:** (1984 census) Tunis (capital) 596,654; Sfax (Safaqis) 231,911; Ariana 98,655; Bizeria (Bizerie) 94,509; Djerba 92,269.

People Population: 8,726,562 (1994 est.). **Nationality:** noun—Tunisian(s); adjective—Tunisian. **Ethnic groups:** 98% Arab, 1% European, less than 1% Jewish. **Languages:** Arabic (official), Arabic and French (commerce). **Religions:** 98% Muslim, 1% Christian, less than 1% Jewish.

Government Type: republic. **Independence:** Mar. 20, 1956 (from France). **Constitution:** June 1, 1959. **National holiday:** Independence Day, June 1. **Heads of government:** Zine el-Abidine Ben Ali, president (since Nov. 1987); Dr. Hamed Karoui, prime minister (since Sept. 1989). **Structure:** executive dominant; unicameral legislative (National Assembly) largely advisory; judiciary patterned on French and Koranic systems.

Economy Monetary unit: Tunisian dinar. **Budget:** (1993 est.) ***income:*** $4.3 bil.; ***expend.:*** $5.5 bil. **GDP:** $34.3 bil., $4,000 (1993 est.). **Chief crops:** cereals (barley and wheat), olives, grapes, citrus fruits, vegetables; not self-sufficient in food. **Livestock:** sheep, goats, cattle, asses, camels. **Natural resources:** crude oil, phosphates, iron ore, lead, zinc, salt. **Major industries:** petroleum, mining (particularly phosphates and iron ore), textiles. **Labor force:** 2.25 mil.; 32% agriculture; 18% unemployment (1987 est.); shortage of skilled labor. **Exports:** $4.1 bil. (f.o.b., 1993); 40% hydrocarbons, 18% agricultural, 18% phosphates and chemicals. **Imports:** $6.4 bil. (c.i.f., 1993); 57% industrial goods, 13% hydrocarbons, 12% food. **Major trading partners:** ***exports:*** 73% EU, 9% Middle East, U.S., Turkey, former USSR. ***imports:*** 68% EU, 7% U.S., Canada, Japan, China.

Intl. Orgs. AfDB, Arab League, FAO, G-77, IAEA, IBRD, ICAO, IDA, IFAD, IFC, ILO, IMF, IMO, INTELSAT, INTERPOL, ITU, NAM, OAU, UN, UNESCO, UPU, WHO, WIPO, WMO.

The Phoenicians, an ancient seafaring people from the eastern Mediterranean, founded settlements in Tunisia dating back to 1000 B.C. The most important of these was Carthage, which dominated trade in the central Mediterranean until it was conquered and destroyed by Rome in 146 B.C. Tunisia remained part of the Roman Empire until it was conquered by the Vandals in the mid-fifth century A.D. The Byzantine Empire reconquered Tunisia in the sixth century.

Tunisia became part of the Arab world with the expansion of Islam in the seventh century and soon emerged as a principal center of Islamic culture in North Africa. Tunisia was incorporated into the Ottoman Empire in 1574 and was ruled from Constantinople by Turkish governors, or beys.

With the waning of Ottoman power in the 19th century, Tunisia became a French protectorate in 1881. Nationalist movements began in the early 20th century. During World War II Tunisia was under Vichy French rule and was the scene of fighting between the Axis and Allies in 1942–43. Nationalist unrest resumed when France reestablished its rule in the postwar period. Widespread popular unrest in the early 1950s led to a French grant of self-rule in 1954. Full independence was proclaimed on Mar. 20, 1956; large numbers of French settlers returned to France. The French-sponsored monarchy was abolished in 1957, and the Neo-Destour (New Constitution) party under the leadership of Habib Bourguiba took power. Bourguiba was elected president in 1959 without opposition and was later named president for life. Under Bourguiba's rule, political parties ranging from Communist to monarchist flourished, leading to both democratic politics and political confusion.

Relations with France were strained in 1964 when Tunisia nationalized foreign assets but have since improved. The basic thrust of Tunisian government was socialist, with state ownership of principal industries and heavy subsidies of basic commodities. In foreign affairs Tunisia has been closely tied to France and has been a moderate voice within the Arab League.

Popular unrest and labor strife have characterized Tunisia's internal situation in the 1980s, as political maneuvering began in anticipation of the end of the Bourguiba era, which came in 1987 when the aged leader was overthrown by Ben Ali. In 1989 the World Bank approved a loan of $130 million to Tunisia, and new elections were planned as part of a political and economic restructuring. Ben Ali has been elected president twice (1989, 1994) winning 99 percent of the vote, while his party won virtually all the seats in the National Assembly. In 1994 and 1995, however, the political stability was threatened by radical Muslim groups both from within and from Algeria. Rumors of brutal repression were rife.

Tunisia's economy, though plagued by labor difficulties, has developed rapidly, led by textiles, food processing and other light industry, tourism, phosphate mining, and other mineral processing. The large agricultural sector includes grain, olives, dates, and winter fruits and vegetables for export to Europe.

Turkey

Republic of Turkey

Geography Location: partly in southeastern Europe and partly in western Asia. **Boundaries:** Black Sea to N; Georgia and Armenia to NE; Iran to E; Iraq, Syria, Mediterranean Sea to S; Aegean Sea, Greece to W; and Bulgaria to NW. **Total land area:** 301,382 sq. mi. (780,580 sq km). **Coastline:** 4,471 mi. (7,200 km). **Comparative area:** about twice size of California. **Land use:** 30% arable land; 4% permanent crops; 12% meadows and pastures; 26% forest and woodland; 28% other; includes 3% irrigated. **Major cities:** (1990 census) Ankara (capital) 2,559,471; Istanbul 6,620,240; Izmir 1,757,414; Adana 916,150; Bursa 834,576.

People Population: 62,153,898 (1994 est.). **Nationality:** noun—Turk(s); adjective—Turkish. **Ethnic groups:** 85% Turkish, 12% Kurd, 3% other.

Languages: Turkish (official), Kurdish, Arabic. **Religions:** 98% Muslim (mostly Sunni), 2% other (mostly Christian and Jewish).

Government Type: republican parliamentary democracy. **Independence:** Oct. 29, 1923 (from Ottoman Empire). **Constitution:** Nov. 7, 1982. **National holiday:** Republic Day, Oct. 29. **Heads of government:** Suleyman Demirel, president (since Apr. 1993); Tansu Ciller, prime minister (since June 1993). **Structure:** executive—president empowered to call new elections, promulgate laws (elected for seven-year term); unicameral legislature (450-member Grand National Assembly); independent judiciary.

Economy Monetary unit: Turkish lira. **Budget:** (1994) ***income:*** $36.5 bil.; ***expend.:*** $47.6 bil. **GDP:** $312.4 bil., $5,100 per capita (1993). **Chief crops:** cotton, tobacco, cereals, sugar beets, fruits; self-sufficient in food in average years; legal producer of opium poppy for pharmaceutical trade. **Livestock:** sheep, cattle, goats, asses, horses. **Natural resources:** antimony, coal, chromium, mercury, copper. **Major industries:** textiles, food processing, mining (coal, chromite, copper, boron minerals). **Labor force:** 20.7 mil.; 56% agriculture, 30% services, 14% industry; about one million Turks work abroad; 15.3% unemployment (1987). **Exports:** $14.9 bil. (f.o.b., 1992); 78% industrial products, 20% crops and livestock products. **Imports:** $22.9 bil. (c.i.f., 1992); crude oil, machinery, transport equipment, metals, pharmaceuticals. **Major trading partners:** ***exports:*** 18% Germany, 9% Iraq, 8% Italy, 7% U.S., 5% UK, 5% Iran; ***imports:*** 14% Germany, 11% U.S., 10% Iraq, 7% Italy, 6% France.

Intl. Orgs. EU (associate member), FAO, IAEA, IBRD, ICAO, IDA, IFAD, IFC, ILO, IMF, IMO, INTELSAT, INTERPOL, ITU, NATO, UN, UNESCO, UPU, WHO, WIPO, WMO, WTO.

The Hittites, an Indo-European people, created an empire in Anatolia before 2000 B.C. and controlled most of what is modern-day Turkey for nearly 1,000 years. The rise of Troy and other Hellenic city-states on the coast of Asia Minor and the expansion of the Assyrian empire led to the collapse of Hittite power by around 900 B.C. Except for some Hellenic enclaves on the Aegean Coast (Ionia), all of Turkey was incorporated into the Persian empire of Cyrus and Darius in the sixth century B.C. Alexander the Great conquered Turkey, but it returned to Persian rule following the collapse of his empire, c. 300 B.C.

All of Turkey, comprising Thracia, Galatia, Cappadocia, Cilicia, and other provinces, was incorporated into the Roman Empire by the end of the first century A.D. Constantine the Great founded the city of Constantinople on the site of ancient Byzantium in 330 as the empire's eastern capital. Following the decline of the western Roman Empire in the seventh century, Constantinople became the capital of the independent Eastern Roman (Byzantine) Empire. The Byzantine Empire fought off repeated attacks by Arab Islamic forces in the seventh and eighth centuries but lost control of central Anatolia to the Seljuk Turkish rulers of Persia after 1038.

The 13th-century Mongol invasions left Turkey largely untouched but weakened both Byzantine and Seljuk power. At the end of the 13th century, the Ottomans, a small Turkish tribe, expanded from their stronghold in western Anatolia and within a century captured most of Turkey, Bulgaria, and Serbia. Constantinople fell to the Ottomans in 1453. By the middle of the 16th century, the Ottoman Empire extended from southeastern Europe into the Crimea and Iran and included most of the Middle East, Egypt, and Arabia.

At its height the Ottoman Empire was a great world power and a substantial participant in European international relations. But beginning in the 18th century, the empire lost much of its autonomy through unequal treaties with European powers, and throughout the 19th century, parts of the empire were detached and either granted independence or placed under European protection. The Ottoman Empire became the "Sick Man of Europe." A liberal constitution was adopted in 1876 but largely ignored until the Young Turk Rebellion of 1908 forced the sultan to accept its provisions.

Siding with the Central Powers in World War I, the Ottoman Empire lost most of its non-Turkish possessions to the Allies. The Treaty of Sèvres (1920) reduced the Ottoman state to a small part of northern Anatolia. Before the treaty was ratified, however, Kemal Ataturk seized power and regained much territory in a series of campaigns with Soviet assistance. The Treaty of Lausanne (1923) established the present boundaries of Turkey, and Turkey was proclaimed a republic in October 1923. The Caliphate was renounced in 1924, ending the Ottoman claim of spiritual leadership in the Islamic world.

The Turkish Republic became officially a secular and multiethnic state. Large numbers of Armenians had been killed or driven from the country in widespread campaigns of persecution in the late 19th and early 20th centuries; after 1923 most Greek and Bulgarian residents were forcibly repatriated. The large minority of Kurds in southeastern Turkey were pressured to abandon their ethnic identity. Today more than 85 percent of the population is Turkish, ultimately of Central Asian origin. Islam is widely practiced, but the veil and other Islamic dress are prohibited, as are religious political parties. In 1928 the Latin alphabet was adopted in place of Arabic script for writing Turkish. In 1930 Constantinople was officially renamed Istanbul.

Turkey joined the League of Nations in 1932. A series of treaties in the 1930s made small adjustments to Turkey's borders and confirmed Turkey's status as a European nation. Under Ismet Inonu, who became president upon Ataturk's death in 1938, Turkey remained neutral throughout most of World War II but was on friendly terms with the Allied powers. Turkey declared war against Germany in January 1945 and became a founding member of the United Nations at the end of the war.

Following World War II, Turkish relations with the Soviet Union cooled; Turkey became a major recipient of American aid under the Truman Doctrine. Turkish troops joined UN forces in the Korean War. Continuing the Europe-oriented policy instituted by Ataturk, Turkey joined both NATO and the OECD and is seeking membership in the European Union.

In 1974, long-standing discord with Greece erupted over the status of Cyprus, an independent nation with strong ties to Greece. On July 20, 1974, Turkish troops invaded Cyprus, occupying the northeastern 40 percent of the island. The United States cut off military aid to Turkey in 1975. Turkey forced resettlement of Greek and Turkish Cypriot residents; the Turkish sector seceded from Cyprus and became a Turkish federated state on July 8, 1975. American aid was restored in 1978. Despite many attempts at reconciliation, relations between Turkey and Greece remain strained.

Politically, postwar Turkey has alternated between civil and military governments. In the wake of mounting violence, martial law was imposed in 1978, and a military takeover of the government occurred on Sept. 12, 1980. Civil government was restored in 1983, and martial law lifted in 1984.

Turkey has tried to remain aloof from the political turmoil of the Middle East, but it was a crucial member of the anti-Iraq coalition in the Persian Gulf War. It supported the UN trade embargo and allowed the Allies to use Turkish bases. Turkey's Kurdish problem was aggravated after the war as the country tried to offer humanitarian assistance to Kurdish refugees from Iraq without encouraging Kurdish nationalists at home. A continuing insurgency in the southeast has led to sporadic but serious violence (an estimated 1,300 people died in 1992). Several serious incidents occurred again in 1993. In addition, Muslim fundamentalists became more active and several violent episodes resulted in deaths and destruction.

Pres. Turgut Özal died of a heart attack on Apr. 17, 1993. He was succeeded as president by Prime Minister Suleyman Demirel. On June 14 the ruling True Path party elected as its leader, and thus as the new prime minister, Mrs. Tansu Ciller, Turkey's first-ever woman prime minister, and the first since 1923 to be born on the European side of the Bosporous. While the economy was her first concern (inflation hit 70 percent in 1994), military operations against the Kurdish rebels intensified greatly, culminating in March 1995 with the launching of an attack into Iraq by 50,000 Turkish troops who aimed to end guerrilla raids by the Kurds.

Turkmenistan

Republic of Turkmenistan

Geography Location: southwestern central Asia. **Boundaries:** Kazakhstan to N, Uzbekistan to N and E, Iran to S, Afghanistan to SE, Caspian Sea to W. **Total land area:** 188,456 sq. mi. (488,100 sq km). **Coastline:** Caspian Sea. **Comparative area:** about the size of Virginia and Montana combined. **Land use:** 2% cropland; 60% permanent pasture; 5% forest and woodland;

33% other (mostly urban and mountain). **Major cities:** (1990 est.) Ashkhabad (capital) 407,200; Chardzou (Carzou) 161,000.

People Population: 3,995,122 (1994 est.). **Nationality:** noun—Turkmen; adjective—Turkmen. **Ethnic groups:** 72% Turkmen, 9.5% Russian, 9% Uzbek, 2.5% Kazakh, Tatar, Ukrainian, Azerbaijani. **Languages:** Turkmen (official), member of southern Turkic language group written in Cyrillic script since 1940; Russian, ethnic languages. **Religions:** Muslim—Sunni, Sufi mysticism, shamanism.

Government Type: republic. **Independence:** declared Oct. 27, 1991 (from USSR). **Constitution:** being drafted. **National holiday:** Independence Day, Oct. 27. **Head of government:** Saparmurat A. Niyazov, president (since Dec. 1991). **Structure:** executive—president, Council of Ministers; legislative—Supreme Soviet; judicial—Supreme Court.

Economy Monetary unit: ruble. **Budget:** N.A. ***income:*** N.A.; ***expend.:*** N.A. **GNP:** $13 bil., $3,300 per capita (1993 est.). **Chief crops:** seed cotton, vegetables, grain, grapes, fruit. **Livestock:** sheep, goats, cattle, pigs. **Natural resources:** petroleum, natural gas, potassium, sulfur, sodium chloride. **Major industries:** chemical processing, textiles, cotton-ginning, breeding Karakul sheep, Turkoman horses, and camels. **Labor force:** 1.542 mil. (1990). **Exports:** $1.2 bil. outside former USSR (1993); natural gas, oil, chemicals, cotton, textiles. **Imports:** $490 mil. outside former USSR (1993); machinery and parts, plastics, rubber, consumer durables, textiles. **Major trading partners:** other republics.

Intl. Orgs. CIS, IBRD, IMF, OSCE, UN, UNCTAD, World Bank; applying for membership in other international organizations.

Turkmenistan, long a battleground for warring Asian empires, is bordered on the north by Uzbekistan and Kazakhstan, and on the west by the Caspian Sea. It also has a long international border with Iran and Afghanistan. About 90 percent of Turkmenistan is covered by the Kara Kum (Black Sand) desert, one of the largest in the world, and the southern areas are mountainous and prone to serious earthquakes.

A very remote and sparsely populated country, Turkmenistan has been inhabited since prehistoric times, first by Iranian-speaking people, then by Turkic tribes. In the 10th century A.D., Oghuz tribes (from Mongolia) arrived, bringing Islam with them. Although the Turkmen had emerged as a distinct ethnic group by the 15th century, they were ruled by the Persians in the south and the Uzbek khanates in the north for about 200 years. In the 19th century, Russian expansionism into Turkmen territory had begun, culminating in the Russian victory in the famous 1881 battle of Gok Tepe that killed an estimated 150,000 Turkmen.

In 1917 the Bolsheviks unsuccessfully attempted to seize power in Turkmen territory. By Apr. 30, 1918, the Soviets succeeded in creating the Turkestan Autonomous Soviet Socialist Republic (ASSR) as part of the Russian republic, but in July of the same year, the ASSR was overthrown by nationalist elements with the help of the British. Once the British withdrew, however, the territory of Turkmen fell to the Soviets, and in 1924 the National Delimitation of Central Asian Republics took place. This created several central Asian republics, including the Turkmen Soviet Socialist Republic, which came into being on Oct. 27, 1924.

During the Soviet period, there were advances in medicine and public health, but the nomadic Turkmen people suffered enormously under forced collectivization and the many bloody antireligious campaigns. The purges of Turkmen intelligentsia in the 1930s were widespread. The Soviets undertook a small-scale industrialization campaign in Turkmenistan, but aside from the extraction of natural gas and petroleum, the majority of the population continued to work in agriculture, mainly growing cotton and fruits.

Under Gorbachev, the main issue for Turkmenistan became the environment. Large-scale cotton planting had led to serious environmental and health hazards. The Kara Kum Canal, which carries water from the Amu-Dar'ya to Turkmenistan's arid regions, is one of the main factors leading to the desiccation of the Aral Sea. Turkmenistan's main cultural issue was the status of the Turkmen language, for until May 1990 the official language had been listed as Russian (although only 25% of Turkmen people claimed to speak Russian). Beyond this, due to its remoteness, Turkmenistan did not become involved in the democratic political changes that engaged the other former union republics in the Gorbachev years. Its Communist party dominated and still dominates Turkmen politics, although the Turkmen president, Saparmurat A. Niyazov, stood for popular election and was elected by direct ballot in October 1990 by 98.3 percent of the population. However, the Turkmen government has banned demonstrations, picketing, and strikes, and it censors its media.

Turkmenistan was one of the early supporters of Gorbachev's proposal to form a new Union Treaty. When that led to the August 1991 coup in Moscow, the Turkmen Supreme Soviet adopted a law on independence on Oct. 27, 1991. Turkmenistan was one of the signatories of the Alma-Ata Declaration that created the Commonwealth of Independent States in December 1991. Since then, Turkmenistan has begun to develop political and economic relations with its neighbor Iran and is working on improving its relations with Turkey. Even with economic mismanagement, Turkmenistan does produce many products such as oil, gas, cotton, melons, and carpets, which can bring foreign currency into the country.

Niyazov was overwhelmingly endorsed in the most recent referendum, held Jan. 15, 1994. An astounding 99.9 percent of voters elected to extend his mandate by five years, until the year 2002, thereby bypassing a constitutional requirement for the reelection of a president every five years.

Tuvalu

Geography Location: group of nine small atolls, about 350 mi. (560 km) from N to S, in South Pacific Ocean. Funafuti 8°30'S, 179°12'E. **Boundaries:** surrounded by South Pacific Ocean; Kiribati to N, Fiji to S, Solomon Islands to W. **Total land area:** 10 sq. mi. (26 sq km). **Coastline:** 15 mi. (24 km). **Comparative area:** about one-tenth size of Washington, D.C. **Land use:** 0% arable land; 0% permanent crops; 0% meadows and pastures; 0% forest and woodland; 100% other. **Major cities:** (by atoll; 1985 census) Funafuti (capital) 2,810; Vaitupu 1,231; Niutao 904; Nanumea 879; Nukufetau 694.

People Population: 9,831 (1994 est.). **Nationality:** noun—Tuvaluan(s); adjective—Tuvaluan. **Ethnic groups:** 96% Polynesian. **Languages:** Tuvaluan, English. **Religions:** Christian, predominantly Protestant.

Government Type: independent state, special member of Commonwealth. **Independence:** Oct. 1, 1978 (from UK). **Constitution:** Oct. 1, 1978. **National holiday:** N.A. **Heads of government:** Toaripi Lauti, governor-general (since 1992); Bikenibeu Paeniu, prime minister (since Oct. 1989). **Structure:** executive—prime minister and cabinet; unicameral legislature—12-member House of Parliament; judicial—high court, eight island courts with limited jurisdiction.

Economy (1989) **Monetary unit:** Australian dollar. **Budget:** ***income:*** $4.3 mil.; ***expend.:*** $4.3 mil. **GNP:** $6.4 mil., $700 per capita (1990). **Chief crops:** coconuts, copra. **Livestock:** pigs. **Natural resources:** none. **Major industries:** fishing, tourism, copra. **Labor force:** N.A. **Exports:** $165,000 (f.o.b., 1989); copra. **Imports:** $4.4 mil. (c.i.f., 1989); food, animals, mineral fuels, machinery, manufactured goods. **Major trading partners:** Fiji, Australia, New Zealand.

Intl. Orgs. Commonwealth (special member), SPARTECA, SPC, SPF, UPU.

A British protectorate was established in 1892, and the islands were incorporated into the British colony of the Gilbert and Ellice Islands in 1915. The nine principal islands that make up the Ellice group escaped Japanese occupation in World War II and were used as Allied bases in the campaign to recapture the Pacific.

The Gilbert and Ellice Islands colony was granted self-rule in 1971. In 1975 the Ellice Islands, inhabited mainly by Polynesians, seceded from the other (mainly Micronesian) islands of the colony and became independent as Tuvalu on Oct. 1, 1978. (See also "Kiribati.") In a 1979 U.S.-Tuvalu friendship treaty, the United States relinquished claims, based on 19th-century guano mining, to the four southernmost islands, in return for access to World War II military airfields and veto power over other nations' use of the islands for military purposes.

The economy is based on subsistence farming and fishing. Exports include copra and woven palm-leaf products, and hydroponic agriculture and offshore fisheries are being developed. Tuvalu remains heavily dependent on foreign aid, principally from Australia, New Zealand, and the United Kingdom.

Uganda
Republic of Uganda

Geography **Location:** landlocked equatorial country in eastern Africa. **Boundaries:** Sudan to N, Kenya to E, Tanzania to S, Rwanda to SW, Zaire to W. **Total land area:** 91,135 sq. mi. (236,040 sq km). **Coastline:** none. **Comparative area:** about size of South Dakota. **Land use:** 23% arable land; 9% permanent crops; 25% meadows and pastures; 30% forest and woodland; 13% other; includes negl. % irrigated. **Major cities:** (1980 est.) Kampala (capital) 458,423; Jinja 45,060; Masaka 29,123; Mbale 28,039; Mbarara 23,155.

People **Population:** 19,121,934 (1994 est.). **Nationality:** noun—Ugandan(s); adjective—Ugandan. **Ethnic groups:** 99% African, 1% European, Asian, Arab. **Languages:** English (official), Luganda, Swahili, other Bantu and Nilotic languages. **Religions:** 33% Roman Catholic, 33% Protestant, 16% Muslim, 18% indigenous beliefs.

Government **Type:** republic. **Independence:** Oct. 9, 1962 (from UK). **Constitution:** Sept. 8, 1967, suspended following coup of July 27, 1985. **National holiday:** Independence Day, Oct. 9. **Heads of government:** Yoweri Kaguta Museveni, president (since Jan. 1986); George Kosmas Adyebo, prime minister (since Jan. 1991). **Structure:** president heads National Resistance Council.

Economy **Monetary unit:** Ugandan shilling. **Budget:** (1989 est.) ***income:*** $365 mil.; ***expend.:*** $545 mil. **GDP:** $24.1 bil., $1,200 per capita (1993 est.). **Chief crops:** coffee, cotton, tobacco, tea. **Livestock:** cattle, goats, sheep, pigs, asses. **Natural resources:** copper, cobalt, limestone, salt. **Major industries:** sugar, brewing, tobacco. **Labor force:** 4.5 mil. (1983 est.); 94% subsistence activities, 6% wage earners (est.); 50% of population of working age (1983); N.A. unemployment. **Exports:** $150 mil. (f.o.b., 1992 est.); 97% coffee, cotton, tea. **Imports:** $513 mil. (c.i.f., 1992 est.); petroleum products, machinery, cotton piece goods, metals, transport equipment, food. **Major trading partners:** ***exports:*** 25% U.S., 18% UK, 11% France, 10% Spain; ***imports:*** 25% Kenya, 14% UK, 13% Italy.

Intl. Orgs. Commonwealth, FAO, G-77, IAEA, IBRD, ICAO, IDA, IFAD, IFC, ILO, IMF, INTELSAT, INTERPOL, ITU, NAM, UN, UNESCO, UPU, WHO, WIPO, WMO, WTO.

Prior to 1800 Uganda was the site of several important kingdoms, notably Buganda, centered on Kampala on the northern shore of Lake Victoria. After 1830 Arabs from the sultanate of Oman, based in Zanzibar, asserted loose control over the region and dominated its trade. British explorers, seeking the source of the Nile, reached the Lake Victoria region in the mid-19th century. Mission stations were established in 1877; a Muslim rebellion destroyed the missions and occupied Kampala in 1888.

Buganda was brought under the control of the British East Africa Company in 1890, and Britain established a protectorate in 1894 that was expanded to include neighboring territories in 1896. In 1902 some of the protectorate's territory was transferred to Kenya. British immigrants extensively developed the agricultural potential of Uganda's fertile and temperate highlands, establishing large and prosperous farms. Lake Victoria was the scene of naval battles between Great Britain and Germany (established in neighboring Tanganyika) during World War I.

In 1955 the British administration created a local parliamentary government in which both whites and Africans held ministerial office. Talks on the terms for independence began in 1961 and after some difficulty arrived at a formula for a national structure in which Buganda and other traditional kingdoms would retain local autonomy. Several political parties competed for power; the Uganda People's Congress led by Milton Obote gradually became dominant. Uganda became independent within the British Commonwealth on Oct. 9, 1962.

Several constitutional changes in the early 1960s led to an end to the autonomy of the kingdoms and the effective concentration of all power in Obote's presidency. In 1967 a new constitution proclaimed Uganda an independent republic.

Obote was overthrown on Jan. 25, 1971, by Idi Amin Dada, commander of Uganda's armed forces. Amin declared himself president, dissolved the Parliament, and assumed absolute powers. In 1972 he expelled Uganda's Asians (primarily people of Indian and Pakistani descent), who controlled most of the country's small-scale commerce. The United States broke off diplomatic relations in 1973. In 1976 Amin declared himself president for life. His eight-year reign was marked by extreme violence and persecution of political and tribal opponents; as many as 300,000 Ugandans may have been killed between 1971 and 1979. The country's prosperous agricultural, mining, and commercial economy was devastated, and its infrastructure, including a good road and rail network and Makerere University, one of Africa's preeminent educational institutions, fell into ruins.

On July 3, 1976, Israeli airborne troops landed at Entebbe and rescued 103 hostages who had been captured in a skyjacking carried out by Palestinian and German terrorists.

In 1978 Amin, with the aid of Libyan troops, invaded Tanzania. In the following year, Tanzanian troops countered by invading Uganda; they captured Kampala on Apr. 11, 1979, and drove Amin into exile. Diplomatic relations with the United States resumed. After a series of interim governments, elections in 1981 returned Obote to power. Obote's new regime was marked by fierce repression of opponents and by the outbreak of rebellion in the northern part of the country by the National Resistance Army (NRA) under Yoweri Museveni.

Obote fled into exile in 1985 and was succeeded by Lt. Gen. Basilio Olara-Okello, but the NRA rebellion continued. Kenyan president Daniel arap Moi mediated peace talks between Olara-Okello and the NRA in late 1985; in January 1986 Olara-Okello fled into exile, and Museveni organized a new government. Despite continued insurgencies by rival military factions and a rebellion led by the charismatic religious leader Alice Lakwena, the Museveni government has generally restored order and, with aid from the World Bank and the IMF, has begun to rebuild Uganda's shattered society. In 1987 Uganda joined in talks with Kenya and Tanzania designed to promote closer political and economic relations in East Africa.

Nearly three decades of misrule have left Uganda in desperate economic straits, and despite its resources it is one of the poorest countries in Africa. Inflation, corruption, and public disorder are continuing problems. In addition, the country is threatened by an extensive epi demic of AIDS.

Ukraine
Republic of Ukraine

Geography **Location:** east-central Europe. **Boundaries:** Belarus to N, Russian Federation to NE and E, Sea of Azov and Black Sea to S, Moldova and Romania to SW, Hungary, Slovakia, Poland to W. **Total land area:** 233,089 sq. mi. (603,700 sq km). **Coastline:** Black Sea. **Comparative area:** about twice the size of Arizona. **Land use:** 57% cropland; 11% permanent pasture; 13% forest and woodland; 19% other (mostly urban). **Major cities:** (1990 est.) Kiev (capital) 2,616,000; Kharkov (Kharkiv) 1,618,000; Dnepropetrovsk (Dnipropetrovske) 1,187,000; Odessa (Odesa) 1,106,000; Donetsk (Donetske) 1,117,000.

People **Population:** 51,846,958 (1994 est.). **Nationality:** noun—Ukrainian(s); adjective—Ukrainian. **Ethnic groups:** 72.7% Ukrainian, 22.1% Russian, Belarussian, Moldovian, Polish. **Languages:** Ukrainian (official), Eastern Slavonic language written in Cyrillic script; Russian, ethnic languages. **Religions:** Christianity—Ukrainian Orthodox, Ukrainian Autocephalous Orthodox, Roman Catholic, Protestant; Judaism, Islam.

Government **Type:** republic. **Independence:** Aug. 24, 1991 (from USSR). **Constitution:** being drafted. **National holiday:** Independence Day, Aug. 24. **Heads of government:** Leonid Kuchma, president (since Dec. 1991); Vitali Masol, prime minister (since June 1994). **Structure:** executive—president, Cabinet of Ministers; legislative—Supreme Council (450 deputies); judicial—Supreme Court.

Economy **Monetary unit:** ruble. **Budget:** N.A. ***income:*** N.A.; ***expend.:*** N.A. **GNP:** $205.4 bil., $3,960 per capita (1993 est.). **Chief crops:** wheat, sugar beet, cotton, flax, tobacco, soya, fruit, vegetables. **Livestock:** cattle, pigs, sheep, goats. **Natural resources:** coal, iron ore, manganese, lignite peat, mercury. **Major industries:** chemicals including acids, soda, alkaline dyes, fertilizers, locomotives, railway equipment, tractors. **Labor force:** 25,277,000 (1990). **Exports:** $3 bil. to countries outside of the FSU countries (1993); coal, electric power, ferrous and nonferrous metals, chemicals, machinery and transport equipment. **Imports:** $2.2 bil. from outside of the FSU countries (1993); machinery and parts, transportation equipment, chemicals, textiles. **Major trading partners:** other republics, Poland, Hungary, Canada.

Intl. Orgs. CIS, IAEA, IMF, ITU, OSCE, UN, UNCTAD, UNESCO, UNIDO, UPU, WHO, WIPO, WMO, World Bank.

Ukraine is the center of the original Russian state, known as Kievan Rus, which came into existence in the ninth century A.D. In the 13th and 14th centuries, during the Mongol invasion, Ukraine was controlled by Lithuania and Poland, and in 1654 it first entered the Russian empire. In the latter half of the 17th century, Ukraine was divided, with the eastern regions becoming part of Russia and the western part annexed by Poland; when Poland was subsequently partitioned, the western sections were ceded to Austria.

Until 1917 eastern Ukraine was a province of Russia called "Little Russia," and for two centuries the dominant country tried to Russianize the Ukrainian clergy and upper classes, and twice banned the Ukrainian language. Nevertheless, secret societies for the study of Ukrainian history, language, and culture formed, and when in the 19th century the Russians exiled Ukrainians to Siberia, modern Ukrainian nationalism was officially born.

In 1917, when the Russian empire collapsed, Ukrainian nationalists demanded Ukraine's autonomy by establishing a Ukrainian People's Republic, but within a few months, Red Army troops had occupied Ukraine. For the next few years, however, Ukraine was in the middle of the civil war and was even ceded to Germany under the Brest-Litovsk treaty of 1918, but in December 1920 a Ukrainian Soviet Socialist Republic (SSR) was established. Ukraine again was divided under the 1921 Treaty of Riga, which gave western Ukraine to Poland, Czechoslovakia, and Romania, while eastern Ukraine formed the Ukrainian SSR. Ukraine became one of the original members of the USSR in December 1922.

As in other Soviet republics, the Ukrainians strongly opposed Stalin's policy of forced collectivization of agriculture in the 1930s, and the resulting chaos, famine, and deportation resulted in the deaths of millions of Ukrainians. Likewise, Stalin's great terror of the 1930s hit Ukraine hard, with the first victims being Ukrainian nationalists. World War II largely devastated Ukraine and killed millions of Ukrainians, but as a result of the war, Ukraine regained its old territories from Romania and Poland and was enlarged by the addition of historical Tatar lands in 1954. (The native Tatar inhabitants were forcibly deported to central Asia in the mid-1940s.)

Mikhail Gorbachev's policy of glasnost, or openness, was slow to take root in Ukraine, largely because until 1989 the head of the Communist party in Ukraine was a loyal Brezhnev crony, Vladimir Shcherbitsky. Outwardly, he appeared to agree with Gorbachev's policies, but Ukraine dissidents were still being arrested and cultural groups harassed by secret police. In 1986 a deadly nuclear power explosion at Chernobyl—and Soviet attempts at covering it up—turned international attention to Ukraine and gave rise to a number of new, powerful opposition movements. Rukh (the Ukrainian People's Movement for Restructuring), the most important of these, was founded in Kiev by a prominent group of writers and intellectuals. By 1989 branches of Rukh had been organized in most parts of Ukraine. At the same time, Ukrainian miners became active in strikes, and the Ukrainian Catholic church and the Ukrainian Orthodox church became politically active. Shcherbitsky's failure to contain these groups led to his dismissal in September 1989.

On July 16, 1990, the Ukrainian Supreme Soviet adopted a declaration of sovereignty. Also in July, Communist party Second Secretary Leonid Kravchuk became chairman of the Supreme Soviet. In March 1991 Ukraine participated in the negotiations to form a new union treaty, despite more radical demands by Rukh for complete independence. The Ukrainian Communist party's failure to denounce the attempted coup in Moscow in August 1991 led to significant changes in Ukraine's political situation. After the coup collapsed, the Communist party was banned, and on Aug. 24, 1991, Ukraine adopted a declaration of total independence. In December, Kravchuk was elected president.

That same month, Ukraine, Belarus, and the Russian Federation signed the Minsk Agreement that created the Commonwealth of Independent States, and on Dec. 21, Ukraine and 10 other former union republics officially committed themselves to the union by signing the Alma-Ata Declaration.

Ukraine lacks the extensive ethnic conflicts that plague other former Soviet republics, although the Crimean Tatars seek some form of autonomy, and in some areas the dominant Russians are opposed to full Ukrainian independence. Potentially dangerous conflicts with Russia still remain, however. A dispute over who controls the powerful Black Sea fleet began soon after the fall of the Soviet government and escalated into armed conflict in April 1994, when Russia removed a ship from Odessa laden with marine-research and navigational equipment valued at more than $10 million.

The other conflict involves 2,000 nuclear warheads still present in Ukraine. In January 1994, Kravchuk, Russian president Boris Yeltsin, and U.S. president Bill Clinton negotiated an agreement to dismantle Ukraine's 175 long-range missiles and more than 1,800 warheads. But Ukraine's Parliament continually refused to approve the agreement, even after Clinton made a $350 million U.S. aid package conditional on total disarmament. Parliament's intransigence was seen as an embarrassment to Kravchuk, and in July 1994 he lost the presidential election to reformer Leonid Kuchma. In November Parliament overwhelmingly approved the Nuclear Nonproliferation Treaty and loans from the United States and the IMF ensued.

In early 1995, at the CIS summit Ukraine distanced itself from a security pact and closer economic links with Russia. Kuchma's government passed an austerity budget, thereby ensuring another IMF loan; in May Kuchma visited Pres. Clinton and received further promises of aid.

United Arab Emirates

Geography Location: eastern Arabian peninsula. **Boundaries:** Persian Gulf to N, Gulf of Oman to NE, Oman to E, Saudi Arabia to S and W, short frontier with Qatar to NW. **Total land area:** 29,182 sq. mi. (75,581 sq km). **Coastline:** 899 mi. (1,448 km). **Comparative area:** between South Carolina and Maine. **Land use:** 2% meadows and pastures; 98% other. **Major cities:** (1980 census) Abu Dhabi (capital) 242,975; Dubai 265,702; Sharjah 125,149; Ras al-Khaimah 42,000.

People Population: 2,791,141 (1994 est.). **Nationality:** noun—Emirian(s); adjective—Emirian. **Ethnic groups:** 19% Emirian, 23% other Arab, 50% South Asian (fluctuating), 8% other expatriates (includes Westerners and East Asians); less than 20% of population are UAE citizens (1982). **Languages:** Arabic (official), Hindi, Urdu; Farsi and English widely spoken in major cities. **Religions:** 96% Muslim (16% Shia), 4% Christian, Hindu, and other.

Government Type: federation with specified powers delegated to UAE central government and other powers reserved to member sheikhdoms. **Independence:** Dec. 2, 1971 (from UK). **Constitution::** Dec. 2, 1971 (provisional). **National holiday:** Dec. 2. **Heads of government:** Sheikh Zayed bin Sultan al-Nahyan of Abu Dhabi, president (since Dec. 1971); Maktoum Bin Rashid Al-Makoum, vice president (since Nov. 1990) and prime minister (since July 1979). **Structure:** executive—Supreme Council of Rulers (seven members), from which president and vice president are elected; prime minister and Council of Ministers; unicameral legislature—Federal National Council; judicial—Union Supreme Court.

Economy Monetary unit: Emirian dirham. **Budget:** (1993) ***income:*** $4.3 bil.; ***expend.:*** $4.8 bil. **GDP:** $63.8 bil., $24,000 per capita (1993 est.). **Chief crops:** food imported; some dates, alfalfa, vegetables, fruit, tobacco. **Livestock:** goats, sheep, camels, cattle. **Natural resources:** crude oil, natural gas. **Major industries:** petroleum, fishing, petrochemicals. **Labor force:** 580,000 (1986 est.); 85% industry and commerce; 80% of labor force is foreign; negl. unemployment (1987). **Exports:** $22.6 bil. (f.o.b., 1993 est.); 65% crude oil, natural gas, reexports, dried fish, dates. **Imports:** $18 bil. (f.o.b., 1993 est.); food, consumer and capital goods. **Major trading partners:** ***exports:*** U.S., EU, Japan; ***imports:*** EU, Japan, U.S.

Intl. Orgs. Arab League, FAO, G-77, IAEA, IBRD, ICAO, IDA, IFAD, IFC, ILO, IMF, IMO, INTELSAT, INTERPOL, ITU, NAM, OPEC, UN, UNESCO, UPU, WHO, WIPO, WTO.

In the 1820s Great Britain established protectorates over seven small sheikhdoms along the gulf coast between Qatar and Oman—Abu Dhabi, Dubai, Sharjah, Ajmar, Fujairah, and Umm al-Qaiwain. The region, which had been known as the Pirate Coast, then was generally referred to as the Trucial Coast or Trucial Oman. Under terms of a supplementary treaty in 1892, the sheikhdoms agreed not to enter into relations with any other country.

After Great Britain announced that it would withdraw its forces from the gulf in 1971, the seven sheikhdoms formed a federation and became independent as the United Arab Emirates on Dec. 2, 1971.

The economy is almost entirely dominated by petroleum. Citizens of the UAE receive extensive social services and enjoy one of the world's highest per capita incomes.

Just prior to his invasion of Kuwait in August 1990, Saddam Hussein threatened both the UAE and Kuwait for overproduction of petroleum, and the UAE was an integral part of the Allied coalition against Iraq. In 1995 the government signed a defensive alliance with France, who supplies the army with most of its weapons.

United Kingdom

United Kingdom of Great Britain and Northern Ireland

Geography Location: northwestern Europe, occupying major portion of British Isles. **Boundaries:** Atlantic Ocean to NW and W, North Sea to E; separated from France by English Channel to S; Republic of Ireland to W. **Total land area:** 94,525 sq. mi. (244,820 sq km). **Coastline:** 7,723 mi. (12,429 km). **Comparative area:** slightly smaller than Oregon. **Land use:** 29% arable land; negl. % permanent crops; 48% meadows and pastures; 9% forest and woodland; 14% other; includes 1% irrigated. **Major cities:** (1992 est.) London (capital) 6,904,600; Birmingham 1,009,100; Leeds 721,800; Glasgow 684,300; Sheffield 531,000.

People Population: 58,135,110 (1994 est.). **Nationality:** noun—Briton(s), British (collective pl.); adjective—British. **Ethnic groups:** 81.5% English, 9.6% Scottish, 2.4% Irish, 1.9% Welsh, 1.8% Ulster, 2.8% West Indian, Indian, Pakistani, and other. **Languages:** English, Welsh (about 26% of population of Wales), Scottish form of Gaelic (about 60,000 in Scotland). **Religions:** 27 mil. Anglican, 5.3 mil. Roman Catholic, 2.0 mil. Presbyterian, 760,000 Methodist, 450,000 Jewish (registered).

Government Type: constitutional monarchy. **Independence:** N.A. **Constitution:** unwritten; partly statutes, partly common law and practice. **National holiday:** birthday of queen, June 16. **Heads of government:** Elizabeth II, queen (since Feb. 1952); John Major, prime minister (since Nov. 1990). **Structure:** executive authority lies with collectively responsible cabinet led by prime minister; legislative authority rests with Parliament (House of Lords, House of Commons); House of Lords is supreme judicial authority and highest court of appeals.

Economy Monetary unit: British pound or pound sterling. **Budget:** (1993 est.) ***income:*** $325.5 bil.; ***expend.:*** $400.9 bil. **GDP:** $980.2 bil., $16,900 per capita (1993). **Chief crops:** wheat, barley, potatoes, sugar beets, dairy products; 62.1% self-sufficient (1983); dependent on imports for more than half of consumption of refined sugar, butter, oils and fats, bacon, ham. **Livestock:** chickens, sheep and lambs, cattle, pigs, ducks, geese. **Natural resources:** coal, crude oil, natural gas, tin, limestone. **Major industries:** machinery and transportation equipment, metals, food processing. **Labor force:** 28 mil. (1992); 52.1% services, 23.4% manufacturing and construction, 10.5% self-employed; 8.1% unemployment. **Exports:** $190.1 bil. (f.o.b., 1993); manufactured goods, machinery, fuels, chemicals, semifinished goods, transport equipment. **Imports:** $221.6 bil. (c.i.f., 1993); manufactured goods, machinery, semifinished goods, foodstuffs, consumer goods. **Major trading partners:** ***exports:*** 50% EU (12% Germany, 10% France, 7% Netherlands), 13% U.S., 2% Communist countries; ***imports:*** 53% EU (17% Germany, 9% France, 8% Netherlands), 10% U.S., 2% Communist countries.

Intl. Orgs. Colombo Plan, EU, FAO, IAEA, IBRD, ICAO, IDA, IFAD, IFC, ILO, IMF, IMO, INTELSAT, INTERPOL, ITU, NATO, OECD, OSCE, UN, UPU, WHO, WIPO, WMO, WTO.

Early megalithic and Iron Age peoples of Britain, primarily Celtic, developed tribal petty states that were conquered by Roman invaders in A.D. 43. After Roman legions withdrew from Britain in 410, invasions of Jutes, Angles, and Saxons conquered much of England, while Celtic peoples flourished in Wales, Scotland, and especially Ireland. Viking invaders established settlements in the eighth century. A united Saxon kingdom fell to the Norman invasion of William the Conquerer in 1066.

An aristocratic rebellion against the royal absolutism of King John in 1215 led to the royal acceptance of the Magna Carta, guaranteeing legal rights and laying the foundations of parliamentary government. From the 12th to the 15th century, the Plantagenet dynasty ruled England and claimed overlordship over Ireland; Wales was conquered in 1283. The Plantagenets also controlled sizable territories in France.

The Hundred Years' War (1337–1453) cost England its French possessions; the War of the Roses, (1455–85) ended the Plantagenet dynasty and brought Henry Tudor (Henry VII) to the throne. The Tudors gradually centralized royal control by bringing pressure against both the church and the nobility. Henry VIII broke with Rome in 1534 and established the Church of England. Under Elizabeth I, the last of the Tudors, England defeated Spain at sea and laid the foundations of later worldwide English sea power. The English Renaissance began under Elizabeth I (1533–1603) with the works of Shakespeare and continued into the 17th century with Milton and Newton.

The Stuart dynasty was founded by James I (1566–1625), uniting the crowns of England and Scotland. The English Civil War (1642–49) culminated in the execution of Charles I and the proclamation of the Commonwealth (later the Protectorate) under Oliver Cromwell. The monarchy was restored with Charles II in 1660. In the bloodless Glorious Revolution (1688), James II fled before a Protestant army under the Dutch William of Orange, who married and ruled jointly with James's daughter Mary II. The English Bill of Rights established the supremacy of Parliament and made the government a model of constitutional monarchy.

In the last gasp of the Stuart claimants to the throne, Irish supporters of James II were defeated at the Battle of the Boyne (1690), which temporarily crushed Irish resistance to annexation by England. The United Kingdom was created when Scotland was joined with England in a common Parliament by the Act of Union in 1707. A Scottish uprising led by the Young Pretender, Charles Edward Stuart, was crushed at Culloden Moor in 1745. Ireland was made part of the United Kingdom in 1801.

In the 1700s the United Kingdom became the greatest sea power in the world, controlling an empire that included much of North America and India. Agrarian "enclosures" of the 18th century ruined the British peasantry but created an entrepreneurial revolution in agriculture that ultimately led to greatly increased agricultural productivity. The capital created in the process contributed to the success of the Industrial Revolution, which over the next century made England the wealthiest land on earth.

Despite the loss of the 13 colonies after the American Revolution (1775–83), England consolidated its holdings in the Indian subcontinent, Australia and New Zealand, Malaya, Hong Kong, much of eastern Africa from "Cape to Cairo," and elsewhere. Britain's prosperity and moral purpose were embodied in the person of Victoria, Queen of Great Britain and Ireland (1836–1901) and Empress of India (from 1836).

The repeal of the protectionist Corn Laws in 1846 led to an agricultural depression and hastened the migration of labor from the countryside to the industrial cities. The rise of labor activism led in 1906 to laws granting privileged status to trade unions, which organized the Labour party to promote their interests.

Britain's involvement in the Triple Entente with France and Russia ensured its participation in World War I (1914–18) against Germany, Italy, and Austria-Hungary. Victory came at the cost of an entire generation of British youth, but Britain emerged from the war with its empire at a high point, adding Tanganyika, Jordan, Palestine, and Iraq as part of the postwar division of spoils. Most of Ireland became independent in 1921, however, leaving only Northern Ireland as part of the United Kingdom.

Between the two world wars, Britain's navy and air force were the largest in the world, its army the third largest. Yet its industry was aging, the Great Depression hit especially hard in the British Isles, strikes and labor unrest weakened the social fabric, and colonial ties began to weaken in the 1930s. Economic retrenchment led to a failure to rearm in the face of the rising threat of Hitler's Germany and Mussolini's Italy.

The Munich Pact of 1938 gave Hitler a license for war; his invasion of Poland in 1939 forced Britain into the conflict. When Winston Churchill became prime minister in 1940, Britain was under daily air attack and in danger of an invasion by sea, and the country was dependent on American friendship and lend-lease war materials. But 1941 brought alliance with the United States and the Soviet Union, and a slowly turning tide of war leading to victory in 1945. Still, postwar Britain quickly dropped to the second rank of superpowers.

The coalition between the Conservative and Labour parties that had governed Great Britain during the war seemed no longer necessary in 1945 as the war wound down. Labour won a landslide victory in the 1945 elections; Churchill was recalled in the midst of the Potsdam Conference, and Clement Atlee became prime minister. A brief Labour flirtation with the USSR quickly ended in the postwar 1940s; England became a founding member of the United Nations and also, in 1949, of NATO. As the Cold War took shape, Britain developed its own nuclear arsenal.

The Labour party nationalized the Bank of England along with railroads, public utilities, and heavy industry. A comprehensive welfare state apparatus was created, including a national health service, unemployment and retirement benefits, and free education at all levels. But postwar Britain was in many respects too poor to afford such changes; in order to cut expenditures, the government hastened the process of withdrawal from colonies and military bases around the world. India was granted its independence in 1947, and Palestine, Burma, and Ceylon in 1948 and 1949.

The elections of 1951 brought Churchill back to the prime ministership at the head of a Conservative majority that would last for 13 years. The Conservatives returned steel and trucking to the private sector but in general refrained from undoing the social policies of their Labour predecessors. Economic growth began in the 1950s and held steady at about 2.5 percent per year, a significantly lower rate than in contemporary continental Europe; obsolescence, excessive wage and benefit settlements with labor, and a low savings rate all took their toll. The coronation of Elizabeth II in 1953 added a much-needed element of national celebration.

Churchill retired in 1955 and was succeeded by Anthony Eden. Eden's government fell in 1956 over the failed and bungled Anglo-French invasion of Suez. Eden's fall in 1957 brought to power Harold Macmillan, who pursued close relations with the United States. Most important, he presided over the transformation of an empire to a commonwealth; in the early 1960s, Ghana, Nigeria, Malaya, Singapore, and numerous other colonies were granted independence and Commonwealth status. Immigrants from the Commonwealth promptly flocked to England, straining housing, social services, and the labor market and creating problems of assimilation that remain unsolved.

Britain under Macmillan was the moving force behind the European Free Trade Association in 1960. In 1961 Britain applied for membership in the EEC, but that application was humiliatingly vetoed by France's Charles de Gaulle in 1963. Macmillan's government fell with the Profumo Scandal of 1963, and Douglas Home became a caretaker prime minister pending new elections.

The 1964 elections brought the Labour party to power under Harold Wilson, whose moderate positions made him unpopular with his own party, especially when he sponsored legislation to ban wildcat strikes. Strikes, wage inflation, the steady growth of the public sector (including renationalization of the steel industry), and the rise of turmoil in Northern Ireland in 1968–69 combined to make public support for Labour evaporate.

The Conservative victory in the 1970 elections brought Edward Heath to the office of prime minister. Promising to cut expenditures and taxes, reward initiative, and curb union power, the Conservatives were able to accomplish none of those aims. Heath's government imposed ineffective wage controls in an attempt to slow inflation and passed the 1971 Industrial Relations Act to regulate unions. When unions defied that act, the government fell. Heath's major achievement was the United Kingdom's admission to the EC in 1973. Continued turmoil in Northern Ireland was met with the abolition of Ulster's Stormount Parliament in 1972 and the imposition of direct British rule—a policy that did nothing to stem the growing sectarian violence.

Wilson returned to the prime ministership in 1974 and retired in 1976, passing on the office to James Callaghan, who governed until 1979 at the head of a Labour-Liberal coalition. The continued power of trade unions was seen in the repeal of the Industrial Relations Act and the extension of union privileges. The left wing of the Labour party brought increasing pressure against defense spending, membership in NATO, and the policy of moderation in Rhodesia (now Zimbabwe), and also loudly criticized American involvement in Vietnam.

The OPEC oil price rises of 1972–74 hurt Great Britain in the short run but also encouraged development of oil and gas fields in the North Sea, which made the nation a major petroleum exporter and helped revitalize its economy. Oil exploration in the North Sea also encouraged Scottish nationalism, with some damage to national unity, although in both Scotland and Wales, proposals in 1979 for separate parliaments were soundly defeated by plebiscites.

The 1979 elections brought the Conservatives to power again, behind Margaret Thatcher, Great Britain's (and Europe's) first female prime minister. She proved to be the only British prime minister in modern times to lead her party successfully in three elections. Thatcher took office with an agenda that involved undoing much of the course of postwar British history.

The first target was inflation, attacked through a freeze on expenditures and reduction of government borrowing. The policy was a success; inflation fell from 18 percent in 1980 to 3 percent in 1989. But the austerity program had a high cost in unemployment, which remained at 14 percent in the mid-1980s.

In 1982 national attention turned abruptly to overseas concerns, as Argentina invaded the Falkland ("Malvinas") Islands (only 300 miles east of Argentina), which it had long claimed as Argentine national territory, on Apr. 2. On May 21 British forces launched a counteroffensive, and the invading Argentine forces surrendered on June 14. The nation's success in mounting an amphibious operation 6,500 miles away provoked an upsurge of British patriotism at home that swept Thatcher's party into a second term of office in 1983.

After the election the government turned to denationalization of industry. Over $30 billion in state property—from industrial giants, such as Britoil and British Gas, to individual apartments in municipal housing projects—was sold to private interests. This program was followed in 1986 by tax cuts, in which the top income-tax rate dropped from 98 percent to 40 percent. In foreign affairs, Britain agreed in 1985 to return Hong Kong to Chinese sovereignty in 1997.

The 1987 elections pitted the Conservatives against a weak Labour party that opposed NATO missile deployment in Great Britain, advocating unilateral disarmament and calling for renationalization of industry and a return to higher taxes for the wealthy. The Conservatives easily won their third straight election. By 1989 the "Thatcher Revolution" had produced a decisive long-term economic recovery, but one that was unevenly distributed: the southern part of the country enjoyed an economic boom, while the older industrial cities of the north remained stagnant. In 1990 an economic slowdown and rising inflation led to a strong decline in support for Mrs. Thatcher and her government. The imposition of a per-capita tax, intended to replace property taxes, met with strong public opposition and led to her resignation in November 1990.

Thatcher was replaced by Chancellor of the Exchequer John Major, whose greatest challenge has been Britain's role in a united Europe, to which Britain now has a land link (for the first time in 9,000 years) via the 31-mile Channel Tunnel (Chunnel), completed in 1994.

In the April 1992 elections, the Conservatives, led by Major, won a comfortable 21-seat margin in Parliament despite a recession. Not since the Napoleonic Wars has a British political party been able to form four consecutive governments. Yet only 13 months later Major's ratings in the polls had fallen to 21 percent as the economy stalled and the Conservatives themselves split badly over some elements in the EC's Maastricht Treaty. The Conservatives were further beset in 1994 with a series of tabloid scandals involving adultery, illegitimacy, transvestitism, and suicide, with allegations of political corruption concerning arms sales to Iraq and Malaysia. May elections to 200 municipal council and June elections of delegates to the European Parliament both showed Tory strength at about 28 percent, Labour at about 43 percent despite a steady slow economic recovery. Labour took 48 percent in 1995 local elections, Tories only 25 percent. Conservative chances in parliamentary elections, which need not be called until the spring of 1997, were looking very slim.

The British Empire, now a shadow of its former grandeur, remains a global responsibility for the British government. The governments of Britain and Ireland are actively cooperating to seek a peaceful solution to the perennial "Irish Question." In May 1995 high-level exploratory talks with the IRA—the first since 1973—began in earnest but with little movement over the first few months. Spain continues to call for a referendum aimed at returning Gibraltar to Spanish control.

United States of America

Geography **Location**: 48 conterminous states in North America, between Atlantic and Pacific Oceans; Alaska in northwest North America; Hawaiian Islands in Pacific Ocean about 3,000 miles W of California. **Boundaries**: Canada to N; Atlantic Ocean to E; Gulf of Mexico, Mexico to S; Pacific Ocean to W. Alaska bounded on E by Canada, on S and W by Pacific Ocean, on W and N by Arctic Ocean. **Total land area**: 3,618,770 sq. mi. (9,372,610 sq km). **Coastline**: 11,954 mi. (19,924 km). **Comparative area**: between Brazil and Canada; fourth-largest country. **Land use**: 20% arable land; negl. % permanent crops; 26% meadows and pastures; 29% forest and woodland; 25% other; includes 2% irrigated. **Major cities**: (1992 est.) Washington, D.C. (capital) 585,000; New York 7,311,966; Los Angeles 3,489,779; Chicago 2,768,483; Houston 1,690,180; Philadelphia 1,552,572.

People **Population**: 260,713,585 (1994 est.). **Nationality**: noun—American(s); adjective—American. **Ethnic groups**: 80.3% white, 12.1% black, 2.9% Asian or Pacific Islander, 0.8% American Indian, Eskimo, or Aleut, 3.9% other; 9% Hispanic origin (of any race) (1990 census). **Languages**: predominantly English; sizable Spanish-speaking minority. **Religions**: 61% Protestant (21% Baptist, 12% Methodist, 8% Lutheran, 4% Presbyterian, 3% Episcopalian, 13% other Protestant), 25% Roman Catholic, 7% none, 2% Jewish, 5% other.

Government **Type**: federal republic; strong democratic tradition. **Independence**: July 4, 1776 (from UK). **Constitution**: Sept. 17, 1787, effective June 21, 1788. **National holiday**: Independence Day, July 4 (1776). **Heads of government**: William J. Clinton, president (since Jan. 1993); Albert Gore, Jr., vice president (since Jan. 1993). **Structure**: executive—president, vice president, cabinet; legislative—bicameral Congress (House of Representatives and Senate); judicial—Supreme Court; branches, in principle, independent and maintain balance of power.

Economy **Monetary unit**: United States dollar ($); $1 = 100 cents. **Budget**: (1993 est.) ***income***: $1.1535 trillion; ***expend:*** $1.4082 trillion **GDP**: $6.379 trillion, $24,700 per capita (1993). **Chief crops**: food grains, feed crops, oil-bearing crops; world's second-largest producer and number-one exporter of grain; an illegal producer of cannabis for international drug trade. **Livestock**: cattle, pigs, lamb. **Natural resources**: coal, copper, lead, molybdenum, phosphates, uranium, bauxite, gold, iron, mercury, nickel, potash, silver, tungsten, zinc, crude oil, natural gas, timber. **Major industries:** leading industrial power in the world, highly diversified; petroleum, steel, motor vehicles, aerospace, telecommunications, chemicals, electronics, food processing, consumer goods, fishing, lumber, mining. **Labor force:** 128,548,000 (includes armed forces and unemployed); civilian labor force 126,982,000 (1992); 7% unemployment (1993). **Exports**: $449 bil. (f.o.b., 1993 est.); ***commodities***—capital goods, automobiles, consumer goods, industrial raw materials, food and beverages. **Imports**: $582 bil. (c.i.f., 1993 est.); ***commodities***—crude and partly refined petroleum, machinery, automobiles, consumer goods, industrial raw materials, food and beverages. **Major trading partners**: (1989) ***exports:*** 27% Western Europe, 21% Canada, 12% Japan; ***imports:*** 22% Western Europe, 20% Japan, 19% Canada.

Intl. Orgs. Colombo Plan, FAO, IAEA, IBRD, ICAO, IDA, IFAD, IFC, ILO, IMF, IMO, INTELSAT, INTERPOL, ITU, NATO, OAS, OECD, OSCE, UN, UPU, WHO, WIPO, WMO, WTO.

(For current events and history see Part I: "Major News Stories of the Year," and Part II: "Chronology of American History.")

Uruguay

Oriental Republic of Uruguay

Geography **Location**: southeastern coast of South America. **Boundaries:** Brazil to N, Atlantic Ocean to E and S, Argentina to W. **Total land area:** 68,039 sq. mi. (176,220 sq km). **Coastline:** 410 mi. (660 km). **Comparative area:** slightly smaller than Washington State. **Land use:** 8% arable land; negl. % permanent crops; 78% meadows and pastures; 4% forest and woodland; 10% other; includes 1% irrigated. **Major cities:** (1985 census) Montevideo (capital) 1,246,500; Salto 77,400; Paysandú 75,200; Las Piedras 61,300; Rivera 55,400.

People **Population:** 3,198,910 (1994 est.). **Nationality:** noun—Uruguayan(s); adjective—Uruguayan. **Ethnic groups:** 88% white, 8% mestizo, 4% black. **Languages:** Spanish. **Religions:** 66% Roman Catholic, 2% Protestant, 2% Jewish, 30% nonprofessing or other (less than half adult population attends church regularly).

Government **Type:** republic. **Independence:** Aug. 25, 1828 (from Brazil). **Constitution:** Nov. 27, 1966; effective Feb. 1967; suspended June 27, 1972; new constitution rejected by referendum, Nov. 30, 1980. **National holiday:** Independence Day, Aug. 25. **Head of government:** Julio María Sanguinetti, president (since Mar. 1995). **Structure:** executive, headed by president; bicameral legislature (Senate and House of Deputies); national judiciary headed by Court of Justice.

Economy **Monetary unit:** Uruguayan peso. **Budget:** (1991 est.) ***income:*** $2.9 bil.; ***expend.:*** $3 bil. **GDP:** $19 bil., $6,000 per capita (1993 est.). **Chief crops:** wheat, rice, corn, sorghum; large areas devoted to extensive livestock grazing; self-sufficient in most basic foodstuffs. **Livestock:** sheep, cattle, horses, pigs. **Natural resources:** soil, hydropower potential, minor minerals. **Major industries:** meat processing, wool and hides, sugar. **Labor force:** 1.3 mil. (1988 est.); 25% government; 19% manufacturing; 12% commerce; 12% utilities, construction, transport, and communications; 11% agriculture; 9% unemployment (1988 est.). **Exports:** $1.6 bil. (f.o.b., 1993 est.); 17% hides and leather goods, 10% beef, 9% wool, 7% fish, 4% rice. **Imports:** $2 bil. (f.o.b., 1993 est.); fuels and lubricants (15%), metals, machinery, transportation equipment, industrial chemicals. **Major trading partners:** ***exports:*** 17% Brazil, 15% U.S., 10% Germany, 10% Argentina; ***imports:*** 24% Brazil, 14% Argentina, 8% U.S., 8% Germany.

Intl. Orgs. FAO, G-77, IAEA, IBRD, ICAO, IFAD, IFC, ILO, IMF, IMO, INTELSAT, INTERPOL, ITU, OAS, UN, UNESCO, UPU, WHO, WIPO, WMO, WTO.

Uruguay was known as the Banda Oriental del Uruguay (Eastern Shore of the Uruguay River) during the colonial period. Although the Spanish first explored the area in 1516, they did not immediately settle there. Instead, the Portuguese founded the Colonia de Sacramento, near Buenos Aires, in 1680. They did not permanently establish the settlement of Montevideo until 1726. Under the leadership of José Gervasio Artigas, Uruguayans fought against both the Portuguese and the junta of Buenos Aires between 1811 and 1814 in an effort to establish their independence; in 1815 they proclaimed the Autonomous Government of the Eastern Provinces.

In 1817 the Portuguese again took control of the region, but Uruguayan nationals ousted them in 1828. A new constitution for the country was promulgated in 1830; however, domestic rivalry among elites soon led to civil war. The two contending factions, Liberals (Colorados) and Conservatives (Blancos), wore red and white armbands, respectively. Civil war continued through the 1840s and 1850s, until the victory of the Colorados in 1865. In the War of the Triple Alliance (1865–70), Uruguay allied itself with Argentina and Brazil against Paraguay. The consequence of the war for Uruguay was the definitive establishment of its independence from the other regional powers.

The Colorado party dominated Uruguayan government from 1865 until 1958. Waves of European immigrants transformed Uruguayan society during the latter half of the 19th century, and by 1880 immigrants made up almost half of the population. The last civil war between the Blancos and the Colorados took place in 1904; the Colorados won a definitive victory under Pres. José Batlle y Ordóñez, one of Uruguay's major political figures.

Batlle inaugurated a labor and social-welfare reform program that created Latin America's first eight-hour working day as well as progressive legislation on women's rights. A proposal for the extension of the franchise to women was put forward in 1917. Impressed with the Swiss plural executive Federal Council during his stay in Switzerland, Batlle believed such a structure could help Uruguay avoid the Latin American hazard of *caudillismo* (authoritarian rule). Batlle proposed the idea of a plural executive, and a version of the idea became part of the constitution in 1919. The new constitution provided for both a president and a collegial National Council, both of which would make up the executive structure of the government.

In 1933 a military coup by Pres. Gabriel Terra sought to dissolve both the legislature and the National Council and to reestablish the single executive presidential system. He managed this by sponsoring a constituent assembly that drew up a new constitution in 1934. In a 1951 plebiscite, Uruguayan voters approved a return to the plural executive system, and a new constitutional order reflecting this went into effect the following year. The debate over the form of the executive was not over, however; in 1966 the public voted for yet another constitution, which once again established the single president as the executive power.

Uruguay's economy began to falter during the 1950s. This, combined with the expansion of governmental bureaucracy tied to the country's social welfare programs, led to increasing popular discontent. In 1958 the Blancos won two successive victories at the polls (for the first time in nearly a century). A candidate from the conservative wing of the Colorado party, Jorge Pacheco Areco, regained the presidency for the traditional ruling party in 1967, but neither the Blancos nor the Colorados were able to deal with Uruguay's deteriorating economy or with its growing political unrest.

Uruguay's politics became increasingly polarized during the 1960s and into the 1970s. The leftist National Liberation Movement (MLN or Tupamaros), formed in 1967 and began urban guerrilla activity that included robbery and kidnapping. The Tupamaros, many of whom were young and middle class, embarrassed government officials and the police and were largely successful in eroding the public image of the civilian government. Tupamaro activity generated violence from the military and police, and as the political situation deteriorated in the early seventies, the government granted the military ever-expanding authority to deal with the situation.

By 1973 the military was in control of the country, and they dissolved the Congress. The military allowed Pres. Juan María Bordaberry to remain in office until 1976, at which time they installed Aparicio Méndez in the presidency. It was Bordaberry, however, who proposed the dismantling of the political parties in 1976. Uruguayan military rule was brutally repressive, and the armed forces perpetrated many human rights abuses (kidnapping, torture, murder). By some estimates, the Uruguayan military regime had the world's largest number of political prisoners in proportion to the population.

The military government held a plebiscite in 1980 on a new constitution that would have amounted to continued de facto military control. The popular vote went against the military, and a slow process of political transition began, in which the military tried to bargain with civilian political elites. In 1984 the civilian Colorado candidate Julio María Sanguinetti was elected to the presidency. He took office the following year as the military withdrew from governance, restoring civilian rule.

Luis Alberto Lacalle, a conservative member of the Blanco party, won the November 1989 presidential election, but his party failed to win a legislative majority, forcing the new president into a political pact with some opposition Colorado party members.

Uzbekistan

Republic of Uzbekistan

Geography Location: central Asia. **Boundaries:** Kazakhstan to N, NE, and NW; Kyrgyzstan to E, Tajikistan to SE, Afghanistan to S, Turkmenistan to SW and W. **Total land area:** 172,741 sq. mi. (447,400 sq km). **Coastline:** Aral Sea. **Comparative area:** about the size of Colorado and Washington State combined. **Land use:** 9% cropland; 49% permanent pasture; 18% forest and woodland; 24% other (mostly urban and mountain). **Major cities:** (1990 est.) Tashkent (capital) 2,094,000; Samarkand 370,000; Namangan 312,000; Andizhan 297,000; Bukhara 228,000.

People Population: 22,608,866 (1994 est.). **Nationality:** noun—Uzbek(s); adjective—Uzbek. **Ethnic groups:** 71.4% Uzbek, 8.3% Russian, 4.7% Tadzhik, 4.1% Kazakh, 2.4% Tatar. **Languages:** Uzbek (official), member of Eastern Turk language group written in Cyrillic script since 1940; Russian, ethnic languages. **Religions:** Muslim—Sunni; Orthodox Christian, Judaism.

Government Type: republic. **Independence:** Aug. 31, 1991 (from USSR). **Constitution:** being drafted. **National holiday:** Independence Day, Sept. 1. **Heads of government:** Islam A. Karimov, president (since Dec. 1991); Abdulhashim Mutalov, prime minister (since Jan. 1992). **Structure:** executive—president, Cabinet of Ministers; legislative—Supreme Soviet (550 members); judicial—Supreme Court.

Economy Monetary unit: som. **Budget:** N.A. ***income:*** N.A.; ***expend.:*** N.A. **GNP:** $53.7 bil., $2,430 per capita (1993 est.). **Chief crops:** seed cotton, vegetables, grain, grapes, potatoes. **Livestock:** sheep, goats, cattle, pigs. **Natural resources:** natural gas, coal, petroleum, gold, uranium, copper, tungsten, aluminium ore. **Major industries:** processing minerals, machine building, chemical processing, iron and steel, textiles, cotton-ginning. **Labor force:** 7,941,000. **Exports:** $706.5 mil. outside the former USSR (1993); cotton, gold, textiles, chemical and mineral fertilizers. **Imports:** $947.3 mil. outside the former USSR (1993); machinery and parts, consumer durables, grain, foodstuffs. **Major trading partners:** other republics.

Intl. Orgs. CIS, IMF, OSCE, UN, UNCTAD, World Bank; applying for membership in other international organizations.

Uzbekistan, a land of deserts and steppe, lies in the heart of central Asia. Although the territory has been inhabited since prehistoric times, today's Uzbeks are actually descendants of nomadic Mongol, Iranian, and Turkic tribes who mixed with the sedentary populations there beginning in the 13th century A.D. The Uzbeks take their name from Khan Uzbek (1282–1342), the ruler responsible for converting the Mongol Golden Horde (the westernmost part of the Mongolian empire) to Islam. In the 18th and 19th centuries, the tribal states known as the Uzbek khanates of Bukhara, Samarkand, and Kokand were formed. Russian conquest of the Uzbek lands already began in the 18th century and was completed in 1876 with the conquering of the khanate of Kokand. The Russian empire quickly built the Transcaucasian Railway to connect it with the region's major cities, thus sealing its hold on the area.

As with Kazakhstan, there was a large influx of Russians into Uzbekistan, mainly to its cities. Uzbek resentment of Russian immigrants precipitated a riot in 1898 in Andidzhan and again in 1916, when a decree that drafted central Asians into the Army was promulgated. At the time of the revolution, Soviet power was established in 1917 in the largely Russian city of Tashkent, and after some fighting, the region of Uzbekistan was incorporated into the Russian republic as the Turkestan Autonomous Soviet Socialist Republic (ASSR) in April 1918. In October 1924, the Uzbek Soviet Socialist Republic (SSR) came into being.

During 1924–25, the Soviet government initiated the National Delimitation of the Central Asian Republics to create Uzbek national symbols, to develop a new literary language, and to increase literacy among Uzbeks. It also conducted a brutal campaign against Islam and its believers. The Soviets modernized agriculture and industrialized the territory, although the native Uzbek population for the most part continued to live in rural areas and worked harvesting cotton, while the Russian population worked in industry. During World War II, Uzbekistan's industrial base expanded as many major factories and plants were moved there from the

Russian areas to keep them safe from enemy attack.

Mikhail Gorbachev's policy of glasnost, or openness, did not immediately result in political changes in Uzbekistan. In time, Uzbeks became politically active over many of the same issues that affected their Kazakh neighbors, such as the environmental problems causing the drying up of its rivers, the desiccation of the Aral Sea, and the salinization of the soil. They also demanded that Uzbek (and not Russian) be the official language of Uzbekistan.

In March 1990 the Supreme Soviet elected Islam Karimov as president, and in April 1991 Uzbekistan agreed to sign a new union treaty, which was derailed by the failed August 1991 coup in Moscow. On Aug. 31, 1991, Uzbekistan declared its independence, and in December signed the Alma-Ata Declaration and joined the Commonwealth of Independent States.

In December 1991 Islam Karimov won the presidential election, and he moved to reduce Uzbekistan's dependence on Russia. In 1994 he signed an economic free-trade agreement with Kazakhstan (later joined by Kyrgystan) and he banned use of the ruble in order to strengthen the som, Uzbekistan's monetary unit. In December 1994 Karimov's supporters (calling themselves the Democratic party) won an overwhelming majority in Uzbekistan's first parliamentary elections.

Vanuatu

Republic of Vanuatu

Geography **Location:** chain of 12 principal and some 60 smaller islands in Pacific Ocean, about 500 mi. (800 km) W of Fiji and 1,100 mi. (2,800 km) E of Australia. Port Vila 17°45'S, 168°18'E. **Boundaries:** surrounded by South Pacific Ocean; nearest neighbor is Santa Cruz Islands to N. **Total land area:** 5,699 sq. mi. (14,760 sq km). **Coastline:** 1,571 mi. (2,528 km). **Comparative area:** slightly larger than Connecticut. **Land use:** 1% arable land; 5% permanent crops; 2% meadows and pastures; 1% forest and woodland; 91% other. **Major cities:** (1989 census) Port Vila (capital) 19,311.

People **Population:** 169,776 (1994 est.). **Nationality:** noun—Vanuatuan(s); adjective—Vanuatuan. **Ethnic groups:** 94% indigenous Melanesian, 4% French; remainder Vietnamese, Chinese, and various Pacific Islanders. **Languages:** English and French (official); pidgin (known as Bislama or Bichelam). **Religions:** most at least nominally Christian.

Government **Type:** republic. **Independence:** July 30, 1980 (from France and UK). **Constitution:** July 30, 1980. **National holiday:** July 30. **Heads of government:** Jean Marie Leye, president (since Mar. 1994); Maxime Carlot Korman, prime minister (since Jan. 1993). **Structure:** unicameral legislature (46-member Parliament).

Economy **Monetary unit:** vatu. **Budget:** (1989 est.) ***income:*** $90 mil. ***expend.:*** $103 mil. **GDP:** $142 mil., $1,050 per capita (1990). **Chief crops:** export crops of copra, cocoa, coffee, and fish; subsistence crops of copra, taro, yams, coconuts, fruits, vegetables. **Livestock:** poultry, cattle, pigs, goats, horses. **Natural resources:** manganese, hardwood forests, fish. **Major industries:** food and fish-freezing, forestry processing, meat canning. **Labor force:** N.A. **Exports:** $14.9 mil. (f.o.b., 1991); 37% copra, 11% cocoa, 9% meat, 8% fish, 4% timber. **Imports:** $74 mil. (f.o.b., 1991); 25% machines and vehicles, 23% food and beverages, 18% basic manufactures, 11% raw materials and fuels, 6% chemicals. **Major trading partners:** ***exports:*** 34% Netherlands, 27% France, 17% Japan, 4% Belgium, 3% New Caledonia; ***imports:*** 36% Australia, 13% Japan, 10% New Zealand, 8% France, 5% Fiji.

Intl. Orgs. Commonwealth, FAO, G-77, IBRD, ICAO, IDA, IFC, IMF, ITU, NAM, UN, WHO, WMO.

Formerly known as the New Hebrides, Vanuatu is a rugged, volcanic island chain with heavily forested mountains; peaks rise to over 6,000 feet (on Espiritu Santo, the largest island). The people are Melanesians. In 1887 the islands were placed under the administration of an Anglo-French naval commission, becoming a joint Anglo-French colony (condominium) in 1906. The islands escaped Japanese occupation during World War II; they sided with the Free French and were used as bases for Allied campaigns in the Pacific. The New Hebrides were granted independence as Vanuatu on July 30, 1980, with membership in the British Commonwealth. The government is a parliamentary system, complemented by a National Council of Chiefs to decide matters of tradition and customary law.

The economy is based on subsistence agriculture, cattle raising, and fishing. Tourism is developing rapidly, and the sale of long-term tuna-fishing rights, principally to Japan, Australia, and the United States, is an important earner of foreign exchange.

Venezuela

Republic of Venezuela

Geography **Location:** northern coast of South America. **Boundaries:** Caribbean Sea to N, Guyana to E, Brazil to S, Colombia to W. **Total land area:** 352,144 sq. mi. (912,050 sq km). **Coastline:** 1,739 mi. (2,800 km). **Comparative area:** about 1.3 times size of Texas. **Land use:** 3% arable land; 1% permanent crops; 20% meadows and pastures; 39% forest and woodland; 37% other; includes negl. % irrigated. **Major cities:** (1990 est.) Caracas (capital) 3,435,795; Maracaibo 1,400,643; Valencia 1,274,354; Maracay 956,656; Barquisimeto 787,359.

People **Population:** 20,562,405 (1994 est.). **Nationality:** noun—Venezuelan(s); adjective—Venezuelan. **Ethnic groups:** 67% mestizo, 21% white, 10% black, 2% Indian. **Languages:** Spanish (official), Indian dialects (spoken by about 200,000 Amerindians in remote interior). **Religions:** 96% nominally Roman Catholic, 2% Protestant.

Government **Type:** republic. **Independence:** July 5, 1821 (from Spain). **Constitution:** Jan. 23, 1961. **National holiday:** Independence Day, July 5. **Head of government:** Rafael Caldera, president (since Feb. 1994). **Structure:** executive (president); bicameral legislature (National Congress—Senate, Chamber of Deputies); judiciary.

Economy **Monetary unit:** bolívar. **Budget:** (1993 est.) ***income:*** $9.8 bil.; ***expend.:*** $11.9 bil. **GDP:** $161 bil., $8,000 per capita (1993 est.). **Chief crops:** cereals, fruits, sugar, coffee, rice; illegal producer of cannabis for international drug trade. **Livestock:** cattle, pigs, goats, horses, asses, sheep. **Natural resources:** crude oil, natural gas, iron ore, gold, bauxite. **Major industries:** petroleum, iron ore mining, construction materials. **Labor force:** 5.8 mil. (1985); 56% services, 28% industry, 16% agriculture; 7% unemployment (1988). **Exports:** $14.2 bil. (f.o.b., 1993 est.); 81% petroleum, bauxite, aluminum, iron ore, agricultural products. **Imports:** $11 bil. (f.o.b., 1993 est.); foodstuffs, chemicals, manufactures, machinery, transport equipment. **Major trading partners:** (1989) ***exports:*** 50% U.S., 14% Europe, 4% Japan; ***imports:*** 44% U.S., 8.5% Germany, 7% Italy, 4% Japan, 2% Canada.

Intl. Orgs. FAO, G-77, IAEA, IBRD, ICAO, IFAD, IFC, ILO, IMF, IMO, INTELSAT, INTERPOL, ITU, LAES, LAIA, OAS, OPEC, UN, UNESCO, UPU, WHO, WMO.

At the time of European contact in the early 16th century, coastal Venezuela was home to nearly 50,000 semisedentary Indians. Although the region was "discovered" by Christopher Columbus in 1498, European settlement of the area was slow in comparison with the neighboring region of New Granada. The Spaniards explored and exploited Venezuela in the 1520s, their activity originally characterized by gold and pearl expeditions.

Early attempts at agriculture by the Spaniards failed until they discovered that the area around Caracas (founded in 1567) could sustain the production of both wheat and cocoa. African slave labor was an important part of the economic structure of the area, and as markets for cocoa expanded, Caracas grew in importance. Venezuela became a captaincy general (an administrative region below the level of viceroyalty) with an *audiencia* (high court) established at Caracas in 1777–78.

As early as 1797, Venezuelan society was in rebellion against the Spanish empire. A major hindrance to the revolutionary leadership of Simón Bolívar was the need to accommodate both the conservative landowners of the white elite and the *pardos*, lower class citizens of mixed African and European ancestry.

The wars of independence were particularly destructive in Venezuela, but by 1821 the region had achieved its independence and had become part of the federation of Gran Colombia, which also included New Granada and Ecuador. By 1830 Gran Colombia was in a state of political collapse, and Venezuela became an independent republic.

The military *caudillo* (leader) José Antonio Páez controlled the country for three decades. With the demise of Páez and his conservative allies in the 1860s, the forces of liberalism under the control of Antonio Guzmán Blanco took over. The Guzmán Blanco era ended during a brief civil war in 1889. The victor of the struggle, Gen. Cipriano Castro, proceeded to establish his own rule. In 1908 Gen. Juan Vicente Gómez occupied the presidency, and he controlled the politics of Venezuela until his death in 1935.

The shift from dictatorship to democracy began with the Generation of 28, a student movement that organized urban workers and peasants into a viable political opposition. The Generation of 28 later became the modern Democratic Action party. In 1945 a group of young military officers overthrew the conservative dictatorship and supported the Democratic Action group in writing a new democratic constitution. Democratic Action won the elections of 1947, but conservative military elements overthrew the new government the following year. The conservative coup brought Col. Marcos Pérez Jiménez to power until his ouster in 1958.

The election of Democratic Action candidate Romulo Betancourt as president marked the beginning of multiparty democratic politics in Venezuela. The stability of the system owed much to political possibilities provided by the country's petroleum revenues.

Despite the nationalization of foreign-owned oil and iron firms in 1975 and 1976, Venezuela's dependence on petroleum revenues precipitated economic and political problems for the country in the 1980s. The downturn of the global oil market caused Venezuela's economic base to shrink, and the country's massive foreign debt hindered the expansion of populist political strategies.

The Christian Democrats defeated Democratic Action in 1968 and again in 1978. Pres. Luis Herrera Campíns' administration (1979–84) took the country in a more conservative direction but Democratic Action regained the presidency in 1983 under Jaime Lusinchi.

Venezuela's huge foreign debt in the 1980s led to tight economic controls and a reduction in social spending, which posed serious problems for the government. The administration of Pres. Carlos Andrés Perez, elected in 1989, began with antigovernment riots in which hundreds died.

In February 1992, Latin America's oldest civilian government thwarted an attempted coup by soldiers angered over connections between high-ranking officers and drug traffickers; a second coup in November also failed. But in early 1993, Pres. Perez was suspended after the Senate ordered impeachment proceedings against him on charges he embezzled $17 million from the government; the Congress overwhelmingly elected Sen. Ramon Jose Valasquez Mujica to serve as interim president.

In early 1994 Rafael Caldera became president and immediately faced severe economic problems as the currency depreciated by more than 80 percent in only a few months caused by the collapse of Banco Latino, the nation's second-largest bank. In June Caldera took extraordinary measures, imposing price and currency controls and suspending several constitutional guarantees, including the guarantee against search and arrest without a warrant. This crisis continued through the first half of 1995.

Vietnam

Socialist Republic of Viet Nam

Geography **Location:** Southeast Asia. **Boundaries:** China to N, Gulf of Tonkin to NE, South China Sea to E, Laos and Cambodia to W. **Total land area:** 127,243 sq. mi. (329,560 sq km). **Coastline:** 2,140 mi. (3,444 km) excluding islands. **Comparative area:** between New Mexico and Montana. **Land use:** 22% arable land; 2% permanent crops; 1% meadows and pastures; 40% forest and woodland; 35% other; includes 5% irrigated. **Major cities:** (1989) Hanoi (capital) 1,088,862; Ho Chi Minh City (formerly Saigon) 3,169,135; Haiphong 456,049; Da Nang 370,670; Long Xuyen 217,171.

People **Population:** 73,103,898 (1994 est.). **Nationality:** noun—Vietnamese (sing., pl.); adjective—Vietnamese. **Ethnic groups:** 85–90% Vietnamese, 3% Chinese; ethnic minorities include Muong, Thai, Meo, Khmer, Man, Cham; other mountain groups. **Languages:** Vietnamese (official); French, Chinese, English, Khmer, ethnic langs. (Mon-Khmer and Malayo-Polynesian). **Religions:** Buddhist, Confucian, Taoist, Roman Catholic.

Government **Type:** Communist state. **Independence:** Sept. 2, 1945 (from France). **Constitution:** Dec. 18, 1980. **National holiday:** Sept. 2. **Heads of government:** Le Duc Anh, president, (since Mar. 1992); Vo Van Kiet, prime minister (since August 1991). **Structure:** highest authority of land is technically Council of State, whose chairman serves as country's president; Council of Ministers oversees implementation of party policies—chairman is equivalent of premier; unicameral legislature (National Assembly).

Economy **Monetary unit:** new dong. **Budget:** (1992) ***income:*** $1.9 bil.; ***expend.:*** $2 bil. **GNP:** $72 bil., $1,000 per capita (1993 est.). **Chief crops:** rice, rubber, fruits, vegetables; some corn, manioc, sugarcane; major food imports—wheat, corn, dairy products. **Livestock:** pigs, buffalo, cattle, goats, horses. **Natural resources:** phosphates, coal, manganese, bauxite, apatite. **Major industries:** food processing, textiles, machine building. **Labor force:** 32.7 mil. civilians (1990 est.); 10% unemployment (1988 est.). **Exports:** $2.6 bil. (f.o.b., 1993 est.); agricultural and handicraft products, coal, minerals, ores. **Imports:** $3.1 bil. (c.i.f., 1993 est.); petroleum, steel products, railroad equipment, chemicals, medicines. **Major trading partners:** ***exports:*** Japan, Singapore, Thailand, Hong Kong, Taiwan; ***imports:*** Japan, Singapore, Thailand.

Intl. Orgs. ASEAN, Colombo Plan, FAO, G-77, IAEA, IBRD, ICAO, IDA, IFAD, IFC, ILO, IMF, INTELSAT, ITU, NAM, UN, UNDP, UNESCO, UNICEF, UPU, WHO, WIPO, WMO.

The southward expansion of the Chinese empire in the first millennium B.C. drove the Vietnamese peoples southward into northern Vietnam (Tonkin). The area came under direct Chinese rule in 111 B.C. Chinese rule endured, with some interruptions, until A.D. 948; thereafter, Vietnam was independent under strong Chinese influence.

The Hindu-Buddhist kingdom of Annam, in central Vietnam, gradually increased in size and power at the expense of Tonkin, to the north, and the Khmer empire and Champa, to the west and south. In 1558 the kingdom of Annam split, with independent courts established at Hanoi, controlling Tonkin and the Red River valley, and Hue, in central Vietnam. A remnant of the old Champa state remained independent in the Mekong delta in the south. In 1802 the monarchy was reunited, with the court at Hue controlling all of Vietnam and exercising hegemony over Cambodia.

European penetration of the region began in the 16th century; by the early 19th century, France was the dominant foreign power in Indochina. Efforts to establish French military control began in 1858–59 with the establishment of a colony in Cochin China, in southern Vietnam. Campaigns in the Red River valley in 1873 and 1882 were complicated by Chinese intervention and the determined resistance of the Vietnamese court. In 1884 separate protectorates were established in Tonkin and Annam; in 1887 those, along with Cochin China and Cambodia, were combined into the Union of Indochina under French colonial rule. Rubber plantations were established, and rice and timber exports were under French control. A nationalist rebellion under Phan Boi Chau was suppressed in the early 20th century.

Nationalist resistance to French colonialism continued, resulting in the creation in 1939 of the Vietminh, or Independence League. In 1940 Japanese troops occupied French Indochina, with the collaboration of colonial administrators loyal to the Vichy regime. The Vietminh spearheaded anti-Japanese guerrilla resistance and in 1945 forced the abdication of King Bao Dai, head of a pro-Japanese puppet state. In 1945 France reoccupied Indochina; in 1946 the leader of the Vietminh, Ho Chi Minh, became president of a separatist government at Hanoi. France ceded local autonomy to Tonkin and Annam but sought to retain Cochin China as a colony. Fighting between the French and the Vietminh resumed. On July 1, 1949, the French reinstalled Bao Dai as king of Vietnam, and in February 1950 recognized the independence of Vietnam within the French Union. Ho Chi Minh's republican government also claimed control of all of Vietnam.

Fighting between the two rivals culminated in the French defeat at Dienbienphu on May 7, 1954. An armistice was concluded according to which the country was partitioned at a demilitarized zone at latitude 17° north, the northern part going to the Communist-controlled Vietminh government, the southern to Bao Dai. Nearly one million refugees, including many ethnic Chinese, fled from the north to the south. An international conference in Geneva agreed that elections would be held throughout Vietnam in 1956. In June 1954 Ngo Dinh Diem became premier of South Vietnam; full sovereignty in the south was transferred by France to the Vietnamese government in December 1954. In October 1955 Diem held elections in the south that resulted in the dismissal of Bao Dai as king and the proclamation of an independent Republic of Vietnam.

The scheduled elections of 1956 were never held. French troops completed withdrawal from South Vietnam in that year. Fighting continued in the south, as the Vietminh-backed National Liberation Front (Vietcong) sought to overthrow the Diem government. On Dec. 31, 1959, the Democratic Republic of Vietnam in the north adopted a new constitution calling for the reunification of the country; northern aid to the Vietcong increased significantly, as did American aid to the south. After 1962 American military advisers steadily increased in number and combat exposure.

In 1963 widespread public demonstrations, under Buddhist leadership, led to a coup on Nov. 1–2 in which Diem was deposed and assassinated. A series of short-lived military regimes followed until September 1967, when Nguyen Van Thieu was elected president. U.S. air strikes against North Vietnam began in 1964. In the same year, the flow of troops and supplies from north to south increased. American combat troops entered the war in 1965. Despite U.S.–South Vietnamese superiority in arms and troops, and total control of the air, Vietcong control over the countryside increased. Both Operation Phoenix, in which antigovernment rural leaders were assassinated, and the establishment of fortified strategic hamlets to control the rural population, failed to reverse the tide.

The combined Vietcong–North Vietnamese Tet Offensive in early 1968 resulted in serious losses for South Vietnamese and American forces. The war spread to Laos and to Cambodia, the latter bombed in 1969. American air strikes in North Vietnam were stepped up, and U.S. troop strength reached a maximum of 543,000 in 1969. In July 1969 a series of U.S. troop withdrawals began, and secret talks were initiated in search of a negotiated settlement of the war. Following heavy U.S. bombardment of the north in 1972, a cease-fire agreement was signed in Paris by South Vietnam, North Vietnam, the Vietcong, and the United States on Jan. 27, 1973. It was never implemented, but the American withdrawal continued. In early 1975 South Vietnamese forces collapsed in the face of a series of North Vietnamese–Vietcong offensives. Remaining U.S. personnel were evacuated, and Saigon fell on Apr. 30, 1975. Hundreds of thousands of refugees ("boat people") fled the country over the next decade.

Following the fall of Saigon, the country was occupied by northern troops and administrators. Businesses were nationalized, agriculture collectivized, and tens of thousands of people sent to labor camps for "reeducation." A unified National Assembly met in 1976, and the country was officially reunified on July 2, 1976, under the existing government of the north. Saigon was renamed Ho Chi Minh City. A Soviet naval base was established at the former U.S. base at Cam Ranh Bay.

In 1978 Vietnamese troops occupied Cambodia (called Kampuchea at the time) ousting the government of Pol Pot and installing Heng Samrin as premier. In February 1979 China launched an unsuccessful attack over its border with Vietnam to display displeasure with the invasion of Cambodia and with the treatment of ethnic Chinese in Vietnam. In 1988 Vietnam pledged to withdraw its troops from Cambodia and completed the withdrawal in September 1989.

Vietnam's communist government ruled through the party's powerful Central Committee; no strong personalities emerged to replace the leaders of the wartime generation. The economy functions only at a basic level, with the infrastructure in disrepair and agriculture and small business hampered by excessive collectivization and central planning. The collapse of the Soviet Union brought about a drastic reduction of the Soviet aid that had kept the Vietnamese economy afloat. Facing economic ruin, Vietnam's leadership eventually turned a blind eye to individual private enterprise. By 1992 the government was encouraging foreign investment.

Resumption of contacts with the United States had been precluded by American insistence that Vietnam account more fully for American prisoners of war and troops missing in action. But high-level talks on the normalization of relations and the Cambodian question opened in 1990, and the success of those negotiations helped to open diplomatic channels between Vietnam and the United States.

In July 1993 the Clinton administration, declaring itself satisfied with Vietnam's efforts to account for POW/MIAs, said it would no longer oppose the granting of loans to Vietnam by international organizations. On Feb. 3, 1994, Pres. Clinton, without normalizing relations, ended the 19-year American trade embargo against Vietnam in response to the government's cooperation in the matter of MIAs. The following day American firms were operating in Ho Chi Minh City. In January 1995 low-level diplomatic ties were established and in July full diplomatic recognition was given.

Western Samoa

Independent State of Western Samoa

Geography **Location:** two large and seven small islands (five inhabited) in South Pacific Ocean, about 1,500 mi. (2,400 km) NE of New Zealand. Apia 13°49'S, 171°45'W. **Boundaries:** surrounded by Pacific Ocean; nearest neighbor is American Samoa to E. **Total land area:** 1,104 sq. mi. (2,860 sq km). **Coastline:** 250 mi. (403 km). **Comparative area:** slightly smaller than Rhode Island. **Land use:** 19% arable land; 24% permanent crops; negl. % meadows and pastures; 47% forest and woodland; 10% other. **Major cities:** (1981 census) Apia (capital) 33,170.

People **Population:** 204,447 (1994 est.). **Nationality:** noun—Western Samoan(s); adjective—Western Samoan. **Ethnic groups:** Samoan; about 7% Euronesians (persons of European and Polynesian blood), 0.4% Europeans. **Languages:** Samoan (Polynesian), English. **Religions:** 99.7% Christian (about half of population associated with London Missionary Society; includes Congregational, Roman Catholic, Methodist, Latter-day Saints, Seventh-day Adventist).

Government **Type:** constitutional monarchy under native chief. **Independence:** Jan. 1, 1962 (from UN trusteeship administered by New Zealand). **Constitution:** Jan. 1, 1962. **National holiday:** Independence Day, Jan. 1. **Heads of government:** Malietoa Tanumafili II, head of state (since 1962); Tofilau E. Alesana, prime minister (since Feb. 1988). **Structure:** head of state and executive council; unicameral legislature (47-member Legislative Assembly); Supreme Court, court of appeal, land and titles court, village courts.

Economy **Monetary unit:** WS tala. **Budget:** (1992) **income:** $95.3 mil.; **expend.:** $95.4 mil. **GDP:** $400 mil., $2,000 per capita (1992 est.). **Chief crops:** coconuts, fruit (including bananas, taro, yams). **Livestock:** poultry, pigs, cattle, horses. **Natural resources:** hardwood forests, fish. **Major industries:** timber, tourism, food processing. **Labor force:** about 38,000 (1987 est.); about 22,000 employed in agriculture. **Exports:** $5.7 mil. (f.o.b., 1992 est.); 42% coconut oil and cream, 19% taro, 14% cocoa. **Imports:** $11.5 mil. (c.i.f., 1992 est.); 58% intermediate goods, 17% food, 12% capital goods. **Major trading partners:** ***exports:*** (1987) 30% New Zealand, 24% EU, 21% Australia, 9% U.S., 7% American Samoa; ***imports:*** 31% New Zealand, 20% Australia, 15% Fiji, 15% Japan, 5% U.S., 4% EU.

Intl. Orgs. Commonwealth, FAO, G-77, IBRD, IDA, IFAD, IFC, IMF, UN, UNESCO, WHO.

The Polynesian island group of Samoa (Navigator's Islands) was partitioned in 1899 between the United States, which had established a naval base at Pago Pago on Tutuila in 1878, and Germany, which organized the westerly islands into a colony in 1894. In 1914 New Zealand troops occupied the German-held islands. New Zealand administered Western Samoa under a League of Nations mandate beginning in 1920 and continued to control the islands as a UN Trust Territory after 1945. In 1959 home rule was established under an elected local government. Western Samoa became an independent nation on Jan. 1, 1962. The constitution blends Western parliamentary government and traditional Samoan forms of rule. The parliamentary electorate is limited to the malai, heads of extended families; the malai are wholly responsible for local affairs. The local culture is similarly a blend of Samoan tradition with Christianity.

The economy is based on subsistence agriculture, forestry, fishing, and tourism. Nearly 50 percent of the land area is forested; lumber and wood products (plywood, veneer) are important exports. Offshore fisheries are being developed, along with light industry, particularly food processing.

Yemen

Republic of Yemen

Geography Location: southern shore of Arabian peninsula and southwest corner of Arabian peninsula. **Boundaries:** Saudi Arabia to N, Oman to E, Gulf of Aden to S, Red Sea to W. **Total land area:** 203,850 sq. mi. (527,970 sq km). **Coastline:** 1,184 mi. (1,906 km). **Land use:** 15% arable land; negl. % permanent crops; 31% meadows and pastures; 7% forest and woodland; 53% other; includes 1% irrigated. **Major cities:** (1986 est.) San'a (capital) 427,150; Ta'lz 178,043 (1973 census); Aden 291,000; Hadhramaut 451,000; Abyan 311,000; Lahej 273,000.

People Population: 11,105,202 (1994 est.). **Nationality:** noun—Yemini(s); adjective—Yemeni. **Ethnic groups:** mostly Arab, a few Indians, Somalis, Europeans. **Languages:** Arabic. **Religions:** Muslim (Sunni and Shia), some Christian, Hindu.

Government Type: republic. **Independence:** Nov. 1918 (from Ottoman Empire). **Constitution:** Dec. 28, 1970; suspended June 19, 1974; amended in 1990. **National holiday:** Proclamation of the Republic, Sept. 26. **Heads of government:** Ali Abdullah Saleh, president of Republic of Yemen (since May 1994); Abdulaziz Abdul Ghani, prime minister of Republic of Yemen (since Oct. 1994). **Structure:** executive—president and cabinet; legislative—People's Constituent Assembly; judicial—Supreme Court and lesser courts.

Economy Monetary unit: riyal. **Budget:** (1988 est.) ***income:*** N.A.; ***expend:*** N.A. **GDP:** $9 bil., $800 per capita (1993 est.). **Exports:** $695 mil. (f.o.b., 1993 est.); oil, cotton, coffee, hides; $908 mil. (f.o.b., 1989 est.); cotton, hides, skins, dried and salted fish. **Imports:** $1.6 bil., (f.o.b., 1993 est.); textiles and other manufactured consumer goods, petroleum products, sugar, grain, flour. **Major trading partners: *exports:*** U.S., EU countries, S. Korea, Saudi Arabia; ***imports:*** Japan, Saudi Arabia, Australia, EU countries, China, Russia, U.S.

Intl. Orgs. Arab League, FAO, G-77, IBRD, ICAO, IDA, IFAD, IFC, ILO, IMF, IMO, INTELSAT, INTERPOL, ITU, NAM, UN, UNESCO, UPU, WHO, WIPO, WMO.

Yemen—in ancient times Sheba or Saba—is strategically located in the southwestern corner of the Arabian peninsula, near the southern end of the Red Sea. In biblical times and for many centuries thereafter, Yemen dominated the caravan trade in spices, gold, and other luxury goods from India and Africa to the Middle East.

The Islamic unification of Arabia in 628 resulted in the incorporation of Yemen into Arabia as a whole, but many local uprisings broke out over the course of the following three centuries. In the 10th century, control passed to a line of Yemeni kings who were simultaneously imams of the Zaidi sect of Islam; the Zaidi imams ruled until 1962.

Aden was the most important port of the ancient kingdom of Sheba and retained that status under the Zaidi imams of Yemen. Portuguese activity around Aden began in the 15th century; from the mid-16th century, control of the port was disputed by the Portuguese, the Yemeni kings, the Ottoman Turks, and, later, the British.

In 1839, Aden was made a British Crown Colony; the Hadramaut region of southern Arabia, north and east of Aden, became the British Protectorate of Aden. The colony and protectorate were both administered as part of British India.

Yemen came under the control of the Ottoman Empire from the mid-16th to the mid-17th centuries, and again from 1849 to 1918. The Turks were expelled at the end of World War I, and Yemen became an independent kingdom in 1918. The kingdom's independence was threatened by a Saudi invasion in 1934 and by a 1954 dispute with Great Britain over the status of Aden, which was the key to British military power in the western Indian Ocean and Persian Gulf after India's independence in 1947.

Imam Ahmed came to the throne of Yemen in 1948, following the assassination of his predecessor. Most of Yemen's large Jewish population was evacuated to Israel in 1949–50. A palace coup against the imam in 1955 failed, but after his death in 1962, his successor was quickly ousted and the country was proclaimed the Yemen Arab Republic (North Yemen) under the leadership of Brig. Gen. Abdullah al-Salal.

A struggle for independence began in Aden and the protectorate in 1963, with two rival groups competing for power. The National Liberation Front (NLF) gained the upper hand over the Egyptian-backed Front for the Liberation of Occupied South Yemen, as both groups waged guerrilla war against the British. Most of the country's Jewish population fled to Israel. British forces withdrew in 1967, and South Yemen became independent on Nov. 30 of that year. The nation's territory included Socotra and adjacent islands off the Horn of Africa, which had been British possessions since 1876.

In 1969 a leftist faction of the NLF seized power, nationalized key industries, and instituted a socialist regime. In the mid-1970s, South Yemeni troops aided leftist guerrillas in Oman, and fought in Ethiopia against Eritrean rebels. Subsequently Pres. Salem Robaye Ali took a more moderate stance and improved relations with Oman and Saudi Arabia. He was overthrown in a coup in June 1978 and executed. The succeeding government was overthrown in another coup on Jan. 13, 1986; on Feb. 8, Hasin Said Numan became prime minister.

In North Yemen, civil war between royalist and republican factions lasted until April 1970, when a coalition republican government was formed with the aid of Saudi mediation. Col. Ibrahim al-Hamidi came to power in a military coup on June 13, 1974; he was assassinated on Oct. 11, 1977. Pres. Ali Abdullah Saleh assumed office on July 17, 1978, following the assassination of previously elected Pres. al-Gashmi.

Border skirmishes between North Yemen and South Yemen broke out during 1972–73. After several years of uneasy peace, South Yemen launched a full-scale war against the north on Feb. 24, 1979. Arab League pressure quickly led to a mutual disengagement.

Relations improved during the 1980s and North Yemen and South Yemen merged as the Republic of Yemen on May 22, 1990. Ali Abdullah Saleh, president of North Yemen, became the new country's president; Ali Salem Al-Baidh, secretary of the South Yemeni Socialist party, was elected vice president by the unified Parliament. San'a was proclaimed the capital of the United Yemen, though Aden remained its most important economic center.

The Gulf War forced the repatriation of tens of thousands of Yemeni workers from Kuwait and other Gulf states; later Saudi Arabia expelled 850,000 more to express its displeasure with Yemen's unenthusiastic stance toward the Gulf War. These repatriations deprived Yemen of a most important source of foreign exchange, and severely damaged the economy.

Yemen held its first general election since unification on Apr. 27, 1993, and a coalition government was formed in June. In August 1993, Vice Pres. Baidh left San'a for Aden protesting northern centralization and dominance. Jordanian mediation seemed to bring the crisis to an end in February 1994, but fighting began almost immediately, and by May a full-scale civil war had broken out. But in July the capture of Aden by government troops ended the conflict.

Yemen's economy has remained largely agricultural until recent years. Cotton is the chief agricultural export. Oil was discovered in North Yemen in 1984 and in South Yemen in 1987; commercial deliveries of crude oil from both areas commenced in 1987. Shipping services in the port of Aden form an important part of the country's commercial economy.

Yugoslavia

Federal Republic of Yugoslavia

Geography Location: Southern central Europe. **Boundaries:** Hungary to N, Romania to NE, Bulgaria to E, Macedonia and Albania to S, Adriatic Sea, Bosnia and Herzegovina to W., Croatia to NW. **Total land area:** 39,424 sq. mi. (102,136 sq km). **Coastline:** 124 mi. (199 km). **Comparative area:** Slightly larger than Kentucky. **Land use:** 30% arable land; 5% permanent crops; 20% meadows and pastures; 25% forest and woodland; 20% other (includes 5% irrigated). **Major cities:** (mid-1992 est.) Belgrade (capital) 1,500,000; Nis 300,000; Kragujevac 250,000; Novi Sad 250,000; Podoricj 80,000.

People Population: 10,759,897 (July 1994 est.). **Nationality:** noun—Yugoslav(s); adjective—

Yugoslav. **Ethnic groups:** 63% Serbian, 14% Albanian, 6% Montenegrin, 4% Hungarian, 13% other. **Languages:** Serbo-Croatian (official), Albanian. **Religions:** 65% Christian Orthodox, 19% Islam, 4% Catholic, 1% Protestant, 11% other.

Government Type: republic. **Independence:** Proclaimed itself successor to former Socialist Federal Republic of Yugoslavia Apr. 11, 1992. **Constitution:** Apr. 27, 1992. **National holiday:** N.A. **Heads of government:** Zoran Lillić, president (since June 1993); Radoje Kontić, prime minister (since Feb. 1993). **Structure:** executive—president; legislative—bicameral.

Economy Monetary unit: Yugoslav new dinar. **Budget:** ***income:*** N.A.; ***expend.:*** N.A. **GDP:** $10 bil., $1,000 per capita (1993 est.). **Chief crops:** cereal, cotton, oilseeds, chicory. **Livestock:** sheep, cattle. **Natural resources:** oil, gas, coal, antimony, copper, lead, zinc, nickel, gold, pyrite, chrome. **Major industries:** machine building, metallurgy, mining, consumer goods, electronics, petroleum products, chemicals, pharmaceuticals. **Labor force:** 2,640,909: 40% industry and mining, 5% agriculture (1990). **Exports:** $4.4 billion (f.o.b., 1990); 29% machinery and transport equipment, 28.5% manufactured goods, 13.5% miscellaneous manufactured articles, 11% chemicals, 9% food and live animals, 6% raw materials, 2% fuels and lubricants, 1% beverages and tobacco. **Imports:** $6.4 bil. (c.i.f., 1990); 26% machinery and transport equipment, 18% fuels and lubricants, 16% manufactured goods, 12.5% chemicals, 11% food and live animals, 8% miscellaneous manufactured items, 7% raw materials, 1.5% beverages and tobacco. **Major trading partners:** The former Yugoslav republics, Italy, Germany, former USSR.

Int'l. Orgs. OSCE, UN. (Note: although the UN recognizes the union of Serbia and Montenegro as the successor nation to the former Socialist Federal Republic of Yugoslavia, the U.S. State Department does not, contending that none of the former Yugoslav republics represent the continuation of the former Yugoslavia.)

The lands that composed Yugoslavia until 1991 were incorporated into the Roman Empire as the province of Illyricum in the first century A.D. Christianity became dominant by A.D. 600. Its nucleus was Serbia, settled in the seventh century by South Slav migrants from the Over and Vistula, and converted to Christianity, in its Eastern Orthodox form, in the ninth century. Twice (in 1077 and again in 1202), the Vatican sent royal crowns to Serbian kings, emphasizing their independence, despite the religious differences. Serbia's medieval zenith came during the reign of Stephen Dushan (1331–55), who subjected Albania and Macedonia as well as Thessaly and Epirus to his rule, and who gained the vassalage of Bulgaria in addition. But within 30 years of his death, the Ottoman Turks had overrun his realm, a dominance sealed by the Serbian catastrophe at the Battle of Kosovo (1389). Not until 1878 did Serbia regain its independence.

The complexities of Balkan politics occupied European statesmen throughout the late 19th century, and the Balkan Wars of 1912 and 1913 led directly to the outbreak of World War I. After the collapse of the Austro-Hungarian Empire during the war, the multiethnic and multinational state of Yugoslavia was patched together in 1918–19. To Serbia were annexed the old Austro-Hungarian lands of Slovenia and Croatia, as well as the ethnically Croatian and Serbian lands of Bosnia and Herzegovina in the northwest, and, in the south and southwest, Montenegro, Macedonia, and Kosovo. The last three were Serbian, Bulgarian, and Albanian in nationality, respectively.

The nationalities coexisted in a state of mutual hostility, provoking a royal dictatorship, instituted by King Alexander in 1929 and enduring after his assassination in 1934. Hitler invaded Yugoslavia in 1941; German troops were welcomed in Croatia as liberators from the Serbs. Resistance began almost immediately, split into two mutually hostile groups: Draza Mihajlovic's Serbian royalist Chetniks, and the Partisans, a group of pan-Yugoslav Communists and non-Serbian anti-German forces led by Tito (a.k.a. Josip Broz). By the end of the war, over 2 million Yugoslavs had died, and 3.5 million were homeless. As marshal, backed by both Churchill and Stalin, Tito ruled over a ruined land: the newly created Federal People's Republic of Yugoslavia.

Until World War II, Yugoslavia was primarily agricultural and pastoral, with peasants who were virtual serfs living on a subsistence level in a largely infertile land. Agriculture was more prosperous in the northern river valleys that formerly had been under Austro-Hungarian control, and there was some industrialization in those areas as well. Virtually all of these areas had to be rebuilt after the war.

Tito imposed agricultural collectivization on the Stalinist model, and pushed for the development of industry under state ownership. Politically, harsh repression fell on members of the Chetnik resistance as well as on the Slovene Home Guard and the Croatian Ustasa. But the postwar period of tyranny was short-lived.

Tito had achieved power as an independent Communist leader and refused to permit Yugoslavia to become a Soviet satellite. In March 1948 he expelled Russian military advisers, and was himself expelled from the Comintern.

In the face of economic pressure and military threats, Tito turned westward. Stalinism yielded to decentralized communism. The 1953 Agrarian Reform Law permitted private agricultural smallholdings, and over 80 percent of the land returned to private ownership; in the rest, "self-management" rather than central control was encouraged. Self-management was instituted in the industrial sector as well, with emphasis varying between capital goods and consumer goods. Economic growth averaged over 7 percent per year for three decades, lifting Yugoslavia into the ranks of the semideveloped countries.

Despite a reconciliation with Nikita Khrushchev's Soviet Union in 1955, Tito continued to chart an independent course, providing a political and economic alternative model for Eastern Europe. But Yugoslavian nationalism in foreign affairs masked the development of separate nationalisms within the Yugoslavian federation. By the time Tito died in 1980, there was a real question as to whether the nation could survive without his leadership.

In the 1980s, the country was plagued by an economic slowdown. Inflation and chronic trade deficits led to soaring national debt, bringing austerity measures and a decline in the standard of living.

The post-Tito "collegial rule," whereby the presidency of the country and the chairmanship of the Party Presidium rotated annually among the six republics and two autonomous regions, worked well for most of the 1980s. But in the summer of 1988, ethnic protests and riots broke out in Serbia's autonomous provinces of Kosovo and Vojvodina, in Slovenia, in Serbia, and in Montenegro. Escalating violence between Serbs and Croats, the two largest ethnic groups, and declarations of independence by Slovenia (the richest republic) and Croatia in June 1991, and Bosnia-Herzegovina later, brought a devastating civil war.

The current Yugoslavia is but a fragment of the original creation of World War I peacemakers. The core remains Serbia, with its once-autonomous and now centrally controlled provinces of Vojvodina and Kosovo, the latter having asked in January of 1993 that the UN take it over as a trusteeship or, in effect, a colony. The other remaining republic, Montenegro, ethnically Serbian, shows signs of restiveness under the strain of continued war: Its economy is in ruins worse than that of Serbia, and 70,000 largely Muslim refugees add further strain. NATO air attacks against Bosnian Serbs in February and April 1994, and agreements in Geneva among the EU, the United States, and Russia to partition Bosnia brought outside pressure toward ending the civil war. Combined with the January bilateral accords between Serbia and Croatia, the May confederation of Muslims and Croats in Bosnia, and the June cease-fire, these interventions created some hope for peace, but again these were too optimistic. (For further developments, see Part I: "Major News Stories of the Year.")

Zaire

Republic of Zaire

Geography Location: equatorial country in central Africa. **Boundaries:** Central African Republic, Sudan to N, Uganda, Rwanda, Burundi, Tanzania to E, Zambia to S, Angola to SW, Atlantic Ocean, Cabinda district of Angola, Congo to W. **Total land area:** 905,564 sq. mi. (2,345,410 sq km). **Coastline:** 23 mi. (37 km). **Comparative area:** about 1.5 times size of Alaska. **Land use:** 3% arable land; negl. % permanent crops; 4% meadows and pastures; 78% forest and woodland; 15% other; includes negl. % irrigated. **Major cities:** (1984 census) Kinshasa (capital)

2,653,558; Lubumbashi (Elizabethville) 543,268; Mbuji-Mayi (Bakwanga) 423,363; Kananga (Luluabourg) 290,898; Kisangani (Stanleyville) 282,650.

People **Population:** 42,684,091 (1994 est.). **Nationality:** noun—Zairian(s); adjective—Zairian. **Ethnic groups:** 45% of the people belong to one of four largest groups—Mongo, Luba, Kongo (all Bantu), and Mangbetu-Azande; over 200 other ethnic groups. **Languages:** French (official), English, Lingala, Swahili, Kingwana, Kikongo, Tshiluba. **Religions:** 50% Roman Catholic, 20% Protestant, 10% Kimbanguist, 10% Muslim, 10% other syncretic sects and traditional beliefs.

Government **Type:** republic with strong presidential system. **Independence:** June 30, 1960 (from Belgium). **Constitution:** June 24, 1967, amended Aug. 1974, revised Feb. 15, 1978. **National holiday:** Independence Day, June 30. **Heads of government:** Marshal Mobutu Sese Seko, president (since 1965); Kengo Wa Dondo, prime minister (since July 1994). **Structure:** executive—president elected originally for seven-year term; Marshal Mobutu reelected July 1984 and limits on reelection removed by new constitution; legislative—unicameral National Legislative Council with 310 members elected for five-year terms; official party is supreme political institution.

Economy **Monetary unit:** zaïre. **Budget:** ***income:*** N.A.; ***expend.:*** N.A. **GDP:** $21 bil., $500 per capita (1993 est.). **Chief crops:** cash crops—coffee, palm oil, rubber, quinine; food crops—manioc, bananas, root crops, corn; some provinces self-sufficient; illegal producer of cannabis for international drug trade. **Livestock:** goats, cattle, pigs, sheep. **Natural resources:** cobalt, copper, cadmium, crude oil, industrial and gem diamonds. **Major industries:** mining, mineral processing, consumer products (including textiles, footwear, cigarettes). **Labor force:** about 15 mil., but only 13% wage earners (1985); 75% agriculture, 13% industry, 12% services; 51% of population of working age (1981); N.A. unemployment. **Exports:** $1.5 bil. (f.o.b., 1992 est.); 37% copper, 24% coffee, 12% diamonds, cobalt, crude oil. **Imports:** $1.2 bil. (f.o.b., 1992 est.); consumer goods, foodstuffs, mining and other machinery, transport equipment, fuels. **Major trading partners:** U.S., Belgium, France, Germany, Italy, UK, Japan.

Intl. Orgs. FAO, G-77, IAEA, IBRD, ICAO, IDA, IFAD, IFC, ILO, IMF, IMO, INTELSAT, INTERPOL, ITU, NAM, UN, UNESCO, UPU, WHO, WIPO, WMO, WTO.

Pygmies were probably the earliest inhabitants of the Congo region, followed much later by Bantu and Nilotic peoples. By the eighth century A.D., a number of well-established kingdoms and empires occupied the lower reaches of the Congo (now Zaire) River and the coastal plain; these included Kongo (Bakongo), Kuba, Luba, and Lunda.

Portuguese explorers and merchants arrived along the coast in the 1480s and initially traded with these kingdoms on a basis of relative equality; an indigenous Catholic church became established. Soon, however, the Portuguese established a slave trade that brought turmoil and decline to the native states. Europeans did not penetrate the interior of Zaire until the 19th century, but the slave trade (partly in Arab hands, in inland regions) had repercussions everywhere.

Henry Stanley descended the Congo River from east to west in 1876, opening the area for further exploration. In 1878 Stanley was engaged by King Leopold II of Belgium to establish Belgian trading stations along the river. King Leopold established the Congo Free State in 1885, not as a Belgian colony but as a personal possession of which he was king as well as chief stockholder.

The management corporation that ran the Free State abolished slavery but instituted a harsh and exploitative regime that reduced native peoples to a condition of involuntary servitude. Forced labor and harsh suppression of rebellion resulted in the deaths of unnumbered thousands of people. Protests against these conditions, led by Great Britain and the United States, led to the transformation of the Free State into the colony of the Belgian Congo in 1908 with promises of reforms.

By the 1920s the Belgian Congo had become a major world producer of copper, diamonds, gold, rubber, palm oil, and other commodities. Railroads were developed to bring these goods to market, notably the line from Elizabethville (now Lubumbashi) in the Katanga region through Angola to the Atlantic coast. River navigation on the Congo was also developed. All mining, plantation agriculture, industry, and administration was in Belgian hands with no native participation in government except at the most local level.

In the 1950s agitation for increased native participation in government led, in 1957, to elections for local councils. In 1959 rioting against Belgian rule broke out. Elections were held on May 31 in anticipation of independence. Joseph Kasavubu became president, and Patrice Lumumba, head of the Congolese National Movement, became prime minister. On June 30, 1960, Belgium granted independence to the Congo; many Europeans fled the country. On July 4 the army mutinied, and on July 11 the southern province of Katanga (now Shaba), under the leadership of Moise Tshombe, seceded from the Congo and declared its independence. Belgium sent troops to quell the disorder.

On Aug. 9 the United Nations called on Belgium to withdraw its troops. Kasavubu removed Lumumba as prime minister. Lumumba, with the backing of Ghana, fought for control. He fled to Stanleyville (now Kisangani) but was kidnapped in January 1961 and taken to Katanga, where he was murdered, apparently with American and Belgian complicity. Fighting continued in Katanga, where Tshombe's regime was supported by European mercenaries and opposed by UN peacekeeping forces. The Katangan rebellion ended in late 1963; rebels fled to Angola, and UN forces were withdrawn in June 1964. In a surprising political settlement, Tshombe became president of the Congo on June 30. On Sept. 7 leftist rebels attempted to establish a "people's republic" based in Stanleyville. Tshombe again resorted to the use of mercenaries to put down the rebellion. Many white settlers, as well as Congolese, were killed in fighting and terrorist atrocities. The rebellion ended in July 1965. In November 1965 Tshombe was deposed in a military coup led by Joseph Mobutu, whose government took immediate steps to consolidate its control and reduce European influence.

In 1971 Mobutu changed the country's name to Zaire and renamed Leopoldville Kinshasa. In 1972 he ordered all Zairians with European names to change them to African names; he became Mobutu Sese Seko. Attempts in 1974 to force foreign investors to sell their holdings to Zairians brought economic disruption, and foreign investors were invited back into the country in 1977.

In 1977 another rebellion broke out in Katanga (now Shaba) Province; the government put down the rebellion with the aid of France, Egypt, and Morocco. The rebels fled to Angola, but the province's rich mining economy was again disrupted; many European technical workers fled, and production plummeted.

Although Zaire is rich with minerals, forest products, hydroelectric potential, and agriculture, most of these natural resources remain undeveloped and the country continues to be impoverished by the nearly unprecedented corruption of the Mobutu regime. The president personally is estimated to have amassed a fortune of $3 billion. Rival political leaders attempted to organize opposition to the Mobutu government in late 1987 and 1988, but most were arrested or driven into exile.

In June 1991, Mobutu agreed to have his representatives meet with opposition leaders to draft a new constitution and end a 20-year ban on multiparty elections. Étiene Tshisekedi was elected prime minister by a national conference in 1992, but Mobutu fired him in 1993. France and Belgium dispatched troops to protect their nationals and together with the United States demanded that Mobutu transfer power to Tshisekedi. Mobuto has not complied and, as his nation's economy sinks, he continues to live in luxury, protected by the army and police.

In 1995, in addition to the burden of dealing with refugees from Rwanda, Zaire was afflicted by an outbreak of the deadly Ebola virus in the region of Kikwit, a city of 600,000 that lies 250 miles east of Kinshasa.

Zambia

Republic of Zambia

Geography **Location:** landlocked country in southern central Africa. **Boundaries:** Zaire to N, Tanzania to NE, Malawi to E, Mozambique to SE, Zimbabwe to S, Namibia to SW, Angola to W. **Total land area:** 290,583 sq. mi. (752,610 sq km). **Coastline:** none. **Comparative area:** slightly larger than Texas. **Land use:** 7% arable land; negl. % permanent crops; 47% meadows and pastures; 27% forest and woodland; 19% other;

includes negl. % irrigated. **Major cities:** (1988 est.) Lusaka (capital) 870,030; Kitwe 472,255; Ndola 442,666; Kabwe (Broken Hill) 199,368.

People **Population:** 9,188,190 (1994 est.). **Nationality:** noun—Zambian(s); adjective—Zambian. **Ethnic groups:** 98.7% African, 1.1% European, 0.2% other. **Languages:** English (official), about 70 indigenous languages. **Religions:** 50–75% Christian, 1% Muslim and Hindu, indigenous beliefs.

Government **Type:** one-party state. **Independence:** Oct. 24, 1964 (from UK). **Constitution:** Aug. 25, 1973. **National holiday:** Independence Day, Oct. 24. **Heads of government:** Frederick Chiluba, president (since Nov. 1991). **Structure:** executive—modified presidential system; legislative—unicameral National Assembly; judiciary.

Economy **Monetary unit:** kwacha. **Budget:** (1991 est.) ***income:*** $665 mil.; ***expend.:*** $767 mil. **GDP:** $7.3 bil., $800 per capita (1993 est.). **Chief crops:** corn, tobacco, cotton; net importer of most major agricultural products. **Livestock:** cattle, goats, pigs, sheep. **Natural resources:** copper, cobalt, zinc, lead, coal. **Major industries:** copper mining and processing, transport, construction. **Labor force:** 2.5 mil.; 85% agriculture, 9% transport and services, 6% mining, manufacturing, and construction. **Exports:** $1 bil. (f.o.b., 1992 est.); copper, zinc, cobalt, lead, tobacco. **Imports:** $1.2 bil. (c.i.f., 1992 est.); machinery, transport equipment, foodstuffs, fuels, manufactures. **Major trading partners:** EU, Japan, South Africa, U.S.

Intl. Orgs. Commonwealth, FAO, G-77, IAEA, IBRD, ICAO, IDA, IFAD, IFC, ILO, IMF, INTELSAT, INTERPOL, ITU, NAM, UN, UNESCO, UPU, WHO, WIPO, WMO, WTO.

Bantu peoples—including Luba, Lunda, Ngoni, and others—moved into what is now Zambia between the 15th and the 19th centuries, displacing or absorbing aboriginal populations. Occasional Portuguese explorers from Angola and Mozambique entered the region, and Angolan slave-raiders were active in the late 18th and early 19th centuries, but serious European influence did not begin until the mid-19th century. At that time British missionaries and merchants arrived, most notably David Livingstone and Cecil Rhodes.

Local rulers granted mineral concessions to Rhodes in both Northern and Southern Rhodesia (now Zambia and Zimbabwe). Rhodesia was declared a British sphere of influence in 1888; a British protectorate was established in 1891 and enlarged in 1894–95. The borders of Northern Rhodesia were established in 1911. The country was administered by the British South Africa Co. until 1924, when direct colonial rule began. Large numbers of British settlers arrived and developed extensive farms and ranches and mined the region's substantial copper deposits. A railroad was built linking Northern Rhodesia with Elizabethville in the Belgian Congo (now Lubumbashi, Zaire).

In 1953 Northern and Southern Rhodesia (Zimbabwe) were joined with Nyasaland (now Malawi) to form the Federation of Rhodesia and Nyasaland. The country entered a period of unrest with native peoples demanding greater participation in government, while white settlers clung to their privileged positions.

As the result of an election in 1962, the federation was dissolved in 1963. A National Assembly was created on the basis of a broader, multiracial electorate. Northern Rhodesia became independent as the Republic of Zambia on Oct. 24, 1964. Relations between Zambia and white-ruled Rhodesia (formerly Southern Rhodesia) became strained in 1965 in a dispute over ownership and administration of the railway that spanned both countries. A new constitution was promulgated in 1973, creating a stronger presidency and a unicameral legislature; the United National Independence party was made the sole legal political party. Opposition parties were allowed to form again starting in December 1990.

Pres. Kenneth Kaunda, in office after Zambia's independence, led a generally moderate government that won the support of both whites and blacks, despite some early white emigration from the country. Even when there was only one legal political party, elections were, and are, freely contested, and there is substantial freedom of the press.

Zambia's economy, however, has not fared well under independence. The nation's wildlife supports only a small tourist industry. Although the country has diverse mineral resources, copper is overwhelmingly the nation's main earner of foreign exchange. A steep decline in the world price of copper since the mid-1970s led to massive foreign debt and labor unrest at home. The IMF demanded reforms as a condition for future aid, and in 1987 Pres. Kaunda announced a program of economic restructuring to deal with these problems. In 1990 the government survived an attempted coup precipitated by a doubling in the price of the staple food, maize meal.

In April 1987 South African troops raided Zambian bases of the African National Congress in an action that led to heavy casualties and was condemned by the United Nations. At the end of 1991, Kaunda was defeated by Frederick Chiluba, head of the new Labor party. Chiluba's economic reforms, many prompted by the IMF and other international lenders, have resulted in dramatic increases in foreign aid.

Zimbabwe

Republic of Zimbabwe

Geography **Location:** landlocked country in southern Africa. **Boundaries:** Zambia to NW, Mozambique to E, South Africa to S, Botswana to SW. **Total land area:** 150,803 sq. mi. (390,580 sq km). **Coastline:** none. **Comparative area:** slightly larger than Montana. **Land use:** 7% arable land; negl. % permanent crops; 12% meadows and pastures; 62% forest and woodland; 19% other; includes negl. % irrigated. **Major cities:** (1982 census) Harare (Salisbury, capital) 656,000; Bulawayo 413,800; Chitungwiza 172,600; Gweru (Gwelo) 78,900; Mutare (Umtali) 69,600.

People **Population:** 10,975,078 (1994 est.). **Nationality:** noun—Zimbabwean(s); adjective—Zimbabwean. **Ethnic groups:** 98% African (71% Shona, 16% Ndebele, 11% other), 1% white, 1% mixed and Asian. **Languages:** English (official), ChiShona, Si Ndebele. **Religions:** 50% syncretic (part Christian, part indigenous beliefs), 25% Christian, 24% indigenous beliefs, 1% Muslim.

Government **Type:** presidential system with bicameral legislature. **Independence:** Apr. 18, 1980 (from UK). **Constitution:** Dec. 21, 1979. **National holiday:** Apr. 18. **Head of government:** Robert Gabriel Mugabe, president (since Dec. 1987). **Structure:** executive—cabinet led by president; legislative—Parliament consisting of 100-member House of Assembly and 40-member Senate; judiciary—high court is supreme judicial authority.

Economy **Monetary unit:** Zimbabwean dollar. **Budget:** (1991) ***income:*** $1.7 bil.; ***expend.:*** $2.2 bil. **GDP:** $15.9 bil., $1,400 per capita (1993 est.). **Chief crops:** tobacco, corn, tea, sugar, cotton. **Livestock:** cattle, goats, sheep, pigs, asses. **Natural resources:** coal, chromium ore, asbestos, gold, nickel. **Major industries:** mining, steel, clothing and footwear. **Labor force:** 3.1 mil. (1987); 74% agriculture, 16% transport and services, 10% mining, manufacturing, construction. **Exports:** $1.5 bil. (f.o.b., 1992 est.); 34% agricultural (21% tobacco, 13% other), 19% manufactures, 11% gold, 11% ferrochrome. **Imports:** $1.8 bil. (c.i.f., 1992 est.); 37% machinery and transport equipment, 22% manufactures, 16% chemicals, 15% fuels. **Major trading partners:** ***exports:*** 55% Europe (41% EU, 6% Netherlands, 8% other), 22% Africa (12% S. Africa, 10% other), 6% U.S; ***imports:*** 31% EU, 29% Africa (21% S. Africa, 8% other), 8% U.S., 4% Japan.

Intl. Orgs. Commonwealth, FAO, G-77, IBRD, ICAO, IDA, IFAD, IFC, ILO, IMF, INTERPOL, NAM, UN, UNESCO, UPU, WHO, WMO, WTO.

Massive stone structures at Great Zimbabwe give evidence of a sizable urban society that flourished from the ninth to the 13th centuries and dominated Iron Age trade in southeastern Africa. Bantu peoples migrated into the region beginning in the 15th century; the Mashona dominated until the early 19th century, when they were displaced by the Matebele.

Portuguese slave raiders from Mozambique were active in Zimbabwe from the 16th to the mid-19th centuries. Mineral concessions were granted to Cecil Rhodes by local rulers in the late 19th century, and the region became a British protectorate in 1888. Salisbury (now Harare) was founded in 1890, and the territory comprising Zimbabwe and Zambia was named Rhodesia in 1895. Rhodesia was governed by the British South Africa Co. until 1923, when it was partitioned into Northern and Southern Rhodesia. Northern Rhodesia became a British colony; Southern Rhodesia, rejecting union with

South Africa, became a self-governing (and white-ruled) state within the British Empire.

Southern Rhodesia had been heavily settled by whites from Great Britain, South Africa, and elsewhere, who developed extensive farms and ranches, forest products industries, and the country's rich mines. The country prospered but with little native participation in government except at the most local level.

In 1953 Northern Rhodesia, Southern Rhodesia, and Nyasaland were joined in the Federation of Rhodesia and Nyasaland. Increasing agitation for black participation in government, especially in the north and in Nyasaland, led to the dissolution of the federation in 1963; Northern Rhodesia subsequently became independent as Zambia, Nyasaland as Malawi. In 1961 Southern Rhodesia had adopted a constitution that guaranteed the continuation of white rule. White resistance to black political demands led to the rise of the Rhodesian Front party, whose leader, Ian D. Smith, became prime minister of Rhodesia (formerly Southern Rhodesia). After British-led negotiations for a biracial political compromise broke down, the Smith government on Nov. 11, 1965, issued a unilateral declaration of independence, which was declared illegal and invalid by the British government.

The UN condemned the Smith government and imposed economic sanctions; the government was supported by South Africa and Mozambique (before that country's independence in 1975). In May 1968 the UN voted to impose a trade embargo on Rhodesia.

A constitution adopted in 1970 effectively barred black participation in national politics. A British-initiated political settlement of 1972 was dropped because of black opposition. By 1974 mounting pressure from other African countries led the Smith government to enter into more serious negotiations. Guerrilla warfare pitting black nationalist groups against white settlers and mercenaries raged sporadically throughout the country, and many white settlers emigrated. A conference in Geneva in 1976 broke down, but a 1977 British-American proposal for majority rule provided the basis for a settlement of the crisis. An "internal settlement" was announced in April 1978 by Smith and three major nationalist leaders: Bishop Abel Muzorewa, leader of the United African National Congress, the Rev. Ndabaningi Sithole, former leader of the Zimbabwe African National Union (ZANU), and Chief Jeremiah Chirau. The settlement was rejected by the Patriotic Front that united ZANU (now led by Robert Mugabe) and Joshua Nkomo's Zimbabwe African People's Union (ZAPU).

Elections were held in April 1979 and Bishop Muzorewa assumed office on June 1 as prime minister of "Zimbabwe-Rhodesia," but the Patriotic Front continued to oppose the government. On Dec. 10 the "Zimbabwe-Rhodesia" Parliament dissolved itself, and the country reverted briefly to British colonial rule. On Dec. 21 all parties agreed to a cease-fire and to a period of transitional British rule leading to independence. International economic sanctions were lifted.

Elections held in February 1980 resulted in a clear majority for Mugabe's ZANU party. Zimbabwe became independent, with Mugabe as prime minister, on April 18. As Mugabe embarked on an ambitious program of national reconstruction, Nkomo became leader of the opposition. Guerrillas linked to ZAPU, with Nkomo's tacit (or perhaps active) leadership and with alleged support from South Africa, continued to engage in sporadic warfare against Mugabe's government, and banditry and sabotage disrupted the countryside.

The elections of 1985 increased ZANU's majority in Parliament. In 1987 the constitution was amended to strengthen the presidency and to end the separate role of blacks and whites in government; new elections were held for black members of Parliament to fill seats formerly reserved for whites. Guerrillas renewed attacks on white-owned farms.

In December 1987 Mugabe and Nkomo agreed to merge ZANU and ZAPU (ZANU-PF), creating a de facto one-party state under Mugabe's leadership. In 1989 a new opposition party was organized by Edgar Z. Tekere, but Mugabe's rule remains virtually unchallenged. A presidential election is scheduled in 1996.

Zimbabwe's economy was traditionally one of the strongest in sub-Saharan Africa. Agriculture is the major employer, and mineral resources are the country's major source of foreign earnings. An excellent transportation network and ample electric power (both hydroelectric and coal-fired) support a strong industrial base; major industries include steel, heavy equipment, ore processing, motor vehicle assembly, textiles, and food processing. Drought in the 1980s led to some food shortages, but Zimbabwe exported food to all its neighbors, and as far afield as Ethiopia. A failure of the winter rains in 1992, however, led to widespread crop failures. The government, taken by surprise, was forced to import food to avert starvation in some regions.

TERRITORIES OF THE WORLD

NON-SELF-GOVERNING STATES

The community of nations has long recognized the existence of territories that do not have the status of independent states and that are subordinate in some degree to another power. The United Nations refers to these as "non-self-governing territories." Except for mandates and trusteeships specified by the League of Nations and the UN, the relationships between more and less powerful states have tended to evolve outside any rigid legal framework, and none of the following terms has an absolutely fixed meaning.

Colonies are dependent possessions whose inhabitants are not constitutionally under the dominant state's system of government but whose inhabitants are nationals of that state.

Commonwealths are autonomous states equal in status, united in their allegiance to a central power but not subordinate either to it or to one another in internal or external affairs.

Dependencies are states, provinces, or other places subject to the control of another power of which they do not form an integral part. The best known is Hong Kong, which China ceded to the United Kingdom in perpetuity in 1842, but which reverts to Chinese rule in 1997. The governor is appointed by the British monarch and foreign relations and defense are the responsibility of the UK, but Hong Kong has substantial autonomy in commercial relations.

Mandates were territories surrendered by Turkey and Germany after World War I and, according to the League of Nations, "inhabited by peoples not yet able to stand by themselves" and therefore placed under the "tutelage" of different members of the League as "mandatories on behalf of the League." The last mandate to gain independence was South West Africa, now Namibia.

Protectorates *(associated states)* are states or territories partly under the control of another state but autonomous in domestic and certain external affairs. Protectorates are established by treaties.

Territories are regions (especially of Australia, Canada, and the United States) administered by a federal government and having some degree of self-government but not organized as a province or a state.

Trust territories are administered on behalf of the UN by a designated power. The Trust Territory of the Pacific Islands (Palau) is the only one of the 11 trusteeships established by the UN that has not achieved self-government or independence either as a new sovereign state or by joining a neighboring independent country. (See Part II: "United States Territories and Possessions.")

AUSTRALIA

Christmas Island

Territory of Christmas Island

Geography Location: eastern Indian Ocean; 10°25'S, 105°39'E. **Boundaries:** Java Head, Indonesia, 224 mi. (360 km) to N, North West Cape, Australia, 875 mi. (1,408 km) to SE. **Total land area:** 52 sq. mi. (135 sq km). **Coastline:** 34 mi. (54 km). **Comparative area:** about seven-tenths size of Washington, D.C. **Land use:** 0% arable land; 0% permanent crops; 0% meadows and pastures;

0% forest and woodland; 100% other. **Major cities:** The Settlement (capital).

People **Population:** 973 (July 1994 est.). **Nationality:** noun—Christmas Islander(s); adjective—Christmas Island. **Ethnic groups:** 61% Chinese, 25% Malay, 11% European, 3% other; no indigenous population. **Languages:** English.

Government **Type:** territory of Australia. **Head of government:** M.J. Grimes, administrator. **Structure:** Advisory Council advises appointed administrator.

Economy **Monetary unit:** Australian dollar. **Natural resources:** phosphates. **Major industries:** phosphate extraction (near depletion). **Labor force:** all workers are employees of Phosphate Mining Co. of Christmas Island, Ltd. **Exports:** about 1.2 million metric tons of phosphate exported to Australia, New Zealand, and some Asian nations. **Major trading partners:** Australia, New Zealand.

Cocos (Keeling) Islands

Territory of Cocos (Keeling) Islands

Geography **Location:** 27 islands in eastern Indian Ocean. West Island 12°05'S, 96°53'E. **Boundaries:** island of Sumatra (part of Indonesia) about 932 mi. (1,500 km) to NE; Perth, Australia 1,720 mi. (2,768 km) to SE. **Total land area:** 5.4 sq. mi. (14.0 sq km). **Coastline:** undetermined. **Comparative area:** about 24 times size of the Mall in Washington, D.C. **Land use:** 0% arable land; 0% permanent crops; 0% meadows and pastures; 0% forest and woodland; 100% other. **Major cities:** West Island (capital).

People **Population:** 598 (July 1994 est.). **Nationality:** noun—Cocos Islander(s); adjective—Cocos Islander. **Ethnic groups:** mostly Europeans on West Island and Cocos Malays on Home Island. **Languages:** English.

Government **Type:** territory of Australia. **Head of government:** B. Cunningham, administrator; Haji Wahin bin Bynie, chairman of Islands Council. **Structure:** administrator, appointed by governor-general of Australia; Cocos Malay community is represented by Cocos (Keeling) Islands Council; Supreme Court.

Economy **Monetary unit:** Australian dollar. **Chief crops:** vegetables, bananas, pawpaws, coconuts. **Natural resources:** fish. **Major industries:** copra products. **Exports:** (1984) 202 metric tons of copra. **Imports:** foodstuffs from Australia, fuel, consumer items. **Major trading partners:** Australia.

Norfolk Island

Territory of Norfolk Island

Geography **Location:** island in western Pacific Ocean; 29°04'S, 167°57'E. **Boundaries:** Vanuatu to N, New Zealand to SE, Brisbane, Australia 870 mi. (1,400 km) to W. **Total land area:** 13.3 sq. mi. (34.5 sq km). **Coastline:** 20 mi. (32 km). **Comparative area:** about one-fifth size of Washington, D.C. **Land use:** 0% arable land; 0% permanent crops; 25% meadows and pastures; 0% forest and woodland; 75% other. **Major cities:** Kingston (capital).

People **Population:** 2,710 (July 1994 est.). **Nationality:** noun—Norfolk Islander(s); adjective—Norfolk Islander. **Ethnic groups:** descendants of *Bounty* mutiny; more recently, Australian and New Zealand settlers. **Languages:** English (official), Norfolk (a mixture of 18th-century English and ancient Tahitian). **Religions:** Church of England, Roman Catholic, Uniting Church in Australia, Seventh-day Adventist.

Government **Type:** territory of Australia. **National holiday:** Pitcairners Arrival Day Anniversary, June 8. **Head of government:** A.G. Kerr, administrator (since April 1992); David Ernest Buffett, assembly president (since May 1992). **Structure:** nine-member elected Legislative Assembly; chief executive is Australian administrator named by governor-general.

Economy **Monetary unit:** Australian dollar. **Budget:** (1989) ***income:*** N.A.; ***expend.:*** $4.2 mil. **Chief crops:** Kentia palm seed, cereals, vegetables, fruit. **Natural resources:** fish. **Major industries:** tourism. **Exports:** $1.7 mil. (f.o.b., 1986); postage stamps, seeds of Norfolk Island pine and Kentia Palm, small quantities of avocados. **Imports:** $15.6 mil. (c.i.f., 1986). **Major trading partners:** ***imports and exports:*** Australia, Pacific Islands, New Zealand, Asia, Europe.

Uninhabited Territories

Ashmore Is. (12°15'S, 123°05'E); Cartier Is. (12°30'S, 123°30'E); Coral Sea Is. (18°00'S, 158°00'E); Heard Is. (53°00'S, 73°35'E); McDonald Is. (52°29'S, 72°50'E).

DENMARK

Faeroe Islands

Geography **Location:** group of 18 islands (17 inhabited) in Atlantic Ocean SE of Iceland. Tórshavn 62°02'N, 6°47'W. **Boundaries:** Iceland to NW, Norwegian Sea to N, Norway to E, Shetland Islands to SE, UK to S. **Total land area:** 541 sq. mi. (1,400 sq km). **Coastline:** 475 mi. (764 km). **Comparative area:** slightly less than eight times size of Washington, D.C. **Land use:** 2% arable land; 0% permanent crops; 0% meadows and pastures; 0% forest and woodland; 98% other. **Major cities:** (1991 est.) Tórshavn (capital) 16,223.

People **Population:** 48,427 (July 1994 est.). **Nationality:** noun—Faeroese (sing., pl.); adjective—Faeroese. **Ethnic groups:** homogeneous Scandinavian population. **Languages:** Faeroese (derived from Old Norse), Danish. **Religions:** Evangelical Lutheran.

Government **Type:** self-governing overseas administrative division of Denmark. **Heads of government:** Margrethe II, queen (since Jan. 1972); Marita Petersen, prime minister (since Jan. 1993). **Structure:** legislative authority lies jointly with Crown, acting through appointed high commissioner, and 32-member provincial Parliament (Lagting) in matters of strictly Faeroese concern; executive power vested in Crown, acting through high commissioner, but exercised by provincial cabinet responsible to provincial Parliament.

Economy **Monetary unit:** Danish krone. **Budget:** (1991 est.) ***income:*** $425 mil.; ***expend.:*** $480 mil. **GDP:** $662 mil., $14,000 per capita. **Chief crops:** sheep and cattle grazing. **Natural resources:** fish. **Major industries:** fishing. **Labor force:** 17,585; fishing, manufacturing, transportation, commerce. **Exports:** $386 mil. (f.o.b., 1990 est.); 86% fish and fish products, animal feedstuffs, transport equipment. **Imports:** $322 mil. (c.i.f., 1990 est.); 38% machinery and transport equipment, 11% food and livestock, 10% fuels, 10% chemicals. **Major trading partners:** ***exports:*** 16% Denmark, 14% UK, 13% Germany, 10% U.S., 9% France, 5% Japan; ***imports:*** 44% Denmark, 16% Norway, 6% Germany, 6% Sweden, 3% U.S.

Greenland

Geography **Location:** North Atlantic Ocean, largely within Arctic Circle. Godthåb 64°11'N, 51°44'W. **Boundaries:** Iceland about 190 mi. (300 km) to E across Denmark Strait, Canada to SW and W across Baffin Bay and Davis Strait. **Total land area:** 840,000 sq. mi. (2,175,600 sq km); land area 131,931 sq. mi. (341,700 sq km) ice free. **Coastline:** 27,400 mi. (44,087 km). **Comparative area:** slightly more than three times size of Texas. **Land use:** 0% arable land; 0% permanent crops; 1% meadows and pastures; negl. % forest and woodland; 99% other. **Major cities:** (1992) Godthåb (Nuuk, capital), 12,233.

People **Population:** 57,040 (July 1994 est.). **Nationality:** noun—Greenlander(s); adjective—Greenlandic. **Ethnic groups:** 86% Greenlander (Eskimos and Greenland-born whites), 14% Danish. **Languages:** Danish, Eskimo dialects. **Religions:** Evangelical Lutheran.

Government **Type:** self-governing overseas administrative division of Denmark. **National holiday:** Apr. 16. **Heads of government:** Margrethe II, queen (since Jan. 1972); Lars Emil Johansen, home-rule chairman (since Mar. 1991). **Structure:** executive—home-rule chairman and four-person council; legislative—elected 27-seat Landsting and Danish Parliament.

Economy **Monetary unit:** Danish krone. **Budget:** (1989) ***income:*** $381 mil.; ***expend:*** $381 mil. **GNP:** $500 mil., $9,000 per capita. **Chief crops:** arable land largely in hay; sheep grazing, garden produce. **Natural resources:** zinc, lead, iron ore, coal, molybdenum. **Major industries:** mining, fishing, sealing. **Labor force:** 22,800; largely engaged in fishing, hunting, sheep breeding. **Exports:** $340.6 mil. (f.o.b., 1991); fish and fish products, metallic ores and concentrates. **Imports:** $403 mil. (c.i.f., 1991); petroleum and petroleum products, machinery and transport equipment, food products. **Major trading partners:** ***exports:*** 74% Denmark, 11% Germany, 6% Sweden; ***imports:*** 69% Denmark, Norway, Germany, Japan, U.S.

FRANCE

French Guiana

Department of Guiana

Geography Location: NE coast of South America. **Boundaries:** North Atlantic Ocean to N, Brazil to E and S across Oyapock River, Suriname to W across Maroni River. **Total land area:** 35,135 sq. mi. (91,000 sq km). **Coastline:** 235 mi. (378 km). **Comparative area:** slightly smaller than Indiana. **Land use:** negl. % arable land; negl. % permanent crops; negl. % meadows and pastures; 82% forest and woodland; 18% other. **Major cities:** (1990) Cayenne (capital) 41,637.

People Population: 139,299 (July 1994 est.). **Nationality:** noun—French Guianese (sing., pl.); adjective—French Guiana. **Ethnic groups:** 66% black or mulatto, 12% Caucasian, 12% East Indian, Chinese or Amerindian, 10% other. **Languages:** French. **Religions:** predominantly Roman Catholic.

Government Type: overseas department of France. **Head of government:** Jean-Francois Cordet, prefect (since 1992). **Structure:** executive—prefect appointed by Paris; legislative—popularly elected 16-member General Council and Regional Council composed of members of the local General Council and of the locally elected deputy and senator to the French Parliament; judicial—under jurisdiction of French judicial system.

Economy Monetary unit: French franc. **Budget:** (1987) ***income:*** $735 mil.; ***expend.:*** $735 mil. **GDP:** $421 mil., $4,390 per capita (1986). **Chief crops:** limited vegetables for local consumption; rice, corn, manioc, cocoa, bananas, sugar. **Livestock:** cattle, pigs, goats. **Natural resources:** bauxite, timber, gold, cinnabar, kaolin, fish. **Major industries:** construction, shrimp processing, forestry products. **Labor force:** 23,265 (1980); 60.6% services, government, and commerce, 21.2% industry, 18.2% agriculture; 13% unemployment (1990). **Exports:** $59 mil. (f.o.b., 1992); shrimp, timber, rum, rosewood essence. **Imports:** $1.5 bil. (c.i.f., 1992); food (grains, processed meat), other consumer goods, producer goods, petroleum. **Major trading partners:** (1987) ***exports:*** 52% France, 15% Spain, 12% U.S.; ***imports:*** 77% France, 11% Germany, 5% U.S.

French Polynesia

Territory of French Polynesia

Geography Location: five island groups (Gambier, Marquesas, Society, Tuamotu, and Tubua") in South Pacific Ocean about two-thirds of way from Panama Canal to New Zealand. Papeete (Society Is.) 17°32'S, 149°34'W. **Boundaries:** Kiribati to NE, Cook Islands to E. **Total land area:** 1,522 sq. mi. (3,941 sq km). **Coastline:** 1,569 mi. (2,525 km). **Comparative area:** slightly less than one-third size of Connecticut. **Land use:** 1% arable land; 19% permanent crops; 5% meadows and pastures; 31% forest and woodland; 44% other. **Major cities:** (1983) Papeete (capital) 23,496.

People Population: 215,129 (July 1994 est.). **Nationality:** noun—French Polynesian(s); adjective—French Polynesian. **Ethnic groups:** 78% Polynesian, 12% Chinese, 6% local French, 4% metropolitan French. **Religions:** 55% Protestant, 32% Roman Catholic, 13% other.

Government Type: overseas territory of France. **Heads of government:** Michel Jau, high commissioner; Gaston Flosse, president of territorial government (since May 1991). **Structure:** 30-member Territorial Assembly, popularly elected; five-member Council of Government, elected by assembly; popular election of two deputies to National Assembly and one senator to Senate in Paris.

Economy Monetary unit: Colonial Francs Pacifique (CFP). **Budget:** (1988) ***income:*** $614 mil.; ***expend.:*** $957 mil. **GDP:** $1.5 bil., $7,000 per capita (1993 est.). **Chief crops:** coconuts. **Livestock:** pigs, cattle, goats, sheep, horses. **Natural resources:** timber, fish, cobalt. **Major industries:** tourism, pearls, agricultural processing. **Labor force:** 76,630 employed (1988). **Exports:** $88.9 mil. (f.o.b., 1989); 79% coconut products, 14% mother-of-pearl, vanilla. **Imports:** $765 mil. (c.i.f., 1989); fuels, foodstuffs, equipment. **Major trading partners:** ***exports:*** 44% France, 21% U.S.; ***imports:*** 50% France, 16% U.S., 6% New Zealand.

Guadeloupe

Department of Guadeloupe

Geography Location: eastern Caribbean Sea: Guadeloupe 16°00'N, 61°42'W; St. Barthélemy 17°55'N, 63°50'W; Marie Galante 15°57'N, 61°20'W. **Boundaries:** Antigua to N, Dominica to S. **Total land area:** 687 sq. mi. (1,780 sq km). **Coastline:** 190 mi. (306 km). **Comparative area:** 10 times size of Washington, D.C. **Land use:** 18% arable land; 5% permanent crops; 13% meadows and pastures; 40% forest and woodland; 24% other; includes 1% irrigated. **Major cities:** (1990 census) BasseTerre (capital) 14,107; Les Abymes 62,809; Pointe à Pitre 26,083.

People Population: 428,947 (July 1994 est.). **Nationality:** noun—Guadeloupian(s); adjective—Guadeloupe. **Ethnic groups:** 90% black or mulatto, 5% white, 5% East Indian, Lebanese, Chinese. **Languages:** French, Creole patois. **Religions:** 95% Roman Catholic, 5% Hindu and African.

Government Type: overseas department of France. **Head of government:** Franck Perriez, prefect (since 1992). **Structure:** executive—prefect appointed by Paris; legislative—popularly elected General Council of 36 members and Regional Council composed of members of local General Council and locally elected deputies and senators to French Parliament; judicial—under jurisdiction of French judicial system.

Economy Monetary unit: French franc. **Budget:** (1989) ***income:*** $333 mil.; ***expend:*** $671 mil. **GDP:** $2.9 bil., $8,400 per capita (1991). **Chief crops:** sugarcane, bananas, pineapples, vegetables. **Livestock:** cattle, pigs, goats. **Natural resources:** cultivable land, beaches and climate that foster tourism. **Major industries:** construction, cement, rum. **Labor force:** 120,000; 53% services, government, and commerce, 25.8% industry, 21.2% agriculture; 25% unemployment. **Exports:** $168 mil. (f.o.b., 1988); bananas, sugar, rum. **Imports:** $1.2 bil. (c.i.f., 1988); vehicles, foodstuffs, clothing and other consumer goods, construction materials, petroleum products. **Major trading partners:** (1989) ***exports:*** 72% France, 16% Martinique; ***imports:*** 59% France.

Martinique

Department of Martinique

Geography Location: eastern Caribbean Sea (14°36'N, 61°05'W). **Boundaries:** Dominica to N, St. Lucia to S. **Total land area:** 425 sq. mi. (1,100 sq km). **Coastline:** 180 mi. (290 km). **Comparative area:** slightly more than six times size of Washington, D.C. **Land use:** 10% arable land; 8% permanent crops; 30% meadows and pastures; 26% forest and woodland; 26% other; includes 5% irrigated. **Major cities:** (1990 census) Fort-de-France (capital) 101,540.

People Population: 392,362 (July 1994 est.). **Nationality:** noun—Martiniquais (sing., pl.); adjective—Martiniquais. **Ethnic groups:** 90% African and African-Caucasian-Indian mixture, 5% Caucasian, 5% East Indian, Lebanese, Chinese. **Languages:** French, Creole patois. **Religions:** 95% Roman Catholic, 5% Hindu and African beliefs.

Government Type: overseas department of France. **Head of government:** Michel Morin, prefect. **Structure:** executive—prefect appointed by Paris; legislative—popularly elected General Council of 44 members and Regional Council, including all members of local General Council and locally elected deputies and senators to French Parliament; judicial—under jurisdiction of French judicial system.

Economy Monetary unit: French franc. **Budget:** (1989 est.) ***income:*** $268 mil.; ***expend.:*** $268 mil. **GDP:** $3.3 bil., $9,500 per capita (1991). **Chief crops:** bananas, pineapples, vegetables, flowers, sugarcane for rum. **Livestock:** sheep, cattle, pigs, goats. **Natural resources:** coastal scenery and beaches, cultivable land. **Major industries:** construction, rum, cement. **Labor force:** 100,000; 31.7% service industry, 29.4% construction and public works, 13.1% agriculture; 25–30% unemployment (1985). **Exports:** $201.5 mil. (f.o.b., 1991); refined petroleum products, bananas, rum, pineapples. **Imports:** $1.5 bil. (c.i.f., 1991); petroleum products, crude oil, foodstuffs, construction materials, vehicles, clothing and other consumer goods. **Major trading partners:** (1991) ***exports:*** 57.1% France, 31.5% Guadeloupe, 6.2% French Guiana; ***imports:*** 62.2% France, UK, Italy, Germany, Japan, U.S.

Mayotte

Territorial Collectivity of Mayotte

Geography Location: Comoros archipelago in eastern Indian Ocean (12°47'S, 45°12'E). **Boundaries:** Indian Ocean to N, Madagascar 300 mi. (480 km) to SE, Mozambique Channel to S, Mozambique to W. **Total land area:** 145 sq.

mi. (375 sq km). **Coastline:** 5,798 mi. (9,330 km). **Comparative area:** slightly more than twice size of Washington, D.C. **Land use:** N.A. **Major cities:** (1985 census) Dzaoudzi (capital) 5,865; Mamoudzou 12,026; Pamanzi-Labattoir 4,106.

People **Population:** 93,468 (July 1994 est.). **Nationality:** noun—Mahorais (sing., pl.); adjective—Mahoran. **Languages:** Mahorian (a Swahili dialect), French. **Religions:** 99% Muslim, 1% Christian (mostly Roman Catholic).

Government **Type:** territorial collectivity of France. **Heads of government:** Jean-Jacques Deracq, prefect; Younoussa Bamana, president of General Council (since 1976). **Structure:** elected 17-member General Council; appointed representative.

Economy **Monetary unit:** French franc. **Budget:** (1985). ***income:*** N.A.; ***expend.:*** $37.3 mil. **GDP:** $54 mil., $600 per capita (1993 est.). **Chief crops:** vanilla, ylang-ylang, coffee, copra. **Natural resources:** none. **Major industries:** newly created lobster and shrimp industry. **Exports:** $4 mil. (1984); ylang-ylang, vanilla. **Imports:** $21.8 mil. (1984); building materials, transport equipment, rice, clothing, flour. **Major trading partners:** ***exports:*** 79% France, 10% Comoros, 9% Réunion; ***imports:*** 57% France, 16% Kenya, 11% South Africa, 8% Pakistan.

New Caledonia

Territory of New Caledonia and Dependencies

Geography **Location:** one large and several smaller islands in western South Pacific. Nouméa 22°16'S, 166°26'E. **Boundaries:** Vanuatu to N, Australia about 930 mi. (1,500 km) to W. **Total land area:** 7,359 sq. mi. (19,060 sq km). **Coastline:** 1,401 mi. (2,254 km). **Comparative area:** slightly smaller than Massachusetts. **Land use:** negl. % arable land; negl. % permanent crops; 14% meadows and pastures; 51% forest and woodland; 35% other. **Major cities:** (1989) Nouméa (capital) 65,110.

People **Population:** 181,309 (July 1994 est.). **Nationality:** noun—New Caledonian(s); adjective—New Caledonian. **Ethnic groups:** 42.5% Melanesian, 37.1% European, 8.4% Wallisian, 3.8% Polynesian, 3.6% Indonesian, 1.6% Vietnamese, 3.0% other. **Languages:** French, Melanesian-Polynesian dialect. **Religions:** 60% Roman Catholic, 30% Protestant, 10% other.

Government **Type:** overseas territory of France. **Heads of government:** Alain Christnacht, high commissioner and president of Council of Government (since Jan. 1991). **Structure:** executive—administered by high commissioner, responsible to French Ministry for Overseas France and Council of Government; legislative—56-seat Territorial Assembly; judicial—Court of Appeal.

Economy **Monetary unit:** Colonial Francs Pacifique (CFP). **Budget:** (1985) ***income:*** $224 mil.; ***expend.:*** $211 mil. **GNP:** $1 bil., $6,000 per capita (1991 est.). **Chief crops:** coffee, maize, wheat, vegetables. **Livestock:** cattle, goats, pigs, horses. **Natural resources:** nickel, chrome, iron, cobalt, manganese, silver. **Major industries:** nickel mining. **Labor force:** 50,469 (1980 est.); immigrant labor now coming from Wallis and Futuna, Vanuatu, and French Polynesia; N.A. unemployment. **Exports:** $671 mil. (f.o.b., 1989); 95% nickel metal, nickel ore. **Imports:** $764 mil. (c.i.f., 1989); foodstuffs, fuels and minerals, machines and electrical equipment. **Major trading partners:** ***exports:*** 56.3% France, Japan; ***imports:*** 50.3% France, Australia.

Intl. Orgs. WMO.

Réunion

Department of Réunion

Geography **Location:** southwestern Indian Ocean (20°15'S, 55°27'E). **Boundaries:** 500 mi. (800 km) E of Madagascar. **Total land area:** 969 sq. mi. (2,510 sq km). **Coastline:** 125 mi. (201 km). **Comparative area:** slightly smaller than Rhode Island. **Land use:** 20% arable land; 2% permanent crops; 4% meadows and pastures; 35% forest and woodland; 39% other; includes 2% irrigated. **Major cities:** (1990 census) Saint-Denis (capital) 121,999; Saint-Paul 71,669; Saint-Pierre 58,846.

People **Population:** 652,857 (July 1994 est.). **Nationality:** noun—Réunionese (sing., pl.); adjective—Réunionese. **Ethnic groups:** mostly intermixed French, African, Malagasy, Chinese, Pakistani, Indian ancestry. **Languages:** French (official), Creole. **Religions:** 94% Roman Catholic.

Government **Type:** overseas department of France. **Head of government:** Hubert Fournier, prefect. **Structure:** administered by prefect appointed by French minister of interior, assisted by secretary general and elected 44-member General Council; in 1974 France created an elected 45-member Regional Assembly to coordinate economic and social development policies; in 1981 both General Council and Regional Assembly received greater authority for fiscal policy.

Economy **Monetary unit:** French franc. **Budget:** (1986) ***income:*** $358 mil.; ***expend.:*** $914 mil. **GDP:** $2.5 bil., $3,900 per capita (1993 est.). **Chief crops:** cash crops—almost entirely sugarcane, small amounts of vanilla and perfume plants; food crops—tropical fruit and vegetables, manioc, bananas, corn, market garden produce; most food imported. **Livestock:** pigs, goats, cattle, sheep. **Natural resources:** negl. **Major industries:** sugar, rum, cigarettes, handicraft items. **Labor force:** (1981) 49% services, 30% agriculture, 21% industry; 32% unemployment (1986) (high seasonal unemployment); 63% of population of working age (1983). **Exports:** $166 mil. (f.o.b., 1988); 75% sugar, 4% rum and molasses, 4% perfume essences, 1% vanilla and tea. **Imports:** $1.7 bil. (c.i.f., 1988); manufactured goods, food, beverages, tobacco, machinery and transportation equipment, raw materials, petroleum products. **Major trading partners:** France, Mauritius, Bahrain, S. Africa, Italy.

St. Pierre and Miquelon

Department of St. Pierre and Miquelon

Geography **Location:** North Atlantic off east coast of Canada. St. Pierre 46°46'N, 56°12'W. **Boundaries:** Newfoundland, Canada 16 mi. (25 km) to N, North Atlantic Ocean to E and S. **Total land area:** 93 sq. mi. (242 sq km). **Coastline:** 75 mi. (120 km). **Comparative area:** slightly less than 1.5 times size of Washington, D.C. **Land use:** 13% arable land; 0% permanent crops; 0% meadows and pastures; 4% forest and woodland; 83% other. **Major cities:** (1990 census) St. Pierre (capital) 5,683; Miquelon 709.

People **Population:** 6,704 (July 1994 est.). **Nationality:** noun—Frenchmen; adjective—French. **Ethnic groups:** originally Basques and Bretons (French fishermen). **Languages:** French. **Religions:** 98% Roman Catholic.

Government **Type:** territorial collectivity of France. **National holiday:** National Day, July 14. **Heads of government:** Yves Henry, commissioner (since Dec. 1993); Marc Plante-Genest, president of the General Council. **Structure:** executive—government commissioner appointed by Paris; legislative—popularly elected 19-member General Council elected for six-year terms; judiciary—Superior Tribunal of Appeals.

Economy **Monetary unit:** French franc. **Budget:** (1989) ***income:*** $18.3 mil.; ***expend.:*** $18.3 mil. **GDP:** $65 mil., $10,000 per capita (1992 est.). **Chief crops:** vegetables. **Livestock:** cattle, sheep, pigs. **Natural resources:** N.A. **Major industries:** fishing, supply base for fishing fleets, tourism. **Labor force:** 2,850 (1988). **Exports:** $30.0 mil. (f.o.b., 1991 est.); fish and fish products, fox and mink pelts. **Imports:** $82 mil. (c.i.f., 1991 est.); meat, clothing, fuel, electrical equipment, machinery, building materials. **Major trading partners:** ***exports:*** 58% U.S., 17% France, 11% Canada; ***imports:*** Canada, France, U.S., Netherlands, UK.

Wallis and Futuna

Territory of the Wallis and Futuna Islands

Geography **Location:** two island groups (Wallis to NE, Hooru, incl. Futuna Is., to SW) in South Pacific. Mata-Utu (Wallis group) 13°22'S, 176°12'W. **Boundaries:** Western Samoa to E, Fiji to SW. **Total land area:** 106 sq. mi. (274 sq km). **Coastline:** 80 mi. (129 km). **Comparative area:** slightly larger than Washington, D.C. **Land use:** 5% arable land; 20% permanent crops; 0% meadows and pastures; 0% forest and woodland; 75% other. **Major cities:** Mata-Utu (capital) (1983 census) 815.

People **Population:** 14,338 (July 1994 est.). **Nationality:** noun—Wallisian(s), Futunan(s), or Wallis and Futuna Islander(s); adjective—Wallisian, Futunan, or Wallis and Futuna Islander. **Ethnic groups:** almost entirely Polynesian. **Languages:** French (official). **Religions:** largely Roman Catholic.

Government **Type:** overseas territory of France. **Head of government:** Philippe Legrix, high administrator. **Structure:** Territorial Assembly of 20 members; popular election of one deputy to National Assembly in Paris and one senator. Note: there are three traditional kings with limited powers.

Economy Monetary unit: Colonial Francs Pacifique (CFP). **Budget:** (1983) ***income:*** $2.7 mil.; ***expend.:*** $2.7 mil. **GDP:** $25 mil., $1,500 per capita (1991 est.). **Chief crops:** dominated by coconuts, subsistence crops of yams, taro, bananas. **Livestock:** pigs, goats. **Natural resources:** none. **Major industries:** copra, handicrafts. **Exports:** negl. **Imports:** $13.3 mil. (c.i.f., 1984); largely foodstuffs and some equipment associated with development programs.

Uninhabited Territories

Bassas da India (21°25'S, 39°42'E); Clipperton Is. (10°21'N, 109°13'W); Europa Is. (22°20'S, 40°22'E); French Southern and Antarctic Lands (Kerguelen Is. 49°20'S, 69°30'E); Glorioso Is. (11°30'S, 47°20'E); Tromelin Is. (15°52'S, 54°25'E).

MOROCCO

Western Sahara

Geography Location: northwestern coast of Africa. **Boundaries:** Morocco to N, Algeria, Mauritania to E, Atlantic Ocean to W. **Total land area:** 102,703 sq. mi. (266,000 sq km). **Coastline:** 690 mi. (1,110 km). **Comparative area:** between Wyoming and Colorado. **Land use:** negl. % arable land; 0% permanent crops; 19% meadows and pastures; 0% forest and woodland; 81% other. **Major cities:** (1982) El Aaiun (capital) 93,785.

People Population: 211,877 (July 1994 est.). **Nationality:** noun—Saharan(s), Moroccan(s); adjective—Saharan, Moroccan. **Ethnic groups:** Arab, Berber. **Languages:** Hassaniya Arabic, Moroccan Arabic. **Religion:** Muslim.

Government Type: legal status of territory and question of sovereignty still unresolved. **Independence:** N.A. **Constitution:** N.A. **National holiday:** N.A. **Head of government:** None. **Structure:** N.A.

Economy Monetary unit: Moroccan dirham. **Budget:** N.A. **GDP:** $60 mil., $300 per capita (1991 est.). **Chief crops:** practically none; some barley grown in nondrought years; fruit and vegetables in the few oases; food imports; water shortage. **Livestock:** N.A. **Natural resources:** phosphates, iron ore. **Major industries:** phosphate, fishing, handicrafts. **Labor force:** 12,000; 50% animal husbandry and subsistence farming. **Exports:** $8 mil. (f.o.b., 1982 est.); 62% phosphates. **Imports:** $30 mil. (c.i.f., 1982); fuel for fishing fleet, foodstuffs. **Major trading partners:** Morocco claims administrative control over Western Sahara and controls all trade with country; trade figures are included in overall Moroccan accounts.

NETHERLANDS

Aruba

Geography Location: southern Caribbean Sea (12°32'N, 70°02'W), off NW Venezuela. **Boundaries:** Curaçao, Netherlands Antilles 42 mi. (68 km) to E, Venezuela 16 mi. (25 km) to S. **Total land area:** 75 sq. mi. (193 sq km). **Coastline:** about 45 mi. (about 72 km). **Comparative area:** slightly larger than Washington, D.C. **Land use:** 0% arable land; 0% permanent crops; 0% meadows and pastures; 0% forest and woodland; 100% other. **Major cities:** Oranjestad (capital).

People Population: 65,545 (July 1994 est.). **Nationality:** noun—Aruban(s); adjective—Aruban. **Ethnic groups:** 80% mixed European/Caribbean Indian. **Languages:** Dutch (official), Papiamento (a Spanish-Portuguese-Dutch-English dialect); English widely spoken. **Religions:** 82% Roman Catholic, 8% Protestant; also small Hindu, Muslim, Confucian, Jewish minorities.

Government Type: self-governing until complete independence from Netherlands is granted in 1996. **Heads of government:** Olindo Koolman, governor-general (since 1986); Nelson O. Oduber, prime minister (since Feb. 1989).

Economy Monetary unit: Aruban florin. **Budget:** (1988) ***income:*** $145 mil.; ***expend.:*** $185 mil. **GDP:** $1.2 bil., $17,400 per capita (1993 est.). **Chief crops:** negl. **Livestock:** N.A. **Natural resources:** negl.; white sandy beaches. **Major industries:** tourism, light manufacturing (tobacco, beverages, consumer goods). **Labor force:** (1986) mostly tourism; 14.5% unemployment (1987). **Exports:** $1.3 bil. (f.o.b., 1993 est.); including oil reexports; mostly petroleum products. **Imports:** $1.6 bil. (f.o.b., 1993 est.); including oil for processing and reexport, foodstuffs, consumer goods. **Major trading partners:** ***exports:*** 64% U.S., EU; ***imports:*** 8% U.S., EU.

Netherlands Antilles

Geography Location: two island groups in Caribbean Sea, about 500 mi. (800 km) apart. Curaçao Is. 12°12'N, 68°56'W; St. Maarten Is. 18°03'N, 63°05'W. **Boundaries:** southern group (Curaçao and Bonaire)—Venezuela to S; northern group (St. Eustatius, Saba, and St. Maarten)—Antigua to E, Virgin Islands to W. **Total land area:** 371 sq. mi. (960 sq km). **Coastline:** 226 mi. (364 km). **Comparative area:** slightly less than 5.5 times size of Washington, D.C. **Land use:** 8% arable land; 0% permanent crops; 0% meadows and pastures; 0% forest and woodland; 92% other. **Major cities:** Willemstad (capital).

People Population: 185,790 (July 1994 est.). **Nationality:** noun—Netherlands Antillean(s); adjective—Netherlands Antillean. **Ethnic groups:** 85% mixed African; remainder Carib Indian, European, Latin, Oriental. **Languages:** Dutch (official), Papiamento (a Spanish-Portuguese-Dutch-English dialect) predominates; English widely spoken; Spanish. **Religions:** predominantly Roman Catholic; Protestant, Jewish, Seventh-day Adventist.

Government Type: autonomous part of Netherlands. **Constitution:** Dec. 29, 1954. **Heads of government:** Jaime Saleh, governor-general (since 1989); Miguel Pourier, prime minister (since Feb. 1994). **Structure:** executive—governor (appointed by Crown); actual power exercised by eight-member Council of Ministers or cabinet presided over by minister-president; legislative—23-member Legislative Council; judicial—independent court system under control of chief justice of Supreme Court of Justice; each island territory has island council headed by lieutenant governor.

Economy Monetary unit: Netherlands Antillean guilder or florin. **Budget:** (1992 est.) ***income:*** $209 mil.; ***expend.:*** $232 mil. **GDP:** $1.8 bil., $9,700 per capita (1993 est.). **Chief crops:** corn, pulses. **Livestock:** goats, sheep, cattle, pigs. **Natural resources:** phosphates (Curaçao only), salt (Bonaire only). **Major industries:** tourism on Curaçao and St. Maarten; petroleum refining on Curaçao; petroleum transshipment facilities on Curaçao and Bonaire; light manufacturing on Curaçao. **Labor force:** 89,000 (1983); 65% government, 28% industry and commerce; 8% unemployment (1987). **Exports:** $240 mil. (f.o.b., 1993); 98% petroleum products. **Imports:** $1.2 bil. (f.o.b., 1993); 64% crude petroleum, food, manufactures. **Major trading partners:** ***exports:*** 39% U.S., 9% Brazil, 6% Colombia; ***imports:*** 26% Venezuela, 18% U.S., 6% Colombia, 6% Netherlands, 5% Japan.

NEW ZEALAND

Cook Islands

Geography Location: 15 islands (13 inhabited) in South Pacific. Avarua 21°12'S, 159° 46'W. Boundaries: French Polynesia to E, American Samoa to W. **Total land area:** 93 sq. mi. (240 sq km). **Coastline:** 75 mi. (120 km). **Comparative area:** slightly less than 1.5 times size of Washington, D.C. **Land use:** 4% arable land; 22% permanent crops; 0% meadows and pastures; 0% forest and woodland; 74% other. **Major cities:** Avarua (capital).

People Population: 19,124 (July 1994 est.). **Nationality:** noun—Cook Islander(s); adjective—Cook Islander. **Ethnic groups:** 81.3% Polynesian (full blood), 7.7% Polynesian and European, 7.7% Polynesian and other, 2.4% European, 0.9% other. **Languages:** English. **Religions:** Christian; majority of populace members of Cook Islands Christian church.

Government Type: self-governing in free association with New Zealand; Cook Islands government fully responsible for internal affairs and has right at any time to move to full independence by unilateral action; New Zealand responsible for external affairs, in consultation with Cook Islands government. **Head of government:** Geoffrey Henry, prime minister (since Feb. 1989). **Structure:** New Zealand governor-general appoints representative to Cook Islands, who represents queen of England and New Zealand government; representative appoints prime minister; popularly elected 25-member Parliament; 15-member House of Arikis (chiefs), appointed by representative, is advisory body only.

Economy Monetary unit: New Zealand dollar. **Budget:** (1993) ***income:*** $38 mil.; ***expend.:*** $34.4 mil. **GDP:** $57 mil., $3,000 per capita (1993 est.). **Chief crops:** cash crops—copra, citrus fruits, pineapples, tomatoes, bananas; food crops—yams, taro. **Livestock:** poultry, pigs, horses, goats. **Natural resources:** negl. **Major industries:** fruit processing, tourism. **Exports:** $3.4 mil. (f.o.b., 1990); copra, fresh and canned fruit. **Imports:** $50 mil. (c.i.f., 1990); foodstuffs, textiles, fuels. **Major trading partners:** ***exports:*** 80% New Zealand, Japan; ***imports:*** 49% New Zealand, Japan, Australia, U.S.

Intl. Orgs. IFC, IMF, INTELSAT, UNESCO, WHO.

Niue

Geography Location: coral island in western South Pacific (19°02'S, 169°55'W). **Boundaries:** Tonga 300 mi. (480 km) to W, southern Cook Islands 580 mi. (930 km) to E. **Total land area:** 100 sq. mi. (260 sq km). **Coastline:** 40 mi. (64 km). **Comparative area:** slightly less than 1.5 times size of Washington, D.C. **Land use:** 61% arable land; 4% permanent crops; 4% meadows and pastures; 19% forest and woodland; 12% other. **Major cities:** Alofi (capital).

People Population: 1,906 (July 1994 est.). **Nationality:** noun—Niuean(s); adjective—Niuean. **Ethnic groups:** Polynesian, with about 200 Europeans, Samoans, Tongans. **Languages:** Polynesian dialect closely related to Tongan and Samoan; English. **Religions:** 75% Ekalesia Nieue (Niuean Church)—a Christian Protestant church closely related to London Missionary Society, 10% Mormon, 5% Roman Catholic, Jehovah's Witnesses, Seventh-day Adventist.

Government Type: self-governing territory in free association with New Zealand. **Heads of government:** Frank F. Lui, premier (since March 1993); Kurt Meyer, New Zealand representative. **Structure:** executive cabinet of four members—premier (elected by assembly) and three ministers (chosen by premier from among assembly members); Legislative Assembly consists of 20 members (14 village representatives and six elected on a common roll); if requested by assembly, New Zealand will also legislate for island.

Economy Monetary unit: New Zealand dollar. **Budget:** (1985 est.) ***income:*** $5.5 mil.; ***expend.:*** $6.3 mil. **GNP:** $2.1 mil., $1,000 per capita (1989 est.). **Chief crops:** cash crops—copra, coconuts, passion fruit, honey, limes; food crops—taro, yams, cassava (tapioca). **Livestock:** chickens, pigs, cattle. **Natural resources:** negl. **Major industries:** tourism, handicrafts. **Labor force:** about 1,000 (1981 est.); most Niueans work on family plantations; paid work exists only in government service, small industry, and Niue Development Board. **Exports:** $175,274 (f.o.b., 1985); canned coconut cream, copra, honey, passion fruit products, pawpaw. **Imports:** $3.8 mil. (c.i.f., 1985); food, live animals, manufactured goods, machinery, fuels, lubricants, chemicals, drugs. **Major trading partners:** ***exports:*** New Zealand, Fiji, Cook Islands, Australia; ***imports:*** New Zealand, Fiji, Japan, Western Samoa, Australia, U.S.

Tokelau

Geography Location: three atolls (Atafu, Nukunonu, Fakaofo) in South Pacific. Atafu 8°33'S, 172°30'W. **Boundaries:** northern Cook Islands to E, Western Samoa 300 mi. (480 km) to S, Tuvalu to W. **Total land area:** 4 sq. mi. (10 sq km). **Coastline:** 62 mi. (101 km). **Comparative area:** about 17 times size of the Mall in Washington, D.C. **Land use:** 0% arable land; 0% permanent crops; 0% meadows and pastures; 0% forest and woodland; 100% other. **Major cities:** none; each atoll has own administrative center.

People Population: 1,523 (July 1994 est.). **Nationality:** noun—Tokelauan(s); adjective—Tokelauan. **Ethnic groups:** all Polynesian, with cultural ties to Western Samoa. **Languages:** Tokelauan (a Polynesian language), English. **Religions:** 70% Congregational Christian church, 30% Roman Catholic—on Atafu, all Congregational Christian church of Samoa; on Nukunonu, all Roman Catholic; on Fakaofo, both denominations.

Government Type: territory of New Zealand. **National holiday:** Waitangi Day, Feb. 6. **Head of government:** Graham Ansell, administrator (since 1990). **Structure:** minister of foreign affairs of New Zealand is empowered to appoint administrator to region; powers of administrator are delegated to official secretary at Office of Tokelau Affairs, Apia, Western Samoa.

Economy Monetary unit: New Zealand dollar and Tokelau souvenir coin; Western Samoan tala also used. **Budget:** (1987) ***income:*** $430,830; ***expend.:*** $2.8 mil. **GDP:** $1.4 mil., $800 per capita (1988 est.). **Chief crops:** cash crops—coconuts, copra; food crops—pulaka, breadfruit, pawpaw, bananas. **Livestock:** pigs. **Natural resources:** negl. **Major industries:** small-scale enterprises for copra production, woodwork, plaited craft goods, stamps, coins. **Labor force:** N.A. **Exports:** $98,000 (f.o.b., 1983); stamps, handicrafts. **Imports:** $323,400 (c.i.f., 1983); foodstuffs, machinery, fuel. **Major trading partners:** New Zealand.

NORWAY

Svalbard

Geography Location: nine large and numerous smaller islands in Arctic Ocean. **Boundaries:** Longyearbyen (Spitsbergen Is.) 78° 13'N, 15°38'W; Bear Is. 74°30'N, 19°00'E. Norway to S, Greenland to W. **Total land area:** 24,000 sq. mi. (62,000 sq km). **Coastline:** undetermined. **Comparative area:** slightly smaller than West Virginia. **Land use:** 0% arable land; 0% permanent crops; 0% meadows and pastures; 0% forest and woodland; 100% other; no trees; only bushes are crowberry and cloudberry. **Major cities:** Longyearbyen (capital).

People Population: 3,018 (July 1994 est.). **Ethnic groups:** 64% Russian, 35% Norwegian, 1% other. **Languages:** Russian, Norwegian.

Government Type: territory of Norway. **Head of government:** Odd Blomdal, governor.

Economy Monetary unit: Norwegian krone. **Budget:** (1990) ***income***: $13.3 mil.; ***expend.:*** $13.3 mil. **Natural resources:** coal, copper, iron ore, phosphate, zinc, wildlife, fish. **Major industries:** coal mining; trapping of seal, polar bear, fox, walrus. **Exports:** 507,000 metric tons of coal from Norwegian mines, 500,000 tons of coal from Soviet mines (1987).

Uninhabited Territories

Bouvet Is. (54°26'S, 3°24'E); Jan Mayen Is. (71°00'N, 8°30'W).

PORTUGAL

Macau

Geography Location: peninsula of Macau, on mainland of southern China, and three nearby islands. **Boundaries:** China to N, Hong Kong to NE, South China Sea to S. **Total land area:** 6 sq. mi. (16 sq km). **Coastline:** 25 mi. (40 km). **Comparative area:** about one-tenth size of Washington, D.C. **Land use:** 0% arable land; 0% permanent crops; 0% meadows and pastures; 0% forest and woodland; 100% other. **Major cities:** Macau (capital).

People Population: 484,557 (July 1994 est.). **Nationality:** noun—Macanese (sing., pl.); adjective—Macau. **Ethnic groups:** 95% Chinese, 3% Portuguese, 2% other. **Languages:** Portuguese (official); Cantonese is language of commerce. **Religions:** mainly Buddhist; 17,000 Catholics, of whom half are Chinese.

Government Type: Chinese territory under Portuguese administration. **Head of government:** Vasco Joachim Rocha Vieira, governor-general (since Mar. 1991). **Structure:** governor assisted by five secretaries-adjunct (all appointed by president of Portugal), 17-member Legislative Assembly (five appointed by governor, six elected by direct and universal suffrage, six elected indirectly by various groups and associations).

Economy Monetary unit: pataca. **Budget:** (1989) ***income:*** $305 mil.; ***expend.:*** $298 mil. **GDP:** $3.5 bil., $7,300 per capita (1992). **Chief crops:** rice, vegetables; food shortages—rice, vegetables; not self-sufficient in food production. **Livestock:** pigs, buffalo, cattle. **Natural resources:** none. **Major industries:** clothing, textiles, toys, plastic products, furniture, tourism. **Labor force:** 180,000 (1986); N.A. unemployment. **Exports:** $1.8 bil. (1992 est.); textiles, clothing. **Imports:** $2 bil. (1992 est.); raw materials, foodstuffs. **Major trading partners:** (1987) ***exports:*** 33% U.S., 15% Hong Kong, 12% Germany, 10% France; ***imports:*** 39% Hong Kong, 21% China, Japan 10%.

UNITED KINGDOM

Anguilla

Geography Location: island in northeastern Caribbean (18°03'N, 63°04'W). **Boundaries:** St. Martin 5 mi. (8 km) to S, St. Kitts 70 mi. (113 km) to SE. **Total land area:** 35 sq. mi. (91 sq km). **Coastline:** 38 mi. (61 km). **Comparative area:** about one-half size of Washington, D.C. **Land use:** N.A.; mostly rock with sparse scrub oak, few trees, some commercial salt ponds. **Major cities:** The Valley (capital).

People Population: 7,052 (July 1994 est.). **Nationality:** noun—Anguillan(s); adjective—Anguillan. **Ethnic groups:** mainly of black African descent. **Languages:** English. **Religions:** Anglican, Methodist, Roman Catholic.

Government Type: dependent territory of UK. **Constitution:** Apr. 1, 1982. **Heads of government:** Alan W. Shave, governor (since Aug. 1992). **Structure:** 11-member House of Assembly, seven-member Executive Council.

Economy Monetary unit: East Caribbean dollar. **Budget:** (1992) ***income:*** $13.8 mil.; ***expend.:*** $15.2 mil. **GDP:** $56.5 mil. (1992), $6,800 per capita (1991 est.). **Chief crops:** pigeon peas, corn, sweet potatoes. **Natural resources:** negl.; salt, fish, lobsters. **Major industries:** tourism, boat building, salt, fishing. **Labor force:** 2,780 (1984); 30% unemployment (1985). **Exports:** $556,000 (f.o.b., 1992); lobsters, salt. **Imports:** $33.5 mil. (f.o.b., 1992).

Intl. Orgs. CARICOM (observer), INTERPOL.

Bermuda

Geography Location: archipelago of about 150 islands, in southern North Atlantic Ocean (32° 18'N, 64°47'W). **Boundaries:** Cape Hatteras 580 mi. (933 km) to W. **Total land area:** 19 sq. mi. (50 sq km). **Coastline:** 64 mi. (103 km). **Comparative area:** about three-tenths size of Washington, D.C. **Land use:** 0% arable land; 0% permanent crops; 0% meadows and pastures; 20% forest and woodland; 80% other. **Major cities:** (1990 est.) Hamilton (capital) 6,000; St. George's 3,000.

People Population: 61,158 (July 1994 est.). **Nationality:** noun—Bermudian(s); adjective—Bermudian. **Ethnic groups:** 61% black, 39% white and other. **Languages:** English. **Religions:** 37% Anglican, 14% Roman Catholic, 10% African Methodist Episcopal (Zion), 6% Methodist, 5% Seventh-day Adventist, 28% other.

Government Type: British dependent territory. **Constitution:** June 8, 1968. **Heads of government:** Sir David Waddington, governor (since Oct. 1988); John William David Swan, premier (since 1982). **Structure:** cabinet (Executive Council) appointed by governor, led by government leader; bicameral legislature with 11-member appointed Senate and 40-member directly elected House of Assembly; Supreme Court.

Economy Monetary unit: Bermuda dollar. **Budget:** (1991) ***income:*** $327.5 mil.; ***expend.:*** $308.9 mil. **GDP:** $1.63 bil., $27,100 per capita (1992). **Chief crops:** bananas, vegetables, Easter lilies, dairy products, citrus fruits. **Livestock:** poultry, pigs, cattle. **Natural resources:** limestone, pleasant climate fostering tourism. **Major industries:** tourism, finance, structural concrete products. **Labor force:** 32,000 (1984); 25% clerical, 22% services, 21% laborers, 13% professional and technical, 10% administrative and managerial. **Exports:** $60 mil. (f.o.b., 1991); semitropical produce, light manufactures. **Imports:** $468 mil. (f.o.b., 1991); fuel, foodstuffs, machinery. **Major trading partners:** ***exports:*** 55% U.S., 32% UK, 11% Canada, 2% other; ***imports:*** 60% U.S., 8% UK, 7% Venezuela, 5% Canada, 5% Japan, 15% other.

Intl. Orgs. CARICOM (observer), INTERPOL.

British Virgin Islands

Geography Location: more than 40 mountainous islands (15 inhabited) in northeastern Caribbean. Road Town (Tortola Is.), 18°26'N, 64°32'W. **Boundaries:** Puerto Rico about 100 mi. (161 km) to W. **Total land area:** 58 sq. mi. (150 sq km). **Coastline:** 50 mi. (80 km). **Comparative area:** about four-fifths size of Washington, D.C. **Land use:** 20% arable land; 7% permanent crops; 33% meadows and pastures; 7% forest and woodland; 33% other. **Major cities:** (1987 est.) Road Town (capital), 2,500.

People Population: 12,864 (July 1994 est.). **Nationality:** noun—Virgin Islander(s); adjective—Virgin Islander. **Ethnic groups:** over 90% black, remainder of white and Asian origin. **Languages:** English. **Religions:** majority Methodist; others include Anglican, Church of God, Seventh-day Adventist, Baptist, Roman Catholic.

Government Type: dependent territory of UK. **Constitution:** June 1, 1977. **National holiday:** Territory Day, July 1. **Heads of government:** Peter Alfred Penfold, governor (since Oct. 1991); H. Lavitty Stout, chief minister (since 1986). **Structure:** cabinet (Executive Council) consists of governor as chairman, four ministers of legislature, and ex officio member, who is attorney general; Legislative Council consists of Speaker (elected from outside council), nine elected members, and ex officio member, who is attorney general.

Economy Monetary unit: U.S. dollar. **Budget:** (1991) ***income:*** $51 mil.; ***expend.:*** $88 mil. **GDP:** $133 mil., $10,600 per capita (1991). **Chief crops:** limited—fruit, vegetables. **Natural resources:** negl. **Major industries:** tourism, construction, rum. **Labor force:** 4,911 (1980). **Exports:** $2.7 mil. (f.o.b., 1988); rum, fresh fish, gravel, sand, fruits, vegetables. **Imports:** $11.5 mil. (c.i.f., 1988); building materials, automobiles, foodstuffs, machinery. **Major trading partners:** Virgin Islands (U.S.), Puerto Rico, U.S.

Intl. Orgs. Commonwealth.

Cayman Islands

Geography Location: three main and numerous smaller islands in western Caribbean. George Town (Grand Cayman Is.) 19°20'N, 81°23'W. **Boundaries:** Cuba to N, Jamaica 180 mi. (290 km) to SE. **Total land area:** 100 sq. mi. (260 sq km). **Coastline:** 100 mi. (160 km). **Comparative area:** slightly less than 1.5 times size of Washington, D.C. **Land use:** 0% arable land; 0% permanent crops; 8% meadows and pastures; 23% forest and woodland; 69% other. **Major cities:** (1989 census) Georgetown (capital) 12,921; West Bay 5,632.

People Population: 31,790 (July 1994 est.). **Nationality:** noun—Caymanian(s); adjective—Caymanian. **Ethnic groups:** 40% mixed, 20% white, 20% black, 20% expatriates of various ethnic groups. **Languages:** English. **Religions:** United Church (Presbyterian and Congregational), Anglican, Baptist, Roman Catholic, Church of God, other Protestant denominations.

Government Type: British dependent territory. **National holiday:** Constitution Day, July 8. **Head of government:** Michael Gore, governor and president of Executive Council (since May 1992). **Structure:** executive—governor and Executive Council; legislative—unicameral Legislative Assembly; judicial—Summary Court, Supreme Court, Cayman Islands Court of Appeals, Her Majesty's Privy Council.

Economy Monetary unit: Cayman dollar. **Budget:** (1991) ***income:*** $141.5 mil.; ***expend.:*** $160.7 mil. **GDP:** $670 mil., $23,000 per capita (1991 est.). **Chief crops:** minor production of vegetables; turtle farming. **Natural resources:** fish, climate and beaches that foster tourism. **Major industries:** tourism, banking, insurance, finance. **Labor force:** 8,061 (1979); 18.7% service workers, 18.6% clerical, 12.5% construction. **Exports:** $2.6 mil. (f.o.b., 1991 est.); turtle products, manufactured consumer goods. **Imports:** $262.2 mil. (c.i.f., 1991 est.); foodstuffs, manufactured goods. **Major trading partners:** ***exports:*** mostly U.S.; ***imports:*** U.S., Trinidad and Tobago, UK, Netherlands Antilles, Japan.

Intl. Orgs. CARICOM (observer), INTERPOL.

Falkland Islands

Colony of the Falkland Islands

Geography Location: two large and about 2,000 smaller islands in southwestern Atlantic Ocean. Stanley (East Falkland) 51°45'S, 57° 56'W. **Boundaries:** Cape Horn, South America, about 480 mi. (770 km) to SW. **Total land area:** 4,699 sq. mi. (12,170 sq km). **Coastline:** 800 mi. (1,288 km). **Comparative area:** slightly smaller than Connecticut. **Land use:** 0% arable land; 0% permanent crops; 99% meadows and pastures; 0% forest and woodland; 1% other. **Major cities:** (1989) Stanley (capital) 1,329.

People Population: 2,261 (July 1994 est.). **Nationality:** noun—Falkland Islander(s); adjective—Falkland Island. **Ethnic groups:** mostly British. **Languages:** English. **Religions:** predominantly Anglican.

Government Type: colony of UK. **Constitution:** Oct. 3, 1985. **Head of government:** David Everard Tatham, governor (since Aug. 1992).

Structure: governor advised by Executive Council; Legislative Council.

Economy Monetary unit: Falkland Island pound. **Budget:** (1990) ***income:*** $62.7 mil.; ***expend.:*** $41.8 mil. **GNP:** N.A., N.A. per capita. **Livestock:** sheep, cattle, horses. **Natural resources:** fish, wildlife. **Major industries:** wool processing. **Labor force:** 1,100 (est.); 95% agriculture, mostly sheepherding. **Exports:** at least $14.7 mil. (1987); wool, hides, skins, other. **Imports:** at least $13.9 mil. (1987); food, clothing, fuels, machinery. **Major trading partners:** (1987 est.) ***exports:*** UK, Netherlands, Japan; ***imports:*** UK, Netherlands Antilles (Curaçao), Japan.

Gibraltar
Colony of Gibraltar

Geography Location: narrow peninsula running southward from southwest coast of Spain, to which it is connected by an isthmus. **Boundaries:** Spain to W and N, Mediterranean Sea to E, Morocco to S across Strait of Gibraltar. **Total land area:** 3 sq. mi. (6 sq km). **Coastline:** 7.5 mi. (12 km). **Comparative area:** about 11 times size of the Mall in Washington, D.C. **Land use:** 0% arable land; 0% permanent crops; 0% meadows and pastures; 0% forest and woodland; 100% other. **Major cities:** Gibraltar (capital).

People Population: 31,684 (July 1994 est.). **Nationality:** noun—Gibraltarian(s); adjective—Gibraltar. **Ethnic groups:** Italian, English, Maltese, Portuguese, and Spanish descent. **Languages:** English and Spanish are primary languages; Italian, Portuguese, Russian also spoken; English used in schools and for official purposes. **Religions:** 75% Roman Catholic, 8% Church of England, 2% Jewish.

Government Type: colony of UK. **Constitution:** May 30, 1969. **Heads of government:** Chief Sir John Chapple, governor (since Mar. 1993); Joe Bossano, chief minister (since Mar. 1988). **Structure:** parliamentary system comprising Gibraltar House of Assembly, Council of Ministers headed by chief minister, and Gibraltar Council; governor appointed by Crown.

Economy Monetary unit: Gibraltar pound. **Budget:** (1988) ***income:*** $136 mil.; ***expend.:*** $139 mil. **GNP:** $182 mil., $4,600 per capita (1987). **Chief crops:** N.A. **Livestock:** N.A. **Natural resources:** none. **Major industries:** tourism, banking and finance, construction; support to large UK naval and air bases. **Labor force:** about 14,800 (including non-Gibraltar laborers); UK military establishments and civil government employ nearly 50% of insured labor force. **Exports:** $82 mil. (1988); principally reexports—51% petroleum, 41% manufactured goods, 8% other. **Imports:** $258 mil. (1988); manufactured goods, fuels, foodstuffs. **Major trading partners:** UK, Morocco, Portugal, Netherlands, Spain, U.S., Germany.

Hong Kong

Geography Location: southern coast of China; consists of island of Hong Kong (22°17'N, 114°10'E), Stonecutters Island, Kowloon peninsula, and New Territories, which are partly on mainland. **Boundaries:** China to N, China sea to E, S, and W. **Total land area:** 402 sq. mi. (1,040 sq km). **Coastline:** 456 mi. (733 km). **Comparative area:** slightly less than six times size of Washington, D.C. **Land use:** 7% arable land; 1% permanent crops; 1% meadows and pastures; 12% forest and woodland; 79% other; includes 3% irrigated. **Major cities:** Victoria (capital).

People Population: 5,548,754 (July 1994 est.). **Nationality:** adjective—Hong Kong. **Ethnic groups:** 98% Chinese, 2% other. **Languages:** Chinese (Cantonese), English. **Religions:** 90% eclectic mixture of local religions, 10% Christian.

Government Type: colony of UK; scheduled to revert back to China on June 30, 1997. **Head of government:** Sir Chris Patten, governor (since July 1992). **Structure:** governor, assisted by advisory Executive Council, legislates with advice and consent of Legislative Council; Executive Council composed of governor, four ex officio senior officials, and 12 nominated members; Legislative Council composed of governor, three ex officio members, seven official members, 22 appointed unofficial members, and 24 unofficial members elected indirectly by functional constituencies and by an electoral college; Urban Council, consisting of 15 elected members and 15 appointed by governor, responsible for health, recreation, and resettlement in urban areas; Regional Council (established Apr. 1, 1986)—composed of 12 directly elected members, nine indirectly elected, 12 appointed, and three ex officio—has similar responsibilities in nonurban areas; independent judiciary.

Economy Monetary unit: Hong Kong dollar. **Budget:** (1994) ***income:*** $19.2 bil.; ***expend:*** $19.7 bil. **GDP:** $119 bil., $21,500 per capita (1993 est.). **Chief crops:** rice, vegetables, dairy products; minor part of economy. **Livestock:** chickens, pigeons, quail, ducks. **Natural resources:** Outstanding deepwater harbor, feldspar. **Major industries:** textiles, clothing, tourism, electronics, plastics, toys, watches, clocks. **Labor force:** 2.8 mil. (1990); 28.5% manufacturing, 27.9% wholesale and retail trade, restaurants and hotels, 17.7% services; 9.2% financing, insurance, and real estate; 4.5% transport and communications, 2.5% construction, 9.7% other. **Exports:** $145.1 bil. (1993 est.), including $104.2 bil. reexports; clothing, textiles, yarn, fabric, footwear, electrical appliances, watches and clocks, toys. **Imports:** $149.6 bil. (c.i.f., 1993 est.); foodstuffs, transport equipment, raw materials, semimanufactures, petroleum. **Major trading partners:** (1993) ***exports:*** 32% China, 23% U.S., 5% Germany, 5% Japan, 3% UK; ***imports:*** 36% China, 19% Japan, 9% Taiwan, 7% U.S.

Intl. Orgs. IMO, INTERPOL, WMO, WTO.

Montserrat

Geography Location: eastern Caribbean Sea (16°44'N, 62°14'W). **Boundaries:** Guadeloupe 35 mi. (55 km) to S, Antigua 27 mi. (47 km) to NE. **Total land area:** 39 sq. mi. (100 sq km). **Coastline:** 25 mi. (40 km). **Comparative area:** about three-fifths size of Washington, D.C. **Land use:** 20% arable land; 0% permanent crops; 10% meadows and pastures; 40% forest and woodland; 30% other. **Major cities:** (1980) Plymouth (capital) 3,500.

People Population: 12,701 (July 1994 est.). **Nationality:** noun—Montserratian(s); adjective—Montserratian. **Ethnic groups:** mostly black, with a few Europeans. **Languages:** English. **Religions:** Anglican, Methodist, Roman Catholic, Pentecostal, Seventh-day Adventist, other Christian denominations.

Government Type: colony of UK. **Heads of government:** Frank Savage, governor (since Feb. 1993); Reuben T. Meade, chief minister (since Oct. 1991). **Structure:** Executive Council presided over by governor, consisting of two ex officio members (attorney general and financial officer) and four unofficial members (chief minister and three other ministers); Legislative Council presided over by speaker chosen by council, seven elected, two official, and two nominated members.

Economy Monetary unit: East Caribbean dollar. **Budget:** (1988) ***income:*** $12.1 mil.; ***expend.:*** $14.3 mil. **GDP:** $53.7 mil., $4,300 per capita (1992 est.). **Chief crops:** cotton, limes, potatoes, tomatoes, hot peppers. **Livestock:** sheep, goats, cattle, pigs. **Natural resources:** negl. **Major industries:** tourism, light manufacturing—rum, textiles, electronic appliances. **Labor force:** 5,100 (1983 est.); 40.5% community, social, and personal services, 13.5% construction, 12.3% trade, restaurants, and hotels, 10.5% manufacturing. **Exports:** $2.8 mil. (f.o.b., 1992); plastic bags, electronic parts, textiles, hot peppers, live plants, cattle. **Imports:** $80.6 mil. (f.o.b., 1992); machinery and transport equipment, foodstuffs, manufactured goods, fuels, lubricants, related materials. **Major trading partners:** N.A.

Pitcairn Islands
Pitcairn, Henderson, Ducie, and Oeno Islands

Geography Location: group of islands (one inhabited) in South Pacific. Pitcairn 25°04'S 130°04'W. **Boundaries:** about halfway between Panama and New Zealand; French Polynesia to NW. **Total land area:** 18 sq. mi. (47 sq km). **Coastline:** 32 mi. (51 km). **Comparative area:** three-tenths size of Washington, D.C. **Major cities:** Adamstown (capital).

People Population: 71 (July 1994 est.). **Nationality:** noun—Pitcairn Islander(s); adjective—Pitcairn Islander. **Ethnic groups:** descendants of *Bounty* mutineers. **Languages:** English (official), also a Tahitian/English dialect. **Religion:** 100% Seventh-day Adventist.

Government Type: colony of UK. **Head of government:** David J. Moss, governor and UK high commissioner to New Zealand (since 1990). **Structure:** administered locally by Island Council consisting of four elected island officers, a secretary, and five nominated members.

Economy **Monetary unit:** New Zealand dollar. **Budget:** (1989 est.) ***income:*** $430,440; ***expend.:*** $429,983. **Chief crops:** citrus, sugarcane, watermelons, bananas, yams. **Natural resources:** miro trees (used for handicrafts), fish. **Major industries:** postage stamp sales. **Labor force:** no business community in usual sense; some public works; subsistence farming and fishing. **Exports:** fruits, vegetables, curios. **Imports:** fuel oil, machinery, building materials, flour, sugar, other foodstuffs.

St. Helena

Geography **Location:** eastern South Atlantic (15°58'S, 5°43'W). Dependencies are Ascension Is. (7°56'S, 14°25'W) 700 mi. to NW, and Tristan da Cunha (37°05'S, 12°17'W) 1,500 mi to SSW. **Boundaries:** Angola about 1,200 mi. (1,930 km) to E. **Total land area:** 158 sq. mi. (410 sq km). **Coastline:** 37 mi. (60 km). **Comparative area:** slightly more than 1.5 times size of Washington, D.C. **Land use:** 7% arable land; 0% permanent crops; 7% meadows and pastures; 3% forest and woodland; 83% other. **Major cities:** (1976) Jamestown (capital) 1,516.

People **Population:** 6,741 (July 1994 est.). **Nationality:** noun—St. Helenian(s); adjective—St. Helenian. **Languages:** English. **Religions:** Anglican majority; also Baptist, Seventh-day Adventist, Roman Catholic.

Government **Type:** colony of UK. **Constitution:** Jan. 1, 1967. **Head of government:** A.N. Hoole, governor. **Structure:** Executive Council, 12-member elected Legislative Council.

Economy **Monetary unit:** British pound. **Budget:** (1984) ***income:*** $3.2 mil.; ***expend.:*** $2.9 mil. **Chief crops:** maize, potatoes, vegetables; timber production being developed; crawfishing on Tristan de Cunha. **Livestock:** poultry, goats, sheep, cattle. **Natural resources:** fish; Ascension is sea turtle and sooty tern breeding ground; no minerals. **Major industries:** crafts (furniture, lacework, fancy woodwork), fish. **Labor force:** 2,516; 8.7% professional, technical, and related; 12.8% managerial, administrative, and clerical; 8.1% sales; 5.4% farmers and fishermen; 14.7% production process workers; 50.3% other (1987). **Exports:** $23,900 (f.o.b., 1984); fish (frozen skipjack, tuna, saltdried skipjack), handicrafts. **Imports:** $2.4 mil. (c.i.f., 1984); food, drink, tobacco, fuel oils, animal feed, building materials. **Major trading partners:** UK, South Africa.

Turks and Caicos Islands

Geography **Location:** more than 30 islands forming southeastern end of Bahamas Islands in Caribbean Sea. **Boundaries:** Haiti 90 mi (145 km) to S. **Total land area:** 166 sq. mi. (430 sq km). **Coastline:** about 186 mi. (about 300 km). **Comparative area:** slightly less than 2.5 times size of Washington, D.C. **Land use:** 2% arable land; 0% permanent crops; 0% meadows and pastures; 0% forest and woodland; 98% other. **Major cities:** Jamestown (capital).

People **Population:** 13,552 (July 1994 est.). **Ethnic groups:** mostly African descent. **Languages:** English. **Religions:** Anglican, Roman Catholic, Baptist, Methodist, Church of God, Seventh-day Adventist.

Government **Type:** colony of UK. **Constitution:** introduced on Aug. 30, 1976, suspended in 1986, and at present a constitutional commission is reviewing its contents. **National holiday:** Commonwealth Day, May 31. **Head of government:** Martin Bourke, governor (since Feb. 1993); Washington Missick, chief minister (since Mar. 1991). **Structure:** executive, bicameral legislature (Executive Council, 20-member Legislative Council), judicial (Supreme Court).

Economy **Monetary unit:** U.S. dollar. **Budget:** (1989) ***income:*** $20.3 mil.; ***expend.:*** $44 mil. **GDP:** $80.8 mil., $6,000 per capita (1992 est.). **Chief crops:** corn, beans. **Natural resources:** spiny lobster, conch. **Major industries:** fishing, tourism, offshore financial services. **Labor force:** some subsistence agriculture; majority engaged in fishing and tourist industries. **Exports:** $6.8 mil. (f.o.b., 1992); lobster, dried and fresh conch, conch shells. **Imports:** $42.8 mil. (1992); food and beverages, tobacco, clothing, manufactures, construction materials. **Major trading partners:** U.S., UK.

Uninhabited Territories

British Indian Ocean Territory (Diego Garcia 6°34'S, 72°24'E); South Georgia Is. (54°15'S, 36°45'W); South Orkney Is. (60°35'S, 45°30'W); South Sandwich Is. (56°00'S, 26°30'W); South Shetland Is. (62°00'S, 58°00'W).

THE UNITED NATIONS

STRUCTURE

Establishment Pres. Franklin D. Roosevelt coined the name United Nations, which was first used in the "Declaration by United Nations," Jan. 1, 1942, during World War II, when representatives of 26 countries pledged their governments to continue fighting together against the Axis Powers. From August to October 1944, representatives of China, the Soviet Union, the United Kingdom, and the United States met at Dumbarton Oaks, a mansion in Washington, D.C., to discuss creating an international peacekeeping organization. Out of these meetings came a general outline for the UN.

At the UN Conference on International Organization, which met at San Francisco from Apr. 25 to June 26, 1945, representatives from 50 countries drew up the UN Charter and signed it on June 26, 1945. Poland, not present at the conference, signed on Oct. 15, 1945, and is considered one of the 51 founding member states.

The UN officially came into existence on Oct. 24, 1945, when the charter was ratified by China, France, the Soviet Union, the United Kingdom, the United States, and by a majority of the other signatories.

UN Charter Full text of the charter may be purchased for $1 from the United Nations, Sales Section, New York, N.Y. 10017 U.S. The preamble to the charter sets forth the hopes for the UN:

WE THE PEOPLES OF THE UNITED NATIONS DETERMINED

- to save succeeding generations from the scourge of war . . .
- to reaffirm faith in fundamental human rights, in the dignity and worth of the human person, in the equal rights of men and women and of nations large and small, and
- to establish conditions under which justice and respect for the obligations arising from treaties and other sources of international law can be maintained, and
- to promote social progress and better standards of life in larger freedom,

AND FOR THESE ENDS

- to practice tolerance and live together in peace with one another as good neighbors, and
- to unite our strength to maintain international peace and security, and
- to ensure, by the acceptance of principles and the institution of methods, that armed force shall not be used, save in the common interest, and
- to employ international machinery for the promotion of the economic and social advancement of all peoples,

HAVE RESOLVED TO COMBINE OUR EFFORTS TO ACCOMPLISH THESE AIMS.

Accordingly, our respective Governments, through representatives assembled in the city of San Francisco, who have exhibited their full powers found to be in good and due form, have agreed to the present Charter of the United Nations and do hereby establish an international organization to be known as the United Nations.

Purposes The purposes of the United Nations as set forth in the Charter are: 1. To maintain international peace and security. 2. To develop friendly relations among nations based on respect for the principle of equal rights and self-determination of peoples. 3. To cooperate in solving international problems of an economic, social, cultural, or humanitarian character, and in promoting respect for human rights and fundamental freedoms for all. 4. To be a center for harmonizing the actions of nations in the attainment of these common ends.

UNITED NATIONS MEMBER STATES (185 member states as of July 1995)

Country	Joined UN	Country	Joined UN	Country	Joined UN	Country	Joined UN
Afghanistan	1946	Dominican Republic	1945	Libyan Arab Jamahiriya	1955	Saint Lucia	1979
Albania	1955	Ecuador	1945	Liechtenstein	1990	Saint Vincent and the Grenadines	1980
Algeria	1962	Egypt[3]	1945	Lithuania	1991	San Marino	1992
Andorra	1993	El Salvador	1945	Luxembourg	1945	São Tomé and Princípe	1975
Angola	1976	Equatorial Guinea	1968	Macedonia[4]	1993	Saudi Arabia	1945
Antigua and Barbuda	1981	Eritrea	1993	Madagascar	1960	Senegal	1960
Argentina	1945	Estonia	1991	Malawi	1964	Seychelles	1976
Armenia	1992	Ethiopia	1945	Malaysia[5]	1957	Sierra Leone	1961
Australia	1945	Fiji	1970	Maldives	1965	Singapore[5]	1965
Austria	1955	Finland	1955	Mali	1960	Slovak Republic	1993
Azerbaijan	1992	France	1945	Malta	1964	Slovenia	1992
Bahamas	1973	Gabon	1960	Marshall Islands	1991	Solomon Islands	1978
Bahrain	1971	Gambia	1965	Mauritania	1961	Somalia	1960
Bangladesh	1974	Georgia	1992	Mauritius	1968	South Africa	1945
Barbados	1966	Germany	1973	Mexico	1945	South Korea	1991
Belarus[1]	1945	Ghana	1957	Micronesia	1991	Spain	1955
Belgium	1945	Greece	1945	Moldova	1992	Sri Lanka	1955
Belize	1981	Grenada	1974	Monaco	1993	Sudan	1956
Benin	1960	Guatemala	1945	Mongolia	1961	Suriname	1975
Bhutan	1971	Guinea	1958	Morocco	1956	Swaziland	1968
Bolivia	1945	Guinea-Bissau	1974	Mozambique	1975	Sweden	1946
Bosnia and Herzegovina	1992	Guyana	1966	Myanmar	1948	Syrian Arab Republic[3]	1945
Botswana	1966	Haiti	1945	Namibia	1990	Tajikistan	1992
Brazil	1945	Honduras	1945	Nepal	1955	Tanzania[6]	1961
Brunei Darussalam	1984	Hungary	1955	Netherlands	1945	Thailand	1946
Bulgaria	1955	Iceland	1946	New Zealand	1945	Togo	1960
Burkina Faso	1960	India	1945	Nicaragua	1945	Trinidad and Tobago	1962
Burundi	1962	Indonesia	1950	Niger	1960	Tunisia	1956
Cambodia	1955	Iran	1945	Nigeria	1960	Turkey	1945
Cameroon	1960	Iraq	1945	North Korea	1991	Turkmenistan	1992
Canada	1945	Ireland	1955	Norway	1945	Uganda	1962
Cape Verde	1975	Israel	1949	Oman	1971	Ukraine	1945
Central African Republic	1960	Italy	1955	Pakistan	1947	United Arab Emirates	1971
Chad	1960	Ivory Coast	1960	Palau	1994	United Kingdom	1945
Chile	1945	Jamaica	1962	Panama	1945	United States	1945
China[2]	1945	Japan	1956	Papua New Guinea	1975	Uruguay	1945
Colombia	1945	Jordan	1955	Paraguay	1945	Uzbekistan	1992
Comoros	1975	Kazakhstan	1992	Peru	1945	Vanuatu	1981
Congo	1960	Kenya	1963	Philippines	1945	Venezuela	1945
Costa Rica	1945	Kyrgyzstan	1992	Poland	1945	Vietnam	1977
Croatia	1992	Kuwait	1963	Portugal	1955	Western Samoa	1976
Cuba	1945	Laos	1955	Qatar	1971	Yemen	1947
Cyprus	1960	Latvia	1991	Romania	1955	Yugoslavia	1945
Czech Republic	1993	Lebanon	1945	Russian Federation	1945	Zaire	1960
Denmark	1945	Lesotho	1966	Rwanda	1962	Zambia	1964
Djibouti	1977	Liberia	1945	Saint Kitts and Nevis	1983	Zimbabwe	1980
Dominica	1978						

1. On Sept. 19, 1991, Byelorussia informed the UN that it had changed its name to Belarus. 2. By resolution 2758 (XXVI) of Oct. 25, 1971, the General Assembly decided "to restore all its rights to the People's Republic of China and to recognize the representatives of its Government as the only legitimate representatives of China to the United Nations, and to expel forthwith the representatives of Chiang Kai-shek from the place they unlawfully occupy at the United Nations and in all the organizations related to it." 3. Egypt and Syria were original UN members from Oct. 24, 1945. Following a plebiscite on Jan. 21, 1958, the United Arab Republic was established by a union of Egypt and Syria and continued as a single member. On Oct. 13, 1961, Syria resumed its status as an independent state and simultaneously its UN membership. On Sept. 2, 1971, the United Arab Republic changed its name to Arab Republic of Egypt. 4. Provisionally referred to for all purposes within the UN as "the former Yugoslav Republic of Macedonia" pending settlement of the difference that had arisen with Greek Macedonia over the name. 5.The Federation of Malaya joined the UN on Sept. 17, 1957. On Sept. 16, 1963, its name was changed to Malaysia, following the admission to the new federation of Singapore, Sabah (North Borneo), and Sarawak. Singapore became an independent state on Aug. 9, 1965, and a UN member on Sept. 21, 1965. 6. Tanganyika was a UN member from Dec. 14, 1961, and Zanzibar was a member from Dec. 16, 1963. Following the ratification on Apr. 26, 1964, of Articles of Union between Tanganyika and Zanzibar, the United Republic of Tanganyika and Zanzibar continued as a single member, changing its name to the United Republic of Tanzania on Nov. 1, 1964.

Official languages Originally, there were five official languages of the UN: Chinese, English, French, Russian, and Spanish. Arabic was added to the General Assembly in 1973, to the Security Council in 1982, and to the Economic and Social Council in 1983. All major UN documents and all meetings of the General Assembly, the Security Council, and the Economic and Social Council are translated into the six working languages.

United Nations headquarters United Nations, New York, N.Y. 10017. The UN headquarters covers a 16-acre site in New York City along the East River from 42nd to 48th Streets. It consists of the interconnected General Assembly, Secretariat, and Dag Hammarskjold Library buildings. Across the street are other UN office buildings: One, Two, and Three UN Plaza. Acquisition of the site was made possible by a gift of $8.5 million from John D. Rockefeller, Jr., and one-third of that amount from New York

U.S. REPRESENTATIVES TO THE UN

The U.S. representative to the UN holds the title Ambassador Extraordinary and Plenipotentiary and heads the U.S. Mission to the UN.

Year	Ambassador
1946	Edward R. Stetinius, Jr.
1946–47	Herschel V. Johnson (acting)
1947–53	Warren R. Austin
1953–60	Henry Cabot Lodge, Jr.
1960–61	James J. Wadsworth
1961–65	Adlai E. Stevenson
1965–68	Arthur J. Goldberg
1968	George W. Ball
1968–69	James Russell Wiggins
1969–71	Charles W. Yost
1971–73	George Bush
1973–75	John A. Scali
1975–76	Daniel P. Moynihan
1976–77	William W. Scranton
1977–79	Andrew Young
1979–81	Donald McHenry
1981–85	Jeane J. Kirkpatrick
1985–89	Vernon A. Walters
1989–92	Thomas R. Pickering
1992–93	Edward J. Perkins
1993–present	Madeleine K. Albright

City. The Board of Design who drew the architectural plans consisted of an international team of architects from 10 countries. In the spring of 1951, the 39-story Secretariat building was complete and began functioning as the official UN home. The interiors of the buildings have been decorated by many gifts from governments and peoples from all over the world.

Geneva office United Nations, Palais des Nations, 1211 Geneva 10, Switzerland. The Palais des Nations houses the European offices of the UN. Located in Geneva, Switzerland, and built in 1936, the complex was the headquarters for the League of Nations.

Vienna office United Nations International Centre, A-1400 Vienna, Austria. The Austrian government built the Vienna International Centre at a cost of $700 million and offers the space rent-free to the UN and its agencies.

Permanent observers to the UN at the New York headquarters cannot vote and do not have diplomatic privileges or immunities. They do have free access to the public meetings and distribution of relevant documentation.

Nonmember observer states are the Holy See and Switzerland.

Intergovernmental and other observer organizations are the following: African, Caribbean, and Pacific Group of States; African Development Bank (ADB); Agency for Cultural and Technical Cooperation; Agency for the Prohibition of Nuclear Weapons in Latin America and the Caribbean; Asian-African Legal Consultative Committee; Commonwealth Secretariat; Council of Europe; European Union (EU); International Committee of the Red Cross; Latin American Economic System; League of Arab States; Organization of African Unity (OAU); Organization of American States (OAS); Organization of the Islamic Conference; Palestine.

PRINCIPAL ORGANS

The charter established six principal organs of the UN.

General Assembly

The Assembly is the world's forum for discussing major issues facing the world community, including world peace and security, human rights, global environment, disarmament, health issues, and the rights of women and children.

The Assembly consists of all 179 member states, each having one vote. On important issues a two-thirds majority of those present and voting is required; other questions require a simple majority vote. It usually holds annual sessions from September to December and may call for extra sessions when needed. Its agenda of more than 150 matters for discussion is first dealt with in seven main committees: First Committee—disarmament and related security issues; Second Committee—economic and financial matters; Third Committee—social, humanitarian, and cultural areas; Fourth Committee—decolonization; Fifth Committee—administrative and budgetary issues; Sixth Committee—legal matters; and the Special Political Committee. The Assembly discusses reports from each committee as well as reports from each UN program, other UN bodies, and the secretary-general. It conducts studies and makes recommendations (called resolutions) but has no power to enforce its decisions (resolutions), except the power of world opinion.

The Assembly considers and approves the UN budget and assesses member states according to their ability to pay.

Security Council

The Council may investigate any dispute or situation that might lead to international friction, and may recommend methods for adjusting such disputes or terms for their settlement. While other UN organs make recommendations to governments, the Council alone has the power to make decisions that member states are obligated under the charter to carry out.

The Security Council has 15 members. The charter designated five permanent members, and the General Assembly elects 10 other members for two-year terms. They are not eligible for immediate reelection. The presidency of the General Assembly rotates monthly among each of the members in turn, according to English alphabetical order. The Council may be called into session at any time, and a representative of each member state must be present at UN headquarters at all times.

The five permanent members are China, France, the Russian Federation, the United Kingdom, and the United States.

The terms of office of each current (1995) nonpermanent member end on Dec. 31 of the year indicated in parentheses: Argentina (1995), Botswana (1996), Czech Republic (1995), Germany (1996), Honduras (1996), Indonesia (1996), Italy (1996), Nigeria (1995), Oman (1995), Rwanda (1995).

Decisions on matters of procedure require the approval of at least nine of the 15 members. Decisions on all other matters also require nine votes, including the concurring votes of all five permanent members. A negative vote by any permanent member on a nonprocedural matter is often referred to as the veto, which results in the rejection of the proposal.

Economic and Social Council (ECOSOC)

The ECOSOC is the principal organ that coordinates the economic and social work of the UN and its specialized agencies. It makes recommendations and initiates activities relating to world trade, industrialization, natural resources, human rights, the status of women, population, social welfare, education, health and related matters, science and technology, and many other economic and social questions.

The ECOSOC has 54 members elected for three-year terms by the General Assembly. The term of office of current (1995) members expires on Dec. 31 of the year indicated in parentheses:

Australia (1997), Bahamas (1995), Belarus (1994), Bhutan (1995), Brazil (1997), Bulgaria (1996), Canada (1995), Chile (1996), China (1995), Colombia (1994), Costa Rica (1996), Cuba (1995), Denmark (1995), Egypt (1996), France (1996), Gabon (1995), Germany (1996), Ghana (1996), Greece (1996), India (1997), Indonesia (1996), Ireland (1996), Ivory Coast (1997), Jamaica (1997), Japan (1996), Libya (1995), Luxembourg (1997), Malaysia (1997), Mexico (1995), Netherlands (1997), Nigeria (1995), Norway (1995), Pakistan (1996), Paraguay (1996), Philippines (1997), Poland (1997), Portugal (1996), Romania (1995), Russian Federation (1995), Senegal (1996), South Africa (1997), South Korea (1995), Sri Lanka (1995), Sudan (1997), Tanzania (1996), Thailand (1997), Uganda (1997), Ukraine (1995), United Kingdom (1995), United States (1997), Venezuela (1996), Zaire (1995), Zimbabwe (1996).

The council generally holds two month-long sessions each year, one in New York and the other in Geneva. Its subsidiary bodies carry out year-round work. They consist of six Functional Commissions: Statistical Commission, Population Commission, Commission for Social Development, Commission on Human Rights, Commission on the Status of Women, and Commission on Narcotic Drugs. There are also five Regional Commissions: Economic Commission for Africa (ECA), in Addis Ababa, Ethiopia; Economic and Social Commission for Asia and the Pacific (ESCAP) in Bangkok, Thailand; Economic Commission for Europe (ECE) in Geneva, Switzerland; Economic Commission for Latin America and the Caribbean (ECLAC) in Santiago, Chile; Economic and Social Commission for Western Asia (ESCWA) in Baghdad, Iraq.

Relations with nongovernmental organizations (NGOs) Under the charter, the ECOSOC may consult with nongovernmental organizations (NGOs) concerned with matters within the council's competence. Over 1,200 NGOs have consultative status with the council and may send observers to public meetings of the council and its subsidiary bodies and may submit written statements relevant to the council's work. Examples of NGOs affiliated with ECOSOC include Amnesty International, Catholic Relief Services, Greenpeace International, Rotary International, The Hunger Project, the Sierra Club, and the Salvation Army.

Trusteeship Council

Supervising the administration of trust territories, the Council's goal is to promote the development of a territory toward self-government or independence.

The Trusteeship Council has five members: China, France, Russian Federation, United Kingdom, and the United States. With the independence of the Pacific island of Palau, the last remaining United Nations trust territory, the council successfully completed its mandate, and as such, formally suspended operations on Nov. 1, 1994. By a resolution adopted that day, the council amended its rules of procedure to drop the obligation to meet annually and agreed to meet only as occasion required—by its decision or the decision of its president, or at the request of a majority of its members or the General Assembly or the Security Council. Discussions are under way to determine the council's future.

International Court of Justice (World Court)

Created under the UN Charter as the UN's official judicial organ, the ICJ, or World Court, has its seat at The Hague, Netherlands. All UN member states are automatically members of the court. Nauru and Switzerland are parties to the statute of the court, although they are not members of the United Nations.

The court is not open to individuals. It issues judgments on all questions that states refer to it and all matters provided for in the UN Charter or in treaties or conventions in force. Both the General Assembly and the Security Council can ask the court for an advisory opinion on any legal question, as can other organs of the UN or its specialized agencies when authorized to do so by the assembly.

The court has dealt with a wide variety of subjects, including territorial rights, the delimitation of territorial waters and continental shelves, fishing jurisdiction, questions of nationality and the right of individuals to asylum, territorial sovereignty, and the right of passage through foreign territory.

The judgment of the court is final and without appeal. However, a revision may be applied for within 10 years from the date of the judgment on the ground of a new decisive factor. If a party rejects the judgment, the other party may take the issue to the Security Council.

Judges The International Court of Justice has 15 independent judges, of different nationalities, elected by both the General Assembly and the Security Council. Judges hold nine-year terms and may be reelected. The Court itself elects its president and vice president for three-year terms and is in permanent session, except during vacations. All questions are decided by a majority of the judges present; the president votes only in case of a tie.

The judges are the following (terms end on Feb. 5 of the year indicated in parentheses): *president:* Rosalyn Higgins of the United Kingdom (2000); *vice president:* Shigeru Oda of Japan (2003); *judges:* Andres Aguilar Mawdsley of Venezuela (2000); Mohammed Bedjaoui of Algeria (1997); Carl-August Fleischauter of Germany (2003); Gilbert Guillaume of France (2000); Geza Hercaegh of Hungary (2003); Abdul G. Koroma of Sierra Leone (2003); Raymond Ranjeva of Madagascar (2000); Stephen M. Schwebel of the United States (1997); Mohammed Shahabuddeen of Guyana (1997); Jiuyong Shi of China (2003); Vladlen S. Vereshchetin of the Russian Federation (1997); Christopher G. Weeramantry of Sri Lanka (2000); vacancy.

Secretariat

Servicing the other UN organs and administering the programs and policies they develop, the UN Secretariat is headed by the secretary-general. It consists of an international staff of more than 25,000 men and women from over 150 countries whose work includes administering peacekeeping operations; organizing international conferences on problems of worldwide concern; surveying world economic and social trends and problems; preparing studies on such subjects as human rights, disarmament, and development; interpreting speeches, translating documents, and supplying the world's communications media with information about the UN.

Relations with nongovernmental organizations (NGOs) More than 1,500 nongovernmental organizations (NGOs), committed to disseminating information about the work of the United Nations, are affiliated with the Department of Public Information (DPI). Each September the UN and NGOs hold a major conference on an aspect of the work of the United Nations at UN headquarters in New York City.

Secretary-general The General Assembly elects the secretary-general who may be reelected to terms of office of five years. The secretary-general cannot be from one of the permanent member states of the Security Council. Those who have served in this post are: Trygve Lie, Norway, Feb. 1, 1946, to Nov. 10, 1952; Dag Hammarskjold, Sweden, Apr. 11, 1953, to Sept. 17, 1961; U Thant, Burma, Nov. 3, 1961, to Dec. 31, 1971; Kurt Waldheim, Austria, Jan. 1, 1972, to Dec. 31, 1981; Javier Pérez de Cuéllar, Peru, Jan. 1, 1982, to Dec. 31, 1991; Boutros Boutros-Ghali, Egypt, Jan. 1, 1992, to present.

UNITED NATIONS PROGRAMS

Each UN program was created by the General Assembly and reports to it through the Economic and Social Council (ECOSOC).

UN programs, agencies, and commissions are headquartered around the world.

International Research and Training Institute for the Advancement of Women (INSTRAW) **Estab.**: 1979 (made UN program in 1985); **HQ:** Calle César Nicolas Penson, 102-A, Santo Domingo, Dominican Republic. Carries out research, training, and information activities worldwide to show and increase women's key role in development.

UN Centre for Human Settlements (Habitat) **Estab.**: 1978; **HQ:** P.O. Box 30030, Nairobi, Kenya. Works to provide models and tools so people can improve their housing. Major concerns are planning, financing, and management of human settlements—especially in developing countries.

UN Children's Fund (UNICEF) **Estab.**: 1946; **HQ:** UNICEF House, Three UN Plaza, New York, N.Y. 10017, U.S. Provides care for children in developing countries by working in both rural and urban settings to provide low-cost, community-based services in interrelated fields of maternal and child health, applied nutrition, clean water and sanitation, formal and nonformal education, and supporting services for women and girls. UNICEF has brought about a virtual revolution in child survival at low cost and in relatively short time, by emphasizing immunization, breast-feeding, growth monitoring, and a simple oral rehydration method.

UN Conference on Trade and Development (UNCTAD) **Estab.**: 1964; **HQ:** Place des Nations, 1211 Geneva 10, Switzerland. Formulates international trade policies, mediates multilateral trade agreements, and coordinates trade and development policies of governments and regional economic groups. Seeks to make international financial and monetary system more responsive to needs of developing countries.

UN Development Programme (UNDP) **Estab.**: 1965; **HQ:** One UN Plaza, New York, N.Y. 10017, U.S. Coordinates all development activities within UN system. Operates over 5,000 projects in 150 countries and territories to facilitate development in economic and social sectors, including farming, fishing, forestry, mining, manufacturing, power, transport, communications, housing, trade, health and environmental sanitation, economic planning, and public administration.

UN Disaster Relief Coordinator, Office of the (UNDRO) **Estab.**: 1972; **HQ:** Place des Nations, 1211 Geneva 10, Switzerland. Acts as focal point and clearinghouse for information on relief needs and on supplies sent by donors to meet those needs. Promotes study, prevention, control, and prediction of natural disasters and provides governments requesting it with assistance in predisaster planning.

UN Environment Programme (UNEP) **Estab.**: 1972; **HQ**: P.O. Box 30552, Nairobi, Kenya. Monitors significant changes in environment and encourages and coordinates sound environmental practices. Programs include Earthwatch, an international surveillance network with three main components: (1) Global Environmental Monitoring System, which monitors selected environmental factors and reports them to governments; (2) INFOTERRA, a computerized referral service to 20,000 sources in some 100 countries for environmental information; and (3) International Register of Potentially Toxic Chemicals, which works to provide scientific and regulatory information on chemicals.

UN High Commissioner for Refugees, Office of the (UNHCR) **Estab.**: 1950; **HQ**: Place des Nations, 1211 Geneva 10, Switzerland. Provides food, clothing, and shelter for refugees and works with governments to establish safe conditions whereby refugees may return home, and when that is not possible, seeks to ensure that refugees receive asylum. In 1988 UNHCR provided services for more than 12 million refugees worldwide.

UN Institute for Training and Research (UNITAR) **Estab.**: 1965; **HQ**: 801 UN Plaza, New York, N.Y. 10017, U.S. Provides training for members of UN's permanent missions, including courses on international economics, workshops in drafting and negotiating international legal instruments and in dispute settlement, and training in peace, security, human rights, and humanitarian assistance issues.

UN Population Fund (UNFPA) **Estab.**: 1969; **HQ**: 220 E. 42nd St., New York, N.Y. 10017, U.S. Provides assistance to population programs in developing countries; promotes understanding of key population factors—population growth, fertility, mortality, spatial distribution, and migration.

UN University (UNU) **Estab.**: 1973; **HQ**: Toho Seimei Building, 15–1, Shibuya 2-chome, Shibuya-ku, Tokyo 150, Japan. Has no students of its own, no campus, and no faculty. It is an international community of scholars engaged in research operating through worldwide networks of academic research institutions and is concerned with nine program areas, including peace and conflict resolution; global economy; energy systems and policy; resource policy and management; food-energy nexus; food, nutrition, biotechnology, and poverty; human and social development; and regional perspectives. Operates two research and training centers, one for development economics research, in Finland, and one for natural resources, on the Ivory Coast.

World Food Council (WFC) **Estab.**: 1974; **HQ**: Via delle Terme di Caracalla, 00100 Rome, Italy. Encourages developing countries to adopt national food strategy whereby they assess their food situation—needs, supply, potential for increasing production, storage, processing, transportation, and distribution; not engaged in field operations.

World Food Programme (WFP) **Estab.**: 1963; **HQ**: Via Cristoforo Colombo, 426, 00145 Rome, Italy. (Joint program operated by United Nations and Food and Agriculture Organization [FAO]). Provides food to support development activities and in times of emergencies. Operates projects in forestry, soil erosion control, irrigation, land rehabilitation, and rural settlements.

SPECIALIZED AGENCIES OF THE UNITED NATIONS

The specialized agencies associated with the United Nations are self-governing, independent organizations that work with the UN system and each other through the coordination machinery of the Economic and Social Council (ECOSOC). Each country affiliates with each agency on an individual basis. Membership in an agency is separate from UN membership. Specialized agencies have affiliations with nongovernmental organizations (NGOs) that have expertise in the work of the agency and that have been accepted for association.

Food and Agriculture Organization (FAO) **Member states**: 170; **Estab.**: Oct. 16, 1945; **HQ**: Via delle Terme di Caracalla, 00100 Rome, Italy. Works to increase output of farmlands, forests, and fisheries and to raise nutritional levels. Cosponsors World Food Programme, which uses food, cash, and services donated by member states for programs of social and economic development and for emergency situations.

International Atomic Energy Agency (IAEA) **Member states**: 121; **Estab.**: July 29, 1957; **HQ**: Vienna International Centre, P.O. Box 100, A-1400 Vienna, Austria. (Not regular specialized agency in that it does not report through ECOSOC but directly to General Assembly.) To foster and guide development of peaceful uses of atomic energy, it establishes standards for nuclear safety and environmental protection, aids member countries through technical cooperation, and fosters exchange of scientific and technical information on nuclear energy.

International Civil Aviation Organization (ICAO) **Member states**: 183; **Estab.**: Apr. 4, 1947; **HQ**: 1000 Sherbrooke St. West, Suite 400, Montreal, Quebec H3A 2R2, Canada. Works for safer air travel conditions worldwide. Establishes visual and instrument flight rules for pilots and crews, develops aeronautical charts for navigation, coordinates aircraft radio frequencies, and works with customs procedures.

International Fund for Agricultural Development (IFAD) **Member states**: 157; **Estab.**: Nov. 30, 1977; **HQ**: Via del Serafico 10,00142 Rome, Italy. Lends money to peoples in developing countries for agricultural development projects, including livestock, fisheries, processing and storage, irrigation, research, and training.

International Labour Organisation (ILO) **Member states**: 171; **Estab.**: 1919, under Treaty of Versailles, became UN specialized agency Dec. 14, 1946; **HQ**: 4, route des Morillons, CH-1211 Geneva 22, Switzerland. Promotes social justice for working people everywhere by formulating international policies and programs to help improve working and living conditions; creates international labor standards to serve as guidelines for governments and assists in vocational training, management techniques, occupational safety, and health.

International Maritime Organization (IMO) **Member states**: 149; **Estab.**: Mar. 17, 1958; **HQ**: 4 Albert Embankment, London SE1 SR, England. Works to improve international shipping procedures and encourages highest standards in maritime safety; seeks to prevent and control marine pollution from ships and sets standards for training and certification of seafarers.

International Monetary Fund (IMF) **Member states**: 179; **Estab.**: Dec. 27, 1945; **HQ**: 700 19th St. NW, Washington, D.C. 20431. Makes financing available to members in balance-of-payments difficulties and provides technical assistance to improve their economic management.

International Telecommunication Union (ITU) **Member states**: 182; **Estab.**: 1865 (became UN specialized agency Jan. 1949); **HQ**: Place des Nations, 1211 Geneva 20, Switzerland. Coordinates use of radio frequencies, tracks positions assigned by countries to geostationary satellites, creates telecommunication equipment, promotes safety measures, and conducts studies.

UN Educational, Scientific and Cultural Organization (UNESCO) **Member states**: 183; **Estab.**: Nov. 4, 1946; **HQ**: 7, Place de Fontenoy, 75007 Paris, France. Promotes literacy through programs in teacher training, building schools, and developing textbooks. Natural-science programs include Man and the Biosphere; Intergovernmental Oceanographic Commission; and International Hydrological and International Geological Correlation programs. Other activities include study and development of cultures, and conservation of world's inheritance of books, art, and monuments.

UN Industrial Development Organization (UNIDO) **Member states**: 166; **Estab.**: 1966 (became UN specialized agency Jan. 1, 1986); **HQ**: Wagramerstrasse 5, Vienna XXII, Austria. Promotes and accelerates industrialization of developing countries by providing technical assistance, training programs, and advisory services. Serves as clearinghouse for industrial information; collects, analyzes, publishes, standardizes, and improves industrial statistics.

Universal Postal Union (UPU) **Member states**: 184; **Estab.**: July 1, 1875 (became UN specialized agency July 1, 1948); **HQ**: Weltpoststrasse 4, Bern, Switzerland. Establishes regulations for smooth exchange of mail worldwide.

World Bank Group of three institutions sharing one address. **HQ:** 1818 H St. NW, Washington, D.C. 20433. *International Bank for Reconstruction and Development (IBRD)* **Member states:** 178; **Estab.**: Dec. 27, 1945, to provide loans and technical assistance to developing countries to assist in their reconstruction and development. *International Finance Corporation (IFC)* **Member states:** 161 (membership open only to World Bank members); **Estab.**: July 20, 1956, to stimulate flow of private capital into productive investment in member countries. While closely associated with Bank, IFC is separate legal entity and its funds are distinct from those of Bank. *International Development Association (IDA)* **Member states:** 135; **Estab.**: Sept. 24, 1960. (Affiliate of Bank, IDA has same directors and staff as Bank.) Lends money to poor countries on easier terms than Bank alone could give.

World Health Organization (WHO) Member states: 189; **Estab.**: Apr. 7, 1948; **HQ:** 20, avenue Appia, 1211 Geneva 27, Switzerland. Coordinates programs aimed at solving health problems by working with governments, other UN agencies, and nongovernmental organizations. In 1977 WHO set "Health for All by the Year 2000" as overriding priority and developed eight-point strategy for implementation, including education on current health issues; proper food supply and nutrition; safe water and sanitation; maternal and child health; immunization against major infectious diseases; and prevention and control of local diseases. WHO is coordinating global strategy to control and prevent AIDS (acquired immune deficiency syndrome).

World Intellectual Property Organization (WIPO) **Member states:** 149; **Estab.**: 1883 (became a UN specialized agency Dec. 17, 1974); **HQ:** 34, chemin des Colombettes, 121 Geneva 20, Switzerland. Promotes protection of intellectual property and cooperation in enforcement of agreements on matters such as copyrights, trademarks, industrial designs, and patents.

World Meteorological Organization (WMO) **Member states:** 177; **Estab.**: 1873 (became UN specialized agency Mar. 23, 1950); **HQ:** 41, avenue Giuseppe-Motta, 1211 Geneva 20, Switzerland. Facilitates exchange of weather reports among countries; established World Weather Watch to track global weather conditions.

PEACEKEEPING OPERATIONS

United Nations peacekeeping is the use of multinational forces, under UN command, to keep disputing countries or communities from fighting while efforts are made to help them negotiate a solution. It is undertaken only with the agreement of the parties. UN Peacekeeping Forces received the Nobel Peace Prize in 1988. As of June 1995, the United Nations had 16 peacekeeping operations, comprising approximately 69,000 men and women peacekeepers from more than 75 countries. Current peacekeeping operations are described below.

UN Truce Supervision Organization (UNTSO) **Estab.**: 1948. Mandate has evolved. Currently UN observers (220) assist peacekeeping operations in Middle East. (Fatalities: 28.)

UN Military Observer Group in India and Pakistan (UNMOGIP) **Estab.**: 1948. UN observers (39) are stationed on both sides of Line of Control agreed on by India and Pakistan under Simla agreement of July 1972 to observe the cease-fire. (Fatalities: 6.)

UN Peacekeeping Force in Cyprus (UNFICYP) **Estab.**: 1964. UN troops (1,200) and civilian police (35) control 112-mile (180 km) buffer zone between cease-fire lines agreed on by Cyprus National Guard and Turkish forces. (Fatalities: 165.)

UN Disengagement Observer Force (UNDOF) **Estab.**: 1974. UN troops and observers (1,035) maintain "area of separation" on Golan Heights between Israel and Syria and verify arms limitations on both sides of the area. (Fatalities: 37.)

UN Interim Force in Lebanon (UNIFIL) **Estab.**: 1978. UN troops (5,146) are in southern Lebanon to confirm withdrawal of Israeli forces, restore international peace and security, and assist Lebanese government in ensuring return of its authority in area. (Fatalities: 200.)

UN Iraq-Kuwait Observation Mission (UNIKOM) **Estab.**: 1991. Comprises military observers (251)—including for the first time observers from the five permanent members of the Security Council serving together—to monitor demilitarized zone set up by Security Council on Iraq-Kuwait border and along Khor Abdullah waterway. (Fatalities: 3.)

UN Mission for the Referendum in Western Sahara (MINURSO) **Estab.**: September 1991. Composed of mainly military personnel (344 observers, including support elements). Mandate limited to monitoring and verification of cease-fire, pending agreement between parties on criteria for eligibility to vote in the referendum. (Fatalities: 4.)

UN Observer Mission in Georgia (UNOMIG) **Estab.**: August 1993. Mandated to verify compliance with cease-fire agreement of July 27, 1993, between Republic of Georgia and Abkhazia, a territory in Georgia's northwestern region on Black Sea that had tried to separate from the Republic. Enduring several breakdowns in the cease-fire, a negotiated settlement was reached on Apr. 4, 1994, to end the conflict. (184 observers.)

UN Observer Mission in Liberia (UNOMIL) **Estab.**: September 1993. First UN peacekeeping mission undertaken in cooperation with a peacekeeping operation already set up by another organization. UNOMIL works with Economic Community of West African States (ECOWAS) in implementation of Cotonau Peace Agreement to end civil war in Liberia and to set up transitional government. (84 observers.)

UN Assistance Mission in Rwanda (UNAMIR) **Estab.**: October 1993. Authorized to comprise 5,400 military personnel, 50 military police, and 90 civilian police personnel and mandated to implement Arusha Peace Agreement. Expectations that transitional government and transitional National Assembly would be set up in January 1994 were not met and violence and ethnic fighting broke out. (Fatalities: 16.)

UN Angola Verification Mission III (UNAVEM III) **Estab.**: February 1995. Mandated to oversee implementation of Lusaka Protocol of November 1994. Authorized strength of 7,000 military personnel, 350 military observers, and 260 civilian police observers.

UN Mission of Observation in Tajikistan (UNMOT) **Estab.**: December 1994. Seventeen observers help to implement a cease-fire agreement between the government and opposition forces, negotiated under UN auspices.

UN Mission in Haiti (UNMIH) **Estab.**: March 1995. On Jan. 30, 1995, the Security Council agreed that transfer of responsibility from multinational force to UNMIH was to be completed by Mar. 31, and authorized up to 6,000 troops and 900 civilian police officers to establish an effective national police force, to improve the functioning of Haiti's justice system and to monitor free elections in June.

UNPROFOR On Mar. 31, 1995, Security Council resolutions 981, 982, and 983 divided the role of UN forces in the former Yugoslavia into three separate operations, under three different mandates, but with one central command. *UN Protection Force (UNPROFOR)* **Estab.**: March 1992. Currently consists of 39,789 troops, 593 military observers, and 664 civilian police. UNPROFOR is *inter alia,* deployed in United Nations Protected Areas in Croatia; provides protection for humanitarian convoys and safe areas in Bosnia and Herzegovina, and monitors borders of former Yugoslav Republic of Macedonia as a preventive deployment of United Nations peacekeepers. (Fatalities: 131.) *UN Confidence Restoration Operation in Croatia (UNCRO)* **Estab.**: May 1995. Mandated to monitor cease-fire agreement of March 1994 between Croatia and local Serb authorities to provide protection for delivery of international humanitarian assistance to Bosnia and Herzegovina and provide other support for UN mandates. *UN Preventive Deployment Force in the former Yugoslav Republic of Macedonia (UNPREDEP)* **Estab.**: March 1995. Mandated to cooperate between UNPROFOR and mission of the Organization for Security and Cooperation in Europe (OSCE).

KEY EVENTS IN UN HISTORY

1946 (Jan. 10) First session of General Assembly begins at London with delegates of 51 member states.

1947 (Nov. 29) General Assembly passes Plan of Partition with Economic Union concerning the future government of Palestine, thereby paving way for government of Tel Aviv to declare State of Israel on May 14, 1948.

1948 (Dec. 10) Universal Declaration of Human Rights adopted by General Assembly.
UN pioneers concept of peacekeeping observer missions and peacekeeping forces (1956).
UN technical assistance to developing countries begins with appropriation of $350,000. Today UN Development Program alone helps finance development activities valued at over $2 billion a year.

1949 Mediates cease-fire between India and Pakistan, ending two years of fighting over control of Kashmir.
Mediates cease-fire between Israel and Arab states.

1950 Security Council calls member states to help South Korea repel invasion from North Korea. (USSR absent from Council, protesting exclusion of People's Republic of China from UN.)
Economic and Social Council adopts Standard International Trade Classification as basis for gathering world trade statistics.

1953 UN coordinates first global-census effort and establishes earth's population for first time in history—2.4 billion people.
Signs truce with North Korea ending conflict with South Korea.

1955 First of ongoing congresses of criminologists and police officials draws up international principles and standards of criminal justice.

1959 UN General Assembly adopts Declaration on the Rights of the Child.

1960 Under decolonization program 17 territories become newly independent States, 16 in Africa, and join UN.
UN Educational, Scientific and Cultural Organization coordinates aid from 50 nations to move Egyptian temples at Abu Simbel to higher ground while Aswan High Dam being built.

1962 Secretary-general plays key role in resolving U.S.-Soviet confrontation over issue of nuclear missiles in Cuba.

1963 Security Council calls for voluntary arms embargo against South Africa. (Made mandatory in 1977.)

1964 Having restored law and order, peacekeeping troops withdraw from Congo (now Zaire).

1967 After war erupts in Middle East, Security Council adopts Resolution 242, calling for withdrawal of forces from occupied territories, and recognizes right of all states in area to security.
UN begins international standardization of geographical names and publishes international geographical dictionaries.
Mediates settlement of Six-Day Arab-Israeli War.

1970 General Assembly adopts first internationally agreed-on set of principles on seabed and ocean floor beyond national jurisdiction. Declares area "common heritage" of humanity.

1972 UN Environment Conference meets at Stockholm; adopts declaration to coordinate environmental issues internationally.

1973 Security Council orders cease-fire in 17-day-old Middle East War and sends peacekeeping force to prevent further fighting between Israel and Arab states.

1975 UN conference at Mexico City launches Decade for Women to begin major effort toward women's equality worldwide.

1979 World Health Organization announces smallpox eradicated from all peoples on earth.

1983 Commission on Status of Women establishes procedure to receive and respond to citizens' complaints of sex discrimination by governments.

1985 General Assembly establishes Program of Action for African Recovery and Development, 1986–90.

1987 First International Conference on Drug Abuse and Illicit Trafficking (at Vienna) develops program on international coordination of illicit-drug issues.
General Assembly receives Report of World Commission on Environment and Development ("Our Common Future")—describes environmental threats and plan for "sustainable development."

1988 Mediates ending of Iran-Iraq War. UN mediates Soviet withdrawal from Afghanistan and establishes Operation Salam to rebuild country.

1989 Mediates withdrawal of Cuban troops from Angola and South African troops from Namibia.
UN sends peacekeeping troops and advisers to Namibia to supervise elections aimed at setting up self-government.
UN sends peacekeeping operation to Nicaragua to monitor free elections.
General Assembly adopts Convention on the Rights of the Child.

1990 Monitors demobilization of Nicaraguan rebel forces, and for first time monitors a presidential campaign and election in an independent nation.
World Summit for Children brings together leaders of 70 nations to approve plan to improve lives of children.
Security Council Resolution 678 calls upon member states to restore peace and security in Kuwait by "all necessary means."
Security Council agrees on plan for comprehensive settlement of 11-year civil war in Cambodia, setting stage for UN peacekeeping operation in Cambodia.
Responding to request by Haiti, UN supervises election of Haiti's first freely elected president.

1991 (Apr. 3) Security Council Resolution 687 sets terms of cease-fire in Gulf War and gives UN variety of duties to ensure peace.
UN teams begin to dismantle Iraq's nuclear weapons capability.
Secretary-general negotiates cease fire in 16-year-old civil war in Angola.
UNICEF and WHO certify that 80 percent of all world's one-year-olds are immunized against the six deadly childhood diseases (diphtheria, whooping cough, measles, tuberculosis, polio, and tetanus); spread of these diseases is effectively halted.
General Assembly establishes first register of international arms sales, hoping to curb trafficking by publicizing transactions and to identify potential trouble spots where arms are increasing.
(Dec. 4) Secretary-general negotiates release of last six hostages held in Lebanon, Terry Anderson being the last released.
(Dec. 16) General Assembly rescinds its Resolution 3379 of Nov. 10, 1975, that Zionism is a form of racism.

1992 Secretary-general completes peace negotiations between government of El Salvador and rebel Farabundo Marti National Liberation Front (FMLN).
UN sends some 20,000 staff into Cambodia to manage the government and to set up free elections to be held April/May 1993.
Convenes Earth Summit at Rio de Janeiro with leaders from 170 nations and some 30,000 citizens, opens Convention on Climate Change and Convention on Biological Diversity, and issues Agenda 21 as blueprint to save environment.
General Assembly establishes Commission on Sustainable Development to assist in implementation of Agenda 21.
(Dec. 10) Representatives from world's indigenous people address General Assembly for the first time ever, officially opening UN's International Year of Indigenous Peoples: 1993.

1993 145 nations cosponsor Convention on Prohibition of the Development, Production, Stockpiling and Use of Chemical Weapons, which opens for nations to sign and ratify.
(Feb. 23) Human Rights Commission adopts Resolution 1993/8, which states that "abhorrent practice of rape and abuse of women and children in the former Yugoslavia . . . constitutes a war crime"—this is the first formal statement that explicitly declares rape, conducted during war, an international war crime under the Geneva Convention.
(Dec. 13) General Assembly creates post of High Commissioner for Human Rights with power to intervene wherever basic freedoms are suppressed.

1994 (June 27) Security Council removes South Africa from its agenda, thereby declaring the end of apartheid.
(Nov. 8) Security Council establishes International Tribunal for Rwanda to prosecute persons responsible for genocide and other violations of international humanitarian law committed in Rwanda and by Rwandan citizens for such crimes in neighboring countries between Jan. 1, 1994, and Dec. 31, 1994.

1995 (Feb. 1) Secretary-General launches United Nations 50th anniversary commemoration. International Tribunal for Former Yugoslavia, established May 25, 1993, to prosecute persons

responsible for serious violations of international humanitarian law in former Yugoslavia since 1991, schedules first trials for September with 15 judges from 15 countries.
(March–May) World Health Organization (WHO) organizes countries in Middle East, Caucasus, and Central Asian Republics to immunize 70 million children against polio.
(June) UN supervises free elections in Haiti.

FURTHER UN INFORMATION

General Information UN Information Center, 1889 F St. NW, Washington, D.C. 20006; 202–289–8670—free materials, loans UN films, interlibrary loan program, library. Public Inquiries Unit, UN, Room GA-57, New York, N.Y. 10017; 212–963–4475—general information, free charts, booklets, and study kits on work of the UN.
Sales Publications UN Sales, UN, Room DC-2853, New York, N.Y. 10017; 212–963–8302; 1–800–253–9646—free publications catalog.
United Nations Bookstore Room GA-32, New York, N.Y. 10017; 212–963–7680, 1–800–553–3210; Fax: 212–963–4910. International publications issued by UN bodies and independent publishers.

MODEL UNITED NATIONS

The Model United Nations (MUN) is a simulation of the activities of the UN conducted by high school and college students worldwide. The MUN introduces students to important concepts in international relations and global diplomacy by having them assume the roles of nations' delegates in simulated sessions of the General Assembly, the Security Council, and various UN committees. Current situations are simulated, and the participants must use accurate documentation.

In the United States, more than 70,000 students in approximately 2,500 high schools and colleges participate in MUN simulations, and approximately 100 major annual conferences are held at colleges and universities.

While teachers and students can conduct their simulations informally, the United Nations Association–USA provides coordinating services to those who chose to affiliate. UNA-USA provides a calendar of conferences, teacher and student guides, and training sessions. UNA-USA, 485 Fifth Avenue, New York, N.Y. 10017; 212–697–3232.

MUN documents are provided by the Public Inquiries Unit. Cost is $15 for postage.

UN INFORMATION ON-LINE

More than 40 UN databases can be accessed from:
gopher://gopher.undp.org
http://www.undp.org
gopher://gopher.unicc.org
http://www.unicc.org

INTERNATIONAL ORGANIZATIONS

Only those states having full official membership are listed as members; states having special relations and observer status to an organization are not included. Membership is as of June 1994. Contact headquarters to obtain publications produced by the organization.

Association of South East Asian Nations (ASEAN) HQ: Jalan Sisingamangaraja, P.O. Box 2072, Jakarta, Indonesia. **Estab.:** Aug. 9, 1967, in Bangkok, to promote political and economic cooperation among non-Communist states of region by coordinating policies in trade, transportation, communications, agriculture, science, finance, and culture. **Members** (7): Brunei, Indonesia, Malaysia, Philippines, Singapore, Thailand, Vietnam.

Caribbean Community and Common Market (CARICOM) HQ: Bank of Guyana Building, P.O. Box 10827, Georgetown, Guyana. **Estab.:** By Treaty of Chaguaramas in 1973 (replaced Caribbean Free Trade Association (CARIFTA), founded in 1965). Movement toward unity in the Caribbean that formulates policies and cooperation in services such as education, health, labor matters, and foreign policy. **Members** (14): Bahamas (member of Community but not Common Market), Barbados, Belize, Dominica, Dominican Republic, Grenada, Guyana, Haiti, Jamaica, Montserrat, Saint Christopher and Nevis, Saint Lucia, Saint Vincent and the Grenadines, Trinidad and Tobago.

Colombo Plan for Cooperative Economic and Social Development in Asia and the Pacific (the Colombo Plan) HQ: 12 Melbourne Ave, P.O. Box 596, Colombo 4, Sri Lanka. **Estab.:** 1950, by seven Commonwealth nations to promote development by newly independent Asian members. Plan has expanded to fostering international effort to aid economic and social development of Asian members. Developed member states provide assistance to developing nations, and countries within region promote economic and technical cooperation among themselves. **Members** (26): Afghanistan, Australia, Bangladesh, Bhutan, Cambodia, Canada, Fiji, India, Indonesia, Iran, Japan, Laos, Malaysia, Maldives, Myanmar, Nepal, New Zealand, Pakistan, Papua New Guinea, Philippines, South Korea, Singapore, Sri Lanka, Thailand, UK, U.S.

Commonwealth HQ: Marlborough House, Pall Mall, London, SW1Y 5HX, England. **Estab.:** By some members of British Empire through evolutionary process formalized by Statute of Westminster on Dec. 31, 1931. Modern Commonwealth was born in 1949, when member countries accepted India's intention of becoming republic while continuing "her full membership of the Commonwealth of Nations." Created to promote cooperation among countries presently or formerly part of British Empire, Commonwealth is voluntary association of independent states and has no written constitution and no rigid contractual obligations. Emphasis is on consultation and exchange of views for cooperation, especially in economic affairs, drug trafficking, international terrorism, and technical assistance to less developed states. Some countries that were part of British Empire are not part of Commonwealth. Observer at the UN. **Members** (48) (year of entry): Antigua and Barbuda (1981), Australia (1931), Bahamas (1973), Bangladesh (1972), Barbados (1966), Belize (1981), Botswana (1966), Brunei (1984), Canada (1931), Cyprus (1961), Dominica (1978), Gambia (1965), Ghana (1957), Grenada (1974), Guyana (1966), India (1947), Jamaica (1962), Kenya (1963), Kiribati (1979), Lesotho (1966), Malawi (1964), Malaysia (1957), Maldives (1982), Malta (1964), Mauritius (1968), Namibia (1990), New Zealand (1931), Nigeria (1960), Pakistan (1989), Papua New Guinea (1975), Seychelles (1976), Sierra Leone (1961), Singapore (1965), Solomon Islands (1978), Sri Lanka (1948), St. Kitts and Nevis (1983), St. Lucia (1979), St. Vincent and the Grenadines (1979), Swaziland (1968), Tanzania (1961), Tonga (1970), Trinidad and Tobago (1962), Uganda (1962), UK (1931), Vanuatu (1980), Western Samoa (1970), Zambia (1964), Zimbabwe (1980).

Commonwealth of Independent States (CIS) HQ: Temporary address: Working Group for the CIS, 220016 City of Minsk, Karl Marx Street, 38, Supreme Council of the Rep. of Belarus. **Estab.:** Dec. 8, 1991, by Byelorussia (Belarus), Russian Federation, and Ukraine, which dissolved the USSR and created the CIS. Members agree to broad cooperation, including to maintain current borders, respect ethnic diversity, cooperate in trade and foreign policy, preserve the environment, and develop transport and communication systems. **Members** (10): Armenia, Byelorussia (Belarus), Kazakhstan, Kyrgyzstan, Moldavia (Moldova), Russia, Tajikistan, Turkmenistan, Ukraine, Uzbekistan.

European Union (EU, the Common Market) See Part III: "The International Economy."

International Criminal Police Organization (ICPO/INTERPOL) HQ: 26 rue Armengaud, 92210 Saint-Cloud, France. **Estab.:** By Second International Criminal Police Congress at Vienna in 1923, "to ensure and promote the widest possible mutual assistance between all criminal police authorities within the limits of the law existing in the different countries and in the spirit of the Universal Declaration of Human Rights." **Members** (146): Algeria, Angola, Andorra, Antigua and Barbuda, Argentina, Aruba, Australia, Austria, Bahamas,

Bahrain, Bangladesh, Barbados, Belgium, Belize, Benin, Bolivia, Botswana, Brazil, Brunei, Burkina Faso, Burundi, Cambodia, Cameroon, Canada, Central African Republic, Chad, Chile, China, Colombia, Congo, Costa Rica, Cuba, Cyprus, Denmark, Djibouti, Dominica, Dominican Republic, Ecuador, Egypt, Equatorial Guinea, Ethiopia, Fiji, Finland, France, Gabon, Gambia, Germany, Ghana, Greece, Grenada, Guatemala, Guinea, Guyana, Haiti, Honduras, Hungary, Iceland, India, Indonesia, Iran, Iraq, Ireland, Israel, Ivory Coast, Italy, Jamaica, Japan, Jordan, Kenya, Kiribati, Kuwait, Laos, Lebanon, Lesotho, Liberia, Libya, Liechtenstein, Luxembourg, Madagascar, Malawi, Malaysia, Maldives, Mali, Malta, Mauritania, Mauritius, Mexico, Monaco, Morocco, Myanmar, Nauru, Nepal, Netherlands, Netherlands Antilles, New Zealand, Nicaragua, Niger, Nigeria, Norway, Oman, Pakistan, Panama, Papua New Guinea, Paraguay, Peru, Philippines, Portugal, Qatar, Romania, Rwanda, Saudi Arabia, Senegal, Seychelles, Sierra Leone, Singapore, Somalia, South Korea, Spain, Sri Lanka, St. Kitts and Nevis, St. Lucia, St. Vincent, Sudan, Suriname, Swaziland, Sweden, Switzerland, Syria, Tanzania, Thailand, Togo, Tonga, Trinidad and Tobago, Tunisia, Turkey, Uganda, United Arab Emirates, UK, Uruguay, U.S., Venezuela, Yemen, Yugoslavia, Zaire, Zambia, Zimbabwe.

International Telecommunication Satellite Organization (INTELSAT) HQ: 3400 Internal Drive NW, Washington, D.C. 20008. **Estab.:** Feb. 12, 1973, by two international agreements to maintain and operate the global satellite system used by public international telecommunication services. Operates space equipment and Earth stations owned by telecommunication entities in each country. INTELSAT's 13-satellite system provides about two-thirds of world's international telecommunication services to more than 140 countries. Services include telephone, television, facsimile, data, and telex transmissions. **Members** (120): Afghanistan, Algeria, Angola, Argentina, Australia, Austria, Bangladesh, Bahamas, Barbados, Belgium, Benin, Bolivia, Burkina Faso, Brazil, Cameroon, Canada, Cape Verde, Central African Republic, Chad, Chile, China, Colombia, Congo, Costa Rica, Cyprus, Denmark, Dominican Republic, Ecuador, Egypt, El Salvador, Ethiopia, Fiji, Finland, France, Gabon, Germany, Ghana, Greece, Guatemala, Guinea, Haiti, Holy See, Honduras, Iceland, India, Indonesia, Iran, Iraq, Ireland, Israel, Italy, Ivory Coast, Jamaica, Japan, Jordan, Kenya, Kuwait, Lebanon, Libya, Liechtenstein, Luxembourg, Madagascar, Malawi, Malaysia, Mali, Mauritania, Mauritius, Mexico, Monaco, Morocco, Mozambique, Nepal, Netherlands, New Zealand, Nicaragua, Niger, Nigeria, Norway, Oman, Pakistan, Panama, Papua New Guinea, Paraguay, Peru, Philippines, Portugal, Qatar, Romania, Rwanda, Saudi Arabia, Senegal, Singapore, Somalia, South Africa, South Korea, Spain, Sri Lanka, Sudan, Swaziland, Sweden, Switzerland, Syria, Tanzania, Thailand, Togo, Trinidad and Tobago, Tunisia, Turkey, Uganda, United Arab Emirates, United Kingdom, Uruguay, U.S., Venezuela, Vietnam, Yugoslavia, Yemen, Zaire, Zambia, Zimbabwe.

North Atlantic Treaty Organization (NATO) HQ: 1110 Brussels, Belgium. **Estab.:** By North Atlantic Treaty on Aug. 24, 1949, as international defense organization composed of European countries, Canada, and U.S. Members agree to settle disputes among each other by peaceful means and regard attack on one as attack on all. Members develop joint defense plans, consult on political problems, share science and technology, and organize joint training. NATO attempts to maintain military balance with countries of Warsaw Pact. NATO forces comprise three elements: conventional forces, intermediate and short-range nuclear forces, and strategic nuclear forces of UK and U.S. NATO consists of three commands: European Command, HQ in Casteau, Belgium; Atlantic Ocean Command, HQ in Norfolk, Va., U.S.; and Channel Command, HQ in Northwood, UK. **Members** (16): Belgium, Canada, Denmark, France, Germany, Greece, Iceland, Italy, Luxembourg, Netherlands, Norway, Portugal, Spain, Turkey, UK, U.S.

Organization of African Unity (OAU) HQ: P.O. Box 3243, Addis Ababa, Ethiopia. **Estab.:** By charter on May 25, 1963, at Addis Ababa, to promote unity and solidarity among African states. OAU works to eradicate all forms of colonialism from Africa and to defend their sovereignty, territorial integrity, and independence. Observer at UN. **Members** (52): Algeria, Angola, Benin, Botswana, Burkina Faso, Burundi, Cameroon, Cape Verde, Central African Republic, Chad, Comoros, Congo, Djibouti, Egypt, Equatorial Guinea, Eritrea, Ethiopia, Gabon, Gambia, Ghana, Guinea, Guinea-Bissau, Ivory Coast, Kenya, Lesotho, Liberia, Libya, Madagascar, Malawi, Mali, Mauritania, Mauritius, Mozambique, Namibia, Niger, Nigeria, Rwanda, Sahrawi Arab Democratic Republic (Western Sahara), São Tomé and Príncipe, Senegal, Seychelles, Sierra Leone, Somalia, Sudan, Swaziland, Tanzania, Togo, Tunisia, Uganda, Zaire, Zambia, Zimbabwe.

Organization of American States (OAS) HQ: 1889 F St. NW, Washington, D.C. 20006, U.S. **Estab.:** By charter signed at Bogotá, Colombia, effective Dec. 13, 1951, to work for "order of peace and justice, promoting solidarity among the American states," and to establish "new objectives and standards for the promotion of the economic, social and cultural development of the peoples of the Hemisphere, and to speed the process of economic integration." Programs include promotion of human rights, education, economic and social development, and scientific exchanges. Observer at UN. **Members** (32): Antigua and Barbuda, Argentina, Bahamas, Barbados, Bolivia, Brazil, Chile, Colombia, Costa Rica, Cuba (was suspended from OAS activities but not membership in 1962), Dominica, Dominican Republic, Ecuador, El Salvador, Grenada, Guatemala, Haiti, Honduras, Jamaica, Mexico, Nicaragua, Panama, Paraguay, Peru, St. Kitts and Nevis, St. Lucia, St. Vincent and the Grenadines, Suriname, Trinidad and Tobago, Uruguay, U.S., Venezuela.

Organization for Economic Cooperation and Development (OECD) HQ: 2 rue André Pascal, 75775 Paris Cedex 16, France. **Estab.:** By convention signed at Paris, effective Sept. 30, 1961, to help "member countries promote economic growth, employment, and improved standards of living through the coordination of policy [and] to help promote the sound and harmonious development of the world economy and improve the lot of the developing countries, particularly the poorest." **Members** (24): Australia, Austria, Belgium, Canada, Denmark, Finland, France, Germany, Greece, Iceland, Ireland, Italy, Japan, Luxembourg, Netherlands, New Zealand, Norway, Portugal, Spain, Sweden, Switzerland, Turkey, UK, U.S.

Organization of the Petroleum Exporting Countries (OPEC) HQ: Obere Donaustrasse 93, 1020 Vienna, Austria. **Estab.:** Nov. 14, 1960, by resolution adopted at Baghdad, Iraq, to attempt to set world oil prices by coordinating members' oil production. OPEC countries conduct research on all areas affecting oil, from uses and development to economic and financial issues. In 1985 it was estimated that OPEC members possessed 67.3 percent of world's known reserves of crude petroleum and 34.7 percent of known reserves of natural gas. Observer at UN. **Members** (13): Algeria, Ecuador, Gabon, Indonesia, Iran, Iraq, Kuwait, Libya, Nigeria, Qatar, Saudi Arabia, United Arab Emirates, Venezuela. (See also "World Energy.")

Organization for Security and Cooperation in Europe (OSCE) HQ: 1010 Vienna. Kärntner Ring 5-7, Austria. **Estab.:** As Conference on Security and Cooperation in Europe (CSCE) in 1972 as multinational forum for dialogue and negotiation. Produced Helsinki Final Act of 1975 on East-West relations. In 1990 Charter of Paris for a New Europe transformed CSCE from an ad hoc forum into an organization with permanent institutions addressing human rights, the environment, preservation of cultural heritages, and promotion of social justice and economic liberty. In December 1994 CSCE adopted the new name of OSCE to reflect its changing political role and strengthened secretariat. New focus is on trying to act as early warning system by identifying areas of minority tension, offering its good offices to mediate potential conflicts, and to strengthen security and stability throughout Europe. **Members** (53): Albania, Armenia, Austria, Azerbaijan, Belarus, Belgium, Bosnia and Herzegovina, Bulgaria, Canada, Croatia, Cyprus, Czech Republic, Denmark, Estonia, Finland, France, Georgia, Germany, Greece, Hungary, Iceland, Ireland, Italy, Kazakhstan, Kyrgyzstan, Latvia, Liechtenstein, Lithuania, Luxembourg, Malta, Moldova, Monaco, Netherlands, Norway, Poland, Portugal, Romania, Russia, San Marino, Slovakia, Slovenia, Spain, Sweden, Switzerland, Tajikistan, Turkey, Turkmenistan, Ukraine, UK, U.S., Uzbekistan, Vatican City (Holy See), Yugoslavia.

PART IV SCIENCE AND TECHNOLOGY

SCIENCE

Astronomy

Astronomy is the oldest science, but it continues to be at the forefront of scientific thought. The ancients of the Northern Hemisphere knew the skies, probably better than most of us do. They recognized that most stars appear to rise in the east at night and travel in circular paths across the sky, and that a few are wanderers—planets—that move among the other stars. They named the groups of stars that we call constellations and recognized that constellations visible in winter were different from those visible in summer (although some were visible all year). They recognized that one star, Polaris, or the North Star, was always in the north, and other stars seemed to move around it. They learned how to find the extremities of the sunrise and built giant stone structures, such as Stonehenge, probably to locate certain of the positions of the Sun or other stars.

In 1609 Galileo introduced the first artificial device for exploring the universe—the astronomical telescope. Even in that first year, he saw wonders the ancients never knew. Since then, we have built larger and better telescopes, devices for detecting radio waves, microwaves, X rays, infrared waves, and gamma rays from space, and have even traveled to our own Moon. We have sent space probes to eight of the nine known planets, comets, and asteroids. Astronomers have learned that the universe is vastly more complex than the ancients thought and that it contains many secrets of nature we hope to unlock.

MAJOR DISCOVERIES AND EVENTS IN ASTRONOMY AND SPACE

B.C.

2296 Chinese astronomers begin recording appearance of "hairy stars" (comets).

585 Thales of Miletus (Greek: c. 625–c. 547) predicts solar eclipse in Asia Minor.

c. 480 Astronomer Oenopides of Chios (Greek: 5th cent.) discovers that Earth is tilted with respect to Sun.

c. 410 First horoscopes developed in Mesopotamia.

352 Chinese report "guest star," or supernova, the earliest known sighting.

c. 340 Astronomer Kidinnu (Kidenas; Babylon: c. 379) discovers precession of equinoxes, the apparent change in position of stars caused by Earth's wobbling on its orbit.

c. 300 Chinese astronomers compile accurate star maps.

c. 240 Chinese astronomers observe Halley's comet.
Eratosthenes of Cyrene (Greek: c. 276–c. 194) correctly calculates Earth's size.

165 Chinese astronomers are first to notice sunspots.

c. 130 Astronomer Hipparchus of Nicea (Greek: 147–127) correctly determines distance to Moon and rediscovers precession of equinoxes (see 340 B.C.).

A.D.

c. 140 *Almagest* of Ptolemy (Greek: c. 90–168) develops astronomy of solar system in form based on Sun and planets rotating about Earth.

1543 *De Revolutionibus* by Nicholas Copernicus (Polish: 1473–1543) presents convincing arguments that Earth and other planets orbit Sun.

1577 Tycho Brahe (Danish: 1546–1601) proves that comets are visitors from space, not weather phenomena as previously believed.

1592 David Fabricius (German: 1564–1617) discovers star, later named Mira, that gradually disappears; in studying it in 1638, Phocyclides Holawarda recognizes that it appears and reappears on regular basis—the first-known variable star.

1609 Johannes Kepler (German: 1571–1630) discovers that the planets move in elliptical orbits.

1610 Galileo observes Jupiter's moons, phases of Venus, and (although he does not recognize what they are) rings of Saturn.

1611 Several astronomers simultaneously discover sunspots for first time in West.

1633 Roman Catholic church forces Galileo to recant his support of Copernicus's theory that Earth revolves about Sun.

1671 Giovanni Domenico Cassini (Italian-French: 1625–1712) correctly determines distances of the planets from Sun.

1682 Edmond Halley (English: 1656–1742) describes comet now known by his name and in 1705 correctly predicts its return in 1758.

1718 Halley discovers that stars move with respect to each other.

1755 Immanuel Kant (German: 1724–1804) proposes that many nebulas are actually composed of millions of stars and that solar system formed when giant cloud of dust condensed.

1773 William Herschel (German-English: 1738–1822) shows that solar system is moving toward constellation Hercules.

1781 Herschel discovers planet Uranus.

1785 Herschel demonstrates that Milky Way is disk- or lens-shaped group of many stars, one of which is the Sun.

1801 Guiseppe Piazzi (Italian: 1746–1826) discovers first-known asteroid, Ceres.

1838 Friedrich W. Bessel (German: 1784–1846) is first to determine distance to star other than the Sun.

1846 Johann G. Galle (German: 1812–1910) discovers planet Neptune using predictions of Urbain J.J. Leverrier (French: 1811–77) and John Couch Adams (English: 1819–92).

1924 Edwin Hubble (American: 1889–1953) shows that galaxies are "island universes"—giant aggregations of stars as large as Milky Way.

1929 Hubble establishes that universe is expanding.

1930 Clyde Tombaugh (American: 1906–) discovers planet Pluto.

1931 Karl Jansky (American: 1905–50) discovers that radio waves are coming from space, leading to founding of radio astronomy.

1948 George Gamow (Russian-American: 1904–68), Ralph Alpher (American: 1921–), and Robert Herman (American: 1914–) develop Big Bang theory of origin of universe.
Jan Hendrik Oort (Dutch: 1900–1992) proposes that comets come from a vast cloud of material orbiting far beyond Pluto; the material is now known as the Oort Cloud.

1957 USSR launches *Sputnik I*, the first man-made satellite.

1961 Soviet cosmonaut Yuri A. Gagarin (Russian: 1934–68) is first human to orbit Earth.

1962 U.S. space probe *Mariner 2* is first to reach neighborhood of another planet, Venus.

1963 Maarten Schmidt (Dutch-American: 1929–) is first astronomer to recognize a quasar.

1965 Arno Penzias (German-American: 1933–) and Robert Wilson (American: 1936–) find radio waves proving to most astronomers that Big Bang actually occurred.

1967 Jocelyn Bell (English: 1943–) discovers first-known pulsar while working for Antony Hewish (English: 1924–); Hewish later gets Nobel Prize for discovery.

1969 Neil Armstrong (American: 1930–) and Edwin E. ("Buzz") Aldrin (American: 1930–) walk on Moon.

1971 American spacecraft, *Mariner 9,* is first to orbit another planet, Mars.

1975 Soviet space probe transmits pictures from surface of Venus.

1976 U.S. *Viking* space probes begin transmitting pictures of surface of Mars—unsuccessful in detecting life on planet.

1977 Rings of Uranus are discovered.

1979 U.S. space probe *Voyager 1* discovers that, like Saturn, Jupiter has rings.

1980 Alan Guth (American: 1947–) develops theory of inflationary universe, an explanation of how Big Bang occurred.

1981 U.S. introduces reusable spacecraft, the space shuttle.

1987 The explosion of Supernova 1987A, the nearest supernova that has been visible from Earth since 1604, is observed.

1989 U.S. space probe *Voyager 2* flies by Neptune, farthest planet from the Sun at that time, imaging the planet, its rings, and its moons.

1990 The Hubble Space Telescope is launched; although it has many technical problems, including a misshaped main lens, it still produces large amounts of previously unattainable information.

1992 The *Magellan* Venus orbiter completes mapping 95 percent of the planet's surface with radar. Aleksander Wolszczan and Dale Frail discover planets orbiting pulsar PSR 1257+12, the first planets confirmed to orbit a body other than the Sun.

1993 Observations from the Cosmic Background Explorer Satellite (COBE) confirm the Big Bang theory.
Members of the crew of the Space Shuttle *Endeavour* successfully repair the main lens of the Hubble Space Telescope.

1994 Comet Shoemaker-Levy 9, broken into 21 fragments, some nearly half a kilometer in diameter, slams into the far side of Jupiter in July, causing fireballs and persistent storms, each the size of Earth, when the fragments strike the Jovian atmosphere.

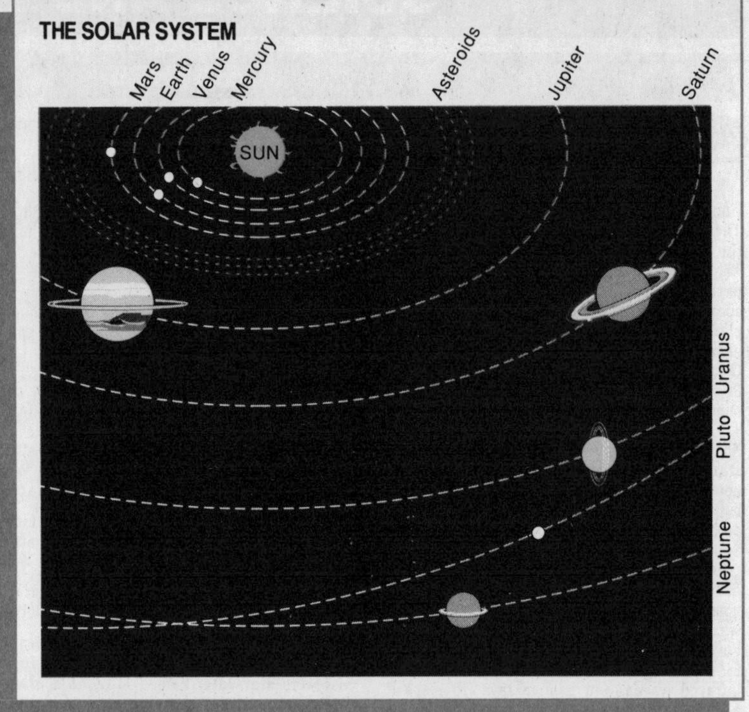

THE SOLAR SYSTEM

Earth is one of nine known planets. A *planet* is a large, fairly cool body traveling in a path, called its orbit, around a star. All of the bodies under the gravitational influence of our local star, the Sun, together with the Sun, form the solar system. All nine of the known planets are in the solar system, although there is evidence for planets around other stars. Many stars are orbited by large, hot bodies—other stars—but these are not considered planets. Cool rocky or metallic bodies smaller than planets that orbit the Sun are called *asteroids*. Small icy bodies are called *comets.* Most comets have orbits that take them from the edge of the system to locations near the Sun (some actually hit the Sun and burn up). Very small objects in space are called *meteoroids*. A meteoroid that burns up in Earth's atmosphere is called a *meteor*. One that reaches Earth's surface without burning completely is a *meteorite*.

Often smaller, cool bodies orbit planets. These are called satellites or moons.

It is currently believed that the solar system formed when a cloud of gas condensed to form the Sun. Parts of the cloud formed small bodies similar to today's asteroids, comets, and meteoroids. Collectively, these small bodies are called *planetesimals* or *planetoids*. Early in the history of the solar system, about 4.6 billion years ago or even before, the planetoids frequently crashed into one another. While this sometimes resulted in one or more of the planetoids breaking up, often a small planetoid would stick to a larger one, making it larger still. The end results of this process, it is proposed, are the nine known planets and their moons, along with the existing asteroids, comets, and meteoroids.

Although six of the nine planets were known to the ancients, and astronomers found the remaining three by early in the 20th century, observations from Earth had not prepared us for what we learned when we began exploring the solar system with space probes in 1962. Radar observations, both from Earth and from space probes, provided still more information. Satellite observation has also told us much we did not know about our own planet, Earth. While this age of exploration is far from over, here is an interim report.

The Terrestrial Planets

In terms of distance from the Sun, these are the first four planets of the solar system—Mercury, Venus, Earth, and Mars. Terrestrial planets all have a comparatively high density, a concentration of metallic elements, and hard, rocky surfaces. Earth is the largest of the terrestrial planets but is dwarfed by the enormous sizes of the outer "gas giant" planets (Jupiter, Saturn, Uranus, and Neptune). Mercury, Earth, and Mars have magnetic fields, but Venus does not. Earth and Venus have thick atmospheres, Mars has a thin atmosphere, and Mercury's atmosphere is almost nonexistent.

Mercury is the planet closest to the Sun and in keeping with its namesake—Mercury, the winged messenger—moves the fastest in its orbit. Usually obscured from view from Earth by the Sun's glare, it is sometimes visible on Earth's horizon just after sunset, when it is called the Evening Star, or just before dawn, when it is called the Morning Star. About 14 times every 100 years, Mercury can also be seen crossing directly in front of the Sun's disk.

Mercury was long thought to be the smallest planet, but better measurements of Pluto's size have shown that Pluto is even smaller.

The U.S. *Mariner 10* space probe provided the first detailed pictures of Mercury's surface during flybys in 1974 and 1975. *Mariner 10* mapped about 35 percent of the planet's heavily cratered, moonlike surface. No space probe has visited the planet since.

Mercury is a waterless, airless world that alternately bakes and freezes as it orbits the Sun. Its tenuous atmosphere is thought to be one-trillionth the density of Earth's atmosphere and largely composed of helium. On Mercury's sunlit side temperatures reach 950°F (510°C) and plummet to –346°F (–210°C) on the dark side. These extremes are largely due to Mercury's slow rate of rotation; one Mercury "day" (or *sol*, as astronomers call a single rotation of a planet or satellite) is two-thirds of one Mercury year. Because it takes 59 Earth days to complete one sol, there is time for the surface to heat up or cool off. In 1990 it was discovered that two spots on the surface are much hotter than other places on the planet. This is caused by the combined action of the planet's rotation and revolution, which have a ratio of 3 to 2. In 1991 research showed that valleys near Mercury's poles could contain water ice.

Mercury's surface is scarred with hundreds of thousands of meteor craters. Many such craters were probably formed during the planetoid showers believed to have occurred soon after the formation of the solar system. Many areas have had the craters smoothed over by ancient lava flows, however. This indicates extensive volcanic activity on Mercury during and after the time of the planetoid showers. The surface is also crisscrossed by huge cliffs, or scarps. These probably formed as Mercury's surface cooled and shrank. Some of the scarps are up to 1.2 miles (1.9 km) high and 932 miles (1,500 km) long.

Mercury is so dense for its size that astronomers think that its rocky outer crust is very thin and that the planet is mostly iron. It probably was once larger. During the early bombardment, it is conjectured that one of the larger planetoids (about a sixth of the size of the early planet) hit Mercury so hard that it blasted most of the rocky crust away.

Venus, as seen in the night sky from Earth, is second only to the Moon in brightness. Venus, named for the Roman goddess of love, is the planet that passes closest to Earth (26,000,000 mi., or 42,000,000 km). Since it is between Earth and the Sun, Venus, like Mercury, is seen either as the Morning Star or the Evening Star.

Because of its closer proximity to Earth and its position between Earth and the Sun, Venus became (in 1962) the first planet beyond Earth to be scanned by a space probe in its neighborhood *(Mariner 2)*. The pull of the Sun's gravity makes Venus and Mercury "downhill" from the Earth; one must travel against the Sun's gravity to reach other planets. Since 1962 Venus has been visited by numerous U.S. and Soviet spacecraft. Soviet space probes *Venera 13* and *Venera 14* were the first to make a soft landing and send back pictures from the Venusian surface.

The Venusian atmosphere is thick with clouds that have shrouded the planet's surface from view, making the planet somewhat mysterious. This dense atmosphere has been studied extensively by a series of U.S. and Soviet space probes. The atmospheric pressure at the surface is 90 times that of Earth, its atmosphere composed of 96 percent carbon dioxide (CO_2) and nitrogen, with small amounts of other substances. The Venusian clouds range from about 28 to 37 miles (45 to 60 km) above the planet's surface and are differentiated into three layers. Droplets of sulfuric acid and water have been identified in the clouds.

The clouds and high level of CO_2 in the atmosphere have combined to trap heat in the lower atmosphere of Venus. This is an extreme form of the greenhouse effect and is responsible for high temperatures in the lower atmosphere, 900°F (482°C)—hot enough to melt lead. Radiation of heat from the lower atmosphere is so inefficient that there is little variation of temperature between night and day.

One feature of the Venusian upper atmosphere is markedly different from that of Earth. The atmosphere superrotates on Venus—that is, the atmosphere above the clouds moves 60 times faster than the planet rotates—whereas the Earth and its atmosphere rotate at the same speed. So, high winds are a dominant part of Venusian weather. Even at only 31 miles (50 km) above the surface, which is just under the cloud layer, the winds blow steadily at 109 miles (175 km) per hour.

Soviet space probes that soft-landed on Venus have provided photographs of the planet's surface. Radar maps of 99 percent of the Venusian surface, completed by the U.S. *Pioneer* spacecraft (from 1978 to 1993), and *Magellan* (from 1989 to 1994), now give a detailed picture of features as small as 350 ft. (100 m) in diameter. More than a thousand Venusian mountains, volcanoes, rifts, basins, impact craters, and other features have been identified.

About 10 percent of the surface is highland terrain, 70 percent rolling uplands, and 20 percent lowland plains. There are two major highland areas: one about half the size of Africa and located in the equatorial region and the other, about the size of Australia, located to the north. The highest mountain on Venus—Maxwell Montes—is in the northern highlands and is higher than Earth's Mt. Everest. Volcanic activity dominates Venus; the planet is covered with volcanic domes and lava channels.

Like Earth, Venus is thought to have an internal structure. The crust, however, is much thicker than that of Earth, perhaps twice as deep on the average, making the crust of Venus about 60 mi. (100 km) thick. Below the crust is a large layer called the mantle; below the mantle is a core thought to be molten nickel-iron, similar to Earth's outer core.

Earth is the third planet from the Sun and the only one in the solar system known to harbor life. From out in space, our planet appears as a bright, blue-and-white sphere—blue because some 70 percent of the surface is covered by water, and white because clouds cover about half the planet's surface.

Earth's atmosphere is composed of about 78 percent nitrogen, 21 percent oxygen, and traces of other gases. The tenuous outer layer of the atmosphere—the thermosphere—begins about 310 miles (500 km) above Earth's surface. Between about 62 miles down to about 31 miles (100 to 50 km) is the mesosphere; below this is the stratosphere (down to about 8 mi., or 13 km); finally, there is the troposphere, the bottom layer. The atmosphere, along with Earth's magnetic field, shields us from nearly all harmful radiation coming from the Sun and from outer space.

The interior consists of three main layers. The outer crust, largely made up of granite and basalt rock, varies from 55 miles (89 km) deep under the continents to 3 miles (5 km) deep under the oceans. The second main layer, the mantle, extends down to about 1,900 miles (3,060 km) below the surface and is composed of silicate rock rich in iron. The top part of the mantle is semiliquid, down to about 150 miles (250 km). The rigid upper crust is broken into large plates that move slowly on this partially fluid layer, which is termed the asthenosphere. Beneath this lies the Earth's iron and nickel core. Scientists believe the temperature at the center of the core could be 7,200°F (4,000°C). The outer core is liquid due to the great heat, while an inner core is solid as a result of the great pressure at Earth's center.

The Moon is Earth's only natural satellite. Just over one-quarter the size of Earth in diameter, it is the brightest object in Earth's nighttime sky. The Moon regularly changes in appearance as seen from Earth. See the discussion of these changes, called "Phases of the Moon," in Part I.

Because the Moon is slightly egg-shaped, the same side of the satellite always faces Earth—this side being the elongated small end. As a result, the Moon rotates once during each revolution. The side we do not see is called the far side (not the dark side—all parts of the moon undergo 14 Earth days of light, followed by 14 days of darkness).

Over a decade of exploration of the Moon by U.S. and Soviet space probes was capped by the landing of two U.S. astronauts on the Moon on July 20, 1969. A total of six two-man crews of American astronauts eventually landed on the Moon between 1969 and 1972, and they brought back some 842 pounds (382 kg) of samples of Moon rocks.

The world these astronauts found was airless, waterless, and devoid of life. Temperatures on the Moon range from up to 273°F (134°C) on the bright side to –274°F (–170°C) on the unlighted side.

The lunar surface is pockmarked with craters up to 56 miles (90 km) across and is broken by

GLOSSARY OF PLANETARY TERMS

Bar A measure of pressure slightly less than Earth's air pressure at sea level under standard conditions, or about 29.92 (76 cm) inches of mercury, the measurement used in giving the weather report of barometric pressure; *bar* is derived from the Greek word for "weight." Standard air pressure at sea level is 1.01325 bars.

Eccentricity A number that measures the shape of a planet's orbit; all the planetary orbits are curves called ellipses, which are "squashed" circles; the smaller the eccentricity, the more an ellipse is like a circle, which has an eccentricity of 0.

Ecliptic The apparent path of the Sun through the stars as viewed from Earth, which is in a plane inclined about 23.5° to Earth's equator. The planets are all roughly in the same plane, so like the Sun, they seem to move through the same groups of stars as the Sun does over the course of a year.

Escape velocity The speed needed for an object to be propelled from the surface of a planet and not fall back. Since the escape velocity for Earth is 6.96 miles (11.2 km) per second, a rocket expected to reach the Moon or another planet must develop a speed of at least 7 miles (12 km) per second.

Inclination of axis The angle that the line about which a planet rotates makes with the plane defined by its path around the Sun.

Inclination of orbit to the ecliptic The angle that the plane defined by a planet's path around the Sun makes with the plane defined by the apparent path of the Sun among the stars as seen from Earth.

Orbital velocity The speed of a planet in its path around the Sun.

BASIC FACTS ABOUT THE PLANETS

Characteristic	Terrestrial planets			
	Mercury	Venus	Earth	Mars
Average distance from Sun	35,900,000 mi. 57,900,000 km	67,200,000 mi. 108,200,000 km	92,960,000 mi. 149,600,000 km	141,600,000 mi. 227,900,000 km
Rotation period (hours)	1,407.6 hrs. (59 d.)	–5,832.2 hrs. (243 d., retrograde)	23.9 hrs.	24.6 hrs.
Period of revolution (in Earth days)	88 d.	224.7 d.	365.26 d.	687 d.
Average orbital velocity in miles per second	29.8	21.75	18.46	14.98
Inclination of axis	2°	3°	23°27'	23°59'
Inclination of orbit to the ecliptic	7°	3.39°	0°	1.9°
Eccentricity of orbit	0.206	0.007	0.017	0.093
Equatorial diameter	3,031 mi. 4,878 km	7,520 mi. 12,104 km	7,926 mi. 12,756 km	4,222 mi. 6,794 km
Diameter relative to Earth	38.2%	94.9%	100%	53.2%
Mass	3.303×10^{23} kg	4.87×10^{24} kg	5.97×10^{24} kg	6.42×10^{23} kg
Mass relative to Earth	5.5%	81.5%	100%	10.74%
Average density	3.13 oz./in.^{3}	3.06 oz./in.^{3}	3.19 oz./in.^{3}	2.27 oz./in.^{3}
Gravity (at equator surface)	12.4 ft./sec.^{2}	28.2 ft./sec.^{2}	32.1 ft./sec.^{2}	12.2 ft./sec.^{2}
Gravity (relative to Earth)	38%	88%	100%	38%
Escape velocity at equator	2.7 mi./sec. 4.3 km/sec.	6.40 mi./sec. 10.3 km/sec.	6.96 mi./sec. 11.2 km/sec.	3.1 mi./sec. 5.0 km/sec.
Average surface temperature	332°F 167°C	854°F 457°C	59°F 15°C	–67°F –55°C
Atmospheric pressure at surface	10^{-14} bar	90 bars	1.013 bars	0.007 bar
Atmosphere (main components)	Virtually none	Carbon dioxide 96%; nitrogen 3.5%	Nitrogen 77%; oxygen 21%; water 1%; argon 0.93%	Carbon dioxide 95%; nitrogen 2.7%; argon 1.6%
Planetary satellites	None	None	1 moon	2 moons

Retrograde In the opposite direction of other planets.

Revolution The trip a planet makes about the Sun.

Rotation The turning of a planet about a line through its center.

The numbers used in tables are sometimes given in scientific notation. A large number, such as 1,840,000,000, might be written as 1.84×10^9. The exponent ^{9} signifies the number of places after the first digit. A small number such as 0.000000000000001 is written as 10^{-15}, where the exponent $^{-15}$ tells the number of zeroes—counting the one before the decimal place—before the numeral *1*.

huge mountain ranges. The near side also has large regions (called maria, or seas) of solidified lava, indicating that the Moon was once volcanically active. Lunar soil, a mixture of fine powder and broken rock, blankets the Moon's surface.

Mars is the outermost of the four terrestrial planets and has a distinctive reddish coloring, coming from iron oxide in the Martian soil. The Romans named the planet after their god of war, and the two irregularly shaped satellites of Mars have been named after the horses—Deimos (terror) and Phobos (fear)—that pulled the war god's chariot. Mars is visible in Earth's nighttime sky and is lined up with Earth between it and the Sun once every 780 days, though its closest approach to Earth (35,000,000 mi., or 56,000,000 km) comes at 15- or 17-year intervals.

The so-called canals on Mars—later found to be optical illusions—were first observed by 19th-century astronomers and led to the widespread belief that there was life on Mars. (In 1900 the French Academy offered a prize to the first person to find life on any planet *except* Mars, presumably because everyone knew that there was life on that planet.) The planet thus became the target of numerous space probes, both U.S. and Soviet, from the early years of interplanetary exploration.

The first successful flyby of Mars was achieved by the U.S. spacecraft *Mariner IV* in 1965. The Soviets became the first to land a probe successfully on the surface of Mars in 1971, but the probe malfunctioned and stopped transmitting after only 20 seconds. It was not until 1976, when the U.S. *Viking 1* and *Viking 2* landers touched down on Mars, that extensive study of the planet from its surface became possible. In fact, the *Viking 1* lander continued to function long after its mission had been completed and sent back information on Martian weather until 1983, when communications with Earth at last failed.

The big question of whether there is (or was) life on Mars has yet to be answered with certainty. The *Viking* landers conducted three experiments on Martian soil to check for biological processes. Some of the tests yielded positive results, but these could also be explained by the soil chemistry. The lack of other evidence of organic molecules adds to the case against life on Mars.

Orbiting satellites have mapped the entire planet down to a resolution of 500–1,000 ft. (150–300 m).

The planet's surface is heavily cratered, and there is extensive evidence of once-active volcanoes. There are also such spectacular features as Olympus Mons (an extinct volcano three times as high as Earth's Mt. Everest); mammoth canyons, one of which is four times deeper than the Grand Canyon; and a gigantic basin (larger than Alaska) in the southern hemisphere that was probably created by a single, huge asteroid. The planet has ice caps at both poles (frozen carbon dioxide with some water), and the ice caps advance and recede with changes in the seasons.

But the most intriguing aspect of the Martian surface is an indication that water once flowed there in great quantities. Parts of the terrain apparently have sedimentary origins, and there are many long channels, complete with smaller tributary channels and islands, that extend for hundreds of kilometers. Scientists speculate that Mars once had a much thicker atmosphere, made up of gases vented during volcanic eruptions, which would have

OUTER PLANETS

	Gas giants				
Characteristic	**Jupiter**	**Saturn**	**Uranus**	**Neptune**	**Pluto**
Average distance from Sun	483,600,000 mi. 778,300,000 km	886,700,000 mi. 1,427,000,000 km	1,783,000,000 mi. 2,869,600,000 km	2,794,000,000 mi. 4,496,600,000 km	3,666,100,000 mi. 5,900,100,000 km
Rotation period (hours)	9.8 hrs.	10.2 hrs.	17.2 hrs.	16.1 hrs.	–153.3 hrs. (6.4 d., retrograde)
Period of revolution (in Earth days)	4,332.6 (11.86 yrs.)	10,759.2 (29.46 yrs.)	30,685.4 (84.01 yrs.)	60,268 (165 yrs.)	90,950 (249 yrs.)
Average orbital velocity	8.1 mi./sec. 13.06 km/sec.	5.99 mi./sec. 9.64 km/sec.	4.2 mi./sec. 6.8 km/sec.	3.35 mi./sec. 5.4 km/sec.	2.9 mi./sec. 4.7 km/sec.
Inclination of axis	3°7'	26°44'	97°54'	28°48'	60°
Inclination of orbit to the ecliptic	1.3°	2.5°	0.8°	1.8°	17.2°
Eccentricity of orbit	0.048	0.056	0.047	0.009	0.25
Equatorial diameter	88,700 mi. 142,800 km	74,800 mi. 120,400 km	32,200 mi. 51,800 km	30,800 mi. 49,500 km	1,423 mi. 2,290 km
Diameter relative to Earth	1,121%	941%	410%	388%	18%
Mass	1.899×10^{27} kg	5.686×10^{26} kg	8.66×10^{25} kg	1.030×10^{26} kg	c. 1.3×10^{22} kg
Mass relative to Earth	31,790%	9,520%	1,460%	1,723%	c. 0.21%
Average density	0.759 oz./in.^{3}	0.40 oz./in.^{3}	0.7 oz./in.^{3}	0.9 oz./in.^{3}	c. 1 oz./in.^{3}
Gravity (at equator surface)	75.06 ft./sec.^{2}	29.69 ft./sec.^{2}	25.5 ft./sec.^{2}	36 ft./sec.^{2}	5.4 ft./sec.^{2}
Gravity (relative to Earth)	234%	92%	79%	112%	16%
Escape velocity at equator	37.0 mi./sec. 59.5 km/sec.	22.1 mi./sec. 35.6 km/sec.	13.2 mi./sec. 21.2 km/sec.	14.66 mi./sec. 23.6 km/sec.	0.8 mi./sec. 1.3 km/sec.
Average temperature in atmosphere	(At surface) –162°F –108°C	(At surface) –208°F –133°C	(Cloud tops) –344°F –209°C	(Cloud tops) –365°F –220°C	(At surface) c. –355°F c. –215°C
Atmospheric pressure at surface	3,000,000 bars	8,000,000 bars	N.A.	N.A.	0.1 millibar (?)
Atmosphere (main components)	(Near cloud tops) hydrogen 90%; helium c. 10%	Hydrogen 94%; helium c. 6%	Hydrogen 85%; helium 15%	Hydrogen, helium, methane % N.A.	Methane, possibly neon % N.A.
Other atmospheric gases	Methane, water, ammonia, ethane, acetylene, phosphine, hydrogen cyanide, carbon monoxide	Methane, ammonia	Unknown	Unknown	Possibly carbon monoxide and argon
Planetary satellites	16	18	15	8	1

made it possible for water in its liquid state to exist on the surface. Martian atmospheric pressure is now so low, however, that surface water would immediately vaporize. It is conjectured that the water in the past flowed through the channels to lowland areas and then sank into the Martian regolith, or upper soil layer, since there is no geologic evidence that standing bodies of water ever existed. Astronomers believe that at least some of the primordial water may still be trapped as ice in the regolith.

Mars is too small to sustain continual volcanic activity. Its atmosphere apparently thinned out after volcanic activity ceased. Atmospheric pressure is now just seven one-thousandths of that on Earth at sea level, and the predominant gas is carbon dioxide, which is relatively heavy. A small amount of water vapor in the atmosphere is enough to form some clouds, small patches of fog in some valleys, and occasionally even patches of frost. Surface temperatures vary from a high of about 70°F (20°C) during summer at the equator to a low of about –220°F (–140°C) during winter at the poles.

By far the most pronounced feature of Martian weather is dust storms, which regularly engulf the entire planet for a period of several months.

The asteroids The asteroid belt—first crossed by the U.S. space probe *Pioneer 10* on its way to Jupiter in 1973—lies between Mars and Jupiter. The name *asteroid* means "starlike" and was given to asteroids because they are so small they appear as points of light (as do stars) even in powerful telescopes. Otherwise, asteroids are not like stars at all. Astronomers once thought the asteroid belt had been formed by the breakup of a planet between Mars and Jupiter, but they now think it is debris left over from the formation of the solar system. For some reason the asteroids did not accrete into a planet, perhaps because of Jupiter's strong gravitational pull.

Not all asteroids are found in the asteroid belt. Some cross Earth's orbit, for example.

The Outer Planets

Beyond Mars and the asteroid belt lie the five known outer planets of our solar system. Four of these planets—Jupiter, Saturn, Uranus, and Neptune—are the so-called gas giants. Many times larger than the terrestrial planets, these planets are huge, dense balls of hydrogen and other gases. Beyond them (most of the time) lies the solar system's outermost and smallest known planet, Pluto, which may be nothing more than a tiny ball of frozen gases.

Jupiter is the largest planet in the solar system. It has 2.5 times more mass than all the other planets of the solar system together and is 11 times as large as Earth in diameter. Jupiter is so large that scientists believe it almost became a star: as the gases and dust contracted to form the planet, gravitational forces created tremendous pressure and temperature inside the core—perhaps as high as tens of thousands of degrees. But there was not enough mass available to create the temperatures needed to start a fusion reaction such as that of the Sun (above 27,000,000°F, or 15,000,000°C, at the Sun's core); thus Jupiter has been slowly cooling down ever since. Even so, Jupiter still radiates about 2.5 times as much heat as it receives from the Sun.

The first object to reach Jupiter from Earth was *Pioneer 10.* It returned the first close-up pictures of the giant planet in 1973. Subsequently, the more sophisticated space probes *Voyager 1* and *Voyager 2* passed by Jupiter in 1979 and sent back images and more data on the planet. One of the most exciting discoveries by *Voyager 1* was that Jupiter has a faint but extensive ring system that extends almost 186,000 miles (300,000 km) out from the planet's surface. And in 1983 a study of *Voyager 2* readings indicated that Jupiter's magnetic field—stretched by solar wind into a long "tail" on the side away from the Sun—had actually reached Saturn when Jupiter and Saturn were aligned with the Sun (which occurs about once every 20 years). *Galileo* is scheduled to arrive at Jupiter at the end of 1995 and should provide further data.

Jupiter's thick atmosphere, which may extend downward by as much as 600 miles (1,000 km), is primarily made up of hydrogen, with some helium and traces of other gases. Because the planet spins so fast (one rotation in just under 10 hours), its clouds tend to form bands that give the planet a striped appearance. Bands of clouds at higher altitudes are carried eastward by jet streams, while those at lower levels are blown westward.

There are numerous eddies and swirls in Jupiter's atmosphere, but none can compare with the Great Red Spot, apparently a massive hurricane (rotating counterclockwise) located in the southern hemisphere near the equator. The Great Red Spot was first observed some 300 years ago, and this storm continues unabated today. Since 1938 three smaller white ovals have been observed to the south of the Great Red Spot.

Jupiter's cloud tops are extremely cold (about –202°F, or –130°C), but temperatures increase deeper inside the atmosphere. Pressure also increases, and at about 620 miles (1,000 km) below the outermost atmospheric layers, great oceans of liquid hydrogen form Jupiter's surface. These may be some 12,000 miles (20,000 km) deep. Beneath them the hydrogen is so densely compacted it is thought to be in a metallic state. Within this is the core, thought to be an iron and silicate rock ball about the size of Earth.

Jupiter is now known to have 16 moons, the four largest being the Galilean moons, so called because they were first observed by Galileo. The Galilean moons are Ganymede, Callisto, Europa, and Io—after the Roman god Jupiter's cupbearer (Ganymede) and three of Jupiter's inamorata. Ganymede is the largest moon in the solar system—although previously this honor was accorded to Saturn's Titan—and is larger even than the planets Pluto and Mercury. It is a huge, cratered ball of ice and may have a core of solid silicate rock. Callisto, with an orbit outside that of Ganymede, is also covered with ice and is riddled with thousands of craters. Europa, which orbits inside Ganymede, is about the size of our Moon and has a smooth surface marked by networks of cracks. The most interesting of Jupiter's moons is Io, which of all four Galilean moon orbits is closest to Jupiter. The *Voyagers* photographed volcanoes erupting on Io. Orange-red patches on Io's mottled surface are apparently molten sulfur beds, but most other parts of Io's surface are apparently very cold (about –229°F, or –145°C). The volcanic activity is caused by gravitational force from Jupiter, Europa, and Ganymede.

Saturn is the sixth planet of the solar system and the second largest, after Jupiter. The outermost of the planets that can be identified easily in Earth's nighttime sky with the unaided eye, Saturn has a pale yellowish color and is not nearly so bright as Mars. Saturn's spectacular ring system, which makes it one of the most interesting of the planets, is visible only through a telescope. Its rings are more extensive than those of any other planet.

Like Jupiter, Saturn is composed of densely compacted hydrogen, helium, and other gases. Liquid or metallic hydrogen probably exists underneath the planet's thick atmosphere, and scientists believe there is a solid core of rock about two times the size of Earth at its center. Saturn's high rotational speed (once every 10 hours, 12 minutes) makes it the most oblate (flattened) of all the planets; it is almost 6,800 miles (11,000 km) wider at the equator than on a line through the poles.

Though exploration of Saturn began in 1979 with the first flyby *(Pioneer 11),* the *Voyager 1* and *Voyager 2* missions in 1980 and 1981, respectively, provided the first detailed look at the planet. Scientists have spent years sifting through the data gathered, and, though there were important new findings, many questions about Saturn remain unanswered.

The *Voyagers* found a huge storm thousands of miles across on Saturn, along with a wide band of extremely high winds—up to 994 miles (1,600 km) per hour—at the equator. Winds in this band all travel in the direction of the planet's rotation (unlike bands of wind on Jupiter). The *Voyagers* also discovered a vast hydrogen cloud circling the planet above the equator.

The *Voyagers'* most exciting discoveries concern the planetary rings. Previously, about six different rings had been identified within the ring system, but *Voyager 1* pictures show as many as 1,000 separate rings. Narrow rings can even be seen within the Cassini Division, once thought to be an empty gap between the two major parts of the ring system. Some rings are not circular, and at least two rings are intertwined, or "braided." A strange new phenomenon was also discovered in the rings. *Voyager 1* pictures clearly show dark, radial fingers—"spokes"—moving inside the rings in the direction of rotation. Scientists speculate that they are made of ice crystals.

Voyager 2 pictures show that Saturn has far more than 1,000 rings—perhaps as many as a hundred thousand or more. One of the brightest rings is shown to be under 152 meters (500 ft.) thick. The pictures do not show signs of moonlets that some scientists had thought were the cause of gaps between individual rings.

Voyager 2 also found seasonal differences between the planet's two hemispheres and photographed a storm some 4,000 miles (6,500 km) wide.

Twelve of Saturn's moons were known before the arrival of the *Voyagers*, and instruments aboard the space probe helped locate five new ones in the 1980s. In 1990 an eighteenth moon, later named Pan, was located in images made by *Voyager 2*. Most of Saturn's moons are relatively small and composed of rock and ice. All but one of the small moons are pockmarked by meteor craters, and in some cases the moons appear to have been cracked by collisions with especially large meteors. But *Voyager* pictures show that one moon, Enceladus, is smooth in large regions apparently unmarked by collisions with meteors. Scientists believe that Enceladus is being pulled and stretched by the combined gravities of a nearby moon and Saturn itself. Tidal forces have apparently heated the core of Enceladus and made its surface soft enough to smooth over any craters formed by meteor impacts.

Titan, Saturn's largest moon (3,000 mi., or 4,800 km in diameter) is the only moon in the solar system known to have an atmosphere of any substance. Scientists suspect that at least some precursors of life may have formed there. For this reason *Voyager 1* was guided to within about 2,500 miles (4,000 km) of Titan during the Saturn flyby. Though Titan's surface was obscured by dense clouds, *Voyager*'s sensors nevertheless returned a considerable amount of information about the moon and its atmosphere. Titan's atmosphere is composed mostly of nitrogen, like that of Earth, with only a small percentage of methane and carbon monoxide. Atmospheric pressure is at least 1.5 times that on Earth and temperatures range around –294°F (–181°C). Titan in fact appears to be a frozen version of Earth before life evolved.

The possibility of oceans of liquid methane (or of nitrogen or methane rain) on Titan was a matter of considerable controversy for some time after *Voyager 1* investigated the moon. But Titan is "dry," at least in the regions investigated. Pools of liquid methane might still exist in other low-lying regions, but it is unlikely that either methane or nitrogen condenses to liquid form on Titan.

Uranus is the seventh planet in the solar system and the third of the gas giants. The planet is barely visible in Earth's nighttime sky (it looks like a faint star) and for that reason, it went undiscovered until 1781.

Nearly the same size as Neptune and only about 5 percent of Jupiter's mass, Uranus is a faintly greenish color, perhaps because its atmosphere contains methane. The planet's axis of rotation is tipped over on its side, and in 1977 a system of nine faint rings was discovered. There are five known moons of Uranus, which range between about 186 and 621 miles (300 and 1,000 km) in diameter.

The atmosphere of Uranus is composed of hydrogen, helium, and methane and is very cold (–355°F, or –215°C). No clouds have been observed.

Scientists speculate that, as on Jupiter and Saturn, temperatures and pressures increase dramatically down through the outer layer of atmosphere. At some point the hydrogen and helium would be sufficiently compressed to form a liquid or slushy surface "crust." Underneath this crust they believe is a mantle of solidified methane, ammonia, and water; and inside this mantle, a rocky core of silicon and iron about 15 times as massive as Earth. The core is hot, probably about 12,000°F (7,000°C).

Neptune, the last of the gas giants, is the eighth planet in the solar system. It was discovered in 1846 after mathematical calculations based on irregularities in the orbit of Uranus provided astronomers with the correct location of the planet. Neptune, like Uranus, has been surrounded by considerable uncertainty because of its enormous distance from Earth. The 1989 visit by *Voyager 2* contributed greatly to improved understanding of the planet.

Neptune is a pale bluish color, and its atmosphere is composed of hydrogen and helium. Unlike Uranus, Neptune's atmosphere is clear, and it is very cold at the cloud tops (about −365°F or −220°C).

Scientists believe that Neptune has a three-layered structure similar to that of Uranus: a crust of solidified or liquid hydrogen and helium that gradually thins outward into an atmosphere; a mantle of solidified gases and water; and a hot, rocky core (about 12,000°F or 7,000°C) some 15 times as massive as Earth. But one aspect of Neptune remains a mystery. Despite similarities with Uranus, Neptune has been found to radiate 2.7 times as much heat as it receives from the Sun (at a rate of 0.03 microwatts per ton of mass). Uranus, on the other hand, does not emit as much excess heat.

Neptune has eight known moons, Triton and Nereid, discovered from Earth, and six others discovered by *Voyager 2,* and a ring system containing three rings and two ringlike features. Triton is the largest moon and has an atmosphere. Triton is unusual in that it travels in a direction opposite that of Neptune's rotation, suggesting that it has a different origin from the planet.

Pluto, the ninth and outermost (most of the time) known planet of the solar system, is a ball of frozen gases probably only about the size of Earth's Moon. Because of its relatively small size and chaotic orbit (which at times crosses inside Neptune's orbit), some scientists think that Pluto is not really a planet at all. Instead, they theorize that Pluto is only a former moon of Neptune that has been pulled out of orbit by some other celestial body.

Pluto was discovered in 1930 as a result of an extensive search by Clyde Tombaugh. Although his search was based on mathematical calculations derived from deviations in the orbit of Neptune, most astronomers now think that Tombaugh found Pluto as a result of a lucky accident.

Frozen methane and a thin atmosphere of methane and some other gases have been detected on Pluto. Pluto has one known moon, Charon, discovered in 1978. Charon is about one-half the size of Pluto. Pluto and Charon rotate and revolve synchronously like a double planet system.

The Sun

Virtually all of the energy used by living things comes from the Sun. The Sun's light causes photosynthesis in green plants, and its heat causes winds. Fossil fuels, such as coal, oil, and natural gas, got their energy originally from photosynthesis, as did wood. Animals derive their energy from plants that photosynthesize, either directly or indirectly. The only natural nonsolar energy sources are nuclear reactions (which also produce geothermal energy), some bacteria that metabolize sulfur, and the tides, which are produced largely by the Moon, but in part by the Sun.

Because the Sun is a ball of gases, it does not rotate as a whole. The equator rotates in about 25 days, while gas near the poles rotates in about 30 days. The period of rotation at each latitude can be found by observing sunspots, which are magnetic storms. Sunspots appear and disappear in a mysterious 22-year cycle that many think influences weather on Earth, although convincing proof is lacking. Sometimes sunspots disappear for tens of years at a time, as during the period from 1645 to 1715. It may or may not be a coincidence that those years coincided with the "Little Ice Age" in Europe, when temperatures were far below average.

Like Earth the Sun is composed of various layers. The part we see is called the photosphere. In the Sun's interior, energy is generated when hydrogen in the core fuses to become helium. Above the photosphere is a region of pinkish gases, the chromosphere. Above that is a large halo, visible only in eclipses, called the corona. Particles from the Sun, the solar wind, stream through the solar system, creating auroras on Earth. Strong increases in solar wind during solar flares can interfere with radio communication.

The Sun will eventually—in about 6.4 billion years—fuse all its hydrogen fuel into helium. Before that happens, the Sun will lose much of its mass, causing the planets, including Earth, to move farther away from the Sun. When the hydrogen is all gone and the Sun begins to rely on fusing helium, the Sun will expand into a red giant star. Even though Earth will be farther from the Sun by then, the expanded Sun will burn Earth and the other planets to cinders. No life will be able to survive on Earth.

CHARACTERISTICS OF THE SUN

Position in solar system	Center
Mean distance from Earth	92,955,600 mi. (149,597,900 km)
Distance from center of Milky Way galaxy	27,710 light-yrs.
Estimated velocity of rotation	175 mi./sec. (282 km/sec.)
Period of rotation	27 d. on average
Inclination (relative to Earth's orbit)	7°
Equatorial diameter	864,930 mi. (1,391,980 km)
Diameter relative to Earth	109 times
Mass	2.2×10^{27} tons (1.989×10^{30} kg)
Gravity relative to Earth's	27.8 times
Temperature at core	27,000,000°F (15,000,000°C)
Temperature at surface	8,700°F (4,800°C)
Main components	Hydrogen and helium
Expected life of hydrogen fuel supply	6.4 billion years

STARS AND THE UNIVERSE

The Constellations

Constellations are small groups of stars that from our vantage point on Earth seem to form some particular shape. In actuality, however, the stars forming a constellation are usually at vastly different distances from the solar system. They only appear to form a particular figure from Earth.

Long ago, before recorded history, people began naming these groups. By Sumerian times (3000–2500 B.C.), stories were already being told about how particular constellations were formed. Most of our present knowledge of such stories comes from the Greeks, much of whose mythology was reflected in the names of stars, planets, and constellations.

One group of constellations has exerted a special influence on human thought, at least since 1500 B.C. As the Sun, Moon, and planets move through the sky, they pass through a group of 12 constellations, called the constellations of the zodiac. Chaldean astronomers believed that the presence of the Sun, a planet, or even the Moon in one of these constellations at a person's birth (or at other significant times) influenced happenings on Earth. We call this belief *astrology*. Because of the precession of the equinoxes (see the section, "The Calendar of the Year"), the traditional 12 constellations are no longer where they were 3,500 years ago. Modern astrologers have divided the year into 12 "houses," based on where the signs of the zodiac used to be. Thus, when an astronomer and an astrologer refer to the zodiac, they mean quite different things.

Today astronomers use constellations for their own purposes, such as for mapping the sky. Each part of the sky is named by a particular constellation. These constellations, especially in the southern hemisphere, may not be traditional ones, but rather, groups of stars astronomers have named so that for reference purposes all of the sky is labeled. The International Astronomical Union has decreed that each such constellation be bounded by straight north-south and east-west lines. As a result, many of the larger traditional constellations extend beyond the boundaries of modern astronomical constellations.

Bright Stars

While astronomers often use the traditional names of stars, most of which come to us from Latin or Arabic sources, they also use another system for naming objects in the sky (galaxies, radio sources, quasars, etc.) that is based on constellations. Generally, the brightest star in a particular astronomical constellation is called alpha (α), the next brightest beta (β), and so on through

25 BRIGHTEST STARS: MAGNITUDES AND DISTANCES FROM EARTH

The following table shows the 25 brightest stars arranged in order of apparent magnitude (i.e., brightness as measured from Earth); thus the star numbered 1, Sirius, is the brightest star as seen from Earth. Rigel and Deneb are the brightest stars in the table in absolute magnitude, however. But Rigel is more than 100 times as far from Earth as Sirius and Deneb is much farther still, so they do not appear as bright.

Rank/ Common name	Star name	Apparent magnitude	Absolute magnitude	Distance from Earth (light-years)
1. Sirius	α CMa	−1.46	1.42	2.65
2. Canopus	α Car	−0.72	−5	70
3. Rigil Kentaurus[1]	α Cen A	−0.01	4.37	1.33
	α Cen B	1.33	5.71	1.33
4. Arcturus	α Boo	−0.04	−0.10	10.3
5. Vega	α Lyr	0.03	0.65	7.5
6. Capella	α Aur A	0.08	−0.40	12.5
7. Rigel	β Ori	0.12	−7	265
8. Procyon	β CMi	0.38	2.71	3.4
9. Achernar	α Eri	0.46	−1.7	27
10. Betelgeuse	α Ori	0.50[2]	−7	320
11. (Unnamed)	β Cen	0.61	−4.3	95
12. Altair	α Aql	0.77	2.30	5.0
13. Aldebaran	α Tau	0.85	−0.49	19
14. Antares	α Sco	0.96	−5.4	190
15. Spica	α Vir	0.98	−3.2	67
16. (Unnamed)[1]	α Cru A	1.58	−3.8	120
	α Cru B	2.09	−3.3	120
17. Pollux	β Gem	1.14	1.00	10.6
18. Fomalhaut	α PsA	1.16	2.02	6.7
19. Deneb	α Cyg	1.25	−7.2	500
20. (Unnamed)	β Cru	1.25	−4.6	150
21. Regulus	α Leo	1.35	−0.38	22
22. Adhara	ε CMa	1.50	−4.9	190
23. Castor	α Gem	1.58	0.72	15
24. Bellatrix	γ Ori	1.64	−1.08	35
25. Elnath	β Tau	1.65	−1.13	36

1. Both components of a binary star contribute significantly to its apparent magnitude. 2. Betelgeuse is a variable star with a magnitude that changes regularly.

several letters of the Greek alphabet. Thus Sirius is also known as alpha Canis Majoris, usually abbreviated to α CMa, which means it is the brightest star in the constellation Big Dog (Sirius has long been known as the dog star). Since Sirius is a binary star (see "The Universe," below), the much brighter main star is officially α CMa A.

All astronomers' constellations are named in Latin. When astronomers refer to a star within its constellation, they use the genitive case, meaning "of the thing." Thus the constellation Big Dog is officially Canis Major, but Sirius is alpha Canis Majoris, or "alpha of Big Dog."

The brightness of a star is designated by a number called its magnitude, although the relationship between size and brightness is complicated. When the magnitude system was first developed, by the early Greek astronomers Hipparchus (c. 190–c. 120 B.C.) and Ptolemy (c. 100–c. 170), astronomers did not know the actual distances to stars, so magnitude always referred to brightness as seen from Earth. They classed the brightest stars as the first magnitude and the dimmest they could see as the sixth. These numbers were somewhat arbitrary until 1856, when George Phillips Bond (American: 1826–65) determined that photographs of stars show magnitude in a way that is directly measurable—bright stars appear as larger spots than dim stars in photographs even though all stars appear as points to the naked eye. Astronomers could use accurate measures to compare two stars and thus measure magnitude with mathematical precision. Under Bond's system, stars with a magnitude of 1.00 are exactly 100 times as bright as those with a magnitude of 5.00. The very brightest stars have negative magnitudes.

CONSTELLATIONS

Name	Genitive	Abbreviation	Translation	Remarks
Andromeda	Andromedae	And	Andromeda	Character in Greek myth
Antlia	Antliae	Ant	Air Pump	Of modern origin
Apus	Apodis	Aps	Bird of Paradise	Of modern origin
Aquarius	Aquarii	Aqr	Water Bearer	In zodiac
Aquila	Aquilae	Aql	Eagle	Contains Altair
Ara	Arae	Ara	Altar	—
Aries	Arietis	Ari	Ram	In zodiac
Auriga	Aurigae	Aur	Charioteer	Contains Capella
Boötes	Boötis	Boo	Herdsman	Contains Arcturus
Caelum	Caeli	Cae	Chisel	Of modern origin
Camelopardalis	Camelopardalis	Cam	Giraffe	Of modern origin
Cancer	Cancri	Cnc	Crab	In zodiac
Canes Venatici	Canum Venaticorum	CVn	Hunting Dogs	Of modern origin
Canis Major	Canis Majoris	CMa	Big Dog	Contains Sirius and Adhara
Canis Minor	Canis Minoris	CMi	Little Dog	Contains Procyon
Capricornus	Capricorni	Cap	Goat	In zodiac
Carina	Carinae	Car	Ship's Keel[1]	Of modern origin; contains Canopus
Cassiopeia	Cassiopeiae	Cas	Cassiopeia	Character in Greek myth
Centaurus	Centauri	Cen	Centaur	Character in Greek myth; contains Rigil Kentaurus and Hadar/Agena
Cepheus	Cephei	Cep	Cepheus	Character in Greek myth
Cetus	Ceti	Cet	Whale	—
Chamaeleon	Chamaeleontis	Cha	Chameleon	Of modern origin
Circinus	Circini	Cir	Compass	Of modern origin
Columba	Columbae	Col	Dove	Of modern origin
Coma Berenices	Comae Berenices	Com	Berenice's Hair	Third-century B.C. Egyptian queen
Corona Australis	Coronae Australis	CrA	Southern Crown	Also Sagittarius's crown
Corona Borealis	Coronae Borealis	CrB	Northern Crown	Also Ariadne's crown
Corvus	Corvi	Crv	Crow	Companion of Orpheus
Crater	Crateris	Crt	Cup	—
Crux	Crucis	Cru	Southern Cross	Of modern origin; contains Beta Crucis and Acrux; smallest constellation
Cygnus	Cygni	Cyg	Swan	Contains Deneb
Delphinus	Delphini	Del	Dolphin	—
Dorado	Doradus	Dor	Goldfish	Of modern origin
Draco	Draconis	Dra	Dragon	—
Equuleus	Equulei	Equ	Little Horse	—
Eridanus	Eridani	Eri	River Eridanus	Contains Achernar
Fornax	Fornacis	For	Furnace	Of modern origin
Gemini	Geminorum	Gem	Twins	In zodiac; contains Pollux
Grus	Gruis	Gru	Crane	Of modern origin
Hercules	Herculis	Her	Hercules	Character from Greek myth
Horologium	Horologii	Hor	Clock	Of modern origin
Hydra	Hydrae	Hya	Hydra	Monster from Greek myth; largest constellation
Hydrus	Hydri	Hyi	Sea Serpent	Of modern origin

Name	Genitive	Abbreviation	Translation	Remarks
Indus	Indi	Ind	Indian	Of modern origin
Lacerta	Lacertae	Lac	Lizard	Of modern origin
Leo	Leonis	Leo	Lion	In zodiac; contains Regulus
Leo Minor	Leonis Minoris	LMi	Little Lion	Of modern origin
Lepus	Leporis	Lep	Hare	—
Libra	Librae	Lib	Scales	In zodiac
Lupus	Lupi	Lup	Wolf	—
Lynx	Lyncis	Lyn	Lynx	Of modern origin
Lyra	Lyrae	Lyr	Harp	Contains Vega
Mensa	Mensae	Men	Table (mountain)	Of modern origin
Microscopium	Microscopii	Mic	Microscope	Of modern origin
Monoceros	Monocerotis	Mon	Unicorn	Of modern origin
Musca	Muscae	Mus	Fly	Of modern origin
Norma	Normae	Nor	Carpenter's Square	Of modern origin
Octans	Octanis	Oct	Octant	Of modern origin
Ophiuchus	Ophiuchi	Oph	Ophiuchus (Serpent Bearer)	Character in Greek myth
Orion	Orionis	Ori	Orion	The hunter, character in Greek myth; contains Rigel, Betelgeuse, and Bellatrix
Pavo	Pavonis	Pav	Peacock	Of modern origin
Pegasus	Pegasi	Peg	Pegasus	Winged horse in Greek myth
Perseus	Persei	Per	Perseus	Character in Greek myth
Phoenix	Phoenicis	Phe	Phoenix	Of modern origin
Pictor	Pictoris	Pic	Painter	Of modern origin
Pisces	Piscium	Psc	Fish	In zodiac
Piscis Austrinus	Piscis Austrini	PsA	Southern Fish	Contains Fomalhaut
Puppis	Puppis	Pup	Ship's Stern[1]	Of modern origin
Pyxis	Pyxidis	Pyx	Ship's Compass[1]	Of modern origin
Reticulum	Reticuli	Ret	Net	Of modern origin
Sagitta	Sagittae	Sge	Arrow	—
Sagittarius	Sagittarii	Sgr	Archer	In zodiac
Scorpius	Scorpii	Sco	Scorpion	In zodiac; contains Antares and Shaula
Sculptor	Sculptoris	Scl	Sculptor	Of modern origin
Scutum	Scuti	Sct	Shield	Of modern origin
Serpens	Serpentis	Ser	Serpent	—
Sextans	Sextantis	Sex	Sextant	Of modern origin
Taurus	Tauri	Tau	Bull	In zodiac; contains Aldebaran and Elnath
Telescopium	Telescopii	Tel	Telescope	Of modern origin
Triangulum	Trianguli	Tri	Triangle	—
Triangulum Australe	Trianguli Australis	TrA	Southern Triangle	Of modern origin
Tucana	Tucanae	Tuc	Toucan	Of modern origin
Ursa Major	Ursae Majoris	UMa	Big Bear	Big Dipper
Ursa Minor	Ursae Minoris	UMi	Little Bear	Little Dipper
Vela	Velorum	Vel	Ship's Sails[1]	Of modern origin
Virgo	Virginis	Vir	Virgin	In zodiac; contains Spica
Volans	Volantis	Vol	Flying Fish	Of modern origin
Vulpecula	Vulpeculae	Vul	Little Fox	Of modern origin

1. Formerly part of the constellation Argo Navis, the Argonauts' ship.

Roughly, each whole number difference in magnitude corresponds to 2.5 times the brightness.

By the time this system was introduced, astronomers already were able to determine the distances of some stars from Earth. Friedrich Wilhelm Bessel was the first to make such a measurement, which he announced in 1838. A closer star appears brighter than a similar star that is farther way. To better understand the relative brightness of stars as they actually are, astronomers imagine viewing all stars from the same distance away. A star's brightness from this distance, which is 10 parsecs or 32.6 light-years, is called its absolute magnitude.

If we could see it clearly, the star Cygnus OB2 #12 would be the brightest star in the Milky Way galaxy (absolute magnitude –9.9), but it is not only far from Earth but also is obscured by dust. The brightest single object known is not a star, but a quasar (see "The Universe," below), BR 1202–07, with an absolute magnitude of about –33. The Sun has the brightest apparent magnitude of any star, –26.8, but its absolute magnitude is only 4.75.

The Universe

Most of the universe was greatly misunderstood until the 20th century. The most common notion from the time of the ancient Greek philosophers until the end of the Middle Ages was that a number of crystal spheres revolved about Earth, and that each of the planets and Earth's Moon occupied one of these spheres. All the stars occupied the farthest sphere. There were only about 6,000 stars known, those visible to the naked eye (and about half of these were south of the equator, so few Europeans had ever seen them).

In 1609 Galileo of Italy turned the first astronomical telescope on the heavens. Galileo's early telescopes were good enough to show that the Milky Way was not merely a whitish band across the sky but consisted of a vast number of stars, far more than the few thousand visible with the naked eye. People began to speculate about astronomical entities beyond a simple sphere of stars. Not until 1924 were telescopes sufficiently powerful to show that many cloudy patches in the sky consisted of millions of stars far away from the Milky Way. This discovery led to the recognition of the enormous complexity and diversity of the universe.

Big Bang The accepted theory of how the universe began is known as the Big Bang theory, since it proposes that the universe began as something like an explosion, which has caused all parts of the universe to rush away from one another (the expansion of the universe). Such an expansion is observed. Other evidence for the Big Bang theory is the discovery of cosmic background radiation, a radiation that seems to come equally from all directions. Cosmic background radiation has the characteristics expected if the universe resulted from a small, dense region exploding.

Binary stars Almost half the stars in the visible universe are actually pairs of stars that orbit each other. Astronomers can sometimes see both stars, but more commonly they recognize that a star is part of a binary because of the influence of the dimmer star's gravitational pull on the other star.

Black holes When a body becomes so massive for its size that not even light can escape the powerful gravitational pull it exerts, it is called a black hole. Black holes were predicted as early as 1784 (by John Michell) and invoked later by various astronomers and physicists to explain many strange astronomical phenomena. It is still not completely clear that any black holes have been found, but they are widely suspected of being at the center of many galaxies, including our own Milky Way.

Brown dwarfs are bodies too small to be stars, but too large to be planets. They glow dimly as a result of energy released by gravitational contraction. A brown dwarf must be between 10 and 80 times the size of Jupiter. None have been positively identified as yet, although several small stars qualify as near misses. Despite the lack of evidence, astronomers think brown dwarfs may be plentiful and may account for the "missing mass" (see below).

Dwarfs All stars can be plotted on a graph where the horizontal axis is spectral class (temperature) and the vertical axis is absolute magnitude (true brightness); such a graph is called a Hertzsprung-Russell (H-R) diagram. On an H-R diagram, most stars fall along the main sequence, a slightly curvy line from the top left to the bottom right of the graph. Stars above the line are giants. White and brown dwarfs fall below the line. Dwarfs are small stars that lie on the main sequence—the brightest are red dwarfs, the dimmest blue dwarfs. The Sun, near the middle of the main sequence, is a yellow dwarf.

Expanding universe When Albert Einstein developed his general theory of relativity, he found it predicted that the universe would expand as if it were exploding. He tried to correct this prediction by inserting a factor in his equations to counteract the prediction, but in the 1920s, Edwin Hubble discovered that the universe actually is expanding. It is easier to measure the speed of recession than the distance, so astronomers commonly use the speed something is moving away as the measure of its distance from us. Of course, it is not just moving away from *us*. In the expanding universe, everything is moving away from everything else.

Galaxies are systems of very many stars separated from one another by largely empty space (sometimes galaxies are called island universes). In the 18th century, William Herschel concluded that many cloudy patches of light seen among the stars were actually giant systems of billions of stars, but so far away from Earth as to look like clouds. Better telescopes proved him right in the early 20th century, and these far-off, great masses of stars became known as galaxies, after our own Milky Way, the galaxy that includes the Sun. Observation with large telescopes in the 20th century has revealed two main types of galaxies—spiral and elliptical—although some galaxies are neither (irregular).

Milky Way This is the galaxy to which the Sun and Earth belong. If you are in a place unafflicted with much light pollution, when you look at the night sky, you can see a faint band crossing it. The ancient Greeks named this the Milky Way (*galaxy* in Greek). Early in the 19th century, William Herschel determined that our Sun was a star in a vast lens-shaped star system, and that the Milky Way was the part of the star system we see from our vantage point inside it. Today, recognizing there are very many other such star systems, scientists often call it the Milky Way galaxy.

Missing mass is matter that is apparently in the universe but that has not been observed. Astronomers note that galaxies are rotating as if they were embedded in larger, invisible bodies. Furthermore, there are theoretical reasons to believe there is even more matter in the universe than can be accounted for by the invisible matter surrounding galaxies. Ideas as to what this "missing mass" might be include everything from brown dwarfs to undiscovered subatomic particles.

Nebulae are patches of gas and dust observable in telescopes. Before Herschel discovered that some cloudy patches seen through telescopes were vast collections of stars, all such patches were called nebulae (meaning *clouds*). Some "clouds" turned out to be galaxies, but many did not. The patches of gas emit light, often by the same mechanism that a fluorescent light does; energy ionizes the gas, which gives off visible light. Some patches of dust also glow, usually reflecting the light of nearby stars. Other patches of dust are opaque or nearly so, blocking out part of the sky. Some of the most striking nebulae consist of glowing gas surrounded by opaque dust or vice versa, which give the nebulae a definite shape, such as the North America Nebula (shaped like the continent of North America) or the Horsehead Nebula (which looks like a black horse's head against a glowing background). Herschel also studied a class of nebulae that looked to be giant spheres. He correctly concluded that these planetary nebulae were balls of gas produced when a star exploded.

Neutron stars are stars that have collapsed in a violent explosion, such as a supernova, so that the force keeping electrons apart is overcome. All the neutrons and protons can touch, forming the equivalent of a giant atomic nucleus. The star is electrically neutral because of the charge of the collapsed electrons. Such a star may be only a dozen miles in diameter but may have a mass twice that of the Sun.

Novae are stars that seem to appear in place of dim stars or out of nowhere. Early peoples were surprised from time to time by the appearance of a new *(nova)* star in the sky. Ancient Chinese astronomers called them guest stars. It is now clear that a truly new star does not appear; instead, a dim, existing star suddenly brightens. In early days, before the telescope, the dim stars could not be seen at all, so it looked as if a star came from nowhere. Today we know that there are two different types of "guest stars," and we reserve the name nova for one type and call the other a supernova (see below). The type referred to today as novae are less bright than supernovae and may appear more than once. It is thought that they occur when material from one star in a binary pair falls on the other star, causing it suddenly to flare up.

Pulsars are neutron stars that emit electromagnetic signals from their magnetic poles in a direction that reaches Earth. All neutron stars emit signals and rotate very rapidly (at least when they are first formed; they gradually slow down). These signals form a tight beam. If the beam intersects Earth, a radio telescope observes a fast pulsing on and off of the signal. The pulses are so regular that when they were first discovered, they were thought to be the work of extraterrestrial beings.

Quasars are distant sources of great energy. The name *quasar* is short for Quasi-Stellar Object, and the objects are so called because they seem to be about the size and general appearance of stars, but produce far too much energy to be stars. No one knows for sure what they are, but there is some evidence that quasars are the central part of distant galaxies. The stars in the galaxies cannot be seen because of the great distance, so we see only the central part, which is the quasar.

Red giants are stars that have used their hydrogen fuel and expanded as a result. Young stars "burn" hydrogen in a nuclear fusion process that leads to helium. When a star has consumed the hydrogen in its core, new fusion reactions that start with helium begin, leading to carbon. The new reactions are hotter than the fusion of hydrogen to helium. This added energy causes the hydrogen and helium outside the core to expand. When the Sun becomes a red giant in the distant future, it will expand almost to the orbit of Earth, completely engulfing Mercury and Venus, and charring Earth to a cinder. The star is red because the outer layers are relatively cool.

Stars are bodies of gas large enough to undergo fusion reactions in their core. As a result of the energy produced by fusion, stars emit visible light, as well as electromagnetic radiation at other wavelengths. The Sun is a star. The hotter or larger a star is, the brighter it is.

Superclusters and clusters of galaxies are groups of galaxies associated in space. There may be just a few members of a cluster or as many as thousands. About two dozen galaxies near us form, with the Milky Way, our Local Group. The members of the Local Group also include the Andromeda galaxy and the Large and Small Magellanic Clouds. All are traveling through the universe together. The Local Group is a member of a supercluster of galaxies, called the Local Supercluster, that contains about 100 clusters. Clusters and superclusters are primarily recognized because the average distance within a cluster or a supercluster from one galaxy or cluster to another is much less than the distance to other galaxies or clusters.

Supernovae are large stars that explode. A supernova explosion is much more dramatic than the brightening of a nova. A supernova reported by Chinese astronomers from A.D. 1054 was visible in the daytime. The remnants of this explosion are known today as the Crab Nebula. At its heart the Crab Nebula has a pulsar, all that is left of the star that exploded.

Variable stars Any star that periodically changes brightness is called a variable (a nova changes brightness but not at regular intervals). The period varies with the cause of the change and the individual star. Some variables are part of a binary system in which one star periodically passes in front of the other. Other kinds of variables are called Mira variables and Cepheid variables, after the first stars known of each type. It is not clear what causes the brightness to vary.

White dwarfs are stars whose cores have collapsed until all the atoms are pressed very close together. A single teaspoonful of the matter in a white dwarf weighs about five tons. The core collapses because a red giant has used all its helium for fuel, but the star is too small to start burning carbon.

Elements in the Universe

Astronomers and physicists believe that the Big Bang produced a universe that contained 80 percent hydrogen, 20 percent helium, and probably no other elements at all. When clouds of hydrogen and helium began to collapse into small spaces as a result of gravitational forces, the nuclei of hydrogen atoms were pressed so close together that they fused into heavier hydrogen (deuterium and tritium), which in turn fused to form helium. The process released energy, and the balls of hydrogen and helium became stars. The energy released balanced the force of gravity, and the stars stabilized in size. This is the source of the Sun's energy, and the process continues today for other small stars. In larger stars the helium and hydrogen continue to fuse, producing nitrogen, carbon, neon, and some oxygen, as well as more helium. Still-larger stars go farther, and are able to produce heavier elements, including magnesium and silicon.

Iron is the end of the line for this process, because fusing iron nuclei takes more energy than the process produces. Gravitational energy, however, causes the star's core to contract with great speed when the fusion process begins to slacken. This contraction provides the necessary energy to fuse iron, but it provides so much energy that the star blows up, becoming a supernova. In the process of exploding, elements heavier than iron are created. Furthermore, the explosion sends all the elements from the supernova into space, creating clouds that contain all elements. The solar system apparently formed from such a cloud, since silicon, oxygen, and iron are abundant, and elements as heavy as uranium occur in smaller amounts.

Since the Big Bang, some hydrogen and helium have remained as interstellar gases, and some have formed smaller stars in which the fusion process does not go beyond fusion of helium. As a result more hydrogen and helium are still present than any other elements. Carbon, nitrogen, and oxygen are the main components of the medium-size star's fusion cycle, so they are the next most abundant elements. After iron is produced, the amount of heavier elements present through supernovae explosions goes down considerably, although nickel occurs in quantities near that of iron. With few exceptions fusion produces elements with even atomic numbers more easily than those with odd atomic numbers. (See "Properties, Abundance, and Discovery of the Elements.")

EXPLORING THE UNIVERSE

Optical Telescopes

Telescopes were first developed in Holland about 400 years ago. The first telescopes used lenses to gather light and focus it. Later in the 17th century, scientists realized that curved mirrors could also gather and focus light. Since the light did not need to pass through the mirror (as light passes through a lens), mirrors proved to be more efficient than lenses for large telescopes.

Year	Type	Importance
1608	Lens	Hans Lippershey in Holland applies for first patent on a telescope
1609	Lens	Galileo builds first astronomical telescopes, eventually reaching 30 power
1611	Lens	Johannes Kepler introduces convex lens, producing greater power
1663	Mirror	James Gregory is first to think that reflecting telescope can be made
1668	Mirror	Isaac Newton builds first telescope to use mirror to collect light, rather than lens
1723	Mirror	John Hadley invents reflecting telescope based on parabola, which concentrates light at a point
1789	Mirror	William Herschel builds telescope with 48-in. (122-cm) mirror, largest for many years
1897	Lens	Alvan Clark builds what is still world's largest telescope to use lens instead of mirror, 40 in. (102 cm)
1917	Mirror	Hooker Telescope at Mount Wilson in California is put into operation; it will be world's largest for about 30 years
1930	Combination	Bernard Schmidt makes first telescopes combining lenses and mirrors; they become workhorse of astronomy
1948	Mirror	Hale Telescope (200 in., or 5 m), located on Mt. Palomar in California, becomes largest and best on Earth
1962	Mirror	Largest telescope devoted to observing the Sun is erected at Kitt Peak in Arizona
1976	Mirror	Soviet Zelenchuksaya becomes largest telescope, but various problems limit effectiveness
1979	Mirrors	MMT on Mt. Hopkins in Arizona uses six mirrors now, but will install two 266-in. (6.5-m) and one 315-in. (8-m) mirrors in mid-1990s
1990	Mirror	Hubble Space Telescope (94 in., or 2.4 m) becomes first optical telescope in space
1991	Mirror	Keck I Telescope in Hawaii uses world's largest mirror, 396 in. in diameter, with 4 times light-gathering capacity of the Hale Telescope; will be joined in 1996 by identical Keck II Telescope, also located on Mauna Kea

Radio Telescopes

Before 1931 all telescopes were optical—i.e., they gathered and focused electromagnetic radiation in the range people can sense with their eyes. Stars, planets, and other objects in the universe also produce other wavelengths of radiation, however. A radio telescope gathers and focuses radiation at long wavelengths, the same kind of electromagnetic radiation used for transmission of radio signals.

Year	Type	Importance
1931	Ordinary antenna	Karl Jansky accidentally discovers, in trying to track down sources of static, that radio waves are coming from space
1937	Parabolic dish	Grote Reber builds first intentional radio telescope dish, Wheaton, Ill.
1957	Steerable dish	Parabolic dish (250 ft., or 75 m) at Jodrell Bank in England is first major radio telescope
1962	Steerable dish	Dish (300 ft., or 90 m) at Green Bank, W.Va., first used to search for extraterrestrial life; it collapses mysteriously on Nov. 15, 1988
1963	Fixed dish	Largest fixed-dish radio telescope, 1,000 ft. (305 m) across, is built in valley at Arecibo, Puerto Rico
1970	Steerable dish	World's largest steerable dish, at Effelsberg, W. Germany, is 328 ft. (100 m) in diameter
1977	Several antennae	First Very Long Baseline Interferometry begins operating at Cal Tech's Owens Valley Radio Observatory
1980	27 antennae	Very Long Array (VLA) is built in 13-mi. (21 km) Y shape near Socorro, New Mexico
1993	10 antennae	Very Long Baseline Array (VLBA) uses techniques that produce a resolution 500 times better than the best optical telescopes
1995	30 antennae	The Giant Meterwave Radio Telescope north of Pune, India, contains 30 parabolic 45-m (148-ft.) antennae arranged in a 25-km (15 mi.) Y

Other Telescopes

Since both short wavelengths and long ones coming from space had been studied by optical and radio telescopes, it seemed likely that other wavelengths could also be detected. The problem was that Earth's atmosphere, relatively transparent to optical and radio waves, is almost opaque to other wavelengths of electromagnetic radiation. The solution to making telescopes that could detect other wavelengths was to put telescopes in satellites traveling above Earth's atmosphere.

MAJOR ACCOMPLISHMENTS OF SATELLITES AND SPACE PROBES, 1957–95

While much attention is focused on human beings in space, most of the serious scientific progress has been made by satellites or probes—the general name for space vehicles that neither carry humans nor orbit Earth—that are directed internally or from Earth. Since 1957 there have been hundreds of such satellites and probes.

Launch date	Name	Accomplishment
10/4/57	Sputnik 1	First satellite to orbit Earth (USSR)
11/3/57	Sputnik 2	Carries Laika, first dog in space; burns in atmosphere 4/14/58
1/31/58	Explorer 1	First satellite to detect Van Allen radiation belts; first U.S. satellite
3/17/58	Vanguard	Demonstrates that Earth is pear shaped with slight bulge in Southern Hemisphere (U.S.)
1/2/59	Mechta	First space probe to go into orbit around Sun, passing 5,000 mi. from Moon (at which it was aimed) (USSR)
3/3/59	Pioneer IV	First American probe aimed at Moon; like Mechta it misses and goes into orbit about Sun
9/12/59	Lunik II	First space probe to reach Moon, where it crash-lands (USSR)
10/4/59	Lunik III	First space probe to return photographs of far side of Moon (USSR)
4/1/60	Tiros I	First weather satellite (U.S.)
6/22/60	Transit I-B	First navigational satellite (U.S.)
8/12/60	Echo I	First communications satellite—actually a large balloon off which radio signals could be bounced (U.S.)
8/18/60	Corona	First U.S. spy satellite
8/19/60	Sputnik 5	Carries dogs Belka and Streika and successfully returns them to Earth; 18 orbits
12/12/61	Venera 1	First space probe intended to reach another planet—Venus (USSR)
3/7/62	OSO I	Orbiting Solar Observatory—first major astronomical satellite (U.S.)
4/23/62	Ranger IV	First U.S. space probe to reach Moon
4/26/62	Cosmos 4	First Soviet spy satellite
7/10/62	Telstar	First active communications satellite, allowing direct television between Europe and U.S. (U.S.)
8/27/62	Mariner II	First space probe to reach vicinity of another planet (Venus) and return scientific information (U.S.)
10/31/62	Anna I-B	First satellite intended for accurately measuring shape of Earth (U.S.)
11/1/62	Mars I	First space probe aimed at Mars; contact lost about 66 million mi. from Earth (USSR)
6/26/63	Syncom II	First communications satellite to go into synchronous orbit with Earth (U.S.)
7/28/64	Ranger VII	Returns close-up photographs of Moon before crashing into it (U.S.)
8/28/64	Nimbus I	First weather satellite to be stabilized so that its cameras always point toward Earth (U.S.)
11/28/64	Mariner IV	Flies by Mars and takes 21 pictures of its surface, successfully transmitting them back to Earth; its closest approach is 6,118 mi. (U.S.)
4/6/65	Early Bird	First commercial satellite (U.S.)
4/23/65	Molniya I	First Soviet communications satellite
7/16/65	Proton I	At 26,896 lbs., it is largest Earth satellite to this date (USSR)
11/16/65	Venera 3	Crash-lands on Venus; first space probe to make physical contact with another planet; radio contact lost before it reaches immediate vicinity of planet (USSR)
11/26/65	A-1	First satellite to be launched by nation other than the USSR or U.S. (France)
12/16/65	Pioneer 6	Launched into solar orbit; still functions today
1/31/66	Luna 9	Although main vehicle crash-lands, ejected capsule lands safely on Moon and transmits photographs to Earth (USSR)
5/30/66	Surveyor 1	First soft landing of complete vehicle on Moon (U.S.)
3/31/66	Luna 10	First space vehicle to go into orbit about Moon (USSR)
8/10/66	Lunar Orbiter 1	First American space vehicle to go into orbit about Moon
6/12/67	Venera 4	Ejects instrument package into atmosphere of Venus; package parachutes toward surface; contact lost before reaching surface (USSR)
6/14/67	Mariner 5	Second American satellite to reach vicinity of Venus
9/15/68	Zond 5	First Soviet satellite to return to Earth from vicinity of Moon
2/11/70	Ohsumi	First satellite to be launched by Japan
4/24/70	Mao 1	First Chinese satellite; it broadcasts song "The East Is Red" once a minute, pausing at the end for other signals
8/17/70	Venera 7	First Venus probe to return signals from planet's surface (USSR)
9/12/70	Luna 16	First space probe to land on Moon without humans aboard, scoop up samples, and return them to Earth (USSR)
11/10/70	Luna 17	Carries roving vehicle to Moon's surface; vehicle roams for 2 weeks at a time (during daylight), then "sleeps"; as it roams, it returns photos and other data to Earth (USSR)
12/12/70	Uhuru	First X-ray satellite telescope (U.S.)
5/28/71	Mars 3	First space probe to soft-land on Mars, although it quickly ceases functioning (USSR)
5/30/71	Mariner 9	First space probe to orbit another planet (Mars); returns 7,329 photographs of planet (U.S.)
3/2/72	Pioneer 10	First space probe to study Jupiter and, on June 13, 1983, first to leave solar system (U.S.)
7/23/72	Landsat I	First Earth resources satellite (U.S.)
3/6/73	Pioneer 11	First space probe to reach vicinity of Saturn (U.S.)
11/3/73	Mariner 10	First space probe to observe 2 planets, Venus and Mercury, and only probe ever to observe Mercury (U.S.)
12/10/74	Helios	First W. German space probe
6/8/75	Venera 9	Returns first photographs from surface of Venus (USSR)
8/20/75	Viking 1	First American space probe to soft-land on Mars; continues to return data until May 1983
9/20/75	Viking 2	Successfully soft-lands on Mars (U.S.)
8/20/77	Voyager 2	After studying Jupiter and Saturn, it becomes first space probe to reach vicinities of Uranus and Neptune (U.S.)
9/5/77	Voyager 1	After studying Jupiter, it becomes first space probe to reach vicinity of Saturn (U.S.)
1/26/78	IUE	International Ultraviolet Explorer—the only astronomical satellite to be placed in geosynchronous orbit; it is still sending back data
5/20/78	Pioneer 12 (Venus 1)	First space probe to go into orbit about Venus; stays in orbit until Oct. 1993 (U.S.)
6/26/78	Seasat	Analyzes ocean currents and ice flow (U.S.)
8/12/78	ISEE-3	Originally the third International Sun-Earth Explorer, space probe is renamed International Cometary Explorer (ICE) when it is redirected to study tail of comet Giacobini-Zinner in 1983 (U.S.)
12/13/78	HEAO-2	High-Energy Astronomy Observatory, also known as the Einstein Observatory—it makes high-resolution X-ray images of the universe (U.S.)
2/24/79	P78-1	Studies solar radiation until purposely shot down by U.S. Air Force 9/13/85; still working at time of its destruction, satellite is deemed by many scientists to be too valuable to be used as target (U.S.)
2/14/80	Solar Max	Studies solar radiation; after failure in Nov. 1980, it is repaired and relaunched from space shuttle in April 1984; finally pushed to its destruction by massive solar flare, Dec. 2, 1989 (U.S.)
1/25/83	IRAS	Infrared Astronomical Satellite studies galactic and extragalactic infrared sources and discovers new stars forming as well as possible planet formation (U.S.)
12/15/84	Vega 1	First Soviet mission to study Halley's comet; along the way it drops balloon probe into atmosphere of Venus
12/21/84	Vega 2	Second Soviet mission to Halley's comet; it also releases a balloon probe at Venus
1/7/85	Sakigake	First Japanese mission to study Halley's comet (this one from far away)

Launch date	Name	Accomplishment
7/2/85	Giotto	Joint European mission to Halley's comet; passes closest to the comet—375 mi.—and later redirected to comet Grigg-Skjellerup, which it passes 7/10/92 at a distance of 125 mi.
8/18/85	Suisei	Japanese mission to Halley's comet
2/21/86	SPOT	French satellite designed to photograph surface details of Earth as small as 30 ft. across
5/4/89	Magellan	American probe orbited Venus and mapped it in detail with radar
10/18/89	Galileo	After passing near Venus and Earth (twice), it will orbit Jupiter, report on Jovian moons, and drop probe into Jupiter's atmosphere (U.S.)
11/18/89	Cosmic Background Explorer (COBE)	Currently studying cosmic background radiation in hopes of learning cause of galaxy formation
4/24/90	Hubble Space Telescope	Flawed optical telescope placed in orbit about Earth by U.S.; successfully repaired 12/10/93
10/6/90	Ulysses	U.S.–European Space Agency to study previously unobserved north and south poles of the Sun
4/5/91	Compton Gamma Ray Observatory	A 17-ton telescope for observing the universe at very short wavelengths
6/7/92	Extreme Ultraviolet Explorer (EUVA)	American satellite to study high range of ultraviolet radiation in universe
7/5/92	Sampex	Solar, Anomalous, and Magnetospheric Particle Explorer. First of the Small Explorer Project satellites; NASA hopes to launch one of these inexpensive scientific satellites every year
7/24/92	Geotail	Japanese satellite launched by NASA to study Earth's magnetosphere
10/6/92	Freja	A Swedish satellite launched by a Chinese rocket from the Gobi Desert, Freja carries experiments from the U.S., Sweden, Canada, France, and Germany; The U.S. experiment is measuring Earth's magnetosphere
2/2/93	Znamya (banner)	Russia's 65-foot-diameter Mylar mirror, which reflects sunlight to nighttime regions of Earth in a feasibility experiment
2/9/93	Pegasus 3	Brazilian satellite to monitor environment in Amazonia, launched by Orbital Sciences Corp. of Fairfax, Va.
2/20/93	Astro-D	Japanese X-ray telescope
11/22/93	Gorizant (horizon)	Russian communications satellite launched into a geostationary orbit controlled by Tonga as a commercial venture by Rimsat Corp. of Fort Wayne, Ind.
1/25/94	Clementine	Joint U.S. military-science mission to map the moon from lunar orbit and later visit the asteroid Geographos
2/9/94	Shijan 4	Chinese space research satellite
3/9/94	Tether experiment	A 15-lb., 12-mi.-long plastic string unwound from a small U.S. satellite is the first space object to be visible from Earth with the naked eye as something other than a point of light
4/14/94	GOES-8	The first of five U.S. Geostationary Operational Environmental Satellites using new technology to track weather in North America
11/1/94	WIND	To go into a figure-8 orbit around the Earth and Moon at first, studying the solar wind; in 1996, will move to a point in Earth's orbit and orbit the Sun itself, staying in the same relation to the Earth as it revolves, about a million miles from Earth

SPACEFLIGHTS CARRYING PEOPLE, 1961–95

The space programs of the Soviet Union and the United States both had dramatic flights by human pilots as an important component, although many scientists felt that most goals of the space program could be achieved without risking lives. The *Vostok, Voskhod,* and *Soyuz* missions are part of the Soviet program; *Mercury, Gemini, Apollo, Skylab,* and the shuttle are part of the U.S. program.

Date	Craft	Duration	Crew	Remarks
Proving that people can venture into space				
4/12/61	*Vostok 1*	1 hr. 48 min.	Yuri A. Gagarin	First spaceflight by human
5/5/61	*Mercury 3*	15 min.	Alan B. Shepard, Jr.	Suborbital
7/21/61	*Mercury 4*	16 min.	Virgil I. Grissom	Suborbital
8/6/61	*Vostok 2*	25 hrs. 18 min.	Gherman S. Titov	First multiorbit flight; 17 orbits
2/20/62	*Mercury 6*	5 hrs. 55 min.	John H. Glenn, Jr.	First orbital flight by American; 3 orbits
5/24/62	*Mercury 7*	4 hrs. 56 min.	M. Scott Carpenter	3 orbits
8/11/62	*Vostok 3*	94 hrs. 24 min.	Andrian G. Nikolayev	64 orbits; landing by parachute
8/12/62	*Vostok 4*	70 hrs. 57 min.	Pavel R. Popovitch	Dual launch with *Vostok 3;* 48 orbits
10/3/62	*Mercury 8*	9 hrs. 13 min.	Walter M. Schirra	6 orbits
5/15/63	*Mercury 9*	34 hrs. 20 min.	L. Gordon Cooper	22 orbits
6/14/63	*Vostok 5*	119 hrs. 6 min.	Valery F. Bikovsky	81 orbits
6/16/63	*Vostok 6*	70 hrs. 50 min.	Valentina V. Tereshkova	First woman cosmonaut; 48 orbits; dual launch with *Vostok 5*
10/12/64	*Voskhod 1*	24 hrs. 17 min.	Vladimir M. Komarov Konstantin P. Feoktistov Boris B. Yegorov	First multihuman crew; 3 cosmonauts make 16 orbits
Planning for operations in space				
3/18/65	*Voskhod 2*	26 hrs.	Aleksei A. Leonov Pavel I. Belyayev	First extravehicular activity (EVA) by Leonov (20 min.); 17 orbits
3/23/65	*Gemini 3*	4 hrs. 53 min.	Virgil I. Grissom John W. Young	First American multi-person crew; 3 orbits
6/3/65	*Gemini 4*	97 hrs. 56 min.	James A. McDivitt Edward H. White II	62 orbits; first American EVA: first use of personal propulsion unit
8/21/65	*Gemini 5*	190 hrs. 56 min.	L. Gordon Cooper Charles Conrad, Jr.	120 orbits; demonstrates feasibility of lunar mission; simulated rendezvous
12/4/65	*Gemini 7*	330 hrs. 35 min.	Frank Borman James A. Lovell, Jr.	206 orbits; extensions of testing and performance; target for first rendezvous
12/15/65	*Gemini 6A*	25 hrs. 51 min.	Walter M. Schirra Thomas P. Stafford	15 orbits; rendezvous with *Gemini 7*

Date	Craft	Duration	Crew	Remarks
3/16/66	*Gemini 8*	10 hrs. 42 min.	Neil A. Armstrong David R. Scott	6.5 orbits; first dual launch and docking; first Pacific landing
6/3/66	*Gemini 9A*	72 hrs. 21 min.	Thomas P. Stafford Eugene A. Cernan	44 orbits; unable to dock with target vehicle; 2 hrs. 7 min. of EVA
7/18/66	*Gemini 10*	70 hrs. 47 min.	John W. Young Michael Collins	43 orbits; first dual rendezvous, docked vehicle maneuvers; umbilical EVA
9/12/66	*Gemini 11*	71 hrs. 17 min.	Charles Conrad, Jr. Richard F. Gordon, Jr.	44 orbits; rendezvous and docking
11/11/66	*Gemini 12*	94 hrs. 34 min.	James A. Lovell, Jr. Edwin E. Aldrin, Jr.	59 orbits; final *Gemini* mission; 5 hrs. of EVA

To the Moon and experiments in space

Date	Craft	Duration	Crew	Remarks
4/23/67	*Soyuz 1*	26 hrs. 48 min.	Vladimir M. Komarov	18 orbits; Komarov is killed when parachute fails, first fatality of space program
10/11/68	*Apollo 7*	260 hrs. 8 min.	Walter M. Schirra Donn F. Eisele R. Walter Cunningham	8 service propulsion firings; 7 live TV sessions with crew; rendezvous with S-IVB stage performed
10/26/68	*Soyuz 3*	94 hrs. 51 min.	Georgi T. Beregovoi	64 orbits; approaches unpiloted *Soyuz 2* to distance of 650 ft. (198 m)
12/21/68	*Apollo 8*	147 hrs.	Frank Borman James A. Lovell, Jr. William A. Anders	First *Saturn-V* propelled flight; first lunar orbital mission (10 orbits); returns good lunar photography
1/14/69	*Soyuz 4*	71 hrs. 14 min.	Vladimir A. Shatalov	48 orbits; docks with *Soyuz 5* in first linkup of 2 space vehicles both carrying people
1/15/69	*Soyuz 5*	72 hrs. 46 min.	Boris V. Volynov Alexei S. Yeliseyev Yevgeni V. Khrunov	3 cosmonauts perform EVA, transferred to *Soyuz 4 in* rescue rehearsal
3/3/69	*Apollo 9*	241 hrs. 1 min.	James A. McDivitt David R. Scott Russell L. Schweickart	First flight of all lunar hardware in Earth orbit, incl. lunar module (LM)
5/18/69	*Apollo 10*	192 hrs. 3 min.	Eugene A. Cernan John W. Young Thomas P. Stafford	Lunar mission development flight to evaluate LM performance in lunar environment; descent to within 50,000 ft. of Moon
7/16/69	*Apollo 11*	165 hrs. 18 min.	Neil A. Armstrong Michael Collins Edwin E. Aldrin, Jr.	First lunar landing; limited inspection, photography, evaluation, and sampling of lunar soil; touchdown: July 20
10/11/69	*Soyuz 6*	118 hrs. 42 min.	Georgi S. Shonin Valery N. Kubasov	First triple launch (with *Soyuz 7* and *8*)
10/12/69	*Soyuz 7*	118 hrs. 41 min.	Anatoly V. Filipchenko Vladislav N. Volkov Viktor V. Gorbatko	With *Soyuz 6* and *8*, conducts experiments in navigation and photography
10/13/69	*Soyuz 8*	118 hrs. 59 min.	Vladimir A. Shatalov Aleksei S. Yeliseyev	80 orbits
11/14/69	*Apollo 12*	244 hrs. 36 min.	Charles Conrad, Jr. Richard F. Gordon, Jr. Alan L. Bean	Second lunar landing; demonstrates point landing capability; samples more area; total EVA time: 15 hrs. 32 min.
4/11/70	*Apollo 13*	142 hrs. 55 min.	James A. Lovell, Jr. Fred W. Haise, Jr. John L. Swigert, Jr.	Third lunar landing attempt aborted owing to loss of pressure in liquid oxygen in service module and fuel cell failure
6/2/70	*Soyuz 9*	424 hrs. 59 min. (17 days 16 hrs.)	Andrian G. Nikolayev Vitaly I. Sevastianov	Longest spaceflight to this time
1/31/71	*Apollo 14*	9 days 42 min.	Alan B. Shepard, Jr. Stuart A. Roosa Edgar D. Mitchell	Third lunar landing, returns 98 lbs. of lunar material
4/23/71	*Soyuz 10*	47 hrs. 46 min.	Vladimir A. Shatalov Alexei S. Yeleseyev Nikolai N. Rukavishnikov	Docks with *Salyut 1*, the first space station
6/6/71	*Soyuz 11*	23 days 18 hrs. 22 min.	Georgi T. Dobrovolsky Viktor I. Patsayev Vladislav N. Volkov	All 3 cosmonauts killed during reentry
7/26/71	*Apollo 15*	12 days 7 hrs. 12 min.	David R. Scott Alfred M. Worden James B. Irwin	Fourth lunar landing; first to carry Lunar Roving Vehicle (LRV); total EVA time: 18 hrs. 46 min.; returns 173 lbs. of material
4/16/72	*Apollo 16*	11 days 14 hrs. 51 min.	John W. Young Thomas K. Mattingly II Charles M. Duke, Jr.	Fifth lunar landing; second to carry LRV; total EVA time: 20 hrs. 14 min.; returns 213 lbs. of material
12/7/72	*Apollo 17*	12 days 13 hrs. 52 min.	Eugene A. Cernan Ronald E. Evans Harrison H. Schmitt	Last manned lunar landing; third with LRV; total EVA time: 44 hrs. 8 min.; returns 243 lbs. of material

Date	Craft	Duration	Crew	Remarks
First stations in space				
5/25/73	*Skylab 2*	28 days 49 min.	Charles Conrad, Jr. Joseph P. Kerwin Paul J. Weitz	First *Skylab* launch; establishes *Skylab Orbital Assembly* in earth orbit; conducts medical and other experiments
7/29/73	*Skylab 3*	59 days 11 hrs. 9 min.	Alan L. Bean Owen K. Garriott Jack R. Lousma	Second *Skylab;* crew performs systems and operational tests, experiments, and thermal shield deployment
9/27/73	*Soyuz 12*	47 hrs. 16 min.	Vasily G. Lazarev Oleg G. Makarov	First Soviet spaceflight to carry humans since the *Soyuz 11* tragedy
11/16/73	*Skylab 4*	84 days 1 hr. 7 min.	Gerald P. Carr Edward G. Gibson William R. Pogue	Third *Skylab;* crew services unmanned Saturn workshop; obtains medical data for extending spaceflights
12/18/73	*Soyuz 13*	7 days 20 hrs. 55 min.	Pyotr I. Klimuk Valentin Lebedev	Performs astrophysical and biological experiments
7/3/74	*Soyuz 14*	15 days 17 hrs. 30 min.	Pavel R. Popovich Yuri P. Artyukhin	Crew occupies *Salyut 3* space station; studies Earth resources
8/26/74	*Soyuz 15*	48 hrs. 12 min.	Gennady Sarafanov Lev Demin	Makes unsuccessful attempt to dock with *Salyut 3*
12/2/74	*Soyuz 16*	5 days 22 hrs. 24 min.	Anatoly V. Filipchenko Nikolai N. Rukavishnikov	Taken to check modifications to *Salyut* system
1/10/75	*Soyuz 17*	29 days 13 hrs. 20 min.	Alexei A. Gubarev Georgi M. Grechko	Docks with *Salyut 4;* sets Soviet endurance record at this time
4/5/75	*Soyuz 18A*	22 min.	Vasily G. Lazarev Oleg G. Makarov	Separation from booster fails, and craft fails to reach orbit, but crew successfully lands in western Siberia
5/24/75	*Soyuz 18B*	63 days	Pyotr I. Klimuk Vitaly I. Sevastyanov	Docks with *Salyut 4*
7/15/75	*ASTP*	9 days 1 hr. 30 min.	Thomas P. Stafford Vance D. Brand Donald K. Slayton	Apollo-Soyuz Test Project, cooperative U.S.-Soviet mission
7/15/75	*Soyuz 19*	5 days 23 hrs. 31 min.	Alexei A. Leonov Valery N. Kubasov	Docks with *ASTP,* the U.S. *Apollo* capsule
The Soviet study of human biology in space				
11/17/75	*Soyuz 20*	90 days	No crew	Biological mission; docks with *Salyut 4*
7/6/76	*Soyuz 21*	49 days	Boris V. Volynov Vitaly Zholobov	Docks with *Salyut 5* and performs Earth resource work
9/15/76	*Soyuz 22*	8 days	Valery F. Bykovsky Vladimir Aksenov	Takes Earth-resources photographs
10/14/76	*Soyuz 23*	2 days	Vyacheslav Zudov Valery Rozhdestvensky	Unsuccessful attempt to dock with *Salyut 5;* first landing in water for Soviet program (in Lake Tengiz; unplanned, but crew survives)
2/7/77	*Soyuz 24*	7 days	Viktor G. Gorbatko Yuri N. Glazkov	Docks with *Salyut 5* for 18 days of experiments
10/9/77	*Soyuz 25*	2 days	Vladimir Kovalyonok Valery Ryumin	Unsuccessful attempt to dock with *Salyut 6*
12/10/77	*Soyuz 26*	96 days	Yuri V. Romanenko Georgi M. Grechko	Docks with *Salyut 6;* crew sets endurance record
1/10/78	*Soyuz 27*	6 days	Valdimir Dzhanibekov Oleg G. Makarov	Carries second crew to dock with *Salyut 6* space station
3/2/78	*Soyuz 28*	8 days	Vladimir Remek Alexi A. Gubarev	Carries third crew to board *Salyut 6;* Remek first non-Russian, non-American in space(Czech)
6/15/78	*Soyuz 29*	140 days	Vladimir Kovalyonok Aleksander S. Ivanchenkov	Docks with *Salyut 6;* crew sets new space endurance record
6/27/78	*Soyuz 30*	8 days	Pyotr I. Klimuk Miroslav Hermaszewski	Carries second international crew to *Salyut 6;* first Polish cosmonaut, Hermaszewski
8/25/78	*Soyuz 31*	8 days	Valery F. Bykovsky Sigmund Jahn	Carries third international crew to *Salyut 6;* first East German, Jahn
2/25/79	*Soyuz 32*	175 days	Vladimir Lyakhov Valery Ryumin	Carries crew to *Salyut 6;* new endurance record set
4/10/79	*Soyuz 33*	2 days	Nikolai N. Rukavishnikov Georgi Ivanov	Engine failure prior to docking forces early termination; first Bulgarian, Ivanov
6/6/79	*Soyuz 34*	74 days	No crew	Launches with no crew; returns with crew from *Salyut 6*
4/9/80	*Soyuz 35*	185 days	Valery Ryumin Leonid Popov	Carries 2 crew members to *Salyut 6*
5/26/80	*Soyuz 36*	8 days	Valery N. Kubasov Bertalan Farkas	Carries 2 crew members to *Salyut 6;* crew returns in *Soyuz 35;* first Hungarian, Farkas
6/5/80	*Soyuz T-2*	4 days	Yuri Malyshev Vladimir Aksenov	Test of modified *Soyuz* craft; docks with *Salyut 6*

Date	Craft	Duration	Crew	Remarks
7/23/80	*Soyuz 37*	8 days	Viktor F. Gorbatko Pham Tuan	Exchanges cosmonauts in *Salyut 6;* returns *Soyuz 35* crew after 185 days in orbit; first Vietnamese in space, Tuan
9/18/80	*Soyuz 38*	8 days	Yuri V. Romanenko Arnaldo Tamayo-Mendez	Ferries to *Salyut 6;* first Cuban in space, Tamayo-Mendez
11/27/80	*Soyuz T-3*	13 days	Leonard Kizim Oleg G. Makarov Gennadi M. Strekalov	Ferries to *Salyut 6;* first 3-person crew since *Soyuz 11*
3/12/81	*Soyuz T-4*	75 days	Vladimer Kovalyonok Viktor Savinykh	Mission to *Salyut 6*
3/22/81	*Soyuz 39*	8 days	Vladimir Dzhanibekov Jugderdemuduyn Gurragcha	Docks with *Salyut 6;* first Mongolian, Gurragcha

The space shuttle: U.S. reentry in space

Date	Craft	Duration	Crew	Remarks
4/12/81	*Columbia*	2 days 6 hrs.	John W. Young Robert L. Crippen	First flight of reusable space shuttle *Columbia;* first landing of U.S. spacecraft on land
5/14/81	*Soyuz 40*	8 days	Leonid Popov Dumitru Prunariu	First Romanian (Prunariu) in space
11/12/81	*Columbia*	2 days 6 hrs.	Joe H. Engle Richard H. Truly	First reuse of space shuttle; ended early due to loss of fuel cell
3/22/82	*Columbia*	8 days	Jack R. Lousma C. Gordon Fullerton	Third shuttle flight; payload includes space science experiments
5/13/82	*Soyuz T-5*	211 days	Anatoly Berezovoy Valentin Lebedev	First flight to *Salyut 7;* space station equipped to measure body functions
6/24/82	*Soyuz T-6*	8 days	Vladimir Dzhanibekov Jean-Loup Chrétien Aleksandr Ivanchenkov	Mission to *Salyut 7;* Soviet/French team; first French cosmonaut, Chrétien
6/27/82	*Columbia*	7 days 1 hr.	Thomas K. Mattingly II Henry W. Hartsfield, Jr.	Fourth shuttle mission; first landing on hard surface
8/16/82	*Soyuz T-7*	8 days	Leonid I. Popov Svetlana Savitskaya Alexander Serebrov	Mission to *Salyut 7;* second Soviet woman in space, Savitskaya
11/11/82	*Columbia*	5 days 2 hrs.	Vance D. Brand Robert F. Overmyer Joseph P. Allen William B. Lenoir	First operational mission; first 4-man crew; first deployment of satellites from shuttle
4/4/83	*Challenger*	5 days	Paul J. Weitz Karol J. Bobko Donald H. Peterson F. Story Musgrave	Second shuttle joins fleet; deploys TDRS tracking satellite; first shuttle EVA
4/20/83	*Soyuz T-8*	48 hrs.	Vladimir G. Titov Gennadi M. Strekalov Aleksandr A. Serebrov	3 cosmonauts fail in planned rendezvous with *Salyut 7*
6/18/83	*Challenger*	6 days 2 hrs.	Robert L. Crippen Frederick H. Hauck John M. Fabian Sally K. Ride Norman E. Thagard	First 5-person crew; first U.S. woman in space; first use of Remote Manipulator Structure ("Arm") to deploy and retrieve satellite
6/27/83	*Soyuz T-9*	150 days	Vladimir Lyakhov Aleksandr Aleksandrov	Crew spends 149 days in *Salyut 7* after *Soyuz 10* fails in relief mission
8/30/83	*Challenger*	6 days	Richard H. Truly Daniel C. Brandenstein William Thornton Guion S. Bluford, Jr. Dale A. Gardner	First night launch; first black American (Bluford); launches weather/communications satellite for India
11/28/83	*Columbia*	10 days	John W. Young Brewster H. Shaw, Jr. Robert A.R. Parker Owen K. Garriott Byron K. Lichtenberg Ulf D. Merbold	Launches Spacelab; crew performs experiments in astronomy and medicine
2/3/84	*Challenger*	8 days	Vance D. Brand Bruce McCandless Robert Stewart Ronald McNair Robert L. Gibson	Jet-propelled backpacks carry 2 astronauts on first untethered space walks; 2 satellites (Western Union and Indonesia) lost; first landing at Kennedy Space Center
2/8/84	*Soyuz T-10B*	237 days	Leonard Kizim Oleg Atkov Vladimir Solovyov	Mission to *Salyut 7* to repair propulsion system; sets new duration-in-space record for crew
4/2/84	*Soyuz T-11*	8 days	Yuri Malyshev Gennadi M. Strekalov Rakesh Sharma	Docks with *Salyut 7;* first Indian cosmonaut, Sharma
4/6/84	*Challenger*	8 days	Robert L. Crippen F. Richard Scobee Terry Hart George Nelson James D. van Hoften	Deploys Long Duration Exposure Facility for experiments in space durability; snares Solar Max satellite and repairs altitude-control system
7/18/84	*Soyuz T-12*	12 days	Svetlana Savitskaya Vladimir Dzhanibekov Igor Volk	Savitskaya becomes first woman to walk in space
8/30/84	*Discovery*	6 days	Henry W. Hartsfield, Jr. Michael L. Coats Steven A. Hawley Judith A. Resnik Richard M. Mullane Charles D. Walker	Third shuttle in fleet; deploys 3 satellites and tests a solar sail

Date	Craft	Duration	Crew	Remarks
10/5/84	*Challenger*	7 days	Robert L. Crippen Jon A. McBride Kathryn D. Sullivan Sally K. Ride Marc Gameau David C. Leestma Paul D. Scully-Power	Carries first Canadian astronaut, Gameau; deploys Earth Radiation Budget Satellite and monitors land formations, ocean currents, and wind patterns; uses Sir-B radar system to see beneath surface of sand
11/8/84	*Discovery*	7 days	Frederick H. Hauck David M. Walker Anna L. Fisher Joseph P. Allen Dale A. Gardner	Salvages 2 inoperative satellites and returns them to Earth
1/24/85	*Discovery*	2 days	Thomas K. Mattingly Loren J. Schriver James F. Buchli Ellison S. Onizuka Gary E. Payton	Secret military mission
4/12/85	*Discovery*	6 days	Karol J. Bobko Donald E. Williams Jake Garn Charles D. Walker Jeffrey A. Hoffman S. David Griggs Margaret Rhea Seddon	First U.S. senator in space, Garn
4/29/85	*Challenger*	7 days	Robert F. Overmyer Frederick D. Gregory Don L. Lind Taylor G. Wang Lodewijk van den Berg Norman E. Thagard William Thornton	Carries European Spacelab module and conducts 15 experiments in space
6/6/85	*Soyuz T-13*	112 days	Vladimir Dzhanibekov Viktor Savinykh	Successful mission to repair damage to *Salyut 7,* which had suffered power failure
6/17/85	*Discovery*	6 days	John O. Creighton Shannon W. Lucid Steven R. Nagel Daniel C. Brandenstein John W. Fabian Salman al-Saud Patrick Baudry	First Arabian in space, Prince Salman al-Saud; successfully launches 4 satellites
7/29/85	*Challenger*	7 days	Roy D. Bridges, Jr. Anthony W. England Karl G. Henize F. Story Musgrave C. Gordon Fullerton Loren W. Acton John-David F. Bartoe	Carries Spacelab 2, a group of scientific experiments
8/27/85	*Discovery*	7 days	John M. Lounge James D. van Hoften William F. Fisher Joe H. Engle Richard O. Covey	Repairs satellite Syncom 3
9/17/85	*Soyuz T-14*	65 days	Vladimir Vasyutin Aleksandr N. Volkov Georgi M. Grechko	Takes supplies to *Salyut 7;* terminates early to return Vasyutin to Earth because he is ill
10/4/85	*Atlantis*	2 days	Karol J. Bobko Ronald J. Grabe David C. Hilmers William A. Pailes Robert C. Stewart	Fourth shuttle brings fleet up to target size
10/30/85	*Challenger*	7 days	Henry W. Hartsfield, Jr. Steven R. Nagel Bonnie J. Dunbar Guion S. Bluford, Jr. Ernst Messerschmid Reinhard Furrer Wubbo J. Ockels	Carries Spacelab 1-D; scientific experiments conducted by Germans
11/26/85	*Atlantis*	7 days	Brewster H. Shaw, Jr. Bryan D. O'Conner Charles D. Walker Rudolfo Neri Vela Jerry L. Ross Sherwood C. Spring Mary L. Cleave	First Mexican in space, Vela; works on assembling structures
1/12/86	*Columbia*	5 days	Robert L. Gibson Charles F. Bolden, Jr. George D. Nelson Franklin R. Chang-Diaz Steven A. Hawley Robert J. Cenker	First U.S. congressman in space, Nelson
1/28/86	*Challenger*	73 seconds	F. Richard Scobee Michael J. Smith Robert E. McNair Ellison S. Onizuka Judith A. Resnik Gregory B. Jarvis Christa McAuliffe	*Challenger* disaster: O-rings in solid-fuel boosters wear through, and fuel supply explodes, killing all 6 regular astronauts and schoolteacher McAuliffe

After the *Challenger* disaster: the first actual space station

Date	Craft	Duration	Crew	Remarks
2/20/86	*Mir*		Variable	Soviet space station, launched without crew
5/5/86	*Soyuz T-15*	125 days	Vladimir Solovyev Leonid Kizim	First cosmonauts to board *Mir* space station
2/7/87	*Soyuz TM-2*	326 days	Yuri Romanenko Aleksandr Laveykin	Romanenko and Laveykin begin marathon tours in space, thought to be leading toward a Mars expedition
7/23/87	*Soyuz TM-3*	8 days	Aleksandr Alexandrov Aleksandr S. Viktorenko Muhammad Faris	First Syrian in space, Faris
12/20/87	*Soyuz TM-4*	366 days	Vladimir G. Titov Musa Manarov Anatoly Levchenko	Cosmonauts set new record of a year in space, mostly in *Mir* space station: 366 days
6/7/88	*Soyuz TM-5*	10 days	Aleksandr Alexandrov Viktor P. Savinykh Anatoly Y. Solovyov	Alexandrov becomes the first Bulgarian in space; not same Alexandrov as *Soyuz TM-3* flight

Date	Craft	Duration	Crew	Remarks
8/29/88	*Soyuz TM-6*	9 days	Vladimir Lyakhov Valery Polyakov (Abdul) Ahad (Mohmand)	Ahad first Afghan in space; on 9/6/88 Lyakhov and Ahad are stranded 24 hrs. as they attempt to return in *Soyuz TM-5*, but land safely on 9/7/88
9/29/88	*Discovery*	4 days	John M. Lounge David C. Hilmers Frederick H. Hauck George D. Nelson Richard O. Covey	Redesigned shuttle makes first flight since the *Challenger* disaster
11/26/88	*Soyuz TM-7*	152 days	Aleksandr Volkov Sergei M. Krikalev Jean-Loup Chrétien	*Mir* is temporarily abandoned for first time after cosmonauts return to Earth
12/2/88	*Atlantis*	4 days	Robert L. Gibson Jerry L. Ross William M. Shepherd Guy S. Gardner Richard M. Mullane	Secret military mission widely known to have deployed radar spy satellite
3/13/89	*Discovery*	4 days	Michael L. Coats John E. Blaha James F. Buchli James P. Bagian Robert C. Springer	Deploys NASA's third relay satellite and tests thermal control system for proposed U.S. space station
5/4/89	*Atlantis*	4 days	David M. Walker Ronald J. Grabe Mary L. Cleave Norman E. Thagard Mark C. Lee	Launches space probe *Magellan* on its way to map Venus with radar
5/9/89	*Soyuz TM-8*	6 days	Alexander S. Viktorenko Alexander A. Serebrov	Reoccupies *Mir*
8/9/89	*Columbia*	5 days	Brewster H. Shaw, Jr. Richard N. Richards David C. Leestma James C. Adamson Mark N. Brown	Secret military mission to launch spy satellite
10/18/89	*Atlantis*	5 days	Donald E. Williams Michael J. McCulley Shannon W. Lucid Franklin R. Chang-Diaz Ellen S. Baker	Launches *Galileo* space probe that travels to Venus, returns twice to vicinity of Earth, and then will take up a long-term orbit around Jupiter
11/22/89	*Discovery*	5 days	Frederick D. Gregory John E. Blaha F. Story Musgrave Kathryn C. Thornton Manley Lanier Carter, Jr.	Secret military mission
1/9/90	*Columbia*	10 days 21 hrs.	Daniel C. Brandenstein Bonnie J. Dunbar Marsha S. Ivens G. David Low James D. Wetherbee	Launches communication satellite Syncom IV and retrieves the Long Duration Exposure Facility (see 4/6/84); longest shuttle flight to date
2/11/90	*Soyuz TM-9*	6 days	Anatoly Solovyev Aleksandr Balandin	To relieve Viktorenko and Serebrov; July 18, Solovyev and Balandin briefly locked out of *Mir* by faulty hatch
2/28/90	*Atlantis*	6 days	John O. Creighton John H. Caspar David C. Hilmers Richard M. Mullane Pierre J. Thuot	Secret military mission launches spy satellite that fails and burns in atmosphere
4/24/90	*Discovery*	5 days	Loren J. Shriver Charles F. Bolden, Jr. Bruce McCandless 2nd Steven H. Hawley Kathryn D. Sullivan	Launches Hubble Space Telescope
5/8/90	*Soyuz TM-10*	6 days	Gennadi Manakov Gennadi Strekalov	To replace Solovyev and Balandin
10/6/90	*Discovery*	4 days	Richard N. Richards Robert D. Cabana Bruce E. Melnick William M. Shepherd Thomas D. Akers	Launches Ulysses space probe into solar orbit
11/15/90	*Atlantis*	6 days	Richard O. Covey Frank L. Culbertson, Jr. Charles D. Gemar Carl J. Meade Robert C. Springer	NASA announces this as last secret military mission
12/2/90	*Columbia*	9 days	Vance D. Brand Guy S. Gardner Jeffrey A. Hoffman John M. (Mike) Lounge Robert A.R. Parker Samuel T. Durrance Ronald A. Parise	Carries set of 3 UV and 1 X-ray telescopes; launch delayed by hydrogen leak
12/2/90	*Soyuz TM-11*	9 days	Viktor Afansev Musa Manarov Toyohiro Akiyama	Journalist Akiyama, sponsored by Japanese corporations, visits *Mir;* others replace Manakov and Strekalov
4/5/91	*Atlantis*	6 days	Steven R. Nagel Kenneth D. Cameron Linda M. Godwin Jerry L. Ross Jerome Apt	Launches 17-ton Gamma Ray Observatory; unscheduled spacewalk required to open properly satellite's antenna; high winds delay landing one day
4/28/91	*Discovery*	5 days	Michael L. Coats L. Blaine Hammond, Jr. Gregory J. Harbaugh Charles Lacy Veach Guion S. Bluford, Jr. Richard J. Hieb Donald R. McMonagle	Tests detection devices developed for space use and recovers Star Wars satellite
5/18/91	*Soyuz TM-12*	8 days	Sergei Krikalev Anatoly Artebarsky Helen Sharman	Political problems in Soviet Union result in Krikalev's spending an unexpected 313 days in space; Sharman is first Briton in space; returns with Manarov and Afansev

Date	Craft	Duration	Crew	Remarks
6/5/91	*Columbia*	10 days	Bryan D. O'Connor Sidney M. Gutierrez James P. Bagian Margaret Rhea Seddon Francis A. Gaffney Millie Hughes-Fulford Tamara E. Jernigan	Performs experiments to test human and animal adaptation to space
8/3/91	*Atlantis*	8 days	John E. Blaha Michael A. Baker Shannon W. Lucid G. David Low James C. Adamson	Performs 22 experiments and launches communications satellite
9/12/91	*Discovery*	5 days	John O. Creighton Kenneth S. Reightler, Jr. Mark N. Brown James F. Buchli Charles D. Gemar	Launches upper-atmosphere research satellite
10/2/91	*Soyuz TM-13*	8 days	Aleksandr Volkov Franz Viehboeck Toktar O. Aubakirov	Viehboeck, first Austrian in space, returns with Artebarsky and Aubakirov
11/24/91	*Atlantis*	7 days	Frederick D. Gregory Terence T. Henricks James S. Voss Mario Runco, Jr. F. Story Musgrave Thomas J. Hennen	First completely nonsecret military flight; studies how well military installations can be seen from space (which turns out to be very well); deploys satellite; lands early as a result of failure of a navigation unit (second time ever that early landing is forced by equipment failure)
1/22/92	*Discovery*	8 days	Ronald J. Grabe Stephen S. Oswald Norman E. Thagard William F. Readdy David C. Hilmers Roberta L. Bondar Ulf D. Merbold	Performs experiments as the First International Microgravity Laboratory
3/17/92	*Soyuz TM-14*	8 days	Klaus-Dietrich Flade Alexsandr S. Viktorenko Aleksandr Kaleri	On March 25, Flade, a German, returns with Sergei Krikalev and Aleksandr Volkov, who were already aboard *Mir*
3/24/92	*Atlantis*	9 days	Charles F. Bolden, Jr. Brian Duffy Kathryn D. Sullivan David C. Leestma Michael Foale Byron K. Lichtenberg Dirk D. Frimout	Inaguaral flight of Mission to Planet Earth studies Earth's atmosphere and auroras despite problems with a blown fuse
5/7/92	*Endeavour*	9 days	Daniel C. Brandenstein Kevin B. Chilton Thomas D. Akers Richard J. Hieb Bruce E. Melnick Kathryn C. Thornton Pierre J. Thout	The first flight of the replacement for *Challenger* features capture and relaunch of an erring communications satellite; after two efforts at rescue fail, the first ever 3-person EVA and manual capture succeeds
6/25/92	*Columbia*	14 days	Richard N. Richards Kenneth D. Bowersox Bonnie J. Dunbar Lawrence J. DeLucas Ellen S. Baker Eugene H. Trinh Carl J. Meade	Sets record for duration of shuttle mission; carries U.S. Microgravity Laboratory for experiments in low gravity
7/27/92	*Soyuz TM-15*	15 days	Anatoly Solovyev Sergei Avdeyev Michael Tognini	The third trip by a French astronaut, Tognini this time, to the Russian (formerly Soviet) space station, costing the French about $12 million.
7/31/92	*Atlantis*	8 days	Loren J. Schriver Andrew M. Allen Marsha S. Ivins Jeffrey A. Hoffman Franklin R. Chang-Diaz Claude Nicollier Franco Mallerba	Main experiment, unrolling of a tethered satellite, fails because of a jammed bolt, but European Retrievable Carrier (Eureca) satellite is launched successfully. Crew includes first Swiss astronaut (Nicollier) and first Italian (Mallerba).
9/12/92	*Endeavour*	8 days	Robert L. Gibson Curtis L. Brown, Jr. Jay Apt N. Jan Davis Mae Carol Jemison Mark C. Lee Mamoru Mohri	Mamoru Mohri is first professional Japanese astronaut in space; Mark Lee and Jan Davis the first married couple in space; and Mae Jemison the first black female astronaut. Japanese-sponsored mission to study biology in space.
10/22/92	*Columbia*	10 days	James D. Wetherbee Michael A. Baker Glenwood MacLean Tamara E. Jernigan William M. Shepherd Charles Lacy Veach	Launches the Italian-made satellite LAGEOS-2, designed to provide information about Earth's gravitational field.
12/2/92	*Discovery*	7 days	Daniel M. Walker Robert D. Cabana Guion S. Bluford, Jr. James S. Voss Michael R. Clifford	Last scheduled military flight for the space shuttle; future military flights, except for emergencies, to use disposable rockets. Launches secret military satellite known as DOD-1.
1/13/93	*Endeavour*	6 days	John H. Caspar Gregory J. Harbaugh Donald R. McMonagle Susan J. Helms Mario Runco, Jr.	Astronauts observe X rays and launch a TDRS (Tracking and Data Relay Satellite).
1/24/93	*Soyuz TM-16*	8 days	Alexander Polishchuk Gennadi Manakov	Docks with *Mir* on Kristall module, using U.S.-compatible port first developed for the joint Soviet-U.S. mission in 1975; Anatoly Solovyov and Sergei Avdeyev return after 6 mo. aboard space station.
4/8/93	*Discovery*	9 days	Kenneth D. Cameron Stephen S. Oswald Kenneth D. Cockrell Michael Foale Ellen Ochoa	Launches and retrieves the Spartan Sun probe, used to study the solar corona, and observes the ozone layer of Earth's atmosphere.
4/26/93	*Columbia*	7 days	Steven R. Nagel Terence T. Henricks Jerry L. Ross Charles Precourt Bernard A. Harris, Jr. Ulrich Walter Hans Schlegel	The European Spacelab with two German scientists (Walter and Schlegel) aboard conducted experiments on weightlessness, mostly paid for by Germany.

Date	Craft	Duration	Crew	Remarks
6/21/93	*Endeavour*	8 days	Ronald J. Grabe Brian Duffy G. Donald Low Peter J.K. Wisoff Nancy Jane Sherlock Janice E. Voss	The crew recovers Europe's Eureca satellite for possible reuse and conducts experiments using a pressurized laboratory called Spacehab, built by McDonnell-Douglas Aerospace for commercial use, although mostly used by NASA for its initial flight.
7/1/93	*Soyuz TM-17*	28 days	Vasily Tsiblyev Alexander Serebrov Jean-Pierre Haignere	Haignere is French astronaut who returns with Anatoly Solovyov and Sergei Andreyev on July 29.
9/12/93	*Discovery*	10 days	Frank L. Culbertson, Jr. William F. Readdy James H. Newman Daniel W. Bursch Carl E. Walz	The crew tried out equipment and procedures to be used in repairing Hubble Space Telescope; first night landing at Kennedy.
10/18/93	*Columbia*	14 days	John E. Blaha Richard A. Searfoss William S. McArthur, Jr. Shannon W. Lucid Martin J. Fettman Margaret Rhea Seddon David Wolf	Conducted biological experiments on humans and rats, including first dissection of animal in space.
12/2/93	*Endeavour*	11 days	Richard O. Covey Kenneth D. Bowersox Claude Nicollier F. Story Musgrave Thomas D. Akers Kathryn C. Thornton Jeffrey A. Hoffman	Installed corrective lenses and other replacement parts on defective Hubble Space Telescope, solving its focusing and stability problems.
1/8/94	*Soyuz TM-18*	21 days	Victor Afanasyev Yuri Usachyov Valery Polyakov	Trip planned to last 14 months; previous crew aboard *Mir* returns to Earth.
2/3/94	*Discovery*	8 days	Charles F. Bolden Sergei M. Krikalev Kenneth S. Reightler, Jr. N. Jan Davis Franklin R. Chang-Diaz Ronald M. Sega	Krikalev first Russian to fly on U.S. space shuttle mission; previously flew missions to and on *Mir*, the Russian space station.
3/4/94	*Columbia*	14 days	John H. Caspar Andrew M. Allen Charles D. Gemar Marsha S. Ivins Pierre J. Thuot	Low-key flight to develop techniques for use in space-station construction; also conducted biological and materials experiments.
4/9/94	*Endeavour*	11 days	Sidney M. Gutierrez Kevin P. Chilton Michael R. Clifford Linda M. Godwin Jay Apt Thomas D. Jones	Used radar to map details of Earth in 3-D and took photographs to check radar against.
7/3/94	*Soyuz TM-19*	16 days	Yuri Malenchenko Talgat Musabayev	Malenchenko from Russia and Musabayev of Kazakhstan travel to *Mir* to relieve Afanasyev and Usachyov.
7/8/94	*Columbia*	14 days 17 hrs. 55 min.	Robert D. Cabana Leroy Chiao James D. Halsell, Jr. Richard J. Hieb Chiaki Naito-Mukai Donald A. Thomas Carl E. Walz	Sets new record for length of time a U.S. space shuttle is in orbit, orbiting Earth 236 times as crew studies biology in space; first Japanese woman in space (heart surgeon Chiaki Naito-Mukai).
9/9/94	*Discovery*	11 days	Richard N. Richards L. Blaine Hammond, Jr. Susan J. Helms Mark C. Lee J.M. Linenger Carl J. Meade	Conducts laser experiments to measure pollution in atmosphere and releases and recaptures satellite that collects data on solar wind; Meade and Lee perform untethered spacewalk to test new jet pack designed for use in building space station.
9/30/94	*Endeavour*	11 days	Michael A. Baker Daniel W. Bursch Thomas D. Jones Steven L. Smith Peter "Jeff" J.K. Wisoff Terrence W. Wukcytt	The Space Radar Laboratory 2 mission is follow-up of nearly identical mission flown in the spring; the purpose is to detect seasonal changes.
10/3/94	*Soyuz TM-20*	1 month	Aleksandr Viktorenko Yelena Kondakova Ulf Merbold	Merbold, from the European Space Agency, studies space biology aboard *Mir* and returns to Earth on 11/4/94 along with Malenchenko and Musabayev, leaving Viktorenko and Kondakova on *Mir*.
11/3/94	*Atlantis*	11 days	Curtis L. Brown Donald R. McMonagle Jean-François Clervoy Scott E. Parazynski Joseph R. Tanner	Third shuttle flight since 1992 to carry the Atlas lab (Atmospheric Laboratory for Applications and Science); Clervoy represents the agency on the mission.
2/3/95	*Discovery*	8 days	James D. Wetherbee Eileen M. Collins C. Michael Foale Bernard A. Harris, Jr. Vladimir G. Titov Janice Voss	Carrying Russian cosmonaut Titov, the shuttle travels to between 11 m and 13 m (37 ft. and 44 ft.) of the space station *Mir*.
3/2/95	*Endeavour*	16 days 15 hrs. 8 min.	Stephen S. Oswald Samuel T. Durrance Tamara E. Jernigan William G. Gregory John M. Grunsfeld Wendy B. Lawrence Ronald A. Parise	Mission carries the lab Astro 2, which centers on 3 ultraviolet telescopes and is used, among other things, to study volcanic eruptions on Jupiter's moon Io. Sets new duration record in space for a shuttle, orbiting Earth 263 times.
3/14/95	*Soyuz TM-21*	8 days	Norman E. Thagard Vladimir Dezhurov Gennady Strekalov	Thagard becomes the first U.S. astronaut to live aboard the Russian space station *Mir*, where he studies the body's reaction to weightlessness; Polyakov, who returns on Mar. 22, 1995, with Kondakova and Viktorenko, sets new space endurance record of 14.5 months in space on one trip.
6/27/95	*Atlantis*	10 days	Robert L. Gibson Charles J. Precourt Ellen S. Baker Gregory J. Harbaugh Bonnie J. Dunbar Anatoly Solovyev Nikolai M. Budarin	Docks with *Mir* for 5 days, giving the space station a temporary crew of 10 and a mass of about 225 tons. Spacelab on *Atlantis* and Spekter module of *Mir* used for biomedical research. Leaves Solovyev and Budarin as crew of *Mir;* returns Thagard, Dezhurov, and Strekalov.

Earth Sciences

Earth sciences include geology (the study of Earth's rocks and interior), oceanography (the study of ocean water, currents, and the ocean floor), paleontology (the study of fossils and ancient life-forms), parts of astronomy, and meteorology (the study of the atmosphere, including weather). Except for astronomy and weather, which are covered elsewhere, this section deals with all of these studies.

MAJOR DISCOVERIES IN EARTH SCIENCES

B.C.

c. 300 Dicaearchus (Greek: c. 320) develops map of Earth on a sphere using lines of latitude.

A.D.

132 Zhang Heng (Chinese: 78–139) develops first crude seismograph.

1600 William Gilbert (English: 1544–1603) suggests that Earth is giant magnet, which is why magnetic compasses indicate north.

1669 Nicolaus Steno (Niels Stensen; Danish: 1638–86) correctly explains origin of fossils.

1777 Nicolas Desmarest (French: 1725–1815) proposes that the rock basalt is formed from lava.

1785 James Hutton (Scottish: 1726–97) explains features of Earth on basis of tiny changes taking place over very long periods of time (uniformitarianism).

1795 Baron Georges Cuvier (French: 1769–1832) shows that giant bones found in Meuse River are remains of extinct giant reptile.

1797 Sir James Hall (Scottish: 1761–1832) shows that melted rocks form crystals upon cooling.

1822 Gideon A. Mantell (English: 1790–1852) and his wife, Mary Ann, are first to discover and recognize dinosaur bones as those of a giant, extinct reptile.

1830 Sir Charles Lyell (Scottish: 1797–1875) begins to publish *Principles of Geology*, the work that convinced geologists that Earth is at least several hundred million years old.

1880 John Milne (English: 1850–1913) invents modern seismograph.

1896 Svante A. Arrhenius (Swedish: 1859–1927) discovers that global temperatures rise with higher levels of carbon dioxide in atmosphere (greenhouse effect).

1902 Léon-Philippe Teisserenc de Bort (French: 1855–1913) discovers the stratosphere.

1906 Richard D. Oldham (English: 1858–1936) establishes existence of Earth's core.

1907 Bertram B. Boltwood (American: 1870–1927) shows that age of rocks containing uranium can be determined by measuring ratio of uranium to lead.

1909 Andrija Mohorovičić (Croatia: 1857–1936) discovers boundary between Earth's crust and mantle, now known as Mohorovičić discontinuity, or "Moho."

1912 Alfred L. Wegener (German: 1880–1930) proposes theory of continental drift, idea that a single continent—Pangaea—split into present-day continents, which have drifted away from each other.

1925 The German *Meteor* expedition discovers Mid-Atlantic Ridge, a giant mountain range in middle of the Atlantic Ocean.

1929 Motonori Matuyama (Japanese: 1884–1958) shows that Earth's magnetic field reverses every few hundred million years.

1943 Mexican farmer discovers volcano—eventually named Mt. Parícutin—in his field; first observation of a volcano's genesis.

1946 Vincent J. Schaefer (American: 1906–93) discovers that dry ice can be used to cause clouds to release rain.

1953 Maurice Ewing (American: 1906–74) discovers rift that runs down middle of Mid-Atlantic Ridge.

1958 James A. Van Allen (American: 1914–) discovers belts of radiation that surround Earth in space, now known as Van Allen belts.

1960 Harry H. Hess (American: 1906–69) develops theory of seafloor spreading—oceans are getting wider as new seafloor is formed at midocean ridges.

1979 American oceanographers discover hot vents in oceans, surrounded by exotic forms of life based on sulfur, not oxygen.

1980 Walter Alvarez (American: 1940–) and coworkers discover geologic layer of iridium in region identified with the demise of the dinosaurs; he attributes both iridium and extinction to impact of a large comet or meteorite on Earth.

1987 NASA determines that continents are moving in ways predicted by theory of plate tectonics, a theory based on idea that Earth's crust is broken into huge plates that are moving with respect to each other.

1990 Kathleen Crane (American) and a Soviet-American team discover hot vents in the floor of Lake Baikal in the USSR, suggesting that this is a "spreading center," a widening crack in the Asian landmass.

1994 Scott R. Woodward extracts DNA from 80-million-year-old dinosaur bones.

COMPOSITION OF THE EARTH

In their study of the Earth, scientists distinguish a number of distinct layers from the inner core—the center of which is about 6,400 km (roughly 4,000 mi.) below the surface—to the farthest limit of the atmosphere, about 1,000 km (620 mi.) above the surface. This section describes these layers, from the innermost to the outermost.

Core The core consists of two parts—one liquid, the other solid—both thought to be a mixture of iron and nickel. The solid inner core begins about 5,000 km (3,100 mi.) from the surface, and the liquid outer core at about 1,100 km (1,800 mi.) from the surface.

Mantle The bulk of the Earth—roughly two-thirds of its mass—is composed of the mantle, which extends from the outer core to within about 90 km (55 mi.) of the Earth's surface below the higher mountains, and to within only 5 to 8 km (3 to 5 mi.) of the Earth's surface below some areas of the oceans. Silicon dioxide constitutes almost half of the mantle, and there is an abundance of magnesium oxide, some iron oxide, and smaller amounts of oxides of other metals. (Although silicon dioxide is known as quartz when found in the Earth's crust, under the heat and pressure of the mantle it may have very different properties from the form we know.) Part of the upper mantle is somewhat liquid and known as the asthenosphere.

Crust The crust is the outermost solid layer of the Earth. Under the continents, the crust varies from 30 to 60 km (19 to 37 mi.) in thickness, while under the oceans it is generally only 5 to 8 km (3 to 5 mi.) thick. Continental and oceanic crust differ from each other in thickness and composition. Continental crust consists of granite and other relatively light rocks, while oceanic crust is made up chiefly of basalt. The crust is separated from the mantle by the Mohorovičić discontinuity, or Moho. The crust that is accessible to accurate measurements contains the following principle elements:

Element	Percent
Oxygen	45.6%
Silicon	27.3
Aluminum	8.4
Iron	6.2
Calcium	4.7
Magnesium	2.8
Sodium	2.3
Potassium	1.8
Hydrogen	1.5
Titanium	0.6

Note: Adds to more than 100% due to independent rounding.

Hydrosphere Water—virtually all of it sea water—covers about 71 percent of the Earth's surface and thereby constitutes a distinct layer of the Earth. Sea water varies in composition from place to place, but on average it is about 3.5 percent salts—that is, evaporating 100 lb. of sea water would yield 3.5 lb. of salt. Sodium chloride (ordinary table salt) constitutes 2.7 percent of sea water, or 77.8 percent of total solids in sea water. The typical composition of solids in sea water is as follows:

Compound	Percent
Sodium chloride	77.8%
Magnesium chloride	10.9
Magnesium sulfide	4.7
Calcium sulfate	3.6
Potassium sulfate	2.5
Calcium carbonate	0.3
Magnesium bromide	0.2
Other compounds	trace

Atmosphere The atmosphere is the gaseous layer that envelopes the Earth. The lower atmosphere consists of the troposphere and the stratosphere. The *troposphere* has an average thickness of about 11 km (7 mi.), although it is only 8 km (5 mi.) at the poles and as much as 16 km (10 mi.) around the equator. Most clouds and weather phenomena occur in this region. The composition of dry air at sea level is: nitrogen, 78.08%; oxygen, 20.05%; argon, 0.93%; and carbon dioxide, 0.03%. There are also lesser amounts of neon, helium, krypton, and xenon. These proportions change with altitude, lighter gases being more common at higher altitudes, but they are approximately the same everywhere on Earth at the same altitude. There are also variable quantities of water vapor, dust particles, and other compounds whose proportions change from place to place at the same altitude—fewer dust particles being found over oceans, and less water vapor over deserts. Temperature decreases with altitude in the troposphere.

The *stratosphere* is found between 11 km and 50 km (7–30 mi.) out from the Earth's surface. Temperatures in this region rise slightly as altitude increases, to a maximum of about 0°C (32°F). Virtually coextensive with the stratosphere is the *ozonosphere*, or ozone layer, the region in which most of the atmosphere's ozone is found. Because ozone absorbs most of the sun's ultraviolet radiation, it is vital to the continued existence of life on the planet.

Beyond the stratosphere is the upper atmosphere, or *ionosphere*, so called because it is the layer in which atmospheric gases have been ionized by solar radiation. The ionosphere reflects certain wavelengths back to the surface, making it possible to transmit radio waves around the curve of the Earth. The ionosphere is further divided into the *mesosphere*, between 50 km and 80 km (30–50 mi.), in which the temperature decreases with altitude to –90°C (–130°F); and the *thermosphere*, from about 80 km to 450 km (50–280 mi.), in which the temperature increases to as much as 1475°C (2690°F). Beyond the thermosphere is the *exosphere*, extending to about 1,000 km (625 mi.). In this layer, temperature no longer has the customary meaning. (See also "Global Warming" and "The Ozone Layer.")

GEOLOGIC TIME SCALE

Geologists and other earth scientists divide the history of the planet into periods of varying length based on the fossils found in rock strata. Geologists often speak of the period before 570 million years ago as Precambrian Time. The eras after 570 million years ago are grouped into the Phanerozoic Eon.

Era or Eon	Period	Epoch	Organisms	Time before present (millions of years)
ARCHEAN EON			Monerans: bacteria and blue-green algae	**4,600**
PROTEROZOIC EON			Protists, algae, and soft-bodied creatures similar to jellyfish and worms	**2,500**
PHANEROZOIC EON PALEOZOIC ERA	Cambrian		Tiny fossils with skeletons followed by animals with shells, notably trilobites	**570**
	Ordovician		Brachiopods (shellfish similar to clams), corals, starfish, and some organisms that have no modern counterparts, called sea scorpions and conodonts.	**500**
	Silurian		Snails, clams and mussels, ammonoids (similar to the nautilus), jawless fish, sea scorpions, first land plants and animals (club mosses, land scorpions); modern groups of algae and fungi	**425**
	Devonian		Spiders, amphibians, jawed fish, lobe-finned fish, sharks, lungfish, and ferns	**395**
	Carboniferous		Insects, land snails, amphibians, early reptiles, sea lilies, giant club mosses, and seed ferns	**350**
	Permian		Mammal-like reptiles and fin-backed reptiles, cycads, ginkgoes, and conifers	**290**
MESOZOIC ERA	Triassic		Marine reptiles (plesiosaurs and ichthyosaurs), crocodiles, frogs, turtles, early mammals, and early dinosaurs	**235**
	Jurassic		Dinosaurs (such as stegosaurus), pterosaurs (such as pterodactyl), early birds, dinoflagellates, diatoms, early flowering plants	**190**
	Cretaceous		Dinosaurs (such as tyrannosaurus, triceratops, and brontosaurus), salamanders, modern bony fishes, mosasaurs (marine lizards), flowering plants, placental and marsupial mammals	**130**
CENOZOIC ERA	Tertiary	Paleocene	Early primates, early horses, rodents, sycamores	**66.5**
		Eocene	Whales, penguins, roses, bats, camels, early elephants, dogs, cats, weasels	**57.8**
		Oligocene	Deer, pigs, saber-toothed cats, monkeys	**36.6**
		Miocene	Seals, dolphins, grasses, daisies, asters, sunflowers, lettuce, giraffes, bears, hyenas, early apes	**23.5**
		Pliocene	Apes, australopithecines (early hominids), *Homo habilis* (first human species), mammoths, giant sloths, and armadillos	**5.2**
	Quaternary	Pleistocene	*Homo erectus* (ancestor of modern humans), modern humans, and Neanderthal humans; large mammals, such as giant bison and beavers; many kinds of hoofed animals	**1.6**
		Holocene	Modern humans and flora and fauna of today	**0.01 (11,000 yrs)**

THE CHANGING EARTH

Despite its apparent solidity, the interior of the Earth is constantly changing. Although most of its movements are slow and seldom affect people, there are some significant exceptions.

Most notable of these are large earthquakes and volcanic eruptions, together with their associated tsunamis and landslides.

Plate tectonics The earth's outer crust is composed of about 20 lithospheric (or tectonic) plates that move from a few millimeters to several centimeters per year. Hundreds of millions of years ago, these plates formed a continuous landmass known as Pangaea and surrounded by ocean. Eventually the plates separated, until they reached the positions they occupy today.

As plates move away from each other, molten rock emerges from the mantle to form oceanic crust. Where they come together, one plate is forced under the other, forming either oceanic trenches or mountain ranges or both. These areas are also the site of greatest volcanic and earthquake activity.

The relative position of the major tectonic plates can be gathered from their names: Antarctic, African, Indo-Australian (including most of the Indian subcontinent), Pacific, South American, North American, and Eurasian (including Southeast Asia). Seven smaller plates are the Nazca, bounded by (in clockwise order) the Cocos, South American, Antarctic, and Pacific; the Cocos, bounded by the North American, Caribbean, South American, Nazca, and Pacific; the Caribbean, bounded by the North American, South American, and Cocos; the Hellenic, bounded by the Eurasian, Arabian, and African; the Arabian, bounded by the Hellenic, Iranian, Indo-Australian, and African; the Iranian, bounded by the Eurasian, Indo-Australian, and Arabian; and the Philippine, bounded by the Pacific to the east and the Eurasian to the west.

Earthquakes and tsunamis Most earthquakes are caused when rock on one side of a fault (or crack) in the Earth's crust moves with respect to the rock on the other side of the fault. The motion causes vibrations in the crust that travel through the rock as shock waves. When these reach the surface, they cause it to move in various ways, which is called seismic motion. (Small earthquakes that accompany volcanic eruptions are caused by the motion of liquid rock, or magma.)

More than 800,000 earthquakes are registered by seismographs each year, but the overwhelming majority go unnoticed by anyone. However, large earthquakes are of great concern to many people living in regions of significant seismic activity. Although research on earthquake prediction has yielded no breakthroughs, death and destruction have been reduced somewhat by improvements in construction codes and techniques. Improvement is needed there as well. The earthquake that struck Kobe, Japan, and nearby regions on Jan. 17, 1995, killed over 5,300, injured more than 35,000, and destroyed nearly 200,000 homes despite construction codes considered to be among the best in the world. Exactly one year earlier, the slightly smaller Northridge earthquake in Los Angeles caused only 57 deaths, but supposedly earthquake-proof steel-frame buildings suffered considerable hidden damage in the earthquake.

MEASURING EARTHQUAKES

The size of an earthquake is generally reported in the United States using the Richter scale, a system developed by American geologist Charles Richter in 1935. The Richter scale measures the magnitude of an earthquake, that is, the size of ground waves generated by an earthquake as shown on a measuring device called a seismograph. Each whole number on the scale represents a tenfold increase (or decrease) in magnitude: a magnitude 6 earthquake produces a ground wave 10 times greater than a magnitude 5.

This does not mean, however, that a magnitude 6 earthquake has 10 times the energy as one of magnitude 5. Measuring the actual energy requires instruments placed at the site of the earthquake. Various methods have been developed for inferring energy from magnitude and these suggest that one magnitude corresponds to a thirty- to sixtyfold change in energy. So the energy of a magnitude 8 earthquake, a very serious event, can be as much as 1 million to 10 million times as much as that of a magnitude 4 earthquake, one that can be felt but causes almost no damage.

A very different scale, developed by Giuseppe Mercalli in 1902 and modified by Harry Wood and Frank Neumann for the United States in the 1930s, is widely used to describe the intensity of earthquakes. The modified Mercalli scale, as it is known, describes the effects of earthquake shocks; comparing the Mercalli and Richter scales helps one to understand the relative energy of earthquakes.

RICHTER AND MERCALLI SCALES COMPARED

Richter scale		Mercalli earthquake intensity scale	
2.5	Generally not felt, but recorded on seismometers.	**I.**	Not felt except by a very few under specially favorable circumstances.
		II.	Felt only by a few persons at rest, especially on upper floors of buildings.
3.5	Felt by many people.	**III.**	Felt quite noticeably indoors, especially on upper floors of buildings, but many people do not recognize as an earthquake.
		IV.	During the day, felt indoors by many; outdoors by few. Sensation like heavy truck striking building.
		V.	Felt by nearly everyone; many awakened. Disturbances of trees, poles, and other tall objects sometimes noticed.
4.5	Some local damage may occur.	**VI.**	Felt by all; many frightened and run outdoors. Some heavy furniture moved; few instances of fallen plaster or damaged chimneys. Damage slight.
		VII.	Everybody runs outdoors. Damage negligible in buildings of good design and construction; slight to moderate in well-built ordinary structures; considerable in poorly built or badly designed structures.
6.0	A destructive earthquake.	**VIII.**	Damage slight in specially designed structures; considerable in ordinary substantial buildings with partial collapse; great in poorly built structures. (Collapse of chimneys, factory stacks, columns, monuments, walls.)
		IX.	Damage considerable in specially designed structures. Buildings shifted off foundations. Ground cracked conspicuously.
7.0	A major earthquake. About 10 occur each year.	**X.**	Some well-built wooden structures destroyed. Most masonry and frame structures destroyed with foundations. Ground badly cracked.
8.0 and above	Great earthquakes. These occur once every five to 10 years.	**XI.**	Few, if any (masonry) structures remain standing. Bridges destroyed. Broad fissures in ground.
		XII.	Damage total. Waves seen on ground surfaces. Objects thrown upward into air.

One common side effect of undersea earthquakes is *tsunamis*—or (incorrectly) tidal waves—against which there is little protection. Tsunamis are caused when an earthquake raises or lowers a section of seabed, thereby producing a wave that, while not generally noticeable at sea, can reach great heights as it approaches land. Similar to and as destructive as tsunamis, harbor waves are generated when a landslide falls into a bay, strait, or other confined body of water causing almost immediate flooding. High waves are also caused by volcanic explosions or collapses, such as the explosion and collapse of Krakatau in 1883.

Volcanoes are openings in the Earth's crust that emit molten or partially molten rock (lava), various hot gases, and ash. (A volcano is also the mountain formed by solidified lava ejected from the opening.) If the opening is like a crack, it is called a vent. If it is larger and fairly circular, it is called a crater. A caldera is a basin formed by the settling of the top of a volcanic mountain, and it may have several vents or craters on its floor.

Most volcanoes are found where two tectonic plates meet, such as along the famous "Ring of Fire" around the Pacific Ocean. A few, such as the volcanoes of the Hawaiian Islands, appear to be over "hot spots" in the Earth's crust where liquid rock flows upward with sufficient force to burn through the crust. Although volcanoes are associated with destruction, they have many positive effects. Minerals from deep within the Earth make the land around many volcanoes extremely fertile; volcanoes can create new landforms in the sea; and the study of volcanoes contributes enormously to our understanding of the Earth's interior.

Although geologists consider a volcano active if it has shown signs of activity in historic times, it is not usually clear whether a volcano is extinct or only dormant and could be active again. (Thus Tambora, which has not erupted since 1815, is considered active.) Some volcanoes once thought to be extinct have become active, and there are now about 600 volcanoes that are considered active. The accompanying list contains about a third of all volcanoes known to have been active in recent years, with special emphasis on volcanoes in the United States and volcanoes that have had famous eruptions.

Although the destruction caused by volcanoes is usually localized, their effects can be felt around the world and take many forms. At their worst, volcanoes can blow themselves to pieces, as the island of Thera did about 1650 B.C. More often, volcanic ash blankets an area (as Mt. Vesuvius did at Pompeii), or clouds of hot gases and dust sweep down the side of the volcano poisoning the air. Although lava generally moves too slowly to be a menace to people, it can sometimes flow too quickly to be outrun. Even more unpredictable, heat from a volcano can melt glaciers or snowcaps, triggering massive mud slides or releasing lakes of boiling water (as happened in Colombia in 1985).

MAJOR EARTHQUAKES, 526–1995

Date	Location and remarks	Estimated deaths	Richter magnitude
May 20, 526	Antioch, Turkey	250,000	—
856	Corinth, Greece	45,000	—
1036	Shanxi, China	23,000	—
1057	Chihli (Hopeh), China	25,000	—
1170	Sicily	15,000	—
1268	Cilicia (Turkey)	60,000	—
Sept. 27, 1290	Chihli (Hopeh), China	100,000	—
May 20, 1293	Kamakura, Japan	30,000	—
Jan. 26, 1531	Lisbon, Portugal	30,000	—
Jan. 24, 1556	Shanxi, China	830,000	—
Nov. 1667	Shemakha, Azerbaijan	80,000	—
June 7, 1692	Port Royal, Jamaica	30,000	—
Jan. 11, 1693	Catania province, Sicily	60,000	—
1693	Naples, Italy	93,000	—
1707	Tsunami hits Japan	30,000	—
Dec. 30, 1730	Hokkaido Island, Japan	137,000	—
1731	Beijing, China	100,000	—
Oct. 11, 1737	Calcutta, India	300,000	—
June 7, 1755	Northern Persia	40,000	—
Nov. 1, 1755	Lisbon, Portugal (earthquake and tsunami)	60,000	8.7
Nov. 19, 1755	Boston, Massachusetts	0	6.0
Feb. 4–5 and Mar. 28, 1783	Calabria, Italy	35,000	—
Feb. 4, 1797	Quito, Ecuador, and Cuzco, Peru	41,000	—
Dec. 16, 1811	New Madrid, Missouri	fewer than 10	8.1
Jan. 23, 1812	New Madrid, Missouri	0	8.2
Feb. 7, 1812	New Madrid, Missouri	0	8.3
Sept. 5, 1822	Aleppo (Syria)	22,000	—
Dec. 28, 1828	Echigo, Japan	30,000	—
June 1838	San Francisco, California	—	—
Dec. 24, 1854	Tokai, Japan	3,000	8.4
Oct. 1855	Tokyo, Japan	2,000+	—
Jan. 9, 1857	Fort Tejon, California	2	8.3
1857	East of Naples, Italy	10,000+	—
Aug. 13–15, 1868	Peru and Ecuador	40,000	—
Mar. 26, 1872	Owens Valley, California	60	—
May 16, 1875	Venezuela and Colombia	16,000	—
Aug. 31, 1886	Charleston, South Carolina	83	7.6
Oct. 28, 1891	Central Japan	7,300	—
June 15, 1896	Sanriku and Kamaishi, Japan (tsunami)	26,000	—
Sept. 3, 1899	Yakatanga, Alaska	0	8.3
Sept. 10, 1899	Yakatanga, Alaska	0	8.6
Apr. 4, 1905	Kangra, India	20,000	—
Apr. 18, 1906	San Francisco, California	667	8.3
Aug. 16, 1906	Valparaiso, Chile	20,000	8.6
1907	Tajikistan	40,000	—
Dec. 28, 1908	Messina, Sicily	75,000	7.5
Jan. 13, 1915	Avezzano, Italy	30,000	—
Oct. 2, 1915	Pleasant Valley, Nevada	0	7.8
Jan. 13, 1916	Avezzano, Italy	29,980	7.5
Oct. 11, 1918	Mona Passage, Caribbean Sea	116	7.5
Dec. 16, 1920	Kansu, China	180,000+	8.6
Sept. 1, 1923	Tokyo and Yokohama, Japan	143,000	7.9
June 27, 1925	Helena, Montana	0	6.8
Mar. 7, 1927	Kita Tango, Japan	2,935	7.3
May 22, 1927	Nan-Shan, China	200,000	8.3
Aug. 16, 1931	Mt. Livermore, Texas	0	6.4
Dec. 20, 1932	Cedar Mountain, Nevada	0	7.3
Dec. 26, 1932	Kansu, China	70,000	7.6
Mar. 2, 1933	Sanriku, Japan (tsunami)	3,064	8.9
Mar. 10, 1933	Long Beach, California	120	6.3
Jan. 15, 1934	India, Bihar, and Nepal	10,700	8.4
Mar. 12, 1934	Great Salt Lake, Utah	0	6.6
May 31, 1935	Quetta, India (Pakistan)	50,000	7.5
Oct.–Nov. 1936	Helena, Montana	2	—
Jan. 24, 1939	Concepción, Chile	30,000	8.3
Dec. 27, 1939	Erzincan, Turkey	30,000	7.9
May 18, 1940	Imperial Valley, California	9	7.1
Apr. 1, 1946	Earthquake at Unimak Island, Alaska, causes tsunami in Hawaii that strikes Hilo	173	7.2
Dec. 21, 1946	Nankai on Honshu Island, Japan	1,330	8.0
June 28, 1948	Fukui, Japan	3,769	7.1
Oct. 1948	Ashkhabad (former USSR)	20,000	—
July 10, 1949	Tajikistan (former USSR)	120,000	7.5
Aug. 5, 1949	Pelileo, Ecuador	6,000	6.8
Aug. 15, 1950	Assam State, India	1,500	8.7
July 21, 1952	Bakersfield, California	12	7.7
Mar. 18, 1953	Northwest Turkey	1,200	7.2
Sept. 9–12, 1954	Orléansville, Algeria	1,660	—
Dec. 16, 1954	Frenchman's Station, Nevada	0	7.1

Date	Location and remarks	Estimated deaths	Richter magnitude
June 10–17, 1956	Northern Afghanistan	2,000	7.7
July 2, 1957	Northern Iran	2,500	7.4
Dec. 13, 1957	Western Iran	2,000	7.1
July 9, 1958	Lituya Bay, Alaska	3	7.9
Aug. 17, 1959	Hebgen Lake, Montana	28	7.1
Feb. 29, 1960	Agadir, Morocco	12,000	8.8
May 21–30, 1960	Southern Chile; on May 22, a tsunami strikes various Pacific islands, including Hawaii, killing 61 in Hilo; greatest earthquake ever recorded	5,700	9.5
Sept. 1, 1962	Northwestern Iran	12,403	7.1
Feb. 21–22, 1963	El Marj, Libya	260	5.0
July 26, 1963	Skopje, Yugoslavia	1,011	5.5
Mar. 27, 1964	Southern Alaska	131	8.5
Mar. 28, 1965	Central Chile	420	—
Aug. 19, 1966	Eastern Turkey	2,520	6.9
July 27, 1967	Caracas, Venezuela	250+	6.5
Dec. 11, 1967	Konya, India (extra pressure from water filling a reservoir caused earth to shift)	117	6.5
Aug. 31, 1968	Khurasan, Iran	12,000	7.8
July 25, 1969	Eastern China	3,000	—
Jan. 5, 1970	Yunnan Province, China	10,000	7.7
Mar. 28, 1970	Gediz, Turkey	1,086	7.4
May 31, 1970	Yungay, Ranrahirca, Huarás, and other cities in Peru	66,794	7.7
Feb. 9, 1971	San Fernando Valley, California	64	6.6
Apr. 10, 1972	Ghir, Iran	5,057	6.9
Dec. 23, 1972	Managua, Nicaragua	10,000+	5.6
Aug. 28, 1973	Puebla, Mexico	527	6.8
Dec. 28, 1974	North Pakistan	5,200+	6.3
Feb. 5, 1975	Liaoning Province, China (predicted)	300	—
Sept. 6, 1975	Lice, Turkey	2,312	6.8
Feb. 4, 1976	Guatemala City, Guatemala	22,778	7.5
May 6, 1976	Northeast Italy	946	6.5
June 26, 1976	New Guinea and Irian Java	8,000+	7.1
July 28, 1976	Tangshan, China	750,000	8.0
Aug. 17, 1976	Philippine island of Mindanao (earthquake and tsunami)	8,000	7.3
Nov. 24, 1976	Eastern Turkey	4,000	7.9
Mar. 4, 1977	Bucharest, Romania	1,541	7.5
Aug. 19, 1977	Indonesia	200	8.0
Nov. 23, 1977	Northwestern Argentina	100	8.2
Dec. 20, 1977	Central Iran	500+	—
Jan. 14, 1978	Tokai region, Japan	25	7.0
June 12, 1978	Sendai, Japan	27+	7.5
June 20, 1978	Salonika, Greece	51	—
Aug. 18, 1978	Tsunami strikes Acajutla, El Salvador	100+	—
Sept. 16, 1978	Northeast Iran	25,000	7.7
Jan. 17, 1979	Eastern Iran	200	6.7–7.5
Apr. 15, 1979	Yugoslavia and Albania	129	7.2
Nov. 14, 1979	Meshed, Iran	500	6.7
Dec. 12, 1979	Colombia and Ecuador	800	7.9
Dec. 18, 1979	Bali, Indonesia	100	6.1
Oct. 10, 1980	Northwestern Algeria	4,500	7.3
Nov. 23, 1980	Southern Italy	4,800	7.2
July 28, 1981	Kerman province, Iran	8,000	—
Dec. 13, 1982	Yemen	2,800	6.0
Mar. 31, 1983	Popayán, Colombia	200,000	5.7
Oct. 28, 1983	Challis, Idaho	2	6.9
Oct. 30, 1983	Erzurum, Turkey	1,330	7.2
Mar. 3, 1985	Algarrobo, Chile	177	7.8
Sept. 19, 21, 1985	Mexico City	4,200	8.1
Oct. 10, 1986	San Salvador, El Salvador	1,000+	7.5
Mar. 5–6, 1987	Ecuador	2,000	7.0
Aug. 20, 1988	Nepal and India	700+	6.5
Nov. 6, 1988	Yunnan Province, China, and Burma	144	7.0
Dec. 6, 1988	Mamasani, Iran	7	5.6
Dec. 7, 1988	Armenia (former USSR)	28,854	6.9
Jan. 22, 1989	Tajikistan (former USSR)	274	5.5
Mar. 10, 1989	Malawi	9	6.2
May 23, 1989	Macquarie Ridge, 300 mi. SE of New Zealand	0	8.2–8.3
Aug. 1, 1989	West Irian, Indonesia	120	5.9
Oct. 17, 1989	Loma Prieta, California (Santa Cruz Mountains), destructive in San Francisco and Oakland	63	7.1
Oct. 18, 1989	Shanxi-Hebei border, China	29+	7.1
Oct. 19, 1989	Cherchell, Algeria	30	6.0
Dec. 15, 1989	Off coast of Mindanao, Philippines	2	7.3
Dec. 27, 1989	Newcastle, Australia	11	5.4
Mar. 4, 1990	West-central Pakistan	11	6.1
Apr. 26, 1990	Qinghai Province, China	126	6.8
May 29, 1990	Northern Peru	137	6.4
June 20, 1990	Caspian Sea, near Rasht, Iran	50,000	7.6
July 16, 1990	Cabanatuan (Luzon I.), Philippines	1,700	7.7
Oct. 25, 1990	Afghanistan and Pakistan	11	6.0
Nov. 6, 1990	Southern Iran	22+	6.8
Dec. 13, 1990	Carlentini, Sicily	15+	5.1
Feb. 1, 1991	Hindu Kush, Afghanistan	600	6.8
Apr. 22, 1991	Cobano, Costa Rica	76	7.4
Apr. 29, 1991	Georgia (former USSR)	144	7.0
June 28, 1991	Los Angeles, California	2	5.9
July 4, 1991	Indonesia	23	6.2
July 23, 1991	Southern Peru	20	5.6
July 24, 1991	Iraq	20+	5.5
Sept. 18, 1991	Guatemala City, Guatemala	25+	6.0
Oct. 20, 1991	India and Nepal	2000+	7.1
Nov. 22, 1991	Yemen	10	4.6
Mar. 13, 1992	Erzincan, Turkey	600+	6.8
June 28, 1992	Landers, California	1	7.5
Aug. 19, 1992	Kyrgyzstan (former USSR)	60	7.5
Sept. 2, 1992	Off coast of Nicaragua	170	7.2
Sept. 11, 1992	Kabala, Zaire	9	6.8
Oct. 12, 1992	Cairo, Egypt	651	5.9
Oct. 18, 1992	Murindo, Colombia	8	7.2
Dec. 13, 1992	Flores Island, Indonesia (tsunami)	2,500	7.5
Apr. 18, 1993	Central Peru	5	6.2
July 12, 1993	Sea of Japan, causing tsunami at Okushiri Islands	200+	7.7
Aug. 9, 1993	Hindu-Kush region, Afghanistan	6	6.4
Sept. 20, 1993	Klamath Falls, Oregon	1	5.4
Sept. 29, 1993	Bombay, India	30,000	6.4
Oct. 13, 1993	Eastern Papua New Guinea	63+	7.2
Dec. 4, 1993	Klamath Falls, Orégon	1	5.4
Jan. 17, 1994	Northridge, California	61	6.8
Feb. 15, 1994	Southern Sumatra, Indonesia	215+	7.2
June 3, 1994	Java and Bali in Indonesia (tsunamis)	218+	7.2
June 6, 1994	Nevada de Huila, Colombia	650+	6.8
Aug. 18, 1994	Northern Algeria	164	6.0
Sept. 1, 1994	Off the coast of northern California, causing a small tsunami at Crescent City	0	7.0
Oct. 4, 1994	Kurile Islands of Japan and Russia	190	8.2
Nov. 14, 1994	Mindoro Island in Philippines	78	7.2
Jan. 17, 1995	Near Kobe, Japan	5,300	7.2
Feb. 8, 1995	Pereira, Colombia	36	6.5
May 28, 1995	Sakhalin Island, Russia	2,000 est.	7.5

VOLCANO ERUPTIONS AND LANDSLIDES, 1628 B.C.–A.D. 1994

Date	Event	Deaths
1628 or 1645 B.C.	Mediterranean volcanic island of Thera (Santorini) explodes.	N.A.
Aug. 24–26, A.D. 79	Mt. Vesuvius, near Naples, Italy, erupts, destroying towns of Pompeii and Herculaneum.	2,000+
260	Mt. Ilopango in El Salvador erupts, apparently destroying the early Maya civilization.	N.A.
Sept. 4, 1618	Landslides hit Chiavenna Valley, Italy.	2,420
Dec. 16, 1631	Mt. Vesuvius erupts.	4,000+
Mar. 25, 1669	Mt. Etna at Catania, Sicily, erupts.	20,000
Jan. 11, 1683	Mt. Etna erupts, accompanied by earthquakes.	60,000
Aug. 11–12, 1772	Mt. Papandayan on Java explodes.	3,000+
June 1783–Feb. 1784	Laki fissure on Mt. Skaptar in Iceland erupts; poisonous gases kill crops and livestock, and thick haze interrupts fishing on oceans.	9,800
1792	Eruption of Mt. Unzen in Japan causes harbor wave.	15,000
Sept. 2, 1806	Rossberg Peak collapses, causing landslides in Goldau Valley, Switzerland.	500
Apr. 5, 1815	Mt. Tambora on Sumbawa in East Indies begins series of eruptions that results in immediate death of about 10,000 people; another 80,000 die of famine and disease locally; eruptions also alter weather around world.	162,000
Oct. 8 and 12, 1822	Mt. Galunggung on Java erupts, causing slides of mud and boiling water.	4,000
1845	Eruption of Nevada del Ruiz in northern Colombia causes mudslides from melting snow.	1,000
July 28, 1883	Epomeo volcano on Italian Isle of Ischia erupts, causing destructive earthquakes.	2,000+
Aug. 26, 1883	Krakatau volcano in East Indies erupts, producing giant waves that strike nearby islands.	37,000
July 15, 1888	Bandai volcano in Japan erupts, causing steaming mud slides.	500+
May 7, 1902	La Soufrière on St. Vincent in West Indies erupts.	1,500–2,000
May 8, 1902	Pelée volcano on neighboring Martinique erupts, pouring cloud of flaming gas on city of St. Pierre.	29,000
Aug. 30, 1902	Mt. Pelée erupts.	2,000
Apr. 18, 1906	Mt. Vesuvius near Naples erupts.	150+
1911	Taal volcano, near Manila, Philippines, erupts.	1,300
May 1919	Crater lake of Mt. Kelut in Indonesia, boiling by volcanic activity, breaks through side of the mountain.	5,000+
Jan. 15, 1951	Mt. Lamington on New Guinea produces cloud of hot gas and dust, similar to that at Mt. Pelée in 1902 and Mt. St. Helens in 1980.	3,000–5,000
Dec. 4, 1951	Mt. Catarman (Hibokhibok) in Philippines releases cloud of hot gas.	500
Sept. 24, 1952	Japanese research ship investigating undersea volcano is destroyed in eruptive event.	29
Dec. 25, 1953	Dam, created by 1945 eruption of Ruapehu volcano on New Zealand, gives way; avalanche of mud and snow strikes passenger train.	150
Sept. 28, 1956	Taal volcano, near Manila, Philippines, erupts.	350
Jan. 10, 1962	Landslide on Mt. Huascarán, Peru.	3,000
Mar. 14, 1962	Two landslides near Paucartambno Hydroelectric Station in Peru.	204
Mar. 17–21, 1963	Mt. Agung volcano in Bali, Indonesia, has second eruption of year.	1,584
Aug. 10, 1963	Landslide in Nepal sweeps villages into Trisuli River.	200
Oct. 9, 1963	Flood occurs when Valont Dam near Langarone, Italy, overflows as result of landslide into its reservoir.	2,200
Aug. 30, 1965	Avalanche near Saas-Fee, Switzerland, from Allalin glacier strikes workers building dam.	40–100
July 22, 1970	Landslide diverts course of Alaknanda River in India, causing sudden flood.	600
Mar. 18, 1971	Landslide into Lake Yanahuani, creates 60-foot wave that sweeps over Chungar, Peru.	200
July 29, 1971	Landslide into high lake in Hindu Kush mountains of Afghanistan, causes instant flood.	1,000+
June 28, 1974	Landslides along Quebrada Blanca Canyon in Eastern Colombia.	200
Jan. 10, 1977	Fast-moving stream of lava from volcano near Goma, Zaire, overtakes fleeing residents.	70
Feb. 21, 1979	Volcano in Java, Indonesia, erupts.	175+
Apr. 30, 1979	Landslide covers side of Marapi volcano in Sumatra, Indonesia.	82+
July 18, 1979	Landslide on Mt. Werung causes wave to strike beach areas on Lomblen Island, Indonesia.	539
May 18, 1980	Mt. St. Helens volcano erupts in Washington.	61
May 20, 1981	Landslides caused by eruption of Semeru in Java, Indonesia.	252
Mar. 28 and Apr. 3–4, 1982	El Chichón in Chiapas State, Mexico, erupts; major blast on Apr. 4 sends cloud of volcanic ash around world.	2,000
Aug. 16, 1984	Carbon dioxide emitted by Lake Monoun, Cameroon, spreads in region around lake.	37
Nov. 13, 1985	Eruption of Nevada del Ruiz in northern Colombia melts snow on its summit, causing massive mud slide that covers town of Armero.	25,000
Aug. 21, 1986	Carbon dioxide from Lake Nyos, Cameroon, caused either by underwater volcano or overturning of water layers, spreads through surrounding region.	1,700+
July 13, 1990	Earthquake triggers landslide in Pamir Mts., Tajikistan, USSR.	40+
Oct. 13, 1990	Geyserlike explosion in the Ahuachapán Geothermal Field, El Salvador, releases wave of carbon dioxide and water.	26
Jan. 5, 1991	Landslide at Zunil Geothermal Field, western Guatemala.	33
June 3, 1991	Eruption of Mt. Unzen on Kyushu, Japan.	43
June 9, 1991	Warned by effective predictions, most are evacuated before major eruption of Mt. Pinatubo on Luzon in the Philippines; 358 of the 745 who die are killed by disease in evacuation camps.	745
Jan. 14, 1993	Galeras in Colombia erupts unexpectedly during a scientific workshop, killing, among others, six volcanologists who had been on the rim studying the volcano.	9
Feb. 2, 1993	An unexpected eruption of Mayon on Luzon in the Philippines produces a cloud of very hot gas and dust that rolls down the slope, killing 70.	70
June 6, 1994	Although the volcano Nevada de Huila in Colombia has not erupted since 1555, it proves a potent force for destruction when an earthquake sends mud landslides that destroy a dozen villages on its slopes.	650+
Nov. 22, 1994	Various flows of hot ash and gases down the slope of Merapi volcano on Java in Indonesia kill workers at a water-treatment plant and sweep through small villages where superstitious villagers had failed to heed a call to evacuate.	c. 50

MAJOR ACTIVE VOLCANOES

Volcano	Location	Height (ft. above sea level)	Last reported eruption
AFRICA AND THE INDIAN OCEAN			
Cameroon Mt.	Cameroon	13,435	1982
Erta-Ale	Ethiopia	1,650	1973
Karthala	Comoros	8,000	1991
Ol Donyo Lengai	Tanzania	9,469	1994
Nyamulagira	Zaire	10,016	1994
Nyirangongo	Zaire	12,381	1994
Piton de la Fournaise	Réunion Island	8,631	1992
ANTARCTICA			
Big Ben	Heard Island	9,007	1986
Deception Island	South Shetland Islands	1,890	1970
Mount Erebus	Ross Island	12,447	1990
ASIA			
Agung	Bali, Indonesia	10,308	1964
Akita Komagatake	Japan	5,449	1970
Alaid	Kuril Islands, Russia	7,674	1972
Amburomrrbi	Indonesia	7,051	1969
Anak Krakatau	Indonesia	330	1993
Asama	Honshu, Japan	8,300	1983
Aso	Kyushu, Japan	5,223	1995
Awu	Indonesia	4,350	1968
Azuma	Honshu, Japan	6,640	1978
Batur	Bali, Indonesia	5,633	1994
Bezymianny	Russia	9,186	1993
Bulusan	Philippines	5,135	1995
Chokai	Honshu, Japan	7,300	1974
Dukono	Indonesia	3,566	1995
Galunggug	Java, Indonesia	7,113	1982
Gamalama	Indonesia	5,625	1994
Gamkonora	Indonesia	5,365	1981
Gerde	Indonesia	9,705	1949
Karymsky	Russia	4,869	1982
Kelimutu	Indonesia	5,381	1968
Kelud	Java, Indonesia	5,679	1967
Kerinci	Sumatra, Indonesia	12,467	1987
Kirisima	Japan	5,577	1994
Kliuchevskoi	Russia	15,912	1990
Koraykskaya	Russia	11,339	1957
Krakatau	Indonesia	2,667	1863
Lewotobi Laki-laki	Indonesia	5,217	1991
Lokon-Empung	Indonesia	5,187	1992
Mayon	Philippines	8,077	1993
Me-akan	Japan	9,846	1966
Merapi	Java, Indonesia	9,550	1995
Nasu	Japan	6,210	1977
Nigata Yakeyama	Japan	8,064	1987
On-Take	Kyushu, Japan	10,049	1979
Oshima	Japan	2,587	1990
Pinatubo	Luzon, Philippines	5,250	1991
Raung	Java, Indonesia	10,932	1991
Rinjani	Lombok Island, Indonesia	12,224	1994
Sakura-jima	Kyushu, Japan	3,665	1995
Sangeang Api	Indonesia	6,351	1988
Sarychev	Kuril Islands, Russia	5,115	1986
Semeru	Java, Indonesia	12,060	1995
Sheveluch	Russia	11,138	1993
Siau	Indonesia	5,853	1976
Sinila	Indonesia	7,000	1979
Slamet	Java, Indonesia	11,260	1989
Soputan	Indonesia	5,994	1984
Suwanose-jima	Japan	2,621	1993
Taal	Luzon, Philippines	1,312	1970
Tambora	Sumbawa, Indonesia	9,354	1815
Tangkuban Prahu	Java, Indonesia	6,637	1967
Tiatia	Kuril Islands, Russia	6,013	1973
Tjarme	Indonesia	10,098	1938
Unzen	Kyushu, Japan	4,921	1995
Usu	Japan	2,390	1978
Yake Dake	Japan	8,052	1963
CENTRAL AMERICA AND THE CARIBBEAN			
Acatenango	Guatemala	12,992	1972
Arenal	Costa Rica	5,436	1995
Concepción	Ometepe Island, Nicaragua	5,106	1986
Conchagua	El Salvador	4,100	1947
El Viejo (San Cristóbal)	Nicaragua	5,840	1977
Fuego	Guatemala	12,582	1987
Irazú	Costa Rica	11,260	1965
Izalco	El Salvador	7,749	1966
Kick-'em-Jenny	subocean, off Grenada	–160	1990
Momotombo	Nicaragua	4,199	1982
Pacaya	Guatemala	8,346	1994
Pelée	Martinique	4,500	1930
Pöas	Costa Rica	8,885	1994
Rincon de la Vieja	Costa Rica	6,286	1992
San Miguel	El Salvador	6,988	1987
San Salvador	El Salvador	6,187	1923
Santiaguito Dome (Santa Maria)	Guatemala	12,362	1993
Soufrière	St. Vincent and the Grenadines	4,048	1979
Tacaná	Guatemala	12,400	1988
Telica	Nicaragua	3,477	1994
EUROPE AND THE ATLANTIC OCEAN			
Askja	Iceland	4,594	1961
Beerenberg	Jan Mayen Island, Norway	7,470	1985
Eldfell	Iceland	327	1973
Etna	Italy	10,794	1993
Fogo	Cape Verde Islands	9,281	1995
Helka	Iceland	4,892	1991
Krafla	Iceland	2,145	1984
Leirhnukur	Iceland	2,145	1975
Stromboli	Italy	3,038	1994
Surtsey	Iceland	568	1967
Tristan da Cunha	St. Helena	6,760	1961
Vesuvius	Italy	4,203	1944
Vulcano	Lipari Island, Italy	1,640	1890
NORTH AMERICA			
Akutan	Alaska	4,265	1992
Amukta	Alaska	3,490	1963
Aniakchak	Alaska	4,450	1934
Augustine	Alaska	3,995	1986
Bogoslof	Alaska	150	1931
Carlisle	Alaska	5,315	1838
Cerberus	Alaska	2,560	1873
Chiginagak	Alaska	7,985	1929
Cinder Cone	California	6,907	1851
Cleveland	Alaska	5,675	1994
Colima	Mexico	13,448	1994
El Chichón	Mexico	7,300	1983
Fisher	Alaska	3,545	1826
Gareloi	Alaska	5,370	1982
Great Sitkin	Alaska	5,775	1974
Iliamna	Alaska	10,140	1978
Isanotski	Alaska	8,185	1845
Kagamil	Alaska	2,945	1929
Kanaga	Alaska	4,288	1994
Katmai	Alaska	7,540	1974
Keniuji	Alaska	885	1828
Kiska	Alaska	4,025	1990
Korovin	Alaska	4,885	1987
Lassen Peak	California	10,453	1921
Little Sitkin	Alaska	3,945	1828
Mageik	Alaska	7,295	1946
Makushin	Alaska	6,680	1987
Martin	Alaska	6,102	1960
Mt. Baker	Washington	10,778	1870
Mt. Hood	Oregon	11,245	1801
Mt. Rainier	Washington	14,410	1882
Mt. St. Helens	Washington	9,671	1991
Mt. Shasta	California	14,160	1855
Novarupta	Alaska	2,759	1912
Okmok	Alaska	3,540	1988
Parícutin	Mexico	1,500	1953
Pavlof	Alaska	8,960	1988
Pavlof Sister	Alaska	7,050	1786
Peulik	Alaska	5,030	1852
Pogromni	Alaska	7,545	1964
Popocatépetl	Mexico	17,930	1995
Redoubt	Alaska	10,265	1990
Sarichef	Alaska	2,015	1812
Seguam	Alaska	3,465	1993
Shishaldin	Alaska	9,430	1987
Spurr	Alaska	11,070	1992
Tanaga	Alaska	7,015	1914
Tobert	Alaska	11,413	1953
Trident	Alaska	6,830	1974
Veniaminof	Alaska	8,225	1994
Vsevidof	Alaska	6,965	1880
Westdahl	Alaska	5,055	1992
Yunaska	Alaska	1,980	1937
OCEANIA—AUSTRALIA, NEW ZEALAND, AND THE PACIFIC ISLANDS			
Ambrym	Vanuatu	4,376	1990
Bagana	Bougainville Island, Papua New Guinea	5,584	1990
Haleakala	Hawaii	10,025	1790
Hualalai	Hawaii	8,251	1801
Karkar	Papua New Guinea	4,920	1979
Kilauea	Hawaii	4,009	1995
Langila	New Britain, Papua New Guinea	4,364	1995
Lopevi	New Hebrides, Vanuatu	4,636	1982
Manam	Papua New Guinea	5,928	1995
Mauna Loa	Hawaii	13,678	1984

Volcano	Location	Height (ft. above sea level)	Last reported eruption
Ngauruhoe	North Island, New Zealand	7,515	1975
Pagan	Mariana Islands	1,870	1993
Rabaul	New Britain, Papua New Guinea	2,257	1995
Ruapehu	New Zealand	9,177	1993
Tarawera	North Island, New Zealand	3,645	1886
Ulawun	New Britain, Papua New Guinea	7,657	1990
White Island	New Zealand	1,053	1994
SOUTH AMERICA			
Alcedo	Galapagos Islands, Ecuador	3,707	1993
Copahue	Argentina/Chile	9,800	1992
Cotacachi	Ecuador	16,204	1955
Cotopaxi	Ecuador	19,347	1975
Galeras	Colombia	14,025	1993
Guagua Pichincha	Ecuador	15,696	1993
Guallatiri	Chile	19,882	1960
Hudson	Chile	8,580	1991
Láscar	Chile	18,372	1995
Llaima	Chile	10,250	1994
Lonquimay	Chile	9,400	1990
Puracé	Colombia	15,604	1977
Reventador	Ecuador	11,434	1976
Ruiz	Colombia	17,720	1991
Sangay	Ecuador	17,159	1976
Shoshuenco	Chile	7,743	1960
Tupungatito	Chile	18,504	1986
Villarica	Chile	9,338	1985

Chemistry

Chemistry is concerned with the way substances interact with one another. These interactions are chiefly the result of outer electrons of an atom interacting with the outer electrons of another atom. It has increasingly become clear that the shapes of the various combinations of atoms (called molecules) also affect chemical reactions, and physical chemistry is one of the most vital parts of chemistry today. Another vital branch is biochemistry, the study of the chemistry of molecules in living organisms. Organic chemistry generally deals with chemicals formed by living organisms and other chemicals containing carbon, but it treats them as chemicals outside the organism. Inorganic chemistry is concerned with chemicals that do not contain carbon.

MAJOR DISCOVERIES IN CHEMISTRY

B.C.

c. 450 Leucippus of Miletus (Greek: 5th cent.) introduces concept of atom, later expanded upon by his pupil Democritus of Abdera (c. 460–c. 370).

A.D.

1662 Robert Boyle (Anglo-Irish: 1627–91) announces what becomes known as Boyle's law: For gas kept at constant temperature, pressure and volume vary inversely.

1755 Joseph Black (Scottish: 1728–99) discovers carbon dioxide.

1766 Henry Cavendish (English: 1731–1810) discovers hydrogen.

1772 Joseph Priestley (English-American: 1733–1804) notes that burning hydrogen produces water.

Daniel Rutherford (Scottish: 1749–1819) and several other chemists discover nitrogen. Karl Wilhelm Scheele (Swedish: 1742–86) discovers oxygen but does not announce discovery until after independent discovery by Joseph Priestley in 1774.

1777 Antoine-Laurent Lavoisier (French: 1743–94) discovers that air is mostly mixture of nitrogen and oxygen.

1784 Cavendish announces water is compound of hydrogen and oxygen.

1789 Lavoisier explicitly states law of conservation of matter: In chemical change, matter is neither created nor destroyed.

1791 Jeremias Benjamin Richter (German: 1762–1807) shows that acids and bases always neutralize each other in same proportion.

1803 John Dalton (English: 1766–1844) establishes atomic theory of matter.

1811 Amedeo Avogadro (Italian: 1776–1856) proposes that equal volumes of gas at same temperature and pressure contain same number of molecules (Avogadro's law).

1824 Joseph-Louis Gay-Lussac (French: 1778–1850) discovers chemical isomers, chemicals with same formula but different structures.

1828 Friedrich Wöhler (German: 1800–1882) prepares organic compound from inorganic chemicals, showing that life is basically same as other matter.

1859 Gustav Robert Kirchhoff (German: 1824–87) and Robert Wilhelm Bunsen (German: 1811–99) introduce use of spectroscope to identify elements from light they give off when heated or burned.

1868 Pierre-Jules-César Janssen (French: 1824–1907) and Sir Joseph Norman Lockyer (English: 1836–1920) discover helium by observing Sun's spectrum.

1869 Dmitry Ivanovich Mendeleyev (Russian: 1834–1907) publishes his first version of periodic table of elements.

1875 Paul-Emile Lecoq de Boisbaudran (French: 1838–1912) discovers gallium, the first discovery of an element predicted by Mendeleyev on basis of his periodic table.

1906 Mikhail Tsvett (Russian: 1872–1919) develops paper chromotography, the beginning of modern methods of chemical analysis.

1908 Fritz Haber (German: 1868–1934) develops cheap process for making ammonia from nitrogen in the air.

1943 Albert Hofmann (Swiss: 1906–) discovers that LSD is hallucinogenic.

1962 Neil Bartlett (English: 1932–) creates xenon, showing that the noble gases can form compounds.

1984 Dany Shechtman (American) and coworkers discover first quasi crystal, a "crystal" that violates the symmetry rules of all other crystals.

1985 Richard E. Smalley (American: 1943–) and Harry Kroto (English) discover buckminsterfullerene, a carbon molecule containing 60 carbon atoms arranged in a geodesic sphere (nicknamed "bucky balls").

1990 Julius Rebeck, Jr., of MIT and coworkers announce creation of a self-replicating molecule, amino adenosine triad ester (AATE).

1993 Using a four-year-old theory, scientists at Harvard create a thin film of a carbon and nitrogen compound believed to be harder than a diamond.

1994 Scientists of the Society for Heavy Ion Research in Darmstadt, Germany, create a few atoms each of elements 110 and 111, continuing a process the society started with the manufacture of elements 107, 108, and 109 in the 1980s.

> ***"Every great advance in science has issued from a new audacity of imagination."***
>
> —John Dewey, *The Quest for Certainty*

PROPERTIES, ABUNDANCE, AND DISCOVERY OF THE ELEMENTS

All ordinary matter is made from one or more substances called elements (because they cannot be changed by chemical means). Ninety elements are found in nature, and people have created others, for a current total of 111. In this table each of the elements is listed in alphabetical order along with several of its important properties. The chemical symbol and the atomic number can be used to locate other information about the elements in the periodic table reprinted below. The relative abundance of the elements is given as parts per million in the Earth's crust—83,600 parts per million for aluminum means that of a million atoms chosen at random from the crust, 83,600 atoms, on average, would be aluminum atoms. Some elements have so few parts per million that they are simply listed as rare, whereas others are "synthetic"—artificial elements not found in the crust at all. Many elements, known from ancient times, are labeled "prehistoric." Others are given with their first discovery—many elements having been independently rediscovered by others. There is significant disagreement among international physicists and chemists around the world about the names of elements 104–111. For example, Soviet chemists agreed to call element 105 Nielsbohrium, while American chemists called it Hahnium and called element 107 Nielsbohrium. Until the disagreement is resolved, the elements are presented as unnamed, with the competing names explained in the "Derivation of name" column.

Element	Symbol/ atomic number	Type[1]	Melting point[1]	Boiling point[1]	Parts per million in crust	Year discovered and by whom	Derivation of name
Actinium	Ac 89	Radioactive metal	1920°F 1050°C	5790°F 3200°C	Rare	1899 André-Louis Debierne	Greek *aktis*, a ray
Aluminum	Al 13	Metal	1220°F 660°C	4473°F 2467°C	83,600	1825 Hans Christian Oersted	Latin *alumen*, a substance having astringent taste
Americium	Am 95	Radioactive metal	1821°F 994°C	4725°F 2607°C	Synthetic	1944 Glenn T. Seaborg & coworkers	For America
Antimony	Sb 51	Metal	1167°F 631°C	3180°F 1750°C	0.2	c. 900 Rhazes	Greek *antimonos*, opposed to solitude; symbol Sb from Latin *stibium*
Argon	Ar 18	Gas	–308.6°F –189.2°C	–302.3°F –185.7°C	Rare	1892 Sir William Ramsay	Greek *argus*, neutral inactive
Arsenic	As 33	Nonmetal	1503°F[2] 817°C[2]	1135°F[2] 613°C[2]	1.8	1649 J. Schroeder & N. Lémery	Latin *arsenicum;* folk etymology connects with yellow and maleness
Astatine	At 85	Radioactive nonmetal	576°F 302°C	639°F 337°C	Synthetic	1940 Emilio Segrè, D.R. Corson, & K.R. MacKenzie	Greek *astatos*, unstable
Barium	Ba 56	Metal	1337°F 725°C	2980°F 1640°C	390	1808 Humphry Davy	Greek *baros*, heavy; because its compounds are dense
Berkelium	Bk 97	Radioactive metal	N.A.	N.A.	Synthetic	1949 Glenn T. Seaborg & coworkers	First made at Univ. of California at Berkeley
Beryllium	Be 4	Metal	2332°F 1278°C	5380°F 2970°C	2	1798 Louis-Nicolas Vauquelin	Latin *beryllus*, Greek *beryllos*, gem
Bismuth	Bi 83	Metal	520°F 271°C	2840°F 1560°C	0.008	1753 Claude J. Geoffrey	German *weisse masse*, white mass; changed to *bismat*
Boron	B 5	Nonmetal	3774°F 2079°C	4620°F 2550°C	9	1808 Joseph-Louis Gay-Lussac & Louis-Jacques Thénard	Arabic *borak* (borax); BORax + carbON
Bromine	Br 35	Liquid nonmetal	19°F –7.2°C	137.8°F 58.8°C	2.5	1825 Carl Löwig	Greek *bromos*, a stench; because of odor of its vapors
Cadmium	Cd 48	Metal	609.6°F 320.9°C	1409°F 765°C	0.16	1817 Friedrich Strohmeyer	Greek *cadmia*, earthy
Calcium	Ca 20	Metal	1542°F 839°C	2703°F 1484°C	46,600	1808 Humphry Davy	Latin *calx, calcis*, lime
Californium	Cf 98	Radioactive metal	N.A.	N.A.	Synthetic	1950 Glenn T. Seaborg & coworkers	First made at Univ. of California
Carbon	C 6	Nonmetal	6420°F 3550°C	8721°F 4827°C	180	Prehistoric	Latin *carbo*, coal
Cerium	Ce 58	Rare earth	1468°F 798°C	5875°F 3246°C	66.4	1803 Martin Klaproth	For asteroid Ceres, discovered in 1801
Cesium	Cs 55	Metal	83.1°F 28.4°C	1236.7°F 669.3°C	2.6	1860 Gustav Kirchhoff & Robert Bunsen	Latin *caesius*, bluish gray
Chlorine	Cl 17	Gas	–150°F –101°C	–30.3°F –34.6°C	126	1774 Karl Wilhelm Scheele	Greek *chloros*, grass-green; from color of gas
Chromium	Cr 24	Metal	3375°F 1857°C	4842°F 2672°C	122	1797 Louis-Nicolas Vauquelin	Greek *chroma*, color; because many of its compounds are colored
Cobalt	Co 27	Metal	2723°F 1495°C	5200°F 2870°C	29	1735 George Brandt	German *Kobalt*, a goblin
Copper	Cu 29	Metal	1981°F 1083°C	4653°F 2567°C	68	Prehistoric	Latin *cuprum;* for island of Cyprus
Curium	Cm 96	Radioactive metal	2444°F 1340°C	N.A.	Synthetic	1944 Glenn T. Seaborg & coworkers	After Pierre and Marie Curie
Dysprosium	Dy 66	Rare earth	2574°F 1412°C	4653°F 2567°C	Rare	1886 Paul-Emile Lecoq de Boisbaudran	Greek *dysprositos*, difficult of access

Element	Symbol/ atomic number	Type[1]	Melting point[1]	Boiling point[1]	Parts per million in crust	Year discovered and by whom	Derivation of name
Einsteinium	Es 99	Radioactive metal	N.A.	N.A.	Synthetic	1952 Albert Ghiorso & coworkers	After Albert Einstein
Element 104	Rf or Unq 104	Radioactive metal	N.A.	N.A.	Synthetic	Claimed by Russian scientists at Dubna in 1964 and by U.S. team led by Albert Ghiorso in 1969	Proposed names include Kurchatovium, Rutherfordium, Unnilquadium (Greek for 104), and Dubnium
Element 105	Ha or Unp 105	Radioactive metal	N.A.	N.A.	Synthetic	Claimed by Russian scientists at Dubna and by U.S. team led by Albert Ghiorso in 1970	Proposed names include Hahnium, Nielsbohrium, Unnilpentium (Greek for 105), and Joliotium
Element 106	Sg or Unh 106	Radioactive metal	N.A.	N.A.	Synthetic	Claimed by Russian scientists at Dubna and by U.S. team from Lawrence Berkeley and Livermore Laboratories in 1974	Proposed names include Seaborgium, Unnilhexium (Greek for 106), and Rutherfordium
Element 107	N.A. 107	Radioactive metal	N.A.	N.A.	Synthetic	Identified by the Society for Heavy Ion Research in 1964 in Darmstadt, Germany	Proposed names include Nielsbohrium and Bohrium
Element 108	N.A. 108	Radioactive metal	N.A.	N.A.	Synthetic	Identified by the Society for Heavy Ion Research in 1964 in Darmstadt, Germany	Proposed names include Hessium and Hahnium
Element 109	N.A. 109	Radioactive metal	N.A.	N.A.	Synthetic	Identified by the Society for Heavy Ion Research in 1964 in Darmstadt, Germany	Proposed name is Meitnerium for the Austrian-Swedish physicist Lee Meitner
Element 110	N.A.	Radioactive metal	N.A.	N.A.	Synthetic	Identified by the Society for Heavy Ion Research in 1964 in Darmstadt, Germany	N.A.
Element 111	N.A.	Radioactive metal	N.A.	N.A.	Synthetic	Identified by the Society for Heavy Ion Research in 1964 in Darmstadt, Germany	N.A.
Erbium	Er 68	Rare earth	2784°F 1529°C	4334°F 2868°C	3.46	1843 Carl Gustav Mosander	For Ytterby, village in Sweden
Europium	Eu 63	Rare earth	1512°F 822°C	2907°F 1597°C	2.1	1896 Eugène-Anatole Demarçay	For Europe
Fermium	Fm 100	Radioactive metal	N.A.	N.A.	Synthetic	1952 Albert Ghioroso & coworkers	After Enrico Fermi, Italian physicist
Fluorine	F 9	Gas	−363.3°F −219.6°C	−306.7°F −188.1°C	544	1886 Ferdinand-Frédéric-Henri Moissan	Latin *fluere,* to flow
Francium	Fr 87	Radioactive metal	80.6°F 27°C	1256°F 677°C	Rare	1939 Marguerite Perey	For France
Gadolinium	Gd 64	Rare earth	2395°F 1313°C	5923°F 3273°C	6.1	1880 Jean-Charles Marignac	After gadolinite, mineral named for Johan Gadolin, Finnish chemist
Gallium	Ga 31	Metal	86.6°F 29.8°C	4357°F 2403°C	19	1875 Paul-Emile Lecoq de Boisbaudran	Latin *Gallia,* France; also Latin *gallus,* a cock—pun on Lecoq de Boisbaudran
Germanium	Ge 32	Metal	1719°F 937°C	5126°F 2830°C	1.5	1886 Clemens Winkler	For Germany
Gold	Au 79	Metal	1947°F 1064°C	5086°F 2808°C	0.002	Prehistoric	Anglo-Saxon *gold;* Sanskrit *juel,* to shine; symbol from Latin *aurum,* shining down
Hafnium	Hf 72	Metal	4041°F 2227°C	8316°F 4602°C	2.8	1923 Dirk Coster & György Hevesy	From *Hafnia,* ancient name of Copenhagen
Helium	He 2	Gas	−458°F −272°C	−452°F −269°C	Rare	1868 Pierre-Jules-César Janssen & Sir Joseph Norman Lockyer	Greek *helios,* the Sun; first observed in Sun's atmosphere
Holmium	Ho 67	Rare earth	2678°F 1470°C	4928°F 2720°C	1.26	1879 Per Teodor Cleve	From *Holmia,* Latinized form of *Stockholm*
Hydrogen	H 1	Gas	−434.6°F −259.1°C	−423.2°F −252.9°C	1520	1766 Henry Cavendish	Greek *hydor,* water, plus *gen,* forming
Indium	In 49	Metal	313.9°F 156.6°C	3776°F 2080°C	0.24	1863 Ferdinand Reich & Hieronymus Theodor Richter	Latin *indicum,* indigo
Iodine[3]	I 53	Nonmetal	236.3°F 113.5°C	363.9°F 184.4°C	0.46	1811 Bernard Courtois	Greek *iodes,* violet; from color of its vapor
Iridium	Ir 77	Metal	4370°F 2410°C	7466°F 4130°C	0.001	1803 Smithson Tennant	Greek *iris,* a rainbow, from changing color of its salts
Iron	Fe 26	Metal	2795°F 1535°C	4982°F 2750°C	62,200	Prehistoric	Anglo-Saxon *iren;* symbol from Latin *ferrum*

Element	Symbol/ atomic number	Type[1]	Melting point[1]	Boiling point[1]	Parts per million in crust	Year discovered and by whom	Derivation of name
Krypton	Kr 36	Gas	−249.9°F −156.6°C	−242.1°F −152.3°C	Rare	1898 Alexander Ramsay & Morris William Travers	Greek *kryptos,* hidden
Lanthanum	La 57	Rare earth	1684°F 918°C	6267°F 3464°C	34.6	1839 Carl Gustav Mosander	Greek *lanthanein,* to be concealed
Lawrencium	Lr 103	Radioactive metal	N.A.	N.A.	Synthetic	1961 Albert Ghiorso & coworkers	After Ernest Lawrence, American physicist
Lead	Pb 82	Metal	621.5°F 327.5°C	3164°F 1740°C	13	Prehistoric	Anglo-Saxon *lead;* symbol from Latin *plumbum*
Lithium	Li 3	Metal	356.9°F 180.5°C	2248°F 1342°C	18	1817 J.A. Arfvedson	Greek *lithos,* stony
Lutetium	Lu 71	Rare earth	3025°F 1663°C	6157°F 3402°C	Rare	1907 Georges Urbain	Latin *Lutetia,* ancient name for Paris
Magnesium	Mg 12	Metal	1200°F 649°C	1994°F 1090°C	27,640	1808 Humphry Davy	Latin *Magnesia,* a district in Asia Minor
Manganese	Mn 25	Metal	2271°F 1244°C	3564°F 1962°C	1060	1774 Johann Gottlieb Gahn	Latin *magnes,* magnet; because of confusion with magnetic iron ores
Mendelevium	Md 101	Radioactive metal	N.A.	N.A.	Synthetic	1955 Albert Ghiorso & coworkers	After Dmitri Mendeléev, Russian chemist
Mercury	Hg 80	Liquid metal	−38.0°F −38.9°C	673.9°F 356.6°C	0.08	Prehistoric	For Roman god Mercurius; symbol from Latin *hydrargyrum*
Molybdenum	Mo 42	Metal	4743°F 2617°C	8334°F 4612°C	1.2	1778 Karl Wilhelm Scheele	Greek *molybdos,* lead
Neodymium	Nd 60	Rare earth	1870°F 1021°C	5565°F 3074°C	39.6	1885 Karl Auer (Baron von Welsbach)	Greek *neo,* new, plus *didymon,* twin (with the element praseodymium)
Neon	Ne 10	Gas	−416.7°F −248.7°C	−411°F −246°C	Rare	1898 Alexander Ramsay & Morris William Travers	Greek *neo,* new
Neptunium	Np 93	Radioactive metal	1184°F 640°C	7056°F 3902°C	Synthetic	1940 Edwin McMillan & Philip Abelson	For planet Neptune
Nickel	Ni 28	Metal	2647°F 1453°C	4950°F 2732°C	99	1751 Axel Cronstedt	German *Nickel,* Satan (Old Nick)
Niobium	Nb 41	Metal	4474°F 2468°C	8568°F 4742°C	20	1801 Charles Hachett	Latin *Niobe,* daughter of Tantalus
Nitrogen	N 7	Gas	−345.8°F −209.9°C	−320.4°F −195.8°C	19	1772 Daniel Rutherford	Latin, forming *niter,* a compound of nitrogen
Nobelium	No 102	Radioactive metal	N.A.	N.A.	Synthetic	1957 P.R. Fields & coworkers	After Alfred Nobel; made at Nobel Institute
Osmium	Os 76	Metal	5513°F 3045°C	9081°F 5027°C	0.005	1803 Smithson Tennant	Greek *osme,* smell; for malodorousness
Oxygen	O 8	Gas	−361°F −218.4°C	−297°F −183°C	456,000	1774 Joseph Priestley	Greek *oxys,* sharp, plus *gen,* forming; from incorrect belief that oxygen forms acids
Palladium	Pd 46	Metal	2829°F 1554°C	5684°F 3140°C	0.015	1803 William Hyde Wollaston	For Greek goddess Pallas; from asteroid Pallas
Phosphorus	P 15	Nonmetal	111.4°F 44.1°C	536°F 280°C	1120	1669 Hennig Brand	Greek *phosphoros,* light-bringer; glows because of rapid oxidation
Platinum	Pt 78	Metal	3222°F 1772°C	6921°F 3827°C	0.01	1735 Antonio de Ulloa	Diminutive of Spanish *plata,* silver, *platina*
Plutonium	Pu 94	Radioactive metal	1186°F 641°C	5850°F 3232°C	Synthetic	1940 Glenn T. Seaborg & coworkers	For planet Pluto
Polonium	Po 84	Radioactive metal	489°F 254°C	1764°F 962°C	Rare	1898 Marie Curie & Pierre Curie	Named by Marie Curie for her native Poland
Potassium	K 19	Metal	145.9°F 63.3°C	1399.8°F 759.9°C	18,400	1807 Humphry Davy	For potash, a compound of potassium; symbol from Latin *kalium*
Praseodymium	Pr 59	Rare earth	6368°F 3520°C	5814°F 3212°C	9.1	1885 Karl Auer (Baron von Welsbach)	Greek *prasios,* green, plus *didymos,* twin (with the element Neodymium)
Promethium	Pm 61	Radioactive rare earth	1908°F 1042°C	5430°F(est.) 3000°C(est.)	Rare	1945 J.A. Marinsky, L.E. Glendenin, & C.D. Coryell	For Greek god Prometheus, who stole fire from heaven
Protactinium	Pa 91	Radioactive metal	2912°F 1600°C	N.A. N.A.	Rare	1917 Otto Hahn & Lise Meitner	Latin *proto,* first, plus actinium, one of the elements
Radium	Ra 88	Radioactive metal	1292°F 700°C	2084°F 1140°C	Rare	1898 Marie Curie & Pierre Curie	Latin *radius,* ray

Element	Symbol/ atomic number	Type[1]	Melting point[1]	Boiling point[1]	Parts per million in crust	Year discovered and by whom	Derivation of name
Radon	Rn 86	Radioactive gas	−96°F −71°C	−79°F −61.8°C	Rare	1900 Friedrich Ernst Dorn	*Radium* plus *on*, as in *neon*
Rhenium	Re 75	Metal	5756°F 3180°C	10,161°F 5627°C	0.0007	1925 Walter Noddack, Ida Tacke, & Otto Berg	Latin *Rhenus*, Rhine
Rhodium	Rh 45	Metal	3571°F 1966°C	6741°F 3727°C	Rare	1803 William Hyde Wollaston	Greek *rhodon*, rose; for red color of its salts
Rubidium	Rb 37	Metal	102°F 38.9°C	1267°F 686°C	78	1861 Gustav Kirchhoff & Robert Bunsen	Latin *rubidus*, red; from red lines in its spectrum
Ruthenium	Ru 44	Metal	4190°F 2310°C	7052°F 3900°C	Rare	1844 Carl Claus	For Ruthenia in Urals, where ore was first found
Samarium	Sm 62	Rare earth	1965°F 1074°C	3261°F 1794°C	7	1879 Paul-Emile Lecoq de Boisbaudran	For Scandinavian mineral samarskite
Scandium	Sc 21	Metal	2806°F 1541°C	5128°F 2831°C	25	1879 Lars Fredrik Nilson	For Scandinavia
Selenium	Se 34	Nonmetal	423°F 217°C	1265°F 685°C	0.05	1817 Jöns Jakob Berzelius	Greek *selene*, the Moon
Silicon	Si 14	Nonmetal	2570°F 1410°C	4271°F 2355°C	273,000	1824 Jöns Jakob Berzelius	Latin *silex*, flint
Silver	Ag 47	Metal	1763.4°F 961.9°C	4014°F 2212°C	0.08	Prehistoric	Anglo-Saxon *sealfor;* symbol is from Latin *argentum*
Sodium	Na 11	Metal	208.0°F 97.8°C	1621.2°F 882.9°C	22,700	1807 Humphry Davy	English soda, compound of sodium; symbol from Latin *natrium*
Strontium	Sr 38	Metal	1416°F 769°C	2523°F 1384°C	384	1808 Humphry Davy	For Strontian, a town in Scotland
Sulfur	S 16	Nonmetal	235.0°F 112.8°C	832.5°F 444.7°C	340	Prehistoric	Sanskrit *solvere*, Latin *sulphur*
Tantalum	Ta 73	Metal	5425°F 2996°C	9797°F 5425°C	1.7	1802 Anders Ekeberg	For mythical king Tantalus, condemned to thirst; because of its insolubility
Technetium	Tc 43	Radioactive metal	3942°F 2172°C	8811°F 4877°C	Synthetic	1937 Emilio Segrè	Greek *technetos*, artificial; first artificial element
Tellurium	Te 52	Metal	841.1°F 449.5°C	1814°F 990°C	Rare	1782 Franz Joseph Müller	Latin *tellus*, the Earth
Terbium	Tb 65	Rare earth	2473°F 1356°C	5846°F 3230°C	1.18	1843 Carl Gustav Mosander	For Ytterby, village in Sweden
Thallium	Tl 81	Metal	578.3°F 303.5°C	2655°F 1457°C	0.7	1861 William Crookes	Greek *thallos*, a young, or green, twig (after color of its spectrum)
Thorium	Th 90	Radioactive metal	3182°F 1750°C	8654°F 4790°C	8.1	1829 Jöns Jakob Berzelius	For Norse god Thor
Thulium	Tm 69	Rare earth	2813°F 1545°C	3542°F 1950°C	0.5	1879 Per Teodor Cleve	Greek *Thule*, Greek name for land north of Britain
Tin	Sn 50	Metal	450°F 232°C	4118°F 2270°C	2.1	Prehistoric	Anglo-Saxon *tin;* symbol from Latin *stannum*
Titanium	Ti 22	Metal	3020°F 1660°C	5949°F 3287°C	6,320	1791 William Gregor	For Titans of classical mythology
Tungsten	W 74	Metal	6170°F 3410°C	10,220°F 5660°C	1.2	1783 Fausto and Juan José d'Elhuyar	Swedish *tung sten*, heavy stone; symbol from German *Wolfram*
Uranium	U 92	Radioactive metal	2070°F 1132°C	6904°F 3818°C	2.3	1789 Martin Klaproth	For planet Uranus
Vanadium	V 23	Metal	3434°F 1890°C	6116°F 3380°C	136	1801 Andrès del Rio	For Scandinavian goddess Vanadis
Xenon	Xe 54	Gas	−169.4°F −111.9°C	−161°F −107°C	Rare	1898 Alexander Ramsay & Morris William Travers	Greek *xenon*, stranger
Ytterbium	Yb 70	Rare earth	1506°F 819°C	2185°F 1196°C	3.1	1907 George Urbain	For Ytterby, a village in Sweden
Yttrium	Y 39	Rare earth	2826°F 1552°C	9640°F 3338°C	31	1794 Johan Gadolin	For Ytterby, a village in Sweden
Zinc	Zn 30	Metal	787.3°F 419.6°C	1665°F 907°C	76	Prehistoric	German *zink*
Zirconium	Zr 40	Metal	3366°F 1852°C	7911°F 4377°C	162	1789 Martin Klaproth	Arabic *zargun*, gold color

1. At a pressure of one atmosphere and, for type, at room temperature. 2. At a pressure of 28 atmospheres. 3. This element sublimes (slowly evaporates from its solid form) at room temperature and one atmosphere.

THE PERIODIC TABLE OF THE ELEMENTS

Key	
6	atomic number
C	chemical number
12.01	atomic mass
Carbon	name of element

	alkali metals I A	alkaline earth metals II A	III B	IV B	V B	VI B	VII B	VIII	VIII	VIII	I B	II B	III A	IV A	V A	VI A	VII A	noble gases O
Period 1	1 H 1.01 Hydrogen																	2 He 4.00 Helium
Period 2	3 Li 6.94 Lithium	4 Be 9.01 Beryllium											5 B 10.81 Boron	6 C 12.01 Carbon	7 N 14.01 Nitrogen	8 O 16.00 Oxygen	9 F 19.00 Fluorine	10 Ne 20.18 Neon
Period 3	11 Na 22.99 Sodium	12 Mg 24.31 Magnesium											13 Al 26.98 Aluminum	14 Si 28.09 Silicon	15 P 30.97 Phosphorus	16 S 32.07 Sulfur	17 Cl 35.45 Chlorine	18 Ar 39.95 Argon
Period 4	19 K 39.10 Potassium	20 Ca 40.08 Calcium	21 Sc 44.96 Scandium	22 Ti 47.88 Titanium	23 V 50.94 Vanadium	24 Cr 52.00 Chromium	25 Mn 54.95 Manganese	26 Fe 55.85 Iron	27 Co 58.93 Cobalt	28 Ni 58.70 Nickel	29 Cu 63.55 Copper	30 Zn 65.39 Zinc	31 Ga 69.72 Gallium	32 Ge 72.61 Germanium	33 As 74.92 Arsenic	34 Se 78.96 Selenium	35 Br 79.90 Bromine	36 Kr 83.80 Krypton
Period 5	37 Rb 85.47 Rubidium	38 Sr 87.62 Strontium	39 Y 88.91 Yttrium	40 Zr 91.22 Zirconium	41 Nb 92.91 Niobium	42 Mo 95.94 Molybdenum	43 Tc (98) Technetium	44 Ru 101.07 Ruthenium	45 Rh 102.91 Rhodium	46 Pd 106.4 Palladium	47 Ag 107.87 Silver	48 Cd 112.41 Cadmium	49 In 114.82 Indium	50 Sn 118.71 Tin	51 Sb 121.74 Antimony	52 Te 127.60 Tellurium	53 I 126.90 Iodine	54 Xe 131.29 Xenon
Period 6	55 Cs 132.91 Cesium	56 Ba 137.33 Barium	Lanthanide series (see below)	72 Hf 178.49 Hafnium	73 Ta 180.94 Tantalum	74 W 183.85 Tungsten	75 Re 186.21 Rhenium	76 Os 190.23 Osmium	77 Ir 192.22 Iridium	78 Pt 195.08 Platinum	79 Au 196.97 Gold	80 Hg 200.59 Mercury	81 Ti 204.38 Thallium	82 Pb 207.2 Lead	83 Bi 208.98 Bismuth	84 Po (209) Polonium	85 At (210) Astatine	86 Rn (222) Radon
Period 7	87 Fr (223) Francium	88 Ra 226.03 Radium	Actinide series (see below)	104 (261)	105 (262)	106 (263)	107 (262)	108 (265)	109 (266)	110 (269)	111 (272)							

transition metals (III B–II B); nonmetals (III A–VII A); other metals

rare earth elements—Lanthanide series

57	58	59	60	61	62	63	64	65	66	67	68	69	70	71
La	Ce	Pr	Nd	Pm	Sm	Eu	Gd	Tb	Dy	Ho	Er	Tm	Yb	Lu
138.91	140.12	140.91	144.24	(145)	150.4	151.96	157.25	158.93	162.50	164.93	167.26	168.93	173.04	174.97
Lanthanum	Cerium	Praseodymium	Neodymium	Promethium	Samarium	Europium	Gadolinium	Terbium	Dysprosium	Holmium	Erbium	Thulium	Ytterbium	Luetium

Actinide series

89	90	91	92	93	94	95	96	97	98	99	100	101	102	103
Ac	Th	Pa	U	Np	Pu	Am	Cm	Bk	Cf	Es	Fm	Md	No	Lr
227.03	232.04	231.04	238.03	237.05	(244)	(243)	(247)	(247)	(251)	(252)	(257)	(258)	(259)	(260)
Actinium	Thorium	Protactinium	Uranium	Neptunium	Plutonium	Americium	Curium	Berkelium	Californium	Einsteinium	Fermium	Mendelevium	Nobelium	Lawrencium

THE PERIODIC TABLE

In the 19th century, chemists began to determine how much one atom of an element weighed with respect to another—the atomic weight (also known as the atomic mass and measured in atomic mass units, or amu, a mass equal to one-twelfth the mass of the most common form of carbon atom). The first comprehensive list was prepared by Jöns Jakob Berzelius in 1828. When chemists made lists of elements in the order of atomic weights, they noticed that every seven or eight elements in the list had similar properties. In 1869 Dmitri Mendeleyev went further and boldly interchanged some elements in the list and left blanks for others to make sure the properties matched for every "period" of eight elements. This was the first periodic table. Mendeleyev had only 63 elements to work with, but he correctly predicted three more that would make his list more complete. Today there are 111 elements in the periodic table.

Early in the 20th century, atoms were discovered to consist of protons and electrons (in 1932 it was discovered that neutrons also are found in atoms). Normally, the number of protons and electrons is equal. This number is the atomic number, which is a different counting number for every element from hydrogen (atomic number 1) to the unnamed element numbered 111. When the concept of atomic number was discovered, it was possible to improve the periodic table by arranging the elements in order of atomic number instead of atomic weight. This did not require the rearrangements Mendeleyev had to make, and it clearly showed where the blanks were—all of which have been filled in since 1940. Any other newly discovered or created elements must go at the end of the table.

Each column of the periodic table includes elements with similar properties, although hydrogen in the first column is less typical in this respect. But the other elements in the first column are all soft metals that react strongly. Similarly, the last column of the table contains only the gases that react only minimally. In general, elements are metals on the left side of the table (except for hydrogen), becoming mostly nonmetals in the last six columns. These last columns include some elements that are metals, such as aluminum. (A broken, heavy line separates the metals from the nonmetals.)

The row of rare-earth elements beginning with lanthanum and the row of actinide elements beginning with actinium do not fit neatly into the rest of the table. Elements from atomic number 57 to 71 are all similar to lanthanum, while elements from atomic number 89 to 103 are similar to actinium. The rare earths are not generally rare, nor do they resemble soil. They are moderately common metals that, because of atomic structure, are very similar chemically. The actinide elements are radioactive metals.

The periodic table also includes the atomic mass as well as the atomic number. The atomic mass is essentially the sum of the protons and neutrons in an atom of an element, although different standards have been used at various times to measure this. As protons and neutrons join to form an atomic nucleus, a little of their energy becomes mass, the amount of which depends on how many protons and neutrons there are (this effect is exploited in nuclear fission, in which the reverse process—splitting the nucleus—releases the energy). Consequently, a particular atom is chosen upon which to base the amu. Today the atomic mass is adjusted to make the most common form of carbon have an atomic mass of exactly 12 (6 protons and 6 neutrons). Most elements occur with several different atomic masses (in addition to carbon-12, for example, there are both carbon-13 and carbon-14; carbon-14 has 6 protons and 8 neutrons and is radioactive). These different forms are called isotopes. Therefore, in the periodic table, the atomic mass given for most elements is the one that would be found by averaging the different isotopes in the amounts they naturally occur. Carbon is given an atomic mass of 12.01 because there is so much more carbon-12 than there is carbon-13 or carbon-14 in an ordinary sample of carbon. For some radioactive elements, natural abundance is meaningless, since there is no stable form. For these, the atomic mass of the most stable form is given, indicated by putting the atomic mass in parentheses.

Physics

Physics is the basis of the other sciences because it is concerned with the fundamental interactions of matter and energy. The first physicists studied how ordinary objects and very large objects (Moon, planets, and stars) moved in response to forces. Their study was extremely successful. Near the end of the 19th century, physicists began to investigate radiation in detail, leading to the discovery of various forms of electromagnetic radiation (of which only forms of light were known previously) and particles smaller than the atom (subatomic particles, such as the electron and proton). In the 20th century, the study of subatomic particles, called particle physics, has become a major branch of the science. Many particle physicists limit their work to the particles in the nucleus of atoms and to the behavior of nuclei. Another major branch, condensed-matter physics, is concerned with the physical behavior of materials—for example, their electrical and magnetic properties. Major successes in condensed-matter physics include development of the transistor and related devices (chips) and superconductivity, a state in which electric currents can be transmitted with no resistance. Today many physicists are also cosmologists, who study how the universe began and is constructed, or astrophysicists, who study processes in stars.

MAJOR DISCOVERIES IN PHYSICS

1586 Simon Stevinus (Belgian-Dutch: 1548–1620) shows that two different weights dropped at same time from same height will reach ground at same time.

1604 Galileo (Italian: 1564–1642) announces his discovery that a body falling freely will increase its distance as square of time.
Johannes Kepler (German: 1571–1630) shows that light diminishes as square of distance from source.

1663 Blaise Pascal (French: 1623–62) proposes what becomes known as Pascal's law: pressure in fluid is transmitted equally in all directions (published year after his death).

1675 Ole Rømer (Danish: 1644–1710) becomes first to measure speed of light, although his value is somewhat too slow by today's standards.

1676 Robert Hooke (English: 1635–1703) discovers what becomes known as Hooke's law: The amount a spring stretches varies directly with its tension.

1678 Christiaan Huygens (Dutch: 1629–95) develops wave theory of light.

1687 Sir Isaac Newton's (English: 1642–1727) *Principia* is published, containing his laws of motion and theory of gravity.

1746 At least two experimenters in Leyden, the Netherlands, invent method for storing static electricity, which becomes known as Leyden jar.

1752 Benjamin Franklin (American: 1706–90) performs kite experiment, demonstrating that lightning is form of electricity.

1787 Jacques A.C. Charles (French: 1746–1823) discovers what is later known as Charles's law: All gases expand same amount with given rise in temperature; e.g., same rise in temperature that will cause hydrogen to double in volume will also cause air to double in volume.

1791 Luigi Galvani (Italian: 1737–98) announces his discovery that when two different metals touch in frog's muscle, they produce electric current.

1798 Benjamin Thompson, Count von Rumford (American-German: 1753–1814) shows that heat is form of motion.
Henry Cavendish (English: 1731–1810) determines gravitational constant and mass of Earth.

1800 William Herschel (German-English: 1738–1822) announces his discovery of infrared light.

1801 Johann W. Ritter (German: 1776–1810) discovers ultraviolet light.

1802 Thomas Young (English: 1773–1829) develops his wave theory of light—more detailed than ideas of Christiaan Huygens and based on convincing experiments.

1819 Hans Christian Oersted (Danish: 1777–1851) discovers that magnetism and electricity are two different manifestations of same force (not published until 1820).

1820 André-Marie Ampère (French: 1775–1836) formulates first laws of electromagnetism.

1831 Michael Faraday (English: 1791–1867) in England and Joseph Henry (American: 1797–1878) in U.S. (in 1830) independently discover principle of electrical dynamo.

1842 Julius Robert von Mayer (German: 1814–78) is first scientist to state law of conservation of energy: In chemical reactions energy is neither created nor destroyed.

1848 William Thompson, Baron Kelvin (Scottish: 1824–1907), proposes concept of absolute zero, the lowest theoretically possible temperature (–460°F, or –273°C).

1850 Rudolf J.E. Clausius (German: 1822–88) makes first clear statement of second law of thermodynamics: Energy in closed system tends to degrade into heat.

1873 James Clerk Maxwell (Scottish: 1831–79) publishes complete theory of electromagnetism, which includes his prediction that radio waves must exist.

1887 Albert A. Michelson (German-American: 1852–1931) and Edward Morley (American: 1838–1923) attempt to measure changes in velocity of light produced by motion of Earth through space; inability to find such changes is later interpreted as helping to establish Einstein's special theory of relativity.

1888 Heinrich P. Hertz (German: 1857–94) produces and detects radio waves.

1895 Wilhelm Konrad Röntgen (German: 1845–1923) discovers X rays.

1896 Henri Becquerel (French: 1852–1908) discovers natural radioactivity.

1897 Sir Joseph John Thomson (English: 1856–1940) discovers electron.

1900 Max K.E.L. Planck (German: 1858–1947) explains behavior of light by proposing that there is smallest step a physical process can take, which he names quantum.

1905 Albert Einstein (German-American: 1879–1955) shows that photoelectric effect—ejection of electrons from metal by action of light—can be explained if light has particle nature as well as wave nature.

Einstein shows that motion of small particles in liquid ("Brownian motion") can be explained by assuming that the liquid is made of molecules. Einstein develops his special theory of relativity and the law $E = mc^2$ (energy equals mass times square of speed of light).

1911 Heike Kamerlingh Onnes (Dutch: 1853–1926) discovers superconductivity in metals cooled near to absolute zero.
Ernest Rutherford (British: 1871–1937) discovers the proton.

1915 Einstein completes his general theory of relativity, a theory of gravity more accurate than that of Sir Isaac Newton, and publishes it the following year.

1919 An expedition led by Sir Arthur S. Eddington (English: 1882–1944) to observe bending of starlight by Sun's gravity during eclipse confirms that Einstein's theory of gravity is more accurate than Newton's in predicting effect of gravity on light.

1924 Louis-Victor de Broglie (French: 1892–1987) publishes his theory that particles, such as electrons, also have wave nature.

1925 Wolfgang Pauli (Austrian-American: 1900–1958) discovers exclusion principal: Two electrons or protons described by same numbers (called quantum numbers) cannot exist in same atom.
Werner Karl Heisenberg (German: 1901–76) develops matrix version of quantum mechanics, a mathematical treatment that explains behavior of electrons and protons.

1926 Erwin Schrödinger (Austrian: 1887–1961) develops wave version of quantum mechanics, a different mathematical treatment of behavior of electrons and protons producing same results as Heisenberg's matrix mechanics.

1927 Heisenberg develops his uncertainty principle: It is impossible to measure accurately position and momentum of electron or proton at same time.

1932 Sir James Chadwick (British: 1891–1974) discovers neutron, a neutral particle about same mass as proton.
Carl D. Anderson (American: 1905–91) discovers positron, a positively charged analog of electron.
Sir John G. Cockcroft (English: 1897–1967) and Ernest Walton (Irish: 1903–) develop first particle accelerator, a device for speeding subatomic particles, which causes them to react more intensely with atoms or other particles (often still known as "atom smasher").

1937 Anderson, with several other physicists, performs the work that culminates in the discovery of the muon.

1938 Otto Hahn (German: 1879–1968) splits uranium atom, opening way for nuclear bombs and nuclear power.

1945 Scientists funded by U.S. government and led by J. Robert Oppenheimer (American: 1904–67) detonate first nuclear-fission explosion (atomic bomb).

1947 Quantum electrodynamics (QED) is born, with many parents: notably, Richard P. Feynman (American: 1918–88), Julian S. Schwinger (American: 1918–94), Schin'ichiro Tomonaga (Japanese: 1906–79), Willis E. Lamb, Jr. (American: 1913–) (all of whom received Nobel Prizes for this concept), and Hans A. Bethe (German-American: 1906–).
Cecil Frank Powell (English: 1903–69) and coworkers discover pion, first-known meson, a subatomic particle involved in holding nucleus of atom together.

1952 Group of scientists in United States led by Edward Teller (Hungarian-American: 1908–) develops first artificial nuclear-fusion device (hydrogen bomb).

1955 Owen Chamberlain (American: 1920–) and Emilio Segrè (Italian-American: 1905–89) produce first-known antiprotons, negatively charged analogs of proton.
Clyde Cowan, Jr. (American: 1919–) and Frederick Reines (American: 1918–) are first to observe neutrino, a subatomic particle with no mass or charge produced in certain forms of radioactive decay (technically, they observe antineutrinos, which have opposite spin of neutrinos).

1957 Experiments by group led by Chien-Shiung Wu (Chinese-American: 1912–) and quickly confirmed by others show that Law of Conservation of Parity does not hold for the weak interaction; broadly speaking, right and left are distinguished by behavior of electrons emitted in certain forms of radioactivity.
John Bardeen (American: 1908–91), Leon Cooper (American: 1930–), and John Schrieffer (American: 1931–) develop a theory explaining superconductivity.

1960 Rudolf Ludwig Mössbauer (German: 1929–) discovers way to make gamma rays with very narrow wavelengths and to measure changes in wavelength; Mössbauer effect confirms Einstein's general relativity theory.

1961 Murray Gell-Mann (American: 1929–) and, independently, Yu'val Ne'eman (Israeli: 1925–) and others develop method of classifying heavy subatomic particles that comes to be known as "eight-fold way."

1964 Gell-Mann introduces concept of quarks as components of heavy subatomic particles, such as protons and mesons.

1967 Steven Weinberg (American: 1933–), Abdus Salam (Pakistani-British: 1926–), and Sheldon Lee Glashow (American: 1932–) independently develop theory that combines electromagnetic force with weak force.

1980 Heinrich Rohrer (Swiss: 1933–) and Gerd Binnig (German: 1947–) invent the scanning-tunneling microscope, a device with which it is possible to produce images of individual atoms or crystal surfaces.

1986 Karl Alexander Müller (Swiss: 1927–) and Johannes Georg Bednorz (German: 1950–) discover first "warm-temperature" superconductor.

1994 Physicists at Fermilab in Batavia, Ill., find evidence for the top quark. (See "Subatomic Particles" later in this chapter.)

THE BASIC LAWS OF PHYSICS

Key Terms

Mass is a measure of the amount of matter; it is proportional to weight. Near the surface of Earth it is roughly equivalent to weight.

Velocity measures how an object changes position with time.

Acceleration is how an object changes velocity with time.

Momentum is the product of mass and velocity.

Energy is the ability to do work.

Law of Gravity

The gravitational force between any two objects is proportional to the product of their masses and inversely proportional to the square of the distance between them. If F is the force, G is the number that represents the ratio (the gravitational constant), m and M are the two masses, and r is the distance between the objects:

$$F = \frac{GmM}{r^2}.$$

In metric measure, the gravitational constant is 0.00000000006672 (6.67×10^{-11}) newton m²/kg², so another way of writing the basic law of gravity is

$$F = \frac{0.0000000000667mM}{r^2}.$$

This law implies that objects falling near the surface of Earth will fall with the same rate of acceleration (ignoring drag caused by air). This rate is 32.174 feet per second per second (ft./sec²), or 9.8 m/sec², and is conventionally labeled g. Applying this rate to falling objects gives the velocity, v, and distance, d, after any amount of time, t, in seconds. If the object starts at rest and 32 ft./sec² is used as an approximation for g,

$$v = 32t$$
$$d = 16t^2.$$

For example, after 3 seconds, a dropped object that is still falling will have a velocity of $32 \times 3 = 96$ feet per second and will have fallen a distance of $16 \times 3^2 = 144$ feet.

If the object has an initial velocity v_0 and an initial height above the ground of a, the equations describing the velocity and the distance, d, above the ground (a positive velocity is *up* and a negative velocity is *down*) become

$$v = v_0 - 32t$$

and

$$d = -16t^2 + v_0 t + a.$$

After 3 seconds, an object tossed in the air from a height of 6 feet with a velocity of 88 feet per second will reach a speed of $88 - 96 = -8$ feet per second, meaning that it has begun to descend, and will have a height of $(-16 \times 9) + (88 \times 3) + 6 = -144 + 264 + 6 = 126$ feet above the ground.

The maximum height, H, reached by the object with an initial velocity v_0 and initial height a is

$$H = a + \frac{v_0^2}{64}.$$

For the object tossed upward at 88 feet per second from a height of 6 feet, the maximum height reached would be $6 + 88^2/64 = 6 + 121 = 127$ feet. Therefore, after 3 seconds, the object has just reached its peak and has fallen back only 1 foot.

Albert Einstein's general theory of relativity introduced laws of gravity more accurate than those just given, which were discovered by Sir Isaac Newton. Newton's gravitational theory is extremely accurate for most practical situations, however. For example, Newton's theory is used to determine how to launch satellites into proper orbits.

Newton's Laws of Motion

Newton's Laws of Motion apply to objects in a vacuum and are not easily observed in the real world, where forces such as friction tend to overwhelm the natural motion of objects. To obtain realistic solutions to problems, however, physicists and engineers begin with Newton's laws and then add in the various forces that also affect motion.

1. *Any object at rest tends to stay at rest. A body in motion moves at the same velocity in a straight line unless acted upon by a force.* This is also known as the law of inertia. Note that this law implies that an object will travel in a curved path only so long as a force is acting on it. When the force is released, the object will travel in a straight line. A weight on a string swung in a circle will travel in a straight line when the string is released, for the string was supplying the force that caused circular motion.

2. *The acceleration of an object is directly proportional to the force acting on it and inversely proportional to the mass of the object.* This law, for an acceleration a, a force F, and a mass m, is more commonly expressed in terms of finding the force when you know the mass and the acceleration. In this form it is written as

$$F = ma.$$

The implication of this law is that a constant force will produce acceleration, which is an increase in velocity. Thus, a rocket, which is propelled by a constant force as long as its fuel is burning, constantly increases in velocity. If there were enough fuel, the rocket would eventually cease to increase in velocity, however, because Einstein's other relativity theory, the special theory of relativity, states that no object can exceed the speed of light in a vacuum (see "Conservation of mass-energy" below). Nevertheless, even a small force, constantly applied, can cause a large mass to reach velocities near the speed of light if enough time is allowed.

3. *For every action there is an equal and opposite reaction.*

Conservation Laws

Many results in physics come from various conservation laws. A conservation law is a rule that a certain entity must not change in amount during a certain class of operations. All such conservation laws treat closed systems. Anything added from outside the system could affect the amount of the entity being conserved.

Conservation of momentum *In a closed system, momentum stays the same.* This law is equivalent to Newton's third law. Since momentum is the product of mass and velocity, if the mass of a system changes, then the velocity must change. For example, consider a person holding a heavy anchor in a stationary rowboat in the water. The momentum of the system is 0, since the masses have no velocity. Now the person in the rowboat tosses the anchor toward the shore. The momentum of the anchor is now a positive number if velocity toward the shore is measured as positive. To conserve momentum, the rowboat is accelerated in the opposite direction, away from the shore. The positive momentum of the anchor is balanced by the negative momentum of the rowboat and its cargo. In terms of two masses, m and M, and matching velocities v and V,

$$mv = MV.$$

Conservation of angular momentum An object moving in a circle has a special kind of momentum, called angular momentum. As noted above, motion in a circle requires some force. Angular momentum combines mass, velocity, and acceleration (produced by the force). For a body moving in a circle, the acceleration depends on both the speed of the body in its path and the square of the radius of the circle. The product of this speed, the mass, and the square of the radius is the angular momentum of the mass.

In a closed system, angular momentum is conserved. This effect is used by skaters to change their velocity of spinning. Angular momentum is partly determined by the masses of a skater's arms combined with the rate of rotation and the square of the radius to the center of mass of each arm (the point that can represent the total mass of the arm). When skaters bring their arms close to their body, this would tend to reduce the angular momentum, because the center of mass is closer to the body. But, since angular momentum is conserved, the rate of rotation has to increase to compensate for the decreased radius. Because the rate depends on the square of the rotation, the rate increases dramatically.

Conservation of mass *In a closed system, the total amount of mass appears to be conserved in all but nuclear reactions and other extreme conditions.*

Conservation of energy *In a closed system, energy appears to be conserved in all but nuclear reactions and other extreme conditions.* Energy comes in very many forms: mechanical, chemical, electrical, heat, and so forth. As one form is changed into another (excepting nuclear reactions and extreme conditions), this law guarantees that the total amount remains the same. Thus, when you change the chemical energy of a dry cell into electrical energy and use that to turn a motor, the total amount does not change (although some becomes heat energy—see "Laws of Thermodynamics" below).

Conservation of mass-energy Einstein discovered that his special theory of relativity implied that energy and mass are related. Consequently, mass and energy by themselves are not conserved, since one can be converted into the other. Mass and energy appear to be conserved in ordinary situations because the effect of Einstein's discovery is very small most of the time. The more general law, then, is the law of conservation of mass-energy: *The total amount of mass and energy must be conserved.* Einstein found the following equation that links mass and energy.

$$E = mc^2$$

In this equation, E is the amount of energy, m is the mass, and c is the speed of light in a vacuum.

One instance of energy changing to mass occurs in Einstein's equation for how the mass increases with velocity. If m_0 is the mass of the object when it is not moving, v is the velocity of the object in relation to an observer who is considered to be at rest, and c is the speed of light in a vacuum, then the mass, m, is given by the equation

$$m = \frac{m_0}{\sqrt{1 - \frac{v^2}{c^2}}}.$$

This accounts for the rule that no object can exceed the speed of light in a vacuum. As the object approaches this speed, so much of the energy is converted to mass that it cannot continue to accelerate.

In both nuclear fission (splitting of the atomic nucleus) and nuclear fusion (the joining of atomic nuclei, producing the energy of a hydrogen bomb), mass is converted into energy.

Conservation for particles Many properties associated with atoms and subatomic particles are also conserved. Among them are charge, spin, isospin, and a combination known as CPT for *charge conjugation, parity,* and *time.*

First and Second Laws of Thermodynamics

First law This is the same as the law of conservation of energy. It is a law of thermodynamics, or the movement of heat, because heat must be treated as a form of energy to keep the total amount of energy constant. All bodies contain heat as energy no matter how cold they are, although there is not much heat at temperatures close to absolute zero.

Second law *Heat in a closed system can never travel from a low temperature region to one of higher temperature in a self-sustaining process. Self-sustaining* in this case means a process that does not need energy from outside the system to keep it going. In a refrigerator, heat from the cold inside of the refrigerator is transferred to a warmer room, but energy from outside is required to make the transfer happen, so the process is not self-sustaining.

The second law has many implications. One of them is that no perpetual motion machine can be constructed. Another is that all energy in a closed system eventually becomes heat that is diffused equally throughout the system, so that one can no longer obtain work from the system.

The equations that describe the behavior of heat also can be applied to order and therefore to information. The word *entropy* refers to diffused heat, disorder, or lack of information. Another form of the second law of thermodynamics is that in a closed system, entropy always increases.

Laws of Current Electricity

Key terms When electrons flow in a conductor, the result is electric *current.* The amount of current is based on an amount of electric charge called the *coulomb,* which is the charge of about 6.25 quintillion (6.25×10^{18}) electrons. When 1 coulomb of charge moves past a point in 1 second, it creates a current of 1 ampere. Just as a stream can carry the same amount of water swiftly through a narrow channel or slowly through a broad channel, the energy of an electric current varies depending on the difference in charge between places along the conductor. This is called *potential difference* and is measured in *volts.* The voltage is affected by the nature of the conductors. Some substances conduct an electric current much more easily than others. This *resistance* to the current is measured in ohms. *Electric power* is the rate at which electricity is used.

Ohm's law *Electric current is directly proportional to the potential difference and inversely proportional to resistance.* If you measure current, I, in amperes, potential difference, V, in volts, and resistance, R, in ohms, then the current is equal to the potential difference divided by the resistance.

$$I = \frac{V}{R}$$

Law of electric power *If electric power,* P, *is measured in watts, then the power is equal to the product of the current measured in amperes and the potential difference measured in volts.*

$$P = IV$$

Laws of Waves, Light, and Electromagnetic Radiation

Key terms Light is a part of a general form of radiation known as *electromagnetic waves,* or, when thought of as particles, *photons.* Here, electromagnetic radiation is considered as a wave phenomenon for the most part. The *velocity* of a wave is how fast the wave travels as a whole. The *wavelength* is the distance between one crest of the wave and the next crest. The *frequency* is how many crests pass a particular location in a unit of time.

Law of wave motion All waves (including water waves and sound waves) obey the wave equation that relates the velocity of the wave to its frequency and wavelength. *For all waves, the velocity is equal to the product of the frequency and wavelength.* The letters traditionally used in this equation have already been used in the equations above to mean something else, so here, W will be used for the velocity of the wave, f for the frequency, and l for the wavelength.

$$W = fl.$$

Law of electromagnetic energy The energy of an electromagnetic wave depends on a small number known as Planck's constant. Measured in joules per hertz (energy per frequency), Planck's constant is 6.626196×10^{-34}. *The energy is equal to the product of Planck's constant and the frequency.* Using E for energy, h for Planck's constant, and f for frequency,

$$E = hf.$$

When thought of in terms of the particles called photons, the energy of a photon obeys the same law. The law of wave motion and the law of electromagnetic energy can be combined with the speed of light in a vacuum *(c)* to give

$$E = \frac{hc}{l}.$$

The energy of a photon is the product of Planck's constant and the speed of light, divided by the wavelength *(l)* of the photon.

Inverse-square law All radiation obeys an inverse-square law, which is similar to the law of gravity. *The intensity of the radiation decreases as the inverse of the square of the distance from a point source radiation.*

Two Basic Laws of Quantum Physics

When one considers effects on very small masses and at very small distances, it is necessary to recognize that objects behave differently than at the sizes and distances one can observe directly. Since these effects occur in discrete steps based upon Planck's constant times the frequency, called the quantum—which is the size by which energy changes in steps (instead of continuously)—the science of such effects is called quantum physics. Small masses act sometimes like particles and sometimes like waves and sometimes like nothing we know about at the scale we live. Two laws in particular that describe the behavior of small masses are basic and easily stated.

Heisenberg's uncertainty principle *It is impossible to specify completely the position and momentum of a particle, such as an electron.*

Pauli's exclusion principle *Two particles of a certain class that are essentially the same cannot be in the same exact state.* This class, the fermions, includes such particles as the electron, neutron, and proton. Bosons, particles of a different class, do not obey Pauli's exclusion principle. (See "Subatomic Particles.")

SUBATOMIC PARTICLES

During the 19th century, most scientists came to believe that everything was made from atoms, even though they had no way then to observe atoms. It is now known they were right, and there are even "photographs" of individual atoms available, images made with the scanning tunneling microscope. At the turn of the 20th century, physicists discovered that atoms themselves were made from smaller pieces—subatomic particles. These smaller pieces seemed at first to be the ultimate limit of matter, but in the 1960s, physicists proposed that many subatomic particles were themselves made from smaller particles that could not be detected. Like the unobserved atoms of the 19th century, the undetectable smaller particles, called quarks, have come to be accepted. Perhaps in the next century, there will be "photographs" of quarks.

Quarks are considered to be "fundamental" in that most scientists believe they are not made up of still smaller pieces. Besides the quarks, various other groups of particles are thought to be fundamental. Among these are the leptons. Together, quarks and leptons form what we think of as matter. They are characterized by a spin of ½, as are the particles made from three quarks, the baryons. *Spin* is a number for each particle that has a behavior similar to angular momentum (see "Basic Laws of Physics"). All particles with a spin of ½ are called fermions. Other apparently fundamental subatomic particles are similar to the photon, the particle that makes up light. Particles such as the photon and other particles with a spin of either 0 or 1 are called bosons, and they act as "glue" that holds matter together. Bosons produce the four known forces: gravity, electromagnetism, the strong force, and the weak force. (Under certain conditions electromagnetism and the weak force become a single force, the electroweak force.)

Many subatomic particles carry charge, which is a unit of electromagnetism. Nearly all charges are counted as either –1 or +1 or 0 (no charge), based on the charge of the electron, which is –1. Quarks, however, have charges in multiples of ⅓. No one knows why charges come only in these particular amounts and do not occur in other amounts. No known law, for example, predicts that the charge of the large proton will be exactly the same amount (but opposite: +1) as the charge of the small electron.

The masses of subatomic particles are measured in terms of the particle's energy, for energy, E, is related to mass, m, and the speed of light, c, by Albert Einstein's famous equation $E = mc^2$. Since c is a very large number, the energy of a particle is much larger than its mass. Even so, the energy is expressed in a very small unit, the MeV, which is a million electron volts. An electron volt is 0.0000000000000000001602 (1.602×10^{-19}) joule.

Recently, many physicists have proposed various other still-undetected particles, such as

WIMPs (for Weakly Interacting Massive Particles); these are far from being fully accepted at this time and are omitted from the following list. Every particle mentioned has an antiparticle whose charge is the opposite (negative particles have positive antiparticles) and whose spin is in the opposite direction. Unless there is something special about the antiparticle, it will not be mentioned.

Fermions

Fundamental particles of matter

The electron (a lepton) Movement of electrons is the source of current electricity, while an excess or deficit of electrons causes static electricity. The properties of the electron form the basis of electronic devices, such as computer chips. Electrons are found in all atoms, where they occupy several shells around the outside of the atom. Interactions between electrons account for all chemical reactions. The electron is stable and very light. Its mass is 0.511 MeV. Its charge is –1. Like all subatomic particles, it has a related particle, or antiparticle, known as the positron. The positron is a mirror image of the electron with a charge of +1. The positron was the first antiparticle to be discovered. It was proposed in 1931 by Paul Adrien Maurice Dirac and discovered (accidentally) in 1932 by Carl David Anderson.

Muons and tauons (leptons) The muon is often described as a "fat electron," since it has all the properties of an electron except that its mass is 200 times as great—105.7 MeV. Similarly, the tauon is a "fat muon," with a mass of 1,750 MeV. No one predicted these particles, and no one knows what their role in the universe is.

Neutrinos (leptons) form a group of leptons associated with electrons, muons, and tauons, with which they form three "families." A family consists of a charged particle, such as an electron, its antiparticle, such as a positron, and an associated neutrino and an antineutrino. Aside from their separate associations, there would seem to be no differences among the three types of neutrino. All have no charge and probably no mass and a spin of ½. (Some evidence suggests that neutrinos have a very small mass.) They do not interact strongly with anything. Neutrinos are passing through your body all the time, and most go on to pass through the Earth and out the other side.

Quarks were first proposed by Murray Gell-Mann in 1964 to account for the relationships between various kinds of baryons (see below). Each baryon is composed of three quarks, and each meson (see below) of two quarks. Common baryons and mesons are composed of quarks known as *up* (charge +⅔ and mass 1.0 MeV) and *down* (charge –⅓ and mass 3.0 MeV). Even though their individual masses are small, the binding energy between them in a baryon produces most of the mass in the universe. Other baryons or mesons have a quality known as "strangeness," which is conferred by the *strange quark* (charge –⅓ and mass 102.2 MeV), or a quality known as "charm," conferred by the *charm quark* (charge –⅔ and mass 1,530 MeV). Two other quarks, now generally known as *top* and *bottom* (formerly sometimes called *truth* and *beauty*) complete the list of six flavors. Bottom has a charge of –⅓ and a mass of 4,700 MeV, while top has a charge of +⅔ and an amazingly high mass for a subatomic particle, measured at about 176,000 MeV in one experiment and as about 199,000 MeV in another, a mass about the same as that of an atom of gold. The six types of quarks and the three types of leptons are often classified as different "flavors." Each quark also comes in one of three "colors," although physicists have yet to settle on what the three colors should be—red, blue, and green are perhaps the most popular combination. In a meson or a baryon, the two or three colors of quarks are always combined to produce an absence of color; thus, color cannot be detected directly, but only inferred. Similarly, since quarks are always confined in mesons or baryons, the cannot be observed directly either; but various experiments confirm that quarks actually exist.

Baryons

The proton is found in the nucleus of the atom. For about 20 years, it was assumed that atoms consisted of a core of protons surrounded by electrons, although the true situation is somewhat more complex. The proton appears to be stable, although recently some theorists have proposed that protons may decay into pure energy after about 10,000,000,000,000,000,000,000,000,000,000 (10^{31}) years. So far, although much watched, no one has seen a proton decay. Protons are heavy particles with a mass of 938.3 MeV, and they have a charge of +1. Every atom contains an equal number of +1 protons and –1 electrons, giving a total charge to the atom of 0. (An atom that has lost or gained an electron—and therefore a charge—is called an ion.)

The neutron is almost exactly like a proton but with no charge and therefore much harder to detect. Neutrons in the nuclei of atoms are stable, but outside the nucleus, each neutron soon decays into a proton, an electron, and an electron antineutrino. All atoms except hydrogen must have neutrons in their nuclei to be stable. Neutrons have a mass of 939.6 MeV.

Other baryons These include two hyperons, three sigmas, two xis, and an omega. Except for the omega, none was predicted. Instead they were found in cosmic-ray and particle-accelerator experiments in the late 1940s and in the 1950s. In 1961 Murray Gell-Mann predicted the omega on the basis of a theory preliminary to the quark theory. The omega was discovered in 1964. None of these particles is stable, decaying after much less than a second into other particles. They are not constituents of ordinary matter; i.e., they do not exist at ordinary energies on Earth.

Bosons

Mesons (bosons made from quarks)

Pions are the bosons that hold the nucleus of atoms together, producing the strong force. Pions come in positive, negative, and neutral forms. In 1935 Hideki Yukawa predicted the pion in his theory of the strong force. When a pion is exchanged between a proton and a neutron, it can change each into the other particle. In the process, it produces the strong force, which is needed to keep the positively charged protons from rushing apart because of the electromagnetic force (positive charges repel each other). When the muon was first discovered in 1937, scientists thought it was the particle Yukawa predicted, but by 1945 it was known that the muon's properties were wrong for that role. In 1947 Cecil Frank Powell and coworkers located the pion in cosmic rays. Each form of the pion has a slightly different mass (positive 139.6 MeV, negative 189.6 MeV, and neutral 135 MeV), and all decay in much less than a second. Pions, like all mesons, are composite particles made from two quarks. Other bosons are thought to be elementary particles, not made up of other particles.

Other mesons Various short-lived mesons heavier than the pion incorporate such quarks as strange, top, and bottom. None of them are constituents of ordinary matter, but the neutral K mesons, or kaons, have been very important in experiments extending basic physical theories.

Bosons not made from quarks

Gluons Although the Yukawa theory of the pion seemed to explain the strong force, the quark theory soon led to the understanding that pions and the strong force are side effects of a more essential strong force, one carried by eight neutral particles called gluons. Exchanging gluons between quarks usually causes quarks to change from one color to another, keeping the quarks attracted to each other. Gluons have no mass and a spin of 1.

The photon is the agent of electromagnetic radiation, including ordinary light, radio waves, microwaves, X rays, and gamma rays. In the 19th century, Thomas Young demonstrated the wave nature of electromagnetic radiation, but in 1905 Albert Einstein showed that it also had a particle nature. The particle, a vector boson (see "Other vector bosons" below), came to be called the photon. Exchanging photons causes charged particles to be attracted (if the charges are unalike) or repelled (if the charges are alike). When an electron absorbs or emits a photon of sufficient energy, it can change into a positron. If a positron and an electron meet, they disappear, leaving an energetic photon. Electrons can emit and absorb photons in other ways as well. The photon has no mass and a spin of 1.

Other vector bosons The *positive and negative W particles* and the *neutral Z particle* were predicted by the electroweak theory and produced and detected by Carlo Rubbia and coworkers in 1983. They are quite massive (W particles 81,000 MeV and Z particle 93,800 MeV) and have a spin of 1. Two other particles of this class have been predicted but not detected: the *Higgs particle,* a massive particle that helps give mass to the W and Z particles, and the massless *graviton,* which should have the same relation to gravity as the photon does to electromagnetism. Both have a spin of 0.

Life Sciences

While the scientific study of living creatures seems to have begun with Aristotle, there was considerable practical experimentation with living things much earlier, going back to the domestication of a species, the dog, around 10,000 B.C. In the years that followed the Scientific Revolution of the 17th century, the science of biology came to include most of the then-known life sciences: zoology (the study of animals), botany (the study of plants), and taxonomy (the classification of living things). In the 19th century, biology began to fragment into other studies: microbiology (the study of creatures visible only through the microscope), genetics (the study of how traits are inherited), biochemistry (the study of molecules in living things), and so forth. At the same time, different ways of studying living organisms were developed, among them anthropology (the study of human beings), ecology (the study of interactions between different living things and their environment), and ethology (the study of animal behavior).

MAJOR DISCOVERIES IN LIFE SCIENCES

B.C.

c. 9000 Agricultural Revolution starts in Near East with domestication of sheep and goats in Persia (Iran) and Afghanistan and of pigs in Anatolia (Turkey); and cultivation of wheat in Canaan (Israel and Jordan).

c. 8000 Agricultural Revolution starts independently in what are now Peru, Central America, and Indochina.

c. 350 Aristotle (Greek: 384–322 B.C.) classifies known animals in system that will continue to be used until 1735.

A.D.

1648 Jan Baptista van Helmont (Flemish: 1580–1644) shows that plants do not obtain large amounts of material for their growth from soil.

1665 Robert Hooke (English: 1635–1703) observes and names the cell.

1668 Francesco Redi (Italian: 1626–97) shows that maggots in meat do not arise spontaneously but are hatched from flies' eggs.

1669 Anton van Leeuwenhoek (Dutch: 1632–1723) discovers microorganisms—creatures too small to see with naked eye—and recognizes that sperm are part of reproduction.

1683 Leeuwenhoek is first to observe bacteria.

1735 Carolus Linnaeus (Carl Linné; Swedish: 1707–78) introduces system in use today for classifying plants and animals.

1779 Jan Ingenhousz (Dutch: 1730–99) discovers that plants release oxygen when exposed to sunlight and they consume carbon dioxide; this is first step in understanding photosynthesis.

1827 John James Audubon (American: 1785–1851) starts publication of *Birds of America*, a collection of engravings of 435 detailed paintings Audubon had made of American birds.

1839 Theodor A.H. Schwann (German: 1810–82), building on work of Matthias Jakob Schleiden (German: 1804–81) in 1838, develops cell theory of life.

1856 First skeleton of what we now call Neanderthals is found in cave in Neander Valley, near Düsseldorf (Germany).
Louis Pasteur (French: 1822–95) discovers that fermentation is caused by microorganisms.

1858 Charles R. Darwin (English: 1809–82) and Alfred R. Wallace (English: 1823–1913) announce their theory of evolution by natural selection to the Linnean Society.

1859 Darwin publishes *On the Origin of Species*.

1865 Gregor Johann Mendel's (Austrian: 1822–84) theory of dominant and recessive genes is published in obscure local journal.

1868 Workers building road in France discover skeletons of first-known Cro-Magnons in cave.

1894 Eugène Dubois (Dutch: 1858–1940) announces discovery of "Java ape-man," now known to be first-discovered specimen of *Homo erectus*.

1898 Mosaic disease of tobacco plants is recognized as being caused by virus, the first identification of a virus (viruses cannot be seen at this time, being known only from their effects).

1900 Three different biologists rediscover laws of genetics originally found by Mendel.

1919 Karl von Frisch (Austrian-German: 1886–1982) discovers that bees have language that can be used to communicate where to find good source of flower nectar.

1924 Raymond A. Dart (Australian–South African: 1893–1988) identifies first fossil of an australopithecine, a close relative of early humans.

1938 First-known live coelacanth, a lobe-finned fish believed to have been extinct for 60 million years, is captured in waters off Comoro Islands.

1952 Eugene Aserinsky (American: 1921–) discovers that sleep with rapid eye movements (REMs) is a distinct stage of sleep, later found to be associated with dreams.

1953 James D. Watson (American: 1928–) and Francis Crick (English: 1916–) determine structure of DNA, the basis of heredity.

1961 Louis S.B. Leakey (English: 1903–72) and Mary D. Leakey (English: 1913–) discover a previously unknown ancestor of humans, *Homo habilis*, in the Olduvai Gorge of northern Tanzania.
Marshall W. Nirenberg (American: 1927–) learns to read one of "letters" of genetic code.

1968 Werner Arber (Swiss: 1929–) discovers restriction enzymes, a class of proteins that will make genetic engineering possible.

1969 Jonathan Beckwith (American: 1935–) and coworkers are first to isolate a single gene.

1970 Har Gobind Khorana (Indian-American: 1922–) and coworkers produce first artificial gene. Howard Temin (American: 1934–94) and David Baltimore (American: 1938–) discover enzyme that causes RNA to be transcribed to DNA, a key step in development of genetic engineering.

1973 Stanley Cohen (American: 1922–) and Herbert Boyer (American: 1936–) succeed in putting specific gene into bacterium, the first instance of true genetic engineering.

1974 Donald C. Johanson (American: 1943–) and coworkers discover Lucy in Afar region of Ethiopia, the nearly complete skeleton—but not the skull—of *Australopithecus afarensis*, an early relative of humans (more than 3 million years old).

1975 César Milstein (Argentine-English: 1927–) announces discovery of how to produce monoclonal antibodies, highly specific chemicals that can be made to react with particular proteins or other chemicals in the body.

1980 Martin Cline (American: 1934–) and coworkers succeed in transferring functioning gene from one mouse to another.
Chinese scientists succeed in cloning a fish.

1983 Kary B. Mullis (American: 1945–) invents the use of the polymerase chain reaction to make copies of DNA sequences, a vital tool in finding specific genes.

1990 Michael T. Clegg (American: 1941–), Edward M. Golenburg (American), and coworkers isolate DNA and a gene for photosynthesis from a fossilized 17-million-year-old magnolia leaf.

1992 An ancestor of modern whales that was able to walk on land is discovered in Pakistan.
Gen Suwa (Japanese), discovers the first fossil of *Australopithecus ramidus*, the oldest known hominid, in Ethiopia.

1993 French geneticists develop first comprehensive map of all the human chromosomes.
V.V. Dyng (Vietnamese), John MacKinnon (UK), and workers discover the forest goat *(Pseudoryx nghetinhensis)*, a new species of large mammal, in the Vietnam forest.

1995 Raúl J. Cano (American), and Monica K. Borucki (American), report that they have revived spores of bacteria 25 to 40 million years old; the bacteria were preserved in bees trapped in amber, but returned to life when put in a growth medium.

MAJOR GROUPS OF LIVING ORGANISMS

Biologists classify all living things (organisms) according to a system first introduced by Carolus Linnaeus in 1735. At that time Linnaeus and other scientists divided all life forms into two kingdoms—plants and animals. Since then, biologists have learned that there are fundamental differences among organisms that go beyond the differences between plants and animals and have added three kingdoms. The five kingdoms recognized today are: Monerans, Protists, Fungi, Plants, and Animals. Many biologists also recognize a sixth kingdom, the Archaebacteria.

Following Linnaeus, all classification terms are usually given in Latin. In the following list, English terms are substituted when they are an exact translation—for example, *animals* instead of *animalia* and *birds* instead of *aves*. If there is no exact translation, the Latin form is kept.

Each kingdom is divided into two or more phyla (singular: phylum). Organisms within one phylum are more closely related to one another than to members of other phyla.

The phyla are also divided into parts, which are then further divided, each time on the basis of closer and closer relationships. In descending order of size, the main divisions are as follows:

- Kingdom
  - Phylum
    - Class
      - Order
        - Family
          - Genus
            - Species

Many biologists add to this list by classifying groups of species with *sub-* or *super-*, as in subphylum or superfamily.

By convention, Latin names except for genus and species are given in Roman type; genus and species are italicized.

Kingdom: Monerans One-celled organisms with simple cells that lack a membrane around the genetic material. Bacteria do not produce their own food; blue-green algae do.

Phylum: Bacteria
Phylum: Blue-green algae, also called blue-green bacteria or cyanobacteria

Kingdom: Protists One-celled or colonial; complex cells that have a membrane around their genetic material; protozoans and slime molds do not produce their own food; all other phyla in this kingdom can.

Phylum: Protozoans
  Class: Ciliophora (ciliated protozoans such as Paramecium)
  Class: Mastigophora (protozoans with flagella such as trypanosomes; the cause of sleeping sickness)
  Class: Sarcodina (protozoans that move by flowing, such as amoebas)
  Class: Sporozoa (parasitic protozoans with no means of motion during most of their lives, such as Plasmodium, the cause of malaria)
Phylum: Euglenas
Phylum: Golden algae and diatoms
Phylum: Fire or golden brown algae
Phylum: Green algae
Phylum: Brown algae
Phylum: Red algae
Phylum: Slime molds

Kingdom: Fungi One-celled or multicelled; cells have nuclei, which stream between cells, giving the appearance that cells have many nuclei; fungi do not produce their own food.

Phylum: Zygomycetes (e.g., black bread mold)
Phylum: Ascomycetes (includes Penicillium, truffles, yeasts)
Phylum: Basidiomycetes (includes mushrooms)

Kingdom: Plants Multicellular organisms that carry out photosynthesis; cells have nuclei and cell walls.

Phylum: Mosses and liverworts
Phylum: Club mosses
Phylum: Horsetails
Phylum: Ferns
Phylum: Conifers
Phylum: Cone-bearing desert plants
Phylum: Cycads
Phylum: The ginkgo
Phylum: Flowering plants
  Subphylum: Dicots (plants with two seed leaves—e.g., most fruits and vegetables, common flowers, and trees)
  Subphylum: Monocots (plants with a single seed leaf—e.g., onions, lilies, and grasses)

Kingdom: Animals Multicellular organisms that get their food by ingestion; most are able to move from place to place; cells have nuclei but not cell walls.

Phylum: Porifera (sponges)
Phylum: Cnidaria (jellyfish, anemones, corals)
Phylum: Platyhelminthes (flatworms)
Phylum: Nematodes (roundworms)
Phylum: Rotifers (microscopic wormlike or spherical animals)
Phylum: Bryozoa (moss animals)
Phylum: Brachiopods (lampshells)
Phylum: Phoronida (tube worms)
Phylum: Annelids (segmented worms, such as earthworms, leeches)
Phylum: Mollusks (soft-bodied animals with a mantle and foot)
  Class: Chitons
  Class: Bivalves (clams, oysters, mussels)
  Class: Scaphopoda (tooth or tusk shells)
  Class: Gastropods (slugs and snails)
  Class: Cephalopods (octopus, squid)
Phylum: Arthropods (segmented animals with an external skeleton)
  Class: Horseshoe crabs
  Class: Crustaceans (lobsters, crabs, shrimp)
  Class: Arachnids (scorpions, spiders, mites, ticks)
  Class: Insects
  Class: Millipedes and centipedes
Phylum: Echinoderms (starfish, brittle stars)
Phylum: Hemichordata (acorn worms)
Phylum: Chordates
  Subphylum: Tunicates
  Subphylum: Lancelets
  Subphylum: Vertebrates (animals with backbones)
    Class: Agnatha (lampreys, hagfish)
    Class: Sharks and rays
    Class: Bony fish
    Class: Amphibians
    Class: Reptiles
    Class: Birds
    Class: Mammals
      Subclass: Monotremes (egg-laying mammals)
      Subclass: Marsupials
      Subclass: Placentals
        Order: Insectivores (shrews, moles, hedgehogs)
        Order: Flying lemurs
        Order: Bats
        Order: Primates (lemurs, monkeys, apes, humans)
        Order: Edentates (anteaters, sloths, armadillos)
        Order: Pangolins
        Order: Lagomorphs (rabbits, hares)
        Order: Rodents (squirrels, rats, mice, porcupines)
        Order: Cetaceans (whales, dolphins)
        Order: Carnivores (wolves, cats, bears, raccoons, weasels, badgers, skunks, otters, hyenas)
        Order: Seals
        Order: The aardvark
        Order: Elephants
        Order: Hyraxes
        Order: Sirenians (dugongs, manatees)
        Order: Odd-toed ungulates (horses, tapirs, rhinoceroses)
        Order: Even-toed ungulates (pigs, hippopotamuses, camels, deer, giraffes, pronghorns, cattle, goats, sheep)

EVOLUTION OF THE HUMAN FAMILY

The understanding of the various relatives of modern human beings and just how they are related is undergoing great changes. Often what seems to be true one year is overturned the next. Currently there is little consensus among paleoanthropologists, the people who study early humans and their relatives, about the details of who is related to whom.

The first column below gives scientific and common names (modern paleoanthropologists shun the use of *man* to mean "human") along with the time and place in which the animal is known to have flourished.

THE HUMAN FAMILY TREE

Catopithecus browni c. 40 million years ago Egypt	Earliest known representative of higher primates, which include Old World monkeys, apes, and humans.
Aegyptopithecus c. 30 million years ago Egypt	Monkeylike creature; may be earliest-known ancestor of hominoids.
Proconsul; three known species c. 20 million years ago East Africa	Oddly named after popular chimpanzee, Consul, in London Zoo (hence, *Proconsul*—"before Consul"); generally recognized as an ancestor of all hominoids.
Dryopithecus c. 12 to 10 million years ago France, Spain, and Hungary	A small ape not much different from *Proconsul*, but identified in 1992 as the common ancestor of all hominids, including the hominid great apes, the australopithecines, and *Homo*.
Sivapithecus c. 10 million years ago India, Pakistan, and Turkey	Once believed to be a direct ancestor of modern humans, *Sivapithecus* ("Shiva's ape," from its discovery in Hindu India) is now considered to be close relative of the orangutan.
Pan troglodytes ***Pan paniscus*** Chimpanzee c. 7 million years ago to present Sub-Saharan African forests	Several studies of proteins and DNA suggest chimpanzee is our closest living relative; some evidence indicates we are more closely related to pygmy chimpanzee or bonobo, *P. paniscus*, than to common chimp.
Australopithecus ramidus c. 4.4 million years ago Ethiopia	Discovered in 1992 at Aramis, Ethiopia, this woodland dweller is the direct ancestor of *A. afarensis* and very close to the common ancestor of the hominid great apes and the human line.
Australopithecus afarensis c. 4 million years ago Ethiopia and East Africa	Many believe *A. afarensis* is ultimate ancestor of humans, but it is not all that clear who ultimate ancestor of *A. afarensis* is. Famous fossil known as "Lucy" is member of this species, as well as group known as "The First Family."
Australopithecus africanus "The Taung Child" c. 2.5 million years ago South Africa	First nonhuman hominid to be discovered (1924) and widely doubted at first. Like all australopithecines, walked upright and had brain much smaller than members of *Homo* of same size. May be an ancestor of humans.
Homo habilis "Handy Man" c. 2.2 million years ago East Africa	First-known member of our own genus, and—if classified correctly—probably direct ancestor; widely believed that stone tools found that date from the same time were made by *H. habilis*. *Not clear whether H. habilis* was hunter or scavenger or both. May actually be two related species.
Paranthropus *or the robust line of* ***Australopithecus*** c. 2.5 million to 1 million years ago Eastern and southern Africa	Recent work has caused both *A. boisei* and *A. robustus* to be reclassified with their original genus name of *Paranthropus*. Several different species are recognized. As these all overlap with the *Homo* line, they are not thought to be direct ancestors of humans.
Homo erectus "Java Ape Man" "Peking Man" c. 2 million–90,000 years ago Africa, Asia, and Europe	Depending on how one classes Neanderthals, this is first nonhuman hominid discovered (1894, by Eugène Dubois). It was successful creature who could make fire and was probably good hunter. That it did not change its basic tool kit for 1.5 million years suggests limited intelligence. Generally thought to be immediate ancestor of *Homo sapiens*. Other hominids became extinct, and by at least million years ago, *H. erectus* was only hominid on Earth, with possible exception of very early archaic *H. sapiens*.
"Neanderthal Man" 100,000–35,000 years ago Mostly European, but some fossils from Africa and Near East	While general sentiment among paleoanthropologists since World War II has classified this well-known group as subspecies of modern humans—*Homo sapiens neandertalis*—current thinking is that this "cave man" of Ice Age may be separate species. They share certain traits with modern human, e.g., large brain and customs such as burial of dead. Anatomical differences between Neanderthals and modern humans not pronounced but are clear.
Archaic ***Homo sapiens*** c. 350,000–40,000 years ago Africa and the Near East at first; Asia and Australia somewhat later	The main reason to call these humans "archaic" is that they precede the well-known Cro-Magnon fossils from Europe and have some primitive features, but otherwise they appear to be the same as modern *H. sapiens*.
Homo sapiens "Cro-Magnon Man" Since 35,000 years ago Worldwide	This is us! We may have started with Archaic *H. sapiens* (see above), and we may—although most think it is not likely—have evolved from Neanderthals around 35,000 years ago. In any case, we replaced all other hominids about 35,000 years ago.

CLASSIFYING HUMANS

KINGDOM: Animals Organisms that use other organisms for food and that sometimes move rapidly.

PHYLUM: Chordates Animals that are partially supported by a rod of cartilage or bone vertebrae and an internal skeleton.

SUBPHYLUM: Vertebrates Chordates that have vertebrae, such as fish, amphibians, reptiles, birds, and mammals.

CLASS: Mammals Vertebrates that have hair and suckle their young.

ORDER: Primates Mammals that use sight more than scent, have nails instead of claws on grasping hands and feet, are mostly active in daylight, and have relatively large brains.

SUPERFAMILY: Hominoids Primates that are tailless, generally large in size, can climb trees, and have relatively flat faces; specifically, the great apes, australopithecines, and human beings.

FAMILY: Hominids Hominoids that walk upright, have small canines, and large brains; specifically, the australopithecines and human beings.

GENUS: *Homo* Hominids with especially large brains that make tools and show other signs of culture; specifically, *Homo habilis, Homo erectus,* and *Homo sapiens.*

SPECIES: *Homo sapiens* Modern human beings.

THE HUMAN BODY

Systems The human body consists of nine main systems: the skeleton, the muscles, the nervous system, the hormonal system, the circulatory system, the digestive system, the respiratory system, the immune system, and the reproductive system.

Organs Each system is made up of a number of organs. An organ is a part of the body with a specific purpose. Some organs, such as the liver or the skin, have more than one function.

Tissues Organs are made from tissues. A tissue is a part of the organ made from similar cells and, in some cases, extracellular material (for example, bone tissue consists of bone cells and extracellular minerals).

Cells are the fundamental components of all organisms. Even they are composed of several different parts—the nucleus, the cytoplasm, the cell membrane, and various smaller parts—that have different functions.

Skeleton

Bones There are 206 bones in the human body, or one or two more or less, depending on how they are counted. Their main function is to provide a structural support for everything else, but they also have other vital functions. Bones might be classified as part of the circulatory system, for example, since they produce all of the body's blood cells within their marrow. Bones are also part of the hormonal system in that they are an important reservoir for calcium, an element necessary for life. If the body's intake of calcium is too low, the bones make up the deficit. This weakens their role as structural support and can result in the condition osteoporosis, or fragile bone structure.

Cartilage is a flexible substance that precedes bone development in children and that is found in adults at joints, places where bones meet, as well as in the nose and ears.

Ligaments Bones are attached to each other by flexible tissues called ligaments. A few bones, such as those in the skull, grow together, forming rigid attachments.

Muscles

There are over 600 muscles in the body that have been named. They occur in three different systems.

Skeletal muscles are used to move various parts of the body. They are what one normally thinks of when one thinks of muscles, and nearly all of them are attached to bones by tendons, long or flat sheets of tough tissue. Made from fibers that are striped (or striated) in appearance under a microscope, each fiber can contract or lengthen when the muscle receives a message from the brain. Because the individual controls the use of these muscles, they are also called voluntary muscles.

Smooth muscles are found in the walls of the stomach and intestines, in the walls of veins and arteries, and in various other internal organs. They are for the most part not controlled by the will, so they also are known as the involuntary muscles. People do have partial control over some of the "involuntary" muscles, however; for example, you can stop the smooth muscle of the diaphragm from causing you to breathe for a time.

Cardiac muscle The muscles of the heart resemble both skeletal muscles in being striped and smooth muscles in their involuntary nature.

Nervous System and Senses

Brain The organ that controls the rest of the body and undertakes thought is composed of three main parts. The cerebrum is the folded, outer part of each half of the brain; it governs thought, the senses, and movement. The cerebellum controls balance and muscle coordination. Deep in the brain is the brain stem, which governs involuntary muscles. A small, but important, part of the human brain is the hypothalamus, which controls the hormonal system (see below). Located in the head, the brain is protected by the bones of the skull.

Spinal cord Extending from the brain to the base of the torso, protected by the vertebrae, the spinal cord is the main highway for messages to and from the brain. The spinal cord can initiate actions on its own, which are known as reflexes.

Nerves Twelve pairs of cranial nerves connect directly to the brain. Ten of these pairs are connected to parts of the head concerned with sight, sound, smell, and taste, such as the optic nerves to the eyes and the auditory nerves to the ears. One part of the eye, the retina, is actually an exposed part of the brain, the only part in direct contact with the outside world. The vagus nerves extend to various organs of the torso, where they control involuntary muscles. The twelfth pair of cranial nerves are connected to the shoulder, where they are mostly involved in the sense of position (e.g., knowing in what position your arms are).

Thirty-one pairs of spinal nerves connect to the spinal cord and are the nerves involved in touch and other sensations, in control of skeletal muscles, and in partial control over internal organs. For example, the median nerve connects from the spinal cord to the finger muscles. Some nerves connected to the cranial and spinal nerves form the autonomic nervous system, one set of nerves that handles stress and another set of nerves that directly controls most of the organs of the body.

Sense organs Specialized organs mediate several of the senses—sight, sound, smell, and taste. The eye contains a lens that focuses light upon the retina, where it sends signals to the rest of the brain. The ear consists of the outer (visible) ear that gathers sounds, a middle ear with an ingenious arrangement for transmitting sound, and an inner ear that uses tiny hairs in a liquid to detect sound waves and transmit them to the auditory nerve. Both the nose and tongue contain cells that detect chemicals, resulting in the senses of smell and taste.

Hormonal System

Hormones are chemicals produced in the body that control various body processes. The important chemicals used to regulate activity of the nervous system (such as dopamine and serotonin) and various other chemical messengers are not considered hormones, however.

Many hormones are produced by organs called glands. Some hormones are produced by organs that have other purposes as well and are not considered glands. For example, the stomach, the heart, and the small intestine all produce important hormones. For the most part, glands come in two varieties—those that release hormones into the blood and those that release chemicals through tubes called ducts. The former are called endocrine glands, and the latter are known as exocrine glands. Some glands, such as the pancreas, have both endocrine and exocrine functions. The exocrine glands are all part of the digestive system, and, with the exception of the pancreas, are included under that heading.

Major endocrine glands are the following:

Pineal Responds to light and helps regulate reproduction. Located in the forehead.

Pituitary Under control of the brain, this "master gland" produces hormones that control many other glands and also produces growth hormone. Located in the head, below the center of the brain.

Thyroid Regulates metabolism, growth, and calcium uptake by bones. Located in the neck or just below it.

Parathyroids Regulate the release of stored calcium from bones. Located on the thyroid gland.

Adrenals Help regulate blood pressure, blood sugar, and the sex drive and also partially control metabolism. Located in the abdomen.

Pancreas Controls blood sugar. The pancreas, located in the abdomen, is also a part of the digestive system; acting as an exocrine gland, it releases chemicals that break down fats, carbohydrates, and proteins in the small intestine.

Ovaries Produce hormones that regulate pregnancy, produce female secondary sexual characteristics, and also help control calcium uptake into bones. Located in the pelvis in women.

Testes Produce secondary sexual characteristics in males and are involved in sperm production. Located in a sack suspended below the penis in men.

Circulatory System

Blood is the main messenger that carries chemicals around the body, although its white cells are essentially part of the immune system and are treated under that heading. If blood flow is cut off from any organ, the organ cannot obtain oxygen, it has no nutrients, and it cannot get rid of wastes. After a short time, the cells of the organ die.

Blood is a complex substance that contains a number of different kinds of cells and extracellular substances. It can be described as the body's only liquid organ. Its red color comes from erythrocytes, commonly known as red blood cells. Unlike true cells, erythrocytes lack nuclei and internal structure. They are produced by true cells in the bone marrow (called stem cells). Erythrocytes carry oxygen needed by cells for metabolism and remove carbon dioxide, produced when cells metabolize. Another component of blood is also made by the bone's stem cells—the platelets, which are even less like cells than erythrocytes. Their function is to keep blood from flowing out of the body when there is a break in the circulatory system—to cause clotting. About half of blood is an extracellular mix of water and chemicals that is called plasma or (when separated from proteins that, with the platelets, are involved in clotting) serum. Lymphocytes and phagocytes (white blood cells) are found in the blood, also (see "Immune System").

Blood vessels are a closed system of tubes that carry blood throughout the body. Vessels carrying blood away from the heart are called arteries. Arteries have strong, four-layered walls to maintain blood under pressure. Arteries connect to very tiny tubes with quite thin walls called capillaries. The walls are so thin that oxygen and nutrients pass through them to reach the cells, while carbon dioxide and wastes from the cells enter through the walls into the blood. The waste-carrying blood then passes into vessels that lead back to the heart, the veins. Most of the blood pressure has been lost by this point, so veins do not need the strong walls of arteries. Instead, veins need and have valves that ensure the blood does not travel in the wrong direction.

Heart Primarily a pump that pushes the blood through blood vessels, it consists of four chambers. Blood from the body enters the chamber known as the right atrium and is pumped through a valve to a larger chamber below the atrium called the right ventricle, which pumps the blood into an artery leading to the lungs. After picking up oxygen and leaving carbon dioxide behind, the blood returns to the heart, entering the left atrium. The blood is pumped through a valve to the left ventricle, which is the largest chamber (and therefore the most powerful pump). The left ventricle sends the blood into the arteries that lead to the body. The heart is also an endocrine gland, secreting a hormone that helps regulate blood pressure.

Spleen This organ is a cleaner and storehouse for blood. Chiefly, it removes damaged red blood cells or platelets. It also stores excess blood and red blood cells until they are needed. Some now believe it may have a role in the immune system. A person can live without a spleen.

Kidneys and the bladder and associated tubes are often considered the urinary system. Technically, however, kidneys are part of the circulatory system in that they remove chemical wastes from blood. They also act as an endocrine gland by secreting hormones that aid in regulating blood pressure. Additionally, they regulate the composition of blood, keeping it from becoming too acid or alkaline. The wastes removed by the kidneys are dissolved in water as urine, which is stored in the bladder before passing through the urethra to leave the body.

Digestive System

The digestive system consists largely of a pathway for food from the mouth to the anus with several ducted or exocrine glands that empty into it (the pancreas, one of these, is treated as part of the hormonal system).

Teeth Thirty-two permanent teeth (if none have been lost) in an adult are used to chop food into small bits.

Salivary glands release saliva, the first of many enzymes (proteins that promote particular chemical reactions) that are used to break down large molecules, such as carbohydrates, proteins, and fats, into smaller molecules that the body can then reassemble to meet its needs. Saliva breaks down some starches into sugars, as you can tell by noticing how much sweeter a cracker becomes if you chew it and then keep it in your mouth for a short while.

Tongue While an important organ of speech in humans, the tongue is basically the part of the digestive system that moves food around and pushes it down the throat.

Esophagus This is a tube through which food moves on its way to the stomach. The pyloric valve at its base prevents food from traveling back up again.

Stomach This organ produces enzymes (and therefore acts as a gland) and hydrochloric acid. These are mixed with the food by churning motions of the stomach, which also tend to break food into smaller particles, even as the stomach enzymes and acid are chemically changing food. From this point forward, one can no longer call this soup of nutrients *food.*

Liver The main chemical factory of the body and, after the skin, the largest organ in the body is the liver. As part of the digestive system, it acts as a ducted, or exocrine, gland that produces bile, a substance that helps reduce the acidity of the nutrient mixture and also helps break down fats. The liver is also part of the circulatory system, since it cleans poisons out of the blood and regulates blood's composition in various other ways. In many cases the liver scavenges unwanted chemicals from the blood, takes them apart, and reassembles the parts into needed chemicals.

Gall bladder This organ simply stores bile from the liver until food is consumed, at which time it releases the bile into the small intestine.

Small intestine Like the stomach, the 21-foot-long small intestine produces enzymes that further break down the nutrients that pass through it. The upper portion of the small intestine is called the duodenum. As nutrients become broken into small enough molecules, they are able to pass through projections, or villi, in the wall of the small intestine into the blood.

Large intestine With most of the nutrients gone, the remains of the food pass into the 5-foot-long large intestine as a kind of soup. Water is transferred to the blood from the soup through the walls of the capillaries that line the large intestine.

Rectum A short tube collects the partially dehydrated waste in preparation for evacuation, which is through a valve called the anus.

Respiratory System

The main purpose of the respiratory system is to get oxygen to the blood and to remove carbon dioxide. Along the way, the air is sampled for chemicals (smelled), partly cleaned, and frequently used to make sounds.

Nose In addition to being an organ of smell, the nose is the place best designed to admit air into the body, for it can warm and moisten it, and hairs in the nose can filter out dust. Often there is a need for more air than can pass through the nose, however, and the mouth is used as a supplemental way to take in air. From either the nose or the mouth, air then passes through the throat (also called the pharynx). The sinuses are air-filled cavities in the skull that are connected to the nose.

Trachea After passing through your throat, air goes into a tube called the trachea. A flap called the epiglottis closes the top of the trachea when food or water is being swallowed and opens to permit air to enter the trachea. The trachea branches into two tubes called bronchi (singular, *bronchus*) that carry the air into the lungs.

Larynx Near the top of the trachea is the larynx, or voice box. The main feature of the larynx is a pair of membranes that stretch across the air passageway. As air is exhaled, these membranes can be tightened across the passage to produce sound.

Lungs, the principal organs of respiration, are two large spongy masses located in the chest that are protected by the ribs. Air enters a lung through a bronchus. The bronchus is divided into smaller bronchial tubes, which continue to divide until they become very fine tubes called bronchioles. Each bronchiole ends in a cluster of tiny round bodies called an air sac. As small as air sacs are, each of these contains even smaller cavities called alveoli. It is in the thin-walled alveoli that the exchange of oxygen to and carbon dioxide from the blood actually takes place. The lungs contain about 300 million alveoli, and although each alveolus is tiny, the total surface area they present is about 40 times the surface area of the skin.

Diaphragm The reason air moves in and out of the body is that the volume of the lungs is continually being changed. The principal agent of change is the diaphragm, a muscle stretched across the abdomen just below the lungs. When the diaphragm is pulled down, the volume of the chest cavity is increased, causing air to enter the lungs. Similarly, when the diaphragm is pulled up, it reduces the volume of the chest cavity and expels air. This process is aided by the muscles of the rib case, which also expand and contract the size of the chest cavity.

Immune System

The immune system was not recognized as a separate system until recently. Although evidence of immune protection was known in ancient times, the first inkling of how the body develops immunity was in 1884, when macrophages (see "Phagocytes" below) were first observed. Since then, many different components of the system have been found. Much still remains to be learned about this system, however.

Skin Although a part of the immune system, skin is often viewed as simply a barrier between the body and the outside world. The largest organ in the body, the skin is far more complex. Its immune functions include not only the barrier against invaders but also production of oil and sweat, both of which kill or retard growth in many bacteria and fungi. On the other hand, the skin harbors millions of helpful bacteria that resist invasion by other bacteria. The skin even has a role in the development of some lymphocytes (white blood cells—see below).

Skin also helps regulate body temperature, helps produce cholesterol (a necessary body chemical, even though it is inadvisable to have too much of it in our blood), and is the location of sensors for heat, cold, and pressure.

Thymus The thymus is a medium-size organ in the upper chest that looks as if it could be an endocrine gland (and was often identified as one in the past). It becomes smaller as a person ages. In some as-yet-unknown way, the thymus "trains" certain lymphocytes to be part of the immune system. If the thymus is removed from a very young animal, the animal does not develop the immune response that causes transplant rejection, for example.

THE HUMAN GENOME PROJECT

Scientists have learned that every organism is almost completely described by its genes, and that the genes are encoded as triplets of bases in long molecules of deoxyribonucleic acid (DNA). The Human Genome Project is an effort to uncover the complete sequence of about 3 billion bases in human DNA, to identify the genes encoded therein, and to recognize the immediate purpose for the genes. Only 2 to 5 percent of the base sequence actually encodes human genes. There are thought to be about 50,000 to 100,000 human genes in all. The average gene consists of a sequence of about 1,500 to 3,000 bases, although genes vary considerably in length. The DNA bases are usually known by the abbreviations T, G, C, and A; thus, the ultimate goal of the project is a string of the letters T, G, C, and A that would fill 510 volumes of a standard-size encyclopedia.

The Human Genome Project can be traced to 1984 when Robert Sinsheimer, chancellor of the University of California at Santa Cruz, first thought of making a map of the human genome. The U.S. Dept. of Energy, the Office of Technology Assessment, the National Research Council, and the National Institutes of Health helped develop the concept. The Human Genome Project started formally on Jan. 3, 1989. The National Institutes of Health became the sponsoring organization with an organization known as the National Center for Human Genome Research. They developed a plan that would start in 1991, run for 15 years, and cost about $3 billion, later revised to $1.5 billion. Scientists from the European Union and the Japanese have also joined the project. An international coordinating group was set up called the Human Genome Organization (HUGO).

After much preliminary work, determination of base sequences began systematically in 1995, primarily by the Genome Sequencing Center at Washington Univ. in St. Louis, Missouri, and the Sanger Centre in the UK. These groups believe that they can complete the sequencing by 2001, five years ahead of schedule, and for a cost of only $100 million.

Meanwhile, private interests have determined that simpler forms of gene maps will be commercially useful and are pursuing these goals. Such a map, based upon a first-generation physical genome map first developed in 1993 by Daniel Cohen and associates of the Centre des Etudes du Polymorphisme Humain in Paris, France, and since improved by French scientists, would probably cost less than $75 million to complete. Many of the genes needed for such use in a map have already been located by Craig Ventner and coworkers at the Institute for Genomic Research, which is funded by the commercial Human Genome Services Inc.

Lymphatic system When blood passes through capillaries, it loses some of its plasma, which becomes part of a liquid between the cells. This liquid is known as lymph. Lymph needs to be returned to the circulatory system to keep the blood volume fairly constant, so a system of tubes called the lymphatic system drains the lymph back into the blood. Along the way it passes through masses of spongy tissue called lymph nodes that filter out any debris, including bacteria, from the lymph. Lymph nodes are made of lymphoid tissue, but they are not the only organs where lymphoid tissue is found; it is found everywhere that bacteria or other germs can easily invade the body, specifically in the linings of the parts of the body exposed to the outside, such as the respiratory system and parts of the digestive system. Most of the action of the immune system takes place in lymphoid tissue.

Lymphocytes Although lymphocytes are known as white blood cells, they are found in the lymph as well as in the blood. Draining all the lymph from an animal's body would remove all the lymphocytes, which would suppress immune reactions. Like red blood cells, lymphocytes are produced in bone marrow, a very well-protected place, suggesting their importance to the body. Scientists have found and continue to find many distinct types of lymphocytes, but there seem to be two main varieties.

The T lymphocytes are those that must mature in the thymus before they can be involved in the immune response. The *T* is for *thymus.* They are the principal cells involved in graft rejection, but they also play a role in fighting bacteria and other invaders. A deficiency of one type of T cell is a major symptom of the disease AIDS, although AIDS seems to affect the immune system in many other ways as well.

The B lymphocytes mature directly in the bone, but the *B* does not stand for *bone.* In birds, B lymphocytes mature in an organ that humans do not have, the bursa of Fabricius, and the *B* stands for *bursa*. B cells react to invaders by releasing chemicals called antibodies. An antibody is a chemical that is specific to a particular protein, sugar, nucleic acid, or fat, but the strongest reaction is with proteins. If, for example, a measles virus is in the blood or lymph, a B lymphocyte will release an antibody that attaches to a protein on the surface of the virus. In some unknown way, one kind of T cell then stimulates the production of many B cells that release the same antibody. The next measles virus that comes along is met with great amounts of the antibody, causing immunity to measles.

Phagocytes There are many other cells produced as part of the immune system by the bone marrow that were formerly grouped under the general heading "white blood cell," including neutrophils, mast cells, and macrophages. When an antibody binds to a protein, it attracts a macrophage, which proceeds to "eat" it, thus removing it. The ability to ingest cells indicates that macrophages are phagocytes, or "eaters of cells." The macrophage also pushes the original protein that triggered the antibody to its surface, where it projects from the cell membrane and causes more B lymphocytes to make the antibody against it. Neutrophils are smaller phagocytes than macrophages, or "big eaters." Mast cells collect near a source of infection and release the chemical histamine, which causes phagocytes to gather and quell the infection.

Reproductive System

The male and female reproductive systems differ in fundamental ways.

Male reproductive system Sperm are formed in the two testes, which hang below the groin, so situated because human body temperature is too high for proper sperm formation. Sperm are stored in the epididymis, just above the testes. During sex the sperm move through tubes and are mixed with secretions from the prostate and Cowper's gland, both ducted glands. The result is called semen. Semen exits the body through a tube in the penis called the urethra, which is otherwise used for excretion of urine.

Female reproductive system Corresponding to the testes in males, the ovaries produce eggs (also known as ova). Unlike sperm, eggs can be produced at human body temperature, allowing for the ovaries and related organs to be located inside the pelvis. Eggs pass through the Fallopian tubes to the uterus, or womb, which is sealed at the other end by the cervix. On the other side of the cervix is a muscular tube called the vagina, or birth canal.

Pregnancy and birth Female physiology changes considerably during pregnancy, although the organs remain the same, with one exception. Sperm that have been implanted in the vagina swim to the uterus, where they fertilize an egg. The egg gradually develops into an embryo attached to a new organ, which consists of the placenta and cord. The placenta has many functions, including the production of hormones, making it an endocrine gland. It is formed from tissue both from the embryo and from the uterus. When the baby is fully formed, the cervix opens and the baby passes through the vagina, still attached to its mother by the cord, which is cut at the navel. The placenta also passes through the vagina and is discarded.

Human Hormones

Hormones are chemicals made in the body that regulate body functions or achieve specific tasks. Some are fairly familiar, such as insulin and estrogen. Others, though less familiar, are clear from their description or name, for example, growth hormone. Increasingly, hormones are available either as products of genetic engineering (human insulin and human growth hormone, for example) or as synthetics. The notorious steroids used for body building are synthetic testosterone. (See "Health and Medicine.") Such manufactured hormones offer both the promise of relief from hormone-deficiency diseases and the possibility of hormone abuse.

Among the main uses for human hormones

today are in regulating reproduction. The familiar birth-control pill and also birth-control implants are hormone delivery systems that are designed to interfere with the female reproductive cycle and prevent pregnancies. Estrogen and progesterone, the hormones used in birth control, also have other common uses. Many older women take estrogen on a continuing basis to replace the hormone, which stops being produced at menopause. Progesterone is often combined with estrogen to enhance its effects. Estrogen supplementation has two main benefits: reduction in heart disease and improved development of skeletal bone. There are some indications, however, that estrogen supplements may increase the likelihood or severity of breast cancers. Physicians monitor older women taking estrogen supplements carefully.

Human growth hormone, which is often prescribed for young people who are deficient in it, is also given by some physicians to increase the height of those who are short for other reasons, although this is controversial. Production of human growth hormone declines with age. Some experiments have suggested that replacement of human growth hormone in older men can help restore muscles and generally remove some of the signs of advanced age.

Elements of the Human Body

The normal human body contains almost all of the chemical elements, mostly in small amounts. Not all are used by the body, and some elements found in tiny quantities in the body are poisonous, such as lead.

The elements that the body uses are necessary for health. For the body to grow, it needs large amounts of elements found in four major nutrients—proteins, carbohydrates, fats, and water—as well as smaller amounts of other elements, known as minerals. When very small amounts are needed, the minerals are called trace elements. Vitamins, the remaining nutrient, are needed compounds that the body cannot make itself in sufficient quantity.

> ***"A human being; an ingenious assembly of portable plumbing."***
>
> —**Christopher Morley,** ***Human Being*** **(1932)**

ELEMENTS IN A 150-POUND INDIVIDUAL

Element	Weight (lbs.)	Use by the body
Oxygen	97.5	Part of all major nutrients, which make up tissues of the body, but also vital to production of energy in the form of elemental oxygen obtained from air.
Carbon	27.0	Essential element for life—most compounds based on carbon are called organic, meaning "from life." An essential part of proteins, carbohydrates, and fats, the building blocks of human cells.
Hydrogen	15.0	Part of each of major nutrients, and thus a building block of every cell. Unlike oxygen, has no part in respiration.
Nitrogen	4.5	Essential part of proteins, DNA, and RNA, the compounds most active in controlling cells; most of the body's functions depend on nitrogen compounds at one stage or another.
Calcium	3.0	Mostly locked into hard compounds that form nonliving parts of bone. One of principal messengers between cells, telling them when to act and when to stay quiet.
Phosphorus	1.8	Important element in bone building, but, like calcium, has another role: it is essential in producing energy in cell.
Potassium	0.3	Regulates contraction of muscle cells (and some other cell functions) along with sodium. In general, potassium is involved with muscle contractions and general maintenance of pressure a cell exerts on its covering membrane.
Sulfur	0.3	Essential to most forms of life. An important constituent of proteins.
Chlorine	0.3	Used in form of chloride ions to transport messages from the body to cells; helps regulate electrical activity.
Sodium	0.165	Required by vertebrates to control fluid pressure in cells.
Magnesium	0.06	Required by both plants (it is in chlorophyll) and animals. In humans, works with enzymes to speed chemical reactions, is involved in transmission of messages between nerves, and has a role in bone structure.
Iron	0.006	Essential for carrying oxygen to cells and carbon dioxide waste away, although present only in small amount; lack of iron causes anemia.
Cobalt	0.00024	Part of vitamin B_{12}, found in meats and dairy products; its exact role in the body is not well understood.
Copper	0.00023	Helps form red blood cells, maintain nervous system, and regulate cholesterol levels.
Manganese	0.00020	Aids in bone formation, helps regulate nervous system, and is part of sex hormones.
Iodine	0.00006	Part of thyroid hormone that controls rate at which food is burned for energy.
Zinc	trace	Needed for some enzymes, for proper sex development, in healing wounds, for sense of taste, and for normal sperm count.
Boron	trace	Low levels required by plants, and hence, element appears in human body, but its role, if any, is not known.
Aluminum	trace	Its role in the body is not clear, but too much aluminum may have role in Alzheimer's disease or other neurological disorders.
Vanadium	trace	Its role, if any, in the body is poorly understood.
Molybdenum	trace	Contained in various enyzmes.
Silicon	trace	Among most abundant elements on Earth, so is not surprising to find silicon in the body, but its necessity to any essential function is unclear.
Fluorine	trace	Strengthens teeth and bones.
Chromium	trace	Used in metabolism of sugar and the regulation of fats.
Selenium	trace	In small amounts, may reduce cell damage and promote growth.

Mathematics

Strictly speaking, mathematics is not considered a science but a separate branch of learning on its own. Because the use of mathematics has been so important to science, however, it is generally treated along with sciences.

Mathematics consists of a set of abstract symbols and of rules for manipulating them, along with the results of that manipulation. Because of this, some have classified mathematics as a kind of language, while others view it as a kind of game. Many mathematicians believe there is a much deeper reality than those classifications, but it is one that is very difficult to explain. Even when mathematics is treated as a game, the results seem to be strongly connected to the real world.

Most people learn numbers, arithmetic, and some geometry in elementary school. In high school more mathematics is taught, perhaps including the calculus. Almost all the mathematics taught in elementary school or high school is at least 300 years old. In the past 300 years, mathematicians have developed many new branches of the subject often requiring years of special training even to understand the basic parts. This section, however, focuses on aspects of mathematics useful in daily life or that may be encountered in school by nonmathematicians.

MILESTONES IN THE HISTORY OF MATHEMATICS

B.C.

c. 20,000 People in Near East begin using notches to record numbers.

c. 3500 Egyptians develop numeration system that can record very large numbers, with different symbols for ones, tens, hundreds, etc.

c. 2400 A numeration system based on place value (similar to Hindu-Arabic system) is introduced in Mesopotamia.

c. 2000 Mesopotamian mathematicians learn how to solve quadratic equations.

c. 1900 Mesopotamian mathematicians discover what we now call the Pythagorean theorem: The sum of the squares of the legs of a right triangle equals the square of the hypotenuse.

c. 470 Mathematician Hippasus of Metapontum (Greek: c. 500) discovers dodecahedron, a regular solid with 12 faces.

c. 450 Pythagoreans show that some lengths, such as the diagonal of a 1 × 1 square ($\sqrt{2}$), cannot be measured exactly; today such lengths are called irrational numbers.

c. 300 Euclid's (Greek: c. 300) *Elements* shows that virtually all parts of mathematics known at the time could be proved from short list of assumptions.

c. 260 In Central America, Maya develop numeration system based on place value.

c. 230 Apollonius of Perga (Greek: c. 262–190) writes *Conics,* an analysis of such curves as parabola, ellipse, and hyperbola.

A.D.

876 The first-known use of a symbol for zero occurs in India.

c. 1100 Poet, mathematician, and astronomer Omar Khayyám (Persian: 1048–c. 1131) develops geometric methods for solving cubic equations.

1321 Levi ben Gershom (Gersonides; French: 1288–1344) is first to use mathematical induction.

c. 1515 Scipione del Ferro (Italian: 1465–1526) discovers algebraic method for solving one form of cubic equations.

1536 Niccolò Tartaglia (Italian: 1499–1557) announces he is able to solve two types of cubic equations.

1545 Girolamo Cardano's (Italian: 1501–76) *Ars Magna* contains Lodovico Ferrari's (Italian: 1522–65) complete solution of the quartic as well as complete solution of the cubic based on Tartaglia's work.

1572 Rafael Bombelli (Italian: 1526–c. 1573) uses complex numbers to solve equations.

1614 John Napier (Scottish: 1550–1617) describes logarithms.

1637 René Descartes (French: 1596–1650) publishes first account of analytic geometry; also discovered by Pierre de Fermat (French: 1601–65).

1639 Gérard Desargues (French: 1591–1661) introduces projective geometry.

1654 Blaise Pascal (French: 1623–62) and Pierre de Fermat develop basic laws of probability.

1666 Sir Isaac Newton (English: 1642–1727) describes his invention of the calculus but does not have it published at this time.

1684 Gottfried Wilhelm Leibniz (German: 1646–1716) publishes first account of his independent discovery of the calculus, the first description to reach print.

1763 Gaspard Monge (French: 1746–1818) invents descriptive geometry, the mathematical techniques that are basis of mechanical drawing and most architects' plans.

1799 Karl Friedrich Gauss (German: 1777–1855) proves fundamental theorem of algebra, which is that every polynomial equation has solution.
Paolo Ruffini (Italian: 1765–1822) offers first proof that not all polynomial equations of fifth degree can be solved by algebraic methods.

1801 Gauss publishes *Disquisitiones arithmeticae,* greatly extending number theory.

1822 Jean-Victor Poncelet (French: 1788–1867) further develops projective geometry.

1826 Nikolai Ivanovich Lobachevski (Russian: 1793–1856) gives first public address concerning non-Euclidean geometry.

1837 Pierre Wantzel (French: 1814–48) proves an angle cannot be trisected with compass and straightedge alone.

1854 Georg F.B. Riemann (German: 1826–66) shows that several non-Euclidean geometries are possible, including one Albert Einstein (German-American: 1879–1955) later demonstrated was the most likely geometry of the universe.

1877 Georg F.L.P. Cantor (German: 1845–1918) shows that number of points in a line segment is same as number in interior of a square.

1881 Josiah Willard Gibbs (American: 1839–1903) introduces vector analysis.

1882 Ferdinand von Lindemann (German: 1852–1939) proves that π is transcendental, implying the circle cannot be squared with straightedge and compass.

1892 Cantor proves there are at least two types of infinities—specifically, that infinity of real numbers (including all infinite decimals) is bigger than infinity of counting numbers (1, 2, 3, . . .).

1900 David Hilbert (German: 1862–1943) proposes his famous list of 23 unsolved problems.

1931 Kurt Gödel (Austrian-American: 1906–78) shows that any formal system strong enough to include laws of arithmetic is either incomplete or inconsistent: *incomplete* if not all true theorems can be proved or *inconsistent* if two contradictory theorems can be proved.

1936 Independently, Alan M. Turing (English: 1912–54) and Alonzo Church (American: 1903–) discover there is no single infallible method for proving whether a statement in mathematics is true or false.

1949 Claude E. Shannon (American: 1916–) publishes his work on information theory, a general approach to handling communications.

1976 In first major computer-assisted proof, it is shown that any map can be colored with four colors in such a way that no two regions of the same color share common border.

1980 Classification of all finite simple groups, started in 1830, is completed, perhaps longest proof in history of mathematics.

1989 Miklos Laczkovich (Hungarian) proves that a circle can be cut into a finite number of pieces that can be reassembled into a square.

1991 Wu-Yi Hsiang (Chinese: 1937–) proves Johannes Kepler's conjecture (1611) that the way to pack spheres with the greatest density is what mathematicians call the face-centered cubic lattice method.

1995 Andrew Wiles (American) publishes a corrected version of his 1993 proof that the equation $x^n + y^n = z^n$ has no solution for n greater than 2 when x, y, and z are counting numbers—known as Fermat's last theorem because Pierre Fermat claimed to have proved it in a note discovered after his death in 1665.

COMMONLY USED MATHEMATICAL FORMULAS

Most formulas needed in solving everyday problems are collected below, with special emphasis on formulas relating to measurements, as these are used in everything from sewing to building a house. However, some important formulas from algebra, graphing, and trigonometry are at the end. Additional formulas can also be found in "Basic Laws of Physics."

General The **distance** d, given the rate r and the time t:

$$d = rt.$$

Length The **perimeter (distance around)** p **of any polygon** (closed plane figure with straight sides that do not cross), given the lengths of the sides a, b, c, and so forth:

$$p = a + b + c + \ldots$$

Perimeter p **of a rectangle**, given the length l and the width w:

$$p = 2l + 2w.$$

Perimeter p **of a square**, given the length of a side s:

$$p = 4s.$$

Circumference (distance around) C **of a circle**, given the diameter d (distance across) or the radius r (distance from the center to the circle):

$$C = \pi d$$

or

$$C = 2\pi r.$$

The number π is an infinite decimal that begins 3.14159 . . . , which is often approximated as either 3.14 or as $22/7$.

Area In each of the following, the area (amount of surface) is A. For three-dimensional figures, A is the total surface area.

Rectangle, given the length l and the width w:

$$A = lw.$$

Square, given the length of a side s:

$$A = s^2.$$

Circle, given the radius r:

$$A = \pi r^2.$$

Triangle, given the base b and the height h:

$$A = \tfrac{1}{2} bh.$$

Right triangle, given the lengths a and b of the two sides (legs) that form the right angle:

$$A = \tfrac{1}{2} ab.$$

Parallelogram, given the base b and the height h:

$$A = bh.$$

Trapezoid, given the two bases B and b and the height h:

$$A = \tfrac{1}{2} h(B + b).$$

Kite, given the lengths of the two diagonals D and d:

$$A = \tfrac{1}{2} Dd.$$

Regular polygon (polygon with all sides of equal length and all angles of equal measure), given the perimeter p and the apothem a (the distance from the center of the regular polygon to one of its sides):

$$A = \tfrac{1}{2} ap.$$

Equilateral triangle (all sides the same length), given the length of a side s:

$$A = \frac{s^2 \sqrt{3}}{4}.$$

Heron's formula Any **triangle**, given half the length of the perimeter (the semiperimeter) s and the lengths of the sides a, b, and c:

$$A = \sqrt{s(s-a)(s-b)(s-c)}.$$

Right circular cylinder (a cylinder with a circular region as its base whose sides make a right angle with the base), given the radius r of the base and the height h of the cylinder:

$$A = 2\pi r(h + r).$$

Right circular cone (a cone with a circular region as its base and whose altitude makes a right angle with the base), given the radius r of the base and the slant height l of the cone (the shortest distance from the tip of the cone to the circle of the base):

$$A = \pi r(l + r).$$

Sphere, given the radius r:

$$A = 4\pi r^2.$$

Volume In each of the following, the volume (space enclosed) is V.

Cube, given the length of an edge e:

$$V = e^3.$$

Right rectangular prism (box), given the length l, the width w, and the height h:

$$V = lwh.$$

Prism, given the area of the base B and the height h:

$$V = Bh.$$

Right circular cylinder, given the radius r of the base and the height h:

$$V = \pi r^2 h.$$

Right circular cone, given the radius r of the base and the height h:

$$V = \tfrac{1}{3} \pi r^2 h.$$

Pyramid, given the area of the base B and the height h:

$$V = \tfrac{1}{3} Bh.$$

Sphere, given the radius r:

$$V = \tfrac{4}{3} \pi r^3.$$

Algebra If a, b, and x are any numbers or variables ("unknowns"):

$$(a + b)^2 = a^2 + 2ab + b^2$$
$$(a - b)^2 = a^2 - 2ab + b^2$$
$$x^2 - a^2 = (x + a)(x - a)$$
$$x^3 - a^3 = (x - a)(x^2 + ax + a^2)$$
$$x^3 + a^3 = (x + a)(x^2 - ax + a^2).$$

If a, b, c, and d are any numbers or variables except that neither b nor d can be zero:

$$a/b + c/d = (ad + bc)/bd$$
$$a/b - c/d = (ad - bc)/bd$$
$$a/b \times c/d = ac/bd$$
$$a/b \div c/d = ad/bc \ (c \neq 0).$$

Quadratic formula for the solutions of a second degree polynomial equation in one variable of the form $ax^2 + bx + c = 0$:

$$x = \frac{-b \pm \sqrt{b^2 - 4ac}}{2a}.$$

Laws of exponents, given that a, b, x, and y are numbers or variables:

$$a^x a^y = a^{x+y}$$
$$(a^x)^y = a^{xy}$$
$$(ab)^x = a^x b^x$$
$$(a/b)^x = a^x/b^x$$
$$a^x/a^y = a^{x-y}$$
$$a^{-x} = 1/a^x$$
$$a^0 = 1$$
$$a^1 = a.$$

Laws of logarithms, given that a, b, x, and y are positive numbers, c is any real number, and $a \neq 1$, $b \neq 1$.

$$\log_a (xy) = \log_a x + \log_a y$$
$$\log_a 1/x = -\log_a x$$
$$\log_a (x/y) = \log_a x - \log_a y$$
$$\log_a (x^c) = c \log_a x$$
$$\log_b x = (\log_a x)/(\log_a b)$$
$$\log_a 1 = 0$$
$$\log_a a = 1$$
$$a^{\log_a x} = x$$
$$\log_a (a^c) = c.$$

Graphs In a rectangular (Cartesian) coordinate plane, where the horizontal axis is x and the vertical axis is y:

Slope of a line, m, given two particular points (x_1, y_1) and (x_2, y_2) where $x_1 \neq x_2$:

$$m = (y_2 - y_1)/(x_2 - x_1).$$

Point-slope equation of a line, given the slope m and a point on the nonvertical line (x_1, y_1):

$$y - y_1 = m(x - x_1).$$

Slope-intercept equation of a line, given the slope m and the y-intercept b (the number on the y axis where the line crosses the y axis):

$$y = mx + b.$$

Distance d **between any two points**, (x_1, y_1) and (x_2, y_2):

$$d = \sqrt{(x_2 - x_1)^2 + (y_2 - y_1)^2}.$$

Trigonometry In a **right triangle** whose two shorter sides (or legs) are a and b, opposite angles A and B respectively, and whose longest side (or hypotenuse, always the side opposite the right angle, C) is c:

Pythagorean theorem:

$$c^2 = a^2 + b^2.$$

Trigonometric functions:

sine: $\sin A = a/c$
cosine: $\cos A = b/c$
tangent: $\tan A = a/b$
cotangent: $\cot A = b/a$
secant: $\sec A = c/b$
cosecant: $\csc A = c/a$.

In any triangle labeled such that side a is opposite angle A, side b is opposite angle B, and side c is opposite angle C:

Angle sum:

$$A + B + C = 180°.$$

Law of sines:

$$(\sin A)/a = (\sin B)/b = (\sin C)/c.$$

Law of cosines:

$$c^2 = a^2 + b^2 - 2ab \cos C.$$

If x is any real number or a measure of an angle in degrees, the following statements are true for all:

Defining trigonometric identities:

$\tan x = \sin x/\cos x$ $\csc x = 1/\sin x$
$\cot x = \cos x/\sin x$ $\cot x = 1/\tan x$
$\sec x = 1/\cos x$

Trigonometric identities of symmetry:

$\sin(-x) = -\sin x$ $\cos(-x) = \cos x$
$\tan(-x) = -\tan x$ $\cot(-x) = -\cot x$
$\sec(-x) = \sec x$ $\csc(-x) = -\csc x.$

Pythagorean identities:

$$\sin^2 x + \cos^2 x = 1$$
$$\tan^2 x + 1 = \sec^2 x$$
$$\cot^2 x + 1 = \csc^2 x.$$

Sum and difference formulas: If x and y are any two real numbers or measures of angles:

$\sin(x + y) = \sin x \cos y + \cos x \sin y$
$\cos(x + y) = \cos x \cos y - \sin x \sin y$
$\tan(x + y) = (\tan x + \tan y)/(1 - \tan x \tan y)$
$\sin(x - y) = \sin x \cos y - \cos x \sin y$
$\cos(x - y) = \cos x \cos y + \sin x \sin y$
$\tan(x - y) = (\tan x - \tan y)/(1 + \tan x \tan y).$

LARGE NUMBERS

There are two primary naming systems for large numbers. The United States and France (among others) use one system, while Germany and Great Britain use the other. (Googol and googolplex, invented by the nephew of mathematician and author Edward Kasner, are rarely used outside the United States.) (See also "Standard Weights and Measures.")

Number of zeroes after 1	American name	British name
6	million	million
9	billion	milliard
12	trillion	billion
15	quadrillion	1,000 billion
18	quintillion	trillion
21	sextillion	1,000 trillion
24	septillion	quadrillion
27	octillion	1,000 quadrillion
30	nonillion	quintillion
33	decillion	1,000 quintillion
100	googol	googol
googol	googolplex	googolplex

FRACTIONS AND DECIMALS

To find the equivalent of a fraction in decimal form, divide the numerator (top number) by the denominator (bottom number). To change from a decimal to a percent, multiply by 100. To change from a percent to a decimal, divide by 100.

Fraction	Decimal	Percent
1/16	0.0625	6.25 %
1/8 (= 2/16)	0.125	12.5
3/16	0.1875	18.75
1/4 (= 2/8; = 4/16)	0.25	25.0
5/16	0.3125	31.25
1/3	$0.\bar{3}$ . . .	$33.\bar{3}$ . . .
3/8 (= 6/16)	0.375	37.5
7/16	0.4375	43.75
1/2 (= 2/4; = 4/8; = 8/16)	0.5	50.0
9/16	0.5625	56.25
5/8 (= 10/16)	0.625	62.5
2/3	$0.\bar{6}$	$66.\bar{6}$
11/16	0.6875	68.75
3/4 (= 6/8; = 12/16)	0.75	75.0
13/16	0.8125	81.25
7/8 (= 14/16)	0.875	87.5
15/16	0.9375	93.75
1 (= 2/2; = 4/4; = 8/8; = 16/16)	1.0	100.0

TECHNOLOGY

In our modern world, most technological advances are closely related to and driven by science, but the inventors of better ways to chip flint or forge iron were not scientists. Even Thomas Alva Edison, perhaps the greatest single contributor to modern technology, made only one scientific discovery (the Edison effect, an electric current produced when a hot wire is near a conductor in a vacuum). Instead, Edison was an inventor. The list of major discoveries in technology is essentially a list of inventions.

Since the Industrial Revolution in the late 18th century, the pace of invention has increased. This is shown dramatically by the rise in the number of U.S. patents issued. At the same time, there are fewer lone inventors—in fact, Edison himself was only a lone inventor in the beginning, and he pioneered the idea of a large group of people working together on new inventions. The creations of the lone inventor gradually have been overtaken by inventions patented by corporations. As technology has become a mainstay of business worldwide, the number of foreign patents issued to corporations has surpassed those obtained by U.S. corporations.

Although the lone inventor is to some degree gone, he or she is not forgotten by the U.S. National Council of Intellectual Property Law, which maintains the Inventors Hall of Fame.

MAJOR DISCOVERIES IN THE HISTORY OF TECHNOLOGY

(See also "Chronology of Information Processing" in "Computers.")

B.C.

2,400,000 Ancestors of human beings begin to manufacture stone tools.

1,000,000 Ancestors of human beings learn to control fire.

90,000 People from the Katranda culture in what is now in Zaire make barbed bone points, probably for use in harpoons.

25,000 People in what is now the Czech Republic were weaving cloth.

23,000 Bow and arrow developed in Mediterranean regions of Europe and Africa.

10,000 The Jomon culture of Japan makes the first known pottery.

5000 Egyptians start mining and smelting copper ore.

3500 Potter's wheel and (shortly after) wheeled vehicles appear in Mesopotamia.

2900 Great Pyramid of Giza and first form of Stonehenge (having only three stones) are built.

2000 Interior bathrooms are built in palaces in Crete.

1500 Earliest glass vessels from Egypt.

522 Eupalinus of Megara (Greek: 6th cent.) constructs 3,600-ft. tunnel on Samos to supply water from one side of Mt. Castro to other.

290 Pharos lighthouse at Alexandria is built.

260 Archimedes (Greek: c. 287–212 B.C.) develops mathematical descriptions of the lever and other simple machines.

200 Romans develop concrete.

140 Chinese start making paper but do not use it for writing.

100 In Illyria (now Yugoslavia and Albania), water-powered mills are introduced.

A.D.

c. 1 Chinese invent centerline rudder for ships and magnetic compass; neither found in West for 1,000 years.

190 Chinese develop porcelain.

600 First windmills are built in what is now Iran.

704 Between 704 and 751, Chinese start printing with woodblocks.

1040 Chinese develop gunpowder.

1041 Between 1041 and 1048, Chinese inventor Bi Sheng develops movable type.

1190 First-known reference to a compass in Europe.

1267 Book written by Roger Bacon (English: c. 1220–92) in 1267 mentions eyeglasses to correct farsightedness.

1288 First-known gun, a small cannon, is made in China.

1310 Mechanical clocks driven by weights begin to appear in Europe.

c. 1440 Johannes Gutenberg (German: c. 1398–1468) reinvents printing with movable type.

1450 Nicholas of Cusa (German: 1401–64) develops eyeglasses for the nearsighted.

1555 Georg Bauer (Georgius Agricola; German: 1494–1555) writes *De re metallica,* a handbook of mining techniques.

c. 1590 Compound microscope (using two lenses) developed in Holland.

1608 Telescope developed in Holland, probably by Hans Lippershey (German-Dutch: c. 1570–1619).

1620 Cornelis Jacobszoon Drebbel (Dutch: 1572–1633) builds first navigable submarine.

1643 Evangelista Torricelli (Italian: 1608–47) makes first barometer, thereby producing first vacuum known to science.

1654 Christiaan Huygens (Dutch: 1629–95) develops pendulum clock.

1658 Robert Hooke (English: 1635–1703) invents balance spring for watches.

1698 Thomas Savery (English: c. 1650– 1715) patents the "Miner's Friend," first practical steam engine.

1701 Jethro Tull (English: 1674–1741), possibly inspired by Chinese devices, invents device for planting seeds called a seed drill.

1709 Daniel Gabriel Fahrenheit (German-Dutch: 1686–1736) invents alcohol thermometer; 1714, mercury thermometer.

1733 John Kay (English: 1704–64) invents flying-shuttle loom, which, along with the steam engine and improvements in making iron, is a key to the start of Industrial Revolution.

1751 Benjamin Huntsman (English: 1704–76) invents crucible process for casting steel.

1762 John Harrison (English: 1693–1776) designs a marine chronometer (clock) accurate enough to enable navigators to calculate longitude at sea.

1764 James Hargreaves (English: 1720–78) introduces spinning jenny, a machine that spins from 8 to 120 threads at once.

1765 James Watt (Scottish: 1736–1819) builds model of his improved steam engine.

1769 Sir Richard Arkwright (English: 1732–92) patents the water frame, a spinning machine that complements spinning jenny.

1783 Joseph-Michel and Jacques-Etienne Montgolfier (French: 1740–1810; 1745–99) develop first hot air balloon. Jacques A.C. Charles (French: 1746–1823) builds first hydrogen balloon.

1785 Edmund Cartwright (English: 1743–1823) invents first form of the power loom.

1792 William Murdock (Scottish: 1754–1839) is first to use coal gas for lighting.

1793 Eli Whitney (American: 1765–1825) invents cotton gin, a machine for separating cotton fibers from seeds.

1800 Alessandro G.A.A. Volta (Italian: 1745–1827) invents first form of chemical battery for producing electric current.

1804 Nicolas-François Appert (French: c. 1750–1841) develops canning as means of preserving food.

1807 Robert Fulton (American: 1765–1815) introduces first commercially successful steamboat.

1816 Sir David Brewster (Scottish: 1781–1868) invents kaleidoscope.

1822 Joseph N. Niepce (French: 1765–1833) produces earliest form of the photograph.

1823 Charles Macintosh (Scottish: 1766–1843) patents a waterproof fabric.

1825 George Stephenson (English: 1781–1848) develops first steam-powered locomotive to carry both passengers and freight.

1835 William Henry Fox Talbot (English: 1800–77) invents photographic negative using silver chloride, essentially how black-and-white pictures are made today.

1837 Samuel Finley Breese Morse (American: 1791–1872) patents first commercially successful version of the telegraph.

1839 Louis J.M. Daguerre (French: 1789–1851) announces his process for making photographs, which come to be called daguerreotypes.
Charles Goodyear (American: 1800–60) discovers how to make rubber resistant to heat and cold, a process called vulcanization.

1842 Sir John Bennet Lawes (English: 1814–99) patents manufacture of superphosphate, the first manufactured fertilizer.

1843 Isambard Kingdom Brunel's (English: 1806–59) *Great Britain* is first iron-hulled screw-propellor ship to cross the Atlantic.

1846 Elias Howe (American: 1819–67) patents lock-stitch sewing machine.
Richard March Hoe (American: 1812–96) invents rotary printing press.

1851 Isaac Merrit Singer (American: 1811–75) patents continuous-stitch sewing machine.

1852 Elisha Graves Otis (American: 1811–61) installs first elevator incorporating safety device that prevents cage from falling if the cable breaks.

1856 Henry Bessemer (English: 1813–98) develops way of making inexpensive steel (Bessemer process).

1859 Edwin L. Drake (American: 1819–80) drills first oil well, in Titusville, Pa.

1862 Richard Jordan Gatling (American: 1818–1903) invents first form of machine gun.

1866 Robert Whitehead (English: 1823–1905) invents naval torpedo.
Georges Leclanché (French: 1839–82) develops first form of dry cell for producing electricity.

1867 Latham Sholes (American: 1819–90) and two others invent first practical typewriter.

1869 Hippolyte Mège Mouriés (French: 1817–80) patents margarine.

1874 Joseph Farwell Glidden (American: 1813–1906) invents the kind of barbed wire used today.

1876 Alexander Graham Bell (Scottish-American: 1847–1922) invents telephone.
Karl von Linde (German: 1842–1934) invents first practical refrigerator.

1877 Nikolaus A. Otto (German: 1832–91) invents type of internal combustion engine still used in most automobiles.
Thomas Alva Edison (American: 1847–1931) invents phonograph, which uses a tinfoil-covered cylinder.

1878 Louis-Marie-Hilaire Bernigaud (French: 1839–1924) develops rayon.
Carl Gustaf Patrik de Laval (Swedish: 1845–1913) invents turbine operated centrifugal cream separator.

1879 Edison and Sir Joseph W. Swan (English: 1828–1914) independently discover how to make practical electric lights.

1885 Karl Benz (German: 1844–1929) builds precursor of modern automobile.
Rover Safety Bicycle, built in England, is first bicycle with essentially modern features.

1886 George Westinghouse (American: 1846–1914) invents air brake for railroad cars.

1888 Emile Berliner (German: 1851–1929) invents phonograph disk.
John B. Dunlop (Scottish: 1840–1921) patents air-filled tire.
George Eastman (American: 1854–1932) develops first camera using roll film.

1889 Gustave Eiffel (French: 1832–1923) builds his famous tower in Paris; at 993 ft. it is tallest freestanding structure of the time.

1893 Rudolf Diesel (German: 1858–1913) describes diesel engine.

1895 First public showing of a motion picture, "Workers Leaving the Lumière Factory" by Auguste and Louis Lumière (French: 1862–1954; 1864–1948), in Paris.

Guglielmo Marconi (Italian: 1874–1937) transmits signals for a mile with his wireless telegraph (a precursor of radio) near Bologna, Italy.

1897 Karl Ferdinand Braun (German: 1850–1918) invents cathode-ray tube oscilloscope.

1898 Valdemar Poulsen (Danish: 1869–1942) invents magnetic wire recorder, the precursor to the modern tape recorder.

1902 Willis H. Carrier (American: 1876–1950) invents air conditioning.

1903 Orville and Wilbur Wright (American: 1871–1948; 1867–1912) fly the first successful airplane at Kitty Hawk, N.C.

1904 John Fleming (English: 1849–1945) develops first vacuum tube, a device for changing alternating current to direct.

1907 Lee De Forest (American: 1873–1961) patents Audion vacuum tube, a device for magnifying weak electronic signals.

1908 Henry Ford (American: 1863–1947) introduces Model T, the first affordable automobile.

1909 Leo Baekeland (Belgian-American: 1863–1944) patents Bakelite, the first truly successful plastic.

1912 Reginald Aubrey Fessenden (Canadian-American: 1866–1932) develops heterodyne circuit, an important improvement in radio reception.

1917 Clarence Birdseye (American: 1886–1956) develops freezing as a means of preserving food.

1919 Sir Arthur W. Brown (British: 1886–1948) and Sir John W. Alcock (British: 1892–1919) make first transatlantic flight, Newfoundland to Ireland.

1924 Vladimir Kosma Zworykin (Russian-American: 1889–1982) develops iconoscope, the beginning of modern television.

1929 Robert H. Goddard (American: 1882–1945) launches first instrumented, liquid-fueled rocket.

1930 Sir Frank Whittle (British: 1907–) patents jet engine.

1931 Ernst A.F. Ruska (German: 1906–) builds first electron microscope.

1934 Wallace Hume Carothers (American: 1896–1937) invents nylon, first marketed in 1938.

1935 Sir Robert Alexander Watson-Watt (Scottish: 1892–1973) begins work on *ra*dio *d*etection *a*nd *r*anging (radar).

1937 Chester F. Carlson (American: 1906–68) invents xerography, the first method of photocopying.

1939 Paul H. Müller (Swiss: 1899–1965) discovers that DDT is potent and long-lasting insecticide.
Igor I. Sikorsky (Russian-American: 1889–1972) designs and flies first helicopter developed for mass production.

1940 Peter Carl Goldmark (Hungarian-American: 1906–77) demonstrates first successful color television system.

1941 John Rex Whinfield (British: 1901–66) invents Dacron.

1942 Enrico Fermi (Italian-American: 1901–54) builds first nuclear reactor.

1947 Dennis Gabor (Hungarian-British: 1900–1979) develops holography, a method of recording and displaying a three-dimensional object.

1948 Goldmark develops the 33⅓ rpm long-playing phonograph record.
Georges de Mestral (Swiss: 1908–90) invents Velcro, patented in 1955.

1957 Gordon Gould (American: 1920–) develops basic idea for the laser, which he succeeds in patenting in 1986 after long struggle.

1958 United States opens first experimental nuclear power plant.

1962 First industrial robot is marketed.
First active communications satellite, Telstar, goes into orbit.

1963 Audiocassettes introduced.

1966 Engineers at ITT demonstrate fiber optics as a method of transmitting data.

1968 The first supersonic airliner, the Soviet Tupolev TU-144, is demonstrated on December 31.

1975 IBM introduces first laser printer.

1982 Compact disc players introduced.

1989 The U.S. Defense Department launches the first satellite in the Global Positioning System.

1990 Leigh T. Canham (British) develops a method for producing light from stimulated silicon.

1991 Woo Paik and coworkers produce the first prototype of digital high-definition television.

1993 Patricia Bianconi and student Glenn Visscher produce a diamond or diamondlike film from a polyacetylene plastic.

1994 The Eurotunnel, also known as the Chunnel, connecting England and France beneath the English Channel, is officially opened.

1995 Scientists at Los Alamos National Laboratory in New Mexico develop a flexible tape that is superconducting at the temperature of liquid nitrogen (about −325°F).

National Inventors Hall of Fame

In 1973 the U.S. National Council of Patent Law Associations (now the National Council of Intellectual Property Law) began the practice of naming inventors who hold U.S. patents to the National Inventors Hall of Fame. Although many of those honored have many patents, the committee selects one patent for each inventor (or group of inventors) as the occasion for the award, which they identify by the title of the original patent application. When an invention is the work of more than one person, the description of the invention is given only for one inventor. The date at the end of each of the following entries denotes the year of induction. The hall is located in Akron, Ohio.

Ernst Alexanderson (Swedish-American: 1878–1975) HIGH FREQUENCY ALTERNATOR This is the basic device that makes it possible for radio (and television) to transmit voices and music, not just dots and dashes. (1983)

Andrew Alford (Russian-American: 1904–) LOCALIZER ANTENNA SYSTEM With this and other inventions, Alford developed the radio system for navigation as well as instrument landing systems for airplanes. (1983)

Luis Walter Alvarez (American: 1911–88) RADIO DISTANCE AND DIRECTION INDICATOR Alvarez is better known for developing methods of studying subatomic particles, which brought him a Nobel Prize for Physics in 1968. (1978)

Edwin Howard Armstrong (American: 1890–1954) METHOD OF RECEIVING HIGH FREQUENCY OSCILLATIONS Armstrong's several inventions connected with radio broadcasting and reception made possible the "radio days" of the 1920s through the 1940s. In 1939 he invented FM broadcasting and reception, which helped lead to another revolution in radio. (1980)

Leo Hendrik Baekeland (Belgian-American: 1863–1944) SYNTHETIC RESINS Baekeland's plastic (synthetic resin) that he named Bakelite was not the first plastic to be manufactured (that was celluloid), but it was the the first to make people realize the potential of plastics in general. (1978)

John Bardeen (American: 1908–91) TRANSISTOR Invented by Bardeen, William Shockley, and Walter Brattain, the transistor is the essential semiconductor device used on microprocessors and other chips. (1974)

Arnold O. Beckman (American: 1900–) APPARATUS FOR TESTING ACIDITY Beckman developed a precise instrument to measure how acid a substance is as well as other precision instruments. (1987)

Alexander Graham Bell (Scottish-American: 1874–1922) TELEGRAPHY Despite the title of this patent, the invention here was the telephone. (1974)

Willard H. Bennett (American: 1903–87) RADIO FREQUENCY MASS SPECTROMETER Measures chemical composition of elements; patented in 1955. (1991)

Emile Berliner (German-American: 1851–1929) MICROPHONE AND GRAMOPHONE Berliner's microphone made it possible to use Alexander Graham Bell's telephone over long distances. With the $50,000 patent rights payment he received from the Bell Telephone Company, Berliner developed the gramophone, the forerunner of the record player. (1994)

Gerd Karl Binnig (German: 1947–) SCANNING TUNNELING MICROSCOPE Traces details as small as 0.1 angstrom, or one-tenth the size of an atom. It opened entirely new views of the study of the structure of atoms and won Binnig and his partner Heinrich Rohrer the Nobel Prize for Physics in 1986. (1994)

Forrest Bird (American: 1921–) MEDICAL RESPIRATORS The little green box known as "The Bird" prevented thousands from dying from cardiopulmonary failure. Its inventor also developed the Babybird respirator for low birth-weight babies, cutting mortality rates for infants with respiratory problems from 70 percent to 10 percent. (1995)

Harold Stephen Black (American: 1898–) NEGATIVE FEEDBACK AMPLIFIER The basic principle of the negative feedback amplifier has become fundamental to many other devices since Black first used it to control distortion. (1981)

Baruch S. Blumberg (American: 1925–) HEPATITIS B VACCINE Since it was patented in 1972, this vaccine (invented with Irving Millman) has protected hundreds of millions of people worldwide against the hepatitis B virus, which is still one of the leading causes of death worldwide. (1993)

Walter H. Brattain (American: 1902–87) TRANSISTOR (See John Bardeen) (1974)

Rachel Fuller Brown (American: 1898–1980) NYSTATIN (See Elizabeth Lee Hazen) (1994)

Luther Burbank (American: 1849–1926) PEACH Burbank's work in developing more than 800 new varieties of plants contributed to the development of the Plant Patent program in 1930. Burbank holds 16 plant patents, all issued posthumously. (1986)

Joseph H. Burckhalter (American: 1912–) FITC Discovered by Burckhalter and Robert J. Seiwald, this yellow-green compound, known to doctors as fluorescein isothiocyanate, has proved invaluable in identifying different antibodies. In addition to helping identify the causes of AIDS, FITC has been used to speed the diagnosis of leukemia and lymphoma. (1995)

William Seward Burroughs (American: 1857–98) CALCULATING MACHINE Although the calculating machine dates from the 17th century, Burroughs's was the first that could be mass produced and easily used. (1987)

William Meriam Burton (American: 1865–1954) MANUFACTURE OF GASOLINE Burton developed the first commercially successful cracking process, a method that yielded twice the amount of gasoline from crude oil than previous methods had. (1984)

Marvin Camras (American: 1916–) METHOD AND MEANS OF MAGNETIC RECORDING Before the tapes currently used to record sound and pictures, sound was recorded on the wire recorder that Camras invented in the 1930s. He went on to develop over 500 inventions, most connected with improvements in recording methods. (1985)

Chester F. Carlson (American: 1906–68) ELECTROPHOTOGRAPHY Carlson invented the dry copying method called xerography. Although patented in 1940, the dry copier was not marketed until 1958, by which time Carlson had patented many improvements. (1981)

Wallace Hume Carothers (American: 1896–1937) DIAMINE-DICARBOXYLIC ACID SALTS AND PROCESS OF PREPARING SAME AND SYNTHETIC FIBER Carothers's invention—known as nylon—contributed an important fiber to the world; he also developed the first commercially successful synthetic rubber. (1984)

NUMBER OF UTILITY PATENTS ISSUED FOR INVENTIONS BY DECADE, 1790–1994

Period	Patents issued	Period	Patents issued
1790–1800	309	1901–10	315,193
1801–10	1,093	1911–20	383,117
1811–20	1,930	1921–30	423,089
1821–30	3,086	1931–40	439,863
1831–40	5,519	1941–50	308,436
1841–50	5,933	1951–60	430,120
1851–60	23,065	1961–70	585,115
1861–70	79,459	1971–80	687,800[1]
1871–80	125,438	1981–90	737,017
1881–90	207,514	1991–94	393,978
1891–1900	220,608		

Note: Excludes patents granted for designs and botanical plants. 1. Numbers rounded in source. **Sources:** U.S. Bureau of the Census, *The Statistical History of the United States* (1976), and U.S. Patent Office, *All Technologies Report* (March 1995).

Willis Haviland Carrier (American: 1876–1950) APPARATUS FOR TREATING AIR Carrier invented the first successful air-conditioning system, and many of the techniques used in modern refrigerators. (1985)

George Washington Carver (American: 1864–1943) PRODUCTS USING PEANUTS AND SWEET POTATOES A successful scientist in Iowa who later taught at the prestigious black Tuskegee Institute, Carver developed over 300 uses for the peanut and 118 sweet potato by-products as an incentive for farmers to plant regenerative crops rather than the traditional soil-destroying cotton and tobacco. (1990)

Frank B. Colton (Polish-American: 1923–) ORAL CONTRACEPTIVES Colton not only developed the first "pill" in 1960, but he also pioneered the development of anabolic steroids. (1988)

Lloyd H. Conover (American: 1923–) TETRACYCLINE Before Conover created tetracycline, no one thought that a natural drug could be chemically modified to improve its action; tetracycline remains the drug of choice for tick-spread diseases such as Rocky Mountain spotted fever and Lyme disease. (1992)

William D. Coolidge (American: 1873–1974) VACUUM TUBE The "Coolidge tube" is actually an X-ray generator. Among his many other inventions was the modern tungsten-filament electric light. (1975)

Frederick G. Cottrell (American: 1877–1948) ELECTROSTATIC PRECIPITATOR Cottrell's invention uses high-voltage electricity to capture the particulates, including fly ash, dust, and droplets of acids or other chemicals, found in smoke from the burning of fossil fuels and many industrial processes; the tons of waste can then be removed from smoke instead of being spread around the countryside. (1992)

Raymond V. Damadian (American: 1936–) APPARATUS AND METHOD FOR DETECTING CANCER IN TISSUE Damadian was the first to realize that the nuclear magnetic resonance technique could be used on living creatures (it was already a success as a laboratory tool used by chemists) and that it could detect cancer cells. (1989)

John Deere (American: 1804–86) PLOW Anyone who grew up near a farm knows the name John Deere. His vastly improved plow was the start of his commercial success, and the company he founded still makes farm tools. (1989)

Lee De Forest (American: 1873–1961) AUDION AMPLIFIER Although he eventually acquired more than 300 patents related to radio, De Forest's invention of the triode was the key to modern radio and later developments in the amplification of signals. (1977)

Rudolf Diesel (German: 1858–1913) INTERNAL COMBUSTION ENGINE The pressure-ignited heat engine is still called the diesel engine. (1976)

Carl Djerassi (Austrian-American: 1923–) ORAL CONTRACEPTIVES A major influence on modern organic chemistry, Djerassi's research into the chemistry of steroids and his synthesis of antihistamines are two of his many contributions. (1978)

Herbert Henry Dow (Canadian-American: 1866–1930) BROMINE Besides new methods of extracting bromine and chlorine from naturally occurring salt deposits, Dow patented over 90 inventions and founded the Dow Chemical Company. (1983)

Charles Stark Draper (American: 1901–87) GYROSCOPIC EQUIPMENT Draper's gyroscopic stabilizer helped both antiaircraft guns and falling bombs hit their targets during World War II. Later he developed gyroscopic systems for air and marine navigation and for guided missiles. (1983)

Graham J. Durant (British-American: 1934–) CIMETIDINE (TAGAMET) With John C. Emmet and C. Robin Ganellin, Durant developed the major drug used to suppress acid in stomach and intestinal ulcers. Introduced in the United States in 1977, by 1980 Tagamet was the best-selling drug in America. (1990)

George Eastman (American: 1854–1932) METHOD AND APPARATUS FOR COATING PLATES FOR USE IN PHOTOGRAPHY Eastman developed the dry plate negative and transparent roll film for still cameras, and a motion picture film for use in the newly invented cinema. (1977)

Harold E. Edgerton (American: 1903–) STROBOSCOPE Edgerton created this device to produce flashes that would stop action in a photograph at regular intervals. (His classic photograph of the crown produced by a drop of milk falling into a bowl of milk dates from the 1930s.) He also contributed inventions to underwater photography. (1986)

Thomas Alva Edison (American: 1847–1931) ELECTRIC LAMP In addition to the carbon-filament electric lamp, Edison patented a phonograph, the mimeograph, the fluoroscope, and motion picture cameras and projectors. (1973)

Gertrude B. Elion (American: 1918–) DNA-BLOCKING DRUGS Crucial to cancer treatment and antiviral research. First woman elected to National Inventors Hall of Fame. (1991)

John C. Emmet (British: 1938–) CIMETIDINE (TAGAMET) (see Graham J. Durant) (1990)

John Ericsson (American: 1803–89) PROPELLOR Ericsson's invention offered a highly efficient, difficult to damage, and easily maintained means of propulsion that sped the transition from wind power to steam power in shipping. (1993)

Philo Taylor Farnsworth (American: 1906–71) TELEVISION SYSTEM Farnsworth patented many components of all-electronic television. He also worked on the electronic microscope, radar, the use of ultraviolet light for seeing in the dark, and nuclear fusion. (1984)

Enrico Fermi (Italian-American: 1901–54) NEUTRONIC REACTOR Fermi's nuclear reactor is the basis of nuclear power today. His many contributions to modern physics include basic theoretical work as well as experimental physics. (1976)

Henry Ford (American: 1863–1947) TRANSMISSION MECHANISM Best remembered for his innovative business practices, Ford also invented and patented numerous mechanisms used in automobiles. (1982)

Jay W. Forrester (American: 1918–) MULTI-COORDINATED DIGITAL INFORMATION STORAGE DEVICE A pioneer in the development of electronic computers after World War II, Forrester's main invention was the magnetic storage of information. Most computers today, from giant mainframes to lightweight laptops, still use magnetic storage to store data even when the computer has been shut off. (1979)

C. Robin Ganellin (British: 1934–) CIMETIDINE (TAGAMET) (see Graham J. Durant) (1990)

Charles P. Ginsburg (American: 1920–) VIDEOTAPE RECORDER The now ubiquitous VCR was originally developed by an engineering team led by Ginsburg. (1990)

Robert Hutchings Goddard (American: 1882–1945) CONTROL MECHANISM FOR ROCKET APPARATUS The father of American rocketry, Goddard devised successful rocket weapons and rocket-assisted take-off mechanisms for carrier-based airplanes for the military. He obtained 214 patents on various aspects of rocketry. (1979)

Charles Goodyear (American: 1800–1860) IMPROVEMENT IN INDIA-RUBBER FABRICS In 1844 Goodyear discovered vulcanization, a process to make rubber resistant to heat and cold. (1976)

Gordon Gould (American: 1920–) OPTICALLY PUMPED LASER AMPLIFIERS Gould envisioned the basic idea for the laser in 1957, but did not win his first patent until 1977. (1991)

Wilson Greatbatch (American: 1919–) MEDICAL CARDIAC PACEMAKER Greatbatch's pacemaker has helped millions of people with heart disease. He also invented batteries to keep the pacemaker running without adverse physical effects from the battery chemicals. (1986)

Leonard M. Greene (American: 1918–) AIRPLANE STALL WARNING DEVICE Patented in 1949. (1991)

Charles Martin Hall (American: 1863–1914) MANUFACTURE OF ALUMINUM In 1886, Hall developed a cheap method to make aluminum (then selling at $5 a pound). That same year, French metallurgist Paul-Louis-Toussaint Héroult discovered the same process. Patent litigation between the two was resolved amicably. (1976)

Robert N. Hall (American: 1919–) HIGH VOLTAGE HIGH POWER SEMICONDUCTOR PIN RECTIFIER This invention greatly reduced the waste of power and dangerous heat buildup that accompanies large-scale power transmission. Hall also invented the first semiconductor laser, which is now commonly found in CD players. (1994)

W.E. "Butch" Hanford (American: 1908–) POLYURETHANE This 1942 patent (won with Donald F. Holmes) remains basis for chemistry used in manufacture of all polyurethanes. (1991)

Elizabeth Lee Hazen (American: 1885–1975) NYSTATIN (with Rachel Fuller Brown), the world's first nontoxic antifungal antibiotic. Not only did this medicine cure many disfiguring and disabling skin, mouth, and throat infections, but it could be combined with other antibacterial drugs to balance their effects. Nystatin has been used to treat Dutch elm disease and to rescue water-damaged artworks from mold. (1994)

William R. Hewlett (American: 1913–) VARIABLE FREQUENCY OSCILLATION GENERATOR The first invention of one of the founders of Hewlett-Packard was the audio oscillator in 1939, a device for generating high-quality audio frequencies that could be used for many different purposes; among the first uses was production of special sounds for the Disney movie *Fantasia*. (1992)

René Alphonse Higonnet (French: 1902–83) PHOTO COMPOSING MACHINE Along with Louis Marius Moyroud, Higonnet developed (in 1946) the first machine to set type by recording the images of letters on film. Film composition became the standard way of setting type, replacing type set from metal for the next 40 years, after which it was replaced by electronic composition. (1985)

James Hillier (Canadian-American: 1915–) ELECTRON LENS CORRECTION DEVICE Although Hillier was not the first to make a microscope using electrons, his microscopes became the standard in the field. Electron microscopes can enlarge much smaller details than light microscopes because the wavelength of an electron is much smaller than the wavelength of a photon of visible light. (1980)

Herman Hollerith (American: 1869–1929) STORAGE AND PROCESSING OF NUMERICAL DATA Hollerith's punched cards and readers, developed for the 1890 U.S. Census, became the basis of modern data processing. (1990) (see also "Chronology of Information Processing")

Donald Fletcher Holmes (American: 1910–80) POLYURETHANE (see W.E. "Butch" Hanford). (1991)

Eugene J. Houdry (French: 1892–1962) CATALYTIC CRACKING OF PETROLEUM Houdry developed a process to make high-grade gasoline and airplane fuel from crude oil, as well as other catalytic processes and devices, including the basic catalytic converter used in automobile mufflers. (1990)

Percy F. Julian (American: 1899–1975) SYNTHESIS OF CORTISONE AND OTHER HORMONES Julian developed many important industrial products derived from soybeans before discovering that soybeans could be used as the basis for synthesizing cortisone, an important hormone with many medical applications. (1990)

Donald B. Keck (American: 1941–) FUSED SILICA OPTICAL WAVEGUIDE (See Robert D. Maurer) (1993)

Charles Franklin Kettering (American: 1875–1958) ENGINE STARTING DEVICES AND IGNITION SYSTEM Kettering's Delco company produced the self-starter for automobiles and a small generator for use in isolated farms. (1980)

Jack S. Kilby (American: 1923–) MINIATURIZED ELECTRONIC CIRCUITS A number of people worked on putting many transistors and other solid-state electronic devices on a single chip, but the monolithic integrated circuit that Kilby developed for Texas Instruments in 1959 was the beginning of the modern integrated circuit. (1982)

Willem J. Kolff (Dutch-American: 1911–) SOFT-SHELL MUSHROOM-SHAPED HEART Although the patent cited is for an early version of an artificial heart, Kolff's most important work was the development of the artificial-kidney dialysis machine. (1985)

Stephanie Kwolek (American: 1923–) KEVLAR This substance is five times as strong as steel and weighs 40 percent less than glass, making it ideal for use in aircraft construction, golf clubs and tennis rackets, fiber-optic cables, and perhaps most importantly, bullet-proof vests. (1995)

Edwin Herbert Land (American: 1909–91) PHOTOGRAPHIC PRODUCT COMPRISING A RUPTURABLE CONTAINER CARRYING A PHOTOGRAPHIC PROCESSING LIQUID Land's first success was the development and application of substances that polarize light. In addition to this and his celebrated instant Polaroid camera, he also made important contributions to the theory of color vision. (1977)

Irving Langmuir (American: 1881–1957) INCANDESCENT ELECTRIC LAMP In 1913 Langmuir realized that filling the original Edison-Swan lightbulb with a nonburning gas would result in a longer-lasting light. His later work on the chemistry of surfaces won him a Nobel Prize in 1932. (1989)

Ernest Orlando Lawrence (American: 1901–58) METHOD AND APPARATUS FOR THE ACCELERATION OF IONS Although Lawrence did not develop the very first particle accelerator (popularly known as an "atom smasher"), his 1930 cyclotron has been the basic pattern for the most successful and powerful machines of its kind ever since. (1982)

William P. Lear (American: 1902–78) AUTOMOBILE RADIO More widely known for his invention of the Learjet, Lear's first claim to fame was in radiotechnology, with a company that went on to become Motorola. His other inventions include the first navigational radio and the first radio direction finder. (1993)

Robert S. Ledley (American: 1926–) WHOLE-BODY CAT SCANNER Ledley's device for making

UTILITY PATENTS GRANTED, BY DATE OF GRANT, 1901–94

Utility patents, also known as patents for inventions, are issued for the invention of a new and useful process, machine, manufacture, or composition of matter, or a new and useful improvement. They permit their owners to prohibit others from making, using, or selling the invention for up to 17 years from the date of the grant. Utility patents represent about 90 percent of all patents. The other 10 percent are divided among *design patents,* issued for a new, original, and ornamental design for an article of manufacture, and which last 14 years; and *plant patents,* issued for a new and distinct, invented, or discovered asexually reproduced plant, lasting 17 years.

		U.S. ownership			Foreign ownership		
Year	**Total patents granted**	**Corporations**	**Government[1]**	**Individuals**	**Corporations**	**Government**	**Individuals**
1901	25,546	4,370	N.A.	20,896[2]	280	N.A.	(2)
1921	37,798	9,860	N.A.	27,098[2]	840	N.A.	(2)
1930	45,226	19,700	N.A.	23,726[2]	1,800	N.A.	(2)
1940	42,238	22,165	40	17,627[2]	2,406	N.A.	(2)
1950	43,040	21,782	622	18,960[2]	1,660	N.A.	(2)
1960	47,170	28,187	1,244	13,069[2]	4,670	N.A.	(2)
1965	62,857	37,158	1,540	16,063[2]	8,096	N.A.	(2)
1970	64,427	36,896	1,726	13,511[2]	12,294	N.A.	(2)
1980	61,819	27,640	1,237	9,956	18,874	254	3,858
1985	71,661	31,181	1,139	9,265	25,957	483	3,636
1990	90,364	36,091	983	12,544	35,547	423	4,776
1991	96,514	39,134	1,183	13,207	37,594	472	4,924
1992	97,444	40,308	1,161	12,751	38,239	463	4,522
1993	98,344	41,827	1,165	12,281	38,402	434	4,234
1994	101,676	44,043	1,251	12,805	38,788	296	4,493

1. Excludes patents issued to Alien Property Custodian until 1942. 2. Patents issued to foreign individuals before 1980 are included with U.S. individuals. **Source:** Department of Commerce, Patent and Trademark Office, *All Technologies Report,* March 1995.

three-dimensional images of living tissues quickly became an established medical technique for looking inside the human body. (1990)

Theodore Harold Maiman (American: 1927–) RUBY LASER SYSTEMS Although there has been much dispute about the invention of the laser, Maiman's ruby laser was the first to be recognized worldwide and to be commercially successful. (1984)

Guglielmo Marconi (Italian: 1874–1937) TRANSMITTING ELECTRICAL SIGNALS Marconi's patent for using radio waves to carry coded messages is best known as wireless telegraphy. (1975)

Robert D. Maurer (American: 1924–) FUSED SILICA OPTICAL WAVEGUIDE (with Donald B. Keck and Peter C. Schultz) This optical fiber helped launch the information age: It carries 65,000 times more information than copper wire 30 to 50 times farther without boosting the signal. (1993)

Cyrus McCormick (American: 1809–84) REAPER McCormick's machine for harvesting grain (patented in 1834) and other inventions revolutionized American agriculture. (1976)

Ottmar Mergenthaler (German-American: 1854–99) MACHINE FOR PRODUCING PRINTING BARS Mergenthaler's invention, known as the Linotype, was the first major improvement in printing since Gutenberg's movable type in the 15th century. This machine, which is controlled by a keyboard, casts individual lines of type from melted lead. (1982)

Irving Millman (American: 1923–) HEPATITIS B VACCINE (See Baruch S. Blumberg) (1993)

Samuel F.B. Morse (American: 1791–1872) TELEGRAPH SIGNALS Morse developed the first commercially successful telegraph. Joseph Henry was the genius behind the electronics, but Morse and his dot-dash code made instantaneous long-distance communications possible. (1975)

Andrew J. Moyer (American: 1899–1959) METHOD FOR PRODUCTION OF PENICILLIN Moyer, a microbiologist at the U.S. Department of Agriculture's Northern Regional Research Laboratory in Peoria, Ill., developed a way of producing penicillin in bulk during World War II. The basic method is still used in manufacture of antibiotics and other substances produced by microorganisms. (1987)

Louis Marius Moyroud (French: 1914–) PHOTO COMPOSING MACHINE (see René Alphonse Higonnet.) (1985)

Robert N. Noyce (American: 1927–90) SEMICONDUCTOR DEVICE-AND-LEAD STRUCTURE Noyce was at the center of development for two important semiconductor producers, the Fairchild and Intel corporations. Intel today makes the most widely used microprocessor chips for personal computers, those at the heart of various IBM models and their clones. (1983)

Kenneth H. Olsen (American: 1926–) IMPROVED MAGNETIC CORE MEMORY Olsen founded Digital Equipment Corp. to manufacture computers based on his new memory devices; he has also contributed extensively to the development of the minicomputer. (1990)

Elisha Graves Otis (American: 1811–61) IMPROVEMENT IN HOISTING APPARATUS Otis devised the safety elevator in 1853, when his employer asked him to build a hoist to lift heavy equipment. Eight years later Otis installed the first passenger elevators. (1988)

Nikolaus August Otto (German: 1832–91) GAS MOTOR ENGINE Otto's four-stroke engine of 1876 is the basis of the modern internal combustion engine. It ran on compressed natural gas instead of gasoline (a development pioneered by Gottlieb Daimler and Wilhelm Maybach in 1889). (1981)

Louis W. Parker (Hungarian-American: 1906–) TELEVISION RECEIVER Parker invented both the basic type of television receiver in common use today, and the type of color television transmission and reception that is most commonly used. (1988)

John T. Parsons (American: 1913–) NUMERICAL CONTROL OF MACHINE TOOLS This 1958 patent introduced automation to manufacturing and design and provided machines that can mill steel with an accuracy of one-tenth the thickness of newsprint. (1993)

Louis Pasteur (French: 1822–95) BREWING OF BEER AND ALE Pasteur's work on beer and ale is generally considered unsuccessful, but he invented several vaccines, and he developed pasteurization, the heating process that protects beverages and food from microbe contamination. (1978)

Charles J. Plank (American: 1915–) CATALYTIC CRACKING OF HYDROCARBONS WITH A CRYSTALLINE ZEOLITE CATALYST COMPOSITE Along with Edward J. Rosinski, Plank discovered in the early 1960s that zeolites (various aluminum silicates, a fairly common kind of mineral) could be used to improve the production of gasoline and other petroleum products. (1979)

Roy J. Plunkett (American: 1910–94) TETRAFLUOROETHYLENE POLYMERS In 1938 Plunkett discovered the tetrafluoroethylene polymer known as Teflon. He later developed many of the hydrofluorocarbons (freons) since found to be eroding the ozone layer. (1985)

Robert H. Rines (American: 1922–) CONTRIBUTIONS TO HIGH RESOLUTION IMAGE-SCANNING RADAR Dr. Rines's patents were the basis for almost all the high-definition radar used to provide the armed forces with early warning radar during the Persian Gulf War. In peacetime, his inventions have been used in underwater archaeology such as locating the *Titanic* and the *Bismarck.* (1994)

Heinrich Rohrer (Swiss: 1933–) SCANNING TUNNELING MICROSCOPE (See Gerd Karl Binnig) (1994)

Edward J. Rosinski (American: 1921–) CATALYTIC CRACKING OF HYDROCARBONS WITH A CRYSTALLINE ZEOLITE CATALYST COMPOSITE (see Charles J. Plank) (1979)

Benjamin A. Rubin (American: 1917–) BIFURCATED VACCINATION NEEDLE Rubin's needle enabled easy use of small amounts of smallpox vaccine, making it possible for vaccine supplies to be stretched and helping the World Health Organization to declare that smallpox as a disease had been eliminated by May 8, 1980. (1992)

Lewis Hastings Sarett (American: 1917–) THE PROCESS OF TREATING PREGNENE COMPOUNDS In 1944 Sarett found a way to produce cortisone as an artificial steroid. By 1949 he and his collaborators had learned to make cortisone from simple inorganic chemicals. Cortisone and related steroids are used for medical treatment of conditions ranging from psoriasis to arthritis. (1980)

Peter C. Schultz (American: 1942–) FUSED SILICA OPTICAL WAVEGUIDE (see Robert D. Maurer) (1993)
Robert J. Seiwald (American: 1925–) FITC (see Joseph H. Burckhalter) (1995)
Waldo Semon (American: 1898–) PVC PLASTISOLS Semon accidentally discovered the first synthetic rubber that bounces. It went on to become the world's second-best-selling plastic and a $30 billion industry. (1995)
John C. Sheehan (American: 1915–92) SEMI-SYNTHETIC PENICILLIN Sheehan's research developed a synthetic pencillin that could be produced cheaply and quickly, in contrast with the slow and expensive natural way of producing it. (1995)
William Bradford Shockley (English-American: 1910–89) TRANSISTOR (see John Bardeen) (1974)
Igor I. Sikorsky (Russian-American: 1889–1972) HELICOPTER CONTROLS Sikorsky designed and built many successful airplanes, but in 1931 he made a critical breakthrough in helicopter design. His continued developments led to the helicopter of today. (1987)
Elmer A. Sperry (American: 1860–1930) SHIP'S GYROSCOPIC COMPASS Patented in 1917. (1991)
William Stanley (American: 1858–1916) ELECTRIC TRANSFORMER This invention allowed for the long-distance transmission of alternating current (AC), which was far less dangerous than transmitting direct current (DC) at very high voltages. (1995)
Charles Proteus Steinmetz (German-American: 1865–1923) SYSTEM OF ELECTRICAL DISTRIBUTION Steinmetz was an important theoretician and inventor whose most significant work was in developing the theory of alternating current that made power grids possible. Among his inventions was a machine that produced "lightning in the laboratory." (1977)
George R. Stibitz (American: 1904–) COMPLEX COMPUTER Stibitz was one of several scientists who developed electromechanical computers in the late 1930s and during World War II. His innovations at Bell Telephone Laboratories and in the U.S. Office of Scientific Research and Development include floating decimal arithmetic and taped computer programs. (1983)
Donalee L. Tabern (American: 1900–1974) THIOBARBITURIC ACID DERIVATIVES Along with Ernest H. Volwiler, Tabern in 1936 discovered Pentothal, anesthetic of choice for short surgical procedures. Tabern later introduced therapeutic use of radioactive chemicals. (1986)
Nikola Tesla (Croatian-American: 1857–1943) ELECTRO-MAGNETIC MOTOR Tesla's induction motor was simpler than previous electric motors and was powered by alternating current (AC), which can be distributed more easily over a long distance than direct current (DC). (1975)
Max Tishler (American: 1906–) RIBOFLAVIN AND SULFAQUINOXALINE In the late 1930s, Tishler developed an economical method for synthesizing riboflavin—vitamin B_2. Later he and his coworkers developed a way to produce sulfaquinoxaline (an antibiotic that prevents and cures a disease common in poultry) commercially. (1982)
Charles Hard Townes (American: 1915–) MASERS The maser, which preceded the better-known laser, is essentially a laser that works at microwave wavelengths instead of at the shorter wavelength of visible light. Masers are used in many applications. Solely responsible for the maser, Townes also contributed to the development of the laser. (1976)
Ernest H. Volwiler (American: 1893–1992) THIOBARBITURIC ACID DERIVATIVES (see Donalee L. Tabern) (1986)
An Wang (Chinese-American: 1920–90) MAGNETIC PULSE CONTROLLING DEVICE Although best known for his state-of-the-art word processor of the 1960s and 1970s, Wang contributed many fundamental ideas to the development of electronic computers, including the principle on which magnetic core memory is built. (1988)
George Westinghouse (American: 1846–1914) STEAM-POWERED BRAKE DEVICES In 1869 Westinghouse patented an air brake for locomotives, his most important contribution to railroad safety. His later work on signals and switches led him to form the Westinghouse Electric Co. in 1884. (1989)
Eli Whitney (American: 1765–1825) COTTON GIN By making it possible to remove seeds from cotton mechanically, the gin made large-scale cotton farming possible. Whitney also introduced interchangeable parts, the beginning of mass production. (1974)
Robert R. Williams (American: 1886–1965) ISOLATION OF VITAMIN B_1 (THIAMINE) He later synthesized thiamine for commercial production in 1935. (1991)
Orville Wright (American: 1871–1948) & **Wilbur Wright** (American: 1867–1912) FLYING MACHINE The Wright brothers not only invented the first airplane in 1903, they also popularized, manufactured, and sold the new machines. (1975)
Vladimir Kosma Zworykin (Russian-American: 1889–1982) CATHODE RAY TUBE The cathode ray tube that Zworykin invented in 1928 is the kinescope, the basic picture tube used in modern television. Ten years later he developed the iconoscope, the first practical television camera. He also contributed to the development of the electron microscope. (1977)

Computers

(For information on multimedia, CD-ROMs, and the Internet, see Part II: "The Media.")

A computer is a machine for storing and processing information. It converts any information that it receives into a binary code—a string of signals, in which each signal is either *1* or *0*. The basic working component of a computer is a series of switches, each of which can be set either "off" or "on" and thus represent 1 or 0 in the binary system. The history of computers is, to some extent, a history of the switching devices that have been used to represent 1 and 0. Early computers were based on mechanical switches; computers based on electronic switches proved much faster. These fall into three main categories: vacuum tubes, transistors, and integrated circuits.

The relative size and power of these three types are so disparate that it is almost impossible to compare them; there is no single scale against which they can be measured. In 1946 the ENIAC (Electronic Numerical Integrator and Calculator)—which occupied 2,000 square feet, weighed 50 tons, and used 18,000 vacuum tubes—could perform about 10,000 multiplications per second and had an internal memory capacity of 200 decimal digits, or about 20 words. By 1992 a silicon chip measuring a quarter of an inch across could outperform ENIAC by a factor of about one million and had a memory capable of storing 800,000 words. As one computer analyst calculated, comparable efficiencies in car manufacturing would have yielded a Rolls Royce costing $1.00 and getting 1 million mpg.

CHRONOLOGY OF INFORMATION PROCESSING

B.C.

500 Bead-and-wire abacus in use in Egypt.

A.D.

200 Computing trays in use in China and Japan.

1340 Double-entry bookkeeping originates in Lombardy.

c. 1621 Mathematician William Oughtred (English: 1574–1660) invents slide rule, which he first describes in 1632.

1642 Blaise Pascal (French: 1623–62) invents "pascaline"—the first calculating machine, capable of addition and subtraction.

1666 Gottfried Wilhelm Leibniz (German: 1646–1716) argues that all reasoning is reducible to an ordered combination of elements—the first principle of computer theory.

1679 Leibniz perfects binary system of notation that eventually will be used by all computers; also develops improved version of pascaline, capable of multiplication and division.

1801 Joseph-Marie Jacquard (French: 1752–1834) uses punched cards to control operation of his mechanical loom—precursor of cards used in early data-storage systems.

1822 Charles Babbage (English: 1792–1871) designs and builds prototype of "Difference Engine" for calculating logarithms.

1833 Babbage designs "Analytical Engine," a computing machine featuring printed card input, memory, and printed output, and capable of being programmed to perform different tasks. Forerunner of modern computer, it never goes beyond design stage.

1847 George Boole (English: 1815–64) publishes *Mathematical Analysis of Logic*, which treats logic as a branch of mathematics (Boolean Algebra).

1853 Pehr Georg Scheutz and his son Edvard G.R. Scheutz (Swedish: 1785–1873; 1821–81) complete version of Babbage's Difference Engine. One client is British government, which uses Scheutz engine to calculate life expectancy tables.

1886 William S. Burroughs (American: 1855–98) develops first commercially successful mechanical adding machine.

1887 U.S. Census Bureau holds competition for device to speed up computation of census information; Herman Hollerith (American: 1860–1929) designs winning tabulating machine. Later develops mechanical sorting machine (1896). His Tabulating Machine Co. (founded 1911) becomes IBM in 1924.

1890 Hollerith's electromechanical machine, using perforated cards, processes U.S. Census results in six weeks—one-third the time taken in 1880.

1894 Otto Steiger develops "Millionaire," the first commercially successful machine capable of direct multiplication, as opposed to multiplication by repeated addition. Nearly 5,000 sold between 1894 and 1935.

1931 Vannevar Bush (American: 1890–1974) completes "differential analyser," first computing machine to use electronic components (vacuum tubes in which values could be stored as voltages).

1936 Mathematician Alan M. Turing (English: 1912–54) publishes "On Computable Numbers," which describes hypothetical computer with infinite storage capacity, capable of performing any conceivable calculation.

1937 John V. Atanasoff (American: 1903–) starts work on first electronic computer.

1938 Konrad Zuse (German: 1910–) builds "Z1," the first computing machine to use binary, instead of decimal, method of operation. Other features include keyboard to input information and system of electric bulbs to signal results of calculations.

1939 Atanasoff and Clifford Berry complete ABC device, first digital computer.

1940 Zuse's Z2 machine introduces electromagnetic relays (as used in telephone switching gear) to store numbers. (Relays were capable of switching, i.e., calculating, five times per second.)

First Generation: Vacuum Tubes

1943 British government uses first fully electronic computer to crack German military codes. Designed by Turing, "Colossus" uses 2,000 vacuum tubes to perform calculations and digest information at rate of 5,000 characters per second.

1944 Completion of "Harvard Mark I," designed by Howard H. Aiken (American: 1900–1973) and built by IBM. Vast, over 50 ft. long, it was obsolete almost immediately because it used electromagnetic relays rather than vacuum tubes.

1946 At press conference at University of Pennsylvania, the ENIAC (Electronic Numerical Integrator and Calculator) multiplies five-digit number by itself 5,000 times in half a second. Designed by J. Presper Eckert, Jr. (American: 1919–) and John W. Mauchly (American: 1907–80) to calculate ballistic trajectories, ENIAC occupies 2,000 sq. ft., weighs 50 tons, uses 18,000 vacuum tubes, and can store about 20 words in its memory.
John von Neumann (Hungarian-American: 1903–57) publishes paper suggesting that instructions given to computer—"programs"—can themselves be stored by computer in numerical form. First use of term *bit* to mean binary digit.

1948 "Mark I," designed by Tom Kilburn (English: 1921–) and Sir Frederic C. Williams (English: 1911–77) at Manchester University, England, is first computer to utilize von Neumann's concept of stored programs. It can thus be "programmed" to perform infinite variety of functions.
John Bardeen (American: 1908–91), Walter H. Brattain (American: 1902–87), and William B. Shockley (English-American: 1910–89) invent the transistor; it will eventually replace vacuum tube and make computers faster and more reliable.
IBM, Bell Telephone, and Sperry-Rand each begin production of commercial computers.
First chess-playing computer built at M.I.T.

1950 Eckert and Mauchly's EDVAC (*E*lectronic *D*iscrete *V*ariable *A*utomatic *C*omputer) is first to use magnetic disks for storage.

1951 Lyons Tea Shop Co. in England uses specially designed computer ("LEO") to perform routine administrative functions.
Eckert and Mauchly's UNIVAC (*Univ*ersal *A*utomatic *C*omputer) is installed at U.S. Bureau of Census. UNIVAC uses magnetic tape for input and becomes first commercially successful machine, selling over 50 models.
Wang Laboratories founded in Boston.

1952 One hour after polls close, CBS television network uses UNIVAC to predict Eisenhower's landslide victory in U.S. presidential election. Prediction was based on less than 10 percent of the votes.

1953 First high-speed printer linked to a computer.
IBM introduces its first stored-program computer, the vacuum-tube–based "701."

1956 First use of term *artificial intelligence*.

Second Generation: Transistors

1958 Control Data Corp. introduces first fully transistorized computer, the CDC 1604, designed by Seymour Cray (American: 1925–).
Jack St.C. Kilby (American: 1923–) of Texas Instruments and Robert Noyce (American: 1927–90) of Intel Corp. independently produce first integrated circuits.

1959 First commercially marketed program.
IBM markets its first transistorized computers, the 1620 and 1790.

1960 The PDP-1, developed by Digital Equipment Corp., is the first commercial computer to use a keyboard and monitor instead of punched cards.
Introduction of removable magnetic disks for data storage.

Third Generation: Integrated Circuits

1965 IBM markets its first integrated-circuit based computer, the 360.
Digital Equipment Corp. markets the first minicomputer, the PDP-8.

1968 Stanley Kubrick's (American: 1928–) *2001: A Space Odyssey* stars supercomputer called "Hal," which critics complain is the most "human" character in film.

1969 Graduate student Alan Kay, later to become top designer with Apple Computer Co., writes doctoral thesis describing hypothetical "personal computer."
First international conference on artificial intelligence.

1970 Lexitron introduces first word processor, a computer designed specifically to handle written text. It features a cathode ray tube (CRT) terminal, as used in television sets, to display information.
Floppy disk is introduced for data storage.

1971 Intel Corp. announces first microprocessor, several integrated circuits contained on one silicon chip.
First electronic pocket calculator produced by Texas Instruments; it weighs about 2½ lbs. and costs about $150.

1973 IBM introduces "Winchester" disc drive, a sealed storage module containing several rotating magnetic discs.
Introduction of "bit-mapped" monitor capable of high-resolution graphics display.
Xerox markets first hand-held "mouse," a time-saving device for giving commands to computer.
Intel introduces 8080 microprocessor, which will become the central processing unit (CPU) of several microcomputers.

1975 First personal computer, the MITS Altair 8800, is marketed in kit form, with memory capacity of 256 bytes.
Cray Research (founded 1972) announces the Cray-1 supercomputer, capable of 100 million operations per second.

1976 Apple Computer Co. founded by Stephen Wozniak and Steven Jobs (American: 1955–) in the Wozniak family garage; first Apple "boards" (self-assembly personal computer kits) go on sale.

1977 Apple markets Apple II—the first widely accepted personal computer. Commodore and Tandy also begin to sell personal computers.
Microsoft Corp. is founded to produce microcomputer operating systems—programs allowing a central processing unit to control and coordinate the different elements of computer's hardware. Microsoft systems used for Radio Shack TRS-80 and Altair PC.

1978 Hayes Microcomputer Products introduces Micromodem 100, the first microcomputer-compatible modem.

1979 Micropro International releases WordStar, popular word-processing program for personal computers.

WordPerfect Corp., producers of rival WordPerfect program, begins operation.

1980 Microsoft adapts UNIX (an operating system for mainframe and minicomputers) for use with microcomputers; paves way for personal computers to begin performing tasks associated with larger machines.

1981 IBM introduces its first personal computer, the IBM PC. Using operating system called PC-DOS, developed by Microsoft, it almost immediately becomes the industry standard.

First fully portable computer, the Osborne 1, is introduced.

Xerox markets the Star, a mouse-driven computer that prefigures many features of Apple Macintosh.

Ashton-Tate introduces dBASE II, the first popular database program for microcomputers.

1982 Microsoft introduces MS-DOS, a version of the PC-DOS operating system designed for IBM PC; allows other manufacturers to produce copies ("clones") of the IBM machine.

Compaq announces its first portable computer (IBM-compatible).

1983 Apple introduces Apple IIe and "Lisa," an important step toward development of the Macintosh.

IBM announces PC Junior, which is commercially unsuccessful.

Radio Shack markets Model 100 portable, weighing just 4 lbs.

First IBM-compatible "laptop" computer introduced by Gavilan Corp.

Lotus Development Corp. introduces 1–2–3, a best-selling program for managing business spreadsheets.

Introduction of optical (laser-readable) storage disks.

1984 Apple introduces Macintosh. With list price of $2,495, it includes Apple's first "Mac" software programs, MacWrite (for text) and MacPaint (for graphics). Fifty thousand are sold within three months.

IBM markets the PC AT (Advanced Technology) model; features include Enhanced Graphics Adapter (EGA) for improved screen resolution.

1985 Apple's LaserWriter printer and Aldus Corp.'s PageMaker program usher in age of desktop publishing—electronic, rather than mechanical, production of documents and books.

Introduction of erasable optical storage disks.

Voice-data entry becomes feasible.

Toshiba markets first widely used laptop computer.

Cray 2 supercomputer is capable of 1.2 billion operations per second.

1986 IBM announces OS/2, a new operating system that allows personal computers to run several programs simultaneously (called multitasking).

1987 Apple introduces Macintosh SE and Macintosh II. IBM introduces Personal System/2 (PS/2), features of which include high-resolution VGA (Video Graphics Array) display.

1988 Computer security becomes an urgent issue when a "worm" program penetrates thousands of systems on Internet information network.

Steven Jobs, now with Next, Inc., unveils "computer workstation," featuring an optical disk drive capable of storing 250 times as much data as floppy disks used by IBM and Apple.

Motorola announces new microprocessor, the 88000, a 32-bit RISC (Reduced Instruction Set Computer) chip.

First IBM PS/2 "clones" announced by rival manufacturers.

Compaq markets SLT/286, the first laptop with VGA display.

IBM and Sears launch Prodigy, an on-line service enabling subscribers with a computer and modem to access a central information bank.

Parallel processing technique introduced that utilizes many inexpensive microprocessors to perform a large number of operations simultaneously.

1989 Intel announces the iPSC/860 chip, containing one million transistors; designed to give a microcomputer the power and speed normally associated with supercomputers.

IBM announces production of commercial quantities of four-megabyte chips.

First portable computers with color liquid crystal displays (LCDs) announced.

1991 The Thinking Machines Inc. CM-200 massively parallel supercomputer can perform 9.03 billion calculations per second.

1993 Intel begins shipping the Pentium chip with 3.1 million transistors on it; it operates twice as fast as the best previous Intel chip for personal computers.

Fujitsu in Japan begins to market a 256-megabit memory chip.

1994 Apple introduces the first personal computers to use the Power PC RISC Chip.

A GLOSSARY OF COMPUTER TERMS

Artificial intelligence (AI) The underlying assumption of artificial intelligence is that machines can be programmed to perform human functions. The primary AI functions are *expert systems,* programs that contain a body of knowledge (contributed by experts) that the machine can draw on to solve specific types of problems; *natural language interfaces* that make it possible for users to access a computer's database with commands entered in ordinary written or spoken language (for example, "Give me a list of countries bordering the Atlantic Ocean"); *speech recognition, speech synthesis,* and *optical recognition* systems that enable computers to understand spoken commands, make speech, and interpret visible images (such as bar codes on retail goods); and *robotics,* machines whose design and systems enable them to imitate complex "eye-hand" coordination of humans.

ASCII (American Standard Code for Information Exchange) Computers work with numbers, not letters. ASCII is the numerical code used by personal computers *(microcomputers).* While many programs also use special codes of their own, data from one computer to another are best transmitted in "pure ASCII."

Baud rate A transmission rate used in sending data from one computer to another, with a baud approximately equal to one *bit* per second. Most *modems* use 1,200, 2,400, or 9,600 baud. Rates must be the same between modems for data to be transmitted.

Bit In the binary system, a bit is either of the digits *0* or *1.* The bit (for *bi*nary dig*it*) is the basic unit for storing data, with "off" representing 0 and "on" representing 1.

Buffer Any memory location where data can be stored temporarily while the computer is doing something else; specifically, a memory location in the computer, in a printer, or in a separate storage device *(peripheral)* that stores a file being printed so that the computer is not tied up waiting for the printing to finish.

Bug An error in a *software* program or in the *hardware.*

Byte A group of eight *bits* that together represent one character, whether alphabetic, numeric, or otherwise. A byte is the smallest accessible unit in a computer's memory.

Cathode ray tube (CRT) The display device, or *monitor,* similar to a television screen, used with most desktop computers.

CD-ROM A Compact Disc ("CD") used as a Read-Only-Memory ("ROM"). The CD, essentially the same as an audio CD, stores data in a form readable by a laser, resulting in a storage device of great capacity and quick accessibility.

Central processing unit (CPU) The group of circuits that directs the entire computer system by (1) interpreting and executing *program* instruction and (2) coordinating the interaction of input, output, and storage devices.

Complex Instruction Set chip See "Reduced Instruction Set Computer chip."

Computer-aided design (CAD), engineering (CAE) and **manufacturing (CAM)** Systems that automate many complex tasks such as drafting, computation, or repetitive actions. CAM is closely related to *robotics* (see "Artificial intelligence").

Cursor A marker on the computer display that shows which region of the screen is active.

Database Either a *program* for arranging facts in the computer and retrieving them (the computer equivalent of a filing system) or a *file* set up by such a system. Often databases are central files that can be accessed by a *modem* for a fee.

Desktop publishing The electronic, rather than mechanical, production of books and documents. A combination of *hardware* (laser printers capable of printing a range of type sizes and styles) and *software* (programs such as Aldus's PageMaker and Xerox's Ventura) enables the writer to design, typeset, and print his or her own work.

Disk drive A mechanism for retrieving information stored on a magnetic disk. The drive rotates the disk at high speed and "reads" the data with a magnetic head similar to those used in tape recorders.

COMPUTER LANGUAGES

Name	Source of name	Introduced	Creators	Uses
ADA	For Lady Ada Lovelace, who wrote programs for Charles Babbage's "analytical engine"	1979	Team headed by Jean Ichbiah of Honeywell	Based on Pascal; devised to manage complex computing activities needed by U.S. Army, Navy, and Air Force.
Algol	*Algo*rithmic *L*anguage	1960	International committee	Designed for solving math problems; both readable and practical, forerunner of many other languages, including Pascal.
APL	*A P*rogramming *L*anguage	1961	Kenneth Iverson of IBM	First used for expressing problems in applied mathematics because it can handle large numbers easily; now useful to airlines for complex routing and scheduling.
BASIC	*B*eginners *A*ll-purpose *S*ymbolic *I*nstruction *C*ode	1965	John Kemeny and Thomas Kurtz of Dartmouth College	Most popular and versatile of all computer languages; most often used as introduction to computing.
C	Successor to B language (Bell Computer Programming Language/BCPL)	1974	Dennis Ritchie at Bell Laboratories	Unusually flexible language; in wide use because programs are easily transferable between types of computers.
COBOL	*Co*mmon *B*usiness *O*riented *L*anguage	1959	Grace Murray Hopper and committee of computer manufacturers	Principal language for large-scale data processing in government, banking, and insurance.
Forth	*Fourth* generation language	1970	Charles Moore of National Radio Astronomy Observatory	Originally invented to control telescope at Kitts Peak Observatory, Ariz.; has been adapted for many mini- and microcomputer uses, including robotics and arcade games.
FORTRAN	*For*mula *Tran*slator	1956	John Backus and team at IBM	Standard computer language for scientists and mathematicians; first designed for large computers, now used by microcomputers for many business calculations.
LISP	*Lis*t *P*rocessing	1956	John McCarthy at M.I.T.	Used primarily for research in artificial intelligence; not mathematical, but composed of words.
Logo	From Greek *logos,* meaning "word"	late 1960s	Seymour Papert and others at M.I.T.	A learning language, simple enough for a child to program, but complex enough to use in higher education.
Pascal	For Blaise Pascal, French mathematician and inventor of early computing device	1971	Niklaus Wirth of the Swiss Federal Institute of Technology	Noted for its simplicity, was devised as a tool for teaching but later adapted to many other uses; is becoming most popular language for application software.
PILOT	*P*rogrammed *I*nquiry, *L*earning *o*r *T*eaching	1969	University of California at San Francisco	First language for computer-aided instruction; can be used by teachers with little computer experience to devise learning programs.
PL/1	*P*rogramming *L*anguage One	1964	Team at IBM	Designed by IBM to run its mainframe computer; rich in useful features, but more difficult to master than other languages.

File Any group of data treated as a single entity by the computer, such as a word processor document, a *program,* or a *database*.

Floppy disk A thin, flexible magnetic disk encased in a protective jacket. On the disk's surface are a number of "tracks" on which data may be recorded in the form of magnetic spots.

Graphical user interface (GUI) A system that uses icons (symbols) seen on the screen to represent available functions. These icons are generally manipulated by a mouse and/or a keyboard. This approach contrasts with the more traditional method of using typed commands.

Hard disk A sealed cartridge containing magnetic storage disk(s) that holds much more memory—typically 20 to 200 *megabytes*—than *floppy disks*. Usually a hard disk is built into the computer, but it can be a *peripheral*.

Hardware The physical equipment, as opposed to the *programs* and procedures, used in data processing. It covers not only computers themselves but also *peripherals* (see "Software").

Integrated circuit An entire electronic circuit contained on one piece of material. Originally, electronic components (transistors, capacitors, etc.) were placed on a metal chassis and wired together. The first integrated circuit began with a single board (originally plastic), onto which strips of conducting material were sprayed. Electronic components could then be inserted directly onto the board (see "Silicon chip").

Kilobyte (K) A unit of measurement for storage capacity; equivalent to 1,024 *bytes,* but often rounded to 1,000 (see "Megabyte").

Laptop A portable *microcomputer* small enough to operate in one's lap (for example, on a commuter train or an airplane). Generally a laptop weighs less than 15 pounds and uses a *liquid crystal display* rather than a *cathode ray tube*.

Liquid crystal display (LCD) A type of flat-panel display monitor used in *portable computers*.

Local area networks (LANs) Systems that allow users to connect *PCs* to one another or to *minicomputers* or *mainframes*.

Mainframe computer Generally the largest, fastest, and most expensive kind of computer, usually costing millions of dollars and requiring special cooling. Mainframe computers can accommodate hundreds of simultaneous users and normally are run around the clock; typically they are owned by large companies (see "Microcomputer"; "Minicomputer"; "Supercomputer").

Massively parallel A form of computer architecture that uses hundreds or thousands of inexpensive *microprocessors* to perform many operations simultaneously.

Megabyte (M) A unit of measurement for storage capacity equivalent to one million *bytes*.

Menu-driven A *program* that uses a number of "menus," or lists of possible activities from which the operator chooses in order to activate the appropriate commands. This is the alternative to a command-driven program, for which the operator must remember a number of commands in order to tell the computer what to do.

Microcomputer Generally the smallest and least expensive kind of computer, usually costing hundreds or thousands of dollars and small enough to fit on a desktop. The heart of the microcomputer is the *microprocessor* (see "Mainframe computer"; "Minicomputer").

Microprocessor A complete *central processing unit* assembled on one single *silicon chip*.

Minicomputer A small computer, usually used by medium-size or smaller businesses. Minicomputers often perform scientific or industrial tasks, cost tens or hundreds of thousands of dollars, and are housed in large cabinets (see "Mainframe computer"; "Microcomputer").

MIPS (million instructions per second) A measure of computer processing speed.

Modem (modulator-demodulator) A device capable of converting a digital (computer-compatible) signal to an analog signal, which can be transmitted via a telephone line, reconverted, and then "read" by another computer.

Monitor The display device on a computer, similar to a television screen.

Mouse A small box connected by cable to a computer and featuring one or more button-style switches. When moved around a desk, the mouse causes a symbol on the computer screen to make corresponding movements. By selecting items on the screen and pressing a button on the mouse, the user can perform certain functions much more quickly than by typing commands on the keyboard.

Network An interconnected group of computers that can exchange information or work together on different parts of the same problem.

Notebook A type of full-function *portable computer* that uses miniaturized components, weighs about 4–6 pounds, and can be carried in a briefcase.

Operating system A sequence of programming codes that instructs a computer about its various parts and peripherals and how to operate them. Operating systems deal only with the workings of the *hardware* and are separate from *software* programs.

Peripheral A device connected to the computer that provides communication or auxiliary functions. There are three types of peripherals: input devices, such as keyboards; output devices, such as *monitors* and printers; and storage devices, such as magnetic discs.

Personal computer A *microcomputer* used by an individual at home or in the office.

Portable computer A *personal computer* with all the functions of a desktop computer but which has a full-size keyboard in the same physical unit as the display and some type of mass storage device. (See also *"Laptop"; "Notebook."*)

Program As a noun, a prepared set of instructions for the computer, often with provisions for the operator to choose among various options. As a verb, to create such a set of instructions.

Random access memory (RAM) A temporary storage space in which data may be held on a *chip* rather than being stored on disk or tape. The contents of RAM may be accessed or altered at any time during a session, but will be lost when the computer is turned off (see "Read-only memory").

Read-only memory (ROM) A type of *chip* memory, the contents of which have been permanently recorded in a computer by the manufacturer and cannot be altered by the user (see "Random access memory").

RISC chip Reduced Instruction Set Computer chip, such as the Apple-IBM Power PC chip, which gains speed by using fewer instructions than the more familiar Complex Instruction Set chip.

Silicon chip A special kind of *integrated circuit* in which traditional electronic components have been replaced by chemicals. Tiny wafers (chips) of silicon are covered with layers of chemicals, each of which acts as an electrical component (a *transistor,* capacitor, etc.). The first chips, made in the early 1960s, contained two transistors. By 1992 chips existed that contained 64 million transistors. The industry standard is one million transistors per chip.

Software The *programs* and procedures, as opposed to the physical equipment, used in data processing (see "Hardware").

Spreadsheet A *program,* such as Lotus 1–2–3, that performs mathematical operations on numbers arranged in large arrays; used mainly for accounting and other record keeping.

Supercomputer The fastest of the *mainframe* class of computers, usually used for complex scientific calculations.

Transistor A small piece of semiconducting material (material that conducts electricity better than, say, wood but not as well as metal). Flows of electrons within the transistor can be controlled, enabling it to act as an electronic "switching" device. In other words, it can record information in the form of an "on" or an "off" signal. Early transistors were about one-hundredth the size of *vacuum tubes,* required very little energy, and generated no heat.

Vacuum tube A glass tube, shaped like a light bulb, that contains a heating element that pumps electrons through a vacuum. In the earliest computers, the status of the electrical current—"on" or "off"—was used as a means of storing information. Two major drawbacks of the vacuum tube were that it generated excessive heat and used large amounts of energy.

Window A portion of the screen display used to view simultaneously a different part of the file in use or a part of a different file than the one in use.

Workstation High-performance *microcomputers* with advanced graphics capabilities designed for use by scientists and engineers.

STANDARD WEIGHTS & MEASURES

SYSTEMS OF MEASUREMENT

There are two measurement systems that are widely used. Most of the world uses a system known as the metric system, or the International System (abbreviated SI from *Système internationale,* its name in French). The United States continues to use a system called U.S. customary measure which derives from (and differs from) the British imperial system. From time to time, our government has taken steps to change from the customary system to the International System, but these efforts have failed. Metric measure is legal in the United States, but nearly everyone continues to use the customary system in everyday use. The International System is generally used in scientific pursuits and increasingly in international trade.

The following tables show first the U.S. customary system, then the International System, and finally some important conversion factors between the two.

Length or Distance

U.S. customary system

1 foot (ft.) = 12 inches (in.)
1 yard (yd.) = 3 feet = 36 inches
1 rod (rd.) = 5½ yards = 16½ feet
1 furlong (fur.) = 40 rods = 220 yards
= 660 feet
1 mile (mi.) = 8 furlongs
= 1,760 yards = 5,280 feet

An international nautical mile has been defined as 6,076.1155 feet.

International System

The basic unit for length is the meter, which is the distance light travels in a vacuum in 1/299,792,458 of a second—slightly longer than the customary yard. Other units of length are decimal multiples of the meter.

1 decimeter (dm) = 10 centimeters
= 0.1 meter
1 centimeter (cm) = 0.01 meter
1 millimeter (mm) = 0.1 centimeter
= 0.001 meter
1 micrometer (μm) = 0.001 millimeter
= 0.0001 centimeter
= 0.000001 meter
1 angstrom (Å) = 0.0001 micrometers
= 0.0000001 millimeter
1 dekameter (dam) = 10 meters
1 hectometer (hm) = 10 dekameters
= 100 meters
1 kilometer (km) = 10 hectometers
= 100 dekameters
= 1,000 meters

Conversions

In 1959 the relationship between customary and international measures of length was officially defined as follows:

0.0254 meter (exactly) = 1 inch
0.0254 meter × 12 = 0.3048 meter
= 1 international foot.

This definition, which makes many conversions simple, defines a foot that is shorter (by about 6 parts in 10,000,000) than the survey foot, which had earlier been defined as exactly 1200/3937, or 0.3048006, meter.

Following the international foot standard, the major equivalents are as listed below:

1 in. = 2.54 cm = 0.0254 m
1 ft. = 30.48 cm = 0.3048 m
1 yd. = 91.44 cm = 0.9144 m
1 mi. = 1,609.344 m
= 1.609344 km
1 cm = 0.3937 in.
1 m = 1.093613 yd.
= 3.28084 ft.
1 km = 0.62137 mi.

Area

U.S. customary system

Areas are derived from lengths as follows:

1 square foot = 144 square inches
1 square yard = 9 sq. ft.
1 square rod = 30¼ square yards
= 272¼ sq. ft.

1 acre = 160 square rods
= 4,840 sq. yd.
= 43,560 sq. ft.
1 square mile = 640 acres
1 section = 1 mile square
1 township = 6 miles square
= 36 square miles

International System

1 sq. millimeter (mm^2) = 1,000,000 sq. micrometers
1 sq. centimeter (cm^2) = 100 mm^2
1 sq. meter (m^2) = 10,000 cm^2
1 are (a) = 100 m^2
1 hectare (ha) = 100 ares
= 10,000 m^2
1 sq. kilometer (km^2) = 100 hectares
= 1,000,000 m^2

Conversions

1 sq. inch = 6.4516 cm^2
1 sq. foot = 929.0304 cm^2
= 0.09290304 m^2
1 sq. yard = 8,361.2736 cm^2
= 0.83612736 m^2
1 acre = 4,046.8564 m^2
= 0.40468564 ha
1 sq. mile = 2,589,988.11 m^2
= 258.998811 ha
= 2.58998811 km^2
1 cm^2 = 0.1550003 sq. in.
1 m^2 = 1,550.003 sq. in.
= 10.76391 sq. ft.
= 1.195990 sq. yd.
1 hectare = 107,639.1 sq. ft.
= 11,959.90 sq. yd.
= 2.4710538 acres
= 0.003861006 sq. mi.
1 km^2 = 247.10538 acres
= 0.3861006 sq. mi.

Cubic Measure

U.S. customary system

1 cubic foot (ft.^{3}) = 1,728 cubic inches (in.^{3})
1 cubic yard (yd.^{3})
= 27 cubic feet

International System

1 cubic centimeter (cm^3) = 1,000 cubic millimeters (mm^3)
1 cubic decimeter (dm^3) = 1,000 cm^3
1 cubic meter (m^3) = 1,000 dm^3
= 1,000,000 cm^3

Cubic centimeter is sometimes abbreviated *cc* and is used in fluid measure interchangeably with milliliter (ml).

Conversions

1 in.^{3} = 16.387064 cm^3
1 ft.^{3} = 28,316.846592 cm^3
= 0.028316847 m^3
1 yd.^{3} = 764,554.857984 cm^3
= 0.764554858 m^3
1 cm^3 = 0.06102374 in.^{3}
1 m^3 = 61,023.74 in.^{3}
= 35.31467 ft.^{3}
= 1.307951 yd.^{3}

Fluid Volume

U.S. customary system

A gallon is equal to 231 cubic inches of liquid or capacity.

1 tablespoon (tbs.) = 3 teaspoons (tsp.)
= 0.5 fluid ounce (fl. oz.)
1 cup = 8 fl. oz.
1 pint (pt.) = 2 cups = 16 fl. oz.
1 quart (qt.) = 2 pt. = 4 cups
= 32 fl. oz.
1 gallon (gal.) = 4 qt. = 8 pt. = 16 cups
1 bushel (bu.) = 8 gal. = 32 qt.

International System

Fluid-volume measurements are directly tied to cubic measure. One milliliter of fluid occupies a volume of 1 cubic centimeter. A liter of fluid (slightly more than the customary quart) occupies a volume of 1 cubic decimeter, or 1,000 cubic centimeters.

1 centiliter (cl) = 10 milliliters (ml)
1 deciliter (dl) = 10 cl
= 100 ml
1 liter (L) = 10 dl
= 1,000 ml
1 dekaliter (dal) = 10 L
1 hectoliter (hl) = 10 dal
= 100 L
1 kiloliter (kl) = 100 hl
= 1,000 L

Conversions

1 fluid ounce = 29.573528 ml = 0.02957 L
1 cup = 236.588 ml = 0.236588 L
1 pint = 473.176 ml = 0.473176 L
1 quart = 946.3529 ml
= 0.9463529 L
1 gallon = 3,785.41 ml = 3.78541 L
1 milliliter = 0.0338 fluid ounce
1 liter = 33.814 fluid ounces
= 4.2268 cups = 2.113 pints
= 1.0567 quarts = 0.264 gallon

Dry Volume

Conversions

1 pint, dry = 33.600 cu. in. = 0.551 L
1 quart, dry = 67.201 cu. in. = 1.101 L

Mass & Weight

Mass and weight are often confused. Mass is a measure of the quantity of matter in an object and does not vary with changes in altitude or in gravitational force (as on the Moon or another planet). Weight, on the other hand, is a measure of the force of gravity on an object and so does change with altitude or gravitational force.

U.S. customary system

In customary measure it is more common to measure weight than mass. The most common customary system of weight is avoirdupois:

1 pound (lb.) = 16 ounces (oz.)
1 (short) hundredweight (cwt.) = 100 lb.
1 (short) ton = 20 hundredweights
= 2,000 lb.
1 long hundredweight = 112 lb.
1 long ton = 20 long hundredweights = 2,240 lb.

PREFIXES USED IN THE METRIC SYSTEM

Prefix	Abbreviation	Factor by which unit is multiplied	Scientific notation
Exa-	E	1,000,000,000,000,000,000	10^{18}
Peta-	P	1,000,000,000,000,000	10^{15}
Tera-	T	1,000,000,000,000	10^{12}
Giga-	G	1,000,000,000	10^{9}
Mega-	M	1,000,000	10^{6}
Kilo-	k	1,000	10^{3}
Hecto-	h	100	10^{2}
Deka-	da	10	10^{1}
Deci-	d	0.1	10^{-1}
Centi-	c	0.01	10^{-2}
Milli-	m	0.001	10^{-3}
Micro-	µ	0.000 001	10^{-6}
Nano-	n	0.000 000 001	10^{-9}
Pico-	p	0.000 000 000 001	10^{-12}
Femto-	f	0.000 000 000 000 001	10^{-15}
Atto-	a	0.000 000 000 000 000 001	10^{-18}

A different system called troy weight is used to weigh precious metals. In troy weight the ounce is slightly larger than in avoirdupois, but there are only 12 ounces to the troy pound.

International System

Instead of weight, the International System generally is used to measure mass. The International System's basic unit for measurement of mass is the gram, which was originally defined as the mass of 1 milliliter (= 1 cm^3) of water at 4 degrees Celsius (about 39°F). Today the official standard of measure is the kilogram (1,000 g).

1 centigram (cg) = 10 milligrams (mg)
1 decigram (dg) = 10 cg = 100 mg
1 gram (g) = 10 dg = 100 cg = 1,000 mg
1 kilogram (kg) = 10 hectograms (hg)
= 100 dekagrams (dag)
= 1,000 g
1 metric ton (t) = 1,000 kg

Conversions

Since mass and weight are identical at standard conditions (sea level on Earth), grams and other International System units of mass are often used as measures of weight or converted into customary units of weight. Under standard conditions:

1 ounce = 28.3495 grams
1 pound = 453.59 grams
= 0.45359 kilogram
1 short ton = 907.18 kilograms
= 0.907 metric ton
1 milligram = 0.000035 ounce
1 gram = 0.03527 ounce
1 kilogram = 35.27 ounces
= 2.2046 pounds
1 metric ton = 2,204.6 pounds
= 1.1023 short tons

Time

Customary and International System

The International System in 1967 adopted a second that is based on the microwaves emitted by the vibrations of hot cesium atoms. A second (abbreviated sec. in customary usage, s in SI usage) is the time it takes the atoms to vibrate exactly 9,192,631,770 times. In the customary measure of time, the day is divided into 24 hours, the hour into 60 minutes, and the minute into 60 seconds. Since the Earth's rotation is gradually slowing, scientists must periodically add a second to a day to keep the year in sequence with their clocks (most recently done on June 30, 1994). The change is so small that for almost all practical purposes an International System second and a customary second are the same.

Decimal fractions of time are used to measure smaller time intervals:

millisecond (ms) = 0.001 second (10^{-3})
microsecond (μs) = 0.000001 second (10^{-6})
nanosecond (ns) = 0.000000001 second (10^{-9})
picosecond (ps) = 0.000000000001 second (10^{-12})

Temperature

U.S. customary system

In the United States, temperature is usually measured in degrees Fahrenheit: water freezes at 32°F and boils at 212°F. The basis of the Fahrenheit scale was 0°F, the coldest temperature that its originator, G.D. Fahrenheit (1686–1736), could obtain under laboratory conditions.

International System

The Swedish astronomer Anders Celsius (1701–44) devised the temperature scale that bears his name in 1742. On the Celsius scale water freezes at 0°C and boils at 100°C. Very low temperatures are measured on the Kelvin scale, named for William Thomson, Baron Kelvin (1824–1907). It is also called the absolute scale because absolute zero—0 K (–273.15° C)—is the temperature at which no body can give up heat. The interval of a degree Kelvin equals the interval of a degree Celsius. At very high temperatures, differences between the Kelvin and Celsius scales are insignificant.

Conversions

Fahrenheit to Celsius Subtract 32 from the temperature and multiply the difference by 5; then divide the product by 9. The formula is:
$C = \frac{5}{9}(F - 32)$

Celsius to Fahrenheit Multiply the temperature by 1.8, then add 32. The formula is often given with the fraction $\frac{9}{5}$ instead of the equivalent decimal, 1.8. The formula is: $F = \frac{9}{5}C + 32$

Celsius to Kelvin Add 273.15 to the temperature. The formula is: $K = C + 273.15$

Kelvin, Celsius, and Fahrenheit equivalents

Characteristic	K	C°	F°
Absolute zero	0	–273.15°	–459.7°
Freezing point, water	273.15	0°	32°
Traditional human body temp.	310.15	37°	98.6°
Boiling point, water	373.15	100°	212°

TEMPERATURE CONVERSIONS

Often you need to know only the approximate values to convert a weather report or temperature in a recipe from Celsius to Fahrenheit. The following table can be used to get an approximate conversion between the two scales for temperatures frequently encountered.

Note that –40°F is the same temperature as –40°C.

Celsius	Fahrenheit	Fahrenheit	Celsius
–45°	–49°	–45°	–42.8°
–40	–40	–40	–40.0
–35	–31	–35	–37.2
–30	–22	–30	–34.4
–25	–13	–25	–31.7
–20	–4	–20	–28.9
–15	5	–15	–26.1
–10	14	–10	–23.3
–5	23	–5	–20.6
0	**32**	0	–17.8
5	41	5	–15.0
10	50	10	–12.2
15	59	15	–9.4
20	68	20	–6.7
25	77	25	–3.9
30	86	30	–1.1
35	95	**32**	**0.0**
40	104	35	1.7
45	113	40	4.4
50	122	45	7.2
55	131	50	10.0
60	140	55	12.8
65	149	60	15.6
70	158	65	18.3
75	167	70	21.1
80	176	75	23.9
85	185	80	26.7
90	194	85	29.4
95	203	90	32.2
100	**212**	95	35.0
125	257	100	37.8
150	302	105	40.6
175	347	110	43.3
200	392	**212**	**100.0**
225	437	225	107.2
250	482	250	121.1
275	527	275	135.0
300	572	300	148.9
325	617	325	162.8
350	662	350	176.7
375	707	375	190.6
400	752	400	204.4
425	797	425	218.3
450	842	450	232.2
475	887	475	246.1

Force, Work/Energy, Power

U.S. customary system

The foot/pound/second system of reckoning includes the following units:

slug = the mass to which a force of 1 poundal will give an acceleration of 1 foot per second per second (= approximately 32.17 lbs.)
poundal = fundamental unit of force
foot-pound = the work done when a force of 1 poundal produces a movement of 1 foot
foot-pound/second = the unit of power equal to 1 foot/pound per second.

Another common unit of power is horsepower, which is equal to 550 foot-pounds per second.

Thermal work or energy is often measured in British thermal units (Btu), which are defined as the energy required to increase the temperature of 1 pound of water by 1 degree Fahrenheit. The Btu is equal to about 0.778 foot-pound.

International System

In physics, compound measurements of force, work or energy, and power are essential. There are two parallel systems using International System units: the centimeter/gram/second system (cgs) is used for small measurements, and the meter/kilogram/second system (mks) is used for larger measurements. The mks system is the official one for SI. They are described below.

Measurement of force

cgs unit	dyne (dy)	The force required to accelerate a mass of 1 g 1 cm/s2 (cm/s2 means "centimeter per second per second")
mks unit	newton (N)	The force required to accelerate a mass of 1 kg 1 m/s2

Measurement of work or energy

cgs unit	erg	The dyne-centimeter, i.e., the work done when a force of 1 dy produces a movement of 1 cm
mks unit	joule (j)	The newton-meter, i.e., the work done when a force of 1 N produces a movement of 1 m (= 10,000,000 ergs)

Measurement of power

cgs unit	erg/second	A rate of 1 erg per second
mks unit	watt (w)	The joule/second, i.e., a rate of 1 joule per second (= 10,000,000 erg-seconds)

Heat energy is also measured using the calorie (cal), which is defined as the energy required to increase the temperature of 1 cubic centimeter (1 ml) of water by 1 degree C. One calorie is equal to about 4.184 joules. The kilocalorie (Kcal or Cal) is equal to 1,000 calories and is the unit in which the energy values of food are measured. This more familiar unit, also commonly referred to as a Calorie, is equal to about 4,184 joules.

Conversions

Measurement of force

1 poundal = 13,889 dynes
= 0.13889 newtons
1 dyne = 0.000072 poundals
1 newton = 7.2 poundals

Measurement of work/energy

1 foot-pound = 1,356 joules
British thermal unit = 1,055 joules
= 252 gram calories
1 joule = 0.0007374 foot-pounds
1 (gram) calorie = 0.003968 Btu
1 (kilo) Calorie = 3.968 Btu

Measurement of power

1 foot-pound/second = 1.3564 watts
1 horsepower = 746 watts
= 0.746 kilowatts
1 watt = 0.73725 foot-pound/second
= 0.00134 horsepower
1 kilowatt = 737.25 ft.-lb./sec.
= 1.34 horsepower

SIMPLIFIED CONVERSION TABLE (alphabetical order)

To convert	to	multiply by:
centimeters	feet	0.0328
centimeters	inches	0.3937
cubic cm	cubic in.	0.0610
cubic ft.	cubic m	0.0283
degrees	radians	0.0175
feet	cm	30.48
feet	meters	0.3048
gallons	liters	3.785
gal. water	lb. water	8.3453
grams	ounces	0.0353
inches	cm	2.54
kilograms	pounds	2.205
kilometers	feet	3,280.8
kilometers	miles	0.6214
knots	mi./hr.	1.151
liters	gallons	0.2642
liters	pints	2.113
meters	feet	3.281
miles	km	1.609
ounces	grams	28.3495
pounds	kg	0.4536

Electrical Measure

Originally, the basic unit of quantity in electricity was the coulomb. A coulomb is equal to the passage of 6.25×10^{18} electrons past a given point in an electrical system.

The unit of electrical flow is the ampere, which is equal to a coulomb/second, i.e., the flow of 1 coulomb per second. The ampere is analogous in electrical measure to a unit of flow such as gallons-per-minute in physical measure. In SI, the ampere is taken as the basic unit.

The unit for measuring electrical potential energy is the volt, which is defined as 1 joule/coulomb, i.e., 1 joule of energy per coulomb of electricity. The volt is analogous to a measure of pressure in a water system.

The unit for measuring electrical power is the watt as defined in the previous section. Power in watts *(P)* is the product of the electrical flow in amperes *(I)* and the potential electrical energy in volts *(E)*:

$$P = I \times E.$$

Since the watt is such a small unit for practical applications, the kilowatt (= 1,000 watts) is often used. A kilowatt-hour is the power of 1,000 watts over an hour's time.

The unit for measuring electrical resistance is the ohm, which is the resistance offered by a circuit to the flow of 1 ampere being driven by the force of 1 volt. It is derived from Ohm's law, which defines the relationship between flow or current (amperes), potential energy (volts), and resistance (ohms). It states that the current in amperes *(I)* is proportional to potential energy in volts *(E)* and inversely proportional to resistance in ohms *(R)*. Thus, when voltage and resistance are known, amperage can be calculated by the simple formula

$$I = \frac{E}{R}.$$

Measure of Angles and Arcs

Angles are measured by systems based on arcs (portions) of circles. Arcs of a circle can be measured by length, but they are also often measured by angles. In the latter case, the measure of the arc is the same as the measure of an angle whose vertex is at the center of the circle and whose sides pass through the ends of the arc. Such an angle is said to be subtended by the arc.

The most commonly used angle measure is degree measure. One degree is the angle subtended by an arc that is 1/360 of a circle. This is an ancient system of measurement probably originally developed by Sumerian astronomers. These astronomers used a numeration system based on 60 ($60 \times 6 = 360$), as well as a 360-day year. They divided the day into 12 equal periods of 30 smaller periods each ($12 \times 30 = 360$) and used roughly the same system for dividing the circle. Even when different years and numeration systems were adopted by later societies, astronomers continued to use a variation of the Sumerian system.

1 degree (1°) = 60 minutes (60')
= 3,600 seconds (3,600")
1 minute = 60 seconds

When two lines are perpendicular to each other, they form four angles of the same size, which are called right angles. Two right angles make up a line, which in this context is considered a straight angle.

1 right angle = 90°
1 straight angle = 180°

While this system is workable for most purposes, it is artificial. Mathematicians discovered that using a natural system of angle measurement produces results that make better sense in mathematical and many scientific applications. This system is called radian measure. Radian measure is considered a supplement to SI. One radian is the measure of the angle subtended by an arc of a circle that is exactly as long as the radius of the circle.

1 radian ≐ about 57° 17' 45"

The circumference, *C*, of a circle is given by the formula $C = 2\pi r$, where π is a number (approximately 3.14159) and r is the radius. Therefore, a semicircle whose radius is 1 is π units long, which implies that there are π radians in a straight angle. Many of the angles commonly encountered are measured in multiples of π radians:

0° = 0 radians	90° = $\pi/2$ radians
30° = $\pi/6$ radians	180° = π radians
45° = $\pi/4$ radians	270° = $3\pi/2$ radians
60° = $\pi/3$ radians	360° = 2π radians

To convert from radians to degrees, use the formula t *radians* $= (180/\pi)\ t°$. To convert from degrees to radians, use the formula

$$\omega° = (\pi/180)\omega \text{ radians}.$$

The U.S. artillery uses the mil to measure angles. A mil is the angle subtended by an arc that is 1/6400 of a circle.

1 mil = 0.05625° ≐ 3' 22.5"
1 mil = almost 0.001 radian

Astronomical Distances

One very large measure of distance useful in astronomy is the light-year. It is defined as the distance light travels through a vacuum in a year (approximately 365¼ days). Light travels though a vacuum at the rate of about 186,250 miles per second (exactly 299,792,458 m/s—exact because the meter is defined in terms of the speed of light in a vacuum). A light-year is approximately equivalent to 5,880 billion miles (9,460 billion km).

Astronomers also use a measure even larger than the light-year, the parsec, equal to 3.258 light-years, or about 19,180 billion miles (30,820 billion km).

A smaller unit, for measurements within the solar system, is the astronomical unit, which is the average distance between the Earth and the Sun, or about 93 million miles (150 million km).

THE ENVIRONMENT

The environmental movement in the United States dates from Earth Day 1970, when the American public first began to take stock of the ecological devastation going on around them. Then there were no pollution controls on cars; people and municipalities dumped untreated sewage into the nation's rivers, some of which were so saturated with chemical waste that they actually caught fire; and industrial cities were routinely shrouded with thick acrid smoke.

Many of these problems have been effectively addressed and dramatically diminished. Today the Environmental Protection Agency (EPA), established in 1970, routinely monitors air quality at thousands of sites around the country. Toxic emissions from smokestacks at smelters, factories, and garbage incinerators have been sharply reduced. Mandatory pollution control standards on automobiles have led to an overwhelming drop in lead emissions. Recycling as a way of reducing solid waste has taken hold in cities and towns throughout the country. The 1994 elections, however, triggered an environmental backlash. Powerful business interests found their point of view better received by the new Congress, which went to lengths to reduce both the amount of regulation and spending on the federal level.

Costing the Earth Spending on the environment is one of the fastest growing sectors of the economy. The majority of the environmental cleanup bill is paid by the private sector. State and local governments pick up most of the remaining costs, with the EPA and other federal agencies paying for the remainder.

Assessing environmental risk While expenditures for environmental protection are significant, many feel they are misapportioned. Based on the findings of a scientific advisory group, the EPA has ranked the major environmental issues as follows:

High risk Habitat destruction; global warming; ozone layer depletion; species extinction; biological diversity.

Medium risk Herbicides and pesticides; surface water pollution; airborne toxic substances.

Low risk Oil spills; radioactive materials; groundwater pollution.

Human health risks Indoor air pollution; outdoor air pollution; drinking water; exposure to chemicals.

Despite such findings, the main attack on environmental regulations in 1995 came from developers seeking to overturn laws intended to preserve habitats and species. The most successful reforms in the 1990s involved steps taken toward protection of the ozone layer.

MAJOR EVENTS IN THE HISTORY OF THE ENVIRONMENT

1775 Sir Percival Potts observes that chimney sweeps develop cancer as a result of their contact with soot, the first recognition of environmental factors on cancer.

1864 George Perkins Marsh (American: 1801–81) publishes *Man and Nature,* the first textbook on conservation and the first detailed study of human influence on the environment.

1872 Robert Angus Smith (Scottish: 1817–84) describes acid rain.
Yellowstone, world's first national park, opens.

1885 Canada establishes first national park at Banff, Alberta.

1892 John Muir (Scottish-American: 1838–1914) founds the Sierra Club.

1903 U.S. president Theodore Roosevelt opens the first national refuge, Pelican Island in Florida, to protect nesting sites of brown pelicans.

1905 U.S. Forest Service established.
National Audubon Society founded.

1911 Canada, Japan, Russia, and the United States sign a treaty to limit the annual harvest of northern fur seals.

1914 Passenger pigeon and Carolina parakeet declared extinct.

1916 National Park Service established.

1928 Boulder Canyon project (Hoover Dam) authorized to bring irrigation, electric power, and flood control system to western United States.

1933 Tennessee Valley Authority created to analyze environmental impact of damming the Tennessee River.

1939 Paul Müller (Swiss: 1899–1965) discovers insecticidal properties of DDT.

1952 Smog blamed for 4,000 deaths in London.

1955 Link between exposure to asbestos and lung cancer established.

1957 Nuclear wastes stored by the Soviet Union in a remote mountain region of the Urals explode; radioactive contamination affects thousands of square miles; several villages permanently evacuated.

1961 Investigations in Scandinavia and the U.S. Adirondacks confirm that acid rain kills some species living in lakes.

1962 *Silent Spring* by Rachel Carson (American: 1907–64) attacks pesticide use and stimulates major environmental movement.

1963 Congress passes first Clean Air Act, allocating $95 million to local, state, and national air pollution control efforts.

1964 Congress passes Wilderness Act, setting up the National Wilderness Preservation System.

1965 Congress passes Highway Beautification Act, banning many highway billboards.
Congress passes Water Quality Act, giving federal government power to set water standards in absence of state action.
Congress passes the Solid Waste Disposal Act, its first major solid waste legislation.

1966 Congress passes Rare and Endangered Species Act.

1967 S. Manabe and R.T. Wetherald predict that increased amounts of carbon dioxide in the atmosphere will lead to global warming.

1968 Congress passes Wild and Scenic Rivers Act, identifying areas of scenic beauty for preservation and recreation.

1970 First Earth Day celebrated on April 22.
Environmental Protection Agency created.

1972 Congress passes Clean Water Act, forbidding discharges of pollutants into navigable waters.
Oregon passes the nation's first bottle recycling law.
The EPA bars registration and interstate sales of DDT because of its persistence in the environment and accumulation in the food chain.

1973 Representatives of 80 nations sign the Convention of International Trade in Endangered Species of Wild Fauna and Flora, which prohibits commercial trade in 375 endangered species of wild animals.

1974 F. Sherwood Rowland and Mario Molinas warn that chlorofluorocarbons (CFCs) produced by spray cans and air conditioners are destroying ozone layer.

1976 Congress passes Toxic Substances Control Act to control hazardous industrial chemicals.

1977 United States signs Convention of International Trade in Endangered Species.

1978 Community of Love Canal, near Niagara, N.Y., evacuated after hazardous waste dumps are uncovered. EPA declares site safe in 1990.

1979 Nuclear reactor at Three Mile Island, near Harrisburg, Pa., suffers partial meltdown; radiation confined to reactor dome.
Herbert Needleman demonstrates that low levels of lead reduce intelligence in exposed children.

1980 Congress passes Comprehensive Environmental Response, Compensation and Liability Act (the "Superfund") to clean up hazardous waste sites.

1983 Scientists predict that a large-scale nuclear war could produce a "nuclear winter," cold global temperatures that might destroy most living creatures.

1984 More than 2,000 die and thousands more are injured by toxic gas from an industrial accident at the U.S.-owned Union Carbide plant in Bhopal, India.

1985 British scientists discover that a "hole" in the ozone layer develops over Antarctica each winter.
The U.S. sets up a Conservation Reserve Program to remove enviromentally sensitive farmland from agricultural use.

1986 A worldwide ban on whaling begins.
Chernobyl nuclear reactor number 4 explodes and burns, causing 31 deaths within days, shortening the lives of thousands, and forcing the evacuation of hundreds of square miles in Soviet Ukraine for an unknown length of time.

1987 Last known wild California condor trapped and moved to a zoo in an effort to save species from extinction.
The worst forest fire in history burns more than 3 million acres of China's timber reserve and up to 15 million acres in the Soviet Union.

1988 The U.S. Ocean Dumping Ban Act mandates an end to ocean dumping of industrial waste and sewage sludge.

1989 *Exxon Valdez* grounds, leaking 35,000 tons of oil into Prince William Sound, Alaska.
Thirteen industrial nations agree to halt production of CFCs by the year 2000.

1991 Iraq dumps over a million tons of oil from occupied Kuwait into Persian Gulf.

1992 Representatives from 178 countries attend the first-ever Earth Summit in Rio de Janeiro, where they sign treaties pledging to increase the diversity of animal and plant species and to halt global warming.

1994 U.S. Fish and Wildlife Service recommends that status of American bald eagle be reduced from "endangered" to "threatened" in most of United States.

GLOBAL WARMING

Many scientists today believe that over the past century the Earth has begun to warm significantly—about 1°F (0.5°C)—and that at its current rate, it is likely to warm as much as 3° to 5°F (1.5° to 2.5°C) more over the next 50 to 60 years. The magnitude of such climatic change is staggering—the temperature has risen only 9°F (5°C) since the end of the last ice age 12,000 years ago. Additional warming would cause melting of polar ice caps, setting off a chain of events that begins with a rise in sea level worldwide and could end with the destruction of water supplies, forests, and agriculture in many parts of the world.

Global warming occurs when certain gases in the atmosphere prevent sunlight from being reflected from the Earth. Ordinarily, sunlight that reaches the surface of the Earth is partly absorbed and partly reflected. The absorbed light heats the surface and is later emitted from the surface as infrared radiation. Gases that are not transparent to infrared radiation (carbon dioxide is one) collect this heat and keep it in the atmosphere, hence their name, greenhouse gases. The Earth's atmosphere is only 0.03 percent carbon dioxide, but combined with other gases this is enough to trap 30 percent of the reflected heat (the rest is radiated out to space), and maintain the Earth's average temperature at about 59°F (15°C).

Since the Industrial Revolution, an unprecedented amount of four primary greenhouse gases have been released into the atmosphere. In addition to carbon dioxide, these are chlorofluorocarbons (CFCs), methane, and nitrous oxide. The worst offenders are CFCs, which in addition to contributing to the greenhouse effect also destroy stratospheric ozone which shields the Earth's surface (and inhabitants) from ultraviolet rays. Countries of the European Union, the United States, Russia, and Japan have agreed to a 100 percent phaseout of CFCs by the year 2000.

The sources of methane and nitrogen oxide are neither as easy to identify nor as easy to control. Methane is emitted by decomposing organic waste, natural-gas leaks, and fermenting rice paddies. The primary sources of nitrogen oxide are automobile exhaust and industrial smoke stacks, especially coal-fired plants. The increased presence of carbon dioxide is due primarily to the burning of carbon fuels including oil, coal, and natural gas, as well as burning trees for deforestation.

Global warming produces a domino effect that can spell environmental disaster. Some of the main steps in this chain are as follows:

Weather patterns Climatologists think that global warming is already disrupting local weather in places around the world. In the United States, according to the National Climactic Data Center in Asheville, North Carolina, greenhouse effects have, with at least a 90 percent probability, caused the unusual and extreme weather patterns of the 1980s and 1990s. For example, the expected pattern of wetter winters and occasional wetter summers in the middle of the North American continent have caused great floods in 1993 and flooding conditions in several other years.

Changed weather patterns can have a severe impact on crops and other forms of vegetation, as well as on the animals that depend on them. Rising temperatures also enable insects and fungal pests to migrate to previously unaffected regions. Long-lived plants, however, such as trees, spread much more slowly in the face of climate change.

Warming patterns Average world temperature is rising already, however. In 1994, for example, the average was more than half a degree Fahrenheit warmer than it had been in the period from 1951 through 1980. Thus, 1994 joins 1990 and 1991 as the three warmest years since global records have been kept.

Temperature change from global warming is not expected to be uniform. In general, climatologists expect greater warming during winter months and at high latitudes (closer to the poles than to the equator).

Higher temperatures, especially at the poles, have an even more dire effect than increased numbers of hot days. They can also melt polar ice caps, causing:

Sea level rise Climatologists generally expect the sea level to rise at least a foot (30–40 cm) and possibly as much as 6.6 feet (200 cm) in the next century. Generally speaking, a rise in sea level would be uniform—both geographically and seasonally—because sea level is a global phenomenon. The impact of such a rise, however, would vary greatly from place to place—a three-foot (1 m) rise would inundate 7,000 square miles (18,000 km^2) of dry land—an area the size of Massachusetts—in the United States, mostly in the southeast. It would also destroy a comparable area of coastal wetlands, erode recreational beaches 100 to 200 meters, exacerbate coastal flooding, and increase the salinity of aquifers and estuaries. It is likely that the people of an industrialized continental nation such as the United States could sustain the population shifts caused by such climatic changes. However, an estimated one-third of the world's population—about 1.75 billion people, today—lives within 40 miles of the sea, mostly along low-lying floodplains and estuaries. How the low-lying Netherlands or Bangladesh or the island nations of the Pacific can or will respond to such forces is impossible to see.

THE OZONE LAYER

There are two distinct problems associated with the chemical ozone (O_3): ground-level ozone, the main component of smog, which is discussed under "Air Pollution," and stratospheric ozone. The primary difference between the two problems is that at ground level there is too much ozone, while in the stratosphere there is not enough.

The problem of stratospheric ozone depletion is closely related to global warming in terms of its causes and its remedies. Stratospheric ozone (sometimes referred to as upper-atmosphere or atmospheric ozone) absorbs most of the Sun's ultraviolet radiation. A significant reduction of the ozone layer would lead to sharp increases in the incidence of skin cancer and cataracts in humans. It is also thought that there would be serious losses of small ocean algae, which produce oxygen and break down carbon dioxide, and of bacteria important to crop production.

Complex natural forces are continually at work creating and destroying ozone in the atmosphere. This involves first the breakdown of individual molecules of oxygen (O_2) into atomic oxygen (O), through the absorption of ultraviolet radiation. In turn, each atomic oxygen normally combines with an additional molecule of O_2 to form ozone (O_3). Destruction of ozone can be caused by the occasional recombination of ozone with atomic oxygen to form two molecules of O_2. As long as the Earth's sunlit atmosphere contains molecular oxygen, as it has for more than one billion years, ozone will be maintained in this dynamic balance.

This balance can be altered, however, by the introduction into the atmosphere of ozone-destroying chemicals that shift the equilibrium toward smaller average concentrations of ozone. In 1974, scientists saw the first suggestion that a group of chemicals known as chlorofluorocarbons (CFCs) could be a major avenue for adding chlorine to the atmosphere and disturbing the ozone balance.

CFCs were developed in the 1930s after a search for an ammonia substitute in refrigeration use. The results of this search produced a family of chemicals with properties ideal for many applications beyond refrigeration. Chemically inert, nontoxic, and easily liquified, CFC use became widespread in air conditioning, packaging and insulation, as a solvent for cleaning electronic circuit boards, and as an aerosol propellant.

It is this very absence of chemical reactivity that makes CFCs so dangerous to the ozone layer. Unlike less inert compounds, CFCs are not destroyed or removed in the lower atmosphere by rain, oxidation, or sunlight. Instead they drift into the upper atmosphere, where their chlorine components are released into the atmosphere under the effects of ultraviolet radiation. Almost all of these freed chlorine atoms find and react with the ozone, creating chlorine monoxide. In a subsequent reaction, the chlorine monoxide releases its oxygen atom to form molecular oxygen, and the chlorine atom is freed once again to repeat the process. The atmospheric lifetimes for the most commonly used CFC compounds have been estimated to be between 75 and 110 years, so through this continuing cycle of reactions, each chlorine atom can destroy about 100,000 molecules of ozone before the chain reaction ends. Ice crystals in the Antarctic and Arctic speed up reactions, producing "ozone holes" near both poles. Such "holes" are regions of extremely low levels of atmospheric ozone during winters.

To combat ozone depletion, there have been stringent reductions in CFC use. The United States, Russia, Japan, and the nations of the European Union have agreed to eliminate CFC use and production 100 percent by 2000. Even so, research reported by NASA in 1995 indicates that adverse effects on the ozone layer from human-produced CFCs will continue until at least 2020.

EMISSIONS ESTIMATES FOR EPA-MONITORED POLLUTANTS BY SOURCE, 1985–93 (million short tons)

Year	Transportation	Fuel combustion	Industrial processes	Solid waste	Miscellaneous	Total
			Particulate matter (PM_{10})			
1985	0.63	1.41	0.56	0.30	0.00	2.95
1990	0.61	1.45	0.55	0.30	0.00	2.91
1991	0.59	1.42	0.54	0.30	0.00	2.85
1992	0.59	1.30	0.54	0.30	0.00	2.73
1993	0.59	1.21	0.55	0.30	0.00	2.66
			Sulfur oxides (SO_x)			
1985	0.65	20.02	2.43	0.04	0.01	23.15
1990	0.74	19.60	1.86	0.04	0.01	22.26
1991	0.74	19.53	1.82	0.04	0.01	22.15
1992	0.76	18.96	1.82	0.04	0.01	21.59
1993	0.72	19.27	1.86	0.04	0.01	21.89
			Carbon monoxide (CO)			
1985	91.09	7.65	5.22	1.99	6.12	112.07
1990	77.50	6.72	5.18	1.74	12.62	103.75
1991	76.70	6.58	5.10	1.70	9.83	99.90
1992	74.76	6.02	5.14	1.77	8.68	96.37
1993	75.26	5.44	5.22	1.79	9.51	97.21
			Nitrogen oxides (NO_x)			
1985	10.82	10.83	0.91	0.09	0.20	22.85
1990	10.33	11.50	0.89	0.08	0.38	23.19
1991	10.17	11.54	0.88	0.08	0.30	22.98
1992	10.32	11.41	0.89	0.09	0.27	22.99
1993	10.42	11.69	0.90	0.09	0.30	23.40
			Ozone (O_3)			
1985	11.38	0.79	2.89	9.92	0.43	25.42
1990	8.97	0.74	3.06	10.19	1.32	24.28
1991	8.62	0.73	3.07	10.15	0.94	23.51
1992	8.23	0.69	3.08	10.24	0.78	23.02
1993	8.30	0.65	3.09	10.38	0.89	23.31

Note: The sums of subcategories may not equal due to independent rounding. **Source:** Environmental Protection Agency, *National Air Quality and Emissions Trends Report, 1993* (October 1994).

AIR POLLUTION

Although we tend to think of air pollution as a local problem, studies reported in 1995 demonstrate that there are widespread effects. Air pollution, they report, is so pervasive in industrial regions of northeastern North America, central Europe, and eastern Asia that it partly blocks sunlight, counteracting global warming with regional cooling.

The U.S. Environmental Protection Agency (EPA) monitors air quality at about 3,000 sites for six pollutants: particulate matter (soot and dust), sulfur dioxide (mostly from smokestacks), carbon monoxide (mostly from automobiles), nitrogen dioxide (from any form of combustion), lead (from industrial processes, materials, and formerly from leaded gasoline), and ozone (from processes connected to auto emissions and volatile chemicals). The ozone is ground level ozone that has little to do with the ozone layer in the atmosphere. These pollutants are those for which the EPA has set what they term "National Ambient Air Quality Standards," rules intended to protect public welfare. In addition to health concerns, the effects of air pollution on vegetation, materials, and visibility are monitored.

Particulate matter (PM_{10}) The EPA measures particulate matter with an aerodynamic diameter smaller than 10 micrometers. This includes dust, dirt, soot, smoke, and liquid droplets directly emitted into the air from factories, power plants, cars, construction sites, fires, and natural erosion, as well as particles formed in the atmosphere by condensation or transformation of emitted gases such as sulfur dioxide and volatile organic compounds.

Particulate matter is responsible for most adverse health effects in the lower regions of the respiratory tract. People with chronic obstructive pulmonary or cardiovascular disease, individuals with influenza, asthmatics, the elderly, and children are especially sensitive. PM_{10} also causes material soiling and is responsible for substantial visibility impairment in many parts of the United States.

Sulfur dioxide (SO_2) Ambient sulfur dioxide comes mostly from stationary-source coal and oil combustion, refineries, pulp and paper mills, and nonferrous smelters. The health hazards associated with exposure to SO_2 include impaired breathing, respiratory illness, alterations in the lungs' defenses, and aggravation of existing respiratory and cardiovascular disease. Those most sensitive to SO_2 include asthmatics and people with chronic lung disease or cardiovascular disease, children, and the elderly. Sulfur dioxide also damages leaves on trees and crops and it is an agent of acid rain.

Electric utilities generate two-thirds of all

SO_2 emissions, 95 percent of which come from coal-fired power plants. Sulfur dioxide emissions decreased 6 percent between 1981 and 1990 due to three factors: installation of desulfurization controls at new coal-fired electric-generating stations and a reduction in the average sulfur content of fuels; implementation of emission-reduction controls at sulfuric acid manufacturing plants and nonferrous smelters, and the shutdown of some large smelters; and decreased use of coal by other stationary-source fuel combustors.

Carbon monoxide (CO) Carbon monoxide is a colorless, odorless, and poisonous gas produced by incomplete burning of carbon in fuels. Carbon monoxide enters the bloodstream and disrupts delivery of oxygen to the body's organs and tissues. The health threat from carbon monoxide is serious for those who suffer from cardiovascular diseases. Healthy individuals are also affected, and exposure to elevated carbon monoxide levels is associated with impairment of visual perception and manual dexterity.

Although carbon monoxide emissions from highway vehicles decreased 37 percent between 1981 and 1990 (this despite a 37 percent increase in vehicle miles traveled), CO remains a concern in many urban areas.

Nitrogen dioxide (NO_2) Nitrogen dioxide is a yellowish brown, highly reactive gas that plays a major role, together with volatile organic compounds, in the formation of ozone. Nitrogen oxides form when fuel is burned at high temperatures. When released into the atmosphere, they are one of the major causes of smog. The two major emissions sources are cars and trucks, and stationary fuel-combustion sources such as electric-utility and industrial boilers.

Nitrogen oxides can irritate the lungs and lower resistance to respiratory infections such as influenza. Prolonged exposure to higher than normal concentrations can cause pulmonary angina. Nitrogen dioxide is also an agent of acid rain and plays a key role in nitrogen loading of forests and ecosystems. Over the past decade, Los Angeles is the only urban area that has consistently recorded violations of the EPA's annual NO_2 standards. Many other urban areas violate the EPA's standards on occasional hot summer days, when the Sun cooks hydrocarbons and nitrogen oxides, thus producing smog.

Ozone (O_3) Ground-level ozone is a colorless gas and the main component of smog. Unlike most other air pollutants, ozone is not emitted by factories or automobiles, but is formed by the interaction of volatile organic compounds (VOCs) and nitrous oxide. These reactions are stimulated by sunlight and temperature so that peak ozone levels occur typically during the warmer times of year. The severity of a smog problem in a given locale is directly related to the temperature and ultraviolet radiation intensity in that area. While the problems associated with ozone depletion (see "The Ozone Layer") and ground-level ozone are usually viewed separately, it is worth noting that as upper-atmo sphere ozone is depleted, more ultraviolet radiation reaches the Earth and stimulates the production of ozone/smog.

Both VOCs and nitrous oxide are emitted by transportation and industrial sources as diverse as autos, chemical manufacturing, dry cleaners, paint shops, and other solvent-using industries. High levels of ozone affect people with impaired respiratory systems, such as asthmatics, and exposure to relatively low concentrations of ozone for only a few hours has been found to significantly reduce lung function in normal, healthy people during exercise. This is generally accompanied by symptoms including chest pain, coughing, sneezing, and pulmonary congestion. Ozone is also responsible each year for several billion dollars worth of domestic crop yield losses, and it causes noticeable damage to leaves in many crops and species of trees. Forest and ecosystem damage may result from high ambient ozone levels.

Lead (Pb) People can be exposed to lead via air, diet, and ingestion of lead in soil and dust. Lead accumulates in the body in blood, bone, and soft tissue, and because it is not readily excreted, it also affects the kidneys, nervous system, and blood-forming organs. Excessive exposure to lead may cause seizures, mental retardation, and/or behavioral disorders. Even at low doses, lead exposure is associated with changes in fundamental enzymatic, energy transfer, and homeostatic mechanisms in the body. Infants and children are especially susceptible to low doses of lead and often suffer central nervous system damage. Recent studies have

NUMBER OF UNHEALTHY DAYS IN SELECTED METROPOLITAN AREAS, 1980–93

To measure air quality in urban areas, the Environmental Protection Agency has developed an indicator called the Pollutant Standard Index (PSI). The PSI integrates into a single number emission levels of five major pollutants: particulate matter (PM_{10}), sulfur dioxide (SO_2), carbon monoxide (CO), ground level ozone (O_3), and nitrogen dioxide (NO_2). A PSI of 0–50 reflects good air, 51–100 denotes moderate air, and a PSI of over 100 is classified as unhealthy (200–299 signifies very unhealthy air; 300–500 is hazardous). The following chart lists the number of days in which the PSI exceeded 100 in 30 major urban metropolitan areas.

Metropolitan area	1980	1985	1988	1989	1990	1991	1992	1993	Total 1988–93
Atlanta	7	9	15	3	16	5	4	14	57
Bakersfield, Calif.	N.A.	29	59	34	29	30	5	28	185
Baltimore	N.A.	21	41	7	12	20	4	12	96
Boston	8	3	12	2	1	3	1	3	22
Chicago	34	8	21	3	3	8	6	1	42
Cleveland	N.A.	1	20	4	1	5	0	1	31
Dallas	19	15	3	3	5	0	2	4	17
Denver	35	38	19	11	7	7	7	3	54
Detroit	N.A.	2	17	10	3	7	0	2	39
El Paso	N.A.	24	13	29	20	8	11	5	86
Fresno, Calif.	N.A.	21	12	21	12	18	16	13	92
Hartford, Conn.	N.A.	17	26	8	7	14	9	9	73
Houston	10	48	48	34	48	40	30	26	226
Kansas City	13	3	3	2	2	1	1	2	11
Las Vegas	N.A.	55	30	44	21	14	5	8	122
Los Angeles	220	194	226	212	163	157	169	131	1,058
Miami	N.A.	5	4	4	1	2	0	0	11
Middlesex–Somerset–Hunterdon, N.J.	N.A.	15	24	7	10	8	3	1	53
Minneapolis–St. Paul	N.A.	21	1	5	1	0	1	0	8
New York	119	61	43	16	17	22	4	6	108
Orange County, Calif.	N.A.	69	54	53	39	32	37	17	232
Philadelphia	52	25	34	19	11	24	3	20	111
Phoenix	N.A.	84	22	30	8	4	8	6	78
Pittsburgh	20	9	23	9	11	3	1	5	52
Riverside–San Bernardino, Calif.	N.A.	142	165	155	128	122	128	115	813
St. Louis	N.A.	10	17	12	8	6	2	5	50
San Diego	N.A.	54	49	61	39	25	19	14	207
San Francisco	2	5	1	0	1	0	0	0	2
Seattle	33	24	6	4	2	0	0	0	12
Washington, D.C.	38	15	36	7	5	16	2	12	78
Total	**610**	**1,027**	**1,044**	**809**	**631**	**601**	**478**	**463**	**4,026**

Note: Figures reflect data from selected EPA trend sites. Number of unhealthy days recorded by all active EPA monitoring sites may be slightly higher in some cities. N.A. = not available. **Source:** Environmental Protection Agency, *National Air Quality and Emissions Trends Report, 1993* (October 1994).

also shown that lead may be a factor in high blood pressure and subsequent heart disease.

Lead gasoline additives, nonferrous smelters, and battery plants are the most significant contributors to atmospheric lead emissions. The decline in the share of lead emissions from internal-combustion engines of all kinds is due to the gradual elimination of leaded gasoline that began in the 1970s. Although the original requirement for unleaded gasoline stemmed from the introduction of catalytic control devices on automobiles—which themselves were installed to reduce emission of carbon monoxide, unburned fuel (a volatile organic compound, or VOC), and nitrogen oxides—the recognition that atmospheric lead contributed to lead poisoning furthered the elimination of lead as a gasoline additive. Today more than 99.8 percent of the lead once added to gasoline in the United States has been removed.

OZONE IN METROPOLITAN AREAS, 1991–93

The following areas have been classified by the EPA as severe violations of ozone standards set by the Clean Air Act of 1990 (except for the Los Angeles South Coast Air Basin, Calif., area, which has been classified as an extreme violation). They are ranked by the number of days they exceeded standards in 1993.

	Number of days exceeding standards	
Metropolitan area	**1991–93 avg.**	**1993**
Los Angeles South Coast Air Basin, Calif.	104.3	97.6
Southeast Desert, Calif.	59.3	72.6
Houston–Galveston–Brazoria, Tex.	6.3	10.4
Ventura County, Calif.	15.9	9.0
Baltimore, Md.	4.8	6.2
New York–No. New Jersey–Long Island–Conn.	6.1	6.0
Philadelphia, Pa.–Wilmington, Del.–Trenton, N.J.	10.3	5.2
San Diego, Calif.	11.8	4.0
Chicago, Ill.–Gary, Ind.–Lake Co., Wis.	4.7	2.4
Milwaukee–Racine, Wis.	3.9	2.4

Note: The national ambient air quality standard for ozone is 0.12 parts per million (ppm) daily maximum one-hour average. Severe violations are defined as concentrations of 0.18 ppm–0.279 ppm; extreme violations are defined as concentrations of .28 ppm or more. **Source:** Environmental Protection Agency, *Ozone Nonattainment Areas, 1991–93* (October 1994).

CARBON MONOXIDE IN METROPOLITAN AREAS, 1990–93

The following areas have been classified by the EPA as moderate violations of carbon monoxide standards set by the Clean Air Act of 1990 (except for the Los Angeles South Coast Air Basin, which has been classified as a serious violation). They are listed alphabetically by state.

	Number of days exceeding standards			
Metropolitan area	**1990**	**1991**	**1992**	**1993**
Anchorage, Alaska	12	3	2	2
Fairbanks–North Star Borough, Alaska	2	3	2	5
Phoenix, Ariz.	4	3	4	0
Chico, Calif.	1	0	0	0
Fresno, Calif.	1	1	0	0
Lake Tahoe–South Shore, Calif.	5	0	1	0
Los Angeles South Coast Air Basin, Calif.	47	41	35	20
Modesto, Calif.	2	1	0	0
Sacramento, Calif.	11	5	0	0
San Diego, Calif.	0	0	0	0
San Francisco–Oakland–San Jose, Calif.	2	4	0	0
Stockton, Calif.	2	2	0	0
Colorado Springs, Colo.	0	0	0	0
Denver–Boulder, Colo.	3	4	7	2
Fort Collins, Colo.	0	2	0	0
Longmont, Colo.	0	0	0	0
Hartford–New Britain–Middletown, Conn.	0	1	1	0
Washington, D.C.	0	0	0	0
Boston, Mass.	0	0	0	0
Baltimore, Md.	1	0	0	0
Minneapolis–St. Paul, Minn.	1	2	0	0
Missoula, Mont.	N.A.	5	0	0
Raleigh–Durham, N.C.	2	0	0	0
Winston-Salem, N.C.	0	0	0	0
Albuquerque, N.Mex.	3	2	0	0
Las Vegas, Nev.	17	6	2	3
Reno, Nev.	7	2	0	0
New York–Northern New Jersey–Long Island–Conn.	4	2	2	0
Grant Pass, Oreg.	0	0	0	0
Klamath Falls, Oreg.	0	1	0	0
Medford, Oreg.	3	3	0	0
Portland, Oreg.–Vancouver, Wash.	2	2	0	0
Philadelphia, Pa.–Camden Co., N.J.	0	0	0	0
El Paso, Tex.	4	3	3	2
Ogden, Utah	3	0	0	0
Provo–Orem, Utah	11	6	3	2
Seattle–Tacoma, Wash.	2	1	1	0
Spokane, Wash.	6	13	6	4

Note: The national ambient air quality standards for carbon monoxide is an average of 9 parts per million (ppm) over an eight-hour period. Moderate violations are defined as concentrations of 9.1–16.4 ppm; serious violations are defined as concentrations of 16.5 ppm or more. **Source:** Environmental Protection Agency, *Carbon Monoxide Nonattainment Areas, 1992–93* (October 1994).

ACID RAIN

Acid rain refers to acidic precipitation of all kinds, including rain, snow, and fog, as well as acidic dust particles. The main component of acid rain is sulfuric acid, a product of reactions of sulfur dioxide released by industrial and power plants fueled by coal or oil. Another major agent of acid rain is nitrogen oxides, which form nitric acid and which are found in motor vehicle exhaust and in emissions from industrial plants that burn any fuel at high temperatures. Burning vegetation also produces nitric acid, as well as formic acid and acetic acid. Acid rain can travel great distances from its source: 10 percent to 80 percent increases in acidity have been detected as far away as 2,500 miles from a source.

Acid rain has been implicated in the destruction of lakes, the weathering of man-made structures, and the destruction of forests and crops. When acid rain winds up in lakes, it can increase the level of acidity to such an extent that the lake loses its ability to buffer the acidity with alkaline chemicals from the surrounding soil and rocks. How quickly this occurs is to some extent determined by the nature of the surrounding soil, which means that lakes in some regions are more vulnerable to the effects of acid rain than others.

As lakes become more acidic, small invertebrates die off. This begins a reaction up the food chain: as the smallest organisms disappear, the food supply for larger invertebrates such as fish and frogs is depleted. Because lakes are not closed ecosystems, the demise of fish and other native populations also affects other forms of wildlife that depend on them at some level for their survival.

DEFORESTATION

Rain forests are defined as forests that grow in regions that receive more than 70 inches (1.8 meters) of rain each year. Some rain forests occur in temperate places, such as southern Chile or the northwest coast of North America, but the majority are found in the tropics. Tropical rain forests cover more than 2 billion acres (0.8 billion hectares) or about 7 percent of the Earth's land surface. They are found in Central and South America, equatorial Africa, Southeast Asia, and northeastern Australia.

It is estimated that the world may be losing more than 49 million acres (20 million hectares) of tropical forest each year. As the 1990s began, Brazil was losing 12.5–22.5 million acres (5–9 million hectares) of rain forest annually; India was losing 3.7 million acres (1.5 million hectares); and Indonesia was losing 2.2 million acres (0.9 million hectares). Other countries experiencing rapid losses included Myanmar, Costa Rica, Sri Lanka, Vietnam, Thailand, the Philippines, and Ghana.

Tropical rain forests are lush habitats, filled with a greater variety of organisms than any other type of habitat. According to a U.S. National Academy of Sciences report, a typical patch of rain forest covering four square miles (10.4 km^2) contains 750 species of trees, 750 species of other plants, 125 species of mammals, 400 species of birds, 100 species of reptiles, and 60 species of amphibians.

The dominant plants in a tropical rain forest are broad-leaved evergreens, while northern-hemisphere temperate rain forests are filled with needle-leaved conifers. In both, the tallest trees form a dense canopy high above the forest floor. Vines climb up the trees in search of sunlight. In a tropical rain forest, nonparasitic plants grow high in the canopy, using the large trees as perches. In both types of forest, the floor is in deep shade; comparatively few shrubs and grasses grow there.

The rich plant life supports food chains that include many of the world's most spectacular animals: brightly colored frogs, fierce harpy eagles, agile monkeys, powerful tigers, slow-moving sloths, and huge columns of army ants, among many others.

While the diversity of plant life in rain forests is rich, the soil generally is not. The lush plants take up so much of the nutrients in rain forests that little is left for the soil below. A study of a rain forest in Venezuela found that 75 percent of the nutrients were in living organisms like plants and trees, 17 percent were in debris, and only 8 percent were in the soil. When an organism dies and decomposes in a rain forest, the nutrients in its cells are quickly absorbed by nearby plants.

Many rain forest species cannot survive in any other type of environment. And like all species, each is biologically unique. It is genetically different from any other species. If it becomes extinct, its uniqueness is lost, and so are any benefits it might have provided to people. The destruction of species that accompanies deforestation could have particularly dire consequences on human life. For example, of the 3,000 plant species the U.S. National Cancer Institute has identified as having anticancer properties, 70 percent are found in tropical rain forests.

Rain forests also have a major impact on both local and global climate. They increase humidity and rainfall in the region, and thus cause large amounts of water to be carried by rivers to the oceans, thus affecting the chemistry and ecology of the oceans. The trees in rain forests consume huge quantities of carbon dioxide from the atmosphere, slowing global warming.

Rain forests also help to maintain soil quality. Plant roots anchor the soil, limiting erosion, creating watersheds, and protecting against destructive floods. Studies in the Ivory Coast showed that an acre of forest on a sloping hillside lost 20 pounds (9 kg) of soil a year due to rain. When the forest was cut down, the same amount of rain washed away 120,000 pounds (54,500 kg) of soil.

Deforestation has many sources. Individuals often cut down rain forest trees for firewood and to clear land on which to raise crops, build ranches, and raise cattle. But erosion and poor soil fertility soon make these farms and ranches worthless. Large commercial operations deforest vast areas for lumber, paper, and other products, much of which are exported to pay debts owed to foreign governments and banks. Development projects such as roads, hydroelectric dams, and mines also destroy large areas of rain forest.

TROPICAL FOREST AREA AND RATE OF DEFORESTATION FOR 87 COUNTRIES, 1981–90 (in thousand hectares)

Region/ Subregion	Number of countries studied	Total land area	Forest area 1980	Forest area 1990	Area deforested annually 1981–90
LATIN AMERICA	**32**	**1,675,700**	**923,000**	**839,000**	**8,300**
Central America and Mexico	7	245,300	77,000	63,500	1,400
Caribbean subregion	18	69,500	48,800	47,100	200
Tropical South America	7	1,360,800	797,100	729,300	6,800
ASIA	**15**	**896,600**	**310,800**	**274,900**	**3,600**
South Asia	6	445,600	70,600	66,200	400
Continental Southeast Asia	5	192,900	83,200	69,700	1,300
Insular Southeast Asia	4	258,100	157,000	138,900	1,800
AFRICA	**40**	**2,243,400**	**650,300**	**600,100**	**5,000**
West Sahelian Africa	8	528,000	41,900	38,000	400
East Sahelian Africa	6	489,600	92,300	85,300	700
West Africa	8	203,200	55,200	43,400	1,200
Central Africa	7	406,400	230,100	215,400	1,500
Tropical Southern Africa	10	557,900	217,700	206,300	1,100
Insular Africa	1	58,200	13,200	11,700	200
Total	**87**	**4,815,700**	**1,884,100**	**1,714,800**	**16,900**

Note: Figures are preliminary estimates. **Source:** World Resources Institute, *World Resources 1992–93* (1992).

U.S. WETLANDS

A wetland is a location other than a river, lake, or open ocean in which the soil for at least part of the year contains as much water as it will hold (the soil is *saturated* with water). Saturated soil often slows decomposition of organic matter, resulting in a thin mud or muck, or in the decayed plant remains known as peat. Common names for wetlands include:

Potholes, which are dry land most of the year, but seasonally become shallow ponds;

Tidal flats, which are underwater at high tide but become muddy land at low tide;

Permafrost, which is saturated soil that is frozen most of the year at the surface, and year-round below the surface;

Bogs, which contain saturated soil and organic material all year, but have little or no standing water;

Marshes, which contain standing shallow water and low vegetation; and

Swamps, where trees grow on small hillocks surrounded by standing water.

Often these informal categories overlap in a given wetland.

One exact definition of what is a "wetland" was developed by the U.S. Army Corps of Engineers in 1987: A wetland is any ground that has mucky or peat-based soils, nourishes specific plant life, and is saturated with water at least seven days a year. By 1989 that definition had been accepted by other U.S. government agencies. But this definition became an active area of controversy in the United States throughout the 1990s. Real-estate interests, farmers, and other business interests favored a definition that would require longer periods of soil saturation to classify potholes and boggy areas as wetlands. In 1991, Pres. Bush's administration proposed, but after pressure from environmental groups, later withdrew, a definition that would have greatly reduced the area of legally defined wetlands in the United States. Although the Bush administration continued to seek ways to change the definition, the subsequent Clinton administration provisionally reaffirmed the 1987 definition. In 1994 the Environmental Protection Agency redefined normal logging practices to prohibit clearing forests from wetlands, extending government protection of swamps. The National Research Council, charged with production of a new definition of wetlands, suggested on May 10, 1995, that a wetland is "an ecosystem that depends on constant or recurrent, shallow inundation or saturation at or near the surface of the substrate." This essentially reaffirms the 1987 definition. Meanwhile, the House of Representatives was contemplating HR 961, which would impose an entirely different definition, requiring that the soil be submerged for at least three weeks in the summer and that the area support plants that only live in saturated soil.

Environmental activists are concerned about the definition of wetlands because wetland environments are important ecosystems that also affect the ecosystems around them. Wetlands provide habitats for many species of animals and plants; a third of the endangered or threatened species in the United States live in or are dependent on them. Wetlands are the nurseries for many fish, almost all amphibians, and various birds and mammals.

The economic importance of wetlands is also immense. For much of the country, wetlands filter and purify water and hold it in place. They store water and slow it down, buffering floods and erosion. Coastal wetlands are spawning grounds for between 60 and 90 percent of U.S. commercial fisheries. Hunting of migratory waterfowl depends entirely upon adequate wetland habitats. Wetlands are among the most productive natural ecosystems on earth in terms of total biological mass per unit of area. There is some evidence that wetlands can eliminate pesticides and other organic toxins by speeding up degradation by microbes.

Despite their significance to the environment and economic importance, from colonial times until recent years, wetlands were regarded primarily as barriers to travel; habitats for such pests as mosquitoes and thus as threats to public health; and as impediments to farm productivity or construction. Therefore, wetlands were drained, cleared, filled, exploited for whatever resources could be extracted from them, and altered in every conceivable way. As a result, more than half the approximately 250 million acres of wetlands in the United States outside of Alaska that were present in colonial times are now gone; about 105 million acres remain according to the 1987 definition. California and Ohio, the states hardest hit, have lost as much as 90 percent of their wetlands. Alaska still has most of its 170 million acres of wetlands, although they too have been under attack by industries seeking to develop about 10 percent of them. The definition proposed by HR 961 would dramatically change the acreage of wetlands since it would define away at least three-fifths of the 105 million acres in the lower 48 states, leaving at best 63 million acres of federally protected wetlands.

STATES WITH MOST WETLAND ACREAGE, 1780s–1980s

	Wetlands in 1780s		Wetlands in 1980s		
State	**Acres**	**Percent of area**	**Acres**	**Percent of area**	**Percent lost**
Alaska	170,200,000	45.3%	170,000,000	45.3%	–0.1%
Florida	20,325,013	54.2	11,038,300	29.5	–46
Louisiana	16,194,500	52.1	8,784,200	28.3	–46
Minnesota	15,070,000	28.0	8,700,000	16.2	–42
Texas	15,999,700	9.4	7,612,412	4.4	–52
North Carolina	11,089,500	33.0	5,689,500	16.9	–49
Michigan	11,200,000	30.1	5,583,400	15.0	–50
Wisconsin	9,800,000	27.3	5,331,392	14.8	–46
Georgia	6,843,200	18.2	5,298,200	14.1	–23
Maine	6,460,000	30.4	5,199,200	24.5	–20

Note: Ranked by wetlands acreage in the 1980s. **Source:** U.S. Dept. of Interior, Fish and Wildlife Service, *Wetlands in the United States, 1780s to 1980s* (1990).

WATER POLLUTION

Although the bad effect of air pollution on health was suspected even earlier, the first proven environmental cause of illness was water pollution. In England, a famous demonstration by physician John Snow in 1854 showed that removing the handle of a pump could reduce the incidence of cholera by depriving people living near a contaminated well from using the water. Chlorine used for water purification was already known at that time, and by the 20th century most major cities in the United States provided treated water.

Problems not directly connected to health also were recognized in the 19th century. Mining in California was, in some locations, polluting the water supply so greatly that crops could not be grown; a law against using water in extracting ores was instituted in the state in 1884. Industrial water pollution was also recognized, although not stopped. Five years after Dr. Snow's famous demonstration, a new source of water pollution was introduced when the first oil well was drilled.

The 20th century brought with it new forms of water pollution. A series of revolutions in agriculture included use of artificial fertilizers, introduction of long-lasting pesticides, and concentration of animal wastes. Each change also introduced new forms of water pollution from runoff—water from rain or snow that fails to sink into the soil. "Point sources," such as sewage pipes and factory waste ponds, were now supplemented with the "nonpoint sources" of farming.

Drinking Water

Americans have for many years taken their drinking water for granted, even when they are among the 8 percent of the population who are supplied by private wells instead of municipal systems of treated water. Despite this complacency, there are many threats to the water supply. These include biological threats to health from contamination, dangerous chemicals in the water supply from a variety of sources, and toxic elements introduced by water treatment or defects in plumbing. The 1972 Clean Water Act, intended to solve many of these problems, has been partially effective in doing so; but it is up for renewal in 1995 and its fate is uncertain. The Clean Water Act is primarily aimed at surface water, but in the mid-1990s, 20 years after passage, more than a third of U.S. rivers and almost half the lakes did not meet its standards. The primary cause was no longer industrial pollution, residue from mining, and untreated sewage; nonpoint sources from runoff, both agricultural and municipal, had taken over as the older point sources were eliminated. A related problem is that high water levels during storms overwhelm both industrial and municipal water treatment. This last source is somewhat more easily controlled than other nonpoint pollution, and revisions of the Clean Water Act in 1987, which went into effect in 1992, attack this problem for urban runoff at the city and county level.

The U.S. Natural Resources Defense Council reported in 1993 that their study found nearly a million cases of Americans each year who become ill from water-borne microorganisms, and about one out of a thousand of such illnesses results in death. A recent instance occurred when the water-supply system in Milwaukee, Wis., became infected with an intestinal parasite that is resistant to chlorine. Many municipal water supply systems regularly are found to contain levels of bacterial contamination that exceed EPA standards.

Most, but not all bacterial contamination stems from the use of surface waters—rivers, lakes, and reservoirs. The other major source of water is groundwater—subsurface water contained for the most part in small cavities, or pores, in rock or soil. Wells in most locations are filled when water from the pores seeps into deep or shallow holes. (Some groundwater is under pressure, and wells that tap into such sources produce an upward-flowing stream of water that often shoots into the air; these are known as artesian wells.) One common way to obtain unpolluted groundwater is to dig deeper wells that find "fossil" water that has been at those levels for thousands of years. Most shallow wells obtain their water from groundwater that recently was surface water and therefore subject to greater contamination.

Groundwater pollution is especially difficult to remedy. Almost all solutions are expensive and, in many cases, not feasible at any price. Such remedies include pumping detoxification agents into the ground or treating the water before use. Often the best treatment is to sink a new, and deeper, well.

Groundwater can be contaminated by industrial pollutants stored or released in ways that put them in contact with the water supply; by leakage from underground storage of volatile chemicals, such as gasoline, cleaning fluid, or petroleum; and by seepage into the soil of agricultural pesticides. A privately funded review of federal and state water tests by the Environmental Working Group reported in 1994 that the water supplies used by 14.1 million Americans contain agricultural pesticides in amounts that would be banned if these levels were found in food.

OIL SPILLS OF 100,000 TONS OR MORE

Date	Cause	Location	Tons spilled
Jan.–June/42	German U-boat attacks on tankers after U.S. enters World War II	U.S., East Coast	590,000
3/18/67	Tanker *Torrey Canyon* grounds	English Channel, off Land's End, UK	119,000
3/20/70	Tanker *Othello* collides with another ship	Tralhavet Bay, Sweden	60,000–100,000
12/19/72	Tanker *Sea Star* collides with another ship	Gulf of Oman	115,000
5/12/76	Tanker *Urquiola* grounds	La Coruña, Spain	100,000
3/16/78	Tanker *Amoco Cadiz* grounds	Northwest France	223,000
6/3/79	Itox I oil well blows	Southern Gulf of Mexico	600,000
7/1/79	Tankers *Atlantic Empress* and *Aegean Captain* collide	Off Trinidad and Tobago	300,000
Feb./83	Blowout in Norwuz oil field	Persian Gulf	600,000
8/6/83	Fire aboard tanker *Castillio de Beliver*	Off Cape Town, South Africa	250,000
1/25/91	Iraq begins deliberately dumping oil into Persian Gulf	Sea Island, Kuwait	1,450,000[1]

Note: One ton equals approximately 269 gallons or 6.4 barrels. For comparison, the 1989 *Exxon Valdez* grounding in Prince William Sound, Alaska, spilled 35,000 tons of oil. 1. Based on UN mission estimates.

Formerly one of the main sources of groundwater contamination had been municipal landfills, but most of these are now sealed with clay liners to prevent seepage; and truly hazardous chemicals, such as mercury or lead from batteries or volatile organic compounds, are banned from landfills.

Some drinking water pollution takes place between the time the water comes from the well or from a surface source and the time it leaves faucets. For example, even though water from municipal plants is tested for lead and kept lead-free, service pipes, home plumbing, and some brass fixtures can leach lead into water, especially hot water. People who depend on private wells can have additional problems, as most of the pumps sold in recent years contain lead in brass or bronze parts that seeps into water contained in or surrounding the pump. Lead from plumbing or from pumps can be flushed from drinking or cooking water by letting the water run before use, but for water supplied by submerged pumps in deep wells, it may be necessary to run water for as long as 10 minutes to get to the lead-free supply.

Even municipal treatment of drinking water is suspected of potentially dangerous side effects. About 70 percent of all Americans drink water that has been disinfected by chlorination. But chlorine can react with organic material in water to form compounds such as chloroform that have been implicated in causing cancer in rats and mice. Except possibly for persons who have some reason for extra caution, however, the benefits of chlorination far outweigh any known danger.

Ocean Pollution

Although the main human health problems associated with water pollution involve sources of fresh water, pollution of the oceans is also an environmental problem. In the long run, ocean pollution could become more of a direct hazard for humans. Indirectly, new laws discouraging dumping of sewage or other wastes at sea mean that these wastes must be kept on the land, where they can more readily affect fresh water supplies.

Ocean pollution also affects food supplies. Pollution is thought to be the trigger for the algal growth that has all but eliminated the scallop fishery in Long Island Sound, for example. Other ocean fisheries in protected bays and sounds have also been damaged by pollution.

Ocean pollution from oil is primarily noted by the public when an oil well at sea is damaged or when an oil-carrying ship leaks large amounts of oil into the sea as a result of an accident. For example, the oil tanker *Braer* made headlines in 1993 when it spilled 26 million gallons of oil (more than twice the amount lost in the famous Exxon *Valdez* accident on March 24, 1989) near a wildlife preserve in the Shetland Islands. Despite this perception, most oil pollution in the ocean actually comes from municipal and industrial runoff, cleaning of ships' bilges or tanks, and other routine events.

Ocean pollution is often in evidence on beaches. Tar balls from oil spills, plastic, and sometimes sewage wash up on beaches. Occasionally ocean beaches have to be closed because of high bacteria counts in the water, making swimming hazardous. The problems with beaches are local, but they reflect a growing problem throughout the oceans.

Plastic, which generally does not break down in the ocean, is a hazard to larger organisms, such as endangered sea turtles. Although the U.S. Senate has ratified an international treaty to prohibit disposal of plastic wastes that can kill or maim creatures that become entangled, the treaty is very difficult to enforce.

> *"Industrial vomit . . . fills our skies and seas."*
>
> —**Alvin Toffler,** ***Future Shock***

SOLID WASTE

Many areas of the United States currently face serious problems in safely and effectively managing the garbage they generate. As a nation, we are generating more trash than ever before, and as the generation of municipal solid waste (MSW) increases, the capacity to handle it is decreasing. Limits to traditional trash management practices such as landfills and incineration are forcing many communities to increase source reduction and recycling programs.

Municipal solid waste is distinct from industrial wastes produced by factories, tailings from mines, construction and demolition waste, sludge from sewage treatment, and junked machinery. MSW is characterized either by the source materials or the end products involved; these characterizations are used to highlight opportunities for source reduction and recycling, and provide information on waste-disposal tendencies.

Disposing of Solid Waste

Total generation of municipal solid waste more than doubled between 1960 and 1993, from 88 million to 207 million tons per year, while per capita generation increased more than 50 percent, from 2.7 pounds to 4.4 pounds per person per day. The EPA projects the per capita figure will decrease to 4.3 pounds by 2000. The four primary methods of dealing with solid waste are putting it in landfills, incineration, recycling, and composting.

Landfills By far the greatest amount of MSW is sent to landfills, of which there are more than 9,000 in the United States. Landfill use fluctuates with changes in the use of alternative waste management methods such as incineration and recycling. In 1960 approximately 62 percent of all garbage was sent to landfills; in 1980 this figure grew to 81 percent, but by 1993 it was back down to 63 percent.

Landfills pose a number of problems. Most landfills are dry and preserve garbage by cutting it off from the rotting influences of air and moisture. William L. Rathje, a professor of anthropology at the University of Arizona and director of The Garbage Project, found that even biodegradable material in landfills does not decay. Newspapers 40 years old can still be read, and hot dogs thrown out years before look more or less unchanged. Some food debris and yard wastes do degrade, but very slowly—about 25 percent in the first 15 years, with almost no visible change thereafter for the 65-year period Rathje studied.

EPA regulations favor dry landfills for two reasons. As biodegradation in wet landfills occurs there is a buildup of hazardous methane gas, and contaminated water leaching out of landfills (leachate) can pollute the surrounding groundwater. But wet landfills have their supporters, who argue that by enhancing decay, a landfill's biological life can be compressed from 40-to-50 years to 5-to-10 years. Since landfills can contain up to 200 hazardous

GENERATION AND RECOVERY OF SELECTED MATERIALS IN MUNICIPAL SOLID WASTE, 1960–93 (millions of tons)

Item and material	1960	1965	1970	1975	1980	1985	1990	1993
Gross waste generated[1]								
Paper and paperboard	29.9	38.0	44.2	43.0	54.7	61.5	73.3	77.8
Glass	6.7	8.7	12.7	13.5	15.0	13.2	13.2	13.7
Metals								
Ferrous	9.9	10.1	12.6	12.3	11.6	10.9	12.3	12.9
Aluminum	0.4	0.5	0.8	1.1	1.8	2.3	2.7	3.0
Other nonferrous	0.2	0.5	0.7	0.9	1.1	1.0	1.2	1.2
Plastics	0.4	1.4	3.1	4.5	7.8	11.6	16.2	19.3
Rubber and leather	2.0	2.6	3.2	3.9	4.3	3.8	4.6	6.2
Textiles	1.7	1.9	2.0	2.2	2.6	2.8	5.6	6.1
Wood	3.0	3.5	4.0	4.4	6.7	8.2	12.3	13.7
Other	0.1	0.3	0.8	1.7	2.9	3.4	3.2	3.3
Materials recovered[2]								
Paper and paperboard	5.4	5.7	7.4	8.2	11.9	13.1	20.9	26.5
Glass	0.1	0.1	0.2	0.4	0.8	1.0	2.6	3.0
Metals								
Ferrous	0.1	0.1	0.1	0.2	0.4	0.4	1.9	3.4
Aluminum	0.0	0.0	0.0	0.1	0.3	0.6	1.0	1.1
Other nonferrous	0.0	0.3	0.3	0.4	0.5	0.5	0.8	0.8
Plastics	0.0	0.0	0.0	0.0	0.0	0.1	0.4	0.7
Rubber and leather	0.3	0.3	0.3	0.2	0.1	0.2	0.2	0.4
Textiles	0.0	0.0	0.0	0.0	0.0	0.0	0.2	0.7
Wood	0.0	0.0	0.0	0.0	0.0	0.0	0.4	1.3
Other[3]	0.0	0.3	0.3	0.4	0.5	0.5	0.8	0.7
Percent of gross discards recovered								
Paper and paperboard	18.1%	15.0%	16.7%	19.1%	21.8%	21.3%	28.6%	34.0%
Glass	1.5	1.1	1.6	3.0	5.3	7.6	19.9	22.0
Metals								
Ferrous	1.0	1.0	0.8	1.6	3.4	3.7	15.4	26.1
Aluminum	0.0	0.0	0.0	9.1	16.7	26.1	38.1	35.4
Other nonferrous	0.0	60.0	42.9	44.4	45.5	50.0	67.7	62.9
Plastics	0.0	0.0	0.0	0.0	0.0	0.9	2.2	3.5
Rubber and leather	15.0	11.5	9.4	5.1	2.3	5.3	4.4	5.9
Textiles	0.0	0.0	0.0	0.0	0.0	0.0	4.3	11.7
Wood	0.0	0.0	0.0	0.0	0.0	0.0	3.2	9.6
Other	0.0	100.0	37.5	23.5	17.2	14.7	23.8	22.1

Note: 1. Generation before materials recovery or combustion. Does not include construction or demolition debris or industrial process wastes. 2. Recovery of postconsumer wastes for recyling and composting; does not include converting fabrication scrap. 3. Recovery of electrolytes in batteries; probably not recycled. **Source:** Environmental Protection Agency, *Characterization of Municipal Solid Waste in the United States: 1994 Update* (1995).

chemicals, they require continuous monitoring anyway; so shortening their active life can yield significant savings. Moreover, by decreasing the volume of trash in a landfill through biodegradation, it can be kept open longer. This is important because some estimates indicate that 80 percent of the nation's landfills will be closed within 20 years, and people are increasingly adamant about not having landfills in their communities, which makes it harder to site new landfills.

To create efficient wet landfills, scientists seek to manipulate the levels of three types of bacteria that ultimately convert wood, paper, and other plant wastes to carbon dioxide and methane. The buildup of methane gas, which is produced through the anaerobic decomposition of organic waste, is a hazard the EPA seeks to avoid. Between 1984 and 1989, explosions and fires from high concentrations of methane killed eight people. But despite methane's potential danger, it can be harnessed efficiently, and methane collection projects are in place at approximately 100 landfills for the primary purpose of resource recovery and energy production.

Incineration/combustion One popular method of disposing of municipal waste used to be simply to burn it. In the 1940s there were approximately 700 municipal incinerators in the United States. Despite the efficiency with which they reduced the volume of waste, they stank, their stacks emitted sizable particles of ash, and they produced noxious gases. For these aesthetic rather than environmental reasons, their numbers declined dramatically in the 1950s. By the time of the Clean Air Act of 1970, there were only 67 incinerators still in operation—most with no energy recovery and no air pollution controls.

In the 1980s, as finding sites for landfills became more difficult, the trend reversed and new incinerators were built or planned. By the early 1990s, the number of incinerators had climbed past 100 again and was heading toward 200. The amount of waste burned by incinerators nearly doubled, from about 9 percent in 1980 to 16 percent in 1993.

About one in five incinerators in the United States uses the energy from burning waste to produce electricity, also a legacy of plans made in the 1980s, when energy prices were still seen as high. Lower energy prices and higher costs for incineration have combined to slow the growth of the industry. The high point for new incinerator plants was 1988, when more than 20 new plants opened. In 1993, no new incinerators opened in the United States, although many remained in various planning stages. At that time, 25 plants burned waste for fuel and there were still 40 such plants being planned.

Any remaining trend toward burning waste stopped suddenly in May 1994 when the U.S. Supreme Court ruled that waste from incinerators had to be treated as toxic on the same basis as any other waste. This was a blow because most incinerator ash contains dioxins that are produced by combustion and heavy metals such as lead, cadmium, and mercury, which do not burn.

In that same month, the Court ruled that localities could not prevent landfills from taking waste away from incinerators if the landfills offered better bargains; the market, not the municipality, was to be the controlling force in determining whether waste was burned or handled some other way. Previously, municipalities could support their incinerator investment by directing all wastes within their governmental unit toward the landfill.

The result of these Court decisions, combined with energy prices that in terms of constant dollars continued to decline, was a scaling down for all types of incinerator construction. In 1991 there were 128 U.S. incinerators, but 89 more had been under construction or in various planning stages. Six months after the Supreme Court rulings, in October 1994, plans for 77 of the proposed incinerators had been canceled. Only three new incinerators were still under construction.

Recycling/composting Recycling of manufactured goods (such as paper, cans, and glass) and composting of organic goods (food and yard waste) are two ways of significantly reducing the amount of waste that winds up in landfills or incinerators. Although composting of municipal waste has been practiced in Europe for more than 30 years—Sweden composts over one-fourth of all its solid waste—it has only recently taken root in the United States. Nevertheless, composting accounts for only a tiny percentage of MSW generated, and the proportion is not expected to grow significantly in the future.

MUNICIPAL SOLID WASTE GENERATED, RECOVERED, COMBUSTED, AND DISCARDED, 1960–93

Category	1960	1965	1970	1975	1980	1985	1990	1993
				Millions of tons				
Generation	87.8	103.4	121.9	128.1	151.5	164.4	195.7	206.9
Materials recovery	5.9	6.8	8.6	9.9	14.5	16.4	33.4	45.0
Recovery for recycling	5.9	6.8	8.6	9.9	14.5	16.4	29.2	N.A.
Recovery for composting	0.0	0.0	0.0	0.0	0.0	0.0	4.2	N.A.
Discards after recovery[1]	81.9	96.6	113.3	118.2	137.0	148.1	162.3	N.A.
Combustion	27.0	27.0	25.1	18.5	13.7	11.7	31.9	32.9
With energy recovery	0.0	0.2	0.4	0.7	2.7	7.6	29.7	N.A.
Without energy recovery	27.0	26.8	25.1	17.8	11.0	4.1	2.2	N.A.
Discards to landfill or other[2]	54.9	69.6	88.2	99.7	123.3	136.4	130.4	129.0
				Percent of total generation				
Generation	100.0%	100.0%	100.0%	100.0%	100.0%	100.0%	100.0%	100.0%
Materials recovery	6.7	6.6	7.1	7.7	9.6	9.9	17.1	21.7
Recovery for recycling	6.7	6.6	7.1	7.7	9.6	9.9	14.9	N.A.
Recovery for composting	0.0	0.0	0.0	0.0	0.0	0.0	2.1	N.A.
Discards after recovery[1]	93.3	93.4	92.9	92.3	90.4	90.1	82.9	N.A.
Combustion	30.8	26.1	20.6	14.4	9.0	7.1	16.3	15.9
With energy recovery	0.0	0.2	0.3	0.5	1.8	4.6	15.2	N.A.
Without energy recovery	30.8	25.9	20.3	13.9	7.3	2.5	0.0	N.A.
Discards to landfill or other[2]	62.5	67.3	72.4	77.8	81.4	82.9	66.6	62.4

1. Does not include residues from recyling or composting processes. 2. Does not include residues from recycling, composting, or combustion processes. **Source:** Environmental Protection Agency, *Characterization of Municipal Solid Waste in the United States: 1994 Update* (1995).

Between 1985 and 1993, the amount of recycled materials in municipal waste more than doubled, from 10 percent to 22 percent. Paper and paperboard are recycled more than any other material, with 34 percent of it being used more than once. Aluminum has a slightly higher rate of recycling, but only three million tons of aluminum ever enter the waste stream, as compared with 77.8 million tons of paper. More than 26 million tons of paper are recovered each year. The problem in recent years with paper recycling is that there have been more paper products set aside for recycling than there have been mills to convert the used paper into new products. Moreover, despite the spiraling cost of paper, it's still cheaper to cut down trees and make virgin paper than it is to use recycled paper. Recycling mills increased their capacities to create an additional 1.5 million tons of cartons and 2 million tons of office paper, which should bring the price down. Paper recycling should also be fueled by Pres. Clinton's 1993 executive order requiring federal agencies to buy printing and writing paper with a minimum of 20 percent recycled fibers.

Recycling is considered vital to reducing the nation's waste. In addition to diverting large volumes of waste from landfills and combustors, it also stops the unnecessary depletion of natural resources and raises awareness about solid waste disposal, because people must become conscious of what they do and do not discard. One impediment to increased recycling is the economic disincentives to processing and purchasing secondary materials, such as the cost of developing new or adapting existing technologies to accommodate recycled materials.

A newspaper de-inking plant alone can cost as much as $75 million to build. Moreover, the cost to the consumer of recycled materials may also dissuade recycling. In some parts of the country, recycled paper costs as much as or more than virgin paper, thus retarding demand for recycled goods. On the supply side, the cost of recycling almost always exceeds the cost of dumping materials in landfills.

New materials being targeted for increased recycling are plastics and lead-acid batteries. The problem with plastics is that they are made from a wide variety of chemical mixes that, so far, must be recycled independently of one another. Coloring agents in plastics pose additional problems.

Source reduction Many experts believe that the key to solving the municipal waste problem is source reduction—minimizing the volume of products and the toxics they contain, and extending their useful life. Removal of toxics enhances the safety of recycling, landfilling, and combustion, while volume reduction helps to extend the capacity of existing waste systems.

Waste Characterizations

Glass enters the waste stream primarily as discarded containers for food, beverages, and cosmetics, as well as in some durable goods. The increased use of plastic and aluminum for containers led to a decline in the amount of glass in MSW.

Metals are classified as either ferrous metals (iron and steel), aluminum, or other nonferrous metals. Iron and steel—mostly from durable goods, containers, and packaging—are the largest category of metals in MSW. Recovery rates for iron and steel are increasing. In 1985, less than 4 percent of iron and steel products were recycled; by 1993, that figure had increased to 26 percent.

Aluminum, used primarily in the making of containers, has largely displaced iron and steel in that area. More than 1 million tons of aluminum, or 36 percent of the total generated, were recycled in 1993. Beer and soda cans are responsible for most aluminum recycling.

Other nonferrous metals in the waste stream—chiefly copper, lead, and zinc—amounted to 800,000 tons in 1993. The greatest source of metal waste that is not iron, steel, or aluminum is worn-out car batteries, which are largely lead. It is estimated that 90 percent of all battery lead is recovered.

Plastics are the most rapidly growing segment of MSW, increasing 66 percent from 11.6 million tons in 1985 to 19.3 million tons in 1993. Recycling of plastics is still in its infancy, but out of necessity, it has risen rapidly, from less than 1 percent in 1985 to 3.5 percent in 1993. Plastics are now often labeled with recycling symbols and names so that they can be more easily sorted. The kind in large soda bottles (#1 PET) is the most valuable and in many states is part of a bottle-deposit program, ensuring that a high percentage is recycled (although not usually as soda bottles: instead, most is turned into fiber). About 35 percent of PET bottles were recycled in 1991. Polystyrene, or #6 PS, the familiar foamed plastic of disposable coffee cups and egg cartons, is seldom recycled; manufacturers do not want it.

Food waste includes uneaten food and food scraps from residences, restaurants, and commercial and institutional establishments. A total of 13.8 million tons of food waste was generated in 1993; almost none of it was recovered. This can be attributed to the increased use of garbage disposals, which send food waste straight to sewer systems, and to the increase in prepared foods, since food preparation waste from foods prepared and packaged off-site are classified as industrial waste.

Yard wastes, including grass clippings and leaves from residential, commercial, and industrial sources, made up 32.8 million tons of MSW in 1993. Composting has made its greatest impact in this area, increasing the yard waste recovery rate from 2 percent in 1988 to 6.5 percent in 1993.

> *"Nothing ever goes away."*
>
> —Barry Commoner

HAZARDOUS WASTE

Superfund

In 1980, Congress enacted the Comprehensive Environmental Response, Compensation, and Liability Act (CERCLA), better known as the Superfund, a $1.6 billion, five-year program to clean up thousands of hazardous waste sites. The fund was renewed in 1986 and again in 1991. The EPA, which administers the Superfund, can take two types of action when a hazardous substance is released into the environment. It can remove the threat, in an emergency action limited to one year and/or $2 million. Or it can provide a permanent remedial response; this is generally longer-term and more expensive than removal. The money for cleaning up hazardous waste comes from several sources. The preferred source is the individuals or companies responsible for the problem, who can clean up the site voluntarily or after action has been taken by the government. In cases where the original polluters are bankrupt or cannot be found, the Superfund can be used to pay for the costs entirely. Generally speaking, the EPA estimates the average cost of a long-term solution at $25–$30 million.

Before work begins on a long-term solution to a hazardous-waste site, the site must be listed on the EPA's National Priorities List (NPL). Whether a site makes the NPL depends on its score on a numerically based system that factors in risks to groundwater, surface water, and air. CERCLA also allows states and territories to designate one top-priority site regardless of its score, and there are seven such sites that would not make the NPL on the basis of their numerical score alone.

The Superfund restricts the EPA's authority to respond to certain sites by expressly excluding some substances—most notably petroleum—from the definition of "release." However, in some cases other laws may enable the federal governments to undertake or enforce cleanup actions of these excluded substances. Since Superfund's enactment, it has evaluated 31,000 sites, of which 5 percent to 10 percent have been placed on the NPL. Because many are in regions of high population density, one in four Americans lives within four miles of an NPL site.

In 1990, the EPA revised the way it ranks hazardous waste sites to take into account contamination of soil and to consider how contamination of the aquatic food chain ultimately affects human food supplies. The revised ranking system also weighs contaminants not only by their toxicity, but by their mobility or their ability to migrate in the air and groundwater.

Despite the EPA's best efforts to improve its hazardous waste ranking system, Superfund continues to fall short in its ultimate aim to improve the environment. After increasing by nearly 600 percent in six years, the number of sites added to the National Priorities List has slowed to a trickle. Furthermore, it has taken about 10 years for the average site to be cleaned up, although some sites from the first list in 1981 have yet to be resolved. The average cost per site has been a staggering $28 million, mostly paid by industry. And critics say that a large proportion of the total of $22 billion spent in the fund's first dozen years has gone to environmental lawyers for the polluting companies. All in all, the EPA claims only 346 sites, little more than 1 percent of all sites identified had been cleaned up by 1994, although the most dangerous chemicals have been removed from another 3,300 sites.

THE 50 WORST SUPERFUND WASTE SITES, 1994

State	Site	City/County	Score (rank)	When listed
Arkansas	Vertac, Inc.	Jacksonville	65.46 (32)	Oct. 1981
California	McCormick & Baxter Creosoting Co.	Stockton	74.86 (5)	Feb. 1992
California	Stoker Company	Imperial	65.51 (30)	July 1991
California	Riverbank Army Ammunition Plant	Riverbank	63.94 (36)	June 1988
Colorado	Rocky Flats Plant (USDOE)	Golden	64.32 (35)	Oct. 1984
Delaware	Tybouts Corner Landfill[1]	New Castle County	73.67 (6)	Oct. 1981
Delaware	Army Creek Landfill	New Castle County	69.92 (18)	Oct. 1981
Florida	Stauffer Chemical Co.	Tarpon Springs	70.71 (12)	Feb. 1992
Florida	Stauffer Chemical Co.	Tampa	63.62 (39)	Feb. 1992
Hawaii	Pearl Harbor Naval Complex	Pearl Harbor	70.82 (11)	July 1991
Idaho	Triumph Mine Tailings Piles	Triumph	90.33 (1)	May 1993
Indiana	U.S. Smelter & Lead Refinery Inc.	East Chicago	70.71 (12)	Feb. 1992
Iowa	Mason City Coal Gasification Plant	Mason City	69.33 (20)	Jan. 1994
Maine	Portsmouth Naval Shipyard	Kittery	67.71 (24)	June 1993
Massachusetts	Industri-Plex	Woburn	72.42 (9)	Oct. 1981
Massachusetts	Nyanza Chemical Waste Dump	Ashland	69.22 (21)	Oct. 1981
Massachusetts	Baird & McGuire	Holbrook	66.35 (27)	Dec. 1982
Michigan	Berlin & Farro	Swartz Creek	66.74 (26)	July 1982
Michigan	Liquid Disposal, Inc.	Utica	63.28 (42)	July 1982
Minnesota	FMC Corp. (Fridley Plant)	Fridley	65.50 (31)	July 1982
Missouri	Big River Tailings/St. Joe Minerals	Desloge	84.91 (3)	Feb. 1992
Montana	Silver Bow Creek/Butte Area	Silver Bow/Deer Lodge	63.76 (37)	Dec. 1982
Montana	East Helena Site	East Helena	61.65 (49)	Sept. 1983
New Hampshire	Somersworth Sanitary Landfill	Somersworth	65.56 (29)	Dec. 1982
New Hampshire	Keefe Environmental Services	Epping	65.19 (34)	Oct. 1981
New Hampshire	Sylvester[1]	Nashua	63.28 (42)	Oct. 1981
New Jersey	Lipari Landfill	Pitman	75.60 (4)	Oct. 1981
New Jersey	Helen Kramer Landfill	Mantua Township	72.66 (8)	July 1982
New Jersey	Price Landfill[1]	Pleasantville	71.60 (10)	Oct. 1981
New Jersey	CPS/Madison Industries	Old Bridge Township	69.73 (19)	Dec. 1982
New Jersey	GEMS Landfill	Gloucester Township	68.53 (23)	July 1982
New Jersey	Lone Pine Landfill	Freehold Township	66.33 (28)	Oct. 1981
New York	Pollution Abatement Services[1]	Oswego	70.80 (12)	Oct. 1981
North Carolina	General Electric Co.–Shepherd Farm	East Flat Rock	70.71 (12)	Feb. 1992
Ohio	Arcanum Iron & Metal	Darke County	62.26 (47)	Dec. 1982
Pennsylvania	Bruin Lagoon	Bruin Borough	73.11 (7)	Oct. 1981
Pennsylvania	East Tenth Street	Marcus Hook	67.68 (25)	Jan. 1994
Pennsylvania	Tysons Dump	Upper Merion Township	63.10 (44)	Sept. 1983
Pennsylvania	McAdoo Associates[1]	McAdoo Borough	63.03 (45)	Oct. 1981
South Dakota	Whitewood Creek[1]	Whitewood	63.76 (37)	Oct. 1981
Texas	French, Ltd.	Crosby	63.33 (40)	Oct. 1981
Texas	Motco, Inc.[1]	La Marque	62.66 (46)	Oct. 1981
Texas	Sikes Disposal Pits	Crosby	61.62 (50)	Oct. 1981
Utah	Murray Smelter	Murray City	86.60 (2)	Jan. 1994
Utah	Kennecott (South Zone)	Copperton	70.71 (12)	Jan. 1994
Utah	Wasatch Chemical Co. (Lot 6)	Salt Lake City	63.31 (41)	Jan. 1987
Utah	Petrochem Recycling/Ekotek Plant	Salt Lake City	62.18 (48)	July 1991
Washington	Pacific Sound Resources	Seattle	70.71 (12)	May 1993
Washington	Hanford 200-Area (USDOE)	Benton County	69.05 (22)	June 1988
Washington	Hanford 300-Area (USDOE)	Benton County	65.23 (33)	June 1988

1. Site is also its state's top priority. **Source:** Environmental Protection Agency, *National Priorities List* (February 1994).

Hazardous Chemicals

By law the EPA must determine which substances used in the United States that might be released into the environment are hazardous. Hundreds of substances are classified as hazardous, and releases of more than a specified amount must be reported to the U.S. Coast Guard's National Response Center—the 24-hour toll-free number is 1-800-424-8802—who pass on information to the EPA and other appropriate agencies. Substances are considered hazardous

COMMON HAZARDOUS CHEMICALS REQUIRING NATIONAL RESPONSE CENTER NOTIFICATION (partial list)

Substance	Remarks	Amount to be reported if released
Acetic acid	Vinegar is generally 2% acetic acid, but acetic acid is used in many manufacturing processes; Toxic as vapor at 10 parts per million in air.	5,000 lbs. (2,270 kg)
Acetone	Toxic chemical (1,000 parts per million in air) used in large amounts as solvent for resins and fats.	5,000 lbs. (2,270 kg)
Aluminum sulfate	Used sometimes in dyeing or in foam fire extinguishers.	1,000 lbs. (454 kg)
Ammonia	Use as fertilizer does not need to be reported; however, it is toxic and extremely hazardous; emergency planning required if 500 lbs. possessed.	100 lbs. (45.4 kg)
Benzene	Used in drugs, dyes, explosives, plastics, detergents, and paint remover; can cause cancer; toxic.	10 lbs. (4.54 kg)
Chlorine	Widely used to disinfect water, the gas is toxic at concentration of one part per million in air; extremely hazardous; requires emergency planning if 100 lbs. is possessed.	10 lbs. (4.54 kg)
Cumene	Additive for high-octane fuels; toxic to skin at 50 parts per million in air.	5,000 lbs. (2,270 kg)
Cyclohexane	Petroleum derivative.	1,000 lbs. (454 kg)
Ethylbenzene	Toxic at 100 parts per million in air.	1,000 lbs. (454 kg)
Ethylene dichloride	Additive to gasoline that combines with lead to make "Ethyl" gasoline; also used in making plastics.	100 lbs. (45.4 kg)
Ethylene oxide	Widely used in making plastics; toxic at 50 parts per million in air; extremely hazardous; requires emergency planning if 1,000 lbs. possessed.	1–10 lbs. (0.454 kg–4.54 kg)
Formaldehyde	Used in wood substitutes and plastics; toxic and may cause cancer; extremely hazardous; requires emergency planning if 500 lbs. possessed.	100 lbs. (45.4 kg)
Hydrochloric acid	Used in petroleum, manufacturing, and metals industries; toxic; as the gas hydrogen chloride, it is extremely hazardous and requires emergency planning if 500 lbs. possessed.	5,000 lbs. (2,270 kg)
Methanol	Commonly called wood alcohol; used as antifreeze, solvent, and starting material for other compounds; toxic.	5,000 lbs. (2,270 kg)
Nitric acid	Used in preparing fertilizers and explosives; toxic and extremely hazardous; requires emergency planning if 1,000 lbs. possessed.	1,000 lbs. (454 kg)
Phenol	Used in making plastics; vapor is toxic to skin at 5 parts per million in air; extremely hazardous; requires emergency planning if 500 pounds possessed and further planning if 10,000 pounds possessed.	1,000 lbs. (454 kg)
Phosphoric acid	Used as flavoring agent, in pharmaceuticals, and in manufacturing fertilizers; toxic.	5,000 lbs. (2,270 kg)
Sodium hydroxide	Commonly known as lye or as caustic soda; toxic.	1,000 lbs. (454 kg)
Styrene	Used in manufacture of styrene plastics and artificial rubber; toxic.	1,000 lbs. (454 kg)
Sulfuric acid	Most common chemical used in U.S.; toxic and extremely hazardous; emergency planning required if 1,000 lbs. possessed.	1,000 lbs. (454 kg)
Toluene	Used in making explosives, drugs, and dyes; toxic.	1,000 lbs. (454 kg)
Vinyl chloride	Used to make plastics and aerosols; causes cancer; toxic.	1 lb. (0.454 kg)
Xylene	Used to make other compounds; toxic.	1,000 lbs. (454 kg)

Source: Environmental Protection Agency, *Title 3: List of Lists* (Jan. 1990).

if they catch fire easily, are corrosive, react easily with other chemicals, or are toxic. Some substances are hazardous because they cause cancer, such as asbestos.

Toxic chemicals must also be reported annually, and extremely hazardous substances require emergency planning if you possess over a certain amount, called the Threshold Planning Quantity (TPQ). If you exceed the TPQ, you must have a plan for emergencies.

The accompanying table describes some of the most commonly used substances in the United States, general information about them, and the amount that must be reported to the National Response Center if any are released into the environment.

SUPERFUND HAZARDOUS WASTE SITES, SELECTED YEARS, 1981–95

Year	Number of sites	Year	Number of sites
1981	115[1]	1989	981
1982	418[1]	1990	1,187
1983	406	1992	1,183
1984	538	1993	1,202
1986	703	1994	1,287
1987	802	1995	1,296

1. Proposed sites only. Final sites not calculated until release of first National Priorities list in 1983. **Source:** Environmental Protection Agency, *National Priorities List, Supplementary Materials* (February 1995).

STATES WITH MOST NATIONAL PRIORITY LIST HAZARDOUS WASTE SITES, 1995

State	Nonfederal	Federal	Total
New Jersey	101	6	107
Pennsylvania	96	6	102
California	73	23	96
New York	78	4	82
Michigan	77	1	78
Florida	54	5	59
Washington	35	20	55
Minnesota	38	3	41
Wisconsin	40	0	40
Ohio	33	5	38
Illinois	33	4	37

Source: Environmental Protection Agency, *National Priorities List, Supplementary Materials* (February 1995).

Nuclear Waste

Nuclear waste in the United States comes from nuclear weapons production facilities, nuclear power plants, medical equipment (primarily used in radiation treatments), industrial sources of radioactivity used as a more powerful alternative to X rays, and residues from uranium mining. Nuclear waste is often grouped into two categories, labeled "low-level" and "high-level." Low-level waste is slightly radioactive, often from exposure to a high-level source. High-level waste is often grouped as either civilian, mainly spent fuel from nuclear reactors, or military, wastes produced in the manufacture of nuclear weapons.

Between 1946 and 1970 the United States disposed of nuclear waste by dumping it at sea, but this practice was thought to be dangerous and stopped in 1970. By 1976 both the United States and the Soviet Union were among the nations signing an international convention against ocean dumping. In 1990, however, it was revealed that the Soviet Union had continued to use ocean dumping for nuclear wastes produced by nuclear-powered submarines and icebreakers.

Another early method of disposal of nuclear wastes involved suspending them in a liquid or in cement and injecting the radioactive combination into wells. In the United States this method was stopped in 1984 because some radioactivity from wastes mixed with cement was seeping into water supplies. It had never been a major method of disposal in any case. The situation was different in the Soviet Union. For the past 30 years the Russians have injected liquefied high-level wastes into rock strata at three sites. This practice has resulted in an unknown amount of spreading contamination.

In the United States current plans call for consortiums of states to develop sites for storage of low-level wastes, while the federal government has tried to find a suitable site for storage of high-level wastes from nuclear power plants and for very long-lived radioactive materials from weapons production. No plans are currently in effect, however, with waste being kept on the site where it was generated. In 37 states east of the Rockies, low-level waste has been temporarily (since 1971) shipped to Barnwell County, South Carolina. Perhaps the closest new site to realization is the Ward Valley site in California for low-level wastes from California, Arizona, and the Dakotas, which would, when opened, become the first such site to open since Barnwell County. Studies for a high-level storage facility at Yucca Mountain in Nevada are expected to continue at least until 2001; the facility might open as early as 2010. Another site under discussion for high-level wastes is near Carlsbad, New Mexico. Like the other sites under discussion, political concerns continue to keep the site under study and from being put into use.

Nuclear Weapons Waste

The Nuclear Regulatory Commission is the agency charged with monitoring the disposal of waste generated by civilian-operated nuclear reactors. However, most of the nuclear waste in the United States is the by-product of the federal government's nuclear weapons programs. Disposal and monitoring of this waste—which includes millions of cubic yards of contaminated soil and other debris at more than 100 sites in 32 states and the Marshall Islands—is the responsibility of the Department of Energy, the Department of Defense, the Nuclear Waste Technical Review Board, and the Office of the Nuclear Waste Negotiator. Total cost of the cleanup could be about $300–$400 billion over 30 years, and by 1992 the Department of Energy was the government's largest environmental agency.

The Nuclear Waste Technical Review Board evaluates the technical and scientific validity of the Department of Energy's nuclear waste disposal program undertaken after the enactment of the Nuclear Waste Policy Amendments Act of 1987.

The Office of the Nuclear Waste Negotiator is directed to attempt to find and to negotiate with any state or Indian tribe willing to host a nuclear waste repository or monitored retrievable storage facility at a technically qualified site on reasonable terms.

The Department of Energy thought it had found its first permanent dumping site for waste contaminated by plutonium during the production of nuclear weapons. But a federal district judge in Washington ruled that the dump, the Waste Isolation Pilot Plant, near Carlsbad, New Mexico, must be approved by both Congress and the state of New Mexico. For its part, New Mexico has demanded money to improve the roads over which the trucks carrying the nuclear waste will run, to train hospital and emergency crews in radiation safety, and to provide oversight by the Environmental Protection Agency. These costs have been estimated at $600 million.

ENDANGERED SPECIES

A species is a specific kind of organism, such as the common earthworm, the daffodil, the American opossum, or the human. All told there are about 1.4 million classified species of all kinds, including plants, microorganisms, mammals, and fish. This is thought to represent no more than about 10 percent of all species. (And if the results of some surveys of rain forest canopies in Panama are correct, there may be as many as 30 million insect species alone.) Since life developed more than 600 million years ago, innumerable species have appeared and become extinct. Today, biological diversity faces a rate of species destruction greater than any since the mass extinctions of the dinosaurs 65 million years ago.

Animal and plant species are threatened on a number of fronts. Their natural habitats face destruction through deforestation, wetlands loss, and urban sprawl, and are also affected by processes that derive from global warming such as shifting climate and vegetation zones. Another problem is the shift to "monocultures" in agriculture, producing only one strain of crop for food.

International controls Although we think primarily of the U.S. Endangered Species Act of 1966 as the chief bulwark protecting species, the act came under attack in 1995 and may be much weakened when renewed. But there are also international treaties to which the United States is a signatory that protect species. The Convention on International Trade in Endangered Species of Wild Fauna and Flora (CITES) has been in force since 1975. Signed by 122 nations, it lists species for which international trade in the live organisms, meat, lumber, or other parts of species is banned or restricted. While smugglers are thought to violate CITES restrictions regularly in what is a $5 billion annual illegal trade, CITES continues to be one of the main forces in species preservation.

At the end of 1993, the United States signed a newer treaty dealing with endangered species, the Convention on Biological Diversity, which has 167 members. This treaty commits its members to species and habitat preservation within their own borders, supplementing the CITES bans on international acts against species.

Other international treaties affect more limited interests. The International Whaling Commission, with 40 members currently, has been in business since 1949. The commission has probably saved whales from extinction with its near-total ban on whaling since the late 1980s. Other groups, such as the 10-nation Inter-American Tropical Tuna Commission, are modeled on the whaling group. The Tuna Commission is also involved in efforts to protect dolphins, which have in the past been trapped in tuna nets.

To reverse the trend toward species extinction, governments around the world have set aside a total of about 425 million hectares (about 16.4 million square miles) of protected lands in about 3,500 parks and preserves. In addition, many countries try to identify species threatened with extinction.

SELECTED ENDANGERED SPECIES OF THE WORLD

Mammals

Cheetah *(Acinonyx jubatus)* It is believed the cheetah almost became extinct at some time in the recent past, causing a "genetic bottleneck" when the population contained only a few closely related individuals. One cause of the fragility of the present cheetah population, which ranges from Africa to India, is this lack of genetic variability—although all the big cats are under pressure from changes in the environment and from hunters.

Chimpanzee, African *(Pan troglodytes)* Endangered status applies to chimpanzees in Africa only; the 600 or so chimpanzees in the United States are classified as threatened and may continue to be used in research. Recent studies suggest that the common chimpanzee is actually two different species in different parts of Africa, making each species even more liable to extinction. A third species, *Pan paniscus*, also consists of a small population in Africa.

Dugong, or sea cow *(Dugong dugon)* An inoffensive sea mammal living in shallow waters around the coasts of the Western Pacific, and Indian Ocean from East Africa to Japan, the dugong is easy to capture and desirable as food. Its hide makes excellent leather. It is so vulnerable, however, that any organized hunting soon leads to local extinction. Although the dugong is protected by law in large parts of its range, controlling hunting at sea is difficult.

ENDANGERED AND THREATENED SPECIES, 1995

Group	Endangered U.S.	Endangered Foreign	Threatened U.S.	Threatened Foreign	Total listed
Mammals	55	252	9	19	335
Birds	76	177	16	6	275
Reptiles	14	65	19	14	112
Amphibians	7	8	5	0	20
Fishes	68	11	37	0	116
Snails	15	1	7	0	23
Clams	51	2	6	0	59
Crustaceans	14	0	3	0	17
Insects	20	4	9	0	33
Arachnids	5	0	0	0	5
Total animals	**325**	**520**	**111**	**39**	**995**
Flowering plants	406	1	90	0	497
Conifers	2	0	0	2	4
Ferns and others	26	0	2	0	28
Total plants	**434**	**1**	**92**	**2**	**529**
Total species	**759**	**521**	**203**	**41**	**1,524**[1]

Note: Separate populations of a species, listed both as endangered and threatened, are tallied twice. For example, the grizzly bear is included as threatened in the U.S. and endangered in Mexico. Eight other species are counted twice: leopard, gray wolf, bald eagle, piping plover, roseate tern, chimpanzee, green sea turtle, and olive ridley sea turtle. **Source:** U.S. Fish and Wildlife Service, *Box Score of U.S. List of Endangered and Threatened Species*, Apr. 30, 1995.

Gibbon (*Hylobates,* all species) As recently as 1969, a major list of endangered species failed to include any gibbon species. Today all species of this most primitive of apes are endangered, primarily because of habitat destruction.

Gorilla *(Gorilla gorilla)* The gorilla is thought to have been endangered since 1933, only 31 years after its "discovery." The causes are habitat destruction, the use of gorillas as a food source, and the sale of baby gorillas to people outside Africa. In 1994 research showed that the West African gorilla was a separate species from the mountain gorilla, so each population is smaller and more endangered than previously believed.

Jaguar *(Panthera onca)* It is surprising that an animal with a historic range extending from the U.S. Southwest to practically the southern tip of South America could become endangered. Habitat destruction and hunting for its pelt are the most likely causes.

Leopard *(Panthera pardus, P. uncia,* and *Neofelis nebulosa)* Three species of leopard are endangered, although the common leopard, *P. pardus,* in the southern part of its African range is not endangered, only threatened. The other two are commonly called the clouded leopard *(N. nebulosa),* found in southeast and south central Asia and Taiwan, and the snow leopard *(P. uncia),* found in the Himalaya Mountains and central Asia.

Monkey Many species of monkey, especially those from Latin America, such as the howler monkey *(Alouatta palliata)* and the spider monkey *(Ateles geoffroyi),* are endangered. A few African species, such as some colobus monkeys (e.g., *Colobus kirki*) are also endangered. The colobus monkeys are hunted for their fur, while habitat destruction and collecting for pets have been problems for Latin American monkeys. Another group of endangered Latin American monkeys is the tamarins (*Leontopithecus* ssp.).

Orangutan *(Pongo pygmaeus)* This great ape has seen its range shrink from much of southern Asia to parts of the islands of Sumatra and Borneo. Habitat destruction and the capture of animals for pets or zoos have been factors, but also young orangutans are likely to catch human diseases. Orangutans also have a very low reproductive rate.

Panda, giant *(Ailuropoda melanoleuca)* One of the last large mammals to become known to Western science (brought to its attention in 1869), the giant panda has been one of the favorite creatures of all who have seen it. Its restricted habitat in China's western mountains and restricted diet of bamboo shoots contribute greatly to its endangered status. There are so few individual pandas that collecting them for zoos probably is a factor as well. Some attempts to breed pandas in zoos have been successful, but it is not easy to accomplish.

Rhinoceros Most species of rhinoceros are endangered, with the black rhinoceros *(Diceros bicornis)* and the northern white rhinoceros *(Ceratotherium simum cottoni)* the principal foci of concern. Several other rhinoceros species in Asia have been close to extinction for many years. Poachers kill rhinos for the horns, which are valued in traditional medicine and for knife or sword handles. China officially banned trade in rhinoceros parts in 1993, while Taiwan officially halted rhino horn trading in 1994.

Tiger *(Panthera tigris)* Eight subspecies of tiger roamed temperate and tropical Asia a century ago. Habitat destruction and excessive hunting caused the extinction of three of them and reduced stocks of the others to low levels. Today, however, poachers are the main threat. Tiger parts are widely used in Asian folk medicine, although their use was officially banned in China in 1993, and poachers can get large sums for tiger bones, blood, or body parts. At most there were about 6,000 tigers left in the wild in 1994, although the true number could be half that.

Whale The blue whale *(Balaenoptera musculus),* bowhead whale *(Balaena mysticetus),* finback whale *(Balaenoptera physalus),* gray whale *(Eschrichtius robustus),* humpback whale *(Megaptera novaeangliae),* right whale *(Balaena glacialis),* Sei whale *(Balaenoptera borealis),* and sperm whale *(Physeter catodon)* are all listed as endangered by the United States. Since 1986 the International Whaling Commission has prohibited essentially all whaling, although a few whales are allowed to be taken by traditional whalers such as the Inuit (or Eskimo) or for research purposes (often disputed). Stocks of blue, bowhead, and right whales, the most endangered, are still below 10,000 for each species. In 1994 the International Whaling Commission agreed to institute a permanent ban on all whaling in southern oceans, including all waters south of Africa, Australia, and South America. Whaling is still outlawed everywhere else, but outside the southern sanctuary the ban must be renewed every two years.

Wolf *(Canis lupus)* The gray wolf once had the greatest range of any terrestrial mammal outside of *Homo sapiens.* Perhaps as many as a half million wolves were once found throughout the Northern Hemisphere except in the tropics and the most arid deserts. Only 100,000 to 150,000 remain, nearly all in the wildernesses of the far north, although some are found in such southern nations as Mexico and Italy. The population in the lower 48 states had been nearly eliminated sometime during the 1940s, but a few wolves maintained a permanent population in northern Minnesota and occasional strays from Canada or Mexico have been found in other border states. In 1995 an attempt began to reintroduce wolves to the interior of the lower 48 states at Yellowstone National Park and in Idaho. One of the first wolves released in Idaho was shot soon after release, however.

Other Species

Birds There are 9,672 species of birds currently identified worldwide. According to the International Council on Bird Preservation, more than a thousand of these are threatened or endangered, although the U.S. Fish and Wildlife Service lists fewer than 250. In the United States today, well-known instances of endangered birds include the northern spotted owl, the American condor, the California gnatcatcher, and the red-cockaded woodpecker, each of which has been given special treatment in hopes of saving the species.

Less well known is a general decline in northeastern and midwestern birds that winter in the Caribbean or in Central or South America. Among those, the reduction in numbers of the redstart and most other warblers, the northern (formerly Baltimore) oriole, the scarlet tanager, and the wood thrush has been particularly sharp. Less desirable birds, such as cowbirds and starlings, have increased in numbers.

Birds have been particularly vulnerable to human-caused extinctions. The first extinctions definitely known to be caused by humans were the extinctions of some 20 species of flightless moas in New Zealand by the Maori, who probably arrived around A.D. 800. The last moa of any species was killed about the time of Capt. James Cook's voyage around the islands in 1769–70. Together with the Europeans who colonized the islands, the Maoris caused the extinction of about a third of the 150 bird species.

Some bird extinctions are well known, such as the dodo (late 17th century), the passenger pigeon (1914), and the Carolina parakeet (1914). But these are only the tip of the iceberg, since about 100 species of birds are known to have become extinct since A.D. 1600 (about the time that good worldwide records of species first became available).

Reptiles Many species or subspecies of alligators, crocodiles, iguanas, and sea turtles are endangered. In the United States, protection of alligators has produced a resurgence in the species. Probably the greatest problem is the sea turtles, hunted from the egg to the adult for their food value or their shells. Beaches where they lay their eggs are raided. Another problem contributing to their endangered status is plastic debris in the ocean, which they often ingest with fatal consequences.

Amphibians Since 1989 biologists have known that many species of frogs and other amphibians have declined dramatically, often for no known reason. By 1992 it was clear that about a third of all U.S. frogs and toads were threatened or endangered. Although research showed that in some cases the decline was caused by ultraviolet light streaming through a thinned ozone layer, this could not account for all species. Toxins from pollution were suspected, but not proved.

Fish Few ocean fish are considered to be endangered, but commercially important species have all suffered from overfishing, and some fisheries have been forced to close. The U.S. National Marine Fisheries Service estimates that about 40 percent of commercially important saltwater species have declined as a result of improvements in harvesting methods. Worldwide, four out of 17 major fisheries have been commercially depleted, while nine more are in serious decline, according to a 1993 report by the U.S. Food and Agriculture Office. About 40,000 Canadian workers were unemployed in 1994 as a consequence of the collapse of fishing in the Grand Banks off Newfoundland. The following year nearly all fishing was halted in the Georges Bank off Cape Cod, throwing thousands of U.S. workers off the job.

Atlantic and Pacific salmon live most of their lives in the sea, where they are netted, but return to fresh waters to breed. While in rivers, the salmon face dams that impede travel up or down the stream as well as loss of habitat as a result of logging and grazing in watersheds and additional fishing pressure. The Pacific Fisheries Management Council in 1994 established the strictest regulations ever, removing large regions of the ocean from any fishing at all. These steps may be too late for the Chinook salmon of the Snake River run, which have been classed as threatened since 1992 and endangered since 1994.

Surprisingly, most commercially valuable freshwater fish are doing all right, thanks to stocking efforts. But many freshwater fish that are not fished for food or sport are endangered, especially those confined to single lakes or river systems.

Plants Worldwide the most concern for plant extinctions is in the tropical rain forest. Tropical rain forests have a greater number of species per unit of area than any other type of environment. This is true for all kinds of organisms in tropical rain forests, not just plants, but plant extinctions are of particular concern because of the possibility of extracting useful products, such as medicines, from them.

In the United States a 1993 estimate was that there are some 20,000 native plants. About 21 percent of these, or 4,200 species of plants, are threatened with extinction, according to botanists at a conference on plant conservation under the auspices of the Missouri Botanical Garden in St. Louis. As many as 750 U.S. plant species could become extinct by the first years of the 21st century.

ENDANGERED ANIMALS IN THE UNITED STATES

Although the world's attention is often on large endangered mammals from Africa or the oceans, the United States is home to many endangered species and subspecies. A subspecies, sometimes called a race, is a local population of a given animal that has some distinctive trait, such as size or color, that sets it apart from the main species but is still classed as part of the species because the two populations can and sometimes do breed with each other.

Many endangered species and subspecies, especially birds, live on islands. Of the 100 or so known species of birds that have become extinct since 1600, 85 lived on islands. Because islands have small populations, limited habitats, and allow the introduction of new species easily, they are especially vulnerable environments.

In 1989 the General Accounting Office reported that only 16 percent of endangered or threatened species in the United States were improving their status, while a third were deteriorating. Since the Endangered and Threatened Wildlife and Plants listing was started in 1967, seven listed species have become extinct: the Tecopa pupfish (*Cyprinodon nevadensis calidae*, 1982), the longjaw cisco (*Coregonus alpenae*, 1983), the blue pike (*Stizostedion vitreum glaucum*, 1983), the Santa Barbara song sparrow (*Melospiza melodia graminea*, 1983), Sampson's pearly mussel (*Epioblasma* (=*Dysnomia*) *sampsoni*, 1984), the Amistad gambusia (*Gambusia amistadensis*, 1987), and the dusky seaside sparrow (*Ammodramus* (=*Ammospiza*) *maritimus nigrescens*, 1990). Three species listed as either threatened or endangered have recovered sufficiently to be removed from the list altogether: the Palau dove (*Gallicolumba canifrons*, 1985), the Palau fantail (or Old World fly catcher; *Rhipidura lepida*, 1985), and the Palau owl (*Pyroglaux* (=*Otus*) *podargina*, 1985).

In the United States, species are classified as threatened or endangered by the U.S. Fish and Wildlife service in accordance with the 1973 Endangered Species Act, renewed and extended in 1988. The list of endangered species maintained by the Department of the Interior goes back to the original Endangered Species Act of 1966. The first list of endangered species, in March 1967, included 78 species. The current list contains more than 2,000 species. Species listed are protected in various ways, most specifically by a prohibition against killing them. Also, a critical habitat can be protected against change if the change would contribute to species extinction.

BALD EAGLE REMOVED FROM ENDANGERED SPECIES LIST

The bald eagle, a symbol of American pride, but also the best known American endangered species, was removed from that list on June 30, 1994, and reclassified as threatened. The removal was due to the success of eagle protection and restoration projects that increased the bird's numbers from just over 800 in 1967 to more than 8,000 in 1994. The 1973 Endangered Species Act and the 1972 banning of the pesticide DDT, which caused eagles to lay eggs with shells that cracked before the offspring could survive, were given primary credit for the proliferation of bald eagles.

ENDANGERED AND THREATENED SPECIES IN THE U.S., 1967–95

Year	New listings	Total listings	Year	New listings	Total listings
1967	78	78	1982	13	803
1968	0	78	1983	29	832
1969	0	78	1984	48	880
1970	323	401	1985	61	941
1971	0	401	1986	46	987
1972	9	410	1987	60	1,047
1973	21	431	1988	46	1,093
1974	3	434	1989	35	1,128
1975	10	444	1990	53	1,181
1976	194	638	1991	86	1,267
1977	20	658	1992	82	1,349
1978	36	694	1993	73	1,422
1979	69	763	1994	128	1,550
1980	23	786	1995	49	1,599
1981	4	790			

Note: As of May 31, 1995. Separate populations of a species, listed both as endangered and threatened, are tallied twice. This table includes emergency listings, but does not subtract de-listed species. **Source:** U.S. Fish and Wildlife Service, unpublished data.

ANIMALS IN THE U.S. OFFICIALLY LISTED AS ENDANGERED, 1995

Mammals endangered in the U.S.

Common name	Scientific name	Remarks
Bat, gray	*Myotis grisescens*	Found in central and southeastern U.S.
Bat, Hawaiian hoary	*Lasiurus cinereus semotus*	Related to hairy-tailed bats found on the mainland of the Americas
Bat, Indiana	*Myotis sodalis*	Found both in East and Midwest
Bat, Mexican long-nosed	*Leptonycteris nivalis*	Found in New Mexico, Texas, and Central America, as well as Mexico
Bat, Ozark big-eared	*Plecotus townsendii ingens*	Lives in caves in Missouri, Oklahoma, and Arkansas
Bat, Sanborn's long-nosed	*Leptonycteris sanborni (=yerbabuenae)*	Found in New Mexico, Texas, and Central America, as well as Mexico
Bat, Virginia big-eared	*Plecotus townsendii virginianus*	A subspecies of big-eared bat found in Kentucky, North Carolina, West Virginia, and Virginia
Caribou, woodland	*Rangifer tarandus caribou*	Endangered in Washington, Idaho, and Canada
Deer, Columbian white-tailed	*Odocoileus virginianus leucurus*	Subspecies of white-tailed deer found in Washington and Oregon
Deer, key	*Odocoileus virginianus clavium*	Subspecies of white-tailed deer found in Florida
Ferret, black-footed	*Mustela nigripes*	Found in Western U.S.
Fox, San Joaquin kit	*Vulpes macrotis mutica*	California subspecies of kit fox; smaller than red fox
Jaguarundi	*Felis jagouaroundi cacomitli*	Found in Texas and Mexico; northern subspecies of small wildcat
Jaguarundi	*Felis jagouaroundi tolteca*	Subspecies of small wildcat found in Mexico and Arizona
Manatee, West Indian (=Florida)	*Trichechus manatus*	Large, plant-eating water mammal believed to have been the inspiration for the mermaid legend
Mountain beaver, Point Arena	*Aplodontia rufa nigra*	Found in California
Mouse, Alabama beach	*Peromyscus polionotus ammobates*	Subspecies of white-footed beach mouse found in Alabama
Mouse, Anastasia Island beach	*Peromyscus polionotus phasma*	Subspecies of white-footed beach mouse found in Florida
Mouse, Choctawhatchee beach	*Peromyscus polionotus allophrys*	Subspecies of white-footed beach mouse found in Florida
Mouse, Key Largo cotton	*Peromyscus gossypinus allapaticola*	Subspecies of white-footed beach mouse found in Florida
Mouse, Pacific pocket	*Perognathus longimembris pacificus*	Found in California
Mouse, Perdido Key beach	*Peromyscus polionotus trissyllepsis*	Subspecies of white-footed beach mouse found in Florida and Alabama
Mouse, salt marsh harvest	*Reithrodontomys raviventris*	Species of American harvest mouse found in California
Ocelot	*Felis pardalis*	Small spotted cat found in Arizona and Texas; endangered throughout Central and South America as well
Panther, Florida	*Felis concolor coryi*	Formerly found throughout Southeast, now confined to Florida; estimated that only 30–50 survive
Pronghorn, Sonoran	*Antilocapra americana sonoriensis*	Desert subspecies of the pronghorn found in Arizona and Mexico
Rabbit, Lower Keys	*Sylvilagus palustris hefneri*	Found in Florida Keys
Rat, Fresno kangaroo	*Dipodomys nitratoides exilis*	California subspecies of kangaroo rat, desert rodent not closely related to true rats
Rat, giant kangaroo	*Dipodomys ingens*	California species of kangaroo rat
Rat, Morro Bay kangaroo	*Dipodomys heermanni morroensis*	California subspecies of kangaroo rat
Rat, rice (=silver rice)	*Oryzomus palustris natator (=O. argentatus)*	Species found in Florida Keys west of the Seven-Mile Bridge
Rat, Stephens' kangaroo	*Dipodomys stephensi* (incl. *D. cascus*)	Historic range: California
Rat, Tipton kangaroo	*Dipodomys nitratoides nitratoides*	California subspecies of kangaroo rat
Seal, Hawaiian monk	*Monachus schauinslandi*	Related species in Caribbean and Mediterranean also endangered
Squirrel, Carolina northern flying	*Glaucomys sabrinus coloratus*	Subspecies of northern flying squirrel found in North Carolina and Tennessee
Squirrel, Delmarva Peninsula fox	*Sciurus niger cinereus*	Subspecies of fox squirrel found on Delmarva Peninsula and in eastern Pennsylvania
Squirrel, Mt. Graham red	*Tamiasciurus hudsonicus grahamensis*	Status has prevented construction of telescopes on Mt. Graham, Arizona
Squirrel, Virginia northern flying	*Glaucomys sabrinus fuscus*	Subspecies of northern flying squirrel found in Virginia and West Virginia
Vole, Amargosa	*Microtus californicus scirpensis*	California subspecies of vole
Vole, Florida salt marsh	*Microtus pennsylvanicus dukecampbelli*	Florida subspecies of vole
Vole, Hualapai Mexican	*Microtus mexicanus hualpaiensis*	Arizona subspecies of Mexican vole
Whale, gray	*Eschrichtius robustus*	Found in North Pacific Ocean
Wolf, gray	*Canis lupus*	Most common wolf; endangered in continental U.S. except Minnesota, where it is threatened
Wolf, red	*Canis rufus*	Found in southeastern U.S.; considered endangered except for an experimental population in North Carolina
Woodrat, Key Largo	*Neotoma floridana smalii*	Historic range: Florida

Birds endangered in the U.S.

Common name	Scientific name	Remarks
Akepa, Hawaii (honeycreeper)	*Loxops coccineus coccineus*	Subspecies of 1 of the 22 known species of Hawaiian honeycreepers; 8 species are extinct and 8 are threatened or endangered
Akepa, Maui (honeycreeper)	*Loxops coccineus ochraceus*	Subspecies of Akepa found on Maui
Akialoa, Kauai (honeycreeper)	*Hemignathus procerus*	Species of Hawaiian honeycreeper
Akiapolaau (honeycreeper)	*Hemignathus munroi (=wilsoni)*	Species of Hawaiian honeycreeper
Blackbird, yellow-shouldered	*Agelaius xanthomus*	Relative of common red-winged blackbird found in Puerto Rico
Bobwhite, masked (quail)	*Colinus virginianus ridgwayi*	Subspecies of common bobwhite found in Sonora desert of Arizona and Mexico
Broadbill, Guam	*Myiagra freycineti*	Historic range: Guam
Condor, California	*Gymnogyps californianus*	Species continues only in captivity; there are plans to reintroduce it to the wild
Coot, Hawaiian (=alae keo keo)	*Fulica americana alai*	Hawaiian subspecies of common American coot
Crane, Mississippi sandhill	*Grus canadensis pulla*	Subspecies of sandhill crane found in Mississippi
Crane, whooping	*Grus americana*	Among most famous endangered species; making a comeback, in part due to program in which sandhill cranes hatch and rear whooping cranes
Creeper, Hawaii	*Oreomystis (=Loxops) mana*	Subspecies of either finch or honeycreeper found in Hawaii
Creeper, Molokai (=kakawahie)	*Paroreomyza (=Oreomystis, =Loxops) flammea*	Subspecies of either finch or honeycreeper found in Hawaii
Creeper, Oahu (=alauwahio)	*Paroreomyza (=Oreomystis, =Loxops) maculata*	Subspecies of either finch or honeycreeper found in Hawaii
Crow, Hawaiian (='alala)	*Corvus hawaiiensis (=tropicus)*	Species of crow found in Hawaii
Crow, Mariana	*Corvus kubaryi*	Historic range: Guam, Western Pacific
Crow, white-necked	*Corvus leucognaphalus*	Historic range: Puerto Rico, Dominican Republic, Haiti
Curlew, Eskimo	*Numenius borealis*	One of the rarest birds on Earth; until near turn of the century, large flocks seen and hunted in eastern U.S. during migration from Alaska and Canada to Argentina
Duck, Hawaiian (=koloa)	*Anas wyvilliana*	Closely related to common mallard
Duck, Laysan	*Anas laysanensis*	Historic range: Hawaii
Eagle, bald	*Haliaeetus leucocephalus*	Endangered in all states except Alaska, Washington, Oregon, Minnesota, Wisconsin, and Michigan, where they are threatened
Falcon, American peregrine	*Falco peregrinus anatum*	Subspecies of peregrine falcon endangered throughout Americas
Falcon, northern aplomado	*Falco femoralis septentrionalis*	Found in southwest U.S., Mexico, and Guatemala
Falcon, peregrine	*Falco peregrinus*	Although population declined severely because DDT interferes with breeding, they have been making a comeback; continued concern about use of DDT in their winter range in Latin America
Finch, Laysan (honeycreeper)	*Telespyza (=Psittirostra) cantans*	Found on island of Laysan, in Hawaiian chain
Finch, Nihoa (honeycreeper)	*Telespyza (=Psittirostra) ultima*	Found on island of Nihoa, in Hawaiian chain
Flycatcher, southwestern willow	*Empindonax trailii extimus*	Found in southwestern U.S.
Goose, Hawaiian (=nene)	*Nesochen (=Branta) sandvicensis*	Once almost extinct; captive breeding program successful in preserving species and reintroducing it to the wild
Hawk, Hawaiian (=lo)	*Buteo solitarius*	Found in upland forests on island of Hawaii
Honeycreeper, crested (='akohekohe)	*Palmeria dolei*	Found on Maui in Hawaii; now rarely sighted or heard
Kingfisher, Guam Micronesian	*Halcyon cinnamomina cinnamomina*	Historic range: Guam, Western Pacific
Kite, Everglade snail	*Rostrhamus sociabilis plumbeus*	Loss of habitat in Florida has confined this bird to one small nesting population; also found in Cuba, where it is not endangered
Mallard, Mariana	*Anas oustaleti*	Historic range: Guam, Western Pacific
Millerbird, Nihoa (Old World warbler)	*Acrocephalus familiaris kingi*	Found on Hawaiian island of Nihoa; one of the rarest birds on Earth
Moorhen (=gallinule), Hawaiian common	*Gallinula chloropus sandvicensis*	Revered by Hawaiians as bird that brought fire to islands; extinct on Hawaii and Maui, endangered on other islands
Moorheu (=gallinule), Mariana common	*Gallinula chloropus guami*	Historic range: Western Pacific, Guam
Nightjar (=whippoorwill), Puerto Rican	*Caprimulgus noctitherus*	Puerto-Rican relative of American whippoorwill; once thought extinct
Nukupu'u (honeycreeper)	*Hemignathus lucidus*	Originally found on Maui, Oahu, and Kauai; now only occasional sightings on Kauai
'O'o, Kauai (='O'o 'A'a) (honeyeater)	*Moho braccatus*	Of 5 species of honeyeaters in Hawaii, 4 have become extinct since 1859, leaving only the 'O'o, on Kauai
'O'u (honeycreeper)	*Psittirostra psittacea*	Once common on all Hawaiian islands, 'O'u now extinct on Oahu, Lanai, and Molokai
Palila (honeycreeper)	*Loxioides (=Psittirostra) bailleiu*	Once common throughout islands, now found only on Hawaii
Parrot, Puerto Rican	*Amazona vittata*	Once common on Puerto Rico and nearby islands, sole remaining population is in Luquillo National Forest, P.R.

Common name	Scientific name	Remarks
Parrotbill, Maui (honeycreeper)	*Pseudonestor xanthophrys*	Extremely rare Hawaiian honeycreeper occasionally sighted on Maui
Pelican, brown	*Pelecanus occidentalis*	Endangered along Pacific coast and in Central and South America; has made comeback in southeastern U.S. since ban of DDT
Petrel, Hawaiian dark-rumped	*Pterodroma phaeopygia sandwichensis*	Subspecies of gadfly petrel; endangered because of predation by rats introduced onto Hawaiian islands where it breeds
Pigeon, Puerto Rican plain	*Columba inornata wetmorei*	Subspecies of pigeon related to common pigeons
Plover, piping	*Charadrius melodus*	Endangered in Great Lakes region and part of Canada
Po'ouli (honeycreeper)	*Melamprosops phaeosoma*	One of 28 species of Hawaiian finches, of which 20 are either endangered or threatened
Prairie chicken, Attwater's greater	*Tympanuchus cupido attwateri*	One of 4 subspecies of prairie chickens once found in U.S.; limited to Texas
Rail, California clapper	*Rallus longirostris obsoletus*	Historic range: California
Rail, Guam	*Rallus owstoni*	Historic range: Western Pacific, Guam
Rail, light-footed clapper	*Rallus longirostris levipes*	Historic range: California and Baja California
Rail, Yuma clapper	*Rallus longirostris yumanensis*	One of a trio of clapper rail subspecies; endangered in Arizona and California
Shrike, San Clemente loggerhead	*Lanius ludovicianus mearnsi*	California subspecies of loggerhead shrike
Sparrow, Cape Sable seaside	*Ammodramus (=Ammospiza) maritimus mirabilis*	Subspecies of seaside sparrow, found in Florida
Sparrow, Florida grasshopper	*Ammodramus savannarum floridanus*	Like the Cape Sable seaside sparrow, this subspecies is actually a New World bunting
Stilt, Hawaiian (=Ae'o)	*Himantopus mexicanus (=himantopus) knudseni*	Subspecies of the black-winged stilt, a wading bird
Stork, wood	*Mycteria americana*	Endangered in Southeastern U.S.
Swiftlet, Mariana gray (=Vanikoro)	*Aerodramus (=Collocalia) vanikorensis bartschi*	Historic range: Western Pacific, Marianas, Guam
Tern, California least	*Sterna antillarum (=albifrons) browni*	Historic range: Mexico, California
Tern, least	*Sterna antillarum*	Endangered throughout Mississippi River basin in U.S.
Tern, roseate	*Sterna dougallii dougallii*	Endangered along Atlantic Coast between North Carolina and Newfoundland
Thrush, large Kauai	*Myadestes (=Phaeornis) myadestinus*	Subspecies of this Hawaiian thrush became extinct on Oahu (1825), Lanai (1931), and Molokai (1936); there is a subspecies on Hawaii
Thrush, Molokai (=oloma'o)	*Myadestes (=Phaeornis) lanaiensis (=obscurus) rutha*	Species of the "Hawaiian thrush"; once believed to have become extinct in 1936
Thrush, small Kauai (=puaiohi)	*Myadestes (=Phaeornis) palmeri*	Found only in forests on Kauai; probably rarest of surviving Hawaiian thrushes
Vireo, black-capped	*Vireo atricapillus*	Vireo found in Kansas, Oklahoma, Texas, and Mexico
Vireo, least Bell's	*Vireo bellii pusillus*	Subspecies of Bell's vireo found in California and Mexico
Warbler (wood), Bachman's	*Vermivora bachmanii*	Considered the rarest North American native songbird; Bachman's may have been near extinction when first noticed by science in 1833
Warbler (wood), golden-cheeked	*Dendroica chrysoparia*	Affected range from Texas to Nicaragua
Warbler (wood), Kirtland's	*Dendroica kirtlandii*	Nesting only in Michigan and wintering in the Bahamas, about 1,000 of these birds survive with human help
White-eye, bridled	*Zosterops conspicillatus conspicillatus*	Historic range: Western Pacific, Guam
Woodpecker, ivory-billed	*Campephilus principalis*	Large American woodpecker close to extinction due to destruction of old growth forests in southeast and Cuba
Woodpecker, red-cockaded	*Picoides (=Dendrocopos) borealis*	Woodpecker of Southeast U.S.; related to more common downy and hairy woodpeckers

Reptiles endangered in the U.S.

Common name	Scientific name	Remarks
Anole, Culebra Island giant	*Anolis roosevelti*	Lizard endangered in Puerto Rico and Culebra Island
Boa, Puerto Rican	*Epicrates inornatus*	Boa found in Puerto Rico
Boa, Virgin Islands tree	*Epicrates monensis granti*	Subspecies of boa found in U.S. and British Virgin Islands
Crocodile, American	*Crocodylus acutus*	In U.S., found only in Florida; endangered throughout range in Americas
Gecko, Monito	*Sphaerodactylus micropithecus*	Puerto-Rican lizard
Iguana, Mona ground	*Cyclura stejnegeri*	Large lizard found on Mona Island (Puerto Rico)
Lizard, blunt-nosed leopard	*Gambelia (=Crotaphytus) silus*	California lizard
Lizard, St. Croix ground	*Ameiva polops*	Found in U.S. Virgin Islands
Snake, San Francisco garter	*Thamnophis sirtalis tetrataenia*	California subspecies of garter snake
Turtle, Alabama red-bellied	*Pseudemys alabamensis*	Alabama freshwater turtle
Turtle, green sea	*Chelonia mydas* (incl. *agassizi*)	Florida breeding ground populations endangered
Turtle, Kemp's (=Atlantic) ridley sea	*Lepidochelys kempii*	One of its few remaining breeding grounds is on Padre Island, Texas
Turtle, leatherback sea	*Dermochelys coriacea*	Although it no longer breeds in the U.S., the leatherback is found sometimes in U.S. waters
Turtle, Plymouth red-bellied	*Pseudemys (=Chrysemys) rubriventris bangsi*	Subspecies of freshwater turtle found in Massachusetts

Amphibians endangered in the U.S.

Common name	Scientific name	Remarks
Salamander, desert slender	*Batrachoseps aridus*	Lungless salamander found in California
Salamander, Santa Cruz long-toed	*Ambystoma macrodactylum croceum*	Mole salamander subspecies found in California
Salamander, Shenandoah	*Plethodon shenandoah*	Virginia salamander; classified as endangered in 1989
Salamander, Texas blind	*Typhlomolge rathbuni*	Lives in caves and has external gills, vestigial eyes, and white body
Toad, Houston	*Bufo houstonensis*	True toad found in Texas
Toad, Wyoming	*Bufo hemiophrys baxteri*	Subspecies of true toad found in Wyoming

Fish endangered in the U.S.

Common name	Scientific name	Remarks
Cavefish, Alabama	*Speoplatyrhinus poulsoni*	Found in caves in Alabama
Chub, bonytail	*Gila elegans*	Historic range: Arizona, California, Colorado, Nevada, Utah, and Wyoming
Chub, Borax Lake	*Gila boraxobius*	Historic range: Oregon
Chub, humpback	*Gila cypha*	Historic range: Arizona, Colorado, Utah, and Wyoming
Chub, Mohave tui	*Gila bicolor mohavensis*	Historic range: California
Chub, Owens tui	*Gila bicolor snyderi*	Historic range: California
Chub, Oregon	*Oregonichthys crameri*	Affected range: Oregon
Chub, Pahranagat roundtail	*Gila robusta jordani*	Historic range: Nevada
Chub, Virgin River	*Gila robusta seminuda*	Southwestern subspecies classified as endangered in 1989
Chub, Yaqui	*Gila purpurea*	Historic range: Arizona, Mexico
Cui-ui	*Chasmistes cujus*	Historic range: Nevada
Dace, Ash Meadows speckled	*Rhinichthys osculus nevadensis*	Historic range: Nevada
Dace, Clover Valley speckled	*Rhinichthys osculus oligoporus*	Nevada subspecies classified as endangered in 1989
Dace, Independence Valley speckled	*Rhinichthys osculus lethoporous*	Nevada subspecies classified as endangered in 1989
Dace, Kendall Warm Springs	*Rhinichthys osculus thermalis*	Historic range: Wyoming
Dace, Moapa	*Moapa coriacea*	Historic range: Warm springs in southern Nevada
Darter, amber	*Percina antesella*	Historic range: Georgia, Tennessee
Darter, bluemask (=jewel)	*Etheostoma n. sp.*	Affected range: Tennessee
Darter, boulder (=Elk River)	*Etheostoma wapiti*	Historic range: Alabama, Tennessee
Darter, Cherokee	*Etheostoma (Ulocentra) sp.*	Affected range: Georgia
Darter, dusky tail	*Etheostoma* (catonotus) sp.	Historic range: Tennessee, Virginia
Darter, Etowah	*Etheostoma etowahae*	Affected range: Georgia
Darter, fountain	*Etheostoma fonticola*	Historic range: Texas
Darter, Maryland	*Etheostoma sellare*	Historic range: Maryland
Darter, Okaloosa	*Etheostoma okaloosae*	Historic range: Florida
Darter, relict	*Etheostoma chienense*	Affected range: Kentucky
Darter, watercress	*Etheostoma nuchale*	Historic range: Alabama
Gambusia, Big Bend	*Gambusia gaigei*	Historic range: Two springs near Big Bend National Park in Texas; in 1957 there were only 2 males and 1 female; has recovered somewhat since
Gambusia, Clear Creek	*Gambusia heterochir*	Historic range: Headwaters of 1 creek in Texas; threatened by competition from interbreeding with introduced mosquito fish
Gambusia, Pecos	*Gambusia nobilis*	Historic range: New Mexico, Texas; now confined to region around Toyahvale, Texas
Gambusia, San Marcos	*Gambusia georgei*	Historic range: Texas
Goby, tidewater	*Eucyclogobius newberryi*	Affected range: California
Killifish, Pahrump	*Empetrichthys latos*	Found in 1 spring in western Nevada
Logperch, Conasauga	*Percina jenkinsi*	Historic range: Georgia, Tennessee
Logperch, Roanoke	*Percina rex*	Classified as endangered in 1989
Madtom, pygmy	*Noturus stanauli*	Historic range: Tennessee
Madtom, Scioto	*Noturus trautmani*	Historic range: Ohio
Madtom, Smoky	*Noturus baileyi*	Historic range: Tennessee
Minnow, Rio Grande silvery	*Hybognathus amarus*	Found in New Mexico and Texas
Pupfish, Ash Meadows Amargosa	*Cyprinodon nevadensis mionectes*	Historic range: Nevada
Pupfish, Comanche Springs	*Cyprinodon elegans*	Historic range: Large springs in Pecos County, Texas; these have gone dry and now the pupfish survives only in irrigation ditches
Pupfish, desert	*Cyprinodon macularius*	Historic range: Arizona, California, Mexico
Pupfish, Devils Hole	*Cyprinodon diabolis*	Historic range: One spring hole in Nevada; perhaps most restricted range of any vertebrate
Pupfish, Leon Springs	*Cyprinodon bovinus*	Historic range: Leon Springs, near Fort Stockton, Texas
Pupfish, Owens	*Cyprinodon radiosus*	Historic range: California
Pupfish, Warm Springs	*Cyprinodon nevadensis pectoralis*	Historic range: Nevada
Salmon, chinook	*Oncorhynchus tshawytscha*	Affected range: The Snake River in Pacific Northwest and the Sacramento River in California
Salmon, sockeye	*Oncorhyncus nerka*	Found in Snake River and its tributaries in Idaho, Oregon, and Washington, including the Salmon River, the Columbia River, and Redfish Lake
Shiner, Cahaba	*Notropis cahabae*	Found only in Alabama
Shiner, Cape Fear	*Notropis mekiestocholas*	Minnow found in North Carolina
Shiner, Paleozone	*Notropis sp.*	Historic range: Alabama, Kentucky, Tennessee
Spinedace, White River	*Lepidomeda albivallis*	Historic range: Nevada
Springfish, Hiko White River	*Crenichthys baileyi grandis*	Historic range: Nevada
Springfish, White River	*Crenichthys baileyi baileyi*	Subspecies of springfish found in Nevada
Squawfish, Colorado	*Ptychocheilus lucius*	Historic range: Southwestern U.S., Mexico
Stickleback, unarmored three-spine	*Gasterosteus aculeatus williamsoni*	Historic range: California
Sturgeon, pallid	*Scaphirhynchus albus*	Affected in a broad range from Montana to Mississippi

Common name	Scientific name	Remarks
Sturgeon, shortnose	*Acipenser brevirostrum*	Historic range: Atlantic coast of U.S. and Canada
Sturgeon, white (Kootenai River pop.)	*Acipenser transmontanus*	Historic range: Idaho and Montana
Sucker, June	*Chasmistes liorus*	Historic range: Utah Lake, a spawning run on Provo River; nearly became extinct during droughts of 1930s
Sucker, Lost River	*Deltistes luxatus*	Historic range: California, Oregon
Sucker, Modoc	*Catostomus microps*	Historic range: California
Sucker, razorback	*Xyrauchen texanus*	Found in southwestern U.S.
Sucker, shortnose	*Chasmistes brevirostris*	Historic range: California, Oregon
Topminnow, Gila (incl. Yaqui)	*Poeciliopsis occidentalis*	Historic range: Lower Gila River basin of Arizona and New Mexico and northern Mexico; competition from introduced mosquito fish
Trout, Gila	*Onchorhychus (=Salmo) gilae*	Historic range: Gila River basin of Arizona and New Mexico; suffers from competition with introduced trout and from habitat destruction
Woundfin	*Plagopterus argentissimus*	Historic range: Arizona, Nevada, and New Mexico

Clams, crustaceans, and snails endangered in the U.S.

Common name	Scientific name	Remarks
Acornshell, southern	*Epioblasma othcaloogensis*	Historic range: Alabama, Georgia, Tennessee
Ambersnail, Kanab	*Oxyloma haydeni kanabensis*	Historic range: Utah
Amphipod, Hay's Spring	*Stygobromus hayi*	Historic range: District of Columbia
Clubshell	*Pleurobema clava*	Historic range: Midwestern U.S.
Clubshell, black (=Curtus' mussel)	*Pleurobema curtum*	Historic range: Alabama, Mississippi
Clubshell, ovate	*Pleurobema perovatum*	Historic range: Alabama, Georgia, Mississippi, Tennessee
Clubshell, southern	*Pleurobema decisum*	Historic range: Alabama, Georgia, Mississippi, Tennessee
Combshell, southern (=penitent mussel)	*Epioblasma (=Dysnomia penita)*	Historic range: Alabama, Mississippi
Combshell, upland	*Epioblasma metastriata*	Historic range: Alabama, Georgia, Tennessee
Crayfish (no common name)	*Cambarus zophonastes*	Historic range: Arkansas
Crayfish, Nashville	*Orconectes shoupi*	Historic range: Tennessee
Crayfish, Shasta (=Placid)	*Pacifastacus fortis*	Historic range: California
Elktoe, Appalachian	*Alasmidonta raveneliana*	Historic range: North Carolina, Tennessee
Fairy shrimp, conservancy	*Branchinecta conservatio*	Historic range: California
Fairy shrimp, longhorn	*Branchinecta longiantenna*	Historic range: California
Fairy shrimp, vernal pool	*Branchinecta lynchi*	Historic range: California
Fanshell	*Cyprogenia stegaria (=irrorata)*	Affected range along Ohio and Mississippi valleys from Pennsylvania to Alabama
Heelsplitter, Carolina	*Lasmigona decorata*	Historic range: North and South Carolina
Isopod, Lee County cave	*Lirceus usdagalun*	Historic range: Virginia
Isopod, Socorro	*Thermosphaeroma (=Exosphaeroma) thermophilus*	Historic range: New Mexico
Kidneyshell, triangular	*Ptychobranchus greeni*	Historic range: Alabama, Georgia, Tennessee
Limpet, Banbury Springs	*Lanx*	Historic range: Idaho
Marstonia (snail), royal (=obese)	*Pyrgulopsis (=Marstonia) ogmoraphee*	Historic range: Tennessee
Moccasinshell, Coosa	*Medionidus parvulus*	Historic range: Alabama, Georgia, Tennessee
Mussel, Cumberland pigtoe	*Pleurobema gibberum*	Historic range: Tennessee
Mussel, Curtus'	*Pleurobema curtum*	Historic range: Alabama, Mississippi
Mussel, dwarf wedge	*Alasmidonta heterodon*	Historic range: Mid Atlantic and New England states
Mussel, Judge Tait's	*Pleurobema taitianum*	Historic range: Mid Atlantic and New England states
Mussel, Marshall's	*Pleurobema marshalli*	Historic range: Mid Atlantic and New England states
Mussel, penitent	*Epioblasma (=Dysomia) penita*	Historic range: Mid Atlantic and New England states
Mussel, ring pink (=golf stick pearly)	*Obovaria retusa*	Mississippi mussel, classified as endangered in 1989
Mussel, winged maple leaf	*Quandrula fragosa*	Historic range: Midwestern U.S.
Pearly mussel, Alabama lamp	*Lampsilis virescens*	Historic range: Alabama, Tennessee
Pearly mussel, Appalachian monkeyface	*Quadrula sparsa*	Historic range: Tennessee, Virginia
Pearly mussel, birdwing	*Conradilla caelata*	Historic range: Tennessee, Virginia
Pearly mussel, cracking	*Hemistena (=Lastena) lata*	Mississippi mussel, classified as endangered in 1989
Pearly mussel, Cumberland bean	*Villosa (=Micromya) trabalis*	Historic range: Tennessee, Virginia
Pearly mussel, Cumberland monkeyface	*Quadrula intermedia*	Historic range: Alabama, Tennessee, Virginia
Pearly mussel, Curtis'	*Epioblasma (=Dysnomia) florentina curtsi*	Historic range: Missouri
Pearly mussel, dromedary	*Dromus dromas*	Historic range: Tennessee, Virginia
Pearly mussel, green-blossom	*Epioblasma (=Dysnomia) torulosa gubermaculum*	Historic range: Tennessee, Virginia
Pearly mussel, Higgins' eye	*Lampsilis higginsi*	Historic range: Midwestern U.S.
Pearly mussel, little wing	*Pegias fabula*	Found from Alabama to Virginia
Pearly mussel (=pimple back) orange-footed	*Plethobasus cooperianus*	Historic range: Midwestern U.S.
Pearly mussel, pale lilliput	*Toxolasma (=Carunculina) cylindrellus*	Historic range: Alabama, Tennessee
Pearly mussel, pink mucket	*Lampsilis orbiculata*	Historic range: Midwestern U.S.
Pearly mussel, purple cat's paw	*Epioblasma (=Dysnomia) obliquata (=sulcata) o.*	Affected range: Alabama, Kentucky, Tennessee
Pearly mussel, tubercled-blossom	*Epioblasma (=Dysnomia) torulosa torulosa*	Historic range: Midwestern U.S.
Pearly mussel, turgid-blossom	*Epioblasma (=Dysnomia) turgidula*	Historic range: Alabama, Tennessee
Pigtoe, dark	*Pleurobema furvum*	Historic range: Alabama
Pigtoe, fine-rayed	*Fusconaia cuneolus*	Clamlike mollusk found in Alabama, Tennessee, Virginia
Pigtoe, rough	*Pleurobema plenum*	Historic range: Indiana, Kentucky, Tennessee, Virginia

Common name	Scientific name	Remarks
Pigtoe, shiny	*Fusconaia edgariana*	Historic range: Alabama, Tennessee, Virginia
Pigtoe, southern	*Pleurobema georgianum*	Historic range: Alabama, Georgia, Tennessee
Pocketbook, fat	*Potamilus (=Proptera) capax*	Clamlike mollusk found in Arkansas, Indiana, Missouri, Ohio
Pocketbook, speckled	*Lampsilils streckeri*	Arkansas mussel classified as endangered in 1989
Riffleshell, northern	*Epioblamsa toulosa rangiana*	Historic range: Midwestern U.S.
Riffleshell, tan	*Epioblasma walkeri*	Pearly mussel found in Kentucky, Tennessee, Virginia
Riversnail, Anthony's	*Athearnia anthonyi*	Found in Alabama, Georgia, Tennessee
Rock-pocketbook, Ouachita (=Wheeler's pearly mussel)	*Arkansia (=Arcidens wheeleri)*	Historic range: Arkansas and Oklahoma
Shrimp, Alabama cave	*Palaemonias alabamae*	Historic range: Alabama
Shrimp, California freshwater	*Syncaris pacifica*	Classified endangered in 1988
Shrimp, Kentucky cave	*Palaemonias ganteri*	Found in Mammoth Cave system

Common name	Scientific name	Remarks
Shrimp, Riverside fairy	*Streptocephalus woottoni*	Historic range: California
Snail, Iowa Pleistocene	*Discus macclintocki*	Historic range: Iowa
Snail, Morro shoulderband (=banded dune)	*Helminthoglypta walkeriana*	Historic range: California
Snail, Oahu tree	*Achatinella* (all species)	Historic range: Hawaii
Snail, Snake River physa	*Physa natricina*	Historic range: Idaho
Snail, tulotoma	*Tulotoma magnifica*	Historic range: Alabama
Snail, Utah Valvata	*Valvata utahensis*	Historic range: Idaho
Snail, Virginia fringed mountain	*Polygyriscus virginianus*	Historic range: Virginia
Spinymussel, James (=Virginia)	*Pleurobema (=Fusconaia =Elliptio =Canthyria) collina*	Historic range: Virginia, West Virginia
Spinymussel, Tar River	*Elliptio (Canthyria) steinstansana*	Historic range: North Carolina
Springsnail, Alamosa	*Tryonia alamosae*	Historic range: New Mexico
Springsnail, Bruneau Hot	*Pyrgulopsis bruneauensis*	Historic range: Idaho
Spingsnail, Idaho	*Fontelicella idahoensis*	Historic range: Idaho
Springsnail, Socorro	*Pyrgulopsis neomexicana*	Historic range: New Mexico
Stirrup shell	*Quadrula stapes*	Pearly mussel found in Alabama and Mississippi
Tadpole shrimp, vernal pool	*Lepidurus packardi*	Historic range: California

Insects and arachnids endangered in the U.S.

Common name	Scientific name	Remarks
Beetle, American burying (=giant carrion beetle)	*Nicrophorus americanus*	Midwestern beetle classified as endangered in 1989
Beetle, Coffin Cave mold	*Batrisodes texanus*	Historic range: Texas
Beetle, Hungerford's carlwing water	*Brychius hungerfordi*	Historic range: Michigan
Beetle, Kretschmarr Cave mold	*Texamaurops reddelli*	Historic range: Texas
Beetle, Tooth Cave ground	*Rhadine persephone*	Historic range: Texas
Butterfly, El Segundo blue	*Euphilotes (=Shijimiaeoides) battoides allyni*	Historic range: California
Butterfly, Karner blue	*Lycaeides melissa samuelis*	Historic range: New England, Great Lakes states
Butterfly, Lange's metalmark	*Apodemia mormo langei*	Historic range: California
Butterfly, lotis blue	*Lycaeides argyrognomon lotis*	Historic range: California
Butterfly, mission blue	*Icaricia icarioides missionensis*	Historic range: California
Butterfly, Mitchell's satyr	*Neonympha mitchelli mitchelli*	Historic range: Indiana, Michigan, New Jersey, Ohio
Butterfly, Myrtle's silverspot	*Speyeria zerene myrtleae*	Historic range: California
Butterfly, Palos Verdes blue	*Glaucopsyche lygdamus palosverdesensis*	Historic range: California

Common name	Scientific name	Remarks
Butterfly, Saint Francis' satyr	*Neonympha mitchellii francisci*	Historic range: North Carolina
Butterfly, San Bruno elfin	*Callophrys mossii bayensis*	Historic range: California
Butterfly, Schaus swallowtail	*Heraclides (=Papilio) aristodemus ponceanus*	Historic range: Florida
Butterfly, Smith's blue	*Euphilotes (=Shijimiaeoides) enoptes smithi*	Historic range: California
Butterfly, uncompahgre fritillary	*Boloria acrocnema*	Historic range: Colorado
Dragonfly, Hine's (=Ohio) emerals	*Somatochlora hineana*	Found in states along Great Lakes
Fly, Delhi Sands flower-loving	*Rhaphiomidas teminatus abdominalis*	Historic range: California
Harvestman, Bee Creek Cave	*Texella reddelli*	"Daddy longlegs" found in Texas
Harvestman, Bone Cave	*Texella reyesi*	Historic range: Colorado
Pseudoscorpion, Tooth Cave	*Microcreagris texana*	Historic range: Texas
Spider, spruce-fir moss	*Microhexura montivaga*	Historic range: North Carolina, Tennessee
Spider, Tooth Cave	*Leptoneta myopica*	Historic range: Texas

Source: U.S. Fish and Wildlife Service, *Endangered and Threatened Wildlife and Plants* (1994).

PART V AWARDS AND PRIZES

ARTS AND ENTERTAINMENT

THE ACADEMY AWARDS

The "Oscars" are officially known as the Academy of Motion Picture Arts and Sciences Awards; they were inaugurated in 1928 as part of Hollywood's drive to improve its less-than-respectable image. (The stated aim of the academy, founded in 1927, was to raise the "cultural, educational, and scientific standards" of the motion picture industry.) Membership in the academy (currently over 3,000) is by invitation only, with members divided into 13 branches. Each branch selects up to five nominees for awards in its own area of expertise, with the entire membership making "Best Film" nominations, and then voting on all the categories. Major awards are shown in the chart. The year 1934 marked a growing number of award categories. "Best Foreign Film" awards, which began in 1956, are listed in a separate table at the end of this section. "Best Directors" are named for films winning "Best Picture" except where indicated.

THE ACADEMY AWARDS, 1928–94

Year	Best picture	Best director	Best actor	Best actress	Best supporting actor	Best supporting actress	Best song (from film)	Original score	Best cinematographer
1928	*Wings*	Frank Borzage *Seventh Heaven* Lewis Milestone *2 Arabian Knights*	Emil Jannings *The Way of All Flesh,* *The Last Command*	Janet Gaynor *Seventh Heaven,* *Sunrise,* *Street Angel*	—	—	—	—	Charles Rosher, Karl Struss *Sunrise*
1929	*Broadway Melody*	Frank Lloyd *The Divine Lady*	Warner Baxter *In Old Arizona*	Mary Pickford *Coquette*	—	—	—	—	Clyde DeVinna *White Shadows,* *In the South Seas*
1930	*All Quiet on the Western Front*	Lewis Milestone	George Arliss *Disraeli*	Norma Shearer *The Divorcee*	—	—	—	—	Joseph T. Rucker, Willard Van Der Veer *With Byrd at the South Pole*
1931	*Cimarron*	Norman Taurog *Skippy*	Lionel Barrymore *A Free Soul*	Marie Dressler *Min and Bill*	—	—	—	—	Floyd Crosby *Tabu*
1932	*Grand Hotel*	Frank Borzage *Bad Girl*	Wallace Beery *The Champ* Fredric March *Dr. Jekyll and Mr. Hyde*	Helen Hayes *The Sin of Madelon Claudet*	—	—	—	—	Lee Garmes *Shanghai Express*
1933	*Cavalcade*	Frank Lloyd	Charles Laughton *The Private Life of Henry VIII*	Katharine Hepburn *Morning Glory*	—	—	—	—	Charles Bryant Lang, Jr. *A Farewell to Arms*
1934	*It Happened One Night*	Frank Capra	Clark Gable *It Happened One Night*	Claudette Colbert *It Happened One Night*	—	—	"The Continental" *The Gay Divorcee*	Louis Silvers[1] *One Night of Love*	Victor Milner *Cleopatra*
1935	*Mutiny on the Bounty*	John Ford *The Informer*	Victor McLaglen *The Informer*	Bette Davis *Dangerous*	—	—	"Lullaby of Broadway" *Lullaby of Broadway*	Max Steiner[1] *The Informer*	Hal Mohr *A Midsummer Night's Dream*
1936	*The Great Ziegfeld*	Frank Capra *Mr. Deeds Goes to Town*	Paul Muni *The Story of Louis Pasteur*	Luise Rainer *The Great Ziegfeld*	Walter Brennan *Come and Get It*	Gale Sondergaard *Anthony Adverse*	"The Way You Look Tonight" *Swing Time*	Leo Forbstein[1] *Anthony Adverse*	Gaetano Gaudio *Anthony Adverse*
1937	*The Life of Emile Zola*	Leo McCarey *The Awful Truth*	Spencer Tracy *Captains Courageous*	Luise Rainer *The Good Earth*	Joseph Schildkraut *The Life of Emile Zola*	Alice Brady *In Old Chicago*	"Sweet Leilani" *Waikiki Wedding*	Charles Previn[1] *100 Men and a Girl*	Karl Freund *The Good Earth*
1938	*You Can't Take It with You*	Frank Capra	Spencer Tracy *Boys Town*	Bette Davis *Jezebel*	Walter Brennan *Kentucky*	Fay Bainter *Jezebel*	"Thanks for the Memory" *Big Broadcast of 1938*	Alfred Newman *Alexander's Ragtime Band* Erich Wolfgang Korngold *The Adventures of Robin Hood*	Joseph Ruttenberg *The Great Waltz*

1. From 1934 to 1937, the "Best Original Score" award was presented to the head of the music department of the relevant studio, and not necessarily to the composer of the score.

Year	Best picture	Best director	Best actor	Best actress	Best supporting actor	Best supporting actress	Best song (from film)	Original score	Best cinematographer
1939	*Gone with the Wind*	Victor Fleming	Robert Donat *Goodbye, Mr. Chips*	Vivien Leigh *Gone with the Wind*	Thomas Mitchell *Stagecoach*	Hattie McDaniel *Gone with the Wind*	"Over the Rainbow" *The Wizard of Oz*	Herbert Stothart *The Wizard of Oz* Richard Hageman, Frank Harling, John Leipold, Leo Shuken *Stagecoach*	Gregg Toland *Wuthering Heights* Ernest Haller, Ray Rennahan *Gone with the Wind*
1940	*Rebecca*	John Ford *The Grapes of Wrath*	James Stewart *The Philadelphia Story*	Ginger Rogers *Kitty Foyle*	Walter Brennan *The Westerner*	Jane Darwell *The Grapes of Wrath*	"When You Wish upon a Star" *Pinocchio*	Alfred Newman *Tin Pan Alley* Leigh Harline, Paul J. Smith, Ned Washington *Pinocchio*	George Barnes *Rebecca* George Perinal *Thief of Bagdad*
1941	*How Green Was My Valley*	John Ford	Gary Cooper *Sergeant York*	Joan Fontaine *Suspicion*	Donald Crisp *How Green Was My Valley*	Mary Astor *The Great Lie*	"The Last Time I Saw Paris" *Lady Be Good*	Bernard Herrmann *All That Money Can Buy* Frank Churchill, Oliver Wallace *Dumbo*	Arthur Miller *How Green Was My Valley* Ernest Palmer, Ray Rennahan *Blood and Sand*
1942	*Mrs. Miniver*	William Wyler	James Cagney *Yankee Doodle Dandy*	Greer Garson *Mrs. Miniver*	Van Heflin *Johnny Eager*	Teresa Wright *Mrs. Miniver*	"White Christmas" *Holiday Inn*	Max Steiner *Now, Voyager* Ray Heindorf, Heinz Roemheld *Yankee Doodle Dandy*	Joseph Ruttenberg *Mrs. Miniver* Leon Shamroy *The Black Swan*
1943	*Casablanca*	Michael Curtiz	Paul Lukas *Watch on the Rhine*	Jennifer Jones *The Song of Bernadette*	Charles Coburn *The More the Merrier*	Katina Paxinou *For Whom the Bell Tolls*	"You'll Never Know" *Hello, Frisco, Hello*	Alfred Newman *The Song of Bernadette* Ray Heindorf *This Is the Army*	Arthur Miller *The Song of Bernadette* Hal Mohr, W. Howard Greene *The Phantom of the Opera*
1944	*Going My Way*	Leo McCarey	Bing Crosby *Going My Way*	Ingrid Bergman *Gaslight*	Barry Fitzgerald *Going My Way*	Ethel Barrymore *None But the Lonely Heart*	"Swinging on a Star" *Going My Way*	Max Steiner *Since You Went Away* Carmen Dragon, Morris Stoloff *Cover Girl*	Joseph LaShelle *Laura* Leon Shamroy *Wilson*
1945	*The Lost Weekend*	Billy Wilder	Ray Milland *The Lost Weekend*	Joan Crawford *Mildred Pierce*	James Dunn *A Tree Grows in Brooklyn*	Anne Revere *National Velvet*	"It Might As Well Be Spring" *State Fair*	Miklos Rozsa *Spellbound* Georgie Stoll *Anchors Aweigh*	Harry Stradling *The Picture of Dorian Gray* Leon Shamroy *Leave Her to Heaven*
1946	*The Best Years of Our Lives*	William Wyler	Fredric March *The Best Years of Our Lives*	Olivia de Havilland *To Each His Own*	Harold Russell *The Best Years of Our Lives*	Anne Baxter *The Razor's Edge*	"On the Atchison, Topeka and Santa Fe" *The Harvey Girls*	Hugo Friedhofer *The Best Years of Our Lives* Morris Stoloff *The Jolson Story*	Arthur Miller *Anna and the King of Siam* Charles Rosher, Leonard Smith, Arthur Arling *The Yearling*
1947	*Gentleman's Agreement*	Elia Kazan	Ronald Colman *A Double Life*	Loretta Young *The Farmer's Daughter*	Edmund Gwenn *Miracle on 34th Street*	Celeste Holm *Gentleman's Agreement*	"Zip-A-Dee-Doo-Dah" *Song of the South*	Miklos Rozsa *A Double Life* Alfred Newman *Mother Wore Tights*	Guy Green *Great Expectations* Jack Cardiff *Black Narcissus*
1948	*Hamlet*	John Huston *Treasure of the Sierra Madre*	Laurence Olivier *Hamlet*	Jane Wyman *Johnny Belinda*	Walter Huston *Treasure of the Sierra Madre*	Claire Trevor *Key Largo*	"Buttons and Bows" *The Paleface*	Brian Easdale *The Red Shoes* Johnny Green, Roger Edens *Easter Parade*	William Daniels *The Naked City* Joseph Valentine, William V. Skall, Winton Hoch *Joan of Arc*
1949	*All the King's Men*	Joseph L. Mankiewicz *A Letter to Three Wives*	Broderick Crawford *All the King's Men*	Olivia de Havilland *The Heiress*	Dean Jagger *Twelve O'Clock High*	Mercedes McCambridge *All the King's Men*	"Baby, It's Cold Outside" *Neptune's Daughter*	Aaron Copeland *The Heiress* Roger Edens, Lenny Hayton *On the Town*	Paul C. Vogel *Battleground* Winton Hoch *She Wore a Yellow Ribbon*

Year	Best picture	Best director	Best actor	Best actress	Best supporting actor	Best supporting actress	Best song (from film)	Original score	Best cinematographer
1950	*All About Eve*	Joseph L. Mankiewicz	José Ferrer *Cyrano de Bergerac*	Judy Holliday *Born Yesterday*	George Sanders *All About Eve*	Josephine Hull *Harvey*	"Mona Lisa" *Captain Carey, USA*	Franz Waxman *Sunset Boulevard* Adolph Deutsch, Roger Edens *Annie Get Your Gun*	Robert Krasker *The Third Man* Robert Surtees *King Solomon's Mines*
1951	*An American in Paris*	George Stevens *A Place in the Sun*	Humphrey Bogart *The African Queen*	Vivien Leigh *A Streetcar Named Desire*	Karl Malden *A Streetcar Named Desire*	Kim Hunter *A Streetcar Named Desire*	"In the Cool, Cool, Cool of the Evening" *Here Comes the Groom*	Franz Waxman *A Place in the Sun* Saul Chaplin, Johnny Green *An American in Paris*	William C. Mellor *A Place in the Sun* Alfred Gilks, John Alton (ballet) *An American in Paris*
1952	*The Greatest Show on Earth*	John Ford *The Quiet Man*	Gary Cooper *High Noon*	Shirley Booth *Come Back, Little Sheba*	Anthony Quinn *Viva Zapata!*	Gloria Grahame *The Bad and the Beautiful*	"High Noon (Do Not Forsake Me, Oh My Darlin')" *High Noon*	Dimitri Tiomkin *High Noon* Alfred Newman *With a Song in My Heart*	Robert Surtees *The Bad and the Beautiful* Winton Hoch, Archie Stout *The Quiet Man*
1953	*From Here to Eternity*	Fred Zinnemann	William Holden *Stalag 17*	Audrey Hepburn *Roman Holiday*	Frank Sinatra *From Here to Eternity*	Donna Reed *From Here to Eternity*	"Secret Love" *Calamity Jane*	Bronislau Kaper *Lili* Alfred Newman *Call Me Madam*	Burnett Guffey *From Here to Eternity* Loyal Griggs *Shane*
1954	*On the Waterfront*	Elia Kazan	Marlon Brando *On the Waterfront*	Grace Kelly *The Country Girl*	Edmond O'Brien *The Barefoot Contessa*	Eva Marie Saint *On the Waterfront*	"Three Coins in the Fountain" *Three Coins in the Fountain*	Dimitri Tiomkin *The High and the Mighty* Saul Chaplin, Adolph Deutsch *Seven Brides for Seven Brothers*	Boris Kaufman *On the Waterfront* Milton Krasner *Three Coins in the Fountain*
1955	*Marty*	Delbert Mann	Ernest Borgnine *Marty*	Anna Magnani *The Rose Tattoo*	Jack Lemmon *Mister Roberts*	Jo Van Fleet *East of Eden*	"Love Is a Many-Splendored Thing" *Love Is a Many-Splendored Thing*	Alfred Newman *Love Is a Many-Splendored Thing* Robert Russell Bennett, Jay Blackton, Adolph Deutsch *Oklahoma!*	James Wong Howe *The Rose Tattoo* Robert Burks *To Catch a Thief*
1956	*Around the World in 80 Days*	George Stevens *Giant*	Yul Brynner *The King and I*	Ingrid Bergman *Anastasia*	Anthony Quinn *Lust for Life*	Dorothy Malone *Written on the Wind*	"Whatever Will Be, Will Be (Que Sera, Sera)" *The Man Who Knew Too Much*	Victor Young *Around the World in 80 Days* Alfred Newman, Ken Darby *The King and I*	Joseph Ruttenberg *Somebody Up There Likes Me* Lionel Lindon *Around the World in 80 Days*
1957	*The Bridge on the River Kwai*	David Lean	Alec Guinness *The Bridge on the River Kwai*	Joanne Woodward *The Three Faces of Eve*	Red Buttons *Sayonara*	Miyoshi Umeki *Sayonara*	"All the Way" *The Joker Is Wild*	Malcolm Arnold *The Bridge on the River Kwai*	Jack Hildyard *The Bridge on the River Kwai*
1958	*Gigi*	Vincente Minnelli	David Niven *Separate Tables*	Susan Hayward *I Want to Live!*	Burl Ives *The Big Country*	Wendy Hiller *Separate Tables*	"Gigi" *Gigi*	Dimitri Tiomkin *The Old Man and the Sea* André Previn *Gigi*	Sam Leavitt *The Defiant Ones* Joseph Ruttenberg *Gigi*
1959	*Ben Hur*	William Wyler	Charlton Heston *Ben Hur*	Simone Signoret *Room at the Top*	Hugh Griffith *Ben Hur*	Shelley Winters *The Diary of Anne Frank*	"High Hopes" *A Hole in the Head*	Miklos Rosza *Ben Hur* Andre Previn, Ken Darby *All That Jazz*	William C. Mellor *The Diary of Anne Frank* Robert L. Surtees *Ben Hur*
1960	*The Apartment*	Billy Wilder	Burt Lancaster *Elmer Gantry*	Elizabeth Taylor *Butterfield 8*	Peter Ustinov *Spartacus*	Shirley Jones *Elmer Gantry*	"Never on Sunday" *Never on Sunday*	Ernest Gold *Exodus* Morris Stoloff, Harry Sukman *Song without End*	Freddie Francis *Sons and Lovers* Russell Metty *Spartacus*

Year	Best picture	Best director	Best actor	Best actress	Best supporting actor	Best supporting actress	Best song (from film)	Original score	Best cinematographer
1961	*West Side Story*	Jerome Robbins, Robert Wise	Maximilian Schell *Judgment at Nuremberg*	Sophia Loren *Two Women*	George Chakiris *West Side Story*	Rita Moreno *West Side Story*	"Moon River" *Breakfast at Tiffany's*	Henry Mancini *Breakfast at Tiffany's* Saul Chaplin, Johnny Green, Sid Ramin, Irwin Kostal *West Side Story*	Eugen Shuftan *The Hustler* Daniel L. Fapp *West Side Story*
1962	*Lawrence of Arabia*	David Lean	Gregory Peck *To Kill a Mockingbird*	Anne Bancroft *The Miracle Worker*	Ed Begley *Sweet Bird of Youth*	Patty Duke *The Miracle Worker*	"Days of Wine and Roses" *Days of Wine and Roses*	Maurice Jarre *Lawrence of Arabia*	Jean Bourgoin, Walter Wottitz *The Longest Day* Fred A. Young *Lawrence of Arabia*
1963	*Tom Jones*	Tony Richardson	Sidney Poitier *Lilies of the Field*	Patricia Neal *Hud*	Melvyn Douglas *Hud*	Margaret Rutherford *The V.I.P.s*	"Call Me Irresponsible" *Papa's Delicate Condition*	John Addison *Tom Jones*	James Wong Howe *Hud* Leon Shamroy *Cleopatra*
1964	*My Fair Lady*	George Cukor	Rex Harrison *My Fair Lady*	Julie Andrews *Mary Poppins*	Peter Ustinov *Topkapi*	Lila Kedrova *Zorba the Greek*	"Chim Chim Cher-ee" *Mary Poppins*	Richard M. Sherman, Robert B. Sherman *Mary Poppins*	Walter Lassally *Zorba the Greek* Harry Stradling *My Fair Lady*
1965	*The Sound of Music*	Robert Wise	Lee Marvin *Cat Ballou*	Julie Christie *Darling*	Martin Balsam *A Thousand Clowns*	Shelley Winters *A Patch of Blue*	"The Shadow of Your Smile" *The Sandpiper*	Maurice Jarre *Dr. Zhivago*	Ernest Laszlo *Ship of Fools* Freddie Young *Dr. Zhivago*
1966	*A Man for All Seasons*	Fred Zinnemann	Paul Scofield *A Man for All Seasons*	Elizabeth Taylor *Who's Afraid of Virginia Woolf?*	Walter Matthau *The Fortune Cookie*	Sandy Dennis *Who's Afraid of Virginia Woolf?*	"Born Free" *Born Free*	John Barry *Born Free*	Haskell Wexler *Who's Afraid of Virginia Woolf?* Ted Moore *A Man for All Seasons*
1967	*In the Heat of the Night*	Mike Nichols *The Graduate*	Rod Steiger *In the Heat of the Night*	Katharine Hepburn *Guess Who's Coming to Dinner*	George Kennedy *Cool Hand Luke*	Estelle Parsons *Bonnie and Clyde*	"Talk to the Animals" *Doctor Dolittle*	Elmer Bernstein *Thoroughly Modern Millie*	Burnett Guffey *Bonnie and Clyde*
1968	*Oliver!*	Carol Reed	Cliff Robertson *Charly*	Katharine Hepburn *The Lion in Winter* Barbra Streisand *Funny Girl*	Jack Albertson *The Subject Was Roses*	Ruth Gordon *Rosemary's Baby*	"The Windmills of Your Mind" *The Thomas Crown Affair*	John Barry *The Lion in Winter*	Pasqualino DeSantis *Romeo and Juliet*
1969	*Midnight Cowboy*	John Schlesinger	John Wayne *True Grit*	Maggie Smith *The Prime of Miss Jean Brodie*	Gig Young *They Shoot Horses, Don't They?*	Goldie Hawn *Cactus Flower*	"Raindrops Keep Fallin' on My Head" *Butch Cassidy and the Sundance Kid*	Burt Bacharach *Butch Cassidy and the Sundance Kid*	Conrad Hall *Butch Cassidy and the Sundance Kid*
1970	*Patton*	Franklin Schaffner	George C. Scott *Patton*	Glenda Jackson *Women in Love*	John Mills *Ryan's Daughter*	Helen Hayes *Airport*	"For All We Know" *Lovers and Other Strangers*	Francis Lai *Love Story* The Beatles (music, lyrics) *Let It Be*	Freddie Young *Ryan's Daughter*
1971	*The French Connection*	William Friedkin	Gene Hackman *The French Connection*	Jane Fonda *Klute*	Ben Johnson *The Last Picture Show*	Cloris Leachman *The Last Picture Show*	"Theme from *Shaft*" *Shaft*	Michel Legrand *The Summer of '42*	Oswald Morris *Fiddler on the Roof*
1972	*The Godfather*	Bob Fosse *Cabaret*	Marlon Brando *The Godfather*	Liza Minnelli *Cabaret*	Joel Grey *Cabaret*	Eileen Heckart *Butterflies Are Free*	"The Morning After" *The Poseidon Adventure*	Charles Chaplin, Raymond Rasch, Larry Russell *Limelight*	Geoffrey Unsworth *Cabaret*
1973	*The Sting*	George Roy Hill	Jack Lemmon *Save the Tiger*	Glenda Jackson *A Touch of Class*	John Houseman *The Paper Chase*	Tatum O'Neal *Paper Moon*	"The Way We Were" *The Way We Were*	Marvin Hamlisch *The Way We Were*	Sven Nykvist *Cries and Whispers*
1974	*The Godfather Part II*	Francis Ford Coppola	Art Carney *Harry and Tonto*	Ellen Burstyn *Alice Doesn't Live Here Anymore*	Robert DeNiro *The Godfather Pt. II*	Ingrid Bergman *Murder on the Orient Express*	"We May Never Love Like This Again" *The Towering Inferno*	Nino Rota, Carmine Coppola *The Godfather Pt. II*	Fred Koenekamp, Joseph Biroc *The Towering Inferno*
1975	*One Flew over the Cuckoo's Nest*	Milŏs Forman	Jack Nicholson *One Flew over the Cuckoo's Nest*	Louise Fletcher *One Flew over the Cuckoo's Nest*	George Burns *The Sunshine Boys*	Lee Grant *Shampoo*	"I'm Easy" *Nashville*	John Williams *Jaws*	John Alcott *Barry Lyndon*
1976	*Rocky*	John G. Avildsen	Peter Finch *Network*	Faye Dunaway *Network*	Jason Robards *All the President's Men*	Beatrice Straight *Network*	"Evergreen" (love theme) *A Star Is Born*	Jerry Goldsmith *The Omen*	Haskell Wexler *Bound for Glory*

Year	Best picture	Best director	Best actor	Best actress	Best supporting actor	Best supporting actress	Best song (from film)	Original score	Best cinematographer
1977	*Annie Hall*	Woody Allen	Richard Dreyfuss *The Goodbye Girl*	Diane Keaton *Annie Hall*	Jason Robards *Julia*	Vanessa Redgrave *Julia*	"You Light Up My Life" *You Light Up My Life*	John Williams *Star Wars*	Vilmos Zsigmond *Close Encounters of the Third Kind*
1978	*The Deer Hunter*	Michael Cimino	Jon Voight *Coming Home*	Jane Fonda *Coming Home*	Christopher Walken *The Deer Hunter*	Maggie Smith *California Suite*	"Last Dance" *Thank God It's Friday*	Giorgio Moroder *Midnight Express*	Nestor Almendros *Days of Heaven*
1979	*Kramer vs. Kramer*	Robert Benton	Dustin Hoffman *Kramer vs. Kramer*	Sally Field *Norma Rae*	Melvyn Douglas *Being There*	Meryl Streep *Kramer vs. Kramer*	"It Goes Like It Goes" *Norma Rae*	Georges Delerue *A Little Romance*	Vittorio Storaro *Apocalypse Now*
1980	*Ordinary People*	Robert Redford	Robert DeNiro *Raging Bull*	Sissy Spacek *Coal Miner's Daughter*	Timothy Hutton *Ordinary People*	Mary Steenburgen *Melvin and Howard*	"Fame" *Fame*	Michael Gore *Fame*	Geoffrey Unsworth, Ghislain Cloquet *Tess*
1981	*Chariots of Fire*	Warren Beatty *Reds*	Henry Fonda *On Golden Pond*	Katharine Hepburn *On Golden Pond*	John Gielgud *Arthur*	Maureen Stapleton *Reds*	"Arthur's Theme" (Best That You Can Do) *Arthur*	Vangelis *Chariots of Fire*	Vittorio Storaro *Reds*
1982	*Gandhi*	Richard Attenborough	Ben Kingsley *Gandhi*	Meryl Streep *Sophie's Choice*	Lou Gossett, Jr. *An Officer and a Gentleman*	Jessica Lange *Tootsie*	"Up Where We Belong" *An Officer and a Gentleman*	John Williams *E.T.—The Extra-Terrestrial*	Billy Williams, Ronnie Taylor *Gandhi*
1983	*Terms of Endearment*	James L. Brooks	Robert Duvall *Tender Mercies*	Shirley MacLaine *Terms of Endearment*	Jack Nicholson *Terms of Endearment*	Linda Hunt *The Year of Living Dangerously*	"Flashdance . . . What a Feeling" *Flashdance*	Bill Conti *The Right Stuff*	Sven Nykvist *Fanny and Alexander*
1984	*Amadeus*	Milŏs Forman	F. Murray Abraham *Amadeus*	Sally Field *Places in the Heart*	Haing S. Ngor *The Killing Fields*	Peggy Ashcroft *A Passage to India*	"I Just Called to Say I Love You" *The Woman in Red*	Maurice Jarre *A Passage to India* Prince *Purple Rain*	Chris Menges *The Killing Fields*
1985	*Out of Africa*	Sydney Pollack	William Hurt *Kiss of the Spider Woman*	Geraldine Page *The Trip to Bountiful*	Don Ameche *Cocoon*	Anjelica Huston *Prizzi's Honor*	"Say You, Say Me" *White Nights*	John Barry *Out of Africa*	David Watkin *Out of Africa*
1986	*Platoon*	Oliver Stone	Paul Newman *The Color of Money*	Marlee Matlin *Children of a Lesser God*	Michael Caine *Hannah and Her Sisters*	Dianne Wiest *Hannah and Her Sisters*	"Take My Breath Away" *Top Gun*	Herbie Hancock *'Round Midnight*	Chris Menges *The Mission*
1987	*The Last Emperor*	Bernardo Bertolucci	Michael Douglas *Wall Street*	Cher *Moonstruck*	Sean Connery *The Untouchables*	Olympia Dukakis *Moonstruck*	"(I've Had) the Time of My Life" *Dirty Dancing*	Ryuichi Sakamoto, David Byrne, Cong Su *The Last Emperor*	Vittorio Storaro *The Last Emperor*
1988	*Rain Man*	Barry Levinson	Dustin Hoffman *Rain Man*	Jodie Foster *The Accused*	Kevin Kline *A Fish Called Wanda*	Geena Davis *The Accidental Tourist*	"Let the River Run" *Working Girl*	Dave Grusin *The Milagro Beanfield War*	Peter Biziou *Mississippi Burning*
1989	*Driving Miss Daisy*	Oliver Stone *Born on the Fourth of July*	Daniel Day-Lewis *My Left Foot*	Jessica Tandy *Driving Miss Daisy*	Denzel Washington *Glory*	Brenda Fricker *My Left Foot*	"Under the Sea" *The Little Mermaid*	Alan Menken *The Little Mermaid*	Freddie Francis *Glory*
1990	*Dances With Wolves*	Kevin Costner	Jeremy Irons *Reversal of Fortune*	Kathy Bates *Misery*	Joe Pesci *GoodFellas*	Whoopi Goldberg *Ghost*	"Sooner or Later (I Always Get My Man)" *Dick Tracy*	John Barry *Dances With Wolves*	Dean Semler *Dances With Wolves*
1991	*The Silence of the Lambs*	Jonathan Demme	Anthony Hopkins *The Silence of the Lambs*	Jodie Foster *The Silence of the Lambs*	Jack Palance *City Slickers*	Mercedes Ruehl *The Fisher King*	"Beauty and the Beast" *Beauty and the Beast*	Alan Menken *Beauty and the Beast*	Robert Richardson *JFK*
1992	*Unforgiven*	Clint Eastwood	Al Pacino *Scent of a Woman*	Emma Thompson *Howards End*	Gene Hackman *Unforgiven*	Marisa Tomei *My Cousin Vinny*	"Whole New World" *Aladdin*	Alan Menken *Aladdin*	Philippe Rousselot *A River Runs Through It*
1993	*Schindler's List*	Steven Spielberg	Tom Hanks *Philadelphia*	Holly Hunter *The Piano*	Tommy Lee Jones *The Fugitive*	Anna Paquin *The Piano*	"Streets of Philadelphia" *Philadelphia*	John Williams *Schindler's List*	Janusz Kaminski *Schindler's List*
1994	*Forrest Gump*	Robert Zemeckis	Tom Hanks *Forrest Gump*	Jessica Lange *Blue Sky*	Martin Landau *Ed Wood*	Dianne Wiest *Bullets Over Broadway*	"Can You Feel the Love Tonight" *The Lion King*	Hans Zimmer *The Lion King*	John Toll *Legends of the Fall*

Source: BASELINE II, INC.

ACADEMY AWARDS FOR BEST FOREIGN LANGUAGE FILM, 1956–94

Year	Film	Country	Director
1956	*La Strada*	Italy	Federico Fellini
1957	*The Nights of Cabiria*	Italy	Federico Fellini
1958	*Mon Oncle*	France	Jacques Tati
1959	*Black Orpheus*	France/Italy/Brazil	Marcel Camus
1960	*The Virgin Spring*	Sweden	Ingmar Bergman
1961	*Through a Glass Darkly*	Sweden	Ingmar Bergman
1962	*Sundays and Cybele*	France	Serge Bourgignon
1963	*8½*	Italy	Federico Fellini
1964	*Yesterday, Today and Tomorrow*	Italy/France	Vittorio de Sica
1965	*The Shop on Main Street*	Czechoslovakia	Jan Kadar
1966	*A Man and a Woman*	France	Claude Lelouch
1967	*Closely Watched Trains*	Czechoslovakia	Jiri Menzel
1968	*War and Peace*	USSR	Sergei Bondarchuk
1969	*Z*	France/Algeria	Constantin Costa-Gavras
1970	*Investigation of a Citizen above Suspicion*	Italy	Elio Petri
1971	*The Garden of the Finzi-Continis*	Italy	Vittorio de Sica
1972	*The Discreet Charm of the Bourgeoisie*	France	Luis Buñuel
1973	*Day for Night*	France/Italy	François Truffaut
1974	*Amarcord*	Italy/France	Federico Fellini
1975	*Dersu Uzala*	USSR/Japan	Akira Kurosawa
1976	*Black and White in Color*	France/Switzerland/ Ivory Coast	Jean-Jacques Annaud
1977	*Madame Rosa*	France	Moshe Mizrahi
1978	*Get Out Your Handkerchiefs*	France	Bertrand Blier
1979	*The Tin Drum*	Germany	Volker Scholondorff
1980	*Moscow Does Not Believe in Tears*	USSR	Vladimir Menshov
1981	*Mephisto*	Austria/Germany/ Hungary	Istvan Szabo
1982	*To Begin Again*	Spain	Jose Luis Garci
1983	*Fanny and Alexander*	Sweden	Ingmar Bergman
1984	*Dangerous Moves*	France	Richard Dembo
1985	*The Official Story*	Argentina	Luis Puenzo
1986	*The Assault*	Netherlands	Fons Rademakers
1987	*Babette's Feast*	Denmark	Gabriel Axel
1988	*Pelle the Conqueror*	Denmark	Bille August
1989	*Cinema Paradiso*	Italy	Giuseppe Tornatore
1990	*Journey of Hope*	Switzerland	Xavier Koller
1991	*Mediterraneo*	Italy	Gabriele Salvatores
1992	*Indochine*	France	Regis Wargnier
1993	*Belle Époque*	Spain	Fernando Trueba
1994	*Burnt by the Sun*	Russia	Nikita Mikhalkov

Source: BASELINE II, INC.

CANNES FESTIVAL BEST FILM AWARDS, 1946–95

The Festival International du Film was scheduled to make its debut in September 1939, but was canceled that year due to the outbreak of World War II. The first festival was held in 1946. The official name for the best film award has been Grand Prix (1949–54 and 1964–74) and the Palme d'Or (1955–63 and 1975–present).

Year	Film and director
1946	*La Bataille du Rail*, René Clément[1]
1949[2]	*The Third Man*, Carol Reed
1951	*Miracle in Milan*, Vittorio De Sica
	Miss Julie, Alf Sjöberg
1952	*Two Cents Worth of Hope*, Renato Castellani
	Othello, Orson Welles
1953	*The Wages of Fear*, Georges Clouzot
1954	*Gate of Hell*, Teinosuke Kinugasa
1955	*Marty*, Delbert Mann
1956	*The Silent World*, Jacques Cousteau, Louis Malle
1957	*Friendly Persuasion*, William Wyler
1958	*The Cranes are Flying*, Mikhail Kalatozov
1959	*Black Orpheus*, Marcel Camus
1960	*La Dolce Vita*, Federico Fellini
1961	*Viridiana*, Luis Buñuel
1962	*The Given Word*, Anselmo Duarte
1963	*The Leopard*, Luchino Visconti
1964	*The Umbrellas of Cherbourg*, Jacques Demy
1965	*The Knack, and How to Get It*, Richard Lester
1966	*A Man and a Woman*, Claude Lelouch
1967	*Blow-Up*, Michelangelo Antonioni[1]
1968	No award[3]
1969	*If . . . ,* Lindsay Anderson
1970	*M*A*S*H*, Robert Altman
1971	*The Go-Between*, Joseph Losey
1972	*The Working Class Goes to Heaven*, Elio Petri
	The Mattei Affair, Francesco Rosi
1973	*Scarecrow*, Jerry Schatzberg
	The Hireling, Alan Bridges
1974	*The Conversation*, Francis Ford Coppola
1975	*Chronique des Années de Braise*, M. Lakhdar Hamina
1976	*Taxi Driver*, Martin Scorsese
1977	*Padre Padrone*, Paolo and Vittorio Taviani
1978	*The Tree of Wooden Clogs*, Ermanno Olmi
1979	*The Tin Drum*, Volker Schlöndorff
1980	*Kagemusha*, Akira Kurosawa
1981	*Man of Iron*, Andrzej Wajda
1982	*Missing*, Constantin Costa-Gavras
	Yol, Yilmar Güney
1983	*The Ballad of Narayama*, Shohei Imamura
1984	*Paris, Texas*, Wim Wenders
1985	*When Father Was Away on Business*, Emir Kusturica
1986	*The Mission*, Roland Joffé
1987	*Under Satan's Sun*, Maurice Pialat
1988	*Pelle the Conqueror*, Bille August
1989	*sex, lies, and videotape*, Steven Soderbergh
1990	*Wild at Heart*, David Lynch
1991	*Barton Fink*, Joel Coen
1992	*The Best Intentions*, Bille August
1993	*The Piano*, Jane Campion
	Farewell My Concubine, Chen Kaige
1994	*Pulp Fiction*, Quentin Tarantino
1995	*Underground*, Emir Kusturica

1. Winner of the International Jury Prize. 2. In 1947, there was no "best film" award, but prizes were given to outstanding works in several categories, including "Psychological and Love Films," "Adventure and Police Films," and so on. The festival was canceled in 1948 and 1950. 3. Festival canceled because of student riots in Paris. **Source:** BASELINE II, INC.

AMERICAN FILM INSTITUTE LIFE ACHIEVEMENT AWARDS, 1973–95

Awarded to individuals whose "talent has fundamentally advanced the art of American film or television . . . and whose work has withstood the test of time."

1973 John Ford
1974 James Cagney
1975 Orson Welles
1976 William Wyler
1977 Henry Fonda
1978 Bette Davis
1979 Alfred Hitchcock
1980 James Stewart
1981 Fred Astaire
1982 Frank Capra
1983 John Huston
1984 Lillian Gish
1985 Gene Kelly
1986 Billy Wilder
1987 Barbara Stanwyck
1988 Jack Lemmon
1989 Gregory Peck
1990 David Lean
1991 Kirk Douglas
1992 Sidney Poitier
1993 Elizabeth Taylor
1994 Jack Nicholson
1995 Steven Spielberg

Source: American Film Institute.

THE EMMY AWARDS, 1948–94

The National Academy of Television Arts and Sciences Awards, formed in 1946, presented the first Emmy Awards in 1949. Only a selection is printed here; not only has the number of awards changed from year to year (peaking in 1978 with a total of 75 categories), but the categories themselves have fluctuated to reflect change in the industry. For 1995 Emmy Award winners, see Part I: "The Year in Review."

1948

Outstanding TV Personality: Shirley Dinsdale (and her puppet Judy Splinters) (KTLA)
Most Popular TV Program: *Pantomime Quiz Time* (KTLA)
Best Film Made for Television: "The Necklace," *Your Show Time* (NBC)
Special Award: Louis McManus, original designer of the Emmy

1949

Best Live Show: *The Ed Wynn Show* (CBS)
Best Kinescope[1] Show: *Texaco Star Theater* (NBC)
Outstanding Live Personality: Ed Wynn (CBS)
Outstanding Kinescope Personality: Milton Berle (NBC)
Best Film Made for TV: *The Life of Riley* (NBC)

1950

Best Actor: Alan Young (CBS)
Best Actress: Gertrude Berg (CBS)
Outstanding Personality: Groucho Marx (NBC)
Best Variety Show: *The Alan Young Show* (CBS)
Best Dramatic Show: *Pulitzer Prize Playhouse* (ABC)
Best Game Show: *Truth or Consequences* (CBS)

1951

Best Dramatic Show: *Studio One* (CBS)
Best Comedy Show: *The Red Skelton Show* (CBS)
Best Variety Show: *Your Show of Shows* (NBC)
Best Actor: Sid Caesar (NBC)
Best Actress: Imogene Coca (NBC)
Best Comedian or Comedienne: Red Skelton (NBC)

1952

Best Dramatic Program: *Robert Montgomery Presents* (NBC)
Best Variety Program: *Your Show of Shows* (NBC)
Best Mystery, Action, or Adventure Program: *Dragnet* (NBC)
Best Situation Comedy: *I Love Lucy* (CBS)
Best Actor: Thomas Mitchell
Best Actress: Helen Hayes

1953

Best Dramatic Program: *The U.S. Steel Hour* (ABC)
Best Situation Comedy: *I Love Lucy* (CBS)
Best Variety Program: *Omnibus* (CBS)
Best Male Star of Regular Series: Donald O'Connor, *Colgate Comedy Hour* (NBC)
Best Female Star of Regular Series: Eve Arden, *Our Miss Brooks* (CBS)
Best Mystery, Action, or Adventure Program: *Dragnet* (NBC)

1954

Best Actor Starring in a Regular Series: Danny Thomas, *Make Room for Daddy* (ABC)
Best Actress Starring in a Regular Series: Loretta Young, *The Loretta Young Show* (NBC)
Best Mystery or Intrigue Series: *Dragnet* (NBC)
Best Variety Series Including Musical Varieties: *Disneyland* (ABC)
Best Situation Comedy Series: *Make Room for Daddy* (ABC)
Best Dramatic Series: *The U.S. Steel Hour* (ABC)

1955

Best Action or Adventure Series: *Disneyland* (ABC)
Best Comedy Series: *The Phil Silvers Show* (CBS)
Best Variety Series: *The Ed Sullivan Show* (CBS)
Best Dramatic Series: *Producers' Showcase* (NBC)
Best Actor (Continuing Performance): Phil Silvers, *The Phil Silvers Show* (CBS)
Best Actress (Continuing Performance): Lucille Ball, *I Love Lucy* (CBS)

1956

Best Single Program of the Year: "Requiem for a Heavyweight," *Playhouse 90* (CBS)
Best Series (Half Hour or Less): *The Phil Silvers Show* (CBS)
Best Series (One Hour or More): *Caesar's Hour* (NBC)
Best Continuing Performance by an Actor in a Dramatic Series: Robert Young, *Father Knows Best* (NBC)
Best Continuing Performance by an Actress in a Dramatic Series: Loretta Young, *The Loretta Young Show* (NBC)

1957

Program of the Year: "The Comedian," *Playhouse 90* (CBS)
Best Dramatic Series with Continuing Characters: *Gunsmoke* (CBS)
Best Comedy Series: *The Phil Silvers Show* (CBS)
Best Musical, Variety, Audience Participation, or Quiz Series: *The Dinah Shore Chevy Show* (NBC)
Best Continuing Performance by an Actor in a Leading Role in a Dramatic or Comedy Series: Robert Young, *Father Knows Best* (NBC)
Best Continuing Performance by an Actress in a Leading Role in a Dramatic or Comedy Series: Jane Wyatt, *Father Knows Best* (NBC)

1958–59

Program of the Year: "An Evening with Fred Astaire" (NBC)
Best Dramatic Series (One Hour or Longer): *Playhouse 90* (CBS)
Best Dramatic Series (Less Than One Hour): *Alcoa-Goodyear Theatre* (NBC)
Best Comedy Series: *The Jack Benny Show* (CBS)
Best Musical or Variety Series: *The Dinah Shore Chevy Show* (NBC)
Best Western Series: *Maverick* (ABC)
Best Actor in a Leading Role (Continuing Character) in a Dramatic Series: Raymond Burr, *Perry Mason* (CBS)
Best Actress in a Leading Role (Continuing Character) in a Dramatic Series: Loretta Young, *The Loretta Young Show* (NBC)
Best Actor in a Leading Role (Continuing Character) in a Comedy Series: Jack Benny, *The Jack Benny Show* (CBS)
Best Actress in a Leading Role (Continuing Character) in a Comedy Series: Jane Wyatt, *Father Knows Best* (CBS and NBC)

1959–60

Program Achievement in the Field of Humor: "The Art Carney Special" (NBC)
Program Achievement in the Field of Drama: *Playhouse 90* (CBS)
Program Achievement in the Field of Variety: "The Fabulous Fifties" (CBS)
Performance by an Actor in a Series (Lead or Support): Robert Stack, *The Untouchables* (ABC)
Performance by an Actress in a Series (Lead or Support): Jane Wyatt, *Father Knows Best* (CBS)
Performance in a Variety or Musical Program or Series: Harry Belafonte, "Tonight with Belafonte," *The Revlon Revue* (CBS)

1960–61

Program of the Year: "Macbeth," *Hallmark Hall of Fame* (NBC)
Program Achievement in the Field of Humor: *The Jack Benny Show* (CBS)
Program Achievement in the Field of Drama: "Macbeth," *Hallmark Hall of Fame* (NBC)
Program Achievement in the Field of Variety: "Astaire Time" (NBC)
Performance by an Actor in a Series (Lead): Raymond Burr, *Perry Mason* (CBS)

Performance by an Actress in a Series (Lead): Barbara Stanwyck, *The Barbara Stanwyck Show* (NBC)
Performance in a Variety or Musical Program or Series: Fred Astaire, "Astaire Time" (NBC)

1961–62

Program of the Year: "Victoria Regina," *Hallmark Hall of Fame* (NBC)
Program Achievement in the Field of Humor: *The Bob Newhart Show* (NBC)
Program Achievement in the Field of Drama: *The Defenders* (CBS)
Program Achievement in the Field of Variety: *The Garry Moore Show* (CBS)
Continued Performance by an Actor in a Series (Lead): E.G. Marshall, *The Defenders* (CBS)
Continued Performance by an Actress in a Series (Lead): Shirley Booth, *Hazel* (NBC)
Performance in a Variety or Musical Program or Series: Carol Burnett, *The Garry Moore Show* (CBS)

1962–63

Program of the Year: "The Tunnel" (NBC)
Program Achievement in the Field of Humor: *The Dick Van Dyke Show* (CBS)
Program Achievement in the Field of Drama: *The Defenders* (CBS)
Program Achievement in the Field of Music: "Julie and Carol at Carnegie Hall" (CBS)
Program Achievement in the Field of Variety: *The Andy Williams Show* (NBC)
Continued Performance by an Actor in a Series (Lead): E.G. Marshall, *The Defenders* (CBS)
Continued Performance by an Actress in a Series (Lead): Shirley Booth, *Hazel* (NBC)
Performance in a Variety or Musical Program or Series: Carol Burnett, "Julie and Carol at Carnegie Hall" (CBS) and "Carol and Company" (CBS)

1963–64

Program of the Year: "The Making of the President 1960" (ABC)
Program Achievement in the Field of Comedy: *The Dick Van Dyke Show* (CBS)
Program Achievement in the Field of Drama: *The Defenders* (CBS)
Program Achievement in the Field of Variety: *The Danny Kaye Show* (CBS)
Continued Performance by an Actor in a Series (Lead): Dick Van Dyke, *The Dick Van Dyke Show* (CBS)
Continued Performance by an Actress in a Series (Lead): Mary Tyler Moore, *The Dick Van Dyke Show* (CBS)
Performance in a Variety or Musical Program or Series: Danny Kaye, *The Danny Kaye Show* (CBS)

1964–65

Achievements in Entertainment: *The Dick Van Dyke Show* (CBS); "The Magnificent Yankee," *Hallmark Hall of Fame* (NBC); "My Name Is Barbra" (CBS)
Individual Achievements in Entertainment (Actors and Performers): Lynn Fontanne, "The Magnificent Yankee," *Hallmark Hall of Fame* (NBC); Barbra Streisand, "My Name Is Barbra" (CBS); Dick Van Dyke, *The Dick Van Dyke Show* (CBS)

1965–66

Comedy Series: *The Dick Van Dyke Show* (CBS)
Variety Series: *The Andy Williams Show* (NBC)
Dramatic Series: *The Fugitive* (ABC)
Continued Performance by an Actor in a Leading Role in a Dramatic Series: Bill Cosby, *I Spy* (NBC)
Continued Performance by an Actress in a Leading Role in a Dramatic Series: Barbara Stanwyck, *The Big Valley* (ABC)
Continued Performance by an Actor in a Leading Role in a Comedy Series: Dick Van Dyke, *The Dick Van Dyke Show* (CBS)
Continued Performance by an Actress in a Leading Role in a Comedy Series: Mary Tyler Moore, *The Dick Van Dyke Show* (CBS)

1966–67

Comedy Series: *The Monkees* (NBC)
Variety Series: *The Andy Williams Show* (NBC)
Dramatic Series: *Mission: Impossible* (CBS)
Continued Performance by an Actor in a Leading Role in a Dramatic Series: Bill Cosby, *I Spy* (NBC)
Continued Performance by an Actress in a Leading Role in a Dramatic Series: Barbara Bain, *Mission: Impossible* (CBS)
Continued Performance by an Actor in a Leading Role in a Comedy Series: Don Adams, *Get Smart* (NBC)
Continued Performance by an Actress in a Leading Role in a Comedy Series: Lucille Ball, *The Lucy Show* (CBS)

1967–68

Comedy Series: *Get Smart* (NBC)
Dramatic Series: *Mission: Impossible* (CBS)
Continued Performance by an Actor in a Leading Role in a Dramatic Series: Bill Cosby, *I Spy* (NBC)
Continued Performance by an Actress in a Leading Role in a Dramatic Series: Barbara Bain, *Mission: Impossible* (CBS)
Continued Performance by an Actor in a Leading Role in a Comedy Series: Don Adams, *Get Smart* (NBC)
Continued Performance by an Actress in a Leading Role in a Comedy Series: Lucille Ball, *The Lucy Show* (CBS)

1968–69

Comedy Series: *Get Smart* (NBC)
Dramatic Series: *NET Playhouse* (NET)
Musical or Variety Series: *Rowan and Martin's Laugh-In* (NBC)
Continued Performance by an Actor in a Leading Role in a Dramatic Series: Carl Betz, *Judd, for the Defense* (ABC)
Continued Performance by an Actress in a Leading Role in a Dramatic Series: Barbara Bain, *Mission: Impossible* (CBS)
Continued Performance by an Actor in a Leading Role in a Comedy Series: Don Adams, *Get Smart* (NBC)
Continued Performance by an Actress in a Leading Role in a Comedy Series: Hope Lange, *The Ghost and Mrs. Muir* (NBC)

1969–70

Comedy Series: *My World and Welcome to It* (NBC)
Dramatic Series: *Marcus Welby, M.D.* (ABC)
Variety or Musical Series: *The David Frost Show* (syndicated)
Continued Performance by an Actor in a Leading Role in a Dramatic Series: Robert Young, *Marcus Welby, M.D.* (ABC)
Continued Performance by an Actress in a Leading Role in a Dramatic Series: Susan Hampshire, *The Forsythe Saga* (NET)
Continued Performance by an Actor in a Leading Role in a Comedy Series: William Windom, *My World and Welcome to It* (NBC)
Continued Performance by an Actress in a Leading Role in a Comedy Series: Hope Lange, *The Ghost and Mrs. Muir* (ABC)

1970–71

Series—Comedy: *All in the Family* (CBS)
Series—Drama: *The Senator* (NBC)
Variety Series—Musical: *The Flip Wilson Show* (NBC)
Continued Performance by an Actor in a Leading Role in a Dramatic Series: Hal Holbrook, *The Senator* (NBC)
Continued Performance by an Actress in a Leading Role in a Dramatic Series: Susan Hampshire, *The First Churchills (Masterpiece Theatre)* (PBS)
Continued Performance by an Actor in a Leading Role in a Comedy Series: Jack Klugman, *The Odd Couple* (CBS)
Continued Performance by an Actress in a Leading Role in a Comedy Series: Jean Stapleton, *All in the Family* (CBS)

1971–72

Series—Comedy: *All in the Family* (CBS)
Series—Drama: "Elizabeth R" Masterpiece Theatre (PBS)
Variety Series—Musical: *The Carol Burnett Show* (CBS)
Variety Series—Talk: *The Dick Cavett Show* (ABC)
Continued Performance by an Actor in a Leading Role in a Dramatic Series: Peter Falk, *Columbo* (NBC)
Continued Performance by an Actor in a Leading Role in a Comedy Series: Carroll O'Connor, *All in the Family* (CBS)
Continued Performance by an Actress in a Leading Role in a Comedy Series: Jean Stapleton, *All in the Family* (CBS)

1972–73

Comedy Series: *All in the Family* (CBS)
Drama Series: *The Waltons* (CBS)
Variety Musical Series: *The Julie Andrews Hour* (ABC)
Continued Performance by an Actor in a Leading Role (Drama Series—Continuing): Richard Thomas, *The Waltons* (CBS)
Continued Performance by an Actress in a Leading Role (Drama Series—Continuing): Michael Learned, *The Waltons* (CBS)
Continued Performance by an Actor in a Leading Role in a Comedy Series: Jack Klugman, *The Odd Couple* (ABC)
Continued Performance by an Actress in a Leading Role in a Comedy Series: Mary Tyler Moore, *The Mary Tyler Moore Show* (CBS)

1973–74

Comedy Series: *M*A*S*H* (CBS)
Drama Series: "Upstairs, Downstairs" Masterpiece Theatre (PBS)
Music-Variety Series: *The Carol Burnett Show* (CBS)
Best Lead Actor in a Comedy Series: Alan Alda, *M*A*S*H* (CBS)
Best Lead Actor in a Drama Series: Telly Savalas, *Kojak* (CBS)
Best Lead Actress in a Comedy Series: Mary Tyler Moore, *The Mary Tyler Moore Show* (CBS)
Best Lead Actress in a Drama Series: Michael Learned, *The Waltons* (CBS)

1974–75

Comedy Series: *The Mary Tyler Moore Show* (CBS)
Drama Series: "Upstairs, Downstairs" Masterpiece Theatre (PBS)
Comedy-Variety or Music Series: *The Carol Burnett Show* (CBS)
Lead Actor in a Comedy Series: Tony Randall, *The Odd Couple* (ABC)
Lead Actor in a Drama Series: Robert Blake, *Baretta* (ABC)
Lead Actress in a Comedy Series: Valerie Harper, *Rhoda* (CBS)
Lead Actress in a Drama Series: Jean Marsh, "Upstairs, Downstairs" Masterpiece Theatre (PBS)

1975–76

Comedy Series: *The Mary Tyler Moore Show* (CBS)
Drama Series: *Police Story* (NBC)
Comedy-Variety or Music Series: *Saturday Night Live* (NBC)
Lead Actor in a Comedy Series: Jack Albertson, *Chico and the Man* (NBC)
Lead Actor in a Drama Series: Peter Falk, *Columbo* (NBC)
Lead Actress in a Comedy Series: Mary Tyler Moore, *The Mary Tyler Moore Show* (CBS)
Lead Actress in a Drama Series: Michael Learned, *The Waltons* (CBS)

1976–77

Comedy Series: *The Mary Tyler Moore Show* (CBS)
Drama Series: "Upstairs, Downstairs" Masterpiece Theatre (PBS)
Comedy-Variety or Music Series: *Van Dyke and Company* (NBC)
Lead Actor in a Comedy Series: Carroll O'Connor, *All in the Family* (CBS)
Lead Actor in a Drama Series: James Garner, *The Rockford Files* (NBC)
Lead Actress in a Comedy Series: Beatrice Arthur, *Maude* (CBS)
Lead Actress in a Drama Series: Lindsay Wagner, *The Bionic Woman* (ABC)

1977–78

Comedy Series: *All in the Family* (CBS)
Drama Series: *The Rockford Files* (NBC)
Comedy-Variety or Music Series: *The Muppet Show* (syndicated)
Lead Actor in a Comedy Series: Carroll O'Connor, *All in the Family* (CBS)
Lead Actor in a Drama Series: Ed Asner, *Lou Grant* (CBS)
Lead Actress in a Comedy Series: Jean Stapleton, *All in the Family* (CBS)
Lead Actress in a Drama Series: Sada Thompson, *Family* (ABC)

1978–79

Comedy Series: *Taxi* (ABC)
Drama Series: *Lou Grant* (CBS)
Comedy-Variety or Music Program (Special or Series): *Steve & Eydie Celebrate Irving Berlin* (NBC)
Lead Actor in a Comedy Series (Continuing or Single Performance): Carroll O'Connor, *All in the Family* (CBS)
Lead Actor in a Drama Series (Continuing or Single Performance): Ron Leibman, *Kaz* (CBS)
Lead Actress in a Comedy Series (Continuing or Single Performance): Ruth Gordon, *Taxi* ("Sugar Mama") (ABC)
Lead Actress in a Drama Series (Continuing or Single Performance): Mariette Hartley, *The Incredible Hulk* ("Married") (CBS)

1979–80

Comedy Series: *Taxi* (ABC)
Drama Series: *Lou Grant* (CBS)
Variety or Music Program (Special or Series): *IBM Presents Baryshnikov on Broadway* (ABC)
Lead Actor in a Comedy Series (Continuing or Single Performance): Richard Mulligan, *Soap* (ABC)
Lead Actor in a Drama Series (Continuing or Single Performance): Ed Asner, *Lou Grant* (CBS)
Lead Actress in a Comedy Series (Continuing or Single Performance): Cathryn Damon, *Soap* (ABC)
Lead Actress in a Drama Series (Continuing or Single Performance): Barbara Bel Geddes, *Dallas* (CBS)

1980–81

Comedy Series: *Taxi* (ABC)
Drama Series: *Hill Street Blues* (NBC)
Variety, Music, or Comedy Program: *Lily: Sold Out* (CBS)
Lead Actor in a Drama Series: Daniel J. Travanti, *Hill Street Blues* (NBC)
Lead Actor in a Comedy Series: Judd Hirsch, *Taxi* (ABC)
Lead Actress in a Drama Series: Barbara Babcock, *Hill Street Blues* (NBC)
Lead Actress in a Comedy Series: Isabel Sanford, *The Jeffersons* (CBS)

1981–82

Comedy Series: *Barney Miller* (ABC)
Drama Series: *Hill Street Blues* (NBC)
Variety, Music, or Comedy Program: *Night of 100 Stars* (ABC)
Lead Actor in a Drama Series: Daniel J. Travanti, *Hill Street Blues* (NBC)
Lead Actor in a Comedy Series: Alan Alda, *M*A*S*H* (CBS)
Lead Actress in a Drama Series: Michael Learned, *Nurse* (CBS)
Lead Actress in a Comedy Series: Carol Kane, *Taxi* ("Simka Returns") (ABC)

1982–83

Comedy Series: *Cheers* (NBC)
Drama Series: *Hill Street Blues* (NBC)
Variety, Music, or Comedy Program: *Motown 25: Yesterday, Today, Forever* (NBC)
Lead Actor in a Drama Series: Ed Flanders, *St. Elsewhere* (NBC)
Lead Actor in a Comedy Series: Judd Hirsch, *Taxi* (ABC)
Lead Actress in a Drama Series: Tyne Daly, *Cagney & Lacey* (CBS)
Lead Actress in a Comedy Series: Shelley Long, *Cheers* (NBC)

1983–84

Comedy Series: *Cheers* (NBC)
Drama Series: *Hill Street Blues* (NBC)
Variety, Music, or Comedy Program: "The 6th Annual Kennedy Center Honors: A Celebration of the Performing Arts" (CBS)
Lead Actor in a Drama Series: Tom Selleck, *Magnum, P.I.* (CBS)
Lead Actor in a Comedy Series: John Ritter, *Three's Company* (ABC)
Lead Actress in a Drama Series: Tyne Daly, *Cagney & Lacey* (CBS)
Lead Actress in a Comedy Series: Jane Curtin, *Kate & Allie* (CBS)

1984–85

Comedy Series: *The Cosby Show* (NBC)
Drama Series: *Cagney & Lacey* (CBS)
Variety, Music, or Comedy Program: "Motown Returns to the Apollo" (NBC)
Lead Actor in a Drama Series: William Daniels, *St. Elsewhere* (NBC)
Lead Actor in a Comedy Series: Robert Guillaume, *Benson* (ABC)
Lead Actress in a Drama Series: Tyne Daly, *Cagney & Lacey* (CBS)
Lead Actress in a Comedy Series: Jane Curtin, *Kate & Allie* (CBS)

1985–86

Comedy Series: *The Golden Girls* (NBC)
Drama Series: *Cagney & Lacey* (CBS)
Variety, Music, or Comedy Program: "The Kennedy Center Honors: A Celebration of the Performing Arts" (CBS)
Lead Actor in a Drama Series: William Daniels, *St. Elsewhere* (NBC)
Lead Actor in a Comedy Series: Michael J. Fox, *Family Ties* (NBC)
Lead Actress in a Drama Series. Sharon Gless, *Cagney & Lacey* (CBS)
Lead Actress in a Comedy Series: Betty White, *The Golden Girls* (NBC)

1986–87

Comedy Series: *The Golden Girls* (NBC)
Drama Series: *L.A. Law* (NBC)
Variety, Music, or Comedy Program: "The 1987 Tony Awards" (CBS)
Lead Actor in a Drama Series: Bruce Willis, *Moonlighting* (ABC)
Lead Actor in a Comedy Series: Michael J. Fox, *Family Ties* (NBC)
Lead Actress in a Drama Series: Sharon Gless, *Cagney & Lacey* (CBS)
Lead Actress in a Comedy Series: Rue McClanahan, *The Golden Girls* (NBC)

1987–88

Comedy Series: *The Wonder Years* (ABC)
Drama Series: *thirtysomething* (ABC)
Variety, Music, or Comedy Program: "Irving Berlin's 100th Birthday Celebration" (CBS)
Lead Actor in a Comedy Series: Michael J. Fox, *Family Ties* (NBC)
Lead Actor in a Drama Series: Richard Kiley, *A Year in the Life* (NBC)
Lead Actress in a Comedy Series: Beatrice Arthur, *The Golden Girls* (NBC)
Lead Actress in a Drama Series: Tyne Daly, *Cagney & Lacey* (CBS)

1988–89

Comedy Series: *Cheers* (NBC)
Drama Series: *L.A. Law* (NBC)
Variety, Music, or Comedy Program: *The Tracey Ullman Show* (Fox)
Lead Actor in a Comedy Series: Richard Mulligan, *Empty Nest* (NBC)
Lead Actor in a Drama Series: Carroll O'Connor, *In the Heat of the Night* (NBC)
Lead Actress in a Comedy Series: Candice Bergen, *Murphy Brown* (CBS)
Lead Actress in a Drama Series: Dana Delany, *China Beach* (ABC)

1989–90

Comedy Series: *Murphy Brown* (CBS)
Drama Series: *L.A. Law* (NBC)
Variety, Music, or Comedy Series: *In Living Color* (Fox)
Lead Actor in a Comedy Series: Ted Danson, *Cheers* (NBC)
Lead Actor in a Drama Series: Peter Falk, *Columbo* (ABC)
Lead Actress in a Comedy Series: Candice Bergen, *Murphy Brown* (CBS)
Lead Actress in a Drama Series: Patricia Wettig, *thirtysomething* (ABC)

1990–91

Comedy Series: *Cheers* (NBC)
Drama Series: *L.A. Law* (NBC)
Variety, Music, or Comedy Series: *The 63rd Annual Academy Awards* (ABC)
Lead Actor in a Comedy Series: Burt Reynolds, *Evening Shade* (CBS)
Lead Actor in a Drama Series: James Earl Jones, *Gabriel's Fire* (ABC)
Lead Actress in a Comedy Series: Kirstie Alley, *Cheers* (NBC)
Lead Actress in a Drama Series: Patricia Wettig, *thirtysomething* (ABC)

1991–92

Comedy Series: *Murphy Brown* (CBS)
Drama Series: *Northern Exposure* (CBS)
Variety, Music, or Comedy Series: *The Tonight Show Starring Johnny Carson* (NBC)
Lead Actor in a Comedy Series: Craig T. Nelson, *Coach* (ABC)
Lead Actor in a Drama Series: Christopher Lloyd, *Avonlea* (The Disney Channel)
Lead Actress in a Comedy Series: Candice Bergen, *Murphy Brown* (CBS)
Lead Actress in a Drama Series: Dana Delany, *China Beach* (ABC)

1992–93

Comedy Series: *Seinfeld* (NBC)
Drama Series: *Picket Fences* (CBS)
Variety, Music, or Comedy Series: *Saturday Night Live* (NBC)
Lead Actor in a Comedy Series: Ted Danson, *Cheers* (NBC)
Lead Actor in a Drama Series: Tom Skerritt, *Picket Fences* (CBS)
Lead Actress in a Comedy Series: Roseanne Arnold, *Roseanne* (ABC)
Lead Actress in a Drama Series: Kathy Baker, *Picket Fences* (CBS)

1993–94

Outstanding Comedy Series: *Frasier* (NBC)
Outstanding Drama Series: *Picket Fences* (CBS)
Outstanding Variety, Music, or Comedy Series: *Late Show with David Letterman* (CBS)
Outstanding Lead Actor in a Comedy Series: Kelsey Grammer, *Frasier* (NBC)
Outstanding Lead Actor in a Drama Series: Dennis Franz, *N.Y.P.D. Blue* (ABC)
Outstanding Lead Actress in a Comedy Series: Candice Bergen, *Murphy Brown* (CBS)
Outstanding Lead Actress in a Drama Series: Sela Ward, *Sisters* (NBC)

1. Kinescope was an early method of recording TV shows, before the advent of videotape. A movie camera was placed in front of a monitor in the TV studio and would "film" the show directly from the screen. The finished program could then be broadcast at a later date.

THE GRAMMYS, 1958–94

The "Grammys" are officially known as the National Academy of Recording Arts and Sciences Awards. Winners (in almost 70 categories) are selected yearly by the 6,000 or so voting members of the academy. The five award categories listed below have remained fairly constant over the years, although the overall "Best Vocal Performance" award was phased out in 1968; from that year on, our listing is for "Best Pop Vocal Performance" except where indicated.

Year	Record of the year	Album of the year	Song of the year[1]	Best vocal performance (male)	Best vocal performance (female)
1958	Domenico Modugno *Nel Blu Dipinto di Blu (Volare)*	Henry Mancini *The Music from Peter Gunn*	Domenico Modugno "Nel Blu Dipinto di Blu" *(Volare)*	Perry Como *Catch a Falling Star*	Ella Fitzgerald *Ella Fitzgerald Sings the Irving Berlin Songbook* [2]
1959	Bobby Darin *Mack the Knife*	Frank Sinatra *Come Dance with Me*	Jimmy Driftwood "The Battle of New Orleans"	Frank Sinatra *Come Dance with Me*	Ella Fitzgerald *But Not for Me*
1960	Percy Faith *Theme from a Summer Place*	Bob Newhart *Button-Down Mind*	Ernest Gold "Theme from Exodus"	Ray Charles *Georgia on My Mind*	Ella Fitzgerald *Mack the Knife*
1961	Henry Mancini *Moon River*	Judy Garland *Judy at Carnegie Hall*	Henry Mancini, Johnny Mercer "Moon River"	Jack Jones *Lollipops and Roses*	Judy Garland *Judy at Carnegie Hall* [2]
1962	Tony Bennett *I Left My Heart in San Francisco*	Vaughn Meader *The First Family*	Leslie Bricusse, Anthony Newley "What Kind of Fool Am I?"	Tony Bennett *I Left My Heart in San Francisco* [2]	Ella Fitzgerald *Ella Swings Brightly with Nelson Riddle* [2]
1963	Henry Mancini *The Days of Wine and Roses*	Barbra Streisand *The Barbra Streisand Album*	Henry Mancini, Johnny Mercer "The Days of Wine and Roses"	Jack Jones *Wives and Lovers*	Barbra Streisand *The Barbra Streisand Album* [2]
1964	Stan Getz, Astrud Gilberto *The Girl from Ipanema*	Stan Getz, Astrud Gilberto *Getz/Gilberto*	Jerry Herman "Hello, Dolly!"	Louis Armstrong *Hello, Dolly!*	Barbra Streisand *People*
1965	Herb Alpert & the Tijuana Brass *A Taste of Honey*	Frank Sinatra *September of My Years*	Paul Francis Webster, Johnny Mandel "The Shadow of Your Smile"	Frank Sinatra *It Was a Very Good Year*	Barbra Streisand *My Name Is Barbra* [2]
1966	Frank Sinatra *Strangers in the Night*	Frank Sinatra *A Man and His Music*	John Lennon, Paul McCartney "Michelle"	Frank Sinatra *Strangers in the Night*	Eydie Gorme *If He Walked into My Life*
1967	5th Dimension *Up, Up and Away*	The Beatles *Sgt. Pepper's Lonely Hearts Club Band*	Jim Webb "Up, Up and Away"	Glen Campbell *By the Time I Get to Phoenix*	Bobbie Gentry *Ode to Billie Joe*
1968	Simon & Garfunkel *Mrs. Robinson*	Glen Campbell *By the Time I Get to Phoenix*	Bobby Russell "Little Green Apples"	Jose Feliciano[3] *Light My Fire*	Dionne Warwick[3] *Do You Know the Way to San Jose?*
1969	5th Dimension *Aquarius/Let the Sunshine In*	Blood, Sweat & Tears *Blood, Sweat & Tears*	Joe South "Games People Play"	Harry Nilsson[4] *Everybody's Talkin'*	Peggy Lee[4] *Is That All There Is?*
1970	Simon & Garfunkel *Bridge over Troubled Water*	Simon & Garfunkel *Bridge over Troubled Water*	Paul Simon "Bridge over Troubled Water"	Ray Stevens[4] *Everything Is Beautiful*	Dionne Warwick[4] *I'll Never Fall in Love Again* [2]
1971	Carole King *It's Too Late*	Carole King *Tapestry*	Carole King "You've Got a Friend"	James Taylor[5] *You've Got a Friend*	Carole King[5] *Tapestry* [2]

Year	Record of the year	Album of the year	Song of the year[1]	Best vocal performance (male)	Best vocal performance (female)
1972	Roberta Flack *The First Time Ever I Saw Your Face*	George Harrison, Ravi Shankar, Bob Dylan et al *Concert for Bangladesh*	Ewan McColl "The First Time Ever I Saw Your Face"	Harry Nilsson *Without You*	Helen Reddy *I Am Woman*
1973	Roberta Flack *Killing Me Softly with His Song*	Stevie Wonder *Innervisions*	Norman Gimbel, Charles Fox "Killing Me Softly with His Song"	Stevie Wonder *You Are the Sunshine of My Life*	Roberta Flack *Killing Me Softly with His Song*
1974	Olivia Newton-John *I Honestly Love You*	Stevie Wonder *Fulfillingness' First Finale*	Marilyn & Alan Bergman, Marvin Hamlisch "The Way We Were"	Stevie Wonder *Fulfillingness' First Finale* [2]	Olivia Newton-John *I Honestly Love You*
1975	Captain & Tennille *Love Will Keep Us Together*	Paul Simon *Still Crazy after All These Years*	Stephen Sondheim "Send in the Clowns"	Paul Simon *Still Crazy after All These Years* [2]	Janis Ian *At Seventeen*
1976	George Benson *This Masquerade*	Stevie Wonder *Songs in the Key of Life*	Bruce Johnston "I Write the Songs"	Stevie Wonder *Songs in the Key of Life* [2]	Linda Ronstadt *Hasten Down the Wind* [2]
1977	The Eagles *Hotel California*	Fleetwood Mac *Rumours*	Barbra Streisand, Paul Williams "Evergreen"	James Taylor *Handy Man*	Barbra Streisand *Evergreen*
1978	Billy Joel *Just the Way You Are*	Various Artists *Saturday Night Fever*	Billy Joel "Just the Way You Are"	Barry Manilow *Copacabana (At the Copa)*	Anne Murray *You Needed Me*
1979	The Doobie Brothers *What a Fool Believes*	Billy Joel *52nd Street*	Kenny Loggins, Michael McDonald "What a Fool Believes"	Billy Joel *52nd Street* [2]	Dionne Warwick *I'll Never Love This Way Again*
1980	Christopher Cross *Sailing*	Christopher Cross *Christopher Cross*	Christopher Cross "Sailing"	Kenny Loggins *This Is It*	Bette Midler *The Rose*
1981	Kim Carnes *Bette Davis Eyes*	John Lennon/Yoko Ono *Double Fantasy*	Donna Weiss, Jackie DeShannon "Bette Davis Eyes"	Al Jarreau *Breakin' Away* [2]	Lena Horne *Lena Horne: The Lady and Her Music Live on Broadway* [2]
1982	Toto *Rosanna*	Toto *Toto IV*	Johnny Christopher, Mark James, Wayne Carson "Always on My Mind"	Lionel Richie *Truly*	Melissa Manchester *You Should Hear How She Talks about You*
1983	Michael Jackson *Beat It*	Michael Jackson *Thriller*	Sting "Every Breath You Take"	Michael Jackson *Thriller* [2]	Irene Cara *Flashdance . . . What a Feeling*
1984	Tina Turner *What's Love Got to Do with It?*	Lionel Richie *Can't Slow Down*	Graham Lyle, Terry Britten "What's Love Got to Do with It?"	Phil Collins *Against All Odds (Take a Look at Me Now)*	Tina Turner *What's Love Got to Do with It?*
1985	USA for Africa *We Are the World*	Phil Collins *No Jacket Required*	Michael Jackson, Lionel Richie "We Are the World"	Phil Collins *No Jacket Required* [2]	Whitney Houston *Saving All My Love for You*
1986	Steve Winwood *Higher Love*	Paul Simon *Graceland*	Various Artists "That's What Friends Are For"	Steve Winwood *Higher Love*	Barbra Streisand *The Broadway Album* [2]
1987	Paul Simon *Graceland*	U2 *The Joshua Tree*	Linda Ronstadt, James Ingram "Somewhere Out There"	Sting *Bring On the Night* [2]	Whitney Houston *I Wanna Dance with Somebody (Who Loves Me)*
1988	Bobby McFerrin *Don't Worry, Be Happy*	George Michael *Faith*	Bobby McFerrin "Don't Worry, Be Happy"	Bobby McFerrin *Don't Worry, Be Happy*	Tracy Chapman *Fast Car*
1989	Bette Midler *Wind Beneath My Wings*	Bonnie Raitt *Nick of Time*	Bette Midler "Wind Beneath My Wings"	Michael Bolton *How Am I Supposed to Live Without You*	Bonnie Raitt *Nick of Time*
1990	Phil Collins *Another Day in Paradise*	Quincy Jones *Back on the Block*	Julie Gold "From a Distance"	Roy Orbison *Oh, Pretty Woman*	Mariah Carey *Vision of Love*
1991	Natalie Cole *Unforgettable*	Natalie Cole *Unforgettable*	Irving Gordon "Unforgettable"	Michael Bolton *When a Man Loves a Woman*	Bonnie Raitt *Something to Talk About*
1992	Eric Clapton *Tears in Heaven*	Eric Clapton *Unplugged*	Eric Clapton "Tears in Heaven"	Eric Clapton *Tears in Heaven*	k.d. lang *Constant Craving*
1993	Whitney Houston *I Will Always Love You*	Whitney Houston *The Bodyguard*	Alan Menken, Tim Rice "A Whole New World" (Aladdin's Theme)	Sting *If I Ever Lose My Faith in You*	Whitney Houston *I Will Always Love You*
1994	Sheryl Crow *All I Wanna Do*	Tony Bennett *MTV Unplugged*	Bruce Springsteen "Streets of Philadelphia"	Elton John *Can You Feel the Love Tonight*	Sheryl Crow *All I Wanna Do*

1. Awarded to the composer, rather than the performer, of the song. 2. Awarded for an album, rather than an individual song. 3. Award given for "Best Contemporary Pop Vocal Performance." 4. Award given for "Best Vocal Performance Contemporary." 5. From 1971 on, all awards in these columns are for "Best Pop Vocal Performance." **Source:** National Academy of Recording Arts and Sciences.

MTV VIDEO MUSIC AWARDS, 1984–94

Each year MTV Networks recognizes outstanding achievement in the field of video music with the MTV Video Music Awards. Since their inception in 1984, the number of awards has grown to 21. In addition to those listed below, there are special categories for rap, heavy metal, and dance videos, as well as for technical achievement in choreography, direction, and cinematography. For 1995 winners, see Part I: "The Year in Review."

Year	Best video	Best male video	Best female video	Best group video	Best new artist in a video
1984	Cars, "You Might Think"	David Bowie, "China Girl"	Cyndi Lauper, "Girls Just Want to Have Fun"	ZZ Top, "Legs"	Eurythmics, "Sweet Dreams (Are Made of This)"
1985	Don Henley, "The Boys of Summer"	Bruce Springsteen, "I'm on Fire"	Tina Turner, "What's Love Got to Do With It?"	USA for Africa, "We Are the World"	til' tuesday, "Voices Carry"
1986	Dire Straits, "Money for Nothing"	Robert Palmer, "Addicted to Love"	Whitney Houston, "How Will I Know?"	Dire Straits, "Money for Nothing"	a-Ha, "Take On Me"
1987	Peter Gabriel, "Sledgehammer"	Peter Gabriel, "Sledgehammer"	Madonna, "Papa Don't Preach"	Talking Heads, "Wild Wild Life"	Crowded House, "Don't Dream It's Over"
1988	INXS, "Need You Tonight/ Mediate"	Prince, "U Got the Look"	Suzanne Vega, "Luka"	INXS, "Need You Tonight/ Mediate"	Guns N' Roses, "Welcome to the Jungle"
1989	Neil Young, "This Note's for You"	Elvis Costello, "Veronica"	Paula Abdul, "Straight Up"	Living Colour, "Cult of Personality"	Living Colour, "Cult of Personality"
1990	Sinead O'Connor, "Nothing Compares 2 U"	Don Henley, "The End of the Innocence"	Sinead O'Connor, "Nothing Compares 2 U"	B-52s, "Love Shack"	Michael Penn, "No Myth"
1991	R.E.M., "Losing My Religion"	Chris Isaak, "Wicked Game"	Janet Jackson, "Love Will Never Do Without You"	R.E.M., "Losing My Religion"	Jesus Jones, "Right Here, Right Now"
1992	Van Halen, "Right Now"	Eric Clapton, "Tears in Heaven"	Annie Lennox, "Why"	U2, "Even Better Than the Real Thing"	Nirvana, "Smells Like Teen Spirit"
1993	Pearl Jam, "Jeremy"	Lenny Kravitz, "Are You Gonna Go My Way"	k.d. lang, "Constant Craving"	Pearl Jam, "Jeremy"	Stone Temple Pilots, "Plush"
1994	Aerosmith, "Cryin'"	Tom Petty and the Heartbreakers, "Mary Jane's Last Dance"	Janet Jackson, "If"	Aerosmith, "Cryin'"	Counting Crows, "Mr. Jones"

Source: MTV Networks.

THE ROCK AND ROLL HALL OF FAME, 1986–95

The Rock and Roll Hall of Fame has three categories. Artists are eligible for induction 25 years after the release of their first recording. Early influences are prerock musical pioneers, usually blues or jazz artists. The nonperformance category includes producers, disc jockeys, agents, and others whose work behind the scenes has had a lasting impact on rock and roll. The hall of fame itself is in Cleveland.

1986
Artists:
Chuck Berry
James Brown
Ray Charles
Sam Cooke
Fats Domino
The Everly Brothers
Buddy Holly
Jerry Lee Lewis
Elvis Presley
Little Richard
Early Influences:
Robert Johnson
Jimmie Rodgers
Jimmy Yancey
Nonperformers:
Alan Freed
Sam Philips
Lifetime Achievement:
John Hammond

1987
Artists:
The Coasters
Eddie Cochran
Bo Diddley
Aretha Franklin
Marvin Gaye
Bill Haley
B.B. King
Clyde McPhatter
Ricky Nelson
Roy Orbison
Carl Perkins
Smokey Robinson
Joe Turner
Muddy Waters
Jackie Wilson
Early Influences:
Louis Jordan
T-Bone Walker
Jerry Wexler
Hank Williams
Nonperformers:
Leonard Chess
Ahmet Ertegun
Jerome Lieber and Michael Stoller

1988
Artists:
The Beach Boys
The Beatles
The Drifters
Bob Dylan
The Supremes
Early Influences:
Woody Guthrie
Leadbelly
Les Paul
Nonperformer:
Berry Gordy, Jr.

1989
Artists:
Dion DiMucci
Otis Redding
The Rolling Stones
The Temptations
Stevie Wonder
Early Influences:
The Ink Spots
Bessie Smith
The Soul Stirrers
Nonperformer:
Phil Spector

1990
Artists:
Hank Ballard
Bobby Darin
The Four Seasons
The Four Tops
The Kinks
The Platters
Simon & Garfunkel
The Who
Early Influences:
Louis Armstrong
Charlie Christian
Ma Rainey
Nonperformers:
Gerry Goffin and Carole King
Lamont Dozier, Brian Holland, and Eddie Holland

1991
Artists:
LaVern Baker
The Byrds
John Lee Hooker
The Impressions
Wilson Pickett
Jimmy Reed
Ike and Tina Turner
Early Influence:
Howlin' Wolf
Nonperformers:
Dave Bartholomew
Ralph Bass
Lifetime Achievement:
Nesuhi Ertegun

1992
Artists:
Bobby "Blue" Bland
Booker T. and the MG's
Johnny Cash
The Jimi Hendrix Experience
The Isley Brothers
Sam and Dave
The Yardbirds
Early Influences:
Elmore James
Professor Longhair
Nonperformers:
Bill Graham
Leo Fender
Doc Pomus

1993
Artists:
Ruth Brown
Cream
Creedence Clearwater Revival
The Doors
Etta James
Frankie Lymon and the Teenagers
Van Morrison
Sly and the Family Stone
Early Influence:
Dinah Washington
Nonperformers:
Milt Gabler
Dick Clark

1994
Artists:
The Animals
The Band
Duane Eddy
The Grateful Dead
Elton John
John Lennon
Bob Marley
Rod Stewart
Early Influence:
Willie Dixon
Nonperformer:
Johnny Otis

1995
Artists:
The Allman Brothers Band
Al Green
Janis Joplin
Led Zeppelin
Martha and the Vandellas
Neil Young
Frank Zappa
Early Influence:
The Orioles
Nonperformer:
Paul Ackerman

THE TONY AWARDS, 1947–95

The Tony Awards are presented each year by the American Theatre Wing for distinguished achievement in the Broadway theater. Named for Antoinette Perry, an actress, producer, director, and chairman of the American Theatre Wing who died in 1946, the Tonys were first presented in 1947. Awards are given to performers, authors, producers, directors, composers, and choreographers, and scenic, costume, and lighting designers. Listed here is a selection of major awards for each year: best play (author), best performance by an actor in a play, best performance by an actress in a play, best musical (composer and lyricist), best performance by an actor in a musical, best performance by an actress in a musical.

		PLAY	
Year	**Best play**	**Best actor**	**Best actress**
1947	No award	José Ferrer, *Cyrano de Bergerac;* Fredric March, *Years Ago* (tie)	Ingrid Bergman, *Joan of Lorraine;* Helen Hayes, *Happy Birthday* (tie)
1948	*Mister Roberts,* Thomas Heggen and Joshua Logan	Henry Fonda, *Mister Roberts;* Paul Kelly, *Command Decision;* Basil Rathbone, *The Heiress* (tie)	Judith Anderson, *Medea;* Katharine Cornell, *Antony and Cleopatra;* Jessica Tandy, *A Streetcar Named Desire* (tie)
1949	*Death of a Salesman,* Arthur Miller	Rex Harrison, *Anne of the Thousand Days*	Martita Hunt, *The Madwoman of Chaillot*
1950	*The Cocktail Party,* T.S. Eliot	Sidney Blackmer, *Come Back, Little Sheba*	Shirley Booth, *Come Back, Little Sheba*
1951	*The Rose Tattoo,* Tennessee Williams	Claude Rains, *Darkness at Noon*	Uta Hagen, *The Country Girl*
1952	*The Fourposter,* Jan de Hartog	José Ferrer, *The Shrike*	Julie Harris, *I Am a Camera*
1953	*The Crucible,* Arthur Miller	Tom Ewell, *The Seven Year Itch*	Shirley Booth, *Time of the Cuckoo*
1954	*The Teahouse of the August Moon,* John Patrick	David Wayne, *The Teahouse of the August Moon*	Audrey Hepburn, *Ondine*
1955	*The Desperate Hours,* Joseph Hayes	Alfred Lunt, *Quadrille*	Nancy Kelly, *The Bad Seed*
1956	*The Diary of Anne Frank,* Frances Goodrich and Albert Hackett	Paul Muni, *Inherit the Wind*	Julie Harris, *The Lark*
1957	*Long Day's Journey Into Night,* Eugene O'Neill	Fredric March, *Long Day's Journey Into Night*	Margaret Leighton, *Separate Tables*
1958	*Sunrise at Campobello,* Dore Schary	Ralph Bellamy, *Sunrise at Campobello*	Helen Hayes, *Time Remembered*
1959	*J.B.,* Archibald MacLeish	Jason Robards, *The Disenchanted*	Gertrude Berg, *A Majority of One*
1960	*The Miracle Worker,* William Gibson	Melvyn Douglas, *The Best Man*	Anne Bancroft, *The Miracle Worker*
1961	*Becket,* Jean Anouilh	Zero Mostel, *Rhinoceros*	Joan Plowright, *A Taste of Honey*
1962	*A Man for All Seasons,* Robert Bolt	Paul Scofield, *A Man for All Seasons*	Margaret Leighton, *Night of The Iguana*
1963	*Who's Afraid of Virginia Woolf?* Edward Albee	Arthur Hill, *Who's Afraid of Virginia Woolf?*	Uta Hagen, *Who's Afraid of Virginia Woolf?*
1964	*Luther,* John Osborne	Alec Guiness, *Dylan*	Sandy Dennis, *Any Wednesday*
1965	*The Subject Was Roses,* Frank Gilroy	Walter Matthau, *The Odd Couple*	Irene Worth, *Tiny Alice*
1966	*Marat/Sade,* Peter Weiss	Hal Holbrook, *Mark Twain Tonight!*	Rosemary Harris, *The Lion in Winter*
1967	*The Homecoming,* Harold Pinter	Paul Rogers, *The Homecoming*	Beryl Reid, *The Killing of Sister George*
1968	*Rosencrantz and Guildenstern Are Dead,* Tom Stoppard	Martin Balsam, *You Know I Can't Hear You When the Water's Running*	Zoe Caldwell, *The Prime of Miss Jean Brodie*
1969	*The Great White Hope,* Howard Sackler	James Earl Jones, *The Great White Hope*	Julie Harris, *Forty Carats*
1970	*Borstal Boy,* Frank McMahon	Fritz Weaver, *Child's Play*	Tammy Grimes, *Private Lives* (R)
1971	*Sleuth,* Anthony Shaffer	Brian Bedford, *The School for Wives*	Maureen Stapleton, *Gingerbread Lady*
1972	*Sticks and Bones,* David Rabe	Cliff Gorman, *Lenny*	Sada Thompson, *Twigs*
1973	*That Championship Season,* Jason Miller	Alan Bates, *Butley*	Julie Harris, *The Last of Mrs. Lincoln*
1974	*The River Niger,* Joseph A. Walker	Michael Moriarty, *Find Your Way Home*	Colleen Dewhurst, *A Moon for the Misbegotten* (R)
1975	*Equus,* Peter Shaffer	John Kani, *Sizwe Banzi Is Dead;* Winston Ntshona, *The Island* (tie)	Ellen Burstyn, *Same Time, Next Year*
1976	*Travesties,* Tom Stoppard	John Wood, *Travesties*	Irene Worth, *Sweet Bird of Youth* (R)
1977	*The Shadow Box,* Michael Cristofer	Al Pacino, *The Basic Training of Pavlo Hummel*	Julie Harris, *The Belle of Amherst*
1978	*Da,* Hugh Leonard	Barnard Hughes, *Da*	Jessica Tandy, *The Gin Game*
1979	*The Elephant Man,* Bernard Pomerance	Tom Conti, *Whose Life Is It Anyway?*	Constance Cummings, *Wings;* Carole Shelley, *The Elephant Man* (tie)
1980	*Children of a Lesser God,* Mark Medoff	John Rubenstein, *Children of a Lesser God*	Phyllis Frelich, *Children of a Lesser God*
1981	*Amadeus,* Peter Shaffer	Ian McKellen, *Amadeus*	Jane Lapotaire, *Piaf*
1982	*The Life and Adventures of Nicholas Nickleby,* David Edgar	Roger Rees, *The Life and Adventures of Nicholas Nickleby*	Zoe Caldwell, *Medea* (R)
1983	*Torch Song Trilogy,* Harvey Fierstein	Harvey Fierstein, *Torch Song Trilogy*	Jessica Tandy, *Foxfire*
1984	*The Real Thing,* Tom Stoppard	Jeremy Irons, *The Real Thing*	Glenn Close, *The Real Thing*
1985	*Biloxi Blues,* Neil Simon	Derek Jacobi, *Much Ado About Nothing* (R)	Stockard Channing, *Joe Egg* (R)
1986	*I'm Not Rappaport,* Herb Gardner	Judd Hirsch, *I'm Not Rappaport*	Lily Tomlin, *The Search for Signs of Intelligent Life in the Universe*
1987	*Fences,* August Wilson	James Earl Jones, *Fences*	Linda Lavin, *Broadway Bound*
1988	*M. Butterfly,* David Henry Hwang	Ron Silver, *Speed-The-Plow*	Joan Allen, *Burn This*
1989	*The Heidi Chronicles,* Wendy Wasserstein	Philip Bosco, *Lend Me a Tenor*	Pauline Collins, *Shirley Valentine*
1990	*The Grapes of Wrath,* Frank Galati	Robert Morse, *Tru*	Maggie Smith, *Lettice and Lovage*
1991	*Lost In Yonkers,* Neil Simon	Nigel Hawthorne, *Shadowlands*	Mercedes Ruehl, *Lost in Yonkers*
1992	*Dancing at Lughnasa,* Brian Friel	Judd Hirsch, *Conversations with My Father*	Glenn Close, *Death and the Maiden*
1993	*Angels in America: Millennium Approaches,* Tony Kushner	Ron Leibman, *Angels in America: Millennium Approaches*	Madeline Kahn, *The Sisters Rosensweig*
1994	*Angels in America: Perestroika,* Tony Kushner	Stephen Spinella, *Angels in America: Perestroika*	Diana Rigg, *Medea* (R)
1995	*Love! Valour! Compassion!* Terrence McNally	Ralph Fiennes, *Hamlet* (R)	Cherry Jones, *The Heiress*

MUSICAL

Year	Best musical	Best actor	Best actress
1947	No award	No award	No award
1948	No award	Paul Hartman, *Angel in the Wings*	Grace Hartman, *Angel in the Wings*
1949	*Kiss Me Kate,* Cole Porter (M & L)	Ray Bolger, *Where's Charley?*	Nanette Fabray, *Love Life*
1950	*South Pacific,* Richard Rodgers (M), Oscar Hammerstein, (L)	Ezio Pinza, *South Pacific*	Mary Martin, *South Pacific*
1951	*Guys and Dolls,* Frank Loesser (M & L)	Robert Alda, *Guys and Dolls*	Ethel Merman, *Call Me Madam*
1952	*The King and I,* Richard Rodgers (M), Oscar Hammerstein (L)	Phil Silvers, *Top Banana*	Gertrude Lawrence, *The King and I*
1953	*Wonderful Town,* Leonard Bernstein (M), Betty Comden and Adolph Green (L)	Thomas Mitchell, *Hazel Flagg*	Rosalind Russell, *Wonderful Town*
1954	*Kismet,* Alexander Borodin (M), adapted by Robert Wright and George Forrest (L)	Alfred Drake, *Kismet*	Dolores Gray, *Carnival in Flanders*
1955	*The Pajama Game,* Richard Adler and Jerry Ross (M & L)	Walter Slezak, *Fanny*	Mary Martin, *Peter Pan*
1956	*Damn Yankees,* Richard Adler and Jerry Ross (M & L)	Ray Walston, *Damn Yankees*	Gwen Verdon, *Damn Yankees*
1957	*My Fair Lady,* Frederick Loewe (M), Alan Jay Lerner (L)	Rex Harrison, *My Fair Lady*	Judy Holliday, *Bells Are Ringing*
1958	*The Music Man,* Meredith Willson (M & L)	Robert Preston, *The Music Man*	Thelma Ritter, *New Girl in Town;* Gwen Verdon, *New Girl in Town* (tie)
1959	*Redhead,* Albert Hague (M), Dorothy Fields (L)	Richard Kiley, *Redhead*	Gwen Verdon, *Redhead*
1960	*Fiorello,* Jerry Bock (M), Sheldon Harnick (L); *The Sound of Music,* Richard Rodgers (M), Oscar Hammerstein (L) (tie)	Jackie Gleason, *Take Me Along*	Mary Martin, *The Sound of Music*
1961	*Bye, Bye, Birdie,* Charles Strouse (M), Lee Adams (L)	Richard Burton, *Camelot*	Elizabeth Seal, *Irma la Douce*
1962	*How to Succeed in Business Without Really Trying,* Frank Loesser (M & L)	Robert Morse, *How to Succeed in Business Without Really Trying*	Anna Maria Alberghetti, *Carnival;* Diahann Carroll, *No Strings* (tie)
1963	*A Funny Thing Happened on the Way to the Forum,* Stephen Sondheim (M & L)	Zero Mostel, *A Funny Thing Happened on the Way to the Forum*	Vivien Leigh, *Tovarich*
1964	*Hello, Dolly!* Jerry Herman (M & L)	Bert Lahr, *Foxy*	Carol Channing, *Hello, Dolly!*
1965	*Fiddler on the Roof,* Jerry Bock (M), Sheldon Harnick (L)	Zero Mostel, *Fiddler on the Roof*	Liza Minnelli, *Flora, the Red Menace*
1966	*Man of La Mancha,* Mitch Leigh (M), Joe Darion (L)	Richard Kiley, *Man of La Mancha*	Angela Lansbury, *Mame*
1967	*Cabaret,* John Kander (M), Fred Ebb (L)	Robert Preston, *I Do! I Do!*	Barbara Harris, *The Apple Tree*
1968	*Hallelujah, Baby!* Jule Styne (M), Betty Comden and Adolph Green (L)	Robert Goulet, *The Happy Time*	Patricia Routledge, *Darling of the Day;* Leslie Uggams, *Hallelujah, Baby* (tie)
1969	*1776,* Sherman Edwards (M & L)	Jerry Orbach, *Promises, Promises*	Angela Lansbury, *Dear World*
1970	*Applause,* Charles Strouse (M), Lee Adams (L)	Cleavon Little, *Purlie*	Lauren Bacall, *Applause*
1971	*Company,* Stephen Sondheim (M & L)	Hal Linden, *The Rothschilds*	Helen Gallagher, *No, No, Nannette* (R)
1972	*Two Gentlemen of Verona* [best score: *Follies,* Stephen Sondheim (M & L)]	Phil Silvers, *A Funny Thing Happened on the Way to the Forum* (R)	Alexis Smith, *Follies*
1973	*A Little Night Music,* Stephen Sondheim (M & L)	Ben Vereen, *Pippin*	Glynis Johns, *A Little Night Music*
1974	*Raisin* [best score: *Gigi,* Frederick Loewe (M), Alan Jay Lerner (L)]	Christopher Plummer, *Cyrano*	Virginia Capers, *Raisin*
1975	*The Wiz,* Charlie Smalls (M & L)	John Cullum, *Shenandoah*	Angela Lansbury, *Gypsy* (R)
1976	*A Chorus Line,* Marvin Hamlisch (M), Edward Kleban (L)	George Rose, *My Fair Lady* (R)	Donna McKechnie, *A Chorus Line*
1977	*Annie,* Charles Strouse (M), Martin Charnin (L)	Barry Bostwick, *The Robber Bridegroom*	Dorothy Loudon, *Annie*
1978	*Ain't Misbehavin'* [best score: *On the Twentieth Century,* Cy Coleman (M), Betty Comden and Adolph Green (L)]	John Cullum, *On the Twentieth Century*	Liza Minnelli, *The Act*
1979	*Sweeney Todd,* Stephen Sondheim (M & L)	Len Cariou, *Sweeney Todd*	Angela Lansbury, *Sweeney Todd*
1980	*Evita,* Andrew Lloyd Webber (M), Tim Rice (L)	Jim Dale, *Barnum*	Patti LuPone, *Evita*
1981	*42nd Street,* [best score: *Woman of the Year,* John Kander (M), Fred Ebb (L)]	Kevin Kline, *The Pirates of Penzance*	Lauren Bacall, *Woman of the Year*
1982	*Nine,* Maury Yeston (M & L)	Ben Harney, *Dreamgirls*	Jennifer Holliday, *Dreamgirls*
1983	*Cats,* Andrew Lloyd Webber (M), T.S. Eliot (L)	Tommy Tune, *My One and Only*	Natalia Makarova, *On Your Toes* (R)
1984	*La Cage Aux Folles,* Jerry Herman (M & L)	George Hearn, *La Cage Aux Folles*	Chita Rivera, *The Rink*
1985	*Big River,* Roger Miller (M & L)	No award	No award
1986	*The Mystery of Edwin Drood,* Rupert Holmes (M & L)	George Rose, *The Mystery of Edwin Drood*	Bernadette Peters, *Song and Dance*
1987	*Les Misérables,* Claude-Michel Schönberg (M), Herbert Kretzmer and Alain Boublil (L)	Robert Lindsay, *Me and My Girl* (R)	Maryann Plunkett, *Me and My Girl* (R)
1988	*The Phantom of the Opera* [best score: *Into the Woods,* Stephen Sondheim (M & L)]	Michael Crawford, *The Phantom of the Opera*	Joanna Gleason, *Into the Woods*
1989	*Jerome Robbins' Broadway* [best score: no award]	Jason Alexander, *Jerome Robbins' Broadway*	Ruth Brown, *Black and Blue*
1990	*City of Angels,* Cy Coleman (M), David Zippel (L)	James Naughton, *City of Angels*	Tyne Daly, *Gypsy* (R)
1991	*The Will Rogers Follies,* Cy Coleman (M); Betty Comden and Adolph Green (L)	Jonathan Pryce, *Miss Saigon*	Lea Salonga, *Miss Saigon*

Year	Best musical	Best actor	Best actress
1992	*Crazy for You* [best score: *Falsettos*, William Finn (M & L)]	Gregory Hines, *Jelly's Last Jam*	Faith Prince, *Guys and Dolls* (R)
1993	*Kiss of the Spider Woman* [best score: *Kiss of the Spider Woman*, John Kander (M) and Fred Ebb (L); *Tommy*, Pete Townshend (M & L) (tie)]	Brent Carver, *Kiss of the Spider Woman*	Chita Rivera, *Kiss of the Spider Woman*
1994	*Passion*, Stephen Sondheim (M & L)	Boyd Gaines, *She Loves Me*	Donna Murphy, *Passion*
1995	*Sunset Boulevard*, Andrew Lloyd Webber (M & L)	Matthew Broderick, *How to Succeed in Business Without Really Trying*	Glenn Close, *Sunset Boulevard*

Note: M = music; L = lyrics; R = revival. Since 1971 "Musical" and "Score" have been separate categories. See listing for 1972, 1974, 1978, 1981, 1988, 1989, 1992, and 1993. **Source:** Isabelle Stevenson, *The Tony Award*. Reprinted with permission.

THE NATIONAL BOOK AWARDS, 1950–94

The National Book Awards are given annually for outstanding literary works by American citizens. The number of prizes awarded has varied and has included such categories as poetry, fiction, biography, science, philosophy, religion, and history.

National Book Awards for fiction, 1950–94

Year	Author/Title
1950	Nelson Algren, *The Man with the Golden Arm*
1951	William Faulkner, *The Collected Stories*
1952	James Jones, *From Here to Eternity*
1953	Ralph Ellison, *Invisible Man*
1954	Saul Bellow, *The Adventures of Augie March*
1955	William Faulkner, *A Fable*
1956	John O'Hara, *Ten North Frederick*
1957	Wright Morris, *Field of Vision*
1958	John Cheever, *The Wapshot Chronicle*
1959	Bernard Malamud, *The Magic Barrel*
1960	Philip Roth, *Goodbye, Columbus*
1961	Conrad Richter, *The Waters of Kronos*
1962	Walker Percy, *The Moviegoer*
1963	J.F. Powers, *Morte d'Urban*
1964	John Updike, *The Centaur*
1965	Saul Bellow, *Herzog*
1966	Katherine Anne Porter, *The Collected Stories*
1967	Bernard Malamud, *The Fixer*
1968	Thornton Wilder, *The Eighth Day*
1969	Jerzy Kosinski, *Steps*
1970	Joyce Carol Oates, *Them*
1971	Saul Bellow, *Mr. Sammler's Planet*
1972	Flannery O'Connor, *The Complete Stories*
1973	John Barth, *Chimera*
	John Williams, *Augustus*
1974	Thomas Pynchon, *Gravity's Rainbow*
	Isaac Bashevis Singer, *A Crown of Feathers & Other Stories*
1975	Robert Stone, *Dog Soldiers*
	Thomas Williams, *The Hair of Harold Roux*
1976	William Gaddis, *JR*
1977	Wallace Stegner, *The Spectator Bird*
1978	Mary Lee Settle, *Blood Ties*
1979	Tim O'Brien, *Going After Cacciato*
1980	William Styron, *Sophie's Choice*
1981	Wright Morris, *Plains Song*
1982	John Updike, *Rabbit Is Rich*
1983	Alice Walker, *The Color Purple*
1984	Ellen Gilchrist, *Victory Over Japan*
1985	Don DeLillo, *White Noise*
1986	E.L. Doctorow, *World's Fair*
1987	Larry Heinemann, *Paco's Story*
1988	Pete Dexter, *Paris Trout*
1989	John Casey, *Spartina*
1990	Charles Johnson, *The Middle Passage*
1991	Norman Rush, *Mating*
1992	Cormac McCarthy, *All the Pretty Horses*
1993	E. Annie Proulx, *The Shipping News*
1994	William Gaddis, *A Frolic of His Own*

National Book Awards for nonfiction, 1950–94

Year	Author/Title
1950	Ralph L. Rusk, *Ralph Waldo Emerson*
1951	Newton Arvin, *Herman Melville*
1952	Rachel Carson, *The Sea Around Us*
1953	Bernard De Voto, *Course of Empire*
1954	Bruce Catton, *A Stillness at Appomattox*
1955	Joseph Wood Krutch, *The Measure of Man*
1956	Herbert Kubly, *An American in Italy*
1957	George F. Kennan, *Russia Leaves the War*
1958	Catherine Drinker Bowen, *The Lion and the Throne*
1959	J. Christopher Herold, *Mistress to an Age*
1960	Richard Ellman, *James Joyce*
1961	William L. Shirer, *The Rise and Fall of the Third Reich*
1962	Lewis Mumford, *The City in History*
1963	Leon Edel, *Henry James*, vols. 2 and 3
1964	Aileen Ward, *John Keats: The Making of a Poet*
1965	Louis Fisher, *The Life of Lenin*
1966	Arthur M. Schlesinger, Jr., *A Thousand Days: JFK in the White House*
1967	Justin Kaplan, *Mr. Clemens and Mark Twain*
1968	Jonathan Kozol, *Death at an Early Age*
1969	Norman Mailer, *The Armies of the Night*
1970	Lillian Hellman, *An Unfinished Woman, a Memoir*
1971	James MacGregor Burns, *Roosevelt: The Soldier of Freedom*
1972	Joseph P. Lash, *Eleanor and Franklin*
1973	Frances Fitzgerald, *Fire in the Lake: The Vietnamese and the Americans in Vietnam*
1974	Pauline Kael, *Deeper into the Movies*
1975	Richard B. Sewall, *The Life of Emily Dickinson*
	Lewis Thomas, *The Lives of a Cell*
1976	Paul Fussell, *The Great War and Modern Memory*
1977	Bruno Bettelheim, *The Uses of Enchantment: The Meaning and Importance of Fairy Tales*
1978	Walter Jackson Bate, *Samuel Johnson*
1979	Arthur M. Schlesinger, Jr., *Robert Kennedy and His Times*
1980	Tom Wolfe, *The Right Stuff*
1981	Maxine Hong Kingston, *China Men*
1982	Tracy Kidder, *The Soul of a New Machine*
1983	Fox Butterfield, *China: Alive in the Bitter Sea*
1984	Robert V. Remini, *Andrew Jackson and the Course of American Democracy, 1833–1845*, vol. 5
1985	J. Anthony Lukas, *Common Ground: A Turbulent Decade in the Lives of Three American Families*
1986	Barry Lopez, *Arctic Dreams*
1987	Richard Rhodes, *The Making of the Atom Bomb*
1988	Neil Sheehan, *A Bright and Shining Lie: John Paul Vann and America in Vietnam*
1989	Thomas L. Friedman, *From Beirut to Jerusalem*
1990	Ron Chernow, *The House of Morgan: An American Banking Dynasty and the Rise of Modern Finance*
1991	Orlando Patterson, *Freedom*
1992	Paul Monette, *Becoming a Man: Half a Life*
1993	Gore Vidal, *United States: Essays 1952–1992*
1994	Sherwin B. Nuland, *How We Die: Reflections on Life's Final Chapter*

National Book Awards for poetry, 1950–84, 1991–94[1]

Year	Author/Title
1950	William Carlos Williams, *Paterson: Book III* and *Selected Poems*
1951	Wallace Stevens, *The Auroras of Autumn*
1952	Marianne Moore, *Collected Poems*
1953	Archibald MacLeish, *Collected Poems 1917–1952*
1954	Conrad Aiken, *Collected Poems*
1955	Wallace Stevens, *The Collected Poems*
1956	W.H. Auden, *The Shield of Achilles*
1957	Richard Wilbur, *Things of this World*
1958	Robert Penn Warren, *Promises: Poems, 1954–56*
1959	Theodore Roethke, *Words for the Wind*
1960	Robert Lowell, *Life Studies*
1961	Randall Jarrell, *The Woman at the Washington Zoo*
1962	Alan Dugan, *Poems*
1963	William Stafford, *Traveling Through the Dark*

Year	Author/Title
1964	John Crowe Ransom, *Selected Poems*
1965	Theodore Roethke, *The Far Field*
1966	James Dickey, *Buckdancer's Choice*
1967	James Merrill, *Nights and Days*
1968	Robert Bly, *The Light Around the Body*
1969	John Berryman, *His Toy, His Dream, His Rest*
1970	Elizabeth Bishop, *The Complete Poems*
1971	Mona Van Duyn, *To See, To Take*
1972	Howard Moss, *Selected Poems*
1973	A.R. Ammons, *Collected Poems: 1951–1971*
1974	Allen Ginsberg, *The Fall of America: Poems of These States, 1965–71*
	Adrienne Rich, *Diving into the Wreck: Poems, 1971–72*
1975	Marilyn Hacker, *Presentation Piece*
1976	John Ashbery, *Self-Portrait in a Convex Mirror*
1977	Richard Eberhart, *Collected Poems, 1930–1976*
1978	Howard Nemerov, *The Collected Poems*
1979	James Merrill, *Mirabell: Books of Number*
1980	Philip Levine, *Ashes*
1981	Lisel Mueller, *The Need to Hold Still*
1982	William Bronk, *Life Supports*
1983	Galway Kinnell, *Selected Poems*
1984	Charles Wright, *Country Music*
1991	Philip Levine, *What Work Is*
1992	Mary Oliver, *New and Selected Poems*
1993	A.R. Ammons, *Garbage*
1994	James Tate, *Worshipful Company of Fletchers*

1. No award given, 1985–90. **Source:** National Book Awards, Inc.

THE NATIONAL BOOK CRITICS CIRCLE AWARD, 1975–94

Selected by a 24-member board of critics (who serve three-year terms) from around the country, this award has been increasingly important in the last few years. Books are often recommended to the board by the more than 500 general members of the Circle.

Fiction, 1975–94

Year	Author/Title
1975	E.L. Doctorow, *Ragtime*
1976	John Gardner, *October Light*
1977	Toni Morrison, *Song of Solomon*
1978	John Cheever, *The Stories of John Cheever*
1979	Thomas Flanagan, *The Year of the French*
1980	Shirley Hazzard, *The Transit of Venus*
1981	John Updike, *Rabbit is Rich*
1982	Stanley Elkin, *George Mills*
1983	William Kennedy, *Ironweed*
1984	Louise Erdrich, *Love Medicine*
1985	Anne Tyler, *The Accidental Tourist*
1986	Reynolds Price, *Kate Vaiden*
1987	Phillip Roth, *The Counterlife*
1988	Bharati Mukherjee, *The Middleman and Other Stories*
1989	E.L. Doctorow, *Billy Bathgate*
1990	John Updike, *Rabbit at Rest*
1991	Jane Smiley, *A Thousand Acres*
1992	Cormac McCarthy, *All the Pretty Horses*
1993	Ernest J. Gains, *A Lesson Before Dying*
1994	Carol Shields, *The Stone Diaries*

General nonfiction, 1975–94

Year	Author/Title
1975	R.W.B. Lewis, *Edith Wharton*
1976	Maxine Hong Kingston, *The Woman Warrior: Memoirs of a Girlhood Among Ghosts*
1977	Walter Jackson Bate, *Samuel Johnson*
1978	Maureen Howard, *Facts of Life*
1979	Telford Taylor, *Munich: The Price of Peace*
1980	Ronald Steel, *Walter Lippmann and the American Century*
1981	Stephen Jay Gould, *The Mismeasure of Man*
1982	Robert A. Caro, *The Path of Power: The Years of Lyndon Johnson*
1983	Seymour M. Hersh, *The Price of Power: Kissinger and the Nixon White House*
1984	Freeman Dyson, *Weapons and Hope*
1985	J. Anthony Lukas, *Common Ground: A Turbulent Decade in the Lives of Three American Families*
1986	John W. Dower, *War Without Mercy: Race and Power in the Pacific War*
1987	Richard Rhodes, *The Making of the Atomic Bomb*
1988	Taylor Branch, *Parting the Waters: America in the King Years, 1954–63*
1989	Michael Dorris, *The Broken Cord*
1990	Shelby Steele, *The Content of Our Character: A New Vision of Race in America*
1991	Susan Faludi, *Backlash: The Undeclared War Against American Women*
1992	Norman Maclean, *Young Men and Fire*
1993	Alan Lomax, *The Land Where Blues Began*
1994	Lynn H. Nicholas, *The Rape of Europa: The Fate of Europe's Treasures in the Third Reich and the Second World War*

Biography/Autobiography, 1983–94

Year	Author/Title
1983	Joyce Johnson, *Minor Characters*
1984	Joseph Frank, *Dostoevsky: The Years of Ordeal: 1850–1859*
1985	Leon Edel, *Henry James: A Life*
1986	Theodore Rosengarten, *Tombee: Portrait of a Cotton Planter*
1987	Donald R. Howard, *Chaucer: His Life, His Works, His World*
1988	Richard Ellman, *Oscar Wilde*
1989	Geoffrey C. Ward, *A First-Class Temperament: The Emergence of Franklin Roosevelt*
1990	Robert A. Caro, *Means of Ascent: The Years of Lyndon Johnson, Vol. 2*
1991	Philip Roth, *Patrimony*
1992	Carol Brightman, *Writing Dangerously: Mary McCarthy and Her World*
1993	Edmund White, *Genet*
1994	Mikal Gilmore, *Shot in the Heart*

Poetry, 1975–94

Year	Author/Title
1975	John Ashbery, *Self-Portrait in a Convex Mirror*
1976	Elizabeth Bishop, *Geography III*
1977	Robert Lowell, *Day by Day*
1978	L.E. Sissman, *Hello Darkness: The Collected Poems of L.E. Sissman*
1979	Philip Levine, *Ashes and Seven Years from Somewhere*
1980	Frederick Seidel, *Sunrise*
1981	A.R. Ammons, *A Coast of Trees*
1982	Katha Pollitt, *Antarctic Traveler*
1983	James Merrill, *The Changing Light at Sandover*
1984	Sharon Olds, *The Dead and the Living*
1985	Louise Glück, *The Triumph of Achilles*
1986	Edward Hirsch, *Wild Gratitude*
1987	C.K. Williams, *Flesh and Blood*
1988	Donald Hall, *The One Day*
1989	Rodney Jones, *Transparent Gestures*
1990	Amy Gerstler, *Bitter Angel*
1991	Albert Goldbarth, *Heaven and Earth*
1992	Hayden Carruth, *Collected Shorter Poems*
1993	Mark Doty, *My Alexandria*
1994	Mark Rudman, *Rider*

Year	Author/Title
	Criticism, 1975–94
1975	Paul Fussell, *The Great War and Modern Memory*
1976	Bruno Bettelheim, *The Uses of Enchantment: The Meaning and Importance of Fairy Tales*
1977	Susan Sontag, *On Photography*
1978	Meyer Schapiro, *Modern Art: 19th and 20th Centuries, Selected Papers*
1979	Elaine Pagels, *The Gnostic Gospels*
1980	Helen Vendler, *Part of Nature, Part of Us: Modern American Poets*
1981	Virgil Thompson, *A Virgil Thompson Reader*
1982	Gore Vidal, *The Second American Revolution and Other Essays, 1976–82*
1983	John Updike, *Hugging the Shore*
1984	Robert Hass, *Twentieth Century Pleasures: Prose on Poetry*
1985	William H. Gass, *Habitations of the Word: Essays*
1986	Joseph Brodsky, *Less Than One: Selected Essays*
1987	Edwin Denby, *Dance Writings*
1988	Clifford Geertz, *Works and Lives: The Anthropologist as Author*
1989	John Clive, *Not by Fact Alone: Essays on the Writing and Reading of History*
1990	Arthur C. Danto, *Encounters and Reflections: Art in the Historical Present*
1991	Lawrence L. Langer, *Holocaust Testimonies*
1992	Garry Wills, *Lincoln At Gettysburg: The Words That Remade America*
1993	John Dizikes, *Opera in America*
1994	Gerald Early, *The Culture of Bruising: Essays on Prizefighting, Literature and Modern American Culture*

Source: The National Book Critics Circle.

BOLLINGEN PRIZE FOR POETRY, 1949–95

First awarded annually, and biennally since 1965, the Bollingen Prize for Poetry is given by Yale University to an American citizen for a distinguished book of poetry, or in recognition of a poet's entire achievement. The award now carries a purse of $25,000.

Year	Recipient
1949	Wallace Stevens
1950	John Crowe Ransom
1951	Marianne Moore
1952	Archibald MacLeish
	William Carlos Williams
1953	W.H. Auden
1954	Leonie Adams
	Louise Bogan
1955	Conrad Aiken
1956	Allen Tate
1957	e.e. cummings
1958	Theodore Roethke
1959	Delmore Schwartz
1960	Ivor Winters
1961	Richard Eberhart
	John Hall Wheelock
1962	Robert Frost
1965	Horace Gregory
1967	Robert Penn Warren
1969	John Berryman
	Karl Shapiro
1971	Richard Wilbur
	Mona Van Duyn
1973	James Merrill
1975	A.R. Ammons
1977	David Ignatow
1979	W. S. Merwin
1981	May Swenson
	Howard Nemerov
1983	Anthony E. Hecht
	John Hollander
1985	John Ashbery
	Fred Chappel
1987	Stanley Kunitz
1989	Edgar Bowers
1991	Laura Riding Jackson
	Donald Justice
1993	Mark Strand
1995	Kenneth Koch

Source: Yale University.

CHILDREN'S BOOK AWARDS

THE NEWBERY MEDAL, 1922–95

The Newbery Medal, presented by the American Library Association, is awarded annually to the author of the most distinguished contribution to American literature for children published in the United States during the previous year. The award is named in honor of John Newbery (1713–67), the first English publisher of books for children.

Year	Author/Title
1922	Willem Van Loon, *The Story of Mankind*
1923	Hugh Lofting, *The Voyages of Doctor Dolittle*
1924	Charles Hawes, *The Dark Frigate*
1925	Charles Finger, *Tales from Silver Lands*
1926	Arthur Bowie Chrisman, *Shen of the Sea*
1927	Will James, *Smoky, The Cowhorse*
1928	Dhan Gopal Mukerji, *Gayneck, The Story of a Pigeon*
1929	Eric P. Kelly, *The Trumpeter of Krakow*
1930	Rachel Field, *Hitty, Her First Hundred Years*
1931	Elizabeth Coatsworth, *The Cat Who Went to Heaven*
1932	Laura Adams Armer, *Waterless Mountain*
1933	Elizabeth Foreman Lewis, *Young Fu of the Upper Yangtze*
1934	Cornelia Meigs, *Invincible Louisa*
1935	Monica Shannon, *Dobry*
1936	Carol Brink, *Caddie Woodlawn*
1937	Ruth Sawyer, *Roller Skates*
1938	Kate Seredy, *The White Stag*
1939	Elizabeth Enright, *Thimble Summer*
1940	James Daugherty, *Daniel Boone*
1941	Armstrong Sperry, *Call It Courage*
1942	Walter D. Edmonds, *The Matchlock Gun*
1943	Elizabeth Janet Gray, *Adam of the Road*
1944	Esther Forbes, *Johnny Tremain*
1945	Robert Lawson, *Rabbit Hill*
1946	Lois Lenski, *Strawberry Girl*
1947	Carolyn Sherwin Bailey, *Miss Hickory*
1948	William Pène du Bois, *The Twenty-One Balloons*
1949	Marguerite Henry, *King of the Wind*
1950	Marguerite de Angeli, *The Door in the Wall*
1951	Elizabeth Yates, *Amos Fortune, Free Man*
1952	Eleanor Estes, *Ginger Pye*
1953	Ann Nolan Clark, *Secret of the Andes*
1954	Joseph Krumgold, *. . . And Now Miguel*
1955	Meindert DeJong, *The Wheel on the School*
1956	Jean Lee Latham, *Carry On, Mr. Bowditch*
1957	Virginia Sorensen, *Miracles on Maple Hill*
1958	Harold Keith, *Rifles for Watie*
1959	Elizabeth George Speare, *The Witch of Blackbird Pond*
1960	Joseph Krumgold, *Onion John*
1961	Scott O'Dell, *Island of the Blue Dolphins*
1962	Elizabeth George Speare, *The Bronze Bow*
1963	Madeleine L'Engle, *A Wrinkle in Time*
1964	Emily Cheney Neville, *It's Like This, Cat*
1965	Maia Wojciechowska, *Shadow of a Bull*
1966	Elizabeth Borten de Trevino, *I, Juan de Pareja*
1967	Irene Hunt, *Up a Road Slowly*
1968	E.L. Konigsburg, *From the Mixed-up Files of Mrs. Basil E. Frankweiler*
1969	Lloyd Alexander, *The High King*
1970	William H. Armstrong, *Sounder*
1971	Betsy Byars, *Summer of the Swans*
1972	Robert C. O'Brien, *Mrs. Frisby and the Rats of NIMH*
1973	Jean George, *Julie of the Wolves*
1973	Paula Fox, *The Slave Dancer*
1975	Virginia Hamilton, *M.C. Higgins the Great*
1976	Susan Cooper, *The Grey King*
1977	Mildred D. Taylor, *Roll of Thunder, Hear My Cry*
1978	Katherine Paterson, *Bridge to Terabithia*
1979	Ellen Raskin, *The Westing Game*
1980	Joan Blos, *A Gathering of Days: A New England Girl's Journal, 1830–32*
1981	Katherine Paterson, *Jacob Have I Loved*
1982	Nancy Willard, *A Visit to William Blake's Inn: Poems for Innocent and Experienced Travelers*
1983	Cynthia Voigt, *Dicey's Song*
1984	Beverly Cleary, *Dear Mr. Henshaw*
1985	Robin McKinley, *The Hero and the Crown*
1986	Patricia MacLachlan, *Sarah, Plain and Tall*
1987	Sid Fleischman, *The Whipping Boy*
1988	Russell Freedman, *Lincoln: A Photobiography*
1989	Paul Fleischman, *Joyful Noise: Poems for Two Voices*
1990	Lois Lowry, *Number the Stars*
1991	Jerry Spinelli, *Maniac Magee*
1992	Phyllis Reynolds Naylor, *Shiloh*
1993	Cynthia Rylant, *Missing May*
1994	Lois Lowry, *The Giver*
1995	Sharon Creech, *Walk Two Moons*

Source: American Library Association.

THE CALDECOTT MEDAL, 1938–95

The Caldecott Medal, presented by the American Library Association, is awarded annually to the illustrator of the most distinguished picture book for children published in the United States during the preceding year. The award is named in honor of the English illustrator Randolph Caldecott (1846–86). In cases where only one name is given, the book was written and illustrated by the same person.

Year	Illustrator/Author/Title
1938	Dorothy Lathrop; Helen Dean Fish, *Animals of the Bible*
1939	Thomas Handforth, *Mei Li*
1940	Ingri and Edgar Parin d'Aulaire, *Abraham Lincoln*
1941	Robert Lawson, *They Were Strong and Good*
1942	Robert McCloskey, *Make Way for Ducklings*
1943	Virginia Lee Burton, *The Little House*
1944	Louis Slobodkin; James Thurber, *Many Moons*
1945	Elizabeth Orton Jones; Rachel Jones, *Prayer for a Child*
1946	Maude and Miska Petersham, *The Rooster Crows* (traditional Mother Goose)
1947	Leonard Weisgard; Golden MacDonald, *The Little Island*
1948	Roger Duvoisin; Alvin Tresselt, *White Snow, Bright Snow*
1949	Bert and Elmer Hader, *The Big Snow*
1950	Leo Politi, *Song of the Swallows*
1951	Katherine Milhous, *The Egg Tree*
1952	Nicolas Mordvinoff; Will Mordvinoff, *Finders Keepers*
1953	Lynd Ward, *The Biggest Bear*
1954	Ludwig Bemelmans, *Madeline's Rescue*
1955	Marcia Brown; Charles Perault, *Cinderella, or the Little Glass Slipper*
1956	Feodor Rojankovsky; John Langstaff, *Frog Went A-Courtin'*
1957	Marc Simont; Janice May Udry, *A Tree is Nice*
1958	Robert McCloskey, *Time of Wonder*
1959	Barbara Cooney, *Chanticleer and the Fox* (adapted from Geoffrey Chaucer)
1960	Marie Hall Ets and Aurora Labastida, *Nine Days to Christmas*
1961	Nicolas Sidjakov; Ruth Robbins, *Baboushka and the Three Kings*
1962	Marcia Brown, *Once a Mouse . . .*
1963	Ezra Jack Keats, *The Snowy Day*
1964	Maurice Sendak, *Where the Wild Things Are*
1965	Beni Montresor; Beatrice Schenk de Regniers, *May I Bring a Friend?*
1966	Nonny Hogrogian; Sorche Nic Leodhas, *Always Room for One More*
1967	Evaline Ness, *Sam, Bangs & Moonshine*
1968	Ed Emberley; Barbara Emberley, *Drummer Hoff*
1969	Uri Shulevitz; Arthur Ransome, *The Fool of the World and the Flying Ship*
1970	William Steig, *Sylvester and the Magic Pebble*
1971	Gail E. Haley, *A Story—A Story*
1972	Nonny Hogrogian, *One Fine Day*
1973	Blair Lent; retold by Arlene Mosel, *The Funny Little Woman*
1974	Margot Zemach; Harve Zemach, *Duffy and the Devil*
1975	Gerald McDermott, *Arrow to the Sun*
1976	Leo and Diane Dillon; retold by Verna Aardema, *Why Mosquitoes Buzz in People's Ears*
1977	Leo and Diane Dillon; Margaret Musgrove, *Ashanti to Zulu: African Traditions*
1978	Peter Spier, *Noah's Ark*
1979	Paul Goble, *The Girl Who Loved Wild Horses*
1980	Barbara Cooney; Donald Hall, *Ox-Cart Man*
1981	Arnold Lobel, *Fables*
1982	Chris Van Allsburg, *Jumanji*
1983	Marcia Brown, *Shadow*
1984	Martin and Alice Provensen, *The Glorious Flight*
1985	Trina Schart Hyman, *Saint George and the Dragon*
1986	Chris Van Allsburg, *The Polar Express*
1987	Richard Egielski; Arthur Yorinks, *Hey, Al*
1988	John Schoenherr, *Owl Moon*
1989	Stephen Gammell; Karen Ackerman, *Song and Dance Man*
1990	Ed Young, *Lon Po Po: A Red-Riding Hood Story from China*
1991	David Macaulay, *Black and White*
1992	David Wiesner, *Tuesday*
1993	Emily Arnold McCully, *Mirette on the High Wire*
1994	Allen Say, *Grandfather's Journey*
1995	David Diaz; Eve Bunting, *Smoky Night*

Source: American Library Association.

AMERICAN INSTITUTE OF ARCHITECTS GOLD MEDALISTS, 1907–95

First awarded in 1907, the American Institute of Architects Gold Medal recognizes outstanding lifetime achievement by an architect.

Year	Medalists
1907	Sir Aston Webb, London
1909	Charles Follen McKim, New York
1911	George B. Post, New York
1914	Jean Louis Pascal, Paris
1922	Victor Laloux, Paris
1923	Henry Bacon, New York
1925	Sir Edwin Landseer Lutyens, London
1925	Bertram Grosvenor Goodhue, New York
1927	Howard Van Doren Shaw, Chicago
1929	Milton Bennett Medary, Philadelphia
1933	Ragnar Ostberg, Stockholm
1938	Paul Philippe Cret, Philadelphia
1944	Louis Henri Sullivan, Chicago
1947	Eliel Saarinen, Bloomfield Hills, Mich.
1948	Charles Donagh Maginnis, Boston
1949	Frank Lloyd Wright, Spring Green, Wis.
1950	Sir Patrick Abercrombie, London
1951	Bernard Ralph Maybeck, San Francisco
1952	Auguste Perret, Paris
1953	Williams Adams Delano, New York
1955	Willem Marinus Dudok, Hilversum, Holland
1956	Clarence S. Stein, New York
1957	Ralph Walker, New York
1957	Louis Skidmore, New York
1958	John Wellborn Root, Chicago
1959	Walter Gropius, Cambridge, Mass.
1960	Ludwig Mies van der Rohe, Chicago
1961	Le Corbusier (Charles Edouard Jeanneret-Gris), Paris
1962[1]	Eero Saarinen, Bloomfield Hills, Mich.
1963	Alvar Aalto, Helsinki
1964	Pier Luigi Nervi, Rome
1966	Kenzo Tange, Tokyo
1967	Wallace K. Harrison, New York
1968	Marcel Breuer, New York
1969	William Wilson Wurster, San Francisco
1970	Richard Buckminster Fuller, Carbondale, Ill.
1971	Louis I. Kahn, Philadelphia
1972	Pietro Belluschi, Boston
1977[1]	Richard Joseph Neutra, Los Angeles
1978	Philip Johnson, New York
1979	Ieoh Ming Pei, New York
1981	Josep Lluis Sert, Cambridge, Mass.
1982	Romaldo Giurgola, New York
1983	Nathaniel A. Owings, San Francisco
1985[1]	William Caudill, Houston
1986	Arthur Erickson, Canada
1989	Joseph Esherick, San Francisco
1990	Fay Jones, Fayetteville, Ark.
1991	Charles Willard Moore, Austin, Tex.
1992	Benjamin Thompson, Boston
1993	Kevin Roche, New Haven, Conn.
1994	Sir Norman Foster, London
1995	Cesar Pelli, New Haven, Conn.

1. Awarded posthumously. **Source:** American Institute of Architects.

PULITZER PRIZES

The Pulitzer Prizes are named for their benefactor, Joseph Pulitzer (1847–1911), a Hungarian-born journalist. Pulitzer founded the *St. Louis Post-Dispatch* (1878) and later purchased the *New York World* (1883), under whose banner he revolutionized journalism for mass readership. He bequeathed $2 million to found the Columbia School of Journalism, whose trustees make annual awards ($3,000 in 1990) for outstanding achievement in journalism (14 prizes), literature and drama (6 prizes), and musical composition (1 prize).

PULITZER PRIZES IN JOURNALISM, 1917–95

MERITORIOUS PUBLIC SERVICE, 1918–95

Year	Winner	Distinction
1918	New York Times	Reports, documents, and speeches relating to World War I.
1919	Milwaukee Journal	Campaign for Americanism.
1920	No award	
1921	Boston Post	Articles exposing operations and leading to arrest of Charles Ponzi.
1922	New York World	Articles exposing operations of Ku Klux Klan.
1923	Memphis Commercial Appeal	News and cartoons about Ku Klux Klan.
1924	New York World	Exposure of Florida peonage evil.
1925	No award	
1926	Columbus (Ga.) Enquirer Sun	Articles decrying Ku Klux Klan, dishonest public officials, lynching, and a law barring teaching of evolution.
1927	Canton (Ohio) Daily News	Articles about collusion between city government and organized crime, resulting in assassination of editor, Don R. Mellett.
1928	Indianapolis Times	Exposure of political corruption in Indiana.
1929	New York Evening World	Campaign to correct evil and corruption in administration of justice.
1930	No award	
1931	Atlanta Constitution	Municipal graft exposure leading to convictions.
1932	Indianapolis News	Campaign to eliminate waste in city management and reduce tax levy.
1933	New York World-Telegram	Series of articles on veterans' relief, real estate bond evil, campaign urging New York City voters to "write in" name of Joseph V. McKee, and articles exposing lottery schemes of various fraternal organizations.
1934	Medford (Oreg.) Mail Tribune	Campaign against unscrupulous politicians in Jackson County, Oreg.
1935	Sacramento (Calif.) Bee	Campaign against political machine influence in appointment of two federal judges in Nevada.
1936	Cedar Rapids (Iowa) Gazette	Crusade against corruption and misgovernment in state of Iowa.
1937	St. Louis Post-Dispatch	Exposure of registration fraud in St. Louis resulting in invalidation of more than 40,000 fraudulent ballots and appointment of new election board.
1938	Bismarck (N.Dak.) Tribune	News reports and editorials entitled "Self Help in the Dust Bowl."
1939	Miami Daily News	Campaign for recall of Miami City Commission.
1940	Waterbury (Conn.) Republican & American	Campaign exposing municipal graft.
1941	St. Louis Post-Dispatch	Campaign against city smoke nuisance.
1942	Los Angeles Times	Campaign resulting in clarification and confirmation of freedom of press rights for all American newspapers.
1943	Omaha (Nebr.) World-Herald	Campaign for collection of scrap metal for war effort. Plan was adopted on national scale by daily newspapers.
1944	New York Times	Survey of teaching of American history.
1945	Detroit Free Press	Investigation of legislative graft and corruption at Lansing, Mich.
1946	Scranton (Pa.) Times	Fifteen-year investigation of judicial practices in U.S. District Court for middle district of Pennsylvania, resulting in removal of district judge and indictment of many others.
1947	Baltimore Sun	Series of articles by Howard M. Norton dealing with administration of unemployment compensation in Maryland, resulting in 93 criminal convictions and/or guilty pleas.
1948	St. Louis Post-Dispatch	Coverage of Centralia, Ill., mine disaster and follow-up articles resulting in reforms in mine safety laws and regulations.
1949	Nebraska State Journal	Campaign establishing "Nebraska All-Star Primary" that called attention to issues early in presidential campaign.
1950	Chicago Daily News and St. Louis Post-Dispatch	Work of George Thiem and Roy J. Harris, respectively, in exposing presence of 37 Illinois newspapermen on an Illinois state payroll.
1951	Miami Herald and Brooklyn Eagle	Crime reporting during year.
1952	St. Louis Post-Dispatch	Investigation and disclosures of corruption in Internal Revenue Bureau and other government departments.
1953	Whiteville (N.C.) News Reporter and Tabor City (N.C.) Tribune	Campaign against Ku Klux Klan by two weekly North Carolina newspapers.
1954	Newsday (Garden City, L.I., N.Y.)	Exposé of New York State's racetrack scandals and labor racketeering, leading to extortion indictment, guilty plea, and imprisonment of racketeer William C. DeKoonig, Sr.
1955	Columbus (Ga.) Ledger and Sunday Ledger-Enquirer	News coverage and editorial attack on corruption in neighboring Phenix City, leading to destruction of racket-ridden city government.
1956	Watsonville (Calif.) Register-Pajaronion	Exposure of corruption in public office leading to resignation of a district attorney and conviction of one of his associates.
1957	Chicago Daily News	Exposure of $2.5 million in office of Illinois state auditor, resulting in his indictment and reorganization of state procedures.
1958	Arkansas Gazette	Civic leadership, journalistic responsibility, and moral courage during school integration crisis of 1957.
1959	Utica (N.Y.) Observer-Dispatch and Utica Daily Press	Campaign against corruption, gambling, and vice and achievement of sweeping civic reforms.
1960	Los Angeles Times	Attack on narcotics traffic; reporting of Gene Sherman, which led to opening of negotiations between U.S. and Mexico to halt flow of illegal drugs into California and other border states.

Year	Winner	Distinction
1961	Amarillo (Tex.) Globe-Times	Exposure of lax law enforcement resulting in punitive action sweeping officials from their posts and creating election of reform slate.
1962	Panama City (Fla.) News-Herald	Three-year campaign against entrenched power and corruption, resulting in reforms in Panama City and Bay County.
1963	Chicago Daily News	Articles calling public attention to providing birth control services in public health programs.
1964	St. Petersburg (Fla.) Times	Investigation of illegal activity within Florida Turnpike Authority, resulting in major reorganization of state's road construction program.
1965	Hutchinson (Kans.) News	Campaign for more equitable reapportionment of Kansas legislature.
1966	Boston Globe	Campaign to prevent confirmation of Francis X. Morrissey as federal district judge in Massachusetts.
1967	Louisville Courier Journal and Milwaukee Journal	Campaign to control Kentucky strip-mining industry; campaign to stiffen water pollution laws in Wisconsin.
1968	Riverside (Calif.) Press-Enterprise	Exposure of corruption in courts in connection with handling of property and estates of an Indian tribe in California.
1969	Los Angeles Times	Exposure of wrongdoing within Los Angeles city government commissions, resulting in criminal convictions, resignations, and sweeping reforms.
1970	Newsday (Garden City, L.I., N.Y.)	Three-year investigation and exposure of secret land deals in eastern Long Island, leading to criminal convictions, resignations, and discharges among public and political officials.
1971	Winston-Salem (N.C.) Journal and Sentinel	Coverage of environmental problems, as exemplified by campaign to block a strip-mining operation that would have caused irreparable damage to northwest North Carolina hill country.
1972	New York Times	Publication of Pentagon Papers.
1973	Washington Post	Investigation of Watergate case.
1974	Newsday (Garden City, L.I., N.Y.)	Definitive report on illicit narcotics traffic in U.S. and abroad, entitled "The Heroin Trail."
1975	Boston Globe	Coverage of Boston school desegregation crisis.
1976	Anchorage Daily News	Disclosures of impact and influence of Teamsters Union on Alaska's economy and politics.
1977	Lufkin (Tex.) News	Obituary of local man who died in Marine training camp, which grew into investigation of that death and fundamental reform in Marine Corps' recruiting and training practices.
1978	Philadelphia Inquirer	Series of articles showing abuses of power by Philadelphia police.
1979	Point Reyes (Calif.) Light	Investigation of Synanon.
1980	Gannett News Service	Series on financial contributions to Pauline Fathers.
1981	Charlotte (N.C.) Observer	Series called "Brown Lung: A Case of Deadly Neglect."
1982	Detroit News	Series by Sydney P. Freedberg and David Ashenfelter exposing U.S. Navy's cover-up of circumstances surrounding deaths of seamen aboard ship and leading to significant reforms in naval procedures.
1983	Jackson (Miss.) Clarion-Ledger	Campaign supporting Gov. Winter in his legislative battle for reform of Mississippi's public education system.
1984	Los Angeles Times	In-depth examination of southern California's growing Latino community.
1985	Fort Worth (Tex.) Star-Telegram	Reporting by Mark J. Thompson revealing that nearly 250 U.S. servicemen died because of a design problem in helicopters built by Bell Helicopter—causing the army to ground almost 600 Huey helicopters pending their modification.
1986	Denver Post	In-depth study of "missing children," revealing that most are involved in custody disputes or are runaways, and helping to mitigate national fears stirred by exaggerated statistics.
1987	Pittsburgh Press	Reporting by Andrew Schneider and Matthew Brelis, revealing inadequacy of FAA's medical screening of airline pilots, and leading to reform.
1988	Charlotte (N.C.) Observer	Revealing misuse of funds by the PTL television ministry, despite massive campaign by PTL to discredit the newspaper.
1989	Anchorage Daily News	For series revealing high incidence of alcoholism and suicide among Native Alaskans.
1990	Philadelphia Inquirer	For series by Gilbert M. Gaul disclosing shortcomings in federal regulation of the nation's blood banks.
	Washington (N.C.) Daily News	For series by Betty Gray and Mike Voss revealing contamination of the municipal water supply in the town of 9,000 and the eight-year cover-up by elected officials.
1991	Des Moines Register	For series by Jane Schorer about a rape and its aftermath that reopened debate over whether rape victims should be identified by name.
1992	Sacramento Bee	For series by Tom Knudson about pollution, overdevelopment, and overpopulation along the Sierra Nevada.
1993	Miami Herald	For helping readers cope with Hurricane Andrew's devastation and for showing "how lax zoning, inspection, and building codes had contributed to the destruction."
1994	Akron (Ohio) Beacon Journal	For two-part examination of race relations.
1995	Virgin Islands Daily News	For 10-part series on crime that examined why crime was so prevalent on the islands, questioned the responses of police and prosecutors to crime, and ultimately led to major reforms.

REPORTING, 1917–95

The Pulitzer Prize for Reporting is the oldest given in journalism. Various journalism prizes have been established over the years, reflecting the changing nature and public perception of reporting. Originally, the reporting prize recognized excellence irrespective of the journalist's beat; it could be local, national, or international. Also, the prize could be awarded for reporting under the pressure of a deadline or investigative reporting carried out over a longer period. In 1929 a correspondence category was created to distinguish reporters stationed in Washington or abroad from local journalists. From 1942 to 1947 two prizes were added for national and international telegraphic reporting. In 1948, these categories and the correspondence category were consolidated into two—national reporting and international reporting. These categories are still recognized today.

In 1953, the original reporting category was broken down into reporting, on deadline; and reporting, not on deadline. The names of these two categories have changed over the years. From 1964 to 1983, they were known as local general or spot news reporting, and local investigative or specialized reporting, respectively. In 1984, they became general local reporting and special local reporting. The following year, general local reporting was changed to general news reporting, and special local reporting was split into three categories: investigative reporting, explanatory journalism, and specialized reporting.

Year	Winner, Newspaper
1917	Herbert Bayard Swope, New York World
1918	Harold A. Littledale, New York Evening Post
1919	No award
1920	John J. Leary, Jr., New York World
1921	Louis Seibold, New York World
1922	Kirke L. Simpson, Associated Press
1923	Alva Johnston, New York Times
1924	Magner White, San Diego Sun
1925	James W. Mulroy and Alvin H. Goldstein, Chicago Daily News
1926	William Burke Miller, Louisville Courier-Journal
1927	John T. Rogers, St. Louis Post-Dispatch
1928	No award
1929	Paul Y. Anderson, St. Louis Post-Dispatch
1930	Russell D. Owen, New York Times
1931	A.B. MacDonald, Kansas City Star
1932	W.C. Richards, D.D. Martin, J.S. Pooler, F.D. Webb, J.N.W. Sloan, Detroit Free Press
1933	Francis A. Jameson, Associated Press
1934	Royce Brier, San Francisco Chronicle
1935	William H. Taylor, New York Herald Tribune
1936	Lauren D. Lyman, New York Times
1937	John J. O'Neill, New York Herald Tribune
	William L. Laurence, New York Times
	Howard W. Blakeslee, Associated Press
	Gobind Behari Lal, Universal Service
	David Dietz, Scripps-Howard Newspaper Alliance
1938	Raymond Sprigle, Pittsburgh Post-Gazette
1939	Thomas Lunsford Stokes, Scripps-Howard Newspaper Alliance (articles published in New York World-Telegram)
1940	S. Burton Heath, New York World-Telegram
1941	Westbrook Pegler, New York World-Telegram
1942	Stanton Delaplane, San Francisco Chronicle
1943	George Weller, Chicago Daily News
1944	Paul Schoenstein and Associates, New York Journal American
1945	Jack S. McDowell, San Francisco Call-Bulletin
1946	William Leonard Laurence, New York Times
1947	Frederick Woltman, New York World-Telegram
1948	George E. Goodwin, Atlanta Journal
1949	Malcolm Johnson, New York Sun
1950	Meyer Berger, New York Times
1951	Edward S. Montgomery, San Francisco Examiner
1952	George de Carvalho, San Francisco Chronicle

REPORTING, EDITION TIME, 1953–63

Year	Winner, Newspaper
1953	Editorial Staff, Providence Journal and Evening Bulletin
1954	Staff, Vicksburg (Miss.) Sunday Post-Herald
1955	Caro Brown, Alice (Tex.) Daily Echo
1956	Lee Hills, Detroit Free Press
1957	Staff, Salt Lake (Utah) Tribune
1958	Staff, Fargo (N.Dak.) Forum
1959	Mary Lou Werner, Evening Star, Washington, D.C.
1960	Jack Nelson, Atlanta Constitution
1961	Sanche de Gramont, New York Herald-Tribune
1962	Robert D. Mullins, Deseret News, Salt Lake City
1963	Sylvan Fox, Anthony Shannon, and William Longgood, New York World-Telegram and Sun

LOCAL GENERAL/SPOT NEWS REPORTING, 1964–83, 1991–95

Year	Winner, Newspaper
1964	Norman C. Miller, Jr., Wall Street Journal
1965	Melvin H. Ruder, Hungry Horse News, Columbia Falls, Mont.
1966	Staff, Los Angeles Times
1967	Robert V. Cox, Chambersburg (Pa.) Public Opinion
1968	Staff, Detroit Free Press
1969	John Fetterman, Louisville Times and Courier-Journal
1970	Thomas Fitzpatrick, Chicago Sun-Times
1971	Staff, Akron (Ohio) Beacon Journal
1972	Richard Cooper and John Machacek, Rochester (N.Y.) Times-Union
1973	Staff, Chicago Tribune
1974	Arthur M. Petacque and Hugh F. Hough, Chicago Sun-Times
1975	Staff, Xenia (Ohio) Daily Gazette
1976	Gene Miller, Miami Herald
1977	Margo Huston, Milwaukee Journal
1978	Richard Whitt, Louisville Courier-Journal
1979	Staff, San Diego Evening Tribune
1980	Staff, Philadelphia Inquirer
1981	Staff, Longview (Wash.) Daily News
1982	Staffs, Kansas City Star and Kansas City Times
1983	Editorial staff, Fort Wayne (Ind.) News-Sentinel
1991	Staff, Miami Herald
1992	Staff, New York Newsday
1993	Staff, Los Angeles Times
1994	Staff, New York Times
1995	Staff, Los Angeles Times

SPECIAL LOCAL REPORTING, 1984

Year	Winner, Newspaper
1984	Kenneth Cooper, Jonathan Kaufman, Joan Fitzgerald, Norman Lockman, Gary McMillan, Kirk Scharfenberg, David Wessel, Boston Globe

REPORTING, NO EDITION TIME, 1953–63

Year	Winner, Newspaper
1953	Edward J. Mowery, New York World-Telegram & Sun
1954	Alvin Scott McCoy, Kansas City Star
1955	Roland Kenneth Towery, Cuero (Tex.) Record
1956	Arthur Daley, New York Times
1957	Wallace Turner and William Lambert, Portland Oregonian
1958	George Beveridge, Evening Star, Washington, D.C.
1959	John Harold Brialin, Scranton (Pa.) Tribune and Scrantonian
1960	Miriam Ottenberg, Evening Star, Washington, D.C.
1961	Edgar May, Buffalo (N.Y.) Evening News
1962	George Bliss, Chicago Tribune
1963	Oscar Griffin, Jr., Pecos (Tex.) Independent and Enterprise

LOCAL INVESTIGATIVE/SPECIALIZED REPORTING, 1964–83

Year	Winner, Newspaper
1964	James V. Magee, Albert V. Gaudiosi, and Frederick A. Meyer, Philadelphia Bulletin
1965	Gene Goltz, Houston Post
1966	John Anthony Frasca, Tampa Tribune
1967	Gene Miller, Miami Herald
1968	J. Anthony Lukas, New York Times
1969	Albert L. Delugach and Denny Walsh, St. Louis Globe-Democrat
1970	Harold Eugene Martin, Montgomery Adviser and Alabama Journal
1971	William Jones, Chicago Tribune
1972	Timothy Leland, Gerard M. O'Neill, Stephen A. Kurkjian, and Ann DeSantis, Boston Globe
1973	Staffs, Sun Newspapers of Omaha
1974	William Sherman, New York Daily News
1975	Staff, Indianapolis Star
1976	Staff, Chicago Tribune
1977	Acel Moore and Wendell Rawls, Jr., Philadelphia Inquirer
1978	Anthony R. Dolan, Stamford (Conn.) Advocate
1979	Gilbert M. Gaul and Elliot G. Jaspin, Pottsville (Pa.) Republican
1980	Stephen A. Kurkjian, Nils Bruzelius, Alexander B. Hawes, Jr., Joan Vennochi, and Robert M. Porterfield, Boston Globe Spotlight
1981	Clark Hallas and Robert B. Lowe, Arizona Daily Star
1982	Paul Henderson, Seattle Times
1983	Loretta Tofani, Washington Post

GENERAL LOCAL REPORTING, 1984

Year	Winner, Newspaper
1984	Team of reporters, Newsday (Garden City, L.I., N.Y.)

GENERAL NEWS REPORTING, 1985–90

Year	Winner, Newspaper
1985	Thomas Turcol, Virginian-Pilot and Ledger-Star (Norfolk, Va.)
1986	Edna Buchanan, Miami Herald
1987	Staff, Akron (Ohio) Beacon Journal
1988	Staff, Alabama Journal
	Staff, Lawrence (Mass.) Eagle-Tribune
1989	Staff, Louisville (Ky.) Courier-Journal
1990	Staff, San Jose (Calif.) Mercury News

INVESTIGATIVE REPORTING, 1985–95

Year	Winner, Newspaper
1985	William K. Marimow, Philadelphia Inquirer
	Lucy Morgan and Jack Reed, St. Petersburg Times
1986	Jeffrey A. Marx and Michael M. York, Lexington (Ky.) Herald Leader
1987	Daniel R. Biddle, H.G. Bissinger, Fredric N. Tulsky, and John Woestendiek, Philadelphia Inquirer
1988	Dean Baquet, William Gaines and Ann Marie Lipinski, Chicago Tribune
1989	Bill Dedman, Atlanta Journal and Constitution
1990	Lon Kilzer and Chris Ison, Minneapolis-St. Paul Star Tribune
1991	Joseph T. Hallinan and Susan M. Headden, Indianapolis Star
1992	Lorraine Adams and Dan Malone, Dallas Morning News
1993	Jeff Brazil and Steve Berry, Orlando Sentinel
1994	Staff, Providence Journal-Bulletin
1995	Stephanie Saul and Brian Donovan, Newsday (Garden City, L.I., N.Y.)

EXPLANATORY JOURNALISM, 1985–95

Year	Winner, Newspaper
1985	Jon Franklin, Baltimore Evening Sun
1986	Staff, New York Times
1987	Jeff Lyon and Peter Gorner, Chicago Tribune
1988	Daniel Hertzberg and James B. Stewart, Wall Street Journal
1989	David Hanners, William Snyder, and Karen Blessen, Dallas Morning News
1990	David A. Vise and Steve Coll, Washington Post
1991	Susan C. Faludi, Wall Street Journal
1992	Robert S. Capers and Eric Lipton, Hartford Courant
1993	Mike Toner, Atlanta Journal-Constitution
1994	Ronald Kotulak, Chicago Tribune
1995	Leon Dash and Lucian Perkins, Washington Post

SPECIALIZED/BEAT REPORTING, 1985–95

Year	Winner, Newspaper
1985	Randall Savage and Jackie Crosby, Macon (Ga.) Telegraph News
1986	Andrew Schneider and Mary Pat Flaherty, Pittsburgh Press
1987	Alex S. Jones, New York Times
1988	Walt Bogdanich, Wall Street Journal
1989	Edward Humes, Orange County (Calif.) Register
1990	Tamar Sieber, Albuquerque Journal
1991	Natalie Angier, New York Times
1992	Deborah Blum, Sacramento Bee
1993	Paul Ingrassia and Joseph B. White, Wall Street Journal
1994	Eric Freeman and Jim Mitzelfeld, Detroit News
1995	David M. Shribman, Boston Globe

CORRESPONDENCE, 1929–47

Year	Winner, Newspaper
1929	Paul Scott Mowrer, Chicago Daily News
1930	Leland Stowe, New York Herald Tribune
1931	H.R. Knickerbocker, Philadelphia Public Ledger and New York Evening Post
1932	Walter Duranty, New York Times
	Charles G. Ross, St. Louis Post-Dispatch
1933	Edgar Ansel Mowrer, Chicago Daily News
1934	Frederick T. Birchall, New York Times
1935	Arthur Krock, New York Times
1936	Wilfred C. Barber (posthumous), Chicago Tribune
1937	Anne O'Hare McCormick, New York Times
1938	Arthur Krock, New York Times
1939	Louis P. Lochner, Associated Press
1940	Otto D. Tolischus, New York Times
1941	Group award[1]
1942	Carlos P. Romulo, Philippines Herald
1943	Hanson W. Baldwin, New York Times
1944	Ernest Taylor Pyle, Scripps-Howard Newspaper Alliance
1945	Harold V. (Hal) Boyle, Associated Press
1946	Arnaldo Cortesi, New York Times
1947	Brooks Atkinson, New York Times

1. Instead of an individual prize, the trustees commissioned the creation of a bronze plaque to symbolize the services and achievements of all American news reporters in the war zones of Europe, Asia, and Africa.

TELEGRAPHIC REPORTING (NATIONAL), 1942–47

Year	Winner, Newspaper
1942	Louis Stark, New York Times
1943	No award
1944	Dewey L. Fleming, Baltimore Sun
1945	James B. Reston, New York Times
1946	Edward A. Harris, St. Louis Post-Dispatch
1947	Edward T. Folliard, Washington Post

TELEGRAPHIC REPORTING (INTERNATIONAL), 1942–47

Year	Winner, Newspaper
1942	Lawrence Edmund Allen, Associated Press
1943	Ira Wolfert, North American Newspaper Alliance, Inc.
1944	Daniel DeLuce, Associated Press
1945	Mark S. Watson, Baltimore Sun
1946	Homer William Bigart, New York Herald Tribune
1947	Eddy Gilmore, Associated Press

NATIONAL REPORTING, 1948–95

Year	Winner, Newspaper
1948	Bert Andrews, New York Herald Tribune
	Nat S. Finney, Minneapolis Tribune
1949	C.P. Trussell, New York Times
1950	Edwin O. Guthman, Seattle Times
1951	No award[1]
1952	Anthony Leviero, New York Times
1953	Don Whitehead, Associated Press
1954	Richard Wilson, Des Moines Register and Tribune
1955	Anthony Lewis, Washington Daily News
1956	Charles L. Bartlett, Chattanooga Times
1957	James B. Reston, New York Times
1958	Relman Morin, Associated Press
	Clark Mollenhoff, Des Moines Register and Tribune
1959	Howard Van Smith, Miami News
1960	Vance Trimble, Scripps-Howard Newspaper Alliance
1961	Edward R. Cony, Wall Street Journal
1962	Nathan G. Caldwell and Gene S. Graham, Nashville Tennessean
1963	Anthony Lewis, New York Times
1964	Merriman Smith, United Press International
1965	Louis M. Kohlmeier, Wall Street Journal
1966	Haynes Johnson, Washington Evening Star
1967	Stanley Penn and Monroe Karmin, Wall Street Journal
1968	Howard James, Christian Science Monitor
	Nathan K. (Nick) Kotz, Des Moines Register and Minneapolis Tribune
1969	Robert Cahn, Christian Science Monitor
1970	William J. Eaton, Chicago Daily News
1971	Lucinda Franks and Thomas Powers, United Press International
1972	Jack Anderson, Syndicated columnist
1973	Robert Boyd and Clark Hoyt, Knight Newspapers
1974	James R. Polk, Washington Star-News
	Jack White, Providence Journal and Evening Bulletin
1975	Donald L. Barlett and James B. Steele, Philadelphia Inquirer
1976	James Risser, Des Moines Register
1977	Walter Mears, Associated Press
1978	Gaylord D. Shaw, Los Angeles Times
1979	James Risser, Des Moines Register
1980	Bette Swenson Orsini and Charles Stafford, St. Petersburg Times
1981	John M. Crewdson, New York Times
1982	Rick Atkinson, Kansas City Times
1983	Staff, Boston Globe
1984	John Noble Wilford, New York Times
1985	Thomas J. Knudson, Des Moines Register
1986	Arthur Howe, Philadelphia Inquirer
	Craig Flournoy and George Rodrigue, Dallas Morning News
1987	Staff, Miami Herald
	Staff, New York Times
1988	Tim Weiner, Philadelphia Inquirer
1989	Donald L. Barlett and James B. Steele, Philadelphia Inquirer
1990	Ross Anderson, Bill Dietrich, Mary Ann Gwinn, and Eric Nalder, Seattle Times
1991	Marjie Lundstrom and Rochelle Sharpe, Gannett News Service
1992	Jeff Taylor and Mike McGraw, Kansas City Star
1993	David Maraniss, Washington Post
1994	Eileen Welsome, Alburquerque Tribune
1995	Tony Horwitz, Wall Street Journal

1. The board decided that Arthur Krock of the *New York Times* deserved the prize for National Reporting, but he could not accept the award because he was a board member.

INTERNATIONAL REPORTING, 1948–95

Year	Winner, Newspaper
1948	Paul W. Ward, Baltimore Sun
1949	Price Day, Baltimore Sun
1950	Edmund Stevens, Christian Science Monitor
1951	Keyes Beech, Chicago Daily News
	Homer William Bigart, New York Herald Tribune
	Marguerite Higgins, New York Herald Tribune
	Relman Morin, Associated Press
	Fred Sparks, Chicago Daily News
	Don Whitehead, Associated Press
1952	John M. Hightower, Associated Press
1953	Austin Wehrwein, Milwaukee Journal
1954	Jim G. Lucas, Scripps-Howard Newspaper Alliance
1955	Harrison E. Salisbury, New York Times
1956	William Randolph Hearst, Jr., Kingsbury Smith, and Frank Conniff, International News Service
1957	Russell Jones, United Press
1958	Staff, New York Times
1959	Joseph Martin and Philip Santora, New York Daily News
1960	A.M. Rosenthal, New York Times
1961	Lynn Heinzerling, Associated Press
1962	Walter Lippmann, New York Herald Tribune Syndicate
1963	Hal Hendrix, Miami News
1964	Malcolm W. Browne, Associated Press
	David Halberstam, New York Times
1965	J.A. Livingston, Philadelphia Bulletin
1966	Peter Arnett, Associated Press
1967	R. John Hughes, Christian Science Monitor
1968	Alfred Friendly, Washington Post
1969	William Tuohy, Los Angeles Times
1970	Seymour M. Hersh, Dispatch News Service
1971	Jimmie Lee Hoagland, Washington Post
1972	Peter R. Kann, Wall Street Journal
1973	Max Frankel, New York Times
1974	Hedrick Smith, New York Times
1975	William Mullen (reporter), Ovie Carter (photographer), Chicago Tribune
1976	Sydney H. Schanberg, New York Times
1977	No award
1978	Henry Kamm, New York Times
1979	Richard Ben Cramer, Philadelphia Inquirer
1980	Joel Brinkely (reporter), Jay Mather (photographer), Louisville Courier-Journal
1981	Shirley Christian, Miami Herald
1982	John Darnton, New York Times
1983	Thomas L. Friedman, New York Times
	Loren Jenkins, Washington Post
1984	Karen Elliott House, Wall Street Journal
1985	Josh Friedman and Dennis Bell (reporters) and Ozier Muhammad (photographer), Newsday (Garden City, L.I., N.Y.)
1986	Lewis M. Simons, Pete Carey, and Katherine Ellison, San Jose (Calif.) Mercury News
1987	Michael Parks, Los Angeles Times
1988	Thomas L. Friedman, New York Times
1989	Glenn Frankel, Washington Post
	Bill Keller, New York Times
1990	Nicholas D. Kristof and Sheryl WuDunn, New York Times
1991	Caryle Murphy, Washington Post
	Serge Schmemann, New York Times
1992	Patrick J. Sloyan, New York Newsday
1993	John F. Burns, New York Times
	Roy Gutman, Newsday (Garden City, L.I., N.Y.)
1994	Team of reporters, Dallas Morning News
1995	Mark Fritz, Associated Press

EDITORIAL WRITING, 1917–95

Year	Winner, Newspaper
1917	Lusitania editorial article, New York Tribune
1918	War editorials and articles, Louisville Courier Journal
1919	No award
1920	Harvey E. Newbranch, Evening World Herald
1921	No award
1922	Frank M. O'Brien, New York Herald
1923	William Allen White, Emporia (Kans.) Gazette
1924[1]	Coolidge editorial, Boston Herald
1925	"Plight of the South" editorial, Charleston (S.C.) News and Courier
1926	Edward M. Kingsbury, New York Times
1927	F. Lauriston Bullard, Boston Herald
1928	Grover Cleveland Hall, Montgomery (Ala.) Advertiser
1929	Louis Isaac Jaffe, Norfolk Virginian-Pilot
1930	No award
1931	Charles S. Ryckman, Fremont (Nebr.) Tribune
1932	No award
1933	Series of editorials, Kansas City Star
1934	E.P. Chase, Atlantic (Iowa) News-Telegraph
1935	No award
1936	Felix Morley, Washington Post
	George B. Parker, Scripps-Howard Newspapers
1937	John W. Owens, Baltimore Sun
1938	William Wesley Waymack, Des Moines Register and Tribune
1939	Ronald G. Callvert, Portland Oregonian
1940	Bart Howard, St. Louis Post-Dispatch
1941	Reuben Maury, New York Daily News
1942	Geoffrey Parsons, New York Herald Tribune
1943	Forrest W. Seymour, Des Moines Register and Tribune
1944	Henry J. Haskell, Kansas City Star
1945	George W. Potter, Providence Journal-Bulletin
1946	Hodding Carter, Delta Democrat-Times (Greenville, Miss.)
1947	William H. Grimes, Wall Street Journal
1948	Virginius Dabney, Richmond Times-Dispatch
1949	John H. Crider, Boston Herald
	Herbert Elliston, Washington Post
1950	Carl M. Saunders, Jackson (Mich.) Citizen Patriot
1951	William Harry Fitzpatrick, New Orleans States
1952	Louis LaCoss, St. Louis Globe Democrat
1953	Vermont Connecticut Royster, Wall Street Journal
1954	Don Murray, Boston Herald
1955	Royce Howes, Detroit Free Press
1956	Lauren K. Soth, Des Moines Register and Tribune
1957	Buford Boone, Tuscaloosa (Ala.) News
1958	Harry S. Ashmore, Arkansas Gazette
1959	Ralph McGill, Atlanta Constitution
1960	Lenoir Chambers, Norfolk Virginian-Pilot
1961	William J. Dorvillier, San Juan (Puerto Rico) Star
1962	Thomas M. Storke, Santa Barbara (Calif.) News-Press
1963	Ira B. Harkey, Jr., Pascagoula (Miss.) Chronicle
1964	Hazel Brannon Smith, Lexington (Miss.) Advertiser
1965	John R. Harrison, Gainesville (Fla.) Daily Sun
1966	Robert Lasch, St. Louis Post-Dispatch
1967	Eugene Patterson, Atlanta Constitution
1968	John S. Knight, Knight Newspapers
1969	Paul Greenberg, Pine Bluff (Ark.) Commercial
1970	Philip L. Geyelin, Washington Post
1971	Horance G. Davis, Jr., Gainesville (Fla.) Sun
1972	John Strohmeyer, Bethlehem (Pa.) Globe-Times
1973	Roger B. Linscott, Berkshire Eagle (Pittsfield, Mass.)
1974	F. Gilman Spencer, Trentonian (Trenton, N.J.)
1975	John Daniell Maurice, Charleston (W.Va.) Daily Mail
1976	Philip P. Kerby, Los Angeles Times
1977	Warren L. Lerude, Foster Church, and Norman F. Cardoza, Reno (Nev.) Evening Gazette and Nevada State Journal
1978	Meg Greenfield, Washington Post
1979	Edwin M. Yoder, Jr., Washington Star
1980	Robert L. Bartley, Wall Street Journal
1981	No award
1982	Jack Rosenthal, New York Times
1983	Editorial board, Miami Herald
1984	Albert Scardino, Georgia Gazette
1985	Richard Aregood, Philadelphia Daily News
1986	Jack Fuller, Chicago Tribune
1987	Jonathan Freedman, San Diego Tribune
1988	Jane Healy, Orlando Sentinel
1989	Lois Wille, Chicago Tribune
1990	Thomas J. Hylton, Pottstown (Pa.) Mercury
1991	Ron Casey, Harold Jackson, and Joey Kennedy, Birmingham (Ala.) News
1992	Maria Henson, Lexington (Ky.) Herald-Leader
1993	No award
1994	R. Bruce Dold, Chicago Tribune
1995	Jeffrey Good, St. Petersburg Times

1. A special prize was awarded to the widow of the late Frank I. Cobb of the *New York World* in recognition of his lifetime of editorial writing and service.

EDITORIAL CARTOONING, 1922–95

Year	Winner, Newspaper
1922	Rollin Kirby, New York World
1923	No award
1924	Jay Norwood Darling, Des Moines Register and Tribune
1925	Rollin Kirby, New York World
1926	Daniel R. Fitzpatrick, St. Louis Post-Dispatch
1927	Nelson Harding, Brooklyn Daily Eagle
1928	Nelson Harding, Brooklyn Daily Eagle
1929	Rollin Kirby, New York World
1930	Charles R. Macauley, Brooklyn Daily Eagle
1931	Edmund Duffy, Baltimore Sun
1932	John T. McCutcheon, Chicago Tribune
1933	H.M. Talburt, Washington Daily News
1934	Edmund Duffy, Baltimore Sun
1935	Ross A. Lewis, Milwaukee Journal
1936	No award
1937	C.D. Batchelor, New York Daily News
1938	Vaughn Shoemaker, Chicago Daily News
1939	Charles G. Werner, Daily Oklahoman
1940	Edmund Duffy, Baltimore Sun
1941	Jacob Burck, Chicago Times
1942	Herbert L. Block ("Herblock"), NEA Service
1943	Jay Norwood Darling, Des Moines Register and Tribune
1944	Clifford K. Berryman, Evening Star (D.C.)
1945	Sgt. Bill Mauldin, United Feature Syndicate, Inc.
1946	Bruce Alexander Russell, Los Angeles Times
1947	Vaughn Shoemaker, Chicago Daily News
1948	Reuben L. Goldberg, New York Sun
1949	Lute Pease, Newark Evening News
1950	James T. Berryman, Evening Star (D.C.)
1951	Reg Manning, Arizona Republic
1952	Fred L. Packer, New York Mirror
1953	Edward D. Kuekes, Cleveland Plain Dealer
1954	Herbert L. Block ("Herblock"), Washington Post & Times Herald
1955	Daniel R. Fitzpatrick, St. Louis Post-Dispatch
1956	Robert York, Louisville (Ky.) Times
1957	Tom Little, Nashville Tennesseean
1958	Bruce M. Shanks, Buffalo (N.Y.) Evening News
1959	William H. ("Bill") Mauldin, St. Louis Post-Dispatch
1960	No award
1961	Carey Orr, Chicago Tribune
1962	Edmund S. Valtman, Hartford (Conn.) Times
1963	Frank Miller, Des Moines Register
1964	Paul Conrad, Denver Post
1965	No award
1966	Don Wright, Miami News
1967	Patrick Oliphant, Denver Post
1968	Eugene Gray Payne, Charlotte (N.C.) Observer
1969	John Fischetti, Chicago Daily News
1970	Thomas F. Darcy, Newsday (Garden City, L.I., N.Y.)
1971	Paul Conrad, Los Angeles Times
1972	Jeffrey K. MacNelly, Richmond News-Leader
1973	No award
1974	Paul Szep, Boston Globe
1975	Garry Trudeau, Universal Press Syndicate
1976	Tony Auth, Philadelphia Inquirer
1977	Paul Szep, Boston Globe
1978	Jeffrey K. MacNelly, Richmond News-Leader
1979	Herbert L. Block ("Herblock"), Washington Post
1980	Don Wright, Miami News
1981	Mike Peters, Dayton (Ohio) Daily News
1982	Ben Sargent, Austin (Tex.) American-Statesman
1983	Richard Locher, Chicago Tribune
1984	Paul Conrad, Los Angeles Times
1985	Jeffrey K. MacNelly, Chicago Tribune
1986	Jules Feiffer, Village Voice (New York City)
1987	Berke Breathed, Washington Post Writers Group
1988	Doug Marlette, Atlanta Constitution and Charlotte Observer
1989	Jack Higgins, Chicago Sun-Times
1990	Tom Toles, Buffalo News
1991	Jim Borgman, Cincinnati Enquirer
1992	Signe Wilkinson, Philadelphia Daily News
1993	Stephen R. Benson, Arizona Republic
1994	Michael P. Ramirez, Commercial Appeal (Memphis)
1995	Mike Luckovich, Atlanta Constitution

PHOTOGRAPHY, 1942–67[1]

Year	Winner, Newspaper
1942	Milton Brooks, Detroit News
1943	Frank Noel, Associated Press
1944	Frank Filan, Associated Press
	Earle L. Bunker, World-Herald (Omaha, Nebr.)
1945	Joe Rosenthal, Associated Press
1946	No award
1947	Arnold Hardy, Amateur; photo distributed by the Associated Press
1948	Frank Cushing, Boston Traveler
1949	Nathaniel Fein, New York Herald-Tribune
1950	Bill Crouch, Oakland (Calif.) Tribune
1951	Max Desfor, Associated Press
1952	John Robinson and Don Ultang, Des Moines Register and Tribune
1953	William M. Gallagher, Flint (Mich.) Journal
1954	Mrs. Walter M. Schau, Amateur; photo published by the Akron (Ohio) Beacon Journal
1955	John L. Gaunt, Jr., Los Angeles Times
1956	Photography staff, New York Daily News
1957	Harry A. Trask, Boston Traveler
1958	William C. Beall, Washington Daily News
1959	William Seaman, Minneapolis Star
1960	Andrew Lopez, United Press International
1961	Yasushi Nagao, Mainichi (Tokyo); photo distributed by United Press International
1962	Paul Vathis, Associated Press
1963	Hector Rondon, La Republica (Caracas, Venezuela); photo distributed by the Associated Press
1964	Robert H. Jackson, Dallas Times-Herald
1965	Horst Faas, Associated Press
1966	Kyoichi Sawada, United Press International
1967	Jack R. Thornell, Associated Press

1. In 1968 the Photography category was divided into two groups: Spot News Photography and Feature Photography.

SPOT NEWS PHOTOGRAPHY, 1968–95

Year	Winner, Newspaper
1968	Rocco Morabito, Jacksonville Journal
1969	Edward T. Adams, Associated Press
1970	Steve Starr, Associated Press
1971	John Paul Filo, Valley Daily News and Daily Dispatch (New Kensington, Pa.)
1972	Horst Faas and Michel Laurent, Associated Press
1973	Huynh Cong Ut, Associated Press
1974	Anthony K. Roberts, Freelance photographer, Beverly Hills, Calif.
1975	Gerald H. Gay, Seattle Times
1976	Stanley Forman, Boston Herald American
1977	Neal Ulevich, Associated Press
	Stanley Forman, Boston Herald American
1978	John H. Blair, United Press International
1979	Thomas J. Kelly III, Pottstown (Pa.) Mercury
1980	Unnamed photographer, United Press International
1981	Larry C. Price, Fort Worth (Tex.) Star-Telegram
1982	Ron Edmonds, Associated Press
1983	Bill Foley, Associated Press
1984	Stan Grossfeld, Boston Globe
1985	Photography staff, Register (Santa Ana, Calif.)
1986	Carol Guzy and Michel duCille, Miami Herald
1987	Kim Komenich, San Francisco Examiner
1988	Scott Shaw, Odessa (Tex.) American
1989	Ron Olshwanger, St. Louis Post-Dispatch
1990	Photography staff, Oakland Tribune
1991	Greg Marinovich, Associated Press
1992	Photography staff, Associated Press
1993	William Snyder and Ken Geiger, Dallas Morning News
1994	Paul Watson, Toronto Star
1995	Carol Guzy, Washington Post

FEATURE PHOTOGRAPHY, 1968–95

Year	Winner, Newspaper
1968	Toshio Sakai, United Press International
1969	Moneta Sleet, Jr., Ebony magazine
1970	Dallas Kinney, Palm Beach Post (West Palm Beach, Fla.)
1971	Jack Dykinga, Chicago Sun-Times
1972	Dave Kennerly, United Press International
1973	Brian Lanker, Topeka Capital-Journal
1974	Slava Veder, Associated Press
1975	Matthew Lewis, Washington Post
1976	Photography staff, Louisville Courier-Journal and Times
1977	Robin Hood, Chattanooga News-Free Press
1978	J. Ross Baughman, Associated Press
1979	Photography staff, Boston Herald American
1980	Erwin H. Hagler, Dallas Times Herald
1981	Taro M. Yamasaki, Detroit Free Press
1982	John H. White, Chicago Sun-Times
1983	James B. Dickman, Dallas Times Heald
1984	Anthony Suau, Denver Post
1985	Stan Grossfeld, Boston Globe
	Larry C. Price, Philadelphia Inquirer
1986	Tom Gralish, Philadelphia Inquirer
1987	David Peterson, Des Moines Register
1988	Michel duCille, Miami Herald
1989	Manny Crisostomo, Detroit Free Press
1990	David C. Turnley, Detroit Free Press
1991	William Snyder, Dallas Morning News
1992	John Kaplan, Pittsburgh Post-Gazette, Block Newspapers
1993	Photography staff, Associated Press
1994	Kevin Carter, freelancer, photo published in New York Times
1995	Photography staff, Associated Press

COMMENTARY, 1970–95

Year	Winner, Newspaper
1970	Marquis W. Childs, St. Louis Post-Dispatch
1971	William A. Caldwell, Record (Hackensack, N.J.)
1972	Mike Royko, Chicago Daily News
1973	David S. Broder, Washington Post
1974	Edwin A. Roberts, Jr., National Observer
1975	Mary McGrory, Washington Star
1976	Walter ("Red") Smith, New York Times
1977	George F. Will, Washington Post Writers Group
1978	William Safire, New York Times
1979	Russell Baker, New York Times
1980	Ellen H. Goodman, Boston Globe
1981	Dave Anderson, New York Times
1982	Art Buchwald, Los Angeles Times Syndicate
1983	Claude Sitton, Raleigh (N.C.) News & Observer
1984	Vermont Royster, Wall Street Journal
1985	Murray Kempton, Newsday (Garden City, N.Y.)
1986	Jimmy Breslin, New York Daily News
1987	Charles Krauthammer, Washington Post
1988	Dave Barry, Miami Herald
1989	Clarence Page, Chicago Tribune
1990	Jim Murray, Los Angeles Times
1991	Jim Hoagland, Washington Post
1992	Anna Quindlen, New York Times
1993	Liz Balsameda, Miami Herald
1994	William Raspberry, Washington Post
1995	Jim Dwyer, New York Newsday

CRITICISM, 1970–95

Year	Winner, Newspaper
1970	Ada Louise Huxtable, New York Times
1971	Harold C. Schonberg, New York Times
1972	Frank Peters, Jr., St. Louis Post-Dispatch
1973	Ronald Powers, Chicago Sun-Times
1974	Emily Genauer, Newsday syndicate
1975	Roger Ebert, Chicago Sun-Times
1976	Alan M. Kriegsman, Washington Post
1977	William McPherson, Washington Post
1978	Walter Kerr, New York Times
1979	Paul Gapp, Chicago Tribune
1980	William A. Henry III, Boston Globe
1981	Jonathan Yardley, Washington Star
1982	Martin Bernheimer, Los Angeles Times
1983	Manuela Hoelterhoff, Wall Street Journal
1984	Paul Goldberger, New York Times
1985	Howard Rosenberg, Los Angeles Times
1986	Donal Henahan, New York Times
1987	Richard Eder, Los Angeles Times
1988	Tom Shales, Washington Post
1989	Michael Skube, Raleigh (N.C.) News and Observer
1990	Allan Temko, San Francisco Chronicle
1991	David Shaw, Los Angeles Times
1992	No award
1993	Michael Dirda, Washington Post
1994	Lloyd Schwartz, Boston Phoenix
1995	Margo Jefferson, New York Times

FEATURE WRITING, 1979–95

Year	Winner, Newspaper
1979	Jon D. Franklin, Baltimore Evening Sun
1980	Madeleine Blais, Miami Herald
1981	Teresa Carpenter, Village Voice (New York City)
1982	Saul Pett, Associated Press
1983	Nan Robertson, New York Times
1984	Peter Mark Rinearson, Seattle Times
1985	Alice Steinbach, Baltimore Sun
1986	John Camp, St. Paul Pioneer Press and Dispatch
1987	Steve Twomey, Philadelphia Inquirer
1988	Jacqui Banaszynski, St. Paul Pioneer Press and Dispatch
1989	David Zucchino, Philadelphia Inquirer
1990	Dave Curtin, Colorado Springs Gazette Telegraph
1991	Sheryl James, St. Petersburg Times
1992	Howell Raines, New York Times
1993	George Lardner, Jr., Washington Post
1994	Isabel Wilkerson, New York Times
1995	Ron Suskind, Wall Street Journal

SPECIAL AWARDS AND CITATIONS, 1930–87

Year	Winner, Newspaper
1930	William O. Dapping, Auburn (N.Y.) Citizen, Prison reporting
1938	Edmonton (Alberta) Journal, Freedom-of-the-press editorials
1941	New York Times, Foreign news reporting
1944	Byron Price, director of the Office of Censorship, Creation and administration of newspaper and radio codes
	Mrs. William Allen White, Services to Advisory Board, Graduate School of Journalism, Columbia University
1945	American press cartographers, Maps of war fronts
1947	Columbia University and Graduate School of Journalism, Governing Pulitzer prizes
	St. Louis Post-Dispatch, Adherence to ideals of journalism
1948	Dr. Frank Diehl Fackenthal, Interest and service
1951	Cyrus L. Sulzberger, New York Times, Interview with Archbishop Stepinac
1952	Max Kase, N.Y. Journal-American, Corruption in basketball
	Kansas City Star, Coverage of regional flood
1953	New York Times, Sunday "Review of the Week" section
1958	Walter Lippmann, New York Herald Tribune, Lifetime achievement
1964	Gannett Newspapers, "The Road to Integration" program
1976	Professor John Hohenberg, Administration of Pulitzer prizes
1978	Richard Lee Strout, Christian Science Monitor, Lifetime achievement
1987	Joseph Pulitzer, Jr., Lifetime services to Pulitzer Board

PULITZER PRIZES IN LETTERS, 1917–95

THE PULITZER PRIZE FOR THE NOVEL/FICTION, 1918–95[1]

Year	Author/Title
1918	Ernest Poole, *His Family*
1919	Booth Tarkington, *The Magnificent Ambersons*
1920	No award
1921	Edith Wharton, *The Age of Innocence*
1922	Booth Tarkington, *Alice Adams*
1923	Willa Cather, *One of Ours*
1924	Margaret Wilson, *The Able McLaughlins*
1925	Edna Ferber, *So Big*
1926	Sinclair Lewis, *Arrowsmith*
1927	Louis Bromfield, *Early Autumn*
1928	Thornton Wilder, *The Bridge of San Luis Rey*
1929	Julia Peterkin, *Scarlet Sister Mary*
1930	Oliver LaFarge, *Laughing Boy*
1931	Margaret Ayer Barnes, *Years of Grace*
1932	Pearl S. Buck, *The Good Earth*
1933	T.S. Stribling, *The Store*
1934	Caroline Miller, *Lamb in His Bosom*
1935	Josephine Winslow Johnson, *Now in November*
1936	Harold L. Davis, *Honey in the Horn*
1937	Margaret Mitchell, *Gone with the Wind*
1938	John Phillips Marquand, *The Late George Apley*
1939	Marjorie Kinnan Rawlings, *The Yearling*
1940	John Steinbeck, *The Grapes of Wrath*
1941	No award
1942	Ellen Glasgow, *In This Our Life*
1943	Upton Sinclair, *Dragon's Teeth*
1944	Martin Flavin, *Journey in the Dark*
1945	John Hersey, *A Bell for Adano*
1946	No award
1947	Robert Penn Warren, *All the King's Men*
1948	James A. Michener, *Tales of the South Pacific*
1949	James Gould Cozzens, *Guard of Honor*
1950	A.B. Guthrie, Jr., *The Way West*
1951	Conrad Richter, *The Town*
1952	Herman Wouk, *The Caine Mutiny*
1953	Ernest Hemingway, *The Old Man and the Sea*
1954	No award
1955	William Faulkner, *A Fable*
1956	MacKinlay Kantor, *Andersonville*
1957	No award
1958	James Agee, *A Death in the Family*
1959	Robert Lewis Taylor, *The Travels of Jaimie McPheeters*
1960	Allen Drury, *Advise and Consent*
1961	Harper Lee, *To Kill a Mockingbird*
1962	Edwin O'Connor, *The Edge of Sadness*
1963	William Faulkner, *The Reivers*
1964	No award
1965	Shirley Ann Grau, *The Keepers of the House*
1966	Katherine Anne Porter, *Collected Stories*
1967	Bernard Malamud, *The Fixer*
1968	William Styron, *The Confessions of Nat Turner*
1969	N. Scott Momaday, *House Made of Dawn*
1970	Jean Stafford, *Collected Stories*
1971	No award
1972	Wallace Stegner, *Angle of Repose*
1973	Eudora Welty, *The Optimist's Daughter*
1974	No award
1975	Michael Shaara, *The Killer Angels*
1976	Saul Bellow, *Humboldt's Gift*
1977	No award
1978	James Alan McPherson, *Elbow Room*
1979	John Cheever, *The Stories of John Cheever*
1980	Norman Mailer, *The Executioner's Song*
1981	John Kennedy Toole,[2] *A Confederacy of Dunces*
1982	John Updike, *Rabbit Is Rich*
1983	Alice Walker, *The Color Purple*
1984	William Kennedy, *Ironweed*
1985	Alison Lurie, *Foreign Affairs*
1986	Larry McMurtry, *Lonesome Dove*
1987	Peter Taylor, *A Summons to Memphis*
1988	Toni Morrison, *Beloved*
1989	Anne Tyler, *Breathing Lessons*
1990	Oscar Hijuelos, *The Mambo Kings Play Songs of Love*
1991	John Updike, *Rabbit at Rest*
1992	Jane Smiley, *A Thousand Acres*
1993	Robert Olen Butler, *A Good Scent from a Strange Mountain*
1994	E. Annie Proulx, *The Shipping News*
1995	Carol Shields, *The Stone Diaries*

1. In 1948 the name of the category was changed to Fiction. 2. Awarded posthumously.

THE PULITZER PRIZE FOR DRAMA, 1918–95

Year	Author/Title
1918	Jesse Lynch Williams, *Why Marry*
1919	No award
1920	Eugene O'Neill, *Beyond the Horizon*
1921	Zona Gale, *Miss Lulu Bett*
1922	Eugene O'Neill, *Anna Christie*
1923	Owen Davis, *Icebound*
1924	Hatcher Hughes, *Hell-Bent Fer Heaven*
1925	Sidney Howard, *They Knew What They Wanted*
1926	George Kelly, *Craig's Wife*
1927	Paul Green, *In Abraham's Bosom*
1928	Eugene O'Neill, *Strange Interlude*
1929	Elmer L. Rice, *Street Scene*
1930	Marc Connelly, *The Green Pastures*
1931	Susan Glaspell, *Alison's House*
1932	George S. Kaufman, Morrie Ryskind, and Ira Gershwin, *Of Thee I Sing*

Year	Author/Title
1933	Maxwell Anderson, *Both Your Houses*
1934	Sidney Kingsley, *Men in White*
1935	Zoe Akins, *The Old Maid*
1936	Robert E. Sherwood, *Idiot's Delight*
1937	Moss Hart and George S. Kaufman, *You Can't Take It with You*
1938	Thornton Wilder, *Our Town*
1939	Robert E. Sherwood, *Abe Lincoln in Illinois*
1940	William Saroyan, *The Time of Your Life*
1941	Robert E. Sherwood, *There Shall Be No Night*
1942	No award
1943	Thornton Wilder, *The Skin of Our Teeth*
1944	No award
1945	Mary Chase, *Harvey*
1946	Russel Crouse and Howard Lindsay, *State of the Union*
1947	No award
1948	Tennessee Williams, *A Streetcar Named Desire*
1949	Arthur Miller, *Death of a Salesman*
1950	Richard Rodgers, Oscar Hammerstein II, and Joshua Logan, *South Pacific*
1951	No award
1952	Joseph Kramm, *The Shrike*
1953	William Inge, *Picnic*
1954	John Patrick, *The Teahouse of the August Moon*
1955	Tennessee Williams, *Cat on a Hot Tin Roof*
1956	Albert Hackett and Frances Goodrich, *The Diary of Anne Frank*
1957	Eugene O'Neill, *Long Day's Journey Into Night*
1958	Ketti Frings, *Look Homeward, Angel*
1959	Archibald MacLeish, *J.B.*
1960	Jerome Weidman and George Abbott (book); Jerry Bock (music); and Sheldon Harnick (lyrics), *Fiorello!*
1961	Tad Mosel, *All the Way Home*
1962	Frank Loesser and Abe Burrows, *How to Succeed in Business Without Really Trying*
1963	No award
1964	No award
1965	Frank D. Gilroy, *The Subject Was Roses*
1966	No award
1967	Edward Albee, *A Delicate Balance*
1968	No award
1969	Howard Sackler, *The Great White Hope*
1970	Charles Gordone, *No Place to Be Somebody*
1971	Paul Zindel, *The Effect of Gamma Rays on Man-in-the-Moon Marigolds*
1972	No award
1973	Jason Miller, *That Championship Season*
1974	No award
1975	Edward Albee, *Seascape*
1976	Michael Bennett; Nicholas Dante and James Kirkwood (book); Marvin Hamlisch (music); and Edward Kleban (lyrics), *A Chorus Line*
1977	Michael Cristofer, *The Shadow Box*
1978	Donald L. Coburn, *The Gin Game*
1979	Sam Shepard, *Buried Child*
1980	Lanford Wilson, *Talley's Folly*
1981	Beth Henley, *Crimes of the Heart*
1982	Charles Fuller, *A Soldier's Play*
1983	Marsha Norman, *'night Mother*
1984	David Mamet, *Glengarry Glen Ross*
1985	Stephen Sondheim (music and lyrics); James Lapine (book), *Sunday in the Park with George*
1986	No award
1987	August Wilson, *Fences*
1988	Alfred Uhry, *Driving Miss Daisy*
1989	Wendy Wasserstein, *The Heidi Chronicles*
1990	August Wilson, *The Piano Lesson*
1991	Neil Simon, *Lost in Yonkers*
1992	Robert Schenkkan, *The Kentucky Cycle*
1993	Tony Kushner, *Angels in America: Millennium Approaches*
1994	Edward Albee, *Three Tall Women*
1995	Horton Foote, *The Young Man from Atlanta*

THE PULITZER PRIZE FOR HISTORY, 1917–95

Year	Author/Title
1917	His Excellency J.J. Jusserand, French ambassador to the U.S., *With Americans of Past and Present Days*
1918	James Ford Rhodes, *A History of the Civil War, 1861–1865*
1919	No award
1920	Justin H. Smith, *The War with Mexico*
1921	William Sowden Sims, with Burton J. Hendrick, *The Victory at Sea*
1922	James Truslow Adams, *The Founding of New England*
1923	Charles Warren, *The Supreme Court in United States History*
1924	Charles Howard McIlwain, *The American Revolution—A Constitutional Interpretation*
1925	Frederic L. Paxson, *A History of the American Frontier*
1926	Edward Channing, *The History of the United States*
1927	Samuel Flagg Bemis, *Pinckney's Treaty*
1928	Vernon Louis Parrington, *Main Currents in American Thought*
1929	Fred Albert Shannon, *The Organization and Administration of the Union Army, 1861–1865*
1930	Claude H. Van Tyne, *The War of Independence*
1931	Bernadotte E. Schmitt, *The Coming of the War: 1914*
1932	John J. Pershing, *My Experiences in the World War*
1933	Frederick J. Turner, *The Significance of Sections in American History*
1934	Herbert Agar, *The People's Choice*
1935	Charles McLean Andrews, *The Colonial Period of American History*
1936	Andrew C. McLaughlin, *The Constitutional History of the United States*
1937	Van Wyck Brooks, *The Flowering of New England*
1938	Paul Herman Buck, *The Road to Reunion 1856–1900*
1939	Frank Luther Mott, *A History of American Magazines*
1940	Carl Sandburg, *Abraham Lincoln: The War Years*
1941	Marcus Lee Hansen, *The Atlantic Migration, 1607–1860*
1942	Margaret Leech, *Reveille in Washington*
1943	Esther Forbes, *Paul Revere and the World He Lived In*
1944	Merle Curti, *The Growth of American Thought*
1945	Stephen Bonsal, *Unfinished Business*
1946	Arthur Meier Schlesinger, Jr., *The Age of Jackson*
1947	James Phinney Baxter III, *Scientists Against Time*
1948	Bernard DeVoto, *Across the Wide Missouri*
1949	Roy Franklin Nichols, *The Disruption of American Democracy*
1950	Oliver W. Larkin, *Art and Life in America*
1951	R. Carlyle Buley, *The Old Northwest, Pioneer Period 1815–1840*
1952	Oscar Handlin, *The Uprooted*
1953	George Dangerfield, *The Era of Good Feelings*
1954	Bruce Catton, *A Stillness at Appomattox*
1955	Paul Horgan, *Great River: The Rio Grande in North American History*
1956	Richard Hofstadter, *The Age of Reform*
1957	George F. Kennan, *Russia Leaves the War: Soviet American Relations, 1917–1920*
1958	Bray Hammond, *Banks and Politics in America*
1959	Leonard D. White, with Jean Schneider, *The Republican Era: 1869–1901*
1960	Margaret Leech, *In the Days of McKinley*
1961	Herbert Feis, *Between War and Peace: The Potsdam Conference*
1962	Lawrence H. Gipson, *The Triumphant Empire, Thunder Clouds in the West*
1963	Constance McLaughlin Green, *Washington, Village and Capital, 1800–1878*
1964	Sumner Chilton Powell, *Puritan Village: The Formation of a New England Town*
1965	Irwin Unger, *The Greenback Era*
1966	Perry Miller, *Life of the Mind in America*
1967	William H. Goetzmann, *Exploration and Empire: The Explorer and the Scientist in the Winning of the American West*
1968	Bernard Bailyn, *The Ideological Origins of the American Revolution*
1969	Leonard W. Levy, *Origins of the Fifth Amendment*
1970	Dean Acheson, *Present at the Creation: My Years in the State Department*
1971	James MacGregor Burns, *Roosevelt, The Soldier of Freedom*
1972	Carl N. Degler, *Neither Black Nor White*
1973	Michael Kammen, *People of Paradox: An Inquiry Concerning the Origins of American Civilization*
1974	Daniel J. Boorstin, *The Americans: The Democratic Experience*
1975	Dumas Malone, *Jefferson and His Time, Vols. I-V*
1976	Paul Horgan, *Lamy of Santa Fe*
1977	David M. Potter[1] (manuscript finished by Don E. Fehrenbacher), *The Impending Crisis*
1978	Alfred D. Chandler, Jr., *The Visible Hand: The Managerial Revolution in American Business*
1979	Don E. Fehrenbacher, *The Dred Scott Case*
1980	Leon F. Litwack, *Been in the Storm So Long*
1981	Lawrence A. Cremin, *American Education: The National Experience, 1783–1876*
1982	C. Vann Woodward (ed.), *Mary Chesnut's Civil War*
1983	Rhys L. Isaac, *The Transformation of Virginia, 1740–1790*
1984	No award
1985	Thomas K. McCraw, *Prophets of Regulation*

1. Awarded posthumously.

Year	Author/Title
1986	Walter A. McDougall, *. . . the Heavens and the Earth: A Political History of the Space Age*
1987	Bernard Bailyn, *Voyagers to the West: A Passage in the Peopling of America on the Eve of the Revolution*
1988	Robert V. Bruce, *The Launching of Modern American Science 1846–1876*
1989	Taylor Branch, *Parting the Waters: America in the King Years, 1954–63*
	James M. McPherson, *Battle Cry of Freedom: The Civil War Era*
1990	Stanley Karnow, *In Our Image: America's Empire in the Philippines*
1991	Laurel Thatcher Ulrich, *A Midwife's Tale: The Life of Martha Ballard, Based on Her Diary 1785–1812*
1992	Mark E. Neely, Jr., *The Fate of Liberty: Abraham Lincoln and Civil Liberties*
1993	Gordon S. Wood, *The Radicalism of the American Revolution*
1994	No award
1995	Doris Kearns Goodwin, *No Ordinary Time: Franklin and Eleanor Roosevelt: The Home Front in World War II*

THE PULITZER PRIZE FOR BIOGRAPHY OR AUTOBIOGRAPHY, 1917–95

Year	Author/Title
1917	Laura E. Richards and Maude Howe Elliott, with Florence Howe Hall, *Julia Ward Howe*
1918	William Cabell Bruce, *Benjamin Franklin, Self-Revealed*
1919	Henry Adams, *The Education of Henry Adams*
1920	Albert J. Beveridge, *The Life of John Marshall*
1921	Edward Bok, *The Americanization of Edward Bok*
1922	Hamlin Garland, *A Daughter of the Middle Border*
1923	Burton J. Hendrick, *The Life and Letters of Walter H. Page*
1924	Michael Idvorsky Pupin, *From Immigrant to Inventor*
1925	M.A. DeWolfe Howe, *Barrett Wendell and His Letter*
1926	Harvey Cushing, *The Life of Sir William Osler*
1927	Emory Holloway, *Whitman*
1928	Charles Edward Russell, *The American Orchestra and Theodore Thomas*
1929	Burton J. Hendrick, *The Training of an American: The Earlier Life and Letters of Walter H. Page*
1930	Marquis James, *The Raven*
1931	Henry James, *Charles W. Eliot*
1932	Henry F. Pringle, *Theodore Roosevelt*
1933	Allan Nevins, *Grover Cleveland*
1934	Tyler Dennett, *John Hay*
1935	Douglas S. Freeman, *R.E. Lee*
1936	Ralph Barton Perry, *The Thought and Character of William James*
1937	Allan Nevins, *Hamilton Fish*
1938	Odell Shepard, *Pedlar's Progress*
	Marquis James, *Andrew Jackson*
1939	Carl Van Doren, *Benjamin Franklin*
1940	Ray Stannard Baker, *Woodrow Wilson, Life and Letters,* vols. 7 & 8
1941	Ola Elizabeth Winslow, *Jonathan Edwards*
1942	Forrest Wilson, *Crusader in Crinoline*
1943	Samuel Eliot Morison, *Admiral of the Ocean Sea*
1944	Carleton Mabee, *The American Leonardo: The Life of Samuel F.B. Morse*
1945	Russell Blaine Nye, *George Bancroft: Brahmin Rebel*
1946	Linnie Marsh Wolfe, *Son of the Wilderness*
1947	William Allen White, *The Autobiography of William Allen White*
1948	Margaret Clapp, *Forgotten First Citizen: John Bigelow*
1949	Robert E. Sherwood, *Roosevelt and Hopkins*
1950	Samuel Flagg Bemis, *John Quincy Adams and the Foundations of American Foreign Policy*
1951	Margaret Louise Coit, *John C. Calhoun: American Portrait*
1952	Merlo J. Pusey, *Charles Evan Hughes*
1953	David J. Mays, *Edmund Pendleton 1721–1803*
1954	Charles A. Lindbergh, *The Spirit of St. Louis*
1955	William S. White, *The Taft Story*
1956	Talbot Faulkner Hamlin, *Benjamin Henry Latrobe*
1957	John F. Kennedy, *Profiles in Courage*
1958	Douglas Southall Freeman,[1] John Alexander Carroll, Mary Wells Ashworth, *George Washington,* vols. 1–4; and vol. 7, written after Dr. Freeman's death in 1953
1959	Arthur Walworth, *Woodrow Wilson, American Prophet*
1960	Samuel Eliot Morison, *John Paul Jones*
1961	David Donald, *Charles Sumner and the Coming of the Civil War*
1962	No award
1963	Leon Edel, *Henry James*
1964	Walter Jackson Bate, *John Keats*
1965	Ernest Samuels, *Henry Adams*
1966	Arthur M. Schlesinger, Jr., *A Thousand Days: JFK in the White House*
1967	Justin Kaplan, *Mr. Clemens and Mark Twain*
1968	George F. Kennan, *Memoirs*
1969	Benjamin Lawrence Reid, *The Man From New York: John Quinn and His Friends*
1970	T. Harry Williams, *Huey Long*
1971	Lawrance Thompson, *Robert Frost: The Years of Triumph, 1915–1938*
1972	Joseph P. Lash, *Eleanor and Franklin*
1973	W.A. Swanberg, *Luce and His Empire*
1974	Louis Sheaffer, *O'Neill, Son and Artist*
1975	Robert A. Caro, *The Power Broker: Robert Moses and the Fall of New York*
1976	R.W.B. Lewis, *Edith Wharton: A Biography*
1977	John E. Mack, *A Prince of Our Disorder: The Life of T.E. Lawrence*
1978	Walter Jackson Bate, *Samuel Johnson*
1979	Leonard Baker, *Days of Sorrow and Pain: Leo Baeck and the Berlin Jews*
1980	Edmund Morris, *The Rise of Theodore Roosevelt*
1981	Robert K. Massie, *Peter the Great: His Life and World*
1982	William S. McFeely, *Grant: A Biography*
1983	Russell Baker, *Growing Up*
1984	Louis R. Harlan, *Booker T. Washington: The Wizard of Tuskegee, 1901–1915*
1985	Kenneth Silverman, *The Life and Times of Cotton Mather*
1986	Elizabeth Frank, *Louise Bogan: A Portrait*
1987	David J. Garrow, *Bearing the Cross: Martin Luther King, Jr. and the Southern Christian Leadership Conference*
1988	David Herbert Donald, *Look Homeward: A Life of Thomas Wolfe*
1989	Richard Ellman,[1] *Oscar Wilde*
1990	Sebastian de Grazia, *Machiavelli in Hell*
1991	Steven Naifeh, Gregory White Smith, *Jackson Pollock: An American Saga*
1992	Lewis B. Puller, Jr., *Fortunate Son: The Healing of a Vietnam Vet*
1993	David McCullough, *Truman*
1994	David Levering Lewis, *W.E.B. Dubois: Biography of A Race, 1868–1919*
1995	Joan D. Hedrick, *Harriet Beecher Stowe: A Life*

1. Awarded posthumously.

THE PULITZER PRIZE FOR POETRY, 1922–95

Pulitzer Prizes in poetry were first awarded in 1922. The Poetry Society awarded prizes in 1918 to Sara Teasdale for *Love Songs,* and in 1919 to Margaret Widdemer for *Old Road to Paradise* and to Carl Sandburg for *Corn Huskers.*

Year	Author/Title
1922	Edward Arlington Robinson, *Collected Poems*
1923	Edna St. Vincent Millay, *The Ballad of the Harp—Weaver; A Few Figs from Thistles; Eight Sonnets in American Poetry, 1922, A Miscellany*
1924	Robert Frost, *New Hampshire: A Poem with Notes and Grace Notes*
1925	Edward Arlington Robinson, *The Man Who Died Twice*
1926	Amy Lowell, *What's O'Clock*
1927	Leonora Speyer, *Fiddler's Farewell*
1928	Edward Arlington Robinson, *Tristram*
1929	Stephen Vincent Benét, *John Brown's Body*
1930	Conrad Aiken, *Selected Poems*
1931	Robert Frost, *Collected Poems*
1932	George Dillon, *The Flowering Stone*
1933	Archibald MacLeish, *Conquistador*
1934	Robert Hillyer, *Collected Verse*
1935	Audrey Wurdemann, *Bright Ambush*
1936	Robert P. Tristram Coffin, *Strange Holiness*
1937	Robert Frost, *A Further Range*
1938	Marya Zaturenska, *Cold Morning Sky*
1939	John Gould Fletcher, *Selected Poems*
1940	Mark Van Doren, *Collected Poems*
1941	Leonard Bacon, *Sunderland Capture*

Year	Author/Title
1942	William Rose Benét, *The Dust Which Is God*
1943	Robert Frost, *A Witness Tree*
1944	Stephen Vincent Benét, *Western Star*
1945	Karl Shapiro, *V–Letter and Other Poems*
1946	No award
1947	Robert Lowell, *Lord Weary's Castle*
1948	W.H. Auden, *The Age of Anxiety*
1949	Peter Viereck, *Terror and Decorum*
1950	Gwendolyn Brooks, *Annie Allen*
1951	Carl Sandburg, *Complete Poems*
1952	Marianne Moore, *Collected Poems*
1953	Archibald MacLeish, *Collected Poems 1917–1952*
1954	Theodore Roethke, *The Waking*
1955	Wallace Stevens, *Collected Poems*
1956	Elizabeth Bishop, *Poems—North & South*
1957	Richard Wilbur, *Things of This World*
1958	Robert Penn Warren, *Promises: Poems 1954–1956*
1959	Stanley Kunitz, *Selected Poems 1928–1958*
1960	W.D. Snodgrass, *Heart's Needle*
1961	Phyllis McGinley, *Times Three: Selected Verse from Three Decades*
1962	Alan Dugan, *Poems*
1963	William Carlos Williams, *Pictures from Breughel*
1964	Louis Simpson, *At the End of the Open Road*
1965	John Berryman, *77 Dream Songs*
1966	Richard Eberhart, *Selected Poems*
1967	Anne Sexton, *Live or Die*
1968	Anthony Hecht, *The Hard Hours*
1969	George Oppen, *Of Being Numerous*
1970	Richard Howard, *Untitled Subjects*
1971	William S. Merwin, *The Carrier of Ladders*
1972	James Wright, *Collected Poems*
1973	Maxine Kumin, *Up Country*
1974	Robert Lowell, *The Dolphin*
1975	Gary Snyder, *Turtle Island*
1976	John Ashbery, *Self-Portrait in a Convex Mirror*
1977	James Merrill, *Divine Comedies*
1978	Howard Nemerov, *Collected Poems*
1979	Robert Penn Warren, *Now and Then*
1980	Donald Justice, *Selected Poems*
1981	James Schuyler, *The Morning of the Poem*
1982	Sylvia Plath,[1] *The Collected Poems*
1983	Galway Kinnell, *Selected Poems*
1984	Mary Oliver, *American Primitive*
1985	Carolyn Kizer, *Yin*
1986	Henry Taylor, *The Flying Change*
1987	Rita Dove, *Thomas and Beulah*
1988	William Meredith, *Partial Accounts: New and Selected Poems*
1989	Richard Wilbur, *New and Collected Poems*
1990	Charles Simic, *The World Doesn't End*
1991	Mona Van Duyn, *Near Changes*
1992	James Tate, *Selected Poems*
1993	Louise Glück, *The Wild Iris*
1994	Yusef Komunyakaa, *Neon Vernacular*
1995	Philip Levine, *Simple Truth*

THE PULITZER PRIZE FOR GENERAL NONFICTION, 1962–95

Year	Author/Title
1962	Theodore H. White, *The Making of the President 1960*
1963	Barbara W. Tuchman, *The Guns of August*
1964	Richard Hofstadter, *Anti-Intellectualism in American Life*
1965	Howard Mumford Jones, *O Strange New World*
1966	Edwin Way Teal, *Wandering Through Winter*
1967	David Brion Davis, *The Problem of Slavery in Western Culture*
1968	Will and Ariel Durant, *Rousseau and Revolution,* vol. 10 of the *Story of Civilization*
1969	René Jules Dubos, *So Human An Animal*
	Norman Mailer, *The Armies of the Night*
1970	Erik H. Erikson, *Gandhi's Truth*
1971	John Toland, *The Rising Sun*
1972	Barbara W. Tuchman, *Stilwell and the American Experience in China, 1911–1945*
1973	Robert Coles, *Children of Crisis,* vols. 2 & 3
	Frances Fitzgerald, *Fire in the Lake: The Vietnamese and the Americans in Vietnam*
1974	Ernest Becker, *The Denial of Death*
1975	Annie Dillard, *Pilgrim at Tinker Creek*
1976	Robert N. Butler, *Why Survive? Being Old in America*
1977	William N. Warner, *Beautiful Swimmers*
1978	Carl Sagan, *The Dragons of Eden*
1979	Edward O. Wilson, *On Human Nature*
1980	Douglas R. Hofstadter, *Gödel, Escher, Bach: An Eternal Golden Braid*
1981	Carl E. Schorske, *Fin-de-Siècle Vienna: Politics and Culture*
1982	Tracy Kidder, *The Soul of a New Machine*
1983	Susan Sheehan, *Is There No Place on Earth for Me?*
1984	Paul Starr, *The Social Transformation of American Medicine*
1985	Studs Terkel, *The Good War: An Oral History of World War Two*
1986	Joseph Lelyveld, *Move Your Shadow: South Africa, Black and White*
	J. Anthony Lukas, *Common Ground: A Turbulent Decade in the Lives of Three American Families*
1987	David K. Shipler, *Arab and Jew: Wounded Spirits in a Promised Land*
1988	Richard Rhodes, *The Making of the Atomic Bomb*
1989	Neil Sheehan, *A Bright Shining Lie: John Paul Vann and America in Vietnam*
1990	Dale Maharidge, Michael Williamson, *And Their Children After Them*
1991	Bert Holldobler, Edward O. Wilson, *The Ants*
1992	Daniel Yergin, *The Prize: The Epic Quest for Oil, Money and Power*
1993	Garry Wills, *Lincoln At Gettysburg: The Words That Remade America*
1994	David Remnick, *Lenin's Tomb: The Last Days of the Soviet Empire*
1995	Jonathan Weiner, *The Beak of the Finch: A Story of Evolution in Our Time*

THE PULITZER PRIZE FOR MUSIC, 1943–95

Year	Composer	Title
1943	William Schuman	Secular Cantata No. 2, *A Free Song*
1944	Howard Hanson	Symphony No. 4, Opus 34
1945	Aaron Copland	*Appalachian Spring*
1946	Leo Sowerby	*The Canticle of the Sun*
1947	Charles Ives	Symphony No. 3
1948	Walter Piston	Symphony No. 3
1949	Virgil Thomson	Music for the film *Louisiana Story*
1950	Gian Carlo Menotti	Music for *The Consul*
1951	Douglas S. Moore	Music for the opera *Giants in the Earth*
1952	Gail Kubik	*Symphony Concertante*
1953	No award	
1954	Quincy Porter	Concerto for Two Pianos and Orchestra
1955	Gian Carlo Menotti	*The Saint of Bleecker Street* (opera)
1956	Ernest Toch	Symphony No. 3
1957	Norman Dello Joio	*Meditations on Ecclesiastes*
1958	Samuel Barber	*Vanessa* (opera)
1959	John LaMontaine	Concerto for Piano and Orchestra
1960	Elliott Carter	Second String Quartet
1961	Walter Piston	Symphony No. 7
1962	Robert Ward	*The Crucible* (opera)
1963	Samuel Barber	Piano Concerto No. 1
1964	No award	
1965	No award	
1966	Leslie Bassett	Variations for Orchestra
1967	Leon Kirchner	Quartet No. 3
1968	George Crumb	*Echoes of Time and the River* (orchestral suite)
1969	Karel Husa	String Quartet No. 3
1970	Charles Wuorinen	*Time's Encomium*
1971	Mario Davidovsky	Synchronisms No. 6 for Piano and Electronic Sound
1972	Jacob Druckman	*Windows*
1973	Elliott Carter	String Quartet No. 3
1974	Donald Martino	*Notturno* (chamber music piece)
1975	Dominick Argento	*From the Diary of Virginia Woolf*
1976	Ned Rorem	*Air Music: Ten Etudes for Orchestra*
1977	Richard Wernick	*Visions of Terror and Wonder*
1978	Michael Colgrass	*Déjà Vu* for Percussion Quartet and Orchestra
1979	Joseph Schwantner	*Aftertones of Infinity*
1980	David Del Tredici	*In Memory of a Summer Day*
1981	No award	
1982	Roger Sessions	Concerto for Orchestra

Year	Composer	Title
1983	Ellen Taaffe Zwilich	Symphony No. 1
1984	Bernard Rands	"Canti del Sole" for Tenor and Orchestra
1985	Stephen Albert	Symphony *RiverRun*
1986	George Perle	Wind Quintet IV
1987	John Harbison	*The Flight into Egypt*
1988	William Bolcom	12 New Etudes for Piano
1989	Roger Reynolds	*Whispers Out of Time*
1990	Mel Powell	*Duplicates: A Concerto for Two Pianos and Orchestra*
1991	Shulamit Ran	*Symphony*
1992	Wayne Peterson	*The Face of the Night, the Heart of the Dark*
1993	Christopher Rouse	*Trombone Concerto*
1994	Gunther Schuller	*Of Reminiscences and Reflections*
1995	Morton Gould	*Stringmusic*

SPECIAL CITATIONS IN MUSIC

Year	Composer	Title
1974	Roger Sessions	Lifetime achievement
1976	Scott Joplin[1]	Contributions to American music
1982	Milton Babbitt	Lifetime achievement
1985	William Schuman	Lifetime achievement

1. Awarded posthumously. **Source:** Columbia University.

PULITZER SPECIAL CITATIONS IN LETTERS

Year	Author/Title
1944	Richard Rodgers and Oscar Hammerstein II, *Oklahoma!*
1957	Kenneth Roberts, for his historical novels
1960	Garret Mattingly, *The Armada*
1961	N.A., *The American Heritage Picture History of the Civil War*
1973	James Thomas Flexner, *George Washington*, vols. 1–4
1977	Alex Haley, *Roots*
1978	E.B. White, lifetime achievement
1984	Theodore Seuss Geisel. (Dr. Seuss), lifetime achievement
1992	Art Spiegelman, *Maus*

Note: N.A. = not applicable. **Source:** Columbia University.

THE NOBEL PRIZES

First awarded in 1901, the Nobel Prizes were established through a bequest of $9.2 million from Alfred Bernhard Nobel (1833–96), a Swedish chemical engineer and the inventor of dynamite and other explosives, and by a gift from the Bank of Sweden. Nobel's will directed that the interest from the fund be divided annually among people who have made significant discoveries or inventions in the fields of chemistry, physics, and physiology or medicine, as well as to that author who has "produced in the field of literature the most outstanding work of an idealistic tendency," and to that individual or group that has "done the most or the best work for fraternity between nations, for the abolition or reduction of standing armies and for the holding and promotion of peace congresses." In 1968, the 300th anniversary of the Bank of Sweden, an additional prize for outstanding work in the economic sciences was established; it was first granted the following year.

Today, all of the prizes are funded with the help of the Bank of Sweden. Final decisions are made for physics, chemistry, and economics by the Royal Swedish Academy of Sciences, Stockholm; for physiology or medicine by the Nobel Assembly at the Karolinska Institute, Stockholm; for literature by the Swedish Academy, Stockholm; and for peace by the Norwegian Nobel Committee, Oslo.

The prizes are formally awarded annually on December 10, the anniversary of Nobel's death, but are announced earlier in the fall. The peace prize is presented in Oslo and other awards are given in Stockholm, by the king of Sweden. The amount of each prize varies according to the interest from the fund. Each 1993 award was approximately $824,000, up from $489,000 in 1989 and $362,500 in 1987. Each prize includes a gold medal, a diploma, and a gift of money which is awarded at a formal ceremony. There were no prizes awarded from 1940 to 1942.

For a list of 1995 winners, See Part I: "The Year in Review."

NOBEL PEACE PRIZE RECIPIENTS

1901 Jean-Henri Dunant (Switzerland) Founder of International Committee of the Red Cross; **Frédéric Passy** (France) Founder of first French peace society.

1902 Elie Ducommun (Switzerland) Director of Permanent International Peace Bureau; **Charles A. Gobat** (Switzerland) Secretary-general of Inter-Parliamentary Union.

1903 Sir William R. Cremer (Great Britain) Founder of International Arbitration League.

1904 Institute of International Law Founded in 1873.

1905 Baroness Bertha S.F. von Suttner (Austria) Author of antiwar novel *Lay Down Your Arms.*

1906 Theodore Roosevelt (U.S.) President; mediated Russo-Japanese War.

1907 Ernesto T. Moneta (Italy) Founder of Lombard League of Peace; **Louis Renault** (France) Leading jurist at Hague Peace Conferences.

1908 Klas P. Arnoldson (Sweden) Founder of Swedish Peace and Arbitration League; **Fredrik Bajer** (Denmark) Writer and peace activist.

1909 Auguste M.F. Beernaert (Belgium) Prime minister and peace activist; **Paul H.B.B. D'Estournelles de Constant (Baron de Constant de Rebecque)** (France) Founder of French parliamentary group for voluntary arbitration.

1910 Permanent International Peace Bureau Founded 1891.

1911 Tobias M.C. Asser (Netherlands) A founder of Institute of International Law; **Alfred H. Fried** (Austria) Journalist and founder of many peace publications.

1912 Elihu Root (U.S.) Secretary of state and originator of several arbitration treaties.

1913 Henri Lafontaine (Belgium) President of Permanent International Peace Bureau in Bern.

1914–16 No award.

1917 International Committee of the Red Cross Founded 1863.

1918 No award.

1919 Thomas Woodrow Wilson (U.S.) President; instrumental in establishing League of Nations.

1920 Léon Victor A. Bourgeois (France) Drafted framework for League of Nations.

1921 Karl H. Branting (Sweden) Prime minister and pacifist; **Christian L. Lange** (Norway) A founder of Inter-Parliamentary Union.

1922 Fridtjof Nansen (Norway) Scientist, explorer, originator of "Nansen passports" for refugees.

1923–24 No award.

1925 Sir Austen Chamberlain (Great Britain) Foreign secretary; worked for Locarno Pact; **Charles G. Dawes** (U.S.) Vice president; drafted Dawes Plan settling German reparations issue.

1926 Aristide Briand (France) and **Gustav Stresemann** (Germany) Creators of Locarno Pact.

1927 Ferdinand Buisson (France) Human rights advocate; **Ludwig Quidde** (Germany) Lifelong peace activist.

1928 No award.

1929 Frank B. Kellogg (U.S.) Secretary of state; a creator of Kellogg-Briand Pact.

1930 L.O. Nathan Söderblom (Sweden) Archbishop; leader in the ecumenical movement.

1931 Jane Addams (U.S.) President of Women's International League for Peace and Freedom; **Nicholas M. Butler** (U.S.) Promoter of Kellogg-Briand Pact.

1932 No award.

1933 Sir Norman Angell (Ralph Lane) (Great Britain) Author of antiwar book *The Great Illusion.*

1934 Arthur Henderson (Great Britain) President of League of Nations World Disarmament Conference 1932.

1935 Carl von Ossietzky (Germany) Journalist and pacifist.

1936 Carlos Saavedra Lamas (Argentina) Secretary of state; president of League of Nations and mediator in a conflict between Paraguay and Bolivia.

1937 Lord Edgar Algernon R.G. Cecil (Great Britain) An architect of League of Nations.

1938 Nansen International Office for Refugees Founded 1921.

1939–43 No award.

1944 International Committee of the Red Cross Founded 1863.

1945 Cordell Hull (U.S.) Secretary of state; instrumental in creating UN.

1946 Emily G. Balch (U.S.) Leader of international women's movement for peace; **John R. Mott** (U.S.) Leader of Christian ecumenical movement.

1947 The Friends Service Council and **The American Friends Service Committee (The Quakers).**

1948 No award.

1949 Lord John Boyd Orr (Great Britain) Nutritionist; worked to eliminate world hunger.

1950 Ralph Bunche (U.S.) Mediator in Middle East war.

1951 Léon Jouhaux (France) Advocate of improved working-class conditions.

1952 Albert Schweitzer (France) Missionary surgeon and founder of Lambarene Hospital in Africa.

1953 George C. Marshall (U.S.) General; originator of Marshall Plan, which provided recovery loans and technical aid to European nations after World War II.

1954 Office of the United Nations High Commissioner for Refugees.

1955–56 No award.

1957 Lester B. Pearson (Canada) Secretary of state; worked to resolve Suez Canal Crisis of 1956.

1958 Georges Pire (Belgium) Dominican priest and leader of relief organization for refugees, l'Europe du Coeur au Service du Monde.

1959 Philip J. Noel-Baker (Great Britain) Lifelong worker for international peace through disarmament.

1960 Albert J. Luthuli (South Africa) President of the African National Congress; led peaceful resistance to apartheid.

1961 Dag Hammarskjöld (Sweden) Secretary-general of UN; worked for peace in the Congo.

1962 Linus C. Pauling (U.S.) Chemist; warned against dangers of radioactive fallout in nuclear weapons testing and war.

1963 International Committee of the Red Cross and **League of Red Cross Societies.**

1964 Martin Luther King, Jr. (U.S.) Leader of American civil rights movement.

1965 United Nations Children's Fund (UNICEF).

1966–67 No award.

1968 René Cassin (France) President of European Court for Human Rights.

1969 International Labour Organization UN agency involved in improving worldwide working and social conditions.

1970 Norman Borlaug (U.S.) Agricultural scientist and developer of high-yield grains credited with helping to alleviate world hunger.

1971 Willy Brandt (Federal Republic of Germany) Chancellor; champion of East-West détente.

1972 No award.

1973 Henry A. Kissinger (U.S.) Secretary of state and **Le Duc Tho** (Democratic Republic of Viet Nam) Foreign minister; negotiated Vietnam cease-fire agreement. Mr. Tho declined the prize.

1974 Seán MacBride (Ireland) President of International Peace Bureau and UN commissioner for Namibia; **Eisaku Sato** (Japan) Prime minister of Japan and campaigner against nuclear weapons.

1975 Andrei Sakharov (USSR) Nuclear physicist and human rights campaigner.

1976 Betty Williams and **Mairead Corrigan** (Northern Ireland) Founders of Northern Ireland Peace Movement.

1977 Amnesty International A human rights organization.

1978 Anwar el-Sadat (Egypt) President and **Menachem Begin** (Israel) Prime minister; negotiated Israeli-Egyptian peace accord.

1979 Mother Teresa (India) Worker for the poor in Calcutta.

1980 Adolfo Pérez Esquivel (Argentina) Architect, sculptor, and human rights leader.

1981 Office of the United Nations High Commissioner for Refugees.

1982 Alva Myrdal (Sweden) and **Alfonso García Robles** (Mexico) Campaigners for disarmament.

1983 Lech Walesa (Poland) Leader of the Solidarity trade union federation.

1984 Desmond M. Tutu (South Africa) Bishop of Johannesburg; a leader of the antiapartheid movement.

1985 International Physicians for the Prevention of Nuclear War Organization jointly headed by a Soviet and an American doctor.

1986 Elie Wiesel (U.S.) Writer on the Holocaust and Nazi death camp survivor.

1987 Oscar Arias Sánchez (Costa Rica) President of Costa Rica; creator of a peace plan for Central America.

1988 United Nations Peacekeeping Forces (see "The United Nations").

1989 Dalai Lama (Tibet) Exiled religious and political leader of Tibet for his nonviolent campaign to end China's domination of his country.

1990 Mikhail Gorbachev (USSR) President of the Soviet Union, "for his leading role in the peace process which today characterizes important parts of the international community."

1991 Aung San Suu Kyi (Myanmar) Leader of opposition to military regime, "for her nonviolent struggle for democracy and human rights."

1992 Rigoberta Menchú (Guatemala) A Quiché Indian who has been an outspoken advocate of human rights during the civil war in her country, "in recognition of her work for social justice . . . based on respect for the rights of indigenous peoples."

1993 Pres. F.W. de Klerk of South Africa and **Nelson Mandela,** black leader of the opposition African National Congress, for negotiating an end to the apartheid policies of the state and their collaboration on the formation of a democracy not based on race.

1994 Yitzhak Rabin (Israel) Prime minister, **Shimon Peres** (Israel) Foreign minister, and **Yasir Arafat,** leader of the Palestinian Liberation Organization, for their negotiation of the historic peace pact allowing Palestinian self-rule in the West Bank and Gaza Strip.

NOBEL PRIZES IN PHYSIOLOGY OR MEDICINE

1901 Emil A. von Behring (Germany) Marburg Univ. "for his work on serum therapy, especially its application against diphtheria, by which he has opened a new road in the domain of medical science and thereby placed in the hands of the physician a victorious weapon against illness and deaths."

1902 Sir Ronald Ross (Great Britain) University College "for his work on malaria, by which he has shown how it enters the organism and thereby has laid the foundation for successful research on this disease and methods of combating it."

1903 Niels R. Finsen (Denmark) Finsen Medical Light Institute "in recognition of his contribution to the treatment of diseases, especially lupus vulgaris, with concentrated light radiation, whereby he has opened a new avenue for medical science."

1904 Ivan P. Pavlov (Russia) Military Medical Academy "in recognition of his work on the physiology of digestion, through which knowledge on vital aspects of the subject has been transformed and enlarged."

1905 Robert Koch (Germany) Institute for Infectious Diseases "for his investigations and discoveries in relation to tuberculosis."

1906 Camillo Golgi (Italy) Pavia Univ., and **Santiago Ramon Y Cajal** (Spain) Madrid Univ. "in recognition of their work on the structure of the nervous system."

1907 Charles L.A. Laveran (France) Institut Pasteur "in recognition of his work on the role played by protozoa in causing diseases."

1908 Il'ja I. Mečnikov (Russia) Institut Pasteur (Paris), and **Paul Ehrlich** (Germany) Goettingen Univ. and Royal Institute for Experimental Therapy "in recognition of their work on immunity."

1909 Emil T. Kocher (Switzerland) Berne Univ. "for his work on the physiology, pathology, and surgery of the thyroid gland."

1910 Albrecht Kossel (Germany) Heidelberg Univ. "in recognition of the contributions to our knowledge of cell chemistry made through his work on proteins, including the nucleic substances."

1911 Allvar Gullstrand (Sweden) Uppsala Univ. "for his work on the dioptrics of the eye."

1912 Alexis Carrel (France) Rockefeller Institute for Medical Research (New York) "in recognition of his work on vascular suture and the transplantation of blood-vessels and organs."

1913 Charles R. Richet (France) Sorbonne Univ. "in recognition of his work on anaphylaxis."

1914 Robert Bárány (Austria) Vienna Univ. "for his work on the physiology and pathology of the vestibular apparatus."

1915–18 No awards.

1919 Jules Bordet (Belgium) Brussels Univ. "for his discoveries relating to immunity."

1920 Schack A.S. Krough (Denmark) Copenhagen Univ. "for his discovery of the capillary motor regulating mechanism."

1921 No award.

1922 Sir Archibald V. Hill (Great Britain) London Univ. "for his discovery relating to the production of heat in the muscle"; **Otto F. Meyerhof** (Germany) Kiel Univ. "for his discovery of the fixed relationship between the consumption of oxygen and the metabolism of lactic acid in the muscle."

1923 Sir Frederick B. Banting (Canada) Toronto Univ., and **John J.R. Macleod** (Canada) Toronto Univ. "for the discovery of insulin."

1924 Willem Einthoven (Netherlands) Leyden Univ. "for his discovery of the mechanism of the electrocardiogram."

1925 No award.

1926 Johannes A.G. Fibiger (Denmark) Copenhagen Univ. "for his discovery of the Spiroptera carcinoma."

1927 Julius Wagner-Jauregg (Austria) Vienna Univ. "for his discovery of the therapeutic value of malaria inoculation in the treatment of dementia paralytica."

1928 Charles J.H. Nicolle (France) Institut Pasteur "for his work on typhus."

1929 Christiaan Eijkman (Netherlands) Utrecht Univ. "for his discovery of the antineuritic vitamin"; **Sir Frederick G. Hopkins** (Great Britain) Cambridge Univ. "for his discovery of the growth-stimulating vitamins."

1930 Karl Landsteiner (Austria) Rockefeller Inst. for Medical Research (New York) "for his discovery of human blood groups."

1931 Otto H. Warburg (Germany) Kaiser-Wilhelm-Institut (now Max-Planck-Institut) "for his discovery of the nature and mode of action of the respiratory enzyme."

1932 Sir Charles S. Sherrington (Great Britain) Oxford Univ., and **Lord Edgar D. Adrian** (Great Britain) Cambridge Univ. "for their discoveries regarding the functions of neurons."

1933 Thomas H. Morgan (U.S.) California Institute of Technology "for his discoveries concerning the role played by the chromosome in heredity."

1934 George H. Whipple (U.S.) Rochester Univ., **George R. Minot** (U.S.) Harvard Univ., and **William P. Murphy** (U.S.) Harvard Univ. "for their discoveries concerning liver therapy in cases of anaemia."

1935 Hans Spemann (Germany) Univ. of Freiburg im Breisgau "for his discovery of the organizer effect in embryonic development."

1936 Sir Henry H. Dale (Great Britain) National Institute for Medical Research, and **Otto Loewi** (Austria) Graz Univ. "for their discoveries relating to chemical transmission of nerve impulses."

1937 Albert Szent-Györgyi von Nagyrapolt (Hungary) Szeged Univ. "for his discoveries in connection with the biological combustion processes, with special reference to vitamin C and the catalysis of fumaric acid."

1938 Corneille J.F. Heymans (Belgium) Ghent Univ. "for the discovery of the role played by the sinus and aortic mechanisms in the regulation of respiration."

1939 Gerhard Domagk (Germany) Munster Univ. "for the discovery of the antibacterial effects of prontosil."

1940–42 No award.

1943 Henrik C.P. Dam (Denmark) Polytechnic Institute "for his discovery of vitamin K"; **Edward A. Doisy** (U.S.) St. Louis Univ. "for his discovery of the chemical nature of vitamin K."

1944 Joseph Erlanger (U.S.) Washington Univ., and **Herbert S. Gasser** (U.S.) Rockefeller Institute for Medical Research "for their discoveries relating to the highly differentiated functions of single nerve fibres."

1945 Sir Alexander Fleming (Great Britain) London Univ., **Sir Ernst B. Chain** (Great Britain) Oxford Univ., and **Lord Howard W. Florey** (Great Britain) Oxford Univ. "for the discovery of penicillin and its curative effect in various infectious diseases."

1946 Hermann J. Muller (U.S.) Indiana Univ. "for the discovery of the production of mutations by means of X-ray irradiation."

1947 Carl F. Cori (U.S.) Washington Univ., and his wife **Gerty T. Cori** (U.S.) Washington Univ. "for their discovery of the course of the catalytic conversion of glycogen"; **Bernardo A. Houssay** (Argentina) Institute for Biology and Experimental Medicine "for his discovery of the part played by the hormone of the anterior pituitary lobe in the metabolism of sugar."

1948 Paul H. Müller (Switzerland) Laboratory of the J.R. Geigy Dye-Factory Co. "for his discovery of the high efficiency of DDT as a contact poison against several arthropods."

1949 Walter R. Hess (Switzerland) Zurich Univ. "for his discovery of the functional organization of the interbrain as a coordinator of the activities of the internal organs; **Antonio Caetano de Abreu F.E. Moniz** (Portugal) Univ. of Lisbon "for his discovery of the therapeutic value of leucotomy in certain psychoses."

1950 Edward C. Kendall (U.S.) Mayo Clinic, **Tadeus Reichstein** (Switzerland) Basel Univ., and **Philip S. Hench** (U.S.) Mayo Clinic "for their discoveries relating to the hormones of the adrenal cortex, their structure, and biological effects."

1951 Max Theiler (Union of South Africa) Laboratories Division of Medicine and Public Health, Rockefeller Foundation (New York) "for his discoveries concerning yellow fever and how to combat it."

1952 Selman A. Waksman (U.S.) Rutgers Univ. "for his discovery of streptomycin, the first antibiotic effective against tuberculosis."

1953 Sir Hans A. Krebs (Great Britain) Sheffield Univ. "for his discovery of the citric acid cycle"; **Fritz A. Lipmann** (U.S.) Harvard Medical School and Massachusetts General Hospital "for his discovery of co-enzyme A and its importance for intermediary metabolism."

1954 John F. Enders (U.S.) Harvard Medical School and Research Division of Infectious Diseases, Children's Medical Center; **Thomas H. Weller** (U.S.) Research Division of Infectious Diseases, Children's Medical Center; and **Frederick C. Robbins** (U.S.) Western Reserve Univ. "for their discovery of the ability of poliomyelitis viruses to grow in cultures of various types of tissue."

1955 Axel H.T. Theorell (Sweden) Nobel Medical Institute "for his discoveries concerning the nature and mode of action of oxidation enzymes."

1956 Andre F. Cournand (U.S.) Cardio-Pulmonary Laboratory, Columbia Univ. Division, Bellevue Hospital; **Werner Forssmann** (Germany) Mainz Univ. and Bad Kreuznach; and **Dickinson W. Richards** (U.S.) Columbia Univ. "for their discoveries concerning heart catheterization and pathological changes in the circulatory system."

1957 Daniel Bovet (Italy) Chief Institute of Public Health "for his discoveries relating to synthetic compounds that inhibit the action of certain body substances, and especially their action on the vascular system and the skeletal muscles."

1958 George W. Beadle (U.S.) California Institute of Technology, and **Edward L. Tatum** (U.S.) Rockefeller Institute for Medical Research "for their discovery that genes act by regulating definite chemical events"; **Joshua Lederberg** (U.S.) Wisconsin Univ. "for his discoveries concerning genetic recombination and the organization of the genetic material of bacteria."

1959 Severo Ochoa (U.S.) New York Univ., College of Medicine, and **Arthur Kornberg** (U.S.) Stanford Univ. "for their discovery of the mechanisms in the biological synthesis of ribonucleic acid and deoxyribonucleic acid."

1960 Sir Frank M. Burnet (Australia) Walter and Eliza Hall Institute for Medical Research, and **Sir Peter B. Medawar** (Great Britain) University College "for discovery of acquired immunological tolerance."

1961 Georg von Békésy (U.S.) Harvard Univ. "for his discoveries of the physical mechanism of stimulation within the cochlea."

1962 Francis H.C. Crick (Great Britain) Institute of Molecular Biology, **James D. Watson** (U.S.) Harvard Univ., and **Maurice H.F. Wilkins** (Great Britain) University of London "for their discoveries concerning the molecular structure of nuclear acids and its significance for information transfer in living material."

1963 Sir John C. Eccles (Australia) Australian National Univ., **Sir Alan L. Hodgkin** (Great Britain) Cambridge Univ., and **Sir Andrew F. Huxley** (Great Britain) University of London "for their discoveries concerning the ionic mechanisms involved in excitation and inhibition in the peripheral and central portions of the nerve cell membrane."

1964 Konrad Bloch (U.S.) Harvard Univ., and **Feodor Lynen** (Germany) Max-Planck-Institut fur Zellchemie "for their discoveries concerning the mechanism and regulation of the cholesterol and fatty acid metabolism."

1965 François Jacob (France) Institut Pasteur, **André Lwoff** (France) Institut Pasteur, and **Jacques Monod** (France) Institut Pasteur "for their discoveries concerning genetic control of enzyme and virus synthesis."

1966 Peyton Rous (U.S.) Rockefeller Univ. "for his discovery of tumor-inducing viruses"; **Charles B. Huggins** (U.S.) Ben May Laboratory for Cancer Research, Univ. of Chicago "for his discoveries concerning hormonal treatment of prostatic cancer."

1967 Ragnar Granit (Sweden) Karolinska Institutet, **Haldan K. Hartline** (U.S.) The Rockefeller Univ., and **George Wald** (U.S.) Harvard Univ. "for their discoveries concerning the primary physiological and chemical visual processes in the eye."

1968 Robert W. Holley (U.S.) Cornell Univ., **Har G. Khorana** (U.S.) Univ. of Wisconsin, and **Marshall W. Nirenberg** (U.S.) National Institutes of Health "for their interpretation of the genetic code and its functions in protein synthesis."

1969 Max Delbrück (U.S.) California Institute of Technology, **Alfred D. Hershey** (U.S.) Carnegie Institution of Washington, and **Salvador Luria** (U.S.) M.I.T. "for their discoveries concerning the replication mechanism and the genetic structure of viruses."

1970 Sir Bernard Katz (Great Britain) University College, **Ulf von Euler** (Sweden) Karolinska Institutet, and **Julius Axelrod** (U.S.) National Institutes of Health "for their discoveries concerning the humoral transmittors in the nerve terminals and the mechanism for their storage, release, and inactivation."

1971 Earl W. Sutherland, Jr. (U.S.) Vanderbilt Univ. "for his discoveries concerning the mechanisms of the action of hormones."

1972 Gerald M. Edelman (U.S.) Rockefeller Univ., and **Rodney R. Porter** (Great Britain) Oxford Univ. "for their discoveries concerning the chemical structure of antibodies."

1973 Karl von Frisch (W. Germany) Zoologisches Institut der Universitat Munchen; **Konrad Lorenz** (Austria) Osterreichische Aka demie der Wissenschaften, Institut fur vergleichende Verhaltensforschung; and **Nikolaas Tinbergen** (Great Britain) Dept. of Zoology, University Museum "for their discoveries concerning organization and elicitation of individual and social behavior patterns."

1974 Albert Claude (Belgium) Université Catholique de Louvain, **Christian de Duve** (Belgium) Rockefeller Univ. (New York), and **George E. Palade** (U.S.) Yale Univ. School of Medicine "for their discoveries concerning the structural and functional organization of the cell."

1975 David Baltimore (U.S.) M.I.T., **Renato Dulbecco** (U.S.) Imperial Cancer Research Fund Laboratory (London), and **Howard M. Temin** (U.S.) Univ. of Wisconsin "for their discoveries concerning the interaction between tumour viruses and the genetic material of the cell."

1976 Baruch S. Blumberg (U.S.) The Institute for Cancer Research, and **D. Carleton Gajdusek** (U.S.) National Institutes of Health "for their discoveries concerning new mechanisms for the origin and dissemination of infectious diseases."

1977 Roger Guillemin (U.S.) The Salk Institute, and **Andrew V. Schally** (U.S.) Veterans Administration Hospital, New Orleans "for their discoveries concerning the peptide hormone production of the brain"; **Rosalyn Yalow** (U.S.) Veterans Administration Hospital, Bronx "for the development of radioimmunoassays of peptide hormones."

1978 Werner Arber (Switzerland) Biozentrum der Universitat, **Daniel Nathans** (U.S.) Johns Hopkins Univ. School of Medicine, and **Hamilton O. Smith** (U.S.) Johns Hopkins Univ. School of Medicine "for the discovery of restriction enzymes and their application to problems of molecular genetics."

1979 Allan M. Cormack (U.S.) Tufts Univ., and **Sir Godfrey N. Hounsfield** (Great Britain) "for the development of computer-assisted tomography."

1980 Baruj Benacerraf (U.S.) Harvard Medical School; **Jean Dausset** (France) Université de Paris, Laboratoire Immuno-Hemetologie; and **George D. Snell** (U.S.) Jackson Laboratory "for their discoveries concerning genetically determined structures on the cell surface that regulate immunological reactions."

1981 Roger W. Sperry (U.S.) California Institute of Technology "for his discoveries concerning the functional specialization of the cerebral hemispheres"; **David H. Hubel** (U.S.) Harvard Medical School, and **Torsten N. Wiesel** (Sweden) Harvard Medical School "for their discoveries concerning information processing in the visual system."

1982 Sune K. Bergström (Sweden) Karolinska Institutet, **Bengt I. Samuelsson** (Sweden) Karolinska Institutet, and **Sir John R. Vane** (Great Britain) The Wellcome Research Laboratories "for their discoveries concerning prostaglandins and related biologically active substances."

1983 Barbara McClintock (U.S.) Cold Spring Harbor Laboratory "for her discovery of mobile genetic elements."

1984 Niels K. Jerne (Denmark) Basel Institute for Immunology (Basel, Switzerland), **Georges J.F. Köhler** (W. Germany) Basel Institute for Immunology, and **César Milstein** (Great Britain and Argentina) Medical Research Council Laboratory of Molecular Biology (Cambridge) "for theories concerning the specificity in development and control of the immune system and the discovery of the principle for production of monoclonal antibodies."

1985 Michael S. Brown (U.S.) Univ. of Texas Health Science Center at Dallas, and **Joseph L. Goldstein** (U.S.) Univ. of Texas Health Science Center at Dallas "for their discoveries concerning the regulation of cholesterol metabolism."

1986 Stanley Cohen (U.S.) Vanderbilt Univ. School of Medicine, and **Rita Levi-Montalcini** (Italy and U.S.) Institute of Cell Biology of the C.N.R. (Rome) "for their discoveries of growth factors."

1987 Susumu Tonegawa (U.S.) M.I.T. "for discovery of the genetic principle for generation of antibody diversity."

1988 Sir James W. Black (United Kingdom) King's College Hospital Medical School, **Gertrude B. Elion** (U.S.) Wellcome Research Laboratories, and **George H. Hitchings** (U.S.) Wellcome Research Laboratories "for their discoveries of Important Principles for Drug Treatment."

1989 J. Michael Bishop and **Harold E. Varmus** (U.S.) Univ. of California School of Medicine, San Francisco "for their discovery of 'The Cellular Origin of Retroviral Oncogenes.'"

1990 Joseph E. Murray (U.S.) Brigham and Women's Hospital, Boston, who performed the first kidney transplant (1954), and **E. Donnall Thomas** (U.S.), Fred Hutchinson Cancer Research Center, Seattle, who performed the first successful bone marrow transplant between two people who were not twins (1970).

1991 Erwin Neher (Germany) Max-Planck Institute for Biophysical Chemistry, Göttingen, and **Bert Sakmann** (Germany) Max-Planck Institute for Medical Research, Heidelberg, for developing a technique that allows detection of "incredibly small electrical currents that pass through an ion channel."

1992 Edmond H. Fischer (U.S.) and **Edwin G. Krebs** (U.S.), both of the Univ. of Washington, for a discovery in the 1950s of a regulatory mechanism in almost all human cells linked to some cancers, to the rejection of transplanted organs, and many other processes.

1993 Richard J. Roberts (UK) New England Bio Labs, and **Phillip A. Sharp** (U.S.) M.I.T., for their discovery in the 1970s that the composition of genes is of several segments, which led to gene splicing and to a better understanding of hereditary diseases and cancer.

1994 Alfred G. Gilbert (U.S.), Univ. of Texas Southwestern Medical Center, and **Martin Rodbell** (U.S.), National Institute of Environmental Health Sciences, for their discovery of natural substances known as G-proteins and for showing how they help cells respond to external stimuli like light and odors.

NOBEL PRIZES IN ECONOMIC SCIENCES

1969 Ragnar Frisch (Norway) Oslo Univ., and **Jan Tinbergen** (Netherlands) The Netherlands School of Economics "for having developed and applied dynamic models for the analysis of economic processes."

1970 Paul A. Samuelson (U.S.) M.I.T. "for the scientific work through which he has developed static and dynamic economic theory and actively contributed to raising the level of analysis in economic science."

1971 Simon Kuznets (U.S.) Harvard Univ. "for his empirically founded interpretation of economic growth which has led to new and deepened insight into the economic and social structure and process of development."

1972 Sir John R. Hicks (Great Britain) All Souls College, and **Kenneth J. Arrow** (U.S.) Harvard Univ. "for their pioneering contributions to general economic equilibrium theory and welfare theory."

1973 Wassily Leontief (U.S.) Harvard Univ. "for the development of the input-output method and for its application to important economic problems."

1974 Gunnar Myrdal (Sweden), **Friedrich A. von Hayek** (Great Britain) "for their pioneering work in the theory of money and economic fluctuations and for their penetrating analysis of the interdependence of economic, social and institutional phenomena."

1975 Leonid Kantorovich (USSR) Academy of Sciences, and **Tjalling C. Koopmans** (U.S.) Yale Univ. "for their contributions to the theory of optimum allocation of resources."

1976 Milton Friedman (U.S.) Univ. of Chicago "for his achievements in the fields of consumption analysis, monetary history and theory, and for his demonstration of the complexity of stabilization policy."

1977 Bertil Ohlin (Sweden) Stockholm School of Economics, and **James E. Meade** (Great Britain) Cambridge Univ. "for their pathbreaking contribution to the theory of international trade and international capital movements."

1978 Herbert A. Simon (U.S.) Carnegie-Mellon Univ. "for his pioneering research into the decision-making process within economic organizations."

1979 Theodore W. Schultz (U.S.) Univ. of Chicago, and **Sir Arthur Lewis** (Great Britain) Princeton Univ. "for their pioneering research into economic development research with particular consideration of the problems of developing countries."

1980 Lawrence R. Klein (U.S.) Univ. of Pennsylvania "for the creation of economic models and their application to the analysis of economic fluctuations and economic policies."

1981 James Tobin (U.S.) Yale Univ. "for his analysis of financial markets and their relations to expenditure decisions, employment, production, and prices."

1982 George J. Stigler (U.S.) Univ. of Chicago "for his seminal studies of industrial structures, functioning of markets, and causes and effects of public regulation."

1983 Gerard Debreu (U.S.) University of California, Berkeley, "for having incorporated new analytical methods into economic theory and for his rigorous reformulation of the theory of general equilibrium."

1984 Sir Richard Stone (Great Britain) Cambridge Univ. "for having made fundamental contributions to the development of systems of national accounts and hence greatly improved [*sic*] the basis for empirical economic analysis."

1985 Franco Modigliani (U.S.) M.I.T. "for his pioneering analyses of saving and of financial markets."

1986 James M. Buchanan, Jr. (U.S.) Center for Study of Public Choice "for his development of the contractual and constitutional bases for the theory of economic and political decision-making."

1987 Robert M. Solow (U.S.) M.I.T. "for his contributions to the theory of economic growth."

1988 Maurice Allais (France) Centre d'analyse économique "for his pioneering contributions to the theory of markets and efficient utilization of resources."

1989 Trygve Haavelmo (Norway) Univ. of Oslo "for his clarification of the probability theory foundations of econometrics and his analyses of simultaneous economic structures."

1990 Harry Markowitz (U.S.) Baruch College of City Univ. of New York, for his Portfolio Theory; **William F. Sharpe** (U.S.) Stanford Univ., for his Capital Asset Pricing Model; and **Merton Miller** (U.S.) Univ. of Chicago, for his work on the Miller-Modigliani Theory. Taken together, their work revolutionized the financial and business industries.

1991 Ronald H. Coase (Great Britain) Univ. of Chicago Law School, for his work on the role of firms in the economy, and the social cost of industry.

1992 Gary S. Becker (U.S.), Univ. of Chicago, for "having extended the domain of economic theory to aspects of human behavior . . ." including crime, family life, and racial bias. His book on education, *Human Capital* (1964), was cited by the Academy as his "most noteworthy contribution."

1993 Robert W. Fogel (U.S.), Univ. of Chicago, and **Douglass C. North** (U.S.), Washington Univ., both economic historians, for "applying economic theory and quarantine methods to historical puzzles." Fogel's work on slavery as an efficient economic system *(Time on the Cross)* caused great controversy.

1994 John F. Nash (U.S.) Princeton Univ., **John C. Harsanyi** (U.S., b. Hungary) Univ. of California, Berkeley, and **Reinhard Selten** (Germany) Univ. of Bonn, for their separate contributions to the field of game theory, which is used to predict how information and competition affect economic outcomes.

NOBEL PRIZES IN CHEMISTRY

1901 Jacobus H. Van't Hoff (Netherlands) Berlin Univ. (Germany) "in recognition of the extraordinary services he has rendered by the discovery of the laws of chemical dynamics and osmotic pressure in solutions."

1902 Hermann E. Fischer (Germany) Berlin Univ. "in recognition of the extraordinary services he has rendered by his work on sugar and purine syntheses."

1903 Svante A. Arrhenius (Sweden) Stockholm Univ. "in recognition of the extraordinary services he has rendered to the advancement of chemistry by his electrolytic theory of dissociation."

1904 Sir William Ramsay (Great Britain) London Univ. "in recognition of his services in the discovery of the inert gaseous elements in air, and his determination of their place in the periodic system."

1905 Johann F.W.A. von Baeyer (Germany) Munich Univ. "in recognition of his services in the advancement of organic chemistry and the chemical industry, through his work on organic dyes and hydroaromatic compounds."

1906 Henri Moissan (France) Sorbonne Univ. "in recognition of the great services rendered by him in his investigation and isolation of the element fluorine, and for the adoption in the service of science of the electric furnace called after him."

1907 Eduard Buchner (Germany) Agricultural College "for his biochemical researches and his discovery of cell-free fermentation."

1908 Lord Ernest Rutherford (Great Britain) Victoria Univ. "for his investigations into the disintegration of the elements, and the chemistry of radioactive substances."

1909 Wilhelm Ostwald (Germany) Leipzig Univ. "in recognition of his work on catalysis, and for his investigations into the fundamental principles governing chemical equilibria and rates of reaction."

1910 Otto Wallach (Germany) Goettingen Univ. "in recognition of his services to organic chemistry and the chemical industry by his pioneer work in the field of alicyclic compounds."

1911 Marie Curie (France) Sorbonne Univ. "in recognition of her services to the advancement of chemistry by the discovery of the elements radium and polonium, by the isolation of radium and the study of the nature and compounds of this remarkable element."

1912 Victor Grignard (France) Nancy Univ. "for the discovery of the so-called Grignard reagent, which in recent years has greatly advanced the progress of organic chemistry"; **Paul Sabatier** (France) Toulouse Univ. "for his method of hydrogenating organic compounds in the presence of finely disintegrated metals whereby the proress of organic chemistry has been greatly advanced in recent years."

1913 Alfred Werner (Switzerland) Zurich Univ. "in recognition of his work on the linkage of atoms in molecules by which he has thrown new light on earlier investigations and opened up new fields of research especially in inorganic chemistry."

1914 Theodore W. Richards (U.S.) Harvard Univ. "in recognition of his accurate determinations of the atomic weight of a large number of chemical elements."

1915 Richard M. Willstätter (Germany) Munich Univ. "for his researches on plant pigments, especially chlorophyll."

1916–17 No award.

1918 Fritz Haber (Germany) Kaiser-Wilhelm-Institut (now Fritz-Haber-Institut) "for the synthesis of ammonia from its elements."

1919 No award.

1920 Walther H. Nernst (Germany) Berlin Univ. "in recognition of his work in thermochemistry."

1921 Frederick Soddy (Great Britain) Oxford Univ. "for his contributions to our knowledge of the chemistry of radioactive substances, and his investigations into the origin and nature of isotopes."

1922 Francis W. Aston (Great Britain) Cambridge Univ. "for his discovery, by means of his mass spectrograph, of isotopes in a large number of nonradioactive elements, and for his enunciation of the whole-number rule."

1923 Fritz Pregl (Austria) Graz Univ. "for his invention of the method of microanalysis of organic substances."

1924 No award.

1925 Richard A. Zsigmondy (Germany) Goettingen Univ. "for his demonstration of the heterogeneous nature of colloid solutions and for the methods he used, which have since become fundamental in modern colloid chemistry."

1926 The (Theodor) Svedberg (Sweden) Uppsala Univ. "for his work on disperse systems."

1927 Heinrich O. Wieland (Germany) Munich Univ. "for his investigations of the constitution of the bile acids and related substances."

1928 Adolf O.R. Windaus (Germany) Goettingen Univ. "for the services rendered through his research into the constitution of the sterols and their connection with the vitamins."

1929 Sir Arthur Harden (Great Britain) London Univ., **Hans K.A. von Euler-Chelpin** (Sweden) Stockholm Univ. "for their investigations on the fermentation of sugar and fermentative enzymes."

1930 Hans Fischer (Germany) Institute of Technology "for his researches into the constitution of haemin and chlorophyll, and especially for his synthesis of haemin."

1931 Carl Bosch (Germany) Heidelberg Univ. and I.G. Farbenindustrie A.G., and **Friedrich Bergius** (Germany) Heidelberg Univ. and I.G. Farbenindustrie A.G. "in recognition of their contributions to the invention and development of chemical high pressure methods."

1932 Irving Langmuir (U.S.) General Electric Co. "for his discoveries and investigations in surface chemistry."

1933 No award.

1934 Harold C. Urey (U.S.) Columbia Univ. "for his discovery of heavy hydrogen."

1935 Frédéric Joliot (France) Institut du Radium, and his wife **Irène Joliot-Curie** (France) Institut du Radium "in recognition of their synthesis of new radioactive elements."

1936 Petrus (Peter) J.W. Debye (Netherlands) Berlin Univ. and Kaiser-Wilhelm-Institut (now Max-Planck-Institut) für Physik (Berlin-Dahlem) "for his contributions to our knowledge of molecular structure through his investigations on dipole moments and on the diffraction of X-rays and electrons in gases."

1937 Sir Walter N. Haworth (Great Britain) Birmingham Univ. "for his investigations on carbohydrates and vitamin C"; **Paul Karrer** (Switzerland) Zurich Univ. "for his investigations on carotenoids, flavins, and vitamins A and B-2."

1938 Richard Kuhn (Germany) Heidelberg Univ. and Kaiser-Wilhelm-Institut (now Max-Planck-Institut) für Medizinische Forschung "for his work on carotenoids and vitamins." (Compelled by the authorities of his country to decline the award, but later received the diploma and the medal.)

1939 Adolf F.J. Butenandt (Germany) Berlin Univ. and Kaiser-Wilhelm-Institut (now Max-Planck-Institut) für Biochemie "for his work on sex hormones." (Compelled by the authorities of his country to decline the award, but later received the diploma and the medal); **Leopold Ruzicka** (Switzerland) Federal Institute of Technology "for his work on polymethylenes and higher terpenes."

1940–42 No award.

1943 George de Hevesy (Hungary) Stockholm Univ. (Sweden) "for his work on the use of isotopes as tracers in the study of chemical processes."

1944 Otto Hahn (Germany) Kaiser-Wilhelm-Institut (now Max-Planck-Institut) für Chemie "for his discovery of the fission of heavy nuclei."

1945 Artturi I. Virtanen (Finland) Helsinki Univ. "for his research and inventions in agricultural and nutrition chemistry, especially for his fodder preservation method."

1946 James B. Sumner (U.S.) Cornell Univ. "for his discovery that enzymes can be crystallized"; **John H. Northrop** (U.S.) Rockefeller Institute for Medical Research, and **Wendell M. Stanley** (U.S.) Rockefeller Institute for Medical Research "for their preparation of enzymes and virus proteins in a pure form."

1947 Sir Robert Robinson (Great Britain) Oxford Univ. "for his investigations on plant products of biological importance, especially the alkaloids."

1948 Arne W.K. Tiselius (Sweden) Uppsala Univ. "for his research on electrophoresis and adsorption analysis, especially for his discoveries concerning the complex nature of the serum proteins."

1949 William F. Giauque (U.S.) Univ. of California, Berkeley, "for his contributions in the field of chemical thermodynamics, particularly concerning the behavior of substances at extremely low temperatures."

1950 Otto P.H. Diels (Germany) Kiel Univ., and **Kurt Alder** (Germany) Cologne Univ. "for their discovery and development of the diene synthesis."

1951 Edwin M. McMillan (U.S.) Univ. of California, Berkeley, and **Glenn T. Seaborg** (U.S.) Univ. of California, Berkeley, "for their discoveries in the chemistry of the transuranium elements."

1952 Archer J.P. Martin (Great Britain) National Institute for Medical Research, and **Richard L.M. Synge** (Great Britain) Rowett Research Institute (Scotland) "for their invention of partition chromatography."

1953 Hermann Staudinger (Germany) State Research Institute for Macromolecular Chemistry "for his discoveries in the field of macromolecular chemistry."

1954 Linus C. Pauling (U.S.) California Institute of Technology "for his research into the nature of the chemical bond and its application to the elucidation of the structure of complex substances."

1955 Vincent du Vigneaud (U.S.) Cornell Univ. "for his work on biochemically important sulphur compounds, especially for the first synthesis of a polypeptide hormone."

1956 Sir Cyril N. Hinshelwood (Great Britain) Oxford Univ., and **Nikolaj N. Semenov** (USSR) Institute for Chemical Physics of the Academy of Sciences of the USSR "for their researches into the mechanism of chemical reactions."

1957 Lord Alexander R. Todd (Great Britain) Cambridge Univ. "for his work on nucleotides and nucleotide co-enzymes."

1958 Frederick Sanger (Great Britain) Cambridge Univ. "for his work on the structure of proteins, especially that of insulin."

1959 Jaroslav Heyrovsky (Czechoslovakia) Polaro-Institute of the Czechoslovak Academy of Science "for his discovery and development of the polarographic methods of analysis."

1960 Willard F. Libby (U.S.) Univ. of California, Los Angeles "for his method to use carbon-14 for age determination in archaeology, geology, geophysics, and other branches of science."

1961 Melvin Calvin (U.S.) Univ. of California, Berkeley, "for his research on the carbon dioxide assimilation in plants."

1962 Max F. Perutz (Great Britain) Laboratory of Molecular Biology, and **Sir John C. Kendrew** (Great Britain) Laboratory of Molecular Biology "for their studies of the structures of globular proteins."

1963 Karl Ziegler (Germany) Max-Planck-Institut for Carbon Research, and **Giulio Natta** (Italy) Institute of Technology "for their discoveries in the field of the chemistry and technology of high polymers."

1964 Dorothy C. Hodgkin (Great Britain) Royal Society, Oxford Univ. "for her determinations by X-ray techniques of the structures of important biochemical substances."

1965 Robert B. Woodward (U.S.) Harvard Univ. "for his outstanding achievements in the art of organic synthesis."

1966 Robert S. Mulliken (U.S.) Univ. of Chicago "for his fundamental work concerning chemical bonds and the electronic structure of molecules by the molecular orbital method."

1967 Manfred Eigen (W. Germany) Max-Planck Institut für Physikalische Chemie, **Ronald G.W. Norrish** (Great Britain) Institute of Physical Chemistry, and **Sir George Porter** (Great Britain) The Royal Institution "for their studies of extremely fast chemical reactions, effected by disturbing the equilibrium by means of very short pulses of energy."

1968 Lars Onsager (U.S.) Yale Univ. "for the discovery of the reciprocal relations bearing his name, which are fundamental for the thermodynamics of irreversible processes."

1969 Sir Derek H.R. Barton (Great Britain) Imperial College of Science and Technology, and **Odd Hassel** (Norway) Kjemisk Institut "for their contributions to the development of the concept of conformation and its application in chemistry."

1970 Luis F. Leloir (Argentina) Institute for Biochemical Research "for his discovery of sugar nucleotides and their role in the biosynthesis of carbohydrates."

1971 Gerhard Herzberg (Canada) National Research Council of Canada "for his contributions to the knowledge of electronic structure and geometry of molecules, particularly free radicals."

1972 Christian B. Anfinsen (U.S.) National Institutes of Health "for his work on ribonuclease, especially concerning the connection between the amino acid sequence and the biologically active conformation"; **Stanford Moore** (U.S.) Rockefeller Univ., and **William H. Stein** (U.S.) Rockefeller Univ. "for their contribution to the understanding of the connection between chemical structure and catalytic activity of the active center of the ribonuclease molecule."

1973 Ernst O. Fischer (W. Germany) Technical Univ. of Munich, and **Sir Geoffrey Wilkinson** (Great Britain) Imperial College "for their pioneering work, performed independently, on the chemistry of the organometallic, so-called sandwich compounds."

1974 Paul J. Flory (U.S.) Stanford Univ. "for his fundamental achievements, both theoretical and experimental, in the physical chemistry of the macromolecules."

1975 Sir John W. Cornforth (Australia and Great Britain) Univ. of Sussex "for his work on the stereochemistry of enzyme-catalyzed reactions"; **Vladimir Prelog** (Switzerland) Eidgenossische Technische Hochschule "for his research into the stereochemistry of organic molecules and reactions."

1976 William N. Lipscomb (U.S.) Harvard Univ. "for his studies on the structure of boranes illuminating problems of chemical bonding."

1977 Ilya Prigogine (Belgium) Université Libre de Bruxelles, (Univ. of Texas, U.S.) "for his contributions to nonequilibrium thermodynamics, particularly the theory of dissipative structures."

1978 Peter D. Mitchell (Great Britain) Glynn Research Laboratories "for his contribution to the understanding of biological energy transfer through the formulation of the chemiosmotic theory."

1979 Herbert C. Brown (U.S.) Purdue Univ., and **Georg Wittig** (Germany) Univ. of Heidelberg "for their development of the use of boron- and phosphorus-containing compounds, respectively, into important reagents in organic synthesis."

1980 Paul Berg (U.S.) Stanford Univ. "for his fundamental studies of the biochemistry of nucleic acids, with particular regard to recombinant-DNA"; **Walter Gilbert** (U.S.) Biological Laboratories, and **Frederick Sanger** (Great Britain) MRC Laboratory of Molecular Biology "for their contributions concerning the determination of base sequences in nucleic acids."

1981 Kenichi Fukui (Japan) Kyoto Univ., and **Roald Hoffmann** (U.S.) Cornell Univ. "for their theories, developed independently, concerning the course of chemical reactions."

1982 Aaron Klug (Great Britain) MRC Laboratory of Molecular Biology "for his development of crystallographic electron microscopy and his structural elucidation of biologically important nucleic acid-protein complexes."

1983 Henry Taube (U.S.) Stanford Univ. "for his work on the mechanisms of electron transfer reactions, especially in metal complexes."

1984 Robert B. Merrifield (U.S.) Rockefeller Univ. "for his development of methodology for chemical synthesis on a solid matrix."

1985 Herbert A. Hauptman (U.S.) The Medical Foundation of Buffalo, and **Jerome Karle** (U.S.) U.S. Naval Research Laboratory "for their outstanding achievements in the development of direct methods for the determination of crystal structures."

1986 Dudley R. Herschbach (U.S.) Harvard Univ., **Yuan T. Lee** (U.S.) Univ. of California, Berkeley, and **John C. Polanyi** (Canada) Univ. of Toronto "for their contributions concerning the dynamics of chemical elementary processes."

1987 Donald J. Cram (U.S.) Univ. of California, Los Angeles, **Jean-Marie Lehn** (France) Université Louis Pasteur, and **Charles J. Pedersen** (U.S.) Du Pont Laboratory "for their development and use of molecules with structure-specific interactions of high selectivity."

1988 Johann Deisenhofer (U.S.) Howard Hughes Medical Institute, **Robert Huber** (W. Germany) Max-Planck-Institut für Biochemie, and **Hartmut Michel** (W. Germany) Max-Planck-Institut für Biophysik "for the determination of the three-dimensional structure of a photosynthetic reaction centre."

1989 Sidney Altman (U.S.) Yale Univ., and **Thomas Cech** (U.S.) Univ. of Colorado "for their discovery of the catalytic properties of RNA." (They worked independently.)

1990 Elias James Coret (U.S.) Harvard Univ., for developing new ways to synthesize complex molecules ordinarily found in nature, work that has contributed to "the high standard of living and health, and the longevity enjoyed at least in the Western world."

1991 Richard R. Ernst (Switzerland) Eidgenössische Technische Hochschule, Zurich, for his work in refining nuclear magnetic resonance spectroscopy for use in chemical analysis.

1992 Rudolph A. Marcus (U.S., b. Canada) Cal Tech, for his mathematical explanation of chemical interactions involving the transfer of electrons between molecules.

1993 Kary B. Mullis (U.S.) who worked for Cetus Corp. in the 1970s when he discovered the polymerase chain reaction (PCR) that allowed scientists to make trillions of copies of DNA from very small amounts. His method has been used in the study of plant and animal fossils and in criminal investigations. **Michael Smith** (Canada) Univ. of British Columbia, for developing the technique that alters the code of genetic molecules that will facilitate new medical therapies and plants that resist disease.

1994 George A. Olah (U.S., b. Hungary) Univ. of Southern California, for his discovery of new ways of breaking apart and rebuilding carbon and hydrogen compounds. He opened a wholly new field of hydrocarbon research, leading to improved fuels based on coal, methane, and petroleum.

NOBEL PRIZES IN PHYSICS

1901 Wilhelm C. Röntgen (Germany) Munich Univ. "in recognition of the extraordinary services he has rendered by the discovery of the remarkable rays subsequently named after him."

1902 Hendrik A. Lorentz (Netherlands) Leyden Univ., and **Pieter Zeeman** (Netherlands) Amsterdam Univ. "in recognition of the extraordinary service they rendered by their researches into the influence of magnetism upon radiation phenomena."

1903 Antoine H. Becquerel (France) Ecole Polytechnique "in recognition of the extraordinary services he has rendered by his discovery of spontaneous radioactivity"; **Pierre Curie** (French) Municipal School of Industrial Physics and Chemistry, and his wife **Marie Curie** (France [born in Poland]) "in recognition of the extraordinary services they have rendered by their joint researches on the radiation phenomena discovered by Professor Henri Becquerel."

1904 Lord Rayleigh (John W. Strutt) (Great Britain) Royal Institution of Great Britain "for his investigations of the densities of the most important gases and for his discovery of argon in connection with these studies."

1905 Philipp E.A. Lenard (Germany) Kiel Univ. "for his work on cathode rays."

1906 Sir Joseph J. Thomson (Great Britain) Cambridge Univ. "in recognition of the great merits of his theoretical and experimental investigations on the conduction of electricity by gases."

1907 Albert A. Michelson (U.S.) Univ. of Chicago "for his optical precision instruments and the spectroscopic and metrological investigations carried out with their aid."

1908 Gabriel Lippmann (France) Sorbonne Univ. "for his method of reproducing colours photographically based on the phenomenon of interference."

1909 Guglielmo Marconi (Italy) Marconi Wireless Telegraph Co., Ltd., and **Carl F. Braun** (Germany) Strasbourg Univ. "in recognition of their contributions to the development of wireless telegraphy."

1910 Johannes D. van der Waals (Netherlands) Amsterdam Univ. "for his work on the equation of state for gases and liquids."

1911 Wilhelm Wien (Germany) Würzburg Univ. "for his discoveries regarding the laws governing the radiation of heat."

1912 Nils G. Dalén (Sweden) Swedish Gas-Accumulator Co. "for his invention of automatic regulators for use in conjunction with gas accumulators for illuminating lighthouses and buoys."

1913 Heike Kamerlingh-Onnes (Netherlands) Leyden Univ. "for his investigations on the properties of matter at low temperatures which led, inter alia, to the production of liquid helium."

1914 Max von Laue (Germany) Frankfurt-am-Main Univ. "for his discovery of the diffraction of X-rays by crystals."

1915 Sir William Henry Bragg (Great Britain) London Univ., and his son **Sir William Lawrence Bragg** (Great Britain) Victoria Univ. "for their services in the analysis of crystal structure by means of X-rays."

1916 No award.

1917 Charles G. Barkla (Great Britain) Edinburgh Univ. "for his discovery of the characteristic Röntgen radiation of the elements."

1918 Max K.E.L. Planck (Germany) Berlin Univ. "in recognition of the services he rendered to the advancement of Physics by his discovery of energy quanta."

1919 Johannes Stark (Germany) Greifswald Univ. "for his discovery of the Doppler effect in canal rays and the splitting of spectral lines in electric fields."

1920 Charles E. Guillaume (Switzerland) International Bureau of Weights and Measures "in recognition of the service he has rendered to precision measurements in physics by his discovery of anomalies in nickel steel alloys."

1921 Albert Einstein (Germany) Kaiser-Wilhelm-Institut für Physik (now Max-Planck-Institut) "for his services to theoretical physics, and especially for his discovery of the law of the photoelectric effect."

1922 Niels Bohr (Denmark) Copenhagen Univ. "for his services in the investigation of the structure of atoms and of the radiation emanating from them."

1923 Robert A. Millikan (U.S.) California Institute of Technology "for his work on the elementary charge of electricity and on the photoelectric effect."

1924 Karl M.G. Siegbahn (Sweden) Uppsala Univ. "for his discoveries and research in the field of X-ray spectroscopy."

1925 James Franck (Germany) Goettingen Univ., and **Gustav Hertz** (Germany) Halle Univ. "for their discovery of the laws of governing the impact of an electron upon an atom."

1926 Jean B. Perrin (France) Sorbonne Univ. "for his work on the discontinuous structure of matter, and especially for his discovery of sedimentation equilibrium."

1927 Arthur H. Compton (U.S.) Univ. of Chicago "for his discovery of the effect named after him"; **Charles T.R. Wilson** (Great Britain) Cambridge Univ. "for his method of making the paths of electrically charged particles visible by condensation of vapour."

1928 Sir Owen W. Richardson (Great Britain) London Univ. "for his work on the thermionic phenomenon and especially for the discovery of the law named after him."

1929 Prince Louis-Victor de Broglie (France) Sorbonne Univ. "for his discovery of the wave nature of electrons."

1930 Sir Chandrasekhara V. Raman (India) Calcutta Univ. "for his work on the scattering of light and for the discovery of the effect named after him."

1931 No award.

1932 Werner Heisenberg (Germany) Leipzig Univ. "for the creation of quantum mechanics, the application of which, has, inter alia, led to the discovery of the allotropic forms of hydrogen."

1933 Erwin Schrödinger (Austria) Berlin Univ., and **Paul A.M. Dirac** (Great Britain) Cambridge Univ. "for the discovery of new productive forms of atomic theory."

1934 No award.

1935 Sir James Chadwick (Great Britain) Liverpool Univ. "for his discovery of the neutron."

1936 Victor F. Hess (Austria) Innsbruck Univ. "for his discovery of cosmic radiation"; **Carl D. Anderson** (U.S.) California Institute of Technology "for his discovery of the positron."

1937 Clinton J. Davisson (U.S.) Bell Telephone Laboratories, and **Sir George P. Thomson** (Great Britain) London Univ. "for their experimental discovery of the diffraction of electrons by crystals."

1938 Enrico Fermi (Italy) Rome Univ. "for his demonstrations of the existence of new radioactive elements produced by neutron irradiation, and for his related discovery of nuclear reactions brought about by slow neutrons."

1939 Ernest O. Lawrence (U.S.) Univ. of California, Berkeley, "for the invention and development of the cyclotron and for results obtained with it, especially with regard to artificial radioactive elements."

1940–42 No award.

1943 Otto Stern (U.S.) Carnegie Institute of Technology (now Carnegie Mellon Univ.) "for his contribution to the development of the molecular ray method and his discovery of the magnetic moment of the proton."

1944 Isidor I. Rabi (U.S.) Columbia Univ. "for his resonance method for recording the magnetic properties of atomic nuclei."

1945 Wolfgang Pauli (Austria) Princeton Univ. "for the discovery of the Exclusion Principle, also called the Pauli Principle."

1946 Percy W. Bridgman (U.S.) Harvard Univ. "for the invention of an apparatus to produce extremely high pressures, and for the discoveries he made therewith in the field of high-pressure physics."

1947 Sir Edward V. Appleton (Great Britain) Dept. of Scientific and Industrial Research "for his investigations of the physics of the upper atmosphere, especially for the discovery of the so-called Appleton layer."

1948 Lord Patrick M.S. Blackett (Great Britain) Victoria Univ. "for his development of the Wilson cloud chamber method, and his discoveries therewith in the fields of nuclear physics and cosmic radiation."

1949 Hideki Yukawa (Japan) Kyoto Imperial Univ. and Columbia Univ. "for his prediction of the existence of mesons on the basis of theoretical work on nuclear forces."

1950 Cecil F. Powell (Great Britain) Bristol Univ. "for his development of the photographic method of studying nuclear processes and his discoveries regarding mesons made with this method."

1951 Sir John D. Cockcroft (Great Britain) Atomic Energy Research Establishment, and **Ernest T.S. Walton** (Ireland) Dublin Univ. "for their pioneer work on the transmutation of atomic nuclei by artifically accelerated atomic particles."

1952 Felix Block (U.S.) Stanford Univ., and **Edward M. Purcell** (U.S.) Harvard Univ. "for their development of new methods for nuclear magnetic precision measurements and discoveries in connection therewith."

1953 Frits (Frederik) Zernike (Netherlands) Groningen Univ. "for his demonstration of the phase contrast method, especially for his invention of the phase contrast microscope."

1954 Max Born (Great Britain) Edinburgh Univ. "for his fundamental research in quantum mechanics, especially for his statistical interpretation of the wave-function"; **Walther Bothe** (Germany) Heidelberg Univ., Max-Planck-Institut "for the coincidence method and his discoveries made therewith."

1955 Willis E. Lamb (U.S.) Stanford Univ. "for his discoveries concerning the fine structure of the hydrogen spectrum"; **Polykarp Kusch** (U.S.) Columbia Univ. "for his precision determination of the magnetic moment of the electron."

1956 William Shockley (U.S.) Semiconductor Laboratory of Beckman Instruments, Inc., **John Bardeen** (U.S.) Univ. of Illinois, and **Walter H. Brattain** (U.S.) Bell Telephone Laboratories "for their researches on semiconductors and their discovery of the transistor effect."

1957 Chen N. Yang (China) Institute for Advanced Study (Princeton, N.J.), and **Tsung-Dao Lee** (China) Columbia Univ. "for their penetrating investigation of the so-called parity laws which has led to important discoveries regarding the elementary particles."

1958 Pavel A. Cherenkov (USSR) Physics Institute of USSR Academy of Sciences, **Il'ja M. Frank** (USSR) Univ. of Moscow and Physics Institute of USSR Academy of Sciences, and **Igor J. Tamm** (USSR) Univ. of Moscow and Physics Institute of USSR Academy of Sciences "for the discovery and the interpretation of the Cherenkov effect."

1959 Emilio G. Segrè (U.S.) Univ. of California, Berkeley, and **Owen Chamberlain** (U.S.) Univ. of California, Berkeley, "for their discovery of the antiproton."

1960 Donald A. Glaser (U.S.) Univ. of California, Berkeley, "for the invention of the bubble chamber."

1961 Robert Hofstadter (U.S.) Stanford Univ. "for his pioneering studies of electron scattering in atomic nuclei and for his thereby achieved discoveries concerning the structure of the nucleons"; **Rudolf L. Mössbauer** (Germany) Technische Hochschule (Munich), and California Institute of Technology "for his researches concerning the resonance absorption of gamma radiation and his discovery in this connection of the effect which bears his name."

1962 Lev D. Landau (USSR) Academy of Sciences "for his pioneering theories for condensed matter, especially liquid helium."

1963 Eugene P. Wigner (U.S.) Princeton Univ. "for his contributions to the theory of the atomic nucleus and the elementary particles, particularly through the discovery and application of fundamental symmetry principles"; **Maria Goeppert-Mayer** (U.S.) Univ. of California, La Jolla, and **J. Hans D. Jensen** (Germany) Univ. of Heidelberg "for their discoveries concerning nuclear shell structure."

1964 Charles H. Townes (U.S.) M.I.T., **Nikolai G. Basov** (USSR) Lebedev Institute for Physics, and **Aleksandre M. Prochorov** (USSR) Lebedev Institute for Physics "for fundamental work in the field of quantum electronics, which has led to the construction of oscillators and amplifiers based on the maser-laser-principle."

1965 Schin'ichiro Tomonaga (Japan) Tokyo Univ. of Education, **Julian Schwinger** (U.S.) Harvard Univ., and **Richard Feynman** (U.S.) California Institute of Technology "for their fundamental work in quantum electrodynamics, with deep-ploughing consequences for the physics of elementary particles."

1966 Alfred Kastler (France) Ecole Normale Supérieure, Université de Paris "for the discovery and development of optical methods for studying hertzian resonances in atoms."

1967 Hans A. Bethe (U.S.) Cornell Univ. "for his contributions to the theory of nuclear reactions, especially his discoveries concerning the energy production in stars."

1968 Luis W. Alvarez (U.S.) Univ. of California, Berkeley, "for his decisive contributions to elementary particle physics, in particular the discovery of a large number of resonance states, made possible through his development of the technique of using hydrogen bubble chamber and data analysis."

1969 Murray Gell-Mann (U.S.) California Institute of Technology "for his contributions and discoveries concerning the classification of elementary particles and their interactions."

1970 Hannes Alfvén (Sweden) Royal Institute of Technology "for fundamental work and discoveries in magneto-hydrodynamics with fruitful applications in different parts of plasma physics"; **Louis Neel** (France) Univ. of Grenoble "for fundamental work and discoveries concerning antiferromagnetism and ferrimagnetism which have led to important applications in solid-state physics."

1971 Dennis Gabor (Great Britain) Imperial College of Science and Technology "for his invention and development of the holographic method."

1972 John Bardeen (U.S.) Univ. of Illinois, **Leon N. Cooper** (U.S.) Brown Univ., and **Robert J. Schrieffer** (U.S.) Univ. of Pennsylvania "for their jointly developed theory of superconductivity, usually called the BCS-theory."

1973 Leo Esaki (Japan) IBM Thomas J. Watson Research Center (Yorktown Heights, N.Y.), and **Ivar Giaever** (U.S.) General Electric Co. "for their experimental discoveries regarding tunneling phenomena in semiconductors and superconductors, respectively"; **Brian D. Josephson** (Great Britain) Cambridge Univ. "for his theoretical predictions of the properties of a supercurrent through a tunnel barrier, in particular those phenomena which are generally known as the Josephson effects."

1974 Sir Martin Ryle (Great Britain) Cambridge Univ., and **Antony Hewish** (Great Britain) Cambridge Univ. "for their pioneering research in radio astrophysics: Ryle for his observations and inventions, in particular of the aperture synthesis technique, and Hewish for his decisive role in the discovery of pulsars."

1975 Aage Bohr (Denmark) Niels Bohr Institute, **Ben Mottelson** (Denmark) Nordita, and **James Rainwater** (U.S.) Columbia Univ. "for the discovery of the connection between collective motion and particle motion in atomic nuclei and the development of the theory of the structure of the atomic nucleus based on this connection."

1976 Burton Richter (U.S.) Stanford Linear Accelerator Center, and **Samuel C.C. Ting** (U.S.) M.I.T. "for their pioneering work in the discovery of a heavy elementary particle of a new kind."

1977 Philip W. Anderson (U.S.) Bell Laboratories, **Sir Nevill F. Mott** (Great Britain) Cambridge Univ., and **John H. van Vleck** (U.S.) Harvard Univ. "for their fundamental theoretical investigations of the electronic structure of magnetic and disordered systems."

1978 Peter L. Kapitsa (USSR) Academy of Sciences "for his basic inventions and discoveries in the area of low-temperature physics; **Arno A. Penzias** (U.S.) Bell Laboratories, and **Robert W. Wilson** (U.S.) Bell Laboratories "for their discovery of cosmic microwave background radiation."

1979 Sheldon L. Glashow (U.S.) Lyman Laboratory, Harvard Univ., **Abdus Salam** (Pakistan) International Centre for Theoretical Physics (Trieste) and Imperial College of Science and Technology (London), and **Steven Weinberg** (U.S.) Harvard Univ. "for their contributions to the theory of the unified weak and electromagnetic interaction between elementary particles, including, inter alia, the prediction of the weak neutral current."

1980 James W. Cronin (U.S.) Univ. of Chicago, and **Val L. Fitch** (U.S.) Princeton Univ. "for the discovery of violations of fundamental symmetry principles in the decay of neutral K-mesons."

1981 Nicolaas Bloembergen (U.S.) Harvard Univ., and **Arthur L. Schawlow** (U.S.) Stanford Univ. "for their contributions to the development of laser spectroscopy"; **Kai M. Siegbahn** (Sweden) Uppsala Univ. "for his contribution to the development of high-resolution electron spectroscopy."

1982 Kenneth G. Wilson (U.S.) Cornell Univ. "for his theory for critical phenomena in connection with phase transitions."

1983 Subrahmanyan Chandrasekhar (U.S.) Univ. of Chicago "for his theoretical studies of the physical processes of importance to the structure and evolution of the stars"; **William A. Fowler** (U.S.) California Institute of Technology "for his theoretical and experimental studies of the nuclear reactions of importance in the formation of the chemical elements in the universe."

1984 Carlo Rubbia (Italy) CERN, Geneva, and **Simon van der Meer** (Netherlands) CERN, Geneva "for their decisive contributions to the large project, which led to the discovery of the field particles W and Z, communicators of weak interaction."

1985 Klaus von Klitzing (W. Germany) Max-Planck-Institut for Solid State Research "for the discovery of the quantized Hall effect."

1986 Ernst Ruska (W. Germany) Fritz-Haber-Institut der Max-Planck-Gesellschaft "for his fundamental work in electron optics, and for the design of the first electron microscope"; **Gerd Binnig** (W. Germany) IBM Zurich Research Laboratory, and **Heinrich Rohrer** (Switzerland) IBM Zurich Research Laboratory "for their design of the scanning tunneling microscope."

1987 Georg J. Bednorz (Switzerland) IBM Zurich Research Laboratory, and **Dr. K. Alex Müller** (Switzerland) IBM Zurich Research Laboratory "for the discovery of new superconducting materials."

1988 Leon M. Lederman (U.S.) Fermi National Accelerator Laboratory, **Melvin Schwartz** (U.S.) Digital Pathways, Inc., and **Jack Steinberger** (Switzerland) CERN "for the neutrino beam method and the demonstration of the doublet structure of the leptons through the discovery of the muon neutrino."

1989 Norman F. Ramsey (U.S.) Harvard Univ. "for the invention of the separated oscillatory fields method and its use in . . . atomic clocks." **Hans G. Dehmelt** (U.S.) Univ. of Washington, and **Wolfgang Paul**, Univ. of Bonn (W. Germany) "for the development of the ion trap technique," which allows detailed study of subatomic particles.

1990 Richard E. Taylor (Canada) Stanford Univ., **Jerome I. Friedman** (U.S.) M.I.T., and **Henry W. Kendall** (U.S.) M.I.T., whose experiments between 1967 and 1973 confirmed the existence of quarks, the fundamental building blocks of matter.

1991 Pierre-Gilles de Gennes (France) Collège de France, Paris, for his discoveries about the ordering of molecules in a variety of substances but especially liquid crystals, where his work has helped in understanding superconductivity.

1992 George Charpak (France, b. Poland) affiliated with CERN, the accelerator complex, where he developed electronic detectors that traced the paths of subatomic particles with lightning speed.

1993 Joseph H. Taylor (U.S.) Princeton Univ., and **Russell A. Hulse** (U.S.) Princeton Plasma Physics Laboratory, for their 1970s discovery of a binary pulsar and their subsequent success in measuring its pulse rate.

1994 Clifford G. Shull (U.S.) M.I.T., and **Bertram N. Brockhouse** (Canada) McMaster Univ., for their experiments in the 1940s and '50s that exploited the penetrating power of low-energy neutron beams produced by nuclear reactors. Neutron beams are much more powerful than X-rays or other forms of radiation, and are now widely used by scientists to explore the atomic structure of matter.

NOBEL PRIZES FOR LITERATURE

1901 Sully Prudhomme (pen name of René F.A. Prudhomme) (France) "in special recognition of his poetic composition, which gives evidence of lofty idealism, artistic perfection, and a rare combination of the qualities of both heart and intellect."

1902 Christian M.T. Mommsen (Germany) "the greatest living master of the art of historical writing, with special reference to his monumental work, *A History of Rome*."

1903 Bjørnstjerne M. Bjørnson (Norway) "as a tribute to his noble, magnificent, and versatile poetry, which has always been distinguished by both the freshness of its inspiration and the rare purity of its spirit."

1904 Frederic Mistral (France) "in recognition of the fresh orginality and true inspiration of his poetic production, which faithfully reflects the natural scenery and native spirit of his people, and, in addition, his significant work as a Provencal philologist"; **José Echegaray y Eizaguirre** (Spain) "in recognition of the numerous and brilliant compositions which, in an individual and original manner, have revived the great traditions of the Spanish drama."

1905 Henryk Sienkiewicz (Poland) "because of his outstanding merits as an epic writer."

1906 Giosuè Carducci (Italy) "not only in consideration of his deep learning and critical research, but above all as a tribute to the creative energy, freshness of style, and lyrical force which characterize his poetic masterpieces."

1907 Rudyard Kipling (Great Britain) "in consideration of the power of observation, originality of imagination, virility of ideas, and remarkable talent for narration which characterize the creations of this world-famous author."

1908 Rudolf C. Eucken (Germany) "in recognition of his earnest search for truth, his penetrating power of thought, his wide range of vision, and the warmth and strength in presentation with which in his numerous works he has vindicated and developed an idealistic philosophy of life."

1909 Selma O.L. Lagerlöf (Sweden) "in appreciation of the lofty idealism, vivid imagination, and spiritual perception that characterize her writings."

1910 Paul J.L. Heyse (Germany) "as a tribute to the consummate artistry, permeated with idealism, which he has demonstrated during his long productive career as lyric poet, dramatist, novelist, and writer of world-renowned short stories."

1911 Count Maurice (Mooris) P.M.B. Maeterlinck (Belgium) "in appreciation of his many-sided literary activities, and especially of his dramatic works, which are distinguished by a wealth of imagination and by a poetic fancy."

1912 Gerhart J.R. Hauptmann (Germany) "primarily in recognition of his fruitful, varied, and outstanding production in the realm of dramatic art."

1913 Rabindranath Tagore (India) "because of his profoundly sensitive, fresh, and beautiful verse, by which, with consummate skill, he has made his poetic thought, expressed in his own English words, a part of the literature of the West."

1914 No award.

1915 Romain Rolland (France) "as a tribute to the lofty idealism of his literary production and to the sympathy and love of truth with which he has described different types of human beings."

1916 Carl G.V. von Heidenstam (Sweden) "in recognition of his significance as the leading representative of a new era in our literature."

1917 Karl A. Gjellerup (Denmark) "for his varied and rich poetry, which is inspired by lofty ideals"; **Henrik Pontoppidan** (Denmark) "for his authentic descriptions of presentday life in Denmark."

1918 No award.

1919 Carl F.G. Spitteler (Switzerland) "in special appreciation of his epic, *Olympian Spring*."

1920 Knut P. Hamsun (Norway) "for his monumental work, *Growth of the Soil*."

1921 Anatole France (pen name of Jacques A. Thibault) (France) "in recognition of his brilliant literary achievements, characterized as they are by a nobility of style, a profound human sympathy, grace, and a true Gallic temperament."

1922 Jacinto Benavente (Spain) "for the happy manner in which he has continued the illustrious traditions of the Spanish drama."

1923 William B. Yeats (Ireland) "for his always inspired poetry, which in a highly artistic form gives expression to the spirit of a whole nation."

1924 Wladyslaw S. Reymont (pen name of Reyment) (Poland) "for his great national epic, *The Peasants*."

1925 George B. Shaw (Great Britain) "for his work which is marked by both idealism and humanity, its stimulating satire often being infused with a singular poetic beauty."

1926 Grazia Deledda (pen name of Grazia Madesani) (Italy) "for her idealistically inspired writings which with plastic clarity picture the life on her native island and with depth and sympathy deal with human problems in general."

1927 Henri Bergson (France) "in recognition of his rich and vitalizing ideas and the brilliant skill with which they have been presented."

1928 Sigrid Undset (Norway) "principally for her powerful descriptions of Northern life during the Middle Ages."

1929 Thomas Mann (Germany) "principally for his great novel *Buddenbrooks*, which has won steadily increased recognition as one of the classic works of contemporary literature."

1930 Sinclair Lewis (U.S.) "for his vigorous and graphic art of description and his ability to create, with wit and humour, new types of characters."

1931 Erik A. Karlfeldt (Sweden) "the poetry of Erik Axel Karlfeldt."

1932 John Galsworthy (Great Britain) "for his distinguished art of narration which takes its highest form in *The Forsythe Saga*."

1933 Ivan A. Bunin (stateless domicile in France) "for the strict artistry with which he has carried on the classical Russian traditions in prose writing."

1934 Luigi Pirandello (Italy) "for his bold and ingenious revival of dramatic and scenic art."

1935 No award.

1936 Eugene G. O'Neill (U.S.) "for the power, honesty, and deep-felt emotions of his dramatic works, which embody an original concept of tragedy."

1937 Roger Martin du Gard (France) "for the artistic power and truth with which he has depicted human conflict as well as some fundamental aspects of contemporary life in his novel-cycle *Les Thibault*."

1938 Pearl Buck (pen name of Pearl Walsh) (U.S.) "for her rich and truly epic descriptions of peasant life in China and for her biographical masterpieces."

1939 Frans E. Sillanpää (Finland) "for his deep understanding of his country's peasantry and the exquisite art with which he has portrayed their way of life and their relationship with Nature."

1940–43 No award.

1944 Johannes V. Jensen (Denmark) "for the rare strength and fertility of his poetic imagination with which is combined an intellectual curiosity of wide scope and bold, freshly creative style."

1945 Gabriela Mistral (pen name of Lucila Godoy y Alcayaga) (Chile) "for her lyric poetry which, inspired by powerful emotions, has made her name a symbol of the idealistic aspirations of the entire Latin American world."

1946 Hermann Hesse (Switzerland) "for his inspired writings which, while growing in boldness and penetration, exemplify the classical humanitarian ideals and high qualities of style."

1947 André P.G. Gide (France) "for his comprehensive and artistically significant writings, in which human problems and conditions have been presented with a fearless love of truth and keen psychological insight."

1948 Thomas S. Eliot (Great Britain) "for his outstanding, pioneer contribution to present-day poetry."

1949 William Faulkner (U.S.) "for his powerful and artistically unique contribution to the modern American novel."

1950 Earl (Bertrand) Russell (Great Britain) "in recognition of his varied and significant writings in which he champions humanitarian ideals and freedom of thought."

1951 Pär F. Lägerkvist (Sweden) "for the artistic vigour and true independence of mind with which he endeavours in his poetry to find answers to the eternal questions confronting mankind."

1952 François Mauriac (France) "for the deep spiritual insight and the artistic intensity with which he has in his novels penetrated the drama of human life."

1953 Sir Winston L.P. Churchill (Great Britain) "for his mastery of historical and biographical description as well as for brilliant oratory in defending exalted human values."

1954 Ernest M. Hemingway (U.S.) "for his mastery of the art of narrative, most recently demonstrated in *The Old Man and the Sea*, and for the influence that he has exerted on contemporary style."

1955 Halldór K. Laxness (Iceland) "for his vivid epic power which has renewed the great narrative art of Iceland."

1956 Juan R. Jiménez (Spain [domicile in Puerto Rico]) "for his lyrical poetry, which in Spanish language constitutes an example of high spirit and artistical purity."

1957 Albert Camus (France) "for his important literary production, which with clearsighted earnestness illuminates the problems of the human conscience in our times."

1958 Boris L. Pasternak (USSR) "for his important achievement both in contemporary lyrical poetry and in the field of the great Russian epic tradition." (Declined the prize.)

1959 Salvatore Quasimodo (Italy) "for his lyrical poetry, which with classical fire expresses the tragic experience of life in our own times."

1960 Saint-John Perse (pen name of Alexis Léger) (France) "for the soaring flight and the evocative imagery of his poetry which in a visionary fashion reflects the conditions of our time."

1961 Ivo Andrić (Yugoslavia) "for the epic force with which he has traced themes and depicted human destinies drawn from the history of his country."

1962 John Steinbeck (U.S.) "for his realistic and imaginative writings, combining as they do sympathetic humour and keen social perception."

1963 Giorgos Seferis (pen name of Giorgos Seferiades) (Greece) "for his eminent lyrical writing, inspired by a deep feeling for the Hellenic world of culture."

1964 Jean-Paul Sartre (France) "for his work which, rich in ideas and filled with the spirit of freedom and the quest for truth, has exerted a far-reaching influence on our age." (Declined the prize.)

1965 Michail A. Solochov (USSR) "for the artistic power and integrity with which, in his epic of the Don, he has given expression to a historic phase in the life of the Russian people."

1966 Shmuel Y. Agnon (Israel) "for his profoundly characteristic narrative art with motifs from the life of the Jewish people; **Nelly Sachs** (Germany [domiciled in Sweden]) "for her outstanding lyrical and dramatic writing, which interprets Israel's destiny with touching strength."

1967 Miguel A. Asturias (Guatemala) "for his vivid literary achievement, deep-rooted in the national traits and traditions of Indian peoples of Latin America."

1968 Yasunari Kawabata (Japan) "for his narrative mastery, which with great sensibility expresses the essence of the Japanese mind."

1969 Samuel Beckett (Ireland) "for his writing, which—in new forms for the novel and drama—in the destitution of modern man acquires its elevation."

1970 Alexandr Solzhjenitsyn (USSR) "for the ethical force with which he has pursued the indispensable traditions of Russian literature."

1971 Pablo Neruda (Chile) "for a poetry that with the action of an elemental force brings alive a continent's destiny and dreams."

1972 Heinrich Böll (W. Germany) "for his writing which through its combination of a broad perspective on his time and a sensitive skill in characterization has contributed to a renewal of German literature."

1973 Patrick White (Australia) "for an epic and psychological narrative art which has introduced a new continent into literature."

1974 Eyvind Johnson (Sweden) "for a narrative art, far-seeing in lands and ages, in the service of freedom"; **Harry Martinson** (Sweden) "for writings that catch the dewdrop and reflect the cosmos."

1975 Eugenio Montale (Italy) "for his distinctive poetry which, with great artistic sensitivity, has interpreted human values under the sign of an outlook on life with no illusions."

1976 Saul Bellow (U.S.) "for the human understanding and subtle analysis of contemporary culture that are combined in his work."

1977 Vicente Aleixandre (Spain) "for a creative poetic writing which illuminates man's condition in the cosmos and in present-day society, at the same time representing the great renewal of the traditions of Spanish poetry between the wars."

1978 Isaac B. Singer (U.S.) "for his impassioned narrative art which, with roots in a Polish-Jewish cultural tradition, brings universal human conditions to life."

1979 Odysseus Elytis (pen name of Odysseus Alepoudhelis) (Greece) "for his poetry, which against the background of Greek tradition, depicts with sensuous strength and intellectual clear-sightedness modern man's struggle for freedom and creativeness."

1980 Czeslaw Milosz (U.S. and Poland) "who with uncompromising clear-sightedness voices man's exposed condition in a world of severe conflicts."

1981 Elias Canetti (Great Britain) "for writings marked by a broad outlook, a wealth of ideas, and artistic power."

1982 Gabriel García Marquez (Colombia) "for his novels and short stories, in which the fantastic and the realistic are combined in a richly composed world of imagination, reflecting a continent's life and conflicts."

1983 William Golding (Great Britain) "for his novels which, with the perspicuity of realistic narrative art and the diversity and universality of myth, illuminate the human condition in the world of today."

1984 Jaroslav Seifert (Czechoslovakia) "for his poetry which, endowed with freshness, sensuality, and rich inventiveness, provides a liberating image of the indomitable spirit and versatility of man."

1985 Claude Simon (France) "who in his novel combines the poet's and the painter's creativeness with a deepened awareness of time in the depiction of the human condition."

1986 Wole Soyinka (Nigeria) "who in a wide cultural perspective and with poetic overtones fashions the drama of existence."

1987 Joseph Brodsky (U.S.) "for his all-embracing authorship imbued with clarity of thought and poetic intensity."

1988 Naguib Mahfouz (Egypt) "who, through works rich in nuance—now clear-sightedly realistic, now evocatively ambiguous—has formed an Arabian narrative art that applies to all mankind."

1989 Camilo José Cela (Spain) a novelist whose "rich and inventive prose, which . . . forms a challenging vision of man's vulnerability." His most famous work is *The Family of Pascual Duarte* (1942).

1990 Octavio Paz (Mexico) poet and social essayist. Volumes include *The Labyrinth of Solitude* (1950), *Sunstone* (1957), and *Sor Juana: Or, the Traps of Faith* (1990).

1991 Nadine Gordimer (South Africa) for her "involvement on behalf of literature and free speech in a police state where censorship and persecution of books and people exist." Novels include *A Guest of Honour, Burger's Daughter,* and *My Son's Story.*

1992 Derek Walcott (West Indies, b. St. Lucia) poet and playwright whose works evoke the cultural diversity of the Carribean "but through them he speaks to each and every one of us." His recent book-length poem, *Omeros,* won worldwide acclaim.

1993 Toni Morrison (U.S.) whose novels about racial prejudice are "characterized by visionary force and poetic import." Her novels include *Sula, Tar Baby, Song of Solomon,* and the Pulitzer Prize–winning *Beloved.*

1994 Kenzaburo Oe (Japan) best known for his accounts of the atomic bombing of Hiroshima and for a novel in which he comes to grips with a mentally handicapped son. The poetic force of his writing "creates an imagined world where life and myth condense to form a disconcerting picture of the human predicament."

For a list of 1995 Nobel Prize winners, see Part I: "The Year in Review."

SCIENCE AWARDS

The National Medal of Science is the highest science award given by the United States government. Since 1962, it has been presented by the president for achievement in physical, biological, mathematical, engineering, behavioral, or social science.

The medal itself is intended to symbolize science. It shows a human being, surrounded by earth, sea, and sky, contemplating and seeking to understand nature. The scientist holds a crystal in one hand, intended to symbolize the universal order and also the basic unit of living things. With the other hand the scientist is sketching a formula in the sand.

The nominees are selected by a presidential committee of 12 members acting with the president's science adviser and the president of the National Academy of Sciences. The medals are not awarded every year.

NATIONAL MEDAL OF SCIENCE AWARDS, 1962–94

Year	Winner, Field, Affiliation
1962	Theodore von Karman, Aeronautics, Cal Tech
1963	Luis Walter Alvarez, Physics, Univ. of California, Berkeley
	Vannevar Bush, Electronics, Carnegie Institute
	John Robinson Pierce, Communications, Bell Labs
	Cornelius B. van Niel, Microbiology, Stanford Univ.
	Norbert Wiener, Mathematics, M.I.T.
1964	Roger Adams, Chemistry, Univ. of Illinois
	Othmar H. Ammann, Engineering, Ammann & Whitney
	Theodosius Dobzhansky, Medicine, Rockefeller Univ.
	Charles Stark Draper, Astronautics, M.I.T.
	Solomon Lefschetz, Mathematics, Princeton Univ.
	Neal Elgar Miller, Psychology, Yale Univ.
	Harold Marston Morse, Mathematics, Institute for Advanced Studies
	Marshall W. Nirenberg, Genetics, National Institutes of Health
	Julian Schwinger, Physics, Harvard Univ.
	Harold C. Urey, Chemistry, Univ. of California, Berkeley
	Robert B. Woodward, Chemistry, Harvard Univ.
1965	John Bardeen, Electronics, Univ. of Illinois
	Peter J.W. Debye, Chemistry, Cornell Univ.
	Hugh L. Dryden, Administration, NASA
	Clarence L. Johnson, Aeronautics, Lockheed
	Leon M. Lederman, Physics, Columbia Univ.
	Warren K. Lewis, Chemical eng., M.I.T.
	Francis Peyton Rous, Medicine, Rockefeller Univ.
	William W. Rubey, Geophysics, UCLA
	George. G. Simpson, Paleontology, Harvard Univ.
	Donald Van Slyke, Chemistry, Brookhaven National Lab
	Oscar Zariski, Mathematics, Harvard Univ.
1966	Jacob Bjerknes, Meteorology, UCLA
	S. Chandrasekhar, Astrophysics, Univ. of Chicago
	Henry Eyring, Administration, Univ. of Utah
	E.F. Knipling, Entomology, U.S. Dept. of Agriculture
	Fritz A. Lipmann, Biochemistry, Rockefeller Univ.
	John W. Minor, Mathematics, Princeton Univ.
	William C. Rose, Chemistry, Univ. of Illinois
	Claude E. Shannon, Science history, M.I.T.
	J.H. Van Vleck, Physics, Harvard Univ.
	Sewall Wright, Genetics, Univ. of Wisconsin
	Vladimir Zworykin, Physics, RCA
1967	J.W. Beams, Physics, Univ. of Virginia
	A. Francis Birch, Geology, Harvard Univ.
	Gregory Breit, Physics, Yale Univ.
	Paul J. Cohen, Mathematics, Stanford Univ.
	Kenneth S. Cole, Biophysics, National Institutes of Health
	Louis P. Hammett, Chemistry, Columbia Univ.
	Harry F. Harlow, Psychology, Univ. of Wisconsin
	Michael Heidelberger, Immunology, New York Univ.
	G.S. Kistiakowsky, Chemistry, Harvard Univ.
	Edwin H. Land, Photography, Polaroid Corporation
	Igor I. Sikorsky, Aeronautics, United Aircraft
	Alfred H. Sturtevant, Biology, Cal Tech
1968	Horace A. Barker, Biochemistry, Univ. of California, Berkeley
	Paul D. Bartlett, Chemistry, Harvard Univ.
	Bernard B. Brodie, Pharmacology, National Institutes of Health
	Detlev W. Bronk, Medicine, Rockefeller Univ.
	J. Presper Eckert, Computer science, Sperry-Rand Corporation
	Herbert Friedman, Astrophysics, Naval Research Lab
	Jay L. Lush, Genetics, Iowa State Univ.
	N.M. Newmark, Civil eng., Univ. of Illinois
	Jerzy Neyman, Mathematics, Univ. of California, Berkeley
	Lars Onsager, Chemistry, Yale Univ.
	B.F. Skinner, Psychology, Harvard Univ.
	Eugene P. Wigner, Physics, Princeton Univ.
1969	Herbert C. Brown, Chemistry, Purdue Univ.
	William Feller, Mathematics, Princeton Univ.
	Robert J. Huebner, Medicine, National Institutes of Health
	Jack S.C. Kilby, Computer science, Texas Instruments
	Ernst Mayr, Zoology, Harvard Univ.
	W.K.H. Panofsky, Physics, Stanford Univ.
1970	Richard D. Brauer, Mathematics, Harvard Univ.
	Robert H. Dicke, Physics, Princeton Univ.
	Barbara McClintock, Genetics, Carnegie Institute
	George E. Mueller, Administration, General Dynamics
	Albert B. Sabin, Medicine, Weizmann Institute
	Allan R. Sandage, Astronomy, Cal Tech
	John C. Slater, Physics, Univ. of Florida
	John A. Wheeler, Physics, Princeton Univ.
	Saul Winstein, Chemistry, UCLA
1973	Daniel I. Arnon, Biochemistry, Stanford Univ.
	Carl Djerassi, Chemistry, Stanford Univ.
	Harold E. Edgerton, Mathematics, M.I.T.
	William M. Ewing, Electrical eng., Univ. of Texas
	Arie J. Haagen-Smit, Biochemistry, Cal Tech
	Vladimir Haensel, Geology, Universal Oil
	Frederick Seitz, Administration, Rockefeller Univ.
	Earl W. Sutherland, Biochemistry, Univ. of Miami
	John W. Tukey, Statistics, Princeton Univ.
	Richard T. Whitcomb, Aeronautics, Langley Center
	Robert P. Wilson, Administration, Fermilab
1974	Nicolaas Bloembergen, Physics, Harvard Univ.
	Britton Chance, Physics, Univ. of Pennsylvania
	Erwin Chargaff, Biochemistry, Columbia Univ.
	Paul J. Flory, Chemistry, Stanford Univ.
	William A. Fowler, Physics, Cal Tech
	Kurt Gödel, Mathematics, Institute for Advanced Study
	Rudolf Kompfner, Physics, Stanford Univ.
	James V. Neel, Genetics, Univ. of Michigan
	Linus Pauling, Chemistry, Stanford Univ.
	Ralph B. Peck, Engineering, Univ. of Illinois
	K.S. Pitzer, Chemistry, Univ. of California, Berkeley
	James A. Shannon, Medicine, Rockefeller Univ.
	Abel Wolman, Engineering, Johns Hopkins Univ.
1975	John Backus, Computer science, San Jose Laboratory
	Manson Benedict, Mathematics, M.I.T.
	Hans A. Bethe, Physics, Cornell Univ.
	Shiing-shen Chern, Mathematics, Univ. of California, Berkeley
	George B. Dantzig, Computer science, Stanford Univ.
	Hallowell Davis, Medicine, Washington Univ.
	Paul Gyorgy, Pediatrics, Univ. of Pennsylvania
	Sterling B. Hendricks, Chemistry, U.S. Dept. of Agriculture
	Joseph O. Hirschfelder, Chemistry, Univ. of Wisconsin
	William H. Pickering, Physics, Jet Propulsion Laboratory
	Lewis H. Sarett, Administration, Merck, Sharp, and Dohme
	Frederick E. Terman, Administration, Stanford Univ.
	Orville A. Vogel, Agronomy, Washington State Univ.
	Wernher von Braun, Administration, NASA
	E. Bright Wilson, Chemistry, Harvard Univ.
	Chien-Shiung Wu, Physics, Columbia Univ.
1976	Morris Cohen, Metallurgy, M.I.T.
	Kurt O. Friedrichs, Mathematics, New York Univ.
	Peter C. Goldmark, Communications, Goldmark Corporation
	Samuel A. Goudsmit, Physics, Univ. of Nevada
	Roger C. Guillemin, Neurology, Salk Institute
	Herbert S. Gutowsky, Chemistry, Univ. of Illinois
	Erwin W. Mueller, Physics, Pennsylvania State Univ.
	Keith R. Porter, Biology, Univ. of Colorado
	Efraim Racker, Biochemistry, Cornell Univ.
	Frederick D. Rossini, Chemistry, Rice Univ.
	Verner E. Suomi, Meteorology, Univ. of Wisconsin
	Henry Taube, Chemistry, Stanford Univ.
	George E. Uhlenbeck, Physics, Rockefeller Univ.
	Hassler Whitney, Physics, Princeton Univ.
	Edward O. Wilson, Zoology, Harvard Univ.

Year Winner, Field, Affiliation

1979 Robert H. Burris, Biochemistry, Univ. of Wisconsin
Elizabeth C. Crosby, Anatomy, Univ. of Michigan
Joseph L. Doob, Mathematics, Univ. of Illinois
Richard P. Feynman, Physics, Cal Tech
Donald E. Knuth, Computer science, Stanford Univ.
Arthur Kornberg, Biochemistry, Stanford Univ.
Emmett N. Leith, Electrical eng., Univ. of Michigan
Herman F. Mark, Administration, Brooklyn Polytech
Raymond D. Mindlin, Civil eng., Columbia Univ.
Robert N. Noyce, Computer science, Intel Corp.
Severo Ochoa, Biochemistry, New York Univ.
Earl R. Parker, Metallurgy, Univ. of California, Berkeley
Edward M. Purcell, Physics, Harvard Univ.
Simon Ramo, Administration, Thompson, Ramo, Wooldridge, Inc.
John H. Sinfelt, Science adviser, Exxon
Lyman Spitzer, Jr., Astronomy, Princeton Univ.
Earl R. Stadtman, Biochemistry, National Institutes of Health
G. Ledyard Stebbins, Genetics, Univ. of California, Davis
Paul A. Weiss, Biology, Rockefeller Univ.
Victor F. Weisskopf, Physics, M.I.T.

1981 Philip Handler, Biochemistry, National Academy of Sciences

1982 Philip W. Anderson, Physics, Bell Labs
Seymour Benzer, Biology, Cal Tech
Glenn W. Burton, Biology, U.S. Dept. of Agriculture
Mildred Cohn, Chemistry, Univ. of Pennsylvania
F. Albert Cotton, Chemistry, Texas A&M
Edward H. Heinemann, Engineering, General Dynamics
Donald Katz, Chemistry, Univ. of Michigan
Yoichiro Nambu, Physics, Univ. of Chicago
Marshall H. Stone, Mathematics, Univ. of Massachusetts
Gilbert Stork, Chemistry, Columbia Univ.
Edward Teller, Physics, Stanford Univ.
Charles H. Townes, Physics, Univ. of California, Berkeley

1985 Howard L. Bachrach, Biochemistry, U.S. Dept. of Agriculture
Paul Berg, Biology, Stanford Univ.
Margaret Burbidge, Astronomy, Univ. of California, San Diego
Maurice Goldhaber, Physics, Brookhaven National Lab
Herman H. Goldstine, Computer science, American Philosophical Society
William R. Hewlett, Electronics, Hewlett-Packard Company
Roald Hoffmann, Chemistry, Cornell Univ.
Helmut Landsberg, Climatology, Resources for the Future
George M. Low, Space science, Rensselaer Polytechnic Inst.
Walter Munk, Geophysics, Univ. of California, San Diego
George C. Pimentel, Chemistry, Univ. of California, Berkeley
Frederick Reines, Physics, Univ. of California, Irvine

Year Winner, Field, Affiliation

Wendell L. Roelofs, Biology, Cornell Univ.
Bruno Rossi, Astronomy, M.I.T.
Berta Scharrer, Medicine, Albert Einstein College of Medicine
Robert Schrieffer, Physics, Univ. of California, Santa Barbara
Isadore Singer, Mathematics, Univ. of California, Berkeley
John G. Trump, Medicine, M.I.T.
Richard N. Zare, Chemistry, Stanford Univ.

1986 Solomon J. Buchsbaum, Physics, Bell Labs
Stanley Cohen, Biochemistry, Vanderbilt Univ.
Horace R. Crane, Biophysics, Univ. of Michigan
Herman Feshbach, Physics, M.I.T.
Harry B. Gray, Chemistry, Cal Tech
Donald A. Henderson, Medicine, Johns Hopkins Univ.
Robert Hofstadter, Physics, Stanford Univ.
Peter D. Lax, Mathematics, New York Univ.
Yuan Tseh Lee, Chemistry, Univ. of California, Berkeley
Hans W. Liepmann, Physics, Cal Tech
Tung Yen Lin, Engineering, T.Y. Lin, International
Carl S. Marvel, Chemistry, Univ. of Arizona
Vernon B. Mountcastle, Medicine, Johns Hopkins Univ.
Bernard M. Oliver, Electronics, NASA
George E. Palade, Biology, Yale Univ.
Herbert A. Simon, Psychology, Carnegie Mellon Univ.
Joan A. Steitz, Biochemistry, Yale Univ.
Frank H. Westheimer, Chemistry, Harvard Univ.
Chen Ning Yang, Physics, State Univ. of N.Y., Stony Brook
Antoni Zygmund, Mathematics, Univ. of Chicago

1987 Philip H. Abelson, Physics, American Association of Allied Sciences
Anne Anastasi, Psychology, Fordham Univ.
Robert Bird, Physics, Univ. of Wisconsin
Raoul Bott, Mathematics, Harvard Univ.
Michael E. DeBakey, Medicine, Baylor College of Medicine
Theodor Diener, Biology, U.S. Dept. of Agriculture
Harry Eagle, Biology, Albert Einstein College of Medicine
Walter M. Elsasser, Physics, Johns Hopkins Univ.
Michael Freedman, Mathematics, Univ. of California, San Diego
William S. Johnson, Biochemistry, Stanford Univ.
Har Gobind Khorana, Biology, M.I.T.
Paul C. Lauterbur, Medicine, Univ. of Illinois
Rita Levi-Montalcini, Medicine, Lab. of Cell Biology, Rome
George E. Pake, Administration, Xerox Corporation
H. Bolton Seed, Engineering, Univ. of California, Berkeley
George J. Stigler, Economics, Univ. of Chicago
Walter H. Stockmayer, Chemistry, Dartmouth College
Max Tishler, Chemistry, Wesleyan Univ.
James A. Van Allen, Astronomy, Univ. of Iowa
Ernest Weber, Engineering, Polytechnic Inst. of N.Y.

Year Winner, Field, Affiliation

1988 William O. Baker, Chemistry, Bell Labs
Konrad E. Bloch, Medicine, Harvard Univ.
D. Allan Bromley, Physics, Yale Univ.
Michael S. Brown, Medicine, Univ. of Texas Medical Center
Paul C.W. Chu, Physics, Univ. of Houston
Stanley N. Cohen, Genetics, Stanford Univ.
Elias J. Corey, Chemistry, Harvard Univ.
Daniel C. Drucker, Engineering, Univ. of Florida
Milton Friedman, Economics, Hoover Institution, Stanford
Joseph L. Goldstein, Medicine, Univ. of Texas Medical Center
Ralph E. Gomery, Mathematics, IBM Corporation
Willis M. Hawkins, Aeronautics, Lockheed Corporation
Maurice R. Hillerman, Medicine, Merck Institute
George W. Housner, Earth science, Cal Tech
Eric R. Kandel, Biochemistry, Columbia Univ.
Joseph B. Keller, Physics, Stanford Univ.
Walter Kohn, Physics, Univ. of California, Santa Barbara
Norman F. Ramsey, Physics, Harvard Univ.
Jack Steinberger, Physics, CERN (European Center for Nuclear Research), Geneva
Rosalyn S. Yalow, Medicine, Mt. Sinai School of Medicine

1989 Arnold O. Beckman, Chemistry, Cal Tech
Richard B. Bernstein, Chemistry, Univ. of California, L.A.
Melvin Calvin, Biochemistry, Univ. of California, Berkeley
Harry G. Drinkamer, Physics, Univ. of Illinois
Katherine Esau, Biology, Univ. of California, Santa Barbara
Herbert E. Grier, Electronics, CER Corporation
Viktor Hamburger, Biology, Washington Univ., St. Louis
Samuel Karlin, Mathematics, Stanford Univ.
Philip Leder, Biochemistry, Harvard Medical School
Joshua Lederberg, Biochemistry, Rockefeller Univ.
Saunders Mac Lane, Mathematics, Univ. of Chicago
Rudolph A. Marcus, Chemistry, Cal Tech
Harden M. McConnell, Biochemistry, Stanford Univ.
Eugene N. Parker, Astrophysics, Univ. of Chicago
Robert P. Sharp, Astronomy, Cal Tech
Donald C. Spencer, Oceanography, Woods Hole
Harland G. Wood, Biochemistry, Case Western Reserve

1990 Baruj Benacerraf, Medicine, Dana-Farber Cancer Inst.
Elkan R. Blount, Medicine, Harvard School of Public Health
Herbert W. Boyer, Biology, Univ. of California
George F. Carrier, Mathematics, Harvard Univ.
Allan M. Cormack, Physics, Tufts Univ.
Mildred S. Dresselhaus, Physics, M.I.T.
Karl Folkers, Biochemistry, Inst. for Biomedical Research, Univ. of Texas
Nick Holonyak, Jr., Physics, Univ. of Illinois

Year	Winner, Field, Affiliation
	Leonid Hurwicz, Economics, Univ. of Minnesota
	Stephen C. Kleene, Mathematics, Univ. of Wisconsin
	Daniel E. Koshland, Jr., Biochemistry, Univ. of Calif., Berkeley
	Edward B. Lewis, Anthropology, Cal Tech
	John McCarthy, Computer science, Stanford Univ.
	Edwin M. McMillan, Physics, Univ. of California, Berkeley
	David G. Nathan, Medicine, The Children's Hospital, Boston
	Robert V. Pound, Physics, Harvard Univ.
	R.D. Revelle, Oceanography, Scripps Institution of Oceanography, Univ. of California, La Jolla
	John D. Roberts, Chemistry, Cal Tech
	Patrick Suppes, Mathematics, Stanford Univ.
	E. Donnall Thomas, Medicine, Fred Hutchinson Cancer Research Center, Seattle
1991	Mary Ellen Avery, Medicine, Harvard Univ.
	Ronald Breslow, Chemistry, Columbia Univ.
	Alberto P. Calderon, Mathematics, Univ. of Chicago
	Gertrude B. Elion, Chemistry, Burroughs Wellcome Co.
	George H. Heilmeier, Engineering, Bellcore Co.
	Dudley R. Herschbach, Chemistry, Harvard Univ.
	G. Evelyn Hutchinson, Ecology, Yale Univ.
	Elvin A. Kabat, Immunology, Columbia Univ.
	Robert W. Kates, Environment, Brown Univ.
	Luna B. Leopold, Geology, Univ. of California, Berkeley
	Salvador E. Luria, Biology, M.I.T.
	Paul A. Marks, Medicine, Memorial Sloan-Kettering Cancer Center
	George A. Miller, Psychology, Princeton Univ.
	Arthur L. Schawlow, Physics, Stanford Univ.
	Glenn T. Seaborg, Chemistry, Univ. of California, Berkeley
	Folke K. Skoog, Botany, Univ. of Wisconsin, Madison
	H. Guyford Stever, Engineering, Washington, D.C.
	Edward C. Stone, Physics, Cal Tech

Year	Winner, Field, Affiliation
	Steven Weinberg, Physics, Univ. of Texas, Austin
	Paul C. Zamecnik, Biochemistry, Worcester Foundation for Experimental Biology
1992	Eleanor J. Gibson, Psychology, Cornell Univ.
	Alan Newell, Computer Science, Carnegie Mellon Univ.
	Calvin F. Quate, Physics, Stanford Univ.
	Eugene M. Shoemaker, Geology, U.S. Geological Survey
	Howard E. Simmons, Jr., Chemistry, E.I. du Pont Nemours
	Maxine F. Singer, Biology, Carnegie Institute of Washington
	Howard M. Temin, Biology, McArdle Laboratory for Cancer Research, Univ. of Wisconsin
	John R. Whinnery, Engineering, Univ. of California, Berkeley
1993	Alfred Y. Cho, Engineering, Semiconductor Research Laboratory, AT&T Bell Laboratories
	Donald J. Cram, Chemistry, Univ. of California, L.A.
	Val. L. Fitch, Physics, Princeton Univ.
	Norman Hackerman, Chemistry, Robert A. Welch Foundation
	Martin D. Kruskal, Mathematics, Rutgers Univ.
	Daniel Nathans, Biology, Johns Hopkins Univ.
	Vera C. Rubin, Physics, Carnegie Institute of Washington
	Salome G. Waelsch, Biology, Albert Einstein College of Medicine
1994	Ray Clough, Engineering, Univ. of California, Berkeley
	John Cooke, Computer Science, IBM
	Thomas Eisner, Chemistry, Cornell Univ.
	George Hammond, Chemistry, Bowling Green State Univ.
	Robert K. Merton, Sociology, Columbia Univ.
	Elizabeth Neufeld, Biochemistry, Univ. of California, L.A.
	Albert Overhauser, Physics, Purdue Univ.
	Frank Press, Physics, Carnegie Institution of Washington

FERMI AWARDS, 1954–93

The Enrico Fermi Award is given by the U.S. Department of Energy for exceptional scientific and technical achievement in the development, use, or control of atomic energy. The award is named for Enrico Fermi, the first recipient and the scientist who constructed the first nuclear reactor (called an atomic pile at the time). Since the award is for a lifetime achievement, a specific work is not cited. The Fermi Award includes a prize of $100,000.

Year	Winners
1954	Enrico Fermi
1956	John von Neumann
1957	Ernest O. Lawrence
1958	Eugene P. Wigner
1959	Glenn T. Seaborg
1961	Hans A. Bethe
1962	Edward Teller
1963	J. Robert Oppenheimer
1964	Adm. Hyman G. Rickover
1966	Otto Hahn, Lise Meitner, and Fritz Strassman
1968	John A. Wheeler
1969	Walter H. Zinn
1970	Norris E. Bradbury
1971	Shields Warren and Stafford L. Warren
1972	Manson Benedict
1976	William L. Russell
1978	Harold M. Agnew and Wolfgang K.H. Panofsky
1980	Alvin M. Weinberg and Rudolf E. Peierls
1981	W. Bennett Lewis
1982	Herbert Anderson and Seth Neddermeyer
1983	Alexander Hollaender and John H. Lawrence
1984	Robert R. Wilson and Georges Vendryés
1985	Norman C. Rasmussen and Marshall N. Rosenbluth
1986	Ernest D. Courant and M. Stanley Livingstone
1987	Luis W. Alvarez and Gerald F. Tape
1988	Richard B. Setlow and Victor F. Weisskopf
1990	George A. Cowan and Robley D. Evans
1992	Leon M. Lederman, Harold Brown, and John S. Foster, Jr.
1993	Freeman Dyson and Liane Russell

PART VI SPORTS

COLLEGE SPORTS

THE NCAA

The NCAA acts as the governing body of intercollegiate athletics, setting the playing rules for each sport and eligibility standards for participating athletes. Its other major functions are to conduct championships and maintain historical records. The organization grew out of a series of meetings convened by President Theodore Roosevelt, who was concerned about the number of serious injuries and deaths in college football games. In 1905 alone, 18 players died.

Football

NCAA NATIONAL FOOTBALL CHAMPIONS

The NCAA Football Guide recognizes as unofficial national champion the team selected each year by press association polls. Where the Associated Press poll (of writers) does not agree with the United Press International poll (of coaches), the guide lists both teams selected.

Year	Team
1936	Minnesota
1937	Pittsburgh
1938	Texas Christian
1939	Texas A&M
1940	Minnesota
1941	Minnesota
1942	Ohio State
1943	Notre Dame
1944	Army
1945	Army
1946	Notre Dame
1947	Notre Dame
1948	Michigan
1949	Notre Dame
1950	Oklahoma
1951	Tennessee
1952	Michigan State
1953	Maryland
1954	Ohio State and UCLA
1955	Oklahoma
1956	Oklahoma
1957	Auburn and Ohio State
1958	Louisiana State
1959	Syracuse
1960	Minnesota
1961	Alabama
1962	Southern California
1963	Texas
1964	Alabama
1965	Alabama and Michigan State
1966	Notre Dame
1967	Southern California
1968	Ohio State
1969	Texas
1970	Nebraska and Texas
1971	Nebraska
1972	Southern California
1973	Notre Dame and Alabama
1974	Oklahoma and Southern California
1975	Oklahoma
1976	Pittsburgh
1977	Notre Dame
1978	Alabama and Southern California
1979	Alabama
1980	Georgia
1981	Clemson
1982	Penn State
1983	Miami (Fla.)
1984	Brigham Young
1985	Oklahoma
1986	Penn State
1987	Miami (Fla.)
1988	Notre Dame
1989	Miami (Fla.)
1990	Colorado and Georgia Tech
1991	Miami (Fla.) and Washington
1992	Alabama
1993	Florida State
1994	Nebraska

Source: NCAA.

NCAA FOOTBALL—MAJOR BOWL GAMES, 1902–95

ROSE BOWL (Pasadena, Calif.)
1902 Michigan 49, Stanford 0
1916 Washington State 14, Brown 0
1917 Oregon 14, Pennsylvania 0
1918 Mare Island 19, Camp Lewis 7
1919 Great Lakes 17, Mare Island 0
1920 Harvard 7, Oregon 6
1921 California 28, Ohio State 0
1922 Washington and Jefferson 0, Cal. 0
1923 Southern Cal. 14, Penn State 3
1924 Navy 14, Washington 14
1925 Notre Dame 27, Stanford 10
1926 Alabama 20, Washington 19
1927 Alabama 7, Stanford 7
1928 Stanford 7, Pittsburgh 6
1929 Georgia Tech 8, California 7
1930 Southern Cal. 47, Pittsburgh 14
1931 Alabama 24, Washington State 0
1932 Southern California 21, Tulane 12
1933 Southern Cal. 35, Pittsburgh 0
1934 Columbia 7, Stanford 0
1935 Alabama 29, Stanford 13
1936 Stanford 7, Southern Methodist 0
1937 Pittsburgh 21, Washington 0
1938 California 13, Alabama 0
1939 Southern California 7, Duke 0
1940 Southern Cal. 14, Tennessee 0
1941 Stanford 21, Nebraska 13
1942 Ore. St. 20, Duke 16 (at Durham)
1943 Georgia 9, UCLA 0
1944 Southern Cal. 29, Washington 0
1945 Southern Cal. 25, Tennessee 0
1946 Alabama 34, Southern Cal. 14
1947 Illinois 45, UCLA 14
1948 Michigan 49, Southern California 0
1949 Northwestern 20, California 14
1950 Ohio State 17, California 14
1951 Michigan 14, California 6
1952 Illinois 40, Stanford 7
1953 Southern California 7, Wisconsin 0
1954 Michigan State 28, UCLA 20
1955 Ohio State 20, Southern Cal. 7
1956 Michigan State 17, UCLA 14
1957 Iowa 35, Oregon State 19
1958 Ohio State 10, Oregon 7
1959 Iowa 38, California 12
1960 Washington 44, Wisconsin 8
1961 Washington 17, Minnesota 7
1962 Minnesota 21, UCLA 3
1963 Southern Cal. 42, Wisconsin 37
1964 Illinois 17, Washington 7
1965 Michigan 34, Oregon State 7
1966 UCLA 14, Michigan State 12
1967 Purdue 14, Southern California 13
1968 Southern California 14, Indiana 3
1969 Ohio State 27, Southern Cal. 16
1970 Southern California 10, Michigan 3
1971 Stanford 27, Ohio State 17
1972 Stanford 13, Michigan 12
1973 Southern Cal. 42, Ohio State 17
1974 Ohio State 42, Southern Cal. 21
1975 Southern Cal. 18, Ohio State 17
1976 UCLA 23, Ohio State 10
1977 Southern California 14, Michigan 6
1978 Washington 27, Michigan 20
1979 Southern Cal. 17, Michigan 10
1980 Southern Cal. 17, Ohio State 16
1981 Michigan 23, Washington 6
1982 Washington 28, Iowa 0
1983 UCLA 24, Michigan 14
1984 UCLA 45, Illinois 9
1985 Southern Cal. 20, Ohio State 17
1986 UCLA 45, Iowa 28
1987 Arizona State 22, Michigan 15
1988 Michigan St. 20, Southern Cal. 17
1989 Michigan 22, Southern Cal. 14
1990 Southern Cal. 17, Michigan 10
1991 Washington 46, Iowa 34
1992 Washington 34, Michigan 14
1993 Michigan 38, Washington 31
1994 Wisconsin 21, UCLA 16
1995 Penn State 38, Oregon 20

COTTON BOWL (Dallas, Tex.)
1937 Texas Christian 16, Marquette 6
1938 Rice 28, Colorado 14
1939 St. Mary's 20, Texas Tech 13
1940 Clemson 6, Boston College 3
1941 Texas A&M 13, Fordham 12
1942 Alabama 29, Texas A&M 21
1943 Texas 14, Georgia Tech 7
1944 Texas 7, Randolph Field 7
1945 Okla. State 34, Texas Christian 0
1946 Texas 40, Missouri 27
1947 Arkansas 0, Louisiana State 0
1948 So. Methodist 13, Penn State 13
1949 Southern Methodist 21, Oregon 13
1950 Rice 27, North Carolina 13
1951 Tennessee 20, Texas 14
1952 Kentucky 20, Texas Christian 7
1953 Texas 16, Tennessee 0
1954 Rice 28, Alabama 0
1955 Georgia Tech 14, Arkansas 6
1956 Mississippi 14, Texas Christian 13
1957 Texas Christian 28, Syracuse 27
1958 Navy 20, Rice 7
1959 Texas Christian 0, Air Force 0

NCAA FOOTBALL—MAJOR BOWL GAMES, 1902–95 *(continued)*

1960 Syracuse 23, Texas 14
1961 Duke 7, Arkansas 6
1962 Texas 12, Mississippi 7
1963 Louisiana State 13, Texas 0
1964 Texas 28, Navy 6
1965 Arkansas 10, Nebraska 7
1966 Louisiana State 14, Arkansas 7
1967 Georgia 24, Southern Methodist 9
1968 Texas A&M 20, Alabama 16
1969 Texas 36, Tennessee 13
1970 Texas 21, Notre Dame 17
1971 Notre Dame 24, Texas 11
1972 Penn State 30, Texas 6
1973 Texas 17, Alabama 13
1974 Nebraska 19, Texas 3
1975 Penn State 41, Baylor 20
1976 Arkansas 31, Georgia 10
1977 Houston 30, Maryland 21
1978 Notre Dame 38, Texas 10
1979 Notre Dame 35, Houston 34
1980 Houston 17, Nebraska 14
1981 Alabama 30, Baylor 2
1982 Texas 14, Alabama 12
1983 Southern Methodist 7, Pittsburgh 3
1984 Georgia 10, Texas 9
1985 Boston College 45, Houston 28
1986 Texas A&M 36, Auburn 16
1987 Ohio State 28, Texas A&M 12
1988 Texas A&M 35, Notre Dame 10
1989 UCLA 17, Arkansas 3
1990 Tennessee 31, Arkansas 27
1991 Miami (Fla.) 46, Texas 3
1992 Florida State 10, Texas A&M 2
1993 Notre Dame 28, Texas A&M 3
1994 Notre Dame 24, Texas A&M 21
1995 Southern Cal 55, Texas Tech 14

ORANGE BOWL (Miami, Fla.)

1935 Bucknell 26, Miami (Fla.) 0
1936 Catholic U. 20, Mississippi 19
1937 Duquesne 13, Miss. State 12
1938 Auburn 6, Michigan State 0
1939 Tennessee 17, Oklahoma 0
1940 Georgia Tech 21, Misouri 7
1941 Miss. State 14, Georgetown 7
1942 Georgia 40, Texas Christian 26
1943 Alabama 37, Boston College 21
1944 Louisiana St. 19, Texas A&M 14
1945 Tulsa 26, Georgia Tech 12
1946 Miami (Fla.)13, Holy Cross 6
1947 Rice 8, Tennessee 0
1948 Georgia Tech 20, Kansas 14
1949 Texas 41, Georgia 28
1950 Santa Clara 21, Kentucky 13
1951 Clemson 15, Miami (Fla.) 14
1952 Georgia Tech 20, Baylor 14
1953 Alabama 61, Syracuse 6
1954 Oklahoma 7, Maryland 0
1955 Duke 34, Nebraska 7
1956 Oklahoma 20, Maryland 6
1957 Colorado 27, Clemson 21
1958 Oklahoma 48, Duke 21
1959 Oklahoma 21, Syracuse 6
1960 Georgia 14, Missouri 0
1961 Missouri 21, Navy 14
1962 Louisiana State 25, Colorado 7
1963 Alabama 17, Oklahoma 0
1964 Nebraska 13, Auburn 7
1965 Texas 21, Alabama 17
1966 Alabama 39, Nebraska 28
1967 Florida 27, Georgia Tech 12
1968 Oklahoma 26, Tennessee 24
1969 Penn State 15, Kansas 14
1970 Penn State 10, Missouri 3
1971 Nebraska 17, Louisiana State 12
1972 Nebraska 38, Alabama 6
1973 Nebraska 40, Notre Dame 6
1974 Penn State 16, Louisiana State 9
1975 Notre Dame 13, Alabama 11
1976 Oklahoma 14, Michigan 6
1977 Ohio State 27, Colorado 10
1978 Arkansas 31, Oklahoma 6
1979 Oklahoma 31, Nebraska 21
1980 Oklahoma 24, Florida State 7
1981 Oklahoma 18, Florida State 17
1982 Clemson 22, Nebraska 15
1983 Nebraska 21, Louisiana State 20
1984 Miami (Fla.) 31, Nebraska 30
1985 Washington 28, Oklahoma 17
1986 Oklahoma 25, Penn State 10
1987 Oklahoma 42, Arkansas 8
1988 Miami (Fla.) 20, Oklahoma 14
1989 Miami (Fla.) 23, Nebraska 3
1990 Notre Dame 21, Colorado 6
1991 Colorado 10, Notre Dame 9
1992 Miami (Fla.) 22, Nebraska 0
1993 Florida State 27, Nebraska 14
1994 Florida State 18, Nebraska 16
1995 Nebraska 24, Miami 17

SUGAR BOWL (New Orleans, La.)

1935 Tulane 20, Temple 14
1936 Texas Christian 3, Louisiana St. 2
1937 Santa Clara 21, Louisiana State 14
1938 Santa Clara 6, Louisiana State 0
1939 Tex. Christian 15, Carnegie Tech 7
1940 Texas A&M 14, Tulane 13
1941 Boston College 19, Tennessee 13
1942 Fordham 2, Missouri 0
1943 Tennessee 14, Tulsa 7
1944 Georgia Tech 20, Tulsa 18
1945 Duke 29, Alabama 26
1946 Oklahoma State 33, St. Mary's 13
1947 Georgia 20, North Carolina 10
1948 Texas 27, Alabama 7
1949 Oklahoma 14, North Carolina 6
1950 Oklahoma 35, Louisiana State 0
1951 Kentucky 13, Oklahoma 7
1952 Maryland 28, Tennessee 13
1953 Georgia Tech 24, Mississippi 7
1954 Georgia Tech 42, West Virginia 19
1955 Navy 21, Mississippi 0
1956 Georgia Tech 7, Pittsburgh 0
1957 Baylor 13, Tennessee 7
1958 Mississippi 39, Texas 7
1959 Louisiana State 7, Clemson 0
1960 Mississippi 21, Louisiana State 0
1961 Mississippi 14, Rice 6
1962 Alabama 10, Arkansas 3
1963 Mississippi 17, Arkansas 13
1964 Alabama 12, Mississippi 7
1965 Louisiana State 13, Syracuse 10
1966 Missouri 20, Florida 18
1967 Alabama 34, Nebraska 7
1968 Louisiana State 20, Wyoming 13
1969 Arkansas 16, Georgia 2
1970 Mississippi 27, Arkansas 22
1971 Tennessee 34, Air Force 13
1972 Oklahoma 40, Auburn 22
1973 Oklahoma 14, Penn State 0
1974 Notre Dame 24, Alabama 23
1975 Nebraska 13, Florida 10
1976 Alabama 13, Penn State 6
1977 Pittsburgh 27, Georgia 3
1978 Alabama 35, Ohio State 6
1979 Alabama 14, Penn State 7
1980 Alabama 24, Arkansas 9
1981 Georgia 17, Notre Dame 10
1982 Pittsburgh 24, Georgia 20
1983 Penn State 27, Georgia 23
1984 Auburn 9, Michigan 7
1985 Nebraska 28, Louisiana State 10
1986 Tennessee 35, Miami (Fla.) 7
1987 Nebraska 30, Louisiana State 15
1988 Syracuse 16, Auburn 16
1989 Florida State 13, Auburn 7
1990 Miami (Fla.) 33, Alabama 25
1991 Tennessee 23, Virginia 22
1992 Notre Dame 39, Florida 28
1993 Alabama 34, Miami 13
1994 Florida 41, West Virginia 7
1995 Florida State 23, Florida 17

HEISMAN MEMORIAL TROPHY—Honoring the outstanding college football player in the United States.

Year	Player	College	Position
1935	Jay Berwanger	Chicago	HB
1936	Larry Kelley	Yale	E
1937	Clint Frank	Yale	HB
1938	Davey O'Brien	Texas Christian	QB
1939	Nile Kinnick	Iowa	HB
1940	Tom Harmon	Michigan	HB
1941	Bruce Smith	Minnesota	HB
1942	Frank Sinkwich	Georgia	HB
1943	Angelo Bertelli	Notre Dame	QB
1944	Les Horvath	Ohio State	QB
1945	Doc Blanchard	Army	FB
1946	Glenn Davis	Army	HB
1947	John Lujack	Notre Dame	QB
1948	Doak Walker	Southern Methodist	HB
1949	Leon Hart	Notre Dame	E
1950	Vic Janowicz	Ohio State	HB
1951	Dick Kazmaier	Princeton	HB
1952	Billy Vessels	Oklahoma	HB
1953	John Lattner	Notre Dame	HB
1954	Alan Ameche	Wisconsin	FB
1955	Howard Cassady	Ohio State	HB
1956	Paul Hornung	Notre Dame	QB
1957	John Crow	Texas A&M	HB
1958	Pete Dawkins	Army	HB
1959	Billy Cannon	Louisiana State	HB
1960	Joe Bellino	Navy	HB
1961	Ernie Davis	Syracuse	HB
1962	Terry Baker	Oregon State	QB
1963	Roger Staubach	Navy	QB
1964	John Huarte	Notre Dame	QB
1965	Mike Garrett	Southern California	HB
1966	Steve Spurrier	Florida	QB
1967	Gary Beban	UCLA	QB
1968	O.J. Simpson	Southern California	HB
1969	Steve Owens	Oklahoma	HB
1970	Jim Plunkett	Stanford	QB
1971	Pat Sullivan	Auburn	QB
1972	Johnny Rodgers	Nebraska	FL
1973	John Cappelletti	Penn State	HB
1974	Archie Griffin	Ohio State	HB
1975	Archie Griffin	Ohio State	HB
1976	Tony Dorsett	Pittsburgh	HB
1977	Earl Campbell	Texas	HB
1978	Billy Sims	Oklahoma	HB
1979	Charles White	Southern California	HB
1980	George Rogers	South Carolina	HB
1981	Marcus Allen	Southern California	HB
1982	Herschel Walker	Georgia	HB
1983	Mike Rozier	Nebraska	HB
1984	Doug Flutie	Boston College	QB
1985	Bo Jackson	Auburn	HB
1986	Vinny Testaverde	Miami (Fla.)	QB
1987	Tim Brown	Notre Dame	WR
1988	Barry Sanders	Oklahoma State	RB
1989	Andre Ware	Houston	QB
1990	Ty Detmer	Brigham Young	QB
1991	Desmond Howard	Michigan	WR
1992	Gino Torretta	Miami	QB
1993	Charlie Ward	Florida State	QB
1994	Rashaan Salaam	Colorado	RB

OUTLAND TROPHY

Honoring the outstanding interior lineman, as selected by the Football Writers Association of America, this trophy commemorates John Outland, a two-time consensus All-American guard for Penn State (1897–98).

Year	Player	College	Position
1946	George Connor	Notre Dame	T
1947	Joe Steffy	Army	G
1948	Bill Fischer	Notre Dame	G
1949	Ed Bagdon	Michigan State	G
1950	Bob Gain	Kentucky	T
1951	Jim Weatherall	Oklahoma	T
1952	Dick Modzelewski	Maryland	T
1953	J.D. Roberts	Oklahoma	G
1954	Bill Brooks	Arkansas	G
1955	Calvin Jones	Iowa	G
1956	Jim Parker	Ohio State	G
1957	Alex Karras	Iowa	T
1958	Zeke Smith	Auburn	G
1959	Mike McGee	Duke	T
1960	Tom Brown	Minnesota	G
1961	Merlin Olsen	Utah State	T
1962	Bobby Bell	Minnesota	T
1963	Scott Appleton	Texas	T
1964	Steve DeLong	Tennessee	T
1965	Tommy Nobis	Texas	G
1966	Loyd Phillips	Arkansas	T
1967	Ron Yary	Southern California	T
1968	Bill Stanfill	Georgia	T
1969	Mike Reid	Penn State	DT
1970	Jim Stillwagon	Ohio State	MG
1971	Larry Jacobson	Nebraska	DT
1972	Rich Glover	Nebraska	MG
1973	John Hicks	Ohio State	OT
1974	Randy White	Maryland	DE
1975	Lee Roy Selmon	Oklahoma	DT
1976	Ross Browner	Notre Dame	DE
1977	Brad Shearer	Texas	DT
1978	Greg Roberts	Oklahoma	G
1979	Jim Ritcher	North Carolina State	C
1980	Mark May	Pittsburgh	OT
1981	Dave Rimington	Nebraska	C
1982	Dave Rimington	Nebraska	C
1983	Dean Steinkuhler	Nebraska	G
1984	Bruce Smith	Virginia Tech	DT
1985	Mike Ruth	Boston College	NG
1986	Jason Buck	Brigham Young	DT
1987	Chad Hennings	Air Force	DT
1988	Tracy Rocker	Auburn	DT
1989	Mohammed Elewonibi	Brigham Young	G
1990	Russell Maryland	Miami (Fla.)	DT
1991	Steve Emtman	Washington	DT
1992	Will Shields	Nebraska	G
1993	Rob Waldrop	Arizona	NG
1994	Zach Weigert	Nebraska	OT

NCAA FOOTBALL CAREER LEADERS

CAREER POINTS (Nonkickers)

Player, team	Years	TD	XPt.	FG	Pts.
Anthony Thompson, Indiana	1986–89	65	4	0	394
Marshall Faulk, San Diego State	1991–93	62	4	0	376
Tony Dorsett, Pittsburgh	1973–76	59	2	0	356
Glenn Davis, Army	1943–46	59	0	0	354
Art Luppino, Arizona	1953–56	48	49	0	337
Steve Owens, Oklahoma	1967–69	56	0	0	336
Wilford White, Arizona State	1947–50	48	27	4	327
Barry Sanders, Oklahoma State	1986–88	54	0	0	324
Allen Pinkett, Notre Dame	1982–85	53	2	0	320
Ed Marinaro, Cornell	1969–71	52	6	0	318
Pete Johnson, Ohio State	1973–76	53	0	0	318

RUSHING, Career yards

Player, team	Years	Carries	Yards	Avg.	Long
Tony Dorsett, Pittsburgh	1973–76	1,074	6,082	5.66	73
Charles White, Southern California	1976–79	1,023	5,598	5.47	79
Herschel Walker, Georgia	1980–82	994	5,259	5.29	76
Archie Griffin, Ohio State	1972–75	845	5,177	6.13	75
Darren Lewis, Texas A&M	1987–90	909	5,012	5.51	84
Anthony Thompson, Indiana	1986–89	1,089	4,965	4.56	52
George Rogers, South Carolina	1977–80	902	4,958	5.50	80
Trevor Cobb, Rice	1989–92	1,091	4,948	4.54	79
Paul Palmer, Temple	1983–86	948	4,895	5.16	78
Steve Bartalo, Colorado State	1983–86	1,215	4,813	3.96	39

CAREER POINTS (Kickers)

Player, team	Years	PAT	Att.	FG	Att.	Pts.
Roman Anderson, Houston	1988–91	213	217	70	101	423
Carlos Huerta, Miami (Fla.)	1988–91	178	181	73	91	397
Jason Elam, Hawaii	1988–92	158	161	79	100	395
Derek Schmidt, Florida State	1984–87	174	178	73	102	393
Luis Zendejas, Arizona State	1981–84	134	135	78	105	368
Jeff Jaeger, Washington	1983–86	118	123	80	99	358
John Lee, UCLA	1982–85	116	117	79	92	353
Max Zendejas, Arizona	1982–85	122	124	77	104	353
Kevin Butler, Georgia	1981–84	122	125	77	98	353
Derek Mahoney, Fresno State	1990–93	216	222	45	63	351

RECEIVING, Career catches

Player, team	Years	Catches	Yards	Avg.	TD
Aaron Turner, Pacific (Calif.)	1989–92	266	4,345	16.3	43
Terance Mathis, New Mexico	1985–87, 1989	263	4,254	16.2	36
Mark Templeton, Long Beach State	1983–86	262	1,969	7.5	11
Howard Twilley, Tulsa	1963–65	261	3,343	12.8	32
David Williams, Illinois	1983–85	245	3,195	13.0	22
Marc Zeno, Tulane	1984–87	236	3,725	15.8	25
Jason Wolf, Southern Methodist	1989–92	235	2,232	9.5	17
Bryan Reeves, Nevada	1991–93	234	3,407	14.6	32
Ryan Yarborough, Wyoming	1990–93	229	4,357	19.0	42
Kenny Hazzard, Houston	1989–90	220	2,635	12.0	31

PASSING, Career yards

Player, team	Years	Att.	Comp.	Int.	Pct.	Yards	TD
Ty Detmer, Brigham Young	1988–91	1,530	958	65	.626	15,031	121
Todd Santos, San Diego State	1984–87	1,484	910	57	.613	11,425	70
Eric Zeier, Georgia	1991–94	1,402	838	37	.598	11,513	67
Alex Van Pelt, Pittsburgh	1989–92	1,463	845	59	.578	10,913	64
Kevin Sweeney, Fresno State	1982–86	1,336	731	48	.547	10,623	66
Doug Flutie, Boston College	1981–84	1,270	677	54	.533	10,579	67
Brian McClure, Bowling Green	1982–85	1,427	900	58	.631	10,280	63
Troy Kopp, Pacific (Calif.)	1989–92	1,374	798	47	.581	10,258	87
Glenn Foley, Boston College	1990–93	1,275	703	60	.551	10,042	72
Ben Bennett, Duke	1980–83	1,375	820	57	.596	9,614	53

Basketball

NCAA DIVISION I MEN'S BASKETBALL FINAL FOUR RESULTS

The first NCAA men's basketball tournament was held in 1939, in Evanston, Ill., with a mere eight teams. Today, 64 teams—30 conference champions and 34 "at-large" teams—compete for the national championship.

Year	Champion	Score	Runner-up	Third place	Fourth place	Champion coach	Outstanding player award	
1939	Oregon	46–33	Ohio State	Oklahoma[1]	Villanova[1]	Howard Hobson	None selected	
1940	Indiana	60–42	Kansas	Duquesne[1]	Southern California[1]	Branch McCracken	Marvin Huffman	Indiana
1941	Wisconsin	39–34	Washington State	Pittsburgh[1]	Arkansas[1]	Harold Foster	John Kotz	Wisconsin
1942	Stanford	53–38	Dartmouth	Colorado[1]	Kentucky[1]	Everett Dean	Howard Dallmar	Stanford
1943	Wyoming	46–34	Georgetown	Texas[1]	DePaul[1]	Everett Shelton	Ken Sailors	Wyoming
1944	Utah	42–40[2]	Dartmouth	Iowa State[1]	Ohio State[1]	Vadal Peterson	Arnold Ferrin	Utah
1945	Oklahoma State	49–45	New York Univ.	Arkansas[1]	Ohio State[1]	Henry Iba	Bob Kurland	Oklahoma State
1946	Oklahoma State	43–40	North Carolina	Ohio State	California	Henry Iba	Bob Kurland	Oklahoma State
1947	Holy Cross	58–47	Oklahoma	Texas	CCNY	Alvin Julian	George Kaftan	Holy Cross
1948	Kentucky	58–42	Baylor	Holy Cross	Kansas State	Adolph Rupp	Alex Groza	Kentucky
1949	Kentucky	46–36	Oklahoma State	Illinois	Oregon State	Adolph Rupp	Alex Groza	Kentucky
1950	CCNY	71–68	Bradley	North Carolina State	Baylor	Nat Holman	Irwin Dambrot	CCNY
1951	Kentucky	68–58	Kansas State	Illinois	Oklahoma State	Adolph Rupp	None selected	
1952	Kansas	80–63	St. John's	Illinois	Santa Clara	Forrest Allen	Clyde Lovellette	Kansas
1953	Indiana	69–68	Kansas	Washington	Louisiana State	Branch McCracken	B.H. Born	Kansas
1954	La Salle	92–76	Bradley	Penn State	Southern California	Kenneth Loeffler	Tom Gola	La Salle
1955	San Francisco	77–63	La Salle	Colorado	Iowa	Phil Woolpert	Bill Russell	San Francisco
1956	San Francisco	83–71	Iowa	Temple	Southern Methodist	Phil Woolpert	Hal Lear	Temple
1957	North Carolina	54–53[3]	Kansas	San Francisco	Michigan State	Frank McGuire	Wilt Chamberlain	Kansas
1958	Kentucky	84–72	Seattle	Temple	Kansas State	Adolph Rupp	Elgin Baylor	Seattle
1959	California	71–70	West Virginia	Cincinnati	Louisville	Pete Newell	Jerry West	West Virginia
1960	Ohio State	75–55	California	Cincinnati	New York Univ.	Fred Taylor	Jerry Lucas	Ohio State
1961	Cincinnati	70–65[2]	Ohio State	St. Joseph's (Pa.)[4]	Utah	Edwin Jucker	Jerry Lucas	Ohio State
1962	Cincinnati	71–59	Ohio State	Wake Forest	UCLA	Edwin Jucker	Paul Hogue	Cincinnati
1963	Loyola (Ill.)	60–58[2]	Cincinnati	Duke	Utah	George Ireland	Art Heyman	Duke
1964	UCLA	98–83	Duke	Michigan	Kansas State	John Wooden	Walt Hazzard	UCLA
1965	UCLA	91–80	Michigan	Princeton	Wichita State	John Wooden	Bill Bradley	Princeton
1966	UTEP	72–65	Kentucky	Duke	Utah	Don Haskins	Jerry Chambers	Utah
1967	UCLA	79–64	Dayton	Houston	North Carolina	John Wooden	Lew Alcindor	UCLA
1968	UCLA	78–55	North Carolina	Ohio State	Houston	John Wooden	Lew Alcindor	UCLA
1969	UCLA	92–72	Purdue	Drake	North Carolina	John Wooden	Lew Alcindor	UCLA
1970	UCLA	80–69	Jacksonville	New Mexico State	St. Bonaventure	John Wooden	Sidney Wicks	UCLA
1971	UCLA	68–62	Villanova[4]	Western Kentucky[4]	Kansas	John Wooden	Howard Porter	Villanova
1972	UCLA	81–76	Florida State	North Carolina	Louisville	John Wooden	Bill Walton	UCLA
1973	UCLA	87–66	Memphis State	Indiana	Providence	John Wooden	Bill Walton	UCLA
1974	North Carolina State	76–64	Marquette	UCLA	Kansas	Norm Sloan	David Thompson	North Carolina State
1975	UCLA	92–85	Kentucky	Louisville	Syracuse	John Wooden	Richard Washington	UCLA
1976	Indiana	86–68	Michigan	UCLA	Rutgers	Bob Knight	Kent Benson	Indiana
1977	Marquette	67–59	North Carolina	UNLV	N. Carolina, Charlotte	Al McGuire	Butch Lee	Marquette
1978	Kentucky	94–88	Duke	Arkansas	Notre Dame	Joe Hall	Jack Givens	Kentucky
1979	Michigan State	75–64	Indiana State	DePaul	Penn	Jud Heathcote	Earvin Johnson	Michigan State
1980	Louisville	59–54	UCLA[4]	Purdue	Iowa	Denny Crum	Darrell Griffith	Louisville
1981	Indiana	63–50	North Carolina	Virginia	Louisiana State	Bob Knight	Isiah Thomas	Indiana
1982	North Carolina	63–62	Georgetown	Houston[1]	Louisville[1]	Dean Smith	James Worthy	North Carolina
1983	North Carolina State	54–52	Houston	Georgia[1]	Louisville[1]	Jim Valvano	Akeem Olajuwon	Houston
1984	Georgetown	84–75	Houston	Kentucky[1]	Virginia[1]	John Thompson	Patrick Ewing	Georgetown
1985	Villanova	66–64	Georgetown	St. John's[1]	Memphis State[1,4]	Rollie Massimino	Ed Pinckney	Villanova
1986	Louisville	72–69	Duke	Kansas[1]	Louisiana State[1]	Denny Crum	Pervis Ellison	Louisville
1987	Indiana	74–73	Syracuse	UNLV[1]	Providence[1]	Bob Knight	Keith Smart	Indiana
1988	Kansas	83–79	Oklahoma	Arizona[1]	Duke[1]	Larry Brown	Danny Manning	Kansas
1989	Michigan	80–79[2]	Seton Hall	Illinois[1]	Duke[1]	Steve Fisher	Glen Rice	Michigan
1990	UNLV	103–73	Duke	Georgia Tech[1]	Arkansas[1]	Jerry Tarkanian	Anderson Hunt	UNLV
1991	Duke	72–65	Kansas	UNLV[1]	North Carolina[1]	Mike Krzyzewski	Christian Laettner	Duke
1992	Duke	71–51	Michigan	Indiana[1]	Cincinnati[1]	Mike Krzyzewski	Bobby Hurley	Duke
1993	North Carolina	77–71	Michigan	Kansas[1]	Kentucky[1]	Dean Smith	Donald Williams	North Carolina
1994	Arkansas	76–72	Duke	Arizona[1]	Florida[1]	Nolan Richardson	Corliss Williamson	Arkansas
1995	UCLA	89–78	Arkansas	North Carolina[1]	Oklahoma State[1]	Jim Harrick	Ed O'Bannon	UCLA

1. Tied for third place. 2. Overtime. 3. Triple overtime. 4. Later declared ineligible.

NCAA BASKETBALL CAREER LEADERS

SCORING

Player, team	Points
Pete Maravich, Louisiana State	3,667
Freeman Williams, Portland St.	3,249
Lionel Simmons, LaSalle	3,217
Alphonzo Ford, Mississippi Valley	3,165
Harry Kelly, Texas Southern	3,066
Hersey Hawkins, Bradley	3,008
Oscar Robertson, Cincinnati	2,973
Danny Manning, Kansas	2,951
Alfredrick Hughes, Loyola (Ill.)	2,914
Elvin Hayes, Houston	2,884

ASSISTS

Player, team	Assists
Bobby Hurley, Duke	1,076
Chris Corchiani, N. Carolina St.	1,038
Keith Jennings, E. Tennessee St.	983
Sherman Douglas, Syracuse	960
Tony Miller, Marquette	956
Greg Anthony, UNLV	950
Gary Payton, Oregon State	938
Orlando Smart, San Francisco	902
Andre Lafleur, Northeastern	894
Jim Les, Bradley	884

REBOUNDS

Player, team	Rebounds
Tom Gola, LaSalle	2,201
Joe Holup, George Washington	2,030
Charlie Slack, Marshall	1,916
Ed Conlin, Fordham	1,884
Dickie Hemric, Wake Forest	1,802
Paul Silas, Creighton	1,751
Art Quimby, Connecticut	1,716
Jerry Harper, Alabama	1,688
Jeff Cohen, William and Mary	1,679
Steve Hamilton, Morehead State	1,675

FIELD GOAL PERCENTAGE

Player, team	Pct.
Ricky Nedd, Appalachian State	69.0
Stephen Scheffler, Purdue	68.5
Steve Johnson, Oregon State	67.8
Murray Brown, Florida State	66.8
Lee Campbell, Southwest Mo. St.	66.5
Warren Kidd, Middle Tenn. State	66.4
Joe Senser, West Chester	66.2
Kevin Magee, U. Cal, Irvine	65.6
Orlando Phillips, Pepperdine	65.4
Bill Walton, UCLA	65.1

NATIONAL INVITATION TOURNAMENT CHAMPIONS

1938 Temple
1939 Long Island Univ.
1940 Colorado
1941 Long Island Univ.
1942 West Virginia
1943 St. John's
1944 St. John's
1945 DePaul
1946 Kentucky
1947 Utah
1948 St. Louis
1949 San Francisco
1950 CCNY
1951 Brigham Young
1952 La Salle
1953 Seton Hall
1954 Holy Cross
1955 Duquesne
1956 Louisville
1957 Bradley
1958 Xavier (Ohio)
1959 St. John's
1960 Bradley
1961 Providence
1962 Dayton
1963 Providence
1964 Bradley
1965 St. John's
1966 Brigham Young
1967 Southern Illinois
1968 Dayton
1969 Temple
1970 Marquette
1971 North Carolina
1972 Maryland
1973 Virginia Tech
1974 Purdue
1975 Princeton
1976 Kentucky
1977 St. Bonaventure
1978 Texas
1979 Indiana
1980 Virginia
1981 Tulsa
1982 Bradley
1983 Fresno State
1984 Michigan
1985 UCLA
1986 Ohio State
1987 S. Mississippi
1988 Connecticut
1989 St. John's
1990 Vanderbilt
1991 Stanford
1992 Virginia
1993 Minnesota
1994 Villanova
1995 Virginia Tech

Other Men's NCAA Champions

SOCCER

Year Champion

1959 St. Louis
1960 St. Louis
1961 West Chester
1962 St. Louis
1963 St. Louis
1964 Navy
1965 St. Louis
1966 San Francisco
1967 Michigan State
St. Louis
1968 Maryland
Michigan State
1969 St. Louis
1970 St. Louis
1971 vacated
1972 St. Louis
1973 St. Louis
1974 Howard
1975 San Francisco
1976 San Francisco
1977 Hartwick
1978 vacated
1979 So. Ill. Univ. at Edwardsville
1980 San Francisco
1981 Connecticut
1982 Indiana
1983 Indiana
1984 Clemson
1985 UCLA
1986 Duke
1987 Clemson
1988 Indiana
1989 Santa Clara
Virginia
1990 UCLA
1991 Virginia
1992 Virginia
1993 Virginia
1994 Virginia

CROSS-COUNTRY

Year Champion

1938 Indiana
1939 Michigan State
1940 Indiana
1941 Rhode Island
1942 Indiana
1944 Drake
1945 Drake
1946 Drake
1947 Penn State
1948 Michigan State
1949 Michigan State
1950 Penn State
1951 Syracuse
1952 Michigan State
1953 Kansas
1954 Oklahoma State
1955 Michigan State
1956 Michigan State
1957 Notre Dame
1958 Michigan State
1959 Michigan State
1960 Houston
1961 Oregon State
1962 San Jose State
1963 San Jose State
1964 Western Michigan
1965 Western Michigan
1966 Villanova
1967 Villanova
1968 Villanova
1969 UTEP
1970 Villanova
1971 Oregon
1972 Tennessee
1973 Oregon
1974 Oregon
1975 UTEP
1976 UTEP
1977 Oregon
1978 UTEP
1979 UTEP
1980 UTEP
1981 UTEP
1982 Wisconsin
1983 vacated
1984 Arkansas
1985 Wisconsin
1986 Arkansas
1987 Arkansas
1988 Wisconsin
1989 Iowa State
1990 Arkansas
1991 Arkansas
1992 Arkansas
1993 Arkansas
1994 Iowa State

WATER POLO

Year Champion

1969 UCLA
1970 U.C., Irvine
1971 UCLA
1972 UCLA
1973 California
1974 California
1975 California
1976 Stanford
1977 California
1978 Stanford
1979 U.C., Santa Barbara
1980 Stanford
1981 Stanford
1982 U.C., Irvine
1983 California
1984 California
1985 Stanford
1986 Stanford
1987 California
1988 California
1989 California
1990 California
1991 California
1992 California
1993 Stanford
1994 Stanford

FENCING

Year Champion[1]

1941 Northwestern
1942 Ohio State
1947 New York University
1948 CCNY
1949 Army
Rutgers
1950 Navy
1951 Columbia
1952 Columbia
1953 Pennsylvania
1954 Columbia
New York University
1955 Columbia
1956 Illinois
1957 New York University
1958 Illinois
1959 Navy
1960 New York University
1961 New York University
1962 Navy
1963 Columbia
1964 Princeton
1965 Columbia
1966 New York University
1967 New York University
1968 Columbia
1969 Pennsylvania
1970 New York University
Columbia
1971 New York University
1972 Detroit
1973 New York University
1974 New York University
1975 Wayne State
1976 New York University
1977 Notre Dame
1978 Notre Dame
1979 Wayne State
1980 Wayne State
1981 Pennsylvania
1982 Wayne State
1983 Wayne State
1984 Wayne State
1985 Wayne State
1986 Notre Dame
1987 Columbia
1988 Columbia
1989 Columbia

1. Since 1990, the NCAA has recognized a joint men's and women's fencing champion.

MEN'S AND WOMEN'S FENCING

Year Champion

1990 Penn State
1991 Penn State
1992 Columbia
1993 Columbia
1994 Notre Dame
1995 Penn State

GYMNASTICS

Year Champion

1938 Chicago
1939 Illinois
1940 Illinois
1941 Illinois
1942 Illinois
1948 Penn State
1949 Temple
1950 Illinois
1951 Florida State
1952 Florida State
1953 Penn State
1954 Penn State
1955 Illinois
1956 Illinois
1957 Penn State

Year	Champion
1958	Michigan State
	Illinois
1959	Penn State
1960	Penn State
1961	Penn State
1962	Southern California
1963	Michigan
1964	Southern Illinois
1965	Penn State
1966	Southern Illinois
1967	Southern Illinois
1968	California
1969	Iowa
	Michigan[1]
1970	Michigan
	Michigan[1]
1971	Iowa State
1972	Southern Illinois
1973	Iowa State
1974	Iowa State
1975	California
1976	Penn State
1977	Indiana State
	Oklahoma
1978	Oklahoma
1979	Nebraska
1980	Nebraska
1981	Nebraska
1982	Nebraska
1983	Nebraska
1984	UCLA
1985	Ohio State
1986	Arizona State
1987	UCLA
1988	Nebraska
1989	Illinois
1990	Nebraska
1991	Oklahoma
1992	Stanford
1993	Stanford
1994	Nebraska
1995	Stanford

1. Trampoline.

ICE HOCKEY

Year	Champion
1948	Michigan
1949	Boston College
1950	Colorado College
1951	Michigan
1952	Michigan
1953	Michigan
1954	Rensselaer
1955	Michigan
1956	Michigan
1957	Colorado College
1958	Denver
1959	North Dakota
1960	Denver
1961	Denver
1962	Michigan Tech
1963	North Dakota
1964	Michigan
1965	Michigan Tech
1966	Michigan State
1967	Cornell
1968	Denver
1969	Denver
1970	Cornell
1971	Boston University
1972	Boston University
1973	Wisconsin
1974	Minnesota
1975	Michigan Tech
1976	Minnesota
1977	Wisconsin
1978	Boston University
1979	Minnesota
1980	North Dakota
1981	Wisconsin
1982	North Dakota
1983	Wisconsin
1984	Bowling Green
1985	Rensselaer
1986	Michigan State
1987	North Dakota
1988	Lake Superior State
1989	Harvard
1990	Wisconsin
1991	Northern Michigan
1992	Lake Superior State
1993	Maine
1994	Lake Superior State
1995	Boston University

INDOOR TRACK

Year	Champion
1965	Missouri
1966	Kansas
1967	Southern California
1968	Villanova
1969	Kansas
1970	Kansas
1971	Villanova
1972	Southern California
1973	Manhattan
1974	UTEP
1975	UTEP
1976	UTEP
1977	Washington State
1978	UTEP
1979	Villanova
1980	UTEP
1981	UTEP
1982	UTEP
1983	Southern Methodist
1984	Arkansas
1985	Arkansas
1986	Arkansas
1987	Arkansas
1988	Arkansas
1989	Arkansas
1990	Arkansas
1991	Arkansas
1992	Arkansas
1993	Arkansas
1994	Arkansas
1995	Arkansas

MEN'S AND WOMEN'S RIFLE

Year	Champion
1980	Tennessee Tech
1981	Tennessee Tech
1982	Tennessee Tech
1983	West Virginia
1984	West Virginia
1985	Murray State
1986	West Virginia
1987	Murray State
1988	West Virginia
1989	West Virginia
1990	West Virginia
1991	West Virginia
1992	West Virginia
1993	West Virginia
1994	Alaska Fairbanks
1995	West Virginia

MEN'S AND WOMEN'S SKIING

Year	Champion
1954	Denver
1955	Denver
1956	Denver
1957	Denver
1958	Dartmouth
1959	Colorado
1960	Colorado
1961	Denver
1962	Denver
1963	Denver
1964	Denver
1965	Denver
1966	Denver
1967	Denver
1968	Wyoming
1969	Denver
1970	Denver
1971	Denver
1972	Colorado
1973	Colorado
1974	Colorado
1975	Colorado
1976	Colorado
	Dartmouth
1977	Colorado
1978	Colorado
1979	Colorado
1980	Vermont
1981	Utah
1982	Colorado
1983	Utah
1984	Utah
1985	Wyoming
1986	Utah
1987	Utah
1988	Utah
1989	Vermont
1990	Vermont
1991	Colorado
1992	Vermont
1993	Utah
1994	Vermont
1995	Colorado

SWIMMING AND DIVING

Year	Champion
1937	Michigan
1938	Michigan
1939	Michigan
1940	Michigan
1941	Michigan
1942	Yale
1943	Ohio State
1944	Yale
1945	Ohio State
1946	Ohio State
1947	Ohio State
1948	Michigan
1949	Ohio State
1950	Ohio State
1951	Yale
1952	Ohio State
1953	Yale
1954	Ohio State
1955	Ohio State
	Michigan
1956	Ohio State
1957	Michigan
1958	Michigan
1959	Michigan
1960	Southern California
1961	Michigan
1962	Ohio State
1963	Southern California
1964	Southern California
1965	Southern California
1966	Southern California
1967	Stanford
1968	Indiana
1969	Indiana
1970	Indiana
1971	Indiana
1972	Indiana
1973	Indiana
1974	Southern California
1975	Southern California
1976	Southern California
1977	Southern California
1978	Tennessee
1979	California
1980	California
1981	Texas
1982	UCLA
1983	Florida
1984	Florida
1985	Stanford
1986	Stanford
1987	Stanford
1988	Texas
1989	Texas
1990	Texas
1991	Texas
1992	Stanford
1993	Stanford
1994	Stanford
1995	Michigan

VOLLEYBALL

Year	Champion
1970	UCLA
1971	UCLA
1972	UCLA
1973	San Diego State
1974	UCLA
1975	UCLA
1976	UCLA
1977	Southern California
1978	Pepperdine
1979	UCLA
1980	Southern California
1981	UCLA
1982	UCLA
1983	UCLA
1984	UCLA
1985	Pepperdine
1986	Pepperdine
1987	UCLA
1988	Southern California
1989	UCLA
1990	Southern California
1991	Cal. St., Long Beach
1992	Pepperdine
1993	UCLA
1994	Penn State
1995	UCLA

WRESTLING

Year	Champion
1928	Oklahoma State[1]
1929	Oklahoma State
1930	Oklahoma State[1]
1931	Oklahoma State[1]
1932	Indiana
1933	Oklahoma State[1]
	Iowa State[1]
1934	Oklahoma State
1935	Oklahoma State
1936	Oklahoma
1937	Oklahoma State
1938	Oklahoma State
1939	Oklahoma State
1940	Oklahoma State
1941	Oklahoma State
1942	Oklahoma State
1946	Oklahoma State
1947	Cornell College
1948	Oklahoma State
1949	Oklahoma State
1950	Northern Iowa
1951	Oklahoma
1952	Oklahoma
1953	Penn State
1954	Oklahoma State
1955	Oklahoma State
1956	Oklahoma State
1957	Oklahoma
1958	Oklahoma State
1959	Oklahoma State
1960	Oklahoma
1961	Oklahoma State
1962	Oklahoma State
1963	Oklahoma
1964	Oklahoma State
1965	Iowa State
1966	Oklahoma State
1967	Michigan State
1968	Oklahoma State
1969	Iowa State
1970	Iowa State
1971	Oklahoma State
1972	Iowa State
1973	Iowa State
1974	Oklahoma
1975	Iowa
1976	Iowa
1977	Iowa State
1978	Iowa
1979	Iowa
1980	Iowa
1981	Iowa
1982	Iowa
1983	Iowa
1984	Iowa
1985	Iowa
1986	Iowa
1987	Iowa State
1988	Arizona State
1989	Oklahoma State
1990	Oklahoma State
1991	Iowa
1992	Iowa
1993	Iowa
1994	Oklahoma State
1995	Iowa

1. Unofficial champions.

BASEBALL

Year	Champion
1947	California
1948	Southern California
1949	Texas
1950	Texas
1951	Oklahoma
1952	Holy Cross
1953	Michigan
1954	Missouri
1955	Wake Forest
1956	Minnesota
1957	California
1958	Southern California
1959	Oklahoma State
1960	Minnesota
1961	Southern California
1962	Michigan
1963	Southern California
1964	Minnesota
1965	Arizona State
1966	Ohio State
1967	Arizona State
1968	Southern California
1969	Arizona State
1970	Southern California
1971	Southern California
1972	Southern California
1973	Southern California
1974	Southern California
1975	Texas
1976	Arizona
1977	Arizona State
1978	Southern California
1979	Cal. St., Fullerton
1980	Arizona
1981	Arizona State
1982	Miami (Fla.)
1983	Texas
1984	Cal. St., Fullerton
1985	Miami (Fla.)
1986	Arizona
1987	Stanford
1988	Stanford
1989	Wichita State
1990	Georgia
1991	Louisiana State

1992 Pepperdine
1993 Louisiana State
1994 Oklahoma
1995 Cal. St., Fullerton

GOLF

Year	Champion
1897	Yale
1898	Harvard (spring)
	Yale (fall)
1899	Harvard
1901	Harvard
1902	Yale (spring)
	Harvard (fall)
1903	Harvard
1904	Harvard
1905	Yale
1906	Yale
1907	Yale
1908	Yale
1909	Yale
1910	Yale
1911	Yale
1912	Yale
1913	Yale
1914	Princeton
1915	Yale
1916	Princeton
1919	Princeton
1920	Princeton
1921	Dartmouth
1922	Princeton
1923	Princeton
1924	Yale
1925	Yale
1926	Yale
1927	Princeton
1928	Princeton
1929	Princeton
1930	Princeton
1931	Yale
1932	Yale
1933	Yale
1934	Michigan
1935	Michigan
1936	Yale
1937	Princeton
1938	Stanford
1939	Stanford
1940	Princeton
	Louisiana State
1941	Stanford
1942	Louisiana State
	Stanford
1943	Yale
1944	Notre Dame
1945	Ohio State
1946	Stanford
1947	Louisiana State
1948	San Jose State
1949	North Texas
1950	North Texas
1951	North Texas
1952	North Texas
1953	Stanford
1954	Southern Methodist
1955	Louisiana State
1956	Houston
1957	Houston
1958	Houston
1959	Houston
1960	Houston
1961	Purdue
1962	Houston
1963	Oklahoma State
1964	Houston
1965	Houston
1966	Houston
1967	Houston
1968	Florida
1969	Houston
1970	Houston
1971	Texas
1972	Texas
1973	Florida
1974	Wake Forest
1975	Wake Forest
1976	Oklahoma
1977	Houston
1978	Oklahoma State
1979	Ohio State
1980	Oklahoma State
1981	Brigham Young
1982	Houston
1983	Oklahoma State
1984	Houston
1985	Houston
1986	Wake Forest
1987	Oklahoma State
1988	UCLA
1989	Oklahoma
1990	Arizona
1991	Oklahoma State
1992	Arizona
1993	Florida
1994	Stanford
1995	Oklahoma State

LACROSSE

Year	Champion
1971	Cornell
1972	Virginia
1973	Maryland
1974	Johns Hopkins
1975	Maryland
1976	Cornell
1977	Cornell
1978	Johns Hopkins
1979	Johns Hopkins
1980	Johns Hopkins
1981	North Carolina
1982	North Carolina
1983	Syracuse
1984	Johns Hopkins
1985	Johns Hopkins
1986	North Carolina
1987	Johns Hopkins
1988	Syracuse
1989	Syracuse
1990	Syracuse
1991	North Carolina
1992	Princeton
1993	Syracuse
1994	Princeton
1995	Syracuse

OUTDOOR TRACK

Year	Champion
1921	Illinois
1922	California
1923	Michigan
1925	Stanford
1926	Southern California
1927	Illinois
1928	Stanford
1929	Ohio State
1930	Southern California
1931	Southern California
1932	Indiana
1933	Louisiana State
1934	Stanford
1935	Southern California
1936	Southern California
1937	Southern California
1938	Southern California
1939	Southern California
1940	Southern California
1941	Southern California
1942	Southern California
1943	Southern California
1944	Illinois
1945	Navy
1946	Illinois
1947	Illinois
1948	Minnesota
1949	Southern California
1950	Southern California
1951	Southern California
1952	Southern California
1953	Southern California
1954	Southern California
1955	Southern California
1956	UCLA
1957	Villanova
1958	Southern California
1959	Kansas
1960	Kansas
1961	Southern California
1962	Oregon
1963	Southern California
1964	Oregon
1965	Oregon
	Southern California
1966	UCLA
1967	Southern California
1968	Southern California
1969	San Jose State
1970	Brigham Young
	Kansas
1971	UCLA
1972	UCLA
1973	UCLA
1974	Tennessee
1975	UTEP
1976	Southern California
1977	Arizona State
1978	UCLA
	UTEP
1979	UTEP
1980	UTEP
1981	UTEP
1982	UTEP
1983	Southern Methodist
1984	Oregon
1985	Arkansas
1986	Southern Methodist
1987	UCLA
1988	UCLA
1989	Louisiana State
1990	Louisiana State
1991	Tennessee
1992	Arkansas
1993	Arkansas
1994	Arkansas
1995	Arkansas

TENNIS

Year	Champion
1946	Southern California
1947	William and Mary
1948	William and Mary
1949	San Francisco
1950	UCLA
1951	Southern California
1952	UCLA
1953	UCLA
1954	UCLA
1955	Southern California
1956	UCLA
1957	Michigan
1958	Southern California
1959	Notre Dame
	Tulane
1960	UCLA
1961	UCLA
1962	Southern California
1963	Southern California
1964	Southern California
1965	UCLA
1966	Southern California
1967	Southern California
1968	Southern California
1969	Southern California
1970	UCLA
1971	UCLA
1972	Trinity (Tex.)
1973	Stanford
1974	Stanford
1975	UCLA
1976	Southern California
	UCLA
1977	Stanford
1978	Stanford
1979	UCLA
1980	Stanford
1981	Stanford
1982	UCLA
1983	Stanford
1984	UCLA
1985	Georgia
1986	Stanford
1987	Georgia
1988	Stanford
1989	Stanford
1990	Stanford
1991	Southern California
1992	Stanford
1993	Southern California
1994	Southern California
1995	Stanford

NCAA Women's Major Sports

NCAA DIVISION I WOMEN'S BASKETBALL CHAMPIONSHIPS

Year	Champion	Coach	Outstanding player	Score	Runner-up
1982	Louisiana Tech	Sonja Hogg	Janice Lawrence	76–62	Cheyney
1983	Southern California	Linda Sharp	Cheryl Miller	69–67	Louisiana Tech
1984	Southern California	Linda Sharp	Cheryl Miller	72–61	Tennessee
1985	Old Dominion	Marianne Stanley	Tracy Claxton	70–65	Georgia
1986	Texas	Jody Conradt	Clarissa Davis	97–81	Southern California
1987	Tennessee	Pat Summitt	Tonya Edwards	67–44	Louisiana Tech
1988	Louisiana Tech	Leon Barmore	Erica Westbrooks	56–54	Auburn
1989	Tennessee	Pat Summitt	Bridgette Gordon	76–60	Auburn
1990	Stanford	Tara VanderVeer	Jennifer Azzi	88–81	Auburn
1991	Tennessee	Pat Summitt	Dawn Staley	70–67	Virginia
1992	Stanford	Tara VanderVeer	Molly Goodenbour	78–62	Western Kentucky
1993	Texas Tech	Marcia Sharp	Sheryl Swoopes	84–82	Ohio State
1994	North Carolina	Sylvia Hatchell	Charlotte Smith	60–59	Louisiana Tech
1995	Connecticut	Geno Auriemma	Rebecca Lobo	70–64	Tennessee

CROSS-COUNTRY

Year	Champion
1981	Virginia
1982	Virginia
1983	Oregon
1984	Wisconsin
1985	Wisconsin
1986	Texas
1987	Oregon
1988	Kentucky
1989	Villanova
1990	Villanova
1991	Villanova
1992	Villanova
1993	Villanova
1994	Villanova

FIELD HOCKEY

Year	Champion
1981	Connecticut
1982	Old Dominion
1983	Old Dominion
1984	Old Dominion
1985	Connecticut
1986	Iowa
1987	Maryland
1988	Old Dominion
1989	North Carolina
1990	Old Dominion
1991	Old Dominion
1992	Old Dominion
1993	Maryland
1994	James Madison

OUTDOOR TRACK

Year	Champion
1982	UCLA
1983	UCLA
1984	Florida State
1985	Oregon
1986	Texas
1987	Louisiana State
1988	Louisiana State
1989	Louisiana State
1990	Louisiana State
1991	Louisiana State
1992	Louisiana State
1993	Louisiana State
1994	Louisiana State
1995	Louisiana State

TENNIS

Year	Champion
1982	Stanford
1983	Southern California
1984	Stanford
1985	Southern California
1986	Stanford
1987	Stanford
1988	Stanford
1989	Stanford
1990	Stanford
1991	Stanford
1992	Florida
1993	Texas
1994	Georgia
1995	Texas

GYMNASTICS

Year	Champion
1982	Utah
1983	Utah
1984	Utah
1985	Utah
1986	Utah
1987	Georgia
1988	Alabama
1989	Georgia
1990	Utah
1991	Alabama
1992	Utah
1993	Georgia
1994	Utah
1995	Utah

SOCCER

Year	Champion
1982	North Carolina
1983	North Carolina
1984	North Carolina
1985	George Mason
1986	North Carolina
1987	North Carolina
1988	North Carolina
1989	North Carolina
1990	North Carolina
1991	North Carolina
1992	North Carolina
1993	North Carolina
1994	North Carolina

FENCING

Year	Champion[1]
1982	Wayne State
1983	Penn State
1984	Yale
1985	Yale
1986	Pennsylvania
1987	Notre Dame
1988	Wayne State
1989	Wayne State

1. Since 1990, the NCAA has recognized a joint men's and women's fencing champion.

SWIMMING AND DIVING

Year	Champion
1982	Florida
1983	Stanford
1984	Texas
1985	Texas
1986	Texas
1987	Texas
1988	Texas
1989	Stanford
1990	Texas
1991	Texas
1992	Stanford
1993	Stanford
1994	Stanford
1995	Stanford

SOFTBALL

Year	Champion
1982	UCLA
1983	Texas A&M
1984	UCLA
1985	UCLA
1986	California State, Fullerton
1987	Texas A&M
1988	UCLA
1989	UCLA
1990	UCLA
1991	Arizona
1992	UCLA
1993	Arizona
1994	Arizona
1995	UCLA

GOLF

Year	Champion
1982	Tulsa
1983	Texas Christian
1984	Miami (Fla.)
1985	Florida
1986	Florida
1987	San Jose State
1988	Tulsa
1989	San Jose State
1990	Arizona State
1991	UCLA
1992	San Jose State
1993	Arizona State
1994	Arizona State
1995	Arizona State

LACROSSE

Year	Champion
1982	Massachusetts
1983	Delaware
1984	Temple
1985	New Hampshire
1986	Maryland
1987	Penn State
1988	Temple
1989	Penn State
1990	Harvard
1991	Virginia
1992	Maryland
1993	Virginia
1994	Princeton
1995	Maryland

INDOOR TRACK

Year	Champion
1983	Nebraska
1984	Nebraska
1985	Florida State
1986	Texas
1987	Louisiana State
1988	Texas
1989	Louisiana State
1990	Texas
1991	Louisiana State
1992	Florida
1993	Louisiana State
1994	Louisiana State
1995	Louisiana State

VOLLEYBALL

Year	Champion
1981	Southern California
1982	Hawaii
1983	Hawaii
1984	UCLA
1985	Pacific
1986	Pacific
1987	Hawaii
1988	Texas
1989	California State, Long Beach
1990	UCLA
1991	UCLA
1992	Stanford
1993	Long Beach State
1994	Stanford

AMATEUR ATHLETIC UNION OF THE U.S. (AAU)

AAU House
3400 West 86th Street
P.O. Box 68207
Indianapolis, IN 46268
(317) 872-2900

President: Richard Harkins Founded: 1888

SULLIVAN AWARD

James E. Sullivan was a longtime official of the Amateur Athletic Union. The AAU awards the trophy annually "to the amateur athlete who, by performance, example, and good influence, did the most to advance the cause of good sportsmanship."

Year	Winner (sport)
1930	Bobby Jones (golf)
1931	Barney Berlinger (track and field)
1932	Jim Bausch (track and field)
1933	Glenn Cunningham (track and field)
1934	Bill Bonthron (track and field)
1935	Lawson Little (golf)
1936	Glenn Morris (track and field)
1937	Don Budge (tennis)
1938	Don Lash (track and field)
1939	Joe Burk (rowing)
1940	Greg Rice (track and field)
1941	Leslie MacMitchell (track and field)
1942	Cornelius Warmerdam (track and field)
1943	Gilbert Dodds (track and field)
1944	Ann Curtis (swimming)
1945	Doc Blanchard (football)
1946	Arnold Tucker (football)
1947	John Kelly, Jr. (rowing)
1948	Robert Mathias (track and field)
1949	Dick Button (figure skating)
1950	Fred Wilt (track and field)
1951	Rev. Robert Richards (track and field)
1952	Horace Ashenfelter (track and field)
1953	Dr. Sammy Lee (diving)
1954	Mal Whitfield (track and field)
1955	Harrison Dillard (track and field)
1956	Patricia McCormick (diving)
1957	Bobby Joe Morrow (track and field)
1958	Glenn Davis (track and field)
1959	Parry O'Brien (track and field)
1960	Rafer Johnson (track and field)
1961	Wilma Rudolph (track and field)
1962	James Beatty (track and field)
1963	John Pennel (track and field)
1964	Don Schollander (swimming)
1965	Bill Bradley (basketball)
1966	Jim Ryun (track and field)
1967	Randy Matson (track and field)
1968	Debbie Meyer (swimming)
1969	Bill Toomey (track and field)
1970	John Kinsella (swimming)
1971	Mark Spitz (swimming)
1972	Frank Shorter (track and field)
1973	Bill Walton (basketball)
1974	Rick Wohlhuter (track and field)
1975	Tim Shaw (swimming)
1976	Bruce Jenner (track and field)
1977	John Naber (swimming)
1978	Tracy Caulkins (swimming)
1979	Kurt Thomas (gymnastics)
1980	Eric Heiden (speed skating)
1981	Carl Lewis (track and field)
1982	Mary Decker (track and field)
1983	Edwin Moses (track and field)
1984	Greg Louganis (diving)
1985	Joan Benoit Samuelson (marathon)
1986	Jackie Joyner-Kersee (track and field)
1987	Jim Abbott (baseball)
1988	Florence Griffith Joyner (track and field)
1989	Janet Evans (swimming)
1990	John Smith (wrestling)
1991	Mike Powell (track and field)
1992	Bonnie Blair (speed skating)
1993	Charlie Ward (football, basketball)
1994	Dan Jansen (speed skating)

Source: Amateur Athletic Union.

INTERNATIONAL SPORTS

THE WORLD CUP, 1994

Brazil became the first team to win four World Cups as it defeated three-time champion Italy in a game that was decided by penalty kicks. After two 45-minute periods and two 15-minute overtime periods, neither team had scored a goal, sending the title game to a shootout for the first time ever. In the shootout, Italy's captain Franco Baresi and star player Roberto Baggio both missed high above the crossbar, ensuring a 3–2 win for Brazil.

The final was typical of the entire tournament, in which defense prevailed and few goals were scored. But despite the lack of offense and the lack of interest by many American sports fans, the 1994 World Cup drew record crowds at eight locations across the United States. More than 3.5 million people attended the 52 games, up from 2.5 million at the 1990 World Cup in Italy. The average of 68,604 fans per game (some paying upwards of $300 face value for a ticket) was significantly higher than the 48,282 four years earlier. Television ratings on ESPN and ABC were also surprisingly high, even after the U.S. team fell to Brazil in the second round.

The U.S. team surprised many by playing Switzerland to a 1–1 tie and then beating a heavily-favored Colombia team 2–1. The United States benefited in that game when Colombian defender Andrés Escobar accidentally kicked the ball into his own goal. Ten days later, Escobar was murdered outside a Bogotá nightclub by unidentified gunmen believed to be drug traffickers who had placed large bets on Colombia's success in the tournament. In another shock, Diego Maradona, the hero of Argentina's 1986 World Cup win, was thrown out of the tournament after failing a drug test. Argentina then went on to lose to Romania in the second round. Other on-the-field suprises included Ireland's 1–0 win over Italy in the first round and Bulgaria's 2–1 triumph over defending champion Germany in the quarterfinals. The 1998 World Cup will be held in France.

Round-by-Round Results

Eliminated in First Round

Team	W	L	T	Team	W	L	T
Bolivia	0	2	1	Morocco	0	2	0
Cameroon	0	2	1	Norway	1	1	1
Colombia	1	2	0	Russia	1	2	0
Greece	0	3	0	South Korea	0	1	2

Second Round

Bulgaria 1, Mexico 1 (PK 3–1)[1]
Germany 3, Belgium 2
Italy 2, Nigeria 1 (OT)
Spain 3, Switzerland 0
Romania 3, Argentina 2
Sweden 3, Saudi Arabia 1
Netherlands 2, Ireland 0
Brazil 1, United States 0

Quarterfinals

Bulgaria 2, Germany 1
Italy 2, Spain 1
Sweden 2, Romania 2 (PK 5–4)[2]
Brazil 3, Netherlands 2

Semifinals

Italy 2, Bulgaria 1
Brazil 1, Sweden 0

Third Place

Sweden 4, Bulgaria 0

Finals

Brazil 0, Italy 0 (PK 3–2)[3]

1. Bulgaria won 3–1 on penalty kicks. 2. Sweden won 5–4 on penalty kicks. 3. Brazil won 3–2 on penalty kicks.

THE WORLD CUP

From its origins in various "football" games dating back to ancient Greece and China, soccer (as it is called in the United States) has become the world's most popular sport, with over 20 million participants in over 140 nations. The World Cup championship, modern soccer's most spectacular event, is staged by the Federation Internationale de Football Association (FIFA). Formally known as the Jules Rimet Trophy, the World Cup is awarded every four years to the victor in a 24-nation, 52-game final tournament. Players must represent their home country, regardless of where they regularly play. Millions attend the Cup's many contests and the televised final is viewed by over a billion people worldwide.

Year	Final score	Leading scorer, country (goals)	Host country	Participating nations
1930	Uruguay 4, Argentina 2	Stabile, Argentina (8)	Uruguay	13
1934	Italy 2, Czechoslovakia 1 (OT)	Conen, Germany (4) Nejedly, Czechoslovakia (4) Schiavo, Italy (4)	Italy	29
1938	Italy 4, Hungary 2	Leonidas, Brazil (8)	France	26
1942	No tournament—World War II			
1946	No tournament—World War II			
1950	Uruguay 2, Brazil 1	Ademir, Brazil (7)	Brazil	28
1954	West Germany 3, Hungary 2	Kocsis, Hungary (11)	Switzerland	36
1958	Brazil 5, Sweden 2	Fontaine, France (13)	Sweden	53
1962	Brazil 3, Czechoslovakia 1	Jerkovic, Yugoslavia (5)	Chile	57
1966	England 4, West Germany 2 (OT)	Eusebio, Portugal (9)	England	71
1970	Brazil 4, Italy 1	Muller, West Germany (10)	Mexico	73
1974	West Germany 2, Netherlands 1	Lato, Poland (7)	West Germany	95
1978	Argentina 3, Netherlands 1 (OT)	Kempes, Argentina (6)	Argentina	105
1982	Italy 3, West Germany 1	Rossi, Italy (6)	Spain	109
1986	Argentina 3, West Germany 2	Lineker, England (6)	Mexico	112
1990	West Germany 1, Argentina 0	Schilacci, Italy (6)	Italy	106
1994	Brazil 0, Italy 0 (Brazil won 3–2 on penalty kicks)	Stoichkov, Bulgaria (6)	United States	140

Source: FIFA.

YACHTING

The America's Cup

In 1851 the Royal Yacht Squadron (United Kingdom) presented a "hundred guinea cup" to the winning yacht in a race around the Isle of Wight in the English Channel. The cup was won by the U.S. schooner *America* and thereafter became known as the America's Cup, which was held by the New York Yacht Club. A fitting name it was, for in 24 challenges held over the next 132 years, it remained in the hands of U.S. yachtsmen.

In 1983, the Australian challenger *Australia II* beat the defender *Liberty,* skippered by San Diego's Dennis Conner, marking the first time America had lost its namesake cup. Conner brought the cup back to San Diego in 1987, defeating a New Zealand team led by financier Michael Fay 4–1 in the final round. Defying the custom of waiting three or four years between Cup races, Fay challenged again in 1988 with an unorthodox 132-foot sloop. Unable to develop as sophisticated a monohull on such short notice, the Americans decided to defend the America's Cup with a catamaran. They handily defeated *New Zealand* on the water, and then again in court in 1990, after Fay protested the Americans' use of the catamaran.

Although Conner lost to another American boat, *America³*, before the finals, the United States successfully defended the cup in 1992 against challengers from several countries. But in 1995, New Zealand's *Black Magic* team spanked Conner 5–0 in the final round to take the cup down under for a second time. This challenge was not without controversy either, as Conner switched boats from *Stars and Stripes*, which he had used in the early rounds, to *Young America* for the final round, claiming that *Stars and Stripes* was too slow to beat *Black Magic*. In the end, though, so was *Young America*.

AMERICA'S CUP RESULTS, 1870–1995

Year	Challenger, rig, country	Defender, rig, country
1870	*Cambria*, schooner, UK	*Magic*, schooner, U.S.
1871	*Livonia*, schooner, UK	*Columbia* and *Sappho*, schooners, U.S.
1876	*Countess of Dufferin*, schooner, Canada	*Madeleine*, schooner, U.S.
1881	*Atalanta*, sloop, Canada	*Mischief*, cutter, U.S.
1885	*Genesta*, cutter, UK	*Puritan*, cutter, U.S.
1886	*Galatea*, cutter, UK	*Mayflower*, cutter, U.S.
1887	*Thistle*, cutter, UK	*Volunteer*, cutter, U.S.
1893	*Valkyrie II*, cutter, UK	*Vigilant*, cutter, U.S.
1895	*Valkyrie III*, cutter, UK	*Defender*, cutter, U.S.
1899	*Shamrock*, cutter, UK	*Columbia*, cutter, U.S.
1901	*Shamrock II*, cutter, UK	*Columbia*, cutter, U.S.
1903	*Shamrock III*, cutter, UK	*Reliance*, cutter, U.S.
1920	*Shamrock IV*, cutter, UK	*Resolute*, cutter, U.S.
1930	*Shamrock V*, J-class sloop, UK	*Enterprise*, J-class sloop, U.S.
1934	*Endeavor*, J-class sloop, UK	*Rainbow*, J-class sloop, U.S.
1937	*Endeavor II*, J-class sloop, UK	*Ranger*, J-class sloop, U.S.
1958	*Sceptre*, 12-m, UK	*Columbia*, 12-m, U.S.
1962	*Gretel*, 12-m, Australia	*Weatherly*, 12-m, U.S.
1964	*Sovereign*, 12-m, UK	*Constellation*, 12-m, U.S.
1967	*Dame Pattie*, 12-m, Australia	*Intrepid*, 12-m, U.S.
1970	*Gretel II*, 12-m, Australia	*Intrepid*, 12-m, U.S.
1974	*Southern Cross*, 12-m, Australia	*Courageous*, 12-m, U.S.
1977	*Australia*, 12-m, Australia	*Courageous*, 12-m, U.S.
1980	*Australia*, 12-m, Australia	*Freedom*, 12-m, U.S.
1983	*Australia II*, 12-m, Australia	*Liberty*, 12-m, U.S.
1987	*Stars & Stripes*, 12-m, U.S.	*Kookaburra III*, 12-m, Australia
1988	*New Zealand*, sloop, New Zealand	*Stars & Stripes*, catamaran, U.S.
1992	*Il Moro*, 75-ft., Italy	*America³*, 75-ft., U.S.
1995	*Black Magic*, 75-ft., New Zealand	*Young America*, 75-ft., U.S.

Note: 12-m = international 12-meter class.

FIGURE SKATING

While the Dutch are credited with inventing ice skating, it was British soldiers stationed in Philadelphia who brought it to colonial America. The nation's first skating club was established there in 1849.

FIGURE SKATING CHAMPIONS

U.S. CHAMPIONS

Year	Men	Women
1952	Richard Button	Tenley Albright
1953	Hayes Jenkins	Tenley Albright
1954	Hayes Jenkins	Tenley Albright
1955	Hayes Jenkins	Tenley Albright
1956	Hayes Jenkins	Tenley Albright
1957	Dave Jenkins	Carol Heiss
1958	Dave Jenkins	Carol Heiss
1959	Dave Jenkins	Carol Heiss
1960	Dave Jenkins	Carol Heiss
1961	Bradley Lord	Laurence Owen
1962	Monty Hoyt	Barbara Roles Pursley
1963	Tommy Litz	Lorraine Hanlon
1964	Scott Allen	Peggy Fleming
1965	Gary Visconti	Peggy Fleming
1966	Scott Allen	Peggy Fleming
1967	Gary Visconti	Peggy Fleming
1968	Tim Wood	Peggy Fleming
1969	Tim Wood	Janet Lynn
1970	Tim Wood	Janet Lynn
1971	John Misha Petkevich	Janet Lynn
1972	Ken Shelley	Janet Lynn
1973	Gordon McKellen, Jr.	Janet Lynn
1974	Gordon McKellen, Jr.	Dorothy Hamill
1975	Gordon McKellen, Jr.	Dorothy Hamill
1976	Terry Kubicka	Dorothy Hamill
1977	Charles Tickner	Linda Fratianne
1978	Charles Tickner	Linda Fratianne
1979	Charles Tickner	Linda Fratianne
1980	Charles Tickner	Linda Fratianne
1981	Scott Hamilton	Elaine Zayak
1982	Scott Hamilton	Rosalynn Sumners
1983	Scott Hamilton	Rosalynn Sumners
1984	Scott Hamilton	Rosalynn Sumners
1985	Brian Boitano	Tiffany Chin
1986	Brian Boitano	Debi Thomas
1987	Brian Boitano	Jill Trenary
1988	Brian Boitano	Debi Thomas
1989	Christopher Bowman	Jill Trenary
1990	Todd Eldridge	Jill Trenary
1991	Todd Eldridge	Tonya Harding
1992	Christopher Bowman	Kristi Yamaguchi
1993	Scott Davis	Nancy Kerrigan
1994	Scott Davis	Tonya Harding[1]
1995	Todd Eldredge	Nicole Bobek

1. Later stripped of title.

WORLD CHAMPIONS

Year	Men	Women
1952	Richard Button, U.S.	Jacqueline du Bief, France
1953	Hayes Jenkins, U.S.	Tenley Albright, U.S.
1954	Hayes Jenkins, U.S.	Gundi Busch, W. Germany
1955	Hayes Jenkins, U.S.	Tenley Albright, U.S.
1956	Hayes Jenkins, U.S.	Carol Heiss, U.S.
1957	Dave Jenkins, U.S.	Carol Heiss, U.S.
1958	Dave Jenkins, U.S.	Carol Heiss, U.S.
1959	Dave Jenkins, U.S.	Carol Heiss, U.S.
1960	Alain Giletti, France	Carol Heiss, U.S.
1961	No champion	No champion
1962	Don Jackson, Canada	Sjoukje Dijkstra, Netherlands
1963	Don McPherson, Canada	Sjoukje Dijkstra, Netherlands
1964	Manfred Schnelldorfer, W. Germany	Sjoukje Dijkstra, Netherlands
1965	Alain Calmat, France	Petra Burka, Canada
1966	Emmerich Danzer, Austria	Peggy Fleming, U.S.
1967	Emmerich Danzer, Austria	Peggy Fleming, U.S.
1968	Emmerich Danzer, Austria	Peggy Fleming, U.S.
1969	Tim Wood, U.S.	Gabriele Seyfert, E. Germany
1970	Tim Wood, U.S.	Gabriele Seyfert, E. Germany
1971	Ondrej Nepela, Czechoslovakia	Beatrix Schuba, Austria
1972	Ondrej Nepela, Czechoslovakia	Beatrix Schuba, Austria
1973	Ondrej Nepela, Czechoslovakia	Karen Magnussen, Canada
1974	Jan Hoffmann, E. Germany	Christine Errath, E. Germany
1975	Sergei Volkov, USSR	Dianne de Leeuw, Netherlands-U.S.
1976	John Curry, Great Britain	Dorothy Hamill, U.S.
1977	Vladimir Kovalev, USSR	Linda Fratianne, U.S.
1978	Charles Tickner, U.S.	Anett Potzsch, E. Germany
1979	Vladimir Kovalev, USSR	Linda Fratianne, U.S.
1980	Jan Hoffmann, E. Germany	Anett Potzsch, E. Germany
1981	Scott Hamilton, U.S.	Denise Biellmann, Switzerland
1982	Scott Hamilton, U.S.	Elaine Zayak, U.S.
1983	Scott Hamilton, U.S.	Rosalynn Sumners, U.S.
1984	Scott Hamilton, U.S.	Katarina Witt, E. Germany
1985	Aleksandr Fadeev, USSR	Katarina Witt, E. Germany
1986	Brian Boitano, U.S.	Debi Thomas, U.S.
1987	Brian Orser, Canada	Katarina Witt, E. Germany
1988	Brian Boitano, U.S.	Katarina Witt, E. Germany
1989	Kurt Browning, Canada	Midori Ito, Japan
1990	Kurt Browning, Canada	Jill Trenary, U.S.
1991	Kurt Browning, Canada	Kristi Yamaguchi, U.S.
1992	Victor Petrenko, Russia	Kristi Yamaguchi, U.S.
1993	Kurt Browning, Canada	Oksana Baiul, Ukraine
1994	Elvis Stojko, Canada	Yuko Sata, Japan
1995	Elvis Stojko, Canada	Lu Chen, China

CHESS

CHESS—WORLD CHAMPIONS

Year(s)	Name	Country
1886–94	Wilhelm Steinitz	Austria
1894–1921	Emanuel Lasker	Germany
1921–27	José R. Capablanca	Cuba
1927–35	Alexander A. Alekhine	France
1935–37	Max Euwe	Netherlands
1937–48	Alexander A. Alekhine	France
1948–57	Mikhail Botvinnik	USSR
1957–58	Vassily Smyslov	USSR
1958–60	Mikhail Botvinnik	USSR
1960–61	Mikhail Tal	USSR
1961–63	Mikhail Botvinnik	USSR
1963–69	Tigran Petrosian	USSR
1969–72	Boris Spassky	USSR
1972–75	Bobby Fischer	U.S.
1975–85	Anatoly Karpov	USSR
1985–	Gary Kasparov[1]	USSR/Russia
1993–	Anatoly Karpov[1]	Russia

1. In 1993, Kasparov started his own chess sanctioning body, the Professional Chess Association, leaving his World Chess Federation (FIDE) championship vacant, whereupon FIDE awarded the title to Karpov. **Source:** U.S. Chess Federation.

U.S. CHESS CHAMPIONS

Year(s)	Name
1845–57	Charles Henry Stanley
1857–71	Paul Morphy
1871–90	Capt. George Mackenzie
1890–91	Jackson Showalter
1891–94	Soloman Lipschutz
1894	Jackson Showalter
1894–95	Albert B. Hodges
1895–97	Jackson Showalter
1897–1906	Harry Nelson Pillsbury
1906–9	Jackson Showalter
1909–36	Frank J. Marshall
1936	Samuel Reshevsky
1938	Samuel Reshevsky
1940	Samuel Reshevsky
1942	Samuel Reshevsky
1944	Arnold Denker
1946	Samuel Reshevsky
1948	Herman Steiner
1951	Larry Evans
1952	Larry Evans
1954	Arthur Bisguier
1957–58	Bobby Fischer
1958–59	Bobby Fischer
1959–60	Bobby Fischer
1960–61	Bobby Fischer
1961–62	Larry Evans
1962–63	Bobby Fischer
1963–64	Bobby Fischer
1965	Bobby Fischer
1966	Bobby Fischer
1968	Larry Evans
1969	Samuel Reshevsky
1972	Robert Byrne
1973	John Grefe, Lubosh Kavalek (tie)
1974	Walter Browne
1975	Walter Browne
1977	Walter Browne
1978	Lubomir Kavalek
1980	Walter Browne, Larry Evans, Larry Christiansen (tie)
1981	Walter Browne, Yasser Seirawan (tie)
1983	Walter Browne, Larry Christiansen, Roman Dzindzichashvili (tie)
1984	Lev Alburt
1985	Lev Alburt
1986	Yasser Seirawan
1987	Joel Benjamin, Nick deFirmian (tie)
1988	Michael Wilder
1989	Roman Dzindzichasvili, Yasser Seirawan, Stuart Rachels (tie)
1990	Lev Alburt
1991	Gata Kamsky
1992	Patrick Wolff
1993	Alexander Shabalaov, Alex Yermolinsky (tie)
1994	Boris Gulko

Note: The U.S. championship is not held every year. **Source:** U.S. Chess Federation.

CYCLING

THE TOUR DE FRANCE

Established in 1903, the world's most important bicycle road race covers between 2,500 and 3,000 miles, including at least one mountain with an elevation of over 7,500 feet.

Year(s)	Champion	Year(s)	Champion
1903	Maurice Garin	1949	Fausto Coppi
1904	Henri Cornet	1950	Ferdi Kubler
1905	Louis Trousselier	1951	Hugo Koblet
1906	Rene Pottier	1952	Fausto Coppi
1907–08	Lucien Petit-Breton	1953–55	Louison Bobet
1909	Francois Faber	1956	Roger Walkowiak
1910	Octave Lapize	1957	Jacques Anquetil
1911	Gustave Garrigou	1958	Charly Gaul
1912	Odile Defraye	1959	Federico Bahamontes
1913–14	Philippe Thijs	1960	Gastone Nencini
1919	Firmin Lambot	1961–64	Jacques Anquetil
1920	Philippe Thijs	1965	Felice Gimondi
1921	Leon Scieur	1966	Lucien Aimar
1922	Firmin Lambot	1967	Roger Pingeon
1923	Henri Pelissier	1968	Jan Janssen
1924–25	Ottavio Bottecchia	1969–72	Eddy Merckx
1926	Lucien Buysse	1973	Luis Ocana
1927–28	Nicolas Frantz	1974	Eddy Merckx
1929	Maurice Dewaele	1975	Bernard Thevenet
1930	Andre Leducq	1976	Lucien Van Impe
1931	Antonin Magne	1977	Bernard Thevenet
1932	Andre Leducq	1978–79	Bernard Hinault
1933	Georges Speicher	1980	Joop Zoetemelk
1934	Antonin Magne	1981–82	Bernard Hinault
1935	Romain Maes	1983–84	Laurent Fignon
1936	Sylvere Maes	1985	Bernard Hinault
1937	Roger Lapebie	1986	Greg Le Mond
1938	Gino Bartali	1987	Stephen Roche
1939	Sylvere Maes	1988	Pedro Delgado
1947	Jean Robic	1989–90	Greg Le Mond
1948	Gino Bartali	1991–95	Miguel Indurain

MARATHON RUNNING

Marathons are 26 miles, 385 yards long, the distance purportedly run by the Athenian messenger who announced his city-state's victory over the Persian Empire on the Plains of Marathon in 490 B.C. The oldest and best-known U.S. marathon covers a route from Hopkinton, Massachusetts, to downtown Boston. For many years, the Boston Athletic Association organized the race on an amateur basis, and winners received only a laurel wreath and the traditional pot of beef stew.

BOSTON MARATHON CHAMPIONS

MEN

Year	Name, city/state/country	Time
1897	John J. McDermott, New York	2:55:10
1898	Ronald J. McDonald, Cambridge, Mass.	2:42:00
1899	Lawrence J. Brignolia, Cambridge, Mass.	2:54:38
1900	James J. Caffrey, Hamilton, Ont.	2:39:44
1901	James J. Caffrey, Hamilton, Ont.	2:29:23
1902	Samuel A. Mellor, Yonkers, N.Y.	2:43:12
1903	John C. Lorden, Cambridge, Mass.	2:41:29
1904	Michael Spring, New York	2:38:04
1905	Fred Lorz, Yonkers, N.Y.	2:38:25
1906	Timothy Ford, Cambridge, Mass.	2:45:45
1907	Thomas Longboat, Hamilton, Ont.	2:24:24
1908	Thomas P. Morrissey, Yonkers, N.Y.	2:25:43
1909	Henri Renaud, Nashua, N.H.	2:53:36
1910	Fred L. Cameron, Amherst, Nova Scotia	2:28:52
1911	Clarence H. DeMar, Melrose, Mass.	2:21:39
1912	Michael J. Ryan, New York	2:21:18
1913	Fritz Carlson, Minneapolis	2:25:14
1914	James Duffy, Hamilton, Ont.	2:25:01
1915	Edouard Fabre, Montreal	2:31:41
1916	Arthur V. Roth, Roxbury, Mass.	2:27:16
1917	William K. Kennedy, Port Chester, N.Y.	2:28:37
1918	(WWI) Service team race won by Camp Devens	
1919	Carl W. A. Linder, Quincy, Mass.	2:29:13
1920	Peter Trivoulidas, Greece	2:29:31
1921	Frank Zuna, Newark, N.J.	2:18:57
1922	Clarence H. DeMar, Dorchester Club, Mass.	2:18:10
1923	Clarence H. DeMar, Melrose, Mass.	2:23:37
1924	Clarence H. DeMar, Melrose, Mass.	2:29:40
1925	Charles L. Mellor, Chicago	2:33:00
1926	John C. Miles, Sidney Mines, Nova Scotia	2:25:40
1927	Clarence H. DeMar, Melrose, Mass.	2:40:22
1928	Clarence H. DeMar, Melrose, Mass.	2:37:07
1929	John C. Miles, Hamilton, Ont.	2:33:08
1930	Clarence H. DeMar, Melrose, Mass.	2:34:48
1931	James P. Henigan, Medford, Mass.	2:46:45
1932	Paul deBruyn, Germany	2:33:36
1933	Leslie Pawson, Pawtucket, R.I.	2:33:01
1934	Dave Komonen, Sudbury, Ont.	2:32:53
1935	John A. Kelley, Arlington, Mass.	2:32:07
1936	Ellison M. (Tarzan) Brown, Alton, R.I.	2:33:40
1937	Walter Young, Verdun, Quebec	2:33:20
1938	Leslie Pawson, Pawtucket, R.I.	2:35:34
1939	Ellison M. (Tarzan) Brown, Alton, R.I.	2:28:51
1940	Gerard Cote, Ste.-Hyacinthe, Quebec	2:33:20
1941	Leslie Pawson, Pawtucket, R.I.	2:30:38
1942	Bernard Joe Smith, Medford	2:26:51
1943	Gerard Cote, Ste.-Hyacinthe, Quebec	2:28:25
1944	Gerard Cote, Ste.-Hyacinthe, Quebec	2:31:50

Year	Name, city/state/country	Time
1945	John A. Kelley, West Acton, Mass.	2:30:40
1946	Stylianos Kyriakides, Greece	2:29:27
1947	Yun Bok Suh, Korea	2:25:39
1948	Gerard Cote, Ste.-Hyacinthe, Quebec	2:31:02
1949	Karle Gosta Leandersson, Sweden	2:31:50
1950	Kee Yong Ham, Korea	2:32:39
1951	Shigeki Tanaka, Japan	2:27:45
1952	Doroteo Flores, Guatemala	2:31:53
1953	Keizo Yamada, Japan	2:18:51
1954	Veikko L. Karvonen, Finland	2:20:39
1955	Hideo Hamamura, Japan	2:18:22
1956	Antti Viskari, Finland	2:14:14
1957	John J. Delley, Boston	2:20:05
1958	Franjo Mihalic, Yugoslavia	2:25:54
1959	Eino Oksanen, Finland	2:22:42
1960	Paavo Kotila, Finland	2:20:54
1961	Eino Oksanen, Finland	2:23:39
1962	Eino Oksanen, Finland	2:23:48
1963	Aurele Vandendriessche, Belgium	2:18:58
1964	Aurele Vandendriessche, Belgium	2:19:59
1965	Morio Shigematsu, Japan	2:16:33
1966	Kenji Kimihara, Japan	2:17:11
1967	David McKenzie, New Zealand	2:15:45
1968	Ambrose Burfoot, Wesleyan University	2:22:17
1969	Yoshiaki Unetani, Japan	2:13:49
1970	Ron Hill, England	2:10:30
1971	Alavaro Mejia, West Valley TC, Calif.	2:18l45
1972	Olavi Suomalainen, Finland	2:15:39
1973	Jon Anderson, Oregon	2:16:03
1974	Neil Cusack, East Tennessee State	2:13:39
1975	Bill Rodgers, Melrose, Mass.	2:09:55
1976	Jack Fultz, Georgetown University	2:20:19
1977	Jerome Drayton, Toronto, Ont.	2:14:46
1978	Bill Rodgers, Melrose, Mass.	2:10:13
1979	Bill Rodgers, Melrose, Mass.	2:09:27
1980	Bill Rodgers, Melrose, Mass.	2:12:11
1981	Toshihiko Seko, Japan	2:09:26
1982	Alberto Salazar, Wayland, Mass.	2:08:52
1983	Gregory A. Meyer, Wellesley, Mass.	2:09:00
1984	Geoff Smith, Rhode Island	2:10:34
1985	Geoff Smith, Massachusetts	2:14:05
1986	Robert de Castella, Australia	2:07:51
1987	Toshihiko Seko, Japan	2:11:50
1988	Ibrahim Hussein, Kenya	2:08:43
1989	Abebe Mekonnen, Ethiopia	2:09:06
1990	Gelindo Bordin, Italy	2:08:20
1991	Ibrahim Hussein, Kenya	2:11:06
1992	Ibrahim Hussein, Kenya	2:08:14
1993	Cosmas N'Deti, Kenya	2:09:33
1994	Cosmas N'Deti, Kenya	2:07:15
1995	Cosmas N'Deti, Kenya	2:09:22

WOMEN

Year	Name, city/state/country	Time
1972	Nina Kuscsik, New York	3:10:26
1973	Jacqueline Hansen, California	3:05:59
1974	Miki Gorman, California	2:47:11
1975	Liane Winter, West Germany	2:42:24
1976	Kim Merritt, Wisconsin	2:47:10
1977	Miki Gorman, California	2:46:22
1978	Gayle Barron, Georgia	2:44:52
1979	Joan Benoit, Maine	2:35:15
1980	Jacqueline Gareau, Canada	2:34:28
1981	Allison Roe, New Zealand	2:26:46
1982	Charlotte Teske, West Germany	2:29:33
1983	Joan Benoit, Massachusetts	2:22:43
1984	Lorraine Moller, New Zealand	2:29:28
1985	Lisa Larsen-Weidenbach, Massachusetts	2:34:06
1986	Ingrid Kristiansen, Norway	2:24:55
1987	Rosa Mota, Portugal	2:25:21
1988	Rosa Mota, Portugal	2:24:30
1989	Ingrid Kristiansen, Norway	2:24:33
1990	Rosa Mota, Portugal	2:25:24
1991	Wanda Panfil, Poland	2:24:18
1992	Olga Markova, Russia	2:23:43
1993	Olga Markova, Russia	2:25:27
1994	Uta Pippig, Germany	2:21:45
1995	Uta Pippig, Germany	2:25:11

Source: Boston Athletic Assn.

NEW YORK MARATHON CHAMPIONS

MEN

Year	Name	Time
1970	Gary Muhrcke	2:31:39
1971	Norman Higgins	2:22:55
1972	Sheldon Karlin	2:27:53
1973	Tom Fleming	2:21:55
1974	Norbert Sander	2:26:31
1975	Tom Fleming	2:19:27
1976	Bill Rodgers	2:10:10
1977	Bill Rodgers	2:11:28
1978	Bill Rodgers	2:12:12
1979	Bill Rodgers	2:11:42
1980	Alberto Salazar	2:09:41
1981	Alberto Salazar	2:08:13
1982	Alberto Salazar	2:09:29
1983	Rod Dixon	2:08:59
1984	Orlando Pizzolato	2:14:53
1985	Orlando Pizzolato	2:11:34
1986	Gianni Poli	2:11:06
1987	Ibrahim Hussein	2:11:01
1988	Steve Jones	2:08:20
1989	Jumo Ikangaa	2:08:01
1990	Douglas Wakiihuri	2:12:39
1991	Salvador Garcia	2:09:28
1992	Willie Mtolo	2:09:29
1993	Andres Espinosa	2:10:04
1994	German Silva	2:11:21

WOMEN

Year	Name	Time
1971	Beth Bonner	2:55:22
1972	Nina Kuscsik	3:08:42
1973	Nina Kuscsik	2:57:08
1974	Katherine Switzer	3:07:29
1975	Kim Merritt	2:46:15
1976	Miki Gorman	2:39:11
1977	Miki Gorman	2:43:10
1978	Grete Waitz	2:32:30
1979	Grete Waitz	2:27:33
1980	Grete Waitz	2:25:41
1981	Allison Roe	2:25:29
1982	Grete Waitz	2:27:14
1983	Grete Waitz	2:27:00
1984	Grete Waitz	2:29:30
1985	Grete Waitz	2:28:34
1986	Grete Waitz	2:28:06
1987	Priscilla Welch	2:30:17
1988	Grete Waitz	2:28:07
1989	Ingrid Kristiansen	2:25:30
1990	Wanda Panfil	2:30:45
1991	Liz McColgan	2:27:32
1992	Lisa Ondieki	2:24:00
1993	Uta Pippig	2:26:24
1994	Tegla Loroupe	2:27:37

Source: New York Roadrunners Club.

TRACK AND FIELD

TRACK AND FIELD WORLD RECORDS (as of July 12, 1995)

These are the recognized records of the IAAF (International Amateur Athletic Federation). Marks pending approval by the IAAF are denoted by "p." All walk records must have been made on a track, and all relay records must be made by teams composed of individuals from the same country. Indoor records must be performed on tracks no larger than 200 m in circumference, and the meet must be subject to drug testing.

MEN

Event	(Min./Sec.)	Record holder (country)	Date
100 m	9.85	Leroy Burrell (U.S.)	7/6/94
200 m	19.72	Pietro Mennea (Italy)	9/17/79
400 m	43.29	Butch Reynolds (U.S.)	8/17/88
800 m	1:41.73	Sebastian Coe (U.K.)	6/10/81
1,000 m	2:12.18	Sebastian Coe (U.K.)	7/11/81
1,500 m	3:27.37	Nourredine Morceli (Algeria)	7/12/95
Mile	3:44.39	Nourredine Morceli (Algeria)	9/5/93
2,000 m	4:47.88p	Nourredine Morceli (Algeria)	7/3/95
3,000 m	7:25.11	Nourredine Morceli (Algeria)	8/2/94
Steeplechase	8:02.08	Moses Kiptanui (Kenya)	8/19/92
5,000 m	12:55.30p	Moses Kiptanui (Kenya)	6/8/95
10,000 m	26:43.63p	Haile Gebreselasie (Ethiopia)	6/5/95
Marathon	2:06:50	Belayneh Densimo (Ethiopia)	4/17/88
110 m hurdles	12.91	Colin Jackson (U.K.)	8/20/93
400 m hurdles	46.78	Kevin Young (U.S.)	8/6/92
20 km walk	1:17:25.50	Bernardo Segura (Mexico)	5/7/94
50 km walk	3:41:28.20	Rene Piller (France)	5/7/94
4 x 100 m	37.40	United States (tie) (Mike Marsh, Leroy Burrell, Dennis Mitchell, Carl Lewis)	8/8/92
	37:40	United States (tie) (John Drummond, Andre Cason, Dennis Mitchell, Leroy Burrell)	8/21/93
4 x 200 m	1:18.68	Santa Monica Track Club (USA) (Mike Marsh 20.0, Leroy Burrell 19.6, Floyd Heard 19.7, Carl Lewis 19.4)	4/17/94
4 x 400 m	2:54.29p	United States (Andrew Valmon 44.5, Quincy Watts 43.6, Butch Reynolds 43.2, Michael Johnson 43.0)	8/22/93

Event	Meters	Ft./In.	Record holder (country)	Date
High jump	2.45	8-0.5	Javier Sotomayor (Cuba)	7/27/93
Pole vault	6.14	20-1.75	Sergey Bubka (Ukraine)	7/31/94
Long jump	8.95	29-4.5	Mike Powell (U.S.)	8/30/91
Triple jump	17.97	58-11.5	Willie Banks (U.S.)	6/16/85
Shot put	23.12	75-10.25	Randy Barnes (U.S.)	5/20/90
Discus	74.08	243-0	Jurgen Schult (East Germany)	6/6/86
Hammer throw	86.74	284-7	Yuriy Syedikh (USSR)	8/30/86
Javelin	95.66	313-10	Jan Zelezny (Czech Republic)	8/29/93
Decathlon	8,891 points		Dan O'Brien (U.S.) (10.43, 8.08, 16.69, 2.07, 48.51, 13.98, 48.56, 5.00, 62.58, 4:42.10)	9/5/92

WOMEN

Event	(Min./Sec.)	Record holder (country)	Date
100 m	10.49	Florence Griffith Joyner (U.S.)	7/16/88
200 m	21.34	Florence Griffith Joyner (U.S.)	9/29/88
400 m	47.60	Marita Koch (East Germany)	10/6/85
800 m	1:53.28	Jarmila Kratochvilova (Czech.)	7/26/83

Event	(Min./Sec.)	Record holder (country)	Date
1,000 m	2:30.67	Christine Wachtel (E. Germany)	8/17/90
1,500 m	3:50.46	Qu Yunxia (China)	9/11/93
Mile	4:15.61	Paula Ivan (Romania)	7/10/89
2,000 m	5:25.36	Sonia O'Sullivan (Ireland)	7/9/94
3,000 m	8:06.11	Wang Junxia (China)	9/13/93
5,000 m	14:37.33	Ingrid Kristiansen (Norway)	8/5/86
10,000 m	29:31.78	Wang Junxia (China)	9/8/93
Marathon	2:21:06	Ingrid Kristiansen (Norway)	4/21/85
100 m hurdles	12.21	Yordanka Donkova (Bulgaria)	8/20/88
400 m hurdles	52.74	Sally Gunnell (U.K.)	8/19/93
4 x 100 m	41.37	East Germany	10/6/85
		(Silke Moller, Sabine Rieger, Ingrid Auerswald, Marlies Gohr)	
4 x 200 m	1:28.15	East Germany	8/9/80
		(Marlies Gohr, Romy Muller, Barbel Wocker, Marita Koch)	
4 x 400 m	3:15.17	Soviet Union	10/1/88
		(Tatyana Ledovskaya 50.12, Olga Nazarova 47.82, Maria Pinigina 49.43, Olga Bryzgina 47.78)	
5 km walk	20:17.19	Kerry Saxby (Australia)	1/14/90
10 km walk	41:37.90p	Gao Hongmiao (China)	4/7/94

Event	Meters	Ft./In.	Record holder (country)	Date
High jump	2.09	6-10.25	Stefka Kostadinova (Bulgaria)	8/30/87
Pole vault	4.15p	13-7.25p	Daniela Bartova (Czech Republic)	7/5/95
Long jump	7.52	24-8.25	Galina Chistyakova (USSR)	6/11/88
Triple jump	15.09	49-6.25	Ann Biryukova (Russia)	8/21/93
Shot put	22.63	74-3	Natalya Lisovskaya (USSR)	6/7/87
Discus	76.80	252-0	Gabriele Reinsch (East Germany)	7/9/88
Hammer throw	68.16p	223-7p	Olga Kuzenkova (Russia)	6/18/95
Javelin	80.00	262-5	Petra Felke (East Germany)	9/9/88
Heptathlon	7,291 points		Jackie Joyner-Kersee (U.S.)	9/24/88
	(12.69, 1.6, 15.80, 22.56, 7.27, 45.66, 2:08.51)			

Source: International Amateur Athletic Federation.

WORLD INDOOR RECORDS

MEN

Event	Min./Sec.	Record holder (country)	Date
50 m	5.61	Manfred Kokot (W. Germany)	2/4/73
	5.61	James Sanford (U.S.)	2/20/81
60 m	6.41	Andre Cason (U.S.)	2/14/92
100 m	10.16	Eugene Ray (W. Germany)	1/25/76
200 m	20.25	Linford Christie (United Kingdom)	2/19/95
300 m	32.19	Robinson da Silva (Brazil)	2/24/89
400 m	44.63	Michael Johnson (U.S.)	3/4/95
800 m	1:44.84	Paul Ereng (Kenya)	3/4/89
1,000 m	2:15.26	Nourredine Morceli (Algeria)	2/22/92
1,500 m	3:34.16	Nourredine Morceli (Algeria)	2/28/91
Mile	3:49.78	Eamonn Coghlan (Ireland)	2/27/83
3,000 m	7:35.12p	Moses Kiptanui (Kenya)	2/12/95
5,000 m	13:20.40	Sulëiman Nyambui (Tanzania)	2/6/81
50 m hurdles	6.25	Mark McKoy (Canada)	3/5/86
60 m hurdles	7.30	Colin Jackson (United Kingdom)	3/6/94
5,000 m walk	18:07.08	Mikhail Shchennikov (Russia)	2/14/95
4 x 200 m	1:22.11	Great Britain	3/3/91
4 x 400 m	3:03.05	Germany	3/10/91
4 x 800 m	7:17.80	USSR	3/14/71

Event	Meters	Ft./In.	Record holder (country)	Date
High jump	2.43	7-11.5	Javier Sotomayor (Cuba)	3/4/89
Pole vault	6.15	20-2	Sergey Bubka (Ukraine)	2/21/93
Long jump	8.79	28-10.25	Carl Lewis (U.S.)	1/27/84
Triple jump	17.77	58-3.75	Leonid Voloshin (Russia)	2/6/94
Shot put	22.66	74-4.25	Randy Barnes (U.S.)	1/20/89
Heptathlon	6,476 points		Dan O'Brien (U.S.)	3/14/93

WOMEN

Event	Min./Sec.	Record holder (country)	Date
50 m	5.96p	Irina Privalova (Russia)	2/9/95
60	6.92	Irina Privalova (Russia)	2/9/95
100 m	11.15	Marita Koch (East Germany)	1/12/80
200 m	21.87	Merlene Ottey (Jamaica)	2/13/93
400 m	49.59	Jarmila Kratochvilova (Czech.)	3/7/82
800 m	1:56.40	Christine Wachtel (East Germany)	2/13/88
1,000 m	2:34.41	Lyubov Kremlyova (Russia)	2/15/95
1,500 m	4:00.27	Doina Melinte (Romania)	2/9/90
Mile	4:17.14	Doina Melinte (Romania)	2/9/90
3,000 m	8:33.82	Elly van Hulst (Holland)	3/4/89
5,000 m	15:03.17	Liz McColgan (U.K.)	2/22/92
50 m hurdles	6.58	Cornelia Oschkenat (East Germany)	2/20/88
60 m hurdles	7.69	Lyudmila Narozhilenko (USSR)	2/4/90
1,500 m walk	5:54.35	Debbie Lawrence (U.S.)	2/8/91
3,000 m walk	11:44.00	Alina Ivanova (CIS)	2/7/92
4 x 200 m	1:32.55	SC Eintracht Hamm (West Germany)	2/20/88
4 x 400 m	3:27.22	Soviet National Team	3/10/91
4 x 800 m	8:18.71	Russia	2/4/94

Event	Meters	Ft./In.	Record holder (country)	Date
High jump	2.07	6-9.5	Heike Henkel (Germany)	2/8/92
Pole vault	4.15	13-7.25p	Sun Caiyun (China)	2/15/95
Long jump	7.37	24-2.25	Heike Drechsler (East Germany)	2/13/88
Triple jump	15.03	49-3.75p	Yolanda Chen (Russia)	3/11/95
Shot put	22.50	73-10	Helena Fibingerova (Czech.)	2/19/77
Pentathlon	4,991 points		Irina Belova (Unified Team)	2/15/92

Source: International Amateur Athletic Federation.

THE OLYMPIC GAMES

1994 Winter Olympics
Lillehammer, Norway, February 12–27, 1994

Event	Gold	Silver	Bronze
Alpine skiing—men			
Downhill	Tommy Moe, United States 1:45.75	Kjetil Andre Aamodt, Norway 1:45.79	Edward Podivinsky, Canada 1:45.87
Giant slalom	Markus Wasmeier, Germany 2:52.46	Urs Kaelin, Switzerland 2:52.48	Christian Mayer, Austria 2:52.58
Super giant slalom	Markus Wasmeier, Germany 1:32.53	Tommy Moe, United States 1:32.61	Kjetil Andre Aamodt, Norway 1:32.93
Slalom	Thomas Stangassinger, Austria 2:02.02	Alberto Tomba, Italy 2:02.17	Jure Kosir, Slovenia 2:02.53
Combined (downhill/slalom)	Lasse Kjus, Norway 3:17.53	Kjetil Andre Aamodt, Norway 3:18.55	Harald Strand Nilsen, Norway 3:19.14
Alpine skiing—women			
Downhill	Katja Seizinger, Germany 1:35.93	Picabo Street, United States 1:36.59	Isolde Kostner, Italy 1:36.85
Giant slalom	Deborah Compagnoni, Italy 2:30.97	Martina Ertl, Germany 2:32.19	Vreni Schneider, Switzerland 2:32.97
Super giant slalom	Diann Roffe-Steinrotter, United States 1:22.15	Svetlana Gladischeva, Russia 1:22.44	Isolde Kostner, Italy 1:22.45
Slalom	Vreni Schneider, Switzerland 1:56.01	Elfriede Eder, Austria 1:56.35	Katja Koren, Slovenia 1:56.61
Combined (downhill/slalom)	Pernilla Wiberg, Sweden 3:05.16	Vreni Schneider, Switzerland 3:05.29	Alenka Dovzan, Slovenia 3:06.64

Event	Gold	Silver	Bronze
Biathlon (cross-country skiing and riflery)—men			
10K (6.21 mi.)	Sergei Tchepikov, Russia 28:07.0	Ricco Gross, Germany 28:13.0	Sergei Tarasov, Russia 28:27.4
20K (12.4 mi)	Sergei Tarasov, Russia 57:25.3	Frank Luck, Germany 57:28.7	Sven Fischer, Germany 57:41.9
4 x 7.5K (18.6 mi.) relay	Germany 1:30:22.1	Russia 1:31:23.6	France 1:32:31.3
Biathlon (cross-country skiing and riflery)—women			
7.5K (4.65 mi.)	Myriam Bedard, Canada 26:08.8	Svetlana Paramygina, Belarus 26:09.9	Valentyna Tserbe, Ukraine 26:10.0
15K (9.3 mi.)	Myriam Bedard, Canada 52:06.6	Anne Briand, France 52:53.3	Ursula Disl, Germany 53:15.3
4 x 7.5K (18.6 mi.) relay	Russia 1:47:19.5	Germany 1:51:16.5	France 1:52:28.3
Bobsled			
Two-man	Switzerland 1 3:30.81	Switzerland 2 3:30.86	Italy 1 3:31.01
Four-man	Germany 2 3:27.78	Switzerland 1 3:27.84	Germany 1 13:28.01
Figure skating			
Men	Aleksei Urmanov, Russia	Elvis Stojko, Canada	Philippe Candeloro, France
Women	Oksana Baiul, Ukraine	Nancy Kerrigan, United States	Chen Lu, China
Pairs	Yekaterina Gordeeva and Sergei Grinkov, Russia	Natalya Mishkutienok and Artur Dmitriev, Russia	Isabelle Brasseur and Lloyd Eisler, Canada

Event	Gold	Silver	Bronze
Ice dancing	Oksana Gritschuk and Evgeni Platov, Russia	Maya Usova and Alexandr Zhulin, Russia	Jayne Torvill and Christopher Dean, United Kingdom
Freestyle skiing—men			
Moguls	Jean-Luc Brassard, Canada 27.24 pts.	Sergei Shoupletsov, Russia 26.90	Edgar Grospiron, France 26.64
Aerials	Andreas Schoenbaechler, Switzerland 234.67	Philippe Laroche, Canada 228.63	Lloyd Langlois, Canada 222.44
Freestyle skiing—women			
Moguls	Stine Lise Hattestad, Norway 25.97 pts.	Liz McIntyre, United States 25.89	Elizaveta Kojevnikova, Russia 25.81
Aerials	Lina Cherjazova, Uzbekistan 166.84	Marie Lindgren, Sweden 165.88	Hilde Synnove Lid, Norway 164.13
Ice hockey	Sweden	Canada	Finland
Luge			
Singles—men	Georg Hackl, Germany 3:21.571	Markus Prock, Austria 3:21.584	Armin Zoggeler, Italy 3:21.833
Two-seater—men	Kurt Brugger and Wilfried Huber, Italy 1:36.720	Hansjorg Raffl and Norbert Huber, Italy 1:36.769	Stefan Krausse and Jan Behrendt, Germany 1:36.945
Singles—women	Gerda Weissensteiner, Italy 3:15.517	Susi Erdmann, Germany 3:16.276	Andrea Tagwerker, Austria 3:16.652
Nordic skiing and jumping—men			
10K (6.2 mi.) cross country	Bjorn Daehlie, Norway 24:20.1	Vladimir Smirnov, Kazakhstan 24:38.3	Marco Albarello, Italy 24:42.3
15K (9.3 mi.) pursuit method	Bjorn Daehlie, Norway 1:00:08.8	Vladimir Smirnov, Kazakhstan 1:00:38.0	Silvio Fauner, Italy 1:01:48.6
30K (18.6 mi.) cross country	Thomas Alsgaard, Norway 1:12:26.4	Bjorn Daehlie, Norway 1:13:13.6	Mika Myllyla, Finland 1:14:14.0
40K (24.8 mi.) cross country relay	Italy 1:41:15.0	Norway 1:41.15.4	Finland 1:42:15.6
50K (31.2 mi.) cross country	Vladimir Smirnov, Kazakhstan 2:07:20.3	Mika Myllyla, Finland 2:08:41.9	Sture Sivertsen, Norway 2:08:49.0
90-meter (295.3 ft.) ski jump, normal hill	Espen Bredesen, Norway 282.0	Lasse Ottesen, Norway 268.0	Dieter Thoma, Germany 260.5
120-meter (393.7 ft.) ski jump, large hill	Jens Weissflog, Germany 274.5	Espen Bredesen, Norway 266.5	Andreas Goldberger, Austria 255.0
120-meter (393.7 ft.) ski jump, team	Germany, 970.1	Japan, 956.9	Austria 918.9
Nordic combined (cross country/ski jump)	Fred Lundberg, Norway	Takanori Kono, Japan	Bjarte Vik, Norway
Nordic combined, team	Japan	Norway, 4:49.1 behind	Switzerland, 7:48.1 behind
Nordic skiing—women			
5K (3.1 mi.) cross country	Lyubov Egorova, Russia 14:08.8	Manuela di Centa, Italy 14:28.3	Marja-Liisa Kirvesniemi, Finland 14:36.0
10K (6.2 mi.) pursuit method	Lyubov Egorova, Russia 41:38.1	Manuela di Centa, Italy 41:46.4	Stefania Belmondo, Italy 42:21.1
15K (9.3 mi.) cross country	Manuela di Centa, Italy 39:44.5	Lyubov Egorova, Russia 41:03.0	Nina Gavriluk, Russia 41:10.4
20K (12.4 mi.) cross country relay	Russia 57:12.5	Norway 57:42.6	Italy 58:42.6
30K (18.6 mi.) cross country	Manuela di Centa, Italy 1:25:41.6	Marit Wold, Norway 1:25:57.8	Marja-Liisa Kirvesniemi, Finland 1:26.13.6
Speed skating (long track)—men			
500 meters (1,641 ft.)	Aleksandr Golubev, Russia 36.33	Sergei Klevchenya, Russia 36.39	Manabo Horii, Japan 36.53
1,000 meters (3,281 ft.)	Dan Jansen, United States 1:12.43	Igor Zhelzovsky, Russia 1:12.72	Sergei Klevchenya, Russia 1:12.85
1,500 meters (4,922 ft.)	Johann Olav Koss, Norway 1:51.29	Rintje Ritsma, Netherlands 1:51.99	Falko Zandstra, Netherlands 1:52.38
5,000 meters (16,405 ft.)	Johann Olav Koss, Norway 6:34.96	Kjell Storelid, Norway 6:42.68	Rintje Ritsma, Netherlands 6:43.94
10,000 meters (32,810 ft.)	Johann Olav Koss, Norway 13:30.55	Kjell Storelid, Norway 13:49.25	Bart Veldkamp, Netherlands 13:56.73
Speed skating (long track)—women			
500 meters (1,641 ft.)	Bonnie Blair, United States 39.25	Susan Auch, Canada 39.61	Franziska Schenk, Germany 39.70
1,000 meters (3,281 ft.)	Bonnie Blair, United States 1:18.74	Anke Baier, Germany 1:20.12	Quiaobo Ye, China 1:20.22
1,500 meters (4,922 ft.)	Emese Hunyady, Austria 2:02.19	Svetlana Fedotkina, Russia 2:02.69	Gunda Niemann, Germany 2:03.41
3,000 meters (9,843 ft.)	Svetlana Bazhanova, Russia 4:17.43	Emese Hunyady, Austria 4:18.14	Claudia Pechstein, Germany 4:18.34
5,000 meters (16,405 ft.)	Claudia Pechstein, Germany 7:14.37	Gunda Niemann, Germany 7:14.88	Hiromi Yamamoto, Japan 7:19.68
Speed skating (short track)—men			
500 meters (1,641 ft.)	Ji-Hoon Chae, South Korea 43.45	Mirko Vuillermin, Italy 43.47	Nicholas Gooch, Great Britain 43.68
1,000 meters (3,281 ft.)	Ki-Hoon Kim, South Korea 1:34.57	Ji-Hoon Chae, South Korea 1:34.92	Marc Gagnon, Canada 1:33.03
5,000 meters (16,405 ft.) relay	Italy 7:11.74	United States 7:13.37	Australia 7:13.68
Speed skating (short track)—women			
500 meters (1,641 ft.)	Cathy Turner, United States 45.98	Yanmei Zhang, China 46.44	Amy Peterson, United States 46.76
1,000 meters (3,281 ft.)	Lee Kyung Chun, South Korea 1:36.87	Nathalie Lambert, Canada 1:36.97	So Hee Kim, South Korea 1:37.09
3,000 meters (9,843 ft.) relay	South Korea, 4:26.64	Canada, 4:32.04	United States, 4:39.34

THE WINTER GAMES

Olympics	Year	Place	Competitors: Men	Competitors: Women	Nations represented
I	1924	Chamonix, France	281	13	16
II	1928	St. Moritz, Switzerland	468	27	25
III	1932	Lake Placid, U.S.	274	32	17
IV	1936	Garmisch-Partenkirchen, Germany	675	80	28
V	1948	St. Moritz, Switzerland	636	77	28
VI	1952	Oslo, Norway	623	109	30
VII	1956	Cortina D'Ampezzo, Italy	686	132	32
VIII	1960	Squaw Valley, U.S.	521	144	30
IX	1964	Innsbruck, Austria	986	200	36
X	1968	Grenoble, France	1,081	212	37
XI	1972	Sapporo, Japan	1,015	217	35
XII	1976	Innsbruck, Austria	900	228	37
XIII	1980	Lake Placid, U.S.	833	234	37
XIV	1984	Sarajevo, Yugoslavia	1,002	276	49
XV	1988	Calgary, Canada	1,445 (total)		57
XVI	1992	Albertville, France	2,174 (total)		64
XVII	1994	Lillehammer, Norway	1,216	521	67
XVIII	1998	Nagano, Japan			

Sources: David Wallechinsky, *The Complete Book of the Olympics* (1988), reprinted by permission; U.S. Olympic Committee.

OLYMPICS MEDAL COUNT, BY NATION

Country	Gold	Silver	Bronze	Total
SUMMER, 1992				
Unified Team	45	38	29	112
United States	37	34	37	108
Germany	33	21	28	82
China	16	22	16	54
Cuba	14	6	11	31
Hungary	11	12	7	30
South Korea	12	5	12	29
France	8	5	16	29
Australia	7	9	11	27
Spain	13	7	2	22
Japan	3	8	11	22
Great Britain	5	3	12	20
Italy	6	5	8	19
Poland	3	6	10	19
Canada	6	5	7	18
Romania	4	6	8	18
Bulgaria	3	7	6	16
Netherlands	2	6	7	15
Sweden	1	7	4	12
New Zealand	1	4	5	10
North Korea	4	0	5	9
Kenya	2	4	2	8
Czech and Slovak Federal Republic	4	2	1	7
Norway	2	4	1	7
Turkey	2	2	2	6
Denmark	1	1	4	6
Indonesia	2	2	1	5
Finland	1	2	2	5
Jamaica	0	3	1	4
Nigeria	0	3	1	4
Brazil	2	1	0	3
Morocco	1	1	1	3
Ethiopia	1	0	2	3
Latvia	0	2	1	3
Belgium	0	1	2	3
Croatia	0	1	2	3
Independent Olympic participants[1]	0	1	2	3
Iran	0	1	2	3
Greece	2	0	0	2
Ireland	1	1	0	2
Algeria	1	0	1	2
Estonia	1	0	1	2
Lithuania	1	0	1	2
Austria	0	2	0	2
Namibia	0	2	0	2
South Africa	0	2	0	2
Israel	0	1	1	2
Mongolia	0	0	2	2
Slovenia	0	0	2	2
Switzerland	1	0	0	1
Chinese Taipei	0	1	0	1
Mexico	0	1	0	1
Peru	0	1	0	1
Argentina	0	0	1	1
Bahamas	0	0	1	1
Colombia	0	0	1	1
Ghana	0	0	1	1
Malaysia	0	0	1	1
Pakistan	0	0	1	1
Philippines	0	0	1	1
Puerto Rico	0	0	1	1
Qatar	0	0	1	1
Surinam	0	0	1	1
Thailand	0	0	1	1
WINTER, 1994				
Norway	10	11	5	26
Germany	9	7	8	24
Russia	11	8	4	23
Italy	7	5	8	20
United States	6	5	2	13
Canada	3	6	4	13
Switzerland	3	4	2	9
Austria	2	3	4	9
South Korea	4	1	1	6
Finland	0	1	5	6
Japan	1	2	2	5
France	0	1	4	5
Netherlands	0	1	3	4
Sweden	2	1	0	3
Kazakhstan	1	2	0	3
China	0	1	2	3
Slovenia	0	0	3	3
Ukraine	1	0	1	2
Belarus	0	2	0	2
Great Britain	0	0	2	2
Uzbekistan	1	0	0	1
Australia	0	0	1	1

1. Athletes from Serbia, Macedonia, and Montenegro were not permitted to compete under the Yugoslavian flag. **Source:** United States Olympic Committee.

THE SUMMER GAMES

Olympics	Year	Place	Competitors: Men	Competitors: Women	Nations represented
I	1896	Athens, Greece	311	—	13
II	1900	Paris, France	1,319	11	22
III	1904	St. Louis, U.S.	681	6	12
—[1]	1906	Athens, Greece	877	7	20
IV	1908	London, UK	1,999	36	23
V	1912	Stockholm, Sweden	2,490	57	28
VI[2]	1916	Berlin, Germany	—	—	—
VII	1920	Antwerp, Belgium	2,543	64	29
VIII	1924	Paris, France	2,956	136	44
IX	1928	Amsterdam, Holland	2,724	290	46
X	1932	Los Angeles, U.S.	1,281	127	37
XI	1936	Berlin, Germany	3,738	328	49
XII[2]	1940	Tokyo, Japan	—	—	—
XIII[2]	1944	London, UK	—	—	—
XIV	1948	London, UK	3,714	385	59
XV	1952	Helsinki, Finland	4,407	518	69
XVI	1956	Melbourne, Australia	3,342	(total)	67
XVII	1960	Rome, Italy	4,738	610	83
XVIII	1964	Tokyo, Japan	4,457	683	93
XIX	1968	Mexico City, Mexico	4,750	781	112
XX	1972	Munich, W. Germany	5,848	1,299	122
XXI	1976	Montreal, Canada	4,834	1,251	92
XXII	1980	Moscow, USSR	4,265	1,088	81
XXIII	1984	Los Angeles, U.S.	5,458	1,620	141
XXIV	1988	Seoul, South Korea	7,105	2,476	160
XXV	1992	Barcelona, Spain	7,555	3,008	172
XXVI	1996	Atlanta, U.S.			
XXVII	2000	Sydney, Australia			

1. Not recognized as an official Olympiad. 2. Canceled due to war. **Source:** United States Olympic Committee.

Olympic Champions, 1896–1994

WINTER OLYMPICS

ALPINE SKIING—MEN

DOWNHILL

Year	Champion	Time
1948	Henri Oreiller, France	2:55.00
1952	Zeno Colo, Italy	2:30.80
1956	Anton Sailer, Austria	2:52.20
1960	Jean Vuarnet, France	2:06.00
1964	Egon Zimmerman, Austria	2:18.16
1968	Jean-Claude Killy, France	1:59.85
1972	Bernhard Russi, Switzerland	1:51.43
1976	Franz Klammer, Austria	1:45.73
1980	Leonhard Stock, Austria	1:45.50
1984	William Johnson, U.S.	1:45.59
1988	Pirmin Zurbriggen, Switzerland	1:59.63
1992	Patrick Ortlieb, Austria	1:50.37
1994	Tommy Moe, United States	1:45.75

GIANT SLALOM

Year	Champion	Time
1952	Stein Eriksen, Norway	2:25.00
1956	Anton Sailer, Austria	3:00.10
1960	Roger Staub, Switzerland	1:48.30
1964	François Bonlieu, France	1:46.71
1968	Jean-Claude Killy, France	3:29.28
1972	Gustavo Thöni, Italy	3:09.62
1976	Heini Hemmi, Switzerland	3:26.97
1980	Ingemar Stenmark, Sweden	2:40.74
1984	Max Julen, Switzerland	2:41.18
1988	Alberto Tomba, Italy	2:06.37
1992	Alberto Tomba, Italy	2:06.98
1994	Markus Wasmeier, Germany	2:52.46

SUPER GIANT SLALOM

Year	Champion	Time
1988	Frank Piccard, France	1:39.66
1992	Kjetil Andre Aamodt, Norway	1:13.04
1994	Markus Wasmeier, Germany	1:32.53

SLALOM

Year	Champion	Time
1948	Edi Reinalter, Switzerland	2:10.30
1952	Othmar Schneider, Austria	2:00.00
1956	Anton Sailer, Austria	3:14.70
1960	Ernst Hinterseer, Austria	2:08.90
1964	Josef Stiegler, Austria	2:11.13
1968	Jean-Claude Killy, France	1:39.73
1972	Francisco Fernandez Ochoa, Spain	1:49.27
1976	Piero Gros, Italy	2:03.29
1980	Ingemar Stenmark, Sweden	1:44.26
1984	Philip Mahre, U.S.	1:39.41
1988	Alberto Tomba, Italy	1:39.47
1992	Finn Christian Jagge, Norway	1:44.39
1994	Thomas Stangassinger, Austria	2:02.02

COMBINED (DOWNHILL/SLALOM)

Year	Champion	Time
1992	Josef Polig, Italy	(14.58 pts.)
1994	Lasse Kjus, Norway	3:17.53

ALPINE SKIING—WOMEN

DOWNHILL

Year	Champion	Time
1948	Hedi Schlunegger, Switzerland	2:28.30
1952	Trude Jochum-Beiser, Austria	1:47.10
1956	Madeleine Berthod, Switzerland	1:40.70
1960	Heidi Biebl, Germany	1:37.60
1964	Christl Haas, Austria	1:55.39
1968	Olga Pall, Austria	1:40.87
1972	Marie-Theres Nadig, Switzerland	1:36.68
1976	Rosi Mittermaier, West Germany	1:46.16
1980	Annemarie Moser-Pröll, Austria	1:37.52
1984	Michela Figini, Switzerland	1:13.36[1]
1988	Marina Kiehl, West Germany	1:25.86
1992	Kerrin Lee-Gartner, Canada	1:52.55
1994	Katja Seizinger, Germany	1:35.93

1. Race shortened by weather conditions.

GIANT SLALOM

Year	Champion	Time
1952	Andrea Mead Lawrence, U.S.	2:06.80
1956	Ossi Reichert, Germany	1.56.50
1960	Yvonne Rüuegg, Switzerland	1:39.90
1964	Marielle Goitschel, France	1:52.24
1968	Nancy Greene, Canada	1:51.97
1972	Marie-Theres Nadig, Switzerland	1:29.90
1976	Kathy Kreiner, Canada	1:29.13
1980	Hanni Wenzel, Liechtenstein	2:41.66
1984	Debbie Armstrong, U.S.	2:20.98
1988	Vreni Schneider, Switzerland	2:06.49
1992	Pernilla Wiberg, Sweden	2:12.74
1994	Deborah Compagnoni, Italy	2:30.97

SUPER GIANT SLALOM

Year	Champion	Time
1988	Sigrid Wolf, Austria	1:19.03
1992	Deborah Compagnoni, Italy	1:21.22
1994	Diann Roffe-Steinrotter, U.S.	1:22.15

SLALOM

Year	Champion	Time
1948	Gretchen Fraser, U.S.	1:57.20
1952	Andrea Mead Lawrence, U.S.	2:10.60
1956	Renée Colliard, Switzerland	1:52.30
1960	Anne Heggtveigt, Canada	1:49.60
1964	Christine Goitschel, France	1:29.86
1968	Marielle Goitschel, France	1:25.86
1972	Barbara Cochran, U.S.	1:31.24
1976	Rosi Mittermaier, West Germany	1:30.54
1980	Hanni Wenzel, Liechtenstein	1:25.09
1984	Paoletta Magoni, Italy	1:36.47
1988	Vreni Schneider, Switzerland	1:36.69
1992	Petra Kronberger, Austria	1:32.68
1994	Vreni Schneider, Switzerland	1:56.01

COMBINED (DOWNHILL/SLALOM)

Year	Champion	Time
1992	Petra Kronberger, Austria	(2.55 pts.)[1]
1994	Permilla Wiberg, Sweden	3:05.16

1. Point System changed to Time System in 1994.

BIATHLON—MEN (Cross-country skiing and riflery)

10-KILOMETER (6.2 MI.)

Year	Champion	Time
1980	Frank Ulrich, East Germany	32:10.69
1984	Eirik Kvalfoss, Norway	30:53.80
1988	Frank-Peter Roetsch, East Germany	25:08.10
1992	Mark Kirchner, Germany	26:02.30
1994	Sergei Tchepikov, Russia	28:07.00

20-KILOMETER (12.4 MI.) INDIVIDUAL

Year	Champion	Time
1960	Klas-Lestander, Sweden	1:33:21.60
1964	Vladimir Melanin, USSR	1:20:26.80
1968	Magnar Solberg, Norway	1:13:45.90
1972	Magnar Solberg, Norway	1:15:55.50
1976	Nikolai Kruglov, USSR	1:14:12.26
1980	Anatoli Alabyev, USSR	1:08:16.31
1984	Peter Angerer, West Germany	1:11:52.70
1988	Frank-Peter Roetsch, East Germany	0:56:33.33
1992	Evgueni Redkine, Unified Team	0:57:34.04
1994	Sergei Tarasov, Russia	0:57:25.30

30-KILOMETER (18.6 MI.) RELAY (4 x 7.5 km)[1]

Year	Champion	Time
1968	USSR,Norway, Sweden	2:13:02.40
1972	USSR, Finland, East Germany	1:51:44.92
1976	USSR, Finland, East Germany	1:57:55.64
1980	USSR, East Germany, West Germany	1:34:03.27
1984	USSR, Norway, West Germany	1:38:51.70
1988	USSR, West Germany, Italy	1:22:30.00
1992	Germany, Unified Team, Sweden	1:24:43.50
1994	Germany, Russia, France	1:30:22.10

1. 40 km (4 x 10 km) until 1980.

BIATHLON—WOMEN (Cross-country skiing and riflery)

7.5-KILOMETER (4.6 MI.)

Year	Champion	Time
1992	Anfissa Restzova, Unified Team	24:29.2
1994	Myriam Bedard, Canada	26:08.8

15-KILOMETER (9.3 MI.)

Year	Champion	Time
1992	Antje Misersky	51:47.2
1994	Myriam Bedard, Canada	52:06.6

30-KILOMETER (18.6 MI.) RELAY (4 x 7.5 km)

Year	Champion	Time
1992	France, Germany, Unified Team (3 x 7.5)	1:15:55.6
1994	Russia, Germany, France	1:47:19.5

BOBSLEDDING

TWO-MAN		Time	FOUR-MAN		Time
1932	U.S.	8:14.74	1924	Switzerland	5:45.54
1936	U.S.	5:29.29	1928	U.S. (5-Man)	3:20.50
1948	Switzerland	5:29.20	1932	U.S.	7:53.68
1952	Germany	5:24.54	1936	Switzerland	5:19.85
1956	Italy	5:30.14	1948	U.S.	5:20.10
1964	Great Britain	4:21.90	1952	Germany	5:07.84
1968	Italy	4:41.54	1956	Switzerland	5:10.44
1972	West Germany	4:57.07	1964	Canada	4:14.46
1976	East Germany	3:44.42	1968	Italy (2 races)	2:17.39
1980	Switzerland	4:09.36	1972	Switzerland	4:43.07
1984	East Germany	3:25.56	1976	East Germany	3:40.43
1988	USSR	3:54.19	1980	East Germany	3:59.42
1992	Switzerland	4:03.26	1984	East Germany	3:20.22
1994	Switzerland	3:30.81	1988	Switzerland	3:47.51
			1992	Austria	3:53.90
			1994	Germany	3:27.78

FIGURE SKATING

MEN

1908 Ulrich Salchow, Sweden
1920 Gillis Grafstrom, Sweden
1924 Gillis Grafstrom, Sweden
1928 Gillis Grafstrom, Sweden
1932 Karl Schafer, Austria
1936 Karl Schafer, Austria
1948 Richard Button, U.S.
1952 Richard Button, U.S.
1956 Hayes Alan Jenkins, U.S.
1960 David W. Jenkins, U.S.
1964 Manfred Schnelldorfer, West Germany
1968 Wolfgang Schwartz, Austria
1972 Ondrej Nepela, Czechoslovakia
1976 John Curry, Great Britain
1980 Robin Cousins, Great Britain
1984 Scott Hamilton, U.S.
1988 Brian Boitano, U.S.
1992 Viktor Petrenko, Unified Team
1994 Aleksei Urmanov, Russia

WOMEN

1908 Madge Syers, Great Britain
1920 Magda Julin-Mauroy, Sweden
1924 Heima von Szabo-Planck, Austria
1928 Sonja Henie, Norway
1932 Sonja Henie, Norway
1936 Sonja Henie, Norway
1948 Barbara Ann Scott, Canada
1952 Jeanette Altwegg, Great Britain
1956 Tenley Albright, U.S.
1960 Carol Heiss, U.S.
1964 Sjoukje Dijkstra, Netherlands
1968 Peggy Fleming, U.S.
1972 Beatrix Schuba, Austria
1976 Dorothy Hamill, U.S.
1980 Annett Pötzsch, East Germany
1984 Katarina Witt, East Germany
1988 Katarina Witt, East Germany
1992 Kristi Yamaguchi, U.S.
1994 Oksana Baiul, Ukraine

PAIRS

1908 Germany—Anna Hubler, Heinrich Burger
1920 Finland—Ludovika & Walter Jakobsson
1924 Austria—Helene Engelman, Alfred Berger
1928 France—Andrée Joly, Pierre Brunet
1932 France—Andrée Joly, Pierre Brunet
1936 Germany—Maxie Herber, Ernst Baier
1948 Belgium—Micheline Lannoy, Pierre Baugniet
1952 Germany—Ria & Paul Falk
1956 Austria—Elisabeth Schwartz, Kurt Oppelt
1960 Canada—Barbara Wagner, Robert Paul
1964 USSR—Ludmila Beloussova, Oleg Protopopov
1968 USSR—Ludmila Beloussova, Oleg Protopopov
1972 USSR—Irina Rodnina, Alexei Ulanov
1976 USSR—Irina Rodnina, Aleksandr Zaitsev
1980 USSR—Irina Rodnina, Aleksandr Zaitsev
1984 USSR—Elena Valova, Oleg Vassiliev
1988 USSR—Ekaterina Gordeeva, Sergei Grinkov
1992 Unified Team—Natalya Mishkutienok, Artur Dmitriev
1994 Russia—Ekaterina Gordeeva, Sergei Grinkov

ICE DANCING

1976 USSR—Lyudmila Pakhomova, Aleksandr Gorshkov
1980 USSR—Natalia Linichuk, Gennadi Karponosov
1984 Great Britain—Jayne Torvill, Christopher Dean
1988 USSR—Natalia Bestemianova, Andrei Bukin
1992 Unified Team—Marina Klimova, Sergei Ponomarenko
1994 Russia—Oksana Gritschuk, Evgeni Platov

FREESTYLE SKIING—MEN

MOGULS

Year	Champion	Points
1992	Edgar Grospiron, France	25.81
1994	Jean-Luc Brassard, Canada	27.24

AERIALS

Year	Champion	Points
1994	Andreas Schoenbaechler, Switzerland	234.67

FREESTYLE SKIING—WOMEN

MOGULS

Year	Champion	Points
1992	Donna Weinbrecht, U.S.	23.69
1994	Stine Lise Hattestad, Norway	25.97

AERIALS

Year	Champion	Points
1994	Lina Cherjazova, Uzbekistan	166.84

ICE HOCKEY

1920 Canada, U.S., Czechoslovakia
1924 Canada, U.S., Great Britain
1928 Canada, Sweden, Switzerland
1932 Canada, U.S., Germany
1936 Great Britain, Canada, U.S.
1948 Canada, Czechoslovakia, Switzerland
1952 Canada, U.S., Sweden
1956 USSR, U.S., Canada
1960 U.S., Canada, USSR
1964 USSR, Sweden, Czechoslovakia
1968 USSR, Czechoslovakia, Canada
1972 USSR, U.S., Czechoslovakia
1976 USSR, Czechoslovakia, W. Germany
1980 U.S., USSR, Sweden

1984	USSR, Czechslovakia, Sweden	
1988	USSR, Finland, Sweden	
1992	Unified Team, Canada, Czechoslovakia	
1994	Sweden, Canada, Finland	

LUGE

SINGLES (MEN)

Year	Winner	Time
1964	Thomas Köhler, East Germany	3:26.77
1968	Manfred Schmid, Austria	2:52.48
1972	Wolfgang Scheidel, East Germany	3:27.58
1976	Dettlef Günther, East Germany	3:27.68
1980	Bernhard Glass, Easter Gamny	2:54.79
1984	Paul Hildgartner, Italy	3:04.25
1988	Jens Mueller, East Germany	3:05.54
1992	Georg Hackl, Germany	3:02.36
1994	Georg Hackl, Germany	3:21.57

TWO-SEATER (MEN)

Year	Winner	Time
1964	Austria	1:41.62
1968	East Germany	1:35.85
1972	Italy, East Germany (tie)	1:28.35
1976	East Germany	1:25.60
1980	East Germany	1:19.33
1984	West Germany	1:23.62
1988	East Germany	1:31.94
1992	Germany	1:32.05
1994	Italy	1:36.72

SINGLES (WOMEN)

Year	Winner	Time
1964	Ortrun Enderlein, East Germany	3:24.67
1968	Erica Lechner, Italy	2:28.66
1972	Anna M. Müller, East Germany	2:59.18
1976	Margit Schumann, East Germany	2:50.62
1980	Vera Zozulya, USSR	2:36.53
1984	Steffi Martin, East Germany	2:46.57
1988	Steffi Walter, East Germany	3:03.97
1992	Doris Neuner, Austria	3:06.69
1994	Gerda Weissensteiner, Italy	3:15.52

NORDIC SKIING AND JUMPING—MEN

10-KILOMETER (6.21 MI.) CROSS-COUNTRY

Year	Winner	Time
1992	Vegard Ulvang, Norway	27:36.00
1994	Bjorn Dahlie, Norway	24:20.10

15-KILOMETER (9.3 MI.) PURSUIT METHOD[1]

Year	Winner	Time
1924	Thorleif Haug, Norway	1:14:31.00
1928	Johan Gröttumsbraaten, Norway	1:37:01.00
1932	Sven Utterstrom, Sweden	1:23:07.00
1936	Erik-August Larsson, Sweden	1:14:38.00
1948	Martin Lundström, Sweden	1:13:50.70
1952	Hallgeir Brenden, Norway	1:01:34.00
1956	Hallgeir Brenden, Norway	0:49:39.00
1960	HakonBrusveen, Norway	0:51:55.50
1964	Eero Mäntyranta, Finland	0:50:54.10
1968	Harald Grönningen, Norway	0:47:54.20
1972	Sven-Ake Lundbäck, Sweden	0:45:28.24
1976	Nikolai Bazhukov, USSR	0:43:58.47
1980	Thomas Wassberg, Sweden	0:41:57.63
1984	Gunde Svan, Sweden	0:41:25.60
1988	Mikhail Deviatiarov, USSR	0:41:18.90
1992	Bjorn Dahlie, Norway	1:05:37.90
1994	Bjorn Dahlie, Norway	1:00:08.80

1. 18 km until 1956.

30-KILOMETER (18.6 MI.) CROSS-COUNTRY

Year	Winner	Time
1956	Veikko Hakulinen, Finland	1:44:06.00
1960	Sixten Jernberg, Sweden	1:51:03.90
1964	Eero Mäntyranta, Finland	1:30:50.70
1968	Franco Nones, Italy	1:35:39.20
1972	Vyacheslav Vedenin, USSR	1:36:31.15
1976	Sergei Saveliev, USSR	1:30:29.38
1980	Nikolai Zimyatov, USSR	1:27:02.80
1984	Nikolai Zimyatov, USSR	1:28:56.30
1988	Aleksei Prokourorov, USSR	1:24:26.30
1992	Vegard Ulvang, Norway	1:22:27.80
1994	Thomas Alsgaard, Norway	1:12:26.40

50-KILOMETER (31.2 MI.) CROSS-COUNTRY

Year	Winner	Time
1924	Thorleif Haug, Norway	3:44:32.00
1928	Per Erik Hedlund, Sweden	4:52:03.00
1932	Veli Saarinen, Finland	4:28:00.00
1936	Elis Viklund, Sweden	3:30:11.00
1948	Nils Karlsson, Sweden	3:47:48.00
1952	Veikko Hakulinen, Finland	3:33:33.00
1956	Sixten Jernberg, Sweden	2:50:27.00
1960	Kalevi Hamalainen, Finland	2:59:06.30
1964	Sixten Jernberg, Sweden	2:43:52.60
1968	Ole Ellefsaeter, Norway	2:28:45.80
1972	Pål Tyldum, Norway	2:43:14.75
1976	Ivar Formo, Norway	2:37:30.05
1980	Nikolai Zimyatov, USSR	2:27:24.60
1984	Thomas Wassberg, Sweden	2:15:55.80
1988	Gunde Svan, Sweden	2:04:30.90
1992	Bjorn Daehlie, Norway	2:03:41.50
1994	Valdimir Smirnov, Kazakhstan	2:07:20.30

40-KILOMETER (24.8 MI.) CROSS-COUNTRY RELAY (4 × 10)

Year	Winner	Time
1936	Finland, Norway, Sweden	2:41:33.00
1948	Sweden, Finland, Norway	2:32:08.00
1952	Finland, Norway, Sweden	2:20:16.00
1956	USSR, Finland Sweden	2:15:30.00
1960	Finland, Norway, USSR	2:18:45.60
1964	Sweden, Finland, USSR	2:18:34.60
1968	Norway, Sweden, Finland	2:08:33.50
1972	USSR, Norway, Switzerland	2:04:47.94
1976	Finland, Norway, USSR	2:07:59.72
1980	USSR, Norway, Finland	1:57:03.46
1984	Sweden, USSR, Finland	1:55:06.30
1988	Sweden, USSR, Czechoslovakia	1:43:58.60
1992	Norway, Italy, Finland	1:39:26.00
1994	Italy, Norway, Finland	1:41:15.00

SKI JUMP

90-METER (295.3 FT.) JUMP[1]

Year	Winner	Points
1964	Veikko Kankkonen, Finland	229.90
1968	Jiri Raska, Czechoslovakia	216.50
1972	Yukio Kasaya, Japan	244.20
1976	Hans-Georg Aschenbach, East Germany	252.00
1980	Anton Innauer, Austria	266.30
1984	Jens Weissflog, East Germany	215.20
1988	Matti Nykänen, Finland	229.10
1992	Ernst Vettori, Austria	222.80
1994	Espen Bredesen, Norway	282.00

1. 70 meters until 1992.

120-METER (393.7 FT.) JUMP[1]

Year	Winner	Points
1924	Jacob Tullin Thambs, Norway	18.960
1928	Alf Andersen, Norway	19.208
1932	Birger Ruud, Norway	228.10
1936	Birger Ruud, Norway	232.00
1948	Petter Hugsted, Norway	228.10
1952	Arnfinn Bergmann, Norway	226.00
1956	Antti Hyvarinen, Finland	227.00
1960	Helmut Recknagel, East Germany	227.20
1964	Toralf Engan, Norway	230.70
1968	Vladimir Beloussov, USSR	231.30
1972	Wojiech Fortuna, Poland	219.90
1976	Karl Schnabl, Austria	234.80
1980	Jouko Tormanen, Finland	271.00
1984	Matti Nykänen, Finland	231.20
1988	Matti Nykänen, Finland	224.00
1992	Toni Nieminen, Finland	239.50
1994	Jens Weissflog, Germany	274.50

1. 90 meters until 1992.

120-METER (393.7 FT.) JUMP, TEAM[1]

Year	Winner	Points
1988	Finland, Yugoslavia, Norway	634.40
1992	Finland, Austria, Czechoslovakia	644.40
1994	Germany, Japan, Austria	970.10

1. 90 meters until 1992.

NORDIC COMBINED (15-KM [9.3 MI.] CROSS-COUNTRY AND 70-METER [229.7 FT.] SKI JUMP)[1]

Year	Winner	Points
1924	Thorleif Haug, Norway	18.906
1928	Johan Gröttumsbraaten, Norway	17.833
1932	Johan Gröttumsbraaten, Norway	446.00
1946	Oddbjörn Hagen, Norway	430.30
1952	Simon Slåttvik, Norway	451.62
1956	Sverre Stenersen, Norway	455.00
1960	George Thoma, West Germany	457.95
1964	Tormod Knutsen, Norway	469.28
1968	Franz Keller, West Germany	449.04
1972	Ulrich Wehling, East Germany	413.34
1976	Ulrich Wehling, East Germany	423.39
1980	Ulrich Wehling, East Germany	432.20
1984	Torn Sandberg, Norway	422.59
1988	Hippolyt Kempf, Switzerland	235.80
1992	Fabrice Guy, France	426.47
1994	Fred Lundberg, Norway	—

1. 18 km until 1956.

NORDIC COMBINED, TEAM

Year	Winner
1988	W. Germany, Switzerland, Austria
1992	Japan, Norway, Austria
1994	Japan, Norway, Switzerland

NORDIC SKIING—WOMEN

5-KILOMETER (3.1 MI.) CROSS-COUNTRY

Year	Winner	Time
1964	Claudia Boyarskikh, USSR	17:50.50
1968	Toini Gustafsson, Sweden	16:45.20
1972	Galina Kulakova, USSR	17:00.50
1976	Helena Takalo, Finland	15:48.69
1980	Raisa Smetanina, USSR	15:06.92
1984	Marja-Liisa Hämäläinen, Finland	17:04.00
1988	Marjo Matikainen, Finland	15:04.00
1992	Lyubov Egorova, Unified Team	14:08.80
1994	Lyubov Egorova, Russia	14:08.80

10-KILOMETER (6.2 MI.) CROSS-COUNTRY PURSUIT METHOD

Year	Winner	Time
1952	Lydia Wideman, Finland	41:40.00
1956	Lyubov Kosyreva, USSR	38:11.00
1960	Maria Gusakova, USSR	39:46.60
1964	Claudia Boyarskikh, USSR	40:24.30
1968	Toini Gustafsson, Sweden	36:46.50
1972	Galina Kolakova, USSR	34:17.82
1976	Raisa Smetanina, USSR	30:31.54
1980	Barbara Petzold, East Germany	30:31.54
1984	Marja-Liisa Hämäläinen, Finland	31:44.20
1988	Vida Ventsene, USSR	30:08.20
1992	Lyubov Egorova, Unified Team	40:07.70
1994	Lyubov Egorova, Russia	41:38.10

15-KILOMETER (9.3 MI.) CROSS-COUNTRY

Year	Winner	Time
1992	Lyubov Egorova, Unified Team	42:20.80
1994	Manuela di Centa, Italy	39:44.50

30-KILOMETER (18.6 MI.) CROSS-COUNTRY[1]

Year	Winner	Time
1984	Marja Liisa Hämäläinen, Finland	1:01:45.00
1988	Tamara Tikhonova, USSR	0:55:53.60
1992	Stefania Belmondo, Italy	1:22:30.10
1994	Manuela di Centa, Italy	1:25:41.60

1. 20 km until 1992.

20-KILOMETER (12.4 MI.) RELAY (4 x 5 km)[1]

Year	Winner	Time
1956	Finland	1:09.01.00
1960	Sweden	1:04.21.00
1964	USSR	0:59:20.00
1968	Norway	0:57:30.00
1972	USSR	0:48:46.15
1976	USSR	1:07:49.75
1980	East Germany	1:02:11.10
1984	Norway	1:06:49.70
1988	USSR	0:59:51.10
1992	Unified Team	0:59:34.80
1994	Russia	0:57:12.50

1. 15 km (3 x 5 km) until 1976.

SPEED SKATING—MEN

LONG TRACK — Time

500 METERS (1,641 FT.)

Year	Winner	Time
1924	Charles Jewtraw, U.S.	0:44.00
1928	Clas Thunberg, Finland, and Bernst Evensen, Norway (tie)	0:43.40
1932	John A. Shea, U.S.	0:43.40
1936	Ivar Ballangrud, Norway	0:43.40
1948	Finn Helgesen, Norway	0:43.10
1952	Ken Henry, U.S.	0:43.20
1956	Yevgeny Grishin, USSR	0:40.20
1960	Yevgeny Grishin, USSR	0:40.20
1964	Terry McDermott, U.S.	0:40.10
1968	Erhard Keller, West Germany	0.40.30
1972	Erhard Keller, West Germany	0.39.44
1976	Yergeny Kulikov, USSR	0:39.17
1980	Eric Heiden, U.S.	0:38.03
1984	Sergei Fokichev, USSR	0:38.19
1988	Uwe-Jens May, East Germany	0:36.45
1992	Uwe-Jens May, Germany	0:37.14
1994	Aleksandr Golubev, Russia	0:36.33

1,000 METERS (3,281 FT.)

Year	Winner	Time
1976	Peter Mueller, U.S.	1:19.32
1980	Eric Heiden, U.S.	1:15.18
1984	Gaétan Boucher, Canada	1:15.80
1988	Nikolai Guiliaev, USSR	1:13.03
1992	Olaf Zinke, Germany	1:14.85
1994	Dan Jansen, U.S.	1:12.43

1,500 METERS (4,922 FT.)

Year	Winner	Time
1924	Clas Thunberg, Finland	2:20.80
1928	Clas Thunberg, Finland	2:21.10
1932	John A. Shea, U.S.	2:57.50
1936	Charles Mathisen, Norway	2:19.20
1948	Sverre Farstad, Norway	2:17.60
1952	Hjalmar Andersen, Norway	2:20.40
1956	Yevgeni Grishin and Yuri Mikhailov, USSR (tie)	2:08.60
1960	Roald Aas, Norway, and Yevgeni Grishin, USSR (tie)	2:10.40
1964	Ants Anston, USSR	2:10.30
1968	Cornelis Verkerk, Netherlands	2:03.40
1972	Ard Schenk, Netherlands	2:02.96
1976	Jan Egil Storholt, Norway	1:59.38
1980	Eric Heiden, U.S.	1:55.44
1984	Gaétan Boucher, Canada	1:58.36
1988	Andre Hoffmann, East Germany	1:52.06
1992	Johann Koss, Norway	1:54.81
1994	Johann Koss, Norway	1:51.29

5,000 METERS (16,405 FT.)

Year	Winner	Time
1924	Clas Thunberg, Finland	8:39.00
1928	Ivar Ballangrud, Norway	8:50.50
1932	Irving Jaffee, U.S.	9:40.80
1936	Ivar Ballangrud, Norway	8:19.60
1948	Reidar Liaklev, Norway	8:29.40
1952	Hjalmar Andersen, Norway	8:10.60
1956	Boris Shilkov, USSR	7:48.70
1960	Viktor Kosichkin, USSR	7:51.30
1964	Knut Johannesen, Norway	7:38.40
1968	F. Anton Maier, Norway	7:22.40
1972	Ard Schenk, Netherlands	7:23.61
1976	Sten Stensen, Norway	7:24.48
1980	Eric Heiden, U.S.	7:02.29
1984	Sven Tomas Gustafson, Sweden	7:12.28
1988	Tomas Gustafson, Sweden	6:44:63
1992	Geir Karlstad, Norway	6:59.97
1994	Johann Koss, Norway	6:34.96

10,000 METERS (32,810 FT.)

Year	Winner	Time
1924	Julien Skutnabb, Finland	18:04.80
1928	(ice thawed, so event canceled)	
1932	Irving Jaffee, U.S.	19:13.60
1936	Ivar Ballangrud, Norway	17:24.30
1948	Ake Seyffarth, Sweden	17:26.30
1952	Hjalmar Andersen, Norway	16:45.80
1956	Sigvard Ericsson, Sweden	16:35.90
1960	Knut Johannessen, Norway	15:46.60
1964	Jonny Nilsson, Sweden	15:50.10
1968	Johnny Hoeglin, Sweden	15:23.60
1972	Ard Schenk, Netherlands	15:01.35
1976	Piet Kleine, Netherlands	14:50.59
1980	Eric Heiden, U.S.	14:28.13
1984	Igor Malikov, USSR	14:39.90
1988	Tomas Gustafson, Sweden	13:48.20
1992	Bart Veldkamp, Netherlands	14:12.12
1994	Johann Koss, Norway	13:30.55

SHORT TRACK — Time

500 METERS (1,641 FT.)

Year	Winner	Time
1994	Ji-Hoon Chae, South Korea	0:43.45

1,000 METERS (3,281 FT.)

Year	Winner	Time
1994	Ki-Hoon Kim, South Korea	1:34.57

5,000 METERS (16,405 FT.) RELAY

Year	Winner	Time
1994	Italy, U.S., Australia	7:11.74

SPEED SKATING—WOMEN

LONG TRACK — Time

500 METERS (1,641 FT.)

Year	Winner	Time
1960	Helga Haase, Germany	0:45.90
1964	Lydia Skoblikova, USSR	0:45.00
1968	Ludmila Titova, USSR	0:46.10
1972	Anne Henning, U.S.	0:43.33
1976	Sheila Young, U.S.	0:42.76
1980	Karin Enke, East Germany	0:41.78
1984	Christa Rothenburger, East Germany	0:41.02
1988	Bonnie Blair, U.S.	0:39.10
1992	Bonnie Blair, U.S.	0:40.33
1994	Bonnie Blair, U.S.	0:39.25

1,000 METERS (3,281 FT.)

Year	Winner	Time
1960	Klara Guseva, USSR	1:34.10
1964	Lydia Skoblikova, USSR	1:33.20
1968	Carolina Geiissen, Netherlands	1:32.60
1972	Monika Pflug, West Germany	1:31.40
1976	Tatiana Averina, USSR	1:28.43
1980	Natalia Petruseva, USSR	1:24.10
1984	Karin Enke, East Germany	1:21.61
1988	Christa Rothenburger, East Germany	1:17.65
1992	Bonnie Blair, U.S.	1:21.90
1994	Bonnie Blair, U.S.	1:18.74

1,500 METERS (4,922 FT.)

Year	Winner	Time
1960	Lydia Skoblikova, USSR	2:25.20
1964	Lydia Skoblikova, USSR	2:22.60
1968	Kaija Mustonen, Finland	2:22.40
1972	Dianne Holum, U.S.	2:20.85
1976	Galina Stepanskaya, USSR	2:16.58
1980	Annie Borchink, Netherlands	2:10.95
1984	Karin Enke, East Germany	2:03.42
1988	Yvonne Van Gennip, Netherlands	2:00.68
1992	Jacqueline Boerner, Germany	2:05.87
1994	Emese Hunyady, Austria	2:02.19

3,000 METERS (9,843 FT.)

Year	Winner	Time
1960	Lydia Skoblikova, USSR	5:14.30
1964	Lydia Skoblikova, USSR	5:14.90
1968	Johanna Schut, Netherlands	4:56.20
1972	Christina Baas-Kaiser, Netherlands	4:52.14
1976	Tatiana Averina, USSR	4:45.19
1980	Bjoerg Eva Jensen, Norway	4:32.13
1984	Andrea Schöne, East Germany	4:24.79
1988	Yvonne Van Gennip, Netherlands	4:11.94
1992	Gunda Niemann, Germany	4:19.90
1994	Svetlana Bazhanova, Russia	4:17.43

5,000 METERS (16,405 FT.)

Year	Winner	Time
1992	Gunda Niemann, Germany	7:31.57
1994	Claudia Pechstein, Germany	7:14.37

SHORT TRACK — Time

500 METERS (1,641 FT.)

Year	Winner	Time
1992	Cathy Turner, U.S.	0:47.04
1994	Cathy Turner, U.S.	0:45.98

1,000 METERS (3,281 FT.)

Year	Winner	Time
1994	Lee-Kyung Chun, South Korea	1:36.87

3,000 METERS (9,843 FT.) RELAY

Year	Winner	Time
1992	Canada, U.S., Unified Team	4:36.62
1994	South Korea, Canada, U.S.	4:26.64

SUMMER OLYMPICS

SWIMMING AND DIVING—MEN

50-METER FREESTYLE

Year	Winner	Time
1988	Matt Biondi, U.S.	0:22.14
1992	Alexandre Popov, Unified Team	0:21.91

100-METER FREESTYLE

Year	Winner	Time
1896	Alfred Hajos, Hungary	1:22.20
1904	Zoltan de Halmay, Hungary (100 yds.)	1:02.80
1908	Charles Daniels, U.S.	1:05.60
1912	Duke Kahanamoku, U.S.	1:03.40
1920	Duke Kahanamoku, U.S.	1:01.40
1924	John Weissmuller, U.S.	0:59.00
1928	John Weissmuller, U.S.	0:58.60
1932	Yasuji Miyazaki, Japan	0:58.20
1936	Ferenc Csik, Hungary	0:57.60
1948	Walter Ris, U.S.	0:57.30
1952	Clarke Scholes, U.S.	0:57.40
1956	Jon Hendricks, Australia	0:55.40
1960	John Devitt, Australia	0:55.20
1964	Donald A. Schollander, U.S.	0:53.40
1968	Michael Wenden, Australia	0:52.20
1972	Mark Spitz, U.S.	0:51.22
1976	Jim Montgomery, U.S.	0:49.99
1980	Jorg Woithe, East Germany	0:50.40
1984	Ambrose ("Rowdy") Gaines, U.S.	0:49.80
1988	Matt Biondi, U.S.	0:48.63
1992	Alexandre Popov, Unified Team	0:49.02

200-METER FREESTYLE

Year	Winner	Time
1968	Michael Wenden, Australia	1:55.20
1972	Mark Spitz, U.S.	1:52.78
1976	Bruce Furniss, U.S.	1:50.29
1980	Sergei Kopliakov, USSR	1:49.81
1984	Michael Gross, West Germany	1:47.44
1988	Duncan Armstrong, Australia	1:47.25
1992	Evgueni Sadovyi, Unified Team	1:46.70

400-METER FREESTYLE

Year	Winner	Time
1896	Paul Neumann, Austria (500 m)	8:12.60
1904	Charles Daniels, U.S. (440 yds.)	6:16.20
1908	Henry Taylor, Great Britain	5:36.80
1912	George Hodgson, Canada	5:24.40
1920	Norman Ross, U.S.	5:26.80
1924	John Weissmuller, U.S.	5:04.20
1928	Albert Zorilla, Argentina	5:01.60
1932	Clarence "Buster" Crabbe, U.S.	4:48.40
1936	Jack Medica, U.S.	4:44.50
1948	William Smith, U.S.	4:41.00
1952	Jean Boiteux, France	4:30.70
1956	Murray Rose, Australia	4:27.30
1960	Murray Rose, Australia	4:18.30
1964	Donald A. Schollander, U.S.	4:12.20
1968	Michael Burton, U.S.	4:09.00
1972	Bradford Cooper, Australia	4:00.27
1976	Brian Goodell, U.S.	3:51.93
1980	Vladimir Salnikov, USSR	3:51.31
1984	George DiCarlo, U.S.	3:51.23
1988	Ewe Dassler, East Germany	3:46.95
1992	Evgueni Sadovyi, Unified Team	3:45.00

1,500-METER FREESTYLE

Year	Winner	Time
1896	Alfred Hajos, Hungary (1,200 m)	18:22.20
1900	John Jarvis, Great Britain (1,000 m)	13:40.20
1904	Emil Rausch, Germany (1,609 m)	27:18.20
1908	Henry Taylor, Great Britain	22:48.40
1912	George Hodgson, Canada	22:00.00
1920	Norman Ross, U.S.	22:23.20
1924	Andrew Charlton, Australia	20:06.60
1928	Arne Borg, Sweden	19:51.80
1932	Kusuo Kitamura, Japan	19:12.40
1936	Noboru Terada, Japan	19:13.70
1948	James P. McLane, U.S.	19:18.50
1952	Ford Konno, U.S.	18:30.30
1956	Murray Rose, Australia	17:58.90
1960	John Konrads, Australia	17:19.60
1964	Robert Windle, Australia	17:01.70
1968	Michael Burton, U.S.	16:38.90
1972	Michael Burton, U.S.	15:52.58
1976	Brian Goodell, U.S.	15:02.40
1980	Vladimir Salnikov, USSR	14:58.27
1984	Michael O'Brien, U.S.	15:05.20
1988	Vladimir Salnikov, USSR	15:00.40
1992	Kieren Perkins, Australia	14:43.48

100-METER BACKSTROKE

Year	Winner	Time
1904	Walter Brack, Germany (100 yds.)	1:16.80
1908	Arno Bieberstein, Germany	1:24.60
1912	Harry Hebner, U.S.	1:21.20
1920	Warren Kealoha, U.S.	1:15.20
1924	Warren Kealoha, U.S.	1:13.20
1928	George Kojac, U.S.	1:08.20
1932	Masaji Kiyokawa, Japan	1:08.60
1936	Adolph Kiefer, U.S.	1:05.90
1948	Allen Stack, U.S.	1:06.40
1952	Yoshinobu Oyakawa, U.S.	1:05.40
1956	David Thiele, Australia	1:02.20
1960	David Thiele, Australia	1:01.90
1964	Not on program	
1968	Roland Matthes, East Germany	0:58.70
1972	Roland Matthes, East Germany	0:56.58
1976	John Naber, U.S.	0:55.49
1980	Bengt Baron, Sweden	0:56.33
1984	Richard Carey, U.S.	0:55.79
1988	Daichi Suzuki, Japan	0:55.05
1992	Mark Tewksbury, Canada	0:53.98

200-METER BACKSTROKE

Year	Winner	Time
1900	Ernest Hoppenberg, Germany	2:47.00
1964	Jed R. Graef, U.S.	2:10.30
1968	Roland Matthes, East Germany	2:09.60
1972	Roland Matthes, East Germany	2:02.82
1976	John Naber, U.S.	1:59.19
1980	Sandor Wladar, Hungary	2:01.93
1984	Richard Carey, U.S.	2:00.23
1988	Igor Polianski, USSR	1:59.37
1992	Martin Zubero, Spain	1:58.47

100-METER BUTTERFLY

Year	Winner	Time
1968	Douglas Russell, U.S.	0:55.90
1972	Mark Spitz, U.S.	0:54.27
1976	Matt Vogel, U.S.	0:54.35
1980	Par Arvidsson, Sweden	0:54.92
1984	Michael Gross, West Germany	0:53.08
1988	Anthony Nesty, Suriname	0:53.00
1992	Pablo Morales, U.S.	0:53.32

200-METER BUTTERFLY

Year	Winner	Time
1956	William Yorzyk, U.S.	2:19.30
1960	Michael Troy, U.S.	2:12.80
1964	Kevin Berry, Australia	2:06.60
1968	Carl Robie, U.S.	2:08.70
1972	Mark Spitz, U.S.	2:00.70
1976	Michael Bruner, U.S.	1:59.23
1980	Sergei Fesenko, USSR	1:59.76
1984	Jon Sieben, Australia	1:57.04
1988	Michael Gross, West Germany	1:56.94
1992	Mel Stewart, U.S.	1:56.26

100-METER BREASTSTROKE

Year	Winner	Time
1968	Donald McKenzie, U.S.	1:07.70
1972	Nobutaka Taguchi, Japan	1:04.94
1976	John Hencken, U.S.	1:03.11
1980	Duncan Goodhew, Great Britain	1:03.44
1984	Steve Lundquist, U.S.	1:01.99
1988	Adrian Moorhouse, Great Britain	1:02.04
1992	Nelson Diebel, U.S.	1:01:50

200-METER BREASTSTROKE

Year	Winner	Time
1908	Frederick Holman, Great Britain	3:09.20
1912	Walter Bathe, Germany	3:01.80
1920	Haken Malmroth, Sweden	3:04.40
1924	Robert Skelton, U.S.	2:56.60
1928	Yoshiyuki Tsuruta, Japan	2:48.80
1932	Yoshiyuki Tsuruta, Japan	2:45.40
1936	Tetsuo Hamuro, Japan	2:41.50
1948	Joseph Verdeur, U.S.	2:39.30
1952	John Davies, Australia	2:34.40
1956	Masura Furukawa, Japan	2:34.70
1960	William Mulliken, U.S.	2:37.40
1964	Ian O'Brien, Australia	2:27.80
1968	Felipe Muñoz, Mexico	2:28.70
1972	John Hencken, U.S.	2:21.55
1976	David Wilkie, Great Britain	2:15.11
1980	Robertas Zhulpa, USSR	2:15.85
1984	Victor Davis, Canada	2:13.34
1988	Jozsef Szabo, Hungary	2:13.52
1992	Mike Barrowman, U.S.	2:10.16

200-METER INDIVIDUAL MEDLEY

Year	Winner	Time
1968	Charles Hickcox, U.S.	2:12.00
1972	Gunnar Larsson, Sweden	2:07.17
1984	Alex Baumann, Canada	2:01.42
1988	Tamas Darnyi, Hungary	2:00.17
1992	Tamas Darnyi, Hungary	2:00.76

400-METER INDIVIDUAL MEDLEY

Year	Winner	Time
1964	Richard W. Roth, U.S.	4:45.40
1968	Charles Hickcox, U.S.	4:48.40
1972	Gunnar Larsson, Sweden	4:31.98
1976	Rod Strachan, U.S.	4:23.68
1980	Aleksandr Sidorenko, USSR	4:22.89
1984	Alex Baumann, Canada	4:17.41
1988	Tamas Darnyi, Hungary	4:14.75
1992	Tamas Darnyi, Hungary	4:14,23

400-METER FREESTYLE RELAY

Year	Winner	Time	Year	Winner	Time
1964	U.S.	3:33.20	1984	U.S.	3:19.03
1968	U.S.	3:31.70	1988	U.S.	3:16.53
1972	U.S.	3:26.42	1992	U.S.	3:16.74

400-METER MEDLEY RELAY

Year	Winner	Time	Year	Winner	Time
1960	U.S.	4:05.40	1980	Australia	3:45.70
1964	U.S.	3:58.40	1984	U.S.	3:39.30
1968	U.S.	3:54.90	1988	U.S.	3:36.93
1972	U.S.	3:48.16	1992	U.S.	3:36.93
1976	U.S.	3:42.22			

800-METER FREESTYLE RELAY

Year	Winner	Time	Year	Winner	Time
1908	Great Britain	10:55.60	1960	U.S.	8:10.20
			1964	U.S.	7:52.10
1912	Australia	10:11.60	1968	U.S.	7:52.33
1920	U.S.	10:04.40	1972	U.S.	7:35.78
1924	U.S.	9:53.40	1976	U.S.	7:23.22
1928	U.S.	9:36.20	1980	USSR	7:23.50
1932	Japan	8:58.40	1984	U.S.	7:15.69
1936	Japan	8:51.40	1988	U.S.	7:12.69
1948	U.S.	8:46.00	1992	Unified Team	7:11.95
1952	U.S.	8:31.10			
1956	Australia	8:23.60			

SPRINGBOARD DIVING

Year	Winner	Points
1908	Albert Zurner, Germany	85.50
1912	Paul Guenther, Germany	79.23
1920	Louis Kuehn, U.S.	675.00
1924	Albert C. White, U.S.	696.40
1928	Pete Desjardins, U.S.	185.04
1932	Michael Galitzen, U.S.	161.38
1936	Richard Degener, U.S.	163.57
1948	Bruce Harlan, U.S.	163.64
1952	David Browning, U.S.	205.29
1956	Robert L. Clotworthy, U.S.	159.56
1960	Gary Tobian, U.S.	170.00
1964	Kenneth R. Sitzberger, U.S.	159.90
1968	Bernard Wrightson, U.S.	170.15
1972	Vladimir Vasin, USSR	594.09
1976	Phil Boggs, U.S.	619.05
1980	Aleksandr Portnov, USSR	905.02
1984	Gregory Louganis, U.S.	754.41
1988	Gregory Louganis, U.S.	730.80
1992	Mark Lenzi, U.S.	676.53

PLATFORM DIVING

Year	Winner	Points
1904	Dr. G. E. Sheldon, U.S.	12.75
1908	Hjalmar Johansson, Sweden	83.75
1912	Erik Adlerz, Sweden	73.94
1920	Clarence Pinkston, U.S.	100.67
1924	Albert C. White, U.S.	97.46
1928	Pete Desjardins, U.S.	98.74
1932	Harold Smith, U.S.	124.80
1936	Marshall Wayne, U.S.	113.58
1948	Dr. Samuel Lee, U.S.	130.05
1952	Dr. Samuel Lee, U.S.	156.28
1956	Joaquin Capilla, Mexico	152.44
1960	Robert Webster, U.S.	165.56
1964	Robert Webster, U.S.	148.58
1968	Klaus DiBiasi, Italy	164.18

1972 Klaus DiBiasi, Italy 504.12
1976 Klaus DiBiasi, Italy 600.51
1980 Falk Hoffmann, East Germany 835.65
1984 Gregory Louganis, U.S. 710.91
1988 Gregory Louganis, U.S. 638.61
1992 Sun Shuwei, China 677.31

SWIMMING AND DIVING—WOMEN Time

50-METER FREESTYLE
1988 Kristin Otto, East Germany 0:25.49
1992 Yang Wenji, China 0:24.79

100-METER FREESTYLE
1912 Fanny Durack, Australia 1:22.20
1920 Ethelda Bleibtrey, U.S. 1:13.60
1924 Ethel Lackie, U.S. 1:12.40
1928 Albina Osipowich, U.S. 1:11.00
1932 Helene Madison, U.S. 1:06.80
1936 Hendrika Mastenbroek, Netherlands 1:05.90
1948 Greta Andersen, Denmark 1:06.30
1952 Katalin Szoke, Hungary 1:06.80
1956 Dawn Fraser, Australia 1:02.00
1960 Dawn Fraser, Australia 1:01.20
1964 Dawn Fraser, Australia 0:59.50
1968 Margo Jan Henne, U.S. 1:00.00
1972 Sandra Neilson, U.S. 0:58.59
1976 Kornelia Ender, East Germany 0:55.65
1980 Barbara Krause, East Germany 0:54.79
1984 Nancy Hogshead, U.S. 0:55.92
1988 Kristin Otto, East Germany 0:54.93
1992 Zhuang Yong, China 0:54.65

200-METER FREESTYLE
1968 Deborah Meyer, U.S. 2:10.50
1972 Shane Gould, Australia 2:03.56
1976 Kornelia Ender, East Germany 1:59.26
1980 Barbara Krause, East Germany 1:58.33
1984 Mary Wayte, U.S. 1:59.23
1988 Heike Friederich, East Germany 1:57.65
1992 Nicole Haislett, U.S. 1:57.90

400-METER FREESTYLE
1920 Ethelda Bleibtrey, U.S. (300 m) 4:34.00
1924 Martha Norelius, U.S. 6:02.20
1928 Martha Norelius, U.S. 5:42.80
1932 Helene Madison, U.S. 5:28.50
1936 Hendrika Mastenbroek, Netherlands 5:26.40
1948 Ann Curtis, U.S. 5:17.80
1952 Valeria Gyenge, Hungary 5:12.10
1956 Lorraine Crapp, Australia 4:54.60
1960 S. Chris Von Saltza, U.S. 4:50.60
1964 Virginia Duenkel, U.S. 4:43.30
1968 Deborah Meyer, U.S. 4:31.80
1972 Shane Gould, Australia 4:19.44
1976 Petra Thuemer, East Germany 4:09.89
1980 Ines Diers, East Germany 4:08.76
1984 Tiffany Cohen, U.S. 4:07.10
1988 Janet Evans, U.S. 4:03.85
1992 Dagmar Hase, Germany 4:07.18

800-METER FREESTYLE
1968 Deborah Meyer, U.S. 9:24.00
1972 Keena Rothhammer, U.S. 8:53.68
1976 Petra Thuemer, East Germany 8:37.14
1980 Michelle Ford, Australia 8:28.90
1984 Tiffany Cohen, U.S. 8:24.95
1988 Janet Evans, U.S. 8:20.20
1992 Janet Evans, U.S. 8:25.52

100-METER BACKSTROKE
1924 Sybil Bauer, U.S. 1:23.20
1928 Marie Braun, Netherlands 1:22.00
1932 Eleanor Holm, U.S. 1:19.40
1936 Dina Senff, Netherlands 1:18.90
1948 Karen Harup, Denmark 1:14.40
1952 Joan Harrison, South Africa 1:14.30
1956 Judy Grinham, Great Britain 1:12.90
1960 Lynn Burke, U.S. 1:09.30
1964 Cathy Ferguson, U.S. 1:07.70
1968 Kaye Hall, U.S. 1:06.20
1972 Melissa Belote, U.S. 1:05.78
1976 Ulrike Richter, East Germany 1:01.83
1980 Rica Reinisch, East Germany 1:00.86
1984 Theresa Andrews, U.S. 1:02.55
1988 Kristin Otto, East Germany 1:00.89
1992 Krisztina Egerszegi, Hungary 1:00.68

200-METER BACKSTROKE
1968 Lillian "Pokey" Watson, U.S. 2:24.80
1972 Melissa Belote, U.S. 2:19.19
1976 Ulrike Richter, East Germany 2:13.43
1980 Rica Reinisch, East Germany 2:11.77
1984 Jolanda de Rover, Netherlands 2:12.38
1988 Krisztina Egerszegi, Hungary 2:09.29
1992 Krisztina Egerszegi, Hungary 2:07.06

100-METER BUTTERFLY
1956 Shelley Mann, U.S. 1:11.00
1960 Carolyn Schuler, U.S. 1:09.50
1964 Sharon Stouder, U.S. 1:04.70
1968 Lynn McClements, Australia 1:05.50
1972 Mayumi Aoki, Japan 1:03.34
1976 Kornelia Ender, East Germany 1:00.13
1980 Caren Metschuck, East Germany 1:00.42
1984 Mary T. Meagher, U.S. 0:59.26
1988 Kristin Otto, East Germany 0:59.00
1992 Qian Hong, China 0:58.62

200-METER BUTTERFLY
1968 Ada Kok, Netherlands 2:24.70
1972 Karen Moe, U.S. 2:15.57
1976 Andrea Pollack, East Germany 2:11.41
1980 Ines Geissler, East Germany 2:10.44
1984 Mary T. Meagher, U.S. 2:06.90
1988 Kathleen Nord, East Germany 2:09.51
1992 Summer Sanders, U.S. 2:08.67

100-METER BREASTSTROKE
1968 Djurdjica Bjedov, Yugoslavia 1:15.80
1972 Cathy Carr, U.S. 1:13.58
1976 Hannelore Anke, East Germany 1:11.16
1980 Ute Geweniger, East Germany 1:10.22
1984 Petra Van Staveren, Netherlands 1:09.69
1988 Tania Dangalakova, Bulgaria 1:07.95
1992 Elena Roudkovskaia, Unified Team 1:08.00

200-METER BREASTSTROKE
1924 Lucy Morton, Great Britain 3:33.20
1928 Hilde Schrader, Germany 3:12.60
1932 Clare Dennis, Australia 3:06.30
1936 Hideko Maehata, Japan 3:03.60
1948 Nelly Van Vliet, Netherlands 2:57.20
1952 Eva Szekely, Hungary 2:51.70
1956 Ursula Happe, Germany 2:53.10
1960 Anita Lonsbrough, Great Britain 2:49.50
1964 Galina Prozumenshikova, USSR 2:46.40
1968 Sharon Wichman, U.S. 2:44.40
1972 Beverly Whitfield, Australia 2:41.71
1976 Marina Koshevaya, USSR 2:33.35
1980 Lina Kaciusyte, USSR 2:29.54
1984 Anne Ottenbrite, Canada 2:30.38
1988 Silke Hoerner, East Germany 2:26.71
1992 Kyoko Iwasaki, Japan 2:26.65

200-METER INDIVIDUAL MEDLEY
1968 Claudia Kolb, U.S. 2:24.70
1972 Shane Gould, Australia 2:23.07
1984 Tracy Caulkins, U.S. 2:12.64
1988 Daniela Hunger, East Germany 2:12.59
1992 Lin Li, China 2:11.65

400-METER INDIVIDUAL MEDLEY
1964 Donna de Varona, U.S. 5:18.70
1968 Claudia Kolb, U.S. 5:08.50
1972 Gail Neall, Australia 5:02.97
1976 Ulrike Tauber, East Germany 4:42.77
1980 Petra Schneider, East Germany 4:36.29
1984 Tracy Caulkins, U.S. 4:39.24
1988 Janet Evans, U.S. 4:37.76
1992 Krisztina Egerszegi, Hungary 4:36.54

400-METER FREESTYLE RELAY
1912 Great Britain 5:52.80
1920 U.S. 5:11.60
1924 U.S. 4:58.80
1928 U.S. 4:47.60
1932 U.S. 4:38.00
1936 Netherlands 4:36.00
1948 U.S. 4:29.20
1952 Hungary 4:24.40
1956 Australia 4:17.10
1960 U.S. 4:08.90
1964 U.S. 4:03.80
1968 U.S. 4:02.50
1972 U.S. 3:55.19
1976 U.S. 3:44.82
1980 East Germany 3:42.71
1984 U.S. 3:43.43
1988 East Germany 3:40.63
1992 U.S. 3:39.46

400-METER MEDLEY RELAY
1960 U.S. 4:41.10
1964 U.S. 4:33.90
1968 U.S. 4:28.30
1972 U.S. 4:20.75
1976 East Germany 4:07.95
1980 East Germany 4:06.67
1984 U.S. 4:08.34
1988 East Germany 4:03.74
1992 U.S. 4:02.54

SPRINGBOARD DIVING Points
1920 Aileen Riggin, U.S. 539.90
1924 Elizabeth Becker, U.S. 474.50
1928 Helen Meany, U.S. 78.62
1932 Georgia Coleman, U.S. 87.52
1936 Marjorie Gestring, U.S. 89.27
1948 Victoria Draves, U.S. 108.74
1952 Patricia McCormick, U.S. 147.30
1956 Patricia McCormick, U.S. 142.36
1960 Ingrid Kramer, Germany 155.81
1964 Ingrid Engle-Kramer, East Germany 145.00
1968 Sue Gossick, U.S. 150.77
1972 Micki King, U.S. 450.03
1976 Jennifer Chandler, U.S. 506.19
1980 Irina Kalinina, USSR 725.91
1984 Sylvie Bernier, Canada 530.70
1988 Gao Min, China 580.23
1992 Gao Min, China 572.40

PLATFORM DIVING
1912 Greta Johansson, Sweden 39.90
1920 Stefani Fryland-Clausen, Denmark 34.60
1924 Caroline Smith, U.S. 33.20
1928 Elizabeth Pinkston, U.S. 31.60
1932 Dorothy Poynton, U.S. 40.26
1936 Dorothy Poynton Hill, U.S. 33.93
1948 Victoria Draves, U.S. 68.87
1952 Patricia McCormick, U.S. 79.37
1956 Patricia McCormick, U.S. 84.85
1960 Ingrid Kramer, Germany 91.28
1964 Lesley Bush, U.S. 99.80
1968 Milena Duchkova, Czechoslovakia 109.59
1972 Ulrika Knape, Sweden 390.00
1976 Yelena Vaitsekhovskaya, USSR 406.59
1980 Martina Jäschke, East Germany 596.25
1984 Zhou Jihong, China 435.51
1988 Xu Yahmei, China 445.20
1992 Fu Mingxia, China 461.43

TRACK AND FIELD—MEN Time

100-METER DASH
1896 Thomas E. Burke, U.S. 12.00
1900 Francis W. Jarvis, U.S. 10.80
1904 Archie Hahn, U.S. 11.00
1908 Reginald E. Walker, South Africa 10.80
1912 Ralph C. Craig, U.S. 10.80
1920 Charles W. Paddock, U.S. 10.80
1924 Harold M. Abrahams, Great Britain 10.60
1928 Percy Williams, Canada 10.80
1932 Eddie Tolan, U.S. 10.30
1936 Jesse Owens, U.S. 10.30
1948 Harrison Dillard, U.S. 10.30
1952 Lindy J. Remigino, U.S. 10.40
1956 Bobby J. Morrow, U.S. 10.50
1960 Armin Hary, Germany 10.20
1964 Robert L. Hayes, U.S. 10.00
1968 James Hines, U.S. 9.90
1972 Valery Borzov, USSR 10.14
1976 Hasely Crawford, Trinidad and Tobago 10.06
1980 Allan Wells, Great Britain 10.25
1984 Carl Lewis, U.S. 9.99
1988 Carl Lewis, U.S. 9.92
1992 Linford Christie, Great Britain 9.96

200 METERS
1900 John W.B. Tewksbury, U.S. 22.20
1904 Archie Hahn, U.S. 21.60
1908 Robert Kerr, Canada 22.60
1912 Ralph C. Craig, U.S. 21.70
1920 Allan Woodring, U.S. 22.00
1924 Jackson V. Scholz, U.S. 21.60
1928 Percy Williams, Canada 21.80
1932 Eddie Tolan, U.S. 21.20
1936 Jesse Owens, U.S. 20.70
1948 Melvin Patton, U.S. 21.10
1952 Andrew W. Stanfield, U.S. 20.70
1956 Bobby J. Morrow, U.S. 20.60
1960 Livio Berruti, Italy 20.50
1964 Henry Carr, U.S. 20.30
1968 Tommie Smith, U.S. 19.80
1972 Valery Borzov, USSR 20.00
1976 Donald Quarrie, Jamaica 20.23
1980 Pietro Mennea, Italy 20.19
1984 Carl Lewis, U.S. 19.80
1988 Joe DeLoach, U.S. 19.75
1992 Mike Marsh, U.S. 20.01

400 METERS
1896 Thomas E. Burke, U.S. 54.20
1900 Maxwell W. Long, U.S. 49.40
1904 Harry I. Hillman, U.S. 49.20
1908 Wyndham Halswelle, Great Britain 50.00
1912 Charles D. Reidpath, U.S. 48.20
1920 Bevil G.D. Rudd, South Africa 49.60
1924 Eric H. Liddel, Great Britain 47.60
1928 Ray Barbuti, U.S. 47.80
1932 William A. Carr, U.S. 46.20
1936 Archie Williams, U.S. 46.50
1948 Arthur Wint, Jamaica 46.20
1952 George Rhoden, Jamaica 45.90
1956 Charles L. Jenkins, U.S. 46.70
1960 Otis Davis, U.S. 44.90
1964 Michael D. Larrabee, U.S. 45.10
1968 Lee Evans, U.S. 43.80
1972 Vince Matthews, U.S. 44.66
1976 Alberto Juantorena, Cuba 44.26
1980 Viktor Markin, USSR 44.60
1984 Alonzo Babers, U.S. 44.27
1988 Steven Lewis, U.S. 43.87
1992 Quincy Watts, U.S. 43.50

800 METERS
1896 Edwin H. Flack, Australia 2:11.00
1900 Alfred E. Tysoe, Great Britain 2:01.40
1904 James D. Lightbody, U.S. 1:56.00
1908 Melvin W. Sheppard, U.S. 1:52.80
1912 James E. Meredith, U.S. 1:51.90
1920 Albert G. Hill, Great Britain 1:53.40
1924 Douglas G.A. Lowe, Great Britain 1:52.40
1928 Douglas G.A. Lowe, Great Britain 1:51.80
1932 Thomas Hampson, Great Britain 1:49.80
1936 John Woodruff, U.S. 1:52.90
1948 Malvin Whitfield, U.S. 1:49.20
1952 Malvin Whitfield, U.S. 1:49.20
1956 Thomas W. Courtney, U.S. 1:47.70
1960 Peter Snell, New Zealand 1:46.30
1964 Peter Snell, New Zealand 1:45.10
1968 Ralph Doubell, Australia 1:44.30
1972 Dave Wottle, U.S. 1:45.90
1976 Alberto Juantorena, Cuba 1:43.50
1980 Steven Ovett, Great Britain 1:45.40
1984 Joaquim Cruz, Brazil 1:43.00
1988 Paul Ereng, Kenya 1:43.45
1992 William Tanui, Kenya 1:43.66

1,500-METER RUN
1896 Edwin H. Flack, Australia 4:33.20
1900 Charles Bennett, Great Britain 4:06.20
1904 James D. Lightbody, U.S. 4:05.40
1908 Melvin W. Sheppard, U.S. 4:03.40
1912 Arnold N.S. Jackson, Great Britain 3:56.80
1920 Albert G. Hill, Great Britain 4:01.80
1924 Paavo Nurmi, Finland 3:53.60
1928 Harry E. Larva, Finland 3:53.20
1932 Luigi Beccali, Italy 3:51.20
1936 Jack E. Lovelock, New Zealand 3:47.80
1948 Henry Eriksson, Sweden 3:49.80
1952 Joseph Barthel, Luxembourg 3:45.20
1956 Ronald Delany, Ireland 3:41.20
1960 Herbert Elliott, Australia 3:35.60
1964 Peter Snell, New Zealand 3:38.10
1968 Kipchoge Keino, Kenya 3:34.90
1972 Pekka Vasala, Finland 3:36.30
1976 John Walker, New Zealand 3:39.17
1980 Sebastian Coe, Great Britain 3:38.40
1984 Sebastian Coe, Great Britain 3:32.53
1988 Peter Rono, Kenya 3:35.96
1992 Fermin Cacho Ruiz, Spain 3:40.12

5,000 METERS
1912 Hannes Kolehmainen, Finland 14:36.60

1920 Joseph Guillemot, France 14:55.60
1924 Paavo Nurmi, Finland 14:31.20
1928 Willie Ritola, Finland 14:38.00
1932 Lauri Lehtinen, Finland 14:30.00
1936 Gunnar Hocket, Finland 14:22.20
1948 Gaston Reiff, Belgium 14:17.60
1952 Emil Zatopek, Czechoslovakia 14:06.60
1956 Vladimir Kuts, USSR 13:39.60
1960 Murray Halberg, New Zealand 13:43.40
1964 Robert K. Schul, U.S. 13:48.80
1968 Mohamed Gammoudi, Tunisia 14:05.10
1972 Lasse Viren, Finland 13:26.40
1976 Lasse Viren, Finland 13:24.76
1980 Miruts Yifter, Ethiopia 13:21.00
1984 Said Aouita, Morocco 13:05.59
1988 John Ngugi, Kenya 13:11.70
1992 Dieter Baumann, Germany 13:12.52

10,000 METERS

1912 Hannes Kolehmainen, Finland 31:20.80
1920 Paavo Nurmi, Finland 31:45.80
1924 Willie Ritola, Finland 30:23.20
1928 Paavo Nurmi, Finland 30:18.80
1932 Janusz Kusocinski, Poland 30:11.40
1936 Ilmari Salminen, Finland 30:15.40
1948 Emil Zatopek, Czechoslovakia 29:59.60
1952 Emil Zatopek, Czechoslovakia 29:17.00
1956 Vladimir Kuts, USSR 28:45.60
1960 Petr Bolotnikov, USSR 28:32.20
1964 William Mills, U.S. 28:24.40
1968 Naftali Temu, Kenya 29:27.40
1972 Lasse Viren, Finland 27:38.40
1976 Lasse Viren, Finland 27:40.38
1980 Miruts Yifter, Ethiopia 27:42.70
1984 Alberto Cova, Italy 27:47.54
1988 Brahim Boutaib, Morocco 27:21.46
1992 Khalid Skah, Morocco 27:46.70

MARATHON

1896 Spyros Loues, Greece 2:58:50.00
1900 Michel Theato, France 2:59:45.00
1904 Thomas J. Hicks, U.S. 3:28:53.00
1908 John J. Hayes, U.S. 2:55:18.40
1912 Kenneth McArthur, South Africa 2:36:54.80
1920 Hannes Kolehmainen, Finland 2:32:35.80
1924 Albin Stenroos, Finland 2:41:22.60
1928 A.B. El Quafi, France 2:32:57.00
1932 Juan Zabala, Argentina 2:31:36.00
1936 Kitei Son, Japan 2;29:19.20
1948 Delfo Cabrera, Argentina 2:34:51.60
1952 Emil Zatopek, Czechoslovakia 2:23:03.20
1956 Alain Mimoun, France 2:25:00.00
1960 Abebe Bikila, Ethiopia 2:15:16.20
1964 Abebe Bikila, Ethiopia 2:12:11.20
1968 Mamo Wolde, Ethiopia 2:20:26.40
1972 Frank Shorter, U.S. 2:12:19.70
1976 Waldemar Cierpinski, East Germany 2:09:55.00
1980 Waldemar Cierpinski, East Germany 2:11.03.00
1984 Carlos Lopes, Portugal 2:09.21.00
1988 Gelindo Bordin, Italy 2:10.32.00
1992 Young-Cho Hwang, South Korea 2:13:23.00

110-METER HURDLES

1896 Thomas P. Curtis, U.S. 17.60
1900 Alvin E. Kraenzlein, U.S. 15.40
1904 Frederick W. Schule, U.S. 16.00
1908 Forrest Smithson, U.S. 15.00
1912 Frederick W. Kelley, U.S. 15.10
1920 Earl J. Thomson, Canada 14.80
1924 Daniel C. Kinsey, U.S. 15.00
1928 Sydney Atkinson, South Africa 14.80
1932 George Saling, U.S. 14.60
1936 Forrest Towns, U.S. 14.20
1948 William Porter, U.S. 13.90
1952 Harrison Dillard, U.S. 13.70
1956 Lee Q. Calhoun, U.S. 13.50
1960 Lee Q. Calhoun, U.S. 13.80
1964 Hayes W. Jones, U.S. 13.60
1968 Willie Davenport, U.S. 13.30
1972 Rod Milburn, U.S. 13.24
1976 Guy Drut, France 13.30
1980 Thomas Munkelt, East Germany 13.39
1984 Roger Kingdom, U.S. 13.20
1988 Roger Kingdom, U.S. 12.98
1992 Mark McKoy, Canada 13.12

400-METER HURDLES

1900 John W.B. Tewksbury, U.S. 57.60
1904 Harry L. Hillman, U.S. 53.00
1908 Charles J. Bacon, U.S. 55.00
1920 Frank F. Loomis, U.S. 54.00
1924 F. Morgan Taylor, U.S. 52.60
1928 Lord David Burghley, Great Britain 53.40
1932 Robert Tisdall, Ireland 51.80
1936 Glenn Hardin, U.S. 52.40
1948 Roy Cochran, U.S. 51.10
1952 Charles Moore, U.S. 50.80
1956 Glenn A. Davis, U.S. 50.10
1960 Glenn A. Davis, U.S. 49.30
1964 Warren "Rex" Cawley, U.S. 49.60
1968 David Hemery, Great Britain 48.10
1972 John Akii-Bau, Uganda 47.82
1976 Edwin Moses, U.S. 47.64
1980 Volker Beck, East Germany 48.70
1984 Edwin Moses, U.S. 47.75
1988 Andre Phillips, U.S. 47.19
1992 Kevin Young, U.S. 46.78

3,000-METER STEEPLECHASE

1920 Percy Hodge, Great Britain 10:00.40
1924 Willie Ritola, Finland 9:33.60
1928 Toivo A. Loukola, Finland 9:21.80
1932 Volmari Iso-Hollo, Finland 10:33.40
(3,460 m—extra lap by official error)
1936 Volmari Iso-Hollo, Finland 9:03.80
1948 Thore Sjostrand, Sweden 9:04.60
1952 Horace Ashenfelter, U.S. 8:45.40
1956 Chris Brasher, Great Britain 8:41.20
1960 Zdzislaw Krzyszkowiak, Poland 8:34.20
1964 Gaston Roelants, Belgium 8:30.80
1968 Amos Biwott, Kenya 8:51.00
1972 Kipchoge Keino, Kenya 8:23.60
1976 Anders Gärderud, Sweden 8:08.20
1980 Bronislaw Malinowski, Poland 8:09.70
1984 Julius Korir, Kenya 8:11.80
1988 Julius Karuiki, Kenya 8:05.51
1992 Matthew Birer, Kenya 8:08.84

20-KILOMETER WALK

1956 Leonid Spirine, USSR 1:31:27.4
1960 Vladimir Golubnichy, USSR 1:34:07.2
1964 Kenneth Matthews, Great Britain 1:29:34.0
1968 Vladimir Golubnichy, USSR 1:33:58.4
1972 Peter Frenkel, East Germany 1:26:42.4
1976 Daniel Bautista, Mexico 1:24:40.6
1980 Maurizio Damilano, Italy 1:23:35.5
1984 Ernesto Canto, Mexico 1:23:13.0
1988 Josef Pribilinec, Czechoslovakia 1:19:57.0
1992 Daniel Montero, Spain 1:21:45.0

50-KILOMETER WALK

1932 Thomas W. Green, Great Britain 4:50:10.0
1936 Harold Whitlock, Great Britain 4:30:41.4
1948 John A. Ljunggren, Sweden 4:41:52.0
1952 Giuseppe Dordoni, Italy 4:28:07.8
1956 Norman Read, New Zealand 4:30:42.8
1960 Donald Thompson, Great Britain 4:25:30.0
1964 Abdon Pamich, Italy 4:11:12.4
1968 Christoph Kohne, East Germany 4:20:13.6
1972 Bernd Kannenberg, West Germany 3:56:11.6
1980 Hartwig Gauter, East Germany 3:49:24.0
1984 Raul Gonzalez, Mexico 3:47:26.0
1988 Vayachselav Ivanenko, USSR 3:38:29.0
1992 Andrei Perlov, Unified Team 3:50:13.0

400-METER RELAY

1912	Great Britain	42.40	1960	W. Germany	39.50
1920	U.S.	42.20	1964	U.S.	39.00
1924	U.S.	41.00	1968	U.S.	38.20
1928	U.S.	41.00	1972	U.S.	38.19
1932	U.S.	40.00	1976	U.S.	38.33
1936	U.S.	40.00	1980	USSR	38.26
1948	U.S.	40.30	1984	U.S.	37.83
1952	U.S.	40.10	1988	USSR	38.19
1956	U.S.	39.50	1992	U.S.	37.40

1,600-METER RELAY

1908	U.S.	3:29.40	1956	U.S.	3:04.80
1912	U.S.	3:16.60	1960	U.S.	3:02.20
1920	Great Britain	3:22.20	1964	U.S.	3:00.70
			1968	U.S.	2:56.10
1924	U.S.	3:16.00	1972	Kenya	2:59.80
1928	U.S.	3:14.20	1976	U.S.	2:58.65
1932	U.S.	3:08.20	1980	USSR	3:01.10
1936	Great Britain	3:09.00	1984	U.S.	2:57.91
			1988	U.S.	2:56.16
1948	U.S.	3:10.40	1992	U.S.	2:55.74
1952	Jamaica	3:03.90			

POLE VAULT — **Height**

1896 William W. Hoyt, U.S. 10'9¾"
1900 Irving K. Baxter, U.S. 10'9 9/10"
1904 Charles E. Dvorak, U.S. 11'6"
1908 Albert C. Gilbert, U.S. 12'2"
Edward T. Cook, Jr., U.S.
1912 Harry S. Babcock, U.S. 12'11½"
1920 Frank K. Foss, U.S. 12'5 9/16"
1924 Lee S. Barnes, U.S. 12'11½"
1928 Sabin W. Carr, U.S. 13'9⅜"
1932 William Miller, U.S. 14'1⅞"
1936 Earle Meadows, U.S. 14'3¼"
1948 O. Guinn Smith, U.S. 14'1¼"
1952 Robert Richards, U.S. 14'11¼"
1956 Robert Richards, U.S. 14'11½"
1960 Donald Bragg, U.S. 15'5⅛"
1964 Fred M. Hansen, U.S. 16'8¾"
1968 Robert Seagren, U.S. 17'8½"
1972 Wolfgang Nordwig, East Germany 18'½"
1976 Tadeusz Slusarki, Poland 18'½"
1980 Wladyslaw Kozakiewicz, Poland 18'11½"
1984 Pierre Quinon, France 18'10¼"
1988 Sergei Bubka, USSR 19'9¼"
1992 Maksim Tarassov, Unified Team 19'0¼"

HIGH JUMP

1896 Ellery Clark, U.S. 5'11¼"
1900 Irving K. Baxter, U.S. 6'2⅘"
1904 Samuel Jones, U.S. 5'11"
1908 Harry Porter, U.S. 6'3"
1912 Almer Richards, U.S. 6'4"
1920 Richmond Landon, U.S. 6'4¼"
1924 Harold Osborn, U.S. 6'5 15/16"
1928 Robert W. King, U.S. 6'4⅜"
1932 Duncan McNaughton, Canada 6'5⅝"
1936 Cornelius Johnson, U.S. 6'7 15/16"
1948 John Winter, Australia 6'6"
1952 Walter Davis, U.S. 6'8¼"
1956 Charles E. Dumas, U.S. 6'11¼"
1960 Robert Shavlakadze, USSR 7'1"
1964 Valery Brumel, USSR 7'1¾"
1968 Richard Fosbury, U.S. 7'4¼"
1972 Juri Tarmak, USSR 7'3¾"
1976 Jacek Wszola, Poland 7'4½"
1980 Gerd Wessig, East Germany 7'8¾"
1984 Dietmar Mogenburg, W. Germany 7'8½"
1988 Guennadi Avdeenko, USSR 7'9½"
1992 Javier Sotomayor, Cuba 7'8"

LONG JUMP — **Distance**

1896 Ellery Clark, U.S. 20'10"
1900 Alvin Kraenzlein, U.S. 23'6⅞"
1904 Meyer Prinstein, U.S. 24'1"
1908 Francis Irons, U.S. 24'6½"
1912 Albert Gutterson, U.S. 24'11¼"
1920 William Pettersson, Sweden 23'5½"
1924 DeHart Hubbard, U.S. 24'5⅛"
1928 Edward Hamm, U.S. 25'4¾"
1932 Edward Gordon, U.S. 25'¾"
1936 Jesse Owens, U.S. 26'5⅜"
1948 Willie Steel, U.S. 25'8"
1952 Jerome Biffle, U.S. 24'10"
1956 Gregory C. Bell, U.S. 25'8¼"
1960 Ralph H. Boston, U.S. 26'7¾"
1964 Lynn Davies, Great Britain 26'5¾"
1968 Robert Beamon, U.S. 29'2½"
1972 Randy Williams, U.S. 27'½"
1976 Arnie Robinson, U.S. 27'4¾"
1980 Lutz Dombrowski, E. Germany 28'¼"
1984 Carl Lewis, U.S. 28'¼"
1988 Carl Lewis, U.S. 28'7¼"
1992 Carl Lewis, U.S. 28'5½"

TRIPLE JUMP

1896 James B. Connolly, U.S. 45'0"
1900 Myer Prinstein, U.S. 47'4¼"
1904 Myer Prinstein, U.S. 47'0"
1908 Timothy Ahearne, Great Britain 48'11¼"
1912 Gustaf Lindblom, Sweden 48'5⅛"
1920 Vilho Tuulos, Finland 47'6⅞"
1924 Archibald Winter, Australia 50'11⅛"
1928 Mikio Oda, Japan 49'10 13/16"
1932 Chuhei Nambu, Japan 51'7"
1936 Naoto Tajima, Japan 52'5⅞"
1948 Arne Ahman, Sweden 50'6¼"
1952 Adhemar Ferreira da Silva, Brazil 53'2½"
1956 Adhemar Ferreira da Silva, Brazil 53'7½"
1960 Jozef Schmidt, Poland 55'1¾"
1964 Jozef Schmidt, Poland 55'3¼"
1968 Viktor Saneyev, USSR 57'¾"
1972 Viktor Saneyev, USSR 56'11"
1976 Viktor Saneyev, USSR 56'8¾"
1980 Jaak Uudmae, USSR 56'11¼"
1984 Al Joyner, U.S. 56'7½"
1988 Hristo Markov, Bulgaria 57'9¼"
1992 Mike Conley, U.S. 57'10¼"

16-POUND SHOT PUT

1896 Robert Garrett, U.S. 36'9¾"
1900 Richard Sheldon, U.S. 46'3⅛"
1904 Ralph Rose, U.S. 48'7"
1908 Ralph Rose, U.S. 46'7½"
1912 Patrick McDonald, U.S. 50'4"
1920 Ville Porhola, Finland 48'7⅛"
1924 Clarence Houser, U.S. 49'2½"
1928 John Kuck, U.S. 52'13/16"
1932 Leo Sexton, U.S. 52'6 3/16"
1936 Hans Woellke, Germany 53'1¾"
1948 Wilbur Thompson, U.S. 56'2"
1952 William Parry O'Brien, Jr., U.S. 57'1½"
1956 William Parry O'Brien, Jr., U.S. 60'11"
1960 William Nieder, U.S. 64'6¾"
1964 Dallas C. Long, U.S. 66'8½"
1968 James Randel Matson, U.S. 67'4¾"
1972 Wladyslaw Komar, Poland 69'6"
1976 Udo Beyer, East Germany 69'6 7/10"
1980 Vladimir Kiselyov, USSR 70'½"
1984 Allesandro Andrei, Italy 69'9"
1988 Ulf Timmermann, East Germany 73'8¾"
1992 Mike Stulce, U.S. 71'2½"

DISCUS THROW

1896 Robert Garrett, U.S. 95'7½"
1900 Rudolf Bauer, Hungary 118'2 9/10"
1904 Martin Sheridan, U.S. 128'10½"
1908 Martin Sheridan, U.S. 134'2"
1912 Armas Taipale, Finland 145'9/16"
1920 Elmer Niklander, Finland 146'7"
1924 Clarence Houser, U.S. 151'5¼"
1928 Clarence Houser, U.S. 155'2⅘"
1932 John Anderson, U.S. 162'4⅞"
1936 Kenneth Carpenter, U.S. 165'7½"
1948 Adolfo Consolini, Italy 173'2"
1952 Sim Iness, U.S. 180'6½"
1956 Alfred A. Oerter, U.S. 184'10½"
1960 Alfred A. Oerter, U.S. 194'2"
1964 Alfred A. Oerter, U.S. 200'1½"
1968 Alfred A. Oerter, U.S. 212'6½"
1972 Ludwick Danek, Czechoslovakia 211'3½"
1976 Mac Wilkins, U.S 221'5⅖"
1980 Viktor·Raschupkin, USSR 218'8"
1984 Rolf Danneberg, West Germany 218'6"
1988 Jurgen Schult, East Germany 225'9¼"
1992 Romas Ubartas, Lithuania 213'8"

16-POUND HAMMER THROW

1900 John Flanagan, U.S. 167'4"
1904 John Flanagan, U.S. 168'1"
1908 John Flanagan, U.S. 170'4¼"
1912 Matthew McGrath, U.S. 179'7⅛"
1920 Patrick Ryan, U.S. 173'5⅝"

1924 Frederick Tootell, U.S. 174'10¼"
1928 Patrick O'Callaghan, Ireland 168'7½"
1932 Patrick O'Callaghan, Ireland 176'11⅛"
1936 Karl Hein, Germany 185'4¼"
1948 Imre Nemeth, Hungary 183'11½"
1952 Jozsef Csermak, Hungary 197'11¾"
1956 Harold V. Connolly, U.S. 207'3½"
1960 Vasiliy Rudenkov, USSR 220'1⅝"
1964 Romuald Klim, USSR 229'9½"
1968 Gyula Zsivotzky, Hungary 240'8"
1972 Anatol Bondarchuk, USSR 247'8"
1976 Yuri Sedykh, USSR 254'4"
1980 Yuri Sedykh, USSR 268'4"
1984 Juha Tiainen, Finland 256'2"
1988 Sergei Litinov, USSR 278'2½"
1992 Andrei Abduvaliyev, Unified Team 270'9"

JAVELIN THROW

1908 Erik Lemming, Sweden 179'10½"
1912 Erik Lemming, Sweden 198'11¼"
1920 Jonni Myyra, Finland 215'9¾"
1924 Jonni Myyra, Finland 206'6¾"
1928 Erik Lundquist, Sweden 218'6⅛"
1932 Matti Jarvinen, Finland 238'7"
1936 Gerhard Stock, Germany 235'8 5/16"
1948 Tapio Rautavaara, Finland 228'10½"
1952 Cyrus Young, U.S. 242'¾"
1956 Egil Danielson, Norway 281'2¼"
1960 Viktor Tsibulenko, USSR 277'8⅜"
1964 Pauli Nevala, Finland 271'2¼"
1968 Janis Lusis, USSR 295'7¼"
1972 Klaus Wolfermann, West Germany 296'10"
1976 Miklos Nemeth, Hungary 310'4½"
1980 Dainis Kula, USSR 299'2"
1984 Arto Harkonen, Finland 284'8"
1988 Tapio Korjus, Finland 276'6"
1992 Jan Zelezny, Czechoslovakia 294'2"

DECATHLON — Points

(Old point system, 1912–32)
1912 Hugo Wieslander, Sweden 7,724.49
1920 Helge Lovland, Norway 6,804.35
1924 Harold Osborn, U.S. 7,710.77
1928 Paavo Yrjola, Finland 8,053.29
1932 James Bausch, U.S. 8,462.23
(Revised point system, 1936–60)
1936 Glenn Morris, U.S. 7,900.00
1948 Robert Mathias, U.S. 7,139.00
1952 Robert Mathias, U.S. 7,887.00
1956 Milton G. Campbell, U.S. 7,937.00
1960 Rafer Johnson, U.S. 8,392.00
(New scoring system, 1964–present)
1964 Willi Holdorf, West Germany 7,887.00
1968 William Toomey, U.S. 8,193.00
1972 Nikolai Avilov, USSR 8,454.00
1976 Bruce Jenner, U.S. 8,618.00
1980 Francis Thompson, Great Britain 8,495.00
1984 Francis Thompson, Great Britain 8,798.00
1988 Christian Schenk, East Germany 8,488.00
1992 Robert Zmelik, Czechoslovakia 8,611.00

TRACK AND FIELD—WOMEN

Time

100-METER DASH

1928 Elizabeth Robinson, U.S. 12.20
1932 Stanislawa Walasiewicz, Poland 11.90
1936 Helen Stephens, U.S. 11.50
1948 Francina Blankers-Koen, Netherlands 11.90
1952 Marjorie Jackson, Australia 11.50
1956 Betty Cuthbert, Australia 11.50
1960 Wilma Rudolph, U.S 11.00
1964 Wyomia Tyus, U.S. 11.40
1968 Wyomia Tyus, U.S. 11.00
1972 Renate Stecher, East Germany 11.07
1976 Annegret Richter, West Germany 11.01
1980 Lyudmila Kondratyeva, USSR 11.06
1984 Evelyn Ashford, U.S. 10.97
1988 Florence Griffith-Joyner, U.S. 10.54
1992 Gail Devers, U.S. 10.82

200 METERS

1948 Francina Blankers-Koen, Netherlands 24.40
1952 Marjorie Jackson, Australia 23.70
1956 Betty Cuthbert, Australia 23.40
1960 Wilma Rudolph, U.S. 24.00
1964 Edith McGuire, U.S. 23.00
1968 Irena Kirszenstein Szewinska, Poland 22.50
1972 Renate Stecher, East Germany 22.40
1976 Bärbel Eckert, East Germany 22.37
1980 Bärbel Wöckel (Eckert), East Germany 22.03
1984 Valerie Brisco-Hooks, U.S. 21.81
1988 Florence Griffith-Joyner, U.S. 21.34
1992 Gwen Torrence, U.S. 21.81

400 METERS

1964 Betty Cuthbert, Australia 52.00
1968 Colette Besson, France 52.00
1972 Monika Zehrt, East Germany 51.08
1976 Irena Szewinska, Poland 49.29
1980 Marita Koch, East Germany 48.88
1984 Valerie Brisco-Hooks, U.S. 48.83
1988 Olga Bryzgina, USSR 48.65
1992 Marie-Jose Perec, France 48.83

800 METERS

1928 Linda Radke-Batschauer, Germany 2:16.80
1960 Lyudmila Shevcova-Lysenko, USSR 2:04.30
1964 Ann Packer, Great Britain 2:01.10
1968 Madeline Manning, U.S. 2:00.90
1972 Hildegard Falck, West Germany 1:58.55
1976 Tatyana Kazankina, USSR 1:54.94
1980 Nadezhda Olizarenko, USSR 1:53.42
1984 Doina Melinte, Romania 1:57.60
1988 Sigrun Wodars, East Germany 1:56.10
1992 Ellen Van Langen, Netherlands 1:55.54

1,500 METERS

1972 Lyudmila Bragina, USSR 4:01.40
1976 Tatyana Kazankina, USSR 4:05.48
1980 Tatyana Kazankina, USSR 3:56.60
1984 Gabrielle Dorio, Italy 4:03.25
1988 Paula Ivan, Romania 3:53.96
1992 Hassiba Boulmerka, Algeria 3:55.30

3,000 METERS

1984 Maricica Puica, Romania 8:35.96
1988 Tatyana Samolenko, USSR 8:26.53
1992 Elena Romanova, Unified Team 8:46.04

10,000 METERS

1988 Olga Boldarenko, USSR 31:44.69
1992 Derartu Tulu, Ethiopia 31:06.02

MARATHON

1984 Joan Benoit, U.S. 2:24.52
1988 Rosa Mota, Portugal 2:25.40
1992 Valentina Yegorova, Unified Team 2:32.41

400-METER RELAY

1928 Canada 48.40
1932 U.S. 47.00
1936 U.S. 46.90
1948 Netherlands 47.50
1952 U.S. 45.90
1956 Australia 44.50
1960 U.S. 44.50
1964 Poland 43.60
1968 U.S. 42.80
1972 West Germany 42.81
1976 East Germany 42.55
1980 East Germany 41.60
1984 U.S. 41.65
1988 U.S. 41.98
1992 U.S. 42.11

1,600-METER RELAY

1972 East Germany 3:23.00
1976 East Germany 3:19.23
1980 USSR 3:20.02
1984 U.S. 3:18.29
1988 USSR 3:15.18
1992 Unified Team 3:20.20

100-METER HURDLES

1972 Annelie Erhardt, East Germany 12.59
1976 Johanna Schaller, East Germany 12.77
1980 Vera Komisova, USSR 12.56
1984 Benita Brown-Fitzgerald 12.84
1988 Jordanka Donkova, Bulgaria 12.38
1992 Paraskevi Patoulido, Greece 12.64

HIGH JUMP — Height

1928 Ethel Catherwood, Canada 5'3"
1932 Jean Shiley, U.S. 5'5¼"
1936 Ibolya Csak, Hungary 5'3"
1948 Alice Coachman, U.S. 5'6⅛"
1952 Esther Brand, South Africa 5'5¾"
1956 Mildred McDaniel, U.S. 5'9¼"
1960 Iolanda Balas, Romania 6'¼"
1964 Iolanda Balas, Romania 6'2¾"
1968 Miloslava Rezkova, Czechoslovakia 5'11¾"
1972 Ulrika Meyfarth, West Germany 6'3½"
1976 Rosemarie Ackermann, East Germany 6'4"
1980 Sara Simeoni, Italy 6'5½"
1984 Ulrike Meyfarth, West Germany 6'7½"
1988 Louise Ritter, U.S. 6'8"
1992 Heike Henkel, Germany 6'7½"

LONG JUMP — Distance

1948 Olga Gyarmati, Hungary 18'8¼"
1952 Yvette Williams, New Zealand 20'5¾"
1956 Elizbieta Krzeskinska, Poland 20'9¾"
1960 Vyera Krepkina, USSR 20'10¾"
1964 Mary Rand, Great Britain 22'2"
1968 Viorica Viscopoleanu, Romania 22'4½"
1972 Heidemarie Rosendahl, West Germany 22'3"
1976 Angela Voigt, East Germany 22'2½"
1980 Tatiana Kolpakova, USSR 23'2"
1984 Anisoara Cusmir-Stanciu, Romania 22'10"
1988 Jackie Joyner-Kersee, U.S. 24'3½"
1992 Heike Drechsler, Germany 23'5¼"

DISCUS THROW

1928 Helena Konopacka, Poland 129'11⅞"
1932 Lillian Copeland, U.S. 133'2"
1936 Gisela Mauermayer, Germany 156'3 3/16"
1948 Micheline Ostermeyer, France 137'6½"
1952 Nina Romaschkova, USSR 168'8½"
1956 Olga Fikotova, Czechoslovakia 176'1½"
1960 Nina Ponomareva, USSR 180'8¼"
1964 Tamara Press, USSR 187'10¾"
1968 Lia Manoliu, Romania 191'2½"
1972 Faina Melnik, USSR 218'7"
1976 Evelin Schlaak, East Germany 226'4½"
1980 Evelin Jahl (Schaak), East Germany 229'6"
1984 Ria Stalman, Netherlands 214'5"
1988 Martina Hellmann, East Germany 237'2¼"
1992 Maritz Marten, Cuba 229'10"

8-LB. 13-OZ. SHOT PUT

1948 Micheline Ostermeyer, France 45'1½"
1952 Galina Zybina, USSR 50'1½"
1956 Tamara Tishkyevich, USSR 54'5"
1960 Tamara Press, USSR 56'9¾"
1964 Tamara Press, USSR 59'6"
1968 Margitta Gummel, East Germany 64'4"
1972 Nadezhda Chizhova, USSR 69'0"
1976 Ivanka Khristova, Bulgaria 69'5"
1980 Ilona Slupianek, East Germany 73'6¼"
1984 Claudia Losch, West Germany 67'2¼"
1988 Natalya Lisovskaya, USSR 72'11½"
1992 Svetlana Krivaleva, Unified Team 69'1¼"

JAVELIN THROW

1932 Mildred Didrikson, U.S. 143'4"
1936 Tilly Fleischer, Germany 148'2¾"
1948 Herma Bauma, Austria 149'6"
1952 Dana Zatopekova, Czechoslovakia 165'7"
1956 Inessa Janzeme, USSR 176'8"
1960 Elvira Ozolina, USSR 183'8"
1964 Mihaela Penes, Romania 198'7½"
1968 Angela Nemeth, Hungary 198'½"
1972 Ruth Fuchs, East Germany 209'7"
1976 Ruth Fuchs, East Germany 216'4"
1980 Maria Colon Ruenes, Cuba 224'5"
1984 Theresa Sanderson, Great Britain 228'2"
1988 Petra Felke, East Germany 245'0"
1992 Silke Renke, Germany 224'2"

PENTATHLON — Points

1964 Irina Press, USSR 5,246
1968 Ingrid Becker, West Germany 5,098
1972 Mary Peters, Great Britain 4,801
1976 Siegrun Siegl, East Germany 4,745
1980 Nadezhda Tkachenko, USSR 5,083

HEPTATHLON

1984 Glynis Nunn, Australia 6,390
1988 Jackie Joyner-Kersee, U.S. 7,215
1992 Jackie Joyner-Kersee, U.S. 7,044

GYMNASTICS—MEN

Points

ALL-AROUND

1900 Gustave Sandras, France 302.000
1904 Julius Lenhart, Austria 69.800
1908 Alberto Braglia, Italy 317.000
1912 Alberto Braglia, Italy 135.000
1920 Giorgio Zampori, Italy 88.350
1924 Leon Stukelj, Yugoslavia 110.340
1928 Georges Miez, Switzerland 247.500
1932 Romeo Neri, Italy 140.625
1936 Alfred Schwarzmann, Germany 113.100
1948 Veikko Huhtanen, Finland 229.700
1952 Viktor Chukarin, USSR 115.700
1956 Viktor Chukarin, USSR 114.250
1960 Boris Shakhlin, USSR 115.950
1964 Yukio Endo, Japan 115.950
1968 Sawao Kato, Japan 115.900
1972 Sawao Kato, Japan 114.650
1976 Nikolai Andrianov, USSR 116.650
1980 Aleksandr Dityatin, USSR 118.650
1984 Koji Gushiken, Japan 118.700
1988 Vladimir Artemov, USSR 119.125
1992 Vitali Scherbo, Unified Team 59.025

HORIZONTAL BAR

1896 Herman Weingärtner, Germany —
1904 Anton Heida, U.S. 40.000
Edward Hennig, U.S. (tie)
1924 Leon Stukelj, Yugoslavia 19.730
1928 Georges Miez 19.170
1932 Dallas Bixler, U.S. 18.330
1936 Aleksanteri Saarvala, Finland 19.367
1948 Josef Stalder, Switzerland 19.850
1952 Jack Günthard, Switzerland 19.550
1956 Takashi Ono, Japan 19.600
1960 Takashi Ono, Japan 19.600
1964 Boris Shakhlin, USSR 19.625
1968 Akinori Nakayama, Japan 19.550
1972 Mitsuo Tsukahara, Japan 19.725
1976 Mitsuo Tsukahara, Japan 19.675
1980 Stoyan Deltchev, Bulgaria 19.825
1984 Shinji Morisue, Japan 20.000
1988 Vladimir Artemov, USSR 19.900
Valeri Lioukine, USSR (tie)
1992 Trent Dimas, U.S. 9.875

PARALLEL BARS

1896 Alfred Flatow, Germany —
1904 George Eyser, U.S. 44.000
1924 August Güttinger, Switzerland 21.630
1928 Ladislav Vácha, Czechoslovakia 18.830
1932 Romeo Neri, Italy 18.970
1936 Konrad Frey, Germany 19.067
1948 Michael Reusch, Switzerland 19.750
1952 Hans Eugster, Switzerland 19.650
1956 Viktor Chukarin, USSR 19.200
1960 Boris Shakhlin, USSR 19.400
1964 Yukio Endo, Japan 19.675
1968 Akinori Nakayama, Japan 19.475
1972 Sawao Koto, Japan 19.475
1976 Sawao Koto, Japan 19.675
1980 Aleksandr Tkachyov, USSR 19.775
1984 Bart Conner, U.S. 19.950
1988 Vladimir Artemov, USSR 19.925
1992 Vitali Scherbo, Unified Team 9.900

LONG HORSE VAULT

1896 Karl Schumann, Germany —
1904 George Eyser, U.S. 36.000
Anton Heida, U.S. (tie)
1924 Frank Kriz, U.S. 9.980
1928 Eugen Mack, Switzerland 9.580

Year	Winner	Points
1932	Savino Guglielmetti, Italy	18.030
1936	Alfred Schwarzmann, Germany	19.200
1948	Paavo Aaltonen, Finland	19.550
1952	Viktor Chukarin, USSR	19.200
1956	Helmut Bantz, West Germany	18.850
1960	Takashi Ono, Japan	19.350
1964	Haruhiro Yamashita, Japan	19.600
1968	Mikhail Voronin, USSR	19.000
1972	Klaus Köste, East Germany	18.850
1976	Nikolai Andrianov, USSR	19.450
1980	Nikolai Andrianov, USSR	19.825
1984	Lou Yun, China	19.950
1988	Lou Yun, China	19.875
1992	Vitali Scherbo, Unified Team	9.856

SIDE HORSE (POMMEL HORSE)

Year	Winner	Points
1896	Jules Zutter, Switzerland	—
1904	Anton Heida, U.S.	42.000
1924	Josef Wilhelm, Switzerland	21.230
1928	Hermann Hänggi, Switzerland	19.750
1932	István Pelle, Hungary	19.070
1936	Konrad Frey, Germany	19.333
1948	Paavo Aaltonen, Finland	19.350
1952	Viktor Chukarin, USSR	19.500
1956	Boris Shakhlin, USSR	19.250
1960	Eugene Ekman, Finland	19.375
1964	Miroslav Cerar, Yugoslavia	19.525
1968	Miroslav Cerar, Yugoslavia	19.325
1972	Viktor Klimenko, USSR	19.125
1976	Zoltán Magyar, Hungary	19.700
1980	Zoltán Magyar, Hungary	19.925
1984	Li Ning, China	19.950
1988	Lyubomir Gueraskov, Bulgaria	19.958
	Dmitri Bilozertchev, USSR	
	Zsolt Borkai, Hungary (tie)	
1992	Vitali Scherbo, Unified Team	9.925
	Gil Su Pae, North Korea (tie)	

RINGS

Year	Winner	Points
1896	Ioannis Mitropoulos, Greece	—
1904	Hermann Glass, U.S.	45.000
1924	Francesco Martino, Italy	21.553
1928	Leon Stukelj, Yugoslavia	19.250
1932	George Gulack, U.S.	18.970
1936	Alois Hudec, Czechoslovakia	19.433
1948	Karl Frei, Switzerland	19.800
1952	Grant Shaginyan, USSR	19.750
1956	Albert Azaryan, USSR	19.350
1960	Albert Azaryan, USSR	19.725
1964	Takuji Haytta, Japan	19.475
1968	Akinori Nakayama, Japan	19.450
1972	Akinori Nakayama, Japan	19.350
1976	Nikolai Andrianov, USSR	19.650
1980	Aleksandr Dityatin, USSR	19.875
1984	Koji Gushiken, Japan	19.850
1988	Holger Behrendt, East Germany	19.925
	Dmitri Bilozertchev, USSR (tie)	
1992	Vitali Scherbo, Unified Team	9.937

FLOOR EXERCISE

Year	Winner	Points
1932	István Pelle, Hungary	9.600
1936	Georges Miez, Switzerland	18.666
1948	Ferenc Pataki, Hungary	19.350
1952	K. William Thoresson, Sweden	19.250
1956	Valentin Muratov, USSR	19.200
1960	Nobuyuki Aihara, Japan	19.450
1964	Franco Menichelli, Italy	19.450
1968	Sawao Koto, Japan	19.475
1972	Nikolai Andrianov, USSR	19.175
1976	Nikolai Andrianov, USSR	19.450
1980	Roland Brückner, East Germany	19.750
1984	Li Ning, China	19.925
1988	Sergei Kharikov, USSR	19.925
1992	Xiaosahuang Li, China	9.925

TEAM COMBINED EXERCISES

Year	Winner	Points
1908	Sweden	438.000
1912	Italy	266.750
1920	Italy	359.855
1928	Switzerland	1,718.625
1932	Italy	541.850
1936	Germany	657.430
1948	Finland	1,358.300
1952	USSR	574.400
1956	USSR	568.250
1960	Japan	575.200
1964	Japan	577.950
1968	Japan	575.900
1972	Japan	571.250
1976	Japan	576.850
1980	USSR	598.600
1984	United States	591.400
1988	USSR	593.350
1992	Unified Team	585.450

GYMNASTICS—WOMEN Points

ALL-ROUND

Year	Winner	Points
1952	Maria Gorokhovskaya, USSR	76.780
1956	Larissa Latynina, USSR	74.933
1960	Larissa Latynina, USSR	77.031
1964	Vera Cáslavská, Czechoslovakia	77.564
1968	Vera Cáslavská, Czechoslovakia	78.250
1972	Lyudmila Tourischeva, USSR	77.025
1976	Nadia Comaneci, Romania	79.275
1980	Yelena Davydova, USSR	79.150
1984	Mary Lou Retton, United States	79.175
1988	Elena Shushunova, USSR	79.662
1992	Tatiana Goutsou, Unified Team	39.737

VAULT

Year	Winner	Points
1952	Yekaterina Kalinchuk	19.200
1956	Larissa Latynina, USSR	18.833
1960	Margarita Nikolayeva, USSR	19.316
1964	Vera Cáslavská, Czechoslovakia	19.483
1968	Vera Cáslavská, Czechoslovakia	19.775
1972	Karin Janz, East Germany	19.525
1976	Nelli Kim, USSR	19.800
1980	Natalya Shaposhnikova, USSR	19.725
1984	Ecaterina Szabó, Romania	19.875
1988	Svetlana Boguinskaya, USSR	19.905
1992	Henrietta Onodi, Romania	9.925
	Lavinia Milosovici, Romania (tie)	

UNEVEN BARS

Year	Winner	Points
1952	Margit Korondi, Hungary	19.400
1956	Agnes Keleti, Hungary	18.966
1960	Polina Astakhova, USSR	19.616
1964	Polina Astakhova, USSR	19.332
1968	Vera Cáslavská, Czechoslovakia	19.650
1972	Karin Janz, East Germany	19.675
1976	Nadia Comaneci, Romania	20.000
1980	Maxi Gnauck, East Germany	19.875
1984	Ma Yanhong, China	19.950
1988	Daniela Silivas, Romania	20.000
1992	Li Lu, China	10.000

BALANCE BEAM

Year	Winner	Points
1952	Nina Bocharova, USSR	19.220
1956	Agnes Keleti, Hungary	18.800
1960	Eva Bosáková, Czechoslovakia	19.283
1964	Vera Cáslavská, Czechoslovakia	19.449
1968	Natalya Kuchinskaya, USSR	19.650
1972	Olga Korbut, USSR	19.400
1976	Nadia Comaneci, Romania	19.950
1980	Nadia Comaneci, Romania	19.800
1984	Simona Pauca, Romania	19.800
1988	Daniela Silivas, Romania	19.924
1992	Tatiana Lyssenko, Unified Team	9.975

FLOOR EXERCISE

Year	Winner	Points
1952	Agnes Keleti, Hungary	19.360
1956	Agnes Keleti, Hungary	18.733
1960	Larissa Latynina, USSR	19.583
1964	Larissa Latynina, USSR	19.599
1968	Vera Cáslavská, Czechoslovakia	19.675
1972	Olga Korbut, USSR	19.575
1976	Nelli Kim, USSR	19.850
1980	Nadia Comaneci, Romania	19.875
1984	Ecaterina Szabó, Romania	19.975
1988	Daniela Silivas, Romania	19.937
1992	Lavina Milosovici, Romania	10.000

TEAM COMBINED EXERCISES

Year	Winner	Points
1928	Holland	316.750
1936	West Germany	506.500
1948	Czechoslovakia	445.450
1952	USSR	527.030
1956	USSR	444.800
1960	USSR	382.320
1964	USSR	280.890
1968	USSR	382.850
1972	USSR	380.500
1976	USSR	466.000
1980	USSR	394.900
1984	Romania	392.020
1988	USSR	395.475
1992	Unified Team	198.159

TEAM SPORTS (since 1948)

BASKETBALL—MEN

Year	Winner	Year	Winner
1948	U.S.	1972	USSR
1952	U.S.	1976	U.S.
1956	U.S.	1980	Yugoslavia
1960	U.S.	1984	U.S.
1964	U.S.	1988	USSR
1968	U.S.	1992	U.S.

BASKETBALL—WOMEN

Year	Winner	Year	Winner
1976	USSR	1988	U.S.
1980	USSR	1992	Unified Team
1984	U.S.		

SOCCER (FOOTBALL)

Year	Winner	Year	Winner
1948	Sweden	1976	East Germany
1952	Hungary		
1956	USSR	1980	Czechoslovakia
1960	Yugoslavia		
1964	Hungary	1984	France
1968	Hungary	1988	USSR
1972	Poland	1992	Spain

VOLLEYBALL—MEN

Year	Winner	Year	Winner
1964	USSR	1980	USSR
1968	USSR	1984	U.S.
1972	Japan	1988	U.S.
1976	Poland	1992	Brazil

VOLLEYBALL—WOMEN

Year	Winner	Year	Winner
1964	Japan	1980	USSR
1968	USSR	1984	China
1972	USSR	1988	USSR
1976	Japan	1992	Cuba

WATER POLO

Year	Winner	Year	Winner
1948	Italy	1972	USSR
1952	Hungary	1976	Hungary
1956	Hungary	1980	USSR
1960	Italy	1984	Yugoslavia
1964	Hungary	1988	Yugoslavia
1968	Yugoslavia	1992	Italy

ALL-TIME OLYMPIC MEDAL WINNERS

Mark Spitz, swimming, U.S.

Spitz set the record for gold medals in one Olympics in 1972 with seven (100m and 200m freestyle, 100m and 200m butterfly, 400m and 800m freestyle relays, and the 400m medley relay). These he added to the four medals he won at the 1968 Olympics: a bronze in the 100m freestyle, a silver in the 100m butterfly, and gold in both the 400m and 800m freestyle relays.

Paavo Nurmi, track and field, Finland

Nurmi won the 10,000m in 1920 and 1928 and might have won in 1924 had he not been prevented by Finnish officials, who felt he had entered too many events. That year Nurmi had already won gold medals in the 1,500m, the 5,000m, the 3,000m team race (a discontinued event), and the individual and team cross-country races, two events he had also won in 1920 (since discontinued). Nurmi also earned three silver medals to go with his nine golds.

Larissa Latynina, gymnastics, Soviet Union

No athlete has won more Olympic medals than this Ukrainian, who won 18 between 1956 and 1964. In addition to nine gold medals—in vault (1956), floor exercise (1956, 1960, and 1964), team combined (1956, 1960, and 1964), and all-around (1956 and 1960)—Latynina won five silver and four bronze medals.

Eric Heiden, speed skating, U.S.

Heiden is the only athlete to win five individual gold medals in one Olympics. He dominated the 1980 Winter Olympics by taking gold in the 500m, 1000m, 1,500m, 5,000m, and 10,000m (breaking the world record by over six seconds).

PROFESSIONAL SPORTS

Basketball

National Basketball Association

Olympic Tower, 645 Fifth Avenue
New York, NY 10022
(212) 826-7000

Commissioner: David Stern
Founded: 1946
Number of teams: 29

Dr. James Naismith invented basketball in 1891 only after his indoor versions of lacrosse, rugby, and soccer proved too violent for the intended use in a YMCA fitness program. Yet even his "noncontact" amateur sport proved too rough for many YMCAs, which dropped basketball. Teams were forced to rent halls; they charged an admission fee to pay the rent, and split any leftover cash among the players. Thus was born professional basketball.

The first pro game was played in 1896 in Trenton, New Jersey, and by 1898 the fledgling National Basketball League and several others were organized. The Buffalo Germans were the first powerhouse, winning 792 games against only 86 losses from 1895 to 1925. In 1914 the New York Celtics (later renamed the Original Celtics) were organized, playing a "modern" style of basketball using zone defenses, the fast break, and a pivot man.

Other "ethnic" teams dominated in the 1930s, including the Philadelphia SPHAs (South Philadelphia Hebrew Association) under Eddy Gottlieb, and the black barnstorming New York Renaissance—the Rens. Several weak leagues continued to compete until the end of World War II. The Basketball Association of America was formed in 1946 by hockey arena managers seeking additional tenants. By 1949, it had merged with its biggest rival to form the modern NBA.

The American Basketball Association, an alternative pro league known for its three-point shots and its red, white, and blue ball, lasted for nine seasons (1968–76) and featured such future NBA All-Stars as Julius Erving and Artis Gilmore. When the league folded after the 1975–76 season, four of its teams—the Denver Nuggets, Indiana Pacers, New York (now New Jersey) Nets, and San Antonio Spurs—were admitted into the NBA.

NBA FINAL STANDINGS, 1994–95

EASTERN CONFERENCE	W	L	Pct.	Home	Away	1993–94
1. Orlando Magic	57	25	.695	39–2	18–23	50–32
2. New York Knicks	55	27	.671	29–12	26–15	57–25
3. Indiana Pacers	52	30	.634	33–8	19–22	47–35
4. Charlotte Hornets	50	32	.610	29–12	21–20	41–41
5. Chicago Bulls	47	35	.573	28–13	19–22	55–27
6. Cleveland Cavaliers	43	39	.524	26–15	17–24	47–35
7. Atlanta Hawks	42	40	.512	24–17	18–23	57–25
8. Boston Celtics	35	47	.427	20–21	15–26	32–50
9. Milwaukee Bucks	34	48	.415	22–19	12–29	20–62
10. Miami Heat	32	50	.390	22–19	10–31	42–40
11. New Jersey Nets	30	52	.366	20–21	10–31	45–37
12. Detroit Pistons	28	54	.341	22–19	6–35	20–62
13. Philadelphia 76ers	24	58	.293	14–27	10–31	25–57
14. Washington Bullets	21	61	.256	13–28	8–33	24–58

WESTERN CONFERENCE	W	L	Pct.	Home	Away	1993–94
1. San Antonio Spurs	62	20	.756	33–8	29–12	55–27
2. Utah Jazz	60	22	.732	33–8	27–14	53–29
3. Phoenix Suns	59	23	.720	32–9	27–14	56–26
4. Seattle SuperSonics	57	25	.695	32–9	25–16	63–19
5. Los Angeles Lakers	48	34	.585	29–12	19–22	33–49
6. Houston Rockets	47	35	.573	25–16	22–19	58–24
7. Portland Trail Blazers	44	38	.537	26–15	18–23	47–35
8. Denver Nuggets	41	41	.500	23–18	18–23	42–40
9. Sacramento Kings	39	43	.476	27–14	12–29	28–54
10. Dallas Mavericks	36	46	.439	19–22	17–24	13–69
11. Golden State Warriors	26	56	.317	15–26	11–30	50–32
12. Minnesota Timberwolves	21	61	.256	13–28	8–33	20–62
13. Los Angeles Clippers	17	65	.207	13–28	4–37	27–55

Note: The top eight teams in each conference qualified for the playoffs. **Source:** National Basketball Association.

NBA CHAMPIONSHIP COMPOSITE BOX, 1995

HOUSTON ROCKETS

Player	G.	Min.	FG M-A	FG Pct.	FT M-A	FT Pct.	Reb. O-T	A	Pts.	Avg.
Olajuwon	4	179	56–116	.483	18–26	.692	11–46	22	131	32.8
Drexler	4	162	27–60	.450	30–38	.789	13–38	27	86	21.5
Horry	4	187	23–53	.434	14–21	.667	9–40	15	71	17.8
Elie	4	161	24–37	.649	9–10	.900	4–17	13	65	16.3
Cassell	4	93	15–35	.429	20–24	.833	1–7	12	57	14.3
Smith	4	105	11–29	.379	0–0	—	2–7	16	30	7.5
Brown	4	38	5–11	.455	2–2	1.000	3–11	0	12	3.0
Jones	4	57	1–2	.500	2–2	1.000	1–7	0	4	1.0
Chilcutt	4	3	0–0	—	0–0	—	0–0	0	0	0.0
Totals	**4**	**985**	**162–343**	**.472**	**95–123**	**.772**	**44–173**	**105**	**456**	**114.0**

3-Point Goals: 37-92, .402 (Horry 11-29, Elie 8-14, Smith 8-19, Cassell 7-15, Drexler 2-13, Olajuwon 1-1, Brown 0-1).

ORLANDO MAGIC

Player	G.	Min.	FG M-A	FG Pct.	FT M-A	FT Pct.	Reb. O-T	A	Pts.	Avg.
O'Neal	4	180	44–74	.595	24–42	.571	11–50	25	112	28.0
Hardaway	4	172	35–70	.500	21–23	.913	6–19	32	102	25.5
Grant	4	168	25–47	.532	4–5	.800	19–48	6	54	13.5
Shaw	4	84	20–47	.426	0–0	—	4–13	13	50	12.5
Anderson	4	161	18–50	.360	3–10	.300	6–34	17	49	12.3
Scott	4	150	13–42	.310	9–9	1.000	2–14	9	42	10.5
Bowie	4	26	6–10	.600	0–0	—	0–2	6	13	3.3
Turner	4	43	2–10	.200	0–0	—	0–4	2	6	1.5
Royal	1	1	0–0	—	0–0	—	0–0	0	0	0.0
Totals	**4**	**985**	**163–350**	**.466**	**61–89**	**.685**	**48–184**	**110**	**428**	**107.0**

3-Point Goals: 41-118, .347 (Hardaway 11-24, Shaw 10-26, Anderson 10-31, Scott 7-29, Turner 2-6, Bowie 1-2).

NBA PLAYOFF RESULTS, 1994–95

FIRST ROUND

EASTERN CONFERENCE

Orlando vs. Boston
ORLANDO 124, Boston 77
Boston 99, ORLANDO 92
Orlando 82, BOSTON 77
Orlando 95, BOSTON 92
(Orlando wins series 3–1)

New York vs. Cleveland
NEW YORK 103, Cleveland 79
Cleveland 90, NEW YORK 84
New York 83, CLEVELAND 81
New York 93, CLEVELAND 80
(New York wins series 3–1)

Indiana vs. Atlanta
INDIANA 90, Atlanta 82
INDIANA 105, Atlanta 97
Indiana 105, ATLANTA 89
(Indiana wins series 3–0)

Chicago vs. Charlotte
Chicago 108, CHARLOTTE 100 (OT)
CHARLOTTE 106, Chicago 89
CHICAGO 103, Charlotte 80
CHICAGO 85, Charlotte 84
(Chicago wins series 3–1)

WESTERN CONFERENCE

San Antonio vs. Denver
SAN ANTONIO 104, Denver 88
SAN ANTONIO 122, Denver 96
San Antonio 99, DENVER 95
(San Antonio wins series 3–0)

Utah vs. Houston
UTAH 102, Houston 100
Houston 140, UTAH 126
Utah 95, HOUSTON 82
HOUSTON 123, Utah 106
Houston 95, UTAH 91
(Houston wins series 3–2)

Phoenix vs. Portland
PHOENIX 129, Portland 102
PHOENIX 103, Portland 94
Phoenix 117, PORTLAND 109
(Phoenix wins series 3–0)

Seattle vs. Los Angeles Lakers
SEATTLE 96, Los Angeles 71
Los Angeles 84, SEATTLE 82
LOS ANGELES 105, Seattle 101
LOS ANGELES 114, Seattle 110
(Los Angeles wins series 3–1)

CONFERENCE SEMIFINALS

Orlando vs. Chicago
ORLANDO 94, Chicago 91
Chicago 104, ORLANDO 94
Orlando 110, CHICAGO 101
CHICAGO 106, Orlando 95
ORLANDO 103, Chicago 95
Orlando 108, CHICAGO 102
(Orlando wins series 4–2)

New York vs. Indiana
Indiana 107, NEW YORK 105
NEW YORK 96, Indiana 77
INDIANA 97, New York 95 (OT)
INDIANA 98, New York 84
NEW YORK 96, Indiana 95
New York 92, INDIANA 82
Indiana 97, NEW YORK 95
(Indiana wins series 4–3)

San Antonio vs. Los Angeles
SAN ANTONIO 100, Los Angeles 94
SAN ANTONIO 97, Los Angeles 90 (OT)
LOS ANGELES 92, San Antonio 85
San Antonio 80, LOS ANGELES 71
Los Angeles 98, SAN ANTONIO 96 (OT)
San Antonio 100, LOS ANGELES 88
(San Antonio wins series 4–2)

Phoenix vs. Houston
PHOENIX 130, Houston 108
PHOENIX 118, Houston 94
HOUSTON 118, Phoenix 85
Phoenix 114, HOUSTON 110
Houston 103, PHOENIX 97
Houston 116, PHOENIX 103
Houston 115, PHOENIX 114
(Houston wins series 4–3)

CONFERENCE FINALS

Orlando vs. Indiana
ORLANDO 105, Indiana 101
ORLANDO 119, Indiana 114
INDIANA 105, Orlando 100
INDIANA 94, Orlando 93
ORLANDO 108, Indiana 106
INDIANA 123, Orlando 96
ORLANDO 105, Indiana 81
(Orlando wins series 4–3)

San Antonio vs. Houston
Houston 94, SAN ANTONIO 93
Houston 106, SAN ANTONIO 96
San Antonio 107, HOUSTON 102
San Antonio 103, HOUSTON 81
Houston 111, SAN ANTONIO 90
HOUSTON 100, San Antonio 95
(Houston wins series 4–2)

NBA CHAMPIONSHIP SERIES

Houston 120, ORLANDO 118 (OT)
HOUSTON 106, Orlando 103
Houston 117, ORLANDO 106
HOUSTON 113, Orlando 101
(Houston wins series 4–0)

Note: Home team in CAPS.

NBA WORLD CHAMPIONSHIP SERIES

Year	Winner	Loser	Games	Series
1947	Philadelphia Warriors	Chicago Stags	4–1	WWWLW
1948	Baltimore Bullets	Philadelphia Warriors	4–2	LWWWLW
1949	Minneapolis Lakers	Washington Capitols	4–2	WWWLLW
1950	Minneapolis Lakers	Syracuse Nationals	4–2	WLWWLW
1951	Rochester Royals	New York Knicks	4–3	WWWLLLW
1952	Minneapolis Lakers	New York Knicks	4–3	WLWLWLW
1953	Minneapolis Lakers	New York Knicks	4–1	LWWWW
1954	Minneapolis Lakers	Syracuse Nationals	4–3	WLWLWLW
1955	Syracuse Nationals	Fort Wayne Pistons	4–3	WWLLLWW
1956	Philadelphia Warriors	Fort Wayne Pistons	4–1	WLWWW
1957	Boston Celtics	St. Louis Hawks	4–3	LWLWWLW
1958	St. Louis Hawks	Boston Celtics	4–2	WLWLWW
1959	Boston Celtics	Minneapolis Lakers	4–0	WWWW
1960	Boston Celtics	St. Louis Hawks	4–3	WLWLWLW
1961	Boston Celtics	St. Louis Hawks	4–1	WWLWW
1962	Boston Celtics	Los Angeles Lakers	4–3	WLLWLWW
1963	Boston Celtics	Los Angeles Lakers	4–2	WWLWLW
1964	Boston Celtics	San Francisco Warriors	4–1	WWLWW
1965	Boston Celtics	Los Angeles Lakers	4–1	WWLWW
1966	Boston Celtics	Los Angeles Lakers	4–3	LWWWLLW
1967	Philadelphia 76ers	San Francisco Warriors	4–2	WWLWLW
1968	Boston Celtics	Los Angeles Lakers	4–2	WLWLWW
1969	Boston Celtics	Los Angeles Lakers	4–3	LLWWLWW
1970	New York Knicks	Los Angeles Lakers	4–3	WLWLWLW
1971	Milwaukee Bucks	Baltimore Bullets	4–0	WWWW
1972	Los Angeles Lakers	New York Knicks	4–1	LWWWW
1973	New York Knicks	Los Angeles Lakers	4–1	LWWWW
1974	Boston Celtics	Milwaukee Bucks	4–3	WLWLWLW
1975	Golden State Warriors	Washington Bullets	4–0	WWWW
1976	Boston Celtics	Phoenix Suns	4–2	WWLLWW
1977	Portland Trail Blazers	Philadelphia 76ers	4–2	LLWWWW
1978	Washington Bullets	Seattle SuperSonics	4–3	LWLWLWW
1979	Seattle SuperSonics	Washington Bullets	4–1	LWWWW
1980	Los Angeles Lakers	Philadelphia 76ers	4–2	WLWLWW
1981	Boston Celtics	Houston Rockets	4–2	WLWLWW
1982	Los Angeles Lakers	Philadelphia 76ers	4–2	WLWWLW
1983	Philadelphia 76ers	Los Angeles Lakers	4–0	WWWW
1984	Boston Celtics	Los Angeles Lakers	4–3	LWLWWLW
1985	Los Angeles Lakers	Boston Celtics	4–2	LWWLWW
1986	Boston Celtics	Houston Rockets	4–2	WWLWLW
1987	Los Angeles Lakers	Boston Celtics	4–2	WWLWLW
1988	Los Angeles Lakers	Detroit Pistons	4–3	LWWLLWW
1989	Detroit Pistons	Los Angeles Lakers	4–0	WWWW
1990	Detroit Pistons	Portland Trail Blazers	4–1	WLWWW
1991	Chicago Bulls	Los Angeles Lakers	4–1	LWWWW
1992	Chicago Bulls	Portland Trail Blazers	4–2	WLWLWW
1993	Chicago Bulls	Phoenix Suns	4–2	WWLWLW
1994	Houston Rockets	New York Knicks	4–3	WLWLLWW
1995	Houston Rockets	Orlando Magic	4–0	WWWW

NBA LEADERS, 1994–95

SCORING	G	Pts.	Avg.
Shaquille O'Neal, Orlando	79	2,315	29.3
Hakeem Olajuwon, Houston	72	2,005	27.8
David Robinson, San Antonio	81	2,238	27.6
Karl Malone, Utah	82	2,187	26.7
Jamal Mashburn, Dallas	80	1,926	24.1
Patrick Ewing, New York	79	1,886	23.9
Charles Barkley, Phoenix	68	1,561	23.0
Mitch Richmond, Sacramento	82	1,867	22.8
Glen Rice, Miami	82	1,831	22.3
Glenn Robinson, Milwaukee	80	1,755	21.9
Clyde Drexler, Portland–Houston	76	1,653	21.8
Scottie Pippen, Chicago	79	1,692	21.4
Cliff Robinson, Portland	75	1,601	21.3
Alonzo Mourning, Charlotte	77	1,643	21.3
Anfernee Hardaway, Orlando	77	1,613	20.9
Gary Payton, Seattle	82	1,689	20.6
Latrell Sprewell, Golden State	69	1,420	20.6
Dana Barros, Philadelphia	82	1,686	20.6
Isiah Rider, Minnesota	75	1,532	20.4
Grant Hill, Detroit	70	1,394	19.9

REBOUNDS	G	Tot.	Avg.
Dennis Rodman, San Antonio	49	823	16.8
Dikembe Mutombo, Denver	82	1,029	12.5
Shaquille O'Neal, Orlando	79	901	11.4
Patrick Ewing, New York	79	867	11.0
Tyrone Hill, Cleveland	70	765	10.9
Shawn Kemp, Seattle	82	893	10.9
David Robinson, San Antonio	81	877	10.8
Hakeem Olajuwon, Houston	72	775	10.8
Karl Malone, Utah	82	871	10.6
Popeye Jones, Dallas	80	844	10.6

FIELD GOAL PERCENTAGE	FGM	FGA	Pct.
Chris Gatling, Golden State	324	512	.633
Shaquille O'Neal, Orlando	930	1,594	.583
Horace Grant, Orlando	401	707	.567
Otis Thorpe, Houston–Portland	385	681	.565
Dale Davis, Indiana	324	576	.563
Gheorge Muresan, Washington	303	541	.560
Dikembe Mutombo, Denver	349	628	.556
Shawn Kemp, Seattle	545	997	.547
Danny Manning, Phoenix	340	622	.547
Olden Polynice, Sacramento	376	691	.544

FREE THROW PERCENTAGE	FTM	FTA	Pct.
Richmond Webb, Sacramento	226	242	.934
Mark Price, Cleveland	148	162	.914
Dana Barros, Philadelphia	347	386	.899
Reggie Miller, Indiana	383	427	.897
Tyrone Bogues, Charlotte	160	180	.889
Scott Skiles, Washington	179	202	.886
Mahmoud Abdul-Rauf, Denver	138	156	.885
B.J. Armstrong, Chicago	206	233	.884
Jeff Hornacek, Utah	284	322	.882
Keith Jennings, Golden State	134	153	.876

3-POINT FIELD GOALS	FGM	FGA	Pct.
Steve Kerr, Chicago	89	170	.524
Detlef Schrempf, Seattle	93	181	.514
Dana Barros, Philadelphia	197	425	.464
Hubert Davis, New York	131	288	.455
John Stockton, Utah	102	227	.449
Hersey Hawkins, Charlotte	131	298	.440
Wesley Person, Phoenix	116	266	.436
Kenny Smith, Houston	142	331	.429
B.J. Armstrong, Chicago	108	253	.427
Del Curry, Charlotte	154	361	.427

ASSISTS	G	No.	Avg.
John Stockton, Utah	82	1,011	12.3
Kenny Anderson, New Jersey	72	680	9.4
Tim Hardaway, Golden State	62	878	9.3
Rod Strickland, Portland	64	562	8.8
Tyrone Bogues, Charlotte	78	675	8.7
Nick Van Exel, Los Angeles Lakers	80	660	8.3
Avery Johnson, San Antonio	82	67	8.2
Pooh Richardson, L.A. Clippers	80	632	7.9
Mookie Blaylock, Atlanta	80	616	7.7
Jason Kidd, Dallas	79	607	7.7

STEALS	G	No.	Avg.
Scottie Pippen, Chicago	79	232	2.94
Mookie Blaylock, Atlanta	80	200	2.50
Gary Payton, Seattle	82	204	2.49
John Stockton, Utah	82	194	2.37
Nate McMillan, Seattle	80	165	2.06
Eddie Jones, Los Angeles Lakers	64	131	2.05
Jason Kidd, Dallas	79	151	1.91
Elliot Perry, Phoenix	82	156	1.90
Hakeem Olajuwon, Houston	72	133	1.85
Dana Barros, Philadelphia	82	149	1.52

BLOCKED SHOTS	G	No.	Avg.
Dikembe Mutombo, Denver	82	321	3.91
Hakeem Olajuwon, Houston	72	242	3.36
Shawn Bradley, Philadelphia	82	274	3.34
David Robinson, San Antonio	81	262	3.23
Alonzo Mourning, Charlotte	77	225	2.90
Shaquille O'Neal, Orlando	79	192	2.43
Vlade Divac, Los Angeles Lakers	80	174	2.18
Patrick Ewing, New York	79	159	2.01
Bo Outlaw, Los Angeles Clippers	81	151	1.86
Oliver Miller, Detroit Pistons	64	116	1.81

Source: NBA.

NBA MOST VALUABLE PLAYERS

Year	Name	Team	Pts.	Avg.	Reb.
1955–56	Bob Pettit	St. Louis Hawks	1,849	25.7	1,164
1956–57	Bob Cousy	Boston Celtics	1,319	20.6	309
1957–58	Bill Russell	Boston Celtics	1,142	16.6	1,564
1958–59	Bob Pettit	St. Louis Hawks	2,105	29.2	1,182
1959–60	Wilt Chamberlain	Philadelphia Warriors	2,207	37.6	1,941
1960–61	Bill Russell	Boston Celtics	1,322	16.9	1,868
1961–62	Bill Russell	Boston Celtics	1,436	18.9	1,790
1962–63	Bill Russell	Boston Celtics	1,309	16.8	1,843
1963–64	Oscar Robertson	Cincinnati Royals	2,480	31.4	783
1964–65	Bill Russell	Boston Celtics	1,102	14.1	1,878
1965–66	Wilt Chamberlain	Philadelphia 76ers	2,649	33.5	1,943
1966–67	Wilt Chamberlain	Philadelphia 76ers	1,956	24.1	1,957
1967–68	Wilt Chamberlain	Philadelphia 76ers	1,992	24.3	1,952
1968–69	Wes Unseld	Baltimore Bullets	1,131	13.8	1,491
1969–70	Willis Reed	N.Y. Knicks	1,755	21.7	1,126
1970–71	Kareem Abdul-Jabbar	Milwaukee Bucks	2,596	31.7	1,311
1971–72	Kareem Abdul-Jabbar	Milwaukee Bucks	2,822	34.8	1,346
1972–73	Dave Cowens	Boston Celtics	1,684	20.5	1,329
1973–74	Kareem Abdul-Jabbar	Milwaukee Bucks	2,191	27.0	1,178
1974–75	Bob McAdoo	Buffalo Braves	2,831	34.5	1,155
1975–76	Kareem Abdul-Jabbar	L.A. Lakers	2,275	27.7	1,383
1976–77	Kareem Abdul-Jabbar	L.A. Lakers	2,152	26.2	1,090
1977–78	Bill Walton	Portland Trail Blazers	1,097	18.9	766
1978–79	Moses Malone	Houston Rockets	2,031	24.8	1,444
1979–80	Kareem Abdul-Jabbar	L.A. Lakers	2,034	24.8	886
1980–81	Julius Erving	Philadelphia 76ers	2,014	24.6	657
1981–82	Moses Malone	Houston Rockets	2,520	31.1	1,188
1982–83	Moses Malone	Philadelphia 76ers	1,908	24.5	1,194
1983–84	Larry Bird	Boston Celtics	1,908	24.2	796
1984–85	Larry Bird	Boston Celtics	2,295	28.7	842
1985–86	Larry Bird	Boston Celtics	2,115	25.8	805
1986–87	Magic Johnson	L.A. Lakers	1,909	23.9	504
1987–88	Michael Jordan	Chicago Bulls	2,868	35.0	449
1988–89	Magic Johnson	L.A. Lakers	1,730	22.5	607
1989–90	Magic Johnson	L.A. Lakers	1,765	22.3	525
1990–91	Michael Jordan	Chicago Bulls	2,580	31.5	492
1991–92	Michael Jordan	Chicago Bulls	2,404	30.1	511
1992–93	Charles Barkley	Phoenix Suns	1,944	25.6	928
1993–94	Hakeem Olajuwon	Houston Rockets	2,184	27.3	955
1994–95	David Robinson	San Antonio Spurs	2,238	27.6	877

NBA CAREER LEADERS

Games		Rebounds		Field goals made		Assists		Points	
Kareem Abdul-Jabbar	1,560	Wilt Chamberlain	23,924	Kareem Abdul-Jabbar	15,837	John Stockton[1]	10,394	Kareem Abdul-Jabbar	38,387
Robert Parish[1]	1,413	Bill Russell	21,620	Wilt Chamberlain	12,681	Magic Johnson	9,921	Wilt Chamberlain	31,419
Moses Malone[1]	1,312	Kareem Abdul-Jabbar	17,440	Elvin Hayes	10,976	Oscar Robertson	9,887	Moses Malone[1]	27,409
Elvin Hayes	1,303	Elvin Hayes	16,279	Alex English	10,659	Isiah Thomas	9,061	Elvin Hayes	27,313
John Havlicek	1,270	Moses Malone[1]	16,212	John Havlicek	10,513	Maurice Cheeks	7,392	Oscar Robertson	26,710
Paul Silas	1,254	Nate Thurmond	14,464	Dominique Wilkins[1]	9,516	Len Wilkens	7,211	John Havlicek	26,395
Alex English	1,193	Robert Parish[1]	14,323	Oscar Robertson	9,508	Bob Cousy	6,955	Alex English	25,613
Tree Rollins[1]	1,156	Walt Bellamy	14,241	Moses Malone[1]	9,435	Guy Rodgers	6,917	Dominique Wilkins[1]	25,389
James Edwards[1]	1,140	Wes Unseld	13,769	Robert Parish[1]	9,424	Nate Archibald	6,476	Jerry West	25,192
Hal Greer	1,122	Jerry Lucas	12,942	Jerry West	9,016	John Lucas	6,454	Adrian Dantley	23,177

Note: At the end of 1994–95 season. 1. Player active during 1994–95 season. **Source:** NBA.

NBA ROOKIES OF THE YEAR

Year(s)	Name	Team
1952–53	Don Meineke	Fort Wayne Pistons
1953–54	Ray Felix	Baltimore Bullets
1954–55	Bob Pettit	Milwaukee Hawks
1955–56	Maurice Stokes	Rochester Royals
1956–57	Tom Heinsohn	Boston Celtics
1957–58	Woody Sauldsberry	Philadelphia Warriors
1958–59	Elgin Baylor	Minneapolis Lakers
1959–60	Wilt Chamberlain	Philadelphia Warriors
1960–61	Oscar Robertson	Cincinnati Royals
1961–62	Walt Bellamy	Chicago Bulls
1962–63	Terry Dischinger	Chicago Bulls
1963–64	Jerry Lucas	Cincinnati Royals
1964–65	Willis Reed	N.Y. Knicks
1965–66	Rick Barry	San Francisco Warriors
1966–67	Dave Bing	Detroit Pistons
1967–68	Earl Monroe	Baltimore Bullets
1968–69	Wes Unseld	Baltimore Bullets
1969–70	Kareem Abdul-Jabbar	Milwaukee Bucks
1970–71	Dave Cowens	Boston Celtics
	Geoff Petrie (tie)	Portland Trail Blazers
1971–72	Sidney Wicks	Portland Trail Blazers
1972–73	Bob McAdoo	Buffalo Braves
1973–74	Ernie DiGregorio	Buffalo Braves
1974–75	Keith Wilkes	Golden State Warriors
1975–76	Alvin Adams	Phoenix Suns
1976–77	Adrian Dantley	Buffalo Braves
1977–78	Walter Davis	Phoenix Suns
1978–79	Phil Ford	Kansas City Kings
1979–80	Larry Bird	Boston Celtics
1980–81	Darrell Griffith	Utah Jazz
1981–82	Buck Williams	New Jersey Nets
1982–83	Terry Cummings	San Diego Clippers
1983–84	Ralph Sampson	Houston Rockets
1984–85	Michael Jordan	Chicago Bulls
1985–86	Patrick Ewing	N.Y. Knicks
1986–87	Chuck Person	Indiana Pacers
1987–88	Mark Jackson	N.Y. Knicks
1988–89	Mitch Richmond	Golden State Warriors
1989–90	David Robinson	San Antonio Spurs
1990–91	Derrick Coleman	New Jersey Nets
1991–92	Larry Johnson	Charlotte Hornets
1992–93	Shaquille O'Neal	Orlando Magic
1993–94	Chris Webber	Golden State Warriors
1994–95	Grant Hill	Detroit Pistons
	Jason Kidd (tie)	Dallas Mavericks

1995 NBA FIRST-ROUND DRAFT PICKS

Rank/Team	Player	College	Position
1. Golden State	Joe Smith	Maryland	Forward
2. Los Angeles Clippers	Antonio McDyess[1]	Alabama	Forward
3. Philadelphia	Jerry Stackhouse	North Carolina	Guard
4. Washington	Rasheed Wallace	North Carolina	Forward
5. Minnesota	Kevin Garnett	*Farragut High School*	Center
6. Vancouver	Bryant Reeves	Oklahoma State	Center
7. Toronto	Damon Stoudamire	Arizona	Guard
8. Portland	Shawn Respert[2]	Michigan State	Guard
9. New Jersey	Ed O'Bannon	UCLA	Forward
10. Miami	Kurt Thomas	Texas Christian	Forward
11. Milwaukee	Gary Trent[2]	Ohio	Forward
12. Dallas	Cherokee Parks	Duke	Center
13. Sacramento	Corliss Williamson	Arkansas	Forward
14. Boston	Eric Williams	Providence	Forward
15. Denver	Brent Barry[1]	Oregon State	Guard
16. Atlanta	Alan Henderson	Indiana	Forward
17. Cleveland	Bob Sura	Florida State	Guard
18. Detroit	Theo Ratliffe	Wyoming	Forward
19. Detroit	Randolph Childress	Wake Forest	Guard
20. Chicago	Jason Caffey	Alabama	Forward
21. Phoenix	Michael Finley	Wisconsin	Forward
22. Charlotte	George Zidek	UCLA	Center
23. Indiana	Travis Best	Georgia Tech	Guard
24. Dallas	Loren Meyer	Iowa State	Center
25. Orlando	David Vaughn	Memphis	Center
26. Seattle	Sherell Ford	Illinois–Chicago	Forward
27. Phoenix	Mario Bennett	Arizona State	Forward
28. Utah	Greg Ostertag	Kansas	Center
29. San Antonio	Cory Alexander	Virginia	Guard

1. The Clippers traded McDyess and Randy Woods to Denver for Brent Barry and Rodney Rogers. 2. Portland traded Respert to Milwaukee for Gary Trent and a No. 1 pick in 1996. **Source:** National Basketball Association.

NAISMITH MEMORIAL BASKETBALL HALL OF FAME

Although the Basketball Hall of Fame elected its first members in 1959, its cornerstone was not laid until 1961. The original Hall of Fame in Springfield, Mass., was opened to the public on Feb. 17, 1968, where it remained for 17 years. On June 30, 1985, the Hall of Fame was reopened in a new, $11.5-million building. Dr. James Naismith, the game's originator, was among the members elected in 1959. Note that the Basketball Hall of Fame includes players from all basketball levels, including college, women's, and foreign leagues. Admission is based on a player's total career, not just his NBA performance. Career statistics are given only for players who played some portion of their career in the NBA.

Player (year elected)		Games	Points	FG%	FT%	Rebs.	Assts.
Archibald, Nate (Tiny) (1991)		876	16,481	.467	.810	2,046	6,476
Averaged 18.8 ppg over 13 seasons; six-time All-Star							
Arizin, Paul J. (1977)		713	16,266	.421	.810	6,129	1,665
NBA scoring leader in 1952 (25.4 ppg) and 1957 (25.6 ppg)							
Barry, Rick (1986–87)		794	18,395	.449	.900	5,168	4,017
	(ABA)	226	6,884	.477	.880	1,695	935
NBA all-time free-throw percentage leader							
Baylor, Elgin (1976)		846	23,149	.431	.780	11,463	3,650
Named to NBA All-Star First Team 10 times							
Bellamy, Walt (1993)		1,043	20,941	.516	.632	14,241	2,544
Averaged 31.6 ppg as a rookie in 1962							
Bing, Dave (1990)		901	18,327	.441	.775	3,420	5,397
NBA rookie of the year, 1967, MVP 1976							
Bradley, Bill (1982)		742	9,217	.448	.840	2,533	2,363
Averaged 30.2 ppg in 83 games at Princeton University							
Chamberlain, Wilt (1978)		1,045	31,419	.540	.511	23,924	4,643
Holds NBA single-game records for points (100) and rebounds (55); led league in scoring 1959–66							
Cousy, Bob (1970)		924	16,960	.375	.803	4,786	6,955
Led NBA in assists eight consecutive seasons (1953–60)							
Cowens, Dave (1991)		766	13,516	.460	.783	10,444	2,950
Seven-time All-Star; three-time All-Defensive team							
Cunningham, Billy (1985–86)		654	13,626	.446	.720	6,638	2,625
	(ABA)	116	2,684	.483	.791	1,343	680
Coached Philadelphia 76ers to 454–196 record in eight years							
Davies, Bob (1969)		462	6,594	.378	.759	980[1]	2,050
NBL MVP, 1947	(NBL)[2]	107	1,177		.747		
DeBusschere, Dave (1982)		875	14,053	.432	.699	2,497	2,801
NBA All-Defensive team six consecutive seasons (1969–74)							
Erving, Julius (Dr. J) (1993)		836	18,364	.507	.777	5,601	3,224
	(ABA)	407	11,662	.504	.778	4,924	1,952
ABA MVP, 1974–76; NBA MVP, 1981							
Frazier, Walt (Clyde) (1986–87)		825	15,581	.490	.786	4,830	5,040
NBA All-Defensive team seven consecutive seasons (1969–75)							
Fulks, Joe (1977)		489	8,003	.302	.766	1,382[1]	587
NBA scoring leader in 1947 (23.2 ppg)							
Gallatin, Harry (1991)		682	8,843	.398	.773	6,684	1,208
Seven-time All-Star							
Gola, Tom (1975)		698	7,871	.431	.760	5,605	2,953
One of only two major-college players with more than 2,000 points and 2,000 rebounds in career							
Greer, Harold (Hal) (1981)		1,122	21,586	.452	.801	5,665	4,540
Scored 19 points in one quarter of 1968 All-Star game							
Hagan, Cliff (1977)		746	13,447	.450	.798	5,019	2,236
	(ABA)	94	1,423	.496	.807	436	398
Helped St. Louis to 1958 championship with 27.7 ppg in playoffs							
Havlicek, John J. (Hondo) (1983)		1,270	26,395	.439	.815	8,007	6,114
Averaged 20.8 ppg; member of eight NBA champion teams							
Hawkins, Connie (1992)		499	8,233	.467	.785	3,971	2,052
	(ABA)	117	3,295	.515	.765	1,479	504
Four-time NBA All-Star; ABA MVP, 1969							
Hayes, Elvin (1990)		1,303	27,313	.452	.670	16,279	2,398
Led league in scoring (1969) and rebounds per game (1970, 1974)							
Heinsohn, Tom (1985–86)		654	12,194	.405	.790	5,749	1,318
Played for eight NBA championship teams and coached two others							
Houbregs, Robert J. (1986–87)		281	2,611	.404	.721	1,552	500
NCAA Player of the Year, 1953							
Issel, Dan (1993)		718	14,659	.506	.797	5,707	1,804
	(ABA)	500	12,823	.488	.786	5,426	1,103
Averaged 33.6 ppg in senior year at Kentucky, 1969–70							
Jabbar, Kareem Abdul (1995)		1,560	38,387	.559	.721	17,440	5,660
Six-time NBA MVP. All-time leader in scoring, games, minutes, and field goals.							
Jeannette, Buddy (1994)	(NBL)[2]	161	1,320	(1)			
	(BAA-NBA)	139	997	.341	.781	—	287
Won NBL MVP three times							
Johnston, Neil (1990)		516	10,023	.444	.768	5,856	1,269
Named to four straight all-NBA First Teams (1953–56)							
Jones, K.C. (1988–89)		676	5,011	.387	.647	2,399	2,908
High scorer in 1955 NCAA finals (24 points); held Tom Gola scoreless for 21 min.							
Jones, Sam (1983)		871	15,411	.456	.803	4,305	2,209
Member of 10 NBA championship teams							
Lanier, Bob (1992)		959	19,248	.514	.767	9,698	3,007
Eight-time NBA All-Star							
Lovellette, Clyde (1987–88)		704	11,947	.443	.756	6,663	1,165
Three-time All-American at University of Kansas (1950–52)							
Lucas, Jerry Ray (Luke) (1979)		829	14,053	.499	.783	12,942	2,730
NBA Rookie of the Year and field-goal percentage leader (.527) in 1964							
Macauley, Edward (Easy Ed) (1960)		641	11,234	.436	.761	2,079	1,667
NBA All-Star Game MVP, 1951							
McGuire, Dick (1993)		738	5,921	.389	.644	2,784	4,205
Averaged 8.0 ppg							
Maravich, Pete (Pistol) (1986–87)		658	15,948	.441	.820	2,747	3,563
NCAA career record holder for points scored (3,667) and average (44.2 ppg)							
Martin, Slater (1981)		745	7,337	.364	.762	2,302[1]	3,160
Played in seven straight All-Star Games, 1953–59							
Mikan, George L. (1959)		439	10,156	.404	.782	4,167[1]	1,245
	(NBL)[2]	81	1,608		.756		
Three-time NBA scoring leader (1949, 1950, 1952)							
Mikkelson, Vern (1995)		699	10,063	.403	.766	5,940[1]	1,515
Six-time NBA All-Star; won 4 NBA Championships: 1950, 1952, 1953, 1954							
Monroe, Earl (The Pearl) (1990)		926	17,454	.464	.807	2,796	3,594
NBA Rookie of the Year, 1968							
Murphy, Calvin (1993)		1,002	17,949	.482	.892	2,103	4,402
Set single-season free throw percentage record with .958 in 1981							
Pettit, Robert L. (1970)		792	20,880	.436	.761	12,849	2,369
Led NBA in scoring (25.7 ppg) and rebounds (1,164) in 1956							
Phillip, Andy (1961)		701	6,384	.368	.695	2,395[1]	3,759
Led NBA in assists, 1951 and 1952							
Pollard, Jim (1977)		438	5,762	.360	.750	2,487[1]	1,417
	(NBL)[2]	59	760		.676		
Started in four NBA All-Star Games							
Ramsey, Frank (1981)		623	8,378	.402	.804	3,410	1,136
Member of seven NBA championship teams							
Reed, Willis (1981)		650	12,183	.476	.747	8,414	1,186
In 1970 was named NBA MVP, All-Star Game MVP, and Playoff MVP							
Robertson, Oscar (1979)		1,040	26,710	.485	.838	7,804	9,887
NBA MVP 1964; member of all-NBA first-team 1961-69							
Russell, Bill (1974)		963	14,522	.440	.561	21,620	4,100
Five-time NBA MVP; 32 rebounds in one half vs. Philadelphia, 1957							
Schayes, Adolph (Dolph) (1972)		996	18,438	.380	.849	11,256[1]	3,072
	(NBL)[2]	63	811		.724		
NBA Coach of the Year (1966)							
Sharman, Bill (1974)		711	12,665	.426	.883	2,779	2,101
Led NBA in free-throw percentage for seven seasons							
Thurmond, Nate (1984)		964	14,437	.421	.667	14,464	2,575
1,000+ rebounds 1964–69, 1970–73							
Twyman, Jack (1982)		823	15,840	.450	.778	5,421	1,969
Led NBA in field-goal percentage, 1958 (.452)							
Unseld, Wes (1987–88)		984	10,624	.509	.633	13,769	3,822
Named NBA MVP and Rookie of the Year in same year (1969)							
Walton, Bill (1993)		468	6,215	.521	.660	4,923	1,590
MVP in 1976							

Player (year elected)	Games	Points	FG%	FT%	Rebs.	Assts.
Wazner, Robert (1986–87)	502	5,891	.388	.800	1,652[1]	1,575
Free-throw percentage leader, 1952 (.904)						
West, Jerry Alan (1979)	932	25,192	.474	.814	5,376	6,238
NBA MVP in 1970; .805 free throw percentage in 13 years in the playoffs						
Wilkens, Lenny (1988–89)	1,077	17,772	.432	.774	5,030	7,211
600+ assists six consecutive seasons						

ELECTED FOR COACHING

Anderson, W. Harold 1984
Auerbach, Arnold J. "Red" 1968
Barry, Justin "Sam" 1978
Blood, Ernest A. 1960
Cann, Howard G. 1967
Carlson, Dr. H. Clifford 1959
Carnesecca, Lou 1992
Carnevale, Ben 1969
Case, Everett 1981
Crum, Denny 1994
Daly, Chuck 1994
Dean, Everett S. 1966
Diddle, Edgar A. 1971
Drake, Bruce 1972
Gaines, Clarence 1981
Gardner, James H. "Jack" 1983
Gill, Amory T. 1967
Harshman, Marv 1984
Hickey, Edgar S. "Eddie" 1978
Hobson, Howard A. 1965
Holzman, William "Red" 1986
Iba, Henry P. 1968
Julian, Alvin F. 1967
Keaney, Frank W. 1960
Keogan, George E. 1961
Knight, Bob 1991
Lambert, Ward L. 1960
Litwack, Harry 1975
Leoffler, Kenneth D. 1964
Lonborg, Arthur C. 1972
McCutchan, Arad A. 1980
McGuire, Al 1992
McGuire, Frank J. 1976
Meanwell, Dr. Walter E. 1959
Meyer, Raymond J. 1978
Miller, Ralph 1987
Ramsay, Jack 1992
Rupp, Adolph F. 1968
Sachs, Leonard D. 1961
Shelton, Everett F. 1979
Smith, Dean 1982
Taylor, Fred R. 1985–86
Wade, L. Margaret 1984
Watts, Stanley H. 1985–86
Wooden, John R. 1972
Woolpert, Phil 1992

Note: All statistics for NBA career unless otherwise noted. NBL = National Basketball League; ABA = American Basketball Association. 1. Does not include seasons played prior to 1950–51, when the NBA first began keeping statistics for rebounds. 2. The National Basketball League did not keep statistics for field-goal percentage, rebounds, or assists.

Football

National Football League

410 Park Avenue, New York, NY 10022
(212) 758-1500

Commissioner: Paul Tagliabue
Founded: 1920—Number of Teams: 30

1994 REGULAR NFL SEASON FINAL STANDINGS

AMERICAN FOOTBALL CONFERENCE

	W	L	T	Pct.	Pts.	Op.
EASTERN DIVISION						
Miami[1]	10	6	0	.625	389	327
New England[2]	10	6	0	.625	351	312
Indianapolis	8	8	0	.500	307	320
Buffalo	7	9	0	.438	340	356
N.Y. Jets	6	10	0	.375	264	320
CENTRAL DIVISION						
Pittsburgh[1]	12	4	0	.750	316	234
Cleveland[2]	11	5	0	.688	340	204
Cincinnati	3	13	0	.188	276	406
Houston	2	14	0	.125	226	352
WESTERN DIVISION						
San Diego[1]	11	5	0	.688	381	306
Kansas City[2]	11	5	0	.688	319	298
L.A. Raiders[2]	9	7	0	.563	303	327
Denver	9	7	0	.563	347	396
Seattle	6	10	0	.375	287	323

NATIONAL FOOTBALL CONFERENCE

	W	L	T	Pct.	Pts.	Op.
EASTERN DIVISION						
Dallas[1]	12	4	0	.750	414	248
N.Y. Giants	9	7	0	.563	279	305
Arizona	8	8	0	.500	235	267
Philadelphia	7	9	0	.438	308	308
Washington	3	13	0	.188	320	412
CENTRAL DIVISION						
Minnesota[1]	10	6	0	.625	356	314
Green Bay[2]	9	7	0	.563	382	287
Detroit[2]	9	7	0	.563	357	342
Chicago[2]	9	7	0	.563	271	307
Tampa Bay	6	10	0	.375	251	351
WESTERN DIVISION						
San Francisco[1]	13	3	0	.813	505	296
New Orleans	7	9	0	.438	348	407
Atlanta	7	9	0	.438	317	385
L.A. Rams	4	12	0	.250	286	365

1. Division champion. 2. Wild Card for playoffs.

1994 NFL POSTSEASON AT A GLANCE

AFC First Round
MIAMI 27, Kansas City 17
CLEVELAND 20, New England 13

AFC Divisional Playoff
PITTSBURGH 29, Cleveland 9
SAN DIEGO 22, Miami 21

NFC First Round
GREEN BAY 16, Detroit 12
Chicago 35, MINNESOTA 18

NFC Divisional Playoff
SAN FRANCISCO 44, Chicago 15
DALLAS 35, Green Bay 9

AFC Championship Game
San Diego 17, PITTSBURGH 13

NFC Championship Game
SAN FRANCISCO 38, Dallas 28

Super Bowl XXIX at Joe Robbie Stadium, Miami, Fla.
SAN FRANCISCO 49ERS 49, San Diego Chargers 26

AFC-NFC Pro Bowl at Honolulu, Hawaii
AFC 41, NFC 13

Note: Home team in capital letters.

NFL LEADERS, 1994

RUSHING

AFC	No.	Yds.	Avg.	Long	TDs
Chris Warren, Seattle	333	1,545	4.6	41	9
Natrone Means, San Diego	343	1,350	3.9	25	12
Marshall Faulk, Indianapolis	314	1,282	4.1	52	11
Thurman Thomas, Buffalo	287	1,093	3.8	29	7
Harvey Williams, L.A. Raiders	282	983	3.5	28	4
Johnny Johnson, N.Y. Jets	240	931	3.9	90	3
Leroy Hoard, Cleveland	209	890	4.3	39	5
Bernie Parmalee, Miami	216	868	4.0	47	6
Barry Foster, Pittsburgh	216	851	3.9	29	5
Bam Morris, Pittsburgh	198	836	4.2	20	7

NFC	No.	Yds.	Avg.	Long	TDs
Barry Sanders, Detroit	331	1,883	5.7	85	7
Emmitt Smith, Dallas	368	1,484	4.0	46	21
Rodney Hampton, N.Y. Giants	327	1,075	3.3	27	6
Terry Allen, Minnesota	255	1,031	4.0	45	8
Jerome Bettis, L.A. Rams	319	1,025	3.2	19	3
Errict Rhett, Tampa Bay	284	1,011	3.6	27	7
Lewis Tillman, Chicago	275	899	3.3	25	7
Ricky Watters, San Francisco	239	877	3.7	23	6
Ron Moore, Phoenix	232	780	3.4	24	4
Craig Heyward, Atlanta	183	779	4.3	17	7

PASSING

AFC	Att.	Comp.	Yds.	TDs	Int.	Rating
Dan Marino, Miami	615	285	4,453	30	17	89.2
John Elway, Denver	494	307	3,490	16	10	85.7
Jim Kelly, Buffalo	448	285	3,114	22	17	84.6
Joe Montana, Kansas City	493	299	3,283	16	9	83.6
Stan Humphries, San Diego	453	264	3,209	17	12	81.6
Jeff Hostetler, L.A. Raiders	455	263	3,334	20	16	80.8
Neil O'Donnell, Pittsburgh	370	212	2,443	13	9	78.9
Boomer Esiason, N.Y. Jets	440	255	2,782	17	13	77.3
Jeff Blake, Cincinnati	306	156	2,154	14	9	76.9
Drew Bledsoe, New England	691	400	4,555	25	27	73.6

PASSING

NFC	Att.	Comp.	Yds.	TDs	Int.	Rating
Steve Young, San Francisco	461	324	3,969	35	10	112.8
Brett Favre, Green Bay	582	363	3,882	33	14	90.7
Jim Everett, New Orleans	540	346	3,855	22	18	84.9
Troy Aikman, Dallas	361	233	2,676	13	12	84.9
Jeff George, Atlanta	524	322	3,734	23	18	83.3
Craig Erickson, Tampa Bay	399	225	2,919	16	10	82.5
Warren Moon, Minnesota	601	371	4,264	18	19	79.9
Steve Walsh, Chicago	343	208	2,078	10	8	77.9
Randall Cunningham, Philadelphia	490	265	3,229	16	13	74.4
Chris Miller, L.A. Rams	317	173	2,104	16	14	73.6

RECEIVING

AFC	No.	Yds.	Avg.	Long	TDs
Ben Coates, New England	96	1,174	12.2	62	7
Andre Reed, Buffalo	90	1,303	14.5	83	8
Tim Brown, L.A. Raiders	89	1,309	14.7	77	9
Shannon Sharpe, Denver	87	1,010	11.6	44	4
Brian Blades, Seattle	81	1,086	13.4	45	4
Rob Moore, N.Y. Jets	78	1,010	12.9	41	6
Glyn Milburn, Denver	77	549	7.1	33	3
Michael Timpson, New England	74	941	12.7	37	3
Irving Fryar, Miami	73	1,270	17.4	54	7
Carl Pickens, Cincinnati	71	1,127	15.9	70	11

NFC	No.	Yds.	Avg.	Long	TDs
Cris Carter, Minnesota	122	1,256	10.3	65	7
Jerry Rice, San Francisco	112	1,499	13.4	69	13
Terance Mathis, Atlanta	111	1,342	12.1	81	11
Sterling Sharpe, Green Bay	94	1,119	11.9	49	18
Jake Reed, Minnesota	85	1,175	13.8	59	4
Quinn Early, New Orleans	82	894	10.9	33	4
Andre Rison, Atlanta	81	1,088	13.4	69	8
Michael Irvin, Dallas	79	1,241	15.7	65	6
Fred Barnett, Philadelphia	78	1,127	14.4	54	5
Edgar Bennett, Green Bay	78	546	7.0	40	4

1995 NFL FIRST-ROUND DRAFT CHOICES

Team	Selection	Pos.	School
1. Cincinnati	Ki-Jana Carter	RB	Penn State
2. Jacksonville	Tony Boselli	OT	Southern California
3. Houston	Steve McNair	QB	Alcorn State
4. Washington	Michael Westbrook	WR	Colorado
5. Carolina	Kerry Collins	QB	Penn State
6. St. Louis	Kevin Carter	DE	Florida
7. Philadelphia	Mike Mamula	DE	Boston College
8. Seattle	Joey Galloway	WR	Ohio State
9. New York Jets	Kyle Brady	TE	Penn State
10. San Francisco	J.J. Stokes	WR	UCLA
11. Minnesota	Derrick Alexander	DE	Florida State
12. Tampa Bay	Warren Sapp	DT	Miami
13. New Orleans	Mark Fields	LB	Washington State
14. Buffalo	Reuben Brown	OT	Pittsburgh
15. Indianapolis	Ellis Johnson	DT	Florida
16. New York Jets	Hugh Douglas	DE	Central State
17. New York Giants	Tyrone Wheatley	RB	Michigan
18. Los Angeles	Napoleon Kaufman	RB	Washington
19. Jacksonville	James Stewart	RB	Tennessee
20. Detroit	Luther Elliss	DE	Utah
21. Chicago	Rashaan Salaam	RB	Colorado
22. Carolina	Tyrone Poole	CB	Fort Valley
23. New England	Ty Law	CB	Michigan
24. Minnesota	Korey Striner	OT	Ohio State
25. Miami	Billy Milner	OT	Houston
26. Atlanta	Devin Bush	S	Florida State
27. Pittsburgh	Mark Breuner	TE	Washington
28. Tampa Bay	Derrick Brooks	LB	Florida State
29. Carolina	Blake Brockmeyer	OT	Texas
30. Cleveland	Craig Powell	LB	Ohio State
31. Kansas City	Trezelle Jenkins	OL	Michigan
32. Green Bay	Craig Newsome	DB	Arizona State

NFL NUMBER-ONE DRAFT PICKS, 1936–95

Year	Player	Team	Pos.	College
1936	Jay Berwanger	Philadelphia Eagles	RB	Chicago
1937	Sam Francis	Philadelphia Eagles	RB	Nebraska
1938	Corbett Davis	Cleveland Rams	RB	Indiana
1939	Charles Aldrich	Chicago Cardinals	OL	Texas Christian
1940	George Cafego	Chicago Cardinals	QB	Tennessee
1941	Tom Harmon	Chicago Bears	RB	Michigan
1942	Bill Dudley	Pittsburgh Steelers	RB	Virginia
1943	Frank Sinkwich	Detroit Lions	RB	Georgia
1944	Angelo Bertelli	Boston Yanks	QB	Notre Dame
1945	Charley Trippi	Chicago Cardinals	RB	Georgia
1946	Frank Dancewicz	Boston Yanks	QB	Notre Dame
1947	Bob Fenimore	Chicago Bears	RB	Oklahoma A&M
1948	Harry Gilmer	Washington Redskins	QB	Alabama
1949	Chuck Bednarik	Philadelphia Eagles	OL	Pennsylvania
1950	Leon Hart	Detroit Lions	RB	Notre Dame
1951	Kyle Rote	New York Giants	E/K	Southern Methodist
1952	Bill Wade	Los Angeles Rams	QB	Vanderbilt
1953	Harry Babcock	San Francisco 49ers	E	Georgia
1954	Bobby Garrett	Cleveland Browns	QB	Stanford
1955	George Shaw	Baltimore Colts	QB	Oregon
1956	Gary Glick	Pittsburgh Steelers	QB	Colorado State
1957	Paul Hornung	Green Bay Packers	RB	Notre Dame
1958	King Hill	St. Louis Cardinals	QB	Rice
1959	Randy Duncan	Green Bay Packers	QB	Iowa
1960	Billy Cannon	Los Angeles Rams	RB	Louisiana State
1961	Tommy Mason	Minnesota Vikings	RB	Tulane
1962	Ernie Davis	Washington Redskins	RB	Syracuse
1963	Terry Baker	Los Angeles Rams	QB	Oregon State
1964	Dave Parks	San Francisco 49ers	E	Texas Tech
1965	Tucker Frederickson	New York Giants	RB	Auburn
1966	Tommy Nobis	Atlanta Falcons	LB	Texas
1967	Bubba Smith	Baltimore Colts	DL	Michigan State
1968	Ron Yary	Minnesota Vikings	OL	USC
1969	O.J. Simpson	Buffalo Bills	RB	USC
1970	Terry Bradshaw	Pittsburgh Steelers	QB	Louisiana Tech
1971	Jim Plunkett	Boston Patriots	QB	Stanford
1972	Walt Patulski	Buffalo Bills	DL	Notre Dame
1973	John Matuszak	Houston Oilers	DL	Tampa
1974	Ed Jones	Dallas Cowboys	DL	Tennessee State
1975	Steve Bartkowski	Atlanta Falcons	QB	California
1976	Lee Roy Selmon	Tampa Bay Buccaneers	DL	Oklahoma
1977	Ricky Bell	Tampa Bay Buccaneers	RB	USC
1978	Earl Campbell	Houston Oilers	RB	Texas
1979	Tom Cousineau	Buffalo Bills	LB	Ohio State
1980	Billy Sims	Detroit Lions	RB	Oklahoma
1981	George Rogers	New Orleans Saints	RB	South Carolina
1982	Kenneth Sims	New England Patriots	DL	Texas
1983	John Elway	Baltimore Colts	QB	Stanford
1984	Irving Fryar	New England Patriots	WR	Nebraska
1985	Bruce Smith	Buffalo Bills	DL	Virginia Tech
1986	Bo Jackson	Tampa Bay Buccaneers	RB	Auburn
1987	Vinny Testaverde	Tampa Bay Buccaneers	QB	Miami (Fla.)
1988	Aundray Bruce	Atlanta Falcons	LB	Auburn
1989	Troy Aikman	Dallas Cowboys	QB	UCLA
1990	Jeff George	Indianapolis Colts	QB	Illinois
1991	Russell Maryland	Dallas Cowboys	DT	Miami (Fla.)
1992	Steve Emtman	Indianapolis Colts	DT	Washington
1993	Drew Bledsoe	New England Patriots	QB	Washington State
1994	Dan Wilkinson	Cincinnati Bengals	DT	Ohio State
1995	Ki-Jana Carter	Cincinnati Bengals	RB	Penn State

NFL PLAYER OF THE YEAR, 1957–94

Year		Player	Pos.	Team
1957		Jim Brown	RB	Cleveland Browns
1958		Jim Brown	RB	Cleveland Browns
1959		Johnny Unitas	QB	Baltimore Colts
1960		Norm Van Brocklin	QB	Philadelphia Eagles
1961		Paul Hornung	HB	Green Bay Packers
1962		Y.A. Tittle	QB	New York Giants
1963		Y.A. Tittle	QB	New York Giants
1964		Johnny Unitas	QB	Baltimore Colts
1965		Jim Brown	RB	Cleveland Browns
1966		Bart Starr	QB	Green Bay Packers
1967		Johnny Unitas	QB	Baltimore Colts
1968		Earl Morrall	QB	Baltimore Colts
1969		Roman Gabriel	QB	Los Angeles Rams
1970	NFC:	John Brodie	QB	San Francisco 49ers
	AFC:	George Blanda	QB-PK	Oakland Raiders
1971	NFC:	Roger Staubach	QB	Dallas Cowboys
	AFC:	Bob Griese	QB	Miami Dolphins
1972	NFC:	Larry Brown	RB	Washington Redskins
	AFC:	Earl Morrall	QB	Miami Dolphins
1973	NFC:	John Hadl	QB	Los Angeles Rams
	AFC:	O.J. Simpson	RB	Buffalo Bills
1974	NFC:	Chuck Foreman	RB	Minnesota Vikings
	AFC:	Ken Stabler	QB	Oakland Raiders
1975	NFC:	Fran Tarkenton	QB	Minnesota Vikings
	AFC:	O.J. Simpson	RB	Buffalo Bills
1976	NFC:	Walter Payton	RB	Chicago Bears
	AFC:	Ken Stabler	QB	Oakland Raiders
1977	NFC:	Walter Payton	RB	Chicago Bears
	AFC:	Craig Morton	QB	Denver Broncos
1978	NFC:	Archie Manning	QB	New Orleans Saints
	AFC:	Earl Campbell	RB	Houston Oilers
1979	NFC:	Ottis Anderson	RB	St. Louis Cardinals
	AFC:	Dan Fouts	QB	San Diego Chargers
1980		Brian Sipe	QB	Cleveland Browns
1981		Ken Anderson	QB	Cincinnati Bengals
1982		Mark Moseley	PK	Washington Redskins
1983		Eric Dickerson	RB	Los Angeles Rams
1984		Dan Marino	QB	Miami Dolphins
1985		Marcus Allen	RB	Los Angeles Raiders
1986		Lawrence Taylor	LB	New York Giants
1987		Jerry Rice	WR	San Francisco 49ers
1988		Boomer Esiason	QB	Cincinnati Bengals
1989		Joe Montana	QB	San Francisco 49ers
1990		Jerry Rice	WR	San Francisco 49ers
1991		Thurman Thomas	RB	Buffalo Bills
1992		Steve Young	QB	San Francisco 49ers
1993		Emmitt Smith	RB	Dallas Cowboys
1994		Steve Young	QB	San Francisco 49ers

Note: In 1970–79 a player was selected as Player of the Year for both the NFC and AFC. In 1980 *The Sporting News* reinstated the selection of one player as Player of the Year for the entire NFL. **Source:** *The Sporting News*.

ALL-TIME PRO FOOTBALL RECORDS

RUSHING

Player	League	Years	Yards	Rushes	Avg.
1. Walter Payton	NFL	13	16,726	3,838	4.4
2. Eric Dickerson	NFL	11	13,259	2,996	4.4
3. Tony Dorsett	NFL	12	12,739	2,936	4.3
4. Jim Brown	NFL	9	12,312	2,359	5.2
5. Franco Harris	NFL	13	12,120	2,949	4.1
6. John Riggins	NFL	14	11,352	2,916	3.9
7. O.J. Simpson	AFL–NFL	11	11,236	2,404	4.7
8. Ottis Anderson	NFL	14	10,273	2,562	4.0
9. Joe Perry	AAFC–NFL	16	9,723	1,929	5.0
10. Earl Campbell	NFL	8	9,407	2,187	4.3

RECEIVING

Player	League	Years	Receptions	Yards	Avg.
1. Art Monk[1]	NFL	15	934	12,607	13.5
2. Jerry Rice[1]	NFL	10	820	13,275	16.2
3. Steve Largent	NFL	14	819	13,089	16.0
4. James Lofton	NFL	16	764	14,004	18.3
5. Charlie Joiner	AFL–NFL	18	750	12,146	16.2
6. Andre Reed[1]	NFL	10	676	9,536	14.1
7. Henry Ellard[1]	NFL	12	667	11,158	16.7
8. Gary Clark[1]	NFL	10	662	10,331	15.6
9. Ozzie Newsome	NFL	13	662	7,980	12.1
10. Drew Hill	NFL	14	634	9,831	15.5

SCORING

Player	League	Yrs.	Total	TD	PAT	FG
1. George Blanda	NFL–AFL	26	2,002	9	943	335
2. Jan Stenerud	AFL–NFL	19	1,699	0	580	373
3. Lou Groza	AAFC–NFL	21	1,608	1	810	264
4. Nick Lowery[1]	NFL	16	1,559	0	512	349
5. Pat Leahy	NFL	18	1,470	0	558	304
6. Jim Turner	AFL–NFL	16	1,439	1	521	304
7. Mark Moseley	NFL	16	1,382	0	482	300
8. Jim Bakken	NFL	17	1,380	0	534	282
9. Fred Cox	NFL	15	1,365	0	519	282
10. Eddie Murray[1]	NFL	17	1,359	0	465	298

Note: Through end of 1994 season. AAFC = All America Football Conference. AFL = American Football League. NFL = National Football League. 1. Player active in 1994. **Source:** National Football League, *1994 Record and Fact Book* (1994).

TOTAL PASSES ATTEMPTED

	Player	Attempts
1.	Fran Tarkenton	6,467
2.	Dan Marino[1]	6,049
3.	Dan Fouts	5,604
4.	Joe Montana[1]	5,391
5.	John Elway[1]	5,384
6.	Johnny Unitas	5,186
7.	Warren Moon[1]	5,147
8.	Jim Hart	5,076
9.	John Hadl	4,687
10.	Phil Simms	4,647
11.	Joe Ferguson	4,519
12.	Roman Gabriel	4,498
13.	John Brodie	4,491
14.	Ken Anderson	4,475
15.	Y.A. Tittle	4,395
16.	Dave Krieg[1]	4,390
17.	Norm Snead	4,353
18.	Boomer Esiason[1]	4,291
19.	Sonny Jurgensen	4,262
20.	Ron Jaworski	4,117

TOTAL PASSES COMPLETED

	Player	Completions
1.	Fran Tarkenton	3,686
2.	Dan Marino[1]	3,604
3.	Joe Montana[1]	3,409
4.	Dan Fouts	3,297
5.	John Elway[1]	3,030
6.	Warren Moon[1]	3,003
7.	Steve DeBerg[1]	2,844
8.	Johnny Unitas	2,830
9.	Ken Anderson	2,654
10.	Jim Hart	2,593
11.	Phil Simms	2,576
12.	Dave Krieg[1]	2,562
13.	John Brodie	2,469
14.	Boomer Esiason[1]	2,440
15.	Sonny Jurgensen	2,433
16.	Jim Kelly[1]	2,397
17.	Joe Ferguson	2,369
18.	Roman Gabriel	2,366
19.	John Hadl	2,363
20.	Norm Snead	2,276

TOTAL TOUCHDOWN PASSES

	Player	TD
1.	Fran Tarkenton	342
2.	Dan Marino[1]	328
3.	Johnny Unitas	290
4.	Joe Montana[1]	273
5.	Sonny Jurgensen	255
6.	Dan Fouts	254
7.	John Hadl	244
8.	Len Dawson	239
9.	George Blanda	236
10.	Dave Krieg[1]	217
11T.	John Brodie	214
11T.	Warren Moon[1]	214
13T.	Terry Bradshaw	212
13T.	Y.A. Tittle	212
15.	Jim Hart	209
16.	Boomer Esiason[1]	207
17T.	Roman Gabriel	201
17T.	Jim Kelly[1]	201
19T.	John Elway[1]	199
19T.	Phil Simms	199

TOTAL YARDS PASSING

	Player	Yards
1.	Fran Tarkenton	47,003
2.	Dan Marino[1]	45,173
3.	Dan Fouts	43,040
4.	Joe Montana[1]	40,551
5.	Johnny Unitas	40,239
6.	Warren Moon[1]	37,949
7.	John Elway[1]	37,736
8.	Jim Hart	34,665
9.	Steve DeBerg[1]	33,872
10.	John Hadl	33,513
11.	Phil Simms	34,462
12.	Ken Anderson	32,838
13.	Sonny Jurgensen	32,224
14.	Dave Krieg[1]	32,114
15.	Boomer Esiason[1]	31,874
16.	John Brodie	31,548
17.	Norm Snead	30,797
18.	Joe Ferguson	29,817
19.	Jim Kelly[1]	29,527
20.	Roman Gabriel	29,444

1. Player active in 1993. **Source:** National Foodtball League, *1994 Record and Fact Book* (1994).

NFL ALL-TIME PASSING LEADERS

RATING

Rank/Player	Yrs.	Att.	Comp.	Yards	TD	Int.	Rating
1. Steve Young[1]	10	2,429	1,546	19,869	140	68	96.8
2. Joe Montana[1]	15	5,391	3,409	40,551	273	139	92.3
3. Dan Marino[1]	12	6,049	3,604	45,173	328	185	88.2
4. Jim Kelly[1]	9	3,942	2,397	29,527	201	143	85.8
5. Roger Staubach	11	2,958	1,685	22,700	153	109	83.4
6. Dave Krieg[1]	15	4,390	2,562	32,114	231	166	83.0
7. Neil Lomax	8	3,153	1,817	22,771	136	90	82.7
8. Sonny Jurgensen	18	4,262	2,433	32,224	255	189	82.6
9. Len Dawson	19	3,741	2,136	28,711	239	183	82.6
10. Brett Favre[1]	4	1,580	963	10,412	70	53	82.2

Note: Rating points based on a combination of performances in the following four categories: percentage of completions, percentage of touchdown passes, percentage of interceptions, and average gain per pass attempt. Minimum 1,500 attempts; through end of 1994 season. 1. Active in 1994.

NFL ROOKIE OF THE YEAR, 1970–94

Year		Player	Pos.	Team
1970	NFC:	Bruce Taylor	CB	San Francisco 49ers
	AFC:	Dennis Shaw	QB	Buffalo Bills
1971	NFC:	John Brockington	RB	Green Bay Packers
	AFC:	Jim Plunkett	QB	New England Patriots
1972	NFC:	Chester Marcol	PK	Green Bay Packers
	AFC:	Franco Harris	RB	Pittsburgh Steelers
1973	NFC:	Chuck Foreman	RB	Minnesota Vikings
	AFC:	Boobie Clark	RB	Cincinnati Bengals
1974	NFC:	Wilbur Jackson	RB	San Francisco 49ers
	AFC:	Don Woods	RB	San Diego Chargers
1975	NFC:	Steve Bartkowski	QB	Atlanta Falcons
	AFC:	Robert Brazile	LB	Houston Oilers
1976	NFC:	Sammy White	WR	Minnesota Vikings
	AFC:	Mike Haynes	CB	New England Patriots

Year		Player	Pos.	Team
1977	NFC:	Tony Dorsett	RB	Dallas Cowboys
	AFC:	A.J. Duhe	DT	Miami Dolphins
1978	NFC:	Al Baker	DE	Detroit Lions
	AFC:	Earl Campbell	RB	Houston Oilers
1979	NFC:	Ottis Anderson	RB	St. Louis Cardinals
	AFC:	Jerry Butler	WR	Buffalo Bills
1980		Billy Sims	RB	Detroit Lions
1981		George Rogers	RB	New Orleans Saints
1982		Marcus Allen	RB	Los Angeles Raiders
1983		Dan Marino	QB	Miami Dolphins
1984		Louis Lipps	WR	Pittsburgh Steelers
1985		Eddie Brown	WR	Cincinnati Bengals
1986		Rueben Mayes	RB	New Orleans Saints
1987		Robert Awalt	TE	St. Louis Cardinals
1988		Keith Jackson	TE	Philadephia Eagles
1989		Barry Sanders	RB	Detroit Lions
1990		Richmond Webb	OL	Miami Dolphins
1991		Mike Croel	LB	Denver Broncos
1992		Santana Dotson	DE	Tampa Bay Buccaneers
1993		Jerome Bettis	RB	Los Angeles Rams
1994		Marshall Faulk	RB	Indianapolis Colts

Note: In 1980 *The Sporting News* began selecting one rookie as Rookie of the Year for the entire NFL. **Source:** *The Sporting News.*

NFL CHAMPIONS, 1921–66

Year	Team
1921	Chicago Staleys (10–1–1)[1]
1922	Canton Bulldogs (10–0–2)
1923	Canton Bulldogs (11–0–1)
1924	Cleveland Bulldogs (7–1–1)[2]
1925	Chicago Cardinals (11–2–1)
1926	Frankford Yellowjackets (14–1–1)
1927	New York Giants (11–1–1)
1928	Providence Steamrollers (8–1–2)
1929	Green Bay Packers (12–0–1)
1930	Green Bay Packers (10–3–1)
1931	Green Bay Packers (12–2–0)
1932	Chicago Bears (7–1–6)
1933	Chicago Bears (10–2–1)
1934	New York Giants (8–5–0)
1935	Detroit Lions (7–3–2)
1936	Green Bay Packers (10–1–1)
1937	Washington Redskins (8–3–0)
1938	New York Giants (8–2–1)
1939	Green Bay Packers (9–2–0)
1940	Chicago Bears (8–3–0)
1941	Chicago Bears (10–1–1)
1942	Washington Redskins (10–1–1)
1943	Chicago Bears (8–1–1)
1944	Green Bay Packers (8–2–0)
1945	Cleveland Rams (9–1–0)
1946	Chicago Bears (8–2–1)
1947	Chicago Cardinals (9–3–0)
1948	Philadelphia Eagles (9–2–1)
1949	Philadelphia Eagles (11–1–0)
1950	Cleveland Browns (10–2–0)
1951	Los Angeles Rams (8–4–0)
1952	Detroit Lions (9–3–0)
1953	Detroit Lions (10–2–0)
1954	Cleveland Browns (9–3–0)
1955	Cleveland Browns (9–2–1)
1956	New York Giants (8–3–1)
1957	Detroit Lions (8–4–0)
1958	Baltimore Colts (9–3–0)
1959	Baltimore Colts ((9–3–0)
1960	Philadelphia Eagles (10–2–0)
1961	Green Bay Packers (11–3–0)
1962	Green Bay Packers (13–1–0)
1963	Chicago Bears (11–1–2)
1964	Cleveland Browns (10–3–1)
1965	Green Bay Packers (10–3–1)
1966	Green Bay Packers (12–2–0)

1. Later called the Chicago Bears. 2. Franchise moved from Canton.

SUPER BOWL RESULTS

Super Bowl I

Jan. 15, 1967, Memorial Coliseum
Los Angeles, California

Green Bay Packers 35
Kansas City Chiefs 10

Green Bay's Max McGee was a surprise star, as he filled in for ailing Boyd Dowler. McGee had caught only three passes all year, but in Super Bowl I he caught seven from quarterback Bart Starr for 138 yards and two touchdowns. Starr himself was the game's MVP, as he completed 16 of 23 passes for 250 yards and two touchdowns. Green Bay broke open the game with three second-half touchdowns, the first of which was set up by all-pro safety Willie Wood's 40-yard return of an interception to the Chiefs' five-yard line.

Super Bowl II

Jan. 14, 1968, Orange Bowl
Miami, Florida

Green Bay Packers 33
Oakland Raiders 14

Bart Starr again dominated proceedings with 13 completions in 24 passing attempts, totaling 202 yards and a touchdown, winning his second straight MVP award. The Pack attack was in control all the way after building a 16–7 halftime lead. Don Chandler kicked four field goals and all-pro cornerback Herb Adderley capped the Green Bay scoring with a 60-yard run on an interception.

Super Bowl III

Jan. 12, 1969, Orange Bowl
Miami, Florida

New York Jets 16
Baltimore Colts 7

Joe Namath became a prophet with honor—on the Thursday before the game, he "guaranteed" victory for New York. He did just that, earning MVP honors by completing 17 of 28 passes for 206 yards and directing a steady attack that racked up 337 total yards. Three times in the first half, the Jet defense intercepted Colts quarterback Earl Morrall, who was playing for an injured Johnny Unitas. With the Jets ahead 16–0 in the fourth quarter, Unitas came off the bench and orchestrated Baltimore's sole touchdown.

Super Bowl IV

Jan. 11, 1970, Tulane Stadium
New Orleans, Louisiana

Kansas City Chiefs 23
Minnesota Vikings 7

Superb quarterbacking continued to be the key to Super Bowl victory as MVP Len Dawson called a nearly flawless game for Kansas City, completing 12 of 17 passes and hitting Otis Taylor on a 46-yard pass for the final Chiefs touchdown. The Kansas City defense limited Minnesota's strong rushing game to 67 yards and had three interceptions and two fumble recoveries. The Chiefs rolled up a 16–0 halftime lead and stood off the Vikings after that.

Super Bowl V

Jan. 17, 1971, Orange Bowl
Miami, Florida

Baltimore Colts 16
Dallas Cowboys 13

First-year kicker Jim O'Brien booted a 32-yard field goal to give the Colts a victory over the Cowboys in the final seconds of the Super Bowl. Dallas led 13–6 at halftime, but two Colt interceptions set up a Baltimore touchdown and O'Brien's crucial kick. Earl Morrall relieved an injured Johnny Unitas in the first half. Unitas's lone scoring pass was dramatic—the ball caromed off receiver Eddie Hinton's fingertips, off Dallas defensive back Mel Renfro, and finally settled into the grasp of tight end John Mackey, who went 45 yards to score on a 75-yard play. Dallas linebacker Chuck Howley was the MVP.

Super Bowl VI

Jan. 16, 1972, Tulane Stadium
New Orleans, Louisiana

Dallas Cowboys 24
Miami Dolphins 3

The Cowboys rushed for a record 252 yards, and their defense limited the Dolphins to a record low 185 while not permitting a touchdown. Dallas converted Chuck Howley's recovery of Larry Csonka's first fumble of the season into a 3–0 advantage. At halftime Dallas led 10–3. An eight-play, 71-yard march made it a 17–3 game. Cowboys' quarterback Roger Staubach was voted MVP for his 12 completions in 19 attempts, 119 yards passing, and two touchdowns.

Super Bowl VII
Jan. 14, 1973, Memorial Coliseum
Los Angeles, California
Miami Dolphins 14
Washington Redskins 7

In a game that wasn't as close as the score, the Dolphins thoroughly dominated the Redskins to complete the NFL's only undefeated season. On its third possession, Miami opened its first scoring drive from their own 37-yard line. Quarterback Bob Griese hit Paul Warfield for 18 yards before delivering a 28-yard strike to Howard Twilley for the Dolphins' first score. Just before the first half ended, Dolphins linebacker Nick Buoniconti intercepted a Billy Kilmer pass at the Miami 41 and returned it to the Washington 27, setting up Miami's second touchdown. Safety Jake Scott led the Dolphin defense with two interceptions (one in the end zone killing a Redskins scoring drive) and was the MVP. The Redskins' sole touchdown resulted when Dolphin kicker Garo Yepremian tried to turn a botched field goal into a forward pass. Washington's Mike Bass picked the ball out of the air and returned it 49 yards for the score.

Super Bowl VIII
Jan. 13, 1974, Rice Stadium
Houston, Texas
Miami Dolphins 24
Minnesota Vikings 7

On their first two possessions, Miami scored, on 62- and 56-yard marches. The initial 10-play drive was climaxed by a Larry Csonka touchdown bolt through right guard after 5:27 had elapsed. Four plays later, Miami's second assault sent Jim Kiick bursting one yard through the middle for the second touchdown. By halftime Miami led 17–0. Minnesota came back from its 20 to a second-and-two situation on the Miami seven-yard line with 1:18 left in the half, but Miami limited Minnesota's Oscar Reed to one yard. On the fourth-and-one from the six, Reed went over right tackle, but Dolphin middle linebacker Nick Buoniconti jarred the ball loose and Jake Scott recovered for Miami to end the Minnesota threat. Csonka rushed 33 times for a Super Bowl record 145 yards, winning the MVP.

Super Bowl IX
Jan. 12, 1975, Tulane Stadium
New Orleans, Louisiana
Pittsburgh Steelers 16
Minnesota Vikings 6

Steeler Dwight White downed Fran Tarkenton's fumbled pass attempt in the end zone for a safety to put the Steelers on the board in the second quarter. They took advantage of another break in the second half, when Minnesota's Bill Brown fumbled on the kickoff and Marv Kellum recovered for Pittsburgh on the Vikings' 30. Franco Harris carried three straight times for 27 yards and a touchdown, putting the Steelers in front 9–0. Minnesota was able to block Bobby Walden's punt attempt, and Terry Brown recovered the ball for a touchdown. But the Steelers roared back with a 66-yard march, climaxed by Terry Bradshaw's four-yard scoring pass to Larry Brown. Pittsburgh's defense controlled the game by permitting Minnesota only 119 yards total offense and a record low 17 yards rushing. Franco Harris's record 158 yards rushing on 34 carries won him MVP honors, and paced the Steelers' 333-yard rushing attack.

Super Bowl X
Jan. 18, 1976, Orange Bowl
Miami, Florida
Pittsburgh Steelers 21
Dallas Cowboys 17

Steeler quarterback Terry Bradshaw hurled a 64-yard touchdown pass to Lynn Swann to win the game, while his aggressive defense stopped the Cowboys' last rally with an end-zone interception in the game's final play. It was a battle of quarterbacks, with Cowboy Roger Staubach and Bradshaw both hurling two touchdowns. Lynn Swann earned his MVP award with a record 161 yards gained on his four receptions. The Steelers blasted out in front with a 14-point fourth quarter.

Super Bowl XI
Jan. 9, 1977, Rose Bowl
Pasadena, California
Oakland Raiders 32
Minnesota Vikings 14

A record 81 million TV viewers watched the Raiders gain a record-breaking 429 yards, including running back Clarence Davis's 137 yards rushing. Wide receiver Fred Biletnikoff made four key receptions, which earned him the game's MVP trophy. Oakland scored on three successive possessions in the second quarter to build a 16–0 halftime lead. Minnesota's Fran Tarkenton passed for a touchdown in the third to cut the deficit, but two fourth-quarter interceptions clinched the title for the Raiders. One set up Pete Banaszak's second touchdown run, the other resulted in cornerback Willie Brown's Super Bowl record 75-yard interception return.

Super Bowl XII
Jan. 15, 1978, Louisiana Superdome
New Orleans, Louisiana
Dallas Cowboys 27
Denver Broncos 10

The TV audience climbed to 102 million, a new record, as Dallas converted two interceptions into 10 points and Efren Herrera added a 35-yard field goal for a 12–0 Dallas halftime lead. Butch Johnston made a spectacular diving catch in the end zone of a Roger Staubach pass to make it 20–3. Dallas clinched the victory when running back Robert Newhouse threw a 29-yard touchdown pass to Golden Richards with 7:04 remaining in the game. It was the first pass thrown by Newhouse since 1975. Co-MVPs Harvey Martin and Randy White led the Cowboys' defense, which recovered four fumbles and intercepted four passes.

Super Bowl XIII
Jan. 21, 1979, Orange Bowl
Miami, Florida
Pittsburgh Steelers 35
Dallas Cowboys 31

Terry Bradshaw hurled four touchdown passes to lead the Steelers to victory, making them the first team to win three Super Bowls. Bradshaw completed 17 of 30 passes for 318 yards. Cowboy quarterback Roger Staubach threw two touchdown passes himself. In the fourth quarter, the Steelers broke open the contest with two touchdowns in 19 seconds. Franco Harris rambled 22 yards up the middle to put Pittsburgh in front 28–17. The Steelers got the ball right back when Randy White fumbled the kickoff and Dennis Winston recovered. On first down Bradshaw hit Lynn Swann with an 18-yard scoring pass to boost the Steelers to 35–17. The Cowboys came back with a Staubach touchdown pass to Billy Joe DuPree and by recovering an onside kick. But Rocky Bleier recovered another onside kick with 17 seconds remaining to seal the victory for Pittsburgh—and the MVP award for Bradshaw.

Super Bowl XIV
Jan. 20, 1980, Rose Bowl
Pasadena, California
Pittsburgh Steelers 31
Los Angeles Rams 19

It was all Terry Bradshaw again as he completed 14 of 21 passes for 309 yards and set two passing records as the Steelers became the first team to win four Super Bowls. Despite three interceptions by the Rams, Bradshaw brought the Steelers back from behind twice in the second half. On Pittsburgh's first possession of the final period, Bradshaw lofted a 73-yard scoring pass to John Stallworth to put the Steelers in front to stay, 24–19. Franco Harris scored on a one-yard run later to seal the verdict. Bradshaw was the MVP for the second straight Super Bowl.

Super Bowl XV
Jan. 25, 1981, Louisiana Superdome
New Orleans, Louisiana
Oakland Raiders 27
Philadelphia Eagles 10

Jim Plunkett threw three touchdown passes, including an 80-yarder to Kenny King—the longest play in Super Bowl history—to give Oakland a decisive 14–0 advantage nine seconds before halftime. Oakland linebacker Rod Martin intercepted three passes for a Super Bowl record, as the Raiders completely stifled Eagle quarterback Ron Jaworski's offense. Jaworski managed an eight-yard touchdown pass in the fourth quarter, but the issue had been decided by Plunkett, who completed 13 of the 21 pass attempts for 261 yards and was named MVP.

Super Bowl XVI
Jan. 24, 1982, Pontiac Silverdome
Pontiac, Michigan
San Francisco 49ers 26
Cincinnati Bengals 21

This was a game of a failed comeback, as the 49ers led 20–0 at halftime and barely hung on to their lead. Ray Wersching kicked a record-tying four field goals for San Francisco. Quarterback Joe Montana capped a San Francisco 11-play, 68-yard drive with a one-yard run. Another key was a record 92-yard drive, which ended in a touchdown pass by Montana. The Bengals rebounded in the second half as quarterback Ken Anderson ran in a touchdown and passed for another. He set Super Bowl records for completions, 25, and completion percentage, 73.5% on 25 of 34. With 16 seconds remaining, the Bengals managed to score on an Anderson-to-Dan Ross three-yard pass, but it was too little too late. Ross set a Super Bowl record with 11 receptions for 104 yards. Montana, the MVP, completed 14 of 22 passes for 157 yards. Cincinnati compiled 345 yards to San Francisco's 275, the first time in Super Bowl history that the team that gained more yards lost the game.

Super Bowl XVII

Jan. 30, 1983, Rose Bowl
Pasadena, California

Washington Redskins 27
Miami Dolphins 17

Washington fullback John Riggins ran the ball for a record 166 yards on 38 carries to lead Washington to victory, their first NFL title since 1942. Their 400 total yards offense, a Super Bowl record 276 yards rushing and 124 yards passing, was paced by Riggins, the MVP, and quarterback Joe Theismann, who passed 23 times for 15 completions and two touchdowns. Miami tied the score with help from a 76-yard touchdown pass from quarterback David Woodley to wide receiver Jimmy Cefalo. But the game's main force was Riggins, who took the ball on fourth-and-one and ran 43 yards for a touchdown to put Washington in front.

Super Bowl XVIII

Jan. 22, 1984, Tampa Stadium
Tampa, Florida

Los Angeles Raiders 38
Washington Redskins 9

This hopelessly lopsided victory set records. Raider reserve linebacker Jack Squirek intercepted a Joe Theismann pass at the Redskins' five-yard line and ran the ball in for a touchdown with seven seconds left in the first half. Raiders' Marcus Allen rushed for a record 191 yards on 20 carries, including two touchdowns, one of which was on a record 74-yard run. Allen was voted game MVP. The 38 points was the highest total scored by a Super Bowl team.

Super Bowl XIX

Jan. 20, 1985, Stanford Stadium
Stanford, California

San Francisco 49ers 38
Miami Dolphins 16

The Dolphins led 10–7 at the end of the first period, but 49er running back Roger Craig set a Super Bowl record by scoring three touchdowns. Joe Montana dominated the game with an MVP performance—24 of 35 passes for a record 331 yards and three touchdowns. He also rushed five times for 59 yards and a touchdown. Craig had 56 yards on 15 carries and caught seven passes for 77 yards. Wendell Tyler rushed 13 times for 65 yards, as San Francisco's running game racked up mileage. As a team San Francisco gained 537 yards, setting a new record, while holding the ball for 37:11 as opposed to Miami's 22:49.

Super Bowl XX

Jan. 26, 1986, Louisiana Superdome
New Orleans, Louisiana

Chicago Bears 46
New England Patriots 10

The Patriots took the quickest lead in Super Bowl history when Tony Franklin kicked a 36-yard field goal with 1:19 elapsed in the first period. But the Bears rebounded by mauling the Pats. Chicago tied the record for sacks (seven) and limited the Pats to a record-low seven yards rushing. Total yardage on the day told the story: Chicago 236, New England minus 19. The Bears ran up a fat 23–3 lead by halftime. In the second half, the Bears marched 96 yards in nine plays, capped by quarterback Jim McMahon's one-yard rush for a touchdown. He became the first quarterback in Super Bowl history to rush for two touchdowns. Bears defensive end Richard Dent won the MVP after contributing one-and-a-half sacks and leading the ferocious Chicago defense. McMahon completed 12 of 20 passes for 256 yards before leaving the game with an injury.

Super Bowl XXI

Jan. 25, 1987, Rose Bowl
Pasadena, California

New York Giants 39
Denver Broncos 20

The Broncos got off to a 10–9 lead at halftime, the narrowest such margin in Super Bowl history, backed by the passing of John Elway. He capped a 58-yard scoring drive on six plays with a four-yard touchdown run. But in the second half, the Giants' defense took over, sacking Elway in his end zone for a safety. The Broncos had a first-and-goal but failed to score on three plays and a field goal attempt. After that the Giants took over, scoring 30 points in the second half. MVP Giants' quarterback Phil Simms set Super Bowl records for most consecutive completions (10) and highest completion percentage (88% on 22 completions in 25 attempts). He passed for 268 yards and three touchdowns.

Super Bowl XXII

Jan. 31, 1988, Jack Murphy Stadium
San Diego, California

Washington Redskins 42
Denver Broncos 10

A record 35-point second quarter was the key to Washington's convincing Super Bowl triumph. The Broncos jumped in front early as John Elway hurled a 56-yard touchdown pass to wide receiver Ricky Nattiel on the Broncos' first play from scrimmage. But the Redskins erupted for 35 points on five straight possessions. Redskins' quarterback Doug Williams led the assault, hurling a record-tying four touchdown passes, including 80- and 50 yarders to wide receiver Gary Clark and an eight-yarder to tight end Clint Didier. Washington scored five touchdowns in 18 plays in 5:47 of possession. MVP Williams completed 18 of 29 passes for 340 yards, a new Super Bowl record. Rookie running back Timmy Smith ran 22 times for a record 204 yards.

Super Bowl XXIII

Jan. 22, 1989, Joe Robbie Stadium
Miami, Florida

San Francisco 49ers 20
Cincinnati Bengals 16

San Francisco captured its third Super Bowl of the 1980s by defeating the Bengals in a rematch of Super Bowl XVI. The 49ers thus became the first NFC team to win three Super Bowls. Even though San Francisco held an advantage in total yards (454 vs. 229), they found themselves trailing late in the game. Cincinnati took a 16–13 lead on Jim Breech's 40-yard field goal with 3:20 remaining. Breech's kick capped a 46-yard ball-control effort, which had consumed 5:27. The 49ers started their winning drive at their own eight-yard line. Over the next 11 plays, they drove 92 yards to the winning score, a 10-yard touchdown pass from Joe Montana to wide receiver John Taylor with only 34 seconds remaining. San Francisco's other wide receiver, Jerry Rice, won the MVP after catching 11 passes for a Super Bowl record 215 yards. Montana completed 23 of 36 passes for a record 357 yards and two touchdowns.

Super Bowl XXIV

Jan. 28, 1990, Louisiana Superdome
New Orleans, Louisiana

San Francisco 49ers 55
Denver Broncos 10

San Francisco demolished the Broncos and became the first team to repeat as champions since the 1979–80 Steelers. The 49ers' diverse offense was magnificently orchestrated by quarterback Joe Montana, who completed 22 of 29 passes for 297 yards and five touchdowns, en route to winning the MVP. Montana raised his record to 122 total Super Bowl pass attempts without an interception. His primary receiver was the fleet Jerry Rice, who hauled in seven passes for 148 yards and three touchdowns. Running backs Tom Rathman and Roger Craig ran for three touchdowns, while combining for nine receptions for an additional 77 yards. The San Francisco defense completely dominated John Elway and the Bronco offense, limiting them to 167 total yards while sacking Elway six times, intercepting him twice, and harrying him into numerous mistakes.

Super Bowl XXV

Jan. 27, 1991, Tampa Stadium
Tampa, Florida

New York Giants 20
Buffalo Bills 19

The Giants edged the Bills in a tightly contested, nearly error-free game; victory was secured only when the Bills' Scott Norwood missed what would have been the winning field goal with eight seconds to play. The key ingredient to the Giants' victory was a ball-control offense, led by reserve quarterback Jeff Hostetler and veteran running back Ottis Anderson, which set a Super Bowl record for possession time of 40 minutes, 33 seconds. Anderson, who carried the ball 21 times for 102 yards, was named Most Valuable Player. After falling behind 12–3, the Giants, led by 21 players with Super Bowl experience, refused to panic. Their defense slowed Buffalo's vaunted "hurry-up" offense to a crawl, surrounding Jim Kelly's receivers with extra defensive backs and linebackers playing a physical, "bump and run" style. Kelly finished the day with 18 completions in 30 attempts for 205 yards, but could rarely convert on crucial third down opportunities. Hostetler, substituting for the injured Phil Simms, directed the Giants on touchdown drives of 75 and 87 yards, while completing 20 of 32 passes for 214 yards and allowing no turnovers.

Super Bowl XXVI

Jan. 26, 1992, Hubert H. Humphrey Metrodome
Minneapolis, Minnesota

Washington Redskins 37
Buffalo Bills 24

Washington jumped out to a 17–0 lead in the first half and never looked back in a game that was not as close as the final score suggests. MVP quarterback Mark Rypien, who had passed for 3,564 yards during Washington's 14–2 regular season, completed 18 of 33 passes for 292 yards and two touchdowns. Meanwhile, the blitzing Redskin defense intercepted Buffalo quarterback Jim Kelly four times (tying a Super Bowl record) and sacked the Bills' signal-caller five times. Buffalo's no-huddle offense was also plagued by several dropped passes, including two that would have gone for touchdowns. In all, Kelly threw a record 58 passes, 30 of which went incomplete. Brad Edwards, Washington's free safety, had four tackles and two interceptions and broke up five passes, while linebacker Wilber Marshall had a game-high 11 tackles, a sack, and forced two fumbles. Bills running back Thurman Thomas, the NFL's regular season MVP, missed the first two plays of the game because he couldn't find his helmet, and was limited to 13 yards on 10 rushes.

Super Bowl XXVII

Jan. 31, 1993, Rose Bowl
Pasadena, California

Dallas Cowboys 52
Buffalo Bills 17

Buffalo lost its record third straight Super Bowl in a second consecutive rout. Dallas capitalized on nine Bills turnovers, scoring 35 points following Buffalo miscues. The game's turning point came early in the second quarter, when Buffalo drove inside the Dallas five-yard line twice but came away with only three points, and lost starting quarterback Jim Kelly in the process. Inspired by its defense's two goal line stands, the Cowboys' offense, which had been fairly inept up to this point, came alive for a long scoring drive. The Bills fumbled their first play from scrimmage on the ensuing drive, and one play later, the Cowboys had scored again, this time on a strike from Troy Aikman to Michael Irvin, giving Dallas a 28–10 halftime lead. The Cowboys poured it on in the second half, forcing four more turnovers, three more touchdowns, and a field goal. Aikman, who passed for four touchdowns, also won MVP honors.

Super Bowl XXVIII

Jan. 30, 1994, Georgia Dome
Atlanta, Georgia

Dallas Cowboys 30
Buffalo Bills 13

Buffalo became the first team in U.S. professional sports history to lose four consecutive championship games in this rematch of Super Bowl XXVII. The Bills actually led at halftime 13–6 on the strength of Thurman Thomas's 37 yards rushing and a Super Bowl record 54-yard field goal by Steve Christie. But Thomas fumbled the opening drive of the second half, and Dallas safety James Washington returned the ball 46 yards for a touchdown, tying the game at 13–13. Dallas then drove the length of the field on its next possession, with running back Emmitt Smith grinding out 61 yards. The Cowboys added another touchdown and a field goal to secure the victory, while the Dallas defense held Buffalo scoreless in the second half. Smith, who was the league's most valuable player during the regular season, was named MVP of the Super Bowl as well.

Super Bowl XXIX

Jan. 29, 1995, Joe Robbie Stadium
Miami, Florida

San Francisco 49ers 49
San Diego Chargers 26

Favored by 20 points (the largest margin in Super Bowl history), San Francisco scored early and often to capture a record fifth Super Bowl championship. The 49ers scored on the third play from scrimmage when quarterback Steve Young found wide receiver Jerry Rice wide open inside the San Diego 10-yard line. The touchdown was the fastest in Super Bowl history (1:24). Young went on to throw five more touchdowns (another Super Bowl record), and to chalk up 49 yards on the ground, making him the 49ers' leading rusher as well. Rice and running back Ricky Watters each scored three touchdowns; rookie fullback William Floyd also scored on a five-yard pass from Young early in the second quarter. The outcome was never in doubt after halftime, though the Chargers did go on to score two meaningless touchdowns, and to notch the first two-point conversion in Super Bowl history. On the strength of his 24-for-36 for 325-yard performance, Young was the obvious choice for MVP.

PRO FOOTBALL HALL OF FAME MEMBERS

Alphabetical listing of the members of the Professional Football Hall of Fame. Listing includes enshrinee's name, year of enshrinement, position(s), and pro team(s).

Herb Adderley (1980) CB, Packers, Cowboys.
Lance Alworth (1978) WR, Chargers, Cowboys.
Doug Atkins (1982) DE, Browns, Bears, Saints.
Morris (Red) Badgro (1981) E, Yankees, Giants, Dodgers.
Lem Barney (1992) CB, Lions.
Cliff Battles (1968) HB, QB, Braves, Redskins. Coach, Dodgers.
Sammy Baugh (1963 Charter) QB, Redskins. Coach, Titans, Oilers, Lions.
Chuck Bednarik (1967) C, LB, Eagles.
Bert Bell (1963 Charter) Commissioner, NFL. Founder, Eagles, 1933. Coach Eagles, Steelers. Club president, Eagles, Steelers.
Bobby Bell (1983) LB, DE, Chiefs.
Raymond Berry (1973) E, Colts. Coach, Patriots.
Charles W. Bidwill, Sr. (1967) Owner and president, Chicago Cardinals.
Fred Biletnikoff (1988) WR, Raiders.
George Blanda (1981) QB, PK, Bears, Colts, Oilers, Raiders.
Mel Blount (1989) CB, Steelers.
Terry Bradshaw (1989) QB, Steelers.
Jim Brown (1971) RB, Browns.
Paul E. Brown (1967) Coach and GM, Browns, Bengals.
Roosevelt Brown (1975) OT, Giants.
Willie Brown (1984) CB, Broncos, Raiders.
Buck Buchanan (1990) DT, Chiefs.
Dick Butkus (1979) LB, Bears.
Earl Campbell (1991) RB, Oilers, Saints.
Tony Canadeo (1974) HB, Packers.
Joe Carr (1963) NFL President.
Guy Chamberlin (1965) E, Bulldogs, Staleys, Yellowjackets, Cardinals. Coach, Bulldogs, Yellowjackets, Cardinals.
Jack Christiansen (1970) DB, Spartans, Lions. Coach, 49ers.
Earl (Dutch) Clark (1970) DB, Spartans, Lions, Rams.
George Connor (1975) OT, DT, LB, Bears.
Jimmy Conzelman (1964) QB, Staleys, Independents, Badgers, Panthers. Owner, Steamrollers, Cardinals, Panthers.
Larry Csonka (1987) RB, Dolphins, Giants.
Al Davis (1992) President, owner, general manager, head coach, Raiders. Commissioner, American Football League.
Willie Davis (1981) DE, Browns, Packers.
Len Dawson (1987) QB, Steelers, Browns, Texans, Chiefs.
Mike Ditka (1988) TE, Bears, Eagles, Cowboys. Coach, Bears.
Art Donovan (1968) DT, Colts, Yankees, Texans.
Tony Dorsett (1994) RB, Cowboys, Broncos.
John (Paddy) Driscoll (1965) QB, Pros, Staleys, Cardinals, Bears. Coach, Cardinals, Bears.
Bill Dudley (1966) RB, Steelers, Lions, Redskins.
Albert Glen (Turk) Edwards (1969) OT, Braves, Redskins. Coach, Redskins.
Weeb Ewbank (1978) Coach, Colts, Jets, General manager, Jets.
Tom Fears (1970) E, Rams. Coach, Saints.
Jim Finks (1995) QB, Steelers. President, Vikings, Bears, Saints.
Ray Flaherty (1976) E, Wildcats, Yankees, Giants. Coach, Redskins, Yankees.
Leonard (Len) Ford (1976) DE, OE, Dons. Browns, Packers.
Daniel J. Fortmann, M.D. (1965) G, Bears.
Dan Fouts (1993) QB, Chargers.
Frank Gatski (1985) C, Browns, Lions.
Bill George (1974) LB, Bears, Rams.
Frank Gifford (1977) RB, Giants.
Sid Gillman (1983) Head coach, Rams, Chargers, Oilers.
Otto Graham (1965) QB, Browns. Head coach, Redskins.

Harold (Red) Grange (1963 Charter) RB, Bears, Yankees.
Bud Grant (1994) Coach, Vikings.
(Mean) Joe Greene (1987) DT, Steelers.
Forrest Gregg (1977) OL, Packers, Cowboys. Head coach, Browns, Bengals, Packers.
Bob Griese (1990) QB, Dolphins.
Lou Groza (1974) OT, PK, Browns.
Joe Guyon (1966) RB, Bulldogs, Indians, Independents, Cowboys, Giants.
George Halas (1963) Founder, head coach, player, Staleys. President, head coach, player, Bears.
Jack Ham (1988) LB, Steelers.
John Hannah (1991) G, Patriots.
Franco Harris (1990) RB, Steelers, Seahawks.
Ed Healey (1964) OT, Independents, Bears.
Mel Hein (1963) C, Giants. Head coach, Dons.
Wilbur (Pete) Henry (1963) OT, Bulldogs, Giants, Maroons.
Arnie Herber (1966) QB, Packers, Giants.
Bill Hewitt (1971) E, Bears, Eagles, Phil-Pitt.
Clarke Hinkle (1964) RB, Packers.
Elroy (Crazy Legs) Hirsch (1968) RB, E, Rockets, Rams.
Paul Hornung (1986) RB, Packers.
Ken Houston (1986) DB, Oilers, Redskins.
Robert (Cal) Hubbard (1963) OT, Giants, Packers, Pirates.
Sam Huff (1982) LB, Giants, Redskins.
Lamar Hunt (1972) Founder, AFL. Owner, Texans, Chiefs.
Don Hutson (1963) E, Packers.
Jimmy Johnson (1994) DB, 49ers.
John Henry Johnson (1987) RB, 49ers, Lions, Steelers, Oilers.
David (Deacon) Jones (1980) DE, Rams, Chargers, Redskins.
Stan Jones (1991) G, DT, Bears, Redskins. Asst. coach Browns, Bills, Patriots.
Henry Jordan (1995) DT, Packers.
Sonny Jurgensen (1983) QB, Eagles, Redskins.
Walt Kiesling (1966) G, Eskimos, Maroons, Chicago Cardinals, Bears, Packers, Pirates. Head coach, Pirates, Steelers.
Frank (Bruiser) Kinard (1971) OT, Dodgers, Yankees.
Early (Curly) Lambeau (1963) HB, Packers. Founder, Packers. Head coach, Packers, Cardinals, Washington Redskins.
Jack Lambert (1990) LB, Steelers.
Tom Landry (1990) Head coach, Cowboys.
Dick (Night Train) Lane (1974) DB, Rams, Cardinals, Lions.
Jim Langer (1987) C, Dolphins, Vikings.
Willie Lanier (1986) LB, Chiefs.
Steve Largent (1995) WR, Seahawks.
Yale Lary (1979) DB, Lions.
Dante Lavelli (1975) E, Browns.
Bobby Layne (1967) QB, Bears, Bulldogs, Lions, Steelers.
Alphonse (Tuffy) Leemans (1978) RB, Giants.
Bob Lilly (1980) DT, Cowboys.
Larry Little (1993) G, Chargers, Dolphins.
Vince Lombardi (1971) Head coach, Packers, Redskins.
Sid Luckman (1965) QB, Bears.
William Roy (Link) Lyman (1964) OT, Bulldogs, Yellowjackets, Bears.
John Mackey (1992) TE, Colts, Chargers.
Tim Mara (1963) Founder, president, Giants.
Gino Marchetti (1972) DE, Texans, Colts.
George Preston Marshall (1963) Founder, president, Braves (Redskins).
Ollie Matson (1972) RB, Cardinals, Rams, Lions, Eagles.
Don Maynard (1987) WR, Giants, Titans, Jets, Cardinals.
George McAfee (1966) RB, Bears.
Mike McCormack (1984) OT, Yankees, Browns. Head coach, Eagles, Colts, Seahawks.
Hugh McElhenny (1970) RB, 49ers, Vikings, Giants, Lions.
John (Blood) McNally (1963) RB, Badgers, Eskimos, Maroons, Packers, Pirates. Head coach and player, Pirates.
August (Mike) Michalske (1964) G, Yankees, Packers.
Wayne Millner (1968) E, Redskins. Head coach, Eagles.
Bobby Mitchell (1983) WR, RB, Browns, Redskins.
Ron Mix (1979) OT, Chargers, Raiders.
Leonard (Lenny) Moore (1975) WR, RB, Colts.
Marion Motley (1968) RB, Browns, Steelers.
George Musso (1982) OT, G, Bears.
Bronko Nagurski (1963) RB, Bears.
Joe Namath (1985) QB, Jets, Rams.
Earle (Greasy) Neale (1969) E, Bulldogs. Head coach, Eagles.
Ernie Nevers (1963) RB, Eskimos, Cardinals. Head coach, Eskimos, Cardinals.
Ray Nitschke (1978) LB, Packers.
Chuck Noll (1993) Coach, Steelers.
Leo Nomellini (1969) DT, 49ers.
Merlin Olson (1982) DT, Rams.
Jim Otto (1980) C, Raiders.
Steven Owen (1966) OT, Cowboys, Giants. Head coach, Giants.
Alan Page (1988) DT, Vikings, Bears.
Clarence (Ace) Parker (1972) QB, Dodgers, Yankees.
Jim Parker (1973) G, OT, Colts.
Walter Payton (1993) RB, Bears.
Fletcher (Joe) Perry (1969) RB, 49ers, Colts.
Pete Pihos (1970) E, Eagles.
Hugh (Shorty) Ray (1966) Supervisor of officals.
Dan Reeves (1967) Owner, Rams.
John Riggins (1992) RB, Jets, Redskins.
Jim Ringo (1981) C, Packers, Eagles. Head coach, Bills.
Andy Robustelli (1971) DE, Rams, Giants.
Art Rooney (1964) Founder, president, Pirates, Steelers.
Pete Rozelle (1985) Commissioner, NFL.
Gale Sayers (1977) RB, Bears.
Joe Schmidt (1973) LB, Lions. Head coach, Lions.
Tex Schramm (1991) GM, Cowboys.
Lee Roy Selmon (1995) DE, Buccaneers.
Art Shell (1989) OT, Raiders. Head coach, Raiders.
O.J. Simpson (1985) RB, Bills, 49ers.
Jackie Smith (1994) TE, Cardinals, Cowboys.
Bart Starr (1977) QB, Packers. Head coach, Packers.
Roger Staubach (1985) QB, Cowboys.
Ernie Stautner (1969) DT, Steelers.
Jan Stenerud (1991) PK, Chiefs, Packers, Vikings.
Bob St. Clair (1990) OT, 49ers.
Ken Strong (1967) RB, Stapletons, Giants, Yankees.
Joe Stydahar (1967) OT, Bears. Head coach, Rams, Cardinals.
Fran Tarkenton (1986) QB, Vikings, Giants.
Charley Taylor (1984) WR, RB, Redskins.
Jim Taylor (1976) RB, Packers, Saints.
Jim Thorpe (1963) RB, Bulldogs, Indians, Maroons, Independents, Giants, Cardinals. Head coach, Bulldogs.
Y.A. Tittle (1971) QB, Colts, 49ers, Giants.
George Trafton (1964) C, Staleys, Bears.
Charley Trippi (1968) RB QB, Cardinals.
Emlen Tunnell (1967) DB, Giants, Packers.
Clyde (Bulldog) Turner (1966) C, LB, Bears. Head coach, Titans.
Johnny Unitas (1979) QB, Colts, Chargers.
Gene Upshaw (1987) G, Raiders.
Norm Van Brocklin (1971) QB, Rams, Eagles. Head coach, Vikings, Falcons.
Steve Van Buren (1965) RB, Eagles.
Doak Walker (1986) RB, Lions.
Bill Walsh (1993) Coach, 49ers.
Paul Warfield (1983) WR, Browns, Dolphins.
Bob Waterfield (1965) QB, Rams. Head coach, Rams.
Arnie Weinmeister (1984) DT, Yankees, Giants.
Randy White (1994) DT, Cowboys.
Bill Willis (1977) G, MG, Browns.
Larry Wilson (1978) DB, Cardinals.
Kellen Winslow (1995) TE, Chargers.
Alex Wojciechowicz (1968) C, LB, Lions, Eagles.
Willie Wood (1989) S, Packers.

Ice Hockey

National Hockey League
650 Fifth Avenue
New York, NY 10019
(212) 398-1100

Montreal Address
1155 Metcalfe, Ste. 960
Montreal, Quebec H3B 2W2
(514) 288-9220

Commissioner: Gary Bettman
Chairman of the Board: William W. Wirtz
Number of Teams: 26 Founded: 1917

THE STANLEY CUP

The Stanley Cup, awarded annually to the team winning the National Hockey League's best-of-seven final playoff round, is symbolic of the World Professional Hockey Championship. The oldest trophy competed for by professional athletes in North America, it was donated by Frederick Arthur, Lord Stanley of Preston and son of the Earl of Derby, in 1893. Lord Stanley purchased the trophy for 10 guineas ($50 at that time) for presentation to the amateur hockey champions of Canada. Since 1910, when the National Hockey Association took possession of the Stanley Cup, the trophy has been the symbol of professional hockey supremacy. Since 1926 only NHL teams have competed for the Stanley Cup. It has been under the exclusive control of the NHL since 1946.

STANLEY CUP PLAYOFFS 1995
(All rounds are seven-game series)

ROUND 1

EASTERN CONFERENCE

Winner	Loser
New York Rangers 4	Quebec Nordiques 2
Philadelphia Flyers 4	Buffalo Sabres 1
Pittsburgh Penguins 4	Washington Capitals 3
New Jersey Devils 4	Boston Bruins 1

WESTERN CONFERENCE

Winner	Loser
Detroit Red Wings 4	Dallas Stars 1
San Jose Sharks 4	Calgary Flames 3
Vancouver Canucks 4	St. Louis Blues 3
Chicago Blackhawks 4	Toronto Maple Leafs 3

ROUND 2

EASTERN CONFERENCE

Winner	Loser
Philadelphia Flyers 4	New York Rangers 0
New Jersey Devils 4	Pittsburgh Penguins 1

WESTERN CONFERENCE

Winner	Loser
Detroit Red Wings 4	San Jose Sharks 0
Chicago Blackhawks 4	Vancouver Canucks 0

CONFERENCE CHAMPIONSHIPS

Winner	Loser
New Jersey Devils 4	Philadelphia Flyers 2
Detroit Red Wings 4	Chicago Blackhawks 1

STANLEY CUP CHAMPIONSHIP

Winner	Loser
New Jersey Devils 4	Detroit Red Wings 0

STANLEY CUP CHAMPIONS, 1917–95

Season	Champion	Finalist	GP in final
1917–18	Toronto Arenas	Vancouver Millionaires	5
1918–19	No decision[1]	No decision	5
1919–20	Ottawa Senators	Seattle Metropolitans	5
1920–21	Ottawa Senators	Vancouver Millionaires	5
1921–22	Toronto St. Pats	Vancouver Millionaires	5
1922–23	Ottawa Senators	Edmonton Eskimos	2
1923–24	Montreal Canadiens	Calgary Tigers	2
1924–25	Victoria Cougars	Montreal Canadiens	4
1925–26	Montreal Maroons	Victoria Cougars	4
1926–27	Ottawa Senators	Boston Bruins	2
1927–28	New York Rangers	Montreal Maroons	5
1928–29	Boston Bruins	New York Rangers	2
1929–30	Montreal Canadiens	Boston Bruins	2
1930–31	Montreal Canadiens	Chicago Blackhawks	5
1931–32	Toronto Maple Leafs	New York Rangers	3
1932–33	New York Rangers	Toronto Maple Leafs	4
1933–34	Chicago Blackhawks	Detroit Red Wings	4
1934–35	Montreal Maroons	Toronto Maple Leafs	3
1935–36	Detroit Red Wings	Toronto Maple Leafs	4
1936–37	Detroit Red Wings	New York Rangers	5
1937–38	Chicago Blackhawks	Toronto Maple Leafs	4
1938–39	Boston Bruins	Toronto Maple Leafs	5
1939–40	New York Rangers	Toronto Maple Leafs	6
1940–41	Boston Bruins	Detroit Red Wings	4
1941–42	Toronto Maple Leafs	Detroit Red Wings	7
1942–43	Detroit Red Wings	Boston Bruins	4
1943–44	Montreal Canadiens	Chicago Blackhawks	4
1944–45	Toronto Maple Leafs	Detroit Red Wings	7
1945–46	Montreal Canadiens	Boston Bruins	5
1946–47	Toronto Maple Leafs	Montreal Canadiens	6
1947–48	Toronto Maple Leafs	Detroit Red Wings	4
1948–49	Toronto Maple Leafs	Detroit Red Wings	4
1949–50	Detroit Red Wings	New York Rangers	7
1950–51	Toronto Maple Leafs	Montreal Canadiens	5
1951–52	Detroit Red Wings	Montreal Canadiens	4
1952–53	Montreal Canadiens	Boston Bruins	5
1953–54	Detroit Red Wings	Montreal Canadiens	7
1954–55	Detroit Red Wings	Montreal Canadiens	7
1955–56	Montreal Canadiens	Detroit Red Wings	5
1956–57	Montreal Canadiens	Boston Bruins	5
1957–58	Montreal Canadiens	Boston Bruins	6
1958–59	Montreal Canadiens	Toronto Maple Leafs	5
1959–60	Montreal Canadiens	Toronto Maple Leafs	4
1960–61	Chicago Blackhawks	Detroit Red Wings	6
1961–62	Toronto Maple Leafs	Chicago Blackhawks	6
1962–63	Toronto Maple Leafs	Detroit Red Wings	5
1963–64	Toronto Maple Leafs	Detroit Red Wings	7
1964–65	Montreal Canadiens	Chicago Blackhawks	7
1965–66	Montreal Canadiens	Detroit Red Wings	6
1966–67	Toronto Maple Leafs	Montreal Canadiens	6
1967–68	Montreal Canadiens	St. Louis Blues	4
1968–69	Montreal Canadiens	St. Louis Blues	4
1969–70	Boston Bruins	St. Louis Blues	4
1970–71	Montreal Canadiens	Chicago Blackhawks	7
1971–72	Boston Bruins	New York Rangers	6
1972–73	Montreal Canadiens	Chicago Blackhawks	6
1973–74	Philadelphia Flyers	Boston Bruins	6
1974–75	Philadelphia Flyers	Buffalo Sabres	6
1975–76	Montreal Canadiens	Philadelphia Flyers	4
1976–77	Montreal Canadiens	Boston Bruins	4
1977–78	Montreal Canadiens	Boston Bruins	6
1978–79	Montreal Canadiens	New York Rangers	5
1979–80	New York Islanders	Philadelphia Flyers	6
1980–81	New York Islanders	Minnesota North Stars	5
1981–82	New York Islanders	Vancouver Canucks	4
1982–83	New York Islanders	Edmonton Oilers	4
1983–84	Edmonton Oilers	New York Islanders	5
1984–85	Edmonton Oilers	Philadelphia Flyers	5
1985–86	Montreal Canadiens	Calgary Flames	5
1986–87	Edmonton Oilers	Philadelphia Flyers	7
1987–88	Edmonton Oilers	Boston Bruins	4
1988–89	Calgary Flames	Montreal Canadiens	6
1989–90	Edmonton Oilers	Boston Bruins	5
1990–91	Pittsburgh Penguins	Minnesota North Stars	5
1991–92	Pittsburgh Penguins	Chicago Blackhawks	4
1992–93	Montreal Canadiens	Los Angeles Kings	5
1993–94	New York Rangers	Vancover Canucks	7
1994–95	New Jersey Devils	Detroit Red Wings	4

1. In the spring of 1919 the Montreal Canadiens traveled to Seattle to meet Seattle, champs of the Pacific Coast Hockey League. After five games had been played—teams were tied at 2 wins and 1 tie—the series was called off by the local Department of Health because of the influenza epidemic.

TOP 10 ALL-TIME NHL SCORING LEADERS

GOALS

Player	Seasons	Games	Goals	Goals/ Game
Wayne Gretzky[1]	16	1,173	814	.694
Gordie Howe	26	1,767	801	.453
Marcel Dionne	18	1,348	731	.542
Phil Esposito	18	1,282	717	.572
Mike Gartner[1]	16	1,208	625	.517
Bobby Hull	16	1,063	610	.574
Mike Bossy	10	752	573	.762
Jari Kurri[1]	14	1,028	566	.550
Guy Lafleur	17	1,126	560	.497
John Bucyk	23	1,540	556	.361

ASSISTS

Player	Seasons	Games	Assists	Assts./ Game
Wayne Gretzky[1]	16	1,173	1,692	1.442
Gordie Howe	26	1,767	1,049	.593
Marcel Dionne	18	1,348	1,040	.771
Paul Coffey[1]	15	1,078	978	.907
Stan Mikita	22	1,394	926	.664
Ray Bourque[1]	16	1,146	908	.792
Bryan Trottier	18	1,279	901	.704
Mark Messier[1]	16	1,127	877	.778
Phil Esposito	18	1,282	873	.681
Bobby Clarke	15	1,144	852	.745

POINTS

Player	Seasons	Games	Goals	Assists	Points
Wayne Gretzky[1]	16	1,173	814	1,692	2,458
Gordie Howe	26	1,767	801	1,049	1,850
Marcel Dionne	18	1,348	731	1,040	1,771
Phil Esposito	18	1,282	717	873	1,590
Stan Mikita	22	1,394	541	926	1,467
Bryan Trottier	18	1,279	524	901	1,425
Mark Messier[1]	16	1,127	492	877	1,369
John Bucyk	23	1,540	556	813	1,369
Guy Lafleur	17	1,126	560	793	1,353
Gilbert Perreault	17	1,191	512	814	1,326

Note: As of end of 1994–95 season. 1. Player active in 1994–95. **Source:** The National Hockey League.

NHL STANDINGS, 1994–95

EASTERN CONFERENCE

NORTHEAST DIVISION	W	L	T	Pts.
Quebec Nordiques	30	13	5	65
Pittsburgh Penguins	29	16	3	61
Boston Bruins	27	18	3	57
Buffalo Sabres	22	19	7	51
Hartford Whalers	19	24	5	43
Montreal Canadiens	18	23	7	43
Ottawa Senators	9	34	5	23

ATLANTIC DIVISION	W	L	T	Pts.
Philadelphia Flyers	28	16	4	60
New Jersey Devils	22	18	8	52
Washington Capitals	22	18	8	52
New York Rangers	22	23	3	47
Florida Panthers	20	22	6	37
Tampa Bay Lightning	17	28	3	37
New York Islanders	15	28	5	35

WESTERN CONFERENCE

CENTRAL DIVISION	W	L	T	Pts.
Detroit Red Wings	33	11	4	70
St. Louis Blues	28	15	5	61
Chicago Blackhawks	24	19	5	53
Toronto Maple Leafs	21	19	8	50
Dallas Stars	17	23	8	42
Winnipeg Jets	16	25	7	39

PACIFIC DIVISION	W	L	T	Pts.
Calgary Flames	24	17	7	55
Vancouver Canucks	18	18	12	48
San Jose Sharks	19	25	4	42
Los Angeles Kings	16	23	9	41
Edmonton Oilers	17	27	4	38
Anaheim Mighty Ducks	16	27	5	37

Note: Because of the hockey strike, each team played only 48 regular season games. **Source:** National Hockey League.

TOP 10 SCORERS, 1994–95

Player	Team	GP	G	A	Pts.
Jaromir Jagr	Pittsburgh	48	32	38	70
Eric Lindros	Philadelphia	46	29	41	70
Alexei Zhamnov	Winnipeg	48	30	35	65
Joe Sakic	Quebec	47	19	43	62
Ron Francis	Pittsburgh	44	11	48	59
Theoren Fleury	Calgary	47	29	29	58
Paul Coffey	Detroit	45	14	44	58
Mikael Renberg	Philadelphia	47	26	31	57
John LeClair	Philadelphia	46	26	28	54
Mark Messier	New York Rangers	46	14	39	53

Source: National Hockey League.

CONN SMYTHE TROPHY WINNERS, 1965–95

The Conn Smythe Trophy is an annual award "to the most valuable player for his team in the playoffs." The winner is selected by the Professional Hockey Writers' Association at the conclusion of the final game in the Stanley Cup Finals and receives $3,000.

Season	Player	Team
1965	Jean Béliveau	Montreal
1966	Roger Crozier	Detroit
1967	Dave Keon	Toronto
1968	Glenn Hall	St. Louis
1969	Serge Savard	Montreal
1970	Bobby Orr	Boston
1971	Ken Dryden	Montreal
1972	Bobby Orr	Boston
1973	Yvan Cournoyer	Montreal
1974	Bernie Parent	Philadelphia
1975	Bernie Parent	Philadelphia
1976	Reggie Leach	Philadelphia
1977	Guy Lafleur	Montreal
1978	Larry Robinson	Montreal
1979	Bob Gainey	Montreal
1980	Bryan Trottier	New York Islanders
1981	Butch Goring	New York Islanders
1982	Mike Bossy	New York Islanders
1983	Bill Smith	New York Islanders
1984	Mark Messier	Edmonton
1985	Wayne Gretzky	Edmonton
1986	Patrick Roy	Montreal
1987	Ron Hextall	Philadelphia
1988	Wayne Gretzky	Edmonton
1989	Al MacInnis	Calgary
1990	Bill Ranford	Edmonton
1991	Mario Lemieux	Pittsburgh
1992	Mario Lemieux	Pittsburgh
1993	Patrick Roy	Montreal
1994	Brian Leetch	New York Rangers
1995	Claude Lemieux	New Jersey

HART TROPHY WINNERS, 1924–95

The Hart Trophy is an annual award "to the player adjudged the most valuable to his team." The winner is selected in a poll of the Professional Hockey Writers' Association in the 21 NHL cities at the end of the regular schedule. The winner receives $3,000 and the runner-up $1,500.

Season	Player	Team
1924	Frank Nighbor	Ottawa Senators
1925	Billy Burch	New York Americans
1926	Nels Stewart	Montreal Maroons
1927	Herb Gardiner	Montreal
1928	Howie Morenz	Montreal
1929	Roy Worters	New York Americans
1930	Nels Stewart	Montreal Maroons
1931	Howie Morenz	Montreal
1932	Howie Morenz	Montreal
1933	Eddie Shore	Boston
1934	Aurel Joliat	Montreal
1935	Eddie Shore	Boston
1936	Eddie Shore	Boston
1937	Babe Siebert	Montreal
1938	Eddie Shore	Boston
1939	Toe Blake	Montreal
1940	Ebbie Goodfellow	Detroit
1941	Bill Cowley	Boston
1942	Tom Anderson	New York Americans
1943	Bill Cowley	Boston
1944	Babe Pratt	Toronto
1945	Elmer Lach	Montreal
1946	Max Bentley	Toronto
1947	Maurice Richard	Montreal
1948	Buddy O'Connor	N.Y. Rangers
1949	Sid Abel	Detroit
1950	Charlie Rayner	N.Y. Rangers
1951	Milt Schmidt	Boston
1952	Gordie Howe	Detroit
1953	Gordie Howe	Detroit
1954	Al Rollins	Toronto
1955	Ted Kennedy	Toronto
1956	Jean Béliveau	Montreal
1957	Gordie Howe	Detroit
1958	Gordie Howe	Detroit
1959	Andy Bathgate	N.Y. Rangers
1960	Gordie Howe	Detroit
1961	Bernie Geoffrion	Montreal
1962	Jacques Plante	Montreal
1963	Gordie Howe	Detroit
1964	Jean Béliveau	Montreal
1965	Bobby Hull	Chicago
1966	Bobby Hull	Chicago
1967	Stan Mikita	Chicago
1968	Stan Mikita	Chicago
1969	Phil Esposito	Boston
1970	Bobby Orr	Boston
1971	Bobby Orr	Boston
1972	Bobby Orr	Boston
1973	Bobby Clarke	Philadelphia
1974	Phil Esposito	Boston
1975	Bobby Clarke	Philadelphia
1976	Bobby Clarke	Philadelphia
1977	Guy Lafleur	Montreal
1978	Guy Lafleur	Montreal
1979	Bryan Trottier	N.Y. Islanders
1980	Wayne Gretzky	Edmonton
1981	Wayne Gretzky	Edmonton
1982	Wayne Gretzky	Edmonton
1983	Wayne Gretzky	Edmonton
1984	Wayne Gretzky	Edmonton
1985	Wayne Gretzky	Edmonton
1986	Wayne Gretzky	Edmonton
1987	Wayne Gretzky	Edmonton
1988	Mario Lemieux	Pittsburgh
1989	Wayne Gretzky	Los Angeles
1990	Mark Messier	Edmonton
1991	Brett Hull	St. Louis
1992	Mark Messier	N.Y. Rangers
1993	Mario Lemieux	Pittsburgh
1994	Sergei Federov	Detroit
1995	Eric Lindros	Philadelphia

ART ROSS TROPHY WINNERS, 1918–95

The Art Ross Trophy is an annual award "to the player who leads the league in scoring points at the end of the regular season." The overall winner receives $3,000, and the runner-up $1,500.

Season	Player	Team
1918	Joe Malone	Montreal
1919	Newsy Lalonde	Montreal
1920	Joe Malone	Quebec
1921	Newsy Lalonde	Montreal
1922	Punch Broadbent	Ottawa
1923	Babe Dye	Toronto
1924	Cye Denneny	Ottawa
1925	Babe Dye	Toronto
1926	Nels Stewart	Montreal Maroons
1927	Bill Cook	New York Rangers
1928	Howie Morenz	Montreal
1929	Ace Bailey	Toronto
1930	Cooney Weiland	Boston
1931	Howie Morenz	Montreal
1932	Harvey Jackson	Toronto
1933	Bill Cook	New York Rangers
1934	Charlie Conacher	Toronto
1935	Charlie Conacher	Toronto
1936	Dave Shriner	New York Americans
1937	Dave Shriner	New York Americans
1938	Gordie Drillon	Toronto
1939	Toe Blake	Montreal
1940	Milt Schmidt	Boston
1941	Bill Cowley	Boston
1942	Bryan Hextall	New York Rangers
1943	Doug Bentley	Chicago
1944	Herbie Cain	Boston
1945	Elmer Lach	Montreal
1946	Max Bentley	Chicago
1947	Max Bentley	Chicago
1948	Elmer Lach	Montreal
1949	Roy Conacher	Chicago
1950	Ted Lindsay	Detroit
1951	Gordie Howe	Detroit
1952	Gordie Howe	Detroit
1953	Gordie Howe	Detroit
1954	Gordie Howe	Detroit
1955	Bernie Geoffrion	Montreal
1956	Jean Béliveau	Montreal
1957	Gordie Howe	Detroit
1958	Dickie Moore	Montreal
1959	Dickie Moore	Montreal
1960	Bobby Hull	Chicago
1961	Bernie Geoffrion	Montreal
1962	Bobby Hull	Chicago
1963	Gordie Howe	Detroit
1964	Stan Mikita	Chicago
1965	Stan Mikita	Chicago
1966	Bobby Hull	Chicago
1967	Stan Mikita	Chicago
1968	Stan Mikita	Chicago
1969	Phil Esposito	Boston
1970	Bobby Orr	Boston

Season	Player	Team
1971	Phil Esposito	Boston
1972	Phil Esposito	Boston
1973	Phil Esposito	Boston
1974	Phil Esposito	Boston
1975	Bobby Orr	Boston
1976	Guy Lafleur	Montreal
1977	Guy Lafleur	Montreal
1978	Guy Lafleur	Montreal
1979	Bryan Trottier	New York Islanders
1980	Marcel Dionne	Los Angeles
1981	Wayne Gretzky	Edmonton
1982	Wayne Gretzky	Edmonton
1983	Wayne Gretzky	Edmonton
1984	Wayne Gretzky	Edmonton
1985	Wayne Gretzky	Edmonton
1986	Wayne Gretzky	Edmonton
1987	Wayne Gretzky	Edmonton
1988	Mario Lemieux	Pittsburgh
1989	Mario Lemieux	Pittsburgh
1990	Wayne Gretzky	Los Angeles
1991	Wayne Gretzky	Los Angeles
1992	Mario Lemieux	Pittsburgh
1993	Mario Lemieux	Pittsburgh
1994	Wayne Gretzky	Los Angeles
1995	Jaromir Jagr	Pittsburgh

JAMES NORRIS MEMORIAL TROPHY WINNERS, 1954–95

The James Norris Memorial Trophy is an annual award "to the defense player who demonstrates throughout the season the greatest all-round ability in the position." The winner is selected in a poll of the Professional Hockey Writers' Association at the end of the regular schedule. The winner receives $3,000, and the runner-up $1,500.

Season	Player	Team
1954	Red Kelly	Detroit
1955	Doug Harvey	Montreal
1956	Doug Harvey	Montreal
1957	Doug Harvey	Montreal
1958	Doug Harvey	Montreal
1959	Tom Johnson	Montreal
1960	Doug Harvey	Montreal
1961	Doug Harvey	Montreal
1962	Doug Harvey	New York Rangers
1963	Pierre Pilote	Chicago
1964	Pierre Pilote	Chicago
1965	Pierre Pilote	Chicago
1966	Jacques Laperrière	Montreal
1967	Harry Howell	New York Rangers
1968	Bobby Orr	Boston
1969	Bobby Orr	Boston
1970	Bobby Orr	Boston
1971	Bobby Orr	Boston
1972	Bobby Orr	Boston
1973	Bobby Orr	Boston
1974	Bobby Orr	Boston
1975	Bobby Orr	Boston
1976	Denis Potvin	New York Islanders
1977	Larry Robinson	Montreal
1978	Denis Potvin	New York Islanders
1979	Denis Potvin	New York Islanders
1980	Larry Robinson	Montreal
1981	Randy Carlyle	Pittsburgh
1982	Doug Wilson	Chicago
1983	Rod Langway	Washington
1984	Rod Langway	Washington
1985	Paul Coffey	Edmonton
1986	Paul Coffey	Edmonton
1987	Ray Bourque	Boston
1988	Ray Bourque	Boston
1989	Chris Chelios	Montreal
1990	Ray Bourque	Boston
1991	Ray Bourque	Boston
1992	Brian Leetch	New York Rangers
1993	Chris Chelios	Chicago
1994	Ray Bourque	Boston
1995	Paul Coffey	Detroit

VEZINA TROPHY WINNERS, 1927–95

The Vezina Trophy is an annual award "to the goalkeeper adjudged to be the best at his position" as voted by the general managers of the 21 clubs. The overall winner receives $3,000, and the runner-up $1,500.

Season	Player	Team
1927	George Hainsworth	Montreal
1928	George Hainsworth	Montreal
1929	George Hainsworth	Montreal
1930	Tiny Thompson	Boston
1931	Roy Worters	New York Americans
1932	Charlie Gardiner	Chicago
1933	Tiny Thompson	Boston
1934	Charlie Gardiner	Chicago
1935	Lorne Chabot	Chicago
1936	Tiny Thompson	Boston
1937	Normie Smith	Detroit
1938	Tiny Thompson	Boston
1939	Frank Brimsek	Boston
1940	Dave Kerr	New York Rangers
1941	Turk Broda	Toronto
1942	Frank Brimsek	Boston
1943	Johnny Mowers	Detroit
1944	Bill Durnan	Montreal
1945	Bill Durnan	Montreal
1946	Bill Durnan	Montreal
1947	Bill Durnan	Montreal
1948	Turk Broda	Toronto
1949	Bill Durnan	Montreal
1950	Bill Durnan	Montreal
1951	Al Rollins	Toronto
1952	Terry Sawchuk	Detroit
1953	Terry Sawchuk	Detroit
1954	Harry Lumley	Toronto
1955	Terry Sawchuk	Detroit
1956	Jacques Plante	Montreal
1957	Jacques Plante	Montreal
1958	Jacques Plante	Montreal
1959	Jacques Plante	Montreal
1960	Jacques Plante	Montreal
1961	Johnny Bower	Toronto
1962	Jacques Plante	Montreal
1963	Glenn Hall	Chicago
1964	Charlie Hodge	Montreal
1965	Terry Sawchuk	Toronto
	Johnny Bower	
1966	Lorne Worsley	Montreal
	Charlie Hodge	
1967	Glenn Hall	Chicago
	Denis Dejordy	
1968	Lorne Worsley	Montreal
	Rogie Vachon	
1969	Jacques Plante	St. Louis
	Glenn Hall	
1970	Tony Esposito	Chicago
1971	Ed Giacomin	N.Y. Rangers
	Gilles Villemure	
1972	Tony Esposito	Chicago
	Gary Smith	
1973	Ken Dryden	Montreal
1974	Bernie Parent	Philadelphia
	Tony Esposito	Chicago
1975	Bernie Parent	Philadelphia
1976	Ken Dryden	Montreal
1977	Ken Dryden	Montreal
	Michel Larocque	
1978	Ken Dryden	Montreal
	Michel Larocque	
1979	Ken Dryden	Montreal
	Michel Larocque	
1980	Bob Sauvé	Buffalo
	Don Edwards	
1981	Richard Sevigny	Montreal
	Denis Herron	
	Michel Larocque	
1982	Bill Smith	N.Y. Islanders
1983	Pete Peeters	Boston
1984	Tom Barrasso	Buffalo
1985	Pele Lindbergh	Philadelphia
1986	John Vanbiesbrouck	N.Y. Rangers
1987	Ron Hextall	Philadelphia
1988	Grant Fuhr	Edmonton
1989	Patrick Roy	Montreal
1990	Patrick Roy	Montreal
1991	Ed Belfour	Chicago
1992	Patrick Roy	Montreal
1993	Ed Belfour	Chicago
1994	Dominik Hasek	Buffalo
1995	Dominik Hasek	Buffalo

LADY BYNG TROPHY WINNERS, 1925–95

The Lady Byng Trophy is an annual award "to the player adjudged to have exhibited the best type of sportsmanship and gentlemanly conduct combined with a high standard of playing ability." The winner is selected in a poll of the Professional Hockey Writers' Association at the end of the regular schedule. The winner receives $3,000, and the runner-up $1,500.

Season	Player	Team
1925	Frank Nighbor	Ottawa
1926	Frank Nighbor	Ottawa
1927	Billy Burch	N.Y. Americans

Season	Player	Team
1928	Frank Boucher	New York Rangers
1929	Frank Boucher	New York Rangers
1930	Frank Boucher	New York Rangers
1931	Frank Boucher	New York Rangers
1932	Joe Primeau	Toronto
1933	Frank Boucher	New York Rangers
1934	Frank Boucher	New York Rangers
1935	Frank Boucher	New York Rangers
1936	Doc Romnes	Chicago
1937	Marty Barry	Detroit
1938	Gordie Drillon	Toronto
1939	Clint Smith	New York Rangers
1940	Bobby Bauer	Boston
1941	Bobby Bauer	Boston
1942	Syl Apps	Toronto
1943	Max Bentley	Chicago
1944	Clint Smith	Chicago
1945	Bill Mosienko	Chicago
1946	Toe Blake	Montreal
1947	Bobby Bauer	Boston
1948	Buddy O'Connor	New York Rangers
1949	Bill Quackenbush	Detroit
1950	Edgar Laprade	New York Rangers
1951	Red Kelly	Detroit
1952	Sid Smith	Toronto
1953	Red Kelly	Detroit
1954	Red Kelly	Detroit
1955	Sid Smith	Toronto
1956	Earl Reibel	Detroit
1957	Andy Hebenton	New York Rangers
1958	Camille Henry	New York Rangers
1959	Alex Delvecchio	Detroit
1960	Don McKenney	Boston
1961	Red Kelly	Toronto
1962	Dave Keon	Toronto
1963	Dave Keon	Toronto
1964	Ken Wharram	Chicago
1965	Bobby Hull	Chicago
1966	Alex Delvecchio	Detroit
1967	Stan Mikita	Chicago
1968	Stan Mikita	Chicago
1969	Alex Delvecchio	Detroit
1970	Phil Goyette	St. Louis
1971	John Bucyk	Boston
1972	Jean Ratelle	New York Rangers
1973	Gilbert Perreault	Buffalo
1974	John Bucyk	Boston
1975	Marcel Dionne	Detroit
1976	Jean Ratelle	New York Rangers-Boston
1977	Marcel Dionne	Los Angeles
1978	Butch Goring	Los Angeles
1979	Bob MacMillan	Atlanta
1980	Wayne Gretzky	Edmonton
1981	Rick Kehoe	Pittsburgh
1982	Rick Middleton	Boston
1983	Mike Bossy	N.Y. Islanders
1984	Mike Bossy	N.Y. Islanders
1985	Jari Kurri	Edmonton
1986	Mike Bossy	New York Islanders
1987	Joe Mullen	Calgary
1988	Mats Naslund	Montreal
1989	Joe Mullen	Calgary
1990	Brett Hull	St. Louis
1991	Wayne Gretzky	Los Angeles
1992	Wayne Gretzky	Los Angeles
1993	Pierre Turgeon	New York Islanders
1994	Wayne Gretzky	Los Angeles
1995	Ron Francis	Pittsburgh

CALDER MEMORIAL TROPHY WINNERS, 1933–95

The Calder Memorial Trophy is an annual award "to the player selected as the most proficient in his first year of competition in the National Hockey League." The winner is selected in a poll of the Professional Hockey Writers' Association at the end of the regular schedule. The winner receives $3,000, and the runner-up $1,500.

Season	Player	Team
1933	Carl Voss	Detroit
1934	Russ Blinko	Montreal Maroons
1935	Dave Schriner	New York Americans
1936	Mike Karakas	Chicago
1937	Syl Apps	Toronto
1938	Cully Dahlstrom	Chicago
1939	Frank Brimsek	Boston
1940	Kilby MacDonald	New York Rangers
1941	Johnny Quilty	Montreal
1942	Grant Warwick	New York Rangers
1943	Gaye Stewart	Toronto
1944	Gus Bodnar	Toronto
1945	Frank McCool	Toronto
1946	Edgar Laprade	New York Rangers
1947	Howie Meeker	Toronto
1948	Jim McFadden	Detroit
1949	Pentti Lund	New York Rangers
1950	Jack Gelineau	Boston
1951	Terry Sawchuk	Detroit
1952	Bernie Geoffrion	Montreal
1953	Lorne Worsley	New York Rangers
1954	Camille Henry	New York Rangers
1955	Ed Litzenberger	Chicago
1956	Glenn Hall	Detroit
1957	Larry Regan	Boston
1958	Frank Mahovlich	Toronto
1959	Ralph Backstrom	Montreal
1960	Bill Hay	Chicago
1961	Dave Keon	Toronto
1962	Bobby Rousseau	Montreal
1963	Kent Douglas	Toronto
1964	Jacques Laperrière	Montreal
1965	Roger Crozier	Detroit
1966	Brit Selby	Toronto
1967	Bobby Orr	Boston
1968	Derek Sanderson	Boston
1969	Danny Grant	Minnesota
1970	Tony Esposito	Chicago
1971	Gilbert Perreault	Buffalo
1972	Ken Dryden	Montreal
1973	Steve Vickers	New York Rangers
1974	Denis Potvin	N.Y. Islanders
1975	Eric Vail	Atlanta
1976	Bryan Trottier	N.Y. Islanders
1977	Willie Plett	Atlanta
1978	Mike Bossy	N.Y. Islanders
1979	Bobby Smith	Minnesota
1980	Raymond Bourque	Boston
1981	Peter Stastny	Quebec
1982	Dale Hawerchuk	Winnipeg
1983	Steve Larmer	Chicago
1984	Tom Barrasso	Buffalo
1985	Mario Lemieux	Pittsburgh
1986	Gary Suter	Calgary
1987	Luc Robitaille	Los Angeles
1988	Joe Nieuwendyk	Calgary
1989	Brian Leetch	New York Rangers
1990	Sergei Makarov	Calgary
1991	Ed Belfour	Chicago
1992	Pavel Bure	Vancouver
1993	Teemu Selanne	Winnipeg
1994	Martin Brodeur	New Jersey
1995	Petr Forsberg	Quebec

FRANK J. SELKE TROPHY WINNERS, 1978–95

The Frank J. Selke Trophy is an annual award "to the forward who best excels in the defensive aspects of the game." The winner is selected in a poll of the Professional Hockey Writers' Association at the end of the regular schedule. The winner receives $3,000, and the runner-up $1,500.

Season	Player	Team
1978	Bob Gainey	Montreal
1979	Bob Gainey	Montreal
1980	Bob Gainey	Montreal
1981	Bob Gainey	Montreal
1982	Steve Kasper	Boston
1983	Bobby Clarke	Philadelphia
1984	Doug Jarvis	Washington
1985	Craig Ramsay	Buffalo
1986	Troy Murray	Chicago
1987	Dave Poulin	Philadelphia
1988	Guy Carbonneau	Montreal
1989	Guy Carbonneau	Montreal
1990	Rick Meagher	St. Louis
1991	Dirk Graham	Chicago
1992	Guy Carbonneau	Montreal
1993	Doug Gilmour	Toronto
1994	Sergei Federov	Detroit
1995	Ron Francis	Pittsburgh

Boxing

Although many governing bodies now issue and certify their own boxing championships, the three most widely accepted are the World Boxing Association (WBA), World Boxing Council (WBC), and the International Boxing Federation (IBF). Years given indicate the year the championship belt changed hands.

HEAVYWEIGHTS (over 195 lbs.)

Year(s)	Name
1882–92	John L. Sullivan
1892–97	James J. Corbett
1897–99	Robert Fitzsimmons
1899–1905	James J. Jeffries
1905–06	Marvin Hart
1906–08	Tommy Burns
1908–15	Jack Johnson
1915–19	Jess Willard
1919–26	Jack Dempsey
1926–28	Gene Tunney[1]
1928–30	Vacant
1930–32	Max Schmeling
1932–33	Jack Sharkey
1933–34	Primo Carnera
1934–35	Max Baer
1935–37	James J. Braddock
1937–49	Joe Louis[1]
1949–51	Ezzard Charles
1951–52	Joe Walcott
1952–56	Rocky Marciano[1]
1956–59	Floyd Patterson
1959–60	Ingemar Johansson
1960–62	Floyd Patterson
1962–64	Sonny Liston
1964–67	Cassius Clay[1] (Muhammad Ali)
1970–73	Joe Frazier
1973–74	George Foreman
1974–78	Muhammad Ali
1978–79	Leon Spinks, Muhammad Ali[1]
1978	Ken Norton (WBC), Larry Holmes (WBC)
1979	John Tate (WBA)
1980	Mike Weaver (WBA)
1982	Michael Dokes (WBA)
1983	Gerrie Coetzee (WBA)
1984	Tim Witherspoon (WBC), Pinklon Thomas (WBC), Greg Page (WBA)
1985	Tony Tubbs (WBA)
1986	Tim Witherspoon (WBA), Trevor Berbick (WBC), Mike Tyson (WBC), James "Bonecrusher" Smith (WBA)
1987–89	Mike Tyson
1990	Buster Douglas, Evander Holyfield
1991–92	Evander Holyfield
1993	Riddick Bowe, Lennox Lewis (WBC)
1994	Michael Moorer (WBA, IBF), Oliver McCall (WBC)
1995	George Foreman (WBA, IBF), Bruce Seldon (WBA)

CURRENT BOXING CHAMPIONS

Class	WBA	WBC	IBF
Heavyweight	Bruce Seldon, United States	Oliver McCall, United States	George Foreman, United States
Cruiserweight	Orlin Norris, United States	Anaclet Wamba, France	Alfred Cole, United States
Light heavyweight	Virgil Hill, United States	Fabrice Tiozzo, France	Henry Maske, Germany
Supermiddleweight	Frank Liles, United States	Nigel Benn, Great Britain	Roy Jones, United States
Middleweight	Jorge Castro, Argentina	Julian Jackson, Virgin Islands	Bernard Hopkins, United States
Junior middleweight	Carl Daniels, United States	Luis Santana, Dominican Republic	Vincent Pettway, United States
Welterweight	Ike Quartey, Ghana	Pernell Whitaker, United States	Felix Trinidad, Puerto Rico
Junior welterweight	Frankie Randall, United States	Jualio Cesar Chavez, Mexico	Kosta Tszyu, Australia
Lightweight	Orzubek Nazarov, Japan	Miguel Angel Gonzalez, Mexico	Oscar de la Hoya, United States
Junior lightweight	Genaro Hernández, United States	Gabriel Ruelas, United States	Ed Hopson, United States
Featherweight	Eloy Rojas, Venezuela	Alejandro Gonzalez, Mexico	Tom Johnson, United States
Junior featherweight	Antonio Cermeno, Venezuela	Hector Acero-Sanchez, Mexico	Vuyani Bungu, South Africa
Bantamweight	Daorung Petroleum, Thailand	Yasuei Yakushiji, Japan	Mbulelo Botile, South Africa
Flyweight	San Sow Ploenchit, Thailand	Yuri Arbachakov, Russia	Danny Romero, United States

Note: As of July 1995. **Source:** *Ring Magazine.*

LIGHT HEAVYWEIGHTS (175–194 lbs.)

Year(s)	Name
1903	Jack Root, George Gardner
1903–05	Bob Fitzsimmons
1905–12	Philadelphia Jack O'Brien[1]
1912–16	Jack Dillon
1916–20	Battling Levinsky
1920–22	Georges Carpentier
1922–23	Battling Siki
1923–25	Mike McTigue
1925–26	Paul Berlenbach
1926–27	Jack Delaney[1]
1927–29	Tommy Loughran[1]
1930–34	Maxie Rosenbloom
1934–35	Bob Olin
1935–39	John Henry Lewis[1]
1939	Melio Bettina
1939–41	Billy Conn[1]
1941	Anton Christoforidis
1941–48	Gus Lesnevich, Freddie Mills
1948–50	Freddie Mills
1950–52	Joey Maxim
1952–60	Archie Moore
1961–62	Vacant
1962–63	Harold Johnson
1963–65	Willie Pastrano
1965–66	Jose Torres
1966–68	Dick Tiger
1968–74	Bob Foster,[1] John Conteh (WBA)
1975–77	John Conteh (WBC), Miguel Cuello (WBC), Victor Galindez (WBA)
1978	Mike Rossman (WBA), Mate Parlov (WBC), Marvin Johnson (WBC)
1979	Victor Galindez (WBA), Matthew Saad Muhammad (WBC)
1980	Eddie Mustava Muhammad (WBA)
1981	Michael Spinks (WBA), Dwight Braxton (WBC)
1983	Michael Spinks undisputed
1986	Marvin Johnson (WBA), Dennis Andries (WBC)
1987	Thomas Hearns (WBC), Leslie Stewart (WBA), Virgil Hill (WBA), Don Lalonde (WBC)
1988	Ray Leonard (WBC)[2], Dennis Andries
1989	Virgil Hill (WBA), Jeff Harding (WBC)
1990	Dennis Andries (WBC), Prince Charles Williams (IBF)
1991	Thomas Hearns (WBA)
1992	Jeff Harding (WBC)
1993	Bobby Czyz (WBA), Henry Maske (IBF), Mike McCallum (WBC)
1995	Fabrice Tiozzo (WBC)

MIDDLEWEIGHTS (160–174 lbs.)

Year(s)	Name
1884–91	Jack "Nonpareil" Dempsey
1891–97	Bob Fitzsimmons[2]
1897–1907	Tommy Ryan[2]
1907–08	Stanley Ketchel, Billy Papke

Year(s)	Name
1908–10	Stanley Ketchel
1911–13	Vacant
1913	Frank Klaus, George Chip
1914–17	Al McCoy
1917–20	Mike O'Dowd
1920–23	Johnny Wilson
1923–26	Harry Greb
1926–31	Tiger Flowers, Mickey Walker
1931–32	Gorilla Jones (NBA)
1932–37	Marcel Thil
1938	Al Hostak (NBA), Solly Krieger (NBA)
1939–40	Al Hostak (NBA)
1941–47	Tony Zale
1947–48	Rocky Graziano
1948	Tony Zale, Marcel Cerdan
1949–51	Jake LaMotta
1951	Ray Robinson, Randy Turpin, Ray Robinson[2]
1953–55	Carl "Bobo" Olson
1955–57	Ray Robinson
1957	Gene Fullmer (NBA), Ray Robinson, Carmen Basilio
1958	Ray Robinson
1959	Gene Fullmer (NBA), Ray Robinson (N.Y.)
1960	Gene Fullmer (NBA), Paul Pender (N.Y. & Mass.)
1961	Gene Fullmer (NBA), Terry Downes (N.Y., Mass., and Europe)
1962	Gene Fullmer (NBA), Dick Tiger (NBA), Paul Pender (N.Y. and Mass.)
1963	Dick Tiger
1963–65	Joey Giardello
1965–66	Dick Tiger
1966–67	Emile Griffith
1967	Nino Benvenuti
1967–68	Emile Griffith
1968–70	Nino Benvenuti
1970–77	Carlos Monzon
1977–78	Rodrigo Valdez
1978–79	Hugo Corro
1979–80	Alan Minter, Marvin Hagler
1987	Ray Leonard[2] (WBC), Thomas Hearns (WBC), Sumbo Kalambay (WBA)
1988	Iran Barkley (WBC)
1989	Sumbo Kalambay (WBA), Mike McCallum (WBA), Roberto Duran (WBC)
1990	Julian Jackson (WBC), James Toney (IBF)
1991	Reggie Johnson (WBA)
1993	Gerald McClellan (WBC), John David Jackson (WBA), Roy Jones (IBF)
1995	Jorge Castro (WBA), Julian Jackson (WBC), Bernard Hopkins (IBF)

WELTERWEIGHTS (147–153 lbs.)

Year(s)	Name
1892–94	Billy Smith
1894–96	Tommy Ryan
1896	Kid McCoy[2]
1900	Rube Ferns, Matty Matthews
1901	Rube Ferns
1901–04	Joe Walcott
1904–06	Dixie Kid, Joe Walcott, Honey Mellody
1907–11	Mike Sullivan
1911–15	vacant
1915–19	Ted Lewis
1919–22	Jack Britton
1922–26	Mickey Walker
1926	Pete Latzo
1927–29	Joe Dundee
1929	Jackie Fields
1930	Jack Thompson, Tommy Freeman
1931	Tommy Freeman, Jack Thompson, Lou Brouillard
1932	Jackie Fields
1933	Young Corbett, Jimmy McLarnin
1934	Barney Ross, Jimmy McLarnin
1935–38	Barney Ross
1938–40	Henry Armstrong
1940–41	Fritzie Zivic
1941–46	Fred Cochrane
1946	Marty Servo,[2] Ray Robinson
1946–50	Ray Robinson[2]
1951	Johnny Bratton (NBA)
1951–54	Kid Gavilan
1954–55	Johnny Saxton
1955	Tony De Marco, Carmen Basilio
1956	Carmen Basilio, Johnny Saxton, Carmen Basilio
1957	Carmen Basilio[2]
1958–60	Virgil Akins, Don Jordan
1960	Benny Paret
1961	Emile Griffith, Benny Paret
1962	Emile Griffith
1963	Luis Rodriguez, Emile Griffith
1964–66	Emile Griffith[2]
1966–69	Curtis Cokes
1969–70	Jose Napoles, Billy Backus
1971–75	Jose Napoles
1975–76	John Stracey (WBC), Angel Espada (WBA)
1976–79	Carlos Palomino (WBC), Jose Cuevas (WBA)
1979	Wilfredo Benitez (WBC), Sugar Ray Leonard (WBC)
1980	Roberto Duran (WBC), Thomas Hearns (WBA) Sugar Ray Leonard (WBC)
1981–82	Sugar Ray Leonard[2]
1983	Donald Curry (WBA), Milton McCrory (WBC)
1985	Donald Curry
1986	Lloyd Honeyghan (WBC)
1987	Mark Breland (WBA), Marlon Starling (WBA), Jorge Vaca (WBC)
1988	Thomas Molinares (WBA), Lloyd Honeyghan (WBC)
1989	Thomas Molinares (WBA),[1] Mark Breland (WBA), Marlon Starling (WBC)
1990	Aaron Davis (WBA), Maurice Blocker (WBC), Meldrick Taylor (WBA)
1991	Simon Brown (WBC, IBF), James McGirt (WBC)
1992	James McGirt (WBC)
1993	Crisanto España (WBA), Pernell Whitaker (WBC), Maurice Blocker (IBF)
1994	Felix Trinidad (IBF)
1995	Ike Quartey (WBA)

LIGHTWEIGHTS (131–135 lbs.)

Year(s)	Name
1896–99	Kid Lavigne
1899–1902	Frank Erne
1902–08	Joe Gans
1908–10	Battling Nelson
1910–12	Ad Wolgast
1912–14	Willie Ritchie
1914–17	Freddie Welsh
1917–25	Benny Leonard[2]
1925	Jimmy Goodrich, Rocky Kansas
1926–30	Sammy Mandell
1930	Al Singer, Tony Canzoneri
1930–33	Tony Canzoneri
1933–35	Barney Ross[2]
1935–36	Tony Canzoneri
1936–38	Lou Ambers
1938	Henry Armstrong
1939	Lou Ambers
1940	Lew Jenkins
1941–43	Sammy Angott
1944	Sammy Angott (NBA), J. Zurita (NBA)
1945–51	Ike Williams
1951–52	James Carter
1952	Lauro Salas, James Carter
1953–54	James Carter
1954	Paddy De Marco, James Carter
1955	James Carter, Bud Smith
1956	Bud Smith, Joe Brown
1956–62	Joe Brown
1962–65	Carlos Ortiz
1965	Ismael Laguna
1965–68	Carlos Ortiz
1968–69	Teo Cruz
1969–70	Mando Ramos
1970	Ismael Laguna, Ken Buchanan (WBA)
1971	Mando Ramos (WBC), Pedro Carrasco (WBC)
1972–79	Roberto Duran[1] (WBA)
1972	Pedro Carrasco, Mando Ramos, Chango Carmona, Rodolfo Gonzalez (all WBC)
1974–76	Guts Ishimatsu (WBC)
1976–77	Esteban De Jesus (WBC)
1979	Jim Watt (WBC), Ernesto Espana (WBA)
1980	Hilmer Kenty (WBA)
1981	Alexis Arguello (WBC), Sean O'Grady (WBA), Arturo Frias (WBA)
1982–84	Ray Mancini (WBA)
1983	Edwin Rosario (WBC)
1984	Livingstone Bramble (WBA), Jose Luis Ramirez (WBC)
1985	Hector (Macho) Camacho (WBC)
1986	Edwin Rosario (WBA), Jose Luis Ramirez (WBC)
1987	Julio Cesar Chavez (WBA)
1988	Julio Cesar Chavez[1] (WBA)
1989	Edwin Rosario (WBA)
1990	Juan Nazario (WBA), Pernell Whitaker
1991	Vacant (WBA, WBC, IBF)
1993	Orzubek (Gusshie) Nazarov (WBA), Miguel Angel Gonzalez (WBC), Fred Pendleton (IBF)
1994	Rafael Ruelas (IBF)
1995	Oscar de la Hoya (IBF)

FEATHERWEIGHTS (126–129 lbs.)

Year(s)	Name
1900–01	Terry McGovern, Young Corbett[2]
1901–12	Abe Attell
1912–23	Johnny Kilbane
1923	Eugene Criqui, Johnny Dundee
1923–25	Johnny Dundee[2]

Year(s)	Name
1925–27	Kid Kaplan[2]
1927–28	Benny Bass, Ton Canzoneri
1928–29	Andre Routis
1929–32	Battling Battalino[2]
1932–34	Tommy Paul
1933–36	Freddie Miller
1936–37	Petey Sarron
1937–38	Henry Armstrong[2]
1938–40	Joey Archibald
1940–41	Harry Jeffra
1942–48	Willie Pep
1948–49	Sandy Saddler
1949–50	Willie Pep
1950–57	Sandy Saddler[2]
1957–59	Hogan (Kid) Bassey
1959–63	Davey Moore
1963–64	Sugar Ramos
1964–67	Vicente Saldivar[2]
1968–71	Paul Rojas (WBA), Sho Saijo (WBA)
1971	Antonio Gomez (WBA), Kuniaki Shibada (WBC)
1972	Ernesto Marcel[2] (WBA), Clemente Sanchez[2] (WBC), Jose Legra (WBC)
1973	Eder Jofre (WBC)
1974	Ruben Olivares (WBA), Alexis Arguello (WBA), Bobby Chacon (WBC)
1975	Ruben Olivares (WBC), David Kotey (WBC)
1976	Danny Lopez (WBC)
1977	Rafael Ortega (WBA)
1978	Cecillio Lastra (WBA), Eusebio Pedrosa (WBA)
1980	Salvador Sanchez (WBC)
1982	Juan LaPorte (WBC)
1984	Wilfredo Gomez (WBC), Azumah Nelson (WBC)
1985	Barry McGuigan (WBA)
1986	Steve Cruz (WBA)
1987	Antonio Esparragoza (WBA)
1988	Jeff Fenech (WBC)
1990	Park Young-Kyun (WBA)
1991	Troy Dorsey (IBF)
1992	Paul Hodkinson (WBC), Manuel Medina (IBF)
1993	Gregorio Vargas (WBC), Tom Johnson (IBF)
1994	Kevin Kelley (WBC), Eloy Rojas (WBA)
1995	Alejandro Gonzalez (WBC)

Note: WBC = World Boxing Council; WBA = World Boxing Assn.; NBA = National Boxing Assn. IBF = International Boxing Federation. 1. Stripped of title. 2. Abandoned title. **Sources:** *KO* magazine; *Ring* magazine.

Bowling—Men

PBA LEADING MONEY WINNERS, 1959–94

Year	Name	Winnings
1959	Dick Weber	$ 7,672
1960	Don Carter	22,525
1961	Dick Weber	26,280
1962	Don Carter	49,972
1963	Dick Weber	46,333
1964	Bob Strampe	33,592
1965	Dick Weber	47,675
1966	Wayne Zahn	54,720
1967	Dave Davis	54,165
1968	Jim Stefanich	67,375
1969	Billy Hardwick	$ 64,160
1970	Mike McGrath	52,049
1971	Johnny Petraglia	85,065
1972	Don Johnson	56,648
1973	Don McCune	69,000
1974	Earl Anthony	99,585
1975	Earl Anthony	107,585
1976	Earl Anthony	110,833
1977	Mark Roth	105,583
1978	Mark Roth	134,500
1979	Mark Roth	124,517
1980	Wayne Webb	116,700
1981	Earl Anthony	164,735
1982	Earl Anthony	134,760
1983	Earl Anthony	135,605
1984	Mark Roth	158,712
1985	Mike Aulby	201,200
1986	Walter Ray Williams, Jr.	145,550
1987	Pete Weber	179,516
1988	Brian Voss	225,485
1989	Mike Aulby	298,237
1990	Auleto Monacelli	204,775
1991	David Ozio	225,585
1992	Marc McDowell	174,215
1993	Walter Ray Williams, Jr.	296,370
1994	Norm Duke	273,753

Professional Bowlers Association

The PBA was founded by 33 charter members who competed in three 1959 tournaments for prizes worth a total of $49,500. The traditional Winter Tour, which has been augmented and expanded into three separate seasonal tours, now pays more than $8 million in prize money.

Source: Professional Bowlers Assn.

Bowling—Women

LADIES PRO BOWLING TOUR (LPBT) LEADING CAREER MONEY WINNERS

Rank/Bowler	Winnings
1. Aleta Sill	$656,931
2. Tish Johnson	585,605
3. Lisa Wagner	575,442
4. Robin Romeo	512,539
5. Nikki Gianulias	477,557
6. Donna Adamok	473,984
7. Lorrie Nichols	460,841
8. Leanne Barrette	454,014
9. Anne Marie Duggan	413,929
10. Cindy Coburn-Carroll	389,516
11. Jeanne Naccarato	373,050
12. Dana Miller-Mackie	362,793
13. Cheryl Daniels	355,369
14. Wendy Macpherson	338,487
15. Carol Gianotti	337,056
16. Betty Morris	336,417
17. Dede Davidson	283,287
18. Pat Costello	253,281
19. Patty Costello	240,705
20. Michelle Mullen	223,097

Note: As of Dec. 19, 1994. **Source:** Ladies Pro Bowling Tour.

Automobile Racing

Indianapolis 500

A number of U.S. states and cities banned automobile racing on public roads during the early 1900s, leading to the development of closed-circuit courses. The Indianapolis Motor Speedway, a 2.5-mile macadam oval, was built in 1909 (it was paved with brick in 1911). The first Indy 500 was run two years later. The American Automobile Association, troubled by a series of fatal crashes, stopped sanctioning races, and in 1956, the United States Auto Club (USAC) took over the Indy 500.

INDY 500, 1911–95

Year	Winner	Time	MPH
UNDER AAA SANCTION			
1911	Ray Harroun	6:42:08	74.602
1912	Joe Dawson	6:21:06	78.719
1913	Juses Goux	6:35:05	75.933
1914	Rene Thomas	6:03:45	82.474
1915	Ralph DePalma	5:33:55	89.840
1916	Dario Resta	3:34:17[1]	84.001
1919	Howard Wilcox	5:40:42	88.050
1920	Gaston Chevrolet	5:38:32	88.618
1921	Tommy Milton	5:34:34	89.621
1922	Jimmy Murphy	5:17:30	94.484
1923	Tommy Milton	5:29:50	90.954
1924	L.L. Corum and Joe Boyer	5:05:23	98.234
1925	Peter DePaolo	4:56:39	101.127
1926	Frank Lockhart	4:10:14[2]	95.904
1927	George Souders	5:07:33	97.545
1928	Louis Meyer	5:01:33	99.482
1929	Ray Keech	5:07:25	97.585
1930	Billy Arnold	4:58:39	100.448
1931	Louis Schneider	5:10:27	96.629
1932	Fred Frame	4:48:03	104.144
1933	Louis Meyer	4:48:00	104.162
1934	William Cummings	4:46:05	104.863
1935	Kelly Petillo	4:42:22	106.240
1936	Louis Meyer	4:35:03	109.069
1937	Wilbur Shaw	4:24:07	113.580
1938	Floyd Roberts	4:15:58	117.200
1939	Wilbur Shaw	4:20:47	115.035
1940	Wilbur Shaw	4:22:31	114.277
1941	Floyd Davis and Mauri Rose	4:20:36	115.117
1946	George Robson	4:21:16	114.820
1947	Mauri Rose	4:17:52	116.338
1948	Mauri Rose	4:10:23	119.814
1949	Bill Holland	4:07:15	121.327
1950	Johnnie Parsons	2:46:55[3]	124.002
1951	Lee Wallard	3:57:38	126.244
1952	Troy Ruttman	3:52:41	128.922
1953	Bill Vukovich	3:53:01	128.740
1954	Bill Vukovich	3:49:17	130.840
1955	Bob Sweikert	3:53:59	128.209
UNDER USAC SANCTION			
1956	Pat Flaherty	3:53:28	128.490
1957	Sam Hanks	3:41:14	135.601
1958	Jim Bryan	3:44:13	133.791
1959	Rodger Ward	3:40:49	135.857
1960	Jim Rathmann	3:36:11	138.767
1961	A.J. Foyt, Jr.	3:35:37	139.131

Year	Winner	Time	MPH
1962	Rodger Ward	3:33:50	140.293
1963	Parnelli Jones	3:29:35	143.137
1964	A.J. Foyt, Jr.	3:23:35	147.350
1965	Jim Clark	3:19:05	150.686
1966	Graham Hill	3:27:52	144.317
1967	A.J. Foyt, Jr.	3:18:24	151.207
1968	Bobby Unser	3:16:13	152.882
1969	Mario Andretti	3:11:14	156.867
1970	Al Unser	3:12:37	155.749
1971	Al Unser	3:10:11	157.735
1972	Mark Donohue	3:04:05	162.962
1973	Gordon Johncock	2:05:26[4]	159.036
1974	Johnny Rutherford	3:09:10	158.589
1975	Bobby Unser	2:54:55[5]	149.213
1976	Johnny Rutherford	1:42:52[6]	148.725
1977	A.J. Foyt, Jr.	3:05:57	161.331
1978	Al Unser	3:05:54	161.363
1979	Rick Mears	3:08:47	158.899
1980	Johnny Rutherford	3:29:59	142.862
1981	Bobby Unser	3:35:41	139.084
1982	Gordon Johncock	3:05:09	162.029
1983	Tom Sneva	3:05:03	162.117
1984	Rick Mears	3:30:21	163.612
1985	Danny Sullivan	3:16:06	152.982
1986	Bobby Rahal	2:55:43	170.722
1987	Al Unser	3:04:59	162.175
1988	Rick Mears	3:27:10	144.809
1989	Emerson Fittipaldi	2:59:01	167.581
1990	Arie Luyendyk	2:41:18	185.984[7]
1991	Rick Mears	2:50:01	176.457
1992	Al Unser, Jr.	3:43:05	134.477
1993	Emerson Fittipaldi	3:10:50	157.207
1994	Al Unser, Jr.	3:06:29	160.872
1995	Jacques Villeneuve	3:15:18	153.616

1. 300 miles (scheduled). 2. 400 miles (rain). 3. 345 miles (rain). 4. 332.5 miles (rain). 5. 435 miles (rain). 6. 255 miles (rain). 7. Track record. **Source:** Indianapolis Motor Speedway Hall of Fame and Museum.

NASCAR

The National Association for Stock Car Auto Racing (NASCAR) first sponsored a Grand National championship in 1949. The 31 Winston Cup races, covering between 400 and 600 miles each, are contested on 17 designated speedways around the country.

WINSTON CUP WINNERS, 1959–94

Year	Driver	Points
1959	Lee Petty	11,792
1960	Rex White	21,164
1961	Ned Jarrett	27,272
1962	Joe Weatherly	30,836
1963	Joe Weatherly	33,398
1964	Richard Petty	40,252
1965	Ned Jarrett	38,824
1966	David Pearson	35,638
1967	Richard Petty	42,472
1968	David Pearson	3,499
1969	David Pearson	4,170
1970	Bobby Isaac	3,911
1971	Richard Petty	4,435
1972	Richard Petty	8,701
1973	Benny Parsons	7,173
1974	Richard Petty	5,037
1975	Richard Petty	4,783
1976	Cale Yarborough	4,644
1977	Cale Yarborough	5,000
1978	Cale Yarborough	4,841
1979	Richard Petty	4,830
1980	Dale Earnhardt	4,661
1981	Darrell Waltrip	4,880
1982	Darrell Waltrip	4,489
1983	Bobby Allison	4,667
1984	Terry Labonte	4,508
1985	Darrell Waltrip	4,292
1986	Dale Earnhardt	4,468
1987	Dale Earnhardt	4,696
1988	Bill Elliott	4,488
1989	Rusty Wallace	4,176
1990	Dale Earnhardt	4,430
1991	Dale Earnhardt	4,287
1992	Alan Kulwicki	4,078
1993	Dale Earnhardt	4,562
1994	Dale Earnhardt	4,694

Stock Car Racing

DAYTONA 500 WINNERS, 1959–95

Year	Driver	Avg. speed (mph)
1959	Lee Petty	135.521
1960	Junior Johnson	124.740
1961	Marvin Panch	149.601
1962	Fireball Roberts	152.529
1963	Tiny Lund	151.566
1964	Richard Petty	154.334
1965	Fred Lorenzen	141.539
1966	Richard Petty	160.627
1967	Mario Andretti	146.926
1968	Cale Yarborough	143.251
1969	LeeRoy Yarbrough	157.950
1970	Pete Hamilton	149.601
1971	Richard Petty	144.462
1972	A.J. Foyt, Jr.	161.550
1973	Richard Petty	157.205
1974	Richard Petty	140.894
1975	Benny Parsons	153.649
1976	David Pearson	152.181
1977	Cale Yarborough	153.218
1978	Bobby Allison	159.730
1979	Richard Petty	143.977
1980	Buddy Baker	177.602
1981	Richard Petty	169.651
1982	Bobby Allison	153.991
1983	Cale Yarborough	155.979
1984	Cale Yarborough	150.994
1985	Bill Elliott	172.265
1986	Geoff Bodine	148.124
1987	Bill Elliott	176.263
1988	Bobby Allison	137.531
1989	Darrell Waltrip	148.466
1990	Derrike Cope	165.761
1991	Ernie Irvan	148.148
1992	Davey Allison	160.260
1993	Dale Jarrett	154.972
1994	Sterling Marlin	156.931
1995	Sterling Marlin	141.710

Source: NASCAR.

Grand Prix Racing

The tradition of road racing in Formula One cars developed in Europe, with the French inaugurating the Grand Prix in 1906; the winner averaged about 12 miles per hour.

"Formula One" refers to certain weight and engine size restrictions intended to emphasize competitiveness and driving skill. The cars today are powered by rear-mounted, V-8 gasoline engines producing 450–475 horsepower, and can attain speeds of approximately 200 miles per hour.

FORMULA ONE CHAMPIONS, 1950–94

Year	Driver	Country	Car
1950	Giuseppe Farina	Italy	Alfa Roméo
1951	Juan Manuel Fangio	Argentina	Alfa Roméo
1952	Alberto Ascari	Italy	Ferrari
1953	Alberto Ascari	Italy	Ferrari
1954	Juan Manuel Fangio	Argentina	Mercedes/Maserati
1955	Juan Manuel Fangio	Argentina	Mercedes
1956	Juan Manuel Fangio	Argentina	Lancia/Ferrari
1957	Juan Manuel Fangio	Argentina	Maserati
1958	Mike Hawthorne	Great Britain	Ferrari
1959	Jack Brabham	Australia	Cooper Climax
1960	Jack Brabham	Australia	Cooper Climax
1961	Phil Hill	United States	Ferrari
1962	Graham Hill	Great Britain	BRM
1963	Jim Clark	Great Britain	Lotus Climax
1964	John Surtees	Great Britain	Ferrari
1965	Jim Clark	Great Britain	Lotus Climax
1966	Jack Brabham	Australia	Brabham Repco
1967	Denis Hulme	New Zealand	Brabham Repco
1968	Graham Hill	Great Britain	Lotus Ford
1969	Jackie Stewart	Great Britain	Matra Ford
1970	Jochen Rindt	Austria	Lotus Ford
1971	Jackie Stewart	Great Britain	Tyrrell Ford
1972	Emerson Fittipaldi	Brazil	Lotus Ford
1973	Jackie Stewart	Great Britain	Tyrrell Ford
1974	Emerson Fittipaldi	Brazil	McLaren Ford
1975	Niki Lauda	Austria	Ferrari
1976	James Hunt	Great Britain	McLaren Ford
1977	Niki Lauda	Austria	Ferrari
1978	Mario Andretti	United States	Lotus Ford
1979	Jody Scheckter	South Africa	Ferrari
1980	Alan Jones	Australia	Williams Ford
1981	Nelson Piquet	Brazil	Brabham Ford
1982	Keke Rosberg	Finland	Williams Ford
1983	Nelson Piquet	Brazil	Brabham BMW Turbo
1984	Niki Lauda	Austria	McLaren TAG Porsche Turbo
1985	Alain Prost	France	McLaren TAG Porsche Turbo
1986	Alain Prost	France	McLaren TAG Porsche Turbo
1987	Nelson Piquet	Brazil	Williams Honda Turbo
1988	Ayrton Senna	Brazil	McLaren Honda Turbo
1989	Alain Prost	France	McLaren Honda Turbo
1990	Ayrton Senna	Brazil	McLaren Honda Turbo
1991	Ayrton Senna	Brazil	McLaren Honda Turbo
1992	Nigel Mansell	England	Williams Renault
1993	Ayrton Senna	Brazil	McLaren Honda Turbo
1994	Michael Schumacher	Germany	Benetton

Thoroughbred Racing

The Triple Crown

KENTUCKY DERBY, 1900–1995

Site: Churchill Downs, Louisville, Kentucky
Distance: 1¼ miles

Year	Horse	Jockey	Time
1900	Lt. Gibson	J. Boland	2:06¼
1901	His Eminence	J. Winkfield	2:07¾
1902	Alan-a-Dale	J. Winkfield	2:08¾
1903	Judge Himes	H. Booker	2:09.0
1904	Elwood	F. Prior	2:08½
1905	Agile	J. Martin	2:10¾
1906	Sir Huon	R. Troxler	2:08.4
1907	Pink Star	A. Minder	2:12.3
1908	Stone Street	A. Pickens	2:15.1
1909	Wintergreen	V. Powers	2:08.1
1910	Donau	F. Herbert	2:06.2
1911	Meridan	G. Archibald	2:05.0
1912	Worth	C. H. Shilling	2:09.2
1913	Donerall	R. Goose	2:04.4
1914	Old Rosebud	J. McCabe	2:03.2
1915	Regret	J. Notter	2:05.2
1916	George Smith	J. Loftus	2:04.3
1917	Omar Khayyam	C. Borel	2:04.0
1918	Exterminator	W. Knapp	2:10.4
1919	Sir Barton	J. Loftus	2:09.4
1920	Paul Jones	T. Rice	2:09.0
1921	Behave Yourself	C. Thompson	2:04.1
1922	Morvich	A. Johnson	2:04.3
1923	Zev	E. Sande	2:05.2
1924	Black Gold	J.D. Mooney	2:05.1
1925	Flying Ebony	E. Sande	2:07.3
1926	Bubbling Over	A. Johnson	2:03.4
1927	Whiskery	L. McAtee	2:06.0
1928	Reigh Count	C. Lang	2:10.2
1929	Clyde Van Dusen	L. McAtee	2:10.4
1930	Gallant Fox	E. Sande	2:07.3
1931	Twenty Grand	C. Kurtsinger	2:01.4
1932	Burgoo King	E. James	2:05.1
1933	Brokers Tip	D. Meade	2:06.4
1934	Cavalcade	M. Garner	2:04.0
1935	Omaha	W. Saunders	2:05.0
1936	Bold Venture	I. Hanford	2:03.3
1937	War Admiral	C. Kurtsinger	2:03.1
1938	Lawrin	E. Arcaro	2:04.4
1939	Johnston	J. Stout	2:03.2
1940	Gallahadion	C. Bierman	2:05.0
1941	Whirlaway	E. Arcaro	2:01.2
1942	Shut Out	W.D. Wright	2:04.2
1943	Count Fleet	J. Longden	2:04.0
1944	Pensive	C. McCreary	2:04.1
1945	Hoop Jr.	E. Arcaro	2:07.0
1946	Assault	W. Mehrtens	2:06.3
1947	Jet Pilot	E. Guerin	2:06.3
1948	Citation	E. Arcaro	2:05.2
1949	Ponder	S. Brooks	2:04.1
1950	Middleground	W. Boland	2:01.3
1951	Count Turf	C. McCreary	2:02.3
1952	Hill Gail	E. Arcaro	2:01.3
1953	Dark Star	H. Moreno	2:02.0
1954	Determine	R. York	2:03.0
1955	Swaps	W. Shoemaker	2:01.4
1956	Needles	D. Erb	2:03.2
1957	Iron Liege	W. Hartack	2:02.1
1958	Tim Tam	I. Valenzuela	2:05.0
1959	Tommy Lee	W. Shoemaker	2:02.1
1960	Venetian Way	W. Hartack	2:02.2
1961	Carry Back	J. Sellers	2:04.0
1962	Decidedly	W. Hartack	2:00.2
1963	Chateaugay	B. Baeza	2:01.4
1964	Northern Dancer	W. Hartack	2:00.0
1965	Lucky Debonair	W. Shoemaker	2:01.1
1966	Kauai King	D. Brumfield	2:02.0
1967	Proud Clarion	R. Ussery	2:00.3
1968	Forward Pass[1]	R. Ussery	2:02.1
1969	Majestic Prince	W. Hartack	2:01.4
1970	Dust Commander	M. Manganello	2:03.2
1971	Canonero II	G. Avila	2:03.1
1972	Riva Ridge	R. Turcotte	2:01.4
1973	Secretariat	R. Turcotte	1:59.2[2]
1974	Cannonade	A. Cordero, Jr.	2:04.0
1975	Foolish Pleasure	J. Vasquez	2:02.0
1976	Bold Forbes	A. Cordero, Jr.	2:01.3
1977	Seattle Slew	J. Cruquet	2:02.1
1978	Affirmed	S. Cauthen	2:01.1
1979	Spectacular Bid	R. Franklin	2:02.2
1980	Genuine Risk	J. Vasquez	2:02.0
1981	Pleasant Colony	J. Velasquez	2:02.0
1982	Gato Del Sol	E. Delahoussaye	2:02.2
1983	Sunny's Halo	E. Delahoussaye	2:02.1
1984	Swale	L. Pincay	2:02.2
1985	Spend A Buck	A. Cordero, Jr.	2:00.1
1986	Ferdinand	W. Shoemaker	2:02.4
1987	Alysheba	C. McCarron	2:03.2
1988	Winning Colors	G. Stevens	2.02.2
1989	Sunday Silence	P. Valenzuela	2:05.0
1990	Unbridled	C. Perret	2:02.0
1991	Strike the Gold	C. Antley	2:03.0
1992	Lil E. Tee	P. Day	2:03.0
1993	Sea Hero	J. Bailey	2:02.2
1994	Go for Gin	C. McCarron	2:03.3
1995	Thunder Gulch	G. Stevens	2:01.1

Note: Race first run in 1875. Prior to 1896 the distance was 1½ miles. 1. In 1968 Dancer's Image finished first but was later disqualified from the purse money, and Forward Pass was declared winner. 2. Record.
Source: *Daily Racing Form.*

THE TRIPLE CROWN WINNERS

In more than 100 years, only 11 horses have won all three jewels of the triple crown, the Kentucky Derby, the Preakness, and the Belmont Stakes:

Horse	Year
Sir Barton	1919
Gallant Fox	1930
Omaha	1935
War Admiral	1937
Whirlaway	1941
Count Fleet	1943
Assault	1946
Citation	1948
Secretariat	1973
Seattle Slew	1977
Affirmed	1978

PREAKNESS STAKES, 1900–1995

Site: Pimlico Racetrack, Baltimore, Maryland
Distance: $1\frac{3}{16}$ miles

Year	Horse	Jockey	Time
1900	Hindus	H. Spencer	1:48.2
1901	The Parader	F. Landry	1:47.1
1902	Old England	L. Jackson	1:45.4
1903	Flocarline	W. Gannon	1:44.4
1904	Bryn Mawr	E. Hildebrand	1:44.1
1905	Cairngorm	W. Davis	1:45.4
1906	Whimsical	W. Miller	1:45.0
1907	Don Enrique	G. Mountain	1:45.2
1908	Royal Tourist	E. Dugan	1:46.2
1909	Effendi	W. Doyle	1:39.4
1910	Layminister	R. Estep	1:40.3
1911	Watervale	E. Dugan	1:51.0
1912	Colonel Holloway	C. Turner	1:56.3
1913	Buskin	J. Butwell	1:53.2
1914	Holiday	A. Schuttinger	1:53.4
1915	Rhine Maiden	D. Hoffman	1:58.0
1916	Damrosch	L. McAtee	1:54.4
1917	Kalitan	E. Haynes	1:54.2
1918	Jack Hare, Jr.	C. Peak	1:53.2
	War Cloud	J. Loftus	1:53.3
1919	Sir Barton	J. Loftus	1:53.0
1920	Man O' War	C. Kummer	1:51.3
1921	Broomspun	F. Coltiletti	1:54.1
1922	Pillory	L. Morris	1:51.3
1923	Vigil	B. Marinelli	1:53.3
1924	Nellie Morse	J. Merimee	1:57.1
1925	Coventry	C. Kummer	1:59.0
1926	Display	J. Maiben	1:59.4
1927	Bostonian	A. Abel	2:01.3
1928	Victorian	R. Workman	2:00.1
1929	Dr. Freeland	L. Schaefer	2:01.3
1930	Gallant Fox	E. Sande	2:00.3
1931	Mate	G. Ellis	1:59.0
1932	Burgoo King	E. James	1:59.4
1933	Head Play	C. Kurtsinger	2:02.0
1934	High Quest	R. Jones	1:58.1
1935	Omaha	W. Saunders	1:58.2
1936	Bold Venture	G. Woolf	1:59.0
1937	War Admiral	C. Kurtsinger	1:58.2
1938	Dauber	M. Peters	1:59.4
1939	Challedon	G. Seabo	1:59.4
1940	Bimelech	F. A. Smith	1:58.3
1941	Whirlaway	E. Arcaro	1:58.4
1942	Alsab	B. James	1:57.0
1943	Count Fleet	J. Longden	1:57.2
1944	Pensive	C. McCreary	1:59.1
1945	Polynesian	W.D. Wright	1:58.4
1946	Assault	W. Mehrtens	2:01.2
1947	Faultless	D. Dodson	1:59.0
1948	Citation	E. Arcaro	2:02.2
1949	Capot	T. Atkinson	1:56.0
1950	Hill Prince	E. Arcaro	1:59.1
1951	Bold	E. Arcaro	1:56.2
1952	Blue Man	C. McCreary	1.57.2
1953	Native Dancer	E. Guerin	1:57.4
1954	Hasty Road	J. Adams	1:57.2
1955	Nashua	E. Arcaro	1:54.3
1956	Fabius	W. Hartack	1:58.2
1957	Bold Ruler	E. Arcaro	1:56.1
1958	Tim Tam	I. Valenzuela	1:57.1
1959	Royal Orbit	W. Harmatz	1:57.0

Year	Horse	Jockey	Time
1960	Bally Ache	R. Ussery	1:57.3
1961	Carry Back	J. Sellers	1:57.3
1962	Greek Money	J. L. Rotz	1:56.1
1963	Candy Spots	W. Shoemaker	1:56.1
1964	Northern Dancer	W. Hartack	1:56.4
1965	Tom Rolfe	R. Turcotte	1:56.1
1966	Kauai King	D. Brumfield	1:55.2
1967	Damascus	W. Shoemaker	1:55.1
1968	Forward Pass	I. Valenzuela	1:56.4
1969	Majestic Prince	W. Hartack	1:55.3
1970	Personality	E. Belmonte	1:56.1
1971	Canonero II	G. Avila	1:54.0
1972	Bee Bee Bee	E. Nelson	1:55.3
1973	Secretariat	R. Turcotte	1:54.2
1974	Little Current	M. Rivera	1:54.3
1975	Master Derby	D. McHargue	1:56.2
1976	Elocutionist	J. Lively	1:55.0
1977	Seattle Slew	J. Cruguet	1:54.2
1978	Affirmed	S. Cauthen	1:54.2
1979	Spectacular Bid	R. Franklin	1:54.1
1980	Codex	A. Cordero, Jr.	1:54.1
1981	Pleasant Colony	J. Velasquez	1:54.3
1982	Aloma's Ruler	J. Kaenel	1:55.2
1983	Deputed Testamony	D. Miller	1:55.2
1984	Gate Dancer	A. Cordero, Jr.	1:53.3
1985	Tank's Prospect	P. Day	1:53.2
1986	Snow Chief	A. Solis	1:54.4
1987	Alysheba	C. McCarron	1:55.4
1988	Risen Star	E. Delahoussaye	1:56.1
1989	Sunday Silence	P. Valenzuela	1:53.4
1990	Summer Squall	P. Day	1:53.3
1991	Hansel	J. Bailey	1:54.0
1992	Pine Bluff	C.J. McCarron	1:55.3
1993	Prairie Bayou	M. Smith	1:56.2
1994	Tabasco Cat	P. Day	1:56.2
1995	Timber Country	P. Day	1:54.2

Note: Race first run in 1873. Distance varied from 1 mile 70 yds to 1⅛ miles until 1925. **Source:** *Daily Racing Form.*

BELMONT STAKES, 1900–1995

Site: Belmont Park, Elmont, New York
Distance: 1½ miles

Year	Horse	Jockey	Time
1900	Ildrim	N. Turner	2:21½
1901	Commando	H. Spencer	2:21.0
1902	Masterman	J. Bullman	2:22½
1903	Africander	J. Bullman	2:23.1
1904	Delhi	G. Odom	2:06.3
1905	Tanya	E. Hildebrand	2:08.0
1906	Burgomaster	L. Lyne	2:20.0
1907	Peter Pan	G. Mountain	No Time
1908	Colin	J. Notter	No Time
1909	Joe Madden	E. Dugan	2:21.3
1910	Sweep	J. Butwell	2:22.0
1913	Prince Eugene	R. Troxler	2:18.0
1914	Luke McLuke	M. Buxton	2:20.0
1915	The Finn	G. Byrne	2:18.2
1916	Friar Rock	E. Haynes	2:22.0
1917	Hourless	J. Butwell	2:17.4
1918	Johren	F. Robinson	2:20.2
1919	Sir Barton	J. Loftus	2:17.2
1920	Man O' War	C. Kummer	2:14.1
1921	Grey Lag	E. Sande	2:16.4
1922	Pillory	C. H. Miller	2:18.4
1923	Zev	E. Sande	2:19.0
1924	Mad Play	E. Sande	2:18.4
1925	American Flag	A. Johnson	2:16.4
1926	Crusader	A. Johnson	2:32.1
1927	Chance Shot	E. Sande	2:32.2
1928	Vito	C. Kummer	2:33.1
1929	Blue Larkspur	M. Garner	2:32.4
1930	Gallant Fox	E. Sande	2:31.1
1931	Twenty Grand	C. Kurtsinger	2:29.3
1932	Faireno	T. Malley	2:32.4
1933	Hurryoff	M. Garner	2:32.3
1934	Peace Chance	W.D. Wright	2:29.5
1935	Omaha	W. Saunders	2:30.3
1936	Granville	J. Stout	2:30.0
1937	War Admiral	C. Kurtsinger	2:28.3
1938	Pasteurized	J. Stout	2:29.2
1939	Johnstown	J. Stout	2:29.2
1940	Bimelech	F.A. Smith	2:29.3
1941	Whirlaway	E. Arcaro	2:31.0
1942	Shut Out	E. Arcaro	2:29.1
1943	Count Fleet	J. Longden	2:28.1
1944	Bounding Home	G.L. Smith	2:32.1
1945	Pavot	E. Arcaro	2:30.1
1946	Assault	W. Mehrtens	2:30.4
1947	Phalanx	R. Donoso	2:29.2
1948	Citation	E. Arcaro	2:28.1
1949	Capot	T. Atkinson	2:30.1
1950	Middleground	W. Boland	2:28.3
1951	Counterpoint	D. Gorman	2:29.0
1952	One Count	E. Arcaro	2:30.1
1953	Native Dancer	E. Guerin	2:28.3
1954	High Gun	E. Guerin	2:30.4
1955	Nashua	E. Arcaro	2:29.0
1956	Needles	D. Erb	2:29.4
1957	Gallant Man	W. Shoemaker	2:26.3
1958	Cavan	P. Anderson	2:30.1
1959	Sword Dancer	W. Shoemaker	2:28.2
1960	Celtic Ash	W. Hartack	2:29.3
1961	Sherluck	B. Baeza	2:29.1
1962	Jaipur	W. Shoemaker	2:28.4
1963	Chateaugay	B. Baeza	2:30.1
1964	Quadrangle	M. Ycaza	2:28.2
1965	Hail to All	J. Sellers	2:28.2
1966	Amberoid	W. Boland	2:29.3
1967	Damascus	W. Shoemaker	2:28.4
1968	Stage Door Johnny	H. Gustines	2:27.1
1969	Arts and Letters	B. Baeza	2:28.4
1970	High Echelon	J.L. Rotz	2:34.0
1971	Pass Catcher	W. Blum	2:30.2
1972	Riva Ridge	R. Turcotte	2:28.0
1973	Secretariat	R. Turcotte	2:24.0
1974	Little Current	M. Rivera	2:29.1
1975	Avatar	W. Shoemaker	2:28.1
1976	Bold Forbes	A. Cordero, Jr.	2:29.0
1977	Seattle Slew	J. Cruguet	2:29.3
1978	Affirmed	S. Cauthen	2:26.4
1979	Coastal	R. Hernandez	2:28.3
1980	Temperance Hill	E. Maple	2:29.4
1981	Summing	G. Martens	2:29.0
1982	Conquistador Cielo	L. Pincay	2:28.1
1983	Caveat	L. Pincay	2:27.4
1984	Swale	L. Pincay	2:27.1
1985	Creme Fraiche	E. Maple	2:27.0
1986	Danzig Connection	C. McCarron	2:29.4
1987	Bet Twice	C. Perret	2:28.1
1988	Risen Star	E. Delahoussaye	2:26.2
1989	Easy Goer	P. Day	2:26.0
1990	Go And Go	M. Kinane	2:27.1
1991	Hansel	J. Bailey	2:28.0
1992	A.P. Indy	E. Delahoussaye	2:26.0
1993	Colonial Affair	J. Krone	2:29.4
1994	Tabasco Cat	P. Day	2:26.4
1995	Thunder Gulch	G. Stevens	2:32.0

Note: Race first run in 1867. Distance varied until 1926. **Source:** *Daily Racing Form.*

HORSE OF THE YEAR (ECLIPSE AWARD)

Year	Horse	Year	Horse
1936	Granville	1966	Buckpasser
1937	War Admiral	1967	Damascus
1938	Seabiscuit	1968	Dr. Fager
1939	Challedon	1969	Arts and Letters
1940	Challedon	1970	Personality
1941	Whirlaway	1971	Ack Ack
1942	Whirlaway	1972	Secretariat
1943	Count Fleet	1973	Secretariat
1944	Twilight Tear	1974	Forego
1945	Busher	1975	Forego
1946	Assault	1976	Forego
1947	Armed	1977	Seattle Slew
1948	Citation	1978	Affirmed
1949	Capot	1979	Affirmed
1950	Hill Prince	1980	Spectacular Bid
1951	Counterpoint	1981	John Henry
1952	Native Dancer	1982	Conquistador Cielo
1953	Tom Fool	1983	All Along
1954	Native Dancer	1984	John Henry
1955	Nashua	1985	Spend a Buck
1956	Swaps	1986	Lady's Secret
1957	Bold Ruler	1987	Ferdinand
1958	Round Table	1988	Alysheba
1959	Sword Dancer	1989	Sunday Silence
1960	Kelso	1990	Criminal Type
1961	Kelso	1991	Black Tie Affair
1962	Kelso	1992	A.P. Indy
1963	Kelso	1993	Kotashaan
1964	Kelso	1994	Holy Bull
1965	Moccasin		

Source: The Jockey Club.

TOP FIVE JOCKEYS, BY EARNINGS, 1995

Jockey	Purses
1. Corey Nakatani	$11,891,226
2. Jerry Bailey	11,491,370
3. Gary Stevens	10,015,313
4. Mike Smith	8,580,614
5. Pat Day	8,338,956

1. Through Oct. 10, 1995. **Source:** *Daily Racing Form.*

THE BREEDERS' CUP

Billed as thoroughbred racing's most glamorous and exciting day of the year, these races (one for each standard category of sex, distance, and surface) attract the finest horses in the world, with unprecedented purses of $1–3 million per race. The site changes from year to year.

JUVENILE

Purse: $1 mil.; distance: 1 1/16 miles (1 mile, 1984–85, 1987–88).

Year	Winner	Jockey	Time
1984	Chief's Crown	Don MacBeth	1:36.1
1985	Tasso	Laffit Pincay, Jr.	1:36.1
1986	Capote	Laffit Pincay, Jr.	1:43.4
1987	Success Express	José Santos	1:35.1
1988	Is It True	Laffit Pincay, Jr.	1:36.3
1989	Rhythm	Craig Perret	1:43.3
1990	Fly So Free	José Santos	1:43.2
1991	Arazi	Pat Valenzuela	1:44.3
1992	Gilded Time	Chris McCarron	1:43.2
1993	Brocco	Gary Stevens	1:42.4
1994	Timber Country	Pat Day	1:44.2

JUVENILE FILLIES

Purse: $1 mil.; distance: 1 1/16 miles (1 mile in 1984, '85, '87).

Year	Winner	Jockey	Time
1984	Outstandingly	Walter Guerra	1:37.4
1985	Twilight Ridge	Jorge Velasquez	1:35.4
1986	Brave Raj	Pat Valenzuela	1:43.1
1987	Epitome	Pat Day	1:36.2
1988	Open Mind	Angel Cordero, Jr.	1:46.3
1989	Go For Wand	Randy Romero	1:44.1
1990	Meadow Star	José Santos	1:44.0
1991	Pleasant Stage	Ed Delahoussaye	1:46.2
1992	Eliza	Pat Valenzuela	1:42.4
1993	Phone Chatter	Laffit Pincay, Jr.	1:43.0
1994	Flanders	Pat Day	1:45.1

Source: Breeders' Cup Limited.

BREEDERS' CUP SPRINT

Purse: $1 mil.; distance: 6 furlongs.

Year	Winner	Jockey	Time
1984	Eillo	Craig Perret	1:10.1
1985	Precisionist	Chris McCarron	1:08.2
1986	Smile	Jacinto Vasquez	1:08.2
1987	Very Subtle	Pat Valenzuela	1:08.4
1988	Gulch	Angel Cordero, Jr.	1:10.2
1989	Dancing Spree	Angel Cordero, Jr.	1:09.0
1990	Safely Kept	Craig Perret	1:09.3
1991	Sheik Albadou	Pat Eddery	1:09.1
1992	Thirty Slews	Ed Delahoussaye	1:08.1
1993	Cardmania	Ed Delahoussaye	1:08.3
1994	Cherokee Run	Mike Smith	1:09.2

BREEDERS' CUP MILE

Purse: $1 mil.; distance: 1 mile, turf.

Year	Winner	Jockey	Time
1984	Royal Heroine	Fernando Toro	1:32.3
1985	Cozzene	Walter Guerra	1:35.0
1986	Last Tycoon	Yves Saint-Martin	1:35.1
1987	Miesque	Freddie Head	1:32.4
1988	Miesque	Freddie Head	1:38.3
1989	Steinlen	José Santos	1:37.1
1990	Royal Academy	Lester Piggott	1:35.1
1991	Opening Verse	Pat Valenzuela	1:37.2
1992	Lure	Mike Smith	1:32.4
1993	Lure	Mike Smith	1:33.2
1994	Barathea	Frankie Dettori	1:34.2

THE DISTAFF

Purse: $1 mil.; distance: 1⅛ miles. (1¼ miles before 1988.)

Year	Winner	Jockey	Time
1984	Princess Rooney	Ed Delahoussaye	2:02.2
1985	Life's Magic	Angel Cordero, Jr.	2:01.0
1986	Lady's Secret	Pat Day	2:01.1
1987	Sacahuista	Randy Romero	2:02.4
1988	Personal Ensign	Randy Romero	1:52.0
1989	Bayakoa	Laffit Pincay, Jr.	1:47.2
1990	Bayakoa	Laffit Pincay, Jr.	1:49.1
1991	Dance Smartly	Pat Day	1:50.4
1992	Paseana	Chris McCarron	1:48.0
1993	Hollywood Wildcat	Ed Delahoussaye	1:48.1
1994	One Dreamer	Gary Stevens	1:50.3

BREEDERS' CUP TURF

Purse: $2 mil.; distance: 1½ miles, turf.

Year	Winner	Jockey	Time
1984	Lashkari	Yves Saint-Martin	2:25.1
1985	Pebbles	Pat Eddery	2:27.0
1986	Manila	José Santos	2:25.2
1987	Theatrical	Pat Day	2:24.2
1988	Great Communicator	Roy Sibille	2:35.1
1989	Prized	Ed Delahoussaye	2:28.0
1990	In The Wings	Gary Stevens	2.29.3
1991	Miss Alleged	Eric Legrix	2:30.4
1992	Fraise	Pat Valenzuela	2:24.0
1993	Kotashaan	Kent Desormeaux	2:25.0
1994	Tikkanen	Mike Smith	2:26.2

CLASSIC

Purse: $3 mil.; distance: 1¼ miles.

Year	Winner	Jockey	Time
1984	Wild Again	Pat Day	2:03.2
1985	Proud Truth	Jorge Velasquez	2:00.4
1986	Skywalker	Laffit Pincay, Jr.	2:00.2
1987	Ferdinand	Bill Shoemaker	2:01.2
1988	Alysheba	Chris McCarron	2:04.4
1989	Sunday Silence	Chris McCarron	2:00.1
1990	Unbridled	Pat Day	2:02.1
1991	Black Tie Affair	Jerry Bailey	2:02.4
1992	A.P. Indy	Ed Delahoussaye	2:00.1
1993	Arcangues	Jerry Bailey	2:00.4
1994	Concern	Jerry Bailey	2:02.2

Harness Racing

HAMBLETONIAN WINNERS

Year	Horse	Driver	Best time	Heats	Purses
1926	Guy McKinney	N. Ray	2:04¾	2	$73,451
1927	Iosola's Worthy	M. Childs	2:03¾	2	54,694
1928	Spenser	W. H. Leese	2:03½	2	66,226
1929	Walter Dear	W. Cox	2:02¾	2	60,310
1930	Hanover's Bertha	T. Berry	2:03.0	3	56,860
1931	Calumet Butler	R. McMahon	2:03¼	3	50,921
1932	The Marchioness	W. Caton	2:01¼	4	48,339
1933	Mary Reynolds	B. White	2:03¾	3	40,461
1934	Lord Jim	H. M. Parshall	2:02¾	4	25,844
1935	Greyhound	S. Palin	2:02¼	2	33,321
1936	Rosalind	B. White	2:01¾	2	35,644
1937	Shirley Hanover	H. Thomas	2:01½	2	37,913
1938	McLin Hanover	H. Thomas	2:02¼	2	37,962
1939	Peter Astra	H. M. Parshall	2:04¼	2	40,502
1940	Spencer Scott	F. Egan	2:02.0	2	43,658
1941	Bill Gallon	L. Smith	2:05.0	3	38,730
1942	The Ambassador	B. White	2:04.0	2	38,854
1943	Volo Song	B. White	2:02½	3	42,298
1944	Yankee Maid	H. Thomas	2:04.0	2	34,427
1945	Titan Hanover	H. Pownall	2:04.0	2	51,047
1946	Chestertown	T. Berry	2:02½	3	51,846
1947	Hoot Mon	S. Palin	2:00.0	3	$ 46,268
1948	Demon Hanover	H. Hoyt	2:02.0	2	59,941
1949	Miss Tilly	F. Egan	2:01.2	2	69,791
1950	Lusty Song	D. Miller	2:02.0	2	75,209
1951	Mainliner	G. Crippen	2:02.3	2	95,264
1952	Sharp Note	B. Shively	2:02.3	3	87,638
1953	Helicopter	H. Harvey	2:01.3	3	117,118
1954	Newport Dream	A. Cameron	2:02.4	2	106,831
1955	Scott Frost	J. O'Brien	2:00.3	2	86,863
1956	The Intruder	W. Bower	2:01.2	3	100,604
1957	Hickory Smoke	J. Simpson, Sr.	2:00.1	5	111,126
1958	Emily's Pride	F. Nipe	1:59.4	3	106,719
1959	Diller Hanover	F. Ervin	2:01.1	2	125,283
1960	Blaze Hanover	J. O'Brien	1:59.3	4	444,590
1961	Harlan Dean	J. Arthur	1:58.2	2	131,573
1962	A.C.'s Viking	S. Russell	1:59.3	2	116,613
1963	Speedy Scot	R. Baldwin	1:57.3	3	115,549
1964	Ayres	J. Simpson, Jr.	1:56.4	2	115,281
1965	Egyptian Candor	A. Cameron	2:03.4	4	122,246
1966	Kerry Way	F. Ervin	1:58.4	2	122,540
1967	Speedy Streak	A. Cameron	2:00.0	2	122,650

Year	Horse	Driver	Best time	Heats	Purses
1968	Nevele Pride	S. Dancer	1:59.2	2	$116,190
1969	Lindy's Pride	H. Beissinger	1:57.3	2	124,910
1970	Timothy T.	J. Simpson, Jr.	1:58.2	3	143,620
1971	Speedy Crown	H. Beissinger	1:57.2	2	129,770
1972	Super Bowl	S. Dancer	1:56.2	2	119,090
1973	Flirth	R. Baldwin	1:57.1	2	144,710
1974	Christopher T.	W. Haughton	1:58.3	3	160,150
1975	Bonefish	S. Dancer	1:59.0	4	232,192
1976	Steve Lobell	W. Haughton	1:56.2	4	263,524
1977	Green Speed	W. Haughton	1:55.3	2	284,131
1978	Speedy Somolli	H. Beissinger	1:55.0	3	241,280
1979	Legend Hanover	G. Sholty	1:56.1	2	300,000
1980	Burgomeister	W. Haughton	1:56.3	3	293,570
1981	Shiaway St. Pat	R. Remmen	2:01.1	3	838,000
1982	Speed Bowl	T. Haughton	1:56.4	2	875,000
1983	Duenna	S. Dancer	1:57.2	2	$1,080,000
1984	Historic Freight	B. Webster	1:56.2	3	1,219,000
1985	Prakas	W. O'Donnell	1:54.3	2	1,272,000
1986	Nuclear Kosmos	J. Campbell	1:55.2	2	1,172,082
1987	Mack Lobell	J. Campbell	1:53.3	2	1,046,300
1988	Armbro Goal	J. Campbell	1:54.3	2	1,156,800
1989[1]	Park Ave Joe	R. Naples	1:55.3	3	565,500
	Probe	W. Fahy	1:54.3	3	282,750
1990	Harmonious	J. Campbell	1:54.1	2	1,346,000
1991	Giant Victory	J. Moiseyev	1:54.4	3	1,238,000
1992	Alf Palema	M. McNichol	1:56.3	3	1,380,000
1993	American Winner	R. Pierce	1:53.2	2	1,200,000
1994	Victory Dream	M. LaChance	1:53.4	2	1,000,000
1995	Tagliabue	J. Campbell	1:54.4	2	1,200,000

1. Cowinners. **Source:** U.S. Trotting Association.

Golf

MEN'S GOLF

No golfer has ever won the four major golf tournaments—the Masters, the U.S. Open, the British Open, and the PGA—in the same year. The player to come closest was Ben Hogan, who won the first three tournaments in 1953, but failed to capture the PGA championship. In fact, only four players have won each of golf's four major tournaments at least once over their entire careers: Hogan, Jack Nicklaus (who won each at least three times), Gary Player, and Gene Sarazen. A total of 10 different players have won two of the major tournaments in the same year, most recently Nick Price, who took the British Open and the PGA in 1994.

MASTERS

Year	Winner
1934	Horton Smith
1935	Gene Sarazen
1936	Horton Smith
1937	Byron Nelson
1938	Henry Picard
1939	Ralph Guldahl
1940	Jimmy Demaret
1941	Craig Wood
1942	Byron Nelson
1943–45	No tournament
1946	Herman Keiser
1947	Jimmy Demaret
1948	Claude Harmon
1949	Sam Snead
1950	Jimmy Demaret
1951	Ben Hogan
1952	Sam Snead
1953	Ben Hogan
1954	Sam Snead
1955	Cary Middlecoff
1956	Jack Burke, Jr.
1957	Doug Ford
1958	Arnold Palmer
1959	Art Wall, Jr.
1960	Arnold Palmer
1961	Gary Player
1962	Arnold Palmer
1963	Jack Nicklaus
1964	Arnold Palmer
1965–66	Jack Nicklaus
1967	Gay Brewer, Jr.
1968	Bob Goalby
1969	George Archer
1970	Billy Casper
1971	Charles Coody
1972	Jack Nicklaus
1973	Tommy Aaron
1974	Gary Player
1975	Jack Nicklaus
1976	Ray Floyd
1977	Tom Watson
1978	Gary Player
1979	Fuzzy Zoeller
1980	Seve Ballesteros
1981	Tom Watson
1982	Craig Stadler
1983	Seve Ballesteros
1984	Ben Crenshaw
1985	Bernhard Langer
1986	Jack Nicklaus
1987	Larry Mize
1988	Sandy Lyle
1989–90	Nick Faldo
1991	Ian Woosnam
1992	Fred Couples
1993	Bernhard Langer
1994	José María Olazábal
1995	Ben Crenshaw

Note: All Masters tournaments are held on the same course at the Augusta National Golf Club, Augusta, Ga.

U.S. OPEN

Year	Winner
1895	Horace Rawlins
1896	James Foulis
1897	Joe Lloyd
1898	Fred Herd
1899	Willie Smith
1900	Harry Vardon
1901	Willie Anderson
1902	Laurie Auchterlonie
1903–05	Willie Anderson
1906	Alex Smith
1907	Alex Ross
1908	Fred McLeod
1909	George Sargent
1910	Alex Smith
1911–12	John McDermott
1913	Francis Ouimet
1914	Walter Hagen
1915	Jerome Travers
1916	Charles Evans, Jr.
1917–18	No championship
1919	Walter Hagen
1920	Edward Ray
1921	James M. Barnes
1922	Gene Sarazen
1923	Robert T. Jones, Jr.
1924	Cyril Walker
1925	W. MacFarlane
1926	Robert T. Jones, Jr.
1927	Tommy Armour
1928	Johnny Farrell
1929–30	Robert T. Jones, Jr.
1931	Billy Burke
1932	Gene Sarazen
1933	Johynny Goodman
1934	Olin Dutra
1935	San Parks, Jr.
1936	Tony Manero
1937–38	Ralph Guldahl
1939	Byron Nelson
1940	Lawson Little
1941	Craig Wood
1942–45	No championship
1946	Lloyd Mangrum
1947	Lew Worsham
1948	Ben Hogan
1949	Cary Middlecoff
1950–51	Ben Hogan
1952	Julius Boros
1953	Ben Hogan
1954	Ed Furgol
1955	Jack Fleck
1956	Cary Middlecoff
1957	Dick Mayer
1958	Tommy Bolt
1959	Billy Casper
1960	Arnold Palmer
1961	Gene Littler
1962	Jack Nicklaus
1963	Julius Boros
1964	Ken Venturi
1965	Gary Player
1966	Billy Casper
1967	Jack Nicklaus
1968	Lee Trevino
1969	Orville Moody
1970	Tony Jacklin
1971	Lee Trevino
1972	Jack Nicklaus
1973	Johnny Miller
1974	Hale Irwin
1975	Lou Graham
1976	Jerry Pate
1977	Hubert Green
1978	Andy North
1979	Hale Irwin
1980	Jack Nicklaus
1981	David Graham
1982	Tom Watson
1983	Larry Nelson
1984	Fuzzy Zoeller
1985	Andy North
1986	Ray Floyd
1987	Scott Simpson
1988–89	Curtis Strange
1990	Hale Irwin
1991	Payne Stewart
1992	Tom Kite
1993	Lee Janzen
1994	Ernie Els
1995	Corey Pavin

BRITISH OPEN

Year	Winner	Year	Winner
1860	Willie Park	1931	Tommy D. Armour
1861–62	Tom Morris, Sr.	1932	Gene Sarazen
1863	Willie Park	1933	Denny Shute
1864	Tom Morris, Sr.	1934	Henry Cotton
1865	Andrew Strath	1935	Alfred Perry
1866	Willie Park	1936	Alfred Padgham
1867	Tom Morris, Sr.	1937	Henry Cotton
1868–70	Tom Morris, Jr.	1938	R.A. Whitcombe
1871	No championship	1939	Richard Burton
1872	Tom Morris, Jr.	1940–45	No championship
1873	Tom Kidd	1946	Sam Snead
1874	Mungo Park	1947	Fred Daly
1875	Willie Park	1948	Henry Cotton
1876	Bob Martin	1949–50	Bobby Locke
1877–79	Jamie Anderson	1951	Max Faulkner
1880–82	Robert Ferguson	1952	Bobby Locke
1883	Willie Fernie	1953	Ben Hogan
1884	Jack Simpson	1954–56	Peter Thomson
1885	Bob Martin	1957	Bobby Locke
1886	David Brown	1958	Peter Thomson
1887	Willie Park, Jr.	1959	Gary Player
1888	Jack Burns	1960	Ken Nagle
1889	Willie Park, Jr.	1961–62	Arnold Palmer
1890	John Ball	1963	Bob Charles
1891	Hugh Kirkaldy	1964	Tony Lema
1892[1]	Harold H. Hilton	1965	Peter Thomson
1893	William Auchterlonie	1966	Jack Nicklaus
1894–95	John H. Taylor	1967	Roberto DeVicenzo
1896	Harry Vardon	1968	Gary Player
1897	Harold H. Hilton	1969	Tony Jacklin
1898–99	Harry Vardon	1970	Jack Nicklaus
1900	John H. Taylor	1971–72	Lee Trevino
1901	James Braid	1973	Tom Weiskopf
1902	Alexander Hord	1974	Gary Player
1903	Harry Vardon	1975	Tom Watson
1904	Jack White	1976	Johnny Miller
1905–06	James Braid	1977	Tom Watson
1907	Arnaud Massy	1978	Jack Nicklaus
1908	James Braid	1979	Seve Ballesteros
1909	John H. Taylor	1980	Tom Watson
1910	James Braid	1981	Bill Rogers
1911	Harry Vardon	1982–83	Tom Watson
1912	Edward ("Ted") Ray	1984	Seve Ballesteros
1913	John H. Taylor	1985	Sandy Lyle
1914	Harry Vardon	1986	Greg Norman
1915–19	No championship	1987	Nick Faldo
1920	George Duncan	1988	Seve Ballesteros
1921	Jock Hutchison	1989	Mark Calcavecchia
1922	Walter Hagen	1990	Nick Faldo
1923	Arthur G. Havers	1991	Ian Baker-Finch
1924	Walter Hagen	1992	Nick Faldo
1925	James M. Barnes	1993	Greg Norman
1926–27	Robert T. Jones, Jr.	1994	Nick Price
1928–29	Walter Hagen	1995	John Daly
1930	Robert T. Jones, Jr.		

1. Championship extended from 36 to 72 holes.

PGA

Year	Winner	Year	Winner
1916	James M. Barnes	1960	Jay Hebert
1917–18	No championship	1961	Jerry Barber
1919	James M. Barnes	1962	Gary Player
1920	Jock Hutchison	1963	Jack Nicklaus
1921	Walter Hagen	1964	Bobby Nichols
1922–23	Gene Sarazen	1965	Dave Marr
1924–27	Walter Hagen	1966	Al Geiberger
1928–29	Leo Diegel	1967	Don January
1930	Tommy Armour	1968	Julius Boros
1931	Tom Creavy	1969	Ray Floyd
1932	Olin Dutra	1970	Dave Stockton
1933	Gene Sarazen	1971	Jack Nicklaus
1934	Paul Runyan	1972	Gary Player
1935	Johnny Revolta	1973	Jack Nicklaus
1936–37	Denny Shute	1974	Lee Trevino
1938	Paul Runyan	1975	Jack Nicklaus
1939	Henry Picard	1976	Dave Stockton
1940	Byron Nelson	1977	Lanny Wadkins
1941	Vic Ghezzi	1978	John Mahaffey
1942	Sam Snead	1979	David Graham
1943	No championship	1980	Jack Nicklaus
1944	Bob Hamilton	1981	Larry Nelson
1945	Byron Nelson	1982	Raymond Floyd
1946	Ben Hogan	1983	Hal Sutton
1947	Jim Ferrier	1984	Lee Trevino
1948	Ben Hogan	1985	Hubert Green
1949	Sam Snead	1986	Bob Tway
1950	Chandler Harper	1987	Larry Nelson
1951	Sam Snead	1988	Jeff Sluman
1952	Jim Turnesa	1989	Payne Stewart
1953	Walter Burkemo	1990	Wayne Grady
1954	Chick Harbert	1991	John Daly
1955	Doug Ford	1992	Nick Price
1956	Jack Burke	1993	Paul Azinger
1957	Lionel Hebert	1994	Nick Price
1958	Dow Finsterwald	1995	Steve Elkington
1959	Bob Rosburg		

PGA LEADING CAREER MONEY WINNERS

Rank/Golfer	Earnings	Rank/Golfer	Earnings
1. Greg Norman	$9,493,579	6. Tom Watson	$7,072,113
2. Tom Kite	9,328,776	7. Paul Azinger	6,930,494
3. Payne Stewart	7,304,599	8. Corey Pavin	6,907,237
4. Nick Price	7,290,119	9. Curtis Strange	6,791,618
5. Fred Couples	7,178,321	10. Ben Crenshaw	6,787,885

Note: As of Sept. 10, 1994. **Source:** Professional Golfers' Association.

THE SENIOR PGA TOUR

The Senior Tour began with two tournaments in 1980, which offered a total of $250,000 in prize money to qualified PGA members over the age of 50. By 1984, the tour had spiraled to 24 tournaments with prize money totaling $5 million. The arrival in 1990 of Jack Nicklaus and Lee Trevino on the Senior Tour helped propel the 50-and-over circuit to unprecedented popularity, surpassing the Ladies' Professional Tour in both prize money and television ratings. That was also the year that Trevino became the first player to win more than $1 million in prize money on the Senior Tour.

LEADING MONEY WINNERS, 1934–94

Year	Name	Winnings
1934	Paul Runyan	$ 6,767
1935	Johnny Revolta	9,543
1936	Horton Smith	7,682
1937	Harry Cooper	14,138
1938	Sam Snead	19,534
1939	Henry Picard	10,303
1940	Ben Hogan	10,655
1941	Ben Hogan	18,358
1942	Ben Hogan	13,143
1943	No statistics compiled	
1944	Byron Nelson	37,967[1]
1945	Byron Nelson	63,335[1]
1946	Ben Hogan	42,556
1947	Jimmy Demaret	27,936
1948	Ben Hogan	32,112
1949	Sam Snead	31,593
1950	Sam Snead	$ 35,758
1951	Lloyd Mangrum	26,088
1952	Julius Boros	37,032
1953	Lew Worsham	34,002
1954	Bob Toski	65,819
1955	Julius Boros	63,121
1956	Ted Kroll	72,835
1957	Dick Mayer	65,835
1958	Arnold Palmer	42,607
1959	Art Wall	53,167
1960	Arnold Palmer	75,262
1961	Gary Player	64,540
1962	Arnold Palmer	81,448
1963	Arnold Palmer	128,230
1964	Jack Nicklaus	113,284
1965	Jack Nicklaus	140,752
1966	Billy Casper	$121,944
1967	Jack Nicklaus	188,998
1968	Billy Casper	205,168
1969	Frank Beard	164,707
1970	Lee Trevino	157,037
1971	Jack Nicklaus	244,490
1972	Jack Nicklaus	320,542
1973	Jack Nicklaus	308,362
1974	Johnny Miller	353,021
1975	Jack Nicklaus	298,149
1976	Jack Nicklaus	266,438
1977	Tom Watson	310,653
1978	Tom Watson	362,428
1979	Tom Watson	462,636
1980	Tom Watson	530,808
1981	Tom Kite	375,698
1982	Craig Stadler	$ 446,462
1983	Hal Sutton	426,668
1984	Tom Watson	476,260
1985	Curtis Strange	542,321
1986	Greg Norman	653,296
1987	Curtis Strange	925,941
1988	Curtis Strange	1,147,644
1989	Tom Kite	1,395,278
1990	Greg Norman	1,165,477
1991	Corey Pavin	979,430
1992	Fred Couples	1,344,188
1993	Nick Price	1,478,557
1994	Nick Price	1,499,927

1. Paid in war bonds. **Source:** Professional Golfers' Association.

WOMEN'S GOLF

LPGA CHAMPIONSHIP

Year	Winner
1955	Beverly Hanson
1956	Marlene Hagge
1957	Louise Suggs
1958	Mickey Wright
1959	Betsy Rawls
1960	Mickey Wright
1961	Mickey Wright
1962	Judy Kimball
1963	Mickey Wright
1964	Mary Mills
1965	Sandra Haynie
1966	Gloria Ehret
1967	Kathy Whitworth
1968	Sandra Post
1969	Betsy Rawls
1970	Shirley Englehorn
1971	Kathy Whitworth
1972	Kathy Ahern
1973	Mary Mills
1974	Sandra Haynie
1975	Kathy Whitworth
1976	Betty Burfeindt
1977	Chako Higuchi
1978	Nancy Lopez
1979	Donna Caponi
1980	Sally Little
1981	Donna Caponi
1982	Jan Stephenson
1983	Patty Sheehan
1984	Patty Sheehan
1985	Nancy Lopez
1986	Pat Bradley
1987	Jane Geddes
1988	Sherri Turner
1989	Nancy Lopez
1990	Beth Daniel
1991	Meg Mallon
1992	Betsy King
1993	Patty Sheehan
1994	Laura Davies
1995	Kelly Robbins

U.S. WOMEN'S OPEN

Year	Winner
1946	Patty Berg
1947	Betty Jameson
1948	Babe Zaharias
1949	Louise Suggs
1950	Babe Zaharias
1951	Betsy Rawls
1952	Louise Suggs
1953	Betsy Rawls
1954	Babe Zaharias
1955	Fay Crocker
1956	Kathy Cornelius
1957	Betsy Rawls
1958–59	Mickey Wright
1960	Betsy Rawls
1961	Mickey Wright
1962	Murle Lindstrom
1963	Mary Mills
1964	Mickey Wright
1965	Carol Mann
1966	Sandra Spuzich
1967	Catherine LaCoste
1968	Susie Berning
1969–70	Donna Caponi
1971	JoAnne Carner
1972–73	Susie Berning
1974	Sandra Haynie
1975	Sandra Palmer
1976	JoAnne Carner
1977–78	Hollis Stacy
1979	Jerilyn Britz
1980	Amy Alcott
1981	Pat Bradley
1982	Janet Anderson
1983	Jan Stephenson
1984	Hollis Stacy
1985	Kathy Baker
1986	Jane Geddes
1987	Laura Davies
1988	Liselotte Neumann
1989–90	Betsy King
1991	Meg Mallon
1992	Patty Sheehan
1993	Lauri Merten
1994	Patty Sheehan
1995	Annika Sorenstam

LPGA LEADING CAREER MONEY WINNERS

Rank/Name	Winnings
1. Betsy King	$5,357,022
2. Pat Bradley	5,107,310
3. Beth Daniel	4,935,597
4. Patty Sheehan	4,788,546
5. Nancy Lopez	4,257,973
6. Amy Alcott	3,135,772
7. Dottie Mochrie	3,055,716
8. JoAnne Carner	2,878,105
9. Ayako Okamoto	2,735,630
10. Rosie Jones	2,583,955
11. Jane Geddes	$2,564,673
12. Jan Stephenson	2,299,024
13. Meg Mallon	2,255,593
14. Colleen Walker	2,246,098
15. Juli Inkster	2,238,901
16. Laura Davies	2,148,652
17. Hollis Stacy	2,079,149
18. Judy Dickinson	2,013,921
19. Tammie Green	1,987,334
20. Danielle Ammaccapane	1,801,166

Note: As of Sept. 18, 1995. **Source:** Ladies' Professional Golfers' Association.

LEADING MONEY WINNERS, 1956–94

Year	Name	Winnings
1956	Marlene Bauer Hagge	$20,235
1957	Patty Berg	16,272
1958	Beverly Hanson	12,629
1959	Betsy Rawls	26,774
1960	Louis Euggs	16,892
1961	Mickey Wright	22,238
1962	Mickey Wright	21,654
1963	Mickey Wright	31,269
1964	Mickey Wright	29,800
1965	Kathy Whitworth	28,658
1966	Kathy Whitworth	33,517
1967	Kathy Whitworth	32,937
1968	Kathy Whitworth	48,379
1969	Carol Mann	49,152
1970	Kathy Whitworth	30,235
1971	Kathy Whitworth	41,181
1972	Kathy Whitworth	65,063
1973	Kathy Whitworth	82,864
1974	JoAnne Carner	87,094
1975	Sandra Palmer	76,374
1976	Judy T. Rankin	$150,734
1977	Judy T. Rankin	122,890
1978	Nancy Lopez	189,813
1979	Nancy Lopez	197,488
1980	Beth Daniel	231,000
1981	Beth Daniel	206,977
1982	JoAnne Carner	310,399
1983	JoAnne Carner	291,404
1984	Betsy King	266,771
1985	Nancy Lopez	416,472
1986	Pat Bradley	492,021
1987	Ayako Okamoto	466,034
1988	Sherri Turner	350,851
1989	Betsy King	654,132
1990	Beth Daniel	863,578
1991	Pat Bradley	763,118
1992	Dottie Mochrie	693,335
1993	Betsy King	595,992
1994	Laura Davies	687,201

Source: Ladies' Professional Golfers' Association.

Tennis

Modern, "open" tennis tournaments, in which both professionals and amateurs compete, began in 1968, when the four major grand slam tournaments opened their ranks to all players.

The Grand Slam: Only five players have won the French Open, the Australian Open, the United States Open, and Wimbledon in the same year. Don Budge became the first "grand slammer" in 1938. Maureen Connolly became the first woman winner in 1953 when she won straight set victories in all four final round matches. Australian Rod Laver won the Grand Slam in 1962 and 1969, making him the only repeat winner. Margaret Court swept through the tournaments in 1970. Steffi Graf became the youngest to accomplish the feat in 1988.

Men's Grand Slam Championships

AUSTRALIAN CHAMPIONSHIPS

Year	Winner	Year	Winner
1905	Rodney Heath	1952	Ken McGregor
1906	Tony Wilding	1953	Ken Rosewall
1907	Horace M. Rice	1954	Mervyn Rose
1908	Fred Alexander	1955	Ken Rosewall
1909	Tony Wilding	1956	Lew Hoad
1910	Rodney Heath	1957–58	Ashley Cooper
1911	Norman Brooks	1959	Alex Olmedo
1912	J. Cecil Parke	1960	Rod Laver
1913	E.F. Parker	1961	Roy Emerson
1914	Pat O'Hara Wood	1962	Rod Laver
1915	Francis G. Lowe	1963–67	Roy Emerson
1916–18	Not held	1968	Bill Bowrey
1919	A.R.F. Kingscote	1969[1]	Rod Laver
1920	Pat O'Hara Wood	1970	Arthur Ashe
1921	Rhys H. Gemmell	1971–72	Ken Rosewall
1922–23	Pat O'Hara Wood	1973	John Newcombe
1924–25	James Anderson	1974	Jimmy Connors
1926	John Hawkes	1975	John Newcombe
1927	Gerald Patterson	1976	Mark Edmondson
1928	Jean Borotra	1977	Roscoe Tanner
1929	John C. Gregory	1977	Vitas Gerulaitis
1930	Gar Moon	1978–79	Guillermo Vilas
1931–33	Jack Crawford	1980	Brian Teacher
1934	Fred J. Perry	1981–82	Johan Kriek
1935	Jack Crawford	1983–84	Mats Wilander
1936	Adrian Quist	1985	Stefan Edberg
1937	Vivian B. McGrath	1986	Not held; moved to Jan. 1987
1938	Don Budge		
1939	John Bromwich	1987	Stefan Edberg
1940	Adrian Quist	1988	Mats Wilander
1941–45	Not held	1989–90	Ivan Lendl
1946	John Bromwich	1991	Boris Becker
1947	Dinny Pails	1992–93	Jim Courier
1948	Adrian Quist	1994	Pete Sampras
1949–50	Frank Sedgman	1995	Andre Agassi
1951	Richard Savitt		

1. Became Open Championships (amateurs and professionals).

FRENCH CHAMPIONSHIPS

Year	Winner	Year	Winner
1925	Rene Lacoste	1931	Jean Borotra
1926	Henri Cochet	1932	Henri Cochet
1927	Rene Lacoste	1933	John H. Crawford
1928	Henri Cochet	1934	Gottfried von Cramm
1929	Rene Lacoste	1935	Fred J. Perry
1930	Henri Cochet	1936	Gottfried von Cramm

Year	Winner	Year	Winner
1937	Henner Henkel	1966	Tony Roche
1938	Don Budge	1967	Roy Emerson
1939	Donald McNeill	1968[1]	Ken Rosewall
1940	Not held	1969	Rod Laver
1941–42	Bernard Destremau	1970–71	Jan Kodes
1943–45	Yvon Petra	1972	Andres Gimeno
1946	Marcel Bernard	1973	Ilie Nastase
1947	Joseph Asboth	1974–75	Bjorn Borg
1948–49	Frank Parker	1976	Adriano Panatta
1950	Budge Patty	1977	Guillermo Vilas
1951–52	Jaroslav Drobny	1978–81	Bjorn Borg
1953	Ken Rosewall	1982	Mats Wilander
1954–55	Tony Trabert	1983	Yannick Noah
1956	Lew Hoad	1984	Ivan Lendl
1957	Sven Davidson	1985	Mats Wilander
1958	Mervyn Rose	1986–87	Ivan Lendl
1959–60	Nicola Pietrangeli	1988	Mats Wilander
1961	Manuel Santana	1989	Michael Chang
1962	Rod Laver	1990	Andrés Gómez
1963	Roy Emerson	1991–92	Jim Courier
1964	Manuel Santana	1993–94	Sergi Bruguera
1965	Fred Stolle	1995	Thomas Muster

1. Became Open Championships (amateurs and professionals).

WIMBLEDON

Year	Winner	Year	Winner
1877	Spencer W. Gore	1946	Yvon Petra
1878	P. Frank Hadow	1947	Jack Kramer
1879–80	John T. Hartley	1948	Bob Falkenburg
1881–86	William Renshaw	1949	Ted Schroeder
1887	Herbert F. Lawford	1950	Budge Patty
1888	Ernest Renshaw	1951	Dick Savitt
1889	William Renshaw	1952	Frank Sedgman
1890	William J. Hamilton	1953	Vic Seixas
1891–92	Wilfred Baddeley	1954	Jaroslav Drobny
1893–94	Joshua Pim	1955	Tony Trabert
1895	Wilfred Baddeley	1956–57	Lew Hoad
1896	Harold S. Mahoney	1958	Ashley Cooper
1897–1900	Reggie F. Doherty	1959	Alex Olmedo
1901	Arthur W. Gore	1960	Neale Fraser
1902–06	H. Laurie Doherty	1961–62	Rod Laver
1907	Norman E. Brooks	1963	Chuck McKinley
1908–09	Arthur W. Gore	1964–65	Roy Emerson
1910–13	Anthony F. Wilding	1966	Manuel Santana
1914	Norman E. Brookes	1967	John Newcombe
1915–18	Not held	1968–69[1]	Rod Laver
1919	Gerald L. Patterson	1970–71	John Newcombe
1920–21	Bill Tilden	1972	Stan Smith
1922	Gerald L. Patterson	1973	Jan Kodes
1923	William M. Johnston	1974	Jimmy Connors
1924	Jean Borotra	1975	Arthur Ashe
1925	Rene Lacoste	1976–80	Bjorn Borg
1926	Jean Borotra	1981	John McEnroe
1927	Henri Cochet	1982	Jimmy Connors
1928	Rene Lacoste	1983–84	John McEnroe
1929	Henri Cochet	1985–86	Boris Becker
1930	Bill Tilden	1987	Pat Cash
1931	Sidney B. Wood, Jr.	1988	Stefan Edberg
1932	Ellsworth Vines	1989	Boris Becker
1933	Jack Crawford	1990	Stefan Edberg
1934–36	Fred J. Perry	1991	Michael Stich
1937–38	Don Budge	1992	Andre Agassi
1939	Bobby Riggs	1993–95	Pete Sampras
1940–45	Not held		

1. Became Open Championships (amateurs and professionals).

U.S. CHAMPIONSHIPS

Year	Winner	Year	Winner	Year	Winner	Year	Winner
1881–87	Richard D. Sears	1920–25	Bill Tilden	1950	Arthur Larsen	1971	Stan Smith
1888–89	H.W. Slocum, Jr.	1926–27	Rene Lacoste	1951–52	Frank Sedgman	1972	Ilie Nastase
1890–92	Oliver S. Campbell	1928	Henri Cochet	1953	Tony Trabert	1973	John Newcombe
1893–94	Robert D. Wrenn	1929	Bill Tilden	1954	E. Victor Seixas, Jr.	1974	Jimmy Connors
1895	Frederick H. Hovey	1930	John H. Doeg	1955	Tony Trabert	1975	Manuel Orantes
1896–97	Robert D. Wrenn	1931–32	H. Ellsworth Vines	1956	Ken Rosewall	1976	Jimmy Connors
1898–1900	Malcolm D. Whitman	1933–34	Fred J. Perry	1957	Malcolm J. Anderson	1977	Guillermo Vilas
1901–02	William A. Larned	1935	Wilmer L. Allison	1958	Ashley J. Cooper	1978	Jimmy Connors
1903	H. Laurie Doherty	1936	Fred J. Perry	1959–60	Neale Fraser	1979–81	John McEnroe
1904	Holcombe Ward	1937–38	Don Budge	1961	Roy Emerson	1982–83	Jimmy Connors
1905	Beals C. Wright	1939	Bobby Riggs	1962	Rod Laver	1984	John McEnroe
1906	William J. Clothier	1940	Donald McNeill	1963	Rafael Osuna	1985–87	Ivan Lendl
1907–11	William A. Larned	1941	Bobby Riggs	1964	Roy Emerson	1988	Mats Wilander
1912–13	Maurice E. McLoughlin	1942	Frederick R. Schroeder, Jr.	1965	Manuel Santana	1989	Boris Becker
1914	Richard N. Williams	1943	Joseph R. Hunt	1966	Fred Stolle	1990	Pete Sampras
1915	William M. Johnston	1944–45	Frank Parker	1967	John Newcombe	1991–92	Stefan Edberg
1916	Richard N. Williams	1946–47	Jack Kramer	1968[1]	Arthur Ashe	1993	Pete Sampras
1917–18	R.L. Murray	1948–49	Pancho Gonzales	1969	Rod Laver	1994	Andre Agassi
1919	William M. Johnston			1970	Ken Rosewall	1995	Pete Sampras

1. Became Open Championships (amateurs and professionals).

Women's Grand Slam Championships

AUSTRALIAN CHAMPIONSHIPS

Year	Winner	Year	Winner
1922–23	Margaret Molesworth	1960–66	Margaret Smith
1924	Sylvia Lance	1967	Nancy Richey
1925–26	Daphne Akhurst	1968	Billie Jean King
1927	Edna Boyd	1969[1]–71	Margaret Smith Court
1928–30	Daphne Akhurst	1972	Virginia Wade
1931–32	Coral Buttsworth	1973	Margaret Smith Court
1933–34	Joan Hartigan	1974–75	Evonne Goolagong
1935	Dorothy Round	1976	Evonne Goolagong Cawley
1936	Joan Hartigan	1977	Kerry Melville Reid
1937	Nancye Wynne Bolton	1977	Evonne Goolagong Cawley
1938	Dorothy Bundy	1978	Chris O'Neil
1939	Emily Westacott	1979	Barbara Jordan
1940	Nancye Wynne Bolton	1980	Hana Mandlikova
1941–45	Not held	1981	Martina Navratilova
1946–48	Nancye Wynne Bolton	1982	Chris Evert Lloyd
1949	Doris Hart	1983	Martina Navratilova
1950	Louise Brough	1984	Chris Evert Lloyd
1951	Nancye Wynne Bolton	1985	Martina Navratilova
1952	Thelma Long	1986	Not held; moved to Jan. 1987
1953	Maureen Connolly		
1954	Thelma Long	1987	Hana Mandlikova
1955	Beryl Penrose	1988–90	Steffi Graf
1956	Mary Carter	1991–93	Monica Seles
1957	Shirley Fry	1994	Steffi Graf
1958	Angela Mortimer	1995	Mary Pierce
1959	Mary Carter Reitano		

1. Became Open Championships (amateurs and professionals).

FRENCH CHAMPIONSHIPS

Year	Winner	Year	Winner
1897–99	Adine Massor	1957	Shirley Bloomer
1900	Y. Prevost	1958	Zsuzsi Kormoczy
1901	P. Girod	1959	Christine Truman
1902–03	Adine Massor	1960	Darlene Hard
1904–05	Katie Gilou	1961	Ann Haydon
1906	Katie Gilou Fenwick	1962	Margaret Smith
1907	Casse De Kerme	1963	Lesley Turner
1908	Katie Gilou Fenwick	1964	Margaret Smith
1909–12	Jeanne Matthey	1965	Lesley Turner
1913–14	Marguerite Broquedis	1966	Ann Jones
1915–19	Not held	1967	Francoise Durr
1920–23	Suzanne Lenglen	1968[2]	Nancy Richey
1924	Diddie Vlasto	1969–70	Margaret Smith Court
1925[1]–26	Suzanne Lenglen	1971	Evonne Goolagong
1927	Kea Bouman	1972	Billie Jean King
1928–29	Helen Wills	1973	Margaret Smith Court
1930	Helen Wills Moody	1974–75	Chris Evert
1931	Cilly Aussem	1976	Sue Barker
1932	Helen Wills Moody	1977	Mima Jausovec
1933–34	Margaret Scriven	1978	Virginia Ruzici
1935–37	Hilde Sperling	1979–80	Chris Evert Lloyd
1938–39	Simone Mathieu	1981	Hana Mandlikova
1940–45	Not held	1982	Martina Navratilova
1946	Margaret Osborne	1983	Chris Evert Lloyd
1947	Patricia Todd	1984	Martina Navratilova
1948	Nelly Landry	1985–86	Chris Evert Lloyd
1949	Margaret Osborne duPont	1987–88	Steffi Graf
1950	Doris Hart	1989	Arantxa Sánchez Vicario
1951	Shirley Fry	1990–92	Monica Seles
1952	Doris Hart	1993	Steffi Graf
1953–54	Maureen Connolly	1994	Arantxa Sánchez Vicario
1955	Angela Mortimer	1995	Steffi Graf
1956	Althea Gibson		

1. Before 1925 the French Championships were limited to residents of France. 2. Became Open Championships (amateurs and professionals).

WIMBLEDON

Year	Winner	Year	Winner
1884–85	Maud Watson	1937	Dorothy Round
1886	Blanche Bingley	1938	Helen Wills Moody
1887–88	Charlotte Dod	1939	Alice Marble
1889	Blanche Bingley Hillyard	1940–45	Not held
1890	Lena Rice	1946	Pauline Betz
1891–93	Charlotte Dod	1947	Margaret Osborne
1894	Blanche Hillyard	1948–50	Louise Brough
1895–96	Charlotte Cooper	1951	Doris Hart
1897	Blanche Hillyard	1952–54	Maureen Connolly
1898	Charlotte Cooper	1955	Louise Brough
1899–1900	Blanche Hillyard	1956	Shirley Fry
1901	Charlotte Cooper Sterry	1957–58	Althea Gibson
1902	Muriel Robb	1959–60	Maria Bueno
1903–04	Dorothea Douglass	1961	Angela Mortimer
1905	May Sutton	1962	Karen Hantze Susman
1906	Dorothea Douglass	1963	Margaret Smith
1907	May Sutton	1964	Maria Bueno
1908	Charlotte Sterry	1965	Margaret Smith
1909	Dora Boothby	1966–68[2]	Billie Jean King
1910–11	Dorothea Lambert Chambers	1969	Ann Jones
		1970	Margaret Smith Court
1912	Ethel Larcombe	1971	Evonne Goolagong
1913–14	Dorothea Lambert Chambers	1972–73	Billie Jean King
		1974	Chris Evert
1915–18	Not held	1975	Billie Jean King
1919–23[1]	Suzanne Lenglen	1976	Chris Evert
1924	Kathleen McKane	1977	Virginia Wade
1925	Suzanne Lenglen	1978–79	Martina Navratilova
1926	Kathleen McKane Godfree	1980	Evonne Goolagong Cawley
		1981	Chris Evert Lloyd
1927–29	Helen Wills	1982–87	Martina Navratilova
1930	Helen Wills Moody	1988–89	Steffi Graf
1931	Cilly Aussem	1990	Martina Navratilova
1932–33	Helen Wills Moody	1991–93	Steffi Graf
1934	Dorothy Round	1994	Conchita Martinez
1935	Helen Wills Moody	1995	Steffi Graf
1936	Helen Jacobs		

1. Through 1921, championship decided on challenge system. If no finalist, holder did not defend. In 1922, challenge round abolished. 2. Became Open Championships (amateurs and professionals).

U.S. CHAMPIONSHIPS

Year	Winner	Year	Winner
1887	Ellen Hensell	1942–44	Pauline Betz
1888–89	Bertha L. Townsend	1945	Sarah Palfrey Cooke
1890	Ellen C. Roosevelt	1946	Pauline Betz
1891–92	Mabe Caty	1947	Louise Brough
1893	Aline Terry	1948–50	Margaret Osborne duPont
1894	Helen Hellwig	1951–53	Maureen Connolly
1895	Juliette Atkinson	1954–55	Doris Hart
1896	Elizabeth Moore	1956	Shirley Fry
1897–98	Juliette Atkinson	1957–58	Althea Gibson
1899	Marion Jones	1959	Maria Bueno
1900	Myrtle McAleer	1960–61	Darlene Hard
1901	Elizabeth Moore	1962	Margaret Smith
1902	Marion Jones	1963–64	Maria Bueno
1903	Elizabeth Moore	1965	Margaret Smith
1904	May Sutton	1966	Maria Bueno
1905	Elizabeth Moore	1967	Billie Jean King
1906	Helen Homans	1968[1]	Virginia Wade
1907	Evelyn Sears	1969–70	Margaret Smith Court
1908	Maud Barger-Wallach	1971–72	Billie Jean King
1909–11	Hazel Hotchkiss	1973	Margaret Smith Court
1912–14	Mary Browne	1974	Billie Jean King
1915–16	Molla Bjurstedt	1975–78	Chris Evert
1917	Not held	1979	Tracy Austin
1918	Molla Bjurstedt	1980	Chris Evert Lloyd
1919	Hazel Hotchkiss Wightman	1981	Tracy Austin
1920–22	Molla Bjurstedt Mallory	1982	Chris Evert Lloyd
1923–25	Helen Wills	1983–84	Martina Navratilova
1926	Molla Bjurstedt Mallory	1985	Hana Mandlikova
1927–29	Helen Wills	1986–87	Martina Navratilova
1930	Betty Nuthall	1988–89	Steffi Graf
1931	Helen Wills Moody	1990	Gabriela Sabatini
1932–35	Helen Jacobs	1991–92	Monica Seles
1936	Alice Marble	1993	Steffi Graf
1937	Anita Lizana	1994	Arantxa Sánchez Vicario
1938–40	Alice Marble	1995	Steffi Graf
1941	Sarah Palfrey Cooke		

1. Became Open Championships (amateurs and professionals).

Baseball

Major League Baseball
Office of the Commissioner
350 Park Avenue
New York, NY 10022
(212) 339-7800
FAX: (212) 355-0007
Acting Commissioner: Allan "Bud" Selig
Number of teams—28

The National League of
Professional Baseball Clubs
350 Park Avenue
New York, NY 10022
(212) 339-7700
FAX: (212) 935-5069
President: Leonard Coleman
Founded: 1876

The American League of
Professional Baseball Clubs
350 Park Ave., 18th Floor
New York, NY 10022
(212) 339-7600
FAX: (212) 593-7138
President: Gene Budig
Founded: 1901

THE 1995 BASEBALL SEASON

The 1995 baseball season was shortened by 18 games due to the inability of players and owners to settle a labor dispute before the scheduled season opener Apr. 2. Up until that point, owners insisted on fielding replacement players in lieu of striking major leaguers who had walked out Aug. 12, 1994, rather than accept a salary cap that the owners had threatened to impose unilaterally if the two sides did not negotiate a new collective bargaining agreement.

But on Mar. 31, two days before the scabs were scheduled to replace the major leaguers for the 1995 season, federal judge Sonia Sotomayor charged the owners with unfair labor practices, and granted the players an injunction restoring the old collective bargaining agreement until the two sides can agree on a new one. When the players immediately voted to end their strike, the owners were left with no choice but to dispatch the replacement players, take the striking players back, and start spring training all over again. After an abbreviated three-week grapefruit league season, major league baseball returned Apr. 25 for a 144-game season.

THE 1995 SEASON

FINAL STANDINGS, 1995

NATIONAL LEAGUE

Division/Team	W	L	Pct.	GB
National League East				
Atlanta[1]	90	54	.625	—
N.Y. Mets	69	75	.479	21
Philadelphia	69	75	.479	21
Montreal	67	76	.469	22.5
Florida	66	78	.458	24
National League Central				
Cincinnati[1]	85	59	.590	—
Houston	76	68	.528	9
Chicago	73	71	.507	12
St. Louis	62	81	.434	22.5
Pittsburgh	58	86	.403	27
National League West				
Los Angeles[1]	78	66	.542	—
Colorado[2]	77	67	.535	1
San Diego	70	74	.486	8
San Francisco	67	77	.465	11

AMERICAN LEAGUE

Division/Team	W	L	Pct.	GB
American League East				
Boston[1]	86	58	.597	—
N.Y. Yankees[2]	79	65	.549	7
Baltimore	71	73	.493	15
Detroit	60	84	.417	26
Toronto	56	88	.389	30
American League Central				
Cleveland[1]	100	44	.694	—
Kansas City	70	74	.486	30
Chicago	68	76	.472	32
Milwaukee	65	79	.451	35
Minnesota	56	88	.389	44
American League West				
Seattle[1]	79	66	.545	—
California	78	67	.538	1
Texas	74	70	.514	4.5
Oakland	67	77	.465	11.5

Note: Season lasted only 144 games because of labor impasse at beginning of year. 1. Division champion. 2. Wild card for playoffs.

1995 POSTSEASON

National League Playoff Summaries

Atlanta v. Colorado
Atlanta 5, COLORADO 4
Atlanta 7, COLORADO 4
Colorado 7, ATLANTA 5 (10 innings)
ATLANTA 10, Colorado 4
(Atlanta wins series 3–1)

Cincinnati v. Los Angeles
Cincinnati 7, LOS ANGELES 2
Cincinnati 5, LOS ANGELES 4
CINCINNATI 10, Los Angeles 1
(Cincinnati wins series 3–0)

American League Playoff Summaries

Seattle v. N.Y. Yankees
N.Y. YANKEES 9, Seattle 6
N.Y. YANKEES 7, Seattle 5 (15 innings)
SEATTLE 7, N.Y. Yankees 4
SEATTLE 11, N.Y. Yankees 8
SEATTLE 6, N.Y. Yankees 5 (11 innings)
(Seattle wins series 3–2)

Cleveland v. Boston
CLEVELAND 5, Boston 4 (13 innings)
CLEVELAND 4, Boston 0
Cleveland 8, BOSTON 2
(Cleveland wins series 3–0)

National League Championship Series

Atlanta 2, CINCINNATI 1 (11 innings)
This pitcher's duel between Tom Glavine and Pete Schourek wasn't settled until the 11th inning, after both starters had departed. The Braves scratched out the decisive run with a walk, a sacrifice, and a single by rightfielder Mike Devereaux, who was only in the game as a defensive replacement for David Justice.

Atlanta 6, CINCINNATI 2 (10 innings)
The second straight pitcher's duel was the second straight extra-inning game and the second straight Braves victory. Reds reliever Mark Portugal threw a bases-loaded wild pitch and then surrendered a three-run homer to Javier Lopez to give the Braves the win.

ATLANTA 5, Cincinnati 2
Charlie O'Brien, a backup catcher playing in his first postseason game, took advantage of his playing time by launching a three-run home run to power the Braves. Atlanta ace Greg Maddux held the Reds to one run and seven hits over eight innings.

ATLANTA 6, Cincinnati 0
Steve Avery, who was ineffective for most of the regular season, compiling a 7–13 record, sparkled in his first postseason start, limiting the Reds offense to just two hits and no runs over six innings. Mike Devereaux again sparked the offense, this time with a three-run homer in the seventh that sealed Cincinnati's fate. Devereaux was named the series MVP. (Atlanta wins series 4–0).

American League Championship Series

SEATTLE 3, Cleveland 2
His pitching staff depleted by the five-game dogfight with the Yankees, Manager Lou Piniella turned to Bob Wolcott, a 22-year-old rookie with just six weeks of major league experience. Wolcott rewarded Piniella's faith in him by limiting the potent Indians lineup to eight hits and two runs over seven innings.

Cleveland 5, SEATTLE 2
Outfielder Manny Ramirez went 4-for-4 with two home runs to power the Indians, while Cleveland starter Orel Hershiser held the Mariners to just one run over eight innings to even the series at a game apiece.

Seattle 5, CLEVELAND 2 (11 innings)
The Mariners liked their chances with fireballer Randy Johnson taking the mound, but Cleveland's Charles Nagy dueled him to a 2–2 tie for the first eight innings. The game wasn't settled until the 11th inning, when Seattle's Jay Buhner, whose error allowed the first Cleveland run, hit his second home run of the night to provide the margin of victory.

CLEVELAND 7, Seattle 0
The Indians jumped all over Seattle starter Andy Benes, scoring three runs in the first inning, one in the second, and two more in the fourth. Eddie Murray and Jim Thome each hit two-run home runs to lead Cleveland's offensive explosion. Meanwhile, Indians' starter Ken Hill shut down the potent Mariner lineup, holding them to five hits over seven innings.

CLEVELAND 3, Seattle 2
Cleveland made four errors and Seattle made two, but the miscues led to only one unearned run for each team. Fine relief pitching by both teams stranded a total of 20 runners on base (9 for Seattle, 11 for Cleveland). Jim Thome's two-run home run in the sixth inning gave the Indians the 3–2 lead in the game and the series.

Cleveland 4, SEATTLE 0
Randy Johnson held the Indians to just one unearned run through seven innings, but the Mariner bats went silent against Dennis Martinez. Cleveland broke through in the eighth, as Ruben Amaro and Kenny Lofton both scored on the same passed ball, and Carlos Baerga poked a solo homer. Orel Hershiser, winner of games 2 and 5, was named MVP. (Cleveland wins series 4–2)

1995 INDIVIDUAL LEADERS

NATIONAL LEAGUE

BATTING AVERAGE		HOME RUNS		RUNS BATTED IN		PITCHING—WINS		PITCHING—ERA	
Gwynn, San Diego	.368	Bichette, Colorado	40	Bichette, Colorado	128	Maddux, Atlanta	19	Maddux, Atlanta	1.63
Piazza, Los Angeles	.346	Sosa, Chicago Cubs	36	Sosa, Chicago Cubs	119	Schourek, Cincinnati	18	Nomo, Los Angeles	2.54
Bichette, Colorado	.340	Walker, Colorado	36	Galarraga, Colorado	106	R. Martinez, Los Angeles	17	Ashby, San Diego	2.94
Bell, Houston	.334	Bonds, San Francisco	33	Conine, Florida	105	Glavine, Atlanta	16	Valdes, Los Angeles	3.05
Grace, Chicago Cubs	.326	Castilla, Colorado	32	Karros, Los Angeles	105	Navarro, Chicago Cubs	14	Glavine, Atlanta	3.08
Larkin, Cincinnati	.319	Karros, Los Angeles	32	Bonds, San Francisco	104	Rapp, Florida	14	Hamilton, San Diego	3.08
Castilla, Colorado	.309	Piazza, Los Angeles	32	Walker, Colorado	101	P. Martinez, Montreal	14	Smolz, Atlanta	3.18
Segui, N.Y.–Montreal	.320	Galarraga, Colorado	31	R. Sanders, Cincinnati	99	Four players tied with	13	Castillo, Chicago Cubs	3.21
Jefferies, Philadelphia	.306	Gant, Cincinnati	29	Caminiti, San Diego	94			Schourek, Cincinnati	3.22
R. Sanders, Cincinnati	.306	R. Sanders, Cincinnati	28	Two players tied with	93			Navarro, Chicago Cubs	3.28

AMERICAN LEAGUE

BATTING AVERAGE		HOME RUNS		RUNS BATTED IN		PITCHING—WINS		PITCHING—ERA	
E. Martinez, Seattle	.356	Belle, Cleveland	50	Belle, Cleveland	126	Mussina, Baltimore	19	R. Johnson, Seattle	2.48
Knoblauch, Minnesota	.333	Buhner, Seattle	40	M. Vaughn, Boston	126	Johnson, Seattle	18	Wakefield, Boston	2.95
Salmon, California	.330	F. Thomas, Chicago	40	Buhner, Seattle	121	Cone, Toronto–New York	18	D. Martinez, Cleveland	3.08
Boggs, New York	.324	McGwire, Oakland	39	E. Martinez, Seattle	113	K. Rogers, Texas	17	Mussina, Baltimore	3.29
Murray, Cleveland	.323	Palmeiro, Baltimore	39	T. Martinez, Seattle	111	Hershiser, Cleveland	16	K. Rogers, Texas	3.38
Surhoff, Milwaukee	.320	M. Vaughn, Boston	39	F. Thomas, Chicago	111	Nagy, Cleveland	16	Cone, Toronto–New York	3.57
Davis, California	.318	Gaetti, Kansas City	35	Edmonds, California	107	Wakefield, Boston	16	K. Brown, Baltimore	3.60
Belle, Cleveland	.317	Salmon, California	34	Ramirez, Cleveland	107	Five players tied with	15	Leiter, Toronto	3.64
Baerga, Cleveland	.314	Edmonds, California	33	Salmon, California	105			Abbott, Chicago–Calif.	3.70
Thome, Cleveland	.314	Tettleton, Texas	32	Palmeiro, Baltimore	104			Gubicza, Kansas City	3.75

MAJOR LEAGUE BASEBALL LEAGUE CHAMPIONSHIP SERIES RESULTS (Divisional play began in 1969)

NATIONAL LEAGUE

Year	Winner	Loser	MVP
1969	N.Y. Mets-3	Atlanta Braves-0	
1970	Cincinnati Reds-3	Pittsburgh Pirates-0	
1971	Pittsburgh Pirates-3	S.F. Giants-1	
1972	Cincinnati Reds-3	Pittsburgh Pirates-2	
1973	N.Y. Mets-3	Cincinnati Reds-2	
1974	L.A. Dodgers-3	Pittsburgh Pirates-1	
1975	Cincinnati Reds-3	Pittsburgh Pirates-0	
1976	Cincinnati Reds-3	Philadelphia Phillies-0	
1977	L.A. Dodgers-3	Philadelphia Phillies-1	Dusty Baker, L.A.
1978	L.A. Dodgers-3	Philadelphia Phillies-1	Steve Garvey, L.A.
1979	Pittsburgh Pirates-3	Cincinnati Reds-0	Willie Stargell, Pittsburgh
1980	Philadelphia Phillies-3	Houston Astros-2	Manny Trillo, Philadelphia
1981	L.A. Dodgers-3	Montreal Expos-2	Burt Hooton, L.A.
1982	St. Louis Cardinals-3	Atlanta Braves-0	Darrell Porter, St. Louis
1983	Philadelphia Phillies-3	L.A. Dodgers-1	Gary Matthews, Philadelphia
1984	San Diego Padres-3	Chicago Cubs-2	Steve Garvey, San Diego
1985[1]	St. Louis Cardinals-4	L.A. Dodgers-2	Ozzie Smith, St. Louis
1986	N.Y. Mets-4	Houston Astros-2	Mike Scott, Houston
1987	St. Louis Cardinals-4	S. F. Giants-3	Jeff Leonard, S.F.
1988	L.A. Dodgers-4	N.Y. Mets-3	Orel Hershiser, L.A.
1989	S.F. Giants-4	Chicago Cubs-1	Will Clark, S.F.
1990	Cincinnati Reds-4	Pittsburgh Pirates-2	Rob Dibble, Randy Myers, Cincinnati
1991	Atlanta Braves-4	Pittsburgh Pirates-3	Steve Avery, Atlanta
1992	Atlanta Braves-4	Pittsburgh Pirates-3	John Smoltz, Atlanta
1993	Philadelphia Phillies-4	Atlanta Braves-2	Curt Schilling, Philadelphia
1994	LCS canceled		
1995	Atlanta Braves-4	Cincinnati Reds-0	Mike Devereaux, Atlanta

AMERICAN LEAGUE

Year	Winner	Loser	MVP
1969	Baltimore Orioles-3	Minnesota Twins-0	
1970	Baltimore Orioles-3	Minnesota Twins-0	
1971	Baltimore Orioles-3	Oakland A's-0	
1972	Oakland A's-3	Detroit Tigers-2	
1973	Oakland A's-3	Baltimore Orioles-2	
1974	Oakland A's-3	Baltimore Orioles-1	
1975	Boston Red Sox-3	Oakland A's-0	
1976	N.Y. Yankees-3	Kansas City Royals-2	
1977	N.Y. Yankees-3	Kansas City Royals-2	
1978	N.Y. Yankees-3	Kansas City Royals-1	
1979	Baltimore Orioles-3	California Angels-1	
1980	Kansas City Royals-3	N.Y. Yankees-0	Frank White, Kansas City
1981	N.Y. Yankees-3	Oakland A's-0	Graig Nettles, N.Y.
1982	Milwaukee Brewers-3	California Angels-2	Fred Lynn, California
1983	Baltimore Orioles-3	Chicago White Sox-1	Mike Boddicker, Baltimore
1984	Detroit Tigers-3	Kansas City Royals-0	Kirk Gibson, Detroit
1985[1]	Kansas City Royals-4	Toronto Blue Jays-3	George Brett, Kansas City
1986	Boston Red Sox-4	California Angels-3	Marty Barrett, Boston
1987	Minnesota Twins-4	Detroit Tigers-1	Gary Gaetti, Minnesota
1988	Oakland A's-4	Boston Red Sox-0	Dennis Eckersley, Oakland
1989	Oakland A's-4	Toronto Blue Jays-1	Rickey Henderson, Oakland
1990	Oakland A's-4	Boston Red Sox-0	Dave Stewart, Oakland
1991	Minnesota Twins-4	Toronto Blue Jays-1	Kirby Puckett, Minnesota
1992	Toronto Blue Jays-4	Oakland Athletics-2	Roberto Alomar, Toronto
1993	Toronto Blue Jays-4	Chicago White Sox-2	Dave Stewart, Toronto
1994	LCS canceled		
1995	Cleveland Indians-4	Seattle Mariners-2	Orel Hershiser, Cleveland

1. In 1985 the League Championship Series was switched to a best-of-seven format.

THE WORLD SERIES

A championship series between the winners of two leagues was held in 1882 between the National League and the American Association and was played at the end of each season until the AA folded in 1890. Following this, the top two NL clubs played each other for the "Temple Cup," but the idea never really caught on with the public. When the American League began operations again in 1901, there was great animosity between the two circuits due to bidding wars for the services of star players. Peace was established before the 1903 season, and when it became clear that Pittsburgh would win the NL and Boston the AL, the owners of each club reached a private agreement to hold a "World Series" in October. Many were surprised when the newer American League won the title.

There was no agreement to play such a series every year, however, and in 1904 the New York Giants refused to meet the Boston club, probably because of John McGraw's dislike of American League president Ban Johnson. But the baseball public wanted a championship series, and by 1905 Giants' owner John Brush proposed rules governing a mandatory series to be played every year. With minute changes, those rules stand to this day.

1903 Boston (A) over Pittsburgh (N), 5–3. The upstart American League emerged victorious in the first World Series, a best-of-nine affair. The "Pilgrims" (Red Sox) staged one of the greatest comebacks in history by sweeping the final four games. Bill Dineen and Cy Young each won two for Boston, and held Pirate immortal Honus Wagner to one harmless single in those four contests.

1904 No series. New York Giants owner John T. Brush and manager John McGraw refused to play the World Champion Boston club, dismissing them as representative of an "inferior league."

1905 New York (N) over Philadelphia (A), 4–1. Every game was won by a shutout, with Christy Mathewson throwing three for the Giants. In 27 innings, he allowed 14 hits, striking out 18 and walking one. The Athletics committed five errors in Game three, the pivotal contest.

1906 Chicago (A) over Chicago (N), 4–2. The first "subway series" was a stunning upset. The "Hitless Wonders" White Sox had batted .230 with seven home runs during the season, while the Cubs were winning 116 games, still the all-time record. Utility man George Rohe hit two game-winning triples for the Sox and Ed Walsh pitched two of their wins.

1907 Chicago (N) over Detroit (A), 4–0. Avenging the past year, the Cubs shut down Ty Cobb, Sam Crawford et al, behind a superb four-man pitching performance, and the hitting of Harry Steinfeldt (.471) and Johnny Evers (.350).

1908 Chicago (N) over Detroit (A), 4–1. Only a little closer this year. Johnny Evers repeated his .350 average of 1907, joining player-manager Frank Chance (.421) and outfielder Wildfire Schulte (.389) in the Cub attack. Ty Cobb led Detroit (.368), to no avail.

1909 Pittsburgh (N) over Detroit (A), 4–3. The Tigers lost their third straight series, as Honus Wagner won the "Battle of the Titans" with Ty Cobb. The Pirate shortstop hit .333 with six RBIs and six stolen bases, and Babe Adams pitched in with three complete-game victories.

1910 Philadelphia (A) over Chicago (N), 4–1. Connie Mack's infielders combined to bat .364 as the A's rolled to an easy title. Jack Coombs pitched three wins and tossed in a .385 batting average. The great Cubs pitching staff was growing old.

1911 Philadelphia (A) over New York (N), 4–2. Regarded by some as the greatest team ever, the A's wrestled down a strong New York club featuring Christy Mathewson and Rube Marquard. Frank "Home Run" Baker got his nickname from game-winning blasts in Games Two and Three.

1912 Boston (A) over New York (N), 4–3. This thrill-a-minute series featured an 11-inning tie in Game Two, and an extra-inning final game. Two Giant errors, by Freds Merkle and Snodgrass, enabled Boston to score two runs in the bottom of the 10th inning of the final contest.

1913 Philadelphia (A) over New York (N), 4–1. Home Run Baker again hammered Giant pitching, batting .450 with seven RBIs. Eddie Collins also starred for the A's, hitting .421 with three stolen bases.

1914 Boston (N) over Philadelphia (A), 4–0. The red-hot "Miracle Braves" swept the heavily favored Athletics, who scored only six runs in the four games. Catcher Hank Gowdy (.545) and second baseman Johnny Evers (.438) led the Boston offense.

1915 Boston (A) over Philadelphia (N), 4–1. The famous Red Sox outfield of Speaker, Lewis, and Hooper combined to bat .364 while Rube Foster pitched two complete-game wins. Foster also batted .500, driving in the winning run in Game Two.

1916 Boston (A) over Brooklyn (N), 4–1. After three one-run games, Boston took charge with 6–2 and 4–1 victories. A young lefthander named Babe Ruth twirled a 14-inning six hitter in Game Two.

1917 Chicago (A) over New York (N), 4–2. The pitching of Red Faber (3–1, 2.33) and the hitting of Eddie Collins, Buck Weaver, and Joe Jackson were too much for the Giants in a sloppy (23 errors) series.

1918 Boston (A) over Chicago (N), 4–2. Every game a pitchers duel, the losing Cubs posted a 1.04 ERA over the six games. The Boston staff allowed but nine runs in the series, led by Babe Ruth, who extended his consecutive scoreless inning streak to 29⅔.

1919 Cincinnati (N) over Chicago (A), 5–3. Results declared invalid after eight Chicago "Black Sox" were found to have acted to lose games intentionally. All eight, plus 14 other major leaguers, were barred from baseball for life in the ensuing scandal.

1920 Cleveland (A) over Brooklyn (N), 5–2. Game Five was surely the most freakish in series history. It featured a) the first World Series grand slam home run (Indians rightfielder Elmer Smith), b) the first World Series home run by a pitcher (Indians Jim Bagby), and c) the first and only unassisted triple play in series action (Indians second baseman Billy Wambsganss).

1921 New York (N) over New York (A), 5–3. Six Giants batted over .300, and their pitchers held Babe Ruth to a .500 slugging average. Giant hurler Jesse Barnes won two games and batted .444.

1922 New York (N) over New York (A), 4–0. The result was said to be final proof that "brains beat brawn." Giant pitching shut down Ruth & Co., allowing only 11 runs in the five contests (one tie).

1923 New York (A) over New York (N), 4–2. The Yankees took the last three to break the spell of their cross-river rivals, behind Babe Ruth's three homers and eight RBIs. Casey Stengel hit two home runs for the losers.

1924 Washington (A) over New York (N), 4–3. A 12-inning seventh game won by Walter Johnson in relief capped an exciting affair. Twenty-seven-year-old player-manager Bucky Harris starred for the Senators (.333, 7 RBIs), as did outfielder Goose Goslin (.344, 7 RBIs).

1925 Pittsburgh (N) over Washington (A), 4–3. Pirate centerfielder Max Carey had 11 hits and three stolen bases, as Pittsburgh became the first team since 1903 to come back from a three games to one deficit.

1926 St. Louis (N) over New York (A), 4–3. Babe Ruth hit three homers in Game Four, but in the seventh inning of the seventh contest Grover Cleveland Alexander struck out Tony Lazzeri with the bases loaded, saving the game and the series for the Cardinals.

1927 New York (A) over Pittsburgh (N), 4–0. Generally regarded as the greatest team of all time, the "Murderers' Row" Yankees disposed of the Pirates behind two more Babe Ruth homers, plus the pitching of Wilcy Moore, Herb Pennock, and George Pipgras.

1928 New York (A) over St. Louis (N), 4–0. Another Yankee sweep. Ruth and Lou Gehrig combined to bat .593, with seven home runs and 13 RBIs. Waite Hoyt pitched two complete-game victories.

1929 Philadelphia (A) over Chicago (N), 4–1. Trailing 8–0 in Game Four, the A's roared back to score 10 runs in the seventh inning, a series record. In the next contest, the Mackmen took the series with a three-run ninth inning.

1930 Philadelphia (A) over St. Louis (N), 4–2. Lefty Grove and George Earnshaw pitched well, while Al Simmons, Jimmie Foxx, and Mickey Cochrane combined for 11 extra-base hits. Cardinal regulars batted only .185 in the six games.

1931 St. Louis (N) over Philadelphia (A), 4–3. Cardinal centerfielder Pepper Martin set a record that stood for 33 years with his 12 hits. Martin also stole five bases and hit a home run. Bill Hallahan and Burleigh Grimes handled the pitching, combining for a 4–0, 1.25 ERA.

1932 New York (A) over Chicago (N), 4–0. The Yankees completed a streak of 12 straight World Series victories in sweeping the Cubs. This time Ruth and Gehrig combined to bat .438, with five homers and 14 RBIs.

1933 New York (N) over Washington (A), 4–1. Same teams as 1924, different result. Bill Terry's Giants defeated Joe Cronin's Senators in a battle of player-managers. Carl Hubbell won two for New York and did not allow an earned run.

1934 St. Louis (N) over Detroit (A), 4–3. Dizzy and Paul Dean hurled the Cardinals to the title, winning all four Redbird victories. A bad defensive series, with 27 errors and 13 unearned runs.

1935 Detroit (A) over Chicago (N), 4–2. The Cubs won 21 straight games in September, but came up short when faced with Mickey Cochrane's Tigers. Charlie Gehringer and Tommy Bridges starred for Detroit, while Lou Warneke (2–0, 0.54) was superb for the losers.

1936 New York (A) over New York (N), 4–2. The Yankees hammered Giant pitching in Games Two and Six, ending with 43 runs for the series. Tony Lazzeri and Bill Dickey each drove in five runs in the second contest, when Joe McCarthy's "Windowbreakers" scored 18 times to set a record.

1937 New York (A) over New York (N), 4–1. Lefty Gomez pitched two of the Yankee wins and drove in the winning run with a single in the final game. The Yanks scored seven runs in the sixth inning of Game One, then coasted to an easy championship.

1938 New York (A) over Chicago (N), 4–0. In a replay of 1932, the Bronx Bombers blew out an overmatched Cub squad. Cub fans are still waiting for their team's first series victory over the Yankees.

1939 New York (A) over Cincinnati (N), 4–0. New York won its fourth straight World Championship the same way they won the first three—easily. Charlie Keller batted .438 with three homers, and scored as many runs as the entire Reds team, eight.

1940 Cincinnati (N) over Detroit (A), 4–3. The Reds repeated as NL champs, then prevailed over the Tigers when Paul Derringer beat Bobo Newsome 2–1 in the seventh game. Derringer and Bucky Walters each won two games.

1941 New York (A) over Brooklyn (N), 4–1. With two outs in the ninth inning of Game Four, Dodger catcher Mickey Owen dropped a third strike on Tommy Henrich, allowing him to reach first base. The Yankees then scored four times to win the ballgame, and finished Brooklyn off the next day.

1942 St. Louis (N) over New York (A), 4–1. The Cardinals, winners of 106 games during the regular season, lost Game One with the tying run at bat. They then swept four in a row, behind the pitching of Johnny Beazley (2–0, 2.50) and Ernie White's shutout in Game Three.

1943 New York (A) over St. Louis (N), 4–1. In a turnaround from 1942, the Yanks held St. Louis to nine runs in the five games. Joe Gordon and Bill Dickey homered, while third baseman Billy Johnson drove in three runs for New York.

1944 St. Louis (N) over St. Louis (A), 4–2. The Browns struggled valiantly in their only World Series appearance, but fell short against a strong Cardinal club left relatively intact by World War II. Ten Brown errors gave the Redbirds seven unearned runs.

1945 Detroit (A) over Chicago (N), 4–3. Tiger Ace Hal Newhouser was hit hard in Game One, but he bounced back to win Games Five and Seven. Doc Cramer (.379) and Hank Greenberg (2 HRs, 7 RBIs) led the Detroit offense.

1946 St. Louis (N) over Boston (A), 4–3. Enos Slaughter scored from first on a base-hit by Harry Walker in the eighth inning of the seventh game, giving St. Louis its third title in five years. Harry Brecheen won three games for the Cardinals, allowing but one run.

1947 New York (A) over Brooklyn (N), 4–3. Yankee pitcher Bill Bevens had a no-hitter for 8⅔ innings in Game Four, but lost the game on a double by Cookie Lavagetto. Tommy Henrich (.323) had the game winning RBIs in Games One, Two, and Seven.

1948 Cleveland (A) over Boston (N), 4–2. The series featured fine pitching on both sides, including the first game, when Boston's Johnny Sain beat Bob Feller 1–0. Cleveland's Gene Beardon did not allow a run in 10⅔ innings.

1949 New York (A) over Brooklyn (N), 4–1. Game One was 0–0 until Tommy Henrich led off the bottom of the ninth with a home run off Don Newcombe. Bobby Brown batted .500 with five RBIs.

1950 New York (A) over Philadelphia (N), 4–0. New York struggled to win the first three contests by scores of 1–0, 2–1, and 3–2, in a series that was closer than it looks. The "Whiz Kid" Phillies held the Yanks to a .222 batting average but managed to hit only .203 themselves.

1951 New York (A) over New York (N), 4–2. A tired Giant pitching staff held the Yankees in check for three games, but the AL champs broke out to score 23 runs in the final three. Eddie Lopat (2–0, 0.50) starred for the winners.

1952 New York (A) over Brooklyn (N), 4–3. Allie Reynolds and Vic Raschi each won two games, combining for a 1.69 ERA. Johnny Mize hit three homers, and Mickey Mantle and Yogi Berra each hit two. Duke Snider batted .345 with four roundtrippers in a losing cause.

1953 New York (A) over Brooklyn (N), 4–2. The Yankees won their fifth straight World Championship as second baseman Billy Martin tied a record with 12 hits. Martin slugged .958 and drove in eight runs.

1954 New York (N) over Cleveland (A), 4–0. The Indians won 111 games during the season, still an AL record. The Giants, sparked by a spectacular Willie Mays catch in the first game, went on to defeat Cleveland easily. Pinch hitter-outfielder Dusty Rhodes drove in seven runs on two homers and two singles in six at bats.

1955 Brooklyn (N) over New York (A), 4–3. The Dodgers finally won a World Series in their eighth try, behind the pitching of series MVP Johnny Podres (2–0, 1.00). Duke Snider hit four homers in a series for the second time, and Dodger leftfielder Sandy Amoros made a game-saving catch in the seventh game.

1956 New York (A) over Brooklyn (N), 4–3. Yankee righthander and series MVP Don Larsen pitched a perfect game in the fifth contest, while Mickey Mantle and Yogi Berra each hit three homers for the winners.

1957 Milwaukee (N) over New York (A), 4–3. Lew Burdette won three times for the Braves, allowing but two runs in 27 innings, and won the MVP. Milwaukee's hitting was led by Hank Aaron (.393, 3 HRs, 7 RBIs).

1958 New York (A) over Milwaukee (N), 4–3. Yankees Hank Bauer and Moose Skowron combined for six homers and 15 RBIs as the Bronx Bombers came back from a 3–1 deficit to sweep the last three games. Yankee pitcher "Bullet" Bob Turley earned MVP honors.

1959 Los Angeles (N) over Chicago (A), 4–2. Los Angeles enjoyed its first World Championship as the transplanted Dodgers prevailed, aided by the relief pitching of MVP Larry Sherry (2 wins, 2 saves). Ted Kluszewski of the "Go-Go" White Sox hit .391, with three homers and 10 RBIs.

1960 Pittsburgh (N) over New York (A), 4–3. Pirate second baseman Bill Mazeroski's home run in the bottom of the ninth in the seventh game capped one of the most exciting contests in history. In the 10–9 ballgame, 10 of the runs were scored in the last two innings. Yankee second baseman Bobby Richardson, a hitting star throughout the series, was named MVP.

1961 New York (A) over Cincinnati (N), 4–1. Whitey Ford tossed two shutouts in winning the MVP, and the Yankee offense pounded out 16 extra-base hits in the five games. Bobby Richardson (.391) and John Blanchard (.400, 2 HRs) starred for New York.

1962 New York (A) over San Francisco (N), 4–3. Ralph Terry's four-hit shutout won the seesaw affair for the Yanks, and earned him the MVP. Whitey Ford completed his series record 33 consecutive scoreless innings in the first game, and for the Giants, Chuck Hiller hit the first National League series grand slam home run in Game Four.

1963 Los Angeles (N) over New York (A), 4–0. Dodger pitchers held New York to four runs, led by Sandy Koufax's two wins and 23 strikeouts, including a record-breaking 15 in the first game. Koufax was the runaway choice for MVP.

1964 St. Louis (N) over New York (A), 4–3. Ten Yankee home runs were not enough to beat the Cardinals. Bob Gibson was the series MVP, and Tim McCarver (.478) also starred. Highlights included Ken Boyer's game-winning grand-slam in Game Four, and Bobby Richardson's record 13 hits.

1965 Los Angeles (N) over Minnesota (A), 4–3. As in 1963, MVP Sandy Koufax again excelled for the Dodgers, allowing only two runs in 24 innings, striking out 29. Jim "Mudcat" Grant won two games and hit a three-run homer for the Twins.

1966 Baltimore (A) over Los Angeles (N), 4–0. The Orioles made the most of their first World Series appearance, as their young pitchers did not allow a run after the third inning of the first game. Slugger Frank Robinson capped a great year with the series MVP award.

1967 St. Louis (N) over Boston (A), 4–3. Bob Gibson pitched three complete game victories, added a home run in Game Seven, and was named MVP. Lou Brock batted .414 and stole seven bases, tying Eddie Collins's record and pacing the Cards.

1968 Detroit (A) over St. Louis (N), 4–3. The Cardinals were rolling behind Bob Gibson's record 17 strikeouts in Game One and his record seventh straight series win in Game Four. Again Lou Brock joined him in the record books with 13 hits and seven stolen bases. But their feats couldn't stop the Tigers, led by the MVP pitching of Mickey Lolich (3–0, 1.67).

1969 New York (N) over Baltimore (A), 4–1. The Mets stunned the baseball world by winning four in a row after dropping the opener. Their young pitchers held the Orioles to only nine runs, aided by the great outfield catches of Ron Swoboda and Tommie Agee. Series MVP Donn Clendenon (.357, 3 HRs) and Al Weis (.455, 1 HR) led the Met attack.

1970 Baltimore (A) over Cincinnati (N), 4–1. Brooks Robinson almost singlehandedly beat the Reds with spectacular defense at third base and a .429 average with two homers and two doubles. His dominance of the series earned the MVP. Also chipping in for the O's were Paul Blair (.474), Frank Robinson, and Boog Powell (two homers each).

1971 Pittsburgh (N) over Baltimore (A), 4–3. Roberto Clemente played in 14 World Series games and hit safely in every one. Here he batted .414, slugged .759, and won MVP honors. Steve Blass, Nelson Briles, and Bruce Kison won all the Pirate victories with a combined ERA of 0.54.

1972 Oakland (A) over Cincinnati (N), 4–3. A's backup catcher Gene Tenace hit home runs in his first two series at bats, then went on to hit two more, becoming the surprise star and MVP selection. Rollie Fingers relieved in six of the contests, winning one and saving two.

1973 Oakland (A) over New York (N), 4–3. The Mets had the worst record of any pennant winner ever (82–79), but they lasted till the seventh game in a sloppily played (19 errors) affair. Darold Knowles pitched in all seven games for the A's, saving two. Reggie Jackson slugged his way to the first of his two series MVP awards.

1974 Oakland (A) over Los Angeles (N), 4–1. The A's won their third straight World Championship behind the three saves and one win of MVP Rollie Fingers. Joe Rudi (.333) and Bert Campaneris (.353) starred with the bats.

1975 Cincinnati (N) over Boston (A), 4–3. Five of the seven games were decided by one run, including the famous twelve-inning sixth contest won on a Carlton Fisk home run. Cincinnati used 23 relief pitchers to set a record. Pete Rose, the heart and soul of the Big Red Machine, hustled his way to MVP honors.

1976 Cincinnati (N) over New York (A), 4–0. The Big Red Machine drove over the Yankees, slugging .522 as a team. Seven of nine Reds hitters batted over .300, led by MVP Johnny Bench's .533 (1.133 slugging average).

1977 New York (A) over Los Angeles (N), 4–2. Reggie Jackson hit five homers, including three in the final game, to equal records set by Babe Ruth and win the MVP for the second time. Mike Torrez won two for the Yankees.

1978 New York (A) over Los Angeles (N), 4–2. Shortstop Bucky Dent and backup infielder Brian Doyle batted .417 and .438 respectively, pacing New York in its second straight six-game triumph. Dent was named MVP. In the last four contests, the Yankees outscored L.A. 28–8.

1979 Pittsburgh (N) over Baltimore (A), 4–3. The Pirates overcame a three games to one deficit as Earl Weaver's Orioles waited for the three-run homer that never came. Led by Willie Stargell (.400, 3 HRs) and Phil Garner (.500), Pittsburgh batted .323 as a team. "Pops" Stargell's on-field performance and team leadership of the Pirates' "family" were honored with the MVP.

1980 Philadelphia (N) over Kansas City (A), 4–2. The two teams batted .292 in a series decided largely by the relief pitching of Tug McGraw (1–1, 2 saves) vs. Dan Quisenberry (1–2, 1 save). Mike Schmidt took MVP honors with a .381 average and seven RBIs.

1981 Los Angeles (N) over New York (A), 4–2. Many observers called this sloppy series a fitting end to this strike-stricken 1981 season. Even the MVP award proved impossible to settle, as Pedro Guerrero, Steve Yeager, and Ron Cey shared the honor.

1982 St. Louis (N) over Milwaukee (A), 4–3. Joaquin Andujar won two games for the Cardinals, and Willie McGee had perhaps the greatest single series game by a rookie, with two homers and two great catches in Game Four. American League MVP Robin Yount batted .414 for the losers.

1983 Baltimore (A) over Philadelphia (N), 4–1. The Phillies couldn't hit Orioles' pitching, scoring but nine runs in the five games. Catcher Rick Dempsey hit four doubles and a home run, held the Phils to one stolen base, and was named MVP.

1984 Detroit (A) over San Diego (N), 4–1. The Tigers belted seven homers and backed them up with the pitching of Jack Morris (2–0, 2.00). Sparky Anderson become the first manager to win World Championships in both leagues. The Tigers' sure-handed shortstop, Alan Trammell, fielded flawlessly and hit with power to earn MVP honors.

1985 Kansas City (A) over St. Louis (N), 4–3. The Cards were one inning away from the title, but a disputed call at first base opened the door for the Royals in Game Six. They won that contest, then blew St. Louis away 11–0 in the finale. Bret Saberhagen won three for Kansas City, and the MVP.

1986 New York (N) over Boston (A), 4–3. As in 1985, misplays in the final inning of Game Six caused the series to turn around, as the Red Sox lost their fourth straight seven-game series. Mets third baseman Ray Knight capped a comeback year with clutch hitting and the series MVP.

1987 Minnesota (A) over St. Louis (N), 4–3. The Twins won their first championship by taking all four games in their exotic home park, the Metrodome. Cardinal pitching held them to five runs in the three games in St. Louis, but in Minnesota the Twins could not be contained, scoring 33 times. Frank Viola (2–1, ERA 3.72) was the MVP.

1988 Los Angeles (N) over Oakland (A), 4–1. Series MVP Orel Hershiser (2–0, 17 Ks) dazzled the powerful A's. Injured Dodger Kirk Gibson's dramatic two-out home run in the bottom of the ninth in Game One set the tone for the unexpected Los Angeles triumph.

1989 Oakland (A) over San Francisco (N), 4–0. The A's thoroughly dominated a weak Giants' pitching staff, pounding out 32 runs, 44 hits (including nine home runs) in only four games. Series MVP Dave Stewart and reliever Dennis Eckersley led an Oakland staff to shut down the Giants. This series will be long remembered for the major earthquake that struck the Bay Area just before Game Three and delayed the contest for 12 days.

1990 Cincinnati (N) over Oakland (A), 4–0. Cincinnati dominated the heavily favored A's in a stunning series sweep. The Reds hit .317 as a team, while their pitchers, led by MVP José Rijo, held Oakland's vaunted offense to a mere .207 series average. Billy Hatcher broke Babe Ruth's World Series record by hitting .750, and he set two other records, with seven consecutive hits and four doubles.

1991 Minnesota (A) over Atlanta (N), 4–3. No team in baseball had ever gone from worst to first. In 1991, it happened twice, as the Twins and Braves, both of whom had finished last in their respective divisions the previous year, met in one of the most exciting fall classics ever. Five games were decided by one run, three went into extra innings, and four were decided on the last at-bat. Perhaps the best of all was Game Seven, a scoreless affair until the bottom of the 10th inning, when the Twins finally scored a run. Jack Morris went the distance for Minnesota and earned MVP honors.

1992 Toronto (A) over Atlanta (N), 4-2. The Blue Jays became the first non-American team to win (or play in) the World Series. Braves closer Jeff Reardon gave up the winning hits in Games Two and Three, making Atlanta manager Bobby Cox reluctant to use him the rest of the series. Dave Winfield's first extra-base hit in World Series play broke a 3–3 tie in the 11th inning of Game Six to send the Braves to their second straight World Series defeat. Toronto catcher Pat Borders was the MVP with a .450 average.

1993 Toronto (A) over Philadelphia (N), 4–2 The Blue Jays became the first team since the 1977–78 Yankees to repeat as World Series champions, battering the Phillies pitching staff for 45 runs (despite being shut out in Game Five). Toronto outfielder Joe Carter's home run in the bottom of the ninth in Game Six marked only the second time the World Series had ended on a home run (Bill Mazeroski's Game Seven shot in 1960 was the other). Toronto DH Paul Molitor went 12 for 24 with six extra-base hits to win MVP honors.

1994 World Series canceled. The longest work stoppage in professional sports history, a 232-day dispute between players and owners over a cap on player salaries, forced the cancellation of the World Series and playoffs for the first time in baseball history.

1995 Atlanta (N) over Cleveland (A), 4–2. Good pitching beats good hitting, as evidenced by this dramatic series. Baseball's best pitching staff (the Braves) held the game's most explosive offense (the Indians) to a .179 average, five home runs, and 19 runs. Five of the six games were decided by one run, including the clincher: a dazzling 1–0 one-hitter by Atlanta's Tom Glavine. The performance earned him the Series MVP honors.

WORLD SERIES RECORDS BATTING

Runs scored

Mickey Mantle	42
Yogi Berra	41
Babe Ruth	37

Hits

Yogi Berra	71
Mickey Mantle	59
Frankie Frisch	58
Most hits in one series:	13

(Bobby Richardson, 1960; Lou Brock, 1968; Marty Barrett, 1986)

Home runs

Mickey Mantle	18
Babe Ruth	15
Yogi Berra	12
Most home runs in one series:	5

(Reggie Jackson, 1977)

Runs batted in

Mickey Mantle	40
Yogi Berra	39
Lou Gehrig	35
Most runs batted in in one series:	12

(Bobby Richardson, 1960)

Source: Major League Baseball.

WORLD SERIES MVP WINNERS

Year	Name	Team
1955	Johnny Podres	Brooklyn Dodgers
1956	Don Larsen	N.Y. Yankees
1957	Lew Burdette	Milwaukee Braves
1958	Bob Turley	N.Y. Yankees
1959	Larry Sherry	L.A. Dodgers
1960	Bobby Richardson	N.Y. Yankees
1961	Whitey Ford	N.Y. Yankees
1962	Ralph Terry	N.Y. Yankees
1963	Sandy Koufax	L.A. Dodgers
1964	Bob Gibson	St. Louis Cardinals
1965	Sandy Koufax	L.A. Dodgers
1966	Frank Robinson	Baltimore Orioles
1967	Bob Gibson	St. Louis Cardinals
1968	Mickey Lolich	Detroit Tigers
1969	Donn Clendenon	N.Y. Mets
1970	Brooks Robinson	Baltimore Orioles
1971	Roberto Clemente	Pittsburgh Pirates
1972	Gene Tenace	Oakland A's
1973	Reggie Jackson	Oakland A's
1974	Rollie Fingers	Oakland A's
1975	Pete Rose	Cincinnati Reds
1976	Johnny Bench	Cincinnati Reds
1977	Reggie Jackson	N.Y. Yankees
1978	Bucky Dent	N.Y. Yankees
1979	Willie Stargell	Pittsburgh Pirates
1980	Mike Schmidt	Philadelphia Phillies
1981	Ron Cey	L.A. Dodgers
	Pedro Guerrero	L.A. Dodgers
	Steve Yeager	L.A. Dodgers
1982	Darrell Porter	St. Louis Cardinals
1983	Rick Dempsey	Baltimore Orioles
1984	Alan Trammell	Detroit Tigers
1985	Bret Saberhagen	Kansas City Royals
1986	Ray Knight	N.Y. Mets
1987	Frank Viola	Minnesota Twins
1988	Orel Hershiser	L.A. Dodgers
1989	Dave Stewart	Oakland A's
1990	José Rijo	Cincinnati Reds
1991	Jack Morris	Minnesota Twins
1992	Pat Borders	Toronto Blue Jays
1993	Paul Molitor	Toronto Blue Jays
1994	World Series canceled	
1995	Tom Glavine	Atlanta Braves

THE 1995 WORLD SERIES

Game	Winner	Loser
Game 1	ATLANTA 3	Cleveland 2

Atlanta ace Greg Maddux was nearly flawless, limiting the Indians to two hits and two unearned runs on 95 pitches. Cleveland starter Orel Hershiser was nearly as good, limiting the Braves to three hits over six innings, but he walked the first two batters he faced in the seventh inning and both came around to score courtesy of a third walk, a fielder's choice, and Rafael Belliard's perfectly executed suicide squeeze. It was Hershiser's first postseason loss after seven consecutive wins.

Game 2 ATLANTA 4 Cleveland 3

Braves catcher Javier Lopez broke a 2–2 tie with a two-run home run in the sixth inning, then nabbed Indians right-fielder Manny Ramirez straying too far off first base to thwart a Cleveland threat in the eighth. Atlanta starter Tom Glavine was less than perfect, but forced the Indians to strand runners in scoring position in both the fourth and fifth innings. Atlanta closer Mark Wohlers got the Braves out of a jam in the eighth and forced Carlos Baerga to pop up with the tying run at second base for the game's final out.

Game 3 CLEVELAND 7 (11 innings) Atlanta 5

The Indians returned home and immediately jumped all over Braves starter John Smoltz, scoring four runs in the first three innings. But the Braves rallied in the eighth against tiring Cleveland starter Charles Nagy and two relievers to take a 6–5 lead. Then the Braves blew their lead in the bottom of the eighth, when Sandy Alomar lashed a run-scoring double off Atlanta closer Mark Wohlers. Alejandro Peña came in in the 11th and failed to retire a batter, giving up a double to Carlos Baerga, an intentional walk to Albert Belle, and the game-winning hit to Eddie Murray.

Game 4 Atlanta 5 CLEVELAND 2

Braves skipper Bobby Cox sent Steve Avery to the hill rather than bringing Greg Maddux back on three days rest. And it worked like a charm. Avery continued his postseason mastery, limiting the Indians to three hits and one run over six innings. Meanwhile, the Braves offense broke open a 1–1 game by scoring three runs in the seventh inning. David Justice capped the rally with a two-run single.

Game 5 CLEVELAND 5 Atlanta 4

The Indians scored four runs over seven innings against Greg Maddux, while Cleveland starter Orel Hershiser returned to the form that had made him unbeaten in postseason play until his Game 1 loss. But the game was again settled by the bullpens. In the eighth, Jim Thome hit a rocket home run off Atlanta reliever Brad Clontz to extend Cleveland's lead to 5–2. It proved to be the difference, as closer Jose Mesa gave up a two-run homer to Ryan Klesko to bring the Braves within one. But they got no closer, as Mesa struck out Mark Lemke to send the series back to Atlanta.

Game 6 ATLANTA 1 Cleveland 0

Only two hits mattered in this game: Tony Peña's soft single in the top of the sixth inning to break up Tom Glavine's no-hitter, and David Justice's solo home run in the bottom of the sixth to provide the game's only run. Braves closer Mark Wohlers pitched a 1-2-3 ninth to preserve the one-hit shutout and bring Atlanta its first World Series championship ever.

MAJOR LEAGUE BASEBALL ALL-TIME CAREER LEADERS

BATTING AVERAGE (minimum 4,000 at bats)

1. Ty Cobb	.367
2. Rogers Hornsby	.358
3. Joe Jackson	.356
4. Ed Delahanty	.346
5. Ted Williams	.344
6. Tris Speaker	.344
7. Billy Hamilton	.344
8. Willie Keeler	.343
9. Dan Brouthers	.342
10. Babe Ruth	.342

TOTAL BASES

1. Hank Aaron	6,856
2. Stan Musial	6,134
3. Willie Mays	6,066
4. Ty Cobb	5,863
5. Babe Ruth	5,793
6. Pete Rose	5,752
7. Carl Yastrzemski	5,539
8. Frank Robinson	5,373
9. Tris Speaker	5,104
10. Lou Gehrig	5,059

SLUGGING AVERAGE (minimum 4,000 at bats)

1. Babe Ruth	.690
2. Ted Williams	.634
3. Lou Gehrig	.632
4. Jimmie Foxx	.609
5. Hank Greenberg	.605
6. Joe DiMaggio	.579
7. Rogers Hornsby	.577
8. Johnny Mize	.562
9. Stan Musial	.559
10. Willie Mays	.557

RUNS BATTED IN

1. Hank Aaron	2,297
2. Babe Ruth	2,211
3. Lou Gehrig	1,990
4. Ty Cobb	1,961
5. Stan Musial	1,951
6. Jimmie Foxx	1,921
7. Willie Mays	1,903
8. Mel Ott	1,861
9. Carl Yastrzemski	1,844
10. Ted Williams	1,839

RUNS

1. Ty Cobb	2,245
2. Babe Ruth	2,174
Hank Aaron	2,174
4. Pete Rose	2,165
5. Willie Mays	2,062
6. Stan Musial	1,949
7. Lou Gehrig	1,888
8. Tris Speaker	1,881
9. Mel Ott	1,849
10. Frank Robinson	1,829

HITS

1. Pete Rose	4,256
2. Ty Cobb	4,191
3. Hank Aaron	3,771
4. Stan Musial	3,630
5. Tris Speaker	3,515
6. Carl Yastrzemski	3,419
7. Honus Wagner	3,418
8. Eddie Collins	3,311
9. Willie Mays	3,283
10. Nap Lajoie	3,244

EXTRA BASE HITS

1. Hank Aaron	1,477
2. Stan Musial	1,377
3. Babe Ruth	1,356
4. Willie Mays	1,323
5. Lou Gehrig	1,190
6. Frank Robinson	1,186
7. Carl Yastrzemski	1,157
8. Ty Cobb	1,139
9. Tris Speaker	1,132
10. Jimmie Foxx	1,117
Ted Williams	1,117

GAMES PLAYED

1. Pete Rose	3,562
2. Carl Yastrzemski	3,308
3. Hank Aaron	3,298
4. Ty Cobb	3,034
5. Stan Musial	3,026
6. Willie Mays	2,992
7. Dave Winfield[1]	2,972
8. Rusty Staub	2,951
9. Brooks Robinson	2,896
10. Robin Yount	2,856

STOLEN BASES

1. Rickey Henderson[1]	1,117
2. Lou Brock	938
3. Ty Cobb	892
4. Tim Raines[1]	777
5. Eddie Collins	743
6. Max Carey	738
7. Honus Wagner	703
8. Joe Morgan	689
9. Willie Wilson	661
10. Bert Campaneris	649

CONSECUTIVE GAMES

1. Cal Ripken, Jr.[1]	2,153
2. Lou Gehrig	2,130
3. Everett Scott	1,307
4. Steve Garvey	1,207
5. Billy Williams	1,117
6. Joe Sewell	1,103
7. Stan Musial	895
8. Eddie Yost	829
9. Gus Sur	822
10. Nellie Fox	798

LIFETIME PITCHING LEADERS

WINS

1. Cy Young	511
2. Walter Johnson	416
3. Christy Mathewson	373
Grover Alexander	373
5. Warren Spahn	363
6. Pud Galvin	361
Kid Nichols	361
8. Tim Keefe	342
9. Steve Carlton	329
10. Eddie Plank	327

INNINGS PITCHED

1. Cy Young	7,356
2. Pud Galvin	5,941
3. Walter Johnson	5,923
4. Phil Niekro	5,403
5. Nolan Ryan	5,387
6. Gaylord Perry	5,351
7. Don Sutton	5,280
8. Warren Spahn	5,244
9. Steve Carlton	5,217
10. Grover Alexander	5,189

EARNED RUN AVG. (minimum 1,500 innings)

1. Ed Walsh	1.82
2. Addie Joss	1.88
3. Mordecai "Three Finger" Brown	2.06
4. Christy Mathewson	2.13
5. Rube Waddell	2.16
6. Walter Johnson	2.17
7. Orval Overall	2.24
8. Ed Reulbach	2.28
9. Jim Scott	2.32
10. Eddie Plank	2.34

STRIKEOUTS

1. Nolan Ryan	5,714
2. Steve Carlton	4,136
3. Bert Blyleven	3,701
4. Tom Seaver	3,640
5. Don Sutton	3,574
6. Gaylord Perry	3,534
7. Walter Johnson	3,508
8. Phil Niekro	3,342
9. Ferguson Jenkins	3,192
10. Bob Gibson	3,117

SHUTOUTS

1. Walter Johnson	110
2. Grover Alexander	90
3. Christy Mathewson	80
4. Cy Young	76
5. Eddie Plank	69
6. Warren Spahn	63
7. Nolan Ryan	61
Tom Seaver	61
9. Bert Blyleven	60
10. Don Sutton	58

Note: For home run leaders, see "Major League Players, 400 or More Home Runs." 1. Player active during 1995 season. **Source:** Major League Baseball.

MAJOR LEAGUE PLAYERS, 400 OR MORE HOME RUNS

Player	HRs	Player	HRs
Hank Aaron	755	Eddie Mathews	512
Babe Ruth	714	Mel Ott	511
Willie Mays	660	Lou Gehrig	493
Frank Robinson	586	Eddie Murray[1]	479
Harmon Killebrew	573	Stan Musial	475
Reggie Jackson	563	Willie Stargell	475
Mike Schmidt	548	Dave Winfield[1]	465
Mickey Mantle	536	Carl Yastrzemski	452
Jimmie Foxx	534	Dave Kingman	442
Willie McCovey	521	Billy Williams	426
Ted Williams	521	Darrell Evans	414
Ernie Banks	512	Duke Snider	407

1. Active during the 1995 season.

MAJOR LEAGUE PLAYERS, 3,000 OR MORE HITS

Player	Hits	Player	Hits
Pete Rose	4,256	George Brett	3,154
Ty Cobb	4,191	Paul Waner	3,152
Hank Aaron	3,771	Robin Yount	3,142
Stan Musial	3,630	Dave Winfield[1]	3,110
Tris Speaker	3,515	Eddie Murray[1]	3,071
Carl Yastrzemski	3,419	Rod Carew	3,053
Honus Wagner	3,418	Cap Anson	3,041
Eddie Collins	3,311	Lou Brock	3,023
Willie Mays	3,283	Al Kaline	3,007
Nap Lajoie	3,244	Roberto Clemente	3,000

1. Active during 1995 season.

A Very Exclusive Club

In 1995, Eddie Murray of the Cleveland Indians became only the sixth man in baseball history to collect 400 homers and 3,000 hits. His teammate Dave Winfield achieved the feat two years earlier as a member of the Minnesota Twins. The last player to turn the trick before him was Carl Yastrzemski, who joined a group that until that point included only Willie Mays, Hank Aaron, and Stan Musial.

Cal Ripken of the Baltimore Orioles joined an even more exclusive club in 1995: one that includes only himself. On Sept. 6, he played in his 2,131st consecutive game, surpassing Lou Gehrig's streak that many thought would never be broken. As the bottom of the fifth inning began (making it an official game), fans at Baltimore's Camden Yards stopped the game for a 22-and-a-half-minute standing ovation to the Orioles' shortstop. To top it off, Ripken hit a home run in the Orioles' victory over the California Angels.

BATTING CHAMPIONS

NATIONAL LEAGUE

Year	Player	Team	Avg.
1876	Roscoe Barnes	Chicago Cubs	.403
1877	James White	Boston Braves	.385
1878	Abner Dalrymple	Milwaukee Brewers	.356
1879	Cap Anson	Chicago Cubs	.407
1880	George Gore	Chicago Cubs	.365
1881	Cap Anson	Chicago Cubs	.399
1882	Dan Brouthers	Buffalo Bisons	.367
1883	Dan Brouthers	Buffalo Bisons	.371
1884	Jim O'Rourke	Buffalo Bisons	.350
1885	Roger Connor	N.Y. Giants	.371
1886	Mike Kelly	Chicago Cubs	.388
1887	Cap Anson	Chicago Cubs	.421
1888	Cap Anson	Chicago Cubs	.343
1889	Dan Brouthers	Boston Braves	.373
1890	Jack Glasscock	N.Y. Giants	.336
1891	Billy Hamilton	Philadelphia Phillies	.338
1892	"Cupid" Childs	Cleveland Spiders	.335
	Dan Brouthers	Brooklyn Dodgers	.335
1893	Hugh Duffy	Boston Braves	.378
1894	Hugh Duffy	Boston Braves	.438
1895	Jesse Burkett	Cleveland Spiders	.423
1896	Jesse Burkett	Cleveland Spiders	.410
1897	Willie Keeler	Baltimore Orioles	.432
1898	Willie Keeler	Baltimore Orioles	.379
1899	Ed Delahanty	Philadelphia Phillies	.408
1900	Honus Wagner	Pittsburgh Pirates	.380
1901	Jesse Burkett	St. Louis Cardinals	.382
1902	C.H. Beaumont	Pittsburgh Pirates	.357
1903	Honus Wagner	Pittsburgh Pirates	.355
1904	Honus Wagner	Pittsburgh Pirates	.349
1905	J. Bentley Seymour	Cincinnati Reds	.377
1906	Honus Wagner	Pittsburgh Pirates	.339
1907	Honus Wagner	Pittsburgh Pirates	.350
1908	Honus Wagner	Pittsburgh Pirates	.354
1909	Honus Wagner	Pittsburgh Pirates	.339
1910	Sherwood Magee	Philadelphia Phillies	.331
1911	Honus Wagner	Pittsburgh Pirates	.334
1912	Heinie Zimmerman	Chicago Cubs	.372
1913	Jake Daubert	Brooklyn Dodgers	.350
1914	Jake Daubert	Brooklyn Dodgers	.329
1915	Larry Doyle	N.Y. Giants	.320
1916	Hal Chase	Cincinnati Reds	.339
1917	Edd Roush	Cincinnati Reds	.341
1918	Zack Wheat	Brooklyn Dodgers	.335
1919	Edd Roush	Cincinnati Reds	.321
1920	Rogers Hornsby	St. Louis Cardinals	.370
1921	Rogers Hornsby	St. Louis Cardinals	.397
1922	Rogers Hornsby	St. Louis Cardinals	.401
1923	Rogers Hornsby	St. Louis Cardinals	.384
1924	Rogers Hornsby	St. Louis Cardinals	.424
1925	Rogers Hornsby	St. Louis Cardinals	.403
1926	Bubbles Hargrave	Cincinnati Reds	.353
1927	Paul Waner	Pittsburgh Pirates	.380
1928	Rogers Hornsby	Boston Braves	.387
1929	Lefty O'Doul	Philadelphia Phillies	.398
1930	Bill Terry	N.Y. Giants	.401
1931	Chick Hafey[1]	St. Louis Cardinals	.349
1932	Lefty O'Doul	Brooklyn Dodgers	.368
1933	Chuck Klein	Philadelphia Phillies	.368
1934	Paul Waner	Pittsburgh Pirates	.362
1935	Arky Vaughan	Pittsburgh Pirates	.385
1936	Paul Waner	Pittsburgh Pirates	.373
1937	Joe Medwick	St. Louis Cardinals	.374
1938	Ernie Lombardi	Cincinnati Reds	.342
1939	Johnny Mize	St. Louis Cardinals	.349
1940	Debs Garms	Pittsburgh Pirates	.355
1941	Pete Reiser	Brooklyn Dodgers	.343
1942	Ernie Lombardi	Boston Braves	.330
1943	Stan Musial	St. Louis Cardinals	.357
1944	Dixie Walker	Brooklyn Dodgers	.357
1945	Phil Cavarretta	Chicago Cubs	.355
1946	Stan Musial	St. Louis Cardinals	.365
1947	Harry Walker	St. Louis-Philadelphia	.363
1948	Stan Musial	St. Louis Cardinals	.376
1949	Jackie Robinson	Brooklyn Dodgers	.342
1950	Stan Musial	St. Louis Cardinals	.346
1951	Stan Musial	St. Louis Cardinals	.355
1952	Stan Musial	St. Louis Cardinals	.336
1953	Carl Furillo	Brooklyn Dodgers	.344
1954	Willie Mays	N.Y. Giants	.345
1955	Richie Ashburn	Philadelphia Phillies	.338
1956	Hank Aaron	Milwaukee Braves	.328
1957	Stan Musial	St. Louis Cardinals	.351
1958	Richie Ashburn	Philadelphia Phillies	.350
1959	Hank Aaron	Milwaukee Braves	.355
1960	Dick Groat	Pittsburgh Pirates	.325
1961	Roberto Clemente	Pittsburgh Pirates	.351
1962	Tommy Davis	L.A. Dodgers	.346
1963	Tommy Davis	L.A. Dodgers	.326
1964	Roberto Clemente	Pittsburgh Pirates	.339
1965	Roberto Clemente	Pittsburgh Pirates	.329
1966	Matty Alou	Pittsburgh Pirates	.342
1967	Roberto Clemente	Pittsburgh Pirates	.357
1968	Pete Rose	Cincinnati Reds	.335
1969	Pete Rose	Cincinnati Reds	.348
1970	Rico Carty	Atlanta Braves	.366
1971	Joe Torre	St. Louis Cardinals	.363
1972	Billy Williams	Chicago Cubs	.333
1973	Pete Rose	Cincinnati Reds	.338
1974	Ralph Garr	Atlanta Braves	.353
1975	Bill Madlock	Chicago Cubs	.354
1976	Bill Madlock	Chicago Cubs	.339
1977	Dave Parker	Pittsburgh Pirates	.338
1978	Dave Parker	Pittsburgh Pirates	.334
1979	Keith Hernandez	St. Louis Cardinals	.344
1980	Bill Buckner	Chicago Cubs	.324
1981[2]	Bill Madlock	Pittsburgh Pirates	.341
1982	Al Oliver	Montreal Expos	.331
1983	Bill Madlock	Pittsburgh Pirates	.323
1984	Tony Gwynn	San Diego Padres	.351
1985	Willie McGee	St. Louis Cardinals	.353
1986	Tim Raines	Montreal Expos	.334
1987	Tony Gwynn	San Diego Padres	.370
1988	Tony Gwynn	San Diego Padres	.313
1989	Tony Gwynn	San Diego Padres	.336
1990	Willie McGee	St. Louis Cardinals	.335
1991	Terry Pendleton	Atlanta Braves	.319
1992	Gary Sheffield	San Diego Padres	.330
1993	Andres Galarraga	Colorado Rockies	.370
1994[2]	Tony Gwynn	San Diego Padres	.394
1995[2]	Tony Gwynn	San Diego Padres	.368

AMERICAN LEAGUE

Year	Player	Team	Avg.
1901	Nap Lajoie	Philadelphia A's	.422
1902	Ed Delahanty	Washington Senators	.376
1903	Nap Lajoie	Cleveland Indians	.355
1904	Nap Lajoie	Cleveland Indians	.381
1905	Elmer Flick	Cleveland Indians	.306
1906	George Stone	St. Louis Browns	.358
1907	Ty Cobb	Detroit Tigers	.350
1908	Ty Cobb	Detroit Tigers	.324
1909	Ty Cobb	Detroit Tigers	.377
1910	Ty Cobb	Detroit Tigers	.385
1911	Ty Cobb	Detroit Tigers	.420
1912	Ty Cobb	Detroit Tigers	.410
1913	Ty Cobb	Detroit Tigers	.390
1914	Ty Cobb	Detroit Tigers	.368
1915	Ty Cobb	Detroit Tigers	.370
1916	Tris Speaker	Cleveland Indians	.386
1917	Ty Cobb	Detroit Tigers	.383
1918	Ty Cobb	Detroit Tigers	.382
1919	Ty Cobb	Detroit Tigers	.407
1920	George Sisler	St. Louis Browns	.407
1921	Harry Heilmann	Detroit Tigers	.394
1922	George Sisler	St. Louis Browns	.420
1923	Harry Heilmann	Detroit Tigers	.403
1924	Babe Ruth	N.Y. Yankees	.378
1925	Harry Heilmann	Detroit Tigers	.393
1926	Heinie Manush	Detroit Tigers	.377
1927	Harry Heilmann	Detroit Tigers	.398
1928	Goose Goslin	Washington Senators	.379
1929	Lew Fonseca	Cleveland Indians	.369
1930	Al Simmons	Philadelphia A's	.381
1931	Al Simmons	Philadelphia A's	.390
1932	Dale Alexander	Detroit-Boston	.367
1933	Jimmie Foxx	Philadelphia A's	.356
1934	Lou Gehrig	N.Y. Yankees	.363
1935	Buddy Myer	Washington Senators	.349
1936	Luke Appling	Chicago White Sox	.388
1937	Charlie Gehringer	Detroit Tigers	.371
1938	Jimmie Foxx	Boston Red Sox	.349
1939	Joe DiMaggio	N.Y. Yankees	.381
1940	Joe DiMaggio	N.Y. Yankees	.352
1941	Ted Williams	Boston Red Sox	.406
1942	Ted Williams	Boston Red Sox	.356
1943	Luke Appling	Chicago White Sox	.328
1944	Lou Boudreau	Cleveland Indians	.327
1945	Snuffy Stirnweiss	N.Y. Yankees	.309
1946	Mickey Vernon	Washington Senators	.352
1947	Ted Williams	Boston Red Sox	.343
1948	Ted Williams	Boston Red Sox	.369
1949	George Kell	Detroit Tigers	.343
1950	Billy Goodman	Boston Red Sox	.354
1951	Ferris Fain	Philadelphia A's	.344
1952	Ferris Fain	Philadelphia A's	.327
1953	Mickey Vernon	Washington Senators	.337
1954	Bobby Avila	Cleveland Indians	.341
1955	Al Kaline	Detroit Tigers	.340
1956	Mickey Mantle	N.Y. Yankees	.353
1957	Ted Williams	Boston Red Sox	.388
1958	Ted Williams	Boston Red Sox	.328
1959	Harvey Kuenn	Detroit Tigers	.353
1960	Pete Runnels	Boston Red Sox	.320
1961	Norm Cash	Detroit Tigers	.361
1962	Pete Runnels	Boston Red Sox	.326

Year	Player	Team	Avg.
1963	Carl Yastrzemski	Boston Red Sox	.321
1964	Tony Oliva	Minnesota Twins	.323
1965	Tony Oliva	Minnesota Twins	.321
1966	Frank Robinson	Baltimore Orioles	.316
1967	Carl Yastrzemski	Boston Red Sox	.326
1968	Carl Yastrzemski	Boston Red Sox	.301
1969	Rod Carew	Minnesota Twins	.332
1970	Alex Johnson	California Angels	.329
1971	Tony Oliva	Minnesota Twins	.337
1972	Rod Carew	Minnesota Twins	.318
1973	Rod Carew	Minnesota Twins	.350
1974	Rod Carew	Minnesota Twins	.364
1975	Rod Carew	Minnesota Twins	.359
1976	George Brett	K.C. Royals	.333
1977	Rod Carew	Minnesota Twins	.388
1978	Rod Carew	Minnesota Twins	.333
1979	Fred Lynn	Boston Red Sox	.333
1980	George Brett	K.C. Royals	.390
1981[2]	Carney Lansford	Boston Red Sox	.336
1982	Willie Wilson	K.C. Royals	.332
1983	Wade Boggs	Boston Red Sox	.361
1984	Don Mattingly	N.Y. Yankees	.343
1985	Wade Boggs	Boston Red Sox	.368
1986	Wade Boggs	Boston Red Sox	.357
1987	Wade Boggs	Boston Red Sox	.363
1988	Wade Boggs	Boston Red Sox	.366
1989	Kirby Puckett	Minnesota Twins	.339
1990	George Brett	K.C. Royals	.329
1991	Julio Franco	Texas Rangers	.341
1992	Edgar Martinez	Seattle Mariners	.343
1993	John Olerud	Toronto Blue Jays	.363
1994[2]	Paul O'Neill	N.Y. Yankees	.359
1995[2]	Edgar Martinez	Seattle Mariners	.356

1. Hafey led with .3489; Bill Terry of N.Y. was second with .3486; Jim Bottomley of St. Louis was third at .3482. 2. Strike-shortened season.

MOST WINS BY MANAGERS

Manager	Wins	Losses	Pct.
1. Connie Mack	3,776	4,025	.484
2. John McGraw	2,840	1,984	.589
3. Bucky Harris	2,159	2,219	.493
4. Joe McCarthy	2,126	1,335	.614
5. Walter Alston	2,040	1,613	.558
6. Sparky Anderson[1]	2,194	1,834	.545
7. Leo Durocher	2,010	1,710	.540
8. Casey Stengel	1,926	1,867	.508
9. Gene Mauch	1,901	2,037	.483
10. Bill McKechnie	1,898	1,724	.524

1. Active during 1995 season.

ROOKIE OF THE YEAR

Year	Name	Team
1947[1]	Jackie Robinson	Brooklyn Dodgers
1948[1]	Alvin Dark	Boston Braves

NATIONAL LEAGUE

Year	Name	Team
1949	Don Newcombe (P)	Brooklyn Dodgers
1950	Sam Jethroe	Boston Braves
1951	Willie Mays	N.Y. Giants
1952	Joe Black (P)	Brooklyn Dodgers
1953	Junior Gilliam	Brooklyn Dodgers
1954	Wally Moon	St. Louis Cardinals
1955	Bill Virdon	St. Louis Cardinals
1956	Frank Robinson	Cincinnati Reds
1957	Jack Sanford (P)	Philadelphia Phillies
1958	Orlando Cepeda	S.F. Giants
1959	Willie McCovey	S.F. Giants
1960	Frank Howard	L.A. Dodgers
1961	Billy Williams	Chicago Cubs
1962	Ken Hubbs	Chicago Cubs
1963	Pete Rose	Cincinnati Reds
1964	Richie Allen	Philadelphia Phillies
1965	Jim Lefebvre	L.A. Dodgers
1966	Tommy Helms	Cincinnati Reds
1967	Tom Seaver (P)	N.Y. Mets
1968	Johnny Bench	Cincinnati Reds
1969	Ted Sizemore	L.A. Dodgers
1970	Carl Morton (P)	Montreal Expos
1971	Earl Williams	Atlanta Braves
1972	Jon Matlack (P)	N.Y. Mets
1973	Gary Matthews	S.F. Giants
1974	Bake McBride	St. Louis Cardinals
1975	John Montefusco (P)	S.F. Giants
1976	Pat Zachry (P)	Cincinnati Reds
	Butch Metzger (P)	San Diego Padres
1977	Andre Dawson	Montreal Expos
1978	Bob Horner	Atlanta Braves
1979	Rick Sutcliffe (P)	L.A. Dodgers
1980	Steve Howe (P)	L.A. Dodgers
1981	Fernando Valenzuela (P)	L.A. Dodgers
1982	Steve Sax	L.A. Dodgers
1983	Darryl Strawberry	N.Y. Mets
1984	Dwight Gooden (P)	N.Y. Mets
1985	Vince Coleman	St. Louis Cardinals
1986	Todd Worrell (P)	St. Louis Cardinals
1987	Benito Santiago	San Diego Padres
1988	Chris Sabo	Cincinnati Reds
1989	Jerome Walton	Chicago Cubs
1990	Dave Justice	Atlanta Braves
1991	Jeff Bagwell	Houston Astros
1992	Eric Karros	L.A. Dodgers
1993	Mike Piazza	L.A. Dodgers
1994	Raul Mondesi	L.A. Dodgers

AMERICAN LEAGUE

Year	Player	Team
1949	Roy Sievers	St. Louis Browns
1950	Walt Dropo	Boston Red Sox
1951	Gil McDougald	N.Y. Yankees
1952	Harry Byrd (P)	Philadelphia A's
1953	Harvey Kuenn	Detroit Tigers
1954	Bob Grim (P)	N.Y. Yankees
1955	Herb Score (P)	Cleveland Indians
1956	Luis Aparicio	Chicago White Sox
1957	Tony Kubek	N.Y. Yankees
1958	Albie Pearson	Washington Senators
1959	Bob Allison	Washington Senators
1960	Ron Hansen	Baltimore Orioles
1961	Don Schwall (P)	Boston Red Sox
1962	Tom Tresh	N.Y. Yankees
1963	Gary Peters (P)	Chicago White Sox
1964	Tony Oliva	Minnesota Twins
1965	Curt Blefary	Baltimore Orioles
1966	Tommie Agee	Chicago White Sox
1967	Rod Carew	Minnesota Twins
1968	Stan Bahnsen (P)	N.Y. Yankees
1969	Lou Piniella	K.C. Royals
1970	Thurman Munson	N.Y. Yankees
1971	Chris Chambliss	Cleveland Indians
1972	Carlton Fisk	Boston Red Sox
1973	Al Bumbry	Baltimore Orioles
1974	Mike Hargrove	Texas Rangers
1975	Fred Lynn	Boston Red Sox
1976	Mark Fidrych (P)	Detroit Tigers
1977	Eddie Murray	Baltimore Orioles
1978	Lou Whitaker	Detroit Tigers
1979	John Castino	Minnesota Twins
	Alfredo Griffin	Toronto Blue Jays
1980	Joe Charboneau	Cleveland Indians
1981	Dave Righetti (P)	N.Y. Yankees
1982	Cal Ripken, Jr.	Baltimore Orioles
1983	Ron Kittle	Chicago White Sox
1984	Alvin Davis	Seattle Mariners
1985	Ozzie Guillen	Chicago White Sox
1986	Jose Canseco	Oakland A's
1987	Mark McGwire	Oakland A's
1988	Walt Weiss	Oakland A's
1989	Greg Olson (P)	Baltimore Orioles
1990	Sandy Alomar, Jr.	Cleveland Indians
1991	Chuck Knoblauch	Minnesota Twins
1992	Pat Listach	Milwaukee Brewers
1993	Tim Salmon	California Angels
1994	Bob Hamelin	K.C. Royals

Note: P = pitcher. 1. One player selected as Major League Rookie of the Year. Policy of naming a player from each league was inaugurated in 1949. **Source:** Baseball Writers Association.

CY YOUNG AWARD WINNERS

BOTH LEAGUES

Year	Name	Team	Won	Lost	ERA
1956	Don Newcombe	Brooklyn Dodgers	27	7	3.06
1957	Warren Spahn	Milwaukee Braves	21	11	2.69
1958	Bob Turley	N.Y. Yankees	21	7	2.97
1959	Early Wynn	Chicago White Sox	22	10	3.17
1960	Vernon Law	Pittsburgh Pirates	20	9	3.08
1961	Whitey Ford	N.Y. Yankees	25	4	3.21
1962	Don Drysdale	L.A. Dodgers	25	9	2.83
1963	Sandy Koufax	L.A. Dodgers	25	5	1.88
1964	Dean Chance	L.A. Angels	20	9	1.65
1965	Sandy Koufax	L.A. Dodgers	26	8	2.04
1966	Sandy Koufax	L.A. Dodgers	27	9	1.73

NATIONAL LEAGUE

Year	Name	Team	Won	Lost	ERA
1967	Mike McCormick	S.F. Giants	22	10	2.85
1968	Bob Gibson	St. Louis Cardinals	22	9	1.12
1969	Tom Seaver	N.Y. Mets	25	7	2.21
1970	Bob Gibson	St. Louis Cardinals	23	7	3.12
1971	Ferguson Jenkins	Chicago Cubs	24	13	2.77
1972	Steve Carlton	Philadelphia Phillies	27	10	1.97
1973	Tom Seaver	N.Y. Mets	19	10	2.08
1974	Mike Marshall[1]	L.A. Dodgers	15	12	2.42
1975	Tom Seaver	N.Y. Mets	22	9	2.38
1976	Randy Jones	San Diego Padres	22	14	2.74
1977	Steve Carlton	Philadelphia Phillies	23	10	2.64
1978	Gaylord Perry	San Diego Padres	21	6	2.72
1979	Bruce Sutter[2]	Chicago Cubs	6	6	2.23
1980	Steve Carlton	Philadelphia Phillies	24	9	2.34
1981	Fernando Valenzuela	L.A. Dodgers	13	7	2.48
1982	Steve Carlton	Philadelphia Phillies	23	11	3.10
1983	John Denny	Philadelphia Phillies	19	6	2.37
1984	Rick Sutcliffe	Chicago Cubs	20	6	3.64
1985	Dwight Gooden	N.Y. Mets	24	4	1.53
1986	Mike Scott	Houston Astros	18	10	2.22
1987	Steve Bedrosian[3]	Philadelphia Phillies	5	3	2.83
1988	Orel Hershiser	L.A. Dodgers	23	8	2.26
1989	Mark Davis[4]	San Diego Padres	4	3	1.85
1990	Doug Drabek	Pittsburgh Pirates	22	6	2.76
1991	Tom Glavine	Atlanta Braves	20	11	2.55
1992	Greg Maddux	Chicago Cubs	20	11	2.18
1993	Greg Maddux	Atlanta Braves	20	10	2.36
1994	Greg Maddux[5]	Atlanta Braves	16	6	1.56

AMERICAN LEAGUE

Year	Name	Team	Won	Lost	ERA
1967	Jim Lonborg	Boston Red Sox	22	9	3.16
1968	Denny McLain	Detroit Tigers	31	6	1.96
1969	Mike Cuellar	Baltimore Orioles	23	11	2.38
	Denny McLain (tie)	Detroit Tigers	24	9	2.80
1970	Jim Perry	Minnesota Twins	24	12	3.03
1971	Vida Blue	Oakland A's	24	8	1.82
1972	Gaylord Perry	Cleveland Indians	24	16	1.92
1973	Jim Palmer	Baltimore Orioles	22	9	2.40
1974	Catfish Hunter	Oakland A's	25	12	2.49
1975	Jim Palmer	Baltimore Orioles	23	11	2.09
1976	Jim Palmer	Baltimore Orioles	22	13	2.51
1977	Sparky Lyle[6]	N.Y. Yankees	13	5	2.17
1978	Ron Guidry	N.Y. Yankees	25	3	1.74
1979	Mike Flanagan	Baltimore Orioles	23	9	3.08
1980	Steve Stone	Baltimore Orioles	25	7	3.23
1981	Rollie Fingers[7]	Milwaukee Brewers	6	3	1.04
1982	Peter Vuckovich	Milwaukee Brewers	18	6	3.34
1983	LaMarr Hoyt	Chicago White Sox	24	10	3.66
1984	Willie Hernandez[8]	Detroit Tigers	9	3	1.92
1985	Bret Saberhagen	K.C. Royals	20	6	2.87
1986	Roger Clemens	Boston Red Sox	24	4	2.48
1987	Roger Clemens	Boston Red Sox	20	9	2.97
1988	Frank Viola	Minnesota Twins	24	7	2.64
1989	Bret Saberhagen	K.C. Royals	23	6	2.16
1990	Bob Welch	Oakland Athletics	27	6	3.06
1991	Roger Clemens	Boston Red Sox	18	10	2.62
1992	Dennis Eckersley[9]	Oakland Athletics	7	1	1.91
1993	Jack McDowell	Chicago White Sox	22	10	3.37
1994	David Cone[5]	K.C. Royals	16	5	2.94

1. In 1974, 21 saves. 2. In 1979, 37 saves. 3. In 1987, 40 saves. 4. In 1989, 44 saves. 5. Strike-shortened season ended Aug. 12. 6. In 1977, 26 saves. 7. In 1981, 28 saves. 8. In 1984, 32 saves. 9. In 1992, 51 saves.

MAJOR LEAGUE PITCHERS, 300 OR MORE VICTORIES

Player	Years	Won	Lost
Cy Young	22	511	315
Walter Johnson	21	416	279
Grover Alexander	20	373	208
Christy Mathewson	17	373	188
Warren Spahn	21	363	245
Pud Galvin	15	361	308
Kid Nichols	15	360	208
Tim Keefe	14	342	225
Steve Carlton	24	329	244
Eddie Plank	17	327	190
John Clarkson	12	326	176
Don Sutton	23	324	256
Nolan Ryan	27	324	292
Phil Niekro	24	318	274
Gaylord Perry	22	314	265
Charles "Old Hoss" Radbourne	11	311	191
Tom Seaver	20	311	205
Mickey Welch	13	308	209
Lefty Grove	17	300	141
Early Wynn	23	300	244

TRIPLE CROWN WINNERS

Only 11 players have led their league in home runs, runs batted in, and batting average in one season.

Player	Team	Year	HRs	RBIs	Avg.
Ty Cobb	Detroit Tigers	1909	9	115	.377
Heinie Zimmerman	Chicago Cubs	1912	14	98	.372
Rogers Hornsby	St. Louis Cardinals	1922	42	152	.401
Rogers Hornsby	St. Louis Cardinals	1925	39	143	.403
Chuck Klein	Philadelphia Phillies	1933	28	120	.368
Jimmie Foxx	Philadelphia A's	1933	48	163	.356
Lou Gehrig	N.Y. Yankees	1934	49	165	.363
Joe Medwick	St. Louis Cardinals	1937	31	154	.374
Ted Williams	Boston Red Sox	1942	36	137	.356
Ted Williams	Boston Red Sox	1947	32	114	.343
Mickey Mantle	N.Y. Yankees	1956	52	130	.353
Frank Robinson	Baltimore Orioles	1966	49	122	.316
Carl Yastrzemski	Boston Red Sox	1967	44	121	.326

MOST VALUABLE PLAYER AWARD WINNERS

Between 1911 and 1914 the Chalmers Award was given to the player judged to be the most valuable in each league. It was not until 1922 that the American League began to select a league MVP. The National League began to do so as well two years later. By the end of the decade, though, both leagues failed to select an MVP. In 1931 the Baseball Writers Association of America began to select the league MVPs, and has continued to do so through today.

NATIONAL LEAGUE

Year	Name	Team	HRs	RBIs	Avg.
1911	Frank Schulte	Chicago Cubs	21	121	.300
1912	Larry Doyle	N.Y. Giants	10	90	.330
1913	Jake Daubert	Brooklyn Dodgers	2	52	.350
1914	Johnny Evers	Chicago Cubs	1	40	.279
1924	Dazzy Vance (P)	Brooklyn Dodgers	28W	6L	2.16 ERA
1925	Rogers Hornsby	St. Louis Cardinals	29	143	.403
1926	Bob O'Farrell	St. Louis Cardinals	7	68	.293
1927	Paul Waner	Pittsburgh Pirates	9	131	.380
1928	Jim Bottomley	St. Louis Cardinals	31	136	.325
1929	Rogers Hornsby	St. Louis Cardinals	39	149	.380
1931	Frankie Frisch	St. Louis Cardinals	4	82	.311
1932	Chuck Klein	Philadelphia Phillies	38	137	.348
1933	Carl Hubbell (P)	N.Y. Giants	23W	12L	1.66 ERA
1934	Dizzy Dean (P)	St. Louis Cardinals	30W	7L	2.66 ERA
1935	Gabby Hartnett	Chicago Cubs	13	91	.344
1936	Carl Hubbell (P)	N.Y. Giants	26W	6L	2.31 ERA
1937	Joe Medwick	St. Louis Cardinals	31	154	.374
1938	Ernie Lombardi	Cincinnati Reds	19	95	.342
1939	Bucky Walters (P)	Cinncinnati Reds	27W	11L	2.29 ERA
1940	Frank McCormick	Cinncinati Reds	19	127	.309
1941	Dolph Camilli	Brooklyn Dodgers	34	120	.285
1942	Mort Cooper (P)	St. Louis Cardinals	22W	7L	1.78 ERA
1943	Stan Musial	St. Louis Cardinals	13	81	.357
1944	Marty Marion	St. Louis Cardinals	6	63	.267
1945	Phil Cavarretta	Chicago Cubs	6	97	.355
1946	Stan Musial	St. Louis Cardinals	16	103	.365
1947	Bob Elliott	Boston Braves	22	113	.317
1948	Stan Musial	St. Louis Cardinals	39	131	.376
1949	Jackie Robinson	Brooklyn Dodgers	16	124	.342
1950	Jim Konstanty (P)[1]	Philadelphia Phillies	16W	7L	2.66 ERA
1951	Roy Campanella	Brooklyn Dodgers	33	108	.325
1952	Hank Sauer	Chicago Cubs	37	121	.270
1953	Roy Campanella	Brooklyn Dodgers	41	142	.312
1954	Willie Mays	N.Y. Giants	41	110	.345
1955	Roy Campanella	Brooklyn Dodgers	32	107	.318
1956	Don Newcombe (P)	Brooklyn Dodgers	27W	7L	3.06 ERA
1957	Hank Aaron	Milwaukee Braves	44	132	.322
1958	Ernie Banks	Chicago Cubs	47	129	.313
1959	Ernie Banks	Chicago Cubs	45	143	.304
1960	Dick Groat	Pittsburgh Pirates	2	50	.325
1961	Frank Robinson	Cincinnati Reds	37	124	.323
1962	Maury Wills	L.A. Dodgers	6	48	.299
1963	Sandy Koufax (P)	L.A. Dodgers	25W	5L	1.88 ERA
1964	Ken Boyer	St. Louis Cardinals	24	119	.295
1965	Willie Mays	San Francisco Giants	52	112	.317
1966	Roberto Clemente	Pittsburgh Pirates	29	119	.317
1967	Orlando Cepeda	San Francisco Giants	25	111	.325
1968	Bob Gibson (P)	St. Louis Cardinals	22W	9L	1.12 ERA
1969	Willie McCovey	San Francisco Giants	45	126	.320
1970	Johnny Bench	Cincinnati Reds	45	148	.293
1971	Joe Torre	St. Louis Cardinals	45	137	.363
1972	Johnny Bench	Cincinnati Reds	40	125	.270
1973	Pete Rose	Cincinnati Reds	5	64	.338
1974	Steve Garvey	L.A. Dodgers	21	111	.312
1975	Joe Morgan	Cincinnati Reds	17	94	.327
1976	Joe Morgan	Cincinnati Reds	27	111	.320
1977	George Foster	Cincinnati Reds	52	149	.320
1978	Dave Parker	Pittsburgh Pirates	30	117	.334
1979	Keith Hernandez	St. Louis Cardinals	11	105	.344
	Willie Stargell	Pittsburgh Pirates	32	82	.281
1980	Mike Schmidt	Philadelphia Phillies	48	121	.286
1981	Mike Schmidt	Philadelphia Phillies	31	91	.316
1982	Dale Murphy	Atlanta Braves	36	109	.281
1983	Dale Murphy	Atlanta Braves	36	121	.302
1984	Ryne Sandberg	Chicago Cubs	19	84	.314
1985	Willie McGee	St. Louis Cardinals	10	82	.353
1986	Mike Schmidt	Philadelphia Phillies	37	119	.290
1987	Andre Dawson	Chicago Cubs	49	137	.287
1988	Kirk Gibson	L.A. Dodgers	25	76	.290
1989	Kevin Mitchell	San Francisco Giants	47	125	.291
1990	Barry Bonds	Pittsburgh Pirates	33	114	.301
1991	Terry Pendleton	Atlanta Braves	22	86	.319
1992	Barry Bonds	Pittsburgh Pirates	34	103	.311
1993	Barry Bonds	San Francisco Giants	46	123	.336
1994	Jeff Bagwell[2]	Houston Astros	39	116	.368

Note: P = pitcher. 1. Twenty-two saves in 1950. 2. Strike-shortened season ended Aug. 12. **Source:** Baseball Writers Association.

AMERICAN LEAGUE

Year	Name	Team	HRs	RBIs	Avg.
1911	Ty Cobb	Detroit Tigers	8	144	.420
1912	Tris Speaker	Boston Red Sox	10	98	.383
1913	Walter Johnson (P)	Washington Senators	36W	7L	1.09 ERA
1914	Eddie Collins	Philadelphia A's	2	85	.344
1922	George Sisler	St. Louis Browns	8	105	.420
1923	Babe Ruth	N.Y. Yankees	41	131	.393
1924	Walter Johnson (P)	Washington Senators	23W	7L	2.72 ERA
1925	Roger Peckinpaugh	Washington Senators	4	64	.294
1926	George Burns	Cleveland Indians	4	114	.358
1927	Lou Gehrig	N.Y. Yankees	47	175	.373
1928	Mickey Cochrane	Philadelphia A's	10	57	.293
1931	Lefty Grove (P)	Philadelphia A's	31W	4L	2.06 ERA
1932	Jimmie Foxx	Philadelphia A's	58	169	.364
1933	Jimmie Foxx	Philadelphia A's	48	163	.356
1934	Mickey Cochrane	Detroit Tigers	2	76	.320
1935	Hank Greenberg	Detroit Tigers	36	170	.328
1936	Lou Gehrig	N.Y. Yankees	49	152	.354
1937	Charley Gehringer	Detroit Tigers	14	96	.371
1938	Jimmie Foxx	Boston Red Sox	50	175	.349
1939	Joe DiMaggio	N.Y. Yankees	30	126	.381
1940	Hank Greenberg	Detroit Tigers	41	150	.340
1941	Joe DiMaggio	N.Y. Yankees	30	125	.357
1942	Joe Gordon	N.Y Yankees	18	103	.322
1943	Spud Chandler (P)	N.Y. Yankees	20W	4L	1.64 ERA
1944	Hal Newhouser (P)	Detroit Tigers	29W	9L	2.22 ERA
1945	Hal Newhouser (P)	Detroit Tigers	25W	9L	1.81 ERA
1946	Ted Williams	Boston Red Sox	38	123	.342
1947	Joe DiMaggio	N.Y. Yankees	20	97	.315
1948	Lou Boudreau	Cleveland Indians	18	106	.355
1949	Ted Williams	Boston Red Sox	43	159	.343
1950	Phil Rizzuto	N.Y. Yankees	7	66	.324
1951	Yogi Berra	N.Y. Yankees	27	88	.294
1952	Bobby Shantz (P)	Philadelphia A's	24W	7L	2.48 ERA
1953	Al Rosen	Cleveland Indians	43	145	.336
1954	Yogi Berra	N.Y. Yankees	22	125	.307
1955	Yogi Berra	N.Y. Yankees	27	108	.272
1956	Mickey Mantle	N.Y. Yankees	52	130	.353
1957	Mickey Mantle	N.Y Yankees	34	94	.365
1958	Jackie Jensen	Boston Red Sox	35	122	.286
1959	Nelson Fox	Chicago White Sox	2	70	.306

Year	Name	Team	HRs	RBIs	Avg.
1960	Roger Maris	N.Y. Yankees	39	112	.283
1961	Roger Maris	N.Y. Yankees	61	142	.269
1962	Mickey Mantle	N.Y. Yankees	30	89	.321
1963	Elston Howard	N.Y. Yankees	28	85	.287
1964	Brooks Robinson	Baltimore Orioles	28	118	.317
1965	Zoilo Versalles	Minnesota Twins	19	77	.273
1966	Frank Robinson	Baltimore Orioles	49	122	.316
1967	Carl Yastrzemski	Boston Red Sox	44	121	.326
1968	Denny McLain (P)	Detroit Tigers	31W	6L	1.96 ERA
1969	Harmon Killebrew	Minnesota Twins	49	140	.276
1970	Boog Powell	Baltimore Orioles	35	114	.297
1971	Vida Blue (P)	Oakland A's	24W	8L	1.82 ERA
1972	Dick Allen	Chicago White Sox	37	113	.308
1973	Reggie Jackson	Oakland A's	32	117	.293
1974	Jeff Burroughs	Texas Rangers	25	118	.301
1975	Fred Lynn	Boston Red Sox	21	105	.331
1976	Thurman Munson	N.Y. Yankees	17	105	.302
1977	Rod Carew	Minnesota Twins	14	100	.388
1978	Jim Rice	Boston Red Sox	46	139	.315
1979	Don Baylor	California Angels	36	139	.296
1980	George Brett	Kansas City Royals	24	118	.390
1981	Rollie Fingers (P)[1]	Milwaukee Brewers	6W	3L	1.04 ERA
1982	Robin Yount	Milwaukee Brewers	29	114	.331
1983	Cal Ripken, Jr.	Baltimore Orioles	27	102	.318
1984	Willie Hernandez (P)[2]	Detroit Tigers	9W	3L	2.48 ERA
1985	Don Mattingly	N.Y. Yankees	35	145	.324
1986	Roger Clemens (P)	Boston Red Sox	24W	4L	2.48 ERA
1987	George Bell	Toronto Blue Jays	47	134	.308
1988	Jose Canseco	Oakland A's	42	124	.307
1989	Robin Yount	Milwaukee Brewers	21	103	.318
1990	Rickey Henderson	Oakland A's	28	61	.325
1991	Cal Ripken, Jr.	Baltimore Orioles	34	114	.323
1992	Dennis Eckersley (P)[3]	Oakland Athletics	7W	1L	1.91 ERA
1993	Frank Thomas	Chicago White Sox	41	128	.317
1994	Frank Thomas[4]	Chicago White Sox	38	101	.353

Note: P = pitcher. 1. Had 28 saves in 1981. 2. Had 32 saves in 1984. 3. Had 51 saves in 1992. 4. Strike-shortened season ended Aug. 12. **Source:** Baseball Writers Association.

ALL STAR GAME RESULTS, 1933–95

Year	Winner	Score	Year	Winner	Score
1933	American	4–2	1963	National	5–3
1934	American	9–7	1964	National	7–4
1935	American	4–1	1965	National	6–5
1936	National	4–3	1966	National	2–1
1937	American	8–3	1967	National	2–1
1938	National	4–1	1968	National	1–0
1939	American	3–1	1969	National	9–3
1940	National	4–0	1970	National	5–4
1941	American	7–5	1971	American	6–4
1942	American	3–1	1972	National	4–3
1943	American	5–3	1973	National	7–1
1944	National	7–1	1974	National	7–2
1945	No game due to wartime		1975	National	6–3
1946	American	12–0	1976	National	7–1
1947	American	2–1	1977	National	7–5
1948	American	5–2	1978	National	7–3
1949	American	11–7	1979	National	7–6
1950	National	4–3	1980	National	4–2
1951	National	8–3	1981	National	5–4
1952	National	3–2	1982	National	4–1
1953	National	5–1	1983	American	13–3
1954	American	11–9	1984	National	3–1
1955	National	6–5	1985	National	6–1
1956	National	7–3	1986	American	3–2
1957	American	6–5	1987	National (10 inn.)	2–0
1958	American	4–3	1988	American	2–1
1959(1)[1]	National	5–4	1989	American	5–3
1959(2)	American	5–3	1990	American	2–0
1960(1)	National	5–3	1991	American	4–2
1960(2)	National	6–0	1992	American	13–6
1961(1)	National	5–4	1993	American	9–3
1961(2)	Tie[2]	1–1	1994	National (10 inn.)	8–7
1962(1)	National	3–1	1995	National	3–2
1962(2)	American	9–4			

1. Two All Star games were played 1959–62. 2. Game was called after nine innings because of rain.

THE BASEBALL HALL OF FAME

National Baseball Hall of Fame and Museum
Main Street, Cooperstown, NY 13326
(607) 547-9988

Hours: From May 1 to Oct. 31—9:00 A.M. to 9:00 P.M.
From Nov. 1 to Apr. 30—9:00 A.M. to 5:00 P.M.
(Every day of the year except Thanksgiving, Christmas, and New Year's.)

The Hall of Fame was established in 1936 and opened in Cooperstown, N.Y., in 1939. From the start there were two ways to be elected: by receiving 75 percent of the votes cast by the Baseball Writers Association of America or 75 percent of the votes cast by a Committee on Old Timers. In the first year, the writers picked the top five players of the post-1900 era: Ty Cobb, Walter Johnson, Christy Mathewson, Babe Ruth, and Honus Wagner. To be elected, a player must have played at least 10 years in the major leagues and been retired for at least five years. The Committee on Old Timers, originally created to consider 19th-century players, was replaced by a Special Veterans Committee whose scope includes all players retired for a minimum of 25 years who may have been overlooked when they were first eligible. In 1971 a Special Committee on the Negro Leagues was set up to consider ballplayers who played in the old Negro Leagues.

BASEBALL HALL OF FAME

Player/Position/Year inducted	Games	At bats	HRs	BA	Hits	RBIs
Aaron, Henry (Hank) OF 1982	3,298	12,364	755	.305	3,771	2,297
All-time leader in home runs and RBIs						
Anson, Adrian (Cap) 1B 1939	2,276	9,108	96	.334	3,041	1,715
Managed 20 years, 1879–98, winning five pennants						
Aparicio, Luis SS 1984	2,599	10,230	83	.262	2,677	791
Led AL in stolen bases nine years in a row (1956–64)						
Appling, Luke SS 1964	2,422	8,857	45	.310	2,749	1,116
Batted .388 in 1936						
Ashburn, Richie OF 1995	2,189	8,365	29	.308	2,574	586
Hit .300 or more nine times						
Averill, Earl OF 1975	1,669	6,358	238	.318	2,020	1,165
232 hits in 1936						
Baker, Frank (Home Run) 3B 1955	1,575	5,985	96	.307	1,838	1,013
Batted .363 in six World Series						
Bancroft, Dave SS 1971	1,913	7,182	32	.279	2,004	591
Handled 984 chances in 1922						
Banks, Ernie SS, 1B 1977	2,528	9,421	512	.274	2,583	1,636
Consecutive MVP awards, 1958–59						
Beckley, Jake 1B 1971	2,386	9,527	88	.308	2,931	1,575
244 career triples, mostly in 19th century						

Player/Position/Year inducted	Games	At bats	HRs	BA	Hits	RBIs
Bench, Johnny C 1989 Hit .529 in 1976 World Series; NL MVP, 1970, 1972	2,158	7,658	389	.267	2,048	1,376
Berra, Lawrence (Yogi) C, OF 1972 Three MVP awards, 1951, 1954, 1955	2,120	7,555	358	.285	2,150	1,430
Bottomley, Jim 1B 1974 Twelve RBIs in one game, 1924	1,991	7,471	219	.310	2,313	1,422
Boudreau, Lou SS 1970 MVP in 1948; managed 16 years	1,646	6,030	68	.295	1,779	789
Bresnahan, Roger C, OF 1945 212 stolen bases; first catcher elected to Hall of Fame	1,430	4,478	26	.279	1,251	530
Brock, Lou OF 1985 938 stolen bases; batted .391 in three World Series	2,616	10,332	149	.293	3,023	900
Brouthers, Dan 1B 1945 Seven slugging and five batting titles during 19th century	1,673	6,716	106	.343	2,304	1,056
Burkett, Jesse OF 1946 Led NL in batting three times and in hits four times	2,072	8,430	75	.341	2,873	952
Campanella, Roy C 1969 Three MVP awards, 1951, 1953, 1955	1,215	4,205	242	.276	1,161	856
Carew, Rod IF 1991 Seven batting titles; 18 All-Star Game appearances	2,469	9,315	92	.328	3,053	1,015
Carey, Max OF 1961 738 stolen bases	2,476	9,363	69	.285	2,665	800
Chance, Frank 1B 1946 Managed Chicago (NL) to four pennants in five years, 1906–10	1,286	4,295	20	.297	1,274	596
Clarke, Fred OF 1945 223 career triples; hit .300 or better 11 times	2,245	8,588	67	.315	2,708	1,015
Clemente, Roberto OF 1973 Career average of over 18 outfield assists per season	2,433	9,454	240	.317	3,000	1,305
Cobb, Ty OF 1936 Batted .320 or better for 23 straight years	3,034	11,429	118	.367	4,191	1,961
Cochrane, Mickey C 1947 Two MVP awards, 1928 and 1934	1,482	5,169	119	.320	1,652	832
Collins, Eddie 2B 1939 Hit .340 or better 10 times; led AL in fielding nine times	2,826	9,949	47	.333	3,311	1,299
Collins, Jimmy 3B 1945 Led NL in home runs, 1898	1,728	6,796	64	.294	1,997	982
Combs, Earle OF 1970 Averaged 127 runs scored per season	1,454	5,748	58	.325	1,866	629
Comiskey, Charles 1B 1939 Manager and owner of Chicago White Sox	1,390	5,796	29	.264	1,531	467
Connor, Roger 1B 1976 Held all-time HR record before Babe Ruth	1,998	7,798	136	.318	2,480	1,078
Crawford, Sam OF 1957 312 triples, best ever	2,517	9,580	97	.309	2,964	1,525
Cronin, Joe SS 1956 MVP in 1930; managed 1933–47	2,124	7,579	170	.301	2,285	1,424
Cuyler, Hazen (Kiki) OF 1968 Led NL in runs scored twice, stolen bases four times	1,879	7,161	127	.321	2,299	1,065
Delahanty, Ed IF, OF 1945 Batted .408 in 1899	1,834	7,502	100	.345	2,591	1,464
Dickey, Bill C 1954 Catcher on eight AL pennant winning teams	1,789	6,300	202	.313	1,969	1,209
DiMaggio, Joe OF 1955 56-game hitting streak in 1941	1,736	6,821	361	.325	2,214	1,537
Doerr, Bobby 2B 1986 Led AL in slugging 1944	1,865	7,093	223	.288	2,042	1,247
Duffy, Hugh OF 1945 Batted .438 in 1894, highest ever	1,736	7,062	103	.328	2,314	1,299
Evers, Johnny 2B 1946 NL MVP in 1914	1,783	6,134	12	.270	1,658	538
Ewing, Buck C, IF, OF 1939 Regarded as greatest player of 19th century	1,315	5,363	70	.303	1,625	733
Ferrell, Rick C 1984 Led AL catchers at times in putouts, assists, fielding average, and double plays	1,884	6,028	28	.281	1,692	734
Flick, Elmer OF 1963 Led AL in triples 1905, 1906, 1907	1,484	5,603	47	.315	1,767	756
Foxx, Jimmie 1B, 3B 1951 Slugged over .700 three seasons	2,317	8,134	534	.325	2,646	1,921
Frisch, Frank 2B, 3B 1947 Hit .300 or better 11 years in a row (1921–31)	2,311	9,112	105	.316	2,880	1,244
Gehrig, Lou 1B 1939 2,130 consecutive games played	2,164	8,001	493	.340	2,721	1,990
Gehringer, Charlie 2B 1949 60 doubles in 1936	2,323	8,860	184	.320	2,839	1,427
Goslin, Leon (Goose) OF 1968 100+ RBIs 11 years	2,287	8,655	248	.316	2,735	1,609
Greenberg, Hank 1B 1956 58 home runs in 1938; 183 RBIs in 1937	1,394	5,193	331	.313	1,628	1,276
Hafey, Charles (Chick) OF 1971 NL batting title (.349) in 1931	1,283	4,625	164	.317	1,466	833
Hamilton, Billy OF 1961 Scored 196 runs in 1894, with a .509 on-base average and 99 stolen bases	1,593	6,284	40	.344	2,163	736
Hartnett, Charles (Gabby) C 1955 Played on four NL pennant winners, managed one	1,990	6,432	236	.297	1,912	1,179
Heilmann, Harry OF, 1B 1952 Batted .403 in 1923	2,146	7,787	183	.342	2,660	1,551
Herman, Billy 2B 1975 57 doubles in 1935	1,922	7,707	47	.304	2,345	839
Hooper, Harry OF 1971 375 career stolen bases	2,308	8,785	75	.281	2,466	817
Hornsby, Rogers 2B, IF 1942 Batted .402 in years 1921–25; nine slugging titles	2,259	8,173	301	.358	2,930	1,584
Huggins, Miller 2B 1964 Managed N.Y. Yankees 1913–29; 1,002 career walks	1,585	5,557	9	.265	1,474	318
Jackson, Reggie OF 1993 Played in five World Series and 11 divisional playoffs; World Series MVP, 1977	2,820	9,864	563	.262	2,584	1,702
Jackson, Travis SS 1982 Batted over .300 six times in 1920s and 1930s	1,656	6,086	135	.291	1,768	929
Jennings, Hugh SS 1945 Managed Detroit 1907–20; batted .398 in 1896	1,285	4,905	18	.312	1,531	840
Kaline, Al OF 1980 3,007 career hits; 11 Gold Gloves	2,834	10,116	399	.297	3,007	1,583
Keeler, Willie OF 1939 Batted .432 in 1897; 495 career stolen bases	2,124	8,591	34	.345	2,962	810
Kell, George 3B 1983 AL batting champ (.343) in 1949	1,795	6,702	78	.306	2,054	870
Kelley, Joe OF 1971 Averaged 151 runs scored, 1894–96	1,845	7,018	65	.319	2,242	1,193
Kelly, George 1B 1973 Led NL in RBIs, 1920 and 1925	1,622	5,993	148	.297	1,778	1,020
Kelly, Mike (King) OF, C 1945 Two batting titles, 1884 and 1886; 315 career stolen bases	1,463	5,923	69	.307	1,820	794
Killebrew, Harmon 1B, 3B, OF 1984 40+ home runs eight years	2,435	8,147	573	.256	2,086	1,584
Kiner, Ralph OF 1975 Second-highest home run per at bat ratio of all-time	1,472	5,205	369	.279	1,451	1,015
Klein, Chuck OF 1980 44 outfield assists in 1930	1,753	6,486	300	.320	2,076	1,201
Lajoie, Napoleon (Larry) 2B 1937 Batted .422 in 1901	2,479	9,589	82	.338	3,244	1,599
Lazzeri, Tony IF 1991 Batted .300 or better five times; clutch hitter in World Series	1,740	6,297	178	.292	1,840	1,191
Lindstrom, Fred 3B, OF 1976 231 hits in 1928	1,438	5,611	103	.311	1,747	779
Lombardi, Ernie C 1986 Two NL batting titles, 1938 and 1942	1,853	5,855	190	.306	1,792	990
Lopez, Al C 1977 Caught 1,918 games over 19 years; managed 17 years	1,950	5,916	52	.261	1,547	652
Mantle, Mickey OF 1974 52 home runs in 1956, 54 in 1961	2,401	8,102	536	.298	2,415	1,509
Manush, Heinie OF 1964 Hit .378 in 1926	2,009	7,653	110	.330	2,524	1,173

Player/Position/Year inducted	Games	At bats	HRs	BA	Hits	RBIs
Maranville, Walter (Rabbit) SS, 2B 1954	2,670	10,078	28	.258	2,605	884
23-year career; hit .308 in two World Series						
Mathews, Eddie 3B 1978	2,388	8,537	512	.271	2,315	1,453
1,444 career walks						
Mays, Willie OF 1979	2,992	10,881	660	.302	3,283	1,903
Slugged over .600 six seasons						
McCarthy, Tommy OF 1946	1,275	5,128	44	.292	1,496	666
Averaged 122 runs scored, 1888–94						
McCovey, Willie 1B, OF 1986	2,588	8,197	521	.270	2,211	1,555
Hit 18 career grand slams						
McGraw, John 3B, SS 1937	1,009	3,922	13	.334	1,308	462
.549 on-base average in 1899; 2,840 career wins as manager						
Medwick, Joe OF 1968	1,984	7,635	205	.324	2,471	1,383
Won NL Triple Crown in 1937						
Mize, Johnny 1B 1981	1,884	6,443	359	.312	2,011	1,337
Four-time NL home run champ						
Morgan, Joe 2B 1990	2,649	9,277	268	.271	2,517	1,133
Won back-to-back MVP awards, 1975, 1976						
Musial, Stan OF, 1B 1969	3,026	10,972	475	.331	3,630	1,951
725 doubles and 177 triples						
O'Rourke, Jim OF 1945	1,774	7,435	51	.310	2,304	830
Batted .300+ 11 times in the 19th century						
Ott, Mel OF 1951	2,732	9,456	511	.304	2,876	1,860
Averaged 121 RBIs 1929–38						
Reese, Harold (Pee Wee) SS 1984	2,166	8,058	126	.269	2,170	885
Finished in top 10 in MVP balloting nine times						
Rice, Sam OF 1963	2,404	9,269	34	.322	2,987	1,078
Only 18 strikeouts per 154 games						
Rizzuto, Phil (Scooter) SS 1994	1,661	5,816	38	.273	1,588	563
AL MVP in 1950; Played in nine World Series						
Robinson, Brooks 3B 1983	2,896	10,654	268	.267	2,848	1,357
16 consecutive Gold Gloves, 1960–75						
Robinson, Frank OF 1982	2,808	10,006	586	.294	2,943	1,812
MVP in both leagues; AL Triple Crown in 1966						
Robinson, Jackie 2B 1972	1,382	4,877	137	.311	1,518	734
First black player in MLB; Rookie of the Year 1947; MVP and batting champ 1949						
Robinson, Wilbert C 1945	1,347	5,077	18	.273	1,399	740
Managed Brooklyn 1914–31, winning two pennants						
Roush, Edd OF 1962	1,967	7,363	68	.323	2,376	981
Two NL batting titles, 1917 and 1919						
Ruth, George (Babe) OF, P 1936	2,503	8,399	714	.342	2,873	2,211
Slugged .847 1920–21						
Schalk, Ray C 1955	1,760	5,306	12	.253	1,345	594
176 stolen bases						
Schmidt, Mike 3B 1995	2,404	8,352	548	.267	2,234	1,595
Led NL in homers eight times; won 10 gold gloves						
Schoendienst, Albert (Red) 1989	2,216	8,479	84	.289	2,449	773
Managed Cards to two pennants and 1967 World Series crown						
Sewell, Joe SS, 3B 1977	1,902	7,132	49	.312	2,226	1,051
Only 22 strikeouts in his last 2,500 at bats, 1929–33						
Simmons, Al OF 1953	2,215	8,761	307	.334	2,927	1,827
Drove in over 100 runs in each of his first 11 years, 1924–34						
Sisler, George 1B 1939	2,055	8,267	100	.340	2,812	1,175
Batted .400 1920–22						
Slaughter, Enos OF 1985	2,380	7,946	169	.300	2,383	1,304
52 doubles in 1939						
Snider, Edwin (Duke) OF 1980	2,143	7,161	407	.295	2,116	1,333
Averaged 41 home runs, 1953–57						
Speaker, Tris OF 1937	2,789	10,208	117	.344	3,515	1,559
Led AL in doubles eight times						
Stargell, Willie OF, 1B 1988	2,360	7,927	475	.282	2,232	1,540
MVP in 1979						
Terry, Bill 1B 1954	1,721	6,428	154	.341	2,193	1,078
Hit .401 in 1930						
Thompson, Sam OF 1974	1,410	6,005	128	.331	1,986	1,299
166 RBIs in 1887, 165 in 1895						
Tinker, Joe SS 1946	1,805	6,441	31	.263	1,695	782
Played in four World Series with Chicago Cubs						
Traynor, Pie 3B 1948	1,941	7,559	58	.320	2,416	1,273
100+ RBIs seven years						
Vaughan, Joseph (Arky) SS 1985	1,817	6,622	96	.318	2,103	926
.385 in 1935						
Wagner, Honus SS 1936	2,786	10,427	101	.327	3,418	1,732
Eight batting titles, four in a row 1906–1909						
Wallace, Bobby SS 1953	2,386	8,652	35	.267	2,314	1,121
Led AL in fielding and assists three times each						
Waner, Lloyd OF 1967	1,992	7,772	28	.316	2,459	598
234 hits in 1929						
Waner, Paul OF 1952	2,549	9,459	112	.333	3,152	1,309
62 doubles in 1932						
Wheat, Zack OF 1959	2,410	9,106	132	.317	2,884	1,261
Batted .375 at age 36 in 1924						
Williams, Billy OF 1987	2,488	9,350	426	.290	2,711	1,475
30+ home runs in five seasons						
Williams, Ted OF 1966	2,292	7,706	521	.344	2,654	1,839
Last .400 hitter in majors, .406 in 1941						
Wilson, Lewis (Hack) OF 1979	1,348	4,760	244	.307	1,461	1,062
56 home runs and 190 RBIs in 1930						
Wright, George SS 1937	329	1,494	2	.256	N/A	N/A
Pioneer of professional baseball						
Yastrzemski, Carl (Yaz) OF, 1B 1989	3,308	11,988	452	.285	3,419	1,844
Won Triple Crown in 1967; three batting titles						
Youngs, Ross OF 1972	1,211	4,627	42	.322	1,491	592
Killed at age 30; .398 on-base average in four World Series, 1921–24						

HALL OF FAME—PITCHERS

Player/Year inducted	Wins	Losses	ERA	Games	IP	SOs
Alexander, Grover Cleveland 1938	373	208	2.56	696	5,189	2,199
Won 30 games three years; led NL in ERA five times						
Bender, Charles (Chief) 1953	210	127	2.46	459	3,017	1,711
Led AL in winning percentage three seasons						
Brown, Mordecai (Three Finger) 1949	239	129	2.06	481	3,172	1,375
1.04 ERA in 1906						
Carlton, Steve (Lefty) 1994	329	244	3.22	741	5,217	4,136
Four-time Cy Young Award winner (1972, '77, '80, '82)						
Chesbro, Jack 1946	198	132	2.68	392	2,897	1,265
41 wins in 1904						
Clarkson, John 1963	326	177	2.81	531	4,536	2,015
53 wins in 1885, with 623 innings pitched						
Coveleski, Stan 1969	215	142	2.88	450	3,093	981
Led AL in ERA in 1925, 2.84						
Cummings, William (Candy) 1939	21	22	2.78	43	372	37
Inventor of the curveball						
Dean, Jay (Dizzy) 1953	150	83	3.03	317	1,966	1,155
30 wins in 1934						
Drysdale, Don 1984	209	166	2.95	518	3,432	2,486
56⅔ consecutive scoreless innings, 1968						
Faber, Urban (Red) 1964	254	212	3.15	669	4,088	1,471
Led AL in ERA in 1921 and 1922						
Feller, Bob 1962	266	162	3.25	570	3,827	2,581
Led AL in wins six times, in shutouts seven						
Fingers, Rollie 1992	114	118	2.90	944	1,701	1,299
341 saves over 17 years; 1981 AL MVP						

Player/Year inducted	Wins	Losses	ERA	Games	IP	SOs
Ford, Edward (Whitey) 1974	236	106	2.75	498	3,170	1,956
25–4 in 1961, 24–7 in 1963						
Galvin, James (Pud) 1965	361	310	2.87	697	5,941	1,799
46 wins in 1883 and 1884						
Gibson, Bob 1981	251	174	2.91	528	3,885	3,117
1.12 ERA in 1968; seven straight wins in World Series play						
Gomez, Vernon (Lefty) 1972	189	102	3.34	368	2,503	1,468
Led AL in shutouts three years						
Grimes, Burleigh 1964	270	212	3.53	617	4,180	1,512
Last legal spitball pitcher; won 20+ five times						
Grove, Robert (Lefty) 1947	300	141	3.06	616	3,941	2,266
Led AL in ERA nine times, in strikeouts seven						
Haines, Jesse 1970	210	158	3.64	555	3,209	981
Twice led NL in shutouts, 1921 and 1927						
Hoyt, Waite 1969	237	182	3.59	674	3,763	1,206
1.83 ERA in 84 World Series innings						
Hubbell, Carl 1947	253	154	2.97	535	3,589	1,678
26–6 in 1936; 1.66 ERA in 1933						
Hunter, Jim (Catfish) 1987	224	166	3.26	500	3,448	2,012
21 or more wins, 1971–75						
Jenkins, Ferguson 1991	284	226	3.34	664	4,499	3,192
Cy Young Award winner (1971); three-time All-Star						
Johnson, Walter 1936	416	279	2.17	802	5,924	3,508
36–7, 1.09 ERA in 1913						
Joss, Addie 1978	160	97	1.88	286	2,336	926
Averaged 21–11, 1.66 ERA in years 1904–08						
Keefe, Tim 1964	344	225	2.62	601	5,072	2,533
Averaged 37 wins 1883–85						
Koufax, Sandy 1972	165	87	2.76	397	2,324	2,396
95–27, 1.85 ERA for seasons 1963–66						
Lemon, Bob 1976	207	128	3.23	460	2,850	1,277
Won 20 or more seven times						
Lyons, Ted 1955	260	230	3.67	594	4,161	1,073
Pitched 27 shutouts						
Marichal, Juan 1983	243	142	2.89	471	3,509	2,303
Only 1.8 walks per nine innings over career						
Marquard, Richard (Rube) 1971	201	177	3.08	536	3,307	1,593
73–23 in years 1911–13						
Mathewson, Christy 1936	373	188	2.13	636	4,782	2,502
80 career shutouts						
McGinnity, Joe 1946	247	144	2.64	466	3,459	1,068
35–8 in 1904, with an ERA of 1.61						
Newhouser, Hal 1992	207	150	3.06	488	2,993	1,796
Led AL in victories three years in a row (1944–46)						
Nichols, Charles (Kid) 1949	360	203	2.94	621	5,084	1,885
Won 30 or more games seven straight seasons, 1891–97						
Palmer, Jim 1990	268	152	2.86	558	3,948	2,212
Won Cy Young Award 1973, 1975, 1976						
Pennock, Herb 1948	240	162	3.61	617	3,558	1,227
162–90 as a New York Yankee, 1923–33						
Perry, Gaylord 1991	314	265	3.10	777	5,352	3,534
Won Cy Young Award in both leagues						
Plank, Eddie 1946	327	193	2.34	622	4,505	2,246
1.32 ERA in seven World Series games						
Radbourn, Charles (Old Hoss) 1939	308	191	2.67	528	4,535	1,830
60–12 in 1884, with 679 innings pitched						
Rixey, Eppa 1963	266	251	3.15	692	4,495	1,350
Won 25 games in 1922						
Roberts, Robin 1976	286	245	3.41	676	4,689	2,357
28–7 in 1952; five-time NL leader in complete games						
Ruffing, Charles (Red) 1967	273	225	3.80	624	4,344	1,987
.645 winning percentage as a New York Yankee						
Rusie, Amos 1977	243	160	3.07	462	3,770	1,957
Won 30+ games three years						
Seaver, Tom 1992	311	205	2.86	656	4,782	3,640
Won 20 or more games five times; won Cy Young Award 1969, 1973, 1975						
Spahn, Warren 1973	363	245	3.09	750	5,244	2,583
Won 20 or more games 13 times, including 23 at age 42						
Spalding, Al 1939	48	13	1.78	65	540	41
First 200-game winner (207–56 from 1871 to 1875 in National Association)						
Vance, Clarence (Dazzy) 1955	197	140	3.24	442	2,697	2,045
60–15 over two years, 1924–25						
Waddell, George (Rube) 1946	191	145	2.16	407	2,961	2,316
349 strikeouts in 1904						
Walsh, Ed 1946	195	126	1.82	430	2,964	1,736
40–15 in 1908 with 11 shutouts						
Ward, Montgomery 1964	161	101	2.10	291	2,462	920
87 wins 1879–80						
Welch, Mickey 1973	311	207	2.71	564	4,802	1,850
44–11 in 1885						
Wilhelm, Hoyt 1985	143	122	2.52	1,070	2,254	1,610
227 career saves; first relief pitcher elected to Hall of Fame						
Wynn, Early 1972	300	244	3.54	691	4,564	2,334
Led AL in shutouts at age 40 in 1960						
Young, Denton (Cy) 1937	511	313	2.63	906	7,359	2,799
All-time leader in wins, losses, complete games, and innings pitched						

ELECTED FOR MANAGING

Alston, Walter 1983
Comiskey, Charles 1939
Durocher, Leo 1994
Griffith, Clark 1946
Harris, Bucky 1975
Huggins, Miller 1964
Lopez, Al 1977
Mack, Connie 1937
McCarthy, Joe 1957
McGraw, John 1937
McKechnie, Bill 1962
Robinson, Wilbert 1945
Stengel, Casey 1966
Wright, George 1937
Wright, Harry 1953

ELECTED FOR MERITORIOUS SERVICE

Barlick, Al
Barrow, Edward
Bulkeley, Morgan
Cartwright, Alexander
Chadwick, Henry
Chandler, Happy
Conlan, John (Jocko)
Connolly, Thomas
Evans, William
Foster, Andrew (Rube)
Frick, Ford
Giles, Warren
Harridge, William
Hubbard, Cal
Johnson, B. Bancroft
Klem, William
Landis, Kenesaw Mountain
McGowan, Bill
MacPhail, Larry
Rickey, W. Branch
Veeck, Bill
Weiss, George
Yawkey, Tom

ELECTED FOR ACHIEVEMENT IN THE NEGRO LEAGUES

In 1971 Satchel Paige became the first player admitted to Cooperstown based on achievement in the old Negro League. Since then, the following men have been granted the same honor.

Gibson, Josh 1972
Leonard, William "Buck" 1972
Irvin, Monte 1973
Bell, James "Cool Papa" 1974
Johnson, Judy 1975
Charleston, Oscar 1976
DiHigo, Martin 1977
Lloyd, John Henry 1977
Dandridge, Ray 1987
Day, Leon 1995

INDEX

A

D

E

H

O

T

Y

Z